Italy's Noble Red Wines

ITALY'S NOBLE RED WINES

SECOND EDITION

Sheldon & Pauline Wasserman

Macmillan Publishing Company, New York
Maxwell Macmillan Canada, Toronto
Maxwell Macmillan International, New York, Oxford, Singapore, Sydney

Macmillan Publishing Company
866 Third Avenue, New York, NY 10022

Maxwell Macmillan Canada, Inc.
1200 Eglinton Avenue East, Suite 200
Don Mills, Ontario M3C 3N1

Macmillan Publishing Company is part of the Maxwell Communication Group of Companies.

Library of Congress Cataloging-in-Publication Data
Wasserman, Sheldon.
Italy's noble red wines/Sheldon and Pauline Wasserman.—2nd ed.
p.   cm.
Includes bibliographical references and index.
ISBN 0-02-624281-8
1. Wine and wine making—Italy.   I. Wasserman, Pauline.
II. Title.
TP559.I8W36   1991
641.2'223'0945—dc20   91-2520
CIP

Macmillan books are available at special discounts for bulk purchases for sales
promotions, premiums, fund-raising, or educational use. For details, contact:

Special Sales Director
Macmillan Publishing Company
866 Third Avenue
New York, NY 10022

10 9 8 7 6 5 4 3 2 1

Designed by Liney Li

Printed in the United States of America

This book is dedicated to

the memory of **GIACOMO BOLOGNA**,
Italy's Grand Ambassador of Wine,
a large man with an enormous heart,

and to
EDOARDO VALENTINI,
scholar, fine winemaker, poet, and friend,

and to
ANGELO CHARLES CASTELLI,
a dear friend, and enthusiastic supporter
in our quest for quality,

and to
the memory of **RENATO RATTI**,
artist, innovator, scholar, and winemaker,
who did so much for his region and fine wine,
and who so generously gave of his time and knowledge, not only to us,
but to anyone who asked.

CONTENTS

PART ONE: NEBBIOLO

Contents

Contents

PART TWO: SANGIOVESE

Contents

Contents

Contents

Contents

Contents

ACKNOWLEDGMENTS

To the late Giacomo Bologna, "Italy's Grand Ambassador of Wine," who said that it would be sufficient thanks for him if we wrote about the wines themselves, making known what quality and greatness Italian wines can achieve, we offer our heartfelt thanks nevertheless—for taking us under his wing and giving us our first real introduction to the fine wines of Piemonte, generously sharing his time, his hospitality, and his ready welcome at the *cantine* of some of the finest producers; for his patience and willingness to repeat and carefully rephrase every explanation, when we could barely speak the language; for the many doors he opened and the many bottles as well, of rare and excellent wines, not only Piemontese, and not only Italian.

Our thanks to the late Renato Ratti, Mr. Nebbiolo, who built the foundation with his historical and original research and work on the crus of Barolo and Barbaresco, which were so useful; also for his time and advice, both invaluable to this work.

Marco Moreschi, of *Unione Italiana Vini,* who came to our rescue with up-to-date statistical data when we were about ready to give up on ever getting that data.

Philip di Belardino did so much to help us that we'd be remiss not to thank him. He answered our countless requests for information in a cheerful and helpful manner. Thanks, Philip.

Giorgio Lingero, who provided much-needed encouragement and some valuable insights and information.

Many thanks to the many importers who gave us much needed cooperation and much-appreciated assistance. The list is long, so we thought it better, and more practicable, to attempt to thank all as a group rather than individually. And considering the number of years involved on this project, we doubt we could remember them all anyway. You know who you are—*mille grazie.*

Sandro Boscaini provided us with a lot of valuable information on Veronese wines, especially the *recioto* wines. He also gave us valuable insights and helped introduce us to producers that we might not have had the chance to meet otherwise.

There are so many producers who deserve special thanks that we decided not to add another whole section to the book in trying to list them all here. Instead we hope the book itself will serve as a small way of saying *grazie tantissimo di cuore* to let them know that we do indeed appreciate their generosity, the time and the opportunity they gave us to better know their wines. Without them there could not have been this book on Italy's noble red wines.

Our thanks to Italian Trade Commissioner Alfonso Barbera. We'd be remiss if we omitted a thanks to Giorgio Lulli of ICE for the help he provided; we are sorry for the problems he encountered to that end, including some in the wee hours of the morning. We also want to thank Augusto Marchini of the Italian Wine Center for the important information he provided for our first edition, and for the invaluable assistance he afforded us; the Sangiovese section in particular was much improved thanks to his efforts. He provided valuable assistance for the second edition as well. And Michelle Jones, as always, was there when we needed her.

Dott. Alessandro Sorrentino and Renato Paparella of ICE Firenze helped organize our last-minute trip to Toscana so that we could taste the 1989s from barrel, as well as other vintages.

The organizers of the *Verona Vinitaly Wine Fair,* especially Dr. Gian Carlo Fochesato, did much to aid our research. They deserve our thanks. Our thanks to "Cicci" Boccoli

Frigerio for her willing and enthusiastic assistance in the field. We also want to thank Carlo Bertolotti, Silvana Genero, and especially Beatrice Mavaracchio of *Torino Esposizioni,* who helped us refine our Piemontese section.

Teobaldo Cappellano, president of the *Enoteca Regionale del Barolo,* did a lot to assist us and came to our rescue when we needed to taste a wide range of Barolos from the 1987, 1988, and 1989 vintages.

Stefano Campatelli, director of the *Consorzio del Brunello di Montalcino,* along with his two able assistants, Giuseppe Gorelli and Maurizo Botarelli, organized a splendid tasting of the five most recent vintages of Brunello for us and provided us with much-needed statistical data. And Maddalena Mazzeschi of the *Consorzio di Vino Nobile di Montalcino* helped us bring our chapter on Vino Nobile up-to-date.

Our thanks to Angelo Charles Castelli, who not only opened many fine Italian wines for us and offered enthusiastic encouragement, but also provided the fine, and much appreciated, translation of Angelo Solci's preface to the first edition.

A special word of thanks to Harry Foulds for his encouragement and invaluable aid during our extended research on this project. A. J. Cosimano also helped us in many ways. Thanks, A. J.

The gentle, soft-spoken, but gentlemanly Dr. Michael Modny helped us in a number of ways that were important to us, and for that we want to thank him.

To Silvano Piacentini of the Istituto Enologico Italiano, who opened some splendid bottles that increased our knowledge and appreciation of Italian wines.

Thanks also to Riccardo Riccardi, who provided us with valuable information and a chance to taste some lovely wines.

To Bud Simon, for his help in getting the first edition published. And we'd like to thank Charles Walther, the publisher of the first edition, who offered us helpful advice and suggestions that we feel contributed to making this a more interesting and valuable book.

A special thanks to Mario Cordero, who cheerfully offered his most valuable services and without whose help we would no doubt still be in Piemonte trying to finish the research on the first edition. To Angelo and Piero Solci, who gave us the opportunity to discover some remarkable Italian wines, and for their very valuable assistance in the office with our attempts to arrange and rearrange our *programma.*

To Claudia and Tonino Verro, who made the lovely La Contea available to us whenever we needed a place for an interview or a tasting in the area, as well as for all the too-good meals that gave us the strength to forge ahead and never let us forget the quality and dedication to be found in Italian wine and the people connected with it. And our thanks to Luigi Veronelli, for introducing us to some fine wines, and some fine producers.

Our agent, Jim Charlton, deserves a thanks for what he did for us.

Our copy editor, Charlotte Gross, deserves a mention for the first-rate job she did. She did much to improve our manuscript.

And last but not least, we'd like to thank our editor, Pam Hoenig, for her helpful suggestions, which did much to improve the second edition. Besides being a knowledgeable and able editor, she is a pleasure to work with.

And for all of those who provided assistance when we needed it, many lost in the cobwebs of time, we want to thank you even if we can't acknowledge you.

PREFACE

Writing a preface for my friends Pauline and Sheldon Wasserman is not an easy task. Many prefaces are done routinely with a description of the subject matter, but such is not possible in this case.

This book is very rich in content. The words and images deal with an area very important and meaningful to Italian agriculture and to the Italian economy. The Wassermans, with their customary professionalism and broad knowledge, have succeeded in putting together a complete and comprehensive treatise that will satisfy the most exacting epicurean. For these reasons, the book in itself has the ability to sustain any preface, thus relieving me somewhat of the responsibility of presenting it.

I will note, however, the feeling of panic that assailed me when I first read the Wassermans' notes, how left behind I felt, as a neophyte, at the unusual competence with which our Italian wines were not only described but also thoroughly understood by them from their thousands, nay millions, of serious and very professional tastings; they went even further, delving into an understanding of the people responsible for the history of the wine and the preservation of its tradition.

Alert and objective critics that they are, the Wassermans have understood the evolution that is taking place in Italian enology for the past decade, how Italian wine in this recent metamorphosis has graduated into a class that compares favorably with the wines of other countries touted for their great wines.

In our country two larger productive categories of wines have gradually emerged: The first is made up of the Great Wines, those that intimately satisfy us in their most praiseworthy sensations and that contain cultural, historical, and artistic aspects of immense interest. These are notably different and superior to the second category, daily table wines, whose main function is to satisfy a single need, that of quenching thirst.

It is this first category of wines that Pauline and Sheldon describe in great depth. Those who are familiar with this dedicated couple know that they write together, they write constantly; even at the table they continue to taste and record in minute detail every sensation, every label.

They never turn down a tasting, nor walk away from a discussion or debate on wine, nor do they bring with them any preconceived attitudes in the quest to satisfy their insatiable curiosity.

The frenetic pen of this couple has now spawned many books that deal with the worldwide panorama of wines, not to mention the numerous articles written for newspapers and magazines. This book is another journey among the wines of Italy, but it is not a simple catalog, nor a classification of one of those erudite solons who judge with pretensions of infallible taste to guide the unenlightened. Theirs are the intimate impressions of two civilized and refined people who share with us their wide experience.

Pauline and Sheldon travel throughout the Italian peninsula in search of our magnificent wines; they take us by the hand and initiate us into both an old and a new art form—that of recognizing, appreciating, and becoming a friend of the wines. The work makes very enjoyable reading and, in my opinion, can be more useful than many other publications, didactic and encyclopedic, in getting to the heart of the matter of wine. It can also be beneficial to those who would venture, with minimal ease, among the many names and labels, the most complicated indications of which are becoming ever more difficult for those in the modest search for a good glass of wine, and perhaps even in putting together a personal wine cellar, modest, but with the stamp of character and imagination.

Their story is always one that begins with the land and the places, with recollections of traditions and human events. This is indeed the preparation required to understand the various crus, the environment, the people and their way of life, the gastronomic customs and their proper matching with the wines.

I encourage you to read this book with confidence: you will learn many things of which you were previously unaware; but above all, you will learn to know and to love the good wine lying in the "religious" silence of your small *cantina*.

Angelo Solci
Milano, Italia
April 1985

PREFACE

to the Second Edition

Italy is the world's largest producer of wine, yet despite this impressive fact a mere fraction of our delightful offerings are understood and appreciated by consumers outside Italy. In the past Italian wines have been perceived as more or less limited to a mainstream triumvirate of tastes—Valpolicella, Bardolino, and Chianti. The reality, however, is that each of our twenty regions produces wines that are a distinctive merging of tradition with technology, wines equally, if not even more, worthy of attention and savoring.

For more than twenty years Pauline and Sheldon Wasserman have tasted Italy's wines as pioneers in opening the minds and palates of wine drinkers to the enjoyment and significance of our vineyards and producers. Without question their meticulous research and tastings have helped immeasurably in promoting a better understanding of Italian wines. Perhaps even more significantly, their work has been accomplished in the spirit of the wines themselves and of the Italian character, with openness, accessibility, and unself-consciousness. All too often self-proclaimed experts serve up their knowledge in a manner that intimidates and even excludes eager seekers of information. Luckily, this is not the case with the Wassermans, who are generous sharers of their information and experience.

I am not a traditionalist about wines, I believe you should always drink what you like, regardless of what anybody else says. Talking about wine is not all that dissimilar from talking about religion or politics—no two people agree. What is important is that you get to know what wines you like and then talk like an expert about them. In this book the Wassermans take a lot of mystery out of Italian wines, which is a very good thing. They explore in detail not only the wines themselves, but also the wineries and the men and women behind them.

A natural consequence of their in-depth descriptive information is the pairing of Italian wines with foods. After all, what we eat is the context in which wine can be enjoyed most fully. A brilliant red Donnaz from the nebbiolo, with its slightly dry, almost bitter flavor and raspberrylike bouquet, is a perfect companion for cheese-based dishes or a veal roast, try a young Merlot throughout a meal, or meditate over a bottle of Sassicaia by your favorite fireplace. Food and wine professionals will find that the information in this book will help them to compile their wine lists and make recommendations to their customers more intelligently, while nonprofessionals will receive a private education that will promote their own enjoyment and connoisseurship.

On a wine-tasting visit to France some years back, Luigi Veronelli, one of Italy's foremost gurus on wines, had a revelatory encounter with an old French winemaker. The two had attended a number of wine tastings together. Pulling Veronelli away at the conclusion of one tasting, the old man leaned forward and announced, "You know, you Italians have golden grapes but make silver wines. We French have silver grapes and make golden wine." This has changed. Today there is no question, Italians are producing golden wines. At long last our potential is finally being realized, recognized, and—most importantly of all—savored by consumers. With Sheldon and Pauline's meticulous explorations of our vineyards, you are about to discover how true it is that the wines of Italy are coming into their own.

Tony May
New York
March 1991

Italy's Noble Red Wines

INTRODUCTION

All the world's wines can be divided into two broad categories—wines *di personalità,* with personality, and wines *senza personalità,* which lack that quality.

The wines in the second category are beverage wines, pure and simple. They are meant to be drunk in drafts to quench thirst and to go with food, no more, no less. If they're well made, they serve their purpose well. They are not wines for contemplation or discussion. At their best, they are balanced, clean and fruity, simple, easy, and undemanding—*non impegnativo,* as they say. Italy, like all the other wine-producing countries of the world, has its fair share of these wines.

Italy also has many wines with personality and character.

A wine of personality tells you something about itself—its nature reflects the soil, the climate, and the grape variety it comes from, and perhaps even the hand of the winemaker who created it. The finer the wine, the more definite and complex its character, its personality, its style.

A NOBLE HERITAGE

Most of the world's fine wines have a noble heritage; they are from the favored regions, from vineyard sites capable of producing grapes of character, warm enough to ripen the grapes fully and cool enough to ripen them slowly, bringing out a panoply of nuances in aroma and flavor. The grape variety itself is often also of noble stock. The noble character of cabernet sauvignon and pinot noir, despite the fickle nature of the latter, has long been recognized by wine lovers; few have noted that Italy is the home of noble varieties as well, varieties capable of producing great

wines given an auspicious combination of nature and man.

The Italians have seldom spoken, or written, of their grape varieties as being noble. As high as the regard for some varieties may be among winemakers and *buongustaii,* they seem better at making, or at appreciating, their viticultural treasures than they are at spreading the word about them. We, as serious students of wine, with experience with wines from all over the world, propose to do that for them, in recognition of Italy's noble varieties and noble wines, which have too long gone unheralded. In appreciation also of the nobility of spirit of Italy's finest producers, we devote this book to their discovery.

Italy has at least three indigenous varieties capable of producing wines of breeding and character, noble varieties—the nebbiolo, sangiovese, and aglianico. We have given a section of this book to each of them.

To fully appreciate these wines, it is important to get a little background on them, to know some of their history, and something about the people who produce the wines, their methods in the vineyards and the cellars, and the winemaking philosophies of some of the best of them.

VINTAGE WINES

Vintages are also important; these fine wines are not wines that are turned out every year, one like the other. They are made from varieties sensitive to changes in each aspect of their environment. And interesting though it is to know how the vintages were regarded initially, it is even more important to know how the wines are now—should you buy, hold, drink, or dump them today?

We discuss both aspects and have asked many producers

to evaluate the vintages for their wines in particular, as different vineyards and microclimates can vary significantly. The character of the same variety varies not only from region to region but also from vineyard to vineyard. Knowing something about the specific crus also tells you something about the wines. The vineyards and crus can play a significant role in the character of the wines they engender.

In this regard it is interesting to note that the differences between the top vineyards and the lesser ones are more pronounced in the lesser years and less evident in the better years. In the better years the sun shines on all the sites and drainage is less important as rain is not a problem. But in the lesser vintages the advantage of the extra sun in those vineyards with better exposure helps the grapes to ripen more fully and the better drainage prevents the grapes from becoming diluted by heavy rains.

OUR RATING SYSTEM

In our evaluation of the vintages, we have used a rating system ranging from four stars to zero: outstanding, excellent, very good, good, average, poor. Brackets around a rating indicate a tentative judgment when we felt our experience was too limited to be more definite or that the vintage was too young to assess fully.

The style and the quality of the wine itself, how it will taste in the glass, is a matter of major importance. We have evaluated the wines of numerous producers in an effort to provide a useful picture of the wines for the wine drinker. Specifics are also helpful, such as actual tasting notes on the wines. As André Simon so aptly put it, "The only way to learn about wines is to taste them, and there is no substitute for pulling a cork."

Our tasting notes, for the most part, are fairly current. In some cases we have gone back as far as a decade. Beyond that we have very rarely included our *schede,* feeling that they are no longer relevant to the discussion of the wines. Although some of the notes we have included are out-of-date, they reflect a point about the wine, producer or vintage that we felt was worth making and so we included them. Whenever possible we have tasted a wine more than once, and although for the most part we give our most recent tasting note, we've relied on previous experiences in making our estimation on drinkability. Tasting notes give the names of the producer and vineyard, with the number of times tasted and date of the most recent tasting in parentheses, and the number of bottles made, when known, followed by the description and rating. In the case of a wine that offers promise of future development, we have given, in parentheses following the rating, the potential increase in the assessment of the wine given sufficient maturity. When its development was in doubt, that was indicated by a question

mark. Where we rated a wine **(*), for example, we felt it deserved ** for the present, but given time could, and probably would, merit ***. A rating of ** + (*** −)—note the space between the ** + and the (*** −)—indicates a ** + for now, with a projection of *** − for the future.

As example of the first, this Montepulciano d'Abruzzo:

Valentini 1985 (*4 times, 10/90, 4,152 bottles*). Deep ruby color; nose is still closed, hints of cherries and spice; sweet and rich, smooth, great mouth feel, already like velvet, some tannin to lose, long, lingering finish; real quality. And to think that less than 4,200 bottles were produced! ***(*)

As an example of the second, this Barbaresco:

Giacosa Bruno 1985 Santo Stefano Riserva (*5 times, 6/90*). A mélange of scents, including tobacco, *tartufi,* berries, flowers; great richness and sweetness; this wine has everything, yet it needs age, what then? Without question the star of the vintage. **** (**** +)

We use the same four-star system in evaluating individual wines and rating the producers.

WHAT THE RATINGS MEAN

****	Great, superb, truly noble
***	Exceptionally fine
**	Very good
*	A good example of its type, somewhat above average
0	Acceptable to mediocre, depending on the context; drinkable
+	Somewhat better than the star category it is put in
−	Somewhat less than the star category it is put in, except for zero where it indicates a wine or producer-wine combination that is badly made or worse
[. .]	*On a producer:* Tentative evaluation based on an insufficient number of wines or based on older, out-of-date vintages, or where the wines we tasted were too difficult to fully judge to give a fair assessment of quality
	On a wine or vintage: Projection for the future. This rating is given to a vintage where we feel that we tasted an insufficient number of wines or those we tasted were too difficult to really judge to give a fair assessment of quality
(. .)	Potential increase in the rating of the wine given sufficient maturity

The ratings of the *aziende,* or producers, are based on overall quality. One bottle from a given producer could merit four stars, while a second is worth only one; the rating for this producer will reflect both. The producers are evaluated for the particular type of wine under discussion—Barolo, Chianti, Cabernet, or whatever. A rating that is above that of the vintage counts positively for a producer, just as a lesser rating in an excellent or great vintage weighs more negatively in the overall rating. If the producer makes multiple kinds of wine and we rank only one, the quality of his other wines is not taken into consideration in that assessment. You should also remember that a three-star Nebbiolo is not equivalent to a three-star Barolo. The Barolo is a better wine, but the Nebbiolo is first-rate vis-à-vis Nebbiolo.

ALLEGRINI AZIENDA AGRICOLA *(Fumane di Valpolicella), 1886.* . . . *Amarone Classico:* ***, Fieramonte **** −; La Poja *vino da tavola* *** +; *Recioto Classico;* ** +, Gardane *** +; *Recioto Bianco* Fiorgardane *** +; *Valpolicella Classico Superiore:* ***, La Grola **** −, Palazzo della Torre ***; *Valpolicella Classico* Lena ***

MASTROJANNI (località *Castelnuovo Abate, zone 2), 1975.* . . . Brunello ***; Rosso di Montalcino ** +.

VIETTI CANTINA DI ALFREDO CURRADO *(Castiglione Falletto), 1960.* . . . *Barolo:* Castiglione ** +, Briacca **** +, Brunate ****, Bussia ****, Lazzarito **** +, Rocche **** +, Villero **** +, non-crus ** +; *Barbaresco:* Masseria *** +, Rabajà ****, non-crus **; *Nebbiolo* ***; *Fioretto* **

In evaluating the producers we relied on our notes about wines tasted since 1972, with the exception of a few rare cases. Where our impressions were based on older tasting notes, we point that out. In some cases we find that a producer's quality has changed. In that case we give him two ratings, one based on our evaluation of wines before a specified time and the other on wines produced since. In some cases the quality of the wines has improved; in others it has declined.

There is naturally a subjective element in tasting wine, but recognizing that, we've tried to be as fair as possible. Whenever there was a question in our minds, and in cases where our experience was limited, we gave the producer the benefit of the doubt, and opted for the higher category, up to three stars. On ratings of three stars or higher, however, we have been more conservative, and to give top marks (four stars) there could be no shadow of a doubt whatsoever in our minds. Any wine or producer awarded three stars or more was a clearcut three stars or more; a doubtful three stars got three stars minus or slightly less, two stars plus.

To be fair to those who will make use of these appraisals in selecting wines, we have been cautious. In cases where we have tasted only one or perhaps two vintages, or only a few unfinished wines from cask, even if the wines were quite impressive, we have hesitated to score the *azienda* overall as highly as the individual wine or wines. There is an exception to that rule. In cases when we have tasted one wine, but one from a great vintage, and that wine proved mediocre, we felt that the one example was sufficient proof of the producer's lack of ability or commitment, and he was scored down. Given one consideration and another, a critic's job is not an easy one.

ON TASTING WINES FROM BARREL: A CAVEAT

We have included our tasting notes on a number of wines that we've tasted from barrel, cask, vat, or *barrique.* It is important to keep in mind that our ratings on these wines are tentative because they are based on unfinished wines and, in some cases, on part of the finished product. It's not uncommon to taste a sample from one or two barrels that are eventually blended together with other barrels. The finished wine is often better than the sum of its parts. We try to project from the sample or samples that we taste based on our knowledge of the area and the producer, and, we might add, based on many years' experience tasting unfinished wine. Incidentally, we have a pretty good track record on this score, but by no means are we infallible.

Another danger in evaluating cask samples is that the wine could have recently been racked or is in need of racking. In either case it wouldn't be at its best. We try to compensate for an out-of-condition wine.

Additionally, as a wine matures in cask, tank, or barrel, its components come together, resulting in a more harmonious product. This is another danger in sampling unfinished wines. One has to learn how to project, from the components, the way the wine will mature and develop as it ages in cask. We have been tasting and evaluating wines from cask since the early 1970s, but even so we make mistakes. Everyone does, except a liar or pretender.

So why do we include tasting notes of unfinished wines? We feel that by including them we can still give you an idea of the wines that we tasted, and of a producer, and the quality of a vintage. *We urge you to read these notes with the utmost caution, though.*

HOW TO INTERPRET OUR TASTING NOTES

The tasting notes, most commonly, are grouped by vintage. In this case the vintage and rating are followed by factual information about the vintage—the weather and crop size, followed by an assessment of the quality of the vintage, first from the producers and then from us. The tasting notes for that vintage follow.

As for that tasting note itself, in the description of the wine, as a general rule, we first describe the color, if it is included; then the aroma; then the flavor, structure, and length (aftertaste); then general quality; and finally ageability. Sometimes the order of the last three components varies, depending on readability. The color and aroma are always first and second, if they appear. In all cases these characteristics are separated by semicolons, just as they are in this paragraph. If we find a discrepancy in the way a particular wine is developing, or among bottles, we include multiple tasting notes for that same wine.

Here are some examples:

EXAMPLE 1

Marcarini (Elvio Cogno), La Serra (*ex-cask, 11/90*). Intense berrylike aroma, nuances suggestive of a forest, raspberry component; great richness and sense of sweetness, a lot of concentration. ***(*)

The components of tasting note 1:

Producer:	**Marcarini (Elvio Cogno)**
Vineyard:	**La Serra**
Times tasted:	If no number given, once is implied
Tasted from:	Cask
Last tasted:	November 1990
Description of the wine	
Color:	Not included
Aroma:	Intense berrylike aroma, nuances suggestive of a forest, raspberry component
Flavor, structure, and length:	Great richness and sense of sweetness, a lot of concentration
General quality:	Implied by comments regarding flavor, structure, and length
Ageability:	Not included
Rating:	***(*)

EXAMPLE 2

Vietti, Rocche (*twice, ex-cask, 11/90*). This wine has everything, real class evident, great richness, concentration and extract, chewy and tannic; this one is for the long haul; most impressive. ****(+)

The components of tasting note 2:

Producer:	**Vietti**
Vineyard:	**Rocche**
Times tasted:	Twice
Tasted from:	Cask
Last tasted:	November 1990
Description of the wine	
Color:	Not included
Aroma:	Not included
Flavor, structure, and length:	This wine has everything, real class evident, great richness, concentration and extract, chewy and tannic
Ageability:	This one is for the long haul
General quality:	Most impressive
Rating:	****(+)

EXAMPLE 3

Barale F.lli, Vigna Castellero (*3 times, 11/90*). We tasted this wine on two different occasions in November 1990 with a surprising variation. *The first and best bottle:* Woodsy, tar and flowers, damp leaves; sense of sweetness, open and appealing fruit. ** — *The second bottle:* Seems older than its years, still it does have nice fruit, tasty, a little dry and firm at the end. * *Bottle of 4/90:* Aroma of nuts and vanilla, camphor and flowers; supple center under moderate tannin, chewy; really forward but could very well tighten up. **

Producer name:	**Barale F.lli**
Vineyard:	**Vigna Castellero**
Times tasted:	3 times
Tasted from:	Bottle implied
Last tasted:	November 1990
Which experience:	*The first and best bottle*
When tasted:	11/90
Description of the wine:	Woodsy, tar and flowers, damp leaves; sense of sweetness, open and appealing fruit
Rating:	** —
Which experience:	*The second bottle*
When tasted:	11/90
Description of the wine:	Seems older than its years, still it does have nice fruit, tasty, a little dry and firm at the end
Rating:	*
Which experience:	*Bottle of 4/90*
Description of the wine:	Aroma of nuts and vanilla, camphor and flowers; supple center under moderate tannin, chewy; really forward but could very well tighten up.
Rating:	**

EXAMPLE 4

Ferrero F.lli (twice, 11/90). Grapey, simple, light tannin, a little dry, very short, dull aftertaste. + *Ex-cask, 4/87:* Open, soft, forward, well balanced, nice fruit, precocious; should be ready early. **

The components of tasting note 4:

Producer:	**Ferrero F.lli**
Vineyard:	None
Times tasted:	Twice
Tasted from:	Bottle implied
Last tasted:	November 1990
Which experience:	Bottle tasted 11/90 implied
Description of the wine	
Color:	Not included
Aroma:	Not included
Flavor, structure, and length:	Grapey, simple, light tannin, a little dry, very short, dull aftertaste
Ageability:	Not included
General quality:	Implied by comments regarding flavor, structure, and length
Rating:	+
Which experience:	*From the cask, 4/87*
Description of the wine	
Color:	Not included
Aroma:	Not included
Flavor, structure, and length:	Open, soft, forward, well balanced, nice fruit, precocious
Ageability:	Should be ready early
General quality:	Implied by comments regarding flavor, structure, and length
Rating:	**

In some cases, where we have tasted a few wines only, we have included the vintage in the heading of the tasting note, instead of breaking the notes out into vintages, as in this Carema:

Ferrando Luigi 1982 black label (8 times, 5/89). Concentrated floral and fruit aroma; big and rich, tasty and open, good structure and balance; still young. ***(+)

The components of the tasting note:

Producer:	**Ferrando Luigi**
Vintage:	**1982**
Qualifier:	**black label**
Times tasted:	8 times
Tasted from:	Bottle implied
Last tasted:	May 1989
Description of the wine	
Color:	Not included
Aroma:	Concentrated floral and fruit aroma
Flavor, structure, and length:	Big and rich, tasty and open, good structure and balance
Ageability:	Still young
General quality:	Implied by comments regarding flavor, structure, and length
Rating:	***(+)

When the production was limited, and we knew the number of bottles produced, we specified that quantity, as in this example:

Valentini 1985 (4 times, 10/90, 4,152 bottles). Deep ruby color; nose is still closed, hints of cherries and spice; sweet and rich, smooth, great mouth feel, already like velvet, some tannin to lose, long, lingering finish; real quality. And to think that less than 4,200 bottles were produced! ***(*)

The components of this tasting note:

Producer name:	**Valentini**
Vintage:	**1985**
Times tasted:	4 times
Tasted from:	Bottle implied
Last tasted:	October 1990
Production:	4,152 bottles
Description of the wine	
Color:	Deep ruby color
Aroma:	Nose is still closed, hints of cherries and spice
Flavor, structure, and length:	Sweet and rich, smooth, great mouth feel, already like velvet, some tannin to lose, long, lingering finish
General quality:	Real quality. And to think that less than 4,200 bottles were produced!
Ageability:	Not included
Rating:	***(*)

OUR ROLE AS CRITICS

In our role as critics, we cannot be totally objective; taste is, after all, a subjective matter. In making a serious assessment, though, it is necessary to have a knowledge of the grape variety and experience with the wines. It is also essential to maintain a sense of fair play.

From some wines you expect more—the possibility is there. Others are more limited; it's not possible for them to rise above a certain level. But if they are honest, well-made wines, although we may not find them to our personal taste, we must admit that they are good for their type. Wines from some varieties—notably the better, and noble, varieties—have a recognizable character; if a wine displays this, it is a plus for the wine—in fact, if it doesn't, it is a fault. If it happens to be a character we personally don't care for, it's a wine not to drink, but not to score down for that reason.

In judging the producers we have considered wines, not personalities. Our opinions of the wines are admittedly affected by our personal tastes, but we cannot, and do not, let our personal reactions to the people color our opinions of their wines.

Although some of the finest producers have become our friends—it is always a pleasure to be in the company of people of integrity who care sincerely about quality—we have been, if anything, a bit more critical of their wines than we would have been otherwise, to offset the natural tendency to want to be generous with friends. And we have a few friends who produce wines that are merely ordinary—from grapes of regions from which excellence is not possible. We've rated their wines so, in person and in print, and they have never tried to influence our judgment. If their reaction had been otherwise, they wouldn't be friends.

In this regard it is perhaps worthwhile to relate three stories.

A few years ago we were introduced to a producer and his wife, a very nice couple whom we both enjoyed meeting. They invited us to come back, to spend an afternoon, come for lunch or dinner. We never did. We found their wine rather mediocre and would not have enjoyed being in the position of wanting to be nice to the people yet not being able to say anything nice about their wine, which they were hoping to hear good things about.

While researching a previous book, we visited a producer who was inhospitable, in fact, downright rude, so much so that we almost left before our interview. When our book was published both the producer and their importer bought a number of copies. They apparently felt that our judgment of their wines was fair.

On one last trip to Italy prior to completing the first edition of this book we visited more than four dozen producers in four weeks, which included nearly one week for the Vinitaly Wine Fair, and tasted over 1,400 wines. Needless to say, upon our return we were rather beat. A few days after we got home the Italian Wine Center invited us to a tasting. We were familiar with all the producers represented, but we went. We had given three producers represented at that tasting zero marks, and we wanted to give them one more chance to be upgraded if possible.

We emphasize that our ratings are our own personal judg-

ments, and we recognize that personal tastes vary; you may agree with us or you may not, but we have tried to be as fair as possible. We have noted our preferences and partialities—for firm acidity and tannin, richness, elegance, personality, etc., which will give you, our readers, a better idea of our standards.

We evaluate wines also for interest, but basically for those aspects of wine judging that can be considered standards for any good, well-made wine—balance, soundness, absence of off-odors or flavors, varietal character, etc.

IT'S JUST A MATTER OF TASTE
OR
THE OBJECTIVE REASONS TASTES ARE SUBJECTIVE

Tastes are subjective, and for at least one objective reason. We all have different palates and different thresholds to all sensory data. Some of us are very sensitive to acidity, others to sugar. A person with a lower threshold to acidity will be unwilling, in most cases, to tolerate a higher level of acidity. One of us (Sheldon) is rather insensitive to carbon dioxide (CO_2) but very sensitive to sulfur dioxide (SO_2). A wine that some find "off" because of the slight spritz from the CO_2 is not off to him, but he finds the slightest amount of SO_2 unpleasant. You cannot take a wine in a lab, analyze it, and conclude that it is unbalanced or well balanced. That is a subjective fact according to our own thresholds. Experience can help you understand the typicity of a wine. But whether it is enjoyable or not is simply a matter of taste. Drink what you like and with what you like it. Remember that there are objective facts of reality but not objective rules of taste. And wine is, or should be, a sensual pleasure. So enjoy!

AN INTERNATIONAL CHARACTER

On a slightly different note, we are of the opinion that it's a pity more and more of the wines produced in the world today are beginning to take on a sameness of character, perhaps becoming more international, but in the process losing their individuality. The trend for producing wines for early drinking, for blending in some cabernet sauvignon, and for aging in *barriques* seems unfortunately to be spreading.

While we love Bordeaux, Burgundy, and Champagne, California Cabernet and Chardonnay, New York State Riesling, Sereksia, and Pinot Gris, Port, German Auslesen, and many other of the world's fine wines, we don't want one wine to taste like another. Tuscan wines should taste like Tuscan wines, and not like imitation California; Piemontese wines should have the character of Piemontese wines, not be copycat Bordeaux.

ANOTHER TROUBLESOME TREND

There is a growing trend to bottle wines from single vineyards. And this trend seems to be growing in areas like the Chianti Classico zone, Montalcino, and Montepulciano. While it makes sense in a wine district like Barolo or Barbaresco, it makes much less sense in Chianti or Montalcino. The Langhe, where Barolo and Barbaresco come from, consists of a number of wine-growing communes with many small vineyards divided, in most cases, by multiple owners. And many, if not most owners have parcels in several vineyards. These vineyards vary from one village to the next, indeed from one slope to the next. It makes sense to keep them separately. The Chianti Classico district, on the other hand, generally consists of large estates owned by a single proprietor and located in a single commune. It seems more reasonable to produce a wine that represents that estate instead of multiple wines that reflect a small part of the estate. Barolo and Barbaresco are, in some ways, like Burgundy, Chianti Classico and Montalcino like Bordeaux. We know of one estate that produces five Chianti Classicos— four single vineyards—and no less than three *vini da tavola*. That is eight red wines. And there are others whose output, in numbers of wine, exceeds that number!

OUR ROLE AS JOURNALISTS

We spent thirteen years researching the first edition of *Italy's Noble Red Wines,* and an additional five to keep our information up-to-date for a revision—this makes a total of nearly two decades. In that time we have made many trips to Italy and have spent many hours talking with producers, tasting wines, and making copious notes. We have checked and rechecked our facts and figures. And when we began writing the book in earnest, in 1984, we designed a questionnaire to get more, and hopefully more accurate, information from people and to ensure that our information was as up-to-date as possible.

We have a profound respect for facts and have made every possible effort to ensure that the least possible margin of error could creep in. We realize that some of our information differs from that which has been published previously, even recently, so we feel that it is worth pointing out that except for history, and where we cite the source of certain information, all of our material is based on first-hand sources.

Producers sometimes gave different figures when asked the same questions more than once, and figures change. To the best of our ability, however, we have been as accurate as possible and turned to the most verifiable, reliable sources for our information.

THE COMPONENTS OF AN ITALIAN WINE LABEL

1. Consortium (*consorzio*) seal: This seal, generally found on the bottle's neck, indicates that the producer belongs to a growers' or producers' consortium. This voluntary association sets qualitative standards that have to be met in order for the wine to carry the seal.

2. Vintage: This tells you the year in which the grapes were harvested. It is an indication of quality as well as age. Frequently the word *annata,* meaning year, appears on the label (as in this example).

3. Wine name: Italian wines are labeled with (a) a geographical name, (b) a combination of grape name and location, or (c) a proprietary or fantasy name.

A *geographical name* is found most often on a wine of quality. This name can be any viticultural area, region, province, zone, village, and/or single vineyard or estate. Frequently, the smaller and more delimited the location the better, or at least the more individual the wine. This information will appear on all, or nearly all, high quality wines. Some examples: del Piemonte, delle Langhe, Chianti Colli Senesi, Colli Berici, Barolo, Barbaresco Santo Stefano, Ornellaia, or Torre Quarto.

Single vineyards are often preceded by a word such as *località, vigna,* or *vigneto.* Other terms that are related to a vineyard are *bric, bricco, capitel, cascina, ciabot, costa,* and *sorì* (see the glossary for definitions). *Vigneti* refers to more than one vineyard.

Oftentimes a geographical name will be combined with a grape name, as in Nebbiolo d'Alba. A *combination grape and location name* generally comes in three parts: (a) the grape variety, (b) the word "of" in the form of *d', dell', della, delle,* or *di,* and (c) the location, as in Brunello di Montalcino, Montepulciano d'Abruzzo, Nebbiolo delle Langhe, Barbera d'Alba, or Cabernet dell'Alto Adige. The "of" always begins with a "d" as in these examples. The most common exceptions to this type of name is the white, red, or rosé of a geographical location such as Bianco di Custoza or Rosso di Montepulciano. Sometimes a name of this type will appear without the "of" and with the grape name as the second part, as in Breganze Cabernet. In general the grape name will be recognizable. In nearly all cases the wine name will be either geographical or a combination of grape and location.

And finally we come to the *proprietary or fantasy name.* These names can take a variety of forms and in general, unless you know the wine or read Italian, they can be difficult to pick out. There are, however, very few of them. Four examples—Corvo (crow), Est! Est!! Est!!! di Montefiascone (It is! It is!! It is!!! of Montefiascone), Lacryma Christi del Vesuvo (the tears of Christ of Vesuvio), and Rosso della Quercia (the red of the oak).

4. Qualifier: This refers to (1) a more delimited part of a geographical zone, such as *classico* or *superiore* (as in the case of Sangiovese di Romagna), (2) something about the way the wine tastes: *secco* (dry) or *amabile* (sweet), or (3) it specifies that the wine was aged longer and/or has more alcohol than the *normale* for the wine, for example, *riserva* or *vecchio.* Other qualifiers include: *abboccato, bianco, cerasuolo, chiaretto, dolce, invecchiato, liquoroso, passito, riserva numerata, riserva speciale, rosato, rosso, rubino, stravecchio* and *vino novello.* (For a definition of these terms and other terms, see the glossary.) Or the label might indicate that it is a limited bottling as in our example: Delle 6020 Bottiglie guesta E' La N° 3980, meaning, of 6,020 bottles this is number 3,980.

5. Name and address of the producer or the marketing firm. Unless you know something about that producer or firm, this only tells you who they are and where they are located. It doesn't tell you a thing about the wine's quality. Sometimes the label tells you who bottled the wine. Our example specifies *imbottigliato da* Vietti Castiglione Falletto Italia. This translates to "bottled by Vietti in Castiglione Falletto, Italy."

Terms relating to the maker-bottler (see glossary for definitions)

az. agr.	*castello*
azienda	*cooperativa*
azienda agricola	*eredi*
azienda vinicola	*fattoria*
az. vin.	*fattorie*
azienda vitivinicola	*f.lli*
az. vit.	*fratelli*
cantina	*imbottigliato da*
cantina sociale	*podere*
cantine	*poderi*
casa	*schloss*
casa vinicola	*tenuta*
cascina	*tenute*
castel	*vignaiolo*

6. Legal category of the wine: Italian wine and grape production are regulated by law. There are four categories of Italian wine—in decreasing amount of regulations (a) wines with a *denominazione di origine controllata,* (b) *vini tipici,* (c) *vino da tavola con indicazione geografica,* and (d) *vino da tavola.*

Wines with a *denominazione di origine controllata* (DOC)— wines that have their origins denominated and controlled— are regulated from the vineyard to the bottle. Regulations govern both the viticultural and vinicultural practices. They specify the allowable grape varieties, and sometimes even the percentages that are permitted, the pruning and yield, and the ripeness of the grapes when harvested, as well as the required aging and type of cooperage to be used, as well as the degree of alcohol, acidity, and dry extract required in the finished wine. The DOC regulations for a particular wine include an organoleptic description as to its color, aroma, and flavor. The wine, to be accepted for the DOC, is subjected to a chemical analysis. And finally, as of 1990, a tasting commission must pass on the wine as well.

There are a handful of wines (nine at the time of this writing) that are subject to even more stringent requirements: these wines have been recognized as *denominazione di origine controllata e garantita* (DOCG). This means that the wine is guaranteed as to its authenticity, but not to its quality. Only a producer can guarantee the quality.

Since the first Italian growing zone came under the DOC

regulations in 1966, the number of regulated growing districts has climbed to more than 230 DOC zones. These zones encompass well over 800 different wines, but only 10 to 12 percent of the country's vast vinicultural output.

The next step below DOC are the *vini tipici,* or wines that have a typical character, not necessarily a historical one. This category was created in 1990. As of this writing we know of no wines that fall into this category.

A number of these wines fall into the superpremium or signature category. They often carry a hefty price and come in a fancy bottle, and not infrequently are of a very high quality as well. This includes Tignanello, Ornellaia, Le Pergole Torte, Coltasala, and Bricco dell'Uccellone.

The next category, *vino da tavola con indicazione geografica,* applies to table wines with an indicated geographical location. The label may specify the vintage and grape variety. The lowest category, *vino da tavola,* may not specify the vintage, variety, or location. The vast majority of these wines are *senza* (without) *personalità.*

As for the wines discussed in this book, many of them have a DOC and many of them do not. Those that don't do specify their geographical origins.

7. Country of origin: Self-explanatory. In the case of the wines discussed herein it will be Italy or Italia.

8. Contents: The quantity of wine in the bottle: 750 centiliters is the most common bottle size.

9. Alcoholic content: United States law allows a leeway of 1.5 percent. That means that a wine labeled as 12.5 percent by volume can be anywhere between 11 and 14 percent, while one labeled "table wine" must be 14 percent or less.

ON QUALITY

While government wine regulations are supposed to guarantee the authenticity of a wine as to its origins and makeup, only a producer can guarantee the quality. If the wine is bad, it's his or her reputation that will suffer. Following the producer's name we would look to the zone and the vintage. If you know the maker, the type of wine, and the year it was born, you know enough to judge the chances of its being good. If it's a Barolo from the likes of Bartolo Mascarello, Bruno Giacosa, Podere Marcarini, or Vietti from a mediocre vintage, you stand a good chance of getting a good wine. If it's a Luigi Cauda, Kiola, or Villadoria from a great vintage, the odds are stacked against you.

What can you do, in the absence of knowing the producer or the wine? In our experience the most reliable guide to quality after the producer name is the guarantee of a voluntary growers' organization founded in 1978—*Associazione Vitivinicoltori Italiani d'Eccellenza.* This organization uses the VIDE (*vitivinicoltori Italiani d'eccellenza*) symbol to promote the wines of its members. VIDE has strict regulations regarding the wines that may display their neck symbol on a bottle. To begin with, the wine must be estate bottled. That is, the estate that produced and bottled the wine had to grow the grapes. Following a chemical analysis the wines must be accepted by a tasting committee. This committee, consisting of five tasters, has no incentive to pass on a wine. A member is obliged to pay his share, based on the amount of his or her production, regardless of whether his wine is accepted or rejected. This, of course, encourages members to be more selective in submitting a wine. All five tasters must find the wine at least good in all fourteen categories that they judge the wine on. If one taster rates a wine less than good in any criterion, the wine is not passed. (The VIDE members are listed in Appendix D.)

A SALUTE TO QUALITY

We believe in quality regardless of the source, which is one of the reasons we wrote this book—to give you, our readers, a greater familiarity and, hopefully, more of an appreciation for the great red wines of Italy, wines that deserve more recognition. Charles Gizelt, one of the first people we met who really cared about Italian wine, used to say, "Great wine knows no borders." He was right. We believe that in the future Italy's great wines will be rated on a par with the other great wines of the world, recognized for the excellence that they represent.

We personally would like to salute those producers who have given their best efforts and never cut corners in their attempts to turn out the finest wines possible, although the fruit of their labors may have often gone unnoticed and unappreciated by the vast majority of wine drinkers, and even wine writers. They have supplied us not only with the material to write this book, but the inspiration to do so as well.

Sheldon and Pauline Wasserman
Piscataway, New Jersey
December 1990

PART ONE

Nebbiolo

CHAPTER 1

Nebbiolo

The early history of the vine in northwestern Italy is lost in the mists of time. When the Greeks arrived in the fifth century B.C., wild vines are believed to have been growing there. The newcomers, though, brought their own vine cuttings as well as their own wine, which was much appreciated by the Liguri Rossi who inhabited the area. They learned from the Greeks how to cultivate the vine, training the plants low to the ground like small bushes and pruning them to concentrate the vine's strength into fewer grape bunches, yielding riper, more concentrated fruit, to produce a sweeter, more alcoholic beverage than the thin wine obtained from their own unpruned vines.

After the Roman conquest in the second century B.C., viticulture and winemaking practices experienced a new influence. The vines were now trained in the Etruscan manner, high on trees or tall poles. The Romans built cellars below ground and into the hills to store the wine. Originally the wine was stored in *amphorae* (earthenware jars) as it was in the south, but they also made use of the wooden casks produced in the region, which seem to have been a Celtic invention.

Pliny noted in his *Natural History* that good wines were produced in the area of Alba and Pollentia, west of Alba near the Tanaro River (now Pollenzo). The fame of the wine of Pollentia spread at least as far as central Italy; *amphorae* stamped with that name have been unearthed in Rome and the region of Romagna.

In his writing of the wines of this region Pliny made note of a vine that he called allobrogica, a late-ripening and cold-resistant black grape. This describes the nebbiolo, a variety that buds early and ripens late, the harvest taking place when the valleys are filled with morning mist, *nebbia,* from which the vine takes the name that it is most commonly known by today. Earlier it was referred to as *Vitis vinifera pedemontana,* later nubiolum.

Renato Ratti, who did extensive research on the wines of the Piemonte, and the nebbiolo in particular, noted references to the "nibiol" in documents from the 1200s.[1] In his *Chronicles,* Oggerio Alfieri recorded that the nebbiolo was being cultivated in 1268 in the area around Rivoli in Piemonte. In 1340 the vine was praised by Pier di'Crescenzi, who referred to the "nubiola" vine in his *Ruralium Commodorum,* describing it as a "marvellously vinous" variety that "makes an excellent wine, very strong, and one to keep."

It was then, as it is now, a highly regarded variety. In 1511, in the local statutes of La Morra, the nebbiolo is referred to as a precious variety, one to be particularly protected. Giovan Battista Croce, court jeweler to Vittorio Emanuele I and a knowledgeable amateur viticulturist who wrote a treatise on the subject, considered the nebbiolo the "queen of the black grapes." Its wines were much appreciated by the House of Savoy. It wasn't long after they had

added Piemonte to their domains that they sent for these wines for the court. Records show that in 1631 they received 6 *carra* (132-gallon/500-liter casks) of the best Barolo. Such was their esteem that the dukes of Savoy sent a shipment of Barolo to Louis XIV of France, reputed to be a lover of the wines of Burgundy and Champagne. The Marquis of St. Maurice recorded that the king, and his prime minister, Colbert, were both favorably impressed with the wine, pronouncing it "excellent."

In Milano, Gattinara wine was much appreciated at the court of the dukes of Sforza.

In the early 1700s the nebbiolo wines of Piemonte were discovered by English merchants seeking an alternative to the wines of Bordeaux, England being involved in a war with France at the time. Old records show that they ordered

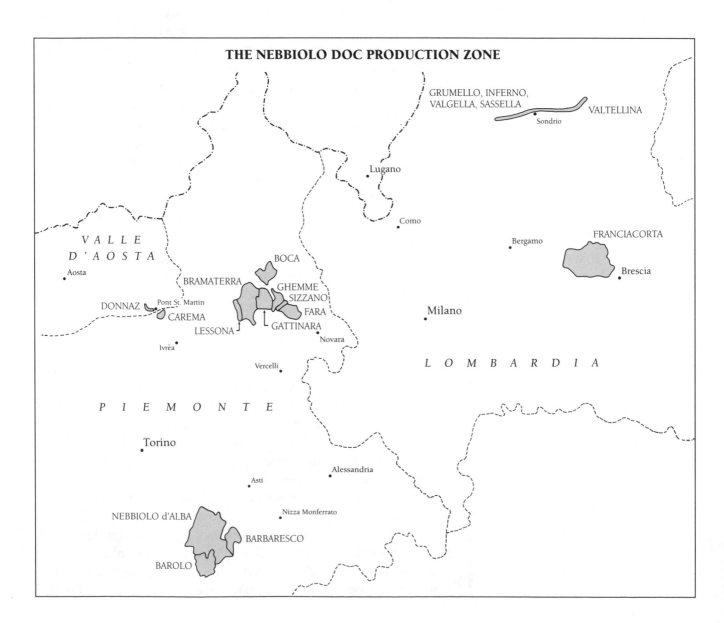

THE NEBBIOLO DOC PRODUCTION ZONE

the wines of Barolo and Gattinara, but the problems of transportation proved insurmountable and the trade was lost. The tariffs levied by the Genovese republic on such shipments were exorbitant, and the sole Piemontese port, Nizza, could be reached only via tortuous mountain tracks impassable by oxcarts laden with the ponderous casks of wine. As a result, the wine was basically unknown outside its own region.

During the struggle for domination of northern Italy, Piemontese wine was singled out for recognition by the Austrian general Melas (remembered best by opera lovers for the splendid opportunity he provides for the tenor in *Tosca* to hit a dramatic high note in a triumphant cry of *"Vittoria! vittoria!"*). Melas ordered supplies of "nebbiolo of Barbaresco" to celebrate a victory over the French in 1799.

Barolo was also accorded recognition by a man of peace when Monsignor Chiaramonti (later Pope Pius VII) visited the Abbazia dell'Annunziata at La Morra in the early nineteenth century. The prelate is reported to have been so impressed with the wine of the abbey that he asked to be supplied with some bottles on an annual basis.

BAROLO AND MARCHESI FALLETTI DI BAROLO

The most important assist to the recognition of Barolo came from the efforts of the Marchesi Falletti di Barolo. According to the famous story, Marchesa Giulia Vittorina Colbert Falletti di Barolo responded to a comment from Carlo Alberto of Savoy, who had expressed an interest in tasting the wines of Barolo by dispatching a train of oxcarts transporting 300 *carra* (39,625 gallons/1,500 hectoliters) of Barolo from the Falletti vineyards in Barolo and Serralunga.

The duke was duly impressed, so much so that he purchased a hunting lodge at Verduno as well and a *cantina* at Pollenzo where he installed the best enologist of the day, General Stangone, to oversee the vineyards and the winemaking on the estate. His son and successor, Vittorio Emanuele II, also bought vineyard property in the zone, at Fontanafredda.

The Marchesa Falletti also deserves credit for changing Barolo, in about 1840, into the dry wine that it is today. A Frenchwoman herself, she brought in enologist Count Oudart of Reims to make the Falletti wines. Previously the wines of the Langhe—and most other viticultural regions—had always contained some residual sugar left from the fermentation. In the 1800s tastes were beginning to change in Europe, and dry wines, first produced in Bordeaux in 1805, began to gain favor over the sweet or semisweet styles that had been preferred previously.

At Castello di Grinzane, Italy's future prime minister, Conte de Cavour, a cousin of the *marchesa,* ran a model farm where he planted experimental vineyards and made a serious study of agriculture. Count Oudart introduced new vinification methods as well as innovations in the vineyards which were considered the most advanced in the Langhe. Cavour worked in collaboration with the Marchesa di Falletti and Oudart to improve the quality of the wine of the zone and to develop the new dry style.

According to Renato Ratti, Barolo was the first wine of the Langhe to be produced as a completely dry wine, followed by Barbaresco, Dolcetto, Barbera, Grignolino, Bonarda, the white Erbaluce and Cortese, Gattinara, Carema, Boca, Sizzano, and finally, over a century later, in the 1950s, Nebbiolo d'Alba. Passito di Caluso, of course, and Asti remained sweet.

In 1873, at the International Exposition of Vienna, the Piemontese wines won eleven medals—seven of them for Barolo—and some praise from foreign experts. Henry Vizetelly, an English journalist, wrote that

Italy, with all its natural advantages, has not yet learned how to produce a truly fine dry wine[,] [w]ith the exception of a limited number of special quality, like the Barolo of Piemonte. . . .

DOMIZIO CAVAZZA AND THE EMERGENCE OF BARBARESCO

The reputation of Barbaresco seems to have always been in the shadow of Barolo. In fact, it wasn't until the late nineteenth century that Barbaresco was sold under that name, previously being known simply as Nebbiolo, or Nebbiolo di Barbaresco.

At Barbaresco, enologist and professor Domizio Cavazza, who was to be the first director of the vinicultural school founded at Alba in 1881, worked on improving the quality and reputation of the nebbiolos of that zone. It was he who turned Barbaresco into a dry wine, suitable for aging. Vinifiers at Alba who bought grapes from the zone followed his example first, before the small growers of Barbaresco, who generally didn't vinify their own wines. Wineries at Bra made most of the Barolo in the zone.

Cavazza founded the first *cantina sociale,* or cooperative winery, in the Langhe, in about 1894. In the cellars of the castle of Barbaresco he aided the members in improving their wines. Today there are 19,000 producers in the Piemonte who belong to 75 cooperative cellars, or *cantina sociale.*

THE VINEYARDS OF PIEMONTE

The vineyards in this area tended to be very small and fragmented among many small growers, who also had to have land for grain and other produce for their families and their livestock to live on. The vine wasn't a specialized culture, rather only a part of the agriculture of the farmers in Piemonte, a situation that existed until this century in some areas.

Even today it is a region of small farms. Of the 130,000 farms in Piemonte today, 110,000 consist of less than 2.5 acres (1 hectare). There are still many small growers in the region, and many sell their grapes, or sell their wine *sfuso,* (in bulk) to wineries that bottle it under their own labels.

Although there was some recognition, especially for Barolo, the wines of the region were not well known or available outside their own area. When more markets opened up for the wines, vine culture became more specialized. The best varieties for making fine dry wine were given greater importance and those for lightly sweet red, *frizzante* (slightly sparkling) wines such as Freisa and Brachetto became less important. Planting an *uvaggio,* or mix of grape varieties, in a single vineyard was also phased out, though there are still a few left, like the Fioretto vineyard of Vietti in the Scarrone district. As a vineyard required replanting, the grower put in vines all of the same variety.

The Regia Scuola Enologica at Alba recommended the Guyot system of training the vines on wires for dry red wines and the moscato for Asti. This method, which replaced the earlier Roman and Etruscan systems, is used throughout the region today. (In the Etruscan system the vines were trained to grow up trees, while the Romans pruned them to grow like little bushes.)

Different grape varieties are grown on the same hillside, but the nebbiolo is generally planted on the slopes with a southern exposure and at the top of the hill, where it gets more sun and where frost and dampness are less of a prob-lem. On the lower slopes, dolcetto, barbera, and the white grapes that can be less ripe are cultivated.

The climate in this region is temperate—fairly warm in summer, humid and cold in autumn. In the Langhe in the fall, the leaves of the various grape varieties form a colorful patchwork on the hillsides—the deep bluish purple of the dolcetto, the gold of the moscato, the rich red of the neb-biolo.

Ninety percent of the vines in the Piemonte are concentrated in the hilly regions of Cuneo, Asti, and Alessandria. The nebbiolo has pride of place among grape varieties, but the others are much more common. By far the most widely planted is barbera, with 51.5 percent of the total acreage under vines. Next is dolcetto with 14.2 percent, followed by moscato at 11.1 percent. Nebbiolo accounts for 5 percent, freisa with 3.9, followed by the white cortese and grignolino and then a number of other varieties.[2] Of the 125 million gallons (4.74 million hectoliters) of wine produced in the Piemonte annually, nebbiolo accounts for about 3.5 million (178,000).

Table wine makes up 34.1 percent of the total Piemontese output, with the 43 DOC and DOCG wines accounting for 33.6 percent and wines with a geographical indication the remaining 32.3 percent.[3]

The nebbiolo is also grown in Lombardia and in the Valtellina, as well as in parts of the Oltrepò Pavese and Franciacorta, where it is blended with other varieties. There are small amounts planted in Liguria and Umbria as well as the islands of Sicilia and Sardegna. Recently the nebbiolo has even migrated to Toscana where Giovannella Stianti Mascheroni planted it at her fine Castello di Volpaia estate in the Chianti Classico district. And plantings seem to be on the increase in California as well.

WINE GRAPES—CULTIVATED AREA AND PRODUCTION

Province	Cultivated Area (Hectares)			Grape Production (x 100 kilograms)	
	Not in Production	In Production	Total	per Producing Hectare	Total
Alessandria	882	21,043	21,925	80.33	1,690,306
Asti	272	22,205	22,477	93.92	2,085,405
Cuneo	530	17,220	17,750	81.52	1,403,700
Novara	15	1,384	1,399	69.92	96,766
Torino	13	5,107	5,120	77.66	396,615
Vercelli	21	1,193	1,214	72.09	86,000
Total	1,733	68,152	69,885	84.50	5,758,792

GRAPE AND WINE PRODUCTION

Province	Grapes Used in Wine Production (x 100 kg)	Wine Production — Wine Produced per 100 Kilograms of Grapes	Total Wine Production (Hectoliters)
Alessandria	1,689,706	70%	1,182,794
Asti	2,085,405	70%	1,459,780
Cuneo	1,398,000	73%	1,020,540
Novara	96,766	70%	67,736
Torino	391,115	73%	285,514
Vercelli	85,800	69%	59,200
Total	5,746,792	70.92%	4,075,565

Source: Piemonte appunti sul vino e dintorni (*Torino: Regione Piemonte, Assessorato Agricoltura e Foreste, October 1989*)

ACREAGE AND PRODUCTION BY GROWING AREA

Growing Area	Total Hectares	DOC Hectares	Total Hectoliters	DOC Hectoliters
Alto Monferrato[a]	12,000	4,462	901,000	301,000
Canavese and Carema[b]	1,500	87	111,000	5,900
Colli Novarese and Vercelli[b]	1,485	309	108,000	20,000
Colli Torinesi[c]	818	94	49,340	6,340
Colli Tortonesi[d]	4,080	653	301,000	44,000
Langhe[b]	14,182	9,182	989,000	620,000
Monferrato Astigiano[e]	24,000	n/a	1,730,000	631,000
Monferrato Casalese[f]	6,590	1,421	387,000	96,000
Roero[b]	3,870	1,335	280,000	90,000
Total	68,525	17,543	4,856,340	1,814,240

NOTES: [a] The 59 *comuni* around the centers of Acqui Terme and Ovada are located in the southern part of the province of Alessandria.
[b] This district is an important nebbiolo production zone and is covered in chapters 2, 3, or 4.
[c] This district, in the province of Alessandria, covering 30 villages, borders on the Oltrepò Pavese zone of Lombardia.
[d] This district, regarded for freisa, encompasses 12 *comuni* in the province of Torino.
[e] This district includes all of the *comuni* in the province of Asti.
[f] This district includes 49 *comuni* around Casalese in the east-central part of Piemonte, north of Alessandria.

Source: Piemonte appunti sul vino e dintorni (*Torino: Regione Piemonte, Assessorato Agricoltura e Foreste, October 1989*)

GROWING CONDITIONS

The nebbiolo is a very demanding grape variety, requiring good drainage and a sunny exposure. Soil is another important consideration. The nebbiolo fares best when planted in calcerous marly soil with admixtures of sand that is low in alkalinity and high in phosphorus, potassium, and magnesium. It is relatively resistant to frost, dampness, and fog. Nebbiolo is the earliest variety in the region to bud and the last to ripen. It requires a lot of care and is a shy bearer, but it produces fruit of excellent quality. The nebbiolo grapes are generally harvested in mid-October or later.

In the Middle Ages the date of the harvest was regulated by the local authorities, who set the opening day of the harvest, announced in the *bando della vendemmia,* a regulation that none dared anticipate. This rule remained in effect until the first years of the twentieth century, and the tradition continued to be followed in some of the more remote areas up until the 1950s, although the rule was no longer enforced.

WINE PRODUCTION BY COLOR

Color	Hectoliters	DOC/DOCG	Vini da tavola	Vini da tavola indic. geografica
Red	2,353,379	583,668	1,098,190	671,521
Rosé	50,110	0	19,027	31,083
White	894,471	610,011*	173,484	110,976
Total	3,297,960	1,193,679	1,290,701	813,580

* Asti Spumante and Moscato d'Asti totaled 554,220 hectoliters.

Source: Piemonte di Vino in Vino, I Segreti di Una Regione D.O.C. (Torino: Regione Piemonte, April 1990)

NEBBIOLO AND ITS SUBVARIETIES

In the various regions where the nebbiolo is grown it has different local names. In Aosta and Torino, it's picotener or pugnet; in Novara-Nercelli, it's called spanna; in the Valtellina, it is known as chiavennasca; in the Langhe-Monferrato, it is the nebbiolo. And then there are its subvarieties, or clones.

The nebbiolo is very sensitive to variations in soil and microclimates, and it clones relatively easily. The cobianco and corosso of Ghemme are believed to be clones of the nebbiolo, as is the prunent of Valvigezzo. In the Langhe there are a number of nebbiolo clones.

Three are accepted in the officially recognized DOC (*Denominazione di Origine Controllata*) for Barolo and Barbaresco wines. Michet, or micot in Piemontese dialect, so named for its small, compact form, which is likened to a small loaf of bread, is the most esteemed subvariety. It produces a small quantity of high-quality fruit, but fares best only in those areas with the most favorable soils and microclimates.

Lampia has longer, more loosely composed clusters. This is said to be the most widely planted subvariety. It has a greater production of consistent quality. Its wines are noted for their elegance and perfume.

There is very little of the rosé subvariety planted. This nebbiolo is similar in appearance to michet, but generally produces a wine with less color and less body than the other two. The Vietti Barolo from the Bricca vineyard (100 percent rosé) and the Barbaresco from Pajorè in Treiso, including the mighty Podere de Pajorè of Giovannini-Moresco, would seem to contradict this opinion. But it may be a vine that must be especially well suited to a particular site to produce its best-quality—in these cases, superb—fruit. (And, of course, in the hands of a talented winemaker. . . .)

Besides these three, there are other less esteemed offshoots, including bolla, rossi, and san luigi.

Recently, we were told by Angelo Gaja, who is doing clonal research on the nebbiolo, that there are almost no plantings of pure michet, lampia, or rosé. It's difficult to find purity and none of these three are found in pure form. What exists are clones of the clones. And, in fact, more than twenty clones have been identified. Still, many growers continue to refer to their plantings of lampia or michet. We are inclined to accept Gaja's view. This point of view is also shared by Roberto Macaluso, who did, or is still doing, clonal experiments at Alba. Further, everyone admits that the nebbiolo is more susceptible to cloning than most varieties. If that is the case, then the lampia and michet subvarieties, for example, are just as susceptible to changing, according to environmental influences.

In the province of Torino and the neighboring region of Valle d'Aosta, nebbiolo wines are produced from three local varieties—nebbiolo spanna, picotener, and pugnet.

The names differ, and the appearance of the vines varies, but the wines are all recognizable as coming from the nebbiolo grape, which is the hallmark of a noble variety. It has a unique, recognizable character, which subtle variations in the wines do not obscure.

THE NEBBIOLO WINES

The nebbiolo is a noble grape variety, its vines producing some of the finest wines of Italy, wines that rank among the world's greats.

They are deeply colored, robust wines, high in tannin and hard, even harsh, in their youth. Their deep ruby color turns to garnet, taking on a brickish hue with maturity which shades to orange and then to onionskin. The youthful aroma of cherries takes on a floral aspect, hinting of violets or roses, and with age developing a complexity of nuances—tobacco, licorice, camphor, *tartufi* (the white truffles of Piemonte), and a particularly characteristic note of *goudron,* or tar.

THE DOC AND DOCG WINES OF PIEMONTE

Piemonte has a wide range of DOCs. Most of the producers that we cover produce more than one wine, and from more than one grape variety. And in each of the nebbiolo growing zones other grape varieties are planted, sometimes in the same vineyard, albeit on a different part of the hillside. To help you better understand the different varieties and the wines they produce, we have included a couple of tables. The first one covers the different DOCs by grape variety or wine type, and the second lists the DOCs by wine-growing district.

BY VARIETY OR TYPE

Barbera

Barbera Colli Tortonesi	Barbera del Monferrato
Barbera d'Alba	Gabiano
Barbera d'Asti	Rubino di Cantavenna

Dolcetto

Dolcetto d'Acqui	Dolcetto delle Langhe Monregalesi
Dolcetto d'Alba	
Dolcetto d'Asti	Dolcetto di Dogliani
Dolcetto d'Ovada	Dolcetto Diano d'Alba

Nebbiolo

Barbaresco	Gattinara
Barolo	Ghemme
Boca	Lessona
Bramaterra	Nebbiolo d'Alba
Carema	Roero
Fara	Sizzano

Others

Brachetto d'Acqui	Malvasia di Casorzo
Freisa d'Asti	Malvasia di Castelnuovo Don Bosco
Freisa di Chieri	
Grignolino d'Asti	Rocche di Castagnole Monferrato
Grignolino del Monferrato Casalese	

White and Dessert Wines

Asti Spumante	Cortese dell'Alto Monferrato
Caluso Passito	
Caluso Passito Liquoroso	Erbaluce di Caluso
Cortese Colli Tortonesi	Gavi or Cortese di Gavi
	Moscato d'Asti
	Roero Arneis

BY DISTRICT

Alto Monferrato

Barbera del Monferrato	Dolcetto d'Acqui
Brachetto d'Acqui	Dolcetto d'Ovada
Cortese dell'Alto Monferrato	Grignolino d'Asti
	Moscato d'Asti

Canavese and Carema

Caluso Passito	Carema
Caluso Passito Liquoroso	Erbaluce di Caluso

Colli Novaresi and Vercellesi

Boca	Ghemme
Bramaterra	Lessona
Fara	Sizzano
Gattinara	

Colli Torinesi

Freisa di Chieri

Colli Tortonesi or Tortonese

Barbera Colli Tortonesi	Cortese Colli Tortonesi

Langhe

Barbaresco	Dolcetto di Dogliani
Barbera d'Alba	Dolcetto Diano d'Alba
Barolo	Moscato d'Asti
Dolcetto d'Alba	Nebbiolo d'Alba
Dolcetto delle Langhe Monregalesi	

Monferrato Astigiano

Asti Spumante	Grignolino d'Asti
Barbera d'Asti	Malvasia di Casorzo
Barbera del Monferrato	Malvasia di Castelnuovo Don Bosco
Brachetto d'Acqui	
Cortese dell'Alto Monferrato	Moscato d'Asti
	Rocche di Castagnole Monferrato
Dolcetto d'Asti	
Freisa d'Asti	

Monferrato Casalese

Barbera del Monferrato	Malvasia di Casorzo
Gabiano	Rubino di Cantavenna
Grignolino del Monferrato Casalese	

Roero

Barbera d'Alba	Roero
Nebbiolo d'Alba	Roero Arneis

CHAPTER 2

The Wines of the Langhe

The Langhe region, in the southern part of Piemonte, is made up of a series of long hills—from which it gets its name, *lingue* in Latin—ranging in altitude from 490 to 1,970 feet (150 to 600 meters) above sea level. The towns, often clustered around medieval castles or towers, are situated on the summits of the hills, whose slopes are blanketed in vines. This region, in the northeastern corner of the province of Cuneo, forms a long triangle around the city of Alba, bordered basically by the Tanaro River and the ridges of the Roero hills on the west, and the Bormida River on the east.

The most important grape varieties here are nebbiolo, dolcetto, barbera, and moscato. There are also plantings of arneis and favorita, pelaverga and brachetto, grignolino and freisa, and even a little pinot bianco, chardonnay, and cabernet sauvignon. There are four important nebbiolo DOCs in the Langhe: Barolo, Barbaresco, Nebbiolo d'Alba, and Roero. Of the vines, 11 percent are nebbiolo, 32 percent barbera, 31 percent dolcetto, 17 percent moscato, and 9 percent the other minor varieties.

The soil here is of maritime origin. The Tanaro River, where it veers east near Bra to flow south and east of the city of Alba, divides the region into two zones. To the left of the Tanaro, in the Roero zone, the soil is yellowish sand with admixtures of limestone and marl. To the right, in the Langa, the soil, grayish or amber in color, is composed of limestone, lightly sandy, with some clay.

The hills of Roero form a continuous series of crests with steeply graded slopes that make cultivation of the vine difficult. In this zone are the vineyards of three DOC wines: Nebbiolo d'Alba, Barbera d'Alba, and Roero.

The vineyards for Barbera d'Alba and Nebbiolo d'Alba extend into the Langa zone on the right bank of the Tanaro. The gentler slopes of the Langa hills are more eroded, their crests forming long, almost horizontal summits. In the northeastern corner of this zone are the vineyards of Barbaresco, Moscato d'Asti, Barbera d'Alba, Dolcetto d'Alba, and Dolcetto di Diano d'Alba. In the southern part of the triangle are the dolcetto vineyards of the Langa Monregalese and Dogliani.

PRODUCTION METHODS

Over the years production methods in the Langhe have undergone a number of changes. This has led some journalists to categorize the producers as either traditional or new wave (modern), dividing them into two camps, which sometimes becomes more misleading than informative. We've tried to sort them out ourselves and it's not all that easy. What characterizes a producer as a modernist? What does it mean to be traditional?

Traditional Winemaking

In the old days wine in the Langhe was made by hand and by foot. There were no machines. Until the 1950s the grapes were commonly brought on oxcarts to the cellars, where they were crushed by men who trod upon them with their bare feet. The whole grape bunches were dumped into the tini, upright wooden vats; stalks and seeds were not broken up in the crushing process.

The must fermented in the open tini for two weeks to a month. The stalks helped to aerate the must, and the cap was punched down periodically.

After the fermented wine was drawn off, its lees were pressed and the juice was combined with the wine. The wine was transferred to large, generally old wooden casks of local chestnut or Slavonian oak where it was periodically racked until it was clear, a relatively short period of one to five years, depending on the vintage and the producer. Then the wine was drawn off and bottled in very large bottles—demijohns (damigiani) and brente—for further aging.

Luciano Rinaldi, of Francesco Rinaldi, told us that fifty or so years ago the wines were aged at most for five to six years in cask, then put into damigiani that were stored sotto portico, under the eaves, for another two to three years. Today this has become too expensive and is rarely done anymore. In the winter of 1929 temperatures dropped so low that half the brente and demijohns broke—a doubly tragic loss, as these bottles are no longer being blown.

Giacomo Bologna of Enoteca Braida, who has a prized collection of old blown-glass brente, asks his favorite producers to bottle their best vintages and crus in them for him for long aging. He bottles some of his especially fine Bricco dell'Uccellone in them as well. (We are fortunate in having one of those rare large bottles of the '85 Bricco dell'Uccellone.) It's a great occasion when Giacomo decides a wine is ready and unstoppers a brenta to enjoy with friends, and with as many friends as Giacomo has, a brenta (13.2 gallons/50 liters) is none too large.

The Advent of Mechanization

During the 1930s machines for crushing were introduced into the zone, although many small producers continued to crush the grapes in the time-honored fashion even into the 1950s. Bartolo Mascarello of Cantina Mascarello said that their entire 1952 harvest was crushed by treading; they didn't buy a crusher until about 1955. Luigi Pira's wine continued to be crushed by foot until his last vintage, in 1979.

With the changeover to machines, other modifications were also made in fermentation methods. The crusher-stemmers removed the stalks before crushing to avoid adding the acid and astringency from the green stems to the wine. The fermentation time was lengthened to about two months to obtain more tannin and extract from the grape skins, which were held submerged under a layer of wooden slats.

Previously the temperature of the wine in the fermentors was controlled—if that is the word—by opening the windows and the doors of the cantina to let in the cool autumn air. If it was Indian summer, more imaginative measures were called for. In 1961, in many cellars in the Langhe, huge chunks of ice were dropped into the fermenting vats in a desperate attempt to cool raging fermentations that threatened to spoil the product of a year's hard work.

The producers were making wines meant to be aged for many years in wooden casks to soften the harsh tannins, but not infrequently it was the fruit that was the first to fade. The best of them were big, dense, tannic wines requiring many years of bottle age to become drinkable—when they did. We are reminded of the observation of a fellow wine drinker who lamented, "These wines never do become ready. When they're young the fruit is covered up by such formidable tannin it takes years to soften; by the time it does, the fruit is gone." It takes a fine vintage, a dedicated winemaker, and severe selection in the vineyards to produce an excellent Barolo or Barbaresco in this style.

A More Drinkable Style

In the late 1960s some producers, following the example of Renato Ratti, started making a different style of Barolo, a softer, fruitier, less tannic wine that developed earlier and was more approachable overall.

Fermentation time was shortened; the must spent less time in contact with the skins. The temperature of the fermentation was lowered and regulated by heat exchangers in the vats or by the use of temperature-controlled stainless steel tanks to reduce the risk of volatile acidity and other problems that confront the traditional producer.

Malolactic fermentation was encouraged, even induced, shortly if not immediately after the first fermentation was complete, in order to convert the sharp malic acid into its softer lactic form.

The wines were given much briefer wood aging. Filters were often employed to clear the wines. And the bottles were released for sale earlier. This style of wine is ready for early consumption; it doesn't need long bottle aging, though the better ones can improve with some time in bottle.

And so the pendulum swung. Some wineries went so far as to turn out wines so streamlined that they were nearly unrecognizable, resembling more a simple Nebbiolo than a Barolo or Barbaresco. These wines have caused a number of producers who use modern techniques to wince when they are referred to as modernists, and to protest that they are traditional, in results, at least, if not in methods.

Fermentation Techniques

There are a variety of winemaking methods used in the Langhe today. As a general rule, the more traditional producers believe in a long fermentation—on the skins—commonly from thirty to sixty days, and they frequently employ *cappello sommerso* ("submerged cap") to obtain fruit, color, and extract from the grapes.

There are, however, notable exceptions. Giuseppe Colla, winemaker and co-proprietor at Prunetto and recognized as one of the most confirmed of the old guard, ferments the grapes for his Barolo and Barbaresco in glass-lined cement tanks for only ten to twenty days at about 77° Fahrenheit (25° centigrade). Giovanni Conterno, of Giacomo Conterno, one of the most staunch traditionalists, macerates his grapes before crushing to extract more fruit and color. He uses *cappello sommerso* and a 25- to 35-day fermentation, which he follows day and night to be sure the temperature doesn't exceed 86° Fahrenheit (30° centigrade). The wine spends forty to sixty days in stainless steel. Mauro Mascarello of Giuseppe Mascarello, another traditionalist, ferments his wine for a full sixty-five days on the skins. Bruno Giacosa ferments his Barolo and Barbaresco for thirty to forty days.

Among the modernists, Paolo Cordero di Montezemolo used to ferment his Barolo in stainless steel tanks for twenty-five to thirty days at controlled temperatures, doing the *rimontaggio,* or pumping over, twice a day. He also used *cappello sommerso.* Today Giovanni and Enrico Cordero di Montezemolo ferment their Barolo for seven to ten days. We don't know if they use *cappello sommerso.* Renato Ratti, the leading spokesman for the new methods, generally ferments his Barolo for eight to twenty days on the skins; in lesser years he reduces the time, in better years he gives it longer. Ratti was one of the first to use a temperature-controlled fermentation. Today Marcello Ceretto ferments his wine for eight to twelve days in temperature-controlled stainless steel tanks. Following fermentation he macerates the wine on the *bucce* for an additional eight to ten days. This represents a change from the way he used to make his wines.

Elvio Cogno of Podere Marcarini ferments for as long as two months in contact with the skins, though generally thirty-five days is the limit; during phase two he holds the cap submerged. Cogno also adds some uncrushed whole berries and stems to the fermenting must. Alfredo Currado of Vietti, leaning more toward the traditional style, though utilizing some modern advances, ferments his Barolo for thirty-five to sixty days, his Barbaresco for thirty to fifty. He uses selected yeast for the fermentation in vats of stainless steel or glass-lined cement. After the initial fermentation, lasting up to three weeks, the cap is submerged and the wine is churned twice a day.

FERMENTATION TECHNIQUES USED BY SELECTED PRODUCERS
(Those marked with an asterisk are considered traditionalists.)

- Giacomo Ascheri ferments his Barbaresco for 15 to 20 days at a maximum of 75° Fahrenheit (24° centigrade).
- Barale* ferments his Barolo for 20 days at 84° to 86° Fahrenheit (29° to 30° centigrade), with submerged cap.
- Bersano ferments his Barolo and Barbaresco for 6 to 8 days.
- Mauro Bianco uses stainless steel for his Barbaresco.
- Bartolomeo Borgogno ferments his Barolo for 15 to 20 days.
- G. Borgogno* ferments their Barolo and Barbaresco for 2 weeks followed by *cappello sommerso.*
- Gianfranco Bovio ferments his Barolo for 20 days.
- F.lli Brovia ferments their Barolo and Barbaresco for 15 to 20 days.
- Cantina del Glicine ferments their Barbaresco for 10 to 15 days.
- Teobaldo e Roberto Cappellano ferments their Barolo and Barbaresco for 15 days.
- Castello di Neive* ferments their Barbaresco 10 to 15 days.
- Cavallotto* has shortened the fermentation time for their Barolo to 15 days from 20 to 25 days. Previously they also followed this with *cappello sommerso* for 15 to 20 days more. We don't know if this is still done.
- Cigliuti ferments his Barbaresco for 25 days.
- Domenico Clerico ferments his Barolo for 20 to 25 days.

- Aldo Conterno ferments his Barolo for up to 60 days, but usually 30.
- Contratto* ferments his Barolo and Barbaresco for 10 to 15 days or longer.
- Luigi Einaudi* ferments his Barolo for 15 days.
- Eredi Lodali ferments their Barolo for 15 to 20 days.
- Giacomo Fenocchio ferments his Barolo for 30 to 40 days.
- Franco Fiorina* ferments their Barolo for 40 to 45 days, and their Barbaresco for 30 to 35 days, both with cappello sommerso and a temperature of 72° to 77° Fahrenheit (22° to 25° centigrade).
- Fontanafredda* ferments their Barolo and Barbaresco for 15 days in temperature-controlled stainless steel tanks.
- Marchese Fracassi ferments her Barolo for 15 days.
- Elio Grasso ferments his Barolo for 40 to 60 days.
- La Spinona ferments their Barbaresco for 15 days.
- Marchesi di Gresy ferments his Barbaresco for 15 days.
- Bartolo Mascarello* ferments his Barolo for 15 to 20 days.
- Massolino ferments his Barolo for 20 days.
- Azienda Agricola "Moccagatta" ferments their Barbaresco for 15 to 20 days.
- Palladino ferments their Barolo for 15 to 23 days in Slavonian oak.
- At her E. Pira winery Chiara Boschis* ferments her Barolo for 15 to 20 days on the skins.
- Produttori del Barbaresco ferments their Barbaresco for 18 days on the skins.
- Punset ferments their Barolo and Barbaresco for 8 to 10 days.
- Francesco Rinaldi* ferments his Barolo and Barbaresco for 15 to 30 days.
- Giuseppe Rinaldi* ferments his Barolo for 10 days.
- Roagna ferments his Barbaresco for 20 to 40 days on the skins.
- Rocche Costamagna ferments their Barolo for 15 to 20 days.
- Scarpa ferments their Barolo for 30 days and their Barbaresco for 25 days.
- Alfonso Scavino ferments his Barolo for 15 to 20 days.
- Paolo Scavino ferments his Barolo for 20 to 40 days at 82° Fahrenheit (28° centigrade), and since 1982 in temperature-controlled stainless steel.
- Seghesio ferments his Barolo for 20 days.
- Sobrero* fermented his Barolo for 15 days.
- Tenuta Carretta* ferments their Barolo for 20 days.
- Roberto Voerzio fermented his '82 Barolo between 86° and 90° Fahrenheit (30° and 32° centigrade), and the '83 at 77° to 82° (25° to 28°).

Malolactic Fermentation

The malolactic fermentation in the old-style wines occurred naturally in the spring, when the temperatures warmed sufficiently to prompt the process, unless for some reason— such as, ironically, too high acidity in the wine—nature didn't take its course.

Modernists make sure the malolactic takes place as soon as possible after the first fermentation by heating the cellars, warming the wine, or inoculating it if necessary.

All of the producers today recognize the importance of the malolactic fermentation and know what to do to bring it about. The only difference among them seems to be not whether, but when the malolactic takes place. Bartolo Mascarello, Alberto Contratto, Aldo Conterno, Giovanni Conterno, and Chiara Boschis's Barolos undergo malolactic in the spring; Renato Ratti, Marcello Ceretto, Alfredo Currado, and Elvio Cogno ensure that it takes place no more than a month after the first fermentation. Of them, Bartolo Mascarello, Alberto Contratto, Giovanni Conterno, and Chiara Boschis are considered traditionalists and Renato Ratti and Marcello Ceretto, modernists, while Alfredo Currado, Aldo Conterno, and Elvio Cogno take a little from both camps.

Wood Aging

The biggest difference between the traditional and the new wave producers is probably the length of time they age their wines in wood. There is no question that the modern producers believe in giving their wines less time in cask. Renato Ratti feels that wine made in the new style is better balanced and has more fruit and more style. Ratti ages his Barolo for the minimum period in wood required by DOCG law, two years. Marcello Ceretto ages his Barbaresco for the minimum, one year in cask, but his Barolos for up to three years, depending on the vineyard and the vintage.

Traditionalist Bartolo Mascarello ages his Barolo three to four years in old oak (and a few chestnut) casks, most fifty years old with a capacity of 660 to 925 gallons (25 to 35 hectoliters). In the better years he puts some of his Barolo in bottiglione of 0.5 to 0.8 gallon (2 to 3 liters) for further aging. Bruno Giacosa ages his Barolo for five to six years in cask, his Barbaresco three to four, although his '64 Barbaresco was in oak for seven to eight. Giovanni Conterno wood-aged his Barolo regular for at least six years; that has since been reduced to four years. Monfortino spends no less than eight years in oak. In November 1984 we tasted the '70 Monfortino from cask. It was bottled in August 1985! It appears that Conterno has since reduced his aging regime for Monfortino as well as his Barolo Riserva.

Alfredo Currado keeps his Barolos for two to four years in 1,190- to 1,585-gallon (45- to 60-hectoliter) Slavonian oak—the better the vintage, the longer in wood. His Barbarescos are given one to three years.

WOOD AGING USED BY SELECTED PRODUCERS
(Those marked with an asterisk are considered traditionalists.)

- Barale* ages his Barolo and Barbaresco for 3 years in Slavonian oak, then to demijohn.
- Mauro Bianco ages his Barbaresco for 1 year in 1,057-gallon (40-hectoliter) oak casks.
- Aldo Conterno ages his Barolo for up to 3 years in 290- to 1,795-gallon (11- to 68-hectoliter) casks, then to 264-gallon (10-hectoliter) stainless steel.
- Contratto* ages his Barolo and Barbaresco for 7 to 8 years in 50-year-old casks of 795- to 1,585-gallon (30- to 60-hectoliter) capacity.
- Luigi Einaudi* ages his Barolo for 8 to 10 years in Yugoslavian oak.
- Franco Fiorina* ages their Barolo for 3 to 4 years and their Barbaresco for 2 years.
- Fontanafredda* ages their Barbaresco for 2 to 3 years and their Barolo for 2 to 4 years.
- Giuseppe Mascarello* ages his Barolo and Barbaresco for 3 to 4 years in 17- to 22-year-old 265- to 3,170-gallon (10- to 120-hectoliter), mostly 2,115-gallon (80-hectoliter), casks.
- La Spinona ages their Barbaresco for at least 2 years in 185- to 1,585-gallon (7- to 60-hectoliter) Slavonian oak casks.
- Giuseppe Rinaldi* ages his Barolo for 5 to 6 years in oak and chestnut casks, some 100 years old; in great vintages, perhaps up to 8 or 9 years.
- Alfonso Scavino ages his Barolo for 3 to 5 years.
- Paolo Scavino ages his Barolo for 2 to 4 years.
- Seghesio ages his Barolo for 4 years.
- Sobrero* aged his Barolo for at least 4 years in old 55- to 130-gallon (2- to 5-hectoliter) Slavonian oak casks.
- Vajra ages his Barolo for a minimum of 3 years in oak and chestnut casks.

Winemaking Styles

It's interesting to see how the producers arrive at their final product. Some winemakers who take advantage of modern technology to produce their wines claim that although they have made changes from the old-fashioned methods to ensure better control over every phase of the winemaking process, they are nevertheless producing a traditional-style Barolo or Barbaresco. Some, like Alfredo Currado and Elvio Cogno, *are* producing grand wines worthy of the best of the old traditions, wines with greater richness and depth than some others that would be classified as traditional.

Although some of the traditional producers make wines of monumental proportions, knife-and-fork wines in their youth, others produce wines that are less imposing in their tannin content and strength but no less impressive in their pedigree. Giacomo Conterno's Monfortino needs a long time to come around but, if stored properly, is definitely worth the wait, becoming a wine of character and style. Bartolo Mascarello's Barolo is more drinkable when young, but with age it develops exceptional quality.

Renato Ratti's 1985s and 1986s are excellent drinking right now, but with time will take on further nuances of bouquet and flavor.

The basic styles can be defined—in basics, but there are still many variations and differences within the categories, as well as may gradations in between. We are dealing with individuals here—hardheaded farmers, college-trained technicians, market-sensitive businessmen, and, in some cases, artists. Even in the past, when fewer options were open to them, when winemakers learned from their fathers and uncles, styles of wines varied, not only from one vineyard area to another but also from cousin to cousin, neighbor to neighbor. Each had his own way of doing things. When producers meet on the *piazza* and chat over a cup of espresso, it isn't necessarily winemaking techniques that they feel impelled to discuss and compare. Soccer is a much more likely topic of debate.

The Quality in the Bottle

The differences in the methods of production are less important than the differences in the wines themselves. To say that a producer is traditional or modern gives only a general idea of what kind of wine it is in terms of style—it tells you nothing about its quality.

Of the best Barolo and Barbaresco that we have tasted, some were made by traditional producers, others were produced by modernists; still others were from winemakers who take advantage of some methods from each. In the final analysis the important thing is, of course, not how the wine is produced, but how it tastes.

Aging in Barrique

Traditionally the wines of Barolo and Barbaresco are aged in *botte,* large chestnut or oaken casks, most commonly today made of Slavonian oak. But many producers in Italy are now trying a new technique. Taking a page from the book of the French producers in Burgundy and Bordeaux, where aging in *barrique* is traditional, and from producers in California, where the art of barrel aging has taken on the dimensions of a practical science, producers in many regions of Italy are experimenting with small-barrel aging for their wines. Piemonte is no exception. Quite a number of producers are putting their Barolo and Barbaresco into *barrique* for varying lengths of time and with various degrees of success.

Without question the most successful is Angelo Gaja, whose achievement, both in the high quality of the wines produced and in the very high prices that he asks for them, has undoubtedly added momentum to the growing trend.

Gaja wasn't the first to try *barrique* aging in the Langhe. A few producers made experiments in the 1950s: Giuseppe Colla tried new oak barrels for aging the wines at Prunotto. Tests were also done in the cellars of Giacomo Borgogno. The resulting wines were not considered to have benefited from the system, however, and it was abandoned.

The traditional casks used in Piemonte are much larger than the *barriques,* and many years old. Over the course of time the wood tannins and flavor components in the wood are drawn out, producing a basically neutral receptacle for the wine which allows a limited exchange of oxygen through the pores of the wood. The surface of wine exposed to the wood in these casks is in a much smaller proportion to the total volume than that in the 60-gallon (225-liter) *barriques.* The wine in the *botti* can be, and is, aged for a much longer period. When new or nearly new small barrels are used, the situation is quite another story.

Barrique aging changes the character of the wine, and to be done to advantage it requires a lot of care and not a little experience. What does the new oak add to the wine, and what does it take away? The wood adds tannin to the wine. It can also create a roundness and a suppleness of texture. The oak also adds its own character, contributing a vanilla aspect to the aroma and flavor of the wine, which if subtle provides a note of complexity, but when strong can be overbearing and obscure the character of the grape variety.

We've tasted some *barrique*-aged Barolo and Barbaresco that was practically unidentifiable as nebbiolo. We find that Barolo and Barbaresco aged in *barrique* nearly always exhibit more of the character of the oak than of the grape variety, although there are exceptions.

Angelo Gaja has learned to control the oakiness, to keep the influence of the *barrique* in the background, to produce a Barbaresco recognizable as a Barbaresco but possessing a suppleness and an added layer of complexity. However, as the nebbiolo is an excellent variety of notable character and structure, it is just possible that we might prefer the Gaja Barbarescos without the influence of the oak. But obviously we couldn't say for certain, not having the chance to compare wines of the two styles against each other.

We must also admit that since the 1978 vintage, when Pio Boffa introduced *barriques* into the Pio Cesare cellars, his Barolos have been of a higher quality. But was it the barrels that made the difference? Or was it rather the other changes he made—cooler fermentation temperatures, reduced skin contact, immediate malolactic fermentation, and consider-

ably shortened wood aging? *Barrique* aging may have added an extra dimension to the wines, but we're inclined to believe that the other changes had a more significant impact on improving the quality.

Colla and Borgogno were dissatisfied with the results of their *barrique* experiments in the 1950s because of the unnecessary tannin added to the already tannic nebbiolo, and because of the way it changed the character of their wines. Others have also tried and abandoned *barriques.* Many producers who were not convinced that *barrique* aging had anything to add to their Barolos or Barbarescos have tried it as a test either to prove to themselves that they were right or to prove to others that their minds were not closed to the possibility, however remote, that it might contribute something worthwhile. The Cerettos are among this group. Marcello Ceretto was dissatisfied with, though not surprised at, the results of his tests with *barriques.*

Other producers, such as Alfredo Currado of Vietti, who has no interest whatever in changing the character of his Barolo and Barbaresco, has made some tests with *barrique* for his Fioretto. He says that while he is using some *barrique* aging for this wine—a nebbiolo-dolcetto-barbera-neirano blend—he will never use them for his Barolo or Barbaresco.

Many are influenced by market pressure, which appears to demand Barolo and Barbaresco in *barrique,* although they would personally prefer their wines without it. Aldo Conterno said that while he has given his Barbera some time in *barriques* of Limousin oak, he does not plan to put his Barolo in small barrels, as he feels it would take away the personality of the nebbiolo, changing its character as well as adding unneeded tannin. He didn't totally rule out the possibility, however. And he does produce a *barrique*-aged nebbiolo, Il Favòt. Armando Cordero, the enologist at Franco Fiorina, opposes *barrique* aging for the nebbiolo, pointing out that this variety has a personality of its own; it has no need of the added flavor or tannin that the oak would provide.

The general feeling among the better producers we have spoken with is that whereas the *barrique* may be well suited to some grape varieties, such as the chardonnay, pinot noir, and cabernet sauvignon, the nebbiolo doesn't need it. And while *barriques* are turning up in *cantina* after *cantina* in the Piemonte, there are still producers like Bartolo Mascarello, who says that he feels no need to prove to others his firm conviction that the nebbiolo is an excellent variety that can stand on its own; he isn't interested in making experiments. A similar view is expressed by Giovanni Conterno, another who has not bowed to the pressure even to make tests with the small barrels.

What can the *barrique* do for the nebbiolo? Can the wines be improved by barrel aging in new oak, or is it only their standing in the international marketplace, where they might frequently be judged by the standards of foreign tasters more accustomed to the oak-aged wines of Bordeaux, Burgundy, or California? In our opinion, based on the rather considerable experience we've had with the wines of Barolo and Barbaresco, as well as the nebbiolo wines from other areas, *barrique* aging doesn't make any significant improvement in these wines. Most often what it adds merely detracts from the character of the wine, making it seem more like a California or French or internationally anonymous wine than it does like one from the Piemonte, a region rich in its own unique winemaking tradition.

If the Piemontese producers want to take advantage of the current marketing demand for oaky wines, we suggest they put their barberas in *barrique*. This grape produces a fruity wine high in acid and low in tannin. Here they have more to gain than to lose. Giacomo Bologna, who ages his Bricco dell'Uccellone and Bricco della Bigotta Barberas in *barrique*, has proved how well this variety takes to new oak.

The nebbiolo is a noble variety, with a unique and well-defined personality. It doesn't need the added character of new oak to produce a wine of depth and complexity.

◁ BAROLO ▷

Barolo is the most majestic of the nebbiolo wines. At its best it is unsurpassed by any other Italian wine and challenged by very few. It is a powerful wine, rich and robust, yet complex and harmonious. In its youth it is hard and austere; with age it takes on a velvety texture, developing a depth of flavor and a grandeur equaled by few wines. This is Barolo at its best; regrettably it doesn't attain these heights often. Too frequently it is lacking in character and structure. Its name is cheapened by a handful of mediocre manufacturers whose wine bears little or no resemblance to a true Barolo, or even a lesser nebbiolo wine.

When the names of wineries such as Luigi Bosca, Cossetti, Kiola, Giovanni Scanavino, and Villadoria are better known than those of the fine Barolo producers, as they unfortunately are in many markets, it is not difficult to understand why many wine drinkers do not recognize Barolo as one of the world's great wines. The rocky road to recognition is made all the more difficult when truckloads of products such as these create a bottleneck at its access. But when the true wine lover, open-minded and persistent in his or her search for quality, discovers the Barolos of producers such as Bartolo Mascarello, Elvio Cogno, Alfredo Currado, Bruno Giacosa, Marcello Ceretto, Aldo Conterno, Giovanni Conterno, Giuseppe Rinaldi, and Luciani Rinaldi, they may find themselves listing the three B's of wine as Burgundy, Bordeaux, and Barolo.

Barolo is a robust wine that complements hearty, flavorful dishes. It goes well with roast red meat, especially game such as venison.

Historian Dalla Chiesa (1568–1621) speculated that San Barolo, martyr of the Thespian League, gave his name to the town and eventually the wine. Another theory suggests that the name Barolo came from the Celtic *brolio* or *bröl,* meaning "wood" or "orchard."[1] Still another agrees with the Celtic origin, but suggests that the name derives from *bas-reul,* meaning *basso luogo,* or low-lying area. However it got its name, the town of Barolo has given its name to the district and the wine.

Barolo is produced in an area encompassing approximately 2,912 acres (1,179 hectares) of vines southwest of Alba, in all or part of 11 *comunis*. First is La Morra, with nearly one-third of the total acreage. Following in decreasing order are Serralunga d'Alba, Monforte d'Alba, Barolo, and Castiglione Falletto, and parts of six other villages. The 1,139 registered growers cultivate an average of about 2.5 acres (1 hectare) each. Maximum production is approximately 8.2 million bottles.

DOC/DOCG REQUIREMENTS FOR BAROLO

	Minimum Aging[a] in Years		Minimum Alcohol	Maximum Yield (Gallons/Acre)[c]
	in Cask[b]	Total		
DOC *normale*	2	3	13%	599
Riserva	2	4	13%	599
Riserva Speciale	2	5	13%	599
DOCG *normale*	2	3	13%	599
Riserva	2	5	13%	599

NOTES: [a] The period of aging begins on the January 1 after the harvest.
[b] Aging can take place in oak or chestnut casks.
[c] The law specifies that no more than 3.57 tons per acre (80 quintali per hectare), or 56 hectoliters per hectare, can be produced. After aging the maximum yield is equivalent to 556 gallons per acre (52 hectoliters per hectare).

BAROLO ACREAGE AND PRODUCTION BY VILLAGE

Village	Number of Growers[a]	Acres	Hectares[b]	Percent of Total	Maximum Annual Production* in Bottles
Barolo	136	370.6138	149.9793	12.7	1,039,830
Castiglione Falletto	87	253.8882	102.7437	8.7	712,339
Cherasco	1	3.1136	1.2600	0.1	8,736
Diano d'Alba	8	42.2452	17.0957	1.5	118,527
Grinzane Cavour	50	72.2409	29.2343	2.5	202,686
La Morra	364	941.4891	381.0000	32.3	2,641,534
Monforte d'Alba	183	478.6686	193.7067	16.4	1,343,000
Novello	62	113.2389	45.8253	3.9	317,714
Roddi d'Alba	24	24.8444	10.4780	0.9	72,646
Serralunga d'Alba	145	487.7183	197.3689	16.7	1,368,390
Verduno	79	123.7124	50.0637	4.2	347,100
Total	1,139	2,911.7734	1,178.7556	99.9†	8,172,502

* Based on a maximum production of 2,806 bottles per acre (52 hectoliters per hectare) after aging
† Error due to rounding

Source: [a] Albo Vigneti '89. Camera di Commercio Industria Artigianato e Agricoltura di Cuneo. December 31, 1989
[b] Associazione Consorzi di Tutela del Barolo, Barbaresco e dei Vini d'Alba, 1988

Between 1967 and 1989, an average of some 1.1 million gallons (41,979 hectoliters) of nebbiolo, equivalent to 5.6 million bottles of Barolo, were produced annually. And the average yield of 445 gallons per acre (41.6 hectoliters per hectare) during this same period demonstrates that the Barolo producers aren't overproducing. This 23-year average is less than 75 percent of the limit allowed by law. The two smallest crops, vis-à-vis the maximum allowable, were those of 1984, when 46.3 percent of the maximum was produced, and 1986, due to hail damage, when 41.1 percent was harvested. The two largest were 1970 with 90.6 percent and 1967 with 90.4—nothing like the overproduction of Burgundy. In the greatest vintages, 1971, 1985, and 1989, 86.3, 77.4, and 58 percent of the maximum were harvested, respectively.

Barolo has been granted DOCG status under Italian wine law, which regulates its production, both in the vineyard and the cellar, and supposedly guarantees its authenticity. Bureaucrats and "there-ought-to-be-a-law" lobbyists notwithstanding, in the real world there is only one real guarantee for a product—the integrity of the producer. The next best indication of the quality of a wine is the vintage, then the vineyard. Let's not forget that the garish red DOCG band stuck over the bottle capsule appears also on some rather abysmal bottles of Barolo.

Producers like Bartolo Mascarello, Elvio Cogno, Giovanni Conterno, Alfredo Currado, and Bruno Giacosa, just to name a few, don't bottle wines unworthy of their names. When some of the wine of a particular vintage doesn't meet their personal standards, they declassify it to Nebbiolo delle Langhe; if they feel that it is not even up to that level, they will not bottle it under their own label at all, but sell it off sfuso. In the worst cases they may judge the grapes not even worth picking. We have no doubt that rejected grapes from Giovanni Conterno's vineyard, left on the vines by harvesters under strict orders not to be picked, have provided anonymous improvement to many barrels in neighboring cellars.

Naive consumers may delude themselves into believing that the government can legislate quality into existence, but there will always be those producers who, though they may squeeze under the government umbrella, will provide the most blatant evidence to prove that you cannot outlaw mediocrity.

Under DOCG regulation, up to 15 percent of a Barolo from a different vintage can be blended in to correct a weak vintage.

Rating: Barolo ****

ANNUAL PRODUCTION OF BAROLO

Year	Maximum Allowed	Actual Amount (Hectoliters)	Actual Number of Bottles	Percentage: Actual to Allowed	Average Yield (Hectoliters/Hectare)
1967	36,108	32,652	4,353,491	90.4	50.62
1968	36,108	30,397	4,052,832	84.2	47.15
1969	38,582	32,562	4,341,491	84.4	47.26
1970	43,685	39,600	5,279,868	90.6	50.74
1971	48,617	41,964	5,595,060	86.3	48.33
1972	54,955		the entire crop was declassified		
1973	56,912	49,821	6,642,633	87.5	49.00
1974	59,428	52,221	6,962,625	87.8	49.17
1975	60,283	37,765	5,035,207	62.6	35.06
1976	59,664	28,496	3,799,371	47.8	26.77
1977	61,194	29,774	3,969,767	48.7	27.27
1978	62,306	31,676	4,223,361	50.8	28.45
1979	62,344	53,193	7,092,222	85.3	47.77
1980	62,255	54,292	7,238,752	87.2	48.83
1981	66,961	46,754	6,233,710	69.8	39.09
1982	66,272	56,096	7,479,279	84.6	47.38
1983	73,192	56,074	7,476,346	76.6	42.90
1984	69,861	32,328	4,310,292	46.3	25.93
1985	70,338	54,454	7,260,351	77.4	43.34
1986	67,650	27,832	3,710,840	41.1	23.02
1987	66,146	47,382	6,317,442	71.6	40.10
1988	66,007	50,329	6,710,365	76.3	42.73
1989	65,304	37,878	5,050,273	58.0	32.48
Average	56,490	41,979	5,597,072	74.3	41.61

Source: *Regione Piemonte*

The Crus of Barolo

The crus (single vineyards) of Barolo have recently received a lot of attention. More and more bottles now carry, besides the name of the production zone and the producer, the name of the vineyard plot where the grapes were grown. It is the latest trend, a trend which is growing.

But this is not a new concept or even a new practice. Much more common, yes, but novel, no. Among the oldest bottles of Barolo still in existence are two labeled simply "1752 Cannubi," the most famous vineyard in the zone. In the cellars of Barolo the wines from the various locations are usually vinified separately and held in different casks marked with the names of the vineyards, even parts of vineyards. This has been done for many years. Bruno Giacosa notes that his grandfather Carlo handled the wines from the various plots individually in the cellar, although he didn't bottle them under the vineyard names.

When we taste the wines from cask in the cellars, the producers will frequently name the vineyard, chalked in abbreviated form on the cask, often offering more than one sample from a particular vintage so that we can note the differences among them, which are sometimes striking.

In the old days, when the oxcarts of grapes from the various locations arrived at the winery, the grapes were fermented as they came in, then pressed in small basket presses and each batch was aged separately. A winemaker would naturally want to know which vineyards provided him with his best fruit, and in the hands of a fine winemaker the grapes from the various plots would be handled differently in the vinification and in the aging to bring out the best in the individual wines. Private customers no doubt selected their wine from the casks they preferred.

But until recently, the wine in the bottle was rarely labeled with the name of the vineyard. If the producer made wine from only one vineyard, the distinction might not have seemed necessary, as that is what his name on the bottle represented. If a small producer made wine from various small plots, it would be hardly worth the extra effort for him to have many different labels for the various crus, unless his wine was from a particularly well-known and highly regarded vineyard, such as Cannubi, in which case it was worth drawing attention to the fact.

There aren't a lot of crus in that category, however. A few have long been recognized but today we see a multitude. Vineyards previously little known outside the zone are popping up like mushrooms after a rainstorm, and just when you think you've got them down, a plethora of subcrus appear on the marketing horizon—crus within the crus that are little known outside the immediate neighborhood, some, it seems, outside the immediate family of the vineyardists themselves. Are these distinctions justified by the differences in the wines?

A significant impetus to labeling the crus separately came from Luigi Veronelli, a writer with a major influence on Italian wine. He encouraged the producers to bottle their best vineyards under cru names, most notably in a major article written in the mid-1960s. Obviously the producers agreed that it was a good idea. Cru labeling emphasizes the special qualities of a particular bottling. The marketing benefits are clear, but perhaps it can be carried too far. We are reminded of Baker's law: "A difference is a difference only if it makes a difference."

AGAINST THE CRUS

Even among the producers who disagree with the concept of cru bottlings, there is a recognition that the wines from the various zones within Barolo have their own characteristics. At Franco Fiorina, Pio Cesare, and Giacomo Borgogno, for example, they point out that it is because of these variations that they make their objection, maintaining that the best Barolos are those made from a balanced blend of wines that take advantages of the particular attributes of the different areas, the wine from one zone providing structure and firmness to the blend, that from another adding body, another contributing delicacy and perfume, and yet another allowing longevity.

FOR THE CRUS

These variations in the wines are derived from various aspects of the land—the composition of the soil, the exposure to the sun, and the incline of the slope, even the particular

subvariety of the nebbiolo grape cultivated. The best vineyards naturally have the best exposure to the sun, which enables the grapes to ripen more completely. Which ones they are can readily be seen after a snowstorm. We could confidently point out the best locations in the zone one winter as we observed the vineyards where the snow had already melted. These obviously received more of the benefit of the sun's warming rays. In some of the less favored spots, as Mario Cordero of Vietti put it, "You'd have to bring down the sun in a basket" to fully ripen the grapes. The best vineyards invariably also have good drainage. This is a twofold benefit; the vines absorb less water after a storm or during a rainy period, and the roots of the vines must dig deeper into the earth in search of moisture where they have a more constant environment.

Major Subdivision

There are two main valleys in the Barolo production zone: the Barolo Valley to the west, and the Serralunga Valley to the east. La Morra and Barolo itself are the major villages in the western valley, which also encompasses Cherasco, Novello, Roddi d'Alba, and Verduno. In the Serralunga Valley, Serralunga d'Alba, Castiglione Falletto, and Monforte are the major towns; Diano d'Alba and Grinzane Cavour are also included in this district.

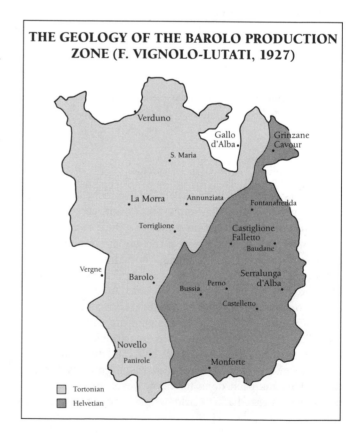

THE GEOLOGY OF THE BAROLO PRODUCTION ZONE (F. VIGNOLO-LUTATI, 1927)

Verduno
Gallo d'Alba
Grinzane Cavour
S. Maria
La Morra
Annunziata
Fontanafredda
Torriglione
Castiglione Falletto
Baudane
Vergne
Barolo
Serralunga d'Alba
Bussia
Perno
Castelletto
Novello
Panirole
Monforte

☐ Tortonian
■ Helvetian

The soil in the Barolo production zone—from the Miocene epoch—is of marine origin, rich in limestone with a high concentration of microelements. According to Renato Ratti, who made a thorough study of the viticultural region, the terrain is divided into two types: tortonian and helvetian. In the Barolo Valley the soil is tortonian, with a basic composition of limestone and marl; in the Serralunga Valley the helvetian soil is characterized by conglomerates of limestone and sand.

As a general rule the wines of the Barolo Valley are noted for their perfume and delicacy; they are lighter in body and develop sooner than those from the Serralunga Valley. The wines of the Serralunga Valley are richer, fuller in body, more tannic and robust; they take longer to come around and are longer lived.

Ratti details the nuances noted in the wines of the various areas: the wines of the Serralunga Valley have suggestions of licorice and tar; the Barolos of Serralunga itself display camphor and mint; those from Castiglione Falletto have a pronounced licorice characteristic and nuances of spice, mint, dried peaches, and prunes; those from Monforte recall spices, mint, hazelnuts, and almonds. The wines from the Barolo Valley bring up underbrush and *tartufi* as well as licorice. Those from the village of Barolo have less of a licorice character but more suggestions of underbrush, truffles, and mint; those from Cannubi display notes of *tartufi,* underbrush, raspberries, and black cherries. The wines of La Morra, especially those from the slopes, combine nuances of *tartufi,* mint, tobacco, spices, cherries, and blackberries.

Ratti lists the major vineyard districts of the Barolo Valley as Brunate, Cannubi-Boschis, Cannubi-Muscatel, Cerequio, Collina Cannubi, Conca dell'Abbazia dell'Annunziata, Le Turnote, Monfalletto, Rocche di La Morra, Rocchette, and Sarmazza. The major vineyard areas of the Serralunga Valley are Baudana, Brea, Bussia Soprana, Bussia Sottana, Cerretta, Cucco, Fontanile, Gautti-Parafada, Lazzarito, Marenca-Rivette, Momprivato, Pian della Polvere, Pugnane, Rocche di Castiglione Falletto, Santo Stefano di Perno, Vigna Arionda, and Villero. Within these areas are the single vineyards, or crus.

Gianfranco Oberto, a regarded authority in Barolo, divides the vineyards of the zone into six major areas. In the *comune* of Barolo he puts Cannubi, Cannubi-Muscatel, and Cannubi-Boschis. In the area between Barolo and La Morra are Cerequio and Brunate; in La Morra are Rocche, Rocchette, Conca dell'Abbazia dell'Annunziata, Le Turnote, Monfalletto, Ciocchini, Serre, and Ornata. In the Serralunga d'Alba district are Brea, Cucco, Lazzarito, Vigna Rionda, Marenga e Rivette, Gabutti-Parafada, and Cerretta. In the area of Monforte are Bussia Soprana, Bussia Sottana, Costa di Rose, Fontanile, Pian delle Polvere, and Santo Stefano. And in the Castiglione Falletto district are Baudana, Momprivato, and Villero. Except for two vineyards, Oberto's six

zones agree with the general view. The two exceptions are Baudana, which others put in Serralunga d'Alba, and Costa di Rose, which is on everyone else's list as being in Barolo. It is also surprising that he lists the Rocche vineyard of La Morra and omits the Rocche of Castiglione Falletto, which is considered to be the most important vineyard of that village.

Lorenzo Fantini, in his *Monografia Sulla Viticoltura ed Enologia Nella Provincia di Cuneo,* lists the following vineyards in the Barolo district.[2]

Barolo

Cannubbio—Le Coste	San Lorenzo
Terlo	Cannubbio Ferreri
Ravera	Cannubbio Boschis
Boschetti	Cannubbio Parrochiale
Castello della Volta	Cascina Bricco
San Pietro	Castellero
Fossati	Zonchei
Zonchetta	Costa di Rose
Bergeisa	Monrobiolo
Sarmassa	Brunata
Fornaci	Rocca
Moscatello	

Perno

Santo Stefano	Colombiro
Disa	

Castiglione Falletto

La Serra	Montanello
Pugnane	Paruzzo
Sobrero	Bricco Boschis

Serralunga d'Alba

Briccolina	Fontanafredda
Sirano	Gallaretto
Cascina Areto	Veglio
Baudana	Collarello
Sorano	Galvagni

Verduno

Madonna del Pilone	Breide
Castagni	

La Morra

San Rocco	Bettola
Pozzo	San Biago
Cascina Nuova	Santa Maria

Alessandria
Roncaglia Soprana
Roncaglia Sottana
Bettolotti
Roggeri
Bojolo

Torriglione
Fontanassa
Pelorosso
Cerequio
Silio

Novello

Soriti del Castello
I Merli
Pratorotondo
Cascina Nuova

Ravera Soprana
Ravera Sottana
Cascina Giordano

Monforte d'Alba

Rovella
Gabutti
Dardi e Piano della Polvere
Bussia Soprana ojo
Ginestra

Mosconi
Gavarrini
Le Coste
Fantini
Bovio

Castelletto-Monforte

Gramolere
Pressenda

Bobessia

The Villages of the Barolo District

The village of **Barolo** at an altitude of 1,015 feet (310 meters) above sea level, which also includes the district of Vergne, is located some 7 miles (12 kilometers) from Alba. There are 136 growers cultivating nebbiolo for Barolo on 371 acres (150 hectares). Here, in the Cannubi vineyard, the tortonian soil of the western Barolo Valley meets and blends with the helvetian terrain of the eastern Serralunga Valley. It produces the ideal mixture, resulting in harmonious wines of great elegance and character.

There is historical evidence to suggest that this territory was once inhabited during prehistoric times. Flint utensils and weapons from the Neolithic age have been found here, and a funeral stone from Roman times was found in the Vergne district.

The village is home to the castle of Barolo, built in the tenth century to stem off attacks from the Saracens of Provence. The castle of Barolo passed into the hands of the Falletti family in the mid-thirteenth century. Marquess Julia Colbert Falletti is credited with the discovery of Barolo. Today her former home is owned by the village of Barolo. It serves as the center for Barolo wine—Enoteca Regionale del Barolo. The Enoteca, with 110 members, including most of the zone's important bottlers, is a good place to taste and buy bottles of Barolo. The *castello* is also home to a hotel

training school, historical museum, and library. There are displays of crystal wineglasses as well as tools and implements used in the cultivation of grapes and the production of wine. The parish church of San Donato is in the courtyard of the Barolo castle.

Barolo is also home to Castello della Volta, the castle of the vault. Local legend has it that wild orgiastic dances were often held here in this castle, and one day the vault that supported the ballroom collapsed. The stones were returned to their original position and no traces of the guests have ever been found. Today the *castello* belongs to the Marchesi di Barolo.

Carnevale, replete with local costumes, takes place in February. The village of Barolo is also the site, at the beginning of September, of "sidewalk" artists who draw wine scenes in chalk, instead of the usual religious portraits. The Barolo wine festival takes place during the second week in September.

Major Vineyards

Cannubi, Collina Cannubi, or Cannubbio	Costa de Rose, or Costa di Rose
Boschetti	Fontanassa, or Fontanazza
Brunate, mostly in La Morra	La Mandorla
	Le Coste
Cannubi-Boschis, or Monghisolfo	Prea
	Ruè
Cannubi-Muscatel	Sarmassa, or Sarmazza, part is in La Morra
Castellero	
Cerequio, mostly in La Morra	

Top Producers

Cantina Mascarello di Bartolo Mascarello	Giuseppe Rinaldi
	Francesco Sandrone
Francesco Rinaldi	Luciano Sandrone

Other Producers of Note

F.lli Barale di Sergio Barale	Cascina Adelaide di G. Terzano (Aie Sottane)
E. Pira & Figli di Chiara Boschis	Chiarlo Michele
G. D. Vajra, Cascina San Ponzio (*località* Vergne)	Azienda Agricola "Ponte Rocca" di Pittatore Cav. Francesco & Figlio
F.lli Serio & Battista Borgogno di Serio Borgogno	Sebaste

Castiglione Falletto, at an altitude of 1,150 feet (350 meters) above sea level, is located some 7 miles (12 kilometers) from Alba. This small village, in the center of the Barolo zone, is home to 87 growers who cultivate 254 acres

(103 hectares) of nebbiolo for Barolo. This village contains the remains of a castle that dates back to at least the ninth century, when it was used as a military fort. The *castello* and the town took its name from the Falletti family, which occupied it from 1225 when Bertoldo Falletti became feudal lord of the Marquis of Monferrato. Since 1860 it has been owned by the Vassallo earls of Castiglione, who have used it as a residence for more than a century. This castle is said to be the most majestic *castello* in the Langhe. It was rebuilt in the twelfth and fourteenth centuries and restored in 1950. A pillar from Roman times has been found in the walls of this castle. During the last week of July the village is host to the feast of Saint Anne.

Major Vineyards

Momprivato, or Monprivato	Rocche di Castiglione Falletto
Pugnane	Villero

Top Producers

Cantina Vietti di Alfredo Currado	Mascarello Giuseppe & Figlio di Mauro Mascarello & C.
Azienda Agricola "Bricco Rocche" di Ceretto	

Other Producers of Note

Azelia di Luigi and Lorenzo Scavino	F.lli Cavallotto Olivio & Gildo, Azienda Agricola "Bricco Boschis"
F.lli Brovia di Giacinto, Raffaele, and Marina Brovia	Paolo Scavino di Enrico Scavino (*località* Garbelletto)

The town of **Cherasco** lies at an altitude of 920 feet (280 meters) above sea level. It is the headquarters of the National Association of Helicutivators. This is probably no surprise for snail lovers, considering that *Helix pomatia cheraschensis* is one of Italy's most appreciated snails. The National Gathering of Snail Breeders takes place here during the second weekend in June. Cherasco is regarded for its woodcraft and antique dealers.

The town was created in the thirteenth century near the ancient Ligurian Clarascum. During the Middle Ages it was an important military stronghold. In 1631 the Cherasco Peace Treaty was signed here between Austria, France, Spain, the Monferrato, and Mantova regions. In 1706 the town was used as a refuge for members of the Savoy royal court. Cherasco was occupied by French General Massena on April 25, 1796. A decade later, in 1806, the peace treaty between Napoleon and the House of Savoy was signed here.

At one time Cherasco was home for the Holy Shroud. In 1706 the Shroud was kept in the "Silent Room" of the Salmatoris Palace. Today Cherasco boasts the fourteenth-century Visconti castle, the 120-foot (36-meter) high civic tower, Saint Peter's Church, and a number of grand houses, including the Brizzo della Veglia Palace dating from 1400 and the Fracassi Palace. Local costumes are worn during *carnevale* and the Feast of Sibla in mid-July.

There is one grower and a grand total of 3.1 acres (1.26 hectares) of nebbiolo for Barolo grown here.

Major Vineyard

Montetetto

Producer of Note

Marchese Maurizio Fracassi Ratti Mentone

Diano d'Alba, at an altitude of 1,625 feet (495 meters), is located some 4 miles (7 kilometers) from Alba. The town's name derives from the Roman and Ligurian hunting goddess, Diana. Diano, which includes the two districts of Ricca and Valle Talloria, is home to 8 growers and 42 acres (17 hectares) of vines for Barolo. The nebbiolo for Barolo is planted in the Valle Talloria section. It is also an important center for dolcetto, with a DOC for Dolcetto Diano d'Alba. The parish church and spired bell tower of Saint John are worth a visit. There is a splendid panorama from the garden in the front of the church.

Major Vineyards

Galleretto	Piadvenza

Producers of Note

Grimaldi & C. (Valle Talloria, *località* Groppone)	Mario Savigliano
	Tenuta Coluè di Massimo Oddero
Porta Rossa di Domenico Berizia e Marilisa Rizzi Artusio	Giovanni Veglio & Figli

Grinzane Cavour, at an altitude of 880 feet (270 meters) above sea level, lies some 3.5 miles (6 kilometers) from Alba. It is divided into two parts: the newer section, Gallo Grinzane, and the old section consisting of twenty houses built on the top of a ridge crowned by a twelfth-century castle. The castle was once the residence of Camillo Benso, Count of Cavour, who from 1800 was mayor of the village. Benso produced wine inside the castle. Today Castello di Grinzane Cavour is the headquarters of the first public wine center in Italy, the Piemontese Regional Wine Center of Cavour, and home to The Order of Knights of the Truffle and Albeisa Wines. Grinzane is also home to a modern viticultural school and 50 registered Barolo growers who cultivate 72 acres (29 hectares) of nebbiolo for Barolo.

Major Vineyards

Case Giuli	Castello

Producers of Note

Cantine Le Ginestre	Guido Molino
Grimaldi Giovanni & C.	Renato Revello

La Morra includes the districts of Annunziata, Berri, Rivalta, and Santa Maria and the hamlet of Serra dei Turchi. The town, at an altitude of 1,685 feet (515 meters) above sea level, is located some 8 miles (13 kilometers) from Alba. The origins of the town of Murra date back to the end of the twelfth century. The name of the town is said to derive from *murra,* a Benedictine place name meaning "a closed place surrounded by low stone walls and used to house animals." Another version suggests that the village takes its name from the blackberry—*mura*—and still another suggests that its name comes from *mola,* the grindstones produced in Croera just below the Bricco del Dente. In 1340 the town came under the domination of the Fallettis. It has had its own constitution since 1402.

With 364 growers and 941 acres (381 hectares) of nebbiolo, La Morra is the largest of the 11 Barolo villages and has nearly one-third of the total acreage for Barolo. The panorama from Belvedere Piazza—the castle square—at the top of the village will provide you with some of the most striking views of the Barolo district. When you look at the Barolo district from here, you will see numerous castles and towers, rolling hills covered with vineyards, and, in the background, the heights of the Langhe, Ligurian Apennines, and Maritime Alps. There's a statue dedicated to the winemaker and a bell tower dating from 1700. And pay a visit to the Cantina Communale, where you can learn more about the wines of La Morra.

If you enjoy art, visit Claudia Ferraresi Locatelli's Ca' dj Amis, where you can see her original paintings and drawings as well as paintings and sculpture from other artists. While you're there, descend into the *cantina* of Rocche Costamagna, where they produce a very good Barolo. Ratti Renato's Antiche Cantine dell'Abbazia dell'Annunziata in the Annunziata district, in the fifteenth-century desanctified Abbey of the Annunciation, houses a small but impressive wine museum and, of course, the excellent *azienda* of Renato Ratti, where you can taste some first-class Dolcetto and Barolo.

Major Vineyards

Annunziata	Le Turnote
Brunate, part is in Barolo	Marcenasco dell'Annunziata
Cerequio, part is in Barolo	Monfalletto
Conca dell'Annunziata	Rocche di La Morra
La Serra	Rocchette

Top Producers

Marcarini di Anna Marcarini & Elvio Cogno	Renato Ratti, Antiche Cantine dell'Abbazia dell'Annunziata

Other Producers of Note

Giovanni Accomasso & Figlio (*località* Annunziata)	Silvio Grasso, Cascina Luciani (*località* Annunziata)
Elio Altare (*località* Annunziata)	F.lli Oddero di Giacomo & Luigi Oddero (*località* Santa Maria in Plaustra)
Gianfranco Bovio (*località* Annunziata)	
Cordero di Montezemolo (*località* Annunziata)	Poderi e Cantine di Marengo-Marenda (Casa Vinicola Piemontese)
Giovanni Corino (*località* Annunziata)	Rocche Costamagna di Claudia Ferraresi Locatelli)
F.lli Ferrero di Renato Ferrero (*località* Annunziata)	Roberto Voerzio

Monforte d'Alba, at an altitude of 1,730 feet (530 meters) above sea level, includes the districts of Bussia, Castelletto, Ginestra, Manzoni, Ornati, Perno, Santa Anna, San Giuseppe, and San Sebastiano. The town at one time was known as Pagus Romanus. It is said that the name of the town derives from the fact that it was at one time a fort at the top of a hill—*mons fortis.* For centuries this fort was strategically important in the continuing struggle between the feudal lords and Alba. This lovely picturesque village is situated in the Serralunga Valley some 10 miles (17 kilometers) from Alba. Here the heights will afford you good views of Barolo.

The town had a castle in the ninth century. Today you will see the remains of an eighteenth-century castle built on the site of that earlier *castello* and a Roman bell tower from the thirteenth century. There is a *castello* at Perno and the Roman chapel of Saint Stephen, which contains a twelfth-century apse. In Monforte, 183 growers cultivate 479 acres (194 hectares) of nebbiolo for Barolo, making it the third largest village for Barolo wine. We've enjoyed many good meals at Ristorante Giardino da Felicin, which serves regional specialties. Trattoria della Poste also offers good local fare. And there are some other good restaurants here as well.

Major Vineyards

Bussia Soprana	Ginestra, or Ginestre
Bussia Sottana, part is in	Pian della Polvere, or
Castiglione Falletto	Pianpolvere
Fontanile	Santo Stefano di Perno

Top Producers

Aldo Conterno (*località*	Domenico Clerico (*località*
Bussia)	Manzoni Cucchi)
Giacomo Conterno di	Elio Grasso
Giovanni Conterno	

Other Producers of Note

Conterno Fantino	Giovanni Manzone (*località*
Giacomo Fenocchio & Figli	Castelletto)
(*località* Bussia Sottana)	Armando Parusso (*località*
Riccardo Fenocchio,	Bussia)
Azienda Agricola	Podere Rocche dei Manzoni
"Pianpolvere Soprano"	di Migliorini Valentino
(*località* Bussia)	(*località* Manzoni Soprani)

The town of **Novello,** located some 11 miles (18 kilometers) from Alba, contains the districts of Bergera, Ciocchini, Corini, Moriglione, Panerole, and Tarditi. A village of crumbling houses built along a ridge, it is located at an altitude of 1,545 feet (470 meters) above sea level, offering a lovely panoramic view of the Barolo Valley. The medieval clock tower is also worth a visit. There are 62 growers cultivating 113 acres (46 hectares) of nebbiolo for Barolo. The crypt of the parish church houses a collection of wines from the producers here.

Major Vineyards

Ciocchini	Vergne
Panerole	

Producers of Note

Francesco Marengo	Ferdinando Roggia
(*località* Ciocchini)	

Roddi d'Alba, located some 2.5 miles (4 kilometers) from Alba, is the first village in the Barolo district that you will pass after leaving Alba. It will be on your right. The town, at an altitude of 930 feet (285 meters) above sea level, was a pre-Roman settlement. The name of the town is said to derive from the Celtic *raud* or *rod,* meaning "river." The plain between Roddi and Pollenzo was said to have been the site of two great battles. The Battle of Campi Raudii in 101 B.C. witnessed the defeat of the Cimbri and Teutons by the Romans, who were led by Caio Mario and Quinto Lutazio Catulo, and in A.D. 403 the Roman forces of Emperor Flavio Onorio defeated the Goths, led by Alarico.

Besides the eleventh-century castle and thirteenth-century bell tower, Roddi is home to the University for Truffle Hounds. Here 24 growers cultivate 25 acres (10 hectares) of nebbiolo for Barolo.

Major Vineyard

Bric Sant'Ambrogio

Producer of Note

Azienda Vinicola Adriano, Cantine Roccabella

Serralunga d'Alba, the second largest Barolo-producing village, is home to 145 growers who cultivate 488 acres (197 hectares) of nebbiolo for Barolo. The village, at an altitude of 1,360 feet (415 meters) above sea level, is huddled near the fourteenth-century *castello,* which towers over the town. The town takes its name from *sera longa,* meaning "a long strip of land stretching across a hilltop."

Major Vineyards

Baudana	Gabutti-Parafada
Brea	Lazzarito
Cascina Francia	Marenca e Rivetti
Cerretta	Vigna Rionda
Cucco	

Producers of Note

Aldo Canale	Azienda Agricola Vigna
Cappellano Teobaldo e	Rionda
Roberto Cappellano	Azienda Vitivinicola
Cascina Bruni di F.lli	Palladino di Maurilio
Veglio	Palladino
Eredi Virginia Ferrero San	Tenimenti di Barolo e di
Rocco	Fontanafredda
Giuseppe Massolino &	Basilio Zunino
Figli Giovanni e Renato,	

Verduno, from *verdun,* meaning "fertile hill," was used as a holiday resort by the noble families of Alba Pompeia and Pollentia. This town, at an altitude of 1,250 feet (380 meters) above sea level, is 6 miles (10 kilometers) from Alba. This village, home to the rare pelaverga grape, has 79 growers who cultivate 124 acres (50 hectares) of nebbiolo for Barolo. The pelaverga is said to have been brought here by the Blessed Sebastian Valfrè in the seventh century.

The medieval castle was reconstructed in the seventeenth century and in 1838 it was bought by King Carlo Albert.

Local legend says that after tasting the Barolo of Marquis Carlo Tancredi Falletti, Lord of Barolo, the king engaged the services of noted enologist General Staglieno so that he could produce Barolo wine.

There are a number of restaurants in Verduno. One that we can recommend personally is Ristorante John Falstaff. And Due Lanterne has a good reputation.

Major Vineyards

Brandini	Monvigliero
Breri	Mosca Brevi
Bricco Fava Ciocchini	Pisapolla
Massara, or Massera, part is in Barolo	Riva
	San Lorenzo

Producers of Note

F.lli Alessandria di G. Battista Alessandria	Burlotto, Antica Casa Vinicola Castello Comm.
Bel Colle di Pontiglione P. & C. e Priola G.	G. B. & Cav. Fran^{sco} di Marina Burlotto
Antonio Brero Cav. Luigi	Castello di Verduno
Andrea Burlotto, Cascina Massara	

Characteristics of the Vineyards

We spoke at length with Renato Ratti about the Barolo district, trying to gain an overall impression of how the wines vary from one village to another, and to pinpoint the particular characteristics of the individual vineyards. In our interviews with the producers we also attempted to gather an overall image of the Barolos of each *comune* and each major vineyard. To this we added our own impressions from personal tastings. Many people were involved in the formulation of this overview, but the evaluations, which we have given where we had sufficient experience to render them, are our own.

The Crus Themselves

The stars given to the cru were compiled by asking the producers to list the best vineyards in the Barolo growing zone. Only one vineyard appeared on everyone's list: Cannubi. We awarded it three stars. The next most frequently listed vineyards were given two stars, and then one star. *No stars simply means that the vineyard didn't appear on anyone's list or appeared only on the list of those producers who bottle it.*

The following notations are used in this section:

[a] Listed by Renato Ratti as a historic subregion for vine growing.

[b] This combination of producer and cru is among our favorites in Barolo.

[c] Labeled with the cru name.

Other owner-producers indicates those who own a piece of this vineyard and/or those who use grapes from this vineyard to produce a Barolo with grapes from here, regardless of whether or not they do a cru bottling.

Albarella (*Barolo*). Marchesi di Barolo owns a piece of this vineyard. Andrea Oberto grows dolcetto here.

Altenazze, or **Altenazzo** (*Castiglione Falletto*). Paolo Scavino owns land in this vineyard.

Altinasso. Cav. Bartolomeo Borgogno owns a piece of this vineyard. It could be part of the Altenazzo vineyard in Castiglione Falletto.

Annunziata (*La Morra*). Many growers own land in the Annunziata district, including Lorenzo Accomasso, Gianfranco Bovio (9.4 acres/3.8 hectares), Angelo Germano, Silvio Grasso, Franco Molino, F.lli Revello, Giovanni Revello, and Settimo Aurelio. F.lli Ferrero grows 3.98 acres (1.61 hectares) of nebbiolo for Barolo and 0.42 (0.17) of barbera here. Renato Ratti finds a hint of tobacco in the aroma of the wines from this district.**

SOME OF THE SUBCRUS OF ANNUNZIATA

Arborina, Arburina, or Arburine	Manzoni
	Marcenasco
Conca dell'Annunziata	Monfalletto
Francesco	Plicotti, or Plucotti
Gancia	Riccardo
Gattera	Rocche di La Morra
Giachini	Rocchette, or Rochetta

Arbarella (*Barolo*). Giacomo Brezza grows dolcetto here.

Arborino, Arburina, or **Arburine dell'Annunziata** (*La Morra*). Elio Altare has produced 4,000 to 5,000 bottles of Barolo a year since 1978 from his 3.7 acres (1.5 hectares) of nebbiolo in this part of **Annunziata**. He also produces a *barrique*-aged nebbiolo, Vigna Arborina, from some of the vines. Gianfranco Bovio started bottling a Barolo cru from his 1.3-acre (0.5-hectare) subplot in Arborina in 1985.*

Arionda (*Serralunga d'Alba*). Another name for **Vigna Rionda.*****

Arione[a] (*Serralunga d'Alba*). Gigi Rosso has bottled a Cascina Arione Barolo from his 7.4 acres (3 hectares) of vines in this historic subregion since 1978.

Arnulfo[a] (*Monforte d'Alba*). Accademia Torregiorgi buys grapes from Arturo Barale to produce his Arnulfo Barolo. And F.lli Felice, Vittorio, and Berardino and Paolina Zabaldano own land here. This cru is in the **Bussia** vineyard district. Carlo Petrini lists it as a separate vineyard in his *Atlante delle grandi vigne di Langa Zona del Barolo, Comune di Monforte.*[3] The vineyard ranges in altitude from 885 to 1,050 feet (270 to 320 meters) above sea level. The vines face south and southwest, with the lower part facing west.*

Baiolo (*La Morra*).

Bartu. Mario Savigliano has vines in this vineyard.

VINEYARD MAP OF BAROLO (BASED ON A MAP PREPARED BY RENATO RATTI, ANTICHE CANTINE DELLA ABBAZIA DELL'ANNUNZIATA, JUNE 1990)

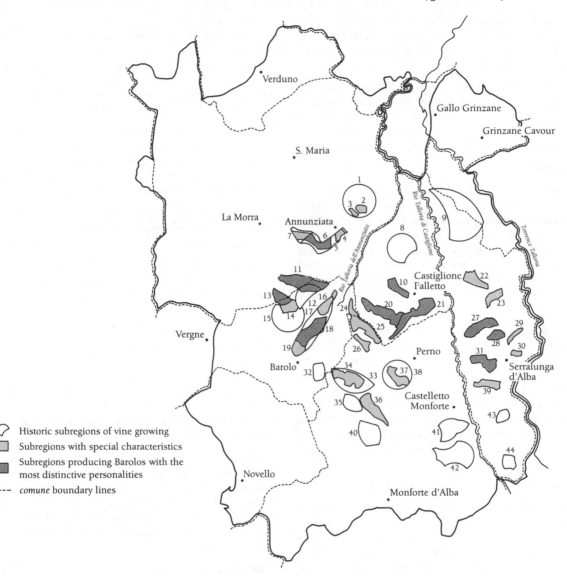

Historic subregions of vine growing

Subregions with special characteristics

Subregions producing Barolos with the most distinctive personalities

---- *comune* boundary lines

1. Monfalletto	16. Cannubi Boschis	31. Marenca-Rivette Iª Categoria
2. Monfalletto	17. Cannubi	32. Costa di Rose
3. Le Turnote	18. Cannubi Iª Categoria	33. Granbussia
4. Conca dell'Abbazia dell'Annunziata	19. Cannubi Muscatel	34. Bussia Soprana
5. Marcenasco	20. Villero Iª Categoria	35. Dardi
6. Rocche Iª Categoria	21. Rocche Iª Categoria	36. Pian della Polvere
7. Rocchette	22. Baudana	37. Santo Stefano
8. Montanello	23. Cerretta	38. S. Stefano di Perno
9. Fontanafredda	24. Pugnane	39. Vigna Rionda
10. Momprivato Iª Categoria	25. Fontanile	40. Arnulfo
11. Brunate Iª Categoria	26. Bussia Sottana	41. Grassi
12. Zonchetta	27. Gabutti-Parafada Iª Categoria	42. Ginestre
13. Cerequio Iª Categoria	28. Lazzarito Iª Categoria	43. Ornato
14. Sarmazza	29. Brea	44. Arione
15. Sarmazza	30. Cucco	

Batasiolo (*La Morra*). F.lli Dogliani has renamed their winery for this vineyard. They produce a Barolo from the 24 acres (9.8 hectares) of nebbiolo that they grow here. They also have 1.2 acres (0.5 hectare) of nebbiolo for Nebbiolo delle Langhe, 2.4 (1) dolcetto, 1.9 (0.8) barbera, and 1.5 (0.6) chardonnay grapes in this vineyard. In total they own 31 acres (12.6 hectares). The vines, planted in clay and marl soil at an altitude of 889 feet (271 meters) above sea level, face southeast.

Baudana (*Serralunga d'Alba*). Teobaldo e Roberto Cappellano buys grapes from this vineyard district. Moscone and Giuseppe Massolino's Azienda Agricola "Vigna Rionda" cultivate vines here, as does Basilio Zunino. Zunino grows nebbiolo for Barolo, dolcetto, and barbera in the section he refers to as **Sorì di Baudana**.**

Bettolotti Para (*La Morra*).

Bianca (*Serralunga d'Alba*). Fontanafredda produces about 3,500 bottles of a Bianca Barolo from their 1.26 acres (0.5 hectare) of nebbiolo vines. These vines, planted at altitudes ranging from 885 to 919 feet (270 to 280 meters), face southwest. The soil is from the Miocene and Helvetian epochs, and consists of limestone and assimilable iron. This Barolo is austere in its youth and is regarded for its bouquet, which Fontanafredda describes as being reminiscent of dried grass and withered flowers. The wine itself is dry and full-bodied.

Bonfani (*Monforte d'Alba and Barolo*). This subcru lies within the Bussia vineyard district. The Doglianis of Batasiolo own 22 acres (8.8 hectares) of vines, which include 18 (7.3) of nebbiolo for Barolo, plus 1.4 (0.6) of nebbiolo for Nebbiolo delle Langhe and 2.3 (0.95) of chardonnay. The vines are planted in clay with calcerous marl and sandstone outcroppings at an altitude of 863 feet (263 meters) above sea level; they face southwest. They produce some 14,000 to 15,000 bottles a year of Barolo from the nebbiolo. In 1979 they produced, under the Dogliani label, a Bonfani-Bussia Barolo.

Borgata di Sorano (*Serralunga d'Alba*). See **Sorano**.

Boscaretto, or **Boscaretti** (*Serralunga d'Alba*). F.lli Dogliani of Batasiolo owns 87 acres (35 hectares) in this vineyard. They have 34 acres (14 hectares) of nebbiolo for Barolo and 2.3 (0.9) for Nebbiolo delle Langhe, plus 1.4 (0.6) of dolcetto, 2.8 (1.1) chardonnay, and 46 (18.6) moscato. The vines, planted in shale and marl at an altitude of 1,381 feet (421 meters) above sea level, face southeast. They have bottled a '79, '82, and '85 Barolo from here. Scarpa buys grapes and produces some 8,000 bottles of I Boscaretti a year from this cru.

Boschetti (*Barolo*). Marchesi di Barolo owns 8.4 acres (3.4 hectares) in this vineyard. They produce a Dolcetto d'Alba from here.

Boschis (*Castiglione Falletto*). The most noted part of this vineyard is the top, **Bricco Boschis,** owned by the Cavallotto brothers.

Brandini (*Verduno*).

Brea (*Serralunga d'Alba*). Brea is a regarded vineyard district.*

Breri (*Verduno*). Members of the Terre del Barolo co-op farm vines here, as do Bel Colle and Marina Burlotto of Comm. G. B. Burlotto.

Briacca (*Castiglione Falletto*). Briacca is a 1-acre (0.4-hectare) parcel of Rocche owned by Basilio Zunino. It faces southeast and was planted 100 percent in nebbiolo rosé. These grapes were vinified by Alfredo Currado of Vietti for his very fine Barolo Briacca.[b] The vines were ripped out in 1984. The vineyard has since been replanted with all three nebbiolo clones. The last Barolo from Briacca was the '83. Briacca produces a softer and more velvety Barolo than Rocche that has less body. Until the grapes reach full maturity they will be blended into Vietti's Castiglione Barolo. They should be producing in 1991. When they are mature enough they will be blended into the Vietti Rocche Barolo.**

Bric del Fiasc (*Castiglione Falletto*). Paolo Scavino owns 6.7 acres (2.7 hectares) of vines in Bricco Fiasco. The vines, at 1,116 feet (340 meters) above sea level, face southwest. Since 1978 he has been bottling a Barolo from his 4.4 acres (1.8 hectares) of nebbiolo vines which he labeled with this dialect name.

Bric in Pugnane (*Castiglione Falletto*). This vineyard is the highest part of the **Pugnane** vineyard district. Giuseppe Mascarello has bought grapes from here for a Barolo cru since 1971.**

Bric Sant'Ambrogio (*Roddi d'Alba*). Eredi Lodali owns 12.4 acres (5 hectares) of vines in this vineyard. They produce three wines from here: 12,000 bottles a year of a Barolo, and a Dolcetto and Barbera d'Alba.

Bricco (*Barolo and La Morra*). F.lli Dogliani of Batasiolo owns 32.4 acres (13.1 hectares) of vines planted on marl with sand strata and sandstone soil at an altitude of 1,575 feet (480 meters) above sea level. The vines face south to southwest. There are 9.6 acres (3.9 hectares) of nebbiolo for Barolo and 8.4 (3.4) for Nebbiolo delle Langhe, plus 5.4 (2.2) for Dolcetto d'Alba, 5.4 (2.2) for Barbera d'Alba, and 3.5 (1.4) for Chardonnay. Bricco di Barolo is actually a part of Bricco di Vergne vineyard.

Bricco (*Castiglione Falletto*). Giuseppe Mascarello owns 1.7 acres (0.7 hectare) of vines here. Silvio Grasso's Cascina Luciani also owns a piece of this vineyard, and the Cavallotto brothers farm a 2.4-acre (1-hectare) portion of Bricco Boschis that they call Bricco. They produce a Barolo from that plot. We don't know if it is the same as this vineyard. Giuseppe Mascarello produces a Dolcetto d'Alba from here.

Bricco Boschis (*Castiglione Falletto*). The top part of the Boschis vineyard. This 50-acre (20-hectare) vineyard is owned in its entirety by F.lli Cavallotto. The Cavallotto brothers have 40 acres (16 hectares) of vines, including 13 (5.3) of nebbiolo. Vines are planted at a median altitude of 1,150 feet (350 meters) above sea level. All of their wines, including their Barolo, are from this vineyard and are labeled with this cru name. They bottle Barolos from four subcrus: Colle Sud-Ovest, Punta Marcello, San Giuseppe, and Bricco.

Bricco Bussia (*Monforte d'Alba*). Aldo Conterno has referred to his holdings in **Bussia** Soprana as Bricco Bussia. He subdivides his Barolo vineyards here into Vigna Ciabot (now Romirasco), Vigna Cicala, and Vigna Colonnello.**

Bricco Cicala (*Monforte d'Alba*). A subcru within the **Bussia** Soprana vineyard district. Aldo Conterno[b] bottles a fine Barolo in

CAVALLOTTO'S BRICCO BOSCHIS BAROLO CRUS

Cru	Acres	Hectares	Average Annual Production in Bottles	Year Planted
Bricco	2.4	0.9800	5,867	1967
Colle Sud-Ovest	2.7	1.1100	6,667	1951
Punta Marcello	1.7	0.6900	4,000	1967
San Giuseppe	10.2	4.1227	24,533	1947
Total	17.0	6.9027	41,067	

some vintages. Carlo Petrini lists Bricco Cicala as a separate vineyard in his *Atlante delle grandi vigne di Langa Zona del Barolo, Comune di Monforte*.[4] Conterno maintains that it is part of Bussia Soprana.**

Bricco Colonello (*Monforte d'Alba*). A subcru within the **Bussia** Soprana vineyard district. Aldo Conterno[b] bottles a fine Barolo in some vintages. According to Carlo Petrini, Colonnello is a separate vineyard.[5] Aldo Conterno disagrees, as do the others who farm grapes here.**

Bricco Fava (*Verduno*).

Bricco Fiasco (*Castiglione Falletto*). This vineyard is more commonly known by its dialect name, **Bric del Fiasc**. Azelia owns 7.4 acres (3 hectares) of vines planted at 787 feet (240 meters) above sea level. They have a southern exposure. Azelia produces between 10,000 and 13,000 bottles of Barolo annually.

Bricco Luciani. Silvio Grasso produced a Barolo cru from his 6 acres (2.5 hectares) of nebbiolo vines here in 1986. He also produces a Barbera d'Alba from here. See **Cascina Luciani.**

Bricco Manescotto (*La Morra*). Angelo Veglio cultivates vines here.

Bricco Mira Langa. Luigi Calissano produced an '82 Barolo Riserva that they labeled as Bricco Mira Langa. This could very well be part of the **Miralanga** vineyard in the *comune* of Barolo.

Bricco Plaustra (*La Morra*). See **Convento di Santa Maria in Plaustra.**

Bricco Punta (*Castiglione Falletto*). Azelia's 3.7 acres (1.5 hectares) of vines here are planted at 978 feet (298 meters) above sea level. Those vines, facing southward, produce 5,000 to 6,000 bottles of Barolo annually.

Bricco Rocche (*Castiglione Falletto*). The Ceretto brothers own a 3.7-acre (1.5-hectare) vineyard on the top part of Rocche known as Bricco Rocche. This part of the vineyard, on the other side of the road from the main part of Rocche, was planted by the Cerettos. The vines, planted at altitudes of 1,107 to 1,116 feet (310 to 340 meters) above sea level, face south.

According to Carlo Petrini, Bricco Rocche is actually part of a vineyard that he calls Serra.[6] Lorenzo Fantini also lists a La Serra vineyard in Castiglione in his *Monografia Sulla Viticoltura ed Enologia Nella Provincia di Cuneo*.[7] Prior to this, we had never heard of a Serra vineyard in Castiglione Falletto. A farm, Cascina Serra, is located in the same area of Bricco Rocche, but no vines were planted there until the Cerettos did so. When we were working on the first edition of this book we were told by a few producers that Bricco Rocche was not part of the Rocche vineyard. These producers said that Rocche was on the eastern side of the road, Bricco Rocche on the western. Second, they argued that prior to the Cerettos having planted this vineyard, it had never been planted before. We asked Renato Ratti, who told us that if you followed the Rocche vineyard you would see that Bricco Rocche was part of that same slope, separated by the road. And yes, the Cerettos planted it, but regardless of whether or not it is planted, if it is part of the same slope and has the same soil and exposure, it is part of that vineyard.

They first produced this Barolo at their Azienda Agricola "Bricco Rocche" in 1982. The second vintage was the '85, followed by the '86, '88, and '89. They plan to produce it in the best vintages only. Production totals some 5,000 bottles in the vintages that they make it.**

Bricco San Biago (*La Morra*). Luigi Oberto has vines here.

Bricco San Martino (*La Morra*). See **San Martino.**

Bricco Viole (*Barolo*). G. D. Vajra owns 3.2 acres (1.3 hectares) of vines here and produces a Barolo. Sebaste produces a *barrique*-aged wine with this name that he said is named for the fourteenth-century San Pietro delle Viole near the winery. We don't know if that wine comes from this vineyard.

Briccolina (*Serralunga d'Alba*). F.lli Dogliani of Batasiolo has 4 acres (1.6 hectares) of nebbiolo planted at 1,326 feet (400 meters) above sea level in clay soil that is rich in gray marl with sand outcroppings. These vines have a southwestern exposure. They produce some 7,000 bottles of Barolo from those vines. F.lli Dogliani sold a '78 Barolo Briccolina under their label. From the 1986 vintage they produced 13,000 bottles of a Barolo in *barrique*. They told us that the Briccolina vineyard is well exposed to the sun, and that their nebbiolo vines here are thirty years old.

Brichet (*La Morra*). Angelo Veglio grows grapes in this vineyard.

Brichetto (*La Morra*). Angelo Veglio cultivates vines here.

Bricotto Bussia e Ciabot (*Monforte d'Alba*). Clerico has bottled a Barolo from his holdings in these two crus since 1978. He makes a scant 1,300 bottles!

Brunate (*mostly in La Morra, a small part is in Barolo*). Brunate, with a southern to southwestern exposure, is about 985 feet (300 meters) in altitude. Among the subdivisions of the Brunate hillside are *Fontanazza, La Serra,* and *Zonchetta,* now Zonchera (as it is called in Piemontese). Elvio Cogno told us that the section containing forty-year-old vines was destroyed by the hail of 1986. Cogno also told us that old-timers here consider Brunate and Fontanazza the two best crus of La Morra. Yet some consider Fontanazza to be a subsection of the Brunate hillside.

Poderi Marcarini's 11.0762 acres (4.4823 hectares) of nebbiolo vines, planted between 1948 and 1985 at an average altitude of about 985 feet (300 meters) above sea level, face south to southwest. Most of Marcarini's holdings here—9.0771 acres (3.6733 hectares)—are in La Morra. The soil is calcareous clay with a predominance of magnesium. Elvio Cogno has vinified a Barolo from here since 1958. Average annual output is 25,000 bottles.[b] Part of the Marcarini holdings are in Barolo. That 1.9769-acre (0.8090-hectare) section has been bottled separately since 1987 and is labeled as Brunate-Canon.[b] Of the four wines produced from this subsection thus far, Cogno has vinified an average of 1,011 gallons (38.25 hectoliters), equivalent to 5,100 bottles of Barolo.

The Ceretto brothers own 15 acres (6 hectares) of vines here planted between 853 and 1,017 feet (260 and 310 meters) above sea level. They have produced an Azienda Agricola "Bricco Rocche" Barolo from here since 1978. They produce 25,000 bottles a year of that Barolo Brunate.

Marchesi di Barolo own 5 acres (2 hectares) here, plus they have an additional 1.7 acres (0.7 hectare) under contract. Their '85 Barolo came from a 4.2-acre (1.69-hectare) section. In 1989 half of their own acreage was replanted.

Renato Ratti notes nuances of licorice, cherries, and *tartufi* in the aroma of Brunate. Luciano Rinaldi finds his Brunate less perfumed but bigger in body than the Cannubi. Elvio Cogno, who vinifies a Brunate and a La Serra, finds the Brunate in its youth more austere and closed, but with age it smooths out and becomes softer, rounder, and more velvety. Indeed it needs age to come into its own. The word *elegant* appeared over and over again from the producers and in our tasting notes. Vietti refers to this Barolo as perfumed. **

OTHER BRUNATE OWNER-PRODUCERS

- Giovanni Bogletti's grapes go to the Terre del Barolo co-op.
- Michele Chiarlo of Cantine Duca d'Asti[c] started producing a Barolo in 1988 from a 1.24-acre (0.5-hectare) plot of 40-year-old vines.
- Luigi Coppo[c]
- F.lli Dogliani of Batasiolo owns a part of Brunate which is in Barolo.

- Franco Fiorina buys grapes.
- Marengo Mario[c]
- F.lli Oddero
- Azienda Agricola "Ponte Rocca" di Francesco Pittatore[c] (we believe that he leases these vines to Michele Chiarlo).
- Francesco Rinaldi[c] owns 5.4 acres (2.2 hectares).
- Giuseppe Rinaldi[b,c] owns 3.7 acres (1.5 hectares) of nebbiolo; he has bottled a Brunate cru since 1971.
- Renzo Roggiero's grapes go to the Terre del Barolo co-op.
- Casa Vinicola San Lorenzo[c]
- Sebaste[c] produced their first Barolo cru in 1989.
- Terre del Barolo[c]
- Vietti[c] has bought grapes from a 2.5-acre (1-hectare) plot of mostly nebbiolo lampia since 1984.
- Roberto Voerzio has leased about 2.5 acres (1 hectare) here since 1988.[c]

Brunate-Canon (*Barolo*). The 1.9769-acre (0.8090-hectare) section of the *Brunate* vineyard in Barolo owned by Anna Marcarini of Podere Marcarini. **

Brunella (*Castiglione Falletto*). Vignolo-Lutati owns vines here and has produced a Barolo Brunella. Francesco Sobrero owns a piece of the section here that they refer to as *Ciabot Tanasio.*

Bruni (*Serralunga d'Alba*). Vezza has a vineyard in Bruni, as does Porta Rossa.

Bussia (*mostly in Monforte d'Alba, a small part is in Castiglione Falletto and in Barolo*). Bussia is actually a series of hills; the highest part, at 1,475 feet (450 meters) above sea level, belongs to Aldo Conterno, who owns 64 acres (26 hectares) here, 28.4 (11.5) in nebbiolo for Barolo. Bussia is subdivided into two sections. The higher part, Bussia Soprana (or Alta), and the lower one, Bussia Sottana (or Bassa). Bussia Soprana borders on Barolo, and Bussia Sottana on Castiglione Falletto. The section in Barolo is known as Monrobiolo. Bartolo Mascarello and, we believe, Sebaste own a piece of this section.

Within Soprana are the crus of Bricco Ciabot now known as *Romirasco, Bricco Cicala,* and *Bricco Colonello.* The Cicala vineyard is situated higher up and at a steeper grade. Aldo Conterno's 2.8 acres (1.1 hectares/3 *giornate*) of vines in Cicala are over thirty-five years old. His plot in Colonello covers 1.9 acres (0.76 hectare/2 *giornate*). Conterno produces some 5,000 bottles of very fine Barolo from each of these last two subcrus as well as 7,200 to 7,500 bottles of Barolo Bussia-Ciabot. His first Ciabot was the '80; he produced 1,000 bottles for the Cavalieri del Tartufi e dei Vini di Alba. His first commercial release was the '82. Since 1986 he has used the Romirasco name, as there were other producers using the Ciabot name. The lampia vines in the Ciabot section were planted about 1970 (*ciabot* means "little house in the country"). Aldo Conterno described the differences of his three '82 crus: the Cicala is the most complete, the Colonello the most forward, and the Romirasco the most tannic. Conterno also produces, in the very best vintages, a Granbussia Barolo. He produced a '71, '74, '78, '82, '85, '88, '89, and, as it now appears, a '90. In all, Aldo Conterno owns some 64 acres (26 hectares) of vines in Bussia Soprana; 28.4 (11.5) are in nebbiolo for Barolo.[b]

Paolo Fenocchio owns a 7.4-acre (3-hectare) subplot in Bricco

Colonello. We suspect that this could adjoin Aldo Conterno's Colonello. He sells the grapes to Alfredo Currado for Vietti's Bussia Barolo. That Barolo is made from a blend of 20-75-5 michet, lampia, and rosé. Currado describes his Bussia Barolo as elegant, with fine perfume, moderate alcohol, and a lot of style. Vietti also produces a Barbera and Dolcetto d'Alba from Bussia.

Giuseppe Mascarello has bought grapes from Bussia Soprana from which he has made a very good Barolo since 1970.

Arnulfo, vinified by Accademia Torregiorgi, is part of Bussia. F.lli Dogliani of Batasiolo owns vines in the subsection of *Bonfani.* Some say *Pianpolvere* is another subcru. Riccardo Fenocchio owns vines in that section, and *Dardi,* too, is said to be within the Bussia district. Angelo Germano cultivates vines in that section.

Carlo Petrini, in his *Atlante delle grandi vigne di Langa Zona del Barolo, Comune di Monforte,* lists Arnulfo, Bricco Cicala, Colonnello, Dardi, and Pianpolvere as separate vineyards.[8]

Giuseppe Colla of Prunotto says that his Bussia cru has better structure and is longer lived than his Cannubi. When he owned the Prunotto winery they bought grapes from a 10-acre (4.1-hectare) plot. Since Antinori acquired the controlling interest of Prunotto, they bought some 20 acres (8 hectares) of Bussia Soprana.

Giacomo Fenocchio owns 14.3 acres (5.8 hectares) of Bussia Sottana—7.9 (3.2) in nebbiolo vines planted between 1,017 and 1,050 feet (310 and 320 meters) above sea level, 1.5 (0.6) in barbera, and 4.9 (2) in dolcetto. He produces a Dolcetto d'Alba from '89 and a Barolo Bussia. Previously his Barolo was labeled Bussia-Bricat Cannubio because it was made from grapes that he grows in Bussia and Cannubio. And Armando Parusso produced a Barolo that he labeled Bussia-Rocche, which we assume was made from grapes grown in those two vineyards.

F.lli Barale own 18.5 acres (7.5 hectares) of vines planted in barbera, chardonnay, dolcetto, and nebbiolo grapes. They are planted at 1,181 feet (360 meters) above sea level at a southwestern exposure.**

OTHER BUSSIA OWNER-PRODUCERS

- Michele Chiarlo of Cantine Duca d'Asti[c] started producing a Barolo from here in 1988. The vines are 18 years old.
- Clerico[c] produces a Barolo **Bricotto Bussia e Ciabot** from his 1.24 acres (0.5 hectare) of nebbiolo vines.
- Bruno Giacosa[c] produced a '79 Barolo Bussia.
- Bartolo Mascarello produces a Dolcetto d'Alba from his 1.8835 acres (0.7622 hectare) of vines here.
- F.lli Oddero own vines in Bussia Soprana.
- Armando Parusso[c] owns 0.9 acre (0.4 hectare) of vines.
- Sebaste[c] owns 16 acres (6.5 hectares) in, we believe, the section of Barolo known as Monrobiolo.
- Terre del Barolo, members of this co-op cultivate vines in Bussia Soprana and Bussia Sottana.

Bussia Soprana and *Bussia Sottana* are discussed under *Bussia.*

Ca' Neire (La Morra). Contratto owns 8.75 acres (3.54 hectares) of nebbiolo planted at 985 feet (300 meters) above sea level. Those vines, facing south, have been used to produce a cru Barolo since 1985. Cà Neire is part of Cerequio.

Camia (Serralunga d'Alba).

Cannubi, or *Cannubbio*[a] (Barolo). If there is a single finest vineyard in Barolo, and the consensus is that there is, that vineyard is Cannubi, or Cannubbio, as it is sometimes called. Being located sort of halfway between two valleys, the Cannubi vineyard is enhanced by the intermingling of both soils, and the wine combines some characteristics from both—"the best of both worlds," as Ratti put it. Cannubi has a southern to southeastern exposure. It ranges in altitude from 755 to 1,015 feet (230 to 309 meters) above sea level and is very steep, with many slopes inclining at a 25 percent grade. Luciano Rinaldi[b] described his Cannubbio as a perfumed wine that ages very well; he noted that it has less body than the Brunate, which he also bottles as a cru. This approximately 75-acre (30-hectare) vineyard is divided into several subsections and among 15 owners.

F.lli Borgogno owns 7 acres (2.8 hectares), 5.2 (2.1) in nebbiolo that they use to produce 1,250 cases of Barolo a year. Their 3.1 acres (1.3 hectares) of lampia were planted in 1981 and the 2 (0.8) of michet in 1945 and 1955. They also have 1.4 acres (0.6 hectare) of barbera that was planted in 1947 and 0.5 (0.2) of dolcetto planted in 1960.

Michele Chiarlo of Duca d'Asti bought 2.5 acres (1 hectare) from Carlo Pittatore in 1988, the steepest part, in the center. It was unplanted and has a 50 percent grade. Chiarlo built terraces and planted vines in March 1990. He estimates that his first vintage will be in 1993. He also rents 1.2 acres (0.5 hectare) from Barale. Chiarlo expects to produce his first Cannubi Barolo from Cannubi in 1990. He told us that he should be able to produce between 2,400 and 2,650 bottles.

Bartolo Mascarello[a] owns 2.8252 acres (1.1433 hectares) of nebbiolo. In 1971, he produced 2,110 bottles of a Cannubi Barolo labeled Giulio Mascarello for his father.

Paolo Scavino rents 2 acres (0.8 hectare) of nebbiolo in the Cannubi district from Michele Fontana from which he produces a Barolo cru. The first was the '84. The vines are planted at 1,198 feet (365 meters) above sea level and face southward.

Scarzello e Abbona of Marchesi di Barolo own 18.1557 acres (7.3472 hectares). They have produced a Barolo from here since 1975. The '85 Barolo came from the grapes grown on a 10.46-acre (4.2324-hectare) plot.***

OTHER CANNUBI OWNER-PRODUCERS

- F.lli Barale owns 2.5 acres (1 hectare).
- Giacomo Borgogno owns 3.7 acres (1.5 hectares).
- Francesco Boschis owns 5 acres (2 hectares).
- Giacomo Brezza produces a cru Barolo from the section that he rents from Beni Parrocchiali.[c] His first Barolo cru from here was the '89.
- Burlotto Comm. G. B. di Marina Burlotto owns a piece.
- Cascina Adelaide di G. Terzano
- Ceretto produced a '71 Barolo Cannubi.
- Dott. Damilano
- Michele Fontana leases his 2.5-acre (1-hectare) plot to Enrico Scavino.
- Franco Fiorina buys grapes from here.

- Lucchini sold their section to Gancia in the spring of 1989.
- E. Pira owns 1.3 acres (0.54 hectare), all in nebbiolo.
- Prunotto[c] buys from 3 acres (1.2 hectares).
- Giuseppe Rinaldi owns 0.094 acre (0.38 hectare) of nebbiolo, in what we believe is the section known as Cannubi San Lorenzo.
- Francesco Sandrone owns or owned a little over an acre (0.5 hectare) of barbera. We heard that he sold it recently to F.lli Barale.
- Tenuta Carretta[b,c] has 6.7 acres (2.71 hectares) of vines here that were planted in 1961.
- Tenuta Coluè owns nebbiolo for Barolo; they don't bottle it as a cru.
- Viberti Mariarosa

Cannubi-Boschis and **Cannubi-Muscatel** (*Barolo*). These two vineyards are not actually within the Cannubi vineyard district, although many producers claim that they are. They are separate districts. Cannubi-Boschis, or Monghisolfo as it is also known, is the northernmost district and Muscatel, just north of Barolo itself, the southernmost one. Some producers also include the **La Valletta** vineyard within the highly esteemed Cannubi district.

Francesco Rinaldi owns 5.4 acres (2.2 hectares) of vines in Boschis. His Barolo from here is labeled as Cannubbio. Marchesi di Barolo owns 8.6 acres (3.5 hectares) of Muscatel and 9.5 (3.9) of La Valletta; the two are bottled separately. They have produced more than 13,000 bottles of a La Valletta Barolo since 1973. They did produce 13,370 bottles of a Barolo Cannubi-Muscatel. The last one they produced was the '82. They are replanting the vineyard with cabernet sauvignon, barbera, and nebbiolo.

F.lli Dogliani of Batasiolo also owns a piece of Muscatel which they call Cannubi-Moscatello. Teobaldo Prandi owns a piece of Monghisolfo and Luciano Sandrone cultivates 3 acres (1.2 hectares) of vines. He labels his Barolo from here Cannubi-Boschis. Giacomo Fenocchio owns 2.5 acres (1 hectare) of nebbiolo vines planted at 951 feet (290 meters) above sea level. Those vines face southeast. Fenocchio produces a Barolo that, although it should be labeled Cannubi-Boschis, is labeled Cannubi.**

Cannubi-Monghisolfo (*Barolo*). This vineyard is discussed under **Cannubi-Boschis**.

Cannubi-Muscatel (*Barolo*). This vineyard is covered under **Cannubi-Boschis**.

Cannubi-San Lorenzo (*Barolo*). See **San Lorenzo** in Barolo.

Capalot (*La Morra*). Azienda Agricola "Santa Maria" bottles a Capalot Barolo from their vines here.

Capalotti (*La Morra*). Silvio Alessandria, Giovanni Roggero, and Azienda Agricola "S. Biagio" cultivate vines in Capalotti which could be the same as Capalot.

Cappellotti (*La Morra*). Azienda Agricola "Santa Maria" has vines in this vineyard.

Carpegna (*Serralunga d'Alba*). This vineyard is in Borgata Sorano. Accademia Torregiorgi buys grapes from Stefano Veglio and produces a cru Barolo from here. Pasquale Veglio of Cascina Bruni

cultivates 7.4 acres (3 hectares) of vines here. F.lli Vaglio of a different Cascina Bruni owns 11.3 acres (4.6 hectares), 8 (3.2) in nebbiolo for Barolo. Cappellano produces a Barolo from here from the grapes he buys from Giovanni Zunino.

Casanere, or **Casenere** (*La Morra*). F.lli Casetta produces a Barolo cru from vines grown here.

Cascina Adelaide (*Barolo*). Terzano-Benvenuti owns this property and bottles their Barolos under its name.

Cascina Alberta (*Treiso d'Alba*). The Contratto winery owns nearly 10 acres (4 hectares) of vines in Treiso from which they produce a cru Barbaresco, Barbera d'Alba, and a Chardonnay delle Langhe. They first produced the Barbaresco in 1985. The vines, planted at altitudes ranging from 985 to 1,150 feet (300 to 350 meters) above sea level, face south-southwest.

Cascina Arione (*Serralunga d'Alba*). Gigi Rosso owns this farm and its 7.4 acres (3 hectares) of vines. He has labeled one of his Barolos with the *cascina* name since the '78.

Cascina Badarina. This *cascina* takes in the vineyard holdings of the Bersano.

Cascina Castelletto (*Perno di Monforte d'Alba*). Gigi Rosso has produced a Barolo from his 9.4 acres (3.79 hectares) of vines in the Castelletto vineyard since the '85.

Cascina Francia (*Serralunga d'Alba*). This 39.5-acre (16-hectare) vineyard has been owned in its entirety by Giacomo Conterno since 1974. This vineyard is planted at an altitude ranging from 1,705 to 1,740 feet (520 to 530 meters) above sea level in various varieties: 12.7 acres (5.1 hectares) are nebbiolo, 6.2 (2.5) barbera, 11.3 (4.6) dolcetto, and 1.4 (0.6) freisa. Conterno uses the vineyard name on the labels of all his wines except Monfortino. **Monfortino**[b] is a Barolo made in the best vintages from some of the best nebbiolo grapes grown here.

Cascina Gagliassi (*Barolo*).

Cascina Gancia (*La Morra*). Angelo Veglio has some holdings in this part of the Annunziata district.

Cascina Luciani (*La Morra*). Silvio Grasso's Cascina Luciani owns 23.5 acres (9.5 hectares), mostly in the Annunziata section of La Morra. He also owns a piece of the Bricco vineyard in Castiglione Falletto, Galinot or Gallinotto and Ciabot di Preve in Barolo. In 1986, Grasso produced a Barolo cru from Cascina Luciani.

Cascina Masante della Bussia Soprana (*Monforte d'Alba*). Aldo Conterno has used this name for some of his Barolos.

Cascina Massara (*Verduno*). Andrea Burlotto bottles his Barolo under this label. At least part of those holdings are in the **Massara** vineyard.

Cascina Mosconi (*Monforte d'Alba*). See **Mosconi.**

Cascina Nuova (*La Morra*). Elio Altare owns this *cascina* in the Annunziata district. Since 1978 Altare has been producing 5,000 to 6,000 bottles of Barolo a year under this label. Angelo Veglio also has some holdings that he calls Cascina Nuova.

Cascina Palazzo. Francesco Rinaldi produced a '78 Barolo Cannubbio e Brunate from his holdings in these two esteemed crus that he labeled Cascina Palazzo.

Cascina Pilone (*Castiglione Falletto*). This 4.7087-acre (1.9055-hectare) estate is owned by Franco Fiorina. They grow dolcetto and barbera and have a small amount of nebbiolo as well.

Cascina Secolo (*Barolo and La Morra*). This *cascina* takes in Contratto's holdings in the part of Cerequio called **Ca' Neire** in La Morra and part of Sarmassa in Barolo.

Cascina Traversa (*La Morra*). This *cascina* is in the Santa Maria area of La Morra.

Cascina Zoccolaio (*Monforte d'Alba*). Franco Fiorina leases 37.7 acres (15.2 hectares) here. The vineyard is planted in nebbiolo.

Case Brusciate (*La Morra*). Franco Fiorina owns 3.7669 acres (1.5244 hectares) of nebbiolo vines. This vineyard is above Cerequio.

Case Giuli (*Grinzane Cavour*).

Castellero (*mostly in Barolo, a small part is in Monforte d'Alba*). F.lli Barale owns 20 acres (8 hectares) of nebbiolo, barbera, and chardonnay planted at an elevation of 1,181 feet (360 meters) above sea level. Those vines face southwest. They produce a Barolo cru from here. Giacomo Brezza and Francesco Pittatore's Azienda Agricola "Ponte Rocca" also have vines here. Brezza does a cru bottling. Marchesi di Barolo owns 1 acre (0.4 hectare) of Castellero; part is in Monforte. The vineyard is being replanted. They produced a Barolo cru in 1979.

Castelletto (*Monforte d'Alba*). F.lli Enrico e Giacomo Saffirio and Stefano Manzone of Azienda Agricola "Ciabot del Preve" own vines in this vineyard district. Manzone produces a Barolo cru that he labels Castelletto-Ciabot del Preve. Giovanni Manzone and Josetta Saffirio also own vines here. Renzo Seghesio buys grapes for his Barolo from Castelletto. Gigi Rosso owns 9.4 acres (3.8 hectares) here in the Perno di Monforte area. He produced a Barolo in 1985 that he labeled Cascina Castelletto.

Castello (*Castiglione Falletto*). Luigi Coppo bottled a Barolo cru from the Castello vineyard. We don't know if they still do.

Castello (*Grinzane Cavour*). Terre del Barolo produces a cru-bottled Barolo from here.

Caudane. See **Le Caudane**.

Cerequio (*mostly in La Morra, part is in Barolo*). Cerequio's exposure is southern to southwestern. Azienda Agricola "Ponte Rossa" told us that La Mandorla is part of Cerequio. Renato Ratti finds notes of tobacco and cherries in the aroma of the Cerequio Barolo.

Poderi e Cantine di Marengo-Marenda & C., formerly Casa Vinicola Piemonte and Tenuta Cerequio, owns 19.4 acres (7.9 hectares) of nebbiolo and barbera. They are the largest holder here and make a cru Barolo from their nebbiolo vines.

Michele Chiarlo of Cantine Duca d'Asti bought 13.6 acres (5.5 hectares) from Ing. Averzme in the spring of 1990. The slopes have an 18 to 20 percent grade. The soil is loose and has a composition of 40 percent clay, 35 percent silt, and 25 percent sand, and contains high amounts of phosphorous and magnesium. The vines, with an average age of sixteen years, face southeast. Chiarlo has vinified a Barolo from this section that he calls Sorì Cerequio since 1987. He didn't bottle the '87 separately. His first Barolo Cerequio will be the '88.

F.lli Dogliani of Batasiolo own 4 acres (1.62 hectares) of vines planted at 1,148 feet (350 meters) above sea level. The vines facing southward are planted in blue marl soil that has straits of sand. Their first cru from here was the '83. **

OTHER CEREQUIO OWNER-PRODUCERS

- Cogno-Marcarini[c] has not produced a Cerequio cru since 1971.
- Contratto (Cascina Secolo) in the part he calls **Ca' Neire**.
- Marchesi di Barolo
- Oberto Egidio di Oberto Giuseppe owns vines in the Cerequio-Canera section.
- F.lli Oddero owns land in Cerequio-Serra.
- Roberto Voerzio has leased about 2.5 acres (1 hectare) here since 1988.[c]

Cerretta (*Serralunga d'Alba*). Basilio Zunino owns vines in this vineyard district.

Cerretta di Perno (*Monforte d'Alba*). Josetta Saffirio cultivates vines in this section of Perno.

Ciabot (*Monforte d'Alba*). Fia Rocca's La Vecchia Cantina has a piece of this vineyard. *Ciabot* means "little house in the country."

Ciabot del Preve (*Monforte d'Alba*). Stefano Manzone grows vines here. He named his Azienda Agricola for the vineyard. Giovanni Manzone also does a Barolo from his vines here.

Ciabot di Preve (*Barolo*). Silvio Grasso produced an '84 Barolo from his 1.5 acres (0.6 hectare) of nebbiolo here.

Ciabot Mentin Ginestra (*Monforte d'Alba*). Clerico has been producing a cru Barolo from his holdings here since 1980.

Ciabot Tanasio (*Castiglione Falletto*). This *cascina* is in the Brunella vineyard. Francesco Sobrero owns some 12 acres (4.9543 hectares/13 giornate) of vines here, 7.5 (3.0488/8) planted in nebbiolo.

Ciocchini (*La Morra*).

Ciocchini (*Novello*). Francesco Marengo farms grapes in this vineyard.

Cö Naive. Giuseppe Oberto of Oberto Egidio produces a Barolo cru from vines grown here.

Codana (*Castiglione Falletto*). Codana has a southwestern exposure. The vines here are planted at an average altitude of 820 feet (250 meters) above sea level. Paolo Scavino owns a piece of this vineyard. In 1971 and again in 1982, Vietti produced 2,900 bottles of Barolo Codana from the 100 percent michet grapes that he bought from a 1.7-acre (0.7-hectare) plot in this cru. Most of the time he blends the grapes into his Castiglione Barolo. Cavallotto owns 3 acres (1.2 hectares), which they use to produce a Dolcetto d'Alba. F.lli Brovia reportedly owns some vines here, as do some members of Terre del Barolo.

Colle Sud-Ovest (*Castiglione Falletto*). A subcru of **Bricco Boschis.**

Collina Cannubi (*Barolo*). This vineyard district is described under **Cannubi.**

Collina Rionda (*Serralunga d'Alba*). Another name for **Vigna Rionda.**

Colonello (*Monforte d'Alba*). This vineyard is actually a section of **Bussia** Soprana more commonly known as **Bricco Colonello.** There are three or four growers here who own vines here. **

Conca dell'Abbazia dell'Annunziata, or **Conca dell'Annunziata** (*La Morra*). This vineyard, named for its shape which curves like a shell, catches the sun's rays from the southeast and southwest. Conca is in the **Marcenasco dell'Annunziata** district. Marino Mauro produces a Barolo Conca in Annunziata. Renato Ratti has produced 5,000 bottles a year of a Conca Barolo since 1978 from the grapes on his own 1.2 acres (0.5 hectare) of vines, plus grapes purchased from another 2.5 acres (1 hectare). The vines have an eastern to southwestern exposure. Ratti finds a pronounced aroma of tobacco in these wines. Ratti's Conca Barolo is softer and lighter than the one he produces from **Rocche di La Morra.** **

Contessa (*La Morra*). Marchese di Fracassi owns 2.8 acres (1.15 hectares) of vines here.

Convento di Santa Maria in Plaustra (*La Morra*). The Oddero brothers own vines here, in the section they call Bricco Plaustra. They produced an '85 Barolo Convento di La Morra from those vines.

Costa di Rose, Costa de Rose, or **Coste della Rose**[a] (*Barolo*). This vineyard is regarded more for dolcetto and barbera than nebbiolo. F.lli Barale has 8.6 acres (3.5 hectares) of dolcetto planted at 853 feet (260 meters) above sea level. Marchesi di Barolo and the Cascina Adelaide of G. Terzano also have vines here. Marchesi produces a Barolo cru from their 7.2 acres (2.9 hectares) of vines here. The '85 was vinified from the grapes of 5.7 acres (2.3105 hectares); they produced 6,958 bottles.

Croera, or **Croesa** (*La Morra*). F.lli Casetta, Giuseppe Oberto of Oberto Egidio, and Roberto and Gianni Voerzio cultivate vines here. Roberto produces a Nebbiolo delle Langhe from his vines.

Crosia (*Barolo*).

Crovera (*La Morra*). Marchesi di Barolo has vines in this vineyard, which we believe is yet another name for **Croera.**

Cucco (*Serralunga d'Alba*). This vineyard district is just north of the town itself.

Dardi[a] (*Monforte d'Alba*). Dardi is a historic subregion of vineyards. Angelo Germano owns 7.1 acres (2.9 hectares). He said that it is part of **Bussia.** F.lli Oddero also owns a piece of Dardi. According to Carlo Petrini, Dardi is about 17 acres (7 hectares) in size and, for the most part, the vines face southwest.[9]

Dei Ville Meriondo (*Castiglione Falletto*). Armando Parusso produced an '85 Barolo from here. We suspect that this is part of **Meriondino.**

Delizia (*Serralunga d'Alba*). Porta Rossa does a Barolo cru from Delizia. We don't know if it is the same as the vineyard that Fontanafredda calls **La Delizia.**

'Dla Roul (*Monforte d'Alba*). Podere Rocche dei Manzoni has done a cru bottling from 'dla Roul since 1978. This vineyard is located in Manzoni Soprana.

Domiano (*Serralunga d'Alba*). Luigi Pira of Pira Secondo & Figli owns 1.4 acres (0.6 hectare).

Enrico VI (*Castiglione Falletto*). See **Villero.**

Falletto (*Serralunga d'Alba*). Bruno Giacosa[b] has owned 20.7 acres (8.3842 hectares/22 *giornate*) of Falletto, mostly planted in nebbiolo, since 1982. He also farms some barbera and dolcetto, but very little. He has bottled a Barolo cru from here since 1982. He produces some 15,000 bottles of Barolo Falletto annually.

Fantini (*La Morra*). Angelo Veglio has vines here.

Farrina (*Serralunga d'Alba*). The Giacomo Ascheri winery owns 3.61 acres (1.46 hectares) from which they produce a Barolo cru.

Fiasco (*Castiglione Falletto*). Lorenzo Scavino of Azelia, Paolo Scavino, and F.lli Oddero own vines here.

Fontana di Croera, or **Fontana di Croesa** (*La Morra*). This is the part of the vineyard known as **Croera,** or **Croesa,** owned by the Fontana brothers. Luigi Veronelli named it.

Fontanafredda[a] (*Serralunga d'Alba, part is in Diano d'Alba*). This name is used to refer to the 250 acres (100 hectares) of land that Fontanafredda owns here; 173 (70) are in vines, 69 (28) of which are planted in nebbiolo.

Fontanassa (*Barolo*). Part of the **Brunate** vineyard district and we suspect a continuation of the Fontanazza vineyard of La Morra.

Fontanazza (*La Morra, part is in Barolo*). Fontanazza is within the **Brunate** district. Old-timers, according to Elvio Cogno, say that Fontanazza and Brunate are the two best crus of La Morra. Poderi Marcarini owns 9.8486 acres (3.9855 hectares) of dolcetto in the Fontanazza Soprana zone. These wines are planted at an altitude averaging 1,050 feet (320 meters) above sea level in calcareous clay soil that contains a predominance of magnesium. These vines have a southern to southwestern exposure and were planted between 1948 and 1985. Marchesi di Barolo also owns a piece of this vineyard.

Fontanile (*Monforte d'Alba*). A vineyard district that adjoins Pugnane to the north. Giacomo Fenocchio at one time farmed nebbiolo here. We're unsure if he still does. Silvio Grasso also owns a plot here.

Fontanin (*Castiglione Falletto*).

Formica (*La Morra*). Stroppiana Oreste has vines here. So does Stefano Oreste, who produces a Barolo cru from here.

Fossati (*La Morra*). F.lli Borgogno owns 2 acres (0.8 hectare) of dolcetto. G. D. Vajra bottles a Barolo Fossati from his 2.7-acre

(1.1-hectare) plot. Giuseppe Oberto of Oberto Egidio produces a Barolo cru from his vines here. Giuseppe Dosio owns vines and bottles a Barolo cru. Giuseppe Finelli and Francesco Boschis also own vines in Fossati. And Franco Fiorina buys grapes from here.

Francesco dell'Annunziata (*La Morra*). "Rocche" Costamagna bottles a cru from their 1.2 acres (0.5 hectare) in Francesco. This subcru is part of the **Rocche** section of Annunziata. *

Gabutti (*Serralunga d'Alba*). Teobaldo e Roberto Cappellano recently bought 10 acres (4 hectares) of Gabutti. Those vines, planted between 820 and 984 feet (250 to 300 meters) above sea level, face south. They produce a Barolo cru. Grignore is a subsection of Gabutti and at one time the Ceretto brothers bottled a Barolo from there, but not since 1974. Giovanni Sordo cultivates vines in the section he calls **Sorì Gabutti**. **

Gabutti della Bussia (*Monforte d'Alba*). Carlo Petrini lists Gabutti della Bussia as a separate vineyard in Monforte.[10] The exposure is southwest to west. Five growers cultivate grapes in this 12.4-acre (5-hectare) vineyard, which is planted between 1,150 and 1,300 feet (350 and 395 meters) above sea level.

Gabutti-Parafada (*Serralunga d'Alba*). This vineyard district, which has a southwestern exposure, includes the adjoining vineyards of Gabutti and Parafada and all of their subsections. The Oddero brothers have produced a cru Barolo from their vines here since 1982. **

Galarei, or **Galleretto** (*Serralunga d'Alba, part is in Diano d'Alba*). Galarei is in the *borgata* of **Sorano** in Serralunga. Giacomo Ascheri has vines in that plot. Fontanafredda produces some 13,500 bottles a year of Galleretto Barolo from their 4.8 acres (2 hectares) of nebbiolo vines. The vines, planted between 787 and 919 feet (240 and 280 meters) above sea level, face south to southwest. The miocenic, helvetian soil is loamy and calcareous, with a high amount of phosphorus and potassium. Fontanafredda's Barolo is regarded for its body and structure. They describe its aromatic and taste characteristics as withered roses, quince, and hazelnuts and say that this Barolo is smooth, warm, and gentle.

Galinot, or **Gallinotto** (*Barolo*). Silvio Grasso's Cascina Luciani owns 1.5 acres (0.6 hectare) of nebbiolo vines here from which they produce a Barolo cru. Francesco Rinaldi also grows vines here.

Gancia in Annunziata (*La Morra*). F.lli Ferrero owns 1.5 acres (0.6 hectare) of nebbiolo for Barolo here. So does Angelo Veglio, in the section he calls Cascina Gancia.

Garbelet Suè (*Castiglione Falletto*). F.lli Brovia own 5 acres (2 hectares) of vines here from which they produced 13,333 bottles of an '85 Barolo. We believe that this vineyard is actually part of the Garbelletto district.

Garbelletto (*Castiglione Falletto*). Bartolomeo Borgogno produces a cru-labeled Barolo from his vines here. F.lli Brovia also grows vines in this district.

Garil (*Serralunga d'Alba*). Fontanafredda produces 2,500 bottles a year of a Barolo Garil from their 0.9 acre (0.4 hectare) of nebbiolo vines grown here. The vines, planted at an altitude of 820 feet (250 meters) above sea level, have a southern exposure.

Garombo (*Serralunga d'Alba*).

Gattera dell'Annunziata (*La Morra*). Bovio owns 4 acres (1.6 hectares) and bottles a Barolo cru. Angelo Germano owns 1.9 acres (0.7 hectare) here, and Marchesi di Barolo owns a small piece as well. *

Gattinera (*Serralunga d'Alba*). Fontanafredda has 11 acres (4.5 hectares) of nebbiolo here from which they produce 31,000 bottles a year of Barolo Gattinera. The vines, with a southern exposure, are planted between 820 and 984 feet (250 and 300 meters) above sea level. The miocenic, helvetian soil is high in limestone and rich in quartz sand, iron, and microelements. Fontanafredda's Gattinera Barolo is austere in its youth, requiring age to round out. It is round, robust, and spicy, with nuances of pepper, nutmeg, and, with age, *goudron*.

Gavarini (*Monforte d'Alba*). The Gavarini vineyard covers some 15 acres (6 hectares). Elio Grasso owns 8.8 acres (3.6 hectares) of vines, 4.1 (1.7) in nebbiolo. He bottles Barolos from his 0.9 acre (0.4 hectare) of Chinera and 2.8 acres (1.2 hectares) of Rüncot. Grasso also produced a Barolo from the top part of his Chinera cru that he labeled as Poggio Chinera. He also has 0.4 acre (0.2 hectare) of vines in the Dei Grassi plot. Giuseppe Mascarello produces a Barbera from grapes grown here.

Giachini in Annunziata (*La Morra*). Giovanni Corino owns and leases some 18.5 acres (7.5 hectares) of vines here, 9.9 (4) in nebbiolo, 4.9 (2) in dolcetto, and 3.7 (1.5) in barbera. Giovanni Revello also owns a section here.

Ginestra, or **Ginestre**[a] (*Monforte d'Alba*). The Ginestra vineyard of nearly 38 acres (15 hectares) has eight owners. The vines here are planted at altitudes ranging from 985 to 1,310 feet (300 to 400 meters) above sea level. Ginestra della Pajana is a 5.7-acre (2.3-hectare) section that is especially esteemed. Giuseppe Colla of Prunotto, who makes wine from Ginestra, characterizes these Barolos as soft. **

OTHER GINESTRA OWNER-PRODUCERS

- Clerico[c] owns 4.7 acres (1.9 hectares) in the section he calls Ciabot Mentin Ginestra.
- Conterno Fantino[c] owns a piece of Ginestra from which they bottle a Barolo Sorì Ginestra and another part that they label as Vigna del Gris (Ginestre).
- Paolo Conterno[c] owns a piece of this vineyard and bottles a Barolo from here that he labels La Ginestra.
- Feyles Maria[c]
- Franco Fiorina buys grapes.
- Grasso[c] owns 6.8 acres (2.7 hectares), 6.1 (2.5) planted in nebbiolo in the Case Matè subcru.
- Giuseppe Mascarello has barbera vines.
- Prunotto[c] buys from 3.3 acres (1.4 hectares).
- Renzo Seghesio buys grapes.

Giuchera, or **Giunchera.** Dialect for **Zonchera,** or **Zonchetta.**

Gramolere (*Monforte d'Alba*). This 33-acre (13.3-hectare) vineyard is planted between 1,150 and 1,475 feet (350 and 450 meters) above sea level at western, southwestern, and southern exposures. Giovanni Manzone owns some vines here in, we suspect, the section he calls Ciabot del Preve. Members of the Terre del Barolo cultivate vines here.

Gramolere Ciabot del Preve (*Monforte d'Alba*). Giovanni Manzone produces a Barolo cru. We suspect that this is part of **Gramolere** and not a separate vineyard.

Gran Bussia, or **Granbussia**[a] (*Monforte d'Alba*). This name is used by Aldo Conterno[b] for his excellent Barolos from his holding in **Bussia** Soprana. He bottles a Gran Bussia Barolo only in great vintages. We have tasted Gran Bussia Barolos from '71, '74, '78, '82, '85, '88, and '89, and there will be a '90 as well. In some vintages Conterno produced up to three Gran Bussia Barolos. We have tasted some from Vigna Bricco Cicala and Vigna Bricco Colonello, and he planned to produce a Gran Bussia Vigna Bricco Ciabot as well. Since 1982 he has blended the different plots together for his Gran Bussia Barolo. The basis of this superb Barolo is the grapes grown in the **Romirasco** cru. ******

Grassi (*Monforte d'Alba*). Accademia Torregiorgi buys grapes from Pietro Iberti to produce his Barolo Grassi. Some producer-owners, notably Elio Grasso, include this subcru as part of **Gavarini.** Carlo Petrini, in his *Atlante delle grandi vigne di Langa Zona del Barolo, Comune di Monforte,* suggests that Grassi is a separate vineyard.[11] This 17-acre (7-hectare) vineyard, planted between 985 and 1,310 feet (300 and 400 meters) above sea level, has four or five owners.

Grignore (*Serralunga d'Alba*). A subsection of **Gabutti.** Ceretto used to produce a Barolo cru from here, and F.lli Giacosa owns a vineyard that they call Grignore-Serra. It might very well be this vineyard or a piece of it.

I Tetti della Morra (*La Morra*). See **Tetti.**

Il Cappallotto (*Serralunga d'Alba*). Villadoria owns vines here.

Il Colombaio. Villadoria owns vines here.

La Cormaretta, or **La Cornaretta** (*Monforte d'Alba*). Podere Rocche dei Manzoni has vines here. Giuseppe Mascarello produces a Barbera from this vineyard. This vineyard is in the *località* Manzoni Soprana.

La Delizia (*Serralunga d'Alba*). Fontanafredda has 8.9 acres (3.6 hectares) of nebbiolo vines planted in this vineyard which they use for their Barolo La Delizia. They produce, on average, 24,000 bottles a year. The vines, facing southward, are planted between 1,116 and 1,247 feet (340 and 380 meters) above sea level. The miocenic, helvetian soil contains assimilable iron, boron, and potassium. Fontanafredda's La Delizia and **La Villa** Barolos mature the soonest. This full-bodied, austere Barolo is, however, for long aging. It is said to have suggestions of spice and cinnamon and, with age, leather and camphor.

La Mandorla (*Barolo*). Azienda Agricola "Ponte Rossa" owns 32.6 acres (13.2 hectares) here, 22.5 (9.1) in vines. They told us that their section of La Mandorla is actually part of Cerequio. Michele Fontana and Ludovico Borgogno have vines in La Mandorla.

La Pria (*La Morra*). Giovanni Accomasso owns vines here.

La Rosa (*Barolo*). Marchesi di Barolo owns vines in La Rosa.

La Rosa (*Serralunga d'Alba*). Fontanafredda produces their Barolo Vigna La Rosa from their 17 acres (6.9 hectares) of nebbiolo vines in this cru. The vines, facing south to southwest, are planted at altitudes ranging from 820 to 1,017 feet (250 to 310 meters) above sea level. In an average year they produce 50,000 bottles. The miocenic, helvetian soil is calcareous and contains quartz sands. La Rosa is perhaps Fontanafredda's most robust Barolo, and one that requires a lot of age. They find in it a bouquet of faded roses, forest leaves, and almonds and, with age, *goudron*.

La Serra (*La Morra*). We were told that this esteemed cru is part of **Brunate,** but Elvio Cogno, who should know, says that La Serra is not really a part of Brunate. Poderi Marcarini owns 7.56 acres (3.0591 hectares) of nebbiolo and, we believe, some dolcetto and barbera vines as well. The vines are planted in calcareous clay soil at an average altitude of 1,245 feet (380 meters) above sea level.

According to Cogno, the La Serra Barolo shows more of the La Morra perfume than Brunate when it is young. It starts off fruitier and is more accessible as well. With age, Cogno points out, their personalities change. Cogno has produced some 20,000 bottles a year of a very fine La Serra Barolo[b] for Marcarini since 1973. Roberto Voerzio owns 4.7 acres (2 hectares) of nebbiolo, all for Barolo, from which he produces a very good La Serra, and his brother Gianni bottles a La Serra Barolo as well. Giuseppe Oberto of Oberto Egidio also owns a piece of La Serra and does a cru bottling that he labels Serre. ******

La Serra dei Turchi (*La Morra*). Gianni Gagliardo owns 20.5 acres (8.3 hectares) of vines from which he produces his Barolo La Serra. The vines, planted at 835 feet (254 meters) above sea level, are in Santa Maria La Morra. Since 1967, Gagliardo has been producing about 6,000 bottles a year from this cru. The new owners of Franco Fiorina have 9.4 acres (3.8 acres) of nebbiolo in this vineyard. Stefano Farina's Cascina Traversa is located in Borgata Serra dei Turchi. We don't know if they own part of the vineyard. This vineyard is not part of La Serra.

La Valletta dei Cannubi (*Barolo*). Marchesi di Barolo owns 9.6 acres (3.9 hectares) of La Valletta. They produce a Barolo cru from their 5.3 acres (2.1 hectares) of nebbiolo vines.

La Villa (*Barolo*). Fontanafredda has 7.9 acres (3.2 hectares) of nebbiolo vines here that they use for their Barolo La Villa. Their production averages 22,000 bottles a year. The vines are planted at altitudes ranging from 1,050 to 1,214 feet (320 to 370 meters) above sea level and face east. The miocenic, tortonian soil is rich in phosphorus, potassium, and copper. Fontanafredda told us that La Villa is actually part of **Cannubi.** Of the Fontanafredda Barolos, La Villa and **La Delizia** are ready the soonest. They find in the aroma of La Villa hints of blackberries, prunes, black cherries, and, with age, licorice, tobacco leaves, old leather, and dried flowers.

La Villa (*Monforte d'Alba*). Carlo Petrini includes a La Villa vineyard in Monforte. The map in his atlas places that vineyard in the eastern part of that village.[12]

Larocca (*Barolo*). Francesco Rinaldi has vines in Larocca.

Lazairasco (*Serralunga d'Alba*). Guido, Giovanni, and Carlo Porro grew grapes in this vineyard. This might be another name for *Lazzarito.*

Lazzarito (*Serralunga d'Alba*). Lazzarito has a southwestern exposure. Fontanafredda owns 6.5 acres (2.63 hectares) of nebbiolo vines that are planted between 1,148 and 1,312 feet (350 and 400 meters) above sea level. The miocenic, helvetian soil is calcareous and dry, containing tufa. They produce 18,000 bottles a year of a Barolo that is, of all their crus, the slowest to mature. It reportedly ages very well. Its aroma is said to recall strawberries, mint, and black cherries. Emilio Noschese of Cantina Lazzarito cultivates grapes in this vineyard. Alfredo Currado of Cantina Vietti produced his first Lazzarito Barolo in 1989, which he expects to release in 1994. And good it is. He made less than 4,390 bottles. In 1990, Alfredo Currado bought 5.7 acres (2.3 hectares/6 *giornate*) from Giovanni di Stefani that is planted 100 percent to lampia. **

Le Caudane (*La Morra*). Monticelli-Olivero of Azienda Agricola "Le Corte" owns 15 acres (6 hectares) of vines in what they say is the best section of Rivalta, Le Caudane. Monticelli produces a Barolo from their 3.8 acres (1.5 hectares) of nebbiolo.

Le Corte (*La Morra*). Monticelli-Olivero of Azienda Agricola "Le Corte" farms 25 acres (10 hectares) of vines here. He produces a Barolo from this cru which is part of *Rivalta.*

Le Coste (*Barolo*). Giuseppe Rinaldi cultivates nebbiolo in his 3.7-acre (1.5-hectare) plot. Marchesi di Barolo and G. D. Vajra farm dolcetto here, the former on 1.5 acres (0.6 hectare), the latter on 2.4 acres (1 hectare). Marchesi di Barolo has recently replanted their section of Le Coste. They last produced a Dolcetto d'Alba cru from here in 1985.

Le Coste (*Monforte d'Alba*). This 19-acre (7.6-hectare) vineyard has eight owners. Carlo Petrini, in his *Atlante delle grandi vigne di Langa Zona del Barolo, Comune di Monforte,* reports that Giuseppe Conterno produced his first Monfortino, the '20, from grapes grown here.[13] Members of the Terre del Barolo cooperative farm grapes here. Renato Anselma owns a plot here. Scarpa buys the grapes for their Le Coste Barolo from this vineyard to produce 12,000 to 14,000 bottles a year of this wine.

Le Turnote (*La Morra*). This vineyard district is in the *Monfalletto* region.

Lipulot (*Castiglione Falletto*). Carlo Petrini includes this vineyard, which we've never heard of before, in his atlas of the Barolo vineyards.[14]

Liste (*Barolo*). Giacomo Borgogno grows grapes here, in both the main vineyard area and the subcru Pascolo.

Magaria (*Serralunga d'Alba*). Other names for this vineyard are Margaria and Margheria. Cantine Duca d'Asti has produced a Barolo cru from here since 1974.

Maniscotto. Ludovico Borgogno produces a Barolo Collina Maniscotto.

Mantoetto (*La Morra*). Marchese di Fracassi owns 5.4 acres (2.2 hectares) of dolcetto vines in Mantoetto.

Manzoni in Annunziata (*La Morra*). Manzoni is in the Rocche di La Morra section of Annunziata. F.lli Ferrero grows nebbiolo on a 0.74-acre (0.3-hectare) section of Manzoni. F.lli Oberto owns a 3-acre (1.2-hectare) plot here.

Marcenasco dell'Annunziata[a] (*La Morra*). This vineyard takes its name from the village and castle built around the fifteenth-century Abbazia dell'Annunziata. Renato Ratti produces some 30,000 bottles of this cru from grapes grown on his 12.4 acres (5 hectares) of Marcenasco, as well as from the subvineyards of *Conca dell'Annunziata* and *Rocche di La Morra.* Ratti's vines have a southern exposure. *

Marenca (*Serralunga d'Alba*). Luigi Pira of Secondo Pira grows vines on a 6.9-acre (2.8-hectare) plot and produces a Barolo cru. This vineyard is included within the *Marenca e Rivetti* district.

Marenca e Rivetti (*Serralunga d'Alba*). This vineyard district, just west of the town itself and facing southwest, includes the vineyards of *Marenca* and Rivetti. Villadoria owned 148 acres (60 hectares) in the Marenca-Rivetti district; in July 1988 they sold 69 acres (28 hectares) to Angelo Gaja. Gaja produced his first Barolo in 1988. In keeping with the policy he established in Barbaresco, Gaja won't use the actual vineyard name on the label, but will use a different name instead. This, of course, will continue to add to the confusion of the vineyard names in Barolo, whereby every producer coins his own, unique name. It's as if the Dômaine de la Romanée Conti decided that too many other producers bottle a Richebourg and Romanée-Saint-Vivant, therefore they'll make up their own name. As they say in the Langhe, *darmagi,* 'tis a pity.

Margaria, or *Margheria* (*Serralunga d'Alba*). Michele Chiarlo's Cantine Duca d'Asti produces a Barolo Margaria from the section of this vineyard that they rent. It has been sold under the Gran Duca label since the '74. Luigi Pira of Secondo Pira owns a piece of the vineyard. Giuseppe Massolino's Azienda Agricola "Vigna Rionda" owns 6.2 acres (2.5 hectares) 5 (2) of which are planted in nebbiolo. They do a cru bottling from here. And the Villadoria-connected DA.I.PI."CM" produced a Barolo from here in 1974. *Söri Margheria* is a subplot.

Maria Luigia (*Serralunga d'Alba*). Pasquale Veglio of Cascina Bruni owns vines here.

Mariondino (*Castiglione Falletto*). See *Meriondino.*

Marzio (*Verduno*).

Massara, or *Massera* (*Verduno, with a small part in Barolo*). Andrea Burlotto's Cascina Massara owns part of this vineyard. Castello di Verduno also has vines here. They produce a Pelaverga di Verduno from this vineyard.

Mentin Ginestra (*Monforte d'Alba*). See *Ciabot Mentin Ginestra.*

Merenda (*Barolo*). This is a subcru of *Sarmassa.*

Meriondino, or *Mariondino* (*Castiglione Falletto*). Meriondino is on the western side of the Alba-Dogliani road, opposite Rocche in the southern part of Castiglione, close to Monforte. Fontana Saverio cultivates vines here. Armando Parusso produced an '86 Barolo from here; he also does a Dolcetto d'Alba. Initially Alfredo Currado of Vietti bought grapes from a 2-acre (0.8-hectare) plot in this vineyard. In 1976 he produced 3,850 bottles of Barolo Meriondino. Today he blends it into his Castiglione Barolo. Next he rented a section of this vineyard, then, at the end of 1990, he bought a 0.4709-acre (0.1906-hectare/0.5-*giornata*) section.

Miralanga (*Barolo*). Gigi Rosso cultivates grapes here.

Molino (*Barolo*). Marchesi di Barolo has vines in Molino.

Momprivato, or **Monprivato** (*Castiglione Falletto*). Momprivato, like most of the best vineyards of Barolo, faces southwest. This approximately 15-acre (6-hectare) vineyard district, north and northwest of the town of Castiglione Falletto itself, is divided among three owners. Giuseppe Mascarello, who owns nearly all of it (12.7 acres/5.15 hectares), produces some 9,000 bottles in an average year when he makes a Monprivato cru. He has been producing this cru since 1970. Sobrero sold his small piece to Giuseppe Mascarello early in 1985. F.lli Brovia owns 1.1 acres (0.46 hectare) of nebbiolo for Barolo. They produced 3,333 bottles of an '85 Monprivato Barolo. Could the third owner be the Cavallotto brothers? If so, the vineyard has to be larger than the reported 15 acres (6 hectares) since the Cavallottos claim to own 5.6 acres (2.3 hectares) of dolcetto vines in a vineyard they call Monprivato from which they produce a Dolcetto d'Alba. Perhaps the nebbiolo plantings amount to the reported 15 acres (6 hectares). **

Mondoca di Bussia (*Monforte d'Alba*). F.lli Oddero produced an '85 cru Barolo from their vines in this section of Bussia.

Monfalletto dell'Annunziata[a] (*La Morra*). This vineyard district also includes Le Turnote. These Barolos are noted more for an aroma of tobacco than of *tartufi*. Cordero di Montezemolo makes a Barolo from their 27 acres (11 hectares) of nebbiolo in Monfalletto. They also own 25 acres (10 hectares) of dolcetto. **

Monfortino[a] (*Serralunga d'Alba*). Giovanni Conterno of Giacomo Conterno makes this wine only in special vintages. Ratti incorrectly lists this as being in Monforte d'Alba, but Conterno owns vineyards only in Serralunga d'Alba. According to Carlo Petrini, Giuseppe Conterno produced his first Monfortino, the '20, from grapes grown in the Le Coste vineyard of Monforte.[15] Other reports suggest that it was made in 1912. Giovanni and Aldo Conterno told us they don't recall the date of the first one, only that it was prior to the First World War.

Contrary to some reports, Conterno does not select his best grapes from his Cascina Francia vineyard to produce this very fine Barolo.[b] There are two differences between Monfortino and the Barolo Riserva produced by Giovanni Conterno. One is the fermentation and the other the aging. The "normal" Conterno Barolo is fermented at temperatures between 80.6° and 82.4° Fahrenheit (27° and 28° centigrade), the Monfortino between 96.8° and 98.6° (36° and 37°)! The former is fermented for thirty to thirty-one days, the latter for thirty-five days. Conterno uses *cappello sommerso* for both wines. While the Cascina Barolo is aged perhaps four years in large *botti* (casks), Monfortino is kept for up to a decade or longer in oak.

Since 1952 there have been 17 Monfortinos: '52, '55, '58, '61, '64, '67, '68, a small amount of '69, '70, '71, '74, '78, '79, '82, '85,

'87, and '88. Conterno told us that the '89 wasn't balanced enough for Monfortino! In 1987 he picked before the rain; consequently the grapes were very ripe. The wine is very good as well.

Monghisolfo (*Barolo*). This vineyard is discussed under **Cannubi-Boschis.**

Monprivato (*Castiglione Falletto*). See **Momprivato.**

Monrobiolo (*Barolo*). This is reportedly the name for the section of **Bussia** Soprana that is in the town of Barolo. Sylla Sebaste and Bartolo Mascarello own vines here. Sebaste labels the Barolo that he produces from here as Bussia.

Montanello[a] (*Castiglione Falletto*). The eastern part of Montanello adjoins Parussi to the north and Bricco Boschis to the south. This vineyard is owned in its entirety by F.lli Monchiero's Tenuta Montanello. About 25 acres (10.2 hectares) are planted in vines; some 10 acres (4 hectares) are in nebbiolo, mostly of the michet subvariety, but there is also some lampia and rosé. Fontana, Pianello, and Pini are subplots of Montanello. *

Montetetto (*Cherasco*).

Monvigliero (*Verduno*). The G. Battista Alessandria winery of F.lli Alessandria, Castello di Verduno, and Comm. G. B. & Cav. Francesco Burlotto all produce Barolo crus from their nebbiolo vines in Monvigliero. Bel Colle produces 6,000 to 7,000 bottles a year of a Barolo cru from here as well. Giacomo Ascheri owns 6.6 acres (2.7 hectares) here also. Members of Terre del Barolo cultivate vines here.

Mosca Brevi (*Verduno*).

Moscatello di Cannubi (*Barolo*). This vineyard is more commonly known as **Cannubi-Muscatel.**

Mosconi (*Monforte d'Alba*). The Mosconi vineyard lies east of the village at an altitude of 1,380 feet (420 meters) above sea level. The vines face south. Four growers share 7.4 acres (3 hectares). Giovanni Scarzello labels his Barolo for his Cascina Mosconi.

Munie, or **Munie Bussia** (*Monforte d'Alba*). This 28-acre (11.4-hectare) vineyard faces west to southwest. Giacomo Fenocchio at one time bottled his Barolo cru labeled Munie Bussia. We suspect that it was from his vines in Bussia Sottana. F.lli Dogliani, Armando Parusso, and Fontana Saverio own vines here.

Muscatel Ruè (*Barolo*). Giacomo Brezza grows barbera here.

Nasön. Giuseppe Oberto of Oberto Egidio produces a Barolo cru from his vines in Nasön.

Nassone. Giuseppe Dosio owns vines here.

Nirane-Sorano Bricco (*Serralunga d'Alba*). Giacomo Ascheri grows grapes in this vineyard, which is located in Sorano Borgata.

Ornata (*La Morra*).

Ornato[a] (*Serralunga d'Alba*). Pio Cesare owns 25 acres (10 hectares) of vines here. He produces a *barrique*-aged Ornato from a blend of nebbiolo and barbera and, since 1985, a single-vineyard Barolo.

Otinasso (*Castiglione Falletto*). F.lli Brovia, who owns 2.5 acres (1 hectare) of vines here, produces an Otinasso Barolo. We don't know if they still produce this wine, or indeed if they still own the vineyard.

Paiagallo, or *Pajagallo* (*Barolo*). Marchesi di Barolo has 5.5 acres (2.2 hectares) of barbera planted here. They have produced a Barbera d'Alba since 1975. Giorgio Scarzello has 2.7 acres (1.1 hectares) of dolcetto in this vineyard. Francesco Boschis owns a piece as well.

Panerole (*Novello*).

Parafada (*Serralunga d'Alba*). Parafada is in the **Gabutti** district. Cappellano buys grapes from this vineyard. Giuseppe Massolino's Azienda Agricola "Vigna Rionda" has 5 acres (2 hectares), 2.5 (1) of which are in nebbiolo. He produces, on average, 13,000 bottles a year of a Barolo cru from here. **Sörì Parafada** is located here. *

Parussi (*Castiglione Falletto*). Parussi is the northernmost vineyard of note in Castiglione Falletto. Its exposure is west-southwest and its altitude between 720 and 985 feet (220 and 300 meters) above sea level. Members of Terre del Barolo cultivate vines here. Vietti had bought nebbiolo grapes, mostly michet, from 2.5 acres (1 hectare) here from 1976 until a few years ago, when he rented a section of the vineyard. At the end of December 1990 he bought a 1.4-acre (0.57-hectare/1.5-*giornate*) plot, 0.94 (0.38/1) of which he will replant with michet. Today there is also 0.47 acre (0.19 hectare/0.5 giornata) of pelaverga. Currado blends the nebbiolo grapes from here into his Castiglione Barolo.

Pascolo (*Barolo*). Pascolo is a subcru of **Liste**. Giacomo Borgogno owns some vines here.

Perias (*Barolo*). This is a subcru of **Sarmassa**.

Pernanno (*Monforte d'Alba*). This 14-acre (5.7-hectare) vineyard, facing east to southeast, is planted at altitudes ranging from 820 to 985 feet (250 to 300 meters) above sea level. This vineyard is separated from Bricco Boschis to the west by the Alba-Dogliani road. Francesco Sobrero cultivates 8.5 acres (3.4 hectares/9 *giornate*), 7.5 (3.0488/8) of which is in nebbiolo for Barolo.

Perno (*Monforte d'Alba*). Renzo Seghesio buys grapes from this vineyard for his Barolo. We suspect that this is part of **Santo Stefano di Perno**. Giovanni Manzone cultivates vines here.

Pian della Polvere, or *Pianpolvere* (*Monforte d'Alba*). Some growers consider Pianpolvere a part of Bussia. Thirty-five of its 50 acres (16 out of 20 hectares) are in vines; 24.6 (10) are in nebbiolo, mostly michet. Riccardo Fenocchio, who owns 8.8 acres (3.6 hectares), two-thirds of which are in nebbiolo, bottles a Barolo Pianpolvere Soprana. F.lli Adriano and Renato Anselma also cultivate vines here. Renzo Seghesio buys grapes from this vineyard. *

Pian Romualdo, or *Pianromualdo* (*Monforte d'Alba*). Ferdinando Principiano's Cascina Nando produces a Barolo from their holding here. Vietti and Porta Rossa both produce Barbera d'Albas from grapes grown here.

Pilone (*Monforte d'Alba*). Pasquale Veglio of Cascina Bruni owns vines here. Pilone, a 6-acre (2.5-hectare) vineyard, is located in the southwestern part of the village.

Pira, or *Poderi Pira* (*Castiglione Falletto*). F.lli Giacosa produces a Barolo cru from their vines here. Sometimes they label it Vigna Pira, other times Poderi Pira. Carlo Petrini, in his *Atlante delle grandi vigne di Langa Zona del Barolo, Comune di Castiglion Falletto,* includes Azienda Agricola "I Paglieri" of Alfredo and Giovanni Roagna as owners here.[16]

Pisapolla (*Verduno*). This 7.4-acre (3-hectare) vineyard is planted mostly in nebbiolo. F.lli Alessandria cultivates vines here.

Plicotti dell'Annunziata, or *Plucotti dell'Annunziata* (*La Morra, part is in Barolo*). Gigi Rosso owns 5 acres (2 hectares) of vines here. Lorenzo Denegri, prior to selling his holdings to Ca' Bianca, made a Barolo from his vines in Plucotti, though it wasn't labeled as a cru. Today Ca' Bianca produces a Barolo from here that they label as Tenuta Denegri. *

Pozzo (*La Morra*). Settimo Aurelio owns some vines here.

Prapò (*Serralunga d'Alba*). Ceretto's Azienda Agricola "Bricco Rocche" owns 7.4 acres (3 hectares) in Prapò. The vines are planted between 886 and 1,050 feet (270 and 320 meters) above sea level and face south to southeast. At one time the Cerettos bottled this cru as Riccardo I; that name has since been dropped. They have produced a Barolo Prapò since 1976. Today they produce 13,000 bottles a year of this Barolo cru. *

Prea (*Barolo*). E. Pira & Figli at one time owned a piece of this vineyard.

Preda (*Barolo*). F.lli Barale owns 5 acres (2 hectares) of vines here.

Pressenda (*Monforte d'Alba*). This approximately 17-acre (7-hectare) vineyard has a southeastern exposure. It is located in the northeastern part of the village, not far from Perno. Cerretta lies to its north and La Villa to the south. Josetta Saffirio and Gigi Rosso cultivate vines here.

Pugnane (*Castiglione Falletto or Monforte d'Alba*). We were told that the Pugnane vineyard is in the *comune* of Castiglione Falletto. Lorenzo Fantini, in his *Monografia Sulla Viticoltura ed Enologia Nella Provincia di Cuneo,* also puts Pugnane in Castiglione Falletto.[17] Carlo Petrini, in his *Atlante delle grandi vigne di Langa Zona del Barolo,* disagrees: he places it in Monforte, albeit on the border with Castiglione.[18] On Renato Ratti's map Pugnane adjoins Fontanile to the south. On Petrini's it lies north of Munie. Petrini doesn't include Fontanile at all. This vineyard has a west-southwest exposure. The four owners cultivate some 22 acres (9 hectares) of vines. Giovanni Sordo owns a section and Giuseppe Mascarello has bought grapes from the part called **Bric Pugnane** and bottled a Barolo cru since 1971. F.lli Sordo of Azienda Agricola "Pugnane" cultivates grapes in the section they call Pugnane Sottana and does a cru bottling from there. **

Punta (*Castiglione Falletto*). Alfonso Scavino bottles a Barolo cru from the nebbiolo vines he grows here.

Punta Marcello (*Castiglione Falletto*). This vineyard is a subcru of **Bricco Boschis**.

Punta Vignolo (*Castiglione Falletto*). This is the name used by the Cavallotto brothers for their section of the **Vignolo** vineyard.

Rabera, or **Ravera** (*Barolo*). Marchesi di Barolo own dolcetto vines in Ravera. G. D. Vajra cultivates 1 acre (0.4 hectare) of nebbiolo here from which he makes a Barolo. He also owns 1.7 acres (0.7 hectare) of barbera. Giuseppe Rinaldi has 5 acres (2 hectares) of nebbiolo, dolcetto, barbera, and freisa vines here as well.

Ravera (*Monforte d'Alba*). Many producers have mentioned the Ravera vineyard in the village of Barolo. Lorenzo Fantini includes it in Barolo in his *Monografia Sulla Viticoltura ed Enologia Nella Provincia di Cuneo.*[19] Carlo Petrini, however, mentions a vineyard of the same name as being in Monforte d'Alba.[20] That vineyard lies between Le Coste and Pilone, and to the east of the town. Since we haven't seen his atlas of Barolo yet, we don't know if he includes a Ravera vineyard there as well.

Riccardo dell'Annunziata (*La Morra*). Rocche Costamagna bottled a '78, '79, and '82 Barolo Riccardo cru from their 1.2-acre (0.55-hectare) plot in this section of the esteemed **Rocche** subsection of Annunziata. They no longer produce it. *

Riccardo I in Prapò (*Serralunga d'Alba*). See **Prapò.**

Rimirasso (*Monforte d'Alba*). See **Romirasco.**

Rionda (*Serralunga d'Alba*). Another name for **Vigna Rionda.**

Riunda (*Serralunga d'Alba*). Another name for **Vigna Rionda.**

Riva (*Verduno*). The 9.4-acre (3.8-hectare) Riva vineyard, to the south of the village, faces southwest.

Rivalta (*La Morra*). Le Caudane owns 15 acres (6 hectares) in the section known as Le Corte. Oreste Stroppiana owns vines in the S. Giacomo section.

Rivassa (*Serralunga d'Alba*). Pasquale Veglio of Cascina Bruni has vines in this vineyard.

Rivassi-Boschetti (*Barolo*). Luciano Sandrone cultivates 3.7 acres (1.5 hectares) of dolcetto here.

Rivera (*Castiglione Falletto*). The Rivera vineyard, southwest of the village, adjoins Scarrone to the east and Pira to the southwest. F.lli Oddero cultivates vines here.

Rivette, or **Rivetti** (*Serralunga d'Alba*). This is part of the **Marenca e Rivetti** vineyard district. *

Rocche di Annunziata (*La Morra*). See **Rocche di La Morra.**

Rocche di Bussia (*Monforte d'Alba*). F.lli Oddero produced an '85 Barolo cru labeled Rocche di Bussia. It seems reasonable to assume that it is a blend of grapes from their holdings in **Bussia** Soprana and **Rocche di Castiglione Falletto.** The section of Rocche owned by the Odderos is in Monforte. We know of one other producer who makes a Barolo that we believe is a blend of grapes from Bussia and Rocche, Armando Parusso. Only he labels his as Bussia-Rocche.

Rocche di Castiglione Falletto (*Castiglione Falletto, with a small section in Monforte d'Alba*). A few years ago we heard that there were some ten owners here. More recently we heard that there are only four or five owners. Giovanni Viberti is the largest proprietor

in the nearly 19-acre (7.6-hectare) vineyard. Rocche lies south of the town of Castiglione Falletto itself, in the southern part of the *comune,* adjoining Villero to the west and separated by the road from Meriondino to the west. Its exposure is southeast. **Briacca** and **Bricco Rocche** are subcrus here. According to Carlo Petrini in his *Atlante delle grandi vigne di Langa Zona del Barolo,* Rocche lies east of Serra, which adjoins Villero to the west.[21]

Until recently Alfredo Currado of Vietti[b] bought grapes from about 1.7 acres (0.7 hectare) of nebbiolo planted in the proportion of 75-20-5 michet, lampia, and rosé. Those grapes came from Natalino Cavallotto. A few years ago Currado rented 1.4 acres (0.57 hectare/1.5 giornate) of vines which, at the end of December 1990, he bought. Currado has produced a Rocche Barolo since 1961, although it wasn't always labeled as such. In our experience it ages the best of the Vietti Barolos. It is full-bodied and robust, high in alcohol and tannin. When young it tends to be harder and more closed than the others and slower to mature. Vietti's Rocche and the offering from Bruno Giacosa,[b] labeled as Le Rocche, are the ultimate expressions of Barolo from here.

Michele Chiarlo of Cantine Duca d'Asti buys grapes from 2 acres (0.8 hectare) of twenty-one-year-old nebbiolo vines. He has produced a Barolo from here since 1982. The soil is 40–60 sand and marly clay, a pale, gray-white marl. The subvarieties found here are lampia and michet. **

OTHER ROCCHE DI CASTIGLIONE FALLOTTO OWNER-PRODUCERS

- F.lli Brovia[c] owns 3.6 acres (1.5 hectares). They have produced this cru since 1971. They produce, on average, 8,666 bottles a year. We have heard that in some years they bottle a Barolo from here as Rocche dei Brovia.
- Bruno Giacosa buys grapes.[b,c] He has produced this Barolo since 1971.
- Elio Icardi sells grapes to Vietti from a 1.7-acre (0.7-hectare) plot of some 70 percent michet.
- Giuseppe Mascarello used to bottle a Barolo from here.
- F.lli Oddero[c] owns a plot in Monforte.
- Paolo Ornato owns 5.7 acres (2.3 hectares).
- Armando Parusso[c] owns 0.9 acre (0.4 hectare).
- F.lli Monchiero of Tenuta Montanello[c] owns 2 acres (0.8 hectare).
- Arnaldo Rivera belongs to the Terre del Barolo co-op.
- Terre del Barolo[c] produces a Barolo from the 4.4 acres (1.8 hectares) owned by their members.

Rocche di La Morra. This vineyard district, facing southwest, lies within the **Marcenasco** area of Annunziata. The wines frequently have a note of *tartufi* in their aroma. Some eight or nine growers own a piece of Rocche.

Renato Ratti has 1.2 acres (0.5 hectare) and buys grapes from another 3.7 (1.5). Ratti's Barolo from Rocche is bigger and more tannic than his softer, more gentle **Conca dell'Abbazia** cru. Ratti has produced 8,000 bottles a year of a Marcenasco-Rocche Barolo since 1978.

Rocche Costamagna owns 11 acres (4.5 hectares), mostly in nebbiolo. Their holdings include the subplots of **Francesco** and

Riccardo. They bottle or have produced Barolo crus from those two subplots. Aurelio Settimo produced an '82 and '83 Rocche di Annunziata from his 5.5 acres (2.2 hectares) of south-southwestern–facing vines. **

OTHER ROCCHE DI LA MORRA
OWNER-PRODUCERS

- Settimo Aurelio[c]
- Andrea Oberto[c]
- F.lli Oberto[c] owns 3 acres (1.2 hectares).
- F.lli Oddero[c] produced an '85 Rocche Annunziata cru.
- Parroco di La Morra
- F.lli Veglio

Rocche di Torriglione (*La Morra*). See **Torriglione**.

Rocchette dell'Annunziata, or *Rochetta dell'Annunziata* (*La Morra*). This vineyard district lies within the **Marcenasco** area of Annunziata. Rocchette could be another name for **Rocche di La Morra** since F.lli Oberto has produced Barolo crus with these two names from two different vintages. Giacomo, and now Giovanni Accomasso and F.lli Oberto, bottle crus from this subplot. F.lli Oberto owns 3 acres (1.2 hectares) of vines. Settimo Aurelio produced a '79 Barolo cru from his 2.2 acres (0.9 hectare) of vines here. Angelo Veglio and Roggeri and Luigi Oberto own part of this vineyard as well. *

Rocchettevino (*La Morra*). F.lli Oddero grows grapes here. This appears to be their name for their part of the Rocchette district of Annunziata.

Roero (*Barolo*). Cantina Bartolo Mascarello owns 0.7 acre (0.3 hectare) of vines here.

Romirasco (*Monforte d'Alba*). This nearly 17-acre (7-hectare) vineyard is located within the **Bussia** district. Carlo Petrini lists it as a separate vineyard.[22] Its exposure is southwestern. Aldo Conterno cultivates 12.4 acres (5 hectares) of vines and produces a cru Barolo from his nebbiolo vines here. The first one that we heard about was the '86. Conterno used to produce a Barolo from here that he labeled Ciabot but dropped the name since other producers used it too. In recent vintages the Barolo Conterno has produced here has been the basis of **Gran Bussia**.

Roncaglia (*La Morra*). Scarpa has produced about 3,400 bottles of Barolo Roncaglia a year since 1978 from the grapes grown in this vineyard. Marchesi di Barolo owns a piece of this vineyard, as does F.lli Viberti fu Giuseppe's Azienda Agricola Breida.

Rotonda (*Serralunga d'Alba*). Another name for **Vigna Rionda**.

Ruè (*Barolo*). Giacomo Borgogno and Bartolo Mascarello grow grapes in this vineyard. Mascarello has some 2 acres (0.8 hectare) of nebbiolo and dolcetto vines. Angelo Germano owns 1.4 acres (0.6 hectare) in Ruè.

San Bernardo (*Serralunga d'Alba*). Cantina Palladino owns 7.4 acres (3 hectares) of vines in this vineyard. They produce 50,000 bottles a year of San Bernardo Barolo from their 3 acres (1.2 hectares) of nebbiolo.

San Biagio (*La Morra*). Giovanni Roggero's Azienda Agricola "S. Biagio" cultivates vines here.

San Giacomo (*La Morra*). See **Rivalta**.

San Giuseppe (*Castiglione Falletto*). A subcru of **Bricco Boschis**.

San Lorenzo (*Barolo*). Cannubi lies to the north and northeast of San Lorenzo and Valletta to the east and south. Bartolo Mascarello owns 1 acre (0.4 hectare) of nebbiolo vines in this vineyard and Chiara Boschis of E. Pira, 2 acres (0.8 hectare). Giuseppe Rinaldi owns some 0.9 acre (0.38 hectare) of nebbiolo in this vineyard, which he and others refer to as Cannubi S. Lorenzo! Giacomo Brezza produces a Dolcetto d'Alba from vines grown here.

San Lorenzo (*Verduno*). The 7.6-acre (19-hectare) San Lorenzo vineyard lies southeast of Monvigliero. The vines here face south. There are some ten owners. F.lli Alessandria and Michele Fontana own a piece of this vineyard and members of the Terre del Barolo cooperative cultivate vines here also.

San Martino (*La Morra*). Aurelio Settimo owns 4 acres (1.6 hectares) of vines in the part of this vineyard that he calls Bricco San Martino. His Barolo from here is an early-maturing one.

San Pietro (*Barolo*). Giacomo Borgogno grows vines in this vineyard.

San Pietro (*Serralunga d'Alba*). Fontanafredda owns 7.3 acres (3 hectares) of nebbiolo vines that are planted between 722 and 853 feet (220 and 260 meters) above sea level and face southwest. The vines are planted in miocenic and tortonian soil, mixed with helvetian. They produce 22,000 bottles of Barolo San Pietro a year. This Barolo ages well and is regarded for a bouquet of prunes, peaches, and dried fruit. Fontanafredda said that it is ready after their La Delizia and La Villa Barolos.

San Pietro delle Viole (*Barolo*). This could very well be part of San Pietro. Sebaste owns 2.47 acres (1 hectare) here from which he produces a Dolcetto delle Langhe.

San Rocco (*Serralunga d'Alba*). Eredi Virginia Ferrero produces 3,000 to 4,000 bottles of Barolo from their 2.47 (1 hectare) of nebbiolo vines.

Santa Caterina (*Serralunga d'Alba*). Guido, Giovanni, and Carlo Porro cultivate vines in this vineyard.

Santa Maria (*La Morra*). Renato Ratti finds in the Barolos of Santa Maria notes of black cherries, prunes, camphor, and mint. Azienda Agricola "Santa Maria" and F.lli Oddero have vines in this vineyard area.

Santo Stefano (*Monforte d'Alba*). This vineyard has a southwesterly exposure. It is within the district of **Santo Stefano di Perno**.

Santo Stefano di Perno[a] (*Monforte d'Alba*). This vineyard lies southwest of Perno in the north-central part of the Monforte district. The 14-acre (5.7-hectare) vineyard averages 1,180 feet (360 meters) above sea level. This property, at one time owned by the church, was until recently not planted in vines. At least one fine producer puts this vineyard on the same level as **Cannubi**. Giuseppe Mascarello told us that he has 1.7 acres (0.68 hectare) planted but not yet in production. We've heard that Poderi Rocche Manzoni also owns a piece of this esteemed vineyard. **

Sarmassa, or **Sarmazza**[a] (*Barolo, partly in La Morra*). There are two subcrus of the Sarmassa vineyard district: Merenda and Perias. Giorgio Scarzello owns 8.2 acres (3.3 hectares) of nebbiolo in Merenda. He has produced some 5,000 bottles a year of a Barolo cru from here since 1979. He owns 1.5 acres (0.6 hectare) of dolcetto in Perias. Marchesi di Barolo has made a Barolo from their 4.8 acres (1.9 hectares) since 1976. They last produced this Barolo in 1982. The vineyard is being replanted. Contratto owns 3.21 acres (1.3 hectares) of nebbiolo planted at an elevation of 820 feet (250 meters) above sea level. Those vines, facing south, have been used to produce a cru Nebbiolo delle Langhe since 1985. **

OTHER SARMASSA OWNER-PRODUCERS

- Alessandria Silvio owns vines in the S. Maria di La Morra area of the Sarmassa vineyard.
- Ludovico Borgogno
- Giacomo Brezza[c]
- Giuseppe Contratto[c]
- Francesco Rinaldi

Scarrone (*Castiglione Falletto*). Scarrone, east of the village and adjoining Rivera to the west, is regarded for its barbera. Alfredo Currado of Vietti owns 5.2 acres (2.1 hectares) in the Fioretto vineyard from which he produces a nebbiolo-barbera-dolcetto-neirano blend. Currado also produces a Barbera d'Alba from Scarrone.

Serra (*Castiglione Falletto*). Carlo Petrini places **Bricco Rocche** in Serra, which he places west of Rocche, divided by the Alba-Dogliani road and east of Villero. This 14 acre (5.7-hectare) vineyard, according to Petrini, faces southeast, at an altitude of 1,215 feet (370 meters) above sea level.[23] The Cerettos report that their vines, planted at altitudes of 1,017 to 1,116 feet (310 to 340 meters) above sea level, face south. Members of the Terre del Barolo co-op also cultivate vines here.

Sillio. F.lli Viberti fu Giuseppe's Azienda Agricola Breida owns vines here.

Sirionato (*Serralunga d'Alba*).

Solanotto (*Castiglione Falletto*). Borgogno Cav. Bartolomeo produces a Barolo from his vines here which he labels Sorì Solanotto.

Sorano (*Serralunga d'Alba*). Sorano, also called Sorano Borgata or Borgata di Sorano, is a *borgata*, or section, of Serralunga. Vineyard areas within this area include **Carpegna, Galarei,** and **Nirane**.

Sorì (*Barolo*). Pasquale Veglio of Cascina Bruni owns about 25 acres (10 hectares) of vines here, 17.3 (7) in nebbiolo, from which he does a cru bottling.

Sorì di Baudana (*Serralunga d'Alba*). Zunino Basilio grows nebbiolo for his very good Barolo, plus dolcetto and barbera, in the proportion of 60-20-20. He owns 7.4 acres (3 hectares) of this section of **Baudana**. **

Sorì Gabutti (*Serralunga d'Alba*). This vineyard area is discussed under **Gabutti**.

Sorì Ginestra (*Monforte d'Alba*). Conterno–Fantino produces a Barolo cru from this section of the **Ginestra** vineyard. **

Sörì Margheria (*Serralunga d'Alba*). Giuseppe Massolino has 3.7 acres (1.5 hectares) of vines planted in this section of **Margaria**. They have a south to southwestern exposure and are planted at an altitude of 918 feet (280 meters) above sea level. He produces some 8,665 bottles a year of Barolo from here.

Sörì Parafada (*Serralunga d'Alba*). Giuseppe Massolino's 3.7 acres (1.5 hectares) of vines are planted at 766 feet (310 meters) above sea level. They face southward. He produces some 8,665 bottles a year of Barolo from this section of **Parafada**. **

Sorì Rionda, or **Sörì Riunda** (*Serralunga d'Alba*). Giuseppe Massolino owns 6.2 acres (2.5 hectares) of vines planted at 984 feet (300 meters) above sea level with a southerly exposure. He produces some 8,665 bottles of Barolo a year from this section of **Vigna Rionda**. **

Specola (*La Morra*). F.lli Oddero cultivates vines here.

Terlo (*Barolo*). Luigi Einaudi grows nebbiolo for his Barolo in this vineyard.

Terra Hera (*Barolo*). F.lli Casetta has vines here and made a Barolo cru from them.

Tetti (*La Morra*). Scarpa produces some 15,000 bottles of Barolo a year from this cru.

Tetti-S. Maria (*La Morra*). Luigi Viberti cultivates vines here.

Torriglione (*La Morra*). Also referred to as Rocche di Torriglione, this vineyard is in the **Annunziata** district of La Morra. Francesco Rinaldi and Bartolo Mascarello own vines in this vineyard. Mascarello has 4.7 acres (1.9 hectares) of nebbiolo. Michele Gagliasso and Giacomo Mascarello also own plots of vines here.

Treccani. Gianni Gagliardo at one time produced a Barolo cru from here for Paolo Colla. We don't know if he continues to produce it under his own label.

Turnalunga (*La Morra*). Angelo Veglio cultivates vines here.

Vergne (*Novello*).

Vezza (*Barolo*). Francesco Rinaldi owns vines here.

Via Nuova (*Barolo*). Chiara Boschis's Azienda Agricola E. Pira owns 1.1 acres (0.4 hectare) of vines in Via Nuova. Teobaldo Prandi also has vines here.

Vigna del Gris (*Monforte d'Alba*). Conterno Fantino produces a Barolo cru from their vines in this section of **Ginestra**.

Vigna Pira (*Castiglione Falletto*). See **Pira**.

Vigna Rionda (*Serralunga d'Alba*). This vineyard, south of Serralunga itself, covers about 30 acres (12 hectares); it is divided among five or six owners. It is also called Arionda, Rionda, and occasionally Rotonda. One section is called **Sorì Rionda.**

Michele Chiarlo's Cantine Duca d'Asti has been producing a Barolo cru from Vigna Rionda since 1982. He leases 1.7 acres (0.7 hectare) of fifteen-year-old vines from Massolino. The vines are planted in sandy, sedimentary subsoils covered with a layer of algae-rich clay; there is a high proportion of chalky marl and it is rich in limestone and magnesium. **

OTHER VIGNA RIONDA OWNER-PRODUCERS

- Aldo Canale[c] owns 4.4 acres (1.8 hectares) of nebbiolo, plus 0.5 (0.2) of barbera and dolcetto. Canale uses the Riunda name.
- Teobaldo and Roberto Cappellano bought grapes until recently from a 1.7-acre (0.7-hectare) plot owned by Massolino.
- Franco Fiorina buys grapes.
- Bruno Giacosa[b,c] buys grapes to produce 6,000 bottles a year of Barolo Collina Rionda.
- Azienda Agricola "Vigna Rionda" di Giuseppe Massolino[c] owns 6.2 acres (2.5 hectares), 5 (2) in nebbiolo.
- Giuseppe Mascarello[c] bought grapes and produced 7,000 to 7,500 bottles a year of Rionda; he no longer produces a Barolo from here.
- F.lli Oddero[c]
- Cantine Palladino[c] produces a Barolo Riunda.

Vignane, or **Vignave** (*Barolo*). Marchesi di Barolo, Francesco Pittatore, and Francesco Rinaldi have vines here. Rinaldi cultivates 6 acres (2.4 hectares).

Vignola, or **Vignolo** (*Castiglione Falletto*). Vignolo, adjoining Codana to the southeast, faces southwest. Giuseppe Mascarello has produced a Barolo from this vineyard since 1974. The Cavallotto brothers own 4.6 acres (1.8681 hectares) of nebbiolo in the section they call Punta Vignolo. They produce more than 11,000 bottles a year of a Barolo cru from here. Reportedly Paolo Scavino also cultivates vines here.

Villero (*Castiglione Falletto*). There are some 10 growers who own a piece of this 37-acre (15-hectare) vineyard, the largest in Castiglione Falletto. Villero is just southwest of the town itself and adjoins Rocche to the east. Carlo Petrini shows it adjoining Serra to the east.[24] It has a south to southwesterly exposure.

Cordero di Montezemolo bottle a Barolo cru from the 5.4 acres (2.2 hectares) of nebbiolo that they own in the section they call Enrico VI. Giuseppe Mascarello bought grapes and produced 7,000 to 15,000 bottles of Barolo annually. Today he owns 1.4 acres (0.6 hectare). He has bottled this cru since 1978. Vietti bought grapes from a 1-acre (0.4-hectare) plot of michet vines that are over thirty-five years old. In 1990 he took out a twenty-year lease of 1.4 acres (0.5717 hectare) of nebbiolo, 100 percent michet. Currado said that his Villero Barolo is high in alcohol and very robust. **

OTHER VILLERO OWNER-PRODUCERS

- Ceretto[c] produced a Barolo from here. They no longer produce it.

- Bruno Giacosa[b,c] buys grapes to produce 14,000 bottles of Barolo annually.
- Armando Parusso owns some 5 acres (2 hectares).
- Sobrero sold his holdings to Giuseppe Mascarello in 1985.
- Sordo Francesco owns 1.8835 acres (0.7622 hectare) here planted in barbera and dolcetto.
- Sordo Giovanni

Visette (*Monforte d'Alba*). This 14-acre (5.7-hectare) vineyard faces south to southwest. Attilio Ghisolfi cultivates vines here.

Zonchetta, or **Zonchera**[a] (*La Morra*). The Cerettos have a lease that expires in the year 2000 on 20 acres (8 hectares) in this part of the **Brunate** vineyard. The vines, planted 689 to 820 feet (210 to 250 meters) above sea level, have a south to southeastern exposure. They have bottled a Barolo Zonchetta since 1968. Today it is labeled Zonchera, and it isn't necessarily from that single vineyard. In some vintages they blend the grapes from their other holdings. Today Zonchera is more of a proprietary wine. Their production of Barolo Zonchera averages 50,000 bottles a year.

F.lli Dogliani of Batasiolo owns 30.6 acres (12.4 hectares) of this vineyard. Their vines are planted at an altitude of 784 feet (240 meters) above sea level and face southeast. The soil is blue marl. They grow nebbiolo for Barolo on 25 acres (10 hectares), 0.8 (0.3) for Dolcetto d'Alba, and 15 (6) for Chardonnay. They have produced an '83 Barolo from here. **

THE BAROLO PRODUCERS RATED

****

+ Mascarello Bartolo (formerly Cantina Mascarello)
+ Giacosa Bruno
+ Marcarini (Elvio Cogno)
+ Vietti, Briacca (Brunate and Bussia ****, non-crus and Castiglione ** +)
+ Vietti, Lazzarito (Brunate and Bussia ****, non-crus and Castiglione ** +)
+ Vietti, Rocche (Brunate and Bussia ****, non-crus and Castiglione ** +)
+ Vietti, Villero (Brunate and Bussia ****, non-crus and Castiglione ** +)
+ Pira E. di Luigi Pira[a]
  Bricco Rocche Azienda Agricola di Ceretto (Casa Vinicola Ceretto, Zonchera ** +)
  Conterno Aldo, Bricco Ciabot (Bussia Soprana ***)
  Conterno Aldo, Bricco Cicala (Bussia Soprana ***)
  Conterno Aldo, Bricco Colonello (Bussia Soprana ***)
  Conterno Aldo, Granbussia (Bussia Soprana ***)
  Conterno Aldo, Romirasco (Bussia Soprana ***)
  Conterno Giacomo, Monfortino (Cascina Francia *** +)
  Rinaldi Francesco
  Rinaldi Giuseppe
  Vietti, Brunate (Briacca, Lazzarito, Rocche, and Villero **** + , non-crus and Castiglione ** +)

Vietti, Bussia (Briacca, Lazzarito, Rocche, and Villero
 ****+, non-crus and Castiglione **+)

***

Barale F.lli, Castellero
Clerico Domenico
Conterno Aldo, Bussia Soprana (Bricco Cicala, Bricco
 Colonello, Granbussia, and Romirasco ****)
+ Conterno Giacomo, Cascina Francia (Monfortino ****)
Grasso Elio (formerly Azienda Agricola Grasso)
Mascarello Giuseppe
Prunotto, Bussia (*normale* *+)
Prunotto, Cannubi (*normale* *+)
Prunotto, Ginestra (*normale* *+)
Ratti Renato, Marcenasco ("Ratti" *)
Sandrone Francesco
− Sandrone Luciano, Cannubi-Boschis
+ Scarpa
− Sobrero Filippo[b]
+ Tenuta Carretta, Cannubi
− Vajra G. D., Fossati (*normale* **+)
− Vajra G. D., Bricco Viole (*normale* **+)

**

Accademia Torregiorgi
+ Accomasso Giacomo (1974)[c] (now Giovanni
 Accomasso)
+ Accomasso Giovanni (1979)[c] (formerly Giacomo
 Accomasso)
Altare Elio
− Azelia (formerly Scavino Alfonso)
Bel Colle, Monvigliero[d]
+ Bel Colle, Vigneti Verduno[d,e]
+ Bergadano Enrico[f]
Borgogno F.lli Serio e Battista, Cannubi (*normale* *)
− Borgogno Giacomo
+ Bovio Gianfranco
Brezza, Cannubi (1989 from barrel)[c] (*normale* 0)
Brezza, Castellero[f] (*normale* 0)
+ Brezza, Sarmassa[f] (*normale* 0)
+ Brovia F.lli
− Burlotto (1974)[g]
Burlotto Andrea, Massara[h]
Canale Aldo
Cantine Duca d'Asti di Chiarlo Michele, Brunate[f]
 (Granduca *)
− Cantine Duca d'Asti di Chiarlo Michele, Bussia[f]
 (Granduca *)
Cantine Duca d'Asti di Chiarlo Michele, Cerequio[f]
 (Granduca *)
+ Cantine Duca d'Asti di Chiarlo Michele, Rocche
 (Granduca *)

Cantine Duca d'Asti di Chiarlo Michele, Vigna Rionda
 (Granduca *)
+ Cappellano Dott. Giuseppe di Teobaldo e Roberto,
 Carpegna
+ Cappellano Dott. Giuseppe di Teobaldo e Roberto,
 Gabutti (1989 from barrel)[c]
− Cascina Adelaide di G. Terzano
Cascina Ballarin di Viberti Luigi[e]
− Cascina Bruni di F.lli Veglio
+ Cavallotto F.lli, Azienda Agricola Bricco Boschis
+ Ceretto Casa Vinicola, Zonchera ("Bricco Rocche"
 Azienda Agricola ****)
+ Conterno Fantino (formerly Colli Monfortesi, *)
− Conterno Paolo, La Ginestra[e]
Contratto Giuseppe
Contratto Giuseppe, Ca' Neire[e]
Contratto Giuseppe, Sarmassa[e]
+ Cordero di Montezemolo
Corino Giovanni
+ Einaudi Luigi
Eredi Virginia Ferrero (formerly Ferrero Virginia)
Fenocchio Giacomo
Fenocchio Riccardo, Azienda Agricola "Pianpolvere
 Soprano"
Feyles Maria, Ginestra
Fontanafredda, crus (*normale* *)
+ Franco Fiorina
+ Gaja[i]
− Gemma
− Giacosa F.lli
Giacosa F.lli, Pira
Manzone Giovanni (1985)[c]
Marchese Maurizio Fracassi Ratti Mentone (1979)[c]
− Marchesi di Barolo, Brunate (*normale* *−)
Marchesi di Barolo, Cannubi (*normale* *−)
Marchesi di Barolo, Costa di Rose (*normale* *−)
Marchesi di Barolo, Valletta (*normale* *−)
Massolino Giuseppe, Sörì Vigna Riunda (*normale* *,
 Margheria *+)
+ Oddero F.lli
− Palladino
− Parusso Armando[j]
Parusso Armando, Bussia-Rocche
+ Parusso Armando, Mariondino
+ Pio Cesare
+ Pira E. di Chiara Boschis
− Poderi e Cantine di Marengo-Marenda (formerly
 Vinicola Piemontese)
Podere Rocche dei Manzoni di Valentino
+ Ponte Rocca Azienda Agricola di Pittatore Cav.
 Francesco[b]
+ Porta Rossa
Revello Renato, Cascina Gustavo

+ Rocche Costamagna
- Saffirio Enrico[f]
- Scavino Alfonso (now Azelia)[k]
+ Scavino Paolo, crus
- Scavino Paolo, *normale*
- Sebaste
- Settimo Aurelio
  Stroppiana Oreste
  Terre del Barolo, Brunate (*normale* *)
  Terre del Barolo, Rocche (*normale* *)
+ Vaira G. D., *normale* (Fossati and Bricco Viole *** −)
- Veglio F. lli, Cascina Bruni
+ Vietti, Castiglione (Briacca, Lazzarito, Rocche, and Villero **** +, Brunate and Bussia ****)
+ Vietti, *normale* (Briacca, Lazzarito, Rocche, and Villero **** +, Brunate and Bussia ****)
- Vinicola Piemontese (now Poderi e Cantine di Marengo-Marenda)
+ Voerzio Giacomo di F.lli Voerzio[b]
+ Voerzio Roberto
+ Zunino Basilio

*
Ascheri Giacomo
+ Asteggiano Vincenzo
  Beni di Batasiolo, Boscareto (*normale* 0, Bonfani +)
  Bersano
  Borgogno Aldo (1971)[c]
+ Borgogno Cav. Bartolomèo
  Borgogno F.lli Serio e Battista, *normale* (Cannubi **)
  Borgogno Ludovico, Cascina Borgognot
- Burlotto Comm. G. B. & Cav. Francesco di Marina Burlotto
- Cabutto Bartolomeo, Tenuta La Volta
  Calissano Luigi
  Cantine Ca' Bianca, Tenuta Denegri
  Cantine Duca d'Asti di Chiarlo Michele, "Granduca" (Brunate **, Bussia ** −, Cerequio **, Rocche ** +, Vigna Rionda **)
  Cantine Le Ginestre (1985)[c]
  Cascina Bruni di Veglio Pasqual
+ Casetta F.lli di Ernesto Casetta & C.
  Castello di Annone, "Viarengo" (1985)[c]
+ Castello di Verduno di Sorelle Burlotto
  Castello Feudale (1971)[c]
  Colli Monfortesi di Fantino Conterno (now Conterno Fantino, ** +)
  Coluè di Massimo Oddero (formerly Tenuta Coluè)
  Coppo Luigi (1979)[g]
- Damilano Dott. Giacomo
  Denegri Lorenzo (now Cà Bianca)
- Dogliani F.lli, crus (now Beni di Batasiolo, *normale* 0)
+ Dosio

Eredi Lodali di Ghione
+ Ferrero F.lli Renato Ferrero
  Fontanafredda, *normale* (crus **)
- Gagliardo Gianni, Ribezzo (1982)[c]
+ Germano Angelo
- Gianolio Tomaso (1985)[c]
  Giri Guido (1970)[g]
+ Grasso Silvio
  Grimaldi Giovanni & C. (1985)[c]
  Lodali Giovanni (1961)[c]
  Manzone Stefano, Azienda Agricola "Ciabot del Preve" (1979)[c]
- Marchesi di Barolo, *normale* (Brunate ** −, Costa di Rose **, Cannubi **, Valletta **)
  Marchesi Spinola[l]
+ Marengo M., Brunate[e]
  Mascarello Giacomo di Alberto Mascarello (1983)[c]
  Massolino Giuseppe (Sörì Vigna Riunda **)
+ Massolino Giuseppe, Margheria (Sörì Vigna Riunda **)
  Mauro Marino (1985)[c]
+ Mirafiore
  Molino Franco, Cascina La Rocca
- Oberto Egidio di Oberto Giuseppe
  Oberto F.lli
  Oberto Severino di Oberto Sisto
+ Oreste Stefano (1974)[c]
+ Ornato Paolo (1979)[g]
  Patrito[m]
  Piazza Cav. Uff. Armando, Podere d'Mugiot (1985)[c]
  Pira Luigi[n] (formerly sold as Pira Secondo)
  Pira Secondo & Figli Luigi Pira (now sold as Luigi Pira)
  Porro Guido[e]
  Principiano Ferdinando, Cascina Nando (1982)[c]
+ Prunotto, *normale* (Bussia, Cannubi, and Ginestra ***)
  Punset, R. Marcarino (1980)[c]
  Ratti (Renato Ratti, Marcenasco ***)
+ Revello F.lli[f]
+ Roggia Ferdinando[f]
  Rolfo Gianfranco (1979)[c]
  Rosso Gigi
  Saffirio F.lli Enrico e Giacomo
  Saffirio Josetta[e]
  San Lorenzo Casa Vinicola (1985)[c]
+ Scarzello Giorgio
+ Scarzello Giovanni (1974)[c]
- Seghesio Renzo
  Severino Oberto di Sesto Severino
+ Sobrero Francesco
+ Sordo F.lli, Azienda Agricola Pugnane
  Sordo Giovanni, Sorì Gabutti[e]
- Tenuta La Volta di Cabutto Bartolomeo[o]
  Tenuta Montanello

Terre del Barolo, *normale* (Brunate and Rocche **)
+ Veglio Angelo
+ Veglio Giovanni[h]
  Voerzio Gianni

0

Abbona Marziamo (1979)[c]
Accornero Flavio (Casa Vinicola Bera)
Aleramici (1983)[c]
+ Alessandria F.lli di G. Battista Alessandro
Ambra[b] (aka F.lli Dogliani) (1980)[c]
Baracco di Baracho (1979)[c]
Beni di Batasiolo (formerly F.lli Dogliani)[p] (Boscareto *)
+ Beni di Batasiolo, Bonfani (Boscareto *)
+ Bianco Michelangelo di F.lli Bianco (1983)[c]
Bonfante e Chiarle in Bazzana di Momburuzzo (1983)[c]
Bongiovanni Giovanni (1985)[c]
Borgogno Wanda Pepino
Bosca Luigi (1974)[g]
Boschis Francesco
Brero Cav. Luigi
+ Brezza, *normale* (Cannubi and Castellero**, Sarmassa** +)
Ca' Romè di Romano Marengo (1982)[c]
+ Camerano G.
+ Cantina Colavolpe (1981)[c]
+ Cantine Bava (1981)[g]
Cantine d'Invecchiamento, "La Brenta d'Oro" (1974)[g]
Cantine Mauro Vini di Osvaldo Mauro
Carnevale Giorgio (1978)[c]
Cauda Luigi (1979)[g]
— Ceste Cav. G.
Colla Paolo (1980)[g] (now Gianni Gagliardo)
— Cossetti Clemente (1971)[g]
DA.I.PI."CM" (1974)[c] (Villadoria connection)
Dellavalle F.lli (1974)[g]
Dogliani F.lli, *normale* (now Beni di Batasiolo; crus * —)
+ Gagliardo Gianni, La Serra
Gagliardo Gianni, Mora
Guasti Clemente (1986 from barrel)[c]
+ Galvagno Ernesto (1982)[c]
Giudice Sergio (1980)[c]
Grimaldi Cav. Carlo e Mario, Azienda Agricola
    Groppone (1978)[g]
Il Vecchio Tralcio (1980)[c]
Kiola[q] (1971)[g] (owned by Beni di Batasiolo)
+ "Le Corte" Azienda Agricola di Monticelli-Olivero
Le Due Torri
Marengo Mario (1983)[c]
Mauro (1982)[c]
Oddero Luigi (1978)[g]
Osvaldo Mauro, Cantine Mauro Vini
Pavese Livio (1978)[g]
Podere Anselma

Ramello Giuseppe (1983)[c]
+ Roche Azienda Vinicola
S. Quirico di Massano
Savigliano Mario
Scanavino Giovanni (1971)[g]
+ Sordo F.lli (1985)[c]
Sordo Giovanni
Troglia Giovanni[l]
Valfieri
Vecchio Piemonte
Vercelli Alessandro (1978)[c]
+ Viberti Giovanni
Villadoria Marchese

Notes:

[a] The last vintage bottled by Luigi Pira was the '75
[b] No longer produced
[c] We base our rating on one vintage
[d] A big and steady improvement since the '85, and we expect this improvement to continue
[e] Based on three barrel samples, the 1987, 1988, and 1989
[f] Based on two barrel samples, the 1988 and 1989
[g] The most recent vintage tasted
[h] Based on four barrel samples, the 1983, 1987, 1988, and 1989
[i] Not produced between 1962 and 1987; we base our rating on barrel samples of the '88 and '89
[j] They have improved since the '85
[k] The last vintage tasted under this label was the '80
[l] We haven't tasted this Barolo in years
[m] Based on four cask samples
[n] Based on seven vintages; six were tasted from cask only
[o] This producer was better in the 1960s and early 1970s
[p] Things have improved since the '82s
[q] The label is still used

Vintage Information and Tasting Notes

THE VINTAGES TODAY

****+	1989
****	1990, 1985, 1971, 1958
****—	1988, 1982
***	1986, 1978, 1947
***—	1970, 1964, 1955
**+	1961, 1957
**	1979, 1967
**—	1987, 1974
*+	1983, 1980
*	1962, 1952, 1950
*—	1984, 1981
0	1977, 1976, 1975, 1973, 1972, 1969, 1968, 1966, 1965, 1963, 1960, 1959, 1956, 1954, 1953, 1949, 1948, 1946, 1945
?	1951

WHAT THE RATINGS MEAN

****   Great, superb, truly noble

***   Exceptionally fine

**   Very good

*   A good example of its type, somewhat above average

0   Acceptable to mediocre, depending on the context; drinkable

+   Somewhat better than the star category it is put in

−   Somewhat less than the star category it is put in, except for zero where it indicates a wine or producer-wine combination that is badly made or worse

[. .]   *On a producer:* Tentative evaluation based on an insufficient number of wines or based on older, out-of-date vintages, or where the wines we tasted were too difficult to fully judge to give a fair assessment of quality.

      On a wine or vintage: Projection for the future. This rating is given to a vintage where we feel that we tasted an insufficient number of wines or those we tasted were too difficult to really judge to give a fair assesment of quality.

(. .)   Potential increase in the rating of the wine given sufficient maturity.

1990 [****]

January and February experienced mild weather. This set the tone for the rest of the growing season. Needed rain fell at the end of July and in early August. Once again the Barolo district was struck by hail; the damage was mild. All varieties ripened early and were harvested in healthy condition. Bartolo Mascarello told us that the harvest was two weeks earlier than normal.

Aldo Conterno produced a Granbussia and Giacomo Conterno a Monfortino. Giovanni Conterno of Giacomo Conterno said that at this stage 1990 seems to be the equal of 1958. Bruno Giacosa said it was exceptional for both Barolo and Barbaresco. Elvio Cogno called it superlative, better even than 1989 or 1988. All the grapes were of high quality.

When we first tasted them in November 1990 the wines displayed a lot of perfume and showed a lot of promise. They have good acidity and good pH. At that time, we tasted a dozen Barolos from seven producers and found them very promising. We tasted, from cask, Aldo Conterno's Bussia Soprana, Colonello, and Romirasco; the Marcarini-Cogno

Brunate; the Marchesi di Barolo Brunate, Cannubi, Coste di Rose, and Valletta crus; Bartolo Mascarello; Renato Ratti's Marcenasco; Ferdinando Roggia; and the Roberto Voerzio Cerequio.

In February and March 1991, we had an opportunity to taste some additional ones. The Vietti Lazzarito and Rocche displayed a lot of potential. They had a lot of perfume, were rich in extract and tannin, and were well balanced with good acidity. The Pio Cesare *normale* and single-vineyard Ornato were highly extracted and had a lot of tannin and structure. The Franco Fiorina also showed promise.

1989 **** +

The winter was very mild. The cold, rainy spring affected the flowering and reduced the crop size. From late June to the end of the harvest on October 14, the weather was warm. The sunshine was punctuated by an occasional storm that provided a welcome relief, always at the right moment for the vines. An early hailstorm hit part of the Barolo area.

The crop size of nearly 1 million gallons (37,878 hectoliters) was equivalent to 5.05 million bottles. This represented 58 percent of the 1.85 million gallons (65,304 hectoliters) allowed by law and is less than the 23-year average of 1.1 million gallons (41,979 hectoliters). It was the third smallest crop of the decade in terms of both size and yield. The yield of 347 gallons per acre (32.5 hectoliters per hectare) was much below the average since 1967 of 445 gallons (41.6 hectoliters).

Aldo Conterno, who produced a Granbussia, said that 1989 was the best of the top four vintages of the 1980s. Giovanni Conterno produced no Monfortino, and only 1,850 gallons (70 hectoliters) of Barolo. Though the wine, he said, wasn't balanced enough for Monfortino, it was still the very best vintage of the decade. Bruno Giacosa called it first rate, and Elvio Cogno said that, according to the analysis, the '89s are better yet the '88s are better balanced. Alfredo Currado of Vietti places it third after 1982 and 1988.

Based on the 99 wines from 66 producers we tasted, we believe that this vintage just might live up to all the hype. There were 6 wines we couldn't rate that showed promise, 10 we rated as simply good (one star), and 6 good plus. That left 77 of 97 wines that were very good or better! We have never tasted more impressive young Barolos, or indeed any young wine. These are wines with great extract and concentration. They have the richness as well as the structure. We expect them to be very long lived.

Thus far the wines that have impressed us the most have been those from Bartolo Mascarello and Vietti's Rocche, followed very closely by Vietti's Lazzarito and the Bricco Rocche cru of the Ceretto's Azienda Agricola Bricco Rocche estate; Aldo Conterno's Colonello, Gran Bussia, and Romi-rasco; Giacomo Conterno's Cascina Francia; Marcarini's Brunate and La Serra; Francesco Rinaldi's Cannubbio; the Barolo from Giuseppe Rinaldi; and Vietti's Villero. We'd be remiss not to mention F.lli Barale's Vigneto Castellero, the Azienda Agricola "Bricco Rocche" Brunate and Prapò crus, Aldo Conterno's Cicala, Bruno Giacosa's Falletto, the Marcarini Brunate-Canon, Tenuta Carretta's Cannubi, and Vietti's Brunate; nor should we omit the Bel Colle Vigneti Verduno, Brezza Castellero, Cantine Duca d'Asti Rocche, Aldo Conterno Bussia Soprana, Luigi Einaudi, Gaja, Elio Grasso Gavarini Vigna Rüncot, Marchesi di Barolo Cannubi, E. Pira, Ratti Renato Marcenasco-Conca and Marcenasco-Rocche, and the Rocche Costamagna Rocche di La Morra.

CAUTION: *Before reading these tasting notes on the wines that we tasted from barrel, please read "On Tasting Wines from Barrel: A Caveat" on page xxv.*

Asteggiano Vincenzo (*ex-cask, 11/90*). Animallike aroma; sweet, grapey and concentrated, berry character, good structure. *(*)

Barale F.lli, Vigneto Castellero (*twice, ex-cask, 11/90*). Lovely nose suggestive of mint and flowers, framboise component; sense of sweetness from the richness and intensity of the fruit, loads of extract, good structure, impressive. ***(+)

Bel Colle, Monvigliero (*ex-cask, 11/90*). Rich, sweet and concentrated, good structure, moderately long aftertaste. **(+)

Bel Colle, Vigneti Verduno (*ex-cask, 11/90*). Packed with flavor, a lot of structure, loads of class, sweet and rich. **(*)

Beni di Batasiolo (F.lli Dogliani), Boscareto (*ex-cask, 3/90*). Open cherry and tobacco aroma; rich, sweet impression, direct and flavorful, rather forward. *

Beni di Batasiolo (F.lli Dogliani), Vigna Bonfani (*ex-cask, 11/90*). Loads of oak on the nose and palate, some fruit, dry, short aftertaste. ?

Bersano (*ex-cask, 11/90*). Good structure and fruit, concentrated, a little lacking in length. *(+)

Borgogno Cav. Bartolomeo (*ex-cask, 11/90*). In a simpler style, light to moderate tannin, sweet berry fruit. *(+)

Borgogno F.lli Serio e Battista, Vigna Cannubi (*ex-cask, 11/90*). Rich fruit aroma and palate, good structure, light to moderate tannin. *(*)

Borgogno Giacomo (*twice, ex-cask, 11/90*). Rich, ripe fruit aroma; firm and tight yet with evident richness and concentration of fruit, lots of tannin as well. *(*)

Borgogno Ludovico, Borgognot (*ex-cask, 11/90*). Open cherry aroma; light tannin, overly simple, good fruit. *

Boschis Francesco (*ex-cask, 11/90*). Tastes a little old!, but there is good fruit, bitter finish. ?

Brezza, Cannubi (*ex-cask, 11/90*). Berry aroma, hint of an *eau de vie*; more sweetness than the Castellero, lots of tannin, hard, firm end. **(+)

Brezza, Castellero (*ex-cask, 11/90*). Dense purple; intense aroma with an overtone that recalls the essence of blueberries; hints of pine resin in the mouth, great richness and concentration, lots of tannin. **(*)

Brezza, Sarmassa (*ex-cask, 11/90*). Aroma of leather and dried fruit; sweet and concentrated, tannic and hard, dry end, rich fruit, again the essence of ripe fruit. *(*+)

"Bricco Rocche" Azienda Agricola (Ceretto), Bricco Rocche (*twice, ex-cask, 11/90*). Open cherry and berry aroma, rich on the nose and in the mouth, with an explosion of ripe fruit flavors that fill the mouth, chewy and tannic yet the extract and weight make it seem less so, at least at first, loads of character, long. ***(*)

"Bricco Rocche" Azienda Agricola (Ceretto), Brunate (*twice, ex-cask, 11/90*). Open cherry aroma, tobacco and cassis nuances; packed with fruit and concentration, the tannin is there as well, chewy, great structure and backbone, very young. ***(+)

"Bricco Rocche" Azienda Agricola (Ceretto), Prapò (*twice, ex-cask, 11/90*). Big, rich with enormous extract and concentration of fruit under the fairly high tannin. **(*+)

Burlotto Andrea, Massara (*ex-cask, 11/90*). Ripe fruit aroma, suggestive of framboise and berries; sweet, rich, open, light tannin. *(*)

Cantine Duca d'Asti (Chiarlo Michele), "Granduca" (*4 times, ex-cask, 6/90*). Lovely fruit aroma; concentrated, good structure, intensely flavored, the components are there to develop into a very good Barolo. **

Cantine Duca d'Asti di Chiarlo Michele, Brunate (*ex-cask, 11/90*). Mintlike nuance, openly fruited aroma; sweet, open and attractive fruit, light to moderate tannin, could use more length. *(*)

Cantine Duca d'Asti di Chiarlo Michele, Bussia (*ex-cask, 11/90*). Quite tannic, more so than the Brunate or Cerequio, firm, a mouthful of flavor, good structure. *(*)

Cantine Duca d'Asti di Chiarlo Michele, Cerequio (*ex-cask, 11/90*). Mintlike aroma and flavor, firm structure, moderate to high tannin, rich fruit, short, dry aftertaste. *(*)

Cantine Duca d'Asti di Chiarlo Michele, Rocche (*ex-cask, 8/90*). Rich, concentrated aroma suggestive of truffles and berries with overtones that recall the woods; great intensity of flavor and fragrance, kirschlike, from the nose through the mouth, a lot of structure and a lot of flavor, impressive richness, most attractive now in spite of the tannin. **(*)

Cantine Duca d'Asti di Chiarlo Michele, Vigna Rionda (*ex-cask, 8/90*). Aroma reveals hints of vanilla, berries, tobacco, camphor, and a woodsy overtone; more structure, weight and tannin than the Rocche, also less appealing, at least at this stage, a richly flavored, full-bodied Barolo with all the components to turn into a very good bottle in time. As good as it is, it's just not up to the Rocche. *(*)

Cappellano, Carpegna (*twice, ex-cask, 11/90*). Beautiful nose, nice fruit, ripe, camphor note; rich and sweet, light to moderate tannin, a tad bitter. *(*)

Cappellano, Gabutti (*ex-cask, 11/90*). Sweet, rich and concentrated, good structure. **(+)

Cascina Adelaide di G. Terzano (*ex-cask, 11/90*). Open fruit, rich and soft under light to moderate tannin. *(+)

Cascina Ballarin Azienda Agricola di Viberti Luigi (*ex-cask, 11/90*). Tar, berries and flowers; rich and concentrated, sweet and ripe. **(+)

Casetta F.lli (*ex-cask, 11/90*). Cherry and berry aroma; open flavor, light tannin, firm, dry end, a tad bitter. *

Cavallotto, Bricco Boschis-Colle Sud-Ovest (*ex-cask, 11/90*). Sense of fruit and richness under a fair amount of tannin, chewy, needs a lot of age, firm at the end. **

Ceretto, Zonchera (*3 times, ex-cask, 11/90*). Complex aroma of resin and vanilla, berries and flowers, mushrooms and truffles; rich and concentrated, moderate to high tannin, sweet impression, fat. *(*+)

Conterno Aldo, Bussia Soprana (*ex-cask, 11/90*). Big, rich and concentrated, wtih lots of tannin, along with the fruit. **(*)

Conterno Aldo, Cicala (*ex-cask, 11/90*). Rich and concentrated with weight and structure. **(*+)

Conterno Aldo, Colonello (*ex-cask, 11/90*). Loads of flavor, a lot of concentration, real class here, the best of the three subcrus and just behind the Granbussia. ***(*)

Conterno Aldo, Granbussia (*ex-cask, 11/90*). Deep color, very dark; intense bouquet; enormous sweetness and extract, a lot of weight, blueberry and woodslike components, ripe and intensely fruited, a great wine that will age for decades. ***(*)

Conterno Aldo, Romirasco (*ex-cask, 11/90*). Great richness, extract and concentration, a lot of structure and weight, loads of tannin. **(**)

Conterno Giacomo (*ex-cask, 11/90*). Deep, even dense color; mushroom and camphor aroma, woodsy component; incredible concentration and extract, this is really impressive. ***(*)

Conterno Paolo, La Ginestra (*ex-cask, 11/90*). Woodsy aroma with a gamy component; odd taste, evident fruit, light tannin, tar. ?

Contratto (*ex-cask, 5/90*). Grapey, tobacco aroma, like nebbiolo grape juice; sweet, rich, open, fruity medium length. **

Contratto Giuseppe, Ca' Neire (*ex-cask, 11/90*). At a difficult stage, sense of fruit evident. ?

Contratto Giuseppe, Sarmassa (*ex-cask, 11/90*). A little simple, a little light and a little disappointing. *

Corino Giovanni (*ex-cask, 4/90*). Loads of new oak, fruit is also evident but as a secondary element, heavy tannin, difficult to be sure. ?

Dosio (*ex-cask, 11/90*). Open cherry and berry aroma; light to moderate tannin, fruity, short, dry end. *(+)

Einaudi Luigi (*ex-cask, 11/90*). Tar, flowers and berries; concentrated, well balanced, sweet. **(*)

Fenocchio Giacomo, Bussia Sottana (*ex-cask, 11/90*). Old-style, tarlike aroma; rich fruit, sense of sweetness, good structure, moderate tannin. **(+)

Fenocchio Riccardo, Pianpolvere Soprano (*twice, ex-cask, 11/90*). Sweet fruit, rich and concentrated, firm, a little difficult, but evident potential. *(*)

Ferrero F.lli (*ex-cask, 11/90*). Firm, moderate to high tannin, evident fruit, short. *(+)

Feyles Maria, Ginestra (*ex-cask, 4/90*). Fresh cherry aroma; sweet, open, full of fruit, some tannin. *(*)

Fontanafredda, Vigna La Rosa (*ex-barrel, 5/90*). Medium dark ruby color, woodsy, mushroom aroma; chewy, sweet impression, rich and concentrated, good structure, tight, evident flavor. **(+)

Franco Fiorina (*twice, ex-cask, 11/90*). Sweet, open fruit, soft under light to moderate tannin. *(*) *Ex-cask 9/90:* Seems to lack the concentration and extract of the '88, could they have reversed the labels? A little unsettled at this stage, still it is good quality. *(*)

Gaja (*3 times, ex-cask, 4/90*). Deep color; intense, deep, rich and concentrated aroma, tobacco, cherries and berries, tar and leather combine with oak; chewy tannin, sweet with great extract and richness, explosive, mouth-filling flavors, a real sense of sweetness in the mouth, long on the palate. ***

Giacosa Bruno, Falletto (*ex-vat, 11/90*). Incredible concentration of fruit, closed in and tannic, great structure, loads of potential. **(*+)

Giacosa F.lli, Pira (*ex-cask, 11/90*). Rich and concentrated, sweet and tannic. *(*)

Grasso Elio, Gavarini Vigna Rüncot (*ex-cask, 11/90*). Nose is a little subdued; sense of sweetness and ripeness, intense, a lot of structure. **(*)

Grasso Silvio, Cascina Luciani (*ex-cask, 11/90*). Nice fruit, open, a little simple, quite attractive. *

Marcarini (Elvio Cogno), Brunate (*ex-cask, 11/90*). Rich nose of resin and vanilla, floral note, scented; real sweetness and flavor, loads of everything. ***(*)

Marcarini (Elvio Cogno), Brunate-Canon (*ex-cask, 11/90*). More berrylike than the Brunate, and with a more intense aroma; seems to have the most tannin of the three. ***(+)

Marcarini (Elvio Cogno), La Serra (*ex-cask, 11/90*). Intense berrylike aroma, nuances suggestive of a forest, raspberry component; great richness and sense of sweetness, a lot of concentration. ***(*)

Marchesi di Barolo, Brunate (*twice, ex-cask, 11/90*). Tartufi, vanilla, resin, berry notes, and fruit; sweet impression, cherry fruit, good concentration, full of tannin, tight and firm, could use more class. *(* −)

Marchesi di Barolo, Cannubi (*twice, ex-cask, 11/90*). Rich and packed with fruit, overtones of flowers, resin, vanilla and berries, big and flavorful, with a softness under moderate tannin. **(*)

Marchesi di Barolo, Costa di Rose (*ex-cask, 11/90*). Camphor note; great richness and extract, a lot of structure, soft tannins, berrylike fruit. **(* −)

Marchesi di Barolo, Valletta (*twice, ex-cask, 11/90*). Sense of ripe raspberry and strawberry fruit, floral note; real sweetness, cassis flavor, tobacco note, rich and packed with fruit, a lot of structure, could use more length, but its richness and flavor make it appealing, lots of tannin as well. **(+)

Marengo M., Brunate (*ex-cask, 11/90*). Rich fruit, moderate to high tannin, tar and berries, firm. *(?)

Mascarello Bartolo (*ex-cask, 11/90*). Expansive aroma, nuances of framboise and flowers; great weight and concentration, enormous extract, rich tannin, good backbone, one for the ages, very long, real class and loads of character. ***(* +)

Massolino, Sörì Vigna Riunda (*ex-cask, 11/90*). Good structure, moderate tannin, nice fruit and concentration. *(*)

Massolino, Vigneto Margheria (*ex-cask, 11/90*). Cherry and berry aroma; light to moderate tannin, attractive fruit. *(*)

Molino Franco, Cascina La Rocca (*ex-cask, 11/90*). Open cherry aroma; light tannin, simple. *

Oberto Severino di Oberto Sisto (*ex-cask, 11/90*). Sweet ripe fruit, concentrated, a little firm and dry at the end. *(*)

Oddero F.lli (*ex-cask, 11/90*). Moderate to high tannin, rich fruit, good weight and concentration, a lot of structure, bitter. *(*)

Parusso Armando, Bussia (*ex-cask, 11/90*). Open and attractive, berry and cherry aroma; moderate tannin, good structure. *(*)

Parusso Armando, Meriondino (*ex-cask, 11/90*). Tar and flowers; good fruit, rich and concentrated, good structure. **(+)

Pira E. (Chiara Boschis) (*ex-cask, 11/90*). Cherry, flowers, licorice and berries; richly concentrated, a lot of potential, Chiara's best to date. ***

Porro Guido (*ex-cask, 11/90*). Sense of fruit evident, a little difficult to evaluate, but the structure and fruit indicate good things for the future. ?

Ratti Renato, Marcenasco (*ex-cask, 11/90*). Rich fruit, a lot of weight and extract, sense of sweetness, rich and concentrated. *(* +)

Ratti Renato, Marcenasco-Conca (*ex-cask, 11/90*). Woodsy aroma, raspberry component; a lot of extract, some elegance, moderate tannin. **(*)

Ratti Renato, Marcenasco-Rocche (*ex-cask, 11/90*). Already displays complexity, woodsy and berry components; good weight and backbone, a lot of structure. **(*)

Ravello Renato, Cascina Gustavo (*ex-cask, 11/90*). Ripe fruit aroma suggestive of framboise and cassis, openly fruity; sweet and rich, medium body, concentrated and firm, dry end. *(*)

Revello F.lli (*ex-cask, 11/90*). Rich in flavor and tannin, loads of fruit, a little short. *(+)

Rinaldi Francesco, Cannubbio (*ex-cask, 11/90*). Perfumed, ripe fruit aroma; rich yet with a gentle touch, moderate tannin, long. ***(*)

Rinaldi Giuseppe (*ex-cask, 11/90*). Ripe aroma, cassis, cherry, the essence of ripe fruit, framboise and strawberries; vein of tannin, packed with flavor, a lot of structure and length. ***(*)

Rocche Costamagna, Rocche di La Morra (*ex-cask, 11/90*). Full of fruit from the nose through the palate, fairly long finish, moderate tannin, the best Costamagna to date. **(*)

Roggia Ferdinando (*ex-cask, 11/90*). Aroma of tobacco and tar; nice fruit, soft under light tannin, short. *

Saffirio Enrico (*ex-cask, 11/90*). Rich fruit aroma, berry characteristic; concentrated, loads of flavor under moderate tannin. *(*)

Saffirio Josetta (*ex-cask, 11/90*). Tobacco, berry fruit; sense of sweetness, good body, rich fruit, moderate tannin, firm finish. *(*)

Sebaste, Bussia (*ex-cask, 11/90*). Open cherry fruit aroma, some oak; good structure, sweet impression. *(*)

Settimo Aurelio (*ex-cask, 11/90*). Framboise and berry aroma; moderate tannin, tight with evident fruit, a tad bitter and very dry at the end. *(*?)

Sordo F.lli, Azienda Agricola "Pugnane" (*ex-cask, 11/90*). Nice fruit and concentration, light tannin, short, tannic end. *

Sordo Giovanni, Sorì Gabutti (*ex-cask, 11/90*). Tobacco and berry aroma; open fruit, a little simple, nice flavor, short. *

Tenuta Carretta, Cannubi (*ex-cask, 11/90*). Packed with sweet, rich ripe fruit, a lot of structure and backbone, high tannin. ***(+)

Vajra G. D., Vigneti Bricco delle Viole (*ex-cask, 11/90*). Lovely fruit on the nose and palate, rich in extract, moderate tannin, good structure, some style, some oak. **(+)

Veglio Giovanni (*ex-cask, 11/90*). Nice fruit, some oak, moderate to high tannin, firm end. *(+)

Vietti, Brunate (*ex-cask, 11/90*). Great richness and concentration, sweetness and class, spicy, peppery even. ***(+)

Vietti, Lazzarito (*ex-cask, 11/90*). If you can believe it, this wine has 15 percent alcohol but carries it very well, the intensity of fruit and concentration gives a real impression of sweetness, loads of flavor, tannin and quality. ****

Vietti, Rocche (*twice, ex-cask, 11/90*). This wine has everything, real class evident, great richness, concentration and extract, chewy and tannic, this one is for the long haul, most impressive. ****(+)

Vietti, Villero (*ex-cask, 11/90*). Great extract and concentration, loads of tannin and structure, robust but with style and length. ***(*)

Voerzio Roberto, Brunate (*ex-cask, 11/90*). Rich fruit, sweet and concentrated, fairly tannic, a lot of promise. **(* −)

Voerzio Roberto, Cerequio (*ex-cask, 11/90*). Great richness and extract, loads of tannin, sense of new oak, at this stage the richness, sweetness, tannin, structure and backbone indicate a long life. **(+)

Voerzio Roberto, La Serra (*ex-cask, 11/90*). Cherry fruit and oak; sweet impression, lovely rich open fruit, cherrylike flavor. **(* −)

1988 **** −

The spring was cool, the summer warm and dry. There was some rain at the end of September. The grapes were harvested under clear skies.

The year's harvest of 1.3 million gallons (50,329 hectoliters), equivalent to 6.7 million bottles, was approximately 20 percent more than the 23-year average, and 76.3 percent of the maximum allowed. In terms of both size and yield it was about average for the decade. It was less than the crops of 1985 and 1982 and greater than that of 1989, the other top vintages of the decade. The average yield was 457 gallons per acre (42.7 hectoliters per hectare), compared to the 599 (56) allowed.

Aldo Conterno said although it was an excellent vintage it was behind 1989, 1982, and 1985 in quality. Bruno Giacosa rated it highly, and Elvio Cogno said that the '88s are better balanced than the '89s. For Vietti, only 1982 was better in the decade. Aldo Conterno produced a Granbussia, and Giacomo Conterno a Monfortino.

Thus far we have tasted more than 90 wines from 66 producers, all from cask, vat, or, in a few cases, *barrique*. The wines are rich but without the concentration and structure of the '89s. They are certainly high-quality Barolos, but they are overshadowed by the very great '89s. At this stage we would rank them fourth in the decade behind 1989, 1985, and 1982. One of the most interesting things about this vintage is the very high level of quality. There have been very few Barolos that we rated less than good (one star). Thus far, the most impressive wine is Giacomo Conterno's Monfortino, followed closely by the Marcarini Brunate-Canon, Giacomo Conterno's Cascina Francia, and the Vietti Rocche; then come a number of first-rate wines—Aldo Conterno's Romirasco, the Marcarini Brunate and La Serra, Bartolo Mascarello, Francesco Rinaldi's Cannubbio, Giuseppe Rinaldi, Vietti's Brunate and Villero, and the Bruno Giacosa Falletto. Other potentially excellent wines include the F.lli

Barale Vigneto Castellero, the three crus from Ceretto's Azienda Agricola "Bricco Rocche"—Bricco Rocche, Brunate, and Prapò—the Cantine Duca d'Asti Rocche, Cappellano's Carpegna, Aldo Conterno's Cicala, the Franco Fiorina, Armando Parusso's Bussia, Renato Ratti's Rocche, and Tenuta Carretta's Cannubi.

> **CAUTION:** *Before reading these tasting notes on the wines that we tasted from barrel, please read "On Tasting Wines from Barrel: A Caveat" on page xxv.*

Asteggiano Vincenzo (*ex-cask, 11/90*). Lovely fruit but an odd note and a bitter edge. ?

Barale F.lli, Vigneto Castellero (*twice, ex-cask, 11/90*). Lovely fruited aroma, framboiselike; light to moderate tannin, rich and sweet, yet gentle, real class. **(*)

Bel Colle, Monvigliero (*ex-cask, 11/90*). Lovely fruit, well balanced, sweet and soft, light tannin, well made *(*)

Bel Colle, Vigneti Verduno (*ex-cask, 11/90*). Attractive fruit, good structure, open, light tannin. **(+)

Beni di Batasiolo (F.lli Dogliani), Boscareto (*ex-cask, 3/90*). Tobacco and cherry aroma; tight and firm after initial entry, a tad light midpalate, forward cherrylike flavor, soft, open and easy, correct. * +

Beni di Batasiolo (F.lli Dogliani), Vigna Bonfani (*ex-cask, 11/90*). Oak then fruit on both the nose and palate, short and a tad dry. +

Bergadano Enrico (*ex-cask, 11/90*). Framboise and flowers; sweet impression, soft, light tannin, gentle. **(+)

Bersano (*ex-cask, 11/90*). Attractive, open, forward fruit. *

Borgogno Cav. Bartolomeo (*ex-cask, 11/90*). Lovely aroma of tar and fruit with a floral note; moderate tannin, good structure. *(*)

Borgogno F.lli Serio e Battista, Vigna Cannubi (*ex-cask, 11/90*). Cherries and berries on both the nose and palate, moderate tannin, good fruit. *(*)

Borgogno Giacomo (*twice, ex-cask, 11/90*). Mushroom and *tartufi* aroma; tight, firm, hard and quite tannic, good structure. *(*?)

Borgogno Ludovico, Borgognot (*ex-cask, 11/90*). Tar and floral aroma combines with fruit; real sweetness, light tannin. *(*)

Boschis Francesco (*ex-cask, 11/90*). Fruit seems a little old, moderate tannin. ?

Brezza, Castellero (*ex-cask, 11/90*). Nice nose, fresh fruit and spice; sense of sweetness, moderate tannin, firm, good fruit, dry, hard, firm finish; could use more style. *(+)

Brezza, Sarmassa (*ex-cask, 11/90*). Raspberry and strawberry aroma; sense of sweetness, rich, moderate tannin, the best Brezza

Barolo we've tasted to date, until we got to the '89s, and a very good wine besides. **(+)

"Bricco Rocche" Azienda Agricola (Ceretto), Bricco Rocche (*twice, ex-cask, 11/90*). Rich nose of fruit, vaguely floral; fairly tannic, chewy, berry fruit and a sweet impression, good concentration of fruit; the best of the three '88 crus. **(*)

"Bricco Rocche" Azienda Agricola (Ceretto), Brunate (*twice ex-cask, 11/90*). Aroma displays mushroom and nebbiolo character; fairly tannic at this stage, a little tight, sense of sweetness; gentle nature. **(*)

"Bricco Rocche" Azienda Agricola (Ceretto), Prapò (*twice ex-cask, 11/90*). Aroma suggestive of mushroom, tar and camphor; moderately tannic, tight, good fruit, good structure. **(*)

Burlotto Andrea, Massara (*ex-cask, 11/90*). Tar, tobacco and berry aroma; light to moderate tannin, well balanced, sweet impression. **(+)

Cantine Duca d'Asti di Chiarlo Michele, Brunate (*ex-cask, 11/90*). Mint and flowers; sweet and open, light tannin, gentle. *(*)

Cantine Duca d'Asti di Chiarlo Michele, Bussia (*ex-cask, 11/90*). Tarlike aroma; sweet impression, a little dull. (*)

Cantine Duca d'Asti di Chiarlo Michele, Cerequio (*ex-cask, 11/90*). Mintlike nuance on the nose and palate, open and attractive fruit, soft, light tannin. *(*)

Cantine Duca d'Asti di Chiarlo Michele, Rocche (*ex-cask, 8/90*). Lovely complex aroma, with hints of vanilla, kirsch and berries and overtones that recall the woods; great sweetness, loaded with flavor, good structure, displays class. **(*)

Cantine Duca d'Asti di Chiarlo Michele, Vigna Rionda (*ex-cask, 8/90*). Aroma of the woods, hints of berries, camphor and tobacco; rich in flavor and extract, more open than the '89 and with less intensity, yet with more class, lots of tannin and fruit. *(*+)

Capellano, Carpegna (*ex-cask, 11/90*). Cassis, cherries and flowers on the nose; rich, open fruit, soft under light to moderate tannin; lovely, the best Cappellano to date, and one with elegance. **(*)

Cascina Adelaide di G. Terzano (*ex-cask, 11/90*). Tobacco and tar aroma; firm, concentrated, flavorful. *(*)

Cascina Ballarin Azienda Agricola di Viberti Luigi (*ex-cask, 11/90*). Tar, tobacco and berry aroma; firm, moderate tannin, attractive fruit. *(*)

Casetta F.lli (*ex-cask, 11/90*). Sweet and gentle, light tannin, simple. *

Cavallotto, Bricco Boschis-Colle Sud-Ovest (*ex-cask, 11/90*). Richly fruited aroma, berrylike note; sense of sweetness, ripe fruit, long. **(*−)

Ceretto, Zonchera (*3 times, ex-cask, 11/90*). Open varietal aroma; lots of nice fruit under moderate tannin, attractive fruit, could use more length. *(*+)

Conterno Aldo, Bussia Soprana (*ex-cask, 11/90*). Lovely fruit on the nose and palate. *(*)

Conterno Aldo, Cicala (*ex-cask, 11/90*). Lovely ripe fruit aroma, strawberry and raspberry components; a little light, really nice fruit, will be ready early, well balanced; some elegance. **(*)

Conterno Aldo, Romirasco (*ex-cask, 11/90*). *Tartufi* and woodsy aroma; fairly tannic, good concentration, a lot of structure, fairly long. ***(+)

Conterno Giacomo (*ex-cask, 11/90*). Perfumed aroma, rich in fruit, ripe, recalls cherries and raspberries, leather and camphor; superbly balanced, ripe fruit flavors, richly concentrated, very long; absolutely first rate, great class and style; has to be among the best of the vintage. ***(*)

Conterno Giacomo, Monfortino (*ex-cask, 11/90*). Deep color; a mélange of ripe fruit nuances, floral backnote; a richly concentrated yet gentle Monfortino, great depth of flavor and enormous length; real class and style, sure to be one of the all-time great Monfortinos. ***(*)

Conterno Paolo, La Ginestra (*ex-cask, 11/90*). Attractive fruit, good structure. *(*)

Contratto Giuseppe, Ca' Neire (*ex-cask, 11/90*). Nose and palate suggestive of grappa without the alcohol, fairly tannic, good sense of fruit. *(*)

Contratto Giuseppe, Sarmassa (*ex-cask, 11/90*). Nice fruit, open and forward, attractive. *(*)

Corino Giovanni (*ex-cask, 4/90*). Heavy oak and tannin, fruit evident, at this stage disjointed. ?

Dosio (*ex-cask, 11/90*). Fruit seems overripe, soft, light tannin. *−

Einaudi Luigi (*ex-cask, 11/90*). This wine was taken from cask and put into bottle for a tasting. It was, surprisingly, oxidized! We include it to point out the hazards of tasting cask samples. Somehow we find it hard to believe that this wine is the same as that we would've tasted had we tasted it directly from cask.

Fenocchio Giacomo, Bussia Sottana (*ex-cask, 11/90*). Good nebbiolo character; light to moderate tannin, sweet impression, fruity. *(+)

Fenocchio Riccardo, Pianpolvere Soprano (*twice, ex-cask, 11/90*). Open nebbiolo fruit aroma, attractive cherry note; open and appealing fruit, tasty. *(*)

Ferrero F.lli (*ex-cask, 11/90*). Ripe berrylike aroma; open fruit, attractive, moderate tannin. *(*)

Franco Fiorina (*ex-cask, 9/90*). Ripe fruit aroma, nuances recall tobacco and berries; great richness and extract, sweet impression, has the sweetness and concentration of an '89. **(*)

Gaja (*ex-cask, 8/90*). Camphor, cherry, berry, resin and vanilla aroma; surprising softness, sweet, even gentle for a Barolo, with the touch perhaps of a Barbaresco maker, could use more length; displays some style. **(+)

Giacosa Bruno, Falletto (*ex-vat, 11/90*). Incredible concentration of fruit in spite of being closed and tannic, a lot of structure and a lot of potential. **(*+)

Giacosa F.lli, Pira (*ex-cask, 11/90*). Open fruit aroma, cherrylike nuance, oak overlay; oak combines with fruit, sweet impression under moderate tannin. *(*)

Grasso Elio, Ginestra Vigna Case Matè (*ex-cask, 11/90*). Loads of fruit, good concentration of flavor, moderate tannin, displays potential. **(*−)

Grasso Silvio, Cascina Luciani (*ex-cask, 11/90*). Firm, hard and tannic, sense of fruit, chewy. *(+)

Marcarini (Elvio Cogno), Brunate (*ex-cask, 11/90*). At a difficult stage to assess the aroma; lovely fruit; the La Morra elegance is evident. **(*?)

Marcarini (Elvio Cogno), Brunate-Canon (*ex-cask, 11/90*). Real elegance on the nose; ripe fruit, a lot of class; has a gentle nature in spite of considerable tannin; very long aftertaste; great quality here. ****

Marcarini (Elvio Cogno), La Serra (*ex-cask, 11/90*). Woodslike and tar aroma; soft under moderate tannin; a lot of elegance. ***(+)

Marchesi di Barolo, Brunate (*twice, ex-cask, 11/90*). Open cherry aroma, floral note; sweet impression under light to moderate tannin, well balanced, quite attractive. **

Marchesi di Barolo, Cannubi (*twice, ex-cask, 11/90*). Open, sweet impression, gentle, good concentration of fruit, forward, attractive flavors. **(+)

Marchesi di Barolo, Costa di Rose (*ex-cask, 11/90*). Floral, cherry, berry fragrance; open, sweet entry, ripe fruit, raspberry flavor; lovely, some elegance; should mature relatively early. **(+)

Marchesi di Barolo, Valletta (*twice, ex-cask, 11/90*). Scented aroma; less open than the other crus, moderate tannin, ripe fruit flavor. *(*)

Marengo M., Brunate (*ex-cask, 11/90*). Open berrylike aroma, framboise overlay; gentle, sweet impression, open and attractive, a tad short. *(*)

Mascarello Bartolo (*ex-cask, 11/90*). Lovely aroma suggestive of forest scents and flowers; soft, supple and packed with flavor, good backbone, very long aftertaste; displays the characteristic Bartolo elegance. ***(+)

Massolino, Sörì Vigna Riunda (*ex-cask, 11/90*). Good structure, moderate tannin, flavorful. *(*)

Massolino, Vigneto Margheria (*ex-cask, 11/90*). Framboise and tar aroma; light to moderate tannin, gentle, short. *(+)

Molino Franco, Cascina La Rocca (*ex-cask, 11/90*). Tar and tobacco aroma, floral note; gentle with the flavor of ripe fruit, light tannin, short. *(+)

Oddero F.lli (*ex-cask, 11/90*). Tar and flowers, berrylike component; open and attractive ripe fruit flavor, light tannin. *(*+)

Parusso Armando, Bussia (*ex-cask, 11/90*). Attractive, open fruit aroma; ripe fruit flavors, sweet impression, good structure. **(*)

Parusso Armando, Meriondino (*ex-cask, 11/90*). Woodsy, berry, tar and tobacco aroma; well made, light to moderate tannin; open and attractive fruit. *(*)

Pira E. (Chiara Boschis) (*ex-cask, 11/90*). Expansive floral aroma, notes of licorice and *tartufi*; open entry, moderate tannin; a lot of potential; some elegance. **(+)

Porro Guido (*ex-cask, 11/90*). Open, forward fruit flavors, light tannin, attractive. *(+)

Ratti Renato, Marcenasco (*ex-cask, 11/90*). Woodslike and mushroom aroma, berrylike nuance; sense of sweetness, rich and concentrated. **

Ratti Renato, Marcenasco-Conca (*ex-cask, 11/90*). Scents recall a forest, damp leaves, mushroom and *tartufi* notes; a lot of extract, moderate tannin. **(+)

Ratti Renato, Marcenasco-Rocche (*ex-cask, 11/90*). Sense of great richness on the nose, framboise component, floral note; sweet impression, open and attractive, good structure; a lot of class here. **(*)

Ravello Renato, Cascina Gustavo (*ex-cask, 11/90*). Framboise and tobacco aroma; good structure, loads of fruit, moderate tannin. **(+)

Revello F.lli (*ex-cask, 11/90*). Floral, fruity, berry aroma; sweet and gentle, light to moderate tannin. *(+)

Rinaldi Francesco, Cannubbio (*ex-cask, 11/90*). Floral and berry aroma; sweet impression, gentle, concentrated, moderate tannin. **(*+)

Rinaldi Giuseppe (*ex-cask, 11/90*). Aroma reveals the concentrated essences of a mélange of fruits; moderate tannin, sweet impression, refined, delicate yet rich at the same time. ***(+)

Rocche Costamagna, Rocche di La Morra (*ex-cask, 11/90*). Ripe fruit aroma, framboise and flowers, berry notes; soft under light tannin, good balance, moderate length. **(+)

Roggia Ferdinando (*ex-cask, 11/90*). Berry and tobacco aroma; attractive ripe fruit flavor, light to moderate tannin. *(*)

Saffirio Enrico (*ex-cask, 11/90*). Tar and tobacco aroma; firm, nice flavor, attractive, appealing fruit, a tad short. *(*)

Saffirio Josetta (*ex-cask, 11/90*). Oak dominates and covers the fruit, which is evident. *?

Sebaste, Bussia (*ex-cask, 11/90*). Attractive fruit aroma and palate, sweet and gentle, moderate tannin. *(*−)

Settimo Aurelio (*ex-cask, 11/90*). Fragrant floral aroma; sweet and gentle; some elegance. **(+)

Sordo F.lli, Azienda Agricola "Pugnane" (*ex-cask, 11/90*). Lovely fruit aroma, tobacco and berry notes; sweet, gentle and flavorful, light tannin. **(+)

Sordo Giovanni, Sorì Gabutti (*ex-cask, 11/90*). Tobacco, tar and floral aroma; moderate tannin, attractive, appealing fruit. *(*)

Tenuta Carretta, Cannubi (*ex-cask, 11/90*). Tar and flowers on the nose; moderate tannin, a lot of structure, rich, ripe fruit flavor. **(*)

Vajra G. D., Vigneti Bricco delle Viole (*ex-cask, 11/90*). Nice fruit, light tannin, forward flavors. *(*)

Veglio Giovanni (*ex-cask, 11/90*). Ripe fruit, concentrated, bitter edge, yet attractive. *(+)

Vietti, Brunate (*twice, ex-cask, 11/90*). Lovely scented aroma, suggestion of mushrooms and *tartufi*; soft under the tannin, berry fruit; real elegance and class. ***(+)

Vietti, Rocche (*twice, ex-cask, 11/90*). Ripe fruit aroma, recalls flowers and berries; great balance, better than the '85 at the same stage, real class and enormous extract and sweetness, long; elegant, a real star. ***(*)

Vietti, Villero (*ex-cask, 11/90*). Good weight and concentration, sweet impression, good structure, lots of tannin, moderately long finish. **(* +)

Voerzio Roberto, Brunate (*ex-cask, 11/90*). Oak evident, sense of sweet fruit, cherry notes, well balanced. *(* −)

Voerzio Roberto, Cerequio (*ex-cask, 11/90*). Rich fruit, full of flavor, good body, structure and backbone, loads of tannin, once again the oak intrudes. *(* −)

Voerzio Roberto, La Serra (*ex-cask, 11/90*). Pretty nose, cherry fruit nuance, new oak overly evident on both the nose and palate, lots of fruit, moderate tannin. *(* −)

1 9 8 7 ** −

Heavy snows blanketed the Piemonte in mid-January, early and mid-February, and again in mid-March. The cold and rain of early April gave way to warm, sunny weather. Early May saw light rain and cool temperatures. The mercury rose toward the month's end. There was rain during the first part of June, then dry weather. A thunderstorm struck the Barolo zone on the 26th. Flowering took place under normal conditions for the nebbiolo. July began very hot. Some heavy thunderstorms struck Barolo on the 3rd, 7th, and 8th of the month and the weather remained cooler than normal for the remainder of July. Storms struck again in the middle of the month and the weather remained unstable for the rest of the month. Toward the latter part of July temperatures rose and remained fairly dry until the 30th, when a storm hit the Roero zone. August started on a favorable note with high temperatures. This didn't last: from the 5th, temperatures dropped and the humidity increased. Mid-month was very hot and humid until the last third of the month, when temperatures dropped and the humidity went up. The rain

on the 23rd and 24th wasn't enough to compensate for the earlier lack of rain. September began hot; the thunderstorm of the 2nd and 3rd brought welcome relief to the Barolo zone. Warm weather continued with another rainfall on the 9th.

The nebbiolo harvest began on October 8 for Barolo, with much of the picking done between the 10th and 15th. Some early reports said that it was an excellent vintage for Barolo. But Barolo was affected by the October rains. Still the grapes came in very healthy with excellent sugar and balance. Some days were sunny, others saw heavy downpours. A lot depends on when the grapes were harvested. White wines were reportedly first rate, especially Gavi. The early picked reds—barbera, dolcetto, grignolino—are reported to be excellent. In some cases, Dolcetto is said to be better than those of '85 and '82.

Quantity at 1.25 million gallons (47,382 hectoliters), or 6.3 million bottles, was nearly 13 percent above the 23-year average of 1.1 million gallons (41,979 hectoliters), but only 71.6 percent of the maximum allowed by law, compared to the 23-year average of 74.3 percent. Both the crop and the average yield per acre (hectare) were about average for the decade. The yield per acre was 429 gallons (40 hectoliters per hectare).

Bruno Ceretto said that although the grapes had high sugar and good acid, they didn't produce any of the Bricco Rocche crus; they put that wine into their Zonchera instead. Giacomo Conterno produced a Monfortino. He picked all his grapes before the rain and told us that they were very ripe. The quality of this wine bears out what he told us.

We have tasted nearly six dozen (69) different wines from 59 producers. There are many good wines as well as a few duds. The best wines thus far are two from Giacomo Conterno—Cascina Francia and Monfortino—and excellent they are. Bruno Giacosa's Rocche is close behind, then the Aldo Conterno Bussia Soprana, Bruno Giacosa Villero, Elio Grasso Rüncot, Bartolo Mascarello, and Tenuta Carretta Cannubi. Other very good Barolos include Andrea Burlotto's Massara, Marcarini's Brunate and Brunate-Canon, F.lli Oddero, Renato Ratti's Marcenasco-Conca, and the Vietti Castiglione. Not to be overlooked are the potentially good Enrico Bergadano, F.lli Borgogno's Cannubi, Renato Ravello, Francesco Rinaldi's Cannubbio, and F.lli Sordo.

> **CAUTION:** *Before reading these tasting notes on the wines that we tasted from barrel, please read "On Tasting Wines from Barrel: A Caveat" on page xxv.*

Asteggiano Vincenzo (*ex-cask, 11/90*). Attractive ripe fruit aroma and flavor, light oak overlay, moderate tannin. *(+)

Azelia, Bricco Fiasco (*ex-cask, 11/90*). Rubber tire aroma and flavor, some fruit, light to moderate tannin. ?

Azelia, Bricco Puna (*ex-cask, 11/90*). Low fruit, dull. ?

Bel Colle, Monvigliero (*ex-cask, 11/90*). Resin, vanilla, tobacco and truffle aroma; nice fruit, forward flavors, light tannin. *(+)

Bel Colle, Vigneti Verduno (*ex-cask, 11/90*). Tobacco and tar aroma; a little dry, good fruit. *(+)

Beni di Batasiolo (F.lli Dogliani), Vigna Bonfani (*ex-cask, 11/90*). Animal fur, fruit and oak define the aroma; soft with fairly good fruit, tastes of oak. * −

Bergadano Enrico (*ex-cask, 11/90*). Lovely fruit on the nose, nuances of tobacco, tar, and flowers; moderate tannin, fairly nice structure. *(*)

Bersano (*ex-cask, 11/90*). Attractive fruit, simple. * −

Borgogno Cav. Bartolomeo (*ex-cask, 11/90*). Moderate tannin, good structure, attractive fruit. *

Borgogno F.lli Serio e Battista, Vigna Cannubi (*ex-cask, 11/90*). Tobacco and tar aroma; good structure and fruit. *(*)

Borgogno Giacomo (*ex-cask, 11/90*). A lot of fruit on the nose, cherry notes, open; hard and firm, with the sense of fruit, is there enough? (*)

Borgogno Ludovico, Borgognot (*ex-cask, 11/90*). Oxidized!

Boschis Francesco (*ex-cask, 11/90*). Dried fruit aroma; light tannin, low fruit.

Brezza (*ex-cask, 11/90*). Light nose, berry note; a little light but agreeable fruit under light to moderate tannin, sense of oak and damp leaves; seems a little tired.

Burlotto Andrea, Massara (*ex-cask, 11/90*). Attractive fruit on the nose and palate, overtones of tar, tobacco and flowers as well. **

Cappellano, Carpegna (*ex-cask, 11/90*). Mushroom and dried fruit aroma; moderate tannin, a little dry, medium body. *(+)

Cascina Adelaide di G. Terzano (*ex-cask, 11/90*). Rubber tire aroma; low fruit, dull. ?

Cascina Ballarin Azienda Agricola di Viberti Luigi (*ex-cask, 11/90*). Tobacco and tar aroma; moderate fruit, very short. +

Casetta F.lli (*ex-cask, 11/90*). Tobacco nuance on the nose; moderate tannin, nice flavor. *

Cavallotto, Bricco Boschis-Colle Sud-Ovest (*ex-cask, 11/90*). Good body, lots of fruit, some tannin, well balanced, firm finish. ** −

Ceretto, Zonchera (*3 times, ex-cask, 11/90*). Mushroom aroma; fairly tannic with a sense of sweetness from the fruit, short. *

Conterno Aldo, Bussia Soprana (*ex-cask, 11/90*). Forestlike aroma, vanilla and berry notes; moderate tannin, good weight and flavor. **(+)

Conterno Giacomo (*twice, ex-cask, 11/90*). Dark color; rich and concentrated, full of fruit, moderate tannin, sense of sweetness. **(*)

Conterno Giacomo, Monfortino (*ex-cask, 11/90*). Deep color; richly fruited nose, hints of cherries and berries, cassis and camphor; surprising richness and concentration, quite tannic, full of fruit and flavor. **(*)

Conterno Paolo, La Ginestra (*ex-cask, 11/90*). A little dry, a tad bitter, open fruit. (*)

Contratto Giuseppe, Cà Neire (*ex-cask, 11/90*). Nice fruit on the nose; light to moderate tannin, attractive, short. (*)

Contratto Giuseppe, Sarmassa (*ex-cask, 11/90*). Evident fruit, light tannin, difficult stage. (*)

Corino Giovanni (*ex-cask, 4/90*). Light tannin, yet chewy, a little difficult to assess. ?

Dosio (*ex-cask, 11/90*). Open fruit aroma and palate, soft, light tannin, forward. *

Einaudi Luigi (*ex-cask, 11/90*). Good structure, sweet impression, open, forward flavors, soft. *(* −)

Fenocchio Giacomo, Bussia Sottana (*ex-cask, 11/90*). Tobacco, tar and flowers; soft, open and attractive. *

Fenocchio Riccardo, Pianpolvere Soprano (*twice, ex-cask, 11/90*). Cherry and berry aroma; soft, fruit evident, light-bodied, light tannin, not a lot of character. *

Ferrero F.lli (*ex-cask, 11/90*). A little coarse but good fruit. *

Giacosa Bruno, Rocche (*ex-vat, 11/90*). Woodslike aroma, tar and floral notes; good structure, sense of sweetness, moderate length. **(* −)

Giacosa Bruno, Villero (*ex-vat, 11/90*). Tar and leather aroma; good body, moderate tannin, flavorful, a little short. **(+)

Giacosa F.lli (*ex-cask, 11/90*). Mushroom, woodsy aroma; fairly good fruit, a little dry, closed, short, firm aftertaste. (* −)

Grasso Elio, Gavarini Vigna Rüncot (*11/90*). Floral, perfumed, scented bouquet; soft, open and forward; elegant. ** +

Grasso Elio, Ginestra Vigna Case Matè (*11/90*). Less nose and more forward than Rüncot, more body and tannin as well, good fruit, short. ** −

Grasso Silvio, Cascina Luciani (*ex-cask, 11/90*). Woodsy and animal fur aroma; low fruit. ?

Marcarini (Elvio Cogno), Brunate (*ex-cask, 11/90*). Light but perfumed aroma; nice entry, sense of sweetness, open forward fruit, nice and easy; it'll close up. **

Marcarini (Elvio Cogno), Brunate-Canon (*ex-cask, 11/90*). Woodsy, mushroom aroma; sense of sweetness, moderate tannin, a little short. **

Marcarini (Elvio Cogno), La Serra (*ex-cask, 11/90*). A little light but with clean fruit; soft under light tannin, raspberry fruit. ** −

Marengo M., Brunate (*ex-cask, 11/90*). Good fruit, moderate to light tannin, attractive flavor. *

Mascarello Bartolo (*ex-cask, 11/90*). Slight nose, a little light, hints of fruit, *cuòio* (leather); light but nice, loads of flavor, moderate length; displays elegance. ** +

Massolino, Sörì Vigna Riunda (*ex-cask, 11/90*). Open fruit aroma and palate, light tannin, good structure, short. *(+)

Molino Franco, Cascina La Rocca (*ex-cask, 11/90*). Open and attractive fruit, sense of sweetness. *

Oberto Severino di Oberto Sisto (*ex-cask, 11/90*). Fruit seems tired and old, light tannin, dull aftertaste.

Oddero F.lli (*ex-cask, 11/90*). Tar, tobacco and berry aroma; well balanced, open, forward fruit, attractive. **

Parusso Armando, Mariondino (*ex-cask, 11/90*). Cherry and small fruit aroma, some oak; chewy tannin, firm and dry aftertaste. (*)

Pira E. (Chiara Boschis) (*ex-cask, 11/90*). Mushroom, woodsy, *tartufi* aroma; a little light, moderate tannin, a bit short and a little dry; will be ready soon. *(+)

Porro Guido (*ex-cask, 11/90*). At a difficult stage, evident fruit. (*)

Ratti Renato, Marcenasco (*11/90*). Nice fruit, clean; a little light, moderate tannin, dry end. *

Ratti Renato, Marcenasco-Conca (*ex-cask, 11/90*). Scented aroma, lovely berrylike fruit, perfumed; some tannin, a lot of nice attractive fruit. **

Ratti Renato, Marcenasco-Rocche (*ex-cask, 11/90*). Mushroom, woodsy and damp leaves aroma, also a vague off note that blew off fairly quickly; dry, evident fruit, short. *

Ravello Renato, Cascina Gustavo (*ex-cask, 11/90*). Lovely fruit, good structure, attractive. *(*)

Rinaldi Francesco, Cannubbio (*ex-cask, 11/90*). Flowers, tobacco and tar; soft, light tannin, nice fruit, gentle. *(*)

Rinaldi Giuseppe (*ex-cask, 11/90*). Dried fruit aroma, hints of raisins and cherries; nice entry then a little dry, pruney, fruit seems a little tired, dull finish. *

Rocche Costamagna, Rocche di La Morra (*ex-cask, 11/90*). Truffle, woodsy and floral aroma; a little dry but nice flavor, light, dry end. *(+)

Saffirio Josetta (*ex-cask, 11/90*). Incredible amount of oak, is there sufficient fruit? Is this a Barolo?

Sebaste, Bussia (*ex-cask, 11/90*). Tar and floral aroma; attractive open fruit on the nose and palate, soft. *(+)

Settimo Aurelio (*ex-cask, 11/90*). Open and attractive fruit, light tannin, short dry aftertaste. (*)

Sobrero Francesco (*11/90*). Nice nose, berrylike; fairly nice fruit on entry, a bit shallow and short but drinkable. * −

Sordo F.lli, Azienda Agricola "Pugnane" (*ex-cask, 11/90*). Lovely nose; firm, good structure, flavorful. *(*)

Sordo Giovanni, Sorì Gabutti (*ex-cask, 11/90*). Some fruit, dull.

Tenuta Carretta, Cannubi (*ex-cask, 11/90*). Flowers and berries; rich, open attractive fruit, has character. **(+)

Vajra G. D. (*ex-cask, 11/90*). Attractive, open fruit aroma, berrylike; gentle and soft. ** −

Veglio Giovanni (*ex-cask, 11/90*). At a difficult stage, the fruit is, however, quite evident. ?

Vietti, Castiglione (*twice, ex-cask, 11/90*). Open attractive aroma, tobacco note; soft, open fruit, for early drinking. **

Voerzio Roberto, La Serra (*ex-cask, 11/90*). Mintlike and leather aroma, nice nose then the oak takes over; heavy oak flavor. * −

1986 ***

On May 29 a major hailstorm struck. Some vineyards were completely affected. Seventy percent of the damage was in the best areas. When it struck La Morra, part of Brunate was destroyed. Elvio Cogno told us that the older vines, those more than forty years old, were affected the most. There won't be any '86 or '87 Barolo from here. Roberto Voerzio produced no wine in 1986, and even worse, he lost 50 percent of his dolcetto vines. Massimo Martinelli of Renato Ratti said that 20 percent of their vines were damaged by the hail. The Ferrero brothers harvested 7 tons (64 quintali) of nebbiolo for Barolo in 1985, and 2.76 (25) in 1986. Fifty percent of their vines suffered hail damage. Cogno said that no one can remember hail as bad. He produced no La Serra, and only 5,000 bottles each of Barolo Brunate and Dolcetto. The part of Brunate near Cannubi was spared.

After wreaking havoc in La Morra, the storm went on to Barolo. Although it passed over Cannubi, the heart of the vineyard was spared. Bartolo Mascarello told us that although more than 90 percent of the village of Barolo was hurt by hail, only 20 percent of Cannubi was damaged. Mascarello had 50 percent of a normal crop. The storm continued on its devastating path into Serralunga and Monforte.

Castiglione Falletto was hurt as well. Cavallotto didn't produce any Punta Marcello and 40 percent of their vines in the Bricco Boschis vineyard suffered damage. Aldo Conterno, practically on the border of Castiglione Falletto, produced 7,926 gallons (300 hectoliters) of Barolo, compared to a normal crop of 9,247 to 9,379 (350 to 355). Vietti experienced very little damage in Bussia and almost none in Rocche, with a 50 percent loss in Brunate, 70 percent in Scarrone, and 100 percent in Pian di Romaldolo. The Cerettos harvested some 14.3 tons (130 quintali) of nebbiolo for Barolo, compared to a normal of 40.8 tons (370 quintali).

Elio Grasso of Monforte told us that at 6 P.M. large hailstones struck the vineyards, and in twenty-one minutes the vines were shredded. Grasso had practically no grapes at all, and consequently produced almost no wine from his own vines. He made 30 to 40 demijohns of 14.3 gallons (54 liters) each and, because of the inferior quality, he sold it *sfuso*. He had no barbera or nebbiolo. It was, he said, the worst hailstorm in more than a hundred years here.

The nebbiolo crop size of 735,321 gallons (27,832 hectoliters), equivalent to 3.7 million bottles of Barolo, was only 41.1 percent of the amount allowed by DOCG regulations and was the smallest percentage since the advent of DOC in 1967. Compare this with the average of 1.1 million gallons (41,979 hectoliters), which is 445 gallons per acre (41.6 hectoliters per hectare), between 1967 and 1989. In terms of both size and yield, 246 gallons per acre (23.02 hectoliters per hectare), it was the smallest of the decade.

Hail is a problem here every six or seven years, but the last major hailstorm, in 1951, did considerably less damage than the brief storm of 1986.

Bruno Ceretto said that what remained was very good. And at least two producers, Bruno Giacosa and Cappellano, rate it higher even than 1985; Cappellano said it was a four-star vintage. Because of a short crop Aldo Conterno produced one Barolo for commercial distribution, a Bussia Soprana, and a limited amount of his Romirasco cru. Giovanni Conterno produced no wine at all.

This vintage has produced some excellent wines. The initial poor press was premature and based more on the quantity rather than the quality. Of the 75 wines from 53 different producers we tasted, we found the top wines to be Ceretto's three "Bricco Rocche" crus, especially the Brunate and Prapò, though the Bricco Rocche was excellent as well; Aldo Conterno's Romirasco, which was produced in a very limited bottling; and two from Bruno Giacosa—Falletto and Villero—followed closely by Marcarini's La Serra and Bartolo Mascarello, and then Marcarini's Brunate, the Giuseppe Mascarello Monprivato, Prunotto Cannubi, and Tenuta Carretta's Cannubi.

Some other very good Barolos were Cappellano's Carpegna, Clerico's Ciabot Mentin Ginestra, Aldo Conterno's Bussia Soprana, Conterno Fantino's Sorì Ginestra and Vigna del Gris (Ginestre), Contratto, Marchesi di Barolo, Armando Parusso's Mariondino, the Renato Ratti Marcenasco, Francesco Rinaldi's Cannubbio, Luciano Sandrone's Cannubi Boschis, Paolo Scavino's Cannubi, and three from Vietti—Brunate, Castiglione, and Rocche. And we would be remiss not to mention Elio Altare's Cascina Nuova and Vigneto Arborina, F.lli Borgogno's Cannubi, Cavallotto's Colle Sud-Ovest, Armando Parusso's Bussia-Rocche, and E. Pira.

Overall, we believe that the '86 Barolos will provide medium-term drinking pleasure, though a few will keep well. Many of the wines are elegant rather than powerful.

CAUTION: *Before reading these tasting notes on the wines that we tasted from barrel, please read "On Tasting Wines from Barrel: A Caveat" on page xxv.*

Altare Elio, Cascina Nuova (4/90, 3,713 bottles). Aroma of truffles and mint; firm and chewy, flavorful, a little tannic at the end. **

Altare Elio, Vigneto Arborina (4/90, 3,900 bottles). Nose is a little closed, vaguely floral; packed with fruit and tannin, oak apparent, tight dry aftertaste. **

Barale F.lli, Vigna Castellero (3 times, 11/90). We tasted this wine on two different occasions in November 1990 with a surprising variation. *The first and best bottle:* Woodsy, tar and flowers, damp leaves; sense of sweetness, open and appealing fruit. ** — *The second bottle:* Seems older than its years, still it does have nice fruit, tasty, a little dry and firm at the end. * *Bottle of 4/90:* Aroma of nuts and vanilla, camphor and flowers; supple center under moderate tannin, chewy, really forward but could very well tighten up. **

Bel Colle, Vigna Monvigliero (twice, 11/90, 6,400 bottles). Woodsy, damp leaves aroma, a slight off note mars the nose; soft, nice fruit, gentle, attractive flavors. * + *Ex-cask, 4/90:* Woodsy, leathery aroma; sweet entry, openly fruited, good structure. **

Beni di Batasiolo (F.lli Dogliani), Vigna Bonfani (11/90, 13,441 bottles and 100 magnums). Soft, open and simple, some structure, off note mars the end. +

Bersano (11/90). Soft, simple and easy. +

Borgogno Bartolomeo (ex-vat, 5/87). Like grape juice, no character but has fruit. * —

Borgogno Giacomo (11/90). Tight, firm and closed, hard. *?

"Bricco Rocche" Azienda Agricola (Ceretto), Bricco Rocche (10/90, 3,794 bottles). Scented bouquet, notes of leather; a little firm in spite of open and attractive flavors, sweet impression, dry, tight finish. **(*)

"Bricco Rocche" Azienda Agricola (Ceretto), Brunate (3 times, 10/90, 19,092 bottles). Delicate scented, perfumed bouquet, fragrant, recalls *tartufi* and underbrush, tobacco and flowers; a delibate, gentle Barolo, soft, open and forward, surprisingly ready now, some tannin remains, supple, lingering finish, elegant, real style and class. ***(+)

"Bricco Rocche" Azienda Agricola (Ceretto), Prapò (10/90, 11,153 bottles). Camphor and berries, a little closed on the nose; firm, still somewhat tight, a lot of structure, the most of the three, very long, class comes through. ***(+)

Brovia F.lli, Monprivato (ex-cask, 4/90). Tar and tobacco aroma; forward, open flavor at first, then tight and dry, still needs time to come together ** —

Brovia F.lli, Rocche (exc-cask, 4/90). Tight nose, unyielding; nice entry, still rather hard though soft in center, needs time. ** —

Ca' Bianca, Cascina Denegri (*twice, 11/90*). Aroma recalls wet animal fur; simple, fruity and sweet, not a lot to it. *Bottle of 4/90— Tenuta Denegri:* Simple, open cherrylike aroma and entry, gives way to some tannin, light fruit midpalate, short dry aftertaste. +

Cantine Duca d'Asti (Chiarlo Michele), "Granduca" (*ex-cask, 4/87*). Fairly dark color; fresh spicy and cherry aroma; moderate to high tannin, fresh fruit palate, rather nice fruit. *(*)

Cappellano, Carpegna (*ex-vat, 11/90*). Good concentration and structure, rich flavor, moderate tannin, a tad bitter. **(+)

Casetta F.lli (*ex-cask, 11/90*). Soft, open entry, moderate tannin, good fruit, clean. * +

Cavallotto F.lli, Bricco Boschis-Colle Sud-Ovest (*3 times, ex-cask, 11/90*). Lovely open fruit aroma, raspberry component; soft, forward, sweet impression and ripe. **

Cavallotto F.lli, Bricco Boschis-San Giuseppe (*ex-cask, 4/87*). Fairly tannic and chewy, good body, soft center, rather tannic end. *(*)

Ceretto, Zonchera (*10/90*). Soft, open and fruity, nice entry, then dry, drink. * +

Clerico, Ciabot Mentin Ginestra (*twice, 4/90, 7,900 bottles*). Lovely but tight nose, leather and tobacco notes, berrylike nuance, some oak, some fruit evident; good structure and fruit, lots of flavor, well made with character and moderately long aftertaste. **(+)

Conterno Aldo, Bussia Soprana (*3 times, 11/90*). Aroma recalls a forest, mushroom note; good body, nice flavor, will be ready early. ** +

Conterno Aldo, Bussia Soprana-Ciabot [Romirasco] (*ex-cask, 4/87*). Intense and rich, full and tannic, lots of structure, the most class of Conterno's Barolo crus. **(*+)

Conterno Aldo, Bussia Soprana-Cicala (*ex-cask, 4/87*). Fullest and most tannic of the three crus, lots of structure. **(*)

Conterno Aldo, Bussia Soprana-Colonello (*ex-cask, 4/87*). A big, rich wine with lots of structure. **(*)

Conterno Fantino, Sorì Ginestra (*twice, 4/90, 8,380 bottles*). Lovely nose recalls ripe fruit and berries; open, forward, soft and round, real smoothness, gentle. ** +

Conterno Fantino, Vigna del Gris (Ginestre) (*4/90, 4,210 bottles*). Mintlike aroma, still a little closed; soft and smooth, almost sweet, some tannin. ** +

Contratto (*ex-cask, 4/87*). Fresh cherrylike fruit from the aroma through the flavor and finish, firm, fairly tannic, good potential. **(+)

Cordero di Montezemolo, Enrico VI in Villero (*4/90*). Mushroom and woodslike aroma, cherry and floral notes; sweet entry, fairly tannic, good structure, seems younger than the Monfalletto, dry firm finish. ** −

Cordero di Montezemolo, Monfalletto (*4/90*). Aroma of the woods and truffles, berries and *tartufi*; chewy, good fruit, will be for early drinking, short. * +

Damilano Dott., Giacomo (*twice, 11/90*). Simple fruit, soft, sweet impression, dull aftertaste. *Bottle of 4/90:* Tar and wet dog aroma; some tannin, forward flavors, soft. * −

Fenocchio Riccardo, Pianpolvere Soprano (*twice, 11/90, 5,241 bottles*). Lovely nose, flowers, berries and vanilla; soft under moderate tannin, good backbone. ** −

Ferrero F.lli (*twice, 11/90*). Grapey, simple, light tannin, a little dry, very short, dull aftertaste. + *Ex-cask, 4/87:* Open, soft, forward, well balanced, nice fruit, precocious, should be ready early. **

Fontanafredda (*twice, 11/90*). Aroma of dried fruit, berries and autumn leaves; open, forward entry, moderate tannin, clean fruit. *

Gagliardo Gianni, La Serra (*4/90*). Not a lot to it, some tannin, some fruit, not bad either! +

Gagliardo Gianni, Mora (*4/90*). Kirschlike aroma; fairly soft and supple, open, light tannin, ready, agreeable, no real character, and no defects.

Germano Angelo (*ex-cask, 4/87*). Fairly nice fruit, on the light side, nice acid, tannic aftertaste. *(+)

Giacosa Bruno, Falletto (*twice, ex-cask, 11/90*). Rich and intense aroma, woodslike, mushroom, leather and camphor components; good body, structure and weight; a big rich wine with a lot of potential. ***(+)

Giacosa Bruno, Villero (*twice, 11/90*). Tar and floral bouquet; sweet impression with a surprising gentle side to it, good structure, very long; great elegance. ***(+)

Giacosa F.lli, Pira (*11/90*). Oak evident from the nose through the palate, there is some fruit but the oak intrudes. +

Grasso Silvio, Bricco Luciani (*twice, 11/90*). Soft, simple and open, agreeable, more forward than the bottle of April 1990. * *Bottle of 4/90:* Clean fruit on the nose; a little light, soft and smooth, clean and open flavors, sense of sweetness, hint of oak, a tad short. * + (** −)

Grasso Silvio, Cascina Luciani (*twice, 4/90*). Tarlike aroma; a little tight, fairly nice fruit, simple. *

Guasti Clemente (*ex-botte, 11/90*). Old nose; sweet impression, soft and open, simple, overly sweet, dull aftertaste.

Marcarini (Elvio Cogno), Brunate (*3 times, 11/90, 5,000 bottles*). Woodsy, damp leaves, resin, dried fruit and berries; open fruit, good structure, moderate tannin. Elvio Cogno thinks this wine will age very well. *** — *Ex-cask, 1/87:* Beautiful color, purple cast; lots of structure, precocious, fruity, light to moderate tannin. **(* −)

Marcarini (Elvio Cogno), La Serra (*11/90; 1,400 bottles*). Lovely nose, woodslike, resin and floral notes; sense of sweetness, fairly long finish; real elegance and class. ***

Marchesi di Barolo (*ex-cask, 3/87*). Fresh, fruity aroma, cherrylike note; rich in fruit, some firmness, good potential. **(+)

Mascarello Bartolo (*11/90*). Lovely fruit aroma with appealing forestlike scents; soft, open and forward, with a sweetness to the fruit. ***

Mascarello Giuseppe, Monprivato (*11/90, 6,628 bottles*). Lovely nebbiolo aroma, woodslike, vague *tartufi* note; lots of flavor and structure, some class. *** −

Massolino Giuseppe (*4/90*). Berry and vanilla aroma; soft with good fruit under hard tannin, needs time, tannin builds up toward the end. * −

Massolino, Sörì Vigna Riunda (*11/90*). Soft, simple, fruity, a slight off quality. * −

Massolino, Vigneto Margheria (*11/90*). Berry aroma; soft, open, forward fruit. *

Oberto F.lli, Vigneto Rocche Annunziata (*4/90*). Slight nose; a sweetness to the fruit on entry then tight and a little firm, dry tannic aftertaste. * −

Parusso Armando, Bussia-Rocche (*3 times, 11/90, 1,664 bottles*). Simple cherrylike aroma, tobacco and dusty notes; good balance, nice fruit from the nose across the palate, sense of sweetness, forward, some tannin, chocolate nuance, should be ready early. **

Parusso Armando, Mariondino (*3 times, 11/90*). Cherry and small fruit aroma, hints of camphor and vanilla; up-front fruit, soft center under moderate tannin, lovely flavors, tobacco note, some tannin, will be ready early. **(+)

Pira E. (Chiara Boschis) (*11/90, 2,692 bottles*). [In an average vintage Chiara Boschis produces 12,000 bottles of Barolo. The nearly 80 percent decline in quantity was due to the severe damage from the hail.] Dried fruit, leather and berry aroma; moderate tannin, good fruit, sense of sweetness, a little short; should mature early; some elegance. **

Prunotto (*11/90*). Tanky, off-putting in spite of the fruit; this was tasted from bottle, not from barrel; a real disappointment from a generally reliable producer.

Prunotto, Bussia (*11/90, 29,600 bottles*). A little tanky; fairly nice fruit, sense of sweetness, unclean; what is happening here? Prunotto has long been one of the zone's more reliable producers! *

Prunotto, Cannubi (*11/90, 5,370 bottles*). Woodslike aroma, flowers, damp leaves and berries; nice fruit, good structure, a lot of quality; more like what we'd expect from Prunotto. **(*)

Ratti Renato, Marcenasco (*ex-cask, 4/87*). Lots of nice fruit, a tad light, good quality, licorice and kirsch. **(+)

Rinaldi Francesco, Cannubbio (*11/90*). Open fruit aroma, floral and tar components; a lot of character, open and soft, seemingly ready. ** +

Rinaldi Giuseppe (*twice, ex-cask, 11/90*). [Rinaldi's Brunate vineyard was the only one of his vineyards to escape the hail.] A little dry and firm, surprisingly tannic, very young, good structure. *(*)

Rocche Costamagna, Rocche di La Morra (*3 times, 11/90*). Open kirschlike fruit aroma, attractive; soft and smooth, light tannin; ready now, could close up but will be for early drinking. *(*)

Sandrone Luciano, Cannubi Boschis (*3 times, 10/90*). Tobacco, truffle and oak aroma, scented berry notes, vaguely floral, loads of oak and a lot of fruit; good structure, some tannin, sense of sweetness, young, quite attractive, good backbone, chocolate notes, tannic aftertaste. **(+)

Scarzello Giorgio (*4/90*). Up-front cherry aroma; sweet and soft entry, kirsch, tobacco, a tad short. * +

Scavino Paolo (*3 times, 4/90*). Up-front fruit on the nose and palate, soft and open, round, some tannin, fairly well balanced, more or less ready at this stage, could very well close down. ** −

Scavino Paolo, Cannubi (*ex-cask, 5/87*). Loaded with nice fruit, sweet impression, medium body, moderate tannin, good quality. **(+)

Sebaste (*4/90*). Nice nose, though a little light, soft entry then somewhat tight, light to moderate tannin, good fruit. * +

Sebaste, Bussia (*4/90*). Tight nose; nice fruit on entry, sense of sweetness, light aftertaste, dusty note. ** −

Seghesio Renzo (*ex-cask, 4/90*). Nice nose, cherrylike fruit; sweet yet tight, some firmness, fairly tannic, sense of sweet ripe fruit, is there enough for the tannin? *?

Settimo Aurelio (*11/90*). Some sulfur on the nose(!); fairly nice fruit on entry, dry aftertaste, a tad bitter. * −

Tenuta Carretta, Poderi Cannubi (*11/90*). Resin, flowers and berries on the aroma; sweet impression, open fruit flavor, and for this producer surprisingly little tannin; overall an attractive and well-made wine. ** + (*** −)

Tenuta Montanello (*4/90*). Tarlike aroma; open, soft, forward, easy style, seems ready. *

Viberti Giovanni (*11/90*). Fairly attractive fruit on the nose and palate, good structure, moderate tannin. *(+)

Vietti, Brunate (*ex-cask, 4/87*). Good structure, a little light, nice fruit, moderate tannin. ** +

Vietti, Castiglione (*4/90, 9,800 bottles*). Leather and tar aroma; open and gentle, on the light side, with style, balanced, seems ready. ** +

Vietti, Rocche (*7 times, 11/90, 5,300 bottles*). Tobacco and tar aroma, vaguely of seaweed; moderate tannin, a little light, but good concentration, forward flavors, for early drinking, nice fruit. **(+)

1985 ****

The weather was very dry; very few days experienced rain. There was a lot of sun. It remained very warm and dry during the harvest. Although it was a very dry year, the grapes didn't suffer. The harvest began on October 16, which was four days earlier than the norm.

The quantity of 1.4 million gallons (54,454 hectoliters),

7.3 million bottles, was 77.4 percent of the amount allowed. Although it was the third largest crop of the decade, it was smaller than 1982 in terms of both production and yield: 463 gallons per acre (43.3 hectoliters per hectare) versus 506 (47.4).

Bartolo Mascarello, Alfredo Currado, and many other producers said that the grapes were even more perfect than in 1982. In November 1990, Mascarello said that these Barolos will be ready sooner than the '82s. Currado of Vietti places it behind 1982, 1988, and 1989. Giuseppe Rinaldi, in November 1985, told us that the year was perfect, even in the less favored positions. He couldn't recall a year with such perfect maturation of the grapes. "It will certainly be as good as 1971," he said, "that is the indication now. It could even be better, but we'll have to wait until after malolactic fermentation to really know. It was certainly the best vintage since 1971." Aldo Conterno, who produced a Granbussia, places it behind 1989 and 1982. Giacomo Conterno produced a Monfortino.

There is no question in our mind that 1985 produced better Barolos than 1982. For the most part, they are extremely well-balanced wines with a lot of perfume and a purity of nebbiolo fruit not often found. They should age well. We have been tasting these wines since January 1986 and have been in the zone on a number of occasions since then. And on every occasion we were more impressed by the vintage than on our previous visit. Thus far we have tasted 160 different Barolos from 105 producers. The vintage is, without question, first rate. For us only 1989 is better in the decade, though a few producers disagree and place 1982 ahead of 1985. There are a lot of stars: the Barolo from Bartolo Mascarello stands out, followed very closely by Aldo Conterno's three Bussia Soprana subcrus—Ciabot, Cicala, and Colonello—as well as his outstanding Granbussia, Monfortino from Giacomo Conterno, Bruno Giacosa's Falletto and Rocche, the Marcarini Brunate, Giuseppe Mascarello's Monprivato, Francesco Rinaldi's Cannubbio, and Vietti's Rocche and Villero Riserva. Also first rate: Bruno Giacosa's Villero, the three Ceretto "Bricco Rocche" crus—Bricco Rocche, Brunate, and Prapò—Aldo Conterno's Bussia Soprana, Elio Grasso's Gavarini Vigna Chinera, the Marcarini La Serra, the Giuseppe Rinaldi Brunate, and the Vietti Brunate. Other excellent '85 Barolos include F.lli Barale Castellero, Clerico's Ciabot Mentin Ginestra, Giacomo Conterno's Cascina Francia, Cordero di Montezemolo's Monfalleto, Bruno Giacosa's Vigna Rionda, Elio Grasso's Gavarini Vigna Rüncot and Ginestra Vigna Case Matè, Pio Cesare *normale* and Ornato, the Brunate from Pittatore Cav. Francesco's Azienda Agricola "Ponte Rocca," Renato Ratti's Marcenasco, Giuseppe Rinaldi, Francesco Sandrone, Scarpa's Tetti di La Morra, Paolo Scavino's Paolo Bric del Fiasc, the Cannubi from Tenuta Carretta, Roberto Voerzio's La Serra, and Basilio Zunino.

Alessandria F.lli di G. B. Alessandro, Monvigliero (4/90). Aroma is suggestive of a combination of leather and damp animal smells; soft, forward, open flavors of dried fruit, short. *

Altare Elio, Cascina Nuova (3 times, 9/89, 7,252 bottles). Somewhat closed aroma displays suggestions of tobacco and fruit, oak component; soft, open and forward, finish is a bit short, though firm, quite attractive now, will be for early drinking. * *Bottle of 4/89:* Seems surprisingly tannic at this stage, good structure, fruit and backbone, firm finish. **

Altare Elio, Vigneto Arborina (4/89). Some oak, chewy and firm with a lot of flavor and richness, young. **

Ascheri Giacomo (4/89). Openly fruity aroma and palate, light tannin, easy and simple, not a lot of character. * −

Ascheri Giacomo, Vigna Farina (3 times, 4/89). Tobacco and fruit aroma; light, open, soft, fruity. *

Azelia, Bricco Fiasco (3 times, 10/90). Tar and dried fruit aroma; a little firm, nice fruit, needs a little more character, could use more weight. *(* −) *Bottle of 4/90:* Woodsy, berry aroma; firm and fairly tannic with a lot of flavor, lacks some length on the palate. * + (** −)

Barale F.lli, Vigna Castellero (twice, 4/90). Perfumed scented bouquet, hints of camphor and leather; real sweetness to the fruit, almost lush, lovely indeed, well balanced. ***

Bel Colle (Monvigliero) (4/89). Tobacco component evident from the must through the flavor, nice fruit, balanced, not special, still, the best Bel Colle to date. *

Bel Colle, Riserva Speciale (4/89). Dry, hard and tannic, though there is sufficient fruit to improve, fairly well balanced. *

Beni di Batasiolo (F.lli Dogliani) (twice, 10/90). A little dry, seems to be losing its fruit. ? *Bottle of 5/90:* Cherry, tobacco aroma; soft and open, forward flavors, simple, some tannin, ready now, should hold, could even improve a bit. *

Beni di Batasiolo (F.lli Dogliani), Bonfani (10/90, 13,180 bottles). Correct but small-scale Barolo, light to moderate tannin, fairly nice fruit. *

Beni di Batasiolo (F.lli Dogliani), Boscareto (3/90). Vaguely cherrylike aroma with notes of tea(!); soft center, a tad low in fruit midpalate, light tannin, soft and easy, quite drinkable. *

Bersano (6/90). Soft, simple, dull, light tannin.

Bongiovanni Giovanni (11/90). Some alcohol and volatile acidity on the nose, harsh edges, medium-bodied, lacks fruit, weight and structure.

Borgogno Bartolomeo (ex-vat, 5/87). Lacks weight but does have fruit, seems a little dirty. ?

Borgogno Bartolomeo, Sorì Solanotto (4/90). Typical tar and floral bouquet; chewy and hard, seems to have the fruit, but the fruit tastes old, firm tannic aftertaste, rustic style. *

Borgogno F.lli Serio e Battista, Vigna Cannubi (twice, 11/90, 19,700 bottles). Nice nose, some complexity; soft, open and fruity, light to moderate tannin, forward flavors, quite attractive. **

Borgogno Giacomo (4/90). Closed nose, nebbiolo character evident; moderate tannin, not quite together, but the components are all there, needs time to meld and soften. *(*)

Borgogno Ludovico, Cascina Borgognot (4/90). Very little nose; has a sweetness to the fruit, kind of old-tasting fruit, lacks distinction, very short finish.

Brezza Giacomo (4/90). Characteristic tarlike aroma; dry, tight and firm, needs time to open and soften. *?

"Bricco Rocche" Azienda Agricola (Ceretto), Bricco Rocche (twice, 5/90, 4,920 bottles). Delicate-scented perfume, woodslike, *tartufi*, raspberries and flowers; at this stage a little tight and closed, sweet, round and supple, great concentration, displays real class and style, harmonious, a cut above the other two crus. There were two bottles when we tasted it in May 1990, one seemed more open, the other seemed tight! ***+

"Bricco Rocche" Azienda Agricola (Ceretto), Brunate (4 times, 5/90, 30,251 bottles). Lovely classic Barolo nose, perfumed raspberry scented, tar and tobacco, berry and cherry notes; soft with a sweet impression, rich, open flavor, some oak, moderate tannin, the most open and forward of the three crus, elegant, on the young side in spite of being so appealing. ***(+)

"Bricco Rocche" Azienda Agricola (Ceretto), Prapò (twice, 5/90, 12,768 bottles). Lovely fragrant nose, reveals nuances of raspberries, *tartufi*, underbrush and camphor; surprisingly open, soft tannins, rich, sweet, ripe fruit, young with real quality and class. ***(+)

Brovia F.lli, Garblèt Suè (4/90). Tight nose, evident fruit; open sweetness makes it the most forward of the three Brovia crus, it even seems a little light by comparison, still, good quality if not special. **

Brovia F.lli, Monprivato (4/90). Nice nose, minty, tobacco nuances; chewy and tannic, with a lot of nice fruit and sweetness, needs time, no question it has the components to age. **+ (***−)

Brovia F.lli, Rocche (4/90). A little closed, yet characteristic tar, woodsy, and tobacco aroma; sweet fruit under firm, chewy tannin, tight toward the end, quite young, the hardness from the firm tannins need time to soften, give it three, perhaps four years. **+ (***−)

Ca' Bianca, Tenuta Denegri (6 times, 11/90). Light but nice nose, of flowers and berries; light to moderate tannin, open, forward flavors, a little dry and short, with some firmness at the end; needs perhaps another year. *

Cabutto, Tenuta La Volta, Vigna Castello (4/89). Light, open nose, cherry and tobacco notes; flavorful, a little short, should improve. *+ (**−)

Calissano Luigi, Vigneti Castelletto Perno di Monforte (11/90). Some oxidation apparent, moderate tannin; lacks the intensity of the vintage; old tasting.

Canale Aldo (ex-cask, 4/86). Just racked yesterday. Deep color; rich fruit, hard and tannic. *(*+)

Cantine Duca d'Asti (Chiarlo Michele), "Granduca" (8 times, 11/90). Cherry and tobacco aroma; soft, fruity and open, ready, precocious, nice fruit; very ready. *

Cantine Duca d'Asti di Chiarlo Michele, Rocche (12/90). Closed on the nose; open fruit on initial entry which then closes up, moderate tannin, good structure, firm, tight end; displays some potential, young. *(*+)

Cantine Duca d'Asti di Chiarlo Michele, Vigna Rionda (12/90). Lovely nose, recalls a forest, notes of *tartufi* and camphor; moderate tannin, evident fruit, good structure; young. *(*)

Cantine Le Ginestre (4/90). Small nose, closed; a little simple, nice entry, some tannin, clean. *

Cappellano Dott. Giuseppe (3 times, 10/90). Tobacco and camphor aroma; soft under light tannin, fairly soft, nice texture, light finish, nice now, could improve. **− (**)

Cascina Adelaide di G. Terzano (ex-cask, 4/86). Dark ruby, grape juice aroma; moderate tannin, quite a lot of fruit, some potential evident. **

Castello d'Annone di G. L. Viarengo (4/90). Light nose, evident varietal, tar and berry components; soft, open and flavorful, fairly nice structure, a little simple, but quite attractive. *+

Cavallotto F.lli, Vigna Bricco Boschis-Colle Sud-Ovest (twice, ex-cask, 4/87). Big, rich, chewy and concentrated, still a little rough. *(*+)

Cavallotto F.lli, Vigna Bricco Boschis-Punta Marcello Riserva (3 times, 4/90). Aroma is somewhat tight yet with an evident richness; full, rich and flavorful with ripe berrylike fruit. **(+)

Cavallotto F.lli, Vigna Bricco Boschis-San Giuseppe (4 times, 10/90). Nice nose, of tobacco, berries and cherries; young, yet with open fruit flavors on the initial impression, giving way to tannin, still surprisingly soft and open, a lot of potential, give it four to five more years. **+ (***−)

Ceretto, Zonchera (twice, 5/90). Open tobacco and fruit aroma, leather nuance, vaguely cherrylike; ready now, soft, a nice wine but without the concentration expected, a tad dry at the end. **+

Clerico, Ciabot Mentin Ginestra (4/89). Light nose at this stage; great structure, richly concentrated and rich, a classy wine, this will be a keeper. ***

Coluè di Massimo Oddero (10/90). *Tartufi* and woodsy aroma; soft under light tannin, a little dry and short. *−

Conterno Aldo, Bussia Soprana (4 times, 4/89). Fruit leaps out of the glass, rich and packed with flavor, real class and elegance. ***+

Conterno Aldo, Bussia Soprana-Ciabot (ex-cask, 4/87). Black cherry component on the nose; richly flavored, great intensity and extract, this has real class. ***(*)

Conterno Aldo, Bussia Soprana-Cicala (ex-cask, 4/87). Fabulous aroma, complex and rich; intensely flavored and rich, with enormous extract and weight, long-lingering finish with sweetness. ***(*)

Conterno Aldo, Bussia Soprana-Colonello (*ex-cask, 4/87*). Woodsy, fruity, cherry aroma, licorice nuance; intensely flavored, full-bodied, rich and concentrated with an extra dimension of quality. ***(*)

Conterno Aldo, Granbussia (*11/90, c. 7,000 bottles*). *Tartufi* and ripe fruit aroma, fragrant scent, berry notes; soft and open, great intensity of flavor, lots of tannin, but soft ones, a lot of texture, impressive. ****– (****)

Conterno Fantino, Sorì Ginestra (*twice, 4/90, 10,532 bottles, plus larger sizes*). Aroma recalls mint, tobacco and tar; soft, round and smooth, moderate tannin, forward flavors; finish is a little harsh. **(+)

Conterno Fantino, Sorì Ginestra Riserva (*4/90*). More body, tannin and extract than the *normale,* young with good potential. **(+)

Conterno Giacomo, Cascina Francia (*6 times, 11/90*). Intense, rich and ripe fruit on the nose and palate; suggestions of underbrush, leather, mint, flowers, camphor and tar on the nose; great richness and extract, lush even, surprisingly soft for Conterno, though with moderate tannin, lovely texture; needs two or three more years as a minimum; real class. ***– (***)

Conterno Giacomo, Monfortino (*ex-cask, 11/90*). Richly fruited aroma, recalls the woods, flowers, tar, leather, camphor and rich fruit; rich in tannin and fruit, great sweetness, and a lot of structure, one for the ages, very long. ***(*)

Contratto (*ex-cask, 6/86*). Fresh and grapey, surprisingly simple at this stage, nice fruit, and fairly well concentrated. **

Cordero di Montezemolo, Enrico VI in Villero (*9/90*). Chewy tannin, has the fruit, but tight and a little earthy, tight dry finish. **(+)

Cordero di Montezemolo, Monfalleto (*4 times, 12/90*). Cherrylike aroma, tobacco and ripe fruit nuances, fragrant; rich core in the center, soft under light to moderate tannin, well balanced, lovely indeed, a tad short, promising. **(*–) *Bottle of 5/90:* Nose is a little tight, woodsy, mushroom components, hint of berries and cassis which carry through on the palate, open fruit flavors display a sweetness of ripe fruit, almost lush. The best Montezemolo in a few years. ***

Corino Giovanni, Vigna Giachini Annunziata (*4/90*). Really closed at this stage, yet the fruit is evident on the nose and palate, a gentle style, balanced and on the young side. **

Damilano Dott. Giacomo (*4/90*). A lightweight, small-scale wine with open, forward flavors, short and tannic finish. *

Eredi Ferrero Virginia, S. Rocco (*3 times, 4/90*). Openly fruity, hints of cherries, camphor and tobacco; sweet and flavorful, supple center, moderate tannin, a little chewy, short, dry finish; should age moderately well. **(+)

Eredi Lodali, Vigneto Bric Sant'Ambrogio (*4/90, 12,247 bottles*). Light, open nose; soft, open berrylike flavors, seemingly ready now, some tannin at the end. *

Fenocchio Giacomo, Vigneti in Bussia Sottana (*3 times, 6/90*). Still closed, suggestions of ripe fruit, vaguely floral; rather tannic with the sense of ripe fruit quite evident, give it three more years. **(+)

Fenocchio Giacomo, Vigneti in Cannubbio (*4/90*). Perfumed, scented bouquet; mouth-filling flavor, tannin evident yet soft, young, and tight finish. **(+?)

Fenocchio Riccardo, Pianpolvere Soprano (*3 times, 6/90, 5,704 bottles*). Tobacco, tar and berry aroma, and an evident *tartufi* component; moderately tannic with the stuffing to carry it to maturity, it still needs a few more years yet with evident potential. **(+)

Ferrero F.lli (*twice, 4/90*). Tight, closed and firm nose; open, attractive fruit flavors. **

Fontanafredda, Vigna La Rosa (*11/90*). Good structure, open, attractive flavors, moderate tannin. **

Franco Fiorina (*10/90*). Fragrant cherry and berry aroma; ripe fruit component, well balanced, soft, light tannin, seemingly ready. **+

Gagliardo Gianni, La Serra (*4/90*). Mushroom and truffle aroma, suggestion of kirsch; chewy tannin, nice fruit on the mid-palate, a surprise for sure. *

Gagliardo Gianni, La Serra Riserva (*4/90*). Slight nose, low fruit, heavy tannin, no character.

Gagliardo Gianni, Mora (*4/90*). Odd nose, a little cooked with dried fruit component; low fruit on the palate, lacks weight and extract, definition and personality, dry, tannic aftertaste.

Gemma (*4/90*). Leathery, woodsy, barnyardy aroma; ripe fruit, open, sweet and soft, round and seemingly ready. **

Germano Angelo (*ex-cask, 4/87*). Nose recalls cherries; fairly grapey flavor, moderate tannin, fruit, tight finish. *(+)

Giacosa Bruno, Falletto (*twice, 11/90*). Classic Barolo aroma of tar and cherries, with notes of licorice, camphor, shaving lotion and flowers; quite tannic, flavorful, a lot of extract and sweetness, packed with fruit. ***(*)

Giacosa Bruno, Rocche (*3 times, 6/90, 7,300 bottles*). Although the nose is closed the great intensity of fruit is quite evident, suggestions of *tartufi,* tobacco and berries with a woodsy overtone, great richness, enormous extract and weight, at this stage it makes the tannin seem rather soft, great structure and balance, enormous length; a true classic. ***(*)

Giacosa Bruno, Vigna Rionda (*twice, ex-cask, 4/86*). Rich in fruit and tannin, very young with evident potential. ***

Giacosa Bruno, Villero (*3 times, 6/90, 19,700 bottles*). A mélange of scents and flavors, sweet and concentrated, mouth-filling, seems more open and forward than expected, we suspect it will close up, great class and elegance. ***(*–)

Giacosa F.lli (*12/90*). Forest scents, vague truffle note; open, soft and forward. *+

Giacosa F.lli, Vigneto Pira (4/90). Ripe cherry aroma, vague *tartufi* nuance; fairly tannic and chewy with the stuffing to carry it, tobaccolike note carries through in the mouth, slightly bitter, a little rustic. ** −

Gianolio Tomaso (Fossano) (4/90). Closed aroma yields very little except oak; fairly sweet upon entry then it gives way to tannin, fruit is quite closed, firm, rather dry, then some sweetness again at the end. * −

Grasso Elio, Gavarini Vigna Chinera (ex-cask, 4/86). Deep purple; berrylike aroma; lots of tannin, chewy, enormous richness of fruit, not the least bit heavy, well balanced. ***(+)

Grasso Elio, Gavarini Vigna Rüncot (4 times, 6/90). Refined, delicate floral bouquet, notes of cherries, tea and tobacco; up-front sweetness, a little firmer than Casa Matè, real flavor, style and class, gentle nature, a tad bitter at this stage. ***

Grasso Elio, Ginestra Vigna Case Matè (twice, 4/90). Lovely floral bouquet, hints of tobacco and truffles; sweet, dusty notes, gentle, lots of character, real class, should improve though attractive now. ***

Grasso Silvio, Cascina Luciani (twice, 4/90). Tobacco and tar aroma; sweet, open entry, moderate tannin, nice fruit, a bit simple, has structure and flavor, and some length. ** −

Grasso Silvio, Ciabot di Preve (ex-cask, 4/87). Nice nose, clean, characteristic, hint of camphor and cherries; fruity, on the light side. *(*)

Grimaldi G. (twice, 4/90). Strawberries and cassis; simple, open and soft, drinkable enough, short. *

"La Corte" Azienda Agricola, Monticelli-Olivero (ex-cask, 4/86). Some volatile acidity; tannic, hard, the fruit is there, the volatile acidity is a problem. (*?)

Mazone Giovanni, Vigna Gramolere Ciabot del Preve (4/90). Woodsy and damp leaves aroma, suggestions of tar, berries and cassis; good structure, rich in extract, young but attractive open flavors. **(+)

Marcarini (Elvio Cogno), Brunate (4 times, 11/90). Lovely fruit on the nose, berry notes; sweet impression from ripe fruit, gentle nature, moderate tannin, very long; young but with real elegance. ***(*) Bottle of 10/89: *Tartufi bianco* is quite pronounced on the aroma, suggestions of berries, tobacco notes; rich, sweet, openly fruity, great richness, weight and extract, real class and style, very long. *** + (****)

Marcarini (Elvio Cogno), La Serra (3 times, 11/90). Woodslike and floral aroma, raspberry nuance; sense of sweetness, light to moderate tannin, yet with a lushness to the fruit; a lot of elegance. ***(+)

Marchesi di Barolo (3 times, 12/90). Small-scale, some flavor, uninteresting(!); the bottle perhaps? *Bottle of 10/90:* Tobacco and tealike aroma; nice entry then firm, could use more weight. * − *Bottle of 5/90:* Nice nose, open; soft, open forward flavors, ready, simple, easy style, lacks the weight and class but certainly drinkable enough. * −

Marchesi di Barolo, Brunate (twice, 11/90). Nice nose, autumn leaves and vanilla; soft entry, moderate yet attractive fruit, firm, very dry finish, overly dry. *(+)

Marchesi di Barolo, Cannubi (11/90). Scented, perfumed, berry and floral aroma; light tannin, soft and open, a good wine, not a great one; doesn't measure up to the vintage or the vineyard. *

Marchesi di Barolo, Costa di Rose (11/90). Dried fruit and autumn leaves aroma, notes of vanilla, oak, seems older than its age; good fruit, short. *

Marchesi di Barolo, Valletta (11/90). Vanilla, open fruit aroma, seems older than it is; ripe fruit flavor, tasty. ** −

Mascarello Bartolo (5 times, 11/90). *Magnum:* Incredible perfume, real fragrance, a mélange of scents, first flowers, then berries, one second raspberries, the next strawberries, then *tartufi*, followed by *cuòio* (leather); explosive, mouth-filling flavors; great class and elegance, a real star. ****(+) *Bottle of 5/90:* Incredible perfume, real fragrance, rich and expansive bouquet, *tartufi* overlay, complex with nuances of berries—strawberries and raspberries—cherries and flowers; sweet, mouth-filling, explosive flavors, great structure, real class and style, young and chewy, impressive, very long; this needs age but will be splendid in time, say from three to five years on; elegant, lots of class. *** + (****)

Mascarello Giuseppe, Monprivato (10/90, 13,730 bottles, plus larger sizes). Expansive aroma, great fragrance, flowers and fruit, tarlike nuance, richly concentrated, great quality, real class though young. ***(*) *Bottle of 4/90:* Tobacco, tar, vaguely floral aroma; a mouthful of tannin and fruit, chewy, great richness and extract, very long, this one needs a lot of age, but it will be worth the wait. ***(+)

Massolino Giuseppe (4/90). Light nose displays a ripe fruit component, some tobacco; chewy tannin, sense of ripe fruit, short, dry aftertaste, tobacco note on the way out. *

Massolino Giuseppe, Sörì Vigna Riunda (twice, 4/90). Scented floral aroma, hint of berries and camphor; a nice sweetness to the fruit, dusty, dry tannin, could use more length. ** −

Massolino Giuseppe, Vigna Margheria (ex-cask, 4/89). Open fruit, good structure, moderate tannin, short. *(+)

Mauro Marino, Vigna Conca (Annunziata) (4/90). Medicinal nose; lightweight but fruity, soft center. *

Mirafiore (6/90). Lovely woodslike aroma, floral and tobacco notes, as well as berries and cassis; perhaps a little too simple in the mouth but balanced, not for aging but for early drinking, like now. * +

Molino Franco, Cascina La Rocca (twice, 4/90). Dried fruit aroma; soft, open, forward flavor, simple.

Oberto Egidio (ex-cask, 4/86). Cherry notes; moderate tannin, sufficient fruit to carry it. *(+)

Oberto Severino (4/89). Light tobacco and fruit aroma; sweet, rich and openly fruity, forward fruit, short, dry aftertaste. *

Oddero F.lli (10/90). *Tartufi* and berry aroma and flavor, light tannin, very drinkable now, room to grow. **

Oddero F.lli, Convento (4/89). Open fruit on the nose and palate, surprisingly accessible, soft center, hard edges. **

Oddero F.lli, Rocche di Bussia (4/89). Tobacco and fruit aroma; ditto the palate, seems a little light but nice flavor, a tad bitter at the end. * +

Oddero F.lli, Vigna Rionda (twice, 4/89). *Tartufi* and tobacco aroma, hint of camphor; sweet entry then closes down, tight yet with richness of fruit quite evident. *** –

Osvaldo Mauro, Cantine Mauro Vini (4/89). Does have fruit, but not a lot.

Parusso Armando (10/90, 13,354 bottles). Open, attractive aroma, nuances of tobacco and tar; ready now, fairly well balanced. **

Parusso Armando, dei Ville Meriondo (ex-vat, 4/86). Richly fruited aroma; moderate tannin, loads of fruit, but a little simple sided, tannin builds at the end. *(*)

Patrito (ex-vat, 4/87). Almost like grape juice, fairly full flavored, simple. *

Piazza Cav. Uff. Armando (Podere d'Mugiot) (4/90). Leather, tobacco and seaweed on the nose; dry, chewy, dusty, moderate tannin, fairly nice fruit, some hardness at the end, overall a rustic wine. *

Pio Cesare (4/90). Thirty percent of this wine spent eighteen months in *barrique*, rich, concentrated aroma, tobacco and vanilla components. Richly fruited with a lot of concentration and a firm structure and backbone, oak from some time in *barrique* adds some smoothness to the texture. **(*)

Pio Cesare, Ornato (3/91). Forty percent of this wine spent 24 months in *barriques* of French oak and the balance spent 36 months in Slavonian oak casks. Some 6,000 bottles were produced. The nose of camphor and flowers had a tar and berry overlay; open entry then a little firm, oak adds softness, good structure. **(*)

Pira E. (Chiara Boschis) (twice, 4/90). Somewhat restrained with suggestions of ripe fruit on the nose which carries through on the palate, at this stage a little tight, some tannin, nice fruit, chocolate nuance, young with good potential, try again in three years. **

Pira Luigi, Marenca (ex-cask, 4/86). Dark ruby color; perfumed, cherry aroma; nice fruit under the astringent tannins. *

Pittatore Cav. Francesco, & E., Azienda Agricola Ponte Rocca, Brunate (ex-cask, 4/86). Deep color; heaps of fruit on the nose and palate, some firmness, loads of tannin as well as flavor, licorice nuance, real concentration. **(*)

Podere Rocche dei Manzoni, Bricco Manzoni (Valentino) (twice, 6/90). The first bottle was oxidized. Tar and cherry aroma; light tannin, soft, fairly good structure. ** –

Poderi e Cantine di Marengo-Marenda, Cerequio, some bottles were labeled Vinicola Piemontese, Cerequio (4 times, 10/90, 42, 729 bottles). Tar and *tartufi* aroma; nice fruit, a mouthful of tannin, firm, dry end. *(* –) *Bottle of 5/90:* Leather and truffle aroma; a little tight, hints of fruit, a little dry, fairly good fruit after the initial tannin, light aftertaste, rather short. *

Porta Rossa, Delizia (ex-cask, 4/86). Deep ruby; tar and floral aroma; richly fruited, some tannin, but at this stage the fruit is dominant, intense, almost jammy, not overripe, flavors, very young indeed. *(* +)

Prunotto (twice, 12/89). Seems forward at this stage, it will most likely close up, well balanced, rather short. * +

"Ratti" (5/90). Tobacco and ripe fruit aroma and flavor, soft entry, then some tannin, forward, easy style. * +

Ratti Renato, Marcenasco (twice, 10/89). Aroma has suggestions of tobacco, tar, berries and cherries; open, and rich with the flavor of sweet ripe fruit, cherrylike nuance, a lot of structure. **(*)

Ratti Renato, Marcenasco-Rocche (12/90, 6,753 bottles). Woodslike scent, truffle and mushroom notes; soft and flavorful with a mushroom nuance. ** +

Rinaldi Francesco, Vigna Cannubbio (4/90, 10,700 bottles). Scented, perfumed bouquet; rich in extract and flavor, loads of style, harmonious, approachable now, don't be deceived, wait, very long finish, real class, splendid. *** + (****)

Rinaldi Giuseppe (magnum, 11/90). Scented, perfumed bouquet combines with ripe fruit; firm backbone, youthful with a real sense of fruit, tight finish; needs a lot of age. **(*)

Rinaldi Giuseppe, Brunate (4 times, 6/90). Lovely tobacco and *tartufi* aroma; fairly tannic, with richness, extract and concentration quite evident, berry flavor, ripe fruit, lingering finish, not as open as the previous bottle. ***(+) *Bottle of 9/89:* The label said *riserva!* Rich, sweet and lush, a classic Barolo with nuances of flowers and *tartufi*, tea and tobacco, at this stage open and flavorful, it will most likely close up, needs age. ***(+)

Rocche Costamagna, Rocche di La Morra (3 times, 4/90). Scented, perfumed bouquet; rich, quite tannic, closed and firm, nice fruit, in spite of being somewhat tight, needs a few years to open and soften up. **

Rocche Costamagna, Vigna Francesco (ex-vat, 4/87). Berrylike aroma, some spice; loads of flavor, good structure, potential for the future quite evident. **(* –)

Roche Azienda Vinicola (4/89). Small-scale with good fruit under moderate tannin. * –

Rosso Gigi, Cascina Arione (4/90, 19,600 bottles). A little seaweed, and some coffee on the nose as well as a touch of oxidization, the bottle perhaps(?); on the palate, open fruit, a lot of tannin. ?

Rosso Gigi, Cascina Castelletto (4/90, 11,900 bottles). Light yet characteristic aroma; fairly tannic and chewy with evident fruit. Needs a few years yet. *(+)

San Lorenzo Casa Vinicola, Vigna Brunate (4/90). Dusty, leathery, tobacco aroma; soft, simple, open style, some tannin, ready now. *

Sandrone Francesco (ex-vat, 4/86). Lovely, richly fruited aroma; rich and concentrated with ripe fruit, refined and elegant. ***

Sandrone Luciano, Cannubi Boschis (twice, 5/90). Lovely bouquet combines floral notes with leather and berries; perfumed and scented, the first impression on the palate is oak, then real richness and sweetness, packed with fruit, lots of structure, quite nice, some firmness especially at the end, if only there was less oak, will certainly improve. **+ (***−)

Savigliano (4/90). Small-scale and simple, open and soft, lacks distinction and weight, could use more backbone and structure, drinkable, no more.

Scarpa, Tetti di La Morra (ex-cask, 4/86). Intense and lush, some elegance, sweet impression from rich, ripe flavors, splendid. ***

Scarzello Giorgio (twice, 4/89). Tobacco and fruit aroma; has fruit, dry finish. *

Scarzello Giorgio, Vigna Merenda (twice, 4/90). Wet dog, fruit evident, on the nose and palate, not pleasant. Both bottles were the same, perhaps a couple of bad bottles.

Scavino Paolo (4 times, 6/90). Open, berrylike aroma; sweet impression, ripe fruit flavors, some tannin, underlying softness. **−

Scavino Paolo, Bric del Fiasc (4 times, 10/90). Tobacco and floral aroma, some tar; soft, open and ready now, light tannin, toward the end, well balanced. **+ *Bottle of 4/90:* Somewhat closed aroma; lush, open, appealing fruit might tempt you to drink it now, resist the temptation, it needs time to develop. **(*)

Scavino Paolo, Cannubi (twice, 4/89). Light nose; soft and round, balanced, good backbone, a little short. **

Sebaste Sylla, Bussia (twice, 12/90). Open tobacco, tar and floral aroma, berry and vanilla notes; nice entry, soft then moderate tannin, a little tight; needs another year or two. *(*+)

Seghesio Renzo (twice, 4/90). Light nose, some fruit evident; nice entry, soft and smooth at first, tobacco note, then some tightness and firmness, fairly tannic, with sufficient ripe fruit to enable it to develop. *

Sordo F.lli, Via Pugnane Sottana (10/90). Open berry aroma; light tannin, soft, not a lot of character, dry end. +

Tenuta Carretta, Podere Cannubi (4/90). Color tending toward brick; dusty aroma, camphor notes; richly concentrated and ripe under moderate, yet soft tannins, attractive and appealing, the tannins build, say three years, perhaps four. ***

Tenuta Montanello (twice, 4/90). Tar, tobacco and camphor aroma; chewy, hard and tannic, firm, tight and closed, old-style. *?

Vajra G. D. (4 times, 9/90). Tobacco and berry aroma; nicely concentrated, still young and firm, closed up a bit. *(*−) *Bottle of*

5/90: Floral and berry aroma, *tartufi* note; rich, open entry, then moderate tannin, well balanced, flavorful, a little light and dry at the end, could use more length. **+ (***−)

Valfieri (9/90). Light nose, tar and flowers; a little dry then some fruit, light tannin, forward and open, ready, dry and short at the end. +

Vecchio Piemonte (4/90). Some fruit, some tannin, very little character.

Veglio Angelo, Cascina Gancia Riserva (4/90). DOCG requires five years for a *riserva*, this would seem to be a pre-release, for tasting purposes perhaps? Rich, characteristic nebbiolo aroma; open, ripe fruit, suggestive of berries, forward flavors, soft and round, good structure, perhaps a little simple. *+

Veglio F.lli, Cascina Bruni, Vigna Carpegna (ex-cask, 4/86). Medium-dark ruby; lots of fruit on the nose and palate, still some sugar, fermentation incomplete(!), moderate tannin, difficult to be sure, but some quality evident. (*+)

Vietti, Brunate (twice, ex-vat, 4/87, c. 12,000 bottles). At this stage the aroma is more open than Rocche or Villero; elegant, almost sweet wine, with less body, and a not surprisingly more gentle nature than the other two crus. ***(+)

Vietti, Castiglione (twice, 5/90, 7,077 bottles). Overall quite nice though without the depth of flavor and structure of the crus, tobacco and berry notes, some tannin, open and forward. **

Vietti, Rocche (7 times, 11/90, 6,020 bottles). *Bottle tasted in Italy at the winery:* Mushroom, floral and woodslike aroma; has closed up since the previous bottle, yet the rich fruit is quite evident. ***(*) *Bottle tasted in the United States, 6/90:* Beautiful, fragrant, complex bouquet, reveals a mélange of scents, suggestive notes of flowers and the characteristic nebbiolo tar, raspberry and *tartufi*, supple under moderate tannins that are soft, great richness, concentration and extract, with an appealing quality due to its harmonious nature, the tannin builds up at the end; make no mistake as tempting as this wine is now it has only one place to go, and that is up, resist, this wine needs three to five years to really show itself. ***+ (****)

Vietti, Villero Riserva (4 times, 11/90, c. 6,000 bottles). *Tartufi* and woodsy aroma, raspberry and leather components; powerful yet with class and elegance; in need of age but tremendous appeal. **** *Ex-cask, 4/87:* Berry, *tartufi* and floral aroma, the nose already displays real character and some complexity; rich, open and concentrated, a lot of structure, very long; great class. ***(*)

Villadoria (twice, 9/90). Awful! *Bottle of 4/90:* Hot, cooked, stewed fruit on the nose and palate, drinkable but lacks definition, weight and character.

Voerzio Gianni, La Serra (twice, 4/90). Dried cherry aroma with suggestions of leather, and fruit; soft, open and fruity, light tannin, seems ready, and somewhat simple, it seemed better three years ago when tasted from cask; this one. *−

Voerzio Roberto, La Serra (5 times, 6/90). Tobacco, cherry and berry aroma; a little closed, but lovely fruit quite evident, all the lushness of the vintage with the elegance of La Morra. **(*)

Zunino Basilio (*ex-cask, 4/86*). Beautiful color; richly fruited aroma; heaps of fruit, well structured, good quality. **(*)

1984 * –

The year began with a wet spring, and the rain continued until June 15, retarding the growth of the vines. The summer, however, was warm and fairly dry. Nevertheless, selection was required during the harvest to obtain good-quality fruit.

The yield of 854,106 gallons (32,328 hectoliters), equivalent to 4.3 million bottles, was 46.3 percent of the maximum allowed and the second smallest crop in terms of the amount allowed since the advent of DOC in 1967. Only 1986 was smaller in crop size and yield per acre—277 gallons per acre (25.93 hectoliters per hectare) versus 246 (23.02)—and that was due to the severe hail damage. It's worth comparing the average yield per acre with the average between 1967 and 1989 of 445 gallons (41.6 hectoliters) as well, keeping in mind that DOC allows a production per acre of 599 gallons (56 hectoliters).

Giovanni Conterno of Giacomo Conterno and the firm of Scarpa didn't produce any Barolo in '84. Conterno, in fact, produced no wine at all. Giacomo Borgogno made only one 10,500-gallon (400-hectoliter) cask. The Cerettos didn't produce any Barolo from their Bricco Rocche estate. The wine, or part of it at least, was put in their proprietary Zonchera. Cavallotto, however, said that for them the vintage was a good one.

There were a number of duds among the four dozen wines we tasted from more than three dozen producers. There were some good ones as well. The best wines—Ceretto's Zonchera, Aldo Conterno's Bussia Soprana, Marcarini's Brunate and La Serra, Bartolo Mascarello, Francesco Sandrone, and Vietti's Brunate and Rocche. The best producers made good wines. We've found the wines light in body and high in acid. One star minus pretty much says it all.

Altare Elio, Cascina Nuova (*10/88*). Tar, cherry and vanilla aroma; fruit seems insufficient, clean.

Azelia, Bricco Fiasco (*3 times, 4/90*). Leather, tobacco and dried fruit aroma; a little light with evident fruit as well as some tannin, not for aging, dry, rather short aftertaste.

Bel Colle, Monfrino (*10/90*). Small-scale, low fruit, dry.

Borgogno Bartolomeo (*twice, 4/90*). Seaweed aroma; light entry, some tannin, low fruit.

Bovio Gianfranco, Gattera dell'Annunziata (*ex-vat, 4/85*). Has a surprising amount of fruit. [**]

Canale Aldo, Riunda (*ex-cask, 4/86*). Aroma recalls varnish; overly tannic for the fruit, or so it seems at this stage, though there is fruit. (?*)

Cantine Duca d'Asti (Chiarlo Michele), "Granduca" (*twice, 12/89*). Could use more fruit, drinkable.

Castello di Verduno, Vigna Massara (*3 times, 4/90*). There was real variation in this wine. One bottle was corked. *A second:* Rubbery, some oxidized, dull. *The third and best:* Light aroma of tar; soft and flavorful, ready, light finish. *

Cavallotto F.lli, Vigna Bricco Boschis-Colle Sud-Ovest (*ex-cask, 4/87*). Fairly tannic, seems to have sufficient fruit. (*)

Cavallotto F.lli, Vigna Bricco Boschis-Punta Marcello (*ex-cask, 4/87*). Rubbery aroma; unbalanced with tannin.

Cavallotto F.lli, Vigna Bricco Boschis-San Giuseppe Riserva (*twice, 4/89*). Some fruit, moderate tannin. * –

Ceretto, Zonchera (*2/89*). Fresh, cherrylike fruit aroma; soft, easy and supple; ready now; for the year very good. ** –

Clerico, Ciabot Mentin Ginestra (*3 times, 10/90, 7,150 bottles*). Real nebbiolo character, tar, flowers and fruit; beginning to dry out, still there is an attractive flavor. * *Bottle of 4/88:* Lots of fruit up front on the nose; tight and tannic, with good fruit; a success. * + (** –)

Conterno Aldo, Bussia Soprana Vigna Cicala (*ex-cask 4/87*). Rich nose; a bit light in body, soft, forward flavors; probably won't be bottled as Cicala. *(*)

Contratto (*5/90*). Light nose; soft, open and ready, short; drink. *

Fenocchio Riccardo, Pianpolvere Soprano (*10/90*). Vaguely stinky, like a barrel sample(!), some fruit; unimpressive, off-putting flavor.

Ferrero F.lli (*3 times, 4/90*). Simple, open, soft and fruity, clean fruit, short; drink now, quite ready. *

Giacosa F.lli (*4/90*). Fresh cherrylike aroma; soft entry then tannin, rather chewy, light-bodied, not to keep, already dry at the end.

Grasso Elio, Gavarini Vigna Rüncot (*4/88*). Nice nose, tar and tobacco; light tannin, light body, nice fruit. * +

Grasso Elio, Ginestra Vigna Case Matè (*4/88*). Tar and underbrush aroma, mushroom note; chewy, moderate tannin, good fruit, light body. * +

Grasso Silvio, Ciabot di Preve (*ex-cask, 4/87*). Low fruit, light body, some tannin, seems to lack the fruit to support it. ?

"La Corte" Azienda Agricola, Monticelli-Olivero (*ex-cask, 4/86*). Lovely aroma, berry fruit; fairly intense, some acid, moderate tannin, seems to have the fruit; good for the year. (*)

Marcarini (Elvio Cogno), Brunate (*3 times, ex-vat, 4/87*). Underbrush, woodslike aroma with nuance of berries and flowers; medium body, some firmness, lots of flavor, some elegance; could be the best of the vintage. **(+)

Marcarini (Elvio Cogno), La Serra (*3 times, ex-vat, 4/87*). Spicy and *tartufi* aroma, tarlike note; light, soft, light tannin, fruity, balanced, displays style; will be for early drinking. **

Mascarello Bartolo (*twice, 4/89*). Cherry and berry aroma, tobacco nuance; soft with light tannin, tasty, a little dry at the end. ** –

Massolino Giuseppe, Riserva (4/90). Leather and dried fruit aroma; dry yet some fruit evident, drink up. +

Massolino Giuseppe, Sörì Vigna Riunda (4/89). Open fruit aroma; fairly tannic for the body and structure. * –

Molino Franco, Cascina La Rocca (4/89). Coffee and chocolate aroma, seaweed note; low fruit.

Palladino (*twice, 4/89*). Open nose; fairly nice fruit, light and soft; drink up. *

Pio Cesare (4/89). Light but correct aroma, good fruit, tobacco and berry nuances; tasty. * +

Pira E. (Chiara Boschis) (*ex-cask, 4/86*). Berrylike aroma; fairly tannic, is there enough fruit(?), hard to be sure. (*?)

Pira Luigi, Marenca (*ex-cask, 4/86*). Pretty nose, with a varnishlike note; fruit seems overly tannic for this stage. (?*)

Rinaldi Giuseppe (4/90). Disappointing for this fine producer, low fruit, unbalanced, some oxidation; an off bottle perhaps?

Rocche Costamagna (*ex-vat, 4/87*). Berrylike fruit on the nose; soft, open flavors, light tannin, will be ready early, short. *(+)

Roche Azienda Vinicola (4/89). Light, it does have fruit, a bit dry at the end.

Sandrone Francesco (*ex-vat, 4/86*). Lovely aroma, *tartufi* note; sweet impression(!), light tannin; well made with style; one of the year's best. ** +

Scavino Paolo (4/88). Nice nose, good fruit evident with underbrush and mushroom notes; a little light, some tannin, open flavor. * +

Scavino Paolo, Bric del Fiasc (*ex-vat, 5/87*). Woodslike aroma, scent of mushrooms; on the light side, nice fruit, forward; will be ready early. *(+)

Severino Oberto (4/89). Soft, light and open, small nose; easy style. +

Tenuta Carretta, Podere Cannubi (4/89). Light nose; firm and hard, seems to have the fruit, tight, firm aftertaste. *(?)

Veglio F.lli, Cascina Bruni, Vigna Carpegna (*ex-cask, 4/86*). Pretty berrylike aroma; some tannin, light up front, soft center; very drinkable now. * +

Vietti, Brunate (*twice, ex-vat, 4/87*). Medium red color; a bit reticent on the nose; a little light but balanced, nice flavor; for early drinking. **

Vietti, Rocche (*twice, ex-vat, 4/87*). Nice nose; light in body, some tannin, good fruit; will be ready early. **

Vinicola Piemontese, Cerequio (*5/90, 4,832 bottles*). Complex dried berry and leather aroma, cassis and framboise notes; a little dry, has a tart edge, some fruit, dry aftertaste.

Voerzio Gianni, La Serra (*twice, 4/89*). Soft, open and ready, tasty.*

Voerzio Roberto, La Serra (*twice, ex-vat, 4/87*). Light nose; light body, good fruit; will make a nice luncheon wine if you like Barolo for lunch. * +

Zunino Basilio (*ex-cask, 4/86*). Difficult stage, good body, but who knows where it will go?

1983 * +

This was a difficult vintage. Many reports cite a very large crop, but the crop size wasn't that large. The yield of 1.5 million gallons (56,074 hectoliters) of nebbiolo for Barolo, equivalent to 7.5 million bottles, versus the 1.1 million-gallon (41,979-hectoliter) average between 1967 and 1989, was 76.6 percent of the amount allowed, yet not unduly high considering that the 23-year average was 74.3 percent. Further, 1982 produced a larger crop and, in terms of yield, 1980, 1982, and 1985 had larger ones. Per acre, the average for 1983 was 459 gallons (42.9 hectoliters) versus the average of 445 (41.6) between 1967 and 1989 and 412 (38.6) for the 1980s.

Many experts rate it three stars; we give it less. Scarpa didn't produce any Barolo. Cavallotto found it a so-so year. Renato Ratti said the wines ranged from okay to good. Alfredo Currado of Vietti considered it a difficult vintage.

We've tasted more than nine dozen wines from over seven dozen producers. The vintage is variable. Very few wines are worth keeping. Some wines are light and perhaps a bit deficient in fruit for their tannin, and then there are those that are simple, light luncheon wines that have matured early and won't last. For the most part, the wines are quite ready, a few will improve, and more than a few are starting to fade or have already. There were many good wines at one time. Initially the wines were fairly light in color and body and displayed a forward fruitiness. Today the best, although light in both color and body, still have elegance and balance. They have soft tannins, open flavor, and are lovely to drink now. There is no need to hold them any longer. The very best include Aldo Conterno's Bussia Soprana, Bruno Giacosa's crus, Marcarini's Brunate and La Serra, Bartolo Mascarello, Renato Ratti's Marcenasco crus, Francesco Rinaldi, and Giuseppe Rinaldi.

Aleramici (2/91). Forget it!

Alessandria F.lli di G. B. Alessandro (*ex-vat, 5/87*). Fresh grapey aroma, some oxidation in the background; light and soft, already old!

Alessandria F.lli di G. B. Alessandro, Monvigliero (4/88). Light nose recalls small fruits, some underbrush; moderate tannin, fairly nice fruit, chewy, could use more weight. +

Ascheri Giacomo (*twice, 5/87*). Fresh grapey aroma, *tartufi* and berry notes; simple, soft, light and fruity; easy to drink. * +

Azelia, Bricco Fiasco (*5/87*). Light smoky nuance on the nose; light, some tannin, rather nice fruit, sense of sweetness, short, some tannin builds up at the end. *(* –)

Barale F.lli, Vigna Castellero (*twice, 5/89*). Berrylike fruit and spice aroma; balanced, nice flavor, light to moderate tannin; almost ready. **(+)

Barale F.lli, Vigna Castellero Riserva (*4/90*). Truffles, chocolate, vanilla, dusty aroma; soft, open, fruity; ready. ** –

Bersano (*twice, 1/89*). Color shows some age at the rim; cooked fruit aroma; lightweight, lacks body and structure, simple, drinkable.

Bianco Michelangelo di F.lli Bianco (*5/87*). Light nose; light body, light tannin, small-scale. +

Bonfante e Chiarle in Bazzana di Momburuzzo (*4/90*). Some oxidation; soft entry, a little light, dull ending.

Borgogno Bartolomeo (*3 times, 4/90*). Soapy smell, it wasn't the glass; soft entry then tannin and an off-putting taste.

Borgogno F.lli Serio e Battista (*ex-cask, 4/85*). Moderate tannin, vaguely bitter.

Borgogno F.lli Serio e Battista, Vigna Cannubi (*11/87, 9,000 bottles*). Dried fruit aroma, vaguely of apricots; soft and tasty, ready, a bit coarse, could use more length. *

Borgogno Giacomo (*ex-vat, 5/87*). Reticent aroma; chewy tannins, on the light side; a bit young. *

Borgogno Ludovico, Cascina Borgognot (*ex-cask, 5/87*). Reticent aroma; some tannin, not a lot of character; should improve. *

Borgogno Ludovico, Cascina Borgognot Riserva (*4/90*). Some seaweed on the nose; light, dry, very short, ready, not to keep.

Borgogno Wanda Pepino, Collina Maniscotto Riserva (*4/90*). Candy, fruit and floral aroma, cherry note; some flavor; drink up.

Bovio Gianfranco, Gattera dell'Annunziata (*ex-cask, 4/85*). The aroma suggests cherries and gingerbread; forward, sweet fruit. **

Brezza Giacomo (*5/87*). Light nose, hint of raspberries; light body, soft and fruity, overly simple. * –

"Bricco Rocche" Azienda Agricola (Ceretto), Brunate (*11 times, 10/90, 24,973 bottles*). Tobacco and tar aroma, some oxidation; starting to dry out, still some flavor interest. * – There was variation among the two bottles we tasted in May 1990. *One bottle:* Lovely scented bouquet, *tartufi* and berry notes; light midpalate, trace of oxidation on the palate suggests it's best to drink up, short, dry finish. * *Another:* Soft, open, very ready, no oxidation apparent. **

"Bricco Rocche" Azienda Agricola (Ceretto), Prapò (*10/90*). Nice nose, tobacco and fruit; still some tannin, tasty, drink, starting to dry out. * + *Bottle of 6/88:* Fairly nice fruit, hard and tight, has the fruit, is there enough? *?

Brovia F.lli, Rocche (*5/87*). Dirty nose, some spice; on the light side, fairly agreeable; young, should be ready soon. *(+)

Burlotto Andrea (*ex-vat, 5/87*). Soft, simple flavor, hint of mushrooms, small-scale. * –

Burlotto Comm. G. B. & Cav. Franc^sco (*5/87*). Awful nose, cheesy; thin, low fruit; rather poor.

Cabutto, Tenuta La Volta (*5/87*). Slight off note mars the aroma, hints of spice and fruit; light body, soft, simple. * –

Canale Aldo, Riunda (*ex-cask, 4/86*). Fresh cherry aroma; soft center under some tannin, balanced, tannic finish. *(*)

Cantine Duca d'Asti di Chiarlo Michele, Rocche di Castiglione Riserva (*twice, 10/90*). Open tobacco and cherry aroma, notes of *tartufi* and tar; soft and ready, fruity, very ready, light tannin; drink. * +

Cantine Duca d'Asti di Chiarlo Michele, Vigna Rionda Riserva (*twice, 10/90, 5,000 bottles*). Light nose, open cherrylike and ripe fruit aroma; moderate tannin after the initial soft entry, open, a little dry, chocolate note, could use more length; drink up. *

Cappellano Dott. Giuseppe (*3 times, 4/88*). Ripe fruit and berry aroma, underbrush component; moderate tannin, tasty; ready. ** –

Cascina Adelaide di G. Terzano (*twice, ex-cask, 5/87*). On the light side, good fruit and structure. *(* –)

Castello di Verduno (Sorelle Burlotto), Vigna Massera (*4/88, 3,714 bottles*). Seems overly tannic for the fruit, there is some fruit though. +

Cavallotto F.lli, Bricco Boschis-Colle Sud-Ovest (*ex-cask, 4/87*). Mushroom aroma; fairly full in body, balanced, lots of flavor under moderate tannin. **(+)

Cavallotto F.lli, Bricco Boschis-Punta Marcello (*ex-cask, 4/87*). Almost Burgundian aroma; full in body, especially for the vintage, some tannin, surprisingly good. ** +

Cavallotto F.lli, Bricco Boschis-San Giuseppe (*ex-cask, 4/87*). Burgundian aroma recalls berries and mushrooms; almost sweet in flavor, balanced, some tannin. ** +

Ceretto, Zonchera (*3 times, 6/88*). The last two times we tasted it we found the wine oxidized and vegetal. The first time, in April 1988, the aroma displayed hints of underbrush and nebbiolo tar; light tannin, flavorful; ready.* +

Clerico, Ciabot Mentin Ginestra (*twice, 10/87, 9,700 bottles*). A nice glass, aroma suggestive of the woods and cherries; soft and tasty, good body, light tannin, enjoyable now. ** –

Conterno Aldo, Bussia Soprana (*5/87*). Rather nice fruit, cassis and berries; light but well balanced, some style and class. ** +

Conterno Giacomo, Cascina Francia Riserva (*3 times, 4/89*). Richly fruited and open aroma; surprisingly open and soft! **

Cordero di Montezemolo Paolo, Enrico VI in Villero (*12/89*). Woodsy, vaguely vegetal aroma; open, tasty and ready now but the harsh edge suggests that it's starting to decline, still in all, good. *

Cordero di Montezemolo Paolo, Monfalletto (*twice, 9/90*). Open cherry aroma, ripe fruit notes, nebbiolo character; a little dry but the fruit is there, clean fruit, some tannin toward the end, still it is good; drink up. * +

Damilano Dott. Giacomo (*twice, 4/90*). Light nose, hint of mint; old tasting, dull, short and dry.

Dogliani F.lli (*5/89*). Drinkable, lacks weight, character and definition.

Dosio, Vigna Fossati (*twice, 4/89, 4,490 bottles*). Ripe berry and cherry aroma; open and soft, light tannin, simple; ready. *

Fenocchio Giacomo, Vigneti in Bussia (*5/87*). Spice and tar, some oxidation; some tannin, tired, old.

Fenocchio Riccardo, Pianpolvere Soprano (*12/86*). Mercaptan and dank, best forgotten.

Ferrero F.lli (*twice, 4/88*). Aroma displays fruit, mushrooms and underbrush; good fruit, moderate tannin, a tad warm at the end. *

Feyles Maria, Vigna della Ginestra (*5/87*). Spicy, fruity aroma; fairly nice structure, on the light side, does have Barolo character. *(* −)

Fontanafredda (*5/87*). Light almost pale color; thin and unbalanced.

Gagliardo Gianni, La Serra (*3 times, 9/89*). Ordinary, lacks character.

Giacosa Bruno (*ex-vat, 4/86*). On the light side, moderate tannin, fruity, will be ready early. *(*)

Giacosa Bruno, Villero (*twice, 10/89*). Rather disappointing, there is fruit, could be an off bottle? *? *Ex-vat, 4/85*: Of those wines we tasted, all from cask, up to this point this was our single favorite, with a cherry and cassis aroma; and a forward, sweet ripe fruitiness, elegant, and stylish. ***

Giacosa F.lli (*4/87*). A bit reticent on the nose; loaded with tannin, harsh and bitter, some fruit. *(?)

Grasso Elio, Gavarini Poggio Chinera (*twice, 5/87*). The wine was bottled one week earlier. When we tasted it from cask a month earlier it showed more. Reticent aroma; seems a little light, closed, some fruit evident, light tannin, moderate length. *(*)

Grasso Elio, Gavarini Vigna Chinera (*twice, 11/87*). Light nose, tobacco nuance; soft, flavorful, light tannin, seems quite ready, an easy-style Barolo. * +

Grasso Elio, Gavarini Vigna Rüncot (*3 times, 5/87*). More color, body and flavor than the Chinera; the aroma is reticent; a little closed, light to moderate tannin, fairly good structure, a touch of alcohol at the end. *(* −)

Grasso Silvio (*5/87*). Unclean aroma and taste, surprisingly poor, unbalanced with tannin.

"La Corte" Azienda Agricola, Monticelli-Olivero (*twice, 5/87*). Simple, fruity aroma, touch of oxidation; could use more weight and fruit. (+)

Le Due Torri (*4/88*). Fairly simple style, some tannin.

Marcarini (Elvio Cogno), Brunate (*4 times, ex-cask, 5/87*). Nicely fruited aroma, suggestive of mushrooms, berries and the woods; lots of flavor, good structure, displays the La Morra class. **(+)

Marcarini (Elvio Cogno), La Serra (*3 times, ex-cask, 4/87*). Spicy, berry aroma; light to moderate tannin, soft center, fruity; should mature early. **(+)

Marchesi di Barolo (*5/87*). Small-scale, some tannin, not much to it.

Marengo M., Brunate (*5/87*). Some oxidation, unbalanced, unimpressive.

Mascarello Bartolo (*7 times, 10/90*). Perfumed, scented bouquet, *tartufi* nuance, fragrant; soft, open, near its peak, full of flavor, lovely, fairly long, elegant; without question the star of the vintage, delicious. ***

Mascarello G^{mo} di Alberto Mascarello (*5/87*). Reticent aroma; light tannin, fruit evident, some character. *(+)

Massolino Giuseppe, Azienda Agricola "Rionda" (*5/87*). Reticent aroma; lightweight, small-scale, simple, nearly ready, very drinkable. *

Massolino Giuseppe, Margheria (*ex-cask, 4/85*). Rather light and a bit simple.

Molino Franco, Cascina La Rocca (*4/89*). Old, dull and tired.

Oberto Egidio (*ex-cask, 4/86*). Difficult to assess, needed to be racked, could use more fruit.

Oberto F.lli (*5/87, 3,786 bottles*). Reticent aroma, vague pickle-like character; overall nice fruit, simple and agreeable. *

Oberto Severino (*5/87*). Unclean, thin.

Oddero F.lli (*5/87*). Dank, mercaptans, and from a normally good producer, the fruit is there, so too is the structure, what happened here?

Parusso Armando (*twice, 4/87*). A harshness intrudes on the nose, some fruit, apparent woodslike nuance carries into the mouth, rather simple and easy, small-scale but drinkable. *

Parusso Armando, Bussia (*5/87*). Some oak evident, *barrique*(?), soft center, good structure and fruit, young, lacks Barolo character but good. *

Pio Cesare, Riserva (*3 times, 5/90*). Mushroom and truffle aroma; soft, open, ready, light aftertaste. ** −

Pira E. (Chiara Boschis) (*3 times, ex-vat, 5/87*). Light nose, spice and fruit components; good structure and flavor, really nice, surprisingly so. Each time we tasted this wine in cask it was better than the last. Chiara, we take our hats off to you. **(+)

Pira Luigi, Marenca (*ex-cask, 4/86*). Hint of *tartufi* and oak on the nose; light tannin, will be ready early. *(+)

Pittatore Cav. Francesco, & E., Azienda Agricola "Ponte Rocca," Brunate (*twice, ex-cask, 5/87*). A little difficult to really be sure, there is a lot of fruit, fairly nice structure. *(+)

Porta Rossa, Delizia (*ex-cask, 4/86*). Aroma recalls camphor, vanilla and cherries; fairly tannic, has the fruit to carry it, sense of richness evident, has an underlying hardness; well made, has character. **(+)

Prunotto, Cannubi Riserva (*11/90*). Complex bouquet offers suggestions of tar, flowers and berries; soft, good body, short finish is a tad dry; good condition for its age and vintage, very ready, near its peak, best to drink. **

Ramello G. (*5/87*). Reticent aroma; light body, moderate tannin, seems to have enough fruit. (?)

Ratti Renato (*10/89*). Soft, easy style, agreeable and correct. *

Ratti Renato, Marcenasco (*twice, 8/90*). Fragrant floral aroma, berry notes; soft and smooth, very ready, nice fruit, a little light but delicious. ** *Bottle of 4/87:* Has an almost Burgundian-like flavor and aroma; the bouquet displays hints of *tartufi*, mushrooms and the woods; soft, fruity and round, smooth, nearly ready, well made, has style and elegance. ** +

Ratti Renato, Marcenasco-Conca (*8/90*). Aroma of tobacco and tar, dried berries and mushrooms; soft like velvet, round; very ready. ** +

Ratti Renato, Marcenasco-Rocche (*twice, 1/89, 4,766 bottles*). Ripe fruit aroma, hints of tobacco and tar, vaguely floral; smooth and soft, flavorful, a little light but very ready and very drinkable. **

Ravello Renato, Cascina Gustavo (*5/87*). Light body, light tannin, soft, fruity and agreeable, simple, ready. *

Rinaldi Francesco, Cannubbio (*twice, 5/87, 15,000 bottles*). Mushroom aroma; sense of sweetness, good fruit, good structure, still a little young, good quality. **(*−)

Rinaldi Giuseppe (*5 times, 12/89*). Characteristic varietal aroma, floral note; some tannin, considerable flavor on entry, starting to fade; best to drink up. *

Rinaldi Giuseppe, Brunate (*10/89*). Open aroma of ripe fruit; soft and tasty, light, displays some class. **

Rocche Costamagna (*3 times, 5/87*). Light but nice nose; light body, fairly soft, light tannin, easy and a little simple; ready. * +

Roche Azienda Vinicola (*4/88*). Nice nose, tar, the woods, licorice; light tannin, nice fruit flavor, ready, short. *

Roche Azienda Vinicola, Riserva (*4/89*). Not a lot of character, light and soft. +

Rosso Gigi, Cascina Arione (*5/87, 19,700 bottles*). Reticent aroma; small-scale, lightweight, lacks some varietal definition, still it is drinkable. * −

S. Quirico (*4/87*). Some fruit, but the tannin is too much for the little there is, lacks definition.

Saffirio F.lli Enrico e Giacomo (*ex-barrel, 5/87*). Spicy, fruity aroma; fairly nice flavor, light to moderate tannin. *(+)

Sandrone Luciano, Cannubi Boschis (*twice, 10/87, 4,650 bottles*). Lovely, perfumed fragrant bouquet; soft, open and fruity, more or less ready. ** −

Scarzello Giorgio (*4/88*). Some fruit on the nose, vague off note in the back; fairly nice fruit under moderate tannin, hot finish. +

Scavino Paolo (*twice, 5/87*). Nice nose of vanilla, berries and flowers; fruity and agreeable, soft; a little young but drinkable now. * +

Scavino Paolo, Bric del Fiasc (*twice, 4/88, 5,933 bottles*). *Tartufi* and berry aroma, vanilla and chocolate notes; light to moderate tannin, light but with nice flavor, short. ** −

Settimo Aurelio, Rocche di Annunziata (*twice, 4/88*). Aroma recalls underbrush; light body, soft, open flavor; ready. *

Severino Oberto di Sesto Severino (*4/88*). Cherrylike aroma; open flavor, some tannin, light. *

Tenuta Carretta, Podere Cannubi (*5/87*). Reticent aroma; a lot of tannin, seems to have the fruit to carry it, but does it(?), on the light side. *(?)

Terre de Barolo (*5/87*). Pale color, mushroom and woodsy aroma; light and simple, ready. *

Vajra G. D. (*3 times, 12/90*). Nice nose; openly fruit, soft entry then dry; drink up. * *Bottle of 9/90:* Old fruit, soft, shows age. + *Bottle of 5/87:* Nice fruit, almost Burgundian with overtones of the woods and mushrooms; good weight and structure. *(*)

Vajra G. D., Bricco Viole (*ex-vat, 4/87*). Truffle aroma; some elegance, a little light, lots of flavor. ** +

Veglio F.lli, Cascina Bruni, Vigna Carpegna (*4/86*). Perfumed berry aroma; light tannin, open flavor, light body, nice fruit, some character. * +

Veglio Giovanni (*ex-vat, 5/87*). Fairly tannic, rather rough, is there enough fruit? (+?)

Viberti Giovanni (*twice, 4/88*). It seemed to offer more a year ago. Mushroom and tobacco aroma; some tannin, light, a bit low in fruit. +

Vietti, Briacca (*ex-cask, 4/87*). Perfumed cherry aroma; soft, seemingly ready now, light tannin, moderate length. ** +

Vietti, Rocche (*12 times, 11/88, 9,261 bottles*). Soft and round, very ready, and tasty too, very good for the vintage. ** +

Vinicola Piemontese, Cerequio (*5/87*). Reticent aroma; moderate tannin, good weight and fruit, still young. *(*−)

Voerzio Giacomo di F.lli Voerzio, La Serra (*twice, ex-cask, 11/85*). Lovely woodsy aroma, floral notes; richer and firmer than the '82, well balanced, good quality, elegance. ***

Voerzio Gianni, La Serra (3 times, 5/87, 1,340 bottles). Fresh, clean fruity aroma; lightweight, small-scale, low in nebbiolo character; what happened? *

Voerzio Roberto, La Serra (twice, 4/87). Lovely nose, fragrant; lots of flavor, elegant, still needs further age. **(*−)

Zunino Basilio, Sorì di Baudana (ex-cask, 4/86). Camphor aroma; rather nice fruit and structure, on the light side. **(+)

1982 **** −

The yield of 1.5 million gallons (56,096 hectoliters), equivalent to 7.5 million bottles, was relatively large. It amounted to 84.6 percent of the maximum allowed, compared to the 74.3 percent average between 1967 and 1989. This made it the largest crop between the advent of DOC in 1967 and 1989. And 1982 produced not only the second highest average yield per acre—506 gallons (47.4 hectoliters)—in the 1980s, but one of the largest since 1967 as well.

Many producers told us that they've never seen such perfect fruit, a statement they were to repeat three years later about the 1985 vintage. Cavallotto said, "The grapes looked so perfect, it seemed a shame to crush them." The weather was exceptional throughout the season and the wines have perfect balance and ripeness. Giovanni Conterno says they have great perfume and are feminine wines, like the 1970s. Pio Boffa finds them very fruity with a softness; he said they will mature sooner than the '78s or '71s. Ratti said they are complete wines that could be grand if allowed to mature. Alfredo Currado said they are better than the '78s, with better structure; if they have any deficiency it is perhaps a touch too little acidity. He believes they'll mature earlier than the higher-acid '78s. Giuseppe Rinaldi thinks that the wines might even be better than the '78s. Production, he said, was small because fertilization wasn't good. Giacomo Conterno produced a Monfortino and Aldo Conterno a Granbussia. Aldo Conterno said that only 1989 was better in the decade, and Alfredo Currado places it first in the decade. Bartolo Mascarello said that the '82s are grand wines for long aging.

Our assessment is based on more than 170 wines from over a hundred producers, many tasted two, three, four, or more times. We rate this vintage very high indeed. But as good as it is—and make no mistake about it, it is a splendid vintage—it doesn't quite measure up to 1985 and 1989. The difference, however, is very small indeed. The vintage is one of the best. These Barolos are exceptionally fine, complete, and finely balanced, with more elegance and fruit than the '78s. While they might not measure up to the '71s or '89s for sheer weight, power, and concentration, or the overall balance of the '85s, there is no question they make up for that with their elegance and finesse. While, at one time, we felt they would mature fairly early, we also believed they would

keep well. These Barolos are, however, maturing slower than we or, for that matter, anyone else thought. The best need further age.

The best wines: Ceretto's Azienda Agricola "Bricco Rocche" crus, Clerico's Ciabot Mentin Ginestra, Aldo Conterno's crus, Giacomo Conterno's Cascina Francia and Monfortino, Bruno Giacosa's crus, Elio Grasso's Gavarini bottlings, Marcarini's Brunate and La Serra, Giuseppe Mascarello's Monprivato, Prunotto's Cannubi, Ratti Renato's Marcenasco, Francesco Rinaldi's Cannubbio, Giuseppe Rinaldi's Brunate, Luciano Sandrone, Scarpa's Tetti di La Morra, Filippo Sobrero, Tenuta Carretta's Podere Cannubi, G. D. Vajra's Bricco delle Viole and Fossati, and Vietti's crus.

Accademia Torregiorgi, Carpegna Riserva (twice, 12/90, 10,700 bottles). Characteristic, old-style aroma of tar, tobacco and camphor, seaweed nuance; rather light but with good fruit, still fairly tannic; seems a little older than its eight years(!), drink. * +

Accornero Flavio (Casa Vinicola Bera) (twice, 10/90). Simple, soft and easy, overly simple, small-scale and one-dimensional. +

Alessandria F.lli di G. B. Alessandro, Monvigliero (4/88). Light woodsy aroma, mushroom notes; chewy tannin, some fruit, lacks the richness of the vintage. +

Altare Elio, Cascina Nuova, Vigneto Arborina (twice, 10/87, 3,970 bottles). Tar and fruit aroma; soft, overly simple and most agreeable. * −

Ascheri Giacomo (ex-cask, 1/86). Fairly deep color; cooked character, fruit evident, rather tannic, fairly nice fruit, could use more character. (*?)

Ascheri Giacomo, Riserva (3/88). Rich nose, concentrated, ripe fruit, berry and woodslike notes; moderate tannin, flavorful, balanced, ripe. * +

Azelia, Bricco Punta (5/87). Reticent aroma; quite tannic, chewy, seems to have sufficient fruit, somewhat hard, bitter finish. *(+)

Azelia, Bricco Punta Riserva (4/90). Tar, leather and woodslike aroma; rich flavor, seems closed(!), still has tannin to shed. ** −

Barale F.lli, Castellero (4/87). Reticent aroma, hint of tobacco; fairly tannic, rich in fruit, good structure; displays quality. **(* −)

Bel Colle (4/87). Some volatile acidity, has fruit, unbalanced, tannin evident, unimpressive.

Bel Colle, Monfrino (9/88). Dullsville(!), unbalanced.

Bel Colle, Riserva Speciale (4/87). Unbalanced, hot, dull, heavy-handed.

Bel Colle, Vigna Monvigliero (ex-cask, 1/86). Some volatile acidity, some fruit, a bit out of balance.

Beni di Batasiolo (F.lli Dogliani) (3/90). Some oxidation, vaguely rubber tire–like, still some flavor, and some tannin, not to keep, short—no, there is no finish of any kind.

Beni di Batasiolo (F.lli Dogliani), Riserva (*twice, 10/90*). Aroma of *tartufi* and tar; correct though lacking weight and character. +

Bersano (*12/87*). Light and simple, easy and drinkable.

Bersano, Riserva (*9/89*). Some varietal character, light to moderate tannin, some fruit, not a lot of character but drinkable, small-scale.

Borgogno Bartolomeo (*twice, 4/90*). Some fruit on the nose, hint of tobacco; nice entry, a little tight, old-style, some fruit, dry aftertaste. *

Borgogno F.lli Serio e Battista, Vigna Cannubi (*ex-cask, 4/85*). Expansive aroma; rich and full with some elegance and a fair amount of tannin. **

Borgogno Giacomo, Riserva (*4 times, 4/90*). Light varietal aroma; a little tight and firm, chewy and tannic, short, dry, tannic aftertaste. *

Borgogno Ludovico, Cascina Borgognot Riserva (*4/90*). Taste of old wood and old fruit, dry and short.

Borgogno Wanda Pepino, Collina Maniscotto (*4/90*). Old fruit, some sweetness, lacks character, rustic.

Boschis Francesco (*4/87*). Oxidized, badly made, lacks structure and weight.

Bovio Gianfranco, Gattera dell'Annunziata (*ex-cask, 4/85*). Intense cherrylike aroma; a mouthful of ripe fruit, moderate tannin, style evident. *** −

Brezza Giacomo, Sarmassa Riserva Speciale (*4/90, 5,600 bottles*). Quite tannic and rustic. +

"Bricco Rocche" Azienda Agricola (Ceretto), Bricco Rocche (*3 times, 11/89, 4,760 bottles*). Surprising, in that we found bottle variation. *Two bottles tasted in 11/89:* Open berrylike aroma; fairly soft and rich in the mouth, sweet, ripe, open, moderate tannin, seems a little simple. ** *Bottle of 11/86:* Tobacco aroma, still closed; rich flavor, a lot of structure, tannin builds, very young with layers of flavor and fruit; give it four or five years as a minimum. ***(+)

"Bricco Rocche" Azienda Agricola (Ceretto), Brunate (*6 times, 11/89, 4,760 bottles*). The last time we tasted it, November 1989, we were disappointed: Light berrylike aroma; seems rather simple, some tannin! * *Bottle of 10/87:* Tobacco and tea, mushroom and woodslike aroma; lots of flavor, elegant, displays class. **(*+)

"Bricco Rocche" Azienda Agricola (Ceretto), Prapò (*5 times, 11/89*). The two most recent bottles were quite similar: Sulfurous, rich fruit, moderate tannin, good structure, tasty. * + *Bottle of 4/89:* Color shows age(!); odd nose, dry and tight, seems unbalanced, the bottle perhaps?

Burlotto Comm. G. B. (*4/88*). Rather tannic with a sense of fruit evident, is there enough? ?* −

Burlotto Comm. G. B., Vigneto Monvigliero (*twice, 4/88, 6,800 bottles*). We were told that 50 percent of this wine was crushed by feet! Old nose; seems to be aging rapidly; not a success.

Ca' Bianca, Tenuta Denegri (*7/87, 13,105 bottles*). Light nose; fairly tannic, could use more weight and substance, short.

Ca' Bianca, Tenuta Denegri, Riserva (*4/90*). Tar, leather and woodsy aroma; old-style, fairly tannic, a bit short, dry aftertaste. *

Ca' Romè, Riserva Speciale (*4/88*). Overly tannic, harsh edge, bitter, some fruit.

Calissano Luigi, Riserva Bricco Mira Langa (*11/90*). Tar, coffee and chocolate aroma; fairly nice fruit, though a little dry; drink. *

Camerano G. (*4/90*). Dusty, leather and tar aroma; chewy, tannic, firm, some fruit evident. * − ?

Canale Aldo, Vigna Riunda (*ex-cask, 4/86*). Lovely aroma, fruit and woodsy components, licorice and cherry notes; a rich mouthful of flavor, tannic over the top and at the end; quality evident. *(*+)

Cantine Duca d'Asti (Chiarlo Michele), "Granduca" (*twice, 3/87*). Cherry aroma, with a hint of the woods; fairly rich, good structure, could use more depth. *(* −)

Cantine Duca d'Asti (Chiarlo Michele), "Granduca" Riserva (*4 times, 10/90*). Open fruit, soft, very ready, simple, correct, easy to drink. * −

Cantine Duca d'Asti di Chiarlo Michele, Rocche di Castiglione Riserva (*twice, 10/90*). *From magnum, 10/90:* Chocolate and fruit aroma; rather dry, not up to the vintage or the previous bottle, still it could improve. *(+) *Bottle of 11/88:* Rich nose, characteristic nebbiolo tar, tobacco and berry notes; fairly nice fruit, moderate tannin that builds, attractive; still young. ** −

Cantine Duca d'Asti di Chiarlo Michele, Vigna Rionda Riserva (*twice, 10/90*). *From magnum, 10/90:* Chocolate, gravelly and camphor aroma; a little dry, nice fruit, though firm at the end. *(+) *Bottle of 11/88:* Somewhat tight aroma, vanilla and berry notes, camphor and chocolate hints; fairly tannic, needs more age than the Rocche. ** −

Cappellano Dott. Giuseppe (*3 times, 4/89*). Some oxidation, drying out, the bottle? A year ago it was considerably better, we find it doubtful that it aged that quickly. *Bottle of 4/88:* Mushroom and vanilla aroma; fairly tannic with evident fruit, perhaps a little too hard at this stage. *

Cappellano Dott. Giuseppe, Parafada (*3 times, ex-cask, 4/86*). Aggressive tannin, the fruit and structure are there to support it if you're willing to wait. *(*)

Cascina Bruni di Veglio Pasqual (*ex-cask, 4/85*). A lot of fruit and a fair amount of tannin, but seems more forward and lighter than many others. *

Casetta F.lli, Vigna Case Nere (*4/87*). Reticent aroma; full of tannin, the sense of fruit is evident, is there enough? We think so even though at this stage it's hard as nails. *(+)

Castello di Verduno, Sorelle Burlotto, Vigna Massara (*twice, 4/90, 2,241 bottles*). Oxidized! *Bottle of 4/88:* Light nose, hints of underbrush; nice flavor, moderate tannin, sufficient fruit to carry it; needs a few years yet. * +

Castello di Verduno, "Cantine del Castello di Re Carlo Alberto" (4/87). Interesting and singular aroma, nuances of seaweed and tar; moderate tannin, good fruit; on the young side; some quality. *(*)

Cavallotto F.lli, Vigna Bricco Boschis-San Giuseppe (ex-cask, 4/85). Heaps of tannin, heaps of fruit, enormous richness, a real mouthful of wine; at this point backward but a lot of quality. **(*)

Cavallotto F.lli, Vigna Bricco Boschis-San Giuseppe Riserva (3 times, 4/90). Rich nose, characteristic; dry, tannic, chewy, is there enough fruit? We think so. *(*?)

Ceretto, Zonchera (twice, 11/89). Simple, open fruit, hint of berries followed by tar and suggestions of the woods; still has tannin to shed, chewy, then soft, good flavor. **

Clerico, Ciabot Mentin Ginestra (1/86, 6,800 bottles). Lovely bouquet, tobacco and floral nuances; tannic with a load of flavor, good structure, and some length; quality evident though young, give it three, perhaps even four more years. **(*)

Colli Monfortesi di Fantino Conterno (9/86). Lots of nice fruit on the nose; moderate tannin, overly simple, good body and very drinkable. *

Colli Monfortesi di Fantino Conterno, Ginestra (4/86, 7,350 bottles). Reticent aroma, displays traces of tobacco and cherries; moderate tannin, balanced, loaded with flavor; needs perhaps four more years. *(+)

Conterno Aldo, Bricco Bussia Vigna Ciabot (ex-vat, 1/86). Tobacco and berry aroma; firm tannin, the most tannic of the three crus, less body than Cicala; displays real style. ***(+)

Conterno Aldo, Bricco Bussia Vigna Cicala (1/86). More color than Colonello and less open and with more body, tobacco nuance, quite tannic, firm, at this stage a knife-and-fork wine, rough and very unready, loads of character and structure. ***(*)

Conterno Aldo, Bricco Bussia Vigna Colonello (4 times, 11/89). Some alcohol evident, classic Barolo bouquet; sweet entry, then a little dry and firm. **(*) *Bottle of 5/88:* Tar and floral bouquet, woodslike; rich and concentrated, great extract and weight; young. ***(+)

Conterno Aldo, Bussia Soprana (twice, 12/88). Classic Barolo bouquet, suggestive of tobacco, tar and berries; rich, packed with flavor under a fair amount of tannin, lots of character. **(*)

Conterno Aldo, "Granbussia" (ex-tank, 4/87). This Barolo was made from the grapes of more than one subcru, most from Ciabot. Cherry, tobacco and floral bouquet; fresh, sweet and rich, good intensity, complex flavors, small stoned fruit, especially plums, the most evident, soft, loads of quality, young, balanced, long. ***(*)

Conterno Fantino (twice, 1/89, 2,638 bottles). Berry notes, kind of an odd, barnyardy aroma; lightweight, flavor evident, short.

Conterno Fantino, Sorì Ginestra Riserva (4/87, 4,152 bottles). Evident fruit, harsh edge, tannic, somewhat astringent, firm, seems to have the fruit but difficult to be sure where it will really go. *(?*)

Conterno Giacomo, Cascina Francia Riserva (13 times, 11/89). Classic old-style Barolo, rich, sweet and packed with fruit and extract, for this producer, forward. **(*) *Ex-cask, 11/84:* Forward aroma of ripe fruit, vague note of *tartufi*, enormous concentration of fruit and tannin, flavor of ripe grapes. ***

Conterno Giacomo, Monfortino (4 times, 4/90). Would you believe Giovanni Conterno made not even 4,000 bottles of this outstanding wine! He said the rest of the fruit didn't quite measure up to his standards (exigent indeed!) for this special reserve. Surely one of the stars of the vintage. Explosive nose reveals a mélange of scents; incredible richness and extract, gobs of tannin and fruit, a turn-of-the-century wine for those willing to wait, we are. ***(*)

Contratto, Riserva (3 times, 11/90). Tobacco and nebbiolo fruit aroma; moderate tannin, soft, light tannin, tasty; on the young side. * + *Bottle of 5/90:* Color and nose are starting to show age; soft, open and surprisingly ready, could use more weight and flavor, quite short. *

Cordero di Montezemolo, Enrico VI in Villero (4/87). Mushroom and truffle aroma; nice fruit under moderate tannin, fairly well made, well balanced. **

Cordero di Montezemolo, Monfalletto (4 times, 11/87). Truffle and woodsy aroma, wet underbrush component; soft under light to moderate tannin, almost a sweetness, has a gentle character, moderately long finish. ** +

Damilano Dott. Giacomo (twice, 4/90). Small-scale, not a lot of structure, some flavor. +

Dogliani F.lli (9/87). Tobacco and fruit aroma; soft and tasty, simple, some varietal character. * —

Dogliani F.lli, Vigneto Bonfani (twice, 2/88). Berries and underbrush on the nose; hard and austere, rough and unready. ?*

Dogliani F.lli, Vigneto Boscareto (3 times, 1/89, 13,700 bottles). Tannin evident, fruit seems to be sufficient. ?*

Dosio, Vigna Fossati (twice, 4/89). Ripe fruit and some tannin. *

Einaudi Luigi (11/89). Old-style Barolo, sweet entry then tight and tannic, real Barolo character. **(+)

Eredi Virginia Ferrero, Riserva "San Rocco" (10/90). Complex bouquet suggestive of flowers, camphor and *tartufi*, nebbiolo fruit character; light tannin, soft, ready now. **

Fenocchio Giacomo, Vigneti in Bussia (3 times, 4/87). Reticent aroma; firm and tannic, good fruit and structure, on the young side. *(*)

Fenocchio Giacomo, Vigneti in Bussia Riserva (4/90). Open, ripe berrylike aroma, strawberry overlay; nice entry, then some tannin, tasty, rich flavor, a little dry at the end, still young but quite attractive with appealing fruit. **

Fenocchio Giacomo, Vigneti in Cannubbio (ex-cask, 4/86). Perfumed; well balanced, fairly tannic, has the stuffing. **(+)

Fenocchio Riccardo, Pianpolvere Soprano (3 times, 10/89). Characteristic tar and woodslike bouquet; nice fruit, forward and open, nearly ready. **

Ferrero F.lli, Riserva (*3 times, 4/88*). Nice nose, underbrush and berries; rich and chewy, young. **

Feyles Maria, Vigna della Ginestra Riserva (*4/90*). Light nose, some delicacy, vaguely floral; sweet impression, light to moderate tannin, nice flavor, finishes a little dry. **

Fontanafredda (*4 times, 1/89*). Characteristic Barolo aroma, hints of camphor, tar and fruit; a bit tight, rather nice flavor, a little short. *

Fontanafredda, Riserva (*3 times, 10/90*). Tobacco, tar and floral aroma; fairly tannic and firm, good fruit. ** − *Bottle of 5/90:* Classic tar and leather aroma; open fruit, soft then some tannin, dry aftertaste. *

Fontanafredda, Vigna La Rosa (*6 times, 5/90*). Tar and tobacco aroma, camphor and truffle notes; rich and flavorful, young, lots of tannin as well as the fruit to back it up. **(+)

Fontanafredda, Vigna San Pietro (*12/88*). Tobacco, tar and ripe fruit, mint and berries; tasty entry with a sweet impression then tight and a little tannic, needs some time. **

Franco Fiorina (*3 times, 11/88*). Still hard but with evident fruit, and a sweetness to the fruit. **

Franco Fiorina, Riserva (*5/90*). Open tobacco and truffle aroma, cherry notes; still some tannin, good body, tasty, a bit short. **

Gagliardo Gianni, La Serra (*4/87*). Hot, baked character, dull, low fruit, some tannin.

Gagliardo Gianni, Riserva Speciale Ribezzo (*twice, 12/90*). Mushroom and fruit aroma; soft, light tannin, correct, a tad dry at the end. * −

Galvagno Ernesto (*4/87*). Tarry aroma, old-style Barolo aroma; fairly tannic, fruit evident, lacks style, does have character; seems a little older than its years. +

Germano Angelo (*ex-cask, 4/87*). Tar and berry aroma; quite a lot of flavor under moderate tannin, lacks depth but makes up for that with its flavor. *(* −)

Giacosa Bruno (*11/89*). Simple berry aroma; simple and straightforward, not up to this producer, rather surprising. *

Giacosa Bruno, Collina Rionda Riserva (*5 times, 10/89*). Tobacco and tar with a component that recalls the woods; great structure, real sweetness and class, first rate, and still in need of age, one of the best young Barolos we've tasted. *** + (****)

Giacosa Bruno, Falletto (*3 times, 10/89, 22,360 bottles*). Tobacco and tar with a woodslike component to the nose; rich and concentrated, a classic Barolo, great richness, young with a lot of quality. **(* +)

Giacosa Bruno, Rocche (*3 times, 2/91*). It's drinking very well now although it is chewy with tannin; loaded with fruit, very well balanced. ***(+)

Giacosa Bruno, Villero (*ex-cask, 4/85*). Enormous concentration and weight, firm and full-bodied; will surely be one of the best of this exceptional vintage. ***(*)

Giacosa F.lli, Poderi Pira (*3 times, 4/90*). Light nose combines fruit and flowers; has a sweetness to the fruit under the tannin, a little rustic, well balanced, dry, tannic finish. ** −

Grasso Elio, Gavarini Vigna Chinera (*6 times, 11/87, 6,555 bottles*). Cherry nuance on the nose, tobacco notes; some tannin, also a sweet, ripe fruit flavor, could use more length; has some elegance. ** (+)

Grasso, Gavarini Vigna Rüncot (*ex-cask, 4/85*). Rich and intense aroma, with cherry and floral notes; soft tannins, some firmness; a gentle, elegant style. **(*)

Grasso Silvio (*ex-cask, 4/87*). Tobacco and camphor aroma; fairly tannic, good stuffing, finish is decidedly tannic, lacks some style perhaps. *(+)

Grimaldi (*4/87*). Rubber tire and seaweed aroma; insufficient fruit.

Grimaldi, Riserva (*4/90*). Old fruit, low character, dull and short.

"La Corte" Azienda Agricola, Monticelli-Olivero (*ex-cask, 4/86*). Overly tannic, is there enough fruit(?), doubtful. ?

Le Due Torri (*4/88*). Tar and woodslike aroma; tannic, doesn't appear to have the fruit to carry the tannin.

Lodali Eredi, Vigneto Bric Santi Ambrogio (*twice, 4/90, 13,593 bottles*). A little stinky, coffee and chocolate, open fruit aroma and palate, fairly well balanced, some tannin; ready; easy style. *

Marcarini (Elvio Cogno), Brunate (*8 times, 11/89*). Wonderful bouquet, great complexity and fragrance; round and lush, very long; real elegance. ***(*)

Marcarini (Elvio Cogno), La Serra (*7 times, 3/89*). Lovely bouquet, floral and ripe fruit; delicate, soft and very attractive; elegant, stylish, great quality. ***(*)

Marchesi di Barolo, Brunate (*twice, 12/90, 19,020 bottles*). Mintlike nuance followed by tar and flowers on the aroma; soft, open and attractive in spite of moderate tannin; more or less ready. **

Marchesi di Barolo, Cannubi Muscatel (*12/90, 17,116 bottles*). Lovely nose of flowers, tobacco, tar and truffles; soft under light to moderate tannin, though open and attractive flavor, finish is decidedly dry, some alcohol at the end; more or less ready in spite of the remaining tannin, sure to be enjoyable with food. ** −

Marchesi di Barolo, Riserva Grande Annata (*3 times, 12/90*). Floral and dried fruit aroma; a little light on the midpalate but fairly nice flavor; best to drink up. *

Marchesi di Barolo, Valletta (*twice, 13,667 bottles*). Though corked some fruit is apparent. ? *Bottle of 3/90:* Small-scale, some evident fruit, no depth. * −

Mascarello Bartolo (*4 times, 11/89*). This wine has become rather tight since it was bottled. The few times we've tasted it in bottle it hasn't shown as well as it did in cask. We suspect that today it would display the same quality it did in cask. Open and expansive berrylike aroma; initially seems really tight and closed, then it opens to some extent and displays a sweetness to the ripe fruit; real class, great elegance, fine quality; still young. *** *Ex-cask, 12/85:* Incredible richness of fruit, cherry and tobacco notes, elegant; very long finish; young, needs time but it will be splendid in time. ***(*)

Mascarello Giuseppe, Monprivato (*twice, 11/89*). Tar and berries on the aroma; rich, flavorful, a tad dry and tannic, needs further age, lots of sweet ripe fruit; lots of class here. **(*)

Massolino Giuseppe, Azienda Agricola "Vigna Rionda," Riserva (*4/90*). Tar, tobacco, berry and camphor aroma; tannic but the fruit is evident albeit tight. * + (**)

Massolino Giuseppe, Sörì Vigna Rionda (*4/89*). Tobacco and cherry aroma; tight under moderate tannin, fairly nice fruit. ** −

Massolino Giuseppe, Sörì Vigna Rionda Riserva (*4/90*). Camphor, tobacco and leather aroma; flavorful, soft center, light to moderate tannin, dryish aftertaste. ** −

Mauro (*4/89*). Chewy tannin, some fruit, dry.

Oberto Egidio (*ex-demijohn, 4/86*). A touch of volatile acidity under the characteristic tar; fairly tannic, seems to lack the richness of the vintage, could use more fruit.

Oddero F.lli (*6 times, 5/89*). Open fruit aroma, flowers and tar; tasty and chewy, quite young, dry aftertaste. *(* +)

Oddero F.lli, Gabutti-Parafada (*4/89*). Tobacco and tar aroma; soft and round, fruity, balanced. ** +

Palladino (*4/87*). Reticent aroma; moderate tannin, fairly rich in fruit, on the young side, fairly well balanced, needs age to round out and soften. *(*)

Palladino, S. Bernardo Riserva (*4/89*). Truffle and tar aroma; chewy, good flavor; can improve. * + (** −)

Parusso Armando (*4/87*). Small and reticent aroma; fairly tannic on entry, rather light and simple, lacks intensity, does have fruit. *

Parusso Armando, Rocche (*ex-cask, 4/86*). Fairly nice nose, some character; light to moderate tannin, good fruit, soft center, seems to lack the intensity of the vintage.

Patrito (*ex-cask, 4/87*). Moderate tannin, nice fruit, on the simple side, a bit firm at the end. *

Pio Cesare, Riserva (*9 times, 12/89*). Characteristic tobacco and woodslike aroma; rich and open, soft, rich, still more to give, chewy, tight, tannic aftertaste. **(+)

Pira E. (Chiara Boschis) (*8 times, 11/90*). Tar, dried fruit and floral aroma, hint of leather and camphor; rich under moderate tannin; in a shell like a number of other '82s, needs more age. *(*?) *Bottle of 4/90:* Dusty tobacco and woodsy aroma; sweet and fairly tannic, flavorful with a dry aftertaste, could use more length. ** −

Pira Luigi (*ex-cask, 4/86*). Reeks of sulfur, seems a bit light for the year, some tannin, does have fruit. ?(*)

Pittatore Cav. Francesco, & E., Azienda Agricola "Ponte Rocca," Brunate (*ex-cask, 4/86*). Intense aroma of ripe and dried fruit, cassis note; firm and tannic, rich with ripe fruit, a big intense wine, heaps of tannin at the end. **(*)

Pittatore Cav. Francesco, & E., Azienda Agricola "Ponte Rocca," Castellero (*ex-cask, 4/86*). Rather nice fruit, quite rich, balanced, moderate tannin, on the soft side, balanced, tannic finish; displays some class. **(*)

Podere Anselma (*4/87*). Tar and nebbiolo fruit aroma; a bit coarse, has varietal character, lacks the richness of the years. *

Podere Rocche dei Manzoni (Valentino), Riserva (*11/89*). Tar and woodsy aroma; sweet and rich, ripe fruit flavor, a bit dry at the end. **

Poderi e Cantine di Marengo-Marenda, Cerequio, some bottles were labeled Vinicola Piemontese, Cerequio (*5 times, 10/90, 31,504 bottles*). Tar and tobacco aroma, mintlike note; moderate tannin, sense of fruit evident, firm and tight. *(* −) *Bottle of 1/89:* Barnyardy and woodsy aroma; light entry then fairly nice flavor, could use more length; it promised more in cask four years ago. * +

Porta Rossa, Delizia (*twice, 4/87, 42,629 bottles*). Somewhat bottle sick, just bottled. Rich flavor, and in tannin, full-bodied, young, firm and tannic at the end. *(* +)

Principiano Ferdinando, Cascina Nando, Pian Romualdo (*5/87*). Reticent aroma; quite tannic, seems to have enough fruit, no real character, could use more weight. *(+)

Prunotto, Bussia Riserva (*twice, 11/90, 21,600 bottles*). Tar, floral and dried fruit aroma, berry note; sweet and soft after initial light tannin; ready, could improve. *** *Bottle of 12/88:* Vague off note in the back, tight and tannic, rich in weight and extract, tasty. **(?)

Prunotto, Cannubi (*ex-cask, 4/85*). Rich, ripe fruit underneath a lot of tannin, already a softness evident but years from ready. **(* +)

"Ratti" (*3/89*). Light nose, tobacco and flowers; tasty, round and soft, light tannin; a simpler but correct style. *

Ratti Renato, Marcenasco (*2/86*). Pretty and very apparent wine, soft, light tannin, acid seems a tad soft, quite drinkable now though can improve, well structured. **(*)

Rinaldi Francesco, Cannubbio (*ex-cask, 4/85*). Perfumed and elegant, with a lot of quality evident, too cold to fully assess. ***

Rinaldi Giuseppe (*twice, ex-cask, 4/86*). Packed with fruit, light tannin, balanced, rich flavor, young but attractive. **(*)

Rinaldi Giuseppe, Brunate Riserva (*twice, 4/87*). Bottled fifteen days ago. Quality evident, rich flavor under moderate tannin, tar and ripe fruit flavor across the palate. **(* +)

Rocche Costamagna (*twice, ex-cask, 11/85*). Aroma displays some delicacy; balanced, moderate tannin, soft tannins; should make a nice glass, and should be ready soon. **(+)

Rocche Costamagna, Vigna Francesco (*4/87, 1,850 bottles*). Aroma a bit reticent, small fruit nuances on the nose; light to medium tannin, lots of flavor, soft in the center, somewhat tannic at the end. **(+)

Rocche Costamagna, Vigna Riccardo (*4/87, 1,850 bottles*). Licorice and berry aroma; moderate tannin, more structure and tannin than the Francesco; needs more age, on the young side, needs perhaps three more years. **(+)

Roche Azienda Vinicola (4/89). Earthy, a bit dry, lacks the richness of the vintage.

Roche Azienda Vinicola, Riserva Speciale (*twice, 4/88*). Old aroma and flavor, some tannin, lacks weight and concentration.

Rosso Gigi, Arione Riserva (4/90). Seaweed character to the aroma; fairly hard and tannic. *(?)

S. Quirico (4/87). Some oxidation, low fruit, harsh aftertaste.

Sandrone Luciano (*twice, 11/89*). Nebbiolo tar and oak aroma, woodslike; sweet, rich and ripe; has an extra dimension, young but with real class. ***

Scarpa, Tetti di La Morra (*3 times, 4/86, 18,100 bottles*). Cherry, berry and licorice aroma; the tannin is there, but the lush fruit at this stage makes it very attractive, young and impressive, rich fruit and good structure. ***(+)

Scarzello Giorgio (*twice, 4/88*). Vanilla and underbrush, hint of mushrooms; rich flavor, moderate to high tannin, some heat at the end. *

Scavino Paolo, Bric del Fiasc (*5/87, 5,200 bottles*). Vanilla and berry aroma, vaguely recalls zinfandel; overall reticent, fairly tannic and hard, moderate tannin, rich fruit, good structure; young, needs perhaps three or so years. *(*)

Sebaste, Bussia (*2/88*). Reticent aroma; moderate tannin, nice fruit, balanced, moderate richness, firm tannic finish. **−

Sebaste, Bussia Riserva (*3 times, 4/87*). Light but characteristic nebbiolo aroma, vaguely of berries; some tannin to shed, fairly nice fruit beneath some oak, a little light in weight, but a good Barolo albeit simple, dry tannic aftertaste. *+

Seghesio Renzo (4/90). Seaweed, tobacco and fruit aroma; incredible tannin, hard, chewy, austere, is there enough fruit?

Settimo Aurelio, Rocche (4/88). Underbrush and tar on the nose; chewy, moderate tannin, fairly nice fruit; young. *

Sobrero Filippo (*twice, 11/89*). Classic old-style Barolo, chewy and tannic, rich and sweet, ripe fruit; real class. **+ (***)

Sobrero Francesco (11/90). Dark color; mintlike nuance; firm but with nice fruit, a little dry but with attractive fruit, tannic finish. *(*)

Stroppiana Oreste (10/90). Old-style but attractive nebbiolo aroma; rich, sweet and concentrated, still some tannin, a lot of flavor, room to improve, quite appealing. **(+)

Tenuta Carretta, Podere Cannubi (*4 times, 4/90*). Lovely scented and refined bouquet, perfumed with flowers and berries, real delicacy; soft, velvety and smooth, lovely mouth feel, surprisingly ready now, enormous length; the best Carretta since the great '71. ***+

Tenuta La Volta di Cabutto Bartolomeo Riserva (*twice, 9/90, 12,130 bottles*). Dried fruit and vanilla aroma; small-scale, simple, light tannin, lacks weight and flavor intensity. +

Tenuta Montanello, Riserva (4/90). Light nose, tar and dried fruit, coffee and chocolate; a lot less interest in the mouth. *

Tenuta Montanello, Rocche (*ex-cask, 4/85*). Lacks the richness of the '78 but does have a lot of fruit. *

Terzano G. (*ex-cask, 4/86*). Fairly tannic, with some fruit beneath, hard finish. **(+)

Vajra G. D. (*twice, 1/89*). Aroma is vaguely of the woods, and a barnyard(!); tight and tannic, surprisingly closed! *(?)

Vajra G. D., Bricco delle Viole (*ex-cask, 4/87*). More closed than the Fossati, bigger and richer as well and with more tannin, rough at this stage, the sense of ripe fruit is evident. **(*−)

Vajra G. D., Vigneto Fossati Riserva (4/87). Closed nose, some fruit; firm and fairly tannic, young with the fruit to carry the tannin, lots of flavor; some style. **(+)

Veglio F.lli, Cascina Bruni, Carpegna (*ex-cask, 4/86*). Berry and tar aroma; fairly tannic, good fruit, well balanced, still rather hard and young. *(*)

Viberti Giovanni (4/88). Slight nose; some tannin, moderate fruit. +

Vietti Briacca (*4 times, 3/88, 2,613 bottles*). Superb bouquet of *tartufi* and tobacco, berries and cherries, camphor and mushrooms; rich and packed with fruit, rich in tannin; very young. ***(+)

Vietti, Bussia (*12 times, 11/90, 9,090 bottles*). Mintlike aroma, cassis and flowers; richly fruited, velvety, smooth and flavorful; still very young. ***(+) *Bottle of 11/89:* This cru is just not up to the others produced by Vietti in 1982. Tar and berry aroma, leather and tobacco; a bit dry, evident fruit and richness, tannic with the stuffing and the structure. **(*)

Vietti, Castiglione (*ex-cask, 4/85*). Fruit evident but still closed and somewhat backward compared to the crus. **

Vietti, Rocche (*4 times, 11/88, 5,964 bottles*). Rich nose, tobacco, mushrooms and berries; sweet impression at first, then tannic, tight flavors; has really closed up since the last time we tasted it; needs a lot of age. **(*+)

Vietti, Villero Riserva (*8 times, 11/90, 8,900 bottles*). Aroma displays suggestions of tar, flowers and berries; full of flavor, great extract and richness, firm and tight; very young. ***(*) *Bottle of 4/90:* Intense woodslike bouquet, dusty and tobacco notes; tannic and rich, sweet and open fruit, starting to round out but still young. ***(+)

Villadoria, Riserva (*3 times, 9/90*). Some fruit and tar on the nose and palate, drinkable but dull and uninteresting, ho hum! *Bottle of 5/87:* Volatile acidity all across this wine from start to finish, to call this wine awful would be a compliment, even for Villadoria it was bad: Ugh! Ugh!! Ugh!!!

Voerzio Giacomo, La Serra (*5 times, 4/87*). Rich and complex aroma, floral, spice and *tartufi* notes; well structured, moderate tannin; elegant. **(*−)

Voerzio Gianni, La Serra (*4 times, 10/90, 3,330 bottles*). Light nose, nebbiolo fruit and tar, vaguely floral; soft entry followed by tannin; will it improve(?), we doubt it, drink up. * *Bottle of 4/87:* Noticeable oxidation from the nose through the palate.

Zunino Basilio (*ex-cask, 4/86*). Good structure, has tannin and rich fruit. **(*)

1 9 8 1   * —

The weather started out fine and was good until the middle of August; then very high humidity and rain created conditions in which the grapes couldn't dry out or ripen. During September it rained on and off. Clearly, careful selection of grapes was in order. The crop size at 1.2 million gallons (46,754 hectoliters) was equivalent to 6.2 million bottles of Barolo. This was 69.8 percent of the quantity allowed. In terms of both size and yield—418 gallons per acre (39 hectoliters per hectare)—it was one of the smallest of the decade, but still surprisingly above the decade's average of 412 gallons per acre (38.6 hectoliters per hectare). Still, it was less than the average between 1967 and 1989 of 445 gallons (41.6 hectoliters).

Ratti told us that he fermented his Barolo for only ten days on the skins, while in the best years he gives them twice as long. Accademia Torregiorgi, Rocche dei Manzoni, Marchese Fracassi, Scarpa, and Voerzio, among others, produced no Barolo, and Giacomo Conterno no wine at all. Bartolo Mascarello declassified all or most of it, selling the wine as Nebbiolo delle Langhe. Bruno Giacosa produced a very small quantity. Rocche Costamagna's quantity was less than 50 percent of normal. Surely a mixed bag of wines.

Of the nearly five dozen different wines we've tasted, 21 rate less than a star and 32 others less than two. The best wines are the crus from Ceretto's "Bricco Rocche" estate, Marcarini, and Vietti. The wines were mixed from the start, many are fading or have already faded. Clearly these are not Barolos to age. Drink up.

Accornero Flavio (Casa Vinicola Bera) (*11/86*). Odd nose; harsh, unbalanced, no character.

Altare Elio, Vigneto Arborino dell'Annunziata (*4/85*). Mushroomy aroma with a flavor to match, unbalanced, some tannin, a bit shallow, finish is all tannin.

Ascheri Giacomo (*3/88*). Old-style Barolo, tar along with fruit on the nose; good flavor on entry, then some tannin, short; ready to drink. *

Azelia, Bricco Punta (*5/87*). Light fruity aroma; some tannin, fairly nice fruit, could use more fruit, on the light side. *

Bel Colle, Vigna Monvigliero (*1/86*). Touch of volatile acidity, moderate tannin, some fruit, insufficient fruit for the tannin; most interesting of the lot from '78 through '81.

Borgogno F.lli Serio e Battista, Vigna Cannubi Riserva (*ex-cask, 11/84*). Surprisingly deep color; aroma still reticent but some fruit already evident; light to moderate tannin, good fruit, medium body; some elegance. *(*)

Borgogno Giacomo, Riserva (*4/87*). Mushroom aroma; well balanced, surprisingly full-flavored, most tannin, lots of fruit, short. ** —

Borgogno Ludovico, Cascina Borgognot (*4/90*). A little volatile, overall soft and very ready. +

"Bricco Rocche" Azienda Agricola (Ceretto), Bricco Rocche (*ex-cask, 11/84*). Mushroomlike aroma; fairly forward on the palate, light-bodied, nice flavor; in all, a nice wine that will be declassified, it doesn't met the Ceretto brothers' standard for the vineyard. *

"Bricco Rocche" Azienda Agricola (Ceretto), Brunate (*twice, 1/85*). Bottled ten days ago, some bottle sickness evident but shows quality and fruit, light to moderate tannin, will be ready early; somewhat less open than the Prapò. **

"Bricco Rocche" Azienda Agricola (Ceretto), Prapò (*6 times, 8/87*). Slight harshness on the nose, also nice nuances of tobacco and cherries; balanced, flavorful; ready now. **

Brovia F.lli, Rocche (*12/89*). Some harshness on the nose, camphor note along with varietal fruit and a touch of volatile acidity; overly tannic, puckery, not a lot of flavor; on the decline.

Burlotto Comm. G. B. & Cav. Franc^{sco} (*twice, 4/86*). Light but nice nose, there seems to be too much tannin for such a lightweight wine, is there enough fruit? We doubt it. (*?)

Canale Aldo, Riunda (*ex-cask, 4/86*). Reticent aroma, fruit evident; overly tannic for the fruit, though there is fruit, perhaps it will soften? *(+?)

Cantina Colavolpe (*4/87*). Small-scale, some fruit and tannin, light-bodied, drinkable. +

Cantine Bava (*1/86*). Nebbiolo fruit character, but more like a wine from Novara-Vercelli than one from the Langhe, light tannin, some fruit, harsh edge, bitter aftertaste; ready, drink. +

Cantine Duca d'Asti (Chiarlo Michele), "Granduca" (*9/86*). Light garnet color; small nose, mineral notes, not characteristic; light body, some tannin, shallow, finish is firm, fell apart in the glass, for present drinking.

Castello di Verduno di Sorelle Burlotto, Vigna Massara (*twice, 4/88, 3,066 bottles*). Underbrush and small fruit aroma; chewy with tannin, the fruit is insufficient.

Cavallotto F.lli, Vigna Bricco Boschis (*ex-cask, 6/82*). Harsh and tannic, not a lot of fruit at this stage, seems unstructured.

Ceretto, Zonchera (*twice, 9/86*). Light to medium body, soft, good flavor, very ready, drink. * +

Clerico (*4/85*). Nice characteristic aroma; fairly tannic, seems to have sufficient fruit beneath; should be ready soon. *(+)

Colli Monfortesi di Conterno Fantino (*twice, 4/86*). Nebbiolo fruit evident along with a touch of oxidation; some tannin and some fruit; seems old before its time, after all it's only five years old!

Damilano Dott. Giacomo (*twice, 4/87*). Light, soft, small-scale.

Fenocchio Giacomo, Vigneti in Bussia Riserva (*twice, 4/87*). Light nose, some oxidation, some fruit. When we last tasted this wine a year ago, from stainless steel, it also displayed some oxidation!

Fenocchio Riccardo, Pianpolvere Soprano (*3 times, 4/87, 1,840 bottles*). Small-scale but with good fruit, best drunk now before the fruit fades, moderate tannin. * +

Germano Angelo (*1/86*). Floral and varietal aroma, touch of volatile acidity; unbalanced with acid, light tannin, fairly nice fruit. * −

Giacosa F.lli (*4/87*). Mushroom and truffle aroma; fairly tannic, sense of fruit evident. *(* −)

Grasso, Gavarini Vigna Chinera (*ex-cask, 2/85*). Open, forward fruity aroma; light tannin, fairly soft already; with a gentle nature; will mature early but, no doubt, it was a success for the vintage. **

Grasso Elio, Ginestra Vigna Case Matè (*twice, 2/86, 6,306 bottles*). A bit light but displays style, berry and vanilla notes, soft; very ready; some elegance. ** −

"La Corte" Azienda Agricola, Monticelli-Olivero (*ex-cask, 4/86*). Unbalanced, lacks fruit, poor.

Marcarini (Elvio Cogno), Brunate (*3 times, 4/86*). Woodslike, *tartufi* and cherry bouquet; seems softer than La Serra(!), elegant and stylish. **(+)

Marcarini (Elvio Cogno), La Serra (*4 times, 4/87*). Bouquet suggestive of *tartufi* and the woods, open fruit; light in body, light tannin, fairly soft, open, forward fruit; for early drinking; some elegance. **

Mascarello Giuseppe, Monprivato (*3 times, 10/90, 7,853 bottles, 24 magnums, and 6 grandi albeise*). Interesting bouquet recalls aftershave and talcum, hints of mint, flowers and woodsy aroma; still some tannin, seems to have sufficient fruit, soft center, short, dry finish, best to drink up. ** −

Oberto Severino (*1/86*). Light to medium brick color; fairly nice fruit on the nose along with notes suggestive of tobacco and tar, follows through in the mouth, a little rough at the end; could improve, say two years. *

Osvaldo Mauro (*4/85*). Unbalanced, high in tannin, low in fruit.

Palladino (*4/87*). Light nose; fairly soft, some tannin; for early drinking; fairly nice, some character. * +

Patrito (*ex-cask, 4/87*). Moderate tannin, simple, seems to have enough fruit. (*)

Pio Cesare, Riserva (*2/88*). Nice nose, good fruit and nebbiolo character; seems overly tannic for the fruit, not bad though. (+)

Pira E. (Chiara Boschis) (*ex-cask, 3 times, 4/86*). Rather light, has fruit under the tannin, is there enough? *?

Pira Luigi (*ex-cask, 4/86*). Odd nose; fairly tannic for its body, lightweight, touch of volatile acidity, still it is drinkable. * −

Pittatore Cav. Francesco, & E., Azienda Agricola "Ponte Rocca" (*4/86*). Licorice and tobacco combine with fruit on the nose; perhaps a touch too tannic for the fruit, but a success for the year. *(+)

Porta Rossa (*4/86, 24,573 bottles*). Woodsy and berry aroma; has tannin, also nice fruit, should be ready soon, tannic end. *(+)

Porta Rossa, Delizia (*4/87*). Cherry and tobacco aroma, tobacco notes; firm tannin, full of flavor, a little astringent, young. *(*)

Ratti Renato (*ex-cask, 5/82*). Somewhat astringent but nice flavor; should make a nice light luncheon wine. *

Rocche Costamagna (*twice, 4/86*). Rather nice fruit, soft and round, easy; some class; nearly ready. * +

Rocche Costamagna, Vigna Francesco Riserva (*12/89*). Some alcohol as well as characteristic nebbiolo aroma, dusty, cherry and tobacco notes; good flavor, soft, rather short, a tad bitter, dry aftertaste; very ready, even a little past its best. *

Roche Azienda Vinicola (*4/88*). Old and tired, very little fruit remains.

Rosso Gigi, "I Tre Merli" (*7/87*). Small-scale, some tannin, not a lot of flavor, drinkable, simple. +

S. Quirico (*4/87*). Some nebbiolo character, too light, unstructured, too much tannin for the fruit.

Sandrone Francesco, Cannubi (*4/86*). Lovely perfumed bouquet; soft and flavorful, elegant. ** −

Sandrone Luciano (*twice, 1/86, 3,870 bottles*). Good color; cherry-like aroma; light tannin, touch of acid, a bit light, nice fruit, fairly well balanced; good for the year; was better a year ago. *

Scarzello Giorgio (*ex-cask, 4/86*). Berrylike aroma; some tannin, light, light tannic finish, trace of bitterness; will be ready soon, and it's still in cask! (*)

Scavino Paolo, Bric del Fiasc (*5/87, 5,026 bottles*). Light woodsy aroma, vague off note—mercaptan—carries into the mouth, on the light side, best to drink now, in spite of the off note there is some flavor, pleasant. * −

Settimo Aurelio (*twice, 4/88*). Underbrush and berry aroma; fruit up front on the entry gives way to tannin. *

Vajra G. D., Riserva (*4/87*). *Tartufi* and licorice notes on the aroma; light body, nice fruit, still some tannin; drinks well now. ** −

Veglio F.lli, Cascina Bruni, Carpegna (*ex-cask, 4/86*). Light but fruity aroma; some tannin but light, open fruit; good for the year, it should be in bottle. * +

Vietti, Briacca (*ex-cask, 6/82*). More color than the Rocche; delicate floral aroma has a vanillalike note; fairly full-flavored but has a softness, should make a nice bottle. *(*)

Vietti, Rocche (*twice, 1/86*). Tar and tobacco aroma; balanced, soft, open fruit, some tannin; coming ready. **

Zunino Basilio (*ex-cask, 4/86*). Perfumed; on the light side, fairly nice fruit, moderate tannin; nearly ready. ** −

1980 * +

The year produced the fourth largest crop of the 1980s—1.4 million gallons (54,292 hectoliters), equivalent to 7.2 million bottles—and the largest average yield of the decade at 522 gallons per acre (48.8 hectoliters per hectare). Still that was 13 percent less than the 599 gallons (56 hectoliters) allowed by law. Overall, the crop was 87.2 percent of what the law allows.

Overall, 1980 is like 1979 in that it is a mixed vintage of fairly light-bodied, early-maturing wines. For us at least, the best wines equaled the best of 1979, but the results are somewhat more mixed. Renato Ratti said the wines range from medium quality to good. The real problem was the snow, which fell prior to the harvest. Scarpa didn't like the quality of the grapes and produced no Barolo in 1980; neither did Rocche dei Manzoni nor Marchese Fracassi. Giovanni Conterno produced a Barolo but no Monfortino. Alfredo Currado told us it was a difficult vintage; one had to select the grapes carefully to make a good wine. Giuseppe Rinaldi said that for him the vintage was a good one, and Pio Boffa found the quality satisfactory.

Many experts gave it three stars. Based on our tastings of more than 100 wines since the mid-1980s, some of them multiple times, we think their state today makes it best to downgrade our original assessment. The best wines certainly merited three stars, but few still do. And more than a few received no marks from us at all; in fact, 30—nearly one-third—received less than one star and 49 others—nearly half—less than two. In all, we rate the vintage today one star plus. The best of these rather light-bodied wines are fully mature and make for pleasant drinking now. A number of wines have faded, many others are fading. While the best will last, we doubt that any will improve further.

Francesco Rinaldi's Cannubbio and Bartolo Mascarello were our two favorites, followed by Aldo Conterno's Bricco Bussia Colonello. A few years ago Azienda Agricola "Bricco Rocche" Brunate, Bruno Giacosa Rionda, and Elio Grasso Gavarini-Chinera all had more in reserve. We suspect that they are at or near their peaks today. Also very good were F.lli Barale Castellero, Gianfranco Bovio Gattera dell'Annunziata, Ceretto Zonchera, Bruno Giacosa Villero, Marcarini Brunate and La Serra, and Ratti Renato Marcenasco-Rocche.

Alessandria F.lli, Monvigliero (*4/85*). Overly tannic, shy of fruit, harsh, tannic finish.

Altare Elio, Cascina Nuova, Vigneto Arborino dell'Annunziata (*4 times, 12/89*). Leather, dried fruit, cherry and woodsy aroma, evident nebbiolo character; harsh edge, still has flavor, rather short and dry, some alcohol, the nose is the best part; best to drink up. * +

Ambra (bottled by FDO [F.lli Dogliani], La Morra) (*12/85*). Southern slant, earthy and minerallike aroma; soft and drinkable, uncharacteristic.

Ascheri Giacomo (*twice, 4/85*). Small nose; has tannin but not a lot of fruit. * −

Asteggiano Vincenzo (*4/85*). Light and fruity, overly simple. +

Azelia (Lorenzo Scavino), Bricco Punta (*4 times, 1/90*). Tobacco and dried fruit aroma; soft, short; at its peak, has held up very well, drink now. ** −

Barale F.lli, Castellero (*3 times, 4/85*). Fairly well balanced, fruit up front gives way to a tannic firmness, has a resinlike aspect; a real success. **(+)

Bel Colle, Vigne Monvigliero (*1/86*). Stinky, hot, lacks varietal definition, not well made, tannin and acid, not a lot of fruit.

Borgogno Bartolomeo (*3 times, 4/90*). All three bottles were oxidized!

Borgogno F.lli Serio e Battista (*ex-vat, 11/84*). Fruity nose that suggests blackberries; light to moderate tannin, lots of flavor, good quality marred only by some alcohol at the end. *

Borgogno F.lli Serio e Battista, Vigna Cannubi Riserva (*twice, 11/87, 10,990 bottles*). Lovely tar and woodslike aroma, hint of mint; well balanced, tasty, soft center; ready. ** −

Bovio Gianfranco, Gattera dell'Annunziata (*twice, 2/85*). Aroma shows some development; moderate tannin, lively acidity, fairly well structured, a lot of flavor, good quality, finishes on a tannic note. **(+)

"Bricco Rocche" Azienda Agricola (Ceretto), Brunate (*twice, 2/85, 24,812 bottles*). Rich, ripe fruit rises out of the glass, with hints of berries, mint, vanilla and flowers—fabulous nose; medium body, light tannin, and a lot of fruit, moderate length; nearly ready. **(*)

"Bricco Rocche" Azienda Agricola (Ceretto), Prapò (*3 times, 2/85, 11,908 bottles*). Nose offers little interest at this point; well balanced, nice fruit, on the light side. *(+)

Burlotto Comm. G. B. (*twice, 4/86*). Old-style Barolo, tar and camphor notes; quite tannic, sense of fruit is there, is it sufficient? We think so. *(+)

Ca' Bianca, Tenuta Denegri [the earlier bottles were labeled Denegri Lorenzo di Ca' Bianca] (*5 times, 1/86*). A bit hot on the nose; light to medium tannin, fairly nice fruit, rough edge, won't last, drink. *

Camerano G. (*4/87*). Oxidized, low fruit, light body, dull and tired.

Cantine Duca d'Asti (Chiarlo Michele), "Granduca" (*1/85*). Tobacco and tea on aroma that is still rather closed; some tannin but a lot of fruit, fairly well balanced, still needs more time to soften, good quality though a bit short, shows promise. *(*)

Cappellano Dott. Giuseppe (*3 times, 1/90*). Open berry aroma, floral component; soft and light, round and ready, short. * +

Casetta F.lli, Vigna Case Nere (*4/87*). Characteristic aroma, truffle and mushroom notes; some tannin, could use more fruit. (*)

Castello di Verduno, "Cantine del Castello di Re Carlo Alberto," Massara (*4/87*). Tar and seaweed aroma; a lighter style, fairly well balanced, good fruit; coming ready. * +

Cavallotto F.lli, Vigna Bricco Boschis (*ex-cask, 2/85*). Fairly rich with a lot of tannin and a lot of fruit, thins out a bit toward the finish. *

Cavallotto F.lli, Vigna Bricco Boschis-Colle Sud-Ovest (*ex-cask, 4/87*). Nice nose; fairly soft under light tannin, balanced; pretty much ready, we wonder why they haven't bottled it. ** −

Cavallotto F.lli, Vigna Bricco Boschis-Conte Vassallo (*ex-cask, 6/82*). Seems overly tannic but the sense of a lot of fruit is there, might make a nice bottle in time, especially considering the way the San Giuseppe has developed over the same period. *

Cavallotto F.lli, Vigna Bricco Boschis-San Giuseppe Riserva (*twice, 12/89*). Typical old-style Barolo aroma; rather astringent, fairly good fruit and nebbiolo character, short, astringent. *

Ceretto, Zonchera (*2/85*). Forward rush of fruit up front, seems almost sweet, a bit light but has style and elegance, light tannin, well balanced, very nice; nearly ready. **(+)

Clerico (*1/85*). Cherrylike aroma, vaguely floral; moderate tannin and a surprising amount of fruit for the vintage; needs a few years yet but potential evident. **

Colla Paolo (*4/85*). Hot and heavy-handed, not unlike a southern wine, low in acid.

Colli Monfortesi di Conterno Fantino (*4/85*). Small cherrylike aroma; light tannin, light body, a bit simple. * −

Conterno Aldo, Bricco Bussia Vigna Cicala (*8/90, 5,650 bottles*). Characteristic nebbiolo bouquet, recalls dried fruit and flowers, mushroom and truffle notes; starting to dry out, fruit still evident, best to drink up. * −

Conterno Aldo, Bricco Bussia Vigna Colonello (*3 times, 11/85, 5,120 bottles*). Soft, smooth and tasty; displays class; one of the real successes of the vintage. *** −

Conterno Giacomo, Cascina Francia Riserva (*7 times, 5/89*). Rich nose, some oak, woodslike, mushroom and camphor notes; surprisingly open and soft, lots of flavor; very drinkable, and nice too. **

Cordero di Montezemolo, Enrico VI in Villero (*2/85*). Forward fruitiness with suggestions of cherries and prunes, light tannin, sweet, ripe fruit, fairly well balanced but quite forward, drinks nicely now. *(*)

Cordero di Montezemolo, Monfalletto (*twice, 11/85*). Cherry and berry aroma, vague tobacco; a bit light, some tannin, almost a sweetness; not quite ready, not far from it, try again in one, perhaps two years. ** −

Fenocchio Giacomo, Vigneti in Bussia Riserva (*twice, 4/90*). Damp leaves, tar and dried fruit aroma; a little dry but nice flavor, best to drink now. * +

Fenocchio Giacomo, Vigneti in Cannubbio Riserva (*ex-cask, 4/86*). Pretty, perfumed aroma; tannic, is there enough fruit? (*)

Fenocchio Riccardo, Pianpolvere Soprano (*twice, 4/85*). Aroma has a forward fruitiness with suggestions of vanilla, almonds, tobacco, cherries, flowers and raspberries; light and fruity, with a hint of cherries, light tannin; in all, a soft, light easy style that should make a nice luncheon wine. * +

Ferrero F.lli, Riserva (*4/87*). Tar, floral and chalk aroma; good structure, moderate tannin, good fruit, well made. *(*)

Fontanafredda (*1/85*). Lovely nose, full and fairly rich with hints of *tartufi*, mint and berries; well balanced, some tannin to shed but also a lot of fruit, young but displays potential. *

Franco Fiorina (*twice, 5/85*). Raspberry aroma with notes of tea and tobacco; entry on palate somewhat astringent, moderate tannin, some fruit, fairly well balanced, drinkable, not for long aging. ** −

Giacosa Bruno, Rocche (*ex-cask, 10/81*). A surprising amount of fruit but also tannin to shed, surprisingly well balanced for the vintage. **

Giacosa Bruno, Vigna Rionda (*twice, 9/86*). Woodslike bouquet; rich and concentrated, tannic, a lot of quality, long; needs time. **(*)

Giacosa Bruno, Villero (*twice, 9/86*). Tobacco, cherry and woodsy aroma; richly flavored, it has so much fruit that it makes the tannin seem soft, long. ** +

Giacosa F.lli (*twice, 4/85*). Aroma a bit reticent, but some fruit evident; light to moderate tannin, some firmness, flavorful, note of licorice, pleasant drinking in spite of the tannin. **

Giudice Sergio (*5/87*). Dirty nose, dirty wine, has tannin, low fruit.

Grasso, Gavarini Vigna Chinera (*twice, 2/85, enormous production of 2,650 bottles!*). Aroma yields hints of cherries and flowers; light tannin, light body but well balanced and elegant, with a lot of flavor. And earlier bottling displayed notes of tobacco and camphor and seemed more closed on the palate. **(*)

Grasso, Gavarini Vigna Rüncot (*twice, 11/86*). Some tar and fruit, off note, fairly soft in the center, moderate tannin, enjoyable but well made; will improve or should. *(* −)

Grasso Silvio (*4/87*). Light nose, reticent; light body, some tannin, fruit seems a bit low, pleasant; small-scale. *

Grimaldi (*4/87*). Weird nose; overly tannic for the fruit, unbalanced.

Il Vecchio Tralcio (1/85). Smallish nose; overly tannic though some fruit evident, a bit shallow; this producer does better with white wines.

"La Corte" Azienda Agricola, Monticelli-Olivero (4/86). Nicely fruited aroma; berrylike, moderate tannin, a little light, needs more fruit. * –

Marcarini (Elvio Cogno), Brunate (6 times, 4/87). Cherry and tobacco aroma, *tartufi* note; almost sweet, a bit more closed and firmer than La Serra; coming ready. ** +

Marcarini (Elvio Cogno), La Serra (5 times, 4/87). Light but nice nose; aftertaste, light tannin, a tad light in body, soft center; ready now. ** +

Marchesi di Barolo, Cannubi Riserva (8/87, 7,252 bottles). Slight varietal aroma; drying out, unbalanced but drinkable.

Marchesi di Barolo, Vigna della Valletta Riserva (5 times, 12/86, 14,625 bottles). This wine has displayed some bottle variation; the most recent bottle was the best: lactic aroma, tobacco notes; bitter and astringent, moderate fruit, some varietal character; young, some potential. *(+)

Mascarello Bartolo [*some bottles were labeled Cantina Mascarello, they are the same wine*] (7 times, 4/87). Tartufi, mushroom and woodslike bouquet; smooth and flavorful, some tannin still evident; lovely now, elegant, very ready, but no need to rush to drink it. ***

Mascarello Giuseppe, Monprivato (4 times, 4/85, 10,422 bottles, plus larger sizes). Lovely nose with notes of tobacco and mushrooms; moderate tannin, sufficient fruit to balance; has an easy nature typical of the vintage. **(+)

Massolino Giuseppe, Vigna Rionda (4 times, 4/89). Old and tired, fading fast. *Bottle of 2/85:* In all, a light, soft, simple wine with a Zinfandel-like raspberry aroma and some spice; light-bodied, soft and easy; for current consumption. *

Oberto Egidio (ex-cask, 4/86). Rather nice fruit on the nose with a berrylike character; tannic entry, then some fruit, and more tannin at the end, could use more body and structure. (*)

Oberto Severino (1/86). Characteristic tar on the nose, touch of camphor; seems to have sufficient fruit for the tannin, drink before the fruit fades. *

Oddero F.lli (twice, 5/85). Lovely bouquet with nuances of cherries, tobacco, mushrooms and flowers; a rush of fruit on entry that carries across the palate, marred by a touch of astringency; for early drinking. **

Osvaldo Mauro (4/85). Structurally and in flavor reminiscent of a southern wine.

Palladino (3 times, 4/87). Tobacco, tar and camphor aroma; light to moderate tannin, soft in the center, fairly well balanced, on the light side. * +

Parusso Armando, Cascina Roella (4/86). Nice nose; has tannin, open fruit, soft, attractive; drink now before it dries out. *

Patrito (ex-demijohn, 4/87). Slight off nose; simple, lacks weight and structure, drinkable.

Pio Cesare, Riserva (3 times, 1/90). Characteristic varietal aroma; harsh edge, could use more fruit, fading, still some interest, short. * –

Pira E. (Chiara Boschis) (6 times, 4/89). Fairly nice nose, open fruit, *tartufi* note; dry but fairly nice fruit, on the light side. *

Pira Luigi (ex-vat, 4/86). Wood dominates the nose, some fruit; moderate tannin, still has fruit; should be in bottle. * –

Pittatore Cav. Francesco, & E., Azienda Agricola "Ponte Rocca," Brunate (3 times, 10/90). Fragrant nose, some mint; fairly soft, has held up quite well, nice flavor, moderate length, a little dry, characteristic tar; no need to keep longer. * + *Bottle of 4/86:* A well-made wine with good structure and some character. ** –

Porta Rossa (4/86, 17,398 bottles). Camphor and ripe fruit; still has harsh tannins, the fruit is there; try in two to three more years. *(+)

Prunotto (10/87). Tough and tannic, has the stuffing, a bit rough. *

Punset, R. Marcarino (4/87). Seaweed and tobacco aroma, some oxidation; has a softness under some tannin, agreeable, small-scale. * –

"Ratti" (10/87). Vaguely recalls caramel and berries on the nose, definite nebbiolo character; soft, round and supple; simple but correct; very ready, drink now. * +

Ratti Renato, Marcenasco (6 times, 10/89). Drink up, starting to dry out, still good. * *Bottle of 1/85:* Tobaccolike aroma; light tannin, fairly nice fruit, a little light but well balanced; will be ready early. **

Ratti Renato, Marcenasco-Conca (1/85, 8,720 bottles). Tobacco and cherry aroma; has tannin and fruit; will be ready early. **

Ratti Renato, Marcenasco-Rocche (1/85, 8,560 bottles). The fruitiest of the three Barolos with nice fruit, fairly forward, quality quite evident. **(+)

Rinaldi Francesco, Cannubbio (1/85, 10,000 bottles). Delicate perfume; a lot of style and elegance, a wine of quality, perhaps the best wine of the vintage. ***

Rinaldi Giuseppe (3 times, 3/90). Lovely classic Barolo aroma; some acidity, some age shows, short, drink. * +

Rocche Costamagna (2/85). Interesting aroma, with a mineral aspect and a hint of almonds, some tannin, rather light and a bit shallow, vaguely bitter, not a success.

Rocche Costamagna, Vigna Francesco (11/88). A bit stinky, losing its fruit, fading.

Roche Azienda Vinicola (1/85). Strange nose; a bit shy on fruit, astringent, not a success.

Roche Azienda Vinicola, Riserva (twice, 4/89). Fairly nice fruit, some tannin, good flavor. *

Rosso Gigi, Vigneti della Cascina Arione (2/88). Nice nose characteristic of nebbiolo, with hints of raspberries and camphor; light tannin, quite approachable, still a bit young, some firmness; needs a few years yet. *

Sandrone Luciano (1/85, 2,940 bottles). A lot of ripe fruit on nose; well balanced and stylish, surprisingly soft, light tannin; nearly ready. **

Scarzello Giorgio (twice, 12/89). Some volatile acidity, some tar, harsh edges, on its way down. *Bottle of 4/85:* Characteristic aroma, more toward the fruity end of the spectrum; fairly good fruit, some acid at the edges, short finish that hints of tobacco. *

Scavino Paolo (twice, 5/87). Vanilla and fruity aroma, vague *tartufi* note, some oak; nice fruit, medium body, fairly ready now, agreeable, small-scale, enjoyable now, could improve. *

Scavino Paolo, Bric del Fiasc (4 times, 5/87, 5,385 bottles). Similar and somewhat richer nose than the *normale*; more weight and structure, nice fruit, still some tannin remains, very drinkable now. ** – *Bottle of 4/85:* Characteristic Barolo aroma, some oak; moderately rich, light tannin, easy, not really ready, still some firmness, but will be soon. ** –

Settimo Aurelio (twice, 4/88). Aroma of tar and underbrush, vaguely suggestive of fossil fuel; light fruit up front, then quite tannic; drying out.

Sobrero Filippo (11/85). Dried out, has some character and interest. *

Sordo Giovanni (1/86). Smell and taste of kerosene, soft if you can get past the flavor.

Tenuta Carretta, Podere Cannubi (twice, 4/87, 12,533 bottles). Mushroom and woodsy aroma; quite a lot of tannin, the fruit is there to carry it; young and in need of age. *(*)

Tenuta Coluè Massimo Oddero (1/85). Typical aroma of fruit and tar; a bit young yet but forward and nearly ready, should keep. *(*)

Tenuta La Volta di Cabutto Bartolomeo (1/85). Mint and berries, rather a nice nose; rather simple flavors and fairly forward, soft and nearly ready. (*)

Tenuta Montanello (1/85). Some tobacco on nose; moderate tannin, fairly nice fruit though a bit light and forward, some tannin at the end. *

Terzano G., Cascina Adelaide (4/86). Rather nice fruit on the nose, recalls raspberries; moderate tannin, soft-centered, well made though light; not for aging but for current drinking, quite nice. ** –

Vajra G. D., Bricco Viole (ex-cask, 2/85). Complex aroma; a fair amount of tannin, a mouthful of fruit, well structured; needs age but forward. **

Veglio F.lli, Cascina Bruni, Carpegna (ex-cask, 4/86). Lovely berry aroma; fairly rich flavor, some tannin; nice now, could even improve; too bad it wasn't in bottle. **

Vietti, Rocche (17 times, 5/90, 10,500 bottles). Light nose, tobacco and light cherry notes; soft, finish is a bit brief, no need to keep any longer; very ready, was better two years ago. ** –

Vinicola Piemontese, Cerequio (4/88, 34,435 bottles). Nose of wet underbrush and a mineral character; some tannin and fruit, light in body. * –

Voerzio Giacomo (2/85). Light cherrylike aroma, touch of vanilla; light but sweet ripe fruit, light and soft even a bit simple, a soft, easy style. *

Zunino Basilio (4/86). Aroma displays the typical camphor of Serralunga; good fruit, moderate tannin; coming ready. * +

1 9 7 9 **

The crop size, at 1.4 million gallons (53,193 hectoliters), equivalent to 7.1 million bottles, was 85.3 percent of the quantity allowed by the DOC and the largest of the decade in size but average in yield. The 511 gallons per acre (47.8 hectoliters per hectare) was 15 percent less than the 599 gallons (56 hectoliters) allowed by law.

Because of rain during the harvest and snow toward the end of it, the results were somewhat mixed. Wines made from grapes picked during the rain were somewhat diluted; those picked before the rain and afterward made more successful Barolo. Overall, 1979 was a good vintage of rather light Barolos that were ready for drinking early. A number of them are starting to fade now, but the best will keep. There are a number of very good wines. Most are near their peaks, a few will continue to improve.

Aldo Conterno considers the vintage on the same level as 1970 and 1974, and says 1983 was also similar. Pio Boffa again found the quality satisfactory. Renato Ratti ranked the vintage as good to very good. Scarpa, however, didn't produce any Barolo; they were dissatisfied with the grapes, which had been snowed on. Giacomo Conterno produced a Monfortino. This vintage has been given three stars; for us two stars, perhaps two minus, seem more appropriate today.

Of 89 wines tasted, 22, or one-quarter, were given less than one star, and 34 others failed to get two stars. No doubt about it, many good and very good wines were made, but so were too many that were not as good.

Our favorites: Cantina Mascarello, Giacomo Conterno Monfortino, Bruno Giacosa Bussia and Rocche, Marcarini La Serra, and Vietti Rocche, followed by "Bricco Rocche" Brunate and Prapò, Marcarini Brunate, Giuseppe Mascarello Monprivato, and Prunotto Cannubi. Some other good Barolos are Accademia Torregiorgi Carpegna, Giovanni Accomasso Rocchette, F.lli Borgogno Cannubi, Gianfranco Bovio Gattera dell'Annunziata, Elio Grasso Ginestra Vigna Case Matè, and Tenuta Carretta Podere Cannubi.

This was the last vintage in which grapes were crushed in

the old-fashioned way, by feet. Luigi Pira, the last producer in the zone to carry on the old tradition, died in 1980.

Abbona Marziano (4/88). Tobacco and underbrush aroma, vague *tartufi* note; dry and tannic, low fruit, alcohol aftertaste.

Accademia Torregiorgi, Carpegna (6/89). Aroma of fairly ripe fruit, vaguely of cherries and a hint of tobacco; light to moderate tannin, somewhat light but with some style, well balanced, has a lot of flavor; a light gentle style; some elegance, nearly ready. **(*)

Accademia Torregiorgi, Carpegna Riserva (2/85). Camphor and tar aroma; soft, flavorful, short; very ready; the *normale* was better when last tasted a few years ago. ** −

Accomasso Giovanni, Vigneto Rocchette Riserva (4/86). Rich tar and vanilla aroma, flowers, vague *tartufi;* rich in tannin as well as fruit, well made, young, **(*−)

Alessandria F.lli (twice, 1/85). Tobacco, tealike aroma; tannic, is there enough fruit? Only time will tell, at this point, it's doubtful.

Ascheri Giacomo (twice, 4/85). Some nebbiolo character evident in aroma; quite tannic but fruit is apparent, is it sufficient? Needs perhaps another four or so years to find out.

Azelia, Bricco Punta (9/86). Nice nose; soft, toward a lighter style; ready. * +

Baracco di Baracho (9/88). Tarry, old-style, drying out, some oxidation.

Barale F.lli, Castellero Riserva (3 times, 2/85). Nice nose though a bit light, vaguely floral, some berry and vanilla notes; light to moderate tannin, fairly nice fruit; already nice though it needs a few more years to develop and round out. **

Bel Colle (1/86). Overripe, baked and dull, atypical, unimpressive.

Bersano (5/84). A simple aroma; light, soft and gentle, a nice little red wine but lacks structure and personality.

Borgogno F.lli Serio e Battista, Riserva (twice, 3/85). Fairly full, typical nose with a *tartufi* note; some tannin, but there seems to be sufficient fruit to support it, alcoholic toward the end. *(+)

Borgogno F.lli Serio e Battista, Vigna Cannubi Riserva (4 times, 10/87, 7,200 bottles). Tobacco and small fruit aroma; good structure, chewy, good weight and flavor. ** +

Borgogno Giacomo, Riserva (twice, 5/85). Nose is undeveloped, notes of tobacco and tea; moderate tannin, a bit light, but soft-centered with nice fruit, finishes on a tannic note, should make a nice bottle in a few years. *(+)

Bovio Gianfranco, Gattera dell'Annunziata (twice, 2/85). Floral perfume over various types of fruit; moderate tannin, medium body, some style and elegance, nice fruit still somewhat closed; say about three years to really show itself. **(+)

"Bricco Rocche" Azienda Agricola (Ceretto), Brunate (9 times, 3/89, 21,813 bottles). Volatile acidity and alcohol intrude, a bad bottle or shot? We suspect the latter. *Bottle of 10/87:* Tobacco, floral bouquet, vaguely woodslike, notes of mint and berries; some tannin, soft-centered, enjoyable now, still could improve a bit, good structure, fairly long finish. *** − *Bottle of 2/85:* A lot of fruit on the nose which has a hint of mint, *tartufi* and cherries; soft tannin, still backward but fuller and richer than is normal for this vintage, has richness of ripe fruit and a lot of style. **(*)

"Bricco Rocche" Azienda Agricola (Ceretto), Prapò (3 times, 11/88, 11,868 bottles). Expansive bouquet has a mintlike note, and suggestions of the woods and tobacco, camphor and tar, and a slight talcum powder nuance; tannin on the entry quickly softens as it goes back with fruit taking over on the midpalate, some length, ready, displays some style. ** + *Bottle of 1/85:* Richly fruited aroma with suggestions of vanilla and raspberries as well as a somewhat floral note; moderate tannin, some elegance, fruit all across the palate, licorice note. *** −

Cantina Mascarello (3 times, 2/85). Aroma has a richness and intensity that's uncommon for the vintage, truffle, cherry and tealike notes; finely made, light to moderate tannin, elegant and stylish, impressive quality, with a very long finish. ***

Cantine Bava (twice, 1/86). One bottle was oxidized. *The other:* The aroma recalls the nebbiolo wines of the Novara-Vercelli hills; light body, light tannin, soft, fruity, simple, easy, a little thin at the end, drinkable not much more. * −

Cascina Bruni di Veglio Pasqual (ex-cask, 1/85). Lovely aroma; ripe fruit flavor, soft, light tannin, some spice; seems ready. * +

Casetta F.lli (twice, 5/85). Brick, orange; not much aroma; has some tannin and also a fair amount of fruit, very tannic at the end, dull but drinkable. * −

Castello di Verduno, "Cantine del Castello di Re Carlo Alberto" (Dott. Lisetta Burlotto e Sorelle Burlotto), Massara (4/87). Light seaweedlike aroma; soft under light to moderate tannin, tarlike flavor, short. * +

Cauda Luigi (1/85). Has tannin, low in acid, a bit shy in fruit, structurally like a southern wine!

Cavallotto F.lli, Vigna Bricco Boschis (ex-cask, 11/84). Vaguely floral aroma; has a fair amount of tannin, but with the fruit to back it up, still needs a few years yet. *(*)

Cavallotto F.lli, Vigna Bricco Boschis-Punta Marcello Riserva (twice, 3/85). Loads of fruit on the nose, some cherries; moderate tannin, fruity, fairly forward for this house, though needs a couple of years yet. ** −

Cavallotto F.lli, Vigna Bricco Boschis-San Giuseppe **normale and Riserva** (twice, ex-cask, 4/87). Ex-cask (Riserva) of 4/87: Perfumed floral aroma; surprisingly big for the year, loaded with flavor under moderate tannin, perhaps a tad lacking in class, but the richness and intensity of flavor compensate. **(*−) *Bottle (normale) of 1/85:* Fairly rich aroma, has a vaguely brambly character; heaps of tannin, but with a lot of fruit beneath; needs perhaps three or four years to soften and show its real quality. *(*)

Ceretto, Zonchetta Brunate (4 times, 3/89, 18,656 bottles). Mushroom and volatile acidity, fading fast, harsh and bitter. *Bottle of*

12/88: Orange toward the rim; tar and tobacco aroma, floral and dried berry notes; still some tannin, good flavor; ready, best to drink up, a little dry at the end. *+ *Bottle of 2/85:* Vaguely floral and richly fruited aroma, has a hint of cassis and tar; moderate tannin, sweet ripe fruit; seems nearly ready, perhaps in 1986. **(+)

Conterno Aldo, Bricco Bussia Vigna Cicala (twice, 10/83, 5,768 bottles). Lovely aroma with an open fruitiness; a mouthful of fruit, light tannin, firm; enjoyable now but with room for improvement. **+

Conterno Giacomo, Cascina Francia Riserva (4 times, 11/85). Nice nose suggestive of camphor and *tartufi*; loaded with fruit under the tannin, packed with flavor, less intensity than the '80(!), long finish. **(*−) *Bottle, twice, 1/85:* Aroma of cinnamon and spice; medium body, somewhat unbalanced with overly high tannin for the fruit and some alcohol, could it develop? It seemed better when tasted in November 1984 from cask **, though that was a different batch, this one was bottled August 1983. ? *Ex-cask, 11/84:* Lovely bouquet suggesting chestnuts and vanilla; young and not surprisingly more forward than the '78 but with a richness and concentration uncommon for the vintage. **(*)

Conterno Giacomo, Monfortino Riserva Speciale (8 times, 10/90). Great richness and concentration, a mouthful of fruit and tannin, mintlike nuance, still more to give. **(*) *Bottle of 10/89:* Chewy, closed up tight, richness of fruit apparent. **+ (***−) *Bottle of 5/89:* Complex bouquet recalls leather, tar, mushrooms and flowers, a mélange of sensations; a big wine, packed with fruit, but dry due to the high tannin, still the flavor is appealing and most attractive; will improve. **+ (***)

Contratto (5 times, 4/89). Light fragrant aroma, floral notes; good body, tasty, balanced, soft, at its peak. **−

Coppo Luigi, Vigneto Brunate (twice, 1/86, 1,310 bottles). Fruity aroma recalls *tartufi* and cherries; some tannin on entry, fruit follows, a tad light midpalate, somewhat simple, could use more weight; ready now, drink. *

Coppo Luigi, Vigneto Castello (twice, 1/86, 1,260 bottles). *Tartufi* and mushroom aroma; moderate intensity, light tannin, nicely fruited center, more body than the Brunate, some tannin at the end; ready. *

Cordero di Montezemolo, Enrico VI-Villero (2/85). Vague off note mars the aroma, which recalls cherries; light-bodied, softer than the Monfalletto with more body and structure, tannin builds up at the end. *(+)

Cordero di Montezemolo, Monfalletto (2/85). Nice nose though rather simple; fairly open, fruity and fresh, light body, light tannin, easy fruity style that can improve, finish is short and rather tannic. *(+)

Dogliani F.lli, Tenuta Bonfani Riserva Speciale (9/87, 10,000 bottles). Tar and vaguely floral aroma; soft, good fruit, could use more weight and structure, chocolate notes. *

Dosio (twice, 5/85). Expansive aroma, varietal character with cherrylike fruit and flowers; moderate tannin, has fruit, somewhat uncomplicated though authentic. *+

Dosio, Riserva Speciale (10/87). Tar and fruit aroma; moderate tannin, nice fruit, open, ready, dry and moderately tannic finish. *−

Fenocchio Riccardo, Pianpolvere Soprano (3 times, 4/85). Lightly fruited aroma, has nuances of tobacco and cherries; some tannin to lose, has the fruit to back it up, coming ready, tannic finish. *+

Ferrero F.lli Giovanni e Renato (4/88). Nice nose, typical; fairly tannic, sense of fruit evident; probably best to drink while some fruit still remains. *

Ferrero F.lli Giovanni e Renato, Riserva Speciale (4/87). Some fruit evident on the nose; firm and tannic, flavorful, a tad light but balanced, tarry flavor, also at end. *(*−)

Feyles Maria, Vigna della Ginestra Riserva Speciale (twice, 4/90). It was better eighteen months ago. Some oxidation and seaweed, chocolate and coffee nuances; still some tannin, and flavor interest; fading. *−

Franco Fiorina, Riserva Speciale (twice, 5/85). Raspberries up front on nose, woodsy scents; still fairly tannic but with the stuffing to support it; try again in, say, three years. **(+)

Gemma (4/85). Mushrooms and cherries on aroma; a bit light, flavorful; quite nice now. *

Giacosa Bruno, Bussia Riserva Speciale (5 times, 10/89, 6,130 bottles). Rich tar- and berry-scented bouquet, somewhat floral, tobacco notes; soft and velvety, although there is some unresolved tannin it is very ready. ***

Giacosa Bruno, Rocche (twice, 11/85, 6,130 bottles). Tobacco and *tartufi* aroma; packed with flavor, well knit, rich in fruit, very long; ready. ***

Giacosa F.lli (3 times, 4/85, 16,800 bottles). Lovely nose with champignons and flowers; moderate tannin, fruity; has quality; needs age. **(+)

Grasso Elio, Ginestra Vigna Case Matè (twice, 2/85, 3,300 bottles). Lovely nose has a suggestion of camphor; fairly soft, light tannin; ready though room for improvement; has a gentle, elegant nature. **+

"La Corte" Azienda Agricola, Monticelli-Olivero (4/86). Shy nose, something vaguely weird; unbalanced, light body, too much tannin for the fruit.

Manzone Stefano, Azienda Agricola "Ciabot del Preve," Castelletto (twice, 4/85). Noticeable fruit on nose and palate, light tannin, fairly forward, some harshness at the end; in all, an agreeable wine. *−

Marcarini (Elvio Cogno), Brunate (5/87, 20,776 bottles). Tobacco, tar, licorice and *tartufi* aroma, vague floral component, and a cherry note; on the light side, soft and flavorful, smooth, fairly long; very ready. ***−

Marcarini (Elvio Cogno), La Serra (twice, 10/86). Lovely bouquet, *tartufi*, tobacco and cherry notes; elegant, stylish. ***

Marchese Maurizio Fracassi Ratti Mentone (*11/84*). Expansive aroma suggestive of *tartufi* and tobacco; a feminine-style Barolo, delicate and elegant, some tannin (Barola). **

Mascarello Giuseppe, Monprivato (*3 times, 4/86, 8,516 bottles, plus larger sizes*). Tobacco, cherry and *tartufi* aroma; similar to the '80 but firmer and more tannic, firm vein of tannin, has the stuffing and balance to carry that tannin; say three years. **(*)

Mascarello Giuseppe, Villero (*5 times, 8/90*). Truffles and berries define the nose; soft and round, near its peak, some alcohol intrudes; no need to keep any longer. **

Massolino Giuseppe, Vigna Rionda (*3 times, 4/89*). Shot. *Bottle of 3/87:* Fruit is there although on the light side, small-scale, drinkable, could use more definition. *

Oberto Egidio (*twice, 4/86*). We had a chance to compare the same wine, one from bottle, one from demijohn. *From bottle:* Oxidized, some fruit, drying out, mishandled somewhere along the way. *From demijohn:* Noticeable oxidation, rather tannic, drying out.

Oddero F.lli (*4 times, 5/85*). Nose has notes of tobacco and fruit, light tannin, sweet ripe fruit, accessible and soft; an easy style but quite nice; will improve over the next two years. **(+)

Ornato Paolo, Rocche (*twice, 2/85*). Aroma of tar and nebbiolo fruit; some tannin, good fruit, forward, some tannin at the end. * +

Palladino (*4/87*). Some oxidized as well as nebbiolo character, kind of dull. *

Pio Cesare, Riserva (*8 times, 8/89*). Intense aroma of tobacco, tar and berries; big entry, lots of fruit, light tannin; very ready. * +

Pira E. (Chiara Boschis) (*4 times, 4/89*). Tobacco and berry aroma; still some fruit, but rather dry. +

Pira Luigi (*twice, 4/86*). We had the opportunity to compare a bottled wine with one still in cask. *Ex-cask:* Woody aroma; still has fruit, moderate tannin; quite nice; should be in bottle. ** − *Bottle:* Characteristic Barolo aroma, notes of camphor and tar; a little light, some tannin; rather nice for drinking now. * +

Podere Rocche dei Manzoni (Valentino), Riserva (*twice, 4/89*). Odd nose, off-putting; harsh edge, drying out and losing its fruit.

Poderi e Cantine di Marengo-Marenda, Cerequio, *some bottles were labeled Vinicola Piemontese, Cerequio* (*5 times, 10/90, 36,533 bottles*). Tobacco and tar aroma; old-style, very ready, soft and tasty. * + *Riserva Speciale of 5/89:* Good fruit, still more to give though ready now, soft center. * +

Porta Rossa, Riserva Speciale (*twice, 10/90, 19,877 bottles*). Open nose, attractive fruit, berry and floral notes; a little dry, still some tannin, best to drink up, it won't keep. * *Bottle of 4/86:* Camphor aroma, vaguely of tobacco; some tannin, open fruit, quite attractive, could improve. **(+)

Prunotto, Bussia Riserva (*twice, 2/87, 13,227 bottles*). Tobacco and camphor aroma; some tannin, fairly soft, firm ending, ready though could improve a bit. ** −

Prunotto, Cannubi Riserva (*1/85, 13,220 bottles*). Perfumed bouquet has a *tartufi* note; well balanced, a mouthful of fruit and a soft center, still with tannin to lose. **(*)

Ratti Renato, Marcenasco (*7 times, 12/87*). Tar and tobacco aroma, dried fruit component—prunes and figs; tasty, some tannin, but well integrated into the wine; nice for current drinking, could possibly improve a bit. **

Ratti Renato, Marcenasco-Conca (*5/83*). Aroma of cherries and tar; a lot of flavor, more tannin than the Marcenasco; still needs two or more years. ** +

Ratti Renato, Marcenasco-Rocche (*6 times, 1/89, 7,074 bottles*). Tobacco, tar, flowers and berries on the nose; sweet impression, soft, round and ready. **

Rocche Costamagna, Vigna Francesco Riserva (*twice, 12/87*). Tobacco, cherry and dried fruit bouquet; vaguely corked, still it does have nice flavor; very ready now. **

Rocche Costamagna, Vigna Riccardo Riserva (*twice, 2/85, 1,450 bottles*). Tobacco, cherry and camphor aroma; light-bodied, moderate tannin, should be ready early, a fair amount of fruit. *(+)

Rolfo Gianfranco (*1/85*). Nice fruit on nose and palate, moderate tannin, a bit light, could use more character but drinkable enough. *

Rosso Gigi, Vigneti della Cascina Arione (*twice, 2/85*). Strawberries rise up out of the glass, touch of camphor; moderate richness, a bit light and forward, exhibits some style, astringent finish, in all a bit light but fairly good. *(+)

Saffirio F.lli Enrico e Giacomo (*11/84*). Big fruited aroma, some cassis and tar; high tannin, moderate fruit, something is missing, but it's not unpleasant.

Savigliano Mario (*1/85*). Old-style Barolo aroma, more tar than fruit, also a tobacco note; overly tannic, has some fruit, but is it enough?

Scavino Paolo, Bric del Fiasc Riserva (*4 times, 4/85, 5,330 bottles*). Nice nose with some depth, richness, nebbiolo character and hints of tobacco, berries and a touch of oak; a bit light with some tannin and nice fruit, nearly ready, well balanced; give it another year or two to soften further. **

Seghesio Renzo (*4/85*). Some oxidation apparent, overly tannic, unstructured.

Settimo Aurelio (*5/85*). Light but nice aroma; some tannin, fruity, easy, some character. **

Settimo Aurelio, Rocchette Riserva (*4/88, 3,000 bottles*). Underbrush and berry aroma; chewy, fairly tannic, good fruit in the center. *

Sobrero Filippo (*11/85*). Volatile acidity, dried out.

Tenuta Carretta, Podere Cannubi (*twice, 4/85, 12,600 bottles*). Aroma is closed in; a mouthful of fruit beneath the gobs of tannin make this a promising bet for long-term growth potential; its style and class are already evident. **(*?)

Tenuta Montanello, Riserva Speciale (twice, 4/90). Tar, fruit, and chocolate aroma; still has flavor but drying out. *−

Tenuta Montanello, Vigneto dei Montello-Pini (ex-cask, 1/85). A bit light but fairly well balanced, some tannin, shows more character than the previous wine. **

Vajra G. D. (twice, 12/89). Characteristic tar and woodslike bouquet; fruit at its best now, soft and tasty, could use more length, a tad astringent at the end. * +

Vajra G. D., Vigneto Fossati (twice, 2/85, 1,760 bottles). Woodsy aroma suggestions of pine, resin and peppermint; soft-centered and supple, still some tannin, peppermint flavor, also on the finish. **(+)

Vietti, Castiglione Falletto (3 times, 11/85). Characteristic aroma; soft and flavorful, very ready now, has character, medium body. ** +

Vietti, Rocche (12 times, 5/86). Lovely rich bouquet suggestive of tobacco, and *tartufi* notes; soft and smooth, light tannin, ready now, will improve, fairly long. ***

1978 ***

This vintage produced highly regarded wines from a very small crop of ripe, mature grapes. The crop size, at 836,879 gallons (31,676 hectoliters), equivalent to 4.2 million bottles, was 50.8 percent of the quantity allowed by law. This compares with the 1.1 million-gallon (41,979-hectoliter) average between 1967 and 1989, with a production that was 74.3 percent of the amount allowed by law. The yield was 304 gallons per acre (28.5 hectoliters per hectare). Only 1977 and 1976 produced smaller crops in the decade. It's also worth comparing this with the yields of the other first-rate vintages: 1971, 517 gallons per acre (48.3 hectoliters per hectare); 1982, 506 (47.4); 1985, 463 (43.3); 1988, 457 (42.7); and 1989, 347 (32.5).

These richly concentrated, fairly high-acid, high-tannin wines should be long-lived. At one time many authorities regarded '78 as equal to or even better than '71. Today this is rarely the case. Very few producers put it on the same level as '71, '82, '85, or '89. The Ceretto brothers are one exception; they consider their '78s even better than their '71s. Aldo Conterno considers it the equal or nearly the equal of 1971, and similar in quality to 1982. Bruno Giacosa said they are grand wines that might equal the '71s but will not be as long-lived. Bartolo Mascarello said '71 is clearly the better vintage. Renato Ratti regards them as fabulous, grand wines on a par with '82, both being wines to lay down. Pio Boffa describes them as bigger than the '74s but with less intensity than the '71s. According to Alfredo Currado, these wines are still closed; they need at least five or six more years to really show their quality. Giuseppe Rinaldi rates the vintage highly, but behind 1985 and 1982. Gio-

vanni Conterno said that in weight and depth of flavor they are in between '71 and '82. He produced a Monfortino, and Aldo Conterno produced a Granbussia.

We disagree with those who rate 1978 at four stars. We have tasted some 110 wines from nearly seven dozen producers. Many of these wines need further age; a lot of unresolved tannin remains. It was the second best vintage of the decade, but not as good as the best vintages of the 1980s: 1989, 1985, or 1982. There is no question, though, that the best wines merit four stars, or will, when they reach maturity. One question for some of the wines: is there sufficient fruit to outlast the tannin? For the best, the answer is yes. For many others, although we have serious doubts, only time will tell.

The Vietti Rocche is marvelous, as is the Giacomo Conterno Monfortino. Also first flight when we last tasted them in the mid-1980s are Bruno Giacosa Collina Rionda, "Bricco Rocche" Brunate, Francesco Rinaldi, Giuseppe Rinaldi Brunate, and Scarpa Le Coste. We should also mention "Bricco Rocche" Prapò, Bruno Giacosa Rocche and Villero, Prunotto Bussia and Cannubi, and Tenuta Carretta Cannubi.

Accademia Torregiorgi, Arnulfo (2/85). Nose somewhat closed with a suggestion of tobacco; moderate tannin, fairly well balanced, more open on palate than on nose, a softer, gentler style with a firm tannic vein, not ready but beginning to open, finish is still tannic. **

Ascheri Giacomo, Riserva (twice, 4/85). Characteristic aroma, vague *tartufi* note; heaps of tannin, seems to have sufficient fruit to support it, time will tell. *

Barale F.lli (6/85). Mineral aroma has suggestions of tobacco and tea as well as a vague cherrylike note; still has considerable tannin, some astringency from the tannin and somewhat high acid, the fruit is there however, quite young; although this bottle seems to be off. *(*)

Barale F.lli, Castellero Riserva (twice, 10/85). Lovely aroma, vague cherry and tobacco notes; some tannin, fairly soft in the center, a bit firm; approachable now. **(+)

Bel Colle (twice, 10/85). Atypical, nothing to it.

Bel Colle, Riserva Speciale (10/85). Some oxidation, unbalanced, poorly made.

Bersano, Riserva Speciale (5/84). Fruity aroma has a sense of oak; lacks depth, rather simple, softer, gentler style; drinkable now, more like a nebbiolo than a Barolo.

Borgogno F.lli Serio e Battista, Riserva Speciale (11/84). Big nose, rich fruit suggestive of blackberries, some alcohol intrudes; rich fruit in mouth, less tannin than expected, balanced, needs a few years but almost drinkable now, finishes short with some alcohol. *(+)

Borgogno F.lli Serio e Battista, Vigna Cannubi Riserva Speciale (3 times, 7/87). Lovely bouquet; showing nicely now, balanced, rich flavor. *** −

Borgogno Giacomo, Riserva (*3 times, 10/85*). Characteristic tar, overly tannic, hot and alcohol, where will it go? *Bottle of 1/85:* Characteristic aroma with a note of *tartufi*, marred by some volatile acidity; a nice wine that lacks the intensity of the vintage, moderate tannin, fairly nice fruit, still undeveloped, some potential, tannic finish. *(+)

Boschis Francesco, Riserva (*4/87*). Oxidized, uninteresting.

"Bricco Rocche" Azienda Agricola (Ceretto), Brunate (*6 times, 1/85, 10,846 bottles*). Aroma has an intensity of ripe fruit, deep and profound; enormous richness, exceptional balance; not ready but tempting. ***(*)

"Bricco Rocche" Azienda Agricola (Ceretto), Prapò (*3 times, 1/85*). Bouquet seems somewhat closed but has the richness of ripe fruit; fairly tannic but the fruit is evident right across the palate, very long finish; young but tempting—resist. ***(+)

Brovia F.lli (*ex-vat, 6/82*). Nice nose with hints of oak and mushroom; moderate intensity, some alcohol evident (14.7%), quite tannic, unstructured, seems to be losing its fruit; not a success.

Burlotto Comm. G. B. (*twice, 4/86*). Reticent aroma; tannic grip, the fruit is sufficient to carry it; needs three to four more years yet. **(+)

Burlotto Comm. G. B. e Cav. Francesco di Burlotto Marina, Riserva (*3/87*). Reticent aroma, fruit closed in; gobs of tannin, the fruit is there. *(*+)

Canale Aldo, Riunda (*4/86*). Rich aroma, tar component; hard and tannic, with a rich core of fruit, needs many years yet, a vague sweetness at the end. **(*−)

Cantina Mascarello (*11/84*). Beautiful robe, garnet with orange reflections; expansive bouquet rises from the glass and fills the room; enormous fruit and concentration, exudes style and elegance, exceptional quality, if this isn't the wine of the vintage it certainly comes close, a wine of meditation, of contemplation. ****

Cantine Bava (*10/85*). Oxidized, dried out.

Cantine Duca d'Asti (Chiarlo Michele), "Granduca" Riserva Speciale (*3 times, 9/86*). A fair amount of fruit on the nose as well as a trace of oxidation, interesting caramellike note and vanilla nuance; fairly nice structure, tannin quite evolved and soft, nice flavor on entry, lacks follow-through and length. * +

Cappellano Dott. Giuseppe (*twice, 10/85*). Camphorlike aroma; still firm and tannic, balanced and flavorful, firm; young. **(+)

Carnevale Giorgio (*10/85*). Mineral aroma; low fruit, high acid. ?

Cascina Bruni di Veglio Pasqual, Vigneto di Sorì (*1/85, 5,200 bottles*). Nebbiolo character and fruit evident on nose, which is still somewhat closed; moderate tannin, nice fruit, fairly forward and surprisingly soft. *

Casetta F.lli (*3 times, 10/85*). Small-scale, old-style, correct, unexciting.

Cauda Luigi (*1/85*). Very reminiscent of a southern wine in aroma, structure and flavor.

Cavallotto F.lli, Vigna Bricco Boschis-Colle Sud-Ovest (*twice, 1/85*). Lovely aroma, fairly rich with suggestions of strawberries and blackberries; quite tannic but with the fruit to support it, will need some time to be ready but should make a good bottle in time. *(*)

Cavallotto F.lli, Vigna Bricco Boschis-San Giuseppe (*6/82*). Fairly rich aroma still somewhat closed, has a hint of mushrooms; rich and full of flavor as well as tannin; young but with potential evident. **(+)

Ceretto, Zonchetta (*4 times, 12/87*). Intense bouquet of tar and the woods; still has a firmness, rich and intense in flavor; approachable, still room to grow. **(+)

Colla Paolo, della Serra (*4/85*). Some oxidation, a lot of tannin, deficient in fruit.

Conterno Aldo, Bussia Soprana (*3/83*). Enormous richness on nose; richly concentrated with a lot of weight and extract, impressive quality; resist the temptation until 1986 or 1987 at least. ***(*)

Conterno Giacomo, Monfortino Riserva Speciale (*3 times, 10/87*). Complex bouquet of camphor, tobacco, berries and mushroom; enormous in all its components, great extract, concentration and weight, chewy, a mouthful of flavor, packed with quality, very long and very young. ***+ (****)

Contratto, Riserva (*3 times, 6/86*). Lovely and characteristic Barolo aroma, tar and fruit; moderate tannin, soft with nice fruit flavor, attractive now, although there is still a firmness; give it another two or three years. **(+)

Cordero di Montezemolo (*ex-cask, 10/80*). Fruity aroma; a forward rush of ripe fruit gives way to light tannin, well balanced; should be a fine bottle in three or four years. **(*)

Damilano Dott. Giacomo (*4/87*). Almost candylike aroma; on the light side, *tartufi* nuance, light and fruity, some tannin. *

Dogliani F.lli, Riserva Speciale (*9/87*). Tobacco, vaguely cherrylike aroma; soft, overripe, coarse.

Dosio, Riserva Speciale (*4 times, 10/85*). Small-scale, light tannin, not much character.

Fenocchio Giacomo, Vigna Munie Bussia Riserva (*4/86, 2,400 bottles*). Brick red color; warm, fairly intense aroma, recalls some kind of root, quinine; similar taste, sufficient fruit to carry the tannin; not up to the vintage; can use a few more years to really soften. (*)

Ferrero F.lli Giovanni e Renato (*4/87*). Richly fruited aroma, tar and small fruit; rich flavor, tannic, a lot of structure; very young, with evident potential, chewy, tannin and fruit indicate long life ahead. **(*)

Fontanafredda (*twice, 6/90*). Seaweedy aroma; a little hard and firm, soft center; say two years. *

Fontanafredda, Vigna Gattinera Riserva Speciale (3 *times*, *12/86*). Big, old-style Barolo, camphor, tar and tobacco; big and full-bodied, still young, the balance and stuffing indicate it will age well. **(*)

Fontanafredda, Vigna La Delizia (12/83). Richly fruited aroma; fairly forward and soft, though tannin still there; quality evident. **(+)

Fontanafredda, Vigna La Rosa (3 *times*, 4/86). Classic Barolo aroma, tobacco and tar; moderate tannin, lots of flavor; more forward than expected but still needs age. **(+)

Fontanafredda, Vigna Lazzarito (*twice*, 1/85). Richly fruited aroma with touches of camphor, mushrooms and *tartufi*; quite tannic and firm, a lot of nice fruit; needs time to soften and develop, quality evident. **(+)

Fontanafredda, Vigna San Pietro Riserva Speciale (9/86). Tar and fruit aroma; fairly tannic, nice fruit and balanced, lots of flavor; nice now with room for improvement. **(+)

Franco Fiorina (5 *times*, 10/85). Lovely nose; almost sweet, firm structure, tannic finish. **(+)

Gemma (*twice*, 4/85). Nice fruit on the nose; some tannin and firmness, flavorful, a bit light at the end. *(+)

Giacosa Bruno, Collina Rionda Riserva Speciale (6 *times*, 4/87, *6,450 bottles*). Fabulous bouquet of flowers, cherries, small fruit and nuts; silky smooth, exceptional balance, velvety texture, very long; young but so appealing due to its richness and concentration. ***(*)

Giacosa Bruno, Rocche (9/86). Woodslike bouquet, tobacco aroma; big and rich, ripe; still very young, loads of potential. ***(+)

Giacosa Bruno, Villero Riserva Speciale (4/86). Deep and intense bouquet, cherries, tobacco and tar; enormous fruit, superb; very young with evident potential. ** + (*** +)

Giacosa F.lli (4 *times*, 10/85). Typical tar and tobacco aroma; light tannin, some firmness, has fruit, short, tannic finish, tannin builds. *(*)

Grasso, Vigna Gavarini-Rüncot (*twice*, 2/85, *3,000 bottles*). Fairly rich and intense aroma of ripe fruit with notes of camphor and tobacco; well balanced, light tannin; more elegant than powerful; tempting now but will certainly improve, well structured. **(*)

Grasso, Vigna Gavarini-Rüncot Riserva Speciale (2/86). Cherry and floral bouquet, touch of grape pips and tobacco; almost sweet; gentle nature. ***

Grimaldi Cav. Carlo e Mario, Azienda Agricola "Groppone" Riserva Speciale (*twice*, 4/87, *4,500 bottles*). Old nose; fairly tannic, harsh even astringent, some varietal character.

Le Due Torri, Riserva (4/88). Characteristic Barolo nose, tar up front then some fruit; some tannin on entry, could use more weight and structure, more character and flavor.

Lodali Eredi di Ghione (10/85). Mineral aroma; light tannin, some firmness, moderate fruit, short, mineral notes, southern slant, tannic finish. * −

Lodali Eredi di Ghione, Vigneto Bric Sant'Ambrogio (10/85, *7,320 bottles*). Southern slant, chocolate component, some tannin, soft center, low acid. * −

Marcarini (Elvio Cogno), Brunate (*ex-cask*, 10/81, *the last cask, all the rest has been bottled*). Expansive aroma recalling raspberries and mushrooms; well structured, has style, balance, flavor and elegance; very well made, classic, impressive. ***(*)

Marchesi di Barolo, Riserva (6 *times*, 11/89). Old-style, tar and vanilla aroma; dry, some firmness, could use more weight; small-scale. * −

Marchesi di Barolo, Riserva Speciale della Casa (12/88). Stinky; some fruit, fairly tannic.

Marchesi di Barolo, Vigna Cannubi Riserva (10/82, *8,450 bottles*). Fairly rich but somewhat reticent aroma vaguely reminiscent of tea; has a sweetness to it; still needs further age but surprisingly forward, although very good it doesn't live up to either the vintage or the vineyard. ** −

Mascarello Giuseppe, Monprivato (*ex-cask*, 6/82). Fairly rich nose suggestive of mushrooms and *tartufi*; full-bodied, with richness and concentration, well balanced, has a lot of tannin but not apparent at first because of the enormous amount of fruit. **(*)

Massolino Giuseppe, Riserva (4/90). Slight nose, hint of fruit and tobacco; still fairly tannic, evident fruit; needs time. * +

Massolino Giuseppe, Vigna Rionda (3 *times*, 4/89). Closed nose, some fruit and tobacco evident; open palate, simple flavor, short and dry ending. *

Oddero F.lli (6 *times*, 10/85). There was noticeable bottle variation. Aroma suggestive of wheat and oats(!); seems overly soft and lacking some style, cherry notes. * + *Bottle of 5/85:* Nose somewhat ungiving though with a tobacco and tarry aspect; fairly tannic but with the fruit to support it, seems almost sweet, somewhat astringent at the end, has quality; give it four to five more years. **(+)

Oddero Luigi (4/85). Lacking in flavor, structure and character.

Ornato Paolo, Rocche (*ex-cask*, 10/81). Very deep color; aroma is rich and concentrated; balanced with considerable flavor and tannin, medium length. * +

Osvaldo Mauro (10/85). Ugh!

Palladino, S. Bernardo Riserva (5/85). Some firmness, moderate tannin, needs some age but potential evident. *(* −)

Palladino, Vigna Riunda (*twice*, 10/85). Some tannin remains but could be drunk in a pinch, soft center. * +

Pavese Livio (1/85). Ripe fruit aroma, some tannin, a lighter, softer style of Barolo that is simple and quite accessible, forward and ready though it might improve somewhat. (*)

Pio Cesare, Riserva (5 *times*, 9/86). Seems closed and hard, even a bit austere, storage? *Bottle of 3/85:* Aroma somewhat reticent, oak, licorice and a hint of chocolate; rich, ripe fruit, moderate tannin; needs a few years but already shows a roundness and smoothness of texture, probably from the *barrique.* **(*)

Pira E. (*4 times, 6/90*). Has fruit, small-scale, best to drink. * The wine tasted from cask in October 1979 had a rich, expansive aroma and exceptional balance with raspberries on the aroma and palate, at the time we expected a lot but. . . .

Podere Anselma, Riserva Speciale (*4/87*). Dank, tarry aroma; unbalanced, harsh and tannic, low fruit.

Podere Rocche dei Manzoni (Valentino), Riserva (*4 times, 9/86*). Tar and leather aroma, woodslike component; nice entry, gives way to tannin, seems to have sufficient fruit, somewhat on the light side, lacks intensity of the year. *(*)

Prunotto, Bussia Riserva (*5 times, 11/90, 12,525 bottles*). Tobacco and tar aroma; a little dry, high acid, very short. * *Bottle of 5/86:* A classic Barolo, fairly tannic, lots of character. ***(+)

Prunotto, Cannubi (*twice, 1/85, 6,195 bottles*). Lovely aroma still somewhat reticent; on the palate gives an initial impression of sweet, ripe fruit that gives way to a lot of tannin; might be ready before the Bussia, but give it also until 1988 or 1989. ***(+)

Prunotto, Ginestra (*twice, 10/83*). Reticent aroma; balanced, firm, a bit rough but a lot of fruit as well as tannin; probably will mature the slowest of the three crus. *(**)

Prunotto, Riserva (*10/86*). Surprising in that it lacks richness and concentration, dull, an off bottle perhaps?

Ratti Renato, Marcenasco (*magnum, 1/85*). Aroma still closed somewhat but has hints of cherries, tobacco, and grape pips; very well balanced with some tannin and a load of fruit; nearly ready but hold off until 1988 or 1989. **(*)

Rinaldi Francesco (*twice, 11/85*). Very deep color; richly fruited aroma, tar and tobacco, floral notes; soft center, moderate tannin, very long, still young, but its style and elegance are apparent; a gentler, more elegant style of Barolo; tempting now but like many other fine wines of this vintage, best held. ***(*)

Rinaldi Giuseppe (*twice, magnum, 11/84*). Richly intense and concentrated bouquet suggests cassis; enormous core of fruit beneath a tannic structure, seems more forward at first due to the rich, sweet mouth-filling fruit; a classic Barolo that needs time and will surely be worth the wait. ***(*)

Rinaldi Giuseppe, Brunate (*9/86*). Lovely woodslike bouquet, berry notes, rich and expansive; lush flavor, chocolate notes, quite young, very good. ***(*)

Rocche Costamagna, Vigna Riccardo Riserva Speciale (*twice, 3/86, 2,000 bottles*). Aroma displays notes of ripe fruit and tobacco, cherry note; firm acid, medium body, good fruit, still young but quite nice. ** +

Roche Azienda Vinicola, Riserva Speciale (*3 times, 4/89*). Interesting nose, dried fruit; fairly tannic; unimpressive.

Rosso Gigi, Vigneti della Cascina Arione (*twice, 2/85*). Vaguely floral, ripe fruit aroma recalls blackberries and a hint of tar; me-dium body, light to moderate tannin, nice flavor; could improve but drinkable enough now. * +

Sandrone Francesco, Vigna Cannubi (*4/86*). Lovely perfumed bouquet, woodslike overtone, floral notes; sweet and elegant, round, seems ready, it's not even though it's quite attractive, long, refined and stylish. ***

Scarpa, Le Coste (*3 times, 4/86, 15,703 bottles*). Rich, deep and intense bouquet; firm with a richness and depth of flavor, with an underlying hardness, velvety texture; needs perhaps three to four years. ***(*)

Scavino Alfonso, della Punta (*10/81*). Reticent aroma offers some fruit and a touch of tar; medium body, has a fair amount of tannin, the fruit is evident; should be ready early, say about 1984 or 1985. *(*)

Scavino Paolo, Bric del Fiasc Riserva (*4 times, 5/87, 2,360 bottles*). Quite a nice nose, characteristic tar, vaguely floral, yet seems older than its years, not old though; still has tannin, beginning to soften and round out; still needs further age; could use more style. *(*)

Seghesio Renzo (*4 times, 4/85*). Has tannin and some fruit but somewhat shallow and unbalanced; not a success though not offensive either.

Sobrero Filippo (*twice, 11/85*). Oxidized, rubber tire, volatile acidity, dried out, the bottle perhaps? *Bottle of 5/84:* Color is black(!); bouquet has a richness and intensity though still somewhat reticent; on the palate an incredible mouthful of refined fruit, exceptional balance; young and full-bodied but tempting now. ***(*)

Sordo Giovanni (*1/86*). Small nose; fairly tannic, moderate fruit, bitter finish, rough edges.

Tenuta Carretta, Podere Cannubi (*twice, 4/85, 7,260 bottles*). Intense aroma, tobacco, vaguely floral with notes of cherries and berries; very well balanced, masses of fruit and gobs of tannin; years from being ready but everything is there to make a splendid bottle; class already evident. ***(+)

Tenuta La Volta di Cabutto Bartolomeo (*1/85*). Aroma of berry-like fruit; light tannin, forward fruit, fairly well balanced, light and surprisingly ready for the vintage, simple, might make a nice luncheon wine. (*)

Tenuta Montanello, Riserva Speciale (*1/85*). Aroma still somewhat closed and undeveloped; ripe fruit seems almost sweet, moderate tannin, finishes with a hint of licorice and a buildup of tannin; give it, say, two to three more years. *(**)

Tenuta Montanello, Selezione (*4/90*). Nice nose, a lot of depth and complexity; drying in the mouth, is there enough fruit?

Vajra G. D. (*twice, 2/85*). Fairly deep color; intensely rich bouquet, vaguely floral; a lot of fruit but still firm; needs a few years yet but quality evident. **(+)

Veglio F.lli, Cascina Bruni, Carpegna (*4/86*). Some oxidation, also varnish; open, moderate tannin, good fruit; drinkable, should improve. **(+)

Vercelli Alessandro (4/89). Shot!

Vietti, Briacca (3 times, 6/82, 2,000 bottles). A shade deeper than the Rocche; delicate floral perfume; lively and richly flavored with superb balance and some elegance, at this point it seems a bit fuller than the Rocche! ***(*)

Vietti, Castiglione Falletto Riserva (4/86). Licorice, cherry and tobacco aroma; rich fruit, has style and balance, firm, tannic finish. **(*)

Vietti, Rocche (14 times, 2/90, 7,200 bottles). Great richness and concentration, complex bouquet suggestive of the woods, mint, camphor, leather, berries and truffles; chewy and firm, packed with flavor, good backbone, long, room to improve, but attractive now. **** – *Bottle of 2/85:* Dense color; bouquet reveals an enormous richness and fragrance with hints of licorice, flowers, tea, tobacco and cherries; incredible concentration of rich, ripe fruit, so well balanced that the tannin hardly seems evident at first; very young but even now a wine of meditation. ***(*)

Villadoria Marchese, Riserva Speciale (4 times, 9/86). A big zero!

Vinicola Piemontese, Cerequio (twice, 10/85). Camphor and vague tar aroma; firm and flavorful, moderate tannin; has potential. **(+)

Zunino Basilio, Sorì di Baudana (twice, 4/86). Rich nose; rich palate, quite tannic, lots of structure; in the old style. **(+)

1977 0

Only 1972 was worse in the decade. There was a lot of rain throughout the growing season of 1977. The vintage yielded an average of 292 gallons per acre (27.3 hectoliters per hectare), for a total of 786,629 gallons (29,774 hectoliters) of nebbiolo for Barolo, equivalent to nearly 4 million bottles. This was 48.7 percent of what the DOC allows and the fourth smallest yield between the advent of DOC in 1967 and 1989. This compares with the average crop in that same period of 1.1 million gallons (41,979 hectoliters), or 74.3 percent of the maximum allowed. And because many producers declassified all or part of their nebbiolo, the actual amount of Barolo produced was considerably less than the amount declared.

Numerous producers didn't bottle a Barolo, choosing to sell it as Nebbiolo delle Langhe or *sfuso* instead. Bartolo Mascarello declassified his entire nebbiolo crop to Nebbiolo delle Langhe. Alfredo Currado didn't produce a Barolo in '77, nor did "Rocche" Costamagna, Marchese Fracassi, or Aldo Conterno. Giovanni Conterno said the vintage was so bad that he didn't even pick his grapes. Luciano Rinaldi rates it as among the worst ever. The best wines were at one time, however, fairly good if not special. The Ceretto brothers selected carefully and managed to produce 6,500 bottles of Prapò sometimes labeled Prapò-Riccardo I (instead of the

usual 13,000 to 15,000). We found it quite nice when last tasted in November 1984. In fact, it was surprisingly good—without question, the Barolo of the vintage. We suspect that it has faded by now.

Although we've tasted only seven '77 Barolos in the past decade, we can confidently say they should have been drunk up years ago. Overall, we give the vintage a rating of zero today. If there are any bottles left, they have almost certainly faded.

Ascheri Giacomo (10/82). Light to pale color; some volatile acidity, light-bodied, some flavor.

"Bricco Rocche" Azienda Agricola (Ceretto), Prapò, or Prapò-Riccardo I (the same wine with two different labels) (6 times, 11/84 at the winery, 6,376 bottles). Bouquet of leather, berries, cherries, underbrush and tobacco; still some tannin over a nicely fruited core, a bit light in body; very good indeed; no need to hold it any longer. **

Cantine Duca d'Asti (Chiarlo Michele), "Granduca" (3/83). Pale garnet; some fruit evident on the nose and palate, but has harsh edges; drinkable, but so what?

Ceretto, Zonchetta (4 times, 3/83, 14,587 bottles). Light to pale garnet; light nose with moderate fruit marred by some alcohol; light-bodied, fairly nice on palate although some roughness, not to keep, some signs of drying out on the finish. * –

Cordero di Montezemolo, Monfalletto (3/83). Nice nose; has a surprising richness but then seems overly tannic; in all, not a bad bottle and certainly a success. * –

Franco Fiorina (3/83). Pale brick color; aroma recalls wheat and toast; moderate to light fruit, some tannin, nice flavors; not to keep, but a nice, drinkable luncheon wine. * –

Ratti Renato (twice, 2/85). Light tawny toward onionskin; characteristic Barolo aroma of tar and flowers, lot of flavor, some alcohol intrudes; fading fast, was better in early 1983 when it merited * –.

Sandrone Francesco, Zona Cannubi (10/81). Aroma has hints of kirsch and tar; a little light, some tannin, fairly nice fruit; not bad for the year. *

1976 0

The total yield of 752,864 gallons (28,496 hectoliters), equivalent to 3.8 million bottles, was one of the smallest crops between 1967 and 1989. The crop size was 47.8 percent of the amount allowed by law; only 1986 and 1984 were smaller. The yield per acre (hectare) at 286 gallons (26.8 hectoliters) was below the 1970s average of 431 (40.3).

The one strong point of the 1976 vintage is perhaps its position between 1975 and 1977; it stands out as the best of this trio of mediocre vintages. Bartolo Mascarello describes the wines as rather similar to those of 1973. Renato Ratti said the wines ranged from so-so to medium. Giuseppe Rinaldi and Marchese Fracassi produced very little Barolo and Giovanni Conterno produced no wine of any kind. Very few wines amounted to much. The wines from Elvio Cogno of Podere Marcarini, Paolo Cordero di Montezemolo, Aldo Conterno, and Renato Ratti were quite interesting at one time.

The wines for the most part should've already been drunk up. It is doubtful if any that might remain hold any interest. We give the vintage zero.

Ascheri Giacomo (*10/82*). Pale garnet; volatile acidity mars the bouquet; better on the palate, though lacks structure and flavor; drying out.

Brovia F.lli, Vigneti di Rocche (*twice, 11/80*). Perfumed bouquet; some tannin but the fruit seems sufficient for it; very good for the vintage. * −

Casetta F.lli (*10/82*). Pale; light nose and palate, not much to it though drinkable.

Cavallotto F.lli, Vigna Bricco Boschis (*5 times, 6/82*). A bit closed, seems overly tannic, not a lot of fruit, some dullness. It was better in cask and should've been bottled sooner.

Conterno Aldo, Bricco Bussia Vigna Colonello (*4/81, 4,970 bottles*). Nice nose; some tannin, well balanced, a lot of flavor. ** −

Contratto, Riserva (*twice, 6/85*). Fragrant, perfumed bouquet, woodsy, tobacco nuances; shows age on the palate, still has flavor but beginning to dry out. * +

Cordero di Montezemolo, Enrico VI-Villero (*12/80*). Good color; aroma is somewhat subdued; soft, nice fruit, fairly well balanced, some style. **

Cordero di Montezemolo, Monfalletto (*3 times, 3/83*). Medum garnet, orange rim; nose yields up hints of cherries, flowers, tar and Barolo character, some refinement; a lot of flavor, well made; very nice now, not to keep. **

Fenocchio Giacomo (*4/80*). Some alcohol intrudes on aroma; rather light, lots of fruit, some tannin, perhaps too much, harsh finish. * −

Marcarini (Elvio Cogno), Brunate (*2/82*). Bouquet of almonds and fruit, also has a touch of *tartufi*; moderately intense, soft and fruity with kirschlike notes, some style, medium length. **

Morando, Riserva (*twice, 2/83 and 3/83*). Very pale color; one bottle had some volatile acidity, the other noticeable oxidation. In all, a dull wine with no future and little or no interest.

Osvaldo Mauro (*4/80*). A big zero, atypical Barolo.

Prunotto, Bussia (*3/83*). Pale; some oxidation and some fruit on aroma; overly tannic, lacks structure and weight but not bad with food.

Prunotto, Bussia Riserva (*10/86*). Mineral, earthy aroma; some fruit but not a lot of trace or depth, simple. +

Ratti Renato (*7 times, 6/85*). Moderate garnet, orange rim; complex aroma of tobacco and tea, fruit and tar; camphor, wood and chamomile on palate, still some tannin, light; still good though starting to fade. *

Roche Azienda Vinicola (*11/80*). Odd aroma; high in tannin, moderate fruit, high acid, in short, unbalanced and light.

Tenuta Montanello (*4/90*). Drying out, no need to say more.

Veglio Angelo (*4/80*). Aroma suggestive of corn; fairly soft, some tannin and fruit; ready. * −

Voerzio Giacomo (*12/80*). Aroma is somewhat alcoholic; rather light and somewhat unbalanced, perhaps too much tannin for the fruit, but drinkable enough.

1975 0

Hail took its toll in some vineyards, reducing the crop in some vineyards by 50 percent or more. The overall nebbiolo crop of 997,751 gallons (37,765 hectoliters) was equivalent to just over 5 million bottles of Barolo. This was 62.6 percent of the amount allowed by the DOC—375 gallons per acre (35 hectoliters per hectare) compared to 599 (56)—and the sixth smallest in yield per acre between 1967 and 1989. And not all of that nebbiolo was bottled as Barolo.

Renato Ratti said the vintage was better even than 1976 or 1977, as did Bartolo Mascarello, who also found it superior to 1973. Alfredo Currado said the wines were not especially good, medium quality perhaps. Marchese Fracassi and Giovanni Conterno, once again, didn't produce a Barolo. Cavallotto, on the other hand, said the wines were good for them. Very few wines amounted to much—Pira and Ratti were two notable exceptions.

We found the wines light and fairly forward, wines that at their best offered pleasant drinking, but not serious wines. For the most part, they should've been drunk up a few years ago. Any still remaining are of questionable value.

Brezza Giacomo (*10/79*). Color shows age; alcohol and volatile acidity evident on aroma; nice entry but shallow, short and alcoholic aftertaste.

Brovia F.lli (*11/80*). Some fruit on nose and palate, somewhat deficient in flavor, a surprising amount of tannin.

Cantine Duca d'Asti (Chiarlo Michele), "Granduca" Riserva (*twice, 12/81 and 2/83*). One bottle was shot, the other, surprisingly drinkable though with an odd nose; quite soft and lacked some character.

Cavallotto F.lli, Vigna Bricco Boschis Riserva Speciale (*5 times, 10/81*). Medium brick red; fairly nice nose, fruity; fairly soft, not at all bad. Some bottles showed noticeable oxidation from overlong wood aging, but the best bottles deserve one star.

Ceretto, Zonchetta (*10/79*). Aroma has some oak and nice fruit; considerable tannin for the fruit, somewhat shallow, short, somewhat alcoholic aftertaste.

Colla Paolo (4/80). Lacks aroma, body substance and distinction, has tannin and moderate flavor.

Fontanafredda (twice, 3/83 and 5/83). One bottle was soft and smooth, quite nice for the vintage *, the other suffered from some oxidation and was unbalanced with tannin.

Gemma (3 times, 3/85). Characteristic tar and floral aroma; vague mushroomlike note, overly tannic on entry, fruit in the center, surprisingly still good. * −

Molino Guido (4/80). Aroma has tarry notes on an alcoholic background; has tannin but insufficient fruit, some alcohol mars the finish.

Pira E. (Luigi Pira) (6 times, 5/87). Age beginning to set in but still surprisingly tasty and good after all these years of a mediocre vintage, character bouquet reveals a refined nature, soft and smooth, thins out a little at the end. ** *Bottle of 2/85:* Dark brickish robe; expansive perfumed bouquet; soft, round and very smooth, has tannin that shows more on the finish; still very good but approaching the end of its useful life. ** +

Ratti Renato, Marcenasco (twice, 11/83). Lovely bouquet suggestive of tobacco, cherries, *tartufi* and vaguely of cassis; soft and round, still some tannin, very ready. **

Tenuta La Volta di Cabutto Bartolomeo (twice, 4/80). Oxidized—both times.

Tenuta Montanello (3/83). Some oxidation, lacking in fruit, harsh.

1974 ** −

The crop size of 1.4 million gallons (52,221 hectoliters), equivalent to nearly 7 million bottles, was the second largest of the 1970s in terms of both size and yield per acre (hectare). It was 87.8 percent of the amount allowed by law. The average yield was 526 gallons per acre (49.2 hectoliters per hectare) compared to the maximum allowed: 599 (56). It was surprisingly larger than 1973's 524 gallons per acre (49 hectoliters per hectare), a year generally said to have produced a crop that was too large.

Many experts and producers rate this vintage highly. Alfredo Currado puts it in the second rank after '71, '78, and the best vintages of the 1980s. Renato Ratti considers it very good to great. Bruno Giacosa places it in the top rank. Giovanni Conterno describes the wines as refined and masculine, while Pio Boffa said the '74s have less tannin and intensity than the '71s. Aldo Conterno produced a Granbussia and Giacomo Conterno a Monfortino.

We've tasted more than six dozen different wines from some 55 producers over the past decade, most in the mid-1980s. Today too many received no marks, and very few rate three stars or more. Most seem ready now and we doubt that any will benefit from further age. The best were still

very good and should continue to hold, but many are starting to fade or have already faded. Very few will improve.

We can recommend Giacomo Accomasso's Rocchette, Aldo Conterno's "Granbussia" Bricco Colonello, Marcarini's Brunate, Renato Ratti's Marcenasco, Giuseppe Rinaldi's Brunate, and Vietti's Rocche. And although variable, Giacomo Conterno's Monfortino can be splendid.

In all, we find the vintage has not lived up to expectations, though without question a few splendid wines were made. Our overall opinion today is summed up by two stars minus.

Accomasso Giacomo, Annunziata Regione Rocchette (4/86). Beautiful warm, brick red color, orange reflections; bouquet suggestive of autumn leaves, hints of licorice and camphor; seems overly tannic, but it still has the sweetness of fruit, with a ripe core in the center, and nice texture; as good as it'll ever be. ** +

Ascheri Giacomo (twice, 10/82). Chocolate note on the aroma; seems overly tannic for the fruit, finishes on a harsh note.

Barale F.lli (6/82). Deep, rich, complex bouquet; palate almost sweet with ripe fruit, still has tannin to shed but quality and style evident; very good indeed. ***

Barale F.lli, Riserva (6/85). Warm nose, some seaweed in the background; high acid, a bit thin; past its best.

Borgogno F.lli Serio e Battista, Riserva Speciale (4 times, 10/87). Odd nose with a medicinal character; odd flavor as well, vegetallike, some nebbiolo fruit; ready; not much character. + *Two bottles were compared in 11/84:* One bottle had been transferred and filtered to remove the sediment, the other still had some. Along with the sediment, the flavor and character were also removed; the wine was shallow and short, offering very little interest. The other bottle, which contained some sediment, had a beautiful brick-orange robe and a fairly rich bouquet, it had tannin and fruit and some character though marred by an alcoholic finish. *

Borgogno F.lli Serio e Battista, Vigna Cannubi Riserva Speciale (3/85). Characteristic nebbiolo aroma; flavorful, tails off toward the finish; ready now. * +

Borgogno Giacomo, Riserva (3 times, 6/90). Old-style Barolo, tar combines with fruit on the nose; some tannin, tasty, chocolate and cherry notes, lovely now, short; best to drink. *

Bosca Luigi (2/80). Very poor—lacks body, flavor, structure and character, mercifully it has no finish either.

Brezza Giacomo (3 times, 4/80). Aroma rather closed though some fruit is evident, along with tealike notes; somewhat light but has fruit and tannin, could use more weight but drinkable, slightly bitter finish. * −

Burlotto, Riserva (4/80). Although the bottle we tasted was slightly corked the wine showed some quality, especially in the structure. Unfortunately we never had an opportunity to try another. **(?)

Cantine d'Invecchiamento, "La Brenta d'Oro" (11/78). Smallish nose; rather light-bodied but nice flavor on entry, shallow, finishes short and alcoholic.

Cantine Duca d'Asti (Chiarlo Michele), "Granduca" Riserva and Riserva Speciale (3 times, 9/86). *Riserva, 9/86:* Some oxidation evident, hint of wheat(!); old-style flavor, soft tannins; lacks real character or definition, drinkable enough. * *Riserva Speciale, 12/84:* Aroma rather light though characteristic with fruity overtones; light tannin, soft, round and fruity; lacks some weight but a drinkable, small-scale Barolo.

Cavallotto F.lli, Vigna Bricco Boschis Riserva Speciale (8 times, 12/83). Aroma recalls tar and varnish over cherrylike fruit; seems overly tannic and drying out though drinkable; the bottles from three years earlier were considerably better, in fact, they even seemed a bit too young.

Ceretto, Grignore (3/80). Expansive bouquet that's richly concentrated; lots of tannin and heaps of flavor; fine quality; still young but quality evident. **(*)

Ceretto, La Morra (1/82, 17,700 bottles). Fairly rich, intense aroma; quite tannic but with sufficient fruit in reserve; give it perhaps three years. **(*)

Ceretto, Zonchetta (1/85, 16,548 bottles and 2,100 magnums). Complex bouquet with lots of woodsy-type nuances; moderate tannin, fruit seems a bit shy but tasty enough; could even improve. *(*)

Colla Paolo (10/78). Lacks aroma; a lightweight little wine with some fruit and some tannin, but overall undistinguished and without character.

Conterno Aldo, "Granbussia" Vigna Bricco Cicala (3 times, 5/82, 5,382 bottles). Richly concentrated bouquet and palate, still has tannin to shed but a full-bodied Barolo that needs time though its splendid quality is apparent now. ***

Conterno Aldo, "Granbussia" Vigna Bricco Colonello (11/85, 5,727 bottles). Intense bouquet; still some tannin but soft and nicely fruited, very long; displays style. ***

Conterno Giacomo, Monfortino Riserva Speciale (7 times, 11/90). The most recent bottle was tasted at the winery. Animal fur and woodsy aroma, notes of camphor; a little tight but with nice fruit, firm and somewhat dry at the end; still seems young. *Bottle of 9/90:* We've tasted this wine seven times with a different impression on each occasion! The bottle of September 1990, tasted in the United States, was the best. Great intensity on the nose and palate, nuances suggestive of tobacco, cherry, berry and *tartufi*, sweet, open and rich; near its peak, and it is good too. *** + *Bottle of 4/89:* Old nose; fairly nice fruit, almost sweet, dry, firm aftertaste. * – *Bottle of 11/85:* Intense bouquet suggestive of camphor and tobacco; a mouthful of fruit and tannin, very well balanced, has a lot of weight and concentration, very long, tannic finish. **(*) *Bottle of 4/85:* Tarry aroma has a touch of oxidation; a mouthful of tannin, is there enough fruit? Difficult to say, hardly seems like the same wine tasted three months earlier, perhaps an off bottle! *Bottle of 1/85:* Intense bouquet with a hint of tobacco, and freshness of

fruit(!); a mouthful of tannin gives way to immense fruit and a hint of licorice, enormous richness but quite tannic, robust, finish is quite long; give it at least four to five years, it should be long-lived. **(* +) *Ex-cask, 11/84:* Aroma is fairly expansive with suggestions of flowers and chestnuts; tannic and firm, with a lot of fruit beneath; seems surprisingly young, with hints of better things to come. **(*)

Conterno Giacomo, Riserva (9/83). Full rich aroma, character of Barolo, with a cherrylike note; still tannic but with considerable substance, bitter cherrylike finish. **(*)

Contratto (8/81). Richly intense bouquet suggestive of tar and flowers; full-bodied, lot of flavor, still has tannin to shed. **(+)

DA.I.PI."CM," Cru Magaria Riserva Speciale (5/87). [Owned by Daniele Lanzavecchia, one of the owners of Villadoria.] Brick red color; light chocolate note adds interest to a wine that displays oxidation and age and very little else.

Damilano Dott. Giacomo (3/84). Ripe fruit aroma with a minty note; has tannin and good fruit but not a lot of Barolo character, finish is quite tannic. * –

Dellavalle F.lli (11/80). Color rather light, not much aroma; some tannin and fruit but lacks distinction and character, finishes on a bitter note.

Dosio, Riserva Speciale (3 times, 5/85). Characteristic Barolo aroma; moderate tannin, still has some fruit but beginning to dry out, overly tannic finish; drink up. *

Einaudi Luigi (twice, 10/83). Some volatile acidity mars the aroma; fairly tannic and fairly fruity; in all, a nice glass of Barolo. *(*)

Fenocchio Giacomo (11/80). Overly tannic, though it does have some fruit, oxidized, it could have been a good bottle.

Fenocchio Giacomo, Bussia Riserva (4/86). Warm brick-red robe, oxidized, still some fruit, fairly tannic; going, not gone. *

Fontanafredda (1/82). Aroma of tar and flowers; fairly rich, has tannin but the amount of fruit makes it enjoyable now, some harshness, tannin builds up at the end. *

Fontanafredda, Vigna La Rosa (5 times, 1/85). Nose offers more fruit than Lazzarito, also a touch of camphor and tar; fairly soft entry, some tannin but nearly ready, medium length. * +

Fontanafredda, Vigna Lazzarito (1/85). Tarry aroma recalls camphor, cheese and wood, vaguely seaweed; tannic entry, soft center over a tannic framework, has a lot of flavor but perhaps too tannic for the fruit. (*)

Franco Fiorina (twice, 4/82). Floral perfume with hints of tar and fruit; well balanced, moderate tannin, tasty; some style, well made. **

Giacosa Bruno, Vigna Rionda (twice, 11/80). Dark color; nose somewhat backward but displays a richness of fruit; exceptional balance with a lot of extract and flavor; quite young but especially fine quality. ***(+)

Marcarini (Elvio Cogno), Brunate (4 times, 1/84). Floral bouquet recalls tobacco and cherries; soft with a tannic vein, a shade astringent but still in all very good. An earlier bottle seemed to offer more depth of flavor without the astringency. ** +

Marchesi di Barolo (11/79). Hot alcoholic nose; light-bodied and unstructured with high acidity, lacks substance and weight, high in tannin, short.

Mascarello Giuseppe, Vignola (11/80). Some fruit on the nose; fairly tannic but with sufficient fruit in reserve to allow aging, aftertaste is long and tannic; give it, say, four to five more years (should be ready now). *(*)

Massolino Giuseppe, Vigna Rionda (10/81). Not well made, rather poor.

Oddero Luigi (4/85). Old, dull and dried out.

Oreste Stefano (1/85). Medium brick; aroma has suggestions of fruit and tar; some tannin on entry, nice fruit flavors; it could improve but there's not much reason to hold it much longer. *(+)

Osvaldo Mauro (11/79). The nose brings up southern wine(!); uncharacteristic Barolo, some tannin, but lacks weight and structure.

Palladino (11/79). Nose brings up aroma of burnt hair(!) but not unpleasantly so; rather nice in the mouth, still has tannin to shed, the finish recalls the unusual aroma. *

Pio Cesare (twice, 1/85). Aroma marred by some volatile acidity; on the palate a lot of tannin but appears to have sufficient fruit, though perhaps not, only real problem is the volatile acidity.

Pira E. (Chiara Boschis) [in an Albeisa bottle] (8 times, 3/88). Fragrant, still a lot of flavor under the tannin, rather nice, the best of the bottles (there was considerable variation; two bottles tasted in November 1987 were dried out and shot). ** + *Bottle of 9/84:* Rubber tire, volatile acidity and tar on the aroma; low in fruit, high in tannin, unbalanced, drinkable no more; questionable future.

Pira E. (Luigi Pira) (3 times, 11/80). Rich and intense on the aroma and palate, heaps of flavor and concentration, very well balanced, a lot of glycerine adds a smoothness and roundness to the wine, very long finish; young but tempting, resist, it still needs time for the tannin to resolve itself, this Barolo displays a lot of style and class. ***(*)

Podere Anselma, Riserva Speciale (4/87). Coarse, unbalanced, overly tannic, low fruit.

Prunotto, San Casciano Riserva (twice, 1/83). Color showing age at rim; bouquet rather dull; astringent and quite tannic, does it have sufficient fruit? Seems to. *(?)

Prunotto, Vigneto Bussia Riserva (1/85, 11,015 bottles). Alcohol all too evident on nose, along with a vague trufflelike note; still a lot of tannin, some volatile acidity but also a lot of fruit—where will it go? ?*

Ratti Renato, Marcenasco (4 times, 3/85). Lovely bouquet suggestive of fruit, tobacco, flowers and *tartufi*; very well balanced, still

some tannin but soft and supple; near its peak; a lot of character. ***

Rinaldi Giuseppe (5 times, 4/87). Complex bouquet reveals nuances of cassis and spice, has a hint of sage; soft though still has some tannin, quite ready with a softness in the center, richly flavored. *** *Bottle of 5/82:* Bouquet of raspberries, cassis and alfalfa; incredible concentration of ripe fruit, has balance, length and style; still room for improvement but superb now. ***(+)

Rinaldi Giuseppe, Brunate (9/86). Classic Barolo bouquet, woodslike; light tannin, soft and smooth, tasty, elegant, almost sweet, long finish. ***

Saffirio F.lli Enrico e Giacomo (4/85). Tar and rubber tire aroma, seaweedy; awful.

Scarzello Giovanni, Cascina Mosconi (10/81). Fairly deep color; richly intense bouquet, well balanced with a lot of fruit and a kirschlike note at the end, which is a bit short; still in all, a good bottle. *(*)

Scavino Alfonso (1/84). Deep color; characteristic aroma; lots of fruit, light tannin, quite ready, medium length. **

Seghesio Renzo (10/81). Aroma of fruit and tar; moderate fruit though somewhat shallow, faintly bitter; undistinguished.

Sobrero Filippo (4/81). Bouquet of tar and flowers with overtones of leather; has tannin but also heaps of flavor, fairly long finish that's overly drying; a very good Barolo overall. **(*)

Stroppiana Oreste (twice, 10/90). Tar and old-style Barolo aroma; some oxidation, yet the flavor is still attractive; best to drink up; seaweed character; still in all, not bad. * +

Tenuta Carretta, Vigna Cannubi (twice, 4/80). Perfumed bouquet; well balanced, some elegance, a lot of flavor; nearly ready. ***(+)

Tenuta La Volta di Cabutto Bartolomeo, Riserva (twice, 1/85). The more recent bottle was far superior to that of April 1980. An aroma of truffles, tobacco, tar and fruit marred by a slight touch of oxidation; light to moderate tannin, good fruit, fairly well balanced; very drinkable though lacks some weight. ** −

Tenuta Montanello (twice, 4/90). Old-style Barolo, fading fast. *Bottle of 5/83:* Aroma recalls oats and wheat; still some tannin, nice fruit; more or less ready. *

Terre del Barolo, Riserva and Riserva Speciale (7 times, 4/80). *Riserva* (3 times): Cheesy aroma with a background of seaweed; softer and more ready than the Riserva Speciale, with good body and a moderately long finish that is marred by some alcohol. * *Riserva Speciale* (4 times): Nose shows some development with considerable fruit and a note of vanilla; still has tannin to shed which is beginning to soften and a surprising amount of fruit, some length and some style. **

Terre del Barolo, Vigna Brunate, Riserva and Riserva Speciale (6 times, 12/80). *Riserva:* Tarlike aroma has a hint of seaweed; flavorful, considerable tannin, the best of the three *riserve.* ** +

Riserva Speciale: Some alcohol lurks beneath the fruit on the nose; softer and more open than Rocche and more ready. **

Terre del Barolo, Vigna Rocche, Riserva and Riserva Speciale (*6 times, 12/80*). *Riserva:* The deepest color of the three *riserve*; tarry, seaweedy aroma; still has tannin to lose, the most tannic of the three. ** *Riserva Speciale:* Fruity aroma over a tarlike background marred by intrusion of alcohol; a chewy wine with loads of flavor and considerable tannin, moderately short, tannic finish. **(+)

Vietti (*12/85*). Lovely bouquet; soft and round, lots of structure, rich in fruit, long; ready. ** +

Vietti, Castiglione Falletto, normale, Riserva, and Riserva Speciale (*13 times, 4/86*). Lovely concentration, berry aroma, reminiscent of pinot noir; sweet impression, smooth, velvety feel; at its peak, no need to keep any longer. ***

Vietti, Rocche, Riserva and Riserva Speciale (*16 times, 11/88, 4,000 bottles*). *Riserva Speciale, 11/88:* Not a lot of nose, some fruit and tobacco notes; still has tannin and nice fruit, almost sweet; has held up but starting to decline, best to drink up. ** — *Bottle of 2/88:* Cherry and tobacco bouquet, lovely, rich and complex; round, velvety and smooth; at its peak. *** — *Bottle of 6/83:* Bouquet of ripe fruit with nuances of cherries, tobacco, tar, mushrooms and flowers; a classic Barolo bouquet, rich and flavorful, very well balanced, still some tannin but more or less ready now; the *riserva speciale* is perhaps somewhat more forward. ***

Villadoria Marchese (*3/81*). A candylike aroma; light-bodied, some tannin, lacks weight and substance, short on the finish; recalls a southern wine.

Vinicola Piemontese, Cerequio Riserva Speciale (*twice, 3/88*). Old-style Barolo nose; starting to dry out, the bottle perhaps, still has flavor, rustic style. * *Bottle of 2/85:* Aroma suggests wheat and hay, plus nebbiolo fruit and tar that emerged with some time in the glass, also a touch of camphor, tobacco and cherries; a lot of good fruit, still some tannin to shed if the fruit holds up, finish is very tannic. **(?)

Voerzio Giacomo normale, Riserva, and Riserva Speciale (*4 times, 3/84*). *Normale of 3/84:* Onionskin; atypical aroma but has interest, and fruit; moderate tannin, a bit shallow though drinkable, some alcohol at the end.

Zunino Basilio, Zona Sorì di Baudana (*10/81*). Characteristic aroma, some oxidation; shows age badly; perhaps only this bottle, we hope so.

1973 0

The year's harvest of 1.3 million gallons (49,821 hectoliters) of nebbiolo, equivalent to 6.6 million bottles of Barolo, was 87.5 percent of the amount allowed and the third largest crop in the decade in both total size and yield per acre (hectare). The 524 gallons per acre (49 hectoliters per hectare) were exceeded only by 1970 and 1974 in the decade.

Renato Ratti said the wines of 1973 were of medium quality. Luciano Rinaldi and Aldo Conterno rated them among the lesser vintages for quality. Conterno, who didn't bottle a '77, rated the '73s as the worst wines he has bottled. Bartolo Mascarello puts the vintage on a par with 1976. Alfredo Currado said the year, like 1975, wasn't very good and he didn't bottle any of his crus. Cavallotto agreed that it wasn't a very good vintage.

Right from the start the wines lacked body and substance. At this point, with very few exceptions—possibly Sobrero—they are too old. They might have been better at one time.

Cavallotto F.lli, Vigna Bricco Boschis (*twice, 12/80*). Light color; fragrant perfume; a little light and soft, some tannin, weak finish; not to keep. *

Conterno Giacomo (*4/80*). Tarlike notes evident but, overall, the aroma is closed and ungiving; light-medium body with insufficient fruit for the tannin.

Fenocchio Giacomo, Bussia (*4/86*). Tawny color; oxidized; still some fruit beneath the tannin; some interest. * —

Osola (*11/79*). Alcoholic aroma; overly tannic for the fruit which is lacking, unbalanced.

Sobrero Filippo (*twice, 5/82*). Must be the wine of the vintage; classic Barolo nose suggestive of tar, alfalfa and flowers; has a surprising intensity of flavor, well structured; has style. ***

1972

Constant rain during the growing season didn't allow the grapes to ripen. There was insufficient alcohol to make the wine. No Barolo was produced. The entire nebbiolo crop was declassified. The worst.

1971 ****

April, May, and June were marked by a lot of rain, which reduced the crop drastically. Then the sun came out and shone warmly almost until Christmas. The weather was consistently good for the rest of the season. The result was, we were told many times, a very small crop of richly intense, highly concentrated wines, rich in extract and very well balanced—overall, splendid wines.

In actuality, 1971's crop of 1.1 million gallons (41,964 hectoliters), 86.3 percent of the amount allowed by law, was the third largest crop of the 1970s in volume and fourth in terms of average yield per acre (hectare). It was larger in per acreage yield than 1978, 1982, 1985, 1988, and 1989, the other first-rate vintages. In terms of average size, it was pretty much equal to the average crop between 1967 and 1989, but considerably higher than the average yield per acre (hectare) of 445 gallons (41.6 hectoliters). The gallon-age was equivalent to 5.6 million bottles of Barolo.

Alfredo Currado described the '71s as complete wines, more consistent than the '78s, at a higher level. Giuseppe Rinaldi said it was the best vintage in memory; Bartolo Mascarello ranks it as the best of the decade. Renato Ratti said the best '71s are at a very high level, and although they will be very long-lived they can be enjoyed now. Pio Boffa said the wines were extremely big and tannic; his wine spent eight years in oak. Giovanni Conterno characterized them as masculine wines like the 74's. He produced a Monfortino, and Aldo Conterno made a Granbussia.

Despite the obvious odds there were many mediocre and even downright poor wines produced; for the most part, these wines came from the likes of Marchese Villadoria, Kiola, Scanavino, and a few others who consistently fail to raise their quality up to the level of mediocrity, frequently even drinkability. After exempting them, we find a preponderance of highly rated Barolos, with many wines meriting two, three, and even four stars. There's no doubt about the high quality of the vintage.

As for now, many are ready. A few are fading, but many others are very fine indeed and show no signs of age. Some of the best ones are starting to come ready. Still others will no doubt improve further; they have a lot more to give. Be patient. This vintage shows all the splendor of Barolo. The best wines, and there are still many that continue to improve, are among the greatest that we've tasted.

Of the more than five dozen wines we've tasted in the past few years, the best ones were Cantina Mascarello, Aldo Conterno, Giacomo Conterno's Monfortino, Bruno Giacosa's Rocche, Marcarini's Brunate, Luigi Pira's bottling of E. Pira, Francesco Rinaldi, Giuseppe Rinaldi, Tenuta Carretta's Cannubi, and Vietti's Briacca and Rocche. Also very good are Ceretto's Cannubi and Zonchetta, Giacomo Conterno's Riserva, Luigi Einaudi, Giuseppe Mascarello's Monprivato, Prunotto's Bussia Riserva di Count Riccardo Riccardi, and Ratti Renato's Marcenasco.

Bersano, Riserva Speciale (5/84). Brick red with orange highlights; not much bouquet; has tannin and a fair amount of flavor, alcohol mars the finish, which is short and somewhat grating; unimpressive.

Borgogno Aldo, Riserva Speciale (3/85). Old-style nebbiolo aroma of tar and fruit, vague touch of oxidation; unbalanced, high acid and volatile acidity, some berrylike fruit, drying out; still drinkable. *

Borgogno F.lli Serio e Battista, Riserva Speciale (twice, 11/84). One bottle had its sediment removed, the other did not. The difference was all too apparent. The first lacked in character and was somewhat shallow, the latter bottle had more aroma, flavor and character. Although some alcohol intruded, the second wine still had a fair amount of tannin and flavor, it was, in short, a more interesting wine. *(+)

Borgogno Giacomo, Riserva (4 times, 1/82). Light-medium brick, light orange rim; tar, fruit and vaguely floral on aroma; has tannin but with sufficient fruit to support it, though out of balance with alcohol which is noticeable on the finish. *

Brezza Giacomo (twice, 10/79). Perfumed aroma marred by the intrusion of alcohol; nice flavor on entry, then shallow, short alcoholic finish; not a success.

Bruzzone (3/81). Some oxidation mars the aroma; unstructured, some tannin, lacks weight, flavor and substance, happily there is no aftertaste.

Cantina Mascarello (3 times, 4/86). Some 80 percent of this Barolo came from Cannubi. Medium-deep brick robe shows age toward the rim; still has tannin, great richness and concentration, liquid velvet, enormous length; still young but so attractive now. ***(*) Magnum of 11/85: This wonderful Barolo was opened about thirty-six hours before we got to drink some! The bouquet was intense and penetrating with suggestions of licorice, tartufi and berries; rich and packed with flavor yet with delicacy and real class, elegant and stylish, velvet texture; truly a great wine; although it's ready there's room for improvement. ****

Cantine Duca d'Asti (Chiarlo Michele), "Granduca" Riserva and Riserva Speciale (twice, 9/86). Riserva of 9/86: Not a lot of nose; good weight and flavor, rather nice palate, some length; room to improve, good but just not up to the year. ** — Riserva Speciale of 3/81: Alcohol intrudes on the tarlike aroma; too much tannin and insufficient flavor to carry it.

Castello Feudale "Flavio Accornero" (11/86). Ripe fruit aroma; rather nice flavor, some tannin; enjoyable now; lacks the richness or intensity of the vintage. * —

Castello Feudale, Riserva Speciale (twice, 4/85). Brick red color shows age; characteristic bouquet of tar and flowers with a chocolate note; beginning to dry out but still has flavor interest. *

Cavallotto F.lli, Vigna Bricco Boschis Riserva Speciale (16 times, 3/88.) (This wine was at its best through 1987.) Interesting bouquet suggestive of chocolate and porcini, woodslike overtone; chocolate carries through in the mouth, still has some tannin; very ready now. **

Ceretto, Cannubi (11/85). Beautiful brick-garnet robe, orange highlights; perfumed bouquet, tobacco and tar, some alcohol; full of flavor, velvet center, still some tannin and firmness, very long; could use more age though certainly enjoyable now; old-style Barolo. ***(+)

Ceretto, Zonchetta (15 times, 2/90, 17,500 bottles). Tobacco, tea and cherries define the bouquet; rich and concentrated, velvety, round and tasty; very ready; it has been better. ***

Colla Paolo (10/78). A big tarry aroma; light-medium body and soft, lacks guts, weight and substance.

Conterno Aldo, Bussia Soprana (11/84). Perfumed bouquet suggesting tartufi and leather with hints of chocolate and flowers; tannic entry, richly fruited center; still young but balance and quality evident, will make a splendid bottle in perhaps four or five years. ***(*)

Conterno Aldo, Cascina Masante della Bussia Soprana (3/85). Smallish nose, vague harshness; quite tannic though sufficient fruit to balance; a real disappointment. **(+)

Conterno Giacomo, Monfortino Riserva Speciale (9 times, 5/90). Rich bouquet with nuances of tobacco, tar and flowers, some volatile acidity only adds complexity; mouth-filling, explosive flavors, great richness and concentration, sweet even, enormously long finish; no need to rush to drink, it will certainly last. ***+ *Bottle of 5/83:* Bouquet beginning to open up, revealing enormous richness and concentration; exceptionally well balanced, an immense concentration of fruit and still a heap of tannin; without question it needs years of age but should make an outstanding bottle; one of the stars of the vintage. ***(*)

Conterno Giacomo, Riserva (5 times, 4/89). Tar and vaguely floral bouquet; packed with flavor; very ready; a bit of an edge. ** *Bottle of 1/88:* Complex bouquet of leather, tar and dried fruit; gobs of tannin, the fruit is there to carry it; seems years from ready. **(* −) *Bottle of 3/85:* Old-style Barolo aroma; considerable tannin remains, the structure and fruit are sufficient to carry it; needs at least five more years, try again in 1990. **(*)

Contratto, Riserva (6 times, 4/89). Lovely bouquet; soft and smooth, at its peak, round and velvetlike, and very nice too. *** − *Bottle of 3/85:* Floral bouquet with the characteristic tarlike note; a full-bodied and fairly rich wine that still has considerable tannin to shed, has the sweetness of ripe fruit; sure to be worth the wait, try in about three years. **(*)

Cossetti Clemente (3/81). Hot, cooked nose reminiscent of a southern wine; low in acid, lacking character, flavor and substance, poor balance, dull, mercifully short.

Dogliani F.lli, Riserva Speciale (9/87). Light nose, some varietal character; drinkable, not much else, unbalanced, some alcohol intrudes.

Dosio, Riserva Speciale (twice, 5/85). Typical floral and tarlike aroma; tannic entry gives way to fruit, could use more weight and definition, not to keep, troublesome tannic ending. * +

Einaudi Luigi (twice, 3/85). Expansive bouquet with some complexity; heaps of flavor, moderate tannin, good weight and concentration, well structured, long finish; has style, enjoyable now. ***

Fontanafredda (11/78). Characteristic Barolo aroma; quite tannic and harsh, but seems to have sufficient fruit to allow it to age and develop; needs perhaps six to eight years.

Fontanafredda, Vigna La Rosa (5 times, 1/85). Aroma is more open, with more fruit than the Lazzarito, has a note of camphor; round and soft; enjoyable now but has room for improvement. **(*)

Fontanafredda, Vigna Lazzarito (1/85). Aroma offers notes of tar and fruit, with a vague note of seaweed; tannic entry gives way to sweet, ripe fruit, finish is very tannic; a full-bodied, robust Barolo that still needs years yet. **(+)

Giacosa Bruno, Rocche Riserva Speciale (3/85, 4,070 bottles). Beautiful brick-red robe shading to orange; toasty, berrylike nu-

ances on the floral bouquet; finely honed, still has tannin but full of flavor and incredible concentration; a real classic. ****

Grimaldi Cav. Carlo e Mario, Azienda Agricola "Groppone" Riserva Speciale (4/87). Tar and tobacco bouquet; soft center, rather simple, but drinkable. *

Kiola (3/81). A soft, light little wine that lacks structure and distinction, has nothing to recommend it.

Marcarini (Elvio Cogno), Brunate (7 times, 9/90, 29,600 bottles). [Some bottles were labeled Brunate, some were not, all came from the Brunate vineyard. Some of the bottles were labeled Dott. Giuseppe Marcarini. We were told that they were all the same wine.] Complex and expansive bouquet with suggestions of leather and tobacco, tar and flowers; a concentrated mouthful of flavor, sweet impression, liquid velvet; real class. **** − *Bottle of 12/87:* (this bottle seemed less impressive than the others): Beautiful brick-garnet robe; nose seems a little closed, hints of berries and mushrooms; richly concentrated, packed with flavor under moderate tannin, still rather young with an attractive nature due to the richness of fruit. *** *Bottle of 6/86:* Tobacco, cherry and berry scent; sweet, richly flavored, harmonious and elegant, long and stylish. **** *Bottle of 3/85:* Brick, almost onionskin robe; richly perfumed bouquet, floral and *tartufi* notes; sweet and flavorful, elegant and stylish; near peak but more to give, a real classic. ***(*) *Bottle of 3/83:* A rich and intense woodsy aroma with a cherrylike nuance; full of flavor, well balanced but not quite as exciting as it should be. **(*) *Bottle of 10/81* tasted at the winery from a magnum that had been opened for 24 hours (*'n fund 'd buta*): Enormous bouquet of flowers, fruit, champignons and raspberries; full and rich with the taste of sweet, ripe fruit, loads of style; coming ready. ***(*)

Marchesi di Barolo, Riserva Speciale della Castellana (8/88). Old nose; tired, old tasting, dry, fading.

Mascarello Giuseppe, Monprivato (6/82, 6,476 bottles, plus some larger sizes). Richly intense aroma marred by some alcohol; full-bodied and thick, with heaps of flavor; will improve but very good even now. **(*)

Massolino, Vigna Rionda (4/89). Drying out.

Oddero F.lli (twice, 4/87). Starting to fade, seaweedy, starting to lose its fruit and dry out. *Bottle of 1/85:* Old-style Barolo bouquet with a lot of tar; still firm and hard and fairly full-bodied; quite young but has the stuffing to enable it to develop. **(*)

Palladino (11/78). Expansive perfumed bouquet; soft and flavorful, still has some tannin, nearly ready, lacks a bit on length. * +

Palladino, Vigneto S. Bernardo Riserva Speciale (twice, 3/85). An almondlike aroma with a hint of Marsala; oxidation is more apparent on the palate; both bottles—tasted two months apart—were the same.

Pio Cesare (twice, 1/85). *Tasted at the winery:* Fresh, well-developed bouquet, fairly rich and intense with suggestions of licorice, flowers and berries; full-bodied and rich with a lot of concentration and tannin, hardly seems it could be the same wine! *** *Bottle of 12/81:* Unbalanced, harsh, tannic and alcoholic.

Pira E. (Luigi Pira) (*twice, 11/80*). Perfumed bouquet with an incredible richness and concentration of rich, ripe fruit and flowers; exceptional balance, enormous flavor, so well balanced the wine at first seems quite accessible but then the high tannin becomes evident; very young but incredible quality. ****

Pira E. (Chiara Boschis) [*in an Albeisa bottle*] (*3 times, 2/90*). There was great bottle variation in this wine. The best, and most recent, bottle displayed great concentration and richness, soft entry, cherry and truffle notes along with the characteristic tar, while it wasn't up to the Pira bottlings it was very good. **

Poderi e Cantine di Marengo-Marenda, Cerequio, *some bottles were labeled Vinicola Piemontese, Cerequio* (*twice, 10/90*). Orange cast, drying out, still some interest. * — *Bottle of 2/85:* Well-developed bouquet recalls raspberries and tar, with a barnyardlike aspect in the background; still has a lot of tannin but seems to have sufficient fruit to support it, finish is somewhat astringent. *(*)

Prunotto, Bussia Riserva di Count Riccardo Riccardi (*one year in wood, 1/85*). Enormous bouquet of ripe fruit and hints of *tartufi;* richly concentrated, a lot of class, sweet and velvety, still has a lot of tannin; a splendid wine. ***(*)

Prunotto, Riserva (*3/85*). Light nose, some fruit; light tannin, has a sweetness to it, some alcohol mars the end; it can improve but ready now. ** +

Ratti Renato, Marcenasco (*twice, 11/83*). Full, rich floral bouquet with hints of cherries, kirsch and *tartufi;* a complete wine; still has some tannin to shed but ready and enjoyable now with the flavor and sweetness of ripe fruit, very long. ***(+)

Rinaldi Francesco (*11/78*). Fairly complex and characteristic Barolo bouquet of tar and flowers overlaid with a suggestion of *tartufi;* well balanced, still somewhat tannic but loads of flavor; young but tempting (by now, it's probably close to ready). ***(+)

Rinaldi Giuseppe (*5 times, 11/85*). Surprising, there was bottle variation here. We suspect bad storage was the culprit. Complex bouquet, characteristic tar and tobacco notes, cassis and blueberries as well; richly fruited, vaguely of *tartufi,* round and soft, velvety, complete with its tannin totally evolved. **** *Bottle of 3/85: Tartufi,* berries and flowers characterize the intense bouquet; still has tannin and a surprising harsh edge, astringent entry, a lot of flavor; not up to previous bottles. ** *Magnum of 11/84:* Complex bouquet of cassis, mushrooms and *tartufi;* still has tannin but underneath is an enormous core of youthful(?) fruit and a firm tannic vein; an elegant Barolo; a delight to drink now but will continue to improve for years. ***(*)

Rinaldi Giuseppe, Brunate Riserva (*3/85*). Deep color; mint and ripe fruit on aroma and more than a hint of almonds; exceptional balance, still has tannin, enormous richness, very long; a stylish Barolo. ***(*)

Scanavino Giovanni (*too many times, 8/82*). Awful nose; light and insipid, no character, flavor or interest, some oxidation on the finish.

Scavino Alfonso, Vigna della Punta (*twice, 6/83*). Fairly nice nose marred by alcohol and volatile acidity—could be an off bottle, or else aging rapidly. *Bottle of 10/81:* Closed-in aroma with a suggestion of fruit and tar; considerable tannin but appears to have sufficient fruit in reserve; seems rather young. *(*)

Scavino Paolo (*5 times, 4/85*). Characteristic old-style Barolo aroma, some champignons; still has some tannin and a firmness remains, but beginning to soften and come ready, flavorful, a bit light at the end. ** —

Stroppiana Oreste (*twice, 3/88*). Some volatile acidity, chocolate note as well on the nose; harsh and unbalanced, alcohol intrudes, the flavor compensates, but unfortunately not enough. *Bottle of 11/85:* Characteristic Barolo aroma, touch of oxidation; dried out a bit, still has flavor interest. *

Tenuta Carretta, Vigna Cannubi (*11 times, 3/85*). Bouquet still somewhat reticent and not fully developed, hints of flowers and *tartufi;* firm, still a lot of tannin, but with the fruit necessary to carry it, long finish; not ready. At a tasting of 17 Barolos from the 1971 vintage in March 1985, this wine was the youngest and needed the most age, it was also one of the most impressive. **(* +)

Tenuta Carretta, Vigna Cannubi Riserva Speciale (*3 times, 11/79*). Bouquet is rich and deep, a faint mustiness in the background; more tannin than the regular bottling and more subdued in flavor; a very good bottle, but doesn't measure up to the regular. **(?)

Tenuta La Volta di Cabutto Bartolomeo (*twice, 1/85*). Odd nose has a vaguely vegetal and cereallike aspect that carries through on the palate, good fruit, ready now, light tannin, lacks some richness and weight but a nice Barolo for current consumption. *

Tenuta Montanello, Riserva Speciale (*magnum, 4/83*). Intensely rich bouquet, has a lot of flavor and some tannin, but quite ripe and ready. ** —

Terre del Barolo, Riserva Speciale (*4/80*). Moderately complex bouquet; nearly ready, soft and round with a lot of flavor, still some tannin. **

Veglio F.lli, Cascina Bruni, Carpegna (*ex-demijohn, 4/86*). Onionskin robe; madeirized-sherrylike aroma; some flavor interest and some sweetness, but alas, it's too old. * —

Vietti, Briacca, normale, Riserva, and Riserva Speciale (*17 times, 11/88, 4,500 bottles*). *Riserva Speciale, 11/88:* Delicate scent, berries and other fruit; sweet and soft, still some tannin, which blends nicely with the fruit; lots of class and style; complete. *** + *Bottle of 3/85:* Mineral aroma, some fruit; more fruit on the palate, still some tannin; seems to have closed up since the previous bottle; has a sweetness to it. **(*) *Bottle of 6/83:* Complex bouquet has floral overtones, notes of cherries and kirsch; still has tannin but richly flavored, with elegance and style, velvety texture, very long finish; tempting now but has more to give, try again in 1986. ***(*)

Vietti, Codana (*4/84*). Moderate garnet, orange at rim; floral bouquet with a suggestion of *tartufi;* well balanced and firm, a lot of flavor; beginning to come ready. ***(+)

Vietti, Rocche (12 times, 2/90, 4,000 bottles). Vaguely of seaweed on the nose, barnyardy and woodsy; but in all attractive, still has tannin, also a lot of fruit, and great length; room to grow but lovely now. **** *Bottle of 3/85:* Refined bouquet offers suggestions of tobacco, tea, cherries and flowers; like liquid velvet on the palate with an enormous richness and concentration of sweet, ripe fruit; this complete and stylish Barolo is near its peak. ****

Vignolo-Lutati (11/78). Lacks aroma; light-bodied and unstructured, overly tannic, lacks substance and length.

Villadoria Marchese (11/79). Hot nose—alcohol and volatile acidity and very little else; on the palate, the same, plus tannin, light-bodied and unstructured, low in fruit, short.

Vinicola Piemontese [bottled by L. C. & F. of Alba, Luigi Calissano perhaps?] (twice, 10/90). *Tartufi* aroma; a little dry but still some fruit, drink. * + *Bottle of 3/88:* Onionskin; delicate, perfumed; still fairly tannic on entry, lightens out in the midpalate, good flavor, short somewhat harsh end. *

1970 *** –

The harvest yielded just over one million gallons of nebbiolo (39,600 hectoliters), equivalent to 5.3 million bottles. It was the fifth largest crop of the decade. The 90.6 percent of the maximum allowed was the highest in the 23 years of DOC production from 1967 through 1989. The 542 gallons per acre (50.7 hectoliters per hectare) were still below the 599 gallons (56 hectoliters) allowed by law.

This vintage was always underrated, though not by Renato Ratti, who called it a grand year. It was unfortunately overshadowed by the spectacular year that followed. It has always been among our favorite vintages. Giacomo Conterno said that the '70s, like the '82s, are feminine wines. He made a Monfortino. Bartolo Mascarello rates only '71 and '78 better in the decade. Overall, it was a good year.

Based on the more than two dozen Barolos we've tasted during the past decade, it seems that the best wines from the best producers are still showing very well, but there are some clear disappointments as well, and we must admit that some poor bottles were produced. The few that we've tasted lately are holding up very well. You don't have to rush to drink them; they will give much pleasure now and in the years ahead.

Our favorite among those tasted in the past few years was Conterno's Monfortino, followed by the very good Bussia Soprana from Giuseppe Mascarello and Prunotto Cascina San Cassiano. Going back over our notes from the mid-1980s, we liked Giuseppe Rinaldi and Francesco Rinaldi and then Contratto and Luigi Einaudi. Giacomo Borgogno was also very good.

Borgogno Giacomo, Riserva (3 times, 3/89). Tar and flowers define the aroma along with spice and raspberries; layers of com-

plexity on the nose, soft, sweet impression; at its peak, and lovely too; could use more length. **

Castello Sperone, Riserva (6/79). The awful stench on the nose carries through on the palate—ugh!

Ceretto, Zonchetta (1/85). Nose shows a lot of age with the characteristic seaweed aroma of an old Barolo; still good on palate; no need to keep any longer. *

Conterno Aldo, "Granbussia" Vigna Bricco Colonello Riserva Speciale (4/80). Expansive bouquet; well balanced with heaps of flavor and a load of tannin still to shed. **(*)

Conterno Giacomo, Monfortino Riserva Speciale (8 times, 11/90). *From magnum, at the winery:* Mintlike aroma, animal fur component, dried fruit and camphor notes, hint of underbrush; soft and smooth, still some tannin, mostly resolved and soft, which adds texture and smoothness, very long; could still improve. *** *Bottle of 4/87:* Intense mushroomlike bouquet; rich and full-flavored, well balanced, great structure, some grip at the end. *** *Bottle of 4/85:* Bouquet suggests mushrooms, *tartufi* and hazelnuts; still has considerable tannin over a core of fruit which is just beginning to come out, firm and flavorful; still young but very good quality, try again in no less than two or three years. **(*) *Ex-cask, 11/84:* Fragrant perfume; very tannic and closed but seems to be a lot of fruit underneath that tannin. Giovanni Conterno has been bottling this wine for three years. **(?)

Contratto Giuseppe, Riserva (3 times, 3/88). Big nose, old-style with tar up front followed by the characteristic Barolo aroma; rich in tannin with the stuffing to carry it; still young. This bottle came from a different cellar than the one tasted three years earlier. **(*) *Bottle of 3/85:* Orange rim; richly intense and fragrant bouquet with hints of flowers and tar; well balanced, soft and smooth, the tannin has resolved itself, lots of flavor, moderately long finish. The bottle of September 1980 needed more time, that of March 1985 is at its peak. *** –

Einaudi Luigi (2/85). Floral bouquet with hints of tar and kirsch and a vague harshness; light tannin, good fruit, soft and round; very ready. *** –

Ferrero Virginia (11/78). Light but fragrant bouquet; lots of tannin, perhaps too much, the wine lacks some stuffing and flavor, rather brief finish.

Fontanafredda (6/79 and 2/82). Lacks fruit, drying out, more or less the same impression from both bottles.

Giri Guido (9/80). Smallish nose with some fruit apparent; flavorful, some tannin to lose, rather short aftertaste (should be ready by now). *

Mascarello Giuseppe (twice, 3/82). Fragrant bouquet with a hint of mint is marred by an off note; some tannin to shed, a bit shy in fruit, harsh, tannic aftertaste; will it ever develop? (*)

Mascarello Giuseppe, Bussia Soprana (4 times, 3/90, 4,702 bottles, plus larger sizes). Brick red, orange toward the rim; vague mint, leather and dustlike nuances, woodsy; harsh edges beginning to set in, starting to break up, yet the richness is appealing; drink up.

+ *Bottle of 3/85:* Floral, fruity aroma has some delicacy and a *tartufi* note; rich and full in the mouth with a lot of flavor, some tannin adds backbone, like velvet; has a gentleness about it. ***

Mascarello Giuseppe, Monprivato *(10/80).* Somewhat reticent aroma with traces of flowers and fruit; good flavor, the tannin is beginning to soften, but there are still some rough edges. (It should be ready by now.) **(*)

Pio Cesare *(11/78).* Backward on aroma; considerable tannin to lose but seems sufficiently well balanced to turn into a good bottle. *(* +)

Prunotto, Cascina San Cassiano Riserva *(7 times, 11/89).* Brick-orange robe; lovely and classic Barolo bouquet; rich and packed with flavor, soft and velvety, dry aftertaste. ** + *Bottle of 2/85:* Aroma somewhat closed, have to work for it, *tartufi*, smoky, tobacco, tar and flowers; full-bodied, still some tannin and lots of fruit, velvet center; ready, could improve. ***

Ratti Renato, Marcenasco *(11/83).* Lovely, well-developed floral bouquet with the characteristic note of tar; fairly well balanced and flavorful, though still some tannin. **(+)

Rinaldi Francesco *(1/85).* Floral bouquet recalls berries and *tartufi*; still quite tannic but with loads of fruit in reserve, firm and well balanced, good quality, long finish; needs a lot of time yet, try in about 1990. **(*)

Rinaldi Giuseppe *(4/86).* Lovely aroma, tar and flowers; velvet center, richly flavored, complete, long finish; at its peak. ***

Sobrero Filippo *(4 times, 2/90).* Bouquet of tobacco, tea and flowers, sweet, ripe and intense, rubberlike. * +

Stroppiana Oreste *(twice, 3/88).* Onionskin color; nice nose, characteristic; good structure, flavorful, some tannin; surprisingly good after the disappointing '71. * +

Tenuta Carretta, Vigna Cannubi *(10/78).* Aroma somewhat closed but some fruit peaking through; considerable tannin to shed but with a richness that bodes well; fine quality. **(*)

Tenuta Montanello *(4/90).* Coffee, toffee and chocolate, oxidized, some fruit. * −

Vinicola Piemontese, Cerequio Riserva Speciale *(6/79).* Vegies dominate the nose; soft and dull on the palate with some tannin, finishes on a bitter note; undistinguished and uninteresting.

Vinicola Piemontese, Riserva Speciale *[bottled by L. C. & F. of Alba, Luigi Calissano perhaps?]* *(twice, 5/90).* Open fruit, tar and floral aroma; soft, open and ready; best to drink now. ** −

1969 0

The 1969 harvest produced 860,288 gallons (32,562 hectoliters) of nebbiolo for Barolo. This was an average of 505 gallons per acre (47 hectoliters per hectare), or 84.4 percent of the amount allowed and the equivalent of 4.3 million bottles. Between 1967 and 1989 the yield was 445 gallons per acre (41.6 hectoliters per hectare), or 74.3 percent of the amount allowed by law.

This vintage was considered from the start to be of average quality. Renato Ratti agreed. Giovanni Conterno of Giacomo Conterno produced a small quantity of Monfortino. Today we doubt there are many wines of interest left. Most of the few we've tasted, mostly in 1982 and 1983, would have been better a few years earlier. Of the few '69s we've had in recent years, only the Vietti was still good.

Barale F.lli, Vigneti Castellero *(twice, 1/82).* Bouquet of vanilla and fruit, some oak; still tannic though it seems to have sufficient fruit to develop. *(*)

Borgogno Giacomo *(1/82).* Light-medium brick orange at rim; moderately intense bouquet marred by the intrusion of some alcohol; fairly nice flavor, still some tannin, tails off at the end; ready now, no need to keep it any longer. *

Conterno Giacomo, Monfortino Riserva Speciale *(4/81).* Tar and alcohol dominate the nose, some fruit comes up with a lot of swirling; unbalanced, high tannin and alcohol dominate on the palate, some fruit, astringent aftertaste.

Contratto *(twice, 3/83).* Still some interest though drying out.

Tenuta Montanello *(4/90).* Starting to fade, still some interest. * −

Terre del Barolo, Riserva *(twice, 1/83).* Chocolate and tar on aroma, marred by some oxidation; still some flavor, but drying out.

Vietti *(4/86).* Oxidation apparent, still has flavor and interest, light tannin, soft center, quite drinkable and agreeable as well. **

1968 0

The crop size of 803,089 gallons (30,397 hectoliters) of nebbiolo was an average of 504 gallons per acre (47 hectoliters per hectare), equivalent to 4.1 million bottles of Barolo. This was 84.2 percent of the maximum allowed.

This vintage was perhaps more highly regarded than 1969 at first. Renato Ratti called it very good. Giacomo Conterno made a Monfortino. We haven't tasted a '68 Barolo since 1984. Those that we tasted in the early 1980s were already fading.

Borgogno Giacomo, Riserva *(3 times, 10/83).* Alcohol and volatile acidity and very little else on the nose; on the palate, the same, plus tannin.

Ceretto, Zonchetta *(6/82, 12,000 bottles).* Bouquet hints of filberts; has fruit and interest but is beginning to dry out. *

Conterno Aldo, Vigna Bussia *(4/80).* Color shades to orange at rim; lovely fragrant bouquet; well structured and smooth in texture with a soft, velvety feel, still some tannin and a lot of flavor; stylish and pretty much at its peak. ** +

Conterno Giacomo, Monfortino (5/81). Not a pleasant wine—stinky and unimpressive; could be a bad bottle.

Contratto (*twice, 2/83*). Showing age on the nose, volatile acidity intrudes; overly tannic, and fruit is fading.

Sobrero Filippo (5/84). Oxidized but still some flavor interest.

1 9 6 7 **

The crop size in 1967, the first year of DOC regulations for Barolo, was 862,666 gallons (32,652 hectoliters). At 90.4 percent of the maximum allowed, this was the second largest between 1967 and 1989. Only 1970 was larger, with a crop that was 90.6 percent of what the law allows. While the yield per acre (hectare) was high—541 gallons (50.6 hectoliters) compared to the 445 (41.6) average between 1967 and 1989—the actual crop was not. It compares with the average between 1967 and 1989 of 1.1 million gallons (41,979 hectoliters). The nebbiolo crop was equivalent to 4.4 million bottles of Barolo.

Renato Ratti said the year was considered very fine at first, but the wines have lost a lot and are generally disappointing today; he advised they be drunk up. Originally he rated 1967 as very good. Bruno Giacosa places them in the top rank. Giacomo Conterno's Monfortino was produced. While there's no question they deserved three stars at one time, many of the wines are fading today. The best, however, are holding, and if well stored, and from a good producer, they can still bring a lot of pleasure. Our favorites are the Marcarini Brunate, then Bruno Giacosa Collina Rionda, Francesco Rinaldi, Giuseppe Rinaldi *normale* and Brunate, and Vietti Rocche.

Borgogno F.lli Serio e Battista, Riserva (11/84). Brick with orange reflections; nose shows some age with a vague oxidation and intrusion of alcohol; still some tannin but fairly nice fruit; ready now, might keep but alcohol on finish is troublesome.

Borgogno Giacomo, Riserva (1/82). Moderately intense bouquet with noticeable alcohol; overly tannic and harsh; too old.

Cantine Duca d'Asti (Chiarlo Michele), "Granduca" Riserva and Riserva (*twice, 9/86*). Slight nose, hints of tar and tobacco; soft, nice mouth feel, fairly well balanced, flavorful, moderate length, the remaining tannin has evolved into the wine, some tannin at the end. ** −

Contratto, Riserva (*4 times, 6/85*). *This bottle came from the winery a few months earlier:* Floral bouquet, woodsy nuance, hints of underbrush; still some tannin, soft-centered, flavorful, like the aroma, the flavor is somewhat woodsy; as ready as it will ever be; somewhat harsh finish. ** *Bottle of 3/85:* Very little of interest left, sadly past its best, alcoholic, drying out, acid finish; it was considerably better when tasted two years earlier, but even then it was drying out but still had some interest: a characteristic aroma of tar and flowers, some nice flavors, but we expected more. * −

Dosio, Riserva Speciale (4/85). Browning; a touch of oxidation on nose, also notes of tobacco and tar; light tannin; very drinkable, not to keep. *

Fontanafredda (*twice, 1/83*). Aroma of tar and rubber; shows age, but still has interest. * −

Fontanafredda, Vigna La Rosa (5/80). Not much aroma; soft, some tannin, not much to it, short aftertaste. * −

Giacosa Bruno, Collina Rionda Riserva Speciale (*twice, 3/86, 5,500 bottles*). Beautiful brick robe, tawny toward the rim; lovely rich and intense bouquet, complex with suggestions of the woods, cherries and a hint of *tartufi*; still has tannin but resolved, making for a velvet mouth feel; real class here. *** +

Marcarini (Elvio Cogno), Brunate (3/85). Beautiful brick robe with orange reflections; expansive, perfumed bouquet; firm tannic vein, texture of liquid velvet; a complete wine, elegant and stylish; very ready, but there's no rush to drink it. ****

Pio Cesare (4/80). Some oxidation on nose; dried out though some flavor remains.

Porta Rossa di Berzia & Rizzi (10/81). High alcohol, noticeable volatile acidity, some flavor; too old.

Prunotto, Bussia Riserva (*8 times, 3/88, 21,355 bottles*). Classic old-style tar and woodsy aroma, floral overtone; fairly tannic, fruit beneath, the finish is decidedly tannic. ** *Bottle of 2/85:* Garnet, orange at rim; characteristic bouquet of flowers and tar, some alcohol; soft, round and flavorful; quite ready, has a slight bite on the finish; a good example of an old-style Barolo at its peak. ***

Ratti Renato (11/83). Lovely, rich floral bouquet shows some refinement; soft and round; near its peak; has some style. ***

Rinaldi Francesco (1/85). Fairly deep color; expansive bouquet, vaguely floral, has some delicacy; still has tannin but a lot of flavor, velvety; nearly ready but with more to give; an elegant gentle Barolo with a very long finish. ***(+)

Rinaldi Giuseppe (2/86). Floral and berry aroma; soft and round, fairly long finish; ready now, no signs of age, sure to keep. ***

Rinaldi Giuseppe, Brunate (9/86). Classic Barolo, from its intense bouquet through the richly flavored palatal impression, smooth and harmonious, very long and complete, displays class. ***

S. Quirico, Massano (4/87). Onionskin; old-style Barolo aroma, seaweed and tar; breaking up; but of the four Barolos tasted from this producer—'83, '82, '81 and '67—this had the most interest!

Veglio F.lli, Cascina Bruni, Carpegna (*ex-demijohn, 4/86*). Pale onionskin color; oxidized; still has flavor interest, but it has faded and is past its best. For the interest. * −

Vietti, Rocche (*magnum, 11/84*). Medium-deep, brick at rim; expansive bouquet; complex and perfumed, with nuances of flowers, kirsch, *tartufi*, mint, leather, licorice, cherries and tobacco; a complete and well-balanced Barolo; velvety and tasty; perfect today but as it sits in the glass it grows and expands, indicating more life ahead; very long finish; five hours later it was even more impressive. ***+

1 9 6 6   0

This vintage never amounted to much. Ratti said it was mediocre. Without question only 1963 was as bad in the decade. We doubt if this vintage holds much interest any longer, although the Guido Giri, the only '66 Barolo that we've tasted recently, was still surprisingly good, though fading.

Borgogno Giacomo, Riserva (1/82). Alcoholic and unbalanced.

Franco, Riserva (12/78). Oxidation and bitter.

Giri Guido (6/90). Fading for sure, yet still some flavor! *

1 9 6 5   0

Some pundits rated this vintage as three stars. Renato Ratti called it average. We had a lot more exposure to it in the early and mid-1970s, but haven't seen any bottles in some time. At their best we wouldn't have given them more than two stars, today zero.

Borgogno Giacomo, Riserva (1/82). Some oxidation, some flavor interest, ends on a bitter note.

Calissano, Riserva Speciale (2/82). Seaweed and oxidation; best forgotten.

Mascarello Giuseppe (twice, 3/82). Volatile acidity and alcohol, harsh edges, some flavor interest; going, but not gone.

1 9 6 4   *** −

This was a very highly thought of vintage. The Marchesi di Barolo classifies it as exceptional. A few years ago Renato Ratti said that they were still holding and should be good for another ten to fifteen years. He rated the vintage as the best between 1947 and 1971. Alfredo Currado puts it on the same level as 1961 and 1967. Giuseppe Rinaldi picks it as the best of the decade and on the same level as 1971. Giacomo Conterno produced a Monfortino.

The only '64 Barolos we've tasted in recent years were the Luigi Calissano—it was still good—and the exceptionally fine Bartolo Mascarello. We expect this vintage could still offer a lot of pleasure if the wines came from a good producer and were well stored.

Bersano, Riserva Speciale (5/84). Some quality evident though beginning to dry out, drinkable but not to keep.

Borgogno F.lli Serio e Battista, Riserva (11/84). Brick red; vaguely resinlike aroma, but pleasant; almost seems sweet, light tannin; ready now, could use more character. *

Borgogno Giacomo, Riserva (6 times, 1/85). Some volatile acidity mars the nose, which has a vague hint of seaweed; still has considerable tannin but also a lot of flavor, smooth texture, fairly well balanced; nice now but can improve further. This is a wine that gave us immense pleasure when it was ten to twelve years old and continues to offer a lot of drinking pleasure even today. **(+)

Calissano Luigi (6/90). Seaweed on the nose; fading but still has some flavor and softness. *

Cantine Duca d'Asti (Chiarlo Michele), "Granduca" Riserva (9/86). Color tending toward brown; nose also shows a lot of age, coffee and oxidation apparent; not shot but fading, some interest remains. * −

Conterno Giacomo, Monfortino Riserva Speciale (many times, 3/81). Nearly every bottle we tasted was shot—either bad or too old. *Most recent bottle:* Tarry notes and a slight harshness (volatile acidity) on the nose; still has tannin but a lot of flavor, where will it go? The volatile acidity is troublesome. *(?)

Dosio, Riserva Speciale (4/85). Browning; oxidized, drying out.

Mascarello Bartolo (magnum, 11/90). Incredible bouquet, rich and complex with a mélange of scents, leather, truffles, flowers and berries; soft, liquid velvet, at its peak, packed with flavor, enormous length; great elegance and class, complete, near perfection. ****

Ratti Renato (10/83). Fairly intense bouquet; still fairly tannic on the palate; it seems to have the fruit to develop—will it? **(?)

1 9 6 3   0

This vintage never amounted to much. Ratti rates the year as bad, making it one of the decade's two worst.

1 9 6 2   [*]

Renato Ratti, as well as many others, considered 1962 an average year from the start, but we've had better experiences than that, especially through the 1970s. Except for the Calissano tasted in 1983 and 1981, we haven't tasted a '62 since 1978, so we put a tentative evaluation on the current state of the vintage.

Borgogno Giacomo (9/78). Has good Barolo character, soft though still some tannin; no need to keep any longer. ** +

Calissano, Riserva Speciale (4 times, 1/83). At one time it was much better, this wine is typical of a Barolo beginning to break up—seaweed aroma and a mouthful of alcohol and tannin though some fruit remains. This Barolo was at its best through the end of the 70s.

1 9 6 1 ** +

Renato Ratti said that although they were very rich wines, the '61s aged quickly and already taste too old. He called it a grand year that was not quite up to the lofty heights of 1964. Alfredo Currado rates the vintage equal to 1964 and after 1971, 1978, and 1982. Some producers, notably Beppe Colla of Prunotto, place it ahead of 1958, as does the Marchesi di Barolo, who classifies it as exceptional. Giacomo Conterno made a Monfortino.

Without question 1961 was one of the two finest vintages of the 1960s. And while some are fading, others are holding up. The only two that we've tasted recently, the Gaja and Vietti, were both splendid indeed. A few years ago the Prunotto Bussia was still excellent as well. We see no need to rush to drink them, nor do we see any need to keep them further. If they are well stored and were made by a good producer, the wines should last. Two stars plus would seem to reflect their current state based on the few wines we've had the opportunity to sample.

Borgogno F.lli Serio e Battista, Riserva (11/84). Onionskin robe; some oxidation on the nose, also some tar; still some tannin but soft, some flavor, not to keep. *(?)

Borgogno Giacomo, Riserva (twice, 1/82). Light brick with an orange rim; characteristic bouquet of moderate intensity; nice entry, almost sweet, velvety, rather short finish but a nice bottle showing no signs of decay. **

Bosca Luigi, Riserva Speciale (too many times, 3/85, 27,000 bottles). Southern aroma, raisins beneath the oxidation. (Bosca has a knack for producing poor wine even in the great years—no surprises here.)

Conterno Giacomo (4/80). Nose is marred by high alcohol and volatile acidity; still has considerable tannin but with fruit beneath; questionable future. (?)

Contratto (10/79). Color shows very little age; aromatic bouquet suggesting *tartufi*; smooth in texture, heaps of flavor, very well balanced; can improve, but near its peak. ***

Contratto, Riserva (twice, 11/85). Delicate aroma, *tartufi* notes; some tannin, has a touch of volatile acidity but no decay, nice flavor midpalate, warm finish. *** — *Bottle of 5/85:* Beautiful brick-orange robe; a lot of nebbiolo character and complexity, berrylike; some volatile acidity and some harsh edges but soft and flavorful, fairly long finish, recalls blackberries, vaguely chalky; ready. ** +

Fontanafredda (1/85, at winery). Beautiful brick-red robe; lovely floral bouquet, with licorice and mint; still some tannin but fairly soft, round and smooth-textured; still has holding power and should improve, but a nice glass right now. **(*)

Gaja (1/90). Brick robe with an orange rim; classic Barolo nose, tar and flowers, vaguely of seaweed; rich and full-flavored, some smoothness of texture, velvety center, rather brief finish; very nice indeed in spite of its dry finish. *** −

Lodali Giovanni (3/85). Caramel candy and a baked character to the aroma; full-bodied, flavorful; lacking in style, coarse but drinkable. *

Prunotto, Bussia Riserva (5 times, 9/86, 26,500 bottles). Beautiful brick-orange robe; lovely floral-scented bouquet, *goudron* with a touch of seaweed; smooth and tasty; at its peak, and holding. ***

Tenuta La Volta di Cabutto Bartolomeo (twice, 1/85). Onionskin; bouquet shows a lot of age, floral with hints of tea and coffee; has a hint of sweetness, also a fullness and yet seems delicate; has held up but is not to keep any longer. ** +

Vietti (4 times, 2/90). (Although not labeled as such, this Barolo is actually from the Rocche vineyard.) There was bottle variation. *The best bottle was also the most recently tasted:* Brick robe; richly intense bouquet suggestive of flowers and berries, hints of the woods; still some tannin, great richness, very long finish; a complete wine that is at its best, one could hardly ask for more. *** +

1 9 6 0 0

The vintage was considered poor from the start. Renato Ratti rated the year as poor and, along with 1963, the worst of the decade. We tasted only one Barolo from this vintage that we can recall.

Gaja (11/84). The color was onionskin; it showed some decay but still offered some interest.

1 9 5 9 0

Like 1960 this vintage was considered a poor one. Renato Ratti classified it mediocre, not quite poor. While we doubt if many '59s hold any interest today, the Pio Cesare, tasted in 1990, was very good.

Gaja (11/84). It was cloudy and alcoholic—in a word, gone.

Pio Cesare (twice, 2/90). Volatile acidity, rich and intense, packed with flavor in spite of the harshness. **

1 9 5 8 ****

Many authorities rate this vintage as one of the all-time greats. Renato Ratti calls it a grand year and therefore not up to 1971 or 1964, and equal to 1961 and 1970. The Marchesi di Barolo classifies it as great and therefore behind 1961 and 1964. Giacomo Conterno made a Monfortino. In our limited experience with it, no vintage has impressed us more, and only '71 and '85 have impressed us as much. Suffice it to say that while we have tasted some very impressive '47s, our experience isn't sufficient to say which is better and, in fact, if '47 is or ever was as good. But make no mistake about it, this was one of the all-time great vintages. The best wines have still more to give. While we tasted many more during the '70s, the few that we've had more recently are still impressive.

Cantina Mascarello's, tasted from *bottiglione* in April 1987, was glorious. We're pleased to report that we were drinking, not tasting! Giacomo Conterno's Monfortino was magnificent as well. Neither wine showed signs of age. We also had the opportunity to enjoy the Pio Cesare, Prunotto, and Fontanafredda. The Giacomo Borgogno and Angelo Germano were both very good as well.

Borgogno Giacomo, Riserva (*numerous times, 1/85*). Medium brick in color; aroma brings up seaweed, beets and cheese and also has a harsh backnote; still has tannin and some firmness, nice flavor and a lot to it; enjoyable now with room for improvement; the only flaw is in the bouquet. **(?)

Cantina Mascarello (bottiglione, 4/87). Beautiful robe; lovely bouquet, rich with overtones of flowers, licorice and tar; intense and concentrated, still some tannin but richness of fruit makes it attractive now, still young, superbly crafted, very long; great quality. ****

Conterno Giacomo, Monfortino (1/88). Beautiful brick-orange robe; ripe fruit, woodslike, berryish component, camphor and leather; superb structure, harmonious, ripe fruit, velvety, complete and long; sheer perfection. ****

Fontanafredda (4 times, 12/85). Seaweed aroma indicates a Barolo that's breaking up; soft center, still fairly tannic; as ready as it will ever be; doesn't match the bottle tasted nearly a year ago. ** + *Bottle of 1/85:* Deep garnet robe, brick at rim, orange reflections; complex bouquet suggesting licorice, camphor, flowers and toast; liquid velvet; seems so ready, though still some tannin. ***(+)

Germano Angelo (4/87). Light tawny color, onionskin toward the rim, seems old though pretty color; oxidized, coffee aroma; still some flavor and a slight sweetness; on the way down but with flavor interest, can still be enjoyed. **

Pio Cesare (twice, 3/91). Oxidation evident; still has flavor interest; dry finish; best to drink up. ** *Bottle of 11/85:* Soft, round and tasty, balanced, still very much alive and packed with fruit; complete and near or at its peak. *** +

Prunotto (1/85). Beautiful robe; brick to orange; some volatile acidity and alcohol intrude on the bouquet; considerably better on the palate, light tannin, velvety and round, an enormously long finish—the palate merits ****, overall, ***

1957 ** + ?

The vintage was always highly regarded but lived in the shadow of 1958. Renato Ratti classified the vintage as very

good, the Marchesi di Barolo as excellent. As for today, we've tasted only one, the Contratto Riserva. It was still excellent in May 1985.

Contratto, Riserva (5/85). Tawny robe, orange reflections; leather, woods, tar and berry notes characterize the bouquet; still some tannin, soft and smooth-textured; very ready, the only flaw is a slight harshness at the end. *** —

1956 [0]

At one time 1956 was considered an average year. Renato Ratti agreed that it was a normal year. Today they're probably too old.

1955 *** —

We always rated this vintage higher than the pundits, who gave it two stars. Renato Ratti called it good. Giacomo Conterno's Monfortino was produced. The few bottles we've tasted were surely better. The Cantina Mascarello we tasted in April 1987 was excellent, though admittedly it was even better five years earlier. The Contratto and Pio Cesare were very good as well.

Borgogno Giacomo, Riserva (many times, 9/83). Orange robe, brick center; light bouquet though quite nice, characteristic; moderate tannin, tasty; more or less ready, with some room for further improvement. **(+)

Cantina Mascarello (3 times, 4/87). Beautiful robe, orange cast; perfumed bouquet; like silk and velvet with a firm finish, loads of flavor, almost sweet; shows age toward the end with a certain hardness. *** *Bottle of 6/82:* This was the best of the three bottles tasted. Each succeeding bottle showed a little more age. Beautiful robe; expansive, perfumed bouquet, has delicacy and elegance; like liquid velvet on the palate, incredible length; nearly perfect. ****

Contratto, Riserva (6/85). Incredible richness and intensity on the nose, tobacco, berry, floral and woodsy nuances, marred by a touch of alcohol and a vague wet dog backnote; soft and velvety, tasty; at its peak and splendid; long, complex finish, has a barnyardy character but in a pleasant way. ***

Pio Cesare (9/86). Classic old-style Barolo tar and flowers; sweet and smooth, balanced; complete; at its peak now. ***

Villadoria Marchese, Riserva Speciale (many times, 2/80). Beautiful orange robe; lovely perfumed bouquet; soft and velvety, seems almost sweet, heaps of flavor and very long finish; at its peak. How could Villadoria have produced such a wine? ***

1954 [0]

At one time this was considered a two-star vintage. Ratti rated it as average. Unfortunately, we've not had the opportunity to taste any '54s. Today the wines are probably too old, although there might be some exceptions.

1953 [0]

This vintage was rated by authorities along with 1959, as the worst of the decade. Ratti said it was bad. The only '53 we tasted was feeble and fading.

Pio Cesare (11/79). Garnet color; oxidized, seaweedy aroma that, however, still offers some interest; nice flavor, still has tannin; on the decline, but surprisingly drinkable for what it is. *

1952 *

Originally rated as a three-star vintage, the best wines merited four. Giacomo Conterno produced a Monfortino. Renato Ratti called it an average vintage. While we know a number of people born in 1952 who are aging very well, we can't say the same for the Barolos. We haven't tasted a '52 Barolo anywhere as impressive as the one produced by Cantina Mascarello and tasted in October 1979 with Giacomo Bologna, Bartolo Mascarello, and his father, Giulio. The few that have come our way in recent years have shown signs of age. It would seem best to drink up those that remain.

Borgogno Giacomo, Riserva (many times, 3/79). Beautiful orange robe; typical seaweed aroma of an old Barolo; round and smooth; at or near its peak; fairly long finish. **

Cantina Mascarello (10/79). Beautiful robe; floral bouquet is deep, rich and intense with hints of fruit and leather; still has tannin, and life; smooth-textured with heaps of flavor, enormously long finish; a classic Barolo. ****

Conterno Aldo, Riserva Speciale (10/78). The bottle had been opened twenty hours earlier, tawny robe; delicately scented bouquet with a suggestion of fennel; soft, round and velvety, fine quality, has style and distinction; nearing its peak. *** +

Conterno Giacomo (4/81). Oxidized, but still has interest on the nose; none on the palate.

Conterno Giacomo, Monfortino (10/79). Intense bouquet with suggestions of *tartufi*; delicate, nice structure, still some tannin, has length, and style. ***

Fontanafredda (2/82). Brick red; seaweed and tar aroma so characteristic of an old Barolo; smooth-textured with a lot of flavor, some harshness at the end; on the way down. *

Franco Fiorina (1/85). Medium brick red; some oxidation on the nose but also a lot of interesting woodsy nuances; very soft and smooth, with a touch of tannin that adds life, and backbone; an old wine but firm, on the way down but still very good. ** +

1951 ?

This vintage was rated three stars by some. Ratti called it good. As for its status today, we couldn't say; we've never tasted a '51 Barolo that we can recall.

1950 *

This year was given two stars by the authorities at the time. Ratti called it an average vintage. The Cantina Mascarello 1950 Cannubi was excellent in April 1987, though it was starting to show age. We suspect that most Barolos from 1950 have faded or are starting to.

Cantina Mascarello, Cannubi (4/87). Opened seven hours ago. Beautiful robe, orange cast toward the rim; vague off note—a slight dankness—in the back, overall the bouquet is lovely and complex; soft and velvety, smooth and long. *** —

Franco Fiorina (1/85, tasted at the winery). Medium brick red color; a bit of oxidation and a vague wheatlike note on the nose; has more interest on the palate, with a smooth texture and almost a sweetness to the flavor, still some tannin; past its prime, but still good. ** —

1949 [0]

The vintage was never highly regarded. Renato Ratti rated 1949 as mediocre. It's probably safe to say that the wines today are probably too old.

1948 [0]

Like the '49s, the '48s were never well thought of. Ratti said it was a bad year. Today the wines are probably gone.

1947 ***

The harvest produced a very small quantity of very ripe grapes. According to Giuseppe Fontana of Franco Fiorina, there might have been 20 producers who bottled Barolo at that time, while today there might just be twenty times that number. For him 1947 was the greatest vintage of the century. His wine, he said, was more than an expression of the vintage; it represented the family's dedication to the wine, the love they had for it. They put everything into it.

Renato Ratti and the Marchesi di Barolo classify 1947 as exceptional and one of the all-time greats. The Ceretto Brunate tasted in November 1986 and the Franco Fiorina tasted in January 1985 were very good indeed. As for the general condition of the remaining wines, we suspect that if they have been cared for in good storage conditions and are from a good maker, the wines can still be magnificent. After all, it was one of the best vintages of the century. Then again, the wines are more than forty years old.

Borgogno Giacomo, Riserva (many times over the past 12 years, 9/83). Brick robe with orange reflections; aspects of seaweed and rubber tire in the bouquet suggest the wine is on the decline, though without question still interesting; fairly soft and enjoyable but not to keep. This wine was better in the late '70s. This bottle **

Ceretto, Brunate (11/86). We were able to taste this one from a number of different bottles; there was some variation. *This was the best bottle:* Deep color; shows age but not fading; big, rich and intense with enormous fruit, almost Port-like, a superb glass of wine, with great intensity of flavor and layers of complexity; nearly perfect, a complete wine. **** –

Franco Fiorina (1/85, tasted at the winery). Medium garnet shading to orange; bouquet has delicacy; on the palate, liquid velvet, has a lot going for it—structure, flavor, style and length, has the sweetness of ripe fruit, still some tannin and a lot of life left, though near its peak; only the bouquet doesn't measure up to the rest— still in all, a great bottle. *** +

Marchesi di Barolo (many times over the past 12 years, 4/82). Medium orange; seaweed and tar on the nose; nice entry gives way to a harsh astringent edge, still has tannin and not much else; breaking up. It was considerably better in the mid- to late '70s.

1946 [0]

This vintage was originally given two stars. Renato Ratti called it average. Today the wines are probably too old.

1945 [0]

The vintage was rated three stars. Ratti rated it good. The only example we've tasted, in November 1979, was, alas, too old.

Marchesi di Barolo (11/79). Tawny robe; oxidized aroma recalls Marsala; still some flavor and interest, and even a touch of tannin; on the way downhill.

OLDER VINTAGES

Renato Ratti rates the vintages:[25]

Exceptional	1931, 1922, 1894, 1868
Grand	1934, 1929, 1927, 1919, 1917, 1912, 1907, 1905, 1898, 1887, 1879

Very good	1925, 1910, 1908, 1897, 1889, 1886, 1873
Good	1937, 1924, 1920, 1911, 1906, 1895, 1890, 1885, 1876, 1870, 1869
Average	1943, 1942, 1938, 1936, 1932, 1930, 1928, 1923, 1921, 1918, 1914, 1913, 1903, 1900, 1899, 1892, 1888, 1883, 1881, 1877, 1872, 1871
Mediocre	1940, 1935, 1926, 1916, 1909, 1901, 1896, 1891, 1882, 1880, 1874
Bad	1944, 1941, 1939, 1933, 1915, 1904, 1902, 1893, 1884, 1878, 1875

Marchesi di Barolo rates the vintages:

Exceptional	1922, 1894, 1861
Great	1934, 1929, 1927, 1919, 1917, 1912, 1907, 1905, 1898, 1892, 1887, 1879
Excellent	1925, 1908, 1897, 1889, 1886, 1873

1931 [****]

Renato Ratti classifies 1931 as exceptional. It is widely considered to be *the* greatest of the century. Going by this one wine, it seems an evaluation well justified.

Conterno Giacomo (4/85). This wine was transferred from a quarter *brenta* (12.5 liters) to a regular bottle 16 to 17 years ago. Aldo Conterno uncorked this bottle in the morning, some four hours before serving it. Beautiful robe, onionskin; fragrant floral bouquet with a suggestion of clover; still has some tannin, seems sweet, impressive depth of flavor, velvety texture; very much alive, showing no signs of fading; still has grip; very long finish, with a hint of licorice; sheer perfection. ****

This magnificent wine demonstrates the grandeur possible in a fine old Barolo. Thank you, Aldo Conterno, for your generosity in sharing it.

1908

Renato Ratti classifies the vintage as very good, the Marchesi di Barolo classifies it as excellent.

Ceretto, Brunate (9/86). Beautiful garnet, brick, tawny robe; lots of personality; sweet and delicate, velvety and elegant; loaded with character and flavor, great class and enormous length; refined, so much to it, complete, sheer perfection. ****

◁ BARBARESCO ▷

The Barbaresco production zone, to the east and north of Alba, is a small area containing about 1,200 acres (488 hectares) of vines cultivated by 475 growers. This name does not describe the character of the wine, which isn't in the least barbaric; in fact, it can be quite refined indeed. The wine takes its name from the town of Barbaresco, a village in the northwestern part of the zone dominated by an eleventh-century tower built as a lookout point and signal tower to warn of barbarian invaders.

Recently we came across an interesting story on the possible origins of the name Barbaresco:

Barbaresco: A strange name of distant origins that recalls the "Barbarica silva," the wild wood, which many centuries ago covered the hillsides where today the Nebbiolo reigns supreme. The name and the wild wood it recalls conjure up images of the life of the savage....[26]

Besides the *comune* of Barbaresco, which contains about 45 percent of the vines, there are two others and a part of a fourth making up the production zone: Neive, with nearly 31 percent of the total, in the northeast; Treiso d'Alba, with about 20 percent, in the south-central part; and, in the west, part of San Rocco Senodelvio d'Alba.

Between 1967 and 1989, an annual average of 444,886 gallons (16,839 hectoliters) of nebbiolo, equivalent to 2.2 million bottles of Barbaresco, were produced. This contrasts with the annual average of 493,024 gallons (18,661 hectoliters) in the most recent five-year period (1985 to 1989). In terms of average yield per acre (hectare), 429 gallons (40 hectoliters) were produced between 1967 and 1989, and 401 gallons (37.5 hectoliters) between 1985 and 1989. This represents 72 percent of the maximum allowed by law for the former period and 67 percent for the latter. And rarely, if ever, is the entire nebbiolo crop bottled as Barbaresco. In some years, like 1987, 1984, and 1977, for example, a significant part of the crop is declassified. Like Barolo, and unlike the Burgundians, the Barbaresco producers aren't prone to overproduction.

Barbaresco is a wine similar to Barolo, though generally lighter and earlier maturing, and often more stylish and elegant. "Lighter" in this context does not mean light; Barbaresco is a full-bodied wine with depth of fruit and character. It has a tannic spine, giving it a youthful hardness that softens with age to a velvety texture and underlying firmness.

Barbaresco has often been referred to as the little brother of Barolo, a description that is misleading as well as disparaging. These are not lesser wines; they can be truly monumental as well as great. The Santo Stefano of Bruno Giacosa or Castello di Neive, Camp Gros-Martinenga of Marchese di Gresy, and the Rabajà of Produttori del Barbaresco, among others, can achieve a grandeur to match the best from Barolo, or, for that matter, from anywhere else.

Barbaresco is a fine wine to accompany roast red meat, game birds such as grouse or woodcock, duck or pigeon. In the medieval upper town of Neive, at Ristorante Contea de Neive, there is an excellent selection of Barbarescos available, as well as a menu of superb regional dishes typical of the Langhe. We can't think of a more enjoyable way to study the wines of Barbaresco than to accompany some fine bottles with a meal prepared by Claudio Verro, the fine chef at Contea.

Barbaresco is drinkable five to eight years after the vintage and can be splendid for twelve to fifteen years, perhaps even longer in better vintages. In the very best vintages the top wines need a decade or more to be drinkable. Bruno Giacosa recommends drinking his after ten to twenty years. And, in our experience, they will live for many years after that.

It's not unusual for a producer's regular Barbaresco to have better fruit and balance than his *riserva* or *riserva speciale,* as these two are frequently given longer wood aging,

DOC/DOCG REQUIREMENTS FOR BARBARESCO

Normale	Minimum Aging[a] in years		Minimum Alcohol	Maximum Yield (Gallons/Acre)[c]
	in Cask[b]	Total		
DOC	1	2	12.5%	599
Riserva	1	3	12.5%	599
Riserva Speciale	1	4	12.5%	599
DOCG *normale*	1	2	12.5%	599
Riserva	1	4	12.5%	599

NOTES: [a] The period of aging begins on the January 1st after the harvest.
    [b] Aging can take place in oak or chestnut casks.
    [c] The law specifies that no more than 3.57 tons per acre (80 quintali per hectare), or 56 hectoliters per hectare, can be produced. After aging the maximum yield is equivalent to 556 gallons per acre (52 hectoliters per hectare).

ANNUAL PRODUCTION OF BARBARESCO

Year	Maximum Allowed (Hectoliters)	Actual Amount (Hectoliters)	Actual Number of Bottles	Percentage Actual to Allowed	Average Yield Hectoliters/Hectare
1967	10,652	9,113	1,215,036	85.6	47.94
1968	10,652	8,887	1,184,903	83.4	46.70
1969	13,046	9,979	1,330,500	76.5	42.84
1970	17,086	13,264	1,768,489	77.6	43.46
1971	18,272	11,297	1,506,229	61.8	34.61
1972	20,995	the crop was declassified			
1973	22,625	20,230	2,697,265	89.4	50.06
1974	24,726	21,953	2,926,993	88.8	49.73
1975	25,455	17,843	2,379,007	70.1	39.26
1976	25,416	12,613	1,681,691	49.6	27.78
1977	26,263	12,538	1,671,691	47.7	26.71
1978	26,426	14,443	1,925,685	54.7	30.63
1979	26,419	23,249	3,099,789	88.0	49.28
1980	26,431	23,568	3,142,321	89.2	49.95
1981	27,722	20,701	2,760,064	74.7	41.83
1982	27,582	22,815	3,041,923	82.7	46.31
1983	29,132	24,121	3,216,052	82.8	46.37
1984	28,658	10,543	1,405,698	36.8	20.61
1985	28,255	19,965	2,661,933	70.7	39.59
1986	28,458	19,994	2,665,800	70.3	39.37
1987	27,832	19,333	2,577,668	69.5	38.92
1988	27,426	17,711	2,361,407	64.6	36.18
1989	27,355	16,304	2,173,812	59.6	33.38
Average	23,778	16,839	2,245,144	71.6	40.10

Source: Regione Piemonte

which tends to diminish their fruit. There are exceptions, of course, particularly from the best producers and the best vintages, wines which have more intensity and concentration of fruit to begin with.

Under the DOCG regulations up to 15 percent of a Barbaresco from a different vintage can be blended in.

Our discussion of the new legal category, DOCG, covered in the Barolo section, applies to Barbaresco also. In buying Barbaresco, the producer is, as always, the most important factor to consider, followed by the vintage and the vineyard, but the general level of quality in Barbaresco is overall quite good. The wines are generally quite reliable; there is more consistency here than in Barolo, for example. This is not unrelated, of course, to the fact that Barolo is a much better known wine. Even a producer such as Villadoria, who makes miserable Barolo, turns out a drinkable Barbaresco. There is obviously not much of a market for a mediocre Barbaresco,

while a poor Barolo can draw on the strength of the Barolo name. And since Barolo generally commands a higher price, there is also more of a temptation to play games.

Rating: Barbaresco ****

The Crus of Barbaresco

It has been said that the differences among the wines from the *communi* of Barbaresco are less evident than those in Barolo and, further, that the wines of a particular hillside evince less variation from one plot to another.

The hills are not as steep in the Barbaresco zone as those in Barolo; they are rounder and gentler, with an average altitude of 655 to 985 feet (200 to 300 meters). The vineyards are planted on the slopes at altitudes of 600 to 1,200 feet (183 to 365 meters) above sea level. The best vineyards generally face southwest, receiving the benefit of the

BARBARESCO ACREAGE AND PRODUCTION BY VILLAGE

Village	Number of Growers[a]	Acres	Hectares[b]	Percent of Total	Maximum Annual Production in Bottles*
Barbaresco	130	542.9921	219.7370	44.98	1,523,472
Neive	227	368.8141	149.2510	30.55	1,034,781
San Rocco Senodelvio	21	64.0027	25.9005	05.30	179,572
Treiso d'Alba	97	231.2641	93.5875	19.16	648,857
Total	475	1207.0730	488.4760	99.99†	3,386,682

* Based on a maximum production of 2,806 bottles per acre (52 hectoliters per hectare) after aging
† Error due to rounding

Source: [a] *Albo Vigneti '89.* Camera di Commercio Industria Artigianato e Agricoltura di Cuneo. December 31, 1989
[b] Associazione Consorzi di Tutela del Barolo, Barbaresco e dei Vini d'Alba, 1988

(warmer) afternoon sun. The soil here is limestone and clayey marl, compact and rich in potassium and other minerals, similar to that in Barolo and of the same marine origin.

Barbaresco is made from 100 percent nebbiolo grapes, in any combination of the three allowable subvarieties: lampia, michet, and rosé. It is said that there is more of the lampia planted in the Barbaresco vineyards than of the other two. But, like Barolo, rarely if ever do these clones exist in pure form.

THE CHARACTER OF THE COMUNI

The Barbarescos of each *comune* vary one from the other. The producers point out that the Barbarescos of Barbaresco itself are lighter in color and body; they are noted for their structure and perfume. Those of Treiso are regarded for their finesse. The wines of Neive, with a less pronounced perfume, are the fullest in body and the most tannic.

San Rocco Senodelvio d'Alba, in the western part of the zone, is home to 21 growers who cultivate 64 acres (25 hectares) of nebbiolo for Barbaresco. It is claimed that the Roman emperor Publius Elvius Pertinace was born here. Then again it is also claimed that he was born in Barbaresco and Liguria, and who knows where else. His brief reign, in 193 B.C., was the shortest of all, eighty-seven days: he was coronated on January 1 and assassinated on March 28. Unlike American politicians, he wanted order and honesty, something that swam against the tide of corruption so prevalent in Rome at the time.

Major Vineyards

Capalot   Montersino

Producer of Note

Piazza Cav. Uff. Armando

Pertinace, in the borough of Treiso, has four houses and a trattoria. They also claim the emperor as their own.

Producer of Note

Cantina Sociale Vignaioli "Elvio Pertinace"

Tre Stelle, is a *frazione* of Treiso. It has a few houses and a *ristorante,* plus a few vines.

Vineyard

Cascina Bruciato

Barbaresco, the village in the northwestern part of the zone, is dominated by the eleventh-century tower that was built as a lookout point and a signal tower to warn of barbarian invaders. The tower stands 118 feet (36 meters) high. The privately owned *castello* of Barbaresco belonged at one time to Domizio Cavazza. Cavazza, the noted professor and agronomist of the nineteenth and twentieth centuries, founded the co-op of Barbaresco in 1894. He is also responsible for making Barbaresco a dry wine. Just off the town hall square stands the mid–nineteenth-century church of the Fraternity of San Donato. It is now used to house the Enoteca Regionale del Barbaresco, which opened in 1986. Barbaresco is home to 130 growers who cultivate 543 acres (220 hectares) of nebbiolo for Barbaresco, about 45 percent of the vines in the entire zone. The Barbarescos of Barbaresco are lighter in color and in body; they are noted for their structure and perfume.

Major Vineyards

Asili	Pora, or Porra
Martinenga	Rabajà, or Rabajat
Montefico	Rio Sordo, or Rivosordo
Montestefano	Secondine
Pajè, or Pagliari	

Top Producers

Azienda Agricola "Brico Asili" de Ceretto	Produttori del Barbaresco
Gaja	Tenuta Cisa Asinari dei Marchesi di Gresy

Other Producers of Note

Cortese Giuseppe (*località* Rabajà)	La Spinoza Azienda Agricola di Pietro Berutti & Figlio (*località* Fassetto)
De Forville	
Giacosa Donato di Carlo Giacosa	Roagna, Azienda Agricola "I Paglieri" di Alfredo e Giovanni

Neive, with nearly 31 percent of the total acreage for Barbaresco, is in the northeast part of the district. There are two sections of Neive, the old and the new. The new section is home to Piemonte's greatest producer, Bruno Giacosa, and to the country's finest grappa maker, Romano Levi. The old section of town contains, as expected, narrow, winding roads, old houses, and palaces. The *castello* belongs to the Stupinos, who produce one of Barbaresco's finest wines. The parish church of Saint Peter and Paul in the Fraternity of Saint Michael is Piemontese baroque. Also, in the medieval upper town, there is the outstanding Ristorante Contea de Neive, where, besides an outstanding meal, you can choose from an excellent selection of Barbarescos. The menu of superb regional dishes, typical of the Langhe, is prepared by chef Claudio Verro. Tonino Verro keeps a watchful eye on the dining room. The 227 growers cultivate 369 acres (149 hectares) of nebbiolo for Barbaresco. The Barbaresco of Neive have a less pronounced perfume, are the fullest in body, and the most tannic.

Major Vineyards

Albesani	Cotta, or Cotà
Basarin	Gallina
Chirra	Santo Stefano

Top Producers

Bruno Giacosa	Cantina del Glicine di Adriana Marzi & Roberto Bruno
Castello di Neive di Familia Stupino	

Other Producers of Note

Accademia Torregiorgi	Parroco di Neive di Benefico Parrocchiale di Neive
Bordino Franco	
Cigliuti F.lli di Renato Cigliuti (Bricco di Neive, *località* Serra Boella)	
	Pasquero-Elia Secondo (Bricco di Neive, *località* Serra Boella)
Giacosa F.lli di Leone, Valerio & Renzo	

Treiso d'Alba, with about 20 percent of the acreage for Barbaresco, is in the south-central part of the zone. These Barbarescos are regarded for their finesse. The 97 growers grow nebbiolo for Barbaresco on 231 acres (95 hectares). For the best view of the valley, look toward the mountains. There is an imposing bell tower here. Just outside the town, in a climb toward the vineyards, you will see a great gorge, *rocche dei sette fratelli,* the rocks of the seven brothers. This gorge, consisting of a series of gullies and overhanging rocks, is the setting for a number of legends dealing with the mysterious happenings that occurred here once upon a time. One account tells of how seven evil and treacherous brothers disappeared into a wide gully that opened onto their courtyard, to repay them for their evil ways, no doubt. This mysterious event took place on the Lord's day. They should've drunk more Barbaresco.

Major Vineyards

Casotto	Marcarini
Giacosa	Pajorè

Producers of Note

Pelissero Luigi & Figlio (*località* Ferrere)	Vezza Sergio (Borgata Ferrere)
Rizzi Azienda Vitivinicola di Ernesto Dellapiana	

THE CRUS THEMSELVES

Lorenzo Fantini, in his *Monografia Sulla Viticoltura ed Enologia Nella Provincia di Cuneo,* lists the following vineyards in the Zona di Barbaresco, all in the *comune* of Barbaresco![27]

Montestefano	Cascina Montà
Ronchi	Ferrere
Cascina Nuova	Cascina Viale
San Teobaldo	Marcarino
Fosetti	Giacosa
Martinenga	Casotto
Cascina Trifolora	Bongivanni (sic)
Cascina Bruciata	S. Stefanetto

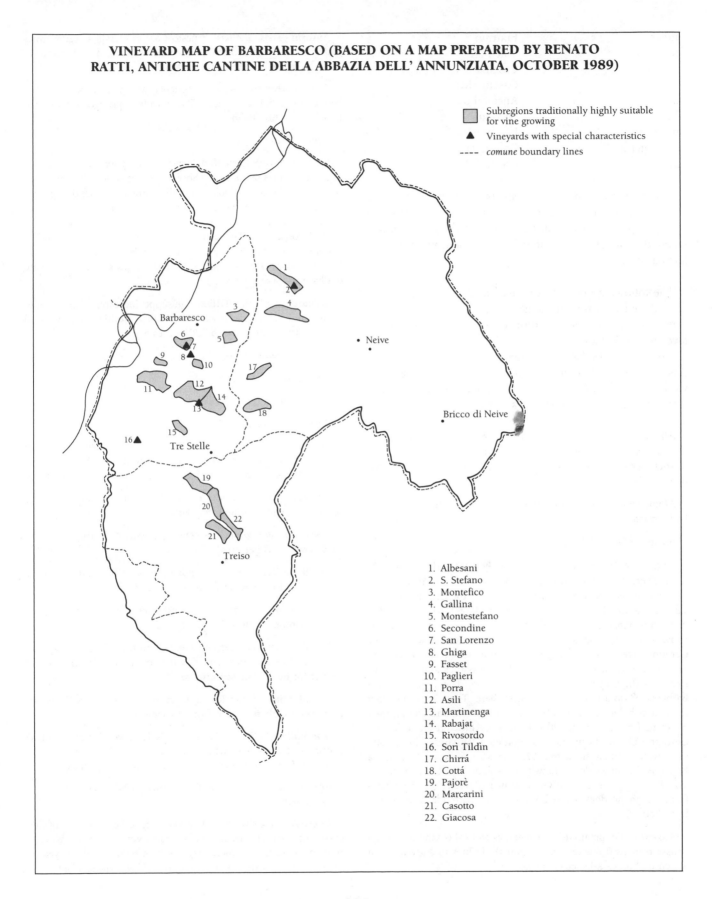

VINEYARD MAP OF BARBARESCO (BASED ON A MAP PREPARED BY RENATO RATTI, ANTICHE CANTINE DELLA ABBAZIA DELL' ANNUNZIATA, OCTOBER 1989)

◻ Subregions traditionally highly suitable for vine growing

▲ Vineyards with special characteristics

---- *comune* boundary lines

Barbaresco

Neive

Bricco di Neive

Tre Stelle

Treiso

1. Albesani
2. S. Stefano
3. Montefico
4. Gallina
5. Montestefano
6. Secondine
7. San Lorenzo
8. Ghiga
9. Fasset
10. Paglieri
11. Porra
12. Asili
13. Martinenga
14. Rabajat
15. Rivosordo
16. Sorì Tildìn
17. Chirrá
18. Cottá
19. Pajorè
20. Marcarini
21. Casotto
22. Giacosa

Cravero	Frattino
Treiso	Valeirano
Pagliere	Cascina del Rio
Montersino	Cascina Rizzi
Reis	Aneairello
Ghiga	Nicolini
Rivosordo	Rambone
Roncaglietta	Roncaglia
Manzola	Corno

The best position in the zone is considered to be La Martinenga, regarded as Barbaresco's top vineyard. This 54-acre (21.8-hectare) vineyard is located at the curve formed where the southeast slope of Asili and the southwest slope of Rabajà meet.

The following notations are used in this section:
[a] Labeled with the cru name.
[b] This combination of producer and cru is among our favorites in Barbaresco.

Other owner-producers indicates those who own a piece of this vineyard and/or those who use grapes from this vineyard to produce a Barbaresco with grapes from here, regardless of whether or not they do a cru bottling.

Albesani (*Neive*). The highly esteemed **Santo Stefano,** owned in its entirety by Castello di Neive, is located within this vineyard district. Bernerdino Gastaldi's Azienda Agricola Gastaldi is located here. *

Albina (*Barbaresco*). This is the same as the **L'Albina** vineyard of La Spinona.

Ansario (*Treiso d'Alba*).

Asili, or **Asij** (*Barbaresco*). This highly esteemed 37-acre (15-hectare) cru adjoins **Martinenga** to the north. **Bricco Asili,** the top part of Asili, is bottled as a Barbaresco cru by the Cerettos. Ceretto also buys grapes from some 10 acres (4 hectares) that they label as Asij. These vines, planted at 853 to 952 feet (260 and 290 meters) above sea level, face southward. Within the past few years the Cerettos have, in some vintages, blended in wine from Bricco Asili as well. On average, they produce 24,000 bottles annually. They have bought grapes from here since 1966. The Produttori del Barbaresco[b] do a cru Barbaresco from here. Their '82 came from the grapes belonging to Conti, Cortese, Giacosa, and Odore, their '85 came from grapes provided by Conti, Aldo and Riccardo Giacosa, and Odore. Bruno Giacosa bottled a Barbaresco from Asili; we haven't seen it since the '67. The Roagnas used to bottle a Barolo Asili, but we don't know if they still do. The last one that we tasted was the '74. Donato Giacosa owns 0.9 acre (0.35 hectare) from which he does a cru bottling. Fontanafredda buys grapes from here. **

Augenta. Fontanafredda buys grapes from this vineyard. Luigi Pelissero owns 6.2 acres (2.5 hectares) of vines in Augenta from which he bottles a Dolcetto d'Alba.

Ausario (*Treiso d'Alba*). Ernesto Casetta of F.lli Casetta grows grapes in this vineyard from which he produces a Barbaresco. In 1978 he made 25,000 bottles of that wine.

Balin (*Barbaresco*). Azienda Agricola "Moccagatta" bottles a Barbaresco from their vines here. They do a *barrique*-aged version that they label as Bric Balin.

Balluri (*Neive*).

Basarin (*Neive*). Castello di Neive owns 2.3 acres (0.94 hectare) of dolcetto vines in Basarin. Those vines face south. They produce some 7,000 bottles of Dolcetto d'Alba annually. Azienda Agricola "Moccagatta" also owns 2.5 acres (1 hectare) here. They have produced a Barbaresco cru from those vines since 1982, when they made 7,000 bottles. Parroco del Neive owns 5 acres (2 hectares) of nebbiolo from which they produce their Barbaresco cru Basarin. Bruno Giacosa produces some 15,000 bottles a year of Dolcetto d'Alba from here.*

Bernardotti (*Treiso d'Alba*). Giuseppe Mascarello buys grapes from here for his Barbaresco cru. He first produced that wine in 1978; today he produces 5,300 bottles a year.

Bernino (*Barbaresco*).

Boito (*Treiso d'Alba*).

Bongiovanni (*Treiso d'Alba*).

Bordini (*Neive*).

Bordino (*Treiso d'Alba*). Azienda Agricola "Le Colline" has 12.4 acres (5 hectares) of nebbiolo vines in Bordino which they use for their Barbaresco. They don't indicate the cru name on the label.

Borgese (*Neive*). Antonio de Nicola of Maria Feyles owns 2.5 acres (1 hectare) nebbiolo for Barbaresco.

Boschetto (*Barbaresco*). Azienda Agricola "Moccagatta" owns 11.8 acres (4.78 hectares) of vines here.

Bric Balin (*Barbaresco*). Azienda Agricola "Moccagatta" bottled a *barrique*-aged Barbaresco from here in 1987.

Bric Buschet (*Barbaresco*). Azienda Agricola "Moccagatta" bottles a Chardonnay delle Langhe from here.

Bric del Cucu (*Barbaresco*). Pietro Berutti of "La Spinona" uses his nebbiolo vines grown in this part of the **La Ghiga** vineyard district for his Barbaresco cru.

Bric Mentina. Dario Rocca of Azienda Agricola "La Ca' Növa" produces a Barbaresco cru from his vines here.

Bric Valtorta (*Neive*). Castello di Neive owns 3.4 acress (1.37 hectares) of vines here which they use to produce some 10,000 bottles of Dolcetto d'Alba annually. The vines face southeast.

Bricco (*Treiso d'Alba*). Pio Cesare owns 19.8 acres (8 hectares) of vines here.

Bricco Asili (*Barbaresco*). Azienda Agricola "Bricco Asili" of Ceretto owns 5 acres (2 hectares) of nebbiolo vines on Bricco Asili, the ridge of **Asili,** from which they produce 8,000 bottles a year of their highly regarded Barbaresco cru.[b] These vines, planted between 952 and 1,083 feet (290 and 330 meters) above sea level, face south. They are the sole owners of this part of Asili. The first Bricco Asili Barbaresco was the '73. This wine is more elegant and has more perfume than their **Faset** or Asij bottlings.**

Bricco Codevilla (*Barbaresco*). Pietro Berutti's "La Spinona" owns vines here.

Bricco del Cucolo (*Barbaresco*). Castello di Verduno produces a Barbera d'Alba from their vines grown here. This could be the Italian name for Bric del Cucu, which is in the **La Ghiga** vineyard district.

Bricco Faset (*Barbaresco*). Pietro Berutti of "La Spinona" has produced a Barbaresco cru from his 6.7 acres (2.7 hectares) of vines in the upper portion of the **Faset** hillside since 1978.

Bricco Malaspina. Luigi Calissano produces a Barbaresco that they label Bricco Malaspina.

Bricco Rio Sordo (*Barbaresco*). See **Rio Sordo**.

Brich. In 1987, Albino Rocca produced a Barbaresco that he labeled as Vigneti Loreto e Brich. We suspect that this wine was made from a blend of grapes from two vineyards, including **Loreto**.

Brichet (*Neive*). A subcru within the **Cotta** vineyard.

Buschet (*Barbaresco*). Azienda Agricola "Moccagatta" bottles a Dolcetto d'Alba from the vines that they farm here. They label their Chardonnay delle Langhe from here as Bric Buschet.

Ca' Növa (*Neive*). See **Cotto**.

Cabanet (*Barbaresco*). Mario Minuto has vines here.

Camp Gros (*Barbaresco*). This plot is in the part of **Martinenga** adjacent to Rabajà.***

Campot (*Barbaresco*). Castello di Verduno produces a Dolcetto d'Alba from the vines they grow here.

Canova (*Barbaresco*). Donato Giacosa owns 2.8 acres (1.15 hectares) of vines in this vineyard. Romualdo Giacosa bottles a cru from his grapes in Canova.

Capalot (*San Rocco Senodelvio d'Alba*). Azienda Agricola "Santa Maria" farms nebbiolo for Barbaresco in this vineyard.

Cars (*Barbaresco*). This vineyard is also known as Don' Cars. The Azienda Agricola "La Spinona" of Pietro Berutti grows dolcetto, barbera, nebbiolo, and freisa here on 10 acres (4 hectares). They use the nebbiolo for a Nebbiolo delle Langhe and also make a Barbaresco cru.

Cascina Alberta (*Treiso d'Alba*). This *cascina* represents Contratto's Barbaresco holdings in Treiso. Since 1985 he has bottled a Barbaresco cru from here.

Cascina Boito (*Treiso d'Alba*).

Cascina Bordino in Langa (*Treiso d'Alba*). See **Bordino**.

Cascina Bricco (*Treiso d'Alba*). See **Bricco**.

Cascina Bruciato (*Treiso d'Alba*). Marino Balbo grows grapes for his Barbaresco here. It is located in the section of Treiso known as Tre Stelle. He does a cru Barbaresco from those holdings.

Cascina Ca' Növa. F.lli Rocca of La Ca' Növa farm vines here.

Cascina Congroia (*Neive*). F.lli Toso produce a Barbaresco from their Cascina Congroia holdings.

Cascina Ghiga (*Barbaresco*). Bersano occasionally bottled a Cascina Ghiga from their vines in Barbaresco. We don't know if they still do.

Cascina La Rocca. Franco Molino produces a Barbaresco from his Cascina La Rocca holdings.

Cascina Nuova (*Neive*).

Cascina Rocca (*Barbaresco*). Riccardo Cortese produces a Barbaresco from his Cascina Rocca holdings.

Cascina Rombone (*Treiso d'Alba*). See **Rombone**.

Cascina Vallegranda Sotto (*Treiso d'Alba*). Ernesto Grasso produced 1,200 bottles of an '87 Barbaresco from his holdings here.

Cascinotta (*Neive*). Parroco del Neive owns vines here.

Casot (*Barbaresco*). Luigi Pelissero owns 1.2 acres (0.5 hectare) of vines here. Vietti bought grapes from the Casot vineyard to produce a small quantity of a Barbaresco Casot in 1980 and 1981. **Vitolotti** and Vecchia Casot are subcrus within this vineyard. Luigi Bianco farms vines in the former section and Carlo Boffa in both. Giuseppe Nada's Poderi Casot produces a Barbaresco cru from here.

Casotto (*Treiso d'Alba*). This vineyard district is close to the Giacosa and Marcarini vineyards. The Cantina Vignaioli "Elvio Pertinace" co-op owns 6.2 acres (2.5 hectares) in this vineyard, 3.7 (1.5) of which are planted in nebbiolo. They did a cru bottling in 1982. Vietti produced 100 bottles of a Barbaresco cru from Casotto from the 1980 and 1981 vintages.*

Castellissano, or **Castellizzano** (*Treiso d'Alba*). Cantina Vignaioli "Elvio Pertinace" owns 8.2 acres (3.3 hectares) in this cru, 3.2 (1.3) in nebbiolo, from which they produced a Barbaresco cru in 1982.

Cavalli (*Neive*).

Cavana, Cavanna (*Barbaresco*). Giovanni Giordano has vines in Cavana from which he bottles a Barbaresco cru. Azienda Agricola "Moccagatta" owns 0.9 acre (0.38 hectare) of vines here as well.

Chirella (*Treiso d'Alba*).

Chirra (*Neive*).*

Ciabot (*Barbaresco*).

Cole (*Barbaresco*). Donato Giacosa owns 0.9 acre (0.4 hectare) of vines here. Mario Minuto of Azienda Agricola "Moccagatta" produced their first Barbaresco Cole from their 1.2 acres (0.47 hectare) of vines here in 1982, making 3,100 bottles.

Cortini-Montebertotto (*Neive*). Castello di Neive owns 2 acres (0.85 hectare) of vines facing south to southwest from which they produce a Grignolino d'Asti. They also cultivate arneis vines in the Montebertotto section.

Costa Russi (*Barbaresco*). A *costa* is the side of a hill that faces the sun and Russi is the name of the former owners. Gaja is the sole owner of this 10.1-acre (4.1-hectare) vineyard. He has bottled a Barbaresco Costa Russi since 1978. His average production from here is 12,000 bottles in the vintages that he makes it. Of his three crus, this one, at 750 feet (230 meters) above sea level, is the lowest in altitude. The vines have a southwestern exposure. The Gajas bought this vineyard in 1950. Although it is a very good Barbaresco, we find it the least of Gaja's three crus, as well as the earliest maturing. It is also the softest and most open, and, according to Gaja, has the most intense perfume and is the sweetest.

Cotta, Cotà, or *Cotto* (*Neive*). Confratelli de San Michele produces a Barbaresco cru from their holdings in this vineyard. Parroco del Neive also owns a piece, and Porta Rossa farms vines here as well in the section known as Ca' Nòva. There are two subcrus: Brichet and La Ca' Nòva or Ca' Nòva. Sottimano owns 1.6 acres (0.67 hectare) of Brichet and has bottled a Barbaresco cru from these vines since 1984. Dario Rocca of Azienda Agricola "La Ca' Nòva" and F.lli Rocca (Giulio and Franco) bottle a Barbaresco Ca' Nòva from their holdings in that subcru. Sottimano owns 0.9 acre (0.4 hectare) in the Ca' Nòva section as well.*

Crichet Pajè (*Barbaresco*). Roagna bottles their best Barbaresco under this name. We believe the grapes are from their vines in the *Pajè* vineyard. They also at one time produced a light, fruity table wine with this name from 100 percent nebbiolo grapes.

Crocetta (*Neive*). Accademia Torregiorgi buys grapes from Giovanni Antona for its Barbaresco Crocetta.

Cubà (*Neive*). Cantina del Glicine bottles, or bottled, a Barbaresco cru from Cubà. The '78 was the last one we tasted.

Curà, or *Curra* (*Neive*). Adriana Marzi, winemaker of Cantina del Glincine, produces some 8,000 bottles a year of Barbaresco Curà from their 7.5339 acres (3.0488 hectares /8 *giornate*) of vines in this vineyard. The vines—mostly nebbiolo, with a little dolcetto—have a southwestern exposure.

Darmagi (*Barbaresco*). Gaja has farmed cabernet sauvignon vines here since 1978 when he first planted them. There are 6.2 acres (2.5 hectares) planted at an elevation of 990 feet (300 meters) above sea level.

Del Sorì (*Treiso d'Alba*). Ernesto Dellapiana of Azienda Vitivinicola "Rizzi" cultivates vines in this vineyard, which seems to be another name for his *Sorì del Noce* vineyard.

Don' Cars (*Barbaresco*). See *Cars.*

Faset, or *Fascet* (*Barbaresco*). Mario Minuto bottles a Barbaresco cru from this vineyard, as does Porta Rossa. F.lli Oddero has vines here and Pietro Berutti owns the top section, *Bricco Faset.* Castello di Verduno farms vines and Luigi Bianco produces a Barbaresco cru from their vines in his section. His '82 was labeled as Fascet, his '83, Faset. The Ceretto brothers own some 6 acres (2.5 hect-

ares) planted at altitudes of 853 to 1,017 feet (260 to 310 meters) above sea level. Their vines face southward. They produced their first Faset Barbaresco in 1985. Bruno Ceretto told us that their Faset bottling matures a little sooner than their Bricco Asili Barbaresco.

Fassetto (*Barbaresco*). We suspect that this is still another name for *Faset.*

Fondetta (*Treiso d'Alba*). The Azienda Vitivinicola "Rizzi" of Ernesto Dellapiana owns 5.9 acres (2.4 hectares) of nebbiolo vines in this vineyard. Reportedly they are all michet. Dellapiana bottles a Barbaresco cru from here.

Gaia, or *Gaja* (*Neive*). Maria Feyles and Cantina del Glicine bottle Barbaresco crus from this vineyard. Glicine owns 0.9 acres (0.4 hectare) of vines and produces some 2,000 bottles a year.

Gaiun (*Barbaresco*). Marchese Alberto di Gresy[b] bottles a cru from this section of La *Martinenga* adjacent to Asili.***

Gallina (*Neive*). Confratelli di San Michele, now just San Michele, and Giuseppe Negro have vines here, as does Parroco del Neive, who owns 3.7 acres (1.5 hectares), 2.5 (1) in nebbiolo. They sell some of the grapes to Bruno Giacosa, and both Parroco and Giacosa produce a Gallina cru. San Michele also does a cru bottling of Barbaresco from here. And Gemma buys grapes to produce a Gallina cru. Cantina del Glicine produces a Barbaresco Gallina as well. While these are all good Barbarescos, we find that from Bruno Giacosa[b] superior to the rest. Giacosa buys grapes from vines that are, on average, nearly twenty years old. At one time Castello de Neive owned 7.4 acres (3 hectares) of vines in Gallina.**

Gallinetta (*Neive*). Sottimano buys grapes from a 3-acre (1.2-hectare) plot here.

Gava Principe. Cantina del Glicine produced an '81 Barbaresco from this vineyard.

Ghiga (*Barbaresco*). See *La Ghiga.*

Giachello (*Treiso d'Alba*).

Giacosa (*Treiso d'Alba*). This vineyard district adjoins Marcarini to the north. Angelo Gaja owns some 4.5 acres (1.8 hectares) of Giacosa, and Gigi Rosso owns a piece as well. Cascina Carlo Viglino produces 9,300 bottles annually of Barbaresco from this vineyard.*

Gresy (*Treiso d'Alba*).

L'Albina (*Barbaresco*). Pietro Berutti of "La Spinona" owns 12.3 acres (5 hectares) of vines here from which he produces his Podere Albina cru. The first was the '86.

La Cà Nòva (*Treiso d'Alba*). A subcru of the *Cotto* vineyard.

La Ghiga (*Barbaresco*). Pietro Berutti of "La Spinona" bottles a very good Barbaresco cru from his 17.6 acres (7 hectares) in La Ghiga. A few years ago he bought this plot from Bersano. Berutti has produced a La Ghiga cru since 1983. He farms the nebbiolo from the section that he calls Bric del Cucu. And *Bricco del Cucolo* could be in this vineyard district as well.

Le Terre Forti (*Barbaresco*). Casa Vinicola Piemontese, now Poderi e Cantine de Marengo-Marenda, produces a Barbaresco cru from vines grown in this vineyard.

Loreto (*Barbaresco*). Paolo de Forville owns vines in this vineyard. Bruno Anfosso de Forville has bottled a Barbaresco Loreto since 1974. And Albino Rocca, in 1987, did a Barbaresco that he labeled as Vigneti Loreto e Brich.

Manzola (*Treiso d'Alba*).

Marcarini, or *Marcarino* (*Treiso d'Alba*). Marcarini is located between the regarded crus of Pajorè, to the north, and Giacosa to the south. Cantina del Glicine produces or produced about 2,000 bottles a year. We haven't tasted it since the '79. Glicine owns 0.94 acre (0.38 hectare) of nebbiolo here. Their Barbera Nebbiolata contains 10 percent nebbiolo for Barbaresco from here. Cantina Vignaioli "Elvio Pertinace" owns 5 acres (2 hectares) and have bottled a Barbaresco from this cru since 1982. And Giuseppe Mascarello also produces or produced a Barbaresco from here. Castello di Neive own 3.2 acres (1.3 hectares) of vines here from which they produce a Moscato d'Asti and a Barbera d'Alba.*

Maringota (*Bricco di Neive*). Giuseppe Traversa of Cascina Chiabotto bottles a Barbaresco Maringota from his vines here.

Martinenga (*Barbaresco*). This 54-acre (21.8-hectare) vineyard, which many consider the finest in the zone, is located at the curve formed where the southeast slope of Asili and the southwest slope of Rabajà meet. La Martinenga is owned by a single proprietor, Marchese Alberto di Gresy. Some 30 acres (12 hectares) are planted in nebbiolo. Di Gresy bottles three Barbarescos from this vineyard, La Martinenga, and two subcrus: Camp Gros (since 1978) and Gaiun. Camp Gros covers 5.2 acres (2.1 hectares) and Gaiun 5.1 (2.05). Of the two, Camp Gros[b], from the plot near Rabajà, has more tannin, structure, acid, and firmness; it matures more slowly and should live longer. Gaiun[b], adjacent to Asili, is softer, rounder, and richer in glycerine; it is a gentle and feminine wine of style and breed with more perfume and elegance. It is, in fact, the essence of the La Martinenga Barbaresco. The two subcru Barbarescos of Martinenga are among our favorites.***

Masseria (*Neive*). Alfredo Currado of Vietti is the sole producer of a Barbaresco from Masseria. He has been buying the grapes from Eugenio Voghera since 1964. Currado produces less than 6,000 bottles a year of this cru. This 5-acre (2-hectare) vineyard, in the *località* Bruciati di Neive, is planted 100 percent in nebbiolo lampia. This Barbaresco, not unexpectedly, is full-bodied and robust as far as Barbarescos go. It requires more time to come around than many Barbarescos.

Messoirano (*Neive*). Castello di Neive owns 10.4 acres (4.2 hectares) here, including 3.2 (1.3) for Barbaresco, 2.2 (0.9) for Barbera d'Alba, and 4.9 (1.97) for Dolcetto d'Alba. Castello di Neive produces a Barbaresco cru from here. They also sell grapes to Accademia Torregiorgi for their Barbaresco cru.

Moccagatta (*Barbaresco*). Carlo Deltetto's il Vecchio Tralcio, Azienda Agricola "Moccagatta," and Produttori del Barbaresco bottle Barbaresco crus from this vineyard. "Moccagatta" owns 25 acres (10 hectares), 15 (6) of which are planted in nebbiolo. Bellora,

Casetta, Lignana, and Viglino provide nebbiolo grapes from 5.9 acres (2.4 hectares) to the Produttori del Barbaresco. In the better vintages the Produttori does a cru bottling of Moccagatta from those grapes.*

Monferrino (*Treiso d'Alba*).

Monprandi (*Bricco di Neive*). Franco Bordino cultivates vines in Monprandi from which he produces a cru bottling.

Monta (*Treiso d'Alba*).

Montarsino (*Treiso d'Alba*). See *Montersino* (*Treiso d'Alba*).

Monte Aribaldo (*Treiso d'Alba*). Marchese di Gresy owns this 16.4-acre (6.6-hectare) vineyard planted in dolcetto for Dolcetto d'Alba and nebbiolo for Barbaresco. We understand that all of the nebbiolo grapes are sold.

Montebertotto (*Neive*). Castello di Neive owns 6.1 acress (2.47 hectares) in this vineyard planted in arneis from which they produce an Arneis delle Langhe.

Montefico (*Barbaresco*). In 1982, Giovanni Rocca and Primo e Romano Rocca delivered their nebbiolo to the Produttori del Barbaresco for their Montefico Barbaresco. The Produttori del Barbaresco produced a Barbaresco cru from those grapes. Ceretto and Bruno Giacosa used to bottle Barbaresco Montefico crus, but neither buys the grapes any longer. The Cerettos haven't produced a Barbaresco from here since 1974. From at least 1969 through 1971, Bruno Giacosa produced some especially fine Barbarescos from here.*

Montersino (*San Rocco Senodelvio d'Alba*). The Azienda Agricola "Santa Maria" of Mario Viberti produces a Barbaresco cru from their vines here.

Montersino (*Treiso d'Alba*). Prunotto bought grapes from this vineyard at one time.

Montesomo (*Barbaresco*). Cantina del Glicine bottles a Barbaresco Montesomo. The only one we've tasted was the '77. Antonio de Nicola of Maria Feyles owns 3.5 acres (1.4 hectares) of nebbiolo.

Montestefano (*Barbaresco*). The Barbarescos of this cru tend to be quite tannic and long-lived, especially those from Prunotto. Montestefano has been called the Barolo of Barbaresco; it is more like a Neive Barbaresco than one from Barbaresco. Produttori del Barbaresco get their grapes for their Barbaresco Montestefano cru from the 9 acres (3.64 hectares) owned by four growers: Gonella, Maffei, Rivella, and Rocca. Bruno Anfosso de Forville has bottled a Barbaresco Montestefano since 1974. Paolo de Forville does a Barbaresco cru from here as well, and so does Prunotto, who buys grapes from a 7.2-acre (2.9-hectare) plot. F.lli Oddero also cultivates vines here.**

Moretti Valfieri buys grapes from here to produce its Barbaresco Moretti.

Munfrina (*Treiso d'Alba*). We believe that Munfrina is Piemontese dialect for Monferrino. Luigi Pelissero does a Dolcetto d'Alba from here.

Muret (*Treiso d'Alba*).

Nervo (*Treiso d'Alba*). Members of the Cantina Vignaioli "Elvio Pertinace" cooperative own a total of 12.4 acres (5 hectares) in the Nervo vineyard. They produced a Barbaresco cru from their 7.4 acres (3 hectares) of nebbiolo in 1982. Torino wine merchant Giovanni Troglia sells a Podere Nervo Barbaresco with his label.

Nicolini (*Treiso d'Alba*). Giuseppe Mascarello produces a cru Barbaresco from here. His first was the '82.

Ovello (*Barbaresco*). Paolo de Forville and members of the Produttori del Barbaresco own vines here. The Produttori del Barbaresco bottles an Ovello cru that is quite good indeed. In certain years that wine can match any other Barbaresco for quality. This wine matures the slowest of all the Produttori crus. Their grapes come from Cravanzola, Maffei, Vacca, and Varaldo. Mauro Bianco owns 2 acres (0.8 hectare) of nebbiolo here.

Paglieri (*Barbaresco*). Roagna used to bottle his Barbaresco with this name. We haven't seen it since his '71. This is another name for **Pajè**. *

Pagliuzzi, or *Pagliuzzo* (*Barbaresco*). F.lli Oddero cultivates vines in this vineyard.

Pajè, Pagliari, or *Payè* (*Barbaresco*). Members of the Produttori del Barbaresco and the Roagnas have vines in this vineyard. Both do a cru bottling. Crichet Pajè is Roagna's best Barbaresco. Franco Giordano and Giuseppe Giordano at one time supplied the Produttori del Barbaresco with their grapes from Pajè for the Produttori's cru Barbaresco.*

Pajorè, or **Payore** (*Treiso d'Alba*). Pajorè, just south of Tre Stelle, adjoins Marcarini on the north. Enrico Giovannini-Moresco[b] at one time owned 23.5 acres (9.5 hectares) of vines here. We were told by Moresco that those vines were 100 percent nebbiolo rosé. Angelo Gaja told us that Moresco's part of this vineyard was planted with only 25 percent, perhaps a bit more, of the nebbiolo rosé clone. Gaja bought 95 percent, or 22 acres (9 hectares), of this vineyard from Moresco's total holding of nebbiolo. The 20,000 bottles of Barbaresco that Moresco produced came from those vines. He produced this outstanding Barbaresco in the good vintages between 1967 and 1981. In 1979 he sold 50 percent of his Pajorè holdings to Angelo Gaja, and 45 percent more in 1985. Today Moresco owns some 1.2 acres (0.5 hectare) of nebbiolo vines here. *

Pas (*Treiso d'Alba*). Luigi Pelissero owns 2.5 acres (1 hectare) of vines in this vineyard.

Pastura (*Neive*). Accademia Torregiorgi and Cantina del Glicine produce good Barbarescos from this vineyard. Glicine produces, on average, 2,000 bottles a year.

Payore-Barberis (*Treiso d'Alba*). Scarpa buys grapes from Sr. Barberis to produce 4,000 bottles a year of their fine Barbaresco cru. They label it Payore so they don't create confusion with Moresco's Pajorè. Both are parts of the same vineyard.*

Podere del Pajorè. See **Pajorè**.

Podere Nervo (*Treiso d'Alba*). See **Nervo**.

Pora, or **Porra** (*Barbaresco*). Sebastiano Musso, F.lli Oddero, and members of the Produttori del Barbaresco own vines in this vineyard. The Produttori bottles a Pora cru. In 1985 they got those grapes from Dellaferrera and Manzone, and in 1982 they also got grapes from Culasso and Veraldo. In 1980, Vietta bought grapes and produced a small quantity of a Barbaresco Pora.*

Pozzo (*Barbaresco*). Bruno Anfosso de Forville has bottled a Barbaresco Pozzo since 1974. Giuseppe Rocca and Severino Oberto have vines here.

Prinsi (*Barbaresco*). Ottavia Lesquio's Azienda Agricola "Cascina Principe" produces a Barbaresco cru from their vines in this vineyard.

Qualin (*Barbaresco*). Qualin is in the **La Ghiga** district. Pietro Berutti of Azienda Agricola "La Spinona" owns 5.4 acres (2.2 hectares) in this vineyard from which he bottles a Barbaresco cru. He also grows dolcetto, barbera, and freisa. Gaja also owns a section of Qualin; at one time he bottled a Freisa from his 2.9-acre (1.2-hectare) plot here.

Rabajà, or **Rabajat** (*Barbaresco*). This fine cru, adjoining Martinenga to the south, is in the **Pora** zone. F.lli Barale has rented 2.5 acres (1 hectare) of fifty-five-year-old vines in this vineyard since 1982. The vines face southward at an average altitude of 1,555 feet (475 meters) above sea level. Barale does a cru Barbaresco from here. Produttori del Barbaresco[b] got their grapes in 1982 from Alutto, Bruno Rocca, Antona, Primo and Romano Rocca, and Vacca. They bottle a Barbaresco from those vines. Vietti buys grapes from a 2.5-acre (1-hectare) plot. He has been producing a Barbaresco Rabajà from 100 percent lampia since 1984. Alfredo Currado describes his Barbaresco from here as more elegant and refined than his Masseria.**

OTHER RABAJA OWNER-PRODUCERS

- Bianco Luigi & Figlio
- Cantina del Glicine[a] owns 0.47 acre (0.2 hectare) from which they produce 1,700 bottles a year.
- Cantine Duca d'Asti[a] has produced a Rabajà Barbaresco since the '82; there was no '84. They contract for the grapes.
- Castello di Verduno
- Cortese Giuseppe[a]
- [Anfosso] de Forville[a] has bottled a Barbaresco Rabajà since 1974.
- Prunotto[a] has produced a Barbaresco cru from here since 1971; they buy nebbiolo grapes from 5 acres (2 hectares).
- Albino Rocca
- Bruno Rocca's Azienda Agricola "Rabajà" bottles a Barbaresco from his holdings in Rabajà.
- Giuseppe Rocca
- Valfieri[a] buys grapes.

Rigo (*Neive*). Parroco del Neive owns vines here.

Rio Sordo, or **Rivosordo** (*Barbaresco*). F.lli Brovia and Produttori del Barbaresco bottle crus from this vineyard. Brovia produces some 3,300 bottles a year from their 1.4 acres (0.58 hectare). They have bottled that Barbaresco since 1978. The grapes for the Produttori's first Rio Sordo Barbaresco came from Francesco Ferrero, Sebastiano Ferrero, and Dante Alutto. Their '82 came from the grapes supplied by the two Ferreros. Fontanafredda buys grapes for their Barbaresco from here. Sebastiano Musso produces a Barbaresco from his vines in the section he calls Bricco Rio Sordo. Bruno Giacosa made a '85 Rio Sordo but not an '86. He first bought grapes from here in 1984 but blended that wine into his *normale* Barbaresco. F.lli Giacosa buy grapes for their Barbaresco cru from here.*

Rivetti (*Neive*).

Rizzi (*Treiso d'Alba*). Ernesto Dellapiana of Azienda Vitivinicola "Rizzi" owns 53.5 acres (21.7 hectares) of vines here for Barbaresco, Dolcetto d'Alba, and Chardonnay.

Rocca del Mattarello (*Neive*). Castello di Neive cultivate 1.2 acres (0.48 hectare) of barbera vines here for their Barbera-in-*barrique*.

Rombone (*Treiso d'Alba*). Giovanni Nada farms vines here. His holdings are labeled as Cascina Rombone. We suspect that there has been a transition at the helm here and the new owner of Cascina Rombone is now Fiorenzo Nada, who does a Barbaresco from here.

Roncaglie (*Barbaresco*). F.lli Giacosa does a Barbaresco cru from grapes they buy from this vineyard.

Roncagliette (*Barbaresco*). F.lli Giacosa owns vines in this vineyard.

Roncalini (*Barbaresco*). Fontanafredda buys grapes from this vineyard for their Barbaresco.

Ronchi (*Barbaresco*). Giuseppe Rocca owns vines in Ronchi, as does Luigi Bianco. Luigi Pelissero produces a Barbera d'Alba from Ronchi.

San Cristoforo (*Neive*). This vineyard is part of the **Basarin** district. San Michele, formerly Confratelli di San Michele, and Parroco del Neive each own a piece. The Confratelli bottles a San Cristoforo Barbaresco cru. Bruno Giacosa used to bottle a cru from here but hasn't done so in some time.

San Giuliano (*Neive*). Parroco del Neive owns 2 acres (0.8 hectare) of nebbiolo vines in this vineyard.

San Lorenzo (*Barbaresco*). This was at one time, according to Angelo Gaja, the name for a vineyard district larger than **Secondine**. Gaja uses the name today along with the Sorì qualifier for the Barbaresco cru he labels as **Sorì San Lorenzo**.

San Stefanetto (*Treiso d'Alba*).

Santa Caterina. Guido, Giovanni, and Carlo Porro own vines here.

Santo Stefano (*Neive*). Castello di Neive[b] owns 100 percent of this vineyard. The 19.4 acres (7.87 hectares) of nebbiolo vines for Barbaresco are approximately eighteen years old. They also own 1.7 acres (0.7 hectare) for Barbera d'Alba. The vines face south to southwest. They sell some of their nebbiolo grapes to Bruno Giacosa,[b] whose Santo Stefano Barbaresco is, without question, *the*

single finest Barbaresco produced today. Castello di Neive also produces one of the greatest and most consistent of all Barbarescos from this vineyard.**

Secondine (*Barbaresco*). This vineyard is just south of Barbaresco itself. Gaja's **Sorì San Lorenzo** is made from grapes grown in this vineyard district. Donato Giacosa bottles a cru Barbaresco from here that he labels Sorì Secondine. Luigi Giordano grows grapes here as well. *

Serra Boella, Serraboella (*Bricco di Neive*). F.lli Cigliuti produces some 4,650 bottles a year of a Barbaresco cru from their 7 acres (2.8 hectares) of vines in Serra Boella. Pasquero-Elia cultivates vines here as well.

Serra del Bricco di Neive (*Bricco di Neive*). F.lli Giacosa produce a Barbera d'Alba from the vines they farm here.

Sorì Ciabot. Giuseppe Traversa first made this Barbaresco in 1982.

Sorì d'Paytin (*Bricco di Neive*). Secondo Pasquero-Elia owns a total of 9 acres (3.6 hectares) of vines in this vineyard. He bottles a fine Barbaresco cru from his 6.9 acres (2.8 hectares) of nebbiolo vines. Of the 21,000 bottles of wine that Pasquero produces annually, 20,000 are Barbaresco. Pasquero bottles that Barbaresco as Sorì Paitin today.

Sorì del Noce (*Treiso d'Alba*). The Azienda Vitivinicola "Rizzi" of Ernesto Dellapiana owns 20 acres (8 hectares) of vines in Sorì del Noce from which he bottles a Barbaresco cru. He has 9.8 acres (3.97 hectares) of dolcetto for Dolcetto d'Alba and 6.2 (2.5) of chardonnay for a Chardonnay delle Lange.

Sorì di Burdin (*Neive*). Fontanabianca produces a Barbaresco from here.

Sorì Paitin. See **Sorì d'Paytin.**

Sorì Secondine (*Barbaresco*). Donato Giacosa does a Barbaresco cru from their vines here which he sometimes labels as **Surì Secondine.** *

Sorì San Lorenzo (*Barbaresco*). Gaja is the sole owner of this 7.9-acre (3.3-hectare) vineyard. He has bottled it as a cru since 1967 and produces an annual average of 10,000 bottles. Its altitude of 820 feet (250 meters) above sea level puts the vineyard between the other two Gaja crus. A *sorì* is a hilltop with a southern exposure. Sorì San Lorenzo, named for the patron saint of Alba, lies within the vineyard district of **Secondine**. Angelo Gaja says that it requires a lot of age to show its real quality, and although it is the slowest maturing it should be the longest lived. This wine is the hardest of all of Gaja's Barbaresco in its youth, and it is less drinkable even after eight years. It really comes into its own after fifteen years.*

Sorì Tildìn (*Barbaresco*). Gaja is the sole owner of this 9.14-acre (3.7-hectare) vineyard. Its name derives from a combination of the nature of the vineyard, a *sorì,* and the nickname of its former owner. The Gajas have owned this vineyard since 1934. Angelo has bottled a Sorì Tildìn Barbaresco since 1970 and produces some 10,000 bottles annually. Of the three Gaja crus, the vines here, at

885 feet (270 meters) above sea level, are grown at the highest altitude. The Sorì Tildìn Barbaresco is more closed and concentrated, with a firm texture, and holds more in reserve than Costa Russi. According to Gaja, wine writers like it because it is ready sooner and is more open than the **Sorì San Lorenzo.**

Sorì Valeriano. Tenuta Coluè bottles a Barbaresco from this vineyard from their 3.7 acres (1.5 hectares) of vines.

Sorj Canta (*Treiso d'Alba*). Eredi Lodali produces a Dolcetto d'Alba here.

Speranza (*Treiso d'Alba*). Ernesto Dellapiana of Azienda Vitivinicola "Rizzi" owns grapes here.

Stella (*Treiso d'Alba*).

Surì (*Barbaresco*). Donato Giacosa owns a 0.9-acre (0.4-hectare) section of this vineyard.

Surì (*Treiso d'Alba*). The Azienda Vitivinicola "Rizzi" of Ernesto Dellapiana owns vines here. It might be still another name for **Sorì del Noce.**

Surì Secondine (*Barbaresco*). Donato Giacosa produces a Barbaresco cru from the vines that he farms in this section of the **Secondine** vineyard district. His '87 Barbaresco from here was labeled as Sorì Secondine. *

Tamburnas (*Neive*). Sottimano buys grapes from a 1-acre (0.4-hectare) piece of this vineyard.

Tetti (*Neive*). Scarpa buys grapes from this vineyard to produce some 10,000 to 12,000 bottles a year of their very fine Barbaresco I Tetti.

Trifolè. Bruno Rocca's Azienda Agricola "Rabajà" does a Dolcetto d'Alba from here.

Trifolera (*Barbaresco*). Sottimano buys grapes from a 1-acre (0.4-hectare) piece of Trifolera.

Valeriano (*Treiso d'Alba*).

Valgrande (*Treiso d'Alba*). Gianni Gagliardo produces a Barbaresco cru from his grapes in the Valgrande vineyard.

Valtorta (*Neive*). Castello di Neive owns 7.4 acres (3 hectares) of dolcetto vines in this vineyard. Cantina del Glicine produces a Barbaresco cru from nebbiolo vines grown here.

Vanotu (*Treiso d'Alba*). Luigi Pelissero produces a Barbaresco cru from his 5 acres (2 hectares) of vines in Vanotu.

Varaldi (*Treiso d'Alba*).

Vecchia Casot (*Barbaresco*). Carlo Boffa produces a Barbaresco cru from his holdings in this vineyard, which is part of the **Casot** vineyard district.

Vedetta. F.lli Giacosa produces a Barbaresco and Barbera d'Alba from grapes grown in this vineyard.

Viglino in Giacosa (*Treiso d'Alba*). Gigi Rosso produces 9,000 bottles of Barbaresco a year from the vines he owns in this section of the **Giacosa** vineyard.

Vigna della Rocca. Orlando Arrigo produces a Barbaresco cru from this vineyard.

Vincenziana (*Barbaresco*). Mauro Bianco owns 0.5 acre (0.2 hectare) of dolcetto in the Vincenziana vineyard.

Vitolotti, or **Vitalotti** (*Barbaresco*). Luigi Bianco and Carlo Boffa own vines here. Boffa produces a Vitolotti cru from his 22 acres (9 hectares) of vines here. This vineyard is part of the **Casot** district.

THE BARBARESCO PRODUCERS RATED

****
+ Giacosa Bruno
  "Bricco Asili" Azienda Agricola di Ceretto, Bricco Asili
      ("Bricco Asili" Azienda Agricola di Ceretto, Faset
      *** −; Ceretto, Asij ** +)
  Castello di Neive
  Gaja, Sorì San Lorenzo (*normale* and Costa Russi ***)
  Gaja, Sorì Tildìn (*normale* and Costa Russi ***)
  Giovannini-Moresco Enrico, Podere del Pajorè[a]
  Marchese di Gresy, Martinenga-Camp Gros
      (Martinenga *** −)
  Marchese di Gresy, Martinenga-Gaiun (Martinenga
      *** −)
  Produttori del Barbaresco, Asili (Pajè, Rio Sordo ***;
  Moccagatta, Montefico, Ovello, and Pora *** +;
      normale **)
  Produttori del Barbaresco, Montestefano (Pajè, and Rio
      Sordo ***; Moccagatta, Montefico, Ovello, and Pora
      *** +; *normale* **)
  Produttori del Barbaresco, Rabajà (Pajè, and Rio Sordo
      ***; Moccagatta, Montefico, Ovello, and Pora
      *** +; *normale* **)
  Vietti, Rabajà (Masseria *** +; *normale* **)

***
− Barale F.lli
− "Bricco Asili" Azienda Agricola di Ceretto, Faset
      ("Bricco Asili" Azienda Agricola di Ceretto, Bricco
      Asili ****; Ceretto, Asij ** +)
  Cantina del Glicine
− Cigliuti F.lli
+ Conterno Giacomo[b]
  Gaja, Costa Russi (Sorì San Lorenzo and Sorì Tildìn
      ****)
  Gaja, *normale* (Sorì San Lorenzo and Sorì Tildìn ****)
  Le Colline
− Marchese di Gresy, Martinenga (Martinenga-Camp
      Gros and Martinenga-Gaiun ****)
  Mascarello Giuseppe
+ Produttori del Barbaresco, Moccagatta (Asili,

Montestefano, and Rabajà ****; *normale* **)
+ Produttori del Barbaresco, Montefico (Asili,
  Montestefano, and Rabajà ****; *normale* **)
+ Produttori del Barbaresco, Ovello (Asili, Montestefano,
  and Rabajà ****; *normale* **)
  Produttori del Barbaresco, Pajè (Asili, Montestefano,
  Rabajà ****; *normale* **)
+ Produttori del Barbaresco, Pora (Asili, Montestefano,
  and Rabajà ****; *normale* **)
  Produttori del Barbaresco, Rio Sordo (Asili,
  Montestefano, and Rabajà ****; *normale* **)
  Prunotto, Montestefano (*normale* *)
  Prunotto, Rabajà (*normale* *)
  Rinaldi Francesco[c]
+ Scarpa
+ Vietti, Masseria (Rabajà ****; *normale* **)

**
− Bianco Mauro, Cascina Morassino (1987)[d]
  Bordino Franco (1974)[d]
  Cantine Duca d'Asti di Chiarlo Michele, Rabajà
  (Granduca *)[e]
− Cappellano Dott. Giuseppe[f]
+ Ceretto, Asij ("Bricco Asili" Azienda Agricola di
  Ceretto, Bricco Asili ****; Faset *** −)
− Contratto
+ Cortese Giuseppe
  De Forville (1980)[c]
  Giacosa Donato
− La Spinona Azienda Agricola di Pietro Berutti
  Oddero F.lli
  Parroco del Neive, Basarin (Gallina *)
+ Pasquero Elia Secondo, Sorì d'Paytin
− Pio Cesare
  Porta Rossa
  Produttori del Barbaresco, *normale* (Asili,
  Montestefano, and Rabajà ****; Pajè and Rio Sordo
  ***; Moccagatta, Montefico, Ovello, Pora *** +)
  Ratti Renato (1980)[c]
  Rizzi Azienda Agricola di Ernesto Dellapiana
  Roagna
+ Vezza Sergio[g]
  Vietti, *normale* (Rabajà ****; Masseria *** +)

*
Accademia Torregiorgi (1980)[c]
− Accornero Flavio
  Arrigo Orlando
  Bianco Luigi
+ Boffa Carlo (1979)[c]
  Borgogno F.lli Serio e Battista[h]
+ Borgogno Giacomo

Brovia F.lli
Ca' Romè di Romano Marengo
− Calissano Luigi
Cantina Vignaioli "Elvio Pertinace," Cantina Sociale
Cantine Ca' Bianca
Cantine Duca d'Asti di Michele Chiarlo, "Granduca"
  (Rabajà **)
Casetta F.lli
Castello d'Annone, "Viarengo" (1985)[d]
+ Castello Feudale (1978)[c]
+ Coluè (formerly Tenuta Coluè di Massimo Oddero)
+ Confratelli di San Michele (now San Michele +)
Coppo Luigi (1978)[c]
De Forville Paolo (1978)[c]
Eredi Lodali
+ Feyles Maria
Fontanabianca (1987)[d]
+ Fontanafredda
+ Franco Fiorina
Gemma (1977)[c]
Giacosa F.lli
Giordano Giovanna (1980)[d]
Giri Guido[c]
+ Grasso F.lli di Emilio Grasso (1985)[d]
Grimaldi G. (1985)[d]
+ La Ca' Növa Azienda Agricola di Dario Rocca
Marchesi Spinola (1967)[d]
"Moccagatta" Azienda Agricola (Bric Balin 0)
Nada Fiorenzo (1986)[d]
Nicolello (1982)[d]
Ottavia Lesquio nell Azienda Agricola "Cascina
Principe" (1985)[d]
Palladino
Parroco del Neive, Gallina (Basarin **)
+ Pelissero Luigi
− Piazza Cav. Uff. Armando
Poderi e Cantine di Marengo-Marenda, Le Terre Forti
Prunotto (Montestefano and Rabajà ***)
Punset di R. Marcarino
Rocca Albino (1987)[d]
Rosso Gigi
Sottimano
− Tomaso Gianolio (1985)[d]
Traversa Giuseppe, Cascina Chiabotto

0
Ascheri Giacomo
Balbo Marino (1974)[d]
Bel Colle (1979)[c]
Beni di Batasiolo (formerly F.lli Dogliani) (1985)[d]
Bersano
Bosca Luigi e Figli[c]

Brero Cav. Luigi (1980)[d]
Bruzzone (1971)[c]
Cabutto Bartolomeo (1976)[c]
Cantina Colavolpe (1981)[d]
Cantine Barbero, "Conte de Cavour" (1974)[d]
Cantine Bava (1979)[d]
Cantine d'Invecchiamento, "La Brenta d'Oro" (1974)[d]
Carra (1973)[c]
— Cauda Cav. Luigi (1979)[d]
— Cavaletto[c]
Colla Paolo (now sold as Gagliardo Gianni) (1981)[c]
Cosetti Clemente[c]
Damilano Dott. Giacomo
Dogliani F.lli (now sold as Beni di Batasiolo) (1983)[c]
Gagliardo Gianni (formerly Colla Paolo) (1982)[d]
Gherzi[c]
Grasso Ernesto, Vallegranda Sotto (1987)[d]
Grazziola[c]
+ Grimaldi Cav. Carlo e Mario (1986)[d]
Il Vecchio Tralcio (1980)[d]
— Kiola[c] (owned by Batasiolo)
Marchesi di Barolo
Mauro (1983)[d]
"Moccagatta" Azienda Agricola, Bric Balin (1987)[d]
  (Other crus *)
+ Musso Sebastiano
Nada Giuseppe, Poderi Casot (1987)[d]
Osvaldo Mauro (1981)[d]
Pavese Livio (1979)[d]
Pippione[c]
Podere Anselma (1980)[d,i]
Podere Casot Nada (1978)[d]
+ Rivetti Guido (1982)[d]
Roche Azienda Vitivinicola
S. Quirico di Massano
+ San Michele (formerly Confratelli di San Michele*)
— Scanavino[c]
Serafino Enrico (1974)[d]
Troglia Giovanni[c]
Valfieri
Vecchio Piemonte Cantine Produttori
Villadoria Marchese
Voerzio Giacomo (1976)[c,i]

Notes:

[a] Not produced since the '81
[b] Not produced since the '71
[c] We haven't tasted it in some time
[d] Based on one vintage only
[e] Based on three wines, including two cask samples
[f] We tasted only the '83, ex-cask
[g] This winery has really improved from the '82
[h] Based on three cask samples, '81 to '83
[i] No longer produced

Vintage Information and Tasting Notes

THE VINTAGES TODAY

****	1990, 1989, 1985
****−	1982
***+	1988, 1978
***	1971, 1964, 1958
**+	1986, 1970, 1961
**	1983, 1967
**−	1974, 1957
*+	1979
*	1980, 1955
*−	1987
0	1984, 1981, 1977, 1976, 1975, 1973, 1969, 1968, 1966, 1965, 1963, 1962, 1960, 1959, 1956, 1954, 1953, 1950, 1949, 1948, 1946
?	1952, 1951, 1947, 1945

1 9 9 0 [* * * *]

The year started out with a mild January and February. The tone was set for the rest of the season. Beneficial rain came at the end of July and in early August. The grapes ripened early.

Bruno Giacosa said it was exceptional for both Barolo and Barbaresco. Alfredo Currado of Vietti produced no Rabajà because of hail damage. The Vietti Masseria, tasted from cask in February 1991, and the Pio Cesare and Franco Fiorina, tasted a month later, showed a lot of structure and fruit. Those three wines, plus the few that we tasted in November 1990, suggest a splendid vintage. At this stage we suspect that it might be the best vintage here since 1985. They seem more like Barbaresco than the 1989s, which are more like Barolo.

1 9 8 9 [* * * *]

Winter was very mild. A wet, cold spring affected the flowering. Then the weather took a turn for the better; from the end of June through the completion of the harvest in mid-October the weather was very dry. This dryness was punctuated by an occasional storm that provided a welcome relief at the right moments. As a result of the poor flowering, quantity was down 8 percent from the 1988 crop, which was also a short crop.

The production of 430,752 gallons (16,304 hectoliters) of nebbiolo, equivalent to 2.2 million bottles of Barbaresco, was 59.6 percent of the maximum allowed by law, compared to the 23-year average of 444,886 gallons (16,839 hectoliters), or 71.6 percent of the amount allowed. This works out to an average of 357 gallons per acre (33.4 hectoliters per hectare) compared to the average between 1967 and 1989 of 428 gallons (40 hectoliters). This was the fifth smallest yield during the same period and just below the 1971 yield, but above that of 1978. In the decade only 1984 had a smaller crop of nebbiolo, and a smaller average yield.

Gaja said that the wines are fantastic; at this stage they appear to be the best of the decade for both Barolo and Barbaresco. It is a little too early to be really sure. But the wines appear to be very promising. Bruno Giacosa calls it a first-rate vintage.

Thus far, based on the 19 Barbarescos that we have tasted from 13 producers, we find a very high level of quality and consistency. The lowest-rated wine that we tasted was good; three others were very good, and all the rest excellent or better. Thus far we single out the Castello di Neive Santo Stefano, followed closely by the Gaja Sorì San Lorenzo, and then the Bricco Asili from Ceretto, Gaja Sorì Tildìn and Bruno Giacosa Santo Stefano

If there is a problem, and there might be, the wines might turn out like the '71s, Barbaresco in the guise of Barolo. For now, though, we rate the vintage a tentative four.

CAUTION: *Before reading these tasting notes on the wines that we tasted from barrel, please read "On Tasting Wines from Barrel: A Caveat" on page xxv.*

Borgogno Giacomo (*ex-cask, 11/90*). Ripe fruit aroma, cherry, strawberry and raspberry notes; concentrated fruit under the tannin, firm, closed, good backbone, hard finish. *(*)

"Bricco Asili" Azienda Agricola (Ceretto), Bricco Asili (*ex-cask, 8/90*). Rich and concentrated, nuances of chocolate and spice; sweet, packed with ripe fruit under enormous chewy tannin. **(*+)

"Bricco Asili" Azienda Agricola (Ceretto), Faset (*ex-cask, 8/90*). Rich, open fruit aroma; rough and tannic, concentrated and rich. **(*)

Cantina del Glicine, Marcorino (*ex-botte, 11/90*). Tight but evident fruit, good structure. **(*−)

Cantina del Glicine, Vigna dei Curà (*ex-botte, 11/90*). Ripe fruit aroma; concentrated, lots of flavor, fairly tannic, good structure; surprisingly big for a Glicine Barbaresco. **(*)

Cantine Duca d'Asti di Chiarlo Michele, Rabajà (*ex-cask, 8/90*). Intense nose displays richness of fruit and nebbiolo character; raspberry and strawberry notes carry through in the mouth, great richness, extract and weight; the best Barbaresco from Chiarlo to date. **(*−)

Castello di Neive, Santo Stefano (*4 times, ex-cask, 11/90*). Deep color; incredible richness on the nose which is already complex, and intensely rich with nuances of tobacco, tar, flowers, berries and truffles; in the mouth there is enormous richness and concentration, extract and weight; this is one of the most impressive Barbarescos that we have tasted from cask. ***(*)

Ceretto, Asij (*twice, 11/90*). Ripe fruit aroma and palate, good concentration of fruit, quite tannic, chewy. *(*+)

Gaja (*ex-cask, 11/90*). At this stage the oak is dominant, but there is no doubt about the ripe fruit as well, a lot of weight and extract. *(**)

Gaja, Costa Russi (*ex-cask, 11/90*). Nebbiolo character quite evident, rich and intense; a lot of potential; very young. **(*)

Gaja, Sorì San Lorenzo (*ex-cask, 11/90*). Rich aroma displays suggestions of berries and flowers under some oak; great richness and extract, sense of real sweetness from ripe fruit, very long ***(+)

Gaja, Sorì Tildìn (*ex-cask, 11/90*). Cherry, berry and oak combine on the nose and carry through on the palate, sense of ripe fruit evident from the nose across the palate, very long; needs a lot of age. **(*+)

Giacosa Bruno, Santo Stefano (*ex-cask, 11/90*). Ripe fruit from the aroma through the palate, great extract and concentration, quite tannic, chewy, full-bodied, great structure, less elegant than the '88 but with more power. **(*+)

Giacosa F.lli (*ex-cask, 11/90*). Sense of ripe fruit from the nose through the palate; cherry and cassis notes on the aroma; full of flavor. *(*)

Parroco del Neive, Vigneto Basarin (*ex-cask, 11/90*). Grapey and ripe fruit aroma; appealing, open, attractive fruit, good body, rich. **

Pasquero Elia Secondo, Sorì Paitin (*twice, ex-vat, 11/90*). Raspberries all over this wine, from the aroma through the flavor; richly fruited, a lot of extract and concentration. *(**−)

San Michele, Vigneto Gallina (*ex-cask, 11/90*). Rich, ripe fruit aroma and palate; the sense of sweetness from ripe fruit very much in evidence, fairly tannic. *

Vietti, Masseria (*ex-cask, 11/90*). A lot of concentration and weight, perhaps too much for a Barbaresco; a Barolo lover's Barbaresco. **(*)

Vietti, Rabajà (*ex-cask, 11/90*). A lot of weight and extract, rich and concentrated; lacks some elegance. **(*)

1988 [*** +]

A very mild and dry winter gave way to a cold and rainy spring. The early part of the summer followed the same pattern as the spring until the end of June. July and August were relatively dry with high daytime temperatures of 90° Fahrenheit (32° centigrade) not uncommon. The autumn days continued dry and warm with dry, cool nights. There was some rain at the end of September and again in the second week of October; the rest of the month was sunny.

The crop, at an average of 387 gallons per acre (36 hectoliters per hectare), was the third smallest in the decade and only 64.6 percent of the 599 gallons per acre (56 hectoliters per hectare) allowed by the DOCG. The total crop size of 467,925 gallons (17,711 hectoliters), equivalent to 2.4 million bottles, was below the 23-year average.

Gaja rates it close to 1985 in quality, though not quite as good. He said that it was more like 1982, though slightly better. It has more tannin than 1985. Bruno Giacosa rates it very highly.

Like 1989 this vintage produced Barbarescos of high quality, and judging by the 19 wines that we tasted from 13 producers, at a very consistent level. We judged only one wine to be less than good and that could have been due more to an out-of-condition cask sample and one other wine as good. All the other Barbarescos were very good or better.

The top wine is Bruno Giacosa's Santo Stefano, followed by the Castello di Neive Santo Stefano, a pair from Gaja—Sorì San Lorenzo and Sorì Tildìn, and the Rabajà from Vietti. Also excellent and potentially better were the Gaja *normale,* followed by the two Ceretto "Bricco Asili" crus of Bricco Asili and Faset, the Gaja Costa Russi, the Glicine Curà, and Vietti Masseria.

CAUTION: *Before reading these tasting notes on the wines that we tasted from barrel, please read "On Tasting Wines from Barrel: A Caveat" on page xxv.*

Borgogno Giacomo (ex-cask, 11/90). Open raspberry aroma, recalls the woods, fragrant; ripe fruit, hard, tight, firm and tannic. *(*)

"Bricco Asili" Azienda Agricola (Ceretto), Bricco Asili (ex-cask, 8/90). Rich and concentrated, ripe, open fruit, floral and berry nuances; a lot of extract, the tannin as well as the fruit is there. **(*)

"Bricco Asili" Azienda Agricola (Ceretto), Faset (ex-cask, 8/90). Fragrant scent, *tartufi* and flowers, also cassis and berrylike notes; a pretty wine, good structure, some spice, a lot of sweetness; real appeal. **(*)

Cantina del Glicine, Marcorino (ex-botte, 11/90). Damp leaves aroma; gentle, a little light, and a tad short. *(*)

Cantina del Glicine, Vigna dei Curà (ex-botte, 11/90). Berry and cherry aroma; well balanced, gentle nature, moderate tannin; elegant. **(*)

Cantine Duca d'Asti di Chiarlo Michele, Rabajà (ex-cask, 8/90). Woods and flowers define the aroma, underbrush, truffle and berry notes; rich yet with a gentle touch, sweet, packed with flavor, could use more length; attractive now. **(+)

Castello di Neive, Santo Stefano (twice, ex-cask, 11/90). Loads of ripe, open fruit apparent on the nose, woodslike, mushroom and underbrush; a lot of structure, moderate tannin, rich and concentrated; very young and very good. ***(+)

Ceretto, Asij (twice, 11/90). At a difficult stage to fully assess, but the fruit is very much in evidence, firm and tannic. *(*?)

Gaja (ex-cask, 12/89). Dense purple color; intense aroma, suggestive of cassis, tobacco and cherries; ripe, rich and sweet, impressive quality, packed with flavor and weight, great concentration; very young and very attractive. **(* +)

Gaja, Costa Russi (ex-cask, 12/89). Deep purple; packed with cherry and blackberry fruit on the nose, oak overlay; big, rich, ripe and sweet, evident and ripe tannins, youthful fruit, firm, tannic, dry end. **(*)

Gaja, Sorì San Lorenzo (ex-cask, 12/89). Deep purple; surprising herbaceous nuance on the nose along with tobacco and berry notes; chewy, more weight and tannin than the others, great richness and sweetness, some alcohol evident at the end. ***(+)

Gaja, Sorì Tildìn (ex-cask, 12/89). Oak and tobacco up front on the nose, blackberry fruit; more open and sweeter than either of the other crus, has richness, body and weight, and the structure to age very well indeed; real class. ***(+)

Giacosa Bruno, Santo Stefano (ex-cask, 11/90). Beautiful color; real fragrance, complex; sweet and gentle, elegant and classy, very long. ***(*)

Giacosa F.lli, Rio Sordo (ex-cask, 11/90). Rich fruit, tannic, a little coarse. *

Parroco del Neive, Vigneto Basarin (ex-cask, 11/90). Ripe, open raspberry aroma; soft, open, sweet impression, appealing and attractive. **

Pasquero Elia Secondo, Sorì Paitin (twice, ex-vat, 11/90). Nice nose; sense of sweetness, fruity, good structure. *(* +)

San Michele, Vigneto Gallina (ex-cask, 11/90). Old-style Barbaresco aroma, tarlike character dominates; full-bodied, good fruit, coarse. *

Vietti, Masseria (twice, ex-cask, 11/90). Dark ruby; ripe, fresh cherrylike aroma, vaguely tobacco, floral notes; great weight and extract, as well as sweetness, very well balanced, long finish; real class. **(*)

Vietti, Rabajà (ex-cask, 11/90). Woodsy aroma, *tartufi* nuances then tightens up on the nose; great richness and extract; real elegance and class, this is special; enormous length and ripeness; perhaps even more impressive than the '85 at the same stage. ***(+)

1987 * −

The winter was cold; snow fell as late as February and March. The spring remained cold until the middle of April.

The remainder of the spring was cooler than normal, and rainy as well. There were a number of 90° Fahrenheit (32° centigrade) days in July, and some cold rainy ones in early August. September was warm. Ceretto said that the vintage looked great until the first Sunday in October: the rains came down and continued for fifteen days. The heavy rain that fell between October 9 and 11 damaged the vineyards that weren't picked.

The crop size was 510,778 gallons (19,333 hectoliters), or 2.6 million bottles. The 416 gallon per acre (39 hectoliter per hectare) yield was 69.5 percent of the maximum allowed by law, but close to the 1967–1989 average of 428 gallons (40 hectoliters).

The Cerettos produced nearly 5,000 bottles of Bricco Asili and 2,500 of Faset from the grapes harvested before the rain. Gaja, as of August 1990, hadn't decided if he would release any of his crus.

We've tasted nearly four dozen Barbarescos from almost three dozen producers and were less than impressed. More than one-third, or 17, received less than one star, meaning they were less than good, and 22 others more than one star or one star plus. Only 7 received our rating of very good or potentially very good. And more than a few are already showing age. Clearly the vintage was less successful in Barbaresco than in Barolo. The two best wines were the Prunotto Rabajà and the Vietti Masseria, followed by the Castello di Neive Santo Stefano, La Spinona Bricco Faset, F.lli Oddero, Prunotto Montestefano, and Vietti Rabajà.

These are Barbarescos for near-term consumption. Only a few will keep.

Bersano (*11/90*). Old!

Bianco Mauro, Cascina Morassino (*3 times, 11/90*). Raspberry, brambly aroma; rather soft, open and attractive, some tannin at the end. * *Bottle of 4/90:* Open cherry and strawberry aroma; open, soft entry, nice on the midpalate, then short, dry and firm, vaguely bitter. ** −

Borgogno Giacomo (*4/90*). Light, floral-scented aroma; cherrylike upon entry, good fruit, a little short. *

"Bricco Asili" Azienda Agricola (Ceretto), Bricco Asili (*8/90, 4,980 bottles*). Light but scented nose; light body, very little tannin, very soft, a little shallow, very forward, lacks length; ready now. *

"Bricco Asili" Azienda Agricola (Ceretto), Faset (*8/90, 2,490 bottles*). Light nose, evident fruit; soft entry, the fruit is there, very ready, won't be a keeper, tasty, short. * +

Calissano Luigi, Bricco Malaspina (*11/90*). Tanky, off-putting!

Cantina del Glicine, Vigna dei Curà (*ex-botte, 11/90*). Mushroomlike aroma, damp earth, some fruit; moderate tannin, fairly good fruit. (*)

Cantina Vignaioli "Elvio Pertinace" (*11/90*). Tanky, unattractive, some fruit.

Cantine Duca d'Asti di Chiarlo Michele, Rabajà (*12/90*). Light nose of leather and forest scents; soft, berrylike character, open fruit, precocious, short; quite ready now. * +

Casetta F.lli (*ex-cask, 11/90*). Nice fruit on the nose and palate, moderate tannin, cherrylike character. * −

Castello di Neive, Santo Stefano (*3 times, 11/90*). Scented bouquet, real nebbiolo character, hints of flowers and mushrooms; soft entry, a little light and dry, moderate tannin, good fruit, a little short; will be ready early. ** −

Ceretto, Asij (*twice, 11/90*). Mintlike nuance on the nose; soft with fairly good fruit, a little dry, light body, very short. * −

Cigliuti, Serra Boella (*twice, 4/90*). Light nose, nice fruit; open entry, a little tight toward the end, still in all not bad, especially considering the vintage. * + *A second bottle tasted two days earlier:* Rubbery character, with firm and hard tannins and a sense of fruit, bitter end.

Cortese Giuseppe, Vigna in Rabajà (*11/90, 8,290 bottles*). A little tanky; sweet impression, soft, light tannin. *

Eredi Lodali, Vigneto Rocche dei 7 Fratelli (*4/90, 5,970 bottles, plus some magnums*). Odd nose; soft, simple and open, drinkable. +

Fontanabianca, Vigneto Sorì di Burdin (*4/90, 3,650 bottles*). Soft and open, forward flavors, light tannin, ready now. *

Gaja (*twice, 8/90*). Some alcohol volatizes, fairly good fruit; nice mouth feel, oak quite evident, has a surprising sweetness, still the end is dry and a little firm, rather short. *

Gaja, Costa Russi (*8/90*). Rather tannic for the fruit, is there enough fruit? Doubtful, some alcohol intrudes. ?

Gaja, Sorì San Lorenzo (*8/90*). Open cherry aroma, truffle and oak components, vegetallike backnote; soft entry, harsh edge, nice flavor, then bitter, still the flavor is attractive. *

Gaja, Sorì Tildìn (*8/90*). Some alcohol, fairly good fruit; nice mouthful, evident oak, with a sweetness, still the end is dry and a little firm, rather short. *

Giacosa Donato, Vigneto Sorì Secondine (*11/90*). Woodslike and berry aroma; soft, open, fruity, a tad short. *

Grasso Ernesto, Cascina Vallegranda Sotto (*11/90, 1,220 bottles*). Tanky nose; sweet impression, open and soft, appealing, not varietal.

"La Ca' Növa," Azienda Agricola Rocca Dario (*twice, 11/90*). Open strawberrylike aroma; soft, open and forward, simple, attractive, good fruit, berrylike, short; for early consumption. * +

"La Ca' Növa," Azienda Agricola Rocca Dario, Bric Mentina (*4/90, 3,000 bottles*). Leathery aroma; nice entry, hint of cherries, then firm and tight, quite flavorful, rather short. * +

La Spinona di Pietro Berutti, Bricco Faset (*ex-botte, 11/90*). Nice fruit, a little unsettled, good body. *(*)

La Spinona di Pietro Berutti, Ghiga and Bric del Cucu (*ex-botte, 11/90*). Attractive fruit, soft under light tannin. *(+)

Marchesi di Barolo (9/90). Light nose, cherry fruit, open and simple, fresh and clean; could use more fruit, harsh, dry finish.

"Moccagatta" Azienda Agricola, Bric Balin (10/90). Oak! oak!! oak!!! and even more oak.

"Moccagatta" Azienda Agricola, Vigneto Balin (twice, 10/90). Shows a lot of age from the color through the palate, a little dry. *Bottle of 4/90:* Some oak evident, cherrylike fruit, vanilla notes; nice midpalate, a tad short. *

"Moccagatta" Azienda Agricola, Vigneto Basarin (11/90). Nice nose; soft, good fruit and structure, appealing, light tannin, noticeable oak. *

"Moccagatta" Azienda Agricola, Vigneto Cole (4/90). Mushrooms, moderate tannin, a bit astringent, fairly nice fruit then tight. *

Nada Giuseppe, Poderi Casot Riserva Speciale (twice, 11/90, 4,500 bottles). DOCG does not recognize *riserva speciale* as a category, and this wine carried the DOCG seal of approval! Both bottles were oxidized!

Oddero F.lli (11/90). Nice fruit on the nose and palate, attractive and open, good structure, flavorful, light tannin, short. ** −

Parroco del Neive, Gallina (twice, 11/90). One bottle showed age and was tired. *The second:* Spice and vanilla aroma, cherrylike nuance; soft and tasty, dull aftertaste. +

Pasquero-Elia Secondo, Sorì Paitin (twice, 11/90, 8,500 bottles). Light nose, some fruit evident; a little dry and tight, fruit seems sufficient, short finish is a little dull. It seemed better when tasted from cask in April 1990; it could be suffering from bottle shock (we don't know when it was bottled). * *Ex-cask, 4/90:* Open cherrylike aroma; soft and fruity, forward flavors. ** −

Pelissero, Vanotu (11/90). Cherrylike aroma; soft and simple, overly simple.

Prunotto (11/90). Dank, some fruit.

Prunotto, Montestefano (11/90). Not a lot of aroma; fairly nice structure and backbone, good fruit, delicious. **

Prunotto, Rabajà (11/90). Floral and woodsy aroma; nice fruit, good structure, complex. ** +

Rocca Albino, Vigneti Loreto e Brich (11/90). A little tanky; fairly nice fruit, soft and open; ready. *

Rosso Gigi, Vigneto Viglino (11/90, 11,980 bottles). Noticeable oxidation, old fruit taste.

San Michele, Vigneto Gallina (twice, 11/90). One bottle was volatile and undrinkable. *The other:* Attractive nose; soft, open and simple, sweet impression. +

Sottimano, Brichet (4/90). Openly fruity, fresh, soft; ready. *

Vecchio Piemonte Cantine Produttori (4/90). Mercaptans, not well made.

Vietti, Masseria (11/90, just bottled). Lovely fruit on the nose and palate, soft, open and attractive, well balanced, moderate length. ** +

Vietti, Rabajà (11/90). Mintlike aroma; a little light but tasty, with good fruit, rather short; will be ready early. **

1 9 8 6 ** +

The winter was long and snowy, the spring rainy, and the summer hot and humid. September was both drier and cooler than normal. On October 2 rain fell, then the weather took a turn for the better, where it remained for the rest of the month. Barbaresco escaped from the hail that ravaged the vineyards of Barolo. The crop size of 528,241 gallons (19,994 hectoliters) of nebbiolo was equivalent to 2.7 million bottles of Barbaresco. This worked out to an average yield of 421 gallons per acre (39.4 hectoliters per hectare), or 70.3 percent of the maximum allowed, and close to the average yield between 1967 and 1989.

Angelo Gaja said that the '86 Barbarescos have more elegance than the '85s. His regular Barbaresco, according to him, should be ready sometime between 1994 and 1995, and the Costa Russi in seven to eight years. The '86s have good intensity of fruit.

Overall, these are light wines for early drinking. They are perhaps along the lines of the '83s and '79s, but better. At this stage, our rating, based on more than three dozen wines from more than two and a half dozen producers, is two stars plus out of four. Just over 17 percent, 7 of 41, were less than good, just over 29 percent, 12 of 41, were good, and 24.4 percent, or 10, were very good.

The best wines are a pair from Bruno Giacosa—Santo Stefano and Gallina—a pair from Marchese di Gresy—Martinenga-Camp Gros and -Gaiun—Ceretto's "Bricco Asili" cru, a pair from Gaja—Sorì San Lorenzo and Sorì Tildìn—and the Rabajà from Vietti, followed by Ceretto's Asij, Gaja's Costa Russi, Donato Giacosa's Asili, and Vietti's Masseria.

Arrigo Orlando, Vigna della Rocca (4/90). Light nose; open, simple and soft, small-scale. *

Barale F.lli, Rabajà (4/90). Floral and cherry aroma; sweet and gentle, elegant nature, short, light finish, has character. ** −

"Bricco Asili" Azienda Agricola (Ceretto), Bricco Asili (3 times, 5/90, 7,576 bottles). Moderately intense berrylike aroma, underbrush component, raspberry and *tartufi* notes; light, soft, open, a little dry, and a tad bitter, attractive now, give it another year, perhaps two, some class evident. *** −

"Bricco Asili" Azienda Agricola (Ceretto), Faset (8/90, 5,898 bottles). Slight corkiness throws the wine off, still some quality as well as flavor is evident, seems a little firm, sense of sweetness, rather short. *?

Ca' Bianca, Tenuta Roncaglie (4/90). Spice, cherries and tobacco; soft, open and fruity, vague taste of truffles and dried fruit. *

Cantine Duca d'Asti di Chiarlo Michele, Rabajà (12/90). Light nose, rather nice fruit, characteristic nebbiolo; soft, open, light tannin, firm, short end; ready. * +

Cappellano (twice, 10/90). Soft and open, then a little tight and dry. * *Bottle of 8/90:* Open tobacco and berry aroma; soft and open, precocious, ready now though some tannin, a tad short. * +

Castello di Neive, Santo Stefano (4 times, 11/90). Floral aroma, vaguely woodsy; sense of sweetness, a little light, soft, open flavors, moderate length. **(+) *Bottle of 4/90:* Cherries up front, overall tight and dry, sense of fruit evident; the wine is in a difficult stage. *? *Bottle of 4/89:* Lovely nose recalls berries and vanilla; loaded with flavor, rich, ripe fruit, tasty, firm aftertaste. ** +

Ceretto, Asij (5/90). Open fruit, fragrant, vaguely floral; soft, open and elegant, supple, ready with room to improve, a tad dry at the end. ** +

Cigliuti, Serra Boella (10/90). Tar and flowers, woodslike impression; agreeable and soft, tasty. **

Cortese Giuseppe, Vigna in Rabajà (4/90). Openly fruity aroma; soft in spite of some tannin, nice fruit, a little light; still needs to age but most attractive. **

Feyles Maria, Vigna dei Gaia in Neive Riserva (4/90). Tobacco, seaweedy aroma; soft, open fruit entry and midpalate, a tad dry and short, but nice. * +

Fontanafredda (twice, 12/90). Tobacco, mint and leather aroma; soft, open, fruity, light tannin; ready. *

Gaja (7 times, 10/90). Nice fruit on the nose and palate, a little dry, and a little young, some smoothness from the oak, firm, dry finish. * + *Bottle of 6/90:* Lovely nebbiolo aroma, recalls the woods, hint of mushrooms; some oak, soft under moderate tannin; should be ready early. **(+)

Gaja, Costa Russi (3 times, 10/90). Fragrant bouquet, some oak, lots of fruit, sweet, ripe nebbiolo impression; smooth feel, vanilla characteristic, appealing and attractive now; will improve. **(+) *Bottle of 1/90:* Vaguely floral scented, some oak and delicacy; a mouthful of oak, noticeable fruit, smooth, more substance than the *normale,* light, dry tannic finish. **(+)

Gaja, Sorì San Lorenzo (4/87). Fragrant ripe fruit aroma; sweet impression on entry, well balanced, good backbone, a little firm yet attractive and chewy toward the end; attractive now, it really needs a few years. **(*)

Gaja, Sorì Tildìn (4/87). Tobacco, tar, flowers and oak; firm yet attractive, open fruit, a little tight, sweet impression from the fruit. **(* −)

Giacosa Bruno, Gallina (twice, 3/91). Lovely fruit on the nose, complex; loads of flavor and character, well balanced. *** − *Exvat, 4/87:* Less body, tannin and structure than Santo Stefano, but by no means lacking in any of those components, lots of fruit, good acidity, potential evident. **(* −)

Giacosa Bruno, Santo Stefano (4 times, 11/90, 13,800 bottles). Cherry and berry aroma, floral component; soft and fruity, smooth, balanced, long finish. ** + *Bottle of 8/90:* Great depth and richness, nuances of tobacco and tea; open and precocious, a little light but elegant. *** *Bottle of 6/90:* Cassis and tobacco aroma; tar and flowers, elegant, open fruit, loads of class and style; seemingly ready, it's not. ***

Giacosa Donato, Vigna Asili (3/90). Tobacco, woodsy and mushroom aroma, not of tar; surprisingly tannic, sense of fruit apparent, young, with a firm, tannic finish; needs age to round out. ** +

Giacosa Donato, Surì Secondine (3/90). Dusty, tobacco and leathery aroma; chewy tannins, some oak apparent, has the stuffing to age and improve, firm, dry aftertaste; a young wine. **

Giacosa F.lli (twice, 11/90). Heavy oak dominates, overdone.

Grimaldi Azienda Vinicola (4/90). Simple, open, soft, ready. +

La Spinona di Pietro Berutti, Podere Albina (4/90). Barnyard and tobacco aroma; fruit seems a little low, fairly well balanced. *

Marchese di Gresy, Martinenga (12/90, 22,613 bottles). Spice and oak combine with forest scents to define the aroma; good body, mouth-filling, light tannin, a little short at the end; ready now. **

Marchese di Gresy, Martinenga-Camp Gros (6/90, 13,453 bottles). Lovely scented, perfumed bouquet, tobacco, cherry and floral notes; soft under light tannin, harmonious and elegant, classy, very long. ***

Marchese di Gresy, Martinenga-Gaiun (6/90, 13,334 bottles). Lovely tobacco and *tartufi* aroma, fruity notes; soft, open and supple, elegant, forward flavors, still some tannin, long; nice now, should be better in two years. *** −

Nada Fiorenzo, Località Rombone (4/90). Light nose, floral and cherry notes; some tannin, good fruit, a little toasty, will be ready early, dry end, a tad simple. *

Parroco del Neive, Vigneto Gallina Riserva (11/90). Like a tank sample, off-putting.

Pasquero-Elia Secondo, Sorì d'Paytin (twice, 11/90, 18,500 bottles). Honeyed nuance(!), nice fruit on the nose; chewy tannins, some firmness, nice finish though a little dry. *(+) *Bottle of 4/90:* Cherry and tobacco aroma; soft, open and ready. **

Pelissero Luigi, Vanotu (4/90). A little alcohol evident, some tar; firm, fairly nice flavor midpalate, dry, chewy and tannic, especially at the end. *

Piazza Cav. Uff. Armando, Poderi d'Mugiot (4/90). Light nose; a little lightweight, some tannin, some fruit, no real backbone or distinction.

Produttori del Barbaresco (twice, 4/90). Woodsy and berry aroma; open, soft, sweet, well balanced; will be ready soon. **

Prunotto (11/90). Not a lot of character, fruit and drinkable. *

Roche Azienda Vinicola (4/89). Lacks personality, some fruit, some tannin.

Rosso Gigi, Vigneto Viglino (4/90, 7,800 bottles). Closed nose; light, soft and open, simple, forward; more or less ready. *

San Michele, Vigneto Gallina (11/90). Mercaptan, tanky, offputting.

Valfieri (9/90). Tar character; unbalanced, insufficient fruit.

Vezza Sergio, Borgato Ferrere (4/90). Buttery(!), vanilla aroma (no *barrique*), *tartufi* background; sweet, soft and smooth, open, forward flavors; ready. ** −

Vietti, Masseria (3 times, 11/90). Tobacco and forest scents; soft, round and ready, moderate length. ** +

Vietti, Rabajà (twice, 4/90, 3,440 bottles). A little closed on the nose, light woodslike and truffle notes; a little chewy, then nice flavor, although a tad light displays elegance, harmonious, fairly long. *** −

1985 ****

Winter was exceptional: it was long, cold, and snowy. Spring came early but was variable. May had very good weather, as did the summer, which was sunny and dry. August was hotter than normal, but the nights were cool. The dry, sunny weather continued into autumn, with high daytime temperatures of 86° Fahrenheit (30° centigrade) and cold nights. There was some rainfall on September 16, and thereafter the climate continued good through mid-November.

The yield of 423 gallons per acre (39.6 hectoliters per hectare) was close to the norm. Total production of 527,475 gallons (19,965 hectoliters) of nebbiolo was equivalent to 2.7 million bottles of Barbaresco. This was 70.7 percent of the amount allowed, which is close to the 1967 to 1989 average of 71.6 percent. Of the best vintages, only 1982 had a higher yield.

Angelo Gaja said he never saw such clean aromas. In April 1986 he thought they fell somewhere between 1982 and 1978. And four years later he described the wines as being opulent with less tannin than either 1982 or 1988, but having real elegance. We asked Bruno Ceretto to compare the big three vintages through 1985: he rated 1985 first, followed by 1978 and then 1982 in that order.

As splendid as 1985 was in Barolo, it might have been even better in Barbaresco. The wines have everything—perfume, harmony, flavor, depth, and length of flavor; the wines were made from perfectly ripe grapes. Until recently we found it hard to choose between 1982 and 1985, but as in Barolo, we give the nod to 1985. It's hard to imagine more perfect Barbarescos.

Thus far we have tasted some four dozen Barbarescos, and one wine, as usual, stands out above the rest: Bruno Giacosa's monumental Santo Stefano Riserva, which we rated at four stars for now and four plus for the future. This stunning wine is the wine of the vintage. Other first-class wines: Ceretto's Bricco Asili, a pair from Castello di Neive—the Santo Stefano *normale* and Riserva—a pair from Gaja—the Sorì San Lorenzo and Sorì Tildìn—Bruno Giacosa's Gallina, Giuseppe Mascarello's Marcarini, a pair of *riserve* from the Produttori del Barbaresco—the Asili and Montestefano—and a pair from Vietti—Masseria and Rabajà. Also first rate are the Martinenga-Camp Gros and Produttori del Barbaresco Moccagatta Riserva, followed closely by the Gaja *normale* and Costa Russi, Marchese di Gresy Martinenga and Martinenga-Gaiun, the Pasquero Elia Secondo Sorì Paitin, four from the Produttori del Barbaresco—Ovello Riserva, Pajè Riserva, Rabajà, and Rio Sordo Riserva—and the Prunotto Montestefano. Also very good were F.lli Barale Vigna Rabajà, Ceretto Asij, Cantina del Glicine Vigna dei Curà, and Produttori del Barbaresco Pora Riserva.

Arrigo Orlando, Riserva (4/90, 1,500 bottles). Light candied fruit aroma; soft, open, fruity, fairly simple and forward, nice flavors. * +

Ascheri Giacomo (twice, 4/89). Hint of cherries; easy style, simple, fairly fruity, not a lot of character.

Barale F.lli, Vigna Rabajà (4/90). Open *tartufi* and cherry aroma; a lot of structure, fairly tannic, rich and packed with flavor. *** −

Batasiolo (3 times, 10/90). Some varietal character, suggestions of leather and the woods; a little light, low intensity flavors, somewhat shallow, small-scale; drink now.

Bianco Luigi, Vigneto Rabajà (twice, 4/90, 4,153 bottles). Skunky nose, chocolate and coffee notes; soft, open, forward. * −

"Bricco Asili" Azienda Agricola (Ceretto), Bricco Asili (twice, 11/90, 5,678 bottles). Forestlike scents, cherry and leathery notes; sense of sweetness from the ripe fruit, fairly long; still quite young but appealing flavors. ***(+) *Bottle of 9/90:* Scented, perfumed aroma, recalls flowers, fruit and leather; a lovely mouthful of wine, rich under moderate but soft tannins, real elegance, very long. ***(* −)

Brovia F.lli, Rio Sordo (4/90). Tobacco up front on the nose; a little dry, fruit evident; on the young side, say one or two years, perhaps three. * +

Ca' Bianca (4/90). Woodsy, mushroomy and dried fruit aroma; tight and dry, sense of fruit evident, firm dry end. *(+)

Ca' Romè, R. Marengo (5/90). Berrylike aroma with suggestions of the woods and tar; soft entry, moderate tannin, dry finish. **

Cantina del Glicine, Vigna dei Curà (3 times, 11/90, 10,680 bottles). Woodslike and damp leaves aroma, nuances of blueberries; moderate tannin, really nice fruit; still a little young, good quality, gentle nature. ***

Cantine Duca d'Asti di Chiarlo Michele, Rabajà (twice, 10/90, 4,500 bottles). Open fruit and floral aroma; soft, round and tasty, very ready, a tad short. ** −

Castello d'Annone di G. L. Viarengo (4/90). Light nose, tobacco, spice, tar, truffles and mushrooms; soft, open, flavor, vaguely of resin in an attractive way. * +

Castello di Neive, Santo Stefano (10 times, 6/90). Tobacco, berry, floral and *tartufi* aroma with suggestions of the woods; rich and concentrated, packed with fruit, long lingering finish; attractive and appealing now yet more to come in the future, resist. ***(+)

Castello di Neive, Santo Stefano Riserva (5 times, 10/90). Tobacco and cherry aroma, *tartufi* note, open fruit; soft under light to moderate tannin; a lot of quality; more open than the bottle tasted four months ago. *** + *Bottle of 6/90*: Tighter with more structure and tannin as well as more concentration and richness than the *normale*, and it needs more age, it is less elegant. **(*)

Ceretto, Asij (twice, 3/89). Still kind of tight, yet lush, open fruit evident, rich flavor, sweet impression, evident potential. **(* −)

Coluè (10/90). *Tartufi* note on the nose, open fruit; soft, a little light; very ready and correct. ** −

Confratelli di San Michele, Vigneto S. Cristoforo (4/89). Good varietal character; heavy tannin, the fruit is there, at this stage quite dry. *

Damilano, Dott. Giacomo (4/90). Soft center, some tannin, no distinction.

Fontanafredda (ex-cask, 6/86). Perfumed aroma at first, then closes up; seems a little light, some tannin that builds at the end. *(*)

Franco Fiorina (9/90). Still a little tight, lots of concentration and fruit, needs some age. *(*)

Gaja (5 times, 12/90). Vanilla and oak combine with nebbiolo on the nose; sweet impression, rich and concentrated, some firmness, yet with a softness; the quality is evident in spite of being more closed than the last time we tasted it. *** *Bottle of 4/89*: Expansive aroma of ripe fruit, blackberry nuance; good structure, packed with flavor of ripe fruit and oak, sweet impression, firm finish. ** + (***)

Gaja, Costa Russi (twice, 12/90). Nose is really closed in; rich flavor, nice texture under light tannin, altogether closed though soft(!), rather short finish; a little disappointing. **(+)

Gaja, Sorì San Lorenzo (3 times, 12/90). Light nose that combines oak and nebbiolo fruit; good structure, a little firm and tight with an evident sense of rich, ripe nebbiolo fruit, and oak; dry finish; young. **(* +)

Gaja, Sorì Tildìn (4 times, 12/90). This wine has closed up since the previous time that we tasted it nearly one year ago. At this stage the oak is dominant on the nose and palate; quite firm but with smooth texture and rich fruit, good concentration. **(* +) *Bottle of 1/90*: Aroma enormously rich in fruit, oak overlay; slightly harsh edge up front, gives way to rich, sweet, ripe fruit, soft, classy. ***(+)

Giacosa Bruno, Gallina (5 times, 11/90). Has closed up since last tasted a year ago; but the fruit is very much in evidence. **(*)

Bottle of 10/89: Dark color; scented perfume, tobacco, berries, vaguely floral; sweet, open, fruity, packed with flavor, supple center, great richness and structure, very long; the class is already evident. ***(+)

Giacosa Bruno, Santo Stefano Riserva (6 times, 11/90). Incredible mélange of scents and flavors, a virtual explosion of fruit that coats the mouth with layers of flavor, voluptuous, enormous length; sheer perfection, yet still very young. **** (**** +) *Bottle of 6/90*: A mélange of scents including tobacco, *tartufi*, berries and flowers; great richness and sweetness; this wine has everything, yet it needs age, what then? Without question the star of the vintage. **** (**** +)

Giacosa F.lli (12/90). Small nose; open fruit entry, fruity, light tannin, short. *

Giacosa F.lli, Vigneto Roccalini (4/89). A little stinky; off note in the mouth, good fruit. * − ?

Giacosa F.lli, Vigneto Roncaglie (4/90). Woodsy, camphor aroma; chewy entry gives way to nice fruit then a chocolate note, dry finish, still young, has structure and extract. **

Grasso F.lli di Emilio Grasso, Valgrande (4/90). Tight nose; open, soft entry, then tannin, good structure, young, has some potential. *(* −)

Grimaldi G. (twice, 4/90). Slight nose, ripe berries; sweet, open fruit, light tannin, a little simple, quite attractive. *

La Spinona di Pietro Berutti, Bricco Faset (4/89). Mushroom, woodsy aroma; ripe and rich, chewy, moderate tannin; a little disappointing, still it is good! ** −

La Spinona di Pietro Berutti, Bricco Faset Riserva (4/90). Tobacco and wet leaves aroma; fairly fruity; has some character, disappointing. *

La Spinona di Pietro Berutti, Vigneto La Ghiga (4/90). Tobacco and camphor aroma; some fruit, overall a disappointing, light-weight wine with a dry, short end. *

Marchese di Gresy, Martinenga (4/89, 12,463 bottles, plus magnums). Tobacco and berry aroma, refined and harmonious, tobacco note carries through on the palate, some elegance, dry, firm finish. ***

Marchese di Gresy, Martinenga-Camp Gros (4/89, 12,364 bottles). Delicate, scented bouquet; soft under moderate tannin, chewy, hard finish. ** + (*** +)

Marchese di Gresy, Martinenga-Gaiun (3 times, 10/89, 12,390 bottles). Some oak evident, then tobacco, cherry, woodsy aroma; firm and chewy, vanilla note. ** + (***)

Marchesi di Barolo (12/90). Small-scale, uninteresting, dull.

Mascarello Giuseppe, Marcarini (4/90, 5,000 bottles). Tar and flowers; some tannin, sweet, rich fruit, very well made, lovely indeed, long finish; elegant. ***(+)

Oddero F.lli (4/89). Light nose, cherry notes; dry, some sweetness, good body, fruity. **

Ottavia Lesquio nell Azienda Agricola "Cascina Principe," Prinsi (4/90). Light nose, some fruit; light tannin, fairly nice fruit; lacks definition and richness of the year, still not bad. *

Pasquero Elia Secondo, Sorì Paitin (twice, 4/89). Nice nose, tobacco note; well balanced, lots of flavor, some length; good quality. ** + (***)

Piazza Cav. Uff. Armando, Poderi d'Mugiot (twice, 4/90). Mushroom, leather and dried fruit aroma; light tannin, open, flavorful, soft center, short; coming ready. *

Piazza Cav. Uff. Armando, Poderi d'Mugiot Riserva (4/90). Barnyardy aroma, some fruit as well; nice flavor, a little light; seems ready now, could improve a bit. *

Pio Cesare (twice, 12/90). [About 15 percent of this wine spent some time in *barrique*.] Oak up front on the nose and palate, some fruit; altogether dull and uninteresting. *Bottle of 4/89:* Closed nose; firm tannin, good fruit, harsh finish. *(*)

Pio Cesare, Riserva (12/90). Kind of simple nose; better in the mouth, fairly good structure, moderate tannin, evident fruit, short. *

Porta Rossa, Faset (ex-vat, 4/86). Expansive aroma, loads of perfume; fairly tannic, the fruit is there, hard finish. *(*)

Produttori del Barbaresco (twice, 4/90). Open, cherrylike fruit on the nose; open and fruity, dry and firm, closed. *(?)

Produttori del Barbaresco, Asili Riserva (twice, 9/90, 18,850 bottles and 1,330 magnums). Open, fragrant, scented bouquet, rich, real class; not ready but certainly appealing with its flavor and concentration; perhaps the most elegant of the crus tasted. ***(+)

Produttori del Barbaresco, Moccagatta Riserva (twice, 9/90, 19,350 bottles). Woodsy, vanilla and floral bouquet; rich and fairly full, tasty along with the tannin; as with the Montestefano, it needs the most age. **(* +)

Produttori del Barbaresco, Montestefano Riserva (3 times, 9/90, 21,210 bottles). Dried fruit and leather aroma, tobacco note; rich, open, ripe fruit entry, sweet impression, harmonious, long finish; in need of age, but very good indeed. ***(+)

Produttori del Barbaresco, Ovello Riserva (twice, 9/90, 24,440 bottles). Complex aroma recalls nuts, flowers, leather, underbrush and vanilla; rich and sweet, packed with flavor; softer than the Montestefano or Moccagatta; still more to give. **(*)

Produttori del Barbaresco, Pajè Riserva (4/90, 12,350 bottles). *Tartufi* up front, then cherries; sweet, openly fruity; more forward than the Moccagatta, still it is young; open and rich, firm aftertaste. **(*)

Produttori del Barbaresco, Pora Riserva (3 times, 9/90, 20,250 bottles). Berry aroma, underbrush component; sweet impression, still some tannin, but attractive at this stage, soft-centered, the end is a tad dry and firm. **(* −)

Produttori del Barbaresco, Rabajà (ex-cask, 4/87). Enormous richness and concentration, full of flavor and body; a little unsettled. **(*)

Produttori del Barbaresco, Rio Sordo Riserva (4/90, 12,970 bottles). Truffle and dried fruit aroma, woodsy component; sweet entry, soft at first then some firmness, good quality though hard, dry aftertaste. **(*)

Prunotto (12/88). Medium intensity, open aroma; ripe fruit flavor then tannin. ** −

Prunotto, Montestefano (twice, 6/90, 12,900 bottles). *Tartufi* note; sweet and rich, good structure, open flavors, fairly long with tannin at the end; lots of class. ***

"Rizzi" Azienda Agricola, Ernesto Dellapiana (twice, 4/90). Damp leaves and woodslike aroma, light vanilla and berry notes; firm and fairly tannic, good structure, rich flavor, young and tight, firm aftertaste. *(*)

Roagna (twice, 5/90). Light but fruity aroma, tobacco notes; sweet, open, ripe berrylike flavor, balanced. **

Roche Azienda Vinicola (4/89). Nice fruit, lacks intensity and ripeness of the vintage, small-scale.

Rosso Gigi, Vigneto Viglino Riserva (4/90, 8,100 bottles). Fragrant scent; soft, open, forward, simple; seems ready though it needs a little more time. * +

Sottimano, Brichet (ex-vat, 4/88). Nice fruit, lacks richness of the vintage, light to moderate tannin. *

Tomaso Gianolio (4/90). *Tartufi* and woodsy aroma; some firmness, fruit evident, no real distinction, dry, tannic aftertaste. * −

Traversa Giuseppe, Sorì Ciabot (4/89). Open, fruity aroma and palate, some oak, moderate tannin, light aftertaste. *

Vietti, Masseria (4 times, 4/90). Mint and menthanollike components, underbrush, tobacco and cherry aroma; richly fruited, light tannin, well made, should be a keeper, very long finish. ***(+)

Vietti, Rabajà (3 times, 4/89). Rich nose, cherrylike fruit; open fruit flavor, soft center, good backbone, sweetness to the fruit; still on the young side, will improve. ***(+)

1 9 8 4 0

The spring of 1984 was the wettest in memory; the rain never seemed to let up from the beginning of April through the first half of June. This, combined with low temperatures, slowed down the growth in the vineyards by at least twenty days and had a major impact on quantity. Rain during the flowering seriously hampered cross-pollination. Crop size was down between 30 and 60 percent from the previous vintage, with the nebbiolo crop being the most affected.

The total yield of nebbiolo was 278,546 gallons (10,543 hectoliters), equivalent to 1.4 million bottles of Barbaresco. This was the smallest crop since the 263,645 gallons (9,979 hectoliters) of 1969. And the average yield of 220 gallons per acre (20.6 hectoliters per hectare), the smallest since the

DOC took effect in 1967, was 36.8 percent of the amount allowed by law and approximately 50 percent of the average between 1967 and 1989. And not all of the declared crop was bottled, making the crop even smaller than these numbers indicate.

Sugars at harvest were satisfactory, but acid levels were fairly high. Some producers—Gaja and Scarpa, for example—didn't produce a Barbaresco. And Ceretto didn't produce their Bricco Asili.

The wines were, from the start, less satisfactory than those of Barolo. Most have passed their best, the few remaining should be consumed now if at all.

Bianco Liugi, Vigneto Faset (4/89). Vegetablelike aroma; fairly nice fruit, soft center, dry end. +

Ceretto, Asij (twice, 6/88). Tobacco and woodslike aroma; light, a bit harsh, some fruit, though not much to it. + *Bottle of 12/87:* Tobacco and fruit aroma; soft and round, a lot of flavor, some style, balanced; has delicacy. **

Eredi Lodali, Vigneto Rocche dei 7 Fratelli (4/89). Light, soft, open, easy. *

Giacosa Bruno (10/89). Real nebbiolo characteristic, well balanced, soft and very ready, quite good, and for the year, very good. ** +

La Spinona di Pietro Berutti (4/88). Lovely, characteristic nebbiolo *tartufi* and underbrush aroma; soft, open flavors, light tannin; a nice easy wine. *

Palladino (4/89). Light, soft, fruity, easy, drink. * —

Pasquero-Elia Secondo, Sorì Paitin (4/89). Nice nose; soft and fruity; easy style. *

Produttori del Barbaresco (twice, 4/89). Open fruit aroma and palate, some tannin, light, fairly soft in center. *

Roche Azienda Vinicola (twice, 4/89). Fairly nice nebbiolo character, light and soft, though a bit dry. * —

S. Quirico (4/87). Small nose; unbalanced with acid and tannin out of kilter; not a lot of character.

Sottimano, Brichet (twice, 4/87). Kind of vegetallike aroma, and the smell of filter paper(!); overly tannic for the fruit. Another bottle, though on the light side, was drinkable and displayed some flavor. +

Vietti, Masseria (12 times, 12/90). *Tartufi* and mushroom aroma, forest scents, lovely nose; drying out but still a lot of attraction, especially on the nose; best to drink up. * *Bottle of 11/89:* This wine was at its best through 1988. Falling apart. *Bottle of 4/89:* Still drinkable but signs of age creeping in. * *Bottle of 11/88:* Tobacco and berry aroma; soft and round; very nice and very ready, best not to keep. ** —

Vietti, Rabajà (twice, 4/88, 2,150 bottles). Aroma of truffles and berries, underbrush and tar; have to work for it but the fruit is there, nice flavor under moderate tannin. **

1983 **

The 1983 harvest of 637,277 gallons (24,121 hectoliters), or 3.2 million bottles, represented 43 percent more than the average produced between 1967 and 1989. This was a large crop, the largest since the DOC took effect in 1967. Its 496 gallon per acre (46.4 hectoliter per hectare) yield, while above the average 428 (40) between 1967 and 1989, was only the seventh largest in this period. In the decade of the 1980s, only 1980 had a larger yield.

The wines are well balanced and tend to be on the light side. Gaja compares them to the '79s, though he rates the year slightly higher in overall quality. The vintage was more successful for Barbaresco than for Barolo. The wines are fairly well balanced and somewhat light-bodied, but can be elegant. They have matured early and are ready now, some are starting to fade. There is no need to hold them any longer.

Bianco Luigi, Vigneto Faset (4/87, 4,980 bottles). Slight off note mars the aroma; fairly nice flavor, on the light side, light tannin, short aftertaste. * —

Bianco Luigi, Vigneto Rabajà (4/87, 4,280 bottles). An off note of mercaptan intrudes on the nose; better in the mouth but it still is a real disappointment after the other two.

Bianco Luigi, Vigneto Ronchi (4/87, 970 bottles). Perfumed aroma is quite nice though light; on the light side with nice flavor; some style. ** —

Borgogno F.lli Serio e Battista (ex-cask, 11/84). Big, fairly rich aroma with hints of *tartufi*; a mouthful of fruit; a Barolo lover's Barbaresco. **(+)

"Bricco Asili" Azienda Agricola (Ceretto), Bricco Asili (5 times, 12/88). Dried fruit aroma; tight entry then a sweetness of flavor, firm tannic aftertaste; disappointing. * + *Bottle of 10/87:* Tobacco, mushroom aroma; soft and round; elegant and stylish. ** +

Cantina del Glicine, Vigna dei Curà (twice, 4/89). Ripe berry aroma; soft, light tannin; well made, gentle. ** —

Cantine Duca d'Asti di Chiarlo Michele, Rabajà Riserva (12/90). Tar and leather aroma, nuances that recall the forest; soft entry, then some dryness; best to drink up. * —

Cappellano Dott. Giuseppe (twice, 4/86). Ripe fruit aroma, toward berries; raspberry flavor, light tannin; still a bit young but balanced and good now. **(+)

Ceretto, Asij (ex-cask, 11/84). A vague mushroomlike note on the aroma; a bit light, but with some elegance; should be ready in two to three years. **(+)

Cortese Giuseppe, Vigna in Rabajà (twice, 8/90). The aroma and flavor recall the woods, nuances of truffles and mushrooms, soft, starting to thin out; showing some age, drink up. +

Dogliani F.lli (9/87). Light varietal aroma, tobacco and fruit backnote; light tannin, a bit shallow, some fruit evident, on the simple and easy side.

Gaja (*3 times, 5/90*). Oak dominates the aroma, notes of tobacco and nebbiolo fruit; soft, and open, supple, very ready, light finish, could use more length; still it is well made. ** −

Gaja, Costa Russi (*8/90*). Characteristic nebbiolo aroma, suggestions of the woods and mushrooms combine with an overlay of oak; still has a fair amount of tannin, harsh edge, vaguely bitter; good but will it improve(?); that harsh edge is troublesome. **

Gaja, Sorì San Lorenzo (*twice, 8/90*). Fruit combines with an oak background; evident tannin, good structure, quite soft on entry and midpalate, a little short, well made, tasty. **

Gaja, Sorì Tildìn (*9/90*). Beautiful bouquet, ripe fruit, cherry, tobacco and oak; soft and smooth, very ready, at its peak now, could use more length, could use more structure, really attractive now. *** −

Giacosa Bruno, Gallina (*3 times, 5/90, 11,780 bottles*). Light somewhat delicate berry- and floral-scented bouquet, hint of *tartufi* and tobacco; light tannin, soft, chocolate note, some elegance, quite ready, moderate length; no need to keep it, it should last. ** +

Giacosa Bruno, Santo Stefano (*3 times, 10/89, 11,630 bottles*). Bouquet suggestive of the woods and tar; tasty, open, well balanced, rich for the year; ready. ** +

Giacosa F.lli (*4/87*). Vague off note intrudes on the nose, also has fruit and tobacco notes; soft center, fairly light, moderate tannin, off note intrudes in the mouth. *(+)

Grimaldi (*4/89*). A bit overripe, some oxidation, rather light, some astringency, dull aftertaste.

La Spinona di Pietro Berutti (*twice, 4/88*). Vanilla, berry notes; moderate tannin, sense of fruit, tight flavors, firm and closed. *
Bottle of 4/87: Fresh floral and cherry aroma; a bit light but nice fruit, almost sweet, attractive. **(+)

La Spinona di Pietro Berutti, Bricco Faset (*3 times, 6/88*). Floral and dried fruit aroma, really fragrant; soft and flavorful, harsh notes at the end; ready, will it keep? We think so. ** +

La Spinona di Pietro Berutti, La Ghiga (*ex-cask, 11/84*). Well balanced, some class, a lot of flavor. **

Marchese di Gresy, Martinenga (*twice, 3/87, 12,300 bottles and 320 magnums*). Light nose, some elegance, *tartufi* component; lots of style, some class. ** +

Marchese di Gresy, Martinenga-Camp Gros (*twice, 9/88*). Floral and ripe berry scent, some delicacy; seems sweet with ripe fruit and some elegance. *** −

Marchese di Gresy, Martinenga-Gaiun (*twice, 3/87, 12,900 bottles and 320 magnums*). An elegant and stylish wine with delicacy and softness, almost sweet, long firm finish, more to give. At this stage it appears to be the wine of the vintage. ***(+)

Marchesi di Barolo (*9/90*). Stinky, harsh and alcoholic; unbalanced.

Mauro (*4/89*). Some oxidation, unclean, very little fruit.

"Moccagatta" Azienda Agricola (*2/85*). This Barbaresco was aged for about ninety days in new *barrique,* which is quite obvious in the oak and fruit aroma and the oaky sweetness on the palate, has some tannin and not much nebbiolo character; a nice red wine, no more. *

Pasquero-Elia Secondo, Sorì d'Paytin (*ex-cask, 10/87*). Lots of fruit, also fairly tannic. *?

Porta Rossa, Faset (*ex-cask, 4/86*). Reticent aroma, vaguely medicinal; quite tannic, sense of fruit evident; seems vaguely oxidized. (?*)

Produttori del Barbaresco (*twice, 4/89*). Mushroom and underbrush aroma; tannic entry, then tight, some fruit. *

Prunotto, Montestefano Riserva (*6/90, 13,219 bottles*). Well-developed bouquet, up-front berries; soft entry, then some tannin; holding up well but a doubtful keeper, drink. ** −

Roche Azienda Vinicola (*4/88*). Not much nose; good fruit, drink. +

S. Quirico (*4/87*). Reticent aroma; lots of tannin, lacks stuffing, low fruit.

Scarpa, Tetti di Neive (*ex-cask, 2/85*). Fairly rich and full, with sweet berrylike fruit, very well balanced. **(*)

Traversa Giuseppe, Sorì Ciabot (*twice, 4/88, 867 bottles*). Hint of berries on the nose; dry, tannic entry, then fruit. *

Vietti, Masseria (*3 times, 5/87, 6,284 bottles*). Almost woodsy aroma, tobacco notes; good structure, soft and elegant; has class. ** +

1982 **** −

As in Barolo the 1982 vintage in Barbaresco was nearly perfect. Cold weather in June slowed down the ripening process, and the harvest took place in the first part of October. The grape bunches were beautiful. And yields were above average, with a crop of 602,772 gallons (22,815 hectoliters), equivalent to 3 million bottles. This was the third largest nebbiolo crop of the decade, and average in yield per acre (hectare). The 495 gallons per acre (46.3 hectoliters per hectare) were still only 80 percent of the amount that the DOC allows. Of all the best vintages between 1967 and 1989, 1982 had the largest average production per acre.

Angelo Gaja says his '82s have more elegance and class than the '78s. Alfredo Currado of Vietti feels the '82s might equal the '71s in quality, a point of view shared by many other producers. Giuseppe Colla of Prunotto said the vintage produced full-bodied wines of very high quality. Pio Boffa of Pio Cesare describes the wines as complex and fruity.

From our experience, based on the uniform high quality of the more than 80 wines that we've tasted, 1982 is better than 1971 and 1978, though not quite as good as 1985. The best wines are Ceretto's Bricco Asili, Castello di Neive Santo Stefano *normale,* the three crus from Gaja—Costa Russi, Sorì San Lorenzo, and Sorì Tildìn—two from Bruno Giacosa—Gallina and Santo Stefano Riserva—a pair from Marchese di Gresy—Martinenga-Camp Gros and Martinenga-Gaiun—a pair from Scarpa—Payore Barberis and Tetti di Neive—and the Vietti Masseria. These were followed closely by Castello di Neive Santo Stefano Riserva, Ceretto Asij, Cigliuti Serra Boella, Bruno Giacosa *normale,* La Spinona *normale,* Le Colline, Pasquero Elia Secondo Sorì d'Paytin Riserva, Prunotto Montestefano, Sergio Vezza, Cantina del Glicine Vigna dei Curà and Vigna Rabajà, and seven *riserve* from the Produttori del Barbaresco—Asili, Moccagatta, Montestefano, Pajè, Pora, Rabajà, and Rio Sordo.

Accornero Flavio (Casa Vinicola Bera) (3 times, 10/90). Alcohol and volatile acidity, fading fast, the bottle or the wine? A second bottle tasted within a week of the first displayed tobacco and tarlike notes; soft and lacking character; certainly drinkable, no more. + *Bottle of 5/89:* Some varietal fruit, open aroma; soft, smooth; very ready, easy to drink; a simple, correct, small-scale Barbaresco. * +

Ascheri Giacomo (4 times, 3/88). Ripe berry fruit; fairly tannic, with a core of fruit beneath; still a little young but good. *

Bianco Luigi, Vigneto Fascet (4/87, 3,330 bottles). Fresh, ripe fruit aroma; moderate tannin, fruity, fairly well balanced, a bit short. *(* −)

Borgogno F.lli Serio e Battista (ex-cask, 11/84). Deep color; oak and blackberries on the nose; a lot of tannin but seems to have sufficient fruit, some alcohol at the end. *

"Bricco Asili" Azienda Agricola (Ceretto), Bricco Asili (4 times, 5/86). Elegant and stylish, *tartufi* and tobacco nuances on the bouquet; soft center, some tannin to shed, loads of flavor, long with a tannic bite at the end. ***(+)

Ca' Romè di Marengo R. (4/87). Tar and floral aroma, slightly cooked character; moderate tannin, fruit evident, alcohol intrudes at the end, with a bite as well. +

Ca' Romè di Marengo R., Riserva Speciale (4/88). Mushrooms on the nose, fairly tannic, some fruit. * −

Cantina del Glicine, Vigna dei Curà (3 times, 4/88, 10,500 bottles). Tobacco and tar aroma with a woodsy component; good structure, loads of flavor under moderate tannin. *** −

Cantina del Glicine, Vigna Rabajà (4/90, 1,405 bottles). Cherry and tobacco bouquet; light tannin; coming ready, certainly approachable. *** −

Cantina del Glicine, Vigneto Gallina (4/89). *Tartufi* note; dry, a bit firm, nice fruit; needs more time. **

Cantina Vignaioli (11/87). Woodslike aroma, dried fruit component; light tannin; a simple style, easy; ready now, could even improve a bit. *

Casetta F.lli, Vigna Ausario (4/87). Floral, fruity aroma; rather nice fruit under a fair amount of tannin, puckery and astringent; is there enough fruit? Difficult to be sure. *(?*)

Castello di Neive, Santo Stefano (8 times, 11/88). Tar and flowers in the background, kind of dusty, leathery note; chewy yet sweet and rich, great concentration of ripe fruit; young but with evident quality. ***(+)

Castello di Neive, Santo Stefano Riserva (3 times, 4/90). Overall, tight on the nose and palate, firm and tannic, tobacco nuance, lots of flavor and richness; real quality and class evident. **(*)

Ceretto, Asij (twice, 5/86). Light aroma, somewhat reticent, tar and underbrush; light to moderate tannin, some elegance; needs a few years to develop and round out. **(*)

Cigliuti, Serra Boella (3 times, 1/86, 5,580 bottles). Nice nose, tobacco notes; fairly tannic entry, gives way to nice fruit; still closed in, needs time to develop. **(*)

Contratto (10/90). Light nose; fairly rich under moderate tannin, balanced, on the young side, tasty. *(* −)

Cortese Giuseppe, Vigna in Rabajà (3 times, 2/86, 10,240 bottles). All three times there was a mercaptan note intruding; fairly tannic, has fruit and structure, black cherry flavor; needs age; if it wasn't for the off note. **?

Damilano, Dott. Giacomo (4/87). Light nose; light body, lacks weight and intensity; simple.

Eredi Lodali, Vigneto Rocche dei 7 Fratelli (twice, 4/90, 5,880 bottles, plus magnums). Seaweedlike aroma, old fruit; tired, soft and easy to drink. +

Gagliardo Gianni, Valgrande (4/87). Raisin aroma; moderate tannin, has a hotness to it, lacks varietal and vintage character, overly tannic.

Gaja (14 times, 12/90, 104,500 bottles, plus larger bottles). Oak and fruit define the light nose; good structure, sweet, ripe and concentrated fruit, oak overlay; seems to have tightened up and gone into a shell at eight years of age, or is it fading? *(*)

Gaja, Costa Russi (4 times, 12/90). Oak is the most pronounced character on the nose and palate, sweetness from the oak apparent; still young. **(*) *Bottle of 11/86:* Deeper color; richer aroma; more body, flavor and tannin than the *normale,* chewy tannins, ripe fruit, somewhat closed, quite long, rich fruit; seems to have closed up since the last time we tasted it. **(* +)

Gaja, Sorì San Lorenzo (3 times, 12/90). Light note suggestive of a forest with an oak component; has the most structure and tannin of the three crus and is in need of the most age. **(* +) *Bottle of 11/86:* Deepest color of the four Barbarescos; the aroma is quite restrained, with the oak being quite pronounced; tannin quite evident, sweetness of ripe fruit; lots of style. ***(*)

Gaja, Sorì Tildìn (3 times, 12/90). Oak and truffle aroma; rather similar in the mouth, moderate tannin, a little tight but apparent richness and concentration; still more to give. ***(+) It's kind of interesting that the previous bottle we tasted some twenty months earlier seemed to be approaching its peak. The most recent bottle, however, came directly from the winery to us. *Bottle of 4/89:* Seems to be rounding out quite nicely, oak blends in with the tobacco character of the nebbiolo; nice texture, harmonious; seems to be quite advanced and near its peak! ***+

Giacosa Bruno (*twice, 5/90*). Bouquet of flowers and cherries; rich and concentrated, well structured, intense and chocolatey. **(*)

Giacosa Bruno, Gallina (*3 times, 10/90*). Scented tobacco and berry aroma, *tartufi*, underbrush and resin nuances; soft under a firm frame, the richness of flavor and its quality quite evident; needs a lot more age! *** *Bottle of 9/86:* Tobacco, cherry and woodslike aroma; rich in tannin and extract, enormous weight, superbly balanced; heaps of style. ***(+)

Giacosa Bruno, Santo Stefano Riserva (*5 times, 11/87*). Reticent aroma, some varietal character; still fairly tannic and tight with a rich sense of fruit, cherry and tobacco notes. ***(+)

Giacosa Donato (*twice, 2/85*). Aroma reminiscent of a Rhone wine, rich fruit and spice, hints of raspberries, tobacco and cherries; moderate tannin but with sufficient fruit to balance, acid a bit low; young, yet some character evident; could be longer on palate. **

Giacosa F.lli (*twice, 4/90*). Tar and leather aroma; old-style Barbaresco; quite tannic, a little coarse, dry tannic aftertaste. *

Giacosa F.lli, Vigneto Roncaglie (*twice, 4/89*). Tar and tobacco aroma, mushroom notes; hard and tannic, seems to have the stuffing. *(+)

La Spinona di Pietro Berutti (*twice, 5/85*). Lovely tobacco, berrylike aroma with hints of flowers and cherries; medium-bodied, some tannin and sweet, ripe fruit; stylish and elegant. **(*)

La Spinona di Pietro Berutti, Bricco Faset (*4 times, 11/87*). *Tartufi* notes come through a reticent aroma; tight flavors, surprisingly closed; the last time we tasted it, some ten months ago, it was quite open and attractive. **(+)

La Spinona di Pietro Berutti, Bricco Faset Riserva (*twice, 4/88*). One bottle had a reticent aroma; was firm, tannic, tight. The other had a woodsy aroma with an almost pinot noir–like sense; tight and tannic, flavorful; closed. **(+)

Le Colline (*4/89*). Delicate perfume; a bit closed, very tannic and tight, good backbone; needs age and has the elements to take age. **+ (***)

Marchese di Gresy, Martinenga (*5 times, 9/88, 13,020 bottles, plus magnums*). Loads of flavor, good structure, more tannin than expected; a bottle tasted two years earlier seemed much more open and ready. This bottle, **

Marchese di Gresy, Martinenga-Camp Gros (*9 times, 3/87, 6,905 bottles and 872 magnums*). Tobacco aroma; still a little closed, has a firmness to it, seems to have closed up since the last time we tasted it, yet the fruit and the style are very much in evidence. **(*+)

Marchese di Gresy, Martinenga-Gaiun (*5 times, 4/86, 5,080 bottles, plus magnums*). Classy bouquet displays cherries, tobacco and flowers; stylish and elegant, heaps of quality; tannic bite at the end. ***(+)

Musso Sebastiano, Bricco Rio Sordo (*4/86*). Shy nose; fairly tannic, some fruit; has a sense of dullness about it, no style or class; some sweetness from ripe fruit; overall, a puzzling wine! (*)

Nicolello (*4/85*). Light nose, some fruit, cherry notes; some tannin with the fruit to support it, tannic finish; quite young. *(+)

Oddero F.lli (*5 times, 5/89*). Rich nose, characteristic nebbiolo flowers and tar; moderate tannin, sweet, ripe fruit, dry aftertaste; some earlier bottles seemed more open. *(*)

Palladino (*4/89*). *Tartufi* nuance on the nose, and some fruit; soft, open, fruity. *

Parroco del Neive, Gallina (*4/87*). Light nose; dry and tannic, firm, good fruit, fairly well balanced, dry, tannic aftertaste. *(*)

Pasquero-Elia Secondo, Sorì d'Paytin (*7 times, 11/87*). Rich tar and tobacco aroma, cherry and mint notes; light tannin, tasty, balanced, lots of flavor; still a little young. **+ (***−)

Pasquero-Elia Secondo, Sorì d'Paytin Riserva (*4/87, 650 bottles*). Very tannic, sense of fruit evident; difficult stage, but its quality is evident. **(*)

Piazza Cav. Uff. Armando (*1/86*). Some barrel stink yet the wine was from bottle(!), tobacco notes; firm and tannic, nice flavor, vaguely bitter, some length, harsh edges. *−

Poderi e Cantine di Marengo-Marenda, Le Terre Forti (*3 times, 10/90*). Aroma of *tartufi* and berries, flowers and tar; fairly tannic, the fruit is beneath, short and a little dry at the end. *+

Porta Rossa, Faset (*twice, 4/87*). Tar and tobacco aroma; balanced, firm, fruity, fairly rich, still some tannin, firm aftertaste. **(+)

Produttori del Barbaresco (*6 times, 4/90*). Open truffle, leather and mint aroma; fruity, good body, some tannin builds at the end. **

Produttori del Barbaresco, Asili Riserva (*3 times, 4/88, 20,480 bottles and 840 magnums*). Earthy aroma, woodsy nuance; chewy with some elegance, on the young side, sense of fruit quite evident. **+ (***)

Produttori del Barbaresco, Moccagatta Riserva (*3 times, 4/88, 20,325 bottles*). Woodsy aroma, underbrush; chewy, well balanced, concentrated with the sense of sweetness. **+ (***)

Produttori del Barbaresco, Montefico Riserva (*4/87, 12,263 bottles*). Woodsy with a minty note; closed and firm, with a lot of fruit beneath the tannin; lacks the richness of the Rio Sordo; very young, give it three to five years. **(*−)

Produttori del Barbaresco, Montestefano Riserva (*4 times, 5/89, 20,318 bottles*). Mushroom and tobacco aroma; rich fruit under moderate tannin, good structure; a bit rough at this stage, seems to be closing up. **+ (***)

Produttori del Barbaresco, Ovella Riserva (*5 times, 5/90, 21,292 bottles*). Animal fur and leather; a little chewy, moderate tannin, good fruit, soft center; a little disappointing. **

Produttori del Barbaresco, Pajè Riserva (*4/87, 8,410 bottles*). Tobacco and mushroom aroma; rich in fruit and tannin, very young. **(*)

Produttori del Barbaresco, Pora Riserva (*3 times, 4/89, 18,986 bottles*). The two bottles of April 1989 were both oxidized, bad storage perhaps. *Bottle of 4/88:* Mushroom and woodsy aroma; sweetness of fruit, and a richness and concentration, bitter note at the end. **+ (***)

Produttori del Barbaresco, Rabajà Riserva (*4 times, 2/90, 21,893 bottles and 1,410 magnums*). Tobacco and cherry aroma; soft and smooth, very ready, finish is a tad light, well balanced; at or close to its peak. ***

Produttori del Barbaresco, Rio Sordo Riserva (*twice, 4/89, 11,102 bottles*). The most recent bottle disappointed. *Bottle of 4/87:* *Tartufi* aroma, moderate intensity; rich and flavorful, at first the fruit masked the tannin that built up; lots of quality evident. **(*)

Prunotto, Montestefano (*ex-cask, 1/85*). Aroma is rich and intense, with hints of *tartufi* and oak; a lot of flavor, a rich, fairly full-bodied Barbaresco. **(*)

Prunotto, Rabajà Riserva (*10/87*). Rough and tannic, closed with the sense of fruit beneath. **(+)

Punset, R. Marcarino (*4/87*). Candy, cherry and tobacco aroma; fairly tannic, almost a sweetness to the fruit, some alcohol at the end. (*)

Rivetti Guido (*4/89*). Fairly nice fruit but seems to be older than its years, tired. *−

Roagna (*1/86*). Closed aroma; lots of tannin upon entry, gives way to nice flavor, quite backward and closed, seems to have sufficient fruit, firm; hopefully it will develop more character and complexity with time; good structure. **(+)

Roagna, Vigna Pajè (*ex-cask, 1/85*). Cherrylike aroma; rich fruit, some tannin; good quality. *(*)

Roche Azienda Vinicola, Riserva Speciale (*4/88*). Underbrush and mushrooms; moderate tannin, good fruit, lacks concentration of the vintage, some heat toward the end. *

Scarpa, Payore Barberis (*twice, 4/86, 7,700 bottles*). Richly fruited aroma, some spice; lush flavor, light tannin; seems ready now, it will improve; has style and class. **(*+)

Scarpa, Tetti di Neive (*twice, 4/86, 14,555 bottles and 566 magnums*). Aroma packed with fruit and a touch of *tartufi*; rich on the palate; at this stage fruit seems lush, giving a sweet impression as well as making it seem drinkable, resist and give it time, perhaps four more years. ***(*)

Traversa Giuseppe, Cascina Chiabotto, Vigneto Maringota (*4/85*). Fruity aroma has peppery notes; some tannin, perhaps a touch too simple, but well made. *

Traversa Giuseppe, Sorì Ciabot (*3 times, 4/88, 867 bottles*). Reticent aroma, berrylike; light, fairly tannic, seems to have the fruit. *+

Vecchio Piemonte Cantine Produttori, Vigna Casotto Riserva (*4/90, 3,150 bottles*). Tobacco, oak and fruit evident, overly dry, short.

Vezza Sergio (*11/85*). Lovely fruit aroma; light tannin, full of flavor, soft, very approachable, round and smooth, fairly long; some style and elegance. ***

Vietti (*11/85*). A blend of grapes from Asili, Pora, Rabajà and other vineyards. Soft, nice flavor, could use more length. **

Vietti, Masseria (*4 times, 4/86, 5,037 bottles*). Aroma seems a little closed, tobacco, cherry and *tartufi* notes; rich in fruit under the tannin, well structured; shows enormous potential, needs perhaps three or four years. **(**)

Villadoria Marchese (*4/90*). Tar and cherries; simple and fruity, open, soft; ready.

1 9 8 1 0

The vintage in 1981 was mixed. Overall, it was not up to the level of 1980, another mixed year, though there were some notable exceptions. The 546,920 gallons (20,701 hecto-liters), equivalent to 2.8 million bottles of Barbaresco, were above the average between 1967 and 1989. It was, at 447 gallons per acre (41.8 hectoliters per hectare), not much above the average yield of 428 gallons (40 hectoliters), however.

Gaja produced all three of his crus in 1981; in 1980 he didn't bottle any. The Cerettos also made better wines in 1981 than 1980. On the other hand, Bruno Giacosa said that for him the '81s were very small wines; he didn't make any Barbaresco, nor did Castello di Neive. Giuseppe Colla described his '81s as medium-bodied wines of average quality.

The '81s were ready early. For the most part, they'd best be drunk up; very few will keep further. Many are starting to fade. The best have some elegance.

Accornero Flavio (Casa Vinicola Bera) (*1/86*). Lacks structure and flavor, harsh.

Ascheri Giacomo (*4/85*). Small nose; some tannin, shy in fruit.

Borgogno F.lli Serio e Battista (*ex-cask, 11/84*). Aroma rather closed, with some alcohol and vague nebbiolo character evident; moderate fruit, moderate tannin, seems to lack a bit of structure.

Cantina del Glicine, Gallina (*8/86*). Nice nose, tobacco nuance; light, elegant, balanced; very drinkable. **

Cantina del Glicine, Gava Principe (*4/89*). Vanilla and floral aroma; dry, has flavor interest though. *

Cantina del Glicine, Vigna dei Curà (*3 times, 1/86, 7,450 bottles*). Fresh fruit aroma, smoky and tobacco notes, cherry fruit; light tannin, elegant; ready now. ** −

Cantina del Glicine, Vigneto Valtorta (*4/87, 4,650 bottles*). Woodsy aroma; fairly light and soft, well made; ready now. ** −

Ceretto, Asij (*twice, 2/85*). Mushrooms on the aroma; a lot of flavor, almost seems sweet, has character and style, some elegance; very good especially for the vintage; moderately long on finish with tannin that indicates it still needs time, though it should be ready early. **

Colavolpe Cantina (*4/87*). Small-scale, some fruit, drinkable, no character.

Colla Paolo, Valgrande (*4/85*). Color shows considerable age; light and fruity nose and palate, soft, undistinguished, lacks structure and weight.

Cortese Giuseppe, Vigna in Rabajà (*3 times, 2/86*). Lovely nose of the woods, mushroom nuance; light tannin, soft, nicely fruited midpalate; quite open and ready, could still improve a bit. **

Fontanafredda (*1/85*). Floral aroma; moderate tannin, a lot of fruit, still young and somewhat astringent, some firmness at the end; shows promise. *(*)

Gaja (*5 times, 9/90*). Aroma of *goudron* and flowers with a touch of oak; soft and smooth in the center though it has a harsh edge; best to drink up; some alcohol intrudes at the end. *

Gaja, Costa Russi (*11/84, 6,800 bottles*). Notes of blackberries and oak on nose; light tannin, forward berrylike fruit; can be enjoyed now though will certainly improve. **(+)

Gaja, Sorì San Lorenzo (*twice, 11/84, 5,870 bottles*). Perfumed, floral bouquet with notes of oak and mushrooms; sweet fruit and oak on palate, elegant and refined, has length; tannin at the end indicates further age needed, though it's tempting now. *** −

Gaja, Sorì Tildìn (*4 times, 11/86, 6,615 bottles*). More substance than the *normale*, good flavor, round, soft, ready, some style. **

Giacosa F.lli (*4/87*). Vague off note intrudes; moderate tannin, moderate fruit, a bit disjointed, no need to keep. *(?)

"La Ca' Növa" Azienda Agricola, Dario Rocca (*twice, 1/85*). Color shows a surprising amount of age; nice fruit on aroma, vaguely floral, tarry notes; tannin seems somewhat high for the fruit; will it soften or dry out first? *(?)

Marchese di Gresy, Martinenga (*twice, 4/87, 14,800 bottles*). Light to moderate tannin, losing its fruit, a bit shallow, some flavor evident, the bottle seems slightly off. * *Bottle of 2/85*: The aroma is there but you have to work for it, then vanilla, cherries and flowers come out; has a fair amount of tannin but seems to have sufficient fruit, some style evident, short, tannic finish. *(*)

Osvaldo Mauro (*twice, 4/85*). Both were oxidized.

Pasquero-Elia Secondo, Sorì d'Paytin (*4 times, 10/87, 14,500 bottles*). Tobacco and tar aroma; soft, light tannin; drink while it still has its fruit. *

Pio Cesare Riserva (*2/88*). Light floral aroma, woodslike component; soft and tasty, a little light, some tannin; ready. *

Poderi e Cantine di Marengo-Marenda, Le Terre Forti (*4/88*). Aroma of mushrooms and underbrush; overly tannic for the fruit, still there is some quality evident; will it develop or dry up? We suspect the latter. * −

Porta Rossa (*twice, 10/90, 8,933 bottles*). Floral and mint aroma; some tannin, starting to dry out but attractive fruit flavors remain; drink up. * −

Produttori del Barbaresco (*1/85*). Fairly nice aroma with a faint suggestion of *tartufi*; light tannin, medium-bodied, good fruit; could improve a bit but is nice drinking now. * +

Punset di R. Marcarino (*1/85*). Cherrylike fruit on nose; moderate tannin, seems to have sufficient fruit, somewhat on the light side; should be ready soon, and won't be a keeper; tannic aftertaste. *

Rosso Gigi, "I Tre Merli" (*7/87*). Too much tannin for the fruit.

S. Quirico di Massano (*4/87*). Off nose, fishy(!); unbalanced, lacks weight, structure and definition.

Scarpa, Payore Barberis (*twice, 4/86, 4,002 bottles*). Aroma of currants and dried fruit, raisins and cinnamon; fairly soft, almost sweet, moderate tannin but nice now, a bit light at the end; some room to improve. **

Scarpa, Tetti di Neive (*4 times, 11/88, 10,575 bottles plus larger sizes*). Dried and ripe fruit aroma, vaguely of berries; soft and smooth, tobacco notes, marred by some oxidation at the end. ** −

Traversa Giuseppe, Cascina Chiabotto, Vigneto Maringota (*4/85*). Light nose; a bit shy on fruit though some is there, not bad considering the year. * −

Vietti, Masseria (*3 times, 2/85, 4,002 bottles*). Perfumed bouquet with suggestions of cherries and tobacco; well balanced, a bit light in body, light tannin, quite a lot of flavor; nearly ready. ** +

1 9 8 0 *

The nebbiolo crop was 622,667 gallons (23,568 hectoliters), equivalent to 3.1 million bottles of Barbaresco. The 534 gallon per acre (50 hectoliter per hectare) average yield was 89.2 percent of the maximum allowed by law and 25 percent greater than the average yield between 1967 and 1989. It was the second largest yield of all; only 1973 was more. And it was the second largest crop produced during this same period; only 1983 was larger.

This was a mixed vintage, overall better than 1981. Angelo Gaja compares it to 1975, not a very impressive year. He bottled no crus. Alfredo Currado noted that the wines have style and perfume. He finds them about equal in quality to the '79s. Giuseppe Colla describes them as well balanced. Pio Boffa found the vintage satisfactory. Castello di

Neive produced very little, choosing instead to sell most of their grapes to the large industrial producers.

The '80s are fully mature and shouldn't be kept much longer. Some of them are starting to fade. The best ones are still fairly good wines.

Accademia Torregiorgi, Messoriano di Neive (1/86). Tar and tobacco aroma is a bit light; fairly tannic entry gives way to some fruit, thins out at the end, with a buildup of tannin; drink, it could be drying out. +

Ascheri Giacomo (1/85). Light aroma, almost candylike; some fruit but atypical, bitter, not a lot of stuffing.

Barale F.lli, Rabajà Riserva (*twice, 4/85*). Up-front fruit on the nose, with suggestions of berries, tobacco, *tartufi* and a vague floral note; firm, a soft center surrounded by tannin, a bit light; could be enjoyed now but it really needs more time, for early drinking. **(+)

Bianco Luigi (*twice, 1/85*). Aroma is closed in though some nebbiolo fruit is evident; a bit light, some tannin, fairly well balanced; will be ready early. *(*)

Borgogno Giacomo, Riserva (*twice, 5/85*). Some volatile acidity and nebbiolo character on the nose; a fair amount of fruit but somewhat unbalanced and harsh, finish is short and somewhat acidic. * −

Brero Cav. Luigi (1/85). Nose has a southern character; same on palate, light tannin, low fruit.

"Bricco Asili" Azienda Agricola (Ceretto), Bricco Asili (*6 times, 8/87, 8,960 bottles*). *Tartufi* and woodslike aroma, vanilla and floral notes; light tannin, soft and round, smooth and spicy, fruity. ** +

Cantina del Glicine, Vigna dei Curà (*4 times, 4/85, 12,525 bottles*). Light floral aroma with hints of *tartufi* and mushrooms; a little light in body, gentle, some tannin, nice flavor; could use another year or two to round out the tannin at the end, not a wine for laying down. **

Cantina del Glicine, Vigna dei Gaja (*3/85, 2,100 bottles*). Nice nose, has fruit and floral aspects, some pine; acid on the high side, light tannin, flavorful; gentle; nearly ready. ** −

Cantina del Glicine, Vigna Rabajà (*twice, 3/85, 2,190 bottles*). Most characteristic varietal aroma of the three crus, cherry note; acid a tad high, overall well balanced; gentle, some elegance; nice now; has length. ** +

Cantina Vignaioli "Elvio Pertinace," Riserva (2/85). Smallish aroma; light-bodied, light tannin, fruit seems almost sweet; lacks some style but drinkable enough; short, tannic aftertaste. (*)

Cantine Duca d'Asti di Chiarlo Michele, "Granduca" (1/85). Aroma displays some richness and vague notes of cherry and tar; tannin up front gives way to fairly decent fruit, fairly well balanced, finishes on a short, tannic note. *

Casetta F.lli (*twice, 5/85*). Cherrylike aroma; moderate tannin, decent fruit; a bit young and simple; should be ready soon. *

Castello di Neive, Santo Stefano (1/85). Aroma reminiscent of cherries; more tannin than expected for the vintage, astringent but the fruit is there, flavor already evident; give it about three years. **(+)

Ceretto, Asili (*2/85, 25,554 bottles*). Aroma reveals less than the '81; somewhat sweet on entry, fairly ripe fruit; some elegance. **(+)

Confratelli di San Michele, Vigneto S. Cristoforo (4/87). Old-style Barbaresco aroma with a seaweedlike character; some fruit; seems old. * −

Contratto (6/85). Pretty, raspberry aroma, fragrant; a nice mouthful of flavor, light tannin; nearly ready, drinkable now. **

Cortese Giuseppe, Vigna in Rabajà (*twice, 2/86*). Mushroom aroma; lots of fruit, balanced, soft center, light tannin, tasty, medium length; ready with room for improvement. ** +

De Forville, Vigneto Loreto (*twice, 4/85*). Aroma of oak and tar; quite tannic with the fruit to back it up, some firmness; fairly nice though still young. **

Franco Fiorina (1/85). Light woodsy aroma; moderate tannin, fairly nice fruit though not a lot of body; should be ready soon; short, tannic aftertaste. *

Franco Fiorina, Riserva (11/87). Woodsy, fruity aroma; some tannin, good fruit; ready now, should last. * +

Giacosa Bruno, Santo Stefano (*3 times, 10/86, 11,300 bottles*). Lovely aroma with suggestions of tobacco, tar and strawberries; soft, smooth and tasty, with backbone, chocolate notes, well made; lots of style, ready with room to improve. *** −

Giacosa F.lli (*3 times, 4/85*). Nice fruit on the nose, vague *tartufi* note; some firmness, well balanced; young but potential evident, some class. **

Giordano Giovanna, Vigneto Cavana (*twice, 1/85*). Ripe, berrylike fruit on aroma; light tannin, fairly soft, medium-bodied; a bit simple; nearly ready. *

Giovannini-Moresco Enrico, Podere del Pajorè (*ex-cask, 10/81, the grapes were picked on November 11*). Very deep color; surprisingly rich and concentrated aroma with hints of blackberries and other fruit; quite tannic but full of fruit; should become a very fine bottle. **(*)

Il Vecchio Tralcio, Moccagatta (*twice, 1/85, 10,000 bottles*). Tobaccolike aroma; fairly tannic—is there enough fruit? Short, tannic aftertaste.

La Spinona di Pietro Berutti (5/85). Aroma recalls resin and berries with a woodsy overtone; some elegance and a lot of style; enjoyable now with room for improvement. *** −

La Spinona di Pietro Berutti, Bricco Faset (11/84). Interesting aroma with a suggestion of wheat and other grain, moderately intense; soft and tasty, light tannin, some sweetness; ready now. **

Marchese di Gresy, Martinenga (*8 times, 4/87, 16,420 bottles*). Light nose of flowers and fruit; a bit light in body, light tannin, nice flavor, soft and ready; some elegance. ** +

"Moccagatta" Azienda Agricola (2/85). Reticent aroma with a faint suggestion of tobacco; moderate tannin, fairly nice fruit, tannic aftertaste with a touch of bitterness; fairly good but lacks style. *

Oddero F.lli (twice, 1/85). Reticent aroma revealing some fruit; moderate tannin but should be ready fairly soon, well balanced; has some character. *(*)

Palladino (2/88). Aroma of the woods, with mushroom and dried berry notes; soft under moderate tannin; drink up.

Pelissero Luigi (twice, 1/85). Lovely, fruity aroma with floral overtones; some tannin, tasty; has a gentleness; good potential. **

Pio Cesare, Riserva (9/86). Good varietal aroma; medium body good fruit, tasty; simple. * −

Podere Anselma (4/87). Earthy aroma has a slight dankness about it; some tannin, unbalanced, on the light side.

Porta Rossa, Riserva Speciale (4/86, 11,351 bottles). Some harshness at the edges, coarse, some tannin over the fruit; not for aging, though needs a year or two if it doesn't dry out first. * −

Produttori del Barbaresco (3 times, 5/85). Moderately intense aroma has a woodsy slant and a note of mushrooms; a bit light, some tannin, fairly well balanced, tasty; nearly ready, should be soon; finish recalls chocolate. **

Prunotto, Montestefano (1/85, 10,400 bottles). Aroma has a harshness to it—volatile acidity, alcohol, or both(?), some fruit; but overly tannic, unbalanced; not a success.

Punset, R. Marcarino (1/85). Cherries on aroma; overly tannic, light-bodied, some fruit.

Punset, R. Marcarino, Riserva (4/87, 2,792 bottles). Seaweed aroma, some oxidation; a bit light, some flavor, tannic aftertaste. * −

Ratti Renato (twice, 10/83). Perfumed bouquet, vague hint of *tartufi*; light tannin, well structured, smooth and tasty, a bit light in body; quite ready. ** −

Roagna, Vigna Pajè (twice, 1/85). Light aroma; moderate tannin, some fruit, soft-centered; not a lot of character; nearly ready. *

Roche Azienda Vinicola (1/85). Flat and dull, some fruit.

Traversa Giuseppe, Cascina Chiabotto, Vigneto Maringota (4/85). Tobacco and mushroom aroma; some tannin, has the fruit to balance; should make a nice little luncheon wine soon. *

Vezza Sergio (twice, 1/85). Aroma suggests strawberries; some tannin, fairly nice fruit; nearly ready, perhaps in a year or two. *

Vietti, Masseria (6 times, 9/87, 4,600 bottles). Aroma of tobacco, flowers and tar; soft center, a bit of an edge; ready now, best to drink up. **

1 9 7 9 * +

This was another uneven vintage; the quality of the wines depends on when the grapes were picked. There was some rain during the harvest. And the nebbiolo crop of 614,239 gallons (23,249 hectoliters), equivalent to 3.1 million bottles of Barbaresco, was large. It was considerably above the 444,886-gallon (16,839-hectoliter) average between 1967 and 1989, but still 12 percent below the amount allowed by DOC. The average yield of 527 gallons per acre (49.3 hectoliters per hectare) was the third largest in the 1970s, with only 1973 and 1974 producing more grapes per acre. And it was the third largest crop between 1967 and 1989; only 1983 and 1980 produced more nebbiolo.

Gaja found the wines more elegant than the '78s and said that they will be ready sooner; they have less body and structure. He felt that Costa Russi was his best wine. For Alfredo Currado the vintage was very good indeed, producing more velvety wines with more glycerine than those of 1980. Giuseppe Colla characterized the '79s as soft and mellow. Pio Boffa found the quality satisfactory. Bruno Ceretto considers them, while not equal to the '78s, certainly very good wines. Bruno Giacosa said although they are easy wines that will be ready early; it was a very good vintage. He also said that the wines won't be long-lived.

For us, the wine of the vintage was Enrico Giovannini-Moresco's Podere del Pajorè. It is truly an outstanding wine, even finer than his excellent '78. Overall, the '79s are soft, easy wines for early drinking; the best have style and elegance and will last. Very few, if any, will improve further. More than a few are starting to decline. We suggest drinking them up.

Ascheri Giacomo (10/82). Lacks structure and weight, some tannin, very little else.

Barale F.lli (twice, 9/86). Soft, ready, fairly well balanced, it was better sixteen months ago. * Bottle of 5/85: Tobacco and flowers on aroma, some fruit in back, light tannin, touch of acid, light-bodied, soft in center, lacks somewhat in depth, ready. ** −

Bava Cantine (1/86). Fruity and vinous aroma, a bit overripe, tannin not high, unbalanced, insufficient fruit, meager in body, unstructured.

Bel Colle (10/82). Pale color, some tannin, in all, an anemic wine.

Bianco Luigi, Riserva (4/87). Aroma displays tar and flowers, light to medium tannin, nice flavor, a bit of a bite at the end, nice flavor. * +

Boffa Carlo, Vigna Vecchia Casot (ex-cask, 4/80). Light to medium in color, some volatile acidity, has some tannin and some fruit but already showing signs of age.

Boffa Carlo, Vigna Vitolotti (ex-cask, 4/80). Fruity aroma, a bit light but nice flavor, some tannin, a lightweight little wine. (*)

Borgogno Giacomo (twice, 11/88). Dried fruit, kind of tired and stale, some alcohol, fading fast.

"Bricco Asili" Azienda Agricola (Ceretto), Bricco Asili (*5 times, 1/85, 7,985 bottles*). Lots of fruit on bouquet—strawberries, raspberries—also mushrooms and a hint of *tartufi*, still somewhat tannic and firm, still young but the quality is already evident, should make a splendid bottle in another three or four years. **(*)

Brovia F.lli (*ex-cask, 6/82*). This wine should've been bottled some time ago, volatile acidity is painfully obvious, still has nice fruit, but a bitter tannic edge, it seems to us it's downhill from here.

Cantina Vignaioli (*11/88*). Characteristic nebbiolo aroma, some warmth, vaguely floral, seems tired, lacks freshness, not a lot of character, still it is drinkable. +

Cantina Vignaioli "Elvio Pertinace" (*3 times, 2/85*). Nice nose, ripe fruit and a note of mushrooms, light to moderate tannin, fairly well balanced, flavor of ripe almost sweet fruit, a bit short and tannic at the end. *(*)

Casetta F.lli (*twice, 5/85*). Small aroma, with a vague hint of tobacco and some nebbiolo fruit, somewhat unbalanced, a bit simple, nice fruit. * −

Castello di Neive, Santo Stefano (*5 times, 9/86*). Classic Barbaresco aroma, *tartufi*, tar and leather, fruit evident, moderate tannin, young, well structured, good fruit. **(* −)

Castello di Neive, Santo Stefano Riserva (*twice, 10/87*). Complex aroma, hints of mint, tar, tobacco and fruit, well balanced, still has tannin, up-front fruit makes it very attractive now, should hold and even improve. *** −

Cauda Cav. Luigi (*1/85*). Wine has a southern character to it, on nose and palate, flat, low in acid.

Ceretto, Asili (*twice, 2/85, 26,550 bottles and 650 magnums*). Big, rich bouquet of ripe fruit, recalls cherries, flowers and *tartufi*, firm tannin, still quite young but a lot of fruit makes it tempting now, the tannin suggests that you resist—give it two or three years at least, has style and some elegance. **(*)

Contratto (*twice, 2/88*). Tar and fruit aroma, soft, light tannin, ready, should hold. * +

Cortese Giuseppe, Vigna in Rabajà Riserva (*twice, 2/86*). Aroma recalls wheat(!), beginning to fade, alcohol intrudes, still has fruit. * *Bottle of 1/86:* Tar and fruit aroma, still some tannin, fairly nice fruit, more body than expected. **

De Forville (*twice, 4/85*). Big, fruity aroma marred by an off-odor vaguely like that of a wet dog, moderate tannin, with sufficient fruit to carry it, needs two to three years. *(+)

Fontanafredda (*12/83*). *Tartufi* and cherries, some vanilla on nose, a surprising mouthful of nice fruit, ready now. **

Franco Fiorina, Riserva and Riserva Speciale (*3 times, 11/86*). Light but nice nose, soft and tasty, still some tannin but soft. * + *Bottle of 5/85:* Lovely bouquet of mushrooms and raspberries seems more suggestive of pinot noir than nebbiolo, medium-bodied, light tannin, soft and round, nice flavor, very well balanced, and nearly ready, fairly long aftertaste. ** +

Gaja (*9 times, 11/85, 118,420 bottles*). Nebbiolo fruit overlaid with oak, tobacco and cherry components, smooth-textured center, light, soft tannins, moderate length, ready now, should hold, could improve. *** −

Gaja, Costa Russi (*5 times, 5/87, 14,487 bottles, plus larger sizes*). Nebbiolo fruit aroma, tobacco notes, soft and flavorful, oak overlay, fairly long finish, displays some style. *** −

Gaja, Sorì San Lorenzo (*4 times, 11/84, 5,281 bottles*). Surprisingly rich Burgundian bouquet(!), a mouthful of flavor, finely balanced and elegant, heaps of style, splendid wine, still has room to improve. ***(+)

Gaja, Sorì Tildìn (*7 times, 2/88, 6,150 bottles, plus larger sizes*). Tight, closed and tannic, hard, surprisingly so, the first time that it's tasted this way! *Bottle of 11/84:* Bouquet already offers some complexity, hints of strawberries, cherries and tobacco over background of oak, lovely, round fruit flavors, some tannin, stylish and elegant, a bit light but well structured, lingers on palate. **(*)

Giacosa F.lli (*4 times, 5/88, 12,400 bottles*). Some oxidized, drying out, still some flavor interest. *Bottle of 9/86:* Not a lot of nose, not a lot to the wine, some acid at the end. What happened? *Bottle of 4/85:* Nice aroma with notes of *tartufi*, fruit and vanilla, well balanced, still has tannin to shed, loads of flavor. ** +

Giovannini-Moresco Enrico, Podere del Pajorè (*17 times, 11/87, 20,765 bottles. Would you believe not often enough?*). This is certainly the wine of the vintage, and more than that—an outstanding wine that might even surpass Moresco's legendary '71—a superstar. Tobacco and cherry aroma has a component that is suggestive of the woods, hints of leather, strawberries and a mélange of other scents, incredible richness and intensity, packed with fruit, great concentration, chocolate notes, this is a great wine. ****

La Spinona di Pietro Berutti (*6/82, bottled 20 days ago*). Still seems tight and ungiving though fruit is evident if you work for it, some elegance, well structured, moderate tannin, a lot of flavor, seems a bit short at this stage, has potential. *(*)

La Spinona di Pietro Berutti, Bricco Faset Riserva Speciale (*twice, 5/84*). Still a bit closed on aroma, sweet ripe fruit flavors in spite of being somewhat light-bodied, has style, well made, firm tannic vein, needs time to soften. **(*)

Le Colline, Riserva Speciale (*twice, 10/87, 18,750 bottles*). Tobacco and cherry aroma, good fruit, moderate tannin, open fruit. ** +

Marchese di Gresy, Martinenga-Camp Gros (*5 times, 3/87, 6,500 bottles*). Some oxidation, still the quality is evident and comes through, slightly bitter, we suspect an off bottle or bad storage. **? *Bottle of 1/86:* Perfumed, elegant, stylish, balanced, loads of quality, long lingering finish, one of the top wines of the vintage. *** +

Marchesi di Barolo (*10/82*). Pale color, not a lot to the aroma, light tannin, fairly nice fruit on entry, light-bodied, lacks some weight and style, rather pedestrian—an industrial wine.

"Moccagatta" Azienda Agricola (*2/85*). Stinky odors, rather light-bodied, moderate tannin, has fruit, bitter on the finish, lacks quality and style.

Musso Sebastiano, Bricco Rio Sordo (4/86). Color showing age, slight nose, some fruit, not much to it, tannic, vaguely bitter aftertaste.

Palladino (twice, 1/85). Vaguely floral bouquet, light-bodied, light tannin, fairly nice fruit up front but tails off as it goes back. (*)

Pasquero-Elia Secondo, Sorì d'Paytin (twice, ex-cask, 11/80). Both times, April and November, overly astringent and rather thin, without much fruit or character, a big surprise from what is normally a very good producer. . . .

Pavese Livio (1/85). Some fruit evident on the nose, moderate tannin, some astringency, fairly forward, marred by intrusion of alcohol at the end.

Pio Cesare (1/85). Light nose, still somewhat reticent, with a suggestion of *barrique* and not much else at this stage, firm tannic vein, seems to be sufficiently well balanced to carry the tannin. *

Produttori del Barbaresco (8 times, 4/90). Leather and tobacco aroma, a little dry, still some fruit, but more of a dried than fresh nature, drink up. *

Produttori del Barbaresco, Asili Riserva (3 times, 5/85, 6,790 bottles). Floral bouquet has a suggestion of *tartufi*, ripe fruit on palate seems sweet and fairly forward, should be ready soon, but drinkable now, stylish. ***

Produttori del Barbaresco, Moccagatta Riserva (twice, 5/85, 13,560 bottles). Quite tannic, fuller and harder than the Asili or Rabajà, quite young, could use more style. *(*)

Produttori del Barbaresco, Montestefano Riserva (3 times, 11/84). Richly fruited aroma, marred by some alcohol, seems overly tannic, a real disappointment. *

Produttori del Barbaresco, Ovello Riserva (3 times, 9/90, 13,565 bottles). Open and characteristic nebbiolo aroma, still has tannin, the fruit is there to support it for now, we wonder if it is sufficient to outlast the tannin, short dry aftertaste suggests that it could be starting to dry out. ** — *Bottle of 1/85:* Aroma has suggestions of cigars, fruit and *tartufi*, well balanced, loads of flavor, a fair amount of tannin, perhaps a bit too much, some length. **(+)

Produttori del Barbaresco, Pora Riserva (twice, 11/85, 27,250 bottles). A lovely, well-balanced wine, soft, round, tasty, a bit light. ** +

Produttori del Barbaresco, Rabajà Riserva (6 times, 6/89, 27,180 bottles). Tar overlays a vaguely floral aroma, good body, tasty, sweet impression, ripe fruit flavor, soft center, some bitterness, very ready. **

Prunotto, Montestefano (1/85, 10,585 bottles). Nose is marred by the intrusion of volatile acidity, some fruit evident but a questionable future. *(?*)

"Rizzi" Azienda Agricola, Ernesto Dellapiana (4/81). Note of cherries on aroma, medium-bodied, well structured, moderate tannin, has some style. *(*)

Rosso Gigi, Riserva (1/85). Expansive bouquet recalls *tartufi*, fresh fruit, strawberries, some tannin, flavorful, almost sweet, very well balanced. **(+)

Scarpa, Payore Barberis (4/86, 4,362 bottles). Brick-colored robe, orange reflections, lovely bouquet suggestive of the woods, berry and mushroom nuances, fairly soft, fruit almost lush, a little on the light side, balanced and smooth, nice now with room to improve. ***

Scarpa, Tetti di Neive (4 times, 2/89, 14,745 bottles). Tobacco notes, overall a light nose, flavorful, some acid, has been better, best to drink up now, a bit harsh at the end. ** —

Vecchio Piemonte Cantine Produttori (1/85). Vague tobaccolike note and some fruit on nose, has a fair amount of fruit, somewhat astringent, rather simple. * —

Vietti, Masseria (4 times, 2/85, 6,070 bottles). Floral bouquet with notes of cherries and *tartufi*, still some tannin but also nice fruit, perhaps a trifle light, can use another two years. **(+)

1 9 7 8   * * * +

The 327 gallon per acre (30.6 hectoliter per hectare) production, 54.7 percent of what the DOC allows, yielded a total crop of 381,584 gallons (14,443 hectoliters), equivalent to 1.9 million bottles of Barbaresco. This was a very small crop indeed. In the 1970s only 1977 and 1976 had smaller yields. And no other topflight vintage had such a small average yield.

Bruno Ceretto calls the '78s wines for poets. Bruno Giacosa said they are grand wines and possibly better than the '71s. And judging by his Santo Stefano—the wine of the vintage for us—we have to concur. Giovannini-Moresco said that for him the vintage produced fat wines that perhaps lack some elegance. Angelo Gaja, in the mid-1980s, said that the very best are better balanced than the '71s and that they should be long-lived wines. Giuseppe Colla considers them outstanding Barbarescos, notable for their harmony and balance. Alfredo Currado also finds them exceptional.

In January 1990, Gaja described the '78 Barbarescos as hard, with green tannins; they need to be kept for another two to three years, and should keep well for a decade after that. The one big question, though: will they really develop? The tannins are intense and more dominant than any other vintage of the 1970s or '80s. The yield was low and the tannins aggressive.

Based on the nearly six dozen Barbarescos that we've tasted, many more than once, we must admit to really being impressed. For us the '78s are simply superb wines, more impressive for their balance and elegance than the '71s. Although we rate them highly, we place them below the topflight vintages of the 1980s. The '78s are definitely Barbarescos to cellar. If there are any questions for their future, they are: Is there sufficient fruit for the tannin? And is the quality of the tannins too hard to soften before the fruit fades? In the case of the top wines, there is no doubt in our minds that the overall structure, weight, and extract are sufficient for the wine to mature properly. As for some others, they have a questionable future.

Accornero Flavio (Casa Vinicola Bera), Riserva Speciale (11/86). Mineral, earthy aroma, thin, low fruit, unimpressive.

Bel Colle (10/82). Pale in color, uncharacteristic aroma, light to moderate tannin, totally undistinctive.

Bersano (5/85). Surprisingly this wine has more class and character, is rounder and smoother on the palate than the *riserva speciale.* *

Bersano, Riserva Speciale (5/84). Straightforward fruity aroma, light tannin, medium-bodied, fruity, grating at the edge, a simple, little agreeable wine that's beneath its class.

Bianco Luigi (twice, 11/82). Lacks weight and substance.

Boffa Carlo, Vigna Vitolotto (ex-cask, 4/80). Simple grapey aroma, some tannin, a bit light in body, tasty, lacks intensity. (*)

"Bricco Asili" Azienda Agricola (Ceretto), Bricco Asili (twice, 1/85, 5,960 bottles). Bouquet still somewhat undeveloped but displays woodsy nuances as well as notes of *tartufi* and raspberries, superbly crafted wine, well structured, tannin is there but the enormous concentration almost makes it seem ready—resist. ***(+)

Cantina del Glicine, Vigna dei Curà (4 times, 11/82). A light aroma with a vague off note, well balanced, nice flavor overall but somewhat weak on the midpalate! *Bottle of 10/81:* Light, soft and tasty with a nice bouquet, some elegance and style evident. Those tasted in April and December 1980 from cask were very good indeed, both merited **(*).

Casetta F.lli (twice, 1/85). Pale, tar and seaweed on aroma, overly tannic, insufficient fruit.

Casetta F.lli, Vigna Ausario (9/86). Good varietal aroma, a bit one-dimensional, simple, nice fruit, fairly well balanced. *

Castello di Neive, Santo Stefano Riserva and Riserva Speciale (5 times, 4/89, 6,150 bottles). *Riserva of 4/89:* Tar and tobacco, loads of fruit, good backbone, rich and tasty, balanced, still more to give. **+ (****) *Riserva Speciale of 9/86:* Classic *tartufi* and leather aroma, rich and full, well balanced, licorice notes, very long, needs more time. ***(*) *Riserva of 2/85:* Richly intense bouquet, expansive, has notes of hazelnuts and *tartufi,* enormous richness and concentration, superbly structured, has a tannic firmness, no doubt that this will make a fine bottle in three or four more years. ***(+)

Castello Feudale, Riserva Speciale (twice, 4/85). Characteristic bouquet, expansive and somewhat floral with a mushroomlike note, medium body, some tannin but soft open fruit, well made, lacks some style, tails off toward the end, more or less ready. * +

Ceretto, Asili (5 times, 11/82, 21,425 bottles). Oaky notes over a background of rich fruit, well structured, supple texture, still some tannin to lose, very good quality. **(*)

Cigliuti, Bricco di Neive (4/81). Fresh fruit and notes of tar on aroma, has tannin, but a lot of fruit, its style is already evident, needs perhaps another three years. **(+)

Cigliuti, Serra Boella (twice, 10/81). Somewhat reticent aroma has a cherrylike note, well balanced, tasty though still rather closed and undeveloped. **(*)

Colla Paolo, Valgrande, Riserva Speciale (4/85). Southern character, low acid, mineral notes, flat and dull.

Contratto, Riserva (6/85, 5,600 bottles). Fairly rich and characteristic aroma, woodsy, floral and berryish nuances, some tannin remains but drinkable now, should improve, well balanced, moderately long finish. *** −

Coppo Luigi (1/85). Tobacco and fruit on aroma, light tannin, fairly forward, soft-centered, nearly ready, aftertaste brings up hints of cherries. *(+)

Coppo Luigi, Riserva Speciale (1/86, 1,440 bottles). Light to medium garnet, characteristic aroma, light tannin, fairly soft, open and quite ready, some tannin at the end, could use more weight. *

Damiliano Dott. G. (4/87). Light and fruity, simple and easy. *

De Forville, Vigneto Montestefano (twice, 4/85). Oak, fruit and tobacco aroma, moderate tannin, firm, chewy, richly flavored, could use more style. **(+)

De Forville Paolo (11/82). Light aroma reminiscent of apricots, light tannin, light body, shallow—fell apart in the glass!

Fontanafredda (twice, 6/86). Medium garnet, characteristic tar and fruit aroma, still quite tannic, but the fruit is there, perhaps lacks some style. *(*)

Franco Fiorina, Riserva (4 times, 5/83). Aroma of nebbiolo fruit and grappa, flavorful, somewhat lean, still has tannin to shed, comes up a bit short. *

Franco Fiorina, Riserva Speciale (11/83). Bouquet still somewhat reticent, has a note of methanol, fairly tannic, is there enough fruit?

Gaja (9 times, 11/84, 82,498 bottles). Bouquet of enormous richness, background of oak and a hint of mushrooms, sweet ripe fruit with a tannic vein, still needs time but tempting. **(*)

Gaja, Costa Russi (4 times, 1/90, 5,804 bottles). Nebbiolo character quite evident on the nose, along with oak, hints of cherries and flowers, good backbone, room to improve, some tannin, especially at the end. ** + (***)

Gaja, Sorì San Lorenzo (twice, 2/82). Richly scented bouquet of spice, fruit and flowers, has tannin and richness, flavorful, supple, lots of style, outstanding pretty much says it all. ***(*)

Gaja, Sorì Tildìn (4 times, 6/82). Bouquet is deep, rich and intense, with a mushroom note and oak in back, rich and harmonious, supple core beneath the tannin, young, but fine quality evident, very long, exudes style. ***(*)

Giacosa Bruno, Gallina (twice, 11/82). Considerable fruit on aroma and a seeming off note that didn't last, well balanced, has richness and concentration, tannin and style, should make a splendid bottle in time. **(*)

Giacosa Bruno, Santo Stefano Riserva (*twice, 5/86*). Complex bouquet, tobacco and woodsy components, rich and concentrated, mushroom notes, superb quality, very long. **** *Bottle of 11/84:* This bottle was tasted seventeen days after it was opened: expansive bouquet virtually leaps out of the glass, offering notes of raspberries, flowers, mushrooms, *tartufi*, leather, almonds, chestnuts, kirsch . . . the bouquet alone is four star, an abundance of flavor, a superbly structured wine of impressive quality, enormously long on finish that leaves reminders of anise, cherries, flowers. . . . This is for us without question the finest wine of a very fine vintage and one of the greatest wines we have ever tasted. ****

Giacosa F.lli (*3 times, 5/88, 4,400 bottles*). Shows age, some oxidized, totally short. *Bottle of 4/85:* Intense aroma, suggestive of cherries, a rush of fruit on entry gives way to a tannic firmness, well structured, loads of potential. **(*)

Giovannini-Moresco Enrico, Podere del Pajorè (*ex-cask, 12/80*). Cherries all over the nose, a big, rich concentrated wine that, as good as it is, falls down somewhat, just not up to the level we expect from Moresco, though it is certainly a very good Barbaresco. ***

La Spinona di Pietro Berutti (*6/82*). Perfumed bouquet though still somewhat reticent, suggests blackberries, seems almost sweet, well structured, gives an impression of being ready at first but it needs a few more years, has elegance. **(+)

La Spinona di Pietro Berutti, Bricco Faset Riserva Speciale (*10/82*). A classic Barbaresco that's still somewhat closed, good balance and weight, comes up to the expectations of the vintage, young, but will surely be a splendid bottle in time. **(*)

Le Colline (*1/86, 10,840 bottles*). Still seems a bit closed in(!), well balanced, well made, has character and style, good structure, needs more time, say three to five years. **(*)

Marchese di Gresy, Martinenga (*11 times, 1/86, 19,580 bottles*). The bottle was slightly corked, and although we can't really assess it, it shows that the wine is holding well, its class still evident. ? *Bottle of 10/81:* Still somewhat closed in but style and elegance are apparent, a lot of potential, well balanced, has class. **(*)

Marchese di Gresy, Martinenga-Camp Gros (*twice, 4/90, 6,400 bottles*). Soft, round and sweet, some firmness, mushrooms and truffles, more or less ready, elegant. ***

Mascarello Giuseppe, Bernadotti (*twice, 11/82*). Fairly rich fruit on bouquet with suggestions of mushrooms and cherries, considerable tannin but has sufficient fruit in reserve to enable it to develop. *(*)

"Moccagatta" Azienda Agricola (*twice, 2/85*). Smallish note, very little on the palate, has tannin and some firmness but not a lot of fruit, where will it go?

Parroco del Neive (*twice, 11/84*). Not at all bad, characteristic Barbaresco but rather slight. *

Parroco del Neive, Vigneto Gallina (*4 times, 3/83*). Very little aroma, tannic but full of flavor, quite young but should make a good bottle in time. *(*+)

Pasquero-Elia Secondo, Sorì d'Paytin (*8 times, 2/85, 3,650 bottles*). Vaguely tobaccolike aroma, richer and more intense than the '82 but with some elegance, has potential. **(*)

Pio Cesare, Riserva (*3/85*). Lovely nose, some oak, light tannin, surprisingly approachable, well balanced, flavorful, has character. **

Podere Casot Nada, Riserva Speciale (*11/84, 4,000 bottles*). Some sulfur on nose, unbalanced, too much tannin for the fruit.

Produttori del Barbaresco, Moccagatta Riserva (*3 times, 11/82*). A well-structured Barbaresco that already shows complexity and style, still young, needs time but fine quality evident. **(*)

Produttori del Barbaresco, Montefico Riserva (*7 times, 11/85, 14,810 bottles*). Mushroom aroma, soft tannins, fruity, more open and rounder than Pora. **(*+)

Produttori del Barbaresco, Montestefano Riserva (*6 times, 6/90, 13,910 bottles*). Cherry, tobacco and *tartufi* aroma, quite tannic, hard and closed, very tight, very much in a shell, needs a lot of age, say three to five years, the fruit is there. **(*)

Produttori del Barbaresco, Ovello Riserva (*3 times, 11/82*). Richly fruity aroma, still has rough tannic edges, but lots of fruit, shows promise. **(+)

Produttori del Barbaresco, Pora Riserva (*9 times, 11/85, 27,910 bottles*). Lovely characteristic aroma, blackberry and tobacco, floral and *tartufi* notes, still has tannin to shed, an underlying hardness, but loads of flavor, approachable. **(*)

Produttori del Barbaresco, Rabajà Riserva (*3 times, 11/82*). Richly fruited bouquet, not fully open yet, still tannic and rough but has the weight and stuffing to carry it, give it at least three, maybe four more years. **(*)

Produttori del Barbaresco, Rio Sordo Riserva (*9/90, 7,000 bottles*). Classic tar and tobacco bouquet with overtones of mushrooms and underbrush, and a vague hint of *tartufi*, tannin evident, so too is the rich fruit needed to carry it, good concentration, attractive, will certainly last and improve. ***(+)

Prunotto, Montestefano Riserva (*3 times, 1/85, 5,754 bottles*). Bouquet still a bit closed but fruit is evident, alcohol intrudes, quite tannic, sensation of ripe fruit in the center indicates it can carry the tannin—if it does, this could be a great wine in time. **(*?)

Punset, R. Marcarino (*twice, 1/85*). Oxidized!!

Ratti Renato (*11/83*). Lovely fragrant bouquet with a faint suggestion of *tartufi*, balanced and stylish, elegant, tasty, enjoyable now, but has room for improvement. **(*)

Roagna, Crichet Pajè (*twice, 1/85*). Lovely bouquet with suggestions of *tartufi*, some tannin, a lot of flavor, not quite ready, finish marred by a touch of alcohol. *(*)

Roagna, Vigna Pajè (*4 times, 2/82*). Color showing age(!); faint off note on aroma, and some alcohol, shallow, not a success, maybe it's the bottle, when we tasted from cask in 1980 the wine showed promise.

Roche Azienda Vinicola, Riserva Speciale (1/85). Light but typical nebbiolo aroma, some tannin, rather light in body, some tannin, astringent finish, lacks character.

Scarpa, Tetti di Neive (4/86, 7,583 bottles). Earthy, mineral aroma, firm and rich in flavor, good structure, tannic, young, say three to five years, evident quality. **(*+)

Vezza Sergio (1/85). Vague off note on aroma—sulfur(?), some tannin, seems to have enough fruit, rather light, an agreeable light wine.

Vietti, Masseria (10 times, 11/85, 6,000 bottles). Tobacco aroma, richly fruited, some tannin, approaching drinkability now, very well balanced, fairly long. ***

Villadoria Marchese (6/85). Unbalanced, harsh, some fruit, overall dull and uncharacteristic.

1977 0

The average yield of 286 gallons per acre (26.7 hectoliters per hectare) was only 47.7 percent of the amount allowed by law. The total nebbiolo crop size of 331,254 gallons (12,538 hectoliters) was equivalent to 1.7 million bottles of Barbaresco. This was the smallest yield of the 1970s and the second smallest of all between 1967 and 1989; only 1984 had a smaller per acre yield. In terms of total crop size, it was the second smallest of the decade; only 1971 produced less nebbiolo.

The 1977 vintage produced poor wines overall, though a few acceptable wines were made; only 1972 was worse in the decade. Italo Stupino of Castello di Neive described the vintage as very poor, as did Angelo Gaja. Bruno Giacosa and Alfredo Currado didn't produce any Barbaresco in 1977. The Cerettos didn't bottle their top cru, Bricco Asili. Giuseppe Colla, on the other hand, rates the vintage as normal. Gaja bottled a small quantity, 2,500 to 2,800 cases, for the home market only.

For the most part, they have long faded and are best forgotten.

Cantina del Glicine, Vigna Montesomo (4/80). Light aroma with suggestions of cherries, light-bodied, some tannin, unbalanced by high acid.

Ceretto, Asili (3 times, 3/83, 24,835 bottles). Pale brick color, lovely perfume, with suggestions of mushrooms and a vaguely Burgundian character, soft, tasty, some tannin, very nice, ready, not to keep, surprisingly good for the vintage. **

Gemma (3/85). Tawny, a surprising amount of fruit on the nose—berries and cassis, drying out, still has flavor. *–

Roagna, Vigna Pajè (3 times, 12/80). Some alcohol on the nose, has fruit on entry, but shallow, ends abruptly with some tannin—was better in cask.

1976 0

The 333,235 gallons (12,613 hectoliters) of nebbiolo was equivalent to 1.7 million bottles of Barbaresco. The 297-gallon per acre (27.8-hectoliter per hectare) yield was 49.6 percent of the 599 gallons (56 hectoliters) allowed by law, and the third smallest yield between 1967, when the DOC took effect, and 1989. Only 1984 and 1977 had a smaller per acre yield. The average yield in 1976 was well below the 1970s average of 417 gallons (39 hectoliters).

Bruno Ceretto said that for them the vintage was quite good; the wines are fine and elegant. Alfredo Currado bottled 20 percent of his Barbaresco as a cru, the remainder as straight Barbaresco. Giuseppe Colla said it was a normal year. Renato Ratti rated it a two stars out of five. Gaja feels the '76s are beginning to decline now and should be drunk up.

Overall, we found the wines ranged from poor to average, more often poor. Very few, if any, hold any interest. For the most part, if you haven't drunk them up, you might as well pour them out.

"Bricco Asili" Azienda Agricola (Ceretto), Bricco Asili (twice, 5/86). Medium brick color, tawny rim, vaguely corked, noticeable oxidation, dried out. *Bottle of 1/85:* Complex floral bouquet with suggestions of mushrooms, raspberries, mint, tobacco and chocolate, has delicacy and elegance, a touch of tannin but velvety, very ready, and very good—impressive. ***!!

Cabutto Bartolomeo (4/80). Pale color, light floral bouquet has a tarlike note, light-bodied, some fruit, not bad for the vintage.

Cantina del Glicine, Vigna Marcarino (5 times, 4/80). Nice nose, light-bodied, light tannin, has fruit, and some length, ready. *

Castello di Neive, Santo Stefano (twice, 12/81). Nice nose, some tannin, light, fairly well balanced for the vintage. *

Ceretto, Asili (1/82, 17,302 bottles). Garnet, orange at rim, some oak on the aroma overlaid with fruit and an almondlike nuance, light-bodied, soft, somewhat unbalanced but not at all bad for the year, nor to keep. *–

Confratelli di San Michele, Vigneto Cotto (10/81). Aroma has some fruit and a faint peppery note, light-bodied and rather shallow.

Contratto, Riserva (1/82). Garnet, tending to orange, moderate varietal aroma, thin and unbalanced, biting aftertaste.

Feyles Maria, Vigna dei Gaia in Neive (4/80). Some alcohol on aroma and not much fruit, has tannin, rather closed, seems to have sufficient fruit in reserve to develop, shows some promise. (*)

Gaja (2/82). Pale garnet, showing age, pretty bouquet of moderate intensity, with hints of cherries and flowers, light-bodied, some tannin, nice flavors, ready. *

Gemma (11/80). Sweet, almost candylike aroma, not much fruit, not enough for the tannin.

La Spinona di Pietro Berutti (3/83). Drying out and showing its age.

Marchese di Gresy, Martinenga (*13 times, 2/84*). This wine was at its best from late 1979 into 1981, the last bottle tasted was beginning to go, showing some volatile acidity and signs of drying out, it still has nice flavor, though, and some class. *

Produttori del Barbaresco (10/81). Some oxidation on the nose, lacks depth and richness, light and soft, tasty, not to keep.

Roagna, Vigna Pajè (*twice, 4/80*). Insufficient fruit for the tannin.

Voerzio Giacomo (*twice, 12/80*). Weird aroma, unbalanced, thin and harsh.

1 9 7 5 0

The nebbiolo harvest yielded an average of 420 gallons per acre (39.3 hectoliters per hectare) for a total crop of 471,412 gallons (17,843 hectoliters), equivalent to 2.4 million bottles of Barbaresco. This was 30 percent less than the amount allowed by law, and just above the 1970s average of 418 gallons per acre (39 hectoliters per hectare).

This vintage produced poor to average Barbarescos, mostly poor. The Cerettos didn't bottle their Bricco Asili cru in 1975. Ratti gave it three stars out of five. Gaja says the '75s are now on the decline.

The wines should have been drunk up: they are fading, if they haven't already.

Cantina del Glicine, Vigna Marcarino Riserva Speciale (*twice, 10/81, 1,866 bottles*). Some fruit on the nose as well as nebbiolo character, soft, light and tasty, very ready, lacks some length, but good. *

Castello di Neive, Santo Stefano (*7 times, 4/89*). Tar and rubber tire aroma, starting to fade but still tasty. *

Ceretto, Asili (1/85). Lovely bouquet with notes of tobacco and raspberry, light-bodied, light tannin, smooth, some style and elegance, very ready. ** +

Damilano, Dott. Giacomo (3/84). Ripe fruit on aroma, a bit shallow, very short—is this a Barbaresco?

De Forville Paolo (11/78). Characteristic aroma, tannic, but seems to have sufficient fruit, young yet and closed, has potential. **

Fontanafredda (3/83). Toasty, caramel aroma with some oxidation, on palate not bad, but not good either.

La Spinona di Pietro Berutti (3/83). Pale brick color, stinky nose, a disappointment from this normally reliable producer.

Marchese di Gresy, Martinenga (*4 times, 3/87*). Oxidation apparent though still some interest, has a softness and flavor, quite short, going but not gone. * +

"Moccagatta" Azienda Agricola, Mario Minuto (11/78). A small-scale, somewhat unbalanced wine, alcoholic aftertaste.

Produttori del Barbaresco (*6 times, 11/80*). Soft, fairly well balanced, has character, light, no need to hold it longer. *

Roagna, Vigna Pajè (*3 times, 12/80*). Too old, was at its best in October 1978 when it had some flavor and character, but even then, not really impressive.

1 9 7 4 ** −

Like Barolo, 1974 produced a large crop of Barbaresco. The 532 gallon per acre (49.7-hectoliter per hectare) yield gave a total production of 579,998 gallons (21,953 hectoliters) of nebbiolo. This was equivalent to 2.9 million bottles of Barbaresco. It was the third largest yield, and nearly 25 percent above the average between 1967 and 1989 and about 89 percent of the maximum allowed by law.

At one time '74 was a highly regarded vintage. And many producers still rate it highly. Others now feel it was overrated. Angelo Gaja is among them; he ranks the year fourth in the decade, after '71, '78, and '79. Bruno Ceretto puts it fifth in the decade after '78, '71, '79, and '70. Giuseppe Colla described it as excellent. Bruno Giacosa said only '71 and '78 were better for him in the decade. Alfredo Currado considers it a very good vintage. Pio Boffa said his wines had less tannin and less intensity than the '71s. Renato Ratti gave the vintage four stars out of five.

We also believe the vintage was originally overrated. Too many wines haven't lived up to expectations, ours as well as many others. While the best of the '74s will hold, most are fully ready by now and some are even beginning to decline. Very few will benefit by further aging.

Accademia Torregiorgi, Pastura di Neive (2/85). Bouquet shows a complexity and mellowness from bottle age, tannin remains, some fruit but beginning to dry out a bit, a drinkable wine though showing some age. *

Balbo Marino, Cascina Bruciato (4/80). Although it's a corked bottle, the quality, which is due to the structure, is quite evident.

Bordino Franco (4/81). Cherrylike notes in the bouquet, moderate tannin, has the fruit to match it, needs perhaps another year or two. **

"Bricco Asili" Azienda Agricola (Ceretto), Bricco Asili (*twice, 1/85*). Floral bouquet with woodsy, mushroomy notes, texture like velvet, ripe fruit and chocolate flavors, near its peak, elegant, still room for improvement. ***(+)

Cantina Vignaioli "Elvio Pertinace" (10/78). Oxidized.

Cantine Barbero, "Conte de Cavour" (10/78). Alcohol and candylike notes define the aroma, light-bodied, out of balance with high alcohol, low fruit and high tannin.

Cantine d'Invecchiamento, "La Brenta d'Oro" Riserva Speciale (*11/78*). Ho hum.

Casetta F.lli (*4/80*). Very light color, browning, alcohol, volatile acidity and some oxidation—gone.

Castello di Neive, Santo Stefano (*4 times, 2/85*). Brick red, vaguely floral bouquet displaying development and complexity of bottle age, still has a fair amount of tannin but with sufficient stuffing to enable it to smooth out, nearly ready. ** +

Castello di Neive, Santo Stefano Riserva (*3 times, 4/89*). Nice nose, lots of fruit apparent, loaded with flavor, tobacco nuance, dry finish suggests drinking up. ** −

Cigliuti F.lli (*twice, 10/78*). Soft and flavorful, some tannin, balanced, has style. ** +

Contratto, Riserva (*12/81*). Color shows some age, characteristic nebbiolo aroma with tar and fruit, some tannin, but fairly soft, vaguely bitter aftertaste. * +

Fontanafredda (*1/85*). Bouquet shows some development, but marred by a harshness, very soft and ready, tasty on entry but tails off toward the end, no need to hold it any longer. *

Franco Fiorina, Riserva Speciale (*twice, 4/82*). Reticent aroma with hints of nebbiolo fruit, tar and flowers, well structured, moderate tannin, tasty, shows some quality. **

Gaja (*10/82*). Moderately rich bouquet, some tannin, flavorful, if it only had more length on the palate. *

Gemma, Riserva (*twice, 10/85*). Light nebbiolo aroma, some rough edges (acid), very little tannin, fairly nice flavor, no finish at all, drink up. *

Giacosa Bruno, Gallina (*10/79*). Perfumed bouquet, well balanced, tannin to shed but with the fruit in reserve. **(+)

Giacosa Bruno, Santo Stefano (*twice, 9/81, 7,200 bottles*). Bouquet is fairly intense and concentrated, has structure and style, and loads of flavor, still some tannin to lose but smooth-textured and drinkable now. **(*)

Giovannini-Moresco Enrico, Podere del Pajorè (*7 times, 5/81*). Expansive, perfumed bouquet recalls cherries and rich ripe fruit, also a touch of alcohol, considerable tannin remaining, enormous weight and extract, young, has potential. **(*)

Marchese di Gresy, Martinenga (*3 times, 2/85*). Not a lot on aroma, some tannin and a lot of flavor, sweet and smooth, at or near its peak. ** −

Palladino (*11/78*). Aroma of burnt hair(!), thin, tannic backbone, short, unpleasant aftertaste.

Parroco del Neive, Vigneto Basarin (*11/80*). Beautiful robe, penetrating aroma, heaps of flavor upon entry that tails off, shallow and short.

Parroco del Neive, Vigneto Gallina (*10/78*). Bouquet of richness and depth, has style and balance, still with tannin to shed, fine quality. ***

Pasquero-Elia Secondo, Sorì d'Paytin (*twice, 11/80*). Reticent aroma reveals some fruit, has tannin to lose but a lot of flavor, holds out some promise, good quality. *(* +)

Pelissero Luigi, Riserva (*4/80*). Nice nose with still more to give, has tannin, flavor and length on the palate. *(*)

Pio Cesare (*twice, 5/83*). Browning, some oxidation and some nebbiolo character on aroma, dried out, too old or else the bottle was better a year ago but seemed perhaps too tannic at the time.

Produttori del Barbaresco, Montestefano Riserva (*3 times, 11/84*). Lovely, fragrant perfume with touches of cherries and tobacco, light tannin, soft, well balanced, at or near its peak. ** +

Produttori del Barbaresco, Pora Riserva (*8 times, 12/83, 14,000 bottles*). Characteristic bouquet with tarlike notes, and a touch of volatile acidity, a mouthful of flavor, light tannin, some alcohol at the end. It was better in 1981. **

Produttori del Barbaresco, Rabajà (*4/80, 14,118 bottles*). Perfumed bouquet, still has tannin but very nice now, a mouthful of nice fruit flavors. ** +

Prunotto, Montestefano (*1/82*). Floral, fruity bouquet with a characteristic hint of *tartufi* in the background, considerable tannin, but seems to have the fruit to back it up, needs a few years yet. **(+)

Punset, R. Marcarino (*3 times, 11/80*). Incredible perfume, has a note of apricots, nice entry, good flavor, but falls down on the finish—short and alcoholic, it was better six months to a year ago, perhaps an off bottle. ** −

"Rizzi" Azienda Agricola, Ernesto Dellapiana (*ex-cask, 4/80*). Nice nose, tannic but with sufficient fruit to develop. *(*)

"Rizzi" Azienda Agricola, Ernesto Dellapiana, Vigna Fondetta (*ex-vat, 4/80*). Aroma of fresh cherries, fairly rich, has tannin and some elegance. **

Roagna, Vigna Pajè Riserva (*8 times, 1/84*). Characteristic bouquet, has a suggestion of cherries, nice flavor, some richness, still some tannin and some elegance, could improve but ready now, as good as it's ever been. **

Roagna, Vigneto Asili Riserva (*12/84*). Shy aroma, some character and varietal nuances, has fruit up front, but without any follow-through, still tannic but losing its fruit.

Scarpa (*10/81*). Bouquet seems subdued, some tannin and a lot of flavor, very good, with room for improvement. **(+)

Scarpa, Payore Riserva (*4/86, 24,800 bottles*). Beautiful color, lovely bouquet, recalls the woods, rich fruit, smooth texture, very appealing, doubtful future, the tannin might overwhelm the fruit, almost a harshness to it, vaguely bitter, drink up. ** +

Serafino Enrico (*4/80*). Aroma of fruit, tar and raisins, has tannin and some fruit, shallow, alcoholic aftertaste.

Tenuta Coluè di Massimo Oddero (2/80). Characteristic aroma of tar and flowers, a little light, some tannin, hollow.

Vietti, Masseria (22 *times*, 8/87, 7,000 *bottles*). Tobacco and cherry bouquet, soft, a bit of an edge, still it is tasty, starting to decline, quite nice, drink up. **

1973 0

The nebbiolo crop yielded an average of 535 gallons per acre (50 hectoliters per hectare) for a total of 534,477 gallons (20,230 hectoliters), which was equivalent to 2.7 million bottles of Barbaresco. This was, however, only 89.4 percent of the amount allowed by DOC. It was larger than the average of 428 gallons per acre (40 hectoliters per hectare) between 1967 and 1989. In fact, it was the largest nebbiolo yield per acre (hectare) during that period. Over-production in 1973 resulted in thin wines that were nevertheless, on balance, better than the poor to middling '75s, '76s, and '77s.

Alfredo Currado bottled very little Barbaresco in 1973; Bruno Giacosa bottled none. Giuseppe Colla rated it as a normal vintage. For Renato Ratti 1973 was a three-star year (out of five). Gaja describes 1973 as a small vintage of medium quality. He bottled a small quantity of Sorì Tildìn and no Sorì San Lorenzo.

Most, if not all, of the '73s are already too old, and there's no reason to keep the rest any longer.

Cantina del Glicine, Vigna Marcorino, Riserva Speciale (*twice*, 10/78). Tar and *tartufi* on aroma, has tannin, also good flavor, a nice bottle. **

Carra (11/79). Awful odor, some tannin, and then. . . .

Castello Feudale, Riserva Speciale (1/85). Bouquet though small shows varietal character, still has tannin and a surprising amount of fruit, not to keep, beginning to dry out, though still good. *

Ceretto, Asili (1/85). Flowers, raspberries, vanilla and spice suggestive of a Rhone wine, the softest and most ready at this vertical tasting from '80 to '73 (at the winery), a soft center and a taste of ripe raspberries. *** —

Colla Paolo (10/78). Nice entry, has tannin, lacks middle body.

Gaja (13 *times*, 11/84). There has been variation, some bottles were too old, others were very nice indeed. *The most recent bottle, tasted at the winery:* Strawberries and mushrooms on the bouquet, quite Burgundian, some alcohol intrudes, a bit light but well balanced, loads of flavor, beginning to dry out a bit but still very good indeed. **

Gaja, Sorì Tildìn (9/83). Bouquet has some interesting nuances though somewhat fleeting, soft, almost sweet, light tannin, might hold for a while but certainly no need to keep it longer. ** —

1972

The weather in 1972 was dismal; the grapes did not ripen. As in Barolo, no Barbaresco was produced in 1972; the entire crop was declassified voluntarily by the producers. When's the last time you heard of an entire crop of Bordeaux or Burgundy being declassified by the producers?

1971 ***

There was rain during the flowering in 1971, which reduced the size of the crop. Toward the end of June the sun came out and the weather took a turn for the better. The remainder of the summer was very hot. The harvest took place early under ideal conditions and was over by the end of September. The average yield of 370 gallons per acre (34.6 hectoliters per hectare) was 38 percent below the maximum allowed by law, and the sixth smallest yield between 1967 and 1989. As far as the top vintages go, only 1989 and 1978 produced a lower per acre yield. The total crop size of 298,467 gallons (11,297 hectoliters) of nebbiolo was equivalent to 1.5 million bottles of Barbaresco.

Giuseppe Colla says the vintage was exceptional. Alfredo Currado agrees, describing it as a first-rate year. For Bruno Giacosa the '71s are the best of all. Angelo Gaja feels that perhaps they're too much of a good thing; they are Barbarescos to cut with a knife, very rich wines that seem more like Barolo than Barbaresco. Renato Ratti gave it five out of five stars.

He pretty much sums up our view too. They are excellent wines, to be sure, but if we have one criticism, it is that they are uncharacteristic. They lack the Barbaresco style, the finesse. If we want a Barolo, we drink Barolo; when we want a more elegant wine, we drink a Barbaresco. Too many of these wines seem to be Barolos in the guise of Barbarescos. They have enormous richness and concentration and very high alcohol. The best will continue to improve for many years, and they will be very long-lived. Rating the wines as Barbarescos we could give them only three stars; as Barolos, we would be tempted to give them four. Overall, we would have to call it a three-star vintage since we are rating them as Barbarescos.

Accornero Flavio (Castello Feudale), Riserva Speciale (11/86). Shows age on the color and the aroma, fading, still some flavor. * —

Bersano, Riserva Speciale (5/84). Fair aroma, lacks the richness and depth expected from this vintage, well balanced, moderate tannin, and the fruit to match, drink it now, it's not going anywhere. *

Boffa Carlo (4/80). Some complexity of bottle age, soft though still has tannin, tasty, ready, moderately long. * +

Castello di Neive, Santo Stefano Riserva (2/85, 4,250 bottles). Complex floral bouquet, enormous richness and concentration, a Barbaresco for Barolo lovers, liquid velvet on palate, sweet, rich ripe fruit, enormous length. *** +

Ceretto, Montefico (5/85, 15,100 bottles). Old-style nebbiolo aroma—tar and rubber tires, alcohol intrudes, dried out, very little of interest remains.

Conterno Giacomo (twice, 4/87). Rich truffle bouquet, of woods and mushrooms, fruity aroma, intense, rich and great concentration, tannin still quite evident but so too is the enormous fruit, superb, very long. *** +

Gaja (5 times, 1/90). Rich bouquet suggestive of the woods and tar, classic nebbiolo, rich tannin, chewy, full-bodied, intense in flavor on the palate, a big, rich and concentrated wine, some alcohol mars the end, still has a hardness, especially at the end. ** + (*** –)

Gaja, Sorì San Lorenzo (10/78). Incredible depth of flavor and richness, needs a lot of age yet but splendid. ***(+)

Gaja, Sorì Tildìn (3 times, 9/83). Age beginning to show in brick color and bouquet with signs of oxidation and seaweed, still has some tannin and fruit, somewhat astringent—was better in 1982, most likely this bottle was not up to par. ** +

Giacosa Bruno, Montefico (4/87, 8,100 bottles). Fabulous bouquet, some delicacy, classic, smooth almost sweet, a big rich concentrated wine, ready but with room to improve. *** +

Giacosa Bruno, Santo Stefano Riserva Speciale (5 times, 1/86, 2,100 bottles). Deep brick robe, intense bouquet of tobacco, berries and perfume, suggestions of the woods and the autumn, blueberry nuance, a profound wine with great concentration and richness, enormous length, still quite a lot of tannin, round, tremendously complex, more to give. ****

Giacosa F.lli (11/78). Expansive bouquet with a note of *tartufi*, well balanced, tasty, still some tannin to shed. ***

Giovannini-Moresco Enrico, Podere del Pajorè (22 times, 6/90, 12,555 bottles, 15.5 percent alcohol). Soft and velvety, some age starting to show, still lovely nevertheless, perhaps not stored as well as other bottles we tasted. *** *Bottle of 2/90:* Great depth on the bouquet, recalls mushrooms and the woods, great richness and concentration, still some tannin and grip. **** *Bottle of 3/85:* Brick robe has an orange cast, floral bouquet is incredibly rich and intense, with suggestions of cherries, tar, tobacco and loads of fruit, a big, rich mouthful of wine, with enormous richness and concentration, velvety almost like an unfortified Port, extremely well structured, a Barbaresco of immense proportions and depth. Right from the first time we tasted it in 1978 this wine has impressed us, and thus far shows no signs of age. Lucky us, we still have a few bottles left. ****

La Spinona di Pietro Berutti (6/82). Vague hint of volatile acidity, also cheese and chocolate, fairly intense and rich, moderate tannin, richly flavored, needs time, has potential. **(+)

Produttori del Barbaresco, Ovello Riserva (17 times, 2/90, 13,260 bottles). Great elegance and class, rich yet delicate and gentle, round, velvety, long, at its peak, heaps of style. **** –

Produttori del Barbaresco, Pora Riserva (twice, 10/79). Cherrylike aroma, well balanced, flavorful, some style, nearly ready. **(+)

Produttori del Barbaresco, Rabajat Riserva (3 times, 1/86). There were three bottles, all were different. We suspect they weren't all well stored. *The best bottle:* Lovely bouquet, complex and mellow, tannic grip, richly fruited center, chewy, long with a bit of an alcohol bite. ***

Prunotto, Montestefano (1/85). Expansive bouquet of ripe blackberries and *tartufi*, soft, round and velvety, still some tannin but hardly seems noticeable, full-bodied and richly concentrated, still has more to give but the quality is already evident. ***(+)

Roagna, Paglieri (5/90). Rich nose, characteristic floral and tar, woodsy, still rich in flavor, with some tannin, holding well. **

1970 ** +

The average production of 465 gallons per acre (43.5 hectoliters per hectare) gave a total nebbiolo crop of 350,435 gallons (13,264 hectoliters), equivalent to 1.8 million bottles of Barbaresco. This was 22.5 percent below the amount allowed by law but greater than the average between 1967 and 1989.

Renato Ratti rated 1970 four stars out of five. The vintage produced very good wines that on balance have been better than the '74s. Some producers equate them with the '62s. The '70s are enjoyable now, and the best will certainly keep.

Borgogno Giacomo, Riserva (3/80). Well-developed bouquet with some complexity, soft and smooth-textured, some tannin, quite ready, short. ** –

Contratto (twice, 2/80). Floral bouquet, characteristic, some depth and complexity, a lot of flavor, still some tannin, very ready, only problem is a touch of alcohol at the end. ** +

Gaja, Sorì Tildìn (11/84). Toasty notes, hint of mushrooms on characteristic nebbiolo bouquet, marred by some alcohol and a touch of volatile acidity, a fair amount of tannin but a lot of fruit in the center, typical old-style Barbaresco, will it develop and soften, or will it dry out first? We think, in spite of the volatile acidity, that it'll improve. **(+)

Giacosa Bruno, Montefico (twice, 10/89). Tar, woods and fruit, complex bouquet, loads of flavor, at its peak, velvety, very long, lots of class. ***

Produttori del Barbaresco, Moccagatta Riserva (4/80). Floral perfume with a tarry note, quite full in the mouth, still has tannin but flavorful and ready. ** +

Produttori del Barbaresco, Rabajà Riserva (4/80). Rich bouquet, intense and full of fruit, has a nutlike aspect, velvety, elegant, heaps of flavor, very nice indeed and quite ready, some tannin and a lot of fruit, should last. ***

1 9 6 9 0

The average yield of 458 gallons per acre (42.8 hectoliters per hectare) resulted in a total crop of 263,645 gallons (9,979 hectoliters) of nebbiolo, or 1.3 million bottles of Barbaresco.

The Barbarescos of 1969 were average at best. Too many never amounted to anything. Italo Stupino of Castello di Neive described it as a very bad year. For Ratti it deserved three stars out of five. Overall, they're too old now, though there are exceptions—the Bruno Giacosa Montefico and Vietti Masseria for two—they should have been drunk up long ago.

Contratto (12/81). In all, a nice glass of wine though past its prime, has flavor but the harsh edges and alcohol aftertaste suggest it's on its last legs. *

Giacosa Bruno, Montefico (3 times, 2/90). Incredible sweetness, richness and surprising intensity, like velvet. ***

Vietti, Masseria (11/90, 2,250 bottles). Lovely, complex bouquet, offers suggestions of chocolate, leather and anise; soft and round, with hints of the same nuances on the nose, very long. ***

1 9 6 8 0

The average of 499 gallons per acre (46.7 hectoliters per hectare) gave a total crop size of 234,795 gallons (8,887 hectoliters) of nebbiolo, equivalent to 1.2 million bottles of Barbaresco.

Renato Ratti gave it three stars out of five. Perhaps average in the beginning, the '68s have faded or are fading now, and there's no point in holding them any longer.

Contratto (twice, 12/81). Still has fruit, but harshness and signs of drying out indicate there's no reason to hold it any longer.

1 9 6 7 **

The average of 512 gallons per acre (48 hectoliters per hectare) gave a total crop size of 240,765 gallons (9,113 hectoliters) of nebbiolo, equivalent to 1.2 million bottles of Barbaresco.

Gaja considers 1967 overall a medium-quality vintage; the wines, he feels, are probably at their peak now. For Bruno Giacosa, on the other hand, it was a very good year, among the best. For Renato Ratti it was on the second level, four stars out of five. We found the '67s to be very good wines. The best are drinking well now and they will last, although not improve. Others are showing signs of decline. For the most part, there's no reason to hold them any longer.

Gaja (3/83). Garnet tending to orange, expansive bouquet with richness and concentration, very tannic but seems to have sufficient fruit given enough time to soften. **(?)

Gaja, Sorì San Lorenzo (twice, 11/84). Brick red, orange reflections, old-style Barbaresco bouquet, loaded with flavor, a firm tannic vein, starting to show age, might hold but future doubtful. * +

Giovannini-Moresco Enrico, Podere del Pajorè (10/79). Bouquet has a lot to it, notes of mushrooms and fruit, falls down on the palate, drying out, too old. (We tasted this wine at the winery. Moresco poured it as a curiosity; it was his first and least successful wine.)

La Spinona di Pietro Berutti (twice, 2/90). On the decline, still has fruit, in fact a surprising amount. ** −

Produttori del Barbaresco (6 times, 3/81). Bouquet of vanilla and nebbiolo fruit, beginning to show some age, soft with a vague harshness that wasn't there a year ago (or the bottle is showing age), tasty, has style, some length on finish, but some alcohol intrudes, still a very good bottle. **

1 9 6 6 0

Renato Ratti gave it two stars out of five. This vintage produced poor wines that never amounted to much.

1 9 6 5 0

It was an average year. Some rated it as good. Ratti gave it three stars out of a possible five. The wines today are too old.

Marchese Villadoria (6/90). Awful, baked, shot.

1 9 6 4 ***

This was an exceptional vintage, perhaps the best of the decade. Renato Ratti gave it his maximum of five stars. Angelo Gaja thinks 1964 was overrated. The wines received a lot of very good press. For Bruno Giacosa it was a topflight year, on a level with 1971. And for anyone fortunate to have tasted his magnificent '64 Santo Stefano they will agree. The best Barbarescos, if well stored, should still be splendid. Although they will certainly last, they are very ready now.

Bersano, Riserva Speciale (5/84). Beginning to dry out though still has flavor interest. * −

Castello di Neive, Santo Stefano (2/85, from a private bottling of 2/70, never in commerce). Lovely, well-developed perfume, rich, round and velvety, at its peak—a superb wine with enormous length. *** +

Gaja (*3 times, 11/84*). Brick red, orange at rim, lovely bouquet, vaguely floral, finely balanced, round and soft, sweet, ripe, elegant, a well-knit Barbaresco of quality. ***

Giacosa Bruno, Santo Stefano (*twice, 12/85, 15 percent alcohol*). Sublime bouquet, great complexity, a cornucopia of scents, liquid velvet, long and complete, wines are rarely better than this, a wine of meditation, glorious. Bruno Giacosa said this wine is medicine, who are we to disagree? **** +

Mascarello Giuseppe (*4 times, 11/82*). Some oxidation and signs of drying out, but still shows quality, mellow and smooth on palate. *

1 9 6 3 0

Ratti gave it his lowest rating, one star out of five. These wines were, for the most part, born too old. They're best forgotten now.

1 9 6 2 0

Renato Ratti saw it as a three-star vintage out of five. This was a mixed vintage. The wines ranged in quality from fair to good. With few, if any exceptions, they should have been drunk up years ago.

1 9 6 1 ** +

Hail at the end of June, during the flowering, reduced the crop size. July turned very hot, and the heat of summer continued into October. The grapes, all picked by the end of September, had very high sugar levels. The grapes themselves were quite warm when brought into the wineries, consequently fermentation started immediately and at very high temperatures.

At Gaja the fermentation got stuck and stayed that way for three and a half months. When it restarted, the must fermented very slowly. In fact, some sugar still remained in the wine for a number of years. The wine was held in the cellar for a long time before it was offered for sale. Angelo Gaja rates this as the best vintage of the decade. Bruno Giacosa considered it, though not quite the equal of 1964, an exceptional vintage. Renato Ratti gave it his maximum of five stars.

For the most part, the '61s are beginning to show their age. If you have any, drink them up while they're still good.

Gaja (*11 times, 2/86*). The variations among bottles have been tremendous, with some wines meriting one star plus, others three stars plus. *The most recent bottle (and one of the better ones):* Complex bouquet, firm, packed with flavor, some volatile acidity mars this tasty wine, still has a sweetness. ***

Giacosa Bruno (*twice, 4/85*). Beautiful brick robe, classic bouquet of flowers, tar and *tartufi*, intense and rich, still has grip and firmness, liquid velvet, incredible length. The first bottle, which we drank in March 1985, was tasted alongside the Gaja. It was, not surprisingly, better. The second and more recent bottle was tasted after chocolate, and it had the richness to follow it!!! Both bottles **** —

Mascarello Giuseppe (*4 times, 4/84*). Orange robe, floral bouquet, characteristic, soft, round and smooth, somewhat past its peak but still very good. ** +

1 9 6 0 A N D 1 9 5 9 0

Ratti gave his 1960 his lowest rating of one star and called 1959 a two-star vintage out of five. Neither vintage amounted to much and both are long gone.

1 9 5 8 [* * *]

Renato Ratti rated it on the second level, four out of five stars. Originally this was a four-star vintage, producing splendid wines overall—full-bodied, rich, and harmonious. Very few remain today, and those few could be very good, but fewer still will deserve full marks. No need to hold them.

Gaja (*5 times, 11/84*). Medium brick shading to orange at rim, complex bouquet, velvety, sweet, lots of style, still has loads of flavor, a complete wine that is still approaching its peak. ***

1 9 5 7 [* * —]

Ratti put it on the second level with four stars out of five. At one time this vintage was rated three stars but today two stars minus is the most one could expect from the '57s; they're undoubtedly showing their age.

1 9 5 6 0

Ratti saw it as a three-star vintage out of five. Most likely the '56s are long gone now.

1 9 5 5 *

The 1955 was never highly regarded by most authorities. Renato Ratti gave it three stars out of five. We have nevertheless tasted some very good bottles. By now, with few exceptions, they would be too old.

Gaja (2/82). Light to medium brick, a musty aspect to the aroma, which blows away to reveal a lovely, fragrant perfume, some age evident on the palate but smooth and sweet, with some style, very good quality, not to keep. ** +

OLDER VINTAGES

While **1954** was better than **1953**, it still wasn't much of a vintage; these Barbarescos are too old today. The vintage of 1953 produced very poor wines, and today these Barbarescos are best forgotten. While **1952** and **1951** originally rated three stars, they are today probably on their last legs. And **1950**, **1949**, **1948**, **1947**, **1946**, and **1945** are, most likely, long past their prime as well. The most highly rated of the lot, at three stars, was 1945, and just possibly if you find a bottle that has been well stored, it could still be good. We doubt if any of the other vintages could offer anything more than academic interest.

From Renato Ratti's vintage chart:[28]

*****	1947
****	1952, 1951
***	1954, 1950, 1946
**	1949, 1948
*	1953

AND ONE STILL OLDER

Giacosa Carlo 1893 (9/86). First we want to thank Bruno Giacosa for his generosity in donating this bottle to a $500 a person black tie dinner that raised $5,500 for the Boys and Girls Club of Newark, New Jersey, and brought both a spiritual and sensual pleasure to about a dozen lucky wine lovers. The superb dinner at Nannina's in the Park, and the reason for the event—to help deprived children from the inner city of Newark—added immensely to our view of the wine. Indeed, when all is said and done, the wine was still a great experience, albeit one whose pleasure was all the more improved by the reason for the event. This wine was made by Bruno's grandfather, Carlo Giacosa.

As for the wine, the cork was loose and fell into the bottle. The sediment was very heavy. The wine in the bottle appeared to have no color, but once it was poured the color, though pale, had a tawny cast to it. The bouquet displayed a sweetness and complexity from its long age in the bottle. Sweet impression, liquid velvet, nutty, complex flavors, surprisingly good, and impressive indeed, not young, but then again, not really old either. The finish is very long and left behind the memory of the subtle flavors of the palate. While it was past its best, the wine was, nevertheless, very impressive, and very good indeed. ***, for the experience *****

O T H E R   N E B B I O L O   W I N E S   O F   T H E   L A N G H E   A N D ◁   M O N F E R R A T O   H I L L S   ▷

There are many nebbiolo-based wines produced in the provinces of Cuneo, Asti, and Alessandria. We discuss a number of them in the following pages. There are, most likely, many others that we don't include. We have tried to include all of the important ones as well as a number of minor ones. Our survey includes the DOC wines of Nebbiolo d'Alba and Roero, as well as a slew of non-DOC wines.

THE WINES RATED

***
Nebbiolo d'Alba, the best ones
Nebbiolo delle Langhe, the best ones

**
+ Arte
Barilòt
Barolino
Bricco del Drago
Bricco Manzoni
Crichet Pajè
Fioretto
Glicinerosso
Il Favòt
Nebbiolo d'Alba
Nebbiolo delle Langhe
Nebbiolo del Piemonte, the best ones
Nebbiolo Passito
Ornato
Roero, the best ones

*
Arborina
Bricco Viole
Mon Pra
Nebbiolo del Piemonte
Opera Prima
Piria
Roero
Zio Giovanni

0
Concerto
Rubello di Salabue
San Mattia
Telià

The Wines

ARBORINA (*Cuneo*). Elio Altare produces this *barrique*-aged nebbiolo at his winery in the Annunziata district of La Morra. Altare owns 3.7 acres (1.5 hectares) of nebbiolo in the Arborina section of Annunziata. From those grapes he produces a Barolo and 2,000 bottles of Vigna Arborina. In 1984, Altare produced all of 567 bottles of Arborina. This wine tastes as if it were made from oak instead of grapes. But since that style of wine is fashionable today, he gets good press and consequently commands overly high prices. Rating *

ARIONE (*Cuneo*). Michele Chiarlo of Cantine Duca d'Asti produces this nebbiolo-barbera blend. Luigi Veronelli reports that the blend is 65–35, with more barbera than nebbiolo. The nebbiolo comes from the Roero area and the barbera from around Nizza Monferrato. The wine is aged for six months in medium-size barrels of Yugoslavian oak and three months in *barrique*. Arione is meant to be drunk between fifteen and eighteen months after the vintage.

ARTE (*Cuneo*). Domenico Clerico, the fine Barolo producer, also makes 6,000 bottles of a *barrique*-aged wine from a blend of 92 percent nebbiolo and 8 percent barbera. He first produced Arte from the 1985 vintage. Besides the richness and structure of Arte, we like its mouth feel. It should take moderate age. Having tasted all of them from the '85 through the '88, we can say with assurance that this is a very well made wine. We especially recommend the '88. Rating ** +

BARILIN (*Cuneo*). Ferrucio Nicolello produces this wine from nebbiolo grapes grown in Borgato Sorano in Serralunga d'Alba. We have heard that some barbera may also be blended in. Barilin is a full-bodied dry red of about 12.5 to 13 percent alcohol.

BARILOT (*Cuneo*). Michele Chiarlo of Cantine Duca d'Asti has produced this barbera-nebbiolo blend since 1982. The first one was made from a blend of 70 percent nebbiolo and 30 percent barbera. Today Chiarlo uses 40 percent of the former and 60 percent of the latter. The grapes come from two vineyards totaling 8.6 acres (3.5 hectares). The vines are fifty years old. The barbera is from the Vincaio vineyard on Chiarlo's Castelgaro estate in Castelboglione, and the nebbiolo from the Margaria vineyard in Serralunga. Barilòt spends one year in *barriques* of Alliers oak. Chiarlo produced 5,920 bottles of the '83, and 13,300 of the '85; there was no '84. Rating **

BAROLINO (*Cuneo*). This "little Barolo" is a wine made in the Langhe from dolcetto grapes fermented on Barolo lees. The only one we can recall tasting was that made by Marchese Fracassi at her winery in Cherasco. It is a medium-bodied dry wine with about 12 percent alcohol, best drunk within a year or two of the vintage. Rating **

BRICCO DEL DRAGO (*Cuneo*). The Giacomi family has owned this estate since 1721. The current owner, Luciano di Giacomi, owns 25 acres (10 hectares) in San Rocco Seno-delvio. His individual vineyards are Bricco, Campo Romano, Mace, Pian, Ranera, and Sgnogna. From those vines he produces between 48,500 and 54,500 bottles of wine a year. This includes from 16,000 to 22,000 bottles of the proprietary Bricco del Drago plus 5,500 of the Riserva Vigna 'd le Mace, although in 1985 he made 6,196 bottles and in 1986, 6,098, so perhaps the production of that wine is increasing. He also produces 8,000 bottles of Dolcetto d'Alba, 4,000 each of Nebbiolo d'Alba and Pinot Nero delle Langhe, 3,500 Freisa della Langhe, and 8,000 Drago Bianco. The pinot and freisa come from the Campo Romano vineyard. The white is made from an interesting blend of riesling renano, freisa, pinot noir, and nebbiolo. At one time Giacomi also produced Campo Romano from freisa with some pinot noir. We don't know if he still does.

Bricco del Drago *normale* is made from dolcetto (85 percent) and nebbiolo (15 percent) grapes grown at the top of the "Dragon Hillside," from which it takes its name. The first Bricco del Drago Riserva was produced in 1971. The *normale* is aged for about one year in cask. Bricco del Drago is at its best within two to five, perhaps six years of the vintage, when it has a fresh cherrylike aroma, is soft and fruity with a zesty nature and some charm. The Riserva is from the best vineyard. And it is aged for a somewhat longer time. The most recent vintage that we tasted was the '86. Both the *normale* and Riserva were very good. We also liked the two '85s. Rating **

BRICCO MANZONI (*Cuneo*). A few years ago we were told that Valentino Migliorini produced about 25,000 bottles of Bricco Manzoni. Yet the label on the bottle of the '82 indicated that there were 34,607 bottles and 607 magnums! This wine is an 80–20 nebbiolo-barbera blend from grapes grown on his Rocche dei Manzoni estate in Monforte. The wine is aged in small barrels for eight to twelve months. We have tasted some from a different mix of the same two grapes. This wine is, generally, medium to full-bodied, with tart acidity and a cherrylike character. Rating **

BRICCO VIOLE (*Cuneo*). This wine takes its name from the fourteenth-century San Pietro delle Viole near the Sebaste winery. Bricco Viole is a *barrique*-aged, 20–80 nebbiolo-barbera blend. The '87 spent four months in *barrique*. Rating *

CASTELLO DI CAMINO (*Alessandria*). This wine is made from barbera, grignolino, and nebbiolo grapes. It is a medium-bodied dry red of about 12 percent alcohol, best drunk within two to three years of the vintage.

CASTELLO DI CURTEIS (*Cuneo*). This is a nebbiolo-dolcetto-pinot blend produced in the Langhe. It is a medium-bodied dry wine of about 12 percent alcohol that is best drunk young.

Colle Sampietro (*Cuneo*). Fontanafredda produced this medium-bodied dry red from nebbiolo grapes; we don't know if they still make it. It is meant for early consumption.

Concerto (*Cuneo*). Gianni Gagliardo of Paolo Colla produces this wine from a 50–50 blend of barbera and nebbiolo. It is a wine meant to be drunk young. We found it simple and one-dimensional, with a raisiny, overripe character. Rating 0

Crebarne (*Asti*). Carlo Quarello in the village of Cossombrato produces Crebarnè from a blend of barbera and nebbiolo grapes.

Crichet Paje (*Cuneo*). Roagna produces some 8,200 bottles of this light, fruity table wine. The first, from 1982, was 100 percent nebbiolo grapes grown in the Barbaresco. It is made from a selection of the best grapes from the best part of their Pajè vineyard. At one time we were told that they made Crichet only in the best vintages, yet 1987 was far from a best vintage! Rating **

Elioro (*Cuneo*). Cordero di Montezemolo produces this blend of nebbiolo (80 percent) and dolcetto (20 percent) grapes at their Azienda Agricola "Monfalletto" winery. Their first was from the 1984 vintage. We haven't seen this wine since January 1985. As for its quality today, we don't know.

Fioretto (*Cuneo*). Alfredo Currado produces this wine at the Vietti winery from a blend of nebbiolo, barbera, dolcetto, and neirano grapes grown in his Fioretto vineyard in the Scarrone district of Castiglione Falletto. The wine is made specifically for the United States market. In the first vintage, 1982, some 4,000 bottles were produced. There was no '83 Fioretto as Currado wasn't satisfied with the quality of the grapes. The '84 was given some time in *barriques* of Alliers oak. But being unhappy with the quality, Alfredo sold it all *sfuso*. Fioretto is a richly colored wine (the local neirano variety adds good color) that has a cherrylike aroma underlaid with notes of tobacco; it is soft, fruity, and balanced, with a lively tartness from the barbera. The '85 was very good, the most successful that we've tasted, though the '88 isn't far behind. The wine ages moderately well. The '82 was at its best from 1984 through 1986. Rating **

Glicinello and Glicinerosso (*Cuneo*). Adriana Marzi and Roberto Bruno, owners of Cantina del Glicine, the fine Barbaresco producer, make 6,000 bottles of a charming rosé from the free-run juice of 20 percent freisa with 80 percent nebbiolo. Their first was the '83. They also produce 2,000 bottles of Glicinerosso, a red wine made from the same combination of nebbiolo and freisa. There were 10,500 bottles of the first one, the '86. In lesser vintages, like 1984, Glicine made no Barbaresco; all their nebbiolo was used for Glicinerosso. We suspect that they have decreased the production since they supplied us with their production figures. Rating: Glicinerosso **

Il Favot (*Cuneo*). Aldo Conterno produces this *barrique*-aged nebbiolo from grapes grown in his Bussia Soprana vineyards. We believe that '83 was the first one. After being fermented in temperature-controlled stainless steel the wine is moved to *barriques*. Part of the '83 was aged for thirteen months in new *barriques* and part spent a year in older *barriques*. Then the two wines were blended together. We really liked the '83, '85, and '87 Il Favòt. Conterno's nebbiolo in *barrique* tasted of the grapes, not the oak. The oak added a note of complexity. Rating **

Lasarin (*Cuneo*). Elvio Cogno produces a delicious Nebbiolo delle Langhe named Lasarin from mostly young nebbiolo vines from the Marcarini La Serra vineyard, although he also uses some of the younger vines from Brunate. In 1989 he made 10,000 bottles and in 1990 even less.

Mon Pra (*Cuneo*). Mon Prà is a *barrique*-aged barbera-nebbiolo blend made by the Conterno Fantino winery in Monforte. Like many others of this ilk, the oak is dominant. The formula—take a few grapes and a lot of oak! Rating *

Nebbiolato (*Cuneo*). This is a nebbiolo wine produced in the early-drinking style.

Nebbiolo d'Alba (*Cuneo*). The growing zone for Nebbiolo d'Alba lies between those of Barolo and Barbaresco, mostly northwest of the city of Alba, with a small part extending to the south. This DOC zone encompasses some 1,371 acres (555 hectares) of vines divided among 1,237 owners.[29] The zone includes 28 *comuni* and three main districts: Roero, the Alba area itself, and Castellinaldo. Roero, now with its own DOC, is discussed under *Roero*. The nebbiolo wines of the Alba area, on the right bank of the Tanaro, are the fullest in body and those of Castellinaldo are the lightest.

The villages in this DOC are Canale, Castellinaldo, Corneliano d'Alba, Govone, Monticello, Piobesi d'Alba, Priocca, Santa Vittoria d'Alba, Sinio, Vezza d'Alba, and parts of Alba, Baldissero d'Alba, Castagnito, Diano d'Alba, Grinzane Cavour, Guarene, La Morra, Magliano Alfieri, Monforte d'Alba, Montà d'Alba, Montaldo Roero, Montelupo Albese, Monteu Roero, Pocapaglia, Roddi, Santo Stefano Roero, Sommariva Perno, and Verduno. Although parts of Bra, Monchiero, Novello, and Roddino are included, there has been no reported production in those villages in recent vintages.

Nebbiolo d'Alba must be aged for at least one year and

THE NEBBIOLO D'ALBA PRODUCTION ZONE

Mascarello Giuseppe, San Rocco	**
Negro Angelo	**
Pasquero Giuseppe, Vigna Dogna	**
Pezzuto F.lli, Vigneto in Vadraman del Roero	***
Prunotto, Bric Rossino di Monteu Roero	**
Prunotto, Ochetti di Monteu Roero	***
Rabezzana Renato	* +
Ratti Renato, Ochetti di Monteu Roero	***
Scarpa, San Carlo di Castellinaldo	***
Tenuta Carretta, Bric' Paradiso	***
Tenuta Carretta, Bric' Tavoleto	***
Tenuta Coluè di Massimo Oddero	**
Terre del Barolo	* +
Verro Tonino, Vigneto Bricchet del Roero	**
Vietti, San Giacomo di Santo Stefano Roero	***
Vietti, St. Michele di Santo Stefano Roero	***

Tenuta Carretta's Bric' Paradiso comes from a 7.4-acre (3-hectare) vineyard. They have produced this fine nebbiolo since 1967. Production averages 14,000 bottles annually. The Bric' Tavoleto vineyard in San Rocco Senodelvio d'Alba covers 5.6 acres (2.3 hectares). Carretta's fine wine from here was the '82. They produce 14,000 bottles a year of this nebbiolo. The '88 of both wines was very good indeed.

THE VINTAGES

Antonio Niederbacher rates the vintages:

1985 ***	1971 ****	1957 **
1984 **	1970 **	1956 **
1983 ***	1969 **	1955 ***
1982 ***	1968 **	1954 *
1981 **	1967 ***	1953 0
1980 ***	1966 0	1952 **
1979 **	1965 **	1951 ***
1978 ***	1964 ***	1950 ***
1977 *	1963 *	1949 *
1976 *	1962 ***	1948 ***
1975 *	1961 ****	1947 **
1974 **	1960 *	1946 **
1973 *	1959 0	1945 ***
1972 0	1958 ***	

The vintages according to Antonio Rossi:

****	1988, 1982, 1978, 1974, 1971
***	1987, 1986, 1985, 1979, 1976, 1970
**	1984, 1983, 1981, 1980, 1975, 1973
*	1977, 1972

NEBBIOLO DEL PIEMONTE. These wines are made from nebbiolo grapes grown anywhere in Piemonte. They range in

attain 12 percent alcohol naturally. Maximum yield per acre is 675 gallons per acre (63 hectoliters per hectare). The average annual production between 1985 and 1989 was just over 1.4 million bottles, up from the 1980–1989 average of 1.2 million.[30]

Besides the dry red nebbiolo wines, there are sweet reds and semisweet sparkling nebbiolos produced in this area. Rating **/***

RECOMMENDED PRODUCERS	RATING
Ascheri Giacomo, Bricco S. Giacomo	*
Baracco F.lli, San Vincenzo di Monteu Roero	** +
Ca' Bianca, Tenuta Denegri	*
Cappellano	** −
Ceretto, Vigneto Bernardine	***
Franco Fiorina	**
Gianni Gagliardo, Roncaglia (we base our rating on the only good Nebbiolo d'Alba that we tasted from Gagliardo, the '88)	*
Gaja, Vignaveja	***
Giacosa Bruno, Valmaggiore di Vezza	***
Malvira, del Roero	**

style from light to full, dry to sweet, fresh, fruity and charming to dull, flat and uninteresting. Your only guide is the producer, and when, really, is it not? Rating */**

NEBBIOLO DELLE LANGHE (*Cuneo*). These wines are similar to Nebbiolo d'Alba but with more body and flavor. Not infrequently those from the better producers are declassified Barolo or Barbaresco. In some vintages, when their wine lacks the weight and structure that they expect their Barolo to have, the most dedicated producers might declassify all of their wine. Rating **/***

RECOMMENDED PRODUCERS	RATING
Accomasso Giovanni	* +
Bel Colle, Monvijè	*
Cascina Rombone di Nada Fiorenzo	**
Clerico	**
Cogno Elvio	***
Conterno Aldo, delle Bussia Conca Tre Pile	***
Conterno Fantino, Ginestrino	** —
De Negri Lorenzo	*
Einaudi Luigi	**
Grasso Elio, di Monforte	**
Marchese di Gresy, della Martinenga	**
Mascarello Bartolo	***
Produttori del Barbaresco	**
Rinaldi Giuseppe	** +
Rocche Costamagna, Roccardo	*
Sebaste	** —
Vajra, Bricco delle Viole	**
Voerzio Roberto, Ciabot della Luna di La Morra	* +
Voerzio Roberto, Croera di La Morra	** —

NEBBIOLO DI TORTONA (*Alessandria*). This wine is produced by Spinetto, Padeira, and Carbonara from nebbiolo grapes grown in the Tortona area.

NEBBIOLO PASSITO (*Cuneo*). This is a semisweet red wine made from late-harvested nebbiolo grapes dried on mats for about three weeks. The wine is a throwback to the old days in the Piemonte before the change was made to dry wines. It is rarely seen today. We tasted one made by Pasquero-Elia Secondo of Neive from the 1976 vintage; another, from Vietti of Castiglione Falletto from the 1980 harvest. The Vietti was from a production of only 300 bottles. Rating [**]

OPERA PRIMA (*Cuneo*). Opera Prima is a *barrique*-aged non-vintage wine made from nebbiolo grapes in the Barbaresco zone. Roagna first produced this wine in 1983. The first one we tasted, in January 1987, was made from a blend of 40 percent each nebbiolo from 1984 and 1983, and 20 percent 1982. It spent one year in *barriques* of Alliers oak. The oak was dominant. Rating *

ORNATO (*Cuneo*). Pio Cesare produces this full-bodied wine from a blend of 60 to 80 percent nebbiolo and 40 to 20 percent barbera grapes grown in their 25-acre (10-hectare) Ornato vineyard in Serralunga d'Alba. In the first year of production, 1982, they made 200 cases. The wine was given eight months of *barrique* aging. Rating **

PAIS (*Alessandria*). Azienda Agricola Colle Manora, located in Quargnento, grows cabernet sauvignon, merlot, sauvignon, and pinot nero alongside barbera and grignolino. They produce Pais from an *uvaggio* of Piemontese grapes, mostly barbera. They made 8,680 bottles of the '88.

PERTINACE ANTICO (*Cuneo*). This wine is produced from nebbiolo grapes grown in the Barbaresco zone. It is a full-bodied dry red of about 13 percent alcohol with an austere nature and a moderate capacity to age.

PIRIA (*Cuneo*). Giuseppe Massolino produced this 50–50 nebbiolo-barbera blend in 1989 from grapes grown in his Vigna Rionda vineyard. It spent three months in *barrique*. The character of both varieties combined with oak to produce an agreeable wine. Rating *

ROERO (*Cuneo*). Roero, DOC from 1985, encompasses all or parts of 19 villages on the left bank of the Tanaro River in the northern part of the Nebbiolo d'Alba area. In 1989,

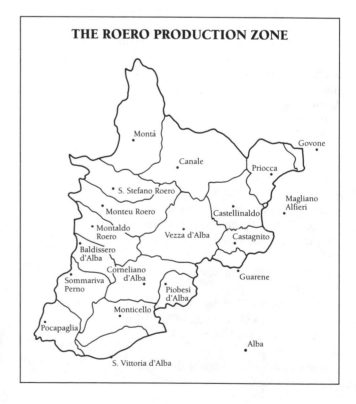

THE ROERO PRODUCTION ZONE

201 growers cultivated some 395 acres (160 hectares).[32] The villages in Roero include Canale, Corneliano d'Alba, Piobesi d'Alba, Vezza d'Alba, and parts of Baldissero d'Alba, Castagnito, Castellinaldo, Govone, Guarene, Montà d'Alba, Montaldo Roero, Monteu Roero, Monticello, Priocca, Santa Vittoria d'Alba, and Santo Stefano Roero. Parts of Magliano Alfieri, Pocapaglia, and Sommariva Perno are also included, although they reported no recent production. The soil here is sandy and cultivation difficult.

Roero must be made from a blend of between 95 and 98 percent nebbiolo and 2 to 5 percent arneis; up to 3 percent of other varieties are allowed. Maximum production per acre is 600 gallons (56 hectoliters per hectare). Between 1985 and 1989 the average yearly production was 554,746 bottles.[33] Minimum alcohol is 11.5 percent. If it attains 12 percent it can carry the Superiore designation on the label. Roero cannot be sold prior to June 1 in the year after the vintage. It is at its best between two and four years after the vintage, but can last five or six. The nebbiolo wines of Roero are noted for their bouquet. The Roero DOC also includes a white wine from the arneis grape. Roero */**

RECOMMENDED PRODUCERS	RATING
Ascheri Giacomo	*
Negro Angelo, Prachiosso	*+
Prunotto	*
Tenuta Carretta, Bricco del Poggio	***

OTHER PRODUCERS WITH A GOOD REPUTATION

Abonna Marziano e Enrico
Almondo Giovanni
Baracco 1871 "Baracco de Baracho"
Ca' du Russ di Sergio Marchisio
Carlo del Tetto
Castello Malabaila
Cornarea
Malvirà
Produttori Montaldesi Associati

The vintages according to Antonio Rossi:[34]

****	1985, 1982, 1978, 1971
***	1988, 1987, 1986, 1983, 1979, 1974, 1970
**	1984, 1981, 1980, 1977, 1976, 1973
*	1975, 1972

ROSALBA (*Cuneo*). This wine is a nebbiolo-dolcetto blend.

ROUVE. Rouvè is still another barbera-nebbiolo blend.

RUBELLO DI SALABUE (*Alessandria*). Carlo Nob. Cassinis produces this light-bodied wine at his 37-acre (15-hectare)

Castello di Salabue in the *località* of Salabue di Ponzano in the *comune* of Ponzano Monferrato from a blend of barbera and nebbiolo grapes. Veronelli reports that the blend is 80 percent barbera and 20 percent nebbiolo and freisa. More recently we heard that it was a blend of nebbiolo with cabernet sauvignon alla Toscana. So perhaps the blend has changed. The '82 we tasted was high in acid and low in fruit. We haven't seen it since. Rating [0]

RUREY (*Cuneo*). The barbera specialist Cantine Bava produced this *barrique*-aged nebbiolo in 1985. The nebbiolo came from La Morra. They made 6,080 bottles. Our only experience with it was when we tasted it from *barrique* in January 1986. It showed a lot of promise. We don't know how it turned out. They expected to keep it in *barrique* for six months. Rating [**]

SAN GUGLIELMO. This medium-bodied wine is made from mostly barbera with nebbiolo and bonarda.

SAN MARZANO (*Asti*). This is one of the many barbera-nebbiolo blends produced in the Asti area.

SAN MATTIA (*Cuneo*). The '85 was made from 70 percent nebbiolo and 15 percent each barbera and grignolino. We hope that Poderi Anselma of Serralunga went back to the drawing boards with this wine. It was, to put it mildly, awful. It went through malolactic fermentation in the bottle. Could it have been designed that way? Rating [0]

TELIA (*Cuneo*). We met Telià on one occasion. There were two bottles. Neither bottle of this nebbiolo-barbera blend was, to be polite, impressive. Rating [0]

VIGNASERRA (*Cuneo*). Roberto Voerzio produces this nebbiolo-barbera blend. We believe that the first one was the '87. And we believe that it is *barrique*-aged.

ZANE (*Asti*). This light-bodied dry red is made in San Desiderlo from a subvariety of the nebbiolo known as zane. It is a soft fruity wine of about 11 percent alcohol, best drunk young while it is still fresh.

ZIO GIOVANNI (*Cuneo*). Azienda Vinicola "Roche" produces this light-bodied wine from a blend of 60 to 65 percent nebbiolo and 35 to 40 percent freisa grapes. It has a fresh, berrylike character, and is best drunk young and cool. Rating *

BAROLO AND ◁ B A R B A R E S C O P R O D U C E R S ▷

Abbona Marziano. The only wine that we tasted from this producer was their unimpressive '79 Barolo. Barolo [0]

Abrigo Orlando Azienda Agricola (*Treiso d'Alba, frazione Cappelletto*), *1937*. The Abrigo family owns 22 acres (9 hectares) of vines in Vigna della Rocca from which they produce 25,000 bottles of wine annually. Besides 5,333 bottles of Barbaresco from Vigna della Rocca plus a regular Barbaresco, they do 3,333 bottles of Barbera d'Alba and 9,333 of Dolcetto d'Alba, 2,667 Pinot delle Langhe, and 667 of a Moscato Passito. Thus far we have tasted two Barolos from Abrigo, both '85s, a regular and the single-vineyard Della Rocca. Barbaresco *

Accademia Torregiorgi (*Neive*), *1976*. This producer owns no vineyards. They buy all of their grapes, selecting at the time of the harvest to get the best fruit and consequently paying a premium. Torregiorgi produces a number of wines, including about 10,000 bottles each of Barolo and Barbaresco. Both of these wines are made in the gentler, more elegant style.

They produce Barolos from Arnulfo di Monforte d'Alba, Carpegna di Serralunga d'Alba, and Grassi di Monforte d'Alba, and Barolos from Crocetta di Neive, Messoriano di Neive, and Pastura di Neive. Not all of these crus are bottled every year. While we have tasted their Barolo in more recent vintages we can't say the same about their Barbaresco. We haven't tasted that wine since the '80. Barolo **; Barbaresco [*]

Accomasso Giacomo. At one time Giacomo Accomasso sold a Barolo under his name; today it is sold under the name of Giovanni Accomasso. The '74 Barolo from Giacomo Accomasso was very good. Barolo ** +

Accomasso Giovanni & Figlio (*Annunziata di La Morra, borgata Pozzo*). Giovanni Accomasso owns vines in the Rocchette and La Pria vineyards. He produces four wines: Barolo, Dolcetto d'Alba, Barbera d'Alba, and Nebbiolo delle Langhe. This highly regarded producer bottles a Barolo from the vineyard of Rocchette dell'Annunziata. We tasted a '74 from Giacomo Accomasso and a '79 from Giovanni Accomasso. Based on those two wines, Barolo ** +

Accornero Flavio (*Neviglie*). Flavio Accornero is a broker and importer. He imports his own wines, as well as others, into the United States. Accornero's family owns vineyards in the Monferrato district, where grignolino and barbera are king. In 1981 he graduated from the enological school at Alba. At that time he began to trade in bulk wine. Shortly thereafter he started buying bulk wine and blending it. After aging it for a sufficient period at Casa Vinicola Bera, the wine, including a Barolo and Barbaresco, is labeled with his name. Walter Bera, the noted Moscato producer, bottles the wine for Accornero. Accornero's first Barolo was the '80, his first Barbaresco the '78. He doesn't always bottle the wine that he buys; sometimes he sells it in bulk. Bera produces Dolcetto, Barbera, and Moscato for Accornero.

In total, Accornero's annual production averages some 3,000 cases of the wines he sells. More than 50 percent of that wine is a mediocre Barolo. His wines are sold only in the United States.

We've also tasted some '71 Barbaresco with Accornero's label that was produced by Castello Feudale. In general, the Barbarescos were better than the Barolos. Recently we tasted an '89 Dolcetto d'Alba with Accornero's label that indicated it was produced by Azienda Agricola "Cascina Palazzo." And the labels of both the '82 Barolo and Barbaresco specified that the wine was bottled by Flavio Accornero. Barolo 0; Barbaresco * –

Adriano Azienda Vinicola (*Roddi d'Alba*). Cantine Roccabella is one of the few Barolo producers in the village of Roddi.

Adriano F.lli Azienda Vinicola (*Monforte d'Alba, località Bussia*). F.lli Adriano owns a piece of the Pianpolvere vineyard. He produces a Barolo.

Aleramici (*Ozzano Monferrato*). The '83 Barolo we tasted was less than impressive. Barolo [0]

Alessandria F.lli di G. Battista Alessandria (*Verduno*). Alessandria produces 15,300 bottles of three different wines: 4,665 of Dolcetto d'Alba, 4,000 of Pelaverga di Verduno, and 6,665 of a Barolo from the Monvigliero vineyard plus a Barbera d'Alba. They also own a piece of the Pisapolla and San Lorenzo and, we heard, the Breri vineyards in Verduno. Thus far we haven't been overly impressed with this producer's Barolo, cru or no. But they are better than they used to be. Barolo +

Alessandria Luigi (*S. Maria di La Morra*). Alessandria has *poderi* in La Morra and Serralunga from which he produces a Barolo.

Alessandria Silvio (*S. Maria di La Morra, borgata Sarmassa*). Silvio Alessandria produces Barolo, Barbera d'Alba, and Dolcetto d'Alba. Besides his vines in the S. Maria district, he owns a piece of the Capalotti vineyard.

Altare Elio (*Annunziata di La Morra*), *1978*. Elio Altare's 15 acres (6 hectares) of vines include the 12.4-acre (5-hectare) Cascina Nuova vineyard, which is planted with 3.7 acres (1.5 hectares) of nebbiolo. Cascina Nuova is in the Arborina section of Annunziata. From those vines he produces between 26,500 and 33,000 bottles of wine a year of which 9,500 to 11,000 are Barolo with the balance being Dolcetto and Barbera. He bottles two Barolos: one from Cascina Nuova and the other from Arborina dell'Annunziata. Altare is also an advocate of *barrique* aging. He makes 2,000 bottles each of a Barbera Vigna Larigi and a Nebbiolo Vigna Arborina that taste as if they were made from oak instead of grapes. But since that style of wine is fashionable today he gets good press and consequently commands overly high prices. And for those who like the taste of grapes, he also produces three Albeisa wines, 4,000 bottles of Barbera, 4,500 each of Dolcetto and Nebbiolo d'Alba. His Barolos have improved. Thus far Altare's '85s and '86s have been his best wines, and they're very good too. Barolo **

Ambra (*La Morra*). This wine was bottled by FDO—F.lli Dogliani—of La Morra. Dogliani informed us that they no longer make it. We doubt that anyone will miss it. Barolo 0

Anforio Vini del Piemonte. The Folonari brothers of Ruffino fame own Premiovini. And that company owns the Anforio brand. Their Barolo is from the good Terre del Barolo co-op. We can't recall tasting it.

Anselma Giacomo (*Serralunga d'Alba*). This could be the same as Podere Anselma, who are also in Serralunga d'Alba.

Anselma Renato (*Monticello d'Alba*). Renato Anselma cultivates vines in the Pianpolvere and Le Coste vineyards of Monforte. He produces a Barolo.

Ascheri Giacomo (*Bra*), *1800*. Maria Teresa Ascheri, Matteo Ascheri, and Maria Cristina Vignola own at least 32 acres (13 hect-

THE CRUS OF GIACOMO ASCHERI

Cru	Location	Acres	Hectares	Average Number of Bottles Per Year	Used for
Vigna Farina	Serralunga d'Alba	3.61	1.46	5,800	Barolo
Vigna Nirane	Verduno	2.32	0.94	7,500	Dolcetto d'Alba
Vigna Gagliassi	Monforte d'Alba	n/a	n/a	5,250	Dolcetto d'Alba
Vigna Fontanelle	La Morra	1.63	0.66	5,500	Barbera d'Alba
Bricco San Giacomo	Montaldo Roero	1.33	0.54	6,000	Nebbiolo d'Alba
Monvigliero	Verduno	6.60	2.67	n/a	Barolo
Total		15.49	6.27		

ares) of vineyards, 16 acres (6.5 hectares) for Barolo, 5.4 (2.2) in La Morra and in Verduno, plus 10.6 (4.3) in Serralunga d'Alba, and produce a wide range of Piemontese wines, including Barolo and Barbaresco. Ascheri produces some 100,000 bottles of wine annually, including some 31,000 bottles of Barolo, 5,000 of Barbaresco, 15,000 of Barbera d'Alba, 27,000 of Dolcetto d'Alba, and 8,000 Nebbiolo d'Alba. More than half of the grapes for their Barolo comes from Verduno, just under a third from Castiglione Falletto and the balance from Serralunga d'Alba and La Morra.

Besides the above crus, Ascheri owns vines in Nirane-Sorano Bricco and Galarei in Serralunga. The wines are honest but could have more style. Barolo *; Barbaresco 0

Asteggiano Vincenzo (*Castiglione Falletto*). Asteggiano produces a good, if unexciting Barolo. Barolo * +

Azelia (*Castiglione Falletto*), 1869. Luigi and Lorenzo Scavino own this estate. The Scavinos have 24.7 acres (10 hectares) in vines.

From these vines they produce between 33,000 and 41,000 bottles of wine annually. They also produce an additional 10,000 to 15,000 bottles of wine from purchased grapes. This includes Barolo, Barbera d'Alba, and Dolcetto d'Alba. They told us that about 50 percent of the Barolo that they produce come from their

own grapes, and 60 percent of the dolcetto. But the numbers don't add up! If they produce between 10,000 and 13,000 bottles of Barolo from their own grapes and 18,000 to 22,000 dolcetto they should be producing an additional 28,000 to 35,000 plus bottles of wine from purchased grapes. And in some years they also produce a Nebbiolo delle Langhe. They used to sell their wines under the Scavino label. Although they changed the label with either the '78 or '79, we tasted an Alfonso Scavino '80 Barolo della Punta. Perhaps they used both labels for a few vintages. In 1980 they produced about 10,000 bottles of Barolo Bricca Punta, and in 1982 some 11,000 bottles. From 1983 to 1986 they replanted the vineyard. Enologist Piero Ballario and Giorgio Barbero consult here. Barolo ** –

Balbo Marino (*Treiso d'Alba*). We haven't tasted their Barbaresco since the '74 vintage, and we found that wanting. Perhaps they have improved. Balbo owns Cascina Bruciato in Tre Stelle. Barbaresco [0]

Baracco 1871 (*Castelinaldo*), 1871. They own 7.5 acres (3 hectares) and produce more than 130,000 bottles of wine annually, including Barolo and Barbaresco, as well as the other Albeisa wines such as Roero, Nebbiolo d'Alba, Barbera d'Alba, and Arneis Roero. They sell their wines under the Baracco de Baracho label. The only

THE CRUS AND VINEYARDS OF AZELIA

Cru	Acres	Hectares	Altitude in		Exposure	Average Number of Bottles Per Year	Used for
			Feet	Meters			
Azelia	6.2	2.5	722	220	SW	10,000–12,000	
Bricco dell'Oriolo	7.4	3.0	1,411	430	S	8,000–10,000	Dolcetto d'Alba
Bricco Fiasco	7.4	3.0	787	240	S	10,000–13,000	Barolo
Bricco Punta*	3.7	1.5	978	298	S	5,000– 6,000	Barolo
Total	24.7	10.0				33,000–41,000	

* These numbers are from 1983; they have since replanted the vineyard.

THE CRUS AND VINEYARDS OF FRATELLI BARALE

Cru/Vineyard	Variety	Acres	Hectares	Altitude in		Exposure
				Feet	Meters	
Bussia	Chardonnay, dolcetto, and nebbiolo	18.5	7.5	1,181	360	SW
Castellero*	Nebbiolo†, chardonnay, and barbera	19.8	8.0	1,181	360	SW
Costa di Rose	Dolcetto	8.6	3.5	1,181	360	E
Rabajà*	Nebbiolo†	2.5	1.0	1,555	474	S

NOTES: * Bottled as a cru
      † Subvariety michet

wine that we have tasted from this producer was their '79 Barolo. It wasn't memorable. Barolo [0]

Baracco de Baracho. See **Baracco 1871.**

Barale F.lli di Sergio Barale (*Barolo*), *1870.* Francesco Barale founded this firm in the last century. At the turn of the twentieth century the company's director Carlo Barale, and his father-in-law, Giovanni Battista Rinaldi, founded the firm of Barale-Rinaldi. A few years later that company was dismantled. Carlo's sons, upon his death in 1918, founded the current firm of Fratelli Barale. Today F.lli Barale is owned by Sergio Barale. He owns some 50 acres (20 hectares) of vineyards from which he produces somewhere between 110,000 to 130,000 bottles of wine a year, including 28,000 to 37,000 bottles of Barolo and 4,665 to 6,266 of Barbaresco. He also produces 13,000 bottles of Nebbiolo delle Langhe from Bussia, 29,300, to 38,600 of Dolcetto d'Alba including one from Costa di Rose, 8,000 of Barbera d'Alba from Castellero, and 16,000 to 20,000 of Pinot Chardonnay. The chardonnay includes from 20 to 30 percent pinot nero. He also does 6,665 bottles of Roero Arneis, 3,600 Moscato d'Asti, and a Grignolino del Monferrato Casalese from the Torrione vineyard.

A few years ago Barale owned a piece of the prized Cannubi vineyard, which we have heard he rents to Michele Chiarlo. And we recently heard that Barale bought a piece of that vineyard from Francesco Sandrone. He recently replanted his 3.7-acre (1.5-hectare) La Preda vineyard.

After aging his Barolo and Barbaresco in oak casks for a sufficient period, Barale transfers the wine to 204-gallon (54-liter) demijohns for further aging. He points out that the wine keeps very well in these large bottles. And in fact he still has some demijohns of old and precious wines.

Overall we have found their wines very good and generally reliable. We can recommend Barale's '82, '83, '85, and '86 Barolo from the Castellero vineyard, and their '85 and '86 Barbaresco Rabajà. Barolo, Castellero ***; Barbaresco *** −

Batasiolo (*Annunziata di La Morra*), *1958.* In 1978 the Dogliani family bought the Kiola brand along with their *cantine* and vine-yards from I.D.V., who had owned the brand since 1974. Dogliani 7 Cascina, Beni di Batasiolo or Batasiolo, as it is now known, own 247 acres (100 hectares) of vineyards including holdings in Barolo, Castiglione Falletto, La Morra, and Serralunga d'Alba. They purchase grapes as well. Some 80 percent of the wine they produce, they are quick to point out, comes from their own grapes. They buy grapes for Barbaresco, Gavi, and Barbera d'Asti. The rest of the wines, including Barolo, are made with their own grapes. Their annual production totals more than 500,000 or 2 million bottles, depending on when we were given the information, of mostly mediocre wine, including more than 265,000 of Barolo. In 1978 they produced 184,380 bottles of Barolo. They produce two Chardonnays, a Gavi, Moscato d'Asti, Asti Spumante, Barolo, Barbaresco, Barbera d'Alba, Dolcetto d'Alba, and Barbera d'Asti. A few years ago they owned a piece of Cannubi-Moscatello. We don't know if they still do.

The Beni di Batasiolo label and fancy bottles date from 1989. Both the label and the bottle are used for older wines as well. The Dogliani label no longer exists. The last wine they bottled as such was the '85 Barolo in 1988. In 1989 F.lli Dogliani was told, according to them, that they could no longer use their own name! Italian law, according to Dogliani, says you can't name a winery for a district! And Dogliani is an area denominated for Dolcetto. In one way this strikes us as odd because the current name that they use, Batasiolo, is the name of a vineyard in La Morra. Kiola is still used for old clients and Ambra is no longer used.

In 1987 they did a Barolo-in-*barrique* experiment using the '86 wine from their Briccolina vineyard. They produced 13,000 bottles of that wine. This thirty-year-old vineyard is well exposed to the sun; the grapes have more sugar and the wines, consequently, more body and alcohol. Still, the oak dominated.

The Batasiolo Barolo is made in a very drinkable style, more like that for a restaurant. It has some structure, but not a lot of tannin or personality. Their cru bottlings are vastly superior to their *normale*. Although even their *normale* has improved since the '82, their Bonfani cru, the most recent ones we sampled, was overoaked; the

THE CRUS OF BATASIOLO

Cru	Acres	Hectares	Altitude in Feet	Altitude in Meters	Exposure	First Vintage	Average Number of Bottles Per Year	Used For
Batasiolo[a]						1983		Barolo
Bonfani[b]	18.1	7.33	863	263	SW	1979	14,000–15,000	Barolo
Bonfani-Bussia[b]						1979		Barolo
Boscaretto[c]	31.9	12.89	1,381	421	SW	1979	15,000–16,000	Barolo
Bricco di Vergne[d]	5.3	2.2	1,575	480	SW	—	12,000	Dolcetto d'Alba
Briccolina[c]	3.9	1.6	1,326	404	SW	1979	7,000	Barolo
Cerequio[a]						1983		
Morino[a]	4.9	2.0	820	250	E	—	9,400[e]	Chardonnay
Zonchetta[d]						1983		

NOTES: [a] in Barolo and Monforte d'Alba
[b] in Serralunga d'Alba
[c] in La Morra and Barolo
[d] in La Morra
[e] Production from this cru has been increasing. The number of bottles here represents the most recent vintage.

THE VINEYARDS OF BATASIOLO

Vineyard	Acres	Hectares	Altitude in Feet	Altitude in Meters	Exposure	Used for
Batasiolo[a]	31.1	12.57	889	271	SE	b, c, d, e, f
Bonfani[g]	21.8	8.83	863	263	SW	b, c, f
Boscaretto[h]	86.8	35.13	1,381	421	SE	b, c, e, f, i
Bricco di Barolo[j, k]	31.3	12.67	1,575	480	SSW	b, c, d, e, f
Briccolina[h]	4.0	1.63	1,326	404	SW	b
Cerequio[a]	4.0	1.62	1,148	350	S	b
Morino[a]	23.6	9.56	820	250	E	b, c, f
Zonchetta[j]	30.6	12.40	784	239	SE	b, e, f

NOTES: [a] in La Morra   [g] in Monforte and Barolo
[b] Barolo   [h] in Serralunga
[c] Nebbiolo delle Langhe   [i] Moscato d'Asti
[d] Barbera d'Alba   [j] in La Morra and Barolo
[e] Dolcetto d'Alba   [k] part of Bricco di Vergne
[f] Chardonnay

fruit was completely covered. Barolo: Beni di Batasiolo Bonfani +, Boscaretto *, *normale* 0, F.lli Dogliani 0, crus * −, Kiola, 0 −; Barbaresco: Beni di Batasiolo 0, Kiola 0

Bel Colle di Pontiglione P. & C e Priola G. (*Verduno, borgata Castagni*), *1978*. Franco Palmino, Carlo Pontiglione, and Giuseppe Priola own this winery and 10 acres (4 hectares) of vineyards. Their cellar has a capacity of more than 105,000 gallons (4,000 hectoliters). Their annual production averages some 150,000 bottles. In the past, we have found these wines, at best, unimpressive, at worst, undrinkable. Striking changes are evident here since they hired the excellent enologist Pier Paolo Torchio. Their white wines have improved dramatically and are among the best being produced in the Langhe today. We have tasted some very good cask samples of Barolos from Monfrino and Monvigliero. But we haven't tasted their Barbaresco since the '79. And considering the dramatic changes here since, it seems best not to rate that wine at this time. Without question Bel Colle is the producer that we will be watching the closest since *we expect them to make the biggest strides*. And judging by the barrel samples that we tasted in November 1990—the 1987, 1988, and 1989—this seems to be the case. They are a producer on the move. They bottle two Barolos that we know of,

THE CRUS AND VINEYARDS OF BEL COLLE

Cru/Vineyard	Average Number of Bottles Per Year	Used For
Monvigliero di Verduno	6,000–7,000	Barolo
Monvijè	10,000	Nebbiolo delle Langhe
Vigne Bosquet and Del Pus di Verduno	13,000	Pelaverga di Verduno[a]
regional	6,000	Barbera d'Alba
Vigna Le Masche	3,700	Barbera d'Alba[b]
Vigneti Verduno	12,000	Dolcetto d'Alba
Vigna Altavilla	7,000	Dolcetto d'Alba
Vigna Madonna Como	11,000	Dolcetto d'Alba
Vigne Marone and Bricco San Michele in Canale	18,000	Roero Arneis
Vigna Bricco San Cristoforo in Santa Vittoria	12,000	Favorita del Piemonte
regional blend	16,000	Melange Bianco[c]
Vigna Palazzo	5,000	Moscato d'Asti

NOTES: [a] Made from the rare pelaverga grape
[b] Aged in *barrique*
[c] The '89 was made from a blend of 60 percent nebbiolo in white with 40 percent chardonnay; reports suggest earlier versions were a 70-15-15 blend of nebbiolo in white, arneis and favorita.

one from their cru Monvigliero, and the other from a few vineyards in Verduno. Barolo (from the '85) Monvigliero, Vigneti Verduno ** +; Barbaresco [0]

Beni di Batasiolo. See **Batasiolo.**

Bera Casa Vinicola (*Neviglie*). They bottle wine for **Flavio Accornero.**

Bergadano Enrico & Figli (*Barolo*). Thus far our experience here has been limited to two very good barrel samples, the '87 and '88. Barolo ** +

Bersano, Antico Podere Conti della Cremosina (*Nizza Monferatto*), *1896*. Probably the most interesting thing about this company is their wine museum. They have 143 acres (58 hectares) of vineyards which provide about 40 percent of their grapes; they buy the balance. Their Barbaresco was produced from grapes grown in their Cascina Ghiga holdings in Treiso and Neive. We don't know where they come from today. A few years ago they sold their holdings in the La Ghiga vineyard to Pietro Berutti of Azienda Agricola La Spinona. Their Barolo is from Cascina Badarina, and Nebbiolo d'Alba from Cascina Cortine. Bersano produce some 355,000 cases of wine a year, in a wide range of types. Their Barolo and Barbaresco are made in the softer, fruitier, more approachable style. But indications, based on the wines we sampled from barrel in November 1990, indicate an improvement here. For the most part, although lacking in structure and personality, they are drinkable enough. Barolo *; Barbaresco 0; Nebbiolo d'Alba *

Bertolo Lorenzo (*Torino*). This merchant sells a wide range of Piemontese wines, including Barolo and Barbaresco, as well as those of the Novara-Vercelli hills.

Bianco Aldo (*Barbaresco*). They produce a Barbaresco.

Bianco Luigi & Figlio Vincenzo (*Barbaresco*). Although we have found their Barbaresco somewhat variable in quality it can be good. Bianco owns vines in Vitolotti, a part of the Casot vineyard district. In 1982 he bottled a Barbaresco from the Faset vineyard as Fascet, and in 1983, Barbarescos from Faset, Rabajà, and Ronchi. Barbaresco *

Bianco Mauro (*Barbaresco*), *1984*. Mauro Bianco owns 12.5 acres (5 hectares) of vines, two-thirds are nebbiolo, in the Barbaresco growing zone. His holdings, in Cascina Morassino, include 0.52 acre (0.21 hectare) of dolcetto in Vigneto Vincenziana and 1.95 (0.79) of nebbiolo for Barbaresco in the Ovello district. His vines are planted at an average altitude of 820 feet (250 meters) above sea level and face south to southeast. Bianco bottled his first Barbaresco from the 1985 vintage. He produces some 37,330 bottles of wine annually, of which 10,665 are Barbaresco, 15,000 Nebbiolo delle Langhe, in both red and rosé, with the balance being Barbera, Dolcetto, and Freisa. Bianco's Barbaresco comes from the Ovello vineyard district. The Barbaresco from this producer tends to be very good. Barbaresco ** −

Bianco Michelangelo di F.lli Bianco. The only wine we tasted from this producer was their decent '83. Barolo [+]

Boffa Carlo & Figli (*Barbaresco*). They produce Barbarescos from the Vecchia Casot and Vitolotti vineyards, both in the Casot vineyard district. Their wines can be fairly good. It could use more style. We haven't tasted it since the '79. Barbaresco [* +]

Bonfante e Chiarle in Bazzana di Momburuzzo. We tasted one wine from this producer, a mediocre '83 Barolo. Barolo [0]

Bongiovanni Giovanni (*Castiglione Falletto*). This small producer grows only nebbiolo grapes. He produced a grand total of 1,920 bottles of Barolo from the fine 1985 vintage. That wine was wanting. Barolo 0

Bonini Romano (*Barbaresco*). Out of Bonini's annual production of some 8,000 bottles of wine, 1,333 are Barbaresco. He also produces an equal amount of five other wines: Arneis, Barbera, Dolcetto d'Alba, Moscato d'Asti, and Roero.

Bordino Franco (*Neive*). We have found their Barbaresco to be quite good. We haven't tasted it in some time, since the '74 vintage to be exact. And that wine was very good. Bordino bottles the Barbaresco cru of Monprandi in Bricco del Neive. Barbaresco **

Borgogno Aldo (*La Morra*). The only bottle of Barolo from this producer we've tasted, a '71, was oxidized. There was some quality still evident, however. Barolo [*]

Borgogno Cav. Bartolomeo & Figlio (*Castiglione Falletto,* frazione *Garbelletto*), *1924.* Mario Borgogno, son of Bartolomeo Borgogno, owns this winery and its 6.2 acres (2.5 hectares) of vines in the vineyards of Altinasso, Fiasco, and Solanotto. His crus are Garbelletto and Sorì Solanotto. We tasted his Barolo from this latter vineyard. Borgogno produces some 26,665 bottles of wines a year, half from Altinasso, and one-quarter each from Fiasco and Solanotto. He has plans to increase his production by 50 percent. Half of his production is Barolo, the other half Dolcetto. In some vintages he also bottles a Nebbiolo delle Langhe. Borgogno has bottled a Barolo since 1970. Barolo * +

Borgogno F.lli Serio & Battista di Serio Borgogno (*Barolo,* località *Crosia*), *1897.* This firm owns 7 acres (2.8 hectares) of Cannubi, a vineyard considered the top cru in Barolo. They have 5.2 acres (2.0903 hectares) planted to nebbiolo. From their nebbiolo—lampia and michet—they produce some 1,250 cases a year of Cannubi Barolo. The balance of their acreage on Cannubi is mostly in barbera, with some dolcetto. They also buy grapes from Barolo, La Morra, Diano d'Alba, and Castiglione Falletto for their other Barolo and from Treiso for their Barbaresco.

They told us that their older vintages of Barolo are aged until they're ready to be shipped; then the wine is *traversato,* drawn out

of the bottles through a rubber tube into a barrel, where it is left for the sediment to settle; then filtered and rebottled. Besides losing their sediment, these wines, not surprisingly, also lose their personality. They are still drinkable, but not much more. Aside from this aberration, the firm is fairly traditional in their methods. Their wines overall are correct for their type and display the character of the grapes they're made from, but we find them unexciting. There is no question that their cru bottling from Cannubi is a superior wine to the regular Barolo, and a very good Barolo besides. Barolo *, Cannubi **; Barbaresco (the most recent one that we tasted, from cask, was the '83) [*]

Borgogno Giacomo e Figli (*Barolo*), *1848.* The firm of Giacomo Borgogno has long been regarded for their Barolo and other wines, so much so that this firm exported their wines to numerous countries including France. In a purely defensive move, in 1955, the French Institut des Appellations d'origine (INAO) instituted a legal action against the Borgogno firm, claiming that they were trading on the reputation of Bourgogne (Burgundy)! Considering the numerous poor wines being sold by the French as Bourgogne we suspect that the wines of this good Piemontese firm, if they had any effect at all on the French region's reputation, would have been to enhance it. Not surprisingly, the French INAO lost their suit. Unfortunately, they didn't learn a lesson from it.

Borgogno, owned by the Boschis family since 1968, produces 300,000 bottles a year, somewhat less than half of which is Barolo. Their own grapes furnish about 35 to 40 percent of their requirements; for the rest they buy grapes, though never must or wine, they point out.

They also produce 18,000 to 20,000 bottles of Barbaresco a year. This wine is made entirely from grapes purchased from the *comune* of Barbaresco. They also produce a Barolo Chinato as well as the standard Albeisa wines.

They own 50 acres (20 hectares) of vineyards, 37 (15) of which are in Barolo: Cannubi, Liste, Pascolo, Ruè, and San Pietro. They also purchase grapes from Barolo, Annunziata di La Morra, Novello, and Verduno. Since the grapes arrive at the winery at different times they are fermented separately, but they are blended and aged together.

At Borgogno they have not considered bottling a separate cru because they want their Barolo to represent the area in general and the house style in particular.

THE CRUS AND VINEYARDS OF FRATELLI BORGOGNO

Cru	Variety	Acres	Hectares	Year Planted	Average Number of Cases Per Year	Used for
Cannubi	Lampia,	3.12	1.2626	1981	1,250	Barolo
	michet,	2.05	0.8277	1945–55		
	barbera, and	1.41	0.5724	1947	440	Barbera d'Alba
	dolcetto	0.46	0.1860	1947	130	Dolcetto d'Alba
Fossati	Dolcetto	2.02	0.8158	1975	600	Dolcetto d'Alba

One policy here, one that is rather uncommon, is to hold back large stocks of Barolo in order to age them for a sufficient period of time. They are released for sale a decade or more later after they have time to age properly. On our most recent visit to their cellars we saw large quantities of Barolos from the best vintages of the 1970s, 1960s, and 1950s. And they still have a fair quantity of '47 Barolo.

For many years this traditional firm was run by Cesare Borgogno. When he died in 1968 his nephew, Franco Boschis, took over at the helm. The house style is for traditional wines, relatively slow-maturing and quite robust and tannic in their youth. They are sometimes overly tannic and deficient in fruit, but honest wines that can be good, even very good. Barolo ** − ; Barbaresco * +

Borgogno Ludovico (*Barolo*), *1925*. Borgogno Ludovico, Cascina Borgognot owned by Wanda Pepino Borgogno has some 62 acres (25 hectares) of vines, including pieces of La Mandrola, La Preda, Maniscotto, San Giovanni, and Sarmassa. The *cantina* has a capacity of 52,800 gallons (2,000 hectoliters). Borgogno produces 27,000 bottles of Barolo, including one from Collina Maniscotto. She also produces Barbera (13,000), Dolcetto (11,000) and Nebbiolo d'Alba (13,000), and Barbaresco. We continue to see Barolo with both labels. The ones with the Ludovico label are superior. Barolo, Cascina Borgognot *, Wanda Pepino Borgogno 0

Borgogno Wanda Pepino. See **Borgono Ludovico.**

Bosca Luigi e Figli (*Canelli*), *1831*. Their best wines, while they can be drinkable, lack character, structure, and interest—and in this regard they are consistent. It's been some time since we tasted their wines. But based on our fairly extensive experience up to that point: Barolo and Barbaresco [0]

Boschis Francesco & Figli (*Barolo*), *1940*. Vittorio Boschis owns this *azienda* and some 6.2 acres (2.5 hectares) of vines, including 5 (2) in the prized Cannubi vineyard. He produces some 14,665 bottles of wines; over half is Barolo. He also produces 6,000 bottles of Barbera d'Alba and 2,000 of Dolcetto d'Alba, as well as some Nebbiolo delle Langhe. In addition, he owns land in Fossati and Pajagallo. We found both the '78 and '82 wanting. Barolo 0

Bosso. There is little that we can say about this producer since we don't know anything about him except for his Barolo, which we haven't tasted since the '71. Barolo [0]

Bovio Gianfranco (*Annunziata di La Morra*). Bovio is the proprietor of Ristorante Belvedere, which offers a beautiful panorama of the La Morra vineyards. He has 9.4 acres (3.8 hectares) of vines in Annunziata di La Morra from which he produces 15,000 to 20,000 bottles of wine a year. Some 8,000 bottles of this are Barolo; the balance, Dolcetto and in some vintages Nebbiolo delle Langhe. Bovio's Barolo is a good example of the La Morra style, tending more toward elegance than bigness. Overall, these are very good wines, with character and balance. He bottles wine from the crus of Arburina, Dabbene for Dolcetto d'Alba, and Gattera for Barolo. Barolo ** +

Brero Cav. Luigi (*Verduno*). There is little we can say about their wines that rating doesn't already say. Barolo and Barbaresco 0

Brezza Giacomo & Figli (*Barolo*). We have found these wines uneven, and at best rather ordinary. Brezza owns vines in the vineyards of Arbarella (dolcetto), San Lorenzo (dolcetto), and Muscatel Ruè (barbera). He bottles Barolos from his holdings in Sarmassa and Castellero, and from the plot he rents in Cannubi. His first Cannubi Barolo was the '89. He also bottles a Dolcetto d'Alba from San Lorenzo and a Barbera d'Alba from Cannubi. His wines have improved, especially the cru bottlings. The first and only Cannubi that we tasted, the '89, was very good, as were the '88 and '89 Castellero, all tasted from barrel. Thus far, also based on barrel samples of the '88 and '89, we find the Sarmassa to be somewhat better than the other two crus. The food at Trattoria Brezza is also good. Barolo: *normale* +, Cannubi **, Castellero **, Sarmassa ** +

"Bricco Asili" Azienda Agricola (*Barbaresco*), *1973*. See **Ceretto.**

"Bricco Boschis" Azienda Agricola. See **Cavallotto F.lli Olivio & Gildo, Azienda Agricola "Bricco Boschis."**

"Bricco Rocche" Azienda Agricola (*Castiglione Falletto*), *1978*. See **Ceretto.**

Brovia F.lli (*Castiglione Falletto*, frazione *Garbelletto*), *1863*. Giacinto, Raffaele, and Marina Brovia own a total of 22 acres (9 hectares) of vines. These vines supply them with some 87 percent of the fruit that they need to produce some 75,000 bottles of wine a year.

Besides the above, from 1988, they have produced a Roero Arneis. At one time they owned part of Otinasso. Their Barolo is fairly consistent in quality, and has improved in quality in the past few years. So too has their Barbaresco, but by a lesser extent. They bottle their Rocche Barolo as Rocche dei Brovia. Barolo ** +; Barbaresco *

Bruzzone (*Strevi*). These wines, from our experience, lack character and structure. We haven't tasted their wine in quite some time, not since the '71 in fact, and don't know if they are still being produced. A few years ago the majority interest of this winery was acquired by the large American importer Villa Banfi. Barolo [0]; Barbaresco [0]

Burlotto. Their '74 Barolo was quite good. Barolo [** −]

Burlotto Andrea, Cascina Massara (*Verduno*). Andrea Burlotto owns a piece of the regarded Massara vineyard. The only wines that we have tasted from Burlotto were his '83, '87, '88, and '89 Barolo, all tasted from cask. Overall, they have been very good Barolos. Barolo **

Burlotto, Antica Casa Vinicola Castello Comm. G. B. & Cav. Franc^sco di Marina Burlotto (*Verduno*), *1850*. Burlotto owns some 20 acres (8 hectares) of vines in the Monvigliero, Breri, and Neirane vineyards in Verduno and Cannubi in Barolo. Their annual production of 70,000 to 80,000 bottles includes nearly 27,000 bottles of Barolo, 6,667 bottles each of Barbera d'Alba and Nebbiolo delle Langhe, 16,000 Dolcetto d'Alba, 8,000 Pelaverga di Verduno, and 2,667 Freisa delle Langhe. The '81 Barolo was labeled Burlotto Comm. G. B. & Cav. Franc., the '83 as Burlotto Comm. G. B. & Cav. Franc^sco, and the '78 Burlotto Comm. G. B. e Cav. Francesco di Burlotto Marina. Burlotto bottles a Barolo from the Monvigliero vineyard. They produce a Dolcetto d'Alba from Neirane. The '78 Barolos, *normale* and Riserva, were very good. We've been less impressed since. Barolo * −

THE CRUS AND VINEYARDS OF FRATELLI BROVIA

Cru/Vineyard	Acres	Hectares	First Vintage	Average Number of Bottles Per Year	Used for
Ciabot del Re	3.7	1.50	—	10,666	Dolcetto
Garbelet Suè	5.0	2.00	1985	13,333	Barolo
Monprivato	1.1	0.46	1985	3,333	Barolo
Rio Sordo	1.4	0.58	1978	3,333	Barbaresco
Rocche	3.6	1.46	1971	8,666	Barolo
Solatio	3l.9	1.56	1985	16,000	Dolcetto
Sorì del Drago	1.9	0.76		n/a	Barbera
Total	20.6	8.32		55,331	

Ca' Bianca. See **Cantine Ca' Bianca.**

Ca' Romè di Romano Marengo (*Barolo,* località *Rabajà*). Romano Marengo owns some 3 acres (1.2 hectares) of vines and produces more than 13,000 bottles of Barbaresco and some 6,700 of Barolo. Their '82 Barolo left us less than impressed. Their Barbaresco is considerably better, especially the '85. Barolo 0; Barbaresco *

Cabutto Bartolomeo—Tenuta "La Volta" (*Barolo,* località *Volta*), 1920. This producer owns about 17.3 acres (7 hectares) of vines, which supply 70 to 75 percent of their grapes. They sell some 6,665 bottles of Barolo with the Tenuta La Volta name. They produce a Barolo from Vigna Castello. The '85 is the best wine that we've tasted from them in years, but then again the vintage was special as well. Besides Barolo and Barbaresco (if the Barbaresco is still made, we haven't tasted it since the '76), they produce the other typical Albeisa wines. Through the years we have found their wines to be somewhat variable. Their Barolo is reasonably good, though not as good as they had been prior to the 1974 vintage. Considering the continual decrease in the quality of their wines, it's not surprising that the last time we wanted to taste them they refused to let us. Good producers are proud of their product and want to show it off, whereas poor ones are ashamed, for they know that they have something to hide. Barolo * −; Barbaresco [0]

Calissano Luigi & Figlio (*Alba*), 1872. This former Winefood-owned company produces some 500,000 cases a year of a wide range of Piemontese wines, including Spumante, and Vermouth. They are part of the Gruppo Vini Italiano spinoff of those holdings. Their wines have been of decent quality and offer good value if not much else. Calissano, like more and more producers here, have jumped aboard the cru bandwagon. They do a Barbaresco from Bricco Malaspina, a Barolo from Castelletto in the Perno district of Monforte, a Barolo from Bricco Mira Langa which could be from the Miralanga vineyard in Barolo, and a Dolcetto d'Alba from the Bricco d'Altavilla vineyards in Rocca di Altavilla d'Alba. Thus far we have been unimpressed with the cru bottlings, finding them no better than their standard offerings, good, no more. Barolo *; Barbaresco * −

Camerano G. Camerano produces Barbera, Nebbiolo, Dolcetto, and Barolo from his own vines. He bottled his first wine from the 1980 vintage with a label. Barolo +

Canale Aldo (*Serralunga d'Alba*). Canale owns some 4.9 acres (2 hectares) in the regarded Vigna Rionda vineyard, of which 4.4 (1.8) are planted in nebbiolo for Barolo. He does a cru bottling that he labels Riunda from those vines. The balance are barbera and dolcetto. He harvests some 13.2 tones (120 *quintali*) of nebbiolo for Barolo, and surprisingly, 5.5 (50) of dolcetto and barbera. His small *cantina* is neat and clean. Canale uses a wooden basket press. Our experience, which has been favorable, has unfortunately, with one exception—the '78—been limited to tasting unfinished wines from cask. In April 1986 we visited Canale and tasted six wines, five from cask. Barolo **

Cantina Colavolpe (*Costigliole d'Asti*). Thus far we've tasted two wines here, both '81s. Barbaresco [0]; Barolo [+]

Cantina del Glicine di Adriana Marzi & Roberto Bruno (*Neive*), 1974. Adriana Marzi and Roberto Bruno have an annual production of 51,000 bottles of wine, of which 15,000 are Barbaresco, including a number of single-vineyard wines, two from their own vineyards of Curà and Marcorino. They don't bottle all of the crus in every vintage. Between 1987 and 1989 Glicine vinified only two Barbarescos, Curà and Marcorino. They produced no Barbaresco in 1968 or 1984. In 1986 they used the nebbiolo grapes for Glicinerosso. The balance includes 6,000 bottles of a charming rosé called Glicinello made from the free-run juice of 20 percent freisa and 80 percent nebbiolo grapes, 2,000 of Glicinerosso, a red wine made from the nebbiolo and freisa grapes in the same proportion, 15,000 of Dolcetto d'Alba, 7,000 of Roero Arneis, 2,000 of Grignolino d'Asti, and 4,000 of Barbera d'Alba Nebbiolata, Barbera made with 10 to 15 percent nebbiolo and refermented on the nebbiolo lees.

Glicine owns a 7.5-acre (3.05-hectare/8-*giornate*) plot of Curà, mostly planted in nebbiolo, with a little dolcetto and a 0.9-acre (0.4-hectare/1-*giornata*) plot in Marcorino, all planted in nebbiolo. They buy dolcetto grapes from Marcorino and other vineyards to produce their Dolcetto d'Alba. The Barbera d'Alba Nebbiolata is made from grapes grown in the Marcarino vineyard from a blend of 90 percent barbera and 10 percent nebbiolo for Barolo. Glicine has produced a Grignolino d'Asti from 1989, Roero Arneis from 1986, Glicinello from 1983, and Glicinerosso from 1986.

THE BARBARESCO CRUS OF CANTINA DEL GLICINE

Cubà	Marcorino
Curà	Montesomo
Gaja	Pastura
Gallina	Rabajà
Gava Principe	Valtora

The Glicine Barbarescos made by Adriana Marzi and Roberto Bruno are in a gentle, elegant style. Some have referred to them as Barbaresca. They are consistent and reliable, even in the lesser vintages. Barbaresco ***

Cantina della Porta Rossa. See **Porta Rossa di Domenico Berizia e Marilisa Rizzi Artusio.**

Cantina Vignaioli "Elvio Pertinace," Cantina Sociale (Treiso d'Alba, località Pertinace), 1973. It is believed that the Roman Emperor Publius Elvio Pertinace was born here. His reign, in 193 B.C., was the shortest of all emperors, just eighty-seven days. The world would be a better place if more politicians had such a brief reign! The 13 members of this co-op own 110 acres (45 hectares) of vines, all in Treiso. From an average harvest they produce some 225,000 bottles of wine annually. They could produce considerably more Barbaresco, but currently make between 50,000 and 60,000 bottles a year. Part of their production is sold sfuso. They also produce more than 13,000 bottles of Barbera d'Alba, nearly 125,000 bottles of Dolcetto d'Alba and delle Langhe, 16,000 Nebbiolo delle Langhe, 9,000 Moscato d'Asti, and 16,000 Chardonnay delle Langhe. A few years ago they began bottling the individual Barbaresco crus of Casotto, Castellizzano, Marcarini, and Nervo. Their Barbaresco is a fairly good one. Barbaresco *

Cantine Barbero (Canale, frazione Valpone). This firm sells a mediocre Barbaresco under the brand name of "Conte de Cavour." We haven't tasted it since the '74. Barbaresco [0]

Cantine Bava (Cocconato Asti). Barbera specialist Cantine Bava produced a wine range of wines, of varying quality, including Barolo and Barbaresco. Their Barberas are better. They also produce a Ruchè di Castagnole Monferrato, which is a new Piemontese DOC from 1989. They produced 6,660 bottles of a very good one from that vintage. They owned a vineyard in Gattinara from which they produced 4,000 bottles of Gattinara as well. Until recently they bought wine for a Barolo which they aged and bottled as they had done since about 1960. And they followed this same practice for Barbaresco. They have produced their Barberas for a considerably longer time. The last Barolo that we tasted from Bava was the '81, the last and only Barbaresco, the '79. We understand that they will no longer produce those wines and will instead stick to their specialty, barbera. Barolo [+]; Barbaresco [0]

Cantine Ca' Bianca (Alice Bel Colle), 1952. Ca' Bianca produces 300,000 bottles of wine a year, as well as 100,000 bottles of a good grappa. They produce a wide range of wines, including the young, fresh Bricchetto; two whites: Pinot Chardonnay and Cortese dell'Alto Monferrato; Claret!, a rosé made from dolcetto grapes; Grignolino d'Asti, Dolcetto d'Acqui, Barbera del Monferrato and d'Asti, Dolcetto d'Alba, Nebbiolo d'Alba, Barolo, and Barbaresco; two dessert wines: Brachetto d'Acqui and Moscato d'Asti; and three sparklers: Asti Spumante, Brachetto Spumante, and Pinot Chardonnay Spumante. They also produce two special wines from their Cascina Polsino holdings in Alice bel Colle: Dolcetto d'Acqui and Barbera d'Asti. Both of these wines spend some time in oak: the former is given a short spell, the latter spends between seven and nine months.

They own 60.5 acres (24.5 hectares) of vines in Alice Bel Colle and La Morra, from which they get 60 percent of their grapes. In August 1984 they purchased the vineyard and winery of Denegri. Besides Tenuta Denegri in the Barolo zone, they own Tenuta Roncaglie, which they bought in 1983. They produced their first Barbaresco in 1983 from this holding in the Barbaresco zone. Barolo *; Barbaresco *

Cantine d'Invecchiamento. The few times that we tasted these wines we've been totally unimpressed. We haven't tasted the Barolo or Barbaresco since their unimpressive '74s. They sell their wines under the "La Brenta d'Oro" label. Barolo [0]; Barbaresco [0]

Cantine Duca d'Asti. See **Chiarlo Michele.**

Cantine Le Ginestre (Grinzane Cavour). They produce more than 37,000 bottles of wine annually—4,000 are Barolo, 3,330 Barbaresco, 10,500 Barbera d'Alba, 8,500 Dolcetto d'Alba, 2,650 Nebbiolo d'Alba, and 8,000 Chardonnay del Piemonte. Thus far the only wine that we tasted from Le Ginestre has been the good '85 Barolo. Barolo *

Cappellano Teobaldo e Roberto Cappellano (Serralunga d'Alba, frazione Bruni), 1870. A few years ago this winery was named Dott. Giuseppe Cappellano. In recent years the name has been changed to that of the current owners. And that is not the only change here. Until recently Cappellano bought all the grapes that they needed for their wines. Recently they acquired some 10 acres (4 hectares) of vines in the Gabutti vineyard of Serralunga d'Alba. They have bought the grapes from that vineyard since 1976. Those vines provide them with 60 percent of the fruit that they need for their annual production of some 40,000 bottles of wine, including 15,000 each of Dolcetto and Barolo. The balance consists of very small quantities of Arneis, Barbera, Favorita, and other wines including a Barbaresco. And like so many others here, they plan to do a Chardonnay. The grapes for their Barolo come from three of the top vineyards in Serralunga d'Alba: Baudana, Gabutti, and Parafada. They did a limited cru bottling from the Parafada vineyard; they don't any longer. Today Cappellano produce two Barolos—one from their holdings in Gabutti and the second from Carpegna. They put the cru name on the former but not on the latter wine. They buy the Carpegna grapes from Giovanni Zunino. Cappellano's annual production includes 7,000 bottles of Dolcetto d'Alba, 5,000 of Barbera d'Alba, and 8,000 of Barolo from their Gabutti vineyard.

Cappellano's Barolo Chinato is simply the finest we have tasted. Admittedly they have had time to perfect their product; they were the first producers to offer a Barolo Chinato in the last century and have been selling it commercially ever since. They produced very good Barolo in '82, '83, and '85. The '89 Gabutti and '88 and '89 Carpegnas tasted from barrel were very good indeed. As for their other wines, we have enjoyed them and can recommend them. Barolo: Carpegna ** +, Gabutti ** +; Barbaresco ** −

Carnevale Giorgio (*Rocchetta Tanaro Cerro*), *1880*. Carnevale produces about 30,000 bottles of wine a year, including Barolo and Barbaresco. They have a very good reputation. The only Barolo that we tasted from this producer was the disappointing '78. Barolo [0]

Carra. The last Carra Barbaresco we tasted was the '73. Consequently it seems unfair to rate them today.

Carretta. See **Tenuta Carretta**.

Cascina Adelaide di G. Terzano (*Barolo*, località *Aie Sottane*). At one time their label read Terzano-Benvenuti. Cascina Adelaide owns 9.3 acres (3.76 hectares), 5.1 (2.06) planted for Barolo, 1.9 (0.75) in barbera, 1.1 (0.45) in dolcetto. This includes a piece of Cannubi, Costa di Rose, and Vignassa. Most of their vines are in Barolo, some are in La Morra. These Barolos are all very good. Barolo ** −

Cascina Ballarin. See **Viberti Luigi**.

Cascina Bruni di Pasquale Veglio (*Serralunga d'Alba*, frazione *Bruni*), *1929*. Giuseppe Veglio owns between 27 and 30 acres (11 and 12 hectares) of vines. His holdings include 17 acres (7 hectares) of nebbiolo vines in Vigneto Sorì which he bottles as a Barolo cru. He also owns 7.4 acres (3 hectares) of Carpegna plus parts of Maria Luigia, Pilone, and Rivassa, all in Serralunga. The average production of nebbiolo, mostly for Barolo, is 22 tones (200 *quintali*) of grapes a year. This Barolo is in the lighter, earlier-maturing style. Our experience with their wines has been limited to the '78 from bottle and the '79 and '82 from cask. Barolo [*]

Cascina Bruni di Veglio F.lli (*Serralunga d'Alba*, frazione *Bruni*). The Veglio brothers own 11.3 acres (4.6 hectares/12 *giornate*) of vines, 8 (3.2/8.5) for Barolo. All of these vines are in the Carpegna vineyard. They produce some 20,000 bottles of Barolo plus 2,665 of Barbera. They also grow dolcetto grapes that are not used for wine. Of the nine vintages of Barolo that we tasted here in April

1986, only two were in bottle, the '78 and '83; two others—the '67 and '71—were in demijohn, and the other five were in cask. They were all quite good, especially the '78, '80, and '82. Barolo ** −

Cascina Gagliassi (*Monforte d'Alba*, località *S. Anna*). They produce some 66,665 bottles of wine annually which includes the normal range of wines from here, Barbera d'Alba and delle Langhe, Dolcetto d'Alba and delle Langhe, and Nebbiolo delle Langhe, and of course Barolo. Barbera makes up 40 percent of their production, and Dolcetto 45 percent. That leaves 5,333 bottles of the Nebbiolo della Langhe and 4,665 of Barolo.

Cascina Traversa (*S. Maria di La Morra*, località *Serra dei Turchi*). Stefano Farina owns Cascina Traversa and Fattoria Le Bocce in the Chianti Classico district. At their Piemontese winery they produce Barolo, Barbaresco, Barbera, Dolcetto and Grignolino d'Asti, Moscato del Piemonte, and La Traversa Brut.

Casetta F.lli di Ernesto Casetta & C. (*Vezza d'Alba*, frazione *Borbore*), *1956*. Ernesto Casetta owns some 150 acres (60 hectares) of vines.

He produces an average of 44,400 cases annually of the characteristic Albeisa wines, including 8,900 each of both Barolo and Roero, and 6,650 of Barbaresco. The grapes for their Barolo come from Serralunga d'Alba, La Morra, and Castiglione Falletto; those for their Barbaresco, from Treiso and S. Rocco Senadelvio d'Alba. We've found their wines overall to be ordinary, though drinkable, regardless of type. At one time Casetta bottled a Barolo that he labelled as being from the Terra Hera vineyard. Today his Barolo carries the name Case Nere on the label. Are these two vineyards in fact the same and did we copy down the name incorrectly, or has the name changed? Casetta's wines have improved. Barolo * +; Barbaresco *

Castello di Neive di Italo Stupino (*Neive*), *1957*. Castello di Neive is owned by Italo, Giulio, Anna, and Pietra Stupino. They produce 186,600 bottles of wine a year, including 54,000 bottles of Barbaresco. The balance is made up of the typical wines of this area: Dolcetto d'Alba, Barbera d'Alba, Grignolino, Arneis delle Langhe, and Moscato d'Asti. All of their wines are produced from their 62 acres (25 hectares) of vines. They also sell grapes to producers such as Bruno Giacosa and Accademia Torregiorgi.

THE CRUS AND VINEYARDS OF FRATELLI CASETTA

Cru/Vineyard	First Vintage	Average Number of Bottles Per Year	Used for
Ausario	1978	25,000	Barbaresco
Case Nere	1980	30,000	Barolo
Delle Mandorle	—	—	—
Lazzaretto	—	—	Barbera d'Alba
Lazzaretto	—	—	Grignolino d'Asti
Magallo	1985	40,000	Dolcetto d'Alba
Pioiero	1985	20,000	Roero

Nearly all of Castello di Neive's wines are cru bottled. They produce Barbera d'Alba from Marcorino, Messoirano and Santo Stefano, a *barrique*-aged Barbera from Rocca del Mattarello, Dolcetto d'Alba from Basarin, Messoirano and Valtorta, Arneis from their Montebertotto vineyard in the Barbaresco zone, as well as two splendid Barbarescos, one from Santo Stefano and the other from Messoirano.

A few years ago Castello di Neive owned 7.4 acres (2.98 hectares) of nebbiolo in Gallina. Evidently they have since sold their share of that vineyard. They also produce a Castelborgo Brut Spumante.

Since the Stupinos live and work in Torino, their cellarman, Talin Brunettini, is in charge of following the wines on a day-to-day basis. Alfonso Carosso is the enologist here.

At our tasting one winter in the beautiful but chilly *castello,* as the old wines sat in decanters near the heat to warm and open up a bit, Italo Stupino also warmed with enthusiasm talking about the wines of Castello di Neive. He is obviously very involved with them, and his care and concern is evident in their quality. The Barbarescos of Castello di Neive are among the most consistent and reliable in the zone. They are full-bodied and concentrated, reflecting the characteristic of the district, but with particular class and distinction; they are harmonious, complex with that extra dimension called style that sets them apart. Their '82 and '85 Santo Stefanos were, as expected, splendid indeed. And we can recommend their '86 and '87 as well. Barbaresco ****

Castello di Verduno (*Verduno*). Gabriella Burlotto and Franco Bianco own this *cantina.* The Burlotto sisters own the *castello,* and Elisa Brilotto and Carlo Buglioni own the Albergo "Real Castello." All three enterprises are, in some way, interconnected. There is some confusion because we have tasted a number of Barolos with different information on the labels that we believe to be from the same Castello di Verduno. This includes Castello di Verduno di Sorelle Burlotto and Castello Verduno "Canine del Castello di Re Carlo Alberto" di Burlotto Dr. Lisetta & Sorelle. This winery produces approximately 40,000 bottles annually of a wide range of wines.

In 1989 the family vinified the wines of Barbaresco for the first time. Previously their wines came from nebbiolo and pelaverga grapes grown in their two vineyards in Verduno—Massara and Monvigliero—in the Barolo zone. Barolo * +

Castello Feudale di Motta Renzo, Cantina del (*Montegrosso d'Asti*). The *castello* itself dates from 1134, but we expect that the winemaking is of a somewhat more recent vintage. The wines are produced in the lighter style. The last vintage that we tasted from this producer was the '78 Barbaresco and the '71 Barolo. Flavio Accornero bought some '71 Barolo, which he sold under his own label. Barolo [*]; Barbaresco [* +]

Castello Sperone. Our experience with these wines has been limited to their '70 Barolo. We think it best to reserve our judgment.

Cauda Cav. Luigi (*Vezza d'Alba, località Montebello*), *1946.* Cauda owned 25 acres (10 hectares) of vineyards planted to nebbiolo and barbera, which supplied him with 30 percent of the grapes he required. His annual production, which included the typical wines of the area plus *spumanti,* was 66,600 bottles. We have rarely tasted such mediocre—make that poor—wines from the Langhe. The last time that we met up with Cauda's wines we tasted, and gladly spit out, the '79 Barolo and Barbaresco, but not

THE CRUS AND VINEYARDS OF CASTELLO DI NEIVE

Vineyard	Acres	Hectares	Exposure	First Vintage	Average Number of Bottles Per Year	Used for
Basarin	2.3	0.94	S	1970	7,000	Dolcetto d'Alba
Bric Valtorta	3.4	1.37	SE	1979	10,000	Dolcetto d'Alba
Cortini-Montebertotto	2.1	0.85	S/SW	—	6,000	Grignolino d'Asti
Marcorino	3.2	1.28	SW	1984	12,000	Moscato d'Asti
				1988*	n/a	Barbera d'Alba
Messoirano	3.2	1.31	S	1970	9,000	Barbaresco
	2.2	0.90	S/SE	1974	8,000	Barbera d'Alba
	4.9	1.97	S	1974	14,000	Dolcetto d'Alba
Montebertotto	6.1	2.47	S	1984	20,000	Arneis delle Langhe
Rocca del Mattarello	1.2	0.48	S/SW	1985	4,200	Barbera in *barrique*
Santo Stefanto	19.4	7.87	S/SW	1967	45,000	Barbaresco
	1.7	0.70	S/SW	1970	6,000	Barbera d'Alba
Total	49.7	20.14			141,200	

* We don't know if this was the first wine from this vineyard.

THE CRUS AND VINEYARDS OF CASTELLO DI VERDUNO

Cru/Vineyard	Comune	Average Number of Bottles Per Year	Used for
Massara	Verduno	5,333	Barolo
Monvigliero	Verduno		
Fascet	Barbaresco	9,333	Barbaresco
Rabajà	Barbaresco		
Bricco del Cucolo	Barbaresco	4,666	Barbera d'Alba
Campot	Barbaresco	6,400	Dolcetto d'Alba
Massara	Verduno	6,000	Pelaverga di Verduno
—	—		Barolo Chinato
—	Barbaresco	4,000	Nebbiolo delle Langhe
—	Barbaresco	933	Pignö

fast enough. We're pleased to report that after being involved in a scandal the winery closed. If you should meet up with the wines we think it best to avoid them. Barolo 0 – ; Barbaresco 0 –

Cavaletto. These wines are as inferior as they are uncharacteristic, the Barbaresco in particular. We would expect their Barolo, if anything, to be even worse. Barbaresco 0 –

Cavallotto F.lli Olivio & Gildo, Azienda Agricola "Bricco Boschis" (Castiglione Falletto), *1948.* This very traditional firm produces Barolo, Barbera, Dolcetto, Grignolino and Favorita from grapes grown in their own vineyards on Bricco Boschis, where approximately 50 acres (20 hectares) are planted in vines. They expect an additional 7.4 acres (3 hectares) to come into production in 1990. From the 23.3 acres (9.4 hectares) of nebbiolo, they produce an average of 52,133 bottles of Barolo. Their total annual

production averages almost 120,000 bottles.

What is quite interesting is the changes taking place in the vineyard. Cavallotto produced a favorita for many years, and a good one at that. But, unfortunately, the world wants still another chardonnay, or so the brothers believe. Out comes the favorita, in goes the chardonnay. We left the older information in for comparison purposes.

We tasted, what we thought was another Barolo cru, from the 1980 vintage, a Conte Vassallo. We haven't heard a thing about it since.

Since the 1978 vintage they have bottled the wines from each sunplot in their Bricco Boschis vineyard separately, indicating the subcru on the label. Punto Marcello, with sandier soil, is in their opinion the best of the original three Barolo crus; this is due in part to its smaller yields. This wine is the more perfumed. The other

THE VARIETIES OF FRATELLI CAVALLOTTO

Variety	Previous Plantings		Current Plantings		Average Annual		Average Number of Bottles Per Year
	Acres	Hectares	Acres	Hectares	Tons	Quintali	
Barbera	9.6407	3.9014	1.4827	0.6000	6.28	(57)	5,333
Chardonnay[a]	—	—	2.2734	0.9200	7.05	(64)	6,000
Dolcetto	13.2429	5.3591	15.4842	6.2661	49.60	(450)	41,866
Grignolino	1.6104	0.6517	0.9884	0.4000	3.31	(30)	2,667
Nebbiolo	13.2023	5.3427	1.6062	0.6500	6.28	(57)	5,333
Nebbiolo[b]	—	—	21.6735	8.7708	61.73	(560)	52,000
Pinot[a]	—	—	2.4167	0.9780	7.05	(64)	6,000
Favorita[c]	1.2237	0.4952	—	—	—	—	—
Total	38.9200	15.7501	45.9251	(18.5849)	141.30	(1,282)	119,199

See chart on page 166 for meaning of notes.

THE CRUS OF FRATELLI CAVALLOTTO

Cru—Barolo	Acres	Hectares	Year Planted	Average Number of Bottles Per Year
Bricco[a]	2.4	0.9800	1967	5,867
Colle Sud-Ovest[d]	2.7	1.1100	1951	6,667
Punta Marcello[a]	1.7	0.6900	1967	4,000
Punta Vignolo[a, e]	4.6	1.8681	—	11,066
San Giuseppe[d]	10.2	4.1227	1947	24,533

Cru—Others	Acres	Hectares	Average Number of Bottles Per Year	Used for
Codana[e]	3.0	1.2000	8,000	Dolcetto d'Alba
Cucolo	1.5	0.6000	—	Barbera d'Alba
Mellera	3.9	1.5900	10,666	Dolcetto d'Alba
Momprivato[c, e, f]	5.6	2.2810	—	Dolcetto d'Alba
Pà[a]	3.0	1.1961	8,000	Dolcetto d'Alba
Pali[c]	3.7	1.4891	—	Dolcetto d'Alba
San Giuseppe	1.6	0.6500	—	Nebbiolo delle Langhe
Scot[a, f]	5.6	2.2800	15,200	Dolcetto d'Alba

NOTES: [a] This information wasn't included in the original information that we received from Cavalotto.
[b] Nebbiolo for Barolo.
[c] This information wasn't included in the most recent information that we received from Cavalotto.
[d] One of their three original Barolo crus.
[e] There are separate vineyards with these names in Castiglione Falletto. We don't know if they own vines in those vineyards or if these are separate plots in the Bricco Boschis vineyard.
[f] These two crus could be the same: they are the same size and one wasn't included in the latest information, and the other wasn't included in the previous information.

two—Colle Sud-Ovest and San Giuseppe—from more calcereous soil, are bigger in body. We find their wines overall to be full-bodied and robust, often high in alcohol and very tannic when young, but in the best vintages they develop well. Cavallotto tends to keep their Barolos very long in cask, sometimes too long, especially in some of the lighter vintages. The oldest Barolo from Cavallotto we've tasted, the '71, is still very good and holding up well with no signs of deterioration. Overall, their wines are good and reliable, if somewhat lacking in style and perhaps even a bit coarse. Their '82, '83, '85, and '86 Barolos were all very good. Barolo ** +

Cella. Their wines, while drinkable enough, lack character and structure. It's been years since we've seen them. Barolo [0]

Ceretto (Alba, località San Cassiano, Barbaresco, and Castiglione Falletto), 1937. The Ceretto brothers, Bruno and Marcello, administrator and winemaker, respectively, are the proprietors of Casa Vinicola Ceretto in Alba, the La Bernardina estate in the San Cassiano area of Alba, Azienda Agricola "Bricco Asili" in Barbaresco, and Azienda Agricola "Bricco Rocche" in Castiglione Falletto. In the early years they bought the grapes for their wines. Later, in order to more closely control the quality of the grapes as well as the wine, they set about acquiring prime vineyard land in Barolo and Barbaresco. In the 1970s they added Bricco Asili in Barbaresco and

Bricco Rocche in Castiglione Falletto to their holdings. They also own a small distillery in Treiso where they make grappa. Today the Cerettos own 116 acres (47 hectares) of vineyards and control 72 (29) others.

The Cerettos produce, on average, more than 570,000 bottles of wine annually. This includes 120,000 bottles of Moscato d'Asti and 200,000 of Arneis plus Barolo, Barbaresco, Nebbiolo d'Alba, Dolcetto d'Alba, and Barbera d'Alba. Their production includes 39,000 bottles of three different Barbarescos: 8,000 of Bricco Asili, 7,000 of Faset, and the rest is Asij. There are some 93,000 bottles of four different Barolos: 7,000 of Bricco Rocche, 25,000 of Brunate, and 13,000 of Prapò, all of which they own; the balance is Zonchera. At one time the Asij Barbaresco and Zonchera Barolo were made from the vineyards that they lease, Asili and Zonchetta respectively. Today they are proprietary wines based on the grapes of those two vineyards. In some vintages, Zonchera includes the declassified grapes from the Bricco Rocche crus, the base is Zonchetta. They produced no 1984 or 1987 crus from their Bricco Rocche winery, all of the grapes were used in their Zonchera Barolo.

At their 175-acre (70-hectare) La Bernardina estate in San Cassiano, previously planted with 75 acres (30 hectares) of nebbiolo, dolcetto, and barbera, they are, like numerous other producers here and elsewhere, experimenting with cabernet sauvignon, chardon-

THE CRUS AND VINEYARDS OF CERETTO

Cru	Acres	Hectares	Altitude		Exposure	Average Number of Bottles Per Year	First Vintage
			Feet	Meters			
BARBARESCO							
Asij[a]	9.9	4.0	853– 951	260–290	S	24,000	1966
Bricco Asili	4.9	2.0	951–1093	290–330	S	7,000	1973
Faset	6.2	2.5	853–1017	260–310	S	8,000	1985
Total	21.0	8.5				39,000	
BAROLO							
Bricco Rocche	34.7	1.5	1,017–1,116	310–340	S	5,000	1982
Brunate	14.8	6.0	853–1,017	260–310	S	25,000	1978
Prapò[b]	7.4	3.0	886–1,050	270–320	S/SE	13,000	1976
Zonchera[c]	19.8	8.0	689– 820	210–250	S/SE	50,000	1968
Total	45.7	18.5				93,000	
OTHER WINES							
Blangè[d]	49.4	20.0	656–1017	200–310	S/SE	200,000	—
Lantasco[e]	4.9	2.0	886– 984	270–300	S	15,000	—
Piana[f]	4.9	2.0	656– 787	200–240	S/SW	15,000	—
Rossana[g]	24.7	10.0	689– 886	210–270	S/SE	65,000	—
Vigna[g]	7.4	3.0	722– 853	220–260	S/E	20,000	—
Total	91.3	37.0				315,000	
Total	158.0	64.0				447,000	

NOTES: [a] At one time bottled as Asili, today it is more of a brand name than a single vineyard.
    [b] At one time bottled as Riccardo I in Prapò
    [c] At one time bottled as Zonchetta, today it is more of a brand name than a single vineyard.
    [d] Arneis, from two vineyards
    [e] Nebbiolo d'Alba
    [f] Barbera d'Alba
    [g] Dolcetto d'Alba

nay merlot, syrah, viognier, and pinot noir. These vines will begin producing from 1991. They have 24.7 acres (10 hectares) planted from which they plan to produce some 30,000 bottles of these vines annually. They also, from 1988, have a new cantina here. There is room to plant another 50 acres (20 hectares); they might plant nebbiolo and dolcetto. The cellar in Alba is now used as a warehouse.

Marcello Ceretto was among the first to adopt, and is still a leading proponent of, the modern style for Barolo and Barbaresco. He began experimenting in 1972 with modern techniques, seeking to produce a finer, more drinkable wine. He shortened the period of skin contact during fermentation and of wood aging for his wines, feeling that Barolo and Barbaresco made in the old style had too much tannin and not enough fruit. In 1973, he began fermenting his red wines in stainless steel tanks. We think few would dispute that the Ceretto wines are among the best in Langhe. Since

the 1979 vintage their Barolos have been produced at their new facilities in Castiglione Falletto, Azienda Agricola "Bricco Rocche."

In February 1985 we had the excellent, and we believe quite rare, opportunity to taste a range of Barbarescos from their Asili and Bricco Asili crus, as well as a number of vintages of two of their Barolo crus, Prapò and Brunate. We were struck by the depth, balance, and style of the wines, as well as the consistency maintained even in some of the lesser years.

The Cerettos are opposed to *barrique* aging, which they feel takes away personality from the wine while giving nothing in return except unnecessary tannin. Marcello demonstrated his point, offering us a couple of samples of his wine which had been put into *barrique*. The wine was harsh, tannic, and lacking in fruit, quite unlike the other wines proudly lined up for us in rows of fine stemware on the long table at the *cantina*.

The Barolo of Brunate has more perfume and complexity than the Prapò. We noted a suggestion of mint in the bouquet. Marcello, who was not commenting on his wines, compared the bouquet to a wild herb similar to mint, which grows wild in the Langhe. Reflecting the character ascribed to the wines from the two valleys, the Brunate is more accessible in its youth, softer, and more open; the Prapò is firmer in structure, somewhat more tannic, and slower maturing.

They also produce a Barolo from their Bricco Rocche vineyard. This Barolo is their signature wine. It falls between the other two in that it matures after the Brunate but before the Prapò. And it has more structure than the former and less than the latter.

The Ceretto brothers own a highly regarded piece of the Asili vineyard in Barbaresco, Bricco Asili, which they bought in 1969, planted in 1970, and built a winery on shortly afterward. They also vinify grapes that they purchase from another part of Asili. Whatever can be said about Asili—perfumed, delicate, elegant—can also be said about Bricco Asili, only more so. This wine has a fine structure and is rich in extract and flavor. And since 1985 they have vinified a Barbaresco from Faset. The Faset matures a little sooner than Bricco Asili. The Bricco Asili is more elegant as well.

Ceretto has also produced Barolos from Villero and Grignore, a part of Baudana. And in 1970 and 1971, even though they didn't label it as such, they produced and sold a Barolo from Cannubi. And in 1971 they produced a Barbaresco from Montefico which they continued to make through the '74.

Barolo: Azienda Agricola "Bricco Rocche" ****, Casa Vinicola Ceretto Zonchera ** + ; Barbaresco: Azienda Agricola "Bricco Asili," Bricco Asili ****, Azienda Agricola "Bricco Asili," Faset *** − , Casa Vinicola Ceretto, Asij ** + ; Nebbiolo d'Alba ***

Ceste Cav. G. These were wretched wines, among the worst in the zone. We don't know if they are still being produced. Barolo 0 −

Chiadò Mario. The most recent Barolo we tasted from Chiadò was his '71 and it was a bad bottle.

Chiarlo Michele Azienda Vitivinicola (*Calamandrana*), *1956*. This firm, owned by Michele Chiarlo, had, for a long time, produced a wide range of fairly reliable and correct, though unexciting

wines, including Barolo and Barbaresco under the Granduca label at his Cantine Duca d'Asti. They bought the grapes for their Barolo from Barolo, Serralunga d'Alba, Castiglione Falletto, and the borderlands, and for their Barbaresco from Barbaresco, Treiso d'Alba, and Neive.

Then Chiarlo decided to make some changes. Beginning with the 1974 vintage he started to produce single-vineyard Barolo and Barbaresco. And those wines have been a significant cut above those that he sells under the Granduca label. His first Barolo cru was the '74 Margaria from lampia and michet subvarieties grown in Vigneto Margaria in Serralunga d'Alba, which he rents. Later he put his name on the label and dropped the Granduca name. Then, on January 1, 1991, he changed the name of his company to Azienda Vitivinicola Michele Chiarlo and dropped the Granduca label.

Since 1982 Chiarlo has been producing Barolos from Rocche di Castiglione Falletto and Vigna Rionda di Serralunga d'Alba. The former Barolo is produced from a 2-acre (0.8-hectare) plot of twenty-one-year-old vines. The later comes from a 1.7-acre (0.7-hectare) plot of fifteen-year-old nebbiolo.

Chiarlo wants to make a classic Barolo. To that end, in 1988 he bought 2.47 acres (1 hectare) of Cannubi from Carlo Pittatore, the steepest part, in the center. It was unplanted, and has a 50 percent grade. Chiarlo built terraces and planted the vineyard in March 1990. He estimates that his first vintage will be in 1993. Additionally he rents 1.2 acres (0.5 hectares) of Cannubi from Barale. He planned to make a Cannubi Barolo in 1990. He has estimated that his production from those vines will be between 2,400 and 2,650 bottles. From 1988 Chiarlo has produced Bussia, Brunate, and Cerequio Barolos from the land that he leases from Pittatore. He has a twenty-year lease on the plots in Brunate and Bussia.

And in the spring of 1990, he bought 13.6 acres (5.5 hectares) of Cerequio in Barolo from Ing. Averzme. Prior to his recent acquisitions Chiarlo owned 7.4 acres (3 hectares) of vines and leased some 300 (120) under special contracts.

From 1982, he has produced a Rabajà Barbaresco from the section of the vineyard that he has under contract. There was no '84.

Chiarlo owns three wineries, the main one in Calamandrana, one in Gavi and a third in Barolo. He produces Barolo, Barbaresco and Dolcetto d'Alba at the winery in Barolo. Besides those wines,

THE CRUS OF MICHELE CHIARLO

Cru	Acres	Hectares	Average Age of Vines	First Vintage	Used for
Brunate	1.24	0.5	40 years	1988	Barolo
Bussia	n/a	n/a	18 years	1988	Barolo
Cannubi	3.71	1.5	n/a	1990	Barolo
Cerequio	13.59	5.5	16 years	1988	Barolo
Magaria	n/a	n/a	n/a	1974	Barolo
Rabajà	1.24	0.5	16 years	1983	Barbaresco
Rocche	1.98	0.8	21 years	1982	Barolo
Valle del Sole	6.18	2.5	35 years	1982	Barbera d'Asti
Vigna Rionda	1.73	0.7	15 years	1982	Barolo

Chiarlo produces a wide range of other wines including Gavi, *spumante,* and three proprietary wines: Arione, Barilot, and Valle del Sole. To celebrate his thirty years as a winemaker, in 1985 he produced 1,210 magnums of a barbera–cabernet sauvignon blend Trentanni. We can't comment on it since we never tasted it.

Thus far we have tasted six different vintages of Chiarlo's Rabajà Barbaresco, two from cask, four from glass. They have left a favorable impression. The '83, '86, and '87 were good, the '85 was very good, and the '88 and '89 showed a lot of promise. As for his Granduca Barbaresco, we haven't tasted that since the '80. It was a good, if unexciting wine. Chiarlo's Barolo cru bottlings, too, are a noticeable cut above his good but simple Granduca bottlings. Of these Granduca Barolos, both the '82 and '85 were very good. Thus far we have tasted, from barrel, in November 1990, the '88 and '89 Brunate, Bussia, Cerequio, Rocche, and Vigna Rionda. Of these last two crus, we have also tasted the '82, '83, and '85 from bottle. The '88 and '89 of the crus were very good, with good potential for the future. The '85s were very good, as were the '82s. Barolo: Granduca *, Brunate **, Bussia ** –, Cerequio **, Rocche ** +, Vigna Rionda **; Barbaresco: Granduca *, Rabajà **

Cigliuti F.lli di Renato Cigliuti (*Bricco Neive*, località *Serra Boella*), *1962.* Renato Cigliuti owns 7.5 acres (3 hectares) of vines. His annual production ranges from 15,000 to 20,000 bottles, which includes 5,500 bottles of Barbaresco; the balance is almost evenly divided between Dolcetto and Barbera. He also produces a small quantity of Freisa delle Langhe. His Barbaresco is somewhat gentler in nature and more elegant than the Barbarescos of Neive in general, being in that respect like others from Bricco Neive that we are familiar with. He bottles his best Barbaresco with the cru name, Serraboella. Barbaresco *** –

Clerico Domenico (*Monforte d'Alba*, località *Manzoni Cucchi*), *1976.* Domenico and Giuliana Clerico own 28.4 acres (11.5 hectares) of vines which supply them with all of the grapes they need. This includes 12.4 acres (5 hectares) of nebbiolo for Barolo in Bussia and 4.7 (1.9) in Ginestra. Their annual production of between 50,000 and 52,000 bottles of wine includes some 10,500 of Barolo, 18,000 of Dolcetto d'Alba, and 11,000 of Barbera d'Alba. Like many other Piemontese producers, Clerico is experimenting with *barriques.* Clerico producers some 6,000 bottles of Arte, a *barrique*-aged wine made from a blend of 92 percent nebbiolo and 8 percent barbera; 1985 was the first vintage. And from 1992 they will produce a Cabernet Sauvignon.

Clerico bottles two Barolo crus: Bricotto Bussia (1,300 bottles), since 1978, and Ciabot Mentin Ginestra (9,000), since 1980. They also own vines in Pajane from which they produce a Nebbiolo, and in Vigna Le Corda from which they bottle a Barbera d'Alba. Clerico also produces a very good Freisa called La Ginestrina. All of the Barolos that we tasted from Clerico have been very good and are getting better. We especially recommend his '82, '83, '85, and '86 Ciabot Mentin Ginestra; the '84 was pretty decent as well. Barolo ***

Cogno Elvio. See *Marcarini di Anna Marcarini & Elvio Cogno.*

Colla Paolo. See *Gagliardo Gianni.*

Colli Monfortesi. See *Conterno Fantino.*

Coluè di Massimo Oddero (*Diano d'Alba*), *1967.* Coluè owns 37 acres (15 hectares) of vines which provide 70 percent of their grapes. They have an annual production of approximately 100,000 bottles, which includes Barolo and Barbaresco as well as the other wines typical of the area plus what is fast becoming typical—a Chardonnay in *barrique*—plus a Dolcetto from Diano d'Alba. Oddero, we have heard, owns a piece of the prized Cannubi vineyard planted in nebbiolo for Barolo, but he doesn't, to our knowledge, do a separate cru bottling from here. There is a cru bottling of Barbaresco from Sorì Valeriano. Their Barolo and Barbaresco are quite good. They also produce a very good fizzy Moscato. Barolo *; Barbaresco * +

Confratelli di San Michele (*Neive*), *1972.* See *San Michele.*

Conte de Cavour. See *Cantine Barbero.*

Conterno Aldo (*Monforte d'Alba*, località *Bussia*), *1968.* Aldo Conterno owns 64 acres (26 hectares) of vines in Bussia Soprana, 28.4 (11.5) are in nebbiolo for Barolo from which he produces almost 50,000 bottles of wine. He selects only the best for his Barolo; the remainder becomes Nebbiolo. Conterno's yearly production averages some 120,000 bottles of wine. This includes some 25,000 to 30,000 bottles of Barolo, more in better vintages. The balance of his production is Barbera d'Alba, Dolcetto d'Alba, "La Bussianella" Freisa delle Langhe, Grignolino delle Langhe, and two Nebbiolo delle Langhes including Il Favòt, a nebbiolo aged in *barrique.*

Conterno also puts his Barbera d'Alba Conca Tre Pile in *barrique* for three months.

Conterno's sons Franco and Stefano work with him. They decided to plant some chardonnay, with their father's permission we assume. The wine we tasted was promising.

When the year justifies it Conterno produces three special sub-crus in Bussia Soprana: about 5,000 bottles each of Bricco Cicala and Bricco Colonello, plus from 7,200 to 7,500 bottles of Romirasco (formerly Bricco Ciabot). Although he did a limited bottling of 1,000 bottles of the '80 Ciabot for the Cavalieri del Tartufi e dei Vini di Alba, he considers the '82 his first. Since 1986 the subplot known as Bricco Ciabot has been changed to Romirasco. Conterno told us that he decided to use the Romirasco name when he realized that other producers used the Ciabot name. Since 1986 he has been producing a Barolo from those holdings that he has labeled Romirasco. Conterno does not always bottle these subplots separately. In 1987, for example, by making a severe selection, he was able to produce 7,000 bottles of one very good Barolo.

In the very best vintages he bottles a Granbussia Barolo as well. Conterno has produced a '71, '74, '78, '82, '85, '88, '89, and '90 Granbussia. From the 1982 harvest, for example, Conterno produced five Barolos: 6,985 bottles and 493 magnums of Granbussia, more than 7,200 bottles of Bricco Bussia Vigna Ciabot, 5,320 bottles and 175 magnums of Bricco Bussia Vigna Cicala, and 4,123 bottles and 170 magnums of Bricco Bussia Vigna Colonello and a Bussia Soprana. Of the three '82 crus, Cicala is the most complete, Colonello the most forward, and Romirasco (Ciabot) the most tannic.

Conterno said that the vines for his Barolo must be at least six years old, fifteen to be used in his cru bottlings. Conterno considers michet his best subvariety; he also has some lampia. He told us that the soil is more important than the variety. The 12.5-acre (5-hectare) Ciabot, or Romirasco, plot was planted in about 1970 with the lampia subvariety. Cicala is 2.8 acres (1.1 hectares) and Colonello 1.9 acres (0.76 hectare). Conterno shares the Colonello with two or three other growers; he owns all of Cicala and Romirasco. We have also seen, on the labels of some of Conterno's Barolos, Cascina Masante della Bussia Soprana.

On our visit to the Piemonte in 1985, Aldo Conterno shared a Barolo with us from his birth year, 1931. The '31 vintage is considered to be the finest of this century, and if this outstanding wine is proof enough, then it certainly was a special year. This wine was produced by Aldo's father, Giacomo. The wine displayed something of the character of Aldo Conterno; it had a firmness about it under its more gentle nature (for our tasting notes see page 106).

Conterno's Barolos are without question among the finest in the zone. They are finely balanced, stylish wines, rich in fruit, displaying depth and class. We find that while they are enjoyable from their sixth year, they approach their peak in their eighth to tenth, depending on the vintage. Barolo: Bussia Soprana ***, Bricco Cicala ****, Bricco Colonello ****, Bricco Ciabot or Romirasco ****, Granbussia ****; Nebbiolo ***

Conterno Fantino (*Monforte d'Alba, regione Fracchia*). Conterno produces between 94,000 and 100,000 bottles of wine annually, which include some 24,000 bottles of Barolo, 14,600 Barbera d'Alba, 26,500 Dolcetto d'Alba, 14,600 Nebbiolo delle Langhe, 10,550 Freisa delle Langhe, 3,300 Chardonnay delle Langhe, and a small amount of the *barrique*-aged Monprà. They used to sell these wines under the Colli Monfortesi label. These Barolos were overly simple and rather unimpressive. Since the label change the wines have improved considerably. They bottle two Barolos from the Ginestre vineyard, one that they label Sorì Ginestra and the other, Vigna del Gris (Ginestre). Of the former, the '82, '85, and '86 were very good, and of the latter, the '86 was disappointing. Barolo: Colli Monfortesi *, Conterno Fantino ** +

Conterno Giacomo di Giovanni Conterno (*Monforte d'Alba*). Unlike his brother, Aldo, Giovanni Conterno is a staunch traditionalist. He speaks somewhat sadly of the push in Italy today toward producing a younger, earlier-maturing wine, affirming that even if the market for the traditional wines should someday no longer exist, his wines will never be made other than by the traditional methods he believes in. His wife nods her head in agreement and support. Conterno realizes that he has chosen the more difficult path, but he believes in his wine.

He wants a full-bodied, ample, and long-lived wine, an old-style Barolo at its best. To achieve this he restricts his production severely, using only the finest fruit from the more favored vintages to produce a dense, robust wine that can stand up to the long wood aging that will smooth it out, rounding off its youthful rough edges.

When the grapes don't measure up to his demanding standards, which unfortunately happens rather frequently, he doesn't produce the wine. For example, in 1984 there was no wine bearing the proud name of Giacomo Conterno; he sold all of his grapes. In 1983 he made very little wine and that only Freisa; in 1977 he didn't pick any grapes. Conterno produced no wine in 1975 or 1976, and although he produced an '81 Barolo and aged it for a time in cask, he decided not to bottle it; he sold it *sfuso*.

His 37-acre (15-hectare) Cascina Francia vineyard in Serralunga d'Alba includes 12.7 acres (5.13 hectares) of nebbiolo for Barolo, 11.3 (4.58) of dolcetto, 6.2 (2.5) of barbera, and 1.4 (0.55) of freisa. His vines are planted between 1,312 and 1,641 feet (400 and 500 meters) above sea level and face southwest. Conterno bought the Cascina Francia vineyard in 1974. Previously he purchased grapes from Serralunga.

Giovanni Conterno made his first Barolo in 1958 with his father. The first Barolo that he produced by himself was the '59; his father consulted. Today his son Roberto works with him. Whether or not it was Roberto's influence we don't know, but recently Giovanni produced a chardonnay.

Conterno produces some 90,000 bottles of wine annually— 32,665 of Barolo, 19,200 of Barbera d'Alba, 35,465 of Dolcetto d'Alba, and 2,667 of Freisa delle Langhe.

Conterno produces two Barolos: the single-vineyard Cascina Francia Riserva and Monfortino. Until recently he aged the former no less than six years in cask and the latter, for at least eight, and ten wasn't uncommon. He began bottling his regular '74 Barolo in 1980, and the Monfortino in 1984. When we visited the *cantina* in November 1984, we tasted a '70 Monfortino still in cask. More recently, since 1985, in a bow to modernity perhaps, Conterno has installed temperature-controlled stainless steel fermenting tanks and reduced his cask-aging regime. He also uses tanks for warming and chilling the wines. The 1985 Barolo spent perhaps four years in cask and the 1982 Monfortino seven or at most eight years.

The Monfortino is not named for a single vineyard; it is from grapes grown in his Cascina Francia holdings. He makes this wine only in special vintages. The first Monfortino was produced, according to both Aldo and Giovanni Conterno, prior to the First World War. Contrary to some reports, Monfortino is not a selection of the best grapes from Conterno's Cascina Francia vineyard. The two differences between Monfortino and the Barolo Riserva have to do with the production: fermentation and aging. The Barolo Riserva is fermented at a temperature between 80.6° and 82.4° Fahrenheit (27° and 28° centigrade) while Monfortino is fermented at a much warmer temperature—will rise to between 96.8° and 98.6° (36° and 37°). The former is fermented for thirty to thirty-one days, the latter for thirty-five days. Conterno uses *cappello sommerso* for both wines. While the Cascina Barolo is aged for perhaps four years in large *botti* (casks), Monfortino is kept for up to a decade or longer in oak. Since 1952 there have been 17 Monfortinos: '52, '55, '58, '61, '64, '67, '68, a small amount of '69, '70, '71, '74, '78, '79, '82, '85, '87, and '88. Conterno told us that although 1989 was a first-rate vintage the wine wasn't balanced enough for Monfortino.

Conterno uses *cappello sommerso* for all of his wines. He ferments the dolcetto for seventeen days, the barbera for twelve, freisa thirteen, Barolo thirty to thirty-one, and Monfortino thirty-five.

Like some of the other Barolos that are given long cask aging, Conterno's wines seem to be more susceptible to damage by improper handling or storage. While we've had many magnificent Barolos from Giovanni Conterno, we've had some that didn't measure up—in fact, they were disappointments. We are convinced, however, that the problems occurred after the wines left the winery. Barolo: Cascina Francia Riserva *** +, Monfortino ****

Conterno Paolo (*Monforte d'Alba*, località *Ginestra*). Paolo Conterno owns a piece of the regarded Ginestra vineyard. Our experience with his Barolos has been limited to three barrel samples, the '87, '88, and '89, in November 1990. They were very good. Barolo [** –]

Contratto Giuseppe di Dott. Alberto Contratto and Contratto Azienda Agricola (*Canelli and La Morra*), *1867*. The Contratto family owns 62 acres (25 hectares) of vineyards, including Cascina Alberta in Treiso, Cascina Secolo in Barolo and La Morra, Cascina Tre Pini and Cascina Pian del Re in Canelli, and Cascina Carmela in Nizza Monferrato. They also buy grapes since their own vines supply them with only 20 percent of their needs.

They produce 1.1 million bottles of a wide range of fairly consistent quality wines, which include 300,000 bottles of champagne-method *spumanti*, 300,000 charmat-method *spumanti*, 250,000 white wines and Moscato d'Asti, and 250,000 of red wines. Contratto's production includes three Barolos, three Barbarescos, a Nebbiolo delle Langhe Sarmassa, Roero, three Barbera d'Astis, Freisa d'Asti, Grignolino d'Asti, a Barbera d'Alba, Dolcetto d'Alba, Barbera del Monferrato, and the whites Cortese dell'Alto Monferrato, Gavi, Gavi di Gavi, Gavi di Gavi San Bartolomeo, Verbesco, and two Chardonnays.

They began to cru bottle in 1985, when they produced a Barolo Ca' Neire di la Morra, Nebbiolo delle Langhe Sarmassa di Barolo, Barbaresco Cascina Alberta di Treiso, Barbera d'Alba Cascina Alberta di Treiso, and Barbera d'Asti Cascina Pian del Re. They own the Azienda Agricola Contratto in La Morra which is used for their two Barolo crus Ca' Neire and Sarmassa.

This serious-minded, traditional firm also produces some of Italy's finest Champagne-method sparkling wines as well as first-rate Asti Spumante. Among these are the Brut Riserva *millesimato*, Brut, Extra Brut Reserve for England, Extra Dry Riserva Bacco d'Oro, Sabauda Imperial Riserva, Brut Riserva Novecento, and a Giuseppe Contratto Brut Rosé. Their dessert wines include the Charmat-method *spumante* Asti Spumante, Brachetto, Gem, and Rubbio, and two Moscato d'Astis, a *normale* and a Cascina Tre Pini, and a *vin santo*. They also produce vermouth, Chiana, grappa, and other such products.

In November 1990, for the first time we had an opportunity to taste, from barrel, Contratto's cru bottlings from their Ca' Neire and Sarmassa crus. The wines—the '87, '88, and '89—were, for the most part, as we expected, very good. Barolo **; Barbaresco ** –

Coppo Luigi e Figli (*Canelli*), *1892*. The Coppo Barolo and Barbaresco are a bit simple, but they can be good. They tend to mature fairly early. Coppo bottles two Barolo crus: Brunate and Castello. The last Coppo Barbaresco that we tasted was the '78, the last Barolo was the '79. More recently we have noticed a significant improvement in Coppo's wines. They produced a good Chardonnay and very good barbera-in-*barrique* Pomorosso. This firm owns 57 acres (23 hectares) of vines. They specialize in Barbera wines. We don't know if they still produce Barolo or Barbaresco. Barolo [*]; Barbaresco [*]

Cordero di Montezemolo (*Annunziata di La Morra*), *1941*. Marchese di Montezemolo produced his first Barolo in 1945. Long an advocate of the modern style of winemaking, he aimed for a

THE CRUS AND VINEYARDS OF GIUSEPPE CONTRATTO

Cru	Location	Acres	Hectares	Altitude in Feet	Meters	Exposure	Average Number of Bottles Per Year	First Vintage	Used for
Alberta	Treiso	2.15	0.87	1,150	350	SW	3,441	1985	Barbaresco
		7.31	2.96	740	300	S	19,362	1985	Barbera d'Alba
		0.42	0.17	1,150	350	SW	2,733	1988	Chardonnay delle Langhe
Ca' Neire	La Morra	8.75	3.54	740	300	S	2,362	1985	Barolo
Carmela	Guargna in Nizza Monferrato	3.48	1.41	395	160	W	11,002	1986	Chardonnay del Piemonte
Pian del Re	Castagnole in Canelli	6.23	2.52	625	190	S/SW	18,113	1985	Barbera d'Asti
San Bartolomeo	Roverto di Gavi	7.41	3.00	820	250	S/SW	20,600	1988	Gavi di Gavi
Sarmassa	Barolo	3.21	1.30	820	250	S	9,736	1985	Nebbiolo delle Langhe
Tre Pini	Monforte in Canelli	5.39	2.18	985–1,170	300–357	S/SW	18,880	1988	Moscato d'Asti

Barolo rich in flavor and fruit, and he succeeded. That forward rush of fruit on the palate was his trademark.

Montezemolo retired on January 1, 1982. Since his sons, Giovanni and Enrico, have taken over the winery, production has more than doubled. Montezemolo produced an average of 30,000 bottles of Barolo and 10,000 of Dolcetto a year. He sold more than 50 percent of his grapes; his sons vinify them all. It shows. The '79 and '80 Barolos were made by Montezemolo, but something happened to the wine somewhere along the line. They were good wines, but they didn't measure up to what we had come to expect from this very serious, dedicated winemaker. Perhaps one of the problems is that the young men chose to vinify the entire crop in 1979 instead of selecting only the better grapes as their father had done. Since the increase in production, they have outgrown the old *cantina* in La Morra. In 1981 they moved to a vastly larger winery in the Monfalletto area of Annunziata.

They currently produce 90,000 bottles of Barolo and 30,000 of Dolcetto a year. There are two Barolos—one from the cru of Monfalletto in La Morra, the other from the part of Villero known as Enrico VI in Castiglione Falletto. The former wine, as is characteristic of their location, matures somewhat sooner.

Today Giovanni and Enrico Montezemolo own 57.4 acres (23.2 hectares) of vines—27.1 (10.9) of nebbiolo for Barolo in Monfalletto, 5.4 (2.2) in Enrico VI, and 24.9 (10.1) of dolcetto in Monfalletto. Over half of their annual production consist of Barolo; the balance is Dolcetto d'Alba. This includes 56,000 bottles each of a Barolo and Dolcetto d'Alba from Monfalletto, and 11,000 of a Barolo from Enrico VI.

According to Luigi Veronelli, their vineyards derive from a 1340 land title belonging to the Falletti family. Cordero di Montezemolo inherited it in 1941 from his great-aunt Countess Luigi Falletti. The first wines sold from these vineyards were made by Giacinto Massimiliano Falletti in 1760.[35]

Montezemolo felt that his Barolos did not show their best until six years after the vintage and could last quite a long time. Unfortunately, we've never tasted one old enough to say whether we agree with this assessment. As for their Barolo today, we're happy to report that things have improved, and we believe that they will continue to do so. Barolo ** +

Corino Giovanni & Figli (*Annunziata di La Morra*). Giovanni Corino produces some 20,000 bottles of wine, including 5,333 of a Barolo from their Vigna Giachini in the Annunziata district, 8,000 of Dolcetto, and 6,667 of Barbera. They farm 18.5 acres (7.5 hectares) of vines—part of which are rented—9.9 (4) in nebbiolo, 4.9 (2) in dolcetto, and 3.7 (1.5) in barbera. Our experience here has been limited to one vintage in bottle, the '85, and three from casks, the '87, '88, and '89. (The cask samples were difficult to taste.) The '85 was very good and the cask samples showed promise. Barolo **

Cortese Giuseppe (*Barbaresco, località Rabajà*). Cortese produces a Barbaresco from the fine Rabajà vineyard and a Nebbiolo delle Langhe. The wines that we've tasted have, for the most part, been very good. Barbaresco ** +

Cortese Riccardo (*Canelli*). This producer owns vineyards in Cascina Rocca in Barbaresco.

Cossetti Clemente & Figli (*Castelnuovo Belbo*). Cossetti produces, or sells under their own label, a wide range of wines varying in quality from nondescript to downright poor. It's been years since we tasted these wines, the most recent Barolo was the '71. Barolo [0]; Barbaresco [0]

Crissante Alessandria & Figli (*S. Maria di La Morra, borgata Roggeri*). Crissante owns vines in Bricco S. Biagio, Capalotti, and Roggeri. He produces Barolo and Dolcetto d'Alba.

DA.I.PI.""CM."" Daniele Lanzavecchia, one of the owners of **Villadoria,** owns this label or winery or both. The wine doesn't belie its connection. The '74 Magaria Barolo that we tasted left a lot to be desired. Barolo 0

Damilano Dott. Giacomo & Figli (*Barolo*). Damilano owns part of the highly prized Cannubi vineyard. He produces more than 250,000 bottles of wine annually, including 113,330 of Barolo, 32,000 Barbaresco, 45,300 Barbera d'Alba, 34,665 Dolcetto d'Alba, and 22,000 Nebbiolo d'Alba. We find this producer's Barolo superior to his Barbaresco, but not by much. We have seen Barolos from Damilano labeled Cantine La Morra. Yet they are in Barolo not La Morra. Barolo * − ; Barbaresco 0

De Forville (*Barbaresco*), *1860*. Bruno Anfosso de Forville owns 25 acres (10 hectares) of vineyards, which supply him with about 40 percent of his grapes. His annual production, of 15,500 to 20,000 cases of wine, includes a good Barbaresco. His two sons, Paolo and Walter, work with him. He believes in long skin contact and long cask aging. Since 1974 De Forville has been bottling Barbaresco from the crus of Loreto, Montestefano, Pozzo, and Rabajà when the vintage justifies it. They also produce a Dolcetto d'Alba from their holdings in the Loreto vineyard as well as a Cortese del Piemonte and a Moscato d'Asti. Somewhat surprisingly, considering De Forville's emphasis on the traditional methods, he has planted chardonnay. The last Barbaresco that we tasted from this producer was the '80. Barbaresco **

De Forville Paolo (*Barbaresco*). At one time these wines had a good reputation, perhaps they still do. Our limited experience hasn't been favorable. There might be a connection between Anfosso and Paolo de Forville, but we don't know. This De Forville has bottled a Barbaresco from Montestefano. They also own vines in Loreto and Ovello. We haven't tasted the wines here since the '78 Barbaresco. Barbaresco [*]

Dellavalle F.lli (*Gattinara*). We have found these wines lacking in personality and structure, though they can be drinkable enough. Dellavalle is primarily a producer of Novara-Vercelli wines. We haven't tasted their Barolo since the mediocre '74. And we don't know if they continue to make it. Barolo [0]

Denegri Lorenzo (*Annunziata di La Morra*), 1953. Sig. Denegri only made two wines: a Barolo and a Nebbiolo. In August 1984, *Ca' Bianca* of Alice Bel Colle bought Denegri's *cantina* and vineyards. Denegri's Barolo was from his holding in Plucotti dell'Annunziata, though the label didn't indicate that. Barolo [*]

Dogliani F.lli. See *Batasiolo.*

Dogliotti Amelio Vincenzo e Figli (*Castagnole Lanze*). This firm produces about 166,650 cases of all the typical wines of this area, including Barolo and Barbaresco.

Dosio Giuseppe (*La Morra*, località *Serradenari*), *1971*. Dosio owns vines in the vineyards of Nassone and Fossati. Casa Vinicola Dosio produces between 65,000 and 70,000 bottles of wine a year; 10,000 to 16,000 are Barolo. They also produce, besides the Albeisa wines from nebbiolo, barbera, and dolcetto, an Arneis, and a *spumante*. The Dosio Barolos are light, early-maturing wines that are overly simple, but they can be quite good nevertheless. At one time—pre-DOCG—they produced a Barolo Riserva Speciale that was aged for five years in oak! From time to time Dosio bottles a Barolo from the Fossati vineyard. Barolo * +

Duca d'Asti Cantine. See *Chiarlo Michele.*

Einaudi Luigi (*Dogliani*), *1907*. This producer is quite traditional. Einaudi has 247 acres (100 hectares), 62 (25) in vines, including 10 acres (4 hectares) of nebbiolo; from 6.2 (2.5) of these in the Terlo di Barolo vineyard he produces a full-bodied, richly-fruited Barolo. Besides this, he makes from 80,000 to 180,000 bottles a year of Barbera, Dolcetto, and Nebbiolo delle Langhe. We have found the Einaudi Barolo consistent and very good. There is a big gap in our experience, however. The last vintage that we tasted until recently had been the '74, now it's the '82. Barolo ** +

Eredi Lodali di Ghione (*Treiso d'Alba*), *1939*. Maria Ghione owns this *cantina* and some 20 acres (8 hectares) of vines.

Besides these wines they also produce 9,300 bottles of Chardonnay delle Piemonte. Barolo *; Barbaresco *

Eredi Virginia Ferrero (*Serralunga d'Alba,* frazione *San Rocco*), *1856*. Over a decade ago we tasted a Barolo sold under the name Ferrero Virginia, the most recent was the '70 and it was unimpressive. More recently we tasted an '85, the only Barolo that we tasted with the Ferrero Eredi Virginia label, it was very good. Since *eredi* means "heirs" we suspect that the new label reflects a change in ownership. The estate today is owned by Mariangela Ferrero. Ferrero produces from 3,000 to 4,000 bottles of Barolo from her 2.47 acres (1 hectare) of vines in the San Rocco vineyard. Barolo **

Fenocchio Giacomo & Figli (*Monforte d'Alba*, località *Bussia Sottana*), *c. 1840*. Claudio Fenocchio owns 35 acres (14.2 hectares) of land, which includes 16.8 acres (6.8 hectares) in vines, 14.3 (5.8) in Bussia Sottana, and 2.5 (1) in Cannubi Boschis. He produces some 43,000 bottles of wine annually—19,000 are a Barolo from Bussia Sottana, 6,000 a Barolo from Cannubi Boschis, 4,000 Barbera d'Alba, and more than 13,000 of Dolcetto d'Alba. At one time

THE CRUS AND VINEYARDS OF EREDI LODALI DI GHIONE

Cru/Vineyard	Location	Acres	Hectares	Average Number of Bottles Per Year	Used for
Bric Sant'Ambrogio	Roddi	12.4	5.0	12,000[a]	Barolo
				10,700[b]	Dolcetto d'Alba
				2,000[c]	Barbera d'Alba
Rocche dei 7 Fratelli	Treiso	3.7	1.5	9,300[d]	Barbaresco
Sorj Canta	Trieso	3.7	1.5	10,000[e]	Dolcetto d'Alba

NOTES: [a] In 1982 they produced 13,593 bottles, plus larger sizes.
[b] In 1987 they produced 4,950 bottles.
[c] In 1985 they produced 3,740 bottles.
[d] In 1982 they produced 5,880 bottles, plus larger sizes.
[e] In 1988 they produced 10,173 bottles.

THE CRUS AND VINEYARDS OF GIACOMO FENOCCHIO

Vineyard	Variety	Acres	Hectares	Altitude in Feet	Meters
Bussia Sottana	Nebbiolo[a]	7.9	3.2	1,017	310
	Dolcetto[b]	4.9	2.0	to	to
	Barbera[a]	1.5	0.6	1,050	320
Cannubbio Boschis	Nebbiolo[c]	2.5	1.0	951	290

NOTES: [a] Bottled as a Bussia or Bussia Sottana cru
[b] Bottled as a Bricat cru; since 1989 as Bussia Sottana
[c] Bottled as a Cannubbio or Cannubi cru

he bottled a Barolo as Vigna Munie Bussia which we suspect was from his holdings in Bussia Sottana although there is a Munie vineyard. He markets his Barolo from Cannubi Boschis as Cannubi and at various times his Barolo from Bussia Sottana as either Bussia or Bussia Sottana. From 1978 he sold his Dolcetto d'Alba as Bussia—Bricat Cannubbio, and later as Bricat, today it's labeled as Bussia Sottana. He also farmed nebbiolo vines in Fontanile. We don't know if he still does.

There is no question that this producer's Barolos have improved. Barolo **

Fenocchio Riccardo, Azienda Agricola "Pianpolvere Soprano" (*Monforte d'Alba*, località *Pianpolvere Soprano*), 1920. Riccardo Fenocchio owns 8.8 acres (3.6 hectares) on Pianpolvere Soprano from which he produces between 22,250 and 27,600 bottles of wine annually. His production today consists of from 5,600 to 6,266 bottles of Barolo, 4,000 to 5,333 of Dolcetto d'Alba, 10,667 to 13,333 of Barbera d'Alba, and 2,000 to 2,667 of Grignolino delle Langhe. When some new vines come into production in the near future, he expects this to increase in the near future to between 40,000 and 53,000 bottles. This will include 14,000 of Barolo, 18,666 of Barbera d'Alba, and 5,600 of Dolcetto d'Alba.

In 1983, Fenocchio vinified all of his grapes for the first time. Previously he had sold his barbera to the Cerettos. His first Barolo, sold in bottle, was produced in 1968; his first Barbera dates from 1974. His vineyard is planted approximately two-thirds in nebbiolo and one-third in barbera; there are also twelve rows of grignolino vines, rather unusual in this area. Fenocchio's Pianpolvere vineyard is, he told us, actually a part of Bussia. We've found his wines to be quite good. Barolo **

Ferrero F.lli di Renato Ferrero (*Annunziata di La Morra*), 1930. The Ferrero brothers, Giovanni and Renato, own less than 4.9 acres (2 hectares) of vines in the Annunziata district of La Morra, 3.98 (1.61) for Barolo and 0.42 (0.17) for barbera. Their vineyards for Barolo include 1.78 acres (0.72 hectare) of Annunziata, 0.74 (0.3) of Manzoni, and 1.46 (0.59) of Gancia. The first wine that they produced with a label was the '64. Today they produce some 20,000 bottles of wine annually, which includes more than 11,000 of Barolo, 1,300 to 3,000 of Nebbiolo delle Langhe, and 1,200 to 1,560 of Barbera d'Alba. On our last visit to their *cantina* in April 1987, they told us that they planned to do a Dolcetto.

At one time the wine from this *cantina* was sold under the Settimo Giuseppe name, next it was sold as Ferrero Lorenzo, and finally, since 1978, F.lli Ferrero. The '78 and '79 were labeled as F.lli Ferrero Giovanni e Renato. Overall, these are well-made Barolos, perhaps lacking the elegance of the *comune*. Barolo * +

Feyles Maria & Figli (*Alba*), 1976. Antonio de Nicola owns this winery and some 6 acres (2.4 hectares) of vineyards. Their vineyards include 3.5 acres (1.4 hectares) of Montesommo and 2.5 (1) of Borgese, both in Neive. They grow nebbiolo in the former and barbera in the latter. Feyles produces a Barbaresco from Vigna dei Gaia in Neive and a Barolo from Vigna della Ginestra in Monforte d'Alba. Just over half, or 51 percent, of their production comes from their own grapes. They produce, on average, 33,300 bottles of wine annually: 10,660 each Barolo and Barbaresco, 6,665 Barbera d'Alba, and 2,665 each Nebbiolo and Dolcetto d'Alba. Their Barbarescos are quite good, their Barolo very good. De Nicola uses

Giuseppe Rinaldi as his consulting enologist. We don't know if that is the exceptionally fine Barolo producer from the *comune* of Barolo, but somehow we doubt it. Barolo **; Barbaresco * +

Finelli Giuseppe (*La Morra*). Giuseppe Finelli owns vines in the Fossati vineyard. He produces a Barolo.

Fontana Michele (*Barolo*). This producer owns part of the very fine Cannubi vineyard as well as part of La Mandorla and San Lorenzo.

Fontana Saverio (*Castiglione Falletto*, frazione *Pugnane*). Fontana Saverio cultivates vines in the Munie vineyard in Monforte and Meriondino in Castiglione. Among the wines that they produce are a Barolo.

Fontanabianca di Capra E. C. (*Neive*). They bottle a Barbaresco from Vigneto Sorì di Burdin in Neive. Our experience here is limited to their good '87. Barbaresco *

Fontanafredda, Tenimenti di Barolo e di (*Serralunga d'Alba*), 1878. The Fontanafredda wine estate was founded by Count Emanuele Guerrieri, son of Vittorio Emanuele II of Italy and his mistress, "La Bela Rosin." The winery and its 250 acres (100 hectares) of vineyards were taken over in 1931 by Monte dei Paschi of Siena, the world's oldest bank. The vineyards on the estate today provide Fontanafredda with only 13 percent of the grapes they need for their annual production of nearly 5 million bottles. Approximately half of this is sparkling wine, including some very good Asti and fine Champagne-method *spumante*. Of the remaining 2.5 million bottles, Barolo and Barbaresco make up 850,000 and 100,000 bottles, respectively; the remainder consists of a wide range of wines, generally reliable and characteristic of their type. Most of their grapes are purchased from growers with whom Fontanafredda has long-term contracts. The grapes for the Barbaresco come from Trieso and Barbaresco. While it is generally a good wine, this Barbaresco often reminds us more of a Barolo in style.

Fontanafredda bottles Barolos from nine crus. They provide the following assessment of each cru. Vigna Bianca has an austere nature, is dry and full-bodied, and is regarded for its bouquet of dried grass and withered flowers. Gallaretto is noted for its body and structure; it is smooth, warm, and gentle with an aroma of withered roses, quince, and hazelnuts. Gattinera is austere in its youth, requiring age to bring it around; it is round, robust, and spicy with an aroma of pepper and nutmeg, and with age *goudron*. (This last cru is also a source of pinot grapes used for their especially fine *metodo champenoise spumante*, Gattinera brut.) La Rosa is perhaps their most noted cru, not necessarily because it's the best, but because it has been the most widely distributed. Barolo La Rosa is perhaps the most robust of the wines, and consequently requires aging to show its quality. Their assessment of the La Rosa Barolo: it is a long-lasting wine, with an aroma of faded roses, forest leaves, almonds, and with age *goudron*. The Barolos of La Delizia and La Villa are ready first and San Pietro shortly afterward. La Delizia, according to Fontanafredda, is full-bodied and austere, and although it matures soon, it ages very well; the aroma is said to be suggestive of spice and cinnamon, and with age, leather and camphor. La Villa, they say, has an aroma of blackberries, prunes, and black cherries, and with age licorice, tobacco leaves, old leather, and dried flowers. The San Pietro also ages well and is regarded for

THE BAROLO CRUS OF FONTANAFREDDA

Barolo Cru	Subvariety	Acres	Hectares	Altitude in Feet	Meters	Exposure	First Vintage	Vines Planted	Average Number of Bottles Per Year
Bianca in Serralunga d'Alba	100% lampia	1.26	0.5080	885–920	270–280	SW	1971	1975	3,500
Galleretto part in Serralunga, part in Diano d'Alba	Lampia, michet	4.84	1.9600	785–920	240–280	S/SW SW	1974	1971	13,500
Garil		0.94	0.3800	820	250	S	1971	n/a	2,500
Gattinera in Serralunga d'Alba	50-50 michet, lampia	11.12	4.5000	820–985	250–300	S	1970	1975	31,000
La Delizia in Serralunga d'Alba	100% michet	8.87	3.5900	1,115–1,245	340–380	S	1967	1964–74	24,000
La Rosa in Serralunga d'Alba	Michet, lampia	17.16	6.9447	820–1,015	250–310	S/SW SW	1975	n/a	50,000
La Villa this cru is in the Cannubi area of Barolo	Lampia	7.89	3.1910	1,050–1,215	320–370	E	1958	1977	22,000
Lazzarito in Serralunga d'Alba	Mostly lampia, some michet	6.50	2.6300	1,150–1,310	350–400	S/SW	1971	1964	18,000
San Pietro in Serralunga d'Alba	Lampia	7.34	2.9700	720–855	220–260	SW	1974	1968	22,000

its bouquet of prunes, peaches, and dried fruit. The Lazzarito Barolo is the slowest to mature and, not surprisingly, ages very well; its aroma recalls strawberries, mint, and black cherry.

Barolo: crus **, *normale* *; Barbaresco * +

Fracchia Provino & Figlio (*Grazzano Badoglio*). Fracchia produces a Barolo and a Gattinara. We've never tasted either one.

Franco. We haven't seen their wine since their mediocre '66 Barolo. Admittedly the vintage was rather mediocre.

Franco Fiorina (*Alba*), *1925*. This firm, founded by Andrea Franco, began bottling their wine in 1947 with Barolo and Barbaresco. They followed with other wines. Franco's daughter, Elsa, and her husband, Giuseppe Fontana, took over the management of the company in 1952. At the beginning of 1990, Corrado Bonino and Carlo Olivero bought the firm. Under the previous ownership

they owned no vineyards, but bought all their grapes from growers with whom they have long-standing agreements.

The Bonino family are well-known industrialists with extensive food processing and agricultural plants. Franco Fiorina's new president, twenty-six-year-old Corrado Bonino, always dreamed of having a winemaking concern. His grandfather devoted more than forty years of his life to winemaking. He took courses in wine in order to prepare himself for a career in wine. When we interviewed him for the revision of our book, we were impressed with his enthusiasm and concern for quality.

The current owners have 13.2 acres (5.3 hectares) in La Morra, 4.7 (1.9) in Castiglione Falletto, and another 37.7 acres (15.2 hectares) that they lease in Monforte d'Alba.

Today Franco Fiorina produces between 250,000 and 300,000 bottles of wine annually of 11 different wines that are consistently

THE CRUS AND VINEYARDS OF FRANCO FIORINA

Vineyard	Comune	Variety	Acres	Hectares
Cascina Pilone	Castiglione Falletto	Dolcetto, barbera, and nebbiolo	4.7	1.9
Cascina Zoccolaio	Monforte d'Alba	Nebbiolo	37.7	15.2
Case Brusciate	La Morra	Nebbiolo	3.8	1.5
Serra dei Turchi	La Morra	Nebbiolo	9.4	3.8

good, wines that sometimes attain great heights. Of these, 60,000 bottles are Barolo and 20,000 are Barbaresco. They also produce 7,000 bottles of Freisa delle Langhe, 40,000 of Dolcetto d'Alba, 10,000 of Nebbiolo d'Alba, 16,000 of Grignolino del Monferrato Casalese, 35,000 Favorita di Monticello d'Alba, 30,000 Primaticcio Vino Novello from 85 percent dolcetto and 15 percent freisa, 20,000 of Chardonnay from the Cars vineyard in Barbaresco which they have made since 1981, 40,000 Barbera d'Alba and 1,000 Pelaverga di Verduno. All of their wines, except for the Primaticcio, are made entirely from one grape. They plan to increase their production to 500,000 bottles in the next five years. Their plans call for them to produce an Arneis and a Gavi as well. And within three years they expect to build a winery at their Cascina Pilone estate in Castiglione Falletto. They'll produce their Barolo there, and perhaps their Barbaresco as well.

At Franco Fiorina, the previous owners didn't believe in the cru concept for Barolo or Barbaresco. They felt they could produce a more balanced wine by blending the grapes from the different *comuni*. Their Barbaresco is made with grapes from Barbaresco itself, which gives structure, and from Treiso for finesse. In their Barolo, they use grapes from four *comuni*. Those from Barolo, they point out, give structure to the wine; those from Castiglione Falletto provide body and strength; the grapes of Serralunga d'Alba provide less alcohol but add perfume; while those from La Morra, which give less color, add delicacy to the blend. The new owners expect to bottle the crus separately.

Franco Fiorina aims to produce a gentle wine—both Barolo and Barbaresco—but also one that can age.

Armando Cordero, the firm's enologist, recognizes the advantages of both the old methods and modern technology, and the disadvantages of both as well. While employing some modern techniques, he produces wines that are basically traditional. Franco Fiorina declassified part of the 1977 and 1976 crops and all of the 1975 harvest, preferring to sell the wine *sfuso* without their label to bottling a wine that didn't come up to their standards. Barolo ** + ; Barbaresco * +

Gagliardo Gianni (*S. Maria di La Morra*, località *Serra dei Turchi*), 1922. Until fairly recently these wines were sold under the Paolo Colla label. The winery was named for Paolo Colla. Gianni Gagliardo, who runs the winery, has changed the label. He produces over 200,000 bottles a year of a wide range of mostly mediocre wines, including 27,000 bottles of Barolo and 3,500 of Barbaresco. Some 65 percent of the grapes come from their own vineyards. Gagliardo owns 47.7 acres (19.3 hectares) of vines, including 20.5 (8.3) of the La Serra dei Turchi vineyard, not to be confused with La Serra, in La Morra, from which he produces 6,000 bottles of Barolo a year. He also produces a Barolo labeled Mora and 7,000 bottles of Barbaresco from their Valgrande vineyard in Treiso. In 1974, Gagliardo bottled a small quantity of Barolo Treccani. He also produced a Barolo under the Ribezzo label which is better than his standard fare.

Gianni Gagliardo produced a good '85 La Serra and a passable '86! We hope that is a good omen. We can't say, however, that his '82 Barbaresco from the Valgrande vineyard was much better than in times past. And the '85 and '86 Barolo Mora failed to impress us as well. Barolo: Colla Paolo (last '80), including La Serra 0; Gagliardo Gianni La Serra + , Mora 0; Ribezzo * − ; Barbaresco: Colla Paolo (last '81), including Valgrande 0; Gagliardo Gianni 0

Gagliasso Michele & Figli (*La Morra*, borgata *Torriglione*). Mario Gagliasso owns a piece of the Torriglione vineyard. He produces Barolo and Dolcetto d'Alba.

Gaja di Angelo Gaja (*Barbaresco*), 1859. The Gaja family moved from Spain in the seventeenth century. In the mid-nineteenth century they began producing wine in the Piemonte. Giovanni Gaja established the winery. Angelo, the fourth generation, joined the family firm in 1961.

This firm has been bottling their wines since the early 1900s. Through the 1961 vintage, they included a Barolo among their production. Since 1964 they have been an *azienda agricola*, making wines only from their own grapes.

Gaja is the largest private owner of vineyards in the Barbaresco zone, with 153 acres (62 hectares) of vines in Barbaresco, Treiso, and Alba, including nearly 75 acres (30 hectares) in Barbaresco itself. Of those vines, 73 (29.5) are planted in nebbiolo for Barbaresco. They own 14 different vineyards in Barbaresco and Treiso for their Barbaresco *normale*. These holdings include 22 acres (9 hectares) of Pajorè, all in nebbiolo, more than 25 percent is nebbiolo rosé, and 11 (4.5) of the Giacosa vineyard in Treiso. Angelo doesn't plan to do a cru bottling from Pajorè. He emphasizes that it is important to maintain a high-quality image for his regular Barbaresco. Pajorè will help maintain that quality.

Gaja's Barbaresco vineyards are planted at an altitude of between 750 and 950 feet (230 to 290 meters) above sea level. The average yield is 2.6 tons per acre (58 quintali per hectare).

Gaja grows 22 different grape varieties. Besides the local varieties, he has 16.3 acres (6.6 hectares) of chardonnay and 6.2 (2.5)

THE CRUS OF GAJA

Barbaresco Cru	Acres	Hectares	Altitude in Feet	Altitude in Meters	First Vintage	Average Number of Bottles Per Year
Costa Russi	10.1315	4.1	755	230	1978	12,000
Sorì San Lorenzo	7.9075	3.2	820	250	1967	10,000
Sorì Tildìn	9.1431	3.7	885	270	1970	10,000

Other Crus	Comune	Acres	Hectares	Altitude in Feet	Altitude in Meters	Used for
Alteni di Brassica	—	3.00	1.20	—	—	Sauvignon Blanc
Bassi	Barbaresco	3.71	1.50	855	260	Chardonnay
Darmagi	Barbaresco	6.18	2.50	990	300	Cabernet Sauvignon
Gaia & Rey	Treiso	9.00	3.64	1,380	420	Chardonnay
Rossj	Barbaresco	3.71	1.50	985	300	Chardonnay
Vignabajla	Alba	17.98	7.28	650	200	Dolcetto d'Alba
Vignarey	Alba	12.45	5.04	650	200	Barbera d'Alba
Vignaveja	Alba	4.94	2.00	700	215	Nebbiolo d'Alba

of cabernet sauvignon. He planted nearly 3 acres (1.2 hectares) of sauvignon blanc in his Alteni di Brassica vineyard in 1983. And some two to four years ago he put in experimental plantings of the Rhône varieties, mourvedre and syrah, as well as some merlot. He expects to produce wines from those grapes in two more years. None of these wines will be bottled under the Gaja label. Angelo feels, and quite strongly, that he must experiment with other grapes.

Gaja has also been experimenting with vine density. In the Barolo and Barbaresco districts, vines are generally planted at an average density of 1,200 vines per acre (3,000 per hectare). He is now planting from 1,500 to 1,800 (3,750 to 4,500) vines of nebbiolo for Barbaresco. He plans to replant one-third of Sorì Tildìn with the higher density. These vineyard experiments are not the first ones for the Gaja winery. In 1961 they experimented with pruning techniques for nebbiolo. They reduced the number of

THE GRAPE VARIETIES PLANTED BY GAJA

Variety	Acres	Hectares	Average Number of Bottles Per Year	Used for
Nebbiolo	72.8974	29.50	128,000	Barbaresco
Nebbiolo	28.6648	11.60	n/a	Barolo
Nebbiolo	4.9422	2.00	12,000	Nebbiolo d'Alba
Barbera	12.4543	5.04	9,000	Barbera d'Alba
Dolcetto	17.9896	7.28	10,000	Dolcetto d'Alba
Freisa	6.6225	2.68	60,000*	Freisa delle Langhe
Cabernet sauvignon	6.1778	2.50	12,000	Cabernet Sauvignon
Chardonnay	16.3093	6.60	25,000	Chardonnay
Sauvignon blanc	2.9653	1.20	n/a	Sauvignon Blanc
To be replanted	29.6532	12.00	n/a	n/a
Total	198.6764	80.40	256,000	

* This includes other wines.

buds to eight to ten from the more common twenty to twenty-four. They wanted to increase the concentration of fruit.

Gaja will try new rootstocks as well in order to reduce vigor. And he is also doing clonal experiments. He points out that the various subvarieties can rarely, if ever, be found in pure form. The michet, for example, is a very rare variety.

In July 1988, Gaja bought 69 acres (28 hectares) in the Marenca-Rivetti district in Serralunga d'Alba from Villadoria, a little more than half planted in nebbiolo for Barolo. He plans to plant 24.7 acres (10 hectares) of chardonnay in that vineyard. Serralunga d'Alba is the only legal area for a moscato DOC in the Barolo area. Gaja will produce a Moscato d'Asti. Like his Barbaresco vineyards, Gaja won't use the Marenca-Rivetti name. He'll come up with one of his own.

Of their annual production, which averages about 264,000 bottles, more than half is Barbaresco. Some 106,000 bottles are *normale,* plus 34,320 of the three crus. Gaja also produces nearly 85,000 bottles of Nebbiolo d'Alba, Dolcetto d'Alba, Barbera d'Alba, and Freisa, plus some 40,000 of Cabernet Sauvignon and Chardonnay, as well as the nouveau-style Nebbiolo Vinot, and since 1988, Barolo. Once his Barolo vineyards are fully utilized, Barbaresco and Barolo could account for two-thirds of his total production.

Angelo Gaja, born in 1940 and present director of this family firm, has, like many of the winemakers of the Langhe, a degree in enology from Alba (1960). And he has a masters in economics from the University of Torino. He also attended schools in Germany and France. In 1974 he went to California, where he presumably fell under the spell of the *barrique.*

Gaja has achieved signal success aging his Barbaresco in small, new oak barrels, where the wine takes on a certain subtlety and suppleness without losing the personality of the nebbiolo grape. While we are not advocates of *barrique* aging for nebbiolo wines, we must give him credit for his accomplishment. There is no question that he is an exceptional winemaker and obviously proud of his achievement and skill.

Despite the oak he wants to make an Italian Barbaresco, but not a typical Barbaresco. Gaja is obviously not interested in making typical wine. Yes, he wants his wine to let the drinker know that it is a Barbaresco, but he wants it to announce that it is a Gaja.

Angelo started working in the cellar in 1967. In 1969 he began his *barrique* experiments. He was completely responsible for the 1970 vintage and has been in charge of the winemaking at the *cantina* since the 1973 vintage. In 1976 he began employing some of these new experimental techniques. These included a shorter fermentation time, at most two weeks on the skins, and the addition of between 40 to 70 percent whole berries to the fermenting must (this is not carbonic maceration, which is whole-berry fermentation in a closed vat). This gives a more evident fruitiness to the wine which balances the tannin and oakiness imparted by the small barrels the wine is aged in. That vintage was the first to be aged in a combination of small barrels and large, old oak casks.

Gaja gives the impression of almost a naive conceitedness when speaking about his wines. He describes himself as "vain," which may sound like a slightly mistaken translation from the Italian; but no, his English is quite good, and vanity is what he is speaking of. When we asked him why he had chosen to plant cabernet sauvignon and chardonnay vines, he replied that they are noble grape varieties that produce excellent wines, and as he is a vain man he wants to work with grape varieties of that proven caliber because it makes it possible for him to produce outstanding wines.

Gaja is an admirer of the fine French wines and the distributor in Italy for the Burgundies of the Dômaine de la Rômanée-Conti, the Champagnes of Gosset, and the Alsatian wines of Léon Beyer. He is quick to point out, however, that he isn't trying to make French wines himself. In 1977 he opened an importing company, Gaja Distribuzione. Today, besides French, German, Spanish, and Australian wines, he imports Californian and Washington State wines, and wine accessories such as Screwpull and Riedl crystal.

He began vinifying Barolo in 1988. He expects to release that wine in late 1992 or 1993 and produce 2,000 cases of it initially. Eventually he will produce 5,000 cases of Barolo, perhaps even 5,500. The nebbiolo for his Barolo is harvested between October 20 and 25, those for Barbaresco are picked earlier. He makes a selection. The grapes are transported to Barbaresco. The wine is kept on the skins between twenty-eight and thirty days. After the malolactic fermentation, the wine is transferred to *barrique* for four months. After that it goes to big, used oak barrels. In total, Angelo expects that his Barolo will spend thirty months in wood.

He aims for a harmonious wine with more aroma and flavor and less tannin. To this end he picks his grapes late, when they are fully mature and richer in extract and color, feeling that it is worth the greater risk for the potentially higher quality to be gained. Of his crus, Sorì San Lorenzo is picked first, Sorì Tildìn last.

Gaja wants an elegant wine, not an opulent one; he wants his Barolo to display delicacy as well. Angelo experimented with *barriques* from 1969 to 1976 for his Barbaresco. Although Barolo is a different wine, he will transfer his experiments to it. Angelo expects that he'll need eight to ten years to get a real handle on Barolo.

In 1970, Angelo started fermenting in stainless steel in order to control the temperature. He started making tests with new *barriques* for aging the wine in 1969. He prefers barrels made from French oak, although he uses some Yugoslavian oak as well. He replaces one-third of his *barriques* with new barrels each year.

Gaja uses French oak from the Massif Central. In 1986 he started having the cut staves aged at his winery. He points out that this is the only way to ensure that the wood is seasoned long enough. He buys the oak and ages it for three years outside his cellar. Then he gives the wood to barrel-maker Gamba, located 18 miles (30 kilometers) from Barbaresco, who coppers the wood. The first *barriques* made from that oak were in 1989. Since 1990, 100 percent of his *barriques* have been made from his own wood. Gaja steams the new barrels for one hour in order to remove 50 percent of the tannin.

The '79s were his first wines made entirely in the new style. While he notes that the wines aren't as rich as the '78s, he finds them more elegant. The '81 Barbaresco spent six months in *barrique* and twelve months in large casks. The '82 was given from eight to nine months in *barrique;* the balance, for two years total in oak, was in large casks. He ages Barbaresco in a combination of new, one- and two-year-old *barriques,* one-third each.

The '85s might be, according to Angelo, his best wines up to that time because of his introduction of new technology. He implemented the changes in 1984, but that vintage wasn't very good. In 1985 he introduced fermentation changes. He lowers the temperature and increases the skin contact. The result is softer tannins. Initially he pushes up the temperature to a high level, 82.4° to 86° Fahrenheit (28° to 30° centigrade) for four to six days. At that stage the sugar has been reduced by 50 percent. Then he lowers the temperature until the fermentation finishes and the temperature is 71.6° Fahrenheit (22° centigrade). Previously he kept the wine from fifteen to twenty days on the skins; now he keeps it from twenty-seven to thirty days at a lower temperature. This avoids the hard tannins and gives softer ones instead. In all, the wine spends three to four weeks on the skins in stainless steel vats at a temperature of 78° to 85° Fahrenheit (25.5° to 29.5° centigrade). It is aged for six months in *barrique,* plus twelve to twenty more months in large oak casks.

Gaja's Barbarescos have a deceptive suppleness in their youth, picked up from the *barriques,* but they seem to have the underlying strength to age quite well, judging from the ones we've tasted thus far, and there have been quite a few.

Besides his regular Barbaresco, Gaja bottles three individual crus. These wines are not made every year, only when he feels the vintage justifies it. He didn't vinify any of the crus, for example, in 1980. In 1973 he made some Sorì Tildìn, but bottled no Sorì San Lorenzo.

Of the three single-vineyard wines, Costa Russi matures the soonest. It is the most open, with a sweeter taste and more intense aroma. Sorì Tildìn is more closed and concentrated; it is firm in texture and holds more in reserve. Sorì San Lorenzo is the hardest of all in its youth, requiring age to show its real quality. It is the slowest maturing of the crus and should be the longest lived. It is less drinkable even after eight years, and more drinkable after fifteen. Gaja thinks wine writers like Sorì Tildìn because it is ready sooner and is more open.

Sorì San Lorenzo and Sorì Tildìn are sold at the same ex-cellar price. It is the distributors that sell them at different prices. Furthermore, Gaja doesn't set the policy that to get a case of any of the crus you have to buy so many cases of the *normale.* He sells whatever the customer wants.

As for his view of some of his own wine, he is happy with the '71 Barbaresco that he helped with, and the '76, he said, "grew up very well." He produced very little '77, and that was only for the Italian market; there were, perhaps, 2,500 to 2,800 cases in total. Today he is concerned about the green, aggressive tannins of the '78. "These wines are aging very slowly, perhaps too slowly. The '78s are very powerful, and they will continue to mature very slowly, but will they really develop?" Angelo likes the '73 Sorì Tildìn and the '79 very much. The '79 is very elegant. He had a problem with the '79 corks. It was the first vintage in which he used extra-long corks. They didn't fit into the bottles very well because the bottles were the old style. The reason Gaja uses a long cork is that "to get a long cork in one piece the corkmaker has to select the best material." The '80 and '81 were from weak vintages. He didn't produce any '84 Barbaresco. And as of October 1990, although he bottled an '87 *normale,* he was unsure if he would sell the crus. Perhaps he will sell 150 to 250 cases of each cru; perhaps he won't sell any of them.

Between 1962 and 1987 the Gaja winery didn't produce a Barolo. Based on the two barrel samples that we tasted—the '88 and '89—we expect good things here. Our rating at this point is tentative. Barolo [** +]; Barbaresco: Sorì San Lorenzo ****, Sorì Tildìn ****, Costa Russi ***, and *normale* ***; Nebbiolo d'Alba ***

Galvagno Ernesto. Thus far we have tasted a single wine from Galvagno, his '82 Barolo. It was passable. Barolo +

Gastaldi Azienda Agricola (*Neive,* borgata *Albesani*). Bernerdino Gastaldi produces Sauvignon del Piemonte, Chardonnay del Piemonte, Dolcetto d'Alba, and Barbaresco. We've never met any.

Gemma (*Barbaresco*). At one time Alfredo Roagna was involved with this winery. Today it is owned jointly by Piemonte's Grand Ambassador of Wine, Giacomo Bologna, and Silvano Piacentini of the Istituto Enologica Italiano of Verona. Although these wines have been good thus far, they haven't come up to our expectations. Considering the source, however, we look forward to better wines in the future. Gemma sometimes bottles the Barbaresco cru Gallina. We haven't tasted the Barbaresco since the '77. As for the Barolo, there has been a gap in our experience. After the '79, we didn't taste it again until the very good '85. Barolo ** −; Barbaresco [*]

Germano Angelo & Figli di Germano G. A. (*Annunziata di La Morra*), 1908. Germano owns 11.3 acres (4.57 hectares/12 *giornate*) of vines, including 7.1 (2.9/7.5) of Dardi in the Bussia zone of Monforte d'Alba, 1.4 (0.6/1.5) of Rué in Barolo, and 1.9 (0.7/2) of Gattera dell'Annunziata plus 0.9 (0.4/1) near the *cantina.* Germano produces from 2,750 to 3,330 cases of wine from his own grapes. He also buys wine from Dogliani and Monforte d'Alba for a total production of between 159,600 and 200,000 cases a year; this includes 20,000 of Barolo, 6,665 Nebbiolo delle Langhe, 17,300 Barbera d'Alba, 13,300 Dolcetto d'Alba, some Grignolino, and a tiny amount of Freisa, as well as from 3,325 to 6,660 cases of Barbaresco. Our experience is somewhat limited here. We tasted the '58 and '81 in bottle, and the '82, '85, and '86 from cask. Based on those wines, Barolo * +

Gherzi. We haven't tasted these wines in some time, but those we have were lacking in structure and character. Barolo [0]; Barbaresco [0]

Ghisolfi Attilio (*Monforte d'Alba*). This grower owns a piece of the Visette vineyard in Monforte. They produce a Barolo.

Giacosa Bruno (*Neive*), 1900. Bruno Giacosa is without question one of Italy's—make that the world's—finest winemakers. A man of few words but eloquent talent, Giacosa has the ability to bring out a richness of flavor and an intensity of character in his wines, to produce wines of meditation. The man is an artist. Besides a profound Barolo and a sublime Barbaresco, he produces superb Barbera, Dolcetto, and Nebbiolo d'Alba, also impressive Arneis and Grignolino d'Asti. And if that isn't enough, his Champagne-method *spumante* just might be Italy's finest. It certainly is as good as many, and better than more than a few, French Champagnes. There are few winemakers able to produce wines as finely honed or as consistent.

His annual production of approximately 400,000 bottles includes 35,000 each of Barolo and Barbaresco. *Poco ma buono* ("little but good") could be his motto. Giacosa has used the phrase fre-

THE CRUS OF BRUNO GIACOSA

Cru	First Vintage	Average Number of Bottles Per Year	Used for
Altavilla	n/a	10,000	Barbera d'Alba
Basarin	n/a	15,000	Dolcetto d'Alba
Collina Rionda	1967	6,000	Barolo
Falletto	1982	15,000	Barolo
Gallina	1974	13,000	Barbaresco
Le Rocche	1971	6,500	Barolo
Plinet	n/a	15,000	Dolcetto d'Alba
Rio Sordo	1985	—	Barbaresco
Santo Stefano	n/a	14,000	Barbaresco
Valmaggiore	n/a	20,000	Nebbiolo d'Alba
Villero	1978	14,000	Barolo
Vineria	n/a	7,000	Dolcetto d'Alba

quently in speaking of his wines with us; it's typical of his tendency toward understatement. He also produces 30,000 bottles of Barbera d'Alba, 90,000 Dolcetto d'Alba, 60,000 Grignolino d'Asti, 30,000 Nebbiolo d'Alba, plus 85,000 Arneis and 25,000 Metodo Champenois Brut Spumante.

Giacosa has been producing an Arneis from 1972 or 1973. It is, as he points out, a very difficult wine to make. He found the arneis vines when he was looking for nebbiolo grapes to make a Nebbiolo d'Alba. He tasted an Arneis from a *contradini*. Although it was poorly made it had a lot of potential. The oldest vines producing these arneis grapes were over sixty years old.

In making his *spumante,* Giacosa selects the grapes, using only the best bunches. He gives them the lightest possible pressing and ferments with wild yeast. His first *spumante* was the '83. That wine was first rate. And he didn't make a test production first.

Giacosa is not an enologist—something that comes as a surprise to most people. He learned by working with his father and grandfather, and became fascinated by what could be created from the grape. Giacosa relates that he fell in love with wine when he was very young and went on to develop a passion for it. He became fascinated by the idea of what could happen with the grape. Bruno drinks wines with his meals. At lunch it's always Dolcetto. He notes that a good palate is necessary to good winemaking.

The Giacosa *cantina* was founded by Carlo Giacosa, Bruno's grandfather. It was Bruno's father, Mario, who began selling the wine in bottle after the war. Although Carlo Giacosa bottled some wine, most was sold *sfuso.*

Bruno feels that wines were better in the past, when there was less sophistication and treatment made to both grapes and wine, less handling. And the yields were smaller as well. In the old days, he points out, things were done more simply and with more care. They used sulfur, but not much else.

As for the best vintages he has made, first is the '61 then '64, '67, '71, '74, '78, '79, '82, '85, and the '58 and '70. As for the best wine he has made? Perhaps the '71 Barbaresco Santo Stefano. The first

vintage he was solely responsible for was 1971. The poor vintages have been the '60, '63, '72, '77, and '81.

Until recently Giacosa owned no vineyards; he bought all the grapes he required, selecting, as he still does, from some of the best sites in the area, and he produces wines that epitomize the vineyards. In 1982 he bought the 20.7-acre (8.4-hectare/22-*giornate*) Falletto vineyard in Serralunga. Falletto is mostly planted in nebbiolo, though there are some barbera and dolcetto but very little. Giacosa believes in the value of single-vineyard bottlings, noting that each vineyard has its own characteristics. Although he's been labeling the crus separately for only about fifteen years, he vinified and aged the wines separately previously. He told us that his grandfather, Carlo, also kept the vineyards separate in the cellar. Bruno bottles the crus only in the better vintages. These wines, under DOC, were bottled with a special label, maroon for the Riserva Speciale and white for the Riserva. On his *normale* Barolo and Barbaresco, with a tan label, he doesn't specify the vineyard name. Since the advent of DOCG here this has changed somewhat. There is no more Riserva Speciale, so the maroon label is used for the Riserva and the white label for the non-Riserva crus.

If the wine doesn't attain a certain very high standard, Bruno doesn't bottle it as a Barbaresco or Barolo; he either declassifies it, selling the wine as a simple Nebbiolo, or he doesn't bottle it at all, but sells it *sfuso.* For example, for Bruno Giacosa there was no '81, '77, or '73 Barolo or Barbaresco; all were sold *sfuso.*

Giacosa observes the Piemontese custom of "'*n fund 'd buta,*" pouring for important guests the end of a previously opened bottle. He feels that his Barbaresco needs at least a few hours of air to open up and show itself. When we had lunch with him in November 1984 and he served us from the half-down bottle of '78 Santo Stefano opened more than two weeks earlier (17 days, to be exact), we were both honored and pleased. This Barbaresco was a knockout, in fact, for us it was the single finest wine produced in that very fine vintage. We told him so. Characteristically, Bruno did not

THE CRUS AND VINEYARDS OF FRATELLI GIACOSA

Cru/Vineyard	Used for
Poderi Pira	Barolo
Grignorè*	
Rio Sordo	Barbaresco
Roccalini	
Roncaglie	
Vedetta*	
Ca' Lunga*	Pinot delle Langhe
Pradonne*	
San Rocco Senodelvio	Dolcetto d'Alba
Bussia	Barbera d'Alba
Serra del Bricco di Neive*	
Vedetta*	

* We don't know if they bottle this vineyard separately.

smile at the compliment. He did acknowledge it, however, in his way; he poured us a generous refill.

Besides the crus, he has from time to time bottled a few others. Until recently he also produced a Barbaresco San Cristoforo di Neive, and a few years ago made a Barbaresco Asili and a Montefico and more recently a Rio Sordo. And from the Barolo zone, in 1979 Giacosa made a Bussia.

Although a few other producers make a Barolo on the same lofty level as Bruno Giacosa, no one produces a Barbaresco the equal of his outstanding Santo Stefano. It is, for us, simply the single finest example of Barbaresco today. The '85 Santo Stefano Riserva, like the '82 and '78, was, without question, the Barbaresco of the vintage. Barolo ****+; Barbaresco ****+; Nebbiolo ***

Giacosa Carlo. See **Giacosa Bruno.**

Giacosa Donato di Carlo Giacosa (*Barbaresco*), *1967.* Carlo Giacosa owns 9.6 acres (3.9 hectares) of vines, including 5.3 acres (2.2 hectares) of nebbiolo in the hills of Barbaresco. He produces some 24,000 bottles of wine a year. Nebbiolo wines, including Barbaresco, account for 15,000 of those bottles. His Silvarosa, made from nebbiolo grapes, is a fresh, clean, fruity rosé. He also produces Barbera and Dolcetto d'Alba and Nebbiolo delle Langhe. Since 1986 he has bottled the two crus of Asili and Surì Secondine separately. Barbaresco **

Giacosa F.lli di Valerio & Silverio (*Neive*), *1895.* The Giacosa brothers own no vineyards; they buy all the grapes they require to produce more than 300,000 bottles of wine a year. This includes 70,000 bottles of Barolo, 35,000 Barbaresco, 40,000 each Barbera and Dolcetto d'Alba, 30,000 Maria Giona, a *barrique*-aged, Barbera d'Alba, 10,000 Nebbiolo d'Alba, 14,000 each Roero Arneis and Gavi, 13,000 Pinot delle Langhe, and 7,000 Freisa delle Langhe.

We have found the F.lli Giacosa wines reliable and very good. They are in the fuller, more tannic style, requiring age to round out and soften. They are correct although sometimes they can be a little coarse. Barolo **−, Pira **; Barbaresco *

Giacosa Romualdo. This Giacosa bottles a Barbaresco cru from his part of the Canova vineyard.

Gianolio Tomaso (*Fossano*). This winery produces 37,300 bottles of wine a year. This includes 5,333 bottles of Barolo, 2,667 Barbaresco, 8,000 Barbera d'Alba, and 21,300 Dolcetto d'Alba. Thus far our experience with Gianolio's wine has been with the '85 Barolo. Based on that wine, Barolo * −

Giordano Giovanni (*Barbaresco*). Giordano owns vines in the Cavana vineyard in Barbaresco; he does a cru bottling from there. To date we have tasted one wine from here, the '80 Barbaresco. Barbaresco [*]

Giordano Luigi (*Barbaresco*). Giordano owns a vineyard in the Secondine district.

Giovannini-Moresco Enrico (*Trieso d'Alba*), *1967.* Moresco's Podere del Pajorè was, without question, one of the most outstanding wines of Barbaresco, and consistently so. It was a full-bodied, richly flavored wine of immense proportions, a fuller, more assertive style of Barbaresco. One of the major reasons for its bigness and intensity is that Moresco believed in harvesting late, waiting until the grapes were totally ripe, despite the obvious hazards, and also in limiting the size of his yields by severe pruning.

His 28.5-acre (11.5-hectare) vineyard produced a yearly average of only 20,000 bottles, which works out to 139.40 gallons per acre (13.04 hectoliters per hectare), or 704 bottles per acre (1,739 per hectare).

The Podere del Pajorè vineyard is, we were told, planted entirely in nebbiolo, the rosé subvariety. That's the one that by reputation produces the lighter nebbiolo wines, if you can believe it. More recently, Angelo Gaja told us that Pajorè contained a little over 25 percent nebbiolo rosé.

Moresco produced his first Barbaresco in 1967, his second from the 1971 vintage (12,500 bottles); these were followed by the '74 (25,000 bottles), '78 (3,500), '79 (3,600), and '80 (1,200). His '71 was, for us, the single finest wine of the vintage, and his '79 was even better. Only the '78, while a very good Barbaresco, did not achieve the heights we expected from it.

From 1979 until Moresco sold 95 percent of his vineyard, his wine was made according to his instructions by Angelo Gaja at Gaja's *cantina*. Angelo Gaja became involved with Giovannini in February 1979. Gaja did all of the vineyard work, picking the grapes for the '79 and each succeeding vintage. At first Gaja rented the vineyard, or part of it at least, from Moresco. He put his share of the grapes in his regular Barbaresco. Later in 1979 he bought 50 percent of Pajorè and 45 percent more in 1985. Moresco owns the remaining 5 percent. The "C" referred to on the label as Podere del Pajorè di Enrico Giovannini-Moresco & C. was Angelo. The '82 was the last one bottled by Angelo. Someone else has bottled the 5 percent of the wine that Moresco keeps since then. As far as we know this splendid Barbaresco is still being made, albeit in minuscule quantities. We haven't seen it in quite some time. In fact, the last Moresco Barbaresco that we tasted was the '80. Barbaresco ****

Giri Guido, Contea di Castiglione (*Alba*), *1969.* Giri owns no vineyards; he buys all the grapes he requires. We have found his wines reliable if unexciting, though admittedly we haven't tasted them in some time. The last wine that we tasted from Giri was the '70 Barolo. Barolo [*]; Barbaresco [*]

Giudice Sergio & Figlio (*Serralunga d'Alba*). We tasted Giudice's '80 Barolo, and that is the only wine that we tasted. Barolo [0]

Glicine. See *Cantina del Glicine di Adriana Marzi & Roberto Bruno.*

Granduca. See *Chiarlo Michele.*

Grasso Elio Azienda Agricola (*Monforte d'Alba*), *1919.* The estate and the original Grasso winery date from 1919, but Elio Grasso, the present proprietor, has been bottling the wines only since 1978. His father sold the wines *sfuso.* All of Grasso's wines—Dolcetto, Barbera, and Gavarini Nebbiolo delle Langhe—are made from his own grapes. He has 15.6 acres (6.3 hectares) of vines, 10.2 (4.1) in nebbiolo. Over 50 percent of his annual production of 4,210 cases is Barolo (2,600).

THE CRUS AND VINEYARDS OF ELIO GRASSO

Gavarini	Gavarini Poggio Chinera
Gavarini-Chinera	Gavarini-Rüncot
Gavarini dei Grassi	Ginestra-Case Matè

Since 1987 Grasso has used temperature-controlled stainless steel fermenting tanks. Although he uses the services of consulting enologist Piero Ballario, Elio Grasso makes the wine.

To ensure top quality, Grasso selects the bunches carefully; any that do not meet his standards are made into an ordinary wine to be sold *sfuso.* We find his wines, especially the Barolos, to be of consistently high quality—elegant wines in a lighter, softer, more gentle style that reflects both the nature of the man who makes the wine and his wife, Marina. Considering the many splendid bottles of Grasso's Barolos that we have enjoyed, we must admit that none have given us as much pleasure as those that accompanied a fine meal prepared by Marina, who is an excellent cook. Barolo ***

Grasso Ernesto & Figlio (*Treiso d'Alba*). Ernesto Grasso owns the Cascina Vallegranda Sotto. He bottled a Barbaresco from there. In 1987 he produced 1,220 bottles. That wine was unimpressive. Barbaresco [0]

Grasso F.lli di Emilio Grasso. Emilio Grasso produces a Barbaresco from the Valgrande cru in Treiso. The only F.lli Grasso wine that we tasted was their good '85 Valgrande. Barbaresco * +

Grasso Silvio, Cascina Luciani (*Annunziata di La Morra*). Silvio Grasso owns the 23.5-acre (9.5 hectare/25-*giornate*) Cascina Luciani. Some 80 percent of his vines are in Annunziata, the rest, he told us, in the Bricco vineyard of Castiglione Falletto. He also reported having nebbiolo vines in the Gallinotto vineyard. Perhaps Gallinotto is part of Bricco. From his vines he produces 33,300 bottles of Barolo, 10,665 of Dolcetto, and 4,000 of Barbera, plus some Nebbiolo delle Langhe and a white wine from a nebbiolo-barbera blend. The small *cantina* is clean and orderly.

Grasso has 1.47 acres (0.6 hectare) of nebbiolo in the Gallinotto or Galinot vineyard, and 1.55 (0.63) in Ciabot di Preve. He also has about 2.5 acres (1 hectare) of barbera in the Fontanile vineyard. Since 1982 he has produced a Barolo from Vigna Galinot and

since 1984, one from Ciabot di Preve. We have also tasted a Barolo labeled as Cascina Luciani—'85 and '86—and another one labeled Bricco Luciani—'86. We understand that the 6.2-acre (2.5-hectare) nebbiolo plot in Bricco Luciani is used to produce this latter Barolo. Barolo * +

Grazziolo (*Canelli*), *1887.* This firm produces the full gamut of Piemontese wines, including *spumanti,* vermouth, and of course Barolo and Barbaresco. Those we've tasted have been rather unimpressive, though we must admit that it's been a while. Barolo [0]; Barbaresco [0]

Grimaldi. This Grimaldi might actually be the same as Grimaldi & C. or Giovanni Grimaldi & C. Whichever, our experience with these wines is limited to three Barolos—an '80, '82, and '82 Riserva—and one Barbaresco—the '83. Barbaresco 0; Barolo 0

Grimaldi & C. (*Diano d'Alba,* frazione *Valle Talloria,* località *Groppone*), *c. 1950.* This *azienda vinicola,* owned by Luigino and Marina Grimaldi, consists of 54 acres (22 hectares) of vines which supply them with 80 percent of their annual production of 325,000 bottles of wine. Their Groppone cru, used for Dolcetto di Diano d'Alba, covers 5.5 acres (2.2 hectares). They produce 29,300 bottles of Barolo, 10,665 each of Barbaresco and Nebbiolo d'Alba, 116,000 of three different Dolcettos, 95,000 of two Barberas, 13,300 each of Gavi and Grignolino d'Asti, 6,665 of Freisa, 10,665 of Moscato del Piemonte, and 20,000 of Cavour Rosé.

Grimaldi Cav. Carlo e Mario, Azienda Agricola Groppone. We're unsure if this is the same as Grimaldi & C., who own vines in the Groppone vineyard. We believe that they are the same. In 1978, Grimaldi produced 4,500 bottles of Barolo. We found it, as well as the '71, not up to the vintage. This Barolo is overly simple, and lacking in both character and interest. The '86 Barbaresco that we tasted wasn't much better. Barolo [0]; Barbaresco +

Grimaldi Giovanni & C. (*Grinzane Cavour*), *1958.* Giovanni Grimaldi owns some 15 acres (6 hectares) of vines. These vines supply him with 50 percent of the grapes he needs. He produces a number of Albeisa wines including, besides 3,333 bottles of Barbaresco and 5,333 of Barolo, 36,665 of Barbera d'Alba, 24,665 of Dolcetto d'Alba, and 6,667 each of Grignolino del Piemonte and Nebbiolo d'Alba. Grimaldi bottles a Dolcetto d'Alba from Vigna S. Martino and a Barbera d'Alba from Vigna Valdisera. And like too many others in the Langhe, he also produces a Chardonnay. We tasted one Barolo and one Barbaresco, both from the splendid '85 vintage. Barolo *; Barbaresco *

Guasti Clemente & Figli (*Nizza Monferrato*). It had been many years since we saw any wines from Guasti. Then, in November 1990, we met up with their '86, from barrel. It was unimpressive. Barolo [0]

Il Vecchio Tralcio di Carlo Deltetto (*Canale*), *1970.* Carlo Deltetto makes Barolo and Barbaresco as well as Arneis, Gavi, and Favorita, and some interesting *spumanti.* In our opinion, the *spumanti* and the white wines are much more interesting than the Barolo and Barbaresco. They own 2.5 acres (1 hectare) in Roero which provides them with 10 percent of their grapes. Deltetto does a Barbaresco cru from Moccagatta. Our experience is limited to the

'80 Barolo and Barbaresco. We don't know if Deltetto still makes these wines. Barolo [0]; Barbaresco [0]

Kiola. The last Kiola that we tasted was the poor '71 Barolo. They are owned by ***Batasiolo***. Barolo 0; Barbaresco 0

La Brenta d'Oro. See ***Cantine d'Invecchiamento.***

La Ca' Növa di Rocca F.lli Pietro, Giulio e Franco (*Barbaresco*). The Rocca brothers produce two wines—4,000 bottles of Dolcetto d'Alba and more than 13,000 of Barbaresco—from their Cascina Ca' Növa holdings.

"La Ca' Növa" Azienda Agricola, Dario Rocca (*Neive*). This producer owns vines in the Ca' Növa part of the Cotto vineyard district in Neive. Our experience is limited to the '81 and two '87 Barbarescos, the regular and the cru Bric Mentina. Barbaresco * +

"La Corte" Azienda Agricola di Monticelli-Olivero (*La Morra, frazione Rivalta Ascheri Soprana*). Monticelli-Oliviero of "La Corte" has 25 acres (10 hectares) of land, 15 (6) in Le Caudane, reportedly the best position of Rivalta. This includes 3.8 acres (1.5 hectares) of nebbiolo. His annual production averages some 33,300 bottles of *vino,* including 10,665 to 12,000 of Barolo, which he sells as Le Caudane di La Morra. Monticelli-Oliviero produced his first Barolo from the 1970 vintage. He also produces Barbera, Dolcetto, and a *bianco* made 100 percent from his 1.4 acres (0.6 hectare) of favorita grapes. We found these wines poorly made when we visited this *cantina* in April 1986. We have found the "La Corte" Barolos to be rather lacking. Those tasted from cask showed more quality than the ones in bottle. Barolo +

La Spinona Azienda Agricola di Pietro Berutti & Figlio (*Barbaresco, località Fassetto*), *1963.* The Beruttis own 54 acres (22 hectares) of vines from which they produce more than 160,000 bottles of wine a year, including 53,000 of Barbaresco. Their other wines are Dolcetto d'Alba (20,000), Barbera d'Alba (16,000), Freisa delle Langhe (16,000), Nebbiolo delle Langhe (16,000), Chardonnay delle Langhe (33,000), and Grignolino delle Langhe (6,665).

Although Pietro Berutti says he personally prefers the older style, like many others in the Langhe he is following the dictates of the market in producing a faster-maturing, more accessible style of Barbaresco. It is however, a well-balanced wine with good fruit and some elegance. But it was better in the past. Barbaresco ** —

"Le Colline" Azienda Agricola (*Neviglie*), *1951.* This traditional firm owns Cascina Bordino in Langa, a 12.4-acre (5-hectare) vineyard in Treiso. From these holdings they produce an excellent Barbaresco as well as a Moscato d'Asti and Dolcetto d'Alba. They also produce "Monsecco" Gattinara and a Ghemme. Their '78, '79, and '82 Barbarescos were all excellent. Barbaresco ***

Le Due Torri. The three Barolos that we tasted from Le Due Torri were wanting, and this included the '78 and '82, two excellent vintages. Barolo 0

Lodali Giovanni & Figlio (*Treiso d'Alba*). The only wine we've tasted from this producer was his '61 Barolo. It wasn't really a bad wine, but it was quite atypical. It reminded us of a southern wine in both aroma and character. Barolo [*]

Manzone Giovanni (*Monforte d'Alba, frazione Castelletto*). Giovanni Manzone produces approximately 13,300 bottles of wines annually; 20 percent is Barbera d'Alba, 30 percent Dolcetto d'Alba, and 50 percent a Barolo from Vigna Gramolere Ciabot del Preive. Reportedly he also owns a piece of the Mosconi vineyard as well as vines in the Perno and Castelletto districts. Besides Barolo he makes a Dolcetto d'Alba. Thus far our experience is limited to the '85 Gramolere Ciabot del Preve Barolo. Barolo **

Manzone Stefano, Azienda Agricola "Ciabot del Preve" (*Monforte d'Alba*). Stefano Manzone cultivates vines in the Castelletto vineyard district. He produces a decent Barolo from the vines he ownes in the part called Ciabot del Preve. Admittedly our experience is limited. We tasted one wine, the '79 "Ciabot del Preve,"

THE CRUS AND VINEYARDS OF LA SPINONA

Cru/Vineyard	Acres	Hectares	Used for
La Spinona Bricco Faset	24.7	10	Barbaresco
Cars			Dolcetto d'Alba,
			Barbera d'Alba,
			Nebbiolo delle Langhe,
			Freisa delle Langhe
Giorgio			Chardonnay delle Langhe
La Ghiga Bric del Cucu	17.3	7	Barbaresco
Qualin			Dolcetto d'Alba,
			Barbera d'Alba,
			Freisa delle Langhe
L'Albina*	12.3	5	Barbaresco

* Barbaresco bottled as Podere Albina

Castelletto Barolo. There could be a connection with Giovanni Manzone. Barolo [*]

Marcarini di Anna Marcarini & Elvio Cogno (*La Morra*), 1958. Elvio Cogno produces the wine, and Anna Marcarini Bava owns and manages the vineyards. Cogno produces some 55,000 bottles of wine annually from Podere Marcarini's 29 acres (11.7 hectares) of vineyards. About 18.4 acres (7.45 hectares) are planted in nebbiolo for Barolo, which yields about 45,000 bottles; there are also 10.5 (4.26) in dolcetto. The nebbiolo plantings include 9 acres (3.7 hectares) of Brunate in La Morra, nearly 2 acres (0.8 hectare) of Brunate-Canon in Barolo, and 7.56 acres (3.06 hectares) of La Serra in La Morra. The dolcetto vines include 9.8 acres (4 hectares) in the Fontanazza Soprana zone. The balance of the dolcetto—0.6741 acre (0.2728 hectare)—is planted in the pre-phylloxera Boschi di Berri vineyard that they lease. This vineyard was planted in dolcetto vines more than a hundred years ago.

A Barolo Brunate-Canon has been bottled separately since 1987. Of the four wines produced from this subsection thus far, Cogno has vinified an annual average of 5,100 bottles of Barolo.

Cogno also produces "Lasarin" Nebbiolo delle Langhe from mosty young nebbiolo vines in La Serra, although some from Brunate are also used. In 1989 he made 10,000 bottles and in 1990 even less. Cogno also produces Barbera, Freisa, and until 1981, Tinello, a proprietary blend made from 80 percent barbera and 20 percent nebbiolo and dolcetto. And under the Elvio Cogno label he bottles a Grignolino del Piemonte, Nebbiolo d'Alba, Freisa, and Barbera.

Cogno, one of the region's truly fine winemakers, produces outstanding wines. His Barolos epitomize balance, elegance, and finesse; they are consistently among the best produced.

In the old and dimly lit, but clean and tidy, aging cellar on one of our many visits, Cogno cheerfully drew samples from various oaken casks of La Serra and Brunate for us to taste and to note the differences between the two crus. They are from different vineyards in La Morra, and each has its own character. Cogno finds that the La Serra starts off fruitier, is more accessible, and shows more of the La Morra perfume than the Brunate, which is more austere and closed when young; but as they develop, their personalities change, and the Brunate, which comes into its own later, smooths out to a softer, rounder, and more velvety wine. Would we like to see for ourselves without any influence? he asks with a twinkle in his eye. Fools rush in. . . . He offers the first glass blind—more closed, must be the Brunate. The second glass is more open, La Serra surely. Wrong, it's just the opposite! We taste again—same. He laughs and shrugs. Wines go through phases, but could it be he mixed them up? Shall we try again? We could spend the whole morning. . . . Barolo **** +

Marchese di Gresy. See *Tenuta Cisa Asinari dei Marchesi di Gresy.*

Marchese Maurizio Fracassi Ratti Mentone (*Cherasco*), 1880. Fracassi owns 15 acres (6 hectares) of vineyards, including 2.8 acres (1.2 hectares) of nebbiolo vines in La Morra. They produce 60,000 bottles of wine annually, all from their own grapes. Of this, a mere 7,000 bottles is Barolo. This Barolo, perhaps Barola, is in a gentle, elegant style, one might even call it a feminine style, which

evidently reflects the taste of the winemaker, the Marchesa. We have tasted only the very good '79. Barolo **

Marchesi di Barolo Già Opera Pia Barolo, Antichi Poderi dei (*Barolo*), 1864. Paolo Abbona, Ernesto Abbona, and Piero Scarzello own the Marchesi di Barolo winery and its vineyards. Marchesi di Barolo owns 86 acres (35 hectares) of vineyards, including some of the best sites in Barolo, a fact unfortunately not always evident in their wines. These vineyards provide less than 20 percent of their grapes, the rest are purchased. The Marchesi produces, on average, more than 1 million bottles of wine annually, 466,000 are Barolo and 46,600 Barbaresco. The rest are the standard Albeisa wines plus a Gavi and Pinot Grigio Oltrepò Pavese. And recently they introduced a new line of wines—the Le Lune series—which includes a Barolo.

At one time the name of Marchesi di Barolo was highly respected; the first Barolo as we know it today was produced in their cellars. Though the label still carries their name, the present winery has been turning out a wide range of wines that for the most part lacked personality. Their single-vineyard Barolos can provide an interesting glass, but are over-priced for their quality. And, they bottle them, seemingly indiscriminately. The 1980s that they bottled from their crus were kind of dull and ordinary. If they cared about quality they wouldn't have put such mediocre Barolos in bottle. As for their standard Barolo and Barbaresco, there are better Nebbiolo d'Alba wines around for a fraction of the price. The wines do offer one thing: consistency. They are, however, consistently ordinary. From time to time they also produce a Barolo Riserva della Casa and della Castellana. Judging by the Barbolos of 1988 and 1989 that we tasted from cask in November 1990, things appear to be changing and, we are happy to report, for the better.

Their Barolo crus can be quite good, rarely more than that. If things continue along the line of the cask samples of the '88 and '89 Barolo crus that we tasted here, this is certainly a winery worth watching. Barolo: Brunate ** −, Cannubi **, Costa di Rose **, Valletta **, *normale* * −; Barbaresco 0

Marchesi Spinola (*Acqui Terme*), 1782. These merchants at one time offered a decent Barolo and Barbaresco under their own label. We don't know if they still do; we haven't seen any in some time. Barolo [*]; Barbaresco [*]

Marengo Mario (*La Morra*). Mario Marengo produces Barolo, Barbera d'Alba, Dolcetto d'Alba, and Nebbiolo. The only wines that we tasted from Marengo were his '83, '87, '88, and '89 Barolos from this Brunate vineyard. The last three wines were tasted from barrel. Barolo * +

Marino Mauro. Mauro Marino produces a Barolo from his Vigna Conca in the Annunziata section of La Morra.

Martinenga. See *Tenuta Cisa Asinari dei Marchesi di Gresy.*

Mascarello Cantina di Bartolo Mascarello (*Barolo*), 1918. Bartolo Mascarello owns 13.7 acres (5.5 hectares) of vines from which he produces between 18,000 and 20,000 bottles a year of what is, in our opinion, the single finest Barolo made. He also produces from 7,000 to 8,000 bottles of a top notch Dolcetto. And since 1985, he has produced 4,000 bottles of a very good Freisa. In

THE CRUS AND VINEYARDS OF MARCHESI DI BAROLO

Barolo Cru/Vineyard	Acres	Hectares	First Vintage	Number of Bottles in 1985
Boschetti[a]	8.4265	3.4100	1989	—
Brunate[b]	4.1762	1.6900	1978	6,169
Cannubi	18.1557	7.3472	1975	25,982
Cannubi-Muscatel[c, d]	8.6464	3.4990	—	13,370
Castellero[d, e]	1.0379	0.4200	—	—
Costa di Rose	7.1415	2.8900	1982	6,958
Le Coste[d, f]	1.4827	0.6000	—	—
Paiagallo[g]	5.5036	2.2272	1975	—
Sarmassa[c, d]	4.7932	1.9397	1976	—
Valletta	9.5864	3.8794	1973	13,441

NOTES: [a] Dolcetto d'Alba
[b] They own 4.9 acres (2 hectares); half was replanted in 1989, and they have another 1.7 (0.69) under contract.
[c] They last produced a Barolo from this cru in 1982. They are replanting the vineyard with cabernet sauvignon, barbera, and nebbiolo.
[d] This vineyard is being replanted.
[e] They produced a Barolo cru in 1979.
[f] They last produced a Dolcetto d'Alba from here in 1985.
[g] Barbera d'Alba

certain vintages Mascarello declassifies all or part of his Barolo, selling it as Nebbiolo delle Langhe.

When we asked Bartolo about vinifying his vineyards separately and doing a cru bottling, he replied with a broad smile that he has one cru: "Bartolo Mascarello"! We doubt if anyone would disagree that Bartolo Mascarello is a *premier grand cru*.

Actually, Bartolo's name didn't, appear on his label, until recently, a situation that concerned us, as we felt it might lead to some confusion with the other Mascarello wines, one that in particular does not begin to approach his in quality. When we asked him about this, he seemed unconcerned. He uses the same label that his father did. The label bears his crest. His customers would remember it. We had to admit he had a point—these are memorable wines. There are no doubt wine lovers searching for that Mascarello label with that crest, perhaps not knowing the producer's name but recognizing his style. (After a scandal broke that concerned another Mascarello, Bartolo started putting his name on the label.)

Bartolo's wines are the epitome of balance, harmony, style, elegance, distinction, and character. Like his father's wines before

THE VINEYARDS OF BARTOLO MASCARELLO

Vineyard	Variety	Acres	Hectares	Giornate
Bussia	Dolcetto[a]	1.8835	0.7622	2.0
Cannubi	Nebbiolo	2.8252	1.1433	3.0
Giardino[b, c]	Freisa	1.4127	0.5717	1.5
Ruè	Nebbiolo and dolcetto	1.8835	0.7622	2.0
San Lorenzo	Nebbiolo	0.9417	0.3811	1.0
Torriglione[d]	Nebbiolo	4.7087	1.9055	5.0
Total		13.6553	5.5260	14.5

NOTES: [a] Mascarello's Dolcetto has always been from Bussia, and since 1985 he has acknowledged that fact on the label. The section of Bussia in the *comune* of Barolo is known as Monrobiolo.
[b] This vineyard is in Monforte d'Alba.
[c] Giardino is actually owned by Alessandro Fantino.
[d] Rocche di Torriglione in Annunziata district of La Morra.

them, every bottle is a wine of meditation, best when shared with good friends who appreciate great wines; no food is necessary as an accompaniment—the wines are food for thought in themselves. The last time we enjoyed his splendid '55 it was served with a plate of fine local cheeses, offered by the mutual friends in whose house we were guests, but nobody paid any attention to the cheese once Bartolo had filled the glasses. The wine was fittingly drunk in an elegantly simple manner, accompanied by the warmth of his smile and our murmured comments of pleasure and appreciation.

The Mascarello Freisa Nebbiolata is refermented in bottle, the Freisa wine is poured over the nebbiolo lees, *passaggio*, which causes a second fermentation to occur, as with the *ripasso* method used in the Veronese zone for special Valpolicella or *vino da tavola*. Bartolo recommends drinking his Freisa with *bagna cauda* and *frittata*, as well as with cheese. *Bagna cauda*, he poitns out, goes well with a young, fresh Dolcetto or Barbera of the latest vintage in the autumn, and Freisa also goes well. As for the ability of these wines to age, Bartolo said that when Dolcetto and Freisa are well made they can take some age. His '85 Dolcetto spent one year in wood.

Freisa is a local grape that had been dying out until Aldo Conterno started to bring it back. Bartolo also mentioned that Vietti was next with a good one, and now a number of producers are making a Freisa. (Among the better ones are Giacomo Conterno, Angelo Gaja, Elvio Cogno, Giuseppe Rinaldi, and Scarpa.) This variety is, compared to the other varieties grown here, a relatively shy bearer. If barbera and dolcetto yield 4.9 tons per acre (110 quintali per hectare), then freisa will give 3.1 (70). As a general rule, nebbiolo yields 2,543 bottles per acre (7,085 per hectare/2,700 per *giornata*), and dolcetto from 2,543 to 3,186 (7,065 to 7,872/2,700 to 3,000). (These numbers are calculated on the basis of 2.2 pounds [1 kilogram] of grapes producing one bottle of wine, more or less.)

Alessandro Fantino, the young enologist who works with Bartolo, told us that he learned more working with Bartolo in a few months than he did during the entire time he spent at the enological school in Alba from which he graduated. And this is the way it has to be: making great wine cannot be taught in the classroom, but can only be learned from those who produce it.

Bartolo Mascarello's winemaking philosophy begins with the rule that the first thing is to make a wine without defects. Volatile acidity, a not uncommon problem in this area, is for Bartolo "public enemy number one," and as he said, it is the winemaker's job "to kill him." This is a simplification of a profound winemaking technique. But Mascarello is an uncomplicated man. He does his work to the best of his considerable ability, laughs easily, and enjoys the simple pleasures, such as the company of friends around a simply marvelous bottle of wine.

Noted Italian wine writer Luigi Veronelli describes Bartolo as ". . . the last of a line of tough men."[36] By this he means self-reliant and fiercely independent. He does things his own way with no concession to change. And for those fortunate enough to taste his Barolo, they'll understand that there is no need to change. For Bartolo Mascarello's Barolo is simply the finest produced today. Barolo ****+

Mascarello Giacomo & Figli (*La Morra*). This Mascarello owns part of the Torriglione vineyard. He produces Barolo, Barbera and Dolcetto d'Alba. We don't know if there is a connection with Alberto Mascarello.

Mascarello Giacomo di Alberto Mascarello. We tasted one wine here, a good '83 Barolo. Barolo *

Mascarello Giuseppe & Figlio di Mauro Mascarello & C. (*Castiglione Falletto and Monchiero*), *1881*. Giuseppe Mascarello bought a piece of the Pian della Polvere vineyard in 1881. In 1904 his son Maurizio bought land in Castiglione Falletto near Monprivato. In 1919, Maurizio purchased an old mansion in Monchiero and established a winery in that town. Maurizio's son Giuseppe took over in 1930, and Giuseppe's son Mauro in 1967.[37] It was Mauro who began bottling the individual vineyards separately.

Today Mauro Mascarello owns about 20 acres (8 hectares) of vines. This includes 12.7 (5.15) of Monprivato, 1.4 (0.58) of Villero, 1.7 (0.67) of Bricco, 2.48 (1.004) of the Toetto vineyards in Castiglione Falletto, and 1.7 (0.68) of Santo Stefano di Perno in Monforte d'Alba. He also buys from some of the other top crus in the Barolo and Barbaresco zones. Mauro prefers to bottle the crus separately, but in years when he feels the quality doesn't justify it, he bottles the wine simply as Barolo; in lesser years he declassifies it to Nebbiolo delle Langhe. And like many fine producers in the Langhe, he has been operating this way since long before the DOCG. At various times he has produced Barolos from Bussia Soprana (from 1970), Monprivato (1970), Pugnane, and Vignola (1974), and Villero (1979), and Barbarescos from Bernardotti (1978), Marcarini (1985), and Nicolini (1982). We haven't seen the Bernardotti Barbaresco since the '78. He still produces Barolos from Monprivato and Villero and a Barbaresco from Nicolini.

Mascarello produces some 30,000 bottles of wine a year from purchased grapes and more than that from his own vines. While we don't have the very latest figures, a few years ago he told us that he produced nearly 27,000 bottles of Barolo, 6,665 of Barbaresco, and 5,300 of Nebbiolo d'Alba. He also made 16,000 each of Barbera d'Alba and Dolcetto d'Alba, and 2,665 of Grignolino Monferrato.

Mauro's wines, especially his Barolos, are well made and have a lot of character; they age quite well. He is traditional in his approach to winemaking. Perhaps our ratings are a little mean. This could be due to a lack of experience here. Barolo ***; Barbaresco ***

Massolino Giuseppe & Figli Giovanni e Renato, Azienda Agricola "Vigna Rionda" (*Serralunga d'Alba*), *1898*. Massolino own 24.7 acres (10 hectares) of vines which provide them with the grapes they require to produce more than 100,000 bottles of wine a year. Some two-thirds are Barolo including 26,000 bottles from the crus of Margheria, Parafada and Vigna Rionda. Besides the other standard Albeisa wines, they produce a Moscato d'Asti and, like more and more producers here, have plans to produce a Chardonnay from the vines that they recently planted. They expect to increase their production by 20 percent. Besides the following crus, they have also produced a Barbera d'Alba from Vigna Margheria.

We have tasted Barolos from this winery labeled as Rionda, Sorì Rionda, and Sorì Riunda. They also have produced a Margheria Barolo. These are Barolos with a forward fruitiness, produced in a soft, easy, uncomplicated style. The wines, we are happy to say,

THE CRUS AND VINEYARDS OF GIUSEPPE MASSOLINO

Cru/Vineyard	Acres	Hectares	Altitude in		Exposure	Average Number of Bottles Per Year
			Feet	Meters		
BAROLO						
Sörì Vigna Margheria	3.7	1.5	920	280	S/SW	8,665
Sörì Vigna Riunda	6.2	2.5	985	300	S	8,665
Sörì Vigna Parafada	3.7	1.5	1,015	310	S	8,665
OTHER WINES						
Barilot*	3.2	1.3	1,050	320	SW	8,000
Rosetta†	2.5	1.0	950	290	S	6,665
Total	19.3	7.8				40,660

* Dolcetto d'Alba
† Barbera d'Alba

especially the cru bottlings, have improved of late. Barolo: *normale* *, Margheria * +, Sörì Vigna Riunda **

Mauro. Our experience with the Barolo is much more extensive than it is for Barbaresco. For that wine the only one that we've tasted was the unimpressive '83. Barolo 0; Barbaresco 0

Mauro Marino. Marino Mauro's '85 Barolo Conca dell'Annunziata was good. Barolo *

Mauro Vini. See **Osvaldo Mauro.**

Minuto Mario (*Barbaresco*). There is more than one Mario Minuto in Barbaresco. This one owns vines in Cabanet and Faset. He does a cru bottling from the latter vineyard.

Mirafiore. At one time Fontanafredda produced a Barolo sold under this label. It was a decent wine, rarely more than that. This label is owned by Gancia. Today the Barolo is produced by Giorgio Grai and Vittoria Gancia. It is well balanced, as one would expect any wine with Giorgio's hand on it to be, but a little too simple for a Barolo. Barolo * +

"Moccagatta" Azienda Agricola di Mario Minuto (*Barbaresco*). This *cantina,* owned by Franco and Sergio Minuto, has some 27 acres (11 hectares) of vines. Their annual production averages 37,600 bottles of Barbaresco, 12,900 of Dolcetto d'Alba, and 6,665 of Barbera d'Alba. They also produce a Freisa and Chardonnay delle Langhe Bric Buschet. Their Dolcetto d'Alba is from their Vigneto Buschet. The Minutos, like many other producers in this area, have jumped aboard the *barrique* bandwagon. They aged a portion of their '82 Barbaresco in small barrels. Judging from the bottle we tasted in January 1985, they would have done better to treat it the same as the rest. The *barrique*-aged Barbaresco that we have tasted since—the '87 Bric Balin—confirmed our original evaluation: it would be better to age their Barbaresco in the more traditional *botte,* or casks. That wine was overoaked. Besides the

THE CRUS AND VINEYARDS OF AZIENDA AGRICOLA "MOCCAGATTA"

Cru/Vineyard	Acres	Hectares	First Vintage	Average Number of Bottles Per Year
Basarin	2.5	1.03	1982	7,000
Boschetto	11.8	4.78	—	—
Cavanna	0.9	0.38	—	—
Cole	1.2	0.47	1982	3,100
Moccagatta	5.9	2.40	—	—

obvious cru bottling from the vineyard which gave Minuto's *azienda* its name they bottle Barbarescos from Basarin, Balin, and Cole. Barbaresco *, Bric Balin 0

Molino Franco & Figli, Cascina La Rocca (*Annunziata di La Morra*, regione *Rocca*). Franco Molino owns vines in La Morra and Castiglione Falletto. They produce a Barolo, Barbera, and Dolcetto d'Alba. He labels his Barolo as Cascina La Rocca. Barolo *

Molino Guido (*Grinzane Cavour*). It's been some time since we tasted Guido Molino's Barolo, not since the '75, in fact. Perhaps they've improved.

"Monfalletto" Azienda Agricola. See **Cordero di Montezemolo.**

Morando (*Boglietto di Costiglione*). Morando produces a Barolo that is light in style with a forward fruitiness; it could use more personality, though it is certainly drinkable. He also produces a Barbaresco which we haven't tasted. Since it's been years since we've tasted it—the '76 was the most recent one—we decided to suspend our judgment. Barolo [0]

Musso Sebastiano (*Barbaresco*). Sebastiano Musso owns vines in the Pora and Rio Sordo vineyards. He produces a Chardonnay delle Langhe and a Barbaresco from the part of Rio Sordo that he calls Bricco Rio Sordo vineyard. That Barbaresco is decent, though not much more. Barbaresco +

Nada Fiorenzo (*Treiso*, località *Rombone*). Nada produced their first wine with a label in 1980. Today their nearly 10 acres (4 hectares) of vines give them sufficient fruit to produce between 15,000 and 20,000 bottles annually. This includes Dolcetto d'Alba, Nebbiolo delle Langhe, and a Barbaresco. Part of their production is *barrique*-aged. The Fiorenzo Nada Barbaresco that we tasted from the Rombone vineyard was good. Barbaresco *

Nada Giovanni (*Treiso d'Alba*). Giovanni Nada produces a Barbaresco from Cascina Rombone. This *casa vinicola* buys grapes. We don't know if they own any vineyards.

Nada Giuseppe (*Treiso d'Alba*). This Nada produces a Barbaresco from the Giacosa vineyard district. The '87 was labeled as Poderi Casot. It was unimpressive. Barbaresco 0

Negro Elio (*Monforte d'Alba*). Elio Negro's Barolo has been recommended to us by a very good producer.

Negro Giuseppe (*Neive*). Giuseppe Negro has vines in the Gallina section of Neive in the Barbaresco zone.

Nicolello Casa Vinicola (*Alba*). Our experience here has been limited to the '82 Barbaresco. They also produce a Barolo. It was a good glass of wine. Barbaresco *

Oberto Andrea (*La Morra*). Oberto produces some 15,000 bottles of wine annually, including a Barolo from Vigneto Rocche in La Morra and a Dolcetto d'Alba from his holdings in the vineyards of Albarella, Lantrino, and San Francesco.

Oberto Egidio di Oberto Giuseppe (*La Morra*, località *Croera*). Giuseppe Oberto owns 10 acres (4 hectares) of vines evenly split between the *comuni* of La Morra and Barolo; some 6 to 7.5 (2.5 to 3) are planted in nebbiolo. About 40 percent of the nebbiolo vines

are planted in the Cerequio-Canera vineyard, and the same amount in La Serra, with the remainder in the Fossati vineyard. The balance is dolcetto and freisa, with a tiny amount of barbera. We also heard that he owns vines in Ca' Najre and Nasön. He vinifies 40 percent of his grapes and sells the rest. His annual production consists of an average of 4,000 bottles each of a Barolo from La Morra and a Dolcetto d'Alba, 933 of Freisa, and 666 of Barbera d'Alba. The first vintage that he put in bottle with a label was the '79. He bottles wines from the crus of Cö Naive, Fossati, Nasön, and Serre. Our experience has been limited to five vintages, four from cask or demijohn. Barolo [* −]

Oberto F.lli (*Annunziata di La Morra*), 1968. Oberto makes one wine, a Barolo, from his 3-acre (1.2-hectare) vineyard in Rocche or Rocchette dell'Annunziata. The two vintages we tasted were good. Barolo *

Oberto Luigi (*La Morra*, regione *Bertone*). Luigi Oberto owns vines in the vineyards of Bricco S. Biago and Roggeri. He produces Barolo, Barbera, Dolcetto and Nebbiolo delle Langhe.

Oberto Severino & Figli di Oberto Sisto (*La Morra*, borgata *Pozzo*). Sisto Oberto owns 11 acres (4.5 hectares) of vines to produce some 34,000 bottles of wine annually, including 13,300 bottles of Barolo, 3,300 Barbera d'Alba, 8,000 Dolcetto d'Alba, and 3,300 Nebbiolo delle Langhe. He uses Azienda Agricola "Erbaluna" for Dolcetto and Barbera d'Alba. Oberto's Barolos are good wines; they could use more style. Barolo *

Oddero F.lli Giacomo & Luigi (*La Morra*, località *Santa Maria in Plaustra*), 1878. Oddero owns 111 acres (45 hectares), half of which is in vines. Their average annual production of 200,000 bottles includes 100,000 bottles of Barolo, 20,000 Barbaresco, and 40,000 Dolcetto d'Alba. In 1982 vintage they started bottling some of their Barolo crus separately. They enjoy a good reputation, and those bottles we've tasted indicate it is deserved.

They cultivate vines in a number of highly regarded vineyards, including in the Barolo district, Brunate, Bussia Soprana, Convento di La Morra, Gabutti-Parafada, Mondoca di Bussia, Rocche di Bussia, Rocche di Castiglione Falletto, Rocchettevino, Vigna Rionda, and Vigneto Rocche Annunziata; and in the Barbaresco zone, Faset, Montestefano, Pagliuzzo, and Pora. They began cru bottling some Barolos from the 1982 vintage with Convento, Mondoca di Bussia, Rocche di Bussia, Vigna Rionda, and Rocche di Annunziata, and in 1985 they added Gabutti-Parafada. Barolo ** +; Barbaresco **

Oddero Luigi & Figli (*Monforte d'Alba*). The few Barolos from this producer that we've tasted we found wanting. We haven't tasted any since the uninspiring '78. Barolo [0]

Oreste Stefano (*La Morra*). Oreste owns vines in the Formica vineyard in La Morra. Our experience is limited to their good '74. Barolo [* +]

Ornato Paolo (*Castiglione Falletto*). We are including Ornato in our survey of producers, although he doesn't sell his wine in bottle. Like numerous other small growers in the area, he produces a Barolo that could be a very good bottle indeed, but because of his small production or lack of interest in the extra work involved in bottling, he prefers to sell his wine *sfuso*. The quality of his wine, however, is indicative of the greatness of this zone. Ornato owns 5.7 acres (2.3 hectares/6 *giornate*) planted mostly in nebbiolo, in the Rocche vineyard, from which he produces the equivalent of 16,650 to 20,000 bottles (125 to 150 hectoliters/250 to 300 *brente*) of wine. Of this, 70 percent is Barolo.

A few years ago we rated his wines two stars; today, probably because of his advanced age, the quality has slipped somewhat although it is still pretty good. We haven't tasted Ornato's Barolo since the '79. Barolo [* +]

Osola. The only Barolo that we tasted from this producer was from the mediocre 1973 vintage.

Osvaldo Mauro (*Castiglione Falletto*). We've found these wines overall rather poor, lacking in structure and character. They are often sold with the Cantine Mauro Vini label. Every Barolo that we tasted, including the most recent, the '85, was pretty poor. We haven't tasted the Barbaresco since the '81, but have no reason to believe that it is any better. Barolo 0 −; Barbaresco 0

Ottavia Lesquio nell Azienda Agricola "Cascina Principe" (*Neive*). Our experience is limited to their good '85 Barbaresco Prinsi. Barbaresco *

Palladino Azienda Vitivinicola di Maurilio Palladino (*Serralunga d'Alba*), *1974.* Palladino owns 7.4 acres (3 hectares) in the San Bernardo vineyard, which supplies them with 26 percent of their Barolo grapes and 67 percent for their Dolcetto. They have an annual production of 84,000 bottles; 45 percent of this is Barolo plus a small amount of Barbaresco. All of the grapes for the Barbaresco are purchased. Palladino produce three different Barolos, a regular and two crus: San Bernardo and Vigna Riunda (his own spelling). They also produce three Albeisa wines from barbera, dolcetto, and nebbiolo grapes. In all, the wines are decent enough though they could use more character, more personality. Barolo ** −; Barbaresco *

Parroco di Neive di Benefico Parrocchiale di Neive (*Neive*). The Parrocchiale was founded in about 1500; we have no idea how long they've been producing wine. They own 37 acres (15 hectares) of vineyards in Neive. This includes their holdings in the vineyards of Cotta, S. Cristoforo, and S. Giuliano, as well as Basarin and Gallina. They bottle two cru Barbarescos from those vineyards. All of their wine is from their own grapes. They also sell a part of their harvest. They produce a total of about 100,000 bottles of wine a year, 46,650 of which is marketed under their label; the balance is sold *sfuso*, or in bulk. Overall, we have found their wines uneven, though the best can be very good. In general, those from Basarin have been better than those from Gallina. Barbaresco: Basarin **, Gallina *

Parusso Armando (*Monforte d'Alba*, località *Bussia*). Parusso's Cascina Roella holdings, including the amount he owns—8.9 to 9.4 acres (3.6 to 3.8 hectares/9.5 to 10 *giornate*)—and the amount he leases, total between 20.2 and 22.6 (8.2 and 9.2/21.5 and 24) of vines. Of this, 5.7 to 6.6 acres (2.3 to 2.7 hectares/6 to 7 *giornate*) are planted in nebbiolo. The balance is barbera and dolcetto. Parusso has between 4.7 and 5.7 acres (1.9 and 2.3 hectares/5 and 6 *giornate*) in Villero and about 0.9 (0.4/1) each in Bussia and Rocche; the balance is in the Meriondina or Mariondino vine-

yard in Castiglione Falletto and Pagliana in Monforte. Besides Barolo, Parusso produces a Dolcetto d'Alba Mariondino, a Grignolino delle Langhe, and a Barbera d'Alba.

We were told by Parusso that he mixes all his vineyards to produce an annual average of 12,000 bottles of a single Barolo. Yet we have tasted a number of single-vineyard Barolos from him: Bussia, Rocche, Bussia-Rocche—which is most probably a blend of grapes from those two vineyards—and Dei Ville Meriondo (the '85) and Mariondino (the '86). Most likely these last two are merely two spellings of the same vineyard. We were also informed that Parusso produced nearly 100,000 bottles of Barolo from the 1980 vintage! It makes us wonder if perhaps there is more than one A. Parusso. He also produces some 6,665 bottles of Dolcetto, 3,333 of Barbera, 5,333 of Grignolino, and a small amount of Freisa. Parusso's Barolo has improved since the '85. Thus far we've found those from Mariondino to be somewhat superior to those from Bussia-Rocche. Barolo: Bussia-Rocche **, Mariondino ** +, *normale* ** −

Pasquero-Elia Secondo Azienda Agricola (*Bricco di Neive*, località *Serra Boella*), *1893.* Secondo Pasquero-Elia produces some 50,000 bottles of wine a year from his 17.3 acres (7 hectares) of vines. This includes 6.9 acres (2.8 hectares) of nebbiolo in the Sorì d'Paytin vineyard, from which he makes about 21,000 bottles of wine; 20,000 are Barbaresco. This Barbaresco is now labeled as Sorì Paitin. In lesser vintages some of the nebbiolo is declassified to Nebbiolo delle Langhe. His other wines: Barbera d'Alba (4,665 bottles), Dolcetto d'Alba (13,335), Chardonnay from the Elisa vineyard (4,000), Moscato d'Asti (13,335), and the *barrique*-aged Paitin (4,665).

On one of our many visits to Piemonte, this genial producer provided us with the answer to the oft-asked question, where is Primo? There is no Primo, she is La Prima, Secondo's better half. Secondo's two sons, Silvano and Giovanni, who work with him, are known as *terzo* and *quarto*.

We have found Pasquero's Barbarescos, tasted over the years, to be well made, medium-bodied, and well balanced, wines. Barbaresco ** +

Patrito di Genesio Sergio & C. (*Barolo*). Patrito owns about 4.9 acres (2 hectares) of vines and produces 3,000 bottles of Barolo annually. In 1986, because of hail damage, he didn't produce any Barolo. The first Barolo that Patrito sold with a label was the '80. Our experience with Patrito's Barolos is limited to four samples from either cask or demijohn. Barolo [*]

Pavese Livio (*Treville Monferrato*). Livio Pavese owns two wineries: Azienda Agricola "Podere Sant' Antonio" and Azienda "Comm. Pavese Livio & C." He has 30 acres (12 hectares) of vineyards which supply him with 20 percent of the grapes he needs. Pavese produces a wide range of reliable, rather simple wines that, while unexciting, are certainly drinkable. Total annual production between the two wineries ranges from 77,700 to 93,300 cases, which includes both Barolo and Barbaresco. The last Barolo we tasted from Pavese was the '78, and the last Barbaresco, the '79. Barolo [0]; Barbaresco [0]

Pelissero Luigi & Figlio (*Treiso d'Alba*, località *Ferrere*), *1970.* Pelissero has 27 acres (11 hectares) of vineyards in the Santo Stefanotto zone which supply all of their grapes. They have an annual production of some 50,000 bottles of wine; 80 to 90 percent is Barbaresco. Pelissero produces Dolcetto d'Alba from the vineyards of Augenta and Munfrina, Barbera d'Alba from Ronchi, and a Barbaresco cru from his Vanotu vineyard. Barbaresco * +

Piazza Cav. Uff. Armando (*Alba,* frazione *S. Rocco Senodelvio d'Alba*), *1970.* Armando Piazzo owns some 49.4 acres (20 hectares) of vines, and leases 74 (30) more. Piazza's holdings in Poderi d'Mugiot provide him with all the fruit that he needs to produce, in an average year, some 168,000 bottles of wine. This includes besides Barbaresco (53,300 bottles) and Barolo (4,000), Barbera (34,665), Dolcetto (40,000), Moscato d'Asti (14,665) Nebbiolo d'Alba (8,000), and Pinot Langhe (13,335). Our experience with this Barolo is limited to the '85. We have considerably more experience with their Barbaresco. Barolo *; Barbaresco * −

Pio Cesare (*Alba*), *1881.* This firm owns 44.5 acres (18 hectares) of vines, including 19.8 acres (8 hectares) in Cascina Bricco in Treiso and 24.7 acres (10 hectares) in the Ornato vineyard in Serralunga d'Alba. They also buy grapes from Castiglione Falletto, Monforte, and La Morra. Of the approximately 6,000 cases of Barolo they produce a year, 60 percent is from their Ornato grapes. They recently acquired another vineyard and told us that in the near future they might be producing as much as 75 percent of their Barolo from their own grapes. And like so many other wine producers, not only in the Langhe but worldwide, they are experimenting with cabernet sauvignon. They planted some cabernet vines in their Treiso vineyard.

Il Nebbio is a Nebbiolo delle Langhe and Piodilei a Chardonnay delle Langhe.

At Pio Cesare they didn't, until recently, believe in making a single-vineyard Barolo. They felt that such a wine would lack what they consider the traditional character of Barolo. They believe that the differences among the subvarieties of nebbiolo are not significant, but that exposure and soil are the determining factors in the character of the wine, particularly the soil. Pio Boffa, who produces

THE WINES OF PIO CESARE

Wine	From Their Own Grapes	Average Number of Cases Per Year
Barbaresco	95%	2,000
Barolo	70%	6,000
Barbera d'Alba	30%	3,000
Dolcetto d'Alba	30%	3,000
Grignolino	—	2,000
Nebbiolo d'Alba	—	2,000
Nebbiolo	—	1,000
Ornato	100%	500
Chardonnay	100%	400
Gavi	—	2,000
Total		21,900

the Pio Cesare wines, along with his father, Giuseppe Boffa, and winemaker Paolo Fenocchio, points out that the grapes from Serralunga d'Alba give their Barolo body, structure, and complexity; the nebbiolo of this area produces wines big in body and rich in tannin. The wines of Castiglione Falletto, he notes, are soft and fruity; they add perfume and finesse to the blend. The Barolos of Monforte are in the middle, with more body than the wines of Castiglione Falletto and more finesse than those of Serralunga d'Alba; and the wine of La Morra provides delicacy. They combine the grapes from the various areas in the fermentation vats to produce a house-style Barolo. From the 1985 vintage they produced the single-vineyard Barolo from their Ornato vineyard in Serralunga.

Their Barbaresco, on the other hand, is made from either 95 or 100 percent grapes grown in their own vineyards, depending on when they replied to our question, with most coming from Treiso and a small part from San Rocco Senodelvio d'Alba. They produce, on average, 2,000 cases a year. They apparently don't discern significant variations between the wines from Barbaresco, Neive, Treiso, and San Rocco. Perhaps that is why they produce a Barbaresco representing mostly one village, with a little from a second thrown in for good measure. Or perhaps they consider single-vineyard Barbarescos to be traditional.

At one time no house was more dedicated to the traditional methods of winemaking than Pio Cesare, and although Boffa says that they still consider themselves a traditional firm, changes have been made in the last few years that have, it seems to us, moved them decidedly closer to the modern camp.

Their Barolo and Barbaresco used to be fermented in wooden vats, where the wine was in contact with the grape skins for two and a half months. Today the fermentation lasts for twenty to twenty-five days, at controlled temperatures, in stainless steel tanks. Whereas previously the malolactic fermentation occurred when it happened to develop, generally within a year or two, under today's more controlled conditions it has always taken place by year's end for all their wines.

After the wine spends some time in 3,965-gallon (150-hectoliter) holding tanks, it is moved to the aging cellar. Previously the wines were kept outside during the winter to precipitate the tartrates, then moved back indoors when the weather warmed. Today the wine is kept indoors and the temperature lowered to effect this cold stabilization. The Barolo and Barbaresco used to be aged in large, old Yugoslavian oak casks for six to nine years. These days they keep the Barolo and Barbaresco up to three or at most four years in a few different kinds and sizes of oak including small barrels, or *barriques,* for some of the wine. They have used these techniques, including small-barrel aging, since 1978. Currently they use half French and half Yugoslavian *barriques.* The *barrique*-aged wine is blended with the rest of the wine before bottling. Part of the '78 Barolo spent six months in *barriques.* Bottling of the '78 Barolo and Barbaresco began in January 1983.

Have these changes affected the wines of Pio Cesare? The answer is clearly yes, and for the better. The wines are more accessible at an earlier age and better balanced. The older Barolos and Barbarescos of Pio Cesare were sometimes—in fact, too often—hurt by overlong cask aging, becoming dried out and high in volatile acidity, though this was less of a problem in great vintages, of course. The Barolos made at Pio Cesare today, while they might not equal those of the greatest producers in the zone, are better than they used to be. Barolo ** + ; Barbaresco ** −

Pippione. It's been some time since we tasted these wines. Barolo [0]; Barbaresco [0]

Pira Azienda Agricola (*Monforte d'Alba,* località *S. Sebastiano*). Pira owns 54 acres (22 hectares), 22 (9) in vines from which they produce some 50,000 bottles of wine annually including Dolcetto di Diano d'Alba, Dolcetto d'Alba, Barbera d'Alba, Barbera delle Langhe, and Barolo.

Pira E. & Figli Azienda Agricola di Chiara Boschis (*Barolo*). When he was still making wine, Luigi Pira was, for us, the single finest producer of Barolo. Pira died in July 1980. Some six months after his death, the *cantina* E. Pira & Figli was purchased by the Boschis family, owners of the Giacomo Borgogno winery.

Luigi Pira, through his last vintage in 1979, maintained the old ways in making his wine, including the crushing of the grapes by feet. As Bartolo Mascarello and others have said, the tradition of *pigiatura a piedi* died with Luigi Pira. The bunches of grapes were brought into his cellar and put into the *tini,* or large, upright oak vats; men trod on them with bare feet and the must fermented. Today at Pira small basket presses are used.

Enrico Pira is now under the management of Chiara Boschis, an energetic and charming young woman in her twenties who was still in school when the *cantina* was purchased. The firm of E. Pira is still an *azienda agricola;* the entire production—12,000 bottles of wine—comes from their own 4.9 acres (2 hectares) of vines in Cannubi, San Lorenzo, and Via Nuova. Some 11,000 bottles are Barolo and 1,000 are Barbera. In some vintages part or all of the Barolo could be declassified to Nebbiolo delle Langhe. Chiara makes the wine and markets it. Her brother, enologist Cesare Boschis, consults for her.

To her credit, Chiara Boschis decided not to use the Pira coat of arms on the labels of their Pira wine; the present crest is a different one. And starting with the 1980 vintage, the words *pigiate a piedi* were removed from the label. Another difference consumers can note in the Pira and post-Pira bottlings is that Luigi Pira's bottles had a longer neck; Boschis uses the Albeisa bottle (stamped "Albeisa" into the glass at the shoulder).

Pira had vines in five vineyards, but shortly before his death he sold his holdings in Prea and Vignane. Boschis owns the plots in Cannubi, San Lorenzo, and Via Nuova.

How are the Pira wines today? Those bottled by Pira are still magnificent; even the '75, from a rather mediocre vintage, is still good. The '74 bottled by Boschis was dried out and lacking in fruit, undoubtedly due to not being cared for, as well as having spent too long in wood. The '78 and '79 we tasted were also disappointing. But with the later vintages, those that Chiara Boschis was fully responsible for, there has been a continuing improvement in quality, although not a return to their previous glory.

Luigi Pira's wines were rich in extract and concentration, with so much fruit that you were tempted to drink them early, but given sufficient age they became truly magnificent, the best that Barolo had to offer.

Chiara Boschis seems determined to produce fine wines here. And considering the noticeable improvement in quality combined with her tenacity since the first edition of this book, she's on the

right track. Each time we visit her *cantina* we watch with amazement as Chiara, in a dress, and looking very elegant and smart, climbs up the ladder, with wine thief and bucket in hand, in order to take a sample first from this cask and then from that. And as we taste the wines, on each visit we can't help noticing that they are better than the last time. Without question the E. Pira winery, along with Bel Colle, has shown the most significant improvement in quality. Barolo: E. Pira di Chiara Boschis ** + , E. Pira di Luigi Pira **** +

Pira Luigi. See *Pira Secondo.*

Pira Secondo & Figli (*Serralunga d'Alba*). Luigi Pira of Secondo Pira owns 12.4 acres (5 hectares) of vines, 7.4 (3) in nebbiolo for Barolo, plus barbera and dolcetto. Pira owns 2.8 acres (1.1 hectares/3 *giornate*) each in the Marenca and Margeria vineyards, 0.94 (0.38/1) in Lobbia, and 1.41 (0.57/1.5) in Domiano. He sells dolcetto and barbera grapes. His annual production of Barolo averages 22,666 bottles. This Pira bottles his Barolo as a cru from Marenca. The wines are now sold under the Luigi Pira label. Our experience here covers seven vintages, six from cask. Barolo *

Pittatore Francesco. See *"Ponte Rocca" Azienda Agricola di Pittatore Cav. Francesco & Figlio.*

Podere Anselma (*Serralunga d'Alba*). Anselma told us that he produces, or bottles, Barolo only in the best vintages. *Fortunato!* Their last Barbaresco was from the 1980 vintage. That was the only one that we tasted. Barbaresco [0]; Barolo 0

Podere Casot Nada. Our limited experience with their Barbaresco has left us unimpressed. We found the only one we tasted, the '78, wanting. Barbaresco [0]

Podere del Pajorè. See *Giovannini-Moresco Enrico.*

Podere Rocche dei Manzoni di Migliorini Valentino & Salomoni Iolanda (*Monforte d'Alba,* località *Manzoni Soprani*), 1971. This firm owns 45 acres (18 hectares) of vineyards. They produce nearly 115,000 bottles of wine a year—42,000 bottles of Barolo, 15,000 of *spumanti* and 55,000 of other wines. Their Barolos are fairly good, reliable enough, but lack intensity and even some character. We find their estate bottled nebbiolo-barbera blend, Bricco Manzoni, more interesting; it has more personality.

In 1978 they bottled a Barolo cru from their 'Dla Roul vineyard. In 1980 and 1981 all of their nebbiolo was vinified for Bricco Manzoni. Barolo **

Poderi e Cantine di Marengo-Marenda (*La Morra*), 1964. In 1985 we were told that Casa Vinicola Piemontese had changed their name to Tenuta Cerequio. Whereas previously they bought grapes and made a range of wines, they would now produce wines only from their Cerequio vineyard: Barolo, Barbera d'Alba, and Dolcetto d'Alba. Now they tell us that the name of their firm is Poderi e Cantine di Marengo-Marenda & C. And they continue to produce wines made from grapes grown outside the Cerequio vineyard. They produce 83,000 bottles of wine annually, some two-thirds of which come from their own grapes. This includes 50,000 bottles of Barolo from Cerequio, 3,000 of Barbera d'Alba from Cerequio, 10,000 Barbaresco, and 20,000 Dolcetto d'Alba. The Barbaresco comes from the Le Terre Forti vineyard.

Poderi e Cantine di Marengo-Marenda are the largest owners in the Cerequio vineyard, with a total of 19.4 acres (7.87 hectares). They grow nebbiolo and barbera vines in that vineyard. This winery is owned by three families, the Marengos, Marendas, and Gilardis.

As Casa Vinicola Piemontese they were a less specialized winery, buying grapes and making a number of Albeisa wines including a Barbaresco and Barolo. They continue to make Barbaresco. We don't know whether or not they own the vineyard that it comes from or if they buy the grapes.

Cerequio is considered one of the top vineyards in the zone. Their Barolos tend to be firm and tannic and have a similar recognizable character. Barolo ** − ; Barbaresco *

"Ponte Rocca" Azienda Agricola di Pittatore Cav. Francesco & Figlio (*Barolo*). Besides the vines that Carlo Pittatore, the proprietor of Ponte Rocca, owns in Brunate, he has 32.6 acres (13.2 hectares/34.58 *giornate*), of which 22.5 (9.09/23.86) are planted in vines in the section of Cerequio known as La Manderla. He also owns vines in Castellero and Vignane, and until recently a piece of Cannubi. On our most recent visit here, in April 1986, Pittatore produced Barolos from Brunate and Castellero, and he planned to do one from Cerequio as well. He produced some 40,000 bottles of Barolo, and 6,665 each of Dolcetto and Nebbiolo, plus 4,665 of Barbera. Of the six Barolos that we tasted here, only two were in bottle, the other four were in cask. All of them were very good. Recently we heard that Pittatore sold his holdings in Cannubi to Michele Chiarlo of Cantine Duca d'Asti and has leased his holdings in Bussia and Brunate for twenty years. We also heard that the *cantina* is closed. Barolo ** +

Porro Guido di Porro Giovanni e Carlo (*Serralunga d'Alba*). Porro owns vines in the vineyards of Lazairasco and Santa Caterina. Our experience with their Barolo has been limited to the '87, '88, and '89 barrel samples we tasted in November 1990. Barolo [*]

Porta Rossa di Domenico Berizia e Marilisa Rizzi Artusio (*Diano d'Alba*), *1973*. Porta Rossa owns less than 12 acres (5 hectares); the rest of the grapes that they require to produce some 800,000 bottles of wine annually is bought. Nearly half of their production is sold in bottle. Besides between 55,000 and 60,000 bottles of Barolo and 20,000 to 25,000 of Barbaresco, they produce Barbera d'Alba, Brachetto d'Acqui, Dolcetto d'Alba, Dolcetto Diano d'Alba, Dolcetto delle Langhe, Gavi, Grignolino d'Asti, Moscato d'Asti, Nebbiolo delle Langhe, and Nebbiolo d'Alba Occhetti di Monteu Roero. They have been doing cru bottlings of Barolo and Barbaresco since 1982. Today they bottle a Barolo Delizia and a Barbaresco Bric Faset, and a Dolcetto d'Alba Sörì Piadvenza from their Piadvenza vineyard in Diano. This vineyard has between 4.9 and 6.2 acres (2 and 2.5 hectares) of vines planted. They also bottle a Barbera Pianromualdo and a Nebbiolo Colombè. Barolo ** + ; Barbaresco **

Prandi Teobaldo (*Barolo*). Prandi owns vines in Monghisolfo and Via Nuova.

Principiano Ferdinando, Cascina Nando (*Monforte d'Alba*, località *S. Giuseppe*). We tasted one wine from this producer, their '82 Barolo Pian Romualdo. It was good. Barolo *

Produttori del Barbaresco (*Barbaresco*), *1958*. In 1894, Domizio Cavazza founded a cooperative winery in Barbaresco; it continued in operation until 1930. In 1958 a new co-op, Produttori del Barbaresco, was organized. Under the able hand of Celestino Vacca, Produttori del Barbaresco became not only the paragon of every other *cantina sociale* in Italy but also the rival of every producer in Barbaresco. There are few producers making Barbaresco in the same class as the wines of the Produttori. Today the wines are made by enologist Gianni Testa.

Initially there were 19 members in the co-op; today there are 66. Among them they own about 272 acres (110 hectares) of vines— some 22.5 percent of the nebbiolo plantings in the Barbaresco zone—in some of the most highly regarded vineyards in the area.

They have an average annual production of 666,650 bottles of wine, all of it from the nebbiolo grape; at most 200,000 to 300,000 bottles are Barbaresco. The grapes from their single vineyards are vinified separately, and when they feel the quality justifies it they are bottled under the cru, *versante* or *sorì*, name. Otherwise, these wines become part of their regular Barbaresco. If the wine doesn't come up to the standards set for the Barbaresco, it is declassified to Nebbiolo delle Langhe. Lesser wine is sold off in bulk, *sfuso*.

Through the years we've found the wines of the Produttori on a consistently high level. They are stylish Barbarescos—elegant, rich, and very well balanced. In fact, with wines this good, each time we pour one for friends and tell them that the producer is a *cantina sociale*, we almost expect an exclamation of "Holy cow!" (which would be particularly fitting, as the name of their founding director, Celestino Vacca, could be loosely translated thus).

In the best vintages they bottle as many as nine crus: Asili, Moccagatta, Montefico, Montestefano, Ovello, Pajè, Pora, Rabajà or Rabajat, and Rio Sordo. The Asili and Rabajà tend to be the most highly regarded of their crus, but we have found their Ovello in some vintages, '71 for example, to be as good or even better. The cru bottlings of the Produttori offer the wine lover an interesting opportunity to compare the individual characteristics of the nine different vineyards. As each wine is made by the same hand, the differences to be noted reflect the attributes contributed by the crus themselves. Barbaresco: Asili ****, Moccagatta *** +, Montefico *** +, Montestefano ****, Ovello *** +, Pajè ***, Pora *** +, Rabajà ****, Rio Sordo ***, *normale* **; Nebbiolo delle Langhe **

Prunotto Alfredo di Colla & Filiberti (*Alba*, località *San Cassiano*), *1904*. Prunotto, until recently, didn't own any vineyards; they bought all of their grapes. They have an annual production of between 16,650 and 19,000 cases of wine, all red. Besides Barolo and Barbaresco, they make Dolcetto, Barbera, Nebbiolo d'Alba, and Roero. When they feel the vintage justifies it, they vinify each vineyard separately and designate the name of the cru on the label. In 1973, 1975, 1977, 1981, and 1984, they blended the crus into their regular Barolo.

Prunotto is considered one of the more traditional of the Barolo and Barbaresco producers. They have experimented with some of the new methods but have generally rejected them. They still age their wines in cask, of chestnut and Slavonian oak, for many years.

Giuseppe Colla, a partner in the firm, is a serious and dedicated winemaker who has produced some truly magnificent wines. We sometimes find the wines, though, to have the typical problems of the old-style Barolos, being high in volatile acidity, dried out, and lacking in fruit. This can be the result of too long wood aging or bad storage or handling somewhere en route to the consumer. In our experience this is a much more common problem with the more traditional-style wines, which tend to have less fruit to begin with. These wines were not made for international shipment; they were styled for the local market and were perfectly suited to local conditions of serving and consumption. The rigors of international transport under conditions, shall we say, less than ideal, sometimes prove too much for them. It's worth noting here that we have been disappointed with these wines much more frequently in the United States than in Italy.

In March 1989, Antinori bought controlling interest, we heard 85 percent, of Prunotto. Shortly afterward they bought 20 acres (8 hectares) of Bussia. Changes will almost certainly be made. We can only hope that they are for the better.

The Prunotto Barolo and Barbaresco are wines that require long age in bottle, but the best vintages, at least, will reward those who are willing to wait.

Prunotto bottles two Barbaresco crus: Montstefano and Rabajà, and three Barolos: Bussia, Cannubi, and Ginestra, and a Nebbiolo d'Alba from Rossino di Monteu Roero. From time to time Prunotto also produces other crus of Barolo and Barbaresco. Barolo: crus ***, *normale* * +; Barbaresco: crus ***, *normale* *; Nebbiolo **

"Pugnane" Azienda Agricola. See *Sordo F.lli.*

Punset di Renzo Marcarino (*Neive*, frazione *Moretta*), 1962. Renzo Marcarino of the Punset winery produces an average of 10,550 cases of wine a year. The Marcarinos own 40 acres (16 hectares) of vines, including 15 acres (6 hectares) planted in nebbiolo, from which they produce 4,450 cases of Barbaresco. We found their wine better and more reliable in the mid-1970s. They have improved slightly. Perhaps with Renzo's daugher Marina's involvement, the quality will continue to improve. Our experience with Punset's Barolo is limited to the '80. Barbaresco *; Barolo *

Ramello Giuseppe (*La Morra*). The only wine that we tasted from this producer was his unimpressive '83 Barolo. Barolo [0]

Ratti Renato, Antiche Cantine dell'Abbazia dell'Annunziata (*Annunziata di La Morra*), 1965. The Renato Ratti winery is in the cellars of the fifteenth-century desanctified Abbey of the Annunciation of La Morra.

Ratti owns 40 acres (16 hectares) of vines which supply about 25 percent of the grapes for their annual production of 100,000 to 120,000 bottles. Of this, 40,000 to 45,000 are Barolo, 4,000 are Barbaresco, and 10,000 to 12,000, Nebbiolo. Their Barolo vineyard, Marcenasco, is in the environs of the village of that name that grew up around the tenth-century Benedictine priory of San Martino. These vineyards are referred to in a deed dated 1162, the earliest documented evidence of vines in this area.

The late Renato Ratti was a scholar and innovator. He made a thoroughly researched study of the wines of the Piemonte and generously shared his findings, unconcerned about being given personal credit for his work but appreciative of the opportunity to see it used to spread knowledge of the wines of his region. Renato noted that his map of the Barolo crus caused some disgruntled comments among growers whose vineyards were not included—"My second scandal," he quipped to us, wide-eyed with a look of mock astonishment at his audacity.

His first: introducing new viticultural techniques to the Langhe, an "outsider" with the temerity to show the Langaroli how to make their own wine! He chuckled at the incongruity of the situation. But, in fact, he was responsible for introducing a number of innovative techniques to the winemaking of the Langhe in the 1960s.

Ratti earned his degree in enology from Alba, as did his nephew Massimo Martinelli, who was responsible for the day-to-day operations of the *cantina* while Renato toured the world as the leading and charismatic spokesman for the wines of Piemonte. Massimo Martinelli continues to make the wines.

Ratti wasn't really a newcomer to the Langhe. He was born and grew up there, but none in his family had made wine previously (although they did own vineyards) and as a young man he worked at his career in Brazil. He returned to the Langhe with a novel, perhaps even a "foreign" point of view, including the notion that these wines should be made in a more drinkable style. Ratti credited his ability to take a fresh approach to winemaking to the fact that he was in one sense an "outsider." He came back to the region with a new appreciation of the wines that he, like many others, had previously tended to take for granted.

This also, he felt, gave him a particular appreciation of the local history and winemaking traditions in the region. Frequently dragging home discarded items no longer considered of value to their owners, but which he recognized as irreplaceable, Ratti began to

THE CRUS OF RENATO RATTI

Cru	Acres	Hectares	Exposure	First Vintage	Average Number of Bottles Per Year	Used for
Marcenasco	12.3555	5.0	S	1965	30,000	Barolo
Marcenasco-Conca	3.7067	1.5	E/SW	1978	5,000	
	owns 1.2356	0.5				
Marcenasco-Rocche	4.9422	2.0	SW	1978	8,000	
	owns 1.2356	0.5				
Colombè	7.4133	3.0	S	1969	25,000–30,000	Dolcetto d'Alba
Ochetti di Monteu Roero	7.4133	3.0		1969	10,000–12,000	Nebbiolo d'Alba

put together what was to become an excellent wine museum. He assiduously and enthusiastically collected old winepresses, other equipment used in the vineyards and cellars, old photographs and documents, and ancient artifacts—valuable testimony tracing the winemaking tradition in the Langhe since the time of the Romans.

In the 1960s, Ratti came to the conclusion—which we feel is quite valid—that too many of the Barolos being produced were overly tannic, low in fruit, and high in volatile acidity. He was convinced that the vineyards of the region produced excellent base material; the problem was in the cellars.

He began producing a Barolo utilizing modern techniques, eventually employing temperature-controlled fermentation in stainless steel. He reduced the period of skin contact, encouraged the malolactic to follow directly after the alcoholic fermentation, and gave the wines shorter cask aging. The result was a more drinkable Barolo that has gained wider acceptance in the world marketplace.

But these are not light, early-maturing wines to be drunk fresh. Ratti's Barolos age quite well, as can be noted in our tasting notes of his '67, for example. The Abbazia wines consistently display a richness of flavor and an intensity of character that put them in the forefront of the wines of the area. Ratti produced good Barolos even in 1975, 1976 and 1977—three rather dismal vintages. He also produced some of the best Dolcetto in the Langhe. The Ratti Colombè is a wine of immense fruit and charm. Their production also includes 12,000 bottles a year of a *barrique*-aged barbera-nebbiolo blend, Villa Pattono.

Noting the obvious as well as the subtle differences among the various growing zones in Barolo, Ratti was one of the first, if not the first to advocate bottling the Barolos as single-vineyard wines. He was, when we last spoke with him, in the process of classifying the Barolo crus, but had hesitated to put it into print, anticipating perhaps a third scandal on his record. The eyebrows over his expressive dark eyes quaked at the thought.

Renato's puckish wit was evident in his marvelous sketches. Dashed off during a boring speech or a dull round-table, they succinctly satirized the improbability of the obtuse statement, the nonsense of the pompous pronouncement. And provided amusement for friends, but to their dismay, the artwork was casually, and perhaps diplomatically, discarded.

A few years ago Ratti introduced a Barolo designed for those who wanted a Barolo to drink as soon as they bought it. It as undemanding, yet correct, albeit small-scale. This wine is sold under the "Ratti" label. Not having tasted Ratti's Barbaresco since the '80, we are not sure if it is still produced.

Barolo: Marcenasco ***, Ratti *; Barbaresco **; Nebbiolo ***

Revello F.lli (*La Morra, Annunziata*). Our experience with F.lli Revello's Barolo has been limited to two barrel samples, the '88 and '89. They were good. Barolo [* +]

Revello Giovanni & Figli (*Annunziata di La Morra*). This *azienda* owns vines in Annunziata including a piece of Giachini. They produce Barolo, Barbera and Dolcetto d'Alba, and Nebbiolo.

Revello Renato (*Grinzane Cavour*). Renato Revello produces a Barolo from his Cascina Gustavo holdings. The Barolos that we have tasted from Revello—the '83, and the '87, '88, and '89 from barrel—were very good. Barolo **

Rinaldi Francesco & Figli (*Alba and Barolo*), *1906*. Luciano Rinaldi owns 25 acres (10 hectares) of vines which supply the grapes for 90 percent of his annual production of 60,000 bottles. Rinaldi buys the grapes for his Barbaresco. He owns vines in the vineyards of Gallinotto, Sarmassa, Vezza, and Vignane as well as in his Barolo crus Brunate and Cannubbio.

At his *cantina* in Barolo he holds a small quantity of older *riserves* in demijohn, as was done commonly in the old days. He keeps some of his Barolo in these 9- and 14-gallon (34- and 54-liter) jugs for ten years or more. The wine is decanted off its sediment into bottles or magnums before being put on sale. Rinaldi still has some '70 and '67 in demijohn and one demijohn of '61. This last, though, will not be sold; it is the private reserve of the family (lucky family!).

At one time it was fairly common for Barolo producers to store their wine this way for aging. But it has become too expensive and is rarely done today. In the winter of 1929 temperatures dropped so low that half the *brente* and demijohns broke—a tragic loss indeed.

Luciano Rinaldi's wines are rich in color and extract, yet gentle and elegant—superb wines. Their quality was eloquently demonstrated to us on one of our visits to his place in Alba. We had just come from Franco Fiorina, where we had an impressive tasting culminating with a superb '47 Barolo. Even though this was our first appointment of the day and we knew full well there would be many wines to come, the '47 was just too good not to indulge in a second glass and to savor every drop. Then it was immediately back to work and off to the next winery, F. Rinaldi. The first wine Rinaldi poured for us was from one of the younger vintages: his '80 Cannubbio. The wine was totally impressive in style, balance, and elegance, even after the splendid '47—a touch act to follow even for an older vintage.

Rinaldi produced a '78 Barolo from Cascina Palazzo labeled as Cannubbio e Brunate, which was a blend of wine from those two fine vineyards.

Rinaldi is a man with a quiet sense of humor and a gentleness of manner. This gentleness is reflected in his wines, which are first class in their elegance, balance, and style. Barolo ****; Barbaresco ***

Rinaldi Giuseppe (*Barolo*), *1890*. Giuseppe Rinaldi owns 20 acres (8 hectares) of vines from which he produces between 35,000 and 40,000 bottles of wine annually—25,000 are Barolo, and the balance is divided nearly evenly between Barbera d'Alba, Dolcetto d'Alba, and Freisa.

Rinaldi has about 1.88 acres (0.7622 hectare) of nebbiolo for Barolo in Le Coste, 3.8 (1.5) in Ravera, about 0.94 acre (0.4 hectare) in San Lorenzo, and 3.8 (1.5) in Brunate, plus 5.7 (2.3) dolcetto, barbera, and freisa in La Ravera.

Rinaldi's Barolos are well-balanced wines with a lot of style and character. They are among our favorites, wines worth lingering over, and it has been our pleasure on a couple of occasions to savor some fine '71 Barolo from *bottiglione* at the house with Rinaldi, who judiciously paired it with some superb parmigiano.

The wine is bottled in standard-size bottles to be sold straightaway and in 0.53-gallon (2-liter) *bottiglioni* that are stored standing up at the *cantina* for anywhere between six and ten years. When the time comes to market the wine, the *bottiglioni* are decanted into regular bottles. Sometimes the bottles are kept standing up, as is the custom in many of the old *cantine* in Barolo, for as long as thirty years with no apparent problem with corks drying out.

We have tasted Rinaldi Barolos from '67, '71, '74, '78, '82, '83, and '85 from his holdings in the Brunate vineyard. At one time he produced a cru bottling from Brunate only in the very best vintages. Nobody would rate '83 as a topflight vintage. Since we see only those wines in the United States and not in Italy, we suspect that his American importer has made a request for them. As a general rule, we don't find much difference between the Barolos. They are both first rate.

There is no doubt about it—Giuseppe Rinaldi's fine Barolos are among the best produced. Barolos like these can convince skeptics that the Langhe does indeed produce world-class wines. Barolo ****

Rivetti Giudo (*Neive*). The only Barbaresco that we tasted from Rivetti was his disappointing '82. Barbaresco +

"Rizzi" Azienda Vitivinicola di Ernesto Dellapiana (*Treiso d'Alba*). Dellapiana has some 74 acres (30 hectares) of vines in the vineyard district of Rizzi from which he produces some 35,000 bottles of wine annually of Barbaresco, Dolcetto, and Chardonnay. Dellapiana produces some 15,000 bottles of Barbaresco from his 19.8-acre (8-hectare) Sorì del Noce vineyard which he currently labels as Vigna Surì, and 4,000 bottles from his 5.9-acre (2.4-hectare) Fondetta vineyards. He also produces some 5,000 bottles each of Dolcetto d'Alba and Chardonnay delle Langhe from the Sorì del Noce vineyard. He has 9.8 acres (3.97 hectares) of the former variety and 6.2 (2.5) of the latter planted. He also owns vines in Speranza. Although his wines are fairly consistent, and pretty good to boot, they could use more style. Barbaresco **

Roagna Alfredo e Giovanni, Azienda Agricola "I Paglieri" (*Barbaresco*), 1960. The Roagnas own some 16 acres (6.5 hectares) of vineyards planted in nebbiolo, chardonnay, dolcetto, and cabernet sauvignon. They produce 5,000 to 6,000 bottles of Dolcetto and 10,000 to 20,000 of Barbaresco. In the mid-1970s their Barbarescos came from the crus of Pajè and Asili. Today they produce two Barbarescos: a *normale* and Crichet Pajè. Besides the Barbaresco named Crichet Pajè, they produce a light, fruity table wine with the same name. We tasted the '82, which was made entirely from nebbiolo grapes, and found it easy and very drinkable, in short a nice little wine. Like many other producers in Piemonte, the Roagnas are experimenting with *barrique*, Chardonnay and Cabernet Sauvignon. His first Chardonnay was the '87, his first Cabernet Sauvignon will be the '90. His *barrique*-aged wine, Opera Prima, is a non-vintage nebbiolo. He first produced this wine in 1983. We recently heard that Roagna owns some nebbiolo in the Pira vineyard in Castiglione Falletto in the Barolo zone.

We have seen Barbarescos from Roagna labeled as Crichet Pajè, I Paglieri, and Vigna Pajè. The last wine that we saw labeled as Paglieri was the '71. At one time he also produced a Barbaresco from his holdings in Asili. We haven't seen that cru here since the '74. The Roagna Barbarescos can be very good, but they lack consistency and some style. Barbaresco **

Rocca Albino & Figlio (*Barbaresco*). Albino Rocca owns vines in the Rabajà vineyard district. In 1987 he produced a Barbaresco labeled Vigneti Loreto e Brich. We assume that this wine was made

from a blend of grapes grown in those two vineyards. It was good. Barbaresco *

Rocca Bruno, Azienda Agricola "Rabajà" (*Barbaresco*). Bruno Rocca produces some 15,000 bottles of wine annually, including Nebbiolo delle Langhe, Chardonnay delle Langhe, Dolcetto d'Alba Vigna Trifolè, and Barbaresco Rabajà.

Rocca Giuseppe (*Barbaresco*). Giuseppe Rocca owns vines in the vineyards of Pozzo, Rabajà, and Ronchi.

Rocche Costamagna di Claudia Ferraresi Locatelli (*La Morra*), *1841*. The Rocche Costamagna *azienda,* owned by Claudia Ferraresi and her son Alessandro Locatelli, has 11 acres (4.5 hectares) of vineyards—mostly planted in nebbiolo—all in the Rocche section of Annunziata district of La Morra, from which they produce 35,500 bottles of wine a year. They expect this to increase to 50,000 bottles annually within two years. Barolo accounts for from 14,000 to 18,000 bottles, Barbera and Dolcetto d'Alba for 4,500 and 9,000 bottles, respectively, and Nebbiolo delle Langhe Vigna Roccardo, 4,000. The Barbera is aged in *barrique*.

Claudia Ferraresi, a well-known and respected artist in Italy, has won recognition and awards for her drawings and paintings. Some of her paintings, as well as other works of art, are in the Ca' dj Amis above the *cantina*.

Her husband, Giorgio Locatelli, makes the wine assisted by their son Alessandro. Piero Ballario is their consulting enologist. The wines are good and getting better, and we can recommend them. In certain vintages they bottle Barolos from two special subcrus— Riccardo and Francesco—with specially designed labels. We have tasted '78, '79, and '82 Riccardo Barolos and '79, '80, '81, '82, and '85 Francesco Barolos. Today they bottle only the one from Vigna Francesco. From that subcru they produce between 1,800 and 2,000 bottles annually. Barolo ** +

Roche Azienda Vinicola di Ferrero Andrea (*Alba*, località *Santa Rosalia*), *1886*. This winery owns 35 acres (14 hectares) from which they produce some 175,000 bottles of wine a year. They make almost 27,000 bottles of Barolo and 16,000 of Barbaresco. Besides the typical Albeisa wines, they produce Arneis, Chardonnay, Malvasia, and an interesting freisa-nebbiolo blend, Zio Giovanni. To date we must admit that although their Barolo has improved it hasn't been by much, and their Barbaresco still fails to impress us. They are, however, honest wines. Barolo +; Barbaresco 0

Roggero Giovanni, Azienda Agricola "S. Biagio" (*S. Maria di La Morra*). Roggero owns vines in S. Biagio and Capalotti. He produces Barolo, Barbera, and Dolcetto d'Alba.

Roggia Ferdinando (*Novello*). We have tasted two good Barolos from Ferdinando Roggia, the '88 and '89 from barrel. Barolo [* +]

Rolfo Gianfranco, 1960. Rolfo owns 12.4 acres (5 hectares) of vines which supply him with between 33 and 39 tons (300 and 350 *quintali*) of grapes, 80 percent of his production. His Barolo was of decent quality. We haven't tasted it since the '79. Barolo [*]

Rosso Gigi (*Castiglione Falletto*), *1979*. Rosso owns 100 acres (40 hectares) of vines, which supplies 95 percent of their grapes. There are 15 acres (6 hectares) of nebbiolo in Barolo. Rosso's production averages more than 300,000 bottles of wine annually. This includes 91,000 bottles of Barolo, 9,000 of Barbaresco, 10,000 of Arneis, 55,000 of Barbera, 113,000 of two Dolcetto, 14,000 Freisa, 20,000 Gavi, 18,000 Grignolino d'Asti, and 15,000 Nebbiolo d'Alba.

They have produced a Barolo from Cascina Arione since at least 1978, and from Cascina Castelletto since the '85. They bottle their Barbaresco from the Viglino vineyard. Rosso has bottled a Barolo and Barbaresco for the New York restaurant I Tre Merli. It carried the "I Tre Merli" label. The ones we tasted—the '81 Barolo and '81 Barbaresco—were totally unimpressive. This is another highly regarded estate that has thus far failed to live up to our expectations. Barolo *; Barbaresco *

S. Quirico di Massano. All we know about this estate is that our experience with their Barolo and Barbaresco has been less than impressive. We have tasted S. Quirico Barolos from '67, '81, '82, and '83, and Barbarescos from '81, '83, and '84. Seven wines, and not one was rated more than zero! Barolo 0; Barbaresco 0

S. Secondo d'Asti di Ghera Graziano (*Tigliole d'Asti*). They produce a Barolo and Barbaresco as well as Asti Spumante, Pinot Spumante, and a Barbera, Dolcetto, and Grignolino d'Asti, Nebbiolo d'Alba, Gavi, and the white *vino da tavola* Rustichello. Their Barolo and Barbaresco are both bottled by B. G. & F. in Calamandrana.

Saffirio Enrico (*Monforte d'Alba*). The two Barolos that we tasted from Enrico Saffirio—the '88 and '89 from barrel—were very good. They promised well for the future. Barolo [** −]

Saffirio F.lli Enrico & Giacomo (*Monforte d'Alba*, località *Castelletto*). Our experience with this Barolo is limited, but we found the '79 and '74 wanting, though the '83 tasted from cask was promising. Perhaps that bodes well for the future. Based on the '83 we decided to upgrade our rating. Barolo *

Saffirio Josetta (*Monforte d'Alba*, frazione *Castelletto*). Josetta Saffirio cultivates vines in the Pressenda and Ceretta di Perno vineyards. She produces an "Alessio" Dolcetto d'Alba, "Sara" Barbera d'Alba, and a Barolo. Her annual production averages some 7,000 bottles. Her husband, Robert Vezza, is an enologist at Marchesi di Barolo. Saffirio ages her Barolo in *barrique*. Based on the three Barolos that we tasted from barrel in November 1990, we conclude that the wines are good, potentially better than our rating suggests. We found the older the wine the more dominant the oak. And in the case of the '87, very little, if any nebbiolo character was evident. Barolo [*]

San Lorenzo Casa Vinicola. The only Barolo that we tasted from San Lorenzo was their good '85 Brunate. Barolo *

San Michele (*Neive*), *1973*. Confratelli di San Michele was, at one time, a cooperative of five who had vineyards in Neive. They had an annual production of 40,000 bottles of wine, which included Barbaresco, Dolcetto d'Alba, and Barbera d'Alba. They bottled cru Barbarescos from the vineyards of Cotta, Gallina, and S. Cristoforo.

Recently Franco Cavallo bought the winery now known as San Michele. Another change here is that the wines have been more variable in recent vintages. Cavallo owns 21.6 acres (8.75 hectares)

THE CASCINA AND CRUS OF GIGI ROSSO

Cascina/Cru	Location	Acres	Hectares	Average Number of Bottles Per Year	Used for
Arione	Serralunga d'Alba	7.4	3.00	21,000	Barolo
Castelletto	Perno di Monforte d'Alba	9.4	3.79	32,000	Barolo
Cortine	Rocca-Giovino in Altavilla d'Alba and Cortine in Guarene d'Alba	4.4	1.80	15,000	Nebbiolo d'Alba[a]
Miralanga and Plucotti[b]	Barolo Annunziata in La Morra	13.6	5.50	38,000	Barolo
Moncolombetto[c]	Diano d'Alba	12.8	5.17	38,000	Dolcetto di Diano d'Alba
Rocca-Giovino	Altavilla d'Alba	14.7	5.93	55,000	Barbera d'Alba
		2.2	8.98	75,000	Dolcetto d'Alba
			n/a	14,000	Freisa Secco
Viglino[d]	Giacosa, Treiso d'Alba		n/a	9,000	Barbaresco

NOTES: [a] At one time this wine was made from grapes grown in Sandri in Monteu Roero and Rocca-Giovino in Altavilla d'Alba.
 [b] There was an '82 Barolo produced from these vineyards.
 [c] In 1988, Rosso produced 3,800 bottles of Dolcetto di Diano d'Alba Vigna Vecchia del Pinnacolo from 50-year-old vines grown in the Pinnacolo vineyard.
 [d] Until recently this vineyard was referred to as Viglino Carlo.

of vines, 9.9 (4) in Cotta, 6.2 (2.5) in Gallina, and 5.6 (2.25) in S. Cristoforo. He produces some 65,000 bottles of wine annually, roughly broken down as follows: 29,335 from Cotta, 18,665 from Gallina, and 16,000 from S. Cristoforo. We know that he produces a Barbera d'Alba from Cotta, a Dolcetto d'Alba from Gallina, and a Barbaresco S. Cristoforo. We don't know what else he produces. The Barbarescos that we have tasted under the San Michele label seem to point to slippage here. The Confratelli di San Michele '80 and '85 S. Cristoforo were good, as was the San Michele '89 Gallina from barrel, while the '87 Vigneto Gallina was another matter, as were the '86 and '88 from barrel. Barbaresco: Confratelli di San Michele S. Cristoforo *, San Michele Gallina +

Sandrone Francesco (*Barolo*). Francesco Sandrone owns about 4.9 acres (2 hectares); this includes a piece of the prized Cannubi vineyard as well as part of Cannubi-Monghisolfo. Some three-quarters of his vines planted in nebbiolo are in the latter vineyard; the balance in barbera for Barbera d'Alba is in the former cru. He sells the barbera grapes. This minuscule producer makes, at most, the gigantic quantity of 1,000 bottles of wine a year, all of it Barolo. 'Tis a pity, *darmaggi* as they say in Piemontese, when one considers the quality. The first one of his Barolos that we tasted, and the first one that he bottled, came from the poor 1977 vintage, and that wine was pretty decent. More recently we found the '78, '81, '84, and '85 to be very well made, rich, and harmonious. Our experience with Francesco Sandrone has been quite favorable. He produces good to very good wines even in vintages like 1977 and 1984, and excellent ones in years like 1978 and 1985. Barolo ***

Sandrone Luciano (*Barolo*), *1978*. Luciano Sandrone, who is an enologist at Marchesi di Barolo, owns 6.7 acres (2.7 hectares) of vines which supply him with all of the grapes he requires to produce 10,000 to 12,000 bottles a year of Dolcetto and Barolo. His holdings are in the vineyards of Monghisolfo, also known as Cannubi-Boschis and Rivassi-Boschetti. He produces a Barolo that he labels as Cannubi Boschis. This is one producer whose wines have been improving in quality. Barolo *** –

"Santa Maria" Azienda Agricola, Cantine di Mario Viberti Figlio (*S. Maria di La Morra*). This *cantina* has 30 acres (12 hectares), half of which are planted in vines. Their Barolo vine-

yards—Cappellotti and S. Maria—are in La Morra; those for Barbaresco in San Rocco Senodelvio d'Alba. All the wine they produce is from their own grapes. They bottle a Barolo cru from Capolot, another name for Cappellotti, and a Barbaresco from Montersino.

Savigliano Mario (*Diano d'Alba*), *1952*. Savigliano owns 27 acres (11 hectares) of vineyards, including some in the Barolo zone, from which they produce 6,650 bottles of Barolo a year. The balance, 60,000 to 66,650 bottles, is made up of other wines typical of the Langhe plus some others. In all, their wines are decent enough though lacking in personality. Barolo 0

Scanavino Comm. Giovanni (*Priocca*). We have always found these wines, at best, mediocre. They are in style, aroma, and structure more like wines from the south than from Piemonte. Needless to say, we cannot recommend them, except as wines to avoid. We can't say that we're sorry that we haven't tasted any since the '71 Barolo. Barolo [0]; Barbaresco [0]

Scarpa, Antiche Casa Vinicola (*Nizzi Monferrato*), *1870*. This firm owns some 124 acres (50 hectares) of vineyards, none of which are in Barolo or Barbaresco. They buy all of their nebbiolo grapes.

They produce some 155,000 bottles of wine a year, which includes 35,000 to 37,000 of Barolo and 14,000 to 16,000 of Barbaresco, as well as three single-vineyard Barbera d'Astis, Brachetto Secco Moirano, Dolcetto Moirano, Freisa Secco Moirano, Grignolino d'Asti, Nebbiolo d'Alba, Rouchet—a rare wine from the homonymous grape variety—Selvarosa, a rosé from a 55–45 trebbiano-dolcetto blend, and Selvarossa from a blend of nebbiolo, rouchet and freisa.

Scarpa is a very serious producer, dedicated to quality. They produced no Barolo in 1981, 1983, or 1984, as they were not satisfied with the quality of the grapes in any of those years. This was after 1980 and 1979, when, as the vines had been snowed on prior to harvest, they didn't vinify a Barolo either year.

The Scarpa wines that we have tasted were strikingly well-balanced, finely-honed, with a richness of flavor and a refined Nebbiolo character. Barolo *** +; Barbaresco *** +; Nebbiolo ***

THE CRUS OF SCARPA

Cru	Average Number of Bottles Per Year	Used for
I Tetti di Neive	10,000–12,000	Barbaresco
Payore Barberis di Treiso	4,000	Barbaresco
Boscaretti di Serralunga d'Alba	8,000	Barolo
Le Coste di Monforte*	12,000–14,000	Barolo
Rongaglia di La Morra	3,400	Barolo
I Tetti della Morra†	15,000	Barolo

* We haven't seen this wine since the '78.
† Also sold as Tetti di La Morria.

Scarzello Giorgio & Figli (*Barolo*), *1903.* Francesco and Gemma Scarzello own 12.4 (5 hectares) of vines from which they produce some 30,000 bottles of wine a year; 45 percent of this is nebbiolo, mostly Barolo. They bottle a Dolcetto d'Alba from Pajagallo and a Barolo cru from Merenda. Their Barolo is a pretty decent wine, one that has even improved a bit. Barolo * +

Scarzello Giovanni, Cascina Mosconi (*Barolo*). Giovanni Scarzello produced quite a good '74 Barolo; that was the most recent vintage we had the opportunity to taste. Barolo [* +]

Scavino Alfonso. This winery has been renamed *Azelia.*

Scavino Paolo Azienda Vitivinicola di Enrico Scavino (*Castiglione Falletto, frazione Garbelletto*), *1921.* Enrico Scavino owns 11 acres (4.5 hectares) of vines from which he produces nearly 50,000 bottles of wine a year; more than half are Barolo. Scavino has 4.4 acres (1.8 hectares) of nebbiolo vines in his 6.7-acre (2.7-hectare) Bric del Fiasc vineyard from which he produces 12,000 bottles of Barolo Bric del Fiasc annually. He has produced that Barolo since 1978. It is quite a good wine. He also owns (or rents) 2 acres (0.8 hectare) of nebbiolo in the prized Cannubi vineyard from which he produces nearly 5,500 bottles of Barolo a year. Scavino first produced that Barolo from the 1984 vintage. Additionally, he produces 4,000 bottles of a Barolo *normale* each year. He also produces 7,200 bottles of Dolcetto d'Alba yearly from his 2.2 acres (0.9 hectare) in Vigneto del Fiasc. His first vintage of that wine was 1982. He also produces some 7,000 bottles of Dolcetto delle Langhe, 4,600 Barbera d'Alba, and 3,335 Nebbiolo delle Langhe each year. Barolo: *normale* ** − , crus ** +

Scrimaglio Franco & Mario (*Nizza Monferrato*). Among the 16 wines that Franco and Mario Scrimaglio produce are a Barolo and Barbaresco.

Sebaste (*Barolo,* località *S. Pietro*), *c. 1960.* Mauro Sebaste Contitolare owns this *cantina* and its vineyards. A few years ago, shortly after Sylla Sebaste passed away, Gancia acquired half interest in this estate. A short time later they sold it back to Sebaste and his partner, Bruno Miretti. The most recent information we have indicates that only Sebaste owns the winery. Sebaste owns 16 acres (6.5 hectares) in Bussia and 2.47 (1) in San Pietro delle Viole. We have heard that Sebaste owns vines in the section of Bussia Soprana in Barolo known as Monrobiolo. Sebaste also buys grapes to supply them with their requirements. Their annual production, according to Sebaste, ranges from 120,000 to 140,000 bottles of wine. Because those figures omitted some of the wines that they produce, we suspect that they actually produce more than the reported amount. Sebaste plans to increase their output to between 200,000 and 250,000 bottles annually within ten years. Besides two Barolos (18,000 to 21,000 bottles), including one from Bussia, and a Barbaresco, they produce Roero Arneis (6,000 to 7,000), Chardonnay Piemonte (12,000 to 14,000), Gavi, Nebbiolo delle Langhe, Freisa Piemonte (18,000 to 21,000), Dolcetto d'Alba (18,000 to 21,000), the *macerazione carbonica* Dolcetto delle Langhe, and their *barrique*-aged, nebbiolo-barbera Bricco Viole (48,000 to 56,000). This wine takes its name from the fourteenth-century San Pietro delle Viole church near the winery. Their first Barolo from Bussia was the 1982; they produce between 8,000 and 12,000 bottles of that wine annually. Since 1989 they have made a Barolo from Brunate. They

made 4,000 bottles of the '89. Sebaste's Barolos can be quite good, although they are somewhat simple and lacking in intensity and style. They are well made, however. Barolo ** −

Seghesio Renzo (*Monforte d'Alba*), *1967.* Seghesio doesn't own any vineyards. He buys either grapes or wine, and produces some 60,000 to 70,000 bottles a year of some rather ordinary wine from barbera, dolcetto, and nebbiolo. About 20 percent is Barolo, mostly from vineyards in Monforte; the balance is the typical Langhe wines. Among the vineyards he buys from are Pianpolvere di Bussia, Perno, Castelletto, and Ginestre. Here is another producer whose wines have improved of late. Barolo * −

Serafino Enrico (*Canale d'Asti*). We haven't tasted Serafino's Barbaresco since the '74, but it left us unimpressed. It could be better. We've never tasted his Barolo. Barbaresco [0]

Settimo Aurelio (*Annunziata di La Morra*). Settimo owns 17 acres (7 hectares) of vines, 70 percent nebbiolo, in the fine vineyard of Rocche di La Morra as well as a part of Bricco San Martino and Pozzo. He produces some 2,200 cases of wine annually, including Barolo, Barbera and Dolcetto d'Alba, Nebbiolo, and Freisa. He produced a '79 Barolo that he labeled as Rocchette and an '82 and '83 as Rocche di Annunziata. They are two different names for the same vineyard. Judging from the Barolos that we've tasted, the Settimo Barolo is reliable and generally very good. Barolo ** −

Severino Oberto di Sesto Severino. We have tasted two Barolos from Oberto Severino, his good '83 and fairly decent '84. Barolo *

Sobrero Filippo & Figli (*Castiglione Falletto*). Sobrero's wines— 12,000 bottles of Barolo plus some Dolcetto and Barbera—were produced from grapes grown on his 7.4 acres (3 hectares) of vines in Monprivato and Villero in Castiglione Falletto. When we visited him in 1982 he opened wine for us to taste, but told us that as he was getting old and had no children and his only nephew wasn't interested in the *cantina,* his wines would not continue to be produced. In 1985 we were told that he was no longer making wine or receiving wine writers. It seems he had even lost interest in his vineyards, which were reportedly overrun with weeds.

Sobrero told us that he felt his wines needed at least eight to ten years to show their quality and that they age well for twenty or more. He is, or was, a very traditional producer. Although we've enjoyed a number of his wines, we have also been quite disappointed with many others. The problem is rather typical and unfortunately quite common with the more traditional Barolos: overlong wood aging, which causes the wines to dry out and develop volatile acidity. When they were good, however, they were magnificent.

The last Barolo that we tasted from Sobrero was his excellent '82. In our experience only his outstanding '78 was better. In 1985, Sobrero sold his vineyards to Mauro Mascarello of Giovanni Mascarello. At least the vineyards will remain in good hands. Barolo *** −

Sobrero Francesco & Figli di Settimo e Pierfranco (*Castiglione Falletto*), *1940.* The Sobreros own some 29.2 acres (11.81 hectares/31 *giornate*) of vines, 13 (5.34/14) in nebbiolo, 0.94 (0.38/1) in chardonnay, with the balance being dolcetto, barbera, and moscato, all in Castiglione Falletto. Their Cascina Ornato holdings encompass 16.95 acres (6.86 hectares, 18 *giornate*), which includes the 5.65-acre (2.29-hectare/6-*giornate*) Amellea vineyard, 8.48 acres (3.43 hectares/9 *giornate*) in Pernanno, 0.94 (0.38/1) in Piantà and 1.88 (0.76/2) in Valentino. The remaining 12.24 acres (4.95 hectares/13 *giornate*) are in the Ciabòt Tanasio in Brunella vineyard. Sobrero also owns 3.77 acres (1.52 hectares/4 *giornate*) in Villero which they didn't originally include in the information they gave us. This would make their actual holding larger than originally reported.

Sobrero produced their first wine with a label in 1982. Today their annual production averages some 80,000 bottles of wine, one-fourth is Barolo. Besides Barolo, and Barbera and Dolcetto d'Alba, Sobrero produces Chardonnay delle Langhe, and Moscato, Nebbiolo, and Freisa del Piemonte. Our experience has been limited to the '82 and '87 Barolo. Barolo * +

Sordo F.lli (*Castiglione Falletto*, località *Pugnane*). F.lli Sordo owns a piece of Pugnane Sottana. Our experience suggests that they can produce some very good Barolos, though the '85 was disappointing. Barolo * +

Sordo Giovanni (*Castiglione Falletto*). Sordo owns a piece of Pugnane and Villero. In our limited experience with Giovanni Sordo's wines we can't say that we are impressed. Both the '80 and '78 left us cold. Barolo [0]

Sordo Giovanni (*Serralunga d'Alba*). This Giovanni Sordo owns a piece of Gabutti that he labels as Sorì Gabutti. The three barrel samples that we tasted in November 1990—the '87, '88, and '89—were promising. Barolo [*]

Sottimano Azienda Vinicola di Sottimano Maggiore (*Neive*, località *Cotta*), 1975. Sottimano owns 3.7 acres (1.5 hectares) of vines which provide them with some 15 percent of the grapes they require to produce over 60,000 bottles of wine a year. They buy from another 5 acres (2 hectares). They produce nearly 7,100 bottles of Barbaresco and we understand that they also do a Barolo. They own part of Ca' Növa and Brichet, two subcrus in Cotta. Sottimano bottle a Barbaresco from Brichet. In 1984 they produced 4,800 bottles of that wine. As we've never tasted it or any of the other Sottimano wines we obviously cannot rate them. They also produce two whites, as more and more producers are doing a

Chardonnay, and a Gavi. Their Barbarescos from the Brichet vineyard are decent enough, especially when you realize that of the three that we tasted two came from the lesser vintages of 1984 and 1987. Barbaresco *

Stroppiana Oreste (*La Morra*, località *Rivalta-S. Giacomo*). Stroppiana owns vines in the San Giacomo di Rivalta vineyard of La Morra. Besides Barolo he produces Barbera and Dolcetto d'Alba, and Nebbiolo d'Alba. His Barolo can be good. Barolo **

Tenuta Carretta (*Piobesi d'Alba*), 1938. Tenuta Carretta is owned by Paolo Dracone, Edoardo Miroglio, and Nicoletta Miroglio. They own 104 acres (42 hectares) of vines, including 6.7 (2.7) in the Cannubi vineyard.

Carretta's annual production is about 227,000 bottles of wine a year. Barolo makes up some 18,000 bottles, another 28,000 are Nebbiolo d'Alba split between their two crus, and 20,000 Roero. They also produce 110,000 bottles of three whites: Roero Arneis, Favorita and Bianco del Poggio. This last wine, formerly known as Bianco del Roero, is an interesting white wine made from a blend of nebbiolo vinified in white and arneis. Besides these, winemaker-enologist Giuseppe Musso also produces Barbera d'Alba, Dolcetto d'Alba, Brachetto and Grignolino at the Carretta winery. The Carretta wines have been both consistent and very good.

Their Barolo is quite hard and tannic when young but matures very well. We have generally found their *normale* bottling superior to their riserva and riserva speciale. At a March 1985, tasting of Barolos from the 1971 vintage, their Cannubi, one of the 17 wines tasted, needed the most further aging. It is a very fine wine but surely not typical of the cru. Their Nebbiolo d'Alba Bric' Paradiso is one of the best Nebbiolos we've tasted, as well as one of the longest-lived. In 1984 we tasted a '71 from gallon; it was superb. As far as recent vintages of Barolo go, the '82 is especially fine and the '85 excellent. Barolo *** +; Nebbiolo d'Alba ***

Tenuta Cerequio. See *Poderi e Cantine di Marengo-Marenda*.

Tenuta Cisa Asinari dei Marchesi di Gresy (*Barbaresco*), 1973. Cisa Asinari di Alberto di Gresy is the owner of four vineyards comprising some 71 acres (28.7 hectares) of vines.

La Martinenga is considered the number one vineyard in the Barbaresco zone by many authorities and producers. It is owned in

THE VINEYARDS OF FRANCESCO SOBRERO

Vineyard	Variety	Acres	Hectares
Amellea	Dolcetto,	0.94	0.38
	barbera	4.71	1.91
Pernanno	Nebbiolo	7.53	3.05
Valentino	Nebbiolo,	0.94	0.38
	dolcetto	0.94	0.38
Villero	Barbera,	1.88	0.76
	dolcetto	1.88	0.76
Ciabòt Tanasio in Brunella	Nebbiolo	7.53	3.05

THE CRUS AND VINEYARDS OF TENUTA CARRETTA

Cru/Vineyard	Comune	Acres	Hectares	First Vintage	Average Number of Bottles Per Year	Used for
Cannubi	Barolo	6.697	2.71	1961	18,000	Barolo
Bric' Paradiso	Alba	7.413	3.00	1967	14,000	Nebbiolo d'Alba
Bric' Tavoleto	San Rocco Senodelvio d'Alba	5.634	2.28	1982	14,000	
Podere Tavoleto		n/a	n/a	—	26,000	Dolcetto d'Alba
Bricco del Poggio	Piobesi	n/a	n/a	—	20,000	Roero
Podere Podio e Carretta	Piobesi	31.136	12.68	—	13,000	Barbera d'Alba
Podere Podio e Carretta	Piobesi	included above		—	6,000	Grignolino delle Langhe
Balin	Piobesi	4.226	1.71	—	—	
Podio	Piobesi	10.354	4.19	—	—	

THE CRUS OF MARCHESI DI GRESY

Cru	Location	Acres	Hectares	Used for
Martinenga	Barbaresco	29.7	12.00	Barbaresco
Martinenga-Camp Gros	Barbaresco	5.2*	2.10	Barbaresco
Martinenga-Gaiun	Barbaresco	5.1*	2.05	Barbaresco
Monte Aribaldo	Treiso	16.4	6.64	Dolcetto d'Alba
La Serra	Cassine	n/a		Moscato d'Asti

* Included in the total for Martinenga

its entirety by Marchese Alberto di Gresy. All 30 acres (12 hectares) are planted to nebbiolo. These grapes are used to produce Barbaresco and Nebbiolo delle Langhe, the latter wine for early drinking. The La Martinenga is a Barbaresco of elegance and finesse rather than power and authority. Its class is evident from the first swallow.

The last time we saw La Martinenga we were not entirely sure we'd recognize it in the daylight, having seen it only at midnight illuminated by the headlights of di Gresy's car both times before. But perhaps the charmingly unconventional proprietor did have his priorities in order; tasting the wine came first.

In the best vintages two parcels of La Martinenga are kept separate and bottled individually: Camp Gros and Gauin. Camp Gros, from the end of the vineyard near Rabajà, has more tannin, structure, acidity, and firmness; it matures more slowly and will probably live longer. Gauin, from the opposite end of La Martinenga near Asili, is softer, richer in glycerine and in perfume. It is, in fact, the essence of La Martinenga Barbaresco—a gentle, feminine wine of elegance and breed.

The Monte Aribaldo vineyard includes a small plot of nebbiolo which can be used to produce Barbaresco. To our knowledge, however, those grapes are sold.

In all, di Gresy produces some 120,000 bottles of wine a year.

He expects this to increase by 50 percent to 180,000 bottles a year by the mid-1990s. The rest of the grapes—some 50 percent or more—are sold. He produces 42,000 bottles of three Barbarescos, 10,000 Nebbiolo delle Langhe, 30,000 Dolcetto d'Alba from Monte Aribaldo, 30,000 of Moscato d'Asti from his La Serra vineyard, and 8,000 Chardonnay. In lesser vintages he will produce more Nebbiolo delle Langhe and less Barbaresco. In 1987, for example, he produced 28,000 bottles of the Martinenga Nebbiolo delle Langhe. From the outstanding 1985 vintage di Gresy produced 12,465 bottles and 498 magnums of Martinenga Barbaresco, 12,364 bottles and 549 magnums of Camp Gros-Martinenga, and 12,390 bottles and 496 magnums of Gaiun-Martinenga.

For us the '74 Martinenga didn't measure up to the vintage. The first to really impress us was the '76, which, although too old today, was at the time possibly the best wine of the vintage. With the '78 vintage and perhaps even more so with the '79, di Gresy has produced a Barbaresco that lives up to the lofty reputation of the vineyard. Since then there have been a number of especially fine Barbarescos, including the '82s, '83s, '85s, and '86s.

Piero Ballario has been the enologist at La Martinenga since 1983. Today he consults here. Enrico Bartolucci is the resident winemaker today.

In the *cantina*, as we tasted the full range of his wines, di Gresy's normal cheerful nonchalance and infectious wit seemed suspended momentarily as we critically evaluated the wines, but returned with a smile of obvious pleasure as we offered our compliments, words he gallantly deflected to his winemaker. Alberto remarked that he's considering taking a few names out of his aristocratic title on the label when the wine becomes a little better known, simplifying it for the consumer by making it simply "Crazy Gresy," a nickname that we (or to be more exact, Sheldon) have tagged him with for his original approach to life. Barbaresco: Martinenga-Camp Gros ****, Martinenga-Gaiun ****, Martinenga *** −; Nebbiolo della Martinenga **

Tenuta Coluè di Massimo Oddero. See *Coluè di Massimo Oddero.*

Tenuta La Volta. See *Cabutto Bartolomeo.*

Tenuta Montanello (*Castiglione Falletto*), *1954.* The Monchiero brothers own this winery and some 50 acres (20 hectares) of vines in Castiglione Falletto, 70 percent in nebbiolo with the remainder in dolcetto, barbera, and freisa. This includes at least 25 acres (10.2 hectares) of vines in the Montanello vineyard, plus 2 acres (0.8 hectare) in Rocche; 11.4 (4.6) are in nebbiolo. Tenuta Montanello produce 33,000 bottles of Barolo a year and 41,000 of other wines. Like many others in Piemonte, they are separating their vineyards into subcrus. Montanello is divided into Fontana, Pianella, and Pini. Although the wines of each plot are kept separate throughout the production and bottled individually, they are not named on the label. Their Barolo is made in a less aggressive, somewhat lighter, simple style. Sometimes they produce a single-vineyard Barolo or a Barolo from a single plot in their Montanello vineyard. There was an '82 Rocche and a '79 Montanello-Pini that we tasted from cask in January 1985. We don't know if they labeled them as such. Barolo *

Terre da Vino (*Moriondo, Torino*). This firm produces a wide range of Piemontese wines including Barolo and Barbaresco.

Terre del Barolo (*Castiglione Falletto*), *1958.* This *cantina sociale,* founded by Arnaldo Rivera, is the largest producer in the Barolo zone. They crush more than 6,000 tones (55,000 quintali) of grapes a year to produce nearly 400,000 cases of wine a year. This includes 1,545 tons (14,000 quintali) of nebbiolo for more than 100,000 cases of Barolo and Nebbiolo d'Alba. This co-op, with the production of approximately a million bottles of Barolo a year, represents a sizeable portion of the zone's annual 5.6 million bottles.

When the co-op was founded there were 40 members; today there are 540, working 2,108 acres (853 hectares) of vineyards. Terre del Barolo provides an important function in the zone in helping to assure a decent income for the grape farmers. By offering their members a reasonable price for their grapes, they furnish a favorable alternative to their selling to the mediocre vinifiers in the district and consequently help raise the average quality of the Barolo produced.

It is somewhat remarkable under the circumstances and at these quantities, but they are able to produce quite a good Barolo. They bottle three very good Barolo crus: Brunate with grapes grown by Giovanni Bogletti and Renzo Roggiero, Castello di Grinzane Cavour, and Rocche di Castiglione Falletto with grapes from Arnaldo Rivera. It is a tribute to their enologists. Barolo: *, crus **

Terzano G., Cascina Adelaide (*Castiglione Falletto*). See *Cascina Adelaide, Terzano G.*

Tomaso Gianolio (*Fossano*), *1960.* Tomaso buys all the grapes that they need to produce some 66,665 bottles of wine annually. Half is Dolcetto d'Alba, 20 percent each are Barbera d'Alba and Nebbiolo d'Alba. They also produce 4,000 bottles of Barolo and 2,667 of Barbaresco. Their '85 Barbaresco, the only wine that we tasted here, was decent enough if not much more. Barbaresco * −

Traversa Giuseppe, Cascina Chiabotto (*Neive*), *1880.* Traversa owns 37 acres (15 hectares) of vines from which he produces more than 105,000 bottles of wine a year. He makes 26,000 bottles of an excellent Moscato d'Asti, 20,000 combined of an Arneis and a Favorita, nearly 21,000 of two Barbera d'Albas, 22,250 of Nebbiolo delle Langhe, and some 10,500 of an agreeable Barbaresco. Traversa does a cru bottling from his holdings in the Maringota vineyard of Bricco di Neive and another one from Sorì Ciabot. The first Sorì Ciabot that we tasted was the '82. Barbaresco *

Troglia Ferrero Mario & Figli di Ferrero M. &. C. (*Ozzano, Torino*). This firm produces at least 15 different wines, including Barolo and Barbaresco as well as Boca, Bramaterra, Carema, Fara, Gattinara, Ghemme, and Sizzano.

Troglia Giovanni (*Torino*). Giovanni Troglia, a wine merchant in Torino, sells under its label Barolo and Barbaresco and a number of other Piemontese wines, packaged in bizarre-shaped bottles. The wines are often just as bizarre. Oxidized wines, in fact, are quite common from them. We found their wines from the 1960s better than those from the more recent vintages. They sell a Barbaresco from Podere Nervo; we haven't tasted it. Barolo 0; Barbaresco 0

Vajra G. D., Cascina San Ponzio (*Barolo,* località *Vergne*), *1972.* Milena and Aldo Vajra own 31 acres (12.5 hectares) 17 (6.9) of which are in vines; this includes 6 acres (2.4 hectares) of nebbiolo for Barolo plus barbera, dolcetto, and freisa.

These vines are planted between 1,150 and 1,475 feet (350 and 450 meters) above sea level. The nebbiolo, barbera, and freisa vines face south to southeast, and part of the dolcetto from south to southwest. Their annual production ranges from 70,000 to 75,000 bottles of wine, all from their own grapes. They bottle two Barolo crus, one from their holdings in the Fossati vineyard the other from their vines in Bricco Viole. Overall their Barolos are quite good and reliable, and they have improved as well. The cru bottlings are somewhat better. Barolo: non-cru ** +, Bricco Viole *** −, Fossati *** −

Valfieri (*Alba*). This firm is part of the Riccadonna group. They have *cantine* in Costigliole d'Asti and Villa Montesino. Since they own no vineyards, they buy all their grapes. We find their Barolo and Barbaresco rather mediocre. They produce two Barbaresco crus: Rabajà and Moretti. Barolo 0; Barbaresco 0

Vecchio Piemonte, Consorzio Cooperativo Soc. Coop. Cantine Produttori (*Grinzane Cavour*). This syndicate is made up of seven cooperative cellars with 2,400 member-growers. They produce 1.4 million cases of wine a year. Their range is wide, as is their quality. The Cantina di Treiso produces Barolo and Barbaresco; the Cantina di Fara Novarese produces Fara and Spanna del Piemonte; and the

THE CRUS AND VINEYARDS OF G. D. VAJRA

Cru/Vineyard	Acres	Hectares	Average Number of Bottles Per Year	Used for
Bergeisa	2.47	1.0	3,000	Barbera d'Alba
Bricco Viole	2.47	1.0	3,000	Barbera d'Alba
	3.21	1.3	7,200	Barolo
Coste di Verne	3.71	1.5	12,000	Dolcetto d'Alba
Fossati	2.72	1.1	6,000	Barolo
San Ponzio	2.47	1.0	7,200	Freisa delle Langhe
Total	17.05	6.9	38,400	

Cantina di Castiglione Falletto makes Nebbiolo d'Alba. They bottle a Barbaresco from the Casotto vineyard. We have more experience with their Barbaresco than their Barolo. All of those we tasted have been unimpressive, including an '85 Barolo and an '82 Barbaresco Casotto. Barolo 0; Barbaresco 0

THE WINES OF VECCHIO PIEMONTE

Wine	Average Number of Cases Per Year
Barolo	88,880
Barbaresco	55,550
Barbera d'Alba	111,100
Barbera del Monferatto	166,650
Dolcetto d'Alba	66,600
Gavi	55,550
Grignolino d'Asti	33,330
Asti Spumante	222,200
Moscato d'Asti	55,550
Total	855,410

Veglio Angelo & Figli (*Annunziata di La Morra*). Veglio owns vines in Bricco Manescotto, Brichetto and Fantinì. He bottles a Barbera d'Alba (6,665 bottles), Dolcetto d'Alba (8,000), and Barolo (13,300) from his Cascina Gancia holdings in the Annunziata section of La Morra. He also produces a Nebbiolo delle Langhe. We have tasted two Barolos from Veglio—one from the mediocre 1976 vintage and it was pretty decent, and a good '85. Barolo * +

Veglio Angelo & Figli (*Annunziata di La Morra, borgata Ciotto*), 1945. This Angelo Veglio is not the same as the one preceding. He also produces Barolo, Barbera and Dolcetto d'Alba, and Nebbiolo delle Langhe. He owns vines in Ricchette, Turnalunga, Cascina Nuova, and Brichet. We've never met his wines.

Veglio F.lli, Cascina Bruni. See **Cascina Bruni di Veglio F.lli**.

Veglio Giovanni & Figli (*Diano d'Alba*, frazione *Talloria*). The Veglios own some 22 acres (9 hectares) of vines and produce more than 93,000 bottles of wine annually. This includes 6,500 bottles of Barolo, 10,500 Barbera d'Alba, 6,000 Dolcetto d'Alba, 33,000 Dolcetto di Diano d'Alba, and 6,000 Chardonnay del Piemonte. Thus far we have tasted four Barolos from Giuseppe, Domenico, and Prospero Veglio, all from cask—the '83, '87, '88, and '89. They were good if not much more. Barolo [* +]

Veglio Pasquale. See **Cascina Bruni di Pasquale Veglio**.

Vercelli Alessandro. Our experience with this producer is limited to their mediocre '78 Barolo. Barolo [0]

Vezza Sergio (*Treiso d'Alba*, borgata *Ferrere*), 1967. Vezza owns 18.5 acres (7.5 hectares) in Treiso from which he produces two wines: Barbera d'Alba and Barbaresco. We found his '78 Barbaresco rather ordinary and his '80 fairly decent! But his '82 was a giant step forward and upward, and his '86 was very good as well. Barbaresco ** +

Viarengo G. L. & Figlio (*Castello di Annone, Asti*), 1883. Giuseppe Viarengo produces 200,000 bottles of wine annually at his estate in Castello di Annone. Castello di Annone is a *località*; there are other producers there as well. Viarengo bottles his wines, his Barolo at least, as Castello d'Annone. He produces, besides Barolo and Barbaresco, a Barbera d'Asti including "Il Fatè" and Morra, Dolcetto d'Alba, and Grignolino d'Asti. Thus far we've tasted two good '85s here, their Barolo and Barbaresco. Barolo *; Barbaresco *

Viberti F.lli fu Giuseppe, Azienda Agricola Breida (*La Morra, borgata Sillio*). Beppe Viberti has vines in the Sillio and Roncaglia vineyards. He produces Barolo, Barbera and Dolcetto d'Alba, and Nebbiolo delle Langhe.

Viberti Giovanni (*Barolo*, frazione *Vergne*). Giovanni Viberti produces some 48,000 bottles of wine annually. This includes

14,000 each of Barolo and Pinot delle Langhe, 6,665 of Barbera d'Alba, 11,300 Dolcetto d'Alba, and 2,000 Nebbiolo delle Langhe. Neither Barolo that we tasted from Viberti—the '82 and '83—really impressed us. Barolo +

Viberti Luigi & Figli, Azienda Agricola "Cascina Ballarin" (*La Morra*, località *Annunziata*). We have tasted three of Luigi Viberti's Barolos from barrel in November 1990—the '87, '88, and '89. The wines, from Viberti's Cascina Ballarin, showed a lot of potential and were, overall, very good. Barolo **

Viberti Luigi & Figlio (*S. Maria di La Morra*, borgata *Tetti*). Barolo accounts for about one-quarter of their annual production of nearly 20,000 bottles of wine, Barbera for more than a third, and Dolcetto the remaining 40 percent.

Vietti Cantina di Alfredo Currado (*Castiglione Falletto*), 1960. Alfredo Currado owns or leases 17.4 acres (7.05 hectares/18.5 *giornate*) of vines which supply 40 percent of the grapes he needs. He buys the rest from growers with whom he has contracts giving him some control over the cultivation of the vines, the pruning in particular. He is looking for a small amount of high quality fruit. Currado produces some 120,000 bottles of wine a year, 80,000 of which are red wines; the balance is mostly Moscato, plus a tiny amount of Arneis. We'd also be remiss if we failed to mention Currado's superb wood-aged grappa from his Rocche vineyard. Unfortunately, quantities are minuscule.

Currado bought a plot in the Lazzarito vineyard from Giovanni di Stefani; it is planted in 100 percent lampia. On December 30, 1990, he bought the sections of Meriondino, Parussi, and Rocche that he had previously rented. Currado will replant the nebbiolo in Parussi with the Michet clone. He has a twenty-year lease in Villero; this plot is planted in 100 percent michet. Currado plans to replant part of this vineyard as an experiment. Currently the Briacca vineyard in Rocche isn't producing; the vineyard was replanted with all three nebbiolo clones and will be in production in 1991. At first Currado will blend the wine into his Castiglione Barolo. When the grapes are fully mature he will blend it into his Rocche.

Although he employs modern technology, Currado considers himself a traditional producer. The changes he has made, he points out, were only to give him a closer control over quality, not to change the character of the wine. He aims for a style of Barolo and Barbaresco that fits into the general concept of traditional wines—big, concentrated wines that improve with age.

Alfredo states with some modesty that his first aim is to produce a wine free of defects, and secondly a wine with style. He succeeds on both counts. Not only are his Barolo and Barbaresco among the zone's finest, but his Barbera, Dolcetto, Freisa, Grignolino, Moscato, and Arneis are as well. Alfredo is a perfectionist who demands the best from himself and elicits the same from his grapes. His family, who work with him, share the same commitment to quality.

Currado graduated from the enological school at Alba in 1952 and went to work first for a *spumante* house. In 1957 he married Luciana Vietti and three years later he began making the Vietti wine. Today he is assisted in the *cantina* by his son Luca, also an enologist with a degree from Alba. The Vietti winery is a family operation. Luciana handles public relations and son-in-law Mario Cordero (husband of daughter Emanuela) is the general manager. He runs the office, is in charge of marketing, and takes care of the vineyards.

Elizabetta, the younger daughter, was the first of the Vietti off-spring to graduate from the enological school at Alba. After graduation Alfredo arranged for her to work in wineries in the United States, in California and Oregon, and in Bordeaux. She then worked in the Vietti cellar with her father applying the benefits of her knowledge and training to the family wines; her father credits Betta with improving the quality of their Arneis. When she was asked whether she had learned a lot from working with her father, Betta's dark, expressive eyes registered her admiration as she replied, "Papa is an artist with the wine." Betta is currently making the wines at Abbazzia di Valle Chiara in Lerna in the province of Alessandria as well as consulting at Poggio Sala in Montepulciano in Toscana. She produces two wines for them, a Dolcetto d'Ovada and the *barrique*-aged Torre Albarola made from a blend of dolcetto and barbera.

Currado is an art lover who has comissioned some fine artists to do his labels. At one time Luciana, a talented artist in her own right, did some of the label designs, but she is too busy today managing the commercial end of the winery and providing (with the very able assistance of the charming Signora "Mama" Vietti) superb hospitality to the frequent guests at the *cantina*. Most of the labels, including all of those for the nebbiolo wines, are done by Gianni Gallo, who is also much in demand by other wineries. But the Vietti wines were the first. As Alfredo tells the story, the idea took shape around a bottle, a dusty bottle of Barolo '64 from his *cantina*. It was a cold winter's evening in 1974, and he and some artist friends had been enjoying each other's company over a few bottles of good wine, when one of them remarked that such a beautiful wine as the '64 merited a beautiful label; it should be the work of an artist. Alfredo recalls with an easy laugh that he, as a good Piemontese, was alert enough to not let such an opportunity slip by; he promptly reached for a piece of paper to get it down in writing. In the euphoria of the moment, he relates, he soon had a list of artists willing to do the job. At first only the crus were bottled with the special labels, but in 1978 he adopted this style for all his wines.

Alfredo Currado is a man firmly rooted in the Langhe, with a love for his region and its wines. But he is also interested in understanding the wines of other fine wine-producing regions. He

THE BAROLO CRUS AND VINEYARDS OF VIETTI

Vineyard	Acres	Hectares
Lazzarito	5.6504	2.2866
Meriondino	0.4709	0.1906 (rented)
Parussi	1.4126	0.5717
Rocche	1.4126	0.5717
Scarrone	5.1795	2.0961
Villero	1.4126	0.5717 (rented)
Others rented	1.8835	0.7622
Total	17.4221	7.0506

THE CRUS AND WINES OF VIETTI

Crus	Nebbiolo Subvariety	Acres	Hectares	First Vintage	Number of Bottles in 1989
BARBARESCO					
Masseria	100% lampia	4.942	2.00	1964	4,340
Rabajà	100% lampia	2.471	1.00	1982	2,670
BAROLO					
Briacca[a]	100% rosé	0.988	0.40	1961	0
Brunate	Mostly lampia	2.471	1.00	1984	3,100
Bussia	70% lampia	7.413	3.00	1982	0
Castiglione[b]	Mostly michet	—	—	—	9,800
Lazzarito	Mostly michet	5.650	2.29	1989	4,390
Meriondino[c]	Mostly michet	0.471	0.19	1971	0
Parussi[c]	Mostly michet	1.413	0.57	1976	n/a
Rocche	70% michet	1.413	0.57	1961	7,000
Villero[d]	100% michet	1.413	0.57	1982	4,200
OTHER CRUS	*WINE PRODUCED*				
Bussia	Barbera d'Alba			—	9,800
Bussia	Dolcetto d'Alba			—	8,350
Disa	Dolcetto d'Alba			—	5,700
Fioretto	*vino da tavola*			1982	n/a
Pian Romualdo	Barbera d'Alba			—	3,500
San Giacomo[e]	Nebbiolo d'Alba			1982	0
San Michele[e]	Nebbiolo d'Alba			1974	6,600
Sant'Anna	Dolcetto d'Alba			—	5,800
Scarrone	Barbera d'Alba			—	6,900

NOTES: [a] Currently not producing, the vineyard was replanted with all three nebbiolo clones and will be in production in 1991.
[b] This is a blend of grapes from various vineyards in Castiglione Falletto.
[c] Not produced as a cru, blended into the Castiglione Barolo.
[d] Only produced as a *riserva* in the better vintages.
[e] Located in S. Stefano Roero.

has visited wineries in France and the United States, where he and Luciana have become good friends of some fine California winemakers since their first visit in 1981. They make regular visits to our shores, and American winemakers enjoy their hospitality in Castiglione. And it's not just makers of wine but wine lovers as well; one of the first English phrases Alfredo mastered, while Luciana was doing a beautiful job of translating nearly all else for him, was a sincere, "My 'ouse is your 'ouse."

Vietti's 1984 production included some 22,000 bottles of Barolo and 7,200 of Barbaresco. There were Barolos from five crus—Briacca, Brunate, Bussia, Rocche, and Villero—and Barbarescos from two—Masseria and Rabajà. Currado points out that the differences in the subvarieties of the nebbiolo can be clearly noted in the crus that he makes, particularly between his Barolo Rocche

(planted 75 percent in michet, 20 percent lampia, and 5 percent rosé) and his Briacca cru (actually a part of the Rocche vineyard, but planted 100 percent in rosé). Both have the same soil and exposure, and as they are vinified the same the only reasonable explanation for the differences between them is in the vines themselves. Currado said that michet gives body to wine as it ages.

Briacca produces a softer, more velvety wine with less body than Rocche. The Rocche Barolo is full-bodied and robust, with more alcohol and tannin, harder and more closed while young, and slower to mature. It ages the best of the Vietti Barolos. Of all the wines Alfredo makes, Barolo is his personal favorite, and of his Barolos he prefers the Rocche, it being the deepest, richest, and most intense.

But it is not only bigness or power that he is aiming for. His

Brunate Barolo is elegant and perfumed. And the Bussia is more elegant still, with a fine perfume, moderate alcohol, and a lot of style. The '82 Bussia Barolo was made from a 20–75–5 blend of nebbiolo michet, lampia, and rosé. His Villero is high in alcohol and very robust. Currado no longer produces a Bussia or Briacca Barolo.

From time to time Currado vinifies other crus. He produced a Barolo from Parussi (100 percent michet) in 1971 and 1982, and from Meriondino (mostly michet), on the other side of the road from Rocche, in 1976, and we also tasted one from Codana. Meriondino is blended into his Castiglione Barolo, which also contains wine from other vineyards in Castiglione Falletto. In 1990 he bought 5.7 acres (2.3 hectares) of the Lazzarito vineyard in Serralunga. His first Barolo from there should be released in 1994. It will be from the very great 1989 vintage.

Alfredo, who describes himself as a *barolista,* produces two excellent Barbarescos as well—Masseria and Rabajà. The Masseria, made from 100 percent lampia, reflects the character of the Neive Barbarescos and is in some respects more like a Barolo than a Barbaresco—fairly full-bodied and rich, requiring more time to come around than many other Barbarescos.

The Rabajà, from Barbaresco itself, is typically more elegant and more refined. It too is made from 100 percent lampia. He has also made small amounts of Barbaresco from other crus including Casotto in 1981, and Pora in his search for the best grapes to produce his wines.

Currado until recently produced two Nebbiolo d'Alba wines, both among the best we have tasted. Today he produces only the S. Michele. He also makes a proprietary blend—Fioretto—from a blend of nebbiolo, barbera and neyrano grapes grown in his Fioretto vineyard in the Scarrone district.

When we first tasted the Vietti wines in 1979 we were struck by their style. These are far from just well-made wines, free of defects; they are wines that exemplify the best style and character of the grape variety they are made from.

Barolo: Castiglione ** +, Briacca **** +, Brunate ****, Bussia ****, Lazzarito **** +, Rocche **** +, Villero **** +, non-crus ** +; Barbaresco: Masseria *** +, Rabajà ****, non-crus **; Nebbiolo ***; Fioretto **

"Vigna Rionda" Azienda Agricola. See *Massolino Giuseppe.*

Vignaioli Piemontese, Soc. Coop. (Asti), 1976. This *cantina sociale* is actually an association of 12 cooperatives made up of 3,500 growers who cultivate 11,100 acres (4,500 hectares) of vines. Their annual production of 2.8 million cases makes them a force in the marketplace. Barolo is one of the many different wines they produce.

Vignolo-Lutati (Castiglione Falletto). This producer owns 25 acres (10 hectares), 20 (8) in vines. Cascina Pilone belonged to them until recently, when they sold it to Franco Fiorina. These wines have enjoyed a good reputation, but unfortunately the one we tasted didn't come up to it. They bottle a Barolo cru from their Brunella di Castiglione Falletto vineyard. The only wine that we can recall tasting was their mediocre '71. Barolo [0]

Villa Ile (Treiso). This winery, owned by Ileana Corradini, has 12.4 acres (5 hectares) of vines from which they produce some 35,000 bottles of wine annually, including Barbaresco, Dolcetto d'Alba, Barbera d'Alba, Moscato Passito, and the *vino da tavola* Garassino. Piero Ballario consults here.

Villadoria (Rivoli). A few years ago they owned 150 acres (61 hectares) of vines and an eyesore winery in Serralunga d'Alba. In July 1988 they sold 69 acres (28 hectares) in the Marenca-Rivetta district to Angelo Gaja, who is sure to make better use of it than Villadoria. They still own vines in that vineyard plus some in Il Colombaio and Il Cappallotto in Serralunga d'Alba.

Until recently the firm sold their mediocre wines under the Marchese Villadoria label. They were not a *marchese* but a trademark of CE.DI.VI. Daniele Lanzavecchia is the managing director as well as one of the partners here.

Villadoria sell their wines in some rather eye-arresting bottles, including a misshapen one with a candle stuck onto it and another bagged in burlap. Perhaps these curiosities are meant to offer some interest for the consumer that the wines are unable to provide. (They certainly do nothing for the image of Italian taste.) The company would do better, we think, to spend more thought on what they put into the bottle. Their Barolo might not be the worst in the zone, but is not far from it. The Barbaresco is not as bad. At one time they sold some Barolo under their label from the 1952, 1955, and 1961 vintages that certainly rose above their current crop of wines; in fact, these wines were very good. Although their current crop of wines rarely achieves the level of mediocrity they are a hair better than they used to be. Perhaps better things are in store here. Another improvement here is that they have finally dropped the pretentious Marchese from the label. Barolo 0; Barbaresco 0

Vinicola Piemontese. See *Poderi e Cantine di Marengo-Marenda.*

Voerzio Giacomo dei F.lli Voerzio (La Morra), 1973. The Giacomo Voerzio firm began bottling wines in 1973, with mixed results. They had an average annual production of 12,000 bottles of Barolo and 70,000 to 85,000 bottles of other Albeisa wines. Their vineyards were Boiolo, Ciabot della Luna, Croera, and Roscaleto—all in the Barolo zone—and La Serra. They owned 21.5 acres (8.7 hectares) of vineyards and bought grapes for some of their wines, but used only their own grapes from La Serra in their Barolo.

With their first cru bottling of La Serra from the 1982 vintage, they discontinued their other Barolos. Their last regular bottling was from the 1980 vintage. They didn't make any Barolo in 1981. The '82 La Serra was very good indeed, but the brothers felt that the 1983 might be superior. They produced 7,000 bottles of the '82 La Serra and 6,700 of the '83. The last Barbaresco was the '76.

F.lli was used on the label from 1978 to 1985. Then in 1986 the brothers, Gianni and Roberto, went their separate ways. Before the brothers split Giovanni managed the vineyards and Roberto the cellar. Today there are two Voerzio *cantine* in La Morra, Roberto and Gianni. As for the wines sold under the F.lli Voerzio label: Barolo ** +; Barbaresco [0].

Voerzio Gianni (La Morra), 1986. Gianni Voerzio and his brother, Roberto, worked together to produce some very good wines from 1980 through 1985. Since 1986, Gianni Voerzio's production has averaged some 100,000 bottles annually. This production consists of 5,300 bottles each of Barolo and Freisa della Langhe, 13,000 each of Barbera d'Alba and Moscato d'Asti, 20,000 to 24,000 Dolcetto d'Alba, 12,000 Nebbiolo delle Langhe, and 26,500 Roero Arneis, plus a small quantity of the *vino da tavola* Serrepiù. Voerzio's Dolcetto d'Alba comes from his Ciabot della Luna vineyard. Having tasted Gianni Voerzio's 82 four times, the '83 La Serra Barolo four times, and the '84 and '85 twice each, we must conclude that while the wines are better than the old Giacomo Voerzio wines, they're not up to what we tasted when the Voerzio brothers were working together. And we must admit to being both surprised and disappointed! Barolo *

Voerzio Roberto (*La Morra*), *1986*. Roberto Voerzio produced his first Arneis in 1986 and his first Freisa in 1985. He produced the Freisa in an autoclave to give it a light fizz and preserve its freshness.

Voerzio farms some 16 acres (6.5 hectares) of vines which in-cludes 4.7 acres (1.9 hectares) of La Serra, all planted for Barolo, and he has leased about 2.5 acres (1 hectare) each in Brunate and Cerequio since 1988. He produced 40,000 bottles of wine in 1987, of which more than 11,000 were Barolo. Today his production averages some 100,000 bottles annually—16,000 Barolo, 3,300 Barbera d'Alba, 26,500 Dolcetto d'Alba Priavino, 8,000 each Nebbiolo delle Langhe and Roero Arneis, 12,300 Freisa delle Langhe, with the balance being Moscato d'Asti. And there is a Favorita from Roero. Since 1987, Roberto Voerzio, like more and more producers here, has aged his Barolo in small, new oak casks, not in *barrique*. Another new wine here, Vignaserra, has been produced from a blend of nebbiolo and barbera; we think the first one was the '87.

Roberto is very serious and determined. He has the heart, and the palate, and is very interested in the wines of other areas and countries. He learned to make wine by reading and doing, and not from his father. He began making wine in the mid-1970s. When Roberto was twenty-seven in 1980, he began to realize how good wine could be. The first wine that he could take full credit for was the '82. The first wines that carry his name on the label are the '83 Barolo and '86 for the others. Barolo ** +

THE CRUS OF ROBERTO VOERZIO

Cru	Used for
Croera di La Morra	Nebbiolo delle Langhe
La Serra di La Morra	Barolo
La Serra di Valdivilla	Moscato d'Asti
Pria S. Francesco Croera	Dolcetto d'Alba
Vigneto del Boiolo	Freisa delle Langhe

Zunino Basilio (*Serralunga d'Alba*, località *Baudana*), *1974*. Zunino, owner of Trattoria del Castello in Serralunga d'Alba, produces a highly acclaimed Barolo from his 7.4 acres (3 hectares) of vines in the part of Baudana known as Sorì di Baudana. These vines are planted in the proportion of 60–20–20 nebbiolo for Barolo, dolcetto, and barbera. In all, he harvests some 16.53 tons (150 quintali) of nebbiolo grapes for Barolo. He also owns vines in the Cerretta vineyard. He sells some grapes to the *cantina sociale*. Of the eight vintages of Barolo that we tasted here, we were most impressed with the '82 and '85, followed by the '78 and, surprisingly, the '83. On our visit during April 1986, we tasted all vintages between the '81 and '85 from cask, plus the '78 and '80 from bottle. Barolo ** +

CHAPTER 3

The Nebbiolo Wines of Torino and Aosta

In the province of Torino and the neighboring region of Valle d'Aosta, nebbiolo wines are produced from three local subvarieties: nebbiolo spanna, picotener, and pugnet. The name *picotener* is from *picciolo tenero,* "tender stem." *Pugnet* is a descriptive term referring to the small, compact "fistlike" shape of the bunches, similar to the michet of the Langhe.

The two major wines from this area, both recognized under DOC, are Carema and Donnaz. Carema is made 100 percent from nebbiolo, or, as it is known locally, picotener. Donnaz is made from at least 85 percent nebbiolo; other local varieties may be blended in.

The vines planted in the morainic terrain of the steep mountainsides rising above the Dora Baltea River are trained on pergolas, the vine leaves spread out over the wooden framework to gain the maximum benefit from the sun needed to ripen the late-maturing nebbiolo. The sturdy supporting pillars of stone and concrete and the pale stones of the dry wall terraces reflect the sun's rays onto the vines and absorb the heat of the day to add an important extra measure of warmth to the vines after the sun has set.

The climate here is rather cold and windy. The picotener wines tend to be lighter in body, less tannic and higher in acidity than the wines of the other major nebbiolo zones. And, not surprisingly, the vintages are more variable.

In the province of Torino there are 12,650 acres (5,120 hectares) of vines producing the equivalent of 3.2 million cases of wine annually. This is down considerably from some six or seven years ago when 22,000 acres (9,000 hectares) produced the equivalent of 5 million cases a year.

There are four wine-producing zones in the province: Canavese and Carema, Chierese, Pineroese, and Valle di Susa. The Canavese and Carema district encompasses 3,700 acres (1,500 hectares), of which 215 (87) are delimited for DOC production.

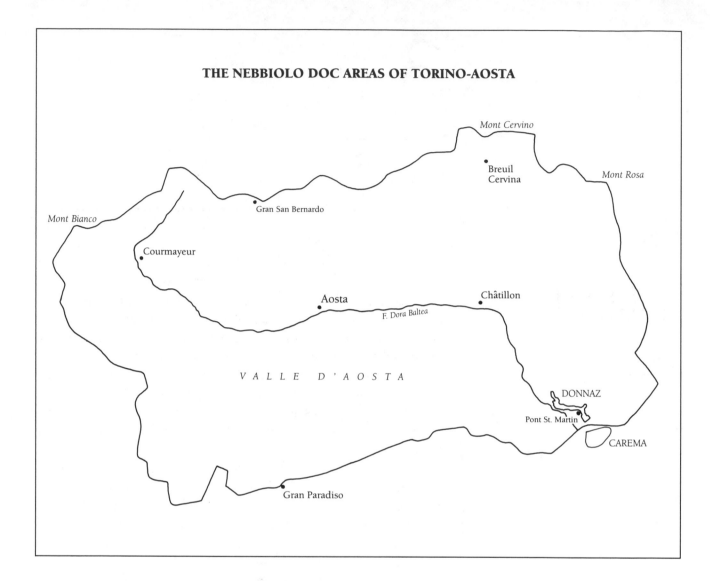

THE NEBBIOLO DOC AREAS OF TORINO-AOSTA

Mont Cervino

• Breuil
Cervina

Mont Rosa

• Gran San Bernardo

Mont Bianco

• Courmayeur

• Aosta

Châtillon •

F. Dora Baltea

V A L L E   D ' A O S T A

DONNAZ

Pont St. Martin •

CAREMA

• Gran Paradiso

Of the 1.2 million cases produced here, 65,550 are DOC.[1] The DOC wines of Torino are Carema, Caluso Passito, Erbaluce di Caluso, both still and sparkling, and Freisa di Chieri.

The Valle d'Aosta region, bordered by some of the highest mountains in Europe—Mont Blanc, the Matterhorn, Monte Rossa, and Gran Paradiso—consists of a series of valleys formed by the tributaries of the Dora Baltea River. French is commonly spoken. In 1988 the DOC zone named for the region had 408 registered growers who cultivated 160 acres (65 hectares) of vines.[2] The Valley d'Aosta DOC has 17 subdenominations. The average annual production of the wines of this DOC, between 1986 and 1988, was 307,860 bottles of wine, of which 211,200 were red.[3]

The Wines Rated

**	*
Carema	Aglie
Donnaz	Arnad-Montjovet
Solativo del Canavese	Campiglione
	Cesnola
	Nebbiolo del Canavese

The Wines

AGLIE (*Torino*). This wine is produced in two styles: semi-sweet and dry. We are concerned only with the dry Aglie,

**** Great, superb, truly noble

*** Exceptionally fine

** Very good

* A good example of its type, somewhat above average

0 Acceptable to mediocre, depending on the context; drinkable

+ Somewhat better than the star category it is put in

− Somewhat less than the star category it is put in, except for zero where it indicates a wine or producer-wine combination that is badly made or worse.

[. .] *On a producer:* Tentative evaluation based on an insufficient number of wines or based on older, out-of-date vintages, or where the wines we tasted were too difficult to fully judge to give a fair assessment of quality.
On a wine or vintage: Projection for the future. This rating is given to a vintage where we feel that we tasted an insufficient number of wines or those we tasted were too difficult to really judge to give a fair assessment of quality.

(. .) Potential increase in the rating of the wine given sufficient maturity.

which is made from 100 percent nebbiolo. It is a medium-bodied wine at about 12 percent alcohol, at its best within four years of the vintage. Rating *

ARNAD-MONTJOVET (*Aosta*), *DOC.* Arnad-Montjovet is part of the Valle d'Aosta DOC. The growing zone takes in the villages of Arnaz, Challand-Saint Victor, Champdepraz, Hone, Issogne, Montjovet, and Verrés. The castle ruins at Montjovet, along with the massive fortress of Bard, command the upper Dora Baltea River. The *castello* at Issogne was built during the fifteenth century. Verrés is home to a fourteenth-century fortress.

Besides a minimum of 70 percent nebbiolo, DOC allows up to 30 percent dolcetto, vien de nus, pinot nero, neyret, and/or freisa. The maximum yield is 600 gallons per acre (56 hectoliters per hectare). This wine must be given at least eight months of age and attain no less than 11 percent alcohol. If it is aged two years and reaches 12 percent it may be labeled as *superiore* or *supérieur*. In 1988 there were 13

growers in this DOC zone, which encompassed 2.7548 acres (1.1148 hectares)! A grand total of 2,933 bottles was produced.[4] This represents a decrease from the 4,933 bottles of 1987, which was down from the 5,467 of 1986. The decrease in production isn't surprising considering the number of growers and acreage in each of those earlier years: 16 growers and 3.4257 acres (1.3863 hectares), and 16 and 4.77 (1.9303), respectively.[5] The only producer that we know of is Vignaiolo Bonin di Dino Bonin.

Arnad is a light-bodied wine that is best drunk within about two to three years of the harvest. Montjovet is a light- to medium-bodied red wine that, prior to DOC, was produced in Montjovet and Saint-Vincent. Surprisingly, Saint-Vincent isn't included in this DOC. Rating *

The vintages according to Antonio Rossi:[6]

**** 1986, 1982

*** 1988, 1987, 1985, 1981, 1979

** 1984, 1983, 1980

CAMPIGLIONE (*Torino*). The Marchesi di San Germano produce this wine in Campiglione Fenile from 100 percent nebbiolo grapes. The vineyards are in the Pelice Valley at altitudes ranging from 2,300 to 3,280 feet (700 to 1,000 meters). It has been reported that a number of other grape varieties are used as well, but we were told that Campiglione is made only from the nebbiolo. The wine has a deep color, is light-bodied and rather low in alcohol at 11 percent. As Campiglione is meant to be drunk young, it wasn't vintage-dated, but in recent years we've seen some that were. The best place to taste this wine is at the very good Ristorante Flipot in Torre Pelice. Chef Walter Eynard will also suggest other hard-to-find wines to accompany his very fine cuisine. During the autumn Flipot offers *funghi* served in a variety of imaginative ways. As for the wine, rating *

CAREMA (*Torino*), *DOC.* Carema has been known since at least the sixteenth century. It is today without a doubt the best-known wine of the Torino-Aosta production zone, and deservedly so. It is the best. This wine is made 100 percent from picotener grapes grown in the terraced mountain vineyards of Carema at altitudes ranging from 1,150 to 2,300 feet (350 to 700 meters) above sea level. The production zone, on the left bank of the Dora Baltea River, east of Ivrea, extends to the Aosta border. In fact, although all the vines are in Piemonte, at least one producer has a *cantina* in a *frazione* of Pont-Saint-Martin called Ivery, which is in Aosta.

The DOC production zone encompasses 94 acres (38.05 hectares), less than half of which is planted. There are 122 growers in Carema, but only 31 declared a crop in 1988.[7] Very few own more than 2.5 acres (1 hectare); most have only about 1.25 acres (0.5 hectare).

Regarded Crus	Owner-Producer
Casetto	n/a
Costa	n/a
Con	n/a
Lavrey	Ferrando
Nusy	Clerino
Paris	n/a
Piole	Ferrando, Morbelli
Rovarey	n/a
Siei	Ferrando, Clerino
Silanc	Ferrando
Villanova	n/a

The climate here is cold and windy, and the picotener is a shy-bearing variety. DOC sets a limit of 599 gallons per acre (56 hectoliters per hectare) and a minimum of 12 percent alcohol. At most, 284,100 bottles of wine a year can be produced. Between 1971 and 1988 the yearly average production of Carema was 114,212 bottles. Between 1985 and 1988 production had dropped to an annual average of 64,200 bottles. And in the excellent vintage of 1988, production was only 26,933 bottles.

Until at least a few years ago, some of the small producers of Carema were still crushing their grapes by foot in the time-honored tradition, but it's difficult today to find men willing to do the work. Usually grapes are destemmed and crushed by machine. When the grapes are to be crushed by feet, the bunches are put into the upright wooden *tini* and left for three or four days to warm up a bit before the men go in, up to their waists in the chilly mass, to do the labo-rious work of crushing the grapes manually—or to be more precise, pedally. The fermentation lasts for three weeks to a month.

Generally, the grapes for Carema crushed by machine are fermented on the skins for seven to ten days, depending on the temperature and how much color is desired. The nebbiolo grape here doesn't attain a very deep color.

In the spring, when the weather warms, the wine undergoes malolactic fermentation—very important as the wines tend to be quite high in acid. In fact, they are sometimes deacidified so that the malolactic won't be inhibited.

Carema is aged for a minimum of four years, at least two of which are in oak or chestnut casks with a capacity of not more than 1,056 gallons (40 hectoliters). The wine is light garnet in color, with a fragrant, often floral perfume that for some recalls roses. It is light in body, with moderate tannin and a firmer acidity than its nebbiolo counterparts to the east in the Novara-Vercelli hills. Carema is a wine esteemed for its delicacy. It is best drunk five to eight years after the vintage, but in exceptional vintages it can live for twenty years, perhaps more.

Carema is a good choice to drink with roast pork or veal or the local fontina or toma cheeses. Rating **

THE PRODUCERS RATED

***
Ferrando Luigi, black label
— Produttori "Nebbiolo di Carema," Carema dei Carema

PRODUCTION OF CAREMA

Year	Gallons	Hectoliters	Year	Gallons	Hectoliters
1971	34,373	1,302	1980	27,192	1,030
1972	15,286	579	1981	27,878	1,056
1973	36,564	1,385	1982	23,628	895
1974	37,118	1,406	1983	30,202	1,144
1975	25,925	982	1984	11,642	441
1976	26,558	1,006	1985	19,457	737
1977	14,494	549	1986	16,368	620
1978	18,295	693	1987	9,689	367
1979	27,060	1,025	1988	5,333	202

Sources: 1971–76: *Regione Piemonte*
1977–86: *Piemonte appunti sul vino e dintori.* Torino: Assessorato Agricoltura e Foreste, October 1989
1976–86, I Vini della Provincia di Torino
1985–88, Piemonte di Vino in Vino

**

Ferrando Luigi
Produttori "Nebbiolo di Carema"

*

+ Morbelli Giovanni

VINTAGE INFORMATION AND TASTING NOTES

The producers we've spoken with rated the best years in Carema as 1961, 1962, 1964, 1967, 1971, 1974, 1978, 1982, and 1983, with 1961 being the best of all. One producer also includes 1968, 1975, 1979, and 1980 on his list. There is general agreement that 1963, 1972, and 1977 were the worst vintages in the zone; 1973 and 1976 were also nominated for this category by at least one producer. Luigi Ferrando singles out 1962 and 1982 as the very best vintages, and 1977 as the worst.

Antonio Niederbacher's chart (adjusted for our four-star system) gives the following ratings:

1985	***	1977	0
1984	*	1976	*
1983	***	1975	**
1982	***	1974	***
1981	*	1973	**
1980	**	1972	*
1979	***	1971	***
1978	***	1970	***

Antonio Rossi rates them:[8]

1988	***	1978	***
1987	***	1977	*
1986	***	1976	**
1985	****	1975	***
1984	**	1974	****
1983	***	1973	**
1982	***	1972	*
1981	**	1971	***
1980	***	1970	***
1979	***		

Our limited experience suggests the following:

1985	***	Based on one wine.
1984	–	None tasted.
1983	**	Soft, open wines that should be drunk up.
1982	***	These will be keepers. One of the best vintages that we've tasted.
1981	0	Based on one wine tasted in 1987.
1980	*	Very ready, some are fading, drink up.

1979	**	For the most part they are ready.
1978	***	Very fine wines that should continue to improve for a few years yet.
1977	0	A poor year from the outset.
1976	*	The best bottles are still good, but are not for keeping. Best to drink.
1975	*	No need to hold any longer.
1974	***	Very fine wines which are holding, the best will last.
1973	0	They never amounted to much.
1972	0	Ditto.
1971	0	Not up to the reputation of the vintage.
1970	0	It's doubtful if any have held.
1968	0	Too old now.
1967	0	The wines are starting to fade.
1964	**	Very good, ready now, perhaps even fading a bit.
1962	**	The one that we tasted in 1988 was still very good. We advise drinking them now.
1957	0	The one that we tasted in 1989, while good, was fading.

Ferrando Luigi 1985 black label (*twice, 4/90*). Big aroma; rich and concentrated, sweet, rich and young; firm and still a little closed. **(*)

Ferrando Luigi 1983 (*5 times, 4/90*). Tarlike component on the nose; soft entry, then some tannin followed by a softness in the center, tasty; a tad light at the end. * +

Produttori "Nebbiolo di Carema" 1983 (*4/89*). More forward than the Carema dei Carema, good flavor, soft. * +

Produttori "Nebbiolo di Carema" 1983 Carema dei Carema (*4/89*). Good fruit, quite young, balanced, tasty. ** +

Ferrando Luigi 1982 black label (*8 times, 5/89*). Concentrated floral and fruit aroma; big and rich, tasty and open, good structure and balance; still young. ***(+)

Morbelli 1982 (*4/89*). Floral perfume; well balanced, soft center, some firmness, good backbone. ** +

Ferrando Luigi 1981 (*4/87*). Dried fruit aroma; moderate tannin, seems to lack the fruit to carry the tannin. (*).

Ferrando Luigi 1980 (*2/87*). Light nose, floral note; soft, yet has an edge to it, light tannin; drinkable, could improve; could use more body. *(+)

Produttori "Nebbiolo di Carema" 1980 (*5 times, 1/86*). Nice fruit aroma; fruity, high acid; nice now, not to keep. *

Produttori "Nebbiolo di Carema" 1980 dove label (*1/86, 19,000 bottles*). A lot of flavor and perfume, acid on the high side which adds zest and liveliness; nice to drink now, doubtful future, drink over the next two years. **

Ferrando Luigi 1979 (*3 times, 4/85*). Perfumed bouquet with suggestions of flowers; somewhat light in body, moderate tannin, good fruit; needs a few years to really soften though can be drunk now, will improve. *(+)

Morbelli 1979 (*twice, 1/85*). A bouquet of flowers and berries; a little light but fairly well balanced, somewhat soft but still has tannin, some acid on the finish. * +

Produttori "Nebbiolo di Carema" 1979 (*10 times, 10/87, 12,500 bottles*). The most recent bottle was the best. Floral, fragrant bouquet; rich and tasty, balanced and complex, lingering finish. ***
Bottle of 1/85: Light-bodied, light tannin, light fruit, rather short, and simple—a disappointment.

Ferrando Luigi 1978 black label (*twice, 2/87*). Good color; good body, some firmness, drinkable now with a nice softness in the center, light tannin; should improve. **(* −)

Morbelli 1978 (*twice, 1/85*). Medium garnet, brick at rim; lovely floral bouquet; still somewhat hard but has good fruit in center; quality already evident; needs perhaps three more years. **

Produttori "Nebbiolo di Carema" 1978 Carema dei Carema (*1/85*). A mineral note on aroma, which is somewhat closed; firm, still has tannin, some acid, medium-bodied, flavorful; still young but quite nice now. **

Ferrando Luigi 1976 (*1/85*). Deepest in color of the '79, '76, '74, and '71 tasted at the same time; fruity, floral aroma but somewhat simple; a fair amount of tannin and acid, insufficient fruit but with food it should be quite drinkable. *

Produttori "Nebbiolo di Carema" 1976 (*6 times, 2/85*). Light color; small but nice floral aroma; somewhat fruity; light-bodied, some tannin, nice flavor; fairly ready.

Ferrando Luigi 1975 (*4/89*). Barnyardy aroma; slight sweetness, good backbone, tasty. ** −

Produttori "Nebbiolo di Carema" 1975 Carema dei Carema (*6 times, 2/85, 40,000 bottles*). Aroma vaguely like that of a rubber tire; a lot better on the palate, light-bodied, nice entry, then a bit shallow; overall quite drinkable. *

Ferrando Luigi 1974 black label (*4 times, 4/89*). Nose off a bit; it seems to be drying out, still it does have fairly nice flavor. ** −
Bottle of 1/88: Light brick color, orange reflections; bouquet recalls faded flowers; still some tannin, lots of flavor, some delicacy, nice texture; lots of life left. ***

Produttori "Nebbiolo di Carema" 1974 (*at least 14 times between 11/79 and 12/83*). Floral aroma with berrylike fruit; soft and smooth, round and fruity; at or very close to its peak. ** +

Produttori "Nebbiolo di Carema" 1974 Carema dei Carema (*4/81, 40,000 bottles*). Expansive bouquet of cherries and flowers; some tannin but soft, almost velvety; has some elegance, and style. ***

Produttori "Nebbiolo di Carema" 1973 (*3 times, 3/80*). Color shows age; some oxidation apparent on aroma; light-bodied, still some tannin, lacks body and fruit; where will it go?

Ferrando Luigi 1971 (*4/89*). Toasty, dried berry flavor, soft, tasty and balanced. **

Ferrando Luigi 1971 black label (*twice, 1/88*). Pale garnet color, orange reflections; lovely floral perfume, with leather and dried berry notes; chewy, and flavorful; could be starting to dry out, best to drink now. **

Ferrando Luigi 1970 (*9/80*). Firm acidity, medium-bodied, still some tannin but very ready now, rather brief on the finish. *

Morbelli 1968 (*1/85*). Fruity, floral aroma; has tannin, good flavor, but beginning to dry out.

Morbelli 1967 (*1/85*). Browning at the rim; showing age, but there's still some interest left. *

Ferrando Luigi 1964 black label (*twice, 3/82*). Fragrant floral bouquet; fruity, still some tannin but fairly soft and ready; nice now and near its peak, no need to hold any longer. **

Ferrando Luigi 1962 black label (*1/88*). Beautiful robe, brick toward garnet with orange highlights; dried fruit and dried flowers, leatherlike notes; still some tannin; could be starting to fade but still a nice glass with a sweetness, dry finish, some alcohol. **

Ferrando Luigi 1957 black label (*4/89*). Though the bouquet is fading, there is still some complexity and interest. Sweet entry, drying out, still some flavor. *

THE PRODUCERS

Bertolo Lorenzo (*Torino*). Bertolo is a negotiant who deals in a wide range of wines, including a Carema that we cannot comment on, never having tasted it.

Calligaris Rino. Calligaris produces a very limited amount of Carema; unfortunately, we've never tasted his wines.

Ferrando Luigi (*Ivrea*), *1900.* Luigi Ferrando is a respected negociant of Carema and other wines, including Fara and Gattinara. He is also a grower, with 17.1 acres (6.9 hectares) of vines, of which 7.4 (3) are in Carema and 9.6 (3.9) in Piverone. Ferrando owns part of some of the better Carema crus: Lavrey, Piole, Siei, and Silanc. His Carema vineyards have a southeastern exposure and are planted at an altitude of 1,280 feet (390 meters) above sea level. He produces about 22,500 bottles of wine per year—15,000 of Carema, 15,000 of Erbaluce, and 2,500 of Solativo. This includes, in some vintages, single-vineyard bottlings as well as a special *riserva* that he distinguishes with a black label, as the term *riserva speciale* is not allowed by DOC regulations for Carema. His black label Carema is the best wine of the area, followed by the Carema dei Carema of the Produttori "Nebbiolo di Carema."

We are not sure if he is still making the cru bottlings, but in 1967 Luigi bottled a Vigneto Nusy from Giuseppe Clerino and a Vigneto Lavrey from his own vines. In 1969 he made a Vigneto Siei, also from Clerino. He also produces some excellent Erbaluce della Serra di Ivrea as well as a fine late-harvest Erbaluce Tardiva, and, from 1986, a *barrique*-aged **Solativo del Canavese**. Carema: **, black label ***

Morbelli Giovanni (*Carema*), *1891.* Morbelli owns 5 acres (2 hectares) of vines, including a piece of the regarded cru of Piole. Some 10 percent of his annual production of Carema (15,000 bottles) is from this vineyard. He also produces 20,000 bottles of the white Erbaluce. We have heard that Morbelli also bottles Arnaz, Donnaz, and Montjovet, three other nebbiolo-based wines. Carema * +

Produttori "Nebbiolo di Carema" (Carema), 1960. This cooperative has 48 members who own 50 acres (20 hectares) of vines. Their annual production is 150,000 bottles. Of this, some 72,000 bottles are Carema, about 59,000 bottles are their regular Carema and another 13,000 bottles are a special selection of their best wine. Until 1978 this wine was sold as Carema dei Carema. Bureaucratic decree has since disallowed this name; they are now required to label their *crème de la crème* simply "Carema." To set it apart from the regular Carema, it is bottled with a dove gray artist's label. This wine, which is not produced every year, was made from the 1974, 1975, and 1978 vintages and we suspect the 1982, 1985, and 1988. Carema: **, dei Carema *** –

Cesnola *(Torino).* Produced in a *frazione* of Settimo Vittone, Cesnola is made from nebbiolo grapes. The wine reputedly often attains 13 percent alcohol. It is not a wine to age but is at its best within four years of the vintage. Rating *

Donnaz *(Aosta), DOC.* Donnaz, or Donnas, is covered under the regional Valle d'Aosta DOC. Some vineyards were planted at altitudes up to 2,000 feet (610 meters) above sea level, making them among the highest grown in Italy. The vines are grown on the sides of the mountains that rise above the valley of the Dora Baltea River in the *comuni* of Donnas, Bard, Perloz, and Pont-Saint-Martin at the border of Carema.

The DOC zone encompasses 371 acres (150 hectares). In 1988, with a scant 32.9672 acres (13.3088 hectares) inscribed for the DOC with 61 growers, production from only 17.3397 acres (7 hectares) was declared by 27 growers.[9] This represents a decrease from the 60 acres (24 hectares) cultivated by 111 growers a few years earlier.

Donnaz must be made from at least 85 percent nebbiolo (locally called pugnet) grapes; the balance may include freisa, neyret, and/or vien de nus. The maximum yield prescribed by DOC is 566 gallons per acre (53 hectoliters per hectare). Production, which has ranged from as little as 9,733 bottles in 1977 to as much as 83,465 in 1979, has generally averaged about 54,130 bottles a year. For the three most recent years that we have data for, 1986 through 1988, production was 46,665, 59,865 and 28,800 bottles, respectively.[10] That's an average of 45,288 bottles per year.

Donnaz has a minimum alcohol of 11.5 percent. It must be aged for at least three years, two in oak or chestnut casks no larger than 790 gallons (30 hectoliters). The wines are light-bodied and meant for early drinking, within three to six years of the harvest. They tend to be somewhat similar to those of Carema, but lighter.

Donnaz, DOC since 1971, was brought under the new regional DOC in 1986, Valle d'Aosta, or Vallée d'Aoste. This DOC covers 17 wines produced in the Aosta Valley from a variety of grapes.

The best Donnaz vintages are considered to be 1983, 1982, 1979, 1978, and 1974. Antonio Rossi rates 1988, 1985, and 1983 as four-star vintages, 1987, 1984, 1981 as three, and 1986 and 1982 at two.[11]

Donnaz is a good choice to accompany white meats such as veal roast or chops, guinea hen, or turkey. Rating **

THE PRODUCERS

Ferrando. Ferrando sold a Donnaz at one time, but we don't know if he still does; we haven't seen any since the 1974 vintage.

F.lli Ghiglieri. This is another Donnaz producer we've heard about, though we've never seen their wine.

Soc. Coop. Caves Cooperatives de Donnaz. Founded in 1971, this co-op has 70 members. It is by far the largest producer in the zone, with an annual output of some 36,000 to 50,000 bottles. In 1979 they produced 48,000 bottles; in 1980, 36,000

Issogne *(Aosta).* Issogne is the product of nebbiolo, gros vien, dolcetto, and vien de nus grapes. It is a light-bodied wine, with about 10.5 percent alcohol, and not meant for aging.

Montjovet *(Aosta).* This wine is now covered under the Valle d'Aosta DOC for **Arnad-Montjovet.**

Nebbiolo del Canavese *(Torino).* The Produttori "Nebbiolo di Carema" produces this wine from grapes grown in vineyards near Carema. It is a wine for early consumption. Rating *

Riserva del Generale *(Torino).* This is a medium-bodied red wine produced from a blend of nebbiolo, barbera, bonarda, dolcetto, and freisa grapes.

Rosso della Serra *(Torino).* This wine is produced by the Cantina Sociale della Serra from a blend of nebbiolo and barbera grapes in about equal proportions. The vineyards are near Ivrea, in the *comuni* of Moncrivello, Roppolo, Viverone, and Zimone. It is a medium-bodied wine, ready to drink shortly after it is released for sale in its third year.

Rosso di Bricherasio *(Torino).* This medium-bodied red wine is made from a blend of nebbiolo, barbera, freisa, and other varieties grown at Bricherasio.

Rosso di Frossasco *(Torino).* Frossasco is produced from nebbiolo with the addition of other local varieties. It is typical of the medium-bodied reds produced in this area.

Rosso di Valperga (*Torino*). This wine, made from nebbiolo and other local grape varieties grown at Valperga, is similar in character to Rosso di Frossasco.

Solativo del Canavese (*Torino*). Luigi Ferrando, the very fine Carema producer, also makes this *barrique*-aged wine. He first produced this wine, 550 bottles and 80 half bottles, in 1986. It spent nine months in *barrique, fusti di rovere*. We rated that wine two stars when we tasted it from barrel in April 1988. It had an aroma and flavor that combined vanilla, flowers, and nuts; it was smooth with a sort of dried fruit overlay. Rating **

Torre Daniele (*Torino*). Torre Daniele, named for the hamlet in Settimo Vittone where it is produced, is made from nebbiolo grapes.

Torre Saint-Pierre (*Aosta*). Doret Esterina produces this wine from a blend of petit rouge (60 percent) and nebbiolo (40 percent). It is a medium-bodied red that should be drunk young.

Vino della Serra (*Torino*). This light-bodied red wine is produced at the Cantina Sociale della Serra from a blend of barbera, freisa, and nebbiolo grapes.

CHAPTER 4

The Nebbiolo Wines of the Novara-Vercelli Hills

The various nebbiolo-based wines of the Novara-Vercelli hills have certain common characteristics. They are generally medium-bodied, dry red wines with a floral bouquet often reminiscent of violets, occasionally roses, sometimes with notes of strawberries or raspberries. They tend to have a firm tannic vein and a slight bitterness on the aftertaste. These wines range in alcohol from 11.5 to 12.5 percent, and have a moderate capacity to age. Few are ready before their fourth year or worth keeping past their eighth to tenth, although there are exceptions, particularly in the better vintages.

These wines make a fine accompaniment to roasted red meat and game birds. Gattinara and Lessona, being bigger wines, also go well with pigeon and duck.

While nebbiolo, known here predominantly as spanna, is the most important grape in these wines, other varieties, especially bonarda, vespolina, and/or croatina, are often blended in. In general, the better the wine, the higher the percentage of spanna and the lesser, the less.

It has frequently been reported that the name spanna is derived from Spagna (Spain) and that the grape variety itself comes from there. Cardinale Mercurino Arborio di Gattinara, who served as Chancellor to Carlo V of Spain from the latter part of the fifteenth to the early part of the sixteenth century, is credited with bringing the spanna grape from Spain to Gattinara. Authorities in Gattinara disagree, however, stating that it was just the reverse. They point out that Cardinal Arborio deserves much credit for promulgating the name of the wine of Gattinara outside the region.

These authorities trace the origins of the grape back to the second century, when the Vercellese were conquered by the Romans, who subsequently restructured the system of agriculture in the area, planting vines on the hillsides and other crops on the plains. Pliny reported that the Romans were responsible for the introduction of the spionia grape—a variety that he noted

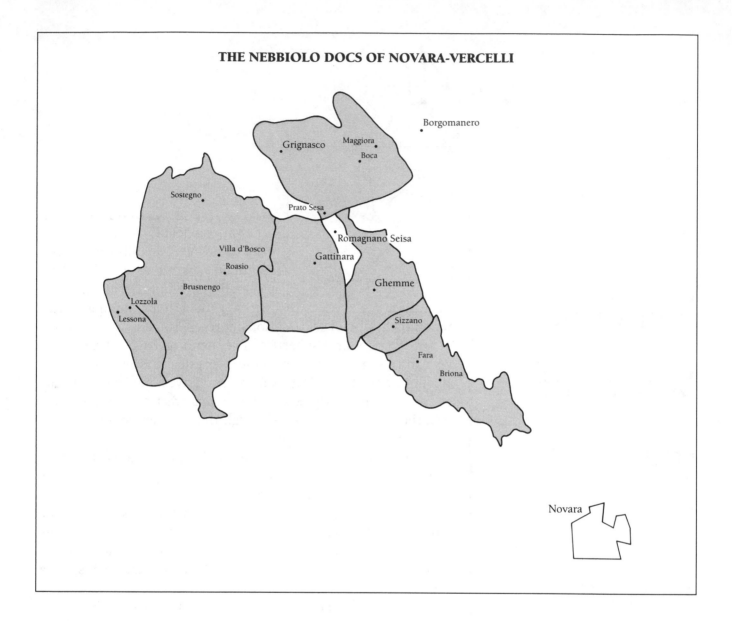

THE NEBBIOLO DOCS OF NOVARA-VERCELLI

thrives in foggy climates—which was cultivated on the plains of Ravenna and in the pre-alpine hills of Lombardia and Piemonte.

Another theory behind the name spanna links it to its method of cultivation, trained *"a spanna"*—at a short distance from the ground—as opposed to the Roman practice of training the vines high on trees or tall poles.

NOVARA

The main growing region of Novara is on the left bank of the Sesia River. The soil here is morainic, of glacial origin, rich in important microelements, and with a bit more limestone than the districts on the opposite bank. The Novara vineyards spread over 3,457 acres (1,399 hectares) of vines which yield an average of 752,500 cases of wine annually.[1] Of these, DOC wines are produced on 400 acres (162 hectares) that, between 1986 and 1988, averaged 30,765 cases,[2] less than 5 percent of the region's total viticultural output. This is down significantly from half a decade ago when 6,700 acres (2,711 hectares) yielded an average annual production of 1.1 million cases with a paltry 60,000 cases of DOC wines. There are 4,000 growers and three cooperative cellars in this region. Four wines have been recognized under DOC, all made basically from spanna: Boca, Fara, Ghemme, and Sizzano.

THE WINES OF THE NOVARA-VERCELLI HILLS—PRODUCTION STATISTICS

Wine	Province	Number of Growers[a]	Extent of Vineyards in Hectares[a]	Maximum Yield per Hectare		Average Yield per Year		Potential Production	
				qli	hl	hl[b]	cases	hl	cases
Boca	Novara	18	14.81	90	63.0	262	2,911	933	10,366
Bramaterra	Vercelli	43	29.18	75	52.5	650	7,222	1,532	17,020
Fara	Novara	35	21.07	110	77.0	868	9,643	1,622	18,020
Gattinara	Vercelli	148	101.97	90	63.0	3,832	42,562	6,424	71,371
Ghemme	Novara	61	85.65	100	70.0	1,578	17,532	5,996	66,616
Lessona	Vercelli	3	6.45	80	56.0	207	2,300	361	4,011
Sizzano	Novara	70	40.47	100	70.0	455	5,055	2,933	32,586
Total		378	299.60	645	451.5	7,852	87,225	19,801	219,990

Abbreviations and conversions:		
	1 hectare	= 2.4711 acres
hl—hectoliter	1 quintal	= 220.4622 pounds
qli—quintali	1 hectoliter	= 26.42 gallons

Sources: [a] ll Corriere Vinicolo, n. 10, March 12, 1990
  [b] *Based on the average production between 1986 and 1988*
  Figures supplied by Regione Piemonte, 1989

VERCELLI

The Gattinara, Lessona, and Bramaterra growing zones are in the province of Vercelli. The major wine-producing area here encompasses 3,000 acres (1,214 hectares) of vines which yield, on average, 657,700 cases of wine a year.[3] The acreage is down considerably from the 4,940 acres (2,000 hectares) planted in vines five years ago, while the average annual production has decreased less significantly from the 777,000 case production. The five DOC wines here produced an annual average of 52,100 cases between 1986 and 1988 from 358 acres (145 hectares) of vines.[4] This, too, shows a significant drop from a few years ago, when the DOCs of Erbaluce di Caluso, Caluso Passito, Lessona, Bramaterra, and Gattinara together accounted for some 77,000 cases annually. Erbaluce di Caluso and Caluso Passito, which extend into the province of Torino not far from Carema, produce white wines. The other three produce spanna-based reds. The Gattinara zone is on the right bank of the Sesia; Lessona is off to the west; between the two is the DOC of Bramaterra.

THE COLLI NOVARESE AND VERCELLI

The Colli Novarese and Vercelli vineyards encompass 3,700 acres (1,485 hectares), 765 (309) of which are DOC. Of an annual production of 1.2 million cases, less than 17 percent, or 222,200 cases, are DOC.[5] Most of the DOC wines are aged for three years, two or so in large, old casks of chestnut or Slavonian oak.

THE WINES

All of the important red wines here are based on the spanna, or nebbiolo. Without question the best one is Gattinara, but those labeled as "Spanna del Piemonte" can, on occasion, match, or even surpass, any other wine produced in this area. At one time wines from points farther south were frequently blended in to add body and structure. This practice is much less common today and in one way it is unfortunate. When it was done judiciously, the resulting wine was far superior to what would have been bottled without it. One advantage to the current state of affairs is that the wines today are purer than in times gone by—that is, they are made from locally grown grapes.

The Wines Rated

***
Gattinara
Spanna [del Piemonte], the best ones

**
Ara
Boca
Bramaterra
Caramino
Fara
Ghemme
Lessona

DOC REQUIREMENTS OF THE WINES OF THE NOVARA-VERCELLI HILLS

							Minimum Aging Years from Harvest		
Wine	Province	Spanna %	Bonarda %	Vespolina %	Others %	Alcohol	Cask Years	Total Years	Best from/to
Boca	Novara	45–75	0–20	20–40	0	12%	2	3[a]	4–12
Bramaterra[b]	Vercelli	50–70	20–30	10–20	20–30	12%	1	2[a]	6–10
Caramino[c]	Novara	30–50	20–40	10–30	0	12%	2	3	4–8
Fara	Novara	30–50	0–40	10–30	0	12%	2	3	4–9
Gattinara[d]	Vercelli	90–100	0–10	0	0	12%	2	4[a]	6–15
Ghemme	Novara	60–85	0–15	10–30	0	12%	3	4[a]	6–12
Lessona	Vercelli	75–100	0–25	0–25	0	12%	2	3	4–10
Sizzano	Novara	40–60	0–25	15–40	0	12%	2	3[a]	4–10
Spanna[e]	Novara–Vercelli	85–100	—	—	0–15	—	—	—	—

NOTES: [a] Aging is from Januiary 1.
[b] Bramaterra: 20 to 30 percent croatina and 10 to 20 percent bonarda and/or vespolina.
[c] Non-DOC: percentages of grape varieties given are estimates only, not requirements.
[d] This information pertains to Gattinara DOC. With its recognition, in March 1991, as DOCG, the alcoholic requirements have been changed to 12.5 percent for the *normale* and 13 percent for the *riserva,* and the total aging to 3 years for the former category and 4 for the latter.
[e] The European Common Market requires that a varietally labeled wine contain at least 85 percent of that grape.

Möt Ziflon
Sizzano
Spanna [del Piemonte]

*
— Agamium
Barengo Rosso
+ Borgo Alto
Fogarin
La Sassaia
Maggiora
Nebbiolo della Serra
Orbello
Piccone
Romagnano Seisa
Spanna [del Piemonte]

AGAMIUM (*Novara*). Antichi Vigneti di Cantalupo produces Agamium (labeled with the Roman name for the village of Ghemme) from a blend of 80 percent spanna, 15 percent vespolina, and 5 percent bonarda after their best grapes have been selected to make their Ghemme. Agamium is aged from twelve to twenty-four months in oak cask. The wine is lightweight and can have a tart edge to it. Rating * —

ARA (*Novara*). This light-bodied, fresh, fruity wine, made predominantly from spanna grapes, is produced in the same area as **Grignasco.** Rating **

BARENGO ROSSO (*Novara*). This wine is produced by the Cantina Sociale dei "Colli Novaresi" from a blend of 50 percent spanna, 30 percent bonarda, and 20 percent vespolina grapes grown in the village of Barengo. Rating *

BOCA (*Novara*), DOC. Boca is made from 45 to 70 percent spanna, with the addition of up to 20 percent bonarda novarese (uva rara), and 20 to 40 percent vespolina grapes. There are 37 acres (15 hectares) of vines delimited for Boca in the *comuni* of Boca, Cavallirio, Grignasco, Maggiora, and Prato Sesia. The vines cannot be planted at an altitude greater than 1,805 feet (550 meters) above sea level. There are 18 authorized growers in the zone and production cannot exceed 10,365 cases, which, considering that the average between 1986 and 1988 was only 2,911 cases, isn't much of a problem.

The aging period begins January 1. This light-bodied, dry red wine is similar to Fara and Sizzano. It is noted for having an aroma of violets, and some find it has an aftertaste of pomegranates. Boca is best consumed within four to twelve years of the vintage. Rating **

Producers

Bertolo Lorenzo
Cantina Ronchetto dei Fornara
* Conti Cav. Ermanno
* Conti Giampero

WHAT THE RATINGS MEAN

****	Great, superb, truly noble
***	Exceptionally fine
**	Very good
*	A good example of its type, somewhat above average
0	Acceptable to mediocre, depending on the context; drinkable
+	Somewhat better than the star category it is put in
−	Somewhat less than the star category it is put in, except for zero where it indicates a wine or producer-wine combination that is badly made or worse.
[. .]	*On a producer:* Tentative evaluation based on · an insufficient number of wines or based on older, out-of-date vintages, or where the wines we tasted were too difficult to fully judge to give a fair assessment of quality.
	On a wine or vintage: Projection for the future. This rating is given to a vintage where we feel that we tasted an insufficient number of wines or those we tasted were too difficult to really judge to give a fair assessment of quality.
(. .)	Potential increase in the rating of the wine given sufficient maturity.

Fornara Benedetta
Poderi ai Valloni di Guido Sertorio
* Ponti
Turba
* Vallana Antonio
Valsesia A.

* Recommended producer

Antonio Vallana's Boca is made from the grapes that used to go into their Montalbano and Traversagna Spannas, which are no longer produced.

VINTAGE INFORMATION AND TASTING NOTES

The vintages according to Antonio Niederbacher:

****	1961, 1950, 1947
***	1985, 1981, 1978, 1974, 1971, 1970, 1969, 1964, 1962, 1959, 1956, 1950, 1945
**	1984, 1982, 1979, 1976, 1975, 1973, 1958, 1955, 1954, 1949, 1948
*	1983, 1980, 1972, 1953, 1946
0	1977, 1968, 1967, 1966, 1965, 1963, 1960, 1957, 1952, 1951

And Antonio Rossi:[6]

****	1982, 1979, 1974
***	1988, 1987, 1986, 1985, 1981, 1978, 1976, 1975, 1973, 1972, 1970
**	1984, 1983, 1980, 1971
*	1977

Based on our somewhat limited experience, we would suspect that all vintages earlier than 1970, with the possible exceptions of 1961, 1950, and 1947, are by now too old. Of the more recent years, 1974, 1978, 1980, 1981, 1982, and 1983 are probably the vintages for present drinking, although 1970 and 1971 could still be good. Vintages to age include 1985 and 1988.

Vallana 1985 (*twice, 4/90*). Fragrant, floral-scented bouquet; open berrylike fruit flavor, long finish; a lot of style and class. ***

Turba 1982 (*4/89*). Some oxidation; fruit fading; some interest remains. +

Vallana 1980 (*4/85*). Floral bouquet with a tarlike component, a slight off note intrudes; some tannin and a lot of fruit; nearly ready. ** −

Vallana 1979 (*4/85*). Stinky; a bit light in body, light tannin, flavorful, short; ready. *

Conti Cav. Ermanno nel suo Castello di Maggiora 1976 (*4/80*). Floral aroma gives way to a slight off-odor; considerable tannin but seems to have the fruit to support it; needs a few years yet. (*)

Vallana 1976 (*4/85*). Browning, aroma has tarlike notes and a vague floral note over a vegetal background; acid too high, has tannin and fruit; doubtful future. (?)

Cantina Ronchetto 1973 (*4/80*). Floral, fruity aroma; soft and flavorful, though slightly alcoholic, short.

Conti Gian Piero 1969 (*4/80*). Floral aroma; fairly soft and flavorful, still some tannin to lose. *

BORGO ALTO (*Vercelli*). Azienda Agricola Monsecco "Le Colline" produces Borgo Alto from mostly spanna grapes. Over half the fruit comes from their own vineyards, the rest is bought. The varietal character is evident in this fairly early-maturing, dry, soft, medium-bodied red wine. We especially enjoyed the '83. Rating * +

DOC REQUIREMENTS OF BOCA

Minimum Aging in Years		Minimum Alcohol	Maximum Yield in	
in Cask	Total		Gallons/Acre	Hectoliters/Hectare
2	3	12%	675	(63)

BRAMATERRA (*Vercelli*), *DOC.* The Bramaterra zone begins at the western edge of the Gattinara district and extends for 12 miles (20 kilometers) to the border of Lessona, with vineyards in the *comuni* of Bramaterra, Brusnengo, Curino, Lozzolo, Masserano, Roasio, Sostegno, and Villa del Bosco. This district, being more protected from the north winds than the neighboring areas, has its own officially recognized microclimate, and the zone given its own DOC. There are 43 growers in the DOC zone which encompasses 72 acres (29 hectares). The maximum allowable production is 17,000 cases. This has never been met. The annual production of Bramaterra, between 1985 and 1988, averaged 7,224 cases.

Bramaterra is made from 50 to 70 percent spanna, 20 to 30 percent croatina, and 10 to 20 percent bonarda novarese (uva rara) and/or vespolina grapes. The aging period begins January 1.

Bramaterra is a medium-bodied wine with a firm, tannic backbone. It is at its best from its sixth to tenth year. Rating **

Recommended Producers

Perazzi Luigi
Sella Tenuta Agricola

Tenuta Agricola Sella owns 15 acres (6 hectares) of vines from which they produce an average of 2,085 cases of Bramaterra a year, making them the largest of Bramaterra's six or so producers. Luigi Perazzi owns 12.4 acres (5 hectares).

VINTAGE INFORMATION AND TASTING NOTES

Antonio Niederbacher rates the vintages:

***	1985, 1983, 1982, 1978, 1974, 1971
**	1980, 1979, 1976, 1975, 1970
*	1984, 1981, 1977, 1972

Antonio Rossi:[7]

***	1988, 1986, 1984, 1983, 1981, 1980, 1974
**	1985, 1982, 1979, 1978, 1977, 1976, 1975, 1973, 1972, 1971, 1970

No rating 1987

And Sella:

Excellent	1985, 1983, 1982, 1978, 1974, 1971
Good	1980, 1979, 1976, 1975, 1970
Medium	1973
Poor	1984, 1981, 1977, 1972

We can't disagree with the vintage ratings, but our experience does indicate that 1971, 1973, 1974, and 1976 *might* at this point be too old to offer further interest. In fact, we wouldn't trust any Bramaterra older than 1982, except for the 1978.

Perazzi Luigi 1985 (4/85). Floral bouquet; good structure, tasty; some character. **

Sella Tenuta Agricola 1983 (*twice*, 4/87). Perfumed, floral bouquet; well balanced, soft, light tannin, smooth center, fruity. ** +

Sella Tenuta Agricola 1980 (*twice*, 1/86). Aroma displays a richness; firm structure, acid a tad high, light to moderate tannin,

DOC REQUIREMENTS OF BRAMATERRA

	Minimum Aging in Years		Minimum Alcohol	Maximum Yield in	
	in Cask	Total		Gallons/Acre	Hectoliters/Hectare
Normale	1	2	12%	561	52.5
Riserva	2	3	12%	561	52.5

flavorful, moderate length, nice but still needs another year, perhaps two. **(+)

Perazzi Luigi 1979 (1/85). Floral, fruity aroma with a touch of tar; a bit rough and tannic but the fruit is there; needs perhaps three to four years. *(*)

Perazzi Luigi 1976 (11/80). Color is showing age; vinous aroma with some varietal character; some tannin, moderate fruit; drinkable.

Sella Tenuta Agricola 1976 (twice, 4/81). Nice aroma, still somewhat reticent; some tannin to lose, but the fruit is there. *

Sella Tenuta Agricola 1974 (twice, 11/78). Tarlike aroma with floral notes; unbalanced with too much tannin, alcohol and acid, some fruit, unpleasant aftertaste; not a success.

Sella Tenuta Agricola 1973 (11/78). Fruity aroma; light and soft, flavorful, moderate length; good quality.*

Sella Tenuta Agricola 1971 (11/78). Fruity aroma; flavorful, but acid is somewhat on the high side. * −

BRIONA (*Novara*). Briona is made from a blend of spanna, vespolina, and bonarda grapes grown in the *comune* of Briona. It is a medium-bodied wine that frequently attains 12.5 percent alcohol.

BRUSCHETT (*Novara*). Bruschett is produced from nebbiolo grapes, known here as prunent, and other local varieties grown in and around Domodossola near the Swiss border. It is a light-bodied red of about 11 percent alcohol, best drunk young and cool.

BRUSNENGO (*Vercelli*). This wine is produced from spanna, bonarda, and vespolina grapes grown in Brusnengo and Curino. Brusnengo is a medium-bodied wine, generally about 12.5 percent alcohol, that ages moderately well.

CARAMINO (*Novara*). The Caramino vineyards are located on a hillside north of Briona, bordering Fara Novarese. Many producers of Caramino use the typical spanna, bonarda, and vespolina blend. Dessilani claims to use 100 percent spanna, although we have heard they include a small amount of the white erbaluce grape. Caramino is usually aged for three years, two in cask. Dessilani departs from the norm, aging

his Caramino for four years in cask. Like the other wines of this area, Caramino generally attains 12 percent alcohol, although 12.5 percent isn't uncommon. This wine is drinkable within three to five years of the vintage and can last longer. Rating **

Producers

Cantina Sociale dei "Colli Novaresi"
Dessilani
Ferrando Luigi

CASTEL D'ANTRINO (*Novara*). This wine is the product of basically spanna grapes, plus some vespolina, grown in Oleggio. It has an alcohol content of 13 percent.

COSSATO ROSSO, OR ROSSO DI COSSATO (*Vercelli*). This wine is the product of spanna and other local grape varieties.

FARA (*Novara*), *DOC*. Fara which takes its name from an ancient village settled by Longobard warriors, is produced from 30 to 50 percent spanna, with up to 40 percent bonarda novarese (uva rara) and between 10 to 30 percent vespolina grapes. The Fara vineyards are located in the *comuni* of Fara Novarese and Briona. Some 35 growers cultivate the 52 acres (21 hectares) of vines in this zone. The annual production of Fara is restricted to 18,000 cases. The average annual production between 1986 and 1988 was 9,643 cases, just over half of that. The local co-op, Cantina Sociale dei "Colli Novaresi," produces, on average, 6,665 cases, or about two-thirds of the total.

Fara has an aroma reminiscent of sweet violets. It is at its best within four to nine years of its vintage. Rating **

Producers

* Bianchi Giuseppe
  Cantina Sociale dei "Colli Novaresi"
  Caldi Luigi
* Castaldi Giuseppe†
* Dessilani Luigi†
* Ferrando Luigi†
  Prolo Giovanni

DOC REQUIREMENTS OF FARA

Minimum Aging in Years		Minimum Alcohol	Maximum Yield in	
in Cask	Total		Gallons/Acre	Hectoliters/Hectare
2	3	12%	823	77

Prolo Luigi
Rusca Attilio
Rusca F.lli

* Recommended producer
† Not tasted in some years

VINTAGE INFORMATION AND TASTING NOTES

Niederbacher rates the vintages:

****	1974, 1967, 1957, 1945
***	1985, 1983, 1979, 1978, 1971, 1970, 1964, 1962, 1961, 1958, 1953, 1947
**	1984, 1982, 1976, 1975, 1973, 1969, 1965, 1960, 1955, 1954, 1951, 1949, 1946
*	1980, 1968, 1973, 1968, 1966, 1963, 1956, 1950, 1948
0	1981, 1977, 1972, 1959

Not rated: 1952

Rossi sees them this way:[8]

****	1988, 1974
***	1987, 1986, 1985, 1984, 1982, 1980, 1978, 1976, 1971
**	1983, 1981, 1979, 1975, 1973, 1972, 1970
*	1977

Our very limited tasting experience with Fara suggests that vintages prior to 1974, except possibly 1945, 1957, and 1967, and perhaps even 1964, 1970, and 1971, are probably too old by now, though there could be some other exceptions.

Bianchi Giuseppe 1985 (4/89). Heavy, cooked, dull character.

Cantina Sociale dei "Colli Novaresi" 1984 (4/89). Oxidized.

Turba 1983 (4/89). Oxidized.

Bianchi Giuseppe 1980 (1/85). Floral bouquet with ripe fruit on a tarlike background, a nice mouthful of fruit under the tannin; give it perhaps three years. *(*)

Cantina Sociale dei "Colli Novaresi" 1980 (1/85). Has a "hot" aroma very reminiscent of a southern wine, though with some nebbiolo character; moderate fruit, perhaps too much tannin; needs age, but will it develop? (?)

Cantina Sociale dei "Colli Novaresi" 1976 (4/81). Somewhat fragrant aroma; has tannin but not a lot of fruit, seems rather shallow and somewhat out of balance.

Cantina Sociale dei "Colli Novaresi" 1974 (4/80). Aroma is a bit closed but nebbiolo fruit and tar evident; balanced, has fruit, tannin to lose, finish is somewhat bitter. (*)

Castaldi Giuseppe 1974 (*twice, 10/78*). Bouquet has suggestions of berries and pine; nice flavor, still has tannin to shed, somewhat bitter aftertaste. *(*)

Dessilani 1974 (4/80). Reticent aroma with a touch of alcohol; undeveloped and backward but fruit and tannin are evident. (*?)

Rusca Attilio 1974 (4/80). Unbalanced and harsh, some fruit, and some tannin; unimpressive.

Ferrando Luigi 1972 (*11/78, from half bottle*). Light, berryish aroma; nice flavor but unbalanced with high acidity; decent quality.

Prolo Giovanni 1972 (4/80). Tar and alcohol on aroma; fruit is insufficient for the tannin, bitter aftertaste.

Dessilani 1970 (12/79). Nice bouquet with complexity of bottle age; soft and flavorful, a touch of tannin; ready; finishes very short. *

FOGARIN (*Novara*). This straightforward, fruity red is best within one to three years of the vintage, while it is still fresh. It is produced by the Ghemme producer Giuseppe Bianchi. Rating *

GATTERA (*Vercelli*). This wine is made from spanna, barbera, spampigno, and bonarda grapes grown in the Gattera area of Serravalle Sesia.

GATTINARA (*Vercelli*), DOC. Much archaeological evidence has been unearthed in the Gattinara area tracing the history of winemaking here to the Roman era. By the time the town of Gattinara was founded in the thirteenth century, the vine was already established as an important part of the agriculture of the region. In an official document dated 1213, reference is made to the vineyards of Guardia, Ronco, and San Lorenzo. Letters in the archives of Milano from the fifteenth century record that requests were received at Romagnano, then part of the Duchy of Milano, to supply wine from Gattinara to the dukes of Sforza for service at court dinners.

With the advent of the DOC for Gattinara in 1967, a number of wine houses bought large parcels of vineyard land to insure their supply of grapes, as production was diminishing. Mechanical methods of cultivation are used on new plantings, but some small growers in the hills continue to produce their wines by the old methods.

The Gattinara zone, on the right bank of the Sesia, is protected from the alpine winds sweeping down from Monte Rosa by a sheltering mountain spur. The vineyards range in altitude from 655 to 985 feet (200 to 300 meters) above sea level, averaging about 865 (263). The vines are mostly spanna. Gattinara is made from at least 90 percent spanna and no more than 10 percent of bonarda di gattinara. The aging period begins January 1. In March 1991, Gattinara was granted DOCG status.

This wine, which has a relatively long aging period for a spanna-based wine, drinks well from five or six years to up to twelve or fifteen years of its vintage. In the best vintages, twenty isn't too old. Gattinara has an aroma of violets that takes on hints of spice with age and a characteristic touch of bitterness on the aftertaste. Rating ***

THE PRODUCERS

There are some 148 growers in Gattinara authorized to cultivate 252 acres (102 hectares) of vineyards. Production cannot exceed 71,350 cases, which is not a problem with an annual average between 1985 and 1988 of 42,562 cases. Seven firms own 65 percent of the area under vines in the DOC zone. The largest producer is the Cantina Sociale, which vinifies 40 percent of all the grapes in Gattinara; not all of this is sold in bottle, however. Travaglini, with an annual production of some 120,000 bottles, is the largest private winery. Italo & Luigi Nervi, with 62 acres (25 hectares), are the largest vineyard owners. Other large producers are Antoniolo, with 37 acres (15 hectares), and Travaglini, with 44.5 (18).

The Gattinara Consorzio, founded in 1962 or 1963, represents 60 percent of the Gattinara sold in bottle. Its 19 members are:

MEMBER	RATING
Albertinetti Pasquale	
Antoniolo Mario	***
Barra Guido & Figlio[a]	** —
Bertolazzi Luigi	
Bertole Ing. Salvatore[b]	*
Bertolo Armando	
Caligaris Guido[b]	* —
Caligaris Ing. Vittorio	
Cametti Felice	
Cantina Sociale Cooperativa	0

Dellavalle F.lli	0
Delsignore Attilio	
Ferretti Carlo	
Franchino Marco[a]	* —
Nervi Livio	
Nervi Luigi & Italo	** +
Patriarca Bruno	
Patriarca Mario[b]	* +
Travaglini Giancarlo	* +

Other Gattinara Producers

Avondo[c]	
Balbiano[b]	**
Bava	+
Bertolo F.lli[b]	**
Bertolo Lorenzo	
Borgo Cav. Ercolo[d]	0
Brugo Agostino[a]	*
Caldi Ditta Cav. Luigi	*
Conti Molini[e]	*
Dessilani Luigi	*
Ferrando Luigi	**
Fiore Umberto	0
Fracchia Provino	
Francoli	
Kiola	0
"Le Colline" Azienda Agricola, Monsecco	***
Orsolani Casa Vinicola[f]	*
Tibalini (EFFEVI)[g]	0
Troglia G.[c]	*
Turba[h]	0
Vallana Antonio	*** —
Villa Antonio[e]	0

NOTES: [a] The last one we tasted was the '79
[b] The only one we tasted was the '79
[c] We haven't tasted it in years
[d] The only one we tasted was the '78
[e] The last one we tasted was the '75
[f] The last one we tasted was the '74
[g] The only one we tasted was the '82
[h] The only one we tasted was the '83

DOC/DOCG REQUIREMENTS OF GATTINARA

	Minimum Aging in Years		Minimum Alcohol	Maximum Yield in	
	in Cask	Total		Gallons/Acre	Hectoliters/Hectare
DOC	2	4	12%	675	63
DOCG *normale*	2	3	12.5%	675	63
DOCG riserva	2	4	13%	675	63

THE CRUS

Vineyard	Owner-Producer
Alice	Barra
Borelle	Bava, recently sold
Casaccia	
Casacolanna	Dellavalle
Castelle	Antoniolo
Galizia	
Guardie	
Lurghe	Marco Franchino, Conti Molini
Molsino	Dellavalle, Nervi, Travaglini
Osso San Gratò	Antoniolo
Podere dei Ginepri*	Nervi
Permolone	Barra, Travaglini
Preludono alla Val Sesia	Barra
Ronchi	Travaglini
San Francesco	Antoniolo
Valferana	Barra, Nervi
Valferrana†	Le Colline "Monsecco"
Vivone	

    * This might not actually be a vineyard
    † We suspect that Valferrana is another name for Valferana

VINTAGE INFORMATION AND TASTING NOTES

Luigi & Italo Nervi see the vintages this way:

Best	1989, 1988, 1986, 1985, 1983, 1982, 1978, 1974, 1972, 1968, 1964, 1961, 1958
Medium	1987, 1981, 1980, 1976, 1973, 1969, 1967, 1962
Worst	1984, 1979, 1977, 1975, 1971, 1970, 1966, 1965, 1963, 1960, 1959

Antonio Niederbacher rates the vintages:

1985 ****	1974 ****	1964 ****	1954 **
1984 ***	1973 *	1963 0	1953 *
1983 **	1972 0	1962 **	1952 ****
1982 ***	1971 *	1961 ***	1951 0
1981 **	1970 ***	1960 *	1950 ***
1980 ***	1969 ***	1959 *	1949 **
1979 ***	1968 ***	1958 ***	1948 *
1978 **	1967 **	1957 **	1947 **
1977 *	1966 *	1956 *	1946 ***
1976 ***	1965 **	1955 ***	1945 ***
1975 **			

The vintages according to Antonio Rossi:[9]

1988 ****	1983 ***	1978 ****	1973 **
1987 **	1982 ****	1977 *	1972 **
1986 ***	1981 ***	1976 **	1971 ***

1989 [* * * *]

Luigi & Italo Nervi rates 1989 as one of the best vintages.

> **CAUTION:** *Before reading these tasting notes on the wines that we tasted from barrel, please read "On Tasting Wines from Barrel A Caveat" on page xxv.*

Nervi Luigi & Italo (*ex-cask, 4 times, 6/90*). Richly concentrated, cherry, floral character; great richness, extract, and flavor; young with evident potential. ***(+)

1988

Luigi & Italo Nervi rates it highly. This vintage has been rated four-stars by Antonio Rossi. We haven't tasted any.

1987

Antonio Rossi rates the year as a two-star vintage. Nervi sees it as a medium-quality vintage. None tasted.

1986 [* *]

Luigi & Italo Nervi calls it one of the best vintages. The vintage has been rated three stars by Antonio Rossi. Based on the one wine that we tasted from the very good Antoniolo winery, we doubt it.

Antoniolo, Vigneto Castelle (*twice, 4/89, 1,860 bottles*). This non-DOC wine from the Gattinara zone was made with Gattinara grapes. It was aged in *barrique* for ten months. Nice fruit, oak overlay, sweet impression, tasty, balanced, short. ** −

1985 * * * ?

Rosanna Antoniolo and Luigi & Italo Nervi said it was one of the best vintages. The consensus here, according to Antonio Niederbacher and Antonio Rossi, is that this is a four-star vintage. Thus far we have tasted eight wines. They displayed a lot of quality.

Antoniolo (*4/90*). Mushroom, woodsy aroma(!), vague floral and tobacco notes; firm, vein of tannin, openly fruity, soft center, moderate length. **

Antoniolo, Vigneto Osso S. Gratò (4/90). Tight, firm and closed, well structured, good backbone, fruity, some tannin to lose; good quality. ***

Barra, Vigna Permolone (6/90). Tobacco and tar aroma, cherry notes; soft, rich flavor, tasty, well balanced, fairly long; ready. ** +

Caldi Ditta Cav. Luigi (10/90). Volatile acidity, unbalanced.

Ferrando Luigi (4/89). Nose seems a little off; better in the mouth, fairly nice fruit. *

Fiore Umberto (ex-cask, 6/86). Fairly deep color; fresh grapey aroma; a bit astringent, seems overly simple at this stage. *

Travaglini (twice, 9/90). Tar and floral aroma; moderate tannin, a little firm, some tannin to lose, but still rather soft, nice fruit. **

Vallana (4/90). Lovely floral scent with a fruity component; sweet, openly fruity, very well balanced, soft center, some tannin, fairly long. *** –

1984 [*]

As in the rest of the Piemonte, this was a very difficult vintage. Very little, if any, wine of quality was produced. Yet it has been rated as a three-star vintage by Antonio Nieder-bacher! Antonio Rossi gives it two, and Luigi & Italo Nervi said it was among the worst vintages. Based on the one wine we tasted, from the very good Vallana winery, we think that it was possible to produce good wine.

Vallana (4/89). Light nose; good fruit, balanced, a bit light, short.*

1983 **

Surprisingly, 1983 is rated lower than 1984 here, with a two-star rating from Antonio Niederbacher. Antonio Rossi gives it three stars. While the wines aren't special, they are certainly very good. Luigi & Italo Nervi puts the year among the best vintages, and Travaglini places it on the second level. We doubt that they will be keepers.

Antoniolo (4/89). Rather a nice nose; a bit light but tasty with good fruit. * +

Antoniolo, Osso San Gratò (4/89). Nice nose, tobacco notes; good backbone and structure, fruit and character, firm and balanced. **

Dellavalle, Casacolanna (4/89). Closed nose, has some fruit; rich fruit flavor on entry, then tight and closed, with a touch of oxidation. *

Nervi Luigi & Italo (5 times, 6/90). The bottles we tasted were uneven. A couple of them seemed to be fading, while the others

were quite good. Complex floral aroma, ripe fruit component; soft entry, firm backbone, lovely fruit, a tad short; ready now. ** –

Nervi Luigi & Italo, Molsino (3 times, 5/90). Floral aroma; dry, hard and firm. *? *A second bottle:* Rich in aromatics and flavor, with cherry and floral components, firm, dry and tannic; this young wine displayed potential. **(+)

Nervi Luigi & Italo, Valferana (twice, 5/90). Openly floral-scented bouquet, suggestive of berries; lovely flavor, soft under light tannin, sweet impression. *** *Another bottle* seemed overly tannic. ?

Travaglini (4/89). Light nose, reticent, some tar and vaguely floral; soft entry, light; not a lot of depth but easy to drink. *

Turba (4/89). Floral notes; still some fruit, dull.

1982 ****

Rosanna Antoniolo, Travaglini, and Luigi & Italo Nervi put it among the best vintages. Antonio Niederbacher gives it three stars, Antonio Rossi, four. Others give it four stars as well. These wines will be long-lived. The better ones still need more age, as they tend toward hardness from the tannin.

Antoniolo, Vigneto San Francesco (4/89). Tar and flowers define the bouquet; flavorful, good structure. **(*)

Caldi Ditta Cav. Luigi (2/88). Floral-scented bouquet, vaguely of vinace and cherries; chewy tannins, good fruit; young, lots of potential; suggestive of an *eau de vie* with tannin and fruit. **

Dessilani (10/87). Small-scale but with varietal and regional character, light tannin. *

Ferrando Luigi (3 times, 4/88). Some tar, some flowers; firm tannic vein, well structured, balanced, rich; some style; young. **(+)

Fiore Umberto (3 times, 12/89). Small-scale, fruity and simple, some varietal character, dry aftertaste.

Le Colline, Monsecco (4/89). Rich floral bouquet, tobacco note; full-bodied, full-flavored, young, a lot of backbone; tremendous potential. ** + (***)

Nervi Luigi & Italo (4/89). Dried fruit aroma, vaguely flora; very tannic, seems to have sufficient fruit. ?

Nervi Luigi & Italo, Molsino (4/89). Even tighter and harder than the '83; is there enough fruit? We think so. ?

Nervi Luigi & Italo, Valferana (4/89). Perfumed scent; hard and tannic, lots of fruit but very tight; needs age. *?

"Tibalini" (EFFEVI) (9/87). Tarlike notes; soft entry, some alcohol intrudes at the end, lacks structure and weight; drinkable, pleasant, simple.

Travaglini, Selezione Numerata (twice, 9/88, 29,700 bottles). Reticent aroma, characteristic floral, tar and fruit components;

good structure, full of flavor and body, soft tannins, has backbone, moderate length; attractive now, could improve. ** +

1981 * +

This vintage has been rated two stars by Antonio Nieder-bacher. Antonio Rossi surprisingly gives it three. Luigi & Italo Nervi sees it as a medium-quality vintage. While we found some good '81s, others have been unbalanced, with high acid. The wines, for the most part, are ready. The better ones will keep.

Ferrando Luigi (4/88). Floral, fruity aroma; moderate tannin, flavorful, tasty, coming ready, balanced. ** −

Nervi Luigi & Italo (ex-cask, 5/82). Fresh cherrylike aroma; high acidity throws off the balance, light-bodied, somewhat un-structured and deficient in fruit.

Vallana (4/90). Toasty notes, dried fruit; still with moderate tannin, some development and mellowness; nice but can improve. **

1980 *

The vintage has been rated three stars by Antonio Nieder-bacher. We'd be more inclined to agree with Antonio Rossi, who rates it two stars. Travaglini said it was on the second level. Luigi & Italo Nervi rates it as a medium vintage. Our limited experience suggests that they won't last.

Fiore Umberto (twice, 12/86). Southern slant to the aroma and flavor, has fruit; lacks the character of the wine.

Travaglini (12/85). Typical aroma, vaguely floral; nice fruit, some firmness, a bit short, thin finish; some character. * +

1979 *** −

This vintage was rated above 1978. Antonio Niederbacher and Antonio Rossi give it three stars. We agree with the three stars, but better than 1978? No! Luigi & Italo Nervi, surprisingly, places 1979 among the worst vintages. The wines are lighter in body and lack the richness and balance of the '78s. They are pretty much ready today—even the normally slow-maturing Monsecco is ready—and while the good ones should last, we doubt they'll improve, nor will they last as well as the '78s.

Antoniolo (1/85). Floral, fruity aroma; light-bodied, soft, agree-able enough but seems overly simple and a bit one-dimensional. *

Antoniolo, Osso San Gratò (3 times, 1/86, 6,000 bottles). Lovely floral bouquet, tarlike suggestion; fairly intense, loaded with flavor, well structured, tannic vein; some class and style evident; lots of character, some complexity; quite young. **(*)

Antoniolo, San Francesco (3 times, 1/86, 3,860 bottles). Floral, almond perfume; not as full, nor as firm and tannic, though, like the Osso San Gratò, there is still some tannin to lose, but has more elegance. **(*)

Balbiano (3 times, 11/87). Some oxidation, starting to face. *Bottle of 1/85:* Floral bouquet with a touch of *goudron;* a bit light, but well balanced, light tannin; ready now though could improve. **

Barra Guido (ex-cask, 7/80). Lovely nose with a suggestion of kirsch; has a fair amount of tannin but also the fruit to support it; should make a nice bottle. **

Barra Guido, Preludono alla Val Sesia (twice, 1/85). Floral bou-quet with a touch of tar; tannin up front gives way to a lot of fruit, fairly soft in the center, ends on a tannic note; overall somewhat simple. *(*)

Barra Guido, Vigna Permolone (4 times, 11/87, 4,500 bottles). Odd nose (recalls a cream puff!), also suggestive of a southern wine; soft though still some tannin, fairly nice flavor; drink. * +

Bertole Ing. Salvatore (twice, 1/85). Typical bouquet, fruit and flowers over a tarry background; fairly soft but a bit out of balance with acid. *

Bertolo F. lli (twice, 1/85). Characteristic bouquet of flowers and tar; still has a firm tannic vein but the fruit is evident; needs two, perhaps three years. **

Brugo Agostino (1/85). Some oxidation on aroma, recalls Mar-sala; moderate fruit; not much character or style. (*)

Caligaris Guido (twice, 1/85). Aroma still closed; fairly well balanced but with noticeable acid and tannin, fruit is also evident; needs a few years to come together. (*)

Dellavalle F. lli, Vigneto Molsino (twice, 1/85). Aroma reminis-cent of a southern wine; rather soft and forward, light tannin; ready; lacks personality.

Franchino Marco & Figlio (twice, 1/85). Rubber tire aroma with a hint of flowers beneath; low fruit, overly tannic; not a success.

Le Colline, Monsecco (4/89). Tobacco, floral aroma; round, sweet impression, soft, well balanced. **

Nervi Luigi & Italo (3 times, 6/85). Floral bouquet, with notes of berries and spice; firm, tannic vein, a lot of flavor; potential is evident. **(+)

Patriarca Mario fu Cesare (1/85). A nice aroma with some richness; a fair amount of tannin but has the stuffing to carry it, firm, tannic finish; try in about three more years. *(*)

Vallana (4/85). Lovely floral bouquet with a hint of licorice; rich fruit, almost sweet; has style. ***

1978 *** +

Rosanna Antoniolo, Travaglini, and Luigi & Italo Nervi place 1978 among the best vintages. We strongly disagree with Antonio Niederbacher's two-star rating and agree more with Antonio Rossi's four. This was, from our experience, a splendid vintage. We've found the wines richly flavored and well balanced, with a fair amount of tannin. A few '78s are fading, but a number of them are good today, and the best still have more to give.

Antoniolo, Osso San Gratò (1/85). A shade deeper in color than the San Francesco; a vague chocolatey note on aroma; a big wine, more forward than the San Francesco, firm, tannic vein, well structured, has weight and concentration; needs time but has so much flavor you might find it enjoyable now in a pinch. ***(+)

Antoniolo, San Francesco (1/85). Perfumed aroma with some fruit; firmly structured with a tannic vein, full of fruit and flavor, but somewhat more backward than the Osso San Gratò. **(*)

Brugo Agostino (4 times, 6/86). Medium garnet, tawny rim; vague perfumed floral aroma; fairly light-bodied, somewhat unbalanced with high acidity, has fruit, could use more weight, moderate tannin.

Cantine Bava, Vigneto Borelle (1/86, 4,060 bottles). Characteristic floral aroma; firm, tannic vein, a bit meager in body, has flavor yet palate not up to the bouquet. * −

Conti Molini, Le Lurghe (4/89). Floral and tar aroma; good backbone, tasty and tannic, some spice. * +

Dessilani (11/85). Nice nose, cherry fruit; light tannin, lacks intensity; simple yet drinkable. * −

Dessilani, Riserva (12/85). Old-style varietal aroma, tarlike component; a bit astringent, moderate fruit, has a bite at the end. * −

Ferrando Luigi (1/88). Perfumed, violet-scented bouquet, like a bouquet of flowers; has firmness along with extract and weight, ripe fruit flavors fill the mouth; the richness of flavor and intensity of fruit make it enjoyable now; resist the temptation, this will make a splendid bottle in a few years. ***

Fiore Umberto (3 times, 6/86). Shows age; hot nose has a trace of oxidation and is suggestive of Marsala.

Fiore Umberto, Lurghe (Marco Franchino) (4 times, 12/86, 5,285 bottles). Either the cooperage this wine was aged in was dirty or three bottles were corked! A fourth bottle, tasted a year earlier, was dull, tired and stale, shallow and short, not a success.

Le Colline, Monsecco (1/86, 17,600 bottles). Orange-garnet rim; expansive bouquet with characteristic floral component; firm vein of tannin and firm acidity, has the structure and stuffing to age gracefully, very rich, very young and very good. ***(+)

Travaglini (12/85). Has some fruit, but rather dull and tired.

Travaglini, Selezione Numerata (9/88). Old, tired aroma; still has fruit but on its last legs, dull, short finish. * −

1977 0

Luigi & Italo Nervi and Travaglini said 1977 was among the worst vintages of all. Perhaps at one time the rating of one star given by Antonio Niederbacher and Antonio Rossi would have been justified. Not so today. It's not likely these wines hold any further interest.

1976 *

Antonio Niederbacher rated this vintage at three stars, higher than we did. Antonio Rossi gave it two and Luigi & Italo Nervi classify it as a medium-quality vintage. We've found the '76s to be unbalanced, with high acid, and felt that one star, perhaps one and a half, was a more accurate rating. They are starting to show age. Drink them up.

Antoniolo (twice, 12/85). Shows a lot of age, mint and eucalyptus notes(!); some acid intrudes, fairly nice fruit; not to keep. *

Fiore Umberto (twice, 12/85). Astringent, still some fruit, but fading fast.

Franchino Marco, Vigna Lurghe [selected by Umberto Fiore] (3/85, 4,950 bottles). Orange at rim; rubber tires on aroma; some fruit, light tannin, soft, a bit shallow; very ready. * −

Le Colline, Monsecco (3 times, 4/89). Rich tobacco, floral bouquet; although it is starting to show age and dry out a bit, it still has flavor interest. * +

Nervi Luigi & Italo (5/82). Berries on aroma; acid a bit on the high side but reasonably well balanced, tasty, a bit lacking in middle body, moderate length with a tannic bite. *

Nervi Luigi & Italo, Podere dei Ginepri (7 times, 6/85). Fragrant, floral perfume; a bit out of balance with high acid, firm structure, a lot of flavor, vaguely acid bite at the end, long finish. ** −

Vallana (4/85). Aroma has notes of tar and a mineral aspect, also a vague dankness; light tannin, light body, lacks some weight and character; drinkable. *

1975 0

The wines are too old. It was considered, surprisingly, a two-star vintage by Antonio Niederbacher and Antonio Rossi. Luigi & Italo Nervi puts 1975 among the worst vintages.

Antoniolo (5/82). Nose displays considerable complexity, and a slight touch of oxidation only adds to it at this point, though making its future doubtful; soft and flavorful with some underlying tannin; enjoyable now, not to keep. * +

Barra Guido (3 times, 5/82). Garnet color showing age; sweet aroma with a candylike note; gives an impression of sweetness upon entry, soft, some tannin, moderate fruit, ends on a somewhat bitter note; more or less ready now. *

Borgo Cav. Ercolo (twice, 12/85). Stinky; hot, old, drying out.

Brugo Agostino (twice, 5/82). Bouquet displays some complexity; fairly well balanced, acid a bit on the high side, moderate tannin; ready now. *

Dellavalle (11/80). Nice nose; some fruit, but dull and unbalanced.

Nervi Luigi & Italo (10/80). Almond notes on aroma and some oxidation; light, unbalanced, harsh, bitter aftertaste.

Travaglini (5/82). Volatile acidity and anchovies(?!) on the nose and palate.

Villa Antonio (twice, 12/85). Old, dull and tired.

1974 ** +

A very highly touted vintage that was given four stars by Antonio Niederbacher and Antonio Rossi, and included among the best by Rosanna Antoniolo and Luigi & Italo Nervi. Travaglini places it on the second level in quality. For us, though, they rarely come up to the four stars of the very best vintages; we rated it two plus. The best are still holding.

Antoniolo (1/85). Lovely bouquet with complexity and richness, floral and fruity; the wine doesn't deliver what the nose promises, some tannin, short, tannic aftertaste; still rather young. *(*)

Antoniolo, San Francesco (5/82, 7,426 bottles). Straightforward nebbiolo aroma marred by the intrusion of alcohol; perhaps too much tannin for the fruit, but some potential evident; needs at least three or four more years. *(+)

Barra Guido (4/82). Perfumed bouquet; firm vein of tannin, lots of fruit; very good indeed. **(*)

Borgo Cav. Ercolo (11/79). Lightly scented aroma; rather light-bodied, some tannin, lacks substance.

Brugo Agostino (3 times, 5/82). Closed-in aroma with some fruit beginning to emerge; still has tannin to lose, but also a lot of nice fruit, soft-centered; can be enjoyed now but it will improve. ** −

Dessilani, Riserva (1/83). Weird, off-putting aroma; much nicer on the palate, some tannin, has flavor but could use more length and style.

Le Colline, Monsecco (4/89). Superb bouquet reminiscent of flowers and ripe fruit, chocolate component; rich and flavorful, good structure, long, lingering finish. *** −

Nervi Luigi & Italo (8 times, 9/86). Perfumed bouquet; full of flavor, light tannin, soft center, well balanced, richly flavored, sweet impression, long finish. *** *Bottle of 12/84:* Light aroma showing some fruit but still closed and surprisingly backward; medium- to full-bodied, still quite tannic but with a richly fruited center, good length; give it perhaps two more years. **(*)

Nervi Luigi & Italo, violet label (10/80). Intense floral bouquet; fairly rich in flavor but without the elegance of the regular. **(+)

Orsolani (twice, 12/85). Not a lot of aroma; fairly nice fruit in the mouth, vaguely bitter; still good. * −

Travaglini (5/80). Simple, fruity aroma; soft and tasty, a bitter finish. *

Travaglini, Selezione Numerata (9/88). Oldish nose, dried fruit; fading but still some interest. *

1973 0

We never agreed with Antonio Rossi's two stars. At one time we would have gone along with Antonio Niederbacher's one-star rating, but no more. Nervi sees it as a medium vintage in quality.

Barra Guido (11/79). Perfumed bouquet; soft and smooth, some tannin, nice flavor, a little light, but has some style. * +

Conte Ravizza, Monsecco (4/89). Chocolate and cocoa aroma, some oxidation; drying out and fading. *

Fiore Umberto (2/85). Too old—alcohol, volatile acidity and tannin are all that remain.

Travaglini, Selezione Numerata (9/88). Some oxidation; some flavor; on its last legs. +

1972 0

Travaglini places 1972 with the worst years and Luigi & Italo Nervi ranks it, surprisingly, among the best. Antonio Rossi gave the vintage two stars and Antonio Niederbacher and nearly everyone else gave it zero. Zero was almost a consensus, and zero it still is.

Barra Guido (6 times, 12/83). Floral, berrylike aroma with a pungent, tarlike aspect; some oxidation and volatile acidity on the palate but still offers interest (other bottles were barely drinkable).

Brugo Agostino (9/82). Some complexity on aroma, marred by a vague off note; thin, shallow, unbalanced.

Fiore Umberto (2/85). High acid, low fruit, vile.

1971 0

Luigi & Italo Nervi places 1971 among the worst vintages and Travaglini puts it with the best! Antonio Rossi gave it three stars, Niederbacher, one. Obviously a controversial vintage. We never agreed with the three-star rating. Nevertheless, we find that all are too old now. At Le Colline they consider their '71 Monsecco on a par with the '64, so it should still be very good.

Antoniolo (11/78). Light nose; acid on the high side, has nice flavor, ready, short.

Brugo Agostino (9 times, 11/82). Lovely floral bouquet; somewhat acidic but has good flavor; was better in 1979. *

Nervi Luigi & Italo, Riserva (twice, 9/82). Very small aroma; overly tannic for the fruit, shallow, short, dull aftertaste; was better in September 1979 when it merited one star, this bottle zero.

1970 **

At one time we agree with Antonio Niederbacher's original three-star rating; these wines have given us a lot of pleasure. Antonio Rossi gave it two stars, a rating that seems fair today. Luigi & Italo Nervi, surprisingly, places it with the worst vintages.

Barra Guido (10 times, 2/85). Garnet with orange reflections; floral bouquet; tannic backbone, round and flavorful, finish is short and tannic; beginning to fade, though it's still good. **

Le Colline Azienda Agricola, Conte Ravizza, Monsecco Riserva Speciale (4/81, 7,935 bottles). Rich bouquet with suggestions of flowers and tar; well-balanced, has tannin, a lot of flavor and some style. **(*)

1969 0

Luigi & Italo Nervi classifies it as a medium-quality vintage. This vintage was rated three stars by Antonio Niederbacher. Perhaps at one time, but no longer though.

Caldi Ditta Cav. Luigi (10/90). Oxidized.

Le Colline Azienda Agricola, Conte Ravizza, Monsecco Riserva Speciale (twice, 3/83). Color showing age; old-style nebbiolo nose with some oxidation; nice flavor, some tannin; not to keep (a bottle tasted a year earlier was similar but perhaps a bit better). *

1968 0

Antonio Niederbacher rated 1968 at three stars and Luigi & Italo Nervi places it among the best vintages. We dissent. The bottles we tasted through the late 1970s, and there were a fair number, never merited more than one star, and many weren't that good.

Antoniolo (9/82). Bouquet has floral and fruity notes; acid a touch high, soft-centered and smooth; quite agreeable; ready. *

Brugo Agostino (3 times, 9/82). Aroma has vegetal overtones and a barnyardy backnote; shallow, short and offensive; was better in November 1979, though not a lot.

Le Colline Azienda Agricola, Conte Ravizza, Monsecco Riserva Speciale (7 times, 4/86, 10,993 bottles). Beautiful garnet robe; floral bouquet, intense character of the zone, nuances of tobacco and vanilla; richly flavored, velvety, spice and fruit, very long. The best bottle we've tasted to date, and the first one without any appreciable oxidation. For the bouquet ****, overall *** *Bottle of 5/83*: Aroma of cherries but with a rubbery, somewhat oxidized aspect; still has loads of tannin but seems to have the stuffing to support it—the only problem is the oxidation (nearly every bottle tasted was similar). ** (?)

1967 **

We have consistently been amazed at the high quality in the bottles of this vintage we've been fortunate enough to drink. We have personally found 1967 to be an especially fine vintage and think three stars would have been a fairer rating at one time, yet most critics, including Antonio Niederbacher, gave it two stars! Luigi & Italo Nervi calls it a medium vintage and Travaglini places it in the second rank. Rosanna Antoniolo, however, names it as one of the best vintages. The wines are admittedly getting on a bit in age now, perhaps deserving a rating of two stars today.

Antoniolo (7 times, 1/87). The most recent bottle was totally oxidized. *Bottle of 7/86*: Orange, tawny robe; some alcohol volatizing, complex bouquet; some tannin, soft center; perhaps just past its best but loads of flavor and interest. *** — *Bottle of 1/85*: Orange cast; expansive floral bouquet with incredible richness; some tannin adds life, sweet, ripe fruit; has the structure to last and probably even improve but ready now. (This bottle, tasted in Torino, was brought directly from the winery; it was very similar to a bottle tasted a month earlier in the United States, but had more life left in it.) ***

Le Colline Azienda Agricola, Conte Ravizza, Monsecco Riserva Speciale (4/89). Lovely floral fragrance; deep, intensely flavored, velvety, harmonious, long. ***

1966 0

Luigi & Italo Nervi places 1966 among the worst of all vintages. Antonio Niederbacher gave the year one star. Today they are most likely too old.

1 9 6 5 0

Luigi & Italo Nervi places the year among the worst. The vintage was given two stars by Antonio Niederbacher.

1 9 6 4 **

Rosanna Antoniolo and Luigi & Italo Nervi place 1964 among the best years. We agree with the original four-star rating. Antonio Niederbacher did too. This was an outstanding vintage. Our experiences suggest the wines have passed their peak. Perhaps, if well stored, some wines can still merit four stars, but caution is advised as they are over twenty five years old now. Perhaps two stars is more realistic today.

Antoniolo (*5 times, 7/86*). Orange, tawny robe; mellow and complex bouquet; starting to fade but still shows a lot of class and style, smooth center, some tannin, fairly long. *** *Bottle of 1/85:* The wine is like a bouquet of flowers, from the lovely fragrant aroma through the mouth-filling flavors and incredibly long finish, a wine of elegance and style—superb now and shows no signs of age. (This bottle, tasted in Torino, was brought directly from the cellars; a bottle tasted October 1984 in the United States was quite similar and very good indeed but not up to the same level, and showed some signs of age—it merited two stars plus.) ****

Brugo Agostino (*12/80*). Lovely bouquet; well balanced, soft and tasty; some style and elegance—very good indeed. ***

Caldi Ditta Cav. Luigi (*10/90*). Dried out, off-putting flavor, shot.

Le Colline Azienda Agricola, Conte Ravizza, Monsecco (*11/78*). Deep color; some harsh edges on aroma; soft and velvety, good length on palate but marred by a touch of volatile acidity. **

1 9 6 2 0

Antonio Niederbacher rated 1962 as a two-star vintage and Luigi & Italo Nervi sees it as a medium-quality year. Though it's been some time since we tasted any '62s, we suspect that any bottles remaining today are long past their prime.

1 9 6 1 **

Rosanna Antoniolo and Luigi & Italo Nervi place 1961 among the best vintages. Antonio Niederbacher gave the year three stars. The few bottles we've tasted suggest that it's a vintage to drink now and not to keep any longer; they're beginning to fade.

Antoniolo 1961 (*twice, 1/85*). Garnet, brick at rim; floral bouquet has a vague Marsala-like note; a bit unbalanced with alcohol,

but overall soft, round and smooth-textured; age is beginning to show, but very good still. **

OLDER VINTAGES

Luigi & Italo Nervi puts **1960** and **1959** with the worst vintages and Antonio Niederbacher gave those vintages one star. While it's been more than a decade since we tasted any '59 Gattinaras, we remember fondly the Antoniolo '59 Gattinaras that we tasted from both bottle and half bottle; all were very fine wines, so for us one star for 1959 seems rather severe. They are, most likely, too old today, however.

Niederbacher rated **1958** at three, and Luigi & Italo Nervi places it with the best years. The '58 Spannas of Vallana rose above this rating. Niederbacher gave **1957** two, **1956** one, and **1955** three. Though we've never tasted any '55 Gattinaras that we can recall, we've tasted some '55 Spannas from Antonio Vallana that were very good indeed and are still holding very well.

Niederbacher rates **1954** at two. The Vallana Spannas that we've tasted, reputedly from the area around Gattinara, have been very fine indeed. Perhaps the '54 vintage was better than the rating. Those wines are still good today. Niederbacher gives **1953** one, and **1952** four. The 1952 was considered outstanding; the wines could very well still be good if they have been properly stored.

GHEMME (*Novara*) *DOC.* The wines of Ghemme have a long history. In the medieval manuscript of St. Julius of Orta, dating from the eleventh to the thirteenth century, mention is found of the wine of the Counts of Biandrate, feudal lords of Ghemme.

The Ghemme vineyards are cultivated high on the slopes that rise above the Sesia River, at an average altitude of 790 feet (240 meters) above sea level. There are 61 registered growers authorized to cultivate 212 acres (86 hectares) of vines in the *comune* of Ghemme and the part of Romagnano Sesia known as Mauletto. The average annual production of 17,532 cases of Ghemme is just over 26 percent of the 66,600 cases allowed by the DOC.

Ghemme is made from a blend of 60 to 85 percent spanna, 10 to 30 percent vespolina (ughetta di Ghemme), and up to 15 percent bonarda novarese (uva rara). The period of aging begins January 1.

This medium-bodied wine is typically described as having an aroma of violets; some tasters also find notes of roses and resin and nebbiolo tar, or *goudron,* is also evident. Ghemme frequently has a vaguely bitter aftertaste. Best drunk within five or six years to ten or twelve years of its vintage; it can last longer in the best vintages. Rating **

DOC REQUIREMENTS OF GHEMME

Minimum Aging in Years		Minimum Alcohol	Maximum Yield in	
in Cask	Total		Gallons/Acre	Hectoliters/Hectare
3	4	12%	748	70

THE PRODUCERS

Ponti, with an annual production of 100,000 bottles, nearly half the overall total, is the largest producer of Ghemme.

PRODUCERS	RATING
Antichi Vigneti di Cantalupo	*
Collis Breclemae, Collis Carelle	** +
Bertinetti, Uglioni dei	
Bertolo Lorenzo	
Bianchi Giuseppe	*
Borgo Cav. Ercolo[a]	0
Brugo Agostino[b]	*
Cantina Sociale dei Colli Novaresi	
Cantina Sociale di Sizzano e Ghemme[b]	*
Dellavalle F.lli[a]	*
Ferrari Azienda Agricola[c]	**
Ferrari F.lli Romano & Guido	
Fiore Umberto[a]	0
Fontana Allesandria	
Francoli Cantine	
Ioppa F.lli	
Le Colline Azienda Agricola[d]	**
Nervi Luigi & Italo[e]	0
Paganotti Alberto e Giuseppe	
Patti Angela	
Ponti	** −
Rovellotti, A. F.	** −
Sebastiani Antonio	
Sebastiani Giovanni Giuseppe[f]	**
Tenuta San Vi' di Ferrante Dante	
Troglia G.[a]	*
Turba[g]	* −
Vallana[g]	* +

Notes: [a] We haven't tasted it in years
[b] The last one we tasted was the '79
[c] The only one we tasted was the '85
[d] The last one we tasted was the '78
[e] The last one we tasted was the '70
[f] The only one we tasted was the '74
[g] The only one we tasted was the '83

VINTAGE INFORMATION AND TASTING NOTES

Niederbacher's vintage chart rates them:

****	1978, 1974, 1947
***	1985, 1983, 1982, 1980, 1979, 1973, 1971, 1970, 1964, 1962, 1957, 1956, 1952
**	1984, 1976, 1975, 1972, 1969, 1967, 1961
*	1981, 1968, 1958, 1955, 1951, 1948, 1945
0	1977, 1966, 1965, 1963, 1960, 1959, 1954, 1953, 1950, 1949, 1946

Antonio Rossi rates them:[10]

****	1988, 1982, 1978, 1974
***	1986, 1985, 1983, 1981, 1979, 1971
**	1987, 1984, 1980, 1976, 1975, 1973, 1972, 1970
*	1977

Of the vintages tasted in recent years, we've found that, except for '64 and '67—and even they should be drunk up—anything earlier than '74 was too old or not very good from the start. Even the '74s are showing age today. The '78s and '79s, while still good, are very ready. Of more recent vintages—1985 shows promise, 1984 offers little to recommend it, and 1983 is very good.

Judging by the number of vintages that have gotten ratings of zero or one star, one has to wonder if it is really worth the effort to make these wines.

Antichi Vigneti di Cantalupo 1985 Collis Carelle (9/90). Lovely floral and spice aroma; suggestions of fruit and mint, good structure; real class; still young. ***

Ferrari Azienda Agricola 1985 Vigneti del Podere "Rossini" (4/90). Floral, strawberry aroma; some tannin, balanced, loads of fruit. **

Bianchi Giuseppe 1984 (4/89). Oxidized!

Cantina Sociale dei Colli Novaresi 1984 (4/89). Shot.

Antichi Vigneti di Cantalupo 1983 (1/86). Aroma of fresh grapes and flowers; meager body, fruity, light tannin, light finish, some alcohol at the end. *

Antichi Vigneti di Cantalupo 1983 Collis Breclemae (twice, 10/89, 10,540 bottles). A lovely glass of wine; fruity, well balanced, tasty. ** + *Bottle of 1/86:* Pretty floral bouquet; soft and tasty, light tannin, fruity, on the short side, but appealing flavor, fairly well balanced. **

Ponti Guido 1983 (4/90). Light open and forward, ready, short. *

Rovellotti A. F. 1983 (4/90). Aroma of tar and flowers; tannic; is there enough fruit? ?

Sebastiani 1983 (4/90). Lots of flavor and structure, tannic finish. **

Turba 1983 (4/89). Still some fruit, dry and firm. * −

Vallana 1983 (4/89). Aroma of tar and flowers; dry and firm, fruity, on the light side. * +

Antichi Vigneti di Cantalupo 1979 (twice, 3/85). Fragrant aroma with a raisinlike aspect; nice fruit, almost sweet, seems overripe, acid on the high side, some tannin, overall a fairly nice bottle. *

Antichi Vigneti di Cantalupo 1979 Collis Breclemae (1/85, 14,271 bottles). Small nose with some fruit; soft-centered, still has some tannin; potential to improve. *(*)

Bianchi Giuseppe 1979 (1/85). Stinky nose though varietal character is evident; has tannin and some fruit but a doubtful future; a disappointment from a generally good producer.

Brugo Agostino 1979 (1/85). Aroma has notes of chocolate and fruit; some tannin; lacks style and character; not up to the vintage.

Cantina Sociale di Sizzano e Ghemme 1979 (1/85). Characteristic nebbiolo bouquet with floral notes; firm tannic vein, has fruit; give it two or three more years. *(*)

Rovellotti A. F. 1979 (twice, 1/85). Floral bouquet with notes of tar; light tannin, firm nice fruit; needs a few years. *(*)

Cantina Sociale di Sizzano e Ghemme 1978 (4/85). Reticent aroma offers hints of things to come; a lot of flavor, well structured, firm; needs time to soften, should make a nice glass in a few years. **(+)

Le Colline 1978 (1/86, 11,349 bottles). This one spent twelve months in French barriques. Brick color; light to moderate intensity, expansive, oaky, vanilla aroma; oak and tannin combine with fruit flavors and high acidity, thins out at the end. * −

Brugo Agostino 1976 (6/85). Corked.

Le Colline 1976 (twice, 4/89, 15,560 bottles). Fragrant perfume; drying out, still some fruit. * − Bottle of 1/86: Lightish color; penetrating tarlike aroma; firm, acidic, full of tannin, puckery, seems to have the fruit; quite closed. *(* +)

Brugo Agostino 1975 (5/82). Complex floral bouquet with notes of spice and tar, marred by a faint off note in back; light-bodied and agreeable, drying on finish; seems to be beginning to go. *

Ponti Guido 1975 (5/82). Bouquet marred by a slight dankness that blows off with airing; not much going for it but not really flawed; no reason to keep it any longer.

Brugo Agostino 1974 (twice, 6/85). Dull nose, a bit stale; cooked, jammy taste. Bottle of 5/82: Berrylike aroma; acid on the high side, lots of flavor; nearly ready. *

Dellavalle 1974 (11/80). Floral bouquet; some tannin to lose but structure and fruit indicate it should improve. *(+)

Le Colline 1974 (1/86, 7,500 bottles). Color beginning to show age, light to medium brick; typical tarlike aroma, vaguely floral; fairly tannic, seems to have the fruit, acid on the high side, tannic finish. ** − (*** −)

Sebastiani G. 1974 (4/80). Oxidized—too bad, the quality was evident in the structure.

Brugo Agostino 1973 (twice, 11/81). Floral bouquet, characteristic nebbiolo; somewhat light, soft, falls off abruptly at the end.

Cantina Sociale di Sizzano e Ghemme 1972 (10/79). Fragrant nebbiolo aroma; a bit light in body, has tannin; needs some time to soften (will it?). *

Brugo Agostino 1971 (11/81). Light, floral, fruity aroma; some tannin, some harshness, lacks structure, weight and flavor, alcoholic aftertaste.

Nervi Luigi & Italo 1970 (10/79). Pale color; volatile acidity and alcohol on aroma; unbalanced with tannin, alcoholic aftertaste.

Cantina Sociale di Sizzano e Ghemme 1967 (3 times, 4/85). Browning; some oxidation sadly apparent; past its peak. Bottle of 5/82: Characteristic bouquet of flowers, tar and fruit; smooth-textured, tannic backbone; ready, but should hold. ** +

Brugo Agostino 1964 (10/80). Orange hue; tarlike notes on aroma; some tannin, considerable fruit; very ready; moderate length. **

GRIGNASCO (Novara). This wine is produced from a blend of spanna, vespolina and bonarda grapes. Grignasco is a soft, light-bodied wine of about 12 percent alcohol. It ages moderately well.

LA SASSAIA (Vercelli). Luigi Perazzi produces this non-DOC, aged-in-barrique Bramaterra from 70 percent nebbiolo, 15 percent croatina, 10 percent bonarda, and 5 percent vespolina. This wine is made from his holdings in Podere La Motta in La Sassaia in Roasio. Perazzi produced 5,000 bottles from the first vintage in 1985. Rating *

TASTING NOTES

Perazzi Luigi 1986 La Sassaia, Podere La Motta (4/89). Under the moderate tannin the wine is flavorful, and has structure and character. ** −

Perazzi Luigi 1985 La Sassaia, Podere La Motta (4/89). Odd, stinky nose; not a lot of fruit; not as good as the '86.

LANGHERINO (Novara). Langherino is the product of croatina, spanna, and vespolina grapes. It is a medium-bodied red wine of 12 percent alcohol, at its best drunk young and fresh.

LESSONA (*Vercelli*), DOC. In the nineteenth century the most respected name in Lessona was that of Villa Sperino. This property is owned by the de Marchi family, proprietors of the noted Chianti Classico estate of Isole e Olena. Villa Sperino was sold in bottle from the nineteenth century, until 1970. The vines continued to be cultivated by the grower-producer Sella until a few years ago, when they were uprooted. For Villa Sperino the great vintages were 1865, 1870, 1879, 1892, 1894, and 1900. Paolo de Marchi, the very able winemaker at Isole e Olena, hopes, one day, to produce the Villa Sperino wines again. We look forward to it.

This DOC zone delimited for Lessona encompasses 16 acres (6.5 hectares) of vineyards on southwest-facing hills. These vineyards can produce up to 4,010 cases of Lessona a year. The three grower-producers in the growing zone produce, on average, about 2,300 cases annually.

Lessona must be made from at least 75 percent spanna; vespolina and/or bonarda may be blended in. The Lessona of Maurizio Ormezzano is made from 100 percent spanna, while Sella uses 75 to 80 percent spanna, plus vespolina and bonarda. We've never tasted the Lessona of Clerico Sandrino. The aging period for Lessona begins January 1.

Lessona goes well with steaks and chops. It ages up to a decade, longer in the best vintages. Rating **

VINTAGE INFORMATION AND TASTING NOTES

Sella rates the vintages:

Excellent	1986, 1985, 1983, 1982, 1981, 1978, 1974, 1971, 1970
Good	1976
Average	1980, 1979, 1975, 1973
Mediocre	1984, 1977, 1972

Niederbacher sees the vintages:

***	1985, 1983, 1982, 1981, 1978, 1974, 1971, 1970
**	1980, 1979, 1976, 1975, 1973
*	1972
0	1984, 1977

Antonio Rossi rates the vintages:[11]

***	1988, 1986, 1985, 1981, 1980, 1974, 1970
**	1984, 1983, 1982, 1979, 1978, 1977, 1976, 1975, 1973, 1972, 1971

No rating 1987

Our experience is too limited to comment on many vintages, but we've found that anything earlier than 1974 was too old or was not good to begin with.

Sella Tenuta Agricola 1982 (*twice, 4/87*). Rich, almost toasty aroma; complex, firm, well balanced, loads of flavor; on the young side, well made. **(*)

Sella Tenuta Agricola 1980 (*twice, 1/85*). Lovely floral bouquet with a note of cherries, varietal character evident; very well balanced, some tannin to shed but overall fairly soft; nearly ready, could improve a bit. **(+)

Ormezzano Tenuta Eredi di Mario 1975 (*ex-cask, 11/78*). Fragrant bouquet; light-bodied, fairly well balanced, nice flavor, forward; for early drinking. **

Sella Tenuta Agricola 1975 (*5 times, 1/86*). Bottle age evident from the complex bouquet that displays a woodslike component through the mellow flavor, high acidity, the fruit is still there; best to drink up. ** +

Sella Tenuta Agricola 1974 (*4 times, 4/80*). Fruity bouquet with hints of cassis and flowers has still more to give; tannin to lose, well balanced, a lot of flavor; some class. ***

Sella Tenuta Agricola 1971 (*11/78*). Bouquet brings up *tartufi*(*!*); unbalanced with high acidity, low fruit.

Sella Tenuta Agricola 1970 (*11/78*). Similar nose to the '71; also unbalanced with high acid and low fruit—not a success.

LOZZOLO (*Vercelli*). Lozzolo is the product of 50 to 70 percent spanna, 20 percent croatina, and 10 to 20 percent bonarda grapes. It is a dry, tannic wine of 12.5 percent alcohol that reputedly ages well.

MAGGIORA (*Novara*). Conti Cav. Ermanno produces this medium-bodied wine from a blend of spanna, vespolina, and bonarda grapes. We haven't tasted it in over a decade. Rating *

DOC REQUIREMENTS OF LESSONA

Minimum Aging in Years		Minimum	Maximum Yield in	
in Cask	Total	Alcohol	Gallons/Acre	Hectoliters/Hectare
1	2	12%	600	56

MASSERANO (*Vercelli*). This wine is made from mostly spanna grapes with a small amount of bonarda blended in. Masserano is a soft, medium-bodied wine of about 12 percent alcohol. It can take moderate age.

MESOLONE (*Vercelli*). Mesolone is produced from an *uvaggio,* or blend, of 50 percent spanna, 30 percent bonarda, and 20 percent vespolina grapes grown on the Colline della Measola in Barengo. It is a medium- to full-bodied wine with about 13 percent alcohol that is reputedly at its best between its fifth and eighth year of vintage. It is produced by Avv. Armando Beccaro e Figlio.

MOT ZIFLON (*Novara*). Luciano Brigatti, the sole producer of this wine, makes about 15,000 bottles a year. It is the product of 70 percent spanna, 20 percent bonarda, and 10 percent vespolina grapes, grown in the Möt Ziflon district of Suno. The wine is fairly full-bodied, with a generous, warm, fruity aroma, and 13 percent alcohol. It is at its best within three to four years of the vintage, perhaps up to six in the better years. Rating **

Best vintages: 1988, 1985, 1983, 1974, 1964
Worst vintages: 1973, 1966, 1965

MOTTALCIATA (*Vercelli*). This wine is produced from spanna grapes grown in the *comuni* of Mottalciata and Castellengo. It is a medium-bodied wine of about 12 percent alcohol.

NEBBIOLO DELLA COLLINE NOVARESI (*Novara*). Rovellotti produces this wine. The only one we tasted was the '80—it left us less than impressed.

NEBBIOLO DELLA SERRA (*Vercelli*). This wine is produced from grapes grown in the *comuni* of Moncrivello, Roppolo, Viverone, and Zimone. It is light to medium in body, and best drunk young. Rating *

ORBELLO (*Vercelli*). There are two producers of Orbello; each uses a different formula, but both versions are based on the spanna grape. Sella blends in 20 to 30 percent cabernet sauvignon and franc, plus freisa, bonarda, and other local varieties. Luigi Perazzi adds 10 percent each of vespolina, bonarda, and croatina. Orbello is at its best drunk within two to five years of the vintage. Rating *

PICCONE (*Vercelli*). Sella produces this wine basically from spanna, with the addition of merlot, freisa, neretto di bairo, and barbera grapes. Piccone is a wine to be consumed young. Rating *

PRUNENT (*Novara*). This wine is produced from spanna grapes, known in Domodossola as prunent. It is light and soft, with about 11 percent alcohol, and at its best within four years, perhaps five, of the vintage.

ROASIO (*Vercelli*). This wine is rather similar to many of the other spanna-based wines of this area.

ROMAGNANO SESIA (*Novara*). Brugo produces this wine from bonarda, croatina, spanna, and vespolina grapes grown in the Ghemme region. It is a medium-bodied wine of 11.5 to 12.5 percent alcohol with a floral aroma and a light bitter-almond finish. It ages moderately well. Rating *

RONCO DEL FRATE (*Novara*). This wine is produced in the Ghemme zone from bonarda, spanna, and vespolina grapes. It is a medium-bodied red of about 12.5 percent alcohol that can take moderate age.

ROSSO DELLA SERRA (*Vercelli*). Another name for the **Nebbiolo della Serra**.

ROSSO DI GRIGNASCO (*Novara*). This wine is produced from a blend of nebbiolo, bonarda, and other local grapes. (See also **Grignasco**.)

SIZZANO (*Novara*), DOC. The vineyards of Sizzano are on the left bank of the Sesia between Ghemme and Fara. This district covers 100 acres (40.5 hectares). The vineyards are planted at an average altitude of 740 feet (225 meters) above sea level. DOC allows an annual production of 31,465 cases. Until 1983 the vineyards of Sizzano were cultivated by 69 growers; annual production averaged 13,300 cases. Between 1985 and 1988 production averaged 5,055 cases, less than half, with 70 authorized growers. One producer, Giuseppe Bianchi, accounts for some 20 percent of the total.

Sizzano is made from a blend of 40 to 60 percent spanna, 15 to 40 percent vespolina, and up to 25 percent bonarda novarese (uva rara). The aging period begins on January 1.

Sizzano is at its best within four to ten years of its vintage. Like many of the spanna-based wines of this area, it is medium in body and has a floral aroma frequently described as reminiscent of violets. Rating **

PRODUCERS	RATING
Bianchi Giuseppe	**
Cantina Sociale di Sizzano e Ghemme	**
Dellavalle F.lli	0
Dessilani	
Fontana Francesco	
Ponti	**
Turba	* —
Zanetta Ercolana	**

DOC REQUIREMENTS OF SIZZANO

Minimum Aging in Years		Minimum Alcohol	Maximum Yield in	
in Cask	Total		Gallons/Acre	Hectoliters/Hectare
2	3	12%	748	70

VINTAGE INFORMATION AND TASTING NOTES

Niederbacher's vintage chart rates them:

****	1957, 1947
***	1985, 1980, 1978, 1974, 1970, 1964, 1961, 1945
**	1984, 1983, 1981, 1979, 1976, 1975, 1973, 1971, 1969, 1967, 1953, 1950
*	1972, 1962, 1960, 1958, 1956, 1948
0	1982, 1977, 1968, 1966, 1965, 1963, 1959, 1955, 1954, 1952, 1951, 1949, 1946

Rossi sees them:[12]

****	1988, 1985, 1978, 1974
***	1983, 1982, 1981, 1979, 1976, 1975, 1971
**	1987, 1986, 1984, 1980, 1973, 1972, 1970
*	1977

While we have tasted very few Sizzanos in the past few years, we suspect that any wines older than 1978 are now too old. The vintages to age are 1988 and 1985. Sizzano isn't a long-lived wine.

Bianchi Giuseppe 1987 Valfrè (4/89). This *barrique*-aged, non-DOC Sizzano showed a heavy hand with the oak, it dominated.

Bianchi Giuseppe 1985 (4/89). Fairly nice fruit, floral notes; tasty, finish is slightly off. * —

Turba 1983 (*twice, 6/90*). Aroma of flowers and fruit; a little hard, fairly nice fruit. *

Bianchi Giuseppe 1980 (1/85). Aroma suggests Marsala; forward fruit, light to moderate tannin, flavor is somewhat floral; drinkable though a bit pedestrian.

Cantina Sociale di Sizzano e Ghemme 1978 (3 times, 4/85). Vaguely floral aroma; moderate tannin, has a tart edge, some firmness, nice fruit; should improve over the next year or two. **(+)

SPANNA [DEL PIEMONTE] (*Novara and Vercelli*). Spanna, the local name for the nebbiolo grape in the Novara-Vercelli production zone, is also the name of a wine—in fact, many wines—of varying styles and qualities. Most today are labeled Spanna del Piemonte, and most are rather unimpressive. Generally they are medium-bodied red wines with the characteristic tannic vein typical of the nebbiolo-based wines of this area. Many spannas carry a more specific denomination of origin. Among the more regarded Spannas of Vercelli are the Spanna di Bosca, di Casa del Bosco, and di Sant'-Emiliano from Sostengo, di Vigliano from Vigliano Biellese, and di Villa del Bosco from Villa del Bosco; from Novara, Spanna di Maggiora from Maggiora.

The regulations promulgated by the Common Market bureaucrats in Brussels who don't make wine, only wine laws, decree that a wine labeled with the name of a grape variety must be made from no less than 85 percent of that variety. Many producers use that prescribed minimum in their Spanna and blend in bonarda, vespolina, croatina, or anything they have handy, including wines and/or grapes trucked in from southern parts of the peninsula. This is not a new practice; it is something of a tradition here, where the name Spanna on a wine came to mean pretty much whatever the producer wanted it to, no more, no less.

Many of the best wines labeled Spanna in days gone by were made with a high proportion of fine southern varieties, like aglianico, which contributed body and richness to the wines. The local Spannas are very often thin and flavorless, especially in the lesser vintages, which are unfortunately all too common in this region. While the best Spannas can be very long-lived, most should be consumed with not more than two to four years of age. The best Spannas can equal any wine of the Novara-Vercelli hills. Rating */***

PRODUCERS	RATING
Vallana Antonio (older vintages)[a]	
Campi Raudii	****
Cinque Castelli	**
Del Camino	**
Montalbano	***
San Lorenzo	***
Traversagna	****
Vallana Antonio (since 1968)	**
Antoniolo, Santa Chiara[b]	** —
Avondo[c]	0
Barra Guido[d]	*
Bertolo Lorenzo	

Borgo Cav. Ercolo[b]   0
Brugo Agostino   *
   Riserva Cantina dei Santi[e]   *
Caldi Ditta Cav. Luigi[f]   *
Cantina Sociale dei "Colli Novaresi"[g]   *
Cantina Sociale Sizzano e Ghemme   *
Conti Cav. Ermanno
Cosseti Clemente[c]   0
Curti
Dellavalle F.lli   0
Dessilani Luigi   *
Ferrando Luigi   *
Fiore Umberto   0
   Sogno del Bacco[h]   0
Francoli Cantine[i]   *
Nervi Livio
Nervi Luigi & Italo   *
Ponti   *
Tibalini (EFFEVI)[j]   0
Travaglini   *
Troglia G.   *
Villa Antonio[b]   0
Villa Era di Vigliano, Tenuta Ermanno Rivetti[k]   *
Villadoria Marchese[i]   * —

NOTES: [a] These wines are no longer being produced
   [b] The last one we tasted was the '76
   [c] We haven't tasted it in years
   [d] The last one we tasted was the '78
   [e] The last one we tasted was the '75
   [f] The last one we tasted was the '86
   [g] The last one we tasted was the '79
   [h] The last one we tasted was the '81
   [i] The last one we tasted was the '74
   [j] The last one we tasted was the '83
   [k] The last one we tasted was the '64

TASTING NOTES

All of these wines are Spanna del Piemonte unless otherwise noted.

Nervi Luigi & Italo 1987 (4/90). A little cooked; some fruit, overly dry.

Travaglini 1987 (9/88). Fresh, forward, open fruit; nice entry, soft, moderate fruit, some tannin toward the back, short. *

Vallana 1987 (twice, 4/90). Berrylike fruit up front; a little tart, light, dryish aftertaste. *

Brugo Agostino 1986 (5/90). Hot, overripe and dull.

Caldi Ditta Cav. Luigi 1986 (10/90). Open fruit aroma, vaguely flora; some tannin, tasty. *

Nervi Luigi & Italo 1986 (4/89). Light nose; fairly nice entry, then very dry. * —

Ferrando Luigi 1985 (6 times, 5/89). Floral, berry, cassis and spice aroma; open fruit, sweet impression, tasty, very good indeed for what it is. **

Nervi Luigi & Italo 1985 (6/90). Some fruit, some tannin, dry, very drinkable. * —

Vallana 1985 (twice, 6/90). Lovely, open tobacco and cherry aroma; soft and tasty, well balanced; a splendid bottle. *** — *Bottle of 4/90:* Floral, berrylike aroma; nice fruit, light tannin, medium length, dry finish, no real distinction. *

Fiore Umberto 1983 (11/89). Unimpressive, hot.

Tibalini (EFFEVI) 1983 (9/87). Overly fruity, like grape juice; soft, lacks distinction or personality; drinkable.

Vallana 1983 (5/90). Earthy, tar and tobacco aroma; open fruit, soft; ready. **

Dessilani 1982 (10/86). Fresh berrylike aroma; fruity, balanced. * +

Fiore Umberto 1982 (12/86). Light nose; nice fruit, some acid, a bit rough at the end. +

Fiore Umberto 1981 "Sogno di Bacco" (6/83). Light, fruity, rather simple aroma; light-bodied, light tannin, fairly fruity and straightforward.

Nervi Luigi & Italo 1980 (6/85). Expansive floral aroma, vaguely peppery; high acid, fruity, light tannin; good with a light chill. *

Cantina Sociale dei "Colli Novaresi" 1979 (4/81). A tarlike aroma with an alcoholic backnote; light to medium body, some tannin, moderate fruit, tannic aftertaste.

Dessilani 1979 (1/83). Pale color; Marsala-like notes on nose and palate—oxidized, lacks structure, flavor, and style.

Ferrando Luigi 1979 (5/82). Musty, stinky odors in background; somewhat unbalanced, with high acidity, rather shallow, short, bitter aftertaste.

Travaglini 1979 (5/82). Straightforward, fresh fruity aroma with a floral note; moderate fruit; agreeable now but with potential to improve. *(+)

Barra Guido 1978 (12/80). Nice aroma though small; light-bodied, soft, fruity and simple, marred by a slight harshness at the end. *

Brugo Agostino 1978 (6/85). Fruity, harsh edges, clumsy, a bit tired, has seen better days.

Vallana 1977 "Traversagna" (4/85). Floral aroma, fruity notes; some tannin, heaps of flavor; drinkable now but should improve, a surprise for the vintage. **(+)

Antoniolo 1976 "Santa Chiara" (5/82). Fresh berrylike aroma with a peppery note; lots of flavor, some tannin; enjoyable now. * +

Borgo Cav. Ercolo 1976 (5/82). Berrylike aroma; moderate fruit; a simple little wine in a straightforward fruity style. *

Brugo Agostino 1976 (5/82). Moderately intense aroma; some tannin to shed, has fruit; enjoyable now but can improve. * +

Dessilani 1976 (5/82). Complex bouquet offers suggestions of blueberries, black pepper and more; blueberries carry through on flavor; a nice bottle. **

Nervi Luigi & Italo 1976 (3 times, 5/82). Characteristic aroma marred by a faint dankness in the back; acid and tannin on the high side, sufficient fruit to make it drinkable, even enjoyable, but drink it now. *

Vallana 1976 (4/85). Floral bouquet with fruity notes; soft, round and tasty, some tannin; very nice. ** +

Villa Antonio 1976 (5/82). A rubbery aroma that carries through on the palate—an awful wine.

Antoniolo 1975 "Santa Chiara" (12/85). Still some interest and fruit, starting to fade, bitter. * −

Brugo Agostino 1975 (5/82). Straightforward fruity aroma; some tannin, a bit shallow; ready as it will ever be.

Brugo Agostino 1975 Cantina dei Santi (1/85). Characteristic old-style spanna aroma with a lot of tar; tannin up front but has the fruit; could get better in a year or two. *

Nervi Luigi & Italo 1975 (11/79). Fragrant, fruity aroma; some tannin, soft and flavorful; ready. *

Brugo Agostino 1974 (twice, 3/83). Garnet, orange at rim; nice fruit on aroma, carries through on palate, unbalanced and showing age; drinkable but not to keep.

Brugo Agostino 1974 Cantina dei Santi Riserva (5/82). Floral bouquet with berrylike notes; acid on the high side; a quaffable wine that's quite ready. *

Francoli 1974 (5/82). Fairly rich bouquet with some complexity; firm tannin, lots of flavor; ready now. * +

Vallana 1974 (2/86). Deep color; rich and intense, blueberry aroma, vaguely recalls figs; acid out of balance, thin at the end, still the bouquet is very attractive. * +

Villadoria Marchese 1974 (5/82). Moderately intense aroma with berries and spice though an off note intrudes; has fruit, acid somewhat on the high side; enjoyable now, not to keep. * −

Brugo Agostino 1973 Cantina dei Santi (twice, 11/82). Tar and flowers on aroma; unbalanced, a bit shallow, some volatile acidity. (The bottle tasted March 1980 was better, and merited one star.)

Fiore Umberto 1973 "Sogno di Bacco" (5/82). Characteristic aroma, floral with some complexity; full of flavor, some tannin, ready now. * +

Vallana 1973 Castello di Montalbano (11/78). High volatile acidity, in fact undrinkable, a wine for the salad.

Vallana 1972 Podere Due Torri di Traversagna (11/78). A ghastly taste of sour seaweed, oxidized.

Brugo Agostino 1971 (10/81). Characteristic aroma; flavorful but acidity throws the balance off; shows signs of drying out; tails off to a bitter ending.

Brugo Agostino 1971 Cantina dei Santi (6/79). Fragrant aroma; soft and mellow with some tannin, acid on the high side; enjoyable now but not to keep.

Vallana 1971 Castello di Montalbano (3/80). Characteristic spanna nose with flowers and tar; considerable tannin but with the fruit to back it up; needs three or four years. *(*)

Nervi Luigi & Italo 1970 (10/79). Fruity aroma marred by some oxidation; fairly nice flavor. * −

Vallana 1970 Campi Raudii (11/78). Awful flavor; must be an off bottle.

Vallana 1969 (twice, 9/83). *More recent bottle:* An off note, like bad fruit; mars the aroma; tannic, shy of fruit—a bad bottle? *Earlier bottle:* Complex bouquet with suggestions of cherries and tobacco; firm and flavorful, still some tannin but with the fruit in reserve. **

Vallana 1969 Spanna di Montalbano (twice, 9/83). Light, fruity, floral aroma; still has a fair amount of tannin, medium-bodied, tasty; should improve; short. *

Brugo Agostino 1967 (twice, 11/82). *From gallon:* Deep color; richer, more intense bouquet; soft and smooth and most agreeable; has potential for improvement perhaps, it'll certainly hold. ** *From bottle:* Soft and smooth but has nowhere to go, as ready as it will ever be. * +

Vallana 1967 Cinque Castelli (1/87). Orange-brick robe; age beginning to set in, some oxidation apparent but at this stage adds complexity; vaguely floral; soft and smooth, rich and flavorful; lovely for current consumption. *** −

Vallana 1967 Podere Due Torri di Traversagna (4 times, 5/85). Barnyardy aroma carries through on the palate, not offensive, just different; light tannin, soft; no sign of age, ready. * + *Bottle of 9/84:* Nice bouquet, well developed and complex; soft entry, a lot of flavor; indications of drying out at the end, it was better a year earlier, could be the bottle. **

Vallana 1966 Castello di Montalbano (twice, 9/83). Floral, fruity bouquet; fairly rich and intense, full-bodied, well balanced, full of flavor; ready. **

Vallana 1964 Castello di Montalbano (3 times, 12/84). Deep red, garnet rim; deep, rich, intense bouquet with hints of vanilla and cherries—somewhat reminiscent of a late-harvest California wine; full-bodied, full of flavor, light tannin, lacks some delicacy but makes up for it in richness; as it sits in the glass, it begins to resemble a late-harvest zinfandel with a brambly, raspberry character. ***

Vallana 1964 Castello San Lorenzo (3 times, 2/89). Cherry and tobacco aroma, floral overtone; smooth and velvety, a bit harsh at the end with an alcoholic bite. ** + *Bottle of 3/82:* Medium dark red shading to orange; big, rich, expansive bouquet; full of flavor, still some tannin to shed; give it two to three more years. **(*)

Villa Era di Vigliano (Tenuta Ermanno Rivetti) 1964 Cru Viola Riserva Speciale (9/86). Volatile acidity under an aroma of tar and fruit; moderate tannin, some fruit. * −

Borgo Cav. Ercolo 1962 (11/78). Characteristic spanna nose; then nothing left but tannin, dried out.

Vallana 1961 Campi Raudii (twice, 2/87). Some volatile acidity apparent and lots of fruit in the aroma; nice fruit on the palate with a richness and concentration of flavor, marred by volatile acidity at the end. ** − *Bottle of 9/80:* Intense floral bouquet; soft and velvety, full of flavor, elegant, long on the finish; can still improve. ***(*)

Vallana 1961 Castello San Lorenzo (5/79). Expansive bouquet; rich concentration of fruit, loads of flavor and loads of tannin; needs age, but the potential is quite evident. ***(+)

Vallana 1961 Podere Traversagna (9/87). Rich cherrylike aroma, suggestions of flowers and peaches; rich, intense and concentrated, packed with enormous fruit and extract; still quite young. ***(+)

Vallana 1958 Campi Raudii (3/83). Deep brick robe; complex bouquet with a touch of oxidation; rich and flavorful; probably best drunk up now. ***

Vallana 1958 Castello San Lorenzo (twice, 1/88, 5,490 bottles). Rich bouquet, floral notes; full of flavor and structure, loads of character, smooth-textured, full-bodied, nuances of leather, figs and prunes, fairly long finish. **** *Bottle of 1/84:* Richly intense bouquet; mouth-filling flavors, enormous richness and concentration, Port-like but without the alcohol and sweetness, perfectly balanced, a complete wine. ****

Vallana 1955 Campi Raudii (6 times, 11/86 6,250 bottles). Deep brick-garnet robe, orange reflections; big, rich, intensely fruited bouquet, complex, suggestions of tar, mushrooms and blueberries; loads of flavor and class, still some tannin, but soft tannin, very long finish, a tad rough. *** *Bottle of 5/85:* Tawny, orange robe; floral, toasty bouquet with grainlike notes; full-bodied, some tannin, sweet berrylike flavors, finishes with a hint of raisins. *** *Bottle of 1/82:* Medium deep red, garnet rim; rich bouquet with suggestions of cassis; very rich, very full and still young, firm, tannic vein; not yet at peak but very good drinking now. ***(*)

Vallana 1955 Podere Due Torri di Traversagna (twice, 1/89, 5,983 bottles). Rich color; expansive bouquet recalls mint and flowers with herbal notes; fruity, rich and velvety; loads of class and style. *** + *Bottle of 11/82:* Richly fruited bouquet with a hint of mint and floral overtones; a rich concentration of ripe fruit flavors, velvety and elegant, enormous length. *** +

Vallana 1954 Campi Raudii (twice, 5/85). Delicate, refined floral bouquet with a berrylike nuance; full-flavored and velvety, rich and intense, still some tannin, very long finish has a vague raisinlike note; no signs of age. *** + *Bottle of 9/78:* Fragrant bouquet with floral notes; soft and smooth, heaps of flavor; quite ready; impressive quality. *** +

VALDENGO ROSSO, OR ROSSO DI VALDENGO (*Vercelli*). Valdengo Rosso is the product of spanna, bonarda, and vespolina grapes. It is a soft, medium-bodied wine of about 12 percent alcohol that can take moderate age.

VECCHIA COLLINA (*Novara*). The Cantina Sociale Coop. di Oleggio produces this wine from a blend of spanna, vespolina, and croatina grapes grown in Oleggio, Mezzomerico, and Barengo. It is a medium- to full-bodied wine of about 13 percent alcohol. At its best with at least four years of age, it drinks well until about its eighth.

VERCELLI ROSSO, OR ROSSO DI VERCELLI (*Vercelli*). This wine is the product of spanna, vespolina, and bonarda grapes.

VIGLIANO (*Vercelli*). Vigliano is made from spanna, bonarda, and vespolina grapes grown in Vigliano Biellese. It is a firm-textured wine that sometimes attains 13 percent alcohol. It ages moderately well.

VILLA DEL BOSCO (*Vercelli*). Villa del Bosco is the product of spanna, bonarda, and vespolina grapes grown in the villages of Bosco and Lozzolo. It is a light- to medium-bodied wine of about 12 percent alcohol, best drunk within four to five years of the vintage.

THE PRODUCERS OF NOVARA-VERCELLI

Albertinetti Pasquale. Pasquale Albertinetti produces a Gattinara.

Antichi Vigneti di Cantalupo di Alberto e Maurizio Arlunno (*Ghemme*), 1977. Antico Vigneti di Cantalupo owns 50 acres (20 hectares) of vines; 30 (12) are currently in production and the remainder they told us a few years ago, should have been by 1985 or 1986. Their main vineyard, at an altitude of about 985 feet (300 meters) above sea level, overlooks Breclema, the site of a once important castle and village. On the sunniest slopes of the vineyard is their 7.4 acre (3-hectare) cru, Collis Breclemae. Since 1979 they have produced about 13,300 bottles annually of this Ghemme cru. And since 1985, they have bottled their Collis Carelle cru as well. Their other vineyards are Baraggiola, Rossini, and Valera.

Antico Vigneti di Cantalupo produces all of its wines from its own grapes. Its Ghemme is made from 75 to 80 percent spanna, 15 percent vespolina (also known as ughetta di Ghemme) which they say adds mildness and delicacy, and 5 to 10 percent bonarda novarese (uva rara). They also make a specialty wine called Agamium. They put their wines in the *champagnotta* bottle seen fairly frequently in Ghemme.

Their best vintages: 1985, 1983, 1982, 1978, and 1974. Today they are the finest producer in the zone. Ghemme: *, crus ** +; Agamium * −

Antoniolo Azienda Vitivinicola di Mario Antoniolo (*Gattinara*), 1955. Antoniolo owns 37 acres (15 hectares) of vineyards which include the two crus of Osso San Gratò and San Francesco. Since 1974 they have kept aside a small part of the crop for these single-vineyard bottlings. The wine from San Francesco us generally softer and rounder than the bigger, more tannic Osso San Gratò. Recently they began bottling a wine from their Castelle vineyard.

THE CRUS OF ANTONIOLO

Cru	Nebbiolo Grapes		Average Number of Bottles Per Year
	Acres	Hectares	
Osso San Gratò	9.9	4	3,000–6,000
San Francesco	7.4	3	3,000–4,000
Total	17.3	7	6,000–10,000

Antoniolo produces an average of 60,000 bottles a year of Gattinara plus "Santa Chiara" Spanna del Piemonte. This wine is named for the fifteenth-century monastery where they have an aging cellar. Approximately 90 percent of their production comes from their own grapes.

We had been quite impressed with the Antoniolo Gattinaras up until the '68; from that vintage on the wines seem to have slipped. We are glad to report now that since 1978 they seem to be back in form. When we spoke with Rosanna Antoniolo about the changes she noted that beginning in 1968 the fermentation time was shortened and stems omitted. With the 1978 vintage, they started adding back up to 50 percent of the stems and lengthened the fermentation time again to fifteen days.

Rosanna names as the best vintages 1985, 1982, 1978, 1974, 1967, 1964, and 1961. We haven't tasted the Santa Chiara Spanna since the '76. Gattinara ***; Spanna ** −

Avondo. It's been a number of years since we've tasted the Gattinara and Spanna of Avondo, but when we did, we found them mediocre at best.

Balbiano Azienda Vitivinicola. (*Andezeno, Torino*), *1935.* Balbiano produces 135,000 bottles of wine a year, 40 percent from their own grapes. They have long been regarded for their Freisa di Chiera and Malvasia Castelnuovo Don Bosco, both still and sparkling. They own 7.4 acres (3 hectares) of vines, none in Gattinara. In 1979, though, they did a limited bottling of Gattinara. We found the wine quite good. We don't know if they still bottle a Gattinara. Gattinara **

Barra Guido & Figlio Azienda Vinicola (*Gattinara*). Barra owns 28 acres (11.3 hectares); 11 (4.5) are planted to vines, mostly nebbiolo (95 percent) with some bonarda (5 percent). They have an annual production of more than 36,000 bottles of Gattinara. They also produce 72,000 bottles of Spanna del Piemonte made from purchased grapes, in a blend of 85 percent spanna and 15 percent bonarda. In their own vineyards they have three crus.

In 1979, Barra bottled their first single-vineyard Gattinara, 4,500 bottles of Permolone. In 1980, this was increased to 6,000 bottles. That same year they also bottled two additional crus: Permolone Valferana (4,500 bottles) and Alice (7,500). The remainder of the grapes went into their regular Gattinara. They also produce some 4,000 bottles of Boca, 5,000 Fara, 7,000 Ghemme, and 6,000 Sizzano, plus a Spanna and Bonarda del Piemonte. The Barra wines, on occasion, like many in the region, have a taste that is suggestive of southern grapes. We haven't tasted the Barra Gattinara since the '79, nor the Spanna since the '78. Gattinara [** −]; [Spanna *]

Bava (*Cocconato Asti, Asti*). Until recently, this Barbera specialist owned the Borelle vineyard in Gattinara, from which they produced 4,000 bottles a year. They also age and market a Barolo and Barbaresco. For those two wines they buy the wine, not the grapes. Gattinara +

Beccaro Armando Azienda Vitivinicola Beccaro is the only producer, as far as we know, that bottles Mesolone.

Bertinetti, Uglioni dei. Bertinetti produces a Ghemme that we've never met.

THE CRUS OF BARRA

Cru	Acres	Hectares	Altitude in		Year Planted	Average Number of Bottles Per Year
			Feet	Meters		
Alice	4.04	1.6338	1,380–1,475	420–450	1970	13,000
Permolone	4.14	1.6780	1,180–1,310	360–400	1968	14,000
Permolone Valferana	2.84	1.1510	1,180–1,280	360–390	1971	9,500
Total	11.02	4.4628				36,500

Bertolazzi Luigi. They produce a Gattinara.

Bertole Ing. Salvatore (*Gattinara*). Our experience is limited to the '79, but it was decent enough. Gattinara [*]

Bertolo Armando. Armando Bertolo produces a Gattinara.

Bertolo F.lli. We found their '79 Gattinara to be very good. Gattinara [**]

Bertolo Lorenzo (*Torino*). This producer-merchant bottles Boca, Gattinara, Ghemme, and Spanna. We have never had the opportunity to taste any of them.

Bianchi Giuseppe Azienda Agricola di Bianchi Eva (*Sizzano*), *1785.* Bianchi owns 30 acres (12 hectares) of vines from which are produced the spanna-based Fara, Ghemme, and Sizzano. They produce an average of 1,110 cases of Sizzano a year, 335 of Fara, 665 of Ghemme, and 445 of Erbaluce. They also make a small quantity of Fogarin del Piemonte from the rare fogarina grape grown on the hilltops of Sizzano, a varietal Bonarda, a white Greco, and a non-DOC, *barrique*-aged Valfrè from the Sizzano zone. Fara **; Ghemme *; Sizzano **; Fogarin *; Valfrè * –

Borgo Cav. Ercolo. While we haven't tasted many of the Borgo wines and the most recent one we've had was the '76 Spanna del Piemonte, we can't say that we've been impressed with those we have. Gattinara [0]; Ghemme [0]; Spanna [0]

Brigatti Luciano (*Suno*), *1938.* Brigatti owns 12.4 acres (5 hectares) of vines from which he produces about 3,000 bottles of the white Costabella and 15,000 bottles of the spanna-based Möt Ziflon. Möt Ziflon **

Brugo Agostino Antica Casa Vinicola (*Romagnano Sesia*), *1894.* Brugo claims to be the oldest wine firm in Novara, but Azienda Agricola Giuseppe Bianchi, owned by Eva Bianchi of Sizzano, gives a founding date of 1785, which would make them even older. We know of at least two other *cantina* that are older: Casa Vinicola Umberto Fiore, owned by Silvana & Mauro Fiore of Gattinara, give a founding date of 1880, and Cooperativa Intercomunale Oleggio Cantina Sociale of Oleggio claims 1891 for the year of their startup. Brugo owns 50 acres (20 hectares) of vineyards, including the cru Cantina dei Santi. From this 5-acre (2-hectare) plot in Ronchi and Panagallo, they produce 30,000 to 40,000 bottles of Spanna del Piemonte. Their annual production is 600,000 to 800,000 bottles, which includes the standard Piemontese varietals—standard both in type and quality. Besides their Spanna cru, they make Spanna del Piemonte from spanna plus bonarda and vespolina grapes, Romagnano Sesia, Gattinara, and Ghemme. Their wines are aged in oak and chestnut casks. The most recent Gattinara and Ghemme that we tasted here were the '79s. Gattinara [*]; Ghemme [*]; Romagnano Sesia [*]; Spanna (both) [*]

Caldi Ditta Cav. Luigi. Caldi produces a Fara, Gattinara, and Spanna. Of the four Gattinaras that we tasted, one, the '82 Gattinara, was very good. Gattinara *; Spanna *

Caligaris Guido (*Gattinara*). Our experience with their Gattinara has been limited to the '79. The wine was certainly drinkable, if not much else. Gattinara [* –]

Caligaris Ing. Vittorio. Vittorio Caligaris produces a Gattinara.

Cametti Felice. This producer makes a Gattinara.

Cantina Ronchetto dei Fornara. Cantina Ronchetto produces a Boca.

Cantina Sociale Cooperativa. See *Cooperativa di Gattinara Cantina Sociale.*

Cantina Sociale dei "Colli Novaresi" (*Fara Novarese*), *1954.* This cooperative of 854 members produces a fairly wide range of wines, including the spanna-based Barengo, Caramino, Fara, and Spanna del Piemonte. Sixty percent of their production is sold in bottle. In 1983 they harvested 4,400 tons (40,000 quintali) of grapes, equivalent to more than 300,000 cases of wine. Their vineyards are in the *comuni* of Barengo, Briona, Cavaglietto, Cavaglio d'Agogna, Fara Novarese, Romagnano Sesia, and Suno. They produce, on average, 6,666 cases of Fara and 1,665 of Ghemme. Barengo *; Caramino *; Fara *; Spanna *

Cantina Sociale di Sizzano e Ghemme (*Sizzano*), *1960.* This co-op has 244 members in Ghemme and Sizzano who provide them with the grapes to produce the characteristic wines of this area. We don't know their average production of the spanna-based wines, but we do know that in 1979 they produced 50,000 bottles of Ghemme, and in 1980, 20,000 bottles of Sizzano. They also make a Spanna del Piemonte that is aged for two years prior to sale. Ghemme *; Sizzano **; Spanna *

Castaldi Giuseppe. Our experience with Castaldi's Fara has left us with a good impression. Fara **

Conte Ravizza. See *Monsecco Azienda Agricola "Le Colline."*

Conti Cav. Ermanno nel suo Castello di Maggiora (*Maggiora*). Our experience with these wines is somewhat limited, and unfortunately not recent. As far as we know they are the only producer of Maggiora. Boca [*]; Maggiora [*]

Conti Gian Piero (*Maggiora*). Their reputation is higher than our rating suggests. It's been some time that we've tasted them. Perhaps they are better. Boca [*]

Conti Molini. Conti Molini owns a piece of the highly regarded Le Lurghe vineyard in Gattinara. They produced a good '79. Gattinara [*]

Cooperativa di Gattinara Cantina Sociale (*Gattinara*), *1908.* This co-op has nearly 200 members in Casa del Bosco, Lozzolo, Roasio, and Sostegno. They produce some 466,000 bottles of wine a year, which includes about 40 percent of the total of DOC Gattinara. Much of this wine, Gattinara and otherwise, is not bottled but sold *sfuso*, or in bulk. Gattinara 0

Cooperativa Intercomunale Oleggio Cantina Sociale (*Oleggio*), *1891.* They are the oldest cooperative in the region. Among their spanna-based wines are Vecchia Collina and Spanna del Piemonte. We have never tasted either of them.

Cossetti Clemente. Cossetti is primarily a producer of mediocre Langhe wines such as Barolo. In our experience, admittedly not recent, these wines have sometimes risen to the level of drinkability, though barely. Spanna [0]

Curti. Curti produces a Spanna del Piemonte.

Dellavalle Cantine F.lli di Osvaldo & Adriano (*Gattinara*). Dellavalle owns 6.3 acres (2.5 hectares) of the Gattinara cru Molsino, planted in spanna. From the 1983 vintage they produced 8,425 bottles of Gattinara from this vineyard as Mursino. They also bottle a second Gattinara cru, Casacolanna. They also buy most of the grapes they use. They produce a wide range of fairly ordinary wines, including Gattinara, Spanna del Piemonte, Sizzano, and Barolo. It's been years since we tasted their Ghemme, which was the best wine that we've tasted from them. Gattinara 0; Ghemme [*]; Spanna del Piemonte 0; Sizzano 0

Delsignore Attilio. They produce a Gattinara.

Dessilani Luigi & Figlio (*Fara Novarese*). Dessilani owns 50 acres (20 hectares) of vines and buys grapes under long-term contracts from another 150 acres (60 hectares). Their average annual production of 600,000 bottles includes four nebbiolo-based wines, three made from 100 percent nebbiolo—Caramino (14,400 bottles), Gattinara (21,600), and Spanna del Piemonte (14,400)—as well as 14,400 bottles of Fara, made from a 60-30-10 nebbiolo, bonarda, vespolina blend. They also make a Sizzano.

Despite their reputation, and although the wines are good, we have been unimpressed with the Dessilani wines we've tasted. Discounting the bad bottles, we find the wines coarse and lacking in both style and distinction. Caramino *; Fara *; Gattinara *; Spanna *

Ferrando Luigi (*Ivrea, Torino*). Ferrando is a producer and merchant of the wines of Aosta-Torino and Novara-Vercelli. Besides Carema and Donnaz, he sells Caramino, Fara, and Spanna del Piemonte. His best wines come from the Aosta-Torino zone. Overall his wines from this zone are reliable, and the Gattinara can be very good. Caramino *; Fara *; Gattinara **; Spanna del Piemonte *

Ferrari Azienda Agricola. They produce a very good Ghemme from Vigneti del Podere "Rossini," or at least the '85 was. Ghemme **

Ferrari F.lli Romano & Guido. F.lli Ferrari produces a Ghemme.

Ferretti Carlo. Carlo Ferretti produces a Gattinara.

Fiore Umberto Casa Vinicola di Silvana & Mauro Fiore (*Gattinara*), *1980.* The Fiore line encompasses a very wide range of wines, mostly mediocre, including whites from Veneto and the Oltrepò Pavese in Lombardia. Their spanna-based wines include Gattinara, Ghemme, Sizzano, and two spannas—the regular Spanna del Piemonte and the fantasy-named Sogno di Bacco, or dream of Bacchus. We have found them all unimpressive. Gattinara 0; Ghemme 0; Sizzano 0; Spanna (both) 0

Fontana Allesandria. Allesandria Fontana produces a Ghemme.

Fontana Francesco. Francesco Fontana produces a Sizzano.

Fornara Benedetta. Benedetta Fornara produces a Boca.

Fracchia Provino (*Grazzano Badoglio*). Fracchia produces two nebbiolo-based wines, a Gattinara and a Barolo.

Franchino Marco (*Gattinara*). Franchino owns a piece of the regarded Lurghe vineyard. Umberto Fiore has from time to time offered the Franchino Lurghe cru under his own label. The only wine that we tasted under the Marco Franchino label was the '79 Gattinara. It was a shade better than the one sold under the Fiore label. Gattinara [* −]

Francoli. Francoli offers a Gattinara, Ghemme, and Spanna under his label. The only one we've tasted was the Spanna and it was, while decent enough, not much else. The most recent Francoli wine that we tasted was the '74. Spanna *

Ioppa F.lli Gianpiero e Giorgio Azienda Agricola e Vitivinicola. (*Romagnano Sesia*). Their Ghemme is highly regarded by other producers in the zone.

Kiola (*La Morra, Cuneo*). This label, owned by F.lli Dogliani's Batasiolo firm in the Langhe, also sold a Gattinara. We don't know if they still do. It was, like all of their wines, mediocre at best. Gattinara 0

Monsecco Azienda Agricola "Le Colline" (*Gattinara*), *1951.* The Monsecco winery produces between 80,000 and 95,000 bottles a year of three nebbiolo-based wines—Barbaresco, Gattinara, and Ghemme—in about equal quantities. A few years ago they were buying about a quarter of their grapes, but told us that when all of their own vineyards are in full production, sometime in the mid-1980s, they expected to make all of their wines from their own grapes. They have 10 acres (4 hectares) in the Valferrana vineyard in Gattinara and 5 acres (2 hectares) in Pelizzane, in Ghemme. They also produce a Barbaresco from their own grapes grown in the 12.5-acre (5-hectare) vineyard in Treiso. In all, they own 40 acres (16 hectares).

Besides these wines, they produce Borgo Alto, mostly from their own grapes (60 percent), a Dolcetto, Moscato, and Pinoir. This last wine is a white made from a blend of pinot noir and chardonnay. Their wines are given fairly long oak aging—the Barbaresco and Gattinara about five years in cask, and the Ghemme four. Their Gattinara is made from 100 percent spanna; the Ghemme contains 30 percent vespolina.

The estate derives its name from previous owner Conte Don Ugo Ravizza's *mon vin sec* ("my dry wine"). Until a few years ago Monsecco didn't use the name Gattinara on the label, proudly flying its own colors. The new owners (since 1979) added that denomination to their labels with the 1974 vintage.

The Monsecco Gattinara can be magnificent, but frequently overlong wood aging dries the wine out, robbing it of fruit and creating problems with volatile acidity. When it is good, there is no finer wine in the zone. The wines continue to be very good under the new ownership. Ghemme **; Gattinara "Monsecco" ***

Nervi Livio (*Gattinara*). Besides their Gattinara, they produce a Spanna. There is no connection between them and Luigi & Italo Nervi, which is another firm.

Nervi Luigi & Italo Casa Vinicola (*Gattinara*), *1920.* Nervi is the largest vineyard owner in Gattinara, with 62 acres (25 hectares) of vines which supply them with 60 percent of their grapes. Their annual production of Gattinara averages 66,660 bottles a year. Their vineyards include 24 acres (10 hectares) in Molsino and 10 (4) in Valferana. In 1978 they produced 1,500 bottles of each. Today they produce an annual average of 20,000 bottles of Molsino and 14,000 of Valferana.

For a time from 1976 they bottled their best Gattinara as Podere dei Ginepri. We preferred their regular Gattinara, especially the one sold in the Bordeaux-type bottle. And, somewhat surprisingly, at one time we found the Gattinara sold in the United States superior to the one sold in Italy. Today their best Gattinaras are sold as single-vineyard wines.

Nervi Luigi & Italo rate the vintages for their wines this way:

Best	1989, 1988, 1986, 1985, 1983, 1982, 1978, 1974, 1972, 1968, 1964, 1961, 1958
Medium	1987, 1981, 1980, 1976, 1973, 1969, 1967, 1962
Worst	1984, 1979, 1977, 1975, 1971, 1970, 1966, 1965, 1963, 1960, 1959

The Nervi wines can be the best in the zone, but in some years they don't quite measure up. We haven't tasted the Ghemme since the '70 and don't know if they still make it. Gattinara ** +; Ghemme [0]; Spanna *

Oleggio Cantina Sociale. See **Cooperativa Intercomunale Oleggio.**

Ormezzano Maurizio (*Mossa S. Maria*). Ormezzano produces a fine Lessona from 100 percent Spanna aged for two years in cask. No Lessona is better. Lessona **

Orsolani Casa Vinicola. Our experience with their Gattinara, although limited, has left a favorable impression. We haven't seen it for a few years, not since the '74. Gattinara [*]

Paganotti Alberto e Giuseppe. Paganotti produces a Ghemme.

Patriarca Bruno. Bruno Patriarca produces a Gattinara.

Patriarca Mario fu Cesare (*Gattinara*). Based on the '79, the only one we tasted, their Gattinara is fairly good. Gattinara [* +]

Patti Angela. Angela Patti produces a Ghemme.

Perazzi Luigi (*Roasio S. Maria*). Perazzi has 12.4 acres (5 hectares) of vineyards from which he produces a Bramaterra made with the maximum amount of nebbiolo allowed under the law (70 percent) and the minimum levels of the other three grapes (20 percent croatina and 5 percent each bonarda and vespolina). He also produces some 15,000 bottles of Orbello, and since 1985, La Sassaia Podere La Motta, a non-DOC, aged-in-*barrique* Bramaterra of which he produced 5,000 bottles from the first vintage. He produces some 10,000 bottles of DOC Bramaterra a year. We've never tasted better Bramaterra than those produced by Perazzi. Bramaterra **; La Sassaia *; Orbello *

Poderi ai Valloni. Poderi ai Valloni is owned by Guido Sertorio. They produce a Boca we've never met.

Ponti Guido (*Ghemme*). Ponti have the largest vineyard holdings in Ghemme, 42 acres (17 hectares), and at an annual production of 100,000 bottles they are, by far, the zone's largest producer. They also make Sizzano and Boca, as well as a Nebbiolo del Piemonte Rosato. We have found both their Ghemme and Sizzano quite reliable. Ghemme ** −; Sizzano **; Spanna *

Prolo Giovanni. Giovanni Prolo makes a Fara.

Prolo Luigi. Luigi Prolo produces a Fara.

Rivetti Ermanno. See **Villa Era di Vigliano.**

Rovellotti A. F. (*Ghemme*), *1971.* Rovellotti owns 12.4 acres (5 hectares) of vines from which they produce a Ghemme and a white Greco. Their vineyards include the 2.5-acre (1-hectare) cru Baraggiola and 5 acres (2 hectares) of Civetta. They have bottled a Ghemme Braggiole since 1974. The best vintages for Rovellotti's Ghemme have been 1974, 1978, 1979, 1982, and 1983; this last vintage, Rovellotti feels, was exceptional. Ghemme ** −

Rusca Attilio. Perhaps their Fara is better than our limited experience suggests. Fara [0]

Rusca F.lli. F.lli Rusca makes a Fara.

Sebastiani Antonio. Antonio Sebastiani produces a Ghemme.

Sebastiani Giuseppe Azienda Agricola (*Ghemme*), *1896.* Sebastiani owns parts of the Baraggiole, Pelizzane, and Ronco Tavoline crus in Ghemme. Their Ghemme, at least the '74 labeled as Giovanni Giuseppe Sebastiani, was quite good. Ghemme [**]

Sella Bramaterra Tenuta Agricola (*Roasio*). Sella owns 22 acres (9 hectares) of vines, some 15 (6) in the DOC Bramaterra zone, from which they produce about 25,000 bottles of Bramaterra and 15,000 of Orbello each year. Bramaterra **; Orbello *

Sella Lessona Azienda Agricola, Tenuta S. Sebastiano allo Zoppo (*Lessona Castello*), *1931.* This winery produces some 52,000 to 53,300 bottles of wine a year, including 20,000 to 30,000 of Lessona from their 24.7 acres (10 hectares) of vines in that zone. They own 47 acres (19 hectares) of vineyards in total. Lessona **; Piccone *

Tenuta San Vi' di Ferrante Dante. Dante Ferrante's Tenuta San Vi' produces a Ghemme.

Tibalini (EFFEVI). We have found their wines, based on the '82 Gattinara and the '83 Spanna, mediocre. Gattinara 0; Spanna 0

Travaglini Giancarlo (*Gattinara*), *1959.* Giancarlo Travaglini owns 44.5 acres (18 hectares) of vineyards in Gattinara, plus 42 additional acres (17 hectares) not planted. This includes parts of the crus of Ronchi, Permolone, and Molsino. Some 85 percent of the vines are spanna; the balance is bonarda, croatina, and vespolina. They produce 16,665 cases of wine a year that include 10,000 cases of Gattinara.

Since 1980 fermentation has been done in small 1,320-gallon (50-hectoliter) stainless steel tanks that are tall and thin. Since 1982 a few *barriques* were added.

They claim to be the first to sell Gattinara in bottle. In 1959 they commercialized the 1952 vintage.

In exceptional vintages Travaglini produces a *riserva numerata* from the best grapes from his best vineyards. While Gattinara *normale* is aged for at least three years in cask, the *numerata* is given an additional year. The first *riserva numerata* was from the 1967 vintage; they also made a 1974, 1978, 1980, 1982, 1983, and 1985. Besides Gattinara they produce a Spanna del Piemonte that contains some 15 percent dolcetto. Their wines can be good, if not much more.

Travaglini picks 1982, 1978, and 1971 as the best vintages, followed closely by 1983, 1980, 1974, and 1967. For the worst years, 1977 and 1972. Gattinara * + ; Spanna *

Troglia Ferrero Mario & Figli di Ferrero M. & C. (*Ozzano, Torino*). This firm produces at least 15 different wines, including Barolo and Barbaresco, as well as Boca, Bramaterra, Carema, Fara, Gattinara, Ghemme, and Sizzano.

Troglia G. (*Torino*). This merchant sells a wide range of wines from the Novara-Vercelli area in weird-shaped bottles. Troglia wines were better in the early to mid-1970s when he was selling vintages from the 1960s. They also sell wines from the Langhe. We haven't had that much experience of late and so give them the benefit of the doubt. Gattinara *; Ghemme *; Spanna *

Turba (*Gattinara*). They bottle a Boca, Fara, Gattinara, Ghemme, and Sizzano. Those few that we've tasted failed to impress. Thus far we haven't tasted their Boca and Fara. Of the ones we have tasted, we found their Ghemme the best. Gattinara 0; Ghemme * − ; Sizzano * − ; Spanna 0

Vallana Antonio & Figlio (*Maggiore*). Vallana used to produce six Spannas—Cinque Castelli, and the single-vineyard Campi Raudii, Traversagna, S. Lorenzo, Montalbano, and del Camino. The single vineyards were labeled "Castello di" followed by the name of each, but as there are no actual castles, the law no longer allows this terminology. Since the inauguration of DOC, Vallana has dropped their individual Spanna bottlings and started producing Gattinara, Spanna del Piemonte, and Boca.

Vallana was a master blender who produced some very fine and long-lived Spannas worthy of three and four stars. His wines underwent a change sometime in the late 1960s or early 1970s; sadly, they are not at the same high level as previously. Rumor has it that Vallana used to blend aglianico grapes from Basilicata into his wines to give them the body and strength they needed to age and develop. (The law today requires Spanna to contain 85 percent of that grape variety.) Whatever he did, the wines were magnificent; today they are a mere shadow of their former glory. If the story is true, we think it would have been preferable to drop the denomination Spanna from the label; the name Vallana meant much more.

Vallana has an annual production of 240,000 bottles—20,000 bottles of Boca, 6,650 to 8,000 of Gattinara, and 80,000 of Spanna del Piemonte, the balance being used for various other wines, red and white. Within the past few years the wines of Vallana have improved. While they don't match the exceptional quality and glory of times past, they are beginning to take their place among the zone's best.

Spanna (single vineyard): Campi Raudii ****, Cinque (5) Castelli **, Del Camino **, Montalbano ***, San Lorenzo ***, Traversagna ****; Boca **; Gattinara *** − ; Ghemme * + ; Spanna del Piemonte **

Valsesia A. Valsesia produces a Boca.

Villa Antonio. The few bottles we've tasted from this producer were, to put it mildly, poor. Admittedly it's been years since we've tasted any. The most recent wines we tasted from Villa Antonio were the '75 Gattinara and '76 Spanna. Gattinara [0]; Spanna [0]

Villa Era di Vigliano (*Tenuta Ermanno Rivetti*). At one time Rivetti bottled a single-vineyard Spanna from the Viola vineyard. The last one we tasted, the '64, was good. Spanna [*]

Villadoria (*Rivoli*). This firm is primarily a mediocre producer of Langhe wines. None of their wines have impressed us; some are worse than others. Spanna 0

Zanetta Ercolana in Giroldi. Our limited experience suggests that they just might be the best producer in the zone. Sizzano **

THE VINEYARDS AND WINES OF ANTONIO VALLANA

Spanna	Last Vintage	Now Used for
Campi Raudii	1973 or 1974	Gattinara
Cinque (5) Castelli	n/a	Spanna del Piemonte
Del Camino	n/a	Spanna del Piemonte
Montalbano	1980	Boca
San Lorenzo	1973 or 1974	Gattinara
Traversagna	1977	Boca

CHAPTER 5

The Nebbiolo Wines of the Valtellina

In the Valtellina area of northern Lombardia, vines are planted on steep terraced hillsides on either side of the Adda River valley to altitudes of over 2,000 feet (610 meters) above sea level. On the north the vineyards are sheltered from the cold northern winds by the Rhaetian Alps; to the south the Orobie Pre-Alps hold back the humidity and fog of the Padana Plains. Situated on the northern end of Lake Como, the vineyards receive the benefit of the lake's moderating winds, which also help to dry the moisture on the vines after rain.

The growing zone of the Valtellina, entirely in the province of Sondrio, extends 24 miles (40 kilometers) east from Ardenno to Tirano, encompassing 5,930 acres (2,400 hectares). 2,972 (1,203) of which are in the DOC zone.[1] The vines in the DOC zone are planted at altitudes ranging from 985 to 2,625 feet (300 to 800 meters) above sea level. The average annual yield here totals some 1.7 million cases, more than half a million of which are DOC Valtellina and Valtellina Superiore. The former accounts for some 60 percent of the total. Average production of the two Valtellina DOCs between 1986 and 1988 was 80 percent as much as the combined output of Barolo and Barbaresco (6.4 million bottles versus 8.1 million) from an area slightly larger than that planted in Barolo—2,973 acres versus 2,912 acres. (1,203 hectares versus 1,179).[2] Overproduction is a problem.

The vine is believed to have been cultivated in the Valtellina since before the Roman era. Some claims have been made that the Etruscans cultivated vines here. The wines of this general area, called Rhaetia by the Romans, were praised by Virgil. Svetonio recorded that Augustus counted these wines among his favorites. Pliny also wrote of the Rhaetian wines, and very likely referred to the Valtellina wines in particular, which he should have known well, being a native of Como. Other ancients who praised this wine include Catullo, Martial, Columello, and Strabone. Leonardo da Vinci noted in his Codice Atlantico that the "Voltolina

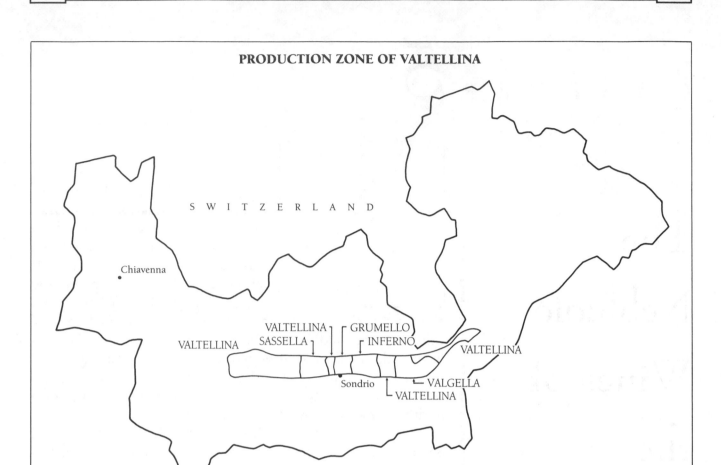

PRODUCTION ZONE OF VALTELLINA

S W I T Z E R L A N D

Chiavenna

VALTELLINA

VALTELLINA
SASSELLA

GRUMELLO
INFERNO

VALTELLINA

Sondrio

VALGELLA
VALTELLINA

. . . valley surrounded by high and terrible mountains makes powerful wines . . ."

The defining grape, the one that gives the character and personality to the Valtellina wines, is the nebbiolo, here known as chiavennasca, apparently taking its name from the town of Chiavenna, to the north and east of the DOC zone. The wines of the Valtellina are made from at least 70 percent chiavennasca; the *superiore,* from 95 percent. Brugnola, merlot, pignola, pinot nero (pinot noir), and rossola grapes, in varying proportions, make up the difference. Fifteen percent grapes, must, or wine from outside the zone may be blended into the *normale,* 10 percent to the *superiore.*

The normal harvest generally occurs during the second half of October, from about mid-month through the end of the month. In some years it extends into November. In the years in which sfursàt is produced, some of the grapes are harvested into December. The harvest begins in the area from Ardenno to Berbenno with the grapes that will be used for Valtellina, followed by those from Castione to Sondrio, then Tresivio, Teglio, and Tirano.

The *normale* Valtellina is a wine best drunk within one to three years of the vintage, though there are a few exceptions which will live a bit longer. The better, more serious wines from the area carry the designation *superiore* and, generally speaking, are superior to those labeled simply Valtellina. Unfortunately, though, they are rarely on a par with—never mind superior to—the other nebbiolo wines to the west, in the Piemonte and Valle d'Aosta. Rating *

Recommended Producers	Rating
Nera, Tellino	*
Rainoldi Aldo	*
non-DOC Ghebellino	** −
Tona di Gianluigi Bonisolo	
La Taberna	*
Perla Villa	*
Triacca F.lli	
La Gatta	* +
Tradizione	**

DOC REQUIREMENTS OF VALTELLINA

	Minimum Aging* in Years		Minimum	Maximum Yield in	
	in Cask	Total	Alcohol	Gallons/Acre	Hectoliters/Hectare
Valtellina	0	1	11%	900	84
Superiore	1	2	12%	750	70
Riserva	1	4	12%	750	70

* The aging period starts on January 1

◁ VALTELLINA SUPERIORE ▷

The Valtellina Superiore wines have higher alcohol than the regular—12 percent—and are aged at least two years, one of which must be in oak. They have a fruity, floral bouquet, sometimes displaying a nutlike nuance. These wines are usually at their best between five and ten years of the vintage. The *superiore* wines often carry the name of the subregion where the grapes are grown: Grumello, Inferno, Sassella, Valgella. These vineyards are all on the right bank of the Adda facing south. Some 1,200 acres (486 hectares) of vines are in the DOC zone. Although there are 1,341 growers authorized to produce grapes in this district, in 1988 only 419 reported any DOC output.[3] From 1977 to 1984 production here averaged 265,000 cases a year, slightly above the 235,000 average for the three most recent vintages we have data for, 1986 through 1988.[4]

Grumello

The Grumello district, located between Sondrio and Montagna, has vineyards covering 250 acres (101 hectares). There are 299 growers in this DOC zone; 186 reported output in 1988.[5] Average annual production between 1986 and 1988 was nearly 50,000 cases.[6]

The regarded crus of Grumello include Castèl Grumello, Sassorosso, and Stangone. Enologica Valtellinese owns the 5.2-acre (2.1-hectare) Castèl Grumello plot, located in Montagna, from which they have been bottling a cru since 1975. They produce an average of 18,000 bottles a year from this vineyard.

Grumello has an aroma that recalls strawberries and, for some, faded roses. It is at its best about five or six years after the vintage. Grumello is a good wine to accompany pork roast and chops or poultry such as quail or guinea hen. Rating **

Recommended Producers	Rating
Bettini F.lli	*
Enologica Valtellinese	*
Nera	**
Riserva	** +
Nino Negri	**
Pelizatti Arturo	*
Riserva Sassorosso	***
Polatti F.lli	*
Rainoldi Aldo	**
San Carlo, Vigna Stangone	** +
Triacca F.lli	** −

OTHER REGARDED WINES

Enologica Valtellinese, Castèl Grumello

Inferno

The Inferno district extends from Poggiridenti east to Tresivio. With only 158 acres (64 hectares) of vines, it is the smallest of the four subregions. There are 184 growers in the Inferno district; 170 produced grapes for this DOC wine.[7] The average production of Inferno between 1986 and 1988 was just under 34,000 cases a year.[8] It is perhaps also the warmest district, taking its name, they say, from the intense summer heat in its steeply terraced vineyards. Inferno has the steepest slopes in the Valtellina.

Al Carmine and Paradiso are two regarded crus of Inferno. The Paradiso vineyard extends into Sassella as well, but its wine is generally described as being more similar in character to the Inferno wines than those of Sassella. Enologica Valtellinese owns 8.9 acres (3.6 hectares) of the Paradiso vineyard, from which they have been bottling a Paradiso Riserva since 1968. Their vineyard site, located in the eastern part of Poggiridenti overlooking Tresivio, is entirely in the Inferno subdistrict. Enologica Valtellinese produces about 35,000 bottles annually. They age this wine for four years in Slavonian oak casks.

The bouquet of the Inferno wines is noted for suggestions of strawberries, violets, and hazelnuts. It is at its best within six to eight years of the vintage. Rating **

Recommended Producers	Rating
Bettini F.lli	*
Enologica Valtellinese	*
Riserva della Casa	** +
Nera	**
Nino Negri	**
Pelizatti Arturo	*
Polatti F.lli	*
Rainoldi	**
San Carlo, Vigna Al Carmine	** +

OTHER REGARDED WINES

Enologica Valtellinese, Paradiso

Sassella

Historically, the name Sassella comes from the small church situated on the promontory. Sassella, the only subregion west of the town of Sondrio, takes in 395 acres (160 hectares) of vines between Castione Andevenno and Sondrio. There are 366 growers here; 260 reported DOC output in 1988.[9] The average annual production between 1986 and 1988 was more than 70,000 cases.[10]

Regarded crus of Sassella include Ai Grigioni, Paradiso (see Inferno), and Sasso dal Corvo.

Sassella is the fullest in body of the Valtellina wines and matures somewhat more slowly than the others; it is also the longest lived. It is at its best from about seven to nine years of the vintage. Some tasters find notes of hazelnuts and spice in these wines. Sassella makes a good accompaniment to pork or lamb chops and steak. Rating **

Recommended Producers	Rating
Bettini F.lli	*
Enologica Valtellinese	*
Riserva	**
Nera	**
Riserva	** +
Nino Negri	**
Pelizatti Arturo	*
Riserva	** +
Polatti F.lli	*
Rainoldi	*
Riserva	**

San Carlo, Vigna Stangone	** +
Tona di Gianluigi Bonisolo	*
Triacca F.lli	**

OTHER REGARDED WINES

La Castellina
Triacca, Paradiso

Valgella

Valgella, barely the largest subregion with 398 acres (161 hectares) of vines, is in the comuni of Chiuro, Tresenda, and Teglio. Of the 492 authorized growers, 285 reported Valgella output in 1988.[11] Between 1986 and 1988 the average annual production of nearly 82,000 cases was down 12,000 from a few years earlier.[12] Caven is a regarded cru.

The wines of Valgella mature within three to four years of the vintage. In aroma they are said to recall strawberries, hazelnuts, and goudron, or tar. Valgella is the lightest in body of the Valtellina Superiore wines and the shortest lived and, many would add, the most variable in quality. About ten or eleven years ago, when we were drinking a lot more Valtellina Superiore wines, however, we found Valgella, contrary to its reputation, to be the most consistent in quality and generally the best, with the exception of some special selections from the other districts. Valgella goes well with pork, veal, or turkey. Rating **

Recommended Producers	Rating
Bettini F.lli	*
Enologica Valtellinese	*
Nera	*
Nino Negri	** +
Rainoldi	**
San Carlo, Vigna Caven	**

Riserva

The term riserva on Valtellina Superiore indicates the wine has been given four years of aging, with at least one in oak. The riserve tend to be fuller in body and richer in flavor than the regular Valtellina Superiore wines. We have enjoyed a number of fine riserve from Pelizatti, especially the '61 and '64 Riserva della Casa, and many bottles of Nino Negri's Castel Chiuro Riserva. This last wine, because of a ruling by the Common Market bureaucrats in Brussels, can no longer be labeled Castel Chiuro but simply Nino Negri Riserva, since Negri doesn't own an actual castle. (A castel must be a castle, it seems but a château may be only a shed.) The wine, however, is none the worse for the name change.

It's interesting to note that we have tasted more *riserve* from Sassella than from any of the other subzones. And we cannot remember ever tasting a Valgella Riserva. Grumello Riserva, in our experience, appears to be more commonly seen than Inferno Riserva.

Some other Valtellina Superiore special selections that we've enjoyed are Nera's Signorie and Negri's Fracia. Signorie comes from a vineyard located between Inferno and Valgella.

The Perla Villa of Tona is a regular Valtellina (not a *riserva*), being produced from 70 percent chiavennasca and 30 percent pignola grapes. Pelizatti's Runchet Valtellina is a blend of all six allowable grape varieties, at least 70 percent being chiavennasca. Rating **/***

Recommended Producers	Rating
Enologica Valtellinese, Inferno Riserva della Casa	** +
Enologica Valtellinese, Sassella Riserva	**
Nino Negri, Castel Chiuro Riserva, now Riserva	***
Nino Negri Fracia	** +
Nera, Grumello Riserva	** +
Nera, Sassella Riserva	** +
Nera, Signorie	*** −
Pelizatti, Grumello Riserva Sassorosso	***
Pelizatti, Sassella Riserva	** +
Rainoldi, Sassella Riserva	**

Sfursàt

Sfursàt, Sfurzàt, or Sforzato is similar in some ways to an Amarone. It is made from late-harvested grapes—in this case, mostly chiavennasca—which are left to dry on frames or mats for a month or two after the harvest, sometimes until the end of January or February. The very sweet, concentrated grapes are fermented until there is no sugar left, producing a dry wine of at least 14.5 percent alcohol.

A. D. Francis, in *The Wine Trade,* writes of a "Valtelline wine" from the seventeenth century made from dried grapes, but unlike the Sfursàt of today, at least, this wine was aged quite differently. He notes that Gilbert Burnet, Bishop of Salisbury, described it as

. . . an aromatic wine tasting like a strong water drawn off spices and, though a natural wine, as strong as brandy. The grapes were left on the vines until November to ripen thoroughly and then kept in garrets for two or three months before pressing. The liquor was then put into an open vessel, where it threw off a scum twice a day for a week or a fortnight, after which it was put into a closed vessel and for

the first year was very sweet and luscious, but at the end of the year about a third was drawn off and replaced with newer wine and so on every year. Every March it fermented and for a long time became undrinkable, but each year it slowly became stronger. Burnet met a lady named Madame de Salis who had kept such wine for forty years. It had become so strong that one could not drink more than a thimbleful.[13]

Sfursàt is full-bodied wine, tannic, and robust, with a richness of flavor and a complex aroma with suggestions of raisins, figs, nuts, and spices. It can age for up to seven or eight years, occasionally longer. It is a good wine to accompany hearty stews, braised meats, and strong cheeses, especially Gorgonzola. Rating ** +

Recommended Producers	Rating
Enologica Valtellinese	** +
Nino Negri	*** −
Nera	**
Pelizatti Arturo	*
Rainoldi	**
Tona di Gianluigi Bonisolo	**
Triacca F.lli	**

VINTAGE INFORMATION AND TASTING NOTES

In rating the vintages in the Valtellina, we unfortunately have had to rely on the evaluations of others more often than on our own sometimes very limited experience. We have noted where our own opinions differ.

The most highly regarded vintages (four stars) since World War II have been 1983, 1964, 1952, and 1947. We have greatly enjoyed quite a number of '64s, including the Negri Castel Chiuro Riserva, Pelizatti Riserva della Casa, and Grumello Riserva, as well as the Inferno Riserva and Sassella Riserva of Enologica Valtellinese. These wines were the finest Valtellina wines we have tasted. We can't comment on the '47s and '52s except to say that most likely the wines are too old today. The '64s could still be holding their own if they have had proper storage. As for the '83s, they certainly show a lot of promise.

Vintages on the next level, rated very good (three stars), are 1982, 1978, 1971, 1970, 1969, 1961, 1959, 1957, and 1954. We are not familiar with the '54s. We've tasted only one bottle of '57, an Enologica Valtellinese Inferno Riserva—insufficient to judge the overall quality of the vintage. We've had a number of '59s and '61s and concur that these were very good years indeed, though they didn't quite come up to 1964. A number of years ago we very much enjoyed the '59

**** Great, superb, truly noble
*** Exceptionally fine
** Very good
* A good example of its type, somewhat above average
0 Acceptable to mediocre, depending on the context; drinkable
+ Somewhat better than the star category it is put in
− Somewhat less than the star category it is put in, except for zero where it indicates a wines or producer-wine combination that is badly made or worse
[. .] *On a producer:* Tentative evaluation based on an insufficient number of wines or based on older, out-of-date vintages, or where the wines we tasted were too difficult to fully judge to give a fair assessment of quality
On a wine or vintage: Projection for the future. This rating is given to a vintage where we feel that we tested an insufficient number of wines or those we tasted were too difficult to really judge to give a fair assessment of quality
(. .) Potential increase in the rating of the wine given sufficient maturity

Negri Castel Chiuro Riserva and the '61 Riserva della Casa, Grumello and Sassella of Pelizatti.

The Enologica Valtellinese lists 1983, 1980, 1978, 1969, 1964, 1961, 1957, and 1954 as excellent vintages, and 1972 as the worst.

Antonio Niederbacher rates the vintages this way:

*** 1985, 1983, 1964, 1952, 1947
*** 1984, 1982, 1978, 1971, 1970, 1969, 1961, 1959, 1957, 1954
** 1981, 1980, 1979, 1975, 1973, 1967, 1945
* 1976, 1974, 1972, 1968, 1966, 1963, 1962, 1958, 1956, 1955, 1951, 1950, 1949, 1948, 1946
0 1977, 1965, 1960, 1953

Antonio Rossi's ratings:[14]

**** 1988, 1986
*** 1985, 1983, 1978, 1975, 1973
** 1987, 1982, 1981, 1980, 1979, 1971, 1970
* 1984, 1977, 1976, 1974, 1972

1989 ?

None tasted.

1988 ?

Antonio Rossi gives it four stars. None tasted.

1987 [* −]

The Valtellina had a rash of problems in 1987. Rain and cold during flowering was a prelude of things to come. A violent hailstorm on July 25 resulted in losses in some vineyards of up to 70 percent and torrential rains took a further toll. The harvest began on October 20 with the weather alternating between sun and heavy rain. Overall crop size was down 20 percent and the quality was, reportedly, mediocre. Antonio Rossi gives 1987 two stars. The one wine we tasted was good.

Valtellina 1987 Nera, Tellino (4/89). Open, fresh, cherrylike aroma; soft and easy; a good quaff. * +

1986 ?

Antonio Rossi calls it a four-star vintage. Thus far we've tasted one wine.

Sassella 1986 Nino Negri (5/90). Open fruit aroma; a little dry in the mouth, does have flavor; short. *

1985 *** +

Antonio Niederbacher rates the year as four stars, Antonio Rossi three. The wines, are for the most part, ready, and very good as well.

Ghebellino 1985 Rainoldi (9/87, 2,496 bottles). This non-DOC wine is a nebbiolo in *barrique*. Lovely bouquet combines vanilla from the oak with the varietal character of the nebbiolo; attractive fruit overlaid with an oak component. ** −

Grumello 1985 Nera (twice, 4/89). Spicy and fruity, moderate tannin; could use more character. *

Inferno 1985 Nera (twice, 4/89). Light floral aroma combines with ripe fruit; light tannin, balanced, fresh; dry finish. * +

Sassella 1985 Nera (twice, 4/89). Open, ripe fruit aroma; good body, tasty, sweetness of ripe fruit. **

Valgella 1985 Nera (twice, 4/89). Light nose, recalls fresh berries; tasty, a little light, some sweetness, moderate tannin; needs a year or so. ** −

Valtellina 1985 Nera (twice, 5/89). Open fruit on the aroma and palate, light, tasty. * +

Valtellina 1985 Rainoldi (6/90). Small-scale but drinkable; not to keep. *

1984 [0]

Antonio Niederbacher rates the year as a three-star vintage and Antonio Rossi as a one. If the one wine that we tasted is any guide, the vintage is unimpressive. The wine was too old three years after the vintage. As elsewhere in Italy, it was a difficult vintage.

Valtellina 1984 Nera (9/87). Odd nose, recalls chop suey(!); earthy taste, some fruit; drying out; unimpressive.

1983 ****

Many good wines were made, most of them are ready now. Rarely has a vintage achieved such a high level of success here. The Enologica Valtellinese puts the vintage on the first level, Niederbacher gives it four stars, and Rossi three.

Grumello 1983 Negri (twice, 9/87). Reticent aroma; dry, tannic, fairly nice fruit beneath; needs some age. *(*)

Grumello 1983 Nera (4 times, 5/89). Tasty, more interest and flavor than the inferno. **

Grumello 1983 Rainoldi (9/87). Aroma suggestive of nuts and fruit; dry flavor; young, good potential, needs say, two or three years. *(*)

Grumello 1983 Triacca (4/87). Light nose; medium body, some tannin, good fruit; on the young side; well balanced. *(*)

Grumello Riserva 1983 Nera (4/89). Tobacco, berry aroma; dry, good body, fairly tannic with the fruit to support it; dry finish. **

Inferno 1983 Nera (4 times, 5/89). A bit dry, does have fruit and structure. * +

Inferno 1983 Rainoldi (9/87). Nice fruit on the nose; tannic and rough on the palate, sense of fruit quite evident. *(*)

Inferno Riserva 1983 Rainoldi (5/90). Rainoldi aged this wine in *barrique* for eighteen months. It shows. Lots of oak on the nose and palate, soft, sweet vanilla flavor, does have evident fruit; short. ** −

Sassella 1983 Negri (9/87). Nutlike aroma; fairly nice fruit, dry, moderate tannin, the fruit is sufficient to carry it, medium body. **(+)

Sassella 1983 Nera (4/88). Fairly nice fruit; soft, forward flavors, round; ready. * +

Sassella 1983 Rainoldi (twice, 5/90). Lovely nose, cherry and floral components; soft, sweet, and open; at its peak; a lovely glass.

*** − *Bottle of 9/87:* Lovely nose, floral component; rough and unready, with evident potential. **(+)

Sassella 1983 Triacca (4/87). Small nose; fairly well balanced, moderate tannin; some firmness and tannin at the end. *(+)

Sassella Riserva 1983 Nera (4/89). Open berry aroma; dry, moderate tannin, seems to have sufficient fruit; light, dry aftertaste. * +

Sforzato 1983 Nera (twice, 4/89). Rich and concentrated with good structure, quite tannic, gobs of fruit, sweet impression, chocolate notes. **(* −)

Sforzato 1983 Triacca (4/87). Slightly corked, yet the quality comes through; vaguely of seaweed on the nose along with a cherry note; cherrylike flavor, tannic, yet with a sweetness to it. *(*)

Sfursàt 1983 Negri (twice, 9/87). Reticent aroma, hint of dried fruit; full-bodied, firm, young, sense of fruit beneath the tannin, closed. **(* −)

Valgella 1983 Rainoldi (9/87). Odd nose at first, then the fruit is evident; comes up dry, with moderate tannin and evident fruit, good structure. **(+)

Valtellina 1983 F.lli Triacca, Villa di Tirano, La Gatta (4/87). This wine was made from between 95 and 98 percent nebbiolo; light nose; fairly soft, open; drinkable and easy; light-bodied. * +

Valtellina Superiore 1983 Negri, Fracia (twice, 9/87). Perfumed scent, nutlike nuance; balanced, nice fruit; a little young, perhaps two years should do it. **(+)

Valtellina Superiore 1983 Nera, Signorie (4/89). Light nose, vaguely floral; full-flavored and tasty under moderate tannin; rather young but has the quality and structure to age. **(* −)

1982 ***

Niederbacher calls it a three-star vintage, Rossi a two. As good as they are, 1983 is superior. The wines, for the most part, are ready.

Grumello 1982 Nera (twice, 9/87). Lacks nose though some fruit evident; lots of fruit in the mouth, also acid and tannin, somewhat disjointed. *

Inferno 1982 Negri (4/87). Woodsy aroma; nice flavor, light tannin, some softness, fairly well balanced. ** −

Inferno 1982 Nera (3 times, 9/87). Nice up-front on the nose, though with a slight background dankness—corked?; dry, tannic and shallow. *Bottle of 4/87:* Fragrant, floral aroma; light- to medium-bodied, well balanced, flavorful; nearly ready. ** +

Inferno 1982 Rainoldi (9/87). Nutlike aroma, fruity component; tannic entry gives way to fruit; young but with evident potential. *(* +)

Sassella 1982 Nino Negri (4/87). Aroma suggestive of nuts; fruity, well balanced, good structure; a bit dry and tannic at the end. **

Sassella 1982 Nino Negri, Le Botti d'Oro (*10/90*). This wine spent two years in oak. Light, fragrant aroma; soft and round, lovely flavor; fairly long finish; at its peak. ***

Sassella Riserva 1982 Rainoldi (*9/87*). Reticent aroma; full of tannin and flavor; loads of potential, has the structure, and extract. **(*−)

1 9 8 1 **

Antonio Niederbacher gives 1981 two stars, Antonio Rossi agrees. The wines are very good, and very ready. There's no need to hold them any longer.

Grumello Riserva 1981 Nera (*4/89*). Berry, tobacco aroma, dried fruit component; light to moderate tannin, tasty; ready now; good body. **−

Sassella Riserva 1981 Nera (*4/89*). Open, ripe fruit, berry aroma and taste, tobacco component, balanced, some smoothness. **

Sforzato 1981 Nera (*3 times, 4/88*). Old and drying out; still some aroma and flavor interest. All three bottles tasted between September 1987 and April 1988 gave the same impression. *

1 9 8 0 **

The Enologica Valtellinese called 1980 an excellent vintage. Most other authorities rated this vintage two stars. Those we tasted seem to bear out that rating. They are ready. Some are fading, or worse, have faded.

Sassella 1980 Nera (*4/85*). Small nose; not a lot of tannin, a bit light in body, tasty; needs two or three years yet to be at its best. *(*)

Sassella 1980 Tona di Gianluigi Bonisolo (*9/83*). Unexpectedly full in aroma and flavor, light tannin, good fruit; ready. *

Sforzato 1980 Enologica Valtellinese (*10/87*). Concentrated, dried fruit aroma; chocolate nuance that carries through in the mouth, rich in flavor; nice now with room to grow. **(+)

Sforzato 1980 Tona di Gianluigi Bonisolo (*9/83*). Lacks the characteristic richness of a Sforzato though has nice enough flavor, light tannin; quite forward, more or less ready. *

Sfursàt 1980 Rainoldi (*twice, 9/87*). Dried fruit and raisin aroma; moderate tannin, vaguely sweet, full of flavor; a bit short; best to drink now. *+

Valtellina 1980 Tona di Gianluigi Bonisolo, Perla Villa (*9/83*). Light-bodied, light in tannin, simple, fruity; agreeable; ready. *

Valtellina 1980 Triacca, Tradizione (*4/87, 12,340 bottles*). This 100 percent nebbiolo has a dried fruit aroma; moderate tannin, good body and a lot of flavor; surprisingly on the young side with a firm, tannic finish. *(*−)

1 9 7 9 ** +

Once again Antonio Niederbacher and Antonio Rossi agree; they place 1979 with the two-star vintages. There was some very good Sforzato made that year. The other wines were generally good, but there is no need to hold them any longer.

Riserva 1979 Negri (*4/87, 30,000 bottles*). Light woodsy aroma; light- to medium-bodied, light tannin, flavorful; moderately long finish. **

Riserva 1979 Negri, barrique-aged (*4/87, 10,000 bottles*). This one spent six months in *barrique*. Small nose, some oak, in fact too much; light-bodied, dry. +

Sassella Riserva 1979 Nera (*twice, 4/88*). Typical old-style nebbiolo, nutty component; losing its fruit; drink up. *− *Bottle of 4/87*: This one had a lot more going for it, it was complex and flavorful, and at its peak. ** +

Sforzato 1979 Enologica Valtellinese (*3 times, 6/89*). Scented, almost floral bouquet with characteristic dried fruit character; rich and dry, still some tannin; enjoyable but best to drink up; a tad bitter. It was at its best when tasted in April 1987. That bottle merited ***, this one, * +

Sforzato 1979 Nera (*6 times, 7/84*). Medium brick; an aroma of cherries and raisins; fairly full-bodied, good fruit; should be ready soon. **

Valtellina 1979 Nera, Tellino (*4/81*). Fresh, fruity, peppery aroma; simple, high acidity, moderate fruit; marred by alcohol on the aftertaste.

Valtellina 1979 Tona di Gianluigi Bonisolo, La Taberna (*9/83*). Pale garnet; small aroma; tasty, light tannin, a nice glass of wine now. *

1 9 7 8 ***

The Enologica Valtellinese lists 1978 as an excellent vintage. The two Antonios, Niederbacher and Rossi, place it at three stars. Splendid wines, the best of the decade, and surely the best since the great '64s. The regular Valtellina *superiori* are showing very well now, including the *riserve,* which are very ready as well.

Grumello 1978 Rainoldi (*9/83*). Full, rich bouquet with suggestions of nuts and flowers; moderate tannin, has the stuffing and backbone; drinks well now but can, and should, improve with two to three more years. **(*)

Inferno 1978 Nera (*9/82*). Bouquet has notes of vanilla and fruit; well balanced, light tannin, lots of flavor; ready now though room for improvement. **

Inferno 1978 Rainoldi (*9/83*). Light garnet; well balanced, some tannin, light-bodied, tasty; ready but should improve yet. **

Inferno Riserva della Casa 1978 Enologica Valtellinese (6/85, 10,600 bottles). Fairly rich, floral, nutty aroma; light tannin, flavorful; quite ready; tails off toward the end. ** +

Sassella 1978 Rainoldi (9/83). Pale garnet; not much aroma; more forward on the palate than the Grumello or Inferno, nice fruit, light-bodied, even a bit simple.

Valgella 1978 Rainoldi (9/83). Nose has a suggestion of nuts; light tannin, well balanced, lots of flavor; enjoyable now. **

Valtellina 1978 Rainoldi (*twice*, 9/83). Small aroma; light-bodied, not a lot of tannin; enjoyable now, and very ready. A bottle tasted one year earlier was better, and also merited *.

1 9 7 7   0

Niederbacher gives it zero, Rossi one. A vintage that should have been declassified.

Sassella 1977 Enologica Valtellinese (9/81). Pale color; small nose; light-bodied, high in acid, some fruit; drinkable; finish is rather harsh.

Sfursàt 1977 Negri (*twice*, 9/82). Lacks the expected richness and intensity on aroma and palate, some glycerine, nice flavor; not to keep. A bottle tasted eighteen months earlier seemed to need more age; this one shows signs of fading.

1 9 7 6   0

Both Niederbacher and Rossi rated the vintage one star. Only 1977 was worse in the decade.

Grumello 1976 Rainoldi (3/81). Floral bouquet with a nutlike note; very good for the vintage; fairly well balanced, nice flavor; some style; for present drinking. *

Inferno 1976 Nera (4/80). Berrylike aroma; light-bodied, some tannin, fruity; very ready now, but it should hold for a year, possibly two. *

Sassella 1976 Rainoldi (9/82). Small aroma; light-bodied, some tannin, lacks weight, unstructured.

1 9 7 5   0

Niederbacher rated it two stars, Rossi three. Most of the '75s are probably too old now. Sforzato, which should be still showing well, deserves two stars.

Inferno 1975 Enologica Valtellinese (11/79). Pale color; a hot, alcoholic aroma; more flavor than the nose suggests, but gives way to too much tannin; short, dull aftertaste—already too old.

Inferno 1975 San Carlo, Vigna Al Carmine (6 times, 12/83). Brick red; some berrylike fruit on nose; high acid, drying out a bit but still has some flavor and interest. Bottles tasted a few years earlier, though better, never amounted to a lot either.

Sassella 1975 Nera (4/80). Fruity aroma marred by alcohol; light to medium body, somewhat off-balance with too much tannin.

Sassella 1975 San Carlo, Vigna Ai Grigioni (6 times, 12/83). Brick red; small floral aroma; somewhat light in body, decent balance, some tannin, acid a trifle high but adds a liveliness; in all, a nice bottle, but not one to keep. *

Sforzato 1975 Nera (7 times, 2/85). Tawny orange at rim; moderately intense aroma with a floral character and notes of nuts and raisins; fairly nice fruit, moderately rich, some alcohol intrudes; very ready. *

Sforzato 1975 Tona (10/78). Fairly rich, concentrated bouquet that recalls raisins and figs; some tannin, a lot of fruit, touch of bitterness on the aftertaste; needs some time yet, but nice now. **(+)

Valtellina 1975 Nera (4/80). Floral aroma with fruit and a touch of tar; soft and fruity but rather light; has held up rather well but is not to keep. *

1 9 7 4   * * *

Niederbacher and Rossi rated 1974 one star. We found these wines better than others did. In fact, many of the '74s were the best Valtellinas we had tasted since the '64s. The best *riserve* should still be good, and there's a good chance that the best of the regular Valtellina *superiori* are also holding, though there's probably no point in keeping them any longer.

Grumello 1974 Nera (6 times, 12/83). Brick red; fruity, vaguely floral aroma; still has fruit but is beginning to dry out. * (It was considerably better in 1980 and 1981, when we gave it ** + .)

Grumello 1974 San Carlo, Vigna Stangone (9 times, 12/83). This wine was at its best from late 1979 through 1982 when it merited four stars. The most recent bottle tasted had a fruity, berrylike aroma; there was still flavor interest but it was showing signs of drying out. *

Inferno 1974 Enologica Valtellinese (10/79). Light-bodied, soft, has fruit; quite ready; perhaps a bit too simple, finish is rather short. * –

Inferno 1974 Nera (10/79). Characteristic aroma; well balanced, nice flavor; good quality; very nice wine. **

Inferno 1974 Rainoldi (11/79). Somewhat backward and closed in but displays a lot of fruit, still has some tannin to shed. *(*)

Inferno 1974 San Carlo, Vigna Al Carmine (10/79). Pleasants characteristic aroma; fuller than the Nera and more flavorful, some tannin but nice now; could even improve. **(*)

Sassella 1974 Nera (10/79). Has body, flavor and balance, some tannin; nearly ready. **(*)

Sfursàt 1974 Enologica Valtellinese (twice, 2/80). Rich and intense on aroma but lacks intensity on the palate, surprisingly soft; not to keep. It was better a year earlier. *

Sfursàt 1974 Negri (11/83). Deep, rich, intense bouquet, recalls almonds; full and robust with the concentrated character of dried fruit; fairly long on the finish. **

Sfursàt 1974 Rainoldi (10/82). Raisiny, concentrated aroma; full-bodied, moderate tannin, some alcohol intrudes but has a lot of fruit. *(*)

Valgella 1974 Nera (8 times, 12/83). This wine was at its best from October 1978 to April 1980 when it merited two stars plus. The bottles tasted in March 1981 showed signs of fading. The last bottle was drying out, with noticeable volatile acidity, though still some flavor interest.

Valgella 1974 San Carlo, Vigna Caven (9 times, 12/83). This wine was at its best in 1979 and 1980, when it merited two stars plus. By 1981 it was showing signs of senility and by December 1983 it was already somewhat oxidized and, although some flavor remained, the wine was falling apart.

Valtellina 1974 Nera (10/78). Seems too light, lacking substance and weight; probably was better a year or two ago.

Valtellina Superiore 1974 Nera, Signorie (9 times, between 10/78 and 11/82). The more recent bottles were better than the earlier ones, having the benefit of more age. *Latest bottle:* Color shading to tawny; lovely bouquet with some delicacy; smooth texture, well balanced and stylish; a long finish; ready. ***

1973 0

Antonio Rossi rates 1973 at three stars, Antonio Niederbacher slightly less at two. Light wines overall. Though better than the Novara-Vercelli and Aosta-Torino nebbiolos, they still weren't much better than average. They're most likely too old now.

Grumello 1973 Nera (10/78). Nice nose; medium-bodied, still some tannin to lose, seems to have the fruit to develop, but . . . *(*?)

Inferno 1973 Negri (11/78). Alcoholic nose; light to medium in body, some oxidation—was it ever better?

Inferno 1973 Nera (10/78). Some varietal character on nose; light- to medium-bodied, some tannin, nice flavor. **

Inferno 1973 Pelizatti (11/78). Pale color; some oxidation.

Sassella 1973 Nera (twice, 11/82). Corked. *Bottle of 10/78:* Light-bodied, but has good flavor; at its peak. ** −

Sassella 1973 Polatti (3/81). Color showing age; some fruit and oak on nose; but alcohol intrudes; palate impressions are favorable but lacks some style; acceptable, no more.

Sassella 1973 San Carlo, Vigna Ai Grigioni (4 times, 7/81). Has developed a nice bouquet with a nutlike nuance; quite soft, a touch of tannin; good, but not up to the earlier bottles. * *Bottle of 10/79:* Well balanced with nice flavor; even perhaps a bit young. **

Sforzato 1973 Enologica Valtellinese (11/78). Big, rich, fruity aroma that brings up cherries; light-bodied, flavorful, some tannin, bitter finish. *

Sfursàt 1973 Negri (twice, 11/79). Nice flavor, some concentration and tannin; nearly ready. ** −

1972 0

The Enologica Valtellinese lists 1972 as the worst year. Antonio Niederbacher and Antonio Rossi rates it slightly higher at one star, but judging from our experience the '72s should never have been bottled. We tasted many '72s from about 1974 through 1978.

Sforzato 1972 Pelizatti (11/78). One-dimensional aroma with the characteristic raisiny note; some tannin, perhaps too much, good flavor; touch of bitterness on finish. *

1971 0

Some authorities, namely Niederbacher, gave this vintage three stars, while others, like Rossi, gave it two. Based on our own experiences with numerous '71s, though no Sfursàt, many were high in acidity and rather thin. It's possible that a few *riserve* have held up and the Sfursàts could still be good.

Grumello 1971 Rainoldi (11/79). Some oxidation, thin, off balance.

Sassella Riserva 1971 Nera (twice, 4/80). The more recent bottle was better—fruity aroma with hints of nuts; a mouthful of tannin but seems to have the fruit to outlast it, a knife-and-fork wine; try again in two, perhaps three years. *(* +)

Sassella Riserva 1971 Pelizatti (11/78). Lightish color; some oxidation, alcoholic, not a lot of fruit, bitter finish.

Valtellina Superiore 1971 Nera, Signorie (1/88). Light red toward garnet; aroma suggestive of leather and dried fruit, vaguely floral; still some tannin, but well integrated with the fruit, flavorful, recalls dried fruit and leather in the mouth with characteristic nebbiolo flavor components. ** +

Valtellina Superiore Riserva 1971 Negri, Fracia (11/78). Note of hazelnuts on aroma, marred by some alcohol; has tannin and nice flavor, but where will it go? Some alcohol also intrudes on the finish, which is short. * −

1970 *

Antonio Niederbacher gave 1970 three stars, Antonio Rossi two. As with the other nebbiolo wines, this was a very good vintage for the Valtellinas. The best *riserve* could still be holding. As for the rest, probably not; fifteen years is too long for most Valtellinas, *superiore* or no.

Grumello Riserva 1970 Pelizatti, Sassorosso (11/78). Pale garnet; some oxidation and alcohol on the nose; little else, some flavor interest on entry, and then, as they would say—*nulla*.

Sassella Riserva 1970 Enologica Valtellinese (4/80). Dried out!!!

1969 0

The Enologica Valtellinese lists 1969 with the top vintages and calls it excellent. Antonio Niederbacher puts it a notch lower at three stars. Some excellent Sforzato was produced. The best *riserve* could still be good. The regular Valtellina *superiore* wines are most likely gone.

Sassella Riserva 1969 Nera (twice, 4/89). Old nose, tired and faded; some flavor interest. * *Bottle of 1/88:* Clear color with orange reflections; dried fruit, leather and prunes; fairly rich and flavorful, moderate tannin; a bit dry at the end. ** +

Sfursàt 1969 Negri (6 times, 11/82). Some oxidation, but also a dried, concentrated raisiny note; some tannin; drying out but not totally gone. Without question it was better three to four years ago when it merited two stars plus.

1968 0

Antonio Niederbacher rates 1968 at one star. We've enjoyed some very good bottles and at one time might have given the vintage two, even three stars. Now the wines are probably too old.

1967 0

Authorities, like Antonio Niederbacher, gave the vintage two stars. We dissented, it was a very fine vintage. The best *riserve* should still be holding, but it is doubtful whether any others are.

Valtellina Superiore Riserva 1967 Nino Negri (11/78). [This wine is made from a selection of Negri's best grapes from Grumello, Inferno, and Sassella.] Fruity aroma; seems to have still more to give, a bit light in body, some tannin, a lot of fruit; should improve yet. **(+)

1964 **

The Enologica Valtellinese classifies 1964 as an excellent vintage and Antonio Niederbacher gives it his maximum four-star rating. These were magnificent wines. The best *riserve* could still be if they were stored well.

Grumello Riserva 1964 Pelizatti, Sassorosso (3/82). Intense, concentrated bouquet; follows through with the same richness on the palate, smooth and flavorful; very impressive indeed. *** +

Sassella Riserva 1964 Enologica Valtellinese (3/80). Brick with orange reflections; floral aroma marred by some volatile acidity; still some tannin and flavor, but beginning to dry out. * −

Valtellina Superiore Riserva 1964 Negri, Castel Chiuro (12 times, 3/82). The bottles from the 1970s were magnificent, meriting three stars plus. Those tasted since 1980 still offered some interest but were on the way downhill; for the memory, three stars. The wine today: 0

1961 *

The Enologica Valtellinese places 1961 in the first rung; they call it excellent. Antonio Niederbacher classifies it a bit lower at three stars. A very fine vintage, on a par with 1967. In the decade, only 1964 was better. Given proper storage, the *riserve* could still be drinking well. Most of the rest will be too old, as will anything else.

1957

The Enologica Valtellinese places 1957 with the excellent vintages, Antonio Niederbacher puts it with the three-star years.

Inferno 1957 Enologica Valtellinese (11/79). Pale garnet; fragrant nutlike aroma; quite lovely, but with a touch of oxidation, considerable tannin, some fruit; probably was better a few years ago. **

THE PRODUCERS

There are 14 producers that bottle all four denominations of Valtellina *superiore* and one additional producer who bottles Grumello and Sassella, and another one that bottles Sassella only.

THE PRODUCERS OF VALTELLINA SUPERIORE

Producer	Grumello	Inferno	Sassella	Sfursàt	Valgella	Selections
Balgera Rag. Gianfranco	x	x	x	—	x	—
Bettini F.lli	x	Poggiridenti	x	Spina	x	—
Enologica Valtellinese	regular and Castèl Grumello	x	regular and Paradiso	x	x	riserve
Fay Sandro	x	x	x	—	x	—
"La Castellina" Azienda Agricola	—	—	x	—	—	—
Nera Casa Vinicola	x	x	x	x	x	Signorie
Nino Negri	x	x	x	x	x	Riserva and Fracia
Pelizatti Arturo	regular and Riserva della Casa	x	x	x	x	Runchet and Sassorosso
Polatti F.lli	x	x	x	—	—	—
Rainoldi Aldo Casa Vinicola di Giuseppe Rainoldi	x	x	x	x	x	Tzapei and Vecchia Valtellina
San Carlo	Stangone	Al Carmine	Ai Grigioni	—	Caven	—
Tona Casa Vinicola di G. Bonisolo	x	Al Carmine	Sasso dal Corvo	x	—	Perla Villa Valtellina*
Triacca F.lli Tenuta "La Gatta" proprietà F.lli Triacca	x	x	Paradiso	x	—	—
"Villa Bianzone" Cantina Coop	x	x	x	x	x	Villa and riserve

Other Producers
Cantina Coop "Villa de Tirano" (& Bianzone)
Emilio Pola
Pietro Plozza

* 70 percent nebbiolo

Rating the Producers

***

− Nera, Signorie
Nino Negri, Castel Chiuro Riserva, now Riserva
− Nino Negri, Sfursàt
Pelizatti, Grumello Riserva Sassorosso

**

+ Enologica Valtellinese, Inferno Riserva della Casa
Enologica Valtellinese, Sassella Riserva
+ Enologica Valtellinese, Sfurzato
Nera, Grumello
+ Nera, Grumello Riserva
Nera, Inferno

Nera, Sassella
+ Nera, Sassella Riserva
Nera, Sfurzato
+ Nino Negri, Fracia
Nino Negri, Grumello
Nino Negri, Inferno
Nino Negri, Sassella
+ Nino Negri, Valgella
+ Pelizatti, Sassella Riserva
Rainoldi Aldo, Grumello
− Rainoldi Aldo, non-DOC Ghebellino
Rainoldi, Inferno
Rainoldi, Sassella Riserva
Rainoldi, Sfursàt

Rainoldi, Valgella
+ San Carlo, Grumello Vigna Stangone
+ San Carlo, Inferno Vigna Al Carmine
+ San Carlo, Sassella Vigna Stangone
San Carlo, Valgella Vigna Caven
Tona di Gianluigi Bonisolo, Sfurzato
− Triacca F.lli, Grumello
Triacca F.lli, Sassella
Triacca F.lli, Sfurzato
Triacca F.lli, Valtellina Tradizione

*

Bettini F.lli, Grumello
Bettini F.lli, Inferno
Bettini F.lli, Sassella
Bettini F.lli, Valgella
Enologica Valtellinese, Grumello
Enologica Valtellinese, Inferno
Enologica Valtellinese, Sassella
Enologica Valtellinese, Valgella
Nera, Valgella
Nera, Valtellina Tellino
Pelizatti Arturo, Grumello
Pelizatti Arturo, Inferno
Pelizatti Arturo, Sassella
Pelizatti Arturo, Sfurzato
Polatti F.lli, Grumello
Polatti F.lli, Inferno
Polatti F.lli, Sassella
Rainoldi, Sassella
Rainoldi, Valtellina
Tona di Gianluigi Bonisolo, Sassella
Tona di Gianluigi Bonisolo, Valtellina La Taberna
Tona di Gianluigi Bonisolo, Valtellina Perla Villa
+ Triacca F.lli, Valtellina La Gatta

Balgera Rag. Gianfranco. They produce all four Valtellina *superiore* subdenominations. We've never met their wines.

Bettini F.lli. Besides their range of Valtellina and Valtellina *superiore* wines they produce the single-vineyard Inferno Poggiridenti and Spina Sfursàt. We haven't tasted them in some time. Grumello *; Inferno *; Sassella *; Valgella *

Enologica Valtellinese (*Sondrio*), *1873*. Enologica Valtellinese owns the 5.2-acre (2.1-hectare) Castèl Grumello plot in Montagna within the Grumello district and 8.9 acres (3.6 hectares) of the Paradiso vineyard. The latter, located in the eastern part of Poggiridenti overlooking Tresivio, is entirely in the Inferno subdistrict.

They have been bottling a Castèl Grumello cru since 1975, producing an average of 18,000 bottles a year. In 1968 they began bottling a Paradiso Riserva, which they age for four years in Slavonian oak casks. Their production of this Inferno is about 35,000 bottles annually. They also produce the rest of the Valtellina range, including Sfursàt and *riserve*. Antica Rhaetia Valtellina is made

from 5 percent pinot noir and pinola valtellinese with the balance being nebbiolo. Enologica Valtellinese also produces some special *riserva* that they label Riserva della Casa. And then there is La Nebbia Bianco, Orbobio white, and Frisun red. Their wines can be very good indeed. Grumello *; Inferno: *, Riserva della Casa ** +; Sassella: *, Riserva **; Sfursàt ** +; Valgella *

Fay Sandro. Sandro Fay produces wines from all four Valtellina Superiore subzones. We've never tasted them.

"La Castellina" Azienda Agricola. As far as we know La Castellina produces only a Sassella. We've never tasted it.

Nino Negri (*Chiuro*). Nino Negri was part of the Winefood group of wineries that have been spun off and now belong to Gruppo Italiano Vini. Negri is the zone's largest producer and grower. They own 104 acres (42 hectares) in the Superiore zone. This includes 14.8 acres (6 hectares) in Sassella, 32 (13) each in Inferno and Grumello, and nearly 25 (10) in Fracia which is in the Valgella zone. Besides the full range of Valtellina wines, they produce the special selections Fracia and Nino Negri Riserva, both Valtellina Superiore. At one time they labeled the Riserva as Castel Chiuro Riserva, which they had to discontinue doing sine they don't actually own a castle. The wine is as good as always. The Nino Negri Riserva is made from a selection of grapes from Grumello, Inferno, and Sassella. They produced 10,000 bottles of a *barrique*-aged version from the 1979 vintage. It spent six months in oak, and it showed. Their '79 Riserva *normale* was considerably better, of which 30,000 bottles were produced. We don't know if they have produced the *barrique*-aged since the '79.

They do produce a partially *barrique*-aged Sfursàt, 5 Stelle (5 Stars), from their own vineyards. It is aged three or four years in oak casks, plus an additional eight to ten months in small barrels. It is only made in the best vintages. The first might have been the '83. At most they produce 3,000 bottles a year. They do a special Sassella and Inferno as well, Le Botti d'Oro—the golden casks—from grapes grown in their own vineyards. This wine is made entirely from nebbiolo and is aged at least two years in oak casks. It is a selection of the best cask(s). They also produce a Chiavennasca Bianco. Their wines can be as good as anyone's in the zone. Grumello **; Inferno **; Sassella **; Sfursàt *** −; Valgella ** +; Valtellina Superiore: Castel Chiuro Riserva, now Nino Negri Riserva ***, *barrique*-aged +; Fracia ** +

Nera Casa Vinicola (*Chiuro*), *1946*. Pietro Nera and his sons, Stefano, an enologist, and Simone, own 94 acres (38 hectares) of vines in the Valtellina DOC and buy grapes for the rest of their needs. Giovanni Silvestrina has been an enologist here for more than a decade

Besides the full range of Valtellina DOC wines, they also produce two white wines from red grapes: Rezio and Chiavennasco. They also produce a Valtellina labeled Tellino; Signorie; a single-vineyard Valtellina Superiore from a vineyard located between Inferno and Valgella; and a Grumello Riserva and Sassella Riserva. Nera can be relied on as much as anyone in this zone to produce good wines. Grumello: **, Riserva ** +; Inferno **; Sassella: **, Riserva ** +; Sfursàt **; Valgella *; Valtellina Tellino *; Valtellina Superiore: Signorie *** −

Pelizatti Arturo. Pelizatti produces the full range of Valtellina wines as well as a few special bottlings. Their special selections are

THE VALTELLINA WINES OF NERA CASA VINICOLA

DOC Zone	Acres	Hectares
Valtellina	11.86	4.8
Sassella	9.88	4.0
Grumello	2.47	1.0
Inferno	19.77	8.0
Valgella and Signorie	29.65	12.0
Total	73.63	29.8

Grumello Riserva Sassorosso, Riserva della Casa, and Runchet, a DOC Valtellina made from all six allowable grape varieties. A few years ago they were owned by Winefood and now, by Gruppo Italiano Vini. Their wines were considerably better in the 1960s and early 1970s. As for today, we don't know, not having tasted them in some time. Inferno *; Grumello: *, Riserva Sassorosso ***; Sassella: *, Riserva ** +; Sfursàt *

Polatti F.lli. They produce the full range of Valtellina *superiore* wines. We haven't tasted them in years. Grumello *; Inferno *; Sassella *

Rainoldi Aldo Casa Vinicola di Giuseppe Rainoldi (*Chiuro*). Rainoldi is a generally reliable producer. Besides the full line of Valtellina *superiore* wines, they produce a *barrique*-aged nebbiolo,

Ghebellino, that is not produced under the DOC regulations. It is a *vino da tavola*. They produced some 2,500 bottles of the '85. They also produce two special selections—Tzapei and Vecchia Valtellina—and a Brut Rosé and Brut Nature *metodo champenois* from nebbiolo grapes, and a Ghebellino Bianco. Ghebellino ** −; Grumello **; Inferno **; Sassella: *, Riserva **; Sfursàt **; Valgella **; Valtellina *

San Carlo. As far as we know San Carlo produces four wines, one from each of the four Valtellina Superiore subzones, and each one from a single vineyard: Grumello Stangone, Inferno Al Carmine, Sassella Ai Grigioni, and Valgella Caven. At one time we found their wines to be the zone's best. We haven't tasted them in years. Grumello Vigna Stangone ** +; Inferno Vigna Al Carmine ** +; Sassella Vigna Ai Grigioni ** +; Valgella Vigna Caven **

Tona Casa Vinicola di Gianluigi Bonisolo. Tona produces the full range of Valtellina wines as well as two single-vineyard wines: Sassella Sasso dal Corvo and Al Carmine Inferno. They produce the Valtellina DOC wines, La Taberna and Perla Villa, from 70 percent chiavennasca and 30 pignola. Sassella *; Sfursàt **; Valtellina: La Taberna *, Perla Villa *

Triacca F.lli. Triacca owns Villa di Tirano. Besides their line of Valtellina wines, they produce Tradizione, a 100 percent nebbiolo that carries the Valtellina DOC, Valtellina La Gatta from their Tenuta "La Gatta," and the single-vineyard Sassella from their holding in the Paradiso vineyard. Grumello ** −; Sassella **; Sfursàt **; Valtellina: Tradizione **, La Gatta * +

Villa Bianzone Cantina Coop. This co-op produces the standard line of Valtellina wines as well as some riservas and the Valtellina Villa.

PART TWO

Sangiovese

CHAPTER 6

The Sangiovese Grape

Sangiovese, the grape of Brunello di Montalcino, Chianti, Carmignano, Vino Nobile di Montepulciano, Torgiano, and many of the new *barrique*-aged wines of Toscana, is one of the world's noble varieties. Sangiovese is the prominent grape of most red wines of central Italy. It is frequently blended with other varieties, which is the tradition there, but it is the sangiovese that gives the character, perfume, and structure to these wines. The best wines tend to be made from sangiovese only, or a very high proportion of that variety.

This widely grown variety is believed to have originated in Toscana. At various times known as sangioveto, san gioveto, sangioghetto, and s. zoveto, the name in general use for the grape today is sangiovese. This name is, according to one theory, derived from Sanguis Jovis ("blood of Jove"), though the reason is not quite clear. The wines of the sangiovese tend to be medium in color, not dark red. And Jove, though a pleasure-loving deity—the original jovial type—was not the god of wine. However it came to be called as such, the sangiovese today stands for a red wine of medium body, dry and firm, with a tannic spine and a floral bouquet, a wine that, for the most part, ages moderately well.

There are a number of subvarieties of the sangiovese and no less than fourteen clones. Among the more noted are the sangiovese piccolo, or sangiovese, and the sangiovese grosso, known as prugnolo gentile in Montepulciano and brunello in Montalcino. Biondi-Santi claims that their Brunello is a clone of the sangiovese grosso. There is a special clone of the sangiovese in the vineyards of Badia a Coltibuono in Chianti Classico and another at Castello di Nipozzano in Chianti Rùfina. And the old sangiovese di lamole clone can be found at Castellare. A few other Chianti estates also have particular clones. The sangiovese di romagna grown in Emilia-Romagna is yet another.

Sangiovese dominates the red grape plantings not only of Tos-

THE DOC AND DOCG WINES OF TOSCANA

1. Brunello di Montalcino
2. Rosso di Montalcino
3. Vino Nobile di Montepulciano
4. Rosso di Montepulciano
5. Chianti Classico
6. Chianti Montalbano
7. Chianti Rùfina
8. Chianti Colli Fiorentini
9. Chianti Colli Senesi
10. Chianti Colli Aretini
11. Chianti Colline Pisane
12. Chianti
13. Rosso delle Colline Lucchesi
14. Parrina Bianco-Rosso
15. Carmignano
16. Carmignano and Chianti Montalbano
17. Montescudaio Bianco-Rosso
18. Morellino di Scansano
19. Pomino
20. Pomino and Chianti Rùfina

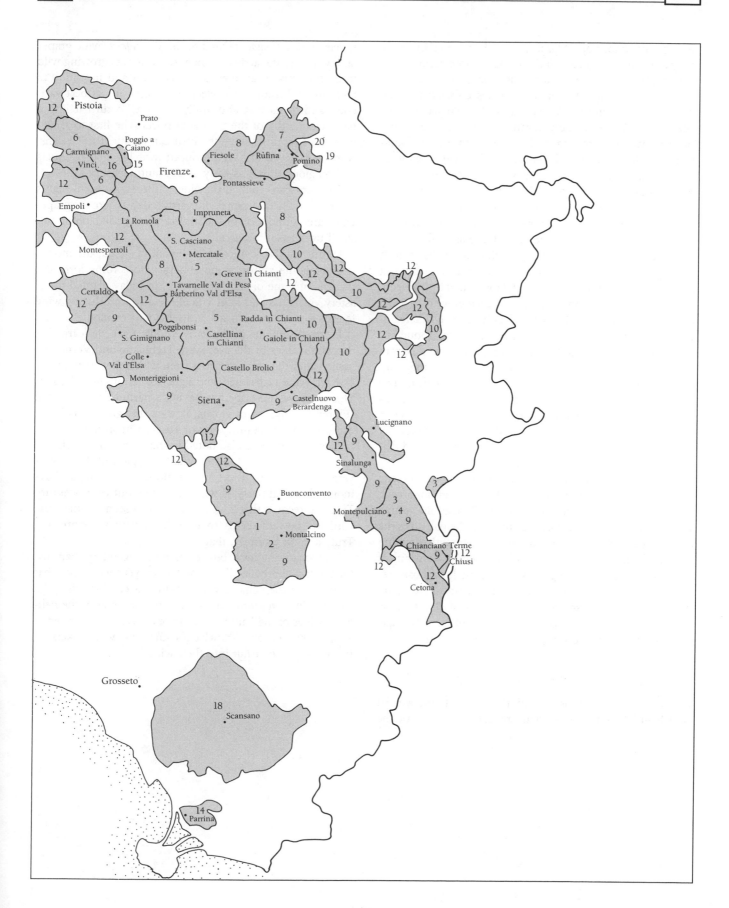

cana, but of Umbria and Marches as well. It is used in nearly every red wine recognized under DOC in those regions. It is widely planted in Emilia-Romagna, Marches, and Lazio. There are a significant number of vines cultivated in the province of Avellino in Campagna, and in Puglia. Sangiovese is also planted in the vineyards of Abruzzo, Basilicata, Calabria, Molise, Sardegna, and Sicilia, and it can be found in the northern reaches of Veneto and Lombardia as well.

The sangiovese grosso is said to have been introduced into Abruzzo from Montepulciano and became known as montepulciano d'abruzzo for the town where it originated. If this is correct, then the sangiovese is also the most important red variety in Abruzzo and Molise as well.

Sangiovese is generally blended with other varieties, as it is in Chianti, Carmignano, Vino Nobile, and Torgiano, but can stand very well on its own, as demonstrated by Brunello, Le Pergole Torte of Monte Vertine, and Sangioveto of Badia a Coltibuono. This noble variety has its own character; it doesn't need to be blended with other grapes to produce an excellent wine. The wines of the sangiovese have a certain subtlety, a delicacy that is lost when some other, more aggressive varieties, such as cabernet, are mixed with it. The personality of the other, more assertive grape tends to dominate, even when only a small proportion is added. When vinified on its own, or with the local varieties traditionally added to it, the characteristic fruity, floral perfume and delicacy of the sangiovese grape shine.

In recent years a number of experiments have been made with aging sangiovese in *barrique,* which, when done well, adds an extra dimension to the wine. Besides interesting nuances of aroma and flavor, the tannin in the oak gives the wine a better capacity to age, developing a smoother texture and more complexity in the course of its evolution. Many of the new *barrique*-aged sangiovese wines, such as those created by enologists Maurizio Castelli and Vittorio Fiore, are especially fine wines (see chapter 12). While we feel that the nebbiolo wines, for example, do not benefit from *barrique* aging, we find that those from the sangiovese can.

Early History

Vine fossils have been discovered in Toscana, to the west of the Chianti Classico zone, that are believed to be of the species *Vitis ausoniae,* related to the *V. vinifera* (wine grape) family. Before the arrival of man, the vine was growing wild in central Italy. It awaited only his talent and ingenuity to cultivate and train it, to select and propagate its best varieties, and to harvest and vinify its fruit, to turn it into a beverage worthy of the paeans of poets. The first to recognize its possibilities were the Etruscan people, the Tuscans, who are believed to have produced wine for their banquets and religious rituals as early as the ninth century B.C.

The Etruscans trained the vines on trees, a system that is still used in the traditional vineyards today, where the grapevines are supported, or garlanded, on wooden poles and small trees called *testucchi.*

During the Dark Ages after the fall of Roma, the monks who built the sturdy stone abbeys whose ruins form the nucleus of some of the wine estates of today planted monastery vineyards and kept viticulture alive, producing wine for solemn refectory meals and religious ceremonies.

From documents of the early Middle Ages we learn that the white wines of the area were Trebbiano and Vernaccia, named after the grape varieties from which they were made. The red wine was called Vermiglio for its bright red color. This wine was described as having a perfume of irises, the "Florentine lily," or of violets, flowers that grow in colorful profusion in the countryside of Toscana in spring.

A scent of irises is also noted in the aroma of the Chianti wine of today. Some folks say that it's typical of the sangiovese, but others attribute it to a more exotic *uvaggio.* Raymond Flower, discussing winemaking in fourteenth-century Toscana, records that ". . . the practice of scenting the wine with iris flowers seems to have been very widespread."[1] Truly a floral bouquet, that.

It's a charming idea, but seems more legendary than historical. It is surely not done any longer, yet there is still that fragrance in the Chianti wines. Many tasters, including the authors, find an aroma of *tartufi* in the bouquet of the nebbiolo wines of the Langhe, but no one has ever suggested—at least not to our knowledge—that the winemakers of Piemonte shave *tartufi* into their wines!

CHAPTER 7

Chianti

Chianti is surely one of the most beautiful viticultural regions of the world. Its rolling hills reveal and conceal pink-roofed gray stone villas and *case coloniche.* On their slopes verdant rows of vines skirt heights crowned with medieval villages and castles. Lines of dark cypresses stand like sentries overlooking valleys dotted with silvery-leaved olive trees, golden poplars, and broad umbrella pines. In the dusky bosks and scrub that fringe the woodlands, brightly feathered pheasants and shaggy wild boar, *cinghiale,* find refuge in the underbrush.

Chianti's fields and forests have been popular hunting grounds, and some people believe the name Chianti may be derived from this activity, first applied to the area where the hunting took place and later to the wine produced there. It's an idea that holds a certain charm for those of us who enjoy a fine Chianti with roast pheasant or *pappardelle* with game sauce, or one of the bigger styles with braised *cinghiale.*

One theory on the origin of the Chianti name, proposed by E. Repetti, suggests that it comes from the Latin word *clangere* or *clango,* which refers to the sounds of the hunt—birdcalls, cries of alarm, and the blast of hunting horns. *Clango* evolved into Clantum or Clanti, in Italian becoming Chianti.[1]

S. Pieri rejects this theory and offers another. He speculates that Clante was an Etruscan family name and that the land which was under their ownership or rule became known by their name, which later evolved into the modern Chianti.[2]

It seems a logical explanation. Historian Alessandro Boglione states, however, that the name Clante has not been found on any of the Etruscan tombs in the area, some of which are marked with stones bearing inscriptions in the Etruscan language (still basically undeciphered) which are believed to be family names.

The earliest-known written reference to the name Chianti is in a twelfth-century copy of a document dating from A.D. 790 in the possession of the Badia di S. Bartolomeo at Ripoli. This parchment confirms a donation of land to the monastery, including a property in Chianti: *"curte in Clanti cum integro salingo."*[3]

Again in the twelfth century, a document from 1148, preserved at Badia a Coltibuono, records that Ildibrandino and his wife gave to his brother Bullitto property in the territory of Chianti inherited from his mother (*"Omnes terras et res quae dicti iugales habent per matrem in Clanti"*) and granted him all rights on the estates and leased properties (*"De omnibus libellariis, feodis e tenimentis suis qui habent in predicto territorio de Clanti."*)[4]

A few other references from the twelfth and thirteenth centuries to the region of Chianti have been found in various deeds and documents, including what perhaps constitutes official recognition of the name in 1260, in the Libro di Montaperti, a register of official records of the Florentine Republic.[5]

CHIANTI WINE

Written reference to the name Chianti being applied to wine is not found until more than a century later. In the book *Compagnia del Banco,* published in December 1398, Francesco Datini and Bartolomeo Cambioni wrote of Francescho di Marcho and Stoldo di Lorenzo, who were in debt to Piero di Tino Riccio for 3 florins, 26 soldi, and 8 denari, the price of six casks of white Chianti wine.[6] It is rather ironic that this first reference is to white wine because contemporary law does not allow the white wine of the region to carry the Chianti name since the inauguration of DOC in 1967.

According to Paronetto[7], the wine of Chianti was named in the miracle play of San Antonio performed during the latter half of the fifteenth century with the lines:

> *Io n'ho di Chianti e vin di San Losino*
> *Trebbian dolci, vernaccia e malvagia....*
> *I have some Chianti and wine of San Losino*
> *Sweet trebbiano, vernaccia and malvasia....*

Written records of the wine being called Chianti, though they have been found, are rather rare. The wine continued to be more commonly known as Vermiglio, or Vin di Firenze (Florence wine), into the seventeenth century.

In England, the wine of Chianti was known as Florence. A. D. Francis notes that in the 1590s

the wines of Florence were well regarded, but were inclined to go off quickly and needed to be shipped promptly through the Strait of Gibraltar before the late autumn winds from the Atlantic held them up.[8]

Andrè Simon cites an entry in Pepys's diary of January 8, 1661, recording that he was served Florence at Lady Sandwich's house. He was apparently appreciative of it (or else remarked that it would be a wine that Mrs. Pepys could enjoy) as her ladyship, he notes, presented him with two bottles of the same wine for his wife.[9]

Others of Pepys's countrymen were less impressed, but the British were in many cases just looking for a temporary substitute for their beloved Claret while they were involved with another war with France.

INTERESTING PARALLELS

The British could have done worse in their choice; there are a number of similarities between the wines of the two regions. Chianti, like Bordeaux, is made from a blend of grape varieties which some wine drinkers feel adds to the wine's complexity. The best Bordeaux and the best Chianti are medium-bodied wines with a certain elegance, firm acidity, and a tannic backbone. They age gracefully, developing nuances of bouquet and flavor. Bordeaux take longer to soften and open up, and they live longer, but at their respective peaks the wines have a similar style. Both are made in two basic styles, one meant to be drunk young and fresh (though not as young for the Bordeaux as is possible for Chianti) and the other to be aged.

The Chianti made for immediate drinking is light and fresh, simple and straightforward. It is meant to quench thirst and to accompany everyday meals. This style of Chianti is the most common, in both senses of the word, and is not the Chianti that concerns us here.

The second style of Chianti is a wine to sip and to savor, to pour at more important meals, at dinners with friends who appreciate fine wine, and on quiet evenings when one relaxes over a glass, giving full attention to the finished product of the winemaker's art.

The more serious style of Chianti is bottled in the shouldered Bordeaux bottle, designed to be laid down to age. It needs five or more years to mature and soften its youthful harshness. At its best—generally from five to eight years of the vintage—it is a stylish, aristocratic wine. From a good vintage it can age ten to fifteen years. Some notable exceptions to this limit are Monsanto Riserva il Poggio, Castello di Nipozzano, Fattoria Montagliari, Fattoria Selvapiana, Badia a Coltibuono Riserva, Castello di Volpaia Riserva, and Ruffino Riserva Ducale gold label. These and a few others can live for decades, developing subtle nuances of aroma and flavor, mellowing to a velvety texture, and leaving a lingering impression on the palate and on the memory. Generally, the best Chiantis for aging come from the Classico and Rùfina zones.

CHIANTI VINTAGES

Vintages in Chianti vary greatly from one area to another. The region is too vast and the exposures and microclimates too diverse to have consistent weather conditions for the year throughout any one zone, let alone the entire region.

Some clue to the quality of a vintage, however, seems better than no idea at all. So we offer here an overall evaluation of the wines of the last decade and a half, with the note that they are, and can be, only generalizations. Since Chiantis rarely live much beyond five years of the vintage, and for the most part are best within a couple of years of their birth, we are including ratings only back to 1985. These refer to the probable condition of the wines today. The 1986 and 1985 ratings apply to *riserve* only; Chianti *normale* from those years would be too old today. Vintage information for the Chianti Classico and Rùfina zones is covered under those zones.

Our rating of the Chianti vintages:

1990 ***	1987 0
1989 0	1986 *
1988 **	1985 ***

Antonio Rossi's ratings:[10]

1988 ****	1978 ***
1987 ***	1977 **
1986 ***	1976 *
1985 ****	1975 ***
1984 **	1974 **
1983 ***	1973 **
1982 **	1972 **
1981 **	1971 ***
1980 **	1970 ***
1979 ***	

THE CHIANTI *UVAGGIO*

From as early as we know, Chianti has been made from an *uvaggio,* or blend of grapes, both red and white. At different periods and in the hands of different producers, the mix has varied.

The Accademia dei Georgofili, a noted agricultural society, experimented with many combinations early in the nineteenth century, and came up with a recommended blend using equal portions of canaiolo, san gioveto, roverusto, and mammolo to produce a wine of body with a capacity to age, while a wine made from occhio di pernice, trebbiano, canaiolo, and mammolo in equal measure was advised for a more delicate wine for drinking young.

Barone Bettino Ricasoli, in the second half of the nineteenth century, developed his own formula. He got the most satisfactory results with a blend of seven to eight parts sangiovese and three to four parts canaiolo. If the wine was to be consumed young, he included a small amount of malvasia. Barone Ricasoli noted in a letter to Professor Studiati of the University of Pisa that the sangiovese contributed bouquet and vigor, the canaiolo added sweetness to soften the acidity of the sangiovese without diminishing the bouquet, and the malvasia added flavor and freshness and made the wine lighter and more accessible for everyday drinking. He noted, though, that this grape should be kept to a minimum in wines for aging.[11]

As tastes in wine change, the *uvaggio* in Chianti has also changed. In earlier days, a light, easy-drinking style was preferred, a young wine of the year that didn't require cellar aging to become soft and ready (one similar to the simple young Chiantis of today). Many modern wine drinkers prefer a more serious wine, a Chianti with more depth, character, and style, one to be laid away to develop complexity and finesse. This means a wine with more sangiovese and less trebbiano. Some canaiolo may still be added to mellow the sangiovese, but trebbiano (Italy's answer to California's ubiquitous thompson seedless), with a lot of juice and little character, has no place here.

The producers, recognizing the shift in consumer demand, have fought for changes in the wine laws to reflect this change in tastes.

Many Chianti producers have openly admitted to us that they use only sangiovese in their wine. Despite the government regulations they are not diluting their wines with other, lesser varieties, especially whites—a situation that the rule makers in Roma have tacitly acknowledged and which is reflected in the nominal amount of white grapes now required in Chianti under the new regulations.

Under DOC the vines could not be used to produce Chianti Classico before their third year; under DOCG this has been changed, to the vines' fifth year.

Canaiolo

Canaiolo nero, canajolo rosso, or canajuolo rosso, as it has variously been known, has been cultivated in Toscana since at least the thirteenth century. Pier de Crescenzi, writing in his monumental twelve-volume *Ruralium Commodorum Libri Duodecum* on agriculture, published in the thirteenth century, described the canaiolo nero. Paronetto[12] cites Giovan Cosimo Villani of Firenze, who wrote in the eighteenth century that Chianti was made predominantly from canaiolo nero plus small amounts of sangioveto, mammolo, and marzemino.

THE *UVAGGIO* FOR CHIANTI

Grape Variety	DOCG		DOC
	Classico	Non-Classico	All Chianti
Sangiovese	75–90%	75–98%	50–80%
Canaiolo nero	5–10	5–10	10–30
Trebbiano	2–5	5–10	10–20
Malvasia			
Other red grapes	0–10	0–10	0–5

Malvasia del Chianti

Malvasia del Chianti, or Malvasia Toscana, is a white variety native to Chianti. It is fruity and perfumed, though less so than the malvasia of the south which is another variety, and oxidizes easily.

Trebbiano

Trebbiano, or trebbiano toscano, grown in Toscana since at least the thirteenth century, has been included in a number of Chianti blends, but not all. Barone Ricasoli, credited for inventing modern Chianti, recommended using a small proportion of white grapes and then only the malvasia variety. He did not advise using trebbiano at all, a grape he considered lacking in character.

Actually, trebbiano wasn't all that common in the *uvaggio* before the advent of DOC in 1967, when a number of producers and growers lobbied for a greater proportion of white grapes, including the trebbiano, to be required in Chianti. Today, with the emergence of Bianco della Lega, Galestro, and a few other new Tuscon whites to take up the slack, the DOCG commission has reduced the white grapes in Chianti to no more than 5 percent.

Trebbiano toscano is the grape known in France and California as saint emilion, or ugni blanc. (The trebbiano di soave, trebbiano giallo, and trebbiano d'abruzzo grown in other regions of Italy are different varieties.) The trebbiano toscano (with very rare exceptions, and those in the hands of some very talented winemakers) produces neutral wines that must be consumed while they are very young and fresh, before they lose their fruit or oxidize, which they do very easily. What does this grape add to the overall blend? You might say that the trebbiano adds elasticity—that is, it allows the wine to be stretched.

GOVERNO

The use of *governo,* a second fermentation created by the addition of dried grapes or the must of dried or concen-

trated grapes, is traditional in Toscana. It was recommended as early as the mid-fourteenth century, though it probably wasn't in widespread use until much later. In a tract published in 1364, Ruberto di Guido Bernardi advised winemakers to employ a governing process, or *governo,* to better control the quality of their vintages. He wrote that a small quantity of grape bunches from the trebbiano nero (a variety virtually unknown today) should be set aside in the *cantina* to dry, then added to the wine to initiate a second fermentation. His colleague, Francesco di Giovanni di Durante, was in basic agreement with the system but differed on the starter. Durante advocated using sun-dried white grapes that had been crushed and heated before being added to the wine.[13]

Governo was not a new idea, although, like many other "innovations" of the Middle Ages, it may have been reinvented. In the second century B.C., Cato advised winemakers to add a small portion of juice from grapes reduced by boiling to their wine. Pliny wrote in *Natural History* of the practice of adding cooked must to counteract harshness. And Columella, in *De Re Rusticus,* included a recipe for it.

What does *governo* do for the wine? It adds needed body, fruit, and glycerine to thin wines. The carbon dioxide it creates gives the wine a freshness and lightness. And the sweet, concentrated berries bring down the total acidity in the wine. It does tend to increase the volatile acidity, however, and produces a wine that is more susceptible to oxidation.

For the *governo toscano,* or *all' uso* Chianti, 10 to 15 percent of must from grapes gathered before the harvest and partially dried on *cannici* (reed trays) or *castelli* (wicker frames) is added to the wine before December 31. The fermentation thus created continues until late January or February, even into March. A *rigoverno* is yet another induced fermentation that, when used, is done in March or April.

Italy, unlike France, is not allowed to chapitalize its wines. As a consequence, Italian wines are more natural than their counterparts from France. They do, however, at least in some regions, in poor years, add concentrated must (*gov-*

erno): 2.2 pounds (1 kilogram) of concentrate contain 19.4 ounces (550 grams) of sugar. As a rule of thumb, 8.6 pounds (3.9 kilos) of concentrate added to 26.4 gallons (1 hectoliter) of wine increases the amount of alcohol by one degree.

Governo is being used less and less commonly today for one reason or another. One of the reasons given is that wines made with *governo* don't age. We find a lot of evidence to contradict this point of view. Ruffino's especially fine Riserva Ducale gold label is made with *governo,* and it is a wine that can take a lot of age, judging by the 1947, as can others we tasted from the 1950s in recent years. The Montagliari Chiantis from the 1940s and 1950s that we recently tasted, also made with *governo,* have aged very well.

We could point to a number of Chianti Classicos from the very fine 1971 and 1975 vintages made without benefit of *governo* that fell apart after a decade, and quite a number of '82s and '83s that are showing age as well. And there is no question that very few of the '85 or '88 Chianti Riservas will live beyond eight or ten years, *governo* or no.

Fabrizio Bianchi of Monsanto, who produces some long-lived Chianti Classico, used *governo* until 1967. He made the wine in the traditional manner, using the whole un-stemmed bunches, crushed by foot in the first years and by hand with a nail-studded cudgel that broke up only a small portion of the grapes. To soften some of the harshness picked up from the stems, he added some white grapes and used *governo* (and made a lovely wine, by the way). When he eliminated the stems, he also stopped using the *governo* (and the white grapes as well in his Il Poggio Riserva).

The colorino is regarded as a good grape to be used in *governo*. It is also used, as its name suggests, to add color to the wine. Both Cappelli and Ruffino, though, use selected bunches of sangiovese in their *governo*.

One reason those no longer using *governo* generally do not give for abandoning the procedure is the extra cost of the labor involved. We are rather more inclined to believe that this has been more of a factor in most decisions to dispense with the process than the ageability of the wines. Many estates that still use *governo* are now adding grape concentrate rather than the grape bunches gathered and sorted, laid out to dry, then tended, collected, and crushed, and added to the wine vats. The concentrate is much cheaper (particularly when bought from the south—up to 15 percent of wine or must from outside the zone was allowed in Chianti); just open the can, add to the wine, and stir!

CHIANTI TERRITORY

Chianti is produced in the Tuscan provinces of Arezzo, Firenze, Pisa, Pistoia, and Siena. This area encompasses 8,650 registered grape-growing farms with 1.2 million acres (466,000 hectares), nearly 150,000 (60,000) of which are in vines. Of these, 4,700 growers are authorized to grow Chianti on just under 58,000 acres (23,400 hectares).[14] The Chianti-growing region is one of large wine estates, as in Bordeaux, instead of small vineyards divided among multiple owners, as in the Langhe and Burgundy. Many of the vineyards in Chianti are planted in *coltura esclusiva,* in specialized vineyards, but there are also still many in *coltura promiscua,* in rows interspersed with olive trees and other crops.

Under *mezzadria,* the feudal system, which lasted until 1967 here when it was prohibited by law, grapes were only one of the variety of crops a tenant farmer needed to provide for the family. When *mezzadria* dried out, many vineyards were replanted exclusively in vines. But many were not replanted, sometimes because of the olive trees, which were too valuable to pull out. (The olive tree, which lives for centuries, takes many years to bear fruit.) With the catastrophic freeze in the winter of 1984–85, which destroyed most of the olive trees in Toscana, the countryside took on a bleaker aspect that will remain for years to come. The loss is more than of the esthetic pleasure of the balanced beauty of the landscape; it is gustatorial as well, with only the rare drop of Toscana's liquid gold to be found until the extensively replanted *oliveti* once again resume production. (Some of the replanted trees have improved the bleakness of the landscape, and some trees, thought to have died, survived.)

More than 23 million gallons (0.9 million hectoliters) of Chianti are produced a year, much of it young Chianti—light, simple, fresh, straightforward wine meant to be drunk within the year. This was the Chianti sold in the rustic straw-covered *fiaschi*. Some of it still is, though considerably less than previously, as the cost of the labor to wrap the flasks in straw is frequently greater than the value of the wine inside. The basket woven around the bottles, originally made to protect the fragile blown-glass containers as they were jostled about in shipment by oxcart, and perhaps also to hold the bulbous flasks upright when set on the table, were later maintained, at least in part, for their picturesque charm. They also made the two styles more obvious to distinguish on the merchant's shelf, as the *fiasco* was obviously not suitable for laying a wine down to age.

CHIANTI AND THE LAW

Some authorities predicted that the production of Chianti under the stricter DOCG regulations would drop to only 5.3 to 8 million gallons (200,000 to 300,000 hectoliters) from the then current 40 million gallons (1.5 million hectoliters). While it has dropped, it was by a considerably smaller amount. Between 1986 and 1988 the annual production of Chianti, in all its forms, averaged 23.69 million gallons (896,634 hectoliters). And we suspect that some of that

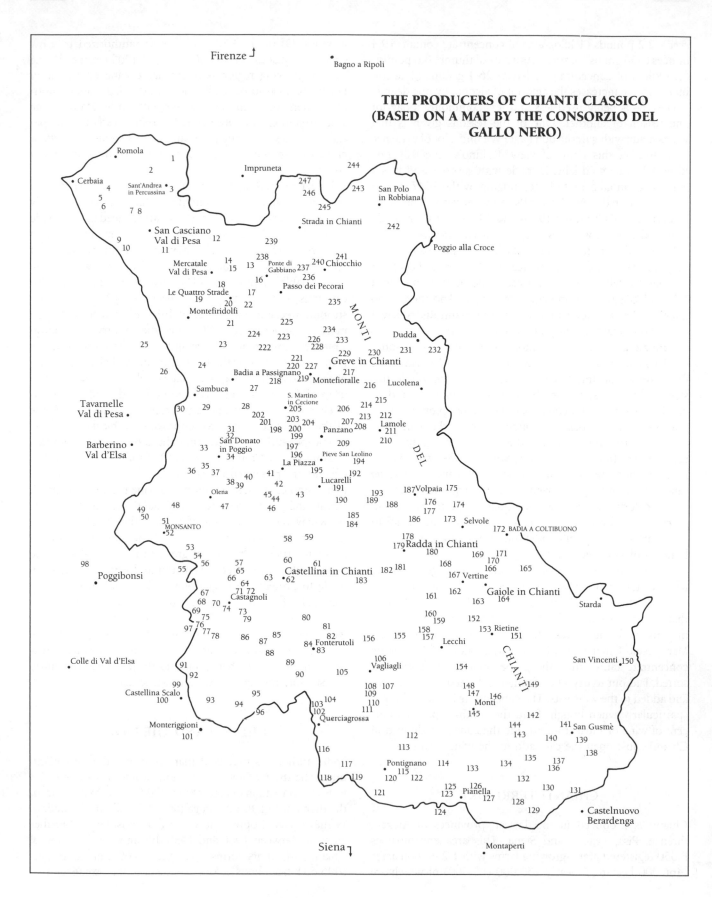

THE PRODUCERS OF CHIANTI CLASSICO
(BASED ON A MAP BY THE CONSORZIO DEL
GALLO NERO)

drop can be attributed to causes other than DOCG. As far as Chianti Classico is concerned, the advent of DOCG has made very little impact on the district's vinicultural output. While the average for the first six years of the DOCG (1984 through 1989) was lower, 78.28 percent of the annual average for the six years preceding the DOCG (1978 through 1983), part of this drop can be attributed to the bad climatic conditions which reduced the crop in 1984 and the spring frost which reduced the output in 1985.

Besides the reduction in allowable yields, there are minimum vine age requirements for the wines in three zones: Classico, Colli Fiorentini, and Rùfina. The grapes used for DOCG Chianti from those three zones must be from vines no less than five years old.

There was speculation that the new regulation requiring that wines be submitted for blind tasting to determine whether or not they are typical in character would further reduce the amount of wine sold as Chianti. It doesn't appear to have made a significant difference.

Under DOC there were no limits on the yield. The law allowed only a certain amount to be used for Chianti. Under DOCG, this has been changed. Now, if the yield exceeds the maximum by 20 percent, the entire crop is declassified. And while the maximum yield can be lowered, unlike in France, it cannot be raised. And with the advent of DOCG, Chianti must be sold in bottles of less than 1.3 gallons (5 liters).

THE CHIANTI VINEYARDS

The soil in Chianti is made up of schistous clay with admixtures of flint, limestone, pebbles, and sand. In the best vineyards there is much *galestro,* a friable rock that breaks easily, cracking from changes in temperature, and crumbling into fragments. The maritime origin of the terrain, formed in the Tertiary period, is evidenced by the fossilized shells of marine creatures that have been found in some of the vineyards.

The Chianti vineyards cannot be situated at altitudes exceeding 1,805 feet (550 meters) above sea level except in certain exceptional cases, where they are allowed up to 2,133 feet (650 meters). The majority are planted between 820 and 1,641 feet (250 and 500 meters).

There are seven delimited Chianti zones: Classico, Colli Aretini, Colli Fiorentini, Colline Pisane, Colli Senesi, Montalbano, and Rùfina. The most famous is, of course, the Classico zone; it is also the largest.

CHIANTI CLASSICO

The Chianti Classico district covers 173,000 acres (70,000 hectares) in the area south of Firenze and north of Siena, most of it wooded. There are 16,878 acres (6,830 hectares) planted in vines for Chianti Classico. Firenze has 7,076 acres (2,864 hectares) and Siena 9,802 (3,967) authorized for the production of Chianti Classico. This is nearly 30 percent of the 57,865 acres (23,417 hectares) registered for Chianti.[15]

This district includes the entire communal territories of Castellina in Chianti, Gaiole in Chianti, Greve in Chianti, and Radda in Chianti, and parts of Barberino Val d'Elsa, Castelnuovo Berardenga, San Casciano Val di Pesa, Tavarnelle Val di Pesa, and Poggibonsi. Of the 4,699 registered growers for Chianti, 965 are in the Classico zone, 533 in Firenze, and 432 in Siena. There are five co-ops and 295 producers who bottle a Chianti Classico. Average annual production of Chianti is 10 million cases, of which nearly 30 percent, or 2.9 million cases, are Classico. Of these more than two-thirds, or 2.1 million cases, come from Siena and 0.9 million from Firenze.[16]

The Classico zone is the original or classic—not necessarily the best—vineyard area in the region. The towns of Radda in Chianti, Gaiole in Chianti, and Castellina in Chianti form the historic center of Chianti Classico. During the turbulent thirteenth century, when constant battles were being waged between Siena and Firenze over control of this territory, these three localities formed a league, the Lega del Chianti, for mutual defense and the administration of lands held in common. The league chose for its standard the sym-

CHIANTI AVERAGE ANNUAL PRODUCTION

	Period	Gallons	Hectoliters	Cases
DOC	1978–83	9,795,796	370,772	4,119,277
DOCG	1984–89	7,668,009	290,235	3,224,511
Average	1980–89	8,442,353	319,544	3,550,134
Average	1970–79	7,245,077	274,227	3,046,662
Average	1967–89	7,275,249	275,369	3,059,350

DOC/DOCG REQUIREMENTS FOR CHIANTI

	DOC		*DOCG*		
	Chianti	Classico	Chianti	Rùfina and Colli Fiorentini	Classico
AGING REQUIREMENTS[a]					
Normale	Cannot be sold prior to March 1 after the harvest		Same as DOC	Cannot be sold prior to June 1 after the harvest	
Vecchio	2 years from Jan. 1			No longer exists under DOCG	
Riserva	3 years from Jan. 1		3 years	3 years	3 years
MINIMUM ALCOHOL					
Normale	11.5%	12.0%	11.5%	11.5%	12.0%
Vecchio	12.0%	12.5%		No longer exists under DOCG	
Riserva	12.0%	12.5%	12.0%[b]	12.5%	12.5%
MAXIMUM YIELD (GALLONS/ACRE)					
	935	861	748[c]	599[d]	561[e]
ADDITION OF CONCENTRATE, MUST, OR GRAPES ALLOWED					
	15%	15%	15%	15%[f]	15%[f]

NOTES: [a] The law does not stipulate the type of receptacle to be used; it can be wooden casks or barrels, stainless steel or cement vats, bottles, or any combination thereof.
[b] If the label bears a geographical designation, the minimum alcohol is 12.5 percent.
[c] 11 pounds (5 kilograms) of grapes per vine up to a maximum of 4.5 tons per acre (100 quintali per hectare). This is equivalent to 70 hectoliters per hectare.
[d] 6.6 pounds (3 kilograms) per vine up to 3.6 tons per acre (80 quintali per hectare). This is equivalent to 56 hectoliters per hectare.
[e] 6.6 pounds (3 kilograms) per vine up to 3.3 tons per acre (75 quintali per hectare). This is equivalent to 52.5 hectoliters per hectare.
[f] Only concentrated must from the production zone in question or purified concentrated must can be added.

bol of a black rooster on a yellow ground, the crest of the *podestà* in charge of the Lega, whose headquarters were in Radda.

In 1932 a ministerial decree defined the modern borders of the Chianti region and the central, Classico, zone. These borders were quite similar to those set down by the Grand Duke of Tuscana in his *bando* of 1716, *Sopra la Dichiarazione de' Confini delle quattro Regioni Chianti, Pomino, Carmignano, e Vald' Arno di Sopra.*

Per il Chianti è restato Determinato sia.
Dalla Spedaluzzo, fino a Greve; di li a Panzano, con tutta la Potesteria di Radda, che contiene tre Terzi, cioè Radda, Gajole, e Castellina, arrivando fino al Confine dello Stato di Siena, &c.

The region of Chianti took in Greve, Panzano, and the three parts of the *podesteria* of Radda—Radda itself, Gaiole, and Castellina in Chianti. Today these areas plus San Casciano Val di Pesa, Barberino Val d'Elsa, Tavarnelle Val di Pesa, Castelnuovo Berardenga, and a small part of Poggibonsi make up the Chianti Classico production zone.

Il Gallo Nero.

There is a rather picturesque legend surrounding the black rooster. According to the story, Firenze and Siena, at one point in their constant dispute over borders, agreed to accept a north-south dividing line established through a rather unusual procedure. They made a pact wherein it was agreed that the point where two horsemen met, one representing each city, would determine the extent of their respective domains. The riders were to set out on a specified day at cock's crow.

The proud Sienese selected a fine strutting cock to do the honors for their city, and they fed their champion well. The

CHIANTI PRODUCTION BY ZONE AND PROVINCE

	Number of Registered Growers	Acres	Hectares	Production in Hectoliters*				Average in Cases
				1988	1987	1986	Average	
CHIANTI								
Arezzo	553	5,258	2,128	73,165	83,880	62,615	73,220	813,474
Firenze	1,373	15,756	6,376	216,354	247,945	242,156	235,485	2,616,238
Pisa	72	1,410	571	15,928	15,534	10,679	14,047	156,062
Pistoia	15	295	119	1,235	1,766	1,328	1,443	16,032
Siena	246	2,403	972	60,534	79,955	76,998	72,496	805,427
Total	2,259	25,122	10,166	367,216	429,080	393,776	396,691	4,407,233
CLASSICO								
Firenze	533	7,076	2,864	74,980	84,752	86,234	81,989	910,894
Siena	432	9,802	3,967	188,279	190,296	182,306	186,960	2,077,129
Total	965	16,878	6,831	263,259	275,048	268,540	268,949	2,988,023
MONTALBANO								
Firenze	17	337	136	4,883	7,116	4,222	5,407	60,072
Pistoia	159	737	298	8,745	12,112	9,353	10,070	111,878
Total	176	1,074	434	13,628	19,228	13,575	15,477	171,950
Colli Aretini	72	1,646	666	32,817	34,585	24,171	30,524	339,125
Colli Fiorentini	170	2,422	980	16,180	23,132	28,412	22,575	250,805
Colline Pisane	60	597	242	8,019	6,290	7,185	7,165	79,599
Colli Senesi	947	8,775	3,551	127,027	142,663	140,913	136,868	1,520,600
Rùfina	50	1,352	547	18,958	17,634	18,567	18,386	204,272
Total	4,699	57,866	23,417	847,104	947,660	895,139	896,635	9,961,607

* 1 hectoliter = 26.42 gallons

Source: Data supplied by *il Corriere Vinicolo*

frugal Florentines secured a scrawny bird and gave him just enough to keep the creature alive and kicking. At daybreak on the appointed day, the overstuffed Sienese chanticleer dozed contentedly, while the hungry Florentine cock awoke early, crowing for chow. Needless to relate, when the riders met, it was almost at the battlements of Siena, at Fonterutoli, where the limits of the zone still are today.

Consorzio Vino Chianti Classico

In 1924, 33 Chianti producers in the Chianti Classico area formed a voluntary growers' organization, the Consorzio Vino Chianti Classico, to defend and promote the Chianti name. Today, of the 970 growers in the Classico district, 642 belong to the *consorzio*. Of these, 281 bottle their own wine. Three of the four largest houses—Ruffino, Brolio, and Antinori—do not belong to the *consorzio*. The *consorzio* members account for some 87.5 percent of the production. According to the *consorzio,* on average, just under 2 million cases of Chianti Classico are bottled annually. The members sell just over half, 51.1 percent, of their wine in Italy; the balance is exported. West Germany takes 30.7 percent, Switzerland 23, the United Kingdom 15.7, and the United States 15 percent.

A few years ago the Consorzio Vino Chianti Classico changed its name to Consorzio del Gallo Nero.

The *consorzio* chose as their emblem the *gallo nero,* the black rooster on a gold background, symbol of the

CHIANTI CLASSICO ACREAGE BY PROVINCE

Province	Number of Registered Growers	Coltura esclusiva		Coltura promiscua	
		Acres	Hectares	Acres	Hectares
Firenze	491	6,081	2,461	796	322
Siena	402	9,195	3,721	356	144
Total	893	15,276	6,182	1,152	466

Source: Consorzio del Gallo Nero, 12/31/87

CHIANTI CLASSICO PRODUCTION OF *CONSORZIO* MEMBERS AND TOTAL

Year	Consorzio Members		Total Production		Members' Percent of Total
	Hectoliters	Cases	Hectoliters	Cases	
1967	95,673	1,062,927	115,677	1,285,171	82.71
1968	109,122	1,212,345	132,122	1,467,875	82.59
1969	132,610	1,473,297	147,968	1,643,924	89.62
1970	174,186	1,935,206	205,074	2,278,372	84.94
1971	155,134	1,723,539	169,619	1,884,467	91.46
1972	169,714	1,885,523	178,157	1,979,324	95.26
1973	264,412	2,937,617	281,980	3,132,798	93.77
1974	281,365	3,125,965	323,029	3,588,852	87.10
1975	226,540	2,516,859	258,027	2,866,680	87.80
1976	223,186	2,479,596	253,216	2,813,230	88.14
1977	266,565	2,961,537	302,565	3,361,497	88.10
1978	280,980	3,121,688	311,765	3,463,709	90.13
1979	402,556	4,472,397	458,838	5,097,690	87.73
1980	299,924	3,332,156	348,133	3,867,758	86.15
1981	296,712	3,296,470	339,745	3,774,567	87.33
1982	342,783	3,808,319	387,684	4,307,169	88.42
1983	324,339	3,603,406	378,469	4,204,791	85.70
1984	214,605	2,384,262	248,015	2,755,447	86.53
1985	227,645	2,529,136	268,612	2,984,279	84.75
1986	258,811	2,875,390	297,715	3,307,614	86.93
1987	279,658	3,107,000	323,378	3,592,730	86.48
1988	255,678	2,840,583	301,499	3,349,654	84.80
1989	253,495	2,816,329	302,190	3,357,331	83.89
Average	240,682	2,673,980	275,369	3,059,345	87.40

Source: Consorzio del Gallo Nero

thirteenth-century Chianti League. They point out that the Chianti League also set standards, as they do now, to protect the wines of the area. The *consorzio* issues a neck label with their *bollino*, or seal, to members' wines that qualify. The border of the *bollino* indicates the category of the wine: a red rim for Chianti Classico *normale*, silver for *vecchio*, and gold for *riserva*.

The Lega del Chianti was the first to set down regulations on winemaking in the territory, along with all the other civil and criminal statutes for the region under the sway of the *podestà*. Their legislation included a decree setting the date when the harvest could begin. A statute from 1444 forbids the harvesting of the grapes before San Michele's Day, September 29, because "the League is damaged by early gathering since the wines cannot be good and cannot be sold."[17]

This power over the picking was one of the methods the Lega's modern-day counterpart chose to enforce their standards for the Classicos of their members, deciding when the harvest could begin for *consorzio* members. Judging by the fiasco of 1973, one wonders what auguries they used to determine when to set the date. It was surely not the ripeness of the grapes.

Fabrizio Bianchi of Fattoria Monsanto told us that as his grapes reached full ripeness in the fall of 1973 and he was looking forward to what appeared to be his best vintage yet, he kept waiting for the *consorzio* to give the approval to harvest, but they remained silent. Finally he called. Wait, they said. He waited. The grapes were perfect, ripe and ready. He called again. Wait, they said. He waited. Finally it started to rain and rain and rain. The vineyards were drenched, the grapes were diluted, and they began to rot. What should have been a vintage to crow over became one to cry over. Bianchi managed to make a good wine only by severe selection, producing about one-fifth of his normal harvest for Il Poggio. Although Fabrizio laughs now at the *consorzio*'s mulishness, he admits he sent them a strong letter at the time.

One has to give the *consorzio* credit for one thing at least—for learning a lesson, albeit at someone else's expense. The following year they decided that perhaps the growers could judge for themselves when their grapes were ripe. Now the decision on when to pick is left up to *consorzio* members.

While we readily admit that the standards maintained by the Consorzio del Gallo Nero are higher than those set down in the DOCG regulations and that they are trying to bring up the minimum level of quality for Chianti Classico, we must point out that they seem to have a ceiling on quality as well. They have told us that certain wines—very fine wines—are rejected at their committee tastings because they are atypical—that is, not modest enough. They have told at least one producer whom we spoke with that his wine was too big, too full-bodied and flavorful, too rich. They suggested that he tone it down, blending in some thin, neutral wine to produce a more representative Chianti Classico. This producer refused to lower his own standards, so they refused to grant him the *bollino* for his wine.

A few years ago many of the better producers felt, and rightly so, that the *consorzio* was a hindrance to quality. They didn't need it, and they left the organization. Capannelle, Monte Vertine, Castello, dei Rampolla and Monsanto are among the better producers that pulled out. Today this attitude has, to some extent, changed. It seems that the *consorzio* finally realized that something was amiss and it appears they have done something about it. On average, the wines of the Chianti Classico district are better today than they were half a decade ago. We don't know whether or not

the *consorzio* can take any credit, but at least they haven't done anything to get in the way.

Key to Quality

The consumer needs some sort of guideline to assist him or her in making the best selections among the different vintages, styles, and levels of Chianti Classico produced. But neither the initials of a government agency nor the seal of a growers' association can guarantee quality. The safest gauge here, besides a good basic knowledge of the wines, is the name of the estate or producer that stands behind the wine.

Naturally, the more knowledge and experience a wine drinker has, the better off he or she is. The grape variety, the region, the vintage—all have an effect on the wine. Whether or not you'll like it in the end depends on your personal taste and preferences, but having an idea of the type of wine you can expect when you pull the cork and pour is a very helpful base to start from.

The Character of the Comuni

In Chianti Classico, the basic style of the wines from the northern part of the region differs from that produced in the southern districts. Going from Firenze toward Siena, the wines become fuller in flavor, firmer in texture, and higher in alcohol and tannin. As a general rule, the Chianti Classicos from the province of Firenze are lighter and more delicate than those of Siena; they have less body and more perfume. Exceptions can be found, but they reflect more the proportions of red and white grapes, yields, and winemaking techniques than geography and climatic differences. All else being equal, one general principle applies: the bigger Chianti Classicos are produced in the southern part of the district, the lighter ones in the northern part.

San Casciano Val di Pesa (*Firenze*). San Casciano, in the Northwestern corner of the Classico zone, takes in the villages of Cerbaia, Mercatale Val di Pesa, Montefiridolfi, and Romola. It covers a series of hills dividing the Val di Pesa from the Val di Greve. The San Casciano district encompasses 41.7 square miles (107.95 square kilometers).

The Chianti wines of San Casciano tend to be light in body and soft. Most of them are best when young, within two to three years of the vintage. The best of them, such as the Palazzo al Bosco, age fairly well. Some critics mention their rich bouquet but thus far that attraction has escaped us. Antinori's Santa Cristina farm is in this district. Some other well-known producers here include Castello di Gabbiano and Conti Serristori.

A harvest festival takes place at Mercatale Val di Pesa during the last week of September.

Greve in Chianti (*Firenze*). Greve, in the northeastern part of the zone, encompasses Dudda, Lucarelli, Lucolena, Montefioralle, Panzano, Passo dei Pecorai, and Strada in Chianti. This zone, on

CHIANTI CLASSICO 1989 PRODUCTION BY *COMUNE*

Comune	Gallons	Hectoliters	Cases
Barberino Val d'Elsa	228,744	8,658	96,190
Greve in Chianti	1,456,561	55,131	612,505
San Casciano Val di Pesa	1,166,466	44,152	490,529
Tavarnelle Val di Pesa	153,077	5,794	64,371
Total for province of Firenze	3,004,848	113,735	1,263,595
Castellina in Chianti	1,342,532	50,815	564,555
Castelnuovo Berardenga	1,298,015	49,130	545,834
Gaiole in Chianti	1,511,752	57,220	635,714
Monteriggioni	65,759	2,489	27,653
Poggibonsi	269,088	10,185	113,155
Radda in Chianti	491,835	18,616	206,824
Total for province of Siena	4,978,981	188,455	2,093,735
TOTAL for both provinces	7,983,829	302,190	3,357,330

Source: *Consorzio del Gallo Nero*

the hills between the Ema and Pesa valleys and the Chianti Mountains, encompasses 65 square miles (169 square kilometers).

The wines of Greve are, by reputation, the most characteristic as well as the most harmonious of the Classicos. They are said to have an aroma of irises. They are not supposed to be long-lived wines, but the Fattoria Montagliari Classico Riservas of Giovanni Cappelli contradict that notion. Other fine estates in this area include Castello dei Rampolla, Castello di Querceto, Fattoria di Fontodi, Le Masse di San Leolino, Savignola Paolina, Vecchie Terre di Montefili, and Villa Cafaggio. The well-known estates of Castello Vicchiomaggio, Castello di Uzzano, Castello di Verrazzano, Tenuta di Nozzole, and Vignamaggio are also in the Greve district.

During the second week of September in Greve there is an exposition of Chianti Classico wines. The *trattoria* at Giovanni Cappelli's Fattoria Montagliari estate in Panzano is an excellent place to eat.

Radda in Chianti (*Siena*). Radda, in the eastern-central part of the Classico zone, is on the hills of the upper Pesa Valley. It includes the towns of Selvole, Villa, and Volpaia. The town of Radda has been known since 1002 when its castle was owned by the Abbey at Firenze. In 1384 it became the capital of the Chianti League. The Radda district takes in 32 square miles (80.6 square kilometers).

The Chiantis of this zone are considered to be well-balanced wines, somewhat similar to those of Greve but fuller in body. They reputedly are also long-lived, a quality we cannot confirm. Castello di Volpaia and Monte Vertine are two *aziende* in this area that produce very good wines. Fattoria Terrabianca is another good estate here. Pian d'Albola, Vignale, and Vignavecchia are among the other well-known estates in Radda.

Gaiole in Chianti (*Siena*). Gaiole is located in the southeastern part of the Classico zone among the hills of the upper Val d'Arbia.

The villages of Lecchi, Monti, Starda, and Vertine are in this district. Gaiole is first mentioned in 1086. The village originated in the Middle Ages as a market for Castello Vertine. Gaiole and its associated villages encompass 50 square miles (129 square kilometers). There is a lot of lime in the soil of Gaiole.

The wines of the Gaiole district are regarded for their richness of flavor and full body. They are fairly tannic, well-structured wines with the capacity to age well. Badia a Coltibuono is a good example. The very fine Capannelle *azienda* is in this *comune*, as are Castello di Ama, Castello Brolio, Castello di Cacchiano, Castello di San Polo in Rosso, Giorgio Regni's Fattoria Valtellina estate, Fattoria San Giusto a Rentennano, Podere Il Palazzino, Riecine, and Rocca di Castagnoli.

Castelnuovo Berardenga (*Siena*). Castelnuovo, in the southernmost part of the Classico zone, is in the upper Ombrone Valley. This district stretches from Pagliaia northwest toward Valiagli and Querciagrossa. It encompasses the villages of San Gusmè, Pianella, Querciagrossa, and Vagliagli. The Frankish nobleman Berardo, in the second half of the tenth century, founded a local dynasty and gave his name to this district. Siena's general council decided to build a castle in 1366. Today the Castelnuovo district covers 68 square miles (177 square kilometers). The soil here is mostly limestone or schistous-clay marl.

Castelnuovo is noted for its full-bodied wines with a pronounced bouquet; they sometimes are a bit low in acid but age quite well. Fine examples of this style of Chianti are produced at Castell'in Villa, Fattoria di Felsina "Berardenga," and Fattoria dei Pagliarese. Some other well-known estates here include Catignano, San Felice, and Villa d'Arceno.

Castellina in Chianti (*Siena*). Castellina, located in the western south-central part of the Classico zone, in the hills overlooking the Elsa, Arbia, and Pesa valleys, takes in the villages of Fonterutoli and Castagnoli. This district covers 38.4 square miles (99.5 square kilometers).

Castellina has been occupied since Etruscan times, but was not mentioned until the twelfth century, when it was controlled by the Guidi counts. Castellina is noted for its local artisans who work with terra-cotta, wood, and wrought iron.

These Classicos are prized for their perfume. It is also claimed that they have the capacity to age. Our experience suggests otherwise. The Castellina Chiantis tend to be fairly full wines, somewhat similar to the wine of the neighboring *comune* of Radda. Regarded estates from Castellina include Castellare, Castello Banfi, Fattoria San Leonino, Melini's Granaio estate, Tenuta di Lilliano, Rocca delle Macìe, Villa Cerna, and Tenuta Villa Rosa. Not one of our top-rated (three stars or higher) Classicos is produced in this area, but that could just be a coincidence.

Barberino Val d'Elsa (*Firenze*). Barberino, in the west-central part of the Classico zone, is on the hills between Pesa and Elsa. It also includes Poggibonsi, located between the hills and plain of the Elsa Valley. This district covers nearly 25.4 square miles (66 square kilometers). Barberino was founded in the thirteenth century as a local judicial center.

This zone boasts two of the top Classico estates—Fattoria Monsanto and Isole e Olena—as well as the very good Villa Francesca and Il Campino di Mondiglia estates. It is a bit difficult to generalize about this area. The wines of Monsanto are among the fullest in body of all the Classicos, yet those produced close by on the estates of Quercia al Poggio and Casa Sola tend to be rather light.

A good place to enjoy local food and good Chianti wine is at the *ristorante* at Villa Francesca in the locality of Cortine in San Donato in Poggio.

Tavarnelle Val di Pesa (*Firenze*). Tavarnelle, north of Barberino, is in the western-central part of the Classico district on the upland hills dividing the Pesa from the Elsa Valley. Badia a Passiagnano, Sambuca, and San Donato in Poggio are in this area. The name is said to derive from *tabernulae* because of the ancient taverns along Via Cassia. Tavarnelle encompasses 22 square miles (57 square kilometers).

Again we find it difficult to generalize about the character of the wines. The best estate here is Poggio al Sole, producing wines that age moderately well. Their wines are high in acid and somewhat austere in nature. Selvoramole is another good estate in San Donato in Poggio, and La Ripa is another well-known property.

A Troublesome Trend

Wine-growing regions can consist of a number of small vineyards, often subdivided among many owners as in Piemonte, or they can be areas of many large estates with a single owner, as in Toscana. That's not to say that there isn't anything in between. There is. But that's not what concerns us at the moment. In the first case, as in Barolo and Barbaresco, or Burgundy, it's reasonable that when the producer harvests, or buys, grapes from multiple vineyards, he keeps them separate when he bottles them. Why? Because each vineyard reveals a different expression of the grape variety. In the second case as in Chianti or Bordeaux, it's

important to produce a unified product that is the expression of the total estate. The differences between the subplots are less evident and the wine should be an expression of that estate.

Can you imagine what would happen to the general quality of Château Latour or Château Lafite if they decided that because one of their plots produced the best fruit on the estate they would bottle it separately? By removing the best part of their estate the whole would suffer. Although it could be true that the single-vineyard bottling would be a superior wine, it would be just as true that the regular bottling, from the rest of the estate, would be a lesser product.

And that is what is happening in the Chianti district. To begin with, most estates produce a *normale* and a *riserva*. Their best fruit is, or should be, reserved for the latter. Now, with the trend to *barrique*-aged wines and single-vineyard Chiantis, the producers are robbing their estate wine of its best fruit, thereby lowering the general quality of what they would have otherwise.

We believe that although the general quality of Chianti Classico has improved in the past few years because of better winemaking, the quality from the estates practicing cru bottling has suffered as a result. Now besides a *normale*, a *riserva*, and a *barrique*-aged wine, some estates produce two, three, and sometimes more separate cru bottlings. What are they leaving for the Chianti Classico *normale* and *riserva*? In some cases the special bottling is actually a selection of the best fruit instead of the product of a single vineyard.

Does this mean that we are against all cru bottlings in Chianti? The answer is no. There are exceptions, the Monsanto Il Poggio being the most notable example. There is no question that the Il Poggio vineyard is special. Consider the high average quality produced there year in and year out. And, no, we wouldn't want to be deprived of that special wine because Fabrizio Bianchi decided to blend it into his regular Monsanto. Actually, when Bianchi began producing Il Poggio in 1962 as a separate wine, it was made as his *riserva*.

And while we commend the exceptions, we find the trend troublesome. Are we headed toward a day when an estate capable of producing 10,000 cases of Chianti Classico will offer ten different Chiantis? Consider that Fattoria Dievole and Castello di Ama produce three cru bottlings each, and Castello Vicchiomaggio does four special Chianti Classicos. Melini, San Felice, and Serristori are other estates that do two or more crus or special bottlings in addition to their standard Chianti Classicos.

Chianti Classico, In Search of an Identity

What is Chianti Classico? Ask a hundred producers, and given the state of affairs in the Chianti Classico district to-

SOME EXAMPLES OF SPECIAL BOTTLINGS

Estate	Special Bottling
Castello Banfi	Il Caggió
Castello di Ama	Vigneto Bellavista
Castello di Ama	Vigneto La Casuccia
Castello di Ama	Vigneto S. Lorenzo
Castello di Cacchiano	Riserva Millennio
Castello di Fonterutoli	Riserva Ser Lapo
Castello Vicchiomaggio	Riserva Paola Matta
Castello Vicchiomaggio	Riserva Prima Vigna
Castello Vicchiomaggio	Riserva Petri
Castello Vicchiomaggio	San Jacopo
Fattoria dei Pagliarese	Riserva Boscardini
Fattoria di Felsina	Vigneto Rancia
Fattoria di Selvole	Riserva Lanfredini
Fattoria di Vistarenni	Podere Bertinga
Fattoria Dievole	Campi Nuovi
Fattoria Dievole	Petrignano
Fattoria Dievole	Sessina Superiore
Fattoria Dievole	Villa Dievole Cuvee
Fattoria Le Filigare	Del Conte
Fattoria San Fabiano Calcinaia	Cellole
Fontodi	Vigna del Sorbo
Melini	Isassi
Melini	Laborel
Melini	Terrarossa
Melini	Vigneti Granaio
Melini	Vigneti La Selvanella
Podere Petroio alla Via della Malpensata	Montetondo
Rocca delle Macìe	Fizzano
Rocca di Castagnoli	Poggio a'Frati
San Felice	Il Grigio
San Felice	Poggio Rosso
Serristori	Machiavelli
Serristori	Machiavelli, Vigna di Fontalle
Serristori	Ser Niccolo
Serristori	Villa Primavera
Tenuta di Nozzole	La Forra
Terrabianca	Scassino
Terrabianca	Vigna della Croce
Vignamaggio	Castello di Monna Lisa

barrique-aged wines and, with more and more frequency, at least one single-vineyard Chianti Classico. They also produce one or more white wines, perhaps a rosé, and a *vin santo,* a *spumante,* and who knows what else. Kind of like a copy of California or Australia, rather than a wine-growing district with a long history and tradition.

Some producers will tell you that their flagship wine is their Chianti Classico *riserva,* yet their *barrique*-aged *vino da tavola* is more expensive. Why would their flagship wine be less expensive? What is happening is that this potentially fine wine-producing district has lost, or is rapidly losing, its identity and thus far has no new identity to offer the world.

Take a Chianti Classico like the one from Castello dei Rampolla which is a blend of sangiovese and cabernet sauvignon. As a *vino da tavola,* we'd have nothing but praise. But as a Chianti Classico we have a problem. The defining grape variety in Chianti Classico is, or should be, sangiovese. In the Rampolla the cabernet sauvignon is dominant. And Rampolla is not the only wine made this way.

Traditionally, Chianti Classico was aged in large Salvonian oak casks. Today more and more producers are using *barrique.* This is not to say that *barrique* is inherently bad. It's not. But it is being overdone, with the result that the regional, or communal, character, as well as the varietal character of the sangiovese, is being submerged beneath the oak. Perhaps a judicious use of oak could improve a wine. But this is rarely the case in the Chianti zone today. To satisfy an international market that is enamored with the taste of wood, the oak is being overdone to the detriment of the wine's personality.

One of the reasons for this situation is that too many owners have relinquished the responsibility for their wines to enologists who want the wines to be recognizable as being made by them. To that enologist, his personality is more important than the character of the estate. The owners should take charge and decide what they want and not let the ego of a consulting enologist get in the way.

We believe that the producers would do well to first improve their Chianti Classico, both the *normale* and the *riserva* before looking to copy the New World by growing every imagined noble variety, red or white. The world is awash in cabernet sauvignon and chardonnay, merlot and sauvignon blanc, and wines-aged-in-*barrique.* What the world needs is more fine wines, wines that proudly display their own varietal and regional characters.

The Chianti Classico district is potentially a great wine-producing region. The producers should work to see that the wines come up to the potential of the region. After all, any wine region can produce cabernet sauvignon, but only one wine district can produce Chianti Classico. The producers in that district should first produce the best Chianti Classico that they can.

day, you might get three, four, or five hundred different answers. Most estates produces two Chianti Classicos, a *normale* and a *riserva.* They also make one or more new-wave,

The Quality of Chianti Classico

As for the quality of Chianti Classico, it is without question variable. But of late, in spite of the identity crisis here, there has been a remarkable improvement in the average quality. And while the best can attain great heights, unfortunately there aren't enough best ones.

Rating the Chianti Classico Producers

****

+ Fattoria Monsanto, Riserva il Poggio

***

+ Badia a Coltibuono, Riserva
  Capannelle di Raffaele Rossetti[a]
+ Castello di Volpaia
  Fattoria di Montagliari (e Castellinuzza), Riserva
+ Fattoria di Montagliari, Riserva Vigna Casaloste
  Fattoria Monsanto
  Fortilizio il Colombaio, Riserva[b]
  Isole e Olena
− Poggio al Sole
  Riecine, Riserva
− Rocca di Castagnoli, Riserva Poggio a 'Fratti
  Ruffino, Riserva Ducale gold label
  Savignola Paolina
− Vecchie Terre di Montefili, Riserva Anfiteatro
  Villa Cafaggio
  Villa Colombaio[b]

**

  Baccio da Gaiuole, Azienda Agricola di Gittori (1977)[c]
+ Badia a Coltibuono, normale
  Berardenga, Fattoria di Felsina normale
+ Berardenga, Fattoria di Felsina Riserva
+ Berardenga, Fattoria di Felsina Riserva Vigneto Rancia
  Brolio, Riserva del Barone
+ Castell'in Villa
− Castellare, normale
+ Castellare, Riserva
  Castello Banfi
+ Castello dei Rampolla
− Castello di Ama
  Castello di Ama, Vigneto Bellavista
− Castello di Ama, Vigneto Bertinga
+ Castello di Ama, Vigneto La Casuccia
+ Castello di Ama, Vigneto S. Lorenzo
  Castello di Cacchiano
+ Castello di Cacchiano, Riserva Millennio
  Castello di Querceto
  Castello di San Polo in Rosso, normale

+ Castello di San Polo in Rosso, Riserva
− Castello di Tizzano
  Castello di Uzzano
  Castello di Verrazzano, Riserva
− Castello Vicchiomaggio, normale
  Castello Vicchiomaggio, Paola Matta
  Castello Vicchiomagggio, Riserva Petri
+ Castello Vicchiomaggio, Riserva Prima Vigna
  Castello Vicchiomaggio, San Jacopo
  Catignano
  Cecchi Luigi, Messer Pietro di Teuzzo
  Conti Serristori, Riserva
− Conti Serristori, Villa Primavera normale
  Conti Serristori, Riserva Villa Primavera
  Fattoria dei Pagliarese
+ Fattoria dei Pagliarese, Boscardini Riserva
  Fattoria di Fontodi, normale
+ Fattoria di Fontodi, Riserva
+ Fattoria di Fontodi, Riserva Vigna del Sorbo
− Fattoria di Selvole
− Fattoria di Vistarenni, Podere Bertinga
− Fattoria Fermignano, "Frimaio"
  Fattoria Le Bocce
  Fattoria Le Filigare
− Fattoria Montiverdi, "Monti Verdi"
− Fattoria Pile e Lamole, Lamole di Lamole
  Fattoria Querciabella
+ Fattoria San Giusto a Rentennano
− Fattoria San Leonino (1988)[c]
− Fattoria Valtellina, Giorgio Regni (1987)[c]
− Fattoria Viticcio
+ Il Campino di Mondiglia
  Le Masse di San Leolino, Riserva
+ Marchesi L. e P. Antinori, Badia a Passignano (1988)[c]
  Marchesi L. e P. Antinori, Pèppoli
− Marchesi L. e P. Antinori, Riserva Marchese
  Marchesi L. e P. Antinori, Tenuta Marchese Riserva
− Marchesi L. e P. Antinori, Villa Antinori Riserva
+ Machiavelli
− Melini, Riserva
  Melini, Riserva Granaio
  Melini, Riserva Laborel
+ Melini, Riserva La Selvanella
  Melini, Riserva Terrarossa
  Monte Vertine[a]
− Monti Verdi (Fattoria Montiverdi)
  Nozzole
  Palazzo al Bosco (1979)[d]
  Paola Matta (Castello Vicchiomaggio)
  Podere Capaccia
+ Podere il Palazzino
  Podere Petroio alla Via della Malpensata
  Podere Petroio alla Via della Malpensata, Cru

Montetondo
- Querciavalle, Riserva
+ Riecine, *normale*
  Rocca delle Macìe, Riserva di Fizzano
+ Rocca di Castagnoli
  Rocca di Castagnoli, Riserva Capraia
  Rocca di Montgegrossi, Riserva
+ Ruffino, Riserva Ducale
  San Felice, Riserva
+ San Felice, Riserva il Grigio
+ San Felice, Riserva Poggio Rosso
  San Jacopo (Castello Vicchiomaggio)
  Selvoramole
  Tenuta di Lilliano, Riserva Eleanora Ruspoli Berlingier (1985)[c]
  Tenuta Villa Rosa
  Terrabianca, Riserva Vigna della Croce
+ Vecchie Terre di Montefili
- Vignamaggio
- Vignamaggio, Riserva Castello di Monna Lisa (1985)[c]
- Villa Antinori, Riserva (Marchesi L. e P. Antinori)
  Villa Cerna
  Villa Francesca
- Villa Terciona[e]

*

Agricoltori del Chianti Geografico Soc. Coop.
Agricoltori del Chianti Geografico Soc. Coop., Castello di Fagnano
Agricoltori del Chianti Georgrafico Soc. Coop., Contessa di Radda
Barfede-Certaldo, Cerbaiola
Barfede-Certaldo, Signoria
Bartali Alberto
Bartali Casa Vinicola
+ Brolio, *normale*
+ Brolio, Riserva
  Carobbio
  Carpineto Casa Vinicola
  Casa Francesco (1985 Riserva)[c]
- Casavecchia di Nittardi
  Castelgreve, Soc. Coop. Castelli del Grevepesa
  Castelgreve, Soc. Coop. Castelli del Grevepesa, Panzano
  Castello d'Albola
  Castello della Paneretta
- Castello di Castelvari
+ Castello di Cerreto
  Castello di Fagnano (Agricoltori del Chianti Geografico Soc. Coop.)
  Castello di Fonterutoli
+ Castelio di Fonterutoli, Riserva Ser Lapo
  Castello di Gabbiano, Riserva

+ Castello di Montegrossi
  Castello di Mugnana (1987)[c]
  Castello di San Polo in Rosso, Castelpolo
  Castello di Verrazzano, *normale*
- Castello Vicchiomaggio, La Lellera (1988 Riserva)[c]
  Cecchi Luigi
  Celli (1987)[c]
  Cennatoio (1985 Riserva)[c]
+ Chiantigiane, Santa Trinita
  Cispiano
  Coli (1987)[c]
  Contessa di Radda (Agricoltori del Chianti Geografico Soc. Coop.)
  Conti Serristori, *normale*
- Fattoria Campomaggio[f]
  Fattoria Casanuova di Nittardi (1987)[c]
  Fattoria Concadoro, Cerasi
  Fattoria di Luiano
- Fattoria di Mocenni (1987)[c]
  Fattoria di Petroio, Riserva
- Fattoria di Valiano
  Fattoria di Vistarenni
  Fattoria Dievole
+ Fattoria il Poggerino
+ Fattoria La Loggia, Terra dei Cavalieri
  Fattoria La Ripa
  Fattoria Le Corti (1988)[c]
  Fattoria Nittardi (1985 Riserva)[c]
+ Fattoria Pile e Lamole, Fattoria Salcetino
- Fattoria Quercia al Poggio
+ Fattoria Salcetino (Fattoria Pile e Lamole)
  Fattoria San Fabiano Calcinaia
+ Fattoria Tregole (1975)[c]
+ Fattoria Vignale
  Fossi
+ Gabbiano
  Giorgio Fico (1988)[c]
- Granducato, Poggibonsi del Consorzio Agrario Provinciale di Siena
  Il Palaggio
  Il Poggiolino
  L'Aja (1987)[c]
  La Brancaia (1987)[c]
+ La Bricola (1988)[c]
- La Lellera (Castello Vicchiomaggio) (1988 Riserva)[c]
  La Quercia, Cappelli Giovanni
- La Sala (1988)[c]
+ Le Chiantigiane, Santa Trinita
  Le Masse di San Leolino, *normale*
  Melini, *normale*
+ Melini, Riserva Isassi
- Monticelli[g]
  Montoro[h]

Podere Campacci
- Podere di Stignano
- Podere di Stignana, San Vicenti
+ Poggiarello
+ Querciavalle, *normale*
   Rocca delle Macìe, *normale*
+ Rocca delle Macìe, Riserva
   Rocca delle Macìe, Tenuta Sant'Alfonso (1988)[c]
   Rocca di Montegrossi, *normale*
+ Rodano
   Ruffino, Aziano
   Ruffino, *normale*
   S. Leonino (Fattoria I Cipressi)
+ Salcetino, Antiche Fattorie Fiorentine
- Salvanza
+ San Felice, *normale*
   Serristori (now Conti Serristori)
   Sicelle da Giovanni Mari
   Straccali
+ Tenuta di Lilliano
   Tenuta di Vignole
   Tenuta Montegiacchi (Agricoltori del Chianti
      Geografico Soc. Coop.)
   Terrabianca, Scassino (1987)[c]
   Villa Calcinaia (Conti Capponi)
   Villa Dievole
   Villa La Pagliaia, Riserva Granduca Ferdinando III
      (1980 Reserva)[d]

0

Casa Sola[i]
Casanuova di Nittardi, Fattoria Nittardi (1987)[c]
Castel Ruggero
+ Castelgreve (Soc. Coop. Castelli del Grevepesa),
   Montefiridolfi
Castello di Meleto
Castello di Monterinaldi
Castello di Radda (1983)[c]
Castello di Rencine[j]
Castello di San Donato in Perano
Cepperellaccio[k]
Chiantigiane
+ Convito (A.C.G.—Gaiole Coop. Agricola Cellars)
Fattoria Barberino (1977)[c]
+ Fattoria della'Aiola
Fattoria di Petroio, *normale*
+ Fattoria La Loggia
Fattoria Le Barone (1977)[c]
Fattoria Montecchio (1987)[c]
- Isabella de'Medici (1975)[c]
+ La Madonnina
Le Grifiere (1983 Riserva)[c]
Montemaggio

Monteropoli (1987)
Piccini
+ Poggio Bonelli
Pomona (1985)[c]
Prunetto
Ricasoli[k]
Rignana (1985)[c]
Riseccoli
Saccardi
Tenuta La Colombaia
Vignavecchia

NOTES: [a] No longer sold as Chianti Classico, sold as *vino da tavola*
[b] No longer produced
[c] Based on one wine
[d] The most recent vintage we tasted
[e] The most recent vintages tasted were the '73 and '74
[f] The most recent vintages tasted were the '80 Riserva and '82 in 1985
[g] Based on one wine, the '81 tasted in 1985
[h] Based on the '84 and '85 tasted from cask in 1986
[i] The most recent vintage tasted was the '78 in 1983
[j] The most recent vintages tasted were the '77 in 1980, and the '75 in 1981
[k] We haven't seen it in years

Vintage Information and Tasting Notes

The Consorzio del Gallo Nero, in their description of the vintages, uses the following technical terms:

	Dry Extract (Grams per Liter)	Total Acidity (Parts per Thousand in Tartaric Acid)
High	more than 26	6.6
Average	24.5 to 26	5.5 to 6.5
Low	less than 24.5	5.5

Our assessment of the vintages today:

****	1990, 1985
**** −	1983
*** +	1988
***	1982
**	1986, 1975, 1971, 1970, 1958, 1947
** −	1979, 1955
* +	1977
*	1987, 1981, 1980, 1978, 1957, 1952
* −	1967, 1964, 1962
0 +	1984
0	1989, 1976, 1974, 1973, 1972, 1969, 1968, 1966, 1965, 1963, 1961, 1960, 1959, 1956, 1954, 1953, 1951, 1950, 1949, 1948, 1946

WHAT THE RATINGS MEAN

**** Great, superb, truly noble
*** Exceptionally fine
** Very good
* A good example of its type, somewhat above average
0 Acceptable to mediocre, depending on the context; drinkable
+ Somewhat better than the star category it is put in
− Somewhat less than the star category it is put in, except for zero where it indicates a wine or producer-wine combination that is badly made or worse
[. .] *On a producer:* Tentative evaluation based on an insufficient number of wines or based on older, out-of-date vintages, or where the wines we tasted were too difficult to fully judge to give a fair assessment of quality.
On a wine or vintage: Projection for the future. This rating is given to a vintage where we feel that we tasted an insufficient number of wines or those we tasted were too difficult to really judge to give a fair assessment of quality.
(. .) Potential increase in the rating of the wine given sufficient maturity.

1990 [****]

The weather during the growing season was warm and very dry. The rain, which fell in August, was welcomed. Picking was supposed to start around September 24. Early reports suggested that the vintage was comparable to 1985. Based on those wines we tasted in June 1991, we believe that 1990 will be better than 1988, though not quite the equal of 1985.

1989 [0]

The dry, mild winter gave way to a damp spring. Vegetation was early. There were frequent summer rains during June, July, and August. Overall, the growing season was cool. The humid weather was conducive to the development of diseases, especially ödium. The high humidity during the first half of August prolonged the vegetation of the vines and slowed the maturity of the grapes. Conditions improved in the latter part of the month and continued to be favorable

through September and October and into November. Atmospheric conditions improved: the humidity dropped, there was almost no rainfall, and the temperatures rose and remained high. Picking got under way at the beginning of October, later than normal. Brolio reported that picking began for their white varieties on October 2, and a full week later for the reds. October was warm and sunny. The harvest of Castello di Verazzano took place between October 20 and November 10.

Production at nearly 8 million gallons (302,190 hectoliters), equivalent to 3.36 million cases, was a little below the ten-year average of 8.4 million gallons (319,544 hectoliters), but slightly above the production of the year earlier.

Thus far, we have tasted more than a dozen wines from cask. The Villa Cerna showed the most promise. Still in all, there will be many unattractive wines. Monsanto will not bottle their Il Poggio, nor Cappelli his Montagliari. And judging by the reluctance on the part of so many producers in letting us taste their '89s from cask, we can only conclude that this won't be a vintage to buy. Of course there will be some exceptions as there often are. But do consider that in the many years we have been visiting the Chianti Classico district to taste wines from cask, rarely has a producer ever refused to let us taste their new wine. And consider that on our last visit in November 1990, one year after the vintage, more producers wanted us to taste their 1990 than would let us taste their '89. Taking this experience into account with the few that we did get to taste, we can only conclude that, for the most part, this will be a vintage to avoid. Our ratings which follow are higher than they would have been if we had rated the vintage higher. We always rate wines more leniently when they come from a lesser vintage since we expect less. On our visit to Chianti in June 1991 we had an opportunity to taste a number of 1989s. They confirmed our suspicions; many bad wines were bottled.

CAUTION: *Before reading these tasting notes on the wines that we tasted from barrel, please read "On Tasting Wines from Barrel: A Caveat" on page xxv.*

Brolio [**Riserva**] (*ex-barrel, 5/90*). Open cherry and ripe fruit aroma; seems sweet, tart edge but good fruit. * +

Cappelli Giovanni, La Quercia (*ex-cask, 11/90*). Fresh spicy, berry aroma; a little dry but fairly attractive fruit, short. *

Castello di Querceto, Caratello (*11/90*). Fresh, grapey, clean. *

Castello di Verrazzano (*ex-barrel, 5/90*). Light and fruity, difficult to be sure, but some quality apparent.

Castello Vicchiomaggio, San Jacopo (*ex-cask, 11/90*). Fresh grapey aroma, peppery and spicy nuances; fresh, quaffable and clean; some charm. * +

Conti Serristori (*ex-cask,11/90*). Soft, open, simple and fruity. *

Fattoria La Loggia (*ex-cask, 11/90*). Surprising amount of fruit on the nose and palate, nice entry, a little short. *(+)

Fattoria Monsanto (*ex-barrel, 4/90*). Fresh pineapple(!) and grape aroma; high acid, sweet, light and fresh. *?

Fattoria Monsanto, del Poggio (*ex-barrel, 4/90*). Open cherry-like aroma; soft, on the light side. **−

Rocca delle Macìe [Riserva] (*ex-barrel, 5/90*). Open, fresh grape aroma and taste, tart edge, short, dry aftertaste

Ruffino (*ex-barrel, 5/90*). Some complexity, vaguely mushroom-like; evident fruit, short, dry aftertaste.

Villa Cafaggio (*ex-cask, 11/90*). Fairly nice fruit, medium body, attractive, short. *

Villa Cerna (*ex-cask, 11/90*). Rich, berrylike aroma, floral backnote; fairly good body, nice fruit, attractive, short; surprisingly good. **(+)

1988 *** +

Winter was mild, with very little precipitation. From the spring through the beginning of the summer, climatic conditions were negative with frequent showers and temperature below normal. The heavy rains of June hindered the blossoming and caused some mildew. This helped to reduce the crop size. From July on there was an almost total lack of rain, and the summer was very hot as well. The harvest began on October 2 and continued, according to Castello di Verrazzano, until October 25. The nearly 8 million–gallon (301,499-hectoliter) yield, equivalent to 3.35 million cases, was 6 percent below the 1980s average.

The *consorzio* gives 1988 top marks, four stars (adjusted for our four-star system) out of four. Thus far we've tasted 93 wines from 69 producers. More than 10 percent were less than good, and another 10 percent no more than good. Some 40 percent were between good and very good. Some 28 wines, 30 percent, were very good or potentially so. The remaining 7 wines were excellent or should be, given sufficient age. The best wines—for the most part, all tasted from cask—were led by Fattoria Monanto's Il Poggio, followed by Antinori's Badia a Passignano, the Badia a Coltibuono Riserva, Castello di Cacchiano *normale*, Castello di Volpaia Riserva, Villa Cafaggio Riserva, and Villa Cerna Riserva; next came three single-vineyard wines from Castello di Ama—Vigneto Bellavista, Vigneto La Casuccia, and Vigneto S. Lorenzo—the Conti Serristori Riserva, Fattoria La Loggia, Fattoria di Montagliari Riserva, Machiavelli Riserva, a pair of *riserve* from Melini—the Granaio and Vigneti La Selvanella—the Rocca di Castagnoli Riserva Poggio a'Fratti, and San Felice Riserva.

> **CAUTION:** *Before reading these tasting notes on the wines that we tasted from barrel, please read "On Tasting Wines from Barrel: A Caveat" on page xxv.*

Antinori, Badia a Passignano (*ex-cask, 11/90*). Oak then fruit on the aroma, chocolate(!) note; good body, firm with evident fruit, real sense of sweetness; undeveloped yet with promise. **(*)

Antinori, Pèppoli (*11/90*). Light nose, peppery; somewhat firm, fairly nice fruit; needs a little age. *(*)

Badia a Coltibuono, Riserva (*ex-cask,11/90*). Rich and concentrated, lots of structure and promise. **(*)

Bartali Alberto (*4/90*). Nice entry, almost sweet, then falls off, a tad shallow, dry aftertaste.

Berardenga, Fattoria di Felsina (*twice, 11/90*). Light nose recalls berries, mushroom note; berrylike flavor, light tannin, short; less attractive than it was nine months ago! * + *Bottle of 2/90:* Flowers and fruit, open, light to medium body, soft and quaffable, very good indeed. ***

Cappelli Giovanni, La Quercia (*11/90*). Fresh, open and attractive aroma; a little dry and surprisingly low in fruit; the bottle perhaps? +

Carobbio (*11/90, 9,000 bottles*). Obviously *barrique*-aged by the dominance of oak, the fruit is there as well but is there enough? +

Castel Ruggero (*4/90*). Light nose, chewy and tannic, sense of fruit evident. ?

Castelgreve, Soc. Coop. Castelli del Grevepesa (*3 times, 11/90*). Open fruit aroma; fruity yet dry, short. It was better five months ago. *Bottle of 6/90:* Soft and fruity, light tannin, simple, short and dry. *-

Castellare (*4 times, 11/90, 62,533 bottles*). Light, fragrant and fruity aroma; nice flavor on entry, easy and simple, open and fruity, a little dry and short. *

Castellare, Riserva (*ex-cask, 11/90*). Light, fragrant aroma; good fruit though dry and firm, really tight and closed, firm, hard finish; seems to have all the ingredients to develop. *(*?)

Castello d'Albola (*11/90*). Small-scale, fairly nice fruit, soft. *

Castello di Ama (*4 times, 11/90, 178,850 bottles*). Vanilla and berry aroma, vaguely floral; nice fruit under light tannin, short and a tad bitter. * + *Bottles of 4/90:* We tasted three bottles with variation. Two bottles revealed an open cherrylike aroma and an intrusive yet vague mercaptan note, it was simple and fruity. * − *The third bottle* had an open fruit aroma with a floral note, was smooth and had good extract. **

Castello di Ama, Vigneto Bellavista (*11/90*). Spice, fruit and oak; sense of sweetness from the oak and ripe fruit combined, a mouthful of fruit, fairly tannic as well. *(* +)

Castello di Ama, Vigneto Bertinga (11/90). Ripe fruit, recalls raspberries; lots of nice fruit on entry before it tightens up, very short and dry ending; the least of the four crus. *(* −)

Castello di Ama, Vigneto La Casuccia (11/90). Rich fruit aroma, berrylike; good structure, oak overlay, firm, dry aftertaste. *(* +)

Castello di Ama, Vigneto S. Lorenzo (11/90). Spice, fruit and oak; sense of sweetness, fairly well balanced, a little short and dry at the end. **(+)

Castello di Cacchiano (ex-barrel, 4/90). Richly fruited aroma, some spice and raspberries, packed with flavor and fruit, real sweetness from ripe fruit, already displays class, moderate length, should make splendid bottle. ***

Castello di Fonterutoli (twice, 6/90). Vaguely floral aroma, some sweetness, soft and fruity, open, cherry nuance, tannin at the end. * +

Castello di Querceto (twice, 11/90). Small nose; fairly nice fruit, dull aftertaste. + *Bottle of 6/90:* Light nose, soft and fruity, open, ready. * +

Castello di San Polo in Rosso, Riserva (ex-cask, 11/90). Rich fruit, good backbone, firm, dry finish. *(*)

Castello di Verrazzano (11/90). Dull, low fruit, dry end.

Castello di Volpaia, Riserva (ex-cask, 11/90). A mouthful of fruit, a lot of structure and extract; great promise. **(*)

Castello Vicchiomaggio, San Jacopo (11/90). Light, floral nose; nice fruit, sense of sweetness. ** −

Cecchi Luigi (twice, 11/90). Open floral aroma, berry notes on the nose and palate, soft under light tannin, good body; ready. * +

Cecchi Luigi, Messer Pietro di Teuzzo (7 times, 11/90). More fragrance and fruit than the regular '88, younger as well; framboise all over this wine from the open and charming aroma through the palate; could improve over the next year or two but very nice now. **

Chiantigiane (4/90). Hot and cooked, totally unimpressive.

Chiantigiane, Santa Trinita (4/90). Fresh, open cherrylike aroma; soft, round and ready. ** −

Conti Serristori, Riserva (ex-cask, 11/90). Nice nose; rich and concentrated, good structure. **(+)

Conti Serristori, Villa Primavera (11/90). Peppery, spicy aroma; clean and simple, fruity. *

Fattoria Concadoro, Cerasi (twice, 4/90). Open fruit aroma, cherrylike; soft, tasty, short and dry. *

Fattoria dei Pagliarese (twice, 6/90). Fresh, floral aroma; light tannin, nice fruit, open and balanced. ** −

Fattoria dell' Aiola (6/90). Cooked quality to the fruit, low fruit, dull and coarse.

Fattoria di Montagliari, Riserva (Cappelli Giovanni) (ex-cask, 11/90). Lovely woodslike aroma, cherry and berry notes; good structure, full of fruit in spite of being tight; very young with good potential. **(+)

Fattoria di Vistarenni (4/90). Mercaptan, off-putting.

Fattoria Il Poggerino (3 times, 6/90). Fragrant aroma suggestive of flowers and berries; soft, light tannin. * +

Fattoria La Loggia (11/90). Lovely nose; full of flavor, good body, tasty. **(+)

Fattoria Le Bocce (4/90). Soft, open, fresh; ready now. *

Fattoria Le Corti (4/90). Fresh, cherrylike aroma; nice fruit, albeit simple, soft, ready. *

Fattoria Le Filigare, Riserva (ex-cask, 11/90). Firm and tight, at a difficult stage, seems to have the fruit. (*?)

Fattoria Monsanto, Il Poggio (ex-cask, 4/90). Open raspberry aroma; great richness, weight and extract, big and concentrated, real sweetness, raspberry and cassis flavor; potentially outstanding. ***(*)

Fattoria Monsanto, Riserva (ex-vat, 4/90). Very big, rich and concentrated, seems rather brief at the end. **?

Fattoria Pile e Lamole, Lamole di Lamole (6/90). Lovely fruit, vanilla overlay, notes of spice and berries; light tannin, good fruit, a little tight and rather short. * +

Fattoria Querciabella (4/90). Light, floral aroma; open and fruity, sweet, vanilla, oak(?); seems ready yet the tannin builds at the end. * +

Fattoria San Fabiano Calcinaia (6/90). Tight nose; lovely fruit, good structure, some tannin. **

Fattoria San Giusto a Rentennano (4/90). Mercaptans intrude, flawed badly, yet fruit is evident.

Geografico (twice, 6/90). Fresh, cherrylike aroma; some tannin, fruity, short and dry at the end. *

Geografico, Castello di Fagnano (10/90). Floral and fruity, soft and tasty, simple and agreeable. *

Giorgio Fico (4/90). Light nose; soft center, light tannin, fruity, short. *

Isole e Olena (6/90). Soft, open and fruity, round, well balanced, flavorful; ready. **

La Bricola (twice, 6/90). Soft, fruity, simple, light tannin, good structure. * +

La Sala (4/90). Light mercaptan note, still there is good fruit, soft and very short, dry. * −

Le Masse di San Leolino (11/90). Mercaptan intrudes, low fruit; a big surprise from what has been a reliable and good producer. ?

Machiavelli, Riserva (ex-cask, 11/90). Berry and floral aroma; good backbone, packed with flavor, soft under moderate tannin. **(+)

Melini, Isassi (3 times, 11/90). Simple, soft and open, notes of cherry and spice on both the nose and palate, clean, short, dry aftertaste. *

Melini, Riserva Vigneti Granaio (*ex-cask, 11/90*). Lovely fragrance; good structure, sweetness of ripe, rich fruit, concentrated. **(+)

Melini, Riserva Vigneti La Selvanella (*ex-cask, 11/90*). Floral and fruit aroma; rich in flavor, good structure. **(+)

Monti Verdi (*11/90*). Fragrant aroma, floral backnote; berrylike flavor, ripe fruit, short and a tad dry. ** —

Paola Matta (Castello Vicchiomaggio) (*11/90*). Fairly nice nose, spice and fruit; soft, light tannin, good fruit, short; attractive. ** —

Piccini (*4/90*). Some fruit, but seems to be drying out!

Podere Capaccia (*4/90*). Flowers and cherries; sweet, soft, supple, ready. *

Podere Capaccia, Riserva (*twice, ex-cask, 11/90*). Nice nose though a little unsettled; good structure, full of flavor, some oak, a little dry at the end. *(*)

Podere di Stignano, San Vicenti (*4/90*). Fresh, openly fruity and simple. *

Podere Petroio alla Via della Malpensata, Cru Montetondo (*4/90*). Fresh, cherrylike aroma; nice fruit, soft, open flavor. **

Querciavalle (*4/90*). Vanilla and cherry aroma; openly fruity and fresh. *

Riecine (*4/90*). Open raspberry scent, mushroomlike backnote; richly flavored, soft and tasty. **

Rocca delle Macìe (*twice, 11/90*). We tasted this one twice in November 1990 with two different impressions. *The most recent bottle:* Floral and cherry nuances, berry notes; very soft and openly fruity; very ready. *** *The earlier bottle:* Peppery, spicy, berry aroma, marred by a slight mercaptan note; sense of sweetness from the ripe fruit, the mercaptan does intrude, still in all it is fruity. *

Rocca delle Macìe, Riserva (*ex-cask, 11/90*). Light nose; chalky taste(!), rather dry and severe, short. (*)

Rocca delle Macìe, Riserva di Fizzano (*ex-cask, 11/90*). Like the Riserva has a chalky taste(!), tight with evident fruit, dry, firm end. *(*)

Rocca delle Macìe, Tenuta Sant'Alfonso (*11/90*). Soft and simple, light tannin, agreeable. *

Rocca di Castagnoli, Riserva Capraia (*ex-cask, 11/90*). Ripe fruit aroma, toward berries, floral note; firm and a little dry, somewhat closed, but the sense of fruit evident. *(+)

Rocca di Castagnoli, Riserva Poggio a'Fratti (*ex-cask, 11/90*). Rich fruit aroma, berry and vanilla components; rich fruit, firm and tight with the components to develop. **(+)

Ruffino, Aziano (*9/90*). Small-scale, simple and fruity. +

Salcetino, Antiche Fattorie Fiorentine (*twice, 4/90*). One bottle seemed old and tired! The second bottle had a light nose, with quite a lot of fruit, light tannin, sweet, good weight. **

San Felice (*3 times, 6/90*). Fragrant-scented aroma; simple, easy and fruity, quaffable style, light tannin. * +

San Felice, Riserva (*twice, 11/90*). *Sample 1:* Fragrant ripe fruit aroma; sweet impression, full-flavored, rich. *(*+) *Sample 2:* Richer nose and more complex than #1; more backbone and structure, could use more length. **(+)

San Leonino (*7 times, 11/90*). A little dry, starting to show some age, still has good fruit; the bottle perhaps. * *Bottle of 9/90:* Fragrant, soft, open and fruity, berry and floral components, light tannin, good body. ** —

Straccali (*4/90*). Floral, fruity aroma; nice entry, then falls off, shallow and short.

Tenuta di Lilliano (*4/90*). Open raspberry aroma; sweet, ripe and fruity, tasty. **

Tenuta di Vignole (*twice, 11/90*). Fragrant, floral and berry aroma, vanilla note; openly fruity, soft, light tannin, has an edge to it, short, dry and bitter; best to drink up. *

Tenuta Villa Rosa (*twice, 4/90*). One bottle was overly tannic for the amount of fruit. The other has a raspberry-scented aroma that vaguely recalled Zinfandel; it was sweet, soft and fruity with light tannin. **

Vecchie Terre di Montefili, Riserva (*11/90*). Good backbone, nice fruit, a little dry and short. * +

Villa Banfi (*4/90*). Simple, soft, open, clean, fresh. *

Villa Cafaggio (*4 times, 11/90*). Floral and berry aroma; full of fruit, good structure; needs age; more substance than the earlier bottles! **(*) We tasted two bottles in June and one in April 1990. *Of these three, the most recent bottle:* Light nose; soft, berrylike fruit; ready. * + *Another bottle:* Cherrylike aroma; fresh, openly fruity, clean and tasty, open, forward flavors with the sweetness of ripe fruit. ** —

Villa Cafaggio, normale (*ex-cask, 11/90*). Rich and flavorful, good structure, sense of sweetness. ** +

Villa Cafaggio, Riserva (*ex-cask, 11/90*). More structure and backbone than the *normale*, good body. **(*)

Villa Calcinaia, Conti Capponi (*twice, 6/90*). Light nose, soft and simple, fruity. *

Villa Cerna (*11/90*). Fresh, berrylike aroma; lovely fruit, ripe, almost sweet, a little short, ** —

Villa Cerna, Riserva (*ex-cask, 11/90*). Fragrant, yet rich, floral aroma; loaded with flavor, some tannin, good structure; should make a nice bottle in time. **(* —)

Villa Dievole (*twice, 6/90*). Soft, open and fruity, small-scale. *

Villa Vignamaggio (*11/90*). Fragrant aroma; good fruit, light tannin, a little dry. +

1987 *

Spring was damp and cold and the summer very dry and warm. September and October were wet. The harvest began on September 20. Some estates reported that picking began even later than that. For example, at Castello di Verrazzano the harvest began on October 5 and ended on November 4. Many vines suffered from lack of water. In some vineyards the vines ripened better than in others. Careful selection was necessary. The 8.5 million-gallon (323,378-hectoliter) production, the equivalent of 3.59 million cases, was slightly above the 1980s average. This was not a year for *riserva* wines. There were many pleasant, light, fairly well-balanced wines. The *consorzio* rates the year two stars out of four.

Based on the 100 wines from 80 producers that we tasted—very few were *riserve*—the vintage was much better than the initial reports. These are fast-maturing, pleasant wines that already give pleasure. Very few will last past their third or fourth year, and more than a few are already fading. Drink them up.

Fully 40 percent of the wines we tasted were less than good, and just over 53.5 percent were good or slightly better. The best two were the Castello di Volpaia Riserva and the Vecchie Terre di Montefili Riserva Anfiteatro, followed by the Badia a Coltibuono Riserva, Fattoria di Selvole *normale*, Fattoria Monsanto Il Poggio, Rodano *normale*, and San Felice Riserva.

CAUTION: *Before reading these tasting notes on the wines that we tasted from barrel, please read "On Tasting Wines from Barrel: A Caveat" on page xxv.*

Antinori, Pèppoli (4 *times*, 11/90). Peppery nose; a little firm, very short and dry; was better six months ago, the bottle perhaps! * −

Antinori, Tenuta Marchese Riserva (11/90). Fragrant, spicy aroma, cabernet and oak quite evident; good body, flavorful, short, dry end. ** −

Badia a Coltibuono (3 *times*, 4/90). A little light on the nose; light- to medium-bodied, dry, short but clean; it was better a year ago. *

Badia a Coltibuono, Riserva (ex-cask, 11/90). Spice and floral aroma; lots of nice fruit, good structure; needs age. *(*)

Bartali (4/89). Aroma recalls varnish and flowers; nice fruit, open and soft under light tannin. *

Berardenga, Fattoria di Felsina (6 *times*, 6/90). *Light, fruity aroma; simple, small-scale, short; ready.* * −

Brolio (11/90). Soft, easy, simple, dry, short end; drink up. * −

Cappelli Giovanni, La Quercia (4/90). Cherry and floral aroma, fresh and clean; light and soft, a nice though simple quaff. *

Carobbio (4/90). Light nose; rather nice fruit in the mouth, a little short. *

Carobbio, barrique-aged (11/90, 21,000 bottles). Some fruit and lot of oak, dry, short end.

Carpineto (3 *times*, 6/90). There was some variation in bottles. *The best bottle, tasted 4/90:* Light, soft and fruity, agreeable and easy. * *The most recent bottle, tasted two months later:* Low fruit and some tannin, unbalanced and uninteresting.

Casanuova di Nittardi, Fattoria Nittardi (4/90). Vegetable aroma; dry, low fruit.

Castel Ruggero (4/90). Light nose; some fruit, a bit tight.

Castelgreve, Soc. Coop. Castelli del Grevepesa (4/89). Light nose; good body, soft, simple, easy. *

Castellare (4 *times*, 6/90, 58,530 bottles). Light and fruity on both the nose and the palate, raspberrylike component, some tannin; could improve a bit. *

Castellare, Riserva (ex-cask, 11/90). Some oak overlays, rather nice fruit; light to moderate tannin, short finish. *(* −)

Castell'in Villa (twice, 6/90). Open, cherrylike fruit aroma; a little dry, yet fruity and soft with light tannin at the end, fairly good body. *

Castello dei Rampolla (twice, 9/90). A lovely glass of well-made, open cherry aroma, herbal overtone; fairly well balanced, soft, herbaceous overtone, short aftertaste; ready now. ** −

Castello di Ama (4/89). Ripe, open berrylike aroma; rich, ripe and concentrated, round and tasty; quite agreeable. ** −

Castello di Ama, Vigneto Bellavista (3 *times*, 11/90, 24,987 bottles). Berrylike fruit combines with oak on the nose; the oak dominates in the mouth (it didn't seven months ago; it spent some twelve to fourteen months in *barrique*); simple, open, soft, short. *

Castello di Ama, Vigneto La Casuccia (4 *times*, 11/90, 22,164 bottles). Open aroma, fruity, oak component overly evident as it is in the mouth (this one, too, displayed less oak seven months ago), soft and simple; drink. +

Castello di Ama, Vigneto S. Lorenzo (twice, 4/90, 22,135 bottles). Mushroom and berry aroma; soft, open and fruity; simple and ready. * +

Castello di Cacchiano (4 *times*, 11/90). Light, spicy nose; lots of flavor, some firmness, light tannin, shirt; drink. *

Castello di Fonterutoli (twice, 4/90). *A bottle tasted one year earlier* had a light but scented aroma, was vaguely floral; tasty and good. * + *The more recent bottle* was stinky and off-putting.

Castello di Montegrossi (4/90). Light, floral aroma; light, soft and open, simple and fruity. *

Castello di Mugnana (4/90). Open fruit, fresh, soft; ready. *

Castello di San Polo in Rosso, Castelpolo (4/89). Dry and fruity, fresh and firm. *

Castello di San Polo in Rosso, Riserva (ex-cask, 11/90). Good body, firm backbone, rather nice flavor on entry which falls away very quickly, dry, tight end. *(+)

Castello di Verrazzano (*4 times, 6/90*). *The most recent bottle* had a simple nose, was a little dry, and seemed to be fading and losing fruit. *Another bottle,* tasted ten days earlier, was soft, fruity, open and ready. *

Castello di Volpaia (*4/90*). Light, floral aroma; some backbone, rather nice fruit, though on the light side. ** −

Castello di Volpaia, Riserva (*ex-cask, 11/90*). Fragrant, floral scent; full of fruit, good body, moderate tannin; well made. **(+)

Castello Vicchiomaggio, San Jacopo (*4/89*). Light nose; open, ripe fruit character; quite ready and agreeable. ** −

Cecchi Luigi (*twice, 6/90*). Soft, simple, fruity, a little short and dry. *

Cecchi Luigi, Messer Pietro di Teuzzo (*twice, 12/89*). Light nose; soft entry then some tannin. *

Celli (*4/89*). Like a barrel sample, so fresh and fruity. *

Cerbaiola (Barfede) (*4/90*). Dull, almost cooked.

Coli (*3 times, 6/90*). Open, soft and fruity; very ready. * *Bottle of 4/90:* Smells like a damp animal, low fruit.

Fattoria Casanuova di Nittardi (*6/90*). Open, soft, sweet impression, fruity; very ready. *

Fattoria dei Pagliarese (*4/89*). Odd nose; seems off, very dry; fair at best.

Fattoria dell'Aiola (*4/89*). This was simply a poor wine; off-putting nose hints of rotten vegetables.

Fattoria di Luiano (*6/90*). Hot, cooked, ugh!

Fattoria di Mocenni (*twice, 4/90*). There was some unevenness. *The best and most recent bottle:* Small-scale, earthy, simple, drinkable. * −

Fattoria di Montagliari, Riserva (Cappelli Giovanni) (*ex-cask, 11/90*). Fragrant, floral scent, berry note; tasty, dried fruit character, medium body, openly fruity, short, dry end. *(+)

Fattoria di Petroio (*4/89*). Low fruit.

Fattoria di Petroio, Lenzi (*4/90*). Not a lot of nose; dry, deficient in fruit.

Fattoria di Selvole (*4/90*). Open cherrylike aroma; sweet, open, soft and quaffable. **

Fattoria di Vistarenni (*5 times, 6/90*). There was a lot of bottle variation. Spicy, fruity, cherry aroma; tails off from the midpalate back, a tad short and dry, lightly bitter. *Bottle of 2/90, the best bottle:* Small-scale, light and soft, quaffable, cherrylike. *

Fattoria Fermignano, "Frimaio" (*twice, 6/90*). Light, soft, open and fruity, dry end; drink. * −

Fattoria Il Poggerino (*4/90*). Nice nose; some fruit on entry, then a little firm and short; still it is agreeable enough. *

Fattoria La Loggia (*4/90*). Light nose; soft and fruity, open at first then dry as it goes back. +

Fattoria La Ripa (*11/90*). Floral, fruity aroma is the best part; dry, low in fruit, bitter.

Fattoria Le Filigare (*twice, 11/90, 20,950 bottles*). Small-scale, nice fruit, dry finish; it was better seven months ago. *

Fattoria Monsanto (*ex-cask, 4/90*). Open fruity aroma; nice fruit, open and forward flavors, short, somewhat light finish. * +

Fattoria Monsanto, Il Poggio (*twice, ex-cask, 4/90*). Spicy, berry aroma; a little light for Il Poggio, some tannin, openly fruity, somewhat short. **

Fattoria Montecchio (*4/89*). Rubber tire; low fruit, dry.

Fattoria Pile e Lamole, Lamole di Lamole (*4/89*). Light nose; rather nice fruit, tasty, light tannin, drinking nice now. *

Fattoria Pile e Lamole, Fattoria Salcetino (*twice, 5/90*). Light nose; soft entry, dry finish. * −

Fattoria San Fabiano Calcinaia (*3 times, 6/90*). Some fruit, rather dry, beginning to thin out at the end. *Bottle of 4/90:* Open, fresh, fruity and warm. *

Fattoria San Giusto a Rentennano (*4/89*). Spicy, fruity and open nose; flavorful, balanced. ** −

Fattoria Valiano (*4/89*). A tad overripe(!), but good fruit. * −

Fattoria Viticcio (*twice, 5/90*). Scented cherry aroma; a little dry, aftertaste is on the light and dry side. * −

Fontodi (*6 times, 4/90*). There has been, surprisingly, some bottle variation. *The most recent bottle:* Open fruit aroma, tar and floral notes; soft, simple, easy. * −

Gabbiano (*twice, 5/90*). One bottle was coarse and dull, the other soft and fruity with a short, dull aftertaste. The best one merits * −

Geografico (*4/89*). Light nose; vague off note in the mouth, somewhat bitter aftertaste.

Giorgio Regni (*twice, 4/89*). Perfumed; soft and flavorful, balanced. * +

Granducato (*4/90*). Soft, fruity; ready. * −

Isole e Olena (*7 times, 9/90*). A little shy on the nose; soft and open, very ready. * + *Bottle of 6/90:* Lovely fruit, cherrylike; soft and balanced; easy style; very ready. **

L'Aia (*4/89*). Light, fruity aroma; soft, easy and simple with nice fruit. *

La Brancaia (*4/90*). Openly fruity aroma; light fruity entry tails off to a dryness at the end. * −

Le Masse di San Leolino (*11/90*). Slight nose; nice fruit on entry, then dry and shallow, very short.

Machiavelli, Vigna di Fontalle (*11/90*). Light, spicy and fruity aroma; sense of sweetness from the fruit, short, dry end. ** −

Melini, Terrarossa (*4/89*). Floral scent; sweet impression, open flavor, soft; simple. * +

Monteropoli (4/89). Hot, overripe.

Monti Verdi (4 times, 11/90). There has been considerable bottle variation. *The most recent bottle:* A little dry and dull; was better five months ago; drink up. +

Paola Matta (Castello Vicchiomaggio) (6/90). Light, open and soft, ready, dryish aftertaste. *

Podere Capaccia (11/90). Spicy aroma; sense of fruit, good body and fruit. * +

Podere Petroio alla Via della Malpensata (4/89). Open cherry-like aroma; openly fruity in the mouth, balanced and fresh. * +

Poggio Bonelli (4/90). Light, cherrylike aroma; nice entry, then a little dry, and tight. *

Riecine (3 times, 4/90). Well made, clean fruit, a little dry but attractive, short, dry finish. * +

Rocca delle Macìe, Riserva (ex-barrel, 11/90). A little light in aroma and body, light tannin, rather nice fruit. *

Rocca delle Macìe, Riserva di Fizzano (ex-barrel, 11/90). Light nose; medium body, nice fruit on entry then a little shallow and short. (*)

Rocca di Castagnoli, Poggio a'Fratti Riserva (3 times, ex-vat, 11/90, 18,660 bottles). Fragrant, floral aroma; raspberry- and cassislike nuances on the nose and palate; it was better in April 1990; we wonder why they don't bottle it. *(+)

Rocca di Castagnoli, Riserva (3 times, ex-vat, 11/90). Floral, vanilla aroma; good backbone, rather nice fruit, a little light, dry, firm ending, could use more age. *(+)

Rocca di Montegrossi (E. Ricasoli) (4/90). Simple cherrylike fruit, easy and light, short finish. *

Rodano (4/90). Fresh, open cherry aroma; some tannin, good fruit, soft-centered. **

Ruffino, Aziano (twice, 7/90). Floral, berry aroma; a little acidic but soft, simple, easy, open, short. *

Salvanza (twice, 4/90). Floral, spicy aroma; nice entry, then falls off, dry end; was better a year earlier. * −

San Felice (3 times, 4/90). Nice fruit, soft, easy, simple. *

San Felice, Riserva (ex-cask, 11/90). Fresh grapey and fragrant aroma; sweet impression, moderate tannin; a surprising amount of promise! *(*)

Serristori, Villa Primavera (4/89). Open, ripe fruit aroma; simple, vague mercaptan note intrudes, still the fruit is nice.*

Terrabianca, Riserva Vigna della Croce (4/90). Leather and dried fruit aroma; moderate tannin, light fruit, slight sweetness, short and dry aftertaste. *

Terrabianca, Scassino (4/90). Small-scale, soft and fruity. +

Vecchie Terre di Montefili (4 times, 11/90). Lovely bouquet, hints of spice and fruit, fresh; open, good body, soft, lots of flavor; very ready. ** −

Vecchie Terre di Montefili, Riserva Anfiteatro (ex-cask, 11/90). Fresh grapey aroma; nice fruit, sense of sweetness; young with good potential. **(+)

Vignamaggio (twice, 6/90). Cooked fruit, coffee nose; dull and tired. *Bottle of 4/90:* Soft, easy and simple. *

Villa Antinori, Riserva (11/90). Fairly nice nose; dry, some fruit under light tannin, dry and short aftertaste. *

Villa Cafaggio (3 times, 4/90). Light nose, clean, fresh and fruity; suggestion of sweetness, soft and ready; well made. ** −

Villa Cafaggio, Riserva (ex-cask, 11/90). Good fruit, fairly full, finish is a little short. * +

Villa Cerna (twice, 11/90). Slight but nice nose; light, soft and open, still has flavor; best to drink up. * −

Villa Dievole (twice, 4/90). Light floral aroma; open, soft, ready. *

1986 **

The rainy, irregular spring gave way to an early summer. The summer was mostly dry, especially August, which experienced very high temperatures as well. This hot, dry weather continued into September. Some reports said that the harvest began one week early. Others suggested otherwise: Castello di Verrazzano reported that, for them, the harvest took place between October 13 and November 5, beginning eight days later than it had in 1987. Production, at 7.9 million gallons (297,715 hectoliters), or 3.31 million cases, was 7 percent below the average between 1980 and 1989.

The *consorzio* reported that the color was very high, the average alcohol was 12.8 percent, acidity was average, and the dry extract high. Their conclusion: these are wines for moderate to long aging. The *consorzio* gives the year four out of four stars. We don't.

Of the 91 wines we tasted from 65 producers, 23, or more than one-fourth, were less than good; 49, or nearly 54 percent, were good to not quite very good; and 16 were very good or slightly better, leaving three wines that were excellent or about excellent. Based on the wines that we tasted, we see the vintage as very good, no more.

The best wine was the Podere Il Palazzino Riserva, followed by the *riserve* from Castello di Volpaia and Podere Capaccia; next came five more *riserve*—Castello Banfi, Fattoria Monsanto Il Poggio, Machiavelli Vigna di Fontalle, Melini La Selvanella, Terrabianca Vigna della Croce, and Vecchie Terre di Montefili Riserva Anfiteatro.

These wines will mature fairly early, many are already good now, and some are showing signs of senility. More than a few have aged quickly between April 1990, when we first tasted them, and six months later, when we next tasted them.

Antinori, Pèppoli (11/90). Open fruit aroma, herbal notes; some tannin, fairly nice fruit, short; drink up. ** −

Antinori, Tenuta Marchese Riserva (11/90). Nice nose, some cabernet herbaceousness evident along with some oak; light tannin, good fruit, a little short and dry. **

Badia a Coltibuono, Riserva (3 times, 11/90). Damp leaves; sweet, rich, concentrated, soft and precocious, light tannin, full of flavor; room to improve. **

Berardenga, Fattoria di Felsina (twice, 4/89). Floral, perfumed; rich and flavorful, balanced, a tad bitter, soft center. * +

Berardenga, Fattoria di Felsina, Riserva (11/90). Floral nose; moderate fruit, a little firm especially at the end. * +

Berardenga, Fattoria di Felsina, Riserva Vigneto Rancia (11/90). Light oak background combines with floral component; on the palate the oak and fruit combine harmoniously, good body, smooth, bitter edge at the end; ready. **

Brolio (twice, 2/90). Fruity aroma; open, good body, fruity; quaffable. * +

Cappelli Giovanni, La Quercia (4/89). Soft, tasty, round, ready. * +

Carpineto, Riserva (6/90). Nice fruit, some oak; soft entry, some tannin, dry, short aftertaste. +

Castelgreve, Soc. Coop. Castelli del Grevepesa, Monte Firidolfi (twice, 6/90). Light tannin, simple, and a tad dull. +

Castelgreve, Soc. Coop. Castelli del Grevepesa, Panzano (twice, 11/90, 46,906 bottles). Dried fruit aroma, vaguely floral, cooked character; really dull and coarse; could this be the same wine? *Bottle of 4/90:* Floral, fruity, sweet impression, open and soft. *

Castellare (4/90). Nose seems older than it is, fruit evident; soft, rather short; drink. * −

Castellare, Riserva (3 times, 11/90, 10,130 bottles). Open berry fragrance, lovely nose, oak component; open fruit flavor, sweet impression, nice mouth feel, light tannin, finish is a little dry, could use more length; ready. ** −

Castell'in Villa (4/89). Light, fruity aroma; simple, tasty, fairly nice structure. *

Castello Banfi, Riserva (11/90). Fragrant aroma; lovely, open, soft, precocious, some oak; ready. ** +

Castello d'Albola (4 times, 6/90). Light, soft and simple, open, fruity, short, dry end. *

Castello della Paneretta (twice, 6/90). Fragrant, floral-scented bouquet; soft and open, fruity; ready. *

Castello di Ama, Vigneto Bellavista (10/89). Openly fruity, berrylike; sweet impression at first then closed and firm. * +

Castello di Cacchiano (4/89). Light, fruity aroma; open entry then some tannin, a tad bitter. * −

Castello di Cacchiano, Riserva Millennio (5 times, 11/90, 17,272 bottles). Fragrant, berry scent, touch of vanilla; a nice mouthful of flavor, smooth texture, some oak combines with the fruit, a little short; very attractive. **

Castello di Fonterutoli, Riserva Ser Lapo (3 times, 6/90, 26,000 bottles and 600 magnums). This wine has displayed some variation—all three bottles were different. *The most recent bottle:* Vague cooked quality, some tannin, soft center, fairly nice fruit, simple, dry finish. ** −

Castello di Querceto (4/89). Nice nose; sweet impression, ripe fruit, tasty, soft. * +

Castello di Querceto, Riserva (5 times, 11/90). Light aroma of flowers and berries; soft and open, fruity, nice fruit, supple, a tad dry at the end, ready. ** −

Castello di Uzzano (4/89). Light nose; richly flavored, supple, some tannin. ** −

Castello di Verrazzano (4/89). Small-scale, good fruit; drinking very well now. * +

Castello di Verrazzano, Riserva (twice, 11/90). Floral, fruity aroma, cherry note; soft under light tannin, a little short and a tad dry. ** −

Castello di Volpaia (twice, 4/89). Light nose, good fruit; open and soft, firm and tasty. * +

Castello di Volpaia, Riserva (twice, 11/90). Scented, fragrant, floral, perfumed bouquet, spicy nuance; well balanced, lots of fruit and spice in the mouth, supple, could use more length; ready; a lot of class. *** −

Castello Vicchiomaggio, Riserva Petri (11/90). Light nose; nice mouth feel, good fruit and balance, could use more length; still a nice glass. **

Castello Vicchiomaggio, Riserva Prima Vigna (11/90). Light nose combines fruit and oak; soft, nice mouth feel, fruit combines with oak, moderate length. **

Cecchi Luigi (4/89). Odd nose, spice and fruit along with a vague resin quality; soft, easy and fruity. *

Conti Serristori, Riserva Villa Primavera (11/90). Fragrant, floral aroma; soft and open fruit, precocious. ** −

Fattoria di Luiano (2/90). Open, light, fruity, simple. *

Fattoria di Luiano, Riserva (twice, 10/90). Openly fruity aroma, some fragrance, vanilla note; soft, open, precocious, lacks depth and structure, overly dry finish. +

Fattoria di Selvole (twice, 4/89). Fragrant aroma; soft, light tannin, tasty. * +

Fattoria di Selvole, Riserva Lanfredini (twice, 5/90). Soft, fruity, easy, lacks concentration, simple; ready. * −

Fattoria Fermignano, "Frimaio" (4/89). Floral, ripe fruit, berry nuance; sweet, open, precocious, tasty. **

Fattoria La Loggia (6/90). Scented floral bouquet, berrylike component; a little dry, starting to fade, shows age, short.

Fattoria La Ripa (4/89). Some oxidation, too old.

Fattoria La Ripa, Riserva (4/90). Open, grapey, simple, soft. *

Fattoria Le Bocce (4/89). Floral scent; soft, open and supple, berrylike fruit. * +

Fattoria Le Filigare (4 times, 6/90). Although there was some variation all four bottles were good. Somewhat complex bouquet, spice and fruit; soft, open, fruity, attractive, round; ready. ** −

Fattoria Monsanto, Riserva (4 times, 4/90). Scented floral bouquet; soft, easy and forward, finishes a little light; not for aging. ** −

Fattoria Monsanto, Riserva Il Poggio (twice, ex-cask, 4/90). Nose displays suggestions of mushroom, vanilla, cassis and spice; open, forward fruit flavors. ** +

Fattoria San Giusto a Rentennano, Riserva (4/90). Light nose; tasty, moderate tannin, soft center, a little short, and a tad dry. ** −

Fattoria Vignale (twice, 4/90). Aroma recalls leather, dried fruit and spice; soft, open fruit, tasty. *

Fattoria Viticcio (4/89). Nice nose; soft and easy. *

Fattoria Viticcio, Riserva (5/90). Light nose; nice entry, a little dry, good fruit midpalate, could use more length. * +

Fontodi (4/89). Fragrant floral scent; fairly tannic but with the fruit to carry it. ** −

Gabbiano Riserva (10/90). The aroma displays some fruit and some oak; a little dry and low in fruit.

Geografico, Contessa di Radda (4 times, 11/90). Overripe, soft and simple, drinkable. + *Bottle of 6/90:* Characteristic floral fragrance, berry component; good fruit, soft, open, precocious; ready. *

Il Poggiolino (3 times, 6/90). Floral fragrance; nice entry, a tad dry, fruity, dry, short finish. * −

Isole e Olena (12/88). Mushroom, woodsy aroma; sweet, open fruit, supple, soft, round and tasty. **

La Lellera (Castello Vicchiomaggio), Riserva (11/90). First sense is herbaceous (cabernet?); fairly tannic, oak and herbal flavor, a little short and dry. * −

Le Masse di San Leolino, Riserva (11/90). Slight nose; a little dry, fairly nice fruit, short finish. * −

Machiavelli, Riserva Vigna di Fontalle (twice, 11/90). Open fruit, berry and floral fragrance, herbal notes; good body, nice fruit and texture, soft, light tannin, moderate length; ready. ** +

Melini, Riserva Laborel (11/90). Light nose, oak overlay; nice fruit in the mouth with an overlay of oak that adds some complexity, a little quick at the end; ready. ** −

Melini, Riserva Vigneti Granaio (11/90). Fragrant floral and fruit aroma; rich and sweet, well balanced, soft under light tannin, could use some length. ** −

Melini, Riserva Vigneti La Selvanella (4 times, 11/90). Floral and fruit aroma; rich fruit, open, nice texture, sense of sweetness, soft, a little dry at the end; ready. ** +

Monte Verdi, Riserva (11/90). Fragrant aroma; good fruit, some backbone, light tannin, short. ** −

Nozzole, Riserva (6/90). Open, simple fruit, supple; ready. * +

Paola Matta (Castello Vicchiomaggio), Riserva (11/90). Light herbal aroma; good fruit, light to moderate tannin, fruity, short. *

Podere Capaccia (4/90). Scented; soft, sweet, fruity. * +

Podere Capaccia, Riserva (11/90). Interesting flowers and fruit; nice fruit, good structure. ** + (***)

Podere Il Palazzino, Riserva (ex-barrel, 4/90). Lovely floral bouquet with components of ripe fruit and oak; rich mouthful of fruit, vanilla overlay, fairly long; will be a winner with more age. ***

Poggiarello, De Rham I Riservati #9 (4/89). Open, fruity, tasty; ready. * +

Poggio al Sole (twice, 4/90). Floral, fruity; soft, light and precocious; ready as it has been for at least a year. ** −

Poggio Bonelli (4/89). Dry, low fruit, firm.

Prunetto (4/90). Small-scale, a little deficient in fruit.

Riecine, Riserva (twice, 4/90). Openly fruity, raspberry and spice components; tasty, some tannin, soft center, attractive. ** −

Rocca delle Macìe, Riserva (3 times, 11/90). Fragrant, nutlike aroma; soft, open fruit, short; drink. * +

Rocca delle Macìe, Riserva di Fizzano (11/90). Open and precocious under light tannin, dry, short end; ready. *

Rocca di Castagnoli (4 times, 4/90). Open raspberry aroma, tobacco nuance; open and richly flavored, packed with flavor, could use more length. ** −

Rocca di Montegrossi, Riserva (E. Ricasoli-Firidolfi) (4/90). Floral, cherrylike aroma; soft, openly fruity, easy. **

Rodano (4/89). Open fruit nose and palate, soft and supple, fruity. * +

Rodano, Riserva (4/90). Overly tannic, some oxidation, the bottle?

Ruffino, Riserva Ducale (5/90). Earthy, mushroom aroma; open and soft; ready. ** −

Saccardi (9/88). Simple, easy, drinkable, light dry aftertaste.

San Felice, Riserva Il Grigio (3 times, 11/90). Open aroma of cherry fruit and vanilla, floral notes; soft, round, supple, precocious; ready. **

Tenuta Villa Rosa (4/89). Dry, some fruit, bitter.

Terrabianca, Riserva Vigna della Croce (*twice, 11/90*). Open floral, raspberry aroma, oak component; soft and open, good body and backbone, light tannin, short; room to improve. **(+)

Vecchie Terre di Montefili (*twice, 6/90*). Rich, toasty, dried fruit aroma; soft under light tannin; drink. *

Vecchie Terre di Montefili, Riserva Anfiteatro (*11/90, 4,182 bottles*). Ripe fruit, grapey, berrylike aroma; sweet impression, rich in flavor under light tannin, precocious; nearly ready. **(+)

Vignamaggio (*2/90*). Small-scale, dry, the bottle seems off.

Villa Antinori, Riserva (*11/90*). Fragrant aroma; light tannin, short. * +

Villa Cafaggio (*4/89*). Open fruit, soft and supple, berrylike. ** −

Villa Cafaggio, Riserva (*4 times, 11/90*). This wine showed some variation between bottles, all were at least very good, some even better. Light floral and fruity aroma; soft, relatively open, forward flavors, short. ** − *Bottle of 6/90:* Lovely nose; tasty, open and supple, a little short. * + *Bottle of 4/90:* Closed nose, cherry background; lots of structure; young and tight with evident class. **(* −)

Villa Calcinaia, Conti Capponi (*4/89*). Skunky; better in the mouth, strawberry fruit. * −

Villa Cerna (*twice, 4/89*). Nice fruit, open and fruity, soft. *

Villa Francesca (*4/89*). Mercaptans intrude, there is some fruit.

Villa Vignamaggio, Riserva (*11/90*). Dried fruit, chocolate; good body, tastes a little cooked.

1985 ****

The winter was extremely cold: in Firenze the temperature plunged to -26° Fahrenheit (-32° centigrade) in January, a new low. The April frost caused damage and killed some vines. This was also the winter that wreaked havoc on the olive trees. Large tracts of trees were decimated. The spring was damp and cool. Then the weather took a fortuitous turn. The very long summer was hot and very dry—in fact, there was a drought. The warm, sunny weather continued into the autumn and lasted beyond the end of the harvest. The harvest, around the middle of September, was early. The grapes were high in sugar and of exceptionally high quality. Only 1984 produced less wine in the decade. The year's output of 7.1 million gallons (268,612 hectoliters), equivalent to 2.98 million cases, was 85 percent of the normal annual production between 1980 and 1989.

Stefano Farkas of Villa Cafaggio said that in some ways it was a difficult vintage to produce. The grapes had too much of everything—color, sugar, and flavor. The *consorzio* reported that the color was very high, the average alcohol was 12.9 percent, the acidity medium-high, and the dry extract high. Their conclusion—these are wines for long aging. The *consorzio* gives it four out of four stars, the same as 1986! While we disagree with their assessment of 1986, we concur with them on 1985. This is a great vintage.

Of the nearly ten dozen (116) wines that we tasted from some seven dozen producers, 20, or just over 17 percent, were less than good; 46, or nearly 40 percent, were between good and not quite very good; and 35, or more than 30 percent, were very good or somewhat better; with the remainder being excellent or above. Clearly this is a first-rate vintage.

First we place the Fattoria Monsanto Riserva Il Poggio, and then the Castello di Volpaia Riserva, followed by Badia a Coltibuono Riserva, the Berardenga Riserva Vigneto Rancia from Fattoria di Felsina, and the *riserve* from Castellare, Castell'in Villa, Castello dei Rampolla, Fattoria di Montagliari, Fattoria Monsanto, Fontodi Vigna del Sorbo, Riecine, Ruffino Riserva Ducale, Savignola Paolina, Vecchie Terre di Montefili, and Villa Cafaggio, and the *normale* of Isole e Olena.

Antinori, Pèppoli (*3 times, 11/90*). Openly fruity aroma, light herbaceous backnote; although still tasty and enjoyable, it's starting to fade, best to drink up. * *Bottle of 12/88:* Fragrant berry-scented aroma, vague herbaceous backnote; rich flavor, good structure, well made; a little young; some firmness at the end. ** +

Antinori, Tenuta Marchese Riserva (*twice, 12/90*). Fruity aroma, herbal and oak components; fairly nice fruit on entry, soft, balanced; nearly ready. **

Badia a Coltibuono, Riserva (*7 times, 11/90*). Lovely, rich nose, of leather and fruit, flowers and cherries, vanilla overlay, and forest-like scents; richly concentrated, full of extract, a lot of structure; very young, should age very well indeed. **(*)

Bartali (*4/89*). Light nose; fairly nice fruit; small-scale. *

Berardenga, Fattoria di Felsina (*2/88*). Dark ruby; cherrylike aroma, some oak; rich fruit; on the young side, needs perhaps two years; good structure. **

Berardenga, Fattoria di Felsina, Riserva (*twice, 6/90*). Vanilla, oak and fruit define the aroma; rich fruit, good concentration, chewy, oak tannin evident, tannic aftertaste. **(+)

Berardenga, Fattoria di Felsina, Riserva Vigneto Rancia (*4 times, 6/90*). Half of this wine spent one year in new *barriques,* the other half spent a year in one-year-old *barrique.* Some oak along with nice rich fruit on the nose, cherry and berry fruit, vaguely recalls the woods; a lot of structure and concentration; young with its class quite evident. **(*)

Brolio (*twice, 12/88*). Warm nose; soft and easy, fruity, short. * +

Brolio, Riserva (*5 times, 11/90*). Fragrant aroma; lots of fruit, soft under light tannin, simple, open and attractive. *

Carobbio (*4/89*). Light-scented nose; fruity, soft, open and ready. *

Carpineto, Riserva (4/90). A little jammy; nice fruit, some sweetness, short, dull aftertaste. * −

Casa Francesco, Riserva (2/90). Simple, fruity, pleasant. *

Casa Vecchia (ex-vat, 4/87). Woodsy aroma; a bit light, some tannin, fairly nice flavor though a bit shallow. * −

Castelgreve, Castelli del Grevepesa, Riserva (3 times, 11/90). Cooked character to this wine; hot and dull, some fruit. *Bottle of 9/90:* Floral, cherry aroma; tasty, fruit seems a little dry, small-scale, somewhat bitter; showing age, it was fresher a year ago. * −

Castellare, Riserva (3 times, 4/90). Tight nose, some fruit evident; a lot of structure, with good backbone, complex, sweet impression, balanced; has class. **(*)

Castell'in Villa, Riserva (6/90). Flowers and berries; sweet, rich and concentrated, well balanced; young; class evident; fairly long. ***

Castello Banfi, Riserva (twice, 6/90). Reticent aroma, floral notes; flavorful, good structure, nice fruit, dry, short aftertaste. * + (** −)

Castello d'Albola, Riserva (5 times, 5/90). Light fruity aroma; good body, soft and tasty, ripe fruit flavor. *

Castello dei Rampolla (twice, 4/89). Nice fruit, good structure, soft and tasty. **

Castello dei Rampolla, Riserva (twice, 2/90). Big, rich and concentrated, herbaceous element, loads of character and quality; the best Rampolla Chianti Classico to date, still young but quality evident. ***

Castello della Paneretta, Riserva (twice, 6/90). Fragrant floral bouquet; soft entry, some alcohol intrudes, light to moderate tannin, nice fruit, short and dry. * *Bottle of 4/90:* Lactic-smelling, chocolate note; rather tannic, fruit seems deficient.

Castello di Ama, Vigneto Bellavista (10/89). Scented floral aroma, berrylike component; rich, round and flavorful, tannin toward the end. ** −

Castello di Cacchiano, Riserva Millennio (twice, 10/89, 1,500 bottles and 600 magnums). Floral scent; good backbone, a bit lean but attractive flavor. * + (** −)

Castello di Fagnano (Geografico) (twice, 2/88). Stinky, though there is a floral component; better in the mouth, slight off note intrudes, hangs at the end.

Castello di Fonterutoli (4/87). Fairly nice fruit, light tannin, simple. *

Castello di Fonterutoli, Riserva Ser Lapo (twice, 4/90). Minerallike component on the nose; dry, firm and tight; could use more character, drinkable. *

Castello di Gabbiano, Riserva (3 times, 5/90). A lot of variation, but each time we tasted it, between February 1990 and May 1990, each bottle was less impressive than the previous one. Overall, a little dry and lacking the richness and concentration of the vintage.

Castello di San Polo in Rosso (twice, 6/90). Flowers, fruit and mushrooms; a little dry, good fruit, somewhat dry finish. ** −

Castello di Uzzano, Riserva (4/89). Rather tight nose; full-flavored, good structure and backbone, young with a firm, hard finish. **

Castello di Verrazzano, Riserva Cinquecentenario (5 times, 11/90). Open, fragrant-scented bouquet, floral; good structure and body, some oak, nice fruit, tasty, moderate tannin, a tad short; should improve. *(*)

Castello di Volpaia, Riserva (5 times, 7/90). Fragrant floral scent, richly fruited aroma with woodsy, mushroom and leather components; soft, open and fruity upon entry, then some tannin, a tad dry at the end; but real class, without question the best Volpaia to date. ***(+)

Castello Vicchiomaggio, Riserva Petri (4/89). Vaguely rubber tire nose, nice oak overlay; flavor combines with berrylike fruit, some tannin. * +

Castello Vicchiomaggio, Riserva Prima Vigna (4/90). This wine spent one year in *barrique,* 20 percent each from new to four-year-old. Flowers, dried fruit and berries, some oak; soft, sweet, smooth texture, balanced, rich and tasty. **

Cecchi Luigi (9/87). Simple, fruity, agreeable. +

Cennatoio, Riserva (4/89). Fairly nice nose; some age, moderate fruit, light tannin. *

Convito (A.C.G.—Gaiole Coop. Agricola Cellars) (twice, 3/88). Simple, fruity, soft, easy and agreeable. *

Fattoria Concadoro, Riserva Cerasi (3 times, 6/90). Cherrylike aroma; soft, open and fruity; no real depth, but quite drinkable. *

Fattoria dei Pagliarese (twice, 6/90). Simple, open cherry aroma; fruity, light tannin, tasty, a little short and dry; was better in 1987. *

Fattoria dei Pagliarese, Riserva (5 times, 6/90). Nice nose; fairly rich, good structure, still some tannin, well balanced, tasty; good quality. ** +

Fattoria di Luiano, Riserva (2/90). Simple, nice fruit, some oak, ready. *

Fattoria di Montagliari, Riserva (Cappelli Giovanni) (twice, ex-cask, 11/90). Pretty floral nose; good structure, moderate tannin, loads of fruit; in need of age, all the components are there, should be a real keeper. **(*)

Fattoria di Petroio, Riserva (twice, 4/90). *The most recent bottle* had a light but fragrant aroma, was light, soft, open, ready and simple. * *A bottle tasted nearly three weeks earlier* had a floral, resin and vanilla aroma; was sweet and openly fruity, had a soft center and some tannin at the end. **

Fattoria di Vistarenni (twice, 4/89). Light nose; soft and fruity, agreeable, dry aftertaste. *

Fattoria La Loggia (4/88). Mineral aroma; good varietal character, some tannin.

Fattoria La Loggia, Riserva (4/90). Floral, fruity aroma; well balanced, open, forward flavors; ready. * +

Fattoria La Loggia, Riserva Terra dei Cavalieri (11/90, 7,200 bottles). Nice nose, fragrant; soft and open, nice flavor, short. ** −

Fattoria La Ripa, Riserva (11/90). Light, berry and floral scent; some fruit, but overall dry and firm, a little light in body, moderate tannin, some acid, rather dry and short; not a lot to it.

Fattoria Le Bocce, Riserva (3 times, 4/90). (Each of the three bottles, tasted between April 1989 and April 1990, was better than the last.) Fragrant floral scent, berry notes; open, soft and flavorful, well balanced. ** +

Fattoria Le Filigare, Riserva (4/90). Open berrylike aroma, vanilla component; firm, a little tight, good concentration, some sweetness. * + (**)

Fattoria Monsanto, Riserva (8 times, 8/90). There has been some bottle variation. Vanilla, floral aroma; lovely, rich under light tannin, a lot of flavor, packed with fruit, still a little young. *** *Bottle of 6/90:* Richly flavored with real concentration, some tannin, dried fruit, leathery. ** *Bottle of 5/90:* Fragrant-scented aroma, suggestions of flowers and berries; well balanced, good concentration, some tannin at the end; displays class. *** −

Fattoria Monsanto, Riserva Il Poggio (5 times, 11/90). Open, expansive aroma of ripe fruit, intense; full of extract and concentration, great structure; very young but class is written all over this wine. **** *Bottle of 4/90:* This just might be the best Il Poggio to date—although closed its richness, extract and concentration are quite evident, great structure, very long; real class here for sure. ***(*)

Fattoria Nittardi, Riserva (twice, 4/90). Openly fruited aroma and palate, ready though it could improve. * +

Fattoria Pile e Lamole, Lamole di Lamole (4/89). Floral perfume; nice fruit, has a sweetness to it, well balanced; ready, could improve. * +

Fattoria Pile e Lamole, Riserva Lamole di Lamole (4 times, 6/90). Lovely bouquet, rich, berries, vanilla and flowers; rich flavor, good body; still a little young. Some bottles have seemed better than others, although all were very good. The most recent was the best: **(+)

Fattoria Querciabella (twice, 9/87). Perfumed fragrance; fairly rich, ripe fruit flavor, soft. **

Fattoria Querciabella, Riserva (3 times, 5/90). Floral perfume; nice backbone, good fruit, soft center, light tannin at the end; ready. *

Fattoria San Fabiano Calcinaia, Cellole, Riserva (3 times, 4/90). All three were unimpressive. A little lactic, chocolate, dull.

Fattoria San Fabiano Calcinaia, Marchese di Gavignano (9/87). Spicy, fruity aroma, immediate appeal; lots of nice fruit, but has a harsh edge, some alcohol intrudes at the end. *

Fattoria San Giusto a Rentennano (10/87). Fairly rich nose; chewy, tannic, richly fruited, flavorful; young. *(*)

Fattoria San Giusto a Rentennano, Riserva (4/90). Vanilla overlay, ripe fruit aroma, light floral note; tight yet with evident fruit, good structure, moderate length. **(+)

Fattoria Valiano, Riserva (twice, 4/90). Dried fruit aroma; fairly tannic, some fruit. * −

Fattoria Vignale, Riserva (twice, 4/90). Tasted twice within four days with noticeable variation. *First bottle:* Light nose; fairly nice fruit, open and soft, ready now. * *Second bottle:* Light nose; a little tight, sweet impression; open and forward, seems ready, yet room to improve; well balanced, moderate length. ** +

Fattoria Viticcio, Riserva (3 times, 6/90). Floral, berry aroma; soft, open and ready, nice fruit. ** −

Fontodi (4 times, 2/88). Floral, fruity aroma; lots of fruit, some tannin, cherry notes, concentrated; will take some age. **

Fontodi, Riserva (4 times, 6/90). Floral perfume; good body, tasty, good structure; has character. **

Fontodi, Riserva Vigna del Sorbo (twice, 6/90, 4,986 bottles). Rich nose, packed with fruit; lots of extract, chocolate note, mouthfilling impression, good structure, long finish; young. **(*)

Gabbiano, Riserva (4/90). Not to be confused with Castello di Gabbiano which is made from estate-grown grapes. This wine is made from bought grapes. Floral, fruity aroma, cherry notes; soft and open. **

Il Campino di Mondiglia (ex-cask, 5/86). Medium dark purplish color; lovely bouquet of flowers and berries; lots of nice fruit, fairly rich, fresh, some tannin; should make a nice glass in time. ** +

Il Palaggio (4/89). Light nose; fairly nice fruit, soft center; drinks nicely now. *

Il Poggiolino (4/89). A bit tight, good body and flavor, moderate tannin. * +

Il Poggiolino, Riserva (4/90). Light nose; tight, dry, firm, evident fruit, short and dry. *

Isole e Olena (4/90). Lots of nice fruit on the nose; packed with flavor, elegant, a lot of structure, the tannins build; very young but very good. ***

Le Masse di San Leolino (twice, 4/89). Rich nose, good varietal character, fragrant and floral slant; sweet impression, balanced, good structure. ** +

Le Masse di San Leolino, Riserva (twice, 11/90). What has happened here? It appears that the oak component of seven months ago has become dominant, overpowering the fruit. * − *Bottle of 4/90:* Floral, berry, vanilla aroma; sweet impression, some oak, good backbone, tasty. ** +

Melini (4/87). Fruity aroma, a bit reticent; nice fruit, a bit simple. *

Melini, Riserva Laborel (3 times, 11/90). Tight nose, ungiving; lots of structure and flavor, rich and concentrated, tasty, oak adds a note of complexity, well balanced. **(+)

Melini, Riserva Vigneti La Selvanella (6 times, 6/90). Floral aroma; open and fruity on entry, moderate tannin, good body, attractive flavors. Some bottles were better than this, the most recent one: **

Montoro (ex-cask, 5/86). Rich and full but unsettled and difficult to assess. Why did we include it? It is instructive: tasting from cask or vat can be difficult. As a rule of thumb, you can't really judge a wine that hasn't undergone malolctic fermentation, or one that needs to be racked or has just been racked.

Paola Matta, Riserva (Castello Vicchiomaggio) (6/90). Soft, sweet, open and ready, some tannin t the end; best to wait another year. ** −

Podere di Stignano, Riserva San Vicenti (4/90). Oxidized!

Podere Il Palazzino (4/89, 10/89). Richly fruited aroma, oak overlay; rich and tasty, very well balanced; has some class. ** +

Podere Il Palazzino, Riserva (twice, 6/90, 6,115 bottles and 240 magnums). Nose displays nice fruit, hint of mushroom, vaguely floral; soft, a tad short. **

Poggio Bonelli, Riserva (twice, 4/90). A little overripe, light tannin, coarse.

Pomona (4/89). Lovely nose, some complexity; full-bodied, nice entry then tannin, dry somewhat bitter at the end.

Prunetto (4/89). Very dry, is there enough fruit?

Querciavalle (twice, 12/90). Showing a lot of age, drying out.

Querciavalle, Riserva (4/90). Light, floral aroma; still some tannin, openly fruity, forward. ** −

Riecine, Riserva (twice, 4/90). Lovely floral aroma, vanilla overlay; packed with fruit, moderate tannin, harmonious; classy; young. ***

Rignana (4/90). Dry tannin, some fruit; past its best.

Rocca delle Macìe, Riserva (4/89). Very nice fruit, dry and firm, dry finish. * +

Rocca delle Macìe, Riserva di Fizzano (6 times, 6/90, 60,835 bottles). Barnyardlike aroma, cherry fruit component; moderate tannin, fruity, good structure; still needs age. *(*)

Rocca di Castagnoli (4/90). Open raspberry aroma; sweet impression, rich flavor, light tannin; attractive. **

Rocca di Castagnoli, Riserva (4/90). Dry, nice fruit, suggestion of mold intrudes.

Rocca di Castagnoli, Riserva Poggio a'Frati (3 times, 4/90, 33,412 bottles). Two bottles had a noticeable smell and taste of mold. The mold character was more pronounced on one bottle than another, but it was noticeable on both, too bad the fruit and structure were there. *The third bottle:* Floral, fruity aroma, tobacco nuance; good structure, tannin to lose, sweetness of ripe fruit. This is the best bottle, ** +

Ruffino (3 times, 2/90). Floral, nutty aroma; a rich mouthful of flavor, round, light tannin; very nice now with room to improve. ** +

Ruffino, Riserva Ducale (11/90). Fragrant, floral-scented bouquet, berry notes; a nice mouthful of fruit, soft tannins, well balanced, sweet impression, open, long aftertaste; still with room to grow though attractive now. ***

San Felice (5/88). Fragrant, some volatile acidity evident in the background; nice entry then the fruit seems a little odd, could it be corked? *

San Felice, Poggio Rosso, Riserva (4 times, 6/90, 39,430 bottles). This wine spent three years in Yugoslavian oak casks plus some two to three months in *barrique*. Some variation was apparent between the bottles, but all were very good. *The most recent bottle:* Open fruit aroma; berry and cherry character on both the nose and palate, soft center, could use more length, nice concentration; young. **(+)

San Felice, Riserva Il Grigio (3 times, 4/90). This wine spent three years in Yugoslavian oak casks. Spicy, floral aroma; nice entry, then fruit seemed odd. * *Bottle of 2/90:* Floral perfume, rich and concentrated; sweet, rich, round and ripe, loads of structure, nice nose, complex; ready now with a lot to offer. ***

Savignola Paolina (ex-vat, 5/86). Rich, perfumed aroma; richly flavored, intense, ripe fruit flavor. ***

Selvoramole (ex-cask, 5/86). Richly fruited aroma, floral aspect; fairly full on the palate, cherry notes, some tannin, seems a little soft at this stage; shows promise. **

Serristori, Riserva Machiavelli, Vigna di Fontalle (4/90). Lovely scented bouquet, some oak; sweet impression, ripe fruit, balanced, some tannin; still a little young. ** +

Serristori, Riserva Villa Primavera (4/89). Fairly nice fruit, good structure. ** −

Tenuta di Lilliano, Riserva Eleanora Ruspoli Berlingier (4/90). Lovely scented bouquet; firm, tight, closed, sense of ripe fruit, short, dry aftertaste. *(* +)

Tenuta di Vignole, Riserva (twice, 4/90). Easy, simple, soft and ready, light tannin at the end builds up. *

Tenuta Montegiacchi, Riserva (Geografico) (twice, 10/90, 32,000 bottles). Dry, fruit seems to be fading. + *Bottle of 6/90:* Full-bodied, moderate tannin, flavorful, a little coarse, but does have fruit. *

Tenuta Villa Rosa, Riserva (twice, 4/90). A little tight and firm, mouth-filling, sweet, fairly firm, and tannic, quite nice indeed. ** +

Terrabianca, Riserva Vigna della Croce (3 times, 11/90). Slight but ripe berrylike aroma; rich, sweet, open and attractive, moderate tannin, a little short and a tad dry. ** −

Vecchie Terre di Montefili (ex-vat, 5/86). Good fruit, light tannin, should be most enjoyable. **

Vecchie Terre di Montefili, Riserva (ex-vat, 5/86). Rich fruit under moderate tannin; some style evident. ***

Vignamaggio (twice, 4/89). Floral, fruity, open aroma and palate, soft and tasty, balanced. ** −·

Vignamaggio, Riserva (*3 times, 4/90*). There was considerable variation between the three bottles, all tasted within two months of each other, and two tasted within two weeks. *The most recent, and best:* Light, fruity aroma, dry, moderate tannin, sense of fruit. *(+)

Vignamaggio, Riserva Castello di Monna Lisa (*twice, 6/90*). Open fruit on the nose and palate, raspberrylike, soft center, dry aftertaste. ** −

Villa Antinori, Riserva (*11/90*). This one is a blend of 80 percent sangiovese, 15 percent canaiolo, trebbiano, and malvasia, and 5 percent cabernet sauvignon and franc. Lovely, fragrant nose of fruit and flowers, light herbaceous note, vanilla component; soft, though still some tannin, sense of sweetness, lacks length; ready. ** −

Villa Cafaggio, Riserva (*4 times, 6/90*). Nose displays nice fruit in spite of being a little closed; richly concentrated, highly extracted, chocolate, cherry nuances; classy. ***

Villa Cerna, Riserva (*7 times, 11/90*). Berry and floral aroma; good body, flavorful, soft, open ripe flavors, some tannin at the end; more or less ready. **

Villa Francesca, Riserva (*twice, 4/90*). Flowers and leather; soft, open and balanced; ready. **

1 9 8 4   0 +

This was a difficult vintage. The very short spring was generally overcast, rainy, and cold. The growth of vegetation was very late; flowering was both late and irregular. The lack of sun, which continued throughout the summer, and the frequent rains through the summer and most of September hindered the ripening process. The heavy rains in early autumn created widespread rot and mildew on the vines. In general, picking took place between October 15 and 20 for sangiovese and October 20 and 30 for canaiolo and the white varieties. Producers who picked early, before the middle of October, got low sugars. Those who felt they could delay the harvest saw sugar levels rise. The best fruit was harvested in November. The crop of 6.6 million gallons (248,015 hectoliters), equivalent to 2.76 million cases, was down 22.4 percent from the decade's annual average. Quality was mixed. In general, the vintage was rather poor. Careful selection was in order; those who selected carefully made some fairly good wines, rarely of *riserva* quality.

The wines, according to the *consorzio*, have a medium-low color, an average of 12.4 percent alcohol, average acidity, and average dry extract. They are pleasant wines that lack flavor intensity. They rate it one star out of four.

Fabrizio Bianchi and Minuccio Cappelli didn't produce any Chianti Classico under their Monsanto and Montagliari labels. Villa Calcinaia described the vintage as poor. Paolo de Marchi said that though their harvest was reduced, it was necessary to make a careful selection. Castello di Vignamaggio considered it a medium vintage.

Though 1984 was generally a poor year, the best wines had a certain elegance. Those wines are as good as they'll ever be. Those that haven't faded would be best drunk up now. We've tasted only one since 1988, and that was showing age.

Badia a Coltibuono (*4/87*). Light nose, good fruit; flavorful, simple. *

Cappelli Giovanni, La Quercia (*5/86*). Fresh, quaffable and light, an easy natured wine. *

Castellare (*ex-cask, 5/85*). Dark color; cherries on aroma and malvasia character; acid a bit high, very fruity. **

Castello dei Rampolla (*5/88*). Surprising richness and structure, quite good. ** −

Castello di Cerreto (*ex-cask, 5/85*). Fairly full-bodied, has fruit; difficult to assess, but shows some potential. (*)

Castello di Querceto, Caratello (*10/87*). Small-scale, small fruit.

Castello di San Polo in Rosso (*ex-vat, 5/85*). A surprising amount of fruit, acid on the high side. *(*)

Castello di Verrazzano (*4/90*). Starting to dry out, still some fruit, shallow, very short.

Catignano (*ex-cask, 5/85*). Aromas of raspberries and spice; a bit light, acid on the high side, fruity. *

Fattoria di Vistarenni (*4 times, 4/87*). Drinkable, some fruit; not a lot of character. +

Fattoria Quercia al Poggio (*ex-vat, 5/85*). Pale color; light, fruity aroma, high acid, low fruit, thin.

Fattoria Querciabella (*4/87*). Perfumed aroma, vaguely of dried fruit; could use more character, but drinkable enough. *

Fontodi (*twice, 9/86*). Vaguely floral, some fruit as well on the nose; a bit light and shallow; drinkable. * −

Isole e Olena (*4/87, 6,000 bottles*). It began life as Cepparello, then Paolo de Marchi changed his mind; the result just might be the Chianti Classico of the vintage. Light oak adds a nice complex note to the nose and some texture; quite good indeed; still a little young. **

La Madonnina (F.lli Triacca) (*4/87*). Cooked, hot aroma and flavor, unbalanced.

Le Masse di San Leolino (*twice, 5/86*). Rich fruit aroma; has a surprising amount of fruit. *(* −)

Melini (*2/87*). Color starting to show age; flavor seems contrived, flat.

Montoro (*ex-cask, 5/86*). Floral perfume; light body, almost sweet, good fruit; for early drinking; simple. * +

Rocca delle Macìe (*9/86*). Some fruit, thin.

San Felice (9/87). Light fruit, light tannin, although a little shy in fruit not all that bad. * —

Savignola Paolina (*twice, ex-cask, 5/86, 4,000 bottles*). Fresh and fruity, cherries and berries; simple, pleasant. *

Tenuta Villa Rosa (4/87). A little deficient in fruit, but does have flavor. * —

Vecchie Terre di Montefili (*ex-vat, 5/86*). Vaguely floral aroma, some fruit as well; light body, fruity, a little short; agreeable. *

Villa Cafaggio (*twice, ex-vat, 5/86*). Pretty nose; soft, light body, balanced, spicy, well made; one of the year's best Chianti Classico. **

1983 **** —

This vintage was characterized by a drought between June and August. In July temperatures soared to over 100° Fahrenheit (38° centigrade), causing some uneven ripening. September rains brought welcome relief. The best grapes were harvested toward the end of October. The crop of nearly 10 million gallons (378,469 hectoliters), equivalent to 4.2 million cases, was 18 percent above the 1980s annual average, but below the 10.2 million gallons (387,684 hectoliters) produced the year before. It was the third largest crop between 1967 and 1989.

According to the *consorzio*, the wines have medium-high color, 12.7 percent alcohol, average acidity, medium-high dry extract, and will have an average to long capacity to age. The *consorzio* gives it four out of four stars.

Niederbacher rates the year three stars. Paolo de Marchi of Isole e Olena said some of their grapes were burnt in the intense heat, giving the resulting wines a slightly raisiny flavor. He describes them, overall, as wines of good color, low acidity, high alcohol, and soft tannins—round wines that will be ready early. Ruffino noted that the wines are very rich and high in alcohol. Villa Cafaggio, Castello di Vignamaggio, Castello di Gabbiano, Castello di Querceto, Fattoria dei Pagliarese, Campomaggio, Castello di Vicchiomaggio, Castellare, Castello di Ama, Catignano, and Minuccio Cappelli of Giovanni Cappelli all rate the vintage as excellent. De Marchi puts it after 1982, but ahead of 1981. Villa Calcinaia, too, puts it on the second level. Castell'in Villa said it was not one of their favorite vintages.

We tasted nearly three dozen Chianti Classicos from the vintage in April and May 1985, and were very impressed. And, based on those wines, our opinions of which have since been corroborated with further tastings, we would rate it the finest vintage since 1971, up to that time. We originally thought that the '83s might not age as well as the bigger '82s. This assessment now appears in doubt; they might, in fact, age better. We still agree with our original assessment that their elegance and style more than compensate for any lack of endurance or strength, and they will give more pleasure in their time. Many are ready, or nearly so. The best will continue to improve.

Of the 92 Chianti Classicos we tasted from 75 producers, more than 27 percent were less than good, nearly 30 percent were good or somewhat better, and nearly 43 percent were very good or better. The star was the potentially outstanding Fattoria Monsanto Riserva Il Poggio, with two wines almost as good—Raffaele Rossetti's Capannelle and the Castello di Volpaia Riserva—with the Badia a Coltibuono *normale* and Riserva, and the *riserve* of Castello di San Polo in Rosso, Fattoria Monsanto, Fontodi, Isole e Olena, Poggio al Sole, Villa Cafaggio, and the Ruffino Riserva Ducale gold label, along with the Villa Cafaggio *normale,* Il Campino di Mondiglia *normale* (actually a *riserva,* though not labeled as such), and the Le Masse di San Leolino Riserva all being excellent or potentially so.

Antinori, Riserva (12/88). Fragrant scent; sweet, almost lush with open fruit flavors; very ready; most attractive. **

Badia a Coltibuono (5/85). Fresh berrylike aroma; moderate tannin, loads of flavor; young but quality is evident. **(*)

Badia a Coltibuono, Riserva (*4 times, 11/90*). Floral and berry aroma; a rich mouthful of fruit, well structured, sweet impression, a lot of extract, and a lot of flavor, long; a young wine in need of age. **(*)

Berardenga, Fattoria di Felsina (9/86). Lovely nose, touch of mint and spice; full of flavor and fruit, smooth, balanced, tasty. **

Berardenga, Fattoria di Felsina, Riserva (*twice, 4/90*). Lovely perfumed, scented bouquet, spicelike component; rich flavors, well balanced, good structure, sweet; ready with room to improve further; a tad short. **(+)

Berardenga, Fattoria di Felsina, Riserva Vigneto di Rancia (*twice, 4/88*). Deep, rich aroma; full-bodied and harmonious, richly fruited with a background of oak; displays class and style. ** +

Brolio, Riserva (12/88). Open floral and fruit aroma, vaguely of nuts and cherries; good body and structure, lots of flavor, attractive, open, the finish is a little dry and firm. *

Brolio, Riserva del Barone (5/90). Lovely nose, albeit a little closed; has a sweetness to it, well balanced and tasty, a tad dry and bitter. **

Capannelle di Raffaele Rossetti (*ex-vat, 5/85*). Big fruity aroma rises out of the glass; rich in flavor, sweet; style already evident; long finish. ***(+)

Cappelli Giovanni, La Quercia (5/85). Light, fruity aroma; some tannin, cherrylike fruit, flavorful; simple. *

Casa Vecchia, Riserva (*twice, ex-cask, 4/87*). [This estate is owned by Francesco Giuntini, proprietor of Fattoria Selvapiana.] Aroma suggestive of the woods; fruity, but lacks character on the palate; no real definition. * —

Castellare (*ex-vat, 5/85*). Simple and fruity, easy, soft, quaffable. *

Castello Banfi, Riserva Il Caggio (*6/90*). Chocolate, cherry aroma; good body, moderate tannin, tasty, open fruit flavors; could improve, ready now. **

Castello d'Albola, Riserva (*11/88*). Light, fragrant, floral aroma, cherrylike note, vaguely pruney; good body; rather coarse but drinkable; hot finish. * –

Castello di Cerreto, Riserva (*ex-cask, 5/85*). Rich aroma; full-bodied, loads of flavor, somewhat astringent; shows promise. **(+)

Castello di Fonterutoli (*10/86*). Fresh, delicate, almost floral scent; light tannin, soft and fruity. easy and simple. *

Castello di Meleto (*5/85*). Aroma lacks freshness; some tannin, shy of fruit; drinkable.

Castello di Montegrossi (*10/87*). Aroma is fairly rich and fruity; soft under light tannin, tasty, easy; ready. * +

Castello di Monterinaldi (*5/85*). Fruity but dull, overly drying at end.

Castello di Querceto (*5/86*). Fresh, fruity, raspberry aroma; ready, will last, could even improve a bit. **(+)

Castello di Querceto, Caratello (*10/86*). Fresh, fruity, grapey and simple. *

Castello di Radda (*5/85*). Simple, fruity, dull, astringent.

Castello di San Donato in Perano (*5/85*). Odd nose; odd flavor, taste recalls filter paper.

Castello di San Polo in Rosso (*twice, 4/88*). Fresh, fruity aroma; open flavor, quite tasty and ready as well. * Bottle of 4/87: Lovely perfumed aroma; has a softness and elegance. ** +

Castello di San Polo in Rosso, Riserva (*ex-cask, 5/85*). Aroma and flavor of sweet ripe fruit, well balanced; already displays style. **(*)

Castello di Uzzano, Riserva (*4/89*). Fragrant nose, dried fruit component; rather dry and tannic. *

Castello di Verrazzano (*10/86*). Fruity, floral aroma; fairly nice fruit, lively, easy and simple. *

Castello di Verrazzano, Riserva (*9/90*). Open, fragrant scent; soft and smooth, fruity; very ready. **

Castello di Volpaia (*twice, 10/87*). Good flavor and weight, nice fruit, well balanced, moderate tannin. **

Castello di Volpaia, Riserva (*twice, 8/90*). Fragrant-scented bouquet; a rich mouthful of flavor, still a little tannin to shed, but a lovely glass now, slight harshness mars the finish, but this wine has real class. ***(+)

Castello Vicchiomaggio (*ex-cask, 5/85*). Raspberries on aroma; a lot of flavor, moderate tannin; young. *(+)

Catignano (*ex-cask, 5/85*). Fragrant and fruity; light and quaffable; quite agreeable. **

Cispiano (*10/87*). Tar up front, fruit seems a little light but drinkable enough. *

Cispiano, Riserva della Serena black label (*10/87*). Floral, fruity aroma; surprisingly full on initial entry, then it seems to lighten up as it goes back.

Contessa di Radda, Riserva (Chianti Geografico) (*twice, 2/88*). Toasty aroma, vaguely suggestive of a sparkling wine(!); some tannin and fruit; lacks definition, kind of diffuse but drinkable.

Conti Serristori, Machiavelli (*10/86*). Perfumed floral bouquet, berrylike note; perhaps a tad overripe, rich, concentrated flavors, some tannin. * +

Convito, Riserva (Coop. Agricola Cellars) (*10/87*). Cooked, hot nose; unbalanced, overly drying.

Fattoria Concadoro, Riserva Cerasi (*4/89*). Oak and fruit aroma; soft, old fruit taste, still it does have interest. *

Fattoria dei Pagliarese (*twice, 5/85*). Fresh aroma with berrylike fruit; some charm, light, fruity; simple and easy. **

Fattoria dell'Aiola, Riserva (*4/89*). Fragrant-scented bouquet; sweet, ripe cherrylike fruit, balanced. **

Fattoria di Luiano (*9/86*). Simple fruity aroma; some fruit on initial entry, then shallow.

Fattoria di Montagliari, Riserva (*11/90*). Complex bouquet reveals floral and berry scents as well as a suggestion of underbrush; rich, open fruit, warm, generous, a little firm at the end. *(*)

Fattoria di Petroio, Riserva (*4/89*). Overly dry, low fruit, hard and tannic.

Fattoria di Selvole (*5/85*). Fruity and quaffable, but rather ordinary, a vague off note at the end.

Fattoria di Vistarenni (*5/86*). Medium ruby; small nose; some fruit, light tannin, some fruit up front, thins out toward the back; drinkable enough if not much else. * –

Fattoria La Loggia (*4/87*). Rubber tire from the nose through the palate, also airplane glue, who said it came only in tubes!

Fattoria La Ripa (*5/85*). Aroma of mushrooms and fruit; light tannin, fruity, simple, agreeable. *

Fattoria Monsanto, Riserva (*twice, ex-vat, 4/88*). Perfumed floral aroma, berrylike fruit; flavorful and rich, light tannin, a lovely mouthful of flavor. ** + (***)

Fattoria Monsanto, Riserva Il Poggio (*8 times, 11/90, 47,660 bottles*). Blueberry and floral aroma; tight but rich fruit and concentration evident; this needs age but the quality is evident. ***(+) Bottle and ex-vat, 4/90: Openly floral bouquet, suggestive of blueberries, cassis, chocolate and cherries; a stylish, well-balanced and elegant wine with real class, extract and weight. Of the two samples we tasted together, from two different bottlings, although one was more forward than the other, both were impressive, the best Il Poggio since 1977, and even better in our view than the richer and weightier '82. We also tasted it at the same time from cask: it was even more open and softer, with great richness, extract and sweetness. *From bottle: ***(+), from cask: **** –*

Fattoria Quercia al Poggio (*ex-vat, 5/85*). Fruity aroma with some tar; still rough and unready but quite a lot of fruit. **(+)

Fattoria Querciabella, Riserva (*4/87*). Perfumed floral aroma; some style and elegance; light to moderate tannin, good richness of flavor. **(+)

Fattoria San Giusto a Rentennano (*10/87*). Tobacco, floral aroma; fairly nice fruit under moderate tannin, then kind of dull. +

Fattoria San Giusto a Rentennano, Riserva (*10/87*). Tobacco and fruit aroma; richly flavored, light to moderate tannin, flavorful; still a little young. *(+)

Fattoria Valiano (*4/85*). Fresh berrylike aroma; light and fruity, acid a bit high, but drinkable enough. *

Fattoria Vignale, Riserva (*4/89*). Starting to dry out, still some flavor.

Fattoria Viticcio (*6/85*). Almost *nouveau*-like in its simplicity and berrylike character, a spritz throws the balance off.

Fattoria Viticcio, Riserva (*2/90*). Floral then dried fruit aroma; dry and firm, lacks richness and concentration; shows age prematurely. * –

Fontodi (*3 times, 1/89*). Floral and nutty aroma, fragrant; full-bodied, fruit is drying a bit, good but fading, not surprising considering that it is a *normale.* The best bottle, from 5/85:* Oak and raspberries on nose; fruity, soft-centered, some tannin, well knit; can be enjoyed today though rather firm on finish. **(*)

Fontodi, Riserva (*4 times, 2/90*). Floral and nutty aroma, oak overlay; rich and tasty, sweet impression, a lot of structure. ***

Fossi, Riserva (*9/89*). Floral, dried fruit aroma; rich and tasty, a bit firm, good body. *

Il Campino di Mondiglia (*3 times, 7/90, 1,000 bottles*). Floral bouquet, spicy nuance; soft, round, smooth, harmonious, rich and warm, fairly long finish. *** –

Il Poggiolino, Riserva (*4/90*). Dried fruit and leather; seems older than seven years; soft, still some tannin; quite ready, best to drink. *

Isole e Olena (*twice, 5/86*). Reticent aroma; richly flavored, balanced, some backbone and structure, fairly long finish. ** +

Isole e Olena, Riserva (*twice, 5/88*). Cherrylike aroma; balanced and elegant, a lot of structure and style. ***

Le Grifiere, Riserva (*4/90*). Oxidized.

Le Masse di San Leolino, Riserva (*twice, 5/86*). Medium dark ruby; floral, mineral aroma; some style; good quality and structure, rich, almost lush. **(* –)

Montemaggio (*4/85*). Fruit and almonds up front; some tannin, dull.

Nozzole, Riserva Vigneto La Forra (*9/90, 34,660 bottles*). This wine spent eight months in *barrique*. Oak up front on the nose followed by fruit; moderate tannin, sweet sense of oak in the mouth, ripe fruit, a little dry; needs another year or two to really soften; a little short. *(*)

Podere Campacci (*ex-cask, 5/85*). Mushrooms on aroma; light and simple. *

Podere Il Palazzino, Riserva (*twice, 10/87*). Floral, berry aroma, light oak backnote; flavorful and rich, full-bodied, could use more length. **

Poggiarello (*4/89*). Floral scent; a bit dry, has fruit, fairly nice. * +

Poggio al Sole (*3 times, 7/87*). Nicely fruited aroma; some acid, good body, light tannin, soft center. **

Poggio al Sole, Riserva (*twice, 4/90, 11,987 bottles*). Lovely floral, berry and vanilla aroma; rich, sweet, concentrated; real character and class. ***

Rocca delle Macìe, Riserva (*12/88*). Nuts and flowers; tasty, soft and balanced. **

Ruffino, Aziano (*6/86*). Slight aroma, vaguely floral; light but balanced, with fruit, and softness; for current consumption; agreeable. *

Ruffino, Riserva Ducale gold label (*3 times, 11/90*). Lovely floral bouquet, suggestions of a forest; rich, warm and ripe, has a sweetness to the fruit; already lovely to drink, some tannin builds at the end, indicates it needs further age, still it is attractive. **(*)

Savignola Paolina (*5 times, 5/88*). Earthy, woodsy, floral aroma; tasty and firm, medium body, sweet impression, could use more length. ** +

Selvoramole (*ex-vat, 5/86*). [To be bottled in June.] Medium red; floral, cherry aroma; soft and fruity, balanced, a nice glass for now, light tannin; some style and length. **

Straccali, Riserva (*4/89*). Scented nose; soft, open and flavorful. ** –

Tenuta di Lilliano, Riserva (*4/90*). Dried fruit, vaguely floral aroma; some tannin, rather short, and a little dry. *

Tenuta Montegiacchi, Riserva (*Chianti Geografico*) (*2/88*). Hot, cooked, overripe aroma, pruney; at best drinkable, real dullsville.

Tenuta Villa Rosa, Riserva (*twice, 4/90*). The bottle of April 1989 was just not comparable to the bottle we tasted a year later: Open berrylike aroma; openly fruity, sweet, rich and ripe, tasty, well balanced, and very good as well. ** +

Terrabianca, Riserva Vigna della Croce (*3 times, 11/90*). Aroma and palate display an oak component, a little dry though still with nice flavor, rather short and dry; best to drink up; going by the last time we tasted it, this seems to be aging quickly. * + *Bottle of 4/90:*

Ripe, berrylike aroma, vanilla, cherry and floral nuances, rich, plump and lush, good backbone, if only it had more length, a little short in finish and a tad dry. ** +

Vecchie Terre di Montefili (*4 times, 10/86*). The best bottle was tasted in May 1986, the worst in October of the same year. Light, fruity, somewhat floral aroma; nice flavor, lively acidity, a touch of tannin at the end. ** −

Vignamaggio, Riserva (*4 times, 4/90*). From the best bottle, tasted in April 1989, each bottle has been less good. Spice and dried fruit aroma, some flowers; fruit seems a little dry; could it be fading and losing fruit? We think so; dry and very short. +

Vignavecchia (*5/85*). Light and fruity; unbalanced, a bit shallow, dull finish.

Villa Banfi, Riserva (*5/89*). Spice and fruit; open, soft center, light tannin; disappointing.

Villa Cafaggio (*4 times, 11/90*). Fairly deep color; light, floral note on a berryish aroma; rich in flavor, still some tannin, smooth texture, long finish; room to improve. *** *Bottle of 6/88:* Oak overlay, vanilla and floral notes, spicy; rich, good structure, tasty and open; could even improve but lovely now. ** + (***)

Villa Cafaggio, Riserva (*5 times, 1/89*). Fragrant perfume, some delicacy; rich and flavorful, good backbone, flavors fill the mouth, has a sweetness about it; very ready although it could improve. ***

Villa Cerna (*12/88*). Floral and dried berry aroma; dry and tight, tannic and young. *

Villa Cerna, Riserva (*11/90*). Dried fruit and floral aroma; could use more fruit, a little short and dry at the end. *

Villa d'Arceno (*twice, 6/90*). Varnishlike aroma; has fruit but drying out. *Bottle of 5/86:* Light, fresh berrylike aroma; a lot of nice fruit, balanced, simple; for current consumption, so why did we save a bottle for four years? To taste for this revision of our book.

1 9 8 2 * * *

Reports pointed out that this was a year destined for a small harvest. The hail that fell in the spring before the flowering curtailed the possible crop size. The hail that struck again in early September reduced the output still further. Still, it was the largest crop of the decade. The 10.2 million gallons (387,684 hectoliters) of wine, equivalent to 4.3 million cases, were 21 percent above the 1980s annual average of 8.4 million gallons (319,544 hectoliters), and the second largest crop between the advent of DOC in 1967 and 1989; only 1979 produced more wine.

The *consorzio* reports that the wines have average color, 12.8 percent alcohol, relatively low acidity, average dry extract, and will age normally. It and Niederbacher rate the vintage three stars out of four.

Paolo de Marchi describes the '82s as hard and tannic, Chianti Classicos to age, and, for them at least, better than the '83s. Minuccio Cappelli, Castello di Querceto, Pagliarese, Catignano, Castello di Ama, Castellare, Vignamaggio, and Campomaggio rate the wines very highly. Castell'in Villa and Villa Calcinaia considered the wines very good.

After tasting nearly four dozen '82s in April and May 1985, we felt that they would be long-lived wines, outlasting the '83s, for example. But, to our surprise, as well as that of many others, they seem to be maturing somewhat faster than the more elegant and stylish '83s. The '82s are big wines, not elegant ones. Most are fully ready now, a few will improve.

Of the approximately seven dozen wines that we tasted, 9 were excellent and 37 very good, 27 good, and only 11 were average or less. Our favorite was Fattoria Monsanto's Riserva Il Poggio, followed by Savignola Paolina Riserva, then Badia a Coltibuono Riserva, Ruffino Riserva Ducale gold label, and Villa Cafaggio Riserva.

Antinori, Tenuta Marchese Riserva (*twice, 12/89*). Cabernet dominates, some oak as well; tannin evident, seems to have enough fruit. * +

Badia a Coltibuono (*5/85*). A lot of berrylike fruit up front, quite rich, a peppery character and notes of spice; room for improvement. ** +

Badia a Coltibuono, Riserva (*6 times, 11/90*). Nice nose; good fruit, some firmness; still a little young; somehow this is much beneath the quality of the previous bottle tasted seven months ago, the bottle perhaps? *(+) *Bottle of 4/90:* Floral, leather aroma, vaguely berries; real sweetness to the fruit, a lot of structure, quite rich, open and flavorful; attractive now, still room to improve; finish is a little short and dry. ** + (*** −)

Badia a Coltibuono, Riserva Old Vines (*ex-cask, 5/85*). Very deep color; intense floral aroma with a berrylike aspect; enormous weight and extact, heaps of tannin; sure to make a very fine bottle in time. ***(+)

Berardenga, Fattoria di Felsina (*5/85*). Lovely aroma with notes of raspberries and flowers; acid a bit high, lively, fruity, tart finish. *

Brolio, Riserva (*5/90*). Light, fragrant aroma; soft, open and fruity, some tannin but enjoyable now, rather short. * +

Brolio, Riserva del Barone (*twice, 12/88*). Warm nose, vaguely suggestive of chestnuts and dried fruit; some firmness, dry, on the young side, attractive flavors, dry finish; overall quite nice. **

Capannelle di Raffaele Rossetti, Vecchio (*3 times, 7/89*). Floral-scented bouquet; good body, some firmness, the fruit has a sweetness to it, good structure, tasty, fairly long finish. ** +

Cappelli Giovanni, La Quercia (*5/85*). Aroma of flowers and cherries; sweet and fruity; simple, quaffable. *

Casavecchia, Riserva (*ex-vat, 4/87*). Woodsy aroma; kind of dull and a tad shallow, bitter aftertaste.

Castellare (3 times, 5/85, 48,336 bottles). Ex-vat, 5/85: Fresh, fruity, simple, easy. * Bottle of 4/85: Nice aroma with floral notes; still a bit closed, well balanced, light tannin, tasty; nice now. ** +

Castell'in Villa (twice, 5/85). Very nice berryish aroma; some tannin, good body, flavorful; too serious for a quaffing wine. * +

Castell'in Villa, Riserva (twice, 4/89). Fragrant perfume; rich, balanced and tasty, sweet impression, then tannin which builds at the end. **(+)

Castello dei Rampolla (5/85). Light, fruity aroma, with cabernet character evident; well balanced; needs another year. *(+)

Castello di Ama (3 times, 10/86, 158,280 bottles). Fresh berrylike aroma; good body and structure, nice fruit; simple and agreeable. * +

Castello di Ama, Riserva Vigneto Bellavista (10/86). A tad overripe but nice berrylike fruit, sweet impression, some firmness, rich. **

Castello di Cerreto (5/85). Floral, fruity aroma, with raspberry notes; light tannin; could soften but nice now. ** −

Castello di Fonterutoli (4 times, 4/87). Three of the four bottles were oxidized, what is going on here? *The fourth bottle:* Floral, fruity aroma; ripe fruit, some tannin, lacks length, perhaps a tad overripe. *

Castello di Gabbiano, Riserva (twice, 4/90). The 65 to 70 percent sangiovese were aged in *barrique,* the rest of the grapes were aged in Yugoslavian oak casks. Flowers, vanilla, berries and cherries define the nose; fruit is dry and tired but there is still some flavor. A bottle tasted three months earlier was rather similar, with the taste of old fruit. * +

Castello di Montegrossi (10/87). Light, fruity aroma; moderate tannin, good weight, lacks length. *

Castello di Monterinaldi (5/85). Insufficient fruit, dull, flat.

Castello di Querceto (5/85). This wine spent six months in barrique. Oak up front with a cherrylike backnote; fruity flavor with an oaky component, has style and structure, finish is all oak; nice now but should improve. ** +

Castello di San Polo in Rosso (5/85). Soft, fruity, quaffable, berrylike, a touch of bitterness at the end. * +

Castello di San Polo in Rosso, Riserva (4 times, 4/89). This wine seemed to be at its best between April 1985 and April 1988. Like a number of other '82s, the wine seems to be aging somewhat more quickly than we expected. Lovely complex nose, licorice note; good structure, balanced, firm and flavorful, dry finish. ** −

Castello di Volpaia (3 times, 10/86). [This wine was made from a blend of 92 to 93 percent sangiovese and 7 to 8 percent canaiolo.] Fresh cherrylike aroma; rich in body, full of flavor. **

Castello di Volpaia, Riserva (3 times, 8/90). Rich and intense bouquet, recalls blueberries and flowers; lovely fruit, open, soft entry; very ready; could use more length; displays class and style. ** +

Catignano (5/85). Flowers and berries on nose; fruity, raspberrylike flavor, light and easy. **

Contessa Radda (Chianti Geografico), Riserva (10/86). Straightforward fruity aroma, a tad overripe; full-bodied, fruity, simple, short. * −

Fattoria Campomaggio (5/85). Notes of tobacco and cherries on aroma; light and fruity, some tannin; in an easy style, perhaps too much so. * −

Fattoria dei Pagliarese (twice, 5/85). Fresh aroma recalls raspberries; still a bit closed, flavorful, sweet fruit, tannic finish. **

Fattoria dei Pagliarese, Riserva (4/87). A bit overripe, full-bodied, a big style, tannic; needs some age. *(*)

Fattoria di Montagliari, Riserva (Cappelli Giovanni) (7 times, 11/90). Light nose but with lovely fruit and a floral note; well balanced and gentle, soft under light tannin, sense of sweetness, fairly long finish though a tad dry; more to give. **(+) *Bottles of 4/90:* In April 1990 we tasted this wine from five different bottles, all of which were surprisingly oxidized. Because Cappelli is one of the most reliable producers of Chianti Classico we were, to say the least, very surprised. Perhaps there was a bad lot. ? Ex-cask, 5/85: Intense aroma of cherries and other fruit; surprisingly full-bodied and rich, rough edges; very young. **(*)

Fattoria di Vistarenni (4/85). A small-scale wine with a touch of astringency.

Fattoria di Vistarenni, Podere Bertinga (5/86). Rich aroma recalls cassis with a touch of licorice; moderate tannin, nice fruit on entry, a bit shy in flavor on the midpalate; could improve, say two years, but drinkable now; short tannic aftertaste. *(+)

Fattoria La Loggia (4/85). Light aroma; astringent, some fruit, unbalanced. * −

Fattoria La Loggia, Riserva (4/87). Airplane glue on the nose (!) as well as a rubber tire aroma and flavor.

Fattoria Le Filigare, Del Conte (3 times, 11/88). Each bottle was less than the previous one. All three times we tasted it—1986, 1987, and 1988—were in November. It was, especially in 1986, quite good. *The most recent bottle:* Kind of tired, still has fruit, drinkable.

Fattoria Monsanto, Riserva (5/88). Berrylike aroma is somewhat reticent(!); good structure, on the young side with nice fruit concentration. **(+)

Fattoria Monsanto, Riserva Il Poggio (9 times, 5/90, 47,320 bottles). Richly concentrated aroma, suggestive of damp leaves, cherries and berries; full-flavored, moderate tannin, chewy, young, great extract and weight; loads of potential for the future. ***(+)

Fattoria Quercia al Poggio (ex-vat, 5/85). Fruity aroma; quite tannic but seems to have sufficient fruit. *(?)

Fattoria Querciabella (4/87). Floral perfume, slight varnish note; rich and flavorful, some tannin, good structure. **

Fattoria Querciabella, Riserva (8/87). Reticent aroma; good body, closed in, but rich fruit evident, some firmness; needs, perhaps, two years. *(*)

Fattoria Viticcio (6/85). Light, floral aroma; fruity, agreeable, quaffable and easy. * +

Fontodi (5/85). Richer and more intense aroma than the '83; full-bodied and full-flavored, still has tannin to shed. **(+)

Fontodi, Riserva (4 times, 10/89, 22,850 bottles). This wine was made from a blend of 90 percent sangiovese, 5 percent canaiolo, and 5 percent trebbiano and malvasia; 10 percent of it spent nine months in *barrique*. Fragrant floral aroma, light spicy character; soft, fruity; very ready. ** +

Fossi, Riserva (twice, 2/90). Older than its years, low fruit. *A bottle tasted six months earlier*: It had more interest; floral aroma; firm and tasty. *

Isole e Olena, Riserva (5/85). Lovely fragrant aroma with a touch of oak; tannic, supple center, lots of character and flavor; needs perhaps three more years. **(* +)

La Madonnina, Riserva (4/87). Fruity, unbalanced with tannin, fruit seems insufficient. (?*)

Le Masse di San Leolino (twice, 5/86). Floral, berry aroma; lush fruit flavors, well balanced, soft center, light tannin; ready; fairly long finish. ** +

Le Masse di San Leolino, Riserva (3 times, 5/86). Floral note, berrylike fruit; moderate tannin, nice fruit, suggestive of raspberries; some style; should improve though nice now. ** +

Melini, Riserva Vigneti Granaio (4/87). Floral, nutty aroma; some oxidation intrudes; drying out.

Melini, Riserva Vigneti La Selvanella (twice, 4/87). Floral, mushroom aroma; fairly full-bodied, nice fruit, light to moderate tannin. *(*)

Monte Vertine (twice, 11/85). A big wine, full of flavor, some tannin, nice texture; room to improve; classy. *** *Bottle of 5/85*: Delicate, floral aroma, light tannin, fruity, well balanced, soft, very drinkable, a trifle short. **

Montemaggio (4/85). Aroma suggestive of amaretto; not a lot of fruit; astringent.

Nozzole, Riserva (3/88). Fragrant floral, cassislike aroma; good structure, concentrated; the best Nozzole since the '64. ** +

Nozzole, Riserva Vigneto La Forra (3 times, 6/90). This one spent eight months in *barrique*, 50 percent were new, they produced 1,000 cases. There was variation among the three bottles. *The most recent, and best*: Floral, berry aroma, oak overlay; soft, openly fruity, good concentration, sweet impression. ** +

Piccini, Riserva (4/89). Hot, lacks freshness, dry.

Podere Campacci (ex-cask, 5/85). Small, vaguely floral aroma; light in body, fruit; simple. * +

Podere Il Palazzino, Riserva (ex-cask, 5/85). Nice fruit on nose and a hint of toffee; tannic entry, has fruity, lacking in structure.

Poggio al Sole (twice, 5/85, 34,559 bottles). Delicate, floral aroma; well balanced, light tannin, lively, some elegance and length; ready. ** +

Poggio al Sole, Riserva (7/87). Lovely floral-scented bouquet; nice fruit, fairly full, light tannin; nice now. **

Riecine (4/90). Some oxidation, still has flavor interest, surprising for an eight-year-old non-*riserva*. *

Rocca delle Macìe, Riserva (5/90). Open, perfumed aroma, vanilla notes; some tannin, soft, good fruit; best to drink up, was better in 1988. *

Rocca delle Macìe, Riserva di Fizzano (9 times, 9/90, 61,093 bottles). This wine was at its best in 1987 and 1988 when we rated it two stars plus out of four. Oak vanilla and floral aroma; drying out, still has some fruit and flavor, overly dry finish. * −

Rocca di Castagnoli, Riserva (4/90). Openly fruity aroma, raspberrylike; sweet impression, a lot of structure, classy, very ready, a tad sweet. ** +

Ruffino, Riserva Ducale gold label (3 times, 5/90). This one was made from a blend of 80 percent sangiovese, 10 percent canaiolo, and 10 percent white grapes; it spent three years in 2,640-gallon (100-hectoliter) oak casks; 5 to 8 percent must was added for the *governo*. Nose is a little light, even diffuse; good body, still tight, dry, the fruit is there. *(*) *Bottle of 11/89*: Suggestions of flowers and cherries; rich and concentrated, a wine of class, very well balanced; still young, but approachable. ** + (***)

San Felice (4/85). Floral aroma; light tannin, fruity, a bit simple, a good quaffing wine. *

San Felice, Riserva Poggio Rosso (twice, 4/90, 29,850 bottles). Woodsy, spice and leather aroma, oak component; soft, open, sweet impression, still some tannin but ready now, although a tad short there is some class. **

Savignola Paolina (twice, 7/86). Lovely floral bouquet; light tannin, lots of fruit, soft and ready, fairly long. ** +

Savignola Paolina, Riserva (twice, 1/89). Corked. *Bottle of 5/86*: Floral perfume, vaguely of honey (!); moderate tannin, nice flavor, firm tannic finish; elegant. **(*)

Selvoramole (5/86). Floral aroma, vaguely of cherries; moderate tannin, with the fruit beneath, medium- to full-bodied; still young, needs one, perhaps two years. *(* −)

Serristori, Riserva Machiavelli (4/87). Fairly nice nose, hint of flowers along with fruit; firm, moderate tannin, nice fruit; youthful but attractive. *(* −)

Sicelle da Giovanni Mari (twice, 5/86). Fresh and fruity, floral aroma; light tannin, balanced, fruity; for current drinking. ** −

Tenuta Villa Rosa (4/85). Floral aroma; fruity, firm vein of tannin; drinkable now, but should be better in a year. *(+)

Vecchie Terre di Montefili (5/85). Floral perfume; fairly full, well balanced, light tannin; good quality. ** +

Vecchie Terre di Montefili, Riserva (5/86, 3,516 bottles). It spent three to four months in *barrique*. Richly fruited aroma, still a little reticent; well balanced, sweet impression, supple, vanilla component, long; has some style; oak adds complexity. **(*)

Vignamaggio (*twice, ex-cask, 5/86*). Fruity aroma and flavor, at this stage the tannin dominates, the fruit is there. **(+)

Vignavecchia (5/85). Berrylike fruit; fresh, simple, quaffable. *

Villa Antinori (2/88). Herbaceous component, light tannin, fruity, firm, could use more weight. *

Villa Cafaggio (*3 times, 4/90*). Corked. *Bottle of 1/87:* Packed with fruit, rich in flavor, balanced, lots of flavor and interest. ** +

Villa Cafaggio Riserva (*5 times, 6/90*). Lovely, fragrant floral scent, vanilla and berries; soft, light tannin, ready now, flavorful, trace of alcohol mars the end. *** −

Villa Calcinaia, Conti Capponi (4/85). Baked character, flat and dull.

Villa Cerna, Riserva (5/89). Warm nose; good body, fruity, open. * +

Villa Francesca, Riserva (4/89). Nice nose; balanced, tasty, good structure. **

1981 *

Winter precipitation was low and temperatures were average. There was very little rain in March and April, both very hot and dry months. This was followed by a rainy May. The first two weeks of June were dry and extremely hot; then, in the second half of the month, rainstorms hit more than once, and there was a significant drop in the temperature. The rest of the summer was dry, with higher than normal temperature. The crop size of nearly 9 million gallons (339,745 hectoliters), equivalent to 3.77 million cases, was a little above the annual average of 8.4 million gallons (319,544 hectoliters) between 1980 and 1989, but considerably above the 1970s average of 7.3 million gallons (274,227 hectoliters).

The wines, the *consorzio* reports, have average color, 12.5 percent alcohol, relative low acidity, medium-high dry extract, and will have a short life. The *consorzio* gives the year three out of four stars; Niederbacher gives it two.

Producers who rated the vintage highly include Castello di Querceto, Minuccio Cappelli, Pagliarese, Catignano, Villa Cafaggio, and Castellare. Raffaele Rossetti of Capannelle said it was top class. Paolo de Marchi describe the '81s as very good wines that are ready now or soon will be. Villa Calcinaia rates it very good and Castell'in Villa said the wines were not bad.

The '81s are somewhat light-bodied, and not wines for long aging. For the most part, they are ready now, and some are beginning to fade or have already faded. Few, if any, will improve. We especially liked the *riserve* from Fattoria di Montagliari, including the single-vineyard Vigna Casaloste, and Fattoria Monsanto's Il Poggio, followed by the *riserve*

from Badia a Coltibuono, Castello di Volpaia, Savignola Paolina, and Tenuta di Lilliano Riserva Eleanora Ruspoli Berlingier, with Ruffino's Riserva Ducale gold label close behind.

Antinori, Santa Cristina (*3 times, 12/85*). Tired, some acid, unbalanced.

Badia a Coltibuono, Riserva (*6 times, 11/90*). Leather and dried fruit aroma; still some tannin, nice fruit, mouth-filling; ready now though could improve a bit. **

Berardenga, Fattoria di Felsina (*twice, 3/87*). Light nose; full-flavored, soft, very ready, also very short. * +

Berardenga, Fattoria di Felsina, Riserva (*twice, 9/86*). Light to medium garnet; floral, berry and toasty notes; almost jammy but still a nice glass. *

Brolio, Riserva del Barone (9/87). Light nose; soft and tasty, short aftertaste; could use more character, surprisingly disappointing. *

Capannelle, Riserva (*twice, 5/85*). Lovely aroma suggests berries and cherries, some oak; light tannin, flavorful, balanced, has a tannic bite at the end. ** +

Cappelli Giovanni, La Quercia (12/83). Light, fresh and fruity with a berrylike character and some charm, very nice. **

Carobbio, Riserva (3/85). Tarlike aroma; fruity, light; not a lot of character or stuffing.

Castellare (*ex-cask, 2/83*). Undeveloped aroma with some fruit evident; tart edge; agreeable, not much more. *

Castello dei Rampolla, Riserva (5/85). Oak and cabernet fruit on nose; well balanced, well made, has style and flavor; but no Chianti character. As a red wine **(*); as a Chianti Classico *

Castello di Ama (*twice, 6/86, 208,870 bottles*). Fragrant floral aroma; fresh and fruity, quaffable, rather short. *

Castello di Ama, Vigneto Bellavista (*twice, 1/89, 13,424 bottles*). Pruney; starting to dry out, still has flavor interest, short. *

Castello di Cacchiano, Riserva (10/86). Straightforward fruity aroma; lacks structure and stuffing; unimpressive.

Castello di Cerreto, Riserva (5/85). Floral aroma; good body, some tannin; should be ready in two or three years. *(* +)

Castello di Montegrossi, Riserva (10/87). Light, slightly over-ripe aroma; soft center, light tannin, flavorful, ready, some tannin at the end. *

Castello di Querceto, Riserva (*twice, 10/86*). [This wine spent eight months in *barrique*.] Some fruit, vaguely floral; more body than expected, lacks depth; could still improve, though it seemed better seventeen months ago. *(+)

Castello di San Polo in Rosso, Castelpolo (5/85). Lovely berrylike aroma, vaguely floral; light tannin, raspberry flavor; easy. * +

Castello di San Polo in Rosso, Riserva (twice, 4/87). Ripe fruit aroma; flavorful, balanced; could improve further. **(+)

Castello di San Polo in Rosso, Vecchio (11/85). Lovely nose; nice nose; some style; ready. ** +

Castello di Verrazzano, Riserva (9/90). Spice and floral aroma, harsh note intrudes; best to drink up; beginning to dry out, still some flavor. * −

Castello di Volpaia, Riserva (6 times, 8/90). Fragrant scent, berry notes; fairly rich and tasty, nice mouth feel on the mid-palate, moderate length; holding up very well, no need to keep any longer. ** +

Castello Vicchiomaggio (5/85, just bottled that day). Vaguely floral aroma with a touch of raspberries; some tannin, flavorful, a bit light, tannin builds up at the end. *(?)

Fattoria dei Pagliarese, Riserva (4 times, 4/90). Fruity aroma; moderate tannin, flavorful; a tad coarse; was at its best in 1985. * +

Fattoria dei Pagliarese, Riserva Boscardini (twice, 7/89). Lovely nose, fragrant scent; some delicacy, tasty, soft, at its peak, a tad bitter, some alcohol mars the finish; drink. * +

Fattoria di Luiano (3 times, 9/86). Insipid, small-scale.

Fattoria di Montagliari, Riserva (5 times, 11/90). Lovely floral bouquet, vanilla, toasty, dried fruit and berry nuances; soft and openly fruity, balanced, sweet impression, warm, moderate to long finish; elegant and stylish; ready, will last. ** +

Fattoria di Montagliari, Riserva Vigna Casaloste (11/90). Floral scent; soft under light to moderate tannin, gentle, finish is a little dry; nice now, can improve. ** +

Fattoria di Vistarenni, Podere Bertinga (4/85). Nice fruit on the nose, vaguely floral; tannic vein, with the stuffing to support it. ** −

Fattoria La Ripa (5/85). Floral, berrylike aroma with a raisiny note; tannic entry, flavor of overripe fruit. * −

Fattoria Monsanto, Riserva Il Poggio (4 times, 6/90, 33,300 bottles). Lovely bouquet suggestive of blueberries and leather; rich, open flavor; seems ready, could improve; fairly long finish. ** +

Fattoria Querciabella, Riserva (4/87). Floral and resin aroma; some firmness, some tannin, fairly nice fruit, though a bit dull. *

Fattoria Querciabella, Vecchio (6/85, 6,000 bottles). Lovely floral aroma, brambly character; fruity, well balanced, somewhat light toward the end. **

Fontodi, Riserva (4 times, 8/89, 5,500 bottles). Perfumed scent; still has nice fruit, but a slight edge as well; best drunk up; was at its best in 1985 and 1986. * +

Isole e Olena, Riserva (5/85). Fragrant aroma with an oaky component; light tannin, well balanced, soft and supple in the center; coming ready but still needs more time. **(+)

Le Masse di San Leolino (twice, 5/85). Fragrant floral bouquet with a touch of resin; elegant; a lot of flavor and style, could be longer on the finish; near its peak. **

Le Masse di San Leolino, Riserva (11/85). Fruity, a bit light, touch of tannin, balanced, fairly nice; very ready. * +

Melini, Riserva Vigneti La Selvanella (twice, 9/87). Nice nose; light tannin, soft center, good structure; on the young side. **(+)

Monte Vertine, Riserva (5/85). Expansive, perfumed floral bouquet, some oak; well knit, soft center; some delicacy; ready though could improve. *** −

Monticelli [Viticola Toscana] (5/85). Simple, fruity, quaffable. * −

Podere Il Palazzino, Riserva (5/85, 3,160 bottles). Floral aroma with a hint of toffee; light tannin, has fruit, unstructured; not a success.

Poggio al Sole (5/85, 30,087 bottles). Floral aroma with some delicacy; light tannin, tart, flavorful, lively finish. * +

Poggio al Sole, Riserva (9/86). Nice nose; a lot of flavor, soft and round, fairly well balanced; very ready. ** +

Riecine (12/86). Fruity, still fresh, good body, balanced; very ready, and very nice too. **

Rocca delle Macìe, Riserva (12/86). Thin, some fruit, dull, nothing to it.

Ruffino (11/83). Light, fruity, fresh and quaffable; a good easy-drinking glass of wine. *

Ruffino, Riserva Ducale gold label (12/88). Rather nice, soft and very open. ** −

San Felice (3/85). Fragrant floral perfume; fairly high acid, has fruit; getting tired, but still drinkable, age shows, especially toward the finish. *

San Felice, Riserva Il Grigio (9/87). Lovely bouquet, flowers and fruit, scented; lots of flavor, good structure; some class. **(+)

San Felice, Riserva Poggio Rosso (9/87). Suggestions of nuts on the nose; fairly nice fruit, a tad light, some tannin toward the end which is somewhat drying. *

Savignola Paolina (twice, 5/85). Nice aroma; flavorful, soft, and smooth with some delicacy and charm. (The bottle of October 1983 was just as nice.) ** +

Savignola Paolina, Riserva (8/89). Fragrant floral scent, perfumed, has delicacy; loads of flavor, balanced, berrylike nuance, fairly long. **

Selvoramole (5/86). Medium garnet red; floral aroma, touch of cherries; still some tannin, the fruit is there, but won't last; beginning to dry out, drink. *

Tenuta di Lilliano (10/86). Fruity with an iodine cooked slant, short and dull.

Tenuta di Lilliano, Riserva Eleanora Ruspoli Berlingier (4/90). Dried fruit aroma, vaguely floral; open, attractive flavor; very ready. **

Tenuta La Colombaia, Riserva (3/87). Light nose, fragrant; unbalanced, lacks freshness, still some tannin.

Vecchie Terre di Montefili, Riserva (5/85). Nice nose, vaguely floral; well knit, quite forward and ready, but room to improve yet. **(+)

Vignavecchia, Riserva (5/85). Low fruit, flat, shallow, dull.

Villa Antinori, Riserva (4 times, 7/88). Cabernet herbaceousness and oak aroma, tobacco note, vague suggestions of flowers and cherries; soft and tasty, easy to drink, not much depth, a bit rough at the end. * +

Villa Antinori, Riserva Marchese (4/88). Oak overlies, fairly nice fruit, some firmness, lean and tasty, short. *

Villa Banfi, Riserva (9/86). Fairly nice nose; moderate fruit, a bit light in the center, and a tad dry at the end. +

Villa Calcinaia, Conti Capponi (4/85). Baked, character.

Villa Cerna, Riserva (11/90). Vanilla and fruit on the nose; a little firm, and a tad dry, short; best to drink up. +

1980 *

Spring was short and the flowering late. The summer was characterized by fluctuating temperatures and long periods of dry weather. Autumn was normal, but the harvest was brought in late, beginning the last week of October and continuing through the first week of November. The production of 9.2 million gallons (348,133 hectoliters), equivalent to 3.87 million cases, was about 9 percent above the 1980s annual average of 8.4 million gallons (319,544 hectoliters) and considerably above the 1970s average of 7.3 million gallons (274,227 hectoliters).

The *consorzio* said that the wines have medium-high color, an average of 12.7 percent alcohol, average acidity, medium-high dry extract, and will take moderate to extended aging. They rate the vintage as a three-star year, out of four.

The wines are medium-bodied and have good color. They are fairly high in acid, more so than the '79s, and are similar to the '78s; they have less tannin than either. Paolo de Marchi found the wines light in body, perhaps even a bit thin. Castello di Gabbiano and Vicchiomaggio considered it an excellent vintage; Antinori gives it four stars out of a possible five. Castello dei Rampolla and Castello di San Polo in Rosso described it as a good vintage, Villa Cafaggio places it about average, Castell'in Villa said it was all right but not one of their favorites, and Villa Calcinaia found it a medium year.

The best wines of the vintage, as far as today goes, are the Fattoria Monsanto Riserva Il Poggio, the *riserve* of Capannelle and Castello di San Polo in Rosso, the Fattoria dei Pagliarese Riserva Boscardini, Fattoria di Montagliari Riserva, Tenuta di Lilliano Riserva Eleanora Ruspoli Berlingier, and Tenuta di Nozzole Riserva La Forra.

While they deserved two stars out of four at one time, they don't any longer. Few Chiantis live more than a decade today. These wines are no exception. More than a few have faded. Drink up.

Brolio (twice, 10/83). Characteristic aroma; light tannin, simple and quaffable, no more. * −

Capannelle, Riserva (twice, 1/88) Peppery, spicy, floral and fruity bouquet; rich in flavor, spice and fruit components, soft-centered, some grip; very ready. **

Cappelli Giovanni, La Quercia (5/82). Fresh and fruity; light and tasty; has some charm. * +

Castellare (2/83). Vaguely toasty note on nose, very little else; moderate fruit, tart edge, a bit thin; not a success; shows more age than the '79.

Castello dei Rampolla, Riserva (5/85). Reticent aroma with hints of oak and cabernet fruit, vaguely floral; firm structure, cabernet herbaceousness more apparent as the wine airs, lean, somewhat austere, but well made and distinctive, if not exactly our idea of a Chianti.** +

Castello di Querceto, Riserva (3/86). Medium red; floral aroma; light tannin, soft center, touch of acid at the end which is fairly long. **(+)

Castello di San Polo in Rosso (4/87). Light nose; lots of fruit on the palate, some tannin; more or less ready. ** −

Castello di San Polo in Rosso, Riserva (5 times, 4/88). Floral aroma with fruity backnote; moderate tannin, drinkable now, medium-bodied, mouth-filling flavors, a bit dry at the end. ** −

Castello di San Polo in Rosso, Vecchio (twice, 5/85). Vaguely musty on aroma; some fruit, light tannin, fruity, a bit short. * +

Castello di Verrazzano, Riserva (9/90). Fragrant-scented bouquet; soft, very ready, actually a tad past its peak, still it is quite drinkable. *

Castello di Volpaia, Riserva (4 times, 4/87). Floral aroma with a fruity component; soft and ready, some age beginning to set in, drink up, tannin finish. * +

Castello Vicchiomaggio, Riserva (5/85). Floral aroma with toasty notes; flavorful, moderate tannin, well balanced, short; needs a few years, shows promise. *(+)

Castello Vicchiomaggio, Riserva Prima Vigna (ex-barrique, 5/85). Oak up front on nose, some fruit in the back, at this point the oak dominates; more tannin and body than the regular *riserva*. *(*)

Fattoria Campomaggio, Riserva (5/85). Aroma of tobacco and cherries, a bit corked; overly tannin for the fruit.

Fattoria dei Pagliarese, Riserva (3 times, 4/89). Dried fruit and floral bouquet; nice fruit; starting to age, drink up. * +

Fattoria dei Pagliarese, Riserva Boscardini (twice, 8/89). Fragrant floral scent; soft yet with an edge, very ready, good body, tasty, round and agreeable. ** −

Fattoria di Luiano, Riserva (7/85). Aroma has a baked character, jammy, overripe, heavy; light tannin, fruit on entry then thins out, tannic aftertaste; not a success.

Fattoria di Montagliari, Riserva (5 times, 4/90). Openly fruity; good structure, some tannin, lacks a little style but nice fruit; drink now. ** −

Fattoria La Loggia, Riserva (4/85). Fruity aroma; astringent, unbalanced.

Fattoria La Ripa (5/85). Somewhat floral aroma; fairly tannic, has fruit, harsh finish. *

Fattoria Monsanto, Riserva (twice, 10/87). Fragrant; balanced, moderate tannin, tasty, nice fruit; could improve with another year or two. **

Fattoria Monsanto, Riserva Il Poggio (4 times, 4/90). Open, scented bouquet suggestive of cassis and berries; still a little firm, rich and concentrated, real sweetness. ** + (*** −)

Fattoria Querciabella, Riserva (6/85, 6,000 bottles). Spicy aroma, black pepper nuance; fruity; seems a trifle tired though quite drinkable. **

Fattoria Vignale, Riserva (10/86). Stale note; drying out, some fruit, short, dull finish.

Fattoria Viticcio, Riserva (twice, 6/85, 10,000 bottles). Similar to the earlier bottle but some age starting to show in the form of acid at the end, drink up. *Bottle of 11/84:* Floral scent, vaguely candylike; some tannin, has fruit, fairly well balanced; nearly ready; some firmness at the end. **

Fontodi, Riserva (twice, 5/85, 13,480 bottles). Floral aroma still somewhat closed; some tannin, a bit light, flavorful; nearly ready, most likely won't keep. **

Fossi, Riserva (10/86). Characteristic Chianti nose with a floral component and a dank background; is there enough for fruit for the tannin? We think so. (*?)

Isole e Olena, Riserva (5/85). Floral aroma with some oak; fairly tannic, supple center, well balanced, some length. **(*)

Le Masse di San Leolino, Riserva (3 times, 11/85). Lovely floral bouquet with a touch of cherries; light tannin, a lot of flavor; some style and character; ready now, with room to improve. **

Melini, Riserva Vigneti La Selvanella (10/86). Perfumed berry aroma; good body, nice flavor, tails off toward the end. *

Monte Vertine (10/83). Light, floral aroma; some fruit, fairly well balanced, light tannin, good flavor; very ready. **

Poggio al Sole, Riserva (5/85, 4,906 bottles). Delicate, floral aroma, vaguely berrylike; firm, well balanced, lively finish. ** +

Riecine (10/83). Straightforward fruity aroma; light tannin, tasty, balanced, quite nice. **

Rocca delle Macìe (4/81). Fruity aroma with some spice; fresh and fruity, high acid, unbalanced.

Rocca delle Macìe, Riserva (9/86). Mineral notes, some fruit; not a lot to it, but drinkable. * −

Ruffino, Riserva Ducale (3/86). Corked.

Ruffino, Riserva Ducale gold label (ex-cask, 7/82). Cherrylike aroma; considerable fruit, well structured; should make a nice bottle. **(?)

San Felice, Riserva Il Grigio (twice, 10/86). Floral aroma with a fruit component; nice fruit, soft center, balanced; has character. ** −

Tenuta di Lilliano (10/83). Very light, though characteristic floral aroma; soft and tasty; most agreeable; very ready. **

Tenuta di Lilliano, Riserva Eleanora Ruspoli Berlingier (4/90). Ripe fruit and oak aroma, delicate scent; good structure, some tannin, openly fruity; ready; dry aftertaste. ** −

Tenuta di Nozzole, Riserva La Forra (11/88). Fragrant floral aroma, nutlike component; flavorful, well balanced; ready with room to grow. ** −

Tenuta La Colombaia, Riserva (3/87). More fruit on the nose than the '81, seems a little tired; better on the palate where fairly nice fruit is evident. *

Tenuta Villa Rosa, Riserva (4/85). Fruity aroma and flavor, rather astringent.

Villa Cerna, Riserva (11/90). Floral, woodsy aroma; still fairly tasty though finish is dry and short; drink. *

Villa La Pagliaia, Riserva Granduca Ferdinando III (5/88, 15,200 bottles). Some age apparent; still has fruit but beginning to dry out, even so there is still interest and character. * −

1 9 7 9 ** −

January was cold. The spring was cooler than normal. The summer was favorable, although the end of August was punctuated by heavy rains. The harvest was long. It was an enormous crop, the largest between the advent of DOC in 1967 and 1989. The production of more than 12 million gallons (458,838 hectoliters), equivalent to 5.1 million cases, was two-thirds more than the average annual output between 1970 and 1979 of 7.3 million gallons (274,227 hectoliters).

Some of the grapes came in overripe. The wines, according to the *consorzio,* have average color, an alcohol level of 12.9 percent, medium-low acidity, and average extract. They rate it as a two-star vintage out of four. Niederbacher gives the year three stars.

Sergio Manetti of Monte Vertine considers this his best Chianti Classico vintage up to that point. Antinori gives it top marks, five stars out of five. Minuccio Cappelli (Fattoria Montagliari), Villa Calcinaia, Pagliarese, and Castello dei Rampolla found it a very good year. Castell'in Villa described it as good, Castello di San Polo in Rosso said it was very good, and Villa Cafaggio rated it average. Vignamaggio and Barone Ricasoli said it was not a good vintage. Paolo de Marchi said overcropping had made his wines light and thin, wines that won't age.

Having tasted nearly four dozen Chianti Classicos, we find that, overall, it was indeed a very good vintage. The wines were for early drinking, though a few will age. As for today, most are getting on in age. The better ones, such as Monsanto and Ruffino, will keep and possibly improve further. We find that two in particular have aged well—Fattoria di Montagliari Riserva and Fattoria Monsanto Riserva Il Poggio—and then the Ruffino Riserva Ducale gold label.

Antinori, Santa Cristina (*twice, 10/82*). Lovely nose; light to medium in body, soft and smooth, an agreeable little wine. * There has been bottle variation. *Bottle of 11/80:* Harsh and unbalanced, and shy of fruit.

Badia a Coltibuono, Riserva (*twice, 10/86*). Garnet, brick orange reflections; light, floral bouquet; soft and balanced, almost sweet, ready now, light tannin. **

Berardenga, Fattoria di Felsina, (*5/85*). Floral aroma with a raspberry note; seems older than its years; good body, tart edge, still some tannin to soften. *(*)

Capannelle, Riserva (*5/85*). Peppermint and fruit on aroma; still some tannin, tasty, long finish that recalls pine and mint; will improve. **(*)

Capannelle, Vecchio (*10/83*). Fruity aroma with a touch of flowers; light tannin, fruity. * +

Cappelli Giovanni, La Quercia (*twice, 12/83*). Has aroma and flavor, but has lost its freshness and charm. The bottle tasted a year earlier was still fairly fresh, meriting *

Castelgreve, Riserva (*10/83*). Still some tannin, decent balance; a bit young but drinkable now.*

Castellare (*twice, 1/87*). Fruit is fading, but still drinkable.

Castell'in Villa, Riserva (*5/85*). Complex bouquet with notes of flowers, pine, mint and raspberries; some tannin, a lot of flavor, good body; quite ready; long, firm finish with notes of blackberries. ** +

Castello dei Rampolla, Riserva (*5/85*). Herbaceous cabernet aroma, some fruit in the back; well made, firm tannin; cabernet character dominates—is this a Chianti? **(+)

Castello di Castelvari (*10/85*). Nice nose with characteristic Chianti flowers; fairly nice flavor, some rough edges, and a bit harsh. * —

Castello di Fonterutoli, Riserva (*10/83*). Fragrant floral aroma; soft and smooth, balanced; quite nice now. **

Castello di Monterinaldi, Riserva (*5/85*). Some fruit, light tannin, unstructured, shallow, short.

Castello di San Polo in Rosso (*3 times, 5/85*). Vaguely woodsy, mushroomlike aroma with a touch of leather; tannin on entry gives way to nice fruit, tannic aftertaste, vaguely bitter. *(*) *Bottle of 7/83:* Softer and more ready to drink. *(*)

Castello di Volpaia, Riserva (*4 times, 4/87*). Floral, cassislike fragrance; soft, seems a tad overripe, fruity; quite ready. ** —

Catignano (*twice, 1/83*). Pale color; fresh and quaffable, seems almost sweet. *

Cellole, Riserva (*twice, 10/83*). Aroma, flavor and structure recall a southern wine.

Cepperellaccio, Principe Kunz d'Asburgo Lorena (*11/80*). A light, unbalanced wine; the most interesting thing about it is the name.

Cispiano Riserva della Serena (*4/85*). Perfumed scent with a spicy note; light-bodied, some fruit, lacks freshness, dull aftertaste.

Fattoria dei Pagliarese, Riserva (*3 times, 5/85*). Floral aroma with raspberrylike fruit; light tannin, fruity, quite ready, soft, vaguely bitter at the end. (Perhaps it was better in October 1983.) **

Fattoria dei Pagliarese, Riserva Boscardini (*twice, 9/87*). Floral-scented bouquet; soft, good structure; nearly ready; attractive. **(+)

Fattoria di Montagliari, Riserva (*8 times, 4/90*). Scented, delicate floral bouquet with dried fruit and leather components, some spice; soft, velvety, round and flavorful, some sweetness; near its peak. *** — *A second bottle, tasted one day later:* Similar, but with less complexity and was a little dry at the end. ** —

Fattoria di Vistarenni (*twice, 10/83 and 4/85*). Both bottles were quite similar: a small, dull wine of no character or style.

Fattoria di Vistarenni, Riserva (*5/86*). Medium garnet; some fruit evident on the nose; some tannin, rather shallow, tannic aftertaste, vaguely bitter, tannin really builds at the end; starting to dry out.

Fattoria La Ripa, Riserva (*twice, 5/85*). Small nose; overly tannic, alcoholic aftertaste. * — *Bottle of 10/83:* Lovely floral bouquet; balanced, some tannin, tasty; ready now. ** +

Fattoria Monsanto, Riserva (*5 times, 11/85*). Fruity, well balanced, light tannin; ready now and very good besides. ** +

Fattoria Monsanto, Riserva Il Poggio (*9 times, 4/90, 32,880 bottles*). Complex bouquet displays tobacco, woodsy and berry components; soft, round and rich, tasty; ready with room to grow, lovely now; fairly long finish. *** — *Bottle of 4/85:* Richly concentrated aroma with suggestions of flowers, berries and apricots; moderate tannin, a bit light for Il Poggio but flavorful with a sweetness to the fruit, long, lingering finish; should be ready in about two to three years. **(*−)

Fattoria Monsanto, Santa Caterina (10/81). Fruity aroma with cherrylike notes; agreeable, fruity, touch of tannin, falls away quickly at the end.

Fattoria Quercia al Poggio (5/85). Pale garnet; fragrant aroma; too much tannin for the fruit, but drinkable enough. *−

Fattoria Querciabella, Riserva (6/85, 2,100 bottles). Spicy aroma bears a resemblance to the '81, brambly note; light tannin, fruity, ready. **

Fontodi, Riserva (twice, 5/85). Floral notes and some berries on aroma that's showing age; still some tannin, flavorful, a bit light, some tannin at the end; ready now. **

Geografico, Riserva (2/88). Off note intrudes from aroma through the palate, some fruit; no real definition or structure.

Isabella de'Medici (twice, 4/83). Pale, anemic color; some character on aroma; light, fruity, simple; could have more weight, but drinkable.

Isole e Olena (5/85, magnum). Lovely bouquet, of fruit and a touch of oak; light tannin, soft and round, smooth, well balanced, light finish; near its peak. **+

Montemaggio, Riserva (4/85). Seaweed on aroma and flavor, awful!

Monte Vertine (5 times, 10/83). Characteristic floral bouquet with some fruit; not to keep but quite enjoyable now. *+

Monte Vertine, Riserva (10/83). Has a richness of bouquet and flavor that makes it seem drinkable now; though still has tannin to shed. **(*)

Palazzo al Bosco (ex-vat, 11/80). Heaps of flavor, well balanced, should make a nice bottle in time. **

Poggio al Sole (5/85, 40,942 bottles). Pale garnet; light, floral aroma with a suggestion of berries; light tannin, soft and flavorful, very ready, moderately long, lively finish. **

Poggio al Sole, Riserva (7/87, 1,390 bottles). This wine spent five years in wood. Medium brick red; floral bouquet, some complexity and mellowness from bottle age; soft, smooth, still some tannin; very ready; fairly long. **+

Poggio Rosso, Riserva [special selection of San Felice] (4/85, 7,536 bottles). Fruity aroma; well balanced, firm tannic vein, flavorful; real quality here. ***−

Riecine (ex-vat, 4/80). Nice aroma, fruity; shows promise. *(*+)

Rocca delle Macìe (11/80). Smallish nose; light bodied, fresh, some fruit, very short.

Ruffino (twice, 11/80). Fresh and fruity, a simple little quaffing wine, goes down easily. *

Ruffino, Riserva Ducale (twice, 6/86). Light to medium garnet; mineral aroma; on the light side, light tannin; enjoyable now, no need to keep further. **−

Ruffino, Riserva Ducale gold label (8 times, 11/89). Typical floral bouquet shows a lot of age, rich, berrylike component; soft center, a bit firm toward the back, a tad short and dry. **−

Tenuta La Colombaia, Riserva (3/87). Fairly rich fruity aroma, slight raisiny note, and somewhat overripe; some tannin remains, fruit seems overripe, could use more structure. +

Vignamaggio, Riserva (5/85). Pretty floral aroma; some tannin, well balanced, a lighter style; still needs some time to soften; tannic ending. **(+)

Vignavecchia, Riserva (5/85). Floral aroma with a touch of cherries; light tannin, low in fruit, unbalanced.

Villa Antinori, Riserva (3 times, 9/85). Flat, shows age, a bit tired at the end. *Bottle of 5/85:* A vague harshness on the nose and some cabernet character evident; fairly soft though has some tannin, a good glass of wine; lacks style and definition but drinkable enough. *+

Villa Antinori, Riserva Marchese (5/85). Herbaceous bell pepper aroma up front with some fruit in the back; moderate tannin beginning to soften, somewhat astringent, flavorful, bell pepper–like notes intrude; needs a few years to really soften. *(*)

Villa Banfi (3/85). Rather shy on aroma, some fruit; medium body, some acid throws the balance off; might soften a bit but hardly seems worth the wait; drinkable now but not a lot to it. *−

Villa Cafaggio, Riserva (twice, 1/87). Garnet toward brick color; some age starting to show; nice flavor; drink up. * *Bottle of 5/85:* Blackberries on aroma; heaps of flavor, light tannin; surprisingly big for a '79; tannic finish. **+

Villa Cerna, Riserva (12/86). Minty, fruity aroma; simple, light tannin. *−

Villa Colombaio (ex-cast, 4/80). Light, perfumed bouquet; very soft and fruity; surprisingly forward; very good. **

1 9 7 8 *

The production of 8.2 million gallons (311,765 hectoliters), equivalent to 3.46 million cases, was 13.7 percent above the annual average between 1970 and 1979 of 7.3 million gallons (274,227 hectoliters). The *consorzio* reported that the wines have medium-high color, 12.7 percent alcohol, high acidity, average dry extract, and are for extended aging. They gave the vintage three stars out of four. Niederbacher gives it four.

Barone Ricasoli rates this as one of the very best vintages. Castell'in Villa said it was a great one. Villa Calcinaia also puts it among the best. Antinori gives it four out of five points. Castello di San Polo in Rosso considers it very good, as does Vicchiomaggio. For Badia a Coltibuono it was better than 1977. Castello di Gabbiano and Catignano describe it as good and Villa Cafaggio calls it about average. Paolo de

Marchi finds the wines not well balanced, in some ways similar to the '80s.

After having tasted over four dozen Chianti Classicos, we find the vintage doesn't live up to the press it received early on. Many are starting to fade; few, if any, will improve. It's best to drink them up now. None really impressed us. They lacked charm from the start. In one way they reminded us of the '74s—there was something missing. It has never been one of our favorite vintages. The Badia a Coltibuono Riserva is our favorite, then the Fattoria Monsanto Riserva Il Poggio.

Badia a Coltibuono, Riserva (5 times, 11/90). The fruit is drying out, showing age; considering the one of seven months ago, it must have been the bottle. *Bottle of 4/90:* Floral and dried fruit scent; moderate tannin, nice structure, soft center, hint of sweetness; very ready. *** −

Bertolli, Riserva (10/83). Small aroma; tasty, lacks somewhat in structure and length, but agreeable.

Brolio (twice, 2/85). Harsh and unbalanced, shallow, dull, thin; was better in January 1980, now too old.

Brolio, Riserva (3 times, 10/83). Simple aroma; some tannin and firmness, simple flavors; drinkable now, could improve. *

Brolio, Riserva del Barone (9/83). Splendid aroma, a lot of fruit, fresh; moderate tannin, well balanced, nice flavor; drinks well now; the best Brolio we've tasted in years. **

Burchino (8/82). Dull, though characteristic aroma; flat; dull and tired, too old.

Capannelle, Riserva (5/85). Woodsy bouquet with notes of mushrooms; fairly rich and tannic, firm, well made, very long finish that recalls pine; needs age yet. **(+)

Cappelli Giovanni, La Quercia (2/85). Floral aroma; almost sweet on entry then thins out; too old.

Casa Sola (11/79). Fresh and grapey yet with a hot, baked character about it!

Casa Sola, Riserva (3/83). Characteristic Chianti aroma; moderate fruit, some tannin; lacks style, not a lot to it.

Castellare (10/83). Simple fruity aroma with a hint of flowers; flavorful, balanced, light tannin; ready now. * +

Castell'in Villa, Riserva (5/85). Floral aroma with a minty note, and something vaguely odd; soft center with a lot of tannin around it, long finish. *(** −)

Castello di Cerreto, Riserva (5/85). Floral, fruity aroma; fairly rich, tannin to shed, finishes on a tannic note. *(*)

Castello di Montegrossi, Riserva (10/87). Fruity aroma, vaguely floral; light tannin; ready now, some age evident, touch of oxidation. *

Castello di Querceto (twice, 1/83). Nice aroma; balanced, fresh and fruity, tasty; some style, quite good. **

Castello di San Polo in Rosso (twice, 5/85). Floral bouquet with berrylike notes; some tannin, and a surprising amount of fruit, quite drinkable, finishes short with some tannic roughness. **

Castello di San Polo in Rosso, Riserva (3 times, 5/85). [Same wine as the regular aged one year in oak.] Aroma of concentrated grapes and figs; some tannin, soft, vaguely bitter, overly tannic finish; drink up now. **

Castello di Volpaia, Riserva (5/85). Floral bouquet with a touch of pine; quite drinkable, light tannin, a bit short. ** −

Castello Vicchiomaggio, Riserva (twice, 5/85). Vague floral notes on nose; moderate tannin, fruity, angular, good but seemed softer when tasted in October 1983. * +

Cerbaiola (Barfede-Certaldo) (4/80). Lightly fruity aroma; a bit light, fruity, some tannin.*

Fattoria dei Pagliarese (twice, 4/89). Old nose; still has fruit, rather dry, and drying out, still with interest. * −

Fattoria dei Pagliarese, Riserva (4/85). Reticent nose with some fruit; still a bit tannic, soft, short. * +

Fattoria dei Pagliarese, Riserva Boscardini (5/85). Floral bouquet with raspberrylike fruit; full-flavored, well balanced, light tannin, long finish; very ready. ***

Fattoria dell'Aiola, Riserva (10/83). Small nose; small wine, not a lot of fruit, lack of fruit makes it seem to have more tannin than it does.

Fattoria di Luiano (2/85). Thin, yeasty, flat, dull, unbalanced.

Fattoria di Montagliari, Riserva (4 times, 1/89). Shy nose, sangiovese character evident; some acid, overall soft; very ready; unexciting, even a bit dull. *

Fattoria La Ripa, Riserva (twice, 5/85). Aroma of prunes and raisins, jammy; overly tannic, alcoholic finish; drying out. *Bottle of 10/83:* Nice fruit initially on the nose gives way to a dullness; good fruit on palate, fair balance. * −

Fattoria Monsanto, Riserva (twice, 5/82). Aroma somewhat closed, hints of tar and fruit; rich flavors, still somewhat backward, loads of flavor, some spiciness. **

Fattoria Monsanto, Riserva Il Poggio (4 times, 4/90, 38,650 bottles). Leather and dried fruit bouquet, floral component; still some tannin, fairly nice fruit, berrylike, could use more length. ** +

Fattoria Valiano, Riserva (10/83). Small nose, moderate fruit; light tannin, moderate fruit, some dullness, but drinkable.

Fossi (2/85). Dull, boring, ho-hum.

Granducato, Riserva Corona (10/83). Light nose, seems closed; good fruit up front, a bit shallow, overly tannic finish; not bad, just unimpressive.

Isole e Olena, Riserva (5/85). Floral bouquet with notes of leather and caramel on a background of oak; some tannin, fruity, evident oak, supple, long. **(+)

La Pagliaia, Riserva Granduca Ferdinando III (4/85). Perfumed bouquet; fruity, peppery flavor, tannic finish. * +

Palazzo al Bosco (*twice, 6/81*). Nose is rather subdued, hints of berries; smooth texture, moderate tannin; quite good; ready. * +

Poggio al Sole (*twice, 5/81*). Lovely perfumed aroma, with fruity overtones; lively acidity, clean, refreshing aftertaste. **

Riecine (4/80). Wild cherries leap out of the glass; well balanced, lots of fruit, some tannin. **

Riseccoli (4/80). A bit light in body, some tannin, short.

Rocca delle Macìe (11/80). Lacking in aroma; some freshness and fruit, rather short, dull aftertaste.

Ruffino (11/80). Fresh fruity aroma; some tannin, soft; pleasant drinking. *

Ruffino, Montemasso (*ex-cask, 11/80*). Nice nose; fruity, some tannin. *

Ruffino, Riserva Ducale gold label (11/90). Lovely, open and fragrant bouquet, scents of flowers and the woods, hint of leather; rich and warm, mellow, full-bodied, very soft and round, could use more length, still it is a lovely glass; at its peak. *** –

S. Leolino, Fattoria I Cipressi, Riserva (*3 times, 2/85*). Thin, some fruit, unbalanced; too old. *Bottle of 10/83:* Floral bouquet; tannin up front, with the fruit to support it; agreeable though not much else. *

San Felice, Riserva Il Grigio (10/83). Lovely fragrant bouquet; a nice mouthful of fruit; needs a few years but is drinkable now. **(*)

Vignamaggio (11/80). Floral, fruity aroma; light- to medium-bodied, fruity, some tannin, balanced; ready. * +

Vignamaggio, Riserva (5/85). Floral aroma with a toffeelike note; firm and tannic, needs time to soften, a bit short. *(*)

Vignavecchia, Riserva (5/85). Seems a lot older than a '78.

Villa Antinori, Riserva (*twice, 10/83*). Fruity aroma with a cabernetlike herbaceousness; tannic, moderate fruit, somewhat unbalanced, short.

Villa Antinori, Riserva Marchese (5/85). Weedy, herbaceous aroma, more like cabernet than sangiovese; moderate tannin, fairly well structured, again cabernet dominates on palate. *(*)

Villa Banfi (*twice, 3/85*). Fragrant floral bouquet with a touch of oak; very well balanced, a lot of flavor; has character and style, one of the better '78s. ***

Villa Calcinaia, Conti Capponi (*3 times, 2/85*). Oxidized. *Bottle of 10/83:* Very dull.

Villa Calcinaia, Riserva Conti Capponi (4/85). Aroma and taste have a cooked quality.

Villa Cerna, Riserva (*twice, 11/90*). Prunelike aroma; sense of sweetness, soft, dry, short end; very ready. * +

Villa Consuelo (*twice, 2/85*). Anemic color; shows age, astringent, thinning out at end.

Villa Francesca (*twice, 5/86*). Medium-dark color; fresh berrylike aroma, perhaps a touch of flowers; sweet fruit impression, round and smooth, loads of flavor, balanced, still some tannin, yet ready, should hold, moderate length; one of the more interesting '78s. *** –

1 9 7 7 * +

The crop of nearly 8 million gallons (302,565 hectoliters), equivalent to 3.36 million cases, was more than 10 percent above the 1970s annual average of 7.3 million gallons (274,227 hectoliters). The *consorzio* said that the wines had average color, 12.8 percent alcohol, medium-high acidity, and medium-high extract. They rated it three stars out of four and said that they were wines for moderate aging.

This vintage was highly regarded from the start, and for good reason: many fine wines were produced. It is possible that Fabrizio Bianchi's Monsanto Il Poggio was his finest to that date, no mean feat when you consider the '75, '71, '66, '64, and '62.

Villa Cafaggio describes it as excellent; Giovanni Cappelli, Catignano, Pagliarese, and Vicchiomaggio all consider it especially fine; La Ripa said for them it was perhaps the best ever. Antinori, Barone Ricasoli, Castell'in Villa and Villa Calcinaia rate it very good. Paolo de Marchi said it was an easy vintage, one with no problems, but the wines are now getting old.

For us, some wines—too many—are showing age badly. But fourteen years is getting on for a Chianti Classico. Many have faded, some are on their last legs. The best, like Fattoria Monsanto Riserva Il Poggio, will continue to improve. And Castello di Volpaia, Fattoria di Felsina's Berardenga, and Fattoria di Montagliari are still very good. In the mid-1980s the *riserve* of Capannelle, Castell'in Villa, and Isole e Olena were all excellent.

Baccio da Gaiuole (3/79). Youthful aroma with character; flavorful, tannin to shed, has structure and style. Out of a group of about 30 Chianti Classicos this was clearly the best. ***

Badia a Coltibuono, Riserva (*twice, 4/89*). Fragrant floral aroma, minty notes; open fruit, a lot of development, nice fruit, firm, dry aftertaste. * +

Barberini (11/79). An undistinguished little wine.

Berardenga, Fattoria di Felsina (9/79). Fresh fruity Chianti aroma; a bit light but tasty, a good quaffing wine. *

Berardenga, Fattoria di Felsina, Riserva (*twice, 3/89*). Fragrant nose, has a richness of fruit and a hint of cassis; rich, sweet impression, round and ripe; very good indeed and very ready. ** +

Brolio (3/82). Fragrant aroma; light-bodied, shows some signs of drying out, dull.

Capannelle, Riserva (5/85). Woodsy bouquet with a touch of strawberries; light tannin, soft, sweet, tasty, impressive, long finish with notes of strawberries and mint. *** +

Cappelli Giovanni, La Quercia (twice, 11/79). Fresh fruity aroma and flavor, some spice on the finish. * +

Carobbio, Vecchio (10/80). Pretty nose, delicate and scented; soft, some tannin, good flavor; ready. *

Castelgreve, Riserva (10/83). Has fruit, moderate tannin, very drinkable though an atypical Chianti. * −

Castell'in Villa (twice, 5/85). Floral bouquet with a vaguely vegetal backnote that adds complexity; light tannin, flavorful, soft, velvety, round, some tannin at the end, finish has a note of blackberries and a touch of mint; enjoyable now. *** −

Castello di Cacchiano (twice, 6/81). On aroma seems more like a California wine than a Chianti, slightly toasty, and a faint off note; soft-centered, harsh edges, something off on flavor as well.

Castello di Cerreto, Riserva (10/83). Smallish nose; some fruit on entry, then shallow.

Castello di Fonterutoli (twice, 6/81). Light nose, some fruit evident; moderate tannin, balanced, flavorful, almost sweet; a small-scale wine. * −

Castello di Meleto, Riserva (5/85). Not much aroma; low in fruit; drying out.

Castello di Rencine (4/80). Floral, fruity aroma; a bit light for the tannin, slightly bitter aftertaste.

Castello di San Donato in Perano, Riserva (5/85). Small nose; unbalanced, no particular character, grating aftertaste.

Castello di Volpaia, Riserva (9/90). Fragrant, floral-scented bouquet; a little dry but lots of flavor; quite attractive; best to drink up. ** −

Castello Vicchiomaggio, Riserva (twice, 5/85). Aroma recalls a bakery, toffee notes, which carry over on the palate; fairly tannic, seems to have sufficient fruit, an angular wine, short tannic finish; will it develop? *(+)

Cerbaiola (Barfede-Certaldo) (4/80). Floral aroma with some fruit; light, fruity, simple. *

Cispiano (11/79). Light aroma; unbalanced, some flavor; not much to it.

Fattoria dei Pagliarese (3 times, 5/81). Somewhat reticent aroma with hints of fruit and flowers; flavorful, soft; has style, a nice bottle. ** +

Fattoria delle Barone (4/81). Floral aroma marred by volatile acidity and lactic overtones; light-bodied and shallow, lacks structure, flavor and length.

Fattoria delle Lodoline (3 times, 6/81). Harsh aroma; some fruit but showing age, drying out; it didn't amount to much in 1979 either.

Fattoria di Montagliari, Riserva (3 times, 4/90). Woodsy, leathery aroma, dried fruit component; a little dry, still some firmness. **

Fattoria di Montagliari e Castellinuzza, Riserva (4 times, 5/84). Floral perfume; soft, light tannin, full of flavor; some elegance. **(+)

Fattoria La Ripa, Riserva (twice, 5/85). Some oxidation, moldy, gone. *Bottle of 10/83:* Light, fruity aroma; some tannin; drinkable now, nowhere to go. *

Fattoria Le Bocce (10/78). Very fresh and fruity, tart, lively, *beverino* (very drinkable). * +

Fattoria Monsanto, Riserva (8 times, 7/86). Medium garnet toward brick; tobacco nuance on the nose, vaguely floral; still some tannin but ready now, moderate length. ** + *Bottle of 9/83:* Big, rich aroma, lots of fruit with hints of spice, blueberries, vanilla and flowers; moderate tannin, heaps of fruit; lovely now but could improve. ***

Fattoria Monsanto, Riserva Il Poggio (16 times, 4/90, 23,730 *bottles*). Complex bouquet reveals a mélange of scents including damp leaves and flowers; still some tannin; a young wine that displays loads of class and character; this bottle, tasted at the winery, was more closed than the bottle we tasted in the States a month ago; it displayed flavors reminiscent of tobacco and chocolate along with ripe fruit. Although we must admit to some bottle variation in the States, most of the bottles from our own cellar have been in fine condition. This bottle ***(+) *Bottle of 4/85:* Big, richly fruited bouquet, expansive and complex, with nuances of flowers, blackberries, blueberries and apricots; enormous extract and weight, richly concentrated, exceptional balance, still quite tannic; full of life and style; superb, it might just be the best Monsanto up to this point. ***(*)

Fattoria Monsanto, Vecchio (4/80). Perfumed bouquet; some tannin but good now, fruity, balanced, some length. **

Fattoria Viticcio, Riserva (7/82, 10,000 *bottles*). Lightly perfumed aroma; light and soft, not a lot to it, shallow, thin, short.

Fossi, Riserva (9/89). Floral aroma; some fruit, a sweetness to the fruit under moderate tannin, tight finish. *

Fossi, Vecchio (5/83). Nice nose; fruity entry, but shallow.

Geografico, Riserva (9/87). Low fruit, dying out, not a lot of tannin.

Il Guerrino (3/79). Hot nose; has weight in the mouth, seems clumsy.

Isole e Olena, Riserva (5/85). Berrylike aroma with a roasted, toasty aspect; some tannin, soft-centered; drinkable but could improve over the next two years. ***

La Pagliaia, Riserva Granduca Ferdinando III (10/83). Light nose; nice flavor, moderate tannin, short. *

Mazzoni [bottled by Villa Cafaggio for Paterno] (11/79). Hot nose; light-bodied, not much to it.

Nozzole, Riserva (10/83). Light, characteristic floral bouquet; soft; ready though could improve. **

Pian d'Albola (*twice, 6/81*). Floral aroma with some fruit; almost sweet on entry, still has tannin, light-bodied, tart edge; ready now, not to keep. *

Poggio al Sole (*twice, 9/82, 39,833 bottle, unfined and unfiltered*). Nice floral aroma; fruity, agreeable flavors, but a harsh acidic edge, a little meager in body, some alcohol intrudes on the finish; old and tired, though still drinkable.

Riecine (*3 times, 11/80*). Characteristic flowers on aroma; refreshing, lively acidity, fruity; well made. **

Riseccoli (*3 times, 6/81*). Aroma has hints of coffee and some oxidation intrudes; harsh edges, some fruit but has seen better days, though we're not sure when; even in March 1979 it seemed old and tired.

Rocca delle Macìe (10/78). Fresh, fruity and simple, low acid, good flavor. * −

Ruffino (11/79). Fresh and fruity, tart, some tannin, quaffable. *

Saccardi (1/82). Has some character and flavor but in all an unimpressive, small wine.

Serristori (11/78). Light, fresh and fruity, quaffable. *

Serristori, Riserva Ser Niccolo (10/83). Smallish nose; unbalanced, not a lot of fruit, moderate tannin; altogether unimpressive.

Tenuta La Colombaia, Riserva (2/83). Small nose; light-bodied, not a lot of flavor, lacks life, harsh edges, bitter aftertaste.

Valiano (11/79). Pale; some fruit, vinous, undistinguished.

Vignale (*twice, 2/80*). Lovely fragrant bouquet, and that's its one real virtue; a bit light, fruity but shallow.

Villa Antinori, Riserva (9/83). Characteristic floral aroma with some fruit; well structured, some tannin to lose, firm acidity; probably needs three years to smooth out the harsh edges. **(+)

Villa Antinori, Riserva Marchese (5/85). Weedy, bell pepper aroma with a touch of fruit, and some oxidation; fruity, herbaceous flavor, is this a Cabernet or a Chianti(?); astringent aftertaste; seems older than its years. *

Villa Cafaggio (3/79). Some fruit on aroma and palate, moderate length. ** −

Villa Cerna, Riserva (11/90). Ripe fruit and berry aroma, floral note; sense of sweetness, attractive flavor, a little short; drink. **

Villa Colombaio (*twice, 4/80*). Perfumed bouquet; soft and fruity, some tannin, balanced tasty. ** −

1976 0

The year's production of 6.7 million gallons (253,216 hectoliters) of wine, equivalent to 2.81 million cases of Chianti Classico, was 8 percent below the 1970s annual average of 7.3 million gallons (274,227 hectoliters). This vintage was without a doubt the worst of the decade. For the most part, it should never have been bottled. And for once the *consorzio* rated a vintage as zero. They described the wines as having low color, an average of 12.1 percent alcohol, average acidity, and low extract.

Bianchi didn't bottle a Monsanto. Minuccio Cappelli didn't offer a Montagliari. He did bottle a small amount of fairly agreeable wine for his own personal use.

Of the two most successful '76s we tasted, both producers—Badia a Coltibuono and Cappelli—considered the vintage very bad, if not downright poor. The best anyone had to say for it was Stefano Farkas of Villa Cafaggio, who said the vintage was "not good." If any remain they would be of academic interest only.

Badia a Coltibuono, Riserva (*twice, 4/89, 7,600 bottles*). Light nose, hint of mint; soft, tasty and balanced, dry finish, still quite nice. This bottle was more attractive than the one tasted four years earlier. ** −

Castello di Gabbiano (3/79). Pale; oxidized, thin, alcoholic.

Cecchi (3/79). Some tannin, lacks substance, weight and length.

Fattoria di Montagliari (5/85). [From a single barrel bottled in 1979–80.] Still has fruit, suggestions of leather; very light and soft, thin finish. *

Fattoria La Ripa (5/85). Off flavors of rotten grapes.

Fattoria Le Bocce (10/78). Fruity, flavorful, light-bodied, a bit clumsy. * −

Monte Vertine (3/79). Small nose; fruity entry gives way to a harshness toward the end.

Montepaldi, Marchese Corsini (3/79). Hot alcoholic nose; touch of oxidation.

1975 **

The production of 6.8 million gallons (258,027 hectoliters), equivalent to 2.88 million cases, was 6 percent below the 1970s annual average. This vintage was highly acclaimed from the outset. The *consorzio* reported that the wines have high color, 12.8 percent alcohol, and medium-high acidity and extract. They gave it four out of four stars and said they are wines for long aging.

Antinori once again gives it five out of five stars. Felsina said it was very, very good, as did Barone Ricasoli. Cispiano considers it one of the great years, and numerous other producers also rate it excellent.

There was rain during the harvest and it made a difference when the grapes were picked. We've tasted some four dozen

'75s; many were fine, but many others were tired, showing age, or poor from the start. The best, once again, was the outstanding Monsanto Riserva Il Poggio. Only second to the Il Poggio was the exceptional Montagliari Riserva Vigna di Casaloste, then the Montagliari e Castellinuzza Riserva. Of those tasted in the mid-1980s, the *riserve* of Badia a Coltibuono, Fattoria di Felsina "Berardenga," Capannelle, Castell'in Villa, Poggio al Sole, and Villa Antinori were all very good to excellent.

For the most part, these wines are fading now; the very best will keep, and a few will improve further. While we gave them three stars out of four at one time, two would seem a more reasonable estimate of their current state.

Badia a Coltibuono, Riserva (7 times, 5/85). Floral bouquet with notes of berries; firm, a mouthful of flavor and a lot of tannin; very young yet but has all the ingredients for a splendid wine. **(*)

Berardenga, Fattoria di Felsina, Riserva (5/85). Aroma still closed; rich in flavor, considerable tannin; needs another three or so years to soften; firm structure; a lot of quality here. **(*+)

Brolio (11/79). Pale garnet; onionlike aspect to aroma; has body and flavor, ready. *

Brolio, Riserva (3 times, 12/88). Brick red; dried fruit aroma; some age apparent, still some tannin, but the attractive open flavors and soft center make it very appealing now, dry finish; drink. *+

Capannelle, Riserva (5/85). Complex floral bouquet with woodsy notes; well balanced, full-flavored, still some tannin, fairly long finish with a suggestion of mint, tannin builds up at the end, too much? **(?*)

Carobbio (10/80). Tired, noticeable oxidation.

Casa Sola, Riserva (11/79). A bit light, has tannin, fruit and backbone; try again in two to three years. *

Castelgreve, Riserva (10/83). Aroma of raisins, oxidation apparent; still has some fruit and tannin; lacks style.

Castell'in Villa, Riserva (5/85). Delicate, floral bouquet with nuances of mint and pine; a rich mouthful of flavor, well structured, very long finish, some tannin at the end; room to improve but very nice now. ***−

Castello di Cacchiano (twice, 6/81). Characteristic aroma, floral and fruity; some tannin, tart edge, shows age, not to keep; it was better in March 1979.

Castello di Fonterutoli (3/79). Floral bouquet marred by intrusion of alcohol; light, flavorful, short, with some alcohol at the end.

Castello di Rencine (twice, 6/81). Small aroma with some fruit, some oxidation; nice entry, mellow, some tannin, a biting sharpness at the end; too old; it was better two years earlier, but still didn't amount to much.

Castello di San Polo in Rosso (5/85). Floral aroma; flavorful, soft; somewhat rustic; has aged surprisingly well for a regular Chianti. **−

Cispiano (11/79). Some fruit, some tannin, not much interest.

Conti Capponi (twice, 11/79). Pale; light-bodied, not much to it except some tannin.

Dom Bruno (ex-demijohn, 5/86). This wine spent two years in wood and was then transferred to demijohn, where it has been ever since. Color and freshness belie its age; light nose, floral note; fruity, very soft and round, a little drying at the end, still it is rather nice. **

Fattoria dei Pagliarese, Riserva (4/89). Lots of age on the nose; dry, moderate tannin, still has a lot of fruit. *+

Fattoria dell'Aiola, Riserva (3/79). Some oxidation, light, harsh; showing age.

Fattoria di Montagliari, Riserva (twice, 5/82). Lightly floral aroma; still tannic but with the stuffing to support it; young yet, has potential. **(*)

Fattoria di Montagliari, Riserva Vigna di Casaloste (5 times, 4/90, 5,500 bottles). Rich bouquet, complex and open, floral component, hint of graphite; richly concentrated, some delicacy; at or near its peak; loads of class; long. ***+

Fattoria di Montagliari e Castellinuzza, Riserva (twice, 6/88). Fragrant-scented bouquet, suggestions of flowers and nuts, light berry note; soft, smooth center, tasty, some tannin; ready now. ***−

Fattoria La Mandria (2/82). Alcoholic nose; drying out.

Fattoria Le Bocce, Vecchio (10/78). Fruity aroma; flavorful, balanced, some tannin but ready. **

Fattoria Monsanto, Riserva (5 times, 10/83). Rich aroma with suggestions of blueberries and toasty notes; flavorful, light tannin, good balance; quite nice now; long finish. ***−

Fattoria Monsanto, Riserva Il Poggio (9 times, 4/90, 35,700 bottles). Lovely bouquet, blueberries and leather; soft and smooth, flavor recalls raspberries and strawberries; seems ready yet with room to improve; still some tannin. ***+ *Bottle of 4/85:* Richly concentrated aroma; lovely, rich, ripe fruit flavors fill the mouth, enormous weight and extract, considerable tannin, beginning to resolve itself and soften, impressive balance and structure, enormous length; this one is bigger and richer than the '77; what it lacks in elegance it makes up in richness. ***(*)

Fattoria Tregole (10/78). Touch of pine and floral notes in aroma; fairly well balanced, flavorful; quite nice. **−

Fattoria Vignale, Riserva (12/82). Nice nose though showing some oxidation; flat, very dull.

Fattoria Viticcio, Riserva (6/85). Nice nose, displays complexity and mellowness from bottle age; soft, round and smooth, flavorful; very ready. **+

Fortilizio Il Colombaio, Riserva (4/80). Light, fruity aroma; well balanced, some tannin to soften, good fruit; give it three, perhaps four years. ***

Fossi, Riserva (5/83). Oxidation is evident, but the structure seems to indicate it was a good wine; could be an off bottle, or perhaps just a bit too old.

Isole e Olena, Riserva (5/85). Well-developed bouquet, floral with some fruit; light tannin, fairly soft, ready, some length; not to keep. ** +

Melini (11/79). Light, fruity aroma; light- to medium-bodied, nice flavor. * +

Nozzole, Riserva (11/80). Blackberries on aroma; some tannin, but richness and concentration make it enjoyable now. ***

Palazzo al Bosco, Riserva (11/80). Somewhat subdued aroma with light fruit; a bit light in body, fruity, some tannin to lose. *(* +)

Pian d'Albola, Riserva (3/79). Hot aroma; some tannin, lacks substance and length.

Poggio al Sole, Riserva (5/85, 1,475 bottles). Berrylike fruit on aroma; flavorful, soft, round and ready. *** −

Riecine (twice, 6/90, 12,500 bottles). Fairly nice nose; but, alas, it's drying out.

Rocca delle Macìe, Riserva (twice, 11/80). Light but characteristic aroma; light- to medium-bodied, some tannin, some fruit; overall unimpressive.

Rocca delle Macìe, Vecchio (10/78). Not much aroma, jammy; some oxidation, unbalanced.

Ruffino, Riserva Ducale (4 times, 11/80). Nose somewhat reticent; good body, a lot of fruit, some tannin to lose; in all, a good bottle. **(+)

Ruffino, Riserva Ducale gold label (twice, 11/90). Light trace of oxidation, hint of flowers and coffee, still at this stage the oxidation adds interest and complexity; soft center, a little dry at the edges and toward the end, still it does have flavor; drink up. **

S. Leolino, Fattoria I Cipressi, Riserva (2/80). Characteristic aroma; some tannin, flavorful; still needs a few more years. *(*)

Saccardi (10/83). Oxidized; still some flavor interest, albeit very little.

Signoria (Barfede-Certaldo) (4/80). Rosé color; floral, fruity aroma; some tannin, moderate length. *

Tenuta La Colombaia (11/79). Small aroma; some tannin and fruity; not bad. * −

Vignavecchia, Riserva (5/85). Floral aroma with a hint of toffee seems older than its years; some fruit remains, but beginning to dry out. * −

Villa Antinori, Riserva (3 times, 5/85). [Part of it was aged eighteen months in *barrique*.] Fruity aroma with an herbaceous backnote; still has tannin but beginning to soften and smooth out nicely, good fruit, well knit; quite enjoyable now; an herbaceous note at the end. *** *Bottle of 11/79*: Herbaceous aroma with some harshness, a nice wine but no depth or class. *

Villa Banfi (twice, 2/80). Pale; light-bodied; undistinguished.

Villa Cafaggio, Vecchio (3/79). Small, scented bouquet; balanced, tasty, some style, good weight and length. ** +

Villa Calcinaia, Riserva Conti Capponi (10/83). Corked.

Villa Colombaio, Riserva (11/79). Lovely perfumed bouquet; some tannin to lose, loads of flavor, good quality; needs some time yet. ** +

1974 0

The crop yielded 8.5 million gallons (323,029 hectoliters) of wine, equivalent to 3.59 million cases. This was 17.8 percent above the 1970s annual average of 7.3 million gallons (274,227 hectoliters) and the second largest of the decade.

This was a year with a very dry summer. The wines had body and tannin, but lacked somewhat in substance and fruit. They were reminiscent in some ways of the '78s; something was missing. The wines, according to *consorzio*, had medium-high color, 12.5 percent alcohol, medium-low acidity, and medium-high extract. They rated it three out of four stars and said it was a very good vintage for aging.

A few producers felt that the vintage was better than 1975. Paolo de Marchi of Isole e Olena feels the wines have aged better than the '75s. Certainly the Monsanto Riserva Il Poggio and Giovanni Cappelli's Montagliari e Castellinuzza Riserva challenge their '75s. Outside these two and the Berardenga from Fattoria di Felsina, there are very few others that we can recommend. For the most part, the '74s are old and getting older. They would have been best drunk up some years ago.

Badia a Coltibuono, Riserva (5/85). Small nose; taste of old wood, moderate tannin, soft-centered; beginning to tire. * +

Berardenga, Fattoria di Felsina, Riserva (twice, 3/87). Brick robe; orange cast; perfumed bouquet, lovely, soft, light tannin; very ready, not to keep, some age at the end. **

Brolio, Riserva (11/79). Hot, alcoholic nose; some tannin, has substance, good body. *

Castello di Cerreto, Riserva (3/79). Some oxidation, could be the bottle.

Castello di Meleto (3/79). Pale garnet; light nose; thin, without substance or length; barely drinkable.

Castello di Verrazzano (twice, 3/81). Fragrant aroma showing bottle age but not much complexity; some tannin, low fruit, acidity on the high side, some alcohol at the end; getting on in age.

Castello di Volpaia, Riserva (5/85). Odd note on aroma; still some tannin, some flavor; drying out, but still good now.*

Castello Vicchiomaggio, Riserva (5/85). Floral aroma; some tannin, soft-centered; shows signs of drying out at end. * +

Fattoria delle Lodoline, Riserva (4/80). Pale; thin, alcoholic.

Fattoria di Montagliari, Riserva (5/85, at the winery). Perfumed bouquet; soft and round, has delicacy; at its peak. ** +

Fattoria di Montagliari e Castellinuzza, Riserva (13 times, 1/88). Perfumed floral bouquet; soft and balanced, long finish; very ready, at its peak, and holding very well indeed; some class and elegance. *** *Bottle of 2/85:* Tawny with orange reflections; lovely fragrant bouquet; well balanced, tasty; elegant and stylish, a real success; at its peak, where it's been for three years. ***

Fattoria La Ripa (5/85). Alcoholic, some oxidation, drying out.

Fattoria Le Bocce, Riserva (10/78). Nice nose; balanced, flavorful, nice texture, some tannin to shed; has style. **(+)

Fattoria Le Pici, Riserva (10/83). Nice fruit up front, then shallow, drying out.

Fattoria Monsanto, normale (twice, 6/83). *From gallon:* Lovely, full rich bouquet with suggestions of blueberries; full of flavor, smooth and round, still some tannin but pretty much ready. ** + *Bottle of 5/83:* Still good, but beginning to fade. *

Fattoria Monsanto, Riserva (twice, 11/80). Fragrant bouquet though a bit reticent; still undeveloped, has some softness. *

Fattoria Monsanto, Riserva Il Poggio (16 times, 4/90, 34,600 bottles). Berrylike aroma recalls blueberries, and components of damp leaves and leather; soft, open and tasty; very ready with some room for further improvement; moderate length, some tannin at the end. ** + *Bottle of 4/85:* Fairly rich bouquet with toasty, berrylike notes, vaguely floral; full of flavor, still some tannin to shed, a big wine; coming ready with still more to give; a slight touch of hotness at the end. ** +

Fattoria Valiano, Riserva (11/79). Hot nose; light-bodied, some tannin and fruit; rather pedestrian.

Fortilizio Il Colombaio, Riserva (twice, 10/81). Lovely fragrant bouquet; well structured, tasty, soft, long finish; elegant. ** +

Fossi, Riserva (twice, 2/90). Age shows, still some flavor. *

Isole e Olena (5/85). Oxidized though still has some interest.

Nozzole, Riserva (3 times, 4/81). Floral bouquet characteristic of Chianti; light-bodied and tart, lacks somewhat in fruit, still has tannin; not a wine to keep.

Rocca delle Macìe, Riserva (10/78). Nice nose though a bit light; good flavor but unbalanced and harsh, especially at the end; not to keep.

Rocca delle Macìe, Riserva Zingarelli (3/79). Oxidation apparent.

Ruffino, Riserva Ducale (7 times, 4/81). Bouquet displays some complexity from bottle age; good body and structure, some acidity and tannin, good fruit; should be better in a year or two. **

Ruffino, Riserva Ducale gold label (twice, 11/90). Woodslike aroma, nuances recall tobacco, dried fruit and flowers; nice flavor, sense of sweetness, starting to lose its fruit, short and dry; drink. ** −

Saccardi (3/79). Not a lot of aroma; flavorful, has tannin and substance, a bit short. *

Serristori, Riserva Machiavelli (11/78). Fragrant scent; a bit light, some tannin to lose, good flavor; enjoyable now. **

Straccali, Riserva (10/78). Bouquet shows development; soft and flavorful, some tannin; ready now. ** +

Tizzano, Riserva (3/79). Pale garnet; small nose with a slight dankness; has substance and weight, only the nose throws it off.

Villa Antinori, Riserva Marchese (5 times, 5/85). *Tasted at the winery:* Pale brick color; weedy, herbaceous notes dominate aroma and palate, showing age but drinkable. * *Bottle of 5/83:* Pale color; showing age, vegetables on aroma that carry through on palate; this wine was at its best in 1980 and 1981.

Villa Terciona (3/79). Small nose marred by intrusion of alcohol; a bit light, still has fruit; no need to hold longer. * −

1973 0

Spring was mild, and the summer hot and dry. Heavy rains close to the harvest only helped stretch the crop. The year's harvest of 7.5 million gallons (281,980 hectoliters), equivalent to 3.13 million cases, was slightly above the 1970s annual average. Overall, the wines were light, even thin, lacking in body, weight, and structure. They matured early and faded fast.

A big problem was the *consorzio*. This was the last vintage they interfered with the grower-producers, telling them when they could harvest. Bureaucratic meddling ruined what might have been a very great vintage. They withheld permission to harvest until too late. While they continued to refuse permission to pick the grapes, heavy rainstorms broke, drenching the vineyards and diluting the fruit.

The wines were, according to the *consorzio*, average in color, acidity, and extract, and had 12.5 percent alcohol. They rated it two stars out of four.

Castello di Gabbiano felt the vintage was very, very good nonetheless. Minuccio Cappelli described his '73s as perfumed wines in which the bouquet makes up for what they lack in body. Cappelli's Montagliari Riserva and Vignamaggio Riserva were still drinking well in the mid-1980s. And the Monsanto Riserva Il Poggio and Villa Francesca Riserva are still very good today. But even they won't improve further. Most '73s have long faded.

Castelgreve, Riserva (10/83). Some oxidation; showing age but still has some interest and fruit. * −

Castello di Uzzano (11/80). Lovely bouquet; soft, nice texture, a bit light but very drinkable. **

Castello di Volpaia, Riserva (5/85). Floral aroma with a touch of pine; still has flavor interest but beginning to dry out. * –

Castello Vicchiomaggio, Riserva (twice, 5/85). Dull nose; overly tannic, drying out.

Fattoria di Montagliari, Riserva (6 times, 5/86). The most recent bottle was the best one. While there was some variation it wasn't major; all six bottles were at least very good. Floral bouquet with a berrylike nuance; soft, round and ready, almost velvety, light but elegant, long finish, vague harshness; very nice now, might last, won't improve. *** –

Fattoria Le Bocce, Riserva (10/78). Complex bouquet showing some development; soft and round; stylish, impressive, particularly for the vintage. ***

Fattoria Monsanto, Riserva (3 times, 3/82). Moderately intense aroma with suggestions of blueberries; some harshness at edges; beginning to fade though still quite good, peaked perhaps two years ago. ** –

Fattoria Monsanto, Riserva Il Poggio (14 times, 4/90, 6,500 bottles). Lovely fragrant bouquet, recalls raspberries, blueberries and flowers; soft, open, tasty, low acid, short, and a tad dry at the end; holding, drink. ** *Bottle of 4/85:* Brickish-orange robe; floral bouquet with berries and a note of apricots; round, smooth, ready and holding well, licorice at the end. ** +

Fortilizio Il Colombaio, Riserva (4 times, 8/82). Floral bouquet; still has flavor and some fruit but showing age, beginning to dry out. *Bottle of 4/80:* Still good, not to keep. * +

Melini, Riserva (twice, 11/79). Small aroma with some volatile acidity and alcohol; nice mouth feel, smooth-textured; as ready as it'll ever be. * +

Palazzo al Bosco, Riserva (twice, 12/80). Smallish nose; light-bodied, nice entry, soft. * –

Straccali, Riserva (10/78). Small nose; unbalanced, alcohol at the end.

Vignamaggio, Riserva (5/85). Light, floral aroma; still has fruit and tannin, some delicacy; shows signs of drying out at the end; drink them up. **

Villa Banfi (twice 3/79). Pale color; oxidized.

Villa Francesca, Riserva (twice, 5/90). Brick, garnet color; complex, mellow bouquet; soft, light tannin, surprisingly good; perhaps a bit over the top but makes an enjoyable glass for now. **

Villa Terciona (10/78). Touch of oxidation on the nose; still some tannin but a surprising amount of fruit; quite good for the year, and its age (not a *riserva*). **

1972 0

The 4.7 million gallons (178,157 hectoliters), equivalent to 1.98 million cases, produced was the second smallest of the decade and only 65 percent of the decade's average. The 1972 vintage was beat out for last place in quality in the decade only by 1976. Many producers described the vintage as bad, others as poor. Yet the *consorzio* rated it as a one-star vintage out of four. The Monsanto Il Poggio was the most notable exception—a big, rich, concentrated wine that has aged gracefully. It is still lovely. Even though it is at its best, there should be no rush to drink it up. The Badia a Coltibuono and Berardenga Riservas are also still good, though starting to go.

Badia a Coltibuono, Riserva (11/90). Forestlike bouquet, damp leaves and animal fair components; soft, sweet impression, very long finish; just past its peak, and very good indeed. ***

Berardenga, Fattoria di Felsina, Riserva (twice, 6/87, 10,655 bottles). Brickish rim, garnet color; earthy aroma, moderate intensity; richly flavored, soft; very ready, and quite good too in spite of a slight harshness at the end. **

Castell'in Villa, Vecchio (10/81). Still has fruit but is beginning to dry out, some alcohol at the end; considering the vintage and its age, not at all bad. *

Fattoria Monsanto, Riserva (9 times, 3/82). Fragrant characteristic bouquet with some delicacy; smooth and tasty; very ready, in fact a bit past its peak (which seemed to be in 1979 and 1980); has a slightly harsh edge to it; in all very enjoyable. * +

Fattoria Monsanto, Riserva Il Poggio (28 times, 4/90, 12,770 bottles). Intensely concentrated bouquet suggestive of leather, cassis, berries and apricots; rich in concentration, packed with fruit, soft and smooth; very ready, and holding well. *** *Bottle of 4/85:* Brickish-orange robe; intensely rich bouquet with nuances of flowers and berries and a note of apricots; a big, richly concentrated wine with a sweetness of ripe fruit, well balanced; very ready. A resounding success for a vintage that was, overall, a disaster, or near disaster. ***

Villa Colombaio (4/80). Small aroma that hints of fruit; light-bodied, some tannin, a surprising amount of fruit. **

1971 **

The flowering took place early, in the second week of March for the sangiovese and a week later for the trebbiano. May was dry and sunny. July and August were mild and extremely dry; a scant 0.087 inch (2.2 millimeters) of rain fell the first month and 0.347 inch (8.8 millimeters) in August. In the first ten days of September, the vineyards were quenched with 1.89 inches (48 millimeters) of much-needed rain. One week before the harvest, hail slashed the crop and made a selection among the damaged vineyards necessary. It was to be, with a production of 4.5 million gallons (169,619 hectoliters), equivalent to 1.88 million cases, the smallest crop of the decade, only 62 percent of the annual average of 7.3 million gallons (274,227 hectoliters) between 1970 and 1979.

Niederbacher and the *consorzio* both give the year their maximum points, four stars. Many producers, including Barone Ricasoli, agreed. Our recent tasting notes indicate that the best are still splendid, but the lesser ones have long since faded. In the mid-1980s, Badia a Coltibuono, Castell'in Villa, Monsanto Uvaggio del Poggio a Sornano, Montagliari, Poggio al Sole, and Vignamaggio were still very good. More recently, Montagliari e Castellinuzza, Montagliari Vigna di Casaloste, Monsanto, and Monsanto Il Poggio were very good indeed, with this last wine absolutely splendid. The Pagliarese and Ruffino Riserva Ducale gold label were fading.

Badia a Coltibuono, Riserva (*3 times, 5/85*). Rich, intense bouquet with notes of berries and pine, a hint of flowers; round and smooth, almost velvety, has style and distinction, a lot of flavor, and still more to give; this wine has opened up a lot since the previous bottle, tasted in October 1982. ***

Berardenga, Fattoria di Felsina, Riserva (*5/85*). Earthy, mineral aroma; tannin, lacks stuffing; not to keep. * −

Castell'in Villa, Riserva (*5/85*). Brick, orange at rim; floral bouquet with berrylike notes; concentrated fruit, smooth and velvety, some tannin, well balanced, long finish; ready. ***

Castello di Cacchiano (*4/80*). Alcoholic nose with some fruit; light-bodied, no fruit left, dried out.

Castello di Fonterutoli, Riserva (*twice, 12/81*). Color showing age; light aroma with some interest; lacks flavor and structure; the wine was better two years ago.

Castello di Volpaia, Riserva (*twice, 9/90*). Light nose, vaguely floral; soft entry, very ready, finish is a bit brief. * +

Fattoria dei Pagliarese, Riserva (*4/89*). Old fruit aroma; drying out, still has flavor, lacks freshness, bitter finish. *

Fattoria di Montagliari, Riserva (*5/86*). Orange toward tawny at the rim; pretty floral bouquet; soft though still some tannin; ready and holding; long and elegant. ***

Fattoria di Montagliari, Riserva Vigna di Casaloste (*6 times, 12/87, 5,500 bottles*). Brick-orange robe; beautiful floral-scented bouquet, displays delicacy and elegance; still some tannin, velvety, has a sweetness from ripe fruit, very long finish; real class. **** *Bottle of 5/85:* Delicate, floral perfume; full-flavored; had delicacy, elegance and style; good now and has a lot of potential. ***(*)

Fattoria di Montagliari e Castellinuzza, Riserva (*13 times, 9/87*). Pale garnet; delicate, scented floral bouquet, berry notes; soft and velvety; elegant, real class; at its peak. *** + *Bottle of 5/85:* Medium garnet, orange reflections; lovely perfumed bouquet; smooth-textured, full of flavor; stylish and elegant; a complete wine, at its peak, where it has been for at least four years. *** +

Fattoria Monsanto, Riserva (*12 times, 8/87*). Richly fruited aroma recalls blueberries, some spice; packed with fruit, full, rich, tasty, still tannin, somewhat dry at the end. *** *Bottle of 8/84:* Lovely bouquet, rich and fragrant; heaps of flavor and concentra-

tion, well structured; most enjoyable. *** *From gallon, 5/84:* Expansive floral bouquet with a note of blueberries; light tannin, soft and full-flavored, velvety, seems sweet; at its peak. *** +

Fattoria Monsanto, Riserva Il Poggio (*12 times, 4/90, 36,700 bottles*). Leather, dried fruit and floral bouquet; sweet entry, round, rich and complete, smooth; room to improve, lovely now; very long finish. *** + (****) *Bottle of 4/85:* Intense aroma with toasty, berrylike notes; heaps of tannin, loads of flavor, has depth and concentration; still very young. ***(*) *Bottle of 10/82:* Floral bouquet with blueberrylike fruit; enormous richness and concentration; still has more to give; should become a great wine. ***(*)

Fattoria Monsanto, Uvaggio del Poggio a Sornano (*twice, 4/85*). [This wine is actually a simple Chianti, the Sornano vineyard is not in the Classico zone.] Deep ruby, garnet at rim; expansive perfumed bouquet with notes of apricots and cassis; smooth-textured, full of flavor, a big, rich wine of very fine quality and enormous length; enjoyable now, will improve. ***(+)

Fattoria Quercia al Poggio (*twice, both 5/85*). *From vat:* Pale, old, drying out. *From bottle:* Some oxidation apparent; still has fairly nice flavor and some interest. *

Fizzano, Riserva (*11/80*). Still has considerable tannin, some fruit evident; is it drying out, or is the fruit masked?

Fossi, Riserva (*5/83*). Dull and flat, shows age.

Isole e Olena, Riserva (*5/85*). Age showing badly, drying out, though some interest remains.

Pandolfini (*8/78*). Characteristic Chianti nose; soft and tasty, a bit short. *

Poggio al Sole, Riserva (*5/85*). Lightly perfumed bouquet with berrylike notes; some tannin, soft, smooth-textured, moderate length; holding but not to keep. **

Riseccoli, Riserva (*3/80*). Perfumed bouquet, its one virtue; somewhat unbalanced, still some fruit and tannin, but showing age, slightly bitter finish.

Rocca delle Macìe, Riserva (*10/78*). Characteristic aroma; somewhat light, high acid throws it out of balance.

Ruffino, Riserva Ducale gold label (*9 times, 6/89*). Brick-orange robe; delicate fragrance; seems to be losing fruit and drying out, still has flavor interest; the bottle perhaps? * *Bottle of 9/83:* Fruity overtones on bouquet and floral notes; still has tannin, rich and concentrated, very well balanced; should make a splendid bottle in four to five years. ***(+)

Vignamaggio, Riserva (*5/85*). Expansive floral aroma showing a lot of development; fairly tannic on entry, with a lot of fruit beneath, quite rich, tannic finish; needs more time. **(*)

Villa Calcinaia, Riserva Conti Capponi (*10/83*). Vaguely mineral note on nose; some age shows, not much tannin left; not to keep. *

Villa Cerna, Riserva (*3 times, 11/90*). It's been seven years since we last tasted this wine, and that is a long time for a Chianti Classico to hold. So we weren't surprised that it was oxidized.

Bottle of 10/83: Floral perfume with some berrylike fruit; still has tannin, soft and round, tasty, a trifle short; ready. ** —

Villa Colombaio, Riserva (4/80). Lovely perfumed bouquet; good body, loads of flavor, well structured, still some tannin to shed; very good quality. ***(+)

1970 **

The yield of 5.4 million gallons (205,074 hectoliters), equivalent to 2.28 million cases, was the largest from 1967 until 1973. This was a good vintage from the start but fell in the shadow of the outstanding 1971. For the most part, the '70s are wines to drink, not to hold. Niederbacher rated the year three stars out of four; the *consorzio* gave it two.

The Castello di Volpaia Riserva is excellent and at its peak. The Berardenga and Castello di Querceto are as good as they'll ever be, which is very good indeed, and the Pagliarese, although past its best, is still good. Badia a Coltibuono and Monsanto Riserva Il Poggio will certainly improve; the '70 Il Poggio has always challenged the younger '71, though we do think that the '71 has pulled ahead.

Badia a Coltibuono, Riserva (4 times, 9/87). Vaguely floral aroma; some tannin remains, most is resolved, good flavor, long; ready now, should hold. *** —

Berardenga, Fattoria di Felsina, Riserva (twice, 12/89). Floral, berry bouquet; soft though seems a little grainy, round and smooth; at its peak but holding, not signs of decline. **

Castelgreve, Riserva (10/83). Raisiny aroma (*governo?*); some intensity; heavy-handed, clumsy.

Castello di Cerreto, Riserva (4 times, 1/84). Oxidized. *Bottle of 9/82:* Some oxidation, but nice flavor and balance; still very good. ** This wine seemed to peak in 1980, at that time it was very, very good.

Castello di Gabbiano, Riserva "La Cagnina" (3 times, 1/84). Brick red, orange at rim; lovely fragrant, characteristic bouquet; soft, smooth and well balanced, some sweetness; at its peak. **+

Castello di Querceto, Riserva (5/85). Floral bouquet with a suggestion of blackberries; tannic entry then a rush of fruit across the palate, almost sweet, hints of leather; not to keep. ***

Castello di Volpaia, Riserva (twice, 9/90). Great class and elegance, soft, liquid velvet, at its peak, very long, real class. ***

Fattoria dei Pagliarese, Riserva (4/89). Starting to lose flavor and fruit, still fairly tannic; drink. *

Fattoria di Montagliari e Castellinuzza, Riserva (twice, 1/84). Light brick red; lovely floral bouquet; light- to medium-bodied, soft, tasty, well balanced; at or near its peak; shows class. **+

Fattoria Monsanto, Riserva (21 times, 10/85). Big, richly fruited aroma, toasty and blueberry nuances; rich, mouth-filling wine; very ready; some acid toward the finish. *** — *Bottle of 11/84:* Floral bouquet with a toasty aspect; fairly full and open, still has tannin and good fruit; more or less ready, though it was better a couple of years ago. *** — *From gallon, 10/79:* Has rounded out nicely, soft, flavorful, moderate length. ***

Fattoria Monsanto, Riserva Il Poggio (16 times, 4/90, 18,630 bottles). Bouquet suggestive of damp leaves, blueberries and flowers; still some tannin to be resolved, but for the most part coming ready; intensely fruited, heaps of flavor and concentration, very long, with a lingering sweetness. ***+ (****—) *Bottle of 4/85:* Deep, rich intense aroma with a concentration of blueberrylike fruit, and toasty, woodsy notes; a big, rich mouthful of wine, enormous weight and extract, still has tannin, suggestions of leather and tobacco; very high quality. ***(*)

Fortilizio Il Colombaio, Riserva (4/80). Aroma is fairly closed but has a suggestion of fruit; tannin to shed, heaps of fruit; still undeveloped but shows impressive quality. **(*+)

Rocca delle Macìe, Riserva (10/78). Browning; some alcohol apparent; overly tannic, low fruit, drying out.

Ruffino, Riserva Ducale gold label (twice, 3/81). Color beginning to show age, floral bouquet with a raisiny note; still has tannin to shed, but the fruit is there to support it. *(*+)

Saccardi, Riserva (10/83). Lightly floral bouquet; drying out, though still has some fruit, a hint of oxidation on the finish.

Straccali, Riserva (10/78). Lovely characteristic bouquet; soft, a bit of tannin, tasty; ready, not to keep, a slight harshness at the end bodes ill for the future. **+

Villa Antinori, Riserva (11/79). Bouquet showing complexity of bottle age; good fruit, still has tannin but quite ready. **

Villa Cerna, Riserva (11/90). Oxidized.

Villa Colombaio, Riserva (3 times, 11/79). Lovely perfumed bouquet; loads of flavor, has some tannin to lose but enjoyable now, has style. *** —

1969 0

Production was 3.9 million gallons (147,968 hectoliters), or 1.64 million cases. The vintage was rated highly from the start; both Niederbacher and the *consorzio* gave it three out of four stars. Barone Ricasoli said it was very good. We never agreed. Today nearly all '69s are too old. Badia a Coltibuono and Berardenga have peaked, but the Monsanto Riserva Il Poggio is still excellent, though there is no reason to hold it any longer.

Badia a Coltibuono, Riserva (6 times, 5/85). Moderately intense floral bouquet, berrylike notes; nice texture, some sweetness, still has some tannin but very ready now, some alcohol mars the finish, no reason to keep any longer. **+

Berardenga, Fattoria di Felsina, Riserva (5/85). Deeper in color than the '70 and '71; perfumed aroma with fruity notes; some tannin, soft and easy, tannic finish. **

Castello di Volpaia, Riserva (twice, 9/90). Light nose, spicy and vaguely floral; has a bit of an edge, still has fruit and flavor, very little tannin; best to drink now. *

Castello Vicchiomaggio, Riserva (5/85, in half bottle). Small aroma; some tannin; beginning to dry out. *

Fattoria Monsanto, Riserva (twice, 12/80). Lovely perfumed bouquet with a suggestion of blueberries; soft and round, intense and flavorful, a touch of acid at the end. ** +

Fattoria Monsanto, Riserva Il Poggio (20 times, 4/90, 13,420 bottles). Lovely scented bouquet, complex with nuances of leather and berries; rich and concentrated, intensely fruited; at or near its peak as it's been for the past few years. *** — *Bottle of 4/85:* Big, rich, expansive bouquet with nuances of berries, leather and toast; soft, round, tasty, the richness makes it seem sweet; near its peak, where it's been for the past few years. ***

Fattoria Quercia al Poggio (5/85). Too old, faded.

Fortilizio Il Colombaio, Riserva (4/80). Lovely perfumed bouquet; some tannin remaining, soft and round; near its peak. ** +

Fossi, Riserva (twice, 2/90). Old, stinky, tired.

Isole e Olena (5/85). Barnyardy, awful!

Poggio al Sole, Riserva (5/85). Nice aroma though showing age; flavorful, beginning to dry out. * +

Rocca delle Macìe, Riserva (10/78). Complex bouquet showing development; soft and velvety, good flavor; peak; the best Rocca delle Macìe we've ever tasted up to this point. ** +

Straccali, Riserva (twice, 11/82). Tawny color; delicate floral perfume; still has some fruit, but beginning to dry out. * —

Villa Antinori, Riserva (twice, 9/83, 1.5-liter bottle). Tawny color, orange at rim; aroma displays some complexity from bottle age, a little light; vaguely floral, soft and smooth, a troublesome dryness at the end; as ready as it will ever be. * +

finish; past its best. * + *Bottle of 10/87:* Lovely floral-scented bouquet, complex; soft and flavorful, tasty and ready, light tannin; a lovely glass for now; this was the best bottle. ** + *Bottle of 5/85:* Onionskin; nice fruit on aroma over a background of old wood, and some oxidation; considerable tannin remaining, and very little fruit, astringent, drying out. ** — (There seems to be bottle variation: one tasted six months earlier was very good, meriting **, while another tasted two years earlier showed signs of drying out.)

Berardenga, Fattoria di Felsina (twice, 5/85, not a riserva, *tasted at the winery*). Awful aroma, ditto on palate.

Castelgreve, Riserva (10/83). Raisiny aroma and flavor, soft, lacks style, though drinkable enough. *

Castello di Volpaia, Riserva (9/90). Open berry aroma, floral component; lovely fruit, soft, tasty, a little short; best to drink, starting to fade. **

Fattoria del Leccio, Riserva "Fratelli Beccaro" (12/78). Characteristic Chianti aroma; still some tannin, a slight harshness, seems a bit shallow, some acid at end.

Fattoria Monsanto, Riserva (3 times, 3/80). Well-developed, expansive bouquet; rich, soft and velvety, very long finish; a very good wine and very ready. *** — (There has been some bottle variation; the lesser bottles seemed to be drying out.)

Fattoria Monsanto, Riserva Il Poggio (16 times, 4/90, 12,550 bottles). Toasty, blueberry bouquet; absolute peak; soft and velvety, rich, with great weight and concentration, complete and long. *** — *Bottle of 4/85:* Lovely bouquet with toasty notes, tobacco, berries and mushrooms; a complete wine that's now at its peak; rich and full-flavored, velvety texture. *** (As with the regular, we've encountered some bottle variation.)

Fortilizio Il Colombaio, Riserva (4/80). Pretty garnet robe; soft and smooth, a lot of flavor; very ready, and very good. ***

Nozzole, Riserva (2/82, in half bottle). Moderately rich bouquet with suggestions of cassis and tar; soft, round and tasty, a touch of tannin but very ready. **

Villa Cerna, Riserva (11/90). Oxidized.

1968 0

There were 3.5 million gallons (132,122 hectoliters), equivalent to 1.47 million cases, produced. Niederbacher gave the year three out of four stars; the *consorzio* gave it two. Badia a Coltibuono said for them it was better than 1971. Giovanni Cappelli, on the other hand, found it not so good. Drink them up now if you have any. Monsanto Il Poggio is still splendid, as is the Castello di Volpaia, but there's no need to keep either of them any longer. The latter wine is starting to fade.

Badia a Coltibuono, Riserva (6 times, 4/89). Floral and fruit aroma; good body, still some tannin, dry and firm, tasty, hard

1967 * —

We have production figures for every year from 1967 to 1989. This vintage was, by far, the smallest crop of all, with a yield of 3.1 million gallons (115,677 hectoliters), equivalent to 1.29 million cases. This is 42 percent of the annual average of 7.3 million gallons (275,369 hectoliters) during that same period.

Without question, 1967 was one of the best vintages of the 1960s. Niederbacher gave it three stars out of four; the *consorzio*, four. Barone Ricasoli said it was very good. At this point most are past their peaks and showing signs of senility. The Monsanto Riserva Il Poggio tasted recently and Giovanni Cappelli's Montagliari Riserva tasted a few years ago are still splendid, although even the Monsanto is starting to fade.

Carpineto, Riserva (10/83). Slight aroma; fairly well balanced, tasty and soft; very ready. *

Fattoria di Montagliari, Riserva (5/85). Brick tending to orange at rim; expansive floral perfume; moderate tannin, sweet fruit, fairly full, soft and velvety, long finish. ***

Fattoria Monsanto, Riserva (10/81). Intense mushroomlike bouquet with a slight earthiness; flavorful, shows signs of drying out at the end. **

Fattoria Monsanto, Riserva Il Poggio (11 times, 4/90, 8,930 bottles). Toast, dried fruit and leather on the nose; fading, starting to dry out, still nice palate feel, and there is flavor. ** This wine seemed to be at its best through August 1987, although we didn't taste it between that date and April 1990. *Bottle of 4/85:* Light though characteristic bouquet with nuances of leather, toast, tobacco and underbrush; full of flavor, some tannin; just coming ready. ***.

Fattoria Viticcio, Riserva (6/85). Vaguely jammy aroma, berrylike fruit, shows age from bottle, old leather; light-bodied, virtually no tannin at all, very drinkable though it falls away at the end. ** –

Fortilizio Il Colombaio, Riserva (4/80). Perfumed bouquet with fruity notes; very soft and smooth, some tannin but good fruit; very ready. ** +

Ruffino, Riserva Ducale gold label (10/80). Perfumed aroma; full-bodied, still has tannin and considerable fruit; surprisingly young, needs more time, though has a troublesome dryness at the end. **(?)

Villa Antinori, Riserva (twice from bottle, 1/82, and twice from 1.5-liter bottle, 9/83). *From bottle:* Browning; some oxidation but also interesting nuances on bouquet; nice flavor, somewhat astringent; certainly on the decline but still a nice glass of wine. ** – *From 1.5-liter:* Tawny, toasty overtones on aroma and a touch of volatile acidity add complexity at this point; well structured, still some tannin; very good drinking now. **

Villa Calcinaia, Riserva, Conti Capponi (twice, 4/85). Onionskin; lovely perfumed bouquet, with some age showing, light tannin, flavorful; very nice now, has held up well. **

1966 0

The 1966 vintage got a lot of bad press, and for good reason—the quality of the goods. There were some remarkable exceptions, though. The Monsanto Riserva Il Poggio is still superb, certainly among the greatest Chiantis we've tasted and among the finest wines from anywhere. The Berardenga, too, was splendid in 1985, and the Badia, in 1989, was very good.

Badia a Coltibuono, Riserva (3 times, 11/90). Light nose, spice and mineral notes; sense of sweetness and a touch of oxidation, nice flavor, short; drink up. *Bottle of 4/89:* Floral, berry aroma; good body, rich, some tannin, a lot of flavor, firm, dry aftertaste. ** – *Bottle of 5/85:* Light nose with some fruit evident; soft and smooth, rather short. **

Berardenga, Fattoria di Felsina (5/85, *not a* riserva!!!, *tasted at the winery*). Perfumed bouquet; still has tannin, loads of flavor, well balanced; very ready. ***

Fattoria Monsanto, Riserva Il Poggio (9 times, 4/90, 5,370 bottles). Intense and complex, expansive blueberrylike overlay; liquid velvet, acidity a little low, sweet, round; complete, nearly perfect. **** *Bottle of 4/85:* Brick robe shading to orange; expansive bouquet with nuances of cassis, flowers, blackberries, almonds and apricots, toasty notes; exceptional balance, superbly crafted, liquid velvet on the palate, enormously long finish; a complete wine. ****

Straccali, Riserva (12/81). Garnet robe, orange at rim; some oak on aroma, very little fruit; still has flavor but showing obvious age, too bad; it was splendid in the mid- to late 1970s.

1965 0

Our experience with the '65s is limited, but as the vintage never amounted to much to begin with, any bottles left now, with very few exceptions, are probably best that way—left.

Badia a Coltibuono, Riserva (1/81). Some oxidation on aroma, berrylike fruit beneath; still flavorful though overly tannic and drying out. +

Fattoria dei Pagliarese (4/89). Fragrant-scented nose shows age but still attractive; drying out, with flavor remaining. *

1964 * –

Barone Ricasoli rates the vintage highly. Niederbacher gave the year three out of four stars; the *consorzio,* four. It was the best vintage of the decade for Chianti. The Monsanto Riserva Il Poggio was superb, at or near its peak in 1985; the bottles tasted in 1986 and 1987 were fading or faded. The Badia is still very good. The Ruffino Riserva Ducale gold label is gone. As for the others, it's hard to say, but we suspect that most have already faded or are starting to fade now.

Badia a Coltibuono, Riserva (3 times, 11/90). As with any old wine—and make no mistake about it, twenty-six years is old for a Chianti Classico—the cork, storage and other factors will result in bottle variation. Of these three bottles, the most recent one came from the winery and was tasted a few miles away at another winery; the bottle of April 1989 came from the winery and was tasted in Verona; and the first bottle was tasted at the winery itself. Floral-scented bouquet, berry note; soft and sweet, round and velvety, very long; lovely; at its absolute peak. *** + *Bottle of 4/89*: Scented, perfumed bouquet; velvety, lots of backbone and structure, richly flavored; still a lot of life left. *** − *Bottle of 5/85*: Floral aroma with toasty notes; smooth, round, full-flavored, moderately long; quite ready. *** −

Fattoria di Montagliari e Castellinuzza, Riserva (12/84). Bouquet shows a lot of depth and complexity from bottle age; soft and smooth; some elegance; lovely now, perhaps even a bit past its peak, but very nice. ** +

Fattoria Monsanto, Riserva (twice, 4/80). Bouquet is the essence of cassis; soft and velvety, enormous extract, very long; still young but so enjoyable now. ***(+)

Fattoria Monsanto, Riserva Il Poggio (8 times, 10/87, 13,760 bottles). Vague touch of oxidation, slightly corked, seems to be losing its fruit, still has interest. ? *Bottle of 11/86*: Medium toward brick red; some oxidation, seems to be drying out. ? *Bottle of 9/85*: Lovely bouquet, recalls cassis; deep, rich and intense, liquid velvet, round and soft, very long; loads of style. *** + *Bottle of 4/85*: Beautiful brick robe with orange reflections; rich, fruity, floral bouquet with nuances of berries, tobacco and leather; has a richness of flavor, a smoothness of texture and a fullness of body, very long finish recalls licorice, evergreen and chocolate; a superb wine; at or near its peak. ****

Fossi, Riserva (6 times, 2/90). Some flavor, old-style, no real depth but still good. * + *Bottle of 1/83*: Pretty floral bouquet with some delicacy; light tannin, tasty; beginning to dry out, drink it now. *

Palazzo al Bosco, Riserva (11/80). Lovely bouquet with some elegance; soft and flavorful, some tannin, good structure; stylish; fairly long on the finish. ** +

Ruffino, Riserva Ducale gold label (twice, 11/90). Oxidized, no interest left.

Serristori, Riserva Machiavelli (3/85). Perfumed floral bouquet, has delicacy; supple center, some acid at the end; just past its peak but still very good. *** −

Tenuta di Lilliano, Riserva (10/83). Browning; bouquet is big and rich with a chocolate note, and a touch of oxidation that adds complexity at this stage; nice flavor; drink up. * +

Villa Antinori, Riserva (1/83, 1.5-liter bottle). Considerable fruit on aroma with suggestions of blueberries; a lot of tannin, is there enough fruit (?), drying at the end. *

Villa Cerna, Riserva (11/90). Some oxidation; still has a lot of flavor and interest. ** −

1963 0

Niederbacher and the *consorzio* agreed; so do we: zero it was and zero it is.

Fossi (6/81). Complex bouquet with overtones of oak, then berrylike fruit and flowers; moderate tannin, moderate fruit; beginning to dry out. *

1962 * −

Only 1964 was better in the decade, though Niederbacher gave 1962 three out of four stars and the *consorzio* four. Barone Ricasoli rates the year highly. The wines are, for the most part, too old now. However, Monsanto and Cappelli's single-vineyard Casaloste, which were still very good a few years ago, could still be good.

Badia a Coltibuono, Riserva (4 times, 1/83). Brick tending to onionskin; well structured and flavorful, moderate tannin; good quality; can still improve. ** (A bottle tasted six months earlier and another, one and a half years earlier, seemed to be drying out!)

Fattoria di Montagliari, Riserva Vigna di Casaloste (14 times, 9/86, 3,500 bottles). Brick red; complex, old-style Chianti aroma; mellow, seems to be losing fruit; starting to show age, the bottle perhaps (a bottle four months earlier was considerably better), still it is quite good. ** *Bottle of 5/86*: Orange, tawny rim, brick center; tar- and blueberry-scented bouquet; soft and smooth, light tannin; holding well; sweet impression, stylish, long; a complete wine. *** + *Bottle of 5/85*: Beautiful orange-garnet robe; expansive floral perfume; silky texture; shows a lot of style and elegance; could be longer on finish. *** (Bottles have been variable: some seemed to show a lot more age, many others were as fine as this.)

Fattoria Monsanto, Riserva Il Poggio (4 times, 4/85, 5,730 bottles). Lovely robe; deep, rich and perfumed bouquet; incredible richness and concentration, fine balance; showing no signs of age, complete, what more can we say? It has been like this for close to five years now. ****

Fossi (6/81). Lovely, elegant refined bouquet; still some tannin, nice flowers; has held up well, but drink them now. **

Ruffino, Riserva Ducale gold label (3 times, 3/81). Fragrant floral bouquet; soft on entry then shows noticeable tannin, well structured; room for improvement; has some length, and style. **(*)

THE OLDER VINTAGES TODAY

**	1958, 1947
** −	1955
*	1957, 1952
0	1961, 1960, 1959, 1956, 1954, 1953, 1951, 1950, 1949, 1948, 1946

1961, 1960, 1959 0

Niederbacher gave the 1961 one star out of four, 1960 and 1959, zero; the *consorzio* gave one star to 1960 and two starts to 1961 and 1959. Barone Ricasoli rates 1960 highly. In our opinion the vintages all started out poor and aged as badly. There are always exceptions; the Badia a Coltibuono '59 Riserva tasted at the winery in May 1985 was still good, and the Nozzole '61 Riserva tasted in June 1990 was very good.

Badia a Coltibuono 1961 Riserva (1/81). Complex bouquet; considerable flavor, some tannin, well knit; very nice, some style, a pleasant surprise. ** +

Fossi 1961 (3 times, 9/89). Southern slant, fairly nice fruit on the nose; soft center, nice fruit; far from a classic Chianti but a nice red wine. * + *Bottle of 6/81:* Cooked aroma; dried out.

Nozzole 1961 Riserva (6/90). Scented bouquet; surprisingly soft and complex, and from such a mediocre vintage(!); lovely indeed, real quality, velvet texture; could use more length. **

Brolio 1960 Riserva (4 times, 12/88). Tawny, brick color; warm nose, floral notes; old but still interesting, starting to dry out, surprising amount of flavor, very dry, hard finish. * *Bottle of 9/83:* Some interesting nuances on aroma but oxidation intrudes; dried out, lacks interest.

Castello d'Albola 1960 Riserva (11/88). A lot of brown in the color; old nose, some decay, also some interest; surprisingly flavorful, still some tannin, drying a bit at the end, but has held up well. * +

Fossi 1960 (6/81). Baked aroma reminiscent of a southern wine; some flavor, clumsy.

Badia a Coltibuono 1959 Riserva (twice, 4/89). Nice nose; a bit light, still it is full-bodied, dry, and has flavor and fruit. * + *Bottle of 5/85:* Aroma of old wood; soft, tasty, short; ready. **

Fossi 1959 (5 times, 2/90). Fading, still has flavor, more typical of the genre than the '61. * *Bottle of 10/83:* Medium brick, browning at edges; light, floral aroma with a candylike note and some oxidation; some fruit, short, but enjoyable still; another surprise. *

Ruffino 1959 Riserva Ducale gold label (4/89). Rather nice indeed, soft and round, high acidity. * +

1958 **

We were always quite pleased with the '58s; we found them superior to the more highly regarded '57s. The few we've been lucky enough to taste in recent years indicate that they can still be very fine if stored properly. Barone Ricasoli said it was an excellent vintage. Niederbacher rated the year two stars out of four; the *consorzio*, three.

Badia a Coltibuono 1958 Riserva (3 times, 11/90). Brick robe, orange at the rim; bouquet recalls underbrush and dried flowers; nice entry, soft and round, silky, nice flavor, has a sweetness to it, fairly long; past its peak but still very nice. *** − *Bottle of 1/88:* Beautiful brick red color, shading toward orange at the rim; perfumed bouquet; some delicacy, dried fruit nuance; good structure, tannin still evident, somewhat austere, moderate length. ** + *Bottle of 5/85:* Fruity aroma recalls old wood, also a piney note; light tannin, soft and round, tasty; very ready; could have more length. *** −

Castello d'Albola 1958 Riserva (11/88). Some volatile acidity, but the rich nose displays a lot of fruit, vague suggestions of berries

and leather, with a barnyardy background; smooth and flavorful, almost velvet texture; starting to dry out, but has held up. * +

Fattoria di Montagliari e Castellinuzza 1958 Riserva Vino Vecchio (5/85). [Label does not say Chianti.] Lovely bouquet somewhat floral with berrylike notes; rich in flavor, velvety, extremely well balanced, sweet finish; a lot of class here. *** +

Fossi 1958 (twice, 6/81). Fragrant bouquet with some refinement; soft, moderate tannin, tasty, shows some signs of drying out at the end; not to keep. **

Ruffino 1958 Riserva Ducale gold label (11/83). Floral, fruity bouquet with a note of cedar; considerable tannin and some astringency, but the flavor is there; needs more age yet. **(*)

Villa Antinori 1958 Riserva (11/79). Lovely bouquet; lots of flavor, well structured; has style; at or near its peak. ***

1957 *

This vintage was highly regarded at one time. The Fattoria di Montagliari e Castellinuzza Vino Vecchio was still very good indeed, but the Fattoria di Querceto Riserva, Palazzo al Bosco Riserva, and Ruffino Riserva Ducale gold label that we tasted in the past decade were fading. And that is how we suspect most other wines are. Barone Ricasoli rates it very good. Niederbacher and the *consorzio* both gave the year three stars out of four.

Fattoria di Montagliari e Castellinuzza 1957 Vino Vecchio (5/86). [Label does not say Chianti.] Beautiful tawny robe, brick rim, green (?) reflections; lovely scented bouquet recalls berries and flowers, vague wet dog note; soft center, moderate tannin; still holding well with room to improve further; fairly long; nice now, has class; almost a sweetness at the end. ***

Fattoria di Querceto 1957 Riserva (3 times, 2/90). Vaguely floral bouquet with a hint of autumn leaves, displays a touch of oxidation; on the decline, drying out; still has flavor and sweetness. ** −

Palazzo al Bosco 1957 Riserva (11/80). Small nose; light tannin, nice flavor, well structured; some elegance; drying a bit at the end. **

Ruffino 1957 Riserva Ducale gold label (twice, 11/83). Some oxidation over a wheatlike aspect and a hint of flowers; drying out though still has some interest. *

1956 0

The '56s never amounted to much and are too old now. Barone Ricasoli said it was a good vintage. Niederbacher and the *consorzio* both gave it one star out of four. The Ruffino Riserva Ducale gold label that we tasted a few years ago, while fading, was still good. We doubt if many others hold any interest.

Ruffino 1956 Riserva Ducale gold label (*twice, 10/87*). Complex bouquet suggestive of leather, dried fruit and flowers; starting to dry out but still has nice flavor. ** –

1955 ** –

The '55s were very fine wines at one time. The vines benefited from a very hot summer and produced some very good fruit. But good as it was, thirty-five years is a long time for Chianti Classico; there is no reason to hold them any longer. Enjoy them now if, in fact, they offer any enjoyment. Both Niederbacher and the *consorzio* rated the year at three stars out of four. Barone Ricasoli picks it as a very fine year. The Ruffino Riserva Ducale gold label, tasted in November 1990, was gone.

Fattoria di Montagliari e Castellinuzza 1955 Chianti Rosso Stravecchio (*twice, 7/88*). Richly concentrated, a bit volatile, some acid but the richness and concentration make it most attractive. ** + *Bottle of 10/83*: Deep color beginning to brown; fairly intense bouquet with some complexity; medium- to full-bodied, soft and round, fairly long. *** –

Ruffino 1955 Riserva Ducale gold label (*7 times, 11/90*). Bouquet vaguely of leather and tobacco with a light berry note, and some oxidation, alcohol also intrudes; fruit has faded, very little interest remains. *Bottle of 1/89*: Floral, minty, chocolate components on the nose; sweet and rich, yet with delicacy, very ready and holding. ** + *Bottle of 11/83*: Deep garnet, brick at rim; lightly floral bouquet with some fruit; complete, well structured, round, full of flavor; very good condition, no signs of age. *** –

1954 0

Barone Ricasoli rated this vintage highly. Niederbacher gave it one star out of four. The only '54 we've tasted in the past few years, in May 1985, Giovanni Cappelli's Fattoria Montagliari, was splendid. As for the rest, we think it doubtful that many have any interest left.

Fattoria di Montagliari e Castellinuzza 1954 Chianti Rosso Stravecchio (*5/85*). Nice delicate floral aroma with a touch of decay in the back; soft and smooth; very ready. And to think that this wine was made with *governo,* 12 percent white grapes, and over thirty years ago! And we keep hearing how Chianti Classico made this way won't age! ***

1953 0

How is the vintage today? Niederbacher rates the year at one star out of four. We doubt that few, if any, are still of much interest, although the Castello d'Albola we tasted in November 1988 had some interest.

Castello d'Albola 1953 Riserva (*11/88*). Skunky at first, some decay; dried out, still some flavor remains, but tannic and harsh; alas, too old, though some interest remains. * –

1952 *

At one time the wines were very good. Now the best of them are beginning to dry out. As for the others, we expect that they have long since faded. Barone Ricasoli said it was an excellent vintage. Although the last three vintages we tasted suggest that the chances of getting an excellent or very good bottle are good, we suspect that they are rare. Niederbacher gave the vintage three of four stars. We think one, at the most, probably reflects those bottles remaining.

Badia a Coltibuono 1952 Riserva (*11/80*). Complex bouquet with just a trace of oxidation; still has tannin and considerable fruit, very good though perhaps drying a bit at the end. *** –

Fattoria di Montagliari e Castellinuzza 1952 Chianti Rosso Stravecchio (*10/83*). Intensely fruity bouquet; heaps of flavor; complete, superb. ***

Fattoria di Montagliari e Castellinuzza 1952 Vino Vecchio (*5/86*). [Label does not say Chianti.] Tawny; lovely complex bouquet of flowers, berries and tar; silky, velvety texture, some tannin, sweetness of ripe fruit, rich and flavorful; still room to grow, very long finish; loads of class and elegance. This wine contained 18 to 20 percent white grapes, and was thirty-four years young. *** + (****)

Ruffino 1952 Riserva Ducale gold label (*11/83*). Lightly perfumed bouquet; round and smooth, loads of flavor though beginning to dry out. **

1951 0

Although the chances of coming up with a good bottle today are doubtful, we managed to ferret out one in July 1988. Oddly enough, the wine came from Minuccio Cappelli, who considered it a poor year. Ruffino felt that the year was a good one. Niederbacher gave the vintage zero.

Fattoria di Montagliari e Castellinuzza 1951 Chianti Rosso Stravecchio (*twice, 7/88*). The bottle of July 1988 was tasted by only one of us. And the circumstance made this bottle incredible. Was it as good as it seemed at the time? The way things turned out we suspect not. For the experience, five stars—the context made it impossible to judge the wine. *Bottle of 10/87*: Floral with fruitlike overtone; good structure, velvety, soft, round and ready; lovely indeed. *** +

Ruffino 1951 Riserva Ducale gold label (*11/83*). Brownish, oxidized.

1950 0

The only '50 we can recall tasting, Giovanni Cappelli's Montagliari, in October 1983, suggests the best can still be good. But most are probably long faded. Barone Ricasoli rates it highly. Niederbacher's rating was two stars out of four.

Badia a Coltibuono 1950 Riserva (twice, 10/82). Light color, browning; a nice bouquet despite some oxidation and some volatile acidity; starting to dry out but still has flavor interest. * +

Brolio 1950 Riserva (12/88). Tawny, orange reflections; old Chianti nose, kind of odd besides; much better in the mouth, with a sweetness of fruit, still some tannin; not to keep; but tasty and a lot of interest. ** −

Fattoria di Montagliari e Castellinuzza 1950 Chianti Rosso Stravecchio (10/83). Floral bouquet; velvety texture, good flavor; very good quality. ** +

Ruffino 1950 Riserva Ducale gold label (10/80). Shows age in color, aroma and flavor; going, though not totally gone.

1949 0

Barone Ricasoli said it was an excellent year. Minuccio Cappelli disagreed. Of the two we've tasted recently, both were getting old. Niederbacher saw 1949 as a three-star vintage out of four stars.

Fattoria di Montagliari e Castellinuzza 1949 Chianti Rosso Stravecchio (2/90). Deep, rich berry and cherry bouquet with a floral component; rich and concentrated with mouth-filling flavors and a velvety texture; at its peak. *** + *Bottle of 5/86:* Tawny robe; floral bouquet, intense and packed with fruit; a rich mouthful of flavor, velvet mouth feel, fine structure and real class; can certainly improve but superb now; very long finish; a complete and nearly perfect wine. ****

1948 [0]

We haven't tasted any. For Niederbacher it was a one-star vintage out of four stars.

1947 **

This vintage was always highly regarded, and the outstanding Ruffino Riserva Ducale we tasted on three different occasions suggests that if they were stored well they can still shine. Niederbacher gave the year three of four stars.

Fattoria di Querceto 1947 Riserva (9/86). Alcohol and volatile acidity, fading and soft, with a smooth mouth feel, better on the palate than the nose, licorice notes. *** −

Ruffino 1947 Riserva Ducale gold label (3 times, 9/83). Brilliant tawny robe with orange edge; lovely almost claretlike bouquet, persistent and expansive, toasty, with a touch of blueberries, refined; a mouthful of wine; lots of class, a classic. ****

1946 0

The '46s were never much regarded; now they're too old. Niederbacher rated it at one star out of four.

Brolio 1946 Riserva (twice, 9/83). Pale brick; some floral notes, but a wet dog smelling the background; drying out, acidic, very little flavor interest; very tired, old and feeble. A second bottle still had some sweetness.

STILL OLDER VINTAGES

Barone Ricasoli said that other very good or excellent vintages this century were **1945, 1943, 1942, 1941, 1938, 1937, 1927, 1923, 1921, 1918, 1917, 1916** and **1909.** Other sources suggest that **1937, 1931, 1929,** and **1923** vintages were all especially fine. As for today, who knows? One never does. A bottle direct from the *cantina* would stand a chance; from the wineshop shelf, we wouldn't be much tempted unless the price was so irresistible that curiosity alone would be enough to satisfy. On the other hand, if you've got one in your cellar that you'd like an expert opinion on, we never turn down an opportunity to add to our experience! ("Indefatigable notetakers," did he calls us?)

Fattoria di Montagliari e Castellinuzza 1940 Chianti Classico Riserva (12/90). The wine was fifty when we opened the bottle. The robe was beautiful with various shadings of color; the bouquet was scented and delicate, offering a mélange of sensations, one moment this, the next moment that; on the palate the wine was like velvet, with lovely mouth-filling flavors; its nature was gentle; its finish long; a classic Chianti of real class and quality; complete and sheer perfection. ****

THE OTHER CHIANTI ZONES

Chianti Colli Aretini

The Colli Aretini production zone is in the easternmost part of the Chianti district, in the province of Arezzo. There are two Chiantis produced in this province: a regional Chianti and Chianti Colli Aretini. There are 553 growers with 5,258 acres (2,128 hectares) registered to produce the former wine, and 72 growers and 1,646 acres (666 hectares) for the latter.[18] The average annual production between 1986 and 1988 for Chianti was 1.9 million gallons (73,220 hectoliters), equivalent to 813,474 cases, and for Colli Aretini,

806,444 gallons (30,524 hectoliters), equivalent to 339,125 cases.[19]

The Chiantis of the Colli Aretini tend to be high in acidity, fresh, and lively. They are best consumed young and with a light chill. One producer really stands out—Villa Cilnia. Their Riserva can take moderate age. The '83 tasted in 1990 was very good indeed. We also recommend Cilnia's excellent '85 Riserva. Rating *

Recommended Producers

* Villa Cilnia (Podere di Cignano)
  Villa La Selva

Chianti Colli Fiorentini

There are five Chiantis produced in the province of Firenze: Chianti Classico, Chianti Montalbano, Chianti Rùfina, a regional Chianti, and Chianti Colli Fiorentini.

The Chianti Colli Fiorentini production zone is located in the Florentine hills south, east, and northeast of the city of Firenze. The best Chiantis of this district are those most like the ones of the Classico zone, which it borders on the north. The Florentine wines, especially the better *riserve,* can be aristocratic, and they age moderately well. Generally, they're at their best between four and six years of the vintage. Rating ** +

Recommended Producers

Castello del Trebbio	Fattoria Lilliano
Castello Guicciardini	Fattoria Pagnana
Poppiano	Pasolini dall'Onda Borghese
Fattoria Giannozzi	Torricino (Oscar Pio)
Fattoria Il Corno	

Chianti Colline Pisane

The Colline Pisane production zone is in the westernmost part of the Chianti district, southeast of Pisa. The two Chiantis produced in this province are a regional one and the Colline Pisane. There are 132 growers and 2,007 acres (813 hectares) registered for the regional Chianti, and 60 growers and 597 acres (242 hectares) registered to produce Chianti Colline Pisane.[20] The average annual production between 1986 and 1988 was 371,122 gallons (14,047 hectoliters), equivalent to 156,062 cases, of the regional Chianti, and 189,299 gallons (7,165 hectoliters), or 79,599 cases, of the Colline Pisane.[21] The Colline Pisane Chiantis are wines to drink young and fresh, preferably with a light chill; they tend to be light and soft. Some tasters detect a scent of hawthorn flowers in the aroma of these wines. Rating *

Chianti Colli Senesi

The province of Siena produces three Chiantis. Besides part of the Classico and regional Chianti zones, the Colli Senesi district is found here. There are 1,625 growers authorized to produce all three Chiantis, on 20,980 acres (8,490 hectares). For Classico there are 432 growers and 9,802 acres (3,967 hectares), for the regional Chianti 246 and 2,403 (972), and for Colli Senesi 947 and 8,775 (3,551).[22] Average annual production for the years 1986 through 1988 was 4.9 million gallons (186,960 hectoliters), equivalent to just over 2 million cases of Chianti Classico; 1.9 million gallons (72,496 hectoliters), or 805,427 cases of regional Chianti; and 3.6 million gallons (136,868 hectoliters), or 1.5 million cases, of Chianti Colli Senesi.[23]

The Colli Senesi, the southernmost of the Chianti zones, is also the largest. It encompasses an area that lies northeast, west, and south of Siena. The two southernmost parts of this district take in the production zones of Brunello di Montal-

ACREAGE AND PRODUCTION OF THE CHIANTIS OF THE PROVINCE OF FIRENZE

Wine	Number of Registered Growers	Acres	Hectares	1986–88 Average Annual Production	
				Hectoliters	Cases
Chianti	1,373	15,756	6,376	235,485	2,616,238
Classico	533	7,076	2,864	81,989	910,894
Colli Fiorentini	170	2,422	980	22,575	250,805
Montalbano	17	337	136	5,407	60,072
Rùfina	50	1,352	547	18,386	204,272
Total	2,143	26,943	10,903	363,842	4,042,281

Source: Il Corriere Vinicolo

ACREAGE AND PRODUCTION OF CHIANTI MONTALBANO

Province	Number of Registered Growers	Acres	Hectares	1986–88 Average Annual Production	
				Hectoliters	Cases
Firenze	17	337	136	5,407	60,072
Pistoia	159	737	298	10,070	111,878
Total	176	1,074	434	15,477	171,950

Source: Il Corriere Vinicolo

cino and Vino Nobile di Montepulciano. Many producers of those wines also make a Chianti Colli Senesi. This situation is changing now that both Rosso di Montalcino and Rosso di Montepulciano are recognized by the DOC, and many producers are making those in preference to a Chianti. Other DOCs in Siena are Bianco Vergine Valdichiana, Moscadello di Montalcino, Val d'Arbia, and Vernaccia di San Gimignano.

The Colli Senesi wines are generally fuller in body and higher in alcohol than most of the other Chiantis. They are generally best drunk young while they are still fresh; the best can take moderate age. F. Bonfio's Il Poggiolo and Le Portine are worth looking for. They have been improving with each vintage and are better than their denomination would suggest. Rating **

Recommended Producers

*Avignonesi
  Barbi Colombini†
*Barone Neri del Nero
  (Castel Pietraio)
*Costanti Emilio††
Falchini Riccardo††
Fattoria Chigi Saracini
Fattoria del Cerro
Fattoria della Talosa
  (Fattoria di Fognano)
Fattoria di Pietrafitta
Fattoria Felsina

Fattoria Il Greppo
  (Biondi-Santi)††
Fattoria Sovestro
Ficomantanino
*F. Bonfio, Il Poggiolo†
*F. Bonfio, Le Portine†
Majnoni Guicciardini
*Pietraserena, Poggio al
  Vento
*Podere Boscarelli
*Villa Cusona
  (Guicciardini-Strozzi)

† Labeled as Chianti
†† We haven't actually tasted their Chianti, but recommend it on the strength of their other wines.

Chianti Montalbano

The Montalbano production zone is in the northwestern corner of the Chianti region. Part of that district is located in the province of Firenze and part in Pistoia. The part in Firenze includes the DOCG production zone of Carmignano. It's not surprising, therefore, to see that some Carmignano producers also make a Chianti Montalbano.

Generally Chianti Montalbano wines are best drunk quite young, within a year or two of the vintage. In the better years—but rarely—some Montalbano is produced that can improve with age. Rating **

Recommended Producers

Fattoria di Artimino
Fattoria di Bacchereto
Fattoria di Calavria†

Fattoria Il Poggiolo†
*Tenuta di Capezzana

† We haven't actually tasted their Chianti, but recommend it on the strength of their other wines.

Chianti Rùfina

The Rùfina production zone, in the northernmost part of the Chianti district, takes in the *comuni* of Rùfina, Dicomano, Londa, Pelago, and Pontassieve in the province of Firenze. Rùfina is the smallest of the Chianti zones. Of the 30,847 acres (12,483 hectares) in the district, some 25 percent are in vines. Of these, 1,352 acres (547 hectares) are registered as Chianti Rùfina vineyards. This is down considerably from the 3,064 acres (1,240 hectares) of a few years ago. That did, however, include 1,236 (500) in *coltura promiscua*. In 1988 there were 50 registered growers. Annual production between 1986 and 1988 averaged some 485,758 gallons (18,386 hectoliters), equivalent to 205,000 cases, a drop in the bucket compared to the nearly 23.7 million gallons (896,634 hectoliters), or 10 million cases, of all Chianti.[24] Approximately 30 producers bottle a Chianti Rùfina.

The Chiantis of Rùfina are the highest in acid, and by reputation are the fullest in body, though our own experience differs on that last point. The Rùfina Chiantis are wines with a good capacity to age, as can be seen by our tasting notes on the outstanding '23, '34, and '45 Nipozzano, and the especially fine '47 and '48 Selvapiana. The Rùfina wines are the most consistent of the Chiantis. No zone produces higher overall quality. They are also among the best. Of all the Chiantis we've tasted, three out of seven of our highest rated Chiantis are in the Rùfina zone—Castello di Nipozzano, Villa Selvapiana, and Montesodi. Rating *** +

RATING THE PRODUCERS OF CHIANTI RUFINA

****
Castello di Nipozzano (Frescobaldi)
Villa Selvapiana (Francesco Giuntini)

***
+ Montesodi (Frescobaldi)

**
Fattoria di Vetrice
Fattoria Il Capitano[a]
Poggio Reale (Spalletti)[b]

*
Fattoria di Grignano[c]
Remole (Frescobaldi)[d]
− Travignoli
Villa di Monte[d]

0
Fattoria di Doccia[e]
Le Coste[f]
Tenuta di Poggio[g]
Villa di Vetrice[d]

NOTES: [a] Based on one wine, the '88 Torricella, tasted from cask in April 1988
  [b] We haven't tasted it since the '75 Riserva, in March 1982
  [c] Based on one wine, the '87
  [d] We haven't tasted it in some time
  [e] We haven't tasted it since the '83, in April 1985
  [f] We haven't tasted it since the '82 and '83, in April 1985
  [g] We haven't tasted it since the '80 Riserva, in April 1985

CONSORZIO VITIRUFINA

This organization was founded in 1980 to defend, protect, and promote the wines of the Chianti Rùfina district.

The members are:

Cerreto	I Poggiolo
Colognole	La Corte
Doccia	Lavacchio
Galiga e Vetrice	Le Coste
Gavignano	Petrognano
Grignano	Poggio Reale
I Veroni	Selvapiana

VINTAGE INFORMATION AND TASTING NOTES

1990 [* * * *]

Leonardo Frescobaldi rates the vintage as outstanding for Castello di Nipozzano and Montesodi and he gave them both five stars out of five. The four cask samples from Selvapiana tasted in June 1991 suggest a first-flight vintage, perhaps on par with 1985.

1989 [* +]

Leonardo Frescobaldi said that it was a very good (four stars out of five) vintage for Castello di Nipozzano, yet not good enough for Montesodi (none was made). The four wines we tasted from cask in April 1990 were all good.

> **CAUTION:** *Before reading these tasting notes on the wines that we tasted from barrel, please read "On Tasting Wines from Barrel: A Caveat" on page xxv.*

Villa Selvapiana 1989 (ex-cask, 4/90). Openly spicy and fruity aroma, cherrylike; fresh, fruity, short. *

Villa Selvapiana 1989 Riserva (ex-vat, 4/90). Open aroma, cherrylike fruit and spicy notes; fresh, fruity, short. * *A second vat:* More flavor, dry, firm and somewhat chewy. *(*)

Villa Selvapiana 1989 Riserva Bucherchiale (ex-vat, 4/90). The most fruit of the four '89s tasted from here, some dryness at the end. *(*)

Villa Selvapiana 1989 Riserva Fornace (ex-vat, 4/90). Tobacco, woodsy aroma; tart, cherrylike fruit. *(*)

1988 [* * * +]

Marchese Leonardo Frescobaldi rates it as an excellent vintage, five stars out of five, for both Castello di Nipozzano and Montesodi. The five wines, tasted from cask in April 1990, were at the least very good; a couple were excellent.

> **CAUTION:** *Before reading these tasting notes on the wines that we tasted from barrel, please read "On Tasting Wines from Barrel: A Caveat" on page xxv.*

Fattoria Il Capitano 1988 Torricella (*ex-cask, 4/90*). Intensely concentrated, well balanced, sweet, long. **

Villa Selvapiana 1988 (*ex-cask, 4/90*). Chewy tannins, quite full and flavorful, more to it than expected for a *normale*. **

Villa Selvapiana 1988 Riserva (*ex-cask, 4/90*). Rich and sweet, lots of structure, a little dry and tannic toward the end, some length; should age very well indeed. **(*)

Villa Selvapiana 1988 Riserva Bucherchiale (*ex-cask, 4/90*). A mouthful of fruit, real sweetness from ripe fruit, chewy tannin; although tight and firm its potential is evident; this has class. ***(+)

Villa Selvapiana 1988 Riserva Fornace (*ex-cask, 4/90*). Chewy, firm and rich, lingering sweetness; lots of potential here. **(*)

1987 *

Leonardo Frescobaldi calls it a favorable year for Castello di Nipozzano and gave it three-stars out of five. No Montesodi was made. The two that we tasted were good. They weren't riserva material, however.

Fattoria di Grignano 1987 (*4/90*). Openly fresh and fruity, soft and quaffable. *

Villa Selvapiana 1987 (*4/90*). Surprising amount of fruit and body, attractive flavors, short, a success. **

1986 ** +

Frescobaldi rates the vintage as excellent and he rated it four stars out of five while he gave Montesodi five stars. The few that we've tasted indicated that this will be a vintage to consume relatively young. The wines display an open and precocious nature about them.

Castello di Nipozzano 1986 Riserva (*twice, 12/90*). Scented bouquet; soft and open, quite forward; should be ready early; displays a lot of style. **

Travignoli 1986 (*4/89*). Light but typical aroma; nice fruit, soft, a bit dry at the end. *

Villa Selvapiana 1986 (*3 times, 4/89*). Nice nose; soft and round, balanced, tasty. ** −

Villa Selvapiana 1986 Riserva (*3 times, 6/90*). Lovely floral, berry aroma; still some tannin, nice fruit; a little young yet. ** +

Villa Selvapiana 1986 Riserva Bucherchiale (*3 times, ex-vat, 4/90*). Intense aroma, floral and berrylike components; sweet, rich and harmonious, long finish; has class. ***

Villa Selvapiana 1986 Riserva Torricella (*twice, ex-vat, 4/87*). Fairly reticent aroma; rich flavor, good structure, nice acid, precocious. **(* −)

1985 ****

It was another excellent vintage (five stars out of five) for Castello di Nipozzano and an excellent (four-star) year for Montesodi according to Marchese de' Frescobaldi. The ones we've tasted have class and structure, depth of flavor, and length on the palate. This is an especially fine vintage. Our personal favorite at this point is the potentially outstanding Villa Selvapiano Riserva Torricella. Also excellent are Marchese di Frescobaldi Montesodi and Villa Selvapiana Bucherchiale. We haven't tasted the Nipozzano as yet!

Marchese di Frescobaldi 1985 Montesodi (*3 times, 12/89*). A young wine that is rich and sweet, concentrated and harmonious, oak and fruit components, ripe fruit; real class. ***(+)

Travignoli 1985 (*twice, 4/89*). There was variation here, one time the wine had a nice nose, but was overly dry, is there enough fruit? The other wine was dull, unbalanced and hot.

Villa Selvapiana 1985 (*twice, ex-vat, 4/87*). Lovely cherrylike aroma, rich, berrylike notes, candyish note(!); chewy, rich flavor, moderate tannin, bitter. ** + (***)

Villa Selvapiana 1985 Riserva (*4 times, 4/90*). Fragrant floral aroma, oak, vanilla component; tannic, tight, good body, a lot of structure and flavor, a little firm at the end. **(*)

Villa Selvapiana 1985 Riserva Bucherchiale (*5 times, 4/90, 7,333 bottles*). Open, ripe fruit aroma, floral and berrylike notes; fairly tannic, lots of fruit and sweetness, mouth-filling. ***(+)

Villa Selvapiana 1985 Riserva Torricella (*4 times, 4/90, 6,650 bottles*). Lovely floral aroma, berry and vanilla nuances, some oak; rich and sweet, open flavor, real ripeness; impressive, lots of class here. ***(*)

1984 0

Leonardo Frescobaldi said the vintage was difficult; no Nipozzano or Montesodi was produced. Francesco Giuntini said that it was poor; he didn't produce a *riserva* at his Villa Selvapiana estate. None tasted.

1983 ****

Marchese de' Frescobaldi called it a very favorable vintage and he gave four stars out of five to Nipozzano and three to Montesodi. Francesco Giuntini called it a first-rate vintage. Our tastings confirm this point of view. The Villa Selvapiana Riserva Bucherchiale is outstanding and should be a keeper. We were also impressed with the Castello di Nipozzano Riserva and Villa Selvapiana Riserva.

Castello di Nipozzano 1983 Riserva (*twice, 10/88*). Perfumed, floral scent; richly flavored and concentrated, good structure, still some tannin, attractive, open flavor, florallike; young, quite nice for now, should improve. ***(+)

Fattoria di Doccia 1983 (4/85). Oxidized.

Fattoria di Vetrice 1983 Riserva (4/89). Nice nose; sweet and ripe on the entry, light finish. * +

Le Coste 1983 (4/85). Dull, flat, uninteresting.

Marchese di Frescobaldi 1983 Remole (11/84). Light and fruity, low acid, somewhat shallow, short.

Villa Selvapiana 1983 Riserva (twice, 4/90). Expansive, openly fruity aroma recalls flowers and berries; packed with sweetness and fruit; this is a class wine that although still young displays a lot of everything. ***(+)

Villa Selvapiana 1983 Riserva in barrique (4/90, 6,750 bottles). Dusty, light oak overlay; chewy firm, sweet; more closed than the other '83s, with less sweetness of fruit; a good wine that doesn't have the class of the other two '83s. **(*)

Villa Selvapiana 1983 Riserva Bucherchiale (5 times, 4/90, 6,650 bottles). Ripe cherrylike aroma; nice entry then tightens up, yet the rich, sweet, ripe fruit is quite evident; real quality and class. ***(*)

Villa Vetrice 1983 (twice, 5/85). Fresh berrylike aroma; some tannin, is there sufficient fruit?

1982 ***

Leonardo Frescobaldi said that it was a two-star (out of five) vintage for Nipozzano yet a four-star year for Montesodi. Francesco Giuntini calls it first rate. The two that impressed us the most were Castello di Nipozzano Riserva and Marchese di Frescobaldi Montesodi.

Castello di Nipozzano 1982 Riserva (twice, 10/88). Open fruit aroma; tasty, some tannin and backbone, rich almost lush fruit; less elegance and more tannin than the '83; should last and develop well. **+ (***)

Le Coste 1982 (4/85). Baked character reminiscent of a southern wine.

Marchese di Frescobaldi 1982 Montesodi (3 times, 12/88). Intense aroma, mint and spice, ripe berrylike fruit; great weight and extract, a lot of structure, sweet, ripe, long; loads of class, perhaps the finest Montosodi to date; needs perhaps three to four more years. ***(+)

Villa Selvapiana 1982 Riserva (5 times, 6/90). We've tasted this wine four times with, surprisingly, some variation. The most recent bottle was bad. *Bottle of 4/90:* Leather and dried fruit aroma; fairly nice fruit; room to improve; light finish. ** + *Bottle of 2/90:* Floral, nutty aroma; a lot of backbone, rich, good structure; young, should be a keeper. **(*)

Villa Selvapiana 1982 Riserva in barrique (4/90, 7,656 bottles). Chocolate and oak aroma, cherry notes; chewy tannin, evident fruit, short; like the '83 in *barrique,* this was just not up to the other wines from Selvapiana. **

Villa Selvapiana 1982 Riserva Bucherchiale (twice, 4/90, 7,980 bottles). Floral, tobacco aroma; sweet, openly fruity, soft center, some tannin, a little short, more fruit and flavor than the other two '82s; seemed to suggest more potential in 1988. ** +

Villa Vetrice 1982 (twice, 5/85). Fruity aroma with a tarlike note; tannic and firm, is there enough fruit?

1981 ***

Leonardo Frescobaldi calls it a very favorable vintage for Nipozzano and Montesodi, and he gave them both three stars out of five. Francesco Giuntini said that it was first rate. There is some indication that it would be best to consume those you still have in your cellar. The best one, as it has been from the beginning, is the Villa Selvapiana Riserva Bucherchiale; there is no need to drink this one, as it is holding well.

Castello di Nipozzano 1981 Riserva (twice, 7/89). Some volatile acidity, some fruit on the nose; tasty, soft and ready, better on the palate than on the nose. * + *Bottle of 10/87:* Floral, fruit and nut aroma; good body, nice balance and structure, young and flavorful. **(* −)

Marchese di Frescobaldi 1981 Montesodi (4/86). Intense aroma recalls cherries and a light background of oak; exudes style; very young, rich, and very good. **(* +)

Villa di Monte 1981 (5/85). Tar and cherries on aroma; a bit unbalanced, fairly nice fruit. * −

Villa Selvapiana 1981 Riserva (10 times, 4/90). Floral and berry aroma; sweet, ripe and elegant; very ready; smooth, moderate length. *** − *Bottle of 5/86:* A touch of oak, less open on aroma than the Bucherchiale; sweet entry, has more tannin and, surprisingly, seems younger than the version not aged in wood. **(+)

Villa Selvapiana 1981 Riserva Bucherchiale (10 times, 4/90, 7,300 bottles). This wine was not aged in wood. Fragrant-scented bouquet, vanilla overlay; velvety texture, smooth and round; real class and elegance. *** + *Bottle of 5/86:* Aroma has notes of underbrush, flowers and cherries; well balanced, sweet ripe fruit on palate, has delicacy and elegance, needs time to soften the tannin though enjoyable now, soft-centered; tannic finish. **(*)

1980 ** −

Leonardo Frescobaldi calls it a favorable vintage for Castello di Nipozzano, and he gave it one star plus. No Montesodi was produced. Francesco Giuntini said it was very good.

Some of the wines are starting to tire. They'd best be consumed now.

Castello di Nipozzano 1980 Riserva (*twice, 5/85*). Complex bouquet, moderately intense, with nuances of flowers, fruit and leather; well balanced, moderate tannin, flavorful; some delicacy and style; young; fairly long finish. ***(+)

Marchese di Frescobaldi 1980 Montesodi (*ex-cask, 5/85*). Rich, intense aroma with berrylike fruit and a touch of tar; very well balanced, full and flavorful, very long on the finish. ***(*)

Tenuta di Poggio 1980 Riserva (*4/85*). Some oxidation, dull and stale, drying out.

Villa di Monte 1980 Riserva (*5/85*). Cherrylike fruit; some tannin, agreeable if a bit young. *(+)

Villa Selvapiana 1980 Riserva (*4 times, 4/90*). Fragrant, leatherlike component; openly fruity on entry, some tannin, finish is a tad short and a little dry. ** −

1 9 7 9 * * *

Frescobaldi said that the vintage was favorable; in the spring of 1985, he gave it three stars out of four. Francesco Giuntini calls it very good for Selvapiana. The wines are ready now.

Castello di Nipozzano 1979 Riserva (*twice, 12/88*). Complex floral and nutty aroma; soft, smooth an tasty, vanilla and ripe fruit, fresh, very long finish; ready, will last. *** *Bottle of 5/85:* Fragrant floral bouquet; well balanced, soft and round; surprisingly ready. **

Fattoria di Vetrice 1979 Riserva (*twice, 5/85*). Cherries and tobacco on aroma and flavor, almost sweet, quite agreeable and should improve. *(*)

Marchese di Frescobaldi 1979 Montesodi (*twice, 12/86*). A lot of class and style; well structured, some oak, flavorful, long. ***

Villa Selvapiana 1979 Riserva (*3 times, 4/90*). Berrylike fruit; ripe, tasty, a little dry, surprising amount of fruit; this bottle was open two days when we tasted it. ** +

Villa Selvapiana 1979 Riserva Bucherchiale (*3/87*). Fragrant, perfumed bouquet; still some tannin, but a lot of nice fruit and structure; lovely now, could improve. ***

1 9 7 8 * * *

Frescobaldi gave the vintage, in the spring of 1985, two stars plus out of four; today he calls it very favorable. Francesco Giuntini said the vintage was very good. There is no need to hold them any longer; few, if any, will improve further. We

suspect that the Montesodi is still holding and can possibly even improve further.

Castello di Nipozzano 1978 Riserva (*twice, 11/83*). Nice nose, some oak and fruit and a vague suggestion of peanut shells; seems a bit rough at this point but well structured, tannic but with the stuffing to support it; give it a few years yet. **(*)

Fattoria di Vetrice 1978 Riserva (*5/85*). Aroma a bit overripe and raisiny, with hints of tobacco and cherries; raisins follow through on palate, flat, tannic aftertaste. * −

Marchese di Frescobaldi 1978 Montesodi (*3 times, 5/85*). Richly fruited aroma with a lot of depth, nuances of flowers, tobacco and oaky notes; enormous richness and weight, has concentration and extract, gobs of fruit, long finish. When we first tasted this wine in May 1983 it was so closed we were not sure where it was going, obviously it was in the right direction. ***(*)

Marchese di Frescobaldi 1978 Tenuta di Pomino (*4/81*). Perfumed aroma with notes of fruit and spice; soft and fruity, could use more acid, a bit dull.

Villa Selvapiana 1978 (*3/87*). Perfumed bouquet; still has a firmness, good body; displays a lot of style; more structure and weight than the '79. *** −

Villa Selvapiana 1978 Riserva (*twice, 4/90*). Lovely fragrant bouquet, open berrylike component, dried fruit and leather; almost sweet, a little chewy, rich and tasty. ***

1 9 7 7 * * * −

Leonardo Frescobaldi called it a one-star vintage (out of four) in the spring of 1985. Francesco Giuntini calls it a top-class vintage. There is no need to give them further age. And some are fading. Drink up.

Castello di Nipozzano 1977 Riserva (*4/81*). Perfumed bouquet with flowers and a touch of spice; some tannin, well balanced, seems to need more fruit, or else it's still closed; some potential evident. *(*)

Fattoria di Vetrice 1977 Riserva (*5/85*). Fruity, a bit simple, some tannin, light, drinkable; room to improve a bit. * +

Villa Selvapiana 1977 Riserva [from a Selected Cask] (*4/87, 7,600 bottles*). Perfumed aroma; still a touch of tannin, fruity, well balanced, soft, almost velvety, still fresh, a tad bitter. ***

Villa Selvapiana 1977 Riserva [no wood aging] (*5/85*). Woodsy, berrylike aroma with a hint of peaches; well balanced, soft, concentrated, tasty, long, complex finish that brings up raspberries and blueberries. ***

Villa Selvapiana 1977 Riserva (*4/90*). This bottle was open two to three days when we got to taste it. Fragrant, floral and damp leaves bouquet, toasty, berry notes; still some tannin, flavorful; holding very well. ***—

Villa Vetrice 1977 Riserva (4/85). Oxidized.

1976 0

We haven't tasted any in too many years to remember them. The weather, as elsewhere in Toscana, was wretched. Frescobaldi gave it zero. Giuntini said the year was very poor and consequently didn't bottle. We don't think there would be any interest to be found in any that might remain.

1975 ***

Leonardo Frescobaldi gave it two stars out of four and Francesco Giuntini called it first class. The best of these wines should last. They are ready. The Villa Selvapiana Riserva is marvelous.

Castello di Nipozzano 1975 Riserva (3/82). Nice nose with some complexity; flavorful, has tannin; needs age, showing good quality. **(+)

Fattoria di Vetrice 1975 Riserva (5/85). Overripe, raisiny aroma; fairly tannic, fruity, harsh aftertaste. *

Poggio Reale (Spalletti) 1975 Riserva (3/82). Stinky, barnyardy; tart edge, drying, and grating on the teeth.

Villa Selvapiana 1975 Riserva (11 times, 4/90). Toasty, dried berrylike aroma, woodsy and damp leaves notes; sweet, velvety, concentrated, a lot of flavor; long and classy. ***+ *Bottle of 5/85:* Floral bouquet with notes of mushrooms and underbrush; very well balanced, ripe fruit flavors, rich and sweet; needs age, but the richness makes it tempting now. ***(+)

1974 ***

We haven't tasted any since 1985. Frescobaldi rated it, in the spring of 1985, three stars out of four. Giuntini called the vintage bad. We suggest drinking them now; although it is possible for the very best ones to last, we doubt they have much left in reserve.

Castello di Nipozzano 1974 Riserva (4 times, 5/85, 198,000 bottles). Lovely complex bouquet, with woodsy, floral and tobacco notes and some delicacy; balanced, light tannin, soft-centered, very long finish with a slight hint of mocha; ready, but has room for improvement. ***

Fattoria di Vetrice 1974 Riserva (5/85). Stinky, drying out.

Marchese di Frescobaldi 1974 Montesodi (4/81). Lovely bouquet with notes of fruit and oak; well knit, some tannin to shed, tasty; stylish. **(*)

1973 0

Leonardo Frescobaldi gave it one star (out of four) in the spring of 1985. Francesco Giuntini calls the vintage bad. If you have any left, pour them out.

Villa Selvapiana 1973 Riserva (twice, 4/90). This bottle was open two to three days; it was clearly fading. Then again, the last time we tasted it in May 1985, it was starting to fade as well. *That bottle:* Brick, orange at rim; overripe aroma with a raisiny note; too old; drinkable but dull.

1972 0

Leonardo Frescobaldi rates it zero, Francesco Giuntini calls it bad. The wines were too old at birth.

Villa Vetrice 1972 Riserva (5/85). It never should've been bottled.

1971 **

Frescobaldi gave it two stars out of four in the spring of 1985. Giuntini called it a first-rate vintage. Drink up while they still have flavor interest. The Villa Selvapiana Riserva is still very good but there is no need to keep it.

Castello di Nipozzano 1971 Riserva (twice, 11/83). Perfumed bouquet with floral notes and a hint of chocolate; still has tannin to shed, seems surprisingly closed in or else is beginning to decline; we suspect the former. **(?) A bottle tasted two years earlier also seemed closed though the fruit was beginning to emerge.

Villa Selvapiana 1971 Riserva (3 times, 4/90). Woodsy, dried fruit and leather bouquet; still some tannin, very good indeed, though seems to be past its best, some smoothness and length. Perhaps another bottle would be better. ***—

1970 **+

Leonardo Frescobaldi rated the vintage two stars out of four. Francesco Giuntini said that it was very good. These wines— the best ones—are fully ready or starting to fade. Drink them now.

Castello di Nipozzano 1970 Riserva (twice, 5/85). Complex fruity bouquet with a touch of tobacco in background; light tannin, velvety texture, rich fruit, complete, fairly long finish; ready now but room to improve further. *** −

Villa Selvapiana 1970 Riserva (5/85). Brickish, orange at rim; lovely nose with strawberry notes; soft, round, sweet fruit, tasty, very nice and very ready. **

1 9 6 9 * * −

Frescobaldi calls it a two-star year (out of four). Giuntini said it was very good for Selvapiana. The '69s won't improve further—drink.

Villa Selvapiana 1969 Riserva (twice, 3/87). Fragrant with a mineral aroma; tannin pretty much evolved, soft and smooth, round, fruity and balanced. ** +

1 9 6 8 * * +

Frescobaldi gave it one star plus out of four. Giuntini rates it very good. The Villa Selvapiana Riserva is holding and, indeed, is very good. As for the rest, drink them up.

Villa Selvapiana 1968 Riserva (4 times, 4/90). Dried fruit aroma, suggestions that recall the woods and underbrush, toasty, berrylike notes; smooth and round, very nice indeed; beginning to decline. *** −

1 9 6 7 * +

It's two stars out of four for Frescobaldi and good for Giuntini. Some are fading or have already faded, and it's doubtful that even the best have a future. It seems best to drink them up while they still have any interest.

Castello di Nipozzano 1967 Riserva (11/83). Perfumed bouquet with some delicacy; light and balanced, still a bit of tannin, nice flavor; beginning to dry out but still quite nice. ** −

Villa Selvapiana 1967 Riserva (twice, 4/87, 24,120 bottles). Perfumed bouquet, slight harsh edge on the nose; rather light in body, very soft, flavorful and ready, a little thin at the end. ** − *Bottle of 5/85:* Complex bouquet with suggestions of underbrush, flowers and berries; soft-centered with tannin around it, loads of flavor; perhaps starting to dry out, but so good now. *** −

1 9 6 6 * * +

We haven't tasted any since 1985. Leonardo Frescobaldi rated 1966 as zero. Francesco Giuntini called it topflight. There's no need to keep them any longer.

Villa Selvapiana 1966 Riserva (5/85). Delicate perfume with woodsy notes; soft and velvety, light tannin, good fruit and balance, could be longer on the palate. *** −

1 9 6 5 *

Frescobaldi rated the vintage one star out of four. Giuntini said that for Selvapiana it was topflight. The wines have faded or are starting to do so. Drink.

Villa Selvapiana 1965 Riserva (3 times, 4/90). Some decay on the nose; much better in the mouth though starting to fade. ** − *Bottle of 5/85:* Berry and woodsy aroma; tannic entry, then soft and flavorful, blueberries on the somewhat tannic finish; beginning to dry out. **

1 9 6 4 * *

The last time we tasted any 1964s was in 1985. Frescobaldi gave the vintage two stars out of four. Giuntini called it good. It seems doubtful if any will improve and we suspect that few will last. Drink them up.

Castello di Nipozzano 1964 Riserva (11/83). Vaguely floral bouquet; a bit light, still has a fair amount of tannin, closed when poured, but opened up in the glass. **

Villa Selvapiana 1964 Riserva (5/85). Brick, tawny at edges; lovely bouquet with a suggestion of underbrush; comes in and goes out with tannin, but soft in center and tasty. ** +

1 9 6 3 [0]

We can't remember tasting any. For Frescobaldi it was a one-star vintage (out of four), for Giuntini it was bad.

1 9 6 2 * *

It was three stars out of four for Frescobaldi and first class for Giuntini. The wines are starting to decline, if they haven't already.

Castello di Nipozzano 1962 Riserva (4 times, 10/88). Color still fairly deep, brick cast; oldish nose, some oxidation; alas, it's gone, a second bottle had more interest but was fading as well. *Bottle of 5/85:* Brick, orange at rim, bouquet of flowers, mushrooms, underbrush and tobacco; still some tannin, medium-bodied, flavorful, hint of raspberries, well structured, smooth, fairly long finish. ***

Villa Selvapiana 1962 Riserva (4 times, 4/90). This wine spent nine years in oak. *The most recent bottle was the best of the four:* Rich bouquet, complex and toasty, woodsy, dried berries, leather and flowers, chocolate component; velvet mouth feel, a little dry at the end; still very good indeed. *** *Bottle of 5/85:* Perfumed bouquet, has delicacy, notes of pine, mint and licorice, later toffee; some tannin still, fairly smooth-textured, tasty, tannic finish. ** +

1961 **

Leonardo Frescobaldi rated the vintage as three stars plus out of four. Francesco Giuntini said it wasn't bad. We haven't had any in years, but we suspect they have either faded or are beginning to do so.

Castello di Nipozzano 1961 Riserva (*11/83*). Expansive bouquet; soft and smooth, loads of flavor; impressive. ***

1960 [0]

We can't recall tasting any. Giuntini said it wasn't a bad vintage.

1959 ** +

We haven't tasted any since 1983. Frescobaldi gave it two stars out of four. Giuntini said it wasn't bad. We suggest that you'd best drink any you have left.

Castello di Nipozzano 1959 Riserva (*twice, 11/83*). Floral bouquet, refined and elegant; soft and velvety, some tannin remains but nearly resolved; a lovely glass of wine, no need to hold longer. ***

1958 ***

Giuntini called it an excellent vintage. The Villa Selvapiana Riserva, tasted in April 1990, was still very good indeed, albeit a little past being a point.

Villa Selvapiana 1958 Riserva (*8 times, 4/90*). Fairly dark robe, orange at the rim; some decay on the nose, leather and fruit; nice flavor, smooth mouth feel, round, still it is starting to decline, although it is very good indeed. We've had better bottles and lesser ones. The best ones were drunk in 1986 and 1987. This one *** *Bottle of 5/85:* Some decay up front on aroma, mint and mushrooms in back; drying out a bit, but still a lot of flavor, overly tannic on finish. **

1957 ?

It's been years since we tasted any '57s. Frescobaldi gave it two stars out of four. Giuntini said it wasn't bad.

1956 ** —

We haven't tasted any since 1985. Giuntini said it was a very good vintage. We suspect that even the best are on their way down.

Villa Selvapiana 1956 Riserva (*5/85*). Complex aroma, rich and intense; sweet ripe fruit flavors, smooth and round. *** —

1955 ***

The last time we tasted any '55s was in 1985. The Nipozzano was holding up very well.

Castello di Nipozzano 1955 Riserva (*5/85*). Lovely tawny robe shading to orange; woodsy bouquet with suggestions of mushrooms and tobacco; ripe fruit, sweet, round, tasty, complete, long finish; real quality here; no signs of fading. *** +

1950 ?

We can't recall tasting any. Leonardo Frescobaldi calls it a three-star vintage (out of four).

1948 ***

Giuntini called the vintage excellent, and indeed the Selvapiana Riserva is proof that it was. It was still excellent when we last tasted it in April 1990.

Villa Selvapiana 1948 Riserva (*3 times, 4/90*). Bouquet recalls damp leaves; rich and flavorful, smooth and satisfying, loaded with flavor, very long; lots of quality. *** *Bottle of 5/85:* Tawny robe shading to onionskin; lovely complex bouquet with a suggestion of mint; velvety texture, tasty, very long; a complete wine, at its peak. *** +

1947 *** +

Another excellent vintage for Selvapiana according to Giuntini and according to the quality of the Villa Selvapiana Riserva we last tasted in July 1988.

Villa Selvapiana 1947 Riserva (*4 times, 7/88*). Fairly deep color; concentrated ripe fruit bouquet, some floral notes; soft, like liquid velvet; exudes class, loads of quality. And who said that Chianti made with *governo* and white grapes doesn't age? *** + *Bottle of 5/85:* Deeper color and richer aroma than the '48; seems younger as well; woodsy bouquet; loads of fruit, still has considerable tannin, velvety texture, very long finish; not at its peak yet. ***(*)

1945 ****

The last '45 we tasted was in 1985. Leonardo Frescobaldi said it was a four-star vintage (perfect marks). The Nipozzano that we tasted in May 1985 was outstanding and still on the young side.

Castello di Nipozzano 1945 Riserva (*twice, 5/85*). Beautiful brick robe, tawny at edge; expansive bouquet with notes of flowers and underbrush; still some tannin, full-bodied, liquid velvet, enormous weight and extract; can still improve, but nearly perfect now. ****

1936 ?

We can't recall ever tasting a '36 Chianti, Rùfina, or any other kind. Frescobaldi gave the vintage two stars out of four.

1934 ***+

The last '34 we tasted was in 1986. Leonardo Frescobaldi rates the year as three stars out of four. The Nipozzano we had was lovely and very ready.

Castello di Nipozzano 1934 Riserva (*9/86*). Beautiful robe; lovely fragrant bouquet; liquid velvet, leathery notes, harmonious, very long; a complete wine of real class. ***+

1923 ****

The last, and only, '23 we tasted was in May 1985. Leonardo Frescobaldi calls it a four-star vintage out of a possible four. The quality of the '23 Nipozzano demonstrates just how right he is.

Castello di Nipozzano 1923 Riserva (*5/85*). Beautiful brick robe shading to orange; full, complex bouquet with suggestions of underbrush and flowers (when it was decanted the bouquet filled the room); still some tannin, sweet and gentle, elegant, incredible length, a touch of tannin at the end. ****

1917 ?

Frescobaldi rates the vintage two stars out of four.

1908 ?

Frescobaldi gives 1908 three stars out of four.

The Chianti Putto Consorzio

This voluntary growers' association has 2,000 members who cultivate some 32,000 acres (13,000 hectares) of vines in Chianti. Some 500 of them bottle their wine; the grapes from another 600 are vinified at co-ops. The members of the Putto Consorzio produce, on average, 18.5 million gallons (700,000 hectoliters) of Chianti a year. The organization was founded in 1927. Today they have members in all of the Chianti zones except Classico, which has its own *consorzio.* The group grants to wines that meet its standards a neck label with the *consorzio* seal depicting a *putto,* or cherub, with a grapevine.

REGIONAL CHIANTI

The Chianti region takes in all of the seven zones as well as some peripheral areas among and around them. Many wines sold simply as Chianti, though, are from one of the delimited zones and could carry that denomination on the label, but, because the names of most of the Chianti zones are not well known, many producers don't bother putting the district name on the label. We hope to see more recognition for the better Italian wines in the future, and perhaps can also look forward to seeing more definitive labeling as a consequence; the more information the wine drinker has, the better.

DOCG REQUIREMENTS FOR CHIANTI VERSUS THOSE FOR THE CHIANTI PUTTO CONSORZIO

	DOCG	*Chianti Putto*
Maximum Yield in Gallons/Acre	935	860
Maximum Yield in Hectoliters/Hectare	87	80
Minimum Alcohol		
Normale	11.5%	12.0%
Riserva	12.0%	12.5%

ACREAGE AND PRODUCTION OF REGIONAL CHIANTI

Province	Number of Registered Growers	Acres	Hectares	1986–88 Average Annual Production Hectoliters	Cases
Arezzo	553	5,258	2,128	73,220	813,474
Firenze	1,373	15,756	6,376	235,485	2,616,238
Pisa	72	1,410	571	14,047	156,062
Pistoia	15	295	119	1,443	16,032
Siena	246	2,403	972	72,496	805,427
Total	2,259	25,122	10,166	396,691	4,407,233
All Chianti	4,699	57,865	23,417	896,634	9,961,607

Source: Il Corriere Vinicolo

Recommended Producers

Coltibuono "La Baida," Cetamura*
Fattoria La Querce
Melini, Borghi d'Elsa
Serristori
Tenuta Il Monte
Tenuta San Vito in Fior di Selva (Roberto Drighi)
Villa Santina

* Made by Badia a Coltibuono from bought grapes

CHIANTI PRODUCERS

Agricoltori del Chianti Geografico Soc. Coop. (*Gaiole in Chianti, Siena*), *1961.* This *cantina sociale* has 125 to 140 members who own some 914 acres (370 hectares) of vines in Castellina, Gaiole, and Radda, 741 (300) in specialized culture and 74 (30) in *coltura promiscua* for Chianti Classico. Some of their associates own *castelli* in Fagnano, Lucignano, Montegiacchi, Tornano, and Vitignano. The Lucignano estate has 74 acres (30 hectares) under vines, and Tornano has 42 (17).

Geografico bottles more than half of its annual production, the equivalent of 33,000 cases, which includes at most 188,000 cases of Chianti Classico. Its aging and vinification cellars are in Gaiole. Like so many others in Toscana, Geografico has installed a *barrique*-aging cellar. Its wines include four still whites—Galestro, Montescudaio, Val d'Arbia, and Vernaccia di San Gimignano—the sparkling white Villa di Gajo, a *vin santo,* four Chianti Classicos, Brunello di Montalcino, Vino Nobile di Montepulciano, Montescudaio Rosso, Sarmento Prime Lucciole, and Predicato di Bitùrica. They market a Vino Nobile di Montepulciano Vigneti alla Cerraia and a Brunello that is bottled for them. The '83 was bottled by Azienda Agricola Il Casello, the '84 by A.A.C., whom we suspect to be Azienda Agricola Camigliano.

Sarmento Prime Lucciole, made from a blend of sangiovese and canaiolo, is meant to be drunk cool while it is still young and fresh. It is best within the year of the vintage.

Geografico's standard quality Chianti Classico is bottled under four labels—Geografico, Castello di Fagnano, Contessa di Radda, and Tenuta Montegiacchi. To our knowledge Lodovico da Montaione, a Chianti Classico they bottled at one time, is no longer produced. All four of the Chianti Classicos are the product of sangiovese, canaiolo, trebbiano, and malvasia grapes grown by their members. The co-op produces, on average, 77,500 cases of the Geografico Chianti Classico and Castello di Fagnano Chiantis combined. The former wine was at one time sold as Chianti Geografico Chianti Classico. The grapes for this wine come from the three *comuni* of Castellina, Gaiole, and Radda. The Castello di Fagnano Chianti Classico is made from the four grape varieties grown in the vineyards of that castle. The castle and its 79 acres (32 hectares) of vines are the property of the Terrosi Vagnoli family. The co-op reports aging this wine for three years in oak casks, but the bottles we have seen have been a *normale,* not a *riserva!* It produces some 11,100 cases of Contessa di Radda from grapes grown around the village of Radda. Tenuta Montegiacchi is a 173-acre (70-hectare) estate owned by Pietro Cinughi de Pazzi. Its *riserva* is aged for three years in oak casks.

In recent years Geografico decided to upgrade its quality, and so secured the services of master enologist Vittorio Fiore. We are watching them with great anticipation. Chianti Classico: *, Castello di Fagnano *, Contessa di Radda *, Tenuta Montegiacchi *

Aiello. They own *Tenuta Canale.* They use this label on another Chianti Classico.

Antiche Fattorie Fiorentine. Adele Giulia Carrara owns Antiche Fattorie Fiorentine and the Lamole di Lamole label, as well as the estates of *Fattoria Salcetino* and *Fattoria Pile e Lamole.*

Antinori. See *Marchese L. e P. Antinori.*

Avignonesi (*Montepulciano, Siena*), *1978.* This fine producer of Vino Nobile di Montepulciano, produces 10,000 to 12,000 bottles a year of Chianti Colli Senesi. It is not wood aged and is meant to be drunk young. Chianti * +

Baccio da Gaiole, Azienda Agricola di Gittori (*Gaiole in Chianti, Siena*). Marchese Ugo di Toscana owned this estate prior to A.D. 1000. The family of sculptor Baccio Bandinelli acquired it in 1488.

Today it is owned by Gianfranco Innocenti. Innocenti has 15 acres (6 hectares) of vineyards on his Gittori estate, 11 (4.5) planted for Chianti Classico at an average altitude of 1,575 feet (480 meters) above sea level. His annual production of that wine averages 33,000 bottles. Our experience with his "Baccio da Gaiuole" is very limited—to one bottle. It was at a tasting of about thirty Chianti Classicos in 1979, and the Baccio da Gaiuole '77 stood out in a lineup that included some quite illustrious names. Unfortunately we've not seen these Chianti Classicos since. Chianti Classico **

Badia a Coltibuono (*Gaiole in Chianti, Siena*). Badia a Coltibuono (the "Abbey of the Good Harvest") was founded in the mid-eleventh century by monks of the Vallombrosian order, who are credited with planting the first vines in this part of Chianti. The Stucchi-Prinetti family has owned Badia since 1847. Today the abbey and property of 2,095 acres (848 hectares) are owned by Piero Stucchi-Prinetti. Surrounding the abbey and its outbuildings are some 1,800 acres (728 hectares) of land ranging in altitude from 1,299 to 2,599 feet (395 to 790 meters) above sea level. It is mostly forestland with some olive groves and vines at the lower elevations. At Monti in Chianti, Badia owns another 300 acres (120 hectares) of land at an average altitude of about 1,299 feet (395 meters). In all, only 133 acres (54 hectares) are planted in vines.

The 6.2-acre (2.5-hectare) La Sorgene vineyard was planted in 1988 and the 3.7-acre (1.5-hectare) Porcelline in 1990. In 1991 the 8.6-acre (3.5-hectare) Boscone vineyard will be planted, and in 1992 they will plant an additional 7.4 acres (3 hectares) on their property.

There is a special clone of the sangiovese at Badia; some of the vines are over forty-five years old. In 1982, for the first time, they produced a very fine Chianti Classico from these old vines. We don't know if they bottled it separately.

Badia produces more than 50,000 cases of wine a year. Besides 10,000 cases each of Chianti Classico *normale* and *riserva*, they produce 15,000 cases of a very good Coltibuono Bianco from trebbiano and malvasia, 10,000 of Coltibuono Rosso from sangiovese, canaiolo, and some cabernet sauvignon, and 3,000 Coltibuono Rosato. At one time the rosso was vinified to be drunk young and fresh, but in recent years it has been modified to take

moderate age. They also produce 800 cases of *vin santo* and 1,250 to 2,500 of the especially fine *barrique*-aged Sangiovese, **Sangioveto di Coltibuono.** Their own vines supply them with 55 percent of their grape requirements. Except for the red, white, and pink Coltibuono, the grapes for all of their other wines come from their own estate. Since 1988 they have produced, from bought grapes, a regional Chianti labeled Cetamura. There were 11,000 cases of that wine. Badia also produces grappa, honey, vinegar, and an exceptionally fine extra virgin olive oil. Roberto Stucchi-Prinetti manages the estate.

Until the end of the 1970s it was possible to have a tasting at Badia of a range of Chianti Classicos going back to 1958, from cask. This, however, has changed. In 1980, Stucchi-Prinetti brought in Dott. Maurizio Castelli, one of Italy's, indeed the world's, finest enologists, to be the winemaker at Badia.

Today the Badia Chianti is fermented in stainless steel and aged for considerably less time than previously in large, very old chestnut and Slavonian oak casks. *Governo* is not used.

At one time we frequently detected an aroma and taste of old wood in the Badia wines, but this is rarely, if ever, the case today. Badia's Chiantis are very fine wines, fairly full-bodied and capable of aging better than most. Among the more impressive recent vintages we've tasted lately were particularly the *riserve* of '85, '83, and '82. The '78, '70, and '64 also showed very well, and the '87 *normale,* and the *riserve* of '86, '81, '77, and '58, and, surprisingly, the '76 and '66, all gave pleasure. Chianti Classico: *normale* ** +, Riserva *** +; Chianti: Cetamura *

Baggiolino (*La Romole, Firenze*), *1950–51.* Ellen Fantoni Sellon Puceinelli owns this estate and its 39.5 acres (16 hectares) of vines in the Chianti Putto district. She has 27.2 acres (11 hectares) planted for Chianti. Her annual production averages 11,665 cases of wine, which include 4,445 of Chianti.

Barberini We haven't seen this Chianti Classico since the '77 that we tasted in 1979. Chianti Classico [0]

Barfede-Certaldo (*S. Donato in Poggio, Firenze*). Barfede-Certaldo owns 12.3 acres (5 hectares) of vines from which it produces 46,500 bottles of Chianti Classico a year. It produces an

THE VINEYARDS OF BADIA A COLTIBUONO

Vineyard	Location	Acres	Hectares	Altitude in Feet	Meters	Soil
Argenina	Monti	11.66	4.72	984–1,083	300–330	*alberese*-clay
Corsignano	Monti	19.72	7.98	919–1,050	280–320	clay
Montebello	Monti	16.28	6.59	984–1,148	300–350	*alberese*
Poggino	Monti	24.39	9.87	1,083–1,181	330–360	*alberese*
Tornano	Gaiole	18.24	7.38	984–1,148	300–350	*alberese*
Valdarno	Coltibuono	13.54	5.48	1,476–1,641	450–500	*galestro*
Vignone	Monti	13.29	5.38	984–1,148	300–350	*alberese*-clay
Total		117.12	47.40			

additional 206,000 bottles of wine a year made from purchased grapes. We found both its '78 and '77 Cerbaiola and '75 Signoria reasonably good. The only wine we've tasted since those bottles has been from the difficult 1987 vintage. It's not enough for us to change our rating. Chianti Classico: Cerbaiola *, Signoria *

Barone Neri del Nero (*Monteriggioni, Siena*). Barone Massimo Neri del Nero, owner of Castel Pietraio, produces 4,200 cases of a good Chianti. Chianti Colli Senesi **

Bartali Casa Vinicola (*Castellina Scalo, Siena*). Attilio Pagli is their enologist. At most they produce a little more than 13,000 cases of Chianti Classico a year, though the winery has a capacity of 194,000 cases. They produced a good '85 and '87, and a disappointing '88. They also sell wines as Alberto Bartali. Chianti Classico *

"Berardenga" Fattoria di Felsina (*Castelnuovo Berardenga, Siena*), *1960*. This estate is made up of thirteen farms including the Felsina farm. It covers 865 acres (350 hectares), 130 (52) planted in vines. More than half of the vineyards, 67 acres (27 hectares), are in the Classico zone; another 23 (9.4) are in the Colli Senesi. The vines, planted at an average altitude of 1,148 feet (350 meters) above sea level, face south to southeast. Felsina produces about 22,000 cases of wine a year, including 12,000 of Chianti Classico and 5,500 of Chianti Colli Senesi.

The first Classico sold in bottle by Felsina was from the 1966 vintage. Highlights of the fine tasting arranged for us in May 1985 at the *azienda* by Giuseppe Mazzocolin, director of the estate, showing most of the vintages they have produced from that date to the most recent, included the '77, '75, '70, and, surprisingly, the '66, a rather mediocre year. The '81, '79, '72, and '69 were also good. We found a consistent quality in these wines. Only the '82, '71, and '68 were disappointing. Of more recent vintages, the '88 is excellent, and the *riserve* of '85 and '83, and '85 *normale* are very good. The '77, '72, and '70 *riserve* tasted fairly recently were all very good.

A few years ago they engaged Franco Bernabei as their consulting enologist, and now, as is becoming so common in Toscana, some of their wines, including a Sangiovese named **Fontalloro**, are aged in *barrique*. Another growing trend, practiced here as well, is the production of single-vineyard Chianti Classicos. At Felsina, beginning in 1983, they have produced one from Vigneto Rancia. Thus far we've tasted the '83 and '85; both were very good. Chianti Classico: *normale* **, Riserva ** +, Riserva Vigneto Rancia ** +

Bertolli (*Castellina in Chianti, Siena*). Bertolli has 81 acres (32.7 hectares) planted at Fattoria di Fizzano, where they produce some 22,000 cases of wine a year. The company, though, sells about three and a half times that amount—about 78,000 cases—nearly half of which is Chianti Classico. Their best wine, which we have not tasted since the '71 vintage, is sold as Fattoria Fizzano.

Our experience with the Bertolli wines of late has been quite limited; we haven't tasted their wines since 1983, when we tasted their less than impressive '78. Consequently, we must suspend judgment on their Chianti Classico. This could very well be the Fizzano estate that was bought by Italo Zingarelli of Rocca delle Macìe in 1982 or 1983. Rocca produces a special single-vineyard Chianti Classico Riserva from that Fizzano property.

Brolio (*Gaiole in Chianti, Siena*). The Brolio castle, on the estate of Barone Ricasoli, the creator of Chianti, dates from 1141. The Canadian liquor giant Seagram's was the owner of the Ricasoli firm from 1959 until the mid-1980s. Then, in 1986, the Lamberth, Grieve, and Ricasoli families bought it, and four years later, in 1990, Hardy's, the large Australian winery, acquired controlling interest in the winery, vineyards, and the Brolio, Ricasoli, and Nicollini brands. Lamberth and the Ricasolis still have a stake here. The Ricasoli family retains control of Castello Brolio, the winery buildings, and the castle vineyards.

There are 618 acres (250 hectares) of vineyards on the property, planted in limestone and marl soil at an average altitude of 1,575 feet (480 meters) above sea level. They replant approximately 37 acres (15 hectares) every year. In 1989, they planted 12.4 acres (5 hectares) of sangiovese and 9.9 (4) each of cabernet sauvignon and chardonnay.

The winery has the capacity to produce 2 million cases a year. Currently they produce an average of approximately 850,000 cases annually. Hardy plans to increase this to its maximum by 1995. They produce 100,000 to 110,000 cases of Chianti Classico (San Ripolo is one of their Classicos), plus 18,000 to 20,000 cases of the Riserva, as well as a regional Chianti and the other standard Tuscan wines, including a very good *vin santo* that ages very well and a line of Veronese wines. They produce a very good white wine, Torricella, made with 75 percent malvasia and 25 percent trebbiano grapes grown on their Torricella vineyard; it is aged in oak for three years. This wine has been produced at Brolio since 1896. Recently they introduced two new wines: the white Nebbiano from 60 percent sauvignon blanc and 40 percent riesling italico, and Tramonto, a sangiovese rosé.

Under the Ricasoli label they sell both Chianti and Chianti Classico. These wines are made basically from grapes they buy. The *uvaggio* is 80 percent sangiovese, 10 percent canaiolo, 5 percent malvasia, and 5 percent other varieties. The Brolio Chianti Classicos, both the *normale* and Riserva, are made from their own grapes. In these wines there is some malvasia in the *uvaggio*, but no trebbiano. The original Barone Ricasoli felt that the malvasia was a variety with some character; the trebbiano, on the other hand, had none, and therefore it couldn't add anything to the blend. (We can't argue with him on that point.) The Brolio Riserva is not made with *governo*. Both Brolio Chiantis are made from a blend of 90 percent sangiovese, 8 percent canaiolo, and 2 percent malvasia toscano, the minimum allowed by law. The *normale* is aged for ten months in oak casks, the Riserva sixteen months.

THE MAIN VINEYARDS OF BROLIO

	Acres	Hectares
Agresto	161	65
La Grotta	111	45
Torricella	74	30
Tremoleto	86	35

Their top wine is the Riserva del Barone, made from 75 percent sangiovese, 12 percent canaiolo, 8 percent malvasia, and 5 percent colorino. The '78 was their first, and a very good wine it was. They produced 546 cases. The '82 was made from a blend of 70 percent sangiovese, 20 percent canaiolo, and 10 percent malvasia. Riserva del Barone is aged for three years in Slavonian oak casks. Since the mid-1970s, about the same time they hired a new enologist, Lugino Casagrande, their Chiantis have been given less wood age.

The present Barone Ricasoli told us that he feels Chianti Classico is not a wine that ages well; it rarely lasts more than twenty years, and is generally best from about five to eight years.

Until the '78 Riserva del Barone, the last really good Brolio Chianti we tasted was the '58. It was a stunning wine. That was, alas, some time ago. Although these wines, under the Seagram reign, were drinkable enough, they had, unfortunately, slipped badly. Things have changed since Lamberth took the reins in 1986. Considering Hardy's plans for expansion, we can only hope they don't slip again.

Of the Brolio Riserva we have tasted recently, we enjoyed the '85, '83, '82, '75, and '50. We can also recommend their *normale* from '86 and '85. Their Riserva del Barone '83, '82, and '81 were all quite good. Chianti: Ricasoli 0; Chianti Classico: Brolio *normale* * +, Brolio Riserva * +, Brolio Riserva del Barone **, Ricasoli [0]

Buracchi (*Montepulciano Stazione, Siena*). This Vino Nobile di Montepulciano producer owns 20 acres (8 hectares) of vineyards, 8.6 (3.5) planted for Chianti.

Burchino. We haven't tasted the Burchino Chianti Classico in a while, not since 1982 when we tasted the '78 vintage. Therefore we think it best not to rate their wine at this time.

Caggiolo, Il Caggio (*Castellina in Chianti, località Caggio, Siena*). Il Caggio has 36.1 acres (14.6 hectares) of land planted in vines at an altitude of 984 feet (300 meters) above sea level. From this acreage they produce 8,330 cases of Chianti Classico a year. The Rivella brothers are involved; Pietro is the enologist, Ezio the export manager.

Caiano (*Castelnuovo Berardenga, località Caiano, Siena*). Their annual production of Chianti Classico averages 4,620 cases from their 19.5 acres (7.9 hectares) of vines.

Campochiarenti (*San Gimignano, località Casaglia, Siena*), 1977. Campochiarenti owns 39.5 acres (16 hectares) of vines from which they produce, besides Chianti Colli Senesi and Vernaccia di San Gimignano, the other wines typical for this area. Their annual production of wine averages between 11,000 and just over 12,000 cases, of which nearly half is Chianti.

Candialle (*Panzano in Chianti, Firenze*). From their 7.9 acres (3.2 hectares) of vines, two-thirds in monoculture, they produce, on average, a little more than 22,000 bottles of Chianti Classico a year.

Cantagalli, Azienda Agricola La Torre (*Barberino Val d'Elsa, località Cortine, Firenze*). Cantagalli has 22 acres (8.9 hectares) of vines planted for Chianti Classico from which it produces an average of 5,150 cases a year.

Cantina Gattavecchi (*Montepulciano, località S. Maria, Siena*), 1958. This firm has no vineyards. They buy wines, and blend, age, and bottle them under their label. They still make a Vino Nobile di Montepulciano, but we don't know if they are continuing to produce a Chianti Colli Senesi.

Cantina Innocenti Vittorio (*Montefollonico, Siena*), 1981. This producer of Vino Nobile di Montepulciano also produces a Chianti Colli Senesi.

Capannelle di Raffaele Rossetti (*Gaiole in Chianti, Siena*), 1974. Rossetti owns 7.4 acres (3 hectares) of vines, planted at an average altitude of 1,180 feet (360 meters) above sea level, facing southwest. Until a few years ago he produced 21,300 bottles a year of very fine Chianti Classico and a *barrique*-aged **Capannelle Rosso**.

Before we visited the *cantina*, Rossetti spoke to us about his wines and his commitment to cleanliness, which includes sterilizing not just the bottles for his wines but also every vat, tube, and machine with which the wine will come in contact. He proudly told us that when a famous surgeon visited his winery a few years ago, the man paid him the highest compliment he could receive: the doctor remarked that the *cantina* was cleaner than his operating room!

We had already accepted an invitation from this quite charming man to visit Capannelle, but must admit we began to fear that his wines would be so clean that they would be not only free of all defects but of all personality and interesting nuances as well. Our trepidations were laid to rest when we tasted the wines. It's true that the Capannelle wines are free from defects, but they are as full of personality and character as the producer himself. In fact, they were among the finest Chiantis produced.

The wines are fermented in stainless steel and aged in fairly small oak casks. They rest again for a period in stainless steel before being bottled, needless to say, under sterile conditions.

Rossetti's Chianti Classico was made from red grapes only. His first wine was from the 1975 vintage.

Among the vintages we tasted at Capannelle we found the '83 to be particularly fine. The '82, '79, and '77 are also very good, followed by '81 and '78. The '75 was also fairly good. There was no '76 Capannelle. Unfortunately we haven't tasted more recent vintages.

Raffaele is proud of his wine, and his packaging reflects this. The wine is bottled with an elegantly simple, hand-stamped silver-colored label. The *vecchio* is available with a silver label, the *riserva* in gold—both done in the noble metal itself. That's surely a bottle one is not likely to soon forget. Fittingly, the wines inside are memorable as well.

Rossetti has dropped out of the *consorzio*, not the first good producer to do so, and just as he told us he would do, he stopped using the Chianti Classico name on his wines. Now he flies with his own colors. His red wines are **Capannelle Riserva** and **Capannelle Barrique**. Chianti Classico ***

Caparsa (*Radda in Chianti, località Caparsa, Siena*), 1966. Reginaldo Cianferoni has owned the Caparsa estate since 1966. He has 29.8 acres (12 hectares) of vines, divided into the 23.5-acre (9.5-hectare) Caparsino vineyard and the 6.3-acre (2.5-hectare) Vigna Vecchia vineyard. The vines, facing southeast, are planted at an altitude of 1,640 feet (500 meters) above sea level. Cianferoni produces some 5,775 cases of wine annually. In 1982 he made 3,300 cases of Caparsino. We've never tasted any of Cianferoni's wines.

Cappelli Giovanni (*Panzano in Chianti, Firenze*), 1730. Giovanni Minuccio Cappelli is the proprietor of the 500-acre (200-hectare) Montagliari farm. Some 64 acres (26 hectares) of the 86 acres (35 hectares) of vines are planted for Chianti Classico. From these vines, some planted in *coltura promiscua*, he produces the Fattoria di Montagliari Chianti.

He also owns Casa Vinicola Socovich and produces a line of wines under the La Quercia label from his own grapes as well as grapes that he buys from other growers. The La Quercia Chianti is a good, fresh red wine meant to be drunk young. Besides the Chianti, he produces a very good sweet *vin santo* and a white wine under this label.

Cappelli has a total production, excluding the La Quercia line, of nearly 25,000 cases of wine a year: 10,000 cases are Chianti Classico, 1,650 *vin santo* (including a very good dry Montagliari *vin santo*), 5,500 white, 2,200 rosé, and 4,260 of a very good *barrique*-aged sangiovese, Brunesco di S. Lorenzo. He also produces up to 22,200 cases of La Quercia Chianti Classico, and a very good *vin santo*, as well as a few other wines under this label.

The Montagliari and Castellinuzza estates were separated into two properties when Cappelli's grandfather died, leaving an estate to each of his two sons. When Minuccio took over, he reunited them. He produces 5,500 cases a year of the Montagliari Riserva, which is labeled either as Fattoria di Montagliari or as Fattoria di Montagliari e Castellinuzza (the second is used in the United States to simplify the name for the American market!). This wine was made from an *uvaggio* of 90 percent sangiovese and 10 percent canaiolo, malvasia, and trebbiano in about equal proportions. The amount of white grapes was decreased a few years ago to comply with the maximum of 5 percent set by DOCG. He uses the same blend for his La Quercia Chianti Classico.

The Montagliari Classico is fermented in oak uprights for seven to eight days on the skins, then continues for an additional fifteen days or more after being drawn off its lees. He adds sangiovese grapes, selected and semidried, for the *governo* to create a second fermentation, which lasts into February or March. He stopped fermenting with the stems for the vintages from 1973 to 1980, but has started adding them again. He finds that including the stems produces a wine with more perfume and body as well as tannin. In March he racks the wine and moves it into oak casks, where it is aged for three to five years before bottling. Cappelli makes the wine with advice from consulting enologist Mario Cortevesio.

Cappelli produces a limited amount of the single-vineyard Casaloste Montagliari Chianti Classico Riserva in vintages that he feels justify it. To date he has produced a '62, '71, '75, and '77—just 2,000 bottles of the '75, and 3,500 bottles each of the other three vintages. He might release an '81 but didn't produce an '82 or '83. He did produce an '85 and '88. He uses the 12.4-acre (5-hectare vineyard) part of the vineyard in *coltura promiscua* planted in sangiovese and colorino grapes.

Coltura promiscua is not as economically viable today as specialized vineyards, but Minuccio says it is in some ways a better system. It is more beneficial to the vines, which, being spaced further apart, get more nutrients from the soil, as well as better ventilation and more sun. Perhaps. Or perhaps there is a touch of nostalgic traditionalism in this brass-tacks businessman.

We recently tasted a wide range of vintages at Montagliari and must admit that while we were very impressed, we were not surprised. Our experience with these very fine Chianti Classicos goes back nearly twenty years and covers vintages from 1940 to the present. Among our favorites of the past twenty years are the '83, '77, '75, and '71, particularly the Casaloste '75 and '71. Cappelli didn't bottle any Montagliari or La Quercia in 1984, 1976, or 1972.

Cappelli rates the vintages for his estate:

Top	1988, 1985, 1975, 1971, 1962
Second	1983, 1981, 1978, 1977, 1964, 1959, 1957, 1947, 1941, 1937
Third	1982, 1979
Fourth	1980, 1974, 1973, 1970, 1969, 1967, 1966, 1960, 1958, 1956, 1955, 1954, 1953, 1950, 1948
Least	1984, 1976, 1972, 1968, 1965, 1963, 1961, 1952, 1951, 1949
Not included	1987, 1986

THE VINTAGES AT FATTORIA MONTAGLIARI

Year	Cappelli's assessment	Our rating
1988	Very big wines, great capacity for aging	Not tasted
1987	No comment	Not tasted
1986	No comment	Not tasted

THE VINEYARDS OF GIOVANNI CAPPELLI

Cru/Vineyard	Acres	Hectares	First Vintage	Used for
Casaloste	22	9	1962 1980	Chianti Classico and Brunesco di San Lorenzo
Dondoli	20	8	—	—
Montagliari	44	18	—	Chianti Classico

1985	Fabulous, full-bodied wines	Not tasted
1984	None made	n/a
1983	Very good now, will improve with age	**(* +)a, b
1982	Very good, better than 1983	?c
1981	Very good (he picked before the rain)	** +
1980	Good	** —
1979	Better than the 1978	***
1978	Might be very good	*
1977	Very good	**
1976	Bad, none was bottled commercially	*b, d
1975	Only 1971 was better in the decade	*** —; cru *** +
1974	Not special	***
1973	The wines had good perfume	*** —e
1972	Terrible, none made	n/a
1971	Outstanding, the best of the decade, and one of the best of all time	*** +f,; cru ***g
1970	Good	** +h
1967	Not described by Cappelli	***b
1964	Not described by Cappelli	** +i
1962	Not described by Cappelli	cru **/*** +j
1958	Not described by Cappelli	*** +b
1957	Not described by Cappelli	***e
1955	Not described by Cappelli	** +
1954	Not described by Cappelli	***b
1952	Not described by Cappelli	*** + (****)e
1951	Not described by Cappelli	*** +
1950	Not described by Cappelli	** +k
1949	Not described by Cappelli	*** +

NOTES: [a] Tasted from cask
[b] Tasted in May 1985
[c] Tasted six times, with mixed results
[d] From a private bottling
[e] Tasted May 1986
[f] Tasted September 1987
[g] Tasted December 1987
[h] Tasted January 1984
[i] Tasted December 1984
[j] Tasted September 1986 and May 1986
[k] Tasted October 1983

On one of our visits to Montagliari, Minuccio set up a fine tasting for us in one of the dining rooms of his trattoria. This research seemed to cause some distraction among the staff, at dinner on the other side of the room. Perhaps it wasn't the number of bottles that Minuccio, always a generous host, was opening that arrested their attention, so much as the fact that though we were tasting them all, we drank nary a one, and such fine wines too. But normalcy returned when the tasting was over. As we left to go into the other room for dinner, we each carried off a couple of bottles for the table. And the tasting broadened, with Minuccio ordering a little of everything on the menu (and off?) that we either expressed an interest in or that he thought we should sample, smiling with satisfaction at our compliments and laughing at the protest that there would be too much when we were so obviously enjoying the fine specialties of the region and of the house.

Friends to whom we recommended the trattoria and rooms at Montagliari were luckier than we, who were traveling on business on a tight-to-bursting schedule. They spent a few idyllic days there in a little house in the midst of the vines, visited the *cantine* at a leisurely pace, ate at the trattoria every day, often with Minuccio, and polished their Italian (after the initial formalities, Cappelli wouldn't hear any English from them, although he speaks it very well when the occasion requires).

Cappelli is without question one of the finest producers of Chianti Classico. His Montagliari is a wine of delicacy, elegance, and balance, and one that ages extremely well. This wine can be relied on for consistency, at a high level. Chianti Classico: La Quercia *, Fattoria di Montagliari Riserva ***, Fattoria di Montagliari e Castellinuzza Riserva ***, Fattoria di Montagliari Riserva Vigna Casaloste *** +

Carobbio (*Greve in Chianti, Firenze*), *1974.* Carlo Novarese owns the 62-acre (25-hectare) Carobbio estate and some 12 acres (4.8 hectares) of vines. The vines, at an altitude of 984 feet (300 meters) above seal level, face southeast. They have three special crus: Del Bosco, Del Pruneto, and La Madonnina. They produce, on average, about 20,000 bottles of Chianti Classico a year, of which 4,000 to 6,200 are a *riserva*. They also produce 4,000 to 4,500 bottles of a white wine. Rather surprising considering the vintage, in 1987 they produced 21,000 bottles of Chianti Classico and in 1985 they produced 6,045 bottles of Chianti Classico Riserva. Both are light, early-maturing Chiantis. Chianti Classico *.

Carpineto Casa Vinicola (*Lucolena, località Dudda, Firenze*). Carpineto owns 20.7 acres (8.4 hectares) of vines, 17.1 (6.9) planted for Chianti Classico. Their vineyards supply some of the grapes for the 38,885 cases of Chianti Classico they sell annually. They buy the rest of the wine they need from wineries in the area. Their cellar has a capacity of 396,000 gallons (15,000 hectoliters). We hear that these wines, in the opinion of some at least, have improved. That, however, has not been our experience. Based on our personal tastings we cannot rate their wine any higher. Chianti Classico *

Casa Emma (*Barberino Val d'Elsa, frazione Cortine, Firenze*), *1973.* Fiorella Bucalossi Lepri owns Casa Emma and its 32 acres (13 hectares) of vines, of which some 26 (10.6) are planted for Chianti Classico. They produce, on average, nearly 72,000 bottles of Chianti Classico annually.

Casa Francesco. All we know about Casa Francesco is that they produced a good '85 Riserva. Chianti Classico *.

Casa Nova della Cappella (*Gaiole in Chianti, Siena*). Casa Nova, at one time, belonged to the family of noted artist Michelangelo Buonarroti. Today they have 8.4 acres (3.4 hectares) of vineyards planted for Chianti Classico at an average altitude of 1,380 feet (420 meters) above sea level, from which they produce 22,660 bottles of wine a year.

Casa Sola (*Barberino Val d'Elsa, frazione Cortine, Firenze*). Casa Sola owns 61 acres (24.5 hectares) of vines, 39 (15.8) of specialized vineyards, plus 5.9 (2.4) in *coltura promiscua* for Chianti Classico. They produce about 19,000 cases a year—somewhat more than 10,000 of Chianti Classico—of fairly mediocre, though drinkable wines including Chianti Classico. We haven't seen their wines since the '78 we tasted in 1983. Chianti Classico [0]

Casa Volterrani (*Vagliagli, Siena*). Volterrani has 79 acres (32 hectares) of vineyards, 62.8 (24.5) of specialized vineyards, and 2 (0.8) planted in mixed culture for Chianti Classico. They produce some 20,000 cases of wine a year, which include 15,275 cases of Chianti Classico, plus Bianco della Lega and *vin santo*. Their Chianti Classico is fermented in stainless steel and aged in *barrique*.

Casalgallo (*Querciagrossa, Siena*). Casalgallo, the rooster house, produces some 19,000 bottles of Chianti Classico annually from its 6.9 acres (2.8 hectares) of vines planted for Chianti. These vines are planted at an average altitude of 1,150 feet (350 meters) above sea level.

Casale. See *Falchini Riccardo*.

Casanova di Pietrafitta (*Castellina in Chianti, Siena*). From their 3.2 acres (1.3 hectares) of vines planted for Chianti Classico, at an average altitude of 1,805 feet (550 meters) above sea level, come 8,666 bottles of wine a year.

Casanuova di Ama (*Lecchi in Chianti, Siena*), *1968*. Ida Carli Vedova Benicini owns this estate and its 14.8 acres (6 hectares) of vines, nearly one-quarter of which, 3.3 (1.3), are planted in *coltura promiscua*. The vines are planted at an average altitude of 1,710 feet (521 meters) above sea level and face southeast. They produce some 32,000 bottles of wine annually, including a Chianti Classico that they label as Casanuova, and a *vin santo*.

Casanuova di Nittardi, Fattoria Nittardi (*Castellina in Chianti, località Nittardi, Siena*). The 245-acre (99-hectare) Nittardi estate is an old property that was once owned by the family of artist Michelangelo Buonarroti, and is consequently known in popular legend as the House of Michelangelo. This estate has 12.4 acres (5 hectares) of vines, of which 7.4 (3) are planted for Chianti Classico at an average altitude of 1,542 feet (470 meters) above sea level. They

produce, at most, 23,330 bottles of Chianti Classico a year. This wine is made from a blend of 95 percent sangiovese with 5 percent canaiolo and white grapes. Pietro Rivella is their consulting enologist. This winery's Chianti Classico is difficult to rate since the only one we tasted was from the mediocre 1987 vintage. Chianti Classico [0]

Casavecchia di Nittardi (*Castellina in Chianti, Siena*). This property belonged at one time to the Buonarroti family. Today they have 5.4 acres (2.2 hectares) of vines planted at 985 feet (300 meters) above sea level, from which they produce some 31,000 bottles of Chianti Classico a year. Pietro Rivella consults here. Thus far our only experience with these wines has been from cask when we visited them in April 1987. Based on that visit and tasting we give their Chianti Classico a tentative rating. Chianti Classico [* −]

Casina di Corina (*Castellina in Chianti, Siena*). Antoine Luginbuhl owns the Casina di Corina estate and its 14 acres (5.7 hectares) of vines. The vineyards face southwest and are planted at an altitude of 1,380 feet (420 meters) above sea level. Besides the standard Chianti grapes they grow cabernet sauvignon, although that variety is becoming standard as well. They produce some 26,600 to 33,300 bottles of wine a year.

Castel Pietraio. See *Barone Neri del Nero*.

Castel Ruggero (*Antella, Strada in Chianti, Firenze*). Castel Ruggero was an early eleventh-century military fortress of the Guidi counts. The Alamanni family turned it into a villa in the fifteenth century. This estate, owned by Ilda d'Afflitto Pecchioli, encompasses 370 acres (150 hectares). Only 7.4 acres (3 hectares) of vines are planted, from which they produce an average of 16,000 bottles of wine annually. We first tasted their Chianti Classico in April 1990. While we didn't expect a lot from the '87, we found the '88 disappointing. Chianti Classico [0]

Castelgreve, Soc. Coop. Castelli del Grevepesa (*Mercatale Val di Pesa, località Ponte Gabbiano, Firenze*), *1966*. The 165 members of the cooperative winery of Castelli del Grevepesa—all in the Florentine section of the zone—own 1,975 acres (800 hectares) of

THE SPECIAL CHIANTI CLASSICOS OF CASTELGREVE, SOC. COOP. CASTELLI DEL GREVEPESA

Cru/Village	Vintage	Tons of Grapes	Number of Bottles Produced
Lamole	1981	77	45,000
	1982		59,827
Montefiridolfi	1983	99	59,960
Panzano	1981	99	51,000
Sant'Angiolo Vico L'Abate	1980	22	9,240
	1982		29,870
	1980		14,000
Vigna Elisa	1983	22	28,668

vines, 1,605 (650) planted for Chianti Classico. They have an annual production of approximately 555,000 cases of wine, one-third of which is exported. At most, they can produce just over 333,000 of Chianti Classico a year.

They actually produce, on average, some 300,000 cases; the balance of their production is *vino da tavola*. This co-op is the largest grape and wine producer in the area. They own cellars in Badia a Passignano and Ponte di Gabbiano. The Castelgreve Chianti Classicos, produced with *governo*, were made from a blend of approximately 80 percent sangiovese, 10 percent canaiolo, 10 percent trebbiano and malvasia, and 5 percent colorino. They were required by law to change this formula to include at most 5 percent white grapes.

They produce a Valgreve rosé and a white made from a blend of trebbiano and malvasia. Under the Castelgreve label they sell a *normale* and a Riserva Chianti Classico, as well as some special single-vineyard and single-village bottlings. They also produce a *vin santo*. Chianti Classico: Castelgreve *, Montefiridolfi +, Panzano *

Castellare (*Castellina in Chianti*, località *Castellare, Siena), 1975.* Milano publisher Paolo Panerai and his wife, Fioretta, have 44.5 acres (18 hectares) of vines, 34.6 (14) for Chianti Classico, on their 148-acre (60-hectare) Castellare estate. The vineyards are planted at an average altitude of 1,000 feet (305 meters) above sea level, with a south to southwestern exposure. The soil is calcareous limestone mixed with marl and sandstone. The vineyard composition for Chianti Classico is 90 percent sangiovese, 5 percent canaiolo, 2 percent trebbiano and malvasia, and 3 percent malvasia nera. Besides these varieties, they have cabernet sauvignon, sauvignon blanc, and semillon vines.

The average annual production at Castellare is more than 100,000 bottles of wine. This includes, besides the 96,000 bottles of Chianti Classico, a *barrique*-aged **I Sodi di S. Niccolò,** the Cabernet Sauvignon **Coniale,** Bianco di Castellare, *vin santo,* and a fresh, light, fruity red, Governo di Castellare. Maurizio Castelli, enologist at Castellare, produced 10,000 bottles of this last wine in 1983, their first vintage. Castellare's pre-DOCG Chianti Classico was made from a blend of about 70 percent sangiovese, 4 percent canaiolo, 13 percent trebbiano, 10 percent malvasia, and 3 percent of other red grapes.

We found the Chianti Classicos of Castellare, at one time, rather uneven, but since Maurizio Castelli became their winemaker in 1981, the wines have displayed more consistency. The *normale* '88, '87, and '86 were all good, and the '86 and '85 *riserve* very good. Chianti Classico: *normale* ** −, Riserva ** +

Castell'in Villa (*Castelnuovo Berardenga, Siena*). Coralia Ghertsos Pignatelli della Leonessa owns 741 acres (300 hectares) of land. Of this, 148 acres (60 hectares) are planted to vines, 133 (54) for Chianti Classico. These vines are planted at an average altitude of 1,410 feet (430 meters) above sea level. Pignatelli produces, on average, some 44,500 cases of wine a year, of which some two-thirds, or 30,000 cases, are Chianti Classico, the balance consisting of the *barrique*-aged Sangiovese **Balsastrada,** a white wine, and a *vin santo*. She also produces an excellent virgin olive oil.

Pignatelli has made the wine here from the first vintage in 1971. Since 1975 her Chianti has been made from sangiovese grapes

only. She produces two Chianti Classicos, a young Chianti sold under the Montecastelli label and the Castell'in Villa *normale* and Riserva.

The Castell'in Villa Chiantis are fairly full-bodied, and stylish, with a characteristic touch of mint in their bouquet. The '87 and '86 *normale,* and the '85, '83, and '82 *riserve* are all worth looking for. Chianti Classico ** +

Castelli del Grevepesa. See **Castelgreve.**

Castellinuzza (*Lamole, Firenze*). Their average annual production of 14,665 bottles of Chianti Classico comes from their 5.2 acres (2.1 hectares) of vines.

Castello Banfi (*Castellina, and Montalcino, Siena*). At one time Rocca delle Macìe produced a mediocre Chianti Classico sold under the Villa Banfi label for this giant American importer based in the Brunello district. Today Banfi is producing their own Chianti Classico, some 22,000 cases of *riserva* only, from their own grapes grown in the Castellina district of the Chianti Classico zone. The grapes are taken to their Montalcino facility, where it is turned into wine. In an average year they produce some 20,000 cases of a *riserva,* plus another 2,000 cases of the single-vineyard Il Caggio Riserva. Ezio Rivella ages the *riserva* for two years in Slavonian oak casks. Until recently this wine was sold under the Villa Banfi label. Today it is sold under the Castello Banfi label. Of more recent vintages we can recommend their '85 Riserva and '83 Riserva Il Caggio. Chianti Classico **

Castello Camigliano (*Camigliano, Montalcino, Siena*), *1956.* This producer, who also makes a Brunello, has some 17 acres (7 hectares) of vines planted for the production of Chianti. They produce about 5,500 cases a year of Chianti Colli Senesi. It's certainly on the same plane as their Brunello. Chianti Colli Senesi 0

Castello d'Albola. See **Fattoria di Albola.**

Castello dei Rampolla (*Panzona in Chianti, Firenze*), *1967.* Principe Alieo di Napoli Rampolla is the proprietor of this 370-acre (150-hectare) castle-estate and its 94 acres (38 hectares) of vines. In the vineyards, planted at altitudes of 985 to 1,310 feet (300 to 400 meters) above sea level, there are 54 acres (22 hectares) of sangiovese, 27 (11) of cabernet sauvignon, 5 (2) of malvasia, and 2.5 (1) each of chardonnay, traminer, and sauvignon blanc. The soil is *galestro* and *alberese*. Recently, like a number of other producers here, they also planted some syrah.

The average annual production at Castello dei Rampolla is 213,000 bottles: about 80,000 of a Chianti Classico *normale* and 53,000 of *riserva,* 40,000 of **Sammarco,** a cabernet sauvignon–sangiovese blend, 20,000 of Malvasia, and 20,000 of Trebianco, an interesting white wine made from three white varieties: chardonnay, traminer, and sauvignon blanc.

The vineyards were planted in 1969. They produced their first Chianti Classico, 15,000 bottles, in 1975. In 1976 they didn't make any wine. They began experimenting with *barriques* with the 1978 vintage. The following year they produced their first Chianti Classico Riserva. That was also the first vintage they included some cabernet sauvignon in the *uvaggio* for their Chianti—8 to 10 percent in the *riserva* and 5 percent in the *normale*. These percentages vary with the vintage. The '81 *normale* again had 5 percent cabernet sauvignon; in the '82 this was reduced to only 1 to 2 percent, while the '81 had a full 10 percent. We've heard, from their importer, that the normal blend for their Chianti is 78 percent sangiovese, 10 percent each canaiolo and cabernet sauvignon, and 2 percent white grapes.

The *normale* Castello dei Rampolla Chianti Classico is aged for one year in stainless steel and one in fairly new oak casks, of 660, 790, and 1,320 gallons (25, 30, and 50 hectoliters). The *riserva* is given an additional year in cask.

The Castello dei Rampolla wines are quite good, although they are certainly not representative of Chianti. We find that, as is the case with many other wines containing cabernet sauvignon in the *uvaggio,* their flavor tends to be dominated by the cabernet, which overpowers the more gentle character of the sangiovese. These wines are Chianti Classico only by virtue of the fact that the vineyards are in the zone. In our opinion, Castello dei Rampolla should fly its own colors and drop the Chianti Classico name. It did drop out of the Chianti Classico *consorzio.*

All of the Castello dei Rampolla wines that we tasted, from '79 to '87, were very good, the '85 Riserva in particular. The '87, '85, and '84 *normale* were also all very good, but as well made as they are, as Chianti Classico we cannot rate them higher than two stars plus. As *vino da tavola* we would rate it three stars. Chianti Classico ** +

Castello del Trebbio (*Santa Brigida, Pontassieve, Firenze*). This 504-acre (204-hectare) estate in the Florentine hills has 79 acres (32 hectares) of specialized vineyards and 2.47 (1) in mixed cultivation. They produce some 16,600 cases of wine a year, which includes a decent Chianti Colli Fiorentini, plus a white, rosé, and *vin santo.* They also produce a regional Chianti with the Torre dei Pazzi label. Chianti Colli Fiorentini *

Castello della Paneretta (*Barberino Val d'Elsa, Firenze*). Maria Carla Musso has owned this estate and its 741 acres (300 hectares) since 1985. There are 37 acres (15 hectares) in vines, from which they produce some 80,000 bottles of wine annually, including Chianti Classico. The individual vineyards are Barbiano, Bossolo, Greppi, Pescina, and Sughera. Those for Chianti Classico are planted with 85 percent sangiovese, 10 percent canaiolo, and 5 percent trebbiano. The '85 Riserva and '86 *normale* were good wines. Chianti Classico *

Castello di Ama. See **Fattoria di Ama.**

Castello di Cacchiano (*Monti in Chianti, Siena*). This 865-acre (350-hectare) estate has been the property of the Ricasoli-Firidolfi family since 1150. Today Elisabetta Ricasoli Balbi Valier owns the estate and its 81.5 acres (33 hectares) of vines planted at an average altitude of 1,475 feet (450 meters) above sea level. The vines face southward. The vineyards for Chianti Classico are planted in 85 percent sangiovese, 10 percent canaiolo, and 5 percent white grapes. They have one special vineyard, the 2.47-acre (1-hectare) Selice vineyard. They produce, on average, some 15,166 cases of wine annually: 11,700 are Chianti Classico, 2,200 a *vino da tavola rosso,* 1,100 a white, and about 166 *vin santo.* They also produce some wines under the Castello di Montegrossi and Rocca di Montegrossi labels, including 20,000 bottles of a Chianti Classico, 900 half bottles of a *vin santo,* and some *barrique*-aged wines. There

were 5,000 bottles of **RF Selice** Rosso from 1985, and 4,000 bottles of **Geremia** Rosso from 1986.

Until fairly recently their wines were totally unimpressive. We are happy to report that things have changed for the better. We recommend their very good '85 and '86 Riserva Millennio and '87 and '88 *normale.* Chianti Classico: **, Riserva Millennio ** +

Castello di Castelvari (*Mercatale Val di Pesa, Firenze*). Our only knowledge of this estate, besides their location, is through their '79 *normale,* which we tasted in October 1985. It was past its best and so it seems safer not to judge them at this point. Chianti Classico [* –]

Castello di Cerreto (*Castelnuovo Berardenga, località Pianella, Siena*). Marchese Emilio Pucci is the proprietor of this Chianti Classico estate and its 71 acres (28.6 hectares) of vines, 60 (24.2) for Chianti Classico. The vines are planted at an average altitude of 1,310 feet (400 meters) above sea level. There is no castle here, though there are the ruins of a tower nearby. Their annual production of 16,000 cases is made up of an average of 12,530 cases of Chianti Classico, with the balance consisting of a *vin santo,* a white, a rosé, and the young red Graniolo.

In the 1940s these wines were sold under the Pianella label, named for the district in which the estate is located. In the nearly 1960s they changed the name to Castello di Cerreto.

The pre-DOCG *uvaggio* used for the Cerreto Chiantis is 80 to 85 percent sangiovese, 10 percent canaiolo, 5 percent malvasia, and a small amount of trebbiano, a blend that was changed with the advent of the DOCG regulations, which doesn't allow more than 5 percent of white grapes in Chianti Classico. The *normale* Cerreto is aged one to two years in oak casks; the Riserva, three to four.

At one time we found these wines considerably better than they are today, particularly in the 1960s and early 1970s. Their '81 is quite good, but the '82 and '83, though good wines, are not really up to the level of those vintages. It is quite possible that Pucci's wines have improved of late since he has brought in consulting enologist Pietro Rivella. These are full-bodied Chiantis, reflecting the style of the district where they are produced. Chianti Classico * +

Castello di Fonterutoli (*Castellina in Chianti, località Fonterutoli, Siena*). The village of Fonterutoli dates back to the eleventh century. The Mazzei family has owned it and its 1,092 acres (442 hectares) since 1435. Today Lapo Mazzei, owner of this estate, has 168 acres (68 hectares) of vines planted at altitudes ranging from 1,050 to 1,805 feet (320 to 500 meters) above sea level in *galestro* and *alberese* soil. The vines have a south to southwestern exposure. The individual vineyards are La Badiola (13.6 acres/5.5 hectares), La Brancaia (18.5/7.5), and Siepi (33.4/13.5).

Mazzei has an annual production of some 200,000 bottles of wine, including no less than three Chianti Classicos. Although these wines seem to enjoy a good reputation, we find them rather disappointing. Even the *riserve* mature quickly and fade shortly afterward. And we can't say that they improved much in spite of the fact that Mazzei hired Franco Bernabei as his consulting enologist. Like most of the other estates Bernabei works with, they use *barriques* here for aging. Since 1985 they have produced a Ser Lapo Chianti Classico Riserva from 80 percent sangiovese, 10 percent canaiolo, malvasia, and trebbiano, and 8 percent other red grapes.

We don't know what the remaining 2 percent is. We found the '85 good and the '86 very good. There were 26,000 bottles, plus 600 magnums, of the '86 vintage. Of the standard Fonterutoli, the '82, '85, '87, and '88 were good, no more, no less. Chianti Classico: *, Riserva Ser Lapo * +

Castello di Gabbiano (*Mercatale Val di Pesa, Firenze*). This estate, named for the twelfth-century castle of Gabbiano, encompasses 125 acres (50 hectares) of vineyards planted at altitudes ranging from 655 to 720 feet (200 to 220 meters) above sea level, facing southeast. Besides the typical Chianti varieties, there are the foreign merlot, cabernet, and chardonnay vines, as well as schioppetino from Friuli–Venezia Giulia, ancellato, and colorino. They use these last three varieties in their Chianti Classico. The annual production at Gabbiano averages 40,000 cases, which includes Chianti Classico, white, *rosato*, and *vin santo*. They also produce a Gabbiano Chianti Classico *normale* and Riserva, as opposed to their estate-bottled Castello di Gabbiano, from non–estate grown grapes. Their Chianti Classico Riserva is made with *governo*, and aged in a combination of one-third *barriques*, oak casks, and stainless steel. Their Chianti Classico gold label Riserva is similar, except that it is aged in French oak. Other wines worth mentioning include **Ania,** a 100 percent *barrique*-aged sangiovese from their own vineyards; **R & R,** a cabernet-merlot blend; and Ariella, a 100 percent chardonnay. Franco Bernabei was, until recently, their consulting enologist. We found the '82 Riserva good; the '86 Riserva, on the other hand, was disappointing. Chianti Classico: Castello di Gabbiano Riserva *, Gabbiano * +

Castello di Meleto (*Gaiole in Chianti, Siena*). Viticola Toscana Agricola Immobiliare owns this estate with its twelfth-century castle and its 514 acres (208 hectares) of vines, 472 (191) planted for Chianti Classico. They produce 133,000 cases of wine a year, including 111,000 cases of Chianti Classico. This wine was bottled, stored at, and sold by the **Storiche Cantine.** Their wine, like that of the others who belong or belonged to the Storiche Cantine, is mediocre at best. We don't know if that organization still exists, but the original estates that made up the group have the same director and enologist. Chianti Classico 0

Castello di Montegrossi (*Monti in Chianti, Siena*). This estate is owned by Elisabetta Ricasoli Balbi Valier. Their mailing address is **Castello di Cacchiano.** Perhaps it is only a second label for the Cacchiano wine. We heard it reported that it is a second estate, but the data we have is identical—estate size, extent of vineyards, percentage of grapes in the vineyard, average annual production, etc.—to that of Castello di Cacchiano. They also sell some wines, including Chianti Classico, under the Rocca di Montegrossi label. The Castello di Montegrossi *normale* '87, '83, and '82 and *riserve* of '81 and '78 were all good. The Rocca di Montegrossi '87 *normale* was good and the '86 Riserva very good. Chianti Classico: Castello di Montegrossi * +, Rocca di Montegrossi *normale* *, Riserva **

Castello di Monterinaldi (*Radda in Chianti, Siena*). Fattoria La Pesanella owns this castle and its 178-acre (72-hectare) vineyard. The vines planted for Chianti Classico encompass 168 acres (68 hectares) at an average altitude of 985 feet (300 meters) above sea level. They produce 55,500 cases of mediocre wine, including 39,700 of Chianti Classico, a year. Castello di Monterinaldi, like Castello di Meleto, belonged to the **Storiche Cantine,** or as it is

sometimes familiarly referred to, hysterical *cantine,* for reasons that will be obvious to anyone who's tasted their wines. Chianti Classico [0]

Castello di Mugnana (*Strada in Chianti, Firenze*). This castle was built in the eleventh century. The entire estate encompasses 740 acres (300 hectares). The vineyards of 74 acres (30 hectares) include 47 (19) planted at an average altitude of 985 feet (300 meters) above sea level for Chianti Classico. They produce, in an average year, 11,000 cases of that wine. They utilize the services of consulting enologist Vittorio Fiore. Thus far the only wine we have tasted from them, the '87, was good. Chianti Classico *

Castello di Nipozzano. See **Frescobaldi.**

Castello di Poppiano. See **Castello Guicciardini Poppiano.**

Castello di Querceto (*Greve*, località *Lucolena, Firenze*), 1895. The François family are the proprietors of this beautiful old castle, dating from the time of the Lombards, and its 457-acre (185-hectare) estate. Their 119 acres (48 hectares) of vines, facing southeast to southwest, are planted at altitudes ranging from 1,475 to 1,640 feet (450 to 500 meters) above sea level. Some 101 acres (41 hectares) are planted for Chianti Classico. The vineyards contain 85 percent sangiovese, 8 percent canaiolo, 2 percent trebbiano and malvasia, and 5 percent other red grapes, including cabernet sauvignon and merlot. They had some chardonnay a few years ago and still might. They have a number of vineyards, or crus, some of which are bottled separately

Alessandro François, in charge of the winemaking here since 1975, produces 260,000 bottles of wine annually. He hopes to increase this to 300,000 within five years. Of these, there are 120,000 bottles of Chianti Classico *normale* and 30,000 of *riserva;* 20,000 each of a *barrique*-aged **La Corte** and Il Picchio; 15,000 each of **Il Querciolaia Predicato di Bitùrica** (a cabernet sauvignon-sangiovese blend), Le Giuncaie (a *vino da tavola* from a blend of chardonnay, trebbiano toscano, and malvasia del chianti), the carbonic maceration Il Quercetino *vino da tavola* from sangiovese, canaiolo, trebbiano, malvasia, and colorino, and François 1er, 10,000 of Cignale, and a *vin santo*. We don't know if they still produce a Bianco della Lega. This *azienda* has three labels for their Chianti Classicos—Caratello for a fresh red wine to drink young, le Capanne, and Castello di Querceto.

OTHER CRUS AND VINEYARDS OF CASTELLO DI QUERCETO

Cru/Vineyard	Acres	Hectares
La Madonnina	9.9	4
Le Capanne	24.7	10
Le Corte	7.4	3
Le Giuncaie	24.7	10
Le Rabatte	7.4	3
Quercetino	14.8	6
Terreni	9.9	4

THE CRUS AND VINEYARDS OF CASTELLO DI QUERCETO

Cru/Vineyard	Acres	Hectares	First Vintage	Average Number of Bottles Per Year
Abetina	7.4	3	n/a	—
Cignale*	n/a	n/a	1986	10,000
Il Picchio	9.9	4	1988	20,000
Quercetino*	14.8	6	n/a	15,000
La Corte	9.9	4	1978	20,000
Le Giuncaie*	24.7	10	n/a	15,000
Querciolaia de'Pitti	14.8	6	1982	15,000

* This information was reported to us five years ago, the information for the other vineyards in 1990. We included these vineyards since the data they gave us in 1990 included production figures for these crus. A number of other vineyards they listed in 1985 were not included in 1990.

François ferments in temperature-controlled stainless steel tanks and ages his Chianti in a combination of oak casks and *barriques*. Even in the better years his Querceto Chianti *normale* is given some time in *barrique*. The *normale* '82, for example, had six months of *barrique* age. The '81 Riserva was given eight months in *barrique*. Giovanni Cappelli is their consulting enologist. We doubt that he is *the* Giovanni Cappelli from Fattoria di Montagliari.

Castello di Querceto has been bottling Chianti Classico since about 1900. These wines are good Chianti Classico. The '86 Riserva is very good, the '86 and '88 *normale* good. Chianti Classico **

Castello di Radda (*Radda in Chianti, Siena*). Montemaggio produces 4,000 cases a year of this Chianti, made from purchased grapes and/or wine. The winery has a capacity of 46,235 gallons (1,750 hectoliters). Our limited experience, based on a bottle from the exceptionally fine 1983 vintage, suggests a rating of zero. Things could very well improve, however, as Vittorio Fiore is their consulting enologist. But for now, Chianti Classico 0

Castello di Rencine (*Castellina in Chianti, Siena*). Around the eleventh-century ruins of the castle of Rencine on this estate are some 68 acres (28 hectares) of vines, 60 (24) for Chianti Classico. The winery has an annual production of about 21,500 cases, of which some 14,000 are Chianti Classico. We haven't tasted their Chianti Classico since 1980 when we tasted the '77, and 1981 when we tasted the '75. Those we did taste, though, never lived up to their reputation. Considering the changes in Toscana, it is possible that their wines have improved sufficiently to garner them a higher rating. Chianti Classico [0]

Castello di San Donato in Perano (*Gaiole in Chianti, Siena*). This winery has 156 acres (63 hectares) of vines, of which 119 (48) are planted for Chianti Classico. They produce 40,000 cases of rather mediocre wine a year; this includes 28,050 cases of Chianti Classico. San Donato was one of the members of the **Storiche Cantine**. We don't know whether or not that organization still exists, but they still have some relationship with the other wineries that belong or belonged to that group: they have the same director and enologist as the other members. Chianti Classico 0

Castello di San Polo in Rosso (*Gaiole in Chianti, località S. Polo, Siena*), 1973. Cesare and Katrin Canessa bought this castle and 1,000-acre (400-hectare) estate a bit over a decade ago to produce Chianti. Today they have some 86.5 acres (35 hectares) of vines at an average altitude of 1,310 feet (400 meters) above sea level. The vineyards, facing south to southwest, are planted with 90 percent sangiovese, about 4 percent canaiolo, with the balance being trebbiano, malvasia, and sauvignon blanc.

Their annual production averages just over 11,000 cases. Chianti Classico makes up 70 percent and the remaining 30 is about evenly divided among their top-of-the-line, *barrique*-aged **Centinaia**, and Bianco and Rosa di Sanpolo. They will make a Sauvignon Blanc from their Le Coccole vineyard.

Maurizio Castelli is the enologist at San Polo in Rosso. He uses the free-run juice only for the two Chianti Classicos that carry the estate name; the Castelpolo contains some press juice. Castelli ferments the wines in stainless steel. When he feels it will add a benefit he uses *governo*. These Chianti Classicos are made from mostly sangiovese. More than 85 percent of their vines are sangiovese, 8.7 percent are canaiolo, 5 percent trebbiano and malvasia, and just a bit more than 1 percent are other varieties.

The San Polo Chianti Classicos are very good wines, wines of style. We especially liked their '85 and '83 *normale*, and '82 and '81 Riserva; we also found the '80 Riserva and *normale* quite good. Chianti Classico: Castello di S. Polo in Rosso *normale* **, Riserva ** +, Castelpolo *

Castello di Tizzano (*Gaiole in Chianti, località San Polo in Chianti, Siena*), 1882. Conte Filippo Pandolfini owns this eleventh-century castle and its 56 acres (22.5 hectares) of vines, which include 31 acres (12.5) for Chianti Classico, 17.3 (7) for Chianti, and 7.4 (3) for white wine. The vines, planted at an average altitude of 870 feet (265 meters) above sea level, face southwest.

Pandolfini produces some 10,000 cases of wine annually, 3,300 of a regional Chianti and 5,555 of a Classico. We haven't tasted this Chianti Classico in some time, but our memory of it is that it was a fairly good one. Chianti Classico [** −]

Castello di Uzzano (*Greve in Chianti, Firenze*). Uzzano own 162 acres (66 hectares) of vines. They produce about 43,000 cases a

THE CRUS OF CASTELLO DI TIZZANO

Cru	Acres	Hectares	Used for
Capanna al Pino	4.9	2.0	Chianti Classico
La Querce	17.3	7.0	Chianti Classico
Massoforte	17.3	7.0	Chianti
Poggerino	8.6	3.5	Chianti Classico
Rapale	7.4	3.0	White wine

year. We hear that they still use *governo*. The '85 Riserva was very good, the '83 Riserva good, and the '86 *normale* very good. They have a good reputation. Chianti Classico **

Castello di Verrazzano (*Greve in Chianti, Firenze*), 1170. This castle was reportedly first Etruscan then Roman. The Verrazzano family acquired it in the seventh century. Giovanni da Verrazzano, navigator, explorer, and possible pirate, was born here in 1485. (Today he is perhaps best known, in the United States at least, for the bridge named for him that spans the narrows in New York harbor, which he explored.) In Greve, capital of Chianti Classico, a memorial statue of Verrazzano dominates the naviform—ship-shaped, to you landlubbers—piazza in the center of town.

The 539-acre (218-hectare) Verrazzano estate, owned by Luigi Cappellini, has 128 acres (52 hectares) of vines, 104 (42) for Chianti Classico. The vines—85 percent sangiovese, 10 percent canaiolo and other red varieties, plus 5 percent trebbiano and malvasia—are planted in calcerous-clay soil at altitudes ranging from 920 to 1,475 feet (280 to 450 meters) above sea level. The vines face south, southeast, east, and northeast. The Verrazzano estate contains six vineyards: three special ones—Querciolina, San Bartolo, and Valdonica—plus Carraia, Casanuova, and Lappole.

The *azienda* has an average annual production of some 300,000 bottles of wine, which include 240,000 of Chianti Classico, plus 4,333 bottles each of Sassello and Bottiglia Particolare, plus 10,000

of white wine, and 2,666 of *vin santo*. Beginning with the 1988 vintage they bottled their San Bartolo and Valdonica crus separately. In 1988 they bottled 12,666 of the former wine and 12,400 of the latter. In 1982, for the first time, they produced *Sassello,* a 100 percent *barrique*-aged sangiovese, as well as a sangiovese-cabernet blend labeled *Bottiglia Particolare.* They produced 2,400 bottles of the 1985 Sassello and 5,000 of Bottiglia Particolare. They also produce a special Chianti Classico Riserva Cinquecentenario. The '85 was made from 85 percent sangiovese, 10 percent canaiolo and mammolo, and 5 percent trebbiano and malvasia. It was aged in casks made of Slavonian oak casks for twenty-eight months. They produced 15,000 cases of that wine. Marco Chellini is their enologist and Mario Cortevesio consults for them.

We have always found their wines agreeable, if a bit simple. They have improved lately. Their '83 Riserva and '85 Riserva Cinquecentenario were very good, and the '86 *normale* and Riserva good. Chianti Classico: *normale* *, Riserva **

Castello di Vertine (*Gaiole in Chianti, Siena*). This producer is a member or former member of the *Storiche Cantine.* They are still associated with the other wineries that were in the group. We've never tasted any of their wines that we can recall, but if they are at the general level of the other wines of the co-op, it has not been a great loss. On the other hand, one never knows, and should the occasion arise to taste them, we would certainly do our duty.

CHIANTI CLASSICO HARVEST OF CASTELLO DI VERRAZZANO

Year	Harvest (from—to)	Hectoliters	Minimum Alcohol	Total Acidity (grams/liter)
1989	October 20–November 10	1,790	12.60%	7.5
1988	October 2–October 25	1,350	13–14%	n/a[a]
1987	October 5–November 4	1,900	12.70%	5.4
1986	October 13–November 5	1,900[b]	13.00%	5.9
1985	October 2–October 25	1,800[c]	13.50%	6.1
1984	October 10–November 8	1,800	12.45%	6.2

NOTES: [a] They reported that the acidity was good
[b] They produced 833 cases (75 hectoliters) of *riserva*
[c] Of this, 5000 cases (450 hectoliters) will be Chianti Classico and 15,000 (1,350) Riserva Cinquecentenario

Castello di Volpaia (*Radda in Chianti,* località *Volpaia, Siena*), *1967.* Giovannella Stianti Mascheroni owns this tenth-century castle and fortified medieval village. The village is practically intact. The deconsecrated Sant'Eufrosino church, the only remaining single-nave Renaissance church in the Florentine countryside, is located here. This church is believed to have been designed by followers of Michelozzo.

With Giovannella Stianti Mascheroni's interest in art it should come as no surprise that she has held annual art exhibits at her Castello di Volpaia estate since 1980. These exhibits begin the second weekend of September and continue for fifteen days. The participating artists are internationally or nationally known. The exhibits, of painting and/or sculpture, take place in the old village. There is no charge to visit the exhibit. If you would like to visit the old village, the *cantina,* or the church you do need to make an appointment in advance.

The Volpaia property covers 808 acres (327 hectares) of land. Of this, 85.7 acres (34.7 hectares) of vines are planted at altitudes ranging from 1,380 to 2,200 feet (420 to 670 meters) above sea level. Plans call for an additional 12.4 acres (5 hectares) to be planted.

Experiments are being conducted with nebbiolo and syrah. They did produce a sangiovese-nebbiolo blend and Giovannella told us that they plan to produce, experimentally at least, a sangiovese-syrah blend as well. They also have pinot noir and merlot.

Giovannella's average annual production of 223,000 bottles is made up of 146,660 bottles of Chianti Classico, 23,325 of the *barrique*-aged sangioveto-mammolo blend **Coltassala,** 23,325 of the sangioveto–cabernet sauvignon–cabernet franc **Balifico,** 10,000 of the *barrique*-aged sauvignon blanc Torniello, 20,000 of the Bianco Val d'Arbia, and a small amount of *vin santo.*

Castello di Volpaia's Chianti Classico is made from a blend of 90 percent sangiovese, 5 percent canaiolo, and 5 percent trebbiano and malvasia. These Chiantis, from the early vintages at least, were not wines for long-aging. We have noticed a definite improvement in the wine over the past few years. These are excellent Chianti Classicos that are getting better and better.

Dott. Maurizio Castelli, who has been the winemaker at Volpaia since 1980, produced an especially fine '85 Riserva and an excellent '83 Riserva. The '79, '81, '82, and '86 *riserve* were very good. Of the older vintages, the '70 Riserva is still splendid, and the '77 Riserva very good. Today there is no question that the Volpaia wines are among the zone's best. Chianti Classico *** +

Castello Guicciardini Poppiano (*Montespertoli, Firenze*). Conte Ferdinando Guicciardini has 593 acres (240 hectares) on his Poppiano estate: 198 (80) are in specialized cultivation, another 54 (22) are in *coltura promiscua.* He produces 66,500 cases of wine a year, including a fairly good Chianti. Chianti Colli Fiorentini *

Castello Vicchiomaggio (*Greve in Chianti, Firenze*). This *castello* was built at least as early as the tenth century; it was described in a document of A.D. 957. According to records, Vicchio dei Longobardi, as it was then known, was built by the Longobards. It was also noted on some of the maps prepared by Leonardo da Vinci. The castle took its current form during the Renaissance. At that time, because it was used for spring festivals, mostly in May (*Maggio*), it took its current name, Vicchiomaggio. The Matta family bought the estate in 1966, and replanted most of the vineyards. (The present owner is John Matta.) They produced their first wine from the 1969 vintage.

The 370-acre (15-hectare) Vicchiomaggio estate has 62 acres (25 hectares) in vines. Because of the reduction of white grapes required by DOCG regulations, only 54 acres (22 hectares) furnish grapes for the Vicchiomaggio Chianti Classico. The vineyards are planted at altitudes ranging from 820 to 950 feet (250 to 290 meters) above sea level. Their 5-acre (2-hectare) Prima Vigna vineyard was planted in mixed cultivation between 1935 and 1940. The vineyard mix consists of 90 percent sangiovese, 5 percent canaiolo, 2 percent trebbiano and malvasia, and the rest in three other varieties. There are seven individual vineyards at Vicchiomaggio.

Vicchiomaggio uses *governo* for all their Chiantis, the Riserva as well as the *normale.* They add unfermented grape juice concentrated from their own grapes to create the second fermentation. In their DOC Chianti Classicos, Vicchiomaggio used 15 to 20 percent white grapes in their *uvaggio;* since the advent of DOCG Vicchiomaggio has reduced that amount to 3 to 5 percent.

At most Vicchiomaggio produces some 12,200 cases of Chianti Classico a year. In the vintages when they make a Riserva, this wine constitutes 25 to 30 percent of the Chianti Classico they produce. Besides these two wines, Vicchiomaggio produces a small amount of *vin santo* and some *barrique*-aged wines. The Vicchiomaggio Chianti Classico Riserva, also aged for a time in *barrique,* is given at most two years in old oak barrels.

The San Jacopo Chianti Classico is made from a blend of 85 percent sangiovese, 10 percent canaiolo, 3 percent colorino, and 2 percent trebbiano and malvasia. The wine is fermented for six to ten days and aged nine months to a year in large oak casks.

Chianti Classico Riserva Petri is fermented nine to twelve days on the skins and aged twelve to eighteen months in a combination of 2,114-gallon (80-hectoliter) oak casks and 60-gallon (225-liter)

THE CRUS AND VINEYARDS OF CASTELLO DI VOLPAIA

Vineyard	Acres	Hectares	First Vintage	Average Number of Bottles Per Year
Balifico	11.1135	4.4974	1985	24,000
Coltassala	12.5480	5.0779	1980	24,000
Torniello	4.8120	1.9473	1986	10,000

THE CRUS AND VINEYARDS OF CASTELLO VICCHIOMAGGIO

Cru/Vineyard	Year(s) Planted	Average Number of Bottles Per Year	Used for
La Lellera*	n/a	40,000	Chianti Classico Riserva
Prima Vigna*	1925–68	13,000	Chianti Classico Riserva
Ripa delle Mandorie†	n/a	n/a	Sangiovese–cabernet sauvignon blend
Ripa delle Mimose†	n/a	n/a	Barrique-fermented Chardonnay
Ripa delle More†	n/a	n/a	Barrique-aged Sangiovese
San Jacopo*	1966–75	53,300	Chianti Classico
Vigna Petri*	1966	26,600	Chianti Classico Riserva

* Bottled as a single-vineyard Chianti Classico
† Bottled as a single-vineyard vino da tavola

barriques. This wine is made from a blend of 88 percent sangiovese, 5 percent canaiolo, 5 percent cabernet sauvignon, and 2 percent trebbiano and malvasia.

Prima Vigna, a barrique-aged Chianti Classico Riserva from this old vineyard, is their flagship wine. It was first produced in 1977 (3,000 bottles). The must is fermented twelve to fifteen days on the skins. The '77 was aged for ten months in previously used barriques. The next vintage they made was the '80; it was aged for three months in new barrels. Currently, Matta ages the wine for at least a year, mostly in barriques.

The first, and the only, Chianti Classico Riserva La Lellera that we tasted was the '88. It was not up to the level of Vicchiomaggio's other wines.

We find the Chiantis of Castello Vicchiomaggio lean, austere, and angular. For those who like this style, we would recommend two '85 riserve, Paola Matta and Prima Vigna, and the '87 San Jacopo normale; the '85 Riserva Petri and '87 Paola Matta are also good. Chianti Classico: normale ** −, Paola Matta **, Riserva La Lellera * −, Riserva Prima Vigna ** +, Riserva Petri **, San Jacopo **

Castiglion del Bosco Azienda Agricola (Montalcino, Siena), 1946. This Brunello di Montalcino producer also makes a Chianti.

Catignano (Pianella, Castelnuovo Berardenga, Siena). This 121-acre (48.8-hectare) estate has 23 acres (9.3 hectares) in vines which yield 93,000 bottles of red wine a year. Of these, 41,000 are a Chianti Classico normale; the balance is a red vino da tavola. They don't produce a riserva. Catignano has been bottling Chianti since about 1960. The pre-DOCG vintages were a blend of 80 percent sangiovese, 15 percent trebbiano and malvasia, and 5 percent canaiolo. By law, the proportion of white grapes was reduced from the 1984 vintage. They still make their Chianti with governo. The wine is aged for two years in old Slavonian oak casks. While theirs is a Chianti Classico ready for early drinking, it can take moderate age. We found both the '82 and '83 quite good, and the '84 tasted from cask in 1985 showed some quality as well. Chianti Classico **

Cecchi Luigi (Castellina in Chianti, località Casina dei Ponti, Siena), 1893. Cecchi produces some 50,000 cases a year of what we had found overall to be mediocre wines. We must admit, though,

that of late there has been a big improvement. This change for the better seems to be the result of young Andrea Cecchi, one of Luigi Cecchi's sons. Andrea impressed us with his concern for quality which has been reflected by the wine he has been putting in the bottle. Cesare, another one of Luigi Cecchi's sons, also works with his father.

The Cecchi winery has a capacity of 1.3 million gallons (50,000 hectoliters) of wine. They also own the 168-acre (68 hectare) Castello di Montauto estate in San Gimignano, which they bought in 1988. That property has 81.5 acres (33 hectares) of vines. Besides the white vernaccia, trebbiano, and malvasia varieties, they have sangiovese and canaiolo planted there.

Among the wines Cecchi produces, besides Chianti and Chianti Classico, are Galestro, Orvieto, Vernaccia di San Gimignano, Vino Nobile di Montepulciano, and the 100-percent sangiovese **Spargolo Predicato di Cardisco**. The '86, '87, and '88 Chianti Classicos were all good. Within the past few years Cecchi began producing Messer Pietro di Teuzzo, a single-vineyard Chianti Classico from their own vineyards in Castellina. We have liked both of those that we tasted, the '87 and '88. But their best Chianti is still the Classico from their **Villa Cerna** estate. Chianti Classico: normale *, Messer Pietro di Teuzzo **

Celli. The only wine that we tasted from Celli was their good '87. Chianti Classico *

Cellole (Castellina in Chianti, località Cellole, Siena). Cellole, until a few years ago, had 35 acres (14 hectares) of vines from which they produced an average of 11,000 cases of Chianti Classico a year. Today their 26.4 acres (10.7 hectares) of vines yield no more than 6,220 cases of Chianti Classico. Our experience with these wines, limited to the '79 Riserva tasted in 1983, has left us less than impressed. It's quite possible that their Chianti Classico has improved. Fairness suggests that we not rate them today. Chianti Classico [0]

Cennatoio (Panzano in Chianti, Firenze). Leandro Alessi owns this 108-acre (43.6-hectare) estate and its 20.5 acres (8.3 hectares) of vines. These vines are planted at an average altitude of 1,575 feet (480 meters) above sea level. In an average year Alessi produces some 56,000 bottles of Chianti Classico. It is made from a blend of

90 percent sangiovese, 8 percent canaiolo, and 2 percent trebbiano and malvasia. Additionally, he produces some 3,000 bottles of **Etrusco Rosso di Panzano,** a 100 percent sangiovese, *barrique*-aged *vino da tavola,* 13,330 bottles of Rosso di Panzano from 92 percent sangiovese and 8 percent canaiolo, 6,667 of Luca della Robbia Spumante Naturale Brut, 4,000 of Brusco Bianco di Panzano, 4,000 of Rosato di Panzano, 3,333 to 4,000 of Vin Santo Secco di Caratello, and all of 267 to 400 of Occhio di Pernice Vin Santo Rosso di Caratello. Alessi produces two Chianti Classicos, a *riserva* and a *normale* with the Cennatoio label and a *normale* under the Braccialini label, from their own grapes, and at least two others—Giaggiolo Rosso Pier delle Vigne and Luca della Robbia—made, we presume, from bought grapes. The labels of these last two Chianti Classicos indicate that they were bottled by Gabriella & Leandro Alessi. The *consorzio* reports that the Luca della Robbia winery has a capacity of 32,000 gallons (1,200 hectoliters). The only one of Alessi's wines that we tasted was the good '85 Riserva. Chianti Classico *

Cepperellaccio (*Barberino Val d'Elsa, Firenze*). Kunz Piast d'Asburgo Lorena, owner of Fattoria Antico Castello di Poppiano, produces this mediocre Chianti Classico. The most interesting thing about it is its rather curious name: it appears to suggest "miserable little vine"! We haven't seen it in years, lucky us. Chianti Classico [0]

Cerbaiola. A label used by **Barfede-Certaldo.**

Cerbaiola (*San Donato in Poggio, Firenze*). Barsottini and Fedeli own this 57-acre (23-hectare) estate. Some 8.9 acres (3.6 hectares) of the 17.3 (7) planted are delimited for Chianti Classico, from which Cerbaiola produces, at most, 25,200 bottles.

Chiantigiane. See **Le Chiantigiane.**

Cispiano (*Castellina in Chianti, Siena*), *1972*. Alceca Corp. of Washington, D.C., an importer of some very good Italian wines, owns this Chianti Classico estate. The annual production from its 25 acres (10 hectares) of vineyards, 21 (8.6) for Chianti Classico, is 5,000 cases of light, drinkable Chiantis. Enologist Pietro Rivella consults for them. We haven't tasted the Cispiano wines since the '83 *normale* and Riserva tasted in 1987. Chianti Classico *

Coli (*Tavarnelle Val di Pesa, località Pontenuovo, Firenze*). F.lli Coli owns 43 acres (17.4 hectares) of vines from which they produce a little more than 10,000 cases of Chianti Classico a year. They also buy grapes to produce another 110,000 cases of Chianti Classico, which they sell under the Della Badessa and San Carlo labels. They've been bottling their Chianti since 1926. Mario Cortevesio consults for them. There is some tie-in with the Pratale and Montignana estates. Thus far the only wine we have tasted from them has been the good '87. Chianti Classico *

Colle Bereto (*Radda in Chianti, località Colle, Siena*). Colle Bereto owns 11 acres (4.5 hectares) of vines in monoculture and another 5 (2.1) in mixed culture. These vines, planted at an average altitude of 1,475 feet (450 meters) above sea level, produce nearly 4,000 cases of Chianti Classico annually.

Conio, Azienda Agricola Immobiliare (*San Donato in Poggio, Firenze*). They have 7 acres (2.9 hectares) of vines, one-third in *coltura promiscua,* planted at an average altitude of 1,310 feet (400

meters) above sea level. Their annual production of Chianti Classico averages almost 1,700 cases.

Conti Capponi. See **Villa Calcinaia.**

Conti Serristori (*San Casciano Val di Pesa, località San Andrea in Percussina, Firenze*). The 185-acre (75-hectare) estate of the Conti Serristori, today owned by Gruppo Italiano Vini, has 64 acres (26 hectares) of vineyards, 54 (22) for Chianti Classico. Their special vineyards are the 15-acre (6-hectare) Fontalle and 4-acre (1.6-hectare) Il Piano vineyards. The varietal breakdown in their vineyards is 85 percent sangiovese, 10 percent canaiolo, and 5 percent white grapes. Until DOCG took effect they had an annual production of about 23,000 cases of Chianti Classico. This has since been reduced to some 13,000 cases. They produce about 3,500 cases of the Chianti Classico Fontalle and 755 of *vino da tavola* Il Piano annually. They first produced Fontalle in 1982, Il Piano in 1988.

Today the Serristori wines are divided into two lines, as it were—the Conti Serristori line and the Machiavelli line. They produce some 1.5 million bottles of Serristori and 400,000 of Machiavelli. All the *riserva* wines come from their own grapes. The *riserve* currently make up some 15 percent of all the Chianti Classicos they produce; this is increasing. In total, their own vineyards supply them with one-third of their needs, but this will increase as their new vineyards come into production.

Under the Serristori line they produce a Chianti from the Solatio, Vigne di Sberla, and Ripe del Lapi vineyards in San Lorenzi. Their Chianti Classico Villa Primavera is made from a blend of sangiovese, canaiolo, malvasia, and trebbiano. Villa Primavera is the name of the entire farm in San Andrea in Percussina. They make this wine as a *normale* and a *riserva*. They also produce Vernaccia di San Gimignano Vigneti di Fullignano, Brunello di Montalcino, Vino Nobile di Montepulciano, and Orvieto.

Under the Machiavelli label they make the single-vineyard Chianti Classico Vigna Fontalle *normale* and Riserva, and Vigne Il Piano *vino da tavola da uve nere,* a white table wine from the black canaiolo.

Their best wine has been the Riserva Machiavelli. We found the '74 tasted in 1978, the '64 tasted in 1985, and the '82 all very good indeed, with the '83 rather good as well. Their single-vineyard Machiavelli '85 Riserva Vigna di Fontalle was also very good. We have found their Villa Primavera, both the '85 Riserva and '87 *normale,* good. Although it's been some time since we tasted their regular Chianti Classicos, we remember them being fairly good, if a bit light in body. The '77 Riserva Ser Niccolo, though, tasted in 1983, was disappointing. They now use the Ser Niccolò name for a *vino da tavola.* Chianti: Serristori *; Chianti Classico: Serristori *normale* *, Serristori Riserva **, Serristori Villa Primavera *normale* ** −, Serristori Riserva Villa Primavera **, Machiavelli *normale* ** +, Machiavelli Riserva ** +

Contucci Azienda Agricola (*Montepulciano*), *1730*. The Contucci family, Gian Stefano, Maria Vittoria, Gigliola, and Alamanno Contucci, own 52 acres (21 hectares) of vineyards, 7.2 (2.9) for Chianti Colli Senesi.

Convito. This Chianti Classico was produced by A.C.G.—the Gaiole Agricola Cooperative Cellars. The '85 was good, the '83 Riserva mediocre. Chianti Classico +

Costanti (*Montalcino, Siena*). This producer of a very fine Brunello produces 2,000 to 2,650 bottles of Chianti Colli Senesi annually. We suspect that he no longer makes it, although we aren't sure. If we can judge from the commitment to quality they display with their Brunello (and, for that matter, their extra virgin olive oil), plus the one Chianti of theirs that we tasted, the '83, we don't doubt it is, or at least was, a very good Chianti. Chianti Colli Senesi ** +

Della Badessa. A label used by *Coli.*

Falchini Riccardo (*San Gimignano, Siena*), *1830*. Riccardo Falchini has 50 acres (20 hectares) of vineyards at his Casale farm. His annual production averages some 15,500 cases of wine, of which 70 percent is a very good Vernaccia di San Gimignano and 30 percent is divided about equally between Chianti Colli Senesi, *vin santo*, and a Champagne-method brut *spumante*. Falchini, like numerous other producers in Toscana, also produces a Cabernet aged in *barrique*. Considering the quality of his Vernaccia, we expect his Chianti to be good.

Fanetti, Comm. Adamo e Giuseppe, Tenuta "S. Agnese" (*Montepulciano, Siena*), *1921*. Fanetti, proprietor of the 306-acre (124-hectare) S. Agnese estate, has 10 acres (4 hectares) planted for Chianti which yield an average of 26,000 bottles annually.

Fassati Casa Vinicola del Chianti (*Pieve di Sinalunga, Siena*), *1913*. Fassati is owned by Fazi Battaglia of Verdicchio fame. About six or seven years ago Fassati bought 50 acres (20 hectares) in the Chianti zone. Since 1986 their Chianti has been produced from their own grapes; previously they bought wine from Chianti and Chianti Classico and aged it in their cellars. They will continue to buy from the Classico zone. Fassati produces, on average, 25,000 bottles of Chianti annually.

Fattoria Barberino (*Barberino Val d'Elsa, Firenze*). Fattoria Barberino produces some 9,450 cases of Chianti Classico a year. The last vintage we tasted from this mediocre producer was the '77, and we found it wanting. Chianti Classico [0]

Fattoria Belvedere Campoli (*Mercatale Val di Pesa, Firenze*). Fattoria Belvedere Campoli has 17.3 acres (7 hectares) of vines for Chianti Classico, planted at an average altitude of 1,310 feet (400 meters) above sea level. Production of DOCG wine averages just over 50,000 bottles a year.

Fattoria Bossi (*Pontassieve, Firenze*). Marchese Bonaccorso Gondi produces 11,000 cases of wine a year from his 40 acres (16 hectares) of vines. He has 13.6 acres (5.5 hectares) in the Chianti Rùfina district, from which he produces 3,300 cases annually, 16 (6.5) in the regional Chianti zone which yield 5,000 cases, and 10 (4) in the Valdisieve area from which he makes 2,600 cases of other wine.

Fattoria Cafaggio di Pesa (*Castellina in Chianti*, località *Molino Novo, Siena*). From their 8.9 acres (3.6 hectares) of vines they produce a little more than 26,000 bottles of Chianti Classico a year.

Fattoria Campomaggio (*Radda in Chianti*, località *Campomaggio, Siena*), *1948*. Campomaggio has 58 acres (23.6 hectares) of vines, 47.4 (19.2) for Chianti Classico. The vineyards are planted at

altitudes ranging from 1,015 to 1,280 feet (310 to 390 meters) above sea level and have a southeastern to southwestern exposure. The grapes for their Riserva come from their Le Vecchie vineyard. The *azienda* has an annual production of 12,000 to 15,500 cases. Besides the 11,000 plus cases of Chianti Classico, they produce a small quantity of *vin santo*.

The Campomaggio Chianti is vinified at their estate, but at one time was bottled and marketed by Fattoria di Ama. We don't know if that is still the case. Campomaggio has sold their Chianti Classico in bottle since the 1967 vintage. In our limited experience, with the '80 Riserva and '82 *normale*, tasted in 1985, we have found their Chianti Classico wanting. Chianti Classico [* −]

Fattoria Casale del Bosco (*Montalcino*, località *Casale del Bosco, Siena*), *1951*. Silvio Nardi has 136 acres (55 hectares) of vines on his Casale del Bosco estate. He produces some 24,000 bottles of Chianti Colli Senesi annually.

Fattoria Casalino (*Querciagrossa, Siena*). Tenuta di Angoris, a large producer of wines in the Friuli–Venezia Giulia region, owns this Chianti Classico farm and its 54 acres (22 hectares) of vines, 35.8 (14.5) planted for Chianti Classico. Casalino produces, on average, 15,500 cases of wine a year, which include just over 7,600 cases of Chianti Classico.

Fattoria Casanuova di Nittardi. The Fattoria Casanuova di Nittardi '87 Chianti Classico was quite good. Chianti Classico *

Fattoria Casenuove (*Greve in Chianti, Firenze*). Most of Casenuove's 63.5 acres (25.7 hectares) of vines are planted in monoculture. They produce, on average, some 15,000 cases of Chianti Classico annually.

Fattoria Castelvecchio (*San Casciano Val di Pesa, Firenze*). Renzo Rocchi produces a Chianti Colli Fiorentini that is, by reputation, for medium-term drinking. He also produces a white and *barrique*-aged wine.

Fattoria Cerreto (*Pontassieve, Firenze*). Fattoria Cerreto owns 198 acres (80 hectares), 31 (12.5) of specialized vineyards and 7.4 (3) in *coltura promiscua* in the Chianti Rùfina zone. They produce some 8,300 cases a year.

Fattoria Concadoro, Cerasi (*Castellina in Chianti, Siena*). The 321-acre (130-hectare) Fattoria Concadoro estate has 49.3 acres (20 hectares) planted in vines, 44.4 (18) for Chianti Classico. Their vineyards are composed of 85 percent sangiovese, 5 percent canaiolo, 5 percent white grapes, and 5 percent other varieties. At most they produce a little more than 125,000 bottles of Chianti Classico a year. Of the three wines that we tasted from them—the '83 and '85 *riserve*, and *normale* of '88—we have found their wines to be good. Chianti Classico *

Fattoria Cusona. See *Villa Cusona.*

Fattoria dei Barbi e del Casato (Francesca Colombini Cinelli) (*Montalcino, Siena*), *c. 1500*. The Colombini estate produces, besides an excellent Brunello di Montalcino, some 20,000 bottles of Chianti a year. Their first Chianti was the '84.

Fattoria dei Pagliarese (*San Gusmè, Siena*), *1810*. The family of Alma Biasiotto in Sanguineti have been the owners of the 247-acre

(100-hectare) Pagliarese estate since 1965. Antonio and Chiara Sanguineti manage the estate. Luciano Bandini is their resident enologist, and Vittorio Fiore, their consulting enologist. There are 62 acres (25 hectares) of vines on the property, planted at an average altitude of 920 feet (280 meters) above sea level. The vineyards, planted in 85 percent sangiovese, 5 percent canaiolo, 5 percent white grapes, and 5 percent malvasia nera, have a south to southwestern exposure. Pagliarese produces 22,000 cases of wine a year, as well as virgin olive oil and honey. At most, 14,555 cases are Chianti Classico.

They make a *normale* Chianti Classico sold under their Pagiatello label and two *riserve*, including a single-vineyard wine from their Boscardini vineyard. Their Classicos produced prior to the new DOCG status for Chianti were made from a blend of 80 percent sangiovese, 12 percent other red varieties, and 8 percent white grapes. They have some cabernet sauvignon in the vineyard and have included 4 to 5 percent in their Chianti for the past few years. Pagliarese bottled their first Chianti Classico under their own label from the 1965 vintage.

The first Boscardini Riserva was the '78. Today they are producing 12,000 bottles a year. This wine, made from sangiovese, canaiolo, and trebbiano grapes grown in their 12.4-acre (5-hectare) Boscardini vineyard, is aged for six months in Alliers *barriques* and another two years in cask. It is their best Chianti Classico. Besides these wines, they make a *barrique*-aged sangiovese grosso, **Camerlengo**.

The Chiantis of Pagliarese are good wines, and quite reliable. Among recently tasted vintages we can recommend the *riserve* of '82 and '85, as well as those of '70, '71, '75, '80, and '81, and the '79, '80, and '81 Boscardini Riserve, and the '85 and '88 *normali*. Chianti Classico: **, Boscardini Riserva ** +

Fattoria del Cerro (Sai Agricola) (*Acquavina di Montepulciano, Siena*), *1922*. This producer of a very fine Vino Nobile makes some 30,000 cases of Chianti Colli Senesi from their 119 acres (48 hectares) of vines in the Sienese hills. They produce two Chiantis: the Del Cerro Chianti, which contains 7 to 8 percent white grapes; and the Baiocchi, which contains little or no white grapes. Chianti Colli Senesi * +

Fattoria del Leccio. At one time they produced a Chianti Classico for Fratelli Beccaro. We haven't seen the wine in years.

Fattoria dell'Aiola (*Vagliagli, Siena*). This 247-acre (100-hectare) estate consists of 89 acres (36 hectares) of vineyards in Castelnuovo Berardenga and Radda, and a thirteenth-century castle. Some 64 acres (26 hectares) are planted in 90 percent sangiovese, 8 percent canaiolo, and 2 percent white grapes for Chianti Classico. They produce some 22,000 cases of wine a year, of which less than 15,000 are Chianti Classico. The only good wine we have tasted from them was the decent '83 Riserva. Chianti Classico +

Fattoria della Talosa. See *Fattoria di Fognano*.

Fattoria delle Corti (*San Casciano Val di Pesa, Firenze*). This *azienda* has 144 acres (58 hectares) of vines, 47 (19) planted in *coltura promiscua*. The vines are planted at an average altitude of 985 feet (300 meters) above sea level. Their annual production of Chianti Classico averages nearly 34,000 cases.

Fattoria delle Fonti (*Poggibonsi*, località *Fonti, Firenze*). Fattoria delle Fonti has 19.3 acres (7.8 hectares) of vines in specialized culture and 5.7 (2.3) mixed. These vines yield nearly 71,000 bottles of Chianti Classico a year.

Fattoria delle Fornacelle (*Mercatale Val di Pesa, Firenze*). Some 85 percent of Fornacelle's 12 acres (5 hectares) of vines are planted in monoculture, the rest mixed. Average annual production of Chianti Classico is 72,000 bottles.

Fattoria delle Lodoline (*Vagliagli, Siena*). Lodoline owns 36.7 acres (14.9 hectares) of vines from which they produce some 10,000 cases of mediocre Chianti Classico a year. The last wine we tasted from them was the '77 in 1981. Considering the major changes in Toscana it would seem that the prudent thing to do would be to reserve judgment. Perhaps they have improved. Chianti Classico [0]

Fattoria di Albola (*Radda in Chianti*, località *Pian d'Albola, Siena*). This tenth-century castle was transformed into a villa in the seventeenth century. The Zonin family of the Veneto has owned this estate with its vineyards and winery since 1979. When they bought it there were 74 acres (30 hectares) planted. According to the Zonins, only one other Chianti Classico estate—Brolio—has a larger, undivided vineyard. This family also owns vineyards in Piemonte, Lombardia, and Friuli, some 2,000 acres (810 hectares) in all.

Today some 375 acres (152 hectares) of the 1,500 (607) on the estate are planted in vines, of which 128 (52) are for Chianti Classico. The vineyards, planted at an altitude ranging from 1,150 to 1,970 feet (350 to 600 meters) above sea level, face south and southeast. The thirteen vineyards on the property are Acciaiolo, Bozzolo, Capaccia, Ellere, Marangole, Mondeggi, Montevertine, Querciola, S. Caterina, S. Michele, Sant'Ilario, Selvole, and Villanova. Besides the grapes for Chianti Classico, they have chardonnay, pinot noir, and cabernet sauvignon and franc. Some 25 additional acres (10 hectares) can be planted. The winery has three aging cellars: De Piazzi and Santa Caterina are used for barrel aging, and San Miniato for bottles.

Albola produces over 1 million bottles of wine annually, most sold with the Castello d'Albola label. Some 650,000 are Chianti Classico, and this number is increasing. They have the capacity to produce 800,000 to 850,000 bottles. They also produce 333,000 of Sant'Ilario *vino novello*, 47,000 of Bianco Val d'Arbia, 13,000 bottles of Chardonnay, 66,000 of Pinot Noir, and 107,000 of a Cabernet made from 80 percent cabernet sauvignon and 20 percent cabernet franc. They can increase the production of these last three wines by 50 percent. They also produce the *barrique*-aged, sangiovese–cabernet sauvignon blend **Acciaiolo** and a barrel-aged Chardonnay from their Le Fagge vineyard. They first made Acciaiolo in 1988, and the Chardonnay in 1989. And they might do a Sauvignon Blanc.

One report they sent us indicated that their '85 and '86 Chianti Classicos—Riserva and *normale*—were made from 90 percent sangiovese, 6 percent canaiolo, 2 percent trebbiano and malvasia, and 2 percent cabernet sauvignon. Another reported that the blend for their '85 and '86 Riservas was the same amount of sangiovese with 8 percent canaiolo and 2 percent malvasia. Their '83 contained 12 to 13 percent white grapes, and the '85, 2 to 3 percent. They don't use *governo*. They age their Chianti Classico in Slavonian oak casks. Malolactic fermentation occurs naturally in the spring after the vintage. Their '85 Riserva and '86 *normale* were both good. Within the past couple of years we also tasted good *riserva* from '60 and '58. Chianti Classico *

Fattoria di Ama (*Ama di Gaiole in Chianti, Siena*), *1976*. The first mention of Ama is from the year A.D. 998. The making of wines here is more recent. The current owners purchased the 556-acre (225-hectare) Fattoria di Ama estate in 1976. Today they have 198 acres (80 hectares) of vineyards planted at altitudes ranging from 1,475 to 1,575 feet (450 to 480 meters) above sea level. Besides the Chianti varieties, they have malvasia nera, chardonnay, pinot grigio, sauvignon, merlot, and pinot noir vines.

Ama produces, on average, some 466,655 bottles of wine a year. We can account for some 333,000 bottles of wine a year, but they produce other wines that were not included in the production statistics with which they supplied us. Their annual production of Chianti Classico averages 235,000 bottles, of which 170,000 are *normale* and 65,000 are the crus. Then there are some 98,000 bottles of three white *vini da tavola*: 30,000 bottles of Chardonnay, 8,000 of Sauvignon Blanc, and 60,000 of a trebbiano toscano–malvasia del chianti blend that they labeled as Colline di Ama. There is also a rosé they sell as Rosato del Toson d'Oro and two other wines they label as either Castello di Ama or Colline di Ama.

They bottled their first Fattoria, or as they generally label it, Castello, di Ama Chianti Classico from the 1977 vintage. Their top wines are labeled for the cru—*vigneto*—where the grapes are grown.

They label two of their *vini da tavola* as "vigna," followed by the vineyard name, and their four single-vineyard Chianti Classicos as "Vigneto." Il Chiuso is used for pinot noir and L'Apparita for merlot. Their Chianti Classico Vigneto Bellavista contains some malvasia nera and Vigneto Bertinga is 100 percent sangiovese, while some merlot is used in their Vigneto La Casuccia and the Vigneto S. Lorenzo *uvaggio* contains some canaiolo.

Since 1982 the cru wines have been given some *barrique*-aging. Today they are aged twelve to fourteen months in *barrique*. Patrick Leon is their consulting enologist. These Chiantis, which are pretty good, have been improving every year. All of their '87s were good, as are their '88s, '86s, and '85s. We'd like to see more style, however. Chianti Classico: ** −, Vigneto Bellavista **, Vigneto Bertinga ** −, Vigneto La Casuccia ** +, Vigneto S. Lorenzo ** +

Fattoria di Artimino (*Artimino, Firenze*), *1936*. This Carmignano producer has 1,810 acres (732 hectares); 210 (85) are planted in vines, of which 86 (35) are for Chianti. They produce 67,000 cases of wine a year, including 8,333 of a fairly good Chianti Montalbano. This wine is aged in oaken casks for six months. Chianti Montalbano *

Fattoria di Bacchereto (*Bacchereto, Firenze*), *1925*. This Carmignano producer also produces a Chianti Montalbano. The *uvaggio* for this Chianti is 60 percent sangiovese, 25 percent canaiolo nero, and 15 percent trebbiano toscano, malvasia, and occhio di pernice. The grapes for that wine come from their 3.7-acre (1.5-hectare) Santuaria and 6.2-acre (2.5-hectare) Vigna Vecchia vineyards. Chianti Montalbano *

Fattoria di Bossi (*Castelnuovo Berardenga, località Bossi in Chianti, Siena*). The Frankish Winigi di Ramieri took possession of Bossi and the surrounding territory around A.D. 800. Today this estate has 107 acres (43.5 hectares) of vines planted at an altitude ranging from 915 to 1,150 feet (280 to 350 meters) above sea level. They produce up to 25,300 cases of Chianti Classico annually.

Fattoria di Calavria (*Comeana di Carmignano*). Conti Michon Pecori produces both Carmignano and Chianti Montalbano.

Fattoria di Calcinaia. See **Villa Calcinaia.**

Fattoria di Calleno (*Castelnuovo Berardenga, Siena*). From their 11 acres (4.5 hectares) of vines they produce up to 30,500 bottles of Chianti Classico a year.

Fattoria di Castelvecchi (*Radda in Chianti, località Castelvecchi, Siena*), *1850*. M.se Carmen and Isabel Cutierrez de la Solona own the Castelvecchi estate. They have 49.4 acres (20 hectares) of vines facing south, planted at an altitude averaging 1,475 feet (450 meters) above sea level. They produce an average of just over 11,000 cases of Chianti Classico annually.

Fattoria di Cinciano (*Poggibonsi, Siena*). Cinciano owns 45 acres (18 hectares) of vines planted at an average altitude of 820 feet (250 meters) above sea level. They produce a little more than 113,000 bottles of Chianti Classico annually.

THE VINO DA TAVOLA OF FATTORIA DI AMA

Vino da Tavola	First Vintage	Variety	Average Number of Bottles Per Year[a]
Bellaria[b,c]	1983	Pinot grigio	3,485
Il Chiuso[d]	—	Pinot nero	6,184
L'Apparita	—	Merlot	n/a

NOTES: [a] Based on 1987 production
  [b] Vinified in *barrique*
  [c] From Vigneto Bellavista
  [d] From Vigneto San Lorenzo

THE SINGLE-VINEYARD CHIANTI CLASSICOS OF FATTORIA DI AMA

Cru/Vineyard	Acres	Hectares	Exposure	First Vintage	Average Number of Bottles Per Year
Bellavista	66.7	27	SE/SW	1978	24,000[a]
Bertinga	n/a		n/a	1988	13,333
La Casuccia	59.3	24	SE/SW	1985	16,000[b]
S. Lorenzo	39.5	16	SW	1982	22,666[c]

NOTES: [a] In 1986 they produced 27,370 bottles
[b] In 1986 they produced 9,970 bottles
[c] In 1986 they produced 27,480 bottles

Fattoria di Corsignano. A second label of **Fattoria di Vistarenni.**

Fattoria di Doccia (*Pontassieve*, località *Molin del Piano, Firenze*). This 519-acre (210-hectare) Chianti Rùfina estate has 141 acres (57 hectares) under vines. Their annual production totals 44,500 cases. The only wine we've tasted from them was the mediocre '83 in April 1985. Chianti Rùfina [0]

Fattoria di Felsina. See "*Berardenga,*" **Fattoria di Felsina.**

Fattoria di Fizzano. See **Bertolli.**

Fattoria di Fognano (*Montepulciano, Siena*), *1873.* Fognano has 160 acres (65 hectares), of which 86 (35) are in vines. Two-thirds are planted for Vino Nobile and one-third for Chianti Colli Senesi. They produce an average of 40,000 bottles of Chianti a year.

Fattoria di Fontodi. See **Tenuta Agricola Fontodi.**

Fattoria di Galiga e Vetrice. See **Villa di Vetrice.**

Fattoria di Gracciano di Dott. Franco Mazzucchelli (*Gracciano di Montepulciano, Siena*), *1864.* Dott. Franco Mazzucchelli owns 17.3 acres (7 hectares) of vineyards planted for Vino Nobile and Chianti Colli Senesi.

Fattoria di Lucignano (*San Casciano Val di Pesa, Firenze*). Conte Ludovico Guicciardini owns this 90-acre (36-hectare) estate with its mid-fifteenth-century home. Guicciardini produces some 100,000 bottles of Chianti Colli Fiorentini annually. This light-bodied, fruity wine is best while young and fresh. It has a good reputation. We've never met it. He uses the Torre di Brugnano label for his *riserva*. In the years that Guicciardini makes that wine, he produces 26,666 to 80,000 bottles.

Fattoria di Luiano (*Mercatale Val di Pesa, Firenze*). The Luiano estate, in the San Casciano area, has 62 acres (25 hectares) of vines planted at altitudes ranging from 820 to 985 feet (250 to 300 meters) above sea level. They produce an average of nearly 16,500 cases of wine a year. This includes 10,000 cases of two Chianti Classico *riserve*: Luiano and S. Andrea a Luiano. These wines are aged for two years in oak casks. The pre-1984 vintages of their *normale* Chianti Classico were made from 65 percent sangiovese, 15 percent canaiolo, 15 percent trebbiano, and 5 percent malvasia; the *uvaggio* of their *riserva* consisted of 70 percent sangiovese, 20 percent canaiolo, plus 10 percent of trebbiano and malvasia. This, of course, has changed with the new DOCG regulations. We were unimpressed recently with their '86 Riserva and '87 *normale*, but found the '85 Riserva and '86 *normale* good. Chianti Classico *

Fattoria di Mocenni (*Vagliagli, Siena*), *1776.* Nicolò Casini owns this 2,470-acre (1,000-hectare) estate, which includes 136 acres (55 hectares) of vines, 94 (38) for Chianti Classico. Some 52 acres (21 hectares) are planted in *coltura promiscua*. The composition of the vineyards for Chianti is 90 percent sangiovese, 8 percent canaiolo, and 2 percent white grapes. The vines are planted at an average altitude of 1,540 feet (470 meters) above sea level. Their annual production, which averages 27,775 cases of wine, includes some 11,000 cases of Chianti Classico. They are associated with Agricola Poggiarello. Other associated estates are Fattoria dei Colli in Monteriggioni; Tenimenti di Macialla, who also produce Chianti Classico; and Fattoria di Marcianella in Chiusi. The only wine we have tasted from them was the uneven '87 from an uneven vintage. Chianti Classico [* −]

Fattoria di Monaciano (*Pianella, Siena*). Monaciano has 66.6 acres (26.9 hectares) of specialized vineyards and 3 (1.2) of mixed ones planted at altitudes ranging from 985 to 1,310 feet (300 to 400 meters) above sea level. Production of the Monaciano Chianti Classico averages some 14,550 cases a year.

Fattoria di Montagliari. See **Cappelli Giovanni.**

Fattoria di Montagliari e Castellinuzza. See **Cappelli Giovanni.**

Fattoria di Paterno (*Montepulciano*), *1975.* Aldo Fresa of Fattoria di Paterno has 19.8 acres (8 hectares) of vines, 5 (2) planted for Chianti.

Fattoria di Petrognano (*Montelupo Fiorentino, Firenze*), *1960.* F.lli Pellegrini own this estate and its 74 acres (30 hectares) of vines. Their best vineyard is the 12.5-acre (5-hectare) Montevago cru where they planted chardonnay. Their annual production of just over 22,000 cases includes a variety of Chiantis from the Colli Fiorentini zone, as well as a Montevago white and rosé. And they have plans for cabernet sauvignon and franc.

Fattoria di Petroio (*Querciagrossa, Siena*). This 321-acre (130-hectare) estate shouldn't be confused with the *Petroio* estate in Radda in Chianti. This one, owned by Gian Luigi Lenzi e Sefral, has 37 acres (15 hectares) in vines, 29.7 (12) planted for Chianti Classico. The vines, facing southwest, are planted at an average altitude of 1,150 feet (350 meters) above sea level. The vineyards consist of 90 percent sangiovese, 5 percent canaiolo, 2 percent white grapes, and 3 percent other varieties. They produce some 7,000 cases of wine annually, including Chianti Classico. Petroio has a fairly good reputation. Of the four wines we have tasted recently, the only one we can recommend is the good '85 Riserva. Chianti Classico *normale* 0, Riserva *

Fattoria di Ripanera (*Cerbaia, Firenze*). Ripanera owns 35.4 acres (14.3 hectares) planted at 625 feet (190 meters) above sea level. They can produce up to 66,665 cases of Chianti Classico a year.

Fattoria di San Fabiano (*Arezzo*), *1890*. Conti Borghini Bladovinetti de Bacci owns this estate and its 180 acres (73 hectares) of vines. The vines, facing south and southeast, range in altitude from 985 to 1,150 feet (300 to 350 meters) above sea level. The annual production here varies between 55,550 and 61,000 cases of wine, nearly 40,000 of which are Chianti, the balance Galestro.

Fattoria di Selvole (*Vagliagli, Siena*). The 403-acre (163-hectare) Selvole estate boasts the eleventh-century Selvoli castle and Church of S. Martino a Selvoli, as well as 54 acres (22 hectares) of vines. They have 42 acres (17 hectares) planted in vines for Chianti Classico. Their annual production of about 16,500 cases of wine includes a little more than 9,900 cases of Chianti Classico. Both '86s that we tasted, the *normale* and Riserva Lanfredini, were good, and the '87 was very good. Chianti Classico ** −

Fattoria di Tizzano. See *Castello di Tizzano.*

Fattoria di Valiano (*Vagliagli*, località *Valiano, Siena*). This 554-acre (224-hectare) estate has 171 acres (69.4 hectares) of vines, 139 (56.3) for Chianti Classico. The composition of these vineyards is 90 percent sangiovese, 8 percent canaiolo, and 2 percent white grapes. Valiano produces some 55,500 cases of wine a year, of which, at most, 32,660 are Chianti Classico. Of recent vintages that we've tasted, while not up to the vintage they came from, the '85 Riserva was agreeable and the '83 was good. Chianti Classico * −

Fattoria di Vetrice. See *Villa di Vetrice.*

Fattoria di Vignole. See *Tenuta di Vignole.*

Fattoria di Vistarenni (*Gaiolo in Chianti*, località *Vistarenni, Siena*). The villa or village of Fisterinne was first mentioned in the *Regesto of Coltibuono* in 1033. The Strozzi family transformed it into a villa in the sixteenth century. Baron Giorgio Sonnino, who acquired the estate in 1895, restored it between 1914 and 1919. The Tognana family bought the 507-acre (205-hectare) Vistarenni estate in 1980. Elisabetta Tognana now manages it. The property and its 28 *poderi* (farms) are located in the communes of Radda and Gaiole. There are either 87, 94.4, or 115 acres (35, 38.2, or 46 hectares) of vines, depending on which set of answers we went by, of which 75.6 (30.6) are planted for Chianti Classico. The vineyards, consisting of 90 percent sangiovese, 8 percent canaiolo, and 2 percent trebbiano and malvasia vines, are planted at altitudes ranging from 1,150 to either 1,475 or 1,640 feet (350 to 450 or 500 meters)—again, depending on which questionnaire we went by—above sea level, in marl, sandstone, and calcerous soil. These vines have a southwestern exposure. They have two special crus.

Vistarenni's annual production of 22,585 cases of wine is down considerably from the 77,500 to 89,000 cases that they reported to us a few years ago. Their current production includes more than 3,100 cases of Fattoria di Lucignano—not to be confused with the Chianti Colli Fiorentini estate of that name—from the Val d'Arbia area which is made from the standard *uvaggio* of trebbiano and malvasia plus 15 percent of riesling renano and chardonnay, 1,300 of the *barrique*-aged **Codirosso**, and some 18,100 cases of five Chianti Classicos—Fattoria di Vistarenni, the second label Fattoria di Corsignano, the single-vineyard Podere Bertinga from the 30-acre (12-hectare) vineyard of that name, the single-vineyard Assolo, and a Chianti in Fiaxo, a wine sold in a ceramic container. This last wine seems like a natural, considering that the Tognana family is well known for their porcelain. A few years ago they told us that they also produced a rosé, a *vin santo*, a *vino novello*, and a brut *spumante*. What their status are today, we don't know.

They continue to use *governo* here. They gave their '85 Chianti Classico, for the first time, a spell in *barrique*. Today they age this wine eight to twelve months in *barrique*. The Assolo Chianti Classico spends twelve to fourteen months in *barriques*, after which it is assembled into large oak casks where it spends two to four more months before it is bottled.

As far as the quality, things seem to have improved here. Their

THE CRUS OF FATTORIA DI VISTARENNI

Cru	Acres	Hectares	First Vintage	Average Number of Bottles Per Year	Used for
Assolo	7.4	3*	1987	4,000	Chianti Classico
Codirosso	7.4	3	1985	3,000	*Barrique*-aged Sangiovese

* They supplied us with two different answers; we received two copies of our questionnaire from them on the same day! The second questionnaire reported that this vineyard is 12.4 acres (5 hectares).

'84 was acceptable, the '85 and '87 were good, but their '88 disappointing. Chianti Classico: Vistarenni *, Podere Bertinga ** —

Fattoria Dievole *(Vagliagli, Siena)*. Mario Schwenn owns the 998-acre (404-hectare) Dievole Estate. He has 237 acres (96 hectares) in vines, including 151 (61) for Chianti Classico, planted at an average altitude of 1,410 feet (430 meters) above sea level, in soil consisting of limestone, tufa, and marl. The composition of the vineyards is 82 percent sangiovese, 6 percent canaiolo, 8 percent malvasia nera, and 4 percent trebbiano and malvasia.

At most Fattoria Dievole produces 32,200 cases of Chianti Classico a year which includes, in years they feel are good enough, three single-vineyard wines—Campi Nuovi, Petrignano, and Sessina Superiore. In 1987, for the first time, they produced a Villa Dievole Cuvee Chianti Classico. They also produce a Bianco Val d'Arbia, and some *vini da tavola*—Broccato Rosso, Maestro, Rosé di Siena, and Vigneto Colombaio Superiore Rosso.

Paolo Vagaggini is their consulting enologist. They ferment in temperature-controlled stainless steel tanks and glass-lined cement, and use the *governo toscano* for their wines. Aging takes place in 185- to 1,320-gallon (7- to 50-hectoliter) Slavonian oak casks and *barrique*. The first wine they released—under the Villa Dievole label—came from the 1987 harvest. It was good, as was the '88. Chianti Classico*

Fattoria Fermignano, "Frimaio" *(San Donato in Poggio, Firenze)*. Andrea Sestini has owned this 4.9-acre (2-hectare) estate and its 3.7 acres (1.5) of vines since 1985. The vineyards are planted in *galestro* and *alberese* soil at an altitude of 985 feet (300 meters) above sea level. Sestini produces 10,000 bottles of the Frimaio Chianti Classico a year. Aging takes place in cement and/or *barrique*. We can recommend the very good '86 and acceptable '87. Sestini also owns the **La Bricola** farm. Chianti Classico ** —

Fattoria I Cipressi. See **S. Leonino.**

Fattoria Il Capitano *(Pontassieve, Firenze)*. Fattoria Il Capitano has 173 acres (70 hectares), 56.8 (23) in vines; 12.4 (5) are in *coltura exclusiva* and 44.4 (18) in *coltura promiscua*. They produce an average of 66,000 cases of wine a year, including Chianti Rùfina. The only wine we've tasted from them has been the very good single-vineyard '88 Torricella, which we tasted from cask in April 1988. Chianti Rùfina **

Fattoria Il Castagno *(Querciagrossa, Siena)*. This *azienda* owns some 56 acres (23 hectares) planted at an average altitude of 985 feet (300 meters) above sea level. Il Castagno produces some 13,300 cases of Chianti Classico annually.

Fattoria Il Corno *(San Casciano Val di Pesa, Firenze)*. This 519-acre (210-hectare) estate has 136 acres (55 hectares) of vines, planted at an average altitude of 655 feet (200 meters) above sea level. The vineyards have a southeastern exposure. Their annual production of 500,000 bottles, all from their own grapes, includes 266,000 to 330,000 bottles of Chianti and 80,000 to 93,000 bottles of Chianti Colli Fiorentini. They also produce 66,000 bottles of white wine and 5,300 of *vin santo*. Vittorio Fiore has been their consulting enologist since 1981. They consider the best vintages at Il

Corno to be 1988, 1985, 1983, 1981, 1980, 1978, 1977, 1975, 1971, 1969, 1967, 1964, 1961, and 1958. We found their '83 quite good; their '80 left something to be desired. Chianti Colli Fiorentini *

Fattoria Il Greppo (Biondi-Santi) *(Montalcino, Siena)*, 1840. The 116-acre (47-hectare) Il Greppo estate of Biondi Santi has a 5.1-acre (2.07-hectare) vineyard planted for Chianti Colli Senesi. Considering the quality of their Brunello, we expect this wine to be very good as well.

Fattoria Il Palagio *(Mercatale Val di Pesa, Firenze)*. The castle here dates from the mid-thirteenth century. Their vines, covering 47 acres (19 hectares) and including some 10 acres (4 hectares) in *coltura promiscua*, are planted at 1,115 feet (340 meters) above sea level. They produce some 133,000 bottles of Chianti Classico a year.

Fattoria Il Paradiso *(San Gimignano, Siena)*, 1972. Graziella Cetti Cappelli is the proprietor of Fattoria Il Paradiso, an estate in the Colli Senesi zone. She has 39.2 acres (15.9 hectares) of vineyards; of which 22 (9) are planted in vines for Chianti, 15 (6) for Vernaccia di San Gimignano, and 2.2 (0.9) in chardonnay. Cappelli produces 80,000 to 93,000 bottles a year of Chianti, and 66,500 to 80,000 of Vernaccia di San Gimignano, including 5,300 bottles of a brut *spumante*. A few years ago she planned to produce a wine from her Paterno II vineyard that was to be called Rosso Paterno II. She planned to make that wine from a familiar *uvaggio*: 80 percent sangiovese, 15 percent cabernet sauvignon, and 5 percent cabernet franc—the same formula as Antinori's Tignanello. We have no idea if that wine was ever produced. She previously made a Chianti Paterno Secondo from those vines.

Fattoria Il Poggerino *(Radda in Chianti, Siena)*. Principi Cori Ginori and Conti Lanza Ginori own this estate. They produced a good '87 and '88 Chianti Classico. Chianti Classico * +

Fattoria Ispoli *(Mercatale Val di Pesa, Firenze)*. Ispoli was, at one time, part of the Serristori and Machiavelli estates. They have some 10.9 acres (4.4 hectares) of vines from which they produce some 17,000 bottles of Chianti Classico annually.

Fattoria La Casaccia *(San Gusmè, Siena)*. Fattoria La Casaccia owns 32.4 acres (13.1 hectares) of vines, including nearly 7 (2.8) planted in *coltura promiscua*. They produce some 92,000 bottles of Chianti Classico annually.

Fattoria La Loggia *(Montefiridolfi, Firenze)*, 1427. Fattoria La Loggia was created by the Buondelmont family in 1427. Later it passed into the hands of the Medicis. Today it is owned by Giulio Baruffaldi and Cuca Roaldi. This Chianti Classico producer in the San Casciano district has 32 acres (13 hectares) of vines, planted at about 1,148 feet (350 meters) above sea level. Their annual production of 113,330 bottles of wine includes Chianti Classico, *bianco*, *rosato*, and *spumante*. They sell a *normale* and a *riserva* Chianti Classico under both the Fattoria La Loggia and the "Terra dei Cavalieri" labels, and non-DOC white, rosé, and red wines under the Tena dei Greppi label. They also sell rosé and white with the "Terra dei Cavalieri" label. In 1986 they produced 33,666 bottles of "Terra dei Cavalieri" Chianti Classico, and in 1983, 5,000 bottles of "Terra dei Cavalieri" Chianti Classico Riserva and 13,334 bottles of Fattoria La Loggia Chianti Classico Riserva.

In 1985, like so many others in Toscana, they produced a barrique-aged sangiovese-cabernet blend from 70 percent of sangiovese and 30 of cabernet.

Neither the '82 Riserva, nor the '83, '85, or '86 normali that we've tasted had much to offer except consistency. The '85 Riserva was good, and the normale '87 acceptable. Chianti Classico: +, Terra dei Cavalieri * +

Fattoria La Mandria (Lecchi in Chianti, Siena). La Mandria has 100 acres (40 hectares) of vines in the Gaiole area, 67 (27) for Chianti Classico. Their vineyards, facing southeast, are planted at an average altitude of 1,710 feet (520 meters) above sea level. They produce, on average, some 16,665 cases of wine annually, most of which is Chianti Classico. The most recent vintage we tasted, in 1982, was their '75; it was quite mediocre. Things, however, are sure to change. Vittorio Fiore, the noted enologist, consults for them. For now we suspend our rating of their Chianti Classico. Chianti Classico [0]

Fattoria La Presura (Strada in Chianti, Firenze). From their 11 acres (4.4 hectares) of vines planted at 655 feet (200 meters) above sea level they produce nearly 20,000 bottles of Chianti Classico annually.

Fattoria La Ripa (San Donato in Poggio, Firenze), 1941. The 346-acre (140-hectare) La Ripa estate, owned by Santa Brigida, has 42 acres (17 hectares) of vines in the S. Donato and Castellina areas of the Classico zone.

The 29.7 acres (12 hectares) planted for Chianti Classico are comprised of 78 percent sangiovese, 8 percent canaiolo, 4 percent white grapes, and 10 percent other red varieties. The vineyards are planted at an average altitude of 1,475 feet (450 meters) above sea level. In 1983 they put in 5 acres (2 hectares) of cabernet sauvignon. This wine will be aged in barrique. Luciano Bandini is their enologist.

In 1985, for the first time, they bottled a Chianti Classico from a single vineyard; they produced 8,000 bottles of Vigna S. Brigida. Their average production of 96,000 bottles of wine a year includes 76,000 of Chianti Classico, 10,665 of Bianco della Lega, 8,000 of Cabernet Sauvignon, and 1,333 of vin santo. They expect their production to increase to 120,000 bottles within three years;

96,000 will be Chianti Classico. They will produce a Chardonnay that will be fermented and aged in barrique, and a Sauvignon Blanc. The first Chianti Classico they bottled was the '67; their first riserva, the '80. Their riserva is aged for at least two years in chestnut casks. Of the vintages that we've tasted recently, the '86 Riserva was good, the '86 normale passable. The La Ripa Chiantis are agreeable wines, though lacking in style. Chianti Classico *

Fattoria Le Barone (Panzano in Chianti, Firenze). This azienda farms 24.7 acres (10 hectares) of vines in specialized cultivation and 17.6 (7.1) in coltura promiscua. They produce nearly 10,000 cases of Chianti Classico a year. Admittedly we have tasted only one vintage, in 1981, the '77, but it was enough. The wine was barely drinkable, although conditions should have been optimum; it was served at the (mediocre) restaurant of this overpriced castle hotel. Perhaps things have changed; we hope so. Chianti Classico [0]

Fattoria Le Bocce (Panzano in Chianti, Firenze). The 86-acre (35-hectare) Le Bocce estate, owned by Stefano Farina, who also owns Cascina Traversa in the Piemonte, has 62 acres (25 hectares) of vineyards, including 39.5 (16) planted for Chianti Classico at an average altitude of 1,970 feet (600 meters) above sea level. They produce up to 9,330 cases of a good Chianti Classico annually. Their '85 Riserva was very good, and the '86 and '88 good. Vittorio Fiore supplies enological advice. Chianti Classico **

Fattoria Le Casalte (Paola Silvestri Barioffi) (Sant' Albino di Montepulciano, Siena), 1975. Paola Silvestri Barioffi owns 20 acres (8 hectares) of vineyards. Until recently, she produced a Vino Nobile and a Chianti, but like many others here, with the new DOC for Rosso di Montepulciano, she dropped the Chianti.

Fattoria Le Corti (Greve in Chianti, Firenze). Angiolo Anchini owns the Le Corti estate and its 16 acres (6.5 hectares) of vines planted at an average altitude of 1,640 feet (500 meters) above sea level. His annual production of Chianti Classico amounts to approximately 45,000 bottles. Franco Bernabei is their consulting enologist. The only wine we've tasted from here was the good '88. Chianti Classico *

Fattoria Le Filigare (San Donato in Poggio, Firenze). This 153-acre (62-hectare) estate has 17.3 acres (7 hectares) of vines, 12.4 (5) for Chianti Classico planted with 90 percent sangiovese, 8

THE VINEYARDS OF FATTORIA LA RIPA

Vineyard	Acres	Hectares	Exposure	Average Annual Yield in	
				Tons/Acre	Quintali/Hectare
Vigna Casa	9.9	4	SW	3.1	70
Vigna Mandria	4.9	2	SE	3.6	80
Vigna S. Brigida	4.9	2	—	2.2	50
Vigna Stalla	17.3	7	SE	3.6	80
Vigna Strada	4.9	2	SW	3.3	75
Total	41.9	17			

percent canaiolo, and 2 percent trebbiano and malvasia. Half of the vines are in monoculture, the rest are mixed with olive trees. These vines—90 percent sangiovese—are planted at 1,310 to 1,640 feet (400 to 500 meters) in altitude. They also have some cabernet sauvignon that they use for their **Podere Le Rocce** wine. Some 90 percent of their production is Chianti Classico *normale,* 5 percent each of a Chianti Classico Riserva and Podere Le Rocce. They produce up to 34,665 bottles of Chianti Classico annually. (In 1987 they produced 20,950 bottles of Chianti Classico.) They also produce a *barrique*-aged *vino da tavola,* Podere Le Rocce. Their Chianti Classico Riserva is aged for ten months in *barrique.* While we were unimpressed with the one vintage of Del Conte that we tasted, the '82, we found the rest of their Chianti Classico—the '85 Riserva, '86, and '87—to be quite good indeed. Vittorio Fiore consults here. Chianti Classico **

Fattoria Le Fioraie (*Castellina in Chianti,* località *Fioraie, Siena*). This estate owns 41 acres (16.7 hectares) of vines. They produce some 52,000 bottles of Chianti Classico annually.

Fattoria Le Pici (*San Gusmè, Siena*). Le Pici produces 58,665 bottles of Chianti Classico a year from their 20.8 acres (8.4 hectares) of vines. We haven't tasted this Chianti since 1983, when we tasted the mediocre '74, so it seems best to suspend our rating. Chianti Classico [0]

Fattoria Le Ripe (*San Casciano Val di Pesa, Firenze*). Le Ripe has 14 acres (5.6 hectares) of vines planted at an average altitude of 820 feet (250 meters) above sea level. Their annual production of Chianti Classico amounts to some 41,600 bottles.

Fattoria Lilliano (*Antella, Firenze*), *1960.* Fattoria Lilliano, not to be confused with the Chianti Classico estate Tenuta di Lilliano, has 178 acres (72 hectares) in the Colli Fiorentini zone; 43 (17.5) are planted in vines for Chianti. A few years ago they reported that they planned to plant 5 acres (2 hectares) of chardonnay. Lilliano produces about 12,000 cases of wine a year. They rate 1983, 1975, and 1970 as their best vintages and 1976 as their worst. We haven't tasted these wines in some time, but with the exception of the '77, we've always had a fairly good impression. Chianti Colli Fiorentini *

Fattoria Monsanto (*Barberino Val d'Elsa*), *1961.* Fabrizio Bianchi, proprietor of Fattoria Monsanto, bought the first part of the estate, then called Azienda Palloni, in 1961. He renamed it Monsanto, taking the name from the district where the property is located. This locality, known in ancient times as Scrutania, was the site of an Etruscan village. It was, according to local legend, given the name Monsanto (holy mount) some time in the early Middle Ages in honor of Sant Ruffiniano, who ended his evangelical mission here. Monsanto is mentioned in ecclesiastical papers from A.D. 998.

Bianchi came to the area to attend the wedding of a friend, he recalls, and seeing the vineyards rekindled his love for the country. He decided he would like to buy some land and produce wine and olive oil for the family. Though he lived and worked near Milano,

PRODUCTION OF THE WINES OF FATTORIA MONSANTO

Wine	First Vintage	Average Number of Cases Per Year
Chianti Classico		
Monsanto Riserva	1962	7,500
Monsanto Riserva Il Poggio	1962	3,000
Chianti		
Santa Caterina	1985	9,000
Barrique-Aged Wines		
Botrytis Bianco Muffato	1977	500
Chardonnay	1990	800
Nemo, Cabernet Sauvignon	1982	800
Sangioveto di Monsanto*	1985	2,000
Tinscvil, Sangioveto-Cabernet	1979	1,500
Other Wines		
Bianco dei Bianchi Spumante	1982	1,500
Vin santo	1962	100
Total		26,700

* This replaced the Sangiovese Grosso di Scanni produced in the 1970s (1974, 1975, and 1977); it is labeled as Fabrizio Bianchi.

PRODUCTION AND RATING OF MONSANTO RISERVA IL POGGIO

Year	Number of Bottles Produced	Our Rating	Fabrizio Bianchi's	
			Rating	Comments
1962*	5,730	****	****	Generally hard wines, ready now.
1963	n/a	—	0	Decent wines that have faded now.
1964†	13,760	***+	***	Lighter than 1962, with more perfume.
1965	—	—	0	Poor vintage, none bottled.
1966	5,370	****	****	Light body, high alcohol, made from young vines.
1967	8,930	**	***	A medium year, lacked body; the last Monsanto with white grapes, stems, and *governo*.
1968	12,550	***−	***	A medium year, very low acid.
1969	13,420	***−	***+	Similar to 1962, needed age but very soft now.
1970	18,630	***+	****	Excellent, close to 1971 in quality, maybe better, and should last longer.
1971	36,700	***(*)	****	Excellent.
1972	12,770	***	****	A success, some botrytis, a lot of rain, but Bianchi waited to pick and the sun came out.
1973	6,500	**	**	Soft, not to age, the least of these vintages in quality.
1974	34,600	**	***	Excellent, to age.
1975	35,700	***+	****	Excellent.
1976	0	—	0	Terrible vintage, none bottled.
1977	23,730	***(+)	****	Best of all the vintages.
1978	38,650	**+	**+	Good.
1979	32,880	***−	***	Better than 1978.
1980	34,550	**(*−)	***	Similar to 1978.
1981	38,300	**+	**	Similar to 1974.
1982	47,320	***(+)	***	Similar to 1970.
1983	47,660	***(+)	***(+)	Similar to 1968.
1984	0	—	0	Terrible vintage, none bottled.
1985	39,630	****	****	Outstanding.
1986	31,970	**+	***	Similar to 1966.
1987	24,240	**	**	Similar to 1973.
1988	36,520	***(*)	***(+)	No comment.
1989	0	—	0	Terrible vintage, none bottled.

* Last tasted April 1985

† Rating based on tasting of September 1985; the two more recent times that we tasted this wine—November 1986 and October 1987—the bottles were out of condition.

in the family textile business, as a boy he had spent many summers in the country with his uncles in Piemonte and worked in their vineyards.

The Pallone property was owned by two sisters who were not on speaking terms and had divided everything, including the house itself, into two parts. The holdings of only one sister were on the market when Bianchi made his original purchase of about half the estate. This included the vineyards of Il Poggio, La Chiesa, Sornano, and part of Fonte del Latte and Scanni. A year later he was able to buy the rest of the property.

At that time the estate was worked under the old feudal system

of *mezzadria*. The *mezzadro* who ran the property made the '61 Monsanto as he had previous vintages; the wine was not bottled but sold in demijohns, except for a small portion that Bianchi took for his personal use and to give as gifts to friends.

In 1962, Fabrizio made the wine with the assistance of his uncle, "in true *contadino* fashion," dumping the grape bunches—whole berries, stems, and all—into large wooden tubs and bashing them about with a wooden club stuck with nails, which broke up only a small portion of the grapes. He recalls that he and his uncle found it funny at the time, but they did it that way, using the local methods. He laughs now at the memory of it.

THE CRUS AND VINEYARDS OF FATTORIA MONSANTO

Cru/Vineyard	Acres	Hectares	Altitude		Exposure	Variety		Year(s) Planted	Zone
			Feet	Meters					
Fonte del Latte	9.56	3.87	950–1,000	290–305	NE	85%	sangiovese	1967, 1968	BVE
						15%	canaiolo		
Il Paretaio	5.78	2.34	985–1,015	300–310	SW	100%	sangiovese	1989, 1990	BVE
Il Poggio[a]	13.15	5.32	920–1,050	280–320	SW	90%	sangiovese	1963, 1964	BVE
						7%	canaiolo		
						3%	colorino		
La Chiesa	4.45	1.80	970–1,000	295–305	NW	75%	sangiovese	1966, 1967	BVE
						25%	malvasia nera		
Mulino[b]	7.17	2.90	820–855	250–260	SW	100%	cabernet s.	1976	BVE
Novoli	4.45	1.80	1,000–1,035	305–315	SW	100%	sangiovese	1988, 1989	BVE
Salcio	5.31	2.15	855–920	260–280	SW	50%	trebbiano t.	1966, 1967	BVE
						50%	vermentino		
Scanni[c]	8.25	3.34	900–985	275–300	SW	100%	sangiovese	1969, 1970	BVE
Sornano[d]	11.69	4.73	920–985	280–300	SW	95%	sangiovese	1966, 1967	PGB
						5%	malvasia nera		
Val di Gallo	8.20	3.32	855–920	260–280	NE	100%	sangiovese	1970, 1971, 1977	PGB
	11.02	4.46				100%	chardonnay	1981	
Total	89.03	36.03							
Other vineyards	29.48	11.93							
Total in vines	118.51	47.96							

NOTES: BVE—Barberino Val d'Elsa
PGB—Poggibonsi
[a] Used for Monsanto, Il Poggio Riserva.
[b] Used for Nemo Cabernet Sauvignon, Vigna Mulino.
[c] Used for Sangioveto di Monsanto in the 1970s and Fabrizio Bianchi today.
[d] Bottled as a Chianti cru in 1971; today the sangiovese is used in Tinscvil.

The must was put with the stems into wooden uprights, *tini di legno,* for the fermentation, which lasted for fifteen days. Wine made by this method tends to pick up harsh tannins from the stems and become rather rough. To soften the wine, they added white grapes and used *governo.* This system of winemaking was employed at Monsanto through the 1967 vintage. In 1966, Fabrizio did some experiments with fermenting without the stems and was pleased with the results. In 1968 he initiated some new vinification methods—no white grapes, *governo,* or stems, and a reduced period of skin contact. Today the Monsanto Chianti Classico is fermented for one week on the skins, the Il Poggio for eight to ten days.

Bianchi taught himself to make wine. With a natural enthusiasm and an eagerness to learn, he read books in French on winemaking and basically learned as he went along. Experience, he feels, is the real teacher. You learn from the wine itself; every vintage is different. Perhaps as a consequence he has more of an open mind about making wine. He was, and still is, willing to experiment, to try new ideas. But he is slow to change; he makes many tests first to be sure of the results and to understand the reasons behind them.

Bianchi sends samples out for analysis and tastes frequently. Tasting, he says, is 90 percent in the aroma; the palate confirms it. When his business requires him to be in Gallarate, he has samples sent up from the farm and is on the phone following the progress of the wine intently. Fabrizio is not an absentee landlord (the bane of many a Chianti *fattoria*).

The most important consideration in making a fine wine, Bianchi believes, is the quality of the fruit. You can't overcrop. While he might get 3 tons of grapes per acre (70 quintali per hectare) for the regular Monsanto, the Il Poggio averages 1.8 to 2 (40 to 45). The

THE VINEYARDS OF FATTORIA MONTIVERDI

Vineyard	Acres	Hectares	Variety		Altitude in		Year Planted
					Feet	Meters	
Carpinaia	4.2	1.7	88%	sangiovese	902–	275–	1972
			10%	cabernet sauvignon	984	300	
			2%	colorino			
Casale	2.2	0.9	97%	sangiovese	968–	295–	1975
			3%	canaiolo	1,001	305	
Cipressone	3.7	1.5	93%	sangiovese	820–	250–	1973–
			5%	canaiolo	886	270	1974
			2%	colorino			
Fontino	1.7	0.7	92%	sangiovese	853–	260–	1972
			8%	cabernet sauvignon	919	280	
Total	11.8	4.8					

Il Poggio vineyard is harvested two weeks later than those for the regular Monsanto. The sweeter must attains three-quarters to one percent more alcohol than the must for the regular *riserva*. Fabrizio echoes the belief of all the finest producers in pointing out that you have to select very carefully and reject all but the best grapes.

The winemaker, he feels, is less important; he should do as little as is necessary and keep the wine as natural as possible. A good wine, Fabrizio says, needs little interference. The less you do, the better. He notes that the farmers made good wine here—surprisingly good considering what they had to work with, using traditional methods and without the benefit of technology. Enology, he feels, has sometimes gotten in the way of good winemaking, taking away the character of the wine.

He does, though, use stainless steel tanks and cultured yeast. These tanks give him better control over the temperature of the fermentation, which is extremely important. He experimented with using cultured yeast in lieu of the wild yeast that forms on the grape skins and found that although it made no difference in the wine, it was a lot more convenient.

The essential things, he says, are to plant the right grapes in the right place, to have a good fermentation, and to bottle at the right time.

They grapes are pressed gently in a Bucher pneumatic press. (No press juice is used in the Il Poggio.) Both Chianti Classicos spend one to two years in stainless after the fermentation and from there are moved to oak. The Il Poggio is aged two to three years in oak casks, the *riserva* for two.

Bianchi doesn't induce the malolactic fermentation. He waits for it to happen, which it always does, sooner or later—sooner when the must is lower in alcohol, later when the gradation is higher. He doesn't fine or filter the wine; he clears it by racking only, twice the first year and once a year after that.

When Fabrizio took over the farm, the vines were in mixed cultivation with olive trees. In 1963 and 1964 he began replanting the vineyards. Barone Ricasoli, then president of the Classico Consorzio, was one of the first to make the changeover to specialized vineyards and advised others to do so also. In 1964, Bianchi replanted the top of the Il Poggio vineyard; two years later he replanted the slope. He had to use dynamite to break up a large stratum of solid rock under part of the vineyard to allow the vines to reach deep into the soil for nutrients and moisture.

The Monsanto estate covers more than 395 acres (160 hectares), 50 (20) in Poggibonsi and 345 (140) in Barberino Val d'Elsa. The 118 acres (48 hectares) of vines produce the equivalent of 30,000 cases annually, of which some 25,000 cases are bottled. This is down from the 35,000 cases of a few years ago.

Besides Chianti Classico, Bianchi produces two whites, a rosé, a small amount of a fine sweet *vin santo*, a **Sangioveto di Monsanto, Nemo Cabernet Sauvignon**, and a sangiovese-cabernet blend called **Tinscvil**, as well as the Champagne-method sparkler Bianco di Bianchi, and, in years that it's possible, a botrytised Bianco Muffato Trebbiano.

Overall, they are good, even very good wines. But the real star is his Monsanto Chianti Classico Riserva from the Il Poggio vineyard. It is in our considerable experience without question the single finest Chianti and one of the world's vinicultural treasures. There are two reasons: its very high level of quality and its very high level of consistency. The worst of the Il Poggios that we've tasted are better than most other Chianti Classicos.

When we say consistency, we are not speaking of a dozen or so bottles, but scores, and not one vertical tasting, but six—of every vintage of Monsanto Il Poggio, from the first in 1962 through the most recent at the time tasted along with a number of other Monsanto Chianti Classicos (missing only two vintages, 1963 and 1965, of which there were only a couple of bottles, one cache saved for sentimental reasons—it was the year of his son's birth—and the other strictly to have a complete library of vintages). And on our most recent visit to Monsanto, in April 1990, we had a chance to taste all the vintages from 1966 through 1989, experiencing once again the same high quality and consistency we've come to expect.

At a tasting of that kind with wines of that level, the tendency is to be more than usually critical. A defect tends to stand out. But we didn't find one wine—that will be bottled—that was less than good.

At a vertical tasting at Monsanto in the spring of 1985, we were joined by Alfredo and Luciana Currado of Piemonte. At the Vietti *cantina* earlier in the trip, Alfredo had said something that rather took us aback: that he found the best wines of Toscana to be—did he say the whites?! Not possible. No, he laughed, not "*i vini bianchi, i vini di Bianchi*." Ah, that was more like it. Alfredo and Luciana were happy to make the trip down despite a busy schedule and a houseful of Americans (Mama and Betta and Emanuele and Mario would take care of them); the tasting was too good an opportunity to miss. And it was. Very impressive indeed.

Fabrizio's wife, the gentle Giuliana, a fashion model before her marriage, came in from the garden in old jeans, her blond hair casually tied back from a face adorned only with a healthy glow and a warm welcoming smile. She joined us just briefly, offering friendly greetings but putting off pleasant conversation until later, in order not to distract anyone from serious tasting. Giuliana, Fabrizio notes, has a very fine palate, and he has a high regard for her opinion. She doesn't care, though, for the harsh young wines, preferring a smooth, round, and ready vintage.

We all enjoyed the older vintages served later at the dinner that Giuliana had prepared. She has a light touch in the kitchen and shares her husband's belief in the importance of the *materia prima*, selecting the best ingredients available and preparing things simply and naturally.

At that tasting, of all the Il Poggio's from 1962 to 1983, not one vintage was fading, though a few had peaked and probably shouldn't be held much longer.

There is still, however, no need to rush to drink the '77 or '75; they will continue to improve. Among the more recent vintages, we recommend laying down the '88 and '85 when they are available, and the '83 and '82 that are. Most will improve with further age, but these four will need more than most. We preferred the '79 to the '78; the '80 is also very good. Both the '70 and '71 can improve yet. The '73 should probably be drunk up.

Of the regular Monsanto Riserva, based on those we tasted recently, we recommend the '82, '83, '85, and '86. The '87 and '88 haven't been bottled; both tasted from cask were good, especially the '88. While we rate the Monsanto Riserva highly, there are other fine Chiantis on that level. The Il Poggio Riserva is simply in a class by itself. This is not a classic Classico, you might say; no, rather it is the epitome of what a Classico can be. It is darker in color, fuller in body, richer in flavor and extract, lower in acid, higher in alcohol, more harmonious and complex, and just downright more impressive overall. This is a wine for contemplation.

We could sit, with the greatest of pleasure, in the *caminetto* at Monsanto on the cushioned benches by the fire—and we have, on frosty spring and autumn evenings—catching the burnished reflections of the ruby wine as it is held up to the flames, inhaling its rich perfume and savoring its nuances.

Lovely as an old vintage is by itself as an after-dinner glass, this wine is an excellent complement to roast meat, *bistecca alla fiorentina* ("*bue americano*," Fabrizio adds with an appreciative grin), with pigeon or duck, or game, especially *cinghiale* (boar) or venison. And tempting as it is to drink young, owing to its depth of fruit and fine balance, Il Poggio should be given age to develop to its full potential, at least eight years and in the best vintages ten to twelve.

It's worth mentioning again that the regular Monsanto Chianti Classico Riserva is a very fine wine, far better than most Chianti Classicos. It has only one real problem—its position, standing as it does in the shadow of the great Il Poggio. Chianti Classico: Santa Caterina *, Monsanto Riserva ***, Monsanto Riserva Il Poggio **** +

Fattoria Montecchio (*San Donato in Poggio, Firenze*). This *azienda* has approximately 36 acres (14.5 hectares) of vines, nearly all in monoculture, for Chianti Classico, from which they produce up to 100,000 bottles of wine. The only Chianti Classico that we tasted from them was from the difficult 1987 vintage; consequently, we can't rate them, considering the nature of the vintage and the quality of the wine. Chianti Classico [0]

Fattoria Montiverdi (*Gaiole in Chianti, Siena*), *1972*. Carmela Maisano, wife of Nicola Longo, has owned this estate since 1972. Shortly after she acquired this land, which had been owned previously by the Stucchi-Prinettis of Badia a Coltibuono, she replanted the vines. Today this 124-acre (50-hectare) estate has nearly 12 acres (4.8 hectares) under vines.

Their first vintage of Chianti Classico was from the 1977 vintage. Today they produce 11,000 cases of "Monti Verdi" Chianti Classicos from a blend of 93 percent sangiovese, 5 percent canaiolo, and 2 percent colorino. They produce 8,000 cases of Chianti Classico *normale*, 1,500 of a *riserva*, and 1,500 of a single-vineyard Chianti Classico that is aged in *barrique*. They also produce a Villa Maisano Brut Spumante and **Vigne**, a *barrique*-aged wine made from a blend of sangiovese with up to 15 percent cabernet sauvignon.

The noted enologist Vittorio Fiore has been consulting here since the 1987 vintage. Thus far the only Chianti Classicos that we tasted from here were the '87 and '88, which were good. Chianti Classico ** —

Fattoria Morrocco (*Tavarnelle Val di Pesa, Firenze*). Morrocco has some 26 acres (10.4 hectares) of vines, 20 percent in mixed culture, planted at an average altitude of 885 feet (270 meters) above sea level. Their average annual production of Chianti Classico amounts to some 6,000 cases.

Fattoria Nittardi (*Castellina in Chianti*, località *Nittardi, Siena*). Anstalt Nittardi owns this 245-acre (99-hectare) estate with its 12.4 acres (5 hectares) of vines, some 7.4 (3) of which are planted for Chianti Classico. They produce about 1,755 cases of Chianti Classico annually. Their '85 Riserva was quite good. Pietro Rivella consults here. Chianti Classico *

Fattoria Ormanni (*Poggibonsi, Siena*). Ormanni produces up to 15,900 cases of wine annually from the nearly 68 acres (27.4 hectares) of vines it has planted for Chianti Classico.

Fattoria Parga (*Molin del Piano, Firenze*). Fattoria Parga, covering 222 acres (90 hectares), has 69 (28) of vineyards, 40 (16) in specialized cultivation. They produce 6,500 cases of wine a year, including a Chianti Rùfina.

Fattoria Pile e Lamole (*Greve in Chianti, Firenze*). This *fattoria* is owned by Antiche Fattorie Fiorentine. They bottle the **Fattoria**

Salcetino and Lamole di Lamole Chianti Classicos. The 334-acre (135-hectare) Pile e Lamole estate consists of 99 acres (40 hectares) of vineyards, of which some 54 (22) are planted for Chianti Classico. These vines—88 percent sangiovese, 10 percent canaiolo, and 2 percent trebbiano and malvasia—are planted at altitudes ranging from 1,150 to 1,640 feet (350 to 500 meters) above sea level. Some 12,245 cases of Chianti Classico are produced with the Lamole di Lamole label annually. Of the wines sold as Lamole di Lamole, we found the '85 Riserva very good, and the '88, '87, and '85 *normali* good. Chianti Classico: Lamole di Lamole ** −

Fattoria Prunatelli (*Pontassieve, Firenze*). Fattoria Prunatelli has 52 acres (21 hectares) of vines, 50 (20) in *coltura promiscua*. They produce 40,000 bottles of wine a year, including a Chianti Rùfina.

Fattoria Quercia al Poggio (*Barberino Val d'Elsa, Firenze*). This *fattoria* has 32 acres (13 hectares) of vines, and produces the equivalent of 120,000 bottles of wine a year, including 86,665 of Chianti Classico. Most of this wine is sold *sfuso*; they bottle only about 26,500. Besides their temperature-controlled stainless steel tanks and cement vats, they have three chestnut casks. They don't believe in giving their wines much wood age but hold some of it in vat for an unusually long duration. In May 1985 we tasted two 1971s at the *cantina,* one from bottle and the other from vat. The cellarman said that the latter was being aged for a client, a restaurant in Roma (sorry, we didn't catch the name) where they go for that sort of wine. We couldn't get excited about either of the '71s, but the '79 and '82 were acceptable. As for the '83 and '84, maybe if they leave them in vat long enough, they can get the restaurant to take them off their hands. Chianti Classico * −

Fattoria Querciabella (*Greve in Chianti*, località *Ruffoli, Firenze*), *1971*. Giuseppe Mazzanti's Agricola Campoverde owns this 210-acre (85-hectare) estate. There are some 39.5 acres (16 hectares) under vines, including 2.5 (1) in *coltura promiscua*. The vineyards, planted at altitudes ranging from 1,510 to 1,575 feet (460 to 480 meters) above sea level, face east to southeast. The vineyards contain 90 percent sangiovese, 5 percent canaiolo, 3 percent white grapes, and 2 percent other varieties. These vines produce the grapes for Querciabella's Chianti Classico Riserva and, at one time, their Vecchio.

At most, Querciabella produces just over 97,000 bottles of Chianti Classico, from a blend of 78 percent sangiovese, 5 percent sangiovese grosso, 4 percent canaiolo, 5 percent cabernet sauvignon, 2 percent cabernet franc, 3 percent trebbiano, 2 percent-

malvasia, and 1 percent colorino. They age their *normale* Chianti Classico for one year in oak, the Vecchio (in times past) for two years, and the Riserva for four. They also produce a *barrique*-aged wine from red grapes only which they call **Casaocci**.

The *riserve* from '81 and '85, and the *normali* from '84 and '88 were good, and the '82 *normale* and Riserva, as well as the '83 Riserva and '85 *normale,* were very good. Mario Cortevesio is their consulting enologist. Chianti Classico **

Fattoria S. Stefano (*Greve in Chianti, Firenze*). The church of Santo Stefano dates from 1137. This estate has 34.6 acres (14 hectares) of vines at 1,150 feet (350 meters) above sea level from which they produce some 98,000 bottles of Chianti Classico annually. Mario Cortevesio consults for them.

Fattoria Salcetino (*Radda in Chianti*, località *Lucarelli, Radda in Chianti, Siena*). This 393-acre (159-hectare) estate is owned by Antiche Fattorie Fiorentine, which also owns **Fattoria Pile e Lamole**. There are 156 acres (63 hectares) of vines planted at altitudes between 985 and 1,310 feet (300 and 400 meters) above sea level. The 74 acres (30 hectares) for Chianti Classico are planted with 88 percent sangiovese, 10 percent canaiolo, and 2 percent trebbiano and malvasia. At most they produce 17,500 cases of Chianti Classico a year. The '87 was good, the '88 very good. Chianti Classico * +

Fattoria San Fabiano Calcinaia (*Castellina in Chianti*, località *Cellole, Siena*). This 420-acre (170-hectare) estate has 79 acres (32 hectares) of vines, 52 (21) for Chianti Classico, planted at altitudes ranging from 985 to 1,640 feet (300 to 500 meters) above sea level. The vineyard is planted with 90 percent sangiovese, 5 percent canaiolo, 3 percent white grapes, and 2 percent other red varieties. Their annual production of Chianti Classico is about 12,200 cases. They age their wines in a combination of oak, including the fashionable *barrique*.

We found all three bottles of the '85 Riserva Cellole we tasted disappointing, the '87 *normale* good, the '88 very good, and the '85 Marchese di Gavignano good. Chianti Classico *

Fattoria San Giusto a Rentennano (*Monti in Chianti, Siena*), *1956*. Enrico Martini di Cigala owns the San Giusto estate and its 61.5 acres (25 hectares) of vines, 49.4 (20) of which are planted for Chianti Classico, 7.4 (3) for the *barrique*-aged, 100 percent sangiovese **Percarlo**, and 3.7 (1.5) for *vin santo*. (The numbers don't add up, but this is the information they supplied us with!)

THE VINEYARDS OF FATTORIA QUERCIABELLA

Vineyard	Acres	Hectares	Year Planted
Il Borro	2.97	1.20	1960
Il Poggio	1.24	0.50	1964
Il Solatio	4.79	1.94	1959
Querciabella	3.71	1.50	1963
S. Lucia	5.44	2.20	1969

These vines, planted at 820 feet (250 meters) above sea level, face south to southwest.

Their first Chianti Classico Riserva was the '75. They produced their first *vin santo* in 1979 and Percarlo in 1983. Today they produce some 40,000 bottles of Chianti Classico annually, including 6,660 of Riserva. They also produce about 10,000 bottles of Percarlo and 1,300 of *vin santo*. Overall, they produce a good Chianti Classico. They ferment the Chianti Classico *normale* for fourteen days, the *riserva* for sixteen, and Percarlo for seventeen. Only the '88 disappointed. The rest of the wines tasted, from '83 through '87, were, at the very least good, and some were very good: the *riserve* of '85 and '86, and *normali* of '85 and '87. Chianti Classico ** +

Fattoria San Leonino (*Castellina in Chianti,* località *I Cipressi, Siena*), *1988.* Fattoria I Cipressi was purchased by Milano businessman Lionello Marchesi in February 1989 at a bankruptcy sale. He renamed it San Leonino, the name used on the label by the previous owners. The estate consists of 272 acres (110 hectares), of which about 116 (47) are in vines, with 94 (38) for Chianti Classico. The vineyards, at altitudes ranging from 920 to 985 feet (280 to 300 meters) above sea level, are planted in 90 percent sangiovese, 5 percent canaiolo, and 5 percent trebbiano and malvasia. They also have 2.5 acres (1 hectare) of cabernet sauvignon and syrah from which they plan to make a *vino da tavola*.

The vineyards here, like Marchesi's two other properties, are being planted with 2,915 vines per acre (7,200 per hectare). Thus far they have replanted 27 acres (11 hectares) in Castellina, 17 (7) in Montepulciano, and 7.5 (3) in Montalcino. In 1991 they will replant 50 (20) more. And after those vines start producing, they will replant still more acreage.

In 1989, Marchesi had the old winery torn down and a new one put up. They produced 5,400 cases of the '88 Chianti Classico, and expect this to increase to about 25,000 cases annually. Marchesi bought the grapes in 1988, since he had an agreement to buy the estate at that time. Rainer Zierock is the viticulturist here and Enzo Tiezzi the enologist, as they are for Marchesi's other two properties, Tenuta Trerose in Montepulciano and ValdiSuga in Montalcino. The San Leonino Chianti Classico spends some time in *barrique;* perhaps 15 percent of the total spends six months in small barrels. The '88 was very good. Based on that one wine, Chianti Classico ** −

Fattoria Selvapiana (*Rùfina, Firenze*), *1827.* The Selvapiana estate was owned by the bishops of Firenze. Banker Michele Giuntini acquired it from Filippo di Lorenzo Corboli as payment on a loan in the early part of the nineteenth century. The current proprietor of the 865-acre (350-hectare) estate, the genial Francesco Giuntini, has managed the Selvapiana farm since 1953. He is the fifth generation of Giuntinis to produce wine here. Today there are some 72 acres (29 hectares) in vines, planted at altitudes ranging between 230 and 655 feet (70 and 200 meters) above sea level; they face northwest. The 10-acre (4-hectare) special cru, Bucherchiale, has a southwestern exposure. Giuntini also has olive trees from which he produces a first-rate extra virgin olive oil.

Giuntini's annual production averages nearly 150,000 bottles of wine—more than 70,000 of Chianti Rùfina, 50,000 Chianti Rùfina *riserva*, 8,000 Rosato della Val di Sieve, a good rosé, 8,000 Bianco della Val di Sieve, 4,000 Bianco Borro Lastricato made from a blend of pinot bianco and pinot grigio, and 3,000 Vin Santo Val di Sieve. He has planted cabernet and pinot nero and plans to produce unblended wines from those varieties.

Selvapiana began cru bottling with the single-vineyard *riserva* from the 11-acre (4.5 hectare) Bucherchiale vineyard, their best one. Their first Bucherchiale Riserva was the '79; they produced it again in '81, '82, '83, '85, '86, and '88. At most they produce 6,500 bottles a year of this splendid Chianti Rùfina *riserva*, although the vineyard could produce 40,000 bottles. The wine they bottle comes from grapes grown in the best part of the vineyard, the central part.

Selvapiana generally uses *governo* for their Chianti Rùfina. They use a combination of concentrated must and dried grapes. The '80 was made with the *governo;* the '78, '79, and '81 were not. Although Franco Bernabei has consulted here since 1977, Giuntini still has the final word. Bernabei, as he does at nearly all his estates, wants to use *barriques*. Giuntini, much to his credit, has resisted thus far. For the sake of the wine we hope he continues to. Consider Bernabei's '82 and '83 *riserve* that were aged in *barrique* versus the regular *riserve*. We had a chance to compare them in April 1990 and there was no question which versions were superior. The regular wines, from both vintages, were much preferred by all present. They had more flavor and were fresher, better structured, and more harmonious than their *barrique*-aged counterparts. Actually it wasn't Bernabei who convinced Giuntini to age these wines in *barrique*. An Austrian customer sent Giuntini the *barriques* and bought the wine on the condition that they be aged in those containers. Considering the way they turned out, we are surprised that Bernabei still wants to make Selvapiana in *barrique!*

We had an opportunity to reassess the Selvapiana wines on more than one of our fairly frequent visits to Toscana. The first time such an opportunity arose was in the spring of 1985. After meeting us at our previous appointment and taking us to the very interesting wine museum at Spalletti's Villa Poggio Reale, Francesco then stopped at another *cantina* that he thought might interest us, and whose wines he described, with astonishing but typical modesty, as on about the same level as his. At our rather definite disagreement, he amended this to say that they should be at about the same level since they had vineyards in very good positions.

Finally, he took us to his own *cantina,* or rather to his house. He had "spared" us the usual visit through the cellar, bringing the wines to us instead. In the comfort of the drawing room, we tasted at our own pace some ten wines from the lineup of bottles he had made ready for us. He had made a selection of vintages, he explained, not wanting to tire us with too many (too many?). It was a very good tasting. During the fine dinner, however, which was accompanied by our favorites from among the bottles opened, our discussion of the Rùfina zone and of Selvapiana brought up other vintages, other wines not tasted. Well, if we wanted to taste them too, we were certainly welcome, Francesco offered, pleased that we should be interested. And before the night was out, he had gone down to the cellar to fetch another dozen bottles, no matter that he hardly drinks wine himself. He does, from time to time, have a sip.

Giuntini, the ever-distinguished gentleman farmer with his large, well-trained white Maremmano-Abruzzese sheepdogs by his side, really cares for his guests and does everything to ensure their comfort.

On our most recent visit, in April 1990, Giuntini gave us the opportunity to taste his splendid wines back to 1947. The young and intelligent Federico Masseti, the estate manager, told us that he had never had the chance to taste the older wines before. And, we noticed, like us, he had a problem spitting them out.

Giuntini's Selvapiana is among the top Chiantis produced. In fact, it is among Italy's top vinicultural gems. The Selvapiana is a wine with balance and class, full of flavor and style. It shows real quality, and consistently so. Our favorite among the recent vintages of Selvapiana *riserve* is the '83 Bucherchiale, followed closely by the '88, tasted from cask, and the '85 and '81. We'd be remiss not to mention the excellent '86 Bucherchiale tasted from tank and, for current drinking pleasure, the '79 Bucherchiale. Among older vintages we enjoyed the superb '75 and the wonderful '47 *riserve* and, for current drinking, the '78 and '77 *riserve* that we tasted from a selected cask, and the *riserve* of '62, '58, and '48. Other excellent wines, though in need of further age, include the '88 and '88 single-vineyard Fornace, both tasted from cask, and the '85 Riserva. And on our final list of highly recommended wines for current enjoyment are the *riserve* of '81, '78, '77, '71, '68, and '66.

Francesco provided us with the following vintage evaluation of his wines the morning after our 1985 tasting. We found it interesting to see how our evaluations stacked up against his own assessments.

Fattoria Selvapiana was a founding member of VIDE. Chianti Rùfina ****

Giuntini's evaluations (from 1985):

Top class	1983, 1982, 1981, 1977, 1975, 1971, 1966, 1965, 1962, 1958, 1948, 1947
Very good	1980, 1979, 1978, 1970, 1969, 1968, 1956
Good	1967, 1964
Average	1984 (no *riserva*), 1961, 1960, 1959, 1957
Bad	1976 (not bottled), 1974, 1973, 1972, 1963

Our evaluations (in Giuntini's terms), based on current tastings:

Top class (*** or ****)
   1990, 1988, 1986, 1985, 1983, 1981, 1977, 1975, 1962, 1958, 1948, 1947

Very good (*** — to **)
   1982, 1979, 1978, 1971, 1970†, 1969, 1968, 1966†, 1964†, 1956†
Good to average (** — to * —)
   1989††, 1987††, 1980, 1967, 1965
Bad (0)   1973

   † Not tasted since 1986 or 1985
   †† Not a *riserva* vintage

Fattoria Talente (*San Casciano Val di Pesa, Firenze*). From their 7.7 acres (3.1 hectares) of vines come some 1,800 cases of Chianti Classico.

Fattoria Terrabianca (*Radda in Chianti,* località *San Fedele a Paterno, Siena*), *1972.* Roberto Guldener acquired this 334-acre (135-hectare) Terrabianca estate in 1988. He has 37 acres (15 hectares) planted in vines, 27 (11) for Chianti Classico.

He produces, with technical assistance from consulting enologist Vittorio Fiore, some 10,555 cases of wine a year—approximately 5,000 of the *barrique*-aged, sangiovese-cabernet sauvignon *vino da tavola rosso* Campaccio, 1,110 each of Piano del Cipresso, *barrique*-fermented and -aged Chardonnay Piano della Cappella, and Chianti Classico Riserva Vigna della Croce. He plans to make a Sauvignon Blanc in 1993. Since 1987 he has also produced another Chianti Classico—the *normale* labeled as Scassino—which is not accounted for in his information to us! Perhaps it is actually the one reported as Piano del Cipresso. We've never seen that wine, or the label, although he has a Lo Scassino cru. He also produces, in very small quantities we assume, "G" Brut Spumante, made from pinot blanc and chardonnay and a *vin santo*.

The Chianti Classico Riserva Vigna della Croce is made mostly from sangiovese with minimal parts of the other required grapes, and the Scassino comes from a blend of sangiovese and canaiolo with a small amount of trebbiano.

Thus far we've tasted five wines; all were good, especially the '83 and '85 Riserva Vigna della Croce, and the '86 and '87 versions of that wine were good as well. The '87 Chianti Classico Scassino was agreeable. Chianti Classico: *, Riserva Vigna della Croce **, Scassino *

THE CRUS OF FATTORIA TERRABIANCA

Cru	First Vintage	Average Number of Cases Per Year	Used for
Campaccio	1987	5,000[a]	Sangiovese-Cabernet Sauvignon
Lo Scassino	1987	n/a	Chianti Classico
Piano del Cipresso	n/a	1,110[a]	n/a
Piano della Cappella	1988	1,110[b]	Chardonnay
Vigna della Croce	1983	1,850[c]	Chianti Classico

NOTES: [a] Based on 1988 production
   [b] Based on 1988 and 1989 production
   [c] Three-year average for 1983, 1985, and 1986

Fattoria Terreno (*Greve in Chianti, Firenze*). This estate has some 24 acres (9.6 hectares) of vines and produces about 5,500 cases of Chianti Classico annually.

Fattoria Tregole (*Castellina in Chianti, località Tregole, Siena*). Fattoria Tregole owns 4.7 acres (1.9 hectares) of vines, 3.7 (1.5) planted for Chianti Classico from which they produce an average of 10,660 bottles of Chianti Classico a year. We haven't tasted any since the '75 vintage, but we did find them fairly good overall. Chianti Classico [* +]

Fattoria Valtellina (Giorgio Regni) (*Gaiole in Chianti, Siena*). Giorgio and Giuseppina Regni own this estate. They have 8.5 acres (3.5 hectares) of vineyards, 5.2 (2.1) planted at 1,475 feet (450 meters) above sea level for Chianti Classico. Their annual production of Chianti averages 14,665 bottles. They also produce some white wine and *vin santo*. Their wines enjoy a high reputation. Our only experience was the two times we tasted the rather good '87. Chianti Classico ** −

Fattoria Vignale (*Radda in Chianti, Siena*). Fattoria Vignale owns 111 acres (45 hectares) of land, of which 59 (24) are planted, 42 (17) for Chianti Classico. The average altitude of the vines is 1,640 feet (500 meters) above sea level. Their vineyard is planted with 90 percent sangiovese, 5 percent canaiolo, and 5 percent white grapes. Their annual production of Chianti Classico cannot exceed 118,665 bottles. Of the more recent vintages of Vignale that we tasted, the '83 Riserva was a disappointment, the '86 *normale* good, and the '85 Riserva very good. Chianti Classico * +

Fattoria Vinicola Riunite La Massa (*Panzano in Chianti, Firenze*). This *azienda* has 57.5 acres (23.3 hectares) of vines planted at an average altitude of 1,310 feet (400 meters) above sea level. Their average annual production of Chianti Classico amounts to some 8,900 cases of wine.

Fattoria Vitiano (*San Polo in Chianti, Firenze*). Vitiano has 49 acres (20 hectares) of vines. Its annual production of Chianti Classico is approximately 11,600 cases. Mario Cortevesio consults for them.

Fattoria Viticcio (*Greve in Chianti, Firenze*). This *azienda* owns 124 acres (50 hectares) of land, of which 49.4 (20) are planted in vines. Viticcio's Chianti Classico vineyards encompass 34.6 acres (14 hectares) and are planted with 88 percent sangiovese, 7 percent canaiolo, 3 percent white grapes, and 2 percent other varieties. The altitude of the vineyards averages 985 feet (300 meters)

above sea level. They produce, at most, some 98,000 bottles of Chianti Classico a year. Mario Cortevesio is their consulting enologist. Our overall experience with these wines has been favorable. The *riserve* from '83, '85, and '86 were all good, as were the '86 and '87 *normali*. Chianti Classico ** −

Filetta, Socci Guido (*Greve in Chianti, località Lamole, Firenze*). Filetta has 19.8 acres (8 hectares) of specialized vines, plus a small amount in *coltura promiscua* planted at altitudes ranging from 1,640 to 1,970 feet (500 to 600 meters) above sea level. Their annual production averages about 40,000 to 53,000 bottles of Chianti Classico. This estate has a good reputation.

Fizzano. This could be the same as the Fattoria di Fizzano estate owned by **Bertolli**. The last wine we tasted from Fizzano, in 1980, was the rather disappointing '71 Riserva. Chianti Classico [0]

Fontevino (*Montalcino, località Camigliano, Siena*). Besides a Brunello they bottle a Chianti Colli Senesi.

Fontodi. See **Tenuta Agricola Fontodi**.

Fortezza di Tuopina (*Castellina in Chianti, Siena*). They have 68 acres (27.6 hectares) of vines and produce some 14,000 cases of Chianti Classico annually.

Fortilizio Il Colombaio. See **Villa Colombaio**.

Fossi (*Campiobbi, Firenze*). The Fossis—Duilio, Gianfranco, and Andrea—don't own any vineyards; they buy grapes and/or wine to produce 40,000 to 66,665 bottles of Chianti Classico a year. Fossi earned something of a reputation with its older wines. On a few different occasions we tasted the Fossi Chiantis from '58 through '77. On the two most recent occasions we found the Riservas of '59, '61, '74, and '77 good. Among the more recent wines, we found the Riservas of '82 and '83 good. Chianti Classico *

Frescobaldi (*Pelago, Rùfina, and Pontassieve, Firenze*). The Frescobaldis, who are among the largest landowners in Europe, own eight *poderi* in Chianti. The most important ones are listed below.

The other five are Castiglioni, Corte, Montagnana, Montecastello, and Valiano. They also have part interest in the Brunello di Montalcino estate of **Castelgiocondo,** which they manage.

At Tenuta di Poggio a Remole in Pontassieve, Frescobaldi produces 400,000 bottles of wine a year. It is a simple young Chianti meant to be drunk young and fresh. This is no sipping wine; it is for drinking in drafts—the younger and fresher, the better. Chianti Rùfina *

THE ESTATES OF FRESCOBALDI

Estate	In Vines		Total		Altitude in	
	Acres	Hectares	Acres	Hectares	Feet	Meters
Castello di Nipozzano	326	132	1,235	500	820–1,247	250–380
Tenuta di Poggio a Remole	136	55	790	320	820–1,300	250–396
Tenuta di Pomino	232	94	2,100	850	984–2,298	300–700

Their Chianti Rùfina Riserva is produced at the Castello di Nipozzano farm in Pelago. (They do not produce a *normale* Chianti Rùfina from Nipozzano.) About half the vineyards on the estate face south, the rest to the west or east. The Nipozzano Riserva is made from a blend of 80 percent sangiovese of the Nipozzano clone, 10 percent canaiolo, 5 percent trebbiano and malvasia, and 5 percent other varieties, including cabernet sauvignon, mammolo, and syrah. Fermentation, on the skins, lasts for seven days. The wine is then aged eighteen months to two years in oak casks; up to 30 percent of the wine is aged in *barrique*. Frescobaldi produces 360,000 to 400,000 bottles of this exceptionally fine Chianti each year.

The Nipozzano Riserva is known for its capacity to age, a reputation that is well deserved. In the spring of 1985 we had the pleasure of sharing a bottle of the '45 and '23 from the cellar of the castle at Nipozzano with Marchese Leonardo Frescobaldi and his fine enologist, Dott. Luciano Boarino. The '23 had coated the sides of the old blue-green blown-glass bottle with sheets of sediment like a Port crust, but the wine had retained a fine color as well as remarkable structure and flavor—an outstanding wine and a memorable experience. The very young '45 was also magnificent. And a few years ago we had an opportunity to taste the wonderful '34. Chianti Rùfina ****

The Montesodi Chianti Rùfina was first produced in 1974 from a special 30-acre (12-hectare) plot on the Nipozzano estate; of that, 4,850 bottles were produced. Today they produce 30,000 to 50,000 bottles a year. The thirty-five-year-old vines in the Montesodi vineyard are planted at an altitude of 1,150 feet (350 meters) above sea level and produce an average of no more than 320 gallons an acre (30 hectoliters a hectare). Thus the maximum potential annual production from the Monteosodi vineyard is 48,000 bottles of wine.

The '85 was made from 75 percent sangiovese of the Nipozzano clone, 10 percent canaiolo, 5 percent trebbiano and malvasia, and 10 percent cabernet sauvignon. The sangiovese is a special clone found here at Nipozzano. Montesodi is produced only in the better vintages. The wine is aged two to four years in small oak barrels; the '78 was given three months of *barrique* aging as well—15,570 bottles were produced. There was also a '79 (18,340 bottles), '81, '82 (18,000), '83 (47,600), and '86. Leonardo picks the '78 and '82 as the two best thus far. The '85 was fermented for ten days at temperatures between 77° and 82° Fahrenheit (25° and 28° centigrade). It spent a total of twelve days on the skins and was aged for twenty-two months in *barrique*. Montesodi is a richly flavored, intense, full-bodied, warm red wine. But as impressed as we are

with Montesodi, for us the sheer elegance and class of Nipozzano Riserva places it ahead. Chianti Rùfina *** +

The Frescobaldis also produce wines at Tenuta di Pomino, at one time in the Rùfina zone and now DOC in its own right. The white is made from a blend of chardonnay, pinot bianco, pinot grigio, and trebbiano. The grapes for the Riserva Il Benefizio are from a 57-acre (23-hectare) vineyard of that name planted at altitudes ranging from 1,970 to 2,300 feet (600 to 700 meters) above sea level. This wine is fermented in wood. They make 10,000 cases of the former and 5,000 of the latter. They also produce 9,000 cases of **Pomino Rosso**, made from a blend of 60 percent sangiovese, 20 percent of cabernet sauvignon and cabernet franc, and 10 percent each of merlot and pinot noir, plus 300 bottles of the very good Tenuta di Pomino Vin Santo.

Besides these wines and a Brunello and Rosso di Montalcino, the Frescobaldis produce a fairly wide range of other wines. This includes 70,000 cases of a simple Chianti from their own vineyards, 3,000 cases of Vergena Predicato del Selvante made from sauvignon blanc grapes grown at the Montalcino estate of Castelgiocondo, 25,000 of Frescobaldi Bianco, and 70,000 of Galestro, plus 10,000 cases of a Champagne-method sparkling brut from a 60-40 blend of chardonnay and pinot noir grapes grown in Trentino, and 2,500 to 3,333 cases of **Mormoreto Predicato di Bitùrica**, a cabernet sauvignon–based wine grown on the 47-acre (19-hectare) Mormoreto plot in the Nipozzano.

Chianti Rùfina: Castello di Nipozzano Riserva ****, Montesodi *** +, Tenuta di Poggio a Remole *

Frigeni Dott. Giulio (*San Gimignano, Siena*), 1960. Dott. Giulio Frigeni owns 37 acres (15 hectares) of vines in the Colli Senesi district, from which he produces 11,000 cases of wine a year, including Chianti Frigeni and Vernaccia di San Gimignano.

Gassini (*San Gimignano, Siena*). The Gassino family owns 39.5 acres (16 hectares) of vines in San Gimignano, 6.8 (2.8) planted for Chianti. Besides the four standard grapes for Chianti, they have colorino in their Chianti vineyards. They also produce the white Vernaccia di San Gimignano, and red and white *vino da tavola*.

Geografico. See **Agricoltori del Chianti Geografico**.

Giorgio Fico. The only wine we have tasted from this producer was the good '88 *normale*. Chianti Classico *

Giorgio Regni. See **Fattoria Valtellina**.

Gittori. See **Baccio da Gaiole**.

THE CHIANTI VINEYARDS OF GASSINI

| Vineyard | Acres | Hectares | Altitude in | | Year Planted | Average Number of Cases Per Year |
			Feet	Meters		
Il Vignone	2.13	0.86	722–820	220–250	1973	650
La Quercia	2.47	1.00	886	270	1968	750
Rigurdi	2.20	0.89	919	280	1966	690

Granducato, Poggibonsi del Consorzio Agrario Provinciale di Siena (*Poggibonsi, Siena*). Enopplio di Poggibonsi bottles some 55,000 cases a year of what is, based on our limited experience, a mediocre Chianti Classico. They have a total capacity of 1 million gallons (40,000 hectoliters), equivalent to 444,400 cases of wine. They also produce a Vino Nobile di Montepulciano that we've never tasted. Things seem to be looking up here; the '87 Chianti was rather good. Chianti Classico * −

Grignano (*Pontassieve, Firenze*). This 1,235-acre (500-hectare) estate has 104 acres (42 hectares) of vines in specialized cultivation and 50 (20) in *coltura promiscua*. Their annual production averages 10,000 cases. They are in the Chianti Rùfina production zone. Based on their good '87, we rate their Chianti Rùfina *.

Grignanello (*Castellina in Chianti, località La Piazza, Siena*). Grignanello has 22 acres (9 hectares) of vines, 40 percent planted in *coltura promiscua*. They produce some 63,000 bottles of Chianti Classico annually.

Il Campino Mondiglia (*Barberino Val d'Elsa, Firenze*). Primo Benelli owns 1.48 acres (0.6 hectare) planted in vines; this is up considerably from the 0.395 acre (0.16 hectare) he had planted in 1986. A scant 0.07413 acre (0.3 hectare) is in vines for Chianti Classico. The balance is located outside the Chianti Classico district. The vineyard, planted at an average altitude of 820 feet (250 meters) above sea level, consists of 80 percent sangiovese, 9 to 11 percent canaiolo, 3 to 4 percent trebbiano, and 6 to 7 percent malvasia. Some of the vines are trained in poplar trees. His vines yield about 2,666 bottles of wine a year, 1,000 of Chianti Classico. In 1983 he produced the equivalent of 1,520 bottles of Chianti Classico, but bottled only 1,000, and in 1985, 960. His first wine sold with a label from here was from the 1974 vintage. His *cantina* consists of two oak casks—one of 198 gallons (7.5 hectoliters), the other 132 (5)—and cement vats. He ages his Classico one year in cement and two in oak. His 1983, for example, was bottled on December 1, 1986. Although he is entitled to label his wine as *riserva*, at least by the length of time he ages it, he chooses not to. We have really liked both of the Benelli wines we have tasted, the '83 and '85. Chianti Classico ** +

Il Capitano. See *Fattoria Il Capitano.*

Il Guerrino (*Montefioralle, Greve in Chianti, Firenze*). This *azienda* owns 27.9 acres (11.3 hectares) of Chianti Classico vineyards, 9.4 (3.8) in monoculture and 18.5 (7.5) mixed. From these vines, planted at an average altitude of 985 feet (300 meters) above sea level, they produce some 77,330 bottles of Chianti a year. We've had limited experience with these wines. The last bottle we tasted, in 1979, was their '77, and many things have happened in Toscana since then. Consequently, we think it best to hold off rating them. Chianti Classico [0]

Il Palaggio. Their '85 Chianti Classico was good. Chianti Classico *

Il Pantano Azienda Agricola (*Chianciano Terme, Siena*). Pantano owns 27 acres (11 hectares) from which it produces a Vino Nobile and a Chianti.

Il Paradiso. See *Fattoria Il Paradiso.*

Il Poggiolino (*Sambuca Val di Pesa, Firenze*). Carlo Pacini owns this 49-acre (20-hectare) estate and its 19.8 acres (8 hectares) of vines, some 14.8 (6) of which are planted for Chianti Classico. The vineyards—composed of 90 percent sangiovese, 5 percent canaiolo, and 5 percent white grapes—are planted at altitudes ranging between 820 and 985 feet (250 and 300 meters) above sea level. Average annual production of Chianti Classico is 42,000 bottles. Thus far we have found their wines good, including the *riserve* of '83, '85, and the *normali* of '85 and '86. Chianti Classico *

Il Poggiolo (*Carmignano, Firenze*). See *Villa Il Poggiolo.*

Il Poggiolo (*Monteriggioni, località Poggiolo, Siena*), 1977. The Bonfio family owns 31.6 acres (12.8 hectares) of vines, 21.6 (8.8) in the Il Poggiolo vineyard and 10 (4) in Le Portine. The vines in Il Poggiolo, facing south, are planted at an average altitude of 985 feet (300 meters) above sea level. Those in Le Portine, facing east to west, are at 1,230 feet (375 meters). They have produced their Il Poggiolo Chianti Colli Senesi since 1977, the Le Portine since 1980. The Bonfios produce an average of about 64,000 bottles of wine annually, 50,000 from Il Poggiolo and 14,000 from Le Portine. They also produce a Proprietor's Reserve in their best vintages from a blend of grapes from the two vineyards. Thus far they have made this Chianti in 1982, 1985, and 1988. Bonfio also rates 1983 and 1981 as excellent; 1980, 1978, and 1977 as very good; and 1979 as good. Giorgio Grai consults here. Our own tastings of the Bonfio wines demonstrate that the wines are getting better and better. This is not surprising considering the seriousness of this producer. Chianti Colli Senesi ** +

Il Villino (*Castellina in Chianti, Siena*). Il Villino owns 7.2 acres (2.9 hectares) of vines, 1 (0.4) in *coltura promiscua*. The vines are planted at altitudes ranging between 1,310 and 1,475 feet (400 and 450 meters) above sea level. Their annual production of Chianti Classico averages 1,667 cases.

Isabella de'Medici (*La Volpaia, Radda in Chianti, Siena*). This *casa vinicola* buys grapes and/or wine to produce over 7,500 cases of really mediocre Chianti Classico a year. They also sell a pretty poor Brunello. We haven't seen any of their wines in a few years. Chianti Classico 0

Isole e Olena (*Barberino Val d'Elsa, Firenze*), 1950. The de Marchi family of Piemonte are the owners of this 717-acre (290-hectare) property, which includes the fourteenth-century village of Olena and the eighteenth-century Isole estate. The de Marchi family also own the Villa Sperino property in Lessona. Paolo told us that he would like someday to restart the winemaking there. We look forward to tasting those wines.

They replanted the Isole e Olena vineyards between 1967 and 1972. Today there are 89 acres (36 hectares) under vines, 63.2 (25.6) for Chianti Classico. These vines are planted at an average altitude of 1,265 feet (385 meters) above sea level. A few years ago the composition of the vineyards was 88 percent sangiovese, 10 percent canaiolo, and 2 percent white grapes. They have since planted syrah, cabernet sauvignon, and chardonnay.

Isole e Olena bottled its first wine sold under this label from the 1969 vintage. Previously it had sold much of its wine to Antinori; it still sells a portion to that firm and to Ruffino. The average annual production at Isole is 20,000 cases; this includes 14,220 cases of Chianti Classico, 1,500 of the *barrique*-aged Sangiovese *Cepparello*, 100 cases of a truly splendid *vin santo*, plus a white, a rosé, and a fresh, young red. And they also do a *barrique*-aged Chardonnay, a Cabernet Sauvignon, and a Syrah.

Since 1976 the estate has been run by Dott. Paolo de Marchi, who is also the enologist. The Isole Chianti Classico is made from 88 percent sangiovese, 10 percent canaiolo, and 2 percent white grapes. The must is fermented in stainless steel and the wine is aged in tanks, casks of chestnut and oak, and *barriques*, in about equal distribution. Currently one-third of their casks are chestnut. De Marchi doesn't want a lot of wood character in the wine; he respects the variety and seeks to maintain its personality. He has been using *barriques* since the 1978 vintage.

At the fine vertical tasting de Marchi set up at the estate in the spring of 1985, we were quite impressed with the style, balance, class, and consistency of the wines. We found his '82 best of all. The '79 and '77 were also quite fine, as were his '83, '81, '80, and '78. The wines here have improved considerably since Paolo's arrival. The older vintages reflect a different style or, shall we say, lack of it. Of the more recent wines tasted, we heartily recommend the excellent '83 Riserva and '85 *normale*, and the very good '84, '86, '87, and '88 *normali*. De Marchi has made this estate one of the most consistent in the zone. Chianti Classico ***

L'Aia (*Radda in Chianti*, località *La Croce, Siena*), *1980*. Milano engineers Angelo and Ugo Contrino own this estate and its 33 acres (13.5 hectares) of vines. These vineyards, planted at altitudes ranging between 1,640 and 1,805 feet (500 and 550 meters) above sea level, face south to southeast. The composition of the vineyards is 85 percent sangiovese, 10 percent canaiolo, and 5 percent trebbiano. They have three individual vineyards: L'Aia, Barlettaio, and Val delle Corti. Their annual production is about 4,400 cases of wine. They made a good '87. Chianti Classico *

La Brancaia (*Castellina in Chianti*, località *La Brancaia, Siena*). This 27-acre (11-hectare) estate, owned by Bruno and Brigitet Widmer, bottles its wine at Castello di Fonterutoli. They own 14.8 acres (6 hectares) of vines, two-thirds for Chianti Classico, planted at an altitude averaging 1,150 feet (350 meters) above sea level. Their annual production of Chianti Classico cannot exceed 2,333 cases. The only wine we've tasted from La Brancaia was the rather good '87. Chianti Classico *

La Bricola (*Sambuca Val di Pesa, Firenze*). Andrea Sestini, who owns **Fattoria Fermignano, "Frimaio"** in San Donato in Poggio, is the proprietor of this 7.4-acre (3-hectare) estate and its 4.4 acres (1.8 hectares) of vineyards. Like the Frimaio estate, he has owned this property since 1985. He produces some 13,000 bottles of La Bricola Chianti Classico annually. He sells this wine with the Vendenniaio label. The '88 was good. Chianti Classico * +

La Capraia (*Castellina in Chianti, Siena*). La Capraia owns 116 acres (47 hectares) of vines planted at an average altitude of 1,640 feet (500 meters) above sea level. They produce some 27,500 cases of Chianti Classico a year.

La Castellina (*Castellina in Chianti, Siena*). The 39 acres (15.7 hectares) of vines here produce approximately 9,150 cases of Chianti Classico annually.

La Cerreta (*Gaiole in Chianti, Siena*). This *cantina sociale* controls 114 acres (46 hectares) of vines. Their average annual production is about 33,000 cases of wine. They belong to the **Storiche Cantine**. We haven't tasted any of the La Cerreta wines, but considering their association with Storiche, our expectations would not be high.

La Ginestra (*Greve in Chianti, Firenze*). La Ginestra produces at least three different regional Chiantis as well as a *vino da tavola rosso dei colli della toscana centrale*.

La Lellera. See **Castello Vicchiomaggio**.

La Loggia. See **Fattoria La Loggia**.

La Madonnina (*Chiocchio, Firenze*). F.lli Triacca of the Valtellina owns this estate and its 151.5 acres (61.3 hectares) of vines. These vines, planted at an average altitude of 855 feet (260 meters) above sea level, yield some 35,775 cases of Chianti Classico a year. We found the '82 Riserva disappointing and the '87 also, but then the vintage wasn't special either. Chianti Classico +

La Montanina (*Monti di Sotto, Siena*). La Montanina has 4.7 acres (1.9 hectares) of vines which yield some 1,110 cases of Chianti Classico annually. More than one-quarter of those vines are in mixed cultivation.

La Pagliaia. See **Villa La Pagliaia**.

La Pesanella. See **Castello di Monterinaldi**.

La Querce (Pinzuti Pino) (*Madonna della Querce, Siena*), *1970*. Lido Pinzi Pinzuti, of the Montepulciano production zone, has 25 acres (10 hectares) on his La Querce farm, 3.7 (1.5) planted for Chianti.

La Quercia. See **Cappelli Giovanni**.

La Ripa. See **Fattoria La Ripa**.

La Sala (*San Casciano Val di Pesa, Firenze*). The 54-acre (22-hectare) La Sala estate has 37 acres (15 hectares) of vines, 29.7 (12) planted for Chianti Classico. They produce up to 7,000 cases of this wine annually. Our experience thus far has been limited to the agreeable '88. Chianti Classico * −

Lamole di Lamole. See **Fattoria Pile e Lamole**.

Le Chiantigiane (*Sambuca Val di Pesa*, località *Ponte Nuovo, Tavarnelle Val di Pesa, Firenze*), *1967*. Le Chiantigiane is an association of ten *cantine sociali*. They have the capacity to produce and age some 265,000 gallons (10,000 hectoliters) of wine, equivalent to 110,000 cases. The co-op's members own 358 acres (145 hectares) of Chianti Classico vineyards from which they are authorized to produce approximately 85,000 cases of DOCG wine per year. It's been a while since we tasted their Chianti Classico; those bottles we did were drinkable, though not much more than that. They sell their Chianti Classico under the Chiantigiane and Santa Trinita labels. We can recommend the '88 Santa Trinita, but not the '88 Chiantigiane. Chianti Classico: Chiantigiane 0, Santa Trinita * +

Le Coste. The most recent wines we have tasted from Le Coste were the '82 and '83 in April 1985. They were unimpressive and uninteresting. Chianti Rùfina 0

Le Grifiere (*Castellina in Chianti, località Gretole, Siena*). This 650-acre (263-hectare) estate has 294 acres (119 hectares) of vineyards, 230 (93) for Chianti Classico. They are allowed to produce up to 54,215 cases of Chianti Classico a year. Our only experience here was with the disappointing Riserva from the very fine 1983 vintage. Chianti Classico 0

Le Lame (*San Casciano Val di Pesa, Firenze*). This *fattoria* produces 4,400 cases of Chianti Classico a year from their 19 acres (7.7 hectares) of vines. Their Vigna di Sorripa Riserva is made from the grapes of that vineyard only.

Le Masse di San Leolino (*Panzano in Chianti, Firenze*). Wine production at this estate was mentioned in the property census of 1427. In 1972, Norman Bain bought the Le Masse property of 34.6 acres (14 hectares). Today Bain has 7.7 acres (3.1 hectares) of vines, 6.4 (2.6) for Chianti Classico, planted at an average altitude of 1,575 feet (480 meters) above sea level. He has planted the maximum amount of sangiovese allowed by law, ditto of canaiolo, and the minimum amount of trebbiano and malvasia. The soil is *galestro*.

His first crop, from the 1977 vintage, was sold off. In 1978, for the first time, he produced wine here, selling it in bulk. In the following year he produced wine again, and again he sold it in bulk. He bottled his first wine from the 1980 vintage. Before the advent of DOCG Bain produced some 2,000 cases of wine annually. Since then his yearly production of Chianti Classico has averaged about 1,500 cases. He bottled about 1,665 cases each year between 1980 and 1983, 720 in 1984, and 1,500 in 1985. In 1980 two-thirds of his bottled wine was sold as *riserva*, 80 percent in 1981, nearly all of the '82 and '83 production, and none of the '84. The only essential difference between the *normale* and the *riserva* is that the latter is aged longer, between one and a half and two years in wood. He uses concentrated must made from his own grapes by **Villa Cafaggio** for the *governo*. Franco Bernabei consults here.

In the past we found Bain's wines to be quite good. The '85 *normale* and Riserva are very good Chianti Classicos. Since then there seems to have been some slippage. The more recent vintages of the *normale* were, while still good, disappointing. Chianti Classico: *normale* *, Riserva **

Le Miccine (*Gaiole in Chianti, località Le Miccine, Siena*). Half of the acreage on this 32-acre (13-hectare) farm is planted in vines, 12 acres (4.8 hectares) for Chianti Classico. They use only organic fertilizer, from sheep, in the vineyards. They have an annual production equivalent to 4,400 cases of Chianti Classico, but bottle only about 20 percent of it (900 cases).

Le Piazze (*Castellina in Chianti, Siena*). This winery has a capacity of 309,000 gallons (11,700 hectoliters), equivalent to 130,000 cases of wine.

Le Pici. See **Fattoria Le Pici.**

Lo Spugnaccio (*San Gusmè, località Santa Chiara, Siena*), 1976. Sergio Marchetti owns this estate and its 24.7 acres (10 hectares) of vines. The vines, planted at 1,194 feet (364 meters) above sea level, face southeast. They produce 4,445 cases of Chianti Classico, 1,090 of Bianco Val d'Arbia, and 890 of *vino da tavola*.

Luca della Robbia (*Panzano in Chianti, Firenze*). See **Cennatoio.**

Machiavelli. See **Conti Serristori.**

Macia (*Vagliagli, località Macia, Cononica, and Cerreto, Siena*). Macia owns 7.4 acres (3 hectares) of vines, one-third in *coltura promiscua*. This yields nearly 21,000 bottles of Chianti Classico annually.

Marchese de' Frescobaldi. See **Frescobaldi.**

Marchesi L. e P. Antinori (*San Casciano Val di Pesa, Firenze*), *1895*. This winemaking family has been producing wine since at least the tenth century. According to family records the Antinoris made wine at Castello di Combiate, near Croci di Calenzano in the Florentine countryside. They brought their winemaking skills to Firenze when they moved there at the beginning on the thirteenth century. Officially, the family has been making wine since 1385. The current firm of Marchesi L. e P. Antinori was founded more recently, however. Brothers Ludovico and Piero Antinori, and their sister's husband, Guglielmo Guerrini, founded the firm toward the latter part of the nineteenth century. The San Casciano cellars were built in 1890. Today Piero Antinori owns 51 percent, his brother, Ludovico, 1 percent, with the remaining 48 percent owned by the English firm of Whitbread.

Antinori owns five estates, three wineries, and more than 5,000 acres (2,000 hectares) of land. Their 1,450-acre (600-hectare) Santa Cristina estate has 370 acres (150 hectares) under vines. This farm includes the famed Tignanello and Solaia plots. Their other vineyard estates, *tenute,* in the Chianti Classico zone are I Pèppoli, which they bought in 1985 from the Saccardi family, and Badia a Passignano. The 370-acre (150-hectare) I Pèppoli vineyard, at one time known as Villa Terciona, currently has 136 acres (55 hectares) under vines; they plan to plant an additional 50 (20). The Badia a Passignano estate has 86.5 acres (35 hectares) under vines. They also own the 1,730-acre (700-hectare) Tenuta Belvedere di Bolghieri in Maremma on the seacoast and the 1,200-acre (485-hectare) Castello della Sala estate outside Orvieto. The former estate has 148 acres (60 hectares) under vines, the latter 321 (130). The Antinoris, in partnership with Bollinger and Whitbread, own the Atlas Peak Vineyard in Napa Valley, and recently they acquired controlling interest in the Prunotto winery in the Langhe.

On average, 25 to 30 percent of Antinori's production of 900,000 cases of wine a year comes from their own estates, the rest from outside growers. They produce about 360,000 cases of Chianti Classico. They also produce 23,000 cases of the sangiovese-cabernet blend **Tignanello,** 4,000 of the cabernet-based **Solàia,** the *vino da tavola rosso* **Santa Cristina**, five white wines including three from their Castello della Sala property in Umbria—Orvieto; Borro della Sala, a sauvignon blanc–pinot bianco–procanico blend; and Cervaro della Sala, a chardonnay-grechetto blend—and two from Toscana—Galestro and Villa Antinori Bianco—plus a Champagne-method Extra Brut Spumante and a *vin santo*.

Antinori doesn't report the figures for the non–estate bottled Santa Cristina. Nearly half of their production is exported. Their Chianti Classicos are made from sangiovese, canaiolo, trebbiano, and malvasia grapes, plus cabernet—both sauvignon and franc—in their *riserva*. They have included cabernet in their *riserva* since 1974 or 1975. We were told a few years ago that the '74 contained

THE ESTATE-BOTTLED WINES OF MARCHESI L. e P. ANTINORI

Wine	First Vintage	Average Number of Cases Per Year
Badia a Passignano	1988	Not yet released
Borro della Sala	1985	13,000
Cervaro della Sala	1985	5,000
Pèppoli	1985	17,000
Scalabrone	1984	8,000
Solaia	1978	4,000
Tignanello	1971	23,000
Tenuta Marchese Antinori	1974	12,000

3 or 4 percent cabernet; more recently they told us the '75 was the first vintage with cabernet in the blend, some 2 to 3 percent.

Antinori produces three Chianti Classicos. At one time Santa Cristina was a *normale* Chianti Classico; today it is a *vino da tavola*. This simple red is meant to be drunk young. It's dependable, if no more. A portion of the Santa Cristina is aged for one year in oak casks.

The I Pèppoli estate is located near Mercatale Val di Pesa. Records indicate that wine was produced here from the beginning of the fourteenth century. The Antinoris first produced a Chianti Classico from here in 1985. The vines, facing south and west, are planted on hills composed of limestone soil. The breakdown is 80 percent sangiovese, 9 percent canaiolo nero, and 4 percent trebbiano and malvasia; the remaining 7 percent is made up of what they define as complementary varieties. The wine is made from a blend of 90 percent sangiovese, 5 percent canaiolo, and 5 percent of other, unspecified varieties. It is aged for nine months in older, more traditional, 1,320- to 1,453-gallon (50- to 55-hectoliter) Slavonian oak casks, instead of the new, more faddish *barrique*. It is made to be drunk while young and fresh. This wine is best within two to three years of the vintage, though they say it will age well for five years. Thus far, based on the two vintages we've tasted, it is a good example of that style of Chianti Classico.

The Antinoris' *riserve* are sold under the Villa Antinori label. These wines are fermented longer—for fourteen instead of nine to twelve days as is the case with the Santa Cristina—to extract more color, flavor, and substance. The *riserva* is aged for about sixteen months in a combination of *barriques* and 1,320-gallon (50-hectoliter) casks of Slavonian oak, some of which is new wood. The casks are at most five to six years old. Less than 50 percent of the wine is aged in small barrels.

The Tenuta Marchese Antinori is their top Chianti. A few years ago it was labeled as Villa Antinori Riserva Marchese. We were told the first time we went to the winery, in May 1982, that this wine was exactly the same as the Villa Antinori Riserva except that it had more bottle age. Perhaps some changes have been made; on our most recent visit we were told that it is a different wine. The *uvaggio* is not the same, nor is the wood aging. For the Riserva Marchese, over 50 percent of the wine goes into *barrique*. The first vintage to be given a signficant period in small barrels was the 1977; 65 percent of that wine was aged in *barrique*.

Giacomo Tachis, enologist at Antinori since 1961, is given a lot of credit for many of Antinori's new wines, such as Tignanello and Solaia.

For a company this size, the quality of the Antinori Chiantis is not bad (not that a small production is any assurance of high quality). The Villa Antinori Riserva is a good Chianti Classico, although not top level. Among the 1970s we found the '75 the best, although there was some variability among bottles. The Villa Antinori Riserva Marchese has been somewhat more consistent, though, to our tastes, not necessarily a better wine. We preferred the regular '77 Riserva, for example. The '79 is a good wine and one that shows promise.

Among the older vintages, we remember the '58 Riserva very well, truly a fine wine. The '64, too, was very good, though the last one we tasted in 1983 was fading. The '67 also gave much pleasure in its time; when last tasted in 1983 it too was getting a bit old. The '70 was quite good, as was the '71 at one time, but somehow these wines just didn't measure up to the vintage. It seems that the '67 was the last first-rate Chianti Classico the Antinoris made for some time, until the 1975 vintage. Of more recent vintages tasted, we found the Villa Antinori Riservas of '81, '82, '85, and '86, and the '81 Riserva Marchese to be good, even very good wines. And we were rather impressed with recent vintages of the Tenuta Marchese Riserva and with the unreleased Badia a Passignano Chianti Classico that we tasted in November 1988. This last Chianti Classico was made from a blend of 90 percent sangiovese and 2 to 5 percent cabernet sauvignon, with the balance being canaiolo.

While it could be argued that the Antinoris make better wines today than they used to, we don't care that much for cabernet in our Chianti. The percentage, as they point out, is not high, but the character of the wine is thrown off—perhaps their cabernet is too aggressive, perhaps the sangiovese they use is deficient in character. As the wine ages it takes on more of a pronounced herbaceous, weedy quality. They say the cabernet adds structure. We can't see that the sangiovese is a grape that lacks structure; look at Monsanto Il Poggio, **Le Pergole Torte**, and Badia **Sangioveto di Coltibuono** for just three fine examples. No, we like the cabernet too, but when we feel like drinking cabernet, we drink a Cabernet, not a Chianti. Chianti Classico: Badia a Passignano ** +, Pèppoli **, Riserva Marchese ** −, Tenuta Marchese Riserva **, Villa Antinori Riserva ** −

Marcialla (*Barberino Val d'Elsa, Firenze*), *1860.* Owner Giovanni Passaponti cultivates 14.8 acres (6 hectares) of vines evenly divided between the vineyards of Le Fate and Montaione. He produces some 4,555 cases of wine annually, of which 1,778 are Chianti Colli Fiorentini, 1,111 of a white wine, and 1,667 of a *vino da tavola rosso.*

Matriolo (*San Donato in Poggio, Firenze*). Matriolo owns 22 acres (8.9 hectares) of vines at an altitude of 1,310 feet (400 meters) above sea level and produces some 5,100 cases of Chianti Classico annually.

Mazzoni. We have tasted this Chianti Classico only once, the unimpressive '77, in 1979. It was bottled by the very fine Chianti Classico producer **Villa Cafaggio**. They also bottled a '78. Stefano Farkas of Villa Cafaggio told us that he never made the wine, he only bottled it.

Melazzano (*Greve in Chianti, Firenze*). This Chianti Classico estate has 44 acres (17.7 hectares), including 6.7 (2.7) in mixed culture, of vines planted at an average altitude of 490 feet (150 meters) above sea level. They produce up to 10,385 cases of Chianti Classico a year.

Melini (*Poggibonsi*, località *Gaggiano, Siena*), *1705*. Melini, one of the largest producers of Chianti Classico, is owned by Gruppo Italiano Vini. Gruppo Italiano Vini (GIV) was created in 1986 when eight cooperative wineries banded together and bought the *cantine* and vineyards owned by Winefood, a subsidiary of the Swiss conglomerate Crosse & Blackwell. The wineries are run independently of each other. GIV handles the marketing. The total output of the ten or so wineries amounts to 7 million cases of wine a year; more than half of that is red. Frascati producer Fontana Candida is the largest firm, followed next by Melini and Lamberti of the Verona area. The other *cantine* are Luigi Calissano in Piemonte, Negri and Pelizatti in the Valtellina, Vaja in Bolzano, Santi in Verona, Conti Serristori and Machiavelli in the Chianti Classico zone, D'Ambra in Campania, Umani Ronchi in Marches, and Bigi in Orvieto. GIV owns the Folonari brand as well.

Melini has 1,406 acres (569 hectares) and a number of *fattorie*. Just over 20 percent of their acreage, or 312 acres (126 hectares), is planted for Chianti Classico. The composition of those vineyards is 85 percent sangiovese, 10 percent canaiolo, and 5 percent white grapes. Melini has four separate cellars that, combined, process 1,100 tons (10,000 quintali) of grapes.

Melini has two wineries, one in Gaggiano in the Chianti Classico zone, and the second in San Gimignano. These cellars have a storage capacity of 2.6 million gallons (100,000 hectoliters) of wine. The one in Gaggiano has a Limousin oak–aging facility with a capacity of 317,040 gallons (12,000 hectoliters). About 35 percent of their annual production is of Chianti Classico (approximately 7 million bottles), another 25 to 27 percent is the regional Chianti Borghi d'Elsa, 10 to 12 percent are some special reds like

the *barrique*-aged, sangiovese-cabernet sauvignon **I Coltri**, a Brunello di Montalcino, and a Vino Nobile di Montepulciano; the balance of production consists of the white Orvieto, Vernaccia di San Gimignano, and Lacrima d'Arno, and a Rosato.

Melini makes five special Chianti Classicos: the *normale* Isassi, the Riserva Laborel, and three single-vineyard *riserve*—Granaio, La Selvanella, and Terrarossa.

Their Borghi d'Elsa Chianti is made from a blend of 80 percent sangiovese, 10 percent canaiolo, and 10 percent trebbiano toscano and malvasia del chianti. The name comes from where the grapes are grown, the boroughs of the Elsa Valley, Monteriggioni, Colle, S. Gimignano, and Certaldo. This Chianti is aged for a minimum of one year in Slavonian oak casks.

Isassi Chianti Classico derives its name from the calcareous stones, *isassi,* found in the Chianti Classico district. This Chianti is made from a blend of 85 percent sangiovese, 10 percent canaiolo nero, and 5 percent trebbiano toscano and malvasia del chianti. Thirty percent of the grapes are from vineyards in the province of Firenze and 70 percent are from Siena. The wine spends more than one year in casks of Limousin oak.

Melini's Laborel Chianti Classico Riserva, named for the company's founder, Adolfo Laborel Melini, who invented the tempered *fiasco*, a bottle that, because it was strong enough to sustain the pressure of a cork, could be shipped to international markets without fear of breakage. This helped create an international market for Chianti Classico. Prior to his invention the fragility of the Chianti bottles made it risky to ship. His namesake is made from a blend of 90 percent sangiovese, 5 percent canaiolo, and 5 percent trebbiano toscano and malvasia del chianti. Thirty percent of the grapes come from vineyards in the province of Firenze and 70 percent are from Siena. Thirty percent of the wine is *barrique*-aged for six months. The wine spends three years in oak casks. This wine was first made in 1983.

Vigneti La Selvanella Chianti Classico Riserva is the product of grapes grown in the Melini vineyard located in Lucarelli and Radda. They produce more than 5,000 cases of this wine a year. The La Selvanella vineyard is planted at an average altitude of 1,133 feet (350 meters) above sea level.

Our experience with the Melini wines goes back many years. We have found their wines, by and large, quite reliable and good. Their

THE CHIANTI CLASSICO VINEYARDS OF MELINI

| Fattoria | Location | *Total* | | *For DOCG Wine* | |
		Acres	Hectares	Acres	Hectares
Granaio*	Castellina	36.67	14.84	32.96	13.34
La Selvanella*	Radda	352.87	142.80	107.47	43.49
San Lorenzo	Castellina	687.36	278.16	87.33	35.34
Terrarossa*	Castellina	328.93	133.11	84.71	34.38
Total		1,405.83	568.91	312.47	126.45

* Bottled separately

Riserva Vigneti La Selvanella often represents good value as well as being a very good Chianti Classico. We found the '80 good, and the '81, '82, '85, and '86 all very good. The '82 Riserva Vigneti Granaio was disappointing, the '85 *normale* good, and the '87 Terrarossa, '85 Riserva Laborel, and '88 Isassi all very good. Chianti: Borghi d'Elsa *, Chianti Classico: *normale* *, Riserva ** −, Riserva Isassi * +, Riserva Laborel **, Riserva Granaio **, Riserva La Selvanella ** +, Riserva Terrarossa **

Mezzuola (*Greve in Chianti, Firenze*). Their 6.4 acres (2.6 hectares) of vines planted for Chianti Classico yield some 18,000 bottles of wine a year. Mario Cortevesio is the consulting enologist.

Miscianello Tomarecchio (*Vagliagli, Siena*). Miscianello Tomarecchio has 11 acres (4.4 hectares) planted for Chianti Classico which yield some 2,545 cases of wine a year.

Monsanto. See **Fattoria Monsanto**.

Montagliari. See **Cappelli Giovanni**.

Montagliari e Castellinuzza. See **Cappelli Giovanni**.

Monte Vertine (*Radda in Chianti, Siena*), *1967*. Sergio Manetti, the proprietor of this estate, has 18.5 acres (7.5 hectares) of vines planted at an average altitude of 1,395 feet (425 meters) above sea level.

Manetti, assisted by Klaus Reimitz, produces 45,000 bottles of wine a year. Until recently he produced two Chianti Classicos, a *normale* and *riserva*. The *normale* was aged for one and half years in oak casks, the *riserva* three years. No white grapes were used in either wine, although at one time it was made with 80 percent sangiovese, 15 percent canaiolo, and 5 percent malvasia and trebbiano. Besides dropping out of the Consorzio del Gallo Nero, Manetti dropped out of the DOCG. Today all of his wines fly by their own colors as **Monte Vertine Rosso**, *vino da tavola*.

The first Chianti Classico produced here was the 1971; the first *riserva* was from the 1974 vintage. Manetti felt that his best Chianti Classico was the '79. We were impressed with it ourselves, the *riserva* especially. The '82, '81, and '80 were also quite good. The last Chianti Classico we saw with the Monte Vertine label was the '82.

Manetti produces two crus: **Il Sodaccio**, from a 4.7-acre (1.9-hectare) plot, and **Le Pergole Torte**, from the 7.9-acre (3.2-hectare) vineyard of that name. He also makes a very fine white wine labeled "M." This quite atypical trebbiano-malvasia blend was first produced in 1982. Chianti Classico **

Montelupo (*Castellina in Chianti, località Montelupo, Siena*). The Mazza brothers acquired the Montelupo estate in 1960. Today they have 86.4 acres (35 hectares) of vines planted at 985 feet (300 meters) above sea level. They produce some 20,000 bottles of wine annually.

Montemaggio (*Radda in Chianti, Siena*). This *azienda* has 37 acres (15 hectares) of vines, 31 (12.5) for Chianti Classico, planted at altitudes ranging from 1,475 to 1,740 feet (450 to 530 meters) above sea level. They produce some 7,500 cases of Monte Maggio Chianti Classico a year from their own vines, plus 4,000 cases of Castello di Radda made from purchased grapes. Montemaggio ferments its wines in stainless steel tanks and ages them in old chest-

nut casks. The '83 Castello di Radda, from that outstanding vintage, was not very good. The Monte Maggio Chianti Classicos were tasted in April 1985—the '83, '82, and '79—were equally unremarkable. Considering that they now use the consulting services of enologist Vittorio Fore they are probably worth watching. For now, Chianti Classico: Castello di Radda 0, Monte Maggio 0

Montepaldi, Marchese Corsini. We haven't seen this Chianti Classico since the '76, which we tasted in 1979.

Monteraponi (*Radda in Chianti*, località *Monteraponi, Siena*). Monteraponi farms 22.5 acres (9 hectares) of vines, some 30 percent planted in *coltura promiscua*. The vineyards are planted, on average, at an altitude of 1,475 feet (450 meters) above sea level. From those vines they produce 5,345 cases of Chianti Classico annually.

Monteropoli. The only Chianti Classico that we've tasted from Monteropoli was from the unexciting 1987 vintage. Chianti Classico [0]

Montessassi (*Castellina in Chianti, Siena*). This estate has 32 acres (13 hectares) of vines planted at an altitude of 1,310 feet (400 meters) above sea level. The vines have a south to southwestern exposure. Some 10 percent of the vines are in mixed culture. Their annual production amounts to some 4,445 cases of Chianti Classico.

Montesodi. See **Frescobaldi**.

Monti Verdi, or **Montiverdi**. See **Fattoria Montiverdi**.

Monticelli. Our experience here is limited to the '81 Monticelli. While it was nothing special, it was drinkable. This wine is produced by **Storiche Cantine** member Viticola Toscana, who also own Castello di Meleto. The '81 tasted in 1985 was agreeable! Chianti Classico* −

Montoro (*Greve in Chianti, Firenze*). Principessa Sobilia Palmieri Nuti in Carafa di Roccella has 6.9 acres (2.8 hectares) of vines, part in *coltura promiscua*, on her Montoro estate, from which she produces, at most, 18,000 bottles of a highly regarded Chianti Classico. In 1986 we visited the estate and tasted from cask a good '84 and a difficult to assess '85. Based on that one experience we give her Chianti Classico a tentative*.

Montoro e Selvole (*Greve in Chianti, Firenze*). They have nearly 5 acres (2 hectares) of vines and produce 1,100 cases of Chianti Classico yearly.

Notorius, La Colombaia (*Chiocchio, Firenze*). This estate has nearly 41 acres (16.5 hectares) of vines from which they produce 9,600 cases of Chianti Classico annually.

Nozzole. See **Tenuta di Nozzole**.

Oliviera (*Vagliagli, Siena*). Oliviera has 8 acres (3.3 hectares) of vines planted at an average altitude of 1,640 feet (500 meters) above sea level. They have an annual production of 1,710 cases of a Chianti Classico that we've never met.

Pagliarese. See **Fattoria dei Pagliarese**.

Pagnana (*Rignano sull'Arno, Firenze*). This 630-acre (255-hectare) Colli Fiorentini estate has 172 acres (70 hectares) of vines in specialized cultivation and 17.2 (7) mixed. They produce between 16,500 ad 22,000 bottles of wine a year. Their Chiantis can be quite agreeable. Chianti Colli Fiorentini *

Pagni Casa Vinicola (*Castelnuovo Berardenga, Siena*). The winery of this negotiant operation has a capacity of 264,000 gallons (10,000 hectoliters). Among their wines is a Chianti Classico.

Palazzo al Bosco (*La Romala, Firenze*). This estate, located in the San Casciano district in the northwestern part of the Classico zone, is owned by Giovanna Querci, who acquired it in 1983. She has 14.6 acres (5.9 hectares) of vines from which she produces 2,450 cases of wine annually, all of it Chianti Classico. At one time the Palazzo al Bosco Classico was good and reliable. We enjoyed many bottles of that Classico in the vintages from the late 1950s through the end of the 1970s. We have rarely seen them since. In fact, the last Chianti Classico we tasted from Palazzo al Bosco was the '79. Chianti Classico [**]

Paneretta (*Barberino Val d'Elsa*). This estate has 28 acres (11.4 hectares) of vines, over 10 percent in mixed cultivation. They produce some 6,645 cases of Chianti Classico a year.

Paola Matta. See **Castello Vicchiomaggio.**

Pasolini dall'Onda Borghese Impresa Agricola (*Imola, Bologna*), *1760; (Barberino Val d'Elsa, Firenze), 1500.* Pasolini has 148 acres (60 hectares) in Barberino Val d'Elsa; not all of them are planted. They produce 40,000 to 45,000 cases of wine a year, including a Chianti Colli Fiorentini *normale* and Riserva. These are reliable wines and generally represent quite good quality. Though the estate is in the Colli Fiorentini zone, the wines, until recently, were sold simply as Chianti, without a more specific denomination. Today they use the Colli Fiorentini denomination. Pasolini also has 104 acres (42 hectares) in Emilia-Romagna from which it produces 33,000 to 40,000 cases of wine a year, including Sangiovese, Trebbiano, and Albana di Romagna. Chianti Colli Fiorentini **

Petriolo (*Rignano sull'Arno, Firenze*). The 346-acre (140-hectare) Petriolo farm has 153 acres (62 hectares) of vineyards, 62 (25) of which are in mixed cultivation. They produce some 22,000 cases of wine a year.

Pian d'Albola (*Radda in Chianti, Siena*). This *fattoria* has 69 acres (28 hectares) of vines from which they produce about 22,000 cases of Chianti Classico a year. Not having tasted any Pian d'Albola Chianti Classicos since 1981 when we had the '77, we decided it best to reserve judgment. Chianti Classico [0]

Pian Del Doccio e Pile di Sotto (*Lamole, Greve in Chianti, Firenze*). Ugo Gianni has owned this estate since 1972. He has 11.4 acres (4.6 hectares) of vines planted at 1,705 feet (520 meters) above sea level. His annual production of wine includes some 26,000 bottles of Chianti Classico.

Piccini Casa Vinicola (*Castellina in Chianti, Siena*). The Piccini winery has a capacity of 309,000 gallons (11,700 hectoliters). They vinify 364 tons (3,300 quintali) of grapes for Chianti Classico. We found both the '82 Riserva and '88 *normale* wanting. Chianti Classico 0

Pietrafitta (*San Gimignano, Siena*), *1500.* Pietrafitta has 100 acres (40 hectares) of vines, 44 (18) planted for Chianti and 54 (22) for Vernaccia di San Gimignano. Their average annual production is 31,000 cases—13,000 of Chianti Colli Senesi and 17,500 of the Vernaccia. In some vintages they bottle a single-vineyard Chianti from their Campidonne vineyard. Pietrafitta names 1983 and 1975 as its two best vintages. Chianti Colli Senesi *

Pietraserena (*San Gimignano, Siena*), *1966.* This *azienda* has 40 acres (16 hectares) of vines, 25 (10) for Chianti Colli Senesi and 15 (6) for Vernaccia di San Gimignano. Their annual production of more than 13,000 cases breaks down to 7,700 of the red and 5,500 of the white. Their '89 Poggio al Vento was very good. Chianti Colli Senesi ** −

Podere Boscarelli (*Cervognano di Montepulciano, Siena*), *1963.* Podere Boscarelli, a good Vino Nobile producer, has 11 acres (4.5 hectares) of vines for Chianti, from which they produce about 30,000 bottles of Chianti a year. At Boscarelli they make a careful selection of the grapes, using only the best for the Vino Nobile. The next level of grapes goes into their Chianti, and the balance is used to produce a wine that is sold in bulk unlabeled. Chianti Colli Senesi **

Podere Campacci (*San Gusmè, Siena*). A few years Remo Migli had 30 acres (12 hectares) of vines from which he produced 60,000 bottles of a wine a year. Most of it was Chianti Classico, both a *normale* and *riserva*. Today, according to the Consorzio del Gallo Nero, he has 14.6 acres (5.9 hectares), 6.7 (2.7) of which are planted in *coltura promiscua* for Chianti Classico. From these he can produce up to 39,065 bottles of Chianti per year. He also produces a tiny amount of *vin santo*.

His Chianti Classico (the pre-1984 vintages, made from 60 percent sangiovese, 20 percent canaiolo, and 10 percent each trebbiano and malvasia) was made with *governo* and aged in casks of oak and chestnut. The Migli Chianti Classicos are decent wines, not bad, though not special either. Of the two vintages we tasted from cask in May 1985, we found the '82 preferable to the '83. Chianti Classico *

Podere Capaccia (*Radda in Chianti, località Capaccia, Siena*). Gianpaolo Pacini has owned this Chianti Classico estate with 7.4 acres (3 hectares) of vines since 1975. The vines, planted at an average altitude of 1,640 feet (500 meters) above sea level, face south to southeast. The soil is sandy-clay. Pacini produces some 6,000 to 7,000 bottles of Chianti Classico a year and 4,000 of the *barrique*-aged, 100 percent sangiovese **Querciagrande** under the watchful eye of consulting enologist Vittorio Fiore. Both the '86 and '88 were good. Chianti Classico **

Podere Castellare. See **Castellare.**

Podere Colle ai Lecci (*San Gusmè, Siena*). From Podere Colle ai Lecci's 15.3 acres (6.2 hectares) of vines come some 3,600 cases of Chianti Classico yearly. They sell their wine under the San Cosma label.

Podere Crognole (*Radda in Chianti, Siena*). The lookout tower here dates back to the thirteenth century. The vineyard and winery are of a more recent vintage. Its 2.37 acres (0.96 hectare) of vines are planted between 1,640 and 1,970 feet (500 and 600 meters) above sea level. The annual production of Chianti Classico there amounts to all of 4,933 bottles.

Podere di Cignano. See **Villa Cilnia.**

Podere di Stignano (*Gaiole in Chianti*, località *San Vicenti, Siena*). This 133-acre (54-hectare) estate has 12.8 acres (5.2 hectares) in vines, 9.9 (4) for Chianti Classico. Its vineyards, composed of 90 percent sangiovese, 8 percent canaiolo, and 2 percent trebbiano and malvasia, are planted at an average altitude of 1,640 feet (500 meters) above sea level. It produces some 2,300 cases of Chianti Classico yearly. Its '85 Riserva San Vicenti was disappointing, the '88 *normale* San Vicenti good. Chianti Classico: * −, San Vicenti * −

Podere I Sodi (*Gaiole in Chianti*, località *Monti in Chianti, Siena*), 1973. F.lli Casini owns the I Sodi estate and its 26.8 acres (10.9 hectares) of vines. It produces 4,645 cases of Chianti Classico and 1,275 of other wines annually.

Podere Il Palazzino (*Monti In Chianti, Siena*). The Sderci brothers have 9.6 acres (3.9 hectares) of vines at their *fattoria*, including the 3.7-acre (1.5-hectare) Grosso Sanese cru. In 1974 they replanted most of their mixed culture vineyards. They still have 1.7 acres (0.7 hectare) in *coltura promiscua*. Their annual production of 24,000 bottles of wine includes 13,000 of Chianti Classico, 3,000 of the *barrique*-aged Sangiovese **Grosso Sanese**, and 2,000 of white wine.

Their Chianti Classico from vintages prior to the advent of the DOCG was made from an *uvaggio* of 70 percent sangiovese, 10 percent canaiolo, and 20 percent white grapes. Since 1984 they have been using a blend of 85 percent sangiovese, 10 percent canaiolo, and 5 percent malvasia. The '77 was the first vintage they bottled under their own label. Their bottling is done by a mobile bottling unit. While their initial releases failed to impress us, we must admit that their more recent offerings have been quite good indeed. We recommend the *riserve* of '83, '85, and '86, as well as the *normale* '85. Chianti Classico ** +

Podere La Casaccia (*Radda in Chianti*, località *Casaccia, Siena*). This wine farm, owned by Nausikaa Ltd., has a mere 1.2108 acres (0.49 hectare) in vines, nearly half of which, 0.5684 (0.23), are in mixed cultivation. These vines are planted at an average altitude of 985 feet (300 meters) above sea level. Their consulting enologist, Pietro Rivella, makes a scant 3,333 bottles of Chianti Classico a year.

Podere La Piaggia (*Castellina in Chianti, Siena*). This estate has 6 acres (2.4 hectares) planted in vines at an average altitude of 1,150 feet (350 meters) above sea level. Less than 40 percent is in monoculture. Their annual production of Chianti Classico doesn't exceed 16,666 bottles. Pietro Rivella is their consulting enologist.

Podere Petroio alla Via della Malpensata (*Radda in Chianti*, località *Petroio, Siena*), 1974. Fausto Cammarata owns 33 acres (13.5 hectares) of vines. These vines, with a north-south exposure, are planted at an altitude of 1,640 feet (500 meters) above sea level. Besides the standard Chianti varieties, Cammarata grows cabernet sauvignon, merlot, pinot noir, and chardonnay. It's kind of like a little bit of California in Radda. He produces a few different wines, including 80,500 bottles of Chianti Classico, 10,000 bottles of the single-vineyard Chianti Classico Montetondo, and **Solo Rosso**, a cabernet-merlot-sangiovese blend. The first Monte-

tondo Chianti Classico was produced in 1987. The '87 Chianti Classico was good, and the '88 Cru Montetondo very good. Chianti Classico: **, Cru Montetondo **

Podere Ripertoli (*Greve in Chianti, Firenze*), 1979. Records of the Ripertoli estate date back to the late tenth century. There are 7.4 acres (3 hectares) of vines on the property, at altitudes of 1,475 to 1,640 feet (450 to 500 meters) above sea level; they have a south to southwesterly exposure. Ripertoli produces two wines: about 6,700 bottles a year of a cabernet sauvignon–sangiovese blend and 13,300 bottles of Chianti Classico. They told us that the first vintage of the Chianti they sold in bottle was the '73. Mario Cortevesio consults here.

Podere Terreno alla Via della Volpaia (*Radda in Chianti*, località *Volpaia, Siena*). Marie Sylvie Haniez has owned Podere Terreno since 1980. She has 7.9 acres (3.2 hectares) of vines from which she produces 12,000 bottles a year of Chianti Classico and 8,000 of the *vino da tavola* **Il Pallaio**, a sangiovese-canaiolo blend that is *barrique*-aged. Paolo Vagaggini consults here.

Poderuzzo (*Panzano in Chianti, Firenze*). Luisa Cappelli owns this estate, and Mario Cortevesio provides the enological advice. Some 40 percent of the 5.1305 acres (2.0762 hectares) of vines are in mixed culture. Cappelli produces about 15,000 bottles of Chianti Classico annually.

Poggerina (*Monti in Chianti, Siena*). The Poggerina estate has 0.3398 acre (0.1375 hectare) under vines at altitudes ranging from 820 to 985 feet (250 to 300 meters) above sea level. Its annual production never exceeds 933 bottles of Chianti Classico. No wonder we've never seen it.

Poggerino (*Radda in Chianti, Siena*). Maria Floriana Ginori Conti owns this 99-acre (40-hectare) estate. Some 12.4 acres (5 hectares) are planted in vines, 11 (4.5) for Chianti Classico. They produce about 2,450 cases of Chianti Classico annually.

Poggiarello (*Poggibonsi, Siena*). Giuseppe Brini owns this estate. The 10 acres (4 hectares) of vines, planted at an average altitude of 1,475 feet (450 meters) above sea level, yield some 7,110 cases of Chianti Classico annually. The Chianti Classico estate of **Fattoria di Mocenni,** Tenimenti di Macialla, as well as Fattoria dei Colli in Monteriggioni and Fattoria di Marcianella in Chiusi, is associated with Poggiarello. Both of the Poggiarello Chianti Classicos that we tasted, the '83 and '86, were good. Chianti Classico * +

Poggio a Remole. See **Frescobaldi.**

Poggio al Sole (*Sambuca Val di Pesa*, località *Badia a Passignano, Firenze*), 1969. The Poggio al Sole farm of Aldo Torrini and family in the Sambuca Val di Pesa area of Chianti Classico, not far from Greve, is on the grounds of the eighteenth-century Vallombrosian Abbey of Passignano. Reportedly there were vines and olive trees growing here in the twelfth century. Torrini put in his first vines in 1969, the year he purchased the 100-acre (40-hectare) estate. Today, according to information supplied by the winery, there are 20 acres (8 hectares) of vines planted at altitudes ranging from 1,475 to 1,640 feet (450 to 500 meters) above sea level with a southern exposure. From those vines Torrini produces 44,600 to 46,700 bottles of wine annually. This includes 30,665 of Chianti

Classico *normale* and 4,000 of *riserva*. (In 1983 he produced 6,477 bottles of Chianti Classico *riserva*.) He also produces 2,000 to 2,660 of Vino della Signora from traminer and 8,000 and 9,300 of a *vino da tavola* meant to be drunk young. (In 1986 he produced 1,350 bottles of the Vino della Signora and in 1988, 6,675 of the *vino da tavola!*)

While waiting for their vines to come into production, the Torrinis bought grapes to produce a wine that they sold in demijohns. Before the DOCG they produced 35,000 to 40,000 bottles of *normale* Chianti Classico and from 1,390 to nearly 12,000 of a *riserva*, as well as 4,000 bottles of Vino della Signora, plus a few other wines.

Their pre-1984 Chianti Classico is made from 75 percent sangiovese, 10 percent canaiolo, and 10 percent trebbiano and malvasia, plus 5 percent colorino, mammolo, and ciliegiolo.

The wine is fermented four to five days on the skins; ten days later they add dried grapes for the *governo*. They use *governo* for all of their Chianti Classico, including the *riserva*. The second fermentation lasts about two and a half months. The *normale* Chianti is aged for two years, the *riserva* for three.

Their Chianti Classico is reliable and good. It has a lively, rather austere nature owing to higher than average acidity. The *riserve* of '83, '82, '80, and '79 were very good indeed, as were the *normali* of '86 and '83. Chianti Classico *** −

Poggio alla Croce (*Monteriggioni, Siena*). This estate has nearly 32 acres (12.8 hectares) of vines and produces some 7,400 cases of Chianti Classico annually.

Poggio Bonelli (*Castelnuovo Berardenga, località Bonelli, Siena*). The 119-acre (48-hectare) Poggio Bonelli estate has 44 acres (18 hectares) of vines, two-thirds planted for Chianti Classico at an altitude of 1,150 feet (350 meters) above sea level. The vineyards consist of 80 percent sangiovese, 5 percent canaiolo, and 15 percent trebbiano and malvasia. Their annual production of 10,000 to 11,100 cases of wine includes 6,665 of Chianti Classico and 1,665 each of Paladino Rosso and Giocoliere Bianco Val d'Arbia. Since 1983 they have been producing 1,665 cases per year of Chianti Classico Tramonto d'Oca from their Cancellino vineyard. Of the three Chianti Classicos we tasted from them—the '85 Riserva, '86 and '87 *normali*—we liked only one, and surprisingly it was the '87 *normale*. Perhaps that wine was made by their consulting enologist, Vittorio Fiore. We doubt that he made the other two. Chianti Classico +

Poggio dell'Oliviera (*Vagliagli, Siena*). About 15 percent of this estate's 5.4 acres (2.2 hectares) of vines are planted in *coltura promiscua*. Their annual production of Chianti Classico amounts to some 1,100 cases.

Poggio Reale. See **Spalletti.**

Poggio Rosso. See **San Felice.**

Poliziano (*Carletti Federico & Della Giovampola*) (*Gracciano, Siena*), *1962*. This fine Vino Nobile producer owns 222 acres (90 hectares) of vines, 124 (50) for Chianti, from which it produces 22,000 cases a year. These grapes, harvested in the middle of October, are fermented in temperature-controlled stainless steel tanks at 82° to 86° Fahrenheit (28° to 30° centigrade) for five to ten days.

Pomona. The only Chianti Classico we tasted from Pomona, the '85, was disappointing. Chianti Classico 0

Pruneto (*Radda in Chianti, località Pruneto, Volpaia, Siena*). Pruneto is a 59-acre (24-hectare) estate owned by Riccardo Lanza. He has 4.9 acres (2 hectares) of vines, 80 percent for Chianti Classico. The vineyards are planted at an altitude of 1,640 feet (500 meters) above sea level in *galestro* soil. Pruneto produces some 12,000 bottles of Chianti Classico annually. The vineyards are planted with 90 percent sangiovese, 5 percent canaiolo, and 5 percent white grapes. Both Chianti Classicos that we tasted—the '85 and '86—failed to impress. Chianti Classico 0

Pucci Emilio. See **Castello di Cerreto.**

Querciavalle (*Vagliagli, località Pontignano, Siena*), *1870*. The Losi family has owned this wine-producing estate since 1954. The 84-acre (34-hectare) Querciavalle estate has 29.7 (12) in vines, 17.3 (7) for Chianti Classico. These vines are planted in limestone, marl, and tufa soil. They produce some 7,750 cases of wine annually, including 4,220 of Chianti Classico, 945 of Bianco Val d'Arbia, and 1,775 of other wines. They continue to use *governo* for their Chianti Classico. The current proprietors, Paolo and Pietro Losi, use the consulting services of Pietro Rivella. Our experience with three wines has left a mixed impression. The '85 *normale* was disappointing, while the Riserva was quite good, and the '86 *normale* good. Chianti Classico: *normale* *, Riserva ** −

Remole. See **Frescobaldi.**

Ricasoli. See **Brolio.**

Riecine (*Gaiole in Chianti, località Riecine, Siena*), *1971*. Documents from 1112 mention the Riecine property. John and Palmina Abbagnano Dunkley have owned this 54-acre (22-hectare) estate since 1971. This farm has 7.4 acres (3 hectares) of vines at an average altitude of 1,475 feet (450 meters) above sea level. The 5.4 acres (2.2 hectares) for Chianti Classico are planted with 90 percent sangiovese, 5 percent canaiolo, and 5 percent white grapes. The exposure is southern and southeastern, and the soil calcerous. John makes, on average, 18,000 bottles of wine a year, including 15,330 of Chianti Classico, 2,000 of the *barrique*-aged 100 percent sangiovese **La Gioia,** and 666 of a *vino da tavola* white.

In our experience, these reasonably consistent and fairly well-made Chianti Classicos have been improving, slowly but steadily. Today the Riecine Riserva stands with the zone's best Chianti Classicos. Dunkley rates '75, '77, '79, '82, '85, '86, and '88 as the best vintages, and '72, '76, and '84 as the worst. The '85 Riserva is excellent, and the '86 Riserva and '88 *normale* are very good. We can also recommend their '87 and '82 *normali*. Chianti Classico: *normale* ** +, Riserva ***

Rietine (*Gaiole in Chianti, Siena*). Less than 90 percent of Rietine's nearly 24 acres (9.6 hectares) are planted in specialized vineyards. It produces approximately 5,600 cases of Chianti Classico each year.

Rignana (*Greve in Chianti, località Rignana, Firenze*). Rignana owns some 3 acres (1.2 hectares) of vines planted at altitudes ranging from 985 to 1,150 feet (300 to 350 meters) above sea level. They produce some 5,555 cases of Chianti Classico annually.

Perhaps with Mario Cortevesio consulting here things will change for the better. The only wine we tasted, from the excellent 1985 vintage, left a lot to be desired. Chianti Classico 0

Riseccoli (*Greve in Chianti, Firenze*). A few years ago we were informed that Riseccoli had 32 acres (13 hectares) of vines and produced 5,500 cases of Chianti Classico a year. Today, the *consorzio* informed us, they have 17 acres (6.9 hectares) of vines and can produce up to 5,700 cases of Chianti Classico annually. The most recent vintages we've tasted of these wines, in the early 1980s, were the '71 Riserva, and the *normale* '77 and '78. None of them amounted to much. They only confirmed our previous dim impression. Perhaps, like elsewhere in Chianti, things have improved. Chianti Classico [0]

Rocca delle Macìe (*Castellina in Chianti, località Le Macìe, Siena*), 1973. Film producer and former actor and stuntman Italo Zingarelli owns this *azienda* and its 1,190 acres (481 hectares) of land. He bought the Le Macìe and Sant'Alfonso farms in 1973 and the Fizzano estate in 1983. Some 593 acres (240 hectares) of vines are planted at altitudes ranging from 1,150 to 1,640 feet (350 to 500 meters) above sea level. Of these, 353 acres (143 hectares) are planted for Chianti Classico. The vineyard composition is 85 percent sangiovese, 10 percent canaiolo and other red varieties, and 5 percent trebbiano and malvasia. They have two special crus, Fizzaoilla and Sant'Alfonso, both 74 acres (30 hectares). They own controlling interest in the Straccali firm.

Their own vines supply them with 60 percent of the grapes they require to achieve an annual production that varies between 122,000 and 133,000 cases. This includes as much as 77,750 cases of Chianti Classico. In the vintages that they make it, they bottle more than 5,000 cases of the Chianti Classico Riserva from the Fizzano estate. The first one was the 1982. They also produce Casato delle Macìe, a chardonnay-trebbiano-malvasia blend, Galestro, Orvieto, Rubizzo, the *barrique*-aged Sangiovese **Ser Gioveto**, and a *vin santo*.

We have tasted a range of their Chiantis, from the '69 to the '89 vintages, and must admit that although few of the early vintages impressed us, there has been a steady improvement in quality, especially from the 1982 vintage on. While the '82 Riserva di Fizzano was at one time very good indeed, it is fading today. The '85 from that vineyard shows good potential. Of the regular *riserve*, we enjoyed the '83 and '85, and found the '86 and '82 good as well. And the first offering—the '88—of their new single-vineyard Chianti Classico, a *normale* from Tenuta Sant' Alfonso, was good. Chianti Classico: *normale* *, Riserva * +, Riserva di Fizzano **, Tenuta Sant' Alfonso *

Rocca di Castagnoli (*Gaiole in Chianti, località Castagnoli, Siena*). This 2,422-acre (980-hectare) estate has 192 acres (78 hectares) in vines—143 (58) for Chianti Classico, plus 24.7 (10) for Bianco Val d'Arbia and 24.7 (10) planted in cabernet sauvignon, chardonnay, and riesling italico—at altitudes ranging from 1,310 to 1,475 feet (400 to 450 meters) above sea level. We have heard, from a very reliable source, that Biondi-Santi was involved. He isn't any longer.

They produce, at most, some 33,300 cases of at least four different Chianti Classicos a year: a *normale* and three Riserve, a regular and two single vineyards—Poggio a'Frati and Capraia. They

produced 33,412 bottles of the '85 Poggio a'Frati and 18,660 of the '87. Both wines were very good. They also produced a very good '85 and '86 *normale*, and '82 and '87 Riservas. Only the '85 Riserva disappointed. Chianti Classico: *normale* ** +, Riserva Capraia **, Riserva Poggio a'Frati *** —

Rocca di Montegrossi. See **Castello di Montegrossi**.

Rodano (*Castellina in Chianti, località Rodano, Siena*). Vittorio Pozzesi owns the 259-acre (105-hectare) Rodano estate and its 47 acres (19 hectares) of vines. The vineyards are composed of 90 percent sangiovese, 8 percent canaiolo, and 2 percent white grapes. From the 38 acres (15.5 hectares) planted for Chianti Classico he produces approximately 8,900 cases of wine annually. Of the three wines we tasted from here, only the '86 Riserva disappointed us, while the '86 *normale* was good and the '87 very good. Chianti Classico * +

Rosso di Massanera (*La Romola, Firenze*). This estate has 4.2 acres (1.7 hectares) of vines planted for Chianti Classico, nearly 1 (0.4) in *coltura promiscua*. The vines are planted at an average altitude of 920 feet (280 meters) above sea level. Their annual production of Chianti Classico amounts to 11,600 bottles.

Ruffino (*Pontassieve, Firenze*), 1877. Ilario and Leopoldo Ruffino founded the Chianti Ruffino firm but it was the Folonaris who brought it fame. Italo and Francesco Folonari bought Ruffino in 1913. Ownership today is in the hands of Ambrogio, Marco, Italo, Paolo, and Alberto Folonari. Ruffino is one of the largest producers of Chianti Classico and one of the largest landowners in the region, with some 4,325 acres (1,750 hectares) of land, 1,235 (500) of it under vines. About 30 percent of the grapes for the standard Ruffino Chianti Classico comes from their own vines; the balance comes from farmers who are under contract to them.

At their Tenuta di Montemasso they produce Sarmento Il Rosolo, Anteprima Il Novello from sangiovese grosso and gamay, Torgaio di San Salvatore Chianti Fresco di Governo, and **Cabreo Vigna Il Borgo (Predicato di Bitùrica)**, a 70-30 sangiovese–cabernet sauvignon blend. They produce the Aziano Chianti Classico at Tenuta Agricola Fattoria di Zano. Their Santedame Chianti Classico wine comes from Tenimenti Agricoli Sant'Agnese. And Tenimenti Agricoli Valdigreve is used for the Nozzole wines. Tenuta di Casa Sala is used for Cabreo Vigna La Pietra (Predicato del Muschio), a barrel-fermented, barrel-aged chardonnay, and Nero del Tondo, a pinot noir.

They own part of an estate located in the Rignana zone between Panzano and Badia a Passignano. Here they have pinto nero, chardonnay, and sauvignon blanc planted. Libaio is a white wine made from a blend of 90 percent chardonnay and 10 percent sauvignon blanc grown on the Castelvecchio estate in which they have an interest. Pinot grigio and vernaccia grapes are also planted there. Their Brunello comes from the Il Greppone Mazzi estate, and shortly they will produce a Vino Nobile di Montepulciano from the Ludola Nuova estate that they acquired in October 1990.

The Folonaris also have production facilities and cellars in Brescia and Cellatica in Lombardia and Negrar in the Veneto. Among their other wines are a Barolo, sold under the Anforio label; a line of Veronese wines; and Monte Rossa, the very good maker of Franciacorta Spumante *metodo champenoise*. They own 50 percent of Monte Rossa and a company called Premiovini. Additional wines

THE FATTORIE OF RUFFINO

Fattoria	Località	In Vines		Total		Altitude in	
		Acres	Hectares	Acres	Hectares	Feet	Meters
Tenuta Agricola Fattoria di Zano	Greve	124	50	371	150	1,150	350
Tenimenti Agricoli Sant'Agnese	Castellina	173	70	618	250	n/a	n/a
Tenimenti Agricoli Valdigreve	Passo dei Pecorai	247	100	1,112	450	n/a	n/a
Tenuta di Casa Sala	Panzano	62	25	64	26	1,150–1,640	350–500
Tenuta di Montemasso	San Polo di Greve	210	85	1,112	450	1,150	350
Rignana*	Rignana	64	26	n/a	n/a		
Castelvecchio*	San Gimignano	185	75	494	200	1,380	420
Il Greppone Mazzi	Montalcino	18.5	7.5	371	150	1,640	500
Ludola Nuova†	Montepulciano	n/a	n/a	n/a	n/a	n/a	n/a
Monte Rossa*	Franciacorta	64	26	247	100	n/a	n/a
Total		1,147.5	464.5	4,390	1,776		

* They own part of this estate.
† They bought this estate in October 1990.

include the white Orvieto, Lugana, and a Galestro made from trebbiano, vernaccia, and chardonnay, the red Il Magnifico, two rosés—Primacuvé di Clivio and Rosatello—and Soliento Vino Liquoroso Bianco.

They produce three Ruffino Chianti Classicos as well as the Chianti Classicos of **Tenuta di Nozzole,** Aziano, and Santedame, Torgaio di San Salvatore Chianti Governato Fresco, and a straight Chianti.

Torgaio, released March 1 after the harvest, is a light and quaffable wine meant to be drunk young and fresh. Their Chianti is made from 90 percent sangiovese and 5 percent each canaiolo and trebbiano. Their regular Ruffino Chianti Classico is also best drunk young and fresh, though it can take a bit more age than the Torgaio. It is reliable and agreeable, no more, no less. And they produce a lot of it.

Their Riserva Ducale, bottled with the beige label, is quite good. It is produced in good vintages only. Their top wine is the Riserva Ducale gold label, and it is very good indeed—in fact, among the best Chianti Classicos. This wine is produced only in the best vintages. They named this wine for the Duke of Aosta, who, when he visited the Ruffino cellars in the nineteenth century, liked their wine. Consequently he arranged for them to be the official supplier to his house. The first Riserva Ducale sold worldwide was the '51; some 30,000 to 35,000 bottles were produced. The gold label, like all their Classicos, is made with *governo*. Ruffino points out that *governo,* when made with dried grapes, gives the typical aroma and taste of Chianti Classico and helps encourage malolactic fermentation. They tried concentrate and found that it wasn't as good. The grapes to be used for *governo* are dried for two months on mats.

They add the equivalent of 6 to 10 percent of these grapes to the wine.

These three Chianti Classicos, pre-1984, were made from an *uvaggio* of 70 percent sangiovese, 15 percent canaiolo, 10 percent malvasia and trebbiano, and 5 percent colorino, ciliegiolo, and cabernet. They were using the cabernet long before it became trendy. It was planted in their vineyard. Since 1982 the cabernet has been added consciously. They ferment it separately and add in the amount they feel is best. Today they use 90 percent sangiovese, 7 to 8 percent canaiolo, and 2 to 3 percent white grapes.

The difference between the wines is in the selection and aging. Only the best grapes from their own vineyards are used for the Riserva Ducale. The gold label is a selection from the best lots of the best vintages of the beige label Riserva Ducale. The beige label Ducale is aged for one year in 185- to 264-gallon (700- to 1,000-liter) oak casks, followed by a year in vats and a further year in oak. The gold label Riserva Ducale is given at least four years in oak.

Ambrogio Folonari describes the aroma of Riserva Ducale as having suggestions of fruit and flowers, especially strawberries in its youth; this turns into forest flowers and underbrush in midlife, and toward leather and tobacco when it is mature.

The Riserva Ducale gold label is a full-bodied, full-flavored, well-balanced wine that requires age (*governo* notwithstanding) and rewards those who have the patience to wait. They have, thus are, released the '83, '82, '81, '80, '79, '75, '71, '70, '67, '64, '62, '59, '58, '57, '56, '55, '52, '51, '50, and '47. Recently we liked the '83 and '82 very much, as well as the '81 and '79. As far as the older vintages go, the '55 was very good, the '56 was uneven, the '59 was still good, and the '71 was, surprisingly, fading.

We have had many bottles of these Chianti Classicos through the years and have rarely been disappointed. Ruffino has been able to maintain a level of quality and consistency unusual for a company of its size. In that regard they are in a class by themself, in Chianti Classico at least.

Since 1981 they have produced a single-vineyard Aziano Chianti Classico from at least 75 percent sangiovese, 12 to 15 percent canaiolo, and 10 to 13 percent trebbiano and malvasia grapes grown on their Villa Zano farm. This estate was referred to in documents from A.D. 963. The earliest name used for this estate was Azzano or Aziano. The three we tasted, the '83, '87, and '88, were all good. With DOCG, the *uvazzio* has changed: it is made with more than 80 percent sangioveto grosso, 8 percent canaiolo, 4 percent white grapes, and 3 percent ciliegiolo, occhio rosso, and capobianco, and, of course, *governo* (the percentages are approximate). The '87 was made from a blend of 90-7-3, sangiovese-canaiolo-trebbiano. They produce some 28,000 cases of Aziano a year. This is a wine to drink in its youth.

Chianti Classico: *normale* *, Torgaio *, Aziano *, Riserva Ducale beige label ** +, Riserva Ducale gold label ***

S. Andrea a Luiano. See Fattoria di Luiano.

S. Leonino (Castellina in Chianti, Siena). Fattoria I Cipressi was a 282-acre (114-hectare) estate that had 131 acres (53 hectares) of vineyards and an annual production of nearly 40,000 cases. Their S. Leonino Chianti Classico was a quite agreeable wine, but rarely more than that. We haven't tasted the Chianti Classico of Fattoria I Cipressi since 1985, when we tasted the '78 Riserva. This is the **Fattoria San Leonino** estate now owned by Lionello Marchesi Chianti Classico [*]

S. Quirico. Vecchione owns this Chianti-producing estate. Our experience with the S. Quirico Chianti has been limited. The most recent one we tasted was the rather unimpressive '87.

Saccardi. The most recent vintage of the Saccardi Chianti that we've tasted is the '86 and, like nearly every wine before it, it left a lot to be desired. Chianti Classico 0

Sagrona e Faule (Greve in Chianti, Firenze). Nello Manetti, the owner here, has 25 acres (10.2 hectares) of vines, some 15 percent in mixed cultivation. Manetti's annual production of Chianti Classico amounts to about 5,900 cases.

Salcetino. See Fattoria Salcetino.

Salvanza. The only Chianti Classico we tasted from Salvanza was the fairly good '87 *normale*. Chianti Classico * −

San Felice (San Gusmè, località San Felice, Siena), 1967. This estate was known in medieval times as the village of San Felice in Pincis. Today this 1,829-acre (740-hectare) farm cultivates 465 acres (188 hectares) of vines in the Chianti Classico zone, planted at altitudes ranging from 1,245 to 1,310 feet (380 to 400 meters) above sea level. The vineyards are planted with 90 percent sangiovese, 4 percent canaiolo, 3 percent other red varieties, and 3 percent white grapes. The vineyards have a southeastern exposure. San Felice produces, on average, 1.85 million bottles of wine annually; 800,000 are Chianti Classico. Besides multiple Chianti Classicos they produce **Vigorello,** a *vino da tavola* made from a

blend of sangiovese, canaiolo, and cabernet sauvignon. After a spell in 793-gallon (30-hectoliter) casks it spends six months in *barriques* of Limousin oak. They also produce a Cabernet Sauvignon, a Champagne-method *spumante,* three white wines—Citerno Chardonnay, Bianco Val d'Arbia, and Galestro—Rosé di Canaiolo, Primanno, and Santuccio Vin Santo. San Felice also owns the Brunello di Montalcino estate of Campogiovanni.

The San Felice Chianti Classico, in pre-1984 vintages, was made from 75 percent sangiovese, 10 percent canaiolo, and 15 percent trebbiano and malvasia. (Under the new regulations, this proportion of white grapes was reduced to, at most, 5 percent.) They also produce two single-vineyard Chianti Classico *riserve*, one from their Poggio Rosso vineyard and the other—Il Grigio—from the best grapes from their 44-acre (18-hectare) Chiesamanti vineyard.

A few years ago San Felice reported to us that Poggio Rosso was a 2.5-acre (1-hectare) vineyard. The first Poggio Rosso Chianti Classico bottled was the '78. Production here has certainly been on the increase since, with 7,536 bottles of the '79, 29,850 of the '82, and 39,430 of the '85. Of the four Riserva Poggio Rosso vintages that we tasted, the '79 remains the best one, followed by the '85, '82, and finally the '81.

THE SPECIAL WINES OF SAN FELICE

Wine	Average Number of Bottles Per Year
Chianti Classico, Riserva Il Grigio	250,000
Chianti Classico, Riserva Poggio Rosso	30,000
Vigorello	48,000
Chardonnay	45,000
Belcarlo	15,000
Vin santo	12,000
Total	400,000

Another one of San Felice's top wines is, without a doubt, the Chianti Classico Riserva Il Grigio. That Chianti is aged for at least three years in Slavonian oak casks. Of those we've tasted, the '85 is excellent, and the '86, '81, '80, and '78 very good.

Their Chianti Classico *normale* is generally consistent and good. Look for the '88; the '87, '86, and '85 were all good as well, though most are, by now, too old. Chianti Classico: *normale* * +, Riserva **, Riserva Il Grigio Riserva ** +, Riserva Poggio Rosso ** +

San Jacopo. See Castello Vicchiomaggio.

San Leonino. See Fattoria San Leonino.

San Piero (Castelnouvo Berardenga, Siena). San Piero owns 14 acres (5.7 hectares) of vines planted at an average altitude of 1,150 feet (350 meters) above sea level. From those vines they produce some 3,300 cases of Chianti Classico annually.

San Vicenti (*Gaiole in Chianti, Siena*). The vineyards here cover 10.6 acres (4.3 hectares) planted at an average altitude of 1,640 feet (500 meters) above sea level. San Vicenti's annual production, from their own vineyards, averages some 2,350 cases of Chianti Classico.

Sanguinetto (*Montepulciano, Siena*), *1979*. Maria and Lucia Monaci own 13.1 acres (5.3 hectares) of vines. They produce a Vino Nobile and a small quantity of Chianti Colli Senesi.

Santa Caterina. See **Fattoria Monsanto.**

Santa Cristina. See **Marchesi L. e P. Antinori.**

Santa Valeria (*Vagliagli, Siena*). Their 15 acres (6.2 hectares) of vines, planted at an altitude averaging 1,540 feet (470 meters) above sea level, yields 3,500 cases of Chianti Classico each year.

Savignola Paolina (*Greve in Chianti, Firenze*), *1780*. Savignola, we were told a few years ago, has 15 acres (6 hectares) of vines planted at altitudes ranging from 1,150 to 1,245 feet (350 to 380 meters) above sea level. Only one-quarter of the vineyards are in specialized cultivation; the other 11 acres (4.5 hectares) are planted in the traditional way, with four to six vines planted around one poplar tree. This is better, according to Paolina Fabbri, because the air and light are all around the vines. Today, according to the *consorzio*, they have 6.7 acres (2.7 hectares) planted for Chianti Classico, 4 (1.6) in monoculture. They produce 22,600 bottles of wine a year—14,600 of the *normale* Chianti Classico, 4,000 *riserva*, 3,300 red and rosé *vino da tavola*, and 660 bottles of white wine.

The winemaker at Savignola is or was Paolina Fabbri, a tiny eighty-eight-year-young dynamo when we last visited here in 1986, whose engagingly enthusiastic yet logically practical outlook was reflected in the quality of her wines. Signora Paolina takes advantage of the services of a consulting enologist, Dott. Mario Cortevesio, but takes charge of making the wines herself. In the past she made the wines with *governo*, but she doesn't do so any longer. In 1986 she purchased a filter, though she hadn't used it as of that visit. Her *riserva* is aged for three years in wood, mostly chestnut. She told us, quite proudly, that she bottles by the phases of the moon. It is best, she says, to bottle when the moon is waning.

The 1942 vintage was the first Chianti Classico she bottled under her label. On the way down to the cellar for a tasting from barrel and bottle conducted at a thoughtfully expeditious pace to keep us on schedule, she made a brief detour to show us some bottles of the older vintages which, though a bit low in fill, seemed to have maintained remarkably good color.

The Savignola Paolina wines are delicate, gentle Chiantis with real style, a characteristic they share with the lady who produces them. They are among the better Chianti Classicos. The '83, '82, and '81 Riservas are all very good or better. Chianti Classico ***

Scopatello (*Chianciano, Siena*). Scopatello has 160 acres (65 hectares) of vineyards from which they produce both a Chianti and a Vino Nobile di Montepulciano.

Selvoramole (*San Donato in Poggio, Firenze*). Selvoramole owns 12.4 acres (5 hectares) of vines planted in sangiovese, canaiolo, trebbiano, and malvasia. When we visited this small Chianti Classico producer in May 1986, they had a small basket press, stainless steel tanks, and one *barrique*. When we asked what they did with the *barrique,* they told us that they might do a Chianti in *barrique.*

They produce, they told us, between 9,247 and 10,568 gallons (350 and 400 hectoliters) of wine a year and bottle at most 7,133 gallons (270 hectoliters), equivalent to 36,000 bottles of Chianti Classico. The rest is for the workers or "whatever." They also sell wine to Brolio. In 1983 they produced 9,247 gallons (350 hectoliters), equivalent to 46,665 bottles of wine, and in 1984 and 1985 they produced 5,284 gallons (200 hectoliters), equivalent to 26,666 bottles of wine. They bottled only a small amount of it in 1983 and 1985 and, we believe, none in 1984.

Their first wine was made from the 1981 vintage, of which they produced 7,000 bottles, the same amount they produced in 1982, 1983, and 1985. Their *normale* is sold after four years of aging! They plan to increase their production to 13,210 gallons (500 hectoliters) of wine, equivalent to 66,665 bottles. To do this they plan to expand the vineyard. They also produce 50 bottles(!) of *vin santo* from a 50-50 blend of trebbiano and malvasia.

They made a good '81 and very good '82, '83, and '85. Chianti Classico **

Serristori. See **Conti Serristori.**

Setriolo (*Castellina in Chianti, Siena*). American Desmond Crawford has 4.7 acres (1.9 hectares) of vines on his Setriolo farm. Half are planted in *coltura promiscua*. He produces 13,200 bottles of Chianti Classico a year. We've heard that it is a pretty good wine, but have not had the opportunity to taste it.

Signoria. A label used by **Barfede-Certaldo.**

Socovich. See **Cappelli Giovanni.**

Sonnino (*Gaiole in Chianti, Siena*). Cantina di Adine owns this estate. They have 5 acres (2.1 hectares) of vines planted at an altitude of 1,640 feet (500 meters) above sea level from which Sonnino produces some 13,300 bottles of Chianti Classico annually.

Spalletti (*Rùfina, Firenze*), *1912*. This *azienda* has 185 acres (75 hectares) of vines which supply them with about 35 percent of the grapes for their wines. They produce a wide range: Veronese wines, Orvieto, a few different Tuscan whites, and Chianti Rùfina. Spalletti owns two estates in the Rùfina zone—Colognole, planted at altitudes ranging from 1,150 to 1,310 feet (350 to 400 meters) above sea level, and Poggio Reale, planted at 330 to 655 feet (100 to 200 meters). The former estate produces 22,000 cases of wine, the latter, 33,000 cases. Their Poggio Reale Riserva, prior to DOCG, was made from 75 percent sangiovese, 12 percent canaiolo, 3 percent colorino, and 5 percent each of trebbiano and malvasia.

A few years ago they considered the best vintages for the Poggio Reale Riserva to be 1983, 1982, 1981, 1979, 1977, 1975, 1971, 1967, 1964, 1959, 1958, 1957, 1955, 1952, 1950, 1949, 1948, and 1946; the worst vintages were 1984, 1973, 1966, 1963, 1956, and 1951.

The wine museum at their Poggio Reale villa is worth a visit.

Their Chiantis were quite good and fairly reliable, though we haven't tasted them in quite some time. Chianti Rùfina **

Storiche Cantine Radda in Chianti (*Radda in Chianti, località Lucarelli, Siena*), *1971*. This cooperative aging cellar stores and markets the wines of its seven members. The *cantina* has a storage capacity of more than 1 million bottles. Their members own some 1,236 acres (500 hectares) of vines and produce over 300,000 cases of wine a year.

As a group these wines are consistent—consistently rather mediocre.

THE CHIANTI CLASSICOS OF STORICHE CANTINE RADDA IN CHIANTI

Chianti Classico	Average Number of Cases Per Year
Castello di Meleto[a, b]	133,000
Castello di Monterinaldi[a, c]	55,500
Castello di S. Donato in Perano[a]	55,500
Castello di Vertine[a]	n/a
La Cerreta[a]	40,000
Montecasi[b]	n/a
Monticelli[b]	n/a

Other Wines

Podere Ferretto Vino Nobile di Montepulciano[a, d]
Podere Scansanaccio

NOTES: [a] See individual entries
[b] Owned by Società Viticola Toscana Agricola Immobiliare "Viticola Toscana"
[c] Owned by La Pesanella Monterinaldi (Fattoria La Pesanella)
[d] Owned by Fattoria delle Maestrelle

Straccali (*Castellina in Chianti, località Le Macìe, Siena*). Casa Vinicola Giulio Straccali, owned mostly by Italo Zingarelli of Rocca delle Macìe, buys grapes and/or wine to produce some 17,000 cases of wine a year. They have a cellar capacity of 211,360 gallons (8,000 hectoliters), and vinify about 275 tons (2,500 quintali) of grapes for Chianti Classico each year. Those wines are made from a blend of 85 percent sangiovese, 10 percent canaiolo, and 5 percent white grapes. In the 1960s we found these Classicos to be quite good, but then the quality slipped and for a time was uneven. We didn't taste any from the '74, which was quite good, until the '83. We have heard, though, that their wines are back in form. The '83 Riserva would attest to that while the '88 *normale* would not. Chianti Classico *

Sugame (*Greve in Chianti, Firenze*). This minuscule Chianti Classico producer has 0.3519 acre (0.1424 hectare) of specialized vineyards and 3.0503 (1.2344) in mixed cultivation. These vines are planted at an altitude of about 1,475 feet (450 meters) above sea level. They produce all of 9,600 bottles of Chianti Classico annually.

Tenuta Agricola Fontodi (*Panzano in Chianti, Firenze*), 1968. Domiziano and Dino Manetti bought the 222-acre (90-hectare) Fontodi estate in 1968. They replanted the vineyards between 1969 and 1974, and produced their first wine in 1970. Marco and Giovanni Manetti manage the estate. Fontodi has 81.5 acres (33 hectares) of vines planted at altitudes ranging from 1,310 to 1,475 feet (400 to 450 meters) above sea level. This includes 47 acres (19 hectares) for Chianti Classico, 5 (2) of sauvignon blanc, traminer, and pinot bianco, and 2.5 (1) of cabernet sauvignon. They have two special crus, the 6.2-acre (2.5-hectare) Del Sorbo and the 18.5-acre (7.5-hectare) Flaccianello vineyards. The vineyards have a southwestern exposure. The vineyards planted for Chianti Classico contain 85 percent sangiovese, 7 percent canaiolo, 3 percent white grapes, and 5 percent complementary varieties.

Their average annual production ranges from 133,000 to 160,000 bottles of wine a year: 93,300 bottles are Chianti Classico: 40,000 each *normale* and *riserva,* and 13,300 Riserva Vigna del Sorbo. They first produced this single-vineyard Chianti Classico in 1985. There were 4,986 bottles of that wine and 32,000 of the '85 Riserva. They also produce 13,300 bottles of a white *barrique*-aged blend called Meriggio from three white varieties, and 26,650 of the *barrique*-aged Sangiovese **Flaccianello.** We don't know if they still produce a Bianco della Lega and a *vin santo*. They plan to increase their annual production to between 266,000 and 300,000 bottles within five years. They have plans to do a cabernet sauvignon–merlot blend.

Their Chianti Classicos prior to the 1984 vintage (when DOCG regulations reduced the proportion of white grapes) were a blend of 80 percent sangiovese, 10 percent canaiolo, and 10 percent white grapes. Their *riserva* already included only 5 percent white grapes. Franco Bernabei is their consulting enologist. Since 1981 about 2 to 3 percent of the wine in their *riserva* has been given some time in *barrique*.

Overall, we find the Fontodi Classicos well-made wines of balance and style. We especially liked their '83 Riserva, and found the '82 and '85, as well as the *normale* '85, very good. We can also recommend the '81 Riserva and '86 *normale*. Chianti Classico: *normale* ** , Riserva ** + , Riserva Vigna del Sorbo ** +

Tenuta Canale (*Castellina in Chianti, località Canale, Siena*). Tenuta Canale is owned by the Aiello estate. They have 15.6 acres (6.3 hectares) of vines at 755 feet (230 meters) above sea level which produce some 3,665 cases of Chianti Classico annually.

Tenuta di Bibbiano (*Castellina in Chianti, Siena*). This twelfth-century castle was part of the feudal domain of the Guidi counts. Their 54 acres (21.8 hectares) of vines yield some 12,665 cases of Chianti Classico annually.

Tenuta di Capezzana (*Carmignano, Firenze*). Conte Ugo Contini Bonacossi's Tenuta di Capezzana produces, besides a very fine Carmignano, a good Chianti Montalbano. The grapes for Chianti Montalbano are planted on 48 acres (19.5 hectares) in soils of clay schists and limestone, medium heavy and rich in chalk. The yields average 427 gallons per acre (40 hectoliters per hectare) for Chianti Montalbano. They use an *uvaggio* of 80 percent sangiovese, 10 percent canaiolo, 5 percent trebbiano, and 5 percent other varieties to make some 8,900 cases of Chianti a year. The wine is aged for six to twelve months in oak casks. Chianti Montalbano *

Tenuta di Gracciano (Della Seta Ferrari Corbelli) (*Gracciano di Montepulciano, Siena*). Corbelli owns 27 acres (11 hectares); 17 (7) are planted in vines for Chianti.

Tenuta di Lilliano (*Castellina in Chianti, Siena*). Conte Ugo, Marquis of Toscana, donated this property to the Abbey of Poggibonsi in A.D. 980. Today Lilliano has some 96 acres (38.7 hectares) of vines producing 30,000 cases of Chianti Classico and other wines a year. Their pre-DOCG vintages are made from 80 percent sangiovese, 6 percent malvasia, 5 percent trebbiano, 4 percent canaiolo, and 5 percent other varieties. The Lilliano Principessa Riserva is made from 100 percent sangiovese. The '83 Riserva was good, the '88 very good. As for the Riserva Eleanora Ruspoli Berlingier, the '85 was very good, as were the '81 and '80. Chianti Classico: * + , Riserva Eleanora Ruspoli Berlingier **

Tenuta di Nozzole (*Passo dei Pecorai, Greve, Firenze*), 1300. The 1,235-acre (500-hectare) Tenimenti Agricoli Valdigreve Chianti Classico estate has been owned by the Folonaris of Ruffino since 1972. There are some 247 acres (100 hectares) of specialized vineyards on the property. Their vineyards for Chianti Classico are planted with 94 percent sangiovese, 3 percent canaiolo, and 3 percent trebbiano. They also grow cabernet and chardonnay. They have three special crus: the 7.9-acre (3.2-hectare) La Forra vineyard for a Chianti Classico Riserva, the 26-acre (10.5-hectare) Le Bruniche vineyard for chardonnay, and the 7.7-acre (3.1-hectare) Paretaio vineyard for cabernet sauvignon. Their first Chianti Classico Riserva La Forra was the '78, the first Chardonnay was the '86, and the first Cabernet the '87. The Cabernet will be released in 1991. Their annual production of Chianti Classico here is 66,600 cases, that of Cabernet 2,775, and Chardonnay 11,100. There were 2,888 cases of the '83 La Forra and 1,000 of the '82. Both vintages spent eight months in *barrique*.

We have found the Nozzole Chiantis to be reliable and fairly good, characteristic of the Greve style. Recently we tasted the surprisingly very good '61 Riserva from half bottle; the vintage was not a success in this district. The bottle was stored in fair conditions by Vicki Breslaw and Alan Ferman. This shows how well good Chianti Classico, even if made with *governo* and white grapes, can age. Of more recent vintages, the '86 Riserva was quite good, and the '80, '82, and '83 single-vineyard Riserva La Forra, made from a blend of sangiovese and canaiolo with a small amount of malvasia, were very good. Chianti Classico **

Tenuta di Poggio a Remole. See *Frescobaldi.*

Tenuta di Pomino. See *Frescobaldi.*

Tenuta di Poneto (*Greve in Chianti*, località *Ferrone, Firenze*). The Poneta estate has almost 44 acres (17.7 hectares) of vines which yield some 10,000 cases of Chianti Classico annually.

Tenuta di San Vito in Fior di Selva (*Montelupo Fino*, località *Camaioni, Firenze*), 1958. Roberto Drighi has 54 acres (22 hectares) of vines on his San Vito farm. He produces 12,500 cases of wine a year, including almost 11,000 of Chianti from the Colli Fiorentini zone. This wine, pre-DOCG, was made from a blend of 69 percent sangiovese, 9 percent canaiolo, and 22 percent trebbiano.

Tenuta di Vignole (*Panzano in Chianti, Firenze*). Tenuta di Vignole has been owned by F.lli Nistri since 1970. This 49-acre (20-hectare) estate has 22 acres (9 hectares) planted in vines, all but 2.47 (1) for Chianti Classico. The vines, planted in *galestro* soil, have a southern to southeastern exposure. They produce

some 4,400 cases of Chianti Classico, plus 10,665 of a white wine. We found both the '85 Riserva and '88 *normale* good. Chianti Classico *

Tenuta Il Monte (*Montespertoli, Firenze*). Ada Montagni owns Tenuta Il Monte. Our experience with her Chianti has been limited to the good '83. Chianti *

Tenuta La Colombaia (*Chiocchio, Firenze*). Our experience with this producer has been less than favorable. Of the five vintages we've tasted from them, only one, the '80 Riserva, was good. Unfortunately we haven't tasted anything more recent than the '81 Riserva. Chianti Classico [0]

Tenuta Montegiacchi. See *Agricoltori del Chianti Geografico Soc. Coop.*

Tenuta Villa Rosa (*Castellina in Chianti*, località *Villarosa, Siena*). The 487-acre (197-hectare) Villa Rosa estate has 91 acres (37 hectares) of vines, 69 (28) for Chianti Classico. Their annual production of wine is 28,000 cases, that of Chianti Classico 16,000 cases. They produced quite a good '83 and '85 Riserva, and '88 *normale*. Chianti Classico **

Terrabianca. See *Fattoria Terrabianca.*

Tiorcia (*Gaiole in Chianti, Siena*). This tiny Chianti Classico producer has 0.6610 acre (0.2675 hectare) planted in monoculture and 1.2474 (0.5048) in mixed at an altitude of 1,705 feet (520 meters) above sea level. They produce 5,333 bottles of Chianti Classico annually.

Torgaio di San Salvatore. See *Ruffino.*

Torre dei Pazzi. See *Castello di Trebbio.*

Torricino (*San Martino alla Palma, Firenze*). Oscar Pio of Torricino produces Chianti in the Colli Fiorentini zone. His '76 was fairly nice, his '77 unimpressive. The Torricino Chianti is made with *governo*; the *uvaggio* used is 60 percent sangiovese, 5 percent canaiolo, and, rather surprisingly, 35 percent white grapes (which is more even than the DOC allowed)—25 percent trebbiano and 10 percent malvasia. Chianti Colli Fiorentini [*]

Travignoli (*Pelago, Firenze*). This estate is owned by Count Busi. Chianti Rùfina * —

Tregole. See *Fattoria Tregole.*

Val delle Corti (*Radda in Chianti*, località *La Croce, Siena*). Val delle Corti's 10.6 acres (4.3 hectares) of vines are planted at an altitude of 1,640 feet (500 meters) above sea level. They produce 2,500 cases of Chianti Classico a year.

Valiano (*Molin del Piano, Firenze*). This 128-acre (52-hectare) estate in the Rùfina zone, not to be confused with Fattoria di Valiano in the Classico district, has 35 acres (14 hectares) of vineyards, 27 (11) in specialized cultivation. They produce 93,000 cases of wine a year.

Vecchia Cantina di Montepulciano, Soc. Coop. (*Montepulciano*, località *Cicolina, Siena*), 1937. This 300-member cooperative winery controls 2,500 acres (1,000 hectares) of vines, of which 1,235

(500) are planted for Chianti. They are better known for their Vino Nobile di Montepulciano.

Vecchie Terre di Montefili (*Greve in Chianti, Firenze*), *1980.* Roccaldo Acuti is the proprietor of this 40.8-acre (16.5-hectare) estate, which was once a farm owned by the Badia a Passignano monastery. Acuti currently has 22 acres (9 hectares) of vineyards, part in *coltura promiscua,* planted at altitudes ranging from 1,475 to 1,640 feet (450 to 500 meters) above sea level with a southwest exposure. The vineyards are planted with approximately 90 percent sangiovese, 5 percent canaiolo, and 5 percent white grapes for Chianti Classico, plus some cabernet sauvignon for the **Bruno di Rocca** *vino da tavola,* and a small amount of pinot noir, pinot gris, and chardonnay.

Acuti's first wine was from the 1980 vintage. The winery is a hobby for him but one that he takes very seriously. He has engaged the noted enologist Vittorio Fiore as consultant. Fiore's philosophy regarding *riserva* is that first the grapes must be selected for that wine or else the wine won't be of *riserva* quality after aging.

The last time we visited Vecchie Terre a few years ago, Acuti told us that he had an annual production of about 30,000 bottles of *normale* Chianti Classico, 3,000 of *riserva* (there were 3,516 bottles of the '82), and 3,000 of Bruno di Rocca, a sangiovese–cabernet sauvignon blend aged in *barrique.* He was aiming for a production of 38,000 bottles of Chianti Classico. The Consorzio del Gallo Nero reports that his production of Chianti Classico today can be as much as 60,000 bottles.

The Vecchie Terre Chianti is made basically from sangiovese; no white grapes are used. The *normale* is made with *governo,* for which they use, Acuti points out, dried grapes, not concentrate, as is now becoming fairly common practice in the area. They dry the grapes for two months, after which they destem them before adding them to the wine. The wine is fermented in stainless steel and aged in oak casks of 795 gallons (30 hectoliters) and in *barriques.*

Since 1986, Vecchie Terre has produced the single-vineyard Riserva Anfiteatro. Both the '86 and '87 showed a lot of promise. Of the most recent vintages we've tasted, both the '86 and '87 were good, especially the '87. Chianti Classico: ** + , Riserva Anfiteatro *** –

Vigna al Sole (*Vagliagli,* località *Oliviera, Siena*). Vigna al Sole has 6.7 acres (2.7 hectares) of vines, nearly all in specialized cultivation, at an average altitude of 1,805 feet (550 meters) above sea level. Their annual production of Chianti Classico is about 1,500 cases.

Vigna di Sorripa. See **Le Lame.**

Vigna Vecchia. See **Vignavecchia.**

Vignamaggio (*Greve in Chianti, Firenze*), *1910.* This estate was owned by the Gherardini family in the 1400s, when Francesco Datini, a successful wine merchant and connoisseur of wine, was one of their best clients. A famous descendent of the Gherardinis, Monna Lisa, who was born here, had her portrait painted by an artist who is said to have had an appreciation for the wines of Chianti, which was perhaps not entirely a sentimental predilection, since he was born in the village of Vinci in the Chianti region.

In 1986, the last time we visited Villa Vignamaggio, the then-owner of this 371-acre (150-hectare) estate was Conte Ranieri

Sanminiatelli. Since then the estate has been sold to the Roma-based lawyer Gianni Nunziante. The 79 acres (32 hectares) of vineyards include 5.4 (2.2) of cabernet sauvignon vines, some of them twenty-three years old. Their annual production averages 200,000 bottles of wine. This includes 10,666 bottles of Vigneto Solatio, a wine first produced in 1985. Besides their regular Chianti Classico, they produce a Chianti Classico Riserva Castello di Monna Lisa. It, too, was first made in 1985.

The first Chianti Classico sold in bottle with the Vignamaggio label was the '26. Under Sanminiatelli's reign, the Vignamaggio Chianti was fermented in oak uprights and aged in oak and chestnut casks. In a move toward modernity, he informed us on our last visit in May 1986, he will be getting some *barriques.* He discontinued the use of *governo* in 1952, with the exception of a couple of weak vintages, the 1976 and 1984. When he did use it, he added concentrate from white grapes to start the second fermentation. He also began to reduce the amount of white grapes in the *uvaggio* in 1952.

One of the first steps the new owner took was to have a new winery built. Today, Vignamaggio uses the advice of consulting enologist Franco Bernabei.

THE CRUS AND VINEYARDS OF VIGNAMAGGIO

Cru/Vineyard	Acres	Hectares
Poggio Asciutto	12.4	5
Poggiarelli	7.4	3
Poggione	9.9	4
Solatio	19.8	8

The Vignamaggio Chianti Classicos are quite good; they have balance and some style. We can recommend the '85 *normale* and the '85 Riserva Castello di Monna Lisa in particular; the '83 and '85 Riservas and the '87 *normale* are also good. Chianti Classico: ** – , Riserva Castello di Monna Lisa ** –

Vignavecchia (*Radda in Chianti, Siena*), *1876.* This *azienda* has 57 acres (23 hectares) planted in vines at altitudes ranging from 1,640 to 1,805 feet (500 to 550 meters) above sea level, and another 5 acres (2 hectares) in *coltura promiscua.* For the most part, the vineyards have a southerly exposure; a small portion faces west.

Vignavecchia has sold wine in bottles since the 1960 vintage. They produce some 12,500 cases of wine a year, most of it Chianti Classico. They also make a small amount of white wine and *vin santo,* plus a *barrique*-aged Sangiovese, **Canvalle,** and Picchio Rosso, a fizzy 100 percent sangiovese with 16 percent alcohol (concentrate is added at bottling to create a second fermentation in the bottle).

This estate has had a fine reputation for years, but we are hard pressed to explain the reason for it. Of the six vintages we tasted during our visit to the estate in May 1985, the '82 and '75 were agreeable, but the '83, '81, '79, and '78 were not. Chianti Classico 0

Villa a Sesta (*San Gusmè, Siena*). There are some 14 acres (5.8 hectares) of vines at Villa a Sesta. Annual production of Chianti Classico approaches about 3,300 cases.

Villa Angiolina (*Via di Pieve a Celle, Pistoia*). They produce two Chiantis, one labeled Bacco, the other Villa Angiolina. The first wine is the product of sangiovese and canaiolo with a small amount of trebbiano toscano, malvasia del chianti, and colorino grapes grown on the Roccolo hill. *Governo* is used. The second Chianti is made from a similar mix of grapes, plus some cabernet sauvignon grown on the Villa Angiolina hillside.

Villa Antinori. See *Marchesi L. e P. Antinori.*

Villa Banfi. See *Castello Banfi.*

Villa Branca (*Mercatale Val di Pesa, Firenze*). Villa Branca has 150 acres (60.6 hectares) of vines planted at an average altitude of 920 feet (280 meters) above sea level. They produce up to 31,665 cases a year of a Chianti Classico that they label Santa Lucia. Mario Cortevesio consults for them.

Villa Cafaggio (*Panzano in Chianti, Firenze*), *1966*. This estate is in the San Martino In Cecione district near Greve. There are references to this property from the Lombard era. *Caffagio* is a Longobard word for "enclosed cultivated fields"—in their case, fields of vines. The oldest part of the villa is the thirteenth-century turret; the rest of the building dates from the sixteenth and seventeenth centuries. The land, at one time the village of Cafaggio, dates from the thirteenth century. It was owned by the Benedictines of Siena in the fourteenth century. The property was bought by the Farkas family in 1965.

The Cafaggio vineyards, facing southward, are planted at an altitude of about 1,575 feet (480 meters) above sea level. They have nearly 72 acres (29 hectares) in cultivation, planted with 90 percent sangiovese, 5 percent canaiolo, 2 percent white grapes, and 3 percent other red varieties.

The '67 was the first Chianti Classico they bottled under the Villa Cafaggio label. They have an annual production of 13,000 to 15,500 cases, which includes 10,250 cases of DOCG Chianti. This will increase to 20,000 cases when their new vineyard, currently being planted, comes into production. A few years ago, Farkas grafted some vines over to cabernet sauvignon. He produced his

first wine—named Cortaccio—from those vines in 1989. He produced some 795 gallons (30 hectoliters) of the '83 and 1,320 (50) of the '90.

He also produces **Solatio Basilica** and **San Martino,** two wines made predominantly from sangiovese. Farkas produces 5,000 to 7,000 bottles of Solatio and 10,000 to 15,000 bottles of San Martino. The Solatio comes from the grapes of three very old vineyards, all planted between 1937 and 1939, the San Martino from the 10-acre (4-hectare) vineyard located near the Church of San Martino in Cecione. The San Martino vineyard contains about 2.5 acres (1 hectare) of sangiovese grosso. In April 1991, Farkas planted an additional 6 acres (2.5 hectares) of sangiovese grosso there.

The modern winery, with its tile floors and stainless steel tanks, presents a marked contrast to the lovely old villa; it appeals to the practical, rather than the romantic in one. The Cafaggio wines, however, satisfy the whole man.

Farkas uses a vaslin press and ferments in temperature-controlled stainless steel tanks. He ferments his red wines twelve to fourteen days at a temperature ranging from 73.4° to 78.8° Fahrenheit (23° to 26° centigrade). He ages his Chianti Classico in Slavonian oak casks. He used to use *governo*, on occasion, but doesn't any longer. In difficult years such as 1981 and 1984, as is commonly done here, he uses some concentrate for the first fermentation. Farkas has a machine that concentrates the must.

We tasted a number of the newer wines in the *cantina*, evaluating the vintages and reevaluating our previous impression of the *azienda*. Stefano was ready to draw samples from whichever vintage or vat we chose, and we were as willing to taste as many as we reasonably had time for. Our tasting of vintages from bottle at the villa on multiple occasions reconfirmed our impressions from the winery. Our experience with these wines goes back many years, and the wines were as we remembered them—very good, and consistently so. A couple of times we had heard the opinion that these wines were not up to their previous high level. We were surprised; this has not been our experience. Since our tasting at Cafaggio in 1985 we are even more surprised, and continue to be impressed.

As a rule of thumb, Farkas produces one Chianti Classico. He bottles it as needed to satisfy the market. If he can keep it long enough it will become a *riserva*, otherwise it will be sold as a *normale*. Our experience suggests that the Cafaggio *normale* ages very well. The '85, '83, and '82 Riservas were excellent, and the '86 was very good. The '87, '86, and '82 *normali* were all very good, the '83 excellent, when tasted either in 1989 or 1990, and the '88 was quite good. The Villa Cafaggio Chiantis are Classicos with body, structure, balance, and style. There are very few finer Chianti Classicos produced. Chianti Classico ***

THE DOCG VINEYARDS OF VILLA CAFAGGIO

Vineyard	Acres	Hectares
Cafaggiolo	7.4	3.0
Canfera	12.4	5.0
Cipressi	6.2	2.5
Vigna Cantina	3.7	1.5
Vigna Nova	11.1	4.5
Villa	14.8	6.0
Total	55.6	22.5

Villa Calcinaia (*Greve in Chianti, Siena*), 1523. Conti Neri Capponi is the proprietor of this 544-acre (220-hectare) estate. He has 82 acres (33 hectares) of vines, 62 (25) for Chianti Classico. The vineyards are planted with 90 percent sangiovese, 5 percent canaiolo, and 5 percent white grapes. Annual production ranges from 19,000 to 21,000 cases: 11,000 to 14,500 are Chianti Classico, which includes a young Chianti sold as Conti Capponi. They also produce 1,650 cases of Casarza and 2,200 of Vindunano, as well as a white wine and a *vin santo*. These Chiantis were better in the 1960s and early 1970s, though there are at least two reasons—the '88 and '86—to believe that they are on an upswing. Chianti Classico: Conti Capponi *, Villa Calcinaia *

Villa Cerna (*Castellina in Chianti, Siena*), 1960. The Cecchi family owns the 297-acre (120-hectare) Villa Cerna estate, at one time the residence of Benedictine monks. The estate was mentioned in a document dated February 4, 1001. Cultivation of vines at the Villa Cerna estate, according to a document of March 12, 1053, dates from at least the mid-eleventh century. Today there are 180 acres (73 hectares) of vines. The vineyards consist of approximately 85 percent sangiovese, 10 percent canaiolo, and 5 percent white grapes. These vines are more than twenty years old. They also grow cabernet sauvignon and pinot blanc. Cecchi produces an average of 44,500 cases of wine a year, 10,000 of white and the balance red.

Of recent vintages, the '85 Riserva and '87 *normale* were very good, the '86, '83, and '82 Riserve all good. Chianti Classico **

Villa Cilnia (*Bagnoro Montoncello, Arezzo*), 1968. Giovanni and Rory Bianchi own this 57-acre (23-hectare) farm in the hills of Arezzo. There are 94 acres (38 hectares) of vines, including 44.5 (18) that they lease. Their vines are planted at an average altitude of 1,215 feet (370 meters) above sea level and have a southern exposure. Their vineyards are planted with 40 percent sangiovese (including some sangiovese grosso) 8 percent cabernet sauvignon, 5 percent canaiolo and montepulciano d'abruzzo, 22 percent chardonnay, 8 percent müller thurgau, and 17 percent other grapes, including pinot nero, trebbiano, malvasia, and riesling. Their annual production here is 220 tons (2,000 quintali) of grapes, of which more than 20 percent become Chianti Colli Aretini.

The Bianchis produce some 200,000 bottles of wine a year, including 50,000 to 60,000 bottles of Villa Cilnia Colli Aretini from an *uvaggio* of 70 percent sangiovese, 15 percent canaiolo, 8 percent malvasia nera, and 7 percent trebbiano. A few years ago they also produced a Chianti Colli Arentini with the Mulino di Salmarega label; we don't know if they still do.

The rest of their production includes some special white wines—25,000 of the single-vineyard Campo del Sasso, made from a blend of 45 percent chardonnay with 40 percent trebbiano toscano and 15 percent malvasia nera; 40,000 of Poggio Garbato, a 40-40-20 chardonnay-trebbiano-malvasia blend from the vineyard of that name; and Sassolato, from a blend of 50 percent malvasia bianca and 25 percent each chardonnay and trebbiano—Le Bizze, a lightly sparkling wine made from 65 percent sangiovese, 20 percent canaiolo, and 15 percent malvasia nera; 10,000 of the single-vineyard Poggio Cicaleto Rosé, made from a malvasia nera–sangiovese-canaiolo blend in the proportion of 40-30-30; Predicato del Muschio; 12,000 of the interesting red **Le Vignacce**, made from a blend of equal parts of cabernet sauvignon, sangiovese grosso, and montepulciano d'abruzzo, from the Le Vignacce vineyard; and **Vocato**, from a blend of sangiovese, canaiolo, malvasia nera and bianca, and cabernet sauvignon grown in the vineyards of Campo del Sasso, Le Vignacce, Poggio Cicaleto, and Poggio Garbato. Chianti Colli Aretini: *normale* *, Riserva ** +

Villa Colombaio (*Quercegrossa, Siena*). This estate was owned by Contessa Isabella Bonucci Ugurgieri della Berardenga until the mid-

1980s. Because of the poor reputation of Chianti wine, the land became worth more for homesites, and consequently the Villa Colombaio winery and vineyards were sold for that purpose. From the point of view of a wine lover, this was a very unfortunate turn of events. The Colombaio wines were, without question, among the most consistent and best of the Chianti Classicos.

Production from their 28 acres (11.3 hectares) of vines was 11,000 cases of wine a year; half was bottled as Chianti Classico. They produced a Villa Colombaio *normale* (also sold as a Riserva in some markets) and a Riserva Fortilizio "Il Colombaio."

If you're lucky, you might find some of these fine, full-bodied Chiantis on the market; they're worth looking for. We've tasted the Colombaio Classicos from the '67s through the '79s and can recommend every vintage. Chianti Classico ***

Villa Consuelo (*Montefiridolfi, Firenze*). The Fattoria di S. Andrea a Fabbrica estate covers 145 acres (58.6 hectares) in the San Casciano Val di Pesa area in the northwestern part of the Classico zone. They produce some 39,000 cases of wine a year. Our limited experience with the Villa Consuelo Chianti Classico has made it too difficult to rate their wine. We haven't tasted any since 1985.

Villa Cusona, Fattoria di Guicciardini-Strozzi (*San Gimignano, località Cusona, Siena*). Roberto Guicciardini and Girolamo Strozzi own 148 (60 hectares) of vineyards at Villa Cusona in the Colli Senesi zone, from which they produce 250,000 bottles a year of Vernaccia di San Gimignano, 150,000 of Chianti, and 7,000 of *vin santo*. They name as the best vintages for their Chianti 1983, 1981, 1979, 1977, 1975, 1971, 1970, 1969, 1967, 1964, 1961, and 1958. Noted enologist Vittorio Fiore consults here. Chianti Colli Senesi ** −

Villa d'Arceno. The only wine of theirs that we met was the '83 Chianti Classico *normale*, which we tested in 1990 when it was too old. We think it best not to judge them. Recently this estate was sold. The new management brought in consultant Maurizio Castelli. They are definitely an estate worth watching.

Villa di Monte. See **Villa di Vetrice.**

Villa di Vetrice (*Rùfina, Firenze*). The Grati brothers own 1,142 acres (462 hectares). They have two estates in the Rùfina zone—Galiga and Vetrice—as well as another 250 acres (100 hectares) of vines. Their average production is more than 111,000 cases of wine a year. Besides the standard white and rosé wines of the area, they produce Chianti Rùfina under a number of labels: Artemide, Fattoria di Vetrice, Villa di Monti, and Villa di Vetrice. These wines vary considerably; some are fair, others good. The best wines seem to be sold under the Fattoria di Vetrice label. We haven't tasted the wines of Villa di Monte in some time. Chianti Rùfina: Fattoria di Vetrice **, Villa di Vetrice 0, Villa di Monte *

Villa Dievole. See **Fattoria Dievole.**

Villa Francesca (*Barberino Val d'Elsa, località Cortine, Firenze*). Giovanni Mari owns this estate and a very good restaurant that serves typical Tuscan food for 300 people. He also has apartments for rent for those wishing to spend time in this beautiful wine region. His 29.7 acres (12 hectares) of vineyards are planted at an altitude averaging 1,310 feet (400 meters) above sea level. Some

80 percent of his vineyards are planted in sangiovese, 10 percent in canaiolo, and 10 percent in white grapes.

Mari produced his first Chianti Classico in 1973. Today he produces approximately 70,000 bottles of Chianti Classico annually, which includes some 5,000 to 6,500 of the Villa Francesca Riserva with the balance being the Sicelle *normale*. He doesn't make a *riserva* every year, nor does he sell a *normale* every year. He is a firm believer in quality, and if the wine doesn't measure up it is either declassified or sold *sfuso*. Between his first vintage in 1973 and 1985 he produced *riserve* in 1973 (5,000 bottles), 1974 (4,000), 1977 (5,000), 1978 (5,000), 1981 (3,500), and 1985 (estimated at 11,500 bottles in 1986), and none in 1975, 1976, 1979, 1980, 1982, 1983, and 1984. His first Chianti Classico *normale* was produced in 1982. In 1983 he sold it to Antinori, and in 1984 he sold it *sfuso*. And in 1985 he produced some 11,500 bottles of *riserva* only; he sold the *normale* Chianti Classico to Antinori.

He also produces some 1,000 cases of *vino da tavola* and minuscule amount of a *vin santo* from 100 percent sangiovese. When we last spoke to Mari, in May 1986, he planned to produce a *barrique*-aged sangiovese–cabernet sauvignon blend to be called Rosso di Eleonora. We don't know if he has produced this wine as yet. It was to be named for his second daughter, who was nine years old at the time. He expected to produce some 110 cases of this wine.

When we visited them in 1986, we tasted a range of wines; all were, at the least, good, including the young and fresh Sicelle da Giovanni Mari. More recently, we liked their *riserve* from '73, '82, and '85, but were disappointed with the *normale* '86. Chianti Classico: Sicelle da Giovanni *, Villa Francesca **

Villa Il Poggiolo (*Carmignano*, località *Poggiolo, Firenze*), 1800. The fine Carmignano producer Giovanni Cianchi Baldazzi also makes a fairly good Chianti Montalbano. That wine is made from an *uvaggio* of 75 percent sangiovese, 10 percent canaiolo nero, 10 percent trebbiano, and 5 percent other varieties. Chianti Montalbano *

Villa La Pagliaia (*Castelnuovo Berardenga, Siena*), 1888. This *azienda* owns either 79 (32) or 115 acres (46.6 hectares) of vines planted 1,150 to 1,245 feet (350 to 380 meters) above sea level from which they produce, at most, 17,775 cases of Chianti Classico a year. Their average annual production of all wines is about 35,500 cases; this includes, besides their Chianti Classico, a Bianco della Lega, a rosé, and a *vin santo*. Their top wine, Chianti Classico Riserva Granduca Ferdinando III, is made from the best grapes from the best parts of their vineyards. The '80, '78, and '77 were all good. They produced 15,200 bottles of the '80. Chianti Classico: Riserva Granduca Ferdinando III *

Villa La Selva (*Montebenichi, Bucine, Arezzo*), 1958. Sergio and Riccardo Carpini have 111 acres (45 hectares) of vineyards on their La Selva farm in the Colli Aretini zone, from which they produce some 35,000 to 40,500 cases of wine a year. This includes three Chiantis, a rosé, and a *spumante*. They make one Chianti meant to be drunk young. The second is aged for two to three years and will live for a few more. Their best wine is the Riserva, which ages fairly well. Reportedly La Selva uses *governo* for all their Chiantis. They use the services of consulting enologist Vittorio Fiore. It's been some time since we've tasted their wines, but we did enjoy them. Chianti **

Villa Montepaldi (*San Casciano Val di Pesa, Firenze*). Montepaldi has 116 acres (47 hectares) of vines, from which it produces 41,000 cases of wine a year. The estate is owned by Marchese Corsini. It's been some years since we tasted this Chianti Classico. Under the circumstances, even though those we tasted left us unimpressed, it seems best to suspend judgment until we taste them again. Chianti Classico [0]

Villa Terciona (*Mecatale Val di Pesa, Firenze*). This estate in the San Casciano area has 138 acres (56 hectares) of vineyards. They produced about 41,000 cases of wine a year. We found both their '73 and '74, the most recent we've tasted, in the late 1970s, surprisingly good for the vintages. The Saccardi family owned Villa Terciona until they sold it, in 1985, to Antinori. We don't know if all or part of the estate was sold, and if there is still a Chianti Classico with this name. Chianti Classico ** —

Vistarenni. See **Fattoria di Vistarenni**.

Vitignano (*Pianella, Siena*). This 46-acre (18.6-hectare) estate produces some 10,000 cases of Chianti Classico annually.

THE SMALLEST CHIANTI CLASSICO ESTATES

Estate	Località	Vineyards		Average Number of Bottles Per Year
		Acres	Hectares	
Casalgallo	Querciagrossa	6.92	2.80	19,000
Casanova di Pietrafitta	Castellina	3.21	1.30	8,666
Casavecchia di Nittardi	Castellina	5.44	2.20	31,000
Castel Ruggero	Strada	7.41	3.00	16,000
Castellinuzza	Lamole	5.19	2.10	14,665
Cerbaiola	San Donato	8.90	3.60	25,200
Conio, Azienda Agricola Immobiliare	San Donato	7.17	2.90	20,000

Estate	Località	Vineyards		Average Number of Bottles Per Year
		Acres	Hectares	
Fattoria Cafaggio di Pesa	Castellina	8.90	3.60	26,000
Fattoria di Calleno	Castelnuovo Berardenga	10.87	4.40	30,500
Fattoria Ispoli	Mercatale	10.87	4.40	17,000
Fattoria La Presura	Strada	10.87	4.40	20,000
Fattoria Nittardi	Castellina	7.41	3.00	21,000
Fattoria Talente	San Casciano	7.66	3.10	21,500
Fattoria Tregole	Castellina	3.71	1.50	10,660
Fattoria Valtellina	Gaiole	5.19	2.10	14,665
Il Campino di Mondiglia	Barberino	0.74	0.30	1,000
Il Villino	Castellina	7.17	2.90	20,000
La Brancaia	Castellina	9.88	4.00	28,000
La Bricola	Sambuca	4.45	1.80	13,000
La Montanina	Monti di Sotto	4.70	1.90	13,300
Le Miccine	Gaiole	11.86	4.80	10,800
Macia	Vagliagli	7.41	3.00	21,000
Mezzuola	Greve	6.42	2.60	18,000
Miscianello Tomarecchio	Vagliagli	10.87	4.40	30,540
Montoro	Greve	6.92	2.80	18,000
Montoro e Selvole	Greve	4.94	2.00	13,200
Oliviera	Vagliagli	8.15	3.30	20,500
Pian Del Doccio e Pile di Sotto	Lamole	11.37	4.60	26,000
Podere Capaccia	Radda	7.41	3.00	6,000–7,000
Podere Crognole	Radda	2.37	0.96	4,933
Podere di Stignano	Gaiole	9.88	4.00	27,600
Podere La Casaccia	Radda	1.21	0.49	3,333
Podere La Piaggia	Castellina	5.93	2.40	16,666
Podere Ripertoli	Greve	7.41	3.00	13,300
Podere Terreno alla Via Della Volpaia	Radda	7.91	3.20	12,000
Poderuzzo	Panzano	5.14	2.08	15,000
Poggerina	Monti	0.35	0.14	933
Poggerino	Radda	11.12	4.50	29,400
Poggio dell'Oliviera	Vagliagli	5.44	2.20	13,200
Pruneto	Radda	3.95	1.60	12,000
Rosso di Massanera	La Romola	0.99	0.40	11,600
San Vicenti	Gaiole	10.63	4.30	28,200
Setriolo	Castellina	4.70	1.90	13,200
Sonnino	Gaiole	5.19	2.10	13,300
Sugame	Greve	3.40	1.38	9,600
Tiorcia	Gaiole	1.91	0.77	5,333
Val delle Corti	Radda	10.63	4.30	30,000
Vigna al Sole	Vagliagli	6.67	2.70	18,000

CHAPTER 8

Brunello di Montalcino

The history of Brunello di Montalcino is very short, going back a little more than one hundred years, but the tradition of winemaking in Montalcino is a long one. The Etruscans may have cultivated the first vines here; many artifacts and tombs from that era have been discovered in the region. Or it may have been the Romans who first planted vineyards on Monte Alcino, which they called Mons Ilcinus. The town takes its name from the holm oak—*ilex*—common in these hills and a symbol on the city's crest and on the seal of the Brunello di Montalcino *consorzio*.

Montalcino was settled by inhabitants of a nearby village seeking refuge from Saracen invaders early in the tenth century. Some believe it was they who terraced its slopes to plant vineyards on the stony hillsides. Their wines would have been quite different, however, from the Brunello of today. Until the 1500s all mention found of the wine of Montalcino refers to white wine. And Francesco Redi in his poem *"Bacco in Toscana,"* written in 1685, praises the Moscadaletto, or "pleasant little Moscadello," which he considered the best wine of the area.

White wine continued to dominate in Montalcino at least until late in the nineteenth century. And the red wine made here included a proportion of white grapes, as the Chianti does today. But that was all changed with the emergence of Brunello, made from only red grapes and only the grapes of a single variety, which would become not only the most noted wine of Montalcino but perhaps the most esteemed wine of Italy.

The grape used is a subvariety of the sangiovese called sangiovese grosso, or brunello, for the brownish cast of its berries. The first reference to Brunello wine, according to Guglielmo Solci, is in a note written in 1842 by Canon Vincenzo Chiarini of Montalcino, in which he gave high praise to the wine from the brunello grape.[1]

At Biondi-Santi, they claim that their brunello vines are a special clone of the sangiovese grosso isolated in the Il Greppo vineyard by Clemente Santi, who recognized its superior qualities and propagated its growth. Nothing has been found in the Biondi-Santi archives noting when he discovered the brunello clone or produced the first wine exclusively from this grape. But by 1860, Santi was producing a wine he called Brunello, and apparently a good one. In 1869 the agrarian committee of the district awarded Santi a silver medal for his Vino Rosso Scelto (Brunello) 1865.

And prior to 1870, we know that others produced a Brunello as well. In the *Prospetto Generale N. 2—Relazione Sui Vini Della Provincia Senese* for the provincial exhibition of August 1870, there is mention of an 1865 and 1869 "brunello" from Tito Costanti. The former wine, we are informed, was 14 percent alcohol and the latter 15 percent.

The subvariety, sangiovese (or sangioveto) grosso, was gaining some recognition outside the region as well. In a technical book on winemaking published in 1871, Alessandro Bizzarri refers to the "Sangioveto grosso and piccolo."[2]

THE BIRTH OF BRUNELLO DI MONTALCINO

Credit for producing the first Brunello wine as we know it today—a 100 percent varietal made without the use of *governo,* traditional in this region—goes to Santi's grandson, Ferruccio Biondi-Santi, who is credited with perfecting Brunello in the 1870s. He planted new vineyards exclusively in this variety and improved the winemaking techniques to produce a wine for long aging. A few bottles of his 1888 and 1891, two exceptional vintages, are still preserved in the *sacristia* of the *cantina* at Fattoria Il Greppo. In 1970, at the second recorking ceremony (Tancredi Biondi-Santi had had the '91 recorked, after thirty years, in 1927), the dignitaries and journalists present are reported to have been impressed with the wine's capacity to age.

Ferruccio Biondi-Santi's son, Tancredi, carried on his father's work, and is responsible for establishing an enviable reputation for the wine through judicious marketing and promotion, emphasizing its importance and quality.

At the Siena Exposition of 1933, four Brunellos were presented: the Biondi-Santi, plus that of Guido Angelini, the Barbi of Giuseppe Colombini, and Roberto Franceschi's Sant' Angelo. According to Emanuele Pellucci,[3] Angelini was the only other producer besides Biondi-Santi bottling a Brunello at that time. Except for occasional special bottles, the others were selling their wine in cask or demijohns. Franceschi began bottling, on a limited basis, in 1936. Colombini was also among the first to offer Brunello in bottle. Later Costanti, Casale del Bosco, Lovatelli, Lisini, Mastro-

paolo, Camigliano, Castiglion del Bosco, and others began doing the same.

Yet, into the 1950s, only Biondi-Santi made a practice of vintage-dating and laying down older vintages in his cellars. The other producers were selling the wine of the year, frequently in *fiaschi.*

The Biondi-Santi Brunello '55 received international attention when it was selected to be poured at a state dinner in honor of Queen Elizabeth II hosted by Italian President Giuseppe Saragat in 1969. With that the reputation of Brunello was made.

THE BRUNELLO PRODUCTION ZONE

Brunello di Montalcino is produced in the hilly region within the Chianti Colli Senesi district, south of Siena, bordered by the Orcia, Ombrone, and Asso rivers. The Montalcino production zone covers 60,200 acres (24,362 hectares); 50 percent of the zone is woodland; large tracts of brush, fields, pastureland, and olive groves make up a major portion of the remaining area. Vines can be planted up to an altitude of 1,970 feet (600 meters) above sea level. At most, 2,470 acres (1,000 hectares) can be planted in vines for Brunello di Montalcino. In 1990, there were 2,100 acres (850 hectares) under vines and an additional 64 acres (25 hectares) registered for Brunello production. There are 142 growers cultivating Brunello vineyards in the zone, and 89 producers who bottle an average of 175,000 cases of Brunello di Montalcino and 166,650 cases of Rosso di Montalcino a year. Production, with the current acreage, cannot exceed 491,062 cases of Brunello and Rosso combined. Interestingly, between 1985 and 1975 less than half—49.87 percent—of the wine declared was bottled as Brunello.

The acreage under vines has been increasing steadily since the recovery from *phylloxera,* which arrived late in this part of Italy, in the 1930s, virtually wiping out the vineyards, which had reached a high of 2,286 acres (925 hectares) in specialized plantings and 3,072 (1,243) in mixed culture in 1929. In 1969 there were just 115 acres (46.6 hectares) of specialized vineyards and 95 (38.4) planted in *coltura promiscua.* By 1974, these figures were 637 (258) and 173 (70), respectively; a decade later, in 1979, there were 1,513 (612) in monoculture and 151 (61) mixed.

The climate in the Brunello production zone is Mediterranean. On the lower slopes the soil is clayey marl, higher up, a combination of limestone and marl with some tufaceous volcanic stone. The best soils are *galestro alberese*—clay with carbonate of lime and friable rock.

The grapes for Brunello di Montalcino are harvested between the latter part of September and the middle of October.

PRODUCERS OF BRUNELLO AND ROSSO DI MONTALCINO (BASED ON A MAP BY THE CONSORZIO DEL VINO BRUNELLO DI MONTALCINO)

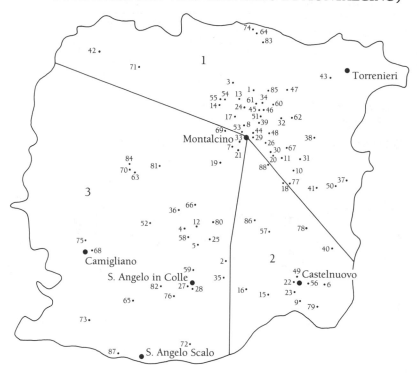

Producer	Winery	Number	Producer	Winery	Number
Abruzzese Vincenzo	Tenuta Valdicava	1	Giannetti Franco	La Fornace*	31
Agricola Centolani S.r.l.	Azienda Agricola Friggiali	66	Giannetti Rino	La Campana	32
Ai Caselli S.r.l.	Castelgiocondo	63	Gorelli Giancarlo	Due Portine*	33
Altesino S.r.l.	Altesi	64	Immobiliare Fortius S.p.A.	Azienda Il Grappolo	76
Anania Giuseppe	La Torre	2	La Lecciaia S.r.l.	Azienda Vallafrico	77
Argiano S.r.l.	Argiano	65	Lambardi Maurizio	Canalicchio di Sotto	34
Azienda Agricola Verbena	Verbena	67	La Velona S.p.A.	La Velona	79
Baricci Nello	Colombaio-Montosoli	3	Lisini Elina	Lisini	35
Bartolomei Alfo	Caprili	4	Machetti Renata	S. Carlo	36
Bellini Roberto	Chiesa di S. Restituta	5	Mantengoli Ennio	Rasa	37
Benocci-Bianchini A.	S. Giorgio	6	Mantengoli Vasco	Rasina	38
Berni Domenico	Pietroso	7	Martini Fort. e Ros.	Paradiso	39
Bianchini Giuseppe	Ciacci Piccolomini	9	Mastrojanni Gabriele	S. Pio e Loreto	40
Bianchini-Mori M.	Marroneto	8	Molinari Diego	Cerbaiona	41
Biliorsi Ruggero	Fornacina	10	Nardi Silvio	Casale del Bosco	42
Biondi-Santi	Fattoria Il Greppo	88	Neri Giovanni	Casanova	43
Burroni Carlo	Ferro*	11	Pacenti Franco e Rosildo	Canalicchio di Sopra	45
Canneta S.r.l.	Podere Canneta	69	Pacenti P.—Ripaccioli P. L.	Canalicchio di Sopra	46
Castelgiocondo S.p.A.	Castelgiocondo	70	Pacenti S. Pieri Graz.	Pelagrilli	47
Castelli Cesare	Villa S. Restituta	12	Padelletti Pier F.	Fontebuia*	44
Castello Camigliano S.r.l.	Camigliano	68	Pallari L.—Mantengoli E.	Pescaia*	48
Castiglion del Bosco S.r.l.	Castiglion del Bosco	71	Poggi-Fabbri Marusca	Le Presi	49
Cencioni Annunziata	Cerbaia	14	Poggio Antico S.r.l.	Poggio Antico	80
Cencioni Giuseppe Ben. Fra.	Capanna	13	Poggio Salvi S.r.l.	Poggio Salvi	81
Ciacci-Bellocci Elisa	Poggio degli Ulivi	16	Rosi Ermanno	S. Filippo	50
Ciacci Giuseppe	Tenuta di Sesta	15	Rossi Sergio	Fattoria La Geria	51
Col d'Orcia S.p.A.	Col d'Orcia	72	Saiagricola S.p.A.	La Poderina	78
Colombini-Cinelli Francesca	Fattoria dei Barbi	18	Salvioni Giulio	Cerbaiola	53
Comp. Agricola Pam	Poggio alle Mura	73	Salvioni Maria Grazia	Quercecchio	52
Corioni A.—Abbarchi F.	Scopetone	17	S. Felice S.p.A.	Azienda Campogiovanni	82
Cosimi Roberto E.	Il Poggiolo	19	Sassetti Angelo	Pertimali	54
Costanti Andrea	Il Colle	20	Sassetti Livio	Pertimali	55
D.A.M. Diffusione Altesino del Montalcino	Altesi	74	Sassetti Vasco	Sassetti	56
Daviddi Enrico	Due Porti	21	Schwarz Herbert	La Magia	57
Eredi Fuligni	Cottimello	29	Soldera Gianfranco	Case Basse	58
Fanti-Baldassarre Filippo	S. Filippo	22	Talenti Pier Luigi	Pian di Conte	59
Fanti Flavio	Palazzetta*	23	Tenuta Caparzo S.r.l.	Caparzo	83
Fastelli Mauro	Paradiso	24	Tiezzi Enzo	Cerrino 1ª	60
Fattoi Ofelio	Capanna	25	Toscovinicola S.r.l.	Castelgiocondo	84
Focacci Gino Antonio	I Comunali	26	Valdisuga S.p.A.	Valdisuga	85
Fontevino S.r.l.	Camigliano	75	Vannini Giancarlo	Le Crete	61
Franceschi Clemente e Roberto	Il Casello	28	Villa a Tolli S.r.l.	Villa a Tolli	86
Franceschi Clemente e Roberto	Tenuta Il Poggione	27	Villa Banfi S.r.l.	Villa Banfi	87
Gianneli-Carli Ernesta	Il Colle 2ª	30	Zannoni G.—Ricciardello F.	La Fortuna	62

*Only bottle Rosso di Montalcino

ACREAGE AND GROWERS REGISTERED TO PRODUCE BRUNELLO DI MONTALCINO

Year	Growers	Acres	Hectares
1989	118	2,250.85	910.87
1988	116	2,163.70	875.60
1987	111	1,911.40	773.50
1986	104	1,864.20	754.40
1985	95	1,762.39	713.20

Source: Consorzio del Vino Brunello di Montalcino

TOTAL PRODUCTION BASED ON HARVEST DECLARATION

Year	Brunello	Rosso Gallons	Total	Brunello	Rosso Hectoliters	Total
1989	1,087,923	37,701	1,125,624	41,178	1,427	42,605
1988	855,163	37,939	893,102	32,368	1,436	33,804
1987	1,066,602	58,996	1,125,598	40,371	2,233	42,604
1986	967,342	56,195	1,023,537	36,614	2,127	38,741
1985	901,450	49,353	950,803	34,120	1,868	35,988
Average	975,696	48,037	1,023,733	36,930	1,818	38,748

Source: Consorzio del Vino Brunello di Montalcino

Subdistricts of the Brunello Zone

Claudio Basla of Altesino points out that the Brunello production zone can be divided into three districts. The first district takes in the area north and to the east of the town of Montalcino, including the town of Torrenieri. This district, Basla says, is noted for producing the most elegant Brunellos. Among the better producers here are Altesino, Costanti, Pertimali, and Tenuta Caparzo.

The second district, the smallest, is a wedge extending southeast from Montalcino and around the town of Castelnuovo. Biondi-Santi, Colombini, and Mastrojanni are located here. This area, the most protected, is considered to be the most favored.

The third zone, the southwestern part of the Brunello region, encompasses the towns of Camigliano, S. Angelo in Colle, and S. Angelo Scalo. This area reportedly produces the most robust Brunellos. Among the better vineyards of this district are those of Case Basse, Il Casello, Il Poggione, and Pian di Conte.

BRUNELLO AND ITALIAN WINE LAW

When Brunello was granted DOCG (*Denominazione di Origine Controllata e Garantita*) status in 1980, some of the regulations regarding its production under DOC were changed.

The Brunello producers were previously allowed to add up to 10 percent of grapes, must, or wine from outside the Brunello production zone to bring up the alcohol in poor years when conditions were less than favorable. Under the new regulations, the correction can be done only with an older vintage of Brunello; up to 15 percent is allowed.

There is one controversial regulation concerning aging requirements. Under DOC, Brunello had to be aged no less than four years in oak or chestnut casks. Some producers protested, and rightly so, that this regulation, especially in the weaker vintages, caused the wine to dry out and be robbed of its fruit. They argued that the producers should be allowed to decide for themselves how long to leave the wine in wood. Other producers, in favor of long cask aging for Brunello, countered that the problem wasn't the time in cask but the wood itself, claiming that if the casks were old enough and large enough there was no problem. The regulation was kept, but modified somewhat. The aging requirement was reduced to three and a half years in oak. And since 1991 that time has been reduced still further, to four years in total with at least three in wood.

Obviously, government officials are not interested in lessening their authority by eliminating regulations, even unnecessary ones. The better producers don't need a government committee to tell them how to make wine; they will continue to make fine wines despite the regulations. And

TOTAL AMOUNT OF BRUNELLO DI MONTALCINO BOTTLED AFTER REQUIRED AGING

| Year | DOC/DOCG PRODUCTION[a] Crop Size Harvested | | Amount Bottled After Aging | | Percentage of Crop Bottled as Brunello |
	Declared Hectoliters[b]	Equivalent Cases	Hectoliters	Cases	
1989	42,605	473,342	The wine is still aging in cask		
1988	33,804	375,562	The wine is still aging in cask		
1987	42,604	473,330	The wine is still aging in cask		
1986	38,741	430,413	The wine is still aging in cask		
1985	35,988	399,827	16,500	183,315	45.85
1984	24,647	273,828	12,054	133,920	48.91
1983	32,063	356,220	16,253	180,571	50.69
1982	28,731	319,201	14,541	161,551	50.61
1981	24,676	274,150	10,058	111,744	40.76
1980	23,960	266,196	13,288	147,630	55.46
1979	25,408	282,283	13,513	150,129	53.18
1978	19,504	216,689	10,381	115,333	53.22
1977	15,571	172,994	8,320	92,435	53.43
1976	10,364	115,144	4,618	51,306	44.56
1975	12,622	140,230	6,905	76,715	54.71
1974	8,388	93,191	Information not available		
Average 1975–85	23,049	256,069	11,494	127,695	49.87

NOTES: [a] Not all of the grapes declared for DOC-DOCG wine are bottled as such. Some of it is bottled as *vino da tavola* or sold in bulk.
[b] Not all wine declared as Brunello is bottled as Brunello. A lot of it is bottled as Rossi di Montalcino.

Sources: 1989–78, Consorzio del Vino Brunello di Montalcino
1977–74, Italian Wine Center, New York

those producers lacking ability or integrity will manage to make poor wines regardless.

We report the DOC and DOCG regulations as part of the description of the wine in general, but are confident that the wine buyer will learn from his or her own experience that the only guarantee of quality is surely not the official government stamp but the name of the producer responsible for the wine. The vintage also affects the quality of the wine, and by vintage-dating the wine the producer gives the consumer a further indication of what to expect, although in the worst cases the topflight producers will not bottle. If the wine doesn't measure up to their own high standards, they will not sell it as Brunello, although it legally qualifies, and if the wine of a particular vintage can't take the required wood aging, it will be declassified.

BRUNELLO IN THE GLASS

Young Brunello di Montalcino has a deep ruby-red color that shades to garnet with age as its harsh, youthful tannins mellow to a velvety texture. It has a rich aroma of cherries and berries which develops nuances of flowers, spices, underbrush, and nutlike notes—that of chestnuts is considered particularly characteristic. It is a firmly structured wine, full in body, with a dry, warm flavor displaying a richness of extract and concentration of fruit. Its finish is long and lingering.

This is Brunello at its best. Unfortunately, such Brunello is not a common enough occurrence. But from producers such as Altesino, Case Basse, Biondi-Santi, Colombini, Costanti, Il Poggione, and Mastrojanni, Brunello di Montalcino

DOC REQUIREMENTS FOR BRUNELLO DI MONTALCINO

	Minimum Aging in Years		Minimum Alcohol	Maximum Yield Gallons/Acre
	in Cask	Total		
DOC *normale*	4.0	4.0[a]	12.5%	748
Riserva	4.0	4.0[a]	12.5%	748
DOCG *normale*	3.5	4.0[b]	12.5%	599/556[c]
Riserva	3.5	5.0[b]	12.5%	599/556[c]
DOCG *normale*	3.0[d]	4.0[b]	12.5%	599/556[c]
Riserva	3.0[d]	5.0[b]	12.5%	599/556[c]
Rosso di Montalcino	n/a	September 1[e]	12.0%	599

Notes: a The aging period begins November 1 in the year of the harvest.
   b The aging period starts on January 1 after the harvest; cask aging begins on April 1.
   c When picked, 599 gallons per acre (56 hectoliters per hectare) are allowed; after aging, only 556 gallons per acre (52 hectoliters per hectare) may be bottled.
   d As of 1991.
   e In the year following the harvest.

can truly be one of the world's viticultural gems, particularly after seven to eight years of aging.

Brunello makes a fine accompaniment to roast beef, pigeon, duck, or goose, and especially game, feathered or furred, such as venison or the local wild boar.

A good place to taste a wide range of Brunellos is *La Cucina di Edgardo, Il Montalcino*, in the town of Montalcino; they offer at least one vintage of all or nearly all the Brunellos bottled.

Rating: ****

ROSSO DI MONTALCINO

At one time many producers of Brunello di Montalcino sold a younger, second wine also made from sangiovese grosso grapes, labeled Rosso dei Vigneti di Brunello, or with some such similar name. Since 1983 this wine, too, has come under DOC regulation and is now officially called Rosso di Montalcino.

Rosso di Montalcino is made from the grapes of younger vines, and/or, in the case of the better producers, from wines that don't quite measure up to the high standards they set for their Brunello.

Rosso di Montalcino cannot be sold prior to September 1 in the year following the harvest. It is generally given six to eighteen months of cask aging. It can be quite a good wine. Though not one for aging, it can take three to five years. Among the better Rosso di Montalcinos we've tasted are those from Altesino, Il Poggione, Mastrojanni, and Pian di Conte. And there are many other good ones as well.

Rosso di Montalcino is a good wine to serve with turkey, Cornish hen, quail or pheasant, cutlets or chops.

Rating: **

SITES WORTH A VISIT

Part of the thirteenth-century walls still surround the town of Montalcino, and the fourteenth-century fortress continues to guard this hillside town. The thirteenth-century town hall and an arcaded gallery built during the fourteenth and fifteenth centuries stand near the Piazza del Popolo.

Some 6 miles (10 kilometers) south of Montalcino, in the second district, near Castelnuovo dell'Abate, stands the ninth-century abbey, Abazzia di Sant' Antimo. The church here, considered to be a good example of Cistercian architecture, dates from the twelfth century.

CONSORZIO DEL VINO BRUNELLO DI MONTALCINO

Of all the *consorzii* that we have dealt with in Italy one stands out as being the most professional and helpful, and that is the *Consorzio del Vino Brunello di Montalcino*. This *consorzio* includes nearly all the growers and bottlers in the zone. They report that its members, which include 130 of the 142 growers in the zone, account for 2,050 acres (830 hectares) of the 2,100 (850) planted, or nearly 98 percent of the vineyards. And 87 of the 89 bottlers belong as well. In the years 1983 through 1989 the *consorzio*'s members produced an average of 131,893 cases of Brunello and 98,571 of Rosso.

OVERALL PRODUCTION OF BRUNELLO AND ROSSO DI MONTALCINO

Year	Brunello (Cases)	Rosso (Cases)	Total (Cases)
1989	175,000	166,667	341,667
1988	170,000	141,607	311,607
1987	154,167	120,833	275,000
1986	120,833	116,667	237,500
1985	155,000	136,444	291,444
1984	121,333	87,167	208,500
1983	100,083	28,167	128,250
Average	142,345	113,936	256,281

Source: Consorzio del Vino Brunello di Montalcino

THE MEMBERS OF THE CONSORZIO

Producer	Winery	DOC/DOCG Vineyard Surface in	
		Acres	Hectares
Abruzzese Vincenzo	Tenuta Valdicava	15.84	6.45
Ai Caselli S.r.l.	Loc. Castelgiocondo	—	—
Altesino S.r.l.	Loc. Altesi	31.73	12.84
Anania Giuseppe	La Torre	7.78	3.15
Argiano S.r.l.	Loc. Argiano	27.43	11.10
Baricci Nello	Colombaio-Montosoli	6.75	2.73
Bartolomei Alfo	Caprili	16.19	(6.55
Bellini Roberto	Chiesa di S. Restituta	28.22	11.42
Benocci-Bianchini A.	S. Giorgio	9.07	3.67
Berni Domenico	Pietroso	1.21	0.49
Bianchini Giuseppe	Ciacci Piccolomini	23.62	9.56
Bianchini-Mori M.	Marroneto	0.99	0.40
Biliorsi Ruggero	Fornacina	2.87	1.16
Burroni Carlo	Ferro	1.43	0.58
Canneta S.r.l. (Angiola Piazzi-Maria)	Podere Canneta	11.74	4.75
Castelgiocondo S.p.A.	Loc. Castelgiocondo	392.66	158.90
Castelli Cesare	Villa S. Restituta	7.02	2.84
Castello Camigliano S.r.l.	Loc. Camigliano	108.95	44.09
Castiglion del Bosco S.r.l.	Castiglion del Bosco	80.80	32.70
Cencioni Annunziata	Cerbaia	2.30	0.93
Cencioni Giuseppe Ben. Fra.	Capanna	18.76	7.59
Centolani S.r.l.	Friggiali Azienda Agricola	11.12	4.50
Ciacci-Bellocci Elisa	Poggio degli Ulivi	20.98	8.49
Ciacci Giuseppe	Tenuta di Sesta	33.71	13.64
Col d'Orcia S.r.l.	Loc. Col d'Orcia	140.80	56.98
Colombini-Cinelli Francesca	Fattoria dei Barbi	81.03	32.79
Comp. Agricola Pam	Poggio alle Mura	—	—
Corioni A.—Abbarchi F.	Scopetone	3.73	1.51
Constanti Andrea	Il Colle	7.73	3.13

Producer	Winery	DOC/DOCG Vineyard Surface in	
		Acres	Hectares
D. A. M. Diffusione Altesino del Montalcino	Loc. Altesi	—	—
Daviddi Enrico	Due Porti	5.68	2.30
E. Cosimi Roberto	Il Poggiolo	6.27	2.54
Eredi Fuligni	Cottimello	8.11	3.28
Fanti Flavio	Palazzetta	4.40	1.78
Fanti-Baldassarre Filippo	S. Filippo	10.38	4.20
Fastelli Mauro	Paradiso	6.70	2.71
Fattoi Ofelio	Capanna	6.87	2.78
Focacci Gino Antonio	I Comunali	13.27	5.37
Fontevino S.r.l.	Loc. Camigliano	4.45	1.80
Franceschi Clemente e Roberto	Il Casello	12.01	4.86
Franceschi Clemente e Roberto	Tenuta Il Poggione	126.67	51.26
Gianneli-Carli Ernesta	Il Colle 2ª	4.62	1.87
Giannetti Franco	La Fornace	1.04	0.42
Giannetti Rino	La Campana	4.32	1.75
Gorelli Giancarlo	Due Portine	1.24	0.50
Immobiliare Fortius S.p.A.	Azienda Il Grappolo	4.45	1.80
La Lecciaia S.r.l.	Azienda Vallafrico	39.51	6.47
La Velona S.r.l.	La Velona	—	—
Lambardi Maurizio	Canalicchio di Sotto	7.41	3.00
Lisini Elina	Lisini	27.92	11.60
Machetti Renata	S. Carlo	5.44	2.20
Mantengoli Ennio	Rasa	1.48	0.60
Mantengoli Vasco	Rasina	2.96	1.20
Martini Fort. e Ros.	Paradiso	1.38	0.56
Mastrojanni Gabriele	S. Pio e Loreto	27.48	11.12
Molinari Diego	Cerbaiona	3.98	1.61
Nardi Silvio	Casale del Bosco	111.40	45.08
Neri Giovanni	Casanova	25.28	10.23
Pacenti Franco e Rosildo	Canalicchio di Sopra	5.56	2.25
Pacenti P.—Ripaccioli P. L.	Canalicchio di Sopra	5.56	2.25
Pacenti S. Pieri Graz.	Pelagrilli	7.07	2.86
Padelletti Pier F.	Fontebuia	1.71	0.69
Pallari L.—Mantengoli E.	Pescaia	4.67	1.89
Poggi-Fabbri Marusca	Le Presi	1.48	0.60
Poggio Antico S.r.l.	Loc. Poggio Antico	50.26	20.34
Poggio Salvi S.r.l.	Poggio Salvi	22.12	8.95
Rosi Ermanno	S. Filippo	9.89	4.00
Rossi Sergio	Fattoria La Gerla	4.94	2.00
S. Felice S.p.A.	Azienda Campogiovanni	23.75	9.61
Saiagricola S.p.A.	La Poderina	20.88	8.45
Salvioni Giulio	Cerbaiola	2.47	1.00
Salvioni Maria Grazia	Quercecchio	9.69	3.92
Sassetti Angelo	Pertimali	6.18	2.50
Sassetti Livio	Pertimali	7.64	3.09
Sassetti Vasco	Sassetti	1.26	0.51
Schwartz Herbert	La Magia	38.55	15.60

Producer	Winery	DOC/DOCG Vineyard Surface in	
		Acres	Hectares
Soldera Gianfranco	Case Basse	15.15	6.13
Talenti Pier Luigi	Pian di Conte	17.92	7.25
Tenuta Caparzo S.r.l.	Caparzo	30.07	12.17
Tiezzi Enzo	Cerrino 1ª	5.31	2.15
Toscovinicola S.r.l.	Loc. Castelgiocondo	—	—
Valdisuga S.p.A.	Valdisuga	61.98	25.08
Vannini Giancarlo	La Crete	1.53	0.62
Villa a Tolli S.r.l.	Villa a Tolli	18.01	7.29
Villa Banfi S.r.l.	Villa Banfi	246.25	99.65
Zannoni G.–Ricciardiello F.	La Fortuna	4.94	2.00

RATING THE MONTALCINO PRODUCERS

****

Altesino
- Case Basse (Soldera Gianfranco)
+ Costanti Andrea (Il Colle al Matrichese)
Fattoria Il Greppo (Biondi-Santi)
Tenuta Il Poggione (Franceschi Clemente e Roberto)

***

+ Fattoria dei Barbi (Colombini-Cinelli Francesca)
- Fattoria La Gerla (Rossi Sergio)
Il Marroneto (M. Bianchini-Mori)[a]
La Chiesa di S. Restituta (Bellini Roberto)
Mastrojanni Gabriele (S. Pio e Loreto)[a]
- Pertimali (Sassetti Livio)
Podere Pian di Conte (Pier Luigi Talenti)
Tenuta Caparzo
Tenuta Caparzo, La Casa
- Tenuta Col d'Orcia, Poggio al Vento (*normale* **, Riserva **)

**

Canalicchio (Lambardi Silvano)
Canalicchio di Sopra (Lambardi Maurizio)
Canalicchio di Sopra (Pacenti Franco e Rosildo)
- Canalicchio di Sopra (Primo Pacenti & Pier Luigi Ripaccioli)
- Canalicchio di Sopra, Le Gode di Montosoli (Primo Pacenti & Pier Luigi Ripaccioli)
- Capanna (Cencioni Giuseppe Ben. Fra.)
- Capanna di S. Restituta (Fattoi Ofelio)
Caprili (Bartolomei Alfo)
- Casanova (Giovanni Neri)
- Castelgiocondo
Castello Banfi (Villa Banfi ** −)
+ Castello Banfi, Riserva Poggio all'Oro (Villa Banfi ** −)
- Castiglion del Bosco

- Cerbaiona (Molinari Diego)
Ciacci Piccolomini d'Aragona (Bianchini Giuseppe)
Comunali (Bartoli-Giusti-Focacci)[b]
Cottimello (Eredi Fuligni)
+ Dei Roseti (Altesino)
- I Verbi di Ferretti R. & Rasconi R.
+ Il Casello (Franceschi Clemente e Roberto)
- Il Paradiso (Manfredi)
- La Fortuna (Zannoni Gioberto)
La Pescaia (Mantengoli Enzo & Pallari Liliana)
Lisini (Lisini Elina)
Pian dei Mercatelli (Fontevino—Camigliano)[c]
+ Podere Cerrino (Enzo Tiezzi)
- Podere Il Poggiolo (Eredi Cosimi Roberto)
- Poggio Antico
Rasina (Mantengoli Vasco)
S. Filippo (Ermanno Rosi)
Tenuta Col d'Orcia (Riserva Poggio al Vento *** −)
+ Tenuta "La Fuga" (Gabriella Cristofolini Attanasio)
Tenuta Valdicava (Vicenzo Abruzzese)[a] (Bramante Martini 0)
+ Tenuta Valdicava, Madonna del Piano (Vicenzo Abruzzese)[a] (Bramante Martini 0)
Valdisuga, since 1981 (pre-1981, 0)
- Vigneti Pacenti Siro di Pacenti S. e Pieri G.
- Villa Banfi (Castello Banfi **, Riserva Poggio all'Oro ** +)
- Villa Niccola (Lee Iacocca, bottled by Tenuta Il Poggione)[d]

*

Argiano
Campogiovanni
Capanna di Fattoi e Minocci "Fattoi"
+ Casa del Cerro[e]
+ Castelli Martinozzi
Centolani Agricola, Tenuta Pietra Focaia[f]

Conti Serristori[f]
Fattoria Casale del Bosco (Nardi Silvio)
− Fattoria Il Grappolo
Fontevino, Villa dei Lecci (Fontevino *normale* 0)
Fornacina (Biliorsi Ruggero)
− Geografico
+ Il Colle
+ La Campana (Mignarri Peris)
+ La Cerbaiola (Salvioni Guido)
+ La Poderina (Saiagricola), since 1982 (pre-1982, 0)
+ La Torre (Giuseppe Anania)
+ Le Due Porti (Daviddi Enrico e Martini Genny)
+ Le Presi (Poggi-Fabbri Marusca)
  Melini
  Paradiso (Mauro Fastelli)
  Podere Scopetone (Abbarchi Federigo & Corioni Angela)
  Poggio Salvi, since 1982[a]
+ Quercecchio (Maria Grazia Salvioni)
  S. Carlo (Machetti Marcucci R.)
+ S. Filippo (Filippo Fanti Baldassarre)
  Tenuta Il Greppone Mazzi
  Verbena (Brigidi e Pascucci)
  Villa a Tolli[f]

0

  Camigliano
+ Castello di Camigliano
  Cecchi Luigi[e]
+ Centolani Friggiali
  Fontevino (Camigliano) (Villa dei Lecci *)
− Isabella de' Medici[g]
+ La Magia (Schwarz Herbert)
  La Poderina, pre-1982 (from 1982, *+)
  La Torre[d]
  Olivieri[g] (Valdicava)
  Pietroso
− Poggio alle Mura[g]
  Poggio degli Ulivi[c]
  Poggio Salvi, pre-1982 (since 1982, *)
  Riguardo (Tosco Vinicola)
  Tenuta di Riguardo (Tosco Vinicola)
  Tenuta di Sesta[c] (Ciacci Giuseppe)
  Tenuta Valdicava (Bramante Martini) (Vicenzo
    Abbruzzese **, Madonna del Piano ** +)
  Valdisuga, pre-1981 (since 1981, **)

NOTES: [a] The producers we expect to improve the most in the next
    few years
    [b] Now Focacci Gino Antonio
    [c] Based on one wine, the '80
    [d] Based on one wine, the '85
    [e] Based on one wine, the '78
    [f] Based on one wine, the '83
    [g] The last vintage tasted was the '75

WHAT THE RATINGS MEAN

****	Great, superb, truly noble
***	Exceptionally fine
**	Very good
*	A good example of its type, somewhat above average
0	Acceptable to mediocre, depending on the context; drinkable
+	Somewhat better than the star category it is put in
−	Somewhat less than the star category it is put in, except for zero, where it indicates a wine or producer-wine combination that is badly made or worse
[. .]	*On a producer:* Tentative evaluation based on an insufficient number of wines or based on older, out-of-date vintages, or where the wines we tasted were too difficult to fully judge to give a fair assessment of quality *On a wine or vintage:* Projection for the future. This rating is given to a vintage where we feel that we tasted an insufficient number of wines or those we tasted were too difficult to really judge to give a fair assessment of quality
(. .)	Potential increase in the rating of the wine given sufficient maturity

VINTAGE INFORMATION AND TASTING NOTES

THE VINTAGES TODAY

****	1990, 1988, 1985
*** +	1983, 1975
***	1970, 1955
*** −	1982
** +	1986, 1977
**	1964
* +	1989, 1969
*	1987, 1978
* −	1984, 1981, 1980, 1979, 1968
0	1976, 1974, 1973, 1972, 1971, 1967, 1966, 1965

1990 [****]

There was a lack of precipitation during the winter. The spring experienced normal rainfall. Summer was very dry and warm. Much needed rain fell toward the end of July and into the early days of August. Picking began early. Some growers reported harvesting their white grapes in late August. The crop was healthy. The vintage has been compared, by a number of producers, to 1985.

On our visit to the zone in November 1990, we tasted a number of Brunellos from cask. Overall, they had deep colors and a lot of weight and extract, with a lot of concentration and flavor. The question we had: was there enough acidity? We feel that one should wait until the spring after the harvest to judge the new vintage. To do so before then makes it too difficult to judge the structure and balance. Yes, the color, fruit, weight, and extract are evident, but not the structure. In March, April, and June 1991 we had the opportunity to sample a handful of 1990 Brunellos. They were impressive wines that, at this stage, appear to be on the same lofty level as 1985 and perhaps a bit better than 1988. We were especially impressed with the *annata* and *riserva* of Tenuta Il Poggione, Pian di Conti, and Biondi-Santi. And while we found the pair from Villa Nicola to be very good, the *annata* showed a touch more class.

1989 * +

The vintage looked bleak until the sun came out during the second half of September; it continued to remain sunny through the end of October. This saved what might have been a disaster. Total crop size at 1.13 million gallons (42,605 hectoliters), equivalent to 473,342 cases of DOC-DOCG wine, was above average. The members of the *consorzio* declared 812,497 gallons (30,753 hectoliters), equivalent to 341,667 cases, of DOC-DOCG wine; of these, 416,157 gallons (15,752 hectoliters), or 175,000 cases, were declared for Brunello and 396,340 (15,002), or 166,667, for Rosso. This was nearly one-third more than the total average production declared by *consorzio* members between 1983 and 1989, and only 23 percent above the average for Brunello, yet nearly 50 percent more than the average for Rosso.

Thus far, the vintage appears to have produced light wines that will mature early, wines that, for the most part, are slightly better than those of the 1987 vintage. While we doubt that high-quality *riserve* will be made, we believe that what was produced will be agreeable, fruity wines. Based on the 43 wines we tasted from barrel, we find that, overall, it is a good vintage, though one that will mature relatively early and not be long-lived. The wines will, however, give short- to medium-term pleasure. One problem remains: how many of these wines will take three or more years in oak? A point worth noting is the number of good wines produced in the zone. We believe that the Montalcino area produced, overall, the best wines in Toscana in 1989. And we also believe that the overall quality here continues to increase.

The best wines, at this stage, appear to be the Tenuta Il Poggione and Tenuta Valdicava Poggio, followed by Altesino, Conti Costanti, Fattoria Il Grepo from Biondi-Santi, La Chiesa di S. Restituta, La Pescaia from Enzo Mantengoli and Liliana Pallari, Podere Pian di Conte, and the Tenuta Valdicava Base. We didn't taste the Case Basse of Gianfranco Soldera, the Il Marroneto of M. Bianchini-Mori, or Mastrojanni.

> **CAUTION:** *Before reading these tasting notes on the wines that we tasted from barrel, please read "On Tasting Wines from Barrel; A Caveat" on page xxv.*

Altesino (*ex-cask, 11/90*). Lovely fruit on the nose; well balanced, should be ready early, most attractive. *(*)

Argiano (*ex-cask, 11/90*). Openly fruity aroma, raspberry nuance; firm, moderate to high tannin, evident sense of fruit, good structure, short, very dry finish. (*)

Canalicchio di Sopra (Pacenti Franco e Rosildo) (*ex-cask, 11/90*). Light to moderate tannin, fairly nice fruit, short finish. *(+)

Canalicchio di Sopra (Primo Pacenti & Pier Luigi Ripaccioli) (*ex-cask, 11/90*). Open fruit aroma, vaguely floral; good structure, nicely fruited, a little short and dry. *(+)

Capanna (Giuseppe Cencioni) (*ex-cask, 11/90*). Nice sense of fruit, moderate tannin, short. (*)

Casanova di Neri (*ex-cask, 11/90*). Attractive fruit, a little light in body, light tannin, attractive fruit, short. A second cask had more tannin and structure. (*)

Castello Banfi (*ex-cask, 11/90*). A slightly dank note; quite dry and firm, closed in, seems to have the fruit, but at this stage difficult to be sure, really tight and dry, short. ?

Castello di Camigliano (*ex-cask, 11/90*). Earthy, mushroom aroma; dry, some fruit, some sweetness. ?

Centolani Friggiali (*ex-cask, 11/90*). Soft entry, then dry, and a little light, rather short. ?

Ciacci Piccolomini d'Aragona (*ex-cask, 11/90*). Barnyardy aroma and flavor, firm, dry end, sense of fruit. (*)

Colombaio di Montosoli (Nello Baricci) (*ex-cask, 11/90*). Seems to be older than an '89; fruit seems tired, perhaps it needs to be racked?

Conti Costanti (*ex-cask, 11/90*). Aroma recalls the woods; good body, sweetness to the fruit, a little light, should be ready early, but the fruit will make it most appealing, short end. *(*)

Cottimello (Eredi Fuligni) (*ex-cask, 11/90*). Floral, cherry, vanilla aroma; nice fruit, a little light, oak evident, sense of sweetness from a combination of oak and ripe fruit, short end. *(*−)

Fattoria Casale del Bosco (Silvio Nardi) (*ex-cask, 11/90*). Sense of sweet, ripe fruit on entry, then it falls off quickly, very short. ?

Fattoria dei Barbi (Colombini) (*twice, ex-barrel, 11/90*). Medium ruby color; open grapey aroma, fresh, ripe cherry note; good body and structure, firm, tasty, balanced, short, dry end. *(+)

Fattoria Il Greppo (Biondi-Santi) (*twice, ex-barrel, 11/90*). Open perfumed scent; a little light, good fruit, a little understated. *(*)

Fattoria La Gerla (*ex-cask, 11/90*). Evident fruit on the nose; nice entry continues with good flavor across the midpalate, then it falls off abruptly. (*)

Fornacina (Biliorsi Ruggero) (*ex-cask, 11/90*). A little firm, moderate tannin, fairly nice fruit, short. (*)

I Verbi di Ferretti R. & Rasconi R. (*ex-cask, 11/90*). Closed nose; firm, moderate tannin, tight and closed, a little light, good fruit; shows potential for medium-term aging. *

Il Poggiolo (E. Cosimi Roberto) (*ex-cask, 11/90*). Raspberrylike aroma; firm, tight, hard, a tad shallow, dry, short end. ?

La Cerbaiola (Salvioni Giulio) (*ex-cask, 11/90*). Openly fruity aroma, cassis and berry notes; a little light, attractive fruit, short, dry finish. *

La Chiesa di S. Restituta (*ex-cask, 11/90*). Nice fruit on the nose; sense of sweet fruit, good structure, a little dry and short at the end *(*)

La Fortuna (Gino e Gioberto Zannoni) (*ex-cask, 11/90*). Open raspberry aroma, a little light; nice entry, openly fruity, then a little shallow, a tad short and dry. ?

La Pescaia (Mantengoli Enzo & Pallari Liliana) (*ex-cask, 11/90*). Lovely scented nose; light to moderate tannin, good structure, really attractive fruit, raspberries across the palate. *(*)

Podere Cerrino (Enzo Tiezzi) (*ex-cask, 11/90*). Fairly soft, attractive fruit, light tannin, short. *(+)

Podere Pian di Conte (Talenti) (*ex-cask, 11/90*). Real sense of sweetness, nice fruit, light to moderate tannin. *(*)

Podere Scopetone (Abbarchi Federigo & Corioni Angela) (*ex-cask, 11/90*). Raspberrylike aroma; nice entry, real flavor on entry then tails off, shallow, rather short; a little light but attractive for its initial impression. (*)

Poggio Antico (*ex-cask, 11/90*). Openly fruity aroma; soft under light tannin, lacks intensity and length, sense of ripe fruit, quite attractive. (*)

Poggio Salvi (*ex-cask, 11/90*). Lovely, open fruit aroma; light, soft, easy, short aftertaste is a tad dry. *

Quercecchio (Maria Grazia Salvioni) (*ex-cask, 11/90*). Openly fruity aroma; a little light, moderate tannin, chocolate nuance, a tad shallow, very short and dry.

Rasina (Mantengoli Vasco) (*ex-cask, 11/90*). Lovely nose, pretty, open fruit, most attractive; sense of sweet, ripe fruit, light tannin, then a softness, finishes a little dry and short. *(+)

San Filippo (Ermanno Rosi) (*ex-cask, 11/90*). Light, fairly nice fruit, should be ready early; will it take three years in oak? (*)

Tenuta Caparzo (*ex-cask, 11/90*). Openly fruity aroma; firm at first, then some tannin, a little closed, evident fruit. *(+)

Tenuta Caparzo, La Casa (*3 times, ex-barrel, 6/90*). Open grapey aroma, cherrylike note, some oak apparent; soft, yet with good backbone; attractive now. * +

Tenuta Col d'Orcia (*ex-cask, 11/90*). Openly fruity aroma, berrylike note; sense of ripe fruit, light to medium body, soft, even supple. *(+)

Tenuta Il Poggione (*ex-cask, 11/90*). Real sense of fruit, moderate tannin, good structure, a little more backbone than most. **(+)

Tenuta La Poderina (Saiagricola) (*ex-cask, 11/90*). Open raspberry aroma; soft, sweet, ripe fruit on entry then rather dull, very short aftertaste. ?

Tenuta Valdicava, Base (*ex-cask, 11/90*). Medium-deep color; open, richly fruited aroma; sense of sweetness, a little lighter and softer than Poggio; a little short. *(*)

Tenuta Valdicava, Poggio (*ex-cask, 11/90*). Medium-deep ruby, toward purple; rich nose suggestive of raspberries, concentrated; surprising richenss, moderate tannin, good structure, a little light at the end. **(+)

Valdisuga (*twice, ex-barrel, 11/90*). Open cherry and grapey aroma; open fruit on entry, sweet impression, then a little dry, moderate tannin, a little light, short aftertaste. (*)

Valdisuga, Vigna del Lago (*twice, 11/90*). Cherry and oak aroma; initial fruit on entry gives way to oak. (*+)

Verbena di Brigidi e Pascucci (*ex-cask, 11/90*). Rather nice fruit, a little light and simple, short, dry finish. (*)

Vigneti Pacenti Siro di Pacenti S. e Pieri G., Pelagrilli (*ex-cask, 11/90*). Talcum powder component on the nose; nice fruit, sweet impression, a little short and dry. *(+)

1988 ****

The winter was mild and there was very little precipitation. Spring came early, as did bud break. From April through the end of June continual rain fell. This affected pollination, which, of course, reduced the eventual crop size. Also, as a result of the rain, some vineyards experienced mildew. Those that sprayed had no problems. July, August, and September were, for the most part, fine. The weather was sunny and warm with hardly any rain. The light rain toward the end of September was welcome. Picking for Brunello began under excellent conditions on October 7 and lasted through October 15. The weather remained perfect.

The total crop size declared was 893,102 gallons (33,804 hectoliters), equivalent to 375,562 cases of DOC-DOCG wine. The declarations included 855,163 gallons (32,368 hectoliters) for Brunello and 37,939 (1,436) for Rosso. The members of the *consorzio* declared the largest crop recorded up to that point for both Brunello and Rosso.

Many producers have compared 1988 with 1985 in terms of quality. And more than a few have said that the '88s are better than the outstanding '85s! Perhaps. Time will tell. Colombini said that the year was among the seven greatest vintages in the past four decades.

Of the 48 Brunellos that we tasted from cask, most in November 1990, we found many good ones, and very few duds. Clearly this is a first-rate vintage. While it might not equal 1985 for sheer elegance, we feel that many of these wines have better structure and might even be longer-lived. It's still early days to be sure, but we feel that any Brunello lover should have a good supply of both vintages in his or her cellar. The faster-maturing '86s, '87s, and '89s will provide a stopgap while we wait for the better and slower-maturing '85s and '88s to come around.

We didn't taste the wines from Case Basse, Il Marroneto, or Mastrojanni. As for those that we did, the top wines offered few surprises. Once again we go with the Conti Costanti, with the Fattoria Il Grepo Riserva of Biondi-Santi a whisker away; close behind were Altesino's Vigna Montosoli, Colombini's Fattoria dei Barbi, and Tenuta Il Poggione. Then came Altesino *normale*, Fattoria Il Greppo *annata*, Roberto Bellini's La Chiesa di S. Restituta, Talenti's Podere Pian di Conte, and a pair from Tenuta Caparzo, the *normale* and their La Casa. We should also mention Enzo Tiezzi's Podere Cerrino, Vasco Mantengoli's Rasina, Tenuta Col d'Orcia, Tenuta Valdicava's Madonna del Piano, and Poggio crus.

CAUTION: *Before reading these tasting notes on the wines that we tasted from barrel, please read "On Tasting Wines from Barrel; A Caveat" on page xxv.*

Altesino (*ex-cask, 11/90*). Good quality, rich fruit, good structure. **(*)

Altesino, Vigna Montosoli (*ex-cask, 11/90*). A big, richly concentrated Brunello, loads of structure and quality; this should be a keeper; displays style. ***(+)

Argiano (*ex-cask, 11/90*). Animal fur on the nose, nice fruit as well; good structure, firm and tight, dry end. *(+)

"Canalicchio," Canalicchio di Sopra (Franco e Rosildo Pacenti) (*ex-cask, 11/90*). Nice fruit on the nose and palate, good structure, quite young. *(*)

Canalicchio di Sopra (Primo Pacenti & Pier Luigi Ripaccioli) (*ex-cask, 11/90*). Sweet, open fruit on entry, followed by moderate tannin; the end is quite firm. *(+)

Capanna (Giuseppe Cencioni) (*ex-cask, 11/90*). Attractive fruit under moderate tannin, hard, firm end. *(+)

Casanova di Neri (*ex-cask, 11/90*). We tasted this Brunello from different casks. Each one was different. Part will be used for a *normale*, part for a *riserva*. The final wines will be blended from these parts. Overall, the wines displayed the richness and concentration, and tannin and structure of the vintage. *(*)

Castello Banfi (*ex-cask, 11/90*). Openly fruity aroma; attractive flavor, supple under light to moderate tannin, tasty. *(*)

Castello di Camigliano (*ex-cask, 11/90*). Moderate tannin, some fruit evident, open flavor. (*)

Castiglion del Bosco (*ex-cask, 11/90*). *Troppo legno*, meaning that there is so much oak in this wine it's like chewing on a barrel; we did keep in mind that this is only one part of the finished wine. ?

Centolani Friggiali (*ex-cask, 11/90*). Spicy, peppery aroma; good body, attractive fruit, firm and tight, rather short. (*)

Ciacci Piccolomini d'Aragona (*ex-cask, 11/90*). Barnyardy aroma; good structure, rich, concentrated, ripe fruit. *(*)

Colombaio di Montosoli (Nello Baricci) (*ex-cask, 11/90*). Nice fruit, open and a little simple. *

Conti Costanti (*ex-cask, 11/90*). Rich, perfumed, fragrant aroma; great richness and flavor intensity, very long; though rich it has a gentle side to it, as well as a lot of elegance and class. ****

Cottimello (Eredi Fuligni) (*ex-cask, 11/90*). Barnyardy, animal fur aroma; rich and concentrated, loaded with fruit and oak; a young Brunello with good potential. *(*)

Fattoria Casale del Bosco (Silvio Nardi) (*ex-cask, 11/90*). Fairly nice fruit, yet lacks the weight and structure of the vintage, a little dry and short. (?*)

Fattoria dei Barbi (Colombini) (*ex-barrel, 11/90*). Sweet, rich, open fruit; berrylike flavor, moderate tannin; displays class and style. ***(+)

Fattoria Il Greppo (Biondi-Santi) (*ex-barrel, 11/90*). Raspberry aroma; a lot of structure and concentration, fairly long; displays elegance. **(*)

Fattoria Il Greppo (Biondi-Santi), Riserva (*ex-barrel, 11/90*). Rich aroma; loaded with flavor and richness, a lot of structure; this will be a great Brunello, the elegance and class are evident. ***(*)

Fattoria La Gerla (*ex-cask, 11/90*). Sense of sweetness from the ripe, concentrated fruit; overall, difficult to assess. *(?)

Fornacina (Biliorsi Ruggero) (*ex-cask, 11/90*). Rather nice fruit on entry, followed by a lot of tannin, sense of fruit evident, short and dry at the end; at a difficult stage. (*)

I Verbi di Ferretti R. & Rasconi R. (*ex-cask, 11/90*). Real sense of sweetness and ripe fruit, good backbone, moderate tannin. *(*)

Il Poggiolo (E. Cosimi Roberto) (*ex-cask, 11/90*). Attractive fruit, moderate tannin, some firmness, especially at the end. *(*−)

La Cerbaiola (Salvioni Giulio) (ex-cask, 11/90). Sense of sweetness on entry gives way to a firmness, tight, closed; fruit seems rather advanced for its age. *(+)

La Chiesa di S. Restituta (ex-cask, 11/90). Real sense of sweetness and ripeness from the concentration and ripeness of the fruit, good structure. **(*)

La Fortuna (Gino e Gioberto Zannoni) (ex-cask, 11/90). Open and attractive fruit, light to moderate tannin. *(* −)

La Pescaia (Mantengoli Enzo & Pallari Liliana) (ex-cask, 11/90). Lovely blueberry aroma; loads of fruit, good structure and backbone. *(*)

Le Due Porti (Daviddi Enrico e Martini Genny) (ex-cask, 11/90). A richly concentrated wine with great richness and sense of sweetness, good structure, lacks some length. *(* −)

Podere Cerrino (Enzo Tiezzi) (ex-cask, 11/90). Closed-in nose; loads of fruit and structure, moderate length; a lot of promise though obviously undeveloped. **(+)

Podere Pian di Conte (Talenti) (ex-cask, 11/90). Lovely fruit on the nose and palate, good structure, a lot of backbone, moderate tannin. **(*)

Podere Scopetone (Abbarchi Federigo & Corioni Angela) (ex-cask, 11/90). Loads of tannin and packed with fruit, firm, tasty and chewy, quite hard; the hard tannins seem to be from oak. *(?)

Poggio Antico (ex-cask, 11/90). Rich, ripe, sweet fruit, good structure, a little firm, moderate tannin. *(* −)

Poggio Salvi (ex-cask, 11/90). Lovely fruited aroma; dry with the sense of fruit, very short and dry, firm end; not up to the vintage. (*)

Quercecchio (Maria Grazia Salvioni) (ex-cask, 11/90). Attractive fruit aroma; open, soft, light tannin, balanced. *(*)

Rasina (Mantengoli Vasco) (ex-cask, 11/90). Lovely, open and attractive fruit aroma and palate, a lot of structure and backbone, real flavor and class, though it could use more length. **(* −)

San Filippo (Ermanno Rosi) (ex-cask, 11/90). Firm and tight, closed, sense of fruit evident, really hard at this stage; the wine is at a difficult stage but the structure and sense of fruit promise well. (**)

Tenuta Caparzo (twice, ex-cask, 11/90). Big, rich and concentrated nose; loads of flavor, sweet impression from the ripe fruit, soft tannins; should age gracefully. **(*)

Tenuta Caparzo, La Casa (twice, ex-barrel, 11/90). Rich and concentrated aroma; sweet, open and ripe, very rich, good backbone; very young and very good. **(*)

Tenuta Col d'Orcia (ex-cask, 11/90). At a difficult stage, good structure and concentration of fruit. *(?*) *Ex-barrel, 7/90:* Deep ruby color; open berry and cherry aroma; richly concentrated, some oak overlays the fruit, a little short and a tad dry; at this stage more appealing than the '85. **(* −)

Tenuta Il Poggione (ex-cask, 11/90). Rich, sweet, ripe and concentrated with a lot of extract, weight and structure; shows quality. ***(+)

Tenuta La Poderina (Saiagricola) (ex-cask, 11/90). Hard and tight, with an evident sense of fruit; at too difficult a stage to assess. ?

Tenuta Valdicava (ex-cask, 11/90). Good structure, nice fruit, tight finish. *(+)

Tenuta Valdicava, Madonna del Piano (ex-cask, 11/90). Lovely, open, ripe fruit aroma; firm, good structure, lots of concentrated fruit; displays potential. *(* +)

Tenuta Valdicava, Poggio (ex-cask, 11/90). Less perfume and more structure than the Madonna del Piano, no less good. *(* +)

Valdisuga (ex-barrel, 11/90). Loaded with fruit, some oak, firm, moderate tannin. *(*)

Valdisuga, Vigna del Lago (ex-barrique, 11/90). We tasted this one from two different *barriques*: the one from the Limousin had more of a vanilla character. Both were, to our taste, overly oaked with the fruit being covered by the oak. Not all of this wine is *barrique*-aged. The part that was will be blended with the part that wasn't. Both samples displayed a richness and concentration. ?

Verbena di Brigidi e Pascucci (ex-cask, 11/90). Chocolate nuance on the nose; a lot of structure, moderate tannin, medium-length finish. *(* −)

Vigneti Pacenti Siro di Pacenti S. e Pieri G., Pelagrilli (ex-cask, 11/90). Chewy entry, gives way to open and attractive fruit. *(*)

1 9 8 7 *

The weather was quite dry through the summer. The harvest began during the first week of October and continued until the 24th. Rains during the harvest affected the quality. The crop size of 1.13 million gallons (42,604 hectoliters), equivalent to 473,330 cases, was the largest crop of the decade at that point. Of this, 1.07 million gallons (40,371 hectoliters) were declared for Brunello and 58,997 (2,233) for Rosso.

Thus far we have tasted 45 Brunellos from the 1987 vintage from cask. Although no great wines were produced, a number of good wines were. Biondi-Santi, which is selective about producing a *riserva*—they produced no '89 or '86 *riserva*—did make one in '87. The wines, for the most part, have open, attractive fruit, light to moderate tannin, and are soft. Most will mature quickly and not last long. But they should bring short- to medium-term pleasure.

Once again we didn't taste Case Basse, Il Marroneto, or Mastrojanni. Of those we did taste, we especially liked the Conti Costanti, and then the Fattoria Il Greppo Riserva, Podere Pian di Conte, and Tenuta Il Poggione. Other potentially very good Brunellos are Castello Banfi, Castiglion del Bosco, Ciacci Piccolomini d'Aragona, Fattoria Il Greppo *annata*, Fattoria La Gerla, Livio Sassetti's Pertimali, Enzo Tiezzi's Podere Cerrino, and the Tenuta Caparzo La Casa.

CAUTION: *Before reading these tasting notes on the wines that we tasted from barrel, please read "On Tasting Wines from Barrel; A Caveat" on page xxv.*

Altesino (*ex-cask, 11/90*). Unsettled, yet the fruit is attractive and the wine soft. *?

Argiano (*ex-cask, 11/90*). Simple, soft, easy and short. (* −)

"Canalicchio," Canalicchio di Sopra (Franco e Rosildo Pacenti) (*ex-cask, 11/90*). Animal fur aroma; attractive fruit in the mouth. *

Canalcchio di Sopra (Primo Pacenti & Pier Luigi Ripaccioli) (*ex-cask, 11/90*). Attractive, berrylike fruit on the nose and palate, light tannin. *(+)

Capanna (Giuseppe Cencioni) (*ex-cask, 11/90*). Soft, open and attractive, light tannin, appealing. *

Casanova di Neri (*ex-cask, 11/90*). Attractive, open and appealing fruit, light tannin, soft; will be for early drinking. A second cask had more structure and more evident oak character. *

Castello Banfi (*ex-cask, 11/90*). A nice mouthful of wine, attractive and well made, light to moderate tannin, short. *(* −)

Castello di Camigliano (*ex-cask, 11/90*). Attractive, open and simple. +

Castiglion del Bosco (*ex-cask, 11/90*). Open fruit; firm, good structure, a little dry and short but well made. *(* −)

Centolani Friggiali (*ex-cask, 11/90*). Nice fruit on entry, ripe impression, then a little firm and dry, very short. ?

Ciacci Piccolomini d'Aragona (*ex-cask, 11/90*). Sense of ripe fruit gives a sweet impression, attractive flavor, moderate tannin. *(*)

Colombaio di Montosoli (Nello Baricci) (*ex-cask, 11/90*). Attractive and appealing flavor, light to moderate tannin, short. *(+)

Conti Costanti (*ex-cask, 11/90*). Lovely perfumed scent, some oak evident; nice mouth feel, good fruit, some oak evident, gentle style. **(+)

Cottimello (Eredi Fuligni) (*ex-cask, 11/90*). A little dry and firm, sense of fruit evident, short. (*)

Fattoria Casale del Bosco (Silvio Nardi) (*ex-cask, 11/90*). Nice fruit on the nose; fairly soft on entry then falls off very quickly, very short.

Fattoria dei Barbi (Colombini) (*ex-barrel, 5/90*). Attractive fruit in entry, then a little dry and short. (*)

Fattoria Il Greppo (Biondi-Santi) (*ex-barrel, 5/90*). Gentle, nice fruit, a little short. *(* −)

Fattoria Il Greppo (Biondi-Santi), Riserva (*ex-barrel, 5/90*). More body than the *annata*, good fruit and structure, a little dry at the end. *(* +)

Fattoria La Gerla (*ex-cask, 11/90*). Good backbone, some oak evident, as well as the fruit, moderate tannin. *(* −)

Fornacina (Biliorsi Ruggero) (*ex-cask, 11/90*). Attractive fruit, open and simple, soft. *

I Verbi di Ferretti R. & Rasconi R. (*ex-cask, 11/90*). Volatile, does have fruit. ?

Il Poggiolo (E. Cosimi Roberto) (*ex-cask, 11/90*). Attractive. open entry, light tannin, very short, a little dry. (* −)

La Campana (Mignarri Peris) (*ex-cask, 11/90*). Nice fruit on entry, a little light, falls off at the end. (*)

La Cerbaiola (Salvioni Giulio) (*ex-cask, 11/90*). Oak evident, a little too much so, still there is attractive fruit; open, simple, easy, fruity. *

La Chiesa di S. Restituta (*ex-cask, 11/90*). Attractive fruit, good structure. *(+)

La Fortuna (Gino e Gioberto Zannoni) (*ex-cask, 11/90*). Unsettled at this stage, quite light, moderate fruit, very short. ?

La Pescaia (Mantengoli Enzo & Pallari Liliana) (*ex-cask, 11/90*). Open cherrylike aroma; appealing and simple fruitiness. (* −)

Le Due Porti (Daviddi Enrico e Martini Genny) (*ex-cask, 11/90*). Dried fruit and raisin aroma; light tannin, simple, open and forward, very short. +

Pertimali (Livio Sassetti) (*ex-cask, 11/90*). Attractive fruit, good backbone, moderate tannin, moderate length. *(*)

Podere Cerrino (Enzo Tiezzi) (*ex-cask, 11/90*). Good structure, nice fruit, short; will be ready early. * + (** −)

Podere Pian di Conte (Talenti) (*ex-cask, 11/90*). Firm, good fruit, surprising structure for a light year; a real success. *(* +)

Podere Scopetone (Abbarchi Federigo & Corioni Angela). Spice, mint and fruit aroma; moderate tannin, seems to have sufficient fruit. (*)

Poggio Antico (*ex-cask, 11/90*). Oak up front on both the nose and palate, soft, seemingly ready. *

Poggio Salvi (*ex-cask, 11/90*). Open fruit on the nose and palate, low fruit, firm, very dry.

Quercecchio (Maria Grazia Salvioni) (*ex-cask, 11/90*). Open, attractive ripe fruit flavor, soft. (*)

San Filippo (Ermanno Rosi) (*ex-cask, 11/90*). Oak dominates on the nose and palate, it seems to be a little too much for the fruit. ?

Tenuta Caparzo (*twice, ex-cask, 11/90*). Open cherrylike aroma; a little dry, soft and simple with attractive fruit; will be ready early. *(+)

Tenuta Caparzo, La Casa (*3 times, ex-cask, 11/90*). Open berry aroma, spice and vanilla notes; fresh, tasty, good fruit and body, most attractive, a little short and dry but appealing and well made. *(* –)

Tenuta Col d'Orcia (*ex-cask, 11/90*). Sense of sweetness from the fruit, soft, light and simple. +

Tenuta Il Poggione (*ex-cask, 11/90*). A mouthful of flavor, good structure, moderate tannin, young with potential. *(* +)

Tenuta La Poderina (Saiagricola) (*ex-cask, 11/90*). A little dry, chocolate notes, very short. ?

Tenuta Valdicava (*ex-cask, 11/90*). Attractive fruit, a little light, soft, easy style, short. (*)

Tenuta Valdicava, Madonna del Piano (*ex-cask, 11/90*). More aroma and structure, more body and flavor than the *normale*; still it will be ready early and not be a keeper. *(+)

Valdisuga (*ex-barrel, 11/90*). Attractive fruit, soft and easy. (*)

Verbena di Brigidi e Pascucci (*ex-cask, 11/90*). Nice nose; open, attractive, ripe fruit flavors, a little simple. (*)

1986 ** +

Spring was cold and wet. Frost in April reduced the size of the crop, affecting those vineyards planted at the lower elevations. Heavy rain in June, during the flowering, affected the set. After an initial rainy period in July, the weather turned favorable. The rest of the summer was hot and dry. The harvest began September 30 and lasted through October 24. The grapes were healthy and mature. Total crop size of 1.02 million gallons (38,741 hectoliters), equivalent to 430,413 cases, consisted of 967,342 gallons (36,614 hectoliters) for Brunello and 56,195 (2,127) for Rosso.

The wines are, according to reports, rich in color and tannin, and have good extract. They will make excellent drinking over the medium term. Colombini includes this among the best vintages.

The wines are precocious and should mature early. The vintage, like 1987, produced wines that tend to be a little light, open, and forward. We doubt if they'll be for long-term aging. For the most part, they will mature early and not last, though there are a few exceptions. While we tasted 44 Brunellos from cask and bottle, including nearly all those of the zone's best producers, we didn't try them from Case Basse, Il Marroneto, or Mastrojanni. The best ones were Altesino, Casanova di Neri Riserva, Castiglion del Bosco, Conti Costanti, La Chiesa di S. Restituta, Podere Pian di Conte, Tenuta "La Fuga," and Tenuta Il Poggione. Also very good, or potentially very good, were Altesino Vigna Montosoli, Castello Banfi Riserva Poggio all'Oro, Ciacci Piccolomini d'Aragona, Fattoria Il Greppo, Podere Cerrino, and Tenuta Col d'Orcia.

CAUTION: *Before reading these tasting notes on the wines that we tasted from barrel, please read "On Tasting Wines from Barrel: A Caveat" on page xxv.*

Altesino (*twice, ex-barrel, 11/80*). Open and rich aroma; good structure, soft and supple; will be ready early; some elegance. **(+)

Altesino, Vigna Montosoli (*ex-cask, 11/90*). This one spent six months in *barrique*. The oak is very obvious, so too is the fruit, soft; like the *normale*, it will be ready early. *(*)

Argiano (*ex-cask, 11/90*). Soft, open and appealing with a forward fruitiness; a little simple. +

"Canalicchio," Canalicchio di Sopra (Franco e Rosildo Pacenti) (*ex-cask, 11/90*). Open and attractive, soft and precocious, dry at the end. *

Canalicchio di Sopra (Primo Pacenti & Pier Luigi Ripaccioli) (*ex-cask, 11/90*). Attractive fruit and soft under light to moderate tannin, dry, short finish; no real depth but appealing. (*)

Capanna (Giuseppe Cencioni) (*ex-cask, 11/90*). Attractive fruit, moderate tannin, short and dry. *(+)

Casanova di Neri (*ex-cask, 11/90*). We tasted this wine from two different casks with a noticeable difference. Our overall impression is a wine with fairly good structure, open and attractive fruit, dry, moderate tannin, short aftertaste. *

Casanova di Neri, Riserva (*ex-cask, 11/90*). A lot of aroma, good structure, rich in fruit and concentration; more body, flavor and structure than the *normale*. **(+)

Castello Banfi (*twice, 11/90*). Openly fruity aroma; nice fruit, open and appealing, no real depth, light tannin; will be ready for early drinking. *(+)

Castello Banfi, Riserva Poggio all'Oro (*11/90*). Attractive berrylike aroma; good structure, more weight than the *normale*, full of ripe fruit flavors. *(*)

Castiglion del Bosco (*ex-cask, 11/90*). Attractive and appealing, soft, fairly good structure, moderate tannin; a little more substance than many of the wines of this vintage. **(+)

Centolani Friggiali (*ex-cask, 11/90*). Firm and dry, there is a sense of fruit. ?

Ciacci Piccolomini d'Aragona (*ex-cask, 11/90*). Soft, open, forward and attractive fruit. *(*)

Colombaio di Montosoli (Nello Baricci) (*ex-cask, 11/90*). Soft, open, simple yet attractive; won't be for aging. *

Conti Costanti (*ex-cask, 11/90*). Lovely fruit, open, attractive and forward; should mature early, quite appealing. **(+)

Cottimello (Eredi Fuligni) (*ex-cask, 11/90*). Evident fruit on the nose; fairly soft under light tannin, short, dry end. (*)

Fattoria Casale del Bosco (Silvio Nardi) (*ex-cask, 11/90*). There is fruit under light to moderate tannin, lacks backbone, very short. ?

Fattoria dei Barbi (Colombini) (*twice, ex-barrel, 11/90*). Moderate tannin, open and attractive fruit, dry, short finish. *(* −)

Fattoria Il Greppo (Biondi-Santi) (*twice, ex-barrel, 11/87*). Nicely scented aroma; fairly nice flavor and structure, moderate tannin; displays good potential; should mature relatively early. *(*)

Fattoria La Gerla (*ex-cask, 11/90*). A little unsettled, still there is good fruit. *?

Fornacina (Biliorsi Ruggero) (*ex-cask, 11/90*). Open, soft, and simple. *

I Verbi di Ferretti R. & Rasconi R. (*ex-cask, 11/90*). Fairly good structure, nice fruit, firm, dry end. (*)

Il Poggiolo (E. Cosimi Roberto) (*ex-cask, 11/90*). Impossible to judge; why did we include it? To point out the hazards of tasting and evaluating cask samples. The wine is out of condition. ?

La Campana (Mignarri Peris) (*ex-cask, 11/90*). Soft, simple, open, seemingly ready. *

La Cerbaiola (Salvioni Giulio) (*ex-cask, 11/90*). Raisin and berry aroma; soft under light tannin, forward, open fruit. *(* −)

La Chiesa di S. Restituta (*ex-cask, 11/90*). Good structure, full of flavor in the mouth, quite tasty. **(+)

La Fortuna (Gino e Gioberto Zannoni) (*ex-cask, 11/90*). Animal and barnyardy aroma and flavor; tight and firm. ?

La Pescaia (Mantengoli Enzo & Pallari Liliana) (*ex-cask, 11/90*). Soft, open, fruity and precocious. *(+)

Le Due Porti (Daviddi Enrico e Martini Genny) (*ex-cask, 11/90*). Raisin notes on the nose and palate; dry, moderate tannin, very short and dry. ?

Pertimali (Livio Sassetti) (*ex-cask, 11/90*). Good structure, tasty, light to moderate tannin, dry, short aftertaste. *(+)

Podere Cerrino (Enzo Tiezzi) (*ex-cask, 11/90*). Openly fruity aroma and palate, attractive, very soft, a little short; will be ready early. **

Podere Pian di Conte (Talenti) (*ex-cask, 11/90*). Good structure, light to moderate tannin, attractive fruit; a little more to it than many '86s. **(+)

Podere Scopetone (Abbarchi Federigo & Corioni Angela) (*twice, ex-cask, 11/90*). One sample was out of condition and difficult to judge. The other displayed good fruit and fairly good structure, light to moderate tannin. (*)

Poggio Antico (*ex-cask, 11/90*). Open, attractive and fruity, yet dry, short aftertaste. * +

Poggio Salvi (*ex-cask, 11/90*). Rather dry, is there enough fruit? ?

Quercecchio (Maria Grazia Salvioni) (*ex-cask, 11/90*). Raspberry and raisin aroma and flavor, soft, open, short. *(+)

San Filippo (Ermanno Rosi) (*ex-cask, 11/90*). Nice nose; good flavor, fairly good structure. (*)

Tenuta Caparzo (*3 times, ex-cask, 11/90*). Open and attractive fruit flavors, cherrylike nuances, soft and precocious; seemingly ready, forward flavors. ** −

Tenuta Caparzo, La Casa (*twice, ex-cask, 11/90*). The oak dominates at this stage; it could very well be the wine we sampled— look at the note of August 1990. *(+) *Ex-cask, 8/90:* Lovely fragrant aroma, cherry fruit; precocious, tasty, balanced and fresh, a little simple. ** −

Tenuta Col d'Orcia (*ex-cask, 11/90*). Good body and structure, fruity, light to moderate tannin. *(*)

Tenuta Il Poggione (*ex-cask, 11/90*). Rich in fruit, good structure, a little dry at the end; more to it than most '86s. **(+)

Tenuta "La Fuga," Gabriella Cristofolini Attanasio (*4/91, 2,300 bottles*). Lovely perfumed aroma, nutlike component; delicious, rich, open fruit; most attractive. ** +

Tenuta La Poderina (Saiagricola) (*ex-cask, 11/90*). Nice nose; light tannin, soft underneath some tannin; short. (*)

Tenuta Valdicava (*ex-cask, 11/90*). Open and attractive, soft, cherrylike nuance. ** −

Valdisuga (*ex-barrel, 5/90*). Moderate tannin, firm, good fruit. *

1 9 8 5 * * * *

The vintage was exceptional. Spring was cold and, according to some reports, relatively dry. Other reports said that the spring was cold and wet. May was hot and rainy, June and July hot and dry. August continued hot but provided much-needed rain. The heat continued into and through September, which was dry as well. The harvest began on September 23, some fifteen days ahead of normal, and lasted until October 14. During the harvest the skies were clear and the weather was perfect.

The total yield produced a crop of 950,803 gallons (35,988 hectoliters) of wine, equivalent to 399,827 cases of DOC-DOCG wine, with 901,450 gallons (34,120 hectoliters) of Brunello and 49,353 (1,868) of Rosso. After the required aging, 183,315 cases of Brunello were bottled, only 45.85 percent of the total declared.

Some producers, taking a page from the French, say that it was the vintage of the century!! (How many vintages of the century can there be? Some producers are calling 1988 another vintage of the century!) Colombini rates it as being among the seven very best vintages since the end of the Second World War, and she suggests that it might be the best of all.

Based on the more than seven dozen Brunellos we've tasted from more than 50 producers, we are confident with our four-star rating. There were a lot of highs. We conssider it the finest overall vintage since 1970. Although some of the '83 Brunellos might reach greater heights, that vintage lacks the high level of consistency displayed by the '85s. These are wines to cellar. We believe that many of them should provide great drinking pleasure beginning somewhere between 1993 and 1995. The best will last for decades.

The best ones were the pair from Conti Costanti, the *normale* and the Riserva, and the Riserva from Biondi-Santi's Fattoria Il Greppo. Close behind were the Altesino Riserva, and then the *normale* and Vigna Montosoli from Altesino, the Fattoria dei Barbi *normale* and Riserva Vigna Fiore from Colombini, the *normali* from the Il Marroneto and Talenti's Podere Pian di Conte, and the *normale* and Riserva from Tenuta Il Poggione. Also excellent, or potentially so, were the Castello Banfi Riserva Poggio all'Oro, Fattoria Il Greppo *annata*, Fattoria La Gerla *normale* and Riserva, Il Marroneto Riserva, the *normale* and Riserva from Roberto Bellini's La Chiesa di S. Restituta and from Livio Sassetti's Pertimali, the Podere Pian di Conte Riserva, three from Tenuta Caparzo—the *normale,* Riserva, and La Casa—the Tenuta Col d'Orcia Riserva Poggio al Vento, and Tenuta Valdicava Riserva Madonna del Piano.

CAUTION: *Before reading these tasting notes on the wines that we tasted from barrel, please read "On Tasting Wines from Barrel: A Caveat" on page xxv.*

Agricola del Geografico (bottled by A.A.C.) (*3 times, 10/90*). Very little to it. *Bottle of 8/90:* Not a lot of character, drinkable, no more. *Bottle of 6/90:* Open cherrylike aroma, berry notes, some tar and tobacco as well, dusty; hint of sweetness, a little simple, short, dry aftertaste. * −

Altesino (*3 times, 4/90*). Subtle aroma, complex; warm, rich and smooth, sweet impression, great structure, very long; a top-class Brunello, and one to age. ***(+)

Altesino, Riserva (*ex-vat, 11/90*). Rich concentration of flavor, a lot of extract, nice mouth feel, great structure, very long; loads of quality and potential. ***(*)

Altesino, Vigna Altesino (*twice, 10/90*). Open, expansive aroma; on the palate the taste of ripe, rich and concentrated fruit, good structure, a little tight especially toward the end; a lot of character. **(*)

Altesino, Vigna Gauggiola (*ex-vat, 5/86*). Deep purple; intensely fruited aroma; moderate tannin; very young, in a difficult stage. ***?

Altesino, Vigna Montosoli (*3 times, 11/90, 8,000 bottles*). This Brunello spent three months in *barrique*. The first time we tasted it in bottle the oak was less evident; the most recent time, seven months later, it was more evident. We believe that eventually the oak and fruit will meld together more harmoniously than they did in November. Oak evident as the initial impression on the nose then gives way to a mélange of scents; richly concentrated with the oak being the first nuance evident, very long finish. ***(+) *Bottle of 4/90:* The wine speaks class from its expansive and intense aroma of cassis, flowers and spice through its rich, smooth, highly extracted flavor and long, lingering finish. Of the three crus that we tasted from barrel in May 1986, we found this one to be the richest and most intense, and while all were impressive, this one was the most impressive. And now that it has been bottled, that class comes through even more. ****

Argiano, Riserva (*ex-botte, 11/90*). Loads of flavor, packed with fruit; the best Argiano in ages. *(*)

Campogiovanni (San Felice) (*6/90*). Open, fresh, grapey aroma; overly simple, very drinkable; is this Brunello?

"Canalicchio," Canalicchio di Sopra (Franco e Rosildo Pacenti) (*twice, 4/90*). Floral, mushroom aroma, vanilla notes; soft, sweet and supple, the structure and tannin are all there, so is an odd off note at the end. ** −

"Canalicchio," Canalicchio di Sopra (Franco e Rosildo Pacenti), Riserva (*ex-cask, 11/90*). Firm, yet with good fruit, a lot of structure. *(*)

Canalicchio di Sopra (Lambardi Maurizio) (*4/90*). Light nose, cherrylike fruit; soft center under moderate tannin, moderate-length finish is a little dry. ** −

Canalicchio di Sopra, Le Gode di Montosoli (Primo Pacenti & Pier Luigi Ripaccioli) (*3 times, 6/90*). Open fruit aroma, hints of cherry, berry, vanilla and spice; a lot of structure, full of flavor, soft, seems ready now, could use more length. **

Capanna (Giuseppe Cencioni), Riserva (*ex-cask, 11/90*). Rich fruit, good structure, attractive; one that needs age. *(*)

Capanna di S. Restituta (Fattoi) (*ex-vat, 5/86*). Medium dark ruby; good fruit, moderate tannin, fairly rich in fruit; has potential. **

Caprili (*4/90*). Floral, earthy, cherry aroma; sweet, rich, open ripe fruit, full of flavor, rich and full, a tad dry at the end; needs a few years yet. ** +

Casanova di Neri (*3 times, 11/90*). Warm, open nose, chestnut component; nice fruit on entry, a little simple, and a tad short. * *Bottle of 4/90:* Light mushroom note on the nose which is a little closed; good structure, moderate tannin, still a little tight. *

Castelgiocondo (*3 times, 11/90*). Is this bottle variation? Two bottles in November 1990 were pretty much the same. Small-scale, openly fruity, simple, very ready. * *Bottle of 4/90:* Lovely, rich, open, ripe fruit aroma, nuances of cherry, cassis, flowers and vanilla; sweet, rich, ripe, open flavors, with structure and extract. ** +

Castelli Martinozzi (*4/90*). Closed nose reveals very little at this stage, rich in flavor and extract, some tannin across the palate builds up at the end; it should age very well, the components are all there. **(+)

Castello Banfi (*3 times, 6/90*). Fragrant aroma of chestnuts and fruit, some vanilla notes; soft light tannin, balanced, good quality, nice fruit, a little short and firm; easy to like. ** −

Castello Banfi, Riserva Poggio all'Oro (*11/90*). A mouthful of concentrated fruit, oak overlay, firm backbone; the best Banfi Brunello to date and very good, too. **(*)

Castello di Camigliano, Riserva (*ex-botte, 11/90*). Small-scale but good fruit. *(+)

Castiglion del Bosco (*3 times, 4/90*). Closed nose; firm, dry and tannic, chewy, sense of fruit evident but very tight, and difficult to be sure. *?

Castiglion del Bosco, Riserva (*ex-cask, 11/90*). Rich, concentrated and tannic, ripe fruit and oak, chewy, very long finish. **(+)

Ciacci Piccolomini d'Aragona (*twice, 4/90*). Richly fruited aroma, suggestive of kirsch; tight and firm with a sweetness to the fruit, fairly tannic and young. ** − (**)

Comunali (Famiglia Bartoli-Giusti-Focacci) (*4/90*). Light, floral aroma, some fruit; rich in the mouth, with a lot of extract, open, ripe fruit flavors, light to moderate tannin, well balanced. **

Conti Costanti (*twice, 11/90*). Fragrant, floral-scented bouquet, with richness and intensity; great weight and extract; this is a class wine, a great Brunello that needs age to develop its evident potential, yet its enormous richness and layers of flavor make it attractive now in spite of some tannin; very long in the mouth, real concentration, packed with flavor, enormous length; if not the star of the vintage then we haven't tasted the star yet, and this one couldn't be far from it; impressive indeed. **** (**** +)

Conti Costanti, Paretaio (*ex-cask, 5/86*). Dark red; richly fruited; with loads of flavor, yet it is difficult to fully assess; the potential seems evident; shows a lot of promise. **? (***?)

Conti Costanti, Riserva (*ex-cask, 11/90*). Subtle bouquet, complex and rich; already displays layers of flavor, sweet, rich, ripe fruit impression, very long; impressive. **** (**** +)

Cottimello (Eredi Fuligni) (*twice, 11/90*). Aromatic; pronounced mintlike nuance on the nose and flavor, good fruit, moderate length. ** *Bottle of 4/90:* Open floral aroma, recalls cassis; sweet, full-flavored, harmonious, good structure, fairly long, youthful; some class. **(+)

Cottimello (Eredi Fuligni), Riserva (*11/90*). Interesting, mintlike aroma; rich, warm, concentrated. **(+)

Fattoria Casale del Bosco (Silvio Nardi) (*3 times, 11/90*). Dusty aroma, tarlike component; light tannin on entry, good flavor; simple. *

Fattoria dei Barbi (Colombini) (*3 times, 11/90*). Nice nose; good fruit, a little firm; has it closed up? **(+) *Bottle of 5/90:* Lovely fruit on the nose and palate; real class and elegance, lovely; still young. ***(+)

Fattoria dei Barbi (Colombini), Riserva Vigna Fiore (*twice, 11/90*). Chestnut aroma combines with rather nice fruit and some oak; real class and sweetness, firm, tight, yet with rich fruit and concentration; has a gentle nature. ***(+)

Fattoria Il Greppo (Biondi-Santi) (*9 times, 11/90*). Two bottles tasted in November 1990—one at the estate, the second in New York—gave the same impression. Fragrant, berrylike aroma, dried fruit component; has closed up since the last time we tasted it; good structure; quality evident. **(*) *Bottle of 6/90:* Nose is a little tight, yet with evident berrylike fruit, fragrant; rich and packed with fruit and tannin, a lot of structure, great concentration and weight, sweet impression from the ripe fruit; very young with a lot of potential here, very long. Surprisingly, a second bottle tasted at the same time seemed to be more open, yet it too displayed loads of potential. And a bottle tasted three months earlier was also firm, hard and tannic. **(*)

Fattoria Il Greppo (Biondi-Santi), Riserva (*twice, ex-cask, 11/90*). Perfumed, scented bouquet; great structure and elegance, young and firm, good backbone, the quality is already evident; it shines from the bouquet through the flavor and the finish. **** (**** +) *Ex-cask, 6/90:* Tight nose, really ungiving, yet the sense of richness is apparent; hard and unyielding, firm and closed in, yet if you look the fruit is there, cherry note peeks out, packed with flavor and extract, tannin builds up at the end; class and quality evident, yet difficult to fully assess. **(*?)

Fattoria La Gerla (*4/90*). Youthful but with great intensity of fruit on the nose and palate, still somewhat tight, chewy, packed with flavor; needs years to be ready. **(*)

Fattoria La Gerla, Riserva (*ex-cask, 11/90*). Sweet, rich and ripe fruit, oak overlay, firm and tannic, a lot of structure. **(*)

Fontevino (*4/90*). Overripe fruit on the nose; dull, low fruit, lacks weight and definition.

Fontevino, Villa dei Lecci (*6/90*). Light nut and floral aroma; moderate tannin, sweet cherrylike fruit, medium length. * +

Fornacina (Biliorsi Ruggero), Riserva (*ex-cask, 11/90*). Seems rather overripe and alcoholic, some fruit evident. ?

Il Marroneto (*twice, 4/90, 3,172 bottles*). Lovely floral-scented bouquet when first poured into the glass, then it closes up; rich and highly extracted, great weight and richness; real class and quality, balanced and stylish. ***(+)

Il Marroneto, Riserva (*11/90*). Forestlike aroma, animal fur; sweet impression, open flavor, attractive, loaded with fruit, moderate length, some alcohol at the end. ** + (***?)

Il Paradiso (Manfredi) (*4/90*). A little barnyardy; some fruit, simple, somewhat off-putting character.

Il Poggiolo (E. Cosimi Roberto) (*twice, 4/90*). Open cherrylike aroma; soft, sweet entry, then some tannin, good backbone and firmness, a tad short and dry. ** −

Il Poggiolo (E. Cosimi Roberto), Riserva (*ex-cask, 11/90*). Good structure, rich, ripe fruit; displays potential. **(+)

Il Poggiolo (E. Cosimi Roberto), "Sassello" (4/90). Oak dominates, some fruit; chewy tannin, a lot of wood, seems to have the fruit, but is this a Brunello di Montalcino? It spent three years in oak, and five months and twenty days in *barrique*. *?

Il Poggiolo (E. Cosimi Roberto), Riserva "Sassello" (ex-cask, 11/90). Oak!, oak!!, oak!!!, and a touch of fruit.

La Campana (Mignarri Peris) (4/90). Kirsch and framboise define the aroma; open, sweet, ripe fruit entry, some tannin, soft center, a tad dry at the end; still in all, nice fruit, though it seems a tad overripe. ** −

La Campana (Mignarri Peris), Riserva (ex-cask, 11/90). Oak dominates the nose and palate, then the fruit; firm, sweet impression not from the fruit, but from the oak. *(+)

La Chiesa di S. Restituta (4/90, 28,700 bottles). Tight nose, really closed in; rich flavor, sweet impression, lots of weight and extract, soft, supple quality in the mouth, well balanced; as it sat in the glass the nose opened and developed a florallike quality. ** + (***)

La Chiesa di S. Restituta, Riserva (twice, 11/90). Closed in on the nose and palate, though the richness and concentration are evident, good backbone, firm and tight; very young. **(*)

La Fortuna (Gino e Gioberto Zannoni), Riserva (11/90). Animal fur combines with fruit; open, soft entry, surprisingly forward, moderate length. *(+)

La Torre (Luigi Anania) (8/90). Rich nose, intense and rich, open fruit; light to moderate tannin, well balanced, open and forward; not a lot of complexity or depth, but attractive fruit makes it appealing. **

Le Due Porti (Daviddi Enrico e Martini Genny) (4/90). Dried fruit aroma, raisins and figs; a little dull in the mouth, moderate tannin, could it be slightly oxidized? Perhaps an off bottle; it was just opened. ?

Le Presi (4/90). Closed aroma; sweet fruit, chewy tannin, a little tight, but overall nice fruit. ** −

Lisini (4 times, 6/90). Open aroma suggestive of nuts, flowers, the woods and mushrooms, some spice; rich and concentrated, sweet impression; seems more forward than the previous bottle tasted two weeks earlier! ** *Bottle of 4/90:* Open fruit aroma and palate, a little simple, and lacking complexity; kind of easy. *

Mastrojanni (ex-vat, 4/86). Fairly dark color; fresh cherrylike aroma; good body, fairly tannic. **

Pertimali (Livio Sassetti) (3 times, 4/90). Lovely bouquet, some complexity, recalls cassis, flowers and vanilla; chewy, yet rich and supple in the center with layers of flavor, until the dry, tight, firm, tannic finish. ** + (***)

Pertimali (Livio Sassetti), Riserva (ex-cask, 11/90). Rich and intense on the nose and flavor; good backbone, sense of sweet ripe fruit, most attractive. **(*)

Podere Cerrino (Enzo Tiezzi) (11/90). Rich nose, nice fruit; moderate tannin, soft, sweet impression; still young. **(+)

Podere Pian di Conte (Talenti) (4/90). Rich nose suggestive of mushrooms and the woods, floral note; great structure, and richly extracted, very long finish; for the future; real class. ***(+)

Podere Pian di Conte (Talenti), Riserva (11/90). Complex aroma, suggestive of berries and flowers; richly extracted, concentrated, loads of tannin; a wine to age. **(*)

Poggio Antico, Riserva (11/90). Rich fruit combines with oak, good backbone, sweet impression. *(*)

Poggio Salvi (twice, 11/90). Light fruit on the nose; evident fruit; unbalanced, very short and dry. ? *Ex-vat, 5/86:* Dark ruby color; packed with fruit; rich and intense, full-bodied, moderate tannin; lots of potential. ** +

Quercecchio (Maria Grazia Salvioni) (4/90). Ripe fruit and floral aroma; rich in flavor; still firm and young. *(* −)

Quercecchio (Maria Grazia Salvioni), Riserva (11/90). Soft, simple, open and fruity; could this be the same wine that we tasted in April? It doesn't seem it. *

Riguardo [Tosco Vinicola] (12/90). Barnyardy aroma, stinky in fact; moderate tannin, shallow, unbalanced, altogether unimpressive.

S. Carlo (R. Machetti Marcucci) (4/90). Flowers, nuts, cherries and vanilla aroma; fairly tannic and chewy, nice fruit midpalate, then dry and firm at the end. *?

San Filippo (Ermanno Rosi) (4/90). Oak, oak and more oak, then some fruit, firm and tannic, tight, *?

San Filippo (Ermanno Rosi), Riserva (11/90). A lot of flavor, moderate tannin, young, moderate length. *(*)

San Filippo, "Fanti" (ex-barrel, 4/90). Fragrant scent; rich entry, then tight and firm, attractive fruit, short aftertaste, a little dry. **

Tenuta Caparzo (twice, 8/90). Leather and cherry aroma, fragrant; soft tannin, well balanced, tasty, nice fruit; has class; very young. **(*) *Bottle of 6/90:* Richly fruited aroma, ripe plummy fruit, with suggestions of nuts, and flowers that define the nose of this wine; great richness and concentration; very young; the components and structure are there; soft tannins, very long finish; the best Caparzo, along with the La Casa, to date. ***(+)

Tenuta Caparzo, La Casa (twice, 8/90). Big, rich and concentrated on the nose and palate, sweet and intense, mouth-filling and young. **(*) *Bottle of 6/90:* Deep ruby; oak overlays the intensely fruited aroma, suggestions of flowers and nuts; a rich mouthful of wine, ripe fruit, great extract and structure; a young but splendid wine. ***(+)

Tenuta Caparzo, Riserva (ex-cask, 11/90). A richly concentrated wine of great structure and extract; still tight and firm. **(*)

Tenuta Col d'Orcia (3 times, 11/90). Nice fruit, open, soft, light tannin; seemingly ready! ** *Bottle of 6/90:* Warm aroma recalls nuts and flowers, vanilla component; open, sweet impression on the entry, then fairly tannic and tight, chewy, firm tannic finish. *(* +)

Tenuta Col d'Orcia, Riserva (twice, ex-barrel, 11/90). Deep ruby color; fairly open and intense aroma, suggestive of ripe fruit and nuts, oak overlay; sweet, rich and ripe, well balanced, chocolate nuance, oak evident, has tannin, very tasty and attractive, moderately long, dry finish; very young. *(* −)

Tenuta Col d'Orcia, Riserva Poggio al Vento (*ex-barrel, 6/90*). Deep color; rich, warm nose, characteristic floral and nut aroma; fairly chewy and tannic, rich, warm and tasty, packed with impressive fruit, chocolate and spice, a lot of structure, rather dry finish; still a baby, time should smooth out the edges and lengthen the finish. ***

Tenuta Il Poggione (*4/90*). Tobacco, cherry, floral aroma; a mouthful of ripe fruit, great weight and extract; loads of quality; needs time. ***(+)

Tenuta Il Poggione, Riserva (*11/90*). Sense of sweetness, rich, concentrated, good structure, chewy; very young indeed. **(*+)

Tenuta La Poderina (Saiagricola) (*4/90*). A little closed on the nose; soft, open and fruity; simple, small-scale but appealing. * +

Tenuta Valdicava (*twice, 4/90*). Light nose; well balanced, good fruit, and a nice sweetness, finish is a little tight; a young wine with some quality. **

Tenuta Valdicava, Riserva Madonna del Piano (*ex-cask, 11/90*). Rich fruit on both the nose and palate; loads of structure and backbone. **(*)

Valdisuga (*6 times, 11/90*). We tasted this twice in November 1990, with a different impression each time. *The most recent bottle:* Rather nice nose; good fruit, some firmness, balanced. ** *The earlier bottle:* Raisins and prunes, overripe; a little coarse, chocolate notes; unimpressive. What is going on here? And the first two bottles that we tasted varied considerably from the previous impression! *Bottle of 9/90:* Fresh cherry aroma; soft under light tannin; lacks intensity of the year. * + *Bottle of 5/90:* Fragrant nose, berry notes; attractive, open fruit, with richness and sweetness, some tannin. **

Valdisuga, Riserva (*ex-cask, 11/90*). Attractive fruit, then oak, good structure. **(+)

Villa Niccola [*estate bottled for Lee Iacocca by Tenuta Il Poggione*] (*2/90*). Cherry and berry aroma, a little closed; though tight the fruit is evident, firm, hard, tannic end; give it three or so years. *(*)

1984 * −

This was a very difficult year. Spring was cold and overcast, and very short. Flowering was both late and irregular. The summer weather continued cold and damp, with the cold continuing into September and October, along with rain. This hindered the ripening process. Then heavy rains in early autumn created widespread rot and mildew on the vines. There were 651,174 gallons (24,647 hectoliters) of DOCG wine declared, equivalent to 273,828 cases. Of this, after the required aging, less than 49 percent was bottled as Brunello.

Biondi-Santi didn't produce a Brunello, and Altesino declassified most of their crop to Rosso. Yet Roberto Bellini of La Chiesa di S. Restituta rates the year as a two-star vintage (out of five). Colombini puts the vintage as among the seven unfortunate ones since the end of the Second World War.

Judging from the two dozen Brunellos we tasted, it appears that with much care and strict selection it was possible to make a good, even a very good wine in 1984. These are fast-maturing wines; even the best are good now. Very few will last. Our favorite is the Case Basse, followed by Il Marroneto, La Chiesa di S. Restituta, and Mastrojanni. The Costanti tasted very good in cask in 1986.

Campogiovanni (San Felice) (*twice, 9/90*). Openly fruity on the nose and palate, soft center, a little dry; best to drink up, drying out. *Bottle of 2/90:* Small-scale, some fruit; more or less ready. *

Canalicchio di Sopra (Lambardi Maurizio) (*4/89*). Open fruit aroma; on the light side; soft and easy. * +

Capanna di Fattoi e Minocci, "Fattoi" (*4/89*). Open fruit, soft and supple, tasty. * +

Capanna di S. Restituta (Fattoi) (*ex-vat, 5/86*). Nicely fruited aroma; light but reasonably well balanced, light tannin, nice fruit; will be ready early. * +

Caprili (*4/89*). Floral aroma, characteristic nutlike nuance; sweet impression, soft, open, tasty, light. * +

Case Basse (*twice, 4/90*). Fairly deep color; dusty, tobacco aroma; a little tight and closed, good backbone, good body and nice fruit, dry finish, on the short side; still in all, a big success for the year; needs a year or two. **(+)

Cerbaiona (Diego Molinari) (*3 times, 9/90*). Light nose, vaguely of tobacco and fruit; a little dry and light, soft center, very short; drinkable if not much more. + *Bottle of 6/90:* Fragrant cherry aroma, tannic entry, then fruit, tight, yet no real body, rather dry finish. * − *Bottle of 2/90:* This bottle was totally different: rich nose, suggestive of flowers and ripe fruit; soft, fruity, open and forward; ready. **

Costanti (*twice, ex-cask, 5/86*). Enormous richness on nose, suggestions of blueberries, tar and licorice; a bit light-bodied but loads of flavor, some acid at the end; the best '84 we tasted. **(+)

Fattoria Casale del Bosco (Silvio Nardi) (*6/90*). Dusty, toasty aroma; soft entry, light tannin; ready now, simple. +

Fattoria Il Grappolo (*4/90*). Light nose; a little odd, but open, soft and fruity, dryish end. * −

Fattoria La Gerla (*twice, 4/89*). Fairly open, some tannin, surprisingly good structure. ** −

Il Marroneto (*4/89*). Gorgeous bouquet, flowers and spice; light, open, forward style, lots of nice fruit. **

Il Paradiso (Manfredi) (*4/89*). Light, nutlike aroma, hints of chestnuts; soft, supple, ripe fruit, ready. * +

La Campana (Mignarri Peris) (4/89). Ripe, berrylike aroma; soft, open and tasty, supple. * +

La Chiesa di S. Restituta (4/90, 17,500 bottles). Slight nose, some fruit; surprisingly full-flavored and balanced, supple, forward; a real success. **

La Fortuna (4/89). Some alcohol on the nose; a bit harsh, some fruit.

Mastrojanni (3 times, 10/90). Fragrant, even-scented bouquet; moderate tannin, evident fruit, a little dry; won't be a keeper, but for the next couple of years it will make a nice glass; attractive fruit, appealing, certainly a success. * + *Bottle of 4/90:* Subtle, scented bouquet; light, open and forward, harmonious, flavorful, nice texture (it spent six months in new 158-gallon/6-hectoliter Alliers oak casks). **

Melini, Vigna Il Comombaione I Gino Antonio Focacci (11/90). Fragrant, nutty aroma; nice mouth feel, good fruit, very short, and very dry end; not bad for the vintage and its age. *

Pietroso (4/90). Harsh, alcoholic nose; overly dry, not a success.

Podere Pian di Conte (Talenti) (4/89). Open fruit aroma; tight and tannic, sense of fruit evident. * +

Podere Scopetone (Abbarchi Federigo & Corioni Angela) (4/90). Light and supple, fruity and clean; for early drinking. *

Poggio Salvi (3 times, 11/90). Light nose; dry, a little severe, low fruit; drying out.

Tenuta Caparzo (ex-cask, 5/85). Surprisingly fruity and well balanced. **

Tenuta Il Poggione (twice, 4/89). Spicy, peppery, fruity aroma; rich and sweet, soft and supple, a bit of tannin at the end. * +

1983 *** +

The vintage was advanced due to the very hot and dry summer, the harvest beginning ten days ahead of normal. Total crop size was 847,104 gallons (32,063 hectoliters), equivalent to 356,220 cases. Nearly 51 percent of the declared crop was bottled as Brunello after the required aging.

This was a vintage of elegant, stylish wines. Many are stunning, particularly the Costanti; it's hard to imagine a better Brunello. The wines lack the richness and fullness of the better '82s, but for their sheer elegance and beauty they will be hard to beat. Initially we thought they might not live as long as the '82s. It now appears that the best will outlive the best 1982s. Based on nearly 50 wines from more than 30 producers, we find that the highs are at least the equal of, and might even exceed, the more consistent 1985s.

Roberto Bellini of La Chiesa di S. Restituta rates the vintage four stars out of five.

The *riserve* from Case Basse, Costanti, and Mastrojanni are all first-rate Brunellos that show their quality, as are the Altesino *normale* and Riserva Vigna Altesino, followed by Fattoria dei Barbi Riserva Vigna del Fiore and Fattoria Il Greppo Riserva. The Tenuta Il Poggione tasted from cask in 1985 showed a lot of promise. We also liked very much Primo Pacenti & P. L. Ripaccioli's Canalicchio di Sopra, Fattoria dei Barbi, Fattoria Il Greppo *normale*, Fattoria La Gerla, and Il Marroneto Riserva.

Altesino (3 times, 4/88). A young but well-balanced and stylish wine, great structure, enormous fruit beneath the tannin. ***(+)

Altesino, Riserva (4/89). Intensely perfumed bouquet, fragrant; chewy, rich and concentrated, very long; loads of class; very young. ***(+)

Altesino, Riserva Vigna Altesino (twice, 6/90). Rich, intense and scented bouquet, vanilla and floral aroma; a mouthful of fruit and tannin, great richness and concentration, sweet impression; seems ready, it's not, there is more to give; real class. ***(+)

Canalicchio di Sopra (4/89). Characteristic aroma; soft, open and tasty; nearly ready. * +

Canalicchio di Sopra (Pacenti Primo & Ripaccioli P. L.) (3 times, 6/90). Fragrant, floral, spicy bouquet, cherry note; light tannin, fairly long; lots of class; ready now. *** −

Capanna (Cencioni), Riserva (4/89). Mushroom note on the nose; sweet impression on entry, good backbone, nice fruit. * +

Capanna di Fattoi e Minocci, "Fattoi" (4/90). Leather, woodsy, barnyardy aroma; fruit seems a tad overripe and a little tired. * −

Capanna di S. Restituta (Fattoi) (ex-vat, 5/86). Medium dark ruby; lovely fruit aroma, nutlike nuance, some spice; some elegance; well balanced, full of flavor. **(+)

Caprili (twice, 2/90). Flowers, vanilla and fruit; soft and round, smooth, good body. ** −

Case Basse (twice, 4/89). Lovely perfumed, scented bouquet; ripe fruit, soft, open, tasty; lots of quality, superbly crafted. ***(+)

Case Basse, Riserva (4/90). Deep color; lovely floral-scented bouquet displays some delicacy, nice fruit; great richness and extract, really sweet and mouth-filling, warm, still some tannin; a young wine, its richness makes it attractive and appealing; very long finish, tannin builds, especially at the end. *** +

Castiglion del Bosco (twice, 4/89). Vanilla, chestnut aroma; rich and flavorful, tasty, lush almost sweet, firm aftertaste. ** −

Centolani, Tenuta Pietra Focaia (4/89). Rather nice nose; lots of fruit, some sweetness. * +

Cerbaiona (Diego Molinari) (9/90). Light but fruity aroma, suggestive of dried berries; sense of sweetness, round and balanced, ready now, rather short, a tad dry at the end. ** −

Comunali (Bartoli-Giusti-Focacci) (ex-cask, 5/85). Lovely aroma; seems sweet, a bit light and simple. *(* −)

Comunali (Bartoli-Giusti-Focacci), Riserva (4/89). Light yet characteristic aroma; soft, open and flavorful, dry aftertaste. *

Conti Serristori (bottled by Agripa) (11/90). Lovely nose; openly fruity, soft under light tannin, attractive flavor, short, dry aftertaste; could use more weight. *

Costanti (ex-cask, 5/85). Already displays elegance and delicacy; should make a splendid bottle. **(*)

Costanti, Riserva (3 times, 9/90). Incredible richness on the nose and palate, great extract and weight; this wine has class, style, balance and flavor, yet it is very young and has so much more to give. We don't believe that we've tasted a more impressive Brunello. It is every bit as stunning as the outstanding '85. **** +

Costanti, Riserva Paretaio (ex-cask, 5/86). Good color; loads of fruit, sweet impression; great elegance and class. ***(*)

Cottimello (Eredi Fuligni), Riserva (4/90). Floral, mineral, vanilla aroma; richly fruited, sweet and open, some tannin, certainly attractive now, well balanced, could use more length. **

Fattoria dei Barbi (Colombini) (twice, 6/90). Lovely nose, real class here; supple; seems ready now, still with room to grow, resist. **(*) *Bottle of 12/88:* Ripe fruit entry, then tightens up; quite nice. **

Fattoria dei Barbi (Colombini), Riserva Vigna del Fiore (7 times, 11/90). Light, floral perfume, nuances suggestive of cherries and dried fruit; richly concentrated, good weight, packed with flavor, real sense of sweetness, intense and tannic; very young but with evident class. ***(+)

Fattoria Il Greppo (Biondi-Santi) (3 times, 10/89). A big, rich, concentrated wine of real flavor and structure. **(*−)

Fattoria Il Greppo (Biondi-Santi), Riserva (6/90). Flowers, nuts and spices, delicately scented bouquet yet richly concentrated; sense of sweetness, packed with flavor and concentration; young, needs age; real class here. **(*+)

Fattoria La Gerla (twice, 4/89). Fragrant vanilla and nut aroma, dried fruit component; rich with nice structure and some class. **(+)

Fattoria La Gerla (4/89). This version spent six months in *barrique*, too bad. Its character and personality were changed, not what we would expect from a Brunello, oak quite evident, more tannin and different aromatics and flavor than the *normale*. *

Il Colle (4/90). Aroma of dried fruit, nuts and berries; openly fruity, soft center; a little simple. *

Il Marroneto, Riserva (4/89, 3,974 bottles). Rich, nutlike aroma, hint of licorice; sweet entry, rich then a bit firm, good structure, round; a lot of class; fairly long. **+ (***)

Il Poggiolo (E. Cosimi Roberto), Riserva (3 times, 4/90). Tight nose; chewy tannins, quite flavorful, good structure. *+

La Chiesa di S. Restituta (4/89). Open fruit aroma; good fruit and structure, young but its open flavors make it attractive now. **−

La Torre, Riserva (4/90, 8,000 bottles). Barnyardlike aroma, leather; lots of fruit, but off-putting flavor intrudes.

Lisini (4 times, 6/90). Floral, mineral, spicy, earthy aroma; almost sweet on entry, big, rich and concentrated, with some tannin to shed, soft center, open flavors; should be ready soon. **+

Mastrojanni (3 times, 4/89). Lovely nose, suggestions of tobacco, cherry, nuts and chestnuts; still some tannin, rich, open attractive flavor, fairly long finish. ***

Mastrojanni, Riserva (twice, 4/90). Aroma displays floral, fruity components; a little closed, packed with fruit, rich and young, but ripeness and extract make it appealing, very long; great elegance. Antonio's best wine to date, and one of the top wines of the vintage. ***+

Mastrojanni, Riserva Schiena d'Asino (ex-vat, 4/86). Deep ruby color; richly fruited aroma, some oak; a rich mouthful of ripe fruit flavors; all the components are there for greatness. ***(+)

Pertimali (Livio Sassetti) (10/88). Floral bouquet; flavorful, firm and rich, fairly long; young. **(+)

Pertimali (Livio Sassetti), Riserva (4/89). Fragrant tobacco and oak aroma; firm and hard, good structure, chewy. *+ (**)

Poggio Salvi (4 times, 5/90). Interesting singular aroma, recalls meat(!); soft entry, a little light, lacks richness and intensity, a little dry at the end. This wine has shown great variation on all four occasions that we tasted it; it ranged from one star in cask to two stars in April 1989. *This bottle* *

S. Filippo (twice, 4/89). Light nose displays nuances of leather and fruit; open fruit, sweet impression; perhaps a tad too simple; coming ready and drinkable now. **−

Tenuta Caparzo (ex-cask, 5/85). Rich aroma with notes of champignons, fruit, nuts and pine; full-flavored, some astringency, vaguely sweet. **(*)

Tenuta Col d'Orcia (twice, 7/90). Mineral and floral bouquet; rich, fairly tannic, a mouthful of fruit, sense of sweetness, dry finish, a tad bitter; should be ready in perhaps two years. **−

Tenuta Col d'Orcia, Riserva (3 times, 7/90). Somewhat reticent aroma, sense of fruit evident; real richness and concentration, more structure and flavor than *normale*, could use more length. **(+) *Bottle of 12/89:* Rich nose, vanilla and nuts, vaguely floral; soft tannins, ripe fruit, full-flavored, soft center, tannin at the end. **

Tenuta Il Poggione (ex-cask, 5/85). Opaque color; a suggestion of licorice on nose; full, rich fruit flavors, tannic; less body than the '82 but more elegance and style. ***(*)

Tenuta Valdicava (Vincenzo Abruzzese) (5 times, 6/90). Fragrant-scented bouquet, leathery component, berry notes; rich in flavor, appealing, well balanced, moderate tannin, nice structure, soft, open forward flavors. **

Valdisuga (3 times, 4/90). Floral and berry aroma; soft entry, then some tannin, a little light, good fruit, well balanced. **−

Valdisuga, Riserva (12/88). Aroma seems to be older than its years; open flavors, soft under some tannin; not a lot of character. An off bottle perhaps?

Valdisuga, Vigna del Lago (*4 times, 5/90, 7,500 bottles*). Intense chocolate and ripe fruit aroma, some oak apparent, vanilla component; great intensity of flavor and ripeness, medium-long finish. ** +

Villa a Tolli, Riserva (*4/91*). Fairly nice aroma, attractive and open; sweet impression with a nice sense of fruit, open and seemingly ready. *

Villa Banfi (*3 times, 8/90*). Characteristic floral and nut aroma, fragrant, vanilla overlay; lots of fruit, has a sweetness to it, tasty and balanced; a little young, quite enjoyable now, it might improve but not by much. ** −

1 9 8 2 *** −

The summer of 1982 was hot and dry with some rain in August. Total crop size was 759,073 gallons (28,731 hectoliters), equivalent to 319,201 cases, of Brunello. Of these, 161,515 cases, or 50.6 percent, were bottled as Brunello.

Altesino, Il Poggione, Colombini, and Castiglion del Bosco rate the vintage as topflight. Biondi-Santi said it was the best vintage of the past fifty years. For Colombini it was first rate. Roberto Bellini of La Chiesa di S. Restituta rates it five stars out of five.

The Brunellos of 1982 are big, fat, rich wines of concentration and extract; what they lack in elegance they make up in power. While at one time we thought they would be long-lived and could outlast the '83s, we have since changed our evaluation. We still believe they'll never match the sheer elegance and beauty of that younger vintage. And although we still believe that some will be long-lived, more than a few are showing age now.

We have tasted some five dozen Brunellos from 45 producers. The wines haven't lived up to our original expectations. The best wines, tasted recently, are Fattoria dei Barbi, Fattoria Il Greppo Riserva, Mastrojanni Riserva, and Tenuta Il Poggione. As good as the Costanti was in barrel, we can't say how it is today, not having tasted it in bottle. We also liked the Case Basse, tasted from cask, very much and Fattoria La Gerla, also from cask.

Altesino (*3 times, 4/87*). Rich, somewhat complex bouquet; layers of fruit, rich, rather tannic; very young. **(*)

Argiano (*4/87*). Aroma suggestive of fruit and nuts; fairly tannic, with the stuffing to support it; the nicest Argiano in some time. *(* −)

Camigliano (*twice, 4/87*). Reticent aroma; rather simple, light tannin, light in fruit as well; lacks weight and definition, still it is drinkable. * −

Canalicchio di Sopra (*3 times, 10/89*). Quite a lot of fruit and character, well balanced, forward; seems ready. **

Capanna (G. Cencioni) (*4/87, 13,300 bottles*). Vaguely seaweedy on the nose; a mouthful of tannin, seems to have the fruit to carry it, a tad bitter. *(* −)

Capanna di Fattoi e Minocci, "Fattoi" (*4/87*). Dank nose, some oxidation; old and tired, tannic, insufficient fruit. A bad bottle?

Capanna di S. Restituta (Fattoi) (*ex-vat, 5/86*). Medium dark ruby; closed-in aroma, with evident fruit; big and rich, with good flavor under moderate tannin; displays some class. **(+)

Caprili (*4/87, 6,000 bottles*). Nuts, flowers and mineral notes; more forward than expected, sweet impression from ripe fruit, balanced; still needs some age. **(+)

Casanova di Neri (Nera Giovanni) (*twice, 4/88*). Nuts and fruit define the aroma; tight and firm, fairly nice flavor, balanced. *

Case Basse (*ex-cask, 5/85*). Delicate, floral aroma with some fruit; sweet, rich and ripe; a lot of quality here, and some elegance. **(*)

Castelli Martinozzi (*4/89*). Nose hints of rubber tire; a bit tight, some fruit.

Castiglion del Bosco (*7 times, 2/90*). Open fruit aroma, suggestions of flowers and dried fruit; some tannin, tasty, balanced; nearly ready. ** −

Cerbaiona (Diego Molinari) (*9/90*). Characteristic aroma displays vanilla and tobacco nuances; tasty, fairly well balanced, some tannin, a little short on the palate and dry, but the fruit is there; needs a couple of years to open up, it should improve. *(* −)

Colombaio di Montosoli (Baricci) (*4/87*). Mercaptans intrude on the nose and palate.

Comunali (Bartoli-Giusti-Focacci) (*ex-cask, 5/85*). At this point harsh, not quite together, but has the stuffing and the potential. *(*?)

Costanti (*twice, ex-cask, 5/86*). Good color; intensity of fruit on the nose, sweet fruit, rich and soft under moderate tannin; lots of potential. ***(+)

Cottimello (Eredi Fuligni) (*4/87*). Floral, berry aroma, perhaps a tad overripe; richness and a sweet impression make it very attractive. *(*)

Dei Roseti (Altesino) (*5/89*). Open chestnut aroma, vanilla component; good structure, tasty; on the young side; good quality; dry aftertaste. **(+)

Fattoria Casale del Bosco (Silvio Nardi) (*5/90*). Characteristic nutlike aroma, vanilla notes; some tannin, ripeness of fruit makes it attractive, soft center, a tad overripe, berrylike flavor recalls zinfandel. *(+)

Fattoria dei Barbi (Colombini) (*3 times, 5/90*). Fragrant-scented bouquet; sweet and concentrated, balanced, fairly long finish; elegant; on the young side, give it two or three years, perhaps four. ***

Fattoria dei Barbi (Colombini), Riserva (*twice, 12/89*). Floral bouquet with a fruit overlay; young, with a sweetness to the fruit, rich yet delicate, good structure. ** + (***)

Fattoria "Il Grappolo" (Prop. Fortius, Loc. Campogiovanni), Riserva (9/90). Slight nose; nice fruit, soft, some tannin, not a lot of character; ready now. +

Fattoria Il Greppo (Biondi-Santi) (5 times, 12/89). Open nut-like aroma; austere, yet with good fruit, firm structure. ** − (**)

Fattoria Il Greppo (Biondi-Santi), Riserva (4 times, 6/90, 13,977 bottles). Rich nose, ripe fruit, concentrated, displays components of nuts and flowers; richly flavored, nice mouth feel, well balanced; still a little young; more forward than the '83. **(*) *Bottle of 12/89:* Rich nose, characteristic nutlike quality; intense and concentrated, more richness and sweetness than the *normale,* also tighter and more closed, a lot of structure and character. **(* −)

Fattoria La Gerla (ex-cask, 5/85). Pepper, cherries and flowers on nose; rich, ripe concentrated fruit under the firm tannic structure; lots of character and potential. **(*)

Fontevino (4/87). Oxidized.

Fontevino, La Torre (3/88). Dark color; leather and prune on the nose; rough and tannic, drying aftertaste; unimpressive.

Fornacina (4/87, 2,150 bottles). Some oxidation painfully evident.

Il Colle (Carli) (4/87). Lovely nose; fairly rich, a nice mouthful of fruit under the tannin, firm tannic aftertaste. **(+)

Il Paradiso (Manfredi) (4/87). Fragrant nutlike aroma, chestnuts; sweet impression, ripe fruit, fairly rich under the tannin, firm, tannic aftertaste. **(+)

La Chiesa di S. Restituta, Riserva (3 times, 11/90, 3,850 bottles). Tight nose, suggestions of chestnuts; rich, nice mouth feel, firm, still fairly tannic, dry, short, tannic finish; needs more age for the tannin to resolve itself and to open and soften. **(+)

La Poderina (5/88). Nuts and rich fruit on the nose; intensely concentrated, sweet, rich, and ripe; displays some class. ** +

Le Due Porti (Daviddi Enrico e Martini Genny) (4/87). Nice nose, suggestion of nuts; good structure, a lighter style, nice fruit, firm aftertaste. *(* +)

Lisini (3 times, 1/89). Coarse nose; lacks flavor intensity; still in all not bad. * − *Bottle of 3/88:* Somewhat reticent but characteristic aroma; moderately high tannin, the fruit is there, some alcohol at the end. * + (** −)

Mastrojanni (6 times, 6/90). Of the two most recent bottles tasted, in June 1990, both had all the components of the earlier bottles, but on one of them an odd note in the aroma was intrusive. For that bottle **?, while the second merited ***. *Bottle of 5/90:* Lovely scented bouquet, recalls cherries and berries; soft with open fruit, and nice concentration, still with tannin to shed; classy. ***

Mastrojanni, Costa Colonna (ex-vat, 4/86). Noticeable oak at this stage, also a lot of fruit, vanilla component; good structure, rich and concentrated. *(*?)

Mastrojanni, Riserva (4/88). Tight nose; ripe fruit evident, excellent structure and flavor, nice texture; a lot of class here. ***

Mastrojanni, Schiena d'Asino (ex-vat, 5/86). Medium dark ruby; a lot of oak evident on the nose along with fruit, but the oak dominates; firm finish; difficult to be sure. *(?)

Paradiso (Mauro Fastelli) (4/89). Odd nose; better in the mouth, fairly nice fruit, firm dry end. *

Podere Il Poggiolo (E. Cosimi Roberto) (4/87, 3,900 bottles). Cherrylike aroma, floral notes; a lot of structure, fairly tannic, with the sense of ripe fruit evident. *(* +)

Podere Pian di Conte (Talenti) (9/88). Floral overtone, with a ripe fruit component; a lot of structure, rich, full-bodied. ** +

Poggio Antico (4/89). Lovely nose, floral up front, then vague odd backnote; could use more fruit.

Poggio Salvi (ex-vat, 5/86). Deep color; maltlike character; a bit rough and tannic, sense of fruit in the background, closed in; displays some potential; not up to the vintage. *

Quercecchio (Maria Grazia Salvioni) (9/87). Dark ruby; nice nose, fruity, vaguely spicy; fairly soft and simple under light tannin, vague off notes intrude toward the finish, except for that an agreeable albeit simple wine. *

S. Filippo (Ermanno Rosi) (4 times, 6/90). Lovely nose, nuts and flowers; good body, sweet impression, soft, light tannin; very ready, drinkable now; moderate-length finish. **

Tenuta Caparzo (twice, 2/89). Nuts and flowers; good weight and structure, flavorful; on the young side. **(+)

Tenuta Caparzo, Riserva (5/90). Some age apparent on the nose, berrylike fruit; fairly tannic at this stage, fruit evident, rather dry and firm, aftertaste. **

Tenuta Col d'Orcia (7 times, 11/90). Nose displays some age, more than expected, hints of nuts and dried fruit; sense of sweetness, moderately tannic, short tannic aftertaste; will it last? ** −

Tenuta Col d'Orcia, Riserva (7/90). More open and richer on the nose than the *normale;* rich and ripe, good structure; a cut above the *normale;* moderate length with tannin at the end. ** +

Tenuta Col d'Orcia, Riserva Poggio al Vento (twice, 11/90). Firm, rather dry, good fruit under light to moderate tannin, a tad bitter even; somehow it seems a lot less than it did a few months earlier. *(*) *Bottle of 7/90:* Nose still a little closed with nuances of fruit and vanilla; concentrated and balanced, chewy, still rather tannic; the youngest of the three wines, and the most tannic. **(+)

Tenuta Il Greppone (6/90, 25,004 bottles). Fragrant aroma, recalls chestnuts and flowers; has a sweetness to the fruit, soft under light to moderate tannin, tasty and quite attractive; will surely improve. **

Tenuta Il Poggione (5 times, 5/90). Lovely nose and flavor, rich and concentrated, ripe fruit, chewy; lots of character, lovely indeed, most attractive; still on the young side. ***

Valdisuga (twice, 12/88). Light nose; tight, fairly nice fruit, firm, could use more weight and extract. *

Valdisuga, Riserva (*twice, 8/90*). Fragrant, earthy aroma; still has tannin to lose, lacks the zest; best to drink though it might last. * *Bottle of 5/90:* Color beginning to brown; vaguely nutlike aroma; some tannin, attractive now, and a little disappointing, fruit seems to be tired, still there is some interest. * −

Villa Banfi (*6 times, 8/90*). Floral nose; a little dry, seems to be losing its fruit, firm and tannic; best to drink. + *Magnum of 12/89:* Nutlike aroma, vaguely floral; firm, some oak, flavorful; still a little closed. * +

1 9 8 1 * −

Total crop size was 651,940 gallons (24,676 hectoliters), equivalent to 274,150 cases, of Brunello. Some 111,744 cases of Brunello were bottled, less than 41 percent of the total declared.

Capanna considers 1981 one of the top vintages. Altesino described it as very good. Colombini and Biondi-Santi also said it was good. Roberto Bellini of La Chiesa di S. Restituta rates it three stars out of five.

We've tasted more than 50 wines, 22 in recent years. Our original assessment was valid: we found the wines to be good, though a trifle light. And we said that they should be ready early. And they were. Many are starting to fade; only a few are still very good. Fattoria dei Barbi Vigna del Fiore and Mastrojanni *normale* and Riserva were the best of those we've tasted, and the Fattoria dei Barbi *normale* and Fattoria Il Greppo Riserva were also very good. We see no point in holding these Brunellos any longer. A few years ago we also liked the Case Basse, Il Casello, and Tenuta Il Poggione.

Altesino (*twice, 4/86*). Lovely aroma; light to moderate tannin, harmonious, a bit light and forward; well made, has character. **

Altesino, Vigna Altesino (*8/90*). Slight nose, suggestions of damp leaves and earth; starting to dry out, the fruit is going. * −

Camigliano (*4/87*). Oxidized.

Camigliano, Riserva (*4/87*). Some oxidation, fruit seems to be fading, unbalanced.

Campogiovanni (*9/87*). Nutlike aroma; seems overly tannic for its weight and fruit. (*)

Canalicchio (Silvano e Maurizio Lambardi) (*4/87*). Aroma displays a richness of ripe fruit; firm and tannic, seems to have the fruit to carry it, tannic aftertaste. *(+)

Canalicchio di Sopra (F.lli Pacenti) (*4 times, 2/87, 7,800 bottles*). Light nose; soft, flavorful, balanced, smooth, light but tasty; ready. * +

Capanna di S. Restituta (Fattoi) (*5/86*). Fairly dark color; nice though light aroma; light body, forward flavors, nice fruit, fairly well balanced, light finish. *(+)

Caprili (*twice, 2/87, 5,200 bottles*). Light nose, suggestive of nuts; on the light side, soft, acid on the high side, a little light in flavor midpalate, short; quite drinkable. *

Casanova (Neri Giovanni) (*4/86*). Chestnut aroma; light tannin; fairly nice though simple; could improve. * +

Casanova di Neri, Riserva (*11/90*). Shows age but still attractive on the nose and palate, dry, short end; drink up. * −

Case Basse (*twice, 4/87*). Lovely nose, recalls nuts and fruit; balanced, still needs more time; elegant and stylish; a cut above most of the other '81s. **(* −)

Castelgiocondo (*twice, 1/88*). Nutlike aroma; still some tannin, attractive open flavor, tasty; enjoyable now; on the light, simple side. *

Cerbaiona (Diego Molinari) (*4/87*). Woodsy, mushroom aroma; moderate tannin, fairly nice fruit, balanced, tannic aftertaste. *(* −)

Chianti Geografico (bottled by A.A.C.) (*2/88*). Light nose; considerable tannin, some fruit, chewy, a mouth of tannin and a sense of fruit. (?*)

Ciacci Piccolomini d'Aragona (*4/87*). Some oxidation.

Comunali (Bartoli-Giusti-Focacci) (*twice, 4/87*). Seaweedlike backnote on the aroma, which is rather tight and ungiving; tannic, some fruit evident. (*)

Costanti (*3 times, ex-cask, 5/86*). Fat and rich for the vintage, forward fruit on the nose and palate, light to medium body, some spice. **(+)

Dei Roseti (Altesino) (*9/87*). Somewhat reticent aroma; moderate tannin, flavorful; good quality; on the young side. **(+)

Fattoria dei Barbi (Colombini) (*3 times, 8/90*). Woodsy, mushroom aroma, fragrant, notes of dried berries and leather; a little dry but nice fruit and nice mouth feel; very ready now, and best to drink. ** − *Bottle of 4/86:* Lovely floral aroma; some tannin, fruit seems a little shy, light body, finish is rather firm and tannic. *(+)

Fattoria dei Barbi (Colombini), Vigna del Fiore (*12/88*). Delicate, fragrant-scented bouquet; sweet and stylish, well made, has class. ** +

Fattoria Il Greppo (Biondi-Santi), Riserva (*8 times, 11/90*). Lovely perfumed, scented aroma recalls chestnuts; nice fruit, a little firm at the end, still has room to improve though attractive now. **(+) *Bottle of 6/90:* Openly fruity aroma recalls chestnuts; soft and flavorful, a little light, nice now and ready though it can still improve, a little short and dry. **

Fattoria La Gerla (*3 times, 10/87*). Nuts and fruit define the nose; moderate tannin, good weight and extract; young, with the stuffing to develop. **

Fornacina (*4/86*). A pretty wine; light tannin, nice fruit, with an almost floral quality to it; light style. ** −

Il Casello (*3 times, 6/87*). Lovely nose, tobacco component; loads of nice fruit, moderate tannin, medium to full body, fairly well balanced. **(+)

Il Paradiso (Manfredi) (4/86). Light aroma, chestnut component; has a sweetness to the fruit and a simpleness about it; nearly ready. *

La Chiesa di S. Restituta (twice, 4/87). Mineral note, some fruit; on the light side, nice flavors. *

La Fortuna (4/87). Rather nice nose; fairly tannic, with enough fruit to carry it, light, tannic finish. *(*)

La Magia (4/87). Vague rubber tire aroma; nice flavor, on the simple side, light finish, some tannin at the end. *

La Poderina (4/87). Touch of oxidation, though fruit still quite evident, rather tannic. (+)

Lisini (4/87). Kind of ripe fruit aroma, suggestion of nuts; balanced and fruity, light tannic aftertaste. *(+)

Mastrojanni (5 times, 4/90). Cassis and cherry bouquet; sweet impression, round and openly fruity; elegant and classy; a tad short. ** +

Mastrojanni, Riserva (twice, 4/88). Floral and kirsch aroma, woodsy and vanilla notes; flavorful, sweet impression, soft; ready or nearly so; could use more length; has class. ** +

Pertimali (Livio Sassetti) (4/87). Stinky off note intrudes on the nose; better in the mouth, firm structure, fairly nice fruit; young with evident potential. *(* −)

Pietroso (4/87). Kind of an odd nose; overly tannic, insufficient fruit.

Podere Pian di Conte (Talenti) (twice, 8/90, 10,600 bottles). Lovely fragrant bouquet; good body, still with tannin, fairly nice fruit, dry, tannic aftertaste; best to drink. * + *Bottle of 4/87:* A bit tight but evident fruit on the nose; a lot of structure, good fruit, fairly tannic, surprisingly fat and rich. **(+)

Poggio Antico (4/87). Light nose; fruity, rather simple, mineral-like aspect to the flavor; no real character.

Poggio Salvi (ex-vat, 5/86). Some oxidation(!), some tannin and some fruit; overall, rather dull and showing age.

Poggio Salvi, Riserva (4/90). Overripe, some oxidation, shot.

Quercecchio (Maria Grazia Salvioni) (4/87). Rather nice nose, woodsy and berrylike; nice fruit, moderately rich, light tannin. *(* −)

S. Carlo (twice, 4/86). Ripe fruit aroma; some tannin, drinkable now, though it should improve; could use more definition and length, say two years. *(+)

S. Filippo (ex-cask, 5/85). Perfumed aroma, pretty, vaguely of pine; well balanced, almost sweet; has some delicacy; should be ready early. **(+)

S. Filippo, Fanti (4/87). Light nose; light body, some tannin, fairly nice fruit, short tannic aftertaste. *(+)

Tenuta Caparzo (4 times, 8/90). Complex bouquet, suggestions of damp leaves, earth, leather and dried berries; sense of sweetness, nice flavor, quite short, still a nice glass; best to drink. * *Bottle of*

8/87: Minty note on the nose, vaguely floral, some spice; very nice for current consumption; soft in the center and balanced, lovely flavors; some class. ** +

Tenuta Caparzo, La Casa (8 times, 8/90). Mushroom, woodsy aroma, with a damp leaves component, similar to the *normale* on the nose at least; tasty, an indication of the fruit fading, perhaps the bottle; drink up. * *Bottle of 6/90:* Well-developed bouquet, complex and mellow, tarlike note, oak component; soft; very ready. ** +

Tenuta Col d'Orcia, Riserva (10/89). Some oxidation, fading or bad storage?

Tenuta Il Greppone Mazzi, Riserva (11/88). Characteristic aroma, fragrant and scented; a bit tight, light to medium body, short with some acid toward the end. * −

Tenuta Il Poggione (twice, 4/87). Reticent aroma; well balanced, still some tannin to shed, flavorful; on the young side. **(+)

Valdicava (4/87). Some oxidation, tired, drying out.

Valdisuga (ex-cask, 7/85). Some fruit evident on the rather shy nose; more apparent on the palate, quite tannic at this stage and rough. *(+)

Valdisuga, Riserva (8/90). Fragrant aroma; a little light in the mouth, nice fruit under some tannin, on the light side, short; quite drinkable, no need to keep. *

Villa Banfi (3 times, 12/88). Characteristic aroma; moderate tannin, nice flavor, dry, hard finish. *

1980 * −

The crop size of 633,023 gallons (23,960 hectoliters) was equivalent to 266,196 cases of Brunello. The 147,630 cases bottled as Brunello amounted to 55.46 percent of the total declared.

Altesino, Castiglion del Bosco, La Fortuna, and Colombini rated the year highly. Biondi-Santi didn't produce a *riserva*. Niederbacher gave it three stars out of four and Roberto Bellini of La Chiesa di S. Restituta gave it four out of five.

We found the vintage mixed. These were wines for early drinking. It's best to drink them up. We've tasted more than 50 wines, about a dozen recently, and without question the '80s are starting to decline. The Mastrojanni is still very good. Those that we tasted a few years ago and really liked included Case Basse, Il Marroneto *normale* and Riserva, and Costanti. Also very good were Altesino, Poggetto Riserva, and Pertimali from Livio Sassetti.

Altesino (4 times, 4/86). Aroma suggestive of nuts, fruit component; soft center, light tannin; enjoyable now, could improve; elegant and stylish. **(* −)

Argiano (4/85). Light nose with a vague off note; tannin seems rather high for the fruit.

Canalicchio di Lambardi (twice, 4/86). Quite a nice nose, vaguely of flowers and fruit; quite tannic, wood tannin(?), firm with evident fruit, astringent at this stage, good structure; very young, say four to five years. **(+)

Canalicchio di Sopra (F.lli Pacenti) (4 times, 8/90, 5,150 bottles). Aroma displays spice and fruit components; some flavor, tasty, very well balanced, very short; drink. * *Bottle of 2/87:* Light but characteristic aroma; more body than the '81 and more structure; nice now with room to improve. ** −

Capanna (G. Cencioni) (5/85, 13,500 bottles). Expansive aroma of flowers and fruit with suggestions of tobacco and licorice; moderate tannin, lots of fruit, firm structure; can be enjoyed now but has potential for improvement. **(+)

Caprili (3 times, 2/87, 5,200 bottles). Minerallike aroma, suggestion of nuts, vaguely vegetal; soft, light; ready. * +

Casanova (4/85). Reticent aroma; light to moderate tannin, lacks some weight and richness, though a pleasant wine; nearly ready. * +

Case Basse (3 times, 4/86). Reticent aroma, fruit in the front, vanilla in the back; rich flavor, quite a nice wine, firm tannins, ripe fruit; real class; very young, needs perhaps four to five years. **(*)

Castiglion del Bosco (twice, 4/87). Light nose, some fruit evident; light in body, chewy with tannin; small-scale. *

Colombaio di Montosoli, "Baricci" (twice, 4/85). Fruity aroma; a richness of flavor under moderate tannin, but no real style; should be ready in two or three years. ** −

Costanti (4/86). Reticent aroma, some fruit evident; has a sweetness and elegance, soft core of fruit; stylish, a lovely glass. ** + (***)

Costanti, Riserva (4 times, 10/87, 4,000 bottles). Full-flavored, with a sweet impression, moderate tannin, good quality; a little young. **(+)

Cottimello (Eredi Fuligni) (4/86). Aroma somewhat unyielding; harsh and tannic, seems to have sufficient fruit; needs a few more years yet. *(?)

Fattoria Casale del Bosco (Silvio Nardi) (3/86). Closed aroma; some tannin, seems to have the fruit to carry it, harsh finish; try in three years. *(+)

Fattoria dei Barbi (Colombini) (5 times, 9/87). Nice nose, recalls nuts; lots of flavor; some elegance and style, a tad young but approachable now. **(+)

Fattoria dei Barbi (Colombini), Riserva (3 times, 8/90). Lovely fragrance, floral and woodslike components; nice entry, then some tannin, nice fruit midpalate, a tad short and dry at the end; best to drink. * + *Bottle of 9/87:* Aroma recalls nuts, some fruit; on the light side, some tannin, could use more structure, lots of flavor which compensates; it seemed better a year ago. This one, *(*)

Fattoria Il Greppo (Biondi-Santi) (twice, 9/88). Vague oxidation, an off bottle perhaps?

Fattoria La Gerla (5/85). Mineral note on aroma; tannic entry, rough and unready but the flavor is there. *(+)

Fontevino, Riserva (4/86). Chestnut aroma; some oxidation, overly tannic for the fruit.

Il Colle (4/86). Reticent aroma; some fruit, moderate tannin, fruit evident beneath; perhaps a tad simple, some character; still a little young. *(* −)

Il Marroneto (4/86). Lovely nose; rich with a sweet impression, well balanced; real character. **(*)

Il Marroneto, Riserva (twice, 4/87, 1,855 bottles). Woodsy, berry aroma; fairly rich, full of flavor, firm, well structured; good quality, some style; give it three to four years. **(*)

La Chiesa di S. Restituta (3 times, 4/85). Nose a bit restrained; nice fruit, some tannin; lacks character, a bit simple. (*)

La Fortuna (10/87). Nuts and fruit define the aroma; lightweight, light to moderate tannin, forward fruit flavors; enjoyable now; a tad dry at the end. ** −

La Magia (Schwarz) (twice, 4/86). Both bottles were corked!

La Poderina (4/86). Cooked and oxidized!

Le Due Porti (4/86). Richly fruited aroma, tobacco nuance; rich in flavor and ripe; perhaps on the simple side; forward; some tannin. ** −

Mastrojanni (5 times, 8/90). Spice and floral bouquet, dried berry nuance; still some tannin, loaded with flavor; very ready, and very nice too; a tad dry at the end; drink. ** +

Mastrojanni, Riserva (twice, 4/87). Light nose; still some tannin to soften, nice fruit, fairly well balanced; needs another two or three years. **(+)

Mastrojanni, Riserva Cru Poggetto (4/87). This wine wasn't filtered. Lovely, perfumed fragrance, floral and fruity; richer than the normal *riserva,* and with more concentration and structure. **(* −)

Melini [bottled by Agrel] (3/87). Fairly rich fruit on the nose; lacks the class of the genre, but quite flavorful. * +

Paradiso (Mauro Fastelli) (twice, 4/87). Woodsy aroma, vague off note intrudes; fairly nice fruit under moderate tannin. *(+)

Pertimali (Livio Sassetti) (4/86). Nose is somewhat closed; rich in flavor, moderate tannin, well made, some style, moderate length; needs perhaps four more years. **(* −)

Pian dei Mercatelli (Azienda Agricola Fontevino—Agricola Camigliano) (twice, 2/86). Color shows age, browning; mercaptan, vague hotness; light tannin, fairly soft, medium length. *The second bottle* was better, displaying hints of chestnuts and berries; soft center; should improve. ** −

Podere Il Poggiolo (4/86). Minerallike aroma; fairly nice fruit under moderate tannin; a bit young yet. *(+)

Poggio Antico (11/87). Small-scale, correct and drinkable, easy, soft, fruity. *

Poggio degli Ulivi, Riserva (4/87). Rubber tire aroma; overly tannic, harsh.

Poggio Salvi (*twice, 4/86*). Both bottles were similar. Some oxidation, dull, flat.

Poggio Salvi, Riserva (4/90). Some oxidation, overly tannic, deficient in fruit.

S. Filippo (*5 times, 4/87*). Has a warmness and slight nuttiness; fairly tannic, good fruit, balanced. *(* −)

Tenuta Caparzo (*3 times, 9/86*). Lovely nose; warm and soft under moderate tannin, balanced; will be ready in a few years, not for long aging. **(+)

Tenuta Caparzo, La Casa (*twice, 8/90*). Oak and vanilla up front on the nose, then some fruit; a little dry, good body, fairly nice fruit; best to drink up. * + *Bottle of 8/87*: Tight nose; good structure, rich flavor, moderate tannin; will improve, fairly young. **(* −)

Tenuta Caparzo, Riserva (8/87). Mushroomlike component to the aroma, vaguely floral; lots of flavor, good body; can improve; tannin at the end. **(+)

Tenuta Col d'Orcia (*4 times, 9/87*). Coarse nose, mineral notes; low fruit, dull. *A bottle tasted 6 months earlier* had an aroma of minerals and flowers; moderate tannin and lots of flavor, while still a little young, rather enjoyable. *(*)

Tenuta di Riguardo [Tosco Vinicola] (4/86). Minty aroma; fairly tannic, sense of fruit while evident, seems insufficient.

Tenuta di Sesta (4/86). Tobacco aroma, also nuts and oxidation; insufficient fruit for the tannin.

Tenuta Il Greppone Mazzi, Riserva (3/88). Mineral aroma; coarse and rustic.

Tenuta Il Poggione (*twice, 5/85*). Reticent aroma with suggestions of licorice and flowers; moderate tannin with nice fruit breath, could have more length on palate; should mature early. **

Valdicava (4/86). Small nose, vaguely chestnut note; fairly nice fruit, light tannin; a bit simple, agreeable; could even improve. *(+)

Valdisuga (4/87). A big nothing, low fruit, some oxidation.

Valdisuga, Riserva (8/90). Pale garnet; baked nose, very little flavor interest, thin, dry and dull.

Villa Banfi (*twice, 4/87*). Some oak, not a lot of fruit, firm, unimpressive.

1979 * −

The harvest gave a yield of 671,279 gallons (25,408 hectoliters), equivalent to 282,283 cases, of Brunello. Of these, 150,129 cases, just over 53 percent, were bottled as Brunello after the requisite aging period.

Altesino and S. Filippo characterized 1979 as a very good year. La Fortuna, Castiglion del Bosco, Castelgiocondo, and Colombini said it was a good vintage. Biondi-Santi didn't produce a *riserva*. Roberto Bellini of La Chiesa di S. Restituta gives it four stars out of five.

There were many splendid and, unfortunately, not so splendid wines produced. It wasn't a vintage to age. We have tasted more than 40 wines, 15 in recent years. We have found that a number of them are fading. We advise drinking them up now; few will improve further.

The Costanti Riserva is still very good, but even that one should be drunk up. The Tenuta Caparzo Riserva is very good. Other wines that we really liked, based on those tasted in the mid-1980s, were Altesino Riserva, Costanti *normale*, Fattoria La Gerla Riserva, Il Casello from Franceschi, Mastrojanni, and Tenuta Il Poggione.

Altesino, Riserva (*11 times, 4/86*). Superbly crafted, elegant and stylish; richly flavored, light to moderate tannin; still needs some age, but tempting now. ***(+) *Bottle of 5/85*: Some oak, a lot of fruit and a vaguely nutty note; tannic, with heaps of flavor to support it, a chewy wine that needs four to five more years to smooth out, but will make a splendid bottle. **(* +)

Camigliano (4/87). Beginning to show age, drying out, some oxidation.

Campogiovanni (4/85). Flowers and nuts on aroma; has tannin and a lot of flavor, with a nutlike note, finish recalls almonds. **

Canalicchio di Sopra (F.lli Pacenti) (*4 times, 8/90, 6,900 bottles*). Characteristic fragrance; a little dry, still has fruit, chocolate note, tasty; drink. * + *Bottle of 2/87*: Not a lot of nose, but what there is is good; well structured, flavorful; could improve, nice now. **

Capanna (G. Cencioni), Riserva (5/85, 720 bottles). Aroma recalls fruit and nuts; moderate tannin, good fruit, light, somewhat tannic finish; seems overly drying at the end, perhaps too long in wood. ** −

Capanna di S. Restituta, Fattoi (*3 times, 4/85*). Vaguely floral aroma; fairly nice fruit on the palate, light tannin, a bit light in body and simple, short. *(+)

Caprili (*twice, 8/90, 5,200 bottles*). Odd nose, recalls cereal and animal fur; tastes the same, really off-putting. *Bottle of 2/87*: Matchstick aroma (sulfur dioxide?) on the nose; soft and ready, though light, and a slight edge.

Casanova di Neri (*twice, 11/90*). Noticeable oxidation, a little dry at the edges, still does have good flavor, rather short; drink up. *

Castelgiocondo (*twice, 5/85*). Aroma somewhat reticent, hints of fruit and vaguely of licorice; still some tannin to soften, a bit light; some tannin at the end; will be ready early. *(*)

Castiglion del Bosco (5/85). Nutty aroma; some tannin, nice fruit; lacks style, a bit pedestrian. * −

Comunali (Bartoli-Giusti-Focacci) (4 times, 8/90). Drying out, still some flavor. *Bottle of 5/85:* Expansive floral bouquet, vaguely nutlike; light tannin, surprisingly forward; perhaps a bit simple; some tannin at the end. * + *Bottle of 4/85:* Lovely complex aroma with nuances of cherries, nuts, flowers and spice; some tannin to shed; a bit young but approachable. **(+)

Costanti (5/85, 11,700 bottles). Lovely bouquet recalls cherries, flowers, vanilla and berries, has delicacy; well balanced, almost sweet, elegant, well made, long finish with a suggestion of nutmeg. **(*)

Costanti, Riserva (3 times, 8/90, 4,400 bottles). Rich, open fruit bouquet, suggestions of nuts and flowers, vaguely of leather; rich and spicy, full-bodied, soft center, some alcohol intrudes at the end; best to drink now. ** + *Bottle of 9/86:* Lovely nose; lush flavors, balanced, moderate tannin; lots of style and quality. **(*)

Fattoria Casale del Bosco (Silvio Nardi) (4/85). Oxidized.

Fattoria dei Barbi (Colombini) (7 times, 6/88). Nutty, floral, fruity aroma; flavorful, some tannin, vague harsh edge, tasty. * +

Fattoria dei Barbi (Colombini), Riserva (7 times, 8/90). Woodslike aroma, leather notes; on the dry side, considerable flavor, short. * *Bottle of 12/86:* Nutlike aroma; good structure, light to medium tannin, with the stuffing, balanced; some class. **(+)

Fattoria Il Greppo (Biondi-Santi) (twice, 6/86). Perfumed, almond bouquet; light body, light tannin, some fruit; ready now, might improve. ** −

Fattoria La Gerla, Riserva (5/85). Closed-in and tannic but shows promise, the stuffing is there, and the structure, finish is a bit light. *(* +)

Il Casello (Franceschi) (twice, 5/85). Floral aroma, a bit closed; well balanced, soft-centered, round, flavorful, tannin to lose, give it perhaps three more years. **(+)

Il Colle (4/85). Tar and nuts on aroma; a fair amount of tannin, with a sense of fruit beneath; lacks style. (*)

La Fortuna (4 times, 8/89). Volatile acidity all too apparent, some tannin, some fruit; fading fast, still with a light chill it does have flavor interest. The previous bottle was better. *Bottle of 4/85:* Aroma of mushrooms and flowers; some tannin, a lot of flavor, soft-centered; young but approaching drinkability. **(+)

La Magia (4/85). Stinky aroma—mercaptans(?); overly tannic for the fruit, harsh finish.

La Poderina (4/85). Notes of chocolate and Marsala on nose; and on palate under the tannin.

Le Presi (4/85). Mineral aroma with suggestions of volcanic earth and black pepper notes; tannic entry gives way to heaps of flavor, short, tannic ending. *(* −)

Mastrojanni, Podere Loreto (4/85). Aroma has a pleasant touch of resin, some flowers and fruit; sweet ripe fruit under the tannin, has style, balance, length; shows real quality. **(*)

Pietroso (4/86). Seaweed, chocolate, off-putting aroma; better in the mouth, tannic, seems to have sufficient fruit to carry the tannin. *?

Poggio Antico (3 times, 4/85). Lacks structure, weight and definition; this was the best bottle of the three!

Poggio Antico, Riserva (4/87). A little overripe, small-scale, drinkable. +

Poggio Salvi (twice, 4/87). Oxidation painfully evident; it was better when tasted a year earlier, but even then it showed signs of aging.

S. Filippo dei Comunali (Ermanno Rosi) (4 times, 8/90). Earthy, leather aroma, floral component; a little dry; best to drink up. * − *Bottle of 5/85:* Aroma a bit reticent, hints of nuts, fruit and flowers; still has tannin to soften, with the fruit to carry it; a nice wine, but could have more style. **

Tenuta Caparzo (3 times, 12/85). Vague nutlike aroma; a little light, some tannin, moderate fruit on entry, a little shallow; short, tannic, aftertaste. *(+)

Tenuta Caparzo, La Casa (6 times, 8/90). Woodsy and mushroom aroma; losing its fruit, drink up. * − *Bottle of 3/89:* Notes of mint and ripe fruit, some vanilla; richly flavored, some tannin, good structure, a bit dry at the end. ** − *Bottle of 5/85:* Fruity aroma with a hint of toffee and overtones of oak; rich, toasty oak flavors on entry give way to tannin, fairly rich, firm, tannic finish; should soften in about three years. **(+)

Tenuta Caparzo, Riserva (twice, 7/89). Richly fruited, spicy, floral aroma, nutlike nuance; full of flavor, rich and intense, very ready, and very good, somewhat harsh at the end. **

Tenuta Col d'Orcia (twice, 3/87). Deep color; reticent aroma; good body, fairly nice structure, some tannin; good potential. **(+)

Tenuta Col d'Orcia, Riserva (7/90). Fairly dark color, showing age on both the color and nose, aroma reveals suggestions of leather and fruit; quite soft on the midpalate, some tannin; best to drink up, short. *

Tenuta Il Poggione (3 times, 9/86). Rich nose, recalls nuts; well structured, a big, rich, flavorful wine, moderate tannin; lots of quality; long. **(*)

Valdicava (4/85). Nutty aroma; a chocolatey flavor, is there enough fruit for the rather considerable tannin?

Valdisuga (4 times, 8/90). Small-scale, drinkable, not much more. *Bottle of 4/87:* Rubber tire; some fruit, drinks nicely; no real regional character, but agreeable.

Valdisuga, Riserva (4 times, 8/90). Aroma of dried fruit and prunes; still some fruit; atypical Brunello, unimpressive.

Villa Banfi (3 times, 8/89). Not a lot of aroma, some fruit evident; soft and fruity; straightforward character; no real depth but drinkable and ready. *

Villa Banfi, Riserva (7/90). Lovely scented nose, suggestions of berries and nuts; warm and mellow, a little dry, starting to lose its fruit, touch of mint; not to keep. *

1978 *

The harvest gave a total crop of 515,296 gallons (19,504 hectoliters), equivalent to 216,689 cases, of Brunello. The 115,333 cases of Brunello bottled were just over 53 percent of the amount declared.

Right from the start, this vintage received a lot of good reviews. We always felt the wines didn't measure up to the acclaim. At this point, our evaluation seems to have been proved correct. It was a mixed vintage. Biondi-Santi, once again, didn't bottle a *riserva*. Roberto Bellini of La Chiesa di S. Restituta rates it at four stars out of five.

Based on some 30 wines, including a baker's dozen tasted recently, we think that it's best to drink them up, as they are fading. Tenuta Il Poggione and Fattoria dei Barbi Riserva are still very good. In the mid-1980s the Altesino Riserva, Lisini, and Mastrojanni were all very good as well. Among the other good ones are La Fortuna, Capanna, and the Caparzo La Casa.

Altesino, Riserva (*3 times, 5/85*). Floral aroma with notes of hazelnuts and cherries; moderate tannin, flavorful; more foward than the 1979(!) though still young; has style and balance; long tannic finish. **(*)

Altesino, Vigna Altesino (*6/84*). Aroma somewhat closed but some richness of fruit comes through; moderate tannin, rich ripe fruit flavors, vaguely bitter on finish. **(+)

Argiano (*1/84*). Not much on nose; light-bodied, unbalanced; altogether unimpressive.

Camigliano (*11/83*). Aroma a bit closed but gives hints of fruit and oak; fairly tannic and astringent, moderate fruit, is there enough? Seems so. (*)

Canalicchio di Sopra (*twice, 2/87, 4,800 bottles*). Small nose; some acid, has flavor, but not up to the quality of the '79; was better in May 1985. *+

Capanna (G. Cencioni) (*1/84*). Full, rich aroma; flavorful, moderate tannin, well structured; a big wine; quite nice. **(+)

Casa del Cerro (*10/85*). Fairly nice nose; still has tannin, but the fruit is there; not far from being ready; a bit short. *(*)

Castiglion del Bosco (*3 times, 6/84*). Ripe cherries on aroma; fairly open, a mouthful of flavor, still has tannin; nearly ready, but will improve. **

Castiglion del Bosco, Riserva (*5/85*). Aroma of licorice, tar, nuts and fruit; a lot of flavor up front, soft-centered, light tannin; a bit coarse, but agreeable. *

Cecchi Luigi [bottled by A.A.T.C.] (*twice, 6/84*). Mineral aspect to aroma; lacks weight, definition and flavor, flat and dull though drinkable.

Comunali (Bartoli-Giusti-Focacci), Riserva (*5/85*). Chestnuts and vanilla on aroma; well knit, a bit light, tasty, chestnuts on palate, tannic finish; could improve. **

Fattoria Casale del Bosco (Silvio Nardi), Riserva (*twice, 4/87*). Has fruit and tannin, but not a lot of structure.

Fattoria dei Barbi (Colombini) (*1/84*). Floral aroma with a nutlike component; tannic, rather closed but holds out some promise, very short, tannic aftertaste. *(*?)

Fattoria dei Barbi (Colombini), Riserva (*4 times, 8/90*). Rich, fragrant nose of ripe berrylike fruit and flowers; soft entry, tasty, goes out a little short. ** — *Bottle of 12/86:* Nice nose, pretty; good body, some style, balanced and flavorful; still young. **(+)

Fattoria Il Greppo (Biondi-Santi) (*3 times, 12/86*). Nice nose, almost minty; firm, some acid; is there enough fruit? (*?)

Lisini (*twice, 4/87*). Lovely mushroom, woodsy aroma; rich, full-bodied Brunello, the fruit is there to carry the tannin. **(*—)

Mastrojanni, Podere Loreto (*5/85*). Some oak and a lot of fruit on nose, vaguely floral with nutlike notes; still undeveloped, fairly rough and tannic but the fruit is there, rich and flavorful. **(*—)

Poggio Antico (*3 times, 4/85*). Quite a lot of bottle variation here. *The best one was the most recent:* Perfumed bouquet; almost sweet on entry, gives way to an astringency, has flavor, some alcohol and a tannic bite on the finish. (*)

S. Filippo dei Comunali (Ermanno Rosi) (*twice, 8/90*). Too old. *Bottle of 5/85:* Aroma of nuts and flowers; quite tannic but with the reserves to carry it; a nice glass though a bit young yet. *(+)

Tenuta Caparzo (*5 times, 8/90*). Lovely fragrant aroma; very soft, nice fruit, short; drink up. * *Bottle of 5/85:* Woodsy aroma with a nutlike aspect; moderate tannin, a trifle shy on fruit, vaguely bitter aftertaste that tails off at the end; shows some potential. *(?)

Tenuta Caparzo, La Casa (*3 times, 8/90*). Lovely nose, combines a touch of oak with fruit and flowers; soft, very ready, short. *+ *Bottle of 5/85:* Hints of toffee on aroma and flavor, fuller, richer and more intense than the '79, also rounder; still young. **(*—)

Tenuta Col d'Orcia, Riserva (*3 times, 7/90*). Fruit and leather aroma, vanilla overlay; some tannin; attractive now, no need to keep; good weight, moderate length. *+ *Bottle of 12/86:* Big nose, nutlike component; rich in flavor but, at this stage, quite astringent. *(*—)

Tenuta di Riguardo [bottled by Tosco Vinicola] (*7/85*). Warm, fruity aroma, slight suggestion of nuts; light tannin, fruity, overly simple; drinkable now; lacks style. * —

Tenuta Il Poggione (*3 times, 8/90*). Interesting nuance on the nose, suggestive of the coolness from methanol, mintlike component as well; rich in flavor, tasty; ready now though no need to rush to drink. **+ *Bottle of 1/84:* Nutty aroma with berrylike notes; well balanced, sweet fruit flavors, supple center. **(+)

Tenuta Il Poggione, Riserva (*twice, 3/85*). Rich, intense floral bouquet with cherrylike notes; surprisingly forward and supple, stylish, has length; still needs age. **(*)

Valdisuga (*9/86*). Overly simple, lacks structure, weight and definition, not bad; not Brunello.

Valdisuga, Riserva (5 times, 8/90). Rather nice nose, recalls dried fruit; small-scale, soft, easy and overly simple, lacks weight and length; drinkable, no more.

Villa Banfi (6/84). Characteristic aroma, flowers and cherries beneath overtones of oak; fairly tannic, lacks structure and definition; not a success.

Villa Banfi, Riserva (3/87). Oak quite pronounced, some fruit evident as well; moderate tannin, fairly nice fruit; no depth, could use more structure, small-scale, coarse.

1 9 7 7 * * +

The vintage produced 411,386 gallons (15,571 hectoliters) of wine, equivalent to 172,994 cases of Brunello. There were 92,435 cases of Brunello bottled, nearly 53.5 percent of the amount declared.

Without question, 1977 produced the best wines between 1975 and 1982. Altesino, Castiglion del Bosco, Biondi-Santi, and La Fortuna rated the vintage highly. Colombini said it was a good year. And once again, Roberto Bellini of La Chiesa di S. Restituta gave it four stars out of five.

We believe, based on the four wines we've tasted in recent years, that the '77 Brunellos from good producers are aging gracefully. The Fattoria Il Greppo Riserva from Biondi-Santi is very good, and the Tenuta Caparzo Riserva good. Our favorites, going back to 1985, were Altesino Riserva and the Fattoria dei Barbi from Colombini. And the Tenuta Caparzo La Casa was very good as well.

Altesino, Riserva (5/85). Floral, fruity bouquet, vaguely nutty; moderate tannin, a complete, well-structured wine of style and elegance; needs two or three years. ***(+)

Argiano (twice, 6/84). Hot nose, with overripe fruit and a mineral aspect; nice fruit, moderate tannin. *

Costanti, Riserva (twice, 5/85, 4,000 bottles). A bit dull and uncharacteristic. The only disappointment we've ever had from this outstanding producer.

Fattoria dei Barbi (Colombini) (3 times, 6/84). Lovely aroma with overtones of cherries and flowers; moderate tannin, well structured; elegant and stylish, good flavor and length. **(*)

Fattoria Il Greppo (Biondi-Santi) (5/83). Full of flavor, round and smooth, surprisingly forward. **

Fattoria Il Greppo (Biondi-Santi), Riserva (twice, 6/90). Floral, mint and spice bouquet; smooth, almost velvet texture, harmonious; some elegance; finish is a little dry, suggestions of kirsch and blueberries, tannic aftertaste. ** *Bottle of 5/85* [decanted two hours earlier following Biondi-Santi's instructions]: Aroma a bit reticent, some fruit evident; moderate tannin, well knit, surprisingly soft, a bit short; should improve. **(+)

La Chiesa di S. Restituta (twice, 6/84, 9,200 bottles). Browning; some oxidation over a hot, baked aroma; better in the mouth, light

tannin, lacking in fruit; nowhere to go; this describes the better bottle. The one tasted eight months earlier was even duller.

Lisini (6/84). A bit reticent on nose though shows some fruit, a mouthful of flavor, light to moderate tannin, well balanced; has style, impressive. **(*)

Riguardo [*bottled by Tosco Vinicola*] (6/84). Browning; a vaguely caramel backnote; light tannin, fruity; simple, agreeable.

Tenuta Caparzo (3 times, 5/85). Fruity aroma, vaguely woodsy; tannic entry, seems to have sufficient fruit but lacks somewhat in weight. *(+)

Tenuta Caparzo, La Casa (5/85). Vaguely toffeelike aroma; moderate tannin, well knit, has a sweetness and lots of fruit, tannic finish; needs a few more years yet. **(*−)

Tenuta Caparzo, Riserva (8/90). Fragrant; nice entry, good body, still some tannin; no need to keep, should hold. *

Tenuta Col d'Orcia (twice, 2/83). Unyielding on nose; fairly well balanced though a bit astringent, has a tannic roughness, but with the stuffing to support it. The bottle tasted a year earlier seemed more forward and softer. *(*)

Tenuta Valdicava, Riserva Madonna del Piano (11/90). Aroma suggestive of a forest, some underbrush and flowers; somewhat firm, still the fruit is fairly nice, moderate length, rather dry at the end; drink up. *

Valdisuga, Riserva (5 times, 8/90). This wine has shown great variation in bottles; some were faded, others fading. None of them displayed much character or interest. Aroma of dried fruit, raisins and prunes; a little light and simple, soft and drinkable, no character.

1 9 7 6 0

The year's output of 273,817 gallons (10,364 hectoliters) was equivalent to 115,144 cases of Brunello. Less than 45 percent of the declared total was bottled as Brunello; this amounted to 51,310 cases.

Altesino, Biondi-Santi, Campogiovanni, Capanna, Castiglion del Bosco, Costanti, Il Poggione, and S. Filippo listed this vintage among the worst ever. Roberto Bellini gave it two stars out of five. Biondi-Santi, much to his credit, didn't bottle. Costanti and Il Poggione produced a limited quantity of surprisingly good wine. Altesino and Canalicchio di Sopra, too, produced pleasant surprises.

We're not sorry to report that we haven't tasted any '76 Brunellos since 1985. We doubt if any would have any interest at all. These wines are past their best; they are, alas, too old today.

Altesino, Vigna Montosoli (6 times, 1/84). Characteristic floral bouquet with fruity overtones; soft, acid a touch high but in all a good glass of wine; not to keep. * +

Canalicchio di Sopra (5/85, at the winery). Aroma shows development and some complexity, nutlike, a hint of fruit; beginning to dry out a bit, but still has a lot of nice fruit; quite drinkable. * +

Costanti (5 times, 3/83). Light-bodied, tasty, very well made; shows some quality; not to keep. ** −

Fattoria dei Barbi (Colombini) (4/86). Medium brick color; mushroom, woodsy aroma; still some fruit, but not to keep, tannin beginning to take over, medium length, tannic aftertaste. *

Riguardo [bottled by Tosco Vinicola] (3/82). Butterscotch and vanilla on aroma that carry through on the palate, lacks structure and weight, but drinkable.

Tenuta Caparzo (3 times, 5/85, at the winery). Pine on aroma that's showing age; still has tannin and a lot of fruit, finish is all tannin; drying out, but still good. * −

Tenuta Il Poggione (3 times, 3/85). Fragrant aroma with a touch of tar and tobacco; still has tannin and a surprising amount of fruit, well made; has held up very well, shows no signs of deterioration! **

1975 *** +

Total crop size was 333,473 gallons (12,622 hectoliters), equivalent to 140,230 cases, of Brunello. The 76,715 cases bottled were less than 55 percent of the amount declared.

Il Poggione rates the vintage among the all-time greats, better even than 1970. Altesino, Biondi-Santi, Camigliano, Campogiovanni, Capanna, Castiglion del Bosco, Castelgiocondo, Costanti, La Fortuna, and Tenuta Caparzo agree it was topflight, one of the very best. And Roberto Bellini gives it top marks, five stars. Colombini said that 1975 was among the seven best since the war.

No question about it, there were some outstanding wines produced in 1975, but the vintage was no guarantee; there were also some losers. The best need more age.

Over the past decade we have tasted some two dozen wines from 16 producers, only three recently but two of them were excellent and showed no signs of age—Altesino Vigna Montosoli and Fattoria Il Greppo Riserva from Biondi-Santi. A few years ago the Tenuta Il Poggione was exemplary and the Costanti Riserva almost as good. And we'd be remiss not to mention Colombini's Fattoria dei Barbi, especially their Riserva.

Altesino (4 times, 10/85). Characteristic nutlike aroma; full of flavor, balanced, has style, long; still has room to improve. **(* −)

Altesino, Vigna Altesino (3 times, 4/81). Chestnuts on aroma; rich and intense though a bit subdued, still has tannin; elegant, well knit, stylish. ***(+)

Altesino, Vigna Montosoli (8 times, 12/89). Floral overtone to a richly fruited bouquet; rich, velvety and round, ready and delicious with the backbone and structure to carry it further. ***

Argiano (twice, 4/81). Some fruit on the nose; a bit pedestrian; nearly ready.

Argiano, Riserva (twice, 11/83). Tawny at rim; some oxidation; better on palate, though low in fruit and a bit shallow.

Castelgiocondo (12/86). Nutlike and floral aroma; soft, smooth and tasty, light tannin, very ready, lacks some weight and intensity, but agreeable. * +

Castiglion del Bosco (3 times, 11/83). Seems to have too much tannin for the fruit, where will it go?

Costanti, Riserva (5/85, 1,200 bottles). Lovely complex bouquet, with nuances of vanilla, toffee, flowers and pine berries; ripe fruit, sweet, some tannin, beginning to resolve itself; finely honed, elegant. ***(+)

Fattoria Casale del Bosco (Silvio Nardi), Riserva (twice, 4/87). Drying out, still has tannin, not a lot of fruit.

Fattoria dei Barbi (Colombini) (7 times, 12/87). The bottle was filled to the upper shoulder. Nuts and dried fruit aroma; fairly rich and concentrated; a big wine that still has some firmness, especially at the end. **(+)

Fattoria dei Barbi (Colombini), Riserva (5 times, 9/83). A wine with everything—richness, elegance, balance, style, flavor and length; it has to be the wine of the vintage. ***(*)

Fattoria Il Greppo (Biondi-Santi) (3 times, 5/83). Real quality—one of the few times the wine has equaled the reputation—not the wine of the vintage, but certainly one of the best. ***

Fattoria Il Greppo (Biondi-Santi), Riserva (6/90). Delicate, floral bouquet; rich and mouth-filling, real class and concentration, fairly long, cherry and berry flavors; still has more to give, should be a keeper; a fine Brunello, and a fine wine by any standard. ***(+)

Isabella de'Medici [bottled by Valdisuga] (4 times, 6/84). We kept on trying, but one bottle was worse than the other.

Lisini, Riserva (4 times, 6/90). Dried fruit, old fruit and leather aroma; drying out, acidic edge, still some fruit but clearly fading. *

Olivieri [bottled by Tenuta Valdicava di Martini Bramante] (twice, 3/82). Soft and easy, lacks style and distinction though pleasant enough; a Chianti-style Brunello.

Poggio alle Mura, Riserva (3 times, 11/83). Pale; unstructured, lacks flavor, weight and definition.

Tenuta Caparzo (6 times, 5/85). Vaguely pinelike aroma showing development and age; some tannin, nice entry and middle palate, has richness of flavor, but going off; not to keep. *

Tenuta Caparzo, Riserva (3 times, 11/83). Pale color; aroma is a bit light, with hints of fruit and flowers; still tannic, flavorful; not up to the vintage, short. *

Tenuta Col d'Orcia (4 times, 2/83). Floral, fruity aroma; seems somewhat young, almost sweet, some tannin to shed, well balanced; displays style and class. **(* −)

Tenuta Col d'Orcia, Riserva (twice, 11/83). More flavor and better structure than the regular; will make a splendid bottle with time. **(*)

Tenuta Il Poggione (5 times, 5/85). Richly perfumed bouquet of flowers, tar and licorice; sweet and ripe, not a big wine but an elegant one, balance is nearly perfect; exudes style; ready but still some room for improvement. ****

Valdisuga, Riserva (3/83). Rather a nice nose; good flavor, surprisingly soft and easy; ready.

1974 0

The vintage produced a yield of 221,611 gallons (8,388 hectoliters), equivalent to 93,191 cases, of Brunello.

At one time the '74s offered pleasant drinking, although many were somewhat low in fruit. Nearly all are too old today. Surprisingly, the Caparzo Riserva was an exception a few years ago. Biondi-Santi didn't produce a *riserva*. It's not a vintage to hold—drink them up, or pour them out.

Argiano (twice, 4/80). Aroma displays some fruit, though a bit closed; light-bodied, some tannin and flavor, very short.

Castelgiocondo, Riserva (4/81). Perfumed scent, with notes of ripe fruit; some tannin, flavorful, a bit light; has some style; a bit young yet but a nice glass. (It has probably faded by now.) **

Castiglion del Bosco (twice, 3/82). Vanilla and ripe fruit on aroma; quite nice, but something unpleasant lurks in the background, considerable tannin; drying out.

Fattoria Casale del Bosco (Silvio Nardi) (10/80). More like a Chianti than a Brunello; a lightweight, small-scale wine.

Fattoria dei Barbi (Colombini) (3 times, 9/81). Perfumed aroma with a nutlike component; nice flavor, a bit light; some style. **−

Fattoria dei Barbi (Colombini), Riserva (11/83). Fruity aroma with cassis and floral notes; light tannin, soft and flavorful; quite ready; a bit short; a pleasant small-scale wine. *+

Fattoria Il Greppo (Biondi-Santi) (11/79). Pale; lacks aroma; thin, low in flavor, a short, sharp finish and this only five years after the vintage!

Olivieri [bottled by Tenuta Valdicava di Martini Bramante] (twice, 12/80). Another Chianti-like Brunello; small-scale and overly simple, with harsh edges.

Tenuta Caparzo (6 times, 12/82). Fruity aroma with a nutty aspect; lacks substance, and somewhat in structure, short finish with noticeable volatile acidity. This wine peaked in 1980 and was enjoyable until early or mid-1981, when it started to decline.

Tenuta Caparzo, Riserva (twice, 5/85, tasted at the winery). Rich aroma with a suggestion of leather, vaguely of figs; surprisingly full, seems younger than a '75, almost sweet. **+

Tenuta Col d'Orcia (3 times, 10/80). Perfumed aroma, some fruit and complexity; considerable tannin, is there enough fruit? We think so. (It is probably too old today.) *(*)

1973 0

Camigliano rated the year highly. Once again the Biondi-Santi *riserva* wasn't produced. For the most part, the '73s are light wines that are fading fast; many are already gone. A real surprise was the Biondi-Santi *annata*, without question the star of this mediocre year and considerably above the vintage. We suspect that even that one has been long gone. Based on eight wines, each from a different producer, we give this vintage zero.

Altesino (5 times, 11/83). Fragrant, vaguely floral bouquet; beginning to dry out, was better in 1979, but still has flavor and interest. *

Campogiovanni, Riserva (3 times, 11/83). Vague coffeelike notes on aroma; some tannin, modest flavors; still good but drying out. *−

Fattoria dei Barbi (Colombini) (8 times, 5/83). Well-developed aroma with some complexity; still drinkable but beginning to dry out; it was at its best between 1978 and 1981. *

Fattoria Il Greppo (Biondi-Santi) (6/84). Surprisingly deep color, garnet; lovely bouquet; some class; has an uncommon richness, well structured; full of style and class; perhaps Biondi-Santi's finest wine of the 1970s after his especially fine '75. **+

Lisini (twice, 11/79). Nice aroma of cherries; light, some tannin, has fruit, short. (We doubt that it has any interest today.) *+

Poggio alle Mura (11/79). Best forgotten. (This producer has trouble in great years.)

Tenuta Caparzo (twice, 5/85). Beginning to brown; shows a lot of age on nose; still has nice flavor and interest but drying out; it was at its peak in 1979 and 1980.

Tenuta Il Poggione (6 times, 2/84). Light but characteristic aroma; fairly well balanced, light-bodied, soft and tasty, moderately long finish with a tannic component; still good though past its peak, which was from 1979 to early 1983. *

1972 0

By reputation, 1972 was among the worst of the Brunello vintages. The only one we tasted, the Colombini, while a decent enough wine, should not have been bottled as a Brunello.

Fattori dei Barbi (Colombini) (3 times, 4/86). Medium brick color; vegetablelike aroma; stalky and stemmy flavor, some fruit evident; drinkable, no more.

1971 0

Biondi-Santi, Camigliano, Campogiovanni, Capanna, and Castiglion del Bosco rate the vintage highly.

High acid and a meagerness of body characterize the '71s, although there were some exceptions. Based on seven wines from as many producers, the '71s are fading or have already faded. The Tenuta Il Poggione was a knockout at one time; we don't know if it still is. The Fattoria dei Barbi Riserva from Colombini was fading when we last tasted it in 1987.

Campogiovanni, Riserva (10/80). Color showing age; some oxidation; still has considerable tannin, but fairly well matched with fruit. (Too old by now.) *(+)

Castiglion del Bosco (4/80). Nice aroma, still a bit closed; tannin to lose, shows some promise. (Too old by now.) *(+)

Fattoria dei Barbi (Colombini), Riserva (25 times, 8/87). Brick color; floral, nutty aroma; high acid, touch of tannin, some heat, short, drink up. * *Bottle of 1/86:* Not to keep, though very nice now, soft and tasty, moderate length. ** *Bottle of 11/84:* Vaguely floral bouquet with nutlike notes; soft, smooth and round, some style; very ready, as good as it ever was; a vague touch of alcohol mars the finish. ** +

Fattoria Il Greppo (Biondi-Santi), Riserva (10 times, 11/90). *The most recent bottle, tasted at the winery:* Tar and fruit on the aroma, damp leaves and vaguely nutty as well; open flavor, warm, a little dry especially at the end, sense of sweetness. ** *Bottle of 6/90:* Aroma suggestive of dried fruit, nuts and leather, complex and mellow; nice mouth feel upon entry then a little dry and lacking on the midpalate, short, tannic aftertaste. * *Bottle of 9/88:* Complex bouquet; quite nice upon entry, then shallow, with some acid at the end. * − *Bottle of 2/84:* Shot. *Bottle of 11/83:* (the best of the nine bottles that we tasted from May 1979 to June 1990): Perfumed bouquet, vaguely nutlike; fairly well balanced, still some tannin, beginning to soften and round out, though a troublesome touch of oxidation intrudes; a good, but not a great bottle. **

Poggio alle Mura, Riserva (4 times, 6/90). Shot! *Bottle of 5/83:* Tawny; aroma offers some interest; still some tannin; as ready as it will ever be.

Tenuta Col d'Orcia (3 times, 11/78). Fragrant scent; light, some tannin, lacks substance and weight.

Tenuta Il Poggione (4 times, 12/85). Lovely fragrant bouquet; fairly soft, still some tannin; ready now, no need to keep any longer. ***

1970 ***

Biondi-Santi, Caparzo, Castiglion del Bosco, Colombini, Costanti, Il Poggione, and La Fortuna rate this year as one of the very best. Il Poggione places it after 1975. Colombini rates this vintage, along with 1975, as among the seven best

between the end of the Second World War and 1989. Judging from the wines we've tasted, the vintage was outstanding, the best in our experience until 1985, and at this point we rate the 1970s higher. Production in 1970 was considerably less than today, as were the number of producers selling Brunello in bottle.

In the past decade we've tasted ten wines from eight producers. Some wines are starting to fade, including the Tenuta Il Poggione, which, although still excellent, was at one time outstanding. Colombini's Fattoria dei Barbi Riserva, a magnificent wine with uncommon elegance and style, is still first rate and can even improve some more. The Il Poggione and Costanti weren't far behind. And, in fact, when last tasted a few years ago, the Costanti Riserva was superb. Among the big names, only Biondi-Santi was disappointing.

Castiglion del Bosco (5/80). Color is browning; volatile acidity on aroma; dried out.

Costanti, Riserva (6 times, 9/87, 2,600 bottles). Complex bouquet, rich and deep, overtones of apricots; full, rich and complete with good structure and loads of flavor, very long; ready now, yet with more room to grow. **** *Bottle of 5/85:* Deep color; intense bouquet with nuances of vanilla, toffee, flowers, resin and leather; still some tannin to shed but heaps of flavor make it tempting now, round and smooth, velvety; real quality here. ***(*)

Fattoria Casale del Bosco (Silvio Nardi) (12 times, 7/83). Hot, almost baked aroma; harsh edges, drying out; this wine was at its best from 1979 to 1980; it started to go over the top in 1981.

Fattoria dei Barbi (Colombini) (3/87). Nutlike aroma; soft and smooth, a slight harshness intrudes, some alcohol at the end; still it is a nice glass now. (The storage that this wine came from was questionable.) ** +

Fattoria dei Barbi (Colombini), Riserva (19 times, 2/90). Rich, intense and expansive bouquet, recalls ripe fruit and nuts; sweet and ripe, still some tannin, with a sweet core of ripe fruit, very long, a tad dry at the end; still more to give. *** + *Bottle of 3/82:* Superb bouquet—deep, rich and complex, with floral overtones; a complete wine, has an uncommon elegance; full of flavor and style, long finish; still room to improve. ****

Fattoria Il Greppo (Biondi-Santi) (17 times, 4/86). Some oxidation intrudes, also some nice nuances; somewhat astringent, and a bit thin on the finish; still some flavor interest. *Bottle of 4/85:* Unbalanced, high acid, very little fruit remaining; it was worth a lot more before we opened it. Of the 17 bottles we tasted only one was good, and that was in 1977. (The bottles came from at least three different shipments, and over half a dozen sources.) And this vintage is considered one of the greatest of all time!

Fattoria Il Greppo (Biondi-Santi), Riserva (4 times, 11/90). *Tasted at the winery:* Toastlike nuance on the nose, berrylike component; soft, rather nice flavor, trace of oxidation, dry, firm finish, trace of acid. ** − *Bottle of 6/90:* Vaguely corked, still there is some flavor as well as tannin; difficult to fully assess; some quality apparent. ? *Two bottles, 10/80, the first*: Completely oxidized. *The second*: Some oxidation, but still offers some interest.

Poggio alle Mura (*10 times, 12/80*). At one time this was a drinkable little wine, with no real character or virtues and no real defects; since 1979 it has shown marked signs of deterioration.

Tenuta Col d'Orcia (*twice, 10/80*). Rich, berrylike aroma; loads of flavor, soft; elegant, stylish; room to improve. ***

Tenuta Il Poggione (*5 times, 6/90*). Fragrant bouquet, vaguely floral with suggestions of leather; light to moderate tannin, chocolate notes, smooth almost velvetlike; very good indeed though it does seem to be on the decline, but it could be the bottle considering that the level was down, there was noticeable ullage. *** *Bottle of 5/85*: Woodsy, floral bouquet with a note of mushrooms; velvety, full-flavored, enormously long finish; a complete wine that while quite ready has room to improve further. ****

1 9 6 9 * +

Castiglion del Bosco described 1969 as a poor year. Biondi-Santi said it was very good. Overall, the vintage wasn't highly thought of. Based on two wines—the Biondi-Santi Il Greppo Riserva tasted in 1990 and the Il Poggione tasted in 1986—the best wines of the vintage appear to be holding. We doubt that many others are; it would seem to be best to drink up what you might still have. We can't see any further improvement.

Fattoria Il Greppo (Biondi-Santi), Riserva (*twice, 6/90*). Lovely and expansive bouquet, suggestive of nuts, plums and flowers, toasty; nice entry, mellow, velvet mouth feel, flavorful, a little short and dry; seems to be drying out a bit, still a nice glass. ** *Bottle of 12/86*: Oxidized, flat, shows age, tired, still some fruit, some acid toward the end, and some interest. ** −

Tenuta Il Poggione (*twice, 4/86*). Medium deep garnet; warm, complex bouquet, nutlike nuance; still some tannin, nice flavor, with a softness in the center and a slight warmness at the end, which is moderately long; drink up. **

1 9 6 8 * −

Castiglion del Bosco, Biondi-Santi, and Camigliano described 1968 as a good to very good year. Overall, it was a medium vintage, and judging from those we've tasted within the past decade, the wines are getting tired. Based on the five wines we've tasted, we advise drinking any that you still have. The Fattoria Il Greppo Riserva from Biondi-Santi is very good, but there is no need to hold it any longer. Tenuta Col d'Orcia Riserva was very good in 1987, as was Colombini's Fattoria dei Barbi Riserva.

Fattoria Casale del Bosco (Silvio Nardi), Riserva (*twice, 4/87*). Drinkable but noticeable oxidation.

Fattoria dei Barbi (Colombini) (*5/80*). Dried out.

Fattoria dei Barbi (Colombini), Riserva (*6 times, 4/86*). Medium brick, garnet rim; rather nice fruit on the nose, vague berrylike nuance; still has fruit, but drying out, interesting raspberry nuance; has character and some sweetness, some elegance. ** *Bottle of 5/85*: Tawny, orange at rim; some oxidation but still has interesting nuances of aroma; soft and tasty, short; still good but going. ** − *Bottle of 9/83*: Light brick color; lovely bouquet, moderately intense; still some tannin, full of flavor; drinkable now though room for improvement. **(+)

Fattoria Il Greppo (Biondi-Santi), Riserva (*6/90*). Fragrant bouquet, recalls flowers and fruit; has delicacy as well as richness, smooth in the center, some tannin still but marries with the fruit; a lovely glass that's near its peak. ** +

Tenuta Col d'Orcia, Riserva (*3/87*). Color shows age; fragrant, perfumed bouquet; soft and smooth, round, nice texture; very ready. *** −

1 9 6 7 0

Camigliano and Costanti called 1967 a very good vintage. Colombini and La Fortuna said it was good. Castiglion del Bosco rated it poor. The '67s are not wines to hold any longer, although it was considered a three-star vintage at one time. Even the Costanti, tasted at the winery in May 1985, showed signs of tiring.

Costanti, Riserva (*5/85*). A trace of oxidation on aroma; still has flavor though drying out. * +

Poggio alle Mura, Riserva (*3/81*). Cooked, somewhat oxidized aroma; unbalanced; poorly made.

1 9 6 6 [0]

Castiglion del Bosco found 1966 rather poor. Biondi-Santi didn't produce their *riserva*. La Fortuna and Colombini, on the other hand, considered it a good year. We can't recall tasting any.

1 9 6 5 0

Castiglion del Bosco said that 1965 was very good. Biondi-Santi didn't bottle any wine in 1965. Colombini places the vintage with the seven most unfortuante years since the Second World War. For the most part, they have probably faded.

Fattoria dei Barbi (Colombini), Riserva (*4/86*). Medium garnet toward brick; warm, nutlike aroma, shows age and development;

beginning to fade, with tannin overpowering the fruit, though soft in the center; some class still evident; it was probably quite nice a few years ago. ** —

Tenuta Col d'Orcia, Riserva (3/87). Brownish color; old nose; tired, still has flavor, alcohol intrudes, a little volatile, still there is interest. *

1964 **

The consensus was that 1964 was a first-class vintage. Biondi-Santi, Castiglion del Bosco, Costanti, Il Poggione, and La Fortuna all gave it high marks. Colombini puts 1964 among the seven best vintages between the end of the Second World War and 1989. Our experience with the Colombini, Costanti, and Biondi-Santi suggests that the wines are getting on in age; they're showing signs of senility. Based on three wines, only one of which we tasted recently, the Biondi-Santi, and the two wines we tasted in 1985—both showed signs of fading—we rate 1964's status today as two stars.

Costanti, Riserva (5/85). Brick red; some oxidation, and a vague figlike note; a lot of age showing, but it still has flavor interest. * +

Fattoria dei Barbi (Colombini), Riserva (4 times, 5/85). Orange, tawny at edge; warm, nutlike aroma, with some oxidation apparent; drying out though some flavor remains. * *Bottle of 11/80:* Deep color; rich, complex bouquet; still has tannin, soft and round, well structured; enjoyable now though can improve yet. **(*)

Fattoria Il Greppo (Biondi-Santi), Riserva (7 times, 11/90). *Bottle of 11/90, at the winery:* Lovely color; lovely nose, complex and rich; sweet impression, rich and flavorful, nice texture, very long; still room to grow; a lot of class. *** + *Bottle of 6/90:* Bouquet displays a richness and concentration, suggestions of dried fruit and leather; velvety, smooth, full of flavor, a little dry at the end; still it is impressive. *** — *Bottle of 9/88:* Complex bouquet, chestnut component; warm and generous, flavorful yet somewhat austere, somewhat dry at the end; still a lot of character, and holding, though age apparent. **

1955 ***

This was considered a first-class vintage. Biondi-Santi, Il Poggione, and La Fortuna gave it top marks. Colombini said that 1955 was one of the seven best vintages between the end of the Second World War and 1989. Niederbacher gave it his top rating, four stars. Biondi-Santi's Fattoria Il Greppo Riserva '55, which we tasted in June 1990, was excellent.

Fattoria Il Greppo (Biondi-Santi), Riserva (twice, 6/90). Bouquet reveals nuances of mint, leather and plums; great concentration and richness of flavor, velvety, very long; a complete wine.

**** — *Bottle of 11/79:* Bouquet has depth and complexity; still has considerable tannin and a richness of flavor, well balanced, has depth, style and length on the palate. ***(+)

OLDER VINTAGES

Niederbacher didn't rate 1963, 1962, 1960, 1959, 1957, 1956, 1954, 1953, 1952, 1950, 1949, 1948, or 1947. Biondi-Santi didn't produce a '62 or a '60. Colombini rated 1963, 1962, 1960, 1959, and 1956 as among the seven most unfortunate vintages between the end of the Second World War and 1989. (The others were 1965 and 1984.) Biondi-Santi, Colombini, and Il Poggione considered 1961 a first-class vintage. Niederbacher rated it his top mark of four stars.

La Fortuna said 1958 was a very good year. Biondi-Santi and Colombini agreed. Niederbacher rated it three stars out of four. La Fortuna rated 1957 as very good. Colombini said it was a good vintage. Biondi-Santi and Colombini characterized 1951 and 1946 as good vintages. Niederbacher rated them both three stars out of four. Biondi-Santi, Colombini, Il Poggione, and La Fortuna rated 1945 as topflight. Niederbacher rated it full marks at four stars. Colombini rates 1932 and 1907 as among the all-time great years.

THE PRODUCERS

Agricoltura del Chianti Geografico. See Geografico.

Ai Caselli (località *Castelgiocondo*, zone 3). They have the same address and phone number as *Castelgiocondo*.

Altesino (località *Altesi*, zone 1), *1970*. Giulio Consonno, a Milanese businessman, is the proprietor of Altesino. There are 55 acres (22.3 hectares) of vineyards on the estate.

A few years ago they also owned the 52-acre (21.1-hectare) Gauggiole vineyard. The vines there are planted at an average altitude of 985 feet (300 meters) above sea level and face from northeast to southwest. They sold it back to Castiglion del Bosco, and in 1989 or 1990 they bought the Due Porti vineyard, which is located in zone 3, just south and a few to the west of the town of Montalcino itself.

Besides the sangiovese grosso and standard white grapes of the zone, they have a few chardonnay and cabernet sauvignon vines.

Altesino produces 113,000 bottles of wine a year, including 40,000 of Brunello, 13,000 of the *barrique*-aged Sangiovese **Palazzo Altesi**, 10,000 of the sangiovese–cabernet sauvignon blend **Alte d'Altesi**, 50,000 of Rosso di Montalcino, plus a minuscule 900 bottles of an exceptional dessert wine, Ambro di Altesi, Moscadello Passito. In 1991 they expect to produce an additional 13,000 bottles of wine, probably a *barrique*-aged Chardonnay. And until recently at least, they produced some 25,000 bottles of a very good white wine from 90 percent trebbiano and 10 percent malvasia. We don't know if they still do.

Claudio Basla manages the estate with a watchful eye on quality.

THE CRUS AND VINEYARDS OF ALTESINO

| Cru/Vineyard | Acres | Hectares | Altitude in | | Exposure |
			Feet	Meters	
Altesino	32.1	13.0	722–820	220–250	S/SW
Due Porti	5.7	2.3	1,475	450	S
Montosoli	17.3	7.0	1,310–1,410	400–430	NW/S

Enologist Pietro Rivella produces the wine and Angelo Solci provides valuable insights and innovations as a second consulting enologist. Antonio Cassisi seems to be a jack-of-all-trades, as well as a master at all of them.

They believe in quality at Altesino and pay the price in reduced quantity. They never plan in the vineyards for the Rosso di Montalcino, for which DOC allows a yield of 748 gallons per acre (70 hectoliters per hectare). Instead, they make the wine as a Brunello at the maximum yield of 599 gallons per acre (56 hectoliters per hectare). Then, after the wine is made and tasted, they select the best for their Brunello and declassify the rest to Rosso di Montalcino. If the wine is not considered up to their standards for Rosso, they sell it off sfuso, in bulk, unlabeled.

The Altesino Brunello is put initially into large, 3,300-gallon (125-hectoliter) Slavonian oak casks for the initial aging period, then moved to progressively smaller casks, down to 790 gallons (30 hectoliters).

In years that justify it, they bottle their crus, Vigna Altesino and Vigna Montosoli. In the best years they also produce a limited amount of riserva, 3,000 bottles at most.

They made a very good '84 Brunello at Altesino by a very careful selection, using only 1.3 tons per acre (29 quintali per hectare) of grapes, in place of the maximum yield of 3.6 tons per acre (80 quintali per hectare).

From their first Brunello in 1972, Altesino has established a reputation for both quality and consistency. We've found their Brunellos to be wines of style and real personality. They are among the top wines of the zone year after year. Their Rosso di Montalcino is also among the best.

Their '83 and '85 are very fine Brunellos, especially their '85 Riserva and Vigna Montosoli, which are among that splendid vintage's finest wines. We can also recommend their '82 and '86. Of their older vintages, the '75 Brunello is still very good indeed, especially the Vigna Montosoli. Brunello ****; Rosso di Montalcino ** +

Argiano (località Argiano, zone 3). Argiano has 741 acres (300 hectares), 40 (16.2) planted in Brunello. Since 1981 they have been connected with the Cinzano group. We have found their wines uneven. At their best, which is unfortunately not often enough, they can be quite good. The '82 is the best Brunello they have made in some time, and the '85 was even better. The '87, '88, and '89, which we tasted from cask in November 1990, suggest that changes have taken place for the better. Brunello *

Bartoli-Giusti-Focacci. See **Comunali.**

Biondi-Santi. See **Fattoria Il Greppo.**

Campogiovanni (zone 3). Campogiovanni is owned by the Chianti Classico producer San Felice, which oversees the winemaking. Their 30-acre (12-hectare) vineyard of sangiovese grosso is planted at an average altitude of 920 feet (280 meters) above sea level, with a southern exposure. Campogiovanni produces some 5,325 cases of wine a year of a Brunello, which they have bottled since 1971, and a Rosso di Montalcino, which is aged for eighteen months in barrel. Their '85 Brunello lacks weight, concentration, and character. It is, to be sure, a disgrace. We tasted it shortly after it was released and found it very light and overly simple. Some producers' Rossos, from 1987 no less, had more structure, character, and depth! Although their wines are good, we haven't been impressed with any of their Brunellos since the very good '79. Brunello *; Rosso di Montalcino *

Canalicchio di Sopra (località Canalicchio di Sopra, zone 1), 1966. The Pacenti brothers, Rosildo and Franco, planted their Brunello vineyards in 1969. Today they have 5.6 acres (2.25 hectares) under vines from which they produce Brunello and Rosso di Montalcino. This is down from the 11 acres (4.5 hectares) under vines a few years ago. They expect another 4.2 acres (1.7 hectares) to come into production in 1992. They produce, on average, some 7,300 bottles of Brunello and 6,600 of Rosso. And they have plans, like so many others, for a vino da tavola aged in barrique.

To ensure better-quality fruit, workers make a pass through the vineyard before the harvest, picking off the bad bunches to concentrate the vines' strength in ripening those that remain, thereby producing better bunches of riper fruit. The best grapes are used for their Brunello. A few figures show the seriousness of their selection. In 1970, 1971, and 1972 they produced a mere 200 to 300 bottles. In 1974 their production had grown to 3,000 bottles, but in 1976, a poor vintage, it dropped to 1,000. Their annual output is increasing as their vineyards come into full production. In 1978 they produced 4,800 bottles; in 1979, 6,900; in 1980, 5,150; and in 1981, 7,800 bottles.

Paolo Vagaggini is their consulting enologist. Until the 1985 vintage, the label carried the names of Primo and Rosildo Pacenti. Our experience with these wines, over eight vintages, shows them to be fairly consistent and generally very good. Even their '76 was good. Brunello **

Canalicchio di Sopra (località Canalicchio di Sopra e Casaccia, zone 1), 1969. Primo Pacenti and Pier Luigi Ripaccioli own 12.4 acres (5 hectares) of vineyards. There is another Canalicchio di

Sopra, owned by the Pacenti brothers, formerly Primo and Rosildo, now Franco and Rosildo. We wonder if this estate is a spinoff of the first, which would help explain the decrease in acreage reported to us by that other Canalicchio di Sopra estate.

The first wine that we tasted with Primo Pacenti and Pier Luigi Ripaccioli's names on the label was the '83. In 1985 they labeled their Brunello Azienda Agricola Canalicchio di Sopra, Le Gode di Montosoli. Their '88 Rosso is labeled Azienda Agricola Canalicchio di Sopra. Paolo Vagaggini consults for them, as he does for the other Canalicchio di Sopra estate. Both the '83 and '85 Brunellos were quite good. Brunello ** −

Canalicchio di Sotto (*zone 1*). Maurizio Lambardi, proprietor of Canalicchio di Sotto, has 8.6 acres (3.5 hectares) of sangiovese grosso vines. Lambardi's labeling can be confusing: the '80 was labeled as Azienda Agricola Canalicchio di Lambardi, the '81 as Azienda Agricola Canalicchio (Silvano e Maurizio Lambardi), and the '84 and '85 as Azienda Agricola Canalicchio di Sopra (Lambardi Maurizio). In spite of that, in our limited experience, Lambardi's Brunello has been a very good one. Brunello **

Canneta (località *Canneta, zone 3*), *1978*. Angiola Piazzi-Maria owns the 11.9-acre (4.8-hectare) Podere Canneta. Canneta produces a Brunello and a Rosso. Enologist Attilio Pagli advises them.

Capanna (località *Capanna, zone 1*), *1957*. Giuseppe Cencioni owns 37 acres (15 hectares) of vines, 24.7 (10) in production, some of it in mixed cultivation with other crops. They have four Brunello crus: Cerro with 10.4 acres (4.2 hectares), Capanna with 4.9 (2), Piemonti 4.9 (2), and Poggio 4.4 (1.8). The vineyards, which face south to southeast, are planted at an average altitude of 985 feet (300 meters) above sea level.

Cencioni produces 26,650 bottles of Brunello annually. He first produced a Brunello in 1970. He also produces 20,000 bottles of Rosso di Montalcino, 9,300 of a red *vino da tavola*, 3,300 to 4,000 of Moscadello di Montalcino, and a small quantity of *vin santo*. Like so many others here, Cencioni plans to produce a Chardonnay and Cabernet Sauvignon. His '78 Brunello was particularly good; we also liked his '79, '80, '82, and '85 *riserve*. Brunello ** −; Rosso di Montalcino *

Capanna di Fattoi e Minocci "Fattoi." This might be a second Fattoi estate; perhaps it is the same as Capanna di S. Restituta. The label reads "Capanna di Fattoi e Minocci 'Fattoi.'" The wines are not equal to those we tasted in tank in May 1986. Based on the three vintages we met in bottle, we rate their Brunello *.

Capanna di S. Restituta (*zone 3*). Ofelio Fattoi has 8.6 acres (3.5 hectares) of brunello vines. He began bottling with the 1979 vintage. Fattoi, on average, produces 4,000 bottles of Brunello and 13,300 of Rosso. In 1985 he produced 8,000 bottles of Brunello.

The Brunellos from Fattoi have been consistently good. We especially liked the '82, '83, and '85 when we tasted them from vat in May 1986. Unfortunately, we've not tasted them from bottle. Brunello for now [** −]

Caparzo. See *Tenuta Caparzo.*

Caprili (*zone 3*). This 5.9-acre (2.4-hectare) vineyard is owned by Alfo Bartolomei. According to the *consorzio*, he has 16.2 acres (6.55 hectares) of land inscribed for the DOC-DOCG. He pro-

duces some 6,000 bottles annually. We've tasted every vintage from Bartolomei between 1979 and 1985. Overall, his wines have been very good and fairly consistent. Of them, we liked the '82 and '85 the best. Brunello **

Casa del Cerro. We believe that this Brunello was produced by Altesino. The only one we tasted, the '78, was pretty good. Brunello [* +]

Casanova, or *Casanova di Neri* (*zone 1*), *1971*. Giovanni Neri owns a total of 25.3 acres (10.23 hectares) of vines planted in three different vineyards. They are the 5.5-acre (2.23-hectare) Cerretalto, 4.9-acre (2-hectare) Fiesole, and the 14.8-acre (6-hectare) Grosseto. In 1992 he expects another 12.4 acres (5 hectares) to come into production. From his vines Neri produces 70,000 bottles of wine per year. Their normal product mix is 40 percent Brunello and 60 percent Rosso, plus 500 bottles of *vin santo*.

The enologist Paolo Vagaggini consults for them, and since 1986 son Giacomo Neri has managed the estate and made the wine. The first wine he vinified was the '81 Riserva, and since 1983 he has been the winemaker. Their first wine in bottle with a label was the '78. They didn't do an '84. Our experience covers most of their Brunellos between 1979 and 1989. Their '86 Riserva, tasted from cask, and their '88, also from cask, suggest things have improved here. The '86, '87, and '89, also from cask, promise good wines. Brunello ** −

Case Basse (*zone 3*), *1972*. Gianfranco Soldera owns some 15.3 acres (6.2 hectares) of brunello vines. A few years ago, at least, he also had 2.5 acres (1 hectare) of white grapes. His brunello vineyards consist of two crus—the 4.4-acre (1.8-hectare) Case Basse and 10.9-acre (4.4-hectare) Intistieti. From 1980 through 1989 Soldera produced an average of 27,000 bottles of wine of a potential 42,400 bottles. He believes that lower yields increase quality. Most of Case Basse's annual production of 37,000 bottles is Brunello; they also make a small quantity of Rosso di Montalcino, and the *vino da tavola* Intistieti. Soldera first produced this table wine from 100 percent sangiovese grosso in 1985; it spent three years in oak casks. Although Case Basse has been bottling their wine since the '75, their first Brunello sold in bottle was from the 1977 vintage.

Gianfranco Soldera produces, without question, one of the zone's best Brunellos. And his Brunello seems to be increasing in quality with each passing year. In fact, we have been impressed with every vintage that Soldera has made from the first one we tasted, the '80, through the most recent, the '84. Even the '84 was a revelation. We especially recommend Soldera's splendid '82 and '83. Although we haven't tasted it, we believe that the '85 might just beat them all. Brunello **** −

Castelgiocondo (località *Castelgiocondo, zone 3*). This 2,150-acre (870-hectare) estate has 545 acres (220 hectares) in vines, 393 (159) for Brunello and Rosso di Montalcino. The vineyards, which have a southern exposure, are planted at altitudes ranging from 920 to 1,310 feet (280 to 400 meters) above sea level.

Their first Brunello was the '74. Today their production of Brunello varies from 160,000 to 250,000 bottles, and that of Rosso from 200,000 to 400,000 bottles. In 1988, Castelgiocondo produced 200,000 bottles of the good Campo ai Sassi Rosso di Montalcino and, from the 1985 vintage, 180,000 bottles of Brunello.

They also produce Vergena, Predicato del Selvante from the 24.7-acre (10-hectare) vineyard of that name. This wine is based on sauvignon blanc. The first vintage of that wine was the '84.

The first Brunello from this estate that impressed us was the '85, although admittedly we never tasted the '82 or '83. We have been a little concerned about the variability of the '85, however.

Among the owners of the Castelgiocondo estate are the Frescobaldis, who have long demonstrated their commitment to quality with their other wines. Brunello ** − ; Rosso di Montalcino **

Castelli Martinozzi (*Villa Santa Restituta, zone 3*), *1700.* Cesare Castelli owns some 10 acres (4 hectares) of vines planted at an average altitude of 1,150 feet (350 meters) above sea level in friable stone (*galestro*) soil. Castelli produces some 40,000 bottles of wine per year. The '82 left us cold, but the '83 was very good, indeed, as was the '85. Our rating, based on those two wines, Brunello * +

Castello Banfi (*zone 3*), *1977.* The Mariani brothers, John and Harry, best known as importers of Riunite Lambrusco, have built a very large, very expensive, and very modern winery in Montalcino. With 7,040 acres (2,850 hectares), they are probably the largest landholders in the area. There are 1,730 acres (700 hectares) of vineyards at Villa or, as it is now known, Castello Banfi; this will eventually reach 2,225 acres (900 hectares). The vines, planted at altitudes ranging from 655 to 1,150 feet (200 to 350 meters) above sea level, have a southern exposure. Their vineyards are planted 20 percent with moscadello. Of the balance, 15 percent each are chardonnay and cabernet sauvignon, 25 percent sangiovese grosso, with the remainder comprising a number of other varieties, including merlot, pinot grigio, pinot noir, sauvignon blanc, and syrah.

Castello Banfi bought another Brunello estate, *Poggio alle Mura,* a few years ago. That label, we were told, was retired after the 1979 vintage, and the vineyards integrated into the Banfi estate. The Banfi castle is, or was, the *castello* of Poggio alle Mura.

Besides the production of Bellagio, a light, sweetish white wine, and Moscadello, they plan to produce 400,000 cases of premium wines. This includes 25,000 cases of Brunello, 30,000 of Rosso di Montalcino, more than 10,000 each of Chardonnay and Cabernet Sauvignon, 40,000 Pinot Grigio, and 30,000 Chianti Classico Riserva. They also produce, or plan to, 50,000 cases of Novello.

Their first Brunello, from the 1973 vintage, was sold in Italy only. They entered the United States market with their first estate-bottled Brunello, the '78. Until the 1985 vintage their Brunello was sold as Villa Banfi; since that vintage the name has been Castello Banfi.

We were unimpressed with Banfi's '78 *normale* and Riserva, and '80 Brunellos, but we liked their '79 and '81, and we must admit that their '82, '83, and '85 are all very good. Their '87 and '88 *normali,* and the '85 and '86 Riserva Poggio all'Oro suggest further improvements have been made here as well. The Marianis and their chief enologist, Ezio Rivella, seem to be on the right track. Brunello: Castello Banfi **, Castello Banfi Riserva Poggio all'Oro ** +, Villa Banfi ** −

Casstello di Camigliano (località *Camigliano, zone 3*), *1956.* This 2,470-acre (1,000-hectare) estate, owned by the Ghezzi family, is located near the medieval village of Camigliano. Of their 173 acres

(70 hectares) of vines, 114 (46) are planted in sangiovese grosso, 35 (14) are for red table wine, 7.5 (3) for white, and 17 (7) for Chianti Colli Senesi. The vines are planted 820 to 985 feet (250 to 300 meters) above sea level. Currently 101 acres (41 hectares) are producing; the remaining 72 acres (29 hectares) should be in production from 1992 through 1993. They have an annual production of 373,000 bottles of wine, which includes Brunello di Montalcino, Chianti, white wine, and *vino da tavola.* They also have some cabernet sauvignon, chardonnay, pinot bianco, and moscadello vines.

They bottled their first Brunello from the 1967 vintage. In 1986 they produced two cru bottlings: 18,600 bottles of Vigna di Fontevecchia and 16,000 of Vigna del Poggiarello. *Fontevino* is another one of their wineries and *Pian dei Mercatelli* another label. Pietro Rivella, the enologist at Camigliano, also consults for some other fine Brunello producers, including Altesino. Our tasting experience with these Brunellos has not been very favorable, though we must admit that those labeled as Castello di Camigliano have been better than those without the Castello designation. Brunello: Camigliano 0, Castello di Camigliano +

Castiglion del Bosco (*zone 1*), *1946.* This firm owns some 5,000 acres (2,000 hectares), 198 (80) in vines, which includes 91 (37) planted in sangiovese grosso. They produce between 6,650 and 7,750 cases of Brunello a year, plus a Rosso di Montalcino, some white wine, and a Chianti. Most of the casks they use for aging are made of chestnut and are of 660-gallon (25-hectoliter) capacity; a few are only 80-gallon (3-hectoliter).

Castiglion del Bosco used to produce the Dei Roseti Brunello, which they began selling in Italy some eleven or twelve years ago. Today it is made by *Altesino.* Castiglion del Bosco bottled their first Brunello from the 1964 vintage.

While these Brunellos can be good, for the most part they are unexciting. But there are changes afoot. They recently hired Maurizio Castelli as their enologist. The '82 and '83 were quite good, but somehow the '85 didn't quite come up to the vintage. The '86, '87, and '88, tasted from barrel, and the '85 Riserva suggest that an improvement has taken place here. Brunello ** − ; Rosso di Montalcino 0

Cecchi Luigi. This Chianti firm sells an undistinguished Brunello. The last one we tasted, the '78, was more like a Chianti, albeit an overpriced one, than a real Brunello. The wine is bottled for Cecchi by A.A.T.C. Brunello 0

Cencioni Giuseppe. See *Capanna.*

Centolani Agricola, Azienda Agricola Friggiali (*zone 3*). Agricola Centolani owns 11.1 acres (4.5 hectares) of vines. Thus far our experience has been limited to four barrel samples—the '86, '87, '88, and '89. Three of the four were rather difficult to evaluate and the '88 suggested a fairly good Brunello would be bottled. Brunello [+]

Centolani Agricola, Tenuta Pietra Focaia. We're unsure if this is the same estate as Agricola Centolani, Azienda Agricola Friggiali. As for this one, we have tasted one wine, their good '83 Brunello. Brunello *

Cerbaia (*zone 1*). Cencioni Annunziata owns 2.3 acres (0.93 hectare) of Brunello vines. We haven't met any of their wines.

Cerbaiola (località *Cerbaiola, zone 1*). Giulio Salvioni owns 3.7 acres (1.5 hectares) of vines. He expects another 6.7 to 7.4 acres (2.7 to 3 hectares) to begin producing about 1995. His first Brunello was produced from the 1985 vintage. The Cerbaiola estate has an average annual production of between 6,600 and 8,000 bottles of wine, which include a Brunello and a Rosso. Attilio Pagli is their consulting enologist. Based on four barrel samples, tasted in November 1990, we can say that their wines are good. Brunello [* +]

Cerbaiona (Molinari Diego) (*zone 1*). Diego Molinari owns 4 acres (1.61 hectares) of brunello vines. We have tasted three vintages here—'81, '83, and '84—and found this Brunellos, overall, to be very good. Brunello ** −

Cerrino 1ª (*zone 1*), 1980. Enzo Tiezzi owns 5.3 acres (2.15 hectares) of brunello vines from which he produces 4,000 bottles of Brunello and 5,000 of Rosso. Tiezzi was, a few years ago, president of the Brunello *consorzio*. He also is resident enologist and winemaker for all three properties of Milano industrialist Lionello Marchesi—Fattoria San Leonino in Chianti Classico, Tenuta Trerose in Montepulciano, and Valdisuga in Montalcino. He bottles his Brunello under the name Podere Cerrino. The '85 was very good, as were the '86, '87, and '88, tasted from barrel. The '89, from barrel, also showed good quality. Brunello ** +

Chianti Geografico. See *Geografico.*

Ciacci Piccolomini d'Aragona (località *Castelnuovo dell'Abate, zone 2*), 1677. Giuseppe Bianchini has owned this estate since 1984. He has 22.2 acres (9 hectares) planted at altitudes ranging from 785 to 1,180 feet (240 to 360 meters) above sea level. He has 23.6 acres (9.6 hectares) inscribed for the DOC-DOCG; perhaps they're not all planted. Bianchini expects another 22.2 acres (9 hectares) of vines to come into production by 1993. He has three vineyards of 7.4 acres (3 hectares) each: Ferraiolo, Pianrosso, and San Martino. The vines, planted in clay and gravel soil of Eocene origin, face southeast. Bianchini uses only organic fertilizers. His annual production averages 13,000 bottles of Brunello and 10,000 of Rosso. He also produces a *vin santo*. The Rosso is aged for eighteen months in oak. He ferments in oak casks at temperatures ranging from 90° to 93° Fahrenheit (32° to 34° centigrade). Bianchini wants the malolactic fermentation to occur as soon as possible after the completion of the first fermentation.

Until ten years ago this estate was owned by the family of Pope Pio (Pius). Pope Pio, who resigned in the seventeenth century, held office for a total of twenty-eight days, the shortest reign for any pope. This palace was his summer home.

This estate enjoys a reputation better than our experience would indicate. Thus far we have tasted six vintages from Ciacci Piccolomini d'Aragona, two from bottle—an unimpressive '81 and a very good '85—and of the four from barrel, the '86, '87, and '88 all showed a lot of promise. Brunello **

Col d'Orcia. See *Tenuta Col d'Orcia.*

Colle al Matrichese. See *Conti Costanti.*

Colombaio di Montosoli (*zone 1*), 1955. Nello Baricci and Ada Nannetti own 10 acres (4 hectares) of vines from which they produce some 21,300 bottles of wine a year, including Brunello and Rosso di Montalcino. Their first Brunello was produced from the 1971 vintage. Paolo Vagaggini is their consulting enologist. Thus far we've tasted their '80 and '82 Brunellos from bottle. The former was pretty good, the latter a disappointment. We also tasted, from barrel, their Brunellos from '86 through '89. Three of the four were good; the '89 was out of condition and couldn't be evaluated fairly. Brunello *

Comunali (Focacci Gino Antonio) (*zone 1*), 1938. Azienda Agricola I Comunali has more than 10 acres (4 hectares) of vineyards planted at altitudes ranging from 985 to 1,475 feet (300 to 450 meters) above sea level. They produce 15,000 bottles each of Brunello and Rosso di Montalcino annually from those vines. Their wine is generally labeled as Comunali di Bartoli-Giusti-Focacci. Their first Brunello, sold in bottle, was the '38. Overall, we find their wines quite good. Their '85, as one would expect, is very good. Brunello **

Conti Costanti (località *Colle al Matrichese, zone 1*), 1950. There are about 15 acres (6 hectares) of vines on Andrea Costanti's Il Colle al Matrichese estate, planted at altitudes ranging from 1,310 to 1,445 feet (400 to 440 meters) above sea level. The vineyards vary in exposure from northeast, to south, to southwest. Recently Costanti acquired some 24.7 acres (10 hectares) of the splendid Montosoli vineyard, and he plans to plant some new vineyards there. The zone's top producer making Brunello from one of the district's finest vineyard areas is certainly worth looking forward to.

THE CRUS AND VINEYARDS OF CONTI COSTANTI

Cru/Vineyard	Acres	Hectares	Used for
Baiocco	2.96	1.2	Brunello *normale*
Paretaio	1.48	0.6	Brunello Riserva
Piano	3.71	1.5	n/a
Sottogiardino	0.49	0.2	n/a
Vignanova	6.18	2.5	n/a
Total	14.82	6.0	

Costanti produces between 13,300 and 14,600 bottles of Brunello a year and 4,000 to 5,300 of Vermiglio from brunello vines. He expects his production to increase to 26,600 to 30,600 bottles a year when the vineyards that were planted between 1986 and 1988 come on-line. He plans to make a Rosso di Montalcino as well.

We know that Tito Costanti produced a Brunello in Montalcino prior to 1870, and Emilio Costanti also produced wines at his Il Colle estate for many years. It wasn't until 1964, however, that he began to produce a Brunello on a regular basis. From that vintage he established a reputation not only for exceptional quality but also for consistency. We've found only one other producer as consistent as Costanti, and that is **Tenuta Il Poggione.** Even in a year like 1976 he produced a good Brunello—in our opinion, the best of the vintage. His '77 never came up to the vintage; in fact, it was not very good. This was quite a surprise until we learned that he had been seriously ill and couldn't give the wines his usual care and attention. Costanti died a few years ago, leaving the estate to his young nephew, Andrea Costanti. Andrea has a high esteem for the wines Emilio Costanti produced, and he is determined to maintain that quality. Enologist Vittorio Fiore was hired as a consultant in 1983. Andrea Costanti, with the help of Fiore, finished the '78 Brunello and made the '83.

When the vintage justifies it, Costanti produces up to 3,000 bottles of Brunello *riserva.* The grapes for the *riserva* come from their Paretaio vineyard. They don't specify the cru name on the label. Their Baiocco vineyard furnishes the grapes for their regular Brunello.

We found the Costanti '70 and '75 top notch, among the very best. The '82, '83, and '85 showed great potential when tasted from cask in May 1986. We haven't tasted the '82 since then. Both the '83 Riserva and '85 *normale* turned out very well, indeed. Both of those wines were quite impressive, with the Riserva being the wine of the vintage. Their '80 Brunello was the best wine of the more than 20 we tasted from that vintage. The '79, '80, and '81 were also good. Even the '84 showed a lot of promise when we last tasted it, from barrel, in May 1985. And the '85 *normale,* like the '83 Riserva, was simply stunning as was the '85 Riserva from cask in November 1990. Brunello **** +

Conti Serristori. The only Brunello that we tasted from this good Chianti Classico producer was the '83, which was bottled by Agripa. Brunello *

Cottimello, or **Vigneti dei Cottimello** (*zone 1*). Eredi Fuligni owns 8.1 acres (3.28 hectares) of brunello vines. The vineyards consist of 12.3 acres (5 hectares) of vines divided into three crus—the 6.2-acre (2.5-hectare) Ginestreto vineyard, the 4.9-acre (2-hectare) Del Piano, and the 1.2-acre (0.5-hectare) Vignaccia. These vines are planted at altitudes ranging from 1,150 to 1,310 feet (350 to 400 meters) above sea level, facing from south to southeast. Production began here in 1969 or 1970. Currently they produce 8,000 bottles of Brunello and 5,300 of Rosso annually. When their new vineyards come into full production this will increase to 10,000 and 12,000 bottles, respectively. Their consulting enologist is Paolo Vagaggini. Eredi Fuligni rates the '70, '75, '80, '82, '83, '85, and '88 as their best wines. They didn't produce any wine in 1972 and 1976. We've tasted his Brunellos from four vintages from bottle and the same number from barrel, and overall found them very

good. Of those wines from bottle, we liked the '83 and '85 *annata* and Riserva. The '80 and '82 also displayed some quality. From barrel we liked the '88 the best, but the '86, '87, and especially the '89 show promise. Brunello **

D. A. M., Diffusione Altesino del Montalcino (località *Altesi, zone 1*). They have the same location and phone number as **Altesino** because they are owned by them. Since 1990 they have produced *aspretto* (vinegar) from fruit, and grappa under the Tre Cerchi label. They make an Aspretto di Lampone (raspberry), Fragola (strawberry), Mirtillo (myrtle), Mora (blackberry), Pesca (peach), and Prugna (plum) . They also produce a Brunello under the Tre Cerchi label.

Dei Roseti. At one time this Brunello was produced by Castiglion del Bosco. Today it is produced by **Altesino.** We have tasted two vintages, a very good '81 and '82. Brunello ** +

Due Portine (*zone 3*). Giancarlo Gorelli owns 2.47 acres (1 hectare) of vines planted at an average altitude of 1,640 feet (500 meters) above sea level, facing northwest. Gorelli expects an additional acre (0.4 hectare) to be producing in 1991. He produces some 5,300 bottles of wine per year. As of now he produces only a Rosso di Montalcino. The '89 was very good indeed. He plans to make a Brunello soon.

Fattoria Casale del Bosco (località *Casale del Bosco, zone 1*), *1951.* Silvio Nardi has 136 acres (55 hectares) of vines on his Casale del Bosco estate, from which he produces 11,000 cases of Brunello a year. Nardi has bottled a Brunello since 1955.

Nardi produces, on average, some 380,000 bottles of wine a year. This includes 18,000 bottles of Brunello, 106,500 of Rosso, 24,000 of Chianti Colli Senesi, 60,000 of Bianco Val d'Arbia, 4,500 of Moscadello della Toscana Spumante, and 2,900 of *vin santo,* plus a small quantity of a dry white Malvasia Toscana.

For the most part, while these wines have tended to lack character and style, they were decent wines, but nothing more. And we've had a few bottles that were considerably less. In 1982, Nardi took a significant step in the direction of quality when he engaged the services of a talented consulting enologist, Vittorio Fiore. That relationship lasted for a few years. Today Paolo Vagaggini is his consulting enologist. Between 1968 and 1979 Nardi's Brunellos were lacking character and quality. The '80, '82, and '85 displayed some quality. Overall, the wines are good, but somehow we expected more. Brunello *

Fattoria dei Barbi e Del Casato (Francesca Colombini Cinelli) (*zone 2*), *c. 1500.* The Colombini estate takes in the 1,000-acre (400-hectare) Fattoria dei Barbi and del Casato properties. They have 420 acres (170 hectares) of grain, 400 (163) of woods, and 128 acres (52 hectares) of vines planted, which include some 20 acres (8 hectares) of new vines and 25 (10) of vineyards that they rent. Brunello is planted on some 50 acres (20 hectares). The vineyards are planted at an average altitude of 1,160 feet (350 meters) above sea level and have a southern exposure.

Donna Francesca Colombini Cinelli, proprietor of the Colombini farm, is also the winemaker. She produces, on average, some 306,600 bottles of wine a year: 133,300 of Brunello, which in the better vintages includes a very small amount, a mere 2,400 to 5,400 bottles, of *riserva* and 10,000 of the single-vineyard Brunello

THE CRUS AND VINEYARDS OF FATTORIA DEI BARBI

Cru/Vineyard	Acres	Hectares	Used for
Barbi Olivetaccio*	1.11	0.45	Sole dei Barbi, Rosso di Montalcino
Casato	11.29	4.57	Brunello di Montalcino
Fiore*	11.00	4.45	Brunello di Montalcino
Pinzina*	5.88	2.38	Brunello di Montalcino
Quercione*	3.76	1.52	Brunello di Montalcino

* Part of the Barbi farm

Vigna Fiore; plus 33,300 of Rosso di Montalcino, 10,000 of the single-vineyard Rosso di Montalcino Sole dei Barbi, 24,000 of a red *vino da tavola*, 61,300 of **Brusco dei Barbi**, 4,000 of **Bruscone dei Barbi**, 20,000 of a Chianti, 5,300 of Bianco del Beato, and 5,300 of *vin santo*.

Colombini has been selling wine in bottle for nearly a century, the first being an unnamed 1892 red table wine. They sold their first Brunello in bottle, with a label, from the 1931 vintage; the next, from the 1957 vintage. In 1981 they produced a single-vineyard Brunello for the first time from the Fiore vineyard; they made 4,256 bottles. They began producing a Rosso di Montalcino and a Chianti in 1984, and a *vin santo* in 1870. In 1986 they made Sole dei Barbi for the first time, a single-vineyard Rosso di Montalcino. The first Bruscone dei Barbi was produced in 1987.

In the great vintages, years like 1970 and 1975, the Colombini Brunellos have an uncommon elegance and finesse, as well as extraordinary balance and style, and are unsurpassed. Indeed, very few are their equal. Those who have tasted Colombini's magnificent '70 and '75 will know what we mean. She produced a very good '71, '77, '78 Riserva, and '80 (we preferred the '80 *annata* to the Riserva). But in some years the wines are disappointing. In lesser vintages—years like 1972, 1973, and 1974, to name some of the more notable examples—the wines just don't seem to be able to rise above the vintage. We find her '78 *normale* and even the '79 wanting. As for more recent vintages, Colombini seems to be more consistent, with more successes and fewer misses. The '81 Vigna Fiore was quite good, as is the '83. The '82—both the *annata* and Riserva—the '83 Riserva Vigna del Fiore, and the '85 *annata* and Riserva Vigna Fiore are splendid Brunellos. And the '88 tasted from cask showed very well, indeed. These are first-rate Brunellos. Brunello *** +

Fattoria dell'Abate. They produce a Brunello and a Rosso di Montalcino. Now you know as much about them as we do.

Fattoria Il Grappolo (*Sant' Angelo in Colle,* località *Campogiovanni, zone 3*), *1974.* Immobiliare Fortius owns Azienda Il Grappolo and some 12.4 acres (5 hectares) of vines. They produce, on average, 42,650 bottles of wine a year. Their Brunello can be good. Brunello * —

Fattoria Il Greppo (Biondi-Santi) (*zone 2*), *1840.* The 116-acre (47-hectare) Il Greppo estate has nearly 37 acres (15 hectares) planted in vines at altitudes ranging from 655 to 1,310 feet (200 to 400 meters) above sea level, facing south.

Contrary to a number of reports, Il Greppo is owned entirely by Franco Biondi-Santi and his son Iacopo. A few years ago they set up a marketing company for their wine and took in a partner, Calogero Cali. Cali owned part of the marketing company, not part of Il Greppo. They have since bought him out. The Biondi-Santis were also, for a time, involved with the very good Chianti Classico producer Rocca di Castagnoli. They have since severed that relationship. Today they have set up a marketing company to commercialize their wine and that of Poggio Salvi with that estate's owner, Pierluigi Tagliabue, who is also Iacopo's father-in-law.

The Biondi-Santis produce an average of 40,000 to 50,000 bottles a year of their Brunello di Montalcino *annata* and 15,000 bottles of the *riserva*. In some years, such as 1984, 1976, 1972, 1965, 1962, and 1960, they have made no Brunello at all. In other years the Biondi-Santis produce an *annata* Brunello but no *riserva;* there was no *riserva* in 1989, 1986, 1980, 1979, 1978, 1974, or 1973.

The difference between the two Brunellos, Biondi-Santi points out, is in the grapes. The Brunello *annata* is from sangiovese grosso vines ten years old or older; the vines for the *riserva* are at least twenty-five years old. Biondi-Santi used to produce a red table wine, labeled Il Greppo, from the vines younger than ten years old. Since 1984 they have made a Rosso di Montalcino from those vines.

According to Franco Biondi-Santi, the great vintages at Il Greppo were 1888 (regarded as the greatest vintage of all), 1891, 1925, 1945, 1946, 1951, 1955, 1958, 1961, 1964, 1968, 1969, 1970, 1971, 1975, 1977, 1981, 1982, 1983, and 1985. They still have three bottles of the 1888, thirteen of the 1891, and four of the 1925.

Of their older vintages, among those we tasted in June 1990, we found the '55 Riserva to be outstanding, and '64 was very good as well. The '68 Riserva was very good and the '69 Riserva was still quite good.

During the 1970s too many bottles from Biondi-Santi were disappointing. They made a splendid '75 Riserva, and a very good '75 and '73 *annata*. The '70, both the *annata* and the Riserva, was a real disappointment. And both of the '77s, and the '79, while very good, didn't measure up to their respective vintages. We can't recommend their '71, '74, '78, or '79.

But we are happy to report that with the new decade the Brunellos of Fattoria Il Greppo seem to be back on track. Thus far, of the wines we tasted in bottle between 1980 and 1985, only the '80 was wanting. They made two splendid '85s, both the *annata* and Riserva, a great '83 Riserva, very good '82 and '83 *annate,* and *reserve* of '81 and '82. And the *reserve* of '85 and '88, which we tasted from cask in November 1990, appear, at this stage, to be stunning Brunellos, while the '86, '87, and '89 *annate,* and the '87 Riserva, all tasted from cask, also show promise. Brunello ****

Fattoria La Gerla (*zone 1*), *1978.* Dott. Sergio Rossi has 12.4 acres (5 hectares) of vines on his La Gerla estate. According to the *consorzio,* some 4.9 acres (2 hectares) are inscribed for DOC-DOCG. The vineyard, planted at altitudes ranging from 820 to 1,245 feet (250 to 380 meters) above sea level, has a western to southern exposure. La Gerla has four crus—Degli Angeli, Tufaia, Boboli, and Pieve. Like so many others here, they are bottling a single-vineyard Brunello. In 1985 they produced a Brunello from Degli Angeli. La Gerla's annual production averages about 30,000 bottles of wine, about evenly divided between Brunello and Rosso di Montalcino. In 1984, 80 percent of the grapes for these two wines were from the vines on the estate; in 1985 all were. They plan to produce a sangiovese–cabernet sauvignon blend that will be *barrique*-aged. Vittorio Fiore, the fine enologist, has been consulting here since 1979. Our experience with their Brunellos, which includes every vintage from 1979 to 1985, indicates that they are a very good Brunello producer. Among those that we tasted recently, we especially recommend their '85 and '83. Their '84 was also quite good. Brunello *** –

Fattoria Poggio Antico (località *Poggio Antico, zone 3*), *1972.* The vineyards on the 495-acre (200-hectare) Poggio Antico estate were for the most part planted in 1970. They have 50 acres (20.3 hectares) of vines planted at altitudes averaging some 1,475 feet (450 meters) above sea level, and they have received permission to plant another 30 acres (12 hectares).

Lamberto Paronetto from the Veronese area is their consulting enologist. They ferment in stainless steel tanks at a controlled temperature of 82° Fahrenheit (28° centigrade). The wine is moved to oak casks in the April after the harvest. Their Brunello spends four years in casks, their Altero two, and the Rosso from one to two. Poggio Antico produced their first Brunello in 1974. Their annual production averages 96,000 bottles of wine, which includes Brunello, Rosso, and Altero. *Altero* is a Brunello that can't be sold as such because of its reduced cask aging. Although the Poggio Antico wines seem to have a fairly good reputation, we have been totally unimpressed with them. To date, we have tasted every Poggio Antico Brunello from '78 through '82, some of them multiple times. Surprisingly, the '80 was the best of all. Of those tasted from cask, in November 1990, the '88 showed, as it should have,

the most promise, but the '86, '87, and '89 also promised good Brunellos. Brunello * –; Rosso di Montalcino 0

Ferro (*zone 1*). Thus far Carlo Burroni produces only a Rosso from his 1.4-acre (0.58-hectare) Ferro estate.

Fontebuia (*zone 1*). Pier F. Padelletti owns 1.7 acres (0.69 hectare) of brunello vines. According to our information, he has bottled only a Rosso.

Fontevino (*Villa dei Lecci, Castello di Camigliano, zone 3*), *1988.* They are owned by the Ghezzi family, who also own **Castello di Camigliano.** This is actually another label used by Camigliano. They own 168 acres (68 hectares) of vines planted at altitudes ranging from 785 to 885 feet (240 to 270 meters) above sea level. The vines have a south to southwestern exposure. They have planted an additional 72 acres (29 hectares) that will come on-line in 1991 and 1992.

Besides a Brunello and Rosso, they bottle a Chianti Colli Senesi, Santa Lucia, and Bianco delle Crete. The Santa Lucia is reportedly made from brunello grapes grown in the vineyard of that name. According to the winery, they also buy grapes! This is surprising since they are an *azienda agricola,* which means that they are supposed to make wine from their own grapes. They also produce a *barrique*-aged sangiovese and, like so many others, plan to produce a sangiovese–cabernet sauvignon blend. Pietro Rivella consults here as he does for numerous other wineries in Montalcino and Chianti.

We've tasted a number of their Brunellos in the past six years and cannot report that we were impressed. The only one that we can recommend is the '85 Villa dei Lecci. Even their '82 La Torre was unimpressive. Brunello: 0, La Torre 0, Villa dei Lecci *

Fornacina (*zone 1*). Ruggero Biliorsi owns 2.9 acres (1.16 hectares) of brunello vines. From the 1982 vintage he produced 2,150 bottles of Brunello. Thus far we've tasted his '81 and '82 Brunellos from bottle, and the '85 Riserva and '86, '87, '88, and '89 *normali* from cask. The '81 was quite good, the '82 disappointing. The '86 though '89 *normali* all showed the potential to be good wines. Brunello *

Geografico (*Gaiole in Chianti*), *1961.* This label and wine are owned by Agricoltura del Chianti Geografico, the large cooperative from the Chianti Classico zone. Their Brunellos, at least the '81 and '85, were bottled by A.A.C., and the '83 by the Il Casello winery of Clemente and Roberto Franceschi. We suspect that A.A.C. stands for Azienda Agricola Camigliano. We tasted the '81 and '85, and found them perhaps a bit better than those of that producer. We

THE CRUS OF FONTEVINO (CAMIGLIANO)

Cru	Acres	Hectares	Average Number of Bottles Per Year
Bellaria	9.4	3.8	n/a
Castelvecchio	—	—	10,000
Fontevecchia	4.9	2.0	6,000
Poggiarello	8.6	3.5	6,000

never tasted the '83, and so can't comment. Overall, the wines were above average. The fine enologist Vittorio Fiore consults for them, so we expect better things in the future. Brunello * –

I Comunali. See **Comunali.**

I Verbi di Ferretti R. & Rasconi R. Their first Brunello was the '86. We tasted that one from cask, along with the '87, '88, and '89. All but the '86 were good; the '86 was too difficult to evaluate. The '88 showed good promise. Brunello [** –]

Il Casello (*zone 3*). This estate is leased by Clemente and Roberto Franceschi, owners of **Tenuta Il Poggione.** Part of the vineyard—5.7 acres (2.3 hectares) of sangiovese grosso vines—is located close to the Il Poggione estate. Pier Luigi Talenti, the fine winemaker at Il Poggione, makes this Brunello as well. Il Casello produces only one wine, Brunello. Their annual production is about 1,325 cases. The only Il Casello Brunellos that we've tasted thus far have been the '79 and '81, and both of them were very good indeed. Brunello ** +

Il Colle (*zone 1*). Il Colle has 4.6 acres (1.9 hectares) of vines, from which they produce a Brunello. Their '79 was unimpressive, yet they did produce a good '82 and '83, and a very good '80. Brunello * +

Il Colle. See **Conti Costanti.**

Il Colle 2ª (*zone 1*). Carli Ernesta Gianneli owns 4.6 acres (1.87 hectares) of brunello vines.

Il Marroneto (località *Madonna delle Grazie, zone 1*), *1974.* This estate is owned by Dott. Maddelana Mori Bianchini. Bianchini owns a mere 1.1 acres (0.45 hectare) of brunello vines which are planted at altitudes averaging 1,970 feet (600 meters) above sea level. The vines have a northwesterly exposure. They report an annual production averaging 2,900 bottles of Brunello! Their first vintage was 1980. In 1980 Bianchini produced a *normale* and Riserva, as he did in 1983. He made 1,855 bottles of the '80 Riserva and 3,974 of the '83. We suspect that he also produced *riserve* in 1982 and 1985. They produced 3,172 bottles of the *normale* '85. Bianchini rates the vintages:1986 excellent; 1985, 1983, 1981, and 1980 good; and 1984 poor. The best of all was 1982. Unfortunately, that is one of the two bottled we haven't tasted. We have been impressed with all of Bianchini's Brunellos that we have tasted, which include the '80, '83, '84, and '85. Brunello ***

Il Paradiso (Manfredi) (*zone 1*). Fortunata and Renata Martini own 3.7 acres (1.5 hectares) of vines planted at altitudes ranging from 1,245 to 1,310 feet (380 to 400 meters) above sea level, with a northern exposure. Enologist Paolo Vagaggini is their consultant. We liked Manfredi's '81, '82, and even their '84, but for some reason we found the '85 wanting. Overall, these are very good Brunellos. Brunello ** –

Il Poggiolo. See **Podere Il Poggiolo.**

Il Poggione. See **Tenuta Il Poggione.**

Isabella de'Medici. Valdisuga produced the '75 Brunello for this mediocre Chianti Classico producer. We do not know if Valdisuga still makes this wine for them, or if anyone else does. It was among the worst in the zone. Brunello 0 –

La Campana (*zone 1*). Rino Giannetti owns 4.3 acres (1.75 hectares) of brunello vines. We never met his Brunellos.

La Campana. We don't know if there is a connection between Rino Giannetti's La Campana and the estate owned by Mignarri Peris. We have found their Brunellos, based on the two vintages we tasted from bottle—the '84 and '85—and three from barrel—the '85 Riserva, and the '86 and '87 *normali*—to be quite good. Brunello * +

La Casa. See **Tenuta Caparzo.**

La Cerbaiola (Salvioni Giulio). See **Cerbaiola.**

La Chiesa di S. Restituta (*zone 3*), *1972.* Roberto Bellini, proprietor of the 173-acre (70-hectare) La Chiesa di S. Restituta estate, planted 20 acres (8 hectares) of vines in 1972. Today there are 45.5 acres (18.42 hectares), 39 (15.82) of brunello vines, and the balance in trebbiano, malvasia, and sauvignon. The vines are planted at altitudes ranging from 820 to 1,150 feet (250 to 350 meters) above sea level.

THE CRUS OF LA CHIESA DI S. RESTITUTA

Cru	Acres	Hectares
Del Campo Santo and Del Pian de' Cerri	9.9	4
Ricciolitto	4.9	2
S. Pietro	9.9	4

Bellini produced his first Rosso di Montalcino in 1974 and his first Brunello the following year. In 1975 he produced 5,000 bottles of Brunello. Today total annual production at S. Restituta ranges from about 70,000 to 80,000 bottles, of which 30,000 to 35,000 each are Brunello and Rosso. Bellini also produces 10,000 bottles of other wines which include Bianco del Vescovo, and 2,000 half bottles of two superb *vin santi*—200 of a very sweet and 1,800 of a moderately sweet one. In 1986 he made 900 bottles of white wine and 2,000 of *vin santo*. Bellini produced 9,200 bottles of Brunello from 1977, 17,500 from 1984, and 28,700 from 1985. In 1982 he produced 3,850 bottles of Brunello Riserva.

Like nearly everyone else here, he plans to produce a sangiovese–cabernet sauvignon blend in *barrique,* and expects to do cru bottlings from Vigna Pian de' Cerri and Campo Ricciolitto. Pietro Rivella consults for him.

Bellini's Brunellos enjoy a good reputation, especially in Germany. Some of the other producers in Montalcino also hold them in regard. While we were unimpressed with the wines we tasted from the 1977 and 1980 vintages, we can recommend those from '81 and '82, which were both good, and the '83 and '84, which were very good. The '85 shows a lot of class. We also tasted a potentially excellent '88 *normale* and '85 Riserva form cask, and very good '86 and '89 *normali*. Brunello ***

La Crete (*zone 1*). Giancarlo Vannini owns 1.5 acres (0.62 hectare) of brunello vines.

La Fornace (*zone 1*). To date, Franco Giannetti has bottled only a Rosso di Montalcino from his 1-acre (0.42-hectare) brunello vineyard.

La Fortuna di Gino e Gioberto Zannoni (*zone 1*), *1974.* Gioberto Zannoni and Felicetta Anna Ricciardiello own 7.4 acres (3 hectares) of vines from which they produce, on average, 20,000 bottles of wine a year. This includes from 8,000 to 9,325 bottles of Brunello and 10,500 to 13,300 bottles of Rosso di Montalcino. Enologist Paolo Vagaggini consults for them. La Fortuna produced good to very good '79, '80, '81, and '85 Riserva Brunellos. Unfortunately, we haven't tasted their '82 or '83. Brunello ** −

La Lecciaia, Azienda Vallafrico (*zone 1*). Azienda Vallafrico owns some 16 acres (6.47 hectares) of brunello vines. They also belong to the *consorzio*. Besides their phone number, we know nothing else about them.

La Magia (*zone 2*). Herbert Schwarz, proprietor of La Magia, owns 38.5 acres (15.6 hectares) planted in sangiovese grosso vines for Brunello. While his '79 and '80 were rather mediocre, he did make a good '81. Brunello [+]

La Pescaia (*zone 1*). Liliana Pallari and Enzo Mantengoli own 5.9 acres (2.39 hectares) of vines. They produce, on average, 16,000 bottles of wine a year. The *consorzio* reports that thus far they have sold only a Rosso di Montalcino. We tasted their '85 Riserva, and '86, '87, '88, and '89 *normali* from cask in November 1990. All of the wines showed promise. Brunello **

La Poderina (*zone 2*). La Poderina has 0.5 acre (0.2 hectare) of brunello vines. All of the vintages we tasted from this estate, from the '79 through the '81, were unimpressive. When we heard that they were owned by Saiagricola we were very surprised, but then again it appears that this acquisition has been recent. And it might also explain the improvement we found with both the '82 and '85; both of those wines were quite good. Brunello: pre-1982, 0, since 1982, * +

La Torre (*S. Angelo in Colle, zone 3*). Giuseppe Anania owns the La Torre estate and its 9.9 acres (4 hectares) of vines. Anania produces, on average, some 11,000 bottles of wine a year. His '85 was good. Brunello * +

La Velona (*zone 2*). All we know about La Velona is that they belong to the *consorzio* and are located in zone 2!

Le Due Porti (*zone 3*), *1970.* Enrico Daviddi and Genny Martini owned this estate and its 7.4 acres (3 hectares) of vines until 1989 or 1990, when they sold the vineyard to **Altesino**. Those vines are planted at altitudes averaging 1,640 feet (500 meters) above sea level. They expected to have an additional 4.9 acres (2 hectares) come on-line in 1993. Their annual production of wine averages between 18,650 and 20,000 bottles. Their '80 and '82 Brunellos were quite good, but the '81 was disappointing. We found the '85 from bottle and the '86 from barrel difficult to judge. The '87 wasn't bad, and the '88 rather good. These last two wines were tasted from cask. The enologist Pietro Rivella consults for them. Their last Brunello from their own vines will be the '89. Brunello * +

Le Presi (*zone 2*). Marusca Poggi-Fabbri has 1.5 acres (0.6 hectare) of brunello vineyards. The two vintages we tasted of Le Presi, the '79 and '85, were good Brunellos. Brunello * +

Lisini (*S. Angelo in Colle, zone 3*). F.lli Lisini's 380-acre (154-hectare) Casanova estate has 25 acres (10 hectares) of vines for Brunello. Some of the vines were put in between 1930 and 1940; others in 1967. The vineyards are Capannelle, Compagnia, S. Biagio, Tufaia, and Vigna Nuova. The oldest part of the vineyards has 200 vines planted in 1880. These plants, unlike the others, which have all been grafted onto phylloxera-resistant rootstock, are still on their own roots. In 1983 they made a special bottling of nearly 80 gallons (300 liters) from the old vines.

Franco Bernabei, a noted enologist, consults for them. Lisini produces, on average, some 62,000 bottles of wine per year. This includes some 30,000 bottles of Brunello and 15,000 of Rosso di Montalcino. The Lisini brothers also produce 3,000 to 4,000 bottles of Brunello *riserva* and a scant 300 bottles of *vin santo*. Lisini's first Brunello sold in bottle was from the 1967 vintage. Their '73 was one of the best produced that year, but the '75 was disappointing. The '77 was, again, one of the best, and the '78 was very good. The '82 was good, and the '83 very good. Thus far, we have found the '85 rather variable, some bottles very good, others merely good. Overall, the Lisini Brunellos are quite good, though somewhat variable. Brunello **

Mastrojanni (località *Castelnuovo dell'Abate, zone 2*), *1975.* Originally this farm was part of the Fattoria dei Barbi estate, which they sold some twenty to twenty-five years ago. After *mezzadria* was eliminated, Colombini sold this farm because it was too far from the main Barbi estate.

The Mastrojanni family owns 222 acres (90 hectares) of land, of which 27.5 (11.1) are in vines at Podere S. Pio and Podere Loreto. Nearly all are planted in brunello vines, although there are a small number of malvasia vines for their own use. The vines, planted at altitudes ranging from 1,150 to 1,310 feet (350 to 400 meters) above sea level, face south to southeast. Mastrojanni planted their first vines in 1975 and bottled their first wine from the 1978 vintage, some 3,000 bottles of Brunello. The next vintage they made 23,000 bottles.

Antonio Mastrojanni manages the estate and makes the wine, and his lovely wife, Concha, helps him in commercializing, and we suspect, in consuming, his splendid product. Antonio has bottled some of the crus since 1979, although he doesn't always indicate this on the label. The best wines of a given year become *riserva*. Mastrojanni produces all of their wine for Brunello di Montalcino; afterward he makes a selection, with the best wine being used for Brunello and the lesser wines for Rosso di Montalcino.

Today they produce 26,600 bottles of Brunello wines, plus 6,600 of a Brunello Riserva, and 40,000 of Rosso di Montalcino. In 1982 and 1987, Mastrojanni's production rose to 80,000 bottles. He makes a splendid single-vineyard Rosso di Montalcino from Costa Colonna. And like so many others, he plans to do a sangiovese–cabernet sauvignon blend.

Mastrojanni is going from strength to strength with each passing year. Antonio is a serious and dedicated producer who believes in quality. We have tasted a wide range of Brunellos and Rossos from Mastrojanni and have found them very good indeed, as well as consistent, and they are getting better. Of those we've tasted, we

THE CRUS OF MASTROJANNI

Cru	Acres	Hectares
Confine	1.73	0.7
Costa Colonna	1.24	0.5
Creta	1.73	0.7
Crocina	2.47	1.0
Piano di Casa	6.18	2.5
Piano Poderino	2.97	1.2
Poggetto	1.24	0.5
Ripi	1.24	0.5
Scesa Poderino	1.24	0.5
Schiena d'Asino	4.94	2.0
Vigna Vecchia	2.47	1.0
Total	27.45	11.1

were most impressed with the '83 and '82 Riservas. We also found all of the *normali*, from the '78 through the '84, and the *riserve* of '81 and '80 very good. Of Mastrojanni's crus we were especially impressed with the '83 Schiena d'Asino Riserva tasted from cask in May 1986, and the '80 Poggetto Riserva. Brunello ***; Rosso di Montalcino ** +

Melini. This reliable Chianti producer bottles a wide range of Tuscan wines, including a Brunello. The only Melini Brunellos that we can recall were the '80 and '84. The '80 was bottled by Agrel. It was good, if not much more. The '84 was labeled Vigna Il Comombaione I Gino Antonio Focacci. For the vintage and its age it was a good wine. Brunello *

Nardi. See *Fattoria Casale del Bosco.*

Oliveri. Marcello Olivieri, who was at one time a producer of a fine Chianti Classico, used to sell 15,000 to 20,000 bottles a year of a simple, almost Chianti-like Brunello that was produced for him by Martini Bramante of Valdicava. We don't know if he still sells this wine. Both of the vintages we tasted, the '74 and '75, were reliable, if unexciting. Brunello [0]

Palazzetta (*zone 2*). Currently Flavio Fanti sells a Rosso from his 4.4 acres (1.78 hectares) of brunello vines. Eventually he will produce a Brunello as well.

Paradiso. See *Il Paradiso (Manfredi).*

Paradiso (*zone 1*). Mauro Fastelli owns 6.7 acres (2.7 hectares) of brunello vines. Our experience with this Paradiso is limited to the good '80 and '82 Brunellos. Brunello *

Pelagrilli, *Azienda Agricola Pacenti Siro & Pieri Graz.* (località *Pelagrilli, 1ª Montalcino, zone 1*), *1970.* Siro Pacenti labels his wines as Vigneti Pacenti Siro. He owns 7.4 acres (3 hectares) of producing vineyards, plus 7.4 of nonbearing vines. Additionally, his grandparents own 12.4 acres (5 hectares), which he leases. His vineyard, Il Poggio, is in the northern zone, while that of his grandparents, Piancornello, is in the southern section. The former

vineyard, with an eastern exposure, is planted at an altitude of 985 feet (300 meters) above sea level; the latter, facing south to southwest, is at 655 feet (200 meters). He produced his first wines that were sold in bottle from the 1988 vintage. Besides a Brunello and a Rosso, he plans to produce a cabernet sauvignon–sangiovese blend in *barrique*. His production averages from 55 to 60 tons (500 to 550 quintali) of sangiovese grosso grapes, 28 (250) from Il Poggio. Currently he has only a Rosso for sale. Paolo Vagaggini is his consulting enologist. The '88 Brunello was potentially very good, and the '89 quite good indeed. We tasted those from barrel in November 1990. We believe that their first Brunello was the '88. Brunello [** −]

Pertimali di Angelo Sassetti (*zone 1*). There are two Pertimali estates, one owned by Angelo Sassetti, the second by Livio. Angelo owns 6.2 acres (2.5 hectares). We've never met his wines.

Pertimali di Livio Sassetti (*zone 1*). Livio Sassetti, who also owns a Pertimali estate, has 7.6 acres (3.1 hectares) of brunello vines. We have found his Brunellos very good and fairly consistent as well. We were especially impressed with the '85 *normale* and Riserva, but also liked his '80, '81, and '83, both the *normale* and Riserva. The '86 and '87 from cask also were quite good. Clearly this is a very good to excellent estate. Brunello *** −

Pian dei Mercatelli (*Azienda Agricola Fontevino—Agricola Camigliano*). The '80 Pian dei Mercatelli Brunello was very good and it was the best wine that we've tasted from Azienda Agricola Fontevino—Agricola Camigliano. It would be nice if all of Camigliano's Brunellos came up to this level. Brunello **

Pietroso (*zone 3*), *1974.* Domenico Berni owns a small farm consisting of 1.2 acres (0.49 hectare) of brunello grapes. On average he produces some 3,300 bottles of wine a year. Attilio Pagli is Berni's consulting enologist. Thus far we've tasted the unimpressive '79, '81, and '84. Brunello 0

Podere Cerrino (*Enzo Tiezzi*). See *Cerrino 1ª.*

Podere Il Poggiolo (*Eredi Cosimi Roberto*) (località *Il Poggiolo, zone 3*), *1969.* This estate includes 12.4 acres (5 hectares) of vines. The Il Poggiolo vineyard covers 7.4 acres (3 hectares); those of Sassello and Vigna del Quercione are 2.47 acres (1 hectare) each. Some 6.3 acres (2.54 hectares) are inscribed for DOC-DOCG. Thus far we have tasted Cosimi's '80, '82, and '83 *riserve*, '85 *annata*, and '85 Sassello from bottle and '85 Riserva, plus '86 through '89 *annata* from cask. Overall, they have been good to very good, if unexciting Brunellos. We've been less impressed with their *barrique*-aged Sassello. Brunello ** −

Podere Pian di Conte (località *Pian di Conte, S. Angelo in Colle, zone 3*), *1980.* Pier Luigi Talenti, the fine enologist at Il Poggione, owns some 18.1 acres (7.25 hectares) of vines at his Pian di Conte estate. The vines are planted at altitudes ranging from 1,245 to 1,310 feet (380 to 400 meters) above sea level, facing south to southwest. The first Brunello he produced here was from the 1981 vintage. Their annual production consists of 40,000 bottles of wine, half Brunello and the other half Rosso di Montalcino. Based on the '81, '82, '84, and '85, we rate this estate as excellent. Not surprisingly, all of these Brunellos have been very good. As we expected, the '85 *annata* and Riserva are both splendid wines, especially the *annata,* that will age very well. And from cask, the '88 was excellent, and the others between '86 and '89 all at least very good. Brunello ***

Podere Scopetone (*zone 1*), *1982.* Federigo Abbarchi and Angela Corioni own a small farm with some 3.7 acres (1.5 hectares) of brunello vines. They produce an average of 9,300 to 10,650 bottles of wine per year. Enologist Attilio Pagli consults for Scopetone. The only Brunello that we've tasted here from bottle was the good '84. We also tasted, from cask, the '86, '87, '88, and '89. They were all potentially good. Brunello [*]

Poderi di Sesta. They sell a Brunello under the Podere della Quercia name. This could be the same winery as **Tenuta di Sesta.**

Poggio alle Mura (*zone 3*). There were 272 acres (110 hectares) in vines on the 4,050-acre (1,639-hectare) Castello Poggio alle Mura farm, 130 (52.5) planted in brunello. There were also 717 acres (290 hectares) planted in olive trees, orchards, and cereals, not to mention pastureland for maintaining livestock. Besides all this, the *fattoria* produced Brunello, Rosso di Montalcino, Chianti, Moscadello, white wine, and *vin santo.* Perhaps their other products were of a higher quality; their wines were without a doubt the worst in the zone. We were less than impressed with all the vintages that we tasted from '67 through '75.

We were told by a noted Brunello producer that Poggio alle Mura used to be one of the two major problems in Montalcino. Fortunately for the other producers, Banfi Vintners (**Castello Banfi**) solved this one by buying the estate. We were also told that effective from the 1979 vintage, Banfi retired the label and that was their last vintage. Soon, we have reason to believe, that label will be reactivated. Although we haven't seen the Poggio alle Mura wines in some time, they are still listed as a member of the *consorzio* under Comp. Agricola Pam. Brunello [0 −]

Poggio Antico. See **Fattoria Poggio Antico.**

Poggio degli Ulivi (*zone 2*). Elisa Ciacci-Bellocci owns 21 acres (8.49 hectares) of brunello vines. Our experience with this estate is very limited. Thus far we've tasted a less than impressive '80 Riserva. Brunello [0]

Poggio Salvi (*zone 3*), *1979.* Pierluigi Tagliabue owns this estate and its 27 acres (11 hectares) of vines. The vines, planted at altitudes ranging from 1,475 to 1,640 feet (450 to 500 meters) above sea level, face southwest. The vineyard is said, by some noted producers in the zone, to be in a very good location. The '78 was the first Brunello they produced for sale. Today they produce 40,000 to 50,000 bottles of Brunello and Rosso di Montalcino a year. Iacopo Biondi-Santi, who is married to Tagliabue's daughter, makes the wine with his father-in-law. We expect an improvement in quality.

Thus far, however, we have been less than impressed with Poggio Salvi's Brunellos. While we must admit to having found the '82, '83, '84, and '85 fairly good, overall we have found their wines disappointing. Look at the '79, and both the *normale* and Riserva from '80 and '81. Brunello: pre-1982, 0, since 1982, *

Quercecchio (*zone 3*). Maria Grazia Salvioni owns 9.7 acres (3.92 hectares) of brunello vines. We liked all three vintages we tasted from bottle—the '81, '82, and '85. Of those we tasted from cask—

the '86, '87, '88, and '89—all, except for the out-of-condition '89, showed quite well. Brunello * +

Rasa (*zone 1*). Ennio Mantengoli owns 1.5 acres (0.6 hectare) of brunello vines.

Rasina (*zone 1*). Vasco Mantengoli has 3 acres (1.2 hectares) of brunello vines planted on his Rasina estate. We believe that his first Brunello was the '88, which we tasted along with the '89 from cask. The '88 showed a lot of promise, and the '89 was quite good. Brunello [**]

Riguardo. Tosco Vinicola bottles this Brunello. It is rather pedestrian, lacking in distinction and class, though admittedly it is drinkable. Thus far we have tasted the '76, '77, '78, '80, and '85. All have left us less than impressed. All we know about Tosco Vinicola is that their address is in care of Castelgiocondo. Some of the wines were bottled as Tenuta di Riguardo, others as Riguardo. Simplifying the name did nothing for the quality. Brunello 0

S. Carlo (*zone 3*), *1974.* Renata Machetti owns 4.4 acres (1.8 hectares) of vines in the Tavernelle district. The vines are planted at an altitude of 985 feet (300 meters) above sea level, facing southwest. Machetti expects to have another 4.9 acres (2 hectares) in production in the future. Enologist Paolo Vagaggini is her consultant. Both the '81 and '85 were good Brunellos. Brunello *

S. Filippo Azienda Agricola di Filippo Fanti Baldassarre (*zone 2*). There are two S. Filippo estates. This one, owned by Filippo Fanti Baldassarre, has 10.4 acres (4.2 hectares) of brunello vines. They produced a good '81 and a very good '85. Brunello * +

S. Filippo di Rosi Ermanno (località *San Filippo, zone 1*), *1972.* Ermanno and Stefano Rosi, proprietors of the other S. Filippo estate, own 54 acres (22 hectares) of land, of which some 14.8 (6) are in vines. These vines are planted at an average altitude of 1,000 feet (305 meters) above sea level. Currently the Rosis produce 32,000 bottles of wine a year. They expect this to increase to 46,600 bottles in 1990. Besides a Brunello and Rosso di Montalcino, they produce a small amount of white wine and *vin santo.* As he is for so many other estates in this area, Paolo Vagaggini is the consulting enologist here.

Overall, the Rosi's S. Filippo Brunellos are very good wines. The first S. Filippo Brunello sold in bottle was the '77. They made a good '78, '80, and '85 *normale* and '85 Riserva, and a very good '79, '81, '82, and '83 *normale,* and, judging by those we tasted in cask in November 1990, a very good '88, and a good '86 and '89. Brunello **; Rosso di Montalcino *

S. Giorgio (*zone 2*). A. Benocci-Bianchini owns this estate with its 9.1 acres (3.67 hectares) of brunello vines.

Sassetti (*zone 2*). Vasco Sassetti has 1.2 acres (0.51 hectare) of brunello vines planted on his estate.

Svetoni. Cantina Svetoni, a producer of Vino Nobile di Montepulciano, sells 10,000 bottles a year of what is probably a mediocre Brunello at best. We haven't tasted it, but at one time they bought the wine from the zone's worst producer, Poggio alle Mura. As for today, we don't know from whom they get it, or indeed if they even continue to sell a Brunello.

Tenuta Caparzo (località *Torrenieri, zone 1*), 1965. The origin of Caparzo derives, it is said, from *ca' pazzo,* meaning "the madman's house." Whether the original owner was mad is difficult to ascertain. The current owners, a group of Milanese businessmen, are not. And we can attest that you don't have to be mad to drink their fine Brunello.

This 150-acre (60-hectare) estate, located in the Torrenieri area, has 62 acres (25 hectares) of vines, including 42 (17) of brunello, 5 (2) of cabernet sauvignon, and 7.5 (3) of chardonnay. The vineyards, planted at altitudes ranging from 720 to 900 feet (220 to 275 meters) above sea level, have a south to southeastern exposure. Their annual production is about 235,000 bottles of wine—66,600 bottles of Brunello; 33,300 of the *barrique*-aged, sangiovese–cabernet sauvignon blend, Ca' del Pazzo; 105,000 of Rosso di Montalcino; 20,000 of the white Le Grance; and 10,000 of a sparkling rosé.

They produce two Brunellos—the Tenuta Caparzo (53,300 bottles) and the single-vineyard La Casa (13,300). La Casa is a 25-acre (10-hectare) plot on the Montosoli hillside north of Montalcino; 14.8 acres (6 hectares) are in vines, including 10 (4) that should be in production in 1991. These new vines were planted at a density of 1,620 vines per acre (4,000 per hectare), as opposed to the 1,090 (2,700) previously planted. Estate manager Nuccio Turone points out that reducing the yield per vine results in juice with more concentration and extract. And, in fact, the increased quality justifies the higher maintenance cost. Altesino, Baricci, Biondi-Santi, Capanna, Costanti, and others also own a piece of the highly regarded Montosoli hillside.

The first Caparzo Brunello was from the 1970 vintage. The La Casa premiered in 1976. The grapes for the La Casa, besides coming from a special vineyard, are handled somewhat differently. This wine spends at least six months of its aging period in French *barriques.* They age their Rosso for a year in Slavonian oak casks, and the Brunello for at least three years, as required by law.

When Caparzo started out, they showed a lot of promise, but they proved inconsistent. One year their wines would be good, the next not so good. The basic material was there, but direction was lacking. Turone decided that something had to be done, and so, in 1980, they hired a consulting enologist, Vittorio Fiore, who has made a significant improvement in these wines. To emphasize their commitment to quality, they also joined VIDE. Today the Caparzo Brunellos are not only consistent but excellent as well. The '79 Riserva, '80 *normale* and Riserva, '81 and '82 *normale* and Riserva, the '83 and '85 *normale* in particular, were all good wines, and we can recommend their La Casa '77, '78, and '79 as well. Of more recent vintages, both '88s showed a lot of promise when tasted from cask, the two '85s are excellent, as is the '85 Riserva, the '86s very good, and the '87s and '89s good. Caparzo also produces a good Rosso di Montalcino. Brunello: ***, La Casa ***; Rosso di Montalcino ** –

Tenuta Col d'Orcia (*Sant'Angelo in Colle,* località *Col d'Orcia, zone 3*). Tenuta Col d'Orcia was at one time part of Franceschi's Azienda Sant' Angelo. When Comm. Franceschi died in 1959, his estate was divided between his two sons, Leopoldo and Stefano. Leopoldo inherited Il Poggione, and Stefano got the 1,485-acre (600-hectare) Col d'Orcia estate. To our knowledge, this Brunello has been sold in bottle, with the Col d'Orcia name, since 1965.

In 1973, Tenuta Col d'Orcia was sold to Cinzano. Today they have nearly 200 acres (80 hectares) in vines for Brunello, making them one of the larger estates in Montalcino. Poggio al Vento, a 10-acre (4-hectare) vineyard, has been bottled as a single-vineyard Brunello since the '82. Each year they produce some 500,000 bottles of Montalcino wines, as well as the Mossa wines from the Collio Goriziano zone in Friuli–Venezia Giulia. In a few years their plans call for an annual production of 800,000 bottles. Of their current production, 150,000 bottles are Brunello, 265,000 are Rosso, 60,000 of the *vino novello* Novembrino, 20,000 Gineprone Chianti, 15,000 Ghiaie Bianco, and 5,000 Moscadello di Montalcino. They plan to produce a *barrique*-aged, brunello–cabernet sauvignon blend and a Cabernet aged in *barrique.* The grapes for all their Brunello, Rosso, and Moscadello come from their own property. They buy 30 percent of what they need for Novembrino, and 100 percent for Ghiaie Bianco.

Enologist Maurizio Castelli consults for Col d'Orcia. Their previous enologist, Pietro Rivella, harvested the grapes for the '85 and made the wine. Maurizio Castelli finished it.

Since the 1982 vintage they have produced a single-vineyard Brunello, Poggio al Vento. They also produced that wine in 1983, 1985, and 1988. This Brunello has more structure, body, flavor, and tannin than their regular wine.

In times past, the Col d'Orcia Brunellos were made in the lighter, more elegant style. This wine, in our opinion, has always been better than its reputation. Signs indicate an improvement in quality here as well as a change in style. Today the Col d'Orcia Brunellos have more body and structure. The '88 from barrel showed a lot of promise, and both of the '85s—*normale* and Riserva—show potential. The '83 and '82 *riserve* and *normali* are very good, and the '85 Riserva Poggio al Vento is excellent, the '82 very good. Brunello: **, Poggio al Vento *** –; Rosso di Montalcino 0

Tenuta di Riguardo. See *Riguardo.*

Tenuta di Sesta (*zone 2*). Giuseppe Ciacci owns 33.7 acres (13.64 hectares) of vines from which he produces a Brunello and, we presume, a Rosso. Thus far the only wine we've tasted was the '80, and it was wanting. Brunello [0]

Tenuta Il Greppone Mazzi. This 370-acre (150-hectare) estate has been owned by the Folonaris of Ruffino fame since 1984. They have 18.5 acres (7.5 hectares) of brunello vines planted at an average altitude of 1,640 feet (500 meters) above sea level. On average, they produce some 23,000 bottles of Brunello a year. They rate as their very best vintages 1964, 1970, 1980, and 1985, and as the worst, 1984; they didn't produce a Brunello that year. Of the three vintages we tasted, we liked the '82 the best. The other two, the '80 and '81, were weak. Brunello *

Tenuta Il Poggione (*S. Angelo in Colle, zone 3*), 1890. The Franceschi family bought this estate in Sant' Angelo in Colle in about 1900. It was then part of Azienda Sant' Angelo. Upon the death of Comm. Franceschi in 1959, the *azienda* was divided between his two sons. The Il Poggione farm went to Leopoldo, and Col d'Orcia to Stefano. When Leopoldo died in 1979, Il Poggione became the property of his sons, Clemente and Roberto.

The estate covers 3,460 acres (1,400 hectares), 182 (73.67) in vines; 127 acres (51.26 hectares) are planted in brunello, 5 (2.01) in moscadello. Those vines are planted at altitudes ranging from

490 to 1,245 feet (150 to 380 meters) above sea level, with a south to southwestern exposure. In 1953 they put in their first specialized vineyards; previously all had been in *coltura promiscua,* with other crops.

Wine was being produced at Il Poggione in the 1920s, but the first Brunello to be sold commercially from the estate was the '65. Previously their Brunello was either drunk at their own table or sold unlabeled.

Il Poggione has an annual production of about 380,000 bottles, of which some 150,000 are Rosso di Montalcino and 160,000 are Brunello. They also produce 12,000 to 16,000 bottles of a very fine Moscadello di Montalcino from their 5-acre (2-hectare) vineyard, and an excellent extra virgin olive oil. The less satisfactory wine is sold *sfuso,* in bulk.

The winemaking at Il Poggione has been in the very capable hands of enologist Pier Luigi Talenti since 1959. Quality control at Il Poggione begins with a careful selection in the vineyard. There is a second selection after the wine is made. Any wine that is judged below their high standards is sold *sfuso.* In the spring after the fermentation, Talenti makes a third selection to decide which wine will become Brunello and which will be sold as Rosso di Montalcino. Both wines start out the same, but the Rosso is aged five to six months in cask while Brunello is given at least three years longer in large Slavonian oak casks.

The Rosso di Montalcino of Il Poggione is, for us, the best in the zone. In 1982, which was exceptional, they produced 5,000 cases. The 1985 was also splendid.

Until 1978 they produced only a regular Brunello. Talenti doesn't believe in overlong wood aging. In that vintage he produced a scant 300 cases of a very fine *riserva* at the request of their American importer.

On our visit in the spring of 1985, we were generously invited to select any bottle we wanted to taste from the fine collection of vintages in the *cantina.* They certainly had no cause for concern about our choosing an off vintage; they don't produce off vintages at Il Poggione. Every year the Brunellos of this producer are among the very best produced in the zone. To our knowledge, they have never produced a Brunello that was less than good. Even in a year like 1976 they made good wine, the result of careful selection and a sharp eye to quality. In 1984, by limiting their production to 25 to 30 percent of normal, they again produced a good Brunello, judging from our cask tasting.

Besides Il Poggione's splendid '70 and '75, we recommend highly their '83 and '85 *annata* and '85 Riserva, followed closely by the '78 Riserva, '79 and '82 *annata.* They also made a very good '78 and '81

annata, and a good '80 and '84. From cask, the '88 was splendid when tasted in November 1990, and the '86, '87, and '89 also showed a lot of promise. For consistency at a very high level Il Poggione is hard to match, never mind beat. As for their Rosso di Montalcino, no one makes a finer one. Brunello ****; Rosso di Montalcino ***

Tenuta "La Fuga." Gabriella Cristofolini Attanasio owns this estate. Our knowledge and experience are limited to the very good '86 Brunello di Montalcino which we tasted in April 1991. Brunello **

Tenuta La Poderina. See *La Poderina.*

Tenuta Valdicava (*zone 1*), *1953.* Vincenzo Abruzzese has owned the 500-acre (200-hectare) Valdicava farm since 1986. Prior to that time it was owned by his grandfather, Bramante Martini. Abruzzese started with the estate in 1980, selling the wine. He finished the '83 Brunello and was fully responsible for the production of the '85. Abruzzese's name first appeared on the label with the '83 Brunello.

The entire estate has 106 acres (43 hectares), of which 24.7 acres (10 hectares) are planted, 19.8 (8) in sangiovese grosso vines. Additionally, he leases 2.47 acres (1 hectare) in the Montosoli vineyard. From those vines Abruzzese produces a Brunello and a Rosso di Montalcino. The balance is some experimental plantings of trebbiano, malvasia, pinot bianco, and cabernet franc. The vines are planted between 985 and 1,150 feet (300 and 350 meters) above sea level. He expects another 5 acres (2 hectares) or so to come into production in the future. He restructured the vineyards and chose the best places for the vines.

Abruzzese vinifies all the vineyards separately. He told us that Madonna del Piano is his best vineyard. In April he blends them together to produce a *normale* or *base.* The best wine goes for Brunello, the rest becomes Rosso. He ages the *base,* Madonna del Piano, Montosoli, and Poggio separately in the years where he thinks he might bottle them individually. Even after or during aging he could still declassify part or all of one or more crus.

To our knowledge, Valdicava produced their first Brunello in 1968. They first produced a Brunello from the Madonna del Piano vineyard in 1975 but didn't sell it. The first to be bottled, labeled, and sold was the '77, and the '88 will be the next one. That vineyard was ripped up in 1978 and replanted. The '81 and '82 wines from there were used in the Rosso and the '83 in the Brunello *base.* The '85 was put in the *riserva.*

Today Abruzzese produces 46,600 bottles of wine annually. Of

THE CRUS AND VINEYARDS OF TENUTA VALDICAVA

Cru/Vineyard	Acres	Hectares	Exposure
Filai Lunghi	4.94	2	North
Imposto	2.47	1	East
Madonna del Piano	4.94	2	West
Montosoli	2.47	1	North
Poggio	7.41	3	South

these, perhaps 22,600 are Brunello and 20,000 Rosso. The balance are, as Abruzzese puts it, experimental. He plans to produce a *barrique*-aged sangiovese grosso–cabernet franc blend from some of the vines in his Madonna del Piano vineyard. And he will also do a Pinot Blanc for himself, which he won't sell.

Abruzzese ferments his Rosso for two weeks and the Brunello for three weeks. His 1985 Brunello, from the crus of Montosoli and Poggio, spent twenty months in Slavonian oak casks of 661 gallons (25 hectoliters) and twenty-two months in Slavonian oak casks of 1,321 gallons (50 hectoliters). Production of that wine totaled 30,000 bottles. Abruzzese's 1988 Rosso, from the Filai Lunghi and Imposto vineyards, spent ten months in 1,321-gallon (50-hectoliter) Slavonian oak casks. He produced 13,300 bottles. Attilio Pagli is his consulting enologist.

Abruzzese wants a balanced and harmonious wine, not a strong one; he aims for a wine that goes with food and is good to drink, not one for wine tastings. He wants character and elegance. Judging from what we have tasted under his label, he is on the right track and succeeding.

A few years ago, when Valdicava was owned by Bramante Martini, they bottled an undistinguished Brunello for Marcello Olivieri as well as for themselves. Since Vincenzo Abruzzese took over, in 1983, the wines have improved considerably. He produced a very good '83 and '85 Brunello. All those we tasted from cask in November 1990—the '86, '87, '88, and '89—showed promise, especially those from the Madonna del Piano and Poggio vineyards. Clearly, this is a Brunello producer worth watching. Brunello: Bramante Martini 0, Vincenzo Abruzzese *normale* **, Madonna del Piano ** +

Tosco Vinicola, Toscovinicola (località *Castelgiocondo, zone 3*). This *azienda* bottles a mediocre Brunello for **Riguardo** and at one time they bottled one for Spalletti as well. We don't know if Spalletti continues to market that wine. Their address and phone number are the same as that of Castelgiocondo.

Tre Cerchi. A label used by **D. A. M., Diffusione Altesino del Montalcino.**

Valdisuga (località *Val di Suga, zone 1*), *1970*. Valdisuga has 89 acres (36 hectares) of vines, planted at altitudes averaging about 985 feet (300 meters) above sea level; 67 (27) currently are in production, and 22 (9) more are scheduled to be in 1991. They have three crus: the 9.9-acre (4-hectare) Vigna del Lago, the 2.5-acre (1-hectare) Vigna Spuntali, and the 9.9-acre (4-hectare) Vigna Poderuccio.

Unusual for the Brunello zone, Valdisuga owns land in two of the three wine-growing districts. Approximately two-thirds of the estate's vineyards are in the northern district, with the remaining third in the southern section. The latter vines benefit from a marine influence. According to Valdisuga, the northern vines contribute rich flavors and delicate aromatics, while the southern fruit adds structure and body. From these vines they produce about 242,000 bottles of wine a year—130,000 bottles of Brunello and 100,000 of Rosso di Montalcino, plus 12,000 of Quercianello, a *vino novello*.

They bottled their first Brunello in 1971. In 1983, Valdisuga began bottling a Brunello from their Lago vineyard. They bottled 7,452 bottles. Unlike their other Brunellos, the Vigna del Lago spent some time in *barriques* of Alliers, Limousin, and Vosges oak.

Since 1988 they have been making a Brunello Vigna Spuntali; there are 7,000 bottles of the original vintage. They expect to make a Poderuccio Brunello from the 1990 vintage.

The Valdisuga Brunellos used to be among the zone's worst. When a new owner took over a few years ago, he brought in Vittorio Fiore as consulting enologist, and things began to improve dramatically. Then the estate went bankrupt and was bought by industrialist Lionello Marchesi. Realizing that he needed someone to look after all three of his estates—including Fattoria San Leonino in the Chianti Classico district and Tenuta Trerose in Montepulciano—Marchesi, shortly after he took over in 1989, brought in Enzo Tiezzi and Professor Rainer Zierock from Germany. Tiezzi has his own Brunello estate, **Cerrino 1ᵃ**, and the professor teaches viticulture at the enological school at St. Michelle dell'Adige.

Tiezzi is in charge of production at all three estates, and Zierock has directed the replanting at all three estates, using high-density planting. With this method they plant some 3,000 vines per acre (7,500 per hectare). Thus far they have planted 7.4 acres (3 hectares) here, plus 17.3 (7) in Montepulciano and 27.2 (11) in Castellina. In 1991 they will plant an additional 49.4 acres (20 hectares) this way. After those vines come into production, they will convert over more land, until eventually all of their vineyards will be in high-density plantings.

While we cannot recommend the Valdisuga *riserve* of '75, '77, and '78, or the *normali* of '78, '79, and '80, we can, and do, recommend their Brunellos since 1981. They produced good wines from 1981 through 1983, and a very good Brunello in 1985, especially the Riserva. Their '86 through '89 showed promise in cask. We must also admit to being impressed with their '83 single-vineyard Brunello, Vigna del Lago. Brunello: pre-1981, 0, since 1981, **

Verbena (*zone 1*), *1972*. Assunta Pascucci and Clara Brigidi Verbena own some 10 acres (4 hectares) of vines. Enologist Attilio Pagli is their consultant. Thus far they have bottled only a Rosso. We tasted three vintages of their Brunello—the '87, '88, and '89—from casks. They were all good, though the '88 is potentially very good. Brunello [*]

Vigneti Pacenti Siro di Pacenti S. e Pieri G. See **Pelagrilli, Azienda Agricola Pacenti Siro & Pieri Graz.**

Villa Tolli (*zone 2*). G. Matteucci owns the Villa a Tolli estate and some 18 acres (7.29 hectares) of brunello vines. Thus far we've tasted one wine, the '83 Riserva. While it was good, it didn't measure up to the vintage. Brunello *

Villa Banfi. See **Castello Banfi.**

Villa Niccola. Lee Iacocca, the great Capitalist Pretender, owns this estate. The wine is made and bottled for him by Tenuta Il Poggione. We don't know if he receives government loan guarantees or subsidies as he did for Chrysler. Nor do we know if he lobbies for tariffs to protect his wine from foreign competition the way he does for his company's cars. Judging from the two wines that we tasted here, the '88 Rosso and the '85 Brunello, he might need some sort of protection. The wines are good to very good. So what! There are many excellent Brunellos and Rossos around for a lot less money. Brunello ** −, Rosso *

CHAPTER 9

Carmignano

The history of Carmignano as a wine region is rooted in ancient times. The Etruscans are believed to have cultivated vines in this area in the eighth century B.C. Later Caesar gave grants of land with vineyards in Carmignano to veterans of his legions.

Francesco Datini, the successful fourteenth-century merchant and connoisseur of wines, wrote of the wine of Charmignano in his letters. He obviously held it in high esteem; he paid four times more for the Carmignano wines than for the others listed in his cellar records.

In the poem "*Bacco in Toscana,*" written in 1685, Aretine poet and noted medical doctor Francesco Redi sang the praises of Carmignano with these lines:

> *Ma se giara io prendo in mano*
> *di brilliante carmignano*
> *cosi grato in sen mi piove*
> *ch'ambrosia e nettar non invidio a Giove.*

> But if I hold a cup in hand
> of brilliant Carmignano
> so much pleasure does it bring to my heart
> that ambrosia and nectar I do not envy of Jove.

In 1716, Grand Duke Cosimo III de' Medici issued his Decreto Motu Proprio, which protected the name of Carmignano, followed by a *bando* prescribing the boundaries of the zone and establishing rules of wine production in Carmignano. Cosimo is said to have sent a gift of Carmignano wine to Queen Anne of England.

THE CARMIGNANO PRODUCTION ZONE

The Carmignano production zone covers a small area a little more than 12 miles (20 kilometers) northwest of Firenze, bor-

PRODUCTION ZONE OF CARMIGNANO

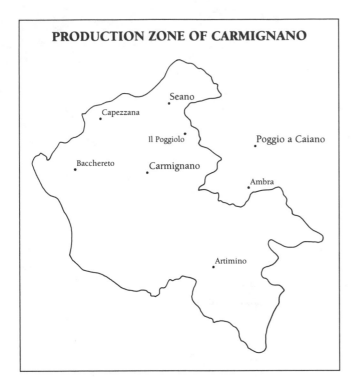

cases a year.[2] There are twelve registered growers in Carmignano, eight of whom bottle the wine and sell it under their own label.

THE CARMIGNANO *UVAGGIO*

Carmignano, like Chianti, is made from a mixture of red and white grapes: 45 to 65 percent sangiovese, 10 to 20 percent canaiolo nero, and 6 to 10 percent cabernet, or as it is better known locally, uva francesca, plus 10 to 20 percent canaiolo bianco, trebbiano toscano, and/or malvasia, and up to 5 percent of other grapes (mammolo, colorino, occhio di pernice, s. colombano, montepulciano, and/or merlot). Most of the cabernet plantings in Carmignano are cabernet sauvignon. Cabernet franc has problems ripening in this area in some vintages, producing very little fruit.

In January 1991, Carmignano was granted DOCG status. This made Carmignano the fourth Tuscan wine, and the seventh Italian wine, to be given the DOCG. The DOCG will be allowed for all wines that are still aging. This will include the exceptionally fine 1988 *riserve*. As far as we know (in January 1991), the DOCG regulations are the same as the DOC requirements.

THE REBIRTH OF CARMIGNANO

In 1932, when the boundaries for the Chianti region were set, including Carmignano in the Chianti Montalbano zone, the wines of this area began to be sold under the better-known Chianti name. This practice continued until the late 1960s, when the producers realized that their wines represented a level of quality higher than that of Chianti and therefore they would do better to sell their wine as Carmignano.

Although the wines of Carmignano had been recognized for centuries, the producers had to demonstrate to govern-

dered by Monte Albano on the southeast and the Arno and Ombrone rivers on the west. The vineyards are in the *comuni* of Carmignano and Poggio a Caiano on the western edge of the Chianti Montalbano zone. Vines are planted on the slopes of the hills at an altitude of up to 1,312 feet (400 meters) above sea level, in marly, calcerous, clayey schists and sandstone soils.

There are 262 acres (106 hectares) under vines for Carmignano.[1] Production of the red wine has been on the increase since the inauguration of DOC in 1975. From just over 10,000 cases in 1975, output had risen two and a half times by 1983, reaching 25,000 cases. Between 1986 and 1988 production increased still further, averaging 31,440

DOC REQUIREMENTS FOR CARMIGNANO

	Minimum Aging in Years		Minimum Alcohol	Maximum Yield (Gallons/Acre)
	in Cask	Total		
Normale	1	1.5[a]	12.5%	599[c]
Riserva	2	3.0[b]	12.5%	599[c]

NOTES: [a] Cannot be sold before June 1 of the second year after the harvest
[b] Aging begins September 29
[c] 56 hectoliters per hectare

ment officials the significant differences between the two in the regulated aspects of the wine's production to be granted a separate DOC. Because there was a tradition in the zone of using foreign grape varieties introduced into the area by the Medicis, the producers decided to use cabernet sauvignon to give their wines a different *uvaggio* from that used in Chianti. Conte Ugo Contini Bonacossi may have been the first to plant cabernet sauvignon in his vineyards at Tenuta di Capezzana. If any of that variety had been planted in the area previously, it was very little indeed.

Since 1975 the wines of the Carmignano zone may be labeled as either Chianti Montalbano or Carmignano. The producers generally take advantage of this situation to make a selection, using their best grapes from their best vineyards for their Carmignano.

THE OTHER WINES OF CARMIGNANO

Besides Carmignano and Chianti Montalbano, many producers in this area make Barco Reale, Vin Ruspo, and *vin santo*. Barco Reale is a younger, lighter version of Carmignano. It is made from the same grapes, but in a style meant to be drunk sooner.

Vin Ruspo is a rosé wine made from the free-run juice of the same grapes used to produce Carmignano. The must is left for a few hours in contact with the skins, just long enough to pick up a little color. This is an old, traditional wine in Carmignano made by the farmers under the old system of *mezzadria*. The *mezzadri* would secretly draw off a portion of the must from the harvested grapes for themselves before they made the wine, which would be divided with the *padrone* of the estate. This "stolen wine" was drunk while young and fresh in the spring following the harvest.

THE CHARACTER OF CARMIGNANO

Of all the DOC-DOCG wines of Toscana, those of Carmignano are possibly the most consistent. The wines are very similar to Chianti, but generally represent a higher-quality product with some refinement. They are noted for a characteristic floral aroma with suggestions of violets and irises; the cabernet frequently adds an herbaceous note.

Carmignano drinks well from its third or fourth year to its tenth or twelfth, though it can live much longer, depending on the vintage and the producer. Rating ***

WHAT THE RATINGS MEAN

****	Great, superb, truly noble
***	Exceptionally fine
**	Very good
*	A good example of its type, somewhat above average
0	Acceptable to mediocre, depending on the context; drinkable
+	Somewhat better than the star category it is put in
−	Somewhat less than the star category it is put in, except for zero where it indicates a wine or producer-wine combination that is badly made or worse
[..]	*On a producer:* Tentative evaluation based on an insufficient number of wines or based on older, out-of-date vintages, or where the wines we tasted were too difficult to fully judge to give a fair assessment of quality
	On a wine or vintage: Projection for the future. This rating is given to a vintage where we feel that we tasted an insufficient number of wines or those we tasted were too difficult to really judge to give a fair assessment of quality
(..)	Potential increase in the rating of the wine given sufficient maturity

Rating the Producers

****
Villa di Capezzana, Riserva

***
Podere Lo Locco

**
+ Fattoria Ambra
− Fattoria di Artimino, Riserva del Granduca
− Fattoria di Artimino, Riserva Villa Medicea
+ Villa di Capezzana
  Villa di Trefiano
+ Villa Il Poggiolo

*
Fattoria di Artimino
Fattoria di Artimino, Vino del Granduca
+ Fattoria di Bacchereto
+ Fattoria di Calavria

Other Carmignano Estates	Location
Azlenda Agricola Landini	Carmignano
Fattoria di Castello	Carmignano
Fattoria "La Farnete"	Comeana
Podere "L'Albanella"	Vergherto di Carmignano
Podere Le Poggiarelle	Fontanaccio di Carmignano
Podere Sasso (they own 7.5 acres [3 hectares] of vines)	Santa Cristina a Mezzana di Carmignano

VINTAGE INFORMATION AND TASTING NOTES

In general, the vintages in Carmignano are quite similar to those of Chianti, though microclimatic differences create some variances. Our personal experience with these wines is insufficient to provide a comprehensive view, but from our survey of some of the more important producers, combined with our tastings, we can offer a guide. In the case of the better producers, their wines from vintages like 1982 and 1979 should be better than our rating for the year. And we suspect that their '77, '71, and '70 would all be quite good if well stored.

THE VINTAGES TODAY

****	1988, 1985
***+	1990, 1983
***	1975
**	1982, 1979
*+	1989, 1987, 1986, 1981, 1980, 1978
*	1969
*−	1984
0	1976, 1974, 1973, 1972
?	1977, 1971, 1970

1990 [***+]

Early reports suggested a favorable vintage. Based on the three that we tasted in January 1991, and again in April 1991, we concur with those reports. The Villa di Trefiano and two Villa di Capezzanas—*normale* and Riserva—showed a lot of promise. All three wines had deep color, a lot of structure, and were full in body and extract. The Capezzana Riserva displayed tremendous potential.

1989 *+

Artimino and Capezzana didn't bottle a Carmignano this year. Based on the three wines we tasted, the wines are good, although not much more. The best ones were the very good Podere Lo Locco and the potentially very good Fattoria Ambra.

CAUTION: *Before reading these tasting notes on the wines that we tasted from barrel, please read "On Tasting Wines from Barrel: A Caveat" on page xxv.*

Fattoria Ambra 1989 (ex-vat, 4/90). Surprisingly full-bodied and fruity(!), light finish. *(*)

Podere Lo Locco 1989 (ex-cask, 4/90). Clean, fresh cherrylike fruit; a little dry, openly fruity. **

Villa Il Poggiolo 1989 (ex-cask, 4/90). This one might not be bottled. Difficult to taste, high acidity, low fruit. ?

1988 ****

The wet spring delayed the flowering. The summer was warm and dry. In early September much-needed rain fell. The harvest was early. Ugo Bonacossi counts this as among the greatest vintages of all. Based on the eight wines we've tasted from seven producers we concur. Thus far the top wines, all tasted from barrel, were the Podere Lo Locco and the Villa di Capezzana Riserva, followed by the Fattoria Ambra and Villa Il Poggiolo. The Fattoria di Bacchereto and Villa di Capezzana were very good indeed, and we'd be remiss if we didn't mention Fattoria di Artimino and Villa di Trefiano.

CAUTION: *Before reading these tasting notes on the wines that we tasted from barrel, please read "On Tasting Wines from Barrel: A Caveat" on page xxv.*

Fattoria Ambra 1988 (ex-vat, 4/90). Deep purple; rich in extract and concentration, packed with flavor, so rich it seems sweet. **(*)

Fattoria di Artimino 1988 (ex-cask, 4/90). Fairly full-bodied, lively acidity, richly concentrated, cherrylike notes, tart, dry aftertaste. *(*)

Fattoria di Bacchereto 1988 (ex-cask, 4/90). Openly grapey, fruity and sweet, rich and chewy with tannin and fruit. **+

Podere Lo Locco 1988 (ex-cask, 4/90). Perfumed scent, suggestive of spice, strawberries and raspberries; great concentration and weight; loads of class and real character, impressive. ***(+)

Villa di Capezzana 1988 (ex-cask, 4/90). Rich fruit on entry then tight, with some firmness, moderate tannin, fruit quite evident from the entry through the midpalate and all the way back. **+

Villa di Capezzana 1988 Riserva (*ex-cask, 4/90, estimated 50,000 bottles*). Really closed on the nose with hints of ripe fruit; a rich mouthful of flavor and tannin, at this stage rather tight and firm but with all the components, this should make a splendid bottle. ***?

Villa di Trefiano 1988 (*ex-cask, 4/90*). Tight, firm and tannic, chewy, sense of sweetness from ripe, rich fruit; somewhat difficult to fully assess. **?

Villa Il Poggiolo 1988 (*ex-cask, 4/90*). Deep color; mouth-filling, chewy and tannic, rich and intense with character; very good indeed. **(*)

1987 * +

Calavria rates this as one of the worst vintages in quality. The best wines of the eight that we've tasted are the Podere Lo Locco 1987 and Villa di Trefiano, followed by Fattoria Ambra *normale* and Riserva, and then Fattoria di Calavria and Villa Il Poggiolo.

> **CAUTION:** *Before reading these tasting notes on the wines that we tasted from barrel, please read "On Tasting Wines from Barrel: A Caveat" on page xxv.*

Fattoria Ambra 1987 (*4/90*). Nice nose, fruit and floral components; open fruit, moderate tannin, a tad short, and a little dry at the end. * +

Fattoria Ambra 1987 Riserva (*4/90, 2,750 bottles*). Herbaceous, raspberry aroma; tasty, moderate tannin, surprisingly fruity, short, dry and tannic. * +

Fattoria di Artimino 1987 (*ex-cask, 4/90*). Spicy, dried cherry aroma, herbaceous component; fairly tannic, fruit seems a little low. ?

Fattoria di Bacchereto 1987 (*4/90*). A little soapy(!), no it wasn't the glass, some fruit; short, dry aftertaste.

Fattoria di Calavria 1987 (*4/90*). Fresh kirschlike aroma with hints of melon and grapefruit(!); some sweetness on entry, then a little tight and unbalanced, open, simple, ready, rather short with a somewhat lingering sweetness. *

Podere Lo Locco 1987 (*4/90*). Light but delicate aroma displays fleeting impressions, kirschlike fruit; flavorful with cassis and berry components; well balanced, quite nice. **

Villa di Trefiano 1987 (*ex-vat, 4/90*). Nice fruit, open and forward, light finish. **

Villa Il Poggiolo 1987 (*ex-cask, 4/90*). Light nose, fairly nice fruit; light tannin, light-bodied, short, dry aftertaste. *

1986 * +

There were heavy rains in August, when some 2 inches (51 millimeters) fell. The harvest began on September 25 and ended on October 17. Ambra rates the year as excellent. Antonio Rossi gave it two stars out of four. We have tasted eight wines from six producers. The wines, while good, are not much more. The best was Villa di Capezzana, followed closely by Fattoria Ambra Riserva and Fattoria di Baccereto Le Vigne di Santuaria, and then Fattoria di Baccereto, Podere Lo Locco, and Villa Il Poggiolo. The Fattoria di Artimino was good as well.

Fattoria Ambra 1986 (*10/90, 7,000 bottles*). Woodsy, mushroom aroma; fruity, soft, precocious, very ready, vague off note intrudes. *

Fattoria Ambra 1986 Riserva (*twice, 10/90, 2,850 bottles*). Woodsy aroma; a little firmer and more tannic than the *normale*, needs perhaps two or three more years. *(*) *Bottle of 4/90:* Fairly delicate, herbal, floral, fruity bouquet; some tannin, forward flavors, short finish is a tad dry. ** —

Fattoria di Artimino 1986 (*3 times, 4/90*). Small-scale, fairly nice fruit, open and soft, some tannin. *

Fattoria di Bacchereto 1986 (*4/89*). Nice nose, fresh, berrylike, some herbaceousness; nice fruit on the palate, fairly soft, vague raisin note. * +

Fattoria di Bacchereto 1986 Le Vigne di Santuaria (*twice, 4/90*). Tight nose; nice fruit on the palate, some tannin, flavorful, of ripe fruit; ready now. ** —

Podere Lo Locco 1986 (*4/89*). Fragrant aroma, suggestive of spice; tasty at first, then tight and hard. * +

Villa di Capezzana 1986 (*3 times, 1/91*). Light fruit, berry, herbal aroma; very soft and open, sweet and supple; quite ready, light tannin at the end, could improve. ** +

Villa Il Poggiolo 1986 (*3 times, 6/90*). Herbaceous background adds complexity to the nose without overpowering the fruit component; soft, open and fruity with some tannin, a little light, ready now, short aftertaste. **

1985 * * * *

Ambra said the vintage was exceptional. Calavria rates this vintage as one of the best, as does Ugo Bonacossi. Antonio Rossi calls it a four-star vintage (out of four), the best. Based on a baker's dozen wines from eight producers, we find the vintage very good indeed, if not quite the equal of 1988. The star is the Villa di Capezzana Riserva, followed closely by Podere Lo Locco. Next come the excellent Villa Il Poggiolo Riserva Villa di Canida, then Fattoria Ambra Riserva and Villa di Capezzana *normale*. We can also recommend Fattoria di Artimino Riserva del Granduca, Fattoria di Bacchereto, Fattoria di Calavria, Villa di Trefiano, and Villa Il Poggiolo *normale* and Riserva.

Fattoria Ambra 1985 (*10/90, 8,200 bottles*). Lovely nose, vanilla and floral aroma, ripe fruit; firm, a lot of structure, and a lot of fruit and concentration; should age very well, give it two or three more years. **(+)

Fattoria Ambra 1985 Riserva (*twice, 10/90, 2,850 bottles*). Reticent aroma, very little at first, you have to work for it, then floral, berry and vanilla notes come out; a mouthful of tannin, some sense of ripe fruit, needs a few years yet. **(*−) *Bottle of 4/90:* Herbaceous, berry aroma; packed with fruit and tannin, the sensation of sweet, rich, ripe fruit; young with evident potential, could use more length. ** +

Fattoria di Artimino 1985 (*twice, 4/89*). Berrylike aroma; vanillalike flavor, fruity yet dry, tight; this wine showed better when tasted from cask in April 1987. This bottle *?

Fattoria di Artimino 1985 Riserva del Granduca (*4/90*). Aroma of dried berries and tobacco, cherry notes; rather nice fruit, still some tannin to soften, chewy. **

Fattoria di Bacchereto 1985 (*twice, 11/90*). Open cherry, tobacco aroma; rich, open and fruity, coming ready though could use a little more time for the light to moderate tannins to soften; well balanced. ** −

Fattoria di Calavria 1985 (*3 times, 4/90*). Woodsy aroma, hints of dried fruit and leather, light herbaceous backnote; rich, mouthful of flavor, some tannin to soften, sense of sweetness, only flaw is that the fruit seems older than its years, dry, chewy finish. *(*)

Podere Lo Locco 1985 (*4/90*). Rather closed nose, hints of tobacco and cherries; balanced, flavors of cherries and kirsch, stylish, real class; quite young. ***, perhaps ***(+)

Villa di Capezzana 1985 (*5 times, 6/90*). A little tight and closed(!), richly fruited, has character. ** + *Bottle of 4/89:* Nose still rather closed; open, forward flavors on entry which quickly tightens up, richness and flavor quite evident. ** +

Villa di Capezzana 1985 Riserva (*6 times, 1/91, 128,876 bottles*). This was the largest production of *riserva* to date. This isn't surprising considering the quality. Real class evident here, has everything going for it, richness, weight and concentration, flavor and extract, backbone and structure, length and style. ***(*)

Villa di Trefiano 1985 (*twice, 6/90*). Light cabernet background, open fruit, herbal and floral components; flavorful, well balanced, still some tannin to soften. ** +

Villa Il Poggiolo 1985 (*4/89*). Berry and vanilla aroma; rich fruit, real flavor, a bit firm and a tad bitter at the end. ** −

Villa Il Poggiolo 1985 Riserva (*3 times, 10/90*). Lovely nose of flowers, vanilla and berries; nice mouth feel, warm and harmonious, still young but richness makes it appealing. **(*) *Bottle of 4/90:* Leather, tobacco, toasty aroma; chewy tannins, good concen-

tration of fruit, fairly tannic, rather dry finish of moderate length, very young. **

Villa Il Poggiolo 1985 Riserva Villa di Canida (*4/90*). Openly fruity aroma; sweet, rich and concentrated, still young, more flavor and extract than the regular *riserva;* real quality. ***

1984 * −

A difficult year that required careful selection; very little *riserva* was produced. Ambra said it was a good vintage. Calavria rates this as one of the worst vintages in quality. Antonio Rossi rates it at two stars out of four. We have tasted six wines, five of which were at least good. The best one was Villa di Capezzana *normale,* followed by Fattoria di Artimino Vino del Granduca, Fattoria di Bacchereto, Podere Lo Locco, and Villa Il Poggiolo.

Fattoria Ambra 1984 (*3 times, 11/87, 8,690 bottles*). Unbalanced, high acid, low fruit, bitter, not a success. *Bottle of 10/87:* Dank nose, some fruit; better in the mouth, fairly nice fruit, soft and ready. * − *Bottle of 4/87:* Floral, fruit aroma; a lot of nice fruit, some tannin; for early drinking. ** −

Fattoria di Artimino 1984 Vino del Granduca (*4/87*). Floral, cherry aroma; fairly full-flavored, perhaps a tad too much tannin for the fruit but should make a nice glass in short order. *

Fattoria di Bacchereto 1984 (*4/89*). Light to medium red, tobacco, floral aroma; soft center, a bit unbalanced but attractive and for early drinking. *

Podere Lo Locco 1984 (*4/87*). Slight nose; chocolate notes in the mouth with nice fruit, perhaps a tad too much tannin for the fruit but, in all, an attractive glass of wine, finish is rather tannic. *(+)

Villa di Capezzana 1984 (*11 times, 11/91*). Floral, berry, herbal aroma; soft, open, attractive flavors, clean fruit, very soft, ready now, short, dry aftertaste. ** − *Ex-vat, 5/85:* Fresh, fruity aroma; has a surprising amount of fruit and body for the vintage; light aftertaste. *(*)

Villa Il Poggiolo 1984 (*twice, 4/90*). Light color, herbaceousness and cassis aroma carry through in the mouth, fruity, some tannin; a lightweight, drinkable wine. *

1983 *** +

Very good; only 1985 and 1988 were better in the decade. Il Poggiolo and Artimino rate it as the best vintage of all. Ambra sees it as excellent. Ugo Bonacossi places it among the best. Antonio Rossi, who rated the vintages between 1970 and 1986, picks this, at four stars out of four, as one of the three best. The best wine of the dozen that we tasted was the excellent Villa di Capezzana Riserva, followed by Villa Il Poggiolo, and then Villa di Trefiano Riserva, Villa di

Capezzana *normale,* and Fattoria Ambra. The Fattoria di Artimino Vino del Granduca, Riserva del Granduca, and Riserva Villa Medicea, along with the Podere Lo Locco, were very good. Fattoria di Bacchereto and Fattoria di Calavria were good as well.

Fattoria Ambra 1983 (4/87, 7,200 bottles). Lovely perfumed bouquet suggestive of flowers; flavorful and attractive, balanced and young. **(+)

Fattoria di Artimino 1983 Riserva del Granduca (4/87). Herbaceous cabernet aroma combines with cherries; moderate tannin with sufficient fruit to age, lacks some style, finish seems a little dull. * –

Fattoria di Artimino 1983 Riserva Villa Medicea (twice, 4/90). Herbal, spicy aroma displays a cassis component; rich, sweet and concentrated, chewy tannins, somewhat short, dry finish, chocolate notes. **

Fattoria di Artimino 1983 Vino del Granduca (4/87). Reticent aroma; rather tannic with evident fruit, firm, tannic aftertaste. *(+)

Fattoria di Bacchereto 1983 (4/87). Floral, mineral aroma; interesting flavor, good structure, light aftertaste. * +

Fattoria di Calavria 1983 (4/87). Lightish red color; mineral notes define the aroma; fairly nice fruit yet seems a little coarse, on the young side. *

Podere Lo Locco 1983 (4/90). Leather, dried fruit aroma; still quite tannic and dry with an evident sense of fruit; lacks the class and balance of the '85. **

Villa di Capezzana 1983 (4 times, 9/88). Nuts and flowers, dried and fresh fruit aroma, vaguely herbaceous backnote; still fairly tannic, rich and concentrated; needs more age; finishes with a slight hardness. **+ (*** –)

Villa di Capezzana 1983 Riserva (14 times, 11/91, 97,200 bottles). Perfumed bouquet displays toasty, woodsy, berry and mushroom components; refined with sweetness of ripe fruit, tannin beginning to smooth out, still it needs more age, packed with flavor and concentration; this is real class. *** +

Villa di Trefiano 1983 (4/87). Floral and fruity aroma, cherrylike; flavorful, has a fair amount of tannin to lose, young. **(*)

Villa di Trefiano 1983 Riserva (4/87, 7,558 bottles). Light aroma seems to be closed up, yet hints of flowers and cherries and some cabernet fruit quite evident; richly flavored with tannin to shed and a softness in the center that makes it attractive, fairly long finish, some elegance. **(* –)

Villa Il Poggiolo 1983 (twice, 4/90). Lovely perfumed bouquet, light herbal note; fairly tannic with the sense of sweet, ripe fruit, well balanced; young but attractive now, wait! ***

1982 **

Very good, though below 1983 in quality. Calavria rates this vintage as one of the best of all. For Antonio Rossi it was a three-star (out of four) year. The best wine was the Villa di Capezzana Riserva, then Fattoria di Artimino Riserva del Granduca and Riserva Villa Medicea, Fattoria di Calavria, and Tenuta di Capezzana.

Fattoria di Artimino 1982 Riserva del Granduca (twice, 4/87). Reticent aroma; loads of flavor, with a richness of fruit in the center; needs a few more years yet but promises well. *(*)

Fattoria di Artimino 1982 Riserva Villa Medicea (3 times, 4/90, 12,325 bottles). Tobacco, strawberry aroma; seems a little dry with some tannin to soften, fruit quite evident, a little short and dry at the end with the tannin building; needs age. *(*)

Fattoria di Bacchereto 1982 (twice, 5/85). Aroma is closed; light to moderate tannin, fruity, a short, tannic finish. (*)

Fattoria di Calavria 1982 (twice, 4/87). Nice nose; rich with a sweet impression, forward flavors; on simple side but enjoyable. ** –

Tenuta di Capezzana 1982 (7 times, 4/90). Open, fruity aroma with evident cabernet herbaceousness; well structured, a lot of flavor, quite ready now, a slightly bitter note evident at the end. **

Villa di Capezzana 1982 Riserva (4 times, 4/90, 20,750 bottles). Dried fruit and leather aroma; soft under some tannin, lighter in body and with less intensity of flavor than the '83; it's doubtful that it'll age as well, still a nice glass. *** –

1981 * +

Elegant wines for early drinking. They are holding well. Antonio Rossi sees it as a three-star (out of four) vintage. The Villa di Capezzana Riserva has given us a lot of pleasure over the past five or six years. The wines aren't big, but they are elegant. The Villa Il Poggiolo Riserva and Tenuta di Capezzana are very good, and Fattoria di Artimino Riserva del Granduca and Fattoria di Bacchereto are good.

Fattoria di Artimino 1981 Riserva del Granduca (4/87). Some oxidation apparent, which we suspect is more the bottle than the wine, flavor and interest quite apparent. *

Fattoria di Bacchereto 1981 (5/85). Cherry aroma with floral notes; lightly tannic, fruity, but a bit simple, and short. *

Tenuta di Capezzana 1981 (5/85). Fruity, a bit simple, some oak, soft and fruity. ** –

Villa di Capezzana 1981 Riserva (10 times, 2/89, 45,570 bottles). Floral, fruity aroma displays elegance and delicacy; well balanced and stylish, flavorful and harmonious, real class here, long finish, very ready. ***

Villa Il Poggiolo 1981 Riserva (twice, 5/85). Floral, berrylike aroma with a touch of oak; medium-bodied, firm acidity, some tannin, flavorful, berrylike fruit, finishes on a tannic note. **(+)

1 9 8 0 * +

Antonio Rossi gave it three out of four stars. Good wines, though not topflight. Our favorite was the Villa di Trefiano Riserva, followed by Fattoria di Artimino Riserva del Granduca, and then Villa Il Poggiolo Riserva and Tenuta di Capezzana.

Fattoria di Artimino 1980 Riserva del Granduca (*twice, 4/85*). Fragrant aroma; quite tannic, but the fruit is evident beneath and is sweet. *(*)

Fattoria di Bacchereto 1980 (*twice, 5/85*). Rich cherrylike aroma with an herbaceous backnote; tannin up front, seems a bit shallow, tannic finish.

Tenuta di Capezzana 1980 (*3 times, 9/86*). Fruit beginning to fade, but still tasty and with interest. ** *Bottle of 9/83:* Somewhat reticent aroma with a vague cherrylike note; firm, some tannin to shed, somewhat astringent, flavorful though still a bit young; in all, a nice bottle. *(*)

Villa di Trefiano 1980 Riserva (*5/86, 7,450 bottles*). Intense aroma combines ripe fruit in the front with cabernet herbaceousness in the background, hints of black cherries and berries add to the complexity; light to moderate tannin, well balanced, still a little young yet its character is evident. **(*)

Villa Il Poggiolo 1980 Riserva (*4 times, 4/87*). Nice nose; soft and fruity, coming ready, some firmness at the end. **

1 9 7 9 **

A topflight vintage, one of the best. Calavria rates this as one of the best vintages in quality, as does Ugo Bonacossi. Antonio Rossi puts it at three stars out of four, one step lower. Once again the Villa di Capezzana Riserva came out on top. The Villa Il Poggiolo Riserva, Villa di Trefiano Riserva, and Tenuta di Capezzana were very good, and the Fattoria di Bacchereto good.

Fattoria di Bacchereto 1979 (*5/85*). Small aroma but nice; tannic entry, fruit follows, give it two or three years. *(*)

Tenuta di Capezzana 1979 (*twice, 5/83*). Moderately rich aroma with notes of tobacco, tea and chocolate, and hints of cherries in the back; tasty, light tannin, well made; needs two years or so though it can be enjoyed now. **(*)

Villa di Capezzana 1979 Riserva (*7 times, 11/91, 40,850 bottles*). Lovely perfumed scent; soft and smooth, velvety, near its peak, very long. *** *Bottle of 6/89:* Lovely bouquet, soft, smooth and round, tasty and harmonious, at its peak. ***

Villa di Trefiano 1979 Riserva (*5/85, 7,045 bottles*). Fruity aroma with flowers and cabernet character; well balanced, moderate tannin, flavorful; still a bit young. **(+)

Villa Il Poggiolo 1979 Riserva (*7 times, 4/87*). Fragrant, fruity aroma; well knit, on the light side with a lot of nice fruit flavors; ready now yet can still improve. ** +

1 9 7 8 * +

A good vintage. Antonio Rossi gives it two stars out of four. The Villa di Capezzana Riserva was excellent, and the Tenuta di Capezzana and Tenuta di Capezzana Riserva, which is supposed to be the same exact wine as the Villa Riserva, were very good.

Tenta di Capezzana 1978 (*1/84*). Aroma has floral and fruity aspects; some acidity, fruity, a bit light but tasty, somewhat simple. * +

Tenuta di Capezzana 1978 Riserva (*twice, 5/83*). Some age evident on aroma; mellow, still has tannin to shed, flavorful, a nice bottle; give it two or three years. **(+)

Villa di Capezzana 1978 Riserva (*4 times, 12/85*). Rich, complex aroma with evident cabernet character; a lot of flavor and character, well knit, tasty and long. ***

1 9 7 7 ?

Elegant wines, similar to the '81s. Antonio Rossi rates it three stars out of four. The only one we've tasted in the past decade—the Tenuta di Capezzana—was bad, the bottle that is.

Tenuta di Capezzana 1977 (*4/80*). Some oxidation apparent; perhaps a bad bottle.

1 9 7 6 0

Very poor; some producers didn't bottle a Carmignano. Ugo Bonacossi rates it with 1966 as the worst in modern times. Antonio Rossi calls it a one-star (out of four) vintage, and along with 1973, one of the two worst between 1970 and 1986.

1 9 7 5 ***

An outstanding year, the best in modern times. Ugo Bonacossi said it was a splendid vintage. Antonio Rossi rates it four stars out of four, and one of the three best between 1970 and 1986. The Villa di Capezzana Riserva showed tremendous potential.

Tenuta di Capezzana 1975 Riserva (*3 times, 9/83*). Berrylike fruit on aroma; still has a fair amount of tannin, but has the fruit beneath to support it, notes of dried apricots and blueberries on this rich mouthful of fruit. **

Villa di Capezzana 1975 Riserva (*3 times, 1/91, 61,200 bottles*). The spice and berries on the bouquet carry through on the palate, well balanced, leathery, real sense of sweetness; lovely now, will certainly last and could well improve too. *** + *Bottle of 5/85:* Beautiful floral bouquet; already nice to drink though with room for further improvement, still has some tannin to shed, well knit, richly flavored, finely honed, long finish—a classic wine. ***(*)

1974 0

Average wines that are beginning to show age. Antonio Rossi rated it two stars out of four.

Villa di Capezzana 1974 Riserva (*4/80*). Tarry notes on aroma and a touch of oxidation, but the fruit is there; well structured, still has tannin; in all, good quality though somewhat off. ** −

1973 0

Rather light-bodied wines of average quality. Antonio Rossi rated it one star out of four, making it, along with 1976, the worst between 1970 and 1986.

1972 0

Generally very poor, though some exceptions can be found. Antonio Rossi, surprisingly, rated it three stars out of four.

1971 ?

Very good. Antonio Rossi rated it three stars out of four.

1970 ?

Good. Antonio Rossi rated it as a three-star year out of a maximum of four.

1969 *

Excellent. Ugo Bonacossi rates it, along with 1961, as among the decade's two best vintages. The best of the few that we've tasted were the Villa Il Poggiolo *normale,* Villa di Capezzana Riserva, and Villa Il Poggiolo Riserva. We suggest, if you have any, to drink them up.

Villa di Capezzana 1969 Riserva (*twice, 1/91, 21,600 each of bottles and half bottles*). Lovely scented, perfumed bouquet, hints of mint and flowers; soft, yet with plenty of life left, real sense of sweetness, very long; has a lot of quality and a lot of class. *** +

Villa Il Poggiolo 1969 (*7/82*). Rich, intense bouquet, thick and full, with heaps of flavor. ** +

Villa Il Poggiolo 1969 Riserva (*4/90*). Beautiful brick, garnet robe with orange reflection; some oxidation, and a tad dry yet flavor and interest remain, starting to dry out. *

OLDER VINTAGES

Ugo Bonacossi also rates 1961, 1941, 1937, and 1930 as being among the best vintages.

Villa di Capezzana 1961 Chianti (*9/86*). This wine was decanted 30 minutes prior to drinking. Rich and intensely concentrated bouquet, superb balance, smooth and velvety texture, leather nuance, still fresh. ****

Villa di Capezzana 1959 Chianti Stravecchio (*3 times, 1/91*). Aroma is slightly like seaweed, with leather and dried fruit nuances; soft, very ready, as good as it will be, low acidity, lovely flavor; drink up. *** − *Bottle of 10/87:* Fading, coffee and chocolate aroma, loads of flavor remains though it is past its best, a little dry at the end with a vague sweetness as well. ** +

Villa di Capezzana 1939 Chianti Very Old Riserva (*5/85*). Onionskin, woodsy, vaguely floral bouquet suggests autumn leaves; still has life left, body and flavor, though drying out, shows no signs of decay. For its stamina **

Villa di Capezzana 1937 Very Old Riserva (*twice, 5/86*). Orange, brick robe, yellow reflections, rich, chocolate aroma, vaguely floral with a trace of oxidation beginning to set in, starting to turn dry on the palate, some tannin remains, flavorful, touch of acid at the end, just past its best but very much alive. *** − *The same bottle tasted 12 hours later:* Still good with nice flavor, the oxidation is apparent but not really intrusive. ** + *Bottle of 5/85:* Onionskin, moldy—over the hill.

Villa di Capezzana 1931 Riserva (*1/91*). Garnet, orange robe; light, fruit bouquet, mintlike notes; soft entry, some acidity, very drinkable, delicate, fragile, a little dry yet a lot of flavor interest; good quality; could last. ** +

Villa di Capezzana 1930 (*twice, 5/86*). Recorked in 1966. Tawny, orange robe, though oxidized the aroma is still attractive with lovely nuances and complexity, sweet and soft like a well-aged gentleman, fragile yet with some firmness of character, a little tired but still kicking. *** *Twelve hours later:* Faded some more but still holding. ** + *Bottle of 5/85:* Onionskin, a lovely floral bouquet with delicacy, sweet and gentle, soft and velvety, elegant, a touch of tannin, long finish, a bit tired but still very, very good. **** −

Villa di Capezzana 1925 (*9/86*). Garnet, brick robe, still has a lot of fruit, which is evident on the nose and palate along with suggestions of mushrooms and a touch of volatile acidity, almost sweet on the palate, a lot of character and flavor, has held up very well indeed. ***

CARMIGNANO PRODUCERS

Fattoria Ambra (*Carmignano*), *1953*. Ludovica Romei Rigoli owns 14.8 acres (6 hectares) of vines planted at 328 to 492 feet (100 to 150 meters) above sea level in *alberese* and *calcare* soil. They have a south to southeast exposure. The 7.4-acre (3-hectare) Santa Cristina in Pilli vineyard is used to produce Carmignano, both the *normale* and the *riserva,* and Barco Reale. Within two years they should have another 7.4 acres (3 hectares) of vines in production.

Their Carmignano is made from 75 percent sangiovese, 15 percent cabernet sauvignon, and 10 percent canaiolo and colorino. They average 2.2 tons per acre (50 quintali per hectare) for sangiovese, 2 (45) for canaiolo nero, 1.3 (30) for cabernet sauvignon, and 1.6 (35) for colorino. Their vineyard composition is 75 percent sangiovese, 8 percent canaiolo nero, 15 percent cabernet sauvignon, and 2 percent colorino.

They bottled their first Carmignano in 1975. Today they average some 10,000 to 15,000 bottles of Carmignano a year—2,666 bottles of the partially *barrique*-aged Carmignano *riserva* and 8,000 to 12,000 bottles of Carmignano—and 5,333 bottles of Barco Reale a year. Of the three *riserve* that we tasted, they produced more than the reported 2,666 bottles: '85, 2,850; '86, 2,850; and '87, 2,750 bottles. They also produce a *bianco*.

They ferment their Carmignano for fifteen to twenty-five days on the skins. Their Carmignano is aged one year in tank and the same of bottle, and their *riserva* is given an additional year in oak casks. Some 30 to 40 percent of the wine for their *riserva* is aged in *barriques* for two years. Their *normale* Carmignano is aged for two years, one in oak casks. And Barco Reale is given one year of age, plus seven months in oak.

The first wine that we tasted from Ambra was their very good '83. And their Carmignanos have been good in every vintage since, their '85 Riserva being, perhaps, their best wine to date. Carmignano ** +

Fattoria di Artimino (*Carmignano*, localitá *Artimino*), *1435*. The beautiful Villa Reale La Ferdinanda or, as it is often called, Villa dei Cento Camini, the villa of a hundred chimneys, built by Ferdinando de' Medici in 1587, is located on the Artimino estate. Artimino also has a hotel, the Paggeria, which was built in about 1596. The hotel restaurant, Biagio Pignatta, serves typical Tuscan specialties.

The wines of Artimino were praised by Francesco Redi, the Medici family's court physician:

> *Ma di quel che sì puretto*
> *si vendemmia in Artimino*
> *vo' trincarne più di un tino*

> Of the wine so pure,
> that is made in Artimino,
> I want to drink more than one full vat.

This 1,810-acre (732-hectare) estate has 297 acres (120 hectares) of vines planted on the hillsides at altitudes ranging from 328 to 984 feet (100 to 300 meters) above sea level. New and future plantings will increase their production of Carmignano. In 1987 they reported an average annual production of 44,440 cases of wine, and surprisingly, in 1990, they reported a considerably lower average of 28,333 cases! This breaks down as 7,500 cases of Carmignano, 4,167 of Vin Ruspo, 8,333 of Chianti, and 8,333 of other wines.

They produce three Carmignanos, a *normale* and two *riserve*: Riserva del Granduca and Riserva Villa Medicea. They produced 12,325 bottles of Riserva Villa Medicea in 1982 and 19,125 bottles in 1983. The 1982 was made from a blend of 58 percent sangiovese from the Valiezzi vineyard, 15 percent canaiolo from Il Barco, 10 percent cabernet sauvignon from Il Querceto, 10 percent trebbiano and malvasia from Il Casotto, 7 percent mammolo, occhio de pernice, and montepulciano from Poggilarca. The must was fermented in 2,640-gallon (100-hectoliter) oak casks. And the resultant wine was aged for two to three years in oak.

They also produce a Rosso dei Comignali from 90 percent canaiolo and 10 percent sangiovese, a Rosso di Artimino from sangiovese, cabernet sauvignon, and montepulciano d'abruzzo grapes and a Chianti Montalbano, plus the usual Vinruspo, Barco Reale, *vin santo,* and a Novello San Leonardo, as well as some white wines. Their Carmignano is aged two to three years in oak casks; the Chianti Montalbano, for six months, and their Rosso, for six to eight months. Artimino round out their line of wines with two styles of Artimino *spumanti,* which they don't produce but buy from others.

The '80, '82, and '85 Riservas del Granduca were all quite good, as were the '82 and '83 Riservas Villa Medicea. Carmignano: *, Riserva del Granduca and Riserva Villa Medicea ** −, Vino del Granduca *

Fattoria di Bacchereto (*Carmignano,* localitá *Bacchereto*), *1925*. The Bacchereto farm has an annual production of 93,000 bottles of wine, all from their own grapes. They make 38.6 acres (15.6) hectares of vines planted at altitudes ranging from 656 to 984 feet (200 to 300 meters) above sea level. Their Carmignano is made from a blend of 60 percent sangiovese, 15 percent canaiolo nero, 10 percent cabernet sauvignon, 10 percent trebbiano toscano and malvasia, plus 5 percent mammolo, san colombano, and occhio di pernice. The *uvaggio* for their Chianti Montalbano is 60 percent sangiovese, 25 percent canaiolo nero, and 15 percent trebbiano toscano, malvasia, and occhio di pernice.

They bottled a single-vineyard Carmignano, Le Vigne di Santuaria, from the 1986 vintage, which was quite good. The best Carmignano we've tasted from Bacchereto was their very good '85, and the '88 tasted from cask was very good as well. Carmignano * +

Fattoria di Calavria (*Comeana di Carmignano*). Conti Michon Pecori put his first Carmignano in bottle in 1978. Pecori has 12.5 acres (5 hectares) of vines, 2.5 (1) devoted to the production of Carmignano. The balance is used for Chianti and *bianco*. From these vines they produce some 25,000 bottles of wine a year, of which 6,000 to 7,000 are Carmignano. We especially liked their '82 and '85. Carmignano * +

CRUS AND VINEYARDS OF FATTORIA DI BACCHERETO

Cru/Vineyard	Acres	Hectares	Used for
Bosco del Martini	12.4	5.0	Carmignano, Barco Reale, Vin Ruspo, *vin santo*
Santuaria	3.7	1.5	Chianti Montalbano
Vigna Sparse	14.8	6.0	Barco Reale
Vigna Vecchio	6.2	2.5	Chianti Montalbano

Podere Lo Locco, Azienda Agricola Pratesi Iolandi (*Seano, Carmignano*), *1828*. Iolanda, Giampiero, and Lorenzo Pratesi produce three wines: Carmignano, Vin Ruspo, and a *vin santo* from their 1.7 acres (0.7 hectare) of grapes. Their vines can, at a yield of 599 gallons per acre (56 hectoliters per hectare), produce 5,227 bottles of wine annually. Their actual annual production averages 2,930 to 3,930 bottles; this includes 2,000 to 3,000 bottles of Carmignano, 900 of Vin Ruspo, and 30 of *vin santo*. The *cantina* is, as you might expect, very small, with a few ovals, a few demijohns, and a few fiberglass vats. They produced their first Carmignano in 1983; it was very good, as are their '85, '87, '88, and '89. Only their '86 disappointed, although it is a good wine. Lo Locco's '84 is a good Carmignano as well. Carmignano ***

Tenuta di Capezzana (*Seano, Carmignano*). Capezzana traces its name to a Roman legionnaire, Capitus, who received a land grant in Carmignano from Julius Caesar in about 60 or 50 B.C. Wine is believed to have been produced at Capezzana since at least that time, if not earlier.

Wine is known to have been produced here during the time of Longobard rule, "in the twenty-first year of [Charlemagne's] reign," when his son Pepin was king of the Longobards and lord of northern Italy. A parchment (now in the archives of the city of Firenze) that was found on the Capezzana estate records an agreement made on December 16, 804 between Dardano, priest of the church of San Pietro in the region called Capezzana ("... *ecclesie in loco qui dicitur Capetiana* ..."), and Martino, son of Johannis, in which Martino gives the priest a lease on the buildings and church land with forests, gardens, vineyards, and olive groves for an annual payment in services and goods including half the olive harvest and half of the wine produced ("... *ecclesie sancti Petri exinde per singulos annus censum reddere deveatis vino et oliva medietate....*").

The Medicis built the villa in the sixteenth century. The property passed through many hands until it was purchased by the Contini Bonacossi family from Baroness Rothschild Franchetti.

The 209 acres (84.64 hectares) of vineyards on the estate are planted at altitudes ranging from 492 to 820 feet (150 to 250 meters) above sea level. Of these, 138 acres (55.65 hectares) are planted for Carmignano and Barco Reale, another 48 acres (19.48 hectares) for Chianti Montalbano, and 23.5 (9.51) for other wines. Their 7.4-acre (3-hectare) Ghiaie della Furba vineyard is planted in cabernet and merlot vines. The soil in this vineyard is alluvial with a fair amount of pebbles. The soils of the vineyards used for Carmignano and Chianti are clay schists and limestone, medium heavy and rich in chalk. Most of the vineyards face southeast or east, with a few, planted in cabernet, having a cooler aspect.

Their new vineyards are planted with greater plant density, 2,226 plants per acre (5,500 per hectare) as compared to 1,214 (3,000) in the older vineyards. Their Santa Valentina vineyard has been planted this way, mostly with sangiovese. They have also planted experimental plots of syrah and zinfandel.

Yields range from 267 to 321 gallons per acre (25 to 30 hectoliters per hectare) for cabernet sauvignon, 427 to 481 (40 to 45) for sangiovese, 534 to 641 (50 to 60) for chardonnay, and 641 to 855 (60 to 80) for trebbiano. By wine, yields average 427 gallons/acre (40 hectoliters/hectare) for Carmignano and Ghiaie, and 534 (50) for Barco Reale and Chianti Montalbano.

This is truly a family operation. Ugo Bonacossi's son Vittorio makes the wine. Daughter Beatrice handles the United States market. And son Filippo manages the vineyards. The gentle and refined Lisa, Ugo's wife, manages the family and household, and makes their many guests feel at home.

VINEYARDS/CRUS OF TENUTA DI CAPEZZANA

USED FOR VILLA DI CAPEZZANA RISERVA		
Vineyard	Acres	Hectares
Baci	3.78	1.5300
Cerreto	9.20	3.7240
Cevoli	7.87	3.1850
Fornace	4.51	1.8250
Isola	3.74	1.5130
Lo Locco	6.73	2.7230
S. Alessandro	8.01	3.2395
S. Valentina	9.09	3.6804
Total	52.93	21.4199

USED FOR VILLA DI TREFIANO RISERVA		
Vineyard	Acres	Hectares
Croci	4.64	1.8765
Pietraia	4.50	1.8228
Trefiano	3.51	1.4186
Total	12.65	5.1179

Tenuta di Capezzana belongs to VIDE, which is no surprise considering that Ugo Bonacossi was a founder and longtime president of this organization.

Carmignano here is made from a blend of 70 percent sangiovese, 15 percent cabernet sauvignon, 10 percent canaiolo, and 5 percent occhio di pernice and other red grapes. Barco Reale is made from the same grape mix. The Vin Ruspo rosé is made from the same blend as the Carmignano. They draw off from 5 to 10 percent of the juice from their Carmignano for Vin Ruspo, which gives it greater concentration, color, and body. All their wines are fermented with the natural yeast found on the grapes.

The juice for Vin Ruspo ferments for fifteen days at temperatures between 60.8° and 64.4° Fahrenheit (16° and 18° centigrade). Malolactic fermentation takes place immediately after. They ferment the sangiovese for Carmignano at 82.4° to 86° Fahrenheit (28° to 30° centigrade) for one week, and cabernet at 77° (25°), also for one week. For both wines the juice macerates for another five days to a week. Malolactic fermentation generally follows immediately after the first fermentation. They use large oak casks for aging their Carmignano and Barco Reale. This last wine spends one year in cask. The '85 Carmignano *riserva* was aged for more than two years in cask. Alberto Bramini consults for Capezzana.

The annual production at Conte Ugo Contini Bonacossi's Tenuta di Capezzana is 50,000 cases a year. Of these, 16,600 cases are Carmignano, 8,900 are Chianti, 2,500 Vin Ruspo, 333 of an excellent *vin santo*, from 945 to 1,225 Ghiaie della Furba, 1,665 to 1,890 Chardonnay, with the balance consisting of a very good Champagne-method sparkler, the white Tremisse, and a few other wines.

They produce three styles of Carmignano: Villa di Capezzana, formerly Tenuta di Capezzana; Villa di Capezzana Riserva (40,000 to 60,000 bottles); and Villa di Trefiano Riserva (5,000 to 8,000 bottles). The Villa di Trefiano contains a higher proportion of cabernet. This last wine, though produced at Capezzana, is the wine of Conte Ugo's son Vittorio.

In some vintages the actual production of these wines, especially the Villa di Capezzana Riserva, exceeds the average by a large margin. Some recent production figures of the Villa di Capezzana Riserva: 1988, estimated 50,000 bottles; 1985, 128,876; 1983, 97,200; 1982, 20,750; 1981, 45,570; 1979, 40,850; and 1975, 61,200. And of Villa di Trefiano Riserva: 1983, 7,558 bottles; 1980, 7,450; and 1979, 7,045.

The *riserva* is produced in the better years only. They produced no Carmignano in 1989, and no *riserva* in 1987, 1986, or 1984. Of recent vintages of Capezzana *riserva,* we rate the '85 as their best wine, with the '83 and '88 close behind; also very good were '79, '81, and '82. Of the non-*riserve,* '83 was the star, with a very good

'85 and '88, '82 and '86 and a most agreeable '84. Without question Villa di Capezzana is the finest Carmignano of all; in certain vintages it reaches exceptional heights of excellence. Carmignano: Villa di Capezzana Riserva ****, Villa (Tenuta) di Capezzana ** +, Villa Trefiano **

Villa Il Poggiolo (*Carmignano,* località *Poggiolo*), *1800.* Giovanni Cianchi Baldazzi has 86.5 acres (35 hectares) of vineyards, 20 (8) in vines for Carmignano. These vines are planted at altitudes ranging from 459 to 558 feet (140 to 170 meters) above sea level. Baldazzi produces 133,000 bottles of wine a year, which includes 35,000 bottles of Carmignano.

A few years ago he had a 2.5-acre (1-hectare) vineyard named Valle, but it wasn't included in the most recent information with which they supplied us.

Il Poggiolo has bottled a Carmignano since the 1860s. Until a few years ago it was made from a blend of 65 percent sangiovese, 15 percent canaiolo nero, 10 percent cabernet sauvignon, and 10 percent white grapes: trebbiano toscano and canaiolo bianco. The white grapes have been eliminated, and since 1979 the cabernet sauvignon for the Carmignano is being aged in small, used Port barrels. Their Carmignano is aged for two to three years in a combination of oak and chestnut casks, mostly oak. The Chianti Montalbano is a blend of 75 percent sangiovese, 10 percent canaiolo nero, 10 percent trebbiano and 5 percent other varieties.

Il Poggiolo also produces a small quantity of very fine *vin santo,* as well as Vin Ruspo and Barco Reale. Like many others in Toscana, they are experimenting with cabernet sauvignon in *barrique*.

Baldazzi considers 1969 his best vintage. The '83 is the best wine that we've tasted here in recent years, followed closely by the '88 from cask. We also liked the '85 Riserva Villa di Canida, and put it equal to the '83. Other very good wines are the '85 Il Poggiolo Riserva and the '85 *normale*. We were told that Villa di Canida is a second label for the exact same wine. Yet in the one vintage that we tasted Carmignanos with both labels, 1985, we found the Canida superior. This producer's Carmignano is a very good one. Carmignano ** +

VINEYARDS OF VILLA IL POGGIOLO

Vineyard	Acres	Hectares
Calcinaia	17.3	7.0
Campisalti	16.1	6.5
Il Poggio delle Monache	3.7	1.15

CHAPTER 10

Vino Nobile di Montepulciano

Vino Nobile di Montepulciano is produced around the walled hilltop town of Montepulciano in the province of Siena in the southern part of Toscana. The village of Montepulciano, which dominates the Valdichiana and Val d'Orcia, is of ancient origin; it may originally have been an Etruscan settlement, although no positive proof of this has been found. This town is said to have been founded in 500 B.C. by the Etruscan king Porsenna. In the sixth century inhabitants from Chiusi, fleeing barbarian invaders, found safety on this hill, then called Mons Politicus or Mons Politanus, which became Montepulciano in Italian. The inhabitants of this village were consequently known as Poliziani or Politians.

When vines were first planted is not known, but documents dating from the eighth and ninth centuries record the sale of lands with vineyards and of payment of rents in money and wine. The earliest document found with evidence of vineyards in Montepulciano, written in A.D. 789, records the donation of land to the church by the cleric Arnipetri, including a vineyard at "*castello pulciani*" on the hill known then as Mons Pulciano. A document from 1350 lays down the conditions for trading in and exporting the wines of Montepulciano.

The wine of Montepulciano was noted outside the zone as early as the 1500s. Sante Lancerio, wine steward to Pope Paul III (1534–49), recorded the prelate's viniferous peregrinations and preferences, and among those the pontiff esteemed highly was the wine of Montepulciano. Sante Lancerio obviously shared his opinion, writing in about 1550:

> *The wine of Montepulciano is absolutely perfect as much winter as in summer. . . . Such wines as these have aroma, color and flavor and His Holiness drinks them gladly, not so much in Rome where they were delivered in* fiaschi *but more so in Perugia. . . .*[1]

ESTATES AND PRODUCERS OF VINO NOBILE DI MONTEPULCIANO (BASED ON A MAP BY THE CONSORZIO DEL VINO NOBILE DI MONTEPULCIANO)

Val di Chiana

2

Pod. Fatt. Pantano
(Fiorini)

Abbadia di
Montepulciano

Az. Poliziano
(Carletti-della Giovampaola)

3

Ascianello

Pod. Gracciano
(Mazzucchelli)

Stazione di Montep

Pod. Gracianello l
(Raspanti)

Tenuta di Gracciano
(della Seta)

Pod. Sanbuono
(Innocenti)

4

Gracciano

Pod. Gracianello-Caggiole
(Casa Vinicola Fassati)

5

Pod. Le Caggiole
(Tiberini)

7

6

Az. Pod. Il Macchione
(Francavilla Agricola)

Az. Pod. Le Caggiole
di Mezzo *(Giordano)*

8

Pod. Badelle
(Farnetani)

Acquav

Pod. Mulinvecchio
(Contucci)

Az. Pod. La Casella *(Carpini)*

Tenuta Valdipiatta

Pod. Fognano
Fatt. Fognano-Talosa

Pod. Cicolina
Vecchia Cantina

Pod. Sanguineto
(Monaci-Crociani)

9

13

14

Pod. Metina
(Buracchi)

Pc
(Ru

10

11

Cervognano

Montepulciano

Villa dei Comizio

Az. Pod. La Querce
(Pinzuti)

Pod. La Grazianella
Fatt. del Cerro
(Sai Agricola)

12

17

Pod. Canneto
Agricola Canneto

16

Pod. Poderuccio
Santavenere *(Romeo)*

Az. Pod. Bertille

Pod. Fonte Al Castagno
Fatt. Il Pulcino
(Ercolani)

Pod. Fatt. Le Casalte *(Silvestri)*

Pod. Bandite
Poggio Alla S
(SAIP

19

Pod. S. Enrico
(Nuova Scopetello)

18

S. Albino

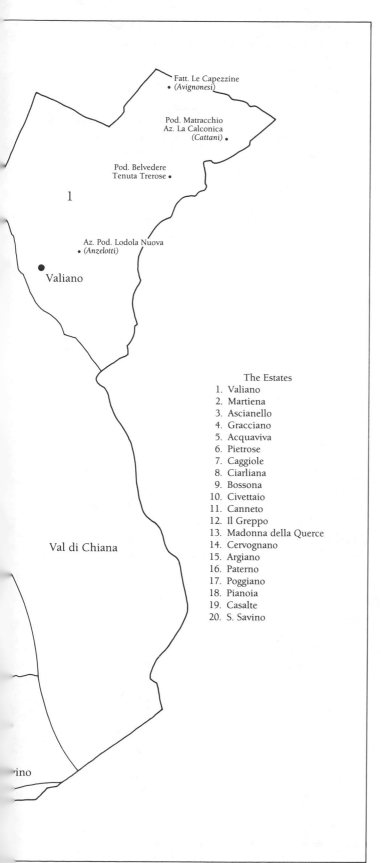

The Estates
1. Valiano
2. Martiena
3. Ascianello
4. Gracciano
5. Acquaviva
6. Pietrose
7. Caggiole
8. Ciarliana
9. Bossona
10. Civettaio
11. Canneto
12. Il Greppo
13. Madonna della Querce
14. Cervognano
15. Argiano
16. Paterno
17. Poggiano
18. Pianoia
19. Casalte
20. S. Savino

In the following century Francesco Redi elevated the wine to regal status. In his poem "*Bacco in Toscana,*" the god of wine, quite overcome by a cup of Montepulciano, declares that "*. . . Montepulciano d'ogni vino è re . . .*" (Montepulciano of all wines is king).

Emanuele Pellucci[2] cites a note written by Giovan Filippo Neri in the mid-1800s referring to "*il vino portato da Monte Pulciano*" (the wine brought from Monte Pulciano) in which it is described as "*vino nobile,*" the first reference found using this term for the Montepulciano wine. This is a description, however, not a name. The origin of the name Vino Nobile di Montepulciano is uncertain. Some think that probably two qualities of wine were being produced in Montepulciano, and the finer one was referred to as the noble wine. Others theorize that the name came from the fact that this wine was drunk by the nobility. It's not unlikely that these two theories go hand in hand. It's only natural that the nobility drank the better wine, in Montepulciano as well as everywhere else. Yet another story suggests that the wine was made from the best grapes, hence the name. And another maintains that the noble quality of the wine and its high price led to the name.

It seems more likely that the name came from the description of the wine of Montepulciano as "the king of all wines" in the famous and much-cited poem by Redi.

Whether the better wines of Montepulciano were ever officially referred to as Vino Nobile in times past, we don't know. On the oldest labels it is simply Rosso Scelto di Montepulciano (selected, or choice, red wine of Montepulciano). We have seen references to a "*Vino rosso scelto detto nobile di seconda qualità*" from "Crociani Germano di Montepulciano," a "*Vino rosso nobile*" from "Crociani Mario di Montepulciano," a "*Vino nobile rosso di detta*" from "Bracci Cav. Pietro di Montepulciano" in a catalog of 1853, and "*Vino rosso detto 'NOBILE'* " from "Colombini Giovanni" in a catalog of 1862. And at the Esposizione Enologica of the provinces of Siena and Grosseto in 1870, the following wines were cited as *Menzione Onorevole* (honorable mention): "Bracci Lucangelo—Vino Nobile 1868—Montepulciano," "Pilacci Oreste—Vino Nobile—Montepulciano," and "Ricci Paracciani—Vino Nobile—Montepulciano." There were other wines entered as "*Rosso nobile*" and "*Rosso c. nobile*" from the *comune* of Montepulciano from Angelotti F., Avignonesi F., Bracci F.lli, Colombi F.lli, Pilacco Oreste, Ricci Paracciani March. Giovanni, and Trecci Teodoro Polic.[3]

In our century Adamo Fanetti was the first to use the name Vino Nobile for the red wine he made at Tenuta Sant' Agnese. In 1933 a wine exhibition was organized at Siena. Fanetti brought some of his best wine to the show, where he shared a stand with Tancredi Biondi-Santi, a friend and producer whose wines he esteemed. Fanetti's wine attracted favorable attention and was sold there at auction for an unusually high price for Montepulciano wine. Encouraged by its reception, he began bottling the wine, labeling it Vino Nobile.

Observing the success of his wine, other producers of Montepulciano began calling their wines Vino Nobile as well. Fanetti sued for the exclusive right to the name, but the judgment went against him. At the second Siena Exhibition a few years later, a number of other *poliziani* producers also presented Vino Nobile, including Baiocchi, Bologna, Bracci Testasecca, Bucelli, Contucci, Pilacci, Ricci Paracciani, and Waldergan. Some of these producers—Bracci, Pilacci, and Ricci Paracciani—had used the designation Nobile in the nineteenth century.

Important foreign recognition came when the Fanetti Vino Nobile won a gold medal in 1937 at the Grand Prix de Paris.

THE VINO NOBILE PRODUCTION ZONE

The vines for Vino Nobile are planted in the municipality of Montepulciano at altitudes ranging from 820 to 1,970 feet (250 to 600 meters) above sea level, though some locations rise to nearly 2,300 feet (700 meters). The flat part of the Valdichiana is excluded from the allowable growing area. There are two major parts of the growing zone: the first section stretches from the plains to the outskirts of Montepulciano, at altitudes ranging from 820 to 1,985 feet (250 to 605 meters) above sea level; the second extends toward Pienza and Chianciano. The vines in this district range from 2,130 to 2,265 feet (650 to 690 meters) in altitude. The soil in the first area is comprised of sand, tufa, and clay; that of the second, silica and siliceous clay.

There are approximately 1,655 acres (670 hectares) of vineyards which are cultivated by 161 growers; another 1,655 (670) are under vines for Chianti Colli Senesi. Today there is very little room for further expansion in the vineyards. Some 1,800 acres (728 hectares) have been delimited for Vino Nobile.

If all the land authorized were planted, as much as 420,580 cases of Vino Nobile could be produced. The average annual production of Vino Nobile di Montepulciano in the period from 1974 to 1983 was 230,000 cases. Production has risen slightly; between 1980 and 1989 it averaged 273,606 cases a year. There are 32 producers in the zone who bottle wine.

The vines, for the most part, face east. Rainfall averages 27.7 inches (740 millimeters) a year, and the temperature averages 57° Fahrenheit (14° centigrade).

THE *UVAGGIO* OF VINO NOBILE

The defining grape variety of Vino Nobile di Montepulciano is prugnolo gentile, a variety known in this area since 1700. According to the Consorzio del Vino Nobile di Montepulciano, Villifranchi, writing in his *Oenologia Toscana, o sia memoria sopra i vini in specie Toscani (Tuscan Enology, or a memoir on wines, especially those of Tuscany)*, in 1773, reported that the prugnolo gentile was selected in this area in 1700.[4]

Previously DOC required an *uvaggio* of 50 to 70 percent prugnolo gentile or sangiovese grosso, a subvariety of sangiovese; 10 to 20 percent canaiolo nero; 10 to 20 percent trebbiano toscano and/or malvasia del chianti; and up to 8 percent mammolo and/or pulcinculo, also known as grechetto bianco. The mammolo vine, fairly common here, gives to the wine, they say, its characteristic scent of sweet violets (*mammola*). Canaiolo nero adds color and tannin.

ANNUAL PRODUCTION OF VINO NOBILE

Year	Gallons	Hectoliters	Cases
1980	767,078	29,034	322,568
1981	484,120	18,324	203,580
1982	704,965	26,683	296,448
1983	661,689	25,045	278,250
1984	357,172	13,519	150,196
1985	674,555	25,532	283,661
1986	711,200	26,919	299,070
1987	625,441	23,673	263,007
1988	708,981	26,835	298,137
1989	811,358	30,710	341,188
Average	650,645	24,627	273,606

Source: Consorzio del Vino Nobile di Montepulciano

Vino Nobile di Montepulciano, then, was a red wine that could be made from as much as 28 percent white grapes, that not including the allowance of 10 percent of must or wine from outside the zone, of unspecified color, that could be added. Under the new DOCG regulations, 60 to 80 percent prugnolo gentile and 10 to 20 percent canaiolo nero are required, and up to 20 percent of other varieties is allowed, but only 10 percent, at most, from white grapes. Only those nonaromatic white varieties permitted in the province of Siena are allowed, with the exception of malvasia del chianti, which is authorized. The percentage of mammolo and/or pulcinculo has been reduced to 5 percent. At one time we were told that the limit on white grapes would be lowered to a maximum of 5 percent, but as far as we know this was never done. The regulation on correcting with must or wine to bring up the alcohol has also been amended; it can be made only with Vino Nobile, up to 15 percent, from another vintage.

ROSSO DI MONTEPULCIANO

From the 1989 harvest Rosso di Montepulciano has been granted DOC status. The delimited area is the same as that for Vino Nobile. DOC authorizes an *uvaggio* of 60 to 80 percent prugnolo gentile, or sangiovese grosso, and 10 to 20 percent canaiolo nero; additionally any white varieties permitted in the province of Siena may be used as long as they don't exceed 10 percent. Aromatic varieties, except for malvasia del chianti, are not permitted. DOC allows a maximum of 748 gallons per acre (70 hectoliters per hectare). Minimum alcohol is 11 percent.

As is done for Rosso di Montalcino, the better producers will use the wine from their young vines as well as certain vats that aren't up to par to be labeled as Vino Nobile. This should have a marked impact on quality. We also suspect that the quantity of wine labeled as such will increase at the expense of Chianti or Chianti Colli Senesi as this lends more recognition to Montepulciano and its wines.

Avignonesi, not surprisingly, produced a good 1989. We can also recommend the Rossos from Contucci and Fattoria del Cerro. Fassati's 1989 Selciaia was agreeable, as were the Rossos from La Calonica and Vecchia Cantina.

THE CHARACTER AND QUALITY OF VINO NOBILE

Vino Nobile can be rough and tannic in its youth but, given five to eight years of aging, mellows to a soft, velvety wine, complex in aroma and rich in flavor. This is Vino Nobile at its best—fortunately a level that is attained more frequently than in times past—Vino Noble is a wine to accompany roasted meats, particularly beef and lamb, and game birds.

Vino Nobile di Montepulciano is produced from a blend of grapes similar to that for Chianti, and the Montepulciano region is within the Chianti Colli Senesi zone. In fact, this wine, despite the name, was too often very common in quality. For many years it was no more than an overrated, overpriced, variable Chianti, and not much else. But changes have taken place here. Since 1982 there has been a dramatic improvement in the overall quality in Montepulciano. We were told that this is due to a more serious effort on the part of the better producers, who came to the realization that the wine wasn't living up to its title.

To begin with, it seems there's a more careful selection of the grapes being made at harvest. The more serious produc-

DOC/DOCG REQUIREMENTS FOR VINO NOBILE DI MONTEPULCIANO

	Minimum Aging in Years		Minimum Alcohol	Maximum Yield (Gallons/Acre)
	in Cask	Total		
DOC *normale*	2	2[a]	12.0%	748[c]
riserva	2	3[a]	12.0%	748[c]
riserva speciale	2	4[a]	12.0%	748[c]
DOCG *normale*	2	2[b]	12.5%	599/556[d]
riserva	2	3[b]	12.5%	599/556[d]
Rosso di Montepulciano	—	5 months	11.0%	748[c]

NOTES: [a] The aging period begins on November 1 in the year of the harvest.
[b] The aging period starts January 1 after the harvest; cask aging begins on April 1.
[c] 70 hectoliters per hectare
[d] When harvested, the equivalent of 599 gallons per acre (56 hectoliters per hectares) is allowed; after aging, not more than 556 gallons per acre (52 hectoliters per hectare) can be bottled.

ers are using the best fruit only in their Vino Nobile and declassifying the rest to Chianti Colli Senesi, Rosso di Montepulciano (since 1989), *vino da tavola,* or, in the worst case, selling the wine off in bulk, unlabeled. The changes can be noted in the marked improvement in quality. In some cases outside help has been brought in. Able enologists, such as Maurizio Castelli, who consults for Boscarelli and Poliziano, and Vittorio Fiore, are sure to make a difference also.

Regrettably, not all the producers have pulled themselves up as firmly. Some of the respected names of the past, such as Contucci and Fanetti, while still producing good wines, have slipped noticeably in recent years. The zone's finest producer, the elderly Bologna Buonsignori, has retired, and the wine, unfortunately, is no longer made. There are, though, some bright new lights appearing on the horizon—Poliziano, since 1982 under the able hand of Dott. Federico Carletti, and Avignonesi are just two. Saiagricola's Fattoria del Cerro and Cantine Baiocchi are also topflight. Although Boscarelli, a longtime favorite, has had its ups and downs, we feel it is one to keep an eye on. Dei, a producer new to us, also shows promise.

The basic material is there. With the new expertise and renewed emphasis on quality, we look forward to more really fine wines from Montepulciano, Vino Nobiles worthy of the name. Rating: Rosso di Montepulciano *; Vino Nobile di Montepulciano ***

THE CONSORZIO DEL VINO NOBILE DI MONTEPULCIANO

In November 1965 the Consorzio del Vino Nobile di Montepulciano was formed. This *consorzio* "promotes and protects" the image of the wine of Montepulciano. In our experience it is one of the better and more valid *consorzii* in Italy. The members, as of 1990, are:

Azienda Agricola, Anzelotti Bruno
Avignonesi
Azienda Agricola "Bertille"
Azienda Agricola Buracchi
Agricola Canneto
Cantina Gattavecchi
Cantina Innocenti Vittorio
Cantina Pulciano (Matassini Ercolani Gabriella)
Cantina "Santavenere" (Massimo Romeo)
Azienda Agricola Contucci
Azienda Agricola Crociani Arnaldo
Dei (Villa Martiena)
Della Seta Ferrari Corbelli "Tenuta di Gracciano"

Farnetani (Cantine Podere Badelle)
Fassati Casa Vinicola del Chianti
"Fattoria del Cerro" (Sai Agricola)
"Fattoria della Talosa" (formerly Fattoria di Fognano)
"Fattoria di Gracciano" (Dott. Franco Mazzucchelli)
"Fattoria di Paterno"
"Fattoria Le Casalte" (Paola Silvestri Barioffi)
"Fattoria Pulciano" (Ercolani Sergio)
Azienda Agricola "Il Macchione," Agricola Fancavilla
  (formerly Agricola Francavilla, Podere Il Macchione)
"Granducato," Enopolio di Poggibonsi
Azienda Agricola "Il Pantano"
Azienda Agricola "La Calonica" (Cattani Fernando)
Azienda Agricola "La Casella" (Alfio Carpini)
Azienda Agricola "La Querce" (Pinzuti Pino)
Azienda Agricola "Le Caggiole di Mezzo" (Giordano & C.)
Nuova Scopetello
Azienda Agricola "Poliziano" (Carletti della Giovampaola)
Azienda Vinicola Raspanti Cav. Giuseppe & Figli
Azienda Agricola "Sanguineto" (Maria e Lucia Monaci)
"Tenuta Valdipiatta"
Azienda Agricola Terre Bindella
Azienda Agricola Tiberini
Vecchia Cantina di Montepulciano, Soc. Coop.

In 1989 there were three other members:

Azienda Agricola Bindella Rudolf (they could be the same
  as Terre Bindella)
Poggio alla Sala
Tenuta Trerose

Rating the Producers

****
Bologna Buonsignori[a, b]

***
Avignonesi
Cantine Baiocchi (Sai Agricola)[c]
Carletti della Giovampaola (Poliziano)
— Dei
Fattoria del Cerro (Sai Agricola)
Poliziano (Carletti & Della Giovampaola)

**
Bindella Rudolf[d]
— Canneto
— Canneto di Sotto
Contucci
Fanetti, Comm. Adamo e Giuseppe[b]

Fassati, Graccianello (*normale* *, Podere Fonte al
　Vescovo *)
Fattoria della Talosa
Fattoria di Fognano, "Talosa"
Il Pantano, pre-1977 (Fattoria del Pantano today, 0)
+ Podere Boscarelli
Poggio alla Sala, Vigna Parceto
Raspanti Cav. Giuseppe
Tenuta Trerose
Terre Bindella

*

Ancilli[e]
Buracchi
Cantina Gattavecchi[f]
Cantina Santavenere (Massimo Romeo)
Cecchi Luigi
Fassati, *normale* (Graccianello **)
Fassati, Podere Fonte al Vescovo (Graccianello **)
+ Fattoria di Fognano
Fattoria di Gracciano (Dott. Franco Mazzucchelli)
Fattoria di Paterno[g]
+ Fattoria Le Casalte (Paola Silvestri Barioffi)
Fattoria Nuova Scopetello[h]
Fiorini - Pantano
+ La Calonica (Cattani Ferrando)
La Casella (Alfio Carpini)
Le Caggiole di Mezzo (Giordano & C.)
Le Pietrose (Sai Agricola)[e]
+ Melini
Monsigliolo[i]
Podere Le Caggiole, "Tiberini"[d]
+ Podere Le Caggiole di Mezzo
Poggio alla Sala (since the '83; previously, 0)
Sanguineto (Maria e Lucia Monaci)
Scopetello
Scopetto[j]
+ Tenuta di Gracciano (Della Seta Ferrari Corbelli)
+ Tenuta Valdipiatta
Vecchia Cantina di Montepulciano
+ Vecchia Cantina di Montepulciano, Riserva

0

Bigi Luigi[k]
Bordini[l]
− Cantina del Redi[m]
Carpineto
Fattoria del Pantano (today, pre-1977, **)
Francavilla, Podere Il Macchione
+ La Querce (Pinzuti Pino Lido)
Le Caggiole (Podere Il Macchione)[n]
Ludola Nuova

+ Podere Badelle
Podere Ferretto, Fattoria delle Maestrelle[l]
Podere Il Macchione, Le Caggiole[n]
Podere Le Caggiole[o]
Poggio alla Sala (pre-1983, since the '83, *)
Tistarelli Mario[e]
Tripusa, Brigatti, Enoteca Europea[p]

NOTES: [a] The last vintage they produced was the 1981
　　　　[b] The last vintage tasted was the '81
　　　　[c] The last vintage tasted was the '82
　　　　[d] Based on one wine, the '86
　　　　[e] Based on one wine, the '79
　　　　[f] They have improved since the '82
　　　　[g] Based on one wine, the '85 Riserva
　　　　[h] Based on one wine, the '85
　　　　[i] Based on one wine, the '83
　　　　[j] Based on one wine, the '80
　　　　[k] The last vintage tasted was the '73
　　　　[l] The last vintage tasted was the '77
　　　　[m] Based on one wine, the '78
　　　　[n] Based on one wine, the '77
　　　　[o] Based on one wine, the '81
　　　　[p] The last vintage tasted was the '79

WHAT THE RATINGS MEAN

****	Great, superb, truly noble
***	Exceptionally fine
**	Very good
*	A good example of its type, somewhat above average
0	Acceptable to mediocre, depending on the context; drinkable
+	Somewhat better than the star category it is put in
−	Somewhat less than the star category it is put in, except for zero where it indicates a wine or producer-wine combination that is badly made or worse
[. .]	*On a producer:* Tentative evaluation based on an insufficient number of wines or based on older, out-of-date vintages, or where the wines we tasted were too difficult to fully judge to give a fair assessment of quality.
	On a wine or vintage: Projection for the future. This rating is given to a vintage where we feel that we tasted an insufficient number of wines or those we tasted were too difficult to really judge to give a fair assessment of quality.
(. .)	Potential increase in the rating of the wine given sufficient maturity

VINTAGE INFORMATION AND TASTING NOTES

THE VINTAGES TODAY

****	1985
***+	1988, 1983
***−	1982
**+	1986
**−	1981
*	1989, 1987, 1979, 1977, 1975, 1970
*−	1984, 1978
0	1980, 1976, 1974, 1973, 1972, 1971, 1969, 1968, 1967
?	1990

1 9 9 0

The weather during the growing season was very dry and warm. Much-needed rain fell during August. Comparisons were being made to 1985. The three Nobiles that we tasted from barrel in November after the vintage—Contucci, and the two Dei crus Bossana and Roccolo—were all opaque in color and displayed a lot of fruit. It was too early to judge them, but they were promising.

1 9 8 9 *

The weather pattern, as well as the reports, suggests it wasn't a successful vintage. Judging by the handful of Rosso di Montepulcianos that we tasted, the wines are light and will be for early drinking, if well selected. Dei rates the vintage as medium.

In November 1990 we tasted 10 Nobiles from barrel. Overall, they were good wines that will, for the most part, mature early; we doubt that they'll keep long. A few were too difficult to evaluate. Of those that we could, we liked the Dei, Fassati, Fiorini - Pantano, and Macchione the best.

> **CAUTION:** *Before reading these tasting notes on the wines that we tasted from barrel, please read "On Tasting Wines from Barrel: A Caveat" on page xxv.*

Avignonesi (*ex-cask, 11/90*). Sense of fruit quite evident, but rather dry and short. ?

Canneto (*ex-cask, 11/90*). Fairly nice fruit on the nose followed by a raisin note; rather dry and bitter; is there enough fruit? ?

Contucci (*twice, ex-cask, 11/90*). Slight nose; a little light and dry, could use more fruit. (*)

Dei (*3 times, ex-cask, 11/90*). Berrylike aroma; dry entry followed by good fruit, some spice, a little light, short, dry aftertaste. *(+)

Fassati (*ex-cask, 11/90*). Open fruit and floral aroma; good structure, quite nice upon entry through midpalate, then a little short and dry and a tad bitter. *(+)

Fattoria della Talosa (*twice, ex-cask, 11/90*). Berrylike aroma; sense of fruit evident, still it is rather dry, light tannin, it could use more fruit; it will mature early. (*)

Fiorini - Pantano (*ex-cask, 11/90*). Lovely nose, open fruit; fairly good fruit, but a little dry, short. *(+)

Macchione (*ex-cask, 11/90*). Floral, fruity aroma; good fruit, somewhat firm, tails off at the end, short and dry. *(+)

Poliziano (*twice, ex-cask, 11/90*). Small nose; fairly good fruit, then rather dry, light tannin, a little short and dry at the end. *

Vecchia Cantina (*twice, ex-cask, 11/90*). Evident fruit on the nose; rather dry on the palate, yet with the sense of fruit; should mature early. ?

1 9 8 8 *** +

The 708,981-gallon (26,835-hectoliter) production, equivalent to 298,137 cases, was above the 1980–88 average of 632,812 gallons (23,952 hectoliters).

Avignonesi, Carletti, and Contucci rate 1988 as among the best. Dei calls it a grand year. Based on the 17 wines we've tasted, all from barrel in November 1990, we have found the wines, overall, very good indeed. The best one was the Poliziano cru Asinone, followed closely by Dei, and then Avignonesi, Contucci *normale* and cru Pietra Rossa, Fassati, Fattoria della Talosa, and Terre Bindella.

> **CAUTION:** *Before reading these tasting notes on the wines that we tasted from barrel, please read "On Tasting Wines from Barrel: A Caveat" on page xxv.*

Avignonesi (*ex-cask, 11/90*). Lovely nose, combines flowers and fruit; good structure, a lot of nice fruit, tasty, firm structure. **(+)

Canneto (*ex-cask, 11/90*). Closed in, sense of ripe fruit evident, firm, tight and dry, slightly bitter. (*)

Contucci (*twice, ex-cask, 11/90*). Richer and more open than the cru, well balanced. **(+)

Contucci, Pietra Rossa (*ex-cask, 11/90*). Rich and concentrated, good structure, a little short and dry; should age well. *(*)

Dei (*twice, ex-cask, 11/90*). Lovely nose, flowers and fruit; good structure, rich, tasty, firm finish; a lot of class, the best Dei to date. **(*)

Fassati (*ex-cask, 11/90*). Evident fruit on the nose; sense of ripe fruit, good structure, a little hard and dry at the end. **(+)

Fattoria della Talosa (*twice, ex-cask, 11/90*). Nice nose, good fruit; lots of structure, a richly concentrated wine, ripe fruit flavor. **(+)

Fattoria di Gracciano (Dott. Franco Mazzucchelli) (*ex-cask, 11/90*). Sense of sweetness from the ripe fruit, could use more depth, a little simple. *(+)

Fattoria Le Casalte (*ex-cask, 11/90*). Fairly nice fruit on the nose; hard, dry and tannic, closed up tight, evident sense of fruit. *(+?)

Fiorini - Pantano (*ex-cask, 11/90*). Hard, tight, firm and tannic. (?*)

Macchione (*ex-cask, 11/90*). Overripe and pruney, does have fruit. *

Poliziano (*twice, ex-cask, 11/90*). A little dry and firm, sense of fruit, but closed. *(+?)

Poliziano, Asinoine (*ex-cask, 11/90*). Firm, hard, rich with a real sense of fruit and sweetness, fairly long finish. **(*)

Tenuta di Gracciano, Della Seta Ferrari Corbelli (*ex-cask, 11/90*). Nice fruit on the nose; firm and dry, good fruit. *(*−)

Tenuta Valdipiatta (*ex-cask, 11/90*). Firm, hard and tannic, again the sense of fruit is evident but the wine is closed and tight. (* + ?)

Terre Bindella (*ex-cask, 11/90*). Lovely rich fruit aroma; well balanced, good structure, sense of sweetness. **(+)

Vecchia Cantina (*twice, ex-cask, 11/90*). Dry, firm and closed, nice sense of fruit; dry, firm end, a tad bitter. *(+)

1987 *

Unlike in most of Toscana, for Vino Nobile the grapes were healthy. The crop size of 625,441 gallons (23,673 hectoliters), equivalent to 263,007 cases, was close to the decade's average.

As elsewhere in Toscana, it was a mixed bag, with mostly mediocre wines, although there were some good ones as well. For the most part, this wine-producing district was more successful than Chianti but less so than Montalcino. Dei calls it a medium vintage.

Based on the 17 Nobiles that we tasted, many more than once, we find the vintage variable, to say the least, even from the same producer. These wines will be ready early and are for short- to mid-term consumption. The best wines have been Carletti and Fassati, along with some bottles of Avignonesi and Poliziano. The Contucci and Canneto were quite

good as well. The Dei tank sample that we tasted in April 1990 showed promise, the one from November didn't.

Avignonesi (*4 times, 11/90*). As with a number of other producers' Nobile from 1987, we have experienced bottle variation. Slight nose hints of animal fur and oak; sense of fruit, is there enough(?), overall, dull and rather uninteresting; perhaps we experienced two off bottles the same day and in two different places, including one at the winery. ? *Bottle of 9/90*: Light nose, fruit evident; open fruit, seems ready at first, but still some tannin to shed; well made. *(*−) *Bottle of 4/90*: Closed-in aroma; open and flavorful in the mouth, soft, balanced and well made. ** +

Buracchi (*twice, 11/90*). Light nose; light-bodied, simple and fruity. * − *Bottle of 4/90*: Light nose; some fruit evident, soft entry, tasty, nice fruit, a bit short. * +

Canneto (*11/90*). Nice fruit on the nose and palate, good structure, a little short and dry. *(+)

Carletti della Giovampaola (*4/90*). Light, fruity aroma; openly fruity, good structure, soft, dry, short aftertaste. ** −

Cecchi (*11/90*). Soft with nice fruit, a tad dry at the end and short. +

Contucci (*twice, 11/90*). Open aroma exhibits components of flowers and fruit; fairly well balanced, a little dry though soft, light tannin, short. * +

Dei (*3 times, ex-vat, 11/90*). Firm and dry, sense of fruit, is there enough? ? *Ex-cask, 4/90*: Chewy, good fruit under the tannin, tight and closed but with evident quality. **?

Fassati (*twice, 11/90*). Nice nose combines oak and fruit; good body, nice fruit, supple. **−

Fattoria della Talosa (*twice, 11/90*). Nice nose suggestive of berries, with tar and fruit components as well that carry over into the mouth, short, a little coarse but quite drinkable. *

Fattoria Le Casalte (*3 times, 11/90, 17,533 bottles*). Good fruit from the nose through the palate, fairly well balanced though a little dry. * *Bottle of 4/90*: Cherrylike aroma; soft, openly fruity, simple and balanced. * +

La Calonica (*3 times, 11/90*). Pruney, overripe, drinkable. *Bottle of 4/90*: Light, fruity aroma; fairly soft, rather nice fruit. * +

Ludola Nuova (*4/90*). Cooked, baked character.

Poliziano (*5 times, 11/90*). There has been some variation here. Nice nose, good fruit; sense of sweetness from the fruit, moderate tannin, short, dry aftertaste. * *A second bottle tasted the same day*: Pruney, overripe aroma; fairly nice fruit on entry, then dry. + *Bottle of 9/90*: Seems hot and overripe, tarlike aroma; full-bodied, coarse and rustic. * *Bottle of 4/90*: Light, fruity aroma, vaguely reminiscent of mushrooms; some tannin, gentle and soft, balanced, some tannin, moderate length with the tannin building up on the finish. **

Tenuta di Gracciano, Della Seta Ferrari Corbelli (*Twice, 11/90*). Tarlike aroma, some fruit; soft, moderate tannin, a little dry, short dry end. (?*) *Bottle of 4/90*: Candied aroma; soft and easy, simple, light tannin. * −

Terre Bindella (11/90). Sense of fruit evident on the nose, which is a little muted; moderate tannin, good fruit. *

Vecchia Cantina (3 times, 11/90). Shy nose; rather dry, some fruit evident under moderate tannin. + *Bottle of 4/90:* Light nose; fairly well balanced, a little light, short, drinkable enough. * −

Villa Martiena (Dei) (11/90). Rather low fruit, dry, firm and short. ?

1986 ** +

There was excellent weather during the harvest. The 1986 yield of 711,200 gallons (26,919 hectoliters), equivalent to 299,070 cases, was 12.5 percent above the 1980–88 average of 632,812 gallons (23,952 hectoliters). It was the second largest crop of the decade, exceeded only by the crop in 1980.

Dei rates the vintage as excellent plus. Some very good wines were produced. Many will mature quickly and not keep well. The best should improve. Overall, it was a very good, albeit light vintage.

Of the 26 wines that we tasted, we found the best wines were the Avignonesi Riserva and Fattoria del Cerro followed by Avignonesi *normale,* Dei Riserva, and Poliziano, then Bindella and Tenuta Trerose. Other very good ones included Carletti della Giovampaola and the Contucci Riserva. The Poggio alla Sala Vigna Parceto that we tasted from cask in 1987 also showed promise.

Avignonesi (4 times, 9/90). A little light on the nose; well balanced, tasty, some tannin to shed, open fruit flavors, soft on the midpalate. ** + (*** −)

Avignonesi, Riserva (twice, 4/90). Vaguely woodsy aroma, noticeable fruit and a light, floral note; overall closed, with some firmness, chewy, evident sweetness of ripe fruit, refined fruit flavors; has style and some elegance. ***

Bindella (twice, 4/89). Fruity, floral, earthy, vanilla aroma; soft center under moderate tannin, well balanced, a tad short. **

Cantina Gattavecchi (4/90). Light nose displays earthy tones; soft, easy, simple. *

Carletti della Giovampaola (twice, 6/90). Open, fruity aroma; a little dry, fruity, could use more length. *(* −)

Carpineto, Riserva (11/90). Light, simple and fruity, dull aftertaste; a Rosso in the guise of a Nobile.

Cecchi Luigi (Della Seta) (2 times, 12/89). Light, floral aroma; sweet entry, then tight. *

Contucci, Riserva (twice, 11/90). A little dry at first, then the fruit, then dry again, rather short finish; it could improve. *(+) *Bottle of 4/90:* Mushroom, woodsy aroma, floral note; chewy tannins, somewhat astringent, but nice mouth feel midpalate, good structure, dry tannic aftertaste. ** −

Dei, Riserva (3 times, 4/90). Cherrylike aroma; dry, loads of fruit beneath moderate tannin, dry and tannic on the fairly long aftertaste; young with evident potential. ** +

Fassati, Podere Fonte al Vescovo (3 times, 5/90, 44,267 bottles). Light and fruity, nose and palate, open, precocious, simple. *

Fattoria del Cerro (4/90). A little restrained on the nose; loaded with flavor, well structured; one of the best '86s. ***

Fattoria della Talosa (4/90). Light nose; soft and openly fruity, balanced. * +

Fattoria della Talosa, Riserva (11/90). Fairly open nose, sense of flowers; suggestion of sweetness, soft, open and fruity, light tannin, very ready, a little dry at the end. ** −

Fattoria di Gracciano, Riserva (4/90). Aroma is vaguely floral, some fruit; good body, flavorful, open. * +

Fattoria Le Casalte (4/89). Woodsy mushroom aroma, carries through into the mouth, unclean.

Fattoria Le Casalte, Riserva (4/90). Floral, earthy aroma, mineral note; fairly nice fruit, a little dry, short, rather dry finish. * +

La Calonica (4/89). Vaguely corked, still the quality is evident. *?

Ludola Nuova (4/90). Cooked, baked character, atypical.

Melini (Vecchia Cantina) (11/90). Pungent aroma, herbaceous; low fruit, dull; a disappointment from a generally reliable producer.

Podere Le Caggiole, Tiberini (4/89). Light, fruity aroma; light tannin, soft, fruity, easy style. *

Poggio alla Sala, Vigna Parceto (ex-cask, 4/87). This wine was fermented in *barrique.* Both the nose and the palate displayed a lot of oak, along with fruit, rich and packed with fruit, good structure, a tad hot at the end; still in all, a good bottle. **(+)

Poliziano (4 times, 11/90). Fragrant nose; still some tannin, on the young side. *(*) *Bottle of 9/90:* Open fruit aroma, floral notes, hint of tar; firm, a little tight on entry, followed by fruit; should improve. **(+)

Tenuta Trerose (11/90). Nice nose; light tannin, good fruit, open flavors, soft, ready. **

Tenuta Valdipiatta (ex-cask, 4/87). Dark purplish color; rich in extract, good acid; potential evident. (**)

Vecchia Cantina (4/89). Light nose; open fruit, soft and easy. +

Vecchia Cantina, Riserva (twice, 1/90). Not a lot of aroma, a little earthy, and vaguely floral; soft and easy under light tannin, short. *

1985 ****

The 674,555 gallons (25,532 hectoliters), equivalent to 283,661 cases, produced was above the decade's average of 632,812 gallons (23,952 hectoliters).

Avignonesi, Carletti, and Contucci place 1985 with the very best vintages. Dei calls it excellent.

As elsewhere in Toscana, many splendid wines were produced, harmonious wines with great structure and extract. The best will be keepers. The best wines were the Avignonesi *normale,* Poliziano *normale* and Riserva, followed closely by the *riserve* of Avignonesi, Canneto, Carletti della Giovampaola, and Dei, as well as the Fattoria del Cerro *normale* and Riserva. Also very good were the Carletti della Giovampaola *normale,* Contucci Riserva, Fattoria della Talosa Riserva, the *normali* of La Calonica, Melini, and Raspanti Cav. Giuseppe, the Tenuta Trerose Riserva, and a pair from Fassati, the Graccianello *normale* and Riserva.

Avignonesi (*4 times, 4/89*). Lovely, open fruit aroma; sweet impression, rich and ripe, well structured, lovely mouth-filling flavors. ***

Avignonesi, Riserva (*4/89*). Intensely fruited aroma; rich in extract and flavor, packed with fruit; still young, but evident potential. **(*)

Buracchi (*4/88*). Hot, baked, dull, heavy.

Buracchi, Riserva (*4/89*). Light nose; fairly tannic and chewy, light tannic aftertaste. (*)

Canneto Agricola, Riserva (*4/90*). Cherrylike fruit, vaguely floral; sweet entry, some oak, firm tannin, good structure, some tannin at the end. *** −

Cantina Gattavecchi (*4/88*). Cherrylike aroma and flavor, chewy, flavorful. *

Carletti della Giovampaola (*4/88*). Nice fruit on the nose, fairly open, some oak; fairly open fruit on entry giving way to tannin, well balanced; not surprisingly young. **(+)

Carletti della Giovampaola, Riserva (*4 times, 12/89*). Oak and ripe fruit; big, rich and ripe, loads of sweet, ripe fruit, good concentration, chewy tannins. ** + (***)

Cecchi Luigi (*twice, 6/90*). Nice fruit aroma, cherry notes; soft under light tannin, simple. * *Bottle of 5/90:* Floral, nutty, fruity aroma; open fruit, sweet impression on entry, then a little firm, flavorful. **

Contucci, Riserva (*twice, 11/90*). Open nose with ripe fruit and floral components, spice and cherry notes; good structure, loads of fruit, firm, tight finish. *(*)

Dei, Riserva (*4/89*). Open, berrylike fruit aroma; moderate tannin, rich and concentrated, sweet impression from ripe fruit, tasty. For their first wine, an auspicious beginning. *** −

Fassati, Graccianello (*11/90*). Nice nose, open and fruity; soft, open fruit, quite ready, light finish. ** −

Fassati, Podere Fonte al Vescovo (*twice, 4/89*). Evident fruit, somewhat earthy; kind of bland; a real disappointment, it promised more from barrel.

Fassati, Riserva Graccianello (*11/90*). Openly fruity aroma, floral and berry notes; nice fruit, soft and open, attractive, ready. **

Fattoria del Cerro (*4/88*). Reticent aroma, hints of tobacco and cherries; good structure; some style and elegance; well made. *** −

Fattoria del Cerro, Riserva (*3 times, 6/90*). Rich and concentrated, still young and backward, but has the elements. **(*) *Bottle of 4/90:* Floral aroma; rich, lots of extract, fairly tannic, sweet impression, rich and flavorful; young, should be a keeper. ** + (***)

Fattoria della Talosa, Riserva (*11/90*). Light nose offers suggestions of flowers and berries; still some firmness, moderate tannin, good fruit and structure, on the young side, firm, dry finish, a tad bitter. *(*)

Fattoria della Talosa (Fattoria di Fognano), Riserva (*twice, 8/90*). Complex aroma, vanilla, flowers and cherries; nice mouth feel under moderate tannin, those tannins are astringent and firm, tight finish; still in all a nice wine that needs two or three years. *(*)

Fattoria di Fognano, Talosa (*3 times, 2/90*). Small-scale aroma; better in the mouth, fairly good body, needs time. *(?) *Bottle of 4/89:* Fruit seems insufficient for the tannin, very little to it. *Bottle of 4/88:* Cherry aroma combines with oak; aggressive tannin, ripe fruit; needs age. *(* −)

Fattoria di Gracciano, Riserva (*4/89*). Moderately intense aroma, nuances of tobacco and fruit; nice entry, then tannin becomes evident, seems to have sufficient fruit. *

Fattoria di Paterno, Riserva (*twice, 4/90*). A little simple, on the light side, soft center. *

Fattoria Le Casalte (*4/88*). Tobacco, cherry aroma, floral notes; seems to have residual sugar, appears unfinished!

Fattoria Nuova Scopetello (*3 times, 4/90*). Earthy, floral aroma; medium weight, nice fruit, some tannin, rather short. There was some bottle variation. This one, *

La Calonica (*twice, 4/89*). Light, fruity aroma; fairly soft, with nice fruit, good structure, tasty, a bit tight at the end. * + (**)

"La Querce" di Pinzi Pinzuti Lido (*4/89*). Aroma smells like an unfinished wine still in barrel(!); open, soft and fruity in the mouth; soft and simple. +

Ludola Nuova (*twice, 4/89*). Lacks freshness, seems stale. Both bottles, tasted a year apart, gave the same impression.

Melini (*twice, 6/90*). Cherry aroma; nice fruit; open, soft and round, tasty, light tannin; could improve. **

Pantano (*4/89*). Fermentation odors, like a barrel sample; ditto the flavor?

Podere Badelle (*4/88*). Hot tasting, some fruit, overall dull and clumsy.

Podere "Le Caggiole" di Mezzo, Riserva (*4/89*). Light nose, fruity; good structure and flavor, moderate tannin. * +

Poggio alla Sala (*twice, 4/88*). Overly simple, sweet and ripe, lacks weight. +

Poliziano (*4/88*). Reticent aroma; rich and flavorful with ripe fruit flavors; very young with evident quality. ***

Poliziano, Riserva (*6/90*). Lovely rich bouquet, scented of flowers with woodsy nuances, vaguely reminiscent of mushrooms; smooth and soft, well balanced and harmonious; some class evident; still needs some time for the tannin to resolve itself. ***

Raspanti Cav. Giuseppe (*4/88*). Chewy and tannic, fruit sufficient to carry it, good structure. ** +

Sanguineto, Riserva (*twice, 12/90*). Very little in the nose; full-bodied, evident fruit under moderate to high tannin, also some alcohol, rather hard at the end, which is very short; will it develop or is it drying out? (?*) *Bottle of 6/90:* Overripe, fruity, lacks weight and extract; simple and drinkable, no more.

Tenuta di Gracciano, Della Seta Ferrari Corbelli (*twice, 4/89*). Mushroomlike aroma; fairly nice fruit, simple, some tannin at the end. *

Tenuta Trerose (*3 times, 4/89*). Open fruit aroma, mushroom note; soft and fruity; a bit simple but quite drinkable. *

Tenuta Trerose, Riserva (*7 times, 9/90*). Nice fruit, open tobacco and cherry aroma; moderate tannin, seems tighter and more closed than before. *(*) *Bottle of 5/90:* Lovely bouquet, scented with floral notes, hints of dried fruit and leather; rich, tasty, open and forward flavors, good extract and backbone. ** +

Tenuta Valdipiatta, Riserva (*twice, 4/90*). Light, grapey aroma; balanced, tasty, short and dry. *

Vecchia Cantina, Riserva (*4/90*). Slight nose, nice fruit; overall soft, flavorful, simple and short. * +

Vecchia Cantina, Riserva numerta (*4/90, 25,000 bottles*). This one is like a *riserva speciale*, a term not allowed by DOCG; they distinguish it from their straight *riserva* by numbering the bottles. Nice nose; fairly nice fruit on the palate, soft, light tannin, a little short; very ready. * +

1984 * −

The crop size at 357,172 gallons (13,519 hectoliters), equivalent to 150,196 cases, was 56.5 percent of normal and the smallest of the nine years between 1980 and 1988.

Right from the beginning the prospects were not good. It was a difficult harvest. Boscarelli, Del Cerro, Poliziano, and Fanetti produced no Vino Nobile, and Avignonesi made no red wine of any kind. Contucci rated it along with 1980 as the decade's worst. Yet in spite of early projections some wines turned out well. For the most part, they should be drunk now; some are already fading.

Fassati (*twice, 4/88*). Light, fairly nice fruit, far from noble. +

Podere Badelle (*4/88*). Kind of light, not a lot of structure, fairly nice fruit. * −

Vecchia Cantina, Riserva (*4/88*). Decent flavor but unbalanced.

1983 *** +

The crop size was just a little above average with a production of 661,689 gallons (25,045 hectoliters), equivalent to 278,250 cases.

We are quite impressed with the style and elegance of the '83s that we tasted. Niederbacher gives the vintage three stars out of four. Avignonesi, Boscarelli, Contucci, and La Querce, among others, rate it highly. Fassati, however, said the weather was too hot for them and that there wasn't enough rain.

The best wines are very impressive. And although they will keep, they can, for the most part, be consumed and enjoyed now. The *riserve* of Avignonesi and Carletti della Giovampaola were the top two wines that we tasted. Others that were very good include Fattoria del Cerro Riserva, Fattoria di Fognano Riserva "Talosa," Fattoria Le Casalte, Poggio alla Sala, Poliziano, Sanguineto Riserva, and Tenuta Valdipiatta.

Avignonesi (*5 times, 5/88*). Tight nose; great structure, intense and rich, ripe and concentrated; young, needs age. ** + (***)

Buracchi, Riserva (*4/87*). Reticent aroma, cherry component; light to moderate tannin, soft center, simple, some tannin at the end. *

Canneto di Sotto (*twice, 4/87*). Nice nose, suggestive of cherries; vaguely dank note on the palate but nice fruit, rather firm on the finish; good potential. (* +)

Carletti della Giovampaola, Riserva (*4 times, 11/88*). Nose seems a little muted, hints of cherries; soft-centered; young yet with evident quality and attractive flavors. ** + (***)

Carpineto (*10/90*). Nothing to it.

Cecchi Luigi (*5/89*). Low in character, moderate tannin, some fruit.

Contucci, Riserva (*4/88*). Reticent aroma, some fruit evident; young and chewy, yet has the fruit. * +

Fassati (*3 times, 12/88, 50,000 bottles*). Small-scale, fruity, soft, light tannin build at the end. *

Fassati, Riserva (*12/90, 63,241 bottles*). Fragrant floral aroma; a little dry, stale taste to the fruit, still some unresolved tannin as well as some acid, bitter edge, does have some flavor interest. +

Fattoria del Cerro, Riserva (*3 times, 11/87*). Richly fruited aroma; tannin up front with a nice mouthful of fruit beneath, tight toward the end; quite young but evident quality, say two to three years. **(+)

Fattoria di Fognano, Riserva "Talosa" (twice, 11/87). Floral, nutty aroma; moderately intense, light tannin, balanced, fruity, soft; ready now; a bit short. ** −

Fattoria Le Casalte (4/87). Cherrylike fruit; loaded with flavor, balanced; some style, good quality. **(+)

Melini (2/87). Nicely fruited aroma; on entry a rich mouthful of fruit, then light to moderate tannin, could use fruit midpalate, but a nice agreeable glass of wine. * +

Monsigliolo (10/87). Tarlike aroma; chewy tannins, nice fruit, good weight across the palate, rather short. *

Poggio alla Sala (12/86). Fairly nice nose, somewhat nutlike; the best Poggio alla Sala to date. **

Poggio alla Sala, Parceto (12/87, 25,000 bottles). This wine spent six months in barrique. Perfumed, yet alcohol gives a hot impression, nail polish–like aroma, not good, perhaps an off bottle?

Poliziano (4 times, 4/87). Reticent aroma; tight, fairly tannic, nice fruit midpalate, firm finish; very young. **(?*)

Sanguineto, Riserva (twice, 2/90). Soft, open and fruity, fairly well balanced. **

Tenuta Valdipiatta (ex-cask, 4/85). Dark, almost opaque; enormous richness on nose; incredible concentration on palate, tannic; a wine of huge proportions. **(+)

Vecchia Cantina, Riserva (4/87). Reticent aroma; fairly tannic for the fruit, has an astringent nature. (*?)

1982 *** −

The crop was large with an output of 704,965 gallons (26,683 hectoliters), equivalent to 296,448 cases. This was more than 10 percent above the average between 1980 and 1988.

Niederbacher rates the year three out of four stars, on the same level as 1983. Carletti rates it among the three best of the decade. Contucci, as well as most producers, also places it about equal to the previous vintage.

We tasted most of these '82 Nobiles in 1985. Avignonesi, Baiocchi, and Poliziano produced excellent wines, while those of Contucci, Fattoria del Cerro, and the Podere Boscarelli normale and Riserva were very good. Some of the wines are fuller, richer, and more concentrated, and might even outlast the '83s (though we prefer the style and elegance of the '83s). Most are ready, a few might improve. Drink now or over the next year or two. With rare exceptions they won't keep.

Avignonesi (ex-cask, 4/85). Some oak, with vague cherry and floral notes; well balanced, has almost a sweetness to it, moderate tannin, some length. **(*)

Baiocchi (twice, 4/85). Richly concentrated aroma with floral overtones; some tannin to shed, flavor of ripe blackberries, licorice

notes from the aroma through the flavor and the finish, richly concentrated; a big wine. **(*)

Cantina Gattavecchi (4/87). Light, cherrylike aroma; soft center, on the simple side yet with a sweetness to the fruit. *

Casella, Riserva (4/87). Light but nice nose; a bit coarse on the palate, fairly tannic, seems to have sufficient fruit. *(+)

Cecchi Luigi (11/86). Vague lactic aroma; moderate tannin with sufficient fruit to support it; needs three to perhaps five years. *(+)

Contucci (4/87). Small nose; fairly tannic, seems to have enough fruit. *(* −)

Fassati (ex-cask, 4/85). Fairly nice fruit on the nose, vaguely cherrylike, fairly full-bodied, a mouthful of flavor, moderate tannin. **

Fattoria del Cerro (4/85). (This is supposed to be the same wine as Baiocchi, but we find a slight difference.) Floral, fruity aroma; seems sweet, fruit is so rich and ripe, acid seems a bit low; has less complexity than the Baiocchi. **(+)

Fattoria di Gracciano (Dott. Franco Mazzucchelli), Riserva (4/87). Seems older than its years, fairly tannic; is there enough fruit? (?*)

Melini, Riserva (4/87). The bottle was off, some fruit was evident. ?

Podere Boscarelli (4/85). Reticent aroma, but with some fruit evident; a touch of oak in back; a mouthful of tannin gives way to sweet vanilla flavor followed by fruit, a firm, tannic finish. **(+)

Podere Boscarelli, Riserva (10/87). Big and rich, moderate to high tannin, good extract, young and chewy. **(+)

Podere Le Caggiole di Mezzo (4/87). Tar and cherry aroma; some oxidation, also some fruit but seems to be fading; the bottle perhaps?

Poggio alla Sala (4/85). Light nose; has tannin and fruit, recalls Marsala!

Poliziano (4 times, 11/90). Lovely nose; lots of nice fruit, and a lot of structure, fairly long; still quite young. **(*) Bottle of 4/87: Rich nose of ripe fruit; rich and flavorful, well structured, at this stage quite tannic, full-bodied and quite young, needs time. **(*)

Tenuta Valdipiatta (twice, 4/87). Touch of oxidation, rather tired, old and fading, disappointing.

1981 ** −

The crop was small, with a total production of 484,120 gallons (18,324 hectoliters), the equivalent of 203,580 cases. This was 76.5 percent of the average between 1980 and 1988, and down 37 percent from the year earlier.

Niederbacher ranks the year at three out of four stars, equal with 1982 and 1983. At Fassati, they considered it the best vintage since 1967. Boscarelli places it after 1982 and 1983. Dott. Federico Carletti of Poliziano said that although the grapes in 1981 were the best of any vintage in the first half of the 1980s, temperatures were too hot during fermentation, and consequently their wines didn't achieve their full potential.

We tasted most of these wines in 1985. The best wines were those from Avignonesi and Bologna Buonsignori. Other very good ones were Fattoria del Cerro Riserva, Fassati, Fattoria di Fognano Riserva, Fattoria Le Casalte, Podere Boscarelli Riserva, Poggio alla Sala Riserva, and Raspanti Cav. Giuseppe. Very few, if any, are worth keeping longer. Many have already faded or are starting to.

Avignonesi (*twice, 4/85*). Fruity, floral aroma with some oak and notes of cherries; well structured; has style, a wine of character. ***

Bologna Buonsignori (*4/86*). Deep ruby color; cherry aroma, vague tobacco note; superbly balanced, rich and intense, very long; has class. ***

Contucci, Riserva (*11/90*). Seems to be drying out.

Fanetti (*4/85*). Richly fruited aroma with hints of flowers and tar; astringent, fairly tannic but has the fruit to back it up, a bit harsh at the end. *(* +)

Fassati (*twice, 3/87*). Quite a nice nose with fruit and floral components; medium body, soft center, light to moderate tannin; rather nice now. ** −

Fassati, Riserva (*8/87*). Simple, fruity and vinous aroma; soft and easy, simple and fruity, agreeable and ready, short. * +

Fattoria del Cerro, Riserva (*4 times, 10/87*). Fruit, tar, blueberries and flowers define the nose; still has tannin, with lots of fruit beneath, rich and packed with flavor, tasty; coming ready; dry finish. *** −

Fattoria di Fognano, Riserva (*twice, 4/85*). Peppery, fruity aroma reminiscent of a Côtes du Rhône, follows through on the palate, light tannin, nice fruit; young, some quality evident. *(*)

Fattoria di Gracciano, Podere Cervognano, Riserva (*twice, 4/85*). A fairly reticent aroma that hints of fruit; light tannin, shallow, tannic finish; a dull wine.

Fattoria Le Casalte (*twice, 4/85*). Nice aroma of spice and berries, recalls a Côtes du Rhône wine, ditto on the flavor, moderate tannin and fruit; shows quality; an off note mars the finish. **(+)

La Querce di Pinzi Pinzuti Lido (*twice, 4/85*). Both times there was some oxidation, dull and flat.

Melini, Riserva (*twice, 9/87*). Fairly nice fruit; light tannin, could use more character, still there is flavor. *

Podere Boscarelli (*twice, 11/85*). Light nose; some tannin, not a lot of stuffing. *(+)

Podere Boscarelli, Riserva (*4/85*). Richly fruited aroma, fairly intense; moderate tannin, a nice mouthful of flavor, well balanced; has some style; give it about three more years. **(+)

Podere Le Caggiole (*4/85*). Small aroma, some fruit evident; dull, wheatlike flavor, astringent, tannic finish.

Poggio alla Sala (*4/85*). Has a cooked fruit character, shallow, short.

Poggio alla Sala, Riserva (*twice, 3/87*). Vanilla and nutlike aroma, hint of varnish in a nice way; loads of fruit, and oak, rather nice; on the young side. * + (**)

Poliziano (*ex-cask, 4/85*). Lots of nice fruit on the nose, also a touch of licorice and a tarlike note; less impressive on the palate, nice entry then shallow, rather short. *

Poliziano, Riserva (*twice, 4/85*). Complex bouquet with nuances of licorice and cherries; nice entry, then a bit shallow, tannic finish. *

Raspanti Cav. Giuseppe (*twice, 4/85*). Pretty floral aroma with notes of pine; has a sweetness to the flavor, a bit light, some tannin, very nice until the finish, which is somewhat bitter. **

Sanguineto, Riserva (*4/87*). Rubber tire aroma; fruity, coarse, moderate tannin. * −

Santavenere (*twice, 4/85*). Flowers, cherries and spice on aroma; some tannin, fruity flavor, perhaps too fruity; lacks Vino Nobile character; three stars as a light, fresh, fruity red, as a Vino Nobile * A second bottle had a problem with hydrogen sulfide.

Tenuta Valdipiatta (*twice, 4/87*). Light nose, fruity, vaguely floral; moderate tannin, good fruit, short with some tannin at the end. *(+)

1 9 8 0   0

The crop of 767,078 gallons (29,034 hectoliters), equivalent to 322,568 cases, was the largest between 1980 and 1988 and more than 21 percent greater than the average of 632,812 gallons (23,952 hectoliters).

This was a mixed vintage. They won't be long-lived wines. Niederbacher gives it two stars out of four. Boscarelli said it was poor and didn't bottle. Contucci, too, rated it as poor. At one time we found it sort of in between the two evaluations. As for now, the wines have, for the most part, faded. And while we gave it one star plus, today zero would be a more reasonable evaluation.

Buracchi, Riserva (*4 times, 4/85*). Two bottles were corked! Another—overly tannic for the low fruit, and lacking in character. *The best bottle:* Nice aroma of fruit with chocolate and spicy aspects; fruity; lacking in length and style. *

Cantina Gattavecchi (*3 times, 4/85*). No variation here—all were unbalanced, low in fruit and lacking personality.

Casella di Carpini (*3 times, 4/87*). Rubber tire aroma; tannic, insufficient fruit remains.

Contucci (*twice, 4/85*). Stinky, reeking of mercaptans(!); a disgusting flavor—barnyards and rubber tires!!! *Another bottle:* Tarry aroma; tannic with a core of almost sweet fruit beneath. *(*)

Fassati, Podere Fonte al Vescovo (*6 times, 9/87, 63,241 bottles*). Low fruit, odd, cheeselike character, was better a year ago.

Fattoria di Fognano, Riserva (*4/85*). Light aroma with fairly nice fruit, somewhat reminiscent of a Côtes du Rhône wine, carries through on palate, moderate tannin; needs another year or two. *(* −)

Poggio alla Sala, Riserva (*6/86*). Medium garnet; chocolate note; has tannin, fruit seems deficient, tannic aftertaste. (*)

Sanguineto di Maria e Lucia Monaci, Riserva (*twice, 9/86*). Vaguely floral, fruity aroma; overly tannic, shallow, short.

Scopetto (*twice, 4/85*). Lightly floral bouquet; some tannin, good fruit in the center, fairly well balanced; a bit simple. *(+)

Tenuta di Gracciano (*twice, 4/87*). Awful nose; drying out.

Tenuta Valdipiatta (*twice, 4/87*). Oxidized, fading fast.

Vecchia Cantina, Riserva (*4/85*). Light aroma with fairly nice fruit, ditto the flavor, marred by an off note at the end. * −

1 9 7 9 *

This was a very good vintage for many producers. Alas, they are showing age. At one time they deserved three stars; today one star or less would seem to be a fairer assessment.

Ancilli, Riserva Speciale (*12/85*). Light to medium color; straightforward, fruit aroma; nicely fruited, flavorful, agreeable, simple, berry character, very short. *

Avignonesi (*4/85*). Expansive floral bouquet with a vague cherrylike note; very well balanced; an elegant, stylish wine; velvety, very long finish; has room for improvement yet. ***

Bologna Buonsignori, Riserva (*4/85*). Pretty nose of ripe fruit and flowers, cherry and tarlike notes; sweet flavor of ripe berries and cherries, soft and round, some tannin; has real style. ***

Cantina Gattavecchi (*twice, 5/85*). Unbalanced, too much tannin for the fruit.

Carletti della Giovampaola [*second label of Poliziano*] (*4/85*). Not much nose, but a lot of flavor, cherrylike fruit, moderate tannin, fairly well balanced. **(+)

Casella, Riserva (*4/85*). Tar and fruit on aroma; fairly nice fruit on entry gives way to tannin—is there enough fruit(?), we suspect not.

Fanetti, Riserva (*3 times, 12/87*). Chocolate nose; fairly full-bodied, could use more fruit, but still it is good. *

Fassati (*11/84*). Reticent aroma; some tannin to lose, flavorful; quite young. *(+)

Fassati, Podere Fonte al Vescovo (*4 times, 6/86, 63,241 bottles*). Rubber tire aroma; dull, even bitter in the mouth; could use more depth though certainly drinkable. *

Fassati, Podere Fonte al Vescovo Riserva (*twice, 8/87*). Lovely nose, floral note; nice fruit, some tannin, flavorful; drink now while there is still fruit, doubtful future, a bit drying at the end. *

Fattoria del Cerro, Riserva Speciale (*4/85*). Aroma shows some development, with vague tarlike and floral nuances; light tannin, fairly fruity, some spice, a vague off note at the end. **

Fattoria di Fognano, Riserva (*4/85*). Spicy, cherry aroma; well balanced, moderate tannin, flavorful, short. *(+)

Le Pietrose, Riserva [*produced by Fattoria del Cerro*] (*4/85*). Nice nose, vaguely floral; overripe, pruney taste, not as good as the del Cerro. *

Podere Boscarelli (*3 times, 9/83*). Rich aroma though not fully open, ripe fruit is evident; flavorful; still needs time to soften. *(*)

Podere Boscarelli, Riserva (*4/85*). Aroma displays some oak over a lot of fruit with a tarlike aspect and a vaguely floral note; loads of tannin but the fruit is there to carry it, has a sweetness to it, a rough, tannic finish. **(*)

Tenuta Valdipiatta (*3 times, 4/87*). Cherry aroma; light to moderate tannin, light-bodied; doubtful future. *(?)

Tistarelli Mario [*bottled by CA.VI.O.T.*] (*4 times, 3/85*). Oxidized. The bottles tasted in 1983 were not oxidized but had very little to offer.

"Tripusa," Brigatti, Riserva (*3/86*). Sangiovese character, unbalanced, fruity, drinkable, no more.

"Tripusa," Enoteca Europea, Riserva (*4/85*). Astringent, low in fruit, unbalanced.

Vecchia Cantina (*twice, 4/85*). Light nose; has tannin and the fruit to carry it, somewhat astringent on aftertaste. *

1 9 7 8 * −

The wines of 1978 were more variable than those of 1979, and like that younger vintage, they have mostly faded. While we rated it two stars once, today at most one star minus would seem to be a more reasonable judgment.

Avignonesi (*4/85*). Floral bouquet, has delicacy; well balanced, light- to medium-bodied, flavorful; quite ready, soft and smooth, room for further improvement; light tannin at the end, which is a bit short. ** +

Cantina del Redi (*4/85*). Baked, cooked, awful.

Cantina Gattavecchi (*twice, 5/85*). Unbalanced with tannin, coarse, no real character.

Casella, Riserva (*4/85*). Overly tannic for the fruit.

Cecchi Luigi (*twice, 1/84*). Awful. A bottle tasted a few months earlier was unstructured and shallow.

Fanetti (*10/81*). Nose is somewhat muted; some tannin, soft, a bit light-bodied, tasty; some style and length. **

Fanetti, Riserva Speciale (*twice, 1/84*). Fruity, floral bouquet; firm and tannic, has structure and fruit; needs two to three more years. *(*)

Fassati (*11/84*). Small nose; astringent, not a lot of fruit; where will it go?

Fattoria del Cerro, Riserva Speciale (*3 times, 4/85*). Aroma shows complexity of bottle age, with nuances of flowers and cherries; well balanced, soft and smooth; some style; ready now; very good indeed. ***

Fattoria di Fognano, Riserva (*1/84*). Almondlike notes on aroma; unbalanced, dull; not a lot to it.

Podere Boscarelli (*6 times, 8/82*). Cherrylike aroma marred by a slight harshness; nice fruit, still needs a few years to soften, short finish. (We have found considerable bottle variation with this wine.) *(+)

Podere Boscarelli, aged in barrique (*4/85*). Some oak on the nose and a lot of fruit; falls down on palate—tannic and lacking in fruit.

Poggio alla Sala (*5 times, 1/84*). None of the bottles amounted to much, all had a baked, cooked character reminiscent of a southern wine (could the 10 percent from outside the zone be showing its nature or did they use concentrate?), dull, unbalanced, flat.

Poliziano, Riserva Speciale (*4/85*). Floral bouquet with some nice fruit in the back; moderate tannin, nice entry, tannic finish that tails off at the end.

Tenuta Valdipiatta (*twice, 5/85*). Fragrant though light aroma; medium-bodied, fruity, a bit simple perhaps, but drinkable enough, short. *

Vecchia Cantina, Riserva (*twice, 3/84*). Nice nose though has a bit of an overripe character; flat and shallow. The bottle tasted two months earlier was considerably better and merited *.

1977 *

The '77s were good wines that failed to live up to their original acclaim. Contucci rates it highly. As for today, at most one star, and our advice is to drink them up. Few will keep and many are already too old.

Bologna Buonsignori, Riserva (*5/85*). Woodsy bouquet with floral and berrylike nuances; still has tannin to lose, well balanced, flavorful; elegant and stylish; needs two years or more, but approachable now. ***(+)

Bordini, Riserva [*bottled by L.B. & F. of Orvieto*] (*9/83*). Nice nose up front, but with an off-putting note lurking in the back; off flavors, thin.

Buracchi (*4/85*). Some oxidation, reminiscent of a wet dog!

Carletti della Giovampaola, Riserva [*second label of Poliziano*] (*4/85*). Showing age on aroma; very shallow, and a bit thin toward the back.

Contucci (*4/80*). Aroma is still closed, but fruit and oak evident; nicely balanced, some tannin, a bit light, good structure; nearly ready. *(+)

Fassati (*3 times, 5/84*). Cherrylike aroma with a floral aspect; good fruit on entry, low acid, has an overripe quality to it and a dull finish.

Fassati, Riserva (*5/85*). Dull and flat, with a somewhat cooked character.

Fattoria del Cerro, Riserva Speciale (*4/85*). Complex bouquet, toasty and fruity; well balanced, soft and round, vaguely sweet, rich blackberrylike fruit, some length. ** +

Fattoria di Fognano, Riserva (*4 times, 9/83*). Pale color shows considerable age, browning; some fruit on nose marred by a vague off note, lacking in structure, weight and definition.

Pantano (*4/85*). Corked.

Podere Boscarelli (*3 times, 8/82*). As with the 1978 Boscarelli we found considerable bottle variation. In this bottle mercaptans were painfully evident. A bottle tasted three weeks earlier—lovely bouquet, nice flavor, well balanced, shows promise. **

Podere Ferretto prop. Fattoria delle Maestrelle [*bottled by Storiche Cantine*] (*5/85, 61,100 bottles*). Toffee notes on aroma, vaguely medicinal; lacks weight, structure and definition.

Podere Il Macchione, Le Caggiole (*4/85*). Stinky, unbalanced, bitter.

Tenuta di Gracciano (*3 times, 8/82*). Nose a bit closed but already shows some fruit; has tannin and the stuffing to support it; lacks style; needs a few years yet. *

Tenuta Valdipiatta (*twice, 4/85*). Lovely bouquet of flowers, fruit and vanilla; light to moderate tannin, fairly nice fruit; short, tannic aftertaste. *

1976 0

This year was very bad from the start. Fassati bottled, Boscarelli and Del Cerro did not. Contucci puts it on a par with that other poor vintage of the 1970s, 1972.

1975 *

Niederbacher gives 1975 four stars out of four, calling it one of the all-time greats. Contucci rates it as one of the best. It's amazing how few wines lived up to expectations. For the most part, they have faded or are starting to fade. There is no need to hold them any longer. Most have turned the corner and are on the decline.

Bologna Buonsignori, Riserva (*4/85*). Vague off note mars a very nice aroma; some tannin to shed, well structured, heaps of flavor; young; shows a lot of quality. **(*)

Carletti della Giovampaola, Riserva Speciale [second label of Poliziano] (4/85). Corked.

Contucci (4/80). Floral bouquet; well balanced, tasty; quite nice. **

Contucci, Riserva (11/90). Nice nose, open fruit and complex, underbrush component; soft, nice texture, smooth, long finish is a tad dry; has aged very well indeed. ** +

Fanetti, Riserva (3 times, 8/82). Fruity aroma; fairly well balanced, flavorful, better on palate than nose but a bit pedestrian. *

Fassati (4 times, 3/82). Mineral notes on aroma; some tannin, some fruit; okay, not special.

Fassati, Riserva (5 times, 5/85). Bottle variation here—the best, and most recent—soft, fruity, easy and agreeable. * +

Fattoria di Fognano (twice, 4/85). A big zero—very little to it, lacks character and structure.

Fattoria di Fognano, Riserva Speciale (twice, 3/82). Good fruit on aroma, some oak; flavorful, fairly well balanced, has tannin to lose, a bit short. *

Fattoria di Gracciano (10/80). Aroma has a hint of chestnuts and a harshness; considerable tannin; some potential. *

Fattoria di Gracciano, Riserva (9/79). Vaguely floral aroma; nice fruit; needs more time; lacks depth. *

Fattoria di Gracciano, Riserva Speciale (12/80). Some complexity on nose; shallow, some alcohol mars the finish.

Melini, Riserva Speciale (3 times, 9/83). Fragrant perfume; good fruit, some tannin to lose, medium-bodied; in all a nice glass of wine. ** −

Podere Boscarelli (5 times, 12/85). Color beginning to show some age; a lot of age apparent on the nose; some tannin; drinkable not much more; over the top. *Bottle of 3/85:* Vaguely floral aroma; some tannin and acid, fairly good fruit, alcohol mars the finish. It was better between two and four years ago when it merited two stars plus; it is showing its age. *

Poggio alla Sala (4/85). Disgusting aroma and flavor.

Poliziano, Riserva (twice, 10/81). Fragrant; some tannin, tasty; ready now. * +

Tenuta di Gracciano (4/85). Odor of mercaptans; overly tannic, low fruit; unimpressive to say the least.

Vecchia Cantina, Riserva (4/85). Toasty, fruity aroma; moderate tannin, flavorful entry, tails off toward the end. * −

1974 0

Most '74s are senile; they offer little or no interest. The Bologna Buonsignori Riserva, tasted in 1985, was still very good. As for its state today, we suspect that even it is over the top.

Bologna Buonsignori, Riserva (twice, 6/86). Beautiful brick red robe, garnet rim; intense, perfumed bouquet; richly flavored, still some tannin, but soft and smooth with a roundness and length. ***

Bordini (twice, 3/82). Slight oxidation mars the nose, which has a raisiny note; taste of overripe, raisined grapes.

Fanetti, Riserva (3 times, 3/82). Floral aroma with tarry notes; overly tannic for the fruit.

Fassati, Podere Fonte al Vescovo (4/85). Honey and berries on the aroma, ripe berrylike fruit; near its peak, surprisingly good. **

Fattoria del Cerro, Riserva Speciale (4/85). A lot of age apparent on the nose; tannin on entry, still a lot of flavor but not to keep, drinkable now, somewhat off at the end. *

Fattoria di Gracciano, Riserva (4/80). Light, fragrant aroma; nice flavor, still has tannin to soften. *

1973 0

This vintage was highly acclaimed at one time. Niederbacher gave it three stars out of four. They are too old today.

Baiocchi (4/85). Medium garnet, brick at rim; light nose, some fruit; light tannin, very soft and smooth; some tannin at the end; quite ready, not to hold. * +

Bigi Luigi, Riserva Speciale (11/78). Light color; small nose; light-bodied, not much tannin; drinkable. *

Bologna Buonsignori, Riserva (5/85). Woodsy, berrylike aroma; well balanced, still some tannin but soft and ready, strawberrylike fruit, fairly long on finish. ***

Fanetti (4 times, 8/82). Awful cardboard smell (dekkra?). The bottles tasted three years earlier were quite nice, with a fragrant bouquet and a hint of sweetness, they merited two stars. This one 0.

Fanetti, Riserva Speciale (4/85). Off-odors; dank.

Fassati (12/79). Light, perfumed aroma; high acid, shallow.

Fassati, Podere Fonte al Vescovo (4/85). Floral bouquet with some fruit, but showing age; still has tannin, nice fruit up front; drying out. *

Fattoria di Gracciano, Riserva (9/79). Some volatile acidity, light, fruity, bitter finish.

Poliziano, Riserva (4/80). Nutty aroma; some fruit, light and tasty, balanced, some tannin. *

Tenuta Valdipiatta (5/85). Corky.

Vecchia Cantina (8/82). Pale garnet; light, fragrant aroma; a bit light in body, tasty, no tannin remains, almost sweet—at its peak. *

1972 0

This was a hopeless vintage. The wines didn't stand a chance. The weather was poor. Contucci rates it along with 1976 as the worst of the decade.

1971 0

The 1971 vintage was another poor one. The wines are too old now.

Fassati (*twice, 8/82*). Tart, lacks flavor; shot.

Fassati, Podere Fonte al Vescovo (*4/85*). Dried berrylike fruit on aroma; tannic, some fruit; drying out.

Fattoria del Pantano (*4/85, 500 bottles*). Vaguely floral bouquet; nice entry, moderate tannin, some sweetness; not to keep but nice now. ** —

Fattoria di Gracciano, Riserva (*10/80*). Browning; alcohol mars the nose, not much flavor left.

Poliziano, Riserva Speciale (*11/80*). Pale; nutty, fruity aroma; light, some tannin and not much beneath it.

1970 *

This was a highly acclaimed vintage, and the wines have lasted well. There is, however, no need to keep them any longer. Niederbacher gave it his maximum of four stars. Few, if any, will offer any interest.

Baiocchi (*4/85*). Floral, vaguely toasty aroma that shows some age; soft and flavorful, a bit past its peak but quite nice now, touch of tannin at the end. **

Contucci, Riserva Speciale (*twice, 4/85*). Aroma of flowers and fruit, shows a lot of development; well balanced, heaps of flavor, soft, lovely now; has some style; could even improve. ***

Fanetti, Riserva Speciale (*9 times, 1/86*). Still a lot of quality, soft, some tannin, lively, well balanced; ready. ** +

Fassati (*4 times, 8/82*). Still some fruit on the nose; nothing left on the palate—it was quite nice a few years ago.

Fassati, Podere Fonte al Vescovo (*4/85*). Small nose with some fruit; drying out though there's still some fruit left.

Melini, Riserva Speciale (*6 times, 3/83*). Some oxidation on the nose; drying on the palate. In 1979 and 1980 this was a very good bottle of wine meriting two stars, today it's too old.

Poliziano (*twice, 4/85*). Floral aroma; light, drying out, fruit on entry, then nothing.

Poliziano, Fattoria Casale, Riserva (*10/81*). Shows age on nose but very little complexity; some dullness; beginning to dry out.

1969 0

Niederbacher gave 1969 two out of four stars. Contucci picks it as one of the worst in quality. Most likely the wines are too old now.

1968 0

The '68s are long gone.

Fassati (*3 times, 8/82*). Some fruit still evident but the wine has dried out.

Fassati, Podere Fonte al Vescovo (*4/85*). Aroma of an old wine; still some flavor interest though drying out.

1967 0

Contucci, among others, rates this year highly. Originally 1967 was one of the all-time great vintages, perhaps deserving four stars. The few we've tasted were completely gone.

Contucci Riserva Speciale (*4/85*). Faded.

Fassati (*twice, 8/82*). Nothing of interest remains.

Fassati, Podere Fonte al Vescovo (*4/85*). Oxidized.

OLDER VINTAGES

Most, if not all, older vintages are too old now. But, for the record, here is how the authorities in the zone rated them:

****	1958
***	1964, 1962, 1954, 1952, 1947
**	1966, 1961, 1957, 1951, 1949, 1945
*	1960, 1956, 1955, 1953, 1950, 1948, 1946
0	1965, 1963, 1959

Baiocchi 1965 Riserva (*4/85*). Nose shows a lot of age, vaguely jammy; drying out but still has flavor interest and fruit. * —

Baiocchi 1964 Riserva (*4/85*). Floral bouquet, vaguely honeyed; light tannin, some delicacy, smooth-textured; some age shows but still very good. **

Contucci 1964 Riserva (*11/90*). Bouquet displays suggestions of dried fruit, flowers and animal fur; loaded with flavor, a tad dry at the end; still in all this wine has aged very well indeed. *** —

Fratelli Baiocchi 1957 Riserva (*4/85*). Brick red robe, orange rim; bouquet has delicacy and floral notes; velvety, round and sweet, very ready, light tannin, complex, long finish with notes of blueberries; perhaps just beginning to dry out. ***

Fratelli Baiocchi 1953 Riserva (*4/85*). Orangish brick robe; toasty, floral bouquet, vaguely berrylike with a hint of leather; soft and round, sweet and delicate; very long finish has a touch of tannin. ***

VINO NOBILE DI MONTEPULCIANO PRODUCERS

Ancilli. The only wine we tasted from them, the '79, was good. Vino Nobile [*]

Antinori. We heard that Antinori, of Chianti fame, bought the Braccisca vineyards in 1989. In 1990 they rented space at Dei and produced their first Nobile. The wine was made by the enologist at their Castello della Sala property. We have high expectations.

Anzelotti Bruno Azienda Agricola (*Valiano di Montepulciano*). They belong to the *consorzio.* We've never met their Nobile.

Avignonesi (*Montepulciano*), *1978.* Avignonesi, managed by the Falvo family, owns 208 acres (84 hectares) of vines; of this 59 acres (24 hectares) are in Montepulciano and 148 (60) in Cortona. Their vineyards in Montepulciano are planted for Vino Nobile and Rosso di Montepulciano. Unlike many others here, they continue to produce a Chianti Colli Senesi. They also have plantings of cabernet franc, chardonnay, cabernet sauvignon, merlot, sauvignon, semillon, pinot noir, traminer, and riesling. Most of their vineyards were replanted in 1972, and a few in 1973 and 1974. The vineyards range in altitude from 950 to 1,085 feet (290 and 330 meters) above sea level and have a southern exposure. The loose soil contains significant amounts of clay.

Avignonesi produces an average of 428 gallons per acre (40 hectoliters per hectare) for Nobile and 374 (35) for their other wines. Their production averages about 400,000 bottles of wine a year. This includes 96,000 bottles of Vino Nobile, 48,000 of the *barrique*-aged sangiovese-cabernet blend *Grifi,* 10,000 to 12,000 of Chianti Colli Senesi, a few white wines—100,000 to 120,000 bottles of Bianco Vergine Valdichiana, 18,000 to 20,000 of Malvasia, and 48,000 of Il Marzocco, a very good barrel-fermented Chardonnay. They also produce the barrel-fermented, sauvignon blanc Il Vignola, Aleatico di Sovana, a Merlot, and a Cabernet Sauvignon, as well as what is without a doubt two of the finest dessert wines that we've ever tasted—a *vin santo* that's simply in a class by itself and Occhio di Pernice, which might be even better. They produce a scant 600 to 800 bottles a year of each of these outstanding dessert wines. And since 1988 a late-harvest botrytis chardonnay–sauvignon blanc blend has been produced. There were 8,000 bottles of the '88 and 9,000 of the '89. The grapes were harvested in November.

Their Vino Nobile ferments for twelve days and is aged in fairly new oak casks. A few years ago they told us that they were exper-imenting with *barriques* for that wine. Since the 1978 vintage their Vino Nobile has been made without white grapes.

Among their Vino Nobiles, the very best ones included the '79, '81, '83, the '85—both the *normale* and Riserva—and the '86 Riserva. We also liked the very good '78, '82, and '86. There is currently no finer producer in the zone. Vino Nobile ***

Baiocchi. See *Fattoria del Cerro.*

Bertille Azienda Agricola (*Montepulciano,* località *Bertile*). They are another member of the *consorzio* whose wines we've never met.

Bigi Luigi. The Bigi Vino Nobile can be good, though unexciting. Many better Chiantis are available. We haven't tasted their Vino Nobile since the mediocre '73. We suspect that they are the L.B. & F. of Orvieto that bottles the mediocre Bordini Vino Nobile. Vino Nobile [0]

Bindella Rudolf Azienda Agricola (*Acquaviva di Montepulciano*). Rudolf Bindella produces three wines, a Vino Nobile di Montepulciano *normale* and *riserva,* and the *vino da tavola* Vallocaia. The only Nobile that we have tasted from Bindella, the '86, was very good. Somehow we suspect that they are the same as *Terre Bindella.* Vino Nobile **

Bologna Buonsignori Nobili F.lli Luigi e Leopoldo, Fattoria Comizio (*Montepulciano*). The few wines we've tasted from this producer have been outstanding wines of style and balance. They are, or were, the zone's finest. Unfortunately Sig. Bologna Buonsignori has retired, and the wine is no longer being produced. The last vintage he bottled was the '81. If you're lucky, you'll be able to find a few bottles that were well kept. We did just a few years ago. Vino Nobile ****

Bordini. We haven't tasted bottles from Bordini since the '77; they were quite mediocre, if not downright poor. They were, at the time, bottled by L.B. & F. of Orvieto—*Bigi Luigi* perhaps. Vino Nobile [0]

Buracchi Azienda Agricola (*Montepulciano Stazione*). Buracchi owns 20 acres (8 hectares) of vineyards, 8.6 (3.5) in vines for Vino Nobile. From the rest of their vines they produce the other typical

THE VINEYARDS OF AVIGNONESI

Vineyard	Location	Acres	Hectares	Altitude in	
				Feet	Meters
La Selva	Cortona località Cignano	148.2	60	985	300
I Poggetti	Montepulciano località Argiano	44.5	18	950	290
Le Capezzine	Montepulciano località Valiano	14.8	6	1,085	330
Total		207.5	84		

wines of the area: Chianti, *vin santo,* and a white wine. Their annual production of Vino Nobile ranges from 20,000 to 26,500 bottles. The wine is aged in a combination of oak and chestnut casks. While we weren't impressed with either the '77 or *normale* '85, we did like the '80, '83, '85 Riserva, and '87. Vino Nobile *

Canneto Agricola, Canneto di Sotto *(Montepulciano).* They first bottled a Vino Nobile from the 1983 vintage; it displayed potential. And the '85 Riserva was very good indeed. The former was labeled Canneto di Sotto, the latter Canneto. And from cask, both the '87 and '88 displayed some potential. Vino Nobile ** –

Cantina del Redi. We haven't tasted their wine since the '78 vintage, and at the time we must admit that they were a disgrace to the name. *Povero* Redi! We recently heard that they sold their winery to Vecchia Cantina, who, we suspect, put it to better use. Vino Nobile [0 –]

Cantina Gattavecchi *(Montepulciano,* località *S. Maria), 1958.* This firm has no vineyards. They buy wines, and blend, age, and bottle them under their label, an average of 30,000 bottles a year. At one time we were less than impressed with their Vino Nobile di Montepulciano, Chianti Colli Senesi, or, for that matter, any of their other wines. But, we are happy to report, while we were disappointed with the wines from the '78 to the '80, from the '82 Nobile things are looking up. We can recommend their '82, '85, and '86 Vino Nobiles. Vino Nobile *

Cantina Innocenti Vittorio *(Montefollonico), 1981.* Innocenti's first Vino Nobile di Montepulciano was produced at Podere Sambono in 1981; they made 500 cases. The wine is aged in chestnut casks. They also produce a Chianti Colli Senesi and a *vin santo.*

Cantina Pulciano *(Matassini Ercolani Gabriella)* *(Montepulciano).* There is also a **Fattoria Pulciano** owned by Sergio Ercolani. Both estates have the same address and the same phone number, so there must be a connection, although we don't know what it is. We've never tasted the wines from either one.

Cantina Santavenere *(Massimo Romeo)* *(Montepulciano), 1979.* Santavenere owns 22 acres (9 hectares) in Montepulciano from which they produce some 30,000 bottles a year. We can recommend the '81. Vino Nobile *

Cantine Baiocchi *(Sai Agricola).* See **Fattoria del Cerro.**

Carletti della Giovampaola. This is a second label used by **Poliziano.**

Carpineto. This mediocre Chianti Classico producer sells, not surprisingly, a mediocre Nobile. Admittedly we've tasted only one wine, the '83. Vino Nobile 0

Castellani, Tenuta La Ciarliana *(Gracciano), 1962.* This firm owns 42 acres (17 hectares), one-third of which is planted in vines for Vino Nobile. The wines are aged in a combination of oak and chestnut casks.

Cecchi Luigi. This Chianti Classico producer markets a Vino Nobile that is drinkable enough, though at one time it was rarely more than that. Like their other wines, it too has improved. We liked their '82, '85, and '86, though not their '83. The '86 was made by Della Seta. Vino Nobile *

Cerraia. This Vino Nobile is marketed by the Agricoltori Geografico of the Chianti Classico area. We've never tasted it.

Contucci Azienda Agricola *(Montepulciano), 1730.* The Contucci family, Gian Stefano, Maria Vittoria, Gigliola, and Alamanno Contucci, own the twelfth-century cellars and some 52 acres (21 hectares) of vineyards, 34 (13.7) in vines for Vino Nobile and 7.2 (2.9) for Chianti Colli Senesi. Their vineyards, in the Salarco section of Montepulciano, are planted at altitudes ranging from 1,310 to 1,640 feet (400 to 500 meters) above sea level. Mulinvecchio and Pietra Rossa are their crus.

They produce, on average, between 133,000 and 180,000 bottles of wine annually, including 60,000 to 80,000 of Vino Nobile; 13,000 to 20,000 of Rosso di Montepulciano; 13,000 to 20,000 of a *vino da tavola,* Rosso del Sansovino, made from prugnolo gentile grapes; 20,000 to 26,000 of Bianco della Contessa; and 26,600 to 33,300 of Rosso and Bianco Tavolo. Contucci also makes 1,067 to 1,333 bottles of *vin santo* from 100 percent malvasia grapes. Their Vino Nobile is aged in a combination of oak and chestnut casks. The Nobile *normale* spends about three years in *botte,* the *riserva* four years. The casks range in age from three to eighteen years. In 1990, Contucci began using French oak; previously the oak was Slavonian. Their '89 Rosso, one of the best that we tasted, was aged in oak casks. And since 1988, Contucci, like many others here, has been producing a Nobile cru from their Pietra Rossa vineyard.

Contucci was among the first to bottle a Vino Nobile and until a few years ago sold the wine under the name Cantine Riunite, Cav. Mario Contucci. At one time we found their wines among the zone's best. Then not only the label changed, but the wine in the bottle as well, and the change was unfortunately not for the better. We can happily recommend their '82, '83 Riserva, '85 Riserva, and '86 Riserva. Perhaps this is an indication that things are returning to normal and the wines are back to form here. In 1981, Alamanno Contucci took over at the helm, and perhaps that explains the improvement here. Vino Nobile **

Crociani Arnaldo *(Montepulciano).* This is still another member of the *consorzio* whose Nobile we've not met.

Dei *(Montepulciano).* Glauco and Galiceo Dei own this estate and its 54 acres (22 hectares) of vines. Claudio Basla, who manages Altesino properties in Montalcino, also manages the commercial affairs of this estate. The aging cellar was the old Bologna Buonsignori property and the vineyards were planted and owned by Dei. They expect another 15 to 25 acres (6 to 10 hectares) to come into production. Previously they sold the grapes to the co-op. The only wine they produce is Vino Nobile di Montepulciano. Their production was 26,000 bottles in 1985, 30,000 in 1986 and 1987, 40,000 in 1988, and 52,000 in 1989. If they continue to expand at the same rate, by the year 2005 they will be producing more than a million bottles a year! They will produce a Rosso di Montepulciano from 1990, and in 1990, for the first time, they produced two crus, Roccolo and Bossona. They also sell wine under the Villa Martiena label. They told us that it is the same exact wine, yet when we visited them in November 1990 the Dei Nobile was still in vat and the Martiena had been in bottle for four months. Perhaps the difference is due more to marketing considerations. Thus far, based on their first three wines, the '85, '86, and '87, and the barrel samples of '88 and '89, we rate them as the producer most worth watching. Vino Nobile *** –

Fanetti, Comm. Adamo e Giuseppe, Tenuta "S. Agnese" (Montepulciano), 1921. Fanetti, proprietor of the 306-acre (124-hectare) S. Agnese estate, has 45 acres (18 hectares) in vines, 35 (14) for Vino Nobile from which he produces 80,000 bottles a year, and 10 (4) for Chianti which yield 26,000 bottles. He also makes *vin santo*, white wine, and a unique *vino da tavola rosso*, **Principesco**. Fanetti's total production is about 120,000 bottles a year. From his 2.5-acre (1-hectare) Vin del Sasso vineyard, planted in 1981, he plans to produce approximately 2,500 bottles of a *barrique*-aged Cabernet. Fanetti, the estate that "made" Vino Nobile, enjoys quite a high reputation, but we find that too often their wines fail to live up to it. On rare occasions, when they do, these wines are among the best in the zone, but too often they are mediocre. The last vintage we tasted from Fanetti was the '81. Vino Nobile **

Farnetani (Sinalunga). They produce 1,000 cases annually of a Nobile that they label Podere Badelle. They also produce a Chianti Colli Senesi. The *cantina* Podere Badelle is in Acquaviva. Their first Nobile was the passable '84. The '85, on the other hand, was mediocre. Vino Nobile +

Fassati Casa Vinicola del Chianti (Pieve di Sinalunga), 1913. This winery has been owned by Fazi Battaglia of Verdicchio fame since 1969. They have two facilities for their Vino Nobile, one in Montepulciano itself, where the cellars are, and one in Sinalunga for bottling and stockage. Their 37 acres (15 hectares) of vines at Podere Fonte al Vescovo are planted at altitudes ranging from 1,310 to 1,575 feet (400 to 480 meters) above sea level. The oldest vines are forty years old. A few years ago they told us that their most recent plantings were put in in 1976. Since 1977 their entire production of Vino Nobile has been made from their own grapes in their Podere Fonte al Vescovo vineyard. In 1985 they acquired vineyards in Graccianello, and in 1988, Gaggiole. They own the Azienda Agricola Graccianello in Gracciano.

About six or seven years ago Fassati bought 50 acres (20 hectares) in the Chianti zone. Since 1986 their Chianti has been produced from their own grapes; previously they bought wine for both Chianti and Chianti Classico and aged it in their cellars. They will continue to buy from the Classico zone.

Their first Vino Nobile was produced in 1967 and, except for 1972, they have bottled one every year since. They make a selection of the grapes, using the best in their *riserva*.

Since 1979, Fassati has been treating their vines against mold with an antibotrytis spray that they say they were the first in the area to use. This treatment, their enologist Amedeo Esposito points out, made it possible for them to produce a Vino Nobile in 1984— and it's a good one—while many other producers had to declassify.

Their grapes are pressed in basket presses, and the wine is aged first in chestnut casks before being moved to oak for the final phase of aging. Some one-third of their casks are chestnut, the rest oak. Fassati produces on average 93,000 bottles of Vino Nobile a year and 25,000 bottles of Chianti.

Our fairly extensive experience with these wines has left us less than impressed. Of those we tasted, we can recommend the '81 *normale* and Riserva, and the '83, '86, and '87. They are fairly good wines, but unexciting, lacking in class and style. The '85 *normale* and Riserva from Graccianello are another matter, however. They represent an improvement in quality. Vino Nobile: *normale* *, Podere Fonte al Vescovo *, Graccianello **

Fattoria del Cerro (Sai Agricola) (Acquaviva di Montepulciano), 1922. Originally founded as F.lli Baiocchi and later renamed Cantine Baiocchi, this winery has been owned since 1978 by Sai Agricola, a company with large land holdings in Umbria, Piemonte, and Toscana.

Del Cerro has 290 acres (117 hectares) of vineyards, planted at altitudes ranging from 885 to 1,180 feet (270 to 360 meters) above sea level, 141 acres (57 hectares) of which are planted for Vino Nobile and 119 (48) for Chianti. They have an average annual production of more than 80,000 cases, 25,000 of the Nobile and 30,000 Colli Senesi Chianti. They also produce a Rosso di Montepulciano. From their other vineyards they produce the other wines typical of the zone: *vin santo* and *vino bianco*. Cerro Bianco is a *barrique*-aged, 50-50 blend of chardonnay and trebbiano. All of their wines are made from their own grapes.

Winery director Marcello Majani told us that the Fattoria del Cerro and Cantine Baiocchi Vino Nobiles are the same wine, with different labels for different markets. There is a difference in the other wines, however; the Del Cerro Rosso contains 15 to 18 percent white grapes, and the Chianti, 7 to 8 percent; the Baiocchi wines contain little or no white grapes. Le Pietrose is another Vino Nobile produced by this firm. Thus far the only one that we've tasted was the '79.

The first Vino Nobile of Del Cerro that we tasted was the '78, the first sold under that label; for us it was best of the vintage. Since then we've tasted many others and, for the most part, they have also been first rate. We especially liked the '82, '85, and '86, and the *riserve* of '81, '83, and '85. The most recent vintage that we've tasted with the Baiocchi label was the '82. Vino Nobile: Cantine Baiocchi ***, Fattoria del Cerro ***, Le Pietrose *

Fattoria del Pantano (Chianciano Terme). Azienda Agricola Il Pantano owns 27 acres (11 hectares), of which 18.5 (7.5) are planted in vines for Vino Nobile. They also produce a Chianti and a *vin santo*. Based on their very good '70 and '71 Nobiles, we felt that they were a producer worth watching. We then lost track of their wines until a bad bottle of the '77 came our way, and an out-of-condition '85. Those early wines were sold as Fattoria del Pantano. Today they are sold as Azienda Agricola Il Pantano. Based on the early vintages, Vino Nobile: Fattoria del Pantano, pre-1977 **, Il Pantano, today 0

Fattoria della Talosa (Montepulciano), 1873. Fognano, now Talosa, has 160 acres (65 hectares), 86 (35) of which are in vines. Two-thirds are planted for Vino Nobile and the rest for Chianti Colli Senesi. They average 93,000 bottles a year of Vino Nobile, 40,000 of Chianti, and about 13,000 of white wine and *vin santo*. Like numerous others, they also plan to produce a wine aged in *barrique*. Their cellars date from A.D. 1000 to 1200. The winemaker here is Enzo Barbi.

After a rocky start they seem now to be on the right track. Their best vintages, according to them, were the 1983, 1981, 1979, 1975, and 1973 Vino Nobile, Fattoria di Fognano, and "Talosa." And we liked their '83, '85, and '86 Talosa bottlings (they began to use the Talosa label with the 1981 vintage, and in November 1988 they changed their name to Fattoria della Talosa). Vino Nobile: Fattoria di Fognano * +, Fattoria della Talosa **

Fattoria di Fognano. They have changed their name to **Fattoria della Talosa.**

THE VINEYARDS OF FATTORIA DEL CERRO

Vineyard	Acres	Hectares	Altitude in Feet	Meters	Variety	Year Planted
Carbonaina	57.82	23.398	1,015	310	a, b, c, d	1973
Grazianella	16.75	6.778	1,150	350	a, c	1969
Le Poggiolo	33.94	13.733	950	290	a, b, c, f	1967
Le Poggiolo Alta	11.24	4.550	1,015	310	a, b, c, f	1965
Manotorta	54.98	22.249	1,050	320	a, b, c, d, e	1973
Palazzolo	7.47	3.023	1,180	360	a, b, c, d, e	1969
Poggio Romito	14.67	5.937	885	270	a, b, c	1969
Sant' Agnese	19.31	7.815	950	290	a, b, c	1973
Vicroce	28.40	11.494	1,015	310	a, b, c, d	1971
Vigna	0.79	0.320	985	300	a	1935
Villa Cappella	43.40	17.565	985	300	a, b, c, d	1971
Total	288.77	116.862				

KEY: a sangiovese
  b canaiolo
  c trebbiano toscano
  d malvasia del chianti
  e grechetto
  f mammolo

Fattoria di Gracciano (Dott. Franco Mazzucchelli) (*Gracciano di Montepulciano*), *1864.* Dott. Franco Mazzucchelli owns 17.3 acres (7 hectares) of vineyards in Cervognano. He plans to plant another 15 acres (6 hectares) between 1991 and 1993. The 17.3-acres (7-hectare) Casella detta Setinaiola-Cervognano cru is planted for Vino Nobile and the balance for a Chianti Colli Senesi sold as a simple Chianti. Mazzucchelli produces about 126,650 bottles a year, which include, besides Vino Nobile, a Chianti, a white wine, and a *vin santo.* These wines, sold under the Fattoria di Gracciano label (not to be confused with **Tenuta di Gracciano,** which is another estate), have been known since the nineteenth century. At one time they bottled their Nobile as Fattoria di Gracciano, Cantina Svetoni. In 1981, Gracciano bottled a Podere Cervognano Riserva. Among more recent wines, we recommend the *riserve* from '82, '85, and '86. They can be quite good, though we find them generally unexciting. Vino Nobile *

Fattoria di Paterno (*Montepulciano*), *1975.* Aldo Fresa owns Fattoria di Paterno and its 19.8 acres (8 hectares) of vines, 14.8 (6) for Vino Nobile, the balance for Chianti. This winery averages some 46,660 bottles per year. Thus far we have tasted one Nobile, a good '85 Riserva. Vino Nobile *

Fattoria Le Casalte (Paola Silvestri Barioffi) (*Sant' Albino di Montepulciano*), *1975.* Paola Silvestri Barioffi owns 20 acres (8 hectares) of vineyards. The first Vino Nobile they bottled was the '79, 2,000 bottles. Until recently, they produced a Vino Nobile and a Chianti, but like many others here, with the new DOC for Rosso di Montepulciano, they dropped the Chianti. Currently they produce about 56,000 bottles of wine a year, 60 percent of which is Vino Nobile, 8 percent Rosso di Montepulciano, the balance white and rosé wine. While we were disappointed with their '85 and '86, we can recommend their '81, '83, '86 Riserva, and '87. Vino Nobile * +

Fattoria Nuova Scopetello (*Chinciano Terme*). The only wine that we tasted from Nuova Scopetello, the '85, was good. Vino Nobile *

Fattoria Pulciano (Ercolani Sergio) (*Montepulciano*). We suspect that there is a connection between Matassini Ercolani Gabriella's **Cantina Pulciano** and this estate since they have the same phone number and address.

Fiorini - Pantano. We first met this Nobile in November 1990 when we tasted their '89 and '88 from barrel. We believe that these Nobiles are produced by Azienda Agricola Il Pantano (see **Fattoria del Pantano**). Vino Nobile [*]

Francavilla Agricola, Podere Il Macchione (*Montepulciano, località Caggiole*). They have changed their name recently to Azienda Agricola "Il Macchione," Agricola Francavilla. We didn't like their '77 Vino Nobile and thus far that is the only wine we've tasted here. (See also **Podere Il Macchione** for a discussion of wines labeled with that name.) Vino Nobile [0]

"Granducato," Enopolio di Poggibonsi (*Siena*). Their full name is Granducato, Poggibonsi del Consorzio Agrario Provinciale di Siena. They are based in Poggibonsi. Enopolio di Poggibonsi bot-

tles some 55,000 cases a year of what is, based on our limited experience, a mediocre Chianti Classico. They also produce a Vino Nobile di Montepulciano that we've never tasted.

Il Macchione. See *Francavilla Agricola, Podere Il Macchione* and *Podere Il Macchione.*

Il Pantano. See *Fattoria del Pantano.*

La Calonica Azienda Agricola (Cattani Fernando) (*Valiano di Montepulciano,* località *Capezzine*). Fernando Cattani's first La Calonica Vino Nobile was the '85. That wine, as well as the '86 and '87, was good. Vino Nobile * +

La Casella Azienda Agricola (Alfio Carpini) (*Gracciano di Montepulciano*), 1969. Alfio Carpini, who also makes the wine for Valdipiatta, has 12.4 acres (5 hectares) of vines on his Casella estate from which he produces about 31,000 bottles of wine a year. We found the '78, '79, and '80 a little disappointing, but we liked the '82. The wines thus far have been fairly good. Vino Nobile *

La Querce Azienda Agricola (Pinzuti Pino) (*Madonna della Querce*), 1970. Lido Pinzi Pinzuti has 25 acres (10 hectares) on his La Querce farm, 17 (7) planted in grapes for Vino Nobile and 3.7 (1.5) for Chianti. His Vino Nobile is aged for three years in oak casks. He also produces a white wine. Average annual production at La Querce is 7,700 cases. Vino Nobile +

Le Caggiole. See *Podere Il Macchione.*

Le Caggiole di Mezzo Azienda Agricola (Giordano & C.) (*Montepulciano*). We tasted two wines from this Le Caggiole. We liked one, the good '85 Riserva, but not the other, the '82. We don't know if there is a connection to the wines labeled as *Podere Il Macchione "Le Caggiole," Podere Le Caggiole,* or *Podere Le Caggiole di Mezzo.* Vino Nobile *

Le Pietrose. A label used by *Fattoria del Cerro.*

Ludola Nuova. In October 1990 the Folonari brothers of Ruffino fame bought this winery. Our experience with the Nobiles of Ludola Nuova prior to that acquisition has been less than impressive. Thus far we have tasted the '87, '86, and '85. We expect some serious changes here, as well as an improvement in quality. Vino Nobile 0

Melini. We have found the Vino Nobile of this Chianti Classico producer to be quite reliable. They bottle it only in the better vintages. We found the '81 Riserva, '83, and '85 quite good. Vino Nobile * +

Monsigliolo. The one Vino Nobile that we tasted from them, the '83, was good. Vino Nobile *

Podere Badelle. See *Farnetani.*

Podere Boscarelli (*Cervognano di Montepulciano*), 1963. Boscarelli was, at one time, considered by many to be the top estate in the zone. That was a view that we never shared. We have found their wines, like nearly every other Vino Nobile di Montepulciano, to be variable. They are nevertheless among the zone's better producers.

They have 22 acres (9 hectares) of vines planted at an altitude of about 655 feet (200 meters) above sea level. Half of the acreage is planted in grapes for Vino Nobile, the other half for Chianti Colli Senesi. They produce about 30,000 bottles of each annually. Since the 1979 vintage their wines have been bottled by a mobile unit, a service used by a number of small producers in the zone. On this bottling-line-on-wheels, the wines are filtered prior to bottling. Previously their wines were not filtered.

At Boscarelli they make a careful selection of the grapes, using only the best for the Vino Nobile. The next quality goes into their Chianti, and the balance is used to produce a wine that is sold, unlabeled, in bulk.

The first wine sold in bottle under their label was the '68. With the 1978 vintage, at the urging of their agent, they experimented with *barrique* aging but were not happy with the results. The white grapes were eliminated from their Vino Nobile after the 1985 vintage. Since the beginning of 1985, enologist Maurizio Castelli has been consulting for Boscarelli. Vino Nobile ** +

Podere Ferretto, Fattoria delle Maestrelle. Storiche Cantine member Fattoria delle Maestrelle produces this wine. They produced over 5,000 cases of mediocre Vino Nobile in 1977. We haven't seen it since. Vino Nobile [0]

Podere Il Macchione "Le Caggiole," Podere Le Caggiole, and *Podere Le Caggiole di Mezzo.* There is a little confusion here. There is a Podere Le Caggiole. They also sell a Nobile with the Tiberini label. Based on the '81 Le Caggiole we rate them as 0, and based on the '86 Podere Le Caggiole "Tiberini," *. There is also a Podere Il Macchione, "Le Caggiole." We don't know if there is a connection. Their '77 was unimpressive. We rate them 0. And there is a Podere Le Caggiole di Mezzo, whose '82 was out of condition. They all share a common thread, however. Most of these wines should, more fittingly, be labeled Vino Ignobile. Vino Nobile: Le Caggiole 0, Podere Le Caggiole "Tiberini" *, Podere Il Macchione, Le Caggiole 0, Podere Le Caggiole di Mezzo ?

Poggio alla Sala (*Montallese di Montepulciano*). This firm has 50 acres (20 hectares) of vines in the Montepulciano zone, plus many other vineyards in Umbria and Lazio. Their annual production at Poggio alla Sala averages about 648,000 bottles, of which some 90,000 are Vino Nobile. This includes a small quantity, about 25,000 to 30,000 bottles of *riserva*. They give that Vino Nobile some six months in *barrique*.

This producer has improved dramatically in recent years. Prior to the '83, we rated them zero. As for their single-vineyard Nobile, Vigna Parceto, we found the '83 lacking, but the '80 and '81 Riservas, and '86 *normale* were quite good, and the '86, tasted from cask, showed a lot of promise. Based on the vintages we have tasted since the '83, we can increase the rating for the Poggio alla Sala Nobile, with an even higher rating for their single-vineyard Nobile, Vigna Parceto.

The new owner Christine Mor hired a consulting enologist. Elizabetta Currado, a graduate of the enological school of Alba and the resident winemaker at Abbazzia di Valle Chiara in Lerna in the province of Alessandria, has worked in wineries in the Piemonte, California, Oregon, and Bordeaux. Under Christine's direction, and with Betta's talent, this is an estate worth watching. Vino Nobile: prior to '83, 0, since '83 *, Vigna Parceto **

Poliziano Azienda Agricola (Carletti Federico & Della Giovampaola) (Gracciano), 1962. Poliziano took its name from a noted local poet, Angelo Ambrogini, called "Il Poliziano" (the man of Montepulciano).

This estate owns 222 acres (90 hectares) of vines, including 124 (50) for Chianti, from which they produce 22,000 cases a year, and 47 (19) for Vino Nobile, yielding nearly 16,665 cases. They also produce 778 cases each of the *barrique*-aged Elegia, and the Cabernet Le Stanze, plus 4,450 of Rosso di Montepulciano. Another development here, since 1988, is the bottling of single-vineyard Nobile.

In 1988 they made two cru bottlings, one from Asinone and the other from Caggiole. They produced 25,000 bottles of the former. These wines will be bottled only under the Poliziano label.

The property was bought by Dino Carletti and Renato della Giovampaola in 1962 and replanted between 1963 and 1975. Today it is owned by Federico Carletti and Renato della Giovampaola.

They blend 80 to 90 percent prugnolo with 5 to 10 percent canaiolo and 3 percent mammolo for their Vino Nobile. They use only 70 percent of the quantity allowed by law for their Vino Nobile, selecting the best grapes to achieve higher quality. The grapes are normally harvested in mid-October and fermented in stainless steel, temperature-controlled tanks at 82° to 86° Fahrenheit (28° to 30° centigrade) ten to fifteen days for the Nobile and five to ten days for both the Rosso and Chianti. The Nobile is aged at least two years in large, fairly new oak casks, none over ten years old. In 1983 they began experimenting with *barriques*. Their *barrique*-aged wine is bottled under the name of Elegia.

At one time the Poliziano wines were rather variable. But since 1982, when Dott. Federico Carletti took charge, there has been a marked improvement. Their '82 Vino Nobile was a very fine wine, the best we've tasted from that vintage. Their '83 was even better. Enologist Maurizio Castelli has been consulting for Poliziano since 1983, but it's Carletti who makes the wine.

Carletti della Giovampaola is another label they use for their Vino Nobile. Carletti told us that this wine is exactly the same as that sold under the Poliziano label. With the Carletti label we can recommended the *normale* of '79, '85, '86 and '87, and the '83 Riserva. With the Poliziano label we liked the '82, '83, '85, '86, and '87 *normali*, as well as the '85 Riserva. That last wine is perhaps the best that we have tasted from Poliziano to date. We rate both labels equal. Vino Nobile: Poliziano ***, Carletti della Giovampaola ***

Raspanti Cav. Giuseppe & Figli, Azienda Vinicola (Gracciano di Montepulciano). Giuseppe Raspanti owns 3.5 acres (1.4 hectares) of vines. Our limited experience with this producer's Vino Nobile—we tasted the '81 and '85—leads us to conclude that the Nobiles of this producer are worth looking for. Vino Nobile **

Sanguineto Azienda Agricola (Maria e Lucia Monaci) (Montepulciano), 1979. The Monacis, Maria and Lucia, own 13.1 acres (5.3 hectares) of vines, 11 (4.5) for Vino Nobile. They produce 32,000 bottles of wine a year which include 8,000 of Nobile plus a small quantity of other wines, including a Chianti Colli Senesi. Our limited experience with the wines has been favorable. We found the '83 Riserva very good and the '81 good. Vino Nobile *

Scopetello (Chianciano). Scopetello has 160 acres (65 hectares) of vineyards from which they produce both a Chianti and a fairly decent Vino Nobile di Montepulciano. Vino Nobile *

Scopetto. It is possible that we goofed and that this is really Scopetello. Thus far we have been unable to verify whether or not we misspelled the name in our notes. We tasted one with this name, the good '80, in 1985. Vino Nobile [*]

Tenuta di Gracciano (Della Seta Ferrari Corbelli) (Gracciano di Montepulciano). Corbelli owns 27 acres (11 hectares), of which 10 (4) are planted in vines for Vino Nobile and 17 (7) for Chianti. He bottles his Vino Nobile under the Tenuta di Gracciano label, which should not be confused with *Fattoria di Gracciano,* which is a different estate. There is little difference in quality, however; like the other Gracciano wines, these can be fairly good. Look for the good '85 and '87. Vino Nobile * +

Tenuta Trerose (Valiano di Montepulciano), 1984. Tenuta Trerose is part of the Velm group owned by Lionello Marchesi. This group also owns Valdisuga in Montalcino and San Leonino in Castellina in Chianti. They own 371 acres (150 hectares), of which some 150 acres (60 hectares) are under vines. These vines are planted at an altitude of 1,085 feet (330 meters) above sea level. They average 2.7 tons per acre (60 quintali per hectare). From this they produce 180,000 bottles of Vino Nobile; 10,000 of the *barrique*-aged chardonnay and sauvignon blend, Salterio; 25,000 of Furfantino, a chardonnay–trebbiano toscano blend; and 3,000 of a very good *vin santo*. Dott. Rainer Zierock and Enzo Tiezzi are their enologists. Zierock consults here, as he does at Marchesi's other Tuscan wineries. Trerose produced their first wine in 1985, and both versions, a *normale* and a *riserva*, were very good.

Some 20 percent of their Vino Nobile is aged in *barriques* of French oak, one-third of which is new. The balance is aged in Slavonian oak casks. Considering their first Nobiles, the '85s, this is clearly an estate worth watching. For now, Vino Nobile **

Tenuta Valdipiatta (Gracciano di Montepulciano), 1973. Giulio Caporali recently acquired this estate from Alex Palenzona. The

THE VINEYARDS OF POLIZIANO

Vino Nobile Vineyards	Acres	Hectares	First Vintage	Average Number of Bottles Per Year
Asinone	17.3	7	1985	15,000
Caggiole	24.7	10	1985	6,000
Casale	37.0	15	n/a	n/a

Valdipiatta estate covers 86 acres (35 hectares), 34.6 (14) in vines—28.4 (11.5) for Nobile and 6.2 (2.5) for Chianti. There are two special vineyards here: the 11.1-acre (4.5-hectare) Sanguineto vineyard and the 8.6 (3.5) Bossona. Valdipiatta's annual production is between 66,665 and 80,000 bottles of wine. A few years ago Vino Nobile di Montepulciano amounted to 54,000 bottles annually. When Palenzona owned the estate, because his work required that he spend much of his time in Milano and Venezuela, Alfio Carpini, proprietor of the neighboring property, La Casella, produced the wines at Valdipiatta as well as his own. Both wineries share the same cellar facilities. We don't know if this is still the case. We do know that Paolo Vagaggini consults here. The first wine at Valdipiatta sold in bottle under their label, was from the 1973 vintage. Overall, their Vino Nobile is good. Vino Nobile * +

Terre Bindella (*Acquaviva di Montepulciano*). Based on three wines, the '88 and '89 from barrel, and the '87, we rate them very good. They could be the same as **Bindella Rudolf,** who also is located in Acquaviva di Montepulciano. Vino Nobile **

Tiberini Azienda Agricola (*Gracciano di Montepulciano*). We have no idea if there is a connection between this Tiberini and Podere Le Caggiole, who sell a Nobile with the Tiberini label. The Podere Le Caggiole 1986 "Tiberini" was a good wine. Assuming that there is a connection we rate them, based on that one wine, good. Vino Nobile: Podere Le Caggiole "Tiberini" *

Tistarelli Mario. This wine is produced for Tistarelli by a firm that doesn't quite identify itself on the label; it does, however, give a clue with their initials: CA.VI.O.T. Perhaps Casa Vinicola O.T. has reason to prefer to be semianonymous, considering the quality of the wine in the bottle. The only wine that we've tasted from Tistarelli was the unimpressive '79. Vino Nobile [0]

Tripusa. From our rather limited experience, Enoteca Europea produces a mediocre Vino Nobile. We haven't tasted any of their wines since the '79 Brigatti Riserva. Vino Nobile [0]

Vecchia Cantina di Montepulciano, Soc. Coop. (*Montepulciano,* località *Cicolina*), *1937.* This 400-member cooperative winery controls some 2,500 acres (1,000 hectares) of vines; 1,000 (400) are planted in vines for Vino Nobile, some 1,100 (450) for Chianti, and the balance for Bianco Vergine Valdichiana. They can produce 634,000 gallons (24,000 hectoliters) of Nobile but produce considerably less. In 1986 they produced 63,400 gallons (2,400 hectoliters), equivalent to 26,600 cases, and in 1988, 216,650 gallons (8,200 hectoliters), or 91,000 cases. They produce, on average, more than 1 million gallons (40,000 hectoliters), equivalent to 444,000 cases, of all types of wine. Among their wines, besides the DOC-DOCG Nobile, Rosso, Chianti Colli Senesi, and Bianco Vergine, are a number of *vini da tavola.* They produce Pulcianello in red and white. They told us that the red, made mostly from sangiovese, is similar to a Chianti. The first wines they sold in bottle were from the 1940 vintage.

Vecchia Cantina produces, when the quality of the vintage justifies it, three Vino Nobiles: *normale, riserva,* and *riserva numerta.* This last wine is what used to be their *riserva speciale,* a term not allowed by DOCG; they distinguish it from their straight *riserva* by numbering their bottles. They produced about 25,000 bottles of the '85. This Vino Nobile di Montepulciano is reliable and can be quite good, though unexciting. Vino Nobile: *normale* *, Riserva * +

CHAPTER **11**

Torgiano

Torgiano is produced around the walled city of that name located between Assisi and Perugia in Umbria. The town takes its name from the ancient Tower of Janus, *Torre di Giano*—the Roman god with two faces—that watches over the town and the vineyards outside.

The excellent wine museum in Torgiano in the Baglioni-Graziani villa which opened in 1974, was put together by the gracious Maria Grazia Lungarotti, wife of the fine producer, and traces the history of the vine in the region from earliest times. Old tools, equipment, and documents, as well as a large selection of wine-related pottery and artifacts from many periods, fill two well-organized floors of museum rooms. There is an excellent collection of old books, as well as Cycladic pitchers, Hittite jars, Etruscan bronzes, and Roman glassware. You can see ceramic containers from the medieval, Renaissance, and baroque periods.

Though references to the wine of Torgiano have been found dating back to the fourteenth and fifteenth centuries, the wine as we know it today is of fairly recent origin.

THE TORGIANO PRODUCTION ZONE

The vineyards are planted at altitudes ranging from 951 to 1,050 feet (290 to 320 meters) above sea level. In 1975 there were 510 acres (206 hectares) of vines in the Torgiano zone with a maximum allowable production by law of 154,000 cases of wine, both red and white. By 1988, this had increased more than threefold to 1,550 acres (627 hectares) under vines with a maximum yield of 543,345 cases.[1] Actual production in 1988 was considerably less than that, however—just over 150,000 cases.[2] There are 113 registered growers in the Torgiano zone; only 35 declared a crop in 1988!

For the ten-year period from 1975 to 1984, production aver-

PRODUCTION ZONE OF TORGIANO

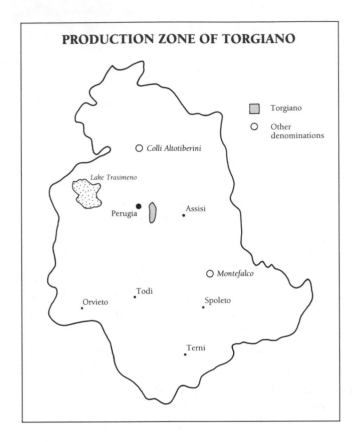

□ Torgiano

○ Other denominations

Colli Altotiberini

Lake Trasimeno

Perugia   Assisi

Montefalco

Todi   Spoleto

Orvieto

Terni

Lungarotti began bottling his wine on a commercial basis only in 1962, at that time just the Rubesco and Torre di Giano. He bottled small amounts of wine in the 1950s, but like his father and uncle before him, he sold virtually all of his production in cask to restaurants in the area. The Lungarotti wines, at that time, were already well known here. Two *cantine sociali* sell Torgiano in bottle under their own labels. A number of small producers also bottle, but mostly for their own use.

TORGIANO IN THE GLASS

Torgiano Rosso has a floral, fruity aroma, is a full-flavored wine with good backbone and structure, and ages very well to a decade or more. Torgiano *riserva* is rather similar but with more body, flavor, and character. It can age for up to two decades. Torgiano Rosso goes well with roasted meats and flavorful birds such as duck or goose. The *riserva* would be a good choice to accompany game birds or venison. Torgiano Rosso **, Riserva ****

RATING THE PRODUCERS

CO.VI.P. Consorzio Vitivinicolo Perugia	* —
Lugarotti, Rubesco	** +
Lungarotti, Rubesco Riserva	**** —
Vignabaldo (Brogal Vini)	0

VINTAGE INFORMATION AND TASTING NOTES

Lungarotti supplied us with the following vintage ratings, from 1955 through 1983. The ratings from 1988 to 1984 are from Antonio Rossi's vintage chart in *Enotria*:[5]

****	1988, 1987, 1986, 1985, 1983, 1982, 1980, 1975, 1971, 1970, 1968, 1966
***	1984, 1981, 1979, 1978, 1977, 1974, 1973, 1969, 1967, 1963, 1962, 1956
**	1972, 1965, 1964
*	1960, 1959, 1957, 1955
0	1976, 1961, 1958

NIEDERBACHER RATES THE OLDER VINTAGES:

***	1953, 1948
**	1954, 1952, 1945
*	1951, 1950, 1949, 1947
0	1946

aged 178,000 cases a year.[3] For the six-year period from 1982 through 1987, production actually decreased, averaging 140,530 cases, 67,326 cases of white and 73,204 cases of red.[4] For now, production appears to have stabilized.

Torgiano Rosso is made from a blend of 50 to 70 percent sangiovese, 15 to 30 percent canaiolo nero, no more than 10 percent trebbiano toscano, and, at most, 10 percent ciliegiolo and montepulciano. The *rosso riserva* was approved DOCG in March 1991. Some changes were made. The *uvaggio* did not change, but the minimum alcohol and maximum yield did.

The aging period begins on November 1 in the year of the vintage.

Lungarotti, the zone's major producer, has an average annual production of between 160,000 and 180,000 cases of Torgiano red and white, 90 percent of it from his own grapes. He has nearly 524 acres (212 hectares) of vines in Torgiano, not all delimited for Torgiano, and buys grapes from another 100 acres (40 hectares) or so. Those vineyards are under contract and are cultivated by Lungarotti. Of the vines cultivated by Lungarotti, 346 acres (140 hectares) are planted for red wines and 178 (72) for white wine.

OUR VINTAGE CHART BASED ON THE CURRENT STATE OF LUNGAROTTI RUBESCO

Vintage	Most Recent Date Tasted	Rating Today	Comment
1989	June 1990	**(+)	We have only tasted the *riserva* from barrel.
1987	October 1990	** +	We have tasted only the *normale;* it is ready.
1986	October 1990	** −	We have tasted only the *normale;* needs further age.
1985	May 1990	** +	We have tasted only the *normale;* ready.
1983	October 1990	**	We have tasted only the *normale.* Best to drink up.
1982	October 1990	** +	The *riserva* should improve, it will hold.
1981	October 1990	**	The *normale* is very ready. The *riserva* is ready.
1980	September 1990	** +	The wines are ready.
1979	October 1990	***	The wines are drinking very nicely now.
1978	June 1990	***	No need to rush to drink, they are ready.
1977	October 1990	*** −	Best to drink them now.
1975	October 1990	***	The *riserva* is excellent, though past its best.
1974	December 1985	**	It was starting to tire when last tasted.
1973	November 1984	**	Drink up.
1971	November 1984	*** −	No need to hold any longer.
1970	February 1982	*** −	Quite ready.
1969	November 1984	**	Drink up.
1968	November 1984	**	No need to hold.
1966	November 1984	**	Drink up.
1964	November 1984	**	We have tasted only the *normale.*
1962	November 1984	*	We have tasted only the *normale.*

PRODUCTION OF TORGIANO IN CASES

Year	White	Red	Total
1986	61,216	53,461	114,677
1987	74,793	87,802	162,595
1988	78,803	72,337	151,140
Average	71,604	71,200	142,804

Source: Il Corriere Vinicolo (*Milano: Unione Italiana Vini*)

DOC/DOCG REQUIREMENTS FOR TORGIANO

	Minimum Aging (years)	Minimum Alcohol	Maximum Yield in	
			Gallons/Acre	Hectoliters/Hectare
DOC *normale*	—	12.0%	834	78.0
DOC Riserva	3	12.0%	834	78.0
DOCG Riserva	3	12.5%	764	71.5

Lungarotti 1989 Rubesco Reserva Vigna Monticchio (*ex-barrel, 4 times, 6/90*). Open cherry and vanilla aroma; sweet impression, open and soft, light tannin, light body, tasty and surprisingly soft; quite appealing. **(+)

Vignabaldo 1988 (*4/91*). Slight cooked quality to the fruit, cherrylike nuance; coarse but fruity, certainly drinkable, if little else.

Lungarotti 1987 Rubesco (*twice, 10/90*). Fragrant, floral and fruit aroma, vanilla nuance; well-balanced, nice fruit soft under light tannin, nice mouth feel; enjoyable now, attractive, ready, should improve. **+

Lungarotti 1986 Rubesco (*twice, 10/90*). Aroma recalls nuts and fruit; firmer and with more body and structure than the '87, but less appeal; at this stage still a little tight and firm, somewhat hard at the end. ** −

CO.VI.P. Consorzio Vitivinicola Perugia 1985 (*4/87*). Cherrylike fruit, light tannin, medium body, fruity, simple. * −

Lungarotti 1985 Rubesco (*3 times, 5/90*). Nice fruit, open on both the nose and the palate, moderate tannin, sweet impression, rich flavors; most attractive. **+

Lungarotti 1983 Rubesco (*10/90*). We tasted this wine twice, both times from the same bottle and on the same day and there was a noticeable difference. *Second time:* A little dry, seems to be losing its fruit, still it does have flavor. *+ *First time:* Fragrant, ripe fruit aroma, floral notes; good structure, lots of flavor, a little dry at the end. **+

Lungarotti 1982 Rubesco (*twice, 10/90*). Lovely, fragrant, aroma more toward the floral end of the spectrum; soft entry, firmer than the '83, and a little lighter, but evident fruit, dry finish. **

Lungarotti 1982 Rubesco Riserva Vigna Monticchio (*10/90*). Lovely nose, dried and ripe fruit, flowers and spice; good body, on the young side but attractive fruit, a little dry at the end. **(+)

Lungarotti 1981 Rubesco (*10/90*). We tasted this wine twice, both times from the same bottle and on the same day, and there was a noticeable difference. *Second time:* Dried fruit aroma, vaguely floral; rather dry, but appealing flavor; best to drink up. *+ *First time:* Fragrant; soft, light tannin, nice fruit, very tasty; holding; finish is a tad dry. **

Lungarotti 1981 Rubesco Riserva Vigna Monticchio (*twice, 10/90*). Light nose, open fruit; attractive flavor, soft, still some tannin; quite appealing. **

Lungarotti 1980 Rubesco (*9/90*). Open, expansive aroma, suggestions of spice and fruit; soft, very ready, appealing flavor, good body; no signs of age; could use more length; still it is very well made. **+

Lungarotti 1980 Rubesco Riserva Vigna Monticchio (*10/90, 10,150 bottles selected*). Floral, open fruit aroma; a nice mouthful of wine, appealing fruit, ready now, light tannin. **+

Lungarotti 1979 Rubesco (*twice, 9/86*). Floral, fruity aroma; good body, light to moderate tannin, well structured; a lovely glass. **+

Lungarotti 1979 Rubesco Riserva Vigna Monticchio (*7 times, 10/90, 9,280 bottles selected*). Lovely floral fragrance; open and round, ripe fruit, soft and tasty, nice mouth feel, well balanced; very ready; fairly long. ***

Lungarotti 1978 Rubesco (*6 times, 9/82*). Rich aroma with suggestions of cassis and blueberries; some tannin to shed, a touch of acid toward the finish, but overall well balanced, richly fruited. **

Lungarotti 1978 Rubesco Riserva Vigna Monticchio (*9 times, 6/90, 14,930 bottles selected*). Fragrant, scented, and perfumed bouquet, berry notes; harmonious, packed with fruit, moderate tannin, rich fruit, some sweetness. ***

Lungarotti 1977 Rubesco (*twice, 10/84*). Fragrant, floral aroma, with some fruit; well balanced, some tannin to lose, good fruit; good quality. **(+)

Lungarotti 1977 Rubesco Riserva Vigna Monticchio (*twice, 10/90*). Delicate, scented aroma; a mouthful of flavor on entry gives way to some tannin, warm, finishes a little dry, best to drink, still quite appealing. *** − *Bottle of 11/84:* Slightly floral aroma with notes of oak and fruit; a bit light in body, very well balanced; young but quality is evident; an elegant wine. **(*)

Lungarotti 1975 Rubesco (*3 times, 2/82*). Fragrant, floral bouquet; smooth-textured, flavorful, vaguely bitter on aftertaste. **(*)

WHAT THE RATINGS MEAN

****	Great, superb, truly noble
***	Exceptionally fine
**	Very good
*	A good example of its type, somewhat above average
0	Acceptable to mediocre, depending on the context; drinkable
+	Somewhat better than the star category it is put in
−	Somewhat less than the star category it is put in, except for zero where it indicates a wine or producer-wine combination that is badly made or worse
[..]	*On a producer:* Tentative evaluation based on an insufficient number of wines or based on older, out-of-date vintages, or where the wines we tasted were too difficult to fully judge to give a fair assessment of quality. *On a wine or vintage:* Projection for the future. This rating is given to a vintage where we feel that we tasted an insufficient number of wines or those we tasted were too difficult to really judge to give a fair assessment of quality.
(..)	Potential increase in the rating of the wine given sufficient maturity

Lungarotti 1975 Rubesco Riserva Vigna Monticchio (*15 times, 10/90*). Lovely complex nose, licorice and floral notes; smooth on the center of the palate, loads of flavor, a little dry at the end; a little past its best, still it is very good. *** *Bottle of 9/90:* Still has an evident richness and concentration, starting to dry out, perhaps an off bottle. *Bottle of 9/88:* Floral, concentrated, dried fruit bouquet with a suggestion of blueberries; richly fruited and sweet with great richness and extract. Very long finish. **** *Bottle of 3/85:* Floral with cherries and a spicy, peppery aspect; exceptional balance, a mouthful of flavor, so much so it's tempting to drink it now, but it will be superb with proper age; say, two to three more years. ***(*)

Lungarotti 1974 Rubesco Riserva Vigna Monticchio (*19 times, 12/85, 29,750 bottles*). Some oxidation, overly astringent. A bad bottle perhaps? *Bottle of 11/84:* Complex bouquet with nuances of flowers, blueberries and black pepper; still has tannin, lovely flavors, round, refined; shows some signs of drying out on the finish. This wine was at its best through early 1984 when we rated it ***. The last three bottles all seemed to be beginning to dry out, though they were still very good. **+

Lungarotti 1973 Rubesco (*twice, 2/81*). Beginning to dry out. *Bottle of 11/80:* Complex bouquet of cherries and flowers with a touch of licorice, full-flavored, has length and style. ***+

Lungarotti 1973 Rubesco Riserva (*4 times, 11/84, 15,820 bottles*). Medium garnet with orange reflections; lovely bouquet has some spice; round and flavorful, a long finish; a wine of quality; ready now but could still improve further. ***

Lungarotti 1971 Rubesco Riserva (*5 times, 11/84, 13,850 bottles*). Complex bouquet with floral and fruity nuances; well balanced, light tannin, full-flavored, smooth texture over a firm frame; a wine of real quality; at or near its peak. ***+

Lungarotti 1970 Rubesco (*2/82*). Deep, rich bouquet brings up almonds and cassis; like velvet on the palate; refined and elegant. ***+

Lungarotti 1970 Rubesco Riserva (*2/86*). Orange, brick color; floral bouquet with suggestions of fruit; soft and round, smooth and velvety; long and complete. ***+

Lungarotti 1969 Rubesco (*2/82*). Floral bouquet; velvety texture; at its peak. ***

Lungarotti 1969 Rubesco Riserva (*11/84, 8,920 bottles*). Beautiful brick red robe; intense bouquet of flowers and fruit with a tarlike note; soft, round, flavorful, light tannin; peak now. ***−

Lungarotti 1968 Rubesco (*twice, 1/83*). Considerable fruit on nose; well balanced, moderately rich, still some tannin; very enjoyable now, can improve. **

Lungarotti 1966 Rubesco Riserva (*11/84, 8,920 bottles*). Beautiful brick red robe; big, richly fruited bouquet with floral notes and a suggestion of tar, velvety texture, very long finish; a complete wine. ***+

Lungarotti 1964 Rubesco Riserva [*the first year a* riserva *was produced*] (*11/84*). Brick robe tending to orange; touch of mint on the bouquet that is beginning to show age; round and smooth,

lovely flavors, full yet subtle, gentle, very long on finish; very close to its peak. ***+

Lungarotti 1962 Rubesco (*11/84*). Color shows a lot of age; also the aroma; tasty upon entry then very little in the center; age evident on finish, tired but still some interest, and quality evident. *

Lungarotti 1956 Rubesco (*11/79*). [This wine was presented at a tasting of about a dozen old vintages organized by the Italian Wine Center in New York. There were some big names present. For us, and many others present, this was the best wine of the show.] Lovely bouquet, floral, delicate; soft, smooth and stylish; an elegant wine of real character. ***+

TORGIANO PRODUCERS

Brogal Vini (*Perugia*). This producer has the distinction of being the third producer whose Torgianos we have tasted. Brogal Vini produces a white and red Torgiano under the Azienda Agricola Vignabaldo label. The pair we tasted—a '90 Bianco and an '88 Rosso—left a lot to be desired. They also produce the red Sagrantino di Montefalco DOC, Sangiovese dell'Umbria, and the white Orvieto Classico DOC, Grechetto and Trebbiano dell'Umbria, plus a Vin Santo Canonico. Torgiano 0

Cantina Lungarotti (*Torgiano*), 1962. Dott. Giorgio Lungarotti graduated in 1935 from the university at Perugia, where he studied enology and specialized in viticulture. He had worked in the vineyards and cellars of his father and uncle since he was a boy and continued to do so while he was studying, creating dust storms on the country roads, he recalls with a smile, as he sped from classes to *cantina* and back.

His enthusiasm for the wine is no less today. This enthusiasm, along with his sincere dedication to quality, is shared by his stepdaughter, Maria Teresa Severini Lungarotti, also a graduate of Perugia, where she was the first woman to receive a degree in enology, in 1979. Teresa began working at the winery in the lab as a winemaker, but has since taken on much greater responsibilities, including marketing.

The Lungarottis have a refreshing attitude toward wine. Dott. Lungarotti says that to open the wine in advance is not very important; if it needs aeration, decanting will take care of that. They make no excuses if the wine arrives at a tasting shaken up from the recent journey. If the wine is well made, it is sound; there is no reason for concern, they feel. Only a very old wine or one with sediment to stir up will be hurt by such treatment, and then only temporarily. We agree (our experiments with a number of batteredabout bottles have borne this out).

The Lungarotti winery has a capacity of 1.6 million gallons (60,000 hectoliters), equivalent to 666,000 cases. Annual production varies from about 200,000 to 230,000 cases, of which 70,000 to 80,000 are Rubesco, 90,000 to 100,000 the white Torre di Giano, 15,000 to 20,000 Chardonnay, 15,000 to 20,000 Pinot Grigio, 5,000 to 6,000 Cabernet Sauvignon, 2,000 San Giorgio, and another 2,000 a Champagne-method brut. He also produces a *vin santo,* a Pinot Noir, a rosé, and a Sherry-type aperitif wine,

Solleone, as well as small amounts of a few other wines. And we'd be remiss if we didn't mention his excellent Salsa Balsamic vinegar and extra virgin olive oil. Lungarotti exports more than 50 percent of his production.

The chardonnay and cabernet sauvignon vines are grown in the Miralduolo area near the Tiber River, outside the DOC zone at an altitude of about 820 feet (250 meters) above sea level, and in other vineyards ranging from 886 to 919 feet (270 to 280 meters). The sangiovese and canaiolo nero are planted higher up on the hillside at 1,148 feet (350 meters), and the trebbiano toscano and grechetto are lower down at 656 to 820 feet (200 to 250 meters).

Lungarotti's average yield is about 855 gallons per acre (80 hectoliters per hectare) for the white grapes, 748 (70) for sangiovese, 513 (48) for canaiolo nero, and 428 (40) for cabernet sauvignon.

Rubesco, for as long as we can remember, has been an underrated wine. While it does receive some recognition today, when you compare its quality to other wines at the same price level, its fine value is even more obvious. And it challenges many that are priced much higher.

The first time we tasted this wine, in 1974 and not under the best of circumstances, it made a memorable impression. We were finishing our first book on Italian wine and had been invited to a private tasting by a small importer of Italian wines. That was good. Then a few days before the tasting a heat wave struck. That was not so good.

When the day arrived the heat had not abated and we frankly would have preferred to go swimming. But there was a deadline to meet and the appointment apparently couldn't be rescheduled. So we went, feeling that we'd give the wines a fair chance; when you taste at the winery or at the importer's, you don't have to be concerned about how long the bottles have been sitting on the merchant's shelf or, hopefully, how they may have been stored.

The heat was sizzling on the asphalt griddle of 125th Street in New York as we approached the importer's office and prepared ourselves for the shock of the air conditioning as we pushed open the door. Shock—there was no air conditioning. We were greeted by a modest drop of perhaps ten degrees. Fortunately, most of the wines were not served at room temperature (optimistically in the high 80s/low 30s), but at the temperature of the somewhat cooler warehouse.

There was one wine there, though, that must have been in the office for a while; when the first wines were poured, the Torgiano from Lungarotti stood out. It was the wine with the steam rising out of the glass; not only were the esters in the wine volatizing but alcohol and acidity as well—our first introduction. The importer noticed it too; he pulled the bottle off the table and jostled it into the fridge with the whites, saying that it should really be tasted under better conditions. We didn't object.

What was this wine, anyway? we asked, never having heard of Torgiano or of Lungarotti. (We had heard of an Italian region called Umbria.) He filled us in with some background, and we went on through the rest of the tasting. What the other wines were we can't recall at this point, but they were probably good. The '66 Rubesco, when they remembered to retrieve it from the icebox, had dipped a few degrees. In fact, it was rather frosty. But despite the less than perfect presentation, its quality shone through. We were impressed. It says a lot for the wine, we think, and for the producer.

Lungarotti's Torgiano Rosso, Rubesco, is made from a blend of about 70 percent sangiovese, 25 percent canaiolo nero, and 5 percent other red grapes. The Rubesco *normale* is aged in large oak casks for about twelve months, the *riserva* for ten to twelve months, partly in new, small oak barrels. Lungarotti's Cabernet Sauvignon, San Giorgio, Rubesco Riserva, Chardonnay, and white Torre di Giano Riserva from the Il Pino vineyard are all given some *barrique* aging. Only a small amount—less than 10 percent—of the Rubesco is *riserva*.

Rubesco has a floral bouquet, often with fruity overtones; it is full-flavored and smooth in texture. The *riserva* is fuller and richer. While it is enjoyable to drink when first released, some eight to ten years after the vintage, it ages well for another ten to fifteen years, taking on nuances of aroma and flavor; in the best vintages it can live even longer.

Rubesco is a fine wine to accompany roast meats, duck, pigeon, or goose; it also goes well with feathered game such as pheasant or quail.

Of the recent vintages of Rubesco *normale,* we recommend the '85 the highest, followed by the '87, and then the '83 and '82; the '80 and '79 are very good as well. The best Riserva Monticchios for

THE CRUS AND VINEYARDS OF CANTINA LUNGAROTTI

Cru	Acres	Hectares	First Vintage	Average Number of Cases Per Year
I Palazzi	29.6	12	1983	2,500
Il Pino	24.7	10	1970	2,500
Monticchio	29.6	12	1964	5,000
Vineyard				
Belvedere	49.4	20		7,000–8,000
Montescosso	39.5	16		—
Montespinello	49.4	20		4,000

current consumption are the '79, '78, '77, and '75, with the '82, '81, and '80 just behind. The '75, although very good indeed, is somewhat past its prime, based on the two most recent times we've tasted it. There is no question about the very high quality of Rubesco, but somehow more recent vintages seem to be a tad less exciting than previous ones. Torgiano Rosso: Rubesco **+, Rubesco Riserva **** —

CO.VI.P. *Consorzio Vitivinicolo Perugia.* The only thing that we know about them is that they bottle a Torgiano Rosso and Bianco. And they have the distinction of being one of only two producers besides Lungarotti whose Torgianos we tasted. Their '85 Rosso was decent enough, if not much more. Rating * —

More Sangiovese-based Wines

One of the unfortunate trends in wine today is the tendency to make wines with a sameness of character, to produce wines that are more international and less individual. They are inoffensive wines, meant for early drinking, and are easy to understand since they imitate wines from other countries or districts that have clearly recognized styles.

One of the great pleasures of wine is its diversity. The trend to eliminate or at least reduce this diversity is a loss to those of us who like wines with individuality and personality. It is true, of course, that many grape varieties used to produce wine are mediocre and incapable of producing fine wines. Even so, there is no reason to reduce the number of varieties to a small handful. In the hands of a skilled maker, many lesser-known varieties often produce wines of class and breeding.

This trend toward what have become international varieties began in California near the end of the sixties and into the seventies, and has since spread to Europe. More and more producers are turning increasingly toward the use of French varieties such as cabernet sauvignon, and chardonnay, pinot noir, and sauvignon blanc. The view appears to be that if it is French it is good. There is no question that the top French varieties are indeed noble, but it just is not true that only French varieties are. Indeed, the Spanish have tempranillo, the Germans riesling, and the Italians nebbiolo, sangiovese, and aglianico. And although there is no question that a number of the world's greatest wines are French, it is just as true that too many of the world's worst wines are also French.

Another growing and, to our mind, unfortunate trend today is the increasing use of new, small oak barrels, or *barriques*, for aging and often fermenting wines. This is not to say that some wines haven't been improved by *barrique* aging. Many have. It's just that the use or misuse of *barriques* has produced a growing sameness in character in many wines.

So widespread is the trend that there are, besides the expected Cabernet Sauvignon and Chardonnay, Soave and Lugana in *barrique* and soon a Frascati and, the ultimate absurdity, a Lambrusco or fruit-flavored wine in *barrique*.

Aging a wine in small barrels of new or fairly new oak changes the character of the wine. The wood adds tannin and can create roundness and suppleness. It also imparts its own character, giving a vanilla component to both the aroma and flavor, and, if used judiciously, can add a note of complexity. On the other hand, it can be overbearing and obscure the character of the grape variety.

The growing trend to plant cabernet and to use *barrique* aging has taken hold from the top of the boot of Italy down to the toe and on the islands of Sicilia and Sardegna as well. Most of these imitation Bordeaux and copycat California wines come from Toscana. We don't mean to imply that all new wines are imitations. Some of the new-wave aged-in-*barrique* wines are improvements over what was made previously.

The International Style of Toscana and Other Central Regions

There is no question that Toscana has its own noble variety—the sangiovese—and its own ignoble one—the trebbiano. The sangiovese is a fairly delicate variety, the trebbiano a neutral one. The sangiovese variety is, with increasing frequency, being blended with cabernet sauvignon, a combination that, for the most part, submerges the sangiovese's somewhat delicate personality beneath the aggressive, sometimes pungent nature of the cabernet.

It is claimed that cabernet adds structure and longevity to the sangiovese and the ability to age. Really! Have you ever tasted the Chianti Classico Riserva Il Poggio from Fattoria Monsanto, a 100 percent sangiovese? No one we know finds that wine lacking in structure or aging ability. "Ah, but that is an exception!" Really!

How about Francesco Guintini's Fattoria Selvapiana Chianti Rùfina Riserva or Giovanni Cappelli's Fattoria Montagliari Chianti Classico Riserva? We have tasted a number of splendid examples from both of these estates going back over forty years. Are these also exceptions? There are, of course, numerous others. The finest Antinori Chianti we've ever tasted was their wonderful '58. In our opinion they haven't equaled it since, even with the use of cabernet and *barrique* aging.

There is also a growing trend toward 100 percent sangiovese in *barrique*. There are also some other nontraditional combinations with a sangiovese base. Most of the new Tuscan wines come from the Chianti area, which isn't surprising considering its large area and the tarnished image of Chianti. (Chianti, we are happy to say, has improved its image in recent years.) Combine this with the fame and high prices

received by Tignanello and the ever-increasing pressures to produce wines of international character, and the result is readily understandable.

But the fame and high prices of Tignanello weren't the only impetus. As the market for Italian wine has become stronger worldwide, the pressures to produce wines of international character have also.

The most important new-wave Tuscan wine for us, is Sergio Manetti's Le Pergole Torte. This wine combines the judicious use of oak and an emphasis on sangiovese to produce a truly first-rate wine. This fine wine is aged in a combination of French *barriques* for about three months and 185- to 265-gallon (7- to 10-hectoliter) Slavonian oak casks. The oak adds some complexity and texture, the sangiovese the basic character and personality.

Another fine example is Badia a Coltibuono's Sangioveto and still another is Villa Cafaggio's Solatio Basilica. These fine wines, it is true, spend a spell in new oak barrels, but they are made from 100 percent sangiovese. Sangiovese, unlike nebbiolo, seems to pick up texture and aromatics from the use of new or fairly new oak that can enhance its own character. No cabernet is added for structure, nor is it needed. Sangiovese, by itself, is quite capable of producing wines with structure. After all, as Giovanni Cappelli said, Toscana "is the area of sangiovese, it's a fine variety, why imitate the French with cabernet?"

And as good as Lungarotti's sangiovese–cabernet sauvignon blend, San Giorgio, is, it just doesn't match his wonderful, rich, and well-balanced "Rubesco" Torgiano Riserva.

The international trend, in our opinion, doesn't bode well for Italian wines. While some of these wines are excellent, it is another step in the leveling of wine quality. We'd much rather see more wines like Le Pergole Torte or Solatio Basilica. These are modern wines, yet they have a clearly recognizable Italian character from the fine sangiovese variety.

One way to improve Italian wines is with better vinification techniques. It isn't necessary to imitate California or Bordeaux in order to make fine wines. Italy produces some of the world's finest wines from its own grapes, and we believe that its producers should place their emphasis on fine wines from Italian varieties.

THE WINES

In discussing the many wines made from the sangiovese, in toto or in part, we have attempted to make our coverage as complete and up-to-date as possible (perhaps up-to-the-minute would be a better word, or, for those computer techies, up-to-the-nanosecond), but it is a task that we have come to consider next to impossible. We have no doubt that new wines are being created even as we write these lines.

We also cover some wines here that are not new and may

even be quite traditional, wines that are not major enough to merit a separate chapter, such as Sangiovese di Romagna and Parrina, but that are too important not to be included in our discussion of the sangiovese-based wines.

Rating the Other Sangiovese-based Wines

****

Le Pergole Torte (Monte Vertine)
Sangioveto di Coltibuono (Badia a Coltibuono)

***

Alte d'Altesi† (Altesino)
Cabreo Vigneto Il Borgo, Predicato di Bitùrica† (Ruffino)
Capannelle Barrique (Raffaele Rossetti)
Capannelle Riserva (Raffaele Rossetti)
Capannelle Rosso (Raffaele Rossetti)
Cepparello (Isole e Olena)
+ Coltassala (Castello di Volpaia)
Grifi† (Avignonesi)
Palazzo Altesi (Altesino)
San Martino (Villa Cafaggio)
Secentenàrio† (Antinori)
+ Solatìo Basilica (Villa Cafaggio)
Tignanello† (Antinori)

**

+ Balifico† (Castello di Volpaia)
− Bel Convento (Dei Roseti, aka Altesino)
Brunesco di San Lorenzo (Giovanni Cappelli)
Bruno di Rocca† (Vecchie Terre de Montefili)
+ Ca' del Pazzo† (Tenuta Caparzo)
Camartina† (Fattoria Querciabella)
+ Castelluccio (Gian Matteo Baldi)
+ Centinàia (Castello di San Polo in Rosso)
Colle Picchioni Rosso, Vigna del Vassallo† (Paola di Mauro)
− Coltibuono Rosso† (Badia a Coltibuono)
Donna Màrzia Rosso (Giuseppe Zecca)
+ Elegia (Poliziano)
Fattoria di Petrognano, Pomino Rosso
+ Flaccianello della Pieve (Tenuta Fontodi)
Fontalloro (Fattoria di Felsina)
Geremia (Castello di Montegrossi di Castello di Cacchiano)
Grattamacco† (Podere Grattamacco)
+ Grosso Sanese (Podere Il Palazzino)
+ I Sodi San Niccolò (Podere Castellare)
− Il Querciolaia, Predicato di Bitùrica† (Castello di Querceto)

Il Sodàccio (Monte Vertine)
Instistietti (Case Basse)
+ La Corte (Castello di Querceto)
Le Vignacce† (Villa Cilnia)
+ Mormoreto, Predicato di Bitùrica† (Frescobaldi)
Monte Antico (Castello di Monte Antico)
Monte Vertine Rosso (Monte Vertine)
− Montenidoli (Podere Montenidoli)
Montescudaio, DOC, the best ones
Morellino di Scansano, DOC
Parrina, DOC
+ Percarlo (Fattoria San Giusto a Rentennano)
Pomino Rosso, DOC†
Pongelli (Bucci)
Predicato di Bitùrica *vino da tavola*†
Predicato di Cardisco *vino da tavola*
Principesco (Fanetti)
Querciagrande (Podere Capaccia)
− Ripa delle More (Castello Vicchiomaggio)
− Rocca di Montegrossi Rosso (Castello di Cacchiano)
Rosso Armentano† (F.lli Vallunga)
San Felice, Predicato di Bitùrica†
+ San Giòrgio† (Lungarotti)
+ Sangiovese di Romagna, DOC, the best ones
+ Sangioveto di Monsanto (Castello di Monsanto)
Santa Croce† (Castell in Villa)
Ser Gioveto (Rocca delle Macìe)
Solo Rosso† (Podere Petroio alla via della Malpensata)
Sono Montenidoli (Podere Montenidoli)
+ Spargolo, Predicato di Cardisco (Cecchi)
Tenuta di Pomino, Pomino Rosso† (Frescobaldi)
Terricci† (Antiche Terre de' Ricci)
+ Tinscvil† (Castello di Monsanto)
Torri (Castello di San Polo in Rosso)
+ Vinattieri Rosso (Maurizio Castelli and Roberto Stucchi-Prinetti)
Vinattieri Rosso II† (Maurizio Castelli and Robert Stucchi-Prinetti)

*

+ Acciaiolo† (Fattoria di Albola)
+ Agricoltori del Geografico, Predicato di Bitùrica†
Ania (Castello di Gabbiano)
− Bottiglia Particolare† (Castello di Verrazzano)
Brusco dei Barbi (Fattoria dei Barbi)
Bruscone dei Barbi (Fattoria dei Barbi)
+ Camerlengo (Fattoria dei Pagliarese)
Codirosso (Fattoria di Vistarenni)
Colli Altotiberini, DOC†
+ Concerto† (Fonterutoli)
+ Convìvo (Giorgio Regni)
Cupido (Fattoria di Valiano)

† Contains cabernet and/or merlot

Elba Rosso, DOC
+ Granchiaia† (Le Macie)
I Coltri Rosso† (Melini)
Isole e Olena Rosso (Isole e Olena)
La Calonica Rosso (La Calonica)
− Le Filgare (Podere Le Rocce)
Leverano Rosso, DOC
+ Liano† (Umberto Cesari)
Logaiolo (Fattoria dell'Aiola)
Marzeno di Marzeno† (Fattoria Zerbina)
+ Masso Tondo (Fattoria Le Corti)
Montecarlo Rosso, DOC
Montescudaio, DOC
Niccolò da Uzzano (Castello di Uzzano)
Pietramora (Fattoria Zerbina)
+ Prunaio (Fattoria Viticcio)
Rango (La Suvera)
RF Selice (Castello di Cacchiano)
Rosso delle Colline Lucchesi, DOC
Sangiovese dei Colli Pesaresi, DOC
Sangiovese di Romagna, DOC
Santa Cristina (Antinori)
− Sassello (Castello di Verrazzano)
+ Ser Niccolò (Conti Serristori)
Stielle (Rocca di Castagnoli)
+ Vigna di Fontevecchia (Agricola Camigliano)
− Vigna Pianacci (Castello di Luiano)
+ Vigorello† (San Felice)
+ Vocato† (Villa Cilnia)

0

Cantinino (Fattoria Sonnino)
+ Castelrapiti Rosso† (Fattoria Montellori)
Granvino di Montemaggio (Giampaolo Bonechi)
Guardiolo Vecchio (Coop. Agricola La Guardinese)
Il Cavaliere† (Castello di Gabbiano)
Montepescali (Cantina Coop. Rosso della Maremma Toscana)
Tegolato (Antico Castello di Poppiano)

† Contains cabernet and/or merlot

ALTERO (*Toscana*). Brunello producer Poggio Antico first produced this wine in 1983, making 4,122 gallons (156 hectoliters), the equivalent of 20,799 bottles. The wine spent two years in 1,585-gallon (60-hectoliter) casks, plus eighteen months in stainless steel vats. It is actually a Brunello with reduced cask aging.

ANIA (*Toscana*). Castello di Gabbiano produces this 100 percent sangiovese grosso. It is aged for eighteen months in *barrique,* a combination of new and one- to three-year-old oak. The first was the '83. The grapes come from a 15-acre

(6-hectare) vineyard. They produce an average of 1,300 cases a year. Thus far, based on two vintages and six bottles, we have found the wine variable. Rating *

TASTING NOTES

1985 (*5 times, 10/90, 19,500 bottles*). Oak dominates, some fruit; hard and tannic, sense of fruit evident, is there enough (?), overly dry center. *? *Bottle of 5/90:* The vanilla from the oak marries well with the berrylike fruit of the sangiovese; still a little tanic, but the fruit is there, soft-centered.**

1983 (*9/88*). Skunky nose, seems old and tired; not a success, unimpressive, lacks definition and character; not well made.

BALSASTRADA (*Toscana*). Castell'in Villa, a good Chianti Classico estate, produced this *barrique*-aged wine from 100 percent sangiovese experimentally in 1982. They used the best grapes from their 10-acre (4-hectare) Balsastrada vineyard. Considering their other wines, we expect it to be a success.

BEL CONVENTO (*Toscana*). Dei Roseti, aka Altesino, produces this 100 percent sangiovese grosso. Altesino told us that it's the same wine as Palazzo Altesi. For some strange reason they bottle it in the same bottle as Alte d'Altesi! Thus far the only one that we tasted was the '87, so our rating is based on that wine. Rating ** —

TASTING NOTE

1987 (*8/90*). Tar and vaguely of rubber tire on the nose; much nicer on the palate, moderate tannin builds at the end. ** —

BONERA ROSSO DI MENFI (*Sicilia*). This wine is a blend of 60 percent of the local nero d'avola with 40 percent sangiovese. We suspect that it is aged in *barrique*.

BORGO AMOROSA (*Toscana*). Carlo Citterio produces this *barrique*-aged sangiovese from grapes grown on his Colli Senesi estate. It spends one year in oak. We've heard that Citterios's Locanda Amorosa is a good place to eat.

BORRO CEPPARELLO. *See* CEPPARELLO.

BOSCARELLI (*Toscana*). Podere Boscarelli, a good Vino Nobile producer, makes this prugnolo gentile–based wine. We've also heard that some canaiolo is used. It spends approximately one year in *barrique*. There were 500 cases of the first, the '83.

BROCCATO (*Toscana*). Chianti Classico producer Villa Dievole produces this sangiovese-canaiolo blend. It is aged for nine months in 185-gallon (7-hectoliter) casks.

BRUNESCO DI SAN LORENZO (*Toscana*). Giovanni Capelli, proprietor of the fine Montagliari estate in Chianti Classico, produces this 100 percent sangiovese wine at his estate in Panzano from the 22-acre (9-hectare) Casaloste vineyard. Brunesco is fermented for fifteen days on the skins. In 1980, the first vintage, he produced 3,000 bottles; in 1981 and 1982, 3,500 each year; and in 1983, 7,000. Today annual production of Brunesco amounts to some 5,000 bottles. Rating **

TASTING NOTES

1988 (*ex-cask, 11/90*). Cherry, berry aroma, oak overlay; rich fruit, moderate tannin, tight; very young. *(*)

1987 (*11/90*). Sangiovese character combines with oak quite nicely; light tannin, fruity, short and dry; a disappointment. *(+)

1985 (*4 times, 11/90*). At this stage the oak dominates on the nose and palate, though there is nice fruit, balanced. ** + *Bottle of*

4/90: Tight nose reveals hints of fruit and chocolate; intense, full-bodied and sweet, closed-in but with evident fruit and intensity of flavor; displays class; on the young side. **(*)

1984 (*4/90*). Dried fruit and floral notes on the nose, some oak; nice fruit, fairly well balanced, a little short. *

1983 (*4 times, 4/90*). Open cherrylike aroma, oak overlay, rich berryish fruit evident; open fruit flavors, mouth-filling sweetness, good structure, some length. Though not up to what we tasted in cask, it still is a very good bottle. *** — *Ex-cask, 5/85:* Richly fruited aroma overlaid with oak; well balanced, a firm vein of tannin, sweet oak and fruit flavors, soft-centered, finish is long and tannic; has a lot of class. **(* +)

1982 (*5 times, 6/90*). Complex aroma, cherry and floral components the most evident; a little tannic, chocolate notes, short and a tad dry, will it last? Could it be the bottle? ** *Bottle of 4/90:* Lovely oak and fruit aroma; sweet, open and ready, though a trifle short. ** — *Bottle of 5/85:* Aroma of oak up front on a fruity background; rich in flavor, sweet and ripe, very long finish; a very young wine. **(*)

1981 (*8 times, 6/90, 3,500 bottles*). Drying out, still has flavor interest. * *Bottle of 5/85;* Aroma is closed, but hints of oak and fruit, perhaps a touch overripe; sweet, fruity and oaky, long finish; needs age. **(+)

1980 (*4 times, 6/90*). Vanilla and flowers, cherry notes; still quite tasty; starting to decline. * *Bottle of 5/85:* Original sensation of oak on the aroma gives way to a cherrylike fruit with a vaguely floral aspect; softly fruited center, loads of tannin, flavor of sweet oak and fruit. **(*)

BRUSCO DEI BARBI (*Toscana*). Brusco dei Barbi is made from a blend of approximately 90 percent sangiovese grosso and 10 percent canaiolo, and in some vintages there is also some trebbiano used. At one time 80 percent sangiovese was used, along with 20 percent canaiolo. The '85 was a 90-5-5 percent blend of sangiovese grosso, canaiolo, and trebbiano. The grapes are destalked and the juice undergoes a two-week fermentation at a controlled temperature. Fermentation continues afterward at a slower pace. *Governo* is used to add glycerine. Around Christmas the wine is racked off after malolactic fermentation has occurred. In February the wine is moved into large Slavonian oak casks where it will stay for six months. For a decade Brusco was made more like a standard wine, but in 1988 they returned to the original formula and have stayed with it.

Production amounts to some 61,300 bottles a year. This wine was first made in 1970 by Giovanni Colombini as a wine to accompany cheese, especially aged pecorino. Brusco dei Barbi is a full-bodied, robust wine that can be rather high in alcohol (14.5 percent). It has a dry, raisiny character, similar to an Amarone. Brusco is a wine to drink with hearty fare. Although it can last for six to eight years, we don't find that it improves with age.

The name derives from an Italian brigand named Bruscone, born into a farm family on May 14, 1864, who didn't like working on the farm. He preferred, instead, hunting, women, and good wine—the legend doesn't tell us in what order. He left home and wandered through the woods of Montalcino with his companion, Baicche. As fate would have it, they both met and fell in love with the same beautiful young woman near the Fattoria dei Barbi estate. On October 7, 1897, they fought a duel of sorts over her. Baicche shot Bruscone and was arrested. Baicche got a jail sentence and Bruscone a bullet wound, and neither got the girl. Bruscone continued to live in the woods and practice the art of hunting and the craft of thievery. He became a legend and is today the symbol of an untamable person with a wild nature who desires liberty and freedom. What the legend doesn't tell us is that while Bruscone wanted independence, he was actually dependent on those he preyed upon for his own survival.

Giovanni Colombini dedicated his wine to the legend, implying that the wine is as wild as Bruscone. And we consider Brusco dei Barbi to be a rustic red, as the name suggests (*brusco*—blunt, brusque) of no particular distinction. Rating *

TASTING NOTES

1988 (*4 times, 11/90*). Rich and concentrated nose, open fruit suggestive of cherries and dried fruit, chocolate notes; soft and fresh, fruity; dry and somewhat short. ** −

1987 (*twice, 6/90*). Openly fruity and soft, tasty. *

1983 (*4 times, 12/87*). A rustic wine with a dried fruit character and a somewhat firm finish. *

1982 (*4 times, 11/89*). Vanilla and dried fruit; richly flavored and full-bodied, has a sweetness about it, fairly long and a tad bitter. **

1981 (*5/85*). Dried, concentrated fruit character, rustic, fruity. * +

1980 (*5/86*). Forthright and fruity aroma, dried fruit character; robust, light tannin, a trifle short. ** −

1978 (*10 times, 4/87*). Drying out, still some flavor. *Bottle of 1/84:* Dark color; aroma has a dried, raisiny character (from *governo?*); quite rich, a mouthful of flavor, the dried fruit flavor recalls Amarone, as does the bitter finish. *

1977 (*3 times, 5/83*). Off notes like a rubber tire smell mar the aroma; flavor is better though an off character is still evident.

1976 (*9 times, 5/85*). Tawny color; some oxidation, old, dull and tired. *Bottle of 4/83:* Dried fruit on aroma similar to an Amarone; full of flavor, somewhat rustic nature, some tannin; no need to hold it. *

1975 (*3 times, 4/81*). Aroma of nuts and raisins; some tannin, alcohol intrudes a bit; drink now.

1974 (*5 times, 4/86*). Dark color; dried fruit aroma has a raspberry nuance; soft center, rather short, almost sweet. * *Bottle of 6/81:* Aroma suggests figs and almonds; a dried, grapey character, some tannin; a rustic wine. *

BRUSCONE DEI BARBI (*Toscana*). Fattoria dei Barbi first produced Bruscone dei Barbi from the 1987 vintage. Bruscone is made from sangiovese grosso grapes grown in the Pinzina dei Barbi vineyard and is vinified in a manner rather similar to Brusco dei Barbi. It is, as they say, an evolution from Brusco dei Barbi. One difference is that Brusco is aged for six months in Slavonian oak casks while Bruscone is aged in *barriques* of Alliers and Tronçais oak for the same length of time. The '87 was made from grapes harvested on October 2 and 3. They made 3,000 bottles of that wine. In an average year they produce 4,000 bottles of Bruscone dei Barbi. Rating *

TASTING NOTE

1988 (*11/90*). Oak and fruit aroma; fairly dry, a little firm, the oak dominates. *

CAMERLENGO (*Toscana*). Fattoria dei Pagliarese, a producer of good Chianti Classico, makes this *barrique*-aged wine from the best sangiovese grosso grapes in their 8-acre (3.25-hectare) Camerlengo vineyard. The wine is put first into large casks, then moved to small barrels for three to four months of further aging. From the initial vintage, 1979, 3,500 bottles were produced; production has since doubled. Rating * +

CANTININO (*Toscana*). Ludovico de Renziss Sonnino produces Cantinino at his Fattoria Sonnino estate in Montespertoli in the province of Firenze. The sangiovese grapes are grown in his Fezzana vineyard. Rating 0

TASTING NOTES

1985 (*9/87*). Deep ruby color; overripe, some spice; unbalanced with alcohol, has fruit, kind of dull, lacks backbone and structure.

1983 (*9/88*). Toasty, dried fruit aroma, raisiny and cereallike, pruney and overripe; unstructured, harsh and hot aftertaste.

CAPANNELLE BARRIQUE, CAPANNELLE RISERVA, CAPANNELLE ROSSO (*Toscana*). Raffaele Rossetti owns 7.4 acres (3 hectares) of vines, planted at an average altitude of 1,180 feet (360 meters) above sea level, facing southwest. Until a few years ago he produced 21,300 bottles a year of very fine Chianti Classico and a *barrique*-aged Capannelle Rosso. Capannelle dropped out of the *consorzio* and out of the DOC. Today the Chianti Classico is sold as Capannelle Rosso. All of his wines are *vino da tavola*. They fly by their own colors.

The wines are fermented in stainless steel and aged in fairly small oak casks. They rest again for a period in stainless steel before being bottled, needless to say, under sterile conditions.

Rossetti produces his *barrique*-aged wine from 100 percent sangiovese grapes. In 1979, the first vintage, there were some 2,000 bottles produced. That wine was aged for three months in *barrique* of Limousin oak, then for a year in oak casks. There was no '80. In 1981 and 1982 he produced 3,000 bottles from each vintage. Capannelle Rosso is aged for four months in *barrique,* followed by five to six months in fairly new oak casks; from the casks it goes to stainless steel tanks before bottling. Rossetti was enthusiastic about the '83, feeling that it will be something really special. When we tasted it a few years ago we agreed. Rating ***

TASTING NOTES

1983 Barrique (*ex*-barrique, 5/85). Aromas of oak and fruit rise out of the glass before swirling; the tannic entry gives way to sweet, ripe fruit; style and class are already evident. ***(+)

1982 Rosso (5 times, 10/89). Floral bouquet; loads of flavor and structure; loads of quality, real class; ready. ***

1981 Rosso (3 times, 9/88). Oak overlay, hint of cherries; soft and round, smooth, well balanced, at its peak, could use more length. ** + *Bottle of 5/85:* Deep red; lovely aroma, blending components of oak and fruit; sweet oak and fruit flavors beneath moderate tannin; drinkable now but give it a few years; has style and length. **(*)

CASTELLUCCIO (*Emilia-Romagna*), 1975. Gian Matteo Baldi's Azienda Agricola Castelluccio estate has 32 acres (13 hectares) presently in vines. The vineyards are cultivated at altitudes ranging from 1,235 to 1,575 feet (375 to 480 meters) above sea level. Some of the vines have a southern to southeastern exposure, while the remainder face north to northeast.

Vittorio Fiore has been their consulting enologist since 1980. He oversees the production of three single-vineyard *barrique*-aged wines made from sangiovese grosso grapes grown on their estate at S. Maria in Casale—Ronco Casone, Ronco dei Ciliegi, and Ronco delle Ginestre. They have plans for a fourth *barrique*-aged sangiovese grosso from their Ronco della Scimma vineyard.

Castelluccio has an annual production of 30,000 to 50,000 bottles of each of the three different sangiovese grosso wines, plus another 600 to 800 bottles of Ronco del Re, an excellent but grossly overpriced white wine made from sauvignon blanc grapes. We saw it in a *ristorante* in Verona for almost the same price as Dom Pérignon and Roederer Cristal! They produced their first wine here in

1979. Castelluccio considers 1979, 1981, and 1983 to be its best vintages to date. (They didn't report on more recent vintages). These wines, judging by the '82s, are best consumed within four years of the vintage. Rating ** +

TASTING NOTES

Ronco Casone 1986 (4/90). Deep ruby color; rich cherrylike aroma, some oak; sweet, lots of fruit, intensely flavored, nice mouth feel. ***

Ronco Casone 1982 (4 times, 5/87). Lots of oak combines with a cherrylike character; high acid, unbalanced; fading fast. *Bottle of 5/85:* Black pepper, spice and cherries on the aroma; light tannin, lots of flavor, well balanced; a bit young yet, but stylish; long finish. *** −

Ronco dei Ciliegi 1982 (6 times, 5/87). Oak dominates, losing its fruit, unbalanced; fading fast. *Bottle of 5/85;* Loads of fruit on aroma overlaid with oak, also a touch of spice and cherries; sweeter and rounder than the Casone, well balanced, flavorful, long. ***

Ronco delle Ginestre 1982 (7 times, 10/87). Rather tannic, oak and fruit evident, the fruit could be fading. * + *Bottle of 5/85:* Aroma has notes of spice and cherries; the fullest, richest and most tannic of the three crus, also the youngest and most closed; cherry flavors across the palate; lots of style. **(*)

Ronco delle Ginestre 1981 (12/84). Floral bouquet with some delicacy and refinement; balanced, lightly tannic, good flavor, almost seems sweet, oak apparent, has length and style. ** + (***)

CASTELPUGNA (*Toscana*). This wine is a sangiovese-canaiolo blend.

CENTINAIA (*Toscana*). Enologist Maurizio Castelli first produced Centinàia from a special selection of mostly sangiovese grapes in 1981. He made 15,000 bottles for Cesare and Katrin Canessa, proprietors of the very good Castello di San Polo in Rosso estate in the Chianti Classico district. Today production of this wine has risen to nearly 20,000 bottles a year. It represents 10 percent of their production. Rating ** +

TASTING NOTES

1988 (ex-barrel, 11/90). A lot of structure, real sense of sweetness, **(*).

1986 (11/90). Nice blend of oak and fruit on the nose and palate, supple; seems ready. **

1985 (11/90). Oak combines with fruit on the nose and in the mouth, nauances of berries and vanilla, balanced, tasty, moderate-length finish is a little firm.**

1982 (3 times, 4/90). Complex aroma combines oak and fruit; sweet impression, flavorful, soft and tasty, a bit dry at the end. * +

Bottle of 4/87: Rich nose; firm backbone, fairly tannic, nice fruit flavors; young; some class. **(*)

1981 (8 times, 10/89). Packed with flavor, oak overall, moderate tannin, good weight. ** *Bottle of 5/85:* Toasty, berryish aroma; soft and mellow, suggestion of sweetness, some tannin, loads of flavor. **(+)

CEPPARELLO (*Toscana*). This *barrique*-aged sangiovese wine is produced at the fine Chianti Classico estate of Isole e Olena under the able hand of Paolo de Marchi. The wine is made with the best grapes selected from their own vineyards and is aged for about one year in *barrique*. Formerly known as Borro Cepparello, this wine is named for a spring torrent, in Italian, *borro,* that runs across the estate. In 1980, the first vintage, about 8,000 bottles were produced. As de Marchi was not satisfied with the '81 Borro Cepparello, it was blended into their Chianti. In 1982 production was nearly double that of the first vintage. Today de Marchi produces 18,000 bottles of this fine wine annually. Rating ***

TASTING NOTES

1986 (twice, 9/90). Lovely, open vanilla and ripe fruit aroma; sweet impression, rich and packed with flavor, supple, harmonious, open; very ready. ***−

1985 (6 times, 9/90). Richly fruited aroma, oaky vanilla component; lots of structure, great richness and extract; loads of quality, the best Cepparello to date; still on the young side but open fruit makes it attractive; real class. **(*+)

1984 (*ex*-barrique, 5/85). Fruity aroma recalls freshly crushed grapes; quite a lot of flavor, acid is on the high side; shows some promise. *(*−)

1983 (twice, 4/87, 15,860 bottles and 300 magnums). Lots of class and style; closed in, yet the flavor and quality are evident. **(*)

1982 (5/82, 14,490 bottles and 265 magnums). Richly fruited aroma overlaid with oak; a mouthful of tannin gives way to a supple center, well structured, a long, tannic finish; impressive. ***(*)

CERCATOIA ROSSO (*Toscana*). Fattoria del Buonamico produces Cercatòia Rosso from a blend of sangiovese and other grapes grown on its vineyards in the Montecarlo zone.

CODIROSSO (*Toscana*). Fattoria di Vistarenni produces this wine from either sangiovese or a blend of sangiovese and sangiovese grosso, in *barrique* from either a single vineyard or a selection of grapes from multiple vineyards, depending on when they answered our questions. They did agree on one point at least, and that was that their first Condirosso was the '85, of which they produced 3,000 bottles—or was it 1,300 cases? They also agreed that Codirosso is a 7.4-acre

(3-hectare) vineyard. The wine spent ten to fourteen months in *carati,* or *barrique,* after which it was assembled and aged for a further two to three months in casks to harmonize the wine, depending on when they answered our question. Rating *

TASTING NOTES

1987 (11/90). Soft, simple and fruity, no particular distinction, but quite agreeable. *−

1986 (4 times, 8/90). Oak and cherry fruit; soft, light tannin, balanced; not a lot of depth or character, a little simple. The four bottles that we've tasted were consistent, even if the information wasn't. *

COLLI MARTANI (*Umbria*), *DOC.* This new DOC zone, since 1989, includes three wines in the discipline, two white and one red. The red is made from a minimum of 85 percent sangiovese, plus up to 15 percent of any or all of the following varieties: the red canaiolo, ciliegiolo, barbera, merlot, and montepulciano, with up to 10 percent of the white trebbiano toscano or spoletino, grechetto, malvasia bianca di candia or del chianti, garganega, and/or verdicchio. The maximum yield is 898 gallons per acre (84 hectoliters per hectare), and the minimum alcohol 11.5 percent. If the wine is aged for at least two years in oak casks and attains at least 12 percent alcohol it may be labeled Riserva.

COLTASSALA (*Toscana*). Maurizio Castelli, consulting enologist for the fine Chianti Classico estate of Castello di Volpaia, first produced this *barrique*-aged wine for proprietor Giovannella Stianti Mascheroni in 1980. It was made from selected sangiovese grapes grown in her 12.5-acre (5.1-hectare) Coltassala vineyard. It also includes 5 percent mammolo, a variety noted for a perfume of sweet violets (*mammole*). The first Coltassala was aged in French oak from three regions. Today the oak comes from the Massif Central in France. In 1980, 19,000 bottles were produced, in 1981, 22,000, and in 1982 and 1983, about 30,000. Annual production now averages 24,000 bottles. This wine seems to be at its best with about four or five years of age, up until six or seven. Rating ***+

TASTING NOTES

1988 (ex-barrel, 11/90). Rich nose; warm and concentrated, lots of structure and extract; a lot of promise for the future; displays class. ***(+)

1987 (11/90). Lovely fruit; balanced, some tannin, sense of sweetness. **

1986 (twice, 9/90, 23,650 bottles, 120 magnums, and 15 imperiali). Oak overlays a tobacco, floral and cherry bouquet; very soft and supple; very ready and very good. **+

1985 (*twice, 9/90, 26,560 bottles, 210 magnums, and 15 imperiali*). Lush fruit, round, soft, near its peak, richly concentrated, ripe fruit flavor, oak overlay; displays some class. *******

1983 (*5 times, 10/90, 28,799 bottles, 1,066 magnums, and 80 imperiali*). Vanilla, cassis and tobacco aroma, vaguely of cherries, overlaid with a light touch of oak; still some tannin, good body and structure, appealing fruit; troublesome dryness at the end, best to drink up. **** −**

1982 (*4 times, 10/90*). Cherrylike aroma over oak; slight edge, nice fruit; best to drink up while the flavor remains. **** −**

1981 (*twice, 9/89*). Open fruit aroma; soft and lively, berry nuance; very ready, sweet impression, at its peak. *******

1980 (*5/85*). Cherrylike aroma over an oaky background; sweet oak flavor mingled with fruit, moderate tannin, well knit; should be ready fairly soon, perhaps two years. ****(+)**

COLTIFREDI (*Toscana*). Chianti Classico producer and *cantina sociale* Castelli di Grevepesa makes this sangiovese and colorino blend. They bottled some 225 cases of the first, the '85.

CONVERTOLE, IL PODERUZZO (*Toscana*). Il Poderuzzo has produced this *barrique*-aged sangiovese since the '85. That wine spent six to eight months in *barrique*. They produced 1,575 bottles.

CONVIVO (*Toscana*). Giorgio Regni produces Convìvo at his Chianti Classico estate. The '86 was made from 100 percent sangiovese and aged in *barrique* for eighteen months. Recently we heard that the blend contained 10 percent merlot. Rating *** +**

TASTING NOTE

1986 (*4/89*). Rich and ripe, full of flavor, round and tasty. *** +**

CUPIDO (*Toscana*). Chianti Classico producer Fattoria di Valiano makes this sangiovese-based wine. Rating *****

TASTING NOTE

1984 (*4/85*). Fresh berrylike aroma; light, a little astringent; serve chilled.*****

DONNA MARZIA ROSSO (*Puglia*). Giuseppe Zecca produces Donna Màrzia Rosso from a blend of negro amaro, sangiovese, montepulciano, and malvasia nera. Ratting ******

ELBA ROSSO (*Toscana*), *DOC*. The island of Elba, noted more for the famous prisoner it once housed than its wine, is located some 7 miles (12 kilometers) southwest of Pi-

ombino. The island is in the province of Livorno. The Etruscans inhabited Elba and some of their tombs can still be seen. DOC recognizes and regulates a white and a red. The Rosso is made from a blend of no less than 75 percent sangiovese and up to 25 percent canaiolo, trebbiano toscano, and biancone. The wine must be vinified on the island. The maximum yield is 673 gallons per acre (63 hectoliters per hectare) and the minimum alcohol 12 percent. In 1988 the 202 registered growers had 506 acres (205 hectares) under vines.[1] Of the 50,000-case production in 1988, 13,500 were red. Production between 1986 and 1988 averaged 16,450 cases.[2] Because of our rather limited experience with this wine, we can recommend only one producer, Tenuta "La Chiusa." Rating *****

Antonio Niederbacher rates the years:

****	1970, 1968, 1964, 1962
***	1983, 1982, 1981, 1979, 1978, 1977, 1973, 1971, 1967, 1961
**	1985, 1980, 1976, 1965, 1963, 1960
*	1984, 1975, 1974, 1972, 1969
No rating:	1966

ELEGIA (*Toscana*). Federico Carletti produces Elegia on his fine Poliziano estate in the Vino Nobile di Montepulciano zone. In 1983, Carletti began experimenting with *barriques*. This wine is a result of those experiments. There were about 250 cases of the '83. Today he produces 778 cases a year of this 100 percent sangiovese grosso, *barrique*-aged wine in an average vintage. It is aged one year to fourteen months in *barrique*. Part of the barrels are new, and part are made of one- and two-year-old wood. Rating **** +**

TASTING NOTES

1988 (*ex*-barrique, *11/90*). This sample was from a new *barrique*. The oak dominated, but the rich, ripe fruit was very evident, firm and chewy, sweet and concentrated. ****(+)**

1983 (*ex-tank, twice, 4/87*). A mouthful of tannin, the fruit is sufficient to carry it, firm, almost astringent; difficult to fully assess, but the quality is evident. ****(?*)**

ETRUSCO (*Toscana*). Leandro Alessi produces 3,000 bottles a year of Etrusco, a 100 percent sangiovese, *barrique*-aged wine at Cennatoio, a Chianti Classico estate in Panzano. He also produces a second *vino da tavola* red named **Panzano Rosso** for the *comune* that his estate is located in.

FABRIZIO BIANCHI (*Toscana*). Fabrizio Bianchi first produced what was originally known as Sangioveto Grosso di Scanni in 1974 from vines planted in his 8.3-acre (3.34-hectare)

Scanni vineyard located in Poggibonsi. The vines in this vineyard, 100 percent sangiovese grosso, were planted in 1969 and 1970 at elevations between 902 and 984 feet (275 and 300 meters) above sea level; they face southwest. Bianchi made 5,200 bottles of that first wine. Today Sangiovese di Monsanto carries the Castello di Monsanto label and the name of its maker. Annual production of Fabrizio Bianchi is up to 24,000 bottles. While it is a very good wine, excellent even, we don't find it up to the admittedly lofty level of his Monsanto Chianti Classico Riserva del Poggio. Rating ** +.

TASTING NOTES

1986 (*ex-vat, 4/90*). At this stage, there's a lot of oak, sweet impression, richly fruited, soft, open, forward flavors. **

1985 (*4 times, 11/90*). Oak dominates the fruit, but there is no question that there is a lot of fruit. *(*)

1977 (*4 times, 4/87*). Still young and tannic, a rich wine that still needs age, it has all the components to develop well; without question the best one to date. We're rather surprised that this wine is developing so slowly, we had expected it to be ready by now. **(*)

1975 (*5 times, 4/89, 3,700 bottles*). Some fruit on the nose, starting to dry out, the bottle perhaps? * *Bottle of 4/85:* Blueberries and vanilla on the bouquet, along with a touch of flowers; full-bodied and rich, still has considerable tannin; quite young but the quality is evident. **(*)

1974 (*10 times, 4/90, 5,200 bottles*). Blueberry aroma, vague dankness in the background; soft, sweet and open, very ready, a little short. ** + *Bottle of 4/85:* Superb bouquet with suggestions of cassis, cherries and blueberries; considerable tannin, is it beginning to dry out(?), it's difficult to say, though sensations of fruit are evident; it seemed more enjoyable two years ago when we gave it ***, for this one **

FLACCIANELLO DELLA PIEVE (*Toscana*). This 100 percent sangiovese wine is produced by the fine Chianti Classico estate of Tenuta Fontodi from the best grapes grown in the 18.5-acre (7.5-hectare) Flaccianello vineyard. That vineyard takes its name from Pieve di San Leolino Flaccianello, which was known as Pagus Flaccianus when it was a Roman settlement. The wine spends eight to nine months in *barriques* of French oak, plus an additional eight to ten months in oak casks. Flaccianello was first made in 1981; there were some 5,000 bottles of that wine. In 1982 production was doubled, and in 1983 it nearly doubled again. We wonder where it will all end. Annual production today averages 26,665 bottles. There was no '84 Flaccianello. The Manettis, who own Fontodi, pick '82, '85, and '88 as the top three Flaccianellos thus far. Rating ** +.

TASTING NOTES

1986 (*4 times, 6/90*). Aroma displays components of cassis and vanilla; open, forward fruit flavor, soft, ready now, moderate length. **

1985 (*3 times, 10/89*). Big, rich and concentrated, packed with fruit over the oak, good structure. ** +

1983 (*3 times, 4/87, 19,800 bottles*). Oak and cherrylike fruit; firm structure, nice core of fruit under some tannin, firm finish. **(*)

1982 (*4 times, 4/89, 10,450 bottles*). Rich, cherrylike aroma combines with vanilla oak; attractive, open fruit flavors, soft, sweet and round, tasty; at or near its peak; nice texture, oak flavor builds at the end. ** +

1981 (*5 times, 5/86, 4,960 bottles*). Medium-dark ruby; aroma and flavor of sweet oak, soft center, pretty, fragrant and supple; nearly ready. **(+)

FONTALLORO (*Toscana*). Felsina, the very good producer of Berardenga Chianti Classico, produces this wine from sangiovese grapes grown in their 15-acre (6.2-hectare) Fontalloro vineyard. The wine, in keeping with the current trend in Toscana today, is put into *barriques*. In 1983 they produced their first Fontalloro, which spent twelve months in *barrique*. Rating **

TASTING NOTES

1985 (*8 times, 6/90*). Oak all over this wine, cherry and berry notes as well, chewy tannin; a little young, it has the structure and fruit to age and develop. ** +

1983 (*twice, 4/87*). Oak dominates on the nose and palate, where's the fruit? It was much more impressive before it was put in *barrique*. *(?*)

GAMAY DI GIOIELLA (*Umbria*). We've heard that Gamay di Gioiella is made from an 80-20 percent blend of gamay and sangiovese, which is odd since both the Common Market and Italian wine law require a varietal-named wine to be made from at least 85 percent of the named grape.

GEREMIA (*Toscana*). Elisabetta Ricasoli-Firidolfi, owner of Castello di Montegrossi on the Castello di Cacchiano estate, produces Geremia under the Rocca di Montegrossi label. This is a *barrique*-aged sangiovese-based wine. The first Geremia, the '86, was made from a 90-10 percent blend of sangiovese and canaiolo and spent one year in oak. Some 4,000 bottles were produced. Rating **

TASTING NOTE

1986 (*4/89*). Oak up front, chewy tannin, good backbone, dry finish. **

GRANVINO DI MONTEMAGGIO (*Toscana*). Giampaolo Bonechi produced 6,000 bottles of this *barrique*-aged sangiovese from the 1981 vintage. Rating 0

TASTING NOTE

1981 (*4/25*). Oak, oak and more oak, a touch of fruit seems somewhat out of place, for interest perhaps.

GROSSO SANESE (*Toscana*). The Sderci brothers produce this *barrique*-aged wine at Podere Il Palazzino, a *fattoria* in the Chianti Classico district. It is made from 100 percent sangiovese grown in their 12.5-acre (5.2-hectare) Grosso Sanese vineyard. It is aged for one year in small barrels and another year in cask. Some 8,000 bottles are produced annually; the first vintage was 1981. We have seen European bottles labeled as Grosso Senese! Recently we heard that they were prohibited from using that name since it seemingly implied Siena! Leave it to the bureaucratic mentality to come up with such an absurdity. Rating ** +

TASTING NOTES

1986 (*6/90*). Lovely blend of oak and fruit, some spice; soft and supple, open and ready. **

1985 (*5 times, 6/90, 8,270 bottles and 200 magnums*). A lovely glass for current consumption; rich and concentrated, nice mouth feel, smooth-textured, richly fruited, open flavor, fairly long. ***

1982 (*ex-vat, 5/85*). Deep color; notes of mint, pine and oak on aroma, with a suggestion of resin in back; oak and resin follow through on the palate, fairly tannic, is there enough fruit(?); seems overoaked. ?

GUARDIOLO VECCHIO (*Campania*). Coop. Agricola La Guardinese produces this 50–25–25 sangiovese-aglianico-piedrosso blend. The '87 that we tasted was totally unimpressive. Rating [0]

I SODI SAN NICCOLO DI CASTELLARE (*Toscana*). This wine is produced from a blend of about three-quarters sangiovese di lamole, a very old clone, and one-quarter malvasia nera grapes grown in the I Sodi San Niccolò vineyard of Podere Castellare. The ruins of the twelfth-century castle-monastery San Niccolò located here give the name to that vineyard. This wine was first made from the 1977 vintage and then again in 1979 and every vintage following that. In 1984 only 2,650 bottles were produced. The malvasia nera, according to consulting enologist Maurizio Castelli, adds color, sweetness, and its personal character to the wine. In 1979 a part of the I Sodi was aged in *barrique*. Today it is put into a combination of new and slightly used French (half from

Alliers) and Slavonian oak *barriques* for an average of about eight months. Rating ** +

TASTING NOTES

1988 (*ex-barrel, 11/90*). A concentrated wine with a lot of backbone and structure, rich fruit, fairly long finish; the best I Sodi to date. **(*)

1987 (*11/90*). Oak dominates the aroma and flavor, evident fruit beneath, a little short. ** −

1986 (*4 times, 6/90, magnum*). Toasty, cherry aroma, cassis notes; soft and round, quite ready, fairly long. ** +

1985 (*twice, 4/89*). Intensely fruited, open, sweet impression, good backbone and structure, sweet; lots of character and quality. ** + (*** −)

1983 (*twice, 2/87, 27,664 bottles*). The nose is kind of odd though the fruit is evident; soft, lacks some flavor on the midpalate, goes out with fruit, rather surprising, the bottle perhaps? * *Ex-barrique, 5/85:* Ripe fruit and oak on aroma; moderate tannin, oak flavors on entry, followed by loads of fruit; still young but shows potential. **(+)

1982 (*twice, 5/85, 18,400 bottles*). Some oak and a lot of fruit; almost sweet, well knit, tannic but soft-centered. **(*)

1981 (*3 times, 5/85, 11,450 bottles*). Floral, fruity aroma with oak and malvasia character the most evident at this stage; moderate tannin, almost sweet, well knit; needs age. **(+)

1979 (*2/83, 2,662 bottles*). A fairly rich, fruity aroma; medium-bodied, flavorful entry; could use more depth; good now though a bit young. *

IL CANNAIO (*Toscana*). Sergio Manetti of Monte Vertine, producer of a very good and reliable *vino da tavola rosso,* as well as the outstanding Le Pergole Torte, created this wine from a blend of sangiovese and canaiolo for Giorgio Pinchiorri, proprietor of the noted Enoteca Pinchiorri in Firenze. Manetti first produced Il Cannaio a few years ago. Our expectations are high, considering Manetti's other wines.

IL LUCOMONE (*Toscana*). Villa Peraio produces this sangiovese-based wine on their estate near Chiusi.

IL PALLAIO (*Toscana*). Podere Terreno alla via della Volpaia, owned by Marie Sylvie Haniez, produces 8,000 bottles annually of the *vino da tavola rosso* Il Pallaio. This sangiovese-canaiolo blend is *barrique*-aged.

IL SODACCIO (*Toscana*). Sergio Manetti of Monte Vertine, producer of a very good and reliable Monte Vertine Rosso, as well as the outstanding Le Pergole Torte, created this wine for Giorgio Pinchiorri, proprietor of the noted Enoteca Pinchiorri in Firenze. Manetti first produced Il Sodàccio in 1980 from an 85-15 percent blend of sangioveto and canaiolo nero grapes grown in his 4.7-acre (1.9-hectare) Il Sodàccio vineyard. The wine is aged in two-year-old 210- to 265-gallon (8- to 10-hectoliter) oak casks. Production is about 12,000 bottles a year, when it is made. No Il Sodàccio was produced from the 1984 vintage. Rating **

TASTING NOTES

1988 (*ex-cask, 4/90*). Rich and concentrated aroma and palate, sweet impression; has an extra dimension compared to past vintages; the best one to date. **(* −)

1987 (*4/90*). Richly fruited, some oak; firm and dry, good fruit; still a little young. *(+)

1986 (*4/89*). Cherry and oak on the nose, firm structure, nice entry then tightens up; quite good. **

1985 (*6/90*). Up-front oak; chewy, good body, nicely balanced, attractive flavor; needs some age. **(* −)

1982 (*5/85*). Cherrylike fruit and some oak on the aroma; moderate tannin, good fruit and structure, has delicacy and flavor, moderate length. ** +

INSTISTIETTI (*Toscana*). Gianfranco Soldera, the very fine Brunello producer, makes Instistietti at his Case Basse estate. Soldera first produced this *vino da tavola* from 100 percent sangiovese grosso in 1985. It spent one and a half years in *barrique,* and the same length of time in bottle prior to its release. There was no '86; it was produced again in 1987. Considering the quality of his Brunello, it's not surprising that the '87 is very good. Rating **

ISOLE E OLENA (*Toscana*). Paolo de Marchi produces this sangiovese-canaiolo blend at his fine Chianti Classico estate. It is not aged in wood and is best drunk young and fresh. Rating *

LA CALONICA (*Toscana*). This wine is made from sangioveto grapes by Fernando Cattani at his La Calonica estate in the Vino Nobile di Montepulciano zone. Rating *

TASTING NOTE

1989 (*4/90*). Light, fresh and fruity, clean; lively acidity; a quaffable wine for drinking young. *

LA CORTE (*Toscana*). La Corte is produced by Alessandro François at his fine Chianti Classico estate of Castello di Querceto. The wine is produced from selected sangiovese grapes (98 percent) grown in their 9.9-acre (4-hectare) Le Corte vineyard, planted in 1973. It is aged eight to nine months in a combination of new and slightly used French *barriques*. In 1978, the first vintage, 6,000 bottles were produced. Today production averages 20,000 bottles a year. Rating ** +

TASTING NOTES

1987 (*11/90*). Nice fruit on the nose, berrylike, scented; rather dry after the initial fruit impression, shallow, very short. +

1982 (*5/86*). This one spent six months in *barrique*. Reticent aroma; hard and firm, richly fruited, light oak and overlay. **(*)

1981 (*5/85*). An aroma of cherries and berries over oak; sweet fruit, moderate tannin; young but enjoyable now; a fairly long finish with a tannic bite. **(*)

1980 (*4 times, 10/86*). Lovely fruit, balanced, moderate richness; still on the young side; some firmness. *(*) *Bottle of 5/85:* Oaky notes overlay the cherries and flowers of the sangiovese grosso; moderate tannin, firm texture, full of flavor; not a big wine but a very pleasant one; needs age but enjoyable now; could have a bit more length. ** +

LA GIOIA DI RIECINE (*Toscana*). La Gioia di Riecine is produced at the Riecine estate located in the Chianti Classico zone and owned by John and Palmina Abbagnano Dunkley. Dunkley first made this *barrique*-aged, 100 percent sangiovese wine in 1982, producing all of 2,000 bottles. La Gioia was produced again in 1985 and 1986.

LE FILGARE (*Toscana*). Fattoria Le Filgare produces the *barrique*-aged Le Filgare from sangiovese grapes grown in their Podere Le Rocce estate in the Chianti Classico district. They produced 2,558 bottles from the 1986 vintage. This wine is aged for fifteen months in *barrique*. Vittorio Fiore consults here. Rating * −

TASTING NOTES

1987 (*11/90*). Oak and then some fruit on both the nose and palate, sense of sweetness from the oak. *

1986 (*twice, 4/95, 2,558 bottles*). Oak! oak!! oak!!! This is a *barrique* lover's answer to est! est!! est!!!. Still, in spite of all the oak, there is some fruit. * −

LE PERGOLE TORTE (*Toscana*). Le Pergole Torte is produced from the twenty-year-old sangiovese vines in the 7.9-acre (3.2-hectare) Le Pergole Torte vineyard on Sergio Manetti's Monte Vertine estate in the Chianti Classico district. The wine is aged in a combination of French *barriques* about three months and 185- to 265-gallon (7- to 10-hectoliter)

Slavonian oak casks. Manetti doesn't want the oak to over-power the subtle character of this 100 percent sangioveto wine. In the first vintage, 1977, fewer than 5,700 bottles were produced. Today annual production averages 20,000 bottles.

Le Pergole Torte is a medium-bodied, stylish dry red wine with a bouquet of flowers and fruit and a touch of oak. It drinks well from its fourth to sixth year on. Manetti told us that 1988 was their best vintage; we agree. He also lists 1979, 1982, 1983, and 1985 as excellent. Le Pergole Torte is not made every year; there was no '84.

Le Pergole Torte is, in our opinion, *the* finest of the new Tuscan wines. It is made solely from the noble sangiovese variety, without the addition of lesser varieties, and shows how fine a purely Italian wine can be, with no need to imitate the wines of California or the Cabernets of France. Rating ****

TASTING NOTES

1988 (*ex*-botte, 4/90). Spice, black cherries and great concentration and sweetness, loads of flavor and character, very long; great quality. ***(*)

1987 (*twice, 6/90*). Lovely nose combines ripe fruit and flowers; light to moderate tannin, some firmness, a lot more body than expected. **

1986 (*3 times, 6/90*). Lovely cherrylike aroma combined with a touch of oak; lots of nice fruit from the initial entry through the midpalate and the finish; displays lots of class and style; still a little young yet. **(*)

1985 (*twice, 6/90*). Spice and flowers, great concentration; still fairly tannic, very young; great quality very evident; needs a few more years but there's no mistaking the quality of this wine. ***(+)

1983 (*twice, 10/87*). Lovely cherry fruit and oak aroma; good structure; lots of class; still a little young, but attractive. ** + (***)

1982 (*6 times, 10/86*). Lovely bouquet; rich and well balanced; stylish; on the young side. ***(+) *Bottle of 5/85:* Beautiful ruby robe; expansive aroma of cherries and flowers with a touch of oak;

a mouthful of flavor, intense, cherrylike, youthful fruit, a firm tannic vein, soft-centered; finely honed. ***(+)

1980 (*3 times, 12/85*). Richly fruited from the aroma through the palate, elegant, soft center. **

1979 (*3 times, 5/83*). More oak than fruit at this point though the fruit is evident; well balanced, has flavor and style, could have more length. **(*)

1978 (*2/82, 9,840 bottles*). Aroma is still backward but suggestions of flowers and fruit evident; still somewhat tannic, but with flavor and structure to match it, a bit short. *(* +)

1977 (*4/81, 5,642 bottles*). Lovely bouquet of fruit and flowers; well structured, some delicacy, moderate tannin; needs another year or two. **(*)

LEVERANO ROSSO (*Puglia*), DOC. Leverano Rosso is produced from no less than 65 percent negro amaro, with up to 35 percent sangiovese, montepulciano, malvasia nera di lecce, and malvasia bianca, either singularly or in combination. These grapes are grown in the *comune* of Leverano. The only producer we can recommend is Giuseppe Zecca, who also produces the good **Donna Màrzia Rosso** from a similar combination of grapes. Rating *

LOGAIOLO (*Toscana*). Fattoria dell'Aiola produces this wine from red grapes only which are grown on the Vagliagli hills in the Chianti Classico zone. Our experience is limited to the '82, which was good. Rating *

TASTING NOTE

1982 (*10/84, 13,930 bottles*). Floral bouquet similar to a Chianti; medium-bodied, soft and round, lacks some backbone, but flavorful; quite ready. *

MASSO TONDO (*Toscana*). Angiolo Anichini produces Masso Tondo at his Fattoria Le Corti estate in Greve. We were told, in April 1990, that the '85 was made from a 85-15 percent blend of sangiovese and canaiolo which was aged for 12 months in *barrique*. One year earlier we were

DOC REQUIREMENTS FOR LEVERANO ROSSO

	Minimum Aging	Minimum Alcohol	Maximum Yield in	
			Gallons/Acre	Hectoliters/Hectare
Normale	none	12.0%	1,122	105
Riserva	2 years	12.5%	1,122	105

told that Masso Tondo was made from 100 percent sangiovese and aged for more than one year in *barrique*. It pays to ask. We wonder what they'll tell us in April 1991. The wine, however, is based on the two vintages that we tasted, quite good. Rating * +

TASTING NOTES

1985 (*twice, 4/90, 3,000 bottles*). Floral and oak aroma, toasty component; spicy and sweet, light tannin. **

1982 (*twice, 4/88, 2,000 bottles*). Floral, vaguely nutlike aroma; tight, light to moderate tannin, fairly nice flavor, light aftertaste. *

MONTE ANTICO (*Toscana*). Monte Antico is produced close to the Brunello zone, in the province of Grosseto, from 95 percent sangiovese grosso grapes. Castello di Monte Antico, the zone's best producer, has 125 acres (50 hectares) of vines, 115 (45) planted in sangiovese grosso. They have an annual production of about 20,000 cases of red wine and another 1,000 of rosé.

They make two reds: a *normale* and a *riserva*. The Monte Antico *normale* is often a good value. Both the *normale* and the *riserva* are quite similar to Chianti in character. The *riserva* is made from vines at least fifteen years old and is aged for about four years in cask. Reputedly it can age for up to twenty years; our experience suggests otherwise. Rating **

TASTING NOTES

1982 (*11/85*). Cherrylike aroma; some tannin; enjoyable now. ** +

1980 (*4/85*). Floral aroma with a touch of oak; tannic on entry, fruit follows. *(+)

1979 (*6 times, 10/83*). Light garnet; small aroma similar to a Chianti; a nice little wine, quite drinkable and correct. *

1975 Riserva (*twice, 2/82*). Delicate bouquet with some refinement; good structure, light tannin, tasty, some length; quite ready now. **

MONTE VERTINE ROSSO (*Toscana*). Sergio Manetti produces a Monte Vertine Rosso from grapes grown on his 3.5-acre (1.4-hectare) Monte Vertine vineyard. Klaus Reimitz is Manetti's able assistant. A few years ago this wine was sold as Chianti Classico. He produces 10,000 bottles a year of this sangioveto-canaiolo blend, as well as three other reds, **Le Pergole Torte, Il Sodàccio,** and **Il Cannaio,** and a very good *vin santo* and an excellent white simply named "M," which could stand for Monte Vertine, Manetti, or Meditation, as some have called it a wine of meditation. Rating **

TASTING NOTES

1988 (*ex-cask, 4/90*). Intensely fruited; enormous richness and extract, firm backbone, light, herbaceous component; Manetti's best *rosso* to date. **(*)

1987 (*4/90*). Openly fruity; soft, a tad dry; very ready, best to drink. *

1986 Riserva (*4/89*). Well made, lots of fruit, good structure, firm aftertaste. ** −

MONTECARLO ROSSO (*Toscana*), *DOC*. Montecarlo, 10 miles (16 kilometers) east of Lucca, is regarded more for its white wine than its red. And, in fact, the DOC has been changed only recently to allow the production of red wine. This wine is made from a blend of sangiovese, canaiolo nero, ciliegiolo, colorino, malvasia nera, and/or syrah. There are 29 growers in this DOC zone with 134 acres (54 hectares) of registered vineyards.[3] The maximum yield is 748 gallons per acre (70 hectoliters per hectare). Between 1986 and 1988 they produced an average of 107,089 cases, of which 32,412 were red.[4] The finished wine must be at least 11.5 percent alcohol. There is no minimum aging requirement. In our experience it's best to consume Montecarlo Rosso when it is relatively young. Rating *

MONTENIDOLI (*Toscana*). This fine producer of Vernaccia di San Gimignano produces this red wine. The '86 was made from a blend of sangiovese and canaiolo, and the '85 was made from 90 percent sangiovese spargolo and grosso, and 10 percent malvasia nera. That wine underwent *governo*. It's meant to be drunk young, while it is still fresh. Rating ** −

MONTEPESCALI (*Toscana*). Cantina Coop. Rosso della Maremma Toscana produces Montepescali, a sangiovese-based red wine that is aged in *barrique*. The '83 that we tasted in 1985 left us less than impressed. Rating 0

MONTESCUDAIO (*Toscana*), *DOC*. Montescudaio is a medium-bodied dry red wine from the Livorno area of Pisa. It is quite similar in character to Chianti, which shouldn't be all that surprising considering the *uvaggio* it is made from—65 to 85 percent sangiovese, 15 to 25 percent trebbiano toscano and/or malvasia del chianti, and up to 10 percent of other varieties. There are 79 registered growers with 603 acres (244 hectares) of vineyards inscribed for the DOC.[5] DOC allows up to 823 gallons per acre (77 hectoliters per hectare). The finished wine must have at least 11.5 percent alcohol. There are no minimum aging requirements. Between 1986 and 1988 they produced an average of 74,230 cases, of which 43,545 were red.[6] Montescudaio is at its best between two and four years of the vintage. The one producer that we can recommend is Fattoria Sorbaiano, which bottles a wine it labels as Rosso delle Miniere. Rating */**

TASTING NOTE

Fattoria Sorbaiano 1988 Rosso delle Miniere (twice, 8/90). Open cherry aroma, vanilla overlay; soft and supple, well balanced, clean fruit; well made. ** +

MORELLINO DI SCANSANO (*Toscana*), DOC. Morellino di Scansano is a Chianti-type wine made from a minimum of 85 percent sangiovese grapes, plus up to 15 percent of other varieties grown in Scansano and parts of Campagnatico, Grosseto, Magliano in Toscana, Manciano, Roccalbegna, and Semproniano, all in the province of Grosseto. In 1988 there were 286 registered growers with 1,051 acres (425 hectares) of vines.[7] Between 1986 and 1988 production averaged 173,546 cases.[8]

The *riserva* is best drunk between its third and sixth year. We've heard that it will last well for up to seven or eight years, but that has not been our experience. Rating **

Recommended Producers

*Banti Erik	Poggio Valente
Fattoria Coltiberto	Poggiolungo
*Fattoria Le Pupille	Val delle Rose
Mantellassi Ezio	

The most interesting producer is Erik Banti. Banti uses a blend of sangiovese, malvasia nera, canaiolo, and alicante for his wines. The black label depicting four birds is *barrique*-aged four to six months with oak from the Massif Central. His beige label with two birds is aged in stainless steel.

Fattoria "Le Pupille" owns 32 acres (13 hectares) and leases nearly 5 (2) others. They produce 60,000 bottles annually of Morellino, two-thirds of which are *riserva*. They told us that they use 5 percent canaiolo. There is certainly no finer producer in the zone.

Poggio Valente owns 17 acres (7 hectares) and produces

12,000 bottles of Morellino annually from 92 percent sangiovese and up to 8 percent mammolo and ciliegiolo. Their wines are not aged in wood.

TASTING NOTES

Poggio Valente 1989 (4/90). Cherry fruit; nice backbone, light tannin; quaffable. **

Poggio Valente 1988 (4/90). Floral and cherry aroma, vague mercaptan note intrudes; open, attractive fruit flavor in the mouth with a slight off note intruding. *

Fattoria Le Pupille 1986 (twice, 4/90). Cherrylike fruit; soft entry then dry. *

Fattoria Le Pupille 1986 Riserva (4/90). Soft-centered, open cherrylike flavor, tobacco note, light tannin. **

Mantellassi Ezio 1986 (4/87). Fresh and fruity, cherrylike; fruity, almost sweet, balanced; on the young side. *(* −)

Fattoria Le Pupille 1985 (4/88). Fairly nice cherrylike character; soft and fruity; ready. * +

Fattoria Le Pupille 1985 Riserva (twice, 2/90). A tad rustic, cherrylike character, light tannin. * +

Mantellassi Ezio 1985 (4/87). Tobacco and cherry aroma and taste, dry and firm, still some tannin; on the young side. *(*)

Fattoria Le Pupille 1984 Riserva (4/88). Floral and dried fruit aroma, berry notes; ditto the palate, some tannin; still it's best to drink it now. **

Cantina Coop. 1983 (4/85). Cooked, southern character—a big zero.

Cantina Coop. del Morellino di Scansano 1983 (4/85). A big zero.

Erik Banti 1983 2 bird label (4/85). Fresh cherrylike fruit and berries on aroma; simple, fruity flavor with a touch of spice. * +

Erik Banti 1983 4 bird label (4/85). Aroma displays oak (110 days in *barrique*); light tannin, simple, fruity and quaffable. *

Erik Banti 1983 Cru Ciabotta (4/86). This wine spent eighteen months in oak. Oxidized! The bottle perhaps?

DOC REQUIREMENTS FOR MORELLINO DI SCANSANO

	Minimum Aging in Years		Minimum Alcohol	Maximum Yield in	
	in Cask	Total		Gallons/Acre	Hectoliters/Hectare
Normale	none	none	11.5%	898	84
Riserva	1	2	12.0%	898	84

Fattoria Coltiberto 1983 (4/85). Corky, but the fruit and structure are still evident. *(?)

Fattoria Le Pupille 1983 Riserva (3 times, 5/88). Perfumed, floral bouquet, nice entry, soft, balanced, agreeable, flavorful. ** +

Mantellassi Ezio 1983 (4/85). Floral aroma with cherrylike fruit; soft, light and quaffable. *

Mantellassi Ezio 1983 Riserva (twice, 4/87). Floral, cherry aroma; dry with moderate tannin, almost sweet, lots of fruit. *(+) *Bottle of 4/85:* Label says "2 years in oak" (plans for the future, maybe?). How can this be a *riserva*. A *riserva* must be aged for at least two years, but this wine isn't even two years old. And if that isn't enough, the wine couldn't have spent two years in oak, but that's what the label says. Oaky, some fruit and tannin; the regular is better.

Poggiolungo 1983 (4/85). Tar, cherries and fruit on aroma; light tannin, simple, quaffable. *

Val delle Rose 1983 (4/85). Nose offers the most interest of the Morellinos tasted—cherry and floral notes; loads of fruit, somewhat tannic, in all a very nice bottle, some tannin on finish. **

Fattoria Le Pupille 1982 Riserva (12/86). Slightly corked, yet the quality is apparent. ?

Fattoria Palazzaccio 1979 (4/80). Stinky on nose; dull, off flavors, though a cherrylike character is evident.

Mantellassi Ezio 1979 (4/80). Cherrylike aroma that carries through on palate, medium body, fruity; enjoyable now though it can improve. *

Poggiolungo 1978 (4/80). Cherries on aroma; medium body, light tannin, soft and fruity. *

Val delle Rose 1978 (4/85). Oxidized.

Azienda di Poggio alla Mozza [Fattoria Moris] NV (4/85). Oxidized.

NICCOLO DA UZZANO (*Toscana*). Castello di Uzzano produces Niccolò da Uzzano from 100 percent sangiovese grosso grapes. The '85, the first they made, spent two years in *barrique*. The label reads Vigna Niccolò Riserva Particolare. Rating *

TASTING NOTE

1985 (4/89, 3,924 bottles). Vanilla oak pronounced, cherry and vanilla character; supple, good fruit, too much oak. *

PALAZZO ALTESI (*Toscana*). Angelo Solci, consulting enologist for Altesino, created this *barrique*-aged 100 percent sangiovese grosso wine. Palazzo Altesi is made in an interesting manner. Grapes from the Montosoli vineyard are crushed and destemmed. Then, 793 gallons (30 hectoliters) of must are put into a 2,642-gallon (100-hectoliter) tank and closed. After the fermentation starts, within a week, carbon dioxide fills the air space. Next Solci takes 2.4 tons (20 quintali) of selected whole bunches from the most recent part of the harvest from Montosoli. Those grapes are funneled into the tank to prevent a loss of carbon dioxide. Consequently, *carbonique maceration* (carbonic maceration) occurs, and continues for seven to eight days. After that, the tank is filled with crushed and stemmed fruit, also from Montosoli from the last picking. The fermentation continues for an additional fifteen days. During this period the tank remains closed, except when they need to push the cap down. When they do, they open the top and push down the cap manually, using a technique called *la follatura*. After another thirty days pass, they combine the free run and the juice obtained from a light pressing, and put it into small Burgundy barrels. The wine is left in these barrels for a year. During the year malolactic fermentation occurs. The wine is racked three times during that year. Around March 1 the wine is egg-white fined and left for a month in tank to settle, after which it is filtered and bottled.

In the first vintage, 1980, 3,000 bottles were produced. That wine was aged in a combination of Slavonian and French oak *barriques* (now they put it all in French oak). Today they produce 13,000 bottles annually. Palazzo Altesi is, for us, one of the most interesting and impressive of Italy's new wines. In fact, if it weren't for the problems we found with a number of bottles of the '85 (the wine refermented in bottle!), we'd give it our highest rating. Be that as it may, the wine still deserves high marks. Rating ***

TASTING NOTES

1989 (twice, *ex*-barrique, 6/90). Vanilla and cherry aroma; medium body, sweet, soft center, good fruit. *(*)

1988 (ex-cask, 11/90). Tarlike aroma combines with berry fruit; open entry, sense of sweetness, good fruit; needs more age yet. **(*)

1987 (5 times, 11/90). Lovely, fragrant aroma, tarlike notes; soft though it has chewy tannins, fairly nice fruit, a little earthy, moderate length; won't be a keeper. **

1986 (twice, *ex*-barrique, 4/88). Rich and concentrated, a mouthful of flavor, good structure. ** + (***)

1985 (12 times, 11/90). This wine has shown tremendous bottle variation! Off aroma and flavors; the wine has refermented in the bottle! *Bottle of 8/90:* Oak, vanilla, tar and berries define the bouquet; packed with flavor, slightly odd note intrudes, good structure; still a little young; not as much as we expected, a disappointment, puzzling. ? *Bottle of 6/90:* Floral, berry aroma, odd backnote; rich and flavorful, sweet impression, supple, good structure. ***? *Bottle of 2/90:* Great richness and concentration, complex, woodsy almost Burgundian slant to the bouquet; and with the structure and backbone of Brunello. ***(+)

1984 (*ex*-barrique, 5/85). A lot of oak (heavy toast) but also a lot of fruit. **(+)

1983 (*7 times, 4/89*). Warm, open bouquet combines fruit and flowers with a light touch of oak; seems a little tight at this stage but the structure and fruit indicate it'll turn out well. **(*)

1982 (*4 times, 4/87*). Complex aroma displays some complexity and mellowness from bottle age; fairly rich and concentrated, good structure, firm; still on the young side. **(*)

1981 (*twice, 4/87*). Almost a Burgundian aroma, recalls the woods with a fruit overlay; seems lush and smooth, some tannin; very ready and very nice. *** −

1980 (4/87). Nutlike and mineral aroma; ready, somewhat dull toward the end, good flavor, lacks the weight and richness displayed by the others—from 1981 through 1986—at this tasting. ** −

PANZANO ROSSO (*Toscana*). Leandro Alessi produces 13,300 bottles annually of Rosso di Panzano from 92 percent sangiovese and 8 percent canaiolo at his Cennatoio estate in Panzano. He also produces **Etrusco,** another *vino da tavola* red.

PARRINA (*Toscana*), *DOC*. The grapes are grown in Parrina and in part of Orbetello in the province of Grosseto. There were 21 registered growers with 273 acres (110 hectares) in 1988.[9] The DOC allows for a red and white, but we are concerned only with the red. This Chianti-style red wine is produced from 80 percent sangiovese and 20 percent canaiolo nero, montepulciano, and/or colorino grapes. The yield cannot exceed 823 gallons per acre (77 hectoliters per hectare). DOC allows up to 10 percent of wine and/or must from outside the zone to be used to correct a weak vintage. Between 1986 and 1988 an average of 35,196 cases were produced, of which 17,395 were red. This included, in 1987 and 1988, 3,110 cases of *riserva*. Maximum production is 99,035 cases.[10] Minimum alcohol for the *normale* is 11.5 percent, for the *riserva* 12 percent. The *normale* cannot be sold prior to December 1 of the following year. The *riserva* must be aged for at least three years. Parrina is best drunk between three and five years of the vintage. Rating **

Recommended Producers

Azienda Agricola Parrina
Vino Etrusco La Parrina di Marchese Spinola Giuntini

Antonio Rossi rates 1988, 1985, 1982, 1978, and 1976 as three-star vintages out of four, and all the rest between 1970 and 1987 as two.[11]

TASTING NOTES

La Parrina Vino Etrusco 1982 (4/85). Fruity, light tannin, balanced, some character; needs another year or two. *(*)

La Parrina Vino Etrusco 1976 (4/80). Floral aroma with a touch of mint; medium-bodied, some tannin, nice flavor and texture; has some style. **

PEPERINO (*Toscana*). Terruzi & Puthod, regarded for their fine Vernaccia di San Gimignano, produce this 70-20-10 blend of sangiovese, montepulciano, and other red grapes grown on their San Gimignano estate.

PERCARLO (*Toscana*). Enrico Martini di Cigala produces Percarlo at his Fattoria San Giusto a Rentennano in the Chianti Classico zone. The wine is made from 100 percent sangiovese grapes grown on a 7.4-acre (3-hectare) vineyard. Martini ferments Percarlo for seventeen days. This wine is *barrique*-aged. The first Percarlo was the '83. We were told that San Giusto produces an average of 10,000 bottles of Percarlo annually, yet there were only 4,077 bottles of the '85 and the equivalent of 6,333 of the '87! Regardless, the wine is very good, and sometimes even better. Rating ** +

TASTING NOTES

1987 (*4/90, 6,033 bottles and 150 magnums*). Floral, cherrylike aroma, oak overlay; rather dry, some fruit, light, dry aftertaste. *

1986 (4/89). Nice nose, ripe berry overlay combines with a judicious touch of oak; well balanced, sweet impression, long finish; displays class. ** +

1985 (*4 times, 9/88, 4,077 bottles*). Complex bouquet combines suggestions of cherries and spice with toasty oak and vanilla; intensely flavored, a lot of structure, good extract, moderately long finish. ** + (***)

PIAN DELLE MURA ROSSO (*Marches*). Pian delle Mura Rosso is a blend of 85 percent sangiovese with 15 percent vernaccia di serrapetrona.

PIETRAMORA (*Emilia-Romagna*). Francesco Geminiani produces Pietramora at his Fattoria Zerbina estate. This wine is the product of 100 percent of a special sangiovese clone grown in their Pietramora vineyard in the vicinity of Marzeno di Faenza in Ravenna. The first, the '85, was aged in *barriques* of Alliers and Vosges oak. Rating *

TASTING NOTE

1985 (6/90). Some oak apparent, cherrylike fruit; simple, soft, small-scale. *

POGGIO BRANDI (*Toscana*). Fattoria Baggiolino in La Romola produces this *barrique*-aged sangiovese. It contains 5 percent ciliegiolo.

PONGELLI (*Marches*). The Bucci family owns the Villa Bucci estate and its nearly 60 acres (24 hectares) of vines, half of which are planted in white verdicchio and half in red varieties. The 12.4-acre (5-hectare) Vigna Passetto di Villa Bucci, the 10-acre (4-hectare) Cupo delle Carne, and the 7.4-acre (3-hectare) Vigna Montefiore–San Fortunato vineyards are planted in verdicchio. The red grapes, 50 percent each, are sangiovese and montepulciano. They produce some 100,000 bottles of wine, white and red, per year.

The legendary Giorgio Grai has consulted here since 1980. The first vintage that was commercialized was the 1982, when they bottled 5,000 bottles of Verdicchio dei Castelli di Jesi. Their first special cuvée was the oak-fermented '83 Villa Bucci Verdicchio, which was in pristine condition when we last tasted it in April 1990. This wine is fermented in casks, not, as is often reported, in *barrique*.

Their first red, the '82, was never bottled. They produced some 6,000 bottles of the '83, no '84—they sold the grapes—and 13,300 bottles of the '85. Pongelli, the product of about half and half sangiovese and montepulciano, is fermented and aged in oak casks. We were told by Ampelio Bucci that the '86 and '87 contained some 4 to 5 percent cabernet sauvignon; we suspect that they all do. The '83 spent two years in wood. Rating **

TASTING NOTES

1987 (*4/90*). Cassis, cherry and herbal nuances; soft and fruity. **

1986 (*twice, 4/90*). Nice nose, herbal notes; good backbone, a tad dry and firm, attractive fruit. ** −

1985 (*twice, 4/90*). Nice fruit on the nose and palate, seems to have more tannin than we expected! *? *Bottle of 4/89:* Light nose; nice fruit, tasty, open, sweet impression. **

PRINCEPESSA (*Toscana*). In 1982 the Chianti Classico producer Tenuta di Lilliano of Castellina in Chianti made 2,200 cases of this wine from 100 percent sangiovese grapes. We've yet to taste it.

PRINCIPESCO (*Toscana*). This wine is made by Fanetti, the Vino Nobile di Montepulciano producer, from a blend of 90 percent sangiovese, 5 percent canaiolo nero, and 5 percent trebbiano and malvasia grapes. We have recently heard that he also uses grechetto bianco and mammolo. It was first produced from the 1979 vintage when Fanetti made 11,600 bottles. The wine is aged for at least five and a half years in most unusual casks—of mulberry wood, one of 605 gallons (23 hectoliters) and another of 1,690 (64). The second Principesco was produced in 1982. It was being aged in two mulberry casks of 820 and 845 gallons (31 and 32 hectoliters) when we wrote these words in the spring of 1985. Rating **

PRUNAIO (*Toscana*). Fattoria Viticcio produces this *barrique*-aged 100 percent sangiovese, or sangiovese grosso, wine. The '85, the first, spent eight months in *barrique*. Viticcio produced 3,618 bottles of the first Prunaio and increased the production in the next vintage more than ninefold. Rating * +

TASTING NOTES

1986 (*3 times, 5/90, 33,840 bottles*). Oak and cherry aroma; firm and dry, nice fruit midpalate, a little dry toward the end. **

1985 (*twice, 4/89, 3,618 bottles*). Open fruit and oak aroma; good structure, tasty, short. * +

PULIGNANO (*Toscana*). Pulignano is produced from a blend of 70 percent sangiovese with 10 percent each canaiolo, trebbiano, and malvasia, with 20 percent white grapes.

QUERCIAGRANDE (*Toscana*). Querciagrande comes from Gianpaolo Pacini's Podere Capaccia estate located in Radda in the Chianti Classico zone. Vittorio Fiore, who consults here, produces 4,000 bottles of this *barrique*-aged 100 percent sangiovese for Pacini. The '83 was the first. It spent twelve months in *barrique*. Rating **

TASTING NOTES

1988 (*ex-barrel, 11/90*). Oak up front then nice fruit; rich, good concentration and structure. *(*)

1987 (*11/90*). Open fruit on the nose and palate; a little dry after the initial fruit impression, fairly well balanced; young. *(*)

1986 (*twice, 4/89*). Oak followed by fruit on the nose; good backbone, almost sweet. **

RANGO (*Toscana*). The La Suvera estate of Marchese Ricci Paracciani Bergamini produces Rango Rosso de Casole d'Elsa on his estate at Pievescola. We were informed that this wine was made from a blend of grapes, the same ones used in Chianti. We've tasted the '83 on two occasions and found the wine good, if a little simple. Rating *

RF SELICE (*Toscana*). Elisabetta Ricasoli-Firidolfi, owner of Castello di Cacchiano, produces RF Selice from her 2.47-acre (1-hectare) Selice vineyard. She produces, on average, 5,000 bottles of this sangiovese-canaiolo blend. It was first made in 1985. We are a little confused, though. Our tasting notes on the name of the '85 read " 'RF' Vigneto Selice," while those for the '86 specify "FR Selice." Perhaps there was a name change. Or perhaps we reversed the R and the F? We liked the '86 and found the '85 disappointing. Rating *

1986 FR Selice (*10/89*). Oak apparent as well as a lot of fruit; good structure, flavorful, could use more length. ** −

1985 "RF" Vigneto Selice (*10/88*). Ripe, berrylike aroma, cherrylike fruit, vague off note in the background (mercaptan?); the fruit flavor recalls the brambly character of a zinfandel, lacks the lushness expected from this vintage, overly dry finish.

RIPA DELLE MORE (*Toscana*). Castello Vicchiomaggio makes the *barrique*-aged, sangiovese-based Ripa delle More. It is aged in a combination of Nevers and Alliers oak. Rating **

1986 (*11/90*). Oak and spice, with a peppery note; good fruit, supple center. ** −

ROCCA DI MONTEGROSSI ROSSO (*Toscana*). Elisabetta Ricasoli-Firidolfi, owner of Castello di Cacchiano, produces this red wine from a blend of 90 percent sangiovese and 10 percent canaiolo. It is aged for one year in oak. She first produced Rocca di Montegrossi Rosso in 1985. Thus far the only one that we tasted was the quite good '87. It is possible that this wine is actually the same as the one labeled Rocca di Montegrossi *Geremia,* since it is made from the same blend of grapes and in the same proportion. We might have inadvertently omitted Geremia from the name in our tasting notes. Be that as it may, the wine, at least the '87, was very good. Rating ** −

1987 (*twice, 4/90*). Delicate nose; a little dry but soft and flavorful, nice fruit; more or less ready. ** −

ROSSO DEI COMIGNALI (*Toscana*). Fattoria di Artimino produces Rosso dei Comignali from a blend of 90 percent canaiolo and 10 percent sangiovese grapes grown on their Carmignano estate. This wine is aged six to eight months in oak casks.

ROSSO DELLA TRAFILA (*Emilia-Romagna*). Rosso della Trafila is made by Azienda Agricola Casetta dei Frati in Forlì from 100 percent sangiovese grapes.

ROSSO DELLE COLLINE LUCCHESI (*Toscana*), DOC. The Rosso delle Colline Lucchesi DOC zone encompasses nearly 500 acres (200 hectares) in Lucca, Capannori, and Pocari. In 1988 there were 54 registered growers and 432 declared acres (175 hectares).[12] The maximum yield is 898 gallons per acre (84 hectoliters per hectare), and the minimum alcohol 11.5 percent. The average production between 1986 and 1988 was 55,339 cases of Rosso delle Colline Lucchesi.[13] There is no minimum aging requirement. This wine is not for aging. Rating *

SALINA ROSSO (*Sicilia*). Salina Rosso is made from a blend of 50 percent sangiovese grosso, 20 percent nerello mascalese, and 30 percent malvasia. We suspect that it is aged in *barrique.*

SAN MARTINO (*Toscana*). The fine Chianti Classico estate of Villa Cafaggio produces San Martino from 100 percent sangiovese grapes, three-quarters sangiovese toscano and one-quarter sangiovese grosso, grown in the 10-acre (4-hectare) vineyard near the Church of San Martino in Cecione. This vineyard, which includes some 2.5 acres (1 hectare) of sangiovese grosso, was planted in 1976. Farkas plans to plant another 6 acres (2.5 hectares) of sangiovese grosso in April 1991, as well as 3.7 (1.5) of regular sangiovese. The plant density will be increased. This wine, which was first produced with the '85, is *barrique*-aged in a combination of Tronçais and Alliers oak. About one-fifth of the *barriques* are new. The other vintages were the '86, '88, and '90. Stefano Farkas, winemaker and estate manager, produces between 10,000 and 15,000 bottles of San Martino per year. Rating ***

1988 (*ex-barrique, 11/90*). Farkas produced some 17,000 bottles of San Martino. At this stage the oak dominates, but there is no doubt about the fruit, which is rich and concentrated. **(*)

1986 (*twice, 11/90, 14,000 bottles*). This one spent nine months in *barrique.* Lovely nose combines ripe fruit and oak; supple, soft and open; fairly long, ready. ** +

1985 (*5 times, 11/90, 12,000 bottles and 667 magnums*). Open fruit aroma, oak overlay, the oak and fruit combine in a harmonious way, cherry and berry notes; rich and concentrated, sweet impression, supple, a lot of structure and character; quite ready though room to improve. ***

SANGIOVESE DEI COLLI PESARESI (*Marches*), DOC. Sangiovese dei Colli Pesaresi is produced from a blend of no less than 85 percent sangiovese and up to 15 percent montepulciano and/or ciliegiolo grapes grown around Pesaro. The maximum yield cannot exceed 823 gallons per acre (77 hectoliters per hectare). In 1988 there were 388 registered growers cultivating 1,930 acres (781 hectares).[14] Between 1986 and 1988 an average of 154,859 cases were produced.[15] The alcoholic content must be no less than 11.5 percent. There is no minimum aging requirement.

This small-scale wine can be agreeable, if rarely more. Rating *

SANGIOVESE DI ROMAGNA (*Emilia-Romagna*), *DOC*. Emilia-Romagna has 14 DOCs and one DOCG. The most important wine, in quantity, is Lambrusco. In wine terms, however, the most important red is Sangiovese di Romagna. Of the average of 15.3 million gallons (580,446 hectoliters) of DOC red produced in Emilia between 1986 and 1988, 3.1 million (115,758), or 20 percent, were Sangiovese di Romagna.[16] The sangiovese grapes for these wines are grown in the provinces of Bologna, Forlì, and Ravenna. Bruno Roncarati said that the best ones come from around Predappio near Forlì; those of Rimini and Cesena are also good. Wines with the Superiore designation come from more delimited areas. In 1988, 1,446 growers cultivated 5,387 acres (2,180 hectares). From this acreage they could produce nearly 2.2 million cases per year.[17] Actual production was considerably less. Between 1986 and 1988 an average of less than 1.3 million cases was produced.[18]

These flavorful dry red wines range from medium to full-bodied and are best drunk with about two to three years of age. Most Sangiovese di Romagna is rather common, but a few producers make a very good one. And a few, but very few, can take up to a decade of age. Rating */** +

Recommended Producers

* Fattoria Paradiso
  Dott. Giuseppe Marabini
  Fattoria Zerbina

Pasolini dall'Onda
* Spalletti, Rocco di Ribiano
  Vallunga

Others with a Good Reputation

Casetto dei Mandorli
Ferrucci Stefano
Foschi Carla

Le Calbane di Cesare Raggi
Muccioli
Zammarchi

Mario Pezzi, without question one of the zone's finest producers (if not the finest), produces 26,600 cases of 10 different wines from 86 acres (35 hectares) of vines at his Fattoria Paradiso winery. This includes 6,100 cases of Sangiovese di Romagna Superiore and 2,775 of Sangiovese di Romagna Superiore Riserva. There are two single-vineyard Sangiovese di Romagnas: Vigna del Molina Superiore, made from sangiovese, is best between one and three years of the vintage; and Vigna delle Lepre Riserva, made from sangiovese grosso, is ready three to four years after the vintage and can last, Pezzi says, for up to ten years.

PRODUCTION OF SANGIOVESE DI ROMAGNA (1986–88)

Province/Wine	1986	1987	1988	Average	Average
		(Hectoliters)*			(Cases)
BOLOGNA					
Sangiovese di Romagna	6,211	6,052	4,174	5,479	60,872
Sangiovese di Romagna Superiore	—	—	—	—	—
FORLI					
Sangiovese di Romagna	79,415	53,243	47,708	60,122	667,955
Sangiovese di Romagna Superiore	46,248	24,256	17,493	29,332	325,882
RAVENNA					
Sangiovese di Romagna	20,952	10,586	6,518	12,685	140,934
Sangiovese di Romagna Superiore	3,224	2,381	2,535	8,140	90,435
Total	156,050	96,518	78,428	115,758	1,286,078

* 1 hectoliter = 26.42 gallons, or 11.11 cases

Source: Data supplied by Il Corriere Vinicolo

DOC REQUIREMENTS FOR SANGIOVESE DI ROMAGNA

	Minimum Aging	Minimum Alcohol	Maximum Yield (Gallons/Acre)
Normale	until April 1	11.5%	764*
Riserva	2 years from January 1	11.5%	764*
Superiore	2 years from January 1	12.0%	764*

* 71.5 hectoliters per hectare

VINTAGE INFORMATION AND TASTING NOTES

The most highly regarded vintages have been 1977, 1961, 1957, and 1956. Also good: 1985, 1983, 1981, 1979, 1978, and 1975. Anything older is sure to be of academic interest only. Mario Pezzi of Fattoria Paradiso lists 1988, 1986, 1985, 1982, 1977, 1970, 1957, and 1956 as the best years, and 1969, 1960, and 1955 as the least.

Antonio Niederbacher's vintage chart:

****	1977, 1961, 1957, 1956
***	1985, 1983, 1981, 1979, 1978, 1975, 1971, 1970, 1968, 1967, 1966, 1965, 1958, 1953, 1952, 1950, 1949, 1946
**	1984, 1982, 1980, 1976, 1974, 1973, 1972, 1964, 1959, 1954, 1948, 1945
*	1969, 1963, 1962, 1960, 1951, 1947
0	1955

Antonio Rossi rates the vintages between 1970 and 1988 as either two- or three-star years out of four, except for 1972, which he rates at one. With three stars he puts 1988, 1985, 1981, 1977, 1974, 1971, and 1970. All the rest get two.[19]

Dott. G. Marabini NV (2/90). Cherries and flowers; light, fresh and easy. *

Fattoria Zerbina (4/89). Open, fresh, cherry and floral aroma; light and tasty, marred by an overly dry finish. *

Cantina Produttori Predappio 1986 Superiore (4/88). Rather ordinary but drinkable, just barely.

Fattoria Paradiso 1985 Vigna delle Lepre Riserva Superiore (twice, 6/90). Cherrylike from the aroma through the flavor, tart and lively, light tannin, lots of fruit. **

San Patrignano 1985 Superiore (4/87). Vinous, fruit, drinkable. +

Fattoria Paradiso 1983 Vigna delle Lepre Riserva Superiore (2/88). Fairly nice fruit, moderate tannin, somewhat tart. *

San Patrignano 1983 Riserva Superiore (4/87). Shows age but drinkable. * —

Fattoria Paradiso 1982 Vigna delle Lepre Riserva Superiore (4 times, 10/87). Fruity but a little coarse. * *Bottle of 4/87:* Cherrylike fruit aroma; some tannin, good structure, nice fruit in the mouth, medium to full body. ** +

Fattoria Paradiso 1981 Vigna delle Lepre Riserva Superiore (2/87). Floral aroma, cherry notes; fruity, soft, well balanced. * +

Fattoria Paradiso 1980 Vigna delle Lepre Riserva Superiore (3 times, 2/87). Nice nose, floral and fruity with suggestions of cherries; starting to fade but still has flavor interest. *

Vallunga 1978 (4/80). Cherries on aroma; light tannin, light body, fruity. *

Fattoria Paradiso 1977 Vigna del Molino Superiore (10/78). Smallish aroma; light tannin, flavorful, bitter almond finish. *

Vallunga 1977 (twice, 11/78). Floral aroma; flavorful, some tannin, ready. * +

Fattoria Paradiso 1976 Vigna delle Lepre Riserva Superiore (twice, 4/85). Pretty bouquet of cherries and flowers; soft and tasty; one of the best Sangiovese di Romagnas we've tasted. *** —

Vallunga 1976 Gran Riserva (9/85, 30,000 bottles). Lots of fresh cherrylike fruit; tart edge, flavorful, shows some age at the end. ** —

Conte G. Battista Spalletti 1975 Rocca di Ribiano Superiore (4/90). Here's an exception to the longevity rule. Rich with a gentle character, soft and round, sweet impression, tasty; no signs of age. *** —

Fattoria Paradiso 1975 Vigna delle Lepre Riserva Superiore (10/78, 2,500 cases). Aroma brings up cherries; a big wine, full of flavor, not a lot of tannin; needs another year or two. **(*)

SANGIOVESE-NEBBIOLO DI VOLPAIA (*Siena*). Although this wine doesn't exactly belong in this chapter, there was no other place to put it that made sense. So here it is. Recently the nebbiolo has even migrated to Toscana where Giovannella Stianti Mascheroni planted it at her fine Castello di

Volpaia estate in the Chianti Classico district. The first sample of the '88, which we tasted from barrel, showed promise. It had a tobacco and cherry aroma, was rich and harmonious, and had the tannin common to the nebbiolo grape. The second sample, tasted many months later, also from barrel, had a more pronounced oak character. The wine was made from a blend of half nebbiolo and half sangiovese. The first experimental wine was produced in 1985. They passed on the '86, '87, and '89, but not on the '88.

SANGIOVETO DI COLTIBUONO (*Toscana*). Enologist Maurizio Castelli created this *barrique*-aged wine at Badia a Coltibuono in 1980. It is made from 100 percent sangiovese, the best grapes from the oldest vines in their vineyards, which are forty to forty-five years old. The wine ferments and is kept on the skins for twenty-one days. It is aged for about nine months in half new and half slightly used French *barriques*. In 1980, 12,000 bottles were produced. Today the annual production ranges from 18,000 to 20,000 bottles. Maurizio Castelli consults with winemaker Roberto Stucchi-Prinetti. They rate '85 as the best vintage and '84, which they didn't bottle, as the worst. Unlike most of Toscana's new-wave *barrique*-aged wines, Sangioveto needs age to soften and harmonize. And indications are that it will keep. Rating ****

TASTING NOTES

1988 (*ex-barrel, 11/90*). Aroma of spice and fruit combine with oak, refined; a rich, concentrated mouthful of fruit, quite tannic; just might be the best Sangioveto to date. ***(*)

1987 (*ex-barrel, 11/90*). Good fruit, oak overlay, well balanced, tannin to shed. *(*)

1986 (*11/90*). Spice and fruit aroma; loads of flavor, good structure, soft under moderate tannin. **(+)

1985 (*twice, 11/90*). A rich mouthful of ripe fruit, sweet impression, open, firm finish; quite young with tannin to shed. ***(+) *Bottle of 4/89*: Floral fragrance, some oak adds a note of complexity without dominating; firm backbone, full of flavor, very young with tannin to shed, good structure and texture; should be splendid in time. **+ (***)

1983 (*5 times, 11/90, 23,680 bottles*). Rich nose displays notes of leather, dried fruit and flowers, complex; tight, rich, concentrated, good extract and concentration, a lot of structure; very young yet; classy. ***+ (****)

1982 (*12 times, 11/90, 24,200 bottles*). Fruit seems a little tight, moderate tannin; it is developing differently than we thought a year ago. *(*) *Bottle of 12/89*: Floral component to the ripe fruit aroma; hard and tannic, firm backbone, rich and concentrated, oak overlay; very young. ***(+)

1981 (*7 times, 11/90*). Lovely complex bouquet, berry, floral and forest scents; sweet impression, somewhat mellow; starting to become ready, but there is some troublesome tannin, the bottle perhaps? *(+) *Bottle of 6/90*: Big and rich, great concentration and structure, aging very well, attractive now. *** −

1980 (*3 times, 11/90*). Seems to be losing its fruit and fading, or is it the bottle. ? *Bottle of 5/85*: Berries, flowers and oak on aroma; oak flavors on entry give way to rich fruit, well knit, long. **(*)

SANGIOVETO DI MONSANTO. See **FABRIZIO BIANCHI.**

SANGIOVETO DI PIOMBINO (*Toscana*). Azienda Agricola Toni Fidenzio produces this Sangioveto from his vineyards in Piombino in the province of Livorno. The vineyards are near the coast, some 7 miles (12 kilometers) northeast of Elba.

SANTA CRISTINA (*Toscana*). Antinori produces this 90-10 percent sangiovese-canaiolo blend. A few years ago it was sold as a Chianti Classico *normale*. Now it is a *vino da tavola*. A portion of the Santa Cristina is aged for one year in oak casks. This simple red, meant to be drunk young, is dependable, if no more. Rating *

SASSELLO (*Toscana*). Castello di Verrazzano produced this *barrique*-aged 100 percent sangiovese for the first time in 1982. They made 2,400 bottles of the '85 Sassello. Rating * −

TASTING NOTE

1985 (*11/90*). Dried fruit, leather and chocolate aroma, floral note; coarse, dry, some fruit, very short; the nose was the best part. * −

SER GIOVETO (*Toscana*). Ser Gioveto is produced by Italo Zingarelli's Rocca delle Macìe winery in the Chianti Classico zone. This *barrique*-aged wine is made from 100 percent sangiovese. It was first produced from the 1985 vintage. There were 13,300 bottles of the '85 and 33,520 of the '87. The wine is good and it ages moderately well. Rating **

TASTING NOTES

1989 (*ex-cask, 6/90*). Mushroom aroma seems a little intrusive; the fruit seems tired! ?

1988 (*11/90, 53,251 bottles*). Aroma of vanilla oak, followed by fruit; good structure, young and a little dry, moderate tannin. *(*)

1987 (*6 times, 11/90, 33,520 bottles*). There was bottle variation. The least of the six we tasted were the two most recent, and the best was the one tasted in May 1990. Warm and fruity aroma; dried fruit, overly dry end, very short. + *Bottle of 9/90*: Fairly nice fruit, yet it seems older than its years. *Bottle of 5/90:* Flowers and tar, dried fruit and leather define the aroma; soft and open, ready now, light tannin. * +

1986 (*3 times, 2/90*). Open fruit and tobacco aroma, cherry notes; soft and supple, oak blends nicely with the fruit; very ready. **

1985 (*4 times, 9/89*). Soft and ready, harmonious blend of sangiovese fruit with the oak from the *barrique;* best not to keep. **

SER NICCOLO (*Toscana*). Initially we were told that Conti Serristori produced Ser Niccolò from a blend of sangiovese grosso, canaiolo, and colorino grapes grown on their Chianti Classico estate. They first produced this *vino da tavola* from the 1981 vintage. The next time we inquired about this wine we were told that it was a blend of 90 percent sangiovese and 10 percent colorino, and that wine—the '85—spent two years in oak. Some 30 percent of that wine spent seven months in *barrique,* the balance in large oak casks. Rating * +

TASTING NOTES

1985 (*11/90*). Fragrant aroma, oak overlay; good structure, rich fruit, sense of sweetness, a little short; young, needs age. *(*)

1981 (*4/87*). Cherrylike aroma, light, herbaceous backnote(!); fruity, some tannin, seems to have sufficient fruit. *(+)

SODOLE (*Toscana*). Guicciardini Strozzi's Fattoria Cusona estate produces the *barrique*-aged Sodolè from sangiovese grapes.

SOLATIO BASILICA (*Toscana*). The very fine Chianti Classico producer Villa Cafaggio produces this wine from 85 to 90 percent sangiovese grapes, which are selected from three very old vineyards, all planted in *coltura promiscua* with olives between 1937 and 1939. The wine is aged for one year in Slavonian oak casks of about 790-gallon (30-hectoliter) capacity. The first Solatìo Basilica was produced in 1981; 7,866 bottles were made. The '82 was blended into their Chianti Classico Riserva. It was produced again in 1983, when 4,000 bottles were made. There was no '84, but it was produced in 1985, 1988, and 1990. Production varies from 5,000 to 7,000 bottles annually. Without question Solatìo Basilica is one of the best of the new-breed sangiovese-based wines. Rating *** +

TASTING NOTES

1988 (*ex-cask, 11/90*). Farkas produced some 8,600 bottles. A big, rich, concentrated wine, lots of structure, lots of flavor, very young, evident promise. **(*)

1985 (*6 times, 11/90, 6,650 bottles*). Complex bouquet, overtones and hints of tobacco, berries and vanilla, floral backnote; richly fruited, with incredible concentration of flavor, deep, rich and complex with layers of flavor, harmonious, very long; quite young, real class. ***(+)

1983 (*ex-cask, twice, 5/86*). Rich, ripe fruit combines with new oak; enormous richness and concentration, lots of tannin; good potential; impressive in all respects. ***(+)

1982 (*ex-cask, 5/85*). Black color; enormous weight and concentration, sweet, rich and ripe. ***(*)

1981 (*5 times, 6/89*). Ripe and dried fruit nuances blend with a vanilla oak overlay, hint of leather; starting to show some age but the attractive flavor makes it quite appealing. (Perhaps the bottle isn't up to snuff. It was much better nine months ago.) ** *Bottle of 5/85:* Deep color; aroma of cherries, flowers and berries; moderate tannin, well balanced, sweet ripe fruit, rich and flavorful. **(*)

SONO MONTENIDOLI (*Toscana*). Elisabetta Fagiuoli produces Sono Montenidoli on her Podere Montenidoli estate in San Gimignano. This very good Vernaccia di San Gimignano producer uses a blend of sangiovese and malvasia nera grapes to make this medium-bodied, fruity red. It can take moderate age. The estate takes its name from the *località* of Montenidoli, where it is situated. Rating **

STIELLE (*Toscana*). The good Chianti Classico producer Rocca di Castagnoli makes this sangiovese-in-*barrique*. Rating *

TASTING NOTES

1988 (*ex-barrel, 11/90*). Ripe berry fruit up front on the nose and palate is quickly followed by gobs of oak, and then more oak, especially in the mouth. *(+)

1987 (*11/90*). Oak dominates on the nose and palate, some fruit is evident. *

TEGOLATO (*Toscana*). This wine is a Chianti, but is sufficiently different—one might even say peculiar—to get its own entry. The name of this wine derives from the word *tegole,* roof tiles. Prinz Kunz Piast d'Asburgo Lorena ages this wine at his Antico Castello di Poppiano estate in small barrels under the *tegole,* from August to December. No, it's not a *vin santo;* it's an oxidized red wine. Rating 0

TORRI (*Toscana*). Castello di San Polo in Rosso produces this 100 percent sangiovese. Some 20 percent of the wine was made with *maceration carbonique* (carbonic maceration). The wine should be consumed while it is young and fresh. Rating **

VALLOCAIA (*Toscana*). This *barrique*-aged wine is produced by the good Vino Nobile producer Rudolf Bindella.

VIGNA DI FONTEVECCHIA (*Toscana*). Agricola Camigliano from the Montalcino zone produces this, what is in effect a non-DOC Rosso di Montalcino in *barrique*. Rating * +

TASTING NOTES

1986 (*ex*-barrique, 4/87). Fresh cherrylike fruit; good fruit, firm tannins. *(*)

1985 (*twice, 10/87, 3,000 bottles*). Cherrylike aroma has a woodsy component; chocolate flavor, moderate tannin, balanced, short, tannic aftertaste. *(+)

VIGNA PIANACCI (*Toscana*). Castello di Luiano produces this wine from 60 percent canaiolo, 10 percent colorino, and 30 percent sangiovese grapes grown in their 10-acre (4-hectare) Pianacci vineyard. It is aged four to six months in *barrique*. We have heard that the colorino has been replaced with cabernet sauvignon. Rating * −

TASTING NOTE

1983 (*3 times, 6/90*). There was considerable variation among the three bottles that we tasted over the course of twenty-one months. Cooked fruit, oxidized. *Bottle of 2/90:* Openly fruity, cherry notes; medium body, soft and tasty. * +

VINATTIERI ROSSO (*Toscana*). The fine enologist Maurizio Castelli created this wine from a blend of sangiovese grapes from two areas, 60 percent from the Chianti Colli Senesi and 40 percent from Montepulciano. It is aged for one year in *barrique*. Vinattieri was produced for the first time from the 1982 vintage. That year Castelli made 7,000 bottles, hardly enough to last him, his friends, and curious journalists until the next harvest. No Vinattieri was produced in 1984. At one time writer Burton Anderson was involved. Today Castelli's partner is Roberto Stucchi-Prinetti of Badia a Coltibuono. There is also a sangiovese–cabernet sauvignon version, **Vinattieri Rosso II,** and a chardonnay, Vinattieri Bianco from Trentino–Alto Adige. Rating ** +

TASTING NOTES

1986 (*11/90*). Cherry and berry fruit combine with oak on the nose and palate, soft, light tannin, precocious. ** +

1985 (*11/90*). Warm and soft, balanced, oak overlay. ** +

1983 (*twice, 11/90*). Complex bouquet from bottle age; rich and warm, moderate length; very ready, perhaps even a trace of age shows. **

1982 (*twice, 11/90*). Near its peak, or perhaps a shade past it, soft and full of flavor; moderate length. ** + *Bottle of 4/85:* Lovely bouquet of cherries and berries, with a nice touch of oak; tannic entry, well knit, sweet fruit and oak flavors; quite young; a well-made wine with real class. ***

◁ THE PREDICATO WINES ▷

A few years ago a group of Chianti's leading producers, led by the Folonaris of Ruffino, got together to create a set of rules for some new wines. These rules today cover four wines known collectively as the Predicato wines. Originally, in 1979, the three firms of Ruffino, Antinori, and Frescobaldi combined their efforts in a *consorzio* for the express purpose of creating a new white wine, namely the light-bodied Galestro. They were joined shortly by Ricasoli, then by a number of other producers, large and small. Since that *consorzio* was already in place, these producers decided to use it for the Predicato wines as well. The *consorzio* Ente Tutela dei Colli della Toscana Centrale has specified the allowable grapes for each of the Predicato wines, where they can come from, minimum alcohol, minimum aging, etc.

The *consorzio* has defined the allowable grape varieties and the location where they can come from. These varieties must be grown in the area known as Terra dei Capitolari, the land between Firenze and Siena. This, the "geographical and enological heart of Toscana," was, they point out, a "land of ecclesiastic rules." The rules were, in the old days, bound in volumes, *capitolari*. The vineyards for the Predicato wines must be planted at an elevation of no less than 490 feet (150 meters) above sea level and 165 feet (50 meters) above the valley floor. The red wines must be aged for no less than six months in wood cask, excluding chestnut, with a maximum capacity of 1,320 gallons (50 hectoliters).

Two of the Predicato wines are white, two red. The white wines are Predicato del Selvante and Predicato del Muschio. The first is made from 100 percent sauvignon blanc, the second from chardonnay and pinot blanc, with up to 20 percent rhine riesling and riesling italico allowed. Originally sauvignon blanc was permitted in the Predicato del Muschio, but this has been changed and that variety is no longer allowed. Frescobaldi produces a good example of Predicato del Selvante with its Vergena, made from sauvignon blanc grapes grown at the Montalcino estate of Castelgiocondo, and Ruffino produces a very good example of a Predicato del Muschio with its Cabreo Vigneto La Pietra, a barrel-fermented chardonnay.

The wines that concern us, however, are the two reds: Predicato di Bitùrica and Predicato di Cardisco.

PREDICATO DI BUTURICA. Predicato di Bitùrica must contain at least 30 percent cabernet; the balance can be sangiovese and/or merlot. The grapes must be planted at an altitude of no less than 600 feet (180 meters) above sea level. Rating **

RECOMMENDED PRODUCERS	RATING
Agricoltori del Geografico	* +
Castello di Querceto, Il Querciolaia	** −
Frescobaldi, Mormoreto	** +
Ruffino, Cabreo Vigneto Il Borgo	***
San Felice	**

Agricoltori del Geografico, a *cantina sociale,* produces a Predicato di Bitùrica from 65 percent sangiovese and 35 percent cabernet grapes grown at vineyards planted at altitudes that range from 1,150 to 1,475 feet (350 to 450 meters) above sea level. Their annual production is 13,300 bottles. Rating * +

Alessandro François of Castello di Querceto produces Il Querciolaia Predicato di Bitùrica, a 70-30 sangiovese–cabernet sauvignon blend, from the 15-acre (6-hectare) Querciolàia de'Pitti vineyard. He produces some 15,000 bottles annually. The first one was the '85. Rating ** −

Frescobaldi's Mormoreto is made mostly from cabernet sauvignon grapes grown in the 47-acre (19-hectare) Mormoreto plot at their Nipozzano estate; a small amount of sangiovese is included. The '83 was 85 percent cabernet sauvignon, 10 percent sangiovese, and 5 percent cabernet franc grapes, the '85 was 90 percent cabernet sauvignon and 10 percent cabernet franc. The '85 was aged eighteen to twenty months in *barrique.* There were 24,000 bottles of the '83 and 33,300 of the '85. Today they produce between 30,000 and 40,000 bottles of this Predicato di Bitùrica annually. Rating ** +

The Ruffino Cabreo Vigneto Il Borgo derives its name from the historical name—*cabreo*—meaning the "the inventory of agricultural land formed from charts and maps." The *cabreo* became identified with a specific family. This Predicato di Bitùrica is a sangiovese–cabernet sauvignon blend made from grapes grown in the Il Borgo vineyard on their Tenuta di Montemasso estate in San Polo di Greve. This 62-acre (25-hectare) vineyard is planted at an altitude of about 1,200 feet (365 meters) above sea level. The blend varies between 60 and 70 percent sangiovese and 40 and 30 percent cabernet sauvignon. The wine is fermented and aged for fourteen months in *barrique.* The '82 was the first one; there was no '84. The Folonaris released the '82 in the spring of 1986. Rating ***

San Felice of Castelnuovo Berardenga produces a 65-35 sangiovese grosso–cabernet sauvignon Predicato di Bitùrica. The '85 spent six months in *barrique,* plus three years in large Slavonian oak casks. Rating **

TASTING NOTES

San Felice 1988 (*ex-barrel, 11/90*). Nice nose, refined cabernet character; good structure, young. **(+)

Castello di Querceto 1987 Il Querciolaia (*11/90*). Aroma is cabernet and oak, cherry and cassis notes; open fruit, moderate tannin, cherry, cassis and tobacco flavors, a little short and dry at the end; still it is quite good. ** −

San Felice 1987 (*11/90*). Open nose, cabernet and oak, nice palate, soft, short finish. ** −

Agricoltori del Geografico 1986 (*6/90*). Herbaceous, cherry aroma; soft, fruity and open, supple, short. * +

Castello di Querceto 1986 Il Querciolaia (*2/90*). Soft, open and tasty, some tannin; needs a few years yet, it should improve. ** −

Ruffino 1986 Cabreo Vigneto Il Borgo (*3 times, 6/90, 60,761 bottles and larger sizes*). Light nose, herbal, green olive components; open fruit flavor, sweet impression, supple, well made and well balanced; should be ready early. **

Frescobaldi 1985 Mormoreto (*11/90*). Refined cabernet aroma; evident fruit in spite of being a little dry; young and in need of age. *(*)

Ruffino 1985 Cabreo Vigneto Il Borgo (*3 times, 5/90*). Loads of vanilla and oak, cassis and tea, green olive; taste of sweet oak evident, richly fruited, nice texture, harmonious. *** − (***)

San Felice 1985 (*3 times, 9/90*). Refined aroma recalls vanilla, floral note; soft, packed with ripe fruit, light tannin, most attractive, quite flavorful; ready, should last. ** +

Frescobaldi 1983 Mormoreto (*twice, 10/89*). A lot to like, cassis aroma and flavor, good structure, well made. ** +

Ruffino 1982 Cabreo Vigneto Il Borgo (*twice, 7/87*). Cabernet dominates, vague cherry note; good body, moderate tannin, fruity with an herbaceous nature, some length, a firm tannic finish; a good first effort. **(+)

San Felice 1982 (*twice, 9/87*). Some cabernet as well as cherry-like fruit evident; rich and flavorful, good structure. *(*)

PREDICATO DI CARDISCO. Thus far the only Predicato di Cardisco that we've seen is Cecchi's Spargolo, made from 100 percent sangiovese grosso and sangiovese toscano. At one time we were told that the wine also contained 5 percent malvasia rosa as well, but recently Andrea Cecchi, who should know, said that this wine was 100 percent sangiovese, right from the beginning. He also told us that the back labels of the original releases were mistaken as to the *uvaggio.* The first one, the '82, spent eighteen months in 1,057-gallon (40-hectoliter) casks, plus six months in *barrique.* Production has varied from 7,000 bottles of the '82 to 20,050 bottles of the '85. Rating ** +

TASTING NOTES

1989 (*ex-barrel, 5/90*). Open grapey aroma; fairly tannic, a little lightweight, lacks structure, does have fruit, short. (*)

1988 (*ex-barrel, 11/90*). At this stage the oak dominates, but the sense of ripe fruit is very much in evidence on both the nose and palate, concentrated, good weight, long; a lot of potential. **(* −)

1986 (*11/90*). Spicy, fruity, berry aroma has an oak overlay; a little firm yet, light to moderate tannin, soft under that tannin; should be ready early. *(*)

1985 (*6 times, 12/90, 20,050 bottles*). A lot of alcohol as well as some fruit on the nose; good structure, a little dry. *(*) *Bottle of 11/90:* Oak and fruit combine very nicely; good fruit, vanilla overlay, seems a little dry in spite of the fruit, firm structure. **(+) *Bottle of 5/90:* Packed with flavor, moderate tannin, a lot of concentration; on the young side; at this stage a little dry at the end. **(* −)

1983 (*6 times, 6/90, 10,130 bottles*). Open cherrylike aroma, vanilla overlay; rich and concentrated, well balanced, moderately long finish. **(+)

1982 (*5 times, 11/90, 7,000 bottles*). Nice nose of oak and fruit; seems to be drying out, could be the bottle. * *Bottle of 5/90:* Perfumed, scented bouquet, ripe fruit and cherrylike component; sweet impression, still a little tannin, fresh, more or less ready, finish is a tad dry. ** +

THE SANGIOVESE-CABERNET ◁ BLENDS ▷

The resounding success of Tignanello created the fad for *barrique*-aged wines made from a blend of sangiovese and cabernet. But that wine was not the first Tuscan wine to intentionally combine sangiovese with cabernet. That "distinction" falls to Carmignano. Conte Ugo Bonacossi planted cabernet sauvignon to blend with sangiovese and other grapes at his Villa Capezzana estate in the 1960s, approximately a decade before Tignanello was created. Still, it was Tignanello that has received the most attention and has had the biggest impact on the current state of affairs in Tuscan viticulture and viniculture.

Rating the Sangiovese-Cabernet Blends

***
Alte d'Altesi (Altesino)
Grifi (Avignonesi)
Secentenàrio (Antinori)
Tignanello (Antinori)

**
+ Balifico (Castello di Volpaia)
Bruno di Rocca (Vecchie Terre de Montefili)
Ca' del Pazzo (Tenuta Caparzo)
Camartina (Fattoria Querciabella)

Colle Picchioni Rosso, Vigna del Vassallo (Paola di Mauro)
− Coltibuono Rosso (Badia a Coltibuono)
Grattamacco (Podere Grattamacco)
Le Vignacce (Villa Cilnia)
Pomino Rosso, DOC
Predicato di Bitùrica *vino da tavola*
Rosso Armentano (F.lli Vallunga)
+ San Giòrgio (Lungarotti)
Santa Croce (Castell'in Villa)
Solo Rosso (Podere Petroio alla via della Malpensata)
Tenuta di Pomino Rosso (Frescobaldi)
Terricci (Antiche Terre de'Ricci)
+ Tinscvil (Castello di Monsanto)
Vinattieri Rosso II

*
+ Acciaiolo (Fattoria di Albola)
− Bottiglia Particolare (Castello di Verrazzano)
Colli Altotiberini, DOC
+ Concerto (Fonterutoli)
+ Granchiaia (Le Macie)
I Coltri Rosso (Melini)
+ Liano (Umberto Cesari)
Marzeno di Marzeno (Fattoria Zerbina)
+ Vigorello (San Felice)
+ Vocato (Villa Cilnia)

0
+ Castelrapiti Rosso (Fattoria Montellori)
Il Cavaliere (Castello di Gabbiano)

ACCIAIOLO (*Toscana*). Acciaiolo derives its name from the Acciaioli family, who created the Castello d'Albola estate in the fourteenth century. This family produced and sold steel swords and *acciaio* is Italian for steel. This wine was not, however, aged in *acciaio*, but in *barrique*. Fattoria di Albola first produced Acciaiolo in 1988 from a blend of 65 percent sangioveto and 35 percent cabernet sauvignon. The grapes were harvested between October 10 and 25. The wine was aged in *barrique* for fourteen months in a combination of 80 percent Alliers and 10 percent each Nevers and Vosges oak. The label depicts Niccolò Acciaioli, who was described in Filippo Villani's *Chronicles,* written in the fourteenth century. Rating * +

TASTING NOTE

1988 (*12/90*). Cabernet herbaceousness and herbal aroma, oak overlay, vague cherry note; open fruit, soft entry, light tannin, forward flavors, hard finish; seemingly ready! * +

ALTE D'ALTESI (*Toscana*). Angelo Solci produces this wine for the excellent Brunello producer Altesino. Solci blends 70 percent sangiovese grosso from the Montosoli vineyard with 30 percent cabernet sauvignon from the Altesino plot. Both varieties are fermented together. The wine is *barrique*-aged. The first Alte d'Altesi was the '85. Today they produce 10,000 bottles annually. Rating ***

TASTING NOTES

1989 (*ex-cask, 6/90*). Cabernet and oak aroma, tarlike note; a little light but tasty and good, soft, light tannin, herbaceous character, short. * +

1988 (*ex-cask, 11/90*). Still closed, but the nose displays a richness; rich and concentrated, attractive fruit, good backbone, well knit, moderate tannin, long finish; very young; the best Alte to date. **(*)

1987 (*twice, 8/90*). Refined cabernet aroma, combines with ripe fruit and vanilla overlay, spicy and cherry notes; soft entry, some tannin, light-bodied, short; room to improve. *(*)

1986 (*9 times, 11/90*). A little closed, herbaceous and tarlike scents; good structure, open, forward flavors, open and tasty, light to moderate tannin, moderate length. **(+)

1985 (*4 times, 11/90*). Open berrylike aroma, combines with vanilla and herbal components, oak overlays the refined cabernet herbaceousness, cassis and cherry notes; soft, lovely fruit flavors, a lot of structure and backbone, long finish; quite ready; impressive first effort. ***

BALIFICO (*Toscana*). Enologist Maurizio Castelli produces this wine for Giovannella Stianti Mascheroni at her very fine Castello di Volpaia estate in the Chianti Classico district. Balifico is made from a 65-25-10 blend of sangioveto, cabernet sauvignon, and cabernet franc grapes grown in the 11-acre (4.5-hectare) Balifico vineyard. It was first produced from the 1985 vintage. This wine is aged in French *barriques*. Production averages 24,000 bottles annually. There were 30,000 bottles of the '86 and less than 20,000 of the '85. Rating ** +

TASTING NOTES

1989 (*ex-barrel, 11/90*). At this stage the wine seems pungent and coarse, the cabernet dominates. This is only one element in the final wine since it came from one barrel.

1988 (*ex-barrel, 11/90*). Firm, tannic and chewy, most pronounced characteristics are the cabernet herbaceousness and the oak; the elements are there to give a good glass in time. *(* +)

1987 (*10/90, 22,950 bottles and 180 magnums*). Tight nose, some oak evident as well as cabernet character; chalky feel, soft under light to moderate tannin. *(+)

1986 (*twice, 5/90, 29,970 bottles*). Herbal, cherry aroma, oak component; soft and round, good balance, sweet oak flavor, a little short; attractive. ** +

1985 (*5 times, 9/90, 19,980 bottles*). Herbal, green olive aroma; sweet taste of oak, soft tannins, smooth and supple, full of fruit; very ready. ***

BOTTIGLIA PARTICOLARE (*Toscana*). In 1982, Castello di Verrazzano, for the first time, produced this 80-20 sangiovese–cabernet blend. They produced 5,000 bottles of that wine. Bottiglia Particolare is aged for six to seven months in *barrique*. Thus far, at least, based on the '85 and '86, the cabernet dominates completely, giving a coarse impression. Rating * –

TASTING NOTES

1986 (*11/90, 3,000 bottles*). Cabernet dominates from the nose through the palate, coarse, could use more fruit. +

1985 (*11/90, 5,000 bottles*). Pungent and aggressive aroma and flavor, evident oak, dry. +

BRUNO DI ROCCA (*Toscana*). Enologist Vittorio Fiore produces the *barrique*-aged Bruno di Rocca at the Chianti Classico estate of Vecchie Terre de Montefili for proprietor Roccaldo Acuti. It is made from a selection of their best sangiovese and cabernet sauvignon grapes. The first, in 1983, was a 50-50 blend. We've heard that the formula has since been changed to 70 percent sangiovese and 30 percent cabernet sauvignon. Bruno di Rocca is aged for about one year in small French oak barrels. In the first vintage some 4,000 bottles were produced. Today, at most 6,000 bottles are produced annually. It wasn't made in 1984. Rating **

TASTING NOTES

1988 (*ex-cask, 11/90*). Sense of sweetness from ripe, rich fruit, harmonious, good backbone, oak and cabernet the most pronounced character; the best Bruno to date. **(*)

1987 (*11/90, 5,448 bottles*). Nice nose; warm, open, tasty; ready. **

1985 (*ex-vat, 5/86*). Full of fruit and tannin, cabernet character dominates; evident potential. **

1983 (*ex-barrique, 5/85*). Aroma of flowers and cherries with overtones of oak, cabernet fruit seems a bit restrained at this point; fruity, well balanced. **

CA' DEL PAZZO (*Toscana*). Enologist Vittorio Fiore created this wine for the noted Brunello di Montalcino producer Tenuta Caparzo from a 50-50 blend of sangiovese grosso and cabernet sauvignon. The wine is aged eight to ten months in French oak, a combination of Limousin, Alliers, and Nevers *barriques*. In the first vintage, 1982, 20,000 bottles were produced. Today they produce 33,300 bottles annually. The origin of Caparzo derives, it is said, from *cà pazzo*, meaning "the madman's house" or "the house of the crazy man." No one would suggest that you had to be crazy to drink this well-crafted wine. Rating **

TASTING NOTES

1988 (*ex-cask, twice, 9/90*). Richly fruited aroma; big, rich and concentrated, soft tannins; the best Ca' del Pazzo that we've tasted. **(*)

1987 (*3 times, 11/90*). Cabernet and oak dominate; soft center, harsh edges, dry, some fruit, chocolate notes, little light; unimpressive. +

1986 (*4 times, 11/90*). Cabernet fruit seems rather pungent, but there is good fruit on the nose and palate, soft. * *Bottle of 6/90:* Rich nose, recalls cassis and cherries; a lot of extract, supple, soft and round, well balanced; a lot of quality; ready. **

1985 (*11/90*). Cabernet dominates, lots of fruit, some dryness, firm, still has tannin. *(*)

1984 (*3 times, 11/90*). Starting to fade, showing age, still some fruit. + *Bottle of 5/89:* Cabernet evident, as well as new oak; nice flavor, but oak is a little dominant, fruity as well, rather short. * +

1983 (*3 times, 6/89*). Oak and cabernet aroma; richly fruited, smooth-textured, too bad there is so much oak. * + (**)

1982 (*3 times, 11/90*). The cabernet fruit, which is pungent, is starting to show age, there is still some fruit left but it is tired and old. * *Bottle of 4/89:* Cabernet dominates, oak overlay, herbaceous notes; round and soft; very ready and tasty too. ** +

CAMARTINA (*Toscana*). Fattoria Querciabella produces Camartina from a blend of 88 percent sangioveto and sangiovese, with 12 percent cabernet sauvignon. We've also heard that there is some cabernet franc in the 12 percent. The first, the '81, spent eight months in *barrique* and some three years in large oak. There were 3,600 bottles produced. The '81 also specified Podere Casaocci on the label. Rating **

TASTING NOTES

1983 (*twice, 4/89*). Warm nose, herbaceous notes; rather tight and firm, the fruit is there. * + (**)

1981 (*4/87*). Oak overlays the fruit; good fruit, moderate tannin, cabernet character, as it usually does, overpowers the sangiovese and dominates. *(*)

CAMPACCIO (*Toscana*). Roberto Guldener produces Campaccio at his Fattoria Terrabianca estate. Consultant Vittorio Fiore provides technical assistance. He uses a 50-50 blend of sangiovese and cabernet sauvignon. The wine is aged for ten months in French oak *barriques*. This wine was first produced in 1987, 2,222 cases. In 1988 there were 5,000 cases. Hmm! What if they continue to increase production at the same rate?

CANVALLE (*Toscana*). Canvalle, an 80-20 sangiovese–cabernet sauvignon blend, is produced by Vignavecchia in the Chianti Classico district. It was aged for three and a half months in *barrique*. It was first produced in 1982. They produced nearly 5,000 bottles.

CAPRIANO DEL COLLE ROSSO (*Lombardia*), *DOC*. This DOC applies to red and white wines produced from grapes grown in Capriano del Colle and Poncarale in the province of Brescia. The *rosso* is made from 40 to 50 percent sangiovese, 35 to 45 percent marzemino, and 3 to 10 percent barbera, with up to a maximum of 15 percent merlot and/or incrocio terzini. The maximum yield is 935 gallons per acre (87.50 hectoliters per hectare). In 1988, 7 growers cultivated 19 acres (7.7 hectares) of red grapes in this relatively new DOC zone. Production between 1986 and 1988 averaged 4,296 cases.[20] DOC requires that the red attain at least 11 percent alcohol. Antonio Rossi rates 1988, 1987, 1986, 1985, 1983, and 1980 as three-star vintages, and 1984, 1982, and 1981 as two out of four.[21]

CASAOCCI (*Toscana*). The good Chianti Classico producer Fattoria Querciabella makes Casaocci from a blend of 75 percent sangiovese, 5 percent sangiovese grosso, and 10 percent each cabernet sauvignon and cabernet franc. It is aged eighteen to twenty-four months in *barrique*. The 1982 was their first vintage. Somehow we suspect that this wine was replaced by **Camartina**. That wine comes from their Podere Casaocci.

CASTELRAPITI ROSSO (*Toscana*). Castelrapiti Rosso is made by Fattoria Montellori from a blend of 60 to 78 percent sangiovese and 40 to 22 percent cabernet sauvignon. It was first made in 1985. The wine is aged in 634-gallon (24-hectoliter) casks, followed by from six to seven months in *barrique*. Rating +

TASTING NOTE

1985 (*4/88*). Cherry and oak aroma, herbaceous background; tannic and tight, fairly nice fruit; not a lot of character. +

COLLE PICCHIONI ROSSO (*Latium*). Paola di Mauro owns the Colle Picchioni estate and its 10 acres (4 hectares) of vines. Her annual production averages 55,000 bottles of wine. This estate, located in the Marino district of the Castelli Romani hills about 12 miles (20 kilometers) southeast of Roma, produces three very good white wines and three good red ones. Colle Picchioni Rosso is made from merlot and sangiovese, with a small amount of montepulciano and cesanese. Annual production averages 10,000 bottles. Vigna Due Santi is made from cesanese and merlot grapes from the Due Santi vineyard. Vigna del Vassallo was, at one time, made from 30 percent each sangiovese and merlot and 40 percent montepulciano grapes grown in the 2.5-acre (1-hectare) cru of that name. Today, we were told, the blend is merlot, cabernet sauvignon, and cabernet franc; sangiovese and montepulciano aren't used. Vigna del Vassallo, which is most likely the best red of the Castelli Romani, is aged in small, 130-gallon (5-hectoliter) casks. The first Vassallo was produced in 1981. In 1982, 3,460 bottles were produced. Today Colle Picchioni produces an average of 5,000 bottles a year. Noted winemaker Giorgio Grai has been their consulting enologist since 1982. (See page 601 for a further discussion of these wines.) Vigna del Vassallo **

COLLI ALTOTIBERINI (*Umbria*), *DOC*. Colli Altotiberini is produced in the villages of Cisterna, Città di Castello, Gubbio, Monte S. Maria Tibernia, Montone, Perugia, San Giustino, and Umbertide in the province of Perugia in Umbria. DOC recognizes this wine in three colors. We are concerned only with the *rosso*. That wine is made from a blend of 55 to 70 percent sangiovese, with 10 to 20 percent merlot, 10 percent trebbiano toscano and/or malvasia del chianti, and up to 15 percent ciliegiolo, gamay, barbera, and other varieties. The maximum yield is 823 gallons per acre (77 hectoliters per hectare). The alcohol level must be at least 11.5 percent. In 1988 there were 126 growers with 911 declared acres (368 hectares) in the DOC zone.[22] Between 1986 and 1988 annual production averaged 27,375 cases of red wine out of an average of 52,954 cases of all colors.[23] There is no minimum aging requirement. This wine is for short-term consumption. Rating *

COLTIBUONO ROSSO (*Toscana*). Coltibuono Rosso is produced at Badia a Coltibuono from a blend of sangiovese, canaiolo, and cabernet sauvignon and franc. When this wine was first made, it was vinified to be drunk young and fresh, but in recent years it has been modified to take moderate age. The '86 contained about 70 percent sangiovese, 25 canaiolo, and about 5 percent cabernet sauvignon and franc. The '83 was made from a blend of 90 percent sangiovese and 10 percent canaiolo. Rating ** −

TASTING NOTES

1987 (*4 times, 11/89*). Noticeable, but restrained, cabernet herbaceousness; lots of fruit, balanced, fresh. ** −

1986 (*twice, 1/88*). Herbaceous component combines with fruit; soft, fruity and round, light tannin. ** −

1983 (*5/85*). Light, fruity, fresh and simple, a good quaff. *

CONCERTO (*Toscana*). Fonterutoli produces Concerto from 75 percent sangiovese and 25 percent cabernet sauvignon. Part is aged in *barrique*, and part in casks. The first was the '81. They made 2,000 cases of the '85. Rating * +

TASTING NOTES

1985 (*4/89*). Cabernet dominates on the nose and palate, good structure. ** −

1983 (*4/89*). Cherry aroma, some cabernet herbaceousness evident; somewhat astringent, does have fruit. *

GHERARDINO (*Toscana*). Gherardino is a *barrique*-aged sangiovese–cabernet sauvignon blend created by consulting enologist Franco Bernabei for the Chianti Classico estate Vignamaggio.

GRANCHIAIA (*Toscana*). Società Agricola Le Macie at Le Macie del Ponte alla Granchiaia in Gaiole in Chianti produces this sangiovese–cabernet sauvignon, *barrique*-aged *vino da tavola*. The first vintage for this wine was the '83. Rating * +

TASTING NOTE

1983 (*4/89*). Oak dominates, tobacco nuance; open fruit, flavorful, soft, smooth-textured. * + (**)

GRATTAMACCO ROSSO (*Toscana*). Pier Mario Meletti Cavallari produces this *vino da tavola rosso* at his Podere Grattamacco estate in Castagneto Carducci in the province of Livorno. At one time Grattamacco Rosso was made from a blend of 85 percent sangiovese with 15 percent colorino and malvasia nera. With the current fad for cabernet sauvignon, it should come as no surprise that the '85 saw the addition of cabernet sauvignon. That wine was made from a blend of 80 percent sangiovese, 5 percent malvasia nera, and 15 percent cabernet sauvignon. It was aged eight to fourteen months in oak, 20 percent in casks of Slavonian oak and 80 percent in *barriques* made of oak from the Massif Central. Between 15,000 and 18,000 bottles are produced annually. Rating **

TASTING NOTES

1985 (*4/87*). The most pronounced characteristics are the cabernet and the *barrique*; firm and tasty, noticeable fruit under the oak. *(* +)

1981 (*2/86*). Fruit and oak combine in a nice way, with the oak at this stage being more dominant. **

GRIFI (*Toscana*). Avignonesi, the fine producer of Vino Nobile di Montepulciano, produces this *barrique*-aged sangiovese-cabernet blend. Originally it was made from a 85-15 blend of prugnolo gentile (as the sangiovese grosso is known locally) and cabernet franc. Today it is more than half cabernet sauvignon. The '89 and '90 were 55 percent cabernet sauvignon; the '88, 40 percent; the '87, 25 percent; and the '86, 15 percent. The '85 was the last vintage where they used cabernet franc. In that vintage they used both cabernets.

The first Grifi, the '81, was aged about a year in French *barriques*; they made more than 12,000 bottles. Production today is 48,000 bottles a year and they age the wine in *barrique* fourteen to sixteen months. At one time this wine was the standard by which we judged other sangiovese-cabernet blends. This is no longer the case. This wine today is clearly in a transition. Rating ***

TASTING NOTES

1988 (*twice, ex*-barrique, *11/90*). Opaque purple; closed in on the nose with a richness of fruit evident, great intensity and extract, sweetness and structure, moderate tannin, firm backbone; a real classic, the best Grifi to date; should be a real keeper. **(*+)

1987 (*twice, 11/90*). Cabernet the most dominant element on both the nose and palate, open fruit, a little too pungent. *

1986 (*6 times, 11/90*). Rich nose, intensely fruited, cabernet evident; chewy, light to moderate tannin, soft center, a little firm, flavorful, could use more length. *(*)

1985 (*5/88*). Complex nose displays a mélange of scents; great structure and extract. ***

1983 (*twice, 4/87*). Floral, fruity aroma, light cabernet herbaceous overlay; well made, flavorful, displays class; needs some age but can be drunk in a pinch. **(*)

1982 (*twice, 3/86*). Aroma of oak up front over a background of cabernet herbaceousness as well as the ripe cherries and flowers of the sangiovese; richly fruited, well balanced and concentrated, soft tannins, very long; nice now with room to improve. ***

1981 (*4/85*). Cabernet and oak aromas dominate, with some tobacco and fruit; a bit light-bodied, fairly well balanced; a nice wine. **

I COLTRI ROSSO (*Toscana*). This *vino da tavola rosso* is produced by Melini from grapes grown in their Granaio vineyard in Castellina in the Chianti Classico district. It was first produced in 1979, and that wine, along with the '80 and '81, was made from a blend of 70 percent sangiovese grosso and 30 percent cabernet sauvignon. The sangiovese grosso was aged for two years in large Slavonian oak casks and the cabernet sauvignon for twelve to eighteen months in *barrique*, much of it used. Rating *

TASTING NOTES

1988 (*ex-barrel, 11/90*). Pungent, aggressive cabernet herbaceousness dominates, still there is fruit. *

1983 (*11/90*). The cabernet is more refined than the '82, good fruit, rich and firm, tight end. *

1982 (*11/90*). Aroma and flavor dominated by pungent cabernet herbaceousness, soft, fairly nice fruit; rather aggressive, but if you like the style. . . .*

1981 (*4/87*). Cabernet character the most pronounced; firm and fairly well balanced, agreeable, small-scale. *

IL CAVALIERE (*Toscana*). Castello di Gabbiano produces Il Cavaliere from a blend of 85 percent sangiovese and 15 percent merlot. We believe that the first one was the rather unimpressive '88. Rating 0

LA LOGGIA (*Toscana*). Chianti Classico producer Fattoria La Loggia produces this *barrique*-aged sangiovese-cabernet blend. The first, in 1985, contained 70 percent sangiovese and 30 cabernet.

LE VIGNACCE (*Toscana*). Giovanni and Rory Bianchi produce Le Vignacce at their Villa Cilnia estate in the Colli Aretini zone. The wine is made from a blend of equal parts of cabernet sauvignon, sangiovese grosso, and montepulciano d'abruzzo grown in their Le Vignacce vineyard. It is aged twelve to fifteen months in ten- to fifteen-year-old Slavonian oak casks of 660 gallons (25 hectoliters). Bianchi produced nearly 7,000 bottles in the first vintage, 1982. Today they make 12,000 bottles annually. Le Vignacce is a fairly full-bodied dry red wine that seems to have the capacity to age moderately well. Rating **

TASTING NOTES

1987 (*3 times, 8/90*). Herbal, grassy, cherry and spicy aroma, floral note; a little light, lots of fruit, some tannin; more or less ready now. **−

1986 (*twice, 2/90*). Cabernet dominates, rich and flavorful, well balanced, some tannin; ready. **

1985 (*7/88*). Complex aroma, mint and eucalyptus, touch of oak; well balanced, harmonious, flavorful, soft, at its peak, a tad short. **

1983 (*4 times, 2/87*). Three out of four bottles were corked. Herbaceous aroma, cabernet dominates; soft, rather light and simple! *

1982 (*4/85*). Fruity aroma, some oak, cherrylike fruit evident on the nose and palate, although the wine is still a bit closed. *

LIANO (*Emilia-Romagna*). Umberto Cesari produces this cabernet sauvignon–sangiovese blend from grapes grown on the hillside vineyards at their Castel Pietro estate. Our experience is limited to one wine, the good '87. Rating * +

TASTING NOTE

1987 (*10/90*). Deep ruby color; kind of oddball aroma and flavor, its own character, not bad, just different, suggestions of spice and herbs. * +

MARZENO DI MARZENO (*Emilia-Romagna*). Vittorio Fiore produces Marzeno di Marzeno for Fattoria Zerbina. The wine is made from a combination of sangiovese and some cabernet grapes grown in Zerbina's Marzeno vineyard located near Marzeno di Faenza. Rating *

TASTING NOTE

1987 (*twice, 6/90*). Herbal notes combine with oak; fairly tannic for the fruit, small-scale. + *Bottle of 4/89:* Oak and cabernet quite apparent, chewy tannins, sweet impression. * +

MONTECORALLO, VIGNA DEL SAUVIGNON (*Emilia-Romagna*). Montecorallo is made from a blend of sangiovese and cabernet sauvignon grapes grown in the Sauvignòn vineyard.

PODERE RIPERTOLI (*Toscana*). Podere Ripertoli produces some 6,700 bottles of a cabernet sauvignon–sangiovese blend.

POMINO ROSSO (*Toscana*), *DOC*. This recent DOC covers a red, a white, and a *vin santo*. We actually prefer the white, which is one of Italy's top white wines, the one from Frescobaldi in particular. The Pomino red was a Chianti Rùfina until 1983. There are some differences in the wine under DOC, though. The *uvaggio* is now 60 to 75 percent sangiovese, 15 to 25 percent canaiolo nero, cabernet sauvignon,

and/or cabernet franc, 10 to 20 percent merlot, and up to 15 percent other varieties. The vineyards cannot be planted at an altitude exceeding 2,133 feet (650 meters) above sea level.

The zone's best and largest producer, the Frescobaldis, produce all three wines allowed by this DOC. Until a few years ago it was made in the style to be drunk young, though it could take moderate age. With the advent of DOC recognition for Pomino, the Frescobaldis have created a new Pomino Rosso. The '85 was made from 60 percent sangiovese, 20 percent sauvignon, and 10 percent each merlot and pinot noir. The use of a little cabernet in the Pomino wines goes back for many years.

In 1988 there were three growers in the Pomino zone with 207 acres (84 hectares) planted.[24] The Frescobaldis' Tenuta di Pomino, with 232 acres (94 hectares) of vines, not all registered for the DOC, is by far the largest estate. Average production for Pomino Rosso, between 1986 and 1988 was 177,672 bottles.[25] The Frescobaldis produced 160,000 bottles of the '86; production today is between 180,000 and 200,000 bottles annually.

The Frescobaldis' Pomino Bianco is made from a blend of chardonnay, pinot bianco, pinot grigio, and trebbiano. The grapes for the Riserva Il Benefizio are from a 57-acre (23-hectare) vineyard of that name planted at altitudes ranging form 1,970 to 2,300 feet (600 to 700 meters) above sea level. This wine is fermented in wood. They make 10,000 cases of the former and 5,000 of the latter. They also produce 300 of the very good Tenuta di Pomino Vin Santo.

The vines for their red wine average twenty years of age. The cabernet and merlot grapes for the '85 Rosso were picked between September 27 and 30, the pinot noir on October 3, and the sangiovese between October 18 and 20. The wine was fermented for ten days in stainless steel tanks at temperatures between 79° and 84° Fahrenheit (26° and 29° centigrade). It was aged for ten months in *barrique*. Rating **

In June 1991 we discovered a second Pomino producer: Fattoria di Petrognano. Their first Pomino to be bottled, the

DOC REQUIREMENTS FOR POMINO ROSSO

	Maximum Aging in Years		Minimum Alcohol	Maximum Yield (Gallons/Acre)
	in Cask[a]	Total		
Normale	6 months	1[b]	12.0%	786[c]
Riserva	18 months	3	12.5%	786[c]

NOTES: [a] Aging can take place in oak or chestnut casks.
  [b] The wine cannot be sold prior to November 1 in the year following the vintage.
  [c] 73.5 hectoliters per hectare

'88, was very good, and their '90 from cask even better. They own 25 acres (10 hectares), of which 15 (6) are planted for Pomino. They used to sell their grapes to the Frescobaldis. Rating **

TASTING NOTES

Frescobaldi 1986 (5 times, 12/90). Herbal, cherry aroma; open flavors, surprisingly soft and ready. ** — *Bottle of 9/90:* Cabernet dominates at the expense of all other elements, a little hard, will it last, is it fading? * *Bottle of 5/90:* Until the bottle of September 1990, we found that each bottle we tasted between November 1989 and May 1990 was better than the last. Herbaceous and cassis aroma, cherry and tobacco nuances; soft under light tannin, nice fruit. **

Frescobaldi 1985 (twice, 10/88). Cabernet herbaceous character dominates, berry and cherry notes, some oak; soft, round, full of flavor, could use more backbone and length. ** —

Frescobaldi 1983 (twice, 1/88). Herbaceous cabernet character is the most pronounced aromatic and flavor component, light tannin, soft; ready now. **

R & R (*Toscana*). This 60-20-20 blend of cabernet sauvignon, merlot, and sangiovese, produced by Castello di Gabbiano in Chianti Classico, is discussed on page 623.

RIPA DELLE MANDORIE (*Toscana*). Castello Vicchiomaggio produces Ripa delle Mandorie, a cabernet sauvignon–sangiovese blend that is discussed on page 623 since it contains mostly cabernet sauvignon.

ROSSO ARMENTANO (*Emilia-Romagna*). F.lli Vallunga produces this medium-bodied dry red wine from a blend of approximately two-thirds sangiovese and one-third cabernet franc. Rating **

ROSSO DI ARTIMINO (*Toscana*). This wine, Rosso di Artimino, is made by Carmignano producer Fattoria di Artimino from a blend of sangiovese, cabernet sauvignon, and montepulciano d'abruzzo grapes. It is aged six to eight months in oak casks.

ROSSO DI ELEONORA (*Toscana*). Giovanni Mari at Villa Francesca planned to produce this *barrique*-aged sangiovese–cabernet sauvignon blend. A few years ago he told us that he was going to call it Rosso di Eleonora. It was to be named for his second daughter, who was nine years old at the time. He expected to produce some 1,320 bottles. We don't know if he has.

ROSSO PATERNO II (*Toscana*). Graziella Cetti Cappelli, proprietor of Fattoria Il Paradiso in the Chianti Colli Senesi zone, produces this Tignanello clone from 80 percent san-

giovese, 15 percent cabernet sauvignon, and 5 percent cabernet franc. We have yet to taste it.

SAMMARCO (*Toscana*). This 75-25 blend of cabernet sauvignon and sangiovese, produced by Castello dei Rampolla in Chianti Classico, is discussed on page 625.

SAN GIORGIO (*Umbria*). San Giòrgio is the creation of the fine winemaker Dott. Giorgio Lungarotti. It is made from a blend of 55 percent sangiovese and 20 percent canaiolo nero, with 25 percent cabernet sauvignon added, he says, to provide backbone and structure (though no one who has tasted Lungarotti's Rubesco *sans* cabernet will think that wine lacks structure). The cabernet adds a firmness to the San Giòrgio, which is a fairly full-bodied wine. It is aged eight to ten months in *barriques* of Slavonian oak. Lungarotti produces 2,000 cases of San Giòrgio a year. Rating ** +

TASTING NOTES

1982 (9/90). Cabernet dominates; fairly tannic, full-bodied, rich fruit, tasty. ** —

1981 (9/90). Open fruit aroma, cabernet dominates; seems a little dry, the fruit is there; best to drink up. ** —

1980 (2/87). Minerallike aroma; some fruit evident, much nicer in the mouth, has tannin, seems to have the fruit, very short; a disappointment. * +

1979 (twice, 9/90). Cabernet quite dominant, drying out, drink up. * — *Bottle of 11/84:* Medium dark red; aroma though somewhat reticent offers suggestions of mushrooms and fruit; richly flavored, some firmness, fairly long aftertaste; still quite young. **(*)

1978 (5 times, 9/90). Pretty much dried out, some interest remains. * — *Bottle of 11/84:* Expansive bouquet with a note of mushrooms and some oak; still has tannin but approachable now, mouth-filling flavors. ***

1977 (7 times, 11/84). Perfumed bouquet, intense and rich, mushroomlike backnote; rich in flavor; a complete wine; lovely now though it will improve. ***

SANTA CROCE (*Toscana*). Castell'in Villa produces this *barrique*-aged wine. The first Santa Croce, the '83, was made from 100 percent sangiovese; it was aged eighteen months in oak. The '86 contained 12 percent cabernet. The only one we've tasted thus far was the very good '83. Rating **

TASTING NOTE

1983 (4/89). Lovely perfumed aroma, ripe fruit and floral components; moderate tannin, sweet impression; quite young. **

SECENTENARIO (*Toscana*). Secentanàrio, which Antinori dubbed as a super Tignanello, was made from a blend of 70 percent sangiovese and 30 percent cabernet sauvignon and franc. They produced it only once, in magnums. It was created to celebrate the Antinoris' six hundredth anniversary as a winemaking family. That wine was aged in a combination of Yugoslavian and French oak *barriques*. The label didn't specify the vintage. Piero Antinori said that is was 100 percent from the 1982 vintage. Rating ***

TASTING NOTE

1982 (9/85). Very deep color; cabernet the most pronounced character; lush fruit, some oak, soft, smooth-textured, firm backbone, nice mouth feel; it is youthful but we feel it is probably at its best now, the flavor and texture are its great appeal. ***

SOLO ROSSO (*Toscana*). Franco Cammarata produces Solo Rosso at his Podere Petroio alla via della Malpensata estate in the Chianti Classico zone. This *vino da tavola* was first made in 1985 from a 50-30-20 blend of sangiovese, cabernet sauvignon, and merlot. It is not *barrique*-aged; instead, it is aged in new, large oak casks. Rating **

TASTING NOTE

1986 (4/90). Fresh floral aroma, green olive, herbaceous underpinning, vanilla component; the flavors are similar, good structure. **

TERRICCI (*Toscana*). Antiche Terre de'Ricci produces this sangiovese *vino da tavola* with the addition of some cabernet sauvignon. There were 9,880 bottles made of the '85. Rating **

TASTING NOTE

1985 (2/90). Cabernet up front; lots of fruit, some tannin. **

TIGNANELLO (*Toscana*). If any one wine can be credited for promoting the fad for *barrique* aging and blending cabernet with other local grape varieties, not only in Italy but worldwide as well, it has to be this one. In 1971, Antinori produced 127,000 bottles of this wine from the 104-acre (42-hectare) Tignanello plot in their Santa Cristina vineyard in the Chianti Classico zone. Since then production has more than doubled, with an annual average of some 276,000 bottles.

The vineyard, at an altitude of 1,310 feet (400 meters) above sea level, faces south. The vines, 80 percent sangiovese, 15 percent cabernet sauvignon, and 5 percent cabernet franc, are planted in rocky soil.

Tignanello today is made from a blend of sangiovese, cabernet sauvignon, and cabernet franc. It is aged in new

60-gallon (225 liter) French oak *barriques* for up to two years. With age the character of the cabernet becomes even more dominant, muting the more delicate personality of the sangiovese.

The wine has, some would say, evolved, from the first vintage, 1971, which was made from sangiovese and canaiolo nero, plus a small amount of malvasia. That wine was aged in new 60-gallon (225-liter) French oak *barriques* until it was bottled, in February 1974. The malvasia caused the wine to age faster than Piero Antinori liked, so it was replaced by cabernet sauvignon and cabernet franc. In the 1975 and 1977 vintages, the proportion of the two cabernets was about 10 percent; by 1978 it had been increased to 12 percent, and in 1979 it was up to 15 percent; today it has reached 20 percent. Of the two cabernet varieties, three-quarters is cabernet sauvignon.

Tignanello is fermented in stainless steel tanks between 78° and 84° Fahrenheit (25° and 29° centigrade) and is given some twenty-two months to two years of *barrique* aging. The French oak barrels originally used for aging the wine were later combined with some Slavonian *barriques*; then more and more of the Slavonian oak was used. Today they use 60 percent brand-new 60-gallon (225-liter) Tronçais oak barrels, 10 percent Nevers and Alliers oak, and 30 percent Slavonian oak.

The Antinoris say that Tignanello is produced only in the best vintages. So far there have been a '71, '75, '77, '78, '79, '80, '81, '82, '83, '85, '86, '87, and '88. We don't know if there was an '84 or '89. Since 1977 the popularity of the wine has been such that nearly every vintage, it seems, is a best vintage for Tignanello.

Piero Antinori told us that in 1967 or 1968 Emile Peynaud, the noted enologist from Bordeaux, consulted at Antinori and in some ways helped to create Tignanello.

Tignanello is certainly a well-made wine; it has structure, balance, and style. The only problem, for us at least, is that the cabernet sauvignon and cabernet franc get in the way. The sangiovese is supposed to be the defining grape, but its character is submerged beneath the aggressive cabernet, even at only 15 to 20 percent.

Tignanello is best drunk from its fifth to eighth year; it can last longer, but at that point the cabernet becomes even more dominant. Recent vintages, like '85 and '86, have shown a marked improvement in quality. Rating ***

TASTING NOTES

1987 (11/90). Herbal and berry aroma, oak overlay; good balance, lots of flavor, moderate length. **

1986 (twice, 11/90). Lovely nose with nuances suggestive of green olives, cassis and oak; sweet impression, supple, nice mouth feel, harmonious, loads of fruit, the oak adds another dimension; very ready. ***

1985 (*3 times, 5/90*). Lovely, richly concentrated bouquet offers layers of complexity; packed with flavor, great extract and concentration, lush, explosive, mouth-filling cassis and berry flavors; this wine has everything going for it, the best Tignanello to date, and the best sangiovese-cabernet blend as well. All three bottles were equally impressive. And to think that Antinori produces 23,000 cases of Tignanello. *** + (****)

1982 (*3 times, 8/88*). The most pronounced characteristic is the cabernet, vaguely nutlike component in the back; dry and firm, moderate tannin, flavorful, a bit firm, finish is overly dry. ** −

1981 (*5 times, 2/87*). Cabernet defines the aroma; nice texture and mouth feel, cabernet herbaceousness more evident in the mouth, firm finish. **

1980 (*4 times, 6/90, 224,500 bottles, plus larger sizes, 18 months in* barrique). Coarse, lacking distinction and class, and fading fast. * −

1979 (*4 times, 5/85, 187,000 bottles*). Cabernet and oak up front on aroma; still has some tannin to shed, supple center, bell pepper flavors across the palate. *(*)

1978 (*11 times, 6/89, 149,850 bottles*). The herbaceous and pungent nature of the cabernet character is the most dominant character; soft entry, an off note intrudes, overall drinkable, not much more. * −

1977 (*6 times, 9/85, 116,334 bottles, plus larger sizes, 17 months in* barrique). Agreeable, soft, ready. **

1975 (*twice, 3/82, 31,200 bottles*). Oak and fruit on aroma, and a suggestion of mint; fine balance, smooth-textured; fairly long finish marred by a touch of alcohol. **(+)

1971 (*7 times, 5/85, 127,000 bottles*). Aroma shows a lot of age, some oxidation, but still has interest; quite soft, beginning to dry out at the end; it was better a few years ago. ** −

TINSCVIL (*Toscana*). Fabrizio Bianchi, proprietor of the very fine Chianti Classico estate of Fattoria Monsanto, produced 6,000 bottles of this wine with the Etruscan name in 1980. It was a blend of grapes—85 percent sangiovese with 15 percent cabernet sauvignon—and of vintages; the sangiovese was from the 1979 harvest, and the cabernet sauvignon, which was aged for one year in *barrique,* from the 1980 crop. Bianchi points out that the cabernet sauvignon vines in 1980 were young and the fruit was not strong, whereas the sangiovese from 1979 was a robust wine, which made for a good balance between the two, with each variety contributing to the overall character of the blend. The '80 was a monovintage but not mono-*cépage*: it contained 20 percent cabernet sauvignon. The blend today is three-quarters sangiovese with one-quarter cabernet sauvignon. Production today averages some 18,000 bottles annually. Tinscvil carries the Castello di Monsanto label. Rating ** +

TASTING NOTES

1986 (*twice, 4/90*). Herbal, cherry aroma, some oak; good structure, a little light, cassis notes; will be ready early. ** +

1985 (*4 times, 6/90*). Cabernet evident on the nose and palate, tobacco and tea, sweet and concentrated, round and harmonious, nice mouth feel. **

1983 (*twice, 4/90*). Hint of green olives, and herbal notes, vague leather nuance; richly flavored, great extract and flavor; young, some firmness. **(+)

1980 (*4 times, 4/90*). Herbaceous, tobacco aroma; soft and flavorful, good structure; well made. *** −

1979 (*10 times, 6/90*). This wine was at its best through 1987. The bottles tasted in 1989 and 1990 were too old, the fruit had faded and there was no interest left.

VENEROSO (*Toscana*). Pierfrancesco Venerosi Pesciolini produces this wine at his Tenuta di Ghizzano estate in Veneroso Ghizzano di Pecciolo, located in the province of Pisa. If you find this a little confusing, fear not, so do we. The blend consists of 65 percent sangiovese with 25 percent cabernet sauvignon and 10 percent malvasia nera.

VIGNE (*Toscana*). Vigne is made by Chianti Classico producer Fattoria Montiverdi from a blend of sangiovese with up to 15 percent cabernet sauvignon. It is aged in *barrique.*

VIGORELLO (*Toscana*). San Felice, the Chianti Classico producer, blends 80 percent sangiovese with 10 percent each of canaiolo and cabernet sauvignon. At one time it was made from an 85-15 blend of sangiovese grosso and cabernet sauvignon. After a spell, at one time up to three years, in a 793-gallon (30-hectoliter) cask it spends six months in *barriques* of Limousin oak, followed by six months in vat. They have produced this wine, albeit with some differences in its production and aging regime, since 1968. San Felice produces, on average, some 48,000 bottles a year. Rating * +

TASTING NOTES

1985 (*5 times, 10/90*). Open cherry and herbaceous aroma; soft under light tannin, well balanced, clean and flavorful; ready. **

1982 (*10/90*). Mellow aroma, components of oak and cabernet; seems to be a little dry, starting to fade and lose its fruit, a little short; best to drink up. * −

1981 (*twice, 10/89*). Cabernet component is the most pronounced, next is the oak, then a sweet fruitiness. * +

1979 (*4/85, 38,880 bottles*). Nice fruit on the nose, rich though somewhat closed; nice fruit on entry gives way to gobs of tannin, is there enough fruit? We doubt it. *?

VINATTIERI ROSSO II (*Toscana*). The fine enologist Maurizio Castelli created this wine from a blend of sangiovese and cabernet sauvignon grapes. It is aged in *barrique.* We believe that the first Vinattieri Rosso II was the '85. Castelli and partner Roberto Stucchi-Prinetti of Badia a Coltibuono also produce a 100 percent sangiovese version **Vinattieri Rosso** and a chardonnay, Vinattieri Bianco, from Trentino–Alto Adige. Rating **

TASTING NOTES

1986 (*11/90*). Open fruit aroma, herbaceous background; soft, good structure, sense of sweetness, oak overlay; very ready. **

1985 (*11/90*). Cabernet pronounced on the nose; sense of sweetness, rich and concentrated, oak and herbal notes, moderate length, a little dry. **

VOCATO (*Toscana*). Villa Cilnia produces this sangiovese, canaiolo, malvasia nera and bianca, and cabernet sauvignon blend from grapes grown in the vineyards of Campo del Sasso, Le Vignacce, Poggio Cicaleto, and Poggio Garbato. The blend is 90 percent sangiovese, canaiolo, and malvasia nera and bianca, and 10 percent cabernet sauvignon. The '87 contained 80 percent sangiovese. Rating * +

TASTING NOTES

1987 (*3 times, 8/90*). There has been some bottle variation. *The most recent, and the best, bottle:* Open fruit, spicy and herbal notes on the nose; nice entry, smooth texture, then a little dry and short. ** −

1986 (*4/89*). Nose seems a little shy; tasty with nice fruit, balanced. * +

1985 (*3 times, 9/87*). Cabernet evident; soft and fruity, tasty, good body; ready. **

CHAPTER 13

Monte-pulciano d'Abruzzo

The montepulciano d'abruzzo grape is said to be the sangiovese grosso, or prugnolo gentile, introduced into Abruzzo during the time of the Florentine Republic in the early nineteenth century by wool merchants from Montepulciano. The Abruzzesi named this grape for its town of origin. Another theory suggests that the Abruzzesi named it montepulciano because they found a similarity between their vine and the sangiovese grosso of Montepulciano. Whether or not this variety was indeed the same sangiovese grosso as was growing in Montepulciano when it was imported into Abruzzo and then to other neighboring regions, it has since adapted to a different environment, creating new clones and becoming transmuted into a different subvariety at least, if not another variety altogether, although one closely related to the sangiovese.

The montepulciano is the most important red variety of Abruzzo and Molise. It is the major variety in the Rosso Conero wines of Marches, as well as a significant part of Rosso Piceno. In Molise it makes up a part of the *uvaggio* in Biferno Rosso and Pentro di Isernia Rosso. It is also used or allowed in Cerveteri, Cori, and Velletri in Latium; Solopaca Rosso in Campania; Cacc'e Mmitte di Lucera, Castèl del Monte Rosso, Gioia del Colle, Leverano, Lizzano, Nardò, Orta Nova, Rosso Canosa, and San Severo in Apulia; Colli Perugini, Montefalco, and Torgiano in Umbria; Colli Bolognesi Monte San Pietro in Emilia-Romagna; Parrina in Toscana; Lacrima di Morro, Kòmaros, and Pongelli in Marches; Rosso della Bissera in Emilia-Romagna; Tenuta Rivera's Il Falcone in Apulia; and many other non-DOC wines in those regions and a number of others.

The montepulciano d'abruzzo grape is frequently blended with sangiovese. Giorgio Grai, consulting enologist for Masseria di Majo Norante in Molise, for example, blends 80 percent montepulciano and 20 percent sangiovese to produce a good Montepulciano del Molise, a wine that is ready to drink within two to

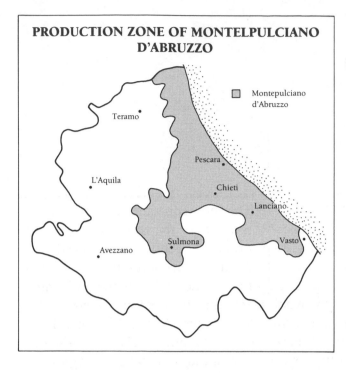

PRODUCTION ZONE OF MONTELPULCIANO D'ABRUZZO

Teramo

Pescara

L'Aquila

Chieti

Lanciano

Sulmona

Avezzano

Vasto

▨ Montepulciano d'Abruzzo

as Gran Sasso d'Italia and Maiella, are among the highest of the Apennines. These mountains dominate the landscape and can be seen for miles. This is a land of narrow gorges and windy plateaus. Wild game abounds in the uninhabited forests. But it is also a land of olive trees, almonds, and vines.

The economy of Abruzzo is based on agriculture. Growing grapes plays an important role, especially along the coast and inland valleys. There are 7,500 grape growers in Abruzzo, with close to 100,000 acres (40,000 hectares) of vines, including some 15,000 (6,000) in mixed cultivation. Montepulciano is planted on 42,130 acres (17,050 hectares) and sangiovese on 4,100 (1,660); there are also plantings of merlot, malbech (malbec), pinot noir, and cabernet sauvignon. In 1988 there were 4,876 growers authorized to produce Montepulciano d'Abruzzo and 18,020 acres (7,293 hectares) registered with the authorities. Wine production here averages some 92.5 million gallons (3.5 million hectoliters), equivalent to nearly 39 million cases. DOC production is considerably less: 1986 production of DOC wines in Abruzzo was 7.6 million gallons (289,503 hectoliters/3.2 million cases), in 1987 nearly 9 million (340,106/3.8 million), and in 1988, 10.3 million (391,418/4.3 million).[1]

Montepulciano vines are planted in the hills at altitudes up to 1,640 feet (500 meters) above sea level in the coastal district and in the valleys near L'Aquila. There are some exceptions made where the vines could be planted at elevations to 1,970 feet (600 meters). The best grapes come from the hillside vineyards in the provinces of Chieti, L'Aquila, Pescara, and Teramo. Chieti is the most important province, with more than two-thirds of the region's total acreage under vines.

The city, more like a large town, of Chieti is also home to the Enoteca Templi Romani, owned by Roberta Giannini and Adriano Scioli. This wineshop, or *enoteca,* has a fine selection of Montepulciano d'Abruzzo wines, including those of Edoardo Valentini and Cantina Zaccagnini. In fact, it was in this shop that we first discovered the wines of

four years of the vintage. Grai also produces the fine Ramitello Rosso for Norante from 80 to 90 percent montepulciano and 20 to 10 percent aglianico.

And we know of at least one wine, Leneo Moro, that blends cabernet sauvignon with montepulciano. This wine is produced in Abruzzo.

Montepulciano, though, is a variety that can stand very well on its own, as demonstrated by the fine Montepulciano d'Abruzzos of Edoardo Valentini and Emidio Pepe.

THE MONTEPULCIANO D'ABRUZZO PRODUCTION ZONE

The Abruzzi is a mountainous land with a wild and rugged landscape and a harsh climate. Some of its mountains, such

PRODUCTION OF MONTEPULCIANO D'ABRUZZO*

Year	Gallons	Hectoliters	Cases
1985	4,840,830	183,226	2,035,641
1986	5,373,458	203,386	2,259,618
1987	6,090,946	230,543	2,561,333
1988	6,754,458	255,657	2,840,349

*This includes the cerasuolo.

Source Il Corriere Vinicolo (Milano: Unione Italiana Vini)

Zaccagnini. This *enoteca* takes its name from the ruins of three small Roman temples nearby.

Forty-one cooperatives, 31 in the province of Chieti alone, vinify 65 percent of the grapes in Abruzzo. Bruno Roncarati, a noted and knowledgeable writer on Italian wines, considers the best Montepulciano d'Abruzzo to come from Francavilla al Mare in Chieti and Sulmona and Pratola Peligna in L'Aquila.

DOC regulations for Montepulciano d'Abruzzo allow up to 15 percent sangiovese grapes in the wine, but the better producers rarely blend, preferring a 100 percent montepulciano.

THE MONTEPULCIANO WINE OF ABRUZZO

The Montepulciano wines in general are light- to medium-bodied, fruity, and common. But in the hands of a producer like Edoardo Valentini or Emidio Pepe, this variety can reach uncommon heights.

On our first visit to Abruzzo some years ago, we stopped for dinner at Albergo di Rocco on the Chieti-Penne highway—make that road—and ordered, as always, local wine to accompany our meal. This wine was about as local as you can get. The restaurant (rooms upstairs, gas station and car wash out front) had a *cantina* below where the proprietor produced his own Montepulciano and Trebbiano. We ordered some of each. When we commented on the food and wine (both good) to the waiter, he told us where we could find the best wine in the area. Having just begun to learn the language, we didn't quite catch the name, but it sounded as if he had said the Tini Valley, or something like that. On a subsequent visit to the region we realized that he had said the wines of Valentini were the best from the area. This was no slight to his employer, who agreed with the evaluation.

MONTEPULCIANO D'ABRUZZO IN THE GLASS

Montepulciano d'Abruzzo runs the entire spectrum, from wines made to consume while young and fresh to those that can live for decades. The former are much more common in both senses of the word. It's the latter that concern us here. As a rule of thumb, the better Montepulciano d'Abruzzos take moderate age and are best drunk within two to four years of the vintage. The Rosso della Quercia of Vinicola Casacanditella epitomizes this style. Drink it with stews and pastas with meat sauce. The exceptional Montepulciano, such as those from Edoardo Valentini or Emidio Pepe, are best drunk from their sixth or seventh year, but are even better after a decade. Drink these with roast meats. Rating */***

The Producers Rated

****
Valentini Edoardo

***
Pepe Emidio

**
Barone Cornacchia
+ Cantina Zaccagnini, Dal Tralcetto
Fattoria Bruno Nicodemi, Colli Venia
− Fattoria Illuminati di Dino Illuminati (includes Ripe Rosse and Vecchio "Zanna")
Montori Camillo Azienda Agricola
Toppi Paltrizi della Marchesi di Torre
+ Vinicola Casacanditella, Riserva Angelo Rosso
Vinicola Casacanditella, Rosso della Quercia

ACREAGE FOR MONTEPULCIANO D'ABRUZZO BY PROVINCE*

Province	Number of Growers	Registered Vineyards		Percentage
		Acres	Hectares	
Chieti	4,046	12,313	4,983	68.33
L'Aquila	246	578	234	3.21
Pescara	313	2,323	940	12.89
Teramo	271	2,807	1,136	15.58
Total	4,876	18,021	7,293	100.01†

*This includes the cerasuolo
†Error due to rounding

Source: Il Corriere Vinicolo, n. 11 (Milano: Unione Italiana Vini, March 19, 1990)

DOC REQUIREMENTS FOR MONTEPULCIANO D'ABRUZZO

Category	Minimum Aging	Minimum Alcohol	Maximum Yield	
			Gallons/Acre	Hectoliters/Hectare
Normale	until March 1 after the vintage	12%	1,050	98
Vecchio	2 years	12%	1,050	98

+ Vinovino, Pianelaroma
  Vinovino, Rodolite

  *
  ‾
  Ántonello, Citra
  Bosco Nestore
  Bottina Davide, Notaresto
– Cantina Sociale "Madonna dei Miracoli"
  Cantina Sociale Tollo
– Cantina Sociale Tollo, Colle Secco
+ Cantina Sociale Tollo, Rubino and Valle d'Oro
  Casal Thaulero
  Dario d'Angelo
  Di Virgilio, Rubino
+ Duchi di Castellucchio
– Fattoria Deapizia
+ "I Vignali" Azienda Agricola, Torre de Passeri
– Monte Antonio e Elio
+ Pietrantori Italo
  Priore
+ Santa Caterina di Cordano
– Scialletti Cologna Paese Azienda Agricola di Roseto
    degli Rosso Sanmarco
  Vinovino, Costarella

OTHER PRODUCERS

Boce
Bove
Cantina Dragani
Contessa Ferrero di Cavallerleone Antonela Giovinazzi
  di Ducentra Azienda Agricola, Rosso di Santandrea
Gabriele & Giovanni Maraville
Masciarelli Azienda Agricola
Pasetti Franco
Peligna

VINTAGE INFORMATION AND TASTING NOTES

Edoardo Valentini, the foremost producer of Montepulciano d'Abruzzo, told us that his best vintages were 1988, 1985,

WHAT THE RATINGS MEAN

**** Great, superb, truly noble
*** Exceptionally fine
** Very good
* A good example of its type, somewhat above average
0 Acceptable to mediocre, depending on the context; drinkable
+ Somewhat better than the star category it is put in
– Somewhat less than the star category it is put in, except for zero where it indicates a wine or producer-wine combination that is badly made or worse
[. .] *On a producer:* Tentative evaluation based on an insufficient number of wines or based on older, out-of-date vintages, or where the wines we tasted were to difficult to fully judge to give a fair assessment of quality
On a wine or vintage: Projection for the future. This rating is given to a vintage where we feel that we tasted an insufficient number of wines or those we tasted were too difficult to really judge to give a fair assessment of quality
(. .) Potential increase in the rating of the wine given sufficient maturity

1974, 1971, and 1968. Other very good years were 1977, 1975, 1973, 1970, 1968, 1965, 1960, 1958, and 1956. The worst: 1989, 1986, 1983, 1981, 1980, 1978, 1976, 1972, 1966, and 1964; in those vintages he didn't produce any red wine. And in 1989, 1976, and 1972 he also didn't bottle any wine. In 1989 it rained continually.

Emidio Pepe, the other top-flight producer of Montepulciano, told us, some five years ago, that the best years for him were 1979, 1975, 1974, 1970, and 1967, and the worst 1976, 1972, and 1969. The 1978, 1973, and 1971 vintages were medium.

Because of the extensive growing region, it is difficult to generalize about vintages; differences can be significant. But on the theory that some information is better than none at all, we provide the following evaluations as a basic guideline. It applies to the small quantity of better wines only; most of the rest are best drunk within a year or two of the vintage. Outside the three- and four-star vintages, we have included only the years from 1970 to 1989, as anything older, with the exception of the Valentini and Pepe wines, would surely be too old today. Actually, except for a handful of wines, mostly from these two producers, anything older than 1980, perhaps even 1985, would be too old today.

From Antonio Niederbacher's vintage chart:

****	1983, 1968, 1958, 1948
***	1985, 1981, 1980, 1979, 1977, 1975, 1974, 1973, 1965, 1963, 1957, 1956
**	1982, 1978, 1967, 1966, 1962, 1961, 1960, 1959
*	1984, 1976, 1972, 1971, 1970, 1954, 1953, 1952, 1951, 1950, 1949, 1947, 1946, 1945
0	1969, 1964, 1955

The way it looks to us:

****	1988, 1985
***	1982, 1979, 1977
**	1987, 1986, 1983, 1980
*	1989, 1984, 1981
0	1978

Antonello 1989 Citra (10/90). Fruity, fresh and clean; a good quaff. *

Monti Antonio e Elio 1989 (8/90). Stinky, some cherries; supple, fruity, no character.

Vinovino 1989 Pianelaroma (twice, ex-barrique, 4/90). Deep purple; rich cherry overlaid with vanilla; aroma carries through on the palate. ** +

Casal Thaulero 1988 (5/90). Dull, some fruit.

Fattoria Illuminati di Dino Illuminati 1988 Ripe Rosse (8/90). Open, fruity, soft. *

Monti Antonio e Elio 1988 (8/90). Simple, cherrylike fruit; agreeable, no more.

Valentini 1988 (4/90). Dense, opaque, purple color; tight nose with characteristic cherry component; chewy, sweet and rich with intensity of flavor and extract; should make a grand wine given sufficient age. (This one combines 14.2 percent alcohol with 6.22 total acidity.) ***(+)

Vinovino 1988 Costarella (4/90). Open cherrylike aroma; soft and fruity, soft and clean. *

Vinovino 1988 Pianelaroma (twice, 4/90, 2,500 bottles). This is the first vintage that this *barrique*-aged wine—it spent six months in small barrels—was produced. It is a non-DOC, 100 percent montepulciano wine from estate-grown grapes. Nice nose that combines cherries with vanilla; smooth-textured, soft, supple and round yet with good backbone, lively acidity; nice now, can improve; one of the better Montepulcianos we've tasted. *** —

Vinovino 1988 Rodolite (4/90, 10,000 bottles). This 100 percent montepulciano, non-DOC wine was produced with cold maceration. It is fresh, clean and lively with the aroma and flavor of Bing cherries. ** —

Barone Cornacchia 1987 (10/89). Soft, cherrylike fruit, quaffable. * +

D'Angelo Dario 1987 (10/89). Simple, cherrylike fruit, soft, easy and quaffable. *

Valentini 1987 (4/90). Deep ruby; cherries evident on the nose which is still a little closed; some tannin to lose, not quite together, the fruit is quite evident though closed in, moderate length, finish is a trifle light. **(+)

Vinicola Casacanditella 1987 Rosso della Quercia (5 times, 4/90). *The one from cask*: Medium- to full-bodied, fruity, somewhat short. *From bottle* (there was some variation, the rating is for the better bottles): Cherrylike aroma; soft and fresh, well balanced; quaffable. ** +

Cantina Zaccagnini 1986 Dal Tralcetto (twice, 4/87). Fresh and fruity aroma; moderate tannin; very nice now. ** —

Santa Caterina di Cordano 1986 (4/87). Fresh cherrylike fruit on the nose and palate, quaffable, easy, simple. * +

Vinicola Casacanditella 1986 Angelo Rosso (4/90). Rich, cherry aroma; lovely, full-flavored and concentrated, round and ready. *** —

Vinicola Casacanditella 1986 Rosso della Quercia (5/89). Open cherrylike aroma; good body, soft, tasty, still fresh. ** —

Azienda Agricola "I Vignali" 1985 Torre de Passeri (10/86). Purple, inky color; rich fruit, some overripeness, richly flavored, full-bodied, soft, still some tannin to shed, low acidity, somewhat flabby. * +

Azienda Agricola Montori Camillo 1985 (4/87). Rather nice cherrylike fruit, light tannin, flavorful, well balanced. **

Barone Cornacchia 1985 (4/87). Fruity aroma, minerallike notes; moderate richness, moderate tannin, a tad bitter. ** —

Bottina Davide 1985 Notaresco (4/87). Fresh cherrylike aroma; medium body, a tad bitter. *

Cantina Sociale "Madonna dei Miracoli" 1985 (4/87). Kind of tobacco, oak aroma; quite fruity and easy. * —

Cantina Zaccagnini 1985 Dal Tralcetto (3 times, 10/87, 4,686 bottles). Deep ruby color; rich, dusty, cherry, fruity aroma; a lot of flavor under light to moderate tannin, quite dry, has the weight and structure. ** +

Di Virgilio 1985 Rubino (4/87). Light, somewhat floral, cherry aroma; light- to medium-bodied, fruity, soft and quaffable. *

Fattoria Illuminati di Dino Illuminati 1985 (4/87). Light, cherrylike aroma; fruity, balanced, medium-bodied. ** –

Fattoria Illuminati di Dino Illuminati 1985 Vecchio "Zanna" (5/90). Open cherry fruit, soft, simple, oak overlay, dry finish. * +

Monti Antonio e Elio 1985 (4/87). Fresh cherrylike aroma; medium body, some tannin, drinkable but could use more fruit mid-palate. * –

Peligna 1985 (*twice*, 4/87). Seems to have undergone malolactic fermentation in bottle. Was it intentional?

Valentini 1985 (*4 times, 10/90, 4,152 bottles*). Deep ruby color; nose is still closed, hints of cherries and spice; sweet and rich, smooth, great mouth feel, already like velvet, some tannin to lose, long, lingering finish; real quality. And to think that less than 4,200 bottles were produced! ***(*)

Vinicola Casacanditella 1985 Rosso della Quercia (4/87). Dried cherry aroma; fruity, soft and balanced, could use more length. ** –

Azienda Agricola Masciarelli 1984 (4/87). Hot, southern nose; baked and coarse.

Azienda Agricola Scialletti Cologna Paese di Roseto degli Abruzzi 1984 Rosso Sanmarco (4/87). Maltlike aroma(!), fruity; not much character; drinkable. +

Bove 1984 (4/87). Fruity but unbalanced with tannin.

Cantina Tollo 1984 Rubino (*Twice, 10/87 and 3/88*). Both bottles were coarse and dull.

Colle Secco 1984 Rubino (3/87). Chocolate notes, fruity; some age starting to show; bitter aftertaste.

Fattoria Deapizia 1984 (4/87). Has fruit and is quite drinkable though has rather drying aftertaste. * –

Maraville Gabriele & Giovanni 1984 (4/87). Fresh cherrylike aroma; a bit low in fruit and unbalanced with tannin.

Pasetti Franco 1984 (4/87). Off nose, hydrogen sulfide carries through on the palate.

Toppi Patrizi della Marchesi di Torre 1984 (4/87). Cherrylike fruit; tannin on the high side for the fruit, but the flavor makes it attractive now. *

Valentini 1984 (*3 times, 4/90*). Full, rich, open bouquet suggestive of ripe cherries, some spice; good structure, open, sweet and appealing with nice fruit; should age moderately well. *** –

Vinicola Casacanditella 1984 Rosso della Quercia (375 ml, 4/90). Tired but still drinkable.

Barone Cornacchia 1983 (4/86). Medium-dark ruby; cherry aroma; full-bodied, full-flavored, balanced, some character, some length, acid on the low side. **

Bosco Nestore 1983 (4/87). Mineral, floral aroma; easy to drink. *

Cantina Tollo 1983 Colle Secco (*twice, 10/87*). Tarry, fruity aroma; a bit rustic, good fruit and weight. A bottle tasted six months earlier was better than this one. * –

Cantina Tollo 1983 Valle d'Oro (4/87). Woodsy, cherry aroma; nice fruit, easy to drink, fairly well balanced. ** –

Duchi di Castellucchio 1983 (4/87). Cherry aroma; moderate tannin, balanced, fruity, could improve, nice now, dry, tannic aftertaste. **

Toppi Patrizi della Marchesi di Torre Città di Chieti Gentile di Toppi 1983 (4/87). Spicy, fruity; fresh, balanced, good structure. ** +

Vinicola Casacanditella 1983 Rosso della Quercia (2/86). Fresh cherrylike aroma; soft and round, smooth and flavorful, some length. **

Boce 1982 (4/87). Coarse, hot, southern.

Duchi di Castellucchio 1982 Oro (*twice, 3/88*). Tar and cherries; chewy, moderate tannin, flavorful. *

Pepe 1982 (*twice, 4/87*). Dark ruby, rich, cherrylike aroma; nice fruit up front, rich and concentrated with good weight and moderate tannin, soft-centered, tannic finish, quite young. **(* –)

Priore 1982 (4/85). Fruity, simple, agreeable, no personality, a few defects. Why did we include it? It's better than most and by that it illustrates a point: while most of these wines are common, a few rise above the ordinary and are worth the serious attention of wine lovers everywhere.

Vinicola Casacanditella 1982 Rosso della Quercia Riserva (*3 times, 4/90, 14,000 bottles*). This one spent fourteen months in barrel. Vanilla and cherry aroma; good body, soft, quite tasty and very ready. ** +

Pepe 1981 (11/87). Some oxidation, unbalanced, still has fruit and a hint of sweetness. *

Vinicola Casacanditella 1981 Rosso della Quercia (*ex-cask, 5/82*). Aroma of chocolate-covered cherries, a little rough but has the fruit. *(+)

Barone Cornacchia 1980 (5/84). Richly fruited aroma recalls cherries; full-bodied, richly flavored, a touch of alcohol mars the finish, not to keep. * +

Fattoria Bruno Nicodemi 1980 Colli Venia (4/83). Rich, cherrylike aroma; full of flavor, some tannin; good quality; good value. **

Pepe 1980 (*3 times, 11/87*). *Bottles of 4/86 and 11/87:* Medium-dark red, alcohol intrudes, some volatile acidity! What happened? *Ex-vat, 1/81:* The color is so dark it's like ink; a nice mouthful of fruit. **(*)

Valentini 1980 (*ex-cask, 4/81*). This wine was never bottled. Cherries all over the nose; some tannin, a bit light; will be ready early. **

Vinicola Casacanditella 1980 Rosso della Quercia (*10 times, 4/85*). Fruity aroma with a dried fruit nuance, still quite fruity but seems to be near the end of its useful life. This wine was considerably better two years ago. This bottle *

Vinicola Casacanditella 1980 Rosso della Quercia Riserva (2/86, 10,000 bottles). This wine spent twenty-four months in barrel. Tobacco, cherry aroma; nice fruit but acid stands apart, unbalanced, nice flavor midpalate, tails off at the end, flat finish, vaguely bitter. *

Azienda Agricola Contessa Ferrero di Cavallerleone Antonela Giovinazzi di Ducentra 1979 Rosso di Santandrea (2/85). Would be that the wine was as much of a mouthful as the name, cooked fruit, prunes and overripe aroma, low acid, full-bodied, beginning to dry out but still has fruit.

Barone Cornacchia 1979 (4/83). Fairly full, quite rich, fairly tannic, has the fruit to back it up, cherry notes from the nose through the finish. ** −

Duchi di Castelluccio 1979 (2/81). Cherry aroma; fruity, some acidity, could use more age, but good. * +

Pepe 1979 (3 times, 11/87). Really off-putting. *Bottle of 9/85:* Very dark color; rich nose with the characteristic cherry character, some complexity; a mouthful of fruit and tannin, but age beginning to creep in. **

Valentini 1979 (9 times, 3/90). Rich, intense bouquet recalls leather, dried fruit, tobacco and a woodsy nuance; rich and full-bodied, full of flavor and extract, a mélange of fruit flavors; real quality; very long. *** +

Vinicola Casacanditella 1979 Rosso della Quercia (8 times, 6/82). Strawberry, cherry aroma; fruity, quaffable; most agreeable. **

Duchi di Costelluccio 1978 (4/80). Dark purplish color; somewhat closed nose; harsh, dried out!

Pepe 1978 (ex-vat, 1/81). Very dark color; some tannin, some astringency, not up to the other wines. * −

Vinicola Casacanditella 1978 Rosso della Quercia (13 times, 4/83). Still has fruit but beginning to fade; this wine was at its best in 1980 and 1981.

Cantina Dragani 1977 (4/81). Lacks flavor, character and structure.

Cantina Tollo 1977 Rubino (10/83). Fruit carries from the aroma across the palate, some firmness; a wine for serious drinking, not serious contemplation, but honest and with some character. **

Duchi di Castelluccio 1977 (3 times, 7/81). Undrinkable. *Bottle of 10/78:* Inky black; aroma leaps out of the glass, cherries; richly flavored; young but drinkable now. **

Pepe 1977 (5 times, 5/81). Cherrylike aroma; some tannin, loads of flavor, moderate length. **

Valentini 1977 (3 times, 4/90). Medium-dark ruby. Rich, cherrylike aroma, some spice; harmonious, has flavor, style, elegance and length. *** + *Bottle of 1/81:* Rich, cherrylike aroma; still with tannin to soften, the fruit is there to carry it, well balanced, some length. **(* −)

Vinicola Casacanditella 1977 Rosso della Quercia (3 times, 10/82). Still has fruit on the nose and palate though it's getting on in years. It was at its best in 1980 and 1981. * +

Duchi di Castelluccio 1975 (twice, 4/80). A big wine, richly fruited, lacks subtlety, but the flavor compensates. **

Pepe 1975 (10 times, 4/87). Complex bouquet reflects bottle age; hints of mushrooms and fruit, loads of flavor, still a fair amount of tannin, enjoyable but should continue to improve. ** + *Bottle of 5/81:* Aroma of cherries; rich flavor, overall fairly well balanced though marred slightly by a touch of alcohol, a nice wine that needs more age. There was some bottle variation; for the best bottles. *** −

Valentini 1975 (7 times, 4/90). Characteristic cherry aroma, hint of tar; rich, full-bodied, round, ready now, will certainly hold, a rich mouthful of flavor. *** *Bottle of 4/89:* Cherrylike aroma, chocolate nuance; displays a richness of fruit, sweet, rich, ripe and round, velvety texture, complete and very long. *** + *Bottle of 1/81:* Black as ink, so big you could cut it with a knife, but not clumsy or lacking in style, a lot of quality and quite young. **(*)

Pepe 1974 (10 times, 11/81). Ripe fruit aroma; soft, round and fruity, ready, though room for improvement, a big, rich wine. ** +

Valentini 1974 (16 times, 2/86). Deep color right to the rim; intense, concentrated cherry aroma; still fairly tannic, richly flavored, full-bodied, well balanced, almost sweet from the ripe fruit, room to improve; a big wine, not a clumsy one; very long. *** *bottle of 5/85:* Opaque color belies its age (it was in our cellar for years); intense, cherrylike aroma; enormous weight and extract, intensely fruited, perhaps lacks some subtlety but makes up for that with its richness of flavor; figlike note at the end. ***

Pepe 1973 (twice, 10/79). Cherry notes, vague yeasty backnote; loads of fruit, moderate length, some style. ** +

Valentini 1973 (twice, 2/86). Raisins, prunes and cherries define the bouquet; loaded with flavor, ready now with light tannin, moderately long finish. ** +

Pepe 1971 (11/79). Fragrant kirschlike aroma; still has tannin, but the fruit is there to carry it. ** +

Valentini 1971 (3 times, 4/87). Rich aroma, full of flavor, soft center, ready now, loads of quality, a tad bitter at the end. *** − *Bottle of 1/81:* Complex bouquet, with the characteristic cherrylike note; soft, round, well structured and tasty, very long finish; very ready. ***

Pepe 1970 (3 times, 1/81). Cherries all over the aroma; flavorful, still has tannin, a bit short. ** +

Valentini 1970 (twice, 2/86). Intense, vaguely floral bouquet, some cherries; big, rich and sweet, well structured, enormous richness, a wine of large proportions, very long; ready now with room to improve further, impressive. *** + *Bottle of 1/81:* Youthful color shows very little age; deep, rich, complex aroma, full-bodied, full-flavored, the finish is marred by a touch of alcohol. ** +

Valentini 1969 (3 times, 2/86, 4,187 bottles). Dark garnet; cherry and grape pips aroma; loads of flavor, still some tannin, ready now with room for improvement, a big wine, rich in flavor; less style than some of the others, perhaps even a bit overripe and jammy. ** + *Bottle of 1/81:* Another deeply colored wine that appears younger than its years; complex bouquet, rich and intense; full-bodied, soft, round and tasty; long on the palate. ** +

Valentini 1968 (twice, 2/86, 4,282 bottles). Deep red toward garnet; somewhat light on the nose, yet with fruit and some spice; has a richness of flavor and a sweetness from ripe fruit, ready yet can still improve. *** *Bottle of 1/81:* Lovely nose, fragrant and fruity; soft, round and velvety; has style. ***

Pepe 1967 (twice, 1/81). Complex bouquet, cherry note; soft and velvety; some style; very ready. ***

Valentini 1967 (twice, 2/86, 3,402 bottles). Medium-dark garnet; fairly nice fruit up front on the nose, with a trace of decay in the back; loads of flavor, well balanced, some sweetness, still has tannin and life; ready; long finish, hint of licorice. *** –

Valentini 1966 (2/86, 1,113 bottles). Medium-dark garnet, woodsy aroma, vaguely of rubber in the back; some tannin, sweet fruit flavor, some softness midpalate; very ready, should hold; long finish. ** +

Valentini 1965 (5 times, 2/86, 1,329 bottles). Fading color, tawny; decayed aroma; really shot, off-putting flavor. *Bottle of 1/81:* Floral bouquet, suggestion of toasted almonds; low acid, tasty; some age beginning to set in. ** –

Valentini 1962 (2/86). Oxidized.

Valentini 1961 (twice, 2/86). Light garnet; a lot of bottle age apparent on the nose, vaguely wet dog background; showing age but still quite drinkable, a bit thin on the midpalate, with a sweetness of age, some tannin at the end. ** *Bottle of 1/81:* Nose shows age, some volatile acidity; harsh edges; beginning to fall apart.

Valentini 1958 (twice, 2/86). Medium brick robe; old, complex, mellow aroma with a trace of oxidation; full-bodied, still some tannin, very much alive; no sign of age; rich in flavor, very long, loaded with class and sweetness. **** – *Bottle of 1/81:* Did we say that Montepulciano d'Abruzzo should be drunk young, or that it is an unserious quaffing wine to wash down hearty fare? Did we also say there are exceptions? Here is one exception that is exceptional as well. Rich and complex, on both the nose and palate, a complete and well-structured wine of real quality, smooth-textured and velvety, very long finish. *** +

Valentini 1957 (2/86). Pale tawny; no tannin left, very little flavor, on the old side but with a complexity and sweetness from age, very drinkable. ** +

Valentini 1956 (2/86). Medium-deep garnet; some decay in the background, still has fruit on the nose; nice flavor on entry gives way to tannin, flavor carries through on the palate, vague decay on the flavor subsided with air, tannin builds at the end. ** + As it sat in the glass it grew in complexity and flavor, a fine wine with real character ***

MONTEPULCIANO PRODUCERS

Barone Cornacchia del Dott. Piero Cornacchia Azienda Agricola (*Torri di Torano Nuovo*). Azienda Agricola Barone Cornacchia says that the Montepulciano wine was created by Barone Filippo Cornacchia in the nineteenth century. The estate's vineyards are in the fertile Vibrata Valley. Their vines, facing south, are planted at an average altitude of 656 feet (200 meters) above sea level. They produce all three types of DOC wines—white, rosé, and red. Their *rosso* is among the better ones of the region. Since at least 1985 they have produced a *barrique*-aged, single-vineyard Montepulciano d'Abruzzo from their Le Coste vineyard. And like so many other producers, they also bottle a Chardonnay. The Barone Cornacchia Montepulciano d'Abruzzo '87 was good, and the '85 and '83 were very good. Montepulciano d'Abruzzo **

Cantina Sociale Tollo. This large co-op produces a wide range of wines, including at least four Montepulciano d'Abruzzos. The two best are the Rubino and Valle d'Oro. Montepulciano d'Abruzzo: *, Colle Secco * –, Rubino and Valle d'Oro * +

Cantina Zaccagnini. Cantina Zaccagnini is quite a small producer. They produced all of 4,686 bottles of their '85 Montepulciano d'Abruzzo dal Tralcetto. Both it and the '86 were very good. Montepulciano d'Abruzzo ** +

Casal Thaulero Soc. Coop. (*Roseto degli Abruzzi*). Casal Thaulero is the largest cooperative in Abruzzo to sell DOC wines in bottle. The members of this co-op cultivate 2,375 acres (961 hectares) of vines. This amounts to more than 13 percent of the total amount of registered vineyards. The vines are grown in the hills above the Adriatic coast. They ferment their wine in temperature-controlled stainless steel tanks and age most of the Montepulciano that they bottle for six months in large oak casks. Small lots are given longer aging. Montepulciano d'Abruzzo *

Dario d'Angelo. The '87 Montepulciano d'Abruzzo from Dario d'Angelo was quite good. Montepulciano d'Abruzzo *

Duchi di Castellucchio. At one time we found the wines of Duchi di Castellucchio much better than they are today. We have no idea what happened. It's not that the wines aren't good, they still are; they just aren't as good as they were. Castellucchio sells their best Montepulciano d'Abruzzo as Oro. The '83 *normale* and '82 Oro were good wines when tasted in 1987. Montepulciano d'Abruzzo * +

Fattoria Bruno Nicodemi. We haven't seen Bruno Nicodemi's Montepulciano d'Abruzzo in some time. We found it consistently good. Nicodemi's wines come from Colli Venia. Montepulciano d'Abruzzo **

Fattoria Illuminati di Dino Illuminati. Fattoria Illuminati produces two special Montepulciano d'Abruzzos; Ripe Rosse and Vecchio "Zanna." Ripe Rosse is from a geographical area and Vecchio Zanna from a 10-acre (4-hectare) single vineyard. The '88 Ripe Rosse and the '85 Vecchio "Zanna" tasted in May 1990 were both good, while the '85 *normale* tasted in April 1987 was very good. Montepulciano d'Abruzzo ** –

Monti Antonio e Elio. We have tasted three wines from Antonio e Elio Monti. Of the three, the only one that was good was the '85, tasted when it was less than two years old. Clearly these Montepulciano wines don't age. Montepulciano d'Abruzzo * −

Montori Camillo Azienda Agricola. The only Montepulciano d'Abruzzo, indeed the only wine, that we tasted from this producer, the '85, was very good. At the time, the wine was less than two years of age. We suspect that Montori produces wine for short- to intermediate-term consumption. Montepulciano d'Abruzzo **

Pepe Emidio (*Torano Nuovo*). Emidio Pepe owns 17.3 acres (7 hectares), 7.4 (3) in vines, of which 4.9 (2) are planted in montepulciano. Pepe produced his first wine from the 1964 vintage. His average production of Montepulciano d'Abruzzo is some 20,000 bottles a year.

Pepe also produces a Trebbiano d'Abruzzo, which undergoes malolactic fermentation in the bottle. It's premeditated; that's the way he likes it. Pepe has some rather atypical ideas about wine and winemaking. He doesn't like the taste of wine aged in wood, and he doesn't drink it. In fact, until a few years ago, he wouldn't drink any producer's wine but his own. At one of the dinners during a wine fair at Foggia, we sat with Pepe. We offered to pour him some wine from the bottles that had been chosen to accompany the buffet. He passed them all up. He had brought a few bottles of his own wine. He offered to pour us some. We accepted. That situation changed when he began to travel to the United States to sell his wine. Now, at least when it comes to wine consumption, Pepe has become more adventurous.

Emidio Pepe must be the most unusual winemaker we've ever met (and we've met quite a few), unusual in the way he makes his wine in particular. He doesn't believe in using machines of any kind, if at all possible.

The grapes for his Montepulciano are first destalked by being pushed by hand through a grid. His wife, Rosa, and daughters help out with the hand labor. Next the grapes are crushed, by feet. Pepe spoke to us about the possibility of being forced to use a hand-operated basket press in the future because of the difficulty of finding men willing to do the treading.

The must is fermented in glass-lined cement tanks, allowed to settle, and then racked. After about a year the wine is racked again and then bottled. Yes, that's right. Pepe doesn't believe in wood aging, you recall. And he doesn't bother with much tank aging either. It's right into the bottles, which are stacked horizontally in long rows where they stay for two or three years (a visit to this part of the *cantina* creates a bit of *déjà-vu à la Champagne*).

At the end of the aging period the bottles are stood upright and the sediment is allowed to settle. A couple of months later they are moved to a small room in a corner of the *cantina* for the final and most curious phase in their rather original handling. Enter a woman with a winged corkscrew. She uncorks the bottle and proceeds to decant it into a fresh bottle. In doing so, she pours, without benefit of a funnel, holding the bottle to the light filtering in through a small window. Not surprisingly, a fair amount of wine misses the bottle. But it is caught in a demijohn topped with a large funnel on the floor at her feet. Do they let the wine left in the bottles settle again and redecant to lose less of it? We asked Pepe.

Only at the table, where it is drunk by his family and by the workers; that wine is not bottled for sale.

We watched the operation in amazement for a while, then suggested to Emidio that things might go a bit faster if he attached a one-arm cork puller to the bench for the woman. *"Mai,"* he protested, that would disturb the wine. It must be opened by hand.

You have to see it to believe it, and if we hadn't, we would be writing about the legend of Emidio Pepe and his twice-bottled Montepulciano, not ever daring to tell you that it is true.

With all the care and concern he invests in his wines, Pepe is bound to produce a fine Montepulciano d'Abruzzo, and he does. To our taste, only Valentini produces a better one, and Pepe's is very close to it in quality. Of all the vintages of Pepe's wines we've tasted, we liked his '70 and '71 the best. Montepulciano d'Abruzzo ***

Rosso della Quercia. See *Vinicola Casacanditella.*

Toppi Patrizi della Marchesi di Torre (*Città di Chieti Gentile di Toppi*). Toppi Patrizi della Marchesi di Torre produced a good '84 and a very good '83 Montepulciano d'Abruzzo. Their wines age moderately well. Montepulciano d'Abruzzo **

Valentini Edoardo (*Loreto Aprutino*), 1964. Valentini produces the finest red and white wines of the region, wines whose quality goes far beyond the borders of Abruzzo. His Montepulciano d'Abruzzo stands with the best wines of Italy. His Trebbiano d'Abruzzo is in a class by itself, the finest Trebbiano we've ever tasted, and a very good white wine by any standard; surprisingly it also ages very well. We've tasted some bottles that were still good after a decade! It is one of Italy's finest and longest lived white wines.

Valentini, a lawyer by profession but a *vignaiolo,* or "little ol' winemaker," by preference, gave up a career in law and city life and moved to the family home in the country in the village of Loreto Aprutino to tend his vines, *oliveti,* and orchards, which he does with a passion, a passion for the land. In one sense, it seems strange that this scholar and intellect would prefer the isolated country life to the activity of the city. But here he has his books, stacked not only by his chair, but on the shelves, tables, cabinets, and all other available spaces not covered with papers, unanswered correspondence, and so on.

When he took the farm over, it was worked under the old system of *mezzadria,* and produced a variety of crops. Edoardo reduced them to three: vines, olives, and fruit trees, all planted in specialized cultivation.

Valentini has 156 acres (63 hectares) of vines, 80 percent planted to montepulciano at altitudes of 919 to 984 feet (280 to 300 meters) above sea level; when we visited him a few years ago, he said he planned to put in another 25 acres (10 hectares).

His first selection is in the vineyards. If it's a rainy, but not too rainy year, he selects the fruit from the vineyards with a southern exposure; in drier years he chooses grapes from vines facing more northerly. He selects the part of the vineyard least affected by the weather and then selects the best bunches. The rest of the grapes are sold. In the years when he produces wine to bottle, about 5 percent of his best grapes are turned into wine, the rest of the fruit is sold. At most he makes 50,000 bottles of wine a year; no more than 35,000 of Trebbiano and 15,000 combined of Montepulciano

THE VINEYARDS OF EDOARDO VALENTINI

Cru	Acres	Hectares	Year(s) Planted	Used for
Camposaero	29.7	12	recently	White
Castelluccio	29.7	12	1964–71	Red, rosé, white
Cavasorge	7.4	3	1965	Red, rosé
Colle Cavaliere	29.7	12	1974–75	Red, rosé, white
Colle Mantello	59.3	24	1978	Red, rosé, white

d'Abruzzo Cerasuolo (rosé) and Montepulciano d'Abruzzo Rosso. Generally, he produces much less. Average production, in the years that he produces, is more like 5,500 bottles of red and 22,000 of white.

He selects from the wine he produces the best to bottle and rejects the rest, usually most of the production. Would that more producers had his integrity.

Although he actually makes wine every year, in order to keep his barrels full he doesn't always bottle it. In the years that he doesn't bottle it, he sells it *sfuso;* the line forms behind us. In the 1970s he didn't bottle any wine in 1972, 1976, or 1978. In the 1980s he didn't bottle a Montepulciano d'Abruzzo in 1980, 1981, 1983, 1986, and 1989. And in the five vintages in that decade that he did bottle one, he produced a grand total of 27,092 bottles, or an average of 2,709 bottles a year!

The first wine Edoardo put in bottle was a Trebbiano and Montepulciano from the 1956 vintage. Before that he produced the wine for himself and a few lucky friends. The first wines he commercialized were the '64 Trebbiano and the '65 Montepulciano. His first *cerasuolo* was the '78.

The first time we visited Edoardo at Loreto we tasted a few wines from cask and some very fine vintages from bottle. He promised if we gave him a couple of days' notice he would set up a tasting for us of all the vintages of Montepulciano d'Abruzzo and Trebbiano d'Abruzzo in his cellar, and his wife, Adriana, would prepare *"la lingua di pappagallo"* and other such delicacies. We gave him ten days' notice.

When we returned ten days later, he had done as he said. And Adriana, a lovely lady whose smile lights up her whole face and those of the people she smiles at, had prepared a menu of regional

and house specialties, one dish more impressive than the last. But before we sated our appetites on the dinner, we had an excellent tasting.

Edoardo had lined up a dozen bottles of his Trebbiano and another dozen of Montepulciano. He says he doesn't care much for the red wine. One wonders what this wine would be like if he did—the only five-star Montepulciano d'Abruzzo? He has raised Trebbiano to heights none would believe possible if they haven't tasted his. He claims he has a special subvariety, the true trebbiano d'abruzzo. (He has all the research and proofs among his papers, and someday when we have lots of time on our hands we've promised to plow through them. In the meantime, we'll take his word for it.)

For each wine Edoardo has a sheet listing all the statistics from the analyses made, as well as much other data in his journal, including the phases of the moon when the wines were racked and bottled. Edoardo is a man of the twentieth century, but he has deep roots in the past. Among his books are the texts of the ancients in the original Latin. (English will be his next language, he assured us.) He spoke of his wines with an enthusiasm that didn't let up for a minute—nor, unfortunately, did his description and explanation, even long enough for a translation. But we couldn't protest too strongly, as the wines themselves spoke volumes, and directly to the tongue.

On one of our trips to Abruzzo, Edoardo staged a gala tasting that included most of the Montepulciano d'Abruzzos he bottled. We're pleased to report that the '56 was included. The lineup of wines also included '57, '58, '61, '65, '66, '67, '68, '69, '70, '71, '73, '74, and '75. The overall quality was striking.

Valentini's Montepulciano d'Abruzzo is aged for one year in old

PRODUCTION OF EDOARDO VALENTINI'S MONTEPULCIANO D'ABRUZZO

Year	Bottles	Year	Bottles	Year	Bottles	Year	Bottles
1970	8,775	1975	12,967	1980	0	1985	4,152
1971	8,182	1976	0	1981	0	1986	0
1972	0	1977	4,637	1982	4,800	1987	9,196
1973	13,027	1978	0	1983	0	1988	4,432
1974	12,779	1979	4,132	1984	4,512	1989	0

casks and is always sold as Vecchio. Of those we've tasted in the past few years we were most impressed with the '88, '85, '77, '75, '74, '71, '68, and '58. Valentini's wines have an uncommon richness and complexity; they are very well balanced and age extremely well, developing nuances of flavor and aroma found only in first-class wines. Montepulciano d'Abruzzo ****

Vinicola Casacanditella (*Casacanditella*). Giuseppe di Camillo, proprietor of Vinicola Casacanditella, has no vineyards. He selects grapes from top-quality sites. At one time they were crushed at a nearby cooperative under the direction of his enologist, and the must was brought to his *cantina,* Vinicola Casacanditella, near Chieti. There it was fermented and the wine aged in oak casks. This has changed recently. In 1983 they began to ferment some grapes at their own winery. Since 1986 they have been buying grapes and crushing them at their own *cantina.*

The winery has a capacity of 118,890 gallons (4,500 hectoliters), equivalent to 600,000 bottles of wine. His young son, Bruno, helps out in the winery; the older son, Peter, handles an important part of the sales. Di Camillo produces red, white, and rosé. His first wine, the *rosso,* was from the 1975 vintage. He didn't make a '76. His production breaks down as 70,000 bottles of Rosso della Quercia Montepulciano d'Abruzzo, 6,000 of the *riserva* Montepulciano d'Abruzzo Angelo Rosso, 20,000 each of Verde Quercia and the *riserva* Bianco della Quercia Trebbiano d'Abruzzo, and 30,000 of Rosa della Quercia, Montepulciano d'Abruzzo Cerasuolo.

The name Rosso della Quercia ("red of the oak tree") does not refer to the origin of the fruit, nor to the type of cooperage used (*rovere*—oak, coincidentally). The *quercia* of the name is a 900-year-old oak tree growing not far from the winery in the village of Casacanditella in the foothills of La Maiella.

Giuseppe is a warm, generous man with a love for his village and region. A few years ago he arranged a special dinner of regional specialties for a small group of journalists and a few other producers attending a wine fair in the area. For the highlight of the meal, he hired a man who could prepare *maccheroni al mugnaio,* a dish that takes all day to make. While the pork, veal, and beef simmered with tomatoes and seasonings in a large kettle on the fire, the man—originally a miller, as the name of the dish indicates—worked a large mound of flour into a long strand of pasta, adding only water, kneading it and rolling it between his palms to form one long piece more than 164 feet (50 meters) long, and coiling it into a tall beehive. This dish was first made, they tell us, at the court of Count Robert d'Anjou at Fiume Fino in 1684.

Our pasta maker cut the *maccherono* with a wooden blade and draped it over his arm to carry it into the kitchen. Then the pasta,

cooked perfectly *al dente,* was spread on a large wooden table and topped with the sauce, and all were invited to dig in, in the traditional manner, eating with the fingers. In our case they made an exception, and those who preferred to be neat and modern were invited to break with tradition and use forks. And to drink the wines passed around from glasses (saves spills from bottles bobbled with slippery fingers!).

Giuseppe's Rosso della Quercia was one of the Montepulciano d'Abruzzos served with the *maccheroni;* it went very well.

Rosso della Quercia is made in two styles, *normale* and *riserva.* The *riserva,* from special vineyards, is aged in Limousin oak casks for about one year. Overall, these are good wines that emphasize the cherrylike fruit of the montepulciano grape. They age moderately well, reaching their peak before their fourth year. The *riserva* has more of a capacity to age. Of recent vintages, the '87, '86, and '85 were very good, and the '86 Angelo Rosso excellent. Montepulciano d'Abruzzio: **, Riserva Angelo Rosso ** +

Vinovino (*Casacanditella*). Giuseppe di Camillo, proprietor of Vinicola Casacanditella, also owns Vinovino. It is a separate company. Di Camillo owns 7.4 acres (3 hectares) of vines and has another 12.4 (5) under lease. The vineyards are planted in cabernet sauvignon and chardonnay, 1.2 acres (0.5 hectare) each, and pinot noir and pinot blanc, 2.5 (1) each. He plans to plant merlot as well.

Di Camillo's first vintage of Vinovino was 1986. Today he produces over 100,000 bottles of wine per year: 10,000 of Costarella Montepulciano d'Abruzzo, 20,000 of Costarella Montepulciano d'Abruzzo Cerasuolo, 50,000 of Costarella Trebbiano d'Abruzzo, 2,500 of the *barrique*-aged, non-DOC *vino da tavola* Montepulciano Pianelaroma, 10,000 bottles of the non-DOC *vino da tavola* Rodolite Montepulciano, 6,000 of Chardonnay, and 12,000 of a white blend.

He plans to increase production a little. And he plans to buy more vineyards in order to maintain better control over fruit quality.

The '89 Pianelaroma, tasted from *barrique,* is very good indeed and the '88 Costarella good. Pianelaroma was first produced in 1988. Di Camillo made 2,500 bottles of this *barrique*-aged *vino da tavola* from 100 percent montepulciano grapes grown on the estate. It spent six months in small barrels. That wine was excellent. Rodolite is a non-DOC *vino da tavola* made from 100 percent montepulciano and produced with cold maceration. There were 10,000 bottles produced from the 1988 vintage. Montepulciano d'Abruzzo: Costarella *; *vino da tavola:* Pianelaroma ** +, Rodolite **

PART THREE

Aglianico

CHAPTER 14

The Aglianico Grape

Aglianico is the third of Italy's excellent native varieties. It is the noble vine of the south, considerably less known and less appreciated than the nebbiolo or the sangiovese. In one sense, the wines of the aglianico are to Italian wines what Italian wines are to the wines of the rest of the world. Edgar Rice Burroughs wrote a book entitled *The Land That Time Forgot*. The aglianico could be called the grape the world forgot.

There are only two really important wines made from the aglianico: Aglianico del Vulture and Taurasi. Outside of these, aglianico is used as part of the *uvaggio* for Cilento, Falerno del Massiccio, Solopaca, Taburno, Vesuvio and the non-DOC Lettere from Campania, and Castel del Monte and Pollino from Puglia, and Biferno and Pentro di Isernia from Molise, as well as a number of other non-DOC wines. One especially fine non-DOC Aglianico worth mentioning is the Majo Norante Aglianico from Molise made by their consulting enologist Giorgio Grai. The '87 was especially good.

Aglianico is grown in Basilicata, Campania, Calabria, Lazio, Molise, and Puglia. Though the variety is a noble one, only a few wines made from it demonstrate its great potential, and even fewer people recognize its pedigree. To those who are wondering what this aglianico is all about, we recommend that they try Fratelli d'Angelo's Aglianico del Vulture or Mastroberardino's Taurasi Radici; we think then they will realize its possibilities.

The aglianico vine was reputedly introduced into the Vulture area of Basilicata by Hellenes from ancient Greece who settled in southern Italy in pre-Roman times. They planted the vine in the volcanic soil on the sunny slopes of Monte Vulturino. From Basilicata, the aglianico was introduced into Calabria, Campania, and other neighboring regions (although one story attributes its introduction here to the Phoenicians).

Some authorities say that the aglianico may have been the first vine brought to Italy by the Greeks and was called *Vitis hellenica*

PRODUCTION ZONE OF AGLIANICO DEL VULTURE

☐ Aglianico del Vulture

Potenza

Matera

Lauria

after them. Later this became ellenico, and in the fifteenth century aglianico, as it is known today. Other names by which it is known include agliatica, ellenico, ellanico, gnanico, and uva nera.

The aglianico of Basilicata is a different clone than the one grown in Campania, the latter having smaller bunches.

BASILICATA

Basilicata is a mountainous region that has very little seacoast; it touches the Ionian Sea at the Gulf of Taranto and the Tyrrhenian Sea at the Gulf of Policastro. Known as Lucania to the ancients, it is the poorest region of Italy and a land of natural disasters.

On November 22, 1980, a major earthquake—not the first, but surely one of the most devastating—brought death and destruction to much of the area, a solemn reminder of the difficulty of eking out a living here. The tremors were felt as far north as Toscana, where chandeliers swayed from the ceilings. Some of the medieval hilltop villages, with their communal ovens and narrow bystreets formed of a series of steps, that we had visited on our trip to the south the previous spring now no longer exist.

Two nights later at the Altesino *cantina* in Montalcino, we met a young man from Basilicata who was on his way south to help the victims of the disaster and to be sure

that his relatives were all right. While he waited for a friend to join him in the early-morning hours to make the trip down, we stayed late in front of the fireplace singing traditional Italian songs as Claudio Basla accompanied us on the guitar.

Basilicata covers 74,000 acres (30,000 hectares), of which 47 percent is mountainous and 43 percent hilly. The approximately 50,000 growers in Basilicata tend some 40,000 acres (16,100 hectares) of vines in specialized cultivation and another 4,000 acres (1,600 hectares) in *coltura promiscua*. Besides aglianico, other important red varieties grown here include barbera, bombino, canosina, colatamburro, malvasia nera, montepulciano, sanginella, sangiovese, and uva di troia.

Cantine sociali—cooperatives—produce approximately half of the region's total vinicultural output. Production averages 11.4 million gallons (430,000 hectoliters), equivalent to 4.8 million cases of wine a year. By far, most of it—8.7 million gallons (330,000 hectoliters)—is produced in the province of Potenza, an area with more than 30,000 acres (12,140 hectares) of vines in specialized vineyards, plus a significant amount planted promiscuously. Some 528,400 gallons (20,000 hectoliters), equivalent to 222,200 cases, come from the Vulture district. A shade over 2 percent of the regional production is DOC wine, and all of that is Aglianico del Vulture.

Besides the one DOC there are two geographical denominations, both from the aglianico grape: Aglianico dei Colli Lucani and Aglianico di Matera.

AGLIANICO DEL VULTURE

Aglianico del Vulture is produced from grapes planted in volcanic soil at altitudes ranging from 650 to 2,300 feet (200 to 700 meters) above sea level in the *comuni* of Acerenza, Atella, Banzi, Barile, Forenza, Genzano di Lucania, Ginestra, Lavello, Maschito, Melfi, Palazzo S. Gervasio, Rapolla, Rionero in Vulture, Ripacandida, and Venosa and the localities of Caldare, Giardino-Macarico, Iatta, Piano Regie, Ponzi, Quercie, S. Croce, S. Maria, and S. Savino in the Vulture area of Basilicata, about midway between the cities of Potenza and Foggia in neighboring Apulia.

The best location for the vines is on the southeastern slope of the now extinct volcano, Monte Vulturino. The soil is rocky and poor. The vines in the best vineyards are trained *al alberello,* as individual head-pruned vines standing separately like "little trees."

The 1,192 registered growers cultivate some 3,550 acres (1,437 hectares) of aglianico vines in the Aglianico del Vulture DOC zone. The maximum production allowed by law of over 2.7 million gallons (100,590 hectoliters), equivalent to 1.1 million cases, is never met. Annual production, which varies considerably, averages less than 8 percent of the amount allowed, a mere 211,600 gallons (8,010 hectoliters), equivalent to 88,993 cases.

AGLIANICO DEL VULTURE PRODUCTION

Vintage	Cases
1975	37,885
1976	71,104
1977	61,105
1978	48,851
1979	142,208
1980	58,883
1981	188,870
1982	96,657
1983	106,656
1984	44,340
1985	60,827
1986	98,768
1987	86,492
1988	92,146

Source: 1975–83, Italian Wine Center, New York City
1984–85, Enotria, June 1987
1986–88, Enotria, March 1990

Italian Wine Law

DOC recognizes Aglianico del Vulture *rosso* and *rosato,* both dry and semisweet, and still and sparkling. The only styles of interest to us here—or, for that matter, in the glass, if you'll pardon our predilection—are the still, dry reds. (The subject *is,* after all, noble wines.)

The aging period for all three types is calculated from November 1; regular Aglianico del Vulture, then, cannot be sold prior to November 1 of the year following the harvest.

The Producers

There are ten individual producers and six cooperatives bottling Aglianico del Vulture. Of the wines we've tasted, those of Fratelli d'Angelo are clearly in a class by themselves. D'Angelo is not only the best producer in the zone but also a fine producer by any standard. He is, in our opinion, one of the two finest producers of wine from aglianico grapes today.

In 1977 the Consorzio Viticoltori Associati del Vulture was formed. As of September 30, 1989, they had eight members.

RECOMMENDED PRODUCERS

Botte
Cantina Coop. della Riforma Fondiaria di Venosa
Consorzio Viticoltori Associati del Vulture
F.lli d'Angelo
Francesco Sasso
Miali
Paternoster
Torre Sveva

Other producers of Aglianico del Vulture are Armando Martino and F.lli Napolitano, who both have good reputations. Carilli and Coop. Vinicola Acheruntina "Covit" also bottle an Aglianico del Vulture.

The Quality of Aglianico del Vulture

Aglianico del Vulture is generally best within five to eight years of the vintage. It makes a good accompaniment to lamb or kid, either chops or roasts; it also goes well with stews and braised red meats.

The poverty of the area, the lack of recognition for the wine, and the consequent low prices discourage many producers from making the sacrifices necessary to create a noble wine from the aglianico. With some recognition, we hope that this situation will change, and we can look forward to tasting a lot of excellent Aglianico del Vulture in the future. Rating ** (the quality is, potentially, much higher)

Vintage Information and Tasting Notes

Donato d'Angelo rates the vintages:

****	1988, 1985, 1978, 1977, 1973, 1968
***½	1987, 1982, 1981, 1975
***	1979, 1969
**	1983, 1971
*	1980, 1976, 1974
0	1989, 1986, 1984, 1972, 1970

Antonio Niederbacher rates them like this (his five-star scale has been adjusted to match our four-star system):

****	1985
***	1981, 1978, 1977, 1975, 1973
**	1984, 1982, 1979, 1974, 1971, 1970
*	1983, 1980
0	1976, 1972

And Antonio Rossi rates them:[1]

****	1988, 1985, 1981, 1975, 1973, 1970
***	1987, 1986, 1984, 1983, 1982, 1980, 1979, 1978, 1977, 1974, 1972, 1971
**	1976

A G L I A N I C O

DOC REQUIREMENTS FOR AGLIANICO DEL VULTURE

| | Minimum Aging in Years | | Minimum Alcohol | Maximum Yield in | |
	in Cask	Total		Gallons/Acre	Hectoliters/Hectare
Normale	0	1	11.5%	748	70
Vecchio	2	3	12.5%	748	70
Riserva	2	5	12.5%	748	70

Of the vintages we've tasted, we liked the '85 and '73 the best; it's doubtful, though, if any bottles of that splendid, earlier vintage are still available today.

D'Angelo 1987 (4/90). This wine was recently bottled. It was tight and closed on the nose with a sweetness of ripe fruit on the palate and a cherrylike component; this well-structured wine should make a fine bottle in time. **(+)

D'Angelo 1987 Canneto (4/90). The fruit of non-DOC Aglianico wine marries well with the *barrique* character; it is firm and dry with an evident sense of fruit. **

Sasso 1986 (4/89). Open, fresh, cherrylike aroma; light, fruity and simple. *

Consorzio Viticoltori Associati del Vulture 1985 (4/89). Fairly tannic and overly dry, yet with a fruity character, perhaps recent bottling made it out of condition?

D'Angelo 1985 (5 times, 4/90). Rich, expansive aroma suggestive of cherries, has notes of tobacco; chewy at first, then a mouth-filling sweetness of ripe, concentrated fruit, very long. ***, perhaps ***(+)

D'Angelo 1985 Canneto (3 times, 4/90). The aroma is closed in; in the mouth, rich, concentrated and sweet, tannic, young and structured; this will make a fine bottle in time. The aglianico character marries nicely with the *barrique*. ***

D'Angelo 1985 Riserva (4/90). Because this wine was bottled two months ago it wasn't surprising how closed and tight it is. Still the richness and concentration, balance and class are quite evident, and while still firm there was no question about its structure and backbone. Perhaps Donato's finest wine to date. ***(+)

Francesco Sasso 1985 (twice, 8/89). Deep color, hints of cherries on the nose; good body, flavorful; though there is some tannin the wine is ready now. *

Paternoster 1985 (twice, 4/89). Off-putting, could be a bad bottle? *Bottle of 7/87:* Nice fruit, dry, fairly tannic; young. *(+)

Cantina Coop. della Riforma Fondiaria di Venosa 1984 (4/89). Agreeable, soft and fruity; best to, drink now. *

Consorzio Viticoltori Associati del Vulture 1982 (4/89). Simple, cherrylike aroma; kind of dull, some fruit. +

D'Angelo 1982 (4 times, 9/88). Complex, yet elusive scent, hint of cherries; open and flavorful, balanced, still some tannin; good quality. *** –

D'Angelo 1981 (4 times, 7/87). Big, richly fruited, expansive aroma, hints of cherries; a well-balanced, tasty wine of good quality; perhaps more elegant than the '82. **+(*** –)

Francesco Sasso 1981 (7/87). Cherrylike fruit aroma with a vanilla component; some alcohol intrudes, yet rather nice fruit, dry finish. *

Martino Armando 1981 (7/87). Cherrylike aroma marred by volatile acidity; nicer in the mouth, especially the initial entry, this gives way to a harsh finish.

D'Angelo 1980 (ex-vat, 1/81). Expansive aroma of fresh cherries; acid on the high side (it hadn't gone through malolactic fermentation yet), loads of flavor. [**]

D'Angelo 1979 Riserva (3 times, 12/84). Ripe cherry aroma; a forward rush of ripe fruit, medium body, balanced, long finish. ** +

D'Angelo 1978 (ex-cask, 5/80). Has the structure and flavor, should make a nice glass with time, though not up to the '79. [**]

Consorzio Viticoltori Associati del Vulture 1978 (6/82). Cherry aroma; balanced, fruity, a bit light; ready. * −

Paternoster 1978 (5/80). Fruity aroma, fennellike note; some tannin; drinkable now. *

Cantina Coop. della Riforma Fondiaria 1977 (5/81). Stinky; has tannin, shallow and bitter. This was better than the '78 (enough said about that wine).

D'Angelo 1977 Riserva (8 times, 6/83). Some oxidation, also some flavor, we suspect an off bottle is the culprit. *Bottle of 4/83:* Characteristic cherry aroma; richly flavored, quite young, good quality. **(+)

D'Angelo 1975 (8 times, 7/85). Cherrylike aroma, vague floral notes; has a rustic side to it, light tannin, a lot of flavor, some astringency setting in; drink up. **

Centrale Cantine Coop. 1974 (6/82). Pretty aroma, fruity, fresh, fragrant; stop there because after that it is awful, it tastes of filter paper!

D'Angelo 1974 Riserva (5 times, 2/81). Cherries all over this wine from the nose through the palate and the long finish, richly flavored and intense. ** +

D'Angelo 1973 (3 times, 5/80). Richly fruited aroma and palate, loads of quality here, very long finish. ***

The Zone's Top Producer

F.lli d'Angelo Casa Vinicola (Rionero in Vulture), 1950. Donato and Lucio d'Angelo produce 200,000 bottles of wine a year. Some 75 percent, 150,000 bottles, of their production is Aglianico del Vulture. They also make a *barrique*-aged non-DOC Aglianico, Canneto, from the Vulture zone, three *spumanti,* plus Moscato, Malvasia, a semisweet red aglianico, the *rosato* Lu Canello from 100 percent aglianico grapes, as well as a red San Savino and a white Lu Canello.

Their *barrique*-aged Canneto was first produced from the 1985 vintage. That wine spent twelve months in a combination of two-thirds Alliers and one-third Slavonian oak *barriques.* Production totaled 20,000 bottles. The '87 spent eleven months in a combination of one-, two-, and three-year-old *barriques.*

Fratelli d'Angelo owns 36.8 acres (15 hectares). Their vineyards, facing east, are planted at an altitude averaging 1,370 feet (450 meters) above sea level in volcanic soils of *calcareo-argilloso.* Their best crus are Sansavino and Valle della Noce. Their own vines, they report, supply them with 60 percent of their needs. They buy the balance of the aglianico grapes that they need from some of the best districts in the zone: Querce, Piano dell'Altare, and Santa Maria. Their aglianico vines produce an average of 2.2 to 2.7 tons per acre (50 to 60 quintali per hectare). The aglianico vines for Canneto average from 1.3 to 1.8 tons per acre (30 to 40 quintali per hectare).

Enologist Donato d'Angelo makes the wine. He ferments the aglianico grapes for seven days and those for Canneto for eight to nine days at 80.6° to 86° Fahrenheit (27° to 30° centigrade).

Until 1958, d'Angelo, like nearly all the other producers here, sold their wine *sfuso.* When they began to bottle the wine they sold it as Rionero Rosso or Vino di Basilicata. In 1964 they began labeling the wine D'Angelo Aglianico del Vulture.

Donato told us that although the wine wasn't labeled as Aglianico del Vulture until 1964, the name was used locally for the wines in the 1940s, although not by them. In 1971, Aglianico del Vulture was granted official DOC status under Italian wine law.

D'Angelo was among the first wineries, if not the first, to export wine from Basilicata to the United States. From 1926 to 1929 they shipped the wines abroad in 55-gallon (2-hectoliter) barrels.

Today F.lli d'Angelo is to our knowledge the finest producer in Basilicata. Aglianico del Vulture ***

FALERNO

Falerno was known in its heyday as Falernian. This was the legendary Roman potation. William Younger describes it as "the Great First Growth of the Roman Empire and . . . the most famous wine in ancient history."[2]

As with the Falernian of ancient times, both red and white Falerno are produced. There was also a sweet version in that age, but if there is one made today we are not aware of it.

The grapes for this wine, today as then, are grown in the region along the border of Lazio (Latium) and Campania, but the modern Falerno is a far cry from the most famous and highly regarded wine of its country.

The Falerno of Lazio

The Falerno produced in Lazio tends to be lower in alcohol—generally under 12 percent—lighter in body, and somewhat earlier maturing than the version south of the border. In Lazio, the aglianico grapes are blended with barbera.

Though it has been some time since we tasted the Falerno of Leone Nannini, he used to make a good one.

The Falerno of Campania

In the Falerno of Campania aglianico was often blended with sangiovese, negro amaro, and/or per'e palumbo. Generally, the higher the proportion of aglianico, the better the wine. With the advent of DOC for Falerno del Massiccio in 1989, the proportion of grapes for the red has been codified as 60 to 80 percent aglianico, 20 to 40 percent piedirosso, and a maximum of 20 percent barbera and/or primitivo. (The DOC covers both red and white.) There is also a DOC for Falerno del Massiccio Primitivo made from at least 85 percent primitivo and no more than 15 percent aglianico.

This new DOC zone encompasses the *comuni* of Falciano del Massico, Carinola, Cellolo, Mondragone, and Sessa Aurunca in the province of Caserta.

At its best, this wine is dry, full-bodied, and somewhat rough when young, requiring a few years of bottle age to soften and mellow. It often attains 13 percent or more of alcohol. The only producers we can recommend are Michele Moio, especially for his fine black label Falerno, and Villa Matilde.

The Producers

Michele Moio. The last time we tasted the Falerno of Michele Moio, his regular label was 12 percent alcohol and the black label 15 percent. Both wines exhibited a floral bouquet. The black label was fuller in body and more robust, with more structure and tannin. Today Moio produces at least three wines of interest here: Metello Red, Falerno, and Vigna Gaurino. The '87 Metello was made from a blend of 60 percent aglianico and 20 percent each piedirosso and primitivo. The '86 red label Falerno would qualify for the DOC Falerno del Massiccio Primitivo. It was made from 85 percent primitivo and 15 percent aglianico. And the '87 Vigna Gaurino, made entirely from primitivo, was 16 percent alcohol.

Villa Matilde. Villa Matilde, owned by Tani and Maria Ida Avallone, has 150 acres (60 hectares) of vines from which they produce between 170,000 and 200,000 bottles of wine annually. Among their vineyards are the 8-acre (3.3-hectare) Vigna Caracci and the 4.4-acre (1.8-hectare) Vigna Camarato, from which they do cru bottlings. They produce 10,000 of the former and 5,000 of the latter. They also produce 50,000 bottles of Falerno del Massiccio Rosso, 70,000 of Falerno del Massiccio Bianco, and 8,000 of a Falerno Riserva. The *riserva* is aged for four years. Their other wines are Cecubo (12,000 bottles), and Tenuta Pietre Bianche red and white (35,000).

AGLIANICO DEL TABURNO

Aglianico del Taburno or Taburno, a new DOC from 1987, is produced from at least 85 percent aglianico grapes grown on the hills of the *comuni* of the province of Benevento at altitudes ranging from 305 to 914 feet (100 to 280 meters) above sea level. Piedirosso, sangiovese, and/or sciascinoso are allowed to 15 percent.

Thus far the only one that we have tasted, and the only one we can recommend, is from Cantina del Taburino. Their '87 was light, soft, easy, and very drinkable. It is a wine for early consumption.

Cantina del Taburino. Cantina del Taburino, founded in 1976, is the largest producer in the zone. Of the 2,011 acres (814 hectares) of vineyards they own, 306 (124) are in the DOC zone. Their vineyards are planted on hillsides at altitudes ranging from 820 to 1,640 feet (250 to 500 meters) above sea level. Besides aglianico they grow piedirosso and falanghina. In an average year they produce 555,500 cases of wine, including 66,660 of DOC red and 22,220 of DOC rosé. The balance is non-DOC red and white. They rate 1987, 1985, 1983, and 1981 as the best vintages, and 1986, 1984, and 1982 as the worst years. Even though they gave us this information in 1990, they didn't comment on 1989 and 1988.

TAURASI

Taurasi takes its name from that village on the site of the ancient Oscan city of Taurasia in the center of the production zone. Wine has been produced here since before 80 B.C. Roman historian Titus Livy, writing of the area a few de-

DOC REQUIREMENTS FOR FALERNO

	Minimum Aging in Years		Minimum Alcohol	Maximum Yield in	
	in Cask	Total		Gallons/Acre	Hectoliters/Hectare
Normale	0	1	12.5%	748	70
Riserva	1	2	13.0%	748	70
Vecchio	1	2	13.0%	748	70

DOC REQUIREMENTS FOR AGLIANICO DEL TABURNO

| | Minimum Aging in Years | | Minimum Alcohol | Maximum Yield in | |
	in Cask	Total		Gallons/Acre	Hectoliters/Hectare
Normale	0	1	11.5%	972	91
Riserva	0	3	12.0%	972	91

cades later in his *History of Rome,* referred to it as a "land verdant with abundant vines."

The DOC growing zone encompasses all or parts of the townships of Aternòpoli, Bonito, Castelfranci, Castelvetere sul Calore, Fontanarosa, Làpio, Luogosano, Mirabella Eclano, Montefalcione, Montemarano, Montemiletto, Pietradefusi, San Mango sul Calore, S. Angelo all'Esca, Taurasi, Torre Le Nocelle, and Venticano.

Aglianico vines are cultivated at altitudes of 1,475 to 2,460 feet (450 to 750 meters) above sea level on slopes with southern and southeastern exposures. Good soil for the aglianico vines, according to Mastroberardino—at one time the zone's only producer, certainly still the most important one—is volcanic earth rich in potassium. This provides higher sugars as well as good acid levels, thereby increasing the wine's capacity to age. The best soils, they feel, are the clay and clay-limestone mixtures in hillside locations.

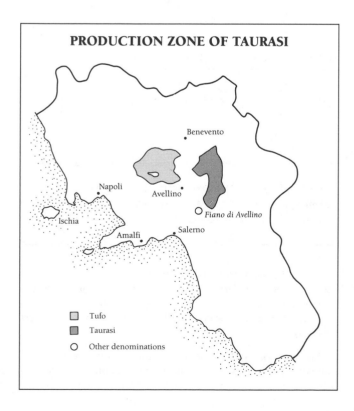

PRODUCTION ZONE OF TAURASI

Benevento

Napoli

Avellino

Ischia

○ Fiano di Avellino

Amalfi • Salerno

☐ Tufo
■ Taurasi
○ Other denominations

The DOC zone encompasses 549 acres (222 hectares) suitable for the planting of vines. This area is cultivated by 158 growers. Production of Taurasi cannot exceed 451,518 gallons (17,090 hectoliters), equivalent to 190,000 cases, a year. Its yearly average, ranging from 25,000 to 30,000 gallons (945 to 1,145 hectoliters), or 10,500 to 12,600 cases, is considerably less.

The *Uvaggio*

DOC regulations for Taurasi allow the addition of up to 30 percent of any combination of piedirosso (reputedly the *Columbina purpurea* referred to by Pliny), sangiovese, and barbera grapes. Mastroberardino uses only aglianico in their Taurasi. They point out that the other varieties not only detract from the character of the wine but shorten its aging potential as well.

DOC allows up to 5 percent concentrated must to be used to bring up the alcohol in weak vintages.

Taurasi may be aged in either oak or chestnut casks. Mastroberardino uses only oak, aging their *riserva* for four years in 795-gallon (30-hectoliter) casks of Slavonian oak.

At Mastroberardino they pick their grapes late to produce wines with greater richness and character. The aglianico is a late ripener, normally reaching maturity in the last ten days of October. When the picking is put off until the middle of November—a harvest between the 15th and 25th of November is normal for Mastroberardino—it is not rare for the first snow to fall while the harvest is still going on. Besides Mastroberardino, the only other bottler we know of is Giovani Struzziero.

The Quality of Taurasi

Taurasi is a fine wine; in topflight vintages it can achieve real distinction and class. It is a wine that deserves greater recognition.

Taurasi goes well with roasted meats, especially beef and lamb; it also is a fine accompaniment to steak or venison chops. A well-aged Taurasi goes very well with a good piece of not too potent provolone and good conversation. And Mastroberardino's new single-vineyard Taurasi from the

DOC REQUIREMENTS FOR TAURASI

| | Minimum Aging in Years | | Minimum | Maximum Yield in | |
	in Cask	Total	Alcohol	Gallons/Acre	Hectoliters/Hectare
Normale	1	3	12%	823	77
Riserva	1	4	12%	823	77

Radici vineyard is food for thought of itself. Rating: **, Riserva ***

Vintage Information and Tasting Notes

VINTAGES EVALUATED BY MASTROBERARDINO
(adjusted for our four-star system)

1990 **** Among the best ever; comparable to 1987, 1985, 1977, 1968, 1961, and 1958

1989 ** Overall it was a good vintage.

1988 **** Along with 1987 and 1985, this was one of the best vintages of the decade.

1987 **** Among the best of the decade

1986 *** Very good

1985 **** Among the best ever

1984 0 Very bad, among the worst. No Taurasi was bottled.

1983 *** Originally rated by Antonio Mastroberardino as four stars, one of the best ever.

1982 ** Originally rated as three stars, very good.

1981 *** Very good

1980 ** Originally declared as a one-star vintage, it has since been upgraded.

1979 *** Quite good, better than 1978

1978 ** Medium

1977 **** One of the best ever

1976 * Originally declared to be a zero vintage, very bad, among the worst, it has been upgraded slightly by Mastroberardino. No Taurasi was bottled.

1975 ** At one time declared to be a three-star year; only 1977 and 1973 were better in the decade. It has since moved down a notch.

1974 ** Medium quality

1973 *** Only 1977 was better in the decade.

1972 ** Fair

1971 *** Very, very good

1970 *** Very good

1969 ** Quite good

1968 **** One of the best ever; only 1961 was better in the decade.

Older vintages:

**** 1961, 1958

*** 1967, 1966, 1964, 1960, 1956, 1955, 1951, 1948

** 1965, 1959, 1954, 1952, 1950, 1949, 1946

* 1957, 1953, 1947

0 1963, 1962, 1945

No Taurasi was bottled in 1984, 1976, 1963, 1962, 1957, 1953, 1947, and 1945.

Niederbacher rates them like this (his five-star scale has been adjusted to match our four-star system):

**** 1985, 1983, 1977, 1968, 1961, 1958

*** 1981, 1979, 1975, 1973, 1971, 1970, 1967, 1966, 1964, 1960, 1956, 1955, 1951, 1948

** 1982, 1980, 1978, 1976, 1974, 1972, 1969, 1965, 1959, 1954, 1952, 1950, 1949, 1946

* 1957, 1953, 1947

0 1984, 1963, 1962, 1945

And Antonio Rossi rates them:

**** 1988, 1987, 1985, 1977

*** 1986, 1983, 1981, 1979, 1973, 1971, 1970

** 1982, 1980, 1978, 1975, 1974, 1972

* 1984, 1976

> **CAUTION:** *Before reading these tasting notes on the wines that we tasted from barrel, please read "On Tasting Wines from Barrel: A Caveat" on page xxv.*

Mastroberardino 1989 Radici (*5 times, ex-cask, 9/90*). Rich aroma of ripe fruit, characteristic cherrylike overtone; rich and intense on the palate with a lot of extract and flavor, seems surprisingly open and appealing at this stage. Could it really get better? We think so. ***(+)

Mastroberardino 1988 Radici (*ex-cask, 10/90*). Great richness and extract, tannic and firm, has all the components to develop well, great concentration and structure. ***(*)

OUR VINTAGE CHART

Year	Most Recent Date Tasted	Rating Today	Comment
1990	April 1991	****	The Radici and *riserva*, both tasted from barrel, were impressive.
1989	September 1990	***	The only wine we tasted was the Radici, and that was from barrel.
1988	October 1990	****	The only wine we tasted was the Radici, and that was from barrel.
1987	September 1990	* +	The only wine we tasted was the Radici, and that was from barrel.
1986	June 1990	** +	The Radici needs a few more years yet.
1985	June 1990	****	The best vintage since 1968.
1983	April 1987	**	We have tasted only the *normale*. It should be ready now.
1982	October 1989	**	Won't be long-lived.
1981	June 1990	*	No need to keep, drink up.
1980	February 1989	*	Drink up, they won't keep.
1979	February 1985	**	Should be ready by now.
1978	February 1985	**	Not for long aging, most likely at its best, or slightly past it.
1977	February 1990	***	Ready now with room to improve.
1975	January 1982	**	We have tasted only the *normale*. No need to keep it any longer.
1974	December 1984	0	We have tasted only the *normale*. It has probably faded.
1973	October 1987	***	Fully ready.
1972	November 1979	0	We have tasted only the *normale*.
1971	September 1983	***	Should be fully ready.
1969	September 1983	**	Probably best to drink up.
1968	May 1990	****	At or near its peak.
1967	January 1967	**	Best to drink up.

Mastroberardino 1987 Radici (*9/90*). Richly fruited aroma of ripe berries and spice; fairly tannic, a little bitter and dry at the end. *(* −)

Mastroberardino 1986 (*6/90*). Lovely open, cherrylike aroma, fragrant; soft entry, packed with flavor, some tannin, balanced, fresh; ready to drink. **

Mastroberardino 1986 Radici (*twice, 6/90*). Lovely nose, rich in fruit; good structure, moderate tannin, sweet and rich; lots of class; long finish has a bit of a bite, cherry fruit lingers in the mouth; give it a few more years yet. *** *Bottle of 3/87:* Spicy, cherry aroma, hint of black pepper; nice structure; displays class and style; very young yet. **(* +)

Mastroberardino 1985 (*6 times, 5/90*). Big, rich and concentrated, on the young side with all the components to develop well over the next couple of years. *** *Bottle of 12/89:* Lovely, scented perfumed bouquet; great richness and flavor, sweet impression, round, well balanced; the best Taurasi in some time. ***

Mastroberardino 1985 Riserva (*6/90*). Open cherry aroma; packed with fruit and flavor, still some tannin to soften, a lot of structure; very young; loads of quality, the best Taurasi since the '68. ***(+)

Mastroberardino 1983 (*4/87*). Nice nose, fruit and flowers; dry, moderate tannin; needs a few years yet. *(*)

Mastroberardino 1982 (*10/89*). Kind of thin and dull.

Mastroberardino 1982 Riserva (*twice, 4/89*). Scented floral aroma displays nuts and cherry notes; some firmness, moderate tannin, tasty. **(+)

Struzziero Giovanni 1982 (*10/90*). This Taurasi, the label said, was made from 50- to 60-year-old vines. Characteristic southern aroma, baked, volcanic character; some alcohol intrudes, fairly tannic, the fruit is there, dry finish; coarse. *

Mastroberardino 1981 (*6 times, 7/85*). Characteristic cherrylike aroma with spicy, black pepper notes; tannic and rough but seems to have sufficient fruit to carry it; try again in three or four years. **(+)

Mastroberardino 1981 Riserva (*6 times, 6/90*). *From magnum:* Seems to be drying out, must be the magnum, the bottle tasted a month earlier was considerably better. * − *Bottle of 5/90:* Lovely open aroma, slight cherry and vanilla notes; soft, well balanced; very ready, while it might hold we doubt that it'll improve. ** − *Bottle of 4/87:* Reticent aroma; full of tannin with sufficient fruit to carry it, firm structure; very young yet. *(**)

Mastroberardino 1980 (*5/86*). Fairly soft and fruity, round and ready, a little light, should hold. ** −

Mastroberardino 1980 Riserva (*15 times, 2/89*). Floral, cherry aroma and flavor, somewhat earthy in nature. * + All of the bottles from June '86 and earlier were better. *Bottle of 4/85 (the best one):* Floral aroma with a hint of almonds, volcanic nuance; a lot of flavor beneath the tannin, quite young, well structured; has potential. **(*)

Mastroberardino 1979 Riserva (9 *times, 2/85*). Floral aroma, vaguely cherrylike backnote; firm and tannic, closed. **

Mastroberardino 1978 Riserva (*twice, 2/85*). Almonds, cherries and flowers on aroma, volcanic backnote; moderate tannin, flavorful; more forward than some of the other vintages but still needs age. ** +

Mastroberardino 1977 Riserva (8 *times, 2/90*). Rich, cherrylike aroma; open, concentrated and soft with a velvet texture; ready now with room to improve. *** *Bottle of 4/85:* Floral bouquet, with notes of cherries and almonds; a mouthful of fruit beneath the tannin, well knit, intense; a lot of class here, has style and real quality. ***(+)

Struzziero 1977 Riserva (*twice, 6/90*). Flowers, spice and cherries; good body, some tannin, soft, fairly nice fruit, short finish. * *Bottles of 5/86:* This estate-bottled Taurasi has a medium ruby color and the characteristic cherry aroma; it is, considering its age, surprisingly fresh(!), although there is light tannin the wine is ready, it is rather simple and lacks intensity and concentration, but it does have some character. ** −

Mastroberardino 1975 (*twice, 1/82*). Aroma of cherries and flowers; still has some tannin to lose, but drinkable now, well balanced; good quality. **(*)

Mastroberardino 1974 (12 *times, 12/84*). Characteristic floral, cherrylike bouquet; full-flavored, has an edge to it, no point in keeping it any longer. ** −

Mastroberardino 1973 Riserva (20 *times, 10/87*). Complex aroma of almonds, cherries and flowers; this wine, tasted from a 1.5-liter bottle, still has some unresolved tannin, but is quite drinkable now, with a lot of distinction and class, its finish lingered for some time, and although ready it is sure to improve; we suspect that the wine in the 750-milliliter bottle is quite ready now. ***

Mastroberardino 1972 (*11/79*). Aroma lacks fruit; some alcohol intrudes, not bad for the year, has body, some tannin, and flavor, very short. * −

Mastroberardino 1971 Riserva (10 *times, 9/83*). Almonds and flowers on bouquet; well structured, still has considerable tannin as well as lots of fruit; young. **(*)

Mastroberardino 1969 Riserva (5 *times, 9/83*). Light, fruity aroma with notes of cherries and flowers; still has a fair amount of tannin but balanced with fruit. ** +

Mastroberardino 1968 Riserva (16 *times, 5/90*). Intense and fragrant bouquet; great richness and concentration, still some tannin, but soft and mellow, nice texture, long finish. *** *Bottle of 2/90:* Complex, perfumed bouquet displays the characteristic cherry component; concentrated and velvety; at or very close to its peak, and it should hold that way for a long time; splendid indeed. ***+ *Bottle of 7/85:* Vaguely floral aroma, cherry notes, some

volatile acidity; still has tannin, and a lot of it, also a smoothness of texture, some alcohol intrudes on the finish. ** *Bottle of 2/85:* Cherries from the first sniff; a rush of fruit across the palate, cassis and floral notes, still firm and tannic, but with the fruit to carry it. It's surprising how slowly this wine is developing. When we first tasted it in 1978, we felt it needed a few more years to soften, now it's been more than a few, and we will wait a few more. **(*)

Mastroberardino 1968 Riserva Montemarano [*bottled after almost seven years in wood*] (*twice, 10/78*). Aroma of cassis; deep, rich flavors under the tannin; shows a lot of potential. **(*)

Mastroberardino 1968 Riserva Piano d'Angelo (*twice, 6/89*). Nose shows a lot of complexity and development with richness and fragrance; sweet and concentrated, yet still some tannin, soft-centered and flavorful with a velvet texture; still has plenty of life ahead of it. The best Taurasi we've tasted. ***+ *Bottle of 4/85:* Rich bouquet with floral notes showing a mellowness and complexity from bottle age; loads of tannin over loads of fruit; very young still; real quality evident. **(*+)

Mastroberardino 1967 Riserva (*1/87*). Some oxidation apparent, but at this stage it adds complexity; soft, smooth and round; quite evolved, drink over the next few years. ** +

Mastroberardino 1961 Riserva (*11/79*). Rich, expansive perfume, with nuances of walnuts, cherries and figs; velvety texture, complexity of flavors; ready. ***

Mastroberardino 1958 Riserva (*11/79*). Lovely aroma; considerable tannin, lots of flavor; still young; could be longer on the aftertaste. ** +

The Zone's Best Producer

Mastroberardino Azienda Vinicola (*Altripalda, Campania*), *1878.* The family can trace its winemaking origins to the early part of the eighteenth century, 1720 in fact, although the Mastroberardinos say that their family was involved with wine in the sixteenth century. The family winery, however, was founded by Michele Mastroberardino at a somewhat more recent vintage. Today it is owned and operated by the two brothers, Antonio and Walter Mastroberardino. Antonio is the winemaker, Walter the viticulturist. The brothers are dedicated to preserving the traditional varieties—aglianico, fiano, and greco—introduced to the Avellino area by the Greeks and Romans.

Mastroberardino has some 495 acres (200 hectares) of vines under their control, including the 260 (105) they own. This supplies them with 50 percent of their grapes. The volcanic soil of these vineyards is rich in clay and microelements. They lie at an altitude ranging from 1,312 to 2,297 feet (400 to 700 meters) above sea level in the Irpinia region and face south to southeast. Yields for their aglianico vines average 598 to 673 gallons per acre (56 to 63 hectoliters per hectare). Irpinia, a hilly region in the Apennine Mountains, lies 30 miles (50 kilometers) east of Napoli.

In the better vintages Mastroberardino bottles selected lots from the best vineyards. In 1986, for the first time they bottled a Taurasi from the single-vineyard Radici. This 49.4-acre (20-hectare) vineyard, planted at an altitude of 1,969 to 2,625 feet (600 to 800

VINEYARDS OF MASTROBERARDINO

Cru	Acres	Hectares	Variety Planted	First Vintage	Average Number of Cases Per Year	Altitude in Feet	Meters
Radici	49.42	20	Aglianico	1986	1,400	1,969–2,625	600–800
	5.81	2.35	and fiano				
Terramajor	39.54	16	Greco	—	—	2,133	650
	39.54	16	Aglianico	—	—	1,969	600
Vignadellacorte	14.83	6	Aglianico	—	—	1,969–2,133	600–650
Vignabosco	2.47	1		—	—		
Vignadangelo	74.13	30	Greco	1982	5,000	1,805	550
Vignadora	24.71	10	Fiano	1983	1,500	1,312	400
Vignamaria	2.47	1	Fiano	—			

meters) above sea level, near Lapio, derives its name from the Italian word meaning "roots." The soil here is rich in clay and poor in organic substances. The average yield for fiano is 1.8 to 2.2 tons per acre (40 to 50 quintali per hectare) and for aglianico 2.2 to 2.7 (50 to 60). In all, there are 12.4 acres (5 hectares) of fiano; the balance isn't in production as yet. Mastroberardino declares that it is "the ultimate expression of Taurasi." We must admit to being impressed with their first effort from the 1986 harvest, as well as the very fine '88 and '89; the '87 was very good as well.

The greco vines in the Terramajor vineyard are planted in the section located in Montefusco. The average yield for those vines is 6 tons per acre (135 quintali per hectare). The aglianico vines are found in the section located in Montemiletto. Those vines are used for Plinius and Lacrimarosa. Aglianico here gives an average yield of 6 tons per acre (135 quintali per hectare).

Vignadora, located in Montelfalcione, has volcanic soil rich in clay. The average yield for the fiano grown here is 5 tons per acre (110 quintali per hectare). The Vignadangelo vineyard, in Santa Paolina, is planted in the greco variety. The soil is rich in clay and limestone, tufa and rock, and has concentrations of calcium, mag-nesium, and potassium. The average yield here is 6 tons per acre (135 quintali per hectare).

Production at Mastroberardino averages 100,000 cases a year.

Against the growing trend to produce wines from cabernet, chardonnay, sauvignon blanc, etc., at Mastroberardino they specialize in producing wines from the ancient varieties and the traditional grapes of the area: aglianico; greco, originally the aminea gemina of Tessaglia; coda di volpe, the alopecis vine called by Pliny *cauda vulpium* ("tail of the fox"); fiano, referred to as *Vitis apiana* (the "bee vine") in Pliny's *Natural History* and the grape of the Roman Apianum wine; and the sangionoso or olivella grape known to Pliny as *Vitis oleagina.*

Their Lacryma Christi del Vesuvio Rosso is made from the pedirosso grape, and in some years they include a small amount of aglianico. Plinius is a white wine made from a blend of 85 percent aglianico and 15 percent code di volpe. Irpinia Rosso is made from a blend of olivella and aglianico grapes.

MASTROBERARDINO'S TAURASI CRU BOTTLINGS

Cru	First Vintage	Average Number of Bottles Per Year
Castelfranci	1968	8,100
Montemarano	1968	7,950
Piano d'Angelo	1968	8,250
Radici	1986	17,000
Tampenne in Argo di Montemarano	1971	2,123

MASTROBERARDINO'S AVERAGE ANNUAL PRODUCTION BY TYPE

Wine	Type	Average Number of Cases Per Year
Avellanio	Red	4,500
Fiano di Avellino	White	3,000– 5,000
Greco di Tufo	White	40,000
Lacrimarosa	Rosé	4,000
Lacryma Christi del Vesuvio	White	15,000
	Red	4,000
Plinius	White	4,000
Taurasi	Red	10,000–15,000
Taurasi Riserva	Red	1,000– 1,500

Mastroberardino's Avellanio Rosso is made from a blend of the second press of the lesser vineyards of piedirosso and aglianico, mostly the latter. Sometimes Avellanio is made entirely from aglianico. We were told that the method used to produce this wine is an ancient one. Part of it is vinified with the skins and reblended back.

They also produce an aglianico rosé called Lacrimarosa d'Irpinia. This wine is made from 100 percent aglianico grapes. Antonio discovered that the ancients had produced a similar wine and reintroduced it in 1966. It is quite a good rosé, with more character than most. It is firm and dry and goes quite well with food, especially luncheon dishes and white meats. Mastroberardino says that it is good from its first through fifth year. Our experience is limited to one- or two-year-old versions only.

Their Taurasi Riserva is produced an average of, perhaps, seven times a decade. The *normale* spends three years in Slavonian oak casks and the *riserva* four years.

The Mastroberardinos are serious about producing fine wines and preserving the ancient traditions of the proud aglianico variety, as well as the other traditional vines of the area. But while they believe in tradition, they are not limited by the past. Where they feel the wines will benefit from it, they take advantage of modern technology. But contrary to the ever-growing trend to use French grapes, such as cabernet, and French methods, such as aging in *barriques,* they are intent on preserving their heritage. Taurasi: **, Riserva ***, Radici *** +

OTHER AGLIANICO WINES

Azienda Agricola Mustilli, owned by Leonardo and Maria Lina Mustilli, is located in Sant'Agata dei Goti in the province of Benevento in Campania. The Mustillis own 50 acres (20 hectares) of vines planted at altitudes between 656 and 984 feet (200 and 300 meters). These vines face northeast. Their annual production varies between 120,000 and 133,000 bottles. All of their wines are *vino da tavola* from Sant'Agata dei Goti, and, appropriately enough, the label specifies the grape of (*di*) S. Agata dei Goti. This includes 20,000 bottles of Aglianico di S. Agata dei Goti, 36,665 La Falanghina, 23,300 Il Greco, 26,665 Il Piedirosso, 16,665 Regina Sofia Aglianico Bianco, and 3,335 Rosato di S. Agata dei Goti from piedirosso grapes. Their range of wines sounds interesting; unfortunately we've never met them.

PART FOUR

Other Noble Reds

CHAPTER 15

Recioto della Valpolicella Amarone

According to archaeological evidence, vines were growing in the Valpolicella area some 40 million years ago. Winemaking in the zone, however, is not quite that ancient. It is known that the Arusnati people living around Tagus Arusnatium, now known as Fumane, were producing wine there in the fifth century B.C. Pliny referred to the Retico wine produced in the territory of Verona. Virgil placed Retico just after Falerno. Suetonius wrote that even though Emperor Augustus didn't drink much, he did enjoy a little Retico. Martial tells us that Retico came from the country of Catullus, Verona. Strabo also wrote about the wines of this region.

In the late Roman period, according to knowledgeable authorities, the name Retico changed to Acinatico. The sweet Acinatico was already being produced during the Roman era. In the sixth century it received high praise from Cassiodorus, or Cassiodoro in Italian, minister to the Ostrogoth king Theodoric. Cassiodoro—scholar, connoisseur, and wine critic—was in charge of ordering provisions for the Veronese court at Ravenna. In a letter to his agents in the countryside, he sent an urgent demand for supplies of this rare wine. It was produced, albeit in very limited quantities, in both red and white versions. Of the red he had this to say:

It has a pure and exceptional taste and a regal colour, so that you may believe either that purple got its colour from the wine or that the wine is the epitome of purple. Its sweetness is of incredible gentleness, its density is accompanied by an indescribable stability and it swells over the tongue in such a way that it seems either a liquid made of solid flesh or else a drink to be eaten.

He also drew their attention to the Acinatico *bianco*:

Nor must you neglect to find that other wine which shines like a milky drink, since it is more marvellous but also more difficult to find. There

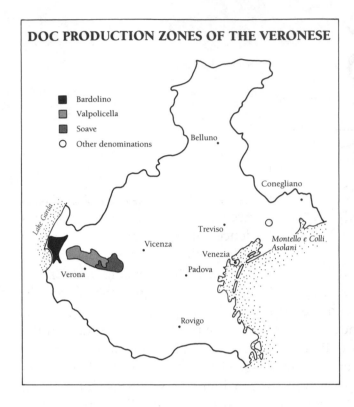

DOC PRODUCTION ZONES OF THE VERONESE

- ■ Bardolino
- ▨ Valpolicella
- ▪ Soave
- ○ Other denominations

Belluno

Conegliano

Treviso

Vicenza

Venezia

Montello e Colli Asolani

Padova

Verona

Lake Garda

Rovigo

is in it a beautiful whiteness and a clear purity, so that whilst the other one may be said to be born of roses, this one seems to be born of the lily.[1]

To his list of credits, we must add poet. One can imagine his agents, even having read such praise, insisting on trying a few glasses of the wine once located, just to be sure they had the real thing.

Based on our very limited experience with this wine, today even rarer than in Cassiodoro's day, the '28 Acinatico from Bertani that we were fortunate to be able to taste twice, once in April 1985 and again in October 1985, we can appreciate his enthusiasms.

The color of the wine, after over half a century, had taken on a warm mahogany hue—born of roses, as the poet would say. Its complex bouquet offered a medley of scents—licorice, berries, chocolate, dried grapes, coffee, nuts, and toffee. It was rich and concentrated, like a liqueur, in some ways reminiscent of an old Madeira, a wine to be sipped and savored. The finish lingered long on the palate, reflecting some of the aromatic chords struck on the aroma. A complete wine, very impressive indeed. ****

Gaetano Bertani told us the wine had 16 to 17 percent alcohol; it was quite well balanced. The high natural sugar content of the wine resulted from the blocking of fermentation when the alcohol got too high for it to continue.

Continuing with the history of Recioto, Rotaro, the Longobard king from A.D. 636 to 652, owned a fief with vineyards and a castle in Valpolicella, Castrum Rotarii, now Castelrotto. He was fond of the Recioto from that area. In 1300, Federico della Scala was appointed Count of Valpolicella by the German emperor Henry VII. His interest in viticulture resulted in his signing a trade agreement with the Prince of Verona in order to protect the vineyards of Valpolicella. The doges of Venice expressed a fondness for Recioto, and as a consequence it became known as a dogal wine.

VALPOLICELLA: THE ORIGIN OF THE NAME

Valpolicella, according to some accounts, means "valley of many cellars," which seems fitting. It is derived, they say, from the Greek word *poli* ("many") and the Latin *cella* ("cellar"). The name Val Polesela used in reference to this area is found, according to Giovanni Vicentini, in a decree issued by Federico Barbarossa on August 24, 1177.[2]

THE GROWING ZONE

The Valpolicella area is a district 27 miles (45 kilometers) long and varying from 3 to 5 miles (5 to 8 kilometers) in breadth, north and west of Verona, extending from the Adige River to the Cazzano Valley. Bardolino and Lake Garda lie to the west and Soave to the east. The land ranges in altitude from 490 to 1,475 feet (150 to 450 meters) above sea level.

The vines in the Classico district, northwest of Verona, are planted on the hillsides and mountain slopes of the valleys of the Adige tributaries and the Fumane, Marano, and Negrar torrents. Some of the vineyards are terraced with stone. The cretaceous, calcareous soil is of glacial origins. And volcanic activity in this area contributed elements to the soil as well.

Some parts of Valpolicella bring to mind the countryside of Toscana, with their vineyards, olive groves, and cypress trees.

There are roughly 15,000 acres (6,000 hectares) under vines in the 19 *comuni* of Valpolicella. More than half of the vineyards are in Valpolicella Classico, the classic or oldest part of the zone, in the western part. This district takes in the villages—from east to west—of Negrar, Marano, S. Pietro Incariano in the Fumane, and S. Ambrogio.

The area around Sant'Ambrogio is considered the heart of the Amarone production zone. Within this area, northeast of Gargagnago, is a valley called Vaio Armaròn, which may have given the wine its name. The Valpolicellas and Amarones of Sant'Ambrogio, including those of San Giorgio and La Grola, have been described as having a bouquet reminiscent of irises. These Amarones have more alcohol, and

ACREAGE OF VALPOLICELLA BY DOC DISTRICT

DOC District	Number of Growers	Acres	Hectares
Valpolicella	1,564	6,205	2,511
Valpolicella Classico	1,401	7,433	3,008
Valpantena	144	1,075	435
Total	3,109	14,713	5,954

Source: Il Corriere Vinicolo, n. 10, (Milano: Unione Italiana Vini, March 12, 1990.)

are bigger in body and smoother in texture than most. They are generally ready to drink from their third or fourth year, though those of San Giorgio reputedly require more time—seven or eight years—to be at their peak. The Valpolicellas and Amarones of Fumane are said to display an aroma of violets; those of Negrar, especially from Jago and Moròn, to have a scent of roses.

THE WINES OF VALPOLICELLA

Average annual production, between 1986 and 1988, of the Valpolicella wines was less than 4 million cases a year. Of this, more than half was produced in the Classico zone. Between 1972 and 1989 less than 4 percent, or about 147,000 cases, was Recioto della Valpolicella, including Amarone.

Sandro Boscaini of Masi Agricola defines the pyramid of quality for Valpolicella as:

The wine of Valpolicella is made in various styles. The most common is the light-bodied, dry, fruity red. This wine is most appealing when drunk young and cool. It is at its best before the end of its second year, in some cases before its third.

Some producers make a more serious style, using a method known as *ripasso*. This word derives from the Italian verb *ripassare*, meaning "to pass over" or "to do something again." In late winter or spring, occasionally later, the new Valpolicella is refermented on the grape pomace from the Amarone, which still contains a lot of sugar. The wine is put into the barrels that had been used to ferment the Amarone immediately after that wine is drawn off. The pomace, still

ANNUAL PRODUCTION OF VALPOLICELLA CLASSICO AND RECIOTO IN CASES

Year	Valpolicella Classico	Recioto and Amarone
1972	1,964,359	87,858
1973	2,095,724	106,067
1974	1,935,551	120,555
1975	1,582,531	98,390
1976	1,808,808	101,290
1977	2,234,665	151,152
1978	1,861,025	100,134
1979	2,443,178	201,935
1980	1,978,002	177,171
1981	1,499,994	141,164
1982	2,219,123	214,656
1983	1,989,923	213,690
1984	1,841,271	202,024
1985	1,955,704	234,265
1986	1,900,499	143,208
1987	2,176,471	108,211
1988	1,911,787	166,006
1989	1,525,090	86,475
Average	1,940,205	147,458

Source: Masi Agricola, 1990

high in sugar, nutrients, and extract, activates an alcoholic refermentation. The temperature increase, due to the warming of the season combined with the warm pomace, causes the development of *Saccharomyces bayanus* yeasts, which bring about the refermentation of the Valpolicella. This adds alcohol, total acidity, dry extract, and glycerine to the wine. The alcohol increases 1.5 to 1.7 percent and total acidity 0.5 to 1 percent. The wine becomes deeper in color, bigger in body, and richer in alcohol, extract, and tannin.

Masi believes that the best *ripasso* wines are made from a

PRODUCTION OF THE WINES OF VALPOLICELLA BY TYPE

Wine	1988	1987	1986	Average Hectoliters	Cases
		Hectoliters			
Valpolicella	136,018	145,358	123,768	135,048	1,500,383
Classico	169,107	195,903	171,062	178,691	1,985,253
Valpantena	24,878	23,947	23,219	24,015	266,803
Superiore	2,972	11,856	7,072	7,300	81,103
Recioto	14,942	9,741	12,891	12,525	139,149
Total	347,917	386,805	338,012	357,579	3,972,691

Source: Data supplied by Il Corriere Vinicolo (Milano: Unione Italiana Vini)

THE CHANGES IN THE BASE WINE DUE TO *RIPASSO*

	Before ripasso	*After* ripasso
Alcohol	11.5–11.8 percent	13.0–13.5 percent
Total acidity	5.5–6.0 ppm	6.0–7.0 ppm
Dry extract	18.0–20.0 ppm	22.0–24.0 ppm
Glycerine	3.0–4.0 g/l	5.0–6.0 g/l

KEY: ppm—parts per million
g/l—grams per liter

Valpolicella grown in vineyards in the classic zone and re-fermented on the pomace of an Amarone from vineyards with a southwestern exposure, and that those vineyards should also be in the Classico zone.

This ancient method was rediscovered by enologist Nino Franceschetti and refined by him in the late 1950s. At that time he created the very fine Campofiorin for Masi. It is still foremost among the wines of that style. Allegrini also uses this traditional method to produce their Valpolicella. We've tasted twenty-year-old and older Campofiorin, as well as ten-year-old Valpolicella from Allegrini, that was still drinking very well. Boscaini, Le Ragose, Quintarelli, and Tedeschi are other producers who use this technique for at least one of their Valpolicellas.

What is interesting here is that although Franceschetti rediscovered the method, it was still in use. The farmers up in the hills had been using this method for decades and many continued to follow the method of their fathers and grandfathers. Change came to the villages and hamlets in the hills of Valpolicella quite late.

At one time the wines of the Veronese hillsides were classified by the farmers according to their degree of sweetness, and the prices that these wines fetched were related to their classification. The sweeter wines were prized the most

and consequently commanded higher prices. The *recioto* wines were the sweetest, *mezzo recioto* was medium sweet, *pastoso* off dry, and *amaro* dry.

At first the *ripasso* technique was used to produce a sweeter wine. The purpose of the resmashing (*ripasso*), as it was referred to, was to obtain a sweeter wine. The wine gained in sweetness from the residual sugar remaining in the *recioto* pomace. At first the pomaces were "washed" with the Valpolicella in order to extract the remaining sugar. Later this process was used for a dry wine in order to increase the glycerine and structure.

Recently we discovered that one producer at least has continued to use the *ripasso* method for a Valpolicella from the Valpantena area since the Bertani brothers produced their first commercial vintage in 1857. That wine, Secco-Bertani Valpolicella-Valpentena, is still made with the *ripasso* technique, though for some reason they have never publicized this fact.

Valpolicella is also made as a full-bodied, semisweet wine, Recioto della Valpolicella; as a semisweet sparkling wine, Recioto della Valpolicella Spumante; and as a full-bodied, robust, characteristically bitter dry wine, Recioto della Valpolicella Amarone.

The producers are waiting for a modification of the labeling laws that would allow them to simplify matters and use the name Recioto della Valpolicella for the sweet style and Amarone della Valpolicella for the dry. Regardless of the style, Italian wine law sets regulations on the allowable grape varieties.

THE *UVAGGIO*

The wine must be made from 40 to 70 percent corvina veronese, 20 to 40 percent rondinella, and 5 to 25 percent molinara; up to 15 percent negrara trentina, rossignola, barbera, and/or sangiovese can also be added. Dindarella is another variety used by some producers. Up to 15 percent of grapes, must, or wine from outside the zone was allowed until the 1989 vintage in order to correct a weak vintage, deficient in alcohol and body. Since 1989 this practice has been prohibited.

The corvina veronese, or cruina as it is also known, has a few subvarieties: these include corvinone, corvina rizza, and corvina gentile. There are also some officially selected clones that have rather official-sounding names, like ISV-CV 7, ISV-CV 13, ISV-CV 48, ISV-CV 78, and ISV-CV 146. The corvina is said to contribute color, body, bouquet, flavor, and the basic Valpolicella character to the wine. Rondinella, resistant to disease and rot, is added for color, strength, tannin, and vigor; it also adds refinement to the aroma. Molinara, or mulinara, also known as rossara veronese and rossanella, is blended in to make the wine lighter and more drinkable; additionally it contributes dryness and acidity, as well as the characteristic bitterness. Negrara, they say, adds softness, freshness, and early drinkability. Rossignola, a minor variety, contributes to the aroma and flavor.

Experiments are being conducted by Masi Agricola and the Stazione Sperimentale Agraria di Verona, Experimental Center of the School of Viticulture, in San Floriano in Valpolicella to find an *uvaggio* that will improve the quality of Valpolicella. Dario Boscaini, the director of the school, is also part of the firm of Boscaini. Besides the clonal experiments, they are experimenting with old, nearly forgotten local varieties like bigolona, dindarella, oseleta, and forselina.

Sandro Boscaini's aim is to make a great Valpolicella. Corvina, he points out, is the major variety, the one that gives the wine its personality and character. It is low in tannin and consequently needs a supporting variety, one that will add to its structure but not diminish its character. Oseleta, an all-but-forgotten local variety, is a low-yielding grape that adds backbone and structure to the corvina. Based on some experiments they have carried out, Boscaini thinks this variety might help improve Valpolicella.

Forselina, which adds a vinous and aromatic quality to the *uvaggio,* is said to be good for Recioto wines. Dindarella, or pelara, a variety that to our knowledge was rediscovered by Giovanni Allegrini over a decade ago, contributes a dry, pleasing quality and adds an aromatic element to the bouquet. Our first experience with this variety was with the very good Allegrini Pelara, a pale red, fresh, fruity wine made from grapes grown in the Cà del Paver vineyard. Dindarella is also good for the *appassimento* process used for Recioto wines.

The aging period for the *superiore* is calculated from January 1 after the harvest. Recioto must contain no less than 14 percent potential alcohol, the level it would reach if fermented dry; actual alcohol must be no less than 12 percent (the balance being unfermented sugar). To qualify as Amarone under the law, this wine cannot contain more than 0.4 percent residual sugar; it is often even drier.

The term *classico* on the label indicates that the grapes came from an area of five villages considered the classic zone. And Recioto della Valpolicella Valpantena comes from the Valpantena Valley to the east of the *zona classica,* in the center of the Valpolicella zone.

RECIOTO

According to Vicentini, the term *recioto* was first used for this wine in the mid-nineteenth century. Various theories are given regarding the origin of the name. The most commonly held one says that it is derived from the dialect word *recia* ("ear") because traditionally the upper and outer parts of the grape bunches were used to produce the wine. An-

DOC REQUIREMENTS FOR VALPOLICELLA

	Minimum Aging	Minimum Alcohol	Maximum Yield in	
			Gallons/Acre	Hectoliters/Hectare
Valpolicella	none	11%	898	84
Superiore	1 year	12%	898	84
Recioto	none	14%	513	48

other explanation points to a possible derivation from the Latin *racemus* ("grape cluster"), or *recisus*, "a harvested cluster hung to dry." Yet another view speculates that *recioto* comes from the ancient name Retico.

Cassiodoro also described the practice of drying the grapes for Retico:

... *the grapes are selected from the trellises around the houses, hung up and turned and then preserved in special jars and kept in ordinary containers. The grapes become hard and do not liquefy. Then the juices seep through, gently sweetening. This process continues until the end of December when the winter weather makes the grapes liquefy and by a miracle the wine begins to be new whilst the wine in the cellars is already old.... It stops bubbling at its origin and when it becomes mature it begins to seem forever young.*[3]

The method was not much changed from that used when Pliny the Elder recorded the method of making the Retico wine from semidried grapes stored in covered amphorae.

The process and the aging potential are noted again in the eighteenth century. Scipione Maffei, the eighteenth-century scholar and historian, explains the process for making the Recioto Bianco:

Store the carefully selected grapes until December; press them delicately during the cold winter season, and decant the must without fermenting. It is the method we are honored to use to this day .... The wine ... can be sweet or not sweet, and has the property of remaining unspoiled however it is kept; it is much like the famous wine of Tocai, and it is often served with this name north of the mountains ...[4]

Basic to the process of making Recioto wines, both the dry amarone and sweet, is the use of corvina for drying because of its susceptibility to the botrytis infection. It also adds glycerine to the wine while it loses tannin and color.

THE DISCOVERY OF AMARONE

The first dry Amarone, according to writer Cesare Marchi, was the result of a fortunate accident. In the early 1950s, Adelino Lucchese, Bertani's cellarmaster, discovered a barrel of wine in the cellar that had been overlooked and neglected for some time. Sure that it had spoiled, he was about to dump it when curiosity prompted him to take a taste just to see what had happened to it. He was astonished to discover that

the forgotten wine had a velvety and penetrating perfume, an all-pervading (but not unpleasant) bitter taste and an austere rounded strength not to be found in the other barrels.[5]

Sandro Boscaini of Masi Agricola points out, however, that the Romans made a type of bitter Recioto for diabetics or other people who couldn't take sugar. This would seem to indicate that Amarone is considerably older than Marchi indicates. An Amaro, a dry Recioto, was produced by the oldest families in Valpolicella. Boscaini, in this connection, mentions the families of Count Campostrini and Count Serègo Alighieri, as well as his own. Most of the Recioto, 90 percent in fact, produced at that time, was sweet, the balance Amaro, or Mandorlato. This is an old-style Amarone, bottled when young and refermented in the bottle. It isn't made anymore, commercially at least. A few years ago we had an opportunity to taste a '58 and '64 Mandorlato from the Boscaini winery.

Boscaini 1964 Mandorlato (4/89). Complex and rich bouquet, fragrant and scented; rich, lovely, long. *** +

Boscaini 1958 Mandorlato (4/89). Woodsy aroma with hints of spice and pine trees; rich and harmonious, complex and round; still fresh. ***

And if this isn't sufficient proof in itself that dry Recioto has a long history, the Stazione Sperimentale Agraria di Verona, in its bulletin number 1 of 1863, lists Reciotos from different valleys along with their analyses—alcohol, sugar, and the like. There were two wines from Gargagnago with 14.5 to 15.6 percent alcohol and almost no residual sugar; a Recioto from Abizzano (Negrar) contained 15 percent alcohol and no residual sugar.

According to Lamberto Paronetto, in his book *Valpolicella, Splendida Contea Del Vino*, the name Amarone has been in use since the eighteenth century. It became popular at the beginning of this century. The name could very well derive from the Italian word *amaro*, meaning "bitter" (scholar Scipione Maffei, writing in the first half of the eighteenth century, refers to an *amaro*, a dry wine from the Valpolicella area), or it could come from Vajo Armaròn, where some highly regarded Amarones have been produced for ages.

AMARONE TODAY

The grapes for Recioto are harvested toward the end of September. They are spread out on *graticci* (trellises), or bamboo trays in large, well-ventilated rooms to evaporate their moisture and concentrate their sugars. During this *appassimento* period of three to five months, the grape clusters are periodically turned and examined for the appearance of unwanted molds. Those bunches that will be used for Amarone and Recioto are left to raisin until January, by which time they have been reduced by two-thirds to three-quarters of their original weight.

Corvina is the grape most susceptible to botrytis during

the *passimento,* or drying, which is why it is favored for Amarone. Rondinella is never affected by botrytis, while negrara and molinara are sometimes susceptible to it. The incidence of botrytis is also influenced by the microclimate of where the *passimento* takes place. Botrytis needs humidity. The drier it is, the lesser the incidence of botrytis.

At Bolla they told us that while they feel it is not necessary to have botrytised grapes to make Amarone, it is necessary for a good Amarone. Bertani also said they want some, though not a lot, of botrytis on the grapes for their wine. At Bertani they keep the grapes from the different vineyards separate during the drying, fermentation, and aging. Their Amarone undergoes a slow fermentation for one month. It is aged for no less than eight years before being offered for sale. At Speri they dry the grapes until January, when they are fermented slowly in stainless steel tanks for one and a half months. After settling, the wine is moved to 528-gallon (20-hectoliter) casks; at that point it still contains some unfermented sugar. The wine is left in the casks until September, by which time it has fermented out and become a dry wine, which is then aged for three years in Slavonian oak.

Amarone needs a very good to great vintage, and a dry season during the *appassimento,* with wide fluctuations between nighttime and daytime temperatures.

AMARONE IN THE GLASS

On aroma, Amarone brings up notes of dried fruit, almonds, and occasionally flowers. Almonds are a quality prized in the bouquet of the best Amarones. This wine has a characteristic bitterness on the finish.

Amarone is full-bodied, dry, rich, and concentrated, a big but not overbearing wine. Though it is quite dry, it hints at sweetness. A good Amarone contains a lot of glycerine, which makes it quite attractive with four or five years of age, when it develops a silky texture.

Many *amatori* of Amarone in Verona believe that it is at its best consumed in its youth, within four to five years of the vintage, while it has all of its fruit. At Bolla they feel their Amarone peaks before its tenth year.

To our taste, good Amarone needs six to ten years to really shine. We've had some bottles thirty years old that were still very good. With this kind of age the Amarone admittedly becomes a different wine; its forthright fruity nature becomes less obvious, and it develops a more subtle, mature mellowness and complexity.

Young Amarone is a good wine to serve with hearty fare like braised meats, stews, even game. An aged wine makes a marvelous accompaniment to Gorgonzola, Stilton, parmigiano reggiano, or other creamy marbled cheeses, as well as walnuts, hazelnuts, or toasted almonds. The ultimate com-

bination would also include a roaring fire and some good conversation. Zeffiro Bocci suggests Amarone

> . . . between meals [when] it is an energetic, invigorating and "solo" wine, the highest expression of Valpolicella's role as a "philosopher's wine." . . . If one abandons oneself to the wine's evocative power, it helps in the clarification of ideas and aids lucid and stimulating meditation.[6]

One of the best places to enjoy the local Veronese treasures, like Allegrini's La Grola Valpolicella, Lena or Pelara, Roberto Bricolo's Bianco di Custoza, especially the single-vineyard San Michelino, Masi's Serègo Alighieri Valpolicella or Col Baraca Soave, is at what just might be the greatest pizzeria in the world: Pizzeria Al Sole in Sommacompagna. When you go there put yourself in Paolo's hands. He will select his finest offerings. And ask him if he has any special bottles. He squirrels away some of the better and rarer ones for special customers.

The best Amarones are among Italy's vinicultural gems. Rating ****

WHAT THE RATINGS MEAN

****	Great, superb, truly noble
***	Exceptionally fine
**	Very good
*	A good example of its type, somewhat above average
0	Acceptable to mediocre, depending on the context; drinkable
+	Somewhat better than the star category it is put in
−	Somewhat less than the star category it is put in, except for zero where it indicates a wine or producer-wine combination that is badly made or worse
[. .]	*On a producer:* Tentative evaluation based on an insufficient number of wines or based on older, out-of-date vintages, or where the wines we tasted were to difficult to fully judge to give a fair assessment of quality *On a wine or vintage:* Projection for the future. This rating is given to a vintage where we feel that we tasted an insufficient number of wines or those we tasted were too difficult to really judge to give a fair assessment of quality
(. .)	Potential increase in the rating of the wine given sufficient maturity

THE WINES AND PRODUCERS RATED

RECOMMENDED PRODUCERS OF VALPOLICELLA

* Allegrini, Classico Superiore
** Allegrini, "La Grola" Classico Superiore
* Allegrini, "Lena" Classico
* Allegrini, "Palazzo della Torre" Classico Superiore
* Bertani, "Secco-Bertani" Valpantena
  Bolla, "Jago" Classico
* Boscaini, "Marano" Classico Superiore
  Brigaldara Azienda Agricola, "Il Vegro" Classico
    Superiore
* Dalforno Romano
  Fulvio Scamperle Azienda Agricola Le Salette, Classico
    Superiore
  Guerrieri-Rizzardi, "Villa Rizzardi Poiega" Classico
  "La Bionda," "Vigneti di Ravazzol Valgatara" Classico
    Superiore
* Le Ragose, Classico Superiore
* Masi, Classico Superiore
* Masi, "Serègo Alighieri" Classico Superiore
* Masi, "Vigneti di Gargagnago" Classico Fresco
  Quintarelli, "Vigneto di Monte Cà Paletta" Classico
    Superiore
  Quintarelli, "Vigneto di Monte Cà Paletta Fiore"
    Classico
* Righetti Luigi, "Campolieti" Classico Superiore
  "San Rustico" di Danilo Campagnola Azienda, Classico
  "San Rustico" di Danilo Campagnola Azienda, "Vigneti
    del Gasso" Classico Superiore
  Santa Sofia, Classico Superiore
  Santi, "Vigneti Castello d'Illasi"
* Tedeschi, Classico Superiore
* Tedeschi, "Vigneto Lucchine" Classico Superiore
  Tommasi, "Vigneto Raffael" Classico Superiore
  Villa Girardi, Classico Superiore
  Zeni F.lli, "Marogne"
  Zeni F.lli, "Vigne Alte" Classico

**Of the highest level
*Highly recommended

RECOMMENDED PRODUCERS OF RECIOTO DELLA VALPOLICELLA RATED

****
Allegrini, Gardane
Masi, Casal dei Ronchi (Serègo Alighieri)
Tedeschi, Capitel Monte Fontana

**
Allegrini

Masi, Riserva degli Angeli
Masi, Mezzanella
Venturini

*
Bergamini[a]
La Crocetta
Lenotti
Tedeschi

RECOMMENDED PRODUCERS OF RECIOTO BIANCO
(VINO DA TAVOLA *AND* DOC)

Allegrini, Fiorgardane Vigna Campogardane *vino da tavola*
Anselmi, Recioto di Soave DOC Dei Capitelli
Leonildo Pieropan, Recioto di Soave DOC
Masi, Campociesca *vino da tavola*
Tedeschi, La Fabriseria de San Rocco *vino da tavola*

RATING THE PRODUCERS OF AMARONE

****
— Allegrini, Fieramonte
— Masi, Campolongo Torbe
  Masi, Mazzano

***
Allegrini
Bertani
Boscaini, Ca' de Loi
Boscaini, Vigneti di Marano
Le Ragose
— Masi, Classico
+ Masi, Serègo Alighieri, Vaio Armaron
  Righetti Luigi, Capitel de'Roari
— San Rustico, Del Gasso[b]
  Tedeschi, Capitel Monte Olmi

**
— Bolla
  Brigaldara
+ Dalforno Romano
+ La Bionda
  Le Salette
  Longo[c]
  Quintarelli
— Santi, Botte Regina[b]
  Tedeschi
+ Tedeschi, Linea Fabriseria[d]
  Tommasi
+ Venturini[e]

*

Aldegheri, "Santambrogio"[f]
− Conati Marco[d]
+ Due Torri[g]
Farina Remo[b]
Guerrieri-Rizzardi
La Croceta[d]
Murari[g]
San Rustico
Santa Sofia
Sartori
Scamperle[h]
+ Tramanal[i]
Villa Spada[j]
Zenato
Zeni

0

Aldegheri[k]
Barberini[l,m]
Burati[m,n]
+ Ca' Merla[d]
Cesari[g]
Corta Vecchia[g]
Fabiano
La Colombaia
+ La Colombaia, Alto Marano[d]
Lamberti
Montresor
Nicolas Angelo
Pasqua
Santi[j]
Speri
Vantini Lorenzo[o]
Villa Girardi[p]
Zardini F.lli[q]

NOTES: [a] This winery is now closed
[b] Based on one vintage, the '85
[c] Not tasted since the '71 in 1978
[d] Based on one vintage, the '83
[e] Not tasted since the '74 in 1978
[f] Based on one vintage, the '81
[g] Based on one vintage, the '82
[h] Not tasted since the '78 in 1985
[i] Not tasted since the '75 in 1981
[j] Based on one vintage, the '80
[k] Based on one vintage, the '84
[l] Not tasted since the '77 in 1983
[m] Private label
[n] Not tasted since the '71 in 1980
[o] Based on one vintage, the '86
[p] Not tasted since the '80 in 1986
[q] Based on one vintage, the '87

The Grasso brothers, Renato Vaona, and Zancote and Aldo Zanotti are highly regarded by some of the other producers. We've never met their wines. F.lli Grasso is in S.

Ambrogio di Valpolicella, Renato Vaona in Noaia di Marano di Valpolicella, and Aldo Zanotti Aldo in Torbe di Negrar.

VINTAGE INFORMATION AND TASTING NOTES

Antonio Niederbacher's vintage chart, possibly more of an evaluation of Valpolicella than Amarone, rates the years as follows (adjusted for our four-star system):

***   1984, 1983, 1979, 1977, 1969, 1967, 1964, 1962, 1961, 1958, 1957, 1955, 1953, 1952, 1948, 1946
**   1985, 1982, 1981, 1980, 1978, 1976, 1974, 1973, 1971, 1970, 1968, 1966, 1959, 1956, 1950, 1949, 1947, 1945
*   1975, 1972, 1965, 1963, 1960, 1954, 1951

Antonio Rossi gives three stars out of four to 1988, 1986, 1985, 1984, 1983, 1981, 1979, 1978, 1977, 1975, 1974, 1973, and 1971, and two stars to 1987, 1982, 1980, 1976, 1972, and 1970.[7]

The Vintages as We See Them Today

****	1990, 1988, 1983
**** −	1985
***	1979, 1977, 1974, 1971
*** −	1981, 1980
**	1986, 1982, 1975, 1970, 1969, 1968
*	1987, 1978, 1976, 1967
* −	1973
0	1972
?	1989, 1984, 1966

1990 [****]

From January through mid-March temperatures were higher than normal. This was followed by cool, rainy weather. Between March 25 and the end of April there were 6.8 inches (172 millimeters) of rain. There was rain in June, followed by a dry July, August, and September. Overall the growing season was warm and dry. The hillsides, unusually, experienced higher temperatures than the lowlands. Harvest began at the end of September in the lowlands and in early October in the hills.

The grapes had high levels of sugar (16.5 to 18.5 percent for the Recioto wines), high concentration of extract, and were uniformly mature. It has been reported that 70 to 80 percent of the hillside grapes were put up to dry for Recioto wines. Production, reportedly, was 10 to 15 percent below that of 1989. The crop size was affected by the hail of the previous year, it having damaged the buds, decreasing fertility. Lower than normal temperatures and rain during the bloom also took their toll on the harvest size.

Early reports compared it to 1962 and 1971. A vintage report issued by Masi Agricola said that "Guido and Battista Boscaini who have experienced at least 70 harvests compare it to the legendary vintages of 1964, 1948 and 1937." High praise indeed.

Thus far, through April 1990, we have tasted a handful of Valpolicellas and Reciotos. The wines have uniformly been impressive. Some still had remaining sugar and consequently were difficult to judge. We do, at this stage, agree with the early enthusiasm for the vintage. The wines that we tasted had great levels of extract and concentration. Indeed the Allegrini and Masi Valpolicellas have been the most impressive that we can recall tasting at a similar stage. And the barrel sample that we tried of a new Masi wine, tentatively called Rosso della Colline Veronese, was extremely impressive.

1 9 8 9 ?

From January to March the weather was mild. This warm, dry weather caused budding to occur ten to fifteen days early. Cold, rainy weather slowed down the vegetation cycle. April was very wet, with eighteen consecutive days of rain. The summer was cold, damp, and wet, with July setting a new record of 10.6 inches (266 millimeters) or rainfall. The high humidity resulted in some peronospora, downy mildew and rot in the corvinone variety. The hillside vineyards were not affected as much. Three major hailstorms struck the area in June and July and took their toll. The storm of June 23 struck the vineyards and damaged 15 to 90 percent of the Veronese vineyards it hit. The storm of July 25 hit the Valpolicella vineyards and its damage varied from 10 to 20 percent. The strong hailstorm of July 31 caused heavy localized damage. The weather, at the end of October, took a decided turn for the better, rewarding those who hung on.

Quantity was below average. And, in general, the quality was not too good. Bola produced 35 percent less Amarone than normal. The Recioto production of 205,653 gallons (7,784 hectoliters), equivalent to 86,475 cases, was considerably below the average between 1972 and 1989 of 350,673 gallons (13,273 hectoliters), or 147,458 cases, and in fact was only 58.6 percent of an average-size Recioto crop. It was the smallest quantity of those wines produced in the period from 1972 through 1989.

Bertani produced one-tenth of their normal quantity of *ripasso* Valpantena-Valpolicella, 20,000 bottles instead of 200,000. Gaetano Bertani told us that you had to select very carefully, the grapes picked bunch by bunch.

Based on the three that we've tasted thus far, we will defer judgment. There is just no way to be able to evaluate wines that haven't finished fermenting and that still contain residual sugar.

> **CAUTION:** *Before reading these tasting notes on the wines that we tasted from barrel, please read "On Tasting Wines from Barrel: A Caveat" on page xxv.*

Bolla (*ex-barrel, 5/90*). Light for the genre, some fruit, difficult to be sure. ?

La Bionda (*ex-barrel, 4/90*). Sugary, seems to have nice fruit; difficult to judge. ?

San Rustico (*ex-barrel, 4/90*). Opaque purple; rich grapey aroma, cherry, berry components; rich and sweet, still some sugar; difficult to be sure, but it does show some promise. ?

1 9 8 8 [* * * *]

Production of Recioto wines, including Amarone, at 394,768 gallons (14,942 hectoliters), the equivalent of 166,006 cases, was 12.6 percent above the average between 1972 and 1989.

Thus far, based on the seven wines we've tasted, this is an impressive vintage. Sandro Boscaini rates it four stars out of four. The Allegrini Fieramonte, and Masi Campolongo di Torbe, Mazzano, and Serègo Alighieri Vaio Armaron all displayed great quality.

> **CAUTION:** *Before reading these tasting notes on the wines that we tasted from barrel, please read "On Tasting Wines from Barrel: A Caveat" on page xxv.*

Allegrini (*ex-barrel, 4/90*). Unfinished but the enormous richness and concentration, weight and extract suggest a wine of real quality; real promise here. (***)

Allegrini, Fieramonte (*ex-barrel, 4/90*). At this stage the oak dominates, but with evident richness and intensity of fruit, similar to the above yet with more of everything. (****)

Boscaini, Classico, Vigneti di Marano (*ex-barrel, 4/90*). Great richness of fruit on the nose; a lot of extract; class evident. ***

Masi, Campolongo di Torbe (*ex-barrel, 4/90*). A little grapey, rich in extract and flavor; real class; should make a splendid bottle. (****−)

Masi, Classico (*twice, ex-barrel, 2/91*). Openly grapey aroma; tight, firm, rich, and concentrated; very young; evident quality. **(*)

Masi, Mazzano (*ex-barrel, 4/90*). Great richness and extract, a lot of weight and class, already displays complexity and layers of flavor, it seems too good to spit; the finest Amarone we've tasted from barrel. The line forms after us. ****(+)

Masi, Serègo Alighieri, Vaio Armaron (*twice, ex-barrel, 4/90*). Up-front grapey aroma with a dried fruit component; sweet and rich with a mouthful of wonderful fruit flavors. (****)

1987 [*]

Growth was slow, the result of a late summer. The weather improved in July as the heat moved in from the south. Crop size was down from the previous year. Masi didn't produce an Amarone. Recioto production, including Amarone, was 73 percent of the 1972–89 average, with 257,331 gallons (9,740 hectoliters), equivalent to 108,211 cases, compared to 350,673 gallons (13,273 hectoliters), or 147,458 cases. It was the second smallest Recioto crop of the decade; only 1989 produced less.

Guerrieri-Rizzardi, Classico (*7/90*). Dried fruit and almond aroma; very light, has flavor, lacks richness and definition, has fruit, moderate length.

Le Ragose (*bottled for Enoteca de Rham, 4/90*). Floral, nutty, spicy aroma and flavor, soft, open and fruity; ready now. *+

Zardini F.lli, Località Pezza-Marano (*4/90*). Alcohol on the nose, some fruit; nice entry, then shallow and lacking flavor mid-palate.

1986 **

Production of Recioto wine, including Amarone, of 340,554 gallons (12,890 hectoliters), equivalent to 143,208 cases, was nearly equal to the 1972–89 average.

Of the 12 wines we tasted, we really liked both of the Allegrinis and Masi's two crus. Sandro Boscaini of Masi rates the vintage three stars out of four.

> **CAUTION:** *Before reading these tasting notes on the wines that we tasted from barrel, please read "On Tasting Wines from Barrel: A Caveat" on page xxv.*

Allegrini (*ex-barrel, 4/90*). A little tight and closed on the nose, yet with lovely fruit evident; dried fruit flavors, suggestion of cher-ries, some tannin, a little firm and dry, especially at the end. **(+)

Allegrini, Fieramonte (*ex-barrel, 4/91*). Fragrant, scented aroma; sense of sweetness; real elegance and style; long finish. ***

Bertani (*ex-barrel, 11/90*). Big, rich and concentrated, with a sense of sweetness from the fruit and glycerine; evident promise though a little difficult to fully assess *(*?)

Boscaini, Classico, Vigneti di Marano (*ex-barrel, 4/90*). Seems a little too precocious, could use more backbone, flavorful with attractive fruit. **

Guerrieri-Rizzardi, Classico (*7/90*). Almond and floral aroma, notes of chocolate and spice; a lightweight Amarone, but attractive fruit; ready. *+

Masi, Campolongo di Torbe (*ex-barrel, 4/90*). Toasty, leathery, fruity aroma; somewhat unsettled, good fruit. **

Masi, Classico (*twice, 10/90*). Berry, floral nose, vaguely nutlike; good fruit, light tannin, room to improve, with the characteristic touch of bitterness at the end. **

Masi, Mazzano (*ex-barrel, 4/90*). Odd tobacco, cigarlike and peanut skin aroma(!); rich and flavorful with some sweetness, good extract, light finish. **+

Masi, Serègo Alighieri, Vaio Armaron (*twice, ex-barrel, 4/90*). Chocolate and dried fruit aroma; sweet entry, soft, openly fruity, gentle nature. **+

Nicolas Angelo (*ex-barrel, 4/90*). Tobacco, smoky, barnyardy aroma; much nicer in the mouth though with the same flavor components as on the nose. *−

San Rustico, Classico (*4/90*). Dried fruit aroma; rich, almost sweet, some tannin, seems a little disjointed, moderate length, chocolate nuance. *(+)

Vantini Lorenzo, Classico (*4/90*). Dried fruit character; some sweetness, nice fruit on entry, somewhat shallow, dry, short aftertaste, with some alcohol apparent.

1985 **** −

Production of Recioto wines, including Amarone, of 561,293 gallons (21,245 hectoliters), equivalent to 234,265 cases, was nearly 60 percent above the 1972–89 average. It was, by far, the largest quantity of these wines produced according to our records, which date back to 1972.

Thus far, we've tasted nearly a dozen and a half wines, more than half from barrel. They were an impressive group indeed. Once again the Allegrini Fieramonte, and Masi Campolongo di Torbe, Mazzano, and Serègo Alighieri were superb. Sandro Boscaini of Masi rates it three stars out of four!

> **CAUTION:** *Before reading these tasting notes on the wines that we tasted from barrel, please read "On Tasting Wines from Barrel: A Caveat" on page xxv.*

Allegrini (3 times, ex-barrel, 4/90). Cherry, black pepper and spice aroma; enormous richness and extract, the ripeness of the fruit gives a sweet impression, great concentration, lots of structure. ***

Allegrini, Fieramonte (3 times, ex-barrel, 4/90). Tight nose, oak evident; real richness and concentration, great weight and extract, with enormous intensity of fruit, this will make a splendid bottle in time. ***(+)

Bertani (ex-cask, 11/90). Characteristic dried fruit aroma; great richness and concentration, a lot of extract; needs age, as it should, will be a keeper. **(*)

Bolla (ex-cask, 6/86). Deep color, not completely clear; fresh, grapey aroma, light almond, floral nuance; slight spritz, some sugar remains, rich in body and fruit. (**)

Boscaini, Classico, Vigneti di Marano (twice, ex-barrel, 4/90). Tobacco, barnyardy aroma, with a nice fruit component; gentle yet rich with nice mouth feel and rich fruit flavors, very long, dryish finish. *** −

Brigaldara, Il Pianeto (4/90). Rich and intense on the nose and palate, berry and cherry notes; young. **(+)

Dalforno Romano (9/90). Leather, dried fruit, almonds and flowers define the aroma; sweet impression, supple, soft and open. **

Farina Remo, Classico (10/90). Floral and dried fruit aroma has an old oak component; lots of flavor, of dried fruit and leather; seems older than its age. *

Guerrieri-Rizzardi, Classico (twice, 7/90). Dried fruit aroma, nuances of tar, leather and flowers; flavorful, a lightweight, soft-styled, simple Amarone, could use more concentration and weight. * +

La Bionda, Classico, Vigneti di Valgatara (twice, 4/90). Scented bouquet; sweet, rich, open, soft; some tannin toward the finish suggests it needs some age. ** +

Le Salette, Classico (twice, 9/90). Aroma of dried fruit, figs and nuts; a medium-weight Amarone, quite flavorful, some tannin, soft, light finish. *

Masi, Campolongo di Torbe (10/90, 10,800 bottles). Enormous richness on the nose, with components suggestive of flowers, dried fruit and spice; great flavor intensity and sweetness, very long; loads of class and style, just might be the most impressive Campolongo di Torbe to date. ***+ (****)

Masi, Classico (3 times, 11/90). Open berry, nutty and floral aroma, spicelike nuance; fruit is sweet and ripe, precocious, good body, long finish; quite ready. *** −

Masi, Mazzano (twice, ex-barrel, 4/90). Leather, dried fruit aroma; rich and concentrated, great extract and weight, harmonious and classy; this one will be a keeper. *** +

Masi, Serègo Alighieri, Vaio Armaron (twice, ex-barrel, 4/90). Somewhat restrained nose; sweet, rich and gentle, loads of flavor, well balanced, long; attractive and inviting. ***(+)

Nicolas Angelo, Classico Superiore (4/90). Barnyardy aroma, dried fruit nuance; some fruit on entry, then shallow, short, dry aftertaste.

Righetti Luigi, Capitel de'Roari (3 times, 6/90). Lovely bouquet of flowers, packed with fruit; rich, and ripe, sweet impression, soft, lots of character, well balanced. ***

San Rustico, Classico, Vigneti del Gasso (4/90). Floral, dried fruit, berry aroma; sweet and rich yet with a lightness, chocolate nuance, some tannin; good quality; long and lingering finish recalls berries and chocolate. ***

Santi, Bottle Regina (11/90). Dried fruit and nut aroma, floral notes; fairly soft, open and tasty; ready. ** −

Sartori, Classico Superiore (11/90). Dried fruit aroma, figlike note; open, fruity style; ready now. * +

Zenato, Classico (twice, 10/90). Characteristic dried fruit and almond aroma; sweet impression, soft, easy style, good fruit concentration, could use more weight, a little short. * +

Zeni, Classico Superiore (6/90). Slight nose; dry, chocolate and dried fruit components, short. * −

1 9 8 4   ?

In this difficult vintage, production was about half of normal. Acid levels were very high. It was, surprisingly, a large crop of Recioto wines, with the production of 480,421 gallons (18,184 hectoliters), equivalent to 202,024 cases, being 37 percent above the 1972–89 average of 350,673 gallons (13,273 hectoliters), or 147,458 cases. Guerrieri-Rizzardi lists this as one of the better vintages. We've tasted only three; only one was good, the Bertani from cask. Masi didn't produce an Amarone.

Aldegheri (12/90). Fruit evident as well as an off-putting character; unbalanced, high acidity, some fruit, chocolate note, very dry finish.

Bertani (ex-botte, 11/90). Scented, fragrant and rich aroma, mintlike nuance; rich flavor, good concentration, moderate tannin. **(+)

Pasqua F.lli, Vigneti Casterna (5/90). Some fruit evident; overall light and soft, open and simple, no depth at all.

1 9 8 3   * * * *

The Recioto crop of 508,162 gallons (19,234 hectoliters), equivalent to 213,690 cases, was almost 45 percent larger than the average between 1972 and 1989. Since 1972 only two vintages—1985 and 1982—saw a larger production of Recioto wines.

Sandro Boscaini of Masi said that 1983 was a great vintage, rating it four stars out of four. Lamberti considers it the best since 1969. For Tedeschi, it was one of the very best, topflight. Bolla and Speri said it was a good year. Based on the more than two dozen Amarones we've tasted, we concur. Only 1988 challenges 1983 for the best of the decade. The best wines of those we tasted: Allegrini Classico Superiore and Fieramonte, Le Ragose, and Masi Campolongo di Torbe, Mazzano, and Serègo Alighieri.

Allegrini, Classico Superiore (*4 times, 4/90*). Dried fruit and nuts define the bouquet; well balanced, sweet impression from ripe fruit, rich, finish is a little dry; still room to improve. **(*−) *Another bottle, tasted a few days earlier:* More complex and impressive; its nose recalled berries and flowers as well as dried fruit and nuts; besides the concentration and extract, this wine had class. ***+

Allegrini, Fieramonte (*6 times, 4/90*). Tight nose yet with an evident intensity and richness, and suggestions of flowers and dried fruit, oak and ripe fruit; the fruit is so ripe and concentrated, cherry notes, superb balance; elegance and length; this is sheer class. ****

Bola (*4 times, 11/90*). Open fruit aroma, light touch of dried fruit and flowers, earthy and nutlike nuances; soft and, for the genre, rather light-bodied, hard finish; very ready, simple but good. *

Boscaini, Classico, Vigneti di Marano (*3 times, 10/90*). Lovely nose suggestive of flowers, almonds and dried fruit; a rich mouthful of fruit, sweet impression; though on the young side, a lot to offer now. *** *Bottle of 4/90:* Barnyardy, tobacco, chocolate aroma, slightly metallic; a real disappointment, light tannin, some flavor, must have been an off bottle. * + *Bottle of 4/89:* Fragrant scent; ripe, packed with fruit, lots of structure and flavor; still young. ***(+)

Brigaldara, Classico (*twice, 4/90*). Light, cherrylike aroma; soft, open and round, some tannin. **

Ca' Merla, Classico (*4/89*). Open and kind of simple, hints of sweetness. +

Conati Marco, Classico (*4/90*). Dried fruit, figs and leather aroma; some tannin and firmness, sense of fruit but lacking flavor on the midpalate, finishes with tannin, short finish with a sense of sweetness. * −

Dalforno Romano (*twice, 12/88*). Rich nose recalls dried fruit and flowers, figs and raisins; sweet impression, well made and well balanced, dry finish. ***

Fabiano (*4 times, 11/90*). Nothing to it; some fruit on the nose and initial entry, lacks concentration and intensity; simple and drinkable though dull.

Guerrieri-Rizzardi, Classico (*7/90*). Leather and dried fruit aroma, berry notes; small-scale, overly dry and shallow; starting to dry out.

La Colombaia (*10/90*). Aroma suggestive of peanuts(!); soft and simple, quite drinkable, not much more. +

La Colombaia, Alto Marano, Barrique (*twice, 10/90, 750 cases*). Mintlike note on the nose; soft, simple and drinkable, lacks weight and concentration, short, dry finish. +

La Crocetta, Classico (*4/88*). Dried fruit, nuts, almonds, figs and prunes; moderate tannin, good fruit, some firmness. *

Le Ragose (*4/90*). Great richness and extract on the nose and palate, complex, floral, nutty components, liquid velvet; enormous depth and length. *** +

Le Salette, Classico (*9/90*). Characteristic aroma; sweet sense of fruit, rich and flavorful under moderate tannin, tasty, a tad short. ** +

Masi, Campolongo di Torbe (*4/89*). Complex bouquet, dried fruit and flowers; sweet, soft, round and rich, great concentration, very long *** +

Masi, Classico (*twice, 4/90*). Dried fruit aroma; rich, and ripe with a sweet impression, loads of character, velvety, dried berry and floral components, could use more length. *** −

Masi, Mazzano (*4/89, 9,600 bottles*). Rather tight nose; in the mouth sweet, open and full, round and packed with flavor; still young but with loads of flavor; this is real quality. ***(+)

Masi, Serègo Alighieri, Vaio Armaron (*4/89*). Ripe fruit, berries and nuts on the nose; real sweetness from ripe fruit, dry, rich and flavorful; young but class quite evident; a classic Amarone. ***(+)

Quintarelli Giuseppe, Classico Superiore, Ca' Paletta beige label (*4/90*). Exotic nose, though somewhat stinky, still it is attractive; lots of tannin with a lot of richness and extract, still firm and tight. **

Righetti Luigi, Capitel de'Roari (*twice, 10/90, 12,500 bottles*). Light nose of ripe and dried fruit; a little light, nice flavor, fairly long with some tannin at the end; either starting to dry out or the bottle is off, if it's not the bottle drink up. ** − *Bottle of 12/87:* Almond, dried fruit aroma; elegant and stylish, real class and delicacy; its only flaw is that it lacks the punch and intensity for its type. ***

Sartori, Classico Superiore (*5/89*). A small-scale Amarone; light and soft.

Tedeschi (*5 times, 5/89*). Big and rich with a concentrated dried fruit character, some sweetness. **

Tedeschi, Linea Fabriseria (*4/87*). A big, rich concentrated wine with firmness and sweetness; still quite young. **(*)

Tedeschi, Vigneto Monte Olmi (*twice, 4/89*). Fragrant, berry, vanilla aroma, floral overtone; tasty with vanilla and berry flavors. ** +

1982 **

The Recioto crop, including Amarone, of 510,461 gallons (19,321 hectoliters), equivalent to 214,656 cases, was slightly above that produced in 1983, and almost 46 percent larger than the 1972–89 average of 147,458 cases. And since 1972 only 1985 saw a larger production of these wines.

Evidently 1982 was a variable vintage, judging from the producers' comments. For Lamberti, it was a medium vintage. Masi noted there was a lot of rain, fog, and humidity after the regular harvest for Valpolicella, and the grapes left to dry were lost due to mold. Bolla said the dryness and heat caused the grapes to mature perfectly. For them the vintage was exceptional, on the same level as 1979, five stars out of five. Bolla rates it as one of the best vintages. Speri found it a good year. Tedeschi ranks it among the worst. Masi didn't produce any Amarone. The Le Ragose is excellent and the Allegrini very good.

Allegrini (*twice, 12/90*). Spice, black pepper, flowers and berries define the bouquet; soft under light tannin, fairly rich, lots of flavor; very ready, tannin fully resolved in the wine. ** +

Bolla (*3 times, 5/90*). Dried fruit and leather; lightweight, some fruit, simple; seems a little tired, drink up. * −

Cesari, Classico Superiore (*7/89*). Totally unimpressive; some fruit, a tad bitter as is characteristic.

Corta Vecchia, Classico (*9/90*). Openly fruited aroma, recalls ripe berry and vanilla; lightweight and simple.

Due Torri (*twice, 12/90*). Simple nose, dried fruit and raisin notes; soft, easy and simple, light tannin, good fruit, characteristic bitter end. * +

Lamberti, Corte Rubini (*5/90, 32,400 bottles*). Dried fruit and leather; high alcohol, unbalanced; lacks class or style.

Le Ragose (*twice, 4/89*). Floral and fruit aroma, berry note; sweet and rich, balanced, a lot of class, vague chocolate nuance. ***

Murari (*4/88*). Dried fruit and cherry aroma, leathery and almond nuances; lightish for the genre, fairly well balanced. *

Santa Sofia, Classico Superiore (*twice, 9/90*). Vaguely vegetal and peanut skin aroma(!); soft under light tannin, could use more weight and character, characteristic bitter end. *

Zeni F.lli, Classico Superiore (*4/88*). Fairly nice nose; soft and round, flavorful, balanced, smooth. **

1 9 8 1 *** −

The 335,693 gallons (12,706 hectoliters), equivalent to 141,164 cases, of Recioto wines produced were just over 4 percent below the average produced between 1972 and 1989.

Lamberti described 1981 as a medium vintage. Tedeschi and Masi both consider it very good, and Bolla said it was good. Masi declassified its Serègo Alighieri Vaio Armaron cru because of hail damage. They gave the year two stars out of four. Allegrini made an excellent pair, the Classico Superiore and Fieramonte, and the Tedeschi Vigneto Monte Olmi was first rate as well.

Aldegheri "Santambrogio" (*12/90*). Dried fruit and almond aroma, vaguely spicy; still has a lot of flavor, characteristic bitterness; shows age, best to drink. * −

Allegrini, Classico Superiore (*3 times, 4/89*). Sweet and rich with ripe fruit aromas and flavor; floral component on the nose; intense and concentrated; very good indeed. ***

Allegrini, Classico Superiore, Fieramonte (*4 times, 4/90*). Intense bouquet, dried fruit and ripe fruit components combine; rich, openly fruity, well balanced, long; has softened considerably since the previous time tasted two years ago, ready now with room to grow. ***

Bertani (*ex-botte, 11/90*). Dried fruit and woodslike aroma; sense of sweetness, rich, moderate tannin, loads of flavor, a tad dry at the end. **(* −)

Boscaini, Classico, Vigneti di Marano (*twice, 4/90*). Barnyard and tobacco aroma; rather similar to the '83 and '85; nice mouth feel, finish is a tad short with a light chocolate note. ** −

Fabiano (*12/88*). Coarse and pedestrian, dry.

Masi, Campolongo di Torbe (*twice, 5/87, 6,200 bottles*). Minty and floral notes; sweet and smooth, round and tasty; good quality. ** +

Masi, Classico (*3 times, 10/90*). Slight nose; a little dry, does have some fruit but seems best to drink up, the fruit could be drying out. * *Bottle of 4/89:* Fragrant, floral aroma; full-flavored, dry and tasty. * *Bottle of 2/88:* Floral, nutty aroma, chocolate nuance; rich in flavor, good structure. *** −

Masi, Mazzano (*twice, 4/89, 8,600 bottles*). Rich, ripe fruit and floral aroma, almonds, berries and figs; full-flavored and dry, round, sweet and full, fairly tannic; a big wine with power and authority. ** +

Montresor (*5/86*). Dried fruit aroma, raisin and berry nuances; on the light side with nice flavors; lacks some character. * −

Tedeschi (*5 times, 11/88*). Almond or other nuts, vaguely of berries and flowers; ripe fruit flavor, soft center, good concentration, characteristic bitter finish. ** +

Tedeschi, Vigneto Monte Olmi (*3 times, 4/88*). Dried fruit, flowers and nuts on the nose; rich and concentrated, chewy, good structure; still young. ***

1 9 8 0 *** −

The 421,320 gallons (15,947 hectoliters), equivalent to 177,171 cases, of Recioto wines produced in 1980 were 20 percent more than the 1972–89 average.

Lamberti rates 1980 very good. Bolla and Speri call it

good. Even those from the better producers are ready. Sandro Boscaini of Masi gave it two out of four stars. Allegrini's Fieramonte and Masi's Vaio Amaron are lovely.

Allegrini, Classico Superiore (4 times, 9/88). Rich nose; flavorful, well structured, some length; stylish, with class. *** −

Allegrini, Classico Superiore, Fieramonte (3 times, 4/89). Intense dried fruit and floral bouquet, tobacco and smoky component; velvet, a lot of structure and class. ***

Bertani (11/90). Lovely nose, rich with nuances that recall flowers and dried fruit, leather note; rich and concentrated, fairly long. ** +

Bolla, Classico (4 times, 2/87). Dried fruit aroma and flavor, full-bodied, ripe fruit with a sweetness to it, very ready, short; lacks the overall impact and power of the genre. * +

Boscaini, Classico, Vigneti di Marano (twice, 10/90). Slight nose, vaguely corked; there is evident fruit and quality; some alcohol at the end. *?

Fabiano, Classico (12/86). Light nose; lightweight, lacks intensity and concentration. +

Le Ragose (4 times, 4/87). Moderately intense aroma, some spice; soft, nice flavor, on the light side, a bit short; some style. ** *Bottle of 4/85:* Characteristic dried fruit on aroma and flavor, full-bodied, richly flavored, intense and concentrated, long finish with the typical bitter note; still has more to give. ***

Masi, Campolongo di Torbe (3 times, 4/87, 6,200 bottles). Dried fruit and floral aroma with notes of leather; rich and concentrated, ready, good backbone, a tad bitter. *** −

Masi, Mazzano (twice, 4/89, 7,500 bottles). Rich and sweet nose and palate, vague trace of oxidation, chocolate, cherry notes, flavorful; drink now. *** −

Masi, Serègo Alighieri, Vaio Armaron (4 times, 4/89). Aroma displays components of figs and raisins, plums and prunes; same style as the '79, even more gentle and elegant; still some tannin. ***

Santi (4/87). Small-scale, light body, lacks weight and definition.

Villa Girardi, Classico (11/86). Dried fruit aroma; fruity and dried fruit flavor, lacks richness and intensity.

Villa Spada, Classico (4/88). Good fruit, soft, lighter style, overly simple but drinkable enough. *

1979 ***

The harvest yielded 480,210 gallons (18,176 hectoliters), equivalent to 201,935 cases, of Recioto wines; this was more than one-third again as much as the 1972–89 average.

Sandro Boscaini of Masi ranks 1979 as excellent, three stars out of four. Tedeschi is pretty much in accord and so too is Guerrieri-Rizzardi. Bolla said it was one of the best years. Many fine wines were produced that can be enjoyed now, though there is no need to rush to drink them. The Allegrini Fieramonte and Masi Mazzano are sure to please Amarone lovers; both are very fine wines. And the Bertani is a standout that, while lovely now, has a lot of room to grow.

Allegrini, Classico (4 times, 4/85). Intense aroma with suggestions of figs and dried fruit; full of flavor, good weight, bitter almonds on finish. *** −

Allegrini, Classico, Vigna Fieramonte (7 times, 4/88, 10,600 bottles). Rich, intense bouquet of berries and flowers, with nuances of figs, raisins and nuts; velvety, the flavor of sweet, rich fruit, almost lush; as impressive as it is now, it should improve. **** −

Bertani, Classico Superiore (4 times, 11/90). Lovely, rich and intense bouquet, recalls berries, flowers, dried fruit and nuts; great richness and concentration, loads of weight and flavor, a lot of length, lovely now with an attractive richness and the backbone to last; real class. *** +

Boscaini, Classico, Vigneti di Marano (twice, 4/89). Spice, tobacco and berries define the bouquet; rich, round and concentrated with a lush quality to the fruit, long. *** −

Guerrieri-Rizzardi, Classico (12/83). Aroma of almonds and raisins; dry, some firmness, light tannin, nice flavor, some alcohol intrudes. * −

La Colombaia (3 times, 9/86). Lacks concentration, intensity, weight and character.

Lamberti (twice, 4/87). Small-scale and lightweight, lacks richness and weight, short.

Le Ragose (twice, 7/85). Dried fruit on aroma; still firm and with tannin to shed, seems to have the fruit to carry it; a nice but disappointing bottle, from a generally very fine producer. ** −

Masi, Campolongo di Torbe (5/87, 6,300 bottles). Light nose with a floral overtone; lovely open fruit flavor, round and smooth. ***

Masi, Classico (twice, 5/87). Aroma recalls cough drops and flowers, mintlike note; loads of flavor, very soft and smooth. *** −

Masi, Mazzano (twice, 4/87, 7,200 bottles). Nose is a bit light, suggestions of berries; a lot of structure, rich and flavorful, with a lot of concentration; should still improve, very attractive now; very long; real class and style. ***(*)

Masi, Serègo Alighieri, Vaio Armaron (4 times, 4/89). Wonderful floral and dried fruit bouquet, nuances of plums and figs; sweet, gentle style with good backbone and structure. ***

Montresor (7/85). Flavorful but no real character or style.

Santa Sofia, Classico Superiore (7/85). Dried fruit character, overall fruity.

Sartori, Classico Superiore (7/85). Off-putting, stinky nose; lacks weight and richness; drinkable.

Speri, Classico Superiore (10/86). Has the body but lacks the depth and structure, harsh, alcoholic and unbalanced.

Tedeschi (4/89). Nicely fruited aroma that carries through in the mouth, flavorful, soft center; ready. **

Tedeschi, Capitel Monte Olmi (4/85). Aroma of figs and raisins, still somewhat reticent; light tannin, gives an impression of sweetness, very long; room for improvement yet. ***

1978 *

The 238,123 gallons (9,013 hectoliters), equivalent to 100,134 cases, of Recioto wines produced were slightly more than two-thirds of the average number of cases produced between 1972 and 1989. Only 1989, 1975, and 1972 produced less Recioto.

Lamberti didn't produce an Amarone in 1978. Sandro Boscaini of Masi considered it a good vintage, giving it two out of four stars. For Speri it was good. All are ready now, though the better ones should last. Masi Classico and Tedeschi Capitel Monte Olmi are very good.

Guerrieri-Rizzardi, Classico (7/90). A lot of age shows on the nose, classic almond and floral aroma; lightweight, soft and tasty, very ready, short. * −

Masi, Classico (4/85). Lovely aroma of almonds and dried fruit; full-flavored, peppery, still has tannin to shed; the richness makes it enjoyable now, but it will improve. ***

Scamperle, Classico (twice, 7/85). Pruney, overripe aroma; straightforward fruitiness, some spice. *

Speri F.lli (1/85). Small-scale, a bit light, has a slight cooked quality to it, and hints of sugar.

Tedeschi, Capitel Monte Olmi (1/88). Characteristic dried fruit aroma, nuts and floral tones; concentrated with rich, ripe fruit flavors, characteristic slightly bitter note at the end. ** +

Tre Rose (4/80). Raisins and dried fruit on aroma; alcoholic, tannic, insufficient fruit.

1977 ***

Production of Recioto wines, including Amarone, at 359,444 gallons (13,605 hectoliters), equivalent to 151,152 cases, was some 2.5 percent above the average produced between 1972 and 1989.

Sandro Boscaini of Masi found the vintage very good, giving it two stars out of four. For Tedeschi it was one of the best. Allegrini rates it tops. Guerrieri-Rizzardi also rates it highly. For the most part, these wines are quite drinkable now. We especially liked the Bertani Classico Superiore, Boscaini Cà de Loi, Luigi Righetti, and Tedeschi Capitel Monte Olmi.

Allegrini, Classico (4 times, 4/81). Aroma quite intense but still somewhat closed; still has tannin to shed, smooth-centered, a lot of glycerine; shows style. **(*)

Barberini (12/83). A cooked, overripe character, overly alcoholic, unbalanced.

Bertani, Classico Superiore (12/88). Dried fruit and almond aroma; rich and sweet, round and ripe, packed with fruit, long finish with characteristic bitterness. *** −

Bolla, Classico (twice, 12/83). Characteristic almondlike aroma; a mouthful of fruit, some tannin, astringent edges; less than expected from this usually good, reliable producer. *A bottle tasted 14 months earlier:* Better, but still below expectations.

Boscaini, Ca' de Loi (4/89). Fragrant scented bouquet, berrylike note along with a dried fruit component; richly concentrated, with a lot of flavor, finish lingers for some time. *** −

Boscaini, Classico, Vigneti di Marano (5 times, 10/90). Dried fruit and floral aroma, vaguely suggestive of peanut skins; lovely entry, soft, sweet impression, smooth, then the tannin which builds at the end; could be starting to dry out. ** + *Bottle of 4/90:* Alcohol intrudes on the nose, toasty, dried fruit notes carry through on the palate, some oxidation, still it does have some interest. Considering the other four bottles, we suspect that this one was an off bottle. * *Bottle of 4/89:* Floral bouquet; rich and concentrated, packed with fruit and extract, dried fruit component, very well balanced and very long. *** −

Guerrieri-Rizzardi, Classico (5 times, 7/90). Vegetal aroma, dried fruit component; faded. *Bottle of 7/85:* Rich and concentrated aroma; could use more weight. *

Le Ragose (twice, 5/83). Intense and rich, so rich it's almost sweet, loads of style. *** −

Masi, Campolongo di Torbe (4/85, 5,700 bottles). Floral aroma with a licorice note; soft-centered, well balanced, tasty, very long. ***

Masi, Classico (4 times, 5/87). Light, berry aroma, minty note; sweet impression, smooth, tasty, packed with flavor. **

Masi, Mazzano (12/83). Flowers on aroma and a hint of wheat; a mouthful of flavor, some astringency at the end; will improve yet. ** +

Pasqua, Classico (3 times, 7/85). Simple and fruity, uncharacteristic.

Righetti Luigi, Classico (9/90). Lovely bouquet of flowers, almonds and dried fruit; sweet, rich and concentrated, soft and round, characteristic bitterness. ***

Sartori, Classico Superiore (12/83). Almonds and flowers on aroma; lots of flavor, medium body, a bit short. * +

Tedeschi (4 times, 9/86). Deep, rich and concentrated, suggestions of almonds and dried fruit, along with a ripe fruit component; tannin at the end suggestive of a wine in decline, drink up. ** −

Tedeschi, Capitel Monte Olmi (*twice, 5/87*). Dried fruit and floral aroma; moderately intense in flavor, dry, some tannin evident, rich, dry and firm. ** +

Tommasi, Classico (*12/83*). Slight, almondlike aroma; balanced, flavorful; a nice bottle of wine. **

Villa Girardi, Classico Superiore (*4 times, 7/85*). A fruity wine that lacks the weight and concentration expected of an Amarone.

Zenato, Classico (*twice, 7/85*). Dried fruit and chocolatey notes, a bit lacking in character, drinkable. * −

Zeni, Classico Superiore (*4/80*). Aroma of dried fruit, figs and raisins; a lightweight but agreeable Amarone. *

1976 *

The spring was very dry, July and August experienced rainfall that was just above normal, and September and October were very wet compared to normal. The 240,871 gallons (9,117 hectoliters), equivalent to 101,290 cases, of Recioto wines produced were slightly more than two-thirds of the average of those wines produced between 1972 and 1989.

For Sandro Boscaini of Masi it was a topflight vintage; he rates it three stars out of four. Bertani didn't produce an Amarone. The '76s are ready to drink, though the best ones will last. Some are showing age. Masi's Mazzano is holding up very well; it is very good indeed.

Allegrini, Classico (*ex-cask, 10/78*). Rich and concentrated, quality quite evident. **

La Colombaia (*7/85*). A waste of time and effort.

Le Ragose (*4/80, 960 bottles*). Aroma is somewhat closed but suggests considerable fruit to come, some tannin, lots of flavor. **

Masi, Campolongo di Torbe (*3 times, 1/82, 3,800 bottles*). Almonds and flowers on aroma; a bit light but characteristic Amarone, typical bitter almond finish. **

Masi, Classico (*twice, 2/91*). Complex bouquet; loads of flavor and glycerine, dry finish; a lovely Amarone at its peak or just ever so slightly past it. ** +

Masi, Mazzano (*twice, 4/90, 5,950 bottles*). This is a big, rich, mouth-filling wine, with a deep and intense bouquet and enormous finish; while it wasn't quite as impressive as the bottle tasted in April 1985, it was still quite splendid. ***

Santa Sofia, Classico Superiore (*twice, 12/83*). Small nose; weak, even a bit thin, some flavor, harsh aftertaste.

Speri, Classico Superiore (*4 times, 7/85*). The bottles tasted in 1983 were clearly superior to the most recent tasted, which was totally uninteresting.

Tommasi, Classico (*4/80*). Dried fruit and raisins, moderate richness, some alcohol evident at the end. *

1975 **

The production of 233,976 gallons (8,856 hectoliters), equivalent to 98,390 cases, of Recioto wines was slightly less than two-thirds of the 1972–89 average. The Recioto crop was the third smallest in this same period, behind 1989 and 1972.

Sandro Boscaini of Masi said 1975 was a good year, rating it at two stars out of four. Bertani made one-tenth their normal production of Amarone, only 6,000 bottles. Tedeschi says it was among their worst vintages, and Guerrieri-Rizzardi agrees. There is no need to hold the '75s any longer. The Boscaini Cà de Loi is excellent.

Allegrini, Classico (*twice, 4/80*). Rich aroma of figs and dried grapes; a rich, full-bodied wine, well structured, robust. ** +

Boscaini, Ca' de Loi (*twice, 4/89*). Open, rich fruit bouquet; round and rich, smooth and tasty, balanced and long. ***

Farina (*4/80*). A lightweight, small-scale wine, shallow.

Lamberti (*11/81*). Tawny color; some oxidation; too old.

Masi, Campolongo di Torbe (*10/78*). Floral, perfumed bouquet, hints of figs and dried fruit; flavorful, seems almost sweet. **

Masi, Classico (*twice, 5/87*). Garnet toward the rim; smooth and soft, nice fruit, typical bitter note at the end. **

Masi, Mazzano (*3 times, 1/82, 3,900 bottles*). Characteristic almond note on the nose; a concentrated wine with loads of flavor, slightly hot at ending. ** −

Quintarelli, Classico, brown label (*11/81*). Nice nose, harsh and shallow on palate, volatile acidity painfully evident.

Quintarelli, Classico, green label (*twice, 3/83*). Rich and intense, full of flavor, almost sweet. ** + *Bottle of 11/81:* Overly drying, more to it than the brown label.

Tommasi, Classico (*3 times, 6/86*). Rich, dried fruit aroma and flavor, firm and dry, balanced and fruity, smooth-textured, long. ** +

Tramanal (*11/81*). Aroma of raisins, almonds and cherries; flavorful, a bit short. * +

1974 ***

Precipitation was about normal during the spring, and June, July, and August were very dry, while rainfall in September was above normal. October was somewhat dryer than normal. Production of Recioto wines, including Amarone, of 286,683 gallons (10,851 hectoliters), equivalent to 120,555 cases, was just about 82 percent of the average of 350,673 gallons (13,273 hectoliters), or 147,458 cases, produced between 1972 and 1989.

Bertani characterized the vintage as exceptional. Both Bolla and Tedeschi put it among the best. Speri rated it good. Sandro Boscaini of Masi rates it three stars out of four. Masi's Mazzano is a real knockout that will certainly improve, and their Campolongo di Torbe and Tedeschi's Capitel Monte Olmi are also very good. Nearly all the others are ready, though at least those from the best producers will certainly last.

Allegrini, Classico (*twice, 10/78*). Almondlike aroma; full-bodied and robust, loads of flavor, very long; a lot of quality here. ***

Bertani, Classico Superiore (*twice, 9/86*). Intense aroma, vaguely floral, some nuts; a lot of fruit, rich and concentrated, sweet impression, smooth and soft, rich and flavorful. ***

Bolla, Classico Superiore (*3 times, 7/85*). Rich and concentrated, dried fruit character; some tannin, characteristic bitterness. ** +

Boscaini, Classico, Vigneti di Marano (*6 times, 10/90*). Characteristic dried fruit and floral bouquet, some spice; warm and soft, smooth and flavorful, quite nice, with style, the finish is a tad dry, still the wine is quite attractive, at, or perhaps just past, its peak. ** + *Bottle of 4/90*: This bottle was, unfortunately, oxidized. *Bottle of 4/89*: Chocolate nuance, flavorful, balanced and round. ** +

Fabiano, Classico Superiore (*twice, 7/85*). Too old, but it didn't offer very much when last tasted in November 1981, either.

Lamberti (*7/85*). Overly simple, some oxidation, on the way down.

Le Ragose (*10/79*). Expansive, aromatic aroma; well balanced, flavorful, good quality. ***

Masi, Campolongo di Torbe (*twice, 5/87, 3,900 bottles*). Lovely bouquet though on the light side; loads of flavor, loads of quality, dry with a lot of glycerine, adds a sweet impression, packed with flavor and character, long, slightly bitter finish. ***

Masi, Classico (*4 times, 2/91*). Some age apparent on the nose: chocolate nuance combines with noticeable oxidation; still has fairly good fruit and a lot of interest, slightly dry finish; best to drink up. ** − *Bottle of 4/85*: Complex aroma recalls figs, raisins, prunes, vaguely floral; dry with an impression of sweetness, some tannin, velvety, long finish. ***

Masi, Mazzano (*4/85, 3,900 bottles*). Intense bouquet, dried fruit, vaguely floral; a big wine with loads of flavor and glycerine; still seems young, impressive quality now with a lot more to give. ***(*)

Montresor, Classico Superiore (*twice, 12/83*). Baked character, shallow, vegetal notes.

Quintarelli, Classico (*twice, 9/84*). Aroma of almonds and dried fruit; loads of flavor, full-bodied, but unbalanced, and alcoholic. * +

Righetti, Classico (*2/86*). Corked. The quality is evident.

Santa Sofia, Classico Superiore (*11/81*). Off notes, shallow, dull.

Sartori, Classico Superiore (*11/81*). Lush, open aroma, with fruit, almonds and raisins that carry over into the mouth; drying out. * −

Speri, Classico Superiore (*twice, 2/82*). Characteristic dried fruit and almonds on aroma; smooth, flavorful, has style, typical note of bitterness at the end. ** +

Tedeschi (*12/83*). Raisins, almonds on aroma; fairly well balanced, characteristic Amarone, good, could be a bit longer on aftertaste. ** −

Tedeschi, Capitel Monte Olmi (*4 times, 1/88*). Rich bouquet, complex, leather, flowers and nuts, dried fruit and berries; chewy, still some tannin, but with great richness and flavor, lingering finish, characteristic bitterness. ***

Venturini (*10/78*). Big, rich, full and concentrated, a lot of quality here. ***

1 9 7 3   * −

The 252,232 gallons (9,547 hectoliters), equivalent to 106,067 cases, of Recioto wines produced were 72 percent of the 1972–89 average of those wines.

Bertani produced very little Amarone in 1973. Sandro Boscaini of Masi rated the vintage as good, giving it one star out of four. We advise drinking them if you have any left; many are fading or already have.

Anselmi (*2/81*). Color shows age; typical note of almonds on nose; a bit thin and drying out.

Bertani, Classico Superiore (*12/83*). Nice nose suggestive of almonds, dried fruit and raisins; flavorful, some tannin, could be longer on aftertaste. * +

Castagna (*10/78*). A lightweight little wine lacking in flavor, concentration and character.

Masi (*10/78*). Aroma of almonds and raisins; balanced, flavorful, somewhat light. ** −

Tedeschi (*12/83*). Caramel candy on aroma, and almondlike notes; dried character to the fruit; very short aftertaste. *

Tedeschi, Capitel Monte Olmi (*4/81*). Typical almond aroma; a lightweight Amarone, fairly nice flavor. *

Tommasi, Classico (*4 times, 7/85*). Fairly nice nose; good fruit in the mouth, thins out at the end; it was better two years ago. * −

1 9 7 2   0

There were 208,929 gallons (7,908 hectoliters), equivalent to 87,858 cases, of Recioto wines produced in 1972, compared to the average of 350,673 gallons (13,273 hecto-liters), or 147,458 cases, produced between 1972 and 1989. This was the second smallest crop of these wines; only 1989 yielded a smaller crop of Recioto.

Masi didn't bottle an Amarone in 1972, nor did Lamberti. Speri considers the vintage the worst and Tedeschi puts it among the worst. Allegrini said it was the worst vintage in memory. Guerrieri-Rizzardi lists this as a mediocre vintage. The only one we've tasted in recent years, the Bertani, indicates these Amarones should have been drunk up already.

Bertani, Classico Superiore (5/83). Has some flavor, but lacks the richness and weight for an Amarone. * −

1971 ***

Sandro Boscaini of Masi gives 1971 three out of four stars. Tedeschi puts it among the finest vintages. Lamberti said it was a very good year. Speri also rated it good. Some wines are beginning to show age. There's no reason to hold them any longer. The Allegrini and Bertani Amarones were splendid in the mid-1980s, and the Masi Mazzano showed the potential to continue to improve further. We also liked the Boscaini Marano and the Righetti.

Allegrini, Classico (6 times, 11/86). Dried fruit and chocolate aroma with flowers, nuts and vanilla; rich, intense and classy; real quality here. *** +

Bertani, Classico Superiore (6 times, 10/85). Concentrated aroma, vague floral component, chocolate and almond notes; a nice mouthful of wine with chocolate and fruit flavors, long, somewhat bitter finish; some style evident. *** +

Bolla (11/79). Lacks weight, flavor and definition; a big disappointment from a firm that usually makes a fairly good Amarone.

Boscaini, Classico, Vigneti di Marano (5/87). Light nose, recalls dried fruit and vaguely floral character; loads of character and flavor, delicate style, well balanced, hint of sweetness. *** −

Burati (2/80). Awful, from the aroma through the bitter end.

Longo (10/78). Characteristic, with dried fruit and almonds all across the wine, flavorful. **

Masi, Classico (5/87). Bouquet displays delicacy and a floral nuance; rich, silky, smooth and concentrated; real class here. ***

Masi, Mazzano (5/87, 3,900 bottles). Aromatic bouquet, seems a little closed; in the mouth great richness and extract, complete and first rate, more to give though certainly attractive now; this wine, although young, has everything going for it. ***(*)

Montresor (10/78). A lightweight wine lacking in flavor and structure.

Righetti (9/90). Oxidation apparent but so too is a chocolate nuance, along with dried fruit, soft and smooth, hint of sweetness, going but not gone. **

Santa Sofia, Classico Superiore (7/85). Stinky aroma; and no improvement on flavor.

Tedeschi (2/83). Richly intense aroma of raisins and almonds; falls down on palate, overly simple and one-dimensional. *

Tommasi, Classico (5 times, 12/83). Typical aroma of raisins and almonds; some tannin, moderate fruit, alcohol at the end; getting a bit old, it was better from 1978 through 1981. * −

1970 **

Sandro Boscaini of Masi considered 1970 a good vintage; he gave it one star out of four. Lamberti rated it very good. It's been years since we've tasted any, but we suspect that those from the better producers are still good.

Bertani, Classico Superiore (twice, 12/83). Dried fruit character, raisins and almonds; a nice mouthful of fruit, chocolatey and rich, fairly long. ** +

1969 **

Nearly all of the producers we spoke to or received replies from on our questionnaire rate this year at the very top, none better. Sandro Boscaini of Masi ranks it as a three-star vintage out of four stars. Bolla said it was one of the best vintages. Some '69s, if stored properly, could still make splendid drinking, but we don't advise holding them. The Boscaini Marano, and Masi Classico and Mazzano were all very good when last tasted.

Bertani, Classico Superiore (twice, 11/81). Almondlike aroma, shows signs of age (same for both bottles, tasted eight months apart); overly drying, though still has some flavor interest.

Bolla (10/82). Lovely, complex aroma from bottle age; intense, dry and firm, richly flavored, could have more length on aftertaste. **

Boscaini, Classico, Vigneti di Marano (twice, 12/87). Nuts and flowers define the bouquet; rich and concentrated, almost sweet, a big wine with a lot of character. *** −

Masi, Classico (4/85). Dried fruit aroma, vaguely floral; soft, almost velvety, full-bodied, tasty, long finish with chocolatey notes. ***

Masi, Mazzano (5/87, 4,100 bottles). Light, yet rich nose(!); still some tannin, rich, smooth and concentrated, fairly long finish, some tannin at the end. ** +

Righetti (9/90). Oxidized but still has flavor interest, very soft, no harshness. *

Santa Sofia, Classico Superiore (twice, 11/81). Bad.

Sartori (10/84). Some oxidation but some quality still evident. *

Tommasi, Classico (3 times, 12/83). Aroma of almonds and raisins; a mouthful of rich fruit, moderate tannin, some alcohol throws the balance off.

1968 **

Sandro Boscaini of Masi considered 1968 a very good vintage; he rates it two out of four stars. These wines are fully ready now. There is no need to hold them any longer.

Bertani, Classico Superiore (twice, 12/83). Slight nose; but a big, rich mouthful of wine, dried fruit character, some alcohol at the end. *

Masi (twice, 4/85). Floral, woodsy bouquet, with mushroomy notes; so smooth and velvety it almost seems sweet, tasty, a very long finish with a hint of chocolate. *** +

1967 *

Sandro Boscaini of Masi gives 1967 three stars out of four. Tedeschi and Guerrieri-Rizzardi consider it among the best; Speri rated it good. The wines are ready now or are fading; there's no reason to hold them any longer.

Bertani, Classico Superiore (twice, 4/81). Rich, raisiny aroma, overlaid with almonds; loads of flavor, quite nice, noticeable alcohol at the end, not to keep. ** –

Righetti (9/90). Brownish cast to the robe, shows a lot of age at the rim; besides the oxidation on the nose there are suggestions of nuts, flowers and dried fruit, with coffee and chocolate nuances; fading and old, but still has a sweet impression; a good glass in spite of being over the top. ** –

Tommasi, Classico (5 times, 12/83). Light nose with almond and vanilla notes; a flavorful wine with some tannin, typical bitterness on finish. * +

1966 ?

Bertani, for one, didn't produce an Amarone in 1966. Sandro Boscaini of Masi rates it two stars out of four.

OLDER VINTAGES

The following ratings apply to the vintages as they were originally evaluated. It is doubtful, of course, that they will reflect the status of the wines today. Our tasting experiences with these vintages are rather limited.

***	1958
*** –	1960
** +	1962
**	1964, 1963, 1959, 1952
** –	1961
0	1965

Guerrieri-Rizzardi also lists 1964, 1962, 1961, 1958, 1957, 1955, 1953, 1952, and 1946 as being very good, and 1965, 1963, 1960, 1954, and 1951 as being mediocre. Renzo Tedeschi rates 1964, 1960, 1959, 1958, and 1952 highly. Bolla rates 1952 as one of the best vintages of all, and 1958 and 1964 as good years. Bertani didn't produce a 1961 Amarone.

Bertani 1965 Classico Superiore (twice, 11/81). Some oxidation, but the richness and intensity of the bouquet shine through; a full-flavored wine with more tannin than we'd expect at this stage, doesn't seem to be drying out. * +

Bertaini 1964 Classico Superiore (6 times, 10/85). Lovely ripe fruit component combines with dried fruit and almonds, vaguely floral; great richness to the flavor, still some tannin and freshness, very long finish. *** +

Masi 1964 Campolongo di Torbe (5/87). Garnet, brick color; besides a touch of oxidation on the nose, there are suggestions of almonds and flowers, beginning to fade, has a sweetness of age; still has a lot of interest and character. ** +

Masi 1964 Classico (twice, 2/91). The older the wine, the greater the risk of bottle variation. Here are two notes tasted nearly four years apart. The earlier bottle was fading, while the more recent one was a lovely bottle indeed. Though the nose shows age, it is quite lovely and complex; lots of richness and concentration, round, very long; loads of quality and interest. *** + *Bottle of 5/87:* Fairly deep color; coffee notes, some oxidation, Amarone character still evident; even though flavor remains, the wine has a dullness; very short, still, some interest remains. *

Masi 1964 Classico, Serègo Alighieri, Vaio Armaron (4/87). Somewhat volatile, with evident fruit, fairly full-bodied, dry finish, difficult to really assess. ?

Tommasi 1964 Classico (3 times, 12/83). Aroma of fruit and almonds, wheatlike notes; round and tasty; very ready, has a lot of character; fairly long, with a touch of bitterness at the end. ** +

Bertani 1963 Classico Superiore (4 times, 4/84). Beautiful robe, garnet with orange reflections; intense bouquet, characteristic; robust and flavorful, full and rich, smooth-textured, very long finish. ***

Bertani 1962 Classico Superiore (6 times, 9/87). Deep color; incredible concentration of fruit on the nose and palate, sweet impression; at its peak now, a complete wine of great quality, very long. **** – *Bottle of 12/82:* Aroma of almonds, dried fruit, figs, prunes, and green olives; a big, rich mouthful of wine, finish is rather short and overly drying, vaguely bitter. **

Masi 1962 Classico (5/87). Brick, amber and orange robe; coffee and oxidation apparent on the nose; much more attractive on the palate, soft and smooth, velvety, lovely flavors, moderately long finish. ** +

Masi 1961 Mazzano (4/87). Apparent oxidation, coffee and chocolate components; some character and flavor add interest; best to drink up. ** –

Bertani 1960 Classico Superiore (*twice, 6/86*). Beautiful robe; rich, intense and concentrated aroma, almond notes, intense, rich, concentrated flavors, packed with attractive fruit, long, and impressive indeed. *** +

Bertani 1959 Classico Superiore (*5 times, 10/85*). Shows a lot of age on the nose, nuances of nuts and flowers; round and smooth-textured, well balanced and long, some tannin at the end; best drunk up. The bottle tasted some months earlier was better. This one, *** – *Bottle of 5/85, in the U.S.A., from a private cellar:* Concentrated bouquet, vaguely floral; richly flavored, intense, dry but almost seems sweet, long, lingering finish. *** *Bottle of 4/85, at the winery:* Bouquet has a lot of complexity and mellowness from bottle age, berry notes; still a lot of tannin, not a lot of fruit left; shows signs of drying out; still some interest left. *

Bertani 1958 Classico Superiore (*4 times, 2/84*). (According to Bertani this wine was never released commercially.) Beautiful brick robe shading to orange; concentrated aroma, with dried fruit; gives an impression of sweetness, smooth-textured, richly flavored, a long, bitter finish. ***

Masi 1958 Campolongo di Torbe (5/87). *From tenth:* Superb bouquet, floral note; supple, sweet impression, loads of flavor and quality, very long finish. *** +

Masi 1958 Classico (2/91). Noticeable oxidation on the nose adds complexity at this stage; a real sense of sweetness though the wine is dry, lots of flavor; real quality. ***

Masi 1958 Classico, Vaio Armaron (4/87). *From tenth:* Lovely, fragrant bouquet suggestive of almonds, dried fruit and flowers, licorice note; rich, smooth, velvetlike; a complete and impressive glass of wine that's still fresh, not a trace of age. ****

Masi 1952 Classico, Vaio Amarone (4/87). Tawny color; chocolate, floral bouquet; smooth entry, sweet impression, nice palate, a bit rough at the edges. *** –

OTHER WINES OF SPECIAL NOTE

Serègo Alighieri 1948 Recioto (4/87). Pale tawny color; some oxidation, chocolate nuance; harsh and unbalanced, still some sugar, and flavor interest; an old wine, fading fast, very heavy sediment. ** –

Serègo Alighieri 1941 Recioto (4/87). Pale tawny robe; some oxidation; still has sweetness and a surprising amount of flavor; good quality and a lot of interest and character. ** +

Serègo Alighieri 1940 Recioto (2/91). Pale color with no indication of brown; bouquet of melon and flowers, banana note; rich yet so delicate yet sweet, very long finish; surprisingly fresh; real elegance and class. *** +

Longo 1911 Recioto (5/87). Its age was questionable, still it was interesting. Medium garnet color; dried fruit aroma; some sugar, nice texture, fruity; surprisingly fresh. ** +

THE PRODUCERS

Aldegheri, Cantine "Le Grolle" (*S. Ambrogio di Valpolicella*), *1958.* Vicenzo, Lorenzo, Fabio, and Adriano Aldegheri own this winery and 74 acres (30 hectares) of vines. Their two vineyards, both on the hills, are located in the Classico zone. Castello di S. Vito di Negrar is 42 acres (17 hectares) and Casterna di Fumane is 32 (13). Just over half of their annual 400,000-gallon (15,000-hectoliter) production, equivalent to 166,650 cases, is *vino da tavola;* the balance is the typical Veronese wines of Bardolino, Bianco di Custoza, Soave, and Valpolicella. They also make *spumante* and *frizzante* wines. They produce, as far as we know, two Amarones: a *normale* and "Santambrogio" Classico Superiore. We've tasted one of each, an '84 of the former and an '81 of the latter. The '84 was fair, no more; the '81 a little past its best but drinkable. Amarone: 0, "Santambrogio" *

Allegrini Azienda Agricola (*Fumane di Valpolicella*), *1886.* This very fine producer specializes in Valpolicella; they do not make Soave or Bardolino. Allegrini has 87 acres (35.24 hectares) of vines from which they produce some 310,000 bottles of fine wine a year. This includes 180,000 bottles of a very good Valpolicella (no Valpolicella is better, and few are its equal), 104,000 of a fine Amarone, 15,200 of Recioto, 5,500 of the single-vineyard Pelara, 2,000 of a still, dry white, and scant 2,900 of the very fine white Recioto Fiorgardane.

Allegrini is family-owned and -operated. Walter oversees the vineyards, Franco is the winemaker, and Marilisa is in charge of exports and administration. When Marilisa makes a marketing trip to the United States Allegrini's sales multiply. This outgoing and enthusiastic young woman could sell her wines on charm alone. But as her charm is based on a sincerity and integrity, she would not be able to do so if they were not excellent wines to begin with—which they are.

Allegrini's vines, planted on the hills at altitudes of 625 to 1,150 feet (190 to 350 meters) above sea level, are mostly in Fumane; all are in the Classico zone. The soil is calcareous. The vineyards are planted in approximately 70 percent corvina, the maximum allowed by law, 17 percent rondinella, 3 percent molinara, and 10 percent sangiovese—the basic composition of their regular Valpolicella and Amarone. The crus differ, and these wines vary according to the makeup of the individual vineyards. The Palazzo della Torre vineyard is planted 60 percent in corvina, 28 percent rondinella, and 12 percent molinara. The Amarone from their Fieramonte cru is 75 percent corvina, 20 percent rondinella, and 5 percent molinara. Allegrini's Gardane Recioto is made from the same combination of grapes.

Yields average 4.5 tons per acre (100 quintali per hectare) for corvina and molinara, 4 (90) for rondinella, 3 (70) for pelara, and 1.8 (40) for garganega. Palazzo della Torre produces, on average, 3.6 tons per acre (80 quintali per hectare), Fieramonte and Cà del Paver 3 (70), while Campogardane and Fiorgardane average only 1.8 (40). The harvest at Allegrini normally begins about the last

THE CRUS AND VINEYARDS OF ALLEGRINI

Cru/Vineyard	Comune	Acres	Hectares	Year(s) Planted	Used for	Cru Since	Cases
Carpanè	Fumane	0.98	0.30	1954	Valpolicella	—	283
Fieramonte	Fumane	8.20	2.50	1975	Amarone	1975	1,667
Gardane	Fumane and			1942	White	—	167
	Marano	9.19	2.80	1942	Valpolicella	—	350
Campogardane		4.59[a]	1.40[a]		Recioto	1969	242
Fiorgardane		4.59[a]	1.40[a]		Recioto, white	1971	100
Giara	Fumane	1.77	0.54	1970	Valpolicella	—	667
La Grola	Sant'Ambrogio	25.49	7.77	1980–84	Valpolicella	1983	4,055
					Amarone and	—	917
La Poja		8.69[b]	2.65[b]		La Poja	1983	358
Lena	Fumane	14.63	4.46	1978	Amarone,	—	1,833
					Recioto, and	—	667
					Valpolicella	1988	667
Mulino	Fumane	1.97	0.60	1963	Amarone,	—	167
					Recioto, and	—	83
					Valpolicella	—	317
Palazzo della Torre	Fumane	23.49	7.16	1967	Valpolicella	1980	4,083
					Amarone	—	2,083
Progni	Fumane	15.52	4.73	1953–63	Amarone and	—	1,000
					Valpolicella	—	2,600
Ca' del Paver	Fumane	1.71[c]	0.52[c]	1968	Pelara	1979	458
Scornocio	Fumane	1.02	0.31	1957	Valpolicella	—	300
Volta	Fumane	11.65	3.55	1958–75	Amarone,	—	1,000
					Recioto, and	—	417
					Valpolicella	—	2,000

NOTES: [a] Included in the total for the Gardane vineyard
[b] Included in the total for the La Grola vineyard
[c] Included in the total for the Progni vineyard.

week of September. The pickers harvesting for the Valpolicella cut off the lower third of the grape bunches of those clusters that will be used for Recioto and Amarone, leaving the top part, in the traditional manner, to ripen longer on the vine before it is gathered.

Their Valpolicella is fermented for eight to ten days, the Amarone and Recioto for twenty to twenty-five, and Pelara for five to six. In March, winemaker Franco Allegrini and consultant Nino Franceschetti referment the Valpolicella on the Recioto lees to produce a bigger, richer, fuller wine, with a better capacity to age. We've tasted Allegrini Valpolicellas with ten years of age that were still very good. Their Valpolicella is aged for a minimum of one year in oak casks, quite a long time by modern standards. But this is not a modern Valpolicella; it is in the traditional *ripasso* style.

Allegrini produces four Valpolicellas, all from the Classico zone; three of them are *superiore,* one is not. Lena, a single-vineyard Valpolicella that is meant to be drunk young, is a very unusual *ripasso;* the wine is passed over the lees of a wine that was fer-mented using carbonic maceration. The three Allegrini Valpolicella Classico *superiore* include a *normale,* the very fine La Grola, and Palazzo della Torre. In 1980 they bottled Palazzo della Torre as Vigna La Torre, producing 10,666 bottles. In 1983 they produced 25,000 bottles, and in 1985, 49,000 bottles.

LA GROLA

La Grola, unlike Allegrini's other Valpolicellas, is not made *ripasso.* The grapes are harvested late and consequently are more concentrated and richer in sugar. La Grola does, however, undergo a second fermentation.

La Grola 1988 Valpolicella Classico Superiore (ex-botte, twice, 4/90). Deep and richly fruited aroma, berries and cherries, vaguely floral; sweet impression; the best one to date, this Valpolicella is the platonic form of the genre, could one possibly be better? ********

OUR ASSESSMENT OF THE ALLEGRINI AMARONES, LA GROLA, AND LA POJA

Year	Wine	Date Tasted	Rating	Comment
1988	Classico	4/90	(***)	From barrel
1988	Classico Fieramonte	4/90	(****)	From barrel. Potentially the best Allegrini Amarone that we've tasted
1988	La Grola Valpolicella Classico Superiore	4/90	****	From barrel. The best La Grola to date
1988	La Poja	4/91	***+ (****)	From barrel. Perhaps the best La Poja to date.
1986	Classico	4/90	**(+)	From barrel
1986	Fieramonte	4/91	***	From barrel
1986	La Grola Valpolicella Classico Superiore	4/90	***+	Ready now, could improve
1986	La Poja	4/91	***	Lighter than the others
1985	Classico	4/90	***	From barrel
1985	Classico Fieramonte	4/90	***(+)	From barrel
1985	La Grola Valpolicella Classico Superiore	4/89	***+ (****−)	Great class, still young. Only the '88 is better
1985	La Poja	4/91	****	From barrel. Rich one moment and delicate the next; truly a great wine
1983	Classico	4/90	**(*−) ***+	The best Allegrini Classico that we've tasted
1983	Classico Fieramonte	4/90	****	The best Allegrini Amarone that we've tasted
1983	La Grola Valpolicella Classico Superiore	4/88	****−	This was the first La Grola. Ready now, could improve
1983	La Poja *vino da tavola*	4/90	***+ (****)	A stunning wine
1982	Classico	12/80	**+	Fully ready now
1981	Classico	4/89	***	Fully ready now
1981	Classico Fieramonte	4/90	***	Ready, could improve
1980	Classico	9/88	***−	Ready
1980	Classico Fieramonte	4/89	***	Ready
1979	Classico	4/85	***−	Ready
1979	Classico Fieramonte	4/88	****−	Ready with room to improve
1977	Classico	4/81	**(*)	Probably best to drink
1976	Classico	10/78	**	From barrel
1975	Classico	4/80	**+	More of a robust style
1974	Classico	10/78	***	More of a robust style
1971	Classico	11/86	***+	Fully ready, best to drink now

La Grola 1986 Valpolicella Classico Superiore (*3 times, 4/90, 48,660 bottles*). Great intensity on the nose, nuances of flowers and spice; loaded with flavor that fills the mouth, smooth-textured, nice mouth feel, a touch of tannin at the end. ***+

La Grola 1985 Valpolicella Classico Superiore (*5 times, 4/89, 32,000 bottles*). Scented bouquet, suggestions of underbrush, mushrooms, flowers and tobacco; richly concentrated, superbly balanced, rich and delicate at the same time; this wine has everything including great class. ***+ (****−)

La Grola 1983 Valpolicella Classico Superiore (*9 times, 4/88, 14,522 bottles*). Floral, almond perfume; berry flavor; loads of class and style, an elegant wine, we can't imagine a Valpolicella being better, and all nine bottles were of the same high quality. ****−

PELARA

The pelara grape was used in Valpolicella before phylloxera. After the scourge devastated the vineyards and the vines were replanted on American roots, this variety wasn't replanted for two reasons. First, the vine is subject to a disease known as floral abortion, which causes problems in fertilization, resulting in low yields; second, its wines have to be consumed young because they mature quickly. The wine is, however, regarded for its perfume. A little more than a decade ago Giovanni Allegrini produced a varietal Pelara. This wine has a coral color, a delicately scented bouquet, and good body, and is fresh and dry yet with a sweet impression.

LA POJA

In 1983, for the first time, they produced 4,296 bottles of the non-DOC La Poja, a wine made 100 percent from corvina graspo rosso grapes grown in the 6.5-acre (2.65-hectare) portion of the La Grola vineyard named La Poja. The grapes were harvested between November 2 and 10. The must was fermented for fifteen days at a temperature between 77 ° and 90 ° Fahrenheit (25 ° and 32 ° centigrade). The wine spent twenty-five months in 2,082-gallon (550-liter) Alliers and Tronçais barrels. We were, to say the least, impressed.

Since then we have tasted the '90, '88, '86, and '85 and found them all impressive. Because we tasted only two wines from bottle, the rest were from barrel, we rate the wine more conservatively at three stars plus.

La Poja 1988 (*ex-barrel, 4/91*). Complex aroma reveals a mélange of scents, floral overtone; great concentration and extract, loads of structure; just might be the best La Poja to date. *** + (****)

La Poja 1986 (*4/91*). Expansive, open aroma, vaguely floral with a berry component; rich and packed with flavor yet lighter than the others; loads of class and style. ***

La Poja 1985 (*twice, ex-barrel, 4/91*). Deep color; Complex aroma, cherrylike up front followed by berries, spice and flowers; combines delicacy and richness with an interesting interplay that makes it seem rich one moment and delicate the next; truly a great wine. ****

La Poja 1983 (*twice, 4/90*). The finished wine has 14 percent alcohol. The wine was simply stunning. The bouquet offered nuances of tobacco and cherry, along with other fruits; it displayed an incredible sweetness, in spite of being dry, and ripeness; the flavor suggested berries. There was great balance and length; impressive indeed. *** + (****)

We rate the vintages for the Allegrini Amarones based on their current state:

****	1988, 1983
*** +	1985, 1979
***	1986, 1981, 1980
*** −	1971
** +	1982, 1977
**	1974
** −	1976, 1975

Each of the Allegrini wines—Valpolicella, Recioto, and Amarone—is among the best of its type; very few are their equal, and none are better. Amarone Classico: ***, Fieramonte **** − ; La Poja *vino da tavola* *** + ; Recioto Classico: ** + , Gardane *** + ; Recioto Bianco Fiorgardane *** + ; Valpolicella Classico Superiore: ***, La Grola **** − , Palazzo della Torre ***; Valpolicella Classico Lena ***

Barberini. We haven't tasted this private label Amarone since the '77 in 1983. Like other Barberini wine, it left us totally unimpressed. Amarone [0]

Bergamini. We've never tasted their Amarone, but their Recioto is good. Recioto *

Bertani Cav. Giov. Batt. (*Grezzana di Valpolicella*), 1857. The firm of Cav. G. B. Bertani is owned by the Bertani family. Their Tenuta di Novare, which has 185 acres (75 hectares) planted in the Valle di Novare, includes three crus: Monteriondo, Ognissanti, and Sereole. They also own the Saccole vineyard in Grezzana in the Valpantena district, the Casetto cru in Bardolino, and a vineyard in Monteforte in Soave. This last is planted in pinot grigio, chardonnay, and sauvignon. Bertani, a long-regarded producer of Veronese wines, produces 140,000 cases a year; this includes an average of 5,000 cases of a very good Amarone Classico Superiore. Their line also includes two Valpolicellas—one from the Valpantena zone which they label Secco-Bertani, and a second Classico Superiore—plus the *vino da tavola ripasso* Catullo, and a Recioto Spumante, also from the Valpantena area. They produce between 20,000 and 22,000 cases of the wine from the Valpolicella-Valpantena zone, 50,000 of the wines from Valle di Novare, between 25,500 and 26,600 of Soave, and 6,200 of Bardolino.

Their own vines supply them with 100 percent of the grapes they require for the Valpolicella Classico and Catullo Rosso, 80 percent for Secco-Bertani, 70 percent for their Amarone, 30 percent each for Bardolino and Soave, and 50 percent each for their Recioto Spumante and Catullo Bianco.

Bertani produces two *ripasso* wines, the Valpantena-Valpolicella and Catullo. The former has been produced with the *ripasso* method since their first in 1857. Since they used the name Secco-Bertani for over a century, after the introduction of DOC prohibited the word *secco,* meaning "dry," on the label, they were allowed to continue to use this copyrighted name. The refined and gentlemanly Gaetano Bertani told us that this wine will last and improve between seven and nine years. Judging by those we've tasted through the years and most recently in November 1990, we would agree. At a tasting arranged for us, we had the opportunity to taste Secco-Bertani '89, '88, and '87 from barrel, and '86, '85, '83, and '81 from bottle. The '86, '85, and '83 were all very good indeed, but the '81, although still very good, was showing some age.

CATULLO

The *ripasso vino da tavola* Catullo is named for Gaius Valerius Catullus, the Roman poet and satirist who lived from 87 to 54 B.C.

The first one, the '83, was produced from selected grapes in their Novare vineyard in the Valpolicella district. The wine is put on the Amarone lees in February. It spends eighteen months in large oak casks. They didn't produce Catullo in 1985 or 1989.

1986 (11/90). Dried fruit aroma, nuances that recall a forest and mushrooms; sense of sweetness from the rich fruit, moderate tannin, nice fruit flavors; on the young side. ** −

1984 (11/90). Dried fruit and forest scents, mushroom component; real sense of sweetness, nice texture, moderate tannin, tasty. ** −

1983 (11/90). Dried fruit character on the nose, floral and raisin notes; rich flavor, good body; still has room to improve. **(+)

They also produce a white Catullo from a blend of garganega, pinot bianco, and chardonnay. They first produced this wine from the 1987 vintage. And their Soave Classico Le Lave, first produced in 1987, is a special selection made with their best grapes, as well as those from a few other growers. Its name derives from the volcanic (*lave*), soil the grapes are grown in. They produced 5,600 bottles of the '87 and 24,500 of the '88.

They produced a *barrique*-aged Valpolicella with the more standard, as opposed to the *ripasso*, method of fermentation. It spent one year in a combination of *barriques* of Alliers and Tronçais oak.

Their Recioto *spumante* is made from dried grapes. The wine is aged in oak three and a half to four years and then moved to tank for its second fermentation where it spends four months. It is made to sparkle with the charmat method. They produce between 15,000 and 20,000 bottles annually of this Valpolicella from the Valpantena district.

Bertani's cellarmaster first produced an Amarone, by accident, in the early 1950s. The firm experimented with this wine over the next few years. Bertaini's first real Amarone was produced in 1958; they made 555 cases. That wine wasn't sold commercially as it wasn't as dry as they wanted it. Their first commercial Amarone, according to Gaetano Bertani, was the '59. They didn't produce a '61 or '66. Bertani, perhaps more than any other Veronese firm, believes in aging its Amarone. Before it is released for sale, it has been aged for no less than eight years. They have supplies of Amarones dating back to 1958 that are still offered for sale from time to time, although in very limited quantities. As of November 1990, Bertani's current vintage for Amarone is the '79. The '80 will be released in April 1991.

The grapes for the Bertani Amarones are processed—crushed and fermented—at their Novare winery. When the wine is separated from the skins it still contains 0.04 percent (4 grams per liter) of residual sugar. It is then moved to oak casks. Gaetano Bertani told us that the Amarone continues to ferment a little, on and off, for four to five years. They produce between 25 and 30 casks per vintage. After the wine finishes fermenting and is dry, it is moved to their other winery, where it is blended to make up the final cuvée.

In 1987 they produced, for the first time, a single-vineyard Amarone from their Ognissanti cru in Tenuta di Novare. This wine spent a year in *barrique*. They plan to release it in 1991! They produced no more than 7,500 bottles of that wine.

Bertani's Amarones age very well. We have tasted some with thirty years of age that were still very good. Generally we find their Amarones to be in a fuller-bodied style. Amarone Classico Superiore ***; Catullo *vino da tavola ripasso* **; Secco-Bertani Valpolicella-Valpantena ***; Recioto di Valpolicella-Valpantena Spumante **

Bolla Fratelli (*Verona*), *1883*. This firm produces well over a million cases of the full range of Veronese wine, including two special Soaves, a Gavi, a White Merlot, the cabernet sauvignon–corvina Creso, a pretty good Amarone and Valpolicella Classico from the vineyards of the Jago area, as well as white and red Rhetico fortified dessert wines. They also produce 1,000 cases of a Recioto Spumante, between 88,000 and 110,000 cases of a Chardonnay from Apulia, and 3,000 cases of a Pinot Grigio from the Alto Adige. One of the Soaves comes from a few vineyards in the Castellero district, the other from Frosca. Both areas are in the Soave Classico zone. The former was first produced in 1976, the latter in 1979. Bolla produces 5,000 to 6,000 cases of the Castellero and fewer than 3,000 of the Frosca.

Since 1989 they have been producing a Recioto di Soave. It is fermented in stainless steel and spends two months in *barrique*. And since 1990 they have been producing a Pinot Grigio from the San Leonardo vineyard in the Valdadige region. Eventually they will produce some 2,500 cases. This Pinot Grigio will eventually replace their Alto Adige version. Some other changes from 1990: Bolla has lightened up its Bardolino by reducing the alcohol degree by half a percent, and they will ship the '90 version in July 1991, and the '91 in May 1992. They plan to ship their regular Soave earlier as well.

Other new Bolla wines include a single-vineyard *ripasso* Valpolicella and Amarone from their 22-acres (9-hectare) San Vito vineyard in the Negrar district. They first produced these two wines from the 1990 vintage. And they also produced a cru Soave from their 41-acre (16.5-hectare) Le Maddelena vineyard in the Castel Cerino district.

Jago comes from 37 acres (15 hectares) of vines in the Negrar Valley in the Classico zone. The vineyards, facing southeast, are planted at an altitude of 820 feet (250 meters) above sea level. Jago is made from a blend of 65 percent corvina, 25 percent rondinella, and 5 percent each molinara and other local varieties. They generally harvest the grapes in mid-October. After a ten-day fermentation, four to five days longer than for their regular Valpolicella, the wine is aged for two years in Slavonian oak casks. They first produced the Jago Valpolicella in 1979. It is not made every year. They also produced it in 1980, 1983, 1985, and 1986. We suspect there will be an '88 as well. When they produce Jago they make between 7,500 and 8,400 cases.

They produced their first Amarone in 1950. It was put on the market in 1955—the first to be sold commercially by any firm. The next one was the '52, followed by the '55. They continue to produce their Amarone in the better vintages; there was no '87, for example. The Bolla Amarone is made from a blend of 65 percent corvina, 25 percent rondinella, and 5 percent each molinara and other local varieties. The grapes undergo the *appassimento* for three months. Fermentation takes place between the second and third week of January in 1,320- to 2,640-gallon (50- to 100-hectoliter) Slavonian oak casks at a controlled temperature of 57° to 59°

Fahrenheit (14° to 15° centigrade). Because the weather, and cellars, are cold, vinification proceeds very slowly, lasting for some two to three months. Malolactic fermentation follows in April or early May, after the weather warms. The resultant wine is aged for four years in twenty-year-old casks. They produce some 100,000 bottles of Amarone a year. Bolla rates 1952, 1969, 1974, 1979, 1982, and 1985 as the best vintages, and 1958, 1964, 1980, 1981, and 1983 as good.

Generally, the Bolla Amarone is good, though unexciting. They feel it is at its best drunk before its tenth year. We can't disagree. Amarone ** − ; Valpolicella Classico *, Jago ** −

Boscaini Paolo Casa Vinicola (*Valgatara di Marano di Valpolicella*), *1948*. The Paolo Boscaini winery is owned by the Boscaini brothers Guido and Battista, cousins of the Boscainis of Masi. They own 49.4 acres (20 hectares) of vineyards; half are in the *comune* of Marano di Valpolicella. The Marano vineyards have been owned by Boscaini for more than a hundred years. From these vineyards they produce five wines that they label with the cru or village name: two Amarones, a Recioto, a Valpolicella Classico Superiore, and a non-DOC *vino da tavola ripasso* wine.

Their average annual production ranges from 500,000 to 550,000 cases. Twenty percent are the Veronese Classico Superiore wines and special cru bottlings, 40 percent are the Veronese DOC wines, and the balance the non-DOC wines from the Veneto. Sixty percent of the grapes for their Valpolicella Classico Superiore wines come from their own vineyards or from growers with whom they have long-term contracts.

The Boscaini vineyards on the Coston hills in the Marano Valley have a southern to southeastern exposure. The Vigneti di Marano, Valpolicella Classico Superiore, comes from compact, chalky, calcerous soil from the Eocene epoch; it is rich is basalt, calcium, iron, and humus. The corvina, molinara, negrara, and a small quantity of nebbiolo grapes are planted on high trellises. The harvest generally occurs about mid-October. The must is fermented for eight to ten days in temperature-controlled stainless steel. In late winter or early spring this *ripasso* wine is refermented on the Amarone lees. It spends two years in large oak barrels. In 1985 they made 68,495 bottles.

Their Amarone Classico from vineyards in the Marano district is made from corvina, rondinella, and molinara grapes generally harvested in mid-October. The grapes are dried on slatted racks until January, during which time they lose about 30 percent of their water content. They are crushed in January and fermented on the skins in large wooden casks until March. The resultant wine is aged for four years in oak casks. In 1981 they produced 5,851 bottles of this Amarone.

From two small vineyards in the hamlet of Valgatara in the Marano Valley they produce two special wines, "Ca' de Loi" Amarone and "Ca' Nicolis" Recioto. The Ca' de Loi Amarone is the product of molinara, corvina, rondinella, and rossignola grapes planted in limestone-based soil. These grapes are harvested in the first half of October. This wine is aged for no less than four years in oak casks. The finished wine has 15.5 to 16 percent alcohol.

The Ca' Nicolis Recioto Classico comes from the same four varieties, plus dindarella and a small amount of garganega planted in red and brown clay on a limestone base. These grapes are picked at the end of September. The wine is aged in small oak barrels for

two years. The finished wine contains 2 to 3 percent residual sugar and 14.5 to 15 percent alcohol.

The Santo Stefano Ripasso Vino da Tavola del Veronese comes from the Santo Stefano vineyard in the Valgatara hamlet of Marano. The soil, from the Eocene epoch, is alluvial on a limestone base. The molinara, corvina, rondinella, and rossignola varieties are harvested in the first two weeks of October. The wine is refermented on the Amarone pomace from the same vineyard in February or March. It spends three to four years in large Slavonian oak casks. This wine was first produced in 1958. It ages well. The '58, tasted in April 1989, was very good indeed; it was produced as an experiment. The '83, '85, and '88 are all very good to excellent as well.

Boscaini also produces a special Bardolino Classico Superiore from the vineyards of—*Vigneti di*—Costermano "Le Canne." These vineyards, Costermano and Cavaion, are planted on the western slopes of Mount Moscal in chalky, calcerous morainal soil with rocks and pebbles; the soil is rich in calcium and somewhat alkaline. The corvina, rondinella, molinara, and rossignola vines are trained on high trellises and receive water by irrigation. The grapes are harvested manually at the end of September and left for a short time in crates to dry. Fermentation takes place for eight to ten days in temperature-controlled stainless steel vats. The resultant wine is aged for one year in large oak casks. Their annual production of this Bardolino is 16,500 bottles.

Their Soave Classico, Vigneti di Costeggiola "Monteleone" comes from garganega, trebbiano di soave, and small amounts of durello and chardonnay grapes planted on Monte Foscarino. The vines, facing southwest, are planted in calcareous soil with volcanic mounds of basalt that is rich in potassium and phosphates. The vines are trained with the pergola Veronese (high trellis) system and are irrigated. The manual harvest takes place in mid-September. The grapes are fermented in temperature-controlled stainless steel at a low temperature. The wine doesn't undergo malolactic fermentation. They make some 43,000 bottles annually.

They also produce single-vineyard wines from the Alto Adige. Monastero di Nostra Signora is made from pinot nero, Castel Firmiano from pinot grigio, and Colle dell'Imperatore from chardonnay.

Boscaini's very good wines include two excellent Amarones. Amarone: Ca' de Loi ***, Marano ***; Valpolicella Classico Superiore Marano ** +; Santo Stefano *ripasso vino da tavola del* Veronese ** +

Brigaldara Azienda Agricola (*San Floriano*), *1933*. Stefano Cesari owns this winery and some 37 acres (15 hectares) of grapes. This includes the 1.2-acre (0.5-hectare) I Filari del Pigno vineyard, the 3.7 (1.5) Il Pianeto, and the 8.6 (3.5) Il Vegro. He expects to plant some new vineyards in the spring of 1991. Cesari's vineyards range in altitude from 490 to 820 feet (150 to 250 meters) above sea level. His annual production of just over 90,000 bottles includes two Valpolicella Classico Superiores, 60,000 of a *normale,* 15,000 of the single-vineyard Il Vegro, 5,000 of a Recioto, two Amarones, 10,000 of a *normale,* and 2,000 of the single-vineyard Il Pianeto, plus 1,500 half bottles of the *vino da tavola* I Filari del Pigno. Il Vegro, first produced in 1985, is a *ripasso* Valpolicella. There were 7,500 bottles of that wine. The first Il Pianeto was also the '85. Brigaldara produces very good wines. Valpolicella Classico Superiore Il Vegro **; Amarone **

Burati. Burati is not a producer. It is a private label used, or that was used, for a rather mediocre range of Veronese wines. We haven't tasted any of their Amarone since the unmemorable '71 tasted in 1980. Amarone [0]

Ca' Merla. We have tasted one Amarone from Ca' Merla, a disappointing '83. Amarone +

Ca' Monte Azienda Agricola di Luigi Zanconte (*Negrar*). Luigi Zanconte's Azienda Agricola Ca' Monte has been recommended to us by two especially fine producers. Unfortunately, we've never met their wines.

Castagna. We haven't tasted any Castagna Amarone since we had their disappointing '73 in 1978. Amarone [0]

Cesari Gerardo Casa Vinicola. Their Valpolicella is Classico Superiore. Their Amarone, based on one vintage, the '82, is *inferiore*. Amarone 0

Conati Marco. Their Recioto failed to impress. Their Amarone, based on one vintage, the '83, was even less impressive. Amarone * −

Corta Vecchia Casa Vinicola (*Cavaion Veronese*). Our experience is limited to their unimpressive '82. Amarone 0

Dalforno Romano Azienda Agricola (*Cellore d'Illasi*). This family-owned winery owns 7 acres (2.8 hectares) of vines, 6 (2.4) of which are planted in corvina. The rest is planted in rondinella and molinara, plus some cabernet sauvignon. Their vineyards are planted at an altitude of 985 feet (300 meters) above sea level. The alluvial soil is pebbly and calcareous. They produce all of 400 cases of Amarone and Valpolicella. They blend 50 percent corvina with 25 percent each rondinella and molinara for both their Amarone and Valpolicella. Dalforno ferments its wines in 264-gallon (10-hectoliter) casks. Since 1983 they have been producing a Valpolicella from the Lodoletta Mountains. The '85 was one of the best Valpolicellas that we have tasted. The grapes for their Amarone are dried on racks until March. They age their Amarone for four years in oak casks of the same size as those they use for fermentation. Valpolicella ***; Amarone ** +

Due Torri (*S. Martino della Battaglia*). We base our rating on one wine, which we tasted twice, their good '82 Amarone. Amarone * +

Fabiano F.lli Azienda Vinicola (*Sona*). This firm produces the full range of Veronese wines, including Amarone. The Fabiano Amarone is made from a blend of 55 percent corvina, 30 percent rondinella, and 15 percent molinara grapes grown around the town of Negrar in the Classico zone. They told us that their '83 was aged for seven years prior to being sold. They produce mediocre Valpolicella and Amarone that are labeled as Classico Superiore. Amarone 0

Farina F.lli Azienda Vinicola (*Pedemonte*). The only Amarone that we can recall tasting from F.lli Farina was the unimpressive '75, and that was a decade ago.

Farina Remo (*Pedemonte*). They use corvina, rondinella, molinara, negrara, and dindarella grapes for their Amarone. The grapes undergo the *passimento* for four months in trays. In February they undergo a slow fermentation. They wine is aged for three years in Slavonian oak casks of 132- to 264-gallon (5- to 10-hectoliter) capacity. Our experience is limited to their '85 Amarone, which, although good, seemed older than its years. Amarone *

Guerrieri-Rizzardi Azienda Agricola (*Bardolino*), *1700*. Rizzardi owns 371 acres (150 hectares) of vines which supply them with all the fruit for their wines. Their vineyards, in Bardolino, Soave, Valpolicella, and the Valadige production zones, are farmed organically. Their annual production averages between 111,000 and 122,000 cases of wine per year.

They produce, on average, 44,440 to 55,550 cases each of Bardolino and Valpolicella, 16,665 to 22,220 cases of Soave, and 11,100 to 16,665 cases of Valadige per year. They make a few special wines in very limited quantities.

Castello Guerrieri is the product of sangiovese, corvinone, rondinella, tenaiol, forcella, and rossara nera grapes grown in their Dògli vineyard in the Bardolino production zone. It is aged in small barrels made of local Venetian oak. The only one we tasted, the '86, was very good. It is, in our opinion, their best wine. They produced 18,200 bottles of that wine.

Besides the typical grapes of the Veronese area, they grow pelara in Valpolicella and semillon, sauvignon, pinot, and malvasia in Bardolino, and chardonnay in Vallagrina. Valpolicella Classico *, Villa Rizzardi Poiega **, Amarone Classico *; Castello Guerrieri *vino da tavola* ***

La Bionda Agricola. La Bionda produces a good Valpolicella Classico Superiore from the vineyards of—*Vigneti di*—Ravazzol Valgatara, and a very good Amarone. Amarone ** +; Valpolicella Classico Superiore Vigneti di Ravazzol Valgatara **

La Colombaia (*Parona di Valpolicella*). We have never been impressed with their Amarones. Their best wine, in our experience,

THE CRUS OF GUERRIERI-RIZZARDI

Cru	Acres	Hectares	Used for
Ca' dell'Ara	24.7	10	Bardolino
Dògli	17.3	7	Bardolino
Villa Rizzardi Poiega	12.4	5	Valpolicella

THE SPECIAL WINES OF GUERRIERI-RIZZARDI

Wine	Location	Type	Average Number of Cases per Year
Costeggiola	n/a	Soave	—
Dògli	Calmasino Bardolino	Moscato d'Italia	—
Tacchetto	—	Bardolino	—
Castello Guerrieri	Dògli	Bardolino	555
S. Pietro	3 localities	White	4,444
	Cavion	Red	2,222
Villa Rizzardi (In 1985 they produced 3,500 bottles.)	Poiega	Valpolicella	555

was the '83 Amarone Alto Marano Barrique. Even that was unimpressive, though a cut above their standard fare. Amarone: 0, Alto Marano Barrique +

La Crocetta Azienda Agricola (*Marano di Valpolicella*). We tasted one Amarone, the '83, one Recioto, the '85, and one Recioto Spumante. The first two wines were good, the *spumante* not. Amarone *; Recioto *

Lamberti. Lamberti is part of the Gruppo Italiano Vini. They produce the full range of Veronese wines. They also produce an Amarone Corte Rubini. In 1982 they made 32,400 bottles of that wine. We found it, like their other Amarone, less than impressive. Amarone 0

Le Ragose Azienda Agricola di Marta Bortoletto Galli (*Arbizzano di Negrar di Valpolicella*). The Galli family bought this property, named for the locality in which it is situated, in 1969. Marta Bortoletto Galli has 30 acres (12 hectares) of vines, including the 8.6-acre (3.5-hectare) Le Sassine vineyard planted with very old vines. The soil in this vineyard is calcareous. In Le Sassine, Marta says that there are nine different clones of molinara. Harvest begins about October 10 and lasts for some six weeks. Yields average 427 gallons per acre (40 hectoliters per hectare) here. From the molinara in that vineyard she produces a very good *ripasso* wine that is aged for two to three years in large oak casks. In 1983 there were a scant 8,000 bottles.

Marta Galli also produces, or did, the very good *vino da davola* Montericco Rosso di Negrar. This wine is also produced with the *ripasso* method of refermenting the wine on the Amarone lees. We haven't tasted or seen it since the '75.

Besides producing a very good *ripasso* Valpolicella Classico Superiore, she makes 4,000 bottles of Recioto Spumante and a very fine Amarone, one of the best and most consistent, in fact. Le Ragose is a member of VIDE. Amarone ***; Le Sassine *vino da tavola ripasso* ***; Valpolicella Classico Superiore ***

Le Salette Azienda Agricola di Fulvio Scamperle (*Fumane*), *1875*. Franco and Fulvio Scamperle own this winery and its 30 acres (12 hectares) of vines. This includes 7.4 acres (3 hectares) each of Ca' Carnocchio and I Progni, 9.9 (4) of La Grola, and 4.9

(2) of La Marega. Their vines, planted at an average altitude of 985 feet (300 meters) above sea level, have a northern exposure. They produce between 10,000 and 12,000 bottles of Amarone Classico La Marega; 8,000 to 10,665 of Recioto Classico; three Valpolicella Classicos, 33,325 to 40,000 of a *normale*, 17,330 to 20,000 of I Progni, and 5,335 to 8,000 of Ca' Carnocchio; plus 1,067 to 1,333 bottles of Cesare Passito Bianco. They plan to increase their production by 30 to 40 percent within five years. They are experimenting with cabernet sauvignon and sangiovese. The two single-vineyard Valpolicellas are Superiore. They use the *ripasso* method for their Valpolicella. Amarone **

Lenotti. They produce a good Recioto. We've never tasted their Amarone that we can recall. Recioto *

Longo Casa Vinicola di Antonio & Fausto Longo (*Buttapietra*). Except for a so-called 1911 Recioto, we haven't tasted Longo's wines since the '71 Amarone in 1978. The wines were very good. Amarone **

Masi Agricola (*Gargagnago di S. Ambrogio*), *1772*. In 1772, Paolo Boscaini bought an estate in Vajo dei Masi, at Torbe between Marano and Negrar. The winery took its name from this small valley. Today the Masi winery and vineyards are still owned by the Boscaini family. Sandro Boscaini, the eldest, is the director of the firm. The Boscaini brothers own or control a total of 435 acres (175 hectares), which include about 158 acres (64 hectares) of some of the finest vineyards in the Valpolicella Classico zone, plus 89 (36) in Bardolino Classico and 49.4 (20) in the hills of Monteforte d'Alpone in the Soave Classico zone.

Masi also buys grapes. It produces, at most, 100,000 cases of very good Veronese wine a year, including a few specialties made from local grape varieties. More than half of their production is of the normal Veronese wines. The remainder is Amarone, Recioto red and white, and a couple of proprietary wines. Some 85 percent of the grapes for their wines are from their own vineyards or from vineyards that they control.

Masi produces three Valpolicella: a *fresco* meant to be drunk young, a regular Classico Superiore that is quite good, and the cru Serègo Alighieri Classico Superiore, which is excellent. The *fresco* is from Vigneti di Gargagnago in the Classico zone. This wine was

THE CRUS OF MASI

Cru	Comune	Acres	Hectares	Exposure	Age of Vines (Years)	Average Number of Cases Per Year	Used for
Campociesca	Torbe di Negrar	8.2	2.5	ESE	18	200	Recioto *bianco*
Campofiorin	Valgatara (near Marrano)	36.1	11.0	NS	25	7,500	*Vino ripasso*
Campolongo di Torbe	Torbe di Negrar	9.8	3.0	SW	15	600	Amarone
Mazzano	Mazzano di Negrar	14.8	4.5	W	20	700	Amarone
Mezzanella	Negrar	9.8	3.0	SE	12	300	Recioto
Serègo Alighieri	S. Ambrosio	45.9	14.0	SSW	20	4,000	Valpolicella
Casal dei Ronchi	*Località* Gargagnano	9.8	3.0	SSW	20	350	Recioto
Vaio Armarom		19.7	6.0	SSW	20	1,000	Amarone

first produced in 1980. The first Serègo Alighieri was from the 1980 vintage as well. They don't produce this wine every year; there was no '82 or '87. They did produce a small quantity of '84. They also produced an '81, '83, '85, '86, and '88. Production averages 41,667 bottles a year. The vineyard is cultivated under Masi's direction but is owned by the Serègo Alighieri family, descendants of Dante Alighieri, father of the modern Italian language and author of *The Divine Comedy*. The son of Dante Alighieri bought land in Gargagnago in 1353 and the Alighieri family has cultivated vineyards here ever since. We have rarely tasted a finer Valpolicella than this one.

In order to improve the quality of Valpolicella Masi has been conducting experiments with many local but forgotten grape varieties. In 1990 they produced a new wine that could one day influence the Valpolicella of the future. We were privileged to be the first people outside the winery to sample this wine, tentatively called Rosso della Colline Veronese. It was impressive indeed. Masi blended the primary local varieties used for Valpolicella with some secondary grapes. Corvina was the major variety since it gives the best results. Molinara is important for its drinkability, though it reduces both body and structure. Rondinella, which is important for the Recioto wines including Amarone, doesn't add much to a wine made from fresh, as opposed to dry, grapes. Some of the secondary varieties that they added—like oseleta—contributed concentration, body, and color. Others—for example, dindarella—added aroma and personality. They used only hillside grapes since they are convinced that those grapes are better than those in the flats. These grapes came from the Torbe hillside in the Negrar Valley. Each variety was fermented separately. An assemblage was then made from corvina, rondinella, and molinara with some of the secondary varieties.

Rosso della Colline Veronese 1990 (ex-barrel, 2/91). The aroma displays great richness of fruit and spice with hints of cherries and berries; a lot of structure, packed with ripe, fruit flavors that fill the mouth; an impressive first effort. ***(+)

They also produce an excellent single-vineyard Bardolino from the La Vegrona vineyard in Costermano. This 67-acre (27-hectare)

cru is on top of a hill, at 915 feet (300 meters) above sea level. The vines, surrounded by a forest, are on terraces; the soil is alluvial. They first produced this wine in 1986; 20,000 bottles were made. Maximum production from La Vegrona is 80,000 bottles. They also make a fine single-vineyard Soave, Col Baraca. And a few years ago they found an old cloister of vineyards in the Alto Adige planted in pinot nero, gewürztraminer, sauvignon, and vernaccia. They have been working with the family who has owned this vineyard since 1987, but haven't as yet decided if they will produce or commercialize the wines from there.

CAMPOFIORIN

The very fine Campofiorin *vino ripasso* was first produced in 1958 from the best grapes selected from Masi's Campofiorin vineyard. This vineyard, in Valgatara di Marano, along the eastern banks of the Progno di Marano torrent contains alluvial soil of coarse siliceous-calcerous material with a topsoil rich in mineral salts and trace elements. Some 70 percent of the vineyard has a northern to southern exposure, the remainder faces east to west. The vines are planted at 560 feet (170 meters) above sea level.

Nino Franceschetti created this wine when he rediscovered a very old method used in these parts many years ago while he was researching the traditions of this zone. The first commercial release was the '64. The *uvaggio* is approximately 55 percent corvina, 25 percent rondinella, 10 percent molinara, and 10 percent rossignola and sangiovese. The grapes are generally harvested during the first two weeks of October. In February or March the wine is refermented on the pomace of the Amarone. This refermentation lasts ten to fifteen days.

The refermentation results in a wine of greater body and better structure, a richer and more complex wine with more alcohol. The wine attains an alcohol level of 13.5 to 14 percent. Following the refermentation the wine is moved to 792- to 2,376-gallon (30- to 90-hectoliter) casks for aging. It will undergo a malolactic fermentation during aging. Campofiorin is aged for four years in cask.

Sandro Boscaini pointed out that Campofiorin is released when they consider it ready, not necessarily in vintage sequence. Campofiorin is ready to enjoy from its fifth or sixth year until its tenth to fifteenth. It can live and improve for more than two decades.

Campofiorin is not produced in bad vintages. The following are Masi's ratings of those vintages (that have been released), adjusted for our four-star system:

****	1988, 1983, 1978, 1964
***	1986, 1985, 1976, 1971, 1969, 1967
**	1981, 1980, 1979, 1977, 1975, 1974, 1968, 1966, 1965
*	1973, 1970
none	1987, 1984, 1982, 1972

We rate them this way, based on their current state:

****	1988
***+	1985, 1967
***	1983, 1969
***−	1986, 1981, 1964
**+	1976
**	1979, 1977, 1974
*	1980, 1978, 1975

Of the 18 vintages of Campofiorin that have been produced between 1964 and 1985, production has averaged 12,995 gallons (491.85 hectoliters) a year, equivalent to 43,833 bottles, and the alcohol level of the 20 vintages produced between 1964 and 1988 has averaged 12.9 percent.

The label on Campofiorin carries the phrase *nectar angelorum hominibus,* "nectar of the angels for men." We couldn't put it any better.

1988 (*twice, ex-cask, 4/90*). Beautiful bouquet, vaguely floral; sweet, rich and concentrated, loads of class already evident, very long. ***(*)

1986 (*twice, ex-cask, 4/90*). Lovely fruit, well structured, grapey, long finish. **(*−)

1985 (*6 times, 12/90*). Lovely and complex bouquet, fragrant, nuances of spice, almonds, flowers, leather, berries and cherries; great richness and intensity, smooth, almost silky, very long finish; a young but appealing wine of real class and quality, should be a real keeper. ***+

1983 (*3 times, 4/90*). Intensely concentrated on the nose and palate, complex, smooth, still some tannin, very long. At this stage the '85 is more impressive, yet the vintage is rated one level down by Masi! ***

1981 (*3 times, 5/90*). Lovely floral bouquet, displays nuances of dried fruit and underbrush; round, sweet and harmonious, rich flavor, long finish, elegant; peak or close to it. ***−

1980 (*4/87*). Nose seems rather tight or lacking; firm, fairly well balanced, a touch of volatile acidity intrudes, still there is fruit. *+

ALCOHOL LEVEL AND PRODUCTION OF CAMPOFIORIN

Year	Alcohol[a]	Hectoliters	Bottles
1988	12.70%	800	[b]
1986	12.65%	750	[b]
1985	12.80%	710	78,000
1983	12.85%	730	90,000[c]
1981	12.70%	650	52,000
1980	12.75%	600	56,000
1979	12.80%	580	58,000
1978	12.85%	550	65,000
1977	12.80%	550	54,000
1976	13.10%	450	40,000
1975	12.80%	250	22,000
1974	12.95%	295	38,000
1973	12.50%	200	20,000
1971	13.50%	400	36,000
1970	12.60%	350	27,000
1969	12.90%	420	41,000
1968	12.90%	390	25,000
1967	12.80%	410	35,000
1965	13.50%	360	32,000
1964	13.45%	392	20,000

NOTES: [a] Alcohol refers to actual alcohol level immediately after the *ripasso.* The wine at this stage has unfermented residual sugar that will ferment out, leaving the resultant wine dry and with an average of 13.5 percent of alcohol.
[b] To be determined.
[c] They also produced 6,000 magnums and 100 double magnums.

1979 (*twice, 4/85*). Peppery aroma, vague almond and cherry note, seems a little stemmy, has a dried fruit character; lots of flavor, some length. **

1978 (*3 times, 4/87*). Dried fruit aroma, somewhat floral; still firm, is it beginning to dry out, or is it an off bottle? * *Bottle of 4/86:* Complex aroma suggestive of dried fruit, spice and black pepper, vaguely chocolate, hint of grape stems; richly flavored, recalls peanuts on the long finish. **(*) *Bottle of 4/85:* Complex bouquet of almonds, dried fruit and black pepper, with a note that hints of chocolate; richly flavored and full, long finish recalls peanuts; this wine has a lot of strength and needs age to tame it. **(*)

1977 (*4 times, 7/85*). Dried fruit character, concentrated, lots of nice fruit, soft. ** *Bottle of 4/85:* Aroma of dried fruit, raisins, figs, prunes and some flowers; richly flavored, soft almost like velvet, long finish is somewhat drying. ***−

1976 (*ex-cask, 10/78*). Big, perfumed aroma; loads of flavor, well structured; has a lot of potential. **(*)

1975 (6 times, 4/85). Dried fruit and chocolate, touch of oxidation; somewhat tired, still has flavor interest. *

1974 (3 times, 4/85). Garnet, orange color; nose displays a lot of complexity with suggestions of dried fruit, almonds, oranges; richly flavored, light tannin, velvety, some age beginning to creep in; very long finish recalls almonds. ** +

1969 (4/87). The label of this wine was interesting in that it read Campo Fiorin Amarone. Dried fruit and floral aroma; smooth-textured, richly fruited, long finish, complex. ***

1967 (4/87). Flowers, almonds and dried fruit define the bouquet; smooth, velvety mouth feel, chocolate notes, still some tannin; very nice indeed. *** +

1964 (4/87). The label on this one read Amarone del Campo Fiorin. Lovely bouquet; smooth and silky, well balanced, loads of flavor; lots of character, displays delicacy and some elegance. *** —

THE RECIOTOS

Masi produces three Recioto della Valpolicellas: a Riserva degli Angeli, a Mezzanella cru, and, since 1983, Casal deì Ronchi from the Serègo Alighieri estate. The Riserva degli Angeli is made from an *uvaggio* of 65 to 70 percent corvina, 5 to 15 percent molinara, 25 to 30 percent rondinella, and no more than 10 percent of dindarella, rossignola, and negrara grapes from vineyards on the Torbe hillside. The harvest generally takes place toward the end of September or beginning of October. The wine is aged for two years in oak casks. The Serègo Alighieri, Casal deì Ronchi Recioto was first produced by Masi in 1983.

Masi also produces the golden Recioto Bianco, Campociesca, a *vino da tavola* from the vineyard of that name, in very limited quantities. It is very rare and very fine. The Campociesca is made basically from garganega and trebbiano di soave grapes, with the addition of some cortese and malvasia. Today Masi refers to this wine as a golden *amabile vino da tavola*.

Masi rates the vintages for their Reciotos (in those years that have been released) as follows (adjusted for our four-star system):

****	1988, 1983
***	1985, 1980, 1979, 1977
**	1986, 1978, 1976
*	1981, 1974, 1973, 1970
0	1975, 1971
None	1987, 1984, 1982, 1972

THE AMARONES

Masi produces four Amarones—a classico and three crus. The Campolongo di Torbe is made from a blend of corvina, rondinella, and molinara, plus some negrara, rossignola, and dindarella grapes. The vineyard is harvested at the end of September or beginning of October. This wine is fermented for fifty days and aged for at least four years in old oak casks. The Mazzano Amarone is made from the same six grapes, plus a small amount of raboso veronese. This wine is given no less than five years of oak aging and achieves a level of 15.8 to 17 percent alcohol.

The Campolongo di Torbe Amarone is made in a gentler, sweeter, and more elegant style. It achieves an alcohol level of 15.5 to 16.5 percent. This wine is, according to the very fine enologist Nino Franceschetti, shorter lived than the Mazzano. He describes Mazzano as "the perfect expression of Amarone." No doubt he knows quite well whereof he speaks; we certainly cannot disagree.

The Vaio Armaron is aged for only three years in oak. This wine is sweeter, softer, and gentler than the Campolongo di Torbe Amarone. Masi first made this exceptionally fine single-vineyard wine in 1979; production is now 12,000 bottles a year.

Masi evaluates the vintages for its Amarones (in those years that have been released) as follows (adjusted for our four-star system):

****	1988, 1983, 1964
***	1986, 1985, 1979, 1976, 1974, 1971, 1969, 1967
**	1981, 1980, 1978, 1977, 1975, 1968, 1966, 1965
*	1973, 1970
None	1987, 1984, 1982, 1972

We rate them this way, based on their current state:

****	1988
*** +	1985, 1983, 1958
***	1979, 1974, 1971, 1969, 1968
*** —	1980, 1952
** +	1986, 1981, 1977, 1962
**	1978, 1976, 1964
** —	1975, 1961
* +	1973

Masi is one of the most serious and dedicated producers of Veronese wines; in fact, no producer is more serious and dedicated to quality than Masi Agricola, and this statement applies to the entire world of wine, not just Verona, or, indeed, Italy. Would that other wine producers take their product as seriously! In years that don't meet their already high standards, they think nothing of declassifying their wines to a lesser level or selling it *sfuso*.

Besides their fine Amarones, Reciotos, and *ripasso* wines, they make a good, and highly reliable, range of Veronese wines. We can especially recommend the Soave Classico from the Col Baraca vineyard, the Bardolino Classico from the La Vegrona vineyard, and their good non-DOC white Masianco. The first two wines are among the best of their type, and the last is among the best whites of the districts.

As for their Amarones, they are unsurpassed by anyone, and one of them, the Mazzano, sets the standards by which we judge all others. Amarone Classico: *** —, Campolongo di Torbe **** —, Mazzano ****, Vaio Armaron *** +; Campofiorin *vino da tavola ripasso* *** +; Recioto: Mezzanella **, Serègo Alighieri Casal deì Ronchi ***, Riserva degli Angeli *** —; Recioto Bianco *vino da tavola* Campociesca *** +; Valpolicella Classico Superiore **, Serègo Alighieri ***; Valpolicella Classico Fresco Vigneti di Gargagnago ** +

Montresor Giacomo (*Verona*). At one time we had a lot more experience with their wines, and they were better than they have shown in recent years. Amarone 0

Murari. The only wine that we can recall tasting from Murari was the good '82 Amarone. Amarone *

Nicolas Angelo Azienda Agricola (*S. Pietro in Cariano*). Nicolas's Valpolicella is Classico Superiore. They produce a decent Recioto Classico. Amarone 0; Recioto +

Pasqua F.lli (*Verona*). Pasqua produces a Valpolicella from grapes grown in the highly regarded Marano district. The '88 was quite good and in 1984 they produced a single-vineyard Amarone from the Casterna vineyard. We found that lacking. Amarone 0

Quintarelli Giuseppe. Quintarelli has a reputation of producing some of the best wines in the zone. He does. But, unfortunately, the bad ones seem to outnumber the good ones. We have tasted some Quintarelli Amarones that had refermented in the bottle! Clearly some quality control is in order here. He makes two Valpolicella Classicos that we know of, a Fiore from Monte Ca' Paletta and a Superiore Monte Ca' Paletta with a beige label. These wines, like his Amarone, are variable. When they are good they are very good indeed, and when not . . . Amarone **; Valpolicella Classico Superiore Vigneto di Monte Ca' Paletta ** +; Valpolicella Classico Vigneto di Monte Ca' Paletta Fiore ** +

Righetti Luigi Azienda Vinicola. (*Valgatara*). Luigi Righetti makes a fine Valpolicella Classico Superiore Campolieti. In 1985 he produced 18,000 bottles. He also makes a single-vineyard Soave Classico Superiore from the Campochiaro vineyard. His Amarone, Capitel de'Roari, is excellent. Valpolicella Classico Superiore Campolieti *** −; Amarone Capitel de'Roari ***

"San Rustico" di Luigi & Danilo Campagnola (*Valgatara di Marano di Valpolicella*), *1870.* In 1973 the Campagnola brothers Luigi & Danilo changed the name of their winery to San Rustico. The brothers own this *cantina* and 99 acres (40 hectares) of vines in Negrar, Marano di Valpolicella, and Fumane, all in the Classico zone. Il Gasso, their special cru, is a 7.4-acre (3-hectare) vineyard in Marano di Valpolicella. They also buy grapes. Their annual production ranges from 27,775 to 33,330 cases.

They began bottling wines from their Gasso vineyard separately in 1985. San Rustico also produces a small quantity of Belfior, a sweet *spumante* from *passito* (dried) grapes, a *vino novello,* using *macerazione carbonica* (whole-berry fermentation), a rosé, Chiaretto del Veneto, and a Soave.

Marco, Danilo's son, and Luigi Campagnola are the winemakers. They ferment their Valpolicella for five to six days and their Amarone for twenty-five to thirty days. The only single-vineyard Amarone that we tasted was their excellent '85. We found it, like their single-vineyard Valpolicella, superior to their *normale.* Amarone *, Gasso *** −; Valpolicella Classico *, Superiore *, Superiore Gasso **; Recioto Spumante **

SAN RUSTICO'S AVERAGE ANNUAL PRODUCTION

Wine	Hectoliters	Cases
Amarone	120	1,333
Amarone, Gasso	30	333
Recioto	50	556
Recioto, Gasso	10	111
Recioto Spumante	30	333
Valpolicella	1,400	15,554
Valpolicella Superiore	800	8,888
Valpolicella Superiore, Gasso	100	1,111

OUR ASSESSMENT OF THE MASI AMARONES AND CAMPOFIORIN

Year	Wine	Date Tasted	Rating	Comment
1988	Classico	2/91	**(*)	From barrel
	Campolongo di Torbe	4/90	(**** −)	From barrel
	Mazzano	4/90	****(+)	The best Amarone we've tasted from barrel
	Serègo Alighieri, Vaio Armaron	4/90	(****)	From barrel
	Campofiorin	4/90	***(*)	From barrel—the best one to date
1986	Classico	10/90	**	
	Campolongo di Torbe	4/90	**	From barrel
	Mazzano	4/90	** +	From barrel
	Serègo Alighieri, Vaio Armaron	4/90	** +	From barrel
	Campofiorin	4/90	**(* −)	From barrrel
1985	Classico	12/90	*** −	Ready now
	Campolongo di Torbe	10/90	*** +	The most impressive CLT to date
			(****)	
	Mazzano	4/90	*** +	From barrel
	Serègo Alighieri, Vaio Armaron	4/90	***(+)	From barrel
	Campofiorin	12/90	*** +	Should keep well

Year	Wine	Date Tasted	Rating	Comment
1983	Classico	4/90	*** —	
	Campolongo di Torbe	4/89	*** +	
	Mazzano	4/89	***(+)	
	Serègo Alighieri, Vaio Armaron	4/89	***(+)	
	Campofiorin	4/90	***	Young, needs age
1981	Clasico	10/90	*	Drink now
	Campolongo di Torbe	5/87	** +	Ready
	Mazzano	4/89	** +	
	Campofiorin	5/90	*** —	Ready
1980	Campolongo di Torbe	4/87	*** —	Ready
	Mazzano	4/89	*** —	Drink now
	Serègo Alighieri, Vaio Armaron	4/89	***	
	Campofiorin	4/87	* +	Drink now
1979	Classico	5/87	*** —	Ready
	Campolongo di Torbe	5/87	***	Ready
	Mazzano	4/87	***(*)	Could improve
	Serègo Alighieri, Vaio Armaron	4/89	***	
	Campofiorin	4/85	**	Drink now
1978	Classico	4/86	***	Should be ready
	Campofiorin	4/87	*	Drink now
1977	Clasico	5/87	**	Ready
	Campolongo di Torbe	4/85	***	Ready
	Mazzano	12/83	** +	Should be ready
	Campofiorin	7/85	**	
1976	Classico	2/91	** +	Ready
	Campolongo di Torbe	1/82	**	Ready
	Mazzano	4/90	***	Ready
	Campofiorin	10/78	**(*)	From cask
1975	Classico	5/87	**	Ready
	Campolongo di Torbe	10/78	**	Should be ready
	Mazzano	1/82	** —	Drink now
	Campofiorin	4/85	*	Drink now
1974	Classico	2/91	** —	Drink now
	Campolongo di Torbe	5/87	***	
	Mazzano	4/85	***(*)	Should be ready
	Campofiorin	4/85	** +	Drink now
1973	Classico	10/78	** —	Drink now
1971	Classico	5/87	***	
	Mazzano	5/87	***(*)	Should be ready
1969	Classico	4/85	***	
	Mazzano	5/87	** +	
	Campofiorin	4/87	***	Drink or hold
1968	Classico	4/85	*** +	Peak
1967	Campofiorin	4/87	*** +	Drink or hold

Year	Wine	Date Tasted	Rating	Comment
1964	Classico	2/91	*** +	At its peak
	Campolongo di Torbe	5/87	** +	Drink now
	Serègo Alighieri, Vaio Armaron	4/87	?	Drink now
	Campofiorin	4/87	*** −	Drink or hold
1962	Classico	5/87	** +	Drink now
1961	Mazzano	4/87	** −	Drink now
1958	Classico	2/91	***	Ready
	Campolongo di Torbe	5/87	*** +	Ready
	Classico, Vajo Armaron	4/87	****	Ready
1952	Classico, Vajo Armaron	4/87	*** −	Ready

Santa Sofia Azienda Agricola di Begnoni G. Carlo (*Pedemonte di Valpolicella*), *1811.* Although Santa Sofia traces the founding of the firm to 1811, the current owner, G. Carlo Begnoni, has owned the firm since 1967. Their annual production varies from 600,000 to 700,000 bottles. They plan to increase this to 1 million bottles in the future.

They produce a decent Valpolicella Classico Superiore and Amarone Classico Superiore. They produce—besides the standard Classico Superiores from Valpolicella, Bardolino, and Soave—Recioto della Valpolicella Classico Superiore; Recioto di Soave Classico; the Soave Classicos Costalta and Montefoscarino; Valpolicella Classico Superiore Monte Gradella; Bardolino Chiaretto; two Bianco di Custozas, Il Vignale and Montemagrinan; and Amarone Classico Superiore Gioé. In 1977, Santa Sofia produced 7,400 bottles of that wine, and in 1986 they produced 14,600 of their Valpolicella Monte Gradella. They also sell a *spumante* brut that is made for them in Valdobbiadene.

Recently Santa Sofia introduced three new non-DOC *vini da tavola*—Predaia, made from cabernet sauvignon, corvina, molinara, and rondinella; Croara, from pinot bianco, altoatesino, garganega, trebbiano di soave, and the trebbiano toscano; and Arléo Chiaretto.

Their wines are correct and good, if not much more. Amarone *

Santi. They are part of Gruppo Italiano Vini and so are in the same stable as Lamberti. Our experience in recent years has been extremely limited. The only one that we've tasted since the disappointing '80 was the very good '85 Botte Regina. Amarone: [0], Botte Regina ** −; Valpolicella Vigneti della Castello d'Illasi *

Sartori Cav. Pietro (*Negrar*). Sartori buys grapes for their Amarone from the valleys of Negrar, Valgatara, and Fumane. They produce a decent Valpolicella Classico Superiore and a good, if unexciting, Amarone. Amarone *

Scamperle F.lli Casa Vinicola do Dino & Gabrielle Scamperle (*Fumane*). We haven't tasted their Amarones since the '78 in 1985. Amarone [*]

Serègo Alighieri. See **Masi.**

Speri F.lli Azienda Agricola (*Pedemonte*), *1874.* The Speri brothers, Carlo, Benedetto, Eliseo, and Giuseppe, own 99 acres (40 hectares) of vines from which they produce 55,000 cases of wine a year, including 23,300 cases of Valpolicella and 8,000 of Amarone. The grapes for their Amarone come from the higher elevations. They also produce 22,000 cases of Soave Classico Superiore and Bianco di Custoza from bought grapes. The grapes for the red wines come from their own vineyards.

The Speri Amarone enjoys a good reputation. In our experience, though they can be good, they have been rather uneven. We have to call them the way we see them. Amarone 0

Tedeschi F.lli Azienda Agricola di Lorenzo Tedeschi (*Pedemonte*), *1890.* In 1824, Nicolo Tedeschi bought some vineyards. This established the Tedeschis as grape growers and winemakers. In 1918, Riccardo purchased the Monte Fontana and Monte Olmi vineyards. Since that time the Tedeschi holdings have continued to increase. Today Lorenzo, or Renzo as he is more commonly known, Tedeschi and his brother Silvino cultivate nearly 30 acres (12

THE CRUS OF F.LLI SPERI

Cru	Località	Altitude in		Cases	First Vintage
		Feet	Meters		
La Roverina	Negrar	490	150	23,000	1978
Monte Sant'Urbano	Fumane	985	300	8,000	1980

hectares) of vines. Two thirds of these are in the hills, the rest in the plains. All of their vineyards except Monte Tenda, which is in Soave, are in the *comune* of S. Pietro Incariano in the Classico zone. These vineyards, planted at an average altitude of 820 feet (250 meters) above sea level, face southwest.

Tedeschi has sold his wines in bottles since 1960. He bottles his best wines under the cru names. Renzo is the winemaker, brother Silvino tends the vineyards. Tedeschi produces nearly 300,000 bottles of wine a year. One-third is Soave and 40 percent Valpolicella. The remaining 27 percent consists of three fine Amarones, two exceptionally fine Reciotos, and a sweet, luscious, golden Recioto *bianco*.

Tedeschi makes a Valpolicella Classico Superiore from a blend of 55 percent corvina, 25 percent rondinella, 10 percent molinara, and 10 percent dindarella and rossignola grapes from his Lucchine vineyard. The grapes are harvested toward the end of September and fermented with the skins for eight to ten days. It spends over a year in large old casks.

Capitel San Rocco Rosso is a red table wine made from the same blend of grapes as the Valpolicella. The vines are planted in alluvial soil that contains limestone deposits in the San Rocco section of the Lucchine vineyard. The grapes are harvested at the end of September or the beginning of October. This *ripasso* wine is refermented in March when the wine is put into the casks containing the Recioto *vinacce* (pomace). Following this refermentation the wine is aged for a minimum of two years in oak casks. At one time this wine was sold as Capitel San Rocco delle Lucchine Rosso, the '83, for example. That wine was, according to the label, a "Valpolicella *ripassato on vinacce di recioto*" in January 1984.

Capitel Monte Olmi Amarone Classico is made from a blend of 65 to 70 percent corvina, 25 to 30 percent rondinella, 5 percent molinara, and 5 percent nevgrara, rossignola, and sangiovese grapes grown in the Monte Olmi vineyard. The grapes are dried on slatted racks until January. They are crushed and the juice runs into oak casks where it will ferment for about a hundred days. After fermentation the wine is racked into oak casks to age three to four years.

Capitel Monte Fontana Recioto is made from 55 to 60 percent corvina, 20 to 25 percent rondinella, 5 to 15 percent molinara, and 5 to 10 percent dindarella, negrara, and rossignola grapes grown in the Monte Fontana vineyard. The grapes are dried until January, when they are crushed and fermented. After the fermentation has reached the point where the sugar is at the desired level, in fifty to sixty days, the wine is racked off the lees into oak casks where it will spend at least two years.

La Fabriseria Recioto Bianco is produced from a combination of garganega, saorin, and other grapes grown in the La Fabriseria de San Rocco vineyard in Pedemonte. This sweet and concentrated *vino da tavola* dessert wine is among the more interesting of its type produced.

The Tedeschi wines can be quite good, but where they really shine is in their single-vineyard bottlings. At their best, these are surely among the zone's finest wines, whether Amarone or Recioto. Amarone: Classico **, Capitel Monte Olmi ***; Recioto: Capitel Monte Fontana ***; Recioto Bianco vino da tavola La Fabriseria de San Rocco ** +; Ripasso vino da tavola Capitel San Rocco [delle Lucchine] Rosso ***; Valpolicella Classico Superiore: ** −, Vigneto Lucchine *** −

Tenuta Villa Girardi (*San Pietro Incariano*). Villa Girardi has 125 acres (50 hectares) of vines which provide them with 70 percent of their grapes. They produce over 75,000 cases a year of a full range of Veronese wine, including Amarone. They produce 5,500 cases of the Amarone cru, Bure Alto, each year. Amarone 0

THE WINES OF TEDESCHI

Wine	Cru	First Vintage	Bottles
Amarone Classico	n/a	—	15,000
Amarone della Fabriseria	Capitel* (La Fabriseria de) San Rocco	—	2,500–3,000
Amarone Monte Olmi	Capitel Monte Olmi	1971	6,000
Capitel S. Rocco Rosso	Capitel (La Fabriseria de) San Rocco	1976	20,000
Recioto Classico	n/a	—	7,500
Recioto Monte Fontana	Capital Monte Fontana	1971	3,500
Valpolicella	n/a	—	70,000
Valpolicella Lucchine	Capitel delle Lucchine	1978	25,000
Valpolicella Nicalò	n/a	—	25,000
Capitel S. Rocco Bianco	Capitel delle Lucchine	1978	20,000
Fabriseria Recioto Bianco	Capitel (La Fabriseria de) San Rocco	—	2,500
Soave	Monte Tenda	1978	100,000
Total			297,000–297,500

*A *capitel* is a stone marker, frequently in the form of a miniature chapel honoring a saint, that is used to mark the corners of a vineyard. It designates the ownership of that land.

Tommasi Azienda Agricola (*Pedemonte*). We have had some very good Amarones from Tommasi and some good Valpolicella. Amarone **; Valpolicella Classico Superiore Vigneto Raffael **

Tramanal. The last time we tasted a Tramanal Amarone, in 1981, we had their good '75. Amarone [* +]

Tre Rose. We haven't tasted their Amarone since 1980, when we tasted their unimpressive '78. Amarone [0]

Vantini Lorenzo. Our experience here is limited to the disappointing '86 Amarone and an equally unimpressive '88 Recioto Classico. Amarone 0

Venturini. We haven't tasted Venturini's Amarone since the very good '74 we tasted in 1978. Amarone [** +]

Villa Girardi. See *Tenuta Villa Girardi.*

Villa Rizzardi. See *Guerrieri-Rizzardi.*

Villa Spada. Our experience with Villa Spada's Amarones is limited to their good '80. Amarone *

Zaconte Luigi. See *Cà Monte Azienda Agricola di Luigi Zanconte.*

Zardini F.lli Azienda Agricola (località *Pezza-Marano*). The only Amarone that we tasted here was the unimpressive '87. Their '87

Recioto was also lacking. We realize that the vintage was unimpressive, but they bottled them. Amarone 0

Zenato Azienda Agricola (*S. Benedetto di Lugana*), *1930.* The Zenato brothers own two wineries and some 118 acres (48 hectares) of vines. This includes Azienda Agricola S. Cristina, which they founded in 1980 and its 50 acres (20 hectares) of vines. At that winery they produce some 200,000 bottles of wine annually. At the second winery, and from its 69 acres (28 hectares) of vines, they produce 600,000 bottles of wine. Among their wines are the full line of Veronese wines, including the white Lugana, Soave, and Bianco di Custoza, and the red Bardolino, Valpolicella, and Amarone. Amarone *

Zeni F.lli (*Bardolino*). Cantina F.lli Zeni produced 6,700 bottles of a single-vineyard Valpolicella from Marogne in 1986. They also produce the single-vineyard Valpolicella Vigne Alte from the Classico zone. We tasted, in 1988, a cask sample of an interesting wine called Cruino. It was a cross, they told us, between corvina and sangiovese, with the former making up 80 percent. Zeni produced 1,280 bottles of this wine, which they aged for four months in *barriques* of Alliers oak and nine months in casks of Slavonian oak. Their Amarone is good. Amarone *

CHAPTER 16

Cabernet and Cabernet Blends

In the early part of the nineteenth century the Bordeaux varieties—cabernet franc, cabernet sauvignon, and merlot—and perhaps some of the other minor varieties, were introduced into Italy, where they were planted in the Tre Venezie (Friuli–Venezia Giulia, Trentino–Alto Adige, and Veneto). The malbec grape was brought to Apulia from Bordeaux in the middle of the century.

After phylloxera wiped out the vines of the northeastern regions in the early part of this century, many vineyards were replanted with grafted Bordeaux varieties, especially merlot and cabernet franc. Today merlot is the major red variety of Friuli–Venezia Giulia and perhaps the Veneto as well.

Cabernet, especially cabernet sauvignon, is becoming more widespread in Italy, with the new plantings in the Piemonte and Toscana. More and more Tuscan producers are introducing some cabernet into their Chianti or blending it with the noble sangiovese to create new wines to satisfy a growing international market with a taste for Cabernet aged in *barrique*. (See page 486 for a more extensive discussion of these wines.) Though we certainly hope that Italian wine will not lose its own identity as a result, which would surely be a loss, with xenophilous producers eschewing their noble native varieties in favor of the more exotic foreign-born, we can't overlook the fact that there are many wines from the Bordeaux varieties being produced in Italy; they make up a significant proportion of the total output, and a number of these wines are very fine ones, and in some areas they are indeed traditional at this point as well—not that a traditional wine is necessarily better than a new and perhaps more innovative one. In the final analysis, it's what's in the glass that counts. In a choice between drinking sentiment and drinking fine wine, we'll take the latter without hesitation.

Sometimes these varieties are blended, as in Grai's Alto Adige Cabernet, from cabernet sauvignon and cabernet franc; sometimes one is used alone to produce a varietal wine such as Maculan's Palazzotto, made from 100 percent cabernet sauvignon; in some wines cabernet is combined with merlot, as in the Ornellaia of Ludovico Antinori; in others they are blended with native varieties, such as is done in the Torre Ercolana of Colacicchi-Anagni, a cesanese-cabernet-merlot blend.

THE GRAPE VARIETIES

CABERNET. Cabernet, which in Italy may mean either cabernet sauvignon or cabernet franc, is recognized under DOC for all six zones of Friuli–Venezia Giulia, two of the zones in Trentino–Alto Adige, and five in the Veneto. It is used as a component in a number of other wines, in both Lombardia and Toscana, for example.

Zones Producing DOC Cabernet Wines

Alto Adige	Colli Orientali del Friuli*
Aquileia*	Grave del Friuli*
Breganze	Isonzo*
Colli Bèrici	Latisana*
Colli Bolognesi (Cabernet Sauvignon)	Lison-Pramaggiore*
	Montello e Colli Asolani
Colli Eugànei	Piave
Collio (Cabernet Franc)†	Trentino*

* *This DOC includes Cabernet, Cabernet Sauvignon, and Cabernet Franc.*
† *As of 1990, the DOC has been changed to Cabernet.*

By far the majority of Italian Cabernet wines should be drunk young, within a year or two of the vintage, at most three. While some can last longer, they generally don't improve with age, and they lose their appealing youthful fruit. The best, though, can live a decade or more.

CABERNET FRANC. This variety is the most widely planted of the cabernet varieties in Italy. Whenever the name Cabernet appears unqualified on a label of an Italian wine, it is virtually always cabernet franc, though in some cases there might be some cabernet sauvignon blended in.

Cabernet franc dominates the cabernet plantings in the Tre Venezie; it is planted as far south as Apulia, also farther north in Lombardia, Emilia-Romagna, and Toscana.

Cabernet franc wines tend to be similar in aroma to those made made from cabernet sauvignon but with a more pronounced herbaceous or bell pepper character. The franc wines are generally softer and rounder with perhaps more body and less refinement.

CABERNET SAUVIGNON. This cabernet is less popular in Italy than cabernet franc, possibly because of its lower yields and

the fact that its wines require more aging. It is, however, becoming more popular as plantings increase in Toscana, Piemonte, Friuli, and other parts of the peninsula. This trend is due more to the internationalization of wine than to any other reason. As in Bordeaux, cabernet sauvignon is more frequently blended, with cabernet franc or with merlot, than it is used on its own as a straight varietal. There is a growing trend to blend it with sangiovese in Toscana or add a dollop or two of it into Chianti, all in order to produce a more acceptable wine in the international marketplace.

Cabernet sauvignon produces deeply colored wines that are hard and tannic in their youth, requiring time to soften and round out. In aroma these wines frequently offer suggestions of green olives, cassis or black currants, or cedar. In the right climate and soil, it produces wines of refinement and breed.

Cabernet sauvignon is the major variety of the Médoc and Graves regions of Bordeaux. In Italy it is planted throughout the three northeastern regions—Trentino–Alto Adige, Friuli–Venezia Giulia, and the Veneto—as well as in Lombardia, Piemonte, Emilia-Romagna, Toscana, and Umbria. Conte Tasca d'Almerita has some cabernet sauvignon planted at his Regaleali estate in Sicilia.

MALBEC. This Bordeaux variety is grown mostly in northeastern Italy, in the regions of Friuli–Venezia Giulia and the Veneto; there are some plantings in Trentino–Alto Adige and Lombardia. It is used mostly in combination with cabernet and merlot. A few producers make a varietal Malbec, or Malbeck as it is sometimes spelled. The one from Duca Badoglia in Friuli–Venezia Giulia, though we haven't tasted it in a few years, was quite a good one and recommendable.

Malbec is grown as far south as Apulia in the Cerignola district between Foggia and Bari. It is a major grape in the *uvaggio* of the very good to excellent Torre Quarto of Fabrizio Cirillo-Farrusi.

Malbec produces wines with good color that tend to be rather soft. It's a variety being grown less today, even in Bordeaux.

MERLOT. This variety, the most important grape in the Bordeaux districts of St. Emilion and Pomerol, is the major red variety in the northeastern corner of Italy. Merlot wines are recognized under DOC in all six zones of Friuli–Venezia Giulia, in six zones in the Veneto (including two labeled not as Merlot, but as Rosso), in two zones in Trentino–Alto Adige, two zones in Emilia-Romagna, and in one zone in Lazio. Merlot is used as a supplemental variety in numerous Italian DOC wines and even more independents. The plantings in Toscana, for a varietal Merlot, have of late been on the increase. Plantings of merlot can be found as far south as Sicilia, where Principessa di Gregorio grows it on her inland estate near Regaleali.

Zones Producing DOC Merlot Wines

Alto Adige	Collio
Aprilia	Grave del Friuli
Aquileia	Isonzo
Bosco Eliceo	Latisana
Breganze ("Rosso")	Lison-Pramaggiore
Colli Bèrici	Montello e Colli Asolani
Colli Bolognesi	Piave
Colli Eugànei*	Trentino
Colli Orientali del Friuli	

* DOC allows for a Merlot and a Rosso that contain between 60 and 80 percent merlot.

The merlot vine tends to be more productive than cabernet. The wines made from the merlot variety tend to be softer, smoother, and rounder than those from cabernet, with less tannin and perhaps more alcohol. The Merlot wines tend to mature sooner than the Cabernets of the same area. As a rule of thumb, most Italian Merlots should be consumed before the end of their second year. The aroma of Merlot, at its textbook best, is reminiscent of tobacco or tea. Italian versions sometimes recall grass.

PETIT VERDOT. There are a few scattered plantings of petit verdot in Italy. This Bordeaux variety produces wines that are high in alcohol and acidity. We are not aware of any Italian wines made exclusively from this grape. There are a few wines that include it in the blend.

THE CABERNET AND MERLOT WINES RATED

****
Bellendorf (Giorgio Grai), Alto Adige DOC Cabernet
Giorgio Grai, Alto Adige DOC Cabernet
Herrnhofer (Giorgio Grai), Alto Adige DOC Cabernet
Kehlburg (Giorgio Grai), Alto Adige DOC Cabernet
Ornellaia (Marchese Ludovico Antinori)

***
Alto Adige DOC Cabernet, the best ones
Breganze DOC Cabernet, the best ones
Campo del Lago (Lazzarini), Colli Bèrici DOC Merlot
Colli Bèrici DOC Merlot, the best ones
Coniale (Castellare)
− Fiorano Rosso (Boncompagni Ludovisi Principe di Venosa)
+ Fratta (Maculan) Breganze DOC Cabernet
Ghiàie della Furba (Conte Ugo Bonacossi)

− Il Roncàt Rosso (Giovanni Dri)
Maurizio Zanella (Cà del Bosco)
Palazzotto (Maculan) Breganze DOC Cabernet
Sammarco (Castello dei Rampolla)
Sassicàia (Tenuta San Guido)
+ Solàia (Antinori)
Torre Ercolana (Cantina Colacicchi-Anagni)
Torre Quarto Riserva (Fabrizio Cirillo-Farrusi)

**
Altesino, Cabernet Sauvignon
Alto Adige, DOC Cabernet
Alto Adige DOC Merlot, the best ones
Avignonesi, Merlot
Avignonesi, Cabernet Sauvignon
− Barbarola (Raffaelle Rino)
Braida Nuova (Borgo Conventi)
Breganze DOC Cabernet
Cabernet del Friuli–Venezia Giulia *vino da tavola*, the best ones
Cabernet del Tre Venezia *vino da tavola*, the best ones
Cabernet del Veneto *vino da tavola*, the best ones
Cabernet Franc del Friuli–Venezia Giulia *vino da tavola*, the best ones
Cabernet Franc del Tre Venezia *vino da tavola*, the best ones
Cabernet Franc del Veneto *vino da tavola*, the best ones
Cabernet Sauvignon del Friuli–Venezia Giulia *vino da tavola*, the best ones
Cabernet Sauvignon del Tre Venezia *vino da tavola*, the best ones
Cabernet Sauvignon del Veneto *vino da tavola*, the best ones
Camoi (Orlandi)
Castel S. Michele (Istituto Agrario Provinciale S. Michele)
Castello di Roncade (Barone Ciani Bassetti)
+ Colle Picchioni, Vigna del Vassallo (Paola di Mauro)
Colli Bèrici DOC Cabernet, the best ones
Colli Bèrici DOC Merlot
− Colli Bolognesi-Monte San Pietro-Castelli Mediovale DOC Cabernet
Colli Eugànei DOC Cabernet, the best ones
Colli Eugànei DOC Merlot, the best ones
Colli Eugànei DOC Rosso, the best ones
− Colli Orientali del Friuli DOC Cabernet
− Colli Orientali del Friuli DOC Cabernet Franc
− Colli Orientali del Friuli DOC Cabernet Sauvignon
− Collio (Goriziano) DOC Merlot
Corbulino Rosso (Afra e Tobia Scarpa)
− Cortaccio (Villa Cafaggio)
− Costa delle Pergole Rosso (Col Sandago)
− Costozza Cabernet Frank (Conte da Schio)

+ Darmaggi (Gaja)
Falchini, Cabernet Sauvignon (Azienda Agricola
  Casale)
+ Faralta (Marina Danieli)
Favònio, Cabernet Franc Riserva (Attilio Simonini)
Foianeghe Rosso (Conti Bossi Fedrigotti)
Franciacorta DOC Rosso, the best ones
− Grave del Friuli DOC Cabernet, the best ones
− Grave del Friuli DOC Cabernet Sauvignon, the best
  ones
I Fossaretti (Alberto Bertelli)
− Le Marne (Volpe Pasini)
+ Le Rive Rosso (Lazzarini), Colli Bèrici DOC Cabernet
− Le Sincette Rosso (Brunori Ruggero)
Linticlarius (Castello Turmhof)
− Lungarotti, Cabernet Sauvignon
Merlot del Friuli–Venezia Giulia *vino da tavola,* the
  best ones
Merlot del Tre Venezia *vino da tavola,* the best
  ones
Merlot del Veneto *vino da tavola,* the best ones
Montsclapade (Girolamo Dorigo)
+ Mori Vecio (Lagaria)
+ Nemo, Cabernet Sauvignon (Castello Monsanto di
  Fabrizio Bianchi)
Quarto Vecchio (Cantine Petternella)
+ R & R (Castello di Gabbiano)
− Rauten (F.Ili Salvetta)
+ Realda (Roberto Anselmi)
− Regaleali, Cabernet Sauvignon (Conte Tasca
  d'Almerita)
+ Riva Rossa (Mario Schiopetto)
+ Ronco dei Roseti (Abbazia di Rosazzo)
+ Rosso del Gnemiz (Ronchi del Gnemiz)
Rosso di Vigne dal Leòn (Tullio Zamò)
San Leonardo (Tenuta San Leonardo)
+ San Zeno (La Vinicola Sociale Aldeno)
+ Tajardino (Gian Paolo & Giovanni Cavalleri)
− Tavernelle, Cabernet Sauvignon (Castello Banfi)
Torre Quarto *normale* (Fabrizio Cirillo-Farrusi)
Trentino DOC Cabernet, the best ones
Trentino DOC Cabernet e Merlot, the best ones
Trentino DOC Cabernet Franc, the best ones
Trentino DOC Cabernet Sauvignon, the best ones
+ Venegazzù, Riserva della Casa black label (Ca' Loredan
  Gasparini)
− Venegazzù, Riserva della Casa white label (Ca' Loredan
  Gasparini)
+ Vigna L'Apparita (Castello di Ama)

*
Alto Adige DOC Merlot

Aquileia DOC Cabernet
Aquileia DOC Cabernet Franc
Aquileia DOC Cabernet Sauvignon
Aquileia DOC Merlot
− Berengario (Domenico Zonin)
Breganze DOC Cabernet
Breganze DOC Rosso
+ Brentino (Maculan) Breganze DOC Rosso
Brume di Monte, Trentino DOC Rossa (Càvit)
− Ca' del Merlot (Quintarelli)
Cabernello (Barone Fini)
Cabernet del Friuli–Venezia Giulia *vino da tavola*
Cabernet del Tre Venezia *vino da tavola*
Cabernet del Veneto *vino da tavola*
Cabernet Franc del Friuli–Venezia Giulia *vino da tavola*
Cabernet Franc del Tre Venezia *vino da tavola*
Cabernet Franc del Veneto *vino da tavola*
Cabernet Sauvignon del Friuli–Venezia Giulia *vino da
  tavola*
Cabernet Sauvignon del Tre Venezia *vino da tavola*
Cabernet Sauvignon del Veneto *vino da tavola*
Colli Bèrici DOC Cabernet
Colli Bèrici DOC Merlot
Colli Bolognesi-Monte San Pietro-Castelli Mediovale
  DOC Merlot
Colli Eugànei DOC Cabernet
Colli Eugànei DOC Merlot
Colli Eugànei DOC Rosso
Colli Morenici Mantovani del Garda DOC
+ Colli Orientali del Friuli DOC Merlot
+ Collio (Goriziano) DOC Cabernet
Creso (Fratelli Bolla)
Favònio, Cabernet Franc *normale* (Attilio Simonini)
+ Formentini Rosso (Contini Formentini)
Franciacorta DOC Rosso
Grave del Friuli DOC Cabernet
Grave del Friuli DOC Cabernet Franc
Grave del Friuli DOC Cabernet Sauvignon
Grave del Friuli DOC Merlot
Grener (F.Ili Dorigati)
Isonzo DOC Cabernet
Isonzo DOC Cabernet Franc
Isonzo DOC Cabernet Sauvignon
Isonzo DOC Merlot
Latisana DOC Cabernet
Latisana DOC Cabernet Franc
Latisana DOC Cabernet Sauvignon
Latisana DOC Merlot
Le Stanze (Poliziano di Carletti)
Lison-Pramaggiore DOC Cabernet
Lison-Pramaggiore DOC Cabernet Franc
Lison-Pramaggiore DOC Cabernet Sauvignon

Lison-Pramaggiore DOC Merlot
Merlot del Friuli–Venezia Giulia *vino da tavola*
Merlot del Tre Venezia *vino da tavola*
Merlot del Veneto *vino da tavola*
Merlot di Cavriana (Azienda Vitivinicola Monte Gallo)
+ Merlot di Sicilia (Principessa di Gregorio)
+ Montello e Colli Asolani DOC Cabernet
+ Montello e Colli Asolani DOC Merlot
Navesèl (Armando Simoncelli)
Piave DOC Cabernet
Piave DOC Merlot
Plazate Rosso (Livon)
Quattro Vicariati (Càvit)
− Quintarelli, Cabernet Franc
Rocca di Castagnoli
S. Cristina, Cabernet Sauvignon
+ Sgreben (La Vinicola Sociale Aldeno)
+ Solesine (Bellavista)
Tebro (Cantina Spagnolli)
Tiarebù (Livon)
Trentino DOC Cabernet
Trentino DOC Cabernet e Merlot
Trentino DOC Cabernet Franc
Trentino DOC Cabernet Sauvignon
Trentino DOC Meriot
+ Valcalèpio Rosso DOC

0

Aprilia DOC Merlot
Borgo di Peuma Russolo
Cabernet del Friuli–Venezia Giulia *vino da tavola*
Cabernet del Tre Venezia *vino da tavola*
Cabernet del Veneto *vino da tavola*
Cabernet Franc del Friuli–Venezia Giulia *vino da tavola*
Cabernet Franc del Tre Venezia *vino da tavola*
Cabernet Franc del Veneto *vino da tavola*
Cabernet Sauvignon del Friuli–Venezia Giulia *vino da tavola*
Cabernet Sauvignon del Tre Venezia *vino da tavola*
Cabernet Sauvignon del Veneto *vino da tavola*
Marago (F.Ili Pasqua)
Merlot del Friuli–Venezia Giulia *vino da tavola*
Merlot del Tre Venezia *vino da tavola*
Merlot del Veneto *vino da tavola*
Stukara (Franco Furlan)

THE WINES

AGRESTO (*Friuli–Venezia Giulia*). Agresto is made by Vigneti Pittaro from an *uvaggio* of 40 percent cabernet franc,

---

WHAT THE RATINGS MEAN

**** Great, superb, truly noble
*** Exceptionally fine
** Very good
* A good example of its type, somewhat above average
0 Acceptable to mediocre, depending on the context; drinkable
+ Somewhat better than the star category it is put in
− Somewhat less than the star category it is put in, except for zero where it indicates a wine or producer-wine combination that is badly made or worse
[. .] *On a producer:* Tentative evaluation based on an insufficient number of wines or based on older, out-of-date vintages, or where the wines we tasted were too difficult to fully judge to give a fair assessment of quality
On a wine or vintage: Projection for the future. This rating is given to a vintage where we feel that we tasted an insufficient number of wines or those we tasted were too difficult to really judge to give a fair assessment of quality
(. .) Potential increase in the rating of the wine given sufficient maturity

---

25 percent cabernet sauvignon, 15 percent tazzelenghe, and 10 percent each pinot noir and refosco.

ALTESINO, CABERNET SAUVIGNON (*Toscana*). This fine Brunello producer has been experimenting with cabernet sauvignon. We tasted a cask sample of Altesino's '84 and '85, both of which showed potential. They expected to market their first Cabernet Sauvignon from the 1986 vintage. Somehow we suspect that they decided to blend it with sangiovese instead for their **Alte d'Altesi.** Rating **

ALTO ADIGE (*Trentino–Alto Adige*), *DOC.* There are 13,600 acres (5,500 hectares) under vines in the Alto Adige, or Süd Tyrol, as the region is known locally. Most of the vineyards are on the slopes and hillsides of the Etsch Valley (Valle d'Isarco) between Meran and Salurn, and in the Eisacktal (Val d'Adige) between Bozen (Bolzano) and Brixen. Two-thirds of the plantings are the prolific vernatsch, or schiava (also known as trollinger), variety.

There are 9,722 growers in Bozen authorized to produce

DOC wine, but most are registered to produce more than one wine, so the actual number of individual growers is lower. These viticulturists cultivate 12,423 registered acres (5,027 hectares) in all of the DOC zones in that province. Twenty-one cooperatives process 54 percent of the grapes and 50 fairly large wineries account for another 42 percent. The remaining 4 percent is vinified by small producers. Total yearly output of all wine in the region averages 6.1 to 6.7 million cases[1]; 3.9 million are DOC.[2]

When we think of this region, like many other wine lovers, we tend to think of the fine white wines made from rülander, gewürztraminer, weissburgunder, and riesling grapes; the Alto Adige does indeed produce some of Italy's finest white wines. But red varieties also do well here, including such international favorites as cabernet sauvignon, cabernet franc, and merlot. These grapes, in the hands of a talented winemaker such as Giorgio Grai, can be the basis of an especially fine wine, one of real quality. These varieties are regulated under the wine law for the Alto Adige.

The official DOC vineyard area covers 4,760 acres (1,927 hectares), in 33 *comuni*; of these, 89 acres (36 hectares) are planted in merlot and 93 (38) in cabernet. The red varieties must be planted at altitudes greater than 2,300 feet (700 meters) above sea level. The maximum yearly output is equivalent to nearly 2 million cases. The annual average between 1986 and 1988 of 1.7 million cases was 85 percent of that. During that same period Merlot accounted for an average of just over 24,000 cases and Cabernet for nearly

26,000—hardly a large production, when one compares it to the total output of some wineries that are considered rather small. In 1988, there were 70 growers registered to produce DOC Cabernet, and 123 for Merlot.[3]

Cabernet sauvignon, cabernet franc, and merlot vines were introduced into the Süd Tyrol over a century ago, so the growers here have had time to find out where each variety fares best.

Alto Adige Cabernet

The major cabernet plantings are in the Bozner Unterland, in the southern part of the zone. The best cabernet grapes, according to Alöis Lageder, who makes a good one, come from Magreid (Magre), an area with a soil composition of sand, limestone, and gravel. This area is almost at the southernmost extent of the vineyards in the region.

Lageder feels that his Cabernet is at its best about ten years after the vintage. He ages it for a year and a half in 530- to 790-gallon (20- to 30-hectoliter) oak casks not made of new wood. Since 1984, though, he has begun using *barriques*. Herbert Tiefenbrunner of Schloss Turmhof has also started giving his Cabernet some *barrique* aging, as have some of the cooperative wineries.

Franco Kettmeir was, until recently, unusual for the region in producing a Cabernet Sauvignon. He produces 50,000 bottles of this wine a year, and half that amount of Merlot. These two wines make up 30 percent of Kettmeir's red wine sold in bottle. He ages the Cabernet for a year, or a year and a half, in 2,100-gallon (80-hectoliter) casks. Beginning with the 1982 vintage he has given the Cabernet Sauvignon *riserva* six months in *barriques*. He produced 2,500 bottles of that wine.

A few years ago Tom O'Toole, who is associated with the Bozen Chamber of Commerce, or was at the time, told us that 40 percent of the Cabernet in the Alto Adige is produced by Schloss Schwanburg; all they make is *riserva*.

Recommended Producers of Alto Adige Cabernet

** Giorgio Grai, who until recently had three labels—Cantina Bellendorf, Herrnhofer, and Kehlburg; he has recently begun selling his wine under his own name
Bauernkelleri
Josef Hofstatter
Kellereigenossenschaft Magreid, from Magre
Kettmeir (Cabernet Sauvignon)
Laimburger
* Alöis Lageder, particularly from the Wurmbrand vineyard
Karl Martini, "Kellermeistertrunk"
Schloss Schwanburg

DOC ZONES OF TRENTINO–ALTO ADIGE

Meran
Bressanone
Alto Adige ○
○ *Colli di Bolzano*
Bozen
Caldaro
Sorni
S. Michele all'Adige
Valdadige
Trento
Riva del Garda
Rovereto

☐ Trentino
▨ Valle Isarco
○ Other denominations

DOC REQUIREMENTS FOR ALTO ADIGE

	Minimum Varietal Component	Minimum Aging	Minimum Alcohol	Maximum Yield in	
				Gallons/Acre	Hectoliters/Hectare
Cabernet	95%	none	11.5%	823	77
Riserva		2 years, from November 1			
Merlot	95%	none	11.0%	973	91
Riserva		1 year, from November 1			

Schloss Turmhof di Tiefenbrunner (Cabernet DOC and Linticlarius *vino da tavola*)

THE LEGENDARY GIORGIO GRAI

Giorgio Grai has become something of a legend in Italy, both for his extraordinary palate and for his ability to craft outstanding wines from the grapes of many different regions. He is frequently asked to consult, and is currently winemaker for *cantine* in Apulia, Friuli, Lazio, Marches, Molise, Piemonte, and Toscana. There might be even more positions, but as one of his (admittedly very satisfied) clients put it, Giorgio can be a *rompicsatole,* or something of a wearisome nitpicker.

We once asked him what his secret is, what he does to create an excellent wine from an area known for its mediocre wines or from a vineyard that was previously the source of nothing more than quite ordinary stuff. "I just make some small changes," he understates. But these small changes are the ones that make the biggest difference. He is admittedly very exacting at the wineries where he consults, insisting first of all on simple cleanliness. "Do you think this barrel is clean?" he asks the cellarmaster. "Yes," comes the reply.

"No. Do you think these hoses are clean?" "Yes." "No." Giorgio is a stickler for taking care of the important details.

Grai has three *cantine* of his own in the vicinity of Bozen where he produces 100,000 to 150,000 bottles of finely honed wines a year. Grai's wines reflect his belief that a wine should have color, body, aroma, flavor, substance, balance, length, and character. "The taster's first reaction," he says, "should not be, 'What is this wine?' but 'This wine is good.' The second reaction: to ask for another glass. Then, 'What variety is it? From where?' Only if the wine is good does the question matter. It's like when you meet a person. First they must be a good person, later you ask, 'Who are they? Where are they from?' "

Giorgio refers to a dinner he attended some time ago with a number of other producers and growers whose wines were being poured. Some of Giorgio's friends asked him if he had any of his wines in the car. He had a few that had been in the back for about a week or so, jostling about as he maneuvered the curves of the mountain road to the house and the intricacies of parking in Bozen—not that he was concerned about the condition of the wines ("To say the wine was shaken up is just a matter of justification if it's not

ALTO ADIGE DOC PRODUCTION

Wine	1988	1987	1986	Average	
	Hectoliters			Hectoliters	Cases
Cabernet	2,346	2,438	2,160	2,315	25,716
Merlot	2,290	1,817	2,388	2,165	24,053
DOC red	94,581	89,707	89,190	90,159	1,001,670
DOC white	67,581	61,496	64,439	64,505	716,654
Total	162,162	151,203	150,629	154,664	1,718,324

Source: Il Corriere Vinicolo

good"). But, he noted, there was plenty of wine on the table. He was urged nevertheless to bring in a few bottles, which he did, and they were poured. The director of a large *cantina sociale* criticized Grai's wines, he notes, "for being too good; they had too much flavor, too much aroma, they were not typical." Giorgio didn't reply. Some of those present felt he should defend his wines. Giorgio responded, "What can I say to this man? He is a big important director; I am just a small producer. So I only pointed out that I arrived late to the dinner, and the other wines had all been poured. 'But if you'll look at the bottles,' I said to them, 'you'll notice that those bottles are all half full. My wines were just poured, and all are finished.' And I sat down."

Grai studied at Congeliano in the late 1940s. After graduating with a degree in enology he did some consulting, at first offering his services without pay to friends and recommended *cantine*. He felt that it furthered his own experience and allowed him the opportunity to follow the progress of a wine and verify his advice.

In 1962 he opened an enology lab where he did analysis. At that time, he says, he overrated the value of technology. "I may do analysis now," he observes, "and I may take down all of the statistics, but I can't tell if a wine will be good without tasting it." He didn't realize until after many mistakes, he adds, that technology and analysis weren't the whole story. "Only when the material is bad is technology important; you can improve bad wine, but you can't make it good. The most important thing is to have good material; that's fifty percent, then you give your best effort."

It's important for a winemaker to know wine, and be honest, and he must taste often. Giorgio frequently tries wines from other parts of Europe.

Tasting, he considered, is 90 percent nose. The palate generally just confirms the original impression gained from the aroma of wine. We visited one winery with Giorgio where he had been asked to consult, at a time when he was just coming down with a head cold. We were tasting the wines from cask when Giorgio looked at us and asked softly, "Do you taste the Sicilian wine?" "It does seem to have some southern wine in it," we noted. "Perhaps about fifteen percent," he commented. "How much Sicilian wine was added to this wine?" he asked the cellarmaster quite matter-of-factly (not "did you," but "how much") *"Che cosa?"* came the astonished reply. Giorgio repeated the question. "Fifteen percent," the *cantiniere* answered.

Timing is also very important, he feels, first to determine when to make the harvest, then when to bottle. "If you bottle the same wine at three different periods of the year, you get three different wines. You must understand how the wine will evolve in the bottle. It can't be bottled when it's ready to drink; it must be too early.

"You can't force the wine, you can't ask it to do what you want; you work with it. It has to come naturally. You don't fight nature—you work with her; you may assist her, but only with her cooperation. Everything is harmony. You have to find the balance in life."

Grai produced small lots of wines for himself in the early years, buying barrels of wine when he found good ones; he left the wine in the cellars as he had no facilities of his own as yet. Kehlburg was his first label. In 1968 he bought Cantine Bellermont Wangen in Appiano. Later he bought the Herrnhofer *cantina* in Caldaro to provide more space. In the mid-1970s he began to use that label for the wines he sold to Enoteca Solci in Milano. Until very recently he had three labels—Bellendorf, Herrnhofer, and Kehlburg. The wines of the same variety from each of the three are the same. Since 1990 he has been selling his wine under his own name. Noted designer and artist Tobia Scarpa designed a label for him.

Grai doesn't own any vineyards. At one time he bought grapes; today he buys new wines and blends them. It's better, he says, to buy young wine, as you have more control, you can choose what you want. He selects lots from different producers in the region, and from various casks and vats. One might be low in acid, he notes, another may be too high; one might have a lovely perfume, another better body. He takes some from each of those that have something to offer, perhaps from four or five different samples, maybe more, and comes up with a balanced blend. He feels this blending also adds complexity to the wine.

We were with him at his bar in Bozen when he was putting together a gewürztraminer from six different lots. He poured us a glass from each of the bottles and asked our opinions of each. Then he gave his impressions. As we talked he was pouring some of the wine from one of the glasses into a measured vial, then adding a little from another, and another. Then he poured that into a glass and offered it for us to taste. Surely the best of the lot. Balanced, interesting, good. Not too bad, he agreed, but could still be better. He poured that out and made a slightly modified blend. Better balanced, more interesting, very good. He had noted the amounts he needed and would buy those quantities from the producers.

Out of Grai's annual production of 100,000 to 150,000 bottles, 15,000 to 20,000 are his Cabernet, a wine of character and style, harmony and breeding. It is made from 40 to 60 percent cabernet sauvignon and the remainder cabernet franc. For us, it is the single finest Cabernet produced in Italy. And we are not alone in that opinion. A few years ago we were asked by another producer of a fine Cabernet if we were going to award four stars to any Italian Cabernets— aside from Grai's, he added.

A few years ago we arranged a tasting in New York of some of Italy's finest cabernet and cabernet-merlot blends. There were 30 wines, including nearly all the best from Trentino–Alto Adige, Friuli–Venezia Giulia, the Veneto, Toscana, and Umbria. Two fine California winemakers were there. When asked to name their favorite from the group, we were not surprised to see they chose Giorgio Grai's Herrnhofer Cabernet. Nor were we surprised at the reason they gave: the wine is a classic of balance and style.

There is only one problem with these wines, as we've told Giorgio many times. He smiles a bit ironically and admits we are right, but. . . . The defect, a grave one: availability, or to be more specific, the lack of it. Once the challenge of making the best wine he possibly can is met, he seems to lose interest in selling it.

Must we go all the way to Bozen to get these wines? True, it's a good excuse to spend a few days with Giorgio, but not really the most convenient method of stocking one's cellar. It's a problem shared by wine lovers, restaurateurs, and wine merchants. The patient and good-natured Solci brothers have been known to throw their hands in the air in exasperation.

Giorgio doesn't decant his wines or open the bottles in advance to give the wine air. He enjoys following the wine's progress as it develops in the glass throughout the meal, inevitably getting better as it goes. When he smiles and gives a short approving nod over the last drops of a wine, you wish you had had the forbearance to drink a little more slowly yourself and still had some left in your own glass to savor. Cabernet ****

THE QUALITY OF ALTO ADIGE CABERNET

Some of Italy's finest Cabernets are produced in this area, Cabernets that age better than most of those produced elsewhere in the country. There are also some good Merlots made in the Alto Adige, though we have considerably less experience with them. Rating: **/***

VINTAGE INFORMATION AND TASTING NOTES

About five years ago we spoke to some producers about their assessment of the vintages here for Cabernet. Giorgio Grai told us that 1969 was surely the finest vintage for Cabernet and 1975 and 1971 were on the next level. Tiefenbrunner picked 1983, 1981, 1979, and 1976 as the best vintages, and 1982 and 1980 as the worst. Franco Kettmeir rated 1983 as the best of the recent vintages and 1981 as the worst.

Antonio Niederbacher rates 1985, 1983, 1981, and 1976 at three stars out of four, and 1984, 1982, 1980, 1979, 1978, 1977, and 1975 at two.

Although we take exception with some of Antonio Rossi's ratings, we include those ratings as being better than none. Our experience is too limited. Our problem with the Rossi ratings is our doubt that there could have been so many good vintages, and no bad ones, in some two decades! Rossi

rated 1983 and 1971 for Cabernet as four-star vintages, and 1988, 1986, 1985, 1982, 1981, 1979, 1976, and 1973 as three out of four, with 1987, 1984, 1980, 1978, 1977, 1975, 1974, 1972, and 1970 getting two stars.[4]

Tiefenbrunner 1987 Schloss Turmhof (6/90, 5,500 bottles). [70 percent cabernet sauvignon, 30 percent cabernet franc.] Pungent, herbaceous aroma; fruity but coarse, and obvious. * —

Alöis Lageder 1986 (4/89). Nice fruit, some herbal notes; soft, balanced and fresh. **

Giorgio Grai 1986 (4/90). Lovely and refined cabernet aroma displays nuances of cassis and tobacco; mouth-filling, explosive flavors, suggestive of cassis, licorice, tobacco and green olives, enormous length; real class. *** +

Hofstatter 1986 Cabernet Sauvignon (4/88). Restrained varietal herbaceousness, hint of berries and green olives; good body, flavorful. ** +

Alöis Lageder 1985 Lowengang (4/89, 8,000 bottles). [The vineyard was planted in 1922. It contains 5 percent cabernet franc.] Rich and intense on both the nose and palate, sweet, round and ripe; lots of style. *** —

Laimburger 1985 (4/87). Herbaceous, low acid, shallow, dull.

Alöis Lageder 1984 (4/87). More refinement than the '84 Riserva, and more flavor and structure as well; some firmness, moderately tannic aftertaste. *

Alöis Lageder 1984 Lowengang (4/89, 7,500 bottles). This was the first vintage for this wine. Refined cassis and berry aroma; round and soft, balanced, a bit light at the end. **

Alöis Lageder 1984 Magreid (ex-cask, 4/85). [100 percent cabernet sauvignon.] Herbaceous, varietal aroma, somewhat grassy; at this point overly fruity, needs to be tamed, fairly well balanced. *

Alöis Lageder 1984 Riserva (4/87). Herbaceous, somewhat pungent and aggressive, though fruity. +

Bauernkelleri 1984 (ex-barrique, 4/85). Bell peppers and new oak on aroma and flavor with sweet vanilla adding an interesting component. * —

Alöis Lageder 1983 Wurmbrand (4/85). [75 percent cabernet sauvignon, 25 percent cabernet franc.] Light, undeveloped aroma, some herbaceousness carries through on the palate; some harshness and astringency but a lot of flavor and potential; needs time to really show its quality, for now *(*)

Alöis Lageder 1982 (4/85). Notes of cassis and grass on aroma; soft, touch of tannin, well balanced. ** —

Alöis Lageder 1982 Riserva Wurmbrand (4/85). [70 to 75 percent cabernet sauvignon, 25 to 30 percent cabernet franc.] Light varietal aroma, some cassislike notes; nice fruit on entry, light tannin, lacks some length. *(*)

Kellereigenossenschaft 1982 Magreid, Magre (4/85). Restrained bell pepper aroma; more aggressive on the palate though nice fruit as well. *

Kettmeir 1982 Cabernet Sauvignon (*4 times, 6/86*). Herbaceous, grassy aroma; soft, bell pepper component along with the fruit flavor, light tannin, low acid. * −

Schloss Schwanburg 1982 Riserva [Rudolf Carl Erben] (*4/85*). Bell pepper and cassis aroma; fairly well balanced, light tannin, fairly soft; some character. * +

Alöis Lageder 1981 Riserva Wurmbrand (*4/85*). Tar and cassis on aroma, lightly grassy notes; medium-bodied, fairly well knit, could be longer on palate, finishes with a touch of tannin. *(+)

H. Lun 1981 non-DOC (*11/84*). Herbaceous; low acid, unbalanced, some fruit.

Tiefenbrunner 1981 Riserva (*11/84*). [70 percent cabernet sauvignon, 30 percent cabernet franc.] Refined cabernet aroma; elegant, well structured, soft, round and flavorful, some length. ** +

Alöis Lageder 1980 (*4 times, 7/85*). Refined cabernet aroma, some herbaceousness, fruity nuances; soft, perhaps too green tasting, but drinkable enough. * +

Alöis Lageder 1980 Riserva Wurmbrand (*4/85*). Lovely bouquet, some cassis over light grassiness; smooth and round, tasty; ready though no need to rush to drink it, it'll hold for some time. **

Bauernkellerei 1980 (*4/85*). Herbaceous aroma with cassis notes; flavorful, light tannin, soft-centered, fairly well balanced, a bit short. * +

Josef Brigl 1980 (*4/85*). Varietal bell peppers; wine settles in the mouth with low acid and hangs at the end.

Kettmeir 1980 Cabernet Sauvignon (*3 times, 6/83*). Light, fruity aroma; light tannin, soft and fruity.*

Alöis Lageder 1979 Riserva (*4/85*). [70 percent cabernet sauvignon, 30 percent cabernet franc.] Bell pepper character, flat, harsh finish, a surprise from a usually quite good producer.

Josef Brigl 1979 (*twice, 4/85*). Bell peppers and still more bell peppers, some nice fruit beneath the vegetables.

Bauernkellerei 1978 (*4/85*). Restrained bell pepper aroma, licorice and cassis notes; nice flavor, soft, finish has a vague dankness. *

Kettmeir 1978 Cabernet Sauvignon (*4/85*). Cassis aroma, some mint; still has tannin; seems to be losing its fruit, drying out.

Giorgio Grai 1977 Bellendorf and Kehlburg (*6 times, 9/89*). [50-50 blend of both cabernets.] Bouquet displays suggestions of mint and tea; round though a bit of an edge; most agreeable and with class. *** −

Kellereigenossenschaft Girlan 1977 "Baron Widmann Kurtatsch" (*10/79*). Characteristic bell pepper aroma, one-dimensional; soft and fruity on entry, shallow, short, harsh, metallic aftertaste.

Giorgio Grai 1975 Bellendorf, Herrnhofer, and Kehlburg (*12 times, 3/90*). Rich bouquet recalls green olives and mint, and has an herbaceous backnote; soft, round and velvety, light tannin, richly flavored, packed with fruit, herbaceous underpinning, lots of style, enormous length; very ready. *** − *Bottle of 4/85:* Intensely rich bouquet recalls cassis and blueberries; soft, round and velvety, light tannin, lots of flavor and style, enormous length; enjoyable now but has potential for further improvement. *** +

Alöis Lageder 1974 Riserva (*4/85*). [85 to 90 percent cabernet sauvignon.] Nice nose, fruity with a cassis note; flavorful, drink up; age shows at the end, but still good. **

Alöis Lageder 1973 Riserva Wurmbrand (*4/85*). [85 percent cabernet sauvignon, 15 percent cabernet franc.] Rich bouquet, light grassiness over cassis; light tannin, velvet center, loads of flavor, well knit, quite long; impressive, some elegance. ***

Giorgio Grai 1973 Herrnhofer and Kehlburg (*6 times, 4/81*). [Two-thirds cabernet franc, one-third cabernet sauvignon.] Herbaceous aroma, with a note of cassis; still some tannin, richly flavored, very long finish. *** − *Bottle of 4/80:* (This wine was opened three days previously in Verona and left in the trunk of our car half full, it was retasted in Abruzzo, after being jostled around for many kilometers.) Expansive aroma rises out of the glass, showing more of an herbaceous aspect than when tasted in Verona; seems softer and smoother as well. ** +

Bauernkellerei 1971 Riserva (*4/85*). Light but nice aroma, licorice and cassis; still flavorful though beginning to dry out a bit. ** −

Giorgio Grai 1971 Herrnhofer (*twice, 2/84*). Richly fruited aroma with the characteristic varietal herbaceousness; rich, ripe fruit flavors, soft and round, fairly long; some age shows at the end which is vaguely bitter. ** +

Alöis Lageder 1970 Riserva (*4/85*). [85 to 90 percent cabernet sauvignon, 15 to 10 percent cabernet franc.] Cassis, bell pepper undertone; the flavor is almost sweet, tastes of ripe fruit, some delicacy, thins out at the end. **

Alöis Lageder 1969 Riserva Wurmbrand (*4/85*). Richly fruited aroma recalls cassis; flavorful, light tannin; beginning to dry out at the end, still good. ** −

Giorgio Grai 1969 Bellendorf (*3 times, 4/85*). Beautiful garnet robe shading to orange; intense bouquet, cassis with an herbaceous backnote; full of style, flavor and elegance, sumptuous; shows no age. ****

Giorgio Grai 1967 Kehlburg (*3 times, 1/84*). Beautiful brick robe, orange at rim; lovely bouquet, recalls mint and cassis; liquid velvet, smooth and supple, richly flavored, a touch of tannin adds life, very long finish; real quality here. *** +

Schloss Schwanburg 1967 Riserva [Rudolf Carl Erben] (*4/85*). Bouquet of concentrated cassis; loaded with flavor, no sign of age, well-balanced light tannin; very ready. ** +

Giorgio Grai 1966 Kehlburg (*5 times, 5/87*). The last three times we tasted it, between March and May 1987, our impression was the same, a great wine of real distinction. Cassis, tobacco and green olive aroma with an herbaceous nuance; finely honed. soft, velvety, complete, enormously long finish; not even a trace of age; great style and elegance, sheer perfection. **** *Bottle of 11/84:* Color shows more age than the rest of the wine; bouquet has an enormous richness, with nuances of blueberries, vanilla and herbaceous elements; finely structured, liquid velvet, full of flavor, enormous length; exudes style and balance. *** +

Alto Adige Merlot

The most important of the merlot plantings in the Alto Adige are in Magreid, Kurtinig, Salurn, Terlan, and Andrian. Tom O'Toole, who is quite knowledgeable about the wines of this, his adopted region, believes the best merlot grapes are grown in Siebeneich, near Terlan. Franco Kettmeir agrees with this; he bottles a Merlot from that area. Rating: */**

Recommended Producers of Merlot

Alöis Lageder
* Josef Hofstatter
Kellereigenossenschaft Gries, Steinhof
Kettmeir, Siebeneich
Liebeneich Kellereigenossenschaft, Schreckbichl

VINTAGE INFORMATION AND TASTING NOTES

Antonio Rossi gave four stars out of four to 1983 and 1971; three to 1988, 1986, 1985, 1982, 1979, 1976, 1975, and 1973; and two to 1987, 1984, 1981, 1980, 1978, 1977, 1974, 1972, and 1970.[5]

Alöis Lageder 1986 (4/89). Berries and green olives define the nose; good fruit, balanced, fresh and soft. **

Hofstatter 1986 (4/88). Nose closed in; flavorful with good fruit, soft and round, smooth-centered under light tannin. **

Alöis Lageder 1984 (4/87). Small-scale, soft and fruity, could use more fruit, dull finish.

Liebeneich Kellereigenossenschaft 1983 Schreckbichl (4/85). Characteristic varietal aroma; fair balance, fruity, good overall though has some harsh edges. * −

Kettmeir 1982 (4/85). Cherrylike fruit, grassy, spicy aroma; light tannin, somewhat unbalanced.

Alöis Lageder 1981 (4/85). Grassy aroma; lacks some structure, light and simple, fruity. * −

Alöis Lageder 1980 (4/85). Fruity aroma, lightly grassy backnotes; well balanced, quite nice now, drink up; starting to show some senility on the finish. * +

Kettmeir 1979 (4/85). Berry, fruity aroma; light tannin, easy to drink; not to keep. *

Kettmeir 1978 Siebeneich (11/84). Varietal aroma; a bit light, fruity; shows signs of age. * −

Hofstatter 1971 (3/80). Rich nose; rich flavor, still has some tannin, well balanced; fine quality. ** +

ALZERO (*Veneto*). Alzero is made from a blend of 90 percent cabernet franc and 10 percent cabernet sauvignon.

APRILIA (*Lazio*), *DOC*. The Aprilia area encompasses the village of that name and parts of Cisterna, Latina, and Nettuno. Viticulture in this area, south of Roma, has a recent history. It dates from 1948, when Italian farmers who fled Tunisia during the Second World War settled here. More recent data, from 1988, report that the region's 203 registered growers have 1,463 acres (592 hectares) planted for Merlot di Aprilia. They have produced, between 1986 and 1988, an annual average of 45,651 cases.[6] DOC also recognizes trebbiano and sangiovese. The Merlot of Aprilia must be made from a minimum of 95 percent merlot grapes. At most 1,050 gallons per acre (98 hectoliters per hectare) can be produced. There is no minimum aging requirement, but the wine must attain at least 12 percent alcohol. This wine at its best is soft and fruity, an everyday quaffable red wine, no more. It is a wine of no particular distinction that is best drunk young, before its second, at most, third year. Rating: 0

Antonio Rossi rates the years:[7]

****	1985, 1980
***	1988, 1983, 1982, 1979, 1977, 1976, 1975, 1972, 1970
**	1987, 1986, 1984, 1981, 1978, 1974, 1973, 1971

AQUILEIA (*Friuli–Venezia Giulia*), *DOC*. Red varieties make up some 55 percent of the plantings, 900 out of 1,630 acres (365 out of 660 hectares) in this region, which encompasses all or part of 18 villages in the province of Udine. Cabernet franc accounts for 165 acres (67 hectares), cabernet sauvignon for 84 (34), and merlot 441 (178). This amounts to over 40 percent of the DOC acreage in Aquileia. Yearly production of Cabernet Franc averaged 36,300 cases between 1986 and 1988, Cabernet Sauvignon 19,300 cases, and Merlot more than 60,000 cases. This is more than 77 percent of the total DOC red wine production for Aquileia, and more than 38 percent of the average DOC production for that district between 1986 and 1988.[8]

A wine from Aquileia labeled Cabernet can be made from any combination of cabernet sauvignon and/or cabernet franc grapes, while one labeled either Cabernet Franc or Cabernet Sauvignon must be made from at least 85 percent of the named variety, ditto the Merlot. There is also a Rosato made from 70 to 80 percent merlot and 20 to 30 percent of one or both of the two cabernets and/or refosco nostrano or dal peduncolo rosso.

The maximum yield for the cabernets is 898 gallons per acre (84 hectoliters per hectare) and 973 (91) for the merlot. There are no minimum aging requirements. The minimum alcohol for any of the Cabernet wines is 11 percent, while the Merlot must contain at least 10.5 percent.

Vanni Tavagnacco, the fine enologist at 1 Moròs, told us that this area is a better one for red wines than for whites. There is a salty character to some of the wines, more pronounced in the whites, which is attributed to the proximity of the sea.

The only producer from Aquileia we can recommend is Ca' Bolani, which produces both a Cabernet and a Merlot. This isn't to suggest that there are no other good producers. It's just that those whose wines we've tasted were not memorable.

Aquileia Cabernet is generally best drunk before its third year; Merlot, before its second. Both wines can be good with an additional year of age. Rating: Cabernet *; Cabernet Franc *; Cabernet Sauvignon *; Merlot *

ANTONIO ROSSI'S RATING OF AQUILEIA'S RED WINE VINTAGES[9]

Vintage	Cabernet	Merlot
1988	****	****
1987	**	**
1986	***	***
1985	****	****
1984	**	**
1983	****	****
1982	***	***
1981	***	****
1980	***	***
1979	***	**
1978	****	****
1977	**	**
1976	***	***
1975	***	***

ARALDO ROSSO (*Friuli–Venezia Giulia*). Luigi Valle produces Araldo Rosso from a blend of cabernet, merlot, and refosco.

AVIGNONESI (*Toscana*). This fine producer, in the Montepulciano zone, produced an '88 Merlot and '88 Cabernet Sauvignon, both of which we tasted from *barrique*. Both were pure varietals and both very good. We found the Merlot the better of the two. The Merlot is *barrique*-aged for fourteen to sixteen months, the Cabernet longer. Rating: Cabernet Sauvignon [**]; Merlot [**]

BARBAROLA (*Trentino–Alto Adige*), *DOC*. Raffaelle Rino produces this merlot-cabernet blend. It is a wine that ages mod-

erately well. The last one we tasted, the '77, was very good. Rating ** −

BAREDO (*Friuli-Venezia Giulia*). Pighin owns vineyards in the Grave del Friuli and Collio zones, and produces a range of reliable and good wines. Among those wines is the *vino da tavola* Baredo, made from a blend of cabernet, merlot, and, we heard, refosco.

BELLAGIO (*Lombardia*). This medium-bodied dry red is produced in the Como area from cabernet franc, malbec, merlot, and a small amount of pinot noir. It drinks well from its second to fourth year.

BERENGARIO (*Friuli–Venezia Giulia*). Domenico Zonin produces Berengario from a blend of two-thirds cabernet sauvignon and one-third merlot. The only one we tasted, the '88, was drinkable enough, if a bit coarse. Rating * −

TASTING NOTE

1988 (12/90). Fairly nice fruit, soft under a light tannic note; somewhat coarse. * −

BORGO DI PEUMA RUSSOLO (*Friuli–Venezia Giulia*). The 1983 was made from a blend of 90 percent merlot with 10 percent cabernet sauvignon and refosco. Ten percent whole berries were added to the must in order to induce a second fermentation, similar to the *governo* of Chianti. The '83 was aged in *barriques* of Tronçais oak. They produced 2,200 bottles of the '83. That wine was fresh, fruity, and vinous, and while it lacked distinction, it was drinkable. Rating 0

BOSCO ELICEO MERLOT (*Emilia-Romagna*), *DOC*. This new DOC includes four wines—a Merlot, Fortana, Sauvignon, and Bianco made from trebbiano. The vineyards are located in the provinces of Ferrara and Ravenna. In 1988 there were 5 growers with 28 registered acres (11.4 hectares) of merlot out of a total of 53 growers and 206 acres (83 hectares) in this DOC zone. All the vines were planted in the province of Ferrara. In 1988, the first year that data was reported, 12,684 cases of Merlot were produced.[10] DOC has set a maximum yield of 1,122 gallons per acre (105 hectoliters per hectare), and a minimum alcohol of 10.5 percent for the Merlot.

BRAIDA NUOVA (*Friuli–Venezia Giulia*). Gianni Vescovo produces this red wine at his Borgo Conventi winery from a blend of 40 percent cabernet sauvignon, 30 to 40 percent cabernet franc, and 20 to 30 percent merlot. The grapes are from a 2-acre (0.8-hectare) vineyard in Farra d'Isonzo in the Collio production zone. His first cabernet-merlot blend was from the 1979 vintage. That wine was made from 85 percent merlot and 15 percent cabernet franc. Like its more recent counterpart, it was aged in small oak barrels. Vescovo gives the Braida Nuova about one year in *barrique*. He produces about 5,000 bottles annually. This is a medium-bodied dry wine with a fruity aroma of cherries and blackberries over an herbaceous background. Rating **

TASTING NOTES

1985 (*twice, 4/89*). Herbaceous, green olive and fruit aroma; soft, pungent yet fruity, balanced. **

1984 (*10/89*). Ripe fruit and cassis aroma, green olive and herbaceous underpinning; soft, fruity and ready. ** –

1983 (*4/85*). Characteristic herbaceousness over oak; a lot of flavor, some harshness suggests it is still young though not a lot of tannin, finish is a bit short; needs two more years yet. *(* –)

1982 (*4,85, 2,810 bottles*). Richly fruited aroma, some cassis and oak, slightly grassy; full of flavor, supple, light tannin, well balanced, could be longer on the finish. **(+)

1979 (*4/81*). Lovely nose, light herbaceousness, suggestions of cherries and blackberries; well structured, lots of flavor, some tannin; some style evident. **(*)

BREGANZE (*Veneto*), *DOC*. The Breganze production zone encompasses the villages of Breganze, Fara Vicentino, Mason Vicentino, Molvena, and parts of nine others, all in the province of Vicenza. There are some 25,000 acres (10,000 hectares) under vines in Breganze, about half on the hillsides and half on the plains.

Two DOC wines from this zone concern us here: Breganze Rosso and Cabernet. In 1988, 1,293 growers cultivated 934 acres (377 hectares) of vines that were delimited for this DOC. For Breganze Cabernet, 294 growers cultivated 183 registered acres (74 hectares).[11]

Breganze Rosso must contain at least 85 percent merlot; the remaining 15 percent can be both or either of the cabernets, marzemino, groppello, and/or freisa. Not all producers follow that regulation, though, and, in some cases at

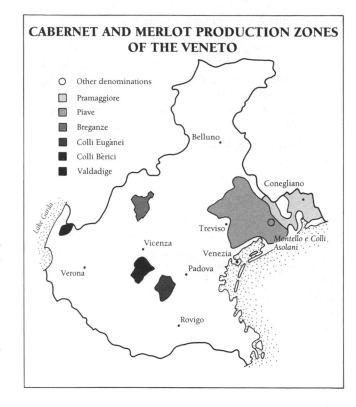

CABERNET AND MERLOT PRODUCTION ZONES OF THE VENETO

- ○ Other denominations
- Pramaggiore
- Piave
- Breganze
- Colli Eugànei
- Colli Bèrici
- Valdadige

least, their wine is no less for it. The Cabernet must be from 100 percent cabernet—cabernet sauvignon and/or cabernet franc.

Annual production, from 1986 through 1988, averaged a little more than 100,000 cases of the Rosso and 37,600 of the Cabernet, not a lot of wine.[12] And, not surprisingly, the best ones are even scarcer. For the most part, the Cabernet is best before its fourth year; the Rosso, or Merlot, before its third. Rating: Cabernet */***; Rosso (Merlot) *

Recommended Producers

Bartolomeo
* Maculan
Villa Magna

DOC REQUIREMENTS FOR BREGANZE

	Minimum Varietal Component	Minimum Alcohol	Maximum Yield in	
			Gallons/Acre	Hectoliters/Hectare
Cabernet	100%	11.5%	903	84.5
Superiore	100%	12.0%	903	84.5
Rosso (Merlot)	85%	11.0%	973	91

From Antonio Niederbacher's vintage chart:

****	1982, 1950
***	1985, 1983, 1981, 1979, 1977, 1972, 1971, 1970, 1967, 1964, 1961, 1957, 1952
**	1984, 1980, 1978, 1976, 1975, 1974, 1973, 1969, 1968, 1966, 1962, 1959, 1958, 1956, 1954
*	1960, 1955
0	1965, 1963, 1953, 1951

ANTONIO ROSSI RATES THE BREGANZE VINTAGES[13]

Vintage	Cabernet	Rosso
1988	***	***
1987	***	***
1986	***	***
1985	***	***
1984	**	**
1983	***	***
1982	****	****
1981	****	****
1980	***	***
1979	****	****
1978	***	***
1977	***	****
1976	***	***
1975	**	**
1974	***	**
1973	**	**
1972	***	***
1971	***	***
1970	***	***

The Breganze Zone's Finest Producer

The finest producer in the zone, and the most innovative, is Maculan. Enologist Fausto Maculan produces a number of very fine wines, white and red, sweet and dry. Among them is the exceptionally fine *barrique*-aged dessert wine Torcolato and the fine white Prato di Canzio. He also makes two red wines of real quality, Fratta and Palazzotto, and a couple of very good, but less grand, ones—Brentino and Breganze Cabernet.

Maculan has 30 acres (12 hectares) of vines which supply 25 percent of their grapes.

The Brentino Breganze Rosso is a blend of both cabernets plus some merlot grapes from various vineyards, the pro-

portions depending on the vintage. The '86 was made from 40 percent each of the two cabernets and 20 percent merlot. The '81 was made from 40 percent cabernet sauvignon and 30 percent each of cabernet franc and merlot; for the '80 Maculan used the same three varieties in a 25-35-40 blend. In the past a small portion of the wine, at most 10 percent, was aged in *barrique*. And in some vintages it is possible, Fausto told us, that none of the wine will be put into *barrique*. It depends on the grapes. Fausto doesn't make wine by a cookbook; he judges his material and works accordingly. Production was some 28,800 bottles in 1981, 10,800 in 1982, and 19,105 in 1986. Brentino is ready to drink from its second year. Drink it soon afterward—it doesn't pay keeping. Breganze Rosso, Brentino * +

TASTING NOTES

1988 *(6/90)*. Herbal, grassy, fruity aroma; light tannin, simple, ready, a tad short. * +

1987 *(twice, 10/89)*. Green olive and tea aroma; soft and round, very ready. * +

1985 *(twice, 2/88)*. Moderately intense aroma, herbaceous background; soft and fruity, balanced. * +

1983 *(4 times, 5/87)*. Light and characteristic herbaceous aroma, cherry note; soft and fruity, ready though light tannin at the end. ** −

1982 *(4/85)*. Light but fruity aroma; some tannin, nice fruit, good balance; the tannin on the aftertaste says it could use another year of age, though it is nice now. *(+)

1981 *(3 times, 7/85)*. Aroma of cabernet fruit, vague bell pepper character; light tannin, fruity, soft and round, short; ready; a nice glass of wine. * +

1980 *(twice, 4/85, 14,870 bottles)*. Light, herbaceous aroma; fruity, more to it than the '81 or '82; moderate length. **

The regular Breganze Cabernet is made from 60 percent cabernet sauvignon and 40 percent cabernet franc. They produced 4,320 bottles in 1983. Maculan also produces two Breganze Cabernet crus, Palazzotto and Fratta.

The Breganze Cabernet Palazzotto is made from 100 percent cabernet sauvignon grapes grown in this 6.4-acre (2.6-hectare) vineyard in Mirabella di Breganze. A few years ago the vineyard wasn't in full production. In 1981, Fausto produced 11,496 regular bottles and 390 magnums; in 1982, 11,400 bottles and 360 magnums; in 1985, 13,440 bottles and 150 magnums. The wine is aged for one year in *barrique*. The '85 had 12.4 percent alcohol; the '82, 12.2, and the '81, 12. In the mid-1980s, Fausto rated the vintages for Palazzotto this way: 1983 with four stars was the best, 1980 at three, and 1982 and 1981 at two. If it wasn't for the Fratta, there is no question that the Palazzotto would be the finest red wine of the zone. Although we prefer the Palazzotto, we must admit that as far as the overall quality is concerned, Fratta is the slightly better wine. Rating ***

1986 (*3 times, 6/90, 12,564 bottles*). Herbal, cassis and tobacco aroma; soft, light tannin, tasty, open, forward fruit; ready. ** +

1985 (*12/87*). Refined varietal aroma has an oak overlay; well balanced, lots of flavor; real elegance; just might be the best Palazzotto to date. *** +

1984 (*4/87*). Refined varietal aroma; balanced, some elegance, a little light, nice fruit, light finish. ** –

1983 (*9 times, 1/90*). Aroma of tobacco and cassis, an oak component; finely crafted with loads of rich fruit flavor, round and ripe, velvety; very ready; real class. *** +

1982 (*3 times, 2/86*). Refined aroma of cassis and oak; lots of flavor, soft, almost sweet, acid a little soft, fairly long; very ready. ** +

1981 (*7/85*). Lovely bouquet, refined and elegant, characteristic cassis and oak nuances; very well balanced, still some rough edges to smooth out but a lot of flavor; in a somewhat understated style, elegant and stylish; sure to improve over the next two or three years but lovely now; and Fausto gave the year only two stars. We gave the wine ***.

1980 (*4/85, 2,768 bottles*). Richly intense aroma of cassis over oak; richly flavored and tasty, smooth-textured. ***

The Breganze Cabernet Fratta is made from 50 to 60 percent cabernet sauvignon and 50 to 40 percent cabernet franc grapes grown in that 2.5-acre (1-hectare) vineyard. Maculan produced 4,368 cases of Fratta in 1981, 3,900 in 1982, and 6,000 in 1983. The wine achieves about half a degree of alcohol more than the Palazzotto. The first Fratta produced was from the 1977 vintage. The '79 was the first aged in *barrique*; it spent six months in Slavonian oak barrels. The '80 was aged for a year in Alliers oak, as was the '81.

A few years ago Fausto said that thus far 1983 was the best vintage for Fratta. He also rated 1980 and 1979 at four stars, and 1982 at three, with 1981 and 1978 getting two, and the worst of all vintages, 1977, receiving one. Fratta is, without question, one of the finest Cabernet wines produced in Italy. Rating *** +

1986 (*twice, 10/89*). Rich and concentrated on the nose and palate, intense flavor, soft; a lot to offer and to like. ** +

1984 (*4/87*). Spicy, cassis aroma, oak overlay; lots of style, good structure and backbone. **(* –)

1983 (*3 times, 4/87*). Somewhat restrained aroma, displays a refined fruit character; rich flavor, still a little young but attractive, good structure; needs time to really develop and round out. ***(+)

1982 (*twice, 9/86*). Rich bouquet of cassis, licorice and oak, vague herbaceous note; full-flavored and rich in extract, though on a leaner frame than the '83; on the young side. **(*)

1981 (*4/85*). Richly fruited aroma, refined; firm with an astringent edge; still young, good potential. **(+)

1980 (*4/85, 4,427 bottles*). Intense bouquet suggesting cassis, vague raspberry note and some oaky vanilla; flavorful, balanced, still needs time for some more tannin to resolve itself. **(*)

1979 (*4/85, 3,985 bottles*). Initial oak aroma gives way to an herbaceous character; nice fruit on entry, firm, lots of flavor; long, needs another year or two. ** +

1978 (*4/80*). Shy nose, some cabernet fruit evident; some tannin with an underlying softness, full finish. *

1977 (*4/85*). Fruity aroma, vague herbaceousness; some tannin, but soft and flavorful; quite nice; no need to hold any longer. **

BRENTINO. *See* **BREGANZE.**

BRUME DI MONTE (*Trentino–Alto Adige*). Since 1988, the large co-op Càvit has been producing Brume di Monte, a Trentino Rosso DOC made from a blend of 70 percent of the two cabernets with 30 percent merlot. Rating *

1988 (*12/90*). Light, herbal aroma; light tannin, tasty though short. *

CABERNELLO (*Trentino–Alto Adige*). Barone Fini produces this 100 percent cabernet sauvignon wine. The '85 was on the pungent side and was agreeable, if not much more. Rating *

CABERNET, CABERNET FRANC, OR CABERNET SAUVIGNON DEL FRIULI–VENEZIA GIULIA, DEL TRE VENEZIA, OR DEL VENETO (*Veneto*). These *vini da tavola* tend to be light- to medium-bodied, dry, and soft. The herbaceous characteristic of the grape variety is quite pronounced, along with an often pungent and sometimes aggressive nature. Many are dull and flabby. They are, as a general rule, best drunk young while their attractive fruitiness is still evident. Afra e Tobia Scarpa produces an excellent example of Cabernet del Veneto, and Orlandi produces a good Cabernet Sauvignon del Veneto. As a rule, most are uninteresting. Some are good, and a few very good. Rating 0/**

CABERNET SAUVIGNON DEL PIEMONTE, OR CABERNET SAUVIGNON DELLE LANGHE (*Piemonte*). In recent years, in a further step toward the internationalization of wine, more and more producers, following the lead of Angelo Gaja, have planted cabernet sauvignon in their Barolo or Barbaresco vineyards. The excellent Barolo producer Domenico Clerico will, from 1992, make a Cabernet Sauvignon. The 8.6-acre (3.5-hectare) section of the Cannubi-Muscatel vineyard owned by the Marchesi di Barolo is being replanted with cabernet sauvignon, barbera, and nebbiolo. Pio Cesare planted some cabernet sauvignon vines in their Treiso vineyard as an experiment. Alfredo e Giovanni Roagna's Azienda Agricola "I Paglieri" produced their first Cabernet Sauvignon from the 1990 vintage. See also *Castello di Salabue, Colle Manora, Darmaggi,* and *I Fossaretti.*

CAMOI (*Veneto*). Orlandi, connected with the very good Prosecco producer Azienda Agricola La Case Bianche, produces this cabernet sauvignon–merlot-wildbacher blend. Camoi is the name of the vineyard. The only one we tasted was the '82. We suspect that this is the same wine that used to be labeled *Costa delle Pergole Rosso.* It was quite good. Rating **

TASTING NOTE

1982 (*9/86*). Intriguing, singular aroma, some cabernet character evident; good balance, flavorful, soft, light tannin. **

CAMPAGNANO (*Lazio*). This wine is made from a blend of the two cabernets and the local cesanese variety. It is a medium-bodied dry red wine best drunk young.

CAMPO DEL LAGO. *See* **COLLI BERICI.**

CANTALEONE (*Trentino–Alto Adige*). Giovanni Visentin produces this wine from a blend of merlot, teroldego, and cabernet grapes grown in the S. Michele d'Adige area. It is a medium-bodied dry red of about 12.5 percent alcohol that ages moderately well.

CASTEL S. MICHELE (*Trentino–Alto Adige*). The Istituto Agrario Provinciale S. Michele produces some 16,000 to 18,000 bottles a year of this wine from 40 to 45 percent merlot, 35 to 40 percent cabernet sauvignon, and 20 percent cabernet franc. We've heard that this blend has changed in recent years to a 60-20-20 combination of merlot, cabernet sauvignon, and cabernet franc. It is dry, soft, and flavorful, with a characteristic herbaceous aspect. Castel San Michele is at its best from its third to sixth year. Rating **

CASTEL SAN GIORGIO (*Lazio*). This wine is made from a blend of cesanese, merlot, and montepulciano grapes grown in the Maccarese area west of Roma. It is a medium-bodied dry red wine that ages moderately well. Castel San Giorgio

is available in the vicinity of Roma, if it can't be found further afield.

CASTELLO DI RONCADE (*Veneto*). Barone Ciani Bassetti produces this wine from cabernet sauvignon, cabernet franc, merlot, and malbec grapes grown on his Villa Giustiniani farm in the Piave River area of Treiso. A normal blend is 40 percent cabernet sauvignon, and 20 percent each cabernet franc, merlot, and malbec. According to some reports, he also adds a little petit verdot. The labels we've seen list the first four grapes, but not the last. We'll take his word for it. Bassetti ages the Castello di Roncade in small barrels for two years. It is a medium-bodied dry soft red with an underlying herbaceous character. The wine drinks well from its fourth to eighth year; in the best vintages, it can live for as much as ten years. We haven't tasted it since the '79 almost a decade ago. Rating [**]

CASTELLO DI SALABUE (*Piemonte*). Carlo Nob. Cassinis produces a Cabernet Sauvignon from grapes grown at his 37-acre (15-hectare) Castello di Salabue estate, which is located at Salabue di Ponzano in the *comune* of Ponzano Monferrato in the province of Alessandria. We've never met the wine.

CASTELVECCHIO (*Veneto*). This wine is made from cabernet and merlot grapes grown in the Portogruaro area west of Friuli. It is a medium-bodied wine of about 12 percent alcohol that can take moderate age.

COGNO (*Trentino–Alto Adige*). Carlo Rossi (no connection to the California wine) produces this wine from a blend of 50 percent merlot and 50 percent of the two cabernets, grown in the Mezza Prada district of Cimone in Trentino. Cogno drinks well from its third or fourth year.

COLLABRIGO ROSSO (*Veneto*). This wine is made from 70 percent cabernet sauvignon and 30 percent merlot.

COLLE DEL CALVARIO (*Lombardia*). Tenuta Castello blends 30 percent merlot with 70 percent cabernet sauvignon grapes grown in their vineyards in Grumello del Monte near Bergamo to produce this medium-bodied dry red wine. Colle del Calvario is aged for about two years in oak barrels. It is a wine that ages moderately well; drink within four to five years of the vintage. This wine is produced within the **Valcalèpio** DOC zone, and within recent vintage is sold under that DOC.

COLLE MANORA (*Piemonte*). Azienda Agricola "Colle Manora," which is located in the *comune* of Quargnento in the province of Alessandria, grows the imported cabernet sauvignon, merlot, sauvignon, and pinot noir vines alongside the local barbera and grignolino. They produce a Cabernet Sauvignon and Merlot. We've never met either one.

COLLE PICCHIONI, VIGNA DEL VASSALLO (*Lazio*). Giorgio Grai produces a number of red and white wines for Paola di Mauro at her Colle Picchioni estate in the Marino zone near Lake Albano, south of Roma. Grai produces a white Marino and three red wines here, first a *rosso* that is soft, fruity, and satisfying, then a bigger, more intense and serious red from the single-vineyard Due Santi. Colle Picchioni's best wine is the red merlot–cabernet sauvignon–sangiovese blend named for the Del Vassallo vineyard where the grapes are grown. The first one was the '81. We were told that the '83 was made from 30 percent each merlot and sangiovese with 40 percent montepulciano. The wine today is a blend of both cabernets with merlot. Vigna del Vassallo is aged in 132- to 264-gallon (5- to 10-hectoliter) oak casks. Colle Picchioni produces some 6,000 to 7,000 bottles of this very good wine per year. (See chapter 12 for a further discussion of this wine.) Rating: Vigna del Vassallo ** +

TASTING NOTES

1985 (*4/87, 5,060 bottles*). Although the nose is closed the richness is evident; young yet with rich, attractive fruit; the tannins need perhaps two more years to soften. **(+)

1984 (*4/88, 5,080 bottles*). A little aggressive yet the attractive fruit and smooth mouth feel make this wine appealing, good weight and structure. ** +

1983 (*7 times, 3/88, 3,460 bottles*). Rich in aroma; rich in flavor, understated yet evident cabernet-merlot character; most attractive. ** + *Bottle of 11/84:* Deep color; big, rich, fruity aroma with notes of cherries; has an uncommon richness for a Roman red, very well balanced, has style, and length. *** −

1982 (*4/86, 3,460 bottles*). Lovely aroma, some complexity; round and smooth, well-made, balanced, long. *** −

COLLI BERICI (*Veneto*), DOC. The Colli Bèrici zone encompasses all or part of 28 *comuni* between the Lessinian Mountains and the Bèrici hills south of the city of Vicenza. Among the wines of this district covered under DOC regulations are Cabernet and Merlot. Both wines must be made from 100 percent of the named variety; the Cabernet can contain either of the two cabernets, alone or in combination.

The vine has quite an ancient history in the Colli Bèrici; grape seeds from the wild species *Vitis silvestris* found here date from the Bronze Age, over 3,000 years ago. Grape growing is referred to in church documents from the eleventh century, and it is known that by 1250 Monte Bèrico was covered with vineyards producing highly regarded wines. In the seventeenth century, Zeffiro Bocci reports, Andrea Scoto wrote about the wines of Barbarano, Costozza, and Lonigo in his Italian itinerary.[14]

Bordeaux varieties were grown here in the nineteenth century, but it wasn't until phylloxera devastated the vineyards in 1929 that these varieties became widely planted. Today the production of Cabernet averages more than 50,000 cases a year, which amounts to 19.7 percent of total red wine production, while the more than 125,000 cases of Merlot account for 48.8 percent of the 257,878 cases of red produced here. In terms of overall production in this DOC zone, annual production between 1986 and 1988 averaged 563,903 cases, with white accounting for 54.4 percent, or 306,205 cases.[15]

With few exceptions, Colli Bèrici Cabernet is best before its fourth year. The Merlot matures a year or two earlier. Rating: Cabernet */**; Merlot */***

Conte da Schio's **Costozza** is a noteworthy wine that is sometimes sold as a Colli Bèrici DOC Cabernet and sometimes not. Ca' Bruzzo produced a good '88 Cabernet. It's the only wine that we've seen from them. The best wines in the zone are produced by Lazzarini.

The Colli Bèrici Zone's Finest Producer

Lazzarini bought the Villa dal Ferro estate located in San Germano dei Bèrici in 1960. He has 32 acres (13 hectares)

DOC REQUIREMENTS FOR COLLI BERICI

	Minimum Varietal Component	Minimum Aging	Minimum Alcohol	Maximum Yield in	
				Gallons/Acre	Hectoliters/Hectare
Cabernet	100%	none	11.0%	834	78
Riserva		3 years, from January 1	12.5%	834	78
Merlot	100%	none	11.0%	973	91

ACREAGE AND AVERAGE PRODUCTION FOR COLLI BERICI

	Growers	Registered Vineyards Acres	Hectares	1986–88 Average Number of Cases
Cabernet	152	320.64	130	50,858
Merlot	381	657.86	266	125,843

Source: *Il Corriere Vinicolo*

FROM ANTONIO ROSSI'S VINTAGE CHART FOR COLLI BERICI:[16]

Vintage	Cabernet	Merlot
1988	***	***
1987	**	**
1986	***	***
1985	****	***
1984	**	**
1983	***	***
1982	***	****
1981	****	***
1980	***	***
1979	****	****
1978	***	***
1977	****	****
1976	***	***
1975	**	**
1974	**	**
1973	**	**
1972	***	***
1971	***	***
1970	***	***

of vines. The Lazzarini wines today are made by enologist Pamela Porro Lazzarini, his daughter.

The Le Rive Rosso is made from both cabernets. It drinks well from four to seven years of the vintage. Rating ** +

TASTING NOTES

1987 (4/87). Refined, fruity aroma, herbaceous and green olive components; soft and flavorful, balanced, well made. **

1986 (4/88). Reticent aroma, notes of spice and green olives; soft, round and smooth. ** +

1978 (4/80). Raspberry aroma, characteristic herbaceous background; loads of fruit, some tannin, concentrated. ** +

1977 (*3 times, 11/82*). Cabernet fruit aroma, light floral note in the back; soft and smooth with light tannin, a bit short. **

1974 (*twice, 4/80*). Nice nose of fruit and spice, bell pepper note in the back; soft, flavorful, light tannin, acid a bit deficient. **

Lazzarini's Campo del Lago is a dry, medium-bodied red wine with a lot of character. It is, in our opinion, the finest wine of the zone and just might be the finest Merlot produced in Italy. This wine is a good accompaniment to steaks and chops. It is at its best drunk between three to six years of age, though it can last eight. Rating ***

THE CRUS AND WINES OF LAZZARINI'S VILLA DAL FERRO

Cru	Variety	Average Number of Bottles Per Year
Bianco del Rocolo	Pinot bianco	13,300
Busa Calcara	Riesling	2,700
Campo del Lago	Merlot	17,300
Costiera Granda	Tocai	5,300
Le Rive Rosso	Cabernet	17,300
Rosso del Roccolo	Pinot nero	8,000
Total		63,900

TASTING NOTES

1986 (4/88). Tobacco and tea along with berrylike notes on the nose; fruity with a light, herbaceous character. ** +

1984 (10/86). A nice glass with the characteristic tobacco and tea components, on the short side. ** −

1980 (1/83). We tasted this wine at a tasting of about three dozen Cabernet and Merlot wines from the Tre Venezia, where it was the only real wine. Fruity, soft; very ready, which seems somewhat of a surprise. ** +

1978 (3 times, 11/82). Light, herbaceous aroma, fruity background; firm texture, flavorful, only defect is a somewhat short finish. **

1977 (3 times, 11/82). Plummy aroma, herbaceous note; firm-textured, full of flavor; a very nice glass of wine. ** +

1975 (3/80). A bit light but tasty and very ready, quite enjoyable. ** +

1972 (11/78). Big and rich on the nose, surprisingly so, green olive notes; soft and flavorful; shows real quality, and from a not very highly regarded vintage. *** −

COLLI BOLOGNESI–MONTE SAN PIETRO–CASTELLI MEDIOVALE (*Emilia-Romagna*), *DOC*. This production zone, southwest of Bologna, covers the villages of Monte San Pietro, Castello di Serravalle, Marzabotto, Monteveglio, Pianoro, Sasso Marconi, and Savigno, and parts of Bazzano, Bologna, Casalecchio di Reno, Crespellano, Monterenzio, S. Lazzaro di Savena, and Zola Predosa in the province of Bologna, and part of Savignano sul Panaro in the province of Modena.

DOC recognizes eight wines. When DOC status was granted to Merlot there was some discussion of also including Cabernet Sauvignon in the discipline. This variety yields the best red wine of the district. Finally, Cabernet Sauvignon is now recognized by the DOC.

In 1988 there were 21 growers in the DOC registry with nearly 50 acres (20 hectares) of cabernet sauvignon and 15 growers with 36 acres (15 hectares) of merlot. Between 1986 and 1988 annual production of DOC wines here has averaged 176,727 case of wine, with nearly 23 percent, or 40,233 cases, of red. Cabernet, with an average of 8,158 cases, and Merlot, with 4,659, account for just over 7 percent of the total and less than 32 percent of the red wine production. In the past decade the production of the Merlot has varied considerably, from a trickle of 1,150 cases in 1981 to 1988's flood of 7,254.[17]

Enrico Vallania produces both a red and a rosé, neither aged in oak. Both are good wines. Bruno Negroni is another good producer. Marchese Malaspina produces good Merlot and Cabernet Sauvignon. He also makes a Cabernet from 80 percent cabernet sauvignon and 20 percent bonarda which we can recommend. And the '87 Cabernet from Santa Rosa was most agreeable.

As a rule these are wines to drink young, the Merlot before its third year, the Cabernet perhaps a year older. Rating: Cabernet ** −; Merlot *

COLLI EUGANEI (*Veneto*), *DOC*. This production zone comprises all or part of 17 villages in the district southwest of Padova. In 1988 there were 752 growers with 1,480 acres (599 hectares) registered for the Colli Eugànei DOC. Of these, 176 growers had cabernet planted on 240 acres (97 hectares) and 165 had 348 acres (141 hectares) of merlot. Production of the Colli Eugànei Rosso averaged more than 103,000 cases a year between 1986 and 1988. Cabernet, during this same period, has averaged more than 44,000 cases, while that of Merlot has been about 67,500 cases. These three wines account for nearly 53 percent of the zone's average annual output of 405,708 cases.[18]

Of the seven wines in the discipline, three concern us here. The Colli Eugànei Rosso is made from a base of 60 to 80 percent merlot; the other grapes in the *uvaggio* may be either or both of the two cabernets, barbera, and/or raboso veronese. The Cabernet must contain at least 90 percent of either or both cabernets and the Merlot 90 percent merlot.

DOC REQUIREMENTS FOR COLLI BOLOGNESI–MONTE SAN PIETRO–CASTELLI MEDIOVALE

Component	Minimum Varietal	Minimum Aging	Minimum Alcohol	Maximum Yield in	
				Gallons/Acre	Hectoliters/Hectare
Cabernet Sauvignon*	85%	none	12.0%	748	70
Riserva	85%	3 years, from November 1	12.5%	748	70
Merlot	85%	none	11.5%	898	84

* Cabernet Sauvignon wines can contain up to fifteen percent merlot.

The remainder for either wine can be any other recommended or authorized variety of the same color.

The maximum yield for the Cabernet is 900 gallons per acre (84 hectoliters per hectare), and for the Merlot and Rosso 1,050 (98). There are no minimum aging requirements for the *normale,* but there are for the *superiore.* Any wine labeled as *superiore* must be aged for a minimum of one year from November 1. The minimum alcohol for the Cabernet *normale* is 11.5 percent, and Merlot and Rosso *normale* must contain at least 11 percent. Any of the *superiori* must be at least 0.5 degree higher. The Rosso and Merlot may be still or sparkling, dry or semisweet. (Make ours dry; we'll take our sweet peppers roasted, thanks.)

ANTONIO ROSSI RATES THE VINTAGES OF COLLI

Year	Cabernet	Merlot	Rosso
1988	***	***	***
1987	***	***	***
1986	**	**	***
1985	***	***	**
1984	**	***	**
1983	***	***	***
1982	—	—	**
1981	—	—	***
1980	—	—	**
1979	—	—	***
1978	—	—	**
1977	—	—	**
1976	—	—	**
1975	—	—	**
1974	—	—	**
1973	—	—	***
1972	—	—	**
1971	—	—	***
1970	—	—	**

The best wine of the Colli Eugànei, by reputation, is Luxardo de Franchi del Venda's Sant'Elmo. This wine is made from a blend of merlot, cabernet franc, and barbera; it is aged for about two years in oak casks. It is at its best within four to six years of the vintage. The La Principesi Colli Eugànei Rosso, too, can be quite good. Like most wines from this district, it is best drunk within two years of the vintage, while it still has its youthful fruit. Rating: Cabernet */**; Merlot */**; Rosso */**

Colli Morenici Mantovani del Garda (*Lombardia*), DOC. This minor red wine from Mantua is made with 20 to 40 percent merlot grapes. It is at best an agreeable everyday beverage wine, to be drunk within two years of the vintage. Rating *

Colli Orientali del Friuli (*Friuli–Venezia Giulia*), DOC. This district takes in the towns of Attimis, Buttrio, Cividale del Friuli, Faedis Manzano, Nimis, Povoletto, Tarcento, and Torreano on the hills east of Udine. The Colli Orientali del Friuli DOC zone includes 20 different wines; 12 are white and one is pink. Among the reds are Cabernet, Cabernet Franc, Cabernet Sauvignon, and Merlot. The rosé is made from merlot. Some 48 percent, or 2,750 acres (1,114 hectares), of the nearly 5,800 acres (2,338 hectares) of vines are red varieties, including 2,165 (875) of merlot and 282 (114) of cabernet sauvignon and franc.[20] Production of Merlot, which averages more than 150,000 cases a year, accounts for just over 20 percent of the district's total, while Cabernet, at just over one-third of that, makes up another 7 percent.[21]

DOC requires that any of the Cabernets and the Merlot be made from at least 90 percent of the named variety. The maximum yield for these wines is 823 gallons per acre (77 hectoliters per hectare). There are no minimum aging requirements for the *normale;* the *riserva* must be aged for at least two years from January 1. The minimum alcohol for all of these wines, *normale* or *riserva,* is 12 percent.

The regular Merlot is at its best before its second, or perhaps third year; the *riserva* can be good for up to four. The Cabernet, made from either or both varieties, is best within four years of the vintage; the *riserva* can age for two, perhaps three years beyond that. Rating: Cabernet, Cabernet Franc, Cabernet Sauvignon ** − ; Merlot * +

Recommended Producers and Wines of the Colli Orientali del Friuli

Abbazia di Rosazzo (Ronco dei Roseti *vino da tavola†*)
Cantine Florio, Tenuta Maseri Florio (Cabernet and Merlot)
* Dorigo Girolamo "Montsclapade" (Cabernet, Merlot, and Montsclapade Rosso *vino da tavola†*)
* Dri Giovanni (Il Roncàt Rosso *vino da tavola†*)
Gianfrano d'Attimis (Merlot)
* I Moròs di Nello Tavagnacco (Cabernet di Ippilis and Merlot)
Livon (Plazate Rosso and Tiarebù *vino da tavola†*)
* Marina Danieli (Cabernet, Merlot, and Faralta *vino da tavola†*)
Rodero (Cabernet Franc)
Ronchi del Gnemiz (Rosso del Gnemiz *vino da tavola†*)
* Specogna Leonardo (Cabernet Sauvignon and Merlot)
V. Nascig di Angelo Nascig (Cabernet Sauvignon and Merlot)

ACREAGE AND AVERAGE PRODUCTION FOR COLLI ORIENTALI DEL FRIULI

| | Growers | Registered Vineyards | | 1986–88 Average Number of Cases |
		Acres	Hectares	
Cabernet	269	282.01	114	54,435
Merlot	567	2,164.21	876	153,440
Red wines		2,753.47	1,114	263,588
White		3,023.62	1,224	496,347
Total red and white DOC production		5,777.09	2,338	759,935

Source: Il Corriere Vinicolo

Villa Belvedere di Taddei (Cabernet Franc and Merlot)

Volpe Pasini, Zuc di Volpe (Merlot)

Zamo Tullio di Ipplis (Merlot and Rosso di Vigne dal Leòn *vino da tavola*†)

† See individual entry.

From Antonio Niederbacher's vintage chart:

**** 1962

*** 1985, 1983, 1979, 1978, 1977, 1975, 1974, 1973, 1972, 1971, 1970, 1969, 1964, 1959, 1957, 1954

** 1984, 1982, 1981, 1976, 1967, 1966, 1963, 1961, 1960, 1958, 1956, 1955, 1953, 1952

* 1980, 1968

0 1965

COLLIO [GORIZIANO] (*Friuli–Venezia Giulia*), DOC. The Collio zone, at the border of Yugoslavia, takes in the hills west of Gorizia. The soil here is of sandstone and marl. Collio is much more highly regarded for its white wines than its reds, and for good reason. But there are some good reds produced here as well. Both Merlot and Cabernet are recognized under DOC, and since 1990, Collio Rosso, a blend of red grapes, has been covered under the DOC regulations. Unlike the other zones of Friuli, here only cabernet franc grapes were allowed in the Cabernet. Since 1990 this has been changed to DOC Cabernet, which may be a blend of both cabernets.

In 1988 there were almost 2,800 acres (1,127 hectares) of vines which included 337 (136) of merlot and 136 (55) of cabernet franc. Of the red vines, which amounted to 16 percent of the total, cabernet accounted for 26 percent and merlot 64 percent. Nearly 15 percent of the total DOC output of more than 800,000 cases, or 115,500 cases, is Merlot and Cabernet; approximately 70 percent of this is Merlot. [23]

The best red wines of Collio, according to Vanni Tava-

ANTONIO ROSSI RATES THE VINTAGES OF COLLI ORIENTALE DEL FRIULI[22]

Vintage	Cabernet	Merlot
1988	****	***
1987	****	****
1986	****	****
1985	***	***
1984	**	**
1983	**	**
1982	**	**
1981	**	**
1980	**	**
1979	***	**
1978	**	**
1977	**	**
1976	***	**
1975	**	**
1974	****	****
1973	**	**
1972	***	***
1971	***	***
1970	**	**

gnacco, the fine enologist at I Moròs in Colli Orientali, are from the vineyards at the lower altitudes in the area of S. Floriano del Collio.

The best Collio reds, which can be quite good, have a definite varietal herbaceousness, but one that is not overbearing. In our experience the Merlot wines tend to be more successful here than the Cabernets. Both wines tend to be soft and fruity. Collio Merlot is best before its second year; the Cabernet before its fourth. Rating: Cabernet * +; Merlot ** –

605

DOC REQUIREMENTS FOR COLLIO GORIZIANO

Component	Minimum Varietal	Minimum Aging	Minimum Alcohol	Maximum Yield in	
				Gallons/Acre	Hectoliters/Hectare
Cabernet	100%	none	12%	823	77
Merlot	100%	none	12%	823	77
Rosso		none	12%	823	77

Recommended Producers and Wines of Collio Goriziano

Attems (Ronco Arcivesco Merlot)
Berlin Fabio (Cabernet Franc)
* Borgo Conventi (Merlot and Braida Nuova *vino da tavola†*)
Ca' Ronesca (Cabernet Franc and Merlot)
Col Rosazzo (Cabernet)
Contini Formentini (Cabernet Franc, Merlot, and Formentini Rosso *vino da tavola†*)
Eno Friulia (Cabernet Franc)
Felluga Livio (Cabernet Franc and Merlot)
* Gradnik (Cabernet Franc and Merlot)
Marco Felluga (Merlot)
Pra di Pradis (Cabernet and Stukara *vino da tavola†*)
* Schiopetto Mario (Cabernet Franc, Merlot, and Riva Rosso *vino da tavola†*)
Scolaris Giovanni (Merlot)
Villa San Giovanni, Marco Felluga (Cabernet)

† See individual entry.

From Antonio Niederbacher's vintage chart:

```
****   1984, 1961, 1959
***    1985, 1983, 1982, 1981, 1980, 1979, 1977, 1973,
         1972, 1971, 1970, 1967, 1966, 1964, 1963,
         1958
**     1978, 1976, 1974, 1969, 1968, 1965, 1962, 1960
*      1975
```

COLLIO PRODUCERS

From Attems comes a very good Collio Merlot, Ronco Arcivesco. The '89 was delicious about a year after the harvest.

Besides producing some very fine white wines, Gianni Vescovo produces a fine *vino da tavola* red, **Braida Nuova,** from a blend of cabernet and merlot, and a good DOC Merlot from grapes grown on his 26-acre (10.5-hectare) Borgo Conventi estate in Farra d'Isonzo.

Contini Formentini produces three good reds from his 240 acres (97 hectares) of vines at San Floriano del Collio: a Cabernet Franc, a Merlot, and a non-DOC merlot-cabernet blend.

ACREAGE AND AVERAGE PRODUCTION FOR COLLIO GORIZIANO

	Growers	Registered Vineyards		1986–88 Average Number of Cases
		Acres	Hectares	
Cabernet Franc	93	136.16	55	38,567
Merlot	280	336.54	136	76,926
DOC red		523.01	212	127,002
DOC white		2,785.98	1,127	679,502
Total red and white DOC production		3,308.99	1,339	806,504

Source: Il Corriere Vinicolo

ANTONIO ROSSI RATES THE VINTAGES OF COLLIO GORIZIONO [24]

Vintage	Cabernet Franc	Merlot
1988	***	***
1987	**	**
1986	**	***
1985	****	***
1984	***	***
1983	**	***
1982	****	***
1981	***	**
1980	***	****
1979	***	***
1978	**	***
1977	***	***
1976	*	*
1975	****	***
1974	**	**
1973	***	**
1972	***	***
1971	***	***
1970	***	***

Eno Friuli, run by Angelo Vittorio Puiatti, produces nearly half a million bottles of 17 different wines a year. Many of these wines are excellent; all are, at the very least, good. While white wines dominate here, Puiatti also produces 7,000 bottles of Cabernet, 9,000 of Cabernet Sauvignon, and 8,500 of Merlot Rosato. A few years ago he produced a very good Cabernet Franc. We suspect that wine is now labeled Cabernet. Puiatti also produces 177,500 bottles of wine under the Puiatti label. Once again, white wines dominate. He produces 13,000 bottles of Cabernet Sauvignon.

It seems that every grape that Mario Schiopetto touches becomes a first-rate wine. This outstanding winemaker, and philosopher, is known, and regarded, for his finely honed whites. Besides his especially fine, often outstanding whites, he produces especially good Cabernet Franc and Merlot, as well as the non-DOC *vino da tavola* **Riva Rosso.**

COMPRINO DI CODEVILLA (*Lombardia*). Comprino di Codevilla is made from merlot grapes. Other than that we are in the dark.

CONIALE (*Toscana*). Maurizio Castelli produces this Cabernet for the Chianti Classico estate of Castellare. There

were a scant 1,435 bottles of the very good '87, but by 1988 production had nearly doubled to 2,826 bottles! Rating ***

TASTING NOTES

1988 (11/90). Lovely, refined aroma; cabernet herbaceousness combines with an oak component to produce an elegant wine with the sweetness of ripe fruit, a lot of structure; has a nice touch and real appeal. ***

1987 (*twice, 11/90*). Dense purple color; on the nose, oak combines with refined cabernet fruit, cassis nuance; a rich mouthful of flavor, a little chewy; even more impressive when one considers the vintage. ** +

CORBULINO ROSSO (*Veneto*). Giorgio Grai produces this wine for Afra and Tobia Scarpa at their winery in Trevignano in the province of Treviso. You can sense the hand of a master craftsman. Corbulino Rosso combines 60 percent cabernet franc and cabernet sauvignon with 40 percent pinot noir, merlot, malbec, and petit verdot, although the grape composition varies with the vintage. For example, the '81 was made from 40 percent cabernet franc, 30 percent cabernet sauvignon, 15 percent merlot, 8 to 10 percent malbec, and 2 to 3 percent petit verdot, with a tiny amount of other varieties. The '79 contained more pinot nero than either the '81 or '85, with the balance being the Bordeaux grapes. The *cantina* is a hobby for the Scarpas. Afra is a noted architect, and Tobia a noted interior designer. Grai also produces very good Cabernet Sauvignon, Merlot, and Pinot Nero, as well as some excellent whites for the Scarpas. Rating **

TASTING NOTES

1988 (4/89). Cassis and green olive aroma with an herbaceous backnote; soft, good body, balanced, fresh. **

1986 (4/88). Characteristic herbaceous, green olive aroma; light tannin, round; ready. **

1985 (*7 times, 3/88*). Lovely perfumed aroma; soft, well balanced, full of flavor. ** +

1983 (4/86). Herbaceous cabernet aroma; flavorful, good backbone, round and full of character. ** −

1981 (4/86). Strong bell pepper character; shows age, still has fruit, drinkable enough. * −

1979 (4/86). This wine had more pinot noir than the '81 or '85. Restrained herbaceous character; has flavor but starting to dry out. +

CORTACCIO (*Toscana*). A few years ago Stefano Farkas grafted some vines over to cabernet sauvignon. He produced his first wine—named Cortaccio—from those vines on his

Villa Cafaggio estate in the Chianti Classico district in 1989. Cortaccio is the name of a vineyard at Cafaggio. There were some 795 gallons (30 hectoliters) of the '89 and 1,320 (50) of the '90. We tasted those two Cabernet Sauvignons from barrel on our visit there in November 1990. It was too soon to judge the '90, but the color was so dense and black it was amazing. The '89 from *barrique* had a lot of fruit and varietal character along with oak; it displayed some potential for development and was a very good first effort. Rating [** —]

Costa delle Pergole Rosso (*Veneto*). Col Sandago produces this wine from a blend of 60 percent cabernet franc, 20 percent merlot, and 10 percent wildbacher grapes, plus a small amount of other varieties, including pinot noir and malbec. It is a medium-bodied dry red wine with an herbaceous, cherrylike character. This wine is best drunk within two to three years of the vintage. Somehow we suspect that this is the same wine as **Camoi**. If that is the case, then this wine, or the name at least, has been discontinued. Rating ** —

Costozza, Cabernet Frank (*Veneto*). Conte da Schio produces this wine from cabernet franc grapes grown in the Colli Bèrici area. It is best drunk between three and four years of the vintage. His 1974 carried the DOC blurb on the label; the 1977 did not. The bottles we've tasted from both vintages were equally variable. The last one we tasted was the '77, and that was in 1983. Rating [** —].

Creso (*Veneto*). F.lli Bolla produces Creso from a blend of 60 percent cabernet sauvignon, 30 percent corvina, and 10 percent selected late-harvested grapes from the Valpolicella district. The vines, with a south to southeastern exposure, are planted on the hillsides at altitudes that range between 655 and 985 feet (200 and 300 meters) above sea level. The first one, the '86, spent thirteen months in *barriques* of Alliers oak, plus an additional five months in Slavonian oak barrels. They produced 54,000 bottles of that wine. The wine is named for King Croesus, who ruled Lydia in the sixth century B.C. The court of Croesus was known for its opulence and vast wealth, giving rise to the saying "as rich as Croesus." The idea behind the name seems clear until you taste the wine. Rating *

TASTING NOTE

1986 (*5 times, 9/90*). Cabernet and oak are the dominant characteristics here; the sweetness from the oak is pervasive, still there is fruit. *

Darmaggi, Cabernet Sauvignon del Piemonte, or delle Langhe, Gaja (*Piemonte*). Angelo Gaja produced his first Cabernet Sauvignon in 1982 from vines grown in his 6.2-acre (2.5-hectare) Darmaggi vineyard in the Barbaresco zone. Gaja planted the cabernet sauvignon here in 1978. The vineyard was named Darmaggi, Piemontese for "what a pity," because Gaja's father and others, when commenting about the sacrilege of planting cabernet in a Barbaresco vineyard, would remark, "*darmaggi.*" The juice ferments for three weeks on the skins in stainless steel at temperatures of 78° to 84° Fahrenheit (25.5° to 29° centigrade). It is aged for six months in a combination of 50-50 new and one-year-old *barriques,* and one year in large casks. Gaja's first Cabernet Sauvignon was the '82, of which 4,800 bottles were produced. The vineyard is planted at an altitude of 990 feet (300 meters) above sea level. The average annual production ranges between 6,500 and 7,000 bottles. Rating ** +

TASTING NOTES

1987 (*11/90*). Refined cabernet aroma combines with vanilla, cassis overlay; well balanced, soft; some elegance. ** +

1986 (*5 times, 11/90*). Lots of oak which combines with refined herbal varietal fruit, nuances of green olives and a light bell pepper note; well balanced, moderate tannins, good body, loaded with flavor, a little short. **

1985 (*3 times, 11/90*). Herbal element on the nose and palate, a little coarse but good fruit. ** —

1984 (*ex-cask, 11/84*). Nose is full and fruity; quite tannic, the fruit is evident; a little too difficult to be sure but potential evident. ?

1983 (*7 times, 4/89*). Rich cabernet aroma, suggestions of cassis and green olives; soft, round and velvety, lots of structure. *** —

1982 (*twice, 3/87*). Refined cabernet herbaceousness, oak component, cassis notes; moderate tannin, supple under a lot of oak flavor, still needs more time to harmonize. **(+)

Dominicale Rosso (*Veneto*). Stepski Doliwa Hans Onno, owner of Agricola Rechsteiner, produces this cabernet-merlot *vino da tavola rosso,* named for the 5.5-acre (2.2-hectare) vineyard of that name on his Piave River district estate.

Dragarska (*Friuli–Venezia Giulia*). Carlo Drufovka, who produces some interesting and very good wines, including Runk, the very good pinot blanc–based wine, makes Dragarska from a blend of merlot and cabernet. It receives good press.

Falchini, Cabernet Sauvignon (*Toscana*). Riccardo Falchini produces this cabernet sauvignon–sangiovese blend at his Azienda Agricola Casale in the San Gimignano zone. The '85 contains 8 percent sangiovese! Wonder what it adds? It spent eighteen months in *barriques* of Limousin and Alliers oak. Falchini made 2,800 bottles. We were told that Giacomo Tachis consulted on this wine. Rating **

TASTING NOTE

1985 (*3 times, 4/89*). Oak overlays cabernet fruit; good backbone chewy and flavorful. **

FARALTA (*Friuli–Venezia Giulia*). Giorgio Grai produces this 40-40-20 cabernet-merlot-tazelenghe blend for Marina Danieli in the Colli Orientali del Friuli zone. The name *faralta* derives from the Longobard word meaning "a high position," appropriate since the grapes for this wine come from the highest part of the estate in Buttrio. Grai made some 10,000 bottles of the first vintage in 1986. Rating ** +

TASTING NOTE

1986 (*twice, 11/90*). Vanilla oak up front on the nose, tobacco and herbaceous components, cherry, berry, herbal, tealike and licorice notes; has real character, very soft, nice mouth feel, fairly long finish; very ready. ** +

FAVONIO, CABERNET FRANC (*Apulia*). Attilio Simonini grows chardonnay, pinot blanc, trebbiano toscano, pinot noir, zinfandel, and cabernet franc on his 41-acre (16.5-hectare) Favònio estate in Donadone on the plains of the Capitanata northeast of Foggia. He has 10 acres (4 hectares) of cabernet franc, which he was warned wouldn't grow here (nor would the other French varieties). He wasn't deterred.

By pruning closely to keep yields low, utilizing extra crop cover to shade the grape clusters, training the vines on wires high above the ground, using a modified drip irrigation system to spurt just enough moisture on the vines at periodic intervals, and picking early, Simonini is able to harvest ripe, but not overripe, healthy bunches of grapes. Any fruit that doesn't meet his standards is not used in his wines.

Simonini established the vineyard and winery in 1970 and produced his first wines commercially in 1974. Today he produces nearly 20,000 cases a year; 5,000 of this is Cabernet. He is happy to say that his daughter Roberta, who is studying viticulture at the University of Padua, will join him at the winery after graduation. (We recently heard that Simonini closed or sold the winery.)

In making his wines Attilio aims for the type of wine he enjoys drinking himself. He prefers a crisp style for his whites (he produces a remarkable Pinot Blanc) and a well-balanced, fruity red with character and style—quite unlike the vast majority of southern reds. But Simonini is an innovator. He sets high standards and works with cheerful determination to achieve them. Though a jovial and good-natured man, inclined to laugh at adversity, Attilio is very

serious about quality and committed to produce the best wines possible. His wines are getting better every year.

He ages his Cabernet for six months to a year in large Slavonian oak casks. His *riserva* is aged for at least a year longer. The *normale* Cabernet is a medium-bodied, warm, dry red wine with an aroma and flavor of bell peppers; the *riserva* is a different matter. This is a wine of some refinement; the extra aging in oak tones down the herbaceousness and brings out a character of oak and cassis. Rating *normale* *; Riserva **

FIORANO ROSSO (*Lazio*). Boncompagni Ludovisi Principe di Venosa produces one red and two white wines on his estate not far from Roma. The production of his Fiorano Rosso, though limited, is greater than one might think. We tasted a number of bottles of the '78, for example, and came across three different lots: from barrel #23 there were 1,366 bottles; from barrel #36, 1,202; and barrel #2, 1,366. We don't know how many lots he bottled from that vintage. Fiorano Rosso is made from a blend of 50 percent each merlot and the two cabernets. It is aged for two years in barrel. Fiorano is an elegant, stylish wine that ages gracefully for eight, even ten years. In our experience, this merlot-cabernet blend has been among the very best produced in Italy, though the most recent that we tasted, the '82, left a lot to be desired. We hope it can be explained by the quality of the vintage, although it seems more of a winemaking flaw. We hope not, but at this point we have no other answer. Rating *** —

TASTING NOTES

1982 (*5 times, 5/87*). The most recent three bottles tasted were all the same: cloudy, pruney, malolactic character!, what happened here? *Bottle of 10/86:* Richly fruited aroma, somewhat overripe, cassis notes; some tannin, nice fruit in the center, some harshness at the end; needs more time. **(*)

1980 (*2/86, barrel #23, 1,390 bottles*). Deep color; cassis up front on the nose; good intensity of fruit, well balanced, vague tarlike component; still young, displays style. ***(+)

1978 (*5 times, 5/89, barrel #23, 1,366 bottles*). Very deep color; still quite tannic, chewy, lots of nice fruit, has a sweetness to it; will the fruit last long enough for the tannin to soften? We think so. **(?) *Bottle of 3/86, barrel #36, 1,202 bottles:* Very deep color; richly fruited aroma, green olive and varietal herbaceous components; fairly tannic, the fruit is there though a little closed in; needs more age. **(*) *Bottle of 8/85, barrel #2, 1,366 bottles:* Deep color is still quite youthful; intense, refined aroma hints of cassis; still full of tannin, well structured, heaps of flavor; quite young but has real class, hold until at least 1988. ***(+)

1973 (*twice, 9/80, 1,398 bottles*). Deep color; refined bouquet recalls flowers, fruit and oak; well knit, tasty, lingers long on the palate; has elegance and a lot of style. ***

FOIANEGHE ROSSO (*Trentino–Alto Adige*). Conti Bossi Fedrigotti produces this soft, round red wine from 60 to 40 percent of the two cabernets and 40 to 60 percent merlot grapes grown on his Foianeghe estate near Rovereto. It is aged for eighteen months to two years in small oak barrels. The wine can take moderate aging—four to six years, perhaps longer in the better vintages. We've heard that Foianeghe has improved of late. Unfortunately we haven't met it in recent years. Rating **

FORMENTINI ROSSO (*Friuli–Venezia Giulia*). Contini Formentini produces this 60 percent merlot and 40 percent cabernet sauvignon blend from vines grown in his San Floriano del Collio estate in the Collio production zone. The wine is aged for about two months in small oak barrels. It is a fairly nice, rather easy style of dry red wine with about twelve percent alcohol. The one that we tasted was not vintage-dated. Rating * +

FRANCIACORTA ROSSO (*Lombardia*), *DOC*. The Franciacorta zone near Brescia, an area best suited to the production of white wines and Champagne-method sparklers, also produces red and rosé wines. The red wines are made from a rather interesting combination of varieties—two from Bordeaux and two from Piemonte. The wine itself is less so. DOC requires a blend of 40 to 50 percent cabernet franc plus 20 to 30 percent barbera, 15 to 25 percent nebbiolo, and 10 to 15 percent merlot. Ten percent of wine and/or must from outside the zone may be used to correct a weak vintage. The grapes are planted at an altitude of at least 1,300 feet (400 meters) above sea level. In 1988 there were 77 growers with 182.54 acres in vines (73.87 hectares). The average annual production between 1986 and 1988 was 114,218 cases.[25]

This medium-bodied, fruity red wine is made in two basic styles. One has a definite character of bell peppers. The Longhi-di Carli Franciacorta is a good example of this type. The second style is less obvious and melds the diverse characters of the different grape varieties better. Gian Paolo e Giovanni Cavalleri produce a good example of this type. Neither style ages well; these wines are best drunk within two, at most three years of the vintage. Rating */**

Recommended Producers of Franciacorta Rosso

Bellavista (Solesine *vino da tavola†*)
Ca' del Bosco (DOC Rosso and Maurizio Zanella *vino da tavola†*)
Catturich Ducco (DOC Rosso)
Cavalleri Gian Paolo e
Giovanni (DOC Rosso and Tajardino *vino da tavola†*)
Lancini Luigi, Vigna Cornaleto (DOC Rosso)
Longhi-di Carli (DOC Rosso)

† See individual entry.

From Antonio Rossi's vintage chart:[26]

****	1985, 1983, 1980, 1974, 1971
***	1988, 1987, 1986, 1982, 1981, 1979, 1978, 1973, 1970
**	1984, 1977, 1975, 1972
*	1976

FRATI PRIORI ROSSO (*Lombardia*). This wine is made from 100 percent cabernet sauvignon grapes.

FRATTA. See **BREGANZE**.

GHIAIE DELLA FURBA (*Toscana*). The very fine Carmignano producer Conte Ugo Bonacossi makes this single-vineyard wine from a blend of 40 percent cabernet sauvignon, 30 percent cabernet franc, and 30 percent merlot grapes grown in a 7.4-acre (3-hectare) plot on his Villa Capezzana estate. This vineyard gives them a yield, in wine, of less than 320 gallons per acre (30 hectoliters per hectare). Their average annual production is 2,140 gallons (81 hectoliters).

In the first vintage, 1979, Capezzana produced about 16,000 bottles. Today they produce between 11,333 and 14,666 bottles. Ghiàie is produced only in selected good vintages. Since the first vintage they produced this wine in 1980, 1981, 1983, 1985, 1987, 1988, and 1990. Although 1982 was generally a good vintage, the fruit was somewhat overripe and consequently wasn't bottled. They haven't as yet decided on the 1989, but, we suspect, judging by the quality of those we tasted from barrel, they will bottle an '89 Ghiàie della Furba.

DOC REQUIREMENTS FOR FRANCIACORTA ROSSO

		Maximum Yield in	
Minimum Aging	Minimum Alcohol	Gallons/Acre	Hectoliters/Hectare
Until June 1 after the harvest	11%	910	85

Fermentation takes place in large wooden casks at a temperature of less than 86° Fahrenheit (30° centigrade) for the must and 95° (35°) for the cap. It lasts for one week. Maceration continues for a further five to six days. The earlier vintages of Ghiàie were aged in 660- to 790-gallon (25- to 30-hectoliter) casks. In 1983, Vittorio Bonacossi, the winemaker here, began experimenting with aging in *barrique*. Today he ages Ghiàie in *barrique* for one year, plus another three months in tank. Since 1985 there has been a definite improvement in this wine. It has become more elegant and less obvious, better balanced and less aggressive. Rating ***

TASTING NOTES

1989 (*4 times, ex-cask, 6/90*). Lovely aroma, oak combines with refined varietal fruit; a lighter, more elegant Ghiàie, one with real class and style, supple. ** +

1988 (*4/90*). This one was made from a 50-15-35 blend of cabernet sauvignon, cabernet franc and merlot. Refined varietal bouquet, herbal and tobacco components; tight yet with a sweetness to it, well structured; perhaps the best Ghiàie to date. ***

1985 (*8 times, 6/90*). Mint, cassis and oak aroma, green olive nuance; rich, round and sweet, harmonious; elegant. ***

1983 (*10 times, 5/90*). Cassis, tobacco and tealike bouquet; nice entry, then a little dry, still there is good fruit; drink up, it was better two or three years ago. ** −

1981 (*4/89*). Refined cabernet and merlot character; somewhat pungent in the mouth, soft, ready, firm ending. *

1980 (*3 times, 6/88*). Vanilla nuance, peppery notes, herbaceous background, hint of cassis; good but rather obvious, pleasant and easy to drink. *

1979 (*3 times, 5/85*). A soft, nicely fruited wine, herbaceous varietal notes; short, a bit simple. * +

GIURAMENTO (*Lombardia*). Cabernet, merlot, barbera, and schiava gentile grapes are the *uvaggio* for this medium-bodied wine from the Bergamo area. It can take moderate aging.

GRAVE DEL FRIULI (*Friuli–Venezia Giulia*), DOC. The wines of Grave del Friuli are produced from vines grown on basically flat terrain in gravelly and sandy-clay soils in 59 *comuni* in the province of Udine and 35 in Pordenone. The soil here is quite porous, and irrigation is commonplace.

Plantings of red varieties make up some 60 percent of the total acreage in the Grave del Friuli district. Merlot, with 6,740 acres (2,727 hectares), represents about 45 percent of the 14,700 acres (5,954 hectares) of vines registered for DOC here. Cabernet plantings total 1,441 acres (583 hectares), or almost 10 percent of the vines in this DOC zone.

DOC ZONES OF FRIULI–VENEZIA GIULIA

- Grave del Friuli
- Colli Orientali del Friuli
- Latisana
- Aquileia
- Isonzo
- Collio Goriziano

Udine

Trieste

Annual production of Merlot averages some 350,000 cases; that of Cabernet, nearly 175,000. Together they account for some 92.5 percent of the red DOC output and 55 percent of all the DOC wine produced in the Grave del Friuli.

The Grave del Friuli zone is, by far, the largest DOC district in Friuli–Venezia Giulia. Plantings of cabernet in the Grave zone represent nearly 58 percent of the 2,478 acres (1,003 hectares) of DOC cabernet in the entire region, while the plantings of merlot represent some 64 percent of the 10,579 acres (4,281 hectares) of DOC merlot in the Friuli. Of the reported 535 acres (216 hectares) of cabernet franc in Friuli, one-quarter are in the Grave zone. And of the 224 acres (91 hectares) of cabernet sauvignon, more than 38 percent are in the Grave.

As in the other DOC zones of Friuli, the Italian wine law recognizes Cabernet and Merlot wines from Grave. Cabernet may be a blend of both cabernets, mostly cabernet franc, or mostly cabernet sauvignon. There is also a *rosato* made from 70 to 80 percent merlot and 30 to 20 percent cabernet franc, cabernet sauvignon, refosco dal peduncolo rosso, and/or pinot nero.

All of these wines—Cabernet, Cabernet Franc, Cabernet Sauvignon, and Merlot—must be made with no less than 85 percent of the named variety, with, at most, 15 percent of refosco nostrano and/or other red varieties. The maximum yield for cabernet, either type, is 898 gallons per acre (84 hectoliters per hectare), for merlot 973 (91). There are no minimum aging requirements. The minimum alcohol is 11 percent for the Cabernet in all forms, and 0.5 less for Merlot, while those labeled Superiore must contain at least 12 percent. Additionally, any of these wines labeled with the qualifier Superiore must be vintage-dated.

ACREAGE AND AVERAGE PRODUCTION FOR GRAVE DEL FRIULI

| | Growers | Registered Vineyards | | 1986–88 Average Number of Cases |
		Acres	Hectares	
Cabernet DOC	641	1,220	494	157,758
Cabernet Franc DOC	34	133	54	10,014
Cabernet Sauvignon DOC	32	88	35	6,588
Total Cabernet DOCs	707	1,441	583	174,360
Merlot DOC	3,191	6,740	2,727	350,913
Total Cabernet-Merlot DOCs	3,898	8,181	3,310	525,273
DOC red		8,842	3,578	781,618
DOC white		5,872	2,376	922,778
TOTAL DOC		14,714	5,954	1,704,396

Source: Il Corriere Vinicolo

Reputedly the best red grapes of the zone—the cabernet, merlot, and refosco in particular—come from the zone near Casarsa. The red wines of Grave tend to be somewhat deficient in acid; they are fruity and overly soft, and have a pronounced herbaceousness. They are, however, moderately priced and can make a good accompaniment to meals. The Cabernet is best before its fourth year; the Merlot, before its second. Rating: Cabernet *: Cabernet Franc *; Cabernet Sauvignon */** −; Merlot *

Recommended Producers and Wines of Grave del Friuli

Antonutti (Cabernet)
Banear (Merlot)

Bollini (Cabernet Sauvignon)

Cantina del Friuli Centrale "La Bora" (Cabernet and Merlot)
Casarsa Coop., "La Delizia" (Cabernet, Cabernet Sauvignon, and Merlot)
Collavini (Cabernet Sauvignon)
Duca Badoglia (Cabernet and Merlot)
Friulivini Cantina Sociale (Cabernet Sauvignon and Merlot)

Lis Gravis (Cabernet Sauvignon)
Pighin F.lli (Cabernet and Merlot)
Plozner (Merlot)
Pradio, Tre Pigne (Cabernet Franc)
Villa Ronche (Cabernet Franc and Merlot)

PLANTINGS IN GRAVE DEL FRIULI BY VARIETAL AS A PERCENTAGE OF DOC PLANTINGS IN FRIULI–VENEZIA GIULIA

| | % of DOC in Grave | Total in Friuli | | Average Number of Cases Per Year |
		Acres	Hectares	
Cabernet	70.98	1,719	696	275,535
Cabernet Franc	25.00	535	216	93,424
Cabernet Sauvignon	38.46	224	91	30,234
Total Cabernet	58.13	2,478	1,003	399,193
Merlot	63.70	10,579	4,281	805,882
TOTAL		13,057	5,284	1,205,075

Source: Il Corriere Vinicolo

From Antonio Niederbacher's vintage chart:

```
****   1962
***    1972, 1964, 1954
**     1985, 1984, 1983, 1980, 1979, 1978, 1975, 1974,
         1973, 1971, 1969, 1961, 1959, 1957, 1956,
         1952
*      1982, 1981, 1977, 1976, 1970, 1967, 1966, 1963,
         1960, 1958, 1955, 1953
0      1968, 1965
```

ANTONIO ROSSI RATES THE VINTAGES OF GRAVE DEL FRIULI [27]

Vintage	Cabernet	Merlot
1988	****	****
1987	***	***
1986	***	***
1985	***	***
1984	***	***
1983	***	**
1982	**	**
1981	**	**
1980	***	***
1979	***	***
1978	***	**
1977	**	**
1976	**	**
1975	***	***
1974	***	***
1973	***	**
1972	***	***
1971	***	***
1970	**	**

Grener (*Trentino–Alto Adige*). F.lli Dorigati blends merlot and cabernet grapes with the local teroldego to produce this soft, fruity, medium-bodied dry red. It is at its best within three to four years of the vintage. It's been about a decade since we've tasted this wine. Rating [*]

Griantino (*Lombardia*). Griantino is produced from a blend of cabernet, malbec, merlot, and pinot noir grapes grown close to Como. It is a medium-bodied dry red wine that can take moderate aging (four to five years).

I Fossaretti (*Piemonte*). Alberto Bertelli, the good Barbera d'Asti producer, makes this cabernet sauvignon at his prop-

erty in S. Carlo di Costigliole d'Asti. The '85 we tasted was very good. Rating **

Il Roncat Rosso (*Friuli–Venezia Giulia*). Giovanni Dri, producer of the superb, contemplative dessert wine Verduzzo di Ramondolo, makes Il Roncàt Rosso from a blend of 50 percent refosco with 20 percent of the two cabernets, 20 percent of schioppettino, and 10 percent of other local varieties. He produced 3,850 bottles of the very good '85. This is not a wine for long aging. Rating *** −

TASTING NOTES

1988 (12/90). Lovely, ripe fruit aroma, cherry and herbal notes; smooth texture, rich and mouth-filling, long finish; a lot of class. ***

1986 (4/89). Herbaceous aroma, green olive nuance; soft and fruity, dry finish. * +

1985 (4/87). Reticent aroma; good concentration and extract, hint of sugar—it's dry—the richness and extract are appealing, the wine is young, long finish. *** −

Isonzo (*Friuli–Venezia Giulia*), *DOC*. The Isonzo production zone takes in the *comuni* of Gradisca d'Isonzo, Romans d'Isonzo, Marino del Friuli, Moraro, San Pier d'Isonzo, Turriaco Medea, Villese, and parts of 13 others in the province of Gorizia. The soil here is rather similar to that of Grave del Friuli. Though less than one-third of the more than 2,500 acres (1,025 hectares) of vines in Isonzo are planted in the red varieties, the red wines of this region are well regarded by a number of producers in Friuli with whom we spoke. Annual production averages approximately 130,000 cases of Merlot and nearly 60,000 of Cabernet—nearly one-third of the entire DOC output of the zone.

The DOC regulations govern the production of Cabernet, Cabernet Franc, Cabernet Sauvignon, and Merlot. Those wines must be made from no less than 100 percent of the named variety. This discipline also includes a Rosso made from 60 to 70 percent merlot and 20 to 30 percent of either or both cabernet franc and cabernet sauvignon, and up to 20 percent refosco dal peduncolo rosso and pinot nero.

The maximum yield for cabernet franc and sauvignon is 898 gallons per acre (84 hectoliters per hectare), and for the merlot and grape for the Rosso 973 (91). There are no minimum aging requirements. The minimum alcohol for the Cabernet in all forms is 11 percent, and for the Merlot and Rosso 0.5 degree less. The Rosso can be still or *frizzante*.

These reds, like those of the Grave zone, are at their best within two or three years of the vintage. There is no reason to cellar them; they don't improve, and since they are soft and ready when released they might as well be enjoyed while they still have all their fruit. Rating: Cabernet *; Cabernet Franc *; Cabernet Sauvignon *; Merlot *

ACREAGE AND AVERAGE PRODUCTION FOR ISONZO

	Growers	Registered Vineyards Acres	Hectares	1986–88 Average Number of Cases
Cabernet	109	99	40	48,077
Cabernet Franc	56	95	39	7,866
Cabernet Sauvignon	29	41	17	3,237
Merlot	383	533	216	132,331
Rosso	3	3.4	1.4	52
DOC red		805	326	194,069
DOC white		1,729	700	414,240
Total DOC		2,534	1,026	608,310

Source: Il Corriere Vinicolo

ANTONIO ROSSI RATES THE VINTAGES OF ISONZO[28]

Vintage	Cabernet	Merlot
1988	***	***
1987	***	***
1986	***	***
1985	**	**
1984	***	***
1983	***	***
1982	**	**
1981	**	**
1980	***	***
1979	***	***
1978	***	***
1977	**	**
1976	**	**
1975	***	***
1974	**	**
1973	***	**
1972	***	***
1971	***	***
1970	**	**

Recommended Producers and Wines of Isonzo

Angoris Riserva Castello (Cabernet)
Conti Attems
Gianni Vescovo (Cabernet Franc)

LA STOPPA (*Emilia-Romagna*). Raffaele Pantaleoni's Azienda Agricola La Stoppa produces a *barrique*-aged Cabernet Sauvignon, as well as a number of other good wines in their winery at Rivergaro in the province of Piacenza.

LA TASSINARA ROSSO (*Lombardia*). Azienda Agricola La Tassinara is named for the *località* where it is situated at Rivoltella del Garda in Brescia. La Tassinara Rosso is a blend of 50 percent merlot, 40 percent cabernet, and 10 percent groppello and sangiovese.

LATISANA (*Friuli–Venezia Giulia*), *DOC*. Latisana includes all or part of 11 *comuni* in the province of Udine, an area of rolling hills and coastal flatlands close to the Adriatic. The soil here is sandy and, as in Aquileia, the wines are said to take on a salty character from its proximity to the sea, the whites in particular. Consequently the red wines are more highly regarded.

Approximately 70 percent of the total acreage under vines in Latisana is planted in red varieties. Annual production of Cabernet and Merlot wines averages nearly 50,000 cases; some two-thirds of this is Merlot. The Cabernet and Merlot wines account for some 52 percent of all DOC wines here.

The Cabernet Franc, Cabernet Sauvignon, and Merlot must be made from no less than 85 percent of the named variety, while the Cabernet must be made from a minimum of 85 percent cabernet franc and/or cabernet sauvignon. There is also a Rosato made from 70 to 80 percent merlot and 30 to 20 percent cabernet franc, cabernet sauvignon, refosco nostrano, and dal peduncolo rosso and/or pinot nero. The maximum yield for cabernet franc and sauvignon is 898 gallons per acre (84 hectoliters per hectare), and for the merlot 973 (91). There are no minimum aging requirements. The minimum alcohol for any of the Cabernets is 11.5 percent, and for the Merlot 11 percent.

These wines are best consumed young while they still

ACREAGE AND AVERAGE PRODUCTION FOR LATISANA

| | Growers | Registered Vineyards | | 1986–88 Average Number of Cases |
		Acres	Hectares	
Cabernet	26	118.0	48.0	15,265
Cabernet Franc	1	5.8	2.3	630
Cabernet Sauvignon	2	12.0	4.8	1,037
Merlot	49	364.0	147.0	32,226
Total Cabernet-Merlot		499.8	202.1	49,158
Red		559.0	226.0	59,590
White		215.0	87.0	34,345
TOTAL		774.0	313.0	93,935

Source: Il Corriere Vinicolo

have all their youthful fruit, which is indeed their only virtue. Rating: Cabernet *; Cabernet Franc *; Cabernet Sauvignon *; Merlot *

Recommended Producer and Wines of Latisana

Isola Augusta (Cabernet and Merlot)

LE GIUNCAIE (*Toscana*). Alessandro François, in charge of the winemaking at the Chianti Classico estate of Castello di Querceto since 1975, produces this cabernet sauvignon–merlot *vino da tavola* from grapes grown in the 24.7-acre (10-hectare) Le Giuncaie vineyard. Production averages 15,000 bottles annually.

LE MARNE (*Friuli–Venezia Giulia*). Azienda Agricola Volpe Pasini, located in Togliano di Torreano in Udine, produces a wide range of wines in the Colli Orientali del Friuli DOC zone. Le Marne is an interesting blend of 40 percent cabernet sauvignon, 30 percent cabernet franc, 20 percent refosco, and 10 percent pinot nero. The '83 was good, not much more. It displayed very little character or personality, though it did have fruit. The '85 was another matter. Rating ** −

TASTING NOTE

1985 (12/90). Nice nose, herbal with a vaguely floral note; soft, nice mouth feel, moderate length. **

LE RIVE ROSSO. See COLLI BERICI.

LE SINCETTE ROSSO (*Lombardia*). Brunori Ruggero produces Le Sincette Rosso at his Cascina La Pertica in Polpenazze del

ANTONIO ROSSI RATES THE VINTAGES OF LATISANA[29]

Vintage	Cabernet	Rosso
1988	****	****
1987	**	**
1986	***	***
1985	***	***
1984	*	*
1983	***	**
1982	**	**
1981	**	**
1980	**	**
1979	***	***
1978	***	***
1977	**	**
1976	**	**
1975	**	***
1974	**	**
1973	**	**
1972	***	**
1971	**	**
1970	**	***

Garda in the province of Brescia. This wine is made from a blend of the local marzemino and groppello with the two cabernets. It is best consumed within two or three years of the vintage, but can still be good with up to four years of age. Rating ** −

LE STANZE (*Toscana*). Federico Carletti produces this 90 percent cabernet sauvignon and 10 percent cabernet franc blend on his very good Poliziano estate in the Vino Nobile di Montepulciano production zone. The '87, which we tasted twice, and the '90 from barrel are the extent of our experience with this wine. Rating *

TASTING NOTE

1987 (*twice, 11/90*). Nice nose; some tannin, tasty, sufficient fruit, a bit short. *

LINTICLARIUS (*Trentino–Alto Adige*). Herbert Tiefenbrunner of Castello or Schloss Turmhof produced 6,500 bottles of the 50-25-25 lagrein-cabernet–pinot noir blend. Both cabernets were used. The '86 spent three months in *barrique*. There were 6,500 bottles of that wine. The first one was the '85. There was none made in 1987. Rating **

TASTING NOTE

1986 (*twice, 6/90*). The most pronounced component on the nose is the herbaceousness of the cabernet, green olive and cassis notes; herbal and fruit flavors, soft until the somewhat dry finish. **

LISON-PRAMAGGIORE (*Veneto*), *DOC*. The Lison-Pramaggiore growing zone is in the easternmost part of the Veneto, with a small section in the westernmost part of Friuli–Venezia Giulia. It takes in all or part of 19 *comuni* between the Livenza and Tagliamento rivers in the provinces of Venezia, Pordenone, and Treviso. Annual production of the Cabernet, in all its forms, between 1986 and 1988, averaged some 118,000 cases a year; that of the Merlot more than 185,000.

Cabernet and merlot vines were introduced here after the First World War. Most of the cabernet plantings are cabernet franc, but there is some cabernet sauvignon. DOC recognizes four red wines from Lison-Pramaggiore that concern us: Cabernet, Cabernet Franc, Cabernet Sauvignon, and Merlot. All of them must be made from no less than 90 percent of the named variety. Up to 10 percent merlot or any other approved red variety can be blended into the Cabernet; and the Merlot may contain 10 percent cabernet or any other allowable red grape.

The maximum yield for the cabernets is 898 gallons per

ACREAGE AND AVERAGE PRODUCTION FOR LISON-PRAMAGGIORE

		Registered Vineyards		1986–88 Average Number of Cases
	Growers	Acres	Hectares	
VENETO				
Cabernet	121	383	155	75,881
Cabernet Franc	57	179	72	31,493
Cabernet Sauvignon	9	31	12.6	4,051
Merlot	550	2,508	1,015	173,435
FRIULI–VENEZIA GIULIA				
Cabernet	33	57	23	2,692
Cabernet Franc	3	12	5	3,626
Cabernet Sauvignon	2	5.2	2	222
Merlot	107	358	145	11,703
TOTAL				
Cabernet	154	440	178	78,574
Cabernet Franc	60	191	77	35,119
Cabernet Sauvignon	11	36.2	14.6	4,274
Merlot	657	2,866	1,160	185,137
TOTAL Cabernet-Merlot	882	3,533	1,430	303,104

Source: Il Corriere Vinicolo

acre (84 hectoliters per hectare), and for the merlot 973 (91). There are no minimum aging requirements for the *normale*; there is one for the *riserva*—three years for the Cabernets and a year less for the Merlot. The aging period for any of the *riserve* is figured from November 1 after the harvest. The minimum alcohol for any of these wines is 11 percent; while those labeled Riserva must contain at least 11.5. Any of these wines can be made with concentrate— but no more than 5 percent and only that made from grapes grown within the zone—to bring up the alcohol to the required minimum in difficult vintages.

These wines can be still or sparkling.

The Lison-Pramaggiore wines tend to be low in acidity; they can take a couple of years of aging, but rarely, if ever, more. They are generally best drunk within two or three years of the vintage. These wines start out with a fairly herbaceous nature that seems to become more aggressive with age. As with the Piave River wines, we feel these wines should be drunk earlier than is generally suggested— between one and three years, at most four, for the Cabernet and one to two, perhaps a year longer, for the Merlot is about right. Rating: Cabernet *; Cabernet Franc *; Cabernet Sauvignon *; Merlot *

Recommended Producers and Wines of Lison-Pramaggiore

De Lorenzi Paolo (Cabernet)	Tenuta Agricola di Lison (Cabernet and Merlot)
"Gruarius," Cantina Sociale di Portogruaro (Merlot)	Tenuta Agricola "La Fattoria" Gli Abbazia Benedettina di Summaga (Merlot)
Guarise (Cabernet)	
Morassutti Giovanni Paolo (Cabernet and Merlot)	
Osvaldo (Cabernet)	Tenuta Sant'Anna (Cabernet and Merlot)
Russolo I Legni (Merlot)	
Santa Margherita (Cabernet Sauvignon and Merlot)	Torresella (Cabernet and Merlot)

The Russolo I Legni '84 Merlot di Pramaggiore was a *barrique*-aged wine produced in very limited quantities. They made 1,496 bottles and 80 magnums.

Santa Margherita produces a DOC Cabernet Sauvignon from Pramaggiore as well as a Cabernet Franc. They bottle a single-vineyard Merlot from Selva Maggiore. They rate 1983, 1982, 1979, 1978, 1974, and 1971 as the best vintages for these wines.

From Antonio Niederbacher's vintage chart for Pramaggiore Cabernet and Merlot:

***	1983, 1979, 1978, 1977, 1971
**	1985, 1984, 1982, 1981, 1980, 1976, 1975, 1974, 1973, 1972, 1970

Antonio Rossi rates the vintages:[30]

***	1988, 1987, 1986, 1985, 1982, 1975, 1973, 1972, 1970
**	1984, 1983, 1981, 1979, 1978, 1977, 1976, 1974, 1971
*	1980

LOGAIOLO (*Toscana*). Fattoria dell'Aiola, in the Chianti Classico district, produces this wine from cabernet sauvignon grapes.

LUNGAROTTI, CABERNET SAUVIGNON (*Umbria*). This fine producer of Rubesco planted cabernet sauvignon vines in 1970 in his vineyards in the Miraduolo district, one of the cooler areas around Torgiano. He produced his first Cabernet Sauvignon from the 1974 vintage. Today Lungarotti produces 5,000 to 6,000 cases a year of this wine. Lungarotti gets only 430 gallons an acre (40 hectoliters a hectare) from the cabernet sauvignon, as compared to 835 (78) from his sangiovese vines. His Cabernet is aged eight to ten months in small oak barrels. The '78 was given one year in *barrique*.

This deeply colored wine has a rich, intense aroma with a characteristic herbaceous aspect. It is full-bodied and soft, having rather low acidity; it ages fairly well, however. Rating ** —

TASTING NOTES

1983 (*9/90*). Aroma displays vanilla and cabernet fruit; soft, good fruit, body and structure, tasty indeed, ready as well, on the short side. **

1982 (*twice, 9/90*). Lovely nose, green olive and herbal notes, vanilla notes; more tannin than the '83, good body, short. ** —

1981 (*twice, 9/90*). Light, varietal aroma; losing its fruit, still has flavor; it was better about sixteen or so months ago, drink up. *

1979 (*9/90*). Old and tired.

1978 (*11 times, 7/85*). Herbaceous, varietal aroma; some though not a lot of tannin, fairly soft and round, could use more acid, tasty; room to improve though drinks well now. **

1977 (*twice, 11/84*). Cassis and oak aroma; soft and flavorful, a bit short. **

1975 (*11/84*). Aroma brings up cassis, some oak in the back; a fair amount of tannin, fruity. **

1974 (*twice, 11/84*). Nice nose, characteristic, with notes of tobacco, tea and bell peppers; still has fruit but is starting to dry out a bit, drink up now. *

MARAGO (*Veneto*). F.lli Pasqua produces this Cabernet Sauvignon. The '87 left a lot to be desired on the two occasions we tasted it. We found it overly pungent and aggressive. Rating 0

MASO LODRON ROSSO (*Trentino–Alto Adige*). Cantina Letrari-Palazzo produces this wine from a blend of both cabernets and merlot. The most recent *uvaggio* is half merlot, 40 percent cabernet franc, and 10 percent cabernet sauvignon. It is aged for about a year and a half in oak barrels, and needs one to three years of bottle age to be at its best.

MAURIZIO ZENELLA (*Lombardia*). Maurizio Zanella, the young producer of the highly esteemed Champagne-method Cà del Bosco *spumanti,* also produces a line of *barrique*-aged wines from French varieties. These wines are made by Zanella himself—very good Chardonnay and pinot noir (Pinero), and a fine Bordeaux blend, made from 35 to 45 percent cabernet sauvignon, 30 percent cabernet franc, and 35 to 25 percent merlot.

The wines are not named for the grape varieties, but simply carry the signature of the producer. The wines are described on the back labels, which also note Maurizio's gratitude to enologist Angelo Solci, with whom the idea for these wines was developed.

The signature wine from the Bordeaux varieties is aged for about a year in *barriques* of Tronçais and Limousin oak. In 1981, the first vintage for this wine, Maurizio made 1,600 bottles and 300 magnums. He was pleased with the wine and within a few years nearly quadrupled the production to 7,000 bottles. He told us the demand is such that he could nearly triple that amount to 20,000 bottles a year if he chose, but he prefers to put a hold on quantity and concentrate on the quality. The '87 vintage saw production increase again, this time more than twofold to more than 15,000 bottles.

The Maurizio Zanella signature wine is a well-balanced wine of character and style, clearly one of the better new wines of Italy. Rating ***

TASTING NOTES

1987 (*3 times, 10/90, 14,268 bottles, plus larger sizes*). Lovely cassis and tea aroma; oak adds a complex overlay and a smoothness to the texture, herbaceous character quite evident, long finish. ** +

1986 (*twice, 4/89*). Herbaceous, bell pepper and cassis aroma; good structure, a little too pungent in the mouth; lacks subtlety. * +

1985 (*twice, 4/88*). Cassis and green olive aroma, some oak; good structure; has a delicate and refined nature, impressive. ***

1984 (*3 times, 5/86*). Aggressive herbaceousness, vaguely of asparagus; moderate tannin, good body, grassy and herbaceous; too aggressive. * + *Bottle of 5/85:* Herbaceous and fruity; sweet impression, rich and concentrated; displays potential. **(+)

1983 (*twice, 5/85*). Aroma of fruit, oak and mint; well balanced, smooth in center, surrounded by tannin, lots of flavor; already shows style. **(* +)

1982 (*twice, 5/85*). Lovely nose, with suggestions of cassis and mint, and an oaky nuance; tannic, rich and ripe, well structured; has personality. **(*)

1981 (*11/84*). Pronounced varietal herbaceousness, plus oak; acid a bit low, some tannin, soft and flavorful. ** +

MAURUS (*Friuli–Venezia Giulia*). Màurus is an 80-20 merlot–cabernet sauvignon blend.

MERLOT DEL FRIULI–VENEZIA GIULIA, DEL TRE VENEZIA, OR DEL VENETO (*Veneto*). These Merlot *vini da tavola* are, generally, light- to medium-bodied, dry and soft, with a pronounced grassy or herbaceous character. Too many are dull and flabby. The better ones are, as a general rule, best drunk young while their attractive fruitiness is still evident. Afra e Tobia Scarpa produce an excellent Merlot del Veneto, and Castelcosa a good Merlot del Friuli–Venezia Giulia. The Castelcosa spent eighteen months in Slavonian oak casks. As a rule, most are uninteresting. Some are good, and a few very good. Rating 0/**

MERLOT DI CAVRIANA (*Lombardia*). Azienda Vitivinicola Monte Gallo produces this richly flavored, well-balanced Merlot from grapes grown on their Mantova estate. Rating *

MERLOT DI SICILIA (*Sicilia*). Principessa di Gregorio produces her Merlot di Sicilia from grapes at her inland estate near Regaleali. The '84 spent one and a half years in wood. Rating * +

MOMPIANO RONCO (*Lombardia*). Pasolini produces this 70-30 marzemino-merlot blend. It is named for the *frazione* of Brescia where their *cantina* is located.

MONT QUARIN (*Friuli–Venezia Giulia*). This wine is produced from cabernet and merlot grapes grown in Cormons, Gorizia. It is fairly characteristic for its type and ages moderately well.

MONTELLO E COLLI ASOLANI (*Veneto*), *DOC*. This growing zone in the province of Treviso in the eastern part of the Veneto encompasses the Asolano and Montello hills around the towns of Montebelluna and Asoli. Documents record that the vine was cultivated in this area as early as A.D. 980. As elsewhere in Veneto, cabernet and merlot grapes became more widely planted here after recovery from phylloxera, which destroyed the vineyards in this district in the period following the First World War.

According to Bocci, the best wines come "from the Montello side, the hills of Montebelluna and Valdobbiadene."[31]

Annual production of the Cabernet has ranged from less than 5,000 cases to the recent average of more than 15,000 cases; there is much more Merlot produced, from the 25,000 cases of a few years ago to recent production of nearly 38,000 cases a year. DOC regulates the production of wines from three grapes in the Montello e Colli Asolani growing district, including Cabernet and Merlot.

ANTONIO ROSSI RATES THE VINTAGES OF MONTELLO E COLLI ASOLANI [32]

Vintage	Cabernet	Merlot
1988	***	****
1987	***	**
1986	***	***
1985	****	***
1984	*	*
1983	****	
1982	****	***
1981	****	****
1980	***	***
1979	***	**
1978	***	***
1977	***	**

The aging period for the *superiore* is calculated from November 1 in the year of the harvest. The Cabernet must be made from no less than 85 percent cabernet, either or both varieties, and the balance, malbec. The Merlot wine may contain up to 15 percent malbec and/or cabernet.

These wines are among the more interesting varietal wines of the Veneto, perhaps because they have more character than most. We have enjoyed a number of bottles of Cabernet Sauvignon from **Venegazzù**. The Merlot and Cabernet of Montelvini can also afford good drinking. Neither of these wines ages very well, though. Some authorities recommend drinking the Cabernet with three to six years of age and the Merlot with two to five. Our experience and taste suggest an earlier timetable. We find the Merlot is at its best within a year or two of the vintage, perhaps three; the Cabernet can take an additional year. Rating: Cabernet * + ; Merlot * +

Azienda Agricola Loredan Gasparini, the zone's finest producer, has 125 acres (50 hectares) of vines on their Venegazzù estate. They produce a good DOC Cabernet Sauvignon as well as two *vini da tavola* made from a blend of the Bordeaux grapes.

Montelvini also makes fairly good wines. This *azienda,* located in Venagazzù di Volpago, has 1,250 acres (500 hectares), 840 (340) in vines. They buy a large proportion of their grapes to produce over half a million cases of wine a year. Of these, 40 percent are Cabernet and 10 percent Merlot. A few years ago they rated 1982 and 1971 as their best vintages and 1983 and 1976 as the least.

MONTEVECCHIA (*Lombardia*). This fairly full-bodied wine comes from the area around Cernusco and Montevecchia north of Milano and west of Bergamo. It is produced from a blend of grapes very similar to that used in Franciacorta—barbera, nebbiolo, and merlot; only cabernet franc is missing.

MONTSCLAPADE (*Friuli–Venezia Giulia*). Girolamo Dorigo produces a wide range of wines under this label but only one of them specifies the name Montsclapade, without a grape name; that wine is a *barrique*-aged Bordeaux variety blend—merlot, cabernet sauvignon, cabernet franc, and malbec. This wine has been produced by Dorigo, a fine producer of wines in the *comune* of Buttrio in the Colli Orientali DOC zone, since 1982. The '84 was made from a

DOC REQUIREMENTS FOR MONTELLO E COLLI ASOLANI

	Minimum Varietal Component	Minimum Aging in Years		Minimum Alcohol	Maximum Yield in	
		in Cask	Total		Gallons/Acre	Hectoliters/Hectare
Cabernet	85%	none	none	11.5%	748	70
Superiore		1	2	12.0%		
Merlot	85%	none	none	11.0%	898	84
Superiore		1	2	11.5%		

ACREAGE AND AVERAGE PRODUCTION FOR MONTELLO E COLLI ASOLANI

| | Growers | Registered Vineyards | | 1986–88 Average Number of Cases |
		Acres	Hectares	
Cabernet	38	111	45	15,469
Merlot	159	321	130	37,741

Source: Il Corriere Vinicolo

blend of about 40-20-40 cabernet sauvignon–cabernet franc–merlot, with a trace of malbec. Some 4,000 bottles and 300 magnums were produced. It was quite a good wine, as was the '87. Rating **

TASTING NOTES

1987 (11/90). Herbal, cassis and tea aroma; acid a little high, good fruit makes it most attractive, very short. ** −

1984 (4/87). Oak and herbaceous character on the aroma; firm and tannic from the oak, good fruit, though the oak does dominate; on the young side. *(*)

MORI VECIO (Trentino–Alto Adige). Lagariavini, or Lagaria as it is labeled for the United States, produces this wine from 50 percent merlot and 25 percent each of the two cabernets. The wine was named for the azienda's 5-acre (2-hectare) vineyard in Mori in the province of Trento. They first produced this wine in 1967. Currently they are producing some 70,000 bottles a year, though not all of the grapes are from the original vineyard. Mori Vecio is given some barrique aging.

Lagaria, when we spoke to them a few years ago, rated 1969 as the best vintage for this wine, and 1972 as the worst. Mori Vecio is ready to drink from its third year and ages well for another three or four. Rating ** +

TASTING NOTES

1986 (4/90). Herbaceous and tobacco aroma; soft and balanced; ready now. **

1983 (11/87). Cassis and gingerbread aroma, herbaceous note; well balanced, rich and soft, tasty, moderate length. ** +

1981 (10/87). Cassis and herbaceous aroma; balanced and fruity, nice texture. **

1979 (7/85). Complex aroma; mellow, smooth and round, good body, nice flavor, marred by a slight harshness at the end. ** −

1977 (3 times, 11/80). Quite a lot of nice fruit, bell pepper note; some tannin; some style; needs one, perhaps two more years. **(+)

1976 (10/79). Has an herbaceous aspect; balanced, soft, some tannin, good fruit. **

1975 (10/78). Distinct varietal character, good quality, flavorful, some length. ** +

1974 (3/80). Herbaceous nature; some tannin; seems to lack some distinction though drinkable. *

1971 (2/79). Small nose, some fruit evident; flavorful; age beginning to show. *

MORLACCO (Trentino–Alto Adige). F.lli Pedrotti produces this wine from a blend of cabernet sauvignon, marzemino, and pinot noir grapes. It ages moderately well, reputedly for up to five or six years.

NAVESEL (Trentino–Alto Adige). Armando Simoncelli produces this wine, one of the many Bordeaux blends from Trentino, from 60 percent cabernet franc and sauvignon and 40 percent merlot. Navesel can be enjoyed from its third year. We haven't tasted this wine for nearly a decade. Rating [*]

NEMO (Toscana). Fabrizio Bianchi produces Nemo from 100 percent cabernet sauvignon grapes grown in the Mulino vineyard on his Fattoria Monsanto estate. It is aged for one year in barrique. The 1980 was his first vintage; today he produces about 6,000 bottles a year. Although it doesn't attain the heights of his outstanding Monsanto Chianti Classico Riserva Il Poggio, it is very good wine and occasionally even better. The 1990 could very well be the best Nemo to date. Rating ** +

TASTING NOTES

1989 (ex-botte, 4/90). Herbaceous and sweet, light, open and forward. *?

1986 (ex-botte, 4/90). Loads of oak and fruit as well, vanilla combines with an herbaceous character. **

1985 (4 times, 4/90). A real surprise and a real disappointment; pungent and coarse the four times we tasted it. *

1984 (4 times, ex-barrique, 5/86). Pale color; light varietal aroma, light-bodied, soft, some oak; some style. **

1983 (6 times, 6/90). Dusty, herbaceous cabernet aroma; after that, tired and fading, probably the bottle. *Bottle of 5/90:* Oak and tar combine with cabernet fruit; rich entry, almost sweet, well balanced, tasty, good concentration, lots of fruit. ** +

1982 (6 times, 5/87, 6,400 bottles). Restrained, though refined varietal aroma, some oak; firm and young, good structure. **(+)

NOVALINE RUBINO (*Trentino–Alto Adige*). Liberio Todesca produces the Novaline Rubino from a blend of 60 percent cabernet sauvignon and 40 percent merlot. It is aged for about a year and a half in barrel. The wine drinks well from three to four years of the vintage till about six or seven.

ORNELLAIA (*Toscana*), *1981.* Marchese Ludovico Antinori, whose labels read Marchese Ludovico A., owns the Tenuta dell'Ornellaia estate in the Bolgheri section of Toscana near Tenuta San Guido where Sassicàia is made. *Ornellaia* is Italian for "ash tree," a name derived from the surrounding groves of ash trees. This estate encompasses 74 acres (30 hectares) of vines first planted in 1981. The vines planted here, at an average altitude of 360 feet (110 meters) above sea level, are sauvignon blanc, semillon, cabernet sauvignon, cabernet franc, and merlot. These vines face south and southwest.

Antinori produces the nonwood-aged Poggio alle Gazze, a sauvignon blanc–semillon wine that seems to get better and better with each passing vintage. Poggio alle Gazze—the hill of the magpies—was first produced in 1987. Antinori produced 30,000 bottles of that wine; today he produces some 45,000 bottles, plus 100,000 of other white wines. The winery's real pride, however, has to be the elegant and polished Ornellaia red. To our mind, this is without question the single finest cabernet-merlot blend in Italy today.

The red grapes in the Ornellaia vineyard are 62 percent cabernet sauvignon, 30 percent merlot, and 8 percent cabernet franc. The cabernets are planted in chalky, gravelly soil and the merlot in clay loam.

The first Ornellaia was the '84, and every vintage since has been impressive. They produced 1,000 bottles of the '84, 10,000 of the '85, 32,000 of the '86, and 50,000 of the '87. Production today has risen to 100,000 bottles. They

hope to reach 150,000 bottles of Ornellaia by 1994, and 90,000 of a Merlot from the Masseto vineyard. The first Masseto Merlot was the '86, of which 800 bottles were produced. They don't put all their grapes in Ornellaia, choosing instead to produce a second wine, Le Sere Nuove, in order to use the best fruit in their flagship wine.

The '85 had 30 percent merlot; today it contains between 15 and 18 percent. The fermentation takes place in temperature-controlled stainless steel tanks; the juice ferments twelve to fifteen days on the skins. Aging begins in oak uprights. In March it is transferred to *barriques* of Alliers, Limousin, Tronçais, and Massif Central oak where it will stay twelve to sixteen months. Approximately 25 to 30 percent of the oak is new. André Tchelistcheff consults here.

From their first vintage in 1985, through the most recent that we tasted, the '89, they haven't produced a single Ornellaia that was less than very good. This is certainly a wine to watch or, better yet, to drink. Rating ****

TASTING NOTES

1989 (ex-cask, 6/90). Oak up front on the nose followed by a richness of cabernet fruit, refined, spicelike component; real elegance and class, loads of flavor, long finish, some tannin at the end. **(*)

1988 (6/90). Deep ruby color, purple toward the rim; oak and spice, complex; great structure and intensity of fruit; has everything including class and length, vaguely of pine, great quality; the finest Tuscan cabernet-based wine that we've tasted to date, real polish and breed. ***(*)

1987 (6/90). Dark color; cassis and tobacco, cherry and oak; moderate tannin, young but quality and elegance evident. ** +

1986 (4 times, 6/90). Lovely, refined and elegant bouquet, cassis and tea, displays delicacy and refinement; great elegance and class, subtle, refined, stylish. **** −

1985 (9/90). Fairly dark ruby color; refined bouquet with green olive, cassis and tobacco notes; soft, smooth, round and harmonious, long finish. A revelation that a wine can be so refined from such young wines. ***

PALAZZOTTO. *See* **BREGANZE.**

PIAVE (*Veneto*), *DOC.* Historical records show that the vine was cultivated in the Piave region during the Roman era, from at least the first century A.D. The vineyards are planted in the lowlands on both sides of the Piave River from Conegliano to the Adriatic Sea in the provinces of Treviso and Venezia in the eastern part of the Veneto. As elsewhere in the region, cabernet and merlot vines were introduced here in the nineteenth century, but didn't become widespread until after recovery from phylloxera, which devastated the vineyards here in the 1920s.

In 1988, 1,293 growers cultivated 3,094 acres (1,252 hectares) of cabernet and 3,643 had 11,040 registered acres

THE VINEYARDS OF THE ORNELLAIA ESTATE

Vineyard	Acres	Hectares
Masseto	16.1	6.5
Ornellaia	37.1	15.0
Poggio alle Gazze	19.8	8.0

(4,468 hectares) of merlot. Average annual production of Cabernet, between 1986 and 1988, averaged about 260,000 cases and that of Merlot exceeded 1 million cases.[33]

DOC regulates the production of eight varietal wines from Piave: four white and four reds, including Cabernet and Merlot.

Aging for the Cabernet Riserva and the Merlot Vecchio is figured from January 1 after the harvest. The Merlot may contain up to 10 percent cabernet and/or raboso grapes. Up to 10 percent of concentrate, if made from grapes grown in the zone, may be used to bring up the alcohol in a weak vintage.

We must disagree with those who suggest these wines will live for five or six years. From our experience, the Cabernet is at its most enjoyable before its third year, though it can last for one year beyond that. The Merlot is best before it is two years old. Rating: Cabernet *; Merlot *

Recommended Producers and Wines of Piave

Enetum (Cabernet and Merlot)
Kunkler Bianchi (Cabernet and Merlot)
Ponte Cantina Sociale (Cabernet Sauvignon and Merlot)
* Rechsteiner (Cabernet and Dominicale Rosso *vino da tavola*†)
Roncade (Cabernet and Castello di Roncade *vino da tavola*†
* Silvestrini (Cabernet)
SO. VI. VE., Società Vini Veneti (Merlot)
Stepski Doliwa (Cabernet)

† See individual entry

Silvestrini's Cabernet is, from our experience, the finest DOC wine of the zone. Agricola Rechsteiner is another first-rate producer in the Piave River district. Kunkler produces some fairly good Piave wines as well. There are also some very good *vini da tavola* produced here. Stepski Doliwa Hans Onno, owner of Agricola Rechsteiner, produces **Dominicale Rosso,** a cabernet-merlot blend. Another noteworthy Bordeaux blend is made by Barone Ciani Bassetti at his **Castello di Roncade** estate and takes its name from the estate.

From Antonio Niederbacher's vintage chart for the red wines:

*** 1979, 1971
** 1983, 1982, 1981, 1980, 1978, 1977, 1976, 1975, 1974, 1972, 1970
* 1985, 1984, 1973

Antonio Rossi rates the vintages:[34]

*** 1987, 1985, 1983, 1982, 1981, 1980, 1979, 1976, 1972, 1971, 1970
** 1988, 1986, 1984, 1978, 1977, 1974
* 1975, 1973

PLAZATE ROSSO (*Friuli–Venezia Giulia*). We were told that Livon produces this red wine from a blend of cabernet franc, cabernet sauvignon, and merlot grapes grown in their Ruttars vineyard in Dolegnano. We were also told that this wine carries the new Colli Orientali del Friuli Rosso DOC. The label indicates that Vigneto Plazate is in Corno di Rosazzo. Perhaps Plazate is part of their Ruttars vineyard; it is also possible that Dolegnano is a *frazione* of Corno. The label also specified that the '87 vine was a *vino da tavola*. Be that as it may, the wine was aged for thirteen months in barrels of Slavonian oak. They produced some 5,300 bottles of the '87 Plazate Rosso. That wine was good, if not much more. Rating *

TASTING NOTE

1987 (9/90). Vaguely herbaceous aroma; open fruit, soft and tasty; lacks personality, but the fruit is attractive. *

PRAGIARA (*Trentino–Alto Adige*). De Tarczal produces this *vino da tavola rosso* from 45 percent merlot, 30 percent cabernet sauvignon, and 25 percent cabernet franc.

PREDAIA (*Veneto*). Veronese producer Santa Sofia produces Predaia from a blend of cabernet sauvignon with the local corvina, molinara, and rondinella.

DOC REQUIREMENTS FOR PIAVE

	Minimum Varietal Component	Minimum Aging	Minimum Alcohol	Maximum Yield in	
				Gallons/Acre	Hectoliters/Hectare
Cabernet	95%	none	11.5%	823	77
Riserva	95%	3 years	12.5%		
Merlot	95%	none	11.0%	973	91
Vecchio	95%	2 years	12.5%		

QUARTO VECCHIO (*Veneto*). Cantine Petternella produces Quarto Vecchio from a blend of 70 percent cabernet sauvignon and 30 percent merlot grown in their Pezzelunghe vineyard. It is best drunk between its third and fourth year, but before its sixth. The wine displays the characteristic herbaceous nature of the cabernet and can be quite agreeable, with nice fruit and a smooth mouth feel. We haven't tasted any since the '78. Rating [**]

QUATTRO VICARIATI (*Trentino–Alto Adige*). The members of Càvit, the large Trentino cooperative, control more than 78 percent—or 16,925 acres (6,850 hectares) out of the 21,620 (8,750) planted—of the region's grape acreage in Trentino. Among the many wines they produce is a special selection of cabernet and merlot grapes from the Quattro Vicariati hills of the Lagarina Valley. It is aged for up to two years in oak casks. Quattro Vicariati is a soft, fairly herbaceous wine of no particular distinction. It is best drunk young, say within three years of the vintage; while it can last beyond that, there's not much, if any, point in keeping it longer. Rating *

QUINTARELLI (*Veneto*). Guiseppe Quintarelli produces a Cà del Merlot and a Cabernet Franc at his winery in Valpolicella. Neither the '77 of the former nor the '83 of the latter was a success. Rating: Cà del Merlot [* −]; Cabernet Franc * −

R & R (*Toscana*). Castello di Gabbiano, the Chianti Classico producer, makes R & R from a blend of 60 percent cabernet sauvignon with 20 percent each merlot and sangiovese. We're unsure of the meaning of the name but do know that it's not rest and recuperation. The '85, the only vintage we've tasted, was very good indeed. Rating ** +

TASTING NOTE

1985 (*twice, 2/90*). Tobacco and berry aroma combines with oak; rich flavor, well balanced and made. ** +

RAUTEN (*Trentino–Alto Adige*). The Salvetta brothers make this wine from 60 percent cabernet sauvignon and 40 percent merlot grapes grown on their farm in the Calavino area of Trentino. It is a fairly good red wine, best drunk within three to six years of the vintage. It's been some time since we met it. Rating [** −]

REALDA (*Veneto*). Roberto Anselmi, the very fine Soave producer, produces Realda from cabernet sauvignon grapes grown in the Dugale Realda vineyard. The label reads "Realda Vigneto Dugale Realda del Veneto." The only one we tasted, the '87, was well balanced and displayed a lot of class. Rating ** +

TASTING NOTE

1987 (*4/89*). Ripe cassis aroma, oak overlay; sweet impression, round and supple, balanced and tasty; lots of class. ** +

REFOLA (*Veneto*). Franca Fiorio, a producer of a good Bianco di Custoza and Bardolino in two colors, red and pink, also produces the 100 percent cabernet Refolà at her Azienda Agricola Le Vigne di San Pietro in Sommacampagna near Verona. This wine is made by Franca's husband, Sergio Nerozzi, from 95 percent cabernet sauvignon and 5 percent cabernet franc. It is aged in a combination of half new oak *barriques* and half one-year-old barrels for one year. Their average annual production of this wine is 6,500 bottles. The *azienda* cites 1984, 1986, and 1988 as the best vintages for Refolà. A good place to drink it is at Pizzeria al Sole in the same town as the *cantina*. Le Vigne di San Pietro belongs to VIDE.

REGALEALI (*Sicilia*). Conte Tasca d'Almerita has some cabernet sauvignon planted at his Regaleali estate in Sicilia. The tank-aged '86s that we tasted in 1987 were both quite good. They were full-bodied and flavorful with tannins that needed time to soften. Rating ** −

RIPA DELLE MANDORIE (*Toscana*). Castello Vicchiomaggio produces Ripa delle Mandorie from 85 percent cabernet sauvignon and 15 percent sangiovese. It is aged in a combination of *barriques* of Nevers and Alliers oak.

RIVA ROSSO (*Friuli–Venezia Giulia*). At one time Mario Schiopetto produced a fine Merlot from vines cultivated in a part of his vineyard in the Collio, a district where the variety does particularly well. In the best vintages he labeled the wine Riva Rossa; in normal years it was simply Merlot. During its next stage Riva Rossa was a blend of approximately 45 percent cabernet, 35 percent merlot, and 20 percent pinot nero. The '88 was made from one-third each of the two cabernets and merlot. Schiopetto is an exceptional winemaker, producing some especially fine white wines. All of his wines, though they tend to be difficult to find, are worth the search. Schiopetto's '79 Riva Rossa remains one of the finest red wines that we have tasted to date from Collio. Rating ** +

TASTING NOTE

1988 (*9/90*). Tobacco and cherry aroma, ripe fruit component, herbal and green olive nuances; soft, well balanced and tasty; nice now with room for improvement. **(+)

ROCCA DI CASTAGNOLI (*Toscana*). As far as we know, the first Cabernet produced at this very good Chianti Classico estate was the '88. The sample we tasted from barrel in November 1990 was good. There was a lot of fruit, as expected from the vintage, and a lot of structure. Rating [*]

ROI (*Friuli–Venezia Giulia*). Röi is a cabernet-refosco-merlot blend produced by Giuseppe Ceschin at Azienda Agricola La Viarte. This *cantina* is located in Prepotto in the province of Udine in the Colli Orientali del Friuli zone.

RONCO DEI ROSETI (*Friuli–Venezia Giulia*). This wine is produced by Abbazia di Rosazzo from cabernet sauvignon, merlot, and the local refosco, franconia, and tazzelenghe varieties grown in their 13.6-acre (5.5-hectare) Ronco dei Roseti vineyard in the Colli Orientali del Friuli district. The wine is *barrique*-aged. They produced 34,666 bottles of this wine in 1986. That wine was very good. Franco Bernabei consults here. Rating ** +

TASTING NOTE

1986 (*3 times, 11/90*). Complex aroma, oak blends in nicely with a mélange of scents; nice structure, medium-bodied, lovely texture, full of attractive fruit, moderate length. ***

RONCO DELLA TORRE (*Friuli–Venezia Giulia*). Torre Rosazza produces this cabernet-merlot wine from grapes grown at their vineyard-estate in the Colli Orientali district.

ROSSO DEI FRATI PRIORI (*Lombardia*). This *vino da tavola rosso* is made from cabernet sauvignon grapes.

ROSSO DEL GNEMIZ (*Friuli–Venezia Giulia*). The *cantina* and vineyards of Ronchi del Gnemiz are in S. Giovanni al Natisone in the Colli Orientali hills in the province of Udine. The first one was from the 1983 vintage. Their annual production of 50,000 to 60,000 bottles includes Rosso del Gnemiz, a cabernet-merlot blend. Both cabernets are used. The '86 was made from 90 percent cabernet and 10 percent merlot. Franco Bernabei is their consulting enologist. Rating ** +

TASTING NOTES

1987 (*twice, 10/90*). Spicy, herbaceous aroma, notes of green olives, tobacco and oak; soft, tasty, light tannin, a little dry and a tad bitter. ** −

1986 (*4/89*). Refined cabernet herbaceousness combined with cassis, cherries, tobacco and oak; sweet impression, rush of ripe fruit across the palate, lots of structure. *** −

ROSSO DEL RIVOLTELLA (*Lombardia*). This wine is produced by Azienda Agricola La Tassinara from merlot and both cabernets. These grapes are grown on their estate near Desenzano del Garda in the Lugana zone. It is aged for a year in cask. Rivoltella is at its best drunk between two and three years of the vintage.

ROSSO DELLA CENTA (*Friuli–Venezia Giulia*). Nicola Manferrari produces Rosso della Centa at his Borgo del Tiglio estate in Collio from a blend of merlot and cabernet.

ROSSO DI FORNAZ (*Friuli–Venezia Giulia*). Ronchi di Fornaz produces this red wine. Three-quarters of the *uvaggio* consists of the two cabernets, the remaining quarter is merlot. The grapes are grown in their vineyards located in the hills east of Udine in the Colli Orientali district.

ROSSO DI PILA (*Trentino–Alto Adige*). Piero Zabini, owner of Trattoria Maso Cantanghel, produces this 100 percent Cabernet Sauvignon at his winery in Civezzano in Trento. It is *barrique*-aged for twelve to fifteen months.

ROSSO DI VIGNE DAL LEON (*Friuli–Venezia Giulia*). Tullio Zamò owns the Vigne dal Leòn winery and its 22 acres (9 hectares) of vines in Premariacco in the Colli Orientali del Friuli district in the province of Udine. Annual production here is 60,000 to 70,000 bottles, 6,000 to 8,000 of which are of this merlot–cabernet sauvignon blend which is produced at their *cantina* in *località* Rocca Bernarda. Both cabernets are blended with merlot. Franco Bernabei is the consulting enologist here. Vigne dal Leòn Rosso is a wine for moderate aging. Rating **

TASTING NOTES

1986 (*4/89*). Herbaceous and green olive aroma, cassis and oak components; sweet impression, ripe fruit, moderate tannin, moderate length. ** −

1985 (*5/88*). Lots of structure, lots of flavor, the wine is rich and tasty. **

ROSSO TORRE ROSAZZA (*Friuli–Venezia Giulia*). Azienda Agricola Torre Rosazza in the Colli Orientali del Friuli zone uses 60 percent merlot and 40 percent cabernet sauvignon to produce this red wine.

ROVERATO, VIGNA DEL SOLZONE (*Emilia-Romagna*). Roverato produces this 100 percent Cabernet Sauvignon from grapes grown in their Solzone vineyard.

ROVETO (*Veneto*). Azienda Agricola La Ripaia produces this Cabernet Franc in their winery located in Selva del Montello in the province of Treviso.

Rujno (*Friuli–Venezia Giulia*). Josko Gravner produces Rujno at the Francesco Gravner estate at Oslavia in the Gorizia hills of the Collio district. We've heard that he labels his Cabernet Sauvignon as Rujno. Other reports suggest that Rujno is a cabernet-merlot blend. In either case, considering Gravner's reputation, we look forward to tasting it.

S. Cristina (*Lombardia*). This *barrique*-aged Cabernet Sauvignon is produced in the Lugana area of the Veneto by Azienda Agricola S. Cristina. Rating *

TASTING NOTES

1987 (*twice, 1/90*). Soft, open and tasty, round and balanced; ready now. *

1985 (*3/88*). Rich fruit, oak backnote, flavorful, oak background, round, light tannin. * +

Sammarco (*Toscana*). Castello dei Rampolla has 25 acres (10 hectares) of cabernet sauvignon vines in their 89-acre (36-hectare) vineyard. They produce Sammarco from a blend of 75 percent cabernet sauvignon and 25 percent sangiovese. The wine is aged in *barrique* for about two years. In 1980, the first vintage for this wine, they made 6,500 bottles; in 1981 production was nearly doubled to 12,500 bottles, and by 1983 production was nearly doubled again to 23,325. The '81 was given twenty-two months of *barrique* aging. Rating ***

TASTING NOTES

1986 (*6/90*). Refined cabernet aroma, oak overlay; supple under moderate tannin, tasty, well balanced; still young. **(+)

1985 (*4 times, 6/90, 30,500 bottles and 762 magnums*). Scented bouquet, rich, the fruit combines with the oak to define a lovely and complex aroma; great concentration and weight, lots of structure and class; needs perhaps two more years to be at its best but certainly attractive now. *** +

1983 (*5 times, 6/90, 23,325 bottles, plus 979 magnums*). Herbal and cassis aroma, tobacco notes; rich and concentrated, still a little young with a lot of structure and flavor. ***

1981 (*3 times, 5/88*). Cabernet combines with oak to define the aroma and palate, lots of structure and extract. ** +

San Leonardo (*Trentino–Alto Adige*). This regarded Bordeaux blend is produced by Marchese Anselmo Guerrieri Gonzaga at his Tenuta San Leonardo estate. It is made from 70 percent cabernet—both types—and 30 percent merlot grapes grown in the Toblino area of Trentino. Giacomo Tachis consults here. San Leonardo is best drunk between four and six years of the harvest. Rating **

TASTING NOTE

1983 (*4/89*). Herbaceous and cassis aroma; soft and tasty; ready. ** _

San Zeno (*Trentino–Alto Adige*). La Vinicola Sociale Aldeno blends 40 percent merlot with 30 percent each of the two cabernets to produce this wine. It ages more gracefully than their other Bordeaux blend, *Sgreben,* five to six years, though it is enjoyable sooner. It's been some time since we tasted it. Rating ** +

Santa Giulia del Poderaccio (*Lazio*). Conte Vaselli, a noted producer of Orvieto, uses merlot and cabernet grapes grown in the Viterbo area to produce this wine. It ages moderately well.

Sariz (*Friuli–Venezia Giulia*). Ca' Ronesca produces this merlot-based red wine from grapes grown in their vineyards in the Collio and Collio Orientali zones.

Sassicaia (*Toscana*), 1942. Tenuta San Guido has some 62 acres (25 hectares) under vines in the Bolgheri zone of Livorno. Some of the vines face north-south, part face east-

THE VINEYARDS OF THE SASSICAIA ESTATE

Vineyard	Acres	Hectares	Altitude in Feet	Meters	Average Age of the Vines
Alianoca	18.0	7.3	280	85	20 years
Castiglioncello	2.5	1.0	1,050	320	this is the oldest vineyard
Sassicàia	25.0	10.0	240	75	20 years

west. They are planted at an average altitude of 295 feet (90 meters) above sea level.

Marchesi Incisa della Roccheta, proprietor of this estate in the Bolgheri zone, first produced Sassicàia in 1948, but the wine wasn't offered commercially until 1968, by the firm of Antinori. About five or six years ago Piero Antinori told us that Sassicàia was always made from a blend of 95 percent cabernet sauvignon and 5 percent cabernet franc. Since then the *uvaggio* has been changed to a combination of 70 percent cabernet sauvignon with 30 percent cabernet franc. The wine is produced at the San Guido estate and was, until the '82 vintage, bottled and marketed by Antinori. Giacomo Tachis continues to consult. Today the Marchesi markets the wine himself.

Sassicàia is macerated for twelve to fourteen days. Vinification is done in 200-gallon (76-hectoliter) stainless steel vats. The wine is aged in a combination of Tronçais and Alliers oak from France and Slavonian oak barrels from Yugoslavia for eighteen to twenty-two months. The bottling, from the '82, has been done by Marchesi Incisa at the estate. Annual production of this Cabernet is 115,000 bottles, considerably more than that of a few years ago. The Marchesi rates 1985 as the very best vintage and 1973 as the worst. A few years ago, for the first edition of this book, we asked Piero Antinori to rate the vintages. Here are those ratings, adjusted for our four-star system:

**** 1981
*** 1982, 1978, 1977, 1975, 1974
** 1979, 1973, 1971
* 1980, 1976
0 1972

He told us that the 1969 was never released because it didn't achieve the level of quality they require. It's interesting to note that at a tasting in London a few years ago, of all the Sassicàia wines, the '80 (a vintage that Antinori considered rather mediocre) was rated best by the tasters present. Which just goes to prove *De gustibus non est disputandum*, there's no disputing about taste. It wouldn't have been our choice either.

The estate says that Sassicàia should not be consumed before its fifth year, and it remains at its best until between its eighth and twelfth years. Rating ***

TASTING NOTES

1987 (10/90). Deep color, nose a little tight and closed, some fruit evident; a mouthful of tannin followed by rich fruit, a lot of structure; young. **(* −)

1986 (6/90, magnum). Cassis and tobacco aroma, rich and intense with an oak overlay; lots of structure and class, long; still young. **(*)

1985 (5/90, magnum). Slightly corked, yet the richness and concentration are still evident; long finish; its class is evident. ***?

1983 (8/88). Refined varietal aroma; tasty, moderate tannin, on the pungent side, has backbone and structure. **

THE SASSICAIA WINES BY VINTAGE

Vintage	Weather	Maceration	Aging (barriques)
1979	Good, not excellent	12 days	65% French and 35% Yugoslavian; 70% were new.
1980	Normal, with modest rainfall, cool average summer and fall temperatures	13 days	20 months in 70% French and 30% Yugoslavian; 50% were new.
1981	Extraordinary	15 days	19 months in 65% French and 35% Yugoslavian.
1982	Normal, dry summer and a good fall	14 days	21 months in 75% French and 25% Yugoslavian; 50% were new.
1983	Slightly abnormal, average rainfall, cool temperatures, moderate sunshine	10 days	22 months in 75% French (70% new) and 30% Yugoslavian (33% new).
1984	Good, average summer temperatures, very little rainfall	13 days	20 months in 75% French and 25% Yugoslavian; 60% were new.
1985	Very hot summer and warm fall, less than average rainfall	14 days	22 months in 60% French and 40% Yugoslavian; 50% were new.

1980 (5/85). Aroma still somewhat closed, some nice nuances beginning to emerge; well structured, flavorful; finish is rather firm. **(+)

1979 (twice, 5/85). Richer but more reticent aroma than the '80; well knit, rich flavor; quite young, yet holds out real promise. **(*)

1978 (4 times, 9/90, 19,027 bottles). Drying out, harsh, has an edge to it, but the richness which is quite evident makes it attractive; drink up. ** — *Bottle of 11/82*: Aroma still closed and undeveloped, some fruit and oak evident; firm-textured, a bit clumsy at this stage, quite a lot of flavor. *(*)

1977 (twice, 9/86). Deep color; lovely rich, fruity aroma, vague tobacco note; a lot of structure, ripe and rich, long; lots of quality. ***(+)

1976 (twice, 3/83). Lacks fruit, balance or style though drinkable; both bottles were similar, allowing for the difference in age, though tasted a couple of years apart.

1975 (twice, 3/80). Aroma of tar and oak; heavy-handed with oak dominating the flavor, overly tannic for the fruit; will it develop?

1970 (twice, 4/81, 9,850 bottles). Richly intense aroma suggestive of cassis; well balanced, full of flavor, still has considerable tannin. **(*−)

1968 (5/81). High volatile acidity, tarry notes, cabernet character evident; full-flavored; where will it go from here? *(?)

SGREBEN (*Trentino–Alto Adige*). This wine, produced by La Vinicola Sociale Aldeno, is made from a blend of 40 percent merlot and 30 percent each of the two cabernets. It is best drunk before its sixth year. We haven't tasted Sgreben for about a decade. Rating [*+]

SIMONINI ATTILIO. See FAVONIO.

SOLAIA (*Toscana*). Antinori first produced this wine from the 1978 vintage; they made 5,000 bottles, which they felt were too few to put on the market. Some were sold, however. In 1979 they tripled their production and commercialized the wine on a wider scale. In 1980 and 1981 they didn't produce any Solàia, preferring instead to use the cabernet grapes in their more profitable Tignanello. In 1982 they produced Solàia again, about 2,000 cases. Eventually they expect to reach an annual production of 4,000 to 5,000 cases. There was no '83 or '84. They did produce an '85, '86, '87, and '88. We don't know if there was an '89.

The grapes for this wine come from the Solàia vineyard on their Santa Cristina property. This vineyard is planted to 60 percent cabernet sauvignon and 20 percent each cabernet franc and sangiovese. The first Solàia, the '78, was made, according to Piero Antinori, from a blend of 50 percent cabernet sauvignon, 30 percent cabernet franc, and 20 per-

cent sangiovese. The current *uvaggio*, we were told, as it has been since the 1982 vintage, contains 75 to 80 percent cabernet sauvignon and 25 to 20 percent cabernet franc. At another time we were informed that the wine still contains some sangiovese! The back label on the '86 agrees. That wine was made from the same combination of grapes, and in the same percentages, as is grown in the vineyard.

Solàia is aged eighteen to twenty-four months in a combination of French *barriques* and Slavonian oak casks. The '86 was aged for eighteen months in Alliers and Slavonian oak. The cabernets for the '85 were aged in *barriques* of Alliers, Tronçais, and Limousin oak for eighteen months; 60 percent were new, the rest were one year old. The sangiovese was kept in older Slavonian oak casks. The cabernet for the '82 was kept in one-, two-, and three-year-old *barriques*; the sangiovese was treated the same.

We've tasted only five vintages of Solàia, but find it Antinori's most interesting wine. In some ways it is more reminiscent of a Bordeaux than the regarded Tuscan Cabernet Sassicàia, which more resembles a California Cabernet. Even though we have more experience with Antinori's other wines, we must admit to being impressed with the style and class of this one, more so than any others. Rating ***+

TASTING NOTES

1987 (11/90). Refined cabernet fruit—tobacco, tea, cassis and green olive—aroma, nice oak overlay; balanced, nice mouth feel, moderate length. **

1986 (twice, 11/90). Deep color; cassis and herbal notes combine with tobacco and green olive nuances, refined; nice mouth feel under moderate tannin, nice texture, rich flavor with an herbaceous underpinning; could use more delicacy and length; a lot of class and style. ***

1985 (twice, 11/90). Refined tobacco and cassis aroma, herbal notes; rich concentration of fruit, velvety texture, moderate tannin; real class and style; the best Solàia to date and an impressive wine besides. ****

1979 (6 times, 7/89). Deep color; tobacco and oak apparent on the nose with some cabernet evident in the back; rich and sweet, good structure, a touch of tannin at the end, still most attractive and well made. ***−

1978 (twice, 4/88). Rich cassis aroma, blueberrylike nuance; fairly tannic, still it does have fruit; starting to dry out. * *Bottle of 5/83*: Nice cabernet fruit up front on the nose, bell pepper backnote; light tannin, well balanced, fairly nice. **−

SOLAROLO (*Lombardia*). Solarolo is made from a blend of 40 percent each merlot and croatina, with 20 percent uva rara.

SOLESINE (*Lombardia*). Bellavista's Champagne-method sparklers are among the country's best. It is located in the

Franciacorta zone near Lake Iseo in the province of Brescia and also produces three *barrique*-aged wines—a chardonnay, a pinot noir, and this cabernet-merlot blend. At one time Solesine was a blend of both cabernets with merlot; today it is made mostly from cabernet sauvignon with some merlot. Solesine, like Bellavista's other *barrique*-aged wines, is given eighteen months in new oak. They produced 850 bottles (about three *barriques*) of the '82 Solesine. The first vintage was the '81. Later vintages saw the production soar to 3,000 bottles! The only one that we tasted, the '82, was good. We suspect that the wine is considerably better today. Bellavista is a first-rate and serious producer. Rating [* +]

TASTING NOTE

1982 (4/85). Understated bell pepper aroma, overlaid with new oak; firm vein of tannin at this stage; beginning to approach drinkability. * +

STUKARA (*Friuli–Venezia Giulia*). Franco Furlan produces this cabernet franc–merlot blend at their Pra di Pradis estate in the hills of Gorizia in the Collio zone, near the border of Yugoslavia. The '87, which we tasted in May 1990, was herbaceous, soft, fruity, and dull. Rating 0

SUD TYROL. See **ALTO ADIGE.**

TAJARDINO (*Lombardia*). Gian Paolo and Giovanni Cavalleri produce this merlot–cabernet sauvignon blend at their Azienda Agricola Cavalleri winery in Erbusco. They also produce method-champenoise Franciacorta *spumanti* that enjoys a good reputation, a very good Franciacorta Rosso, a Novello di Erbusco, and three Franciacorta white wines, a regular one and two single-vineyard chardonnays—Rampanetto and Seradina. Their *spumanti* are fermented and sold in a variety of bottles, from 375 and 750 milliliters, to 1.5-liter magnums, 3-liter jeroboams, 6-liter mathusalems, and 9-liter salmanazars.

The information that they gave us reported that Tajardino was a DOC Franciacorta Rosso made from a blend of 50 percent cabernet sauvignon, 25 percent merlot, 15 percent nebbiolo, and 10 percent barbera. That information applied, we believe, to their first Tajardino. Today, from at least the '87, Tajardino has been a *vino da tavola,* one made from cabernet and merlot without the nebbiolo and barbera. The wine takes its name from the Tajardino vineyard where the grapes are grown. Those vines, planted in 1975, are at an altitude of 815 feet (250 meters) above sea level and face southwest. In 1987 they made 5,600 bottles of Tajardino. Rating ** +

TASTING NOTE

1987 (9/90). Green olive and tobacco aroma with an herbaceous character; well balanced, supple center, good fruit, a tad dry toward the end, toward the pungent end of the flavor spectrum; displays style. ** +

TANCA FARRA (*Sardegna*). Cabernet sauvignon has reached into all sections of the Italian boot, including the remote island of Sardegna. The innovative and reliable Sella & Mosca winery produces Tanca Farrà from a 50-50 blend of the local cannonau with cabernet sauvignon.

TAVERNELLE (*Toscana*). The large American importing firm Villa Banfi produces this wine from vines grown at altitudes averaging 1,100 feet (340 meters) above sea level on their Montalcino estate in the Brunello zone. Their first Cabernet Sauvignon was produced from the 1982 vintage. Tavernelle is aged for one year in *barriques* of Tronçais oak. A few years ago they produced 5,000 cases of Tavernelle. Eventually Banfi plans to produce 70,000 cases a year of this California-style Cabernet. In our experience each vintage has been better than the previous one. Rating ** −

TASTING NOTES

1989 (*twice, ex-vat, 6/90*). Some oak and herbal notes with an understated cabernet fruit component; soft and tasty, a tad light but good quality. ** −

1986 (*ex-vat, 3/87*). Pronounced cabernet herbaceousness, with fresh fruit and oak; no real depth but the fruit is attractive. *(+)

1984 (*6 times, 6/90*). Evident varietal character, cassis and tobacco notes; fairly soft and open, fruity. * +

1983 (*4 times, 9/87*). Fairly tannic, the fruit is there, agreeable; lacks style. *

1982 (*4 times, 8/87*). Characteristic cabernet aroma with an oak overlay; a bit shallow on the midpalate, some flavor on entry and toward the end. * −

TEBRO (*Trentino–Alto Adige*). Cantina Spagnolli produces Tebro from a blend of cabernet, merlot, and teroldego grapes. Our experience here is limited to the '88, which we tasted in April 1990. It had a grassy, herbaceous aroma, and was pungent, soft, simple, and coarse. Rating *

TERRE ROSSO. See **COLLI BOLOGNESI.**

TIAREBU (*Friuli–Venezia Giulia*). Livon produces this *barrique*-aged, cabernet sauvignon–merlot blend. It was aged for thirteen months in Alliers oak *barriques*. They produced some 3,600 bottles of the '85 Tiarebù. This wine is named for the vineyard in the Colli Orientali zone where the grapes are grown. Rating *

TASTING NOTE

1985 (9/90). The oak is evident, then the fruit, unfortunately the oak dominates. *

Torre Alemanna (*Apulia*). This wine is produced from the French malbec and native negro amaro and uva di troia grapes grown in the Cerignola district between Foggia and Bari. Torre Alemanna is a full-bodied wine of 13 percent alcohol that can take a few years of age.

Torre Ercolana (*Lazio*). A few years ago Cantina Colacicchi-Anagni produced a scant 1,200 to 1,400 bottles a year of this wine. It is made from a blend of approximately one-third each cesanese del piglio, cabernet, and merlot grapes grown on their estate in the Frosinone area, and aged for about two years in oak casks. Torre Ercolana is a rich, flavorful, full-bodied, smooth red wine that in our experience ages magnificently for up to ten years, and can probably last longer. Rating ***

TASTING NOTES

1985 (3 times, 4/90). Open herbaceous aroma, a little pungent, cassis notes; soft and smooth, tasty and well balanced, fruit displays a sweetness, some acid at the end. **?

1982 (3 times, 2/88). Tar and dried berry aroma; richly concentrated with an oak overlay. ** +

1980 (3 times, 11/87). Seems older than its years; still the richness of fruit is there. **

1975 Riserva (twice, 3/82, 1,184 bottles). Rich, full bouquet, cassis notes; some tannin, full of flavor, well balanced, very rich; has style. ** +

1973 Riserva (3/81, 1,496 bottles). Richly fruited aroma recalls cassis; full-flavored and velvety. ***

Torre Quarto (*Apulia*). This estate is named for the ruins of a tower dating from A.D. 850 on the property. In 1847, Duc de la Rochefoucauld brought cuttings of the malbec vine from Bordeaux and planted a 2,500-acre (1,000-hectare) vineyard here. Marcello Cirillo-Farrusi, who bought the estate in the early 1930s, restored the winery and replanted part of the vineyard. Today the property is owned jointly by his son Fabrizio Cirillo-Farrusi and the regional government. We heard that controlling interest is in the hands of the regional government but that Cirillo-Farrusi continues to run it.

There are 150 acres (60 hectares) of vines at Torre Quarto planted at 30 feet (9 meters) above sea level. Annual production averages nearly 30,000 cases; over 60 percent of this is red, which includes Torre Quarto and the DOC Rosso di Cerignola. The estate also produces a *bianco* and a *rosato*.

Torre Quarto is made from 75 percent malbec and 25 percent uva di troia grapes. The *normale* is aged for two years in oak cases, the *riserva* for an additional year. That wine is made only in the better vintages, and not more than 2,000 cases a year.

A few years ago Fabrizio rated as his best vintages 1981, 1979, 1977, 1973, and 1971, the 1981 being especially fine, and the 1977 better than the 1979. The 1975 was good, the 1974 and 1970 average years; 1968, he said, was also a good year.

Torre Quarto is a richly flavored, full-bodied wine that can seem a bit coarse in its youth. Given sufficient time, however, it can develop into a very impressive wine, with a richness of flavor and a complexity of character found only in top-quality wines. Torre Quarto drinks well from its fourth or fifth year to up to two decades or longer. We have tasted thirty-year-old vintages that were still in fine condition; they had, in fact, improved with the years. Rating: *normale* **, Riserva ***

TASTING NOTES

1984 (4/86). Fresh fruit aroma; some tannin, good body, rich flavor, at this stage one-dimensional, moderate length. *(*)

1980 (ex-cask, 4/81). Has fruit, but rasping at edges; not up to the level we expect from this wine.

1979 (ex-cask, 4/80). Pruney, raisiny aroma; rich extract, seems a trifle overripe; should make a nice glass of wine with sufficient time. *(*)

1977 (14 times, 7/85). Richly fruited aroma, notes of figs and prunes, and a touch of vanilla; still some tannin, soft-centered, richly flavored; good now but has a lot of potential yet. **(*)

1975 (5 times, 7/85). Nose shows a lot of development and complexity from bottle age; mellow, toasty notes, loads of flavor, full-bodied; still has a lot of life left, no sign of age except in its mellowness. **(+)

1975 Riserva (4/80, from tenth). Very soft, some tannin and a lot of flavor. **

1974 Riserva (5 times, 7/85, 20,000 bottles). Toasty, woodsy aroma, with berry notes; tannin up front gives way to a load of fruit, goes out with tannin; seems as if it's beginning to dry out, but still quite good. ** −

1973 (twice, 5/80). Fruity aroma, some oak beneath; balanced, tasty, full-bodied; could use more age, it seemed younger than the '75 we tasted with it. ** +

1971 Riserva (*4 times, 7/85*). Richly fruited and intense aroma, vague raisiny note, also prunes; smooth-textured, full and flavorful though a bit overripe, finish lingers. ** +

1970 Riserva (*4 times, 1/81*). Lovely, complex bouquet of fruit and flowers; rich in extract and flavor; good quality. ** +

1968 (*8/78*). Fruity aroma, some oak; soft, tasty, balanced. ** −

1961 Riserva (*4 times, 4/83*). Beautiful garnet robe, orange at rim; lovely bouquet, mellow and complex; soft, smooth and round, tasty; very ready, as it has been for at least the past five or six years. ***

1957 Riserva (*twice, 3/85*). Beautiful robe; expansive bouquet recalling cassis and toast; velvety texture, full of flavor, very long; has style. *** +

1953 Riserva (*3 times, 9/83*). Intense, complex bouquet with nuances of figs, blueberries, cassis and apricots; soft and smooth, flavorful, very good and very long. *** +

TRENTANNI (*Piemonte*). Michele Chiarlo of Cantine Duca d'Asti, to commemorate his thirtieth vintage as a wine producer (his first was in 1956), produced this barbera and cabernet sauvignon blend from the 1985 vintage. He fermented the must at temperatures between 77° and 79° Fahrenheit (25° and 26° centigrade), and aged it for twenty-four months in *barriques* of Alliers oak. Chiarlo produced 1,210 magnums that were bottled in March 1988.

TRENTINO (*Trentino–Alto Adige*), DOC. The major part of the Trentino growing zone is along the Adige River from Mezzocorona north of Trento to Belluno Veronese some 15 miles (25 kilometers) north of Verona, in the Lagarina Valley around Rovereto, in the lower Sacra Valley from Vezzano to north of Lake Garda and in the Cembra Valley. There are some 27,000 acres (11,000 hectares) planted in vines, not all of it DOC; over 85 percent of the plantings are of the red varieties.

The Trentino DOC zone includes 48 villages. The 4,329 growers registered under the Trentino DOC in 1988 had 4,984 acres (2,017 hectares) under vines. Besides the Trentino DOC, this includes parts of the DOCs of Caldaro and Valdadige, and all of Casteller, Sorni, and Teroldego. In total, there are 9,451 growers with 13,810 acres (5,588 hectares) of vines registered for all of the DOCs in the province of Trentino. Trentino DOC wines, between 1986 and 1988, averaged some 1.26 million cases a year, of which some 20 percent were cabernet and merlot-based wines.[35]

The Trentino DOC encompasses 20 wines—17 varietals, plus a white and a red blend and a *vin santo*. Cabernet and Merlot wines are included. The Cabernet can be made from either or both franc and sauvignon. An update to the DOC regulations, effective from 1984, allows a blend of cabernet and merlot. These wines are labeled as "Cabernet e Merlot del Trentino" or some such similar phrase, or Trentino Rosso.

Reputedly the best cabernet is grown in the Adige and Sario valleys. Cabernet franc, it is said, fares better on the lower slopes, while cabernet sauvignon does best at the higher elevations. The best merlot vines are considered to be those from the vineyards on the valley floors in the southern part of the region.

The best Cabernets of Trentino are as good as those from any of the other DOC zones; they tend to be fuller in body and not as long-lived as those from the Alto Adige. The Merlots are less interesting. There are also a number of interesting cabernet-merlot blends produced in Trentino, such as **Castel S. Michele, Foianeghe Rosso, Maso Lodron Rosso, Rauten,** and **Vallarom Rosso,** and we may see more, since this category is covered under the DOC recognitions. Rating: Cabernet */**; Cabernet e Merlot */**; Cabernet Franc *; Cabernet Sauvignon */**; Merlot *

ACREAGE AND AVERAGE PRODUCTION FOR TRENTINO

| | Growers | Registered Vineyards | | 1986–88 Average Number of Cases |
		Acres	Hectares	
Rosso	28	51.5	21.0	6,066
Cabernet	449	489.0	198.0	110,963
Cabernet Franc	6	5.8	2.4	970
Cabernet Sauvignon	38	40.7	16.5	8,436
Merlot	475	736.0	298.0	100,612
Total	996	1,323.0	535.9	227,047

Source: Il Corriere Vinicolo

DOC REQUIREMENTS FOR TRENTINO

	Minimum Varietal Component	Minimum Aging*	Minimum Alcohol	Maximum Yield in	
				Gallons/Acre	Hectoliters/Hectare
Cabernet	100%	none	11.0%	973	91
Riserva	100%	2 years	11.5%	973	91
Cabernet Franc	100%	none	11.0%	973	91
Riserva	100%	2 years	11.5%	973	91
Cabernet Sauvignon	100%	none	11.0%	973	91
Riserva	100%	2 years	11.5%	973	91
Merlot	100%	none	11.0%	1,122	105
Riserva	100%	2 years	11.5%	1,122	105
Rosso	†	none	11.5%	1,048	98

* The aging period is calculated from January 1.
† The Rosso is made from a blend of 50 to 85 percent cabernet (either or both) and 50 to 15 percent merlot.

Recommended Producers and Wines of Trentino

Barone de Cles (Cabernet)
Barone Fini (Cabernet and Cabernello†)
Càvit (Cabernet, Brume di Monte,† and Quattro Vicariati†)
Collavinus† (Cabernet)
Conti Bossi Fedrigotti (Cabernet, Merlot, and Foianeghe Rosso†)
Dorigati F.lli (Cabernet and Grener†)
Endrizzi F.lli (Cabernet and Merlot)
Gaierhof (Merlot and Torre di Luna—also sold as Elle & Co.)
Istituto Agrario Provinciale S. Michele (Cabernet and Castel S. Michele†)
Kupelweiser (Cabernet)
La Bottega de Vinai† (Cabernet)
La Vinicola Sociale Aldeno (Cabernet, San Zeno†, and Sgreben†)

Lagaria, I Vini del Concilio (Cabernet, Merlot, and Mori Vecio†)
Lechthaler (Cabernet)
Letrari (Cabernet)
Pedrotti (Cabernet)
Pisoni (Cabernet)
Rino Raffaelli (Cabernet and Barbarola†)
Rocca Mürer†† (*barrique*-aged Cabernet Sauvignon)
Salvetta F.lli (Cabernet and Rauten†)
Santico di Santi (Cabernet Sauvignon)
Simoncelli Armando (Cabernet and Navesèl†)
Tenuta San Leonardo (Cabernet, Merlot, and San Leonardo†)
Vallarom† (*barrique*-aged Cabernet from the Casetta vineyard)

† See individual entry.
†† The same winery with different labels.

NIEDERBACHER RATES THE VINTAGES
Cabernet

****	1985, 1970, 1969, 1964, 1959, 1949, 1947
***	1983, 1971, 1957
**	1984, 1982, 1980, 1979, 1977, 1976, 1975, 1967, 1966, 1963, 1961, 1958, 1954, 1952, 1946
*	1981, 1978, 1974, 1973, 1972, 1968, 1962, 1956, 1955, 1951, 1950, 1948, 1945
0	1965, 1960, 1953

Merlot

****	1985, 1969, 1959, 1947
***	1975, 1971, 1964, 1961, 1957
**	1984, 1983, 1980, 1976, 1974, 1970, 1967, 1966, 1962, 1954, 1952, 1949, 1946
*	1982, 1981, 1979, 1978, 1977, 1968, 1958, 1945
0	1973, 1972, 1965, 1963, 1960, 1956, 1955, 1953, 1951, 1950, 1948

ANTONIO ROSSI RATES THE VINTAGES[36]
Cabernet

****	1988, 1985, 1974, 1971
***	1987, 1986, 1984, 1983, 1982, 1980, 1979, 1976, 1973, 1970
**	1981, 1978, 1977, 1975, 1972

Merlot

****	1988, 1971
***	1987, 1986, 1985, 1984, 1983, 1982, 1980, 1979, 1976, 1974, 1973, 1970
**	1981, 1978, 1977, 1975, 1972

Rosso

****	1988, 1971
***	1985, 1984, 1983, 1980, 1979, 1976, 1974, 1973, 1970
**	1987, 1986, 1982, 1981, 1978, 1977, 1975, 1972

TUSCAN CABERNET AND **TUSCAN CABERNET-BASED BLENDS** (*Toscana*). Cabernet sauvignon is being used to produce more and more wines in Toscana. Frequently it is used in an *uvaggio* with sangiovese; it is also used by itself or in combination with merlot and/or cabernet franc. Those that we recommend and include herein are:

Altesino, Cabernet Sauvignon
Avignonesi, Cabernet Sauvignon
Avignonesi, Merlot
Coniale (Castellare)
Cortaccio (Villa Cafaggio)
Falchini, Cabernet Sauvignon (Azienda Agricola Casale)
Ghiàie della Furba (Conte Ugo Bonacossi)
Le Stanze (Poliziano di Carletti)
Nemo, Cabernet Sauvignon (Castello Monsanto di Fabrizio Bianchi)
Ornellàia (Marchese Ludovico Antinori)
R & R (Castello di Gabbiano)
Rocca di Castagnoli, Cabernet Sauvignon
Sammarco (Castello dei Rampolla)
Sassicàia (Tenuta San Guido)
Solàia (Antinori)
Tavernelle, Cabernet Sauvignon (Castello Banfi)

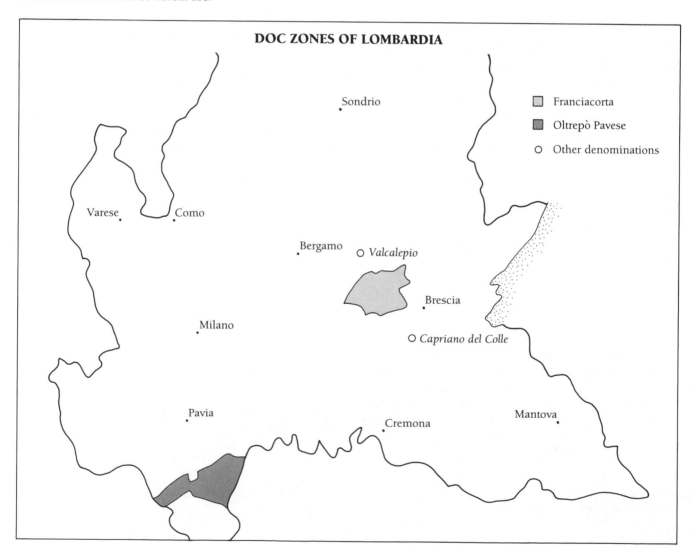

DOC ZONES OF LOMBARDIA

VALCALEPIO (*Lombardia*), *DOC*. In 1988 there were 76 registered growers with 267 acres (108 hectares) in this DOC zone. Between 1986 and 1988 average annual production of Valcalèpio Rosso was 22,613 cases.[37] This wine is produced near Lake Iseo east of Bergamo from a blend of 55 to 75 percent merlot and 45 to 25 percent cabernet sauvignon grapes.

The Bergamasca cooperative cellars, with about 150 members, is the zone's most important producer, and in our limited experience, one of the best. They age their Valcalèpio for two years as required, one in oak casks. They also produce a varietal Merlot meant to be drunk young. The wines of Conte Medolaga Albani and Tenuta Castello can be fairly good. Tenuta Castello's **Colle del Calvario** is very good. They also produce a second Valcalèpio Rosso. Caselle Alte, a producer of some other good wines, enjoys a good reputation, as do Tenuta La Cornasella, Azienda Agricola Corne, and Bortolo Locatelli.

Valcalèpio is best drunk within four years of the vintage, though it can last beyond that. When we visited the zone in 1981 we tasted three vintages, the '78, '76, and '75. The '75 was getting on in age; the other two were fairly enjoyable. In 1989 the '86s were drinking very well. The Valcalèpio wines are light- to medium-bodied dry reds that display the characteristic herbaceousness of the grape varieties from which they are produced. Rating * +

Antonio Rossi rates the Rosso vintages:[38]

****	1988
***	1987, 1986, 1985, 1983, 1981, 1978
**	1984, 1982, 1980, 1979

VALLAROM ROSSO (*Trentino–Alto Adige*). Giuseppina and Ezio Scienza, owners of Azienda Agricola Vallarom, produce this Trentino Rosso DOC from a blend of 80 percent cabernet sauvignon, 10 merlot, 8 percent cabernet franc, and 2 percent petit verdot. It is *barrique*-aged for eight months. They also produce a good *barrique*-aged Trentino Cabernet Sauvignon from their Casetta vineyard.

VALTREBBIOLA (*Emilia-Romagna*). Azienda Agricola Vigneti Casa Rossa blends 50 percent merlot, 40 percent cabernet sauvignon, and 10 percent malbec grapes to produce this wine, which is aged in cask for a year or two.

VECCHIA CASA ROSA (*Emilia-Romagna*). Azienda Agricola Vigneti Casa Rossa produces Vecchia Casa Rosa from a blend of 30 percent each of merlot, cabernet sauvignon, and cabernet franc, plus 10 percent malbec and pinot noir. It is aged for about two years in oak casks.

VENEGAZZU (*Veneto*). Conte Loredan Gasparini, former owner of Venegazzù, planted French varieties on his estate in the Montello e Colli Asolani area in the 1930s. Today the 125-acre (50-hectare) Azienda Agricola Cà Loredan Gasparini estate produces 44,000 to 55,000 cases of wine a year, including 11,000 of the red Venegazzù.

The Venegazzù Riserva della Casa *etichetta bianca,* white label, is made from a blend of cabernet sauvignon, cabernet franc, merlot, and malbec, and the Riserva della Casa *etichetta nera,* black label, combines the first three grapes with petit verdot.

Neil Empson, export agent for the wines, describes the rather unusual method employed to produce the black label. Following the fermentation, 50 percent of the wine is bottled with 5 percent malbec concentrate, and is left for three years in bottle, during which time it referments. At the end of this period, the bottles are opened and emptied into a tank where the wine is combined with the other 50 percent. This wine is then aged in oak for several months.

Some five years ago Venegazzù listed as the best vintages of its Riserva della Casa 1980, 1976, 1972, 1971, 1968, 1964, and 1961.

The Riserva della Casa wines were among the first, and are also among the more interesting, of Italy's Bordeaux blends. Of the two, the black label offers more interest and quality; it also ages better than the white label. The more recent vintages we've tasted suggest that this winery has slipped of late. Rating: white label ** −, black label ** +

TASTING NOTES

1982 black label (5/87). Rubber tire and tarlike aroma; moderate tannin, fairly well balanced, a bit hot at the end. ** −

DOC REQUIREMENTS FOR VALCALEPIO

Minimum Aging in Years		Minimum Alcohol	Maximum Yield in	
in Oak	Total		Gallons/Acre	Hectoliters/Hectare
1	2	12.0%	695	65

1981 white label (10/86). Packed with fruit on entry and toward the end, but could use more flavor on the midpalate. *

1980 white label (11/85, from tenth). Herbaceous aroma; light; past its best.

1979 white label (7/85). Aroma shows some refinement, herbaceous notes evident; well knit and flavorful, still some tannin though quite nice now, moderately long finish; some style. ** +

1978 black label (3 times, 3/83). Pretty nose, characteristic herbaceousness; tasty, has personality and balance. ** +

1978 white label (3 times, 3/83). Some age beginning to show but still has flavor interest. *

1977 black label (5/84). Drinking very nice now though has some roughness. ** −

1977 white label (3/83). Herbaceous aroma; acid on the low side, nice flavor, some dullness at the end. *

1976 (11/80). Lovely nose, oak and characteristic herbaceousness; well structured, tasty, still some tannin; has style. *** −

VIGNA L'APPARITA (*Toscana*). Castello di Ama produces this wine from the merlot grapes grown in their Vigna L'Apparita. This wine has gotten a lot of favorable press. The only one we tasted was very good. Rating ** +

TASTING NOTE

1988 (11/90). Deep color; ripe fruit recalls raspberries; rich flavor, good backbone, delicious, oak component, could use more length. **(+)

VIGNALTA (*Veneto*). Lucio Gomiero and Franco Zanovello, owners of this Colli Eugànei estate, produce all of 4,000 cases of wine annually. They produce two whites—a Pinot Bianco and a barrel-fermented Chardonnay—two reds—a Merlot and Gemola Reserva—and a dessert wine, Orange Blossom Muscat. The only one of their wines that we tasted was the quite impressive 1988 Gemola. We discovered this wine in June 1991 when Gomiero's American importer sent us a half bottle to sample. We were impressed enough to add this wine at the last minute, as it were, to our book.

Vignalta is located at an altitude of about 1,250 feet (380 meters) above sea level. They don't use pesticides or herbicides. Gemola is made by winemakers Gomiero and Zanovello from a blend of merlot and cabernet franc. This wine combines a richness with a delicacy not often found in cabernet and merlot wines. Due to time constraints we decided not to rate the wine. Suffice to say that it is impressive.

VIGNETO DEL FALCONE (*Veneto*). This medium-bodied dry red is made from a blend of cabernet sauvignon, cabernet franc, and merlot.

VIN DEL SASSO (*Toscana*). Vin del Sasso is a 100 percent Cabernet Sauvignon that we've never tasted.

ZUITER ROSSO (*Veneto*). Montelvini produces this wine from merlot, cabernet, marzemino, and pinot noir grapes grown in the Le Zuitere area of Montello e Colli Asolani. Production is 40,000 bottles a year. *Zuitere* is the dialect word for owl; this area was at one time, they say, densely populated by these nocturnal flyers. (We don't imagine, though, that they gave a hoot for the area's wines.)

CHAPTER 17

Other Noble Reds

Besides those wines produced from Italy's three noble grape varieties—nebbiolo, sangiovese, and aglianico—the fine Amarones, and the wines made from the Bordeaux grapes cabernet and merlot, there are a number of other excellent wines produced in Italy. These are the subject of our final chapter.

There are wines that could have been included here but have not been. Undoubtedly there are noble red wines produced in Italy that we haven't yet discovered. Those are pleasures to look forward to.

There are others that we have heard of, but haven't enough information to be able to discuss them. And there are still others for which our information is too out-of-date.

The Producers and Wines Rated

***

Ai Suma Barbera d'Asti (Bologna Giacomo)
— Amanda, Primitivo di Manduria DOC 21°†
— Amanda, Primitivo di Manduria DOC 22°†
— Amanda, Rosso di Sava 21°†
— Amanda, Rosso di Sava 22°†
Bricco dell'Uccellone (Bologna Giacomo), Barbera in *barrique*
Bricco Marun (Correggia Matteo), Barbera d'Alba DOC in *barrique*††
Passum (Cascina Castlet di Maria Borio)
Ronchi di Cialla, Schioppettino
Schioppettino, the best ones

**

— Alfeo (La Stoppa), Pinot Nero
Alto Adige Lagrein DOC, the best ones

Amanda, Primitivo di Manduria†
Amanda, Rosso di Sava†
Bricco della Bigotta (Bologna Giacomo), Barbera in barrique
− Josef Brigl, Alto Adige DOC Pinot Nero, Kreuzbichler
+ Cascina Castlet (Maria Borio), Barbera d'Asti Superiore DOC in barrique, Vigna Policalpo
Castel Cosa (Franco Furlan), Schioppettino
Chambave Rouge (Ezio Voyat)††
Conterno Aldo, Barbera d'Alba DOC in barrique†
+ Creme du Vien de Nus (Don Augusto Pramotton)††
+ Duca Enrico (Duca di Salaparuta)
Franconia, the best ones
Gaja, Barbera d'Alba DOC in barrique, Vignarey
Giarone (A. Bertelli), Barbera d'Asti DOC in barrique
− J. Hofstatter, Alto Adige DOC Pinot Nero Riserva, Barthenau
Martina (Elio Grasso), Barbera in barrique
Maurizio Zanella (Ca' del Bosco), Pinot Nero (now Pinero)
Monsupello, Podere 'La Borla
+ Montsclapade di Girolamo Dorigo, Schioppettino
+ Pignolo, the best ones
+ Refosco, the best ones
+ Rosso del Conte di Regaleali (Conte Tasca d'Almerita)
Pinero (Ca' del Bosco), Pinot Nero (formerly "Maurizio Zanella")
+ Pomorosso (Coppo Luigi), Barbera d'Asti DOC in barrique
Rocca del Mattarello (Castello di Neive), Barbera in barrique
Rosso del Rocolo (Pinot) (Villa dal Ferro di Lazzarini)
Sang des Salasses de Moncenis (Vignoble du Prieure de Montfleury), Pinot Nero††
Schioppettino
Stradivarius (Bava), Barbera d'Asti DOC in barrique
Tazzelenghe, the best ones
Torre Albarola (Abbazzia di Valle Chiara)
Trentino DOC Lagrein, the best ones
Valle del Sole (Cantine Duca d'Asti di Michele Chiarlo), Barbera d'Asti DOC in barrique
+ Vigne dal Leon di Tullio Zamò, Schioppettino
Villa Pattono (Renato Ratti)

*

Barone Felix Longo (Tenuta Schlosshof), Alto Adige DOC Pinot Nero
Bel Colle, Barbera d'Alba DOC in barrique, Vigna Muliasso Le Masche††
+ Bellendorf, Alto Adige DOC Pinot Nero
+ Josef Brigl, Alto Adige DOC Pinot Nero
Casotte (Bellavista), Pinot Nero††
Càvit, Trentino DOC Pinot Nero, Masso S. Valentino††

Corino Giovanni, Barbera in barrique††
Drago, Pinot Nero delle Langhe, Vigneto di Campo Romano††
+ Giorgio Grai, Alto Adige DOC Pinot Nero
+ Herrnhofer, Alto Adige DOC Pinot Nero
J. Hofstatter, Alto Adige DOC Pinot Nero
+ Kehlburg, Alto Adige DOC Pinot Nero
Kellereigenossenschaft Girlan, Alto Adige DOC Pinot Nero
Alöis Lageder, Alto Adige DOC Pinot Nero††
Livon, Schioppettino, Vigneto Cumini in Corno di Rosazzo††
Lungarotti, Pinot Nero††
Maria Giovana (Giacosa F.lli) Barbera d'Alba DOC in barrique
+ Maso Cantanghell, Atesino Pinot Nero Riserva††
Moccagatta, Barbera d'Alba DOC in barrique†
Nero del Tondo (Ruffino), Pinot Nero††
Nostra Signora (Boscaini), Alto Adige DOC Pinot Nero Vigneti di Montan††
Rocche delle Rocche (Rocche Costamagna), Barbera in barrique††
Scarpa Afra e Tobia, Pinot Nero
Scavino Paolo, Barbera affinato in carati††
Schiopetto Mario, Collio DOC Pinot Nero††
Schioppettino, the best ones
Schloss Schwanburg, Alto Adige DOC Pinot Nero
Vigna Il Chiuso (Castello di Ama), Pinot Nero††
− Vigna Larigi (Elio Altare), Barbera in barrique

† No longer produced
†† Tentative rating based on a limited experience or on old experiences

THE WINES

BARBERA IN BARRIQUE (*Piemonte*). Why did we include Barbera in a discussion of Italy's noble reds? How could we include it? When we were working on the first edition of *Italy's Noble Red Wines* we never thought that we could include a Barbera. The truth is we couldn't—until the winter of 1986. In January of that year, we went to VI.PI.85, a fair of Piemontese wines. And there we discovered a Barbera unlike any we had tasted before—Giacomo Bologna's Bricco dell'Uccellone.

We were, of course, familiar with his La Monella, which is a very good Barbera. But good as it is, we could not have included it in the book. The Bricco dell'Uccellone is another story.

When we tasted this wine at the dinner where it had its "debut" (before it was acutally released on the market), we had already tasted it at Giacomo's stand at the fair, and our initial impressions were confirmed—it really was that good.

Giacomo's regular Barbera is very good—superb for its type, just as his Moscato d'Asti is the platonic form for a moscato. But Giacomo, a man who values quality in all of its forms, wanted to do something more.

Those of you who had the opportunity to dine at Giacomo's now defunct and much lamented *Trattoria Braida* will know what we are talking about. Giacomo has an eye for beauty and his palate is just as discriminating. Is it any wonder that when we visit him and his wife, the essential Anna (less outgoing and enthusiastic than Giacomo but no less good-hearted and sincere), we discover not only excellent wines (such as the rare Malvasia, Vigna Sotto La Rocca Bernarda from the exceptionally fine Friulian producer Leonardo Specogna), but also elegant gourmet treats—the dishes produced by Anna and by Mama (ex-chef at Braida), olive oil from all over the country—Tuscan for the salad, Ligurian for the bread, and new specialties (or at least they're new to us) like the excellent goose products of the genial Gioacchino Palestro (delivered in person through the snow and fog to his friend Giacomo and Giacomo's friends)—the best of whatever there is.

It's no surprise that Giacomo also had a desire to offer the best Barbera he could find; and he found it in the Bricco dell'Uccellone vineyard and his own *cantina,* where he turned the grapes into a wine that does no less than create a whole new category of Barbera.

The Bricco dell'Uccellone vineyard has a southern exposure, which allows the grapes to ripen fully. In 1982, a very fine vintage, the grapes were harvested in October at 22 percent sugar and 0.85 total acidity. Giacomo fermented the wine in stainless steel, *cappello sommerso,* with a submerged cap, at 77° Fahrenheit (25° centigrade). The finished wine was aged in *barrique* for about one year, from February 1983 until March 1984, and given a further year of aging in bottle prior to release.

The '82 Bricco dell'Uccellone had 13.7 percent alcohol (and for the Californians among us who like statistics, 5.8 grams per liter of total acidity, 0.4 volatile acidity, and 3.5 pH—all surprising figures for a Barbera). Other vintages had similar stats.

This Barbera is so good that as soon as we began to put words to paper, we felt the need to have a glass to accompany them.

We have tasted every release of Bricco dell'Uccellone since the first, the '82, and we can say that it has gone from strength to strength. So successful has it been that it has helped create this new category of wine for our book— Barbera in *barrique.* For us Bricco dell'Uccellone remains the standard to judge the others by. Rating: Bricco dell'Uccellone ***

Bologna, in 1985, produced a second Barbera in *barrique,* Bricco della Bigotta. This wine spends four extra months in *barrique.* We prefer Bricco dell'Uccellone. The Bigotta has a little too much oak for our taste. Rating: Bricco della Bigotta **

In 1989, Giacomo Bologna created a third Barbera-in-*barrique*: Ai Suma. The barbera grapes came from Bologna's own vineyards on the slopes of Rocchetta Tanaro. Ai Suma spent six months in *barrique.* This is the only one of Giacomo's Barberas-aged-in-*barrique* that is DOC; it is a Barbera d'Asti. Rating [***]

Gaudio Amilcare produces 5,000 bottles of an excellent Barbera d'Asti Vigna Il Bergatino at his Azienda Agricola Bricco Mondalino in Vignale Monferrato, Alessandria in the Piemonte from his 2-acre (0.8-hectare) Il Bergatino vineyard; we'd be remiss not to mention his excellent Grignolino as well. Although it's not aged in *barrique,* we thought it worth a mention to give you an idea of the other face of Barbera. This wine and La Monella are excellent examples of the lighter, fruitier, more quaffable style of Barbera.

Gattaneo Giustiniani, at his Castello di Gabiano estate, produced for many years a Barbera with a different face. His *riserva* was deeper, richer, and more complex. It required time to smooth out. It's been quite a while since we tasted this Barbera. We have memories of many splendid bottles; some kept well for nearly two decades. Gabiano is now a DOC.

Another interesting and very good wine is Elvio Cogno's Tinello, which is made from an *uvaggio* of 80 percent barbera, and 20 percent nebbiolo and dolcetto blend. (This wine has been discontinued.)

For the Alba style of Barbera we recommend Bruno Giacosa, Castello di Neive, Aldo Conterno, Giacomo Conterno, Riccardo Fenocchio, Prunotto, Giuseppe Rinaldi, and Vietti. Fenocchio's Pianpolvere vineyard is a highly regarded place for barbera grapes.

Still another face of barbera is the *nebbiolata*. The only ones that we can recall tasting have been made by Cantina del Glicine. They make from 4,000 to 6,800 bottles a year of a Barbera d'Alba Nebbiolata from a blend of grapes grown in the Curà, Marcorino, and S. Cristoforo vineyards. This very good Barbera is made with 10 to 15 percent nebbiolo and refermented on the nebbiolo lees, a *ripasso* Barbera.

Elio Altare is an advocate of *barrique* aging. He makes 2,000 bottles of a barbera Vigna Larigi that tastes as if it were made from oak instead of grapes. But since that style of wine is fashionable today he gets good press and consequently commands overly high prices. And for those who like the taste of grapes, he also produces 4,000 bottles of Barbera d'Alba. Not being big fans of oak and much preferring the taste of grapes, we must admit that Vigna Larigi is not one of our favorite *barrique*-aged Barberas. Rating *–

Cantine Bava in Cocconato d'Asti has long been a Barbera specialist. They believe that their Barberas can age, but we found them better when young. A few years ago they began producing a Barbera in *barrique*. Stradivarius—Bava is a music fan—is a Barbera d'Asti that spent about nine months in *barrique*. The oak was half Alliers and half Tronçais. The '88 was well made and blended the cherrylike fruit of the barbera with the oak. Rating **

Cascina Barisèl produced all of 1,196 bottles of the '88 *barrique*-aged Barbera d'Asti La Cappelletta.

Mariuccia Borio specializes in Barbera wines at her Cascina Castlet estate in Costiglione d'Asti. She makes a range of interesting, and very good wines, including the *passito* **Passum** and the *barrique*-aged Vigna Policalpo Barbera d'Asti Superiore. This wine, from the Policalpo vineyard, is made from the grapes of forty- to fifty-year-old vines. Borio first experimented with Barbera in *barrique* in 1985. The Policalpo spends between four and twelve months in *barriques* of Alliers, Troçais, and Vosges oak. She produced 11,000 bottles of the '87 and 15,000 of the '88. Her Vigna Zia Litina is a good example of Barbera d'Asti, as is Vigna Malabaila. Rating: Vigna Policalpo ** +

Cascina La Barbatella, located in the Asti zone, produces the Barbera-in-*barrique* Vigna dell'Angelo.

Vigna del Sole is a *barrique*-aged Barbera del Monferrato from Carlo Nob. Cassinis at his 37-acre (15-hectare) Castello di Salabue in the *località* of Salabue di Ponzano in the *comune* of Ponzano Monferrato in Alessandria. Cassinis also produces Rubello di Salabue from barbera and nebbiolo, as well as a Cabernet Sauvignon.

Michele Chiarlo at Cantine Duca d'Asti has also produced some good Barbera through the years. He also makes two Barberas in *barrique*. The grapes for Chiarlo's Valle del Sole Barbera d'Asti come from a 6-acre (2.5-hectare) vineyard of thirty-five-year-old vines on the upper slopes of the southeast hills between Nizza Monferrato and Castelboglione. The vines yield, on average, from 375 to 425 gallons per acre (35 to 40 hectoliters per hectare), as opposed to a normal barbera yield of 750 (70). The grapes are harvested ten to fifteen days later than normal. This *superiore* is aged in *barrique* for twelve to fourteen months. The first was the '82. Rating **

Azienda Agricola Colle Manora grows cabernet sauvignon, merlot, sauvignon, and pinot nero alongside barbera and grignolino on their estate in Quargnento in Alessandria. They produced 8,680 bottles of the '88 Pais, made from an *uvaggio* of Piemontese grapes, mostly barbera, and 5,950 bottles of the '86 Manora, a *barrique*-aged Barbera.

The first Barbera in *barrique* that we tested from Aldo Conterno was the '84. It showed, as one might expect from this fine winemaker, a lot of quality. The grapes come from Conterno's vineyard on Bussia Soprana in Monforte d'Alba. He has 45 *barriques* of Alliers oak for his Barbera d'Alba. Rating [**]

Angelo Gaja's Barbera d'Alba comes from forty-year-old vines grown in his 6-acre (2.5-hectare) Vignarey vineyard just outside of Alba. The vineyard is named for Angelo Gaja's grandmother, Clotilde Rey, and the wine is named for the vineyard. The vines are planted at an altitude of 650 feet (200 meters) above sea level. The yield here averages approximately 375 gallons per acre (35 hectoliters per hectare). The '78 through the '85 were fermented for two to three weeks. They spent two to four months in *barrique* and eight to fifteen months in large oak casks. Rating **

The F.lli Giacosa—Leone, Valerio, and Renzo—produce the *barrique*-aged Maria Gioana Barbera d'Alba. The grapes are harvested later than for their normal Barbera, and they come from a special section of the Vedetta vineyard. The '85 was quite good. Rating *

Elio Grasso, at his Monforte d'Alba winery in the Barolo zone, produces Martina, a *vino da tavola* barbera from grapes grown in his Gavarini vineyard. The first one was the '88; it spent three months in *barriques* of Alliers oak. Grasso produced 4,500 bottles. Rating **

And Tenuta La Tenaglia, also in the province of Alessandria, produces a *barrique*-aged barbera as well.

RATING THE PRODUCERS OF BARBERA IN *BARRIQUE*

* —	Altare Elio, Vigna Larigi
**	Bava, "Stradivarius" Barbera d'Asti
[*]	Bel Colle, Barbera d'Alba Vigna Muliasso Le Masche
**	Bertelli A., Barbera d'Asti Giarone
[***]	Bologna Giacomo, Ai Suma Barbera d'Asti
***	Bologna Giacomo, Bricco dell'Uccellone
**	Bologna Giacomo, Bricco della Bigotta
**	Cantine Duca d'Asti di Michele Chiarlo Barbera d'Asti Valle del Sole
** +	Cascina Castlet, Barbera d'Asti Superiore Vigna Policalpo
**	Castello di Neive, Rocca del Mattarello
[**]	Conterno Aldo, Barbera d'Alba
** +	Coppo Luigi, Barbera d'Asti Pomorosso
[*]	Corino Giovanni
[***]	Correggia Matteo, Barbera d'Alba del Bricco Marun
**	Gaja, Barbera d'Alba Vignarey
*	Giacosa F.lli, Barbera d'Alba "Maria Giovana"
**	Grasso Elio, Martina
[*]	Moccagatta, Barbera d'Alba
[*]	Rocche Costamagna, Rocche delle Rocche
[*]	Scavino Paolo, *affinato in carati*

TASTING NOTES

Bologna Giacomo 1989 Ai Suma Barbera d'Asti (4/91). Lovely cherrylike aroma has a nice oak overlay that adds a vanilla note; rich, has a sweet impression, open, round, and smooth, so well-balanced we didn't notice that it has 14.86 percent alcohol(!), long finish; real class. ***

Corino Giovanni 1989 (ex-barrique, 4/90). At this stage the oak dominates, still there is a sweetness from the fruit. [*]

Correggia Matteo 1989 Barbera d'Alba, del Bricco Marun (ex-barrique, 4/90). Correggia produced 2,200 bottles of this impressive wine. Dense color; rich and packed with fruit; at this stage very impressive indeed. ** + (***)

Moccagatta 1989 Barbera d'Alba (ex-barrique, 4/90). Cherry fruit and oak; tart, vanilla and fruit flavor. *

Altare Elio 1988 Vigna Larigi (4/90). Heavy-handed use of oak, it dominates; if you like the style, you'll like this. * —

Bel Colle 1988 Barbera d'Alba, Vigna Muliasso Le Masche (ex-vat, 4/90). This wine spent nine months in *barrique*. At this stage the oak is dominant, but a richness and concentration of fruit are evident as well. *?

Bertelli A. 1988 Barbera d'Asti, Giarone (ex-barrique, 4/90). Oak dominates, then some fruit, and it's still in *barrique!* * —

Cantine Bava 1988 Barbera d'Asti, Stradivarius (twice, 6/90). Nice blend of oak and cherrylike fruit; a little chewy at this stage, all the elements are there, good acidity, nice mouth feel. **

Grasso Elio 1988 Martina (11/90). Oak blends with the cherrylike fruit of the barbera; nice mouthful of varietal fruit with an oak component. **

Scavino Paolo 1988 affinato in carati (4/90). Heavy oak, some barbera character, chewy, sweet. * —

Altare Elio 1987 Vigna Larigi (3 times, 10/90). Heavy oak dominates, sweet oaky flavor seems contrived. It was better eighteen months ago. * —

Bologna Giacomo 1987 Bricco dell'Uccellone (6 times, 6/90). Harmonious blend of oak and cherrylike fruit; open, appealing fruit flavor combines with a nice oak overlay which adds texture, soft, fairly long in the mouth. *** —

Gaja 1987 Barbera d'Alba, Vignarey (1/90). Deep purple; open cherrylike aroma, then some harshness intrudes on the nose; soft, open and fruity, dry end, tasty. * +

Rocche Costamagna 1987 Rocche delle Rocche (4/89). Twenty percent nebbiolo was blended with 80 percent barbera, and the result was aged in *barrique*. One whiff and you won't doubt it, some fruit is still apparent. * —

Bologna Giacomo 1986 Bricco dell'Uccellone (12 times, 9/90). Cherrylike fruit up front on the nose followed by an oak overlay; lovely texture, rich with a taste of sweet fruit and an evident oak component, very long at the end. ***

Bologna Giacomo 1986 Bricco della Bigotta (3 times, 6/90). Lots of oak as well as fruit on the nose and palate; the oak is more pronounced than it is in the Uccellone, this one also has more body, cherrylike fruit. ** +

Cantine Duca d'Asti di Michele Chiarlo 1986 Barbera d'Asti Superiore, Valle del Sole (twice, 11/90). Oak and cherrylike fruit; soft and tasty, some oak at the end. * +

Castello di Neive 1986 Rocca del Mattarello (4/89). Nice blend of oak with the cherrylike varietal character of the barbera; supple, good structure; ready. **

Coppo Luigi 1986 Barbera d'Asti, Pomorosso (3 times, 10/90). Oak and fruit combine for a nice touch, a little dry, well made. *Bottle of 5/90:* Cherrylike fruit of the barbera marries nicely with the vanilla of the oak on the nose and palate, soft, open, tasty, ready. ** +

Giacosa F.lli 1986 Barbera d'Alba, Maria Giovana (3 times, 11/90). Each succeeding bottle was less interesting than the previous one; the wine was tiring fast and losing its fruit; the oak was all that was left.

Altare Elio 1985 Vigna Larigi (4/87). Oak! oak!! and more oak!!!

Bertelli A. 1985 Barbera d'Asti, Giarone (10/90). Open fruit, some oak adds complexity, soft, quite drinkable. **

Bologna Giacomo 1985 Bricco dell'Uccellone (8 times, 10/89). Rich in both aroma and flavor, packed with fruit, smooth-textured, very long finish. ***

Bologna Giacomo 1985 Bricco della Bigotta (4/88). Light aroma combines oak with leather and animal fur; rich, round, full and warm. ***

Cantine Duca d'Asti di Michele Chiarlo 1985 Barbera d'Asti Superiore, Valle del Sole (12/88). Aroma is complex and rich; sweet impression, round and ripe. ** +

Cascina Castlet 1985 Barbera d'Asti Superiore, Vigna Policalpo (3 times, 10/90). Lovely blend of oak with cherry fruit on both the nose and palate, a harmonious blend, nice mouth feel. ** +

Castello di Neive 1985 Rocca del Mattarello (3 times, 4/89). This, the first one, spent nine months in *barrique.* Lots of cherrylike fruit, oak adds a nice overlay, smooth mouth feel, long. **

Gaja 1985 Barbera d'Alba, Vignarey (11/88). Slight nose, hint of cherries, oak evident; tart and lively; signs of age, best to drink up. *

Giacosa F.lli 1985 Barbera d'Alba, Maria Giovana (twice, 4/90). This one, the first they made, spent six months in *barrique.* Fresh cherrylike aroma, vanilla and chocolate notes; good fruit. *

Bologna Giacomo 1984 Bricco dell'Uccellone (6 times, 8/88). Cherry fruit marries well with the vanilla of the *barrique,* smooth-textured, full of flavor, very long finish. ***

Conterno Aldo 1984 (ex-barrique, 1/86). Oak somewhat dominant at first followed by cherrylike fruit; good acid, sweet oak flavor, should soften a bit, very nice. **(+)

Bologna Giacomo 1983 Bricco dell'Uccellone (9 times, 4/88). Barbera fruit quite evident with a complex overlay of oak; lovely mouth feel, very long finish; starting to show some age. It was better a year ago; perhaps the bottle was off. **

Gaja 1983 Barbera d'Alba, Vignarey (twice, 11/85). This wine spent four months in *barrique.* Oak has become dominant, still the fruit is evident.** − *Bottle of 11/84:* Cherry fruit and oak aroma; round, nice fruit flavor with an oak overlay; a lot of quality. ***

Bologna Giacomo 1982 Bricco dell'Uccellone (11 times, 7/85). Typical barbera cherries plus oaky vanilla notes on the bouquet; rich and expansive, well balanced and supple with a lot of fruit and the complexity and extra dimension from the oak, long lingering finish; displays real style and a lot of quality. ***

Cantine Duca d'Asti di Michele Chiarlo 1982 Barbera d'Asti Superiore, Valle del Sole (1/86). Overoaked, no varietal character left; there is, however, still some fruit. * −

Cascina Castlet 1982 Barbera d'Asti Superiore, Vigna Policalpo (twice, 1/86). Starting to fade but some fruit is still evident.

Gaja 1982 Barbera d'Alba, Vignarey (11/86). Lovely cherrylike fruit on the nose; fresh, lively acidity, good body, a lot of fruit, zesty finish marred by a touch of alcohol. *** −

Gaja 1979 Barbera d'Alba, Vignarey (6 times, 6/84). Characteristic cherrylike fruit aroma; fruity, quite agreeable. **

Gaja 1978 Barbera d'Alba, Vignarey (twice, 9/83). This one has held up very well; lively with nice fruit, no need to keep. **

BRICCO DELL'UCCELLONE. *See* BARBERA IN *BARRIQUE.*

CHAMBAVE ROUGE *(Aosta).* Ezio Voyat, producer of Passito di Chambave, one of the finest sweet wines we've ever tasted, also makes Chambave Rouge. This medium-bodied dry red has an alcohol level of close to 13 percent, which is high for this region. It reputedly ages very well. This wine is made from a blend of the local gros vien variety, with the addition of some dolcetto and barbera. We haven't had it in some time, but what we tasted was very fine indeed. And we don't know if Voyat produces his wine under the regulations set down in the Valle d'Aosta DOC for Chambave Rouge. In 1988 there were 49 registered growers for that denomination, with 12.7326 acres (5.1526 hectares) of vines planted.[1] Rating [**]

CREME DU VIEN DE NUS *(Aosta).* Don Augusto Pramotton produces this wine from a blend of the local vien du nus variety, plus pinot nero grapes from the vineyards of the church of Nus. We've heard that a small amount of merlot and petit rouge are also included in the blend. The wine is aged for about one year in oak casks. Creme du Vien de Nus is a full-bodied, full-flavored, mellow, dry red with a richness and level of glycerine that give it an impression of sweetness. The wine is also known as Vin de la Curé de Nus (wine of the parish priest of Nus). It's been some time since we last tasted it. We don't know whether or not this wine is produced under the regulations set down in the Valle d'Aosta DOC for Nus Rosso. In 1988, 21 registered growers cultivated 8.2211 acres (3.3269 hectares) of vines in the Nus denominated zone.[2] Rating [** +]

DUCA ENRICO *(Sicilia).* Duca di Salaparuta, known for its Corvo wines, produces the *barrique*-aged Duca Enrico, an upscale, finely honed wine. The name *corvo* derives from a legend concerning a noisy crow, a hermit, and a stick given to the hermit by a sympathetic populace to drive away the crow. Besides Corvo whites and a red, Duca di Salaparuta produces three new wines—the *barrique*-aged Bianco di Valguarnera, the partly *barrique*-aged red Terre d'Agala, and Duca Enrico.

Winemaker-enologist Franco Giacosa, who's from the Piemonte, conceived the idea for Duca Enrico in 1983. He first produced it in 1984. That wine, and each subsequent vintage, we have been told, was made from specially selected nero d'avola grown in the best vineyards in the island's finest growing zones. The grapes for the '84 came from sixteen-year-old vines. The wine was given a light maceration of eight days on the skins at a temperature between 77° and 80° Fahrenheit (25° and 26.5° centigrade) and fermented at a relatively cool 70° (21°). It was aged for eighteen months in *barriques* of Tronçais and Alliers oak, plus twelve months in 1,055-gallon (4,000-liter) Slavonian oak casks. Malolactic fermentation took place in *barrique*. They produced just over 50,000 bottles of the '84. Rating ** +

TASTING NOTES

1986 (11/90, 52,308 bottles). Fruit more pronounced than the '84 or '85, both of which displayed the oak more up front; good structure; a little young.*(*)

1985 (12/89). More elegance and complexity than the '84; sweet, rich, ripe fruit, fairly long finish is a tad dry.** +

1984 (6 times, 5/90). Lovely blend of oak and rich fruit, vaguely herbaceous; sweet and rich, well balanced, good structure.** +

FRANCONIA (*Friuli–Venezia Giulia*). The franconia grape variety of the Friuli region, alternatively known as blaufränkisch, blaufraenkisch, or limberger, is said to be the pinot noir. (In Austria blaufränkisch is another name for the gamay. Pierre Galet, in his monumental ampelography *Cépages et Vignobles de France,* does not make any tie-in with either the pinot or the gamay, though he does say that the other three names, as well as a few others, are synonyms for this variety.)

The only DOC zone for franconia is Isonzo, but the respected districts for this variety are in the Collio and Colli Orientali zones. The Cormons district of Gorizia and the Rocca Bernarda and Corno di Rosazzo areas of Udine are highly regarded for their Franconia wines. Angelo Nascig, a fine producer who makes a scant 165 to 220 cases of this wine a year at his *cantina* in Corno di Rosazzo, produces a very good one. Some other regarded producers of Franconia are the Santa Caterina estate of Gianfranco Fantinel in Buttrio, Francesco Lui in Corno di Rosazzo, Azienda Agricola della Roncada in Cormons, and Giuseppe Toti of Prepotto.

In our rather limited experience the Franconia wines are at their best between two and three years of the vintage and last well until four or five. Rating **

LAGREIN (*Trentino–Alto Adige*). The lagrein grape is used to produce a rosé called Lagrein Kretzer, or Lagrein Rosato, and the red Lagrein Dunkel, or Lagrein Scuro, in the Alto Adige. In 1988 there were 641 registered growers authorized to cultivate 756 acres (306 hectares) of lagrein. This acreage was 6 percent of all the vines cultivated in the province of Bozen for all of the province's DOC wines. The average annual production between 1986 and 1988 was some 242,400 cases of wine.[3]

Most of the plantings are in the province of Bozen (Bolzano) in the area stretching from Meran to Salurn in the Etschtal (Valle d'Isarco). The main growing areas are in Gries, Fagen, Bozen Dorf, Auer, Eppan, Kurtatsch, Neumarkt, and Andrian.

The Lagreins from Fagen and Bozen Dorf are particularly prized; those of Auer, Eppan, and Kurtatsch are also regarded. The Lagrein, red and rosé, produced from vineyards on the red cliffs of Gries and Mortizing on the edge of Bozen may be denominated Grieser Lagrein or Lagrein di Gries. There are 454 growers who cultivate 368 acres (149 hectares) of Lagrein for the Alto Adige DOC and 187 with 389 acres (158 hectares) for Grieser Lagrein. Between 1986 and 1988 production of Alto Adige Lagrein averaged nearly 110,000 cases, and that of Grieser Lagrein almost 133,610 cases.[4] The Kellereigenossenschaft Gries produces a Grieser Lagrein, as does the Klosterkellerei Muri-Gries.

DOC regulations for Alto Adige Lagrein require a minimum of 95 percent lagrein to be used. The law allows up to 1,048 gallons per acre (98 hectoliters per hectare) and requires that the alcohol level be at least 11.5 percent. If the wine is aged for at least a year from November 1, it may be labeled *riserva*.

Good vintages for Alto Adige DOC Lagrein were 1964, 1969, 1971, 1974, and 1976. Giorgio Grai rates the 1975 and 1974 vintages highly, and his own Lagreins support that view. (Unfortunately we don't have information on more recent vintages for Lagrein.)

Lagrein is also DOC in the Trentino denomination. In 1988, 189 growers were authorized to cultivate 228 acres (92 hectares) of lagrein for the DOC. This was less than 2 percent of the grapes cultivated there for the DOC. Between 1986 and 1988 the annual production of Trentino Lagrein averaged some 166,475 cases.[5] DOC requires that this wine be made purely from lagrein grapes. The law allows a production of up to 1,048 gallons per acre (98 hectoliters per hectare) and requires that the alcohol level be at least 11 percent. Lagrein can be *rubino* or *dunkel* if red, and *rosato* or *kretzer* if pink. If the wine is aged for at least a year from November 1, it may be labeled *riserva*.

The wines made from this variety have a structure similar to those made from cabernet. Lagrein has a fruity aroma with hints of almonds. It is generally at its best within four to six years of the vintage, but we've had some at ten years that were still in fine condition. Rating **

Recommended Producers of Lagrein

Barone de Cles (Trentino)	Klosterkellerei Muri-Gries,
Bellendorf (Alto Adige)	Grieser Lagrein (Alto
Conti Martini (Trentino)	Adige)
Grai Giorgio (Alto Adige)	Alöis Lageder, Lindenburg
Herrnhofer (Alto Adige)	(Alto Adige)
J. Hofstatter (Alto Adige)	S. Margherita
Kaufmann (Alto Adige)	Schlos Schwanburg (Alto
Kehlburg (Alto Adige)	Adige)
Kellereigenossenschaft	Schlosskellerei Turmhof,
Gries, Grieser Lagrein	especially Lagrein Schmalz
(Alto Adige)	(Alto Adige)

MONSUPELLO, PODERE 'LA BORLA (*Lombardia*). Carlo Boatti, at Azienda Agricola Monsupello, produces what are for us some of the finest wines of the Oltrepò Pavese. Boatti has an annual production of 90,000 to 120,000 bottles of wine, including a very good white—Friday's White Wine—and a good *spumante* from pinot nero. He makes about 21,000 bottles a year of Monsupello, Podere 'La Borla. Boatti has 27 acres (11 hectares) of vineyards, most in Torricella Verzate.

The *cantina* was founded in 1893. Boatti has produced his Monsupello since 1961. It is made from a blend of 45 percent barbera, 25 percent croatina, 24 percent uva rara (bonarda novarese), and 6 percent pinot noir. Boatti uses the free-run juice only and ages the wine for two years in oak casks. 'La Borla needs at least four years of age to soften and smooth out, and can live for up to a decade, developing interesting nuances of aroma and flavor. Rating **

TASTING NOTES

1985 (*4/89*). Open fruit aroma, cherry and vanilla notes; good body. **+

1983 (*4/87*). Spicy and cherry aroma; tart and firm, fruity; seems a tad older than its years! *

1982 (*7/87*). Fruity aroma hints of cherries; nice acid, good fruit. **

1979 (*3 times, 9/83*). Some complexity on aroma, floral and fruity nuances, a vague cherrylike note; well structured, tasty, ready. **

1976 (*4/80*). Fruity aroma; soft, balanced, flavorful, some length. **–

1974 (*twice, 4/81*). Cherry notes on a fruity aroma; tart edge, lively, a bit light, flavorful. **

1971 (*9/81*). Bouquet displays a mellowness and complexity from bottle age, hints of blueberries; soft and round, some age beginning to show but still has a surprising amount of flavor. **

PASSUM (*Piemonte*). Mariuccia Borio is a barbera specialist. At her Cascina Castlet in Costiglione d'Asti in Piemonte she produces a range of barbera wines. One-quarter of the 50-acre (20-hectare) Borio estate is in vines, all barbera. Borio's vineyards—Malabaila, Policalpo, and Zia Litina—are all vinified separately. A number of her vines are more than thirty-five years old, some as old as fifty.

This charming and energetic woman has been involved with wine since she was fifteen years old. Today she produces between 80,000 and 100,000 bottles of Barbera wines annually with the advice of consulting enologist Armando Cordero. Borio produces three single-vineyard Barbera d'Astis, all *superiori*. Her first cru, in 1980, was from her Vigna Zia Litina. She also produces 10,000 bottles of Barbera from

Vigna Malabaila and 11,000 to 15,000 of the *barrique*-aged Vigna Policalpo (see **Barbera in barrique**). Besides those three, she does a straight Barbera d'Asti Superiore; there were 15,000 bottles of the '87.

Borio also produces some extraordinary honey, including one from chestnut blossoms and another from acacia flowers. Those who have had the pleasure of tasting them agree that these first-rate honeys are not quite as sweet as Mariuccia herself.

Other wines here include 5,000 to 6,000 bottles of Castlèt Rosso Frizzante Naturale and 18,000 to 20,000 of the Castlètbianco Frizzante, both of which are given a light sparkle in an autoclave; 5,000 to 6,000 bottles of Castlètbianco su Lievito Attivi, which was first made in 1980; and 4,000 of Castlètbianco *normale*. She told us a few years ago that she planned to increase the production of the su Lievito Attivi.

The wine that concerns us here is Cascinacastlèt "Passum." After the grapes are harvested they are dried in small baskets between three and five months. During this time the sugar level climbs to 27 to 28 percent as the water evaporates and the acid drops. The must is fermented for two months, then stops; it reposes until the summer when the fermentation finishes. It spends two years in stainless steel and is then bottled. The first Passum was the '76. In 1983, Borio made 5,500 bottles; in 1987, 11,000; and in 1988, 20,000. The bottle was created by Studio Congegno and graphic artist Giacomo Bersanetti. The design on the bottle is the artist's conception of an ancient "P," which was inspired by the fanstasy of a pre-alphabetic script. Borio told us that this Passum ages well. Rating ***

TASTING NOTES

1986 (*ex-vat, 5/87*). Restrained aroma, late-harvest character; nice acid balance, long, dry and refreshing finish, still has a sense of sugar. **(*–)

1985 (*ex-cask, 5/87*). Recalls a late-harvest wine, zinfandellike raspberries, vaguely raisinlike note; lively, nice acid, dried fruit flavor; lots of character. ***

1984 (*twice, 10/90*). Singular personality, aroma recalls flowers, varietal cherries, leather and dried fruit; well balanced, lots of character and flavor. ***

1983 (*twice, 7/87*). Dried cherry aroma, nuances suggestive of figs, richly flavored; good weight and concentration, very well balanced, long finish. ***

1982 (*1/86*). Dried fruit character; firm and full, interesting flavor. **

1979 (*5/87*). Some age evident on the nose; some sugar, dried fruit flavor; has held up though starting to fade. *–

PIGNOLO (*Friuli–Venezia Giulia*). Some years ago, on one of our trips to Friuli, a number of producers told us that pignolo was the single finest red variety of the region but very few plantings were left. Today we are happy to report that there is a small but growing interest in the grape. The first Pignolo that we tasted was the '78 from Conte Antonio di Trento. It was fading when we tasted it in 1981—the bottle might have been bad—but it still displayed some quality. Girolamo Dorigo produces the excellent Ronc di Jura at his Montsclapade estate in Buttrio. He made all of 800 bottles of the impressive '85. He has 1,122 pignolo vines planted, or did a few years ago. Another producer we know of that makes one is Abbazia di Rosazzo. The winery-estate is located in Manzano in the province of Udine in the Colli Orientali del Friuli zone. Their '86 was very good, indeed. They produced 2,413 bottles of the '87. Based on the three that we've tasted, the better examples of a wine made from pignolo have herbaceous, strawberry, and floral components, good body, nice texture, and good length in the mouth. Rating ** +

PINOT NERO, PINOT NOIR. When the pinot noir attains its glorious best there are no finer wines in the world—a situation, alas, as rare as it is rarefied. Even in its native Burgundy, where the variety yields its finest wines, the quality it is famous for often eludes wine producers. Innovative winemakers in California, who have had great successes with the other French varieties, have yet to master this difficult variety. But there are signs of strides being made in the Golden State.

Italian winemakers, too, have attempted to produce excellent wine from the noble pinot noir, often to have their efforts treated to its highborn scorn. But, occasionally, as elsewhere, including Burgundy, they have succeeded. Giorgio Grai has had some successes. Lazzarini in the Colli Bèrici has also managed to produce a few Pinot Noirs that demonstrated the nobility of the variety. And Maurizio Zanella in the Franciacorta district of Lombardia has made a few good Pinot Noirs as well. More recent entries have come from Ruffino in Toscana and Lungarotti in Umbria.

Most of the plantings of pinot noir in Italy are in the northeastern regions of Trentino–Alto Adige, the Veneto, and Friuli, and in the Oltrepò Pavese and Franciacorta districts of Lombardia. A significant portion of those vines is used for the production of some of the better Italian sparkling wines. Among the best growing zones are the Alto Adige, Colli Bèrici in the Veneto, Franciacorta in Lombardia, and the Valle d'Aosta. The wine is DOC in various zones in Friuli (Colli Orientali del Friuli, Collio, and Grave del Friuli), the Veneto (Breganze and Piave), the Alto Adige and Trentino, the Oltrepò Pavese, Colli Piacentini, and the Valle d'Aosta. Additionally it is authorized in many other wines. And there are numerous *vini da tavola* made from pinot nero as well, some of which count among the best examples of all.

In the Alto Adige, or Süd Tyrol, where the pinot noir is known as blauburgunder, there are 546 acres (221 hectares) of pinot noir, yielding an average production of over 200,000 cases of wine a year. Most of the plantings are between Meran and Salurn. The best vineyards are considered to be in the Bressanone and Appiano districts; the grapes from Mazzon in the Unterland are also highly prized. Other regarded areas for the pinot noir are Girlan, Pinzon, and Schreckbichl. DOC sets the maximum yield at 898 gallons per acre (84 hectoliters per hectare) and the minimum alcohol at 11.5 percent. To qualify as *riserva* the wine must be aged for at least one year, calculated from November 1.

In Trentino, the best wines by reputation are from Mezzocorona. DOC recognizes and regulates the Pinot Noirs of Trentino. The maximum yield allowed is 748 gallons an acre (70 hectoliters per hectare); the minimum alcohol, 11.5 percent. Trentino Pinot Nero must be aged at least one year, from January 1; with an additional year, it can be labeled *riserva.*

Maurizio Zanella, proprietor of the fine Champagne-method *spumante* house Ca' del Bosco, made his first still red Burgundy-style Pinot Noir from the 1982 vintage, and it was a darned good one. A few years ago Zanella told us that he was producing 3,000 bottles a year and could easily more than double that to 7,000. Today his production of Pinero is 5,460 bottles. Maurizio has made a number of pilgrimages to Burgundy in his attempt to master the intricacies of this enigmatic variety. Given Zanella's commitment to quality for all his wines, perhaps one day he will succeed in producing world-class Pinot Noirs. His initial entry was one of his signature wines, sold with Zanella's name on the label. Today the wine is sold as Ca' del Bosco Pinero. Thus far only one other Pinot Noir in Italy has, in our opinion, managed to surpass his for Burgundian finesse. That wine is Lazzarini's Rosso del Rocolo, which has sometimes achieved real heights.

Nearly a decade ago we went to a dinner with friends at a BYOB restaurant, to which each brought a bottle of Pinot Noir. Burgundy lover Patrice Gourdin brought a fine one. We selected an Italian Pinot Noir. Other wine-knowledgeable friends brought some other fine bottles. Had we known what wines Patrice, Carlo Russo of Ho-Ho-Kus Wine & Spirit World, and Willi Frank of Vinifera Wine Cellars were going to bring, we might have chosen a Burgundy cru rather than Lazzarini's Rosso del Rocolo, excellent as it was. On the other hand, we didn't think that Sig. Lazzarini would have been unhappy; though the others did bring some beautiful bottles, including some lovely Burgundies, his fine Pinot Noir stood up to the competition admirably—not that it was the best wine of the night, but neither was it out of its league.

Rating */**

RECOMMENDED PRODUCERS OF PINOT NERO

**

— Alfeo (La Stoppa), from Veneto
— J. Hofstatter, Alto Adige DOC Riserva, Barthenau
— Josef Brigl, Alto Adige DOC, Kreuzbichler
  Maurizio Zanella (now Pinero)
  Pinero (Ca' del Bosco), from the Franciacorta zone in
    Lombardia
  Rosso del Rocolo (Pinot), (Villa dal Ferro, Lazzarini),
    from the Colli Bèrici zone in Veneto
  Sang des Salasses de Moncenis (Vignoble du Prieure de
    Montfleury), from Aosta

*

  Barone Felix Longo (Tenuta Schlosshof), Alto Adige
    DOC
+ Bellendorf, Alto Adige DOC
  Casotte (Bellavista), from the Franciacorta zone in
    Lombardia
  Drago, Pinot delle Langhe Vigneto di Campo Romano,
    from Piemonte
+ Giorgio Grai, Alto Adige DOC
+ Herrnhofer, Alto Adige DOC
  J. Hofstatter, Alto Adige DOC
+ Josef Brigl, Alto Adige DOC
+ Kehlburg, Alto Adige DOC
  Kellereigenossenschaft Girlan, Alto Adige DOC
  Alöis Lageder (Alto Adige DOC)
  Lungarotti, from the Torgiano zone in Umbria
+ Maso Cantanghell, Riserva, from the Atesino in
    Trentino–Alto Adige
  Masso S. Valentino (Càvit), Trentino DOC
  Nero del Tondo (Ruffino), from Toscana
  Nostra Signora Vigneti di Montan (Boscaini), Alto
    Adige DOC
  Scarpa Afra e Tobia, from Veneto
  Schiopetto Mario, from the Collio zone in
    Friuli–Venezia Giulia
  Schloss Schwanburg, Alto Adige DOC
  Vigna Il Chiuso (Castello di Ama), from Toscana

TASTING NOTES

Castello di Ama 1988 Vigna Il Chiuso (*11/90*). Open berrylike aroma, some oak; firm yet with good fruit, dry, short end. *(*)

La Stoppa 1988 Alfeo (*6/90, 5,400 bottles*). Cherry and berry aroma, oak component; soft, not a lot of varietal definition but a nice red with good fruit. ** –

Lungarotti 1988 (*9/90, c. 7,800 bottles*). Light but openly fruited aroma; not a lot of varietal character but soft, open and fruity. *

Maso Cantanghell 1988 Riserva, Atesino (*9/90*). Some varietal character quite evident, hints of leather, forest nuances with a mushroom overlay; soft and tasty, berry notes, a tad short and a little dry at the end. * +

Scarpa 1988 (*4/90*). Toward the vegetal end of the spectrum with good fruit as well. *

Boscaini 1987 "Nostra Signora" Alto Adige, Vigneti di Montan (*4/89*). Sweet entry, light herbaceous note, not a lot of varietal character. *

Ca' del Bosco 1987 Pinero (*twice, 6/90*). Oak and varietal aroma, hints of berries and the woods; new oak quite evident on the initial entry then the fruit comes out. ** –

Castello di Ama 1987 Vigna Il Chiuso (*4/90, 6,184 bottles*). Ripe aroma, hints of black cherries; nice fruit, good texture, not a lot of varietal character but a good glass of red wine. *

Drago 1987 Pinot delle Langhe, Vigneto di Campo Romano (*10/90*). Kirsch and strawberry aroma; soft, easy, simple and quaffable. *

Hofstatter 1986 Alto Adige Riserva, Villa Barthenau (*4/88*). Reticent aroma, vaguely of strawberries, does have varietal character; soft, fruity, with a strawberry flavor; still a little young but very drinkable. ** –

Scarpa 1986 (*4/89*). A bit stemmy; soft, not a lot of varietal, good fruit, recalls cabernet more than pinot noir! +

Hofstatter 1985 Alto Adige (*10/87*). Berry notes, somewhat vegetal in the background; fruity, could use more acidity, berrylike notes. *

Hofstatter 1985 Alto Adige Riserva, Barthenau (*twice, 4/88*). Vinous and fruity aroma, spice and tar notes; varietal berries in the mouth. **

Maurizio Zanella (Ca' del Bosco) 1985 Pinero (*4/88*). Beautiful pinot aroma; lacks follow-through in the mouth, still in all a good glass. ** –

Ruffino 1985 Nero del Tondo (*twice, 10/89*). Tar and dried fruit aroma; lots of tannin, chewy, some fruit evident, small-scale, soft and agreeable. *

Sarpa 1985 (*4 times, 3/88*). Some evident varietal character; soft, fruity and easy. *

Lageder Alöis 1984 (*4/87*). Spicy and fruity aroma; soft, medium body, kind of dull at the end. +

Maurizio Zanella (Ca' del Bosco) 1984 (*twice, 5/86*). Light, varietal aroma, some spice, a bit undeveloped; medium body, light tannin, balanced; young but displays some class and style. **(*)

Villa dal Ferro (Lazzarini) 1984 Rosso del Rocolo (Pinot) (*twice, 10/87*). Light, varietal aroma, vaguely vegetal; good fruit. *

Bellavista 1983 Casotte (*4/85, 800 bottles*). Some oak, some fruit; tasty, not especially varietal in character. *

Grai Giorgio 1983 Alto Adige (*ex-vat, 11/84*). Undeveloped aroma; well balanced, flavorful; needs time to show its quality. *(*)

Hofstatter 1983 Alto Adige Riserva, Barthenau (4/88). Vague off note on the nose, some varietal character; a little unbalanced, the fruit is attractive. * −

Josef Brigl 1983 Alto Adige (4/85). Vaguely mushroomy aroma; almost sweet, flavorful, a bit short. * +

Maurizio Zanella (Ca' del Bosco) 1983 (3 times, 5/86). Pretty aroma, characteristic pinot noir fruit and champignon aroma, touch of volatile acidity adds complexity as it does in Burgundy; soft and smooth-textured, well balanced, a little light, lacks some follow-through at the end. **

Maurizio Zanella (Ca' del Bosco) 1982 (5/85). Berries and oak on aroma, with a mushroomlike note in the back; seems somewhat heavy-handed, nice flavor. (*)

Kehlburg (Grai Giorgio) 1981 Alto Adige (twice, 3/87). Does have fruit, could use more varietal character, nice acid, will improve. *

Hofstatter 1980 Alto Adige Riserva, Barthenau (10/87). Some varietal character, vaguely vegetal; drying out, still has flavor evident. * −

Herrnhofer (Grai Giorgio) 1979 Alto Adige (twice, 2/84). Characteristic strawberries on aroma; nice flavor but a bit simple; an agreeable wine. * +

Josef Brigl 1979 Alto Adige, Kreuzbichler (4/85). Lovely aroma, berries and flowers; nice flavor, marred by some harshness at the end. *

Hofstatter 1978 Alto Adige Riserva, Barthenau (4/88). Interesting aroma, though not varietal; still has fruit and some softness but a bit drying at the end. * −

Josef Brigl 1978 Alto Adige, Kreuzbichler (4/85). Varietal mushroomlike aroma with berry notes; good fruit, light tannin; a nice glass. ** −

Villa dal Ferro (Lazzarini) 1978 Rosso del Rocolo (Pinot) (3 times, 2/83). Expansive varietal aroma of berries and mushrooms; smooth-textured and supple, a lot of flavor; has some style. ** +

Bellendorf (Grai Giorgio) 1977 Alto Adige (4/80). Raspberry aroma; seems a little low in acid, fruity. *

Sang des Salasses de Moncenis 1977 Vignoble du Prieure de Montfleury (8/79). Lovely perfumed bouquet, hints of berries and mushrooms; lively acidity, nice flavor, a bit light. ** +

Villa dal Ferro (Lazzarini) 1977 Rosso del Rocolo (Pinot) (twice, 5/83). Characteristic pinot aroma, berries, underbrush, tar; some tannin, nice flavor, vaguely bitter finish. **

Villa dal Ferro (Lazzarini) 1976 Rosso del Rocolo (Pinot) (twice, 12/82). Typical strawberries and mushrooms on aroma; soft, round and smooth, harmonious; elegant and stylish, a bit light but full of quality. ***

Villa dal Ferro (Lazzarini) 1974 Rosso del Rocolo (Pinot) (8/79). Deep color; expansive bouquet; intense, flavorful, displays style, long finish. ***

Kehlburg (Grai Giorgio) 1973 Alto Adige (twice, 9/81). Nice aroma, with a note of strawberries; fruity, soft. * +

Josef Brigl 1971 Alto Adige (4/85). Toasty, berry aroma; light tannin, tasty, very nice; signs of drying out at the end, drink up. * +

Herrnhofer and *Kehlburg (Grai Giorgio) 1969 Alto Adige* (twice, 4/85). The bottle of February 1984 seemed to be drying out. *This bottle:* Beautiful brickish-orange robe; champignonlike aroma, complex, toasty notes; liquid velvet, tasty, full of style and class, quite long; impressive indeed ***

Josef Brigl 1969 Alto Adige, Kreuzbichler (4/85). Lovely aroma, toasty, berrylike, age apparent; flavorful; beginning to dry out, still good. * +

Josef Brigl 1964 Alto Adige (4/85). Light, varietal aroma, some vegetal notes; a lot of tannin; is there enough fruit left? It seems so. *(*)

Josef Brigl 1961 Alto Adige (4/85). Lovely pinot bouquet with a berrylike quality; has a sweetness on the palate which gives way to a drying note at the end. ** +

Josef Brigl 1959 Alto Adige (4/85). Toasty, berry notes, lovely bouquet; full-flavored, soft, long; showing no signs of age. ***

Josef Brigl 1955 Alto Adige (4/85). Berry, mushroomy aroma; loads of flavor; a bit drying out at the end, but still good. **

Josef Brigl 1951 Alto Adige, Kreuzbichler (4/85). Deeper color than the younger wines; lovely bouquet recalls mushrooms, berries and underbrush; smooth-textured, well balanced, thinning out a bit toward the back. ***

PRIMITIVO DI MANDURIA (*Apulia*). Following the outbreak of phylloxera in Apulia at the end of the nineteenth century, many grape varieties from other regions and countries were introduced in hopes of renewing the vineyards. Among these, according to the late Dott. Piero Garoglio in his monumental eight-volume *Enciclopedia Vitivinicola Mondiale*, was a variety that became known as primitivo, or primativo.

This vine was planted in the Murge hills of Gioia del Colle, Acquaviva delle Fonti, Casamassima, Turi, and S. Michele. From there it traveled south to the Tarantino plains. Today 70 percent of the vines in the province of Taranto are primitivo.

Vines transplanted from the Gioia del Colle zone were called primitivo di gioia; those from other districts were named for their locality as well—primitivo di lizzano or primitivo del tarantino.

As this is an early-ripening variety that produces a mature crop of grapes in the second or third week of August, it became known as primitivo, from the dialect word *primativus*, "early ripener."

The primitivo yields two crops, the first in August and the second at the end of September or beginning of October. The name *primitivo,* it seems, is not used just for a single

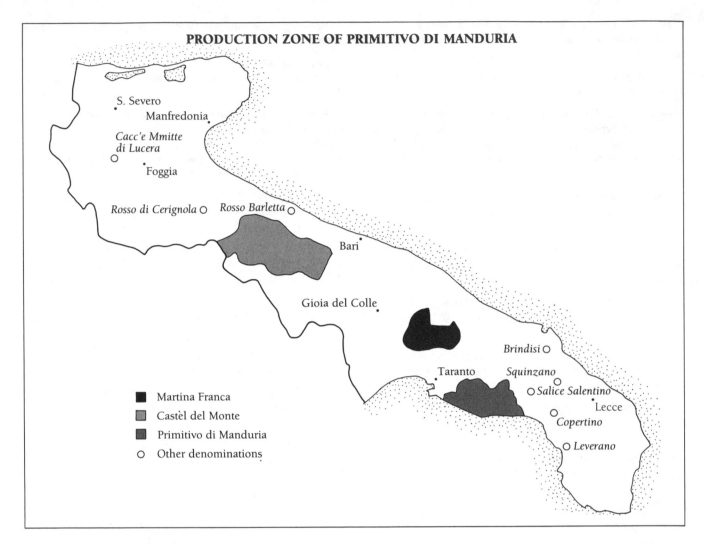

PRODUCTION ZONE OF PRIMITIVO DI MANDURIA

S. Severo
Manfredonia
Cacc'e Mmitte di Lucera
Foggia
Rosso di Cerignola ○   *Rosso Barletta* ○
Bari
Gioia del Colle
Brindisi ○
Taranto   *Squinzano*
Salice Salentino ○
Lecce
Copertino
Leverano ○

■ Martina Franca
▨ Castèl del Monte
▦ Primitivo di Manduria
○ Other denominations

early-ripening variety, but for a number of varieties or sub-varieties. One, at least—unlike the vast majority of grapes—yields red juice, not clear.

The wine produced from the primitivo, especially when the vines are judiciously pruned and trained individually *al alberello,* like "little trees," rather than spread out on wires, is inky black in color, and robust and powerful, achieving a high degree of alcohol. It is made in dry and semisweet styles. On occasion it is fortified to increase the natural high levels of alcohol, sometimes approaching 20 percent, and produce a primitivo *liquoroso.*

DOC requires that Primitivo di Manduria be made from 100 percent primitivo grapes grown in the area around the ancient Mesapican town of Manduria and 16 other *comuni* in the province of Taranto and three in Brindisi.

The aging period for the *liquoroso* wines is figured from the time when the wine is fortified. The regular—both the *secco* and *amabile*—and the *dolce naturale* must be aged at least until June 1 in the year after the vintage.

One of the best zones in the Mandurian district for the

Primitivo di Manduria wine is the area around the village of Sava, where there are some vineyards with vines more than fifty years old. Vittorio Librale's Azienda Vinicola Amanda, in Sava, was the zone's most important winery, both for quantity and quality. Production at Amanda was about 50,000 cases a year. Since the death of Vittorio Librale we have no idea of the status of the winery.

Librale produced his first wine, which he labeled Rosso di Sava, in the mid-1960s. After the introduction of the DOC for these wines, Librale labeled his Rosso di Sava Primitivo as Primitivo di Manduria. He also produced other wines from a blend of primitivo and other local varieties.

Vittorio didn't own any vineyards; he bought all the grapes for his wines mostly from Sava and the nearby villages. He told us that the best vineyards in the area are Casale di Aliano, Contrada Petrose, Pasano, and Contra da Casa Rossa.

From those sites he was able to produce, three times in the 1970s, a wine he called "Ventuno" for its 21 percent potential alcohol (18 percent actual alcohol, plus the po-

DOC REQUIREMENTS FOR PRIMITIVO DI MANDURIA

	Minimum Total Aging	Minimum Potential Alcohol	Minimum Actual Alcohol	Maximum Sugar	Maximum Yield in	
					Gallons/Acre	Hectoliters/Hectare
Regular	June 1	14.0%	14.0%	—	673	63
Amabile	June 1	14.0%	14.0%	1.0%	673	63
Dolce naturale	June 1	16.0%	13.0%	—	673	63
Liquoroso (fortified)						
Dolce naturale	2 years	17.5%	15.0%	—	673	63
Secco	2 years	18.0%	16.5%	—	673	63

tential alcohol of the unfermented sugar). In 1973 he produced 5,496 bottles from Casale di Aliano and 4,752 from Contra da Casa Rossa; in 1974 he made 13,578 bottles. The third was from the 1979 vintage, which actually attained 22 percent; he made 19,840 bottles of that one. In 1980, Vittorio made a "21" and a "22" as well.

This is a wine to enjoy with fruit and nuts, aged *pecorino piccante* or the local fermented cheese, *ricotta ascante*. Vittorio also poured it with wife Nella's homemade *biscotti* seasoned with almonds and fennel.

The Amanda Primitivo has something that the others lack—personality and style. As big and full-bodied as this wine is, it is not coarse.

The regular Amanda Primitivo is at its best from three or four years of the vintage till about eight. This wine, with a touch of sweetness (less than 1 percent) and a robust, fruity nature, goes well with hearty stews and braised red meat or game, as well as assertive cheeses.

We found it also went reasonably well with *cozzimateddi*, some local wildlife hunted down in the vineyards—black snails, actually, that Vittorio found while we were looking over the primitivo vines, wondering if they could be related to the zinfandel. The snails were not exactly needed as a supplement to the banquet of local specialties that Nella, sister Pompea, and Mama had prepared, but Vittorio knew that we'd find them interesting, so another side dish was added.

The subject of zinfandel came up again at the table when brother-in-law Gregorio Contessa spoke about his research into the history of the primitivo. Though they all liked the popular theory that relates it to the zinfandel, he had been unable to find any proof of it, despite a thorough examination of all the old documents and manuscripts in the local archives.

A number of people believe that the primitivo was brought to the United States from Apulia in the nineteenth century and planted in California where it became known as zinfandel. The two varieties have some common characteristics.

A few years ago we organized a blind tasting of Zinfandels and Primitivos. None of the tasters knew how many bottles of each varietal there were. Interestingly, with the exception of a single person, no one there was able to identify the grape variety correctly for all the wines. The matching up was even more difficult when the wine was a Zinfandel made in the late-harvest style.

Dott. Garoglio notes, however, that primitivo wasn't planted in Apulia until 1890 or 1892, fifty years after zinfandel was established in the vineyards of our own West Coast. So although the primitivo is not the missing ancestor of the zinfandel, that's not to say that the zinfandel couldn't be the progenitor of the primitivo. Perhaps along with the American rootstock brought to Italy to do battle against phylloxera, a few zinfandel cuttings also made it to Gioia del Colle.

More recently, about a decade ago, zinfandel cuttings migrated to Puglia to be planted by Attilio Simonini at his Favònio estate near Foggia and Vittorio Librale in Sava. We also know of primitivo cutting vines that were planted by Joseph Swan in his Forestville vineyard in the Sonoma Valley and by Angelo Papagni in his Madera vineyards. So far the most convincing wine came from Swan, but his production was so miniscule that it was enough to satisfy a curiosity only. In his first vintage, sometime in the mid-1980s, he made all of nineteen half bottles! We were privileged to taste it. It was quite delicious.

Amanda Rosso di Sava: *normale* ** , 21° *** − , 22° *** − ; Amanda Primitivo di Manduria: *normale* ** , 21° *** − , 22° *** −

TASTING NOTES

1983 (4/85). Dried fruit character on aroma; full of fruit and concentration, with a richness of flavor that makes it attractive now though it is still quite young, some tannin. **

1980 Liquoroso Secco (18 percent complete, 16.5 percent actual) (5/82). Opaque color; chocolatey, cherry aroma; full-bodied and robust, noticeable sweetness, cherry flavor with a suggestion of chocolate; needs another two years or so. **

1980 "21" (21 percent complete, 17.8 percent actual) (ex-vat, 1/81). The black wine of Sava—if we had a fountain pen we could write indelible tasting notes with it; raisins and nuts on aroma; very full, very rich, very young, has sweetness and tannin both, as thick as fava puree. **(+)

1980 "22" (22 percent complete, 18 percent actual) (ex-vat, 5/81). Blacker even than the 21er!; aroma recalls chocolate, cherries, figs, raisins, nuts and blackberries and this is a baby yet; sweet and intense, full-bodied and rich; a knife and fork wine. **(*)

1979 "22" (22 percent complete, 18 percent actual) (4/85). Opaque; dense, concentrated, raisiny notes, semisweet. **

1978 Liquoroso Secco (18 percent complete, 16.5 percent actual) (6 times, 4/85). Inky; chocolate, cherry aroma; robust and chewy, noticeable sweetness, tannic finish. * +

1977 (16.5 percent) (twice, 1/82). Very dark; cherrylike flavor, very full; very ready. *

1976 (17 percent alcohol, 1 percent sugar) (6 times, 1/81). Deep purple; rich, concentrated aroma recalls figs and raisins; some tannin, sweetness gives it a mellowness, full-bodied and robust. ** +

1974 "21" (21 percent complete) (1/81). Aroma suggests blueberries and raisins; interesting flavors, concentrated. **

1973 (17 percent) (1/82). Opaque; chocolate, cherry aroma, intense; some sweetness, very full. ** +

1973 Contra da Casa Rossa "21" (21 percent complete, 17 percent actual) (6 times, 7/82). Sweet and grapey, reminiscent of freshly crushed grapes, chocolatey notes; beginning to dry out on the finish; was better in 1980. **

1973 Vigneti dell' Antico Casale di Aliano "21" (21 percent complete, 18 percent actual) (6 times, 5/81). Opaque; complex bouquet recalls black cherries, chocolate, figs, nuts and raisins; lovely texture, full of flavor and personality; went perfectly with the anise biscuit. ***

1972 (18 percent complete, 17 percent actual) (5/81). Deep ruby; fruity aroma recalls raisins; noticeable sweetness, but beginning to lose its fruit, almost rasping aftertaste. *

1971 (18 percent complete, 17 percent actual) (1/81). Still has sugar, round, full-bodied and flavored, alcohol starting to intrude at the end. *

REFOSCO (*Friuli–Venezia Giulia*). The refosco variety has been linked to a variety that was planted in Friuli during the Roman era. Today refosco is recognized under DOC for Aquileia, Carso, Colli Orientali del Friuli, Grave del Friuli, Isonzo, and Latisana in Friuli, and Lison-Pramaggiore in the provinces of Venezia and Treiso in the Veneto and Pordenone in Friuli.

The refosco grape has seven or eight subvarities, the two most common being the refosco dal peduncolo rosso and refosco nostrano. The former, also known as pecol ross, so named for its red stalks, is considered the best, and the refoscone is just behind it in quality. It also has a variety of names, depending on where it is grown. The producer Giovanni Collavini told us that this variety was known during the Roman era as pucino. In the Savoie of France it's known as mondeuse, the name by which it is also known in California; in Emilia-Romagna it is called cagnina; and in the Carso zone of Friuli, it goes by the name terrano.

Colli Orientali del Friuli is considered the best district for this variety and the most highly regarded wines are said to come from the *comuni* of Savorgnano and Nimìs. Some producers of Refosco in Colli Orientali make wines of distinction. There are some good Refoscos produced around Casarsa and in the Grave del Friuli zone as well. And there

DOC REGISTERED VINEYARDS FOR REFOSCO

DOC Zone	Growers	Acres	Hectares
Aquileia	60	93.75	37.94
Carso	41	22.22	8.99
Colli Orientali del Friuli	231	233.67	94.56
Grave del Friuli	337	571.80	231.39
Isonzo	9	21.07	8.53
Latisana	13	58.77	23.78
Lison-Pramaggiore	19	95.95	38.83
Total	710	1,097.23	444.02

Source: Il Corriere Vinicolo, n. 10, March 12, 1990.

SYNONYMS FOR REFOSCO VARIETY BY DOC ZONE

DOC Zone	Synonym
Aquileia	Refosco dal peduncolo rosso
Carso	Terrano (aka refosco nostrano)
Colli Orientali del Friuli	Refosco dal peduncolo rosso
Grave del Friuli	Refosco
Isonzo	Refosco dal peduncolo rosso
Latisana	Refosco dal peduncolo rosso
Lison-Pramaggiore	Refosco dal peduncolo rosso

are also regarded refosco wines in the Carso district. In Emilia, Fattoria Paradiso produces a good Cagnina.

The Refosco from the Lison-Pramaggiore zone can be made to sparkle and is sold as a *spumante!* The regulations for the other districts are limited to a more palatable version. In the Corso zone the terrano may be blended with up to 15 percent piccola nera and/or pinot nero.

Generally Refosco has a vinous character with some herbaceousness, sometimes with a touch of spice; it is full-bodied, fruity, and somewhat rustic. The better ones have real character. Rating, for the better ones ** +

SOME PRODUCERS

Giovanni Dri, at Nimis in Udine, who produces the exceptionally fine Verduzzo di Ramondolo, one of Italy's finest dessert wines, also makes a very good Refosco. When we visited him in 1981 he had 9.9 acres (4 hectares) of vineyards, 7.5 (3) planted in verduzzo, 0.7 (0.3) in tocai, and 1.7 (0.7) in refosco dal peduncolo rosso, and had plans, he

told us, to put in another 3.7 acres (1.5 hectares) of verduzzo and refosco. His vines are planted at an altitude of 1,215 feet (370 meters) above sea level, the highest vineyards in Friuli, he told us. Dri's annual production at that time was 14,650 to 16,000 bottles of Verduzzo, 1,325 of Tocai, and 2,650 to 5,325 of Refosco. Today he produces 26,000 bottles of Verduzzo which he labels Ramondolo; 3,650 of Il Roncàt Bianco from verduzzo grapes; 1,000 of Picolit (480 full bottles and 1,040 half bottles); 3,850 Il Roncàt Rosso, made from a blend of refosco, schioppettino, the two cabernets, and other local varieties; and 16,500 bottles of Refosco. Dri feels his Refosco is at its best between four and seven years of the vintage. His best vintages, he told us a few years ago, were 1979, 1978, 1974, and 1972; average years: 1980, 1977, and 1976. Dri's '85 Refosco was excellent; some 9,000 bottles were produced.

Angelo Nascig, in Corno di Rosazzo, has 6.2 acres (2.5 hectares) of vines at his Azienda Agricola V. Nascig, from which he produces 14,400 bottles of very good to excellent wine a year, including 2,640 bottles of Refosco. He produces two Refoscos, one from refosco dal peduncolo rosso and the other from refosco nostrano. In 1980, because he had such a small quantity, he blended the two together.

Ronchi di Cialla, located in Prepotto in the province of Udine, was started by Paolo and Dina Rapuzzi in 1970. The Rapuzzis have 36 acres (14.5 hectares) of vines on their Ronchi di Cialla farm, of which 5 (2) are planted in refosco. They planted an additional 15 acres (6 hectares) of vines in 1989 and 1990. Since his first vintage, in 1977, Rapuzzi has used new *barriques* of Slavonian oak to age all of his wines. He produces 30,665 to 33,325 bottles of wine a year, two whites and two reds, all from native grape varieties—Picolit and Verduzzo, Refosco and Schioppettino. All are very good, and each is among the best of its type made. Since 1982, Rapuzzi has aged his wines in French oak *barriques,* 25 to 30

DOC REQUIREMENTS FOR REFOSCO BY DOC ZONE

DOC Zone	Minimum Variety Component	Minimum Aging	Minimum Alcohol	Maximum Yield in	
				Gallons/Acre	Hectoliters/Hectare
Aquileia	85%	none	10.5%	975	91
Carso	85%	none	10.0%	750	70
Colli Orientali del Friuli	90%	none	12.0%	825	77
Riserva	90%	2 years	12.0%	825	77
Grave del Friuli	85%	none	11.0%	975	91
Isonzo	100%	none	11.0%	975	91
Latisana	85%	none	11.0%	975	91
Lison-Pramaggiore	90%	none	11.0%	900	84

percent new oak for his reds and 100 percent new oak for his whites. Two-thirds of his production is red; of that, 60 percent is schioppettino and 40 percent refosco. Rapuzzi cultivates refosco dal peduncolo rosso on a vineyard that faces south to southeast, and is planted at altitudes ranging between 490 and 540 feet (150 and 165 meters) above sea level. His annual production of Refosco averages 8,000 bottles. The wine is aged between fourteen and sixteen months in *barrique*.

Leonardo Specogna, who produces what is easily the finest Picolit of all, has 14.8 acres (6 hectares) of vines from which he produces some 53,000 bottles of what are surely some of the very best wines of Friuli: 70 percent is white, the balance consists of the reds—cabernet, merlot, and refosco in the proportion of 30 percent each of the two cabernets and 40 percent refosco. The first wine that Specogna bottled was his outstanding Picolit, the '78. His first reds are from the 1983 vintage.

Other good Refoscos are produced by Girolamo Dorigo, Volpe Pasini, and Villa Belvedere di Taddei in the Colli Orientali del Friuli zone, and Giovanni Collavini in the Grave del Friuli zone. Girolamo Dorigo produced 3,500 bottles and 300 magnums of a *barrique*-aged "Montsclapade" Refosco dal Peduncolo Rosso in 1984. That wine, from this normally very fine producer, left us cold. Dorigo produced 9,500 bottles of the '85 "Montsclapade" Refosco dal Peduncolo Rosso. In 1979 he labeled his Refosco as Casa Rossa. Pasini's Zuc Volpe can be very good indeed; the '88 was.

Marina Danieli and her consulting enologist, Giorgio Grai, produced a very good Refosco del Friuli from the 1988 vintage. Livon produces a single-vineyard Refosco from Vigneto di Masarotte in Dolegnano in the Colli Orientali district. We were unimpressed with the '83.

ROSSO DEL CONTE (*Sicilia*). Giuseppe Tasca Conte d'Almerita of the Azienda Agricola Regaleali del Conte Tasca d'Almerita, founded in 1835, owns some 520 acres (210 hectares) of vines. The vines are planted on hilly terrain at altitudes ranging from 1,310 to 2,460 feet (400 to 750 meters) above sea level. Some 85 percent of the grapes that they require come from their own property. Regaleali's production in 1989 was nearly 240,000 cases of wine. They produce some 25,000 cases annually each of Regaleali *rosso* and *rosato,* 3,333 of Rosso del Conte, 4,165 of Nozze d'Oro, and 1,000 each of a cremant and brut champenois.

Conte d'Almerita grows the white sauvignon blanc, inzolia, and catarratto, and the red nerello mascalese, nero d'avola and perricone varieties. The nero d'avola is also known by the name calabrese. The grapes for the first-rate white Nozze d'Oro come from the 23.7-acre (9.6-hectare) Tenuta Sant'-Oliva vineyard. This especially good white wine was created to commemorate the golden wedding anniversary of

Giuseppe and Franca Tasca d'Almerita. They also produce, naturally, a Cabernet Sauvignon and Chardonnay, as experiments.

Rosso del Conte, originally known as Riserva del Conte, was first produced in 1970. The name was changed in 1977. The grapes for that wine are grown at the count's 20-acre (8-hectare) Tenuta San Lucio vineyard. The '77 came from Colline Casa Vecchie, the '75 from Colline Canalotto and Gelso, and the '73 from Piana di S. Lucio. After the harvest the grapes for Rosso del Conte—perricone and calabrese or nero d'avola—are macerated between five and six days at a temperature between 86° and 90° Fahrenheit (30° and 32° centigrade). The wine is then moved to tank to finish fermenting. The Rosso spends between fifteen and twenty days on the skins. The '81 spent eighteen months in cask. Rosso del Conte is not produced every year; there was no '72, '73, '74, or '82.

PRODUCTION OF ROSSO DEL CONTE
(BOTTLES)

1970	8,500
1971	8,000
1975	4,550
1976	12,000
1977	25,000
1978	28,000
1979	24,000
1980	36,500
1981	54,600
1983	40,000
1984	36,000
1985	40,000
1986	40,000

Rosso del Conte is a deeply colored red wine with great weight and concentration of fruit that ages moderately well. Although it can last for more than a decade, it doesn't really improve after eight years or so. Rating ** +

TASTING NOTES

1989 (*twice, ex-barrel, 6/90*). This wine was a blend of 50 percent perricone and 50 percent nero d'avola. Deep color; ripe cherry aroma, touch of spice; rich and concentrated, moderate length. **(+)

1988 (*twice, ex-barrel, 6/90*). Chocolate component, tarlike nuance; has a sweetness to the fruit, fairly tannic; very young. *(*)

1987 (6/90). Rich, cherrylike fruit; a little firm, evident fruit, needs time, short aftertaste. *(* −)

1986 (3 times, 6/90). Deep purple color; deep, rich and intense aroma, ripe, cherry and floral components; concentrated, good weight, moderate tannin, full-bodied, young, a tad bitter. **(+)

1985 (6 times, 11/90). Complex aroma of ripe fruit and flowers, tar and berrylike nuances; good structure, soft, a mouthful of lovely fruit. ** +

1984 (5 times, 9/90). Rich and flavorful, more open than the '85 with good weight and structure; still room to improve though quite attractive now. **

1983 (twice, 12/88). Rich nose, tar and ripe berries; sweet impression, packed with fruit. **

1981 (5 times, 9/90). Lovely bouquet displays suggestions of dried fruit and is vaguely floral; mellow, soft, round, warm and tasty. ** +

1980 (5/87). Deep, youthful color, richly fruited aroma recalls cherries; full-bodied, fairly tannic, even a bit rough but with an evident sense of fruit, we expect this one to soften over the next year or two. **(+)

1979 (twice, 5/87). Chocolate, cherry aroma, fairly intense; a little coarse, fairly tannic; is there enough fruit? (*?)

1977 (twice, 3/87). Thouth the fruit was still evident the wine was coarse and firm with some alcohol intruding. *

1975 (twice, 3/87). Nose is somewhat hot; the flavor is much more interesting, still it displays some coarseness. *

1970 (4/87). Bottle age has added some complexity on the nose; the wine has held up but not really developed; there is some oxidation. *

SCHIOPPETTINO (*Friuli–Venezia Giulia*). Schioppettino, also known as ribolla nera, can produce wines of real quality, especially in the area around Prepotto in Colli Orientali del Friuli. There are perhaps 10 to 15 producers who make a Schioppettino, but, in our experience, no one produces finer ones than Paolo Rapuzzi.

Rapuzzi began producing wines at his Ronchi di Cialla estate in 1977. His wines are very fine, and because of his severe selection, the quantity is always very limited. When we asked him why he pruned so closely, when mother nature restricted production for him every year, he responded with a question: "And what if one year mother nature didn't prune for me? I really don't have a choice if I want to produce top-quality wines." Which he obviously does. Rapuzzi's yield averages 25 percent of that allowed by DOC. Rapuzzi has 7.4 acres (3 hectares) of schioppettino from which he produces about 1,500 bottles a year. From the 1978 harvest he got only 1,400 bottles from his 3,500 vines—one bottle of wine from two and a half vines. From the 1986 he produced 9,895 bottles and 210 magnums, and

from 1987 there were 6,595 bottles and 210 large bottles. Today he produces, on average, some 13,325 bottles of Schioppettino annually. Like all his wines, Rapuzzi's Schioppettino is aged in *barriques;* it spends between twelve and thirteen months in barrel. Up to and including the '82, Rapuzzi used *barriques* of Slavonian oak. He has since switched to French oak. The Ronchi di Cialla Schioppettino comes from two small vineyards—the 1.38-acre (0.56-hectare) Roncjs vineyard and the 7.4-acre (3-hectare) Cjastenet vineyard. The Roncjs vineyard, facing south to southeast, is planted at altitudes ranging between 540 and 590 feet (165 and 180 meters) above sea level. Cjastenet faces south-southwest and is planted at altitudes of 490 to 655 feet (150 to 200 meters).

Collavini, producer of a vast range of Friulian wines, produces some 2,400 bottles of a *barrique*-aged Schioppettino. Girolamo Dorigo's Montsclapade produced a *barrique*-aged '84 from the Premariacco area. He made 1,700 bottles of this very good wine. His first one was the '82. We also found Franco Furlan's Castel Cosa version, especially the '85, to be very good. This wine was aged in a combination of *barrique* (25 percent) and Slavonian oak casks (75 percent). Livon produces a good one from their Vigneto Cumini in Corno di Rosazzo. They made 3,333 bottles of the '88. And Tullio Zamò's Vigne dal Leon estate in the Rocca Bernarda district of the Colli Orientali district produces between 1,500 and 2,500 bottles of a very good Schioppettino. The Schioppettinos of Giorgio Rieppi, Giuseppe Toti, and Gianfranco Fantinel's Santa Caterina estate have received some favorable reviews in the Italian press. It's been reported that Rieppi is a specialist with the Schioppettino.

Rating */***

RATING THE PRODUCERS OF SCHIOPPETTINO

**	Castel Cosa di Franco Furlan
** +	Girolamo Dorigo, "Montsclapade" di Premariacco
*	Livon, Vigneto Cumini in Corno di Rosazzo
***	Ronchi di Cialla

TASTING NOTES

Livon 1988 Vigneto Cumini in Corno di Rosazzo (9/90). Light nose; good body, open fruit, soft, short, not a lot of character, very drinkable and attractive. *

Girolamo Dorigo 1987 Montsclapade (12/90). Cherry, herbal aroma; soft, open, nice fruit, tart edge; ready. ** −

Vigne dal Leon di Tullio Zamò 1986 (4/89). Complex fruit aroma; full, firm and tannic, chewy, ripe fruit; young. **(+)

Franco Furlan 1985 Castel Cosa (7/88). Cherry fruit on the nose; almost sweet, soft and tasty, smooth, balanced. **

Girolamo Dorigo 1984 Montsclapade di Premariacco (4/87). Rhone-like aroma with hints of black pepper and fruit; the same on the palate; a little young yet with evident potential. ** +

Ronchi di Cialla 1984 (3 times, 12/90, 10,240 bottles). Nose packed with fruit, nuances of cherries, berries and spice, herbal and herbaceous notes; cabernetlike flavor, fairly full, soft, well balanced, long finish. *** −

Ronchi di Cialla 1982 (3 times, 10/86, 6,750 bottles). Ripe fruit, cherry and spicy notes; light to moderate tannin, ripe flavor, soft and smooth, nice mouth feel, moderate length. *** −

Ronchi di Cialla 1978 (4 times, 1/83, 1,400 bottles, 3,500 vines). Aroma of cherries and black pepper, spicy, raspberry, walnut, vanilla and cassis notes; richly intense, a nice mouthful of flavor, firm, very long and very nice. ***

Ronchi di Cialla 1977 (7/80). Lovely nose, spice and flowers, black pepper and fruit; soft though some tannin remains, firm acidity, long. ** +

TAZZELENGHE (*Friuli–Venezia Giulia*). The name of the tazzelenghe variety is said to derive from its sharp acidity that cuts the tongue. This variety, with its various names— tazzelenghe, tarcelenghe, tacelenge, or tazzalenga—is planted in the area around Buttrio in Udine. A few years ago four or five producers made a Tazzelenghe wine; that number has increased considerably today.

The most important producer a few years ago, and one whose wine we've tasted, was Cantine Florio. Florio's tazzelenghe vines are over thirty years old. Tazzelenghe makes up only a small part of their annual production, 13,200 bottles out of a total of 174,000. But that's not so little, depending on how you look at it; we understand that the other producers make only about 250 to 400 bottles in a year. Florio ages the Tazzelenghe, like all their reds, for about one year in fifty-year-old casks of 185 to 1,320 gallons (7 to 50 hectoliters). The Florio Tazzelenghe is a wine reminiscent of a Cabernet, though with somewhat higher acidity.

Collavini, who produces a wide number of Friulian wines, also produces a Tarcelenghe in *barrique*. Marina Danieli, with advice from consultant Giorgio Grai, also produces a Tazzelenghe. Girolamo Dorigo, a very fine producer, and Brava have gotten some good press for their Tazzelenghes. Dorigo produces a *barrique*-aged Tazzelenghe that he labels as Ronc di Juri. There were 1,700

bottles and 300 magnums of the very good '84, a wine that displayed the characteristic high acidity of the grape. The reliable Tullio Zamò's Vigne dal Leon in the Rocca Bernarda district produces between 1,500 and 2,500 bottles of this wine annually.

Our experience with Tazzelenghe is limited to just two wines from two different producers. Rating **

TORRE ALBAROLA (*Piemonte*). Elizabetta Currado, a graduate of the enological school at Alba, makes the wines at the Abbazzia di Valle Chiara estate owned by actress Ornella Muti and painter Léon Ribi in Lerna in the province of Alessandria. She also consults at Poggio Sala in Montepulciano in Toscana. After graduation Currardo worked in wineries in California, Oregon and the Bordeaux region, as well as at her father's Vietti winery in the Langhe.

Betta produces two wines for the Abbazzia, an excellent Dolcetto d'Ovada and the very good *barrique*-aged Torre Albarola, made from a blend of dolcetto, barbera, and the ancient lancillotta. The Torre Albarola takes its name from the tenth-century watchtower near the Portofino–San Fruttuoso highway, and its formula from the Benedictine friars who, according to local records, blended these three grape varieties together. Currado aged the '88 Torre Albarola in *barrique* for one year. As for the Dolcetto, it has been produced here since the 1500s, when the friars first made one. Rating **

TASTING NOTE

1988 (11/90). The first scent reveals oak from the *barrique* that the wine was aged in; ripe fruit flavors fill the mouth, then, toward the end, the oak takes over again. **

VILLA PATTONO (*Piemonte*). Renato Ratti produces some 12,000 bottles annually of this partially *barrique*-aged wine. He first produced Villa Pattono in 1982. The wine is aged 50-50 in cask and *barrique*. One part spends nine to twelve months in *barrique*. The blend is 70 to 75 percent barbera, 10 to 12 freisa, and the balance uvalino. The uvalino is a very old variety from the Monferrato. Azienda Agricola Villa Pattono is in Costiglione d'Asti, home to the exceptionally fine Ristorante da Guido and the very fine honey and Barberas of Maria Boria. Rating **

A P P E N D I X   A

THE PRODUCERS AND WINES RATED BY
THE STARS

Where a producer name has been changed, both names are included, the old and the new. This appendix is divided into six parts: (1) the nebbiolo wines, (2) the sangiovese-based wines, (3) aglianico wines, (4) Amarone, Recioto, and Valpolicella, (5) the cabernet-based wines, which includes merlot, and (6) others.

WHAT THE RATINGS MEAN

****	Great, superb, truly noble
***	Exceptionally fine
**	Very good
*	A good example of its type, somewhat above average
0	Acceptable to mediocre, depending on the context; drinkable
+	Somewhat better than the star category it is put in
−	Somewhat less than the star category it is put in, except for zero where it indicates a wine or producer-wine combination that is badly made or worse

---

The Producers and Wines of Nebbiolo Rated

****

Barbaresco DOCG
Barolo DOCG

"Bricco Asili" Azienda Agricola di Ceretto, Barbaresco DOCG Bricco Asili
"Bricco Rocche" Azienda Agricola di Ceretto, Barolo DOCG
Campi Raudii di Vallana Antonio, Spanna del Piemonte
+ Cantina Mascarello, Barolo DOCG
Castello di Neive, Barbaresco DOCG
Conterno Aldo, Barolo DOCG Bricco Ciabot
Conterno Aldo, Barolo DOCG Bricco Cicala
Conterno Aldo, Barolo DOCG Bricco Colonello
Conterno Aldo, Barolo DOCG Romirasco
Conterno Aldo, Granbussia Barolo DOCG
Conterno Giacomo (Giovanni Conterno), Monfortino Barolo DOCG
Gaja, Barbaresco DOCG Sorì San Lorenzo
Gaja, Barbaresco DOCG Sorì Tildìn
+ Giacosa Bruno, Barbaresco DOCG
+ Giacosa Bruno, Barolo DOCG
Giovannini-Moresco Enrico, Barbaresco DOCG Podere del Pajorè
Granbussia di Conterno Aldo, Barolo DOCG
Marchese di Gresy, Barbaresco DOCG Martinenga-Camp Gros
Marchese di Gresy, Barbaresco DOCG Martinenga-Gaiun
+ Mascarello Bartolo, Barolo DOCG
Monfortino di Conterno Giacomo, Barolo DOCG
+ Pira E. (Luigi Pira), Barolo DOCG
Podere del Pajorè di Giovannini-Moresco Enrico, Barbaresco DOCG
+ Podere Marcarini (Elvio Cogno), Barolo DOCG
Produttori del Barbaresco, Barbaresco DOCG Asili
Produttori del Barbaresco, Barbaresco DOCG Montestefano
Produttori del Barbaresco, Barbaresco DOCG Rabajà
Rinaldi Francesco, Barolo DOCG
Rinaldi Giuseppe, Barolo DOCG
Traversagna di Vallana Antonio, Spanna del Piemonte
Vallana Antonio, Campi Raudii Spanna del Piemonte

Vallana Antonio, Traversagna Spanna del Piemonte
Vietti (Alfredo Currado), Barbaresco DOCG Rabajà
+ Vietti (Alfredo Currado), Barolo DOCG Briacca
Vietti (Alfredo Currado), Barolo DOCG Brunate
Vietti (Alfredo Currado), Barolo DOCG Bussia
+ Vietti (Alfredo Currado), Barolo DOCG Lazzarito
+ Vietti (Alfredo Currado), Barolo DOCG Rocche
+ Vietti (Alfredo Currado), Barolo DOCG Villero

***
Antoniolo Mario, Gattinara DOC
— Barale F.lli, Barbaresco DOCG
Barale F.lli, Barolo DOCG Castellero
— "Bricco Asili" Azienda Agricola di Ceretto, Barbaresco DOCG
  Faset
Cantina del Glicine, Barbaresco DOCG
Castel Chiuro di Nino Negri, Valtellina Superiore Riserva
  DOC
Ceretto Casa Vinicola, Nebbiolo d'Alba DOC Vigneto
  Bernardine
— Cigliuti F.lli, Barbaresco DOCG
Clerico Domenico, Barolo DOCG
Conterno Aldo, Barolo DOCG Bussia Soprana
Conterno Aldo, Nebbiolo delle Bussia Conca Tre Pile
+ Conterno Giacomo (Giovanni Conterno), Barbaresco DOCG
+ Conterno Giacomo (Giovanni Conterno), Barolo DOCG
  Cascina Francia
Ferrando Luigi, Carema DOC black label
Gaja, Barbaresco DOCG
Gaja, Barbaresco DOCG Costa Russi
Gaja, Nebbiolo d'Alba DOC Vignaveja
Gattinara DOC
Giacosa Bruno, Nebbiolo d'Alba DOC Valmaggiore di Vezza
Grasso Azienda Agricola (Elio Grasso), Barolo DOCG
Grasso Elio, Barolo DOCG
"Le Colline" Azienda Agricola, Barbaresco DOCG
"Le Colline" Azienda Agricola, Monsecco Gattinara DOC
— Marchese di Gresy, Barbaresco DOCG Martinenga
Mascarello Bartolo, Nebbiolo delle Langhe
Mascarello Giuseppe (Mauro Mascarello), Barbaresco DOCG
Mascarello Giuseppe (Mauro Mascarello), Barolo DOCG
Monsecco (Conte Don Ugo Ravizza)
Montalbano di Vallana Antonio, Spanna del Piemonte
Nebbiolo d'Alba DOC (the best ones)
Nebbiolo delle Langhe *vino da tavola* (the best ones)
— Nera, Signorie Valtellina Superiore DOC
Nino Negri, Castel Chiuro Valtellina Superiore Riserva DOC
— Nino Negri, Sfursàt DOC
Nino Negri, Valtellina Superiore Riserva DOC
Pelizatti Arturo, Grumello Riserva DOC Sassorosso
Pezzuto F.lli, Nebbiolo d'Alba DOC Vigneto in Vadraman del
  Roero
Podere Marcarini (Elvio Cogno), Nebbiolo delle Langhe
+ Produttori del Barbaresco, Barbaresco DOCG Moccagatta
+ Produttori del Barbaresco, Barbaresco DOCG Montefico
+ Produttori del Barbaresco, Barbaresco DOCG Ovello
Produttori del Barbaresco, Barbaresco DOCG Pajè

+ Produttori del Barbaresco, Barbaresco DOCG Pora
Produttori del Barbaresco, Barbaresco DOCG Rio Sordo
— Produttori "Nebbiolo di Carema," Carema DOC dei Carema
Prunotto, Barbaresco DOCG Montestefano
Prunotto, Barbaresco DOCG Rabajà
Prunotto, Barolo DOCG Bussia
Prunotto, Barolo DOCG Cannubi
Prunotto, Barolo DOCG Ginestra
Prunotto, Nebbiolo d'Alba DOC Ochetti di Monteu Roero
Ratti Renato, Barolo DOCG Marcenasco
Ratti Renato, Barolo DOCG Marcenasco-Conca
Ratti Renato, Barolo DOCG Marcenasco-Rocche
Ratti Renato, Nebbiolo d'Alba DOC Ochetti di Monteu Roero
Rinaldi Francesco, Barbaresco DOCG
San Lorenzo di Vallana Antonio, Spanna del Piemonte
Sandrone Francesco, Barolo DOCG
— Sandrone Luciano, Barolo DOCG Cannubi-Boschis
+ Scarpa, Barbaresco DOCG
+ Scarpa, Barolo DOCG
Scarpa, Nebbiolo d'Alba DOC San Carlo di Castellinaldo
— Signorie di Nera, Valtellina Superiore DOC
— Sobrero Filippo, Barolo DOCG
Spanna (del Piemonte) *vino da tavola* (the best ones)
+ Tenuta Carretta, Barolo DOCG Cannubi
Tenuta Carretta, Nebbiolo d'Alba DOC Bric' Paradiso
Tenuta Carretta, Nebbiolo d'Alba DOC Bric' Tavoletto
Tenuta Carretta, Roero DOC Bricco del Poggio
— Vajra G. D., Barolo DOCG Bricco Viole
— Vajra G. D., Barolo DOCG Fossati
— Vallana Antonio, Gattinara DOC
Vallana Antonio, Montalbano Spanna del Piemonte
Vallana Antonio, San Lorenzo Spanna del Piemonte
Valtellina Superiore DOC Grumello Riserva
Valtellina Superiore DOC Inferno Riserva
Valtellina Superiore DOC Sassella Riserva
+ Vietti (Alfredo Currado), Barbaresco DOCG Masseria
Vietti (Alfredo Currado), Nebbiolo d'Alba DOC San Giacomo
  di Santo Stefano Roero
Vietti (Alfredo Currado), Nebbiolo d'Alba DOC St. Michele
  di Santo Stefano Roero

**
Accademia Torregiorgi, Barolo DOCG
+ Accomasso Giacomo, Barolo DOCG
+ Accomasso Giovanni, Barolo DOCG
Altare Elio, Barolo DOCG
+ Antichi Vigneti di Cantalupo, Ghemme DOC Collis
  Breclemae
+ Antichi Vigneti di Cantalupo, Ghemme DOC Collis Carelle
— Antoniolo Mario, Santa Chiara Spanna del Piemonte
Ara
+ Arte (Clerico Domenico)
— Azelia, Barolo DOCG
Balbiano, Gattinara DOC
+ Baracco F.lli, Nebbiolo d'Alba DOC San Vincenzo di Monteu
  Roero
Barilot (Cantine Duca d'Asti di Chiarlo Michele)

Barolino (Marchese Maurizio Fracassi Ratti Mentone)
- Barra Guido, Gattinara DOC
Bel Colle, Barolo DOCG Monvigliero
+ Bel Colle, Barolo DOCG Vigneti Verduno
+ Bergadano Enrico, Barolo DOCG
Bertolo F.lli, Gattinara DOC
Bianchi Giuseppe, Fara DOC
Bianchi Giuseppe, Sizzano DOC
- Bianco Mauro, Cascina Morassino Barbaresco DOCG
Boca DOC
Bordino Franco, Barbaresco DOCG
Borgogno F.lli Serio e Battista, Barolo DOCG Cannubi
- Borgogno Giacomo, Barolo DOCG
+ Bovio Gianfranco, Barolo DOCG
Bramaterra DOC
Brezza, Barolo DOCG Cannubi
Brezza, Barolo DOCG Castellero
+ Brezza, Barolo DOCG Sarmassa
+ "Bricco Boschis" Azienda Agricola di Cavallotto F.lli, Barolo
  DOCG
Bricco del Drago (Cascina Drago)
Bricco Manzoni (Rocche dei Manzoni di Valentino Migliorini)
Brigatti Luciano, Möt Ziflon
+ Brovia F.lli, Barolo DOCG
Burlotto Andrea, Barolo DOCG Massara
- Burlotto, Barolo DOCG
Canale Aldo, Barolo DOCG
Cantina del Glicine, Glicinerosso
Cantina Sociale di Sizzano e Ghemme, Sizzano DOC
Cantine Duca d'Asti di Chiarlo Michele, Barbaresco DOCG
  Rabajà
Cantine Duca d'Asti di Chiarlo Michele, Barilot
Cantine Duca d'Asti di Chiarlo Michele, Barolo DOCG
  Brunate
- Cantine Duca d'Asti di Chiarlo Michele, Barolo DOCG Bussia
Cantine Duca d'Asti di Chiarlo Michele, Barolo DOCG
  Cerequio
+ Cantine Duca d'Asti di Chiarlo Michele, Barolo DOCG
  Rocche
Cantine Duca d'Asti di Chiarlo Michele, Barolo DOCG Vigna
  Rionda
- Cappellano Dott. Giuseppe (Teobaldo e Roberto Cappellano),
  Barbaresco DOCG
+ Cappellano Dott. Giuseppe (Teobaldo e Roberto Cappellano),
  Barolo DOCG Carpegna
+ Cappellano Dott. Giuseppe (Teobaldo e Roberto Cappellano),
  Barolo DOCG Gabutti
- Cappellano Dott. Giuseppe (Teobaldo e Roberto Cappellano),
  Nebbiolo d'Alba DOC
Caramino *vino da tavola*
Carema DOC
- Cascina Adelaide di G. Terzano, Barolo DOCG
Cascina Ballarin di Viberti Luigi, Barolo DOCG
- Cascina Bruni di F.lli Veglio, Barolo DOCG
- Cascina Morassino di Bianco Mauro, Barbaresco DOCG
Cascina Rombone di Nada Fiorenzo, Nebbiolo delle Langhe
Castaldi Giuseppe, Fara DOC

+ Cavallotto F.lli, Barolo DOCG Bricco Boschis
+ Ceretto Casa Vinicola, Barbaresco DOCG Asij
+ Ceretto Casa Vinicola, Barolo DOCG Zonchera
Chiarlo Michele, Cantine Duca d'Asti Barbaresco DOCG
  Rabajà
Chiarlo Michele, Cantine Duca d'Asti Barilot
Chiarlo Michele, Cantine Duca d'Asti Barolo DOCG Brunate
- Chiarlo Michele, Cantine Duca d'Asti Barolo DOCG Bussia
Chiarlo Michele, Cantine Duca d'Asti Barolo DOCG Cerequio
+ Chiarlo Michele, Cantine Duca d'Asti Barolo DOCG Rocche
Chiarlo Michele, Cantine Duca d'Asti Barolo DOCG Vigna
  Rionda
Cinque Castelli di Vallana Antonio, Spanna del Piemonte
+ Clerico Domenico, Arte
Clerico Domenico, Nebbiolo delle Langhe
Conterno Aldo, Il Favòt
+ Conterno Fantino, Barolo DOCG
- Conterno Fantino, Nebbiolo delle Langhe Ginestrino
- Conterno Paolo, Barolo DOCG La Ginestra
- Contratto, Barbaresco DOCG
Contratto Giuseppe, Barolo DOCG
Contratto Giuseppe, Barolo DOCG Ca' Neire
Contratto Giuseppe, Barolo DOCG Sarmassa
+ Cordero di Montezemolo, Barolo DOCG Enrico IV-Villero
+ Cordero di Montezemolo, Barolo DOCG Monfalletto
Corino Giovanni, Barolo DOCG
+ Cortese Giuseppe, Barbaresco DOCG
Crichet Pajè (Roagna)
De Forville, Barbaresco DOCG
Del Camino di Vallana Antonio, Spanna del Piemonte
Donnaz DOC
+ Einaudi Luigi, Barolo DOCG
Einaudi Luigi, Nebbiolo delle Langhe
+ Enologica Valtellinese, Inferno DOC Riserva della Casa
Enologica Valtellinese, Sassella Riserva
+ Enologica Valtellinese, Sforzato
Eredi Virginia Ferrero, Barolo DOCG
Fara DOC
Fenocchio Giacomo, Barolo DOCG
Fenocchio Riccardo, Barolo DOCG Pianpolvere Soprano
Ferrando Luigi, Carema DOC
Ferrando Luigi, Gattinara DOC
Ferrando Luigi, Solativo del Canavese
Ferrari, Ghemme DOC
Feyles Maria, Barolo DOCG Ginestra
Fioretto (Vietti)
Fontanafredda, Barolo DOCG crus
+ Fracia di Nino Negri, Valtellina Superiore DOC
+ Franco Fiorina, Barolo DOCG
Franco Fiorina, Nebbiolo d'Alba DOC
+ Gaja, Barolo DOCG
- Gemma, Barolo DOCG
- Ghebellino (Rainoldi Aldo)
Ghemme DOC
Giacosa Donato, Barbaresco DOCG
- Giacosa F.lli, Barolo DOCG
Giacosa F.lli, Barolo DOCG Pira

Glicinerosso (Cantina del Glicine)
Grasso Elio, Nebbiolo di Monforte
Il Favòt (Aldo Conterno)
− "La Spinona" Azienda Agricola di Piero Berutti, Barbaresco DOCG
"Le Colline" Azienda Agricola, Ghemme DOC
Lessona DOC
Malvira, Nebbiolo d'Alba DOC Del Roero
Manzone Giovanni, Barolo DOCG
Marchese di Gresy, Nebbiolo delle Martinenga
Marchese Maurizio Fracassi Ratti Mentone, Barolino
Marchese Maurizio Fracassi Ratti Mentone, Barolo DOCG
− Marchesi di Barolo, Barolo DOCG Brunate
Marchesi di Barolo, Barolo DOCG Cannubi
Marchesi di Barolo, Barolo DOCG Costa di Rose
Marchesi di Barolo, Barolo DOCG Valletta
Mascarello Giuseppe (Mauro Mascarello), Nebbiolo d'Alba DOC San Rocco
Massolino Giuseppe, Barolo DOCG Söri Vigna Riunda
Möt Ziflon (Luciano Brigatti)
Nada Fiorenzo, Cascina Rombone Nebbiolo delle Langhe
Nebbiolo d'Alba DOC
Nebbiolo del Piemonte *vino da tavola* (the best ones)
Nebbiolo delle Langhe *vino da tavola*
Nebbiolo Passito *vino da tavola*
Negro Angelo, Nebbiolo d'Alba DOC
Nera, Grumello DOC
+ Nera, Grumello Riserva DOC
Nera, Inferno DOC
Nera, Sassella DOC
+ Nera, Sassella Riserva DOC
Nera, Sfurzato DOC
+ Nervi Luigi & Italo, Gattinara DOC
Nino Negri, Grumello DOC
Nino Negri, Inferno DOC
Nino Negri, Sassella DOC
+ Nino Negri, Valgella DOC
Oddero F.lli, Barbaresco DOCG
+ Oddero F.lli, Barolo DOCG
Ormezzano Maurizio, Lessona DOC
Ornato (Pio Cesare)
− Palladino, Barolo DOCG
Parroco del Neive, Barbaresco DOCG Basarin
− Parusso Armando, Barolo DOCG
Parusso Armando, Barolo DOCG Bussia-Rocche
+ Parusso Armando, Barolo DOCG Mariondino
+ Pasquero-Elia Secondo, Barbaresco DOCG Sorì d'Paytin
+ Pasquero-Elia Secondo, Barbaresco DOCG Sorì Paitin
Pasquero Giuseppe, Nebbiolo d'Alba DOC Vigna Dogna
+ Pelizatti Arturo, Sassella Riserva DOC
Perazzi Luigi, Bramaterra DOC
"Pianpolvere Soprano" Azienda Agricola di Fenocchio Riccardo, Barolo DOCG
− Pio Cesare, Barbaresco DOCG
+ Pio Cesare, Barolo DOCG
Pio Cesare, Ornato
+ Pira E. (Chiara Boschis), Barolo DOCG

Podere Rocche dei Manzoni di Valentino Migliorini, Barolo DOCG
− Poderi e Cantine di Marengo-Marenda, Barolo DOCG
+ "Ponte Rocca" Azienda Agricola di Pittatore Cav. Francesco, Barolo DOCG
− Ponti, Ghemme DOC
Ponti, Sizzano DOC
Porta Rossa, Barbaresco DOCG
+ Porta Rossa, Barolo DOCG
Produttori del Barbaresco, Barbaresco DOCG *normale*
Produttori del Barbaresco, Nebbiolo delle Langhe
Produttori "Nebbiolo di Carema," Carema DOC
Prunotto, Nebbiolo d'Alba DOC Bric Rossino di Monteu Roero
− Rainoldi Aldo, Ghebellino
Rainoldi Aldo, Grumello DOC
Rainoldi Aldo, Inferno DOC
Rainoldi Aldo, Sassella Riserva DOC
Rainoldi Aldo, Sfursàt DOC
Rainoldi Aldo, Valgella DOC
Ratti Renato, Barbaresco DOCG
Revello Renato, Cascina Gustavo Barolo DOCG .
+ Rinaldi Giuseppe, Nebbiolo delle Langhe
"Rizzi" Azienda Agricola di Ernesto Dellapiana, Barbaresco DOCG
Roagna, Barbaresco DOCG
Roagna, Crichet Pajè
+ Rocche Costamagna, Barolo DOCG
Rocche dei Manzoni di Valentino Migliorini, Bricco Manzoni Roero DOC (the best ones)
− Rovellotti, A. F., Ghemme DOC
− Saffirio Enrico, Barolo DOCG
+ San Carlo, Grumello DOC Vigna Stangone
+ San Carlo, Inferno DOC Vigna Al Carmine
+ San Carlo, Sassella DOC Vigna Stangone
San Carlo, Valgella DOC Vigna Caven
− Scavino Alfonso, Barolo DOCG
− Scavino Paolo, Barolo DOCG
+ Scavino Paolo, Barolo DOCG crus
− Sebaste, Barolo DOCG
− Sebaste, Nebbiolo delle Langhe
Sebastiani Giovanni Giuseppe, Ghemme DOC
Sella, Bramaterra DOC
Sella, Lessona DOC
− Settimo Aurelio, Barolo DOCG
Sizzano DOC
Solativo del Canavese (Luigi Ferrando)
Spanna (del Piemonte) *vino da tavola*
Stroppiana Oreste, Barolo DOCG
Tenuta Coluè di Massimo Oddero, Nebbiolo d'Alba DOC
Terre del Barolo, Barolo DOCG Brunate
Terre del Barolo, Barolo DOCG Rocche
− Terzano G., Cascina Adelaide Barolo DOCG
Tona di Gianluigi Bonisolo, Sforzato DOC
Tradizione di Triacca F.lli, Valtellina DOC
− Triacca F.lli, Grumello DOC
Triacca F.lli, Sassella DOC

Triacca F.lli, Sforzato DOC
Triacca F.lli, Tradizione Valtellina DOC
+ Vajra G. D., Barolo DOCG *normale*
Vajra, Nebbiolo delle Bricco delle Viole
Vallana Antonio, Boca DOC
Valtellina Superiore DOC
Vallana Antonio, Cinque Castelli Spanna del Piemonte
Vallana Antonio, Del Camino Spanna del Piemonte
Vallana Antonio, Spanna del Piemonte
Valtellina DOC
Valtellina Superiore DOC
Valtellina Superiore DOC Grumello
Valtellina Superiore DOC Grumello Riserva
Valtellina Superiore DOC Inferno
Valtellina Superiore DOC Inferno Riserva
Valtellina Superiore DOC Sassella
Valtellina Superiore DOC Sassella Riserva
+ Valtellina Superiore DOC Sfursàt
Valtellina Superiore DOC Valgella
− Veglio F.lli, Cascina Bruni Barolo DOCG
Verro Tonino, Nebbiolo d'Alba DOC Vigneto Bricchet del Roero
+ Vezza Sergio, Barbaresco DOCG
Viberti Luigi, Cascina Ballarin Barolo DOCG
Vietti (Alfredo Currado), Barbaresco DOCG *normale*
+ Vietti (Alfredo Currado), Barolo DOCG Castiglione
+ Vietti (Alfredo Currado), Barolo DOCG *normale*
Vietti (Alfredo Currado), Fioretto
− Vinicola Piemontese, Barolo DOCG
+ Voerzio Giacomo (F.lli Voerzio), Barolo DOCG
+ Voerzio Roberto, Barolo DOCG
− Voerzio Roberto, Nebbiolo delle Croera di La Mora
Zanetta Ercolina, Sizzano DOC
+ Zunino Basilio, Barolo DOCG

*

Accademia Torregiorgi, Barbaresco DOCG
+ Accomasso Giovanni, Nebbiolo delle Langhe
− Accornero Flavio, Barbaresco DOCG
− Agamium (Antichi Vigneti di Cantalupo)
Aglie
Altare Elio, Vigna Arborina
− Antichi Vigneti di Cantalupo, Agamium
Antichi Vigneti di Cantalupo, Ghemme DOC
Arborina (Altare Elio)
Arnad-Montjovet DOC
Arrigo Orlando, Barbaresco DOCG
Ascheri Giacomo, Barolo DOCG
Ascheri Giacomo, Nebbiolo d'Alba DOC Bricco S. Giacomo
Ascheri Giacomo, Roero DOC
+ Asteggiano Vincenzo, Barolo DOCG
Barengo Rosso (Cantina Sociale dei "Colli Novaresi")
Barra Guido, Spanna del Piemonte
Bel Colle, Nebbiolo delle Langhe Monvijè
Beni di Batasiolo, Barolo DOCG Boscareto
Bersano, Barolo DOCG
Bertole Ing. Salvatore, Gattinara DOC
Bettini F.lli, Grumello DOC

Bettini F.lli, Inferno DOC
Bettini F.lli, Sassella DOC
Bettini F.lli, Valgella DOC
Bianchi Giuseppe, Fogarin
Bianchi Giuseppe, Ghemme DOC
− Bianchi Giuseppe, Valfrè
Bianco Luigi, Barbaresco DOCG
+ Boffa Carlo, Barbaresco DOCG
+ Borgo Alto (Azienda Agricola "Le Colline")
Borgogno Aldo, Barolo DOCG
+ Borgogno Cav. Bartolomeo, Barolo DOCG
Borgogno F.lli Serio e Battista, Barbaresco DOCG
Borgogno F.lli Serio e Battista, Barolo DOCG *normale*
+ Borgogno Giacomo, Barbaresco DOCG
Borgogno Ludovico, Cascina Borgognot Barolo DOCG
Bricco Viole (Sebaste)
Brovia F.lli, Barbaresco DOCG
Brugo Agostino, Gattinara DOC
Brugo Agostino, Ghemme DOC
Brugo Agostino, Romagnano Sesia
Brugo Agostino, Spanna del Piemonte
Brugo Agostino, Spanna del Piemonte Riserva Cantina dei Santi
− Burlotto Comm. G. B. & Cav. Francesco (Marina Burlotto), Barolo DOCG
Ca' Bianca, Tenuta Denegri Nebbiolo d'Alba DOC
Ca' Romè di Romano Marengo, Barbaresco DOCG
− Cabutto Bartolemeo, Tenuta La Volta Barolo DOCG
Caldi Ditta Cav. Luigi, Gattinara DOC
Caldi Ditta Cav. Luigi, Spanna del Piemonte
-- Caligaris Guido, Gattinara DOC
− Calissano Luigi, Barbaresco DOCG
Calissano Luigi, Barolo DOCG
Campiglione (Marchesi di San Germano)
Cantina Sociale dei "Colli Novaresi," Barengo Rosso
Cantina Sociale dei "Colli Novaresi," Caramino
Cantina Sociale dei "Colli Novaresi," Fara DOC
Cantina Sociale dei "Colli Novaresi," Spanna del Piemonte
Cantina Sociale di Sizzano e Ghemme, Ghemme DOC
Cantina Sociale di Sizzano e Ghemme, Spanna del Piemonte
Cantina Vignaioli "Elvio Pertinace," Barbaresco DOCG
Cantine Ca' Bianca, Barbaresco DOCG
Cantine Ca' Bianca, Tenuta Denegri Barolo DOCG
Cantine Duca d'Asti (Chiarlo Michele), "Granduca" Barbaresco DOCG
Cantine Duca d'Asti (Chiarlo Michele), "Granduca" Barolo DOCG
Cantine Francoli, Spanna del Piemonte
Cantine Le Ginestre, Barolo DOCG
Cascina Borgognot di Borgogno Ludovico, Barolo DOCG
Cascina Bruni di Veglio Pasqual, Barolo DOCG
Cascina Chiabotto di Traversa Giuseppe, Barbaresco DOCG
Cascina La Rocca di Molino Franco, Barolo DOCG
Cascina Nando di Principiano Ferdinando, Barolo DOCG
Cascina Principe di Ottavia Lesquio, Barbaresco DOCG
Casetta F.lli (Ernesto Casetta), Barbaresco DOCG
+ Casetta F.lli (Ernesto Casetta), Barolo DOCG

Castello d'Annone, "Viarengo" Barbaresco DOCG
Castello d'Annone, "Viarengo" Barolo DOCG
+ Castello di Verduno (Sorelle Burlotto), Barolo DOCG
+ Castello Feudale, Barbaresco DOCG
Castello Feudale, Barolo DOCG
Cesnola
Colli Monfortesi di Conterno Fantino, Barolo DOCG
+ Coluè di Massimo Oddero, Barbaresco DOCG
Coluè di Massimo Oddero, Barolo DOCG
Confratelli di San Michele, Barbaresco DOCG
Conterno Fantino, Mon Pra
Conti Cav. Ermanno, Boca DOC
Conti Cav. Ermanno, Maggiora
Conti Gian Piero, Boca DOC
Conti Molini, Gattinara DOC
Coppo Luigi, Barbaresco DOCG
Coppo Luigi, Barolo DOCG
− Damilano Dott. Giacomo, Barolo DOCG
De Forville Paolo, Barbaresco DOCG
De Negri Lorenzo, Nebbiolo delle Langhe
Dellavalle F.lli, Ghemme DOC
Denegri Lorenzo, Barolo DOCG
Dessilani Luigi, Caramino
Dessilani Luigi, Fara DOC
Dessilani Luigi, Gattinara DOC
Dessilani Luigi, Spanna del Piemonte
− Dogliani F.lli, Barolo DOCG crus
+ Dosio, Barolo DOCG
Enologica Valtellinese, Grumello DOC
Enologica Valtellinese, Inferno DOC
Enologica Valtellinese, Sassella DOC
Enologica Valtellinese, Valgella DOC
Eredi Lodali di Ghione, Barbaresco DOCG
Eredi Lodali di Ghione, Barolo DOCG
Ferrando Luigi, Caramino
Ferrando Luigi, Fara DOC
Ferrando Luigi, Spanna del Piemonte
+ Ferrero F.lli (Renato Ferrero), Barolo DOCG
+ Feyles Maria, Barbaresco DOCG
Fogarin (Giuseppe Bianchi)
Fontanabianca, Barbaresco DOCG
+ Fontanafredda, Barbaresco DOCG
Fontanafredda, Barolo DOCG *normale*
− Franchino Marco, Gattinara DOC
+ Franco Fiorina, Barbaresco DOCG
− Gagliardo Gianni, Ribezzo Barolo DOCG
Gagliardo Gianni, Nebbiolo d'Alba DOC Roncaglia
Gemma, Barbaresco DOCG
+ Germano Angelo, Barolo DOCG
Giacosa F.lli, Barbaresco DOCG
− Gianolio Tomaso, Barolo DOCG
Giordano Giovanna, Barbaresco DOCG
Giri Guido, Barbaresco DOCG
Giri Guido, Barolo DOCG
Granduca, Cantine Duca d'Asti (Chiarlo Michele), Barbaresco DOCG

Granduca, Cantine Duca d'Asti (Chiarlo Michele), Barolo DOCG
+ Grasso F.lli (Emilio Grasso), Barbaresco DOCG
+ Grasso Silvio, Barolo DOCG
Grimaldi G., Barbaresco DOCG
Grimaldi Giovanni, Barolo DOCG
+ "La Ca' Nova" Azienda Agricola di Dario Rocca, Barbaresco DOCG
+ La Gatta di Triacca F.lli, Valtellina DOC
La Sassaia (Luigi Perazzi)
La Taberna di Tona di Gianluigi Bonisolo, Valtellina DOC
+ Le Colline Azienda Agricola Borgo Alto
Lesquio Ottavia nell Azienda Agricola "Cascina Principe," Barbaresco DOCG
Lodali Giovanni, Barolo DOCG
Maggiora (Conti Cav. Ermanno)
Manzone Stefano, Barolo DOCG Ciabot del Preive
− Marchesi di Barolo, Barolo DOCG *normale*
Marchesi di San Germano, Campiglione
Marchesi Spinola, Barbaresco DOCG
Marchesi Spinola, Barolo DOCG
+ Marengo M., Barolo DOCG Brunate
Mascarello Giacomo di Alberto Mascarello, Barolo DOCG
Massolino Giuseppe, Barolo DOCG
+ Massolino Giuseppe, Barolo DOCG Margheria
Massolino Giuseppe, Piria
Mauro Marino, Barolo DOCG
+ Mirafiore, Barolo DOCG
"Moccagatta" Azienda Agricola, Barbaresco DOCG
Molino Franco, Cascina La Rocca Barolo DOCG
Mon Prà (Conterno Fantino)
+ Morbelli Giovanni, Carema DOC
Nada Fiorenzo, Barbaresco DOCG
Nebbiolo del Canavese (Produttori "Nebbiolo di Carema")
Nebbiolo del Piemonte *vino da tavola*
Nebbiolo della Serra
+ Negro Angelo, Roero DOC Prachiosso
Nera, Tellino Valtellina DOC
Nera, Valgella DOC
Nervi Luigi & Italo, Spanna del Piemonte
Nicolello, Barbaresco DOCG
− Oberto Egidio (Oberto Giuseppe), Barolo DOCG
Oberto F.lli, Barolo DOCG
Oberto Severino (Oberto Sisto), Barolo DOCG
Opera Prima (Roagna)
Orbello
+ Oreste Stefano, Barolo DOCG
+ Ornato Paolo, Barolo DOCG
Orsolani Casa Vinicola, Gattinara DOC
Palladino, Barbaresco DOCG
Parroco del Neive, Barbaresco DOCG Gallina
+ Patriarca Mario, Gattinara DOC
Patrito, Barolo DOCG
+ Pelissero Luigi, Barbaresco DOCG
Pelizzati Arturo, Grumello DOC
Pelizzati Arturo, Inferno DOC
Pelizzati Arturo, Sassella DOC

Pelizatti Arturo, Sforzato DOC
Perazzi Luigi, La Sassaia
Perazzi Luigi, Orbello
Perlavilla di Tona di Gianluigi Bonisolo, Valtellina DOC
− Piazza Cav. Uff. Armando, Barbaresco DOCG
Piazza Cav. Uff. Armando, Podere d'Mugiot Barolo DOCG
Piccone (Sella)
Pira Luigi, Barolo DOCG
Pira Secondo & Figli Luigi Pira, Barolo DOCG
Piria (Giuseppe Massolino)
Podere d'Mugiot di Piazza Cav. Uff. Armando, Barolo DOCG
Poderi e Cantine di Marengo-Marenda, Barbaresco DOCG Le Terre Forti
Polatti F.lli, Grumello DOC
Polatti F.lli, Inferno DOC
Polatti F.lli, Sassella DOC
Ponti Guido, Spanna del Piemonte
Porro Guido, Barolo DOCG
Principiano Ferdinando, Cascina Nando Barolo DOCG
Produttori "Nebbiolo di Carema," Nebbiolo del Canavese
Prunotto, Barbaresco DOCG *normale*
+ Prunotto, Barolo DOCG *normale*
Prunotto, Roero DOC
+ "Pugnane" Azienda Agricola di F.lli Sordo, Barolo DOCG
Punset di R. Marcarino, Barbaresco DOCG
Punset di R. Marcarino, Barolo DOCG
+ Rabezzana Renato, Nebbiolo d'Alba DOC
Rainoldi Aldo, Sassella DOC
Rainoldi Aldo, Valtellina DOC
Ratti, Barolo DOCG
+ Revello F.lli, Barolo DOCG
− Ribezzo di Gagliardo Gianni, Barolo DOCG
Roagna, Opera Prima
Rocca Albino, Barbaresco DOCG
+ Rocca Dario, Azienda Agricola "La Ca' Nova" Barbaresco DOCG
Rocche Costamagna, Roccardo Nebbiolo delle Langhe
Roche Azienda Vinicola, Zio Giovanni
Roero DOC
+ Roggia Ferdinando, Barolo DOCG
Rolfo Gianfranco, Barolo DOCG
Romagnano Seisa (Brugo Agostino)
Rosso Gigi, Barbaresco DOCG
Rosso Gigi, Barolo DOCG
Saffirio F.lli Enrico e Giacomo, Barolo DOCG
Saffirio Josetta, Barolo DOCG
San Lorenzo Casa Vinicola, Barolo DOCG
+ Scarzello Giorgio, Barolo DOCG
+ Scarzello Giovanni, Barolo DOCG
Sebaste, Bricco Viole
− Seghesio Renzo, Barolo DOCG
Sella, Orbello
Sella, Piccone
Severino Oberto (Sesto Severino), Barolo DOCG
+ Sobrero Francesco, Barolo DOCG
+ Sordo F.lli, Azienda Agricola "Pugnane" Barolo DOCG
Sordo Giovanni, Barolo DOCG Sorì Gabutti

Sottimano, Barbaresco DOCG
Spanna (del Piemonte) *vino da tavola*
Tellino di Nera, Valtellina DOC
Tenuta Ermanno Rivetti, Villa Era di Vigliano Spanna del Piemonte
− Tenuta La Volta di Cabutto Bartolemeo, Barolo DOCG
Tenuta Montanello, Barolo DOCG
Terre del Barolo, Barolo DOCG *normale*
+ Terre del Barolo, Nebbiolo d'Alba DOC
− Tomaso Gianolio, Barbaresco DOCG
Tona di Gianluigi Bonisolo, La Taberna Valtellina DOC
Tona di Gianluigi Bonisolo, Perlavilla Valtellina DOC
Tona di Gianluigi Bonisolo, Sassella DOC
+ Travaglini Giancarlo, Gattinara DOC
Travaglini Giancarlo, Spanna del Piemonte
Traversa Giuseppe, Cascina Chiabotto Barbaresco DOCG
+ Triacca F.lli, La Gatta Valtellina DOC
Troglia G., Gattinara DOC
Troglia G., Ghemme DOC
Troglia G., Spanna del Piemonte
− Turba, Ghemme DOC
− Turba, Sizzano DOC
− Valfrè (Bianchi Giuseppe)
+ Vallana Antonio, Ghemme DOC
Valtellina DOC
+ Veglio Angelo, Barolo DOCG
+ Veglio Giovanni, Barolo DOCG
Veglio Pasqual, Cascina Bruni Barolo DOCG
Viarengo, Castello d'Annone Barbaresco DOCG
Viarengo, Castello d'Annone Barolo DOCG
Vigna Arborina (Altare Elio)
Villa Era di Vigliano (Tenuta Ermanno Rivetti), Spanna del Piemonte
Voerzio Gianni, Barolo DOCG
+ Voerzio Roberto, Nebbiolo delle Ciabot della Luna di La Mora
Zio Giovanni (Azienda Vinicola Roche)

0

Abbona Marziano, Barolo DOCG
Accornero Flavio (Casa Vinicola Bera), Barolo DOCG
Aleramici, Barolo DOCG
+ Alessandria F.lli di G. Battista Alessandro, Barolo DOCG
Ambra (dba of F.lli Dogliani), Barolo DOCG
Ascheri Giacomo, Barbaresco DOCG
Avondo, Spanna del Piemonte
Balbo Marino, Barbaresco DOCG
Baracco di Baracho, Barolo DOCG
+ Bava, Gattinara DOC
Bel Colle, Barbaresco DOCG
Beni di Batasiolo, Barbaresco DOCG
Beni di Batasiolo, Barolo DOCG
+ Beni di Batasiolo, Barolo DOCG Bonfani
Bersano, Barbaresco DOCG
+ Bianco Michelangelo di F.lli Bianco, Barolo DOCG
Bonfante e Chiarle in Bazzana di Momburuzzo, Barolo DOCG
Bongiovanni Giovanni, Barolo DOCG

Borgo Cav. Ercole, Gattinara DOC
Borgo Cav. Ercole, Ghemme DOC
Borgo Cav. Ercole, Spanna del Piemonte
Borgogno Wanda Pepino, Barolo DOCG
Bosca Luigi, Barbaresco DOCG
Bosca Luigi, Barolo DOCG
Boschis Francesco, Barolo DOCG
Brero Cav. Luigi, Barbaresco DOCG
Brero Cav. Luigi, Barolo DOCG
+ Brezza, Barolo DOCG *normale*
Bruzzone, Barbaresco DOCG
Ca' Romè di Romano Marengo, Barolo DOCG
Cabutto Bartolomeo, Barbaresco DOCG
+ Camerano G., Barolo DOCG
Cantina Colavolpe, Barbaresco DOCG
+ Cantina Colavolpe, Barolo DOCG
Cantina Sociale Cooperativa di Gattinara, Gattinara DOC
Cantine Barbero, "Conte de Cavour" Barbaresco DOCG
Cantine Bava, Barbaresco DOCG
+ Cantine Bava, Barolo DOCG
Cantine d'Invecchiamento, "La Brenta d'Oro" Barbaresco DOCG
Cantine d'Invecchiamento, "La Brenta d'Oro" Barolo DOCG
Cantine Mauro Vini (Osvaldo Mauro), Barbaresco DOCG
Cantine Mauro Vini (Osvaldo Mauro), Barolo DOCG
Carnevale Giorgio, Barolo DOCG
Carra, Barbaresco DOCG
Castello di Salabue di Carlo Nob. Cassinis, Rubello di Salabue
− Cauda Cav. Luigi, Barbaresco DOCG
Cauda Cav. Luigi, Barolo DOCG
− Cavaletto, Barbaresco DOCG
− Ceste Cav. G., Barolo DOCG
Colla Paolo, Barbaresco DOCG
Colla Paolo, Barolo DOCG
Concerto (Gianni Gagliardo)
Conte de Cavour (Cantine Barbero), Barbaresco DOCG
Cossetti Clemente, Barbaresco DOCG
− Cossetti Clemente, Barolo DOCG
Cossetti Clemente, Spanna del Piemonte
DA.I.PI."CM" (dba of Villadoria), Barolo DOCG
Damilano Dott. Giacomo, Barbaresco DOCG
Dellavalle F.lli, Barolo DOCG
Dellavalle F.lli, Gattinara DOC
Dellavalle F.lli, Sizzano DOC
Dellavalle F.lli, Spanna del Piemonte
Dogliani F.lli, Barbaresco DOCG
Dogliani F.lli, Barolo DOCG *normale*
Fiore Umberto, Gattinara DOC
Fiore Umberto, Ghemme DOC
Fiore Umberto, "Sogno del Bacco" Spanna del Piemonte
Fiore Umberto, Spanna del Piemonte
Gagliardo Gianni, Barbaresco DOCG
+ Gagliardo Gianni, Barolo DOCG La Serra
Gagliardo Gianni, Barolo DOCG Mora
Gagliardo Gianni, Concerto
+ Galvagno Ernesto, Barolo DOCG

Gherzi, Barbaresco DOCG
Giudice Sergio, Barolo DOCG
Grasso Ernesto, Barbaresco DOCG Vallegranda Sotto
Grazziola, Barbaresco DOCG
Grimaldi Cav. Carlo e Mario, Azienda Agricola "Groppone" Barolo DOCG
+ Grimaldi Cav. Carlo e Mario, Barbaresco DOCG
"Groppone" Azienda Agricola di Grimaldi Cav. Carlo e Mario, Barolo DOCG
Guasti Clemente, Barolo DOCG
Il Vecchio Tralcio, Barbaresco DOCG
Il Vecchio Tralcio, Barolo DOCG
− Kiola (dba of Batasiolo), Barbaresco DOCG
Kiola (dba of Batasiolo), Barolo DOCG
Kiola, Gattinara DOC
La Brenta d'Oro (Cantine d'Invecchiamento), Barbaresco DOCG
La Brenta d'Oro (Cantine d'Invecchiamento), Barolo DOCG
+ "Le Corte" Azienda Agricola di Monticelli-Olivero, Barolo DOCG
Le Due Torri, Barolo DOCG
Marchese Villadoria, Barbaresco DOCG
Marchese Villadoria, Barolo DOCG
Marchese Villadoria, Spanna del Piemonte
Marchesi di Barolo, Barbaresco DOCG
Marengo Mario, Barolo DOCG
Mauro, Barbaresco DOCG
Mauro, Barolo DOCG
"Moccagatta" Azienda Agricola, Barbaresco DOCG Bric Balin
+ Monticelli-Olivero, Azienda Agricola "Le Corte" Barolo DOCG
+ Musso Sebastiano, Barbaresco DOCG
Nada Giuseppe, Barbaresco DOCG Poderi Casot
Nervi Luigi & Italo, Ghemme DOC
Oddero Luigi, Barolo DOCG
Osvaldo Mauro, Cantine Mauro Vini Barbaresco DOCG
Osvaldo Mauro, Cantine Mauro Vini Barolo DOCG
Pavese Livio, Barbaresco DOCG
Pavese Livio, Barolo DOCG
Pippione, Barbaresco DOCG
Podere Anselma, Barbaresco DOCG
Podere Anselma, Barolo DOCG
Podere Anselma, San Mattia
Podere Casot Nada, Barbaresco DOCG
Ramello Giuseppe, Barolo DOCG
+ Rivetti Guido, Barbaresco DOCG
+ Roche Azienda Vinicola, Barolo DOCG
Roche Azienda Vitivinicola, Barbaresco DOCG
Rubello di Salabue (Castello di Salabue di Carlo Nob. Cassinis)
Rusca Attilio, Fara DOC
S. Quirico di Massano, Barbaresco DOCG
S. Quirico di Massano, Barolo DOCG
San Mattia (Podere Anselma)
+ San Michele, Barbaresco DOCG
Savigliano Mario, Barolo DOCG
− Scanavino Giovanni, Barbaresco DOCG

Scanavino Giovanni, Barolo DOCG
Serafino Enrico, Barbaresco DOCG
Sogno del Bacco (Fiore Umberto), Spanna del Piemonte
+ Sordo F.lli, Barolo DOCG
Sordo Giovanni, Barolo DOCG
Telia
Tibalini (EFFEVI), Gattinara DOC
Tibalini (EFFEVI), Spanna del Piemonte
Troglia Giovanni, Barbaresco DOCG
Troglia Giovanni, Barolo DOCG
Turba, Gattinara DOC
Turba, Spanna del Piemonte
Valfieri, Barbaresco DOCG
Valfieri, Barolo DOCG
Vecchio Piemonte, Barolo DOCG
Vecchio Piemonte Cantine Produttori, Barbaresco DOCG
Vercelli Alessandro, Barolo DOCG
+ Viberti Giovanni, Barolo DOCG
Villa Antonio, Gattinara DOC
Villa Antonio, Spanna del Piemonte
Villadoria, Barbaresco DOCG
Villadoria, Barolo DOCG
Villadoria, Spanna del Piemonte
Voerzio Giacomo, Barbaresco DOCG

Sangiovese-based Wines and Producers Rated

****
Altesino, Brunello di Montalcino DOCG
Badia a Coltibuono, Sangioveto di Coltibuono
Biondi-Santi, Fattoria Il Greppo Brunello di Montalcino DOCG
Bologna Buonsignori, Vino Nobile di Montepulciano DOCG
Brunello di Montalcino DOCG
Bonacossi Conte Ugo, Villa di Capezzana Carmignano Riserva DOC
− Case Basse, Brunello di Montalcino DOCG
Castello di Nipozzano di Frescobaldi, Chianti Rùfina Riserva DOCG
+ Conti Costanti (Il Colle al Matrichese), Brunello di Montalcino DOCG
+ Costanti Emilio (Il Colle al Matrichese), Brunello di Montalcino DOCG
Fattoria Il Greppo di Biondi-Santi, Brunello di Montalcino DOCG
+ Fattoria Monsanto, Chianti Classico Riserva DOCG Il Poggio
Frescobaldi, Castello di Nipozzano Chianti Rùfina Riserva DOCG
+ Il Colle al Matrichese di Conti Costanti, Brunello di Montalcino DOCG
+ Il Colle al Matrichese di Emilio Costanti, Brunello di Montalcino DOCG
Le Pergole Torte (Monte Vertine)
− Lungarotti, Rubesco Torgiano Rosso Riserva DOC
Monte Vertine, Le Pergole Torte
− Rubesco di Lungarotti, Torgiano Rosso Riserva DOC
Sangioveto di Coltibuono (Badia a Coltibuono)

Tenuta Il Poggione, Brunello di Montalcino DOCG
Torgiano Rosso Riserva DOC
Valentini, Montepulciano d'Abruzzo DOC
Villa di Capezzana di Conte Ugo Bonacossi, Carmignano Riserva DOC
Villa Selvapiana (Francesco Giuntini), Chianti Rùfina Riserva DOCG

***
Alte d'Altesi (Altesino)
Altesino, Alte d'Altesi
Altesino, Palazzo Altesi
Antinori, Secentenàrio
Antinori, Tignanello
Avignonesi, Grifi
Avignonesi, Vino Nobile di Montepulciano DOCG
+ Badia a Coltibuono, Chianti Classico Riserva DOCG
Cabreo di Ruffino, Predicato di Bitùrica Vigneto Il Borgo
Cantine Baiocchi (Sai Agricola), Vino Nobile di Montepulciano DOCG
Capannelle (Raffaele Rossetti), Barrique
Capannelle (Raffaele Rossetti), Chianti Classico DOCG
Capannelle (Raffaele Rossetti), Riserva
Capannelle (Raffaele Rossetti), Rosso
Cappelli Giovanni, Fattoria di Montagliari Chianti Classico Riserva DOCG
+ Cappelli Giovanni, Fattoria di Montagliari Chianti Classico Riserva DOCG Vigna Casaloste
Cappelli Giovanni, Fattoria di Montagliari e Castellinuzza Chianti Classico Riserva DOCG
Carletti della Giovampaola, Vino Nobile di Montepulciano DOCG
+ Castello di Volpaia, Chianti Classico DOCG
+ Castello di Volpaia, Coltassala
Cepparello (Isole e Olena)
Chianti Classico DOCG
+ Chianti Rùfina DOCG
+ Colombini-Cinelli Francesca, Fattoria dei Barbi Brunello di Montalcino DOCG
+ Coltassala (Castello di Volpaia)
− Dei, Vino Nobile di Montepulciano DOCG
+ Fattoria dei Barbi di Colombini-Cinelli Francesca, Brunello di Montalcino DOCG
Fattoria Del Cerro (Sai Agricola), Vino Nobile di Montepulciano DOCG
Fattoria di Montagliari (Giovanni Cappelli), Chianti Classico Riserva DOCG
+ Fattoria di Montagliari (Giovanni Cappelli), Chianti Classico Riserva DOCG Vigna Casaloste
Fattoria di Montagliari e Castellinuzza (Giovanni Cappelli), Chianti Classico Riserva DOCG
− Fattoria La Gerla, Brunello di Montalcino DOCG
Fattoria Monsanto, Chianti Classico DOCG
Fortilizio Il Colombaio (Villa Colombaio), Chianti Classico Riserva DOCG
+ Frescobaldi, Montesodi Chianti Rùfina Riserva DOCG
Grifi (Avignonesi)

Il Marroneto, Brunello di Montalcino DOCG
Isole e Olena, Cepparello
Isole e Olena, Chianti Classico DOCG
La Chiesa di S. Restituta, Brunello di Montalcino DOCG
Marchesi L. e P. Antinori, Secentenàrio
Marchesi L. e P. Antinori, Tignanello
Mastrojanni (S. Pio e Loreto), Brunello di Montalcino DOCG
Montepulciano d'Abruzzo DOC (the best ones)
+ Montesodi di Frescobaldi, Chianti Rùfina DOCG
Palazzo Altesi (Altesino)
Pepe Emidio, Montepulciano d'Abruzzo DOC
− Pertimali (Sassetti Livio), Brunello di Montalcino DOCG
Podere Lo Locco, Carmignano DOC
Podere Pian di Conte di Pier Luigi Talenti, Brunello di Montalcino DOCG
− Poggio al Sole, Chianti Classico DOCG
Poliziano, Vino Nobile di Montepulciano DOCG
Riecine, Chianti Classico Riserva DOCG
− Rocca di Castagnoli, Chianti Classico Riserva DOCG Poggio a'Frati
Ruffino, Cabreo Predicato di Bitùrica Vigneto Il Borgo
Ruffino, Chianti Classico DOCG Riserva Ducale gold label
San Martino (Villa Cafaggio)
Savignola Paolina, Chianti Classico DOCG
Secentenàrio (Antinori)
+ Solatìo Basilica (Villa Cafaggio)
Talenti Pier Luigi, Podere Pian di Conte Brunello di Montalcino DOCG
Tenuta Caparzo, Brunello di Montalcino DOCG
Tenuta Caparzo, Brunello di Montalcino DOCG La Casa
− Tenuta Col d'Orcia, Brunello di Montalcino DOCG Poggio al Vento
Tenuta Il Poggione, Rosso di Montalcino DOC
Tignanello (Antinori)
− Vecchie Terre di Montefili, Chianti Classico Riserva DOCG Anfiteatro
Villa Cafaggio, Chianti Classico DOCG
Villa Cafaggio, San Martino
+ Villa Cafaggio, Solatìo Basilica
Villa Colombaio, Chianti Classico DOCG
Vino Nobile di Montepulciano DOCG

**
+ Altesino, Rosso di Montalcino DOC
+ Angelo Rosso Riserva (Vinicola Casacanditella), Montepulciano d'Abruzzo DOC
+ Antinori, Chianti Classico DOCG Badia a Passignano
Antinori, Chianti Classico DOCG Pèppoli
− Antinori, Chianti Classico DOCG Riserva Marchese
Antinori, Chianti Classico DOCG Riserva Tenuta Marchese
− Antinori, Chianti Classico DOCG Riserva Villa Antinori
Baccio da Gaiuole Azienda Agricola di Gittori, Chianti Classico DOCG
+ Badia a Coltibuono, Chianti Classico DOCG *normale*
− Badia a Coltibuono, Coltibuono Rosso
+ Balifico (Castello di Volpaia)
Barone Cornacchia, Montepulciano d'Abruzzo DOC

Barone Neri del Nero, Castel Pietraio, Chianti Colli Senesi DOCG
− Bel Convento (Dei Roseti, aka Altesino)
Berardenga, Fattoria di Felsina Chianti Classico DOCG
+ Berardenga, Fattoria di Felsina Chianti Classico Riserva DOCG
+ Berardenga, Fattoria di Felsina Chianti Classico Riserva DOCG Vigneto Rancia
Bindella Rudolf, Vino Nobile di Montepulciano DOCG
Brolio, Chianti Classico DOCG Riserva del Barone
Brunesco di San Lorenzo (Giovanni Cappelli)
Bruno di Rocca (Vecchie Terre de Montefili)
Bucci, Pongelli
+ Ca' del Pazzo (Tenuta Caparzo)
Camartina (Fattoria Querciabella)
Canalicchio (Lambardi Silvano), Brunello di Montalcino DOCG
Canalicchio di Sopra (Lambardi Maurizio), Brunello di Montalcino DOCG
Canalicchio di Sopra (Pacenti Franco e Rosildo), Brunello di Montalcino DOCG
− Canalicchio di Sopra (Primo Pacenti & Pier Luigi Ripaccioli), Brunello di Montalcino DOCG
− Canalicchio di Sopra (Primo Pacenti & Pier Luigi Ripaccioli), Le Gode di Montosoli Brunello di Montalcino DOCG
− Canneto, Vino Nobile di Montepulciano DOCG
− Canneto di Sotto, Vino Nobile di Montepulciano DOCG
+ Cantina Zaccagnini, Montepulciano d'Abruzzo DOC "Dal Tralcetto"
− Capanna (Cencioni Giuseppe Ben. Fra.), Brunello di Montalcino DOCG
− Capanna di S. Restituta (Fattoi Ofelio), Brunello di Montalcino DOCG
Cappelli Giovanni, Brunesco di San Lorenzo
Caprili (Bartolomei Alfo), Brunello di Montalcino DOCG
− Casanova di Neri, Brunello di Montalcino DOCG
Castel Pietraio di Barone Neri del Nero, Chianti Colli Senesi DOCG
Case Basse (Instistietti)
− Castelgiocondo, Brunello di Montalcino DOCG
Castelgiocondo, Rosso di Montalcino DOC
+ Castell'in Villa, Chianti Classico DOCG
Castell'in Villa, Santa Croce
− Castellare, Chianti Classico DOCG
+ Castellare, Chianti Classico Riserva DOCG
+ Castellare, I Sodi San Niccolo
Castello Banfi, Brunello di Montalcino DOCG
+ Castello Banfi, Brunello di Montalcino Riserva DOCG Poggio all'Oro
Castello Banfi, Chianti Classico DOCG
+ Castello dei Rampolla, Chianti Classico DOCG
− Castello di Ama, Chianti Classico DOCG
Castello di Ama, Chianti Classico DOCG Vigneto Bellavista
− Castello di Ama, Chianti Classico DOCG Vigneto Bertinga
+ Castello di Ama, Chianti Classico DOCG Vigneto La Casuccia
+ Castello di Ama, Chianti Classico DOCG Vigneto S. Lorenzo
Castello di Cacchiano, Chianti Classico DOCG

+ Castello di Cacchiano, Chianti Classico Riserva DOCG Millennio
  Castello di Cacchiano, Rocca di Montegrossi Chianti Classico Riserva DOCG
- Castello di Cacchiano, Rocca di Montegrossi Rosso
+ Castello di Monsanto, Sangioveto di Monsanto
+ Castello di Monsanto, Tinscvil
  Castello di Montegrossi (Castello di Cacchiano), Geremia
  Castello di Querceto, Chianti Classico DOCG
+ Castello di Querceto, La Corte
- Castello di Querceto, Predicato di Bitùrica Il Querciolaia
+ Castello di San Polo in Rosso, Cetinaia
  Castello di San Polo in Rosso, Chianti Classico DOCG
+ Castello di San Polo in Rosso, Chianti Classico Riserva DOCG
  Castello di San Polo in Rosso, Torri
- Castello di Tizzano, Chianti Classico DOCG
  Castello di Uzzano, Chianti Classico DOCG
  Castello di Verrazzano, Chianti Classico Riserva DOCG
- Castello Vicchiomaggio, Chianti Classico DOCG
  Castello Vicchiomaggio, Chianti Classico DOCG Paola Matta
  Castello Vicchiomaggio, Chianti Classico DOCG San Jacopo
  Castello Vicchiomaggio, Chianti Classico Riserva DOCG Petri
+ Castello Vicchiomaggio, Chianti Classico Riserva DOCG Prima Vigna
- Castello Vicchiomaggio, Ripa delle More
+ Castello di Volpaia, Balifico
+ Castelluccio Azienda Agricola (Gian Matteo Baldi), Ronco Casone
+ Castelluccio Azienda Agricola (Gian Matteo Baldi), Ronco dei Ciliegi
+ Castelluccio Azienda Agricola (Gian Matteo Baldi), Ronco delle Ginestre
- Castiglion del Bosco, Brunello di Montalcino DOCG
  Catignano, Chianti Classico DOCG
  Cecchi Luigi, Chianti Classico DOCG Messer Pietro di Teuzzo
+ Cecchi Luigi, Predicato di Cardisco Spargolo
+ Cetinàia (Castello di San Polo in Rosso)
- Cerbaiona (Molinari Diego), Brunello di Montalcino DOCG
+ Chianti Colli Fiorentini DOCG
  Chianti Colli Senesi DOCG
  Chianti Montalbano DOCG
  Ciacci Piccolomini d'Aragona, Brunello di Montalcino DOCG
+ Colle Picchioni di Paola di Mauro, Vigna del Vassallo
- Coltibuono Rosso (Badia a Coltibuono)
  Comunali (Bartoli-Giusti-Focacci), Brunello di Montalcino DOCG
  Conti Serristori, Chianti Classico Riserva DOCG
  Conti Serristori, Chianti Classico Riserva DOCG Villa Primavera
- Conti Serristori, Chianti Classico DOCG Villa Primavera
  Contucci, Vino Nobile di Montepulciano DOCG
+ Costanti, Chianti Colli Senesi DOCG
  Cottimello (Eredi Fuligni), Brunello di Montalcino DOCG
+ Dei Roseti (dba of Altesino), Brunello di Montalcino DOCG
  Donna Màrzia Rosso (Giuseppe Zecca)

+ Elegia (Poliziano)
  Fanetti Comm. Adamo e Giuseppe, Principesco
  Fanetti Comm. Adamo e Giuseppe, Vino Nobile di Montepulciano DOCG
  Fassati, Vino Nobile di Montepulciano DOCG Graccianello
+ Fattoria Ambra, Carmignano DOC
  Fattoria Bruno Nicodemi, Montepulciano d'Abruzzo DOC Colli Venia
  Fattoria dei Pagliarese, Chianti Classico DOCG
+ Fattoria dei Pagliarese, Chianti Classico Riserva DOCG Boscardini
  Fattoria della Talosa, Vino Nobile di Montepulciano DOCG
- Fattoria di Artimino, Carmignano DOC Riserva del Granduca
- Fattoria di Artimino, Carmignano Riserva DOC Villa Medicea
  Fattoria di Felsina, "Berardenga" Chianti Classico DOCG
+ Fattoria di Felsina, "Berardenga" Chianti Classico Riserva DOCG
+ Fattoria di Felsina, "Berardenga" Chianti Classico Riserva DOCG Vigneto Rancia
  Fattoria di Felsina, Fontalloro
  Fattoria di Fognano, "Talosa" Vino Nobile di Montepulciano DOCG
  Fattoria di Fontodi, Chianti Classico DOCG
+ Fattoria di Fontodi, Chianti Classico Riserva DOCG
+ Fattoria di Fontodi, Chianti Classico Riserva DOCG Vigna del Sorbo
  Fattoria di Petrognano, Pomino DOC
- Fattoria di Selvole, Chianti Classico DOCG
  Fattoria di Vetrice, Chianti Rùfina DOCG
- Fattoria di Vistarenni, Chianti Classico DOCG Podere Bertinga
- Fattoria Fermignano, "Frimaio" Chianti Classico DOCG
  Fattoria Il Capitano, Chianti Rùfina DOCG
- Fattoria Illuminati di Dino Illuminati, Montepulciano d'Abruzzo DOC
- Fattoria Illuminati di Dino Illuminati, Montepulciano d'Abruzzo DOC Ripe Rosse
- Fattoria Illuminati di Dino Illuminati, Montepulciano d'Abruzzo DOC Vecchio "Zanna"
  Fattoria Le Bocce, Chianti Classico DOCG
  Fattoria Le Filigare, Chianti Classico DOCG
- Fattoria Montiverdi, "Monti Verdi" Chianti Classico DOCG
- Fattoria Pile e Lamole, Lamole di Lamole Chianti Classico DOCG
  Fattoria Querciabella, Chianti Classico DOCG
+ Fattoria San Giusto a Rentennano, Chianti Classico DOCG
+ Fattoria San Giusto a Rentennano, Percarlo
- Fattoria San Leonino, Chianti Classico DOCG
- Fattoria Valtellina di Giorgio Regni, Chianti Classico DOCG
- Fattoria Viticcio, Chianti Classico DOCG
+ Flaccianello della Pieve (Tenuta Fontodi)
  Fontalloro (Fattoria di Felsina)
  Fontevino - Camigliano, Brunello di Montalcino DOCG Pian dei Mercatelli
+ Frescobaldi, Predicato di Bitùrica Mormoreto
  Frescobaldi, Tenuta di Pomino Pomino Rosso DOC
  Geremia (Castello di Montegrossi di Castello di Cacchiano)

Grattamacco (Podere Grattamacco)
+ Grosso Sanese (Podere Il Palazzino)
+ I Sodi San Niccolò (Podere Castellare)
− I Verbi di Ferretti R. & Rasconi R., Brunello di Montalcino DOCG
+ Il Campino di Mondiglia, Chianti Classico DOCG
+ Il Casello (Franceschi Clemente e Roberto), Brunello di Montalcino DOCG
Il Pantano, Vino Nobile di Montepulciano DOCG, pre-1977
− Il Paradiso (Manfredi), Brunello di Montalcino DOCG
+ Il Poggiolo, Chianti Colli Senesi DOCG
+ Il Poggiolo, Chianti Colli Senesi DOCG Il Poggiolo
+ Il Poggiolo, Chianti Colli Senesi DOCG Le Portine
− Il Querciolaia (Castello di Querceto), Predicato di Bitùrica
Instistietti (Case Basse)
Il Sodàccio (Monte Vertine)
+ La Corte (Castello di Querceto)
− La Fortuna (Zannoni Gioberto), Brunello di Montalcino DOCG
La Pescaia (Mantengoli Enzo & Pellari Liliana), Brunello di Montalcino DOCG
− Lamole di Lamole (Fattoria Pile e Lamole), Chianti Classico DOCG
Le Masse di San Leolino, Chianti Classico Riserva DOCG
Le Vignacce (Villa Cilnia)
Lisini (Lisini Elina), Brunello di Montalcino DOCG
+ Lungarotti, Rubesco Torgiano Rosso DOC
+ Lungarotti, San Giòrgio
+ Machiavelli, Chianti Classico DOCG
+ Marchesi L. e P. Antinori, Chianti Classico DOCG Badia a Passignano
Marchesi L. e P. Antinori, Chianti Classico DOCG Pèppoli
− Marchesi L. e P. Antinori, Chianti Classico DOCG Riserva Marchese
Marchesi L. e P. Antinori, Chianti Classico DOCG Riserva Tenuta Marchese
− Marchesi L. e P. Antinori, Chianti Classico DOCG Riserva Villa Antinori
+ Mastrojanni, Rosso di Montalcino DOC
− Melini, Chianti Classico Riserva DOCG
Melini, Chianti Classico Riserva DOCG Granaio
+ Melini, Chianti Classico Riserva DOCG La Selvanella
Melini, Chianti Classico Riserva DOCG "Laborel"
Melini, Chianti Classico Riserva DOCG Terrarossa
Monte Antico (Castello di Monte Antico)
Monte Vertine, Chianti Classico DOCG
Monte Vertine, Il Sodaccio
Monte Vertine, Rosso
− Montenidoli (Podere Montenidoli), Rosso
Montepulciano d'Abruzzo DOC
Montescudaio DOC (the best ones)
− Monti Verdi (Fattoria Montiverdi), Chianti Classico DOCG
Montori Camillo Azienda Agricola, Montepulciano d'Abruzzo DOC
Morellino di Scansano DOC
+ Mormoreto (Frescobaldi), Predicato di Bitùrica
Nozzole, Chianti Classico DOCG

Palazzo al Bosco, Chianti Classico DOCG
Paola Matta (Castello Vicchiomaggio), Chianti Classico DOCG
Parrina DOC
Pasolini dall'Onda Borghese, Chianti Colli Fiorentini DOCG
− Pelagrilli (Pacenti Siro & Pieri Graz.), Brunello di Montalcino DOCG
+ Percarlo (Fattoria San Giusto a Rentennano)
Pian dei Mercatelli (Fontevino - Camigliano), Brunello di Montalcino DOCG
+ Pianelaroma (Vinovino)
− Pietraserena, Chianti Colli Senesi DOCG
− Pietraserena, Chianti Colli Senesi DOCG Poggio al Vento
Podere Boscarelli, Chianti Colli Senesi DOCG
+ Podere Boscarelli, Vino Nobile di Montepulciano DOCG
Podere Capaccia, Chianti Classico DOCG
Podere Capaccia, Querciagrande
+ Podere Castellare, I Sodi San Niccolò
+ Podere Cerrino (Enzo Tiezzi), Brunello di Montalcino DOCG
Podere Grattamacco, Grattamacco
+ Podere Il Palazzino, Chianti Classico DOCG
+ Podere Il Palazzino, Grosso Sanese
− Podere Il Poggiolo (Eredi Cosimi Roberto), Brunello di Montalcino DOCG
− Podere Montenidoli, Montenidoli Rosso
Podere Montenidoli, Sono Montenidoli
Podere Petroio alla via della Malpensata, Chianti Classico DOCG
Podere Petroio alla via della Malpensata, Chianti Classico DOCG Cru Montetendo
Podere Petroio alla via della Malpensata, Solo Rosso
Poggio alla Sala, Vino Nobile di Montepulciano DOCG Vigna Parceto
− Poggio Antico, Brunello di Montalcino DOCG
Poggio Reale di Spalletti, Chianti Rùfina Riserva DOCG
+ Poliziano, Elegia
Pomino Rosso DOC
Pongelli (Bucci)
Predicato di Bitùrica *vino da tavola*
Predicato di Cardisco *vino da tavola*
Principesco (Fanetti)
Querciagrande (Podere Capaccia)
− Querciavalle, Chianti Classico Riserva DOCG
Rasina (Mantengoli Vasco), Brunello di Montalcino DOCG
Raspanti Cav. Giuseppe, Vino Nobile di Montepulciano DOCG
− Regni Giorgio, Fattoria Valtellina Chianti Classico DOCG
+ Riecine, Chianti Classico DOCG *normale*
− Ripa delle More (Castello Vicchiomaggio)
Rocca delle Macìe, Chianti Classico DOCG Riserva di Fizzano
Rocca delle Macìe, Ser Gioveto
+ Rocca di Castagnoli, Chianti Classico DOCG
Rocca di Castagnoli, Chianti Classico Riserva DOCG Capraia
Rocca di Montegrossi (Castello di Cacchiano), Chianti Classico Riserva DOCG
− Rocca di Montegrossi (Castello di Cacchiano), Rosso
Rodolite (Vinovino)

Rosso Armentano (F.lli Vallunga)

Rosso della Quercia (Vinicola Casacanditella), Montepulciano d'Abruzzo DOC

Rosso di Montalcino DOC

+ Rubesco di Lungarotti, Torgiano Rosso DOC

+ Ruffino, Chianti Classico DOCG Riserva Ducale

S. Filippo (Ermanno Rosi), Brunello di Montalcino DOCG

San Felice, Chianti Classico Riserva DOCG

+ San Felice, Chianti Classico Riserva DOCG Il Grigio

+ San Felice, Chianti Classico Riserva DOCG Poggio Rosso

San Felice, Predicato di Bitùrica

+ San Giòrgio (Lungarotti)

San Jacopo (Castello Vicchiomaggio), Chianti Classico DOCG

+ Sangiovese di Romagna DOC (the best ones)

+ Sangioveto di Monsanto (Castello di Monsanto)

Santa Croce (Castell'in Villa)

Selvoramole, Chianti Classico DOCG

Ser Gioveto (Rocca delle Macìe)

Solo Rosso (Podere Petroio alla via della Malpensata)

Sono Montenidoli (Podere Montenidoli)

Spalletti, Poggio Reale Chianti Rùfina Riserva DOCG

+ Spargolo di Cecchi, Predicato di Cardisco

+ Tenuta Caparzo, Ca' del Pazzo

− Tenuta Caparzo, Rosso di Montalcino DOC

Tenuta Col d'Orcia, Brunello di Montalcino DOCG

Tenuta di Lilliano, Chianti Classico DOCG Riserva Eleanora Ruspoli Berlingier

Tenuta di Pomino di Frescobaldi, Pomino Rosso DOC

+ Tenuta Fontodi, Flaccianello della Pieve

+ Tenuta "La Fuga" (Gabriella Cristofolini Attanasio), Brunello di Montalcino DOCG

Tenuta Trerose, Vino Nobile di Montepulciano DOCG

Tenuta Valdicava (Vicenzo Abruzzese), Brunello di Montalcino DOCG

+ Tenuta Valdicava (Vicenzo Abruzzese), Brunello di Montalcino DOCG Madonna del Piano

Tenuta Villa Rosa, Chianti Classico DOCG

Terrabianca, Chianti Classico Riserva DOCG Vigna della Croce

Terre Bindella, Vino Nobile di Montepulciano DOCG

Terricci (Antiche Terre de'Ricci)

+ Tinscvil (Castello di Monsanto)

Toppi Patrizi della Marchesi di Torre, Montepulciano d'Abruzzo DOC

Torgiano Rosso DOC *normale*

Torri (Castello di San Polo in Rosso)

Valdisuga, Brunello di Montalcino DOCG since 1981

Vallunga F.lli, Rosso Armentano

+ Vecchie Terre di Montefili, Chianti Classico DOCG

− Vignamaggio, Chianti Classico DOCG

− Vignamaggio, Chianti Classico Riserva DOCG Castello di Monna Lisa

− Vigneti Pacenti Siro di Pacenti S. e Pieri G., Brunello di Montalcino DOCG

− Villa Antinori (Marchesi L. e P. Antinori), Chianti Classico Riserva DOCG

− Villa Banfi, Brunello di Montalcino DOCG

Villa Cerna, Chianti Classico DOCG

+ Villa Cilnia, Chianti Colli Aretini Riserva DOCG

Villa Cilnia, Le Vignacce

− Villa Cusona (Guicciardini-Strozzi), Chianti Colli Senesi DOCG

+ Villa di Capezzana, Carmignano DOC

Villa di Trefiano, Carmignano DOC

Villa Francesca, Chianti Classico DOCG

+ Villa Il Poggiolo, Carmignano DOC

Villa La Selva, Chianti Colli Aretini DOCG

− Villa Niccola di Lee Iacocca, Brunello di Montalcino DOCG

− Villa Terciona, Chianti Classico DOCG

+ Vinattieri Rosso (Maurizio Castelli & Roberto Stucchi-Prinetti)

Vinattieri Rosso II (Maurizio Castelli and Roberto Stucchi-Prinetti)

+ Vinicola Casacanditella, Angelo Rosso Riserva Montepulciano d'Abruzzo DOC

Vinicola Casacanditella, Rosso della Quercia Montepulciano d'Abruzzo DOC

+ Vinovino, Pianelaroma

Vinovino, Rodolite

*

+ Acciaiolo (Fattoria di Albola)

Agricoltori del Chianti Geografico, Castello di Fagnano Chianti Classico DOCG

Agricoltori del Chianti Geografico, Chianti Classico DOCG

Agricoltori del Chianti Geografico, Contessa di Radda Chianti Classico DOCG

Agricoltori del Chianti Geografico, Tenuta Montegiacchi Chianti Classico DOCG

+ Agricoltori del Geografico, Predicato di Bitùrica

Ancilli, Vino Nobile di Montepulciano DOCG

Ania (Castello di Gabbiano)

+ Antiche Fattorie Fiorentine, Salcetino Chianti Classico DOCG

Antinori, Santa Cristina

Antonello, Montepulciano d'Abruzzo DOC Citra

Argiano, Brunello di Montalcino DOCG

+ Avignonesi, Chianti Colli Senesi DOCG

+ Baiocchi (Sai Agricola), Chianti Colli Senesi DOCG

Barfede-Certaldo, "Cerbaiola" Chianti Classico DOCG

Barfede-Certaldo, "Signoria" Chianti Classico DOCG

Bartali Alberto, Chianti Classico DOCG

Bartali Casa Vinicola, Chianti Classico DOCG

Bosco Nestore, Montepulciano d'Abruzzo DOC

− Bottiglia Particolare (Castello di Verrazzano)

Bottina Davide, Montepulciano d'Abruzzo DOC Notaresco

+ Brolio, Chianti Classico DOCG

+ Brolio, Chianti Classico Riserva DOCG

Brusco dei Barbi (Fattoria dei Barbi)

Bruscone dei Barbi (Fattoria dei Barbi)

Buracchi, Vino Nobile di Montepulciano DOCG

+ Camerlengo (Fattoria dei Pagliarese)

Camigliano Agricola, Vigna di Fontevecchia

Campogiovanni, Brunello di Montalcino DOCG

Campogiovanni, Rosso di Montalcino DOC

Cantina Gattavecchi, Vino Nobile di Montepulciano DOCG
Cantina Santavenere (Massimo Romeo), Vino Nobile di Montepulciano DOCG
− Cantina Sociale "Madonna dei Miracoli," Montepulciano d'Abruzzo DOC
Cantina Sociale Tollo, Montepulciano d'Abruzzo DOC
− Cantina Sociale Tollo, Montepulciano d'Abruzzo DOC Colle Secco
+ Cantina Sociale Tollo, Montepulciano d'Abruzzo DOC Rubino
+ Cantina Sociale Tollo, Montepulciano d'Abruzzo DOC Valle d'Oro
Capanna (Giuseppe Cencioni), Rosso di Montalcino DOC
Capanna di Fattoi e Minocci, "Fattoi" Brunello di Montalcino DOCG
Cappelli Giovanni, La Quercia Chianti Classico DOCG
Carobbio, Chianti Classico DOCG
Carpineto Casa Vinicola, Chianti Classico DOCG
+ Casa del Cerro (dba of Altesino), Brunello di Montalcino DOCG
Casa Francesco, Chianti Classico DOCG
Casal Thaulero, Montepulciano d'Abruzzo DOC
− Casavecchia di Nittardi, Chianti Classico DOCG
Castelli del Grevepesa Soc. Coop., "Castelgreve" Chianti Classico DOCG
Castelli del Grevepesa Soc. Coop., "Castelgreve" Chianti Classico DOCG Panzano
+ Castelli Martinozzi, Brunello di Montalcino DOCG
Castello d'Albola, Chianti Classico DOCG
Castello del Trebbio, Chianti Colli Fiorentini DOCG
Castello della Paneretta, Chianti Classico DOCG
Castello di Cacchiano, RF Selice
− Castello di Castelvari, Chianti Classico DOCG
+ Castello di Cerreto, Chianti Classico DOCG
Castello di Fagnano (Agricoltori del Chianti Geografico), Chianti Classico DOCG
Castello di Fonterutoli, Chianti Classico DOCG
+ Castello di Fonterutoli, Chianti Classico Riserva DOCG Ser Lapo
+ Castello di Fonterutoli, Concerto
Castello di Gabbiano, Ania
Castello di Gabbiano, Chianti Classico Riserva DOCG
− Castello di Luiano, Vigna Pianacci
+ Castello di Montegrossi, Chianti Classico DOCG
Castello di Mugnana, Chianti Classico DOCG
Castello di San Polo in Rosso, Castelpolo Chianti Classico DOCG
Castello di Uzzano, Niccolò da Uzzano
− Castello di Verrazzano, Bottiglia Particolare
Castello di Verrazzano, Chianti Classico DOCG *normale*
− Castello di Verrazzano, Sassello
Castello Guicciardini Poppiano (Conte Ferdinando Guicciardini), Chianti Colli Fiorentini DOCG
− Castello Vicchiomaggio, Chianti Classico Riserva DOCG La Lellera
Cecchi Luigi, Chianti Classico DOCG
Cecchi Luigi, Vino Nobile di Montepulciano DOCG

Celli, Chianti Classico DOCG
Cennatoio, Chianti Classico DOCG
Centolani Agricola, Tenuta Pietra Focaia Brunello di Montalcino DOCG
+ Cerbaiola (Giulio Salvioni), Brunello di Montalcino DOCG
+ Cesari Umberto, Liano
Chianti Colli Aretini DOCG
Chianti Colline Pisane DOCG
Chianti DOCG
+ Chiantigiane, Santa Trinita Chianti Classico DOCG
Cispiano, Chianti Classico DOCG
Codirosso (Fattoria di Vistarenni)
Coli, Chianti Classico DOCG
Colli Altotiberini DOC
Colombaio di Montosoli (Nello Baricci), Brunello di Montalcino DOCG
Coltibuono "La Baida," Cetamura Chianti DOCG
+ Concerto (Castello di Fonterutoli)
Contessa di Radda (Agricoltori del Chianti Geografico), Chianti Classico DOCG
Conti Capponi, Villa Calcinaia Chianti Classico DOCG
Conti Serristori, Brunello di Montalcino DOCG
Conti Serristori, Chianti Classico DOCG *normale*
Conti Serristori, Chianti DOCG
+ Conti Serristori, Ser Niccolò
+ Convivo (Giorgio Regni)
Costarella (Vinovino), Montepulciano d'Abruzzo DOC
− CO.VI.P. (Consorzio Vitivinicolo Perugia), Torgiano Rosso DOC
Cupido (Fattoria di Valiano)
D'Angelo Dario, Montepulciano d'Abruzzo DOC
Di Virgilio, Montepulciano d'Abruzzo DOC Rubino
+ Duchi di Castellucchio, Montepulciano d'Abruzzo DOC
Elba Rosso DOC
Fassati, Vino Nobile di Montepulciano DOCG
Fassati, Vino Nobile di Montepulciano DOCG Podere Fonte al Vescovo
− Fattoria Campomaggio, Chianti Classico DOCG
Fattoria Casale del Bosco (Nardi Silvio), Brunello di Montalcino DOCG
Fattoria Casanuova di Nittardi, Chianti Classico DOCG
Fattoria Concadoro, Cerasi Chianti Classico DOCG
− Fattoria Deapizia, Montepulciano d'Abruzzo DOC
Fattoria dei Barbi, Brusco dei Barbi
Fattoria dei Barbi, Bruscone dei Barbi
+ Fattoria dei Pagliarese, Camerlengo
+ Fattoria Del Cerro (Sai Agricola), Chianti Colli Senesi DOCG
Fattoria dell'Aiola, Logaiolo
+ Fattoria di Albola, Acciaiolo
Fattoria di Artimino, Carmignano DOC
Fattoria di Artimino, Carmignano DOC Vino del Granduca
Fattoria di Artimino, Chianti Montalbano DOCG
+ Fattoria di Bacchereto, Carmignano DOC
Fattoria di Bacchereto, Chianti Montalbano DOCG
+ Fattoria di Calavria, Carmignano DOC
+ Fattoria di Fognano, Vino Nobile di Montepulciano DOCG

Fattoria di Gracciano (Dott. Franco Mazzucchelli), Vino Nobile di Montepulciano DOCG

Fattoria di Grignano, Chianti Rùfina DOCG

Fattoria di Luiano, Chianti Classico DOCG

– Fattoria di Mocenni, Chianti Classico DOCG

Fattoria di Paterno, Vino Nobile di Montepulciano DOCG

Fattoria di Petroio, Chianti Classico Riserva DOCG

Fattoria di Pietrafita, Chianti Colli Senesi DOCG

– Fattoria di Valiano, Chianti Classico DOCG

Fattoria di Valiano, Cupido

Fattoria di Vistarenni, Chianti Classico DOCG

Fattoria di Vistarenni, Codirosso

Fattoria Dievole, Chianti Classico DOCG

Fattoria Il Corno, Chianti Colli Fiorentini DOCG

– Fattoria Il Grappolo, Brunello di Montalcino DOCG

+ Fattoria Il Poggerino, Chianti Classico DOCG

Fattoria Il Poggiolo, Chianti Montalbano DOCG

+ Fattoria La Loggia, Terra dei Cavalieri Chianti Classico DOCG

Fattoria La Ripa, Chianti Classico DOCG

+ Fattoria Le Casalte (Paola Silvestri Barioffi), Vino Nobile di Montepulciano DOCG

Fattoria Le Corti, Chianti Classico DOCG

+ Fattoria Le Corti, Masso Tondo

Fattoria Lilliano, Chianti Colli Fiorentini DOCG

+ Fattoria Montellori, Castelrapiti Rosso

Fattoria Nittardi, Chianti Classico DOCG

Fattoria Nuova Scopetello, Vino Nobile di Montepulciano DOCG

Fattoria Pagnana, Chianti Colli Fiorentini DOCG

+ Fattoria Pile e Lamole, Fattoria Salcetino Chianti Classico DOCG

– Fattoria Quercia al Poggio, Chianti Classico DOCG

+ Fattoria Salcetino (Fattoria Pile e Lamole), Chianti Classico DOCG

Fattoria San Fabiano Calcinaia, Chianti Classico DOCG

Fattoria Sonnino, Cantinino

+ Fattoria Tregole, Chianti Classico DOCG

+ Fattoria Vignale, Chianti Classico DOCG

+ Fattoria Viticcio, Prunaio

Fattoria Zerbina, Marzeno di Marzeno

Fattoria Zerbina, Pietramora

Fico Giorgio, Chianti Classico DOCG

Fiorini - Pantano, Vino Nobile di Montepulciano DOCG

Fontevino, Villa dei Lecci Brunello di Montalcino DOCG

Fornacina (Biliorsi Ruggero), Brunello di Montalcino DOCG

Fossi, Chianti Classico DOCG

Frescobaldi, Chianti Rùfina DOCG Remole

+ Gabbiano, Chianti Classico DOCG

– Geografico, Brunello di Montalcino DOCG

+ Granchiaia (Le Macìe)

– Granducato (Poggibonsi del Consorzio Agrario Provinciale di Siena), Chianti Classico DOCG

Grignano, Chianti Rùfina DOCG

I Coltri Rosso (Melini)

+ I Vignali Azienda Agricola, Montepulciano d'Abruzzo DOC Torre de Passeri

+ Il Colle, Brunello di Montalcino DOCG

Il Palaggio, Chianti Classico DOCG

Il Poggiolino, Chianti Classico DOCG

Il Poggiolo, Chianti Montalbano DOCG

Isole e Olena, Rosso

L'Aja, Chianti Classico DOCG

La Brancaia, Chianti Classico DOCG

+ La Bricola, Chianti Classico DOCG

La Calonica (Cattani Fernando), Rosso

+ La Calonica (Cattani Fernando), Vino Nobile di Montepulciano DOCG

+ La Campana (Mignarri Peris), Brunello di Montalcino DOCG

La Casella (Alfio Carpini), Vino Nobile di Montepulciano DOCG

+ La Cerbaiola (Salvioni Giulio), Brunello di Montalcino DOCG

– La Lellera (Castello Vicchiomaggio), Chianti Classico Riserva DOCG

+ La Poderina (Sai Agricola), Brunello di Montalcino DOCG, since 1982

La Quercia (Cappelli Giovanni), Chianti Classico DOCG

– La Sala, Chianti Classico DOCG

La Suvera, Rango

+ La Torre (Giuseppe Anania), Brunello di Montalcino DOCG

Le Caggiole di Mezzo (Giordano & C.), Vino Nobile di Montepulciano DOCG

+ Le Chiantigiane, Santa Trinita Chianti Classico DOCG

+ Le Due Porti (Daviddi Enrico e Martini Genny), Brunello di Montalcino DOCG

– Le Filgare (Podere Le Rocce)

+ Le Macìe, Granchiaia

Le Masse di San Leolino, Chianti Classico DOCG *normale*

Le Pietrose (Sai Agricola), Vino Nobile di Montepulciano DOCG

+ Le Presi (Poggi-Fabbri Marusca), Brunello di Montalcino DOCG

Leverano Rosso DOC

+ Liano (Umberto Cesari)

Logaiolo (Fattoria dell'Aiola)

Marzeno di Marzeno (Fattoria Zerbina)

+ Masso Tondo (Fattoria Le Corti)

Melini, Brunello di Montalcino DOCG

Melini, Chianti Classico DOCG

+ Melini, Chianti Classico Riserva DOCG Isassi

Melini, Chianti DOCG Borghi d'Elsa

Melini, I Coltri Rosso

+ Melini, Vino Nobile di Montepulciano DOCG

Monsigliolo, Vino Nobile di Montepulciano DOCG

Montecarlo Rosso DOC

Montepulciano d'Abruzzo DOC

Montescudaio DOC

– Monti Antonio e Elio, Montepulciano d'Abruzzo DOC

– Monticelli, Chianti Classico DOCG

Montoro, Chianti Classico DOCG

Niccolò da Uzzano (Castello di Uzzano)

Pagnana, Chianti Colli Fiorentini DOCG

Paradiso (Mauro Fastelli), Brunello di Montalcino DOCG

Pietrafitta, Chianti Colli Senesi DOCG

Pietramora (Fattoria Zerbina)
+ Pietrantori Italo, Montepulciano d'Abruzzo DOC
Podere Campacci, Chianti Classico DOCG
− Podere di Stignano, Chianti Classico DOCG
− Podere di Stignano, San Vicenti Chianti Classico DOCG
Podere La Caggiole, "Tiberini" Vino Nobile di Montepulciano DOCG
+ Podere Le Caggiole di Mezzo, Vino Nobile di Montepulciano DOCG
− Podere Le Rocce, Le Filgare
Podere Scopetone (Abbarchi Federigo & Corioni Angela), Brunello di Montalcino DOCG
+ Poggiarello, Chianti Classico DOCG
− Poggibonsi del Consorzio Agrario Provinciale di Siena, "Granducato" Chianti Classico DOCG
Poggio alla Sala, Vino Nobile di Montepulciano DOCG, since the '82
Poggio Salvi, Brunello di Montalcino DOCG, since the '82
Priore, Montepulciano d'Abruzzo DOC
+ Prunaio (Fattoria Viticcio)
+ Quercecchio (Maria Grazia Salvioni), Brunello di Montalcino DOCG
+ Querciavalle, Chianti Classico DOCG *normale*
Rango (La Suvera)
+ Regni Giorgio, Convìvo
Remole di Frescobaldi, Chianti Rùfina DOCG
RF Selice (Castello di Cacchiano)
Rocca delle Macìe, Chianti Classico DOCG
Rocca delle Macìe, Chianti Classico DOCG Tenuta Sant'Alfonso
+ Rocca delle Macìe, Chianti Classico Riserva DOCG
Rocca di Castagnoli, Stielle
Rocca di Montegrossi, Chianti Classico DOCG *normale*
+ Rodano, Chianti Classico DOCG
Rosso delle Colline Lucchesi DOC
Rosso di Montepulciano DOC
Ruffino, Chianti Classico DOCG
Ruffino, Chianti Classico DOCG Aziano
S. Carlo (Machetti Marcucci R.), Brunello di Montalcino DOCG
+ S. Filippo (Filippo Fanti Baldassarre), Brunello di Montalcino DOCG
S. Filippo (Rosi Ermanno), Rosso di Montalcino DOC
S. Leonino (Fattoria I Cipressi), Chianti Classico DOCG
+ Salcetino (Antiche Fattorie Fiorentine), Chianti Classico DOCG
− Salvanza, Chianti Classico DOCG
+ San Felice, Chianti Classico DOCG *normale*
+ San Felice, Vigorello
Sangiovese dei Colli Pesaresi DOC
Sangiovese di Romagna DOC
Sanguineto (Maria e Lucia Monaci), Vino Nobile di Montepulciano DOCG
+ Santa Caterina di Cordano, Montepulciano d'Abruzzo DOC
Santa Cristina (Antinori)
+ Santa Trinita (Chiantigiane), Chianti Classico DOCG
− Sassello (Castello di Verrazzano)

− Scialletti Cologna Paese Azienda Agricola di Roseto degli Rosso Sanmarco, Montepulciano d'Abruzzo DOC
Scopatello, Vino Nobile di Montepulciano DOCG
Scopetto, Vino Nobile di Montepulciano DOCG
+ Ser Niccolò (Conti Serristori)
Serristori, Chianti Classico DOCG
Sicelle da Giovanni Mari, Chianti Classico DOCG
Stielle (Rocca di Castagnoli)
Straccali, Chianti Classico DOCG
Tenuta di Capezzana, Chianti Montalbano DOCG
+ Tenuta di Gracciano (Seta Ferrari Corbelli), Vino Nobile di Montepulciano DOCG
+ Tenuta di Lilliano, Chianti Classico DOCG
Tenuta di Vignole, Chianti Classico DOCG
Tenuta Il Greppone Mazzi, Brunello di Montalcino DOCG
Tenuta Il Monte, Chianti DOCG
Tenuta Montegiacchi (Agricoltori del Chianti Geografico), Chianti Classico DOCG
Tenuta Pietra Focaia (Agricola Centolani), Brunello di Montalcino DOCG
+ Tenuta Valdipiatta, Vino Nobile di Montepulciano DOCG
+ Terra dei Cavalieri (Fattoria La Loggia), Chianti Classico DOCG
Terrabianca, Chianti Classico DOCG Scassino
Tiberini (Podere La Caggiole), Vino Nobile di Montepulciano DOCG
Torricino (Oscar Pio), Chianti Colli Fiorentini DOCG
− Travignoli, Chianti Rùfina DOCG
Vecchia Cantina di Montepulciano, Vino Nobile di Montepulciano DOCG
+ Vecchia Cantina di Montepulciano, Vino Nobile di Montepulciano Riserva DOCG
Verbena (Brigidi e Pascucci), Brunello di Montalcino DOCG
+ Vigna di Fontevecchia (Agricola Camigliano)
− Vigna Pianacci (Castello di Luiano)
+ Vigorello (San Felice)
Villa a Tolli, Brunello di Montalcino DOCG
Villa Calcinaia di Conti Capponi, Chianti Classico DOCG
Villa Cilnia, Chianti Colli Aretini DOCG *normale*
+ Villa Cilnia, Vocato
Villa di Monte, Chianti Rùfina DOCG
Villa Dievole, Chianti Classico DOCG
Villa La Pagliaia, Chianti Classico DOCG Riserva Granduca Ferdinando III
Villa Niccola (Lee Iacocca), Rosso di Montalcino DOC
Vinovino, Costarella Montepulciano d'Abruzzo DOC
+ Vocato (Villa Cilnia)

0

Antico Castello di Poppiano, Tegolato
Barberini, Chianti Classico DOCG
Brogal Vini "Vignabaldo" Torgiano Rosso DOC
Bigi Luigi, Vino Nobile di Montepulciano DOCG
Bonechi Giampaolo, Granvino di Montemaggio
Bordini, Vino Nobile di Montepulciano DOCG
Camigliano, Brunello di Montalcino DOCG
Cantina Coop. Rosso della Maremma Toscana, Montepescali

− Cantina del Redi, Vino Nobile di Montepulciano DOCG
Cantinino (Fattoria Sonnino)
Carpineto, Vino Nobile di Montepulciano DOCG
Casa Sola, Chianti Classico DOCG
Casanuova di Nittardi, Fattoria Nittardi Chianti Classico DOCG
Castel Ruggero, Chianti Classico DOCG
+ Castelli del Grevepesa, "Castelgreve" Chianti Classico DOCG Monte Firidolfi
+ Castello di Camigliano, Brunello di Montalcino DOCG
Castello di Camigliano, Chianti Colli Senesi DOCG
Castello di Gabbiano, Il Cavaliere
Castello di Meleto, Chianti Classico DOCG
Castello di Monterinaldi, Chianti Classico DOCG
Castello di Poppiano, Tegolato
Castello di Radda, Chianti Classico DOCG
Castello di Rencine, Chianti Classico DOCG
Castello di San Donato in Perano, Chianti Classico DOCG
+ Castelrapiti Rosso (Fattoria Montellori)
Castiglion del Bosco, Rosso di Montalcino DOC
Cecchi Luigi, Brunello di Montalcino DOCG
Cellole, Chianti Classico DOCG
+ Centolani Agricola (Azienda Agricola Friggiali), Brunello di Montalcino DOCG
Cepperellaccio, Chianti Classico DOCG
Chiantigiane, Chianti Classico DOCG
+ Convito (A.C.G. Gaiole Coop. Agricola Cellars), Chianti Classico DOCG
Fattoria Barberino, Chianti Classico DOCG
Fattoria del Pantano, Vino Nobile di Montepulciano DOCG
+ Fattoria dell'Aiola, Chianti Classico DOCG
Fattoria delle Lodoline, Chianti Classico DOCG
Fattoria delle Maestrelle, Podere Ferretto Vino Nobile di Montepulciano DOCG
Fattoria di Doccia, Chianti Rùfina DOCG
Fattoria di Petroio, Chianti Classico DOCG *normale*
+ Fattoria La Loggia, Chianti Classico DOCG
Fattoria La Mandria, Chianti Classico DOCG
Fattoria Le Barone, Chianti Classico DOCG
Fattoria Le Pici, Chianti Classico DOCG
Fattoria Montecchio, Chianti Classico DOCG
Fattoria Nittardi, Casanuova di Nittardi Chianti Classico DOCG
Fattoria Poggio Antico, Rosso di Montalcino DOC
Fizzano, Chianti Classico DOCG
Fontevino (Camigliano), Brunello di Montalcino DOCG
Fontevino (Camigliano), Brunello di Montalcino DOCG La Torre
Francavilla Agricola, Podere Il Macchione Vino Nobile di Montepulciano DOCG
Granvino di Montemaggio (Giampaolo Bonechi)
Guardiolo Vecchio (Coop. Agricola La Guardinese)
Il Cavaliere (Castello di Gabbiano)
Il Guerrino, Chianti Classico DOCG
− Isabella de'Medici, Brunello di Montalcino DOCG
− Isabella de'Medici, Chianti Classico DOCG
La Guardinese Coop. Agricola, Guardiolo Vecchio

+ La Madonnina, Chianti Classico DOCG
+ La Magia (Schwarz Herbert), Brunello di Montalcino DCiCG
La Poderina, Brunello di Montalcino DOCG, pre-1982
+ La Querce (Pinzuti Pino Lido), Vino Nobile di Montepulciano DOCG
La Torre, Brunello di Montalcino DOCG
Le Caggiole (Podere Il Macchione), Vino Nobile di Montepulciano DOCG
Le Coste, Chianti Rùfina DOCG
Le Grifiere, Chianti Classico DOCG
Ludola Nuova, Vino Nobile di Montepulciano DOCG
Mazzoni, Chianti Classico DOCG
Montemaggio, Chianti Classico DOCG
Montepaldi (Marchese Corsini), Chianti Classico DOCG
Montepescali (Cantina Coop. Rosso della Maremma Toscana)
Monteropoli, Chianti Classico DOCG
Olivieri (Valdicava), Brunello di Montalcino DOCG
Pian d'Albola, Chianti Classico DOCG
Piccini, Chianti Classico DOCG
Pietroso, Brunello di Montalcino DOCG
+ Podere Badelle, Vino Nobile di Montepulciano DOCG
Podere Ferretto, Fattoria delle Maestrelle Vino Nobile di Montepulciano DOCG
Podere Il Macchione, Le Caggiole Vino Nobile di Montepulciano DOCG
Podere Le Caggiole, Vino Nobile di Montepulciano DOCG
Poggio alla Sala, Vino Nobile di Montepulciano DOCG, pre-1983
− Poggio alle Mura, Brunello di Montalcino DOCG
+ Poggio Bonelli, Chianti Classico DOCG
Poggio degli Olivi, Brunello di Montalcino DOCG
Poggio Salvi, Brunello di Montalcino DOCG, pre-1982
Pomona, Chianti Classico DOCG
Prunetto, Chianti Classico DOCG
Ricasoli, Chianti Classico DOCG
Ricasoli, Chianti DOCG
Rignana, Chianti Classico DOCG
Riguardo (Tosco Vinicola), Brunello di Montalcino DOCG
Riseccoli, Chianti Classico DOCG
Saccardi, Chianti Classico DOCG
Tegolato (Antico Castello di Poppiano)
Tenuta Col d'Orcia, Rosso di Montalcino DOC
Tenuta di Poggio, Chianti Rùfina DOCG
Tenuta di Riguardo (Tosco Vinicola), Brunello di Montalcino DOCG
Tenuta di Sesta (Ciacci Giuseppe), Brunello di Montalcino DOCG
Tenuta La Colombaio, Chianti Classico DOCG
Tenuta Valdicava (Bramante Martini), Brunello di Montalcino DOCG
Tistarelli Mario, Vino Nobile di Montepulciano DOCG
Tosco Vinicola, "Riguardo" Brunello di Montalcino DOCG
Tosco Vinicola, Tenuta di Riguardo, Brunello di Montalcino DOCG
Tripusa, Brigatti (Enoteca Europea), Vino Nobile di Montepulciano DOCG
Valdisuga, Brunello di Montalcino DOCG, pre-1981

Vignabaldo (Brogal Vini), Torgiano Rosso DOC
Vignavecchia, Chianti Classico DOCG
Villa di Vetrice, Chianti Rùfina DOCG

Recommended, Not Rated
Falchini Riccardo, Chianti Colli Senesi DOCG
Fattoria Chigi Saracini, Chianti Colli Senesi DOCG
Fattoria Coltiberto, Morellino di Scansano DOC
Fattoria dei Barbi (Colombini), Chianti Colli Senesi DOCG
Fattoria della Talosa, Chianti Colli Senesi DOCG
Fattoria di Calavria, Chianti Montalbano DOCG
Fattoria Felsina, Chianti Colli Senesi DOCG
Fattoria Fognano, Chianti Colli Senesi DOCG
Fattoria Giannozzi, Chianti Colli Fiorentini DOCG
Fattoria Il Greppo (Biondi-Santi), Chianti Colli Senesi DOCG
Fattoria La Querce, Chianti DOCG
* Fattoria Le Pupille, Morellino di Scansano DOC
* Fattoria Paradiso, Sangiovese di Romagna DOC
Fattoria Sorbaiano, Montescudaio DOC Rosso delle Miniere
Fattoria Sovestro, Chianti Colli Senesi DOCG
Fattoria Zerbina Sangiovese di Romagna DOC
Ficomantanino, Chianti Colli Senesi DOCG
Majnoni Guicciardini, Chianti Colli Senesi DOCG
Mantellassi Ezio, Morellino di Scansano DOC
Marabini Dott. Giuseppe, Sangiovese di Romagna DOC
Marchese Spinola Giuntini, "Vino Etrusco La Parrina" Parrina DOC
Parrina Azienda Agricola, Parrina DOC
Pasolini dall'Onda, Sangiovese di Romagna DOC
Poggio Valente, Morellino di Scansano DOC
Poggiolungo, Morellino di Scansano DOC
* Spalletti, Sangiovese di Romagna DOC Rocco di Ribano
Tenuta La Chiusa, Elba Rosso DOC
Tenuta San Vito in Fior di Selva (Roberto Drighi), Chianti DOCG
Val delle Rose, Morellino di Scansano DOC
Vallunga F.lli, Sangiovese di Romagna DOC
Villa Santina, Chianti DOCG
Zecca Giuseppe, Leverano Rosso DOC

* Especially recommended

The Wines and Producers of Aglianico Rated

***

D'Angelo F.lli, Aglianico del Vulture DOC
D'Angelo F.lli, Canneto
+ Mastroberardino, Taurasi DOC Radici
Mastroberardino, Taurasi Riserva DOC
Taurasi Riserva DOC

**

Aglianico del Vulture DOC
Mastroberardino, Taurasi DOC
Taurasi DOC

*

Struzziero, Taurasi DOC

Recommended, Not Rated
Botte, Aglianico del Vulture DOC
Cantina Coop. della Riforma Fondiaria di Venosa, Aglianico del Vulture DOC
Cantina del Taburino, Aglianico del Taburno DOC
Consorzio Viticoltori Associati del Vulture, Aglianico del Vulture DOC
Francesco Sasso, Aglianico del Vulture DOC
Miali, Aglianico del Vulture DOC
Moio Michele, Falerno
Paternoster, Aglianico del Vulture DOC
Torre Sveva, Aglianico del Vulture DOC
Villa Matilde, Falerno del Massiccio Rosso DOC
Villa Matilde, Falerno del Massiccio Rosso Riserva DOC

The Wines and Producers of Amarone, Recioto, and Valpolicella Rated

****

— Allegrini, Recioto della Valpolicella Amarone DOC Fieramonte
— Allegrini Valpolicella Classico Superiore DOC La Grola
— Masi, Recioto della Valpolicella Amarone DOC Campolongo Torbe
Masi, Recioto della Valpolicella Amarone DOC Mazzano
Recioto della Valpolicella Amarone DOC

***

+ Allegrini, La Poja
+ Allegrini, Recioto Bianco Fiorgardane Vigna Campogardane
Allegrini, Recioto della Valpolicella Amarone DOC
+ Allegrini, Recioto della Valpolicella DOC Gardane
Allegrini, Valpolicella Classico DOC Lena
Allegrini, Valpolicella Classico Superiore DOC
Allegrini, Valpolicella Classico Superiore DOC Palazzo della Torre
Bertani, Recioto della Valpolicella Amarone Classico Superiore DOC
Bertani, "Secco-Bertani" Valpolicella-Valpantena DOC
Boscaini, Recioto della Valpolicella Amarone DOC Cà de'Loi
Boscaini, Recioto della Valpolicella Amarone DOC Vigneti di Marano
+ Campofiorin di Masi, *ripasso vino da tavola* del Veronese
Capitel San Rocco [delle Lucchine] Rosso di Tedeschi, *ripasso vino da tavola* del Veronese
Castello Guerrieri (Guerrieri-Rizzardi)
Dalforno Romano, Valpolicella DOC
Guerrieri-Rizzardi, Castello Guerrieri
Le Ragose, Le Sassine *ripasso vino da tavola* del Veronese
Le Ragose, Recioto della Valpolicella Amarone DOC
Le Ragose, Valpolicella Classico Superiore DOC
Le Sassine di Le Ragose, *ripasso vino da tavola* del Veronese
+ Masi, Campociesa Bianco Dolce
+ Masi, Campofiorin *ripasso vino da tavola* del Veronese
— Masi, Recioto della Valpolicella Amarone Classico DOC
— Masi, Recioto della Valpolicella DOC Riserva degli Angeli

+ Masi, Serègo Alighieri Recioto della Valpolicella Amarone DOC Vaio Armaron
Masi, Serègo Alighieri Recioto della Valpolicella DOC Casal dei Ronchi
Masi, Serègo Alighieri Valpolicella Classico Superiore DOC
Righetti Luigi, Recioto della Valpolicella Amarone DOC Capitel de'Roari
− Righetti Luigi, Valpolicella Classico Superiore DOC Campolieti
Ripasso vino da tavola del Veronese (the best ones)
− San Rustico, Recioto della Valpolicella Amarone DOC Del Gasso
Secco-Bertani di Bertani, Valpolicella-Valpantena DOC
+ Serègo Alighieri di Masi, Recioto della Valpolicella Amarone DOC Vaio Armaron
Serègo Alighieri di Masi, Recioto della Valpolicella DOC Casal dei Ronchi
Serègo Alighieri di Masi, Valpolicella Classico Superiore DOC
Tedeschi, Capitel San Rocco [delle Lucchine] Rosso, *ripasso vino da tavola* del Veronese
Tedeschi, Recioto della Valpolicella Amarone DOC Capitel Monte Olmi
Tedeschi, Recioto della Valpolicella DOC Capitel Monte Fontana
− Tedeschi, Valpolicella Classico Superiore DOC Vigneto Lucchine

**

+ Allegrini, Recioto della Valpolicella DOC
Bertani, Catullo *ripasso vino da tavola* del Veronese
Bertani, Recioto di Valpolicella-Valpantena Spumante DOC
− Bolla, Recioto della Valpolicella Amarone DOC
− Bolla, Valpolicella Classico DOC Jago
+ Boscaini, Valpolicella Classico Superiore DOC Marano
+ Boscaini, Santo Stefano *ripasso vino da tavola* del Veronese
Brigaldara, Recioto della Valpolicella Amarone DOC
Brigaldara, Valpolicella Classico Superiore DOC Il Vegro
Catullo (Bertani), *ripasso vino da tavola* del Veronese
+ Dalforno Romano, Recioto della Valpolicella Amarone DOC
Guerrieri-Rizzardi, Villa Rizzardi Poiega Valpolicella Classico DOC
+ La Bionda, Recioto della Valpolicella Amarone DOC
La Bionda, Valpolicella Classico Superiore DOC Vigneti di Ravazzol Valgatara
+ La Fabriseria de San Rocco (Tedeschi), Recioto Bianco
Le Salette di Fulvio Scamperle, Recioto della Valpolicella Amarone DOC
Longo, Recioto della Valpolicella Amarone DOC
Masi, Recioto della Valpolicella DOC Mezzanella
+ Masi, Valpolicella Classico DOC Fresco Vigneti di Gargagnago
Masi, Valpolicella Classico Superiore DOC
+ Pieropan Leonildo, Recioto di Soave DOC
Quintarelli, Recioto della Valpolicella Amarone DOC
+ Quintarelli, Valpolicella Classico DOC Fiore Vigneto di Monte Ca' Paletta

+ Quintarelli, Valpolicella Classico Superiore DOC Vigneto di Monte Ca' Paletta
San Rustico di Danilo Campagnola, Valpolicella Classico Superiore DOC Vigneti del Gasso
San Rustico di Danilo Campagnola, Valpolicella della Reciote Spumante DOC
− Santi, Recioto della Valpolicella Amarone DOC Botte Regina
Scamperle Fulvio, Le Salette Recioto della Valpolicella Amarone DOC
+ Tedeschi, Recioto Bianco La Fabriseria de San Rocco
Tedeschi, Recioto della Valpolicella Amarone Classico DOC
+ Tedeschi, Recioto della Valpolicella Amarone DOC Linea Fabbriseria
− Tedeschi, Valpolicella Classico Superiore DOC
Tommasi, Recioto della Valpolicella Amarone DOC
Tommasi, Valpolicella Classico Superiore DOC Vigneto Raffael
+ Venturini, Recioto della Valpolicella Amarone DOC
Venturini, Recioto della Valpolicella DOC

*

Aldegheri, "Sant'Ambrogio" Recioto della Valpolicella Amarone DOC
Bergamini, Recioto della Valpolicella DOC
Bolla, Valpolicella Classico DOC
− Conati Marco, Recioto della Valpolicella Amarone DOC
+ Due Torri, Recioto della Valpolicella Amarone DOC
Farina Remo, Recioto della Valpolicella Amarone DOC
Guerrieri-Rizzardi, Recioto della Valpolicella Amarone DOC
Guerrieri-Rizzardi, Valpolicella Classico DOC
La Crocetta, Recioto della Valpolicella DOC
La Crocetta, Recioto della Valpolicella Amarone DOC
Lenotti, Recioto della Valpolicella DOC
Murari, Recioto della Valpolicella Amarone DOC
San Rustico di Luigi & Danilo Campagnola, Recioto della Valpolicella Amarone DOC
San Rustico di Luigi & Danilo Campagnola, Valpolicella Classico
Santa Sofia, Recioto della Valpolicella Amarone DOC
Sant'Ambrogio di Aldegheri, Recioto della Valpolicella Amarone DOC
Santi, Valpolicella Classico Superiore DOC Vigneti Castello d'Illasi
Sartori, Recioto della Valpolicella Amarone DOC
Scamperle, Recioto della Valpolicella Amarone DOC
Tedeschi, Recioto della Valpolicella DOC
+ Tramanal, Recioto della Valpolicella Amarone DOC
Villa Spada, Recioto della Valpolicella Amarone DOC
Zenato, Recioto della Valpolicella Amarone DOC
Zeni F.lli, Recioto della Valpolicella Amarone DOC

0

Aldegheri, Recioto della Valpolicella Amarone DOC
Barberini, Recioto della Valpolicella Amarone DOC
Burati, Recioto della Valpolicella Amarone DOC
+ Ca' Merla, Recioto della Valpolicella Amarone DOC
Castagna, Recioto della Valpolicella Amarone DOC

Cesari, Recioto della Valpolicella Amarone DOC
Corta Vecchia, Recioto della Valpolicella Amarone DOC
Fabiano, Recioto della Valpolicella Amarone DOC
Farina F.lli, Recioto della Valpolicella Amarone DOC
La Colombaia, Recioto della Valpolicella Amarone DOC
+ La Colombaia, Recioto della Valpolicella Amarone DOC Alto Marano
Lamberti, Recioto della Valpolicella Amarone DOC
Montresor, Recioto della Valpolicella Amarone DOC
Nicolas Angelo, Recioto della Valpolicella Amarone DOC
+ Nicolas Angelo, Recioto della Valpolicella DOC
Pasqua, Recioto della Valpolicella Amarone DOC
Santi, Recioto della Valpolicella Amarone DOC
Speri, Recioto della Valpolicella Amarone DOC
Tenuta Villa Girardi, Recioto della Valpolicella Amarone DOC
Tre Rose, Recioto della Valpolicella Amarone DOC
Vantini Lorenzo, Recioto della Valpolicella Amarone DOC
Villa Girardi, Recioto della Valpolicella Amarone DOC
Zardini F.lli, Recioto della Valpolicella Amarone DOC

Recommended, Not Rated
* Anselmi, Recioto di Soave DOC dei Capitelli
Le Salette di Fulvio Scamperle, Valpolicella Classico Superiore DOC
Santa Sofia, Valpolicella Classico Superiore DOC
Villa Girardi, Valpolicella Classico Superiore DOC
Zeni F.lli, Valpolicella Classico Superiore DOC Marogne
Zeni F.lli, Valpolicella Classico Superiore DOC Vigne Alte

* Especially recommended

The Wines and Producers of Cabernet and Merlot Rated

****
Bellendorf (Giorgio Grai), Alto Adige Cabernet DOC
Grai Giorgio, Alto Adige Cabernet DOC
Herrnhofer (Giorgio Grai), Alto Adige Cabernet DOC
Kehlburg (Giorgio Grai), Alto Adige Cabernet DOC
Ornellaia (Marchese Ludovico Antinori)

***
Alto Adige Cabernet DOC (the best ones)
+ Antinori, Solàia
− Boncompagni Ludovisi Principe di Venosa, Fiorano Rosso
Breganze Cabernet DOC (the best ones)
Bonacossi Conte Ugo, Ghiaie della Furba
Ca' del Bosco, Maurizio Zanella
Campo del Lago di Lazzarini, Colli Bèrici Merlot DOC
Castellare, Coniale
Castello dei Rampolla, Sammarco
Cirillo-Farrusi Fabrizio, Torre Quarto Riserva
Colacicchi-Anagni, Torre Ercolana
Colli Bèrici Merlot DOC (the best ones)
Coniale (Castellare)
Conte Ugo Bonacossi, Ghiàie della Furba
− Dri Giovanni, Il Roncàt Rosso
− Fiorano Rosso (Boncompagni Ludovisi Principe di Venosa)

+ Fratta di Maculan, Breganze Cabernet DOC
Ghiàie della Furba (Conte Ugo Bonacossi)
− Il Roncàt Rosso (Giovanni Dri)
Lazzarini, Colli Bèrici Merlot DOC Campo del Lago
+ Maculan, Breganze Cabernet DOC Fratta
Maculan, Breganze Cabernet DOC Palazzotto
+ Marchese, L. e P. Antinori, Solàia
Maurizio Zanella (Ca' del Bosco)
Palazzotto di Maculan, Breganze Cabernet DOC
Sammarco (Castello dei Rampolla)
Sassicàia (Tenuta San Guido)
+ Solàia (Antinori)
Tenuta San Guido, Sassicàia
Torre Ercolana (Cantina Colacicchi-Anagni)
Torre Quarto Riserva (Fabrizio Cirillo-Farrusi)

**
+ Abbazia di Rosazzo, Ronco dei Roseti
Altesino, Cabernet Sauvignon
Alto Adige Cabernet DOC
Alto Adige Merlot DOC (the best ones)
+ Anselmi Roberto, Realda
Avignonesi, Cabernet Sauvignon
Avignonesi, Merlot
− Barbarola (Raffaelle Rino)
Barone Ciani Bassetti, Castello di Roncade
Bertelli Alberto, I Fossaretti Cabernet Sauvignon
Borgo Conventi, Braida Nuova
Braida Nuova (Borgo Conventi)
Breganze Cabernet DOC
− Brunori Ruggero, Le Sincette Rosso
+ Ca' Loredan Gasparini, Venegazzù Riserva della Casa black label
− Ca' Loredan Gasparini, Venegazzù Riserva della Casa white label
Cabernet del Friuli–Venezia Giulia *vino da tavola* (the best ones)
Cabernet del Tre Venezia *vino da tavola* (the best ones)
Cabernet del Veneto vino da tavola (the best ones)
Cabernet Franc del Friuli–Venezia Giulia *vino da tavola* (the best ones)
Cabernet Franc del Tre Venezia *vino da tavola* (the best ones)
Cabernet Franc del Veneto *vino da tavola* (the best ones)
Cabernet Sauvignon del Friuli–Venezia Giulia *vino da tavola* (the best ones)
Cabernet Sauvignon del Tre Venezia *vino da tavola* (the best ones)
Cabernet Sauvignon del Veneto *vino da tavola* (the best ones)
Camoi (Orlandi)
Cantine Petternella, Quarto Vecchio
Casale Azienda Agricola (Falchini), Cabernet Sauvignon
Castel S. Michele (Istituto Agrario Provinciale S. Michele)
− Castello Banfi, Tavernelle Cabernet Sauvignon
+ Castello di Ama, Vigna L'Apparita
+ Castello di Gabbiano, R & R
Castello di Roncade (Barone Ciani Bassetti)
+ Castello Monsanto di Fabrizio Bianchi, Nemo

Castello Turmhof, Linticlarius
+ Cavalleri Gian Paolo & Giovanni, Tajardino
Cirillo-Farrusi Fabrizio, Torre Quarto *normale*
− Col Sandago, Costa delle Pergole Rosso
Colli Bèrici Cabernet DOC (the best ones)
Colli Bèrici Merlot DOC
− Colli Bolognesi-Monte San Pietro-Castelli Mediovale Cabernet DOC
Colli Eugànei Cabernet DOC (the best ones)
Colli Eugànei Merlot DOC (the best ones)
Colli Eugànei Rosso DOC (the best ones)
− Colli Orientali del Friuli Cabernet DOC
− Colli Orientali del Friuli Cabernet Franc DOC
− Colli Orientali del Friuli Cabernet Sauvignon DOC
− Collio (Goriziano) Merlot DOC
− Conte Da Schio, Costozza Cabernet Frank
Conti Bossi Fedrigotti, Foianeghe Rosso
Corbulino Rosso (Afra e Tobia Scarpa)
− Cortaccio (Villa Cafaggio)
− Costa delle Pergole Rosso (Col Sandago)
− Costozza (Conte da Schio), Cabernet Frank
+ Danieli Marina, Faralta
+ Darmaggi di Gaja, Cabernet Sauvignon
Dorigo Girolamo, Montsclapade
Falchini (Azienda Agricola Casale), Cabernet Sauvignon
+ Faralta (Marina Danieli)
Favònio di Attilio Simonini, Cabernet Franc Riserva
Foianeghe Rosso (Conti Bossi Fedrigotti)
Franciacorta Rosso DOC (the best ones)
+ Gaja, Darmaggi Cabernet Sauvignon
− Grave del Friuli Cabernet DOC (the best ones)
− Grave del Friuli Cabernet Sauvignon DOC (the best ones)
I Fossaretti (Alberto Bertelli)
Istituto Agrario Provinciale S. Michele, Castèl S. Michele
+ La Vinicola Sociale Aldeno, San Zeno
+ Lagaria, Mori Vecio
+ Lazzarini, Colli Bèrici Cabernet DOC Le Rive Rosso
− Le Marne (Volpe Pasini)
+ Le Rive Rosso (Lazzarini), Colli Bèrici Cabernet DOC
− Le Sincette Rosso (Brunori Ruggero)
Linticlarius (Castello Turmhof)
− Lungarotti, Cabernet Sauvignon
Merlot del Friuli–Venezia Giulia *vino da tavola* (the best ones)
Merlot del Tre Venezia *vino da tavola* (the best ones)
Merlot del Veneto *vino da tavola* (the best ones)
Montsclapade (Girolamo Dorigo)
+ Mori Vecio (Lagaria)
+ Nemo (Castello Monsanto di Fabrizio Bianchi)
Orlandi, Camoi
− Pasini Volpe, Le Marne
Quarto Vecchio (Cantine Petternella)
+ R & R (Castello di Gabbiano)
− Rauten (F.lli Salvetta)
+ Realda (Roberto Anselmi)
− Regaleali di Conte Tasca d'Almerita, Cabernet Sauvignon
− Rino Raffaelle, Barbarola

+ Riva Rossa (Mario Schiopetto)
+ Ronchi del Gnemiz, Rosso del Gnemiz
+ Ronco dei Roseti (Abbazia di Rosazzo)
+ Rosso del Gnemiz (Ronchi del Gnemiz)
Rosso di Vigne dal Leòn (Tullio Zamò)
− Salvetta F.lli, Rauten
San Leonardo (Tenuta San Leonardo)
+ San Zeno (La Vinicola Sociale Aldeno)
Scarpa Afra e Tobia, Corbulino Rosso
+ Schiopetto Mario, Riva Rossa
Simonini Attilio, Favònio Cabernet Franc Riserva
+ Tajardino (Gian Paolo & Giovanni Cavalleri)
− Tavernelle (Castello Banfi), Cabernet Sauvignon
Torre Quarto (Fabrizio Cirillo-Farrusi), *normale*
Trentino Cabernet DOC (the best ones)
Trentino Cabernet e Merlot DOC (the best ones)
Trentino Cabernet Franc DOC (the best ones)
Trentino Cabernet Sauvignon DOC (the best ones)
+ Venegazzù di Ca' Loredan Gasparini, Riserva della Casa black label
− Venegazzù di Ca' Loredan Gasparini, Riserva della Casa white label
+ Vigna L'Apparita (Castello di Ama)
Vigne dal Leòn (Tullio Zamò), Rosso
− Villa Cafaggio, Cortaccio
Zamò Tullio, Rosso di Vigne dal Leòn

*

Alto Adige Merlot DOC
Aquileia Cabernet DOC
Aquileia Cabernet Franc DOC
Aquileia Cabernet Sauvignon DOC
Aquileia Merlot DOC
Barone Fini, Cabernello
+ Bellavista, Solesine
− Berengario (Domenico Zonin)
Bolla Fratelli, Creso
Breganze Cabernet DOC
Breganze Rosso DOC
+ Brentino (Maculan) Breganze Rosso DOC
Brume di Monte (Càvit), Trentino Rosso DOC
− Ca' del Merlot (Quintarelli)
Cabernello (Barone Fini)
Cabernet del Friuli–Venezia Giulia *vino da tavola*
Cabernet del Tre Venezia *vino da tavola*
Cabernet del Veneto *vino da tavola*
Cabernet Franc del Friuli–Venezia Giulia *vino da tavola*
Cabernet Franc del Tre Venezia *vino da tavola*
Cabernet Franc del Veneto *vino da tavola*
Cabernet Sauvignon del Friuli–Venezia Giulia *vino da tavola*
Cabernet Sauvignon del Tre Venezia *vino da tavola*
Cabernet Sauvignon del Veneto *vino da tavola*
Cantina Spagnolli, Tebro
Càvit, Quattro Vicariati
Càvit, Trentino Rosso DOC Brume di Monte
Colli Bèrici Cabernet DOC
Colli Bèrici Merlot DOC

Colli Bolognesi-Monte San Pietro-Castelli Mediovale Merlot DOC
Colli Eugànei Cabernet DOC
Colli Eugànei Merlot DOC
Colli Eugànei Rosso DOC
Colli Morénici Mantovani del Garda DOC
+ Colli Orientali del Friuli Merlot DOC
+ Collio (Goriziano) Cabernet DOC
+ Conti Formentini, Formentini Rosso
Creso (Fratelli Bolla)
Dorigati F.lli, Grener
Favònio (Attilio Simonini), Cabernet Franc *normale*
+ Formentini Rosso (Contini Formentini)
Franciacorta Rosso DOC
Grave del Friuli Cabernet DOC
Grave del Friuli Cabernet Franc DOC
Grave del Friuli Cabernet Sauvignon DOC
Grave del Friuli Merlot DOC
Grener (F.lli Dorigati)
Isonzo Cabernet DOC
Isonzo Cabernet Franc DOC
Isonzo Cabernet Sauvignon DOC
Isonzo Merlot DOC
+ La Vinicola Sociale Aldeno, Sgreben
Latisana Cabernet DOC
Latisana Cabernet Franc DOC
Latisana Cabernet Sauvignon DOC
Latisana Merlot DOC
Le Stanze (Poliziano di Carletti)
Lison-Pramaggiore Cabernet DOC
Lison-Pramaggiore Cabernet Franc DOC
Lison-Pramaggiore Cabernet Sauvignon DOC
Lison-Pramaggiore Merlot DOC
Livon, Plazate Rosso
Livon, Tiarebù
+ Maculan, Breganze Rosso DOC Brentino
Merlot del Friuli–Venezia Giulia *vino da tavola*
Merlot del Tre Venezia *vino da tavola*
Merlot del Veneto *vino da tavola*
Merlot di Cavriana (Azienda Vitivinicola Monte Gallo)
+ Merlot di Sicilia (Principessa di Gregorio)
Monte Gallo Azienda Vitivinicola, Merlot di Cavriana
+ Montello e Colli Asolani Cabernet DOC
+ Montello e Colli Asolani Merlot DOC
Navesè (Armando Simoncelli)
Piave Cabernet DOC
Piave Merlot DOC
Plazate Rosso (Livon)
Polizano, Le Stanze
+ Principessa di Gregorio, Merlot di Sicilia
Quattro Vicariati (Càvit)
− Quintarelli, Ca' del Merlot
− Quintarelli, Cabernet Franc
S. Cristina, Cabernet Sauvignon
+ Sgreben (La Vinicola Sociale Aldeno)
Simoncelli Armando, Navesèl
Simonini Attilio, Favònio Cabernet Franc *normale*

+ Solesine (Bellavista)
Tebro (Cantina Spagnolli)
Tiarebù (Livon)
Trentino Cabernet DOC
Trentino Cabernet e Merlot DOC
Trentino Cabernet Franc DOC
Trentino Cabernet Sauvignon DOC
Trentino Merlot DOC
+ Valcalèpio Rosso DOC
− Zonin Domenico, Berengario

0
Aprilia Merlot DOC
Borgo di Peuma Russolo
Cabernet del Friuli–Venezia Giulia *vino da tavola*
Cabernet del Tre Venezia *vino da tavola*
Cabernet del Veneto *vino da tavola*
Cabernet Franc del Friuli–Venezia Giulia *vino da tavola*
Cabernet Franc del Tre Venezia *vino da tavola*
Cabernet Franc del Veneto *vino da tavola*
Cabernet Sauvignon del Friuli–Venezia Giulia *vino da tavola*
Cabernet Sauvignon del Tre Venezia *vino da tavola*
Cabernet Sauvignon del Veneto *vino da tavola*
Furlan Franco, Stukara
Marago (F.lli Pasqua)
Merlot del Friuli–Venezia Giulia *vino da tavola*
Merlot del Tre Venezia *vino da tavola*
Merlot del Veneto *vino da tavola*
Pasqua F.lli, Marago
Stukara (Franco Furlan)

Recommended, Not Rated
Angoris, Isonzo Cabernet DOC Riserva Castello
Antonutti, Grave del Friuli Cabernet DOC
Attems, Collio Merlot DOC Ronco Arcivesco
Banear, Grave del Friuli Merlot DOC
Barone de Cles, Trentino Cabernet DOC
Barone Fini, Trentino Cabernet DOC
Bauernkelleri, Alto Adige Cabernet DOC
Bergamasca Coop., Valcalèpio Rosso DOC
Bergamasca Coop., Merlot
Berin Fabio, Collio Cabernet Franc DOC
Bollini, Grave del Friuli Cabernet Sauvignon DOC
* Borgo Conventi, Collio Merlot DOC
Ca' Bolani, Aquileia Cabernet DOC
Ca' Bolani, Aquileia Merlot DOC
Ca' Bruzzo, Colli Bèrici Cabernet DOC
Ca' del Bosco, Franciacorta Rosso DOC
Ca' Ronesca, Collio Cabernet Franc DOC
Ca' Ronesca, Collio Merlot DOC
Cantina del Friuli Centrale "La Bora," Grave del Friuli Cabernet DOC
Cantina del Friuli Centrale "La Bora," Grave del Friuli Merlot DOC
Cantina Sociale Ponte, Piave Cabernet Sauvignon DOC
Cantina Sociale Ponte, Piave Merlot DOC

Cantine Florio (Tenuta Maseri Florio), Colli Orientali del
Friuli Cabernet DOC

Cantine Florio (Tenuta Maseri Florio), Colli Orientali del
Friuli Merlot DOC

Casarsa Coop. "La Delezia," Grave del Friuli Cabernet DOC

Casarsa Coop. "La Delezia," Grave del Friuli Cabernet
Sauvignon DOC

Casarsa Coop. "La Delezia," Grave del Friuli Merlot DOC

Castelcosa, Merlot del Friuli–Venezia Giulia

Catturich Ducco, Franciacorta Rosso DOC

Cavalleri Gian Paolo e Giovanni, Franciacorta Rosso DOC

Càvit, Trentino Cabernet DOC

Col Rosazzo, Collio Cabernet DOC

Collavini, Grave del Friuli Cabernet Sauvignon DOC

Collavinus, Trentino Cabernet DOC

Conte Medolaga Albani, Valcalèpio Rosso DOC

Conti Attems, Isonzo Cabernet DOC

Conti Bossi Fedregotti, Trentino Cabernet DOC

Conti Bossi Fedregotti, Trentino Merlot DOC

Contini Formentini, Collio Cabernet Franc DOC

Contini Formentini, Collio Merlot DOC

* Danieli Marina, Colli Orientali del Friuli Cabernet DOC

* Danieli Marina, Colli Orientali del Friuli Merlot DOC

De Lorenzi Paolo, Lison-Pramaggiore Cabernet DOC

Dorigati F.lli, Trentino Cabernet DOC

Duca Badoglia, Grave del Friuli Cabernet DOC

Duca Badoglia, Grave del Friuli Merlot DOC

Elle (Gaierhof), Trentino Merlot DOC

Endrizzi F.lli, Trentino Cabernet DOC

Endrizzi F.lli, Trentino Merlot DOC

Enetum, Piave Cabernet DOC

Enetum, Piave Merlot DOC

Eno Friulia, Collio Cabernet Franc DOC

Felluga Livio, Collio Cabernet Franc DOC

Felluga Livio, Collio Merlot DOC

Felluga Marco, Collio Merlot DOC

Friulivini Cantina Sociale, Grave del Friuli Cabernet
Sauvignon DOC

Friulivini Cantina Sociale, Grave del Friuli Merlot DOC

Gaierhof, Elle Trentino Merlot DOC

Gaierhof, Trentino Merlot DOC

Gianfrano d'Attimis, Colli Orientali del Friuli Merlot DOC

* Gradnik, Collio Cabernet Franc DOC

* Gradnik, Collio Merlot DOC

Gruarius (Cantina Sociale di Portogruaro), Lison-Pramaggiore
Merlot DOC

Guarise, Lison-Pramaggiore Cabernet DOC

Hofstatter Josef, Alto Adige Cabernet DOC

* Hofstatter Josef, Alto Adige Merlot DOC

* I Moròs di Nello Tavagnacco, Cabernet di Ippilis

* I Moròs di Nello Tavagnacco, Colli Orientali del Friuli
Cabernet DOC

* I Moròs di Nello Tavagnacco, Colli Orientali del Friuli Merlot
DOC

I Vini del Concilio, Trentino Cabernet DOC

I Vini del Concilio, Trentino Merlot DOC

Isola Augusta, Latisana Cabernet DOC

Isola Augusta, Latisana Merlot DOC

Istituto Agrario Provinciale S. Michele, Trentino Cabernet
DOC

Kellereigenossenschaft Gries, Alto Adige Merlot DOC
Steinhof

Kellereigenossenschaft Liebeneich, Alto Adige Merlot DOC
Schreckbichl

Kellereigenossenschaft Magreid, Alto Adige Cabernet DOC

Kettmeir, Alto Adige Cabernet Sauvignon DOC

Kettmeir, Alto Adige Merlot DOC Siebeneich

Kunkler Bianchi, Piave Cabernet DOC

Kunkler Bianchi, Piave Merlot DOC

Kupelweiser, Trentino Cabernet DOC

La Bottega de Vinai, Trentino Cabernet DOC

La Vinicola Sociale Aldeno, Trentino Cabernet DOC

Lagaria, Trentino Cabernet DOC

Lagaria, Trentino Merlot DOC

Lechthaler, Trentino Cabernet DOC

Letrari, Trentino Cabernet DOC

La Principesi, Colli Eugànei Rosso DOC

Lageder Alöis, Alto Adige Cabernet DOC

* Lageder Alöis, Alto Adige Cabernet DOC Wurmbrand

Lageder Alöis, Alto Adige Merlot DOC

Laimburger, Alto Adige Cabernet DOC

Lancini Luigi, Franciacorta Rosso DOC Vigna Cornaleto

Lis Gravis, Grave del Friuli Cabernet Sauvignon DOC

Longhi-di Carli, Franciacorta Rosso DOC

Maculan, Breganze Cabernet DOC

Marchese Malaspina, Colli Bolognesi Cabernet Sauvignon
DOC

Marchese Malaspina, Colli Bolognesi Merlot DOC

Martini Karl, Alto Adige Cabernet DOC Kellermeistertrunk

Montelvini, Montello e Colli Asolani Cabernet DOC

Montelvini, Montello e Colli Asolani Merlot DOC

* Montsclapade di Dorigo Girolamo, Colli Orientali del Friuli
Cabernet DOC

* Montsclapade di Dorigo Girolamo, Colli Orientali del Friuli
Merlot DOC

Morassutti Giovanni Paolo, Lison-Pramaggiore Cabernet DOC

Morassutti Giovanni Paolo, Lison-Pramaggiore Merlot DOC

* Nascig V. di Angelo Nascig, Colli Orientali del Friuli
Cabernet Sauvignon DOC

* Nascig V. di Angelo Nascig, Colli Orientali del Friuli Merlot
DOC

Negroni Bruno, Colli Bolognesi Cabernet Sauvignon DOC

Orlandi, Cabernet Sauvignon del Veneto

Osvaldo, Lison-Pramaggiore Cabernet DOC

Pasini Volpe, Zuc Volpe Colli Orientali del Friuli Merlot
DOC

Pedrotti, Trentino Cabernet DOC

Pighin F.lli, Grave del Friuli Cabernet DOC

Pighin F.lli, Grave del Friuli Merlot DOC

Pisoni, Trentino Cabernet DOC

Plozner, Grave del Friuli Merlot DOC

Pra di Pradis di Franco Furlan, Collio Cabernet DOC

Pradio, Tre Pigne Grave del Friuli Cabernet Franc DOC

* Rechsteiner, Piave Cabernet DOC

Rino Raffaelli, Trentino Cabernet DOC
Rocca Mürer, Trentino Cabernet Sauvignon DOC
Rodero, Colli Orientali del Friuli Cabernet Franc DOC
Roncade, Piave Cabernet DOC
Russolo I Legni, Lison-Pramaggiore Merlot DOC
Salvetta F.lli, Trentino Cabernet DOC
Sant'Elmo (Luxardo de' Franchi del Venda), Colli Eugànei Cabernet DOC
Santa Margherita, Lison-Pramaggiore Cabernet Sauvignon DOC
Santa Margherita, Lison-Pramaggiore Merlot DOC
Santa Rosa, Colli Bolognesi Cabernet Sauvignon DOC
Santico di Santi, Trentino Cabernet Sauvignon DOC
Scarpa Afra e Tobia, Cabernet del Veneto
Scarpa Afra e Tobia, Merlot del Veneto
* Schiopetto Mario, Collio Cabernet Franc DOC
* Schiopetto Mario, Collio Merlot DOC
Schloss Schwanburg, Alto Adige Cabernet DOC
Schloss Turmhof di Tiefenbrunner, Alto Adige Cabernet DOC
Scolaris Giovanni, Collio Merlot DOC
* Silvestrini, Piave Cabernet DOC
Simoncelli Armando, Trentino Cabernet DOC
SO.VI.VE. (Società Vini Veneti), Piave Merlot DOC
* Specogna Leonardo, Colli Orientali del Friuli Cabernet Sauvignon DOC
* Specogna Leonardo, Colli Orientali del Friuli Merlot DOC
Stepski Doliva, Piave Cabernet DOC
Tenuta Agricola di Lison, Lison-Pramaggiore Cabernet DOC
Tenuta Agricola di Lison, Lison-Pramaggiore Merlot DOC
Tenuta Agricola "La Fattoria" Gli Abbazia Benedettina di Summaga, Lison-Pramaggiore Merlot DOC
Tenuta Castello, Valcalèpio Rosso DOC
Tenuta Castello, Valcalèpio Rosso DOC Colle Calvario
Tenuta San Leonardo, Trentino Cabernet DOC
Tenuta San Leonardo, Trentino Merlot DOC
Tenuta Sant'Anna, Lison-Pramaggiore Cabernet DOC
Tenuta Sant'Anna, Lison-Pramaggiore Merlot DOC
Torresella, Lison-Pramaggiore Cabernet DOC
Torresella, Lison-Pramaggiore Merlot DOC
Vallarom, Trentino Cabernet DOC Casetta
Valliana Enrico, Colli Bolognesi Cabernet Sauvignon DOC
Venegazzù di Azienda Agricola Loredan Gasparini, Montello e Colli Asolani Cabernet Sauvignon DOC
Vescovo Gianni, Isonzo Cabernet Franc DOC
Villa Belvedere di Taddei Colli Orientali del Friuli Cabernet Franc DOC
Villa Belvedere di Taddei, Colli Orientali del Friuli Merlot DOC
Villa Ronche, Grave del Friuli Cabernet Franc DOC
Villa Ronche, Grave del Friuli Merlot DOC
Villa San Giovanni (Marco Felluga), Collio Cabernet DOC
Zamò Tullio di Ipplis, Colli Orientali del Friuli Merlot DOC

* Especially recommended

Other Noble Red Wines and Producers Rated

***

Ai Suma (Bologna Giacomo) Barbera d'Asti DOC (in barrique)
— Amanda, Primitivo di Manduria DOC 21°
— Amanda, Primitivo di Manduria DOC 22°
— Amanda, Rosso di Sava 21°
— Amanda, Rosso di Sava 22°
Bologna Giacomo, Ai Suma Barbera d'Asti DOC (in barrique)
Bologna Giacomo, Bricco dell'Uccellone (barbera in barrique)
Bricco dell'Uccellone (Bologna Giacomo) (barbera in barrique)
Bricco Marun (Correggia Matteo), Barbera d'Alba DOC (in barrique)
Cascinacastlèt di Maria Borio, Passum
Correggia Matteo, Barbera d'Alba DOC (in barrique) Del Bricco Marun
Passum (Cascina Castlet di Maria Borio)
Ronchi di Cialla, Schioppettino
— Rosso di Sava 21° (Amanda)
— Rosso di Sava 22° (Amanda)
Schioppettino vino da tavola (the best ones)

**

Abbazzia di Valle Chiara, Torre Albarola
— Alfeo di La Stoppa, Pinot Nero
Alto Adige Lagrein DOC (the best ones)
Amanda, Rosso di Sava
Amanda, Primitivo di Manduria DOC
Bertelli A., Barbera d'Asti (in barrique) Giarone
Bologna Giacomo, Bricco della Bigotta (barbera in barrique)
Bricco della Bigotta (Bologna Giacomo) (barbera in barrique)
— Brigl Josef, Alto Adige Pinot Nero DOC Kreuzbichler
Ca' del Bosco, Pinero
Cantine Bava, "Stradivarius" Barbera d'Asti DOC (in barrique)
Cantine Duca d'Asti di Chiarlo Michele, Barbera d'Asti DOC (in barrique) Valle del Sole
+ Cascina Castlet di Maria Borio, Barbera d'Asti Superiore DOC (in barrique) Vigna Policalpo
Castel Cosa di Franco Furlan, Schioppettino
Castello di Neive, Barbera (in barrique) Rocca del Mattarello
Chambave Rouge (Ezio Voyat)
Conterno Aldo, Barbera d'Alba DOC (in barrique)
+ Coppo Luigi, Barbera d'Asti DOC (in barrique) Pomorosso
+ Creme du Vien de Nus (Don Augusto Pramotton)
+ Dorigo Girolamo, Montsclapade Schioppettino
Duca di Salaparuta, Duca Enrico
Duca Enrico (Duca di Salaparuta)
Franco Furlan, Castel Cosa Schioppettino
Franconia vino da tavola (the best ones)
Gaja, Barbera d'Alba DOC (in barrique) Vignarey
Giarone di A. Bertelli, Barbera d'Asti DOC in barrique
Grasso Elio, Martina Barbera (in barrique)
— Hofstatter J., Alto Adige Pinot Nero Riserva DOC Barthenau
— La Stoppa, Alfeo Pinot Nero
Martina di Elio Grasso, Barbera in barrique

Maurizio Zanella di Ca' del Bosco, Pinot Nero
Monsupello, Podere 'La Borla
+ Montsclapade di Girolamo Dorigo, Schioppettino
+ Pignolo *vino da tavola* (the best ones)
Pinero (Ca' del Bosco)
Podere 'La Borla, Monsupello
+ Pomorosso di Coppo Luigi, Barbera d'Asti DOC (in *barrique*)
Ratti Renato, Villa Pattono
+ Refosco *vino da tavola* (the best ones)
+ Regaleali di Conte Tasca d'Almerita, Rosso del Conte
Rocca del Mattarello di Castello di Neive, Barbera (in *barrique*)
+ Rosso del Conte (Regaleali del Conte Tasca d'Almerita)
Rosso del Rocolo (Pinot) (Villa dal Ferro di Lazzarini)
− Rosso di Sava (Amanda)
Sang des Salasses de Moncenis (Vignoble du Prieure de Montfleury), Pinot Nero
Schioppettino *vino da tavola*
Stradivarius di Cantine Bava, Barbera d'Asti DOC (in *barrique*)
Tazzelenghe *vino da tavola* (the best ones)
Torre Albarola (Abbazzia di Valle Chiara)
Trentino Lagrein DOC (the best ones)
Valle del Sole (Cantine Duca d'Asti di Chiarlo Michele), Barbera d'Asti DOC (in barrique)
+ Vigne dal Leòn di Tullio Zamò, Schioppettino
Vignoble du Prieure de Montfleury, Pinot Nero Sang des Salasses de Moncenis
Villa dal Ferro di Lazzarini, Rosso del Rocolo (Pinot)
Villa Pattono (Renato Ratti)
Voyat Ezio, Chambave Rouge

*

− Altare Elio, Barbera (in *barrique*) Vigna Larigi
Barone Felix Longo (Tenuta Schlosshof), Alto Adige Pinot Nero DOC
Bellavista, Casotte
Bel Colle, Barbera d'Alba DOC (in *barrique*) Vigna Muliasso Le Masche
+ Bellendorf, Alto Adige Pinot Nero DOC
Boscaini, "Nostra Signora" Alto Adige Pinot Nero DOC Vigneti di Montan
+ Brigl Josef, Alto Adige Pinot Nero DOC
Casotte (Bellavista)
Castello di Ama, Pinot Nero Vigna Il Chiuso
Càvit, Trentino Pinot Nero DOC Masso S. Valentino
Corino Giovanni, Barbera (in *barrique*)
Drago (Cascina Drago), Pinot Nero delle Langhe Vigneto di Campo Romano
Giacosa F.lli, "Maria Giovana" Barbera d'Alba DOC (in *barrique*)
+ Grai Giorgio, Alto Adige Pinot Nero DOC
+ Herrnhofer, Alto Adige Pinot Nero DOC
Hofstatter J., Alto Adige Pinot Nero DOC
+ Kehlburg, Alto Adige Pinot Nero DOC
Kellereigenossenschaft Girlan, Alto Adige Pinot Nero DOC
Lageder Alöis, Alto Adige Pinot Nero DOC

Livon, Schioppettino Vigneto Cumini in Corno di Rosazzo
Lungarotti, Pinot Nero
Maria Giovana (F.lli Giacosa), Barbera d'Alba DOC (in *barrique*)
+ Maso Cantanghell, Pinot Nero Riserva Atesino
"Moccagatta" Azienda Agricola, Barbera d'Alba DOC (in *barrique*)
Nero del Tondo (Ruffino), Pinot Nero
Nostra Signora (Boscaini), Alto Adige Pinot Nero DOC Vigneti di Montan
Rocche Costamagna, Rocche delle Rocche Barbera (in *barrique*)
Rocche delle Rocche (Rocche Costamagna), Barbera (in *barrique*)
Ruffino, "Nero del Tondo" Pinot Noir
Scarpa Afra e Tobia, Pinot Nero del Veneto
Scavino Paolo, Barbera *affinato in carati*
Schiopetto Mario, Pinot Nero del Collio
Schloss Schwanburg, Alto Adige Pinot Nero DOC
Tenuta Schlosshof, "Barone Felix Longo" Alto Adige Pinot Nero DOC
Vigna Il Chiuso (Castello di Ama), Pinot Nero
− Vigna Larigi (Elio Altare), Barbera (in *barrique*)

Recommended, Not Rated
* Amilcare Gaudio Azienda Agricola Bricco Mondalino, Barbera d'Asti DOC Vigna Il Bergatino
* Amilcare Gaudio, Barbera del Monferrato DOC
* Banti Erik, Morellino di Scansano DOC
Barone de Cles, Trentino Lagrein DOC
* Bellendorf, Alto Adige Lagrein DOC
Bologna Giacomo, "La Monella" Barbera di Rocchetta Tanaro
Cantine Florio, Tazzelenghe
Castello di Gabiano (Giustiniani Gattaneo, Gabiano DOC)
* Castello di Gabiano (Giustiniani Gattaneo, Gabiano Riserva) DOC
Castello di Neive, Barbera d'Alba DOC
Collavini, Grave del Friuli Refosco DOC
Conte Antonio di Trento, Pignolo
* Conterno Aldo, Barbera d'Alba DOC
* Conterno Giacomo, Barbera d'Alba DOC
Conti Martini, Trentino Lagrein DOC
Danieli Marina, Refosco del Friuli
Dorigo Girolamo, "Montsclapade" Refosco dal Peduncolo Rosso
Dorigo Girolamo, Ronc di Juri Tazzelenghe
Dri Giovanni, Refosco di Ramondolo
Fenocchio Riccardo, Barbera d'Alba DOC Pianpolvere
* Giacosa Bruno, Barbera d'Alba DOC
* Grai Giorgio, Alto Adige Lagrein DOC
* Herrnhofer, Alto Adige Lagrein DOC
Hofstatter Josef, Alto Adige Lagrein DOC
Kaufmann, Alto Adige Lagrein DOC
* Kehlburg, Alto Adige Lagrein DOC
Kellereigenossenschaft Gries, Alto Adige Lagrein DOC Grieser
Klosterkellerei Muri-Gries, Alto Adige Lagrein DOC Grieser
Lageder Alöis, Alto Adige Lagrein DOC Lindenburg

Livon, Refosco Vigneto di Masarotte in Dolegnano
Nascig V. di Angelo Nascig, Refosco dal Peduncolo Rosso
Nascig V. di Angelo Nascig, Refosco Nostrano
Nascig V. di Angelo Nascig, Franconia
Pasini Volpe, Zuc Volpe Colli Orientali del Friuli Refosco DOC
Prunotto, Barbera d'Alba DOC
Rinaldi Giuseppe, Barbera d'Alba DOC
Ronchi di Cialla, Refosco di Cialla

Santa Margherita, Alto Adige Lagrein DOC
Schloss Schwanburg, Alto Adige Lagrein DOC
* Schlosskellerei Turmhof, Alto Adige Lagrein DOC
   Schmalz
Specogna Leonardo, Colli Orientali del Friuli Refosco DOC
* Vietti, Barbera d'Alba DOC
Villa Belvedere di Taddei, Colli Orientali del Friuli Refosco DOC

* Especially recommended

APPENDIX B

THE WINES RATED BY PRODUCER

> ### WHAT THE RATINGS MEAN
>
> ******** Great, superb, truly noble
> ******* Exceptionally fine
> ****** Very good
> ***** A good example of its type, somewhat above average
> **0** Acceptable to mediocre, depending on the context; drinkable
> **+** Somewhat better than the star category it is put in
> **−** Somewhat less than the star category it is put in, except for zero where it indicates a wine or producer-wine combination that is badly made or worse
>
> *especially recommended (esp rec).* Not rated in the book, but they produce an excellent example of this wine
>
> *recommended (rec).* Not rated in the book, but they produce a very good example of this wine

Abbazia di Rosazzo
** + Ronco dei Roseti

Abbazia di Valle Chiara
** Torre Albarola

Abbona Marziano
0 Barolo DOCG

Accademia Torregiorgi
* Barbaresco DOCG
** Barolo DOCG

Accomasso Giacomo
** + Barolo DOCG

Accomasso Giovanni
** + Barolo DOCG
* + Nebbiolo delle Langhe

Accornero Flavio
0 Barolo DOCG
* − Barbaresco DOCG

Agricoltori del Chianti Geografico or Geografico
* − Brunello di Montalcino DOCG
* Castello di Fagnano, Chianti Classico DOCG
* Chianti Classico DOCG
* "Contessa di Radda" Chianti Classico DOCG
* + Predicato di Bitùrica
* Tenuta Montegiacchi, Chianti Classico DOCG

Aldegheri
0 Recioto della Valpolicella Armarone DOC
* "Santambrogio" Recioto della Valpolicella Amarone DOC

Aleramici
0 Barolo DOCG

Alessandria F.lli di G. Battista Alessandria
0 + Barolo DOCG

Allegrini
*** +   La Poja
*** +   Recioto Bianco Fiorgardane Vigna Campogardane
***   Recioto della Valpolicella Amarone DOC
**** −   Recioto della Valpolicella Amarone DOC Fieramonte
** +   Recioto della Valpolicella DOC
*** +   Recioto della Valpolicella DOC Gardane
***   Valpolicella Classico DOC Lena
***   Valpolicella Classico Superiore DOC
**** −   Valpolicella Classico Superiore DOC La Grola
***   Valpolicella Classico Superiore DOC Palazzo della
          Torre

Altare Elio
**   Barolo DOCG
*   Vigna Arborina
* −   Vigna Larigi, Barbera (in *barrique*)

Altesino, Casa del Cerro, or **Dei Roseti**
***   Altesino, Alte d'Altesi
****   Altesino, Brunello di Montalcino DOCG
**   Altesino, Cabernet Sauvignon
***   Altesino, Palazzo Altesi
** +   Altesino, Rosso di Montalcino DOC
* +   Casa del Cerro, Brunello di Montalcino DOCG
** −   Dei Roseti, Bel Convento
** +   Dei Roseti, Brunello di Montalcino DOCG

Amanda (Vittorio Librale)
**   Primitivo di Manduria DOC
*** −   Primitivo di Manduria DOC 21°
*** −   Primitivo di Manduria DOC 22°
**   Rosso di Sava
*** −   Rosso di Sava 21°
*** −   Rosso di Sava 22°

Ambra, see **Beni di Batasiolo**

Amilcare Gaudio Azienda Agricola Bricco Mondalino
esp rec   Barbera d'Asti DOC Vigna Il Bergatino
esp rec   Barbera del Monferrato DOC

Ancilli
*   Vino Nobile di Montepulciano DOCG

Angoris
rec   Isonzo Cabernet DOC Riserva Castello

Anselmi Roberto
** +   Realda
esp rec   Recioto di Soave DOC Dei Capitelli

Antiche Fattorie Fiorentine
* +   "Salcetino" Chianti Classico DOCG

Anitche Terre de' Ricci
**   Terricci

Antichi Vigneti di Cantalupo
* −   Agamium
*   Ghemme DOC
** +   Ghemme DOC Collis Breclemae
** +   Ghemme DOC Collis Carelle

Antico Castello di Poppiano
0   Tegolato

Antinori, see **Marchesi L. e P. Antinori**

Antonello
*   Montepulciano d'Abruzzo DOC Citra

Antoniolo Mario
***   Gattinara DOC
** −   Santa Chiara Spanna del Piemonte

Antonutti
rec   Grave del Friuli Cabernet DOC

Argiano
*   Brunello di Montalcino DOCG

Arrigo Orlando
*   Barbaresco DOCG

Ascheri Giacomo
0   Barbaresco DOCG
*   Barolo DOCG
*   Nebbiolo d'Alba DOC Bricco S. Giacomo
*   Roero DOC

Asteggiano Vincenzo
* +   Barolo DOCG

Attems
rec   Collio Merlot DOC Ronco Arcivesco

Avignonesi
**   Cabernet Sauvignon
* +   Chianti Colli Senesi DOCG
***   Grifi
**   Merlot
***   Vino Nobile di Montepulciano DOCG

Avondo
0   Spanna del Piemonte

Azelia, see also **Scavino Alfonso**
** −   Barolo DOCG

Baccio da Gaiuole Azienda Agricola di Gittori
**   Chianti Classico DOCG

Badia a Coltibuono
rec   "Cetamura" Chianti
**+   Chianti Classico DOCG
***+   Chianti Classico Riserva DOCG
**−   Coltibuono Rosso
****   Sangioveto di Coltibuono

Balbiano
**   Gattinara DOC

Balbo Marino
0   Barbaresco DOCG

Banear
rec   Grave del Friuli Merlot DOC

Banti Erik
esp rec   Morellino di Scansano DOC

Baracco di Baracho
0   Barolo DOCG

Baracco F.lli
**+   Nebbiolo d'Alba DOC San Vincenzo di Monteu Roero

Barale F.lli
***−   Barbaresco DOCG
***   Barolo DOCG Castellero

Barberini
0   Chianti Classico DOCG
0   Recioto della Valpolicella Amarone DOC

Barfede-Certaldo
*   "Cerbaiola" Chianti Classico DOCG
*   "Signoria" Chianti Classico DOCG

Barone Ciani Bassetti
**   Castello di Roncade
rec   Roncade, Piave Cabernet DOC

Barone Cornacchia
**   Montepulciano d'Abruzzo DOC

Barone de Cles
rec   Trentino Cabernet DOC
rec   Trentino Lagrein DOC

Barone Fini
*   Cabernello
rec   Trentino Cabernet DOC

Barone Neri del Nero, Castel Pietraio
**   Chianti Colli Senesi DOCG

Barra Guido
**−   Gattinara DOC
*   Spanna del Piemonte

Bartali Alberto
*   Chianti Classico DOCG

Bartali Casa Vinicola
*   Chianti Classico DOCG

Bauernkellerei
rec   Alto Adige Cabernet DOC

Bel Colle
0   Barbaresco DOCG
*   Barbera d'Alba DOC (in *barrique*) Vigna Muliasso Le Masche
**   Barolo DOCG Monvigliero
**+   Barolo DOCG Vigneti Verduno
*   Nebbiolo delle Langhe Monvijè

Bellavista
*   Casotte
*+   Solesine

Bellendorf, see **Grai Giorgio**

Beni di Batasiolo, Ambra, Dogliani F.lli, or Kiola
0   Ambra, Barolo DOCG
0   Beni di Batasiolo, Barbaresco DOCG
0   Beni di Batasiolo, Barolo DOCG
0+   Beni di Batasiolo, Barolo DOCG Bonfani
*   Beni di Batasiolo, Barolo DOCG Boscareto
0   Dogliani F.lli, Barbaresco DOCG
0   Dogliani F.lli, Barolo DOCG
*−   Dogliani F.lli, Barolo DOCG crus
0−   Kiola, Barbaresco DOCG
0   Kiola, Barola DOCG
0   Kiola, Gattinara DOC

Berardenga, see **Fattoria di Felsina**

Bergadano Enrico
**+   Barolo DOCG

Bergamasca Coop.
rec   Merlot
rec   Valcalèpio Rosso DOC

Bergamini
*   Recioto della Valpolicella DOC

Berin Fabio
rec   Collio Cabernet Franc DOC

Bersano
0   Barbaresco DOCG
*   Barolo DOCG

Bertani
**   "Catullo" *ripasso vino da tavola* del Veronese
***   Recioto della Valpolicella Amarone Classico Superiore
         DOC
**   Recioto di Valpolicella-Valpantena Spumante DOC
***   "Secco-Bertani" Valpolicella-Valpantena DOC

Bertelli Alberto
**   Barbera d'Asti (in *barrique*) Giarone
**   I Fossaretti, Cabernet Sauvignon

Bertole Ing. Salvatore
*   Gattinara DOC

Bertolo F.lli
**   Gattinara DOC

Bettini F.lli
*   Grumello DOC
*   Inferno DOC
*   Sassella DOC
*   Valgella DOC

Bianchi Giuseppe
**   Fara DOC
*   Fogarin
*   Ghemme DOC
**   Sizzano DOC
* –   Valfrè

Bianco Luigi
*   Barbaresco DOCG

Bianco Mauro, see **Cascina Morassino di Bianco Mauro**

Bianco Michelangelo di F.lli Bianco
0+   Barolo DOCG

Bigi Luigi
0   Vino Nobile di Montepulciano DOCG

Bindella Rudolf
**   Vino Nobile di Montepulciano DOCG

Biondi-Santi, Fattoria Il Greppo
****   Brunello di Montalcino DOCG
rec   Chianti Colli Senesi DOCG

Boffa Carlo
* +   Barbaresco DOCG

Bolla Fratelli
*   Creso
** –   Recioto della Valpolicella Amarone DOC
*   Valpolicella Classico DOC
** –   Valpolicella Classico DOC Jago

Bollini
rec   Grave del Friuli Cabernet Sauvignon DOC

Bologna Buonsignori
****   Vino Nobile di Montepulciano DOCG

Bologna Giacomo
***   Ai Suma, Barbera d'Asti DOC (in *barrique*)
***   Bricco dell'Uccellone (Barbera in *barrique*)
**   Bricco della Bigotta (Barbera in *barrique*)
esp rec "La Monella" Barbera di Rocchetta Tanaro

Boncompagni Ludovisi Principe di Venosa
*** –   Fiorano Rosso

Bonechi Giampaolo
0   Granvino di Montemaggio

Bonfante e Chiarle in Bazzana di Momburuzzo
0   Barolo DOCG

Bordini
0   Vino Nobile di Montepulciano DOCG

Bordino Franco
**   Barbaresco DOCG

Borgo Cav. Ercolo
0   Gattinara DOC
0   Ghemme DOC
0   Spanna del Piemonte

Borgo Conventi
**   Braida Nuova
*   Collio Merlot DOC

Borgogno Aldo
*   Barolo DOCG

Borgogno Cav. Bartolomeo
* +   Barolo DOCG

Borgogno F.lli Serio e Battista
*   Barbaresco DOCG
*   Barolo DOCG
**   Barolo DOCG Cannubi

Borgogno Giacomo
* +   Barbaresco DOCG
** –   Barolo DOCG

Borgogno Ludovico, see **Cascina Borgognot**

Borgogno Wanda Pepino
0   Barolo DOCG

Bosca Luigi
0   Barbaresco DOCG
0   Barolo DOCG

Boscaini
*   "Nostra Signora" Alto Adige Pinot Nero DOC
             Vigneti di Montan
***   Recioto della Valpolicella Amarone DOC Ca' de'Loi
***   Recioto della Valpolicella Amarone DOC Vigneti di
             Marano
** +   Santo Stefano *ripasso vino da tavola* del Veronese
** +   Valpolicella Classico Superiore DOC Marano

Boschis Francesco
0   Barolo DOCG

Bosco Nestore
*   Montepulciano d'Abruzzo DOC

Botte
rec   Aglianico del Vulture DOC

Bottina Davide
*   Montepulciano d'Abruzzo DOC Notaresco

Bovio Gianfranco
** +   Barolo DOCG

Brero Cav. Luigi
0   Barbaresco DOCG
0   Barolo DOCG

Brezza
0 +   Barolo DOCG
**   Barolo DOCG Cannubi
**   Barolo DOCG Castellero
** +   Barolo DOCG Sarmassa

"Bricco Asili" Azienda Agricola, see **Ceretto Casa Vinicola**

"Bricco Boschis" Azienda Agricola di F.lli Cavallotto
** +   Barolo DOCG

"Bricco Rocche" Azienda Agricola, see **Ceretto Casa Vinicola**

Brigaldara
**   Recioto della Valpolicella Amarone DOC
**   Valpolicella Classico Superiore DOC Il Vegro

Brigatti Luciano
**   Möt Ziflon

Brigl Josef
* +   Alto Adige Pinot Nero DOC
** −   Alto Adige Pinot Nero DOC Kreuzbichler

Brolio or **Ricasoli**
* +   Brolio, Chianti Classico DOCG
**   Brolio, Chianti Classico DOCG Riserva del Barone
* +   Brolio, Chianti Classico Riserva DOCG
0   Ricasoli, Chianti Classico DOCG
0   Ricasoli, Chianti DOCG

Brovia F.lli
*   Barberesco DOCG
** +   Barolo DOCG

Brugo Agostino
*   Gattinara DOC
*   Ghemme DOC
*   Romagnano Sesia
*   Spanna del Piemonte
*   Spanna del Piemonte Riserva Cantina dei Santi

Brunori Ruggero
** −   Le Sincette Rosso

Bruzzone
0   Barbaresco DOCG

Bucci
**   Pongelli

Buracchi
*   Vino Nobile di Montepulciano DOCG

Burati
0   Recioto della Valpolicella Amarone DOC

Burlotto
** −   Barolo DOCG

Burlotto Andrea
**   Barolo DOCG Massara

Burlotto Comm. G. B. & Cav. Francesco (Marina Burlotto)
* −   Barolo DOCG

Ca' Bolani
rec   Aquileia Merlot DOC

Ca' Bruzzo
rec   Colli Bèrici Cabernet DOC

Cabutto Bartolomeo
0   Barbaresco DOCG
* −   Tenuta La Volta, Barolo DOCG

Ca' del Bosco
***   Maurizio Zanella
**   Pinero
rec   Franciacorta Rosso DOC

Caldi Ditta Cav. Luigi
*   Gattinara DOC
*   Spanna del Piemonte

Caligaris Guido
* −   Gattinara DOC

Calissano Luigi
* −   Barbaresco DOCG
*   Barolo DOCG

Ca' Loredan Gasparini or **Venegazzu di Azienda Agricola**
** +   Venegazzù Riserva della Casa black label
** −   Venegazzù Riserva della Casa white label
rec   Montello e Colli Asolani Cabernet Sauvignon

Camerano G.
0 +   Barolo DOCG

Ca' Merla
0 +   Recioto della Valpolicella Amarone DOC

Camigliano Agricola or **Castello di Camigliano,** also see **Fontevino**
0   Agricola Camigliano, Brunello di Montalcino DOCG
0 +   Castello di Camigliano, Brunello di Montalcino DOCG
0   Chianti Colli Senesi DOCG
* +   Vigna di Fontevecchia

Campogiovanni
*   Brunello di Montalcino DOCG
*   Rosso di Montalcino DOC

Canale Aldo
**   Barolo DOCG

Canalicchio di Sopra (Lambardi Maurizio)
**   Brunello di Montalcino DOCG

Canalicchio di Sopra (Pacenti Franco e Rosildo)
**   Brunello di Montalcino DOCG

Canalicchio di Sopra (Primo Pacenti & Pier Luigi Ripaccioli)
** −   Brunello di Montalcino DOCG
** −   Le Gode di Montosoli, Brunello di Montalcino DOCG

Canalicchio (Lambardi Silvano)
**   Brunello di Montalcino DOCG

Canneto
** −   Vino Nobile di Montepulciano DOCG

Canneto di Sotto
** −   Vino Nobile di Montepulciano DOCG

Cantina Colavolpe
0   Barbaresco DOCG
0 +   Barolo DOCG

Cantina Coop. della Riforma Fondiaria di Venosa
rec   Aglianico del Vulture DOC

Cantina Coop. Rosso della Maremma Toscana
0   Montepescali

Cantina del Friuli Centrale "La Bora"
rec   Grave del Friuli Cabernet DOC
rec   Grave del Friuli Merlot DOC

Cantina del Glicine
***   Barbaresco DOCG
**   Glicinerosso

Cantina del Redi
0 −   Vino Nobile di Montepulciano DOCG

Cantina del Taburino
rec   Aglianico del Taburno DOC

Cantina Gattavecchi
*   Vino Nobile di Montepulciano DOCG

Cantina Mascarello, see **Mascarello Bartolo**

Cantina Santavenere (Massimo Romeo)
*   Vino Nobile di Montepulciano DOCG

Cantina Sociale Cooperativa di Gattinara
0   Gattinara DOC

Cantina Sociale dei "Colli Novaresi"
*   Barengo Rosso
*   Caramino
*   Fara DOC
*   Spanna del Piemonte

Cantina Sociale di Sizzano e Ghemme
*   Ghemme DOC
**   Sizzano DOC
*   Spanna del Piemonte

Cantina Sociale "Madonna dei Miracoli"
* −   Montepulciano d'Abruzzo DOC

Cantina Sociale Ponte
rec   Piave Cabernet Sauvignon DOC
rec   Piave Merlot DOC

Cantina Sociale Tollo
*   Montepulciano d'Abruzzo DOC
* −   Montepulciano d'Abruzzo DOC Colle Secco
* +   Montepulciano d'Abruzzo DOC Rubino
* +   Montepulciano d'Abruzzo DOC Valle d'Oro

Cantina Spagnolli
*   Tebro

Cantina Vignaioli "Elvio Pertinace"
*   Barbaresco DOCG

Cantina Zaccagnini
** +   "Dal Tralcetto" Montepulciano d'Abruzzo DOC

Cantine Baiocchi (Sai Agricola)
* +   Chianti Colli Senesi DOCG
***   Vino Nobile di Montepulciano DOCG

Cantine Barbero
0   "Conte de Cavour" Barbaresco DOCG

Cantine Bava
0   Barbaresco DOCG
0 +   Barolo DOCG
0 +   Gattinara DOC
**   "Stradivarius" Barbera d'Asti DOC (in *barrique*)

Cantine Cà Bianca
*   Barbaresco DOCG
*   Tenuta Denegri, Barolo DOCG
*   Tenuta Denegri, Nebbiolo d'Alba DOC

Cantine d'Invecchiamento
0   "La Brenta d'Oro" Barbaresco DOCG
0   "La Brenta d'Oro" Barolo DOCG

Cantine Duca d'Asti di Chiarlo Michele
**   Barbaresco DOCG Rabajà
**   Barbera d'Asti DOC (in *barrique*) Valle del Sole
**   Barilot
**   Barolo DOCG Brunate
** −   Barolo DOCG Bussia
**   Barolo DOCG Cerequio
** +   Barolo DOCG Rocche
**   Barolo DOCG Vigna Rionda
*   "Granduca" Barbaresco DOCG
*   "Granduca" Barolo DOCG

Cantine Florio (Tenuta Maseri Florio)
rec   Colli Orientali del Friuli Cabernet DOC
rec   Colli Orientali del Friuli Merlot DOC
rec   Tazzelenghe

Cantine Francoli
*   Spanna del Piemonte

Cantine Le Ginestre
*   Barolo DOCG

Cantine Mauro Vini (Osvaldo Mauro)
0   Barbaresco DOCG
0   Barolo DOCG

Cantine Petternella
**   Quarto Vecchio

Capanna (Cencioni Giuseppe Ben. Fra.)
** −   Brunello di Montalcino DOCG
*   Rosso di Montalcino DOC

Capanna di Fattoi e Minocci
*   "Fattoi" Brunello di Montalcino DOCG

Capanna di S. Restituta (Fattoi Ofelio)
** −   Brunello di Montalcino DOCG

Capannelle (Raffaele Rossetti)
***   Barrique
***   Chianti Classico DOCG
***   Riserva
***   Rosso

Cappellano or **Cappellano Dott. Giuseppe**
** −   Barbaresco DOCG
** +   Barolo DOCG Carpegna
** +   Barolo DOCG Gabutti
** −   Nebbiolo d'Alba DOC

Cappelli Giovanni
**   Brunesco di San Lorenzo
***   Fattoria di Montagliari, Chianti Classico Riserva DOCG
*** +   Fattoria di Montagliari, Chianti Classico Riserva DOCG Vigna Casaloste
***   Fattoria di Montagliari e Castellinuzza, Chianti Classico Riserva DOCG
*   "La Quercia" Chianti Classico DOCG

Caprili (Bartolomei Alfo)
**   Brunello di Montalcino DOCG

Carletti or **Carletti della Giovampaola**, see **Polizano**

Carnevale Giorgio
0   Barolo DOCG

Carobbio
*   Chianti Classico DOCG

Ca' Romè di Romano Marengo
*   Barbaresco
0   Barolo DOCG

Ca' Ronesca
rec   Collio Cabernet Franc DOC
rec   Collio Merlot DOC

Carpineto Casa Vinicola
*   Chianti Classico DOCG
0   Vino Nobile di Montepulciano DOCG

Carra
0   Barbaresco DOCG

Casa del Cerro, see **Altesino**

Casa Francesco
*   Chianti Classico DOCG

Casale Azienda Agricola (Falchini)
**   Cabernet Sauvignon

Casal Thaulero
*   Montepulciano d'Abruzzo DOC

Casanova di Neri
** –   Brunello di Montalcino DOCG

Casanuova di Nittardi, see **Fattoria Nittardi**

Casarsa Coop. "La Delezia"
rec   Grave del Friuli Cabernet DOC
rec   Grave del Friuli Cabernet Sauvignon DOC
rec   Grave del Friuli Merlot DOC

Casa Sola
0   Chianti Classico DOCG

Casavecchia di Nittardi
* –   Chianti Classico DOCG

Cascina Adelaide di G. Terzano
** –   Barolo DOCG

Cascina Ballarin di Viberti Luigi
**   Barolo DOCG

Cascina Borgognot di Borgogno Ludovico
*   Barolo DOCG

Cascina Bruni di Veglio F.lli
** –   Barolo DOCG

Cascina Bruni di Veglio Pasqual
*   Barolo DOCG

Cascina Castlet di Maria Borio
** +   Barbera d'Asti Superiore DOC (in *barrique*) Vigna
          Policalpo
***   Passum

Cascina Chiabotto di Traversa Giuseppe
*   Barbaresco DOCG

Cascina Drago
**   Bricco del Drago
*   Pinot Nero delle Langhe Vigneto di Campo Romano

Cascina Gustavo di Revello Renato
**   Barolo DOCG

Cascina La Rocca di Molino Franco
*   Barolo DOCG

Cascina Morassino di Bianco Mauro
** –   Barbaresco DOCG

Cascina Nando di Principiano Ferdinando
*   Barolo DOCG

Cascina Principe di Ottavia Lesquio
*   Barbaresco DOCG

Cascina Rombone, see **Nada Fiorenzo**

Case Basse
**** – Brunello di Montalcino DOCG
**   Instistietti

Casetta F.lli (Ernesto Casetta)
*   Barbaresco DOCG
* +   Barolo DOCG

Castagna
0   Recioto della Valpolicella Amarone DOC

Castaldi Giuseppe
**   Fara DOC

Castelgiocondo
** –   Brunello di Montalcino DOCG
**   Rosso di Montalcino DOC

Castelgreve (Castelli del Grevepesa)
*   Chianti Classico DOCG
0 +   Chianti Classico DOCG Monte Firidolfi
*   Chianti Classico DOCG Panzano

Castell'in Villa
** +   Chianti Classico DOCG
**   Santa Croce

Castellare
** –   Chianti Classico DOCG
** +   Chianti Classico Riserva DOCG
***   Coniale
** +   I Sodi San Niccolò

Castelli del Grevepesa Soc. Coop., see "**Castelgreve**"

Castelli Martinozzi
* +   Brunello di Montalcino DOCG

Castello Banfi or **Villa Banfi**
**   Brunello di Montalcino DOCG
** +   Brunello di Montalcino Riserva DOCG Poggio all'Oro
**   Chianti Classico DOCG
** −   Tavernelle Cabernet Sauvignon
** −   Villa Banfi, Brunello di Montalcino DOCG

Castello d'Albola or **Fattoria di Albola**
* +   Acciaiolo
*   Chianti Classico DOCG

Castello d'Annone, "Viarengo"
*   Barbaresco DOCG
*   Barolo DOCG

Castello dei Rampolla
** +   Chianti Classico DOCG
***   Sammarco

Castello del Trebbio
*   Chianti Colli Fiorentini DOCG

Castello della Paneretta
*   Chianti Classico DOCG

Castello di Ama
** −   Chianti Classico DOCG
**   Chianti Classico DOCG Vigneto Bellavista
** −   Chianti Classico DOCG Vigneto Bertinga
** +   Chianti Classico DOCG Vigneto La Casuccia
** +   Chianti Classico DOCG Vigneto S. Lorenzo
*   Vigna Il Chiuso (Pinot Noir)
** +   Vigna L'Apparita (Merlot)

Castello di Cacchiano, Castello di Montegrossi, or **Rocca di Montegrossi**
**   Castello di Cacchiano, Chianti Classico DOCG
** +   Castello di Cacchiano, Chianti Classico Riserva DOCG Millennio
*   Castello di Cacchiano RF Selice
* +   Castello di Montegrossi, Chianti Classico DOCG
**   Castello di Montegrossi, Geremia
*   Rocca di Montegrossi, Chianti Classico DOCG
**   Rocca di Montegrossi, Chianti Classico Riserva DOCG
** −   Rocca di Montegrossi Rosso

Castello di Camigliano, see **Camigliano Agricola**

Castello di Castelvari
* −   Chianti Classico DOCG

Castello di Cerreto
* +   Chianti Classico DOCG

Castello di Fonterutoli
*   Chianti Classico DOCG
* +   Chianti Classico Riserva DOCG Ser Lapo
* +   Concerto

Castello di Gabbiano or **Gabbiano**
*   Ania
*   Chianti Classico Riserva DOCG
* +   Gabbiano, Chianti Classico DOCG
0   Il Cavaliere
** +   R & R

Castello di Gabiano (Giustiniani Gattaneo)
rec   Gabiano DOC
esp rec   Gabiano Riserva DOC

Castello di Luiano or **Fattoria di Luiano**
*   Chianti Classico DOCG
* −   Vigna Pianacci

Castello di Meleto
0   Chianti Classico DOCG

Castello di Monsanto Fabrizio Bianchi, see **Fattoria Monsanto**

Castello di Monte Antico
**   Monte Antico

Castello di Montegrossi, see **Castello di Cacchiano**

Castello di Monterinaldi
0   Chianti Classico DOCG

Castello di Mugnana
*   Chianti Classico DOCG

Castello di Neive
****   Barbaresco DOCG
**   Barbera (in *barrique*) Rocca del Mattarello
rec   Barbera d'Alba DOC

Castello di Nipozzano, see **Frescobaldi**

Castello di Poppiano
0   Tegolato

Castello di Querceto
**   Chianti Classico DOCG
** +   La Corte
** −   Predicato di Bitùrica Il Querciolaia

Castello di Radda
0   Chianti Classico DOCG

Castello di Rencine
0   Chianti Classico DOCG

Castello di Roncade, see **Barone Ciani Bassetti**

Castello di Salabue di Carlo Nob. Cassinis
0   Rubello di Salabue

Castello di San Donato in Perano
0   Chianti Classico DOCG

Castello di San Polo in Rosso
*   Castelpolo Chianti Classico DOCG
** +   Cetinaia
**   Chianti Classico DOCG
** +   Chianti Classico Riserva DOCG
**   Torri

Castello di Tizzano
** −   Chianti Classico DOCG

Castello di Uzzano
**   Chianti Classico DOCG
*   Niccolo Da Uzzano

Castello di Verduno (Sorelle Burlotto)
* +   Barolo DOCG

Castello di Verrazzano
* −   Bottiglia Particolare
*   Chianti Classico DOCG
**   Chianti Classico Riserva DOCG
* −   Sassello

Castello di Volpaia
** +   Balifico
*** +   Chianti Classico DOCG
*** +   Coltassala

Castello Feudale
* +   Barbaresco DOCG
*   Barolo DOCG

Castello Guicciardini Poppiano (Conte Ferdinando Guicciardini)
*   Chianti Colli Fiorentini DOC

Castello Turmhof di Tiefenbrunner, Schlosskellerei Turmhof, or **Tiefenbrunner**
rec   Alto Adige Cabernet DOC
rec   Alto Adige Lagrein DOC Schmalz
**   Linticlarius

Castello Vicchiomaggio
** −   Chianti Classico DOCG
**   Chianti Classico DOCG Paola Matta
**   Chianti Classico DOCG San Jacopo

* −   Chianti Classico Riserva DOCG La Lellera
**   Chianti Classico Riserva DOCG Petri
** +   Chianti Classico Riserva DOCG Prima Vigna
** −   Ripa delle More

Castelluccio Azienda Agricola (Gian Matteo Baldi)
** +   Ronco Casone
** +   Ronco dei Ciliegi
** +   Ronco delle Ginestre

Castel Pietraio, see **Barone Neri del Nero**

Castel Ruggero
0   Chianti Classico DOCG

Castiglion del Bosco
** −   Brunello di Montalcino DOCG
0   Rosso di Montalcino DOC

Catignano
**   Chianti Classico DOCG

Catturich Ducco
rec   Franciacorta Rosso DOC

Cauda Cav. Luigi
0 −   Barbaresco DOCG
0 −   Barolo DOCG

Cavaletto
0 −   Barbaresco DOCG

Cavalleri Gian Paolo & Giovanni
rec   Franciacorta Rosso DOC
** +   Tjardino

Cavallotto F.lli, see **"Bricco Boschis" Azienda Agricola**

Càvit
*   Quattro Vicariati
rec   Trentino Cabernet DOC
*   Trentino Pinot Nero DOC Masso S. Valentino
*   Trentino Rosso DOC Brume di Monte

Cecchi Luigi, also see **Villa Cerna**
0   Brunello di Montalcino DOCG
*   Chianti Classico DOCG
**   Chianti Classico DOCG Messer Pietro di Teuzzo
** +   Predicato di Cardisco Spargolo
*   Vino Nobile di Montepulciano DOCG

Celli
*   Chianti Classico DOCG

Cellole
*   Chianti Classico DOCG

Cennatoio
*   Chianti Classico DOCG

Centolani Agricola (Azienda Agricola Friggiali)
0+   Brunello di Montalcino DOCG
*   Tenuta Pietra Focaia, Brunello di Montalcino DOCG

Cepperellaccio
0   Chianti Classico DOCG

Cerbaiola (Giulio Salvioni), see **La Cerbaiola**

Cerbaiona (Molinari Diego)
**−   Brunello di Montalcino DOCG

Ceretto Casa Vinicola, Azienda Agricola "Bricco Asili" and Azienda Agricola "Bricco Roche"
****   Azienda Agricola "Bricco Asili," Barbaresco DOCG Bricco Asili
***−   Azienda Agricola "Bricco Asili," Barbaresco DOCG Faset
****   Azienda Agricola "Bricco Rocche," Barolo DOCG Bricco Rocche
****   Azienda Agricola "Bricco Rocche," Barolo DOCG Brunate
****   Azienda Agricola "Bricco Rocche," Barolo DOCG Prapò
**   Barbaresco DOCG Asij
**+   Barolo DOCG Zonchera
***   Nebbiolo d'Alba DOC Vigneto Bernardine

Cesari
0   Recioto della Valpolicella Amarone DOC

Cesari Umberto
*+   Liano

Ceste Cav. G.
0−   Barolo DOCG

Ciacci Piccolomini d'Aragona
**   Brunello di Montalcino DOCG

Cigliuti F.lli
***−   Barbaresco DOCG

Cirillo-Farrusi Fabrizio
**   Torre Quarto
***   Torre Quarto Riserva

Cispiano
*   Chianti Classico DOCG

Clerico Domenico
**+   Arte
***   Barolo DOCG
**   Nebbiolo delle Langhe

Colacicchi-Anagni
***   Torre Ercolana

Coli
*   Chianti Classico DOCG

Colla Paola, also see **Gagliardo Gianni**
0   Barbaresco DOCG
0   Barolo DOCG

Collavini
rec   Grave del Friuli Cabernet Sauvignon DOC
rec   Grave del Friuli Refosco DOC

Collavinus
rec   Trentino Cabernet DOC

Colle Picchioni (Paola di Mauro)
**+   Vigna del Vassallo

Colli Monfortesi, see **Conterno Fantino**

Colombaio di Montosoli (Nello Baricci)
*   Brunello di Montalcino DOCG

Colombini-Cinelli Francesca, see **Fattoria dei Barbi di Colombini−Cinelli Francesca**

Col Rosazzo
rec   Collio Cabernet DOC

Col Sandago, also see **Orlandi**
**−   Costa delle Pergole Rosso

Coluè di Massimo Oddero or **Tenuta Coluè**
*+   Barbaresco DOCG
*   Barolo DOCG
**   Nebbiolo d'Alba DOC

CO. VI.P. Consorzio Vitivinicolo Perugia
*−   Torgiano Rosso DOC

Comunali (Bartoli-Giusti-Focacci)
**   Brunello di Montalcino DOCG

Conati Marco
*−   Recioto della Valpolicella Amarone DOC

Confratelli di San Michele
*   Barbaresco DOCG

Consorzio Viticoltori Associati del Vulture
rec   Aglianico del Vulture DOC

Conte Antonio di Trento
rec   Pignolo

Conte Da Schio
** —   Costozza Cabernet Frank

Conte de Cavour, see **Cantine Barbero**

Conte Medolaga Albani
rec   Valcalèpio Rosso DOC

Conterno Aldo
esp rec   Barbera d'Alba DOC
**   Barbera d'Alba DOC (in *barrique*)
****   Barolo DOCG Bricco Ciabot
****   Barolo DOCG Bricco Cicala
****   Barolo DOCG Bricco Colonello
***   Barolo DOCG Bussia Soprana
****   Barolo DOCG Granbussia
****   Barolo DOCG Romirasco
**   Il Favot
***   Nebbiolo delle Bussia Conca Tre Pile

Conterno Fantino or **Colli Monfortesi**
** +   Barolo DOCG
*   "Colli Monfortesi" Barolo DOCG
*   Mon Pra
** —   Nebbiolo delle Langhe Ginestrino

Conterno Giacomo (Giovanni Conterno)
*** +   Barbaresco DOCG
esp rec   Barbera d'Alba DOC
*** +   Barolo DOCG Cascina Francia
****   "Monfortino" Barolo DOCG

Conterno Paolo
** —   Barolo DOCG La Ginestra

Conte Ugo Bonacossi, see **Villa di Capezzana**

Conti Attems
rec   Isonzo Cabernet DOC

Conti Bossi Fedregotti
**   Foianeghe Rosso
rec   Trentino Cabernet DOC
rec   Trentino Merlot DOC

Conti Capponi
*   Villa Calcinaia Chianti Classico DOCG

Conti Cav. Ermanno
*   Boca DOC
*   Maggiora

Conti Costanti, Il Colle al Matrichese, or **Costanti Emilio**
**** +   Brunello di Montalcino DOCG
** +   Chianti Colli Senesi DOCG

Conti Formentini
rec   Collio Cabernet Franc DOC
rec   Collio Merlot DOC
* +   Formentini Rosso

Conti Gian Piero
*   Boca DOC

Conti Martini
rec   Trentino Lagrein DOC

Conti Molini
*   Gattinara DOC

Conti Serristori or **Serristori**
*   Brunello di Montalcino DOCG
*   Chianti DOCG
*   Chianti Classico DOCG
** —   Chianti Classico DOCG Villa Primavera
**   Chianti Classico Riserva DOCG
**   Chianti Classico Riserva DOCG Villa Primavera
* +   Ser Niccolò

Contratto Giuseppe
**   Barolo DOCG
**   Barolo DOCG Cà Neire
**   Barolo DOCG Sarmassa
** —   Barbaresco DOCG

Contucci
**   Vino Nobile di Montepulciano DOCG

Convito (A.C.G. Gaiole Coop. Agricola Cellars)
0 +   Chianti Classico DOCG

Coppo Luigi
*   Barbaresco DOCG
*   Barolo DOCG
** +   "Pomorosso" Barbera d'Asti DOC (in *barrique*)

Cordero di Montezemolo
** +   Barolo DOCG Enrico IV-Villero
** +   Barolo DOCG Monfalletto

Corino Giovanni
*   Barbera (in *barrique*)
**   Barolo DOCG

Correggia Matteo
***   Barbera d'Alba DOC (in *barrique*) Del Bricco Marun

Corta Vecchia
0   Recioto della Valpolicella Amarone DOC

Cortese Giuseppe
** +   Barbaresco DOCG

Cossetti Clemente
0   Barbaresco DOCG
0 –   Barolo DOCG
0   Spanna del Piemonte

Costanti Emilio, see **Conti Costanti**

Cottimello (Eredi Fuligni)
**   Brunello di Montalcino DOCG

DA.I.PI. "CM", see **Villadoria**

Dalforno Romano
** +   Recioto della Valpolicella Amarone DOC
***   Valpolicella DOC

Damilano Dott. Giacomo
0   Barbaresco DOCG
* –   Barolo DOCG

D'Angelo Dario
*   Montepulciano d'Abruzzo DOC

D'Angelo F.lli
***   Aglianico del Vulture DOC
***   Canneto

Danieli Marina
*   Colli Orientali del Friuli Cabernet DOC
*   Colli Orientali del Friuli Merlot DOC
** +   Faralta
rec   Refosco del Friuli

D'Attimis Gianfrano
rec   Colli Orientali del Friuli Merlot DOC

De Forville Paolo
*   Barbaresco DOCG

Dei
*** –   Vino Nobile di Montepulciano DOCG

Dei Roseti, see **Altesino**

Dellavalle F.lli
0   Barolo DOCG
0   Gattinara DOC
*   Ghemme DOC
0   Sizzano DOC
0   Spanna del Piemonte

De Lorenzi Paolo
rec   Lison-Pramaggiore Cabernet DOC

Denegri Lorenzo
*   Nebbiolo delle Langhe

Denegri Lorenzo
*   Barolo DOCG

Dessilani Luigi
*   Caramino
*   Fara DOC
*   Gattinara DOC
*   Spanna del Piemonte

Di Virgilio
*   Montepulciano d'Abruzzo DOC Rubino

Dogliani F.lli, see **Beni di Batasiolo**

Don Augusto Pramotton
** +   Creme du Vien de Nus

Dorigati F.lli
*   Grener
rec   Trentino Cabernet DOC

Dorigo Girolamo
esp rec   Colli Orientali del Friuli Cabernet DOC
esp rec   Colli Orientali del Friuli Merlot DOC
**   Montsclapade
rec   Montsclapade, Refosco dal Peduncolo Rosso
** +   Montsclapade, Schioppettino
rec   Ronc di Juri Tazzelenghe

Dosio
* +   Barolo DOCG

Dri Giovanni
*** –   Il Roncat Rosso
rec   Refosco di Ramondolo

Duca Badoglia
rec   Grave del Friuli Cabernet DOC
rec   Grave del Friuli Merlot DOC

Duca di Salaparuta
**   Duca Enrico

Duchi di Castellucchio
* +   Montepulciano d'Abruzzo DOC

Due Torri
* +   Recioto della Valpolicella Amarone DOC

Einaudi Luigi
** +   Barolo DOCG
**   Nebbiolo delle Langhe

Endrizzi F.lli
rec   Trentino Cabernet DOC
rec   Trentino Merlot DOC

Enetum
rec   Piave Cabernet DOC
rec   Piave Merlot DOC

Eno Friulia
rec   Collio Cabernet Franc DOC

Enologica Valtellinese
*   Grumello DOC
*   Inferno DOC
** +   Inferno DOC Riserva della Casa
*   Sassella DOC
**   Sassella Riserva
** +   Sforzato
*   Valgella DOC

Eredi Lodali di Ghione
*   Barbaresco DOCG
*   Barolo DOCG

Eredi Virginia Ferrero
**   Barolo DOCG

Fabiano
0   Recioto della Valpolicella Amarone DOC

Falchini Riccardo (Azienda Agricola Casale)
**   Cabernet Sauvignon
rec   Chianti Colli Senesi DOCG

Fanetti Comm. Adamo e Giuseppe
**   Principesco
**   Vino Nobile di Montepulciano DOCG

Farina F.lli
0   Recioto della Valpolicella Amarone DOC

Farina Remo
*   Recioto della Valpolicella Amarone DOC

Fassati
*   Vino Nobile di Montepulciano DOCG
**   Vino Nobile di Montepulciano DOCG Graccianello
*   Vino Nobile di Montepulciano DOCG Podere Fonte al Vescovo

Fattoria Ambra
** +   Carmignano DOC

Fattoria Barberino
0   Chianti Classico DOCG

Fattoria Bruno Nicodemi
**   Montepulciano d'Abruzzo DOC Colli Venia

Fattoria Campomaggio
* −   Chianti Classico DOCG

Fattoria Casale del Bosco (Nardi Silvio)
*   Brunello di Montalcino DOCG

Fattoria Casanuova di Nittardi
*   Chianti Classico DOCG

Fattoria Chigi Saracini
rec   Chianti Colli Senesi DOCG

Fattoria Coltiberto
rec   Morellino di Scansano DOC

Fattoria Concadoro
*   Cerasi Chianti Classico DOCG

Fattoria Deapizia
* −   Montepulciano d'Abruzzo DOC

Fattoria dei Barbi di Colombini-Cinelli Francesca
*** + Brunello di Montalcino DOCG
*   Brusco dei Barbi
*   Bruscone dei Barbi
rec   Chianti Colli Senesi DOCG

Fattoria dei Pagliarese
* +   Camerlengo
**   Chianti Classico DOCG
** +   Chianti Classico Riserva DOCG Boscardini

Fattoria del Cerro (Sai Agricola)
* +   Chianti Colli Senesi DOC
***   Vino Nobile di Montepulciano DOCG

Fattoria dell' Aiola
0 +   Chianti Classico DOCG
*   Logaiolo

Fattoria della Talosa or **Fattoria di Fognano**
rec   Chianti Colli Senesi DOCG
**   Fattoria della Talosa, Vino Nobile di Montepulciano DOCG
* +   Fattoria di Fognano, Vino Nobile di Montepulciano DOCG

Fattoria delle Lodoline
0   Chianti Classico DOCG

Fattoria delle Maestrelle (Podere Ferretto)
0   Vino Nobile di Montepulciano DOCG

Fattoria del Pantano or **Il Pantano**
**   Vino Nobile di Montepulciano DOCG pre-1977
0   Vino Nobile di Montepulciano DOCG since the '77

Fattoria di Albola, see **Castello d'Albola**

Fattoria di Artimino
*   Carmignano DOC
** −   Carmignano DOC Riserva del Granduca
*   Carmignano DOC Vino del Granduca
** −   Carmignano Riserva DOC Villa Medicea
*   Chianti Montalbano DOCG

Fattoria di Bacchereto
* +   Carmignano DOC
*   Chianti Montalbano DOCG

Fattoria di Calavria
* +   Carmignano DOC
rec   Chianti Montalbano DOCG

Fattoria di Doccia
0   Chianti Rùfina DOCG

Fattoria Dievole or **Villa Dievole**
*   Chianti Classico DOCG

Fattoria di Felsina, "Berardenga"
**   Chianti Classico DOCG
** +   Chianti Classico Riserva DOCG
** +   Chianti Classico Riserva DOCG Vigneto Rancia
rec   Chianti Colli Senesi DOCG
**   Fontalloro

Fattoria di Fognano, see **Fattoria della Talosa**

Fattoria di Fontodi or **Tenuta Fontodi**
**   Chianti Classico
** +   Chianti Classico Riserva DOCG
** +   Chianti Classico Riserva DOCG Vigna del Sorbo
** +   Flaccianello della Pieve

Fattoria di Gracciano (Dott. Franco Mazzucchelli)
*   Vino Nobile di Montepulciano DOCG

Fattoria di Grignano
*   Chianti Rùfina DOCG

Fattoria di Luiano, see **Castello di Luiano**

Fattoria di Mocenni
* −   Chianti Classico DOCG

Fattoria di Montagliari, see **Cappelli Giovanni**

Fattoria di Paterno
0   Vino Nobile di Montepulciano DOCG

Fattoria di Petrognano
**   Pomino Rosso DOC

Fattoria di Petroio
0   Chianti Classico DOCG
*   Chianti Classico Riserva DOCG

Fattoria di Pietrafita
*   Chianti Colli Senesi DOCG

Fattoria di Selvole
** −   Chianti Classico DOCG

Fattoria di Valiano
* −   Chianti Classico DOCG
*   Cupido

Fattoria di Vetrice
**   Chianti Rùfina DOCG

Fattoria di Vistarenni
*   Chianti Classico DOCG
** −   Chianti Classico DOCG Podere Bertinga
*   Codirosso

Fattoria Fermignano
** −   "Frimaio" Chianti Classico DOCG

Fattoria Giannozzi
rec   Chianti Colli Fiorentini DOCG

Fattoria Il Capitano
**   Chianti Rùfina DOCG

Fattoria Il Corno
*   Chianti Colli Fiorentini DOCG

Fattoria Il Grappolo
* −   Brunello di Montalcino DOCG

Fattoria Il Greppo, see **Biondi-Santi**

Fattoria Illuminati di Dino Illuminati
** −   Montepulciano d'Abruzzo DOC
** −   Montepulciano d'Abruzzo DOC Ripe Rosse
** −   Montepulciano d'Abruzzo DOC Vecchio "Zanna"

Fattoria Il Poggerino
* +   Chianti Classico DOCG

Fattoria Il Poggiolo
*   Chianti Montalbano DOCG

Fattoria La Gerla
*** − Brunello di Montalcino DOCG

Fattoria La Loggia
0 +   Chainti Classico DOCG
* +   Terra dei Cavalieri Chianti Classico DOCG

Fattoria La Mandria
0   Chianti Classico DOCG

Fattoria La Querce
rec   Chianti DOCG

Fattoria La Ripa
*   Chianti Classico DOCG

Fattoria Le Barone
0   Chianti Classico DOCG

Fattoria Le Bocce
**   Chianti Classico DOCG

Fattoria Le Casalte (Paola Silvestri Barioffi)
* +   Vino Nobile di Montepulciano DOCG

Fattoria Le Corti
*   Chianti Classico DOCG
* +   Masso Tondo

Fattoria Le Filigare
**   Chianti Classico DOCG
* −   Podere Le Rocce, Le Filigare

Fattoria Le Pici
0   Chianti Classico DOCG

Fattoria Le Pupille
esp rec Morellino di Scansano DOC

Fattoria Lilliano
*   Chianti Colli Fiorentini DOCG

Fattoria Monsanto or **Castello di Monsanto (Fabrizio Bianchi)**
***   Chianti Classico DOCG
****+   Chianti Classico Riserva DOCG II Poggio
** +   Fabrizio Bianchi
** +   Nemo
** +   Sangioveto di Monsanto
** +   Tinscvil

Fattoria Montecchio
0   Chianti Classico DOCG

Fattoria Montellori
* +   Castelrapiti Rosso

Fattoria Montiverdi
** −   "Monti Verdi" Chianti Classico DOCG

Fattoria Nittardi
0   Casanuova Nittardi, Chianti Classico DOCG
*   Chianti Classico DOCG

Fattoria Nuova Scopetello
*   Vino Nobile di Montepulciano DOCG

Fattoria Pagnana
esp rec Chianti Colli Fiorentini DOCG

Fattoria Paradiso
esp rec Sangiovese di Romagna DOC

Fattoria Pile e Lamole
* +   Fattoria Salcetino, Chianti Classico DOCG
** −   "Lamole di Lamole" Chianti Classico DOCG

Fattoria Poggio Antico
** −   Brunello di Montalcino DOCG
0   Rosso di Montalcino DOC

Fattoria Quercia al Poggio
* −   Chianti Classico DOCG

Fattoria Querciabella
**   Chianti Classico DOCG

Fattoria Salcetino, see **Fattoria Pile e Lamole**

Fattoria San Fabiano Calcinaia
*   Chianti Classico DOCG

Fattoria San Giusto a Rentennano
** +   Chianti Classico DOCG
** +   Percarlo

Fattoria San Leonino
** −   Chianti Classico DOCG

Fattoria Sonnino
0   Cantinino

Fattoria Sorbaiano
rec   Montescudaio DOC Rosso delle Miniere

Fattoria Sovestro
rec   Chianti Colli Senesi DOCG

Fattoria Tregole
* +   Chianti Classico DOCG

Fattoria Valtellina, see **Regni Giorgio**

Fattoria Vignale
* +   Chianti Classico DOCG

Fattoria Viticcio
** −   Chianti Classico DOCG
* +   Prunaio

Fattoria Zerbina
* Marzeno di Marzeno
* Pietramora
rec Sangiovese di Romagna DOC

Favonio (Attilio Simonini)
* Cabernet Franc
** Cabernet Franc Riserva

Felluga Livio
rec Collio Cabernet Franc DOC
rec Collio Merlot DOC

Felluga Marco
rec Collio Merlot DOC
rec Villa San Giovanni, Collio Cabernet DOC

Fenocchio Giacomo
** Barolo DOCG

Fenocchio Riccardo, Azienda Agricola "Pianpolvere Soprano"
rec Barbera d'Alba DOC Pianpolvere Soprano
** Barolo DOCG

Ferrando Luigi
* Caramino
** Carema DOC
*** Carema DOC black label
* Fara DOC
** Gattinara DOC
** Solativo del Canavese
* Spanna del Piemonte

Ferrari
** Ghemme DOC

Ferrero F.lli
* + Barolo DOCG

Feyles Maria
* + Barbaresco DOCG
** Barolo DOCG Ginestra

Fico Giorgio
* Chianti Classico DOCG

Ficomantanino
rec Chianti Colli Senesi DOCG

Fiore Umberto
0 Gattinara DOC
0 Ghemme DOC
0 "Sogno del Bacco" Spanna del Piemonte
0 Spanna del Piemonte

Fiorini–Pantano
* Vino Nobile di Montepulciano DOCG

Fizzano
0 Chianti Classico DOCG

Fontanabianca
* Barbaresco DOCG

Fontanafredda
* − Barbaresco DOCG
* Barolo DOCG
** Barolo DOCG crus

Fontevino, also see **Camigliano Agricola**
0 Brunello di Montalcino DOCG
0 Brunello di Montalcino DOCG La Torre
** Brunello di Montalcino DOCG Pian dei Mercatelli
* Villa dei Lecci, Brunello di Montalcino DOCG

Fornacina (Biliorsi Ruggero)
* Brunello di Montalcino DOCG

Fossi
* Chianti Classico DOCG

Francavilla Agricola
0 Podere Il Macchione, Vino Nobile di Montepulciano DOCG

Francesco Sasso
rec Aglianico del Vulture DOC

Franchino Marco
* − Gattinara DOC

Franco Fiorina
* + Barbaresco DOCG
** + Barolo DOCG
** Nebbiolo d'Alba DOC

Frescobaldi
**** Castello di Nipozzano, Chianti Rùfina Riserva DOCG
*** + Montesodi, Chianti Rùfina Riserva DOCG
** + Predicato di Bitùrica Mormoreto
* Remole, Chianti Rùfina DOCG
** Tenuta di Pomino, Pomino Rosso DOC

Friulivini Cantina Sociale
rec Grave del Friuli Cabernet Sauvignon DOC
rec Grave del Friuli Merlot DOC

Furlan Franco
rec Castelcosa, Merlot del Friuli Venezia Giulia
** Castelcosa, Schioppettino
rec Pra di Pradis, Collio Cabernet DOC
0 Stukara

Gabbiano, see **Castello di Gabbiano**

Gagliardo Gianni
0	Barbaresco DOCG
0+	Barolo DOCG La Serra
0	Barolo DOCG Mora
0	Concerto
*	Nebbiolo d'Alba DOC Roncaglia
*−	"Ribezzo" Barolo DOCG

Gaierhof
rec	"Elle" Trentino Merlot DOC
rec	Trentino Merlot DOC

Gaja
***	Barbaresco DOCG
***	Barbaresco DOCG Costa Russi
****	Barbaresco DOCG Sorì San Lorenzo
****	Barbaresco DOCG Sorì Tildìn
**	Barbera d'Alba DOC (in *barrique*) Vignarey
**+	Barolo DOCG
**+	Darmaggi, Cabernet Sauvignon
***	Nebbiolo d'Alba DOC Vignaveja

Galvagno Ernesto
0+	Barolo DOCG

Gemma
*	Barbaresco DOCG
**−	Barolo DOCG

Geografico, see **Agricoltori del Chianti Geografico**

Germano Angelo
*+	Barolo DOCG

Gherzi
0	Barbaresco DOCG

Giacosa Bruno
****+	Barbaresco DOCG
esp rec	Barbera d'Alba DOC
****+	Barolo DOCG
***	Nebbiolo d'Alba DOC Valmaggiore di Vezza

Giacosa Donato
**	Barbaresco DOCG

Giacosa F.lli
*	Barbaresco DOCG
**−	Barolo DOCG
**	Barolo DOCG Pira
*	"Maria Giovana" Barbera d'Alba DOC (in *barrique*)

Gianolio Tomaso
*−	Barolo DOCG

Giordano Giovanni
*	Barbaresco DOCG

Giovannini-Moresco Enrico
****	Barbaresco DOCG Podere del Pajorè

Giri Guido
*	Barbaresco DOCG
*	Barolo DOCG

Giudice Sergio
0	Barolo DOCG

Gradnik
esp rec	Collio Cabernet Franc DOC
esp rec	Collio Merlot DOC

Grai Giorgio, Bellendorf, Herrnhofer, or Kehlburg
****	Alto Adige Cabernet DOC
esp rec	Alto Adige Lagrein DOC
*+	Alto Adige Pinot Nero DOC

Granduca, see **Cantine Duca d'Asti di Chiarlo Michele**

Granducato, see **Poggibonsi del Consorzio Agrario Provinciale di Siena**

Grasso Elio or Grasso Azienda Agricola
***	Barolo DOCG
**	"Martina" Barbera (in *barrique*)
**	Nebbiolo di Monforte

Grasso Ernesto
0	Barbaresco DOCG Vallegranda Sotto

Grasso F.lli (Emilio Grasso)
*+	Barbaresco DOCG

Grasso Silvio
*+	Barolo DOCG

Grazziola
0	Barbaresco DOCG

Grignano
*	Chianti Rùfina DOCG

Grimaldi Cav. Carlo e Mario, Azienda Agricola "Groppone"
0+	Barbaresco DOCG
0	Barolo DOCG

Grimaldi G.
*	Barbaresco DOCG

Grimaldi Giovanni
*	Barolo DOCG

Gruarius (Cantina Sociale di Portogruaro)
rec   Lison-Pramaggiore Merlot DOC

Guardiolo Vecchio (Coop. Agricola La Guardinese)
0   Guarise
rec   Lison-Prammaggiore Cabernet DOC

Guasti Clemente
0   Barolo DOCG

Guerrieri-Rizzardi
***   Castello Guerrieri
*   Recioto della Valpolicella Amarone DOC
*   Valpolicella Classico DOC
**   Villa Rizzardi Poiega, Valpolicella Classico DOC

Herrnhofer, see **Grai Giorgio**

Hofstatter Josef
rec   Alto Adige Cabernet DOC
rec   Alto Adige Lagrein DOC
esp rec   Alto Adige Merlot DOC
*   Alto Adige Pinot Nero DOC
** −   Alto Adige Pinot Nero Riserva DOC Barthenau

Il Campino Mondiglia
** +   Chianti Classico DOCG

Il Casello (Franceschi Clemente e Roberto)
** +   Brunello di Montalcino DOCG

Il Colle
* +   Brunello di Montalcino DOCG

Il Colle al Matrichese, see **Conti Costanti**

Il Guerrino
0   Chianti Classico DOCG

Il Marroneto
***   Brunello di Montalcino DOCG

Il Palaggio
*   Chianti Classico DOCG

Il Pantano, see **Fattoria del Pantano**

Il Paradiso (Manfredi)
** −   Brunello di Montalcino DOCG

Il Poggiolino
*   Chianti Classico DOCG

Il Poggiolo
** +   Chianti Colli Senesi DOCG
** +   Chianti Colli Senesi DOCG Il Poggiolo
** +   Chianti Colli Senesi DOCG Le Portine

Il Vecchio Tralcio
0   Barbaresco DOCG
0   Barolo DOCG

I Moròs di Nello Tavagnacco
esp rec   Cabernet di Ippilis
esp rec   Colli Orientali del Friuli Cabernet DOC
esp rec   Colli Orientali del Friuli Merlot DOC

Isabella de' Medici
0 −   Brunello di Montalcino DOCG
0 −   Chianti Classico DOCG

Isola Augusta
rec   Latisana Cabernet DOC
rec   Latisana Merlot DOC

Isole e Olena
***   Cepparello
***   Chianti Classico DOCG
*   Rosso

Istituto Agrario Provinciale S. Michele
**   Castel S. Michele
rec   Trentino Cabernet DOC

I Verbi di Ferretti R. & Rasconi R.
** −   Brunello di Montalcino DOCG

I Vignali Azienda Agricola
* +   Montepulciano d'Abruzzo DOC Torre de Passeri

I Vini del Concilio, Mori Vecio, or Lagaria
** +   Mori Vecio
rec   Trentino Cabernet DOC
rec   Trentino Merlot DOC

Kaufmann
rec   Alto Adige Lagrein DOC

Kehlburg, see **Grai Giorgio**

Kellereigenossenschaft Girlan
*   Alto Adige Pinot Nero DOC

Kellereigenossenschaft Gries
rec   Alto Adige Lagrein DOC Greiser
rec   Alto Adige Merlot DOC Steinhof

Kellereigenossenschaft Liebeneich
rec   Alto Adige Merlot DOC Schreckbichl

Kellereigenossenschaft Magreid
rec   Alto Adige Cabernet DOC

Kettmeir
rec Alto Adige Cabernet Sauvignon DOC
rec Alto Adige Merlot DOC Siebeneich

Kiola, see **Beni di Batasiolo**

Klosterkellerei Muri-Gries
rec Alto Adige Lagrein DOC Greiser

Kunkler Bianchi
rec Piave Cabernet DOC
rec Piave Merlot DOC

Kupelweiser
rec Trentino Cabernet DOC

La Bionda
** + Recioto della Valpolicella Amarone DOC
** Valpolicella Classico Superiore DOC Vigneti di
    Ravazzol Valgatara

La Bottega de Vinai
rec Trentino Cabernet DOC

La Brancaia
* Chianti Classico DOCG

La Brenta d'Oro, see **Cantine d'Invecchiamento**

La Bricola
* + Chianti Classico DOCG

La Calonica (Cattani Fernando)
* Rosso
* + Vino Nobile di Montepulciano DOCG

La Campana (Mignarri Peris)
* + Brunello di Montalcino DOCG

"La Ca' Nova" Azienda Agricola di Dario Rocca
* + Barbaresco DOCG

La Casella (Alfio Carpini)
* Vino Nobile di Montepulciano DOCG

La Cerbaiola (Salvioni Giulio)
* + Brunello di Montalcino DOCG

La Chiesa di S. Restituta
*** Brunello di Montalcino DOCG

La Colombaia
0 Recioto della Valpolicella Amarone DOC
0 + Recioto della Valpolicella Amarone DOC Alto Marano

La Crocetta
* Recioto della Valpolicella Amarone DOC
* Recioto della Valpolicella DOC

La Fortuna (Zannoni Gioberto)
** − Brunello di Montalcino DOCG

Lagaria, see **I Vini del Concilio**

Lageder Alöis
rec Alto Adige Cabernet DOC
esp rec Alto Adige Cabernet DOC Wurmbrand
rec Alto Adige Lagrein DOC Lindenburg
rec Alto Adige Merlot DOC
* Alto Adige Pinot Nero DOC

La Guardinese Coop. Agricola
0 Guardiolo Vecchio

Laimburger
rec Alto Adige Cabernet DOC

L'Aja
* Chianti Classico DOCG

La Madonnina
0 + Chianti Classico DOCG

La Magia (Schwarz Herbert)
0 + Brunello di Montalcino DOCG

Lamberti
0 Recioto della Valpolicel'a Amarone DOC

Lancini Luigi
rec Franciacorta Rosso DOC Vigna Cornaleto

La Pescaia (Mantengoli Enzo & Valdisuga Liliana)
** Brunello di Montalcino DOCG

La Poderina (Sai Agricola)
0 Brunello di Montalcino DOCG pre-1982
* + Brunello di Montalcino DOCG since the '82

La Principesi
rec Colli Eugànei Rosso DOC

La Querce (Pinzuti Pino Lido)
0 + Vino Nobile di Montepulciano DOCG

La Sala
* − Chianti Classico DOCG

"La Spinona" Azienda Agricola di Pietro Berutti
** − Barbaresco DOCG

La Stoppa
** −   Alfeo, Pinto Nero

La Suvera
*   Rango

La Torre (Giuseppe Anania)
* +   Brunello di Montalcino DOCG

La Vinicola Sociale Aldeno
** +   San Zeno
* +   Sgreben
rec   Trentino Cabernet DOC

Lazzarini (Villa dal Ferro)
** +   Colli Berici Cabernet DOC Le Rive Rosso
***   Colli Berici Merlot DOC Campo del Lago
**   Rosso del Rocolo (Pinot)

Le Caggiole di Mezzo (Giordano & C.)
*   Vino Nobile di Montepulciano DOCG

Le Caggiole (Podere Il Macchione)
0   Vino Nobile di Montepulciano DOCG

Le Chiantigiane
0   Chianti Classico DOCG
* +   Santa Trinita Chianti Classico DOCG

Lechthaler
rec   Trentino Cabernet DOC

"Le Colline" Azienda Agricola
***   Barbaresco DOCG
* +   Borgo Alto
**   Ghemme DOC
***   Monsecco, Gattinara DOC

"Le Corte" Azienda Agricola, see **Monticelli-Olivero**

Le Coste
0   Chianti Rùfina DOCG

Le Due Porti (Daviddi Enrico e Martini Genny)
* +   Brunello di Montalcino DOCG

Le Due Torri
0   Barolo DOCG

Le Grifiere
0   Chianti Classico DOCG

Le Macìe
* +   Granchiaia

Le Masse di San Leolino
*   Chianti Classico DOCG
**   Chianti Classico Riserva DOCG

Lenotti
*   Recioto della Valpolicella DOC

Le Pietrose (Sai Agricola)
*   Vino Nobile di Montepulciano DOCG

Le Presi (Poggi-Fabbri Marusca)
* +   Brunello di Montalcino DOCG

Le Ragose
***   Le Sassine *ripasso vino da tavola* del Veronese
***   Recioto della Valpolicella Amarone DOC
***   Valpolicella Classico Superiore DOC

Le Salette (Fulvio Scamperle)
**   Recioto della Valpolicella Amarone DOC
rec   Valpolicella Classico Superiore DOC

Lesquio Ottavia, see **Cascina Principe**

Letrari
rec   Trentino Cabernet DOC

Lis Gravis
rec   Grave del Friuli Cabernet Sauvignon DOC

Lisini
**   Brunello di Montalcino DOCG

Livon
*   Plazate Rosso
rec   Refosco Vigneto di Masarotte in Dolegnano
*   Schioppettino Vigneto Cumini in Corno di Rosazzo
*   Tiarebù

Lodali Giovanni
*   Barolo DOCG

Longhi di Carli
rec   Franciacorta Rosso DOC

Longo
**   Recioto della Valpolicella Amarone DOC

Ludola Nuova
0   Vino Nobile di Montepulciano DOCG

Lungarotti
** −   Cabernet Sauvignon
*   Pinot Nero
** +   "Rubesco" Torgiano Rosso DOC
**** −   "Rubesco" Torgiano Rosso Riserva DOC
** +   San Giòrgio

Luxardo dè Franchi del Venda
rec   Sant' Elmo, Colli Eugànei Cabernet DOC

Machiavelli, see also **Conti Serristori**
** +   Chianti Classico DOCG

Maculan
rec   Breganze Cabernet DOC
*** +   Breganze Cabernet DOC Fratta
***   Breganze Cabernet DOC Palazzotto
* +   Breganze Rosso DOC Brentino

Majnoni Guicciardini
rec   Chianti Colli Senesi DOCG

Malvira
**   Nebbiolo d'Alba DOC Del Roero

Mantellassi Ezio
rec   Morellino di Scansano DOC

Manzone Giovanni
**   Barolo DOCG

Manzone Stefano
*   Barolo DOCG Ciabot del Preive

Marabini Dott. Giuseppe
rec   Sangiovese di Romagna DOC

Marchese di Gresy
*** −   Barbaresco DOCG Martinenga
****   Barbaresco DOCG Martinenga-Camp Gros
****   Barbaresco DOCG Martinenga-Gaiun
**   Nebbiolo delle Martinenga

Marchese Ludovico A. (Marchese Ludovico Antinori)
****   Ornellaia

Marchese Malaspina
rec   Colli Bolognesi Cabernet Sauvignon DOC
rec   Colli Bolognesi Merlot DOC

Marchese Maurizio Fracassi Ratti Mentone
**   Barolino
**   Barolo DOCG

Marchese Villadoria, see **Villadoria**

Marchesi di Barolo
0   Barbaresco DOCG
* −   Barolo DOCG
** −   Barolo DOCG Brunate
**   Barolo DOCG Cannubi
**   Barolo DOCG Costa di Rose
**   Barolo DOCG Valletta

Marchesi di San Germano
*   Campiglione

Marchesi L. e P. Antinori or **Antinori**
** +   Chianti Classico DOCG Badia a Passignano
**   Chianti Classico DOCG Pèppoli
** −   Chianti Classico DOCG Riserva Marchese
**   Chianti Classico Riserva DOCG
*   Santa Cristina
***   Secentenàrio
*** +   Solàia
** −   Tenuta Marchese, Chianti Classico Riserva DOCG
***   Tignanello
** −   Villa Antinori, Chianti Classico Riserva DOCG

Marchesi Spinola
*   Barbaresco DOCG
*   Barolo DOCG

Marchesi Spinola Giuntini
rec   "Vino Etrusco La Parrina" Parrina DOC

Marengo M.
* +   Barolo DOCG Brunate

Marengo Mario
0   Barolo DOCG

Martini Karl
rec   Alto Adige Cabernet DOC Kellermeistertrunk

Mascarello Bartolo or **Cantina Mascarello**
**** +   Barolo DOCG
***   Nebbiolo delle Langhe

Mascarello Giacomo di Alberto Mascarello
*   Barolo DOCG

Mascarello Giuseppe (Mauro Mascarello)
***   Barbaresco DOCG
***   Barolo DOCG
**   Nebbiolo d'Alba DOC San Rocco

Masi
*** +   Campociesa Bianco Dolce
*** +   Campofiorin *ripasso vino da tavola* del Veronese
*** −   Recioto della Valpolicella Amarone Classico DOC
**** −   Recioto della Valpolicella Amarone DOC Campolongo Torbe
****   Recioto della Valpolicella Amarone DOC Mazzano
**   Recioto della Valpolicella DOC Mezzanella
*** −   Recioto della Valpolicella DOC Riserva degli Angeli
*** +   Serègo Alighieri Recioto della Valpolicella Amarone DOC Vaio Armaron
***   Serègo Alighieri Recioto della Valpolicella DOC Casal dei Ronchi
***   Serègo Alighieri Valpolicella Classico Superiore DOC

**+ Valpolicella Classico DOC Fresco Vigneti di
     Gargagnago
** Valpolicella Classico Superiore DOC

Maso Cantanghell
*+ Pinot Nero Riserva Atesino

Massolino Giuseppe
* Barolo DOCG
*+ Barolo DOCG Margheria
** Barolo DOCG Sörì Vigna Riunda
* Piria

Mastroberardino
** Taurasi DOC
***+ Taurasi DOC Radici
*** Taurasi Riserva DOC

Mastrojanni
*** Brunello di Montalcino DOCG
**+ Rosso di Montalcino DOC

Mauro
0 Barbaresco DOCG
0 Barolo DOCG

Mauro Marino
* Barolo DOCG

Mazzoni
0 Chianti Classico DOCG

Melini
* "Borghi d'Elsa" Chianti DOCG
* Brunello di Montalcino DOCG
* Chianti Classico DOCG
**− Chianti Classico Riserva DOCG
** Chianti Classico Riserva DOCG Granaio
*+ Chianti Classico Riserva DOCG Isassi
**+ Chianti Classico Riserva DOCG La Selvanella
** Chianti Classico Riserva DOCG Terrarossa
* I Coltri Rosso
** "Laborel" Chianti Classico Riserva DOCG
*+ Vino Nobile di Montepulciano DOCG

Miali
rec Aglianico del Vulture DOC

Mirafiore
*+ Barolo DOCG

"Moccagatta" Azienda Agricola
* Barbaresco DOCG
0 Barbaresco DOCG Bric Balin
* Barbera d'Alba DOC (in *barrique*)

Moio Michele
rec Falerno

Molino Franco, see **Cascina La Rocca di Molino Franco**

Monsigliolo
* Vino Nobile di Montepulciano DOCG

Monsupello
** Podere 'La Borla

Monte Gallo Azienda Vitivinicola
* Merlot di Cavriana

Montelvini
rec Montello e Colli Asolani Cabernet DOC
rec Montello e Colli Asolani Merlot DOC

Montemaggio
0 Chianti Classico DOCG

Montepaldi (Marchese Corsini)
0 Chianti Classico DOCG

Monteropoli
0 Chianti Classico DOCG

Monte Vertine
** Chianti Classico DOCG
** Il Sodaccio
**** Le Pergole Torte
** Rosso

Monti Antonio e Elio
*− Montepulciano d'Abruzzo DOC

Monticelli
*− Chianti Classico DOCG

Monticelli-Olivero, Azienda Agricola "La Corte"
0+ Barolo DOCG

Montori Camillo
** Montepulciano d'Abruzzo DOC

Montoro
* Chianti Classico DOCG

Montresor
0 Recioto della Valpolicella Amarone DOC

Montsclapade, see **Dorigo Girolamo**

Morassutti Giovanni Paolo
rec Lison-Pramaggiore Cabernet DOC
rec Lison-Pramaggiore Merlot DOC

Morbelli Giovanni
* +   Carema DOC

Murari
*   Recioto della Valpolicella Amarone DOC

Musso Sebastiano
0 +   Barbaresco DOCG

Nada Fiorenzo
*   Barbaresco DOCG
**   Cascina Rombone, Nebbiolo delle Langhe

Nada Giuseppe
0   Barbaresco DOCG Poderi Casot

Nascig V. di Angelo Nascig
esp rec   Colli Orientali del Friuli Cabernet Sauvignon DOC
esp rec   Colli Orientali del Friuli Merlot DOC
rec   Franconia
rec   Refosco dal Peduncolo Rosso
rec   Refosco Nostrano

Negro Angelo
**   Nebbiolo d'Alba DOC
* +   Roero DOC Prachiosso

Negroni Bruno
rec   Colli Bolognesi Cabernet Sauvignon DOC

Nera
**   Grumello DOC
** +   Grumello Riserva DOC
**   Inferno DOC
**   Sassella DOC
** +   Sassella Riserva DOC
**   Sfurzato DOC
*** −   "Signorie" Valtellina Superiore DOC
*   "Tellino" Valtellina DOC
*   Valgella DOC

Nervi Luigi & Italo
** +   Gattinara DOC
0   Ghemme DOC
*   Spanna del Piemonte

Nicolas Angelo
0   Recioto della Valpolicella Amarone DOC
0 +   Recioto della Valpolicella DOC

Nicolello
*   Barbaresco DOCG

Nino Negri
***   "Castel Chiuro" Valtellina Superiore Riserva DOC
***   "Fracia" Valtellina Superiore Riserva DOC
**   Grumello DOC

**   Inferno DOC
**   Sassella DOC
*** −   Sfursàt DOC
** +   Valgella DOC
***   Valtellina Superiore Riserva DOC

Nozzole
**   Chianti Classico DOCG

Oberto Egidio (Oberto Giuseppe)
* −   Barolo DOCG

Oberto F.lli
*   Barolo DOCG

Oberto Severino (Oberto Sisto)
*   Barolo DOCG

Oddero F.lli
**   Barbaresco DOCG
** +   Barolo DOCG

Oddero Luigi
0   Barolo DOCG

Olivieri (Valdicava)
0   Brunello di Montalcino DOCG

Oreste Stefano
* +   Barolo DOCG

Orlandi
rec   Cabernet Sauvignon del Veneto
**   Orlandi, Camoi

Ormezzano Maurizio
**   Lessona DOC

Ornato Paolo
* +   Barolo DOCG

Ornellaia, see Marchese Ludovico A.

Orsolani Casa Vinicola
*   Gattinara DOC

Osvaldo
rec   Lison-Pramaggiore Cabernet DOC

Osvaldo Mauro, see Cantine Mauro Vini

Pagnana
*   Chianti Colli Fiorentini DOCG

Palazzo al Bosco
**   Chianti Classico DOCG

Palladino
*   Barbaresco DOCG
** −   Barolo DOCG

Paradiso (Mauro Fastelli)
*   Brunello di Montalcino DOCG

Parrina Azienda Agricola
rec   Parrina DOC

Parroco del Neive
**   Barbaresco DOCG Basarin
*   Barbaresco DOCG Gallina

Parusso Armando
** −   Barolo DOCG
**   Barolo DOCG Bussia-Rocche
** +   Barolo DOCG Mariondino

Pasini Volpe
** −   Le Marne
rec   Zuc Volpe, Colli Orientali del Friuli Merlot DOC
rec   Zuc Volpe, Colli Orientali del Friuli Refosco DOC

Pasolini dall'Onda Borghese
**   Chianti Colli Fiorentini DOCG
rec   Sangiovese di Romagna DOC

Pasqua F.lli
0   Marago
0   Recioto della Valpolicella Amarone DOC

Pasquero-Elia Secondo
** +   Barbaresco DOCG Sorì d'Paytin
** +   Barbaresco DOCG Sorì Paitin

Pasquero Giuseppe
**   Nebbiolo d'Alba DOC Vigna Dogna

Paternoster
rec   Aglianico del Vulture DOC

Patriarca Mario
* +   Gattinara DOC

Patrito
*   Barolo DOCG

Pavese Livio
0   Barbaresco DOCG
0   Barolo DOCG

Pedrotti
rec   Trentino Cabernet DOC

Pelagrilli (Pacenti Siro & Pieri Graz.)
** −   Brunello di Montalcino DOCG

Pelissero Luigi
* +   Barbaresco DOCG

Pelizatti Arturo
*   Grumello DOC
***   Grumello Riserva DOC Sassorosso
*   Inferno DOC
*   Sassella DOC
** +   Sassella Riserva DOC
*   Sforzato DOC

Pepe Emidio
***   Montepulciano d'Abruzzo DOC

Perazzi Luigi
**   Bramaterra DOC
*   La Sassaia
*   Orbello

Pertimali (Sassetti Livio)
*** −   Brunello di Montalcino DOCG

Pezzuto F.lli
***   Nebbiolo d'Alba DOC Vigneto in Vadraman del Roero

Pian d'Albola
0   Chianti Classico DOCG

Piazza Cav. Uff. Armando, Podere d'Mugiot
* −   Barbaresco DOCG
*   Barolo DOCG

Piccini
0   Chianti Classico DOCG

Pieropan Leonildo
esp rec   Recioto di Soave DOC

Pietrafitta
*   Chianti Colli Senesi DOCG

Pietrantori Italo
* +   Montepulciano d'Abruzzo DOC

Pietraserena
** −   Chianti Colli Senesi DOCG
** −   Chianti Colli Senesi DOCG Poggio al Vento

Pietroso
0   Brunello di Montalcino DOCG

Pighin F.lli
rec   Grave del Friuli Cabernet DOC
rec   Grave del Friuli Merlot DOC

Pio Cesare
** −   Barbaresco DOCG
** +   Barolo DOCG
**   Ornato

Pippione
0   Barbaresco DOCG

Pira E. (Chiara Boschis)
** +   Barolo DOCG

Pira E. (Luigi Pira)
**** +   Barolo DOCG

Pira Luigi
*   Barolo DOCG

Pira Secondo & Figli Luigi Pira
*   Barolo DOCG

Pisoni
rec   Trentino Cabernet DOC

Plozner
rec   Grave del Friuli Merlot DOC

Podere Anselma
0   Barbaresco DOCG
0   Barolo DOCG
0   San Mattia

Podere Badelle
0 +   Vino Nobile di Montepulciano DOCG

Podere Boscarelli
**   Chianti Colli Senesi DOCG
** +   Vino Nobile di Montepulciano DOCG

Podere Campacci
*   Chianti Classico DOCG

Podere Capaccia
**   Chianti Classico DOCG
**   Querciagrande

Podere Casot Nada
0   Barbaresco DOCG

Podere Cerrino (Enzo Tiezzi)
** +   Brunello di Montalcino DOCG

Podere di Stignano
* −   Chianti Classico DOCG
* −   "San Vicenti" Chianti Classico DOCG

Podere Ferretto, Fattoria delle Maestrelle
0   Vino Nobile di Montepulciano DOCG

Podere Grattamacco
**   Grattamacco

Podere Il Macchione
0   Le Caggiole, Vino Nobile di Montepulciano DOCG

Podere Il Palazzino
** +   Chianti Classico DOCG
** +   Grosso Sanese

Podere Il Poggiolo (Eredi Cosimi Roberto)
** −   Brunello di Montalcino DOCG

Podere La Caggiole
*   "Tiberini" Vino Nobile di Montepulciano DOCG
0   Vino Nobile di Montepulciano DOCG

Podere Le Caggiole di Mezzo
* +   Vino Nobile di Montepulciano DOCG

Podere Lo Locco
***   Carmignano DOC

Podere Marcarini (Elvio Cogno)
**** +   Barolo DOCG
***   Nebbiolo delle Langhe

Podere Montenidoli
** −   Montenidoli Rosso
**   Sono Montenidoli

Podere Petroio alla via della Malpensata
**   Chianti Classico DOCG
**   Chianti Classico DOCG Cru Montetondo
**   Solo Rosso

Podere Pian di Conte di Pier Luigi Talenti
***   Brunello di Montalcino DOCG

Podere Rocche dei Manzoni di Valentino Migliorini
**   Barolo DOCG
**   Bricco Manzoni

Podere Scopetone (Abbarchi Federigo & Corioni Angela)
*   Brunello di Montalcino DOCG

Poderi e Cantine di Marengo–Marenda or Vinicola Piemontese
*   Barbaresco DOCG Le Terre Forti
** −   Barolo DOCG
** −   Barolo DOCG Cerequio

Poggiarello
* +   Chianti Classico DOCG

Poggibonsi del Consorzio Agrario Provinciale di Siena
* −   "Granducato" Chianti Classico DOCG

Poggio al Sole
*** −   Chianti Classico DOCG

Poggio alla Sala
0   Vino Nobile di Montepulciano DOCG pre-1983
*   Vino Nobile di Montepulciano DOCG since the '83
**   Vino Nobile di Montepulciano DOCG Vigna Parceto

Poggio alle Mura
0 −   Brunello di Montalcino DOCG

Poggio Bonelli
0 +   Chianti Classico DOCG

Poggio degli Olivi
0   Brunello di Montalcino DOCG

Poggiolungo
rec   Morellino di Scansano DOC

Poggio Reale, see **Spalletti**

Poggio Salvi
0   Brunello di Montalcino DOCG pre-1982
*   Brunello di Montalcino DOCG since the '82

Poggio Valente
rec   Morellino di Scansano DOC

Polatti F.lli
*   Grumello DOC
*   Inferno DOC
*   Sassella DOC

Polizano, Carletti, or **Carletti della Giovampaolo**
** +   Elegia
*   Le Stanze
***   Vino Nobile di Montepulciano DOCG

Pomona
0   Chianti Classico DOCG

"Ponte Rocca" Azienda Agricola di Pittatore Cav. Francesco
** +   Barolo DOCG

Ponti Guido
** −   Ghemme DOC
**   Sizzano DOC
*   Spanna del Piemonte

Porro Guido
*   Barolo DOCG

Porta Rossa
**   Barbaresco DOCG
** +   Barolo DOCG

Pradio
rec   "Tre Pigne" Grave del Friuli Cabernet Franc

Pra di Pradis, see **Furlan Franco**

Principessa di Gregorio
* +   Merlot di Sicilia

Principiano Ferdinando, see **Cascina Nando di Principiano Ferdinando**

Priore
*   Montepulciano d'Abruzzo DOC

Produttori del Barbaresco
**   Barbaresco DOCG
****   Barbaresco DOCG Asili
*** +   Barbaresco DOCG Moccagatta
*** +   Barbaresco DOCG Montefico
****   Barbaresco DOCG Montestefano
*** +   Barbaresco DOCG Ovello
***   Barbaresco DOCG Pajè
*** +   Barbaresco DOCG Pora
****   Barbaresco DOCG Rabajà
***   Barbaresco DOCG Rio Sordo
**   Nebbiolo delle Langhe

Produttori "Nebbiolo di Carema"
**   Carema DOC
*** −   Carema DOC dei Carema
*   Nebbiolo del Canavese

Prunetto
0   Chianti Classico DOCG

Prunotto
*   Barbaresco DOCG
***   Barbaresco DOCG Montestefano
***   Barbaresco DOCG Rabajà
rec   Barbera d'Alba DOC
* +   Barolo DOCG
***   Barolo DOCG Bussia
***   Barolo DOCG Cannubi
***   Barolo DOCG Ginestra
**   Nebbiolo d'Alba DOC Bric Rossino di Monteu Roero
***   Nebbiolo d'Alba DOC Ochetti di Monteu Roero
*   Roero DOC

"Pugnane" Azienda Agricola, see **Sordo F.lli, Azienda Agricola "Pugnane"**

Punset di R. Marcarino
*   Barbaresco DOCG
*   Barolo DOCG

Quercecchio (Maria Grazia Salvioni)
* +   Brunello di Montalcino DOCG

Querciavalle
* +   Chianti Classico DOCG
** −   Chianti Classico Riserva DOCG

Quintarelli
* −   Cabernet Franc
* −   Ca' del Merlot
**   Recioto della Valpolicella Amarone DOC
** +   Valpolicella Classico DOC Fiore Vigneto di Monte
           Ca' Paletta
** +   Valpolicella Classico Superiore DOC Vigneto di Monte
           Ca' Paletta

Rabezzana Renato
* +   Nebbiolo d'Alba DOC

Rainoldi Aldo
** −   Ghebellino
**   Grumello DOC
**   Inferno DOC
*   Sassella DOC
**   Sassella Riserva DOC
**   Sfursàt DOC
**   Valgella DOC
*   Valtellina DOC

Ramello Giuseppe
0   Barolo DOCG

Rasina (Mantengoli Vasco)
**   Brunello di Montalcino DOCG

Raspanti Cav. Giuseppe
**   Vino Nobile di Montepulciano DOCG

Ratti Renato
**   Barbaresco DOCG
***   Barolo DOCG Marcenasco
***   Barolo DOCG Marcenasco-Conca
***   Barolo DOCG Marcenasco-Rocche
*   Nebbiolo d'Alba DOC Ochetti di Monteu Roero
*   "Ratti" Barolo DOCG
**   Villa Pattono

Rechsteiner
esp rec   Piave Cabernet DOC

Regaleali di Conte Tasca d'Almerita
** −   Cabernet Sauvignon
** +   Rosso del Conte

Regni Giorgio, Fattoria Valtellina
* +   Convivo
** −   Chianti Classico DOCG

Revello F.lli
* +   Barolo DOCG

Revello Renato, see **Cascina Gustavo di Revello Renato**

Ribezzo, see **Gagliardo Gianni**

Ricasoli, see **Brolio**

Riecine
** +   Chianti Classico DOCG
***   Chianti Classico Riserva DOCG

Righetti Luigi
***   Recioto della Valpolicella Amarone DOC Capitel
           de'Roari
*** −   Valpolicella Classico Superiore DOC Campolieti

Rignana
0   Chianti Classico DOCG

Riguardo, see **Tosco Vinicola**

Rinaldi Francesco
***   Barbaresco DOCG
****   Barolo DOCG

Rinaldi Giuseppe
****   Barolo DOCG
** +   Nebbiolo delle Langhe
rec   Barbera d'Alba DOC

Rino Raffaelle
** −   Barbarola
rec   Trentino Cabernet DOC

Riseccoli
0   Chianti Classico DOCG

Rivetti Guido
* +   Barbaresco DOCG

"Rizzi" Azienda Agricola di Ernesto Dellapiana
**   Barbaresco DOCG

Roagna
**   Barbaresco DOCG
**   Crichet Pajè
*   Opera Prima

Rocca Albino
*   Barbaresco DOCG

Rocca Dario, see **"La Ca' Nova" Azienda Agricola di Dario Rocca**

Rocca delle Macìe
*   Chianti Classico DOCG
**   Chianti Classico DOCG Riserva di Fizzano
*   Chianti Classico DOCG Tenuta Sant' Alfonso

* +   Chianti Classico Riserva DOCG
**   Ser Gioveto

Rocca di Castagnoli
** +   Chianti Classico DOCG
**   Chianti Classico Riserva DOCG Capraia
*** − Chianti Classico Riserva DOCG Poggio a'Frati
*   Stielle

Rocca di Montegrossi, see **Castello di Cacchiano**

Rocca Mürer
rec   Trentino Cabernet Sauvignon DOC

Rocche Costamagna
** +   Barolo DOCG
*   "Roccardo" Nebbiolo delle Langhe
*   "Rocche delle Rocche" Barbera (in *barrique*)

Roche Azienda Vinicola
0   Barbaresco DOCG
0 +   Barola DOCG
*   Zio Giovanni

Rodano
* +   Chianti Classico DOCG

Rodero
rec   Colli Orientali del Friuli Cabernet Franc DOC

Roggia Ferdinando
* +   Barolo DOCG

Rolfo Gianfranco
*   Barolo DOCG

Roncade, see **Barone Ciani Bassetti**

Ronchi del Gnemiz
** +   Rosso del Gnemiz

Ronchi di Cialla
rec   Refosco di Cialla
***   Schioppettino di Cialla

Rosso Gigi
*   Barbaresco DOCG
*   Barolo DOCG

Rovellotti, A. F.
** −   Ghemme DOC

Ruffino
***   Cabreo, Predicato di Bitùrica Vigneto Il Borgo
*   Chianti Classico DOCG
*   Chianti Classico DOCG Aziano
** +   Chianti Classico DOCG Riserva Ducale

***   Chianti Classico DOCG Riserva Ducale gold label
*   "Nero del Tondo" Pinot Noir

Rusca Attilio
0   Fara DOC

Russolo I Legni
rec   Lison-Pramaggiore Merlot DOC

Saccardi
0   Chianti Classico DOCG

Saffirio Enrico
** −   Barolo DOCG

Saffirio F.lli Enrico e Giacomo
*   Barolo DOCG

Saffirio Josetta
*   Barolo DOCG

Salvanza
* −   Chianti Classico DOCG

Salvetta F.lli
** −   Rauten
rec   Trentino Cabernet DOC

San Carlo
** +   Grumello DOC Vigna Stangone
** +   Inferno DOC Vigna Al Carmine
** +   Sassella DOC Vigna Stangone
**   Valgella DOC Vigna Caven

S. Carlo (R. Machetti Marcucci)
*   Brunello di Montalcino DOCG

Sandrone Francesco
***   Barolo DOCG

Sandrone Luciano
*** − Barolo DOCG Cannubi-Boschis

San Felice
* +   Chianti Classico DOCG
**   Chianti Classico Riserva DOCG
** +   Chianti Classico Riserva DOCG Il Grigio
** +   Chianti Classico Riserva DOCG Poggio Rosso
**   Predicato di Bitùrica
* +   Vigorello

S. Filippo (Ermanno Rossi)
**   Brunello di Montalcino DOCG
*   Rosso di Montalcino DOC

S. Filippo (Filippo Fanti Baldassarre)
* +   Brunello di Montalcino DOCG

Sanguineto (Maria e Lucia Monaci)
*   Vino Nobile di Montepulciano DOCG

S. Leonino (Fattoria I Cipressi)
*   Chianti Classico DOCG

San Lorenzo Casa Vinicola
*   Barolo DOCG

San Michele
0+   Barbaresco DOCG

S. Quirico di Massano
0   Barbaresco DOCG
0   Barolo DOCG

San Rustico di Luigi & Danilo Campagnola
*   Recioto della Valpolicella Amarone DOC
***−   Recioto della Valpolicella Amarone DOC Del Gasso
**   Recioto della Valpolicella Spumante DOC
*   Valpolicella Classico DOC
**   Valpolicella Classico Superiore DOC Vigneti del Gasso

Santa Caterina di Cordano
*+   Montepulciano d'Abruzzo DOC

S. Cristina
*   Cabernet Sauvignon

Santa Margherita
rec   Alto Adige Lagrein DOC
rec   Lison-Pramaggiore Cabernet Sauvignon DOC
rec   Lison-Pramaggiore Merlot DOC

Santa Rosa
rec   Colli Bolognesi Cabernet Sauvignon DOC

Santa Sofia
*   Recioto della Valpolicella Amarone DOC
rec   Valpolicella Classico Superiore DOC

Santi
**−   "Botte Regina" Recioto della Valpolicella Amarone DOC
0   Recioto della Valpolicella Amarone DOC
*   Valpolicella Classico Superiore DOC Vigneti Castello d'Illasi

Santico di Santi
rec   Trentino Cabernet Sauvignon DOC

Sartori
*   Recioto della Valpolicella Amarone DOC

Savigliano Mario
0   Barolo DOCG

Savignola Paolina
***   Chianti Classico DOCG

Scamperle
*   Recioto della Valpolicella Amarone DOC

Scamperle Fulvio, see **Le Salette (Fulvio Scamperle)**

Scanavino Giovanni
0−   Barbaresco DOCG
0   Barolo DOCG

Scarpa
***+   Barbaresco DOCG
***+   Barolo DOCG
***   Nebbiolo d'Alba DOC San Carlo di Castellinaldo

Scarpa Afra e Tobia
rec   Cabernet del Veneto
**   Corbulino Rosso
rec   Merlot del Veneto
*   Pinot Nero del Veneto

Scarzello Giorgio
*+   Barolo DOCG

Scarzello Giovanni
*+   Barolo DOCG

Scavino Alfonso, also see **Azelia**
**−   Barolo DOCG

Scavino Paolo
*   Barbera *affinato in carati*
**−   Barolo DOCG
**+   Barolo DOCG crus

Schiopetto Mario
esp rec   Collio Cabernet Franc DOC
esp rec   Collio Merlot DOC
*   Pinot Nero del Collio
**+   Riva Rossa

Schloss Schwanburg
rec   Alto Adige Cabernet DOC
rec   Alto Adige Lagrein DOC
*   Alto Adige Pinot Nero DOC

Schlosskellerei Turmhof, see **Castello Turmhof di Tiefenbrunner**

Scialletti Cologna Paese Azienda Agricola di Roseto degli Rosso Sanmarco
*−   Montepulciano d'Abruzzo DOC

Scolaris Giovanni
rec   Collio Merlot DOC

Scopatello
*   Vino Nobile di Montepulciano DOCG

Scopetto
*   Vino Nobile di Montepulciano DOCG

Sebaste
** −   Barolo DOCG
*   Bricco Viole
** −   Nebbiolo delle Langhe

Sebastiani Giovanni Giuseppe
**   Ghemme DOC

Seghesio Renzo
* −   Barolo DOCG

Sella
**   Bramaterra DOC
**   Lessona DOC
*   Orbello
*   Piccone

Selvoramole
**   Chianti Classico DOCG

Serafino Enrico
0   Barbaresco DOCG

Serègo Alighieri, see **Masi**

Serristori, see **Conti Serristori**

Settimo Aurelio
** −   Barolo DOCG

Severino Oberto (Sesto Severino)
*   Barolo DOCG

Silvestrini
esp rec   Piave Cabernet DOC

Simoncelli Armando
*   Navesel
rec   Trentino Cabernet DOC

Simonini Attilio, see **Favonio (Attilio Simonini)**

Sobrero Filippo
*** −   Barolo DOCG

Sobrero Francesco
* +   Barolo DOCG

SO.VI.VE. (Società Vini Veneti)
rec   Piave Merlot DOC

Sordo F.lli
0 +   Barolo DOCG

Sordo F.lli, Azienda Agricola "Pugnane"
* +   Barolo DOCG

Sordo Giovanni
0   Barolo DOCG
*   Barolo DOCG Sorì Gabutti

Sottimano
*   Barbaresco DOCG

Spalletti
**   Poggio Reale, Chianti Rùfina Riserva DOCG

Spalletti
esp rec   Sangiovese di Romagna DOC Rocco di Ribano

Specogna Leonardo
esp rec   Colli Orientali del Friuli Cabernet Sauvignon DOC
esp rec   Colli Orientali del Friuli Merlot DOC
rec   Colli Orientali del Friuli Refosco DOC

Speri
0   Recioto della Valpolicella Amarone DOC

Stepski Doliva
rec   Piave Cabernet DOC

Straccali
*   Chianti Classico DOCG

Stroppiana Oreste
**   Barolo DOCG

Struzziero
*   Taurasi DOC

Talenti Pier Luigi, see **Podere Pian di Conte**

Tedeschi
***   Capitel San Rocco delle Lucchine Rosso *ripasso vino da tavola* del Veronese
***   Capitel San Rocco Rosso *ripasso vino da tavola* del Veronese
** +   Recioto Bianco La Fabbriseria de San Rocco
**   Recioto della Valpolicella Amarone Classico DOC
***   Recioto della Valpolicella Amarone DOC Capitel Monte Olmi
** +   Recioto della Valpolicella Amarone DOC Linea Fabbriseria
*   Recioto della Valpolicella DOC
***   Recioto della Valpolicella DOC Capitel Monte Fontana
** −   Valpolicella Classico Superiore DOC
*** −   Valpolicella Classico Superiore DOC Vigneto Lucchine

Tenuta Agricola di Lison
rec   Lison-Pramaggiore Cabernet DOC
rec   Lison-Pramaggiore Merlot DOC

Tenuta Agricola "La Fattoria" Gli Abbazia Benedettina di Summaga
rec   Lison-Pramaggiore Merlot DOC

Tenuta Caparzo
***   Brunello di Montalcino DOCG
***   Brunello di Montalcino DOCG La Casa
**+   Ca' del Pazzo
**–   Rosso di Montalcino DOC

Tenuta Carretta
***+   Barolo DOCG Cannubi
***   Nebbiolo d'Alba DOC Bric' Paradiso
***   Nebbiolo d'Alba DOC Bric' Tavoletto
***   Roero DOC Bricco del Poggio

Tenuta Castello
rec   Valcalèpio Rosso DOC
rec   Valcalèpio Rosso DOC Colle Calvario

Tenuta Col d'Orcia
**   Brunello di Montalcino DOCG
***–   Brunello di Montalcino DOCG Poggio al Vento
0   Rosso di Montalcino DOC

Tenuta Coluè, see Coluè di Massimo Oddero

Tenuta di Gracciano (Seta Ferrari Corbelli)
*+   Vino Nobile di Montepulciano DOCG

Tenuta di Lilliano
*+   Chianti Classico DOCG
**   Chianti Classico DOCG Riserva Eleanora Ruspoli
        Berlingier

Tenuta di Poggio
0   Chianti Rùfina DOCG

Tenuta di Pomino, see Frescobaldi

Tenuta di Riguardo, see Tosco Vinicola

Tenuta di Sesta (Ciacci Giuseppe)
0   Brunello di Montalcino DOCG

Tenuta di Vignole
*   Chianti Classico DOCG

Tenuta Ermanno Rivetti, see Villa Era di Vigliano

Tenuta Fontodi, see Fattoria di Fontodi

Tenuta Il Greppone Mazzi
*   Brunello di Montalcino DOCG

Tenuta Il Monte
*   Chianti DOCG

Tenuta Il Poggione
****   Brunello di Montalcino DOCG
***   Rosso di Montalcino DOC

Tenuta La Chiusa
rec   Elba Rosso DOC

Tenuta La Colombaia
0   Chianti Classico DOCG

Tenuta "La Fuga" (Gabriella Cristofolini Attanasio)
**+   Brunello di Montalcino DOCG

Tenuta La Volta, see Cabutto Bartolemeo

Tenuta Montanello
*   Barolo DOCG

Tenuta Montegiacchi, see Agricoltori del Chianti Geografico

Tenuta Pietra Focaia, see Centolani Agricola

Tenuta San Guido
***   Sassicaia

Tenuta San Leonardo
rec   Trentino Cabernet DOC
rec   Trentino Merlot DOC

Tenuta Sant' Anna
rec   Lison-Pramaggiore Cabernet DOC
rec   Lison-Pramaggiore Merlot DOC

Tenuta San Vito in Fior di Selva (Roberto Drighi)
rec   Chianti DOCG

Tenuta Schlosshof
*   "Barone Felix Longo" Alto Adige Pinot Nero DOC

Tenuta Trerose
**   Vino Nobile di Montepulciano DOCG

Tenuta Valdicava (Abruzzese Vicenzo)
**   Brunello di Montalcino DOCG
**+   Brunello di Montalcino DOCG Madonna del Piano

Tenuta Valdicava (Bramante Martini)
0   Brunello di Montalcino DOCG

Tenuta Valdipiatta
* +   Vino Nobile di Montepulciano DOCG

Tenuta Villa Girardi
0   Recioto della Valpolicella Amarone DOC

Tenuta Villa Rosa
**   Chianti Classico DOCG

Terrabianca
*   Chianti Classico DOCG Scassino
**   Chianti Classico Riserva DOCG Vigna della Croce

Terra dei Cavalieri, see **Fattoria La Loggia**

Terre Bindella
**   Vino Nobile di Montepulciano DOCG

Terre del Barolo
*   Barolo DOCG
**   Barolo DOCG Brunate
**   Barolo DOCG Rocche
* +   Nebbiolo d'Alba DOC

Terzano G., see **Cascina Adelaide di G. Terzano**

Tibalini (EFFEVI)
0   Gattinara DOC
0   Spanna del Piemonte

Tiberini, see **Podere La Caggiole**

Tiefenbrunner, see **Castello Turmhof**

Tistarelli Mario
0   Vino Nobile di Montepulciano DOCG

Tomaso Gianolio
* –   Barbaresco DOCG

Tommasi
**   Recioto della Valpolicella Amarone DOC
**   Valpolicella Classico Superiore DOC Vigneto Raffael

Tona di Gianluigi Bonisolo
*   La Taberna Valtellina DOC
*   Perlavilla Valtellina DOC
*   Sassella DOC
**   Sforzato DOC

Toppi Patrizi della Marchesi di Torre
**   Montepulciano d'Abruzzo DOC

Torre Ercolana, see **Colacicchi-Anagni**

Torre Quarto, see **Cirillo-Farrusi Fabrizio**

Torresella
rec   Lison-Pramaggiore Cabernet DOC
rec   Lison-Pramaggiore Merlot DOC

Torre Sveva
rec   Aglianico del Vulture DOC

Torricino (Oscar Pio)
*   Chianti Colli Fiorentini DOCG

Tosco Vinicola
0   "Riguardo," Brunello di Montalcino DOCG
0   Tenuta di Riguardo, Brunello di Montalcino DOCG

Tramanal
* +   Recioto della Valpolicella Amarone DOC

Travaglini Giancarlo
* +   Gattinara DOC
*   Spanna del Piemonte

Traversa Giuseppe, see **Cascina Chiabotto di Traversa Giuseppe**

Travignoli
* –   Chianti Rùfina DOCG

Tre Rose
0   Recioto della Valpolicella Amarone DOC

Triacca F.lli
** –   Grumello DOC
* +   "La Gatta" Valtellina DOC
**   Sassella DOC
**   Sforzato DOC
**   "Tradizione" Valtellina DOC

Tripusa, Brigatti (Enoteca Europea)
0   Vino Nobile di Montepulciano DOCG

Troglia Giovanni
0   Barbaresco DOCG
0   Barolo DOCG
*   Gattinara DOC
*   Ghemme DOC
*   Spanna del Piemonte

Turba
0   Gattinara DOC
* –   Ghemme DOC
* –   Sizzano DOC
0   Spanna del Piemonte

Vajra G. D.
** +   Barolo DOCG
*** −   Barolo DOCG Bricco Viole
*** −   Barolo DOCG Fossati
**   Nebbiolo delle Bricco delle Viole

Val delle Rose
rec   Morellino di Scansano DOC

Valdisuga
0   Brunello di Montalcino DOCG pre-1981
**   Brunello di Montalcino DOCG since the '81

Valentini
****   Montepulciano d'Abruzzo DOC

Valfieri
0   Barbaresco DOCG
0   Barolo DOCG

Vallana Antonio
**   Boca DOC
****   Campi Raudii, Spanna del Piemonte
**   Cinque Castelli, Spanna del Piemonte
**   Del Camino, Spanna del Piemonte
*** −   Gattinara DOC
* +   Ghemme DOC
***   Montalbano, Spanna del Piemonte
***   San Lorenzo, Spanna del Piemonte
**   Spanna del Piemonte
****   Traversagna, Spanna del Piemonte

Vallarom
rec   Trentino Cabernet DOC Casetta

Valliana Enrico
rec   Colli Bolognesi Cabernet Sauvignon DOC

Vallunga F.lli
**   Rosso Armentano
rec   Sangiovese di Romagna DOC

Vantini Lorenzo
0   Recioto della Valpolicella Amarone DOC

Vecchia Cantina di Montepulciano
*   Vino Nobile di Montepulciano DOCG
* +   Vino Nobile di Montepulciano Riserva DOCG

Vecchie Terre di Montefili
**   Bruno di Rocca
** +   Chianti Classico DOCG
*** −   Chianti Classico Riserva DOCG Anfiteatro

Vecchio Piemonte Cantine Produttori
0   Barbaresco DOCG
0   Barolo DOCG

Veglio Angelo
* +   Barolo DOCG

Veglio F.lli, see **Cascina Bruni di Veglio F.lli**

Veglio Giovanni
* +   Barolo DOCG

Veglio Pasqual, see **Cascina Bruni di Veglio Pasqual**
*   Barolo DOCG

Venegazzù di Azienda Agricola, see **Ca' Loredan Gasparini**

Venturini
** +   Recioto della Valpolicella Amarone DOC
**   Recioto della Valpolicella DOC

Verbena (Brigidi e Pascucci)
*   Brunello di Montalcino DOCG

Vercelli Alessandro
0   Barolo DOCG

Verro Tonino
**   Nebbiolo d'Alba DOC Vigneto Bricchet del Roero

Vescovo Gianni
rec   Isonzo Cabernet Franc DOC

Vezza Sergio
** +   Barbaresco DOCG

Viarengo, see **Castello d'Annone, "Viarengo"**

Viberti Giovanni
0 +   Barolo DOCG

Viberti Luigi, see **Cascina Ballarin di Viberti Luigi**

Vietti (Alfredo Currado)
**   Barbaresco DOCG
*** +   Barbaresco DOCG Masseria
****   Barbaresco DOCG Rabajà
esp rec   Barbera d'Alba DOC
** +   Barolo DOCG
**** +   Barolo DOCG Briacca
****   Barolo DOCG Brunate
****   Barolo DOCG Bussia
** +   Barolo DOCG Castiglione
**** +   Barolo DOCG Lazzarito
**** +   Barolo DOCG Rocche
**** +   Barolo DOCG Villero
**   Fioretto
***   Nebbiolo d'Alba DOC San Giacomo di Santo Stefano
              Roero
***   Nebbiolo d'Alba St. Michele di Santo Stefano Roero

Vignabaldo (Brogal Vini)
0   Torgiano Rosso DOC

Vignamaggio
** −   Chianti Classico DOCG
** −   Chianti Classico Riserva DOCG Castello di Monna Lisa

Vignavecchia
0   Chianti Classico DOCG

Vigne dal Leon di Tullio Zamò
rec   Colli Orientali del Friuli Merlot DOC
**   Rosso
** +   Schioppettino

Vigneti Pacenti Siro di Pacenti S. e Pieri G.
** −   Brunello di Montalcino DOCG

Vignoble du Prieure de Montfleury
**   Pinot Nero Sang des Salasses de Moncenis

Villa Antonio
0   Gattinara DOC
0   Spanna del Piemonte

Villa a Tolli
*   Brunello di Montalcino DOC

Villa Banfi, see **Castello Banfi**

Villa Belvedere di Taddei
rec   Colli Orientali del Friuli Cabernet Franc
rec   Colli Orientali del Friuli Merlot DOC
rec   Colli Orientali del Friuli Refosco DOC

Villa Cafaggio
***   Chianti Classico DOCG
** −   Cortaccio
***   San Martino
*** +   Solatìo Basilica

Villa Calcinaia, see **Conti Capponi**

Villa Cerna, also see **Cecchi Luigi**
**   Chianti Classico DOCG

Villa Cilnia
*   Chianti Colli Aretini DOCG
** +   Chianti Colli Aretini Riserva DOCG
**   Le Vignacce
* +   Vocato

Villa Colombaio
***   Chianti Classico DOCG
***   Fortilizio Il Colombaio, Chianti Classico Riserva DOCG

Villa Cusona (Guicciardini-Strozzi)
** −   Chianti Colli Senesi DOCG

Villa dal Ferro, see **Lazzarini (Villa dal Ferro)**

Villa di Capezzana di Conte Ugo Bonacossi
** +   Carmignano DOC
****   Carmignano Riserva DOC
*   Chianti Montalbano DOCG
***   Ghiaie della Furba

Villa Dievole, see **Fattoria Dievole**

Villa di Monte
*   Chianti Rùfina DOCG

Villa di Trefiano
**   Carmignano DOC

Villa di Vetrice
0   Chianti Rùfina DOCG

Villadoria, DA.I.PI.“CM,” or **Marchese Villadoria**
0   Barbaresco DOCG
0   Barolo DOCG
0   DA.I.PI.“CM,” Barolo DOCG
0   Spanna del Piemonte

Villa Era di Vigliano, Tenuta Ermanno Rivetti
*   Spanna del Piemonte

Villa Francesca
**   Chianti Classico DOCG
*   Sicelle da Giovanni Mari, Chianti Classico DOCG

Villa Girardi
0   Recioto della Valpolicella Amarone DOC
rec   Valpolicella Classico Superiore DOC

Villa Il Poggiolo
** +   Carmignano DOC
*   Chianti Montalbano DOCG

Villa La Pagliaia
*   Chianti Classico DOCG Riserva Granduca Ferdinando III

Villa La Selva
**   Chianti Colli Arentini DOCG

Villa Matilde
rec   Falerno del Massiccio Rosso DOC
rec   Falerno del Massiccio Rosso Riserva DOC

Villa Niccola di Lee Iacocca
** −   Brunello di Montalcino DOCG
*   Rosso di Montalcino DOC

Villa Ronche
rec   Grave del Friuli Cabernet Franc DOC
rec   Grave del Friuli Merlot DOC

Villa San Giovanni, see **Felluga Marca**

Villa Santina
rec   Chianti DOCG

Villa Selvapiana (Francesco Giuntini)
****   Chianti Rùfina Riserva DOCG

Villa Spada
*   Recioto della Valpolicella Amarone DOC

Villa Terciona
** −   Chianti Classico DOCG

Vinattieri (Maurizio Castelli & Roberto Stucchi-Prinetti)
** +   Rosso
**   Rosso II

Vinicola Casacanditella
** +   "Angelo Rosso Riserva," Montepulciano d'Abruzzo
        DOC
**   "Rosso della Quercia," Montepulciano d'Abruzzo DOC

Vinicola Piemontese, see **Poderi e Cantine di Marengo–Marenda**

Vinovino
*   Costarella, Montepulciano d'Abruzzo DOC
** +   Pianelaroma
**   Rodolite

Voerzio Giacomo
0   Barbaresco DOCG

Voerzio Giacomo (F.lli Voerzio)
** +   Barolo DOCG

Voerzio Gianni
*   Barolo DOCG

Voerzio Roberto
** +   Barolo DOCG
* +   Nebbiolo delle Ciabot della Luna di La Mora
** −   Nebbiolo delle Croera di La Mora

Voyat Ezio
**   Chambave Rouge

Zamo Tullio, see **Vigne dal Leon di Tullio Zamò**

Zanetta Ercolina
**   Sizzano DOC

Zardini F.lli
0   Recioto della Valpolicella Amarone DOC

Zecca Giuseppe
**   Donna Marzia Rosso
rec   Leverano Rosso DOC

Zenato
*   Recioto della Valpolicella Amarone DOC

Zeni F.lli
*   Recioto della Valpolicella Amarone DOC
rec   Valpolicella Classico Superiore DOC Marogne
rec   Valpolicella Classico Superiore DOC Vigne Alte

Zonin Domenico
* −   Berengario

Zunino Basilio
** +   Barolo DOCG

A P P E N D I X   C

OUR VINTAGE CHART BASED ON THE CURRENT STATE OF THE VINTAGES†

	Amarone	Barbaresco	Barolo	Brunello	Carema	Carmignano	Chianti Classico	Chianti Rùfina	
1990	****	****	****	****	?	*** +	****	****	1990
1989	?	****	**** +	* +	?	* +	0	* +	1989
1988	****	*** +	**** –	****	?	****	*** +	*** +	1988
1987	*	* –	** –	*	?	* +	*	*	1987
1986	**	** +	*** –	** +	?	* +	**	** +	1986
1985	**** –	****	****	****	***	**** –	****	****	1985
1984	?	0	* –	* –	–	* –	0 +	0	1984
1983	****	**	* +	*** +	**	*** +	**** –	****	1983
1982	**	**** –	**** –	*** –	***	**	***	***	1982
1981	*** –	0	* –	* –	0	* +	*	***	1981
1980	*** –	*	* +	* –	*	* +	*	** –	1980
1979	***	* +	**	* –	**	**	** –	***	1979
1978	*	*** +	***	*	***	* +	*	***	1978
1977	***	0	0	** +	0	?	* +	*** –	1977
1976	*	0	0	0	*	0	0	0	1976
1975	**	0	0	*** +	*	***	**	***	1975
1974	***	** –	** –	0	***	0	0	***	1974
1973	* –	0	0	0	0	0	0	0	1973
1972	0	not produced		0	0	0	0	0	1972
1971	***	***	****	0	0	?	**	**	1971
1970	**	** +	*** –	***	0	?	**	** +	1970
1969	**	0	0	* +	0	*	0	** –	1969
1968	**	0	0	* –	0	–	0	** +	1968
1967	*	**	**	0	**	–	* –	* +	1967
1966	–	0	0	0	0	–	0	** +	1966
1965	–	0	0	0	0	–	0	*	1965

	Amarone	Barbaresco	Barolo	Brunello	Carema	Carmignano	Chianti Classico	Chianti Rùfina	
1964	–	***	*** –	**	**	–	* –	**	1964
1963	–	0	0	0	0	–	0	0	1963
1962	–	0	*	0	**	–	* –	**	1962
1961	–	** +	** +	–	0	–	0	**	1961
1960	–	0	0	0	–	–	0	0	1960
1959	–	0	0	–	–	–	0	** +	1959
1958	–	***	****	–	–	–	**	***	1958
1957	–	** –	** + ?	–	–	–	*	–	1957
1956	–	0	0	–	–	–	0	** –	1956
1955	–	*	*** –	***	–	–	** –	***	1955
1954	–	0	0	–	–	–	0	–	1954
1953	–	0	0	–	–	–	0	–	1953
1952	–	–	*	–	–	–	*	–	1952
1951	–	–	–	–	–	–	0	–	1951
1950	–	0	*	–	–	–	0	–	1950
1949	–	0	0	–	–	–	0	–	1949
1948	–	0	0	–	–	–	0	***	1948
1947	–	–	***	–	–	–	**	*** +	1947
1946	–	0	0	–	–	–	–	–	1946
1945	–	–	0	–	–	–	–	****	1945

	Gattinara	Montepulciano D'Abruzzo	Taurasi	Torgiano	Valtellina Superiore	Vino Nobile	
1990	?	?	****	?	?	?	1990
1989	****	*	***	**	?	*	1989
1988	?	****	****	–	?	*** +	1988
1987	?	**	* +	** +	* –	*	1987
1986	**	**	** +	** –	?	** +	1986
1985	*** ?	****	****	** +	*** +	****	1985
1984	*	*	?	–	0	* –	1984
1983	**	**	**	**	****	*** +	1983
1982	****	***	**	** +	***	*** –	1982
1981	* +	*	*	**	**	** –	1981
1980	*	**	*	** +	**	0	1980
1979	*** –	***	**	***	** +	*	1979
1978	*** +	0	**	***	***	* –	1978
1977	0	***	***	*** –	0	*	1977
1976	*	–	?	–	0	0	1976
1975	0	–	**	***	0	*	1975
1974	** +	–	0	**	***	0	1974
1973	0	–	***	**	0	0	1973
1972	0	–	0	–	0	0	1972
1971	0	–	***	*** –	0	0	1971
1970	**	–	–	*** –	*	0	1970

	Gattinara	Montepulciano D'Abruzzo	Taurasi	Torgiano	Valtellina Superiore	Vino Nobile	
1969	0	—	**	**	0	0	1969
1968	0	—	****	**	0	0	1968
1967	**	—	**	**	0	0	1967
1966	0	—	—	—	**	—	1966
1965	0	—	—	**	0	—	1965
1964	**	—	—	*	—	—	1964
1963	0	—	—	—	0	—	1963
1962	0	—	—	—	0	—	1962
1961	**	—	—	—	*	—	1961

† These ratings are predicated on the condition of the vintage today. If the wine is too young, we rated it for how we believe it will turn out when it is at its best. A vintage that we might have rated four stars at one time, but one that we deem is too old today, received a significantly lower rating.

? We lack the experience or knowledge to evaluate the vintage. See the appropriate section in the book for a further discussion or rating based on other sources. The ratings herein are our ratings, based on our tastings. They do not take into consideration the opinions of others, no matter how highly we regard their knowledge. If we lacked the experience, we passed on a rating. We include the ratings and opinions of others in the specific section dealing with the wine.

− The wine is too old or we are unable to put a rating on it.

A P P E N D I X   D

THE MEMBERS OF VIDE

Vitivinicoltori Italiani d'Eccellenza

Azienda Agricola Bricco Mondalino di Gaudio Amilcare*
Tenute Cisa Asinari dei Marchesi di Gresy di Alberto Cisa Asinari di Gresy & C.*
Tenuta San Pietro di Maria Rosa Gazzaniga
Azienda Agrovitivinicola Giustiniana
Azienda Agricola Ca' dei Fratti di Dal Cero Pietro & Figli
Azienda Agricola Faccoli Lorenzo
Azienda Agricola Monsupello di Carlo Boatti*
Azienda Agricola Le Case Bianche-Orlandi*
Azienda Agricola Le Ragose*
Azienda Agricola Rechsteiner di Stepski Doliwa Hans O.*
Azienda Agricola Le Vigne di San Pietro di Franca Fiorio*
Azienda Agricola Villa dal Ferro Lazzarini*
Azienda Agricola Russiz Superiore*
Azienda Agricola Mario Schiopetto*
Azienda Agricola Volpe Pasini*
Azienda Agricola La Stoppa di Raffaele Pantaleoni*
Azienda Agricola Vitivinicola Fattoria Paradiso*
Azienda Agricola Vigneto delle Terre Rosse*
Fattoria dei Barbi e del Casato*
Tenuta di Capezzana di Ugo Contini Bonacossi*
Azienda Agricola Poggio al Sole*
Azienda Agricola Poggio Bonelli*
Fattoria Selvapiana*
Azienda Agricola Villa Cilnia di Giovanni e Rory Bianchi*
Azienda Agricola F.lli Zaccagnini
Azienda Agricola Mustilli*
Azienda Agricola Villa Matilde*
Azienda Agricola Vecchio Samperi

---

* One or more of their wines are discussed or recommended in this book.

GLOSSARY

a spanna: method of cultivation used in the Novara–Vercelli hills of the Piemonte.

abboccato*:   lightly sweet.

affinato in carati: refined, meaning aged, in small barrels, *barriques*.

al alberello: the vines are head-pruned and trained so that each one stands separately "like a little tree."

alberese: limestone soil.

albeise wines: the wines of the Alba zone in the Piemonte.

amabile*:   semisweet.

amaro: bitter.

annata*:   literally year; refers to the year of the vintage or harvest, or, as in the case of Brunello, the wine of the year as opposed to a *riserva*.

appassimento: the period of drying the grapes.

argilla: clay soil.

argilloso: clayey loam soil.

asciutto*:   very dry.

az. agr.*:   abbreviation for *azienda agricola*.

azienda*:   winery.

azienda agricola*:   a farm; more commonly used for a winery-farm that grows the grapes it needs to produce the wine it makes.

azienda vinicola*:   a winery that buys grapes and/or wine.

azienda vitivinicola*:   like an *azienda agricola*.

az. vin.*:   abbreviation for *azienda vinicola*.

az. vit.*:   abbreviation for *azienda vitivinicola*.

bando della vendemmia: in the Middle Ages the date of the harvest was regulated by the local authorities who set the opening day of the harvest.

barrique: a 60-gallon (225-liter) oak barrel.

bianco*:   white or white wine. Plural is *bianchi*.

bollino: a seal found on a bottle of wine and issued by a *consorzio* to its members for the wines that qualify.

borgata: suburban tenement district.

borgo: small town or village.

botte: a large chestnut or oaken cask; today it is most commonly made of Slavonian oak. Plural is *botti*.

bottiglie: a bottle.

botrytis: gray mold; depending on the grape variety and the degree of development, this type of rot may be considered noble (*Botrytis cinerea* or *Mufa nobile*) or ignoble. In the latter case it affects the grapes and the wine in an undesirable way.

bottiglione: a 0.5- to 0.8-gallon (2- to 3-liter) bottle. Plural is *bottiglioni*.

brenta: a 13.2-gallon or 50-liter container. Plural is *brente*.

bric*:   Piemontese dialect for *bricco*.

bricco*:   in Piemonte, the top part of a hill.

calcare: limestone soil.

calcareo: calcareous soil.

calcareo-argilloso: calcareous-clayey loam soil.

cannici: reed trays used for drying grapes in Toscana.

cantina*:   winery or wine cellar. Plural is *cantine*.

cantina sociale*:   cooperative winery.

capitel*:   a stone marker, frequently in the form of a miniature chapel honoring a Saint, used to mark the corners of a vineyard and designate that the land is owned. It is used to designate a vineyard in the Veronese district.

cappello sommerso: literally, "submerged cap"; during the fermentation the solids, which would normally float to the top and form the cap, are held submerged in the fermenting must.

carati: *barrique.*

carbonique maceration: whole berry fermentation in a closed, often pressurized tank.

carra: a 132-gallon (500-liter) cask.

casa*: house.

casa vinicola*: see *azienda agricola.*

cascina*: literally, "holdings," it could refer to a single vineyard or a group of vineyards owned by a single proprietor or estate; this term is generally used in northern Italy.

castel*: castle.

castello*: castle.

castelli: wicker frames used for drying grapes in Toscana.

cerasuolo*: a light red, more like a rosé.

champagnotta: a specially shaped bottle used in the Ghemme district of the Piemonte.

charmat method: when the second fermentation—the one which results in the sparkle, or carbon dioxide—takes place in a closed, pressurized tank.

chiaretto*: literally, "claret color"; used to refer to a light red or, more often, dark rosé.

ciabot*: house in the country; used to refer to a vineyard in the Piemonte that contains a house or shack.

classico*: the original or classic vineyard area in the region, and the wine produced from the grapes grown there.

cold maceration: the process by which the must remains in contact with the skins at a low temperature.

coltura esclusiva: vineyards in monoculture.

coltura promiscua: the grapevines planted in rows interspersed with olive trees and other crops.

comune: municipality, town. Plural is *comuni.*

consorzio: voluntary wine growers' organization.

contadino: peasant, farmer.

cooperativa*: a cooperative winery.

costa*: side of a hill that faces the sun.

cru: at one time used to refer to a single vineyard with a unique position and/or microclimate; today it is often used generically to refer to a single vineyard.

crusher: a machine that crushes grapes.

crusher-stemmer: a machine that removes stems and crushes the grapes.

damigiani: demijohn, a 50-liter glass container.

denominazione di origine controllata*: see page xxxi in the Introduction for an explanation.

denominazione di origine controllata e garantita*: see page xxxi in the Introduction for an explanation.

DOC: abbreviation of *denominazione di origine controllata.*

DOCG: abbreviation of *denominazione di origine controllata e garantita.*

dolce*: sweet.

dry extract: the higher the degree of dry extract, the greater the wine's body and flavor; it is measured in grams per liter.

enologo: enologist.

enoteca: literally, a wine library; used to indicate a wine shop.

eredi: heirs.

ettaro: a hectare, or 2.4711 acres.

ettolitro: a hectoliter, or 26.42 gallons.

ex-barrel: refers to a wine tasted from the barrel.

ex-barrique: refers to a wine tasted from *barrique.*

ex-botte: refers to a wine tasted from the *botte.*

ex-tank: refers to a wine tasted from tank.

ex-vat: refers to a wine tasted from a vat.

f.lli*: abbreviation for *fratelli,* brothers.

fattoria*: literally, farmhouse; commonly used to refer to a winery located on a wine estate in central Italy.

fiasco: a rustic straw-covered bulbous wine bottle used for Chianti. Plural is *fiaschi.*

filter: to clear the wine.

framboise: raspberries.

fratelli*: brothers.

frazione: literally, a fraction; used to refer to part of a city or village.

frizzante: light sparkle or prickle.

fusti di rovere: small oak barrel.

galestro: a type of soil found in Toscana: a friable rock that breaks easily, cracking from changes in temperature, and crumbling into fragments.

galestro alberese: clay soil with carbonate of lime and friable rock.

giornata: a measure used in the Piemonte to designate the amount of land a man can work in one day or *giorno;* equivalent to 0.3811 hectares or 0.9417 acres. Plural is *giornate.*

goudron: tar.

governo: a second fermentation created by the addition of dried grapes or the must of dried or concentrated grapes.

grappa: a marc distilled from the pomace left after the fermentation.

graticci: trellises or bamboo trays used for drying grapes in the Veronese district.

hectare: equivalent to 2.4711 acres.

hectoliter: equivalent to 26.42 gallons, 11.11 cases, or 133.33 bottles.

imbottigliato da*: bottled by.

invecchiato: aged.

kirsch: cherries.

la follatura: a technique used to push down the cap manually.

liquoroso*: fortified wine.

località*: an area or locality.

macerazione carbonica: see *carbonique maceration*.

magnum: equivalent to two bottles (1,500 milliliters).

malolactic fermentation: a bacterial fermentation that converts the sharp malic acid into its softer lactic form.

mezzadri: the farmers or peasants under *mezzadria*.

mezzadria: the feudal system of tenant farming; cropsharing.

mezzadro: the man who ran the property under *mezzadria*.

meter: equivalent to 3.281 feet.

metodo champenoise*: when the second fermentation—the one which results in the carbon dioxide which creates the sparkle—takes place in the bottle in which the wine is sold.

millesimato*: a sparkling wine of a single year or vintage.

mono-cepage: a wine from a single grape variety.

mono-vintage: a wine from a single vintage.

mufa nobile: see *botrytis*.

must: the grape juice before or during the early stages of fermentation before it becomes wine.

normale: literally, normal; under some of the DOC-DOCG regulations there are categories of wine which depend on its alcohol content and age; a *normale* refers to the basic wine with the minimum alcohol and aging. Plural is *normali*.

nouveau: a wine vinfied to drink young.

novello*: see *nouveau*.

oïdium: powdery mildew.

passimento: the drying process which produces Recioto wines.

passito*: a wine made from dried, or raisined, grapes; it is often, but not always, sweet.

peronospora: downy mildew.

phylloxera: a soil pest that lives on the root of a vine and saps its strength and productivity, eventually killing it; this scourge devastated the vineyards of Europe and most of the rest of the world in the latter part of the nineteenth century and into the twentieth; consequently most *Vitis vinifera* vines are grafted onto phylloxera-resistant rootstock.

pigiate a piedi: crushed by feet, referring to the grapes.

pigiatura a piedi: crushing (treading) grapes with bare feet.

podere*: small farm; term most often used in the Piemonte. Plural is *poderi*.

provincia: province.

quercia: oak.

quintali: equivalent to 100 kilograms or 220.4622 pounds.

racking: to clear the wine by moving it from one vat, cask, or barrel to another, thereby leaving the sediment behind.

ripasso: the wine is refermented on the grape pomace which still contains a lot of sugar. This technique is most commonly found in the Veronese district.

ripassare: to pass over or to do something again.

riserva*: under some of the DOC-DOCG regulations there are categories of wines which depend on its alcohol content and age; a *riserva* generally must attain a higher alcohol degree and be aged for a longer period of time. Plural is *riserve*.

riserva numerata*: a producer's *riserva* that is given a number; that is, the bottles are numbered.

riserva speciale*: under DOC, wines of this category are aged even longer than those wines which qualify as *riserva*. DOC could also require that the wines attain a higher alcohol degree.

rimontaggio: pumping over, whereby the juice—must or new wine—is pumped over the floating cap (see also *cappello sommerso*.)

rigoverno: an induced fermentation that, when used, is done in March or April (see also *governo*).

rosato*: rosé. Plural is *rosati*.

rosso*: red or red wine. Plural is *rossi*.

rubino*: ruby red.

sacristia: where they store prized, old bottles of wine.

schloss*: castle.

secco*: dry.

sfuso: wine sold in bulk; also referred to as open wine.

soprana: top or upper.

sorì*: a hilltop with a southern exposure.

sottana: bottom or lower.

spumante*: sparkling wine. Plural is *spumanti*.

stravecchio*: very old.

superiore*: literally, superior; to qualify, for some DOC wines the grapes must come from a more delimited area; for other wines the requirement specifies longer aging and/or a higher degree of alcohol.

tartufi: white truffles.

tenuta*: farm, estate, property, holding.

testucchi: small trees.

tini: upright wooden vats.

tini di legno: wooden uprights used for fermentation.

total acidity: the total amount of acid in a wine, measured in parts per thousand in tartaric acid.

training of vines:

    Greek system: the Greeks trained the vines like small bushes—*al alberello*—low to the ground; they were pruned to concentrate the vine's strength into fewer grape bunches, thereby yielding riper, more concentrated fruit which produced a sweeter, more alcoholic beverage than the thin wine obtained from unpruned vines.

    Etruscan manner: the Etruscans trained the vines high on trees or tall poles: the grapevines were supported or garlanded on wooden poles and small trees called *testucchi*.

    Roman system: the Romans used the Etruscan manner of training the vines high on trees or tall poles.

traversato: to transfer the wine from vat, cask, or barrel to another vat, cask, or barrel.

treading: to crush the grapes by feet.

uva: grape.

uvaggio: a blend of grape varieties.

vecchio*:   literally, old.

versante: slope, side of a hill.

vigna*:   vineyard.

vignaiolo*:   winemaker.

vigneto*:   vineyard. Plural is *vigneti*.

vino da tavola*:   table wine. Plural is *vini da tavola*.

vino novello*:   a wine made to drink young.

Vitis vinifera: the wine grape family.

zona classica: the classic zone, see *classico*.

* This term is used on an Italian wine label.

CHAPTER NOTES

Chapter 1: Nebbiolo

1 Renato Ratti, *Guida ai Vini del Piemonte* (Torino: Edizioni Eda, 1977). We have relied quite heavily on this book and many articles and discussions with Renato Ratti for much, but not all, of the historical information in this chapter.

2 *Piemonte appunti sul vino e dintorni* (Torino: Regione Piemonte, Assessorato Agricoltura e Foreste, October 1989).

3 *Anagrafe Vitivinicola in Piemonte* (Torino: Regione Piemonte, Assessorato Agricoltura e Foreste, May 1988).

Chapter 2: The Wines of the Langhe

1 Guglielmo Solci, *Barolo, the Wine of Kings* (Milano: *Italian Wine & Spirits,* May 1983).

2 Lorenzo Fantini, *Monografia Sulla Viticoltura Ed Enologia Nella Provincia Di Cuneo* (Alba: Reprinted by Ordine dei Cavalieri del Tartufo e dei Vini di Alba, 1973).

3 Carlo Petrini, *Atlante delle grandi vigne di Langa Zona del Barolo, Commune di Monforte* (Bra: Slow Food Editore, 1990).

4 *Ibid.*

5 *Ibid.*

6 Carlo Petrini, *Atlante delle grandi vigne di Langa Zona del Barolo, Comune di Castiglion Falletto* (Bra: Slow Food Editore, 1990).

7 Fantini.

8 Petrini, *Comune di Monforte.*

9 *Ibid.*

10 *Ibid.*

11 *Ibid.*

12 *Ibid.*

13 *Ibid.*

14 Petrini, *Comune di Castiglion Falletto.*

15 Petrini, *Comune di Monforte.*

16 Petrini, *Comune di Castiglion Falletto.*

17 Fantini.

18 Petrini, *Comune di Monforte.*

19 Fantini.

20 Petrini, *Comune di Monforte.*

21 Petrini, *Comune di Castiglion Falletto.*

22 Petrini, *Comune di Monforte.*

23 Petrini, *Comune di Castiglion Falletto.*

24 *Ibid.*

25 Renato Ratti, *Guida ai Vini del Piemonte* (Torino: Edizioni Eda, 1977).

26 *Barbaresco* (Associazione Consorzi di Tutela del Barolo, Barbaresco e dei Vini d'Alba).

27 Fantini.

28 Ratti.

29 *Albo Vigneti '89* (Camera di Commercio Industria Artigianato e Agricoltura di Cuneo, December 31, 1989).

30 *Ibid.*

31 *Enotria,* n. 62 (Milano: Unione Italiana Vini, December 1989).

32 *Albo Vigneti '89.*

33 Data supplied by *Il Corriere Vinicolo* (Milano: Unione Italiana Vini).

34 *Enotria.*

35 Luigi Veronelli, *I Vignaiolo Storici* (Milano: Mediolanum Editori Associati, 1986), p. 123.

36 *Ibid.,* p. 135.

37 *Ibid.,* p. 123.

Chapter 3: The Nebbiolo Wines of Torino and Aosta

1 *Piemonte appunti sul vino e dintorni* (Torino: Regione Piemonte, Assessorato Agricoltura e Foreste, October 1989).

2 *Il Corriere Vinicolo,* n. 10, March 12, 1990 (Milano: Unione Italiana Vini).

3 Data supplied by *Il Corriere Vinicolo.*

4 *Il Corriere Vinicolo,* n. 10.

5 Data supplied by *Il Corriere Vinicolo.*

6 *Enotria,* n. 62 (Milano: Unione Italiana Vini, December 1989).

7 *Il Corriere Vinicolo,* n. 10.

8 *Enotria.*
9 *Il Corriere Vinicolo.*
10 Data supplied by *Il Corriere Vinicolo.*
11 *Enotria.*

Chapter 4: The Wines of the Novara-Vercelli Hills

1 *Piemonte appunti sul vino e dintorni* (Torino: Regiona Piemonte, Assessorato Agricoltura e Foreste, October 1989).
2 *Il Corriere Vinicolo,* n. 10, March 12, 1990 (Milano: Unione Italiana Vini).
3 *Piemonte appunti sul vino e dintorni.*
4 *Il Corriere Vinicolo,* n. 10.
5 *Piemonte appunti sul vino e dintorni.*
6 *Enotria,* n. 62 (Milano: Unione Italiana Vini, December 1989).
7 *Ibid.*
8 *Ibid.*
9 *Ibid.*
10 *Ibid.*
11 *Ibid.*
12 *Ibid.*

Chapter 5: The Nebbiolo Wines of the Valtellina

1 *Il Corriere Vinicolo,* n. 10, March 12, 1990 (Milano: Unione Italiana Vini).
2 Data supplied by *Il Corriere Vinicolo.*
3 *Il Corriere Vinicolo,* n. 10.
4 Data supplied by *Il Corriere Vinicolo.*
5 *Il Corriere Vinicolo,* n. 10.
6 Data supplied by *Il Corriere Vinicolo.*
7 *Il Corriere Vinicolo,* n. 10.
8 Data supplied by *Il Corriere Vinicolo.*
9 *Il Corriere Vinicolo,* n. 10.
10 Data supplied by *Il Corriere Vinicolo.*
11 *Il Corriere Vinicolo,* n. 10.
12 Data supplied by *Il Corriere Vinicolo.*
13 A. D. Francis, *The Wine Trade* (New York: Harper & Row, 1973).
14 *Enotria,* n. 62 (Milano: Unione Italiana Vini, December 1989).

Chapter 6: The Sangiovese Grape

1 Raymond Flower, *Chianti—The Land, the People and the Wine* (New York: Universe Books, 1979), p. 131.

Chapter 7: Chianti

1 E. Repetti, *Dizionario geografico fisico storico della Toscana* (Firenze, 1833–46). Quoted by Alessandro Boglione in Raymond Flower, *Chianti—The Land, the People and the Wine* (New York: Universe Books, 1979), appendix 6.
2 S. Pieri, *Toponomastica della Valle dell'Arno* (Roma, 1919). Alessandro Boglione.
3 Flower, photo between pp. 40 and 41.
4 *Ibid.,* pp. 279–80.
5 Lamberto Paronetto, *Chianti, The History of Florence and Its Wines* (London: Wine and Spirit Publications, Ltd., 1970).
6 *Ibid.,* p. 65.

7 *Ibid.,* p. 66.
8 A. D. Francis, *The Wine Trade* (New York: Harper & Row, 1973), p. 45.
9 André Simon, *The History of the Wine Trade in England,* Volume III (London: The Holland Press, 1964), p. 359.
10 *Enotria,* n. 62 (Milano: Unione Italiana Vini, December 1989).
11 Paronetto, p. 195.
12 *Ibid.,* p. 169.
13 *Ibid.,* p. 45.
14 *Il Corriere Vinicolo,* n. 11, March 19, 1990 (Milano: Unione Italiana Vini).
15 *Ibid.*
16 Most of this data was supplied by *Il Corriere Vinicolo.*
17 Paronetto, p. 67.
18 *Il Corriere Vinicolo,* n. 11.
19 Data supplied by *Il Corriere Vinicolo.*
20 *Il Corriere Vinicolo,* n. 11.
21 Data supplied by *Il Corriere Vinicolo.*
22 *Il Corriere Vinicolo,* n. 11.
23 Data supplied by *Il Corriere Vinicolo.*
24 *Ibid.*

Chapter 8: Brunello di Montalcino

1 Guglielmo Solci, "Montalcino Pleases the Eye, Brunello Charms the Palate," *Italian Wines & Spirits,* August 1983, p. 65.
2 Alessandro Bizzarri, *Sulla Importanza dell'Esame del Mosto nel Processo di Vinificazione, Mezzi Facili per Esaminarlo* (Milano: A. Lombardi, 1871), pp. 12–13.
3 Emanuele Pellucci, *Brunello di Montalcino* (Fiesole: Ugo Fontana, 1981).

Chapter 9: Carmignano

1 *Il Corriere Vinicolo,* n. 11, March 19, 1990 (Milano: Unione Italiana Vini).
2 Data supplied by *Il Corriere Vinicolo.*

Chapter 10: Vino Nobile di Montepulciano

1 Emanuele Pellucci, *Vino Nobile di Montepulciano* (Fiesole: Ugo Fontana, 1985).
2 *Ibid.*
3 Piero Zoi, *Vino nobile di Montepulciano Dalla storia alla realtà d'oggi* (Sarteano, Siena: Edizioni Lui, 1987), pp. 58–62.
4 Villifranchi, *Oenologia Toscana, o sia memoria sopra i vini in specie Toscani* (Tuscan Enology, or a Memoir on Wines, Especially Those of Tuscany), Vol. II (Firenze: 1773).

Chapter 11: Torgiano

1 *Il Corriere Vinicolo,* n. 11, March 19, 1990 (Milano: Unione Italiana Vini).
2 *Umbria i grandi vini.*
3 Italian Wine Center in New York.
4 *Enotria,* n. 62 (Milano: Unione Italiana Vini, December 1989).
5 *Ibid.*

Chapter 12: More Sangiovese-based Wines

1 *Il Corriere Vinicolo,* n. 11, March 19, 1990 (Milano: Unione Italiana Vini).
2 Data supplied by *Il Corriere Vinicolo.*
3 *Il Corriere Vinicolo,* n. 11.
4 Data supplied by *Il Corriere Vinicolo.*
5 *Il Corriere Vinicolo,* n. 11.
6 Data supplied by *Il Corriere Vinicolo.*
7 *Il Corriere Vinicolo,* n. 11.
8 Data supplied by *Il Corriere Vinicolo.*
9 *Il Corriere Vinicolo,* n. 11.
10 Data supplied by *Il Corriere Vinicolo.*
11 *Enotria,* n. 62 (Milano: Unione Italiana Vini, December 1989).
12 *Il Corriere Vinicolo,* n. 11.
13 Data supplied by *Il Corriere Vinicolo.*
14 *Il Corriere Vinicolo,* n. 11.
15 Data supplied by *Il Corriere Vinicolo.*
16 *Ibid.*
17 *Il Corriere Vinicolo,* n. 11.
18 Data supplied by *Il Corriere Vinicolo.*
19 *Enotria.*
20 *Il Corriere Vinicolo,* n. 11.
21 Data supplied by *Il Corriere Vinicolo.*
22 *Il Corriere Vinicolo,* n. 11.
23 Data supplied by *Il Corriere Vinicolo.*
24 *Il Corriere Vinicolo,* n. 11.
25 Data supplied by *Il Corriere Vinicolo.*

Chapter 13: Montepulciano d'Abruzzo

1 *Enotria,* n. 63 (Milano: Unione Italiana Vini, March 1990).

Chapter 14: The Aglianico Grape

1 *Enotria,* n. 62 (Milano: Unione Italiana Vini, December 1989).
2 William Younger, *Gods, Men, and Wine* (London: The Wine and Food Society, 1966), p. 202.

Chapter 15: Recioto della Valpolicella Amarone

1 Zeffiro Bocci, *Wines of the Veneto with Controlled Specifications of Origin (DOC)* (Verona: ESAV—Ente di Sviluppo Agricolo del Veneto, 1980), p. 142.
2 Giovanni Vicentini, *Veneto Verona Valpolicella Masi 6 Generations in the Shade of the Vine* (Gargagnago, Italy: Masi Agricola, S.P.A., 1982), p. 42.
3 Bocci, p. 143.
4 Vicentini, p. 50.
5 Bocci, p. 142.
6 *Ibid.,* p. 145.
7 *Enotria,* n. 62, (Milano: Unione Italiana Vini, December 1989).

Chapter 16: Cabernet and Cabernet Blends

1 *South Tyrolean Wine Guide* (Bozen: Board of Trade of the Autonomous Province of Bozen).
2 Data supplied by *Il Corriere Vinicolo.*
3 *Ibid.*
4 *Enotria,* n. 62 (Milano: Unione Italiana Vini, December 1989).
5 *Ibid.*
6 *Il Corriere Vinicolo.*
7 *Enotria.*
8 *Il Corriere Vinicolo.*
9 *Enotria.*
10 *Il Corriere Vinicolo.*
11 *Ibid.*
12 *Ibid.*
13 *Enotria.*
14 Zeffiro Bocci, *Wines of the Veneto with Controlled Specifications of Origin (DOC)* (Verona: ESAV—Ente di Sviluppo Agricolo del Veneto, 1980), p. 78.
15 *Il Corriere Vinicolo.*
16 *Enotria.*
17 *Il Corriere Vinicolo.*
18 *Ibid.*
19 *Enotria.*
20 *Il Corriere Vinicolo.*
21 *Enotria.*
22 *Il Corriere Vinicolo.*
23 *Ibid.*
24 *Enotria.*
25 *Il Corriere Vinicolo.*
26 *Enotria.*
27 *Ibid.*
28 *Ibid.*
29 *Ibid.*
30 *Ibid.*
31 Bocci, p. 42.
32 *Enotria.*
33 *Il Corriere Vinicolo.*
34 *Enotria.*
35 *Il Corriere Vinicolo.*
36 *Enotria.*
37 *Il Corriere Vinicolo.*
38 *Enotria.*

Chapter 17: Other Noble Reds

1 *Il Corriere Vinicolo,* n. 10, March 12, 1990 (Milano: Unione Italiana Vini).
2 *Ibid.*
3 Data supplied by *Il Corriere Vinicolo.*
4 *Ibid.*
5 *Ibid.*

SELECTED BIBLIOGRAPHY

Books and Pamphlets

Allen, H. Warner. *A History of Wine*. London: Faber and Faber, 1961.

Anderson, Burton. *The Wine Atlas of Italy & Traveller's Guide to the Vineyards*. New York: Simon and Schuster, 1990.

Bizzarri, Alessandro. *Sulla Importanza dell'Esame del Mosto nel Processo di Vinificazione, Mezzi Facili per Esaminarlo*. Milano: A. Lombardi, 1871.

Bocci, Zeffiro. *Wines of the Veneto with Controlled Specifications of Origin (DOC)*. Verona: ESAV—Ente di Sviluppo Agricolo del Veneto, 1980.

Bonacina, Gianni. *Lo Stivale in Bottiglia Piccola Enciclopedia dei 3811 Vini Italiani*, 3 volumes. Bresca: AEB, 1978.

Canessa, G. *Guida del Chianti*, Vol. 2. Firenze: Arnaud, 1970.

Corato, Riccardo di. *2214 Vini d'Italia Guida Regionale*, edition no. 2. Milano: Sonzogno, 1976.

Fantini, Lorenzo. *Monografia Sulla Viticoltura Ed Enologia Nella Provincia Di Cuneo*. Alba: Reprinted by Ordine dei Cavalieri del Tartufo e dei Vini di Alba, 1973.

Flower, Raymond. *Chianti—The Land, the People and the Wine*. New York: Universe Books, 1979.

Francis, A. D. *The Wine Trade*. New York: Harper & Row, 1973.

Galet, Pierre. *Cépages et Vignobles de France*, Volume III: *Les Cépages de Cuvé*. Montpellier: Paysan du Midi, 1962.

Garoglio, Dott. Piero. *Enciclopedia Vitivinicola Mondiale*, Volume I. Milano: Edizioni Scientifiche UIV, 1973.

Minetti, Gian, and Beppe Rinaldi. *The Regional Barolo Enoteca: Eleven Country-Towns for a Great Wine*. Barolo: Enoteca Regionale del Barolo, January 1985.

Montaldo, Giancarlo. *Highways and Byways of Alba Wines*. Torino: Order of Knights of the Truffle and Alba Wines, 1989.

O'Toole, Tom. *South Tyrol Wine Guide*. Bozen: Chamber of Commerce, 1983.

Paronetto, Lamberto. *Chianti, The History of Florence and Its Wines*. London: Wine and Spirit Publications, Ltd., 1970.

Pellucci, Emanuele. *Brunello di Montalcino*. Fiesole: Ugo Fontana, 1981.

———. *Vino Nobile di Montepulciano*. Fiesole: Ugo Fontana, 1985.

Petrini, Carlo. *Atlante delle grandi vigne di Langa Zona del Barolo, Comune di Castiglion Falletto*. Bra: Slow Food Editore, 1990.

———. *Atlante delle grandi vigne di Langa Zona del Barolo, Comune di Monforte*. Bra: Slow Food Editore, 1990.

———. *Atlante delle grandi vigne di Langa Zona del Barolo, Comune di Verduno*. Bra: Slow Food Editore, 1990.

Ratti, Renato. *Guida ai Vini del Piemonte*. Torino: Edizioni Eda, 1977.

Repetti, E. *Dizionario geografico fisico storico della Toscana*. Firenze, 1833–46.

Roncarati, Bruno. *Viva Vino Doc Wines of Italy*. London: Wine and Spirit Publications, Ltd., 1976.

———. *Viva Vino 200 + DOC + DOCG Wines & Wine Roads of Italy*. London: Wine and Spirit Publications, Ltd., 1986.

S. Pieri. *Toponomastica della Valle dell'Arno*. Roma, 1919.

Simon, André. *The History of the Wine Trade in England*, Volume III. London: The Holland Press, 1964.

Veronelli, Luigi. *Catalogo dei Vini d'Italia*. Torino: Giorgio Mondadori & Associati, 1983.

———. *Catalogo dei Vini del Mondo*. Torino: Giorgio Mondadori & Associati, 1982.

———. *I Vignaiolo Storici*. Milano: Mediolanum Editori Associati, 1986.

———. *Le Cantine di Veronelli*. Torino: Giorgio Mondadori & Associati, 1989.

———. *Vivi d'Italia N. 3*. Torino: Giulio Bolaffi, 1974.

———. *Vini d'Italia N. 4*. Torino: Giulio Bolaffi, 1976.

———. *Vini Rossi d'Italia*. Torino: Giulio Bolaffi, 1980.

Vicentini, Giovanni. *Veneto Verona Valpolicella Masi 6 Generations in the Shade of the Vine*. Garganago, Italy: Masi Agricola, S.P.A., 1982.

Vigliermo, Amerigo. *Carema: Gente e Vino*. Ivrea: Priuli & Verlucca, 1981.

Vignolo-Lutati, Ferdinando. *Sulla delimitazione delle zone a vini tipici in Annali della R. Accademia di Agricoltura di Torino,* Volume LXXII, November 24, 1929. Torino: E. Schioppo, 1930.

Villifranchi. *Oenologia Toscana, o sia memoria sopra i vini in specie Toscani* (Tuscan Enology, or a Memoir on Wines, Especially Those of Tuscany), Volume II. Firenze: 1773.

Younger, William. *Gods, Men, and Wine.* London: The Wine and Food Society, 1966.

Zoi, Piero. *Vino nobile di Montepulciano Dalla storia alla rèaltà d'oggi.* Sarteano, Siena: Edizioni Lui, 1987.

Albo Vigneti. Camera di Commercio Industria Artigianato e Agricoltura di Cuneo. December 31, 1985.

———. Camera di Commercio Industria Artigianato e Agricoltura di Cuneo. December 31, 1986.

Albo Vigneti '89. Camera di Commercio Industria Artigianato e Agricoltura di Cuneo. December 31, 1989.

Almanacco 1978 dei Vini del Piemonte. Torino: Regione Piemonte, 1979.

Almanacco 1979 dei Vini del Piemonte. Torino: Regione Piemonte, 1980.

Almanacco 1980 dei Vini del Piemonte. Torino: Regione Piemonte, 1981.

Almanacco 1981 dei Vini del Piemonte. Torino: Regione Piemonte, 1982.

Almanacco 1982 dei Vini del Piemonte. Torino: Regione Piemonte, 1983.

Almanacco 1983 dei Vini del Piemonte. Torino: Regione Piemonte, 1984.

Almanacco 1984 dei Vini del Piemonte. Torino: Regione Piemonte, 1985.

Anagrafe Vitivinicola in Piemonte. Torino: Regione Piemonte, Assessorato Agricoltura e Foreste, May 1988.

Barbaresco. Associazione Consorzi di Tutela del Barolo, Barbaresco e dei Vini d'Alba.

Barolo. Associazione Consorzi di Tutela del Barolo, Barbaresco e dei Vini d'Alba.

Catalogo dei Confezionatori del Chianti Classico Gallo Nero. Firenze: Consorzio Vino Chianti Classico, 1984.

Disciplinari di Produzione Vini A Denominazione di Origine "Controllata," Volumes I, II, and III. Conegliano: Scarpis, 1968, 1971, 1978.

Guida Turistica di Gattinara. Usmate, Milano: Associazione Culturale di Gattinara, 1981.

I Grandi Vini de l'Albese. Torino: Ordine dei Cavalieri del Tartufo e dei Vini di Alba, 1977.

Il Chianti Classico. Firenze: Consorzio Vino Chianti Classico, 1984. Firenze: Consorzio Vino Chianti Classico, 1984.

Il Mondo del Gallo Nero Un Vino Una Storia. Firenze: Consorzio del Gallo Nero, 1988.

I. L. Ruffino 1877–1977. Firenze: private publication, 1978.

La Morra Guida Vino. La Morra: Cantina Comunale Permanente di La Morra, Spring 1984.

Piemonte appunti sul vino e dintorni. Torino: Regione Piemonte, Assessorato Agricoltura e Foreste, April 1989.

———. Torino: Regione Piemonte, Assessorato Agricoltura e Foreste, October 1989.

South Tyrolean Wine Guide. Bozen: Board of Trade of the Autonomous Province of Bozen.

Vignamaggio e Montagliari dal secolo XIV ai giorni nostri. Firenze: Olimpia.

V.Q.P.R.D. d'Italia. Repubblica Italiana, Minestro dell' Agricoltura e Foreste. Enoteca Italiana Siena.

Magazines

Barolo & Co. *News of Piedmont's Wines.* This magazine contains up-to-date information on the wines of the Piemonte. It is written in Italian with summaries of the highlights in English. It is worthwhile for those wanting to keep abreast of this region and its wines. For information, write to Barolo & Co., Via C. Fossati 6, 10141 Torino, Italy.

Enotria and *Il Corriere Vinicolo* (Milano: Unione Italiana Vini). *Enotria* is a magazine and *Il Corriere* a newspaper. Both offer up-to-date information on Italian wine. The statistical data in particular are invaluable. For further information, contact Unione Italiana Vini, Via S. Vittore al Teatro 3, 20122 Milano, Italy.

TASTING NOTE INDEX

GENERAL INDEX